The Best Books for Academic Libraries

The Best Books for Academic Libraries
10 Volumes (ISBN 0-7222-0014-5)

Volume 1 — Science, Technology, and Agriculture
(ISBN 0-7222-0011-0)
Q   Science
S   Agriculture
T   Technology, Engineering

Volume 2 — Medicine
(ISBN 0-7222-0012-9)
BF   Psychology
R   Medicine
RM-RS   Therapeutics
RT   Nursing

Volume 3 — Language and Literature
(ISBN 0-7222-0013-7)
P   Language and Literature
PA   Classical Language and Literature
PB-PH   Modern European Languages and Slavic
           Languages and Literature
PJ-PL   Oriental Language and Literature
PN   Literature: General and Comparative
PQ   Romance Literatures
PR   English Literature
PS   American Literature
PT   German, Dutch and Scandinavian Literature
PZ   Juvenile Literature

Volume 4 — History of the Americas
(ISBN 0-7222-0014-5)
E   America
E151-E970   United States
F1-975   US Local History
F1001-3799   Canada, Latin America

Volume 5 — World History
(ISBN 0-7222-0015-3)
C   Auxiliary Sciences of History
D   History

Volume 6 — Social Sciences
(ISBN 0-7222-0016-1)
G-GF   Geography, Oceanography, Human Ecology
GN   Anthropology, Ethnology, Archaeology
GR-GT   Folklore, Customs, Costumes
GV   Recreation, Physical Training, Sports
H-HA   Social Sciences. General Statistics
HB-HJ   Economics, Population
HM-HV   Sociology, Social History, Social Pathology
HX   Socialism, Communism, Anarchism

Volume 7 — Political Science, Law, Education
(ISBN 0-7222-0017-X)
J   Political Science
L   Education
K   Law

Volume 8 — Religion and Philosophy
(ISBN 0-7222-0018-8)
B-BJ   Philosophy
BL-BX   Religion

Volume 9 — Music & Fine Arts
(ISBN 0-7222-0019-6)
ML, MT   Music
N-NX   Fine Arts

Volume 10 — General Works, Military Science, Naval Science, Library Science, Author Index, Subject Guide
(ISBN 0-7222-0020-X)
A   General Works
U   Military Science
V   Naval Science
Z   Bibliography, Library Science
           Author Index, Subject Guide

The Best Books for Academic Libraries

General Works, Military Science,
Naval Science, Bibliography,
Library Science,
Author Index & Subject Guide

Volume 10

First Edition

The Best Books, Inc.
P. O. Box 893520
Temecula, CA. 92589-3520

Printed in the United States of America

ISBN 0-7222-0010-2 (10 Volume Set)
ISBN 0-7222-0020-X (Volume 10)

```
Library of Congress Cataloging-in-Publication Data

The best books for academic libraries.-- 1st ed.
      v. cm.
Includes indexes.
Contents: v. 1. Science, technology, and agriculture -- v. 2. Medicine
-- v. 3. Language and literature -- v. 4. History of the Americas -- v.
5. World history -- v. 6. Social sciences -- v. 7. Political science,
law, education - v. 8. Religion and philosophy -- v. 9. Music & fine
arts -- v. 10. General works, military & naval, library science.
    ISBN 0-7222-0020-21-0.(set : alk. paper) -- ISBN 0-7222-0011-0 (v. 1 :
alk. paper. ISBN 0-7222-0012-9 (v. 2 : alk. paper) -- ISBN 0-7222-
0013-7 (v.3 : alk. paper) -- ISBN 0-7222-0014-5 (v. 4 : alk.
paper) -- ISBN 0-7222-0015-3 (v. 5 : alk. paper) ISBN 0-7222-0016-1
(v. 6 : alk. paper) -- ISBN 0-7222-0017-X (v. 7 : alk. paper) -- ISBN
0-7222-0018-8 (v. 8 : alk. paper) -- ISBN 0-7222-0019-6 (v. 9 : alk.
paper) -- ISBN 0-7222-0020-X (v. 10 : alk. paper).
    1.   Academic libraries--United States--Book lists.  I.  Best Books,
Inc.

Z1035 .B545 2002
011'.67—dc21   2002013790
```

For further information, contact:

The Best Books, Inc.
P.O. Box 893520
Temecula, CA 92589-3520
(Voice) 888-265-3531
(Fax) 888-265-3540

For product information/customer service, E-mail: customerservice@thebbooks.net

Visit our Web site: www.bestbooksfor.com

Table of Contents

Introduction xiii
Contributing Advisors xvii
Senior Subject Advisors xix
AC Collections. Series. Collected works 1
AE Encyclopedias 1
    AE1 History, method of use, etc. 1
AG Dictionaries and other general reference works 2
    AG243 Wonders. Curiosities. Eccentric characters, fads, etc. — 1871- 3
    AG250 Pictorial works (Views, events, etc.) 3
AI Indexes 3
    AI3 By language of index — English 3
    AI21 Indexes to individual newspapers, A-Z 3
AM Museums. Collectors and collecting 3
    AM1 Periodicals, societies, collections, etc. 3
    AM3.6 Biography — Individual, A-Z 3
    AM5 General works — 1801- 3
    AM7 General special 4
    AM101 Description and history of museums — Individual museums. By place, A-Z 4
AS Academies and learned societies 5
    AS2 Serial directories. Serial handbooks 5
    AS2.5 International associations, congresses, conferences, etc. — General works 5
    AS8 Directories and lists 5
    AS911 Other associations, "funds," foundations, and institutions 5
AY Yearbooks. Almanacs. Directories 6
AZ History of scholarship and learning. The humanities 6
    AZ103 Philosophy. Theory — Value, aims, influences etc. Addresses, essays, lectures. Pamphlets 6
    AZ182 Study and teaching — General works 6
    AZ183 Study and teaching — By region or country, A-Z 6
    AZ999 Popular errors and delusions 7
U Military science (General) 7
    U11 Army lists. By region or country, A-Z 7
    U19 Addresses, essays, lectures 7
    U22 War. Philosophy. Military sociology — Ethics. Morale 10
    U22.3 War. Philosophy. Military sociology — Military psychology 10
    U24 Dictionaries. Encyclopedias — General works 10
    U26 Military symbols and abbreviations 11
    U27 History of military science — General works 11
    U37 History of military science — Medieval 12
    U43 History of military science — By region or country, A-Z 14
    U51 Biography — Collective 14
    U101 General works — Early through 1788 15
    U102 General works — 1789- 15
    U104 General special 16
    U105 Popular works 16
    U162.6 Strategy — Deterrence 16
    U163 Strategy — Miscellaneous topics (not A-Z) 17
    U167.5 Tactics — Special topics, A-Z 17

    U168 Logistics 17
    U200 Debarkation. Landing maneuvers 17
    U240 Small wars. Guerrilla warfare. Indian fighting 17
    U241 Counterinsurgency. Counter-guerrilla warfare 18
    U260 Joint operations. Combined operations 18
    U262 Commando tactics 18
    U263 Atomic warfare 19
    U264 Atomic weapons — General works 20
    U264.5 Atomic weapons — Other regions or countries, A-Z 21
    U310 War games. Kriegsspiel — General works 21
    U328 Military sports — By region or country, A-Z 21
    U793 Weapons of mass destruction 22
    U800 History of arms and armor — General works 22
    U825 History of arms and armor — Armor 22
UA Armies: Organization, distribution, military situation 23
    UA10 General works 23
    UA10.5 National security 23
    UA11 Military policy 23
    UA12 Mutual security programs 24
    UA12.5 Disarmament inspection. Arms control and nuclear arms control verification 24
    UA15 Armies of the world. Armies and navies of the world 25
    UA15.5 Foreign military bases 25
    UA17 Cost of armaments, budgets, estimates, etc. 25
    UA18 Industrial mobilization for war and defense 25
    UA21 By region or country — America 25
    UA917 Demobilization 45
    UA926 Civil defense — General works 45
    UA990 Military geography — General works 45
UB Military administration 45
    UB23-87 By region or country 45
    UB147 Military service as a profession 46
    UB210 Command of troops. Leadership 46
    UB212 Command and control systems 46
    UB220 Staffs of armies — General works 46
    UB250 Intelligence — General works 46
    UB251 Intelligence — By region or country, A-Z 46
    UB275 Psychological warfare. Propaganda — General works 48
    UB340 Compulsory service. Conscription and exemption — General works 48
    UB416 Minorities, women, etc., in armed forces — General works 50
    UB775 Civil law relating to the military 51
    UB800 Prisons and prisoners — General works 51
    UB825 Military police. Gendarmes — By region or country, A-Z 51
UC Maintenance and transportation 51
    UC267 Supplies and stores — Contracts 52

UD Infantry **52**
    UD59 By region or country 52
UE Cavalry. Armor **52**
UF Artillery **53**
    UF157 Tactics. Maneuvers. Drill regulations —
    General works 53
    UF400 Field artillery — General works 53
    UF500 Weapons systems — General works 53
    UF700 Ordnance material (Ordnance proper)
    — Ammunition 54
    UF860 Military explosives and pyrotechnics —
    General works 54
UG23-612 Military engineering **54**
    UG128 Biography — Individual, A-Z 54
    UG446.5 Attack and defense. Siege warfare —
    Tanks, armored cars, etc. 55
    UG447.8 Attack and defense. Siege warfare —
    Biological warfare. Bacterial warfare 55
    UG460 Military architecture and building 55
    UG475 Military surveillance 55
    UG486.5 Directed-energy weapons 56
    UG626.2 Biography — Individual, A-Z 56
    UG628 Dictionaries. Encyclopedias 56
    UG630 General works 56
    UG635 By region or country — Other regions
    or countries, A-Z 58
    UG700 Tactics — By region or country 58
    UG730 Air defenses — General works 58
    UG740 Ballistic missile defenses — General
    works 58
    UG1520 General works 60
    UG1523 By region or country — United
    States 60
    UG1525 By region or country — Other regions
    or countries, A-Z 61
    UG1530 Space warfare. Interplanetary warfare ..61
UH Other services **61**
    UH630 Protection of morals and health 61
    UH740 Military unions. Union movements in
    armed forces — General works 62
V Naval science (General) **62**
    V23 Dictionaries and encyclopedias —
    General 62
    V25 History and antiquities of naval science —
    Philosophy of history 62
    V27 History and antiquities of naval science —
    General works 62
    V55 History and antiquities of naval science —
    By region or country, A-Z 63
    V165 Naval strategy — General special 64
    V167 Naval tactics — General works 64
    V179 Naval logistics 64
    V182 Convoys 64
    V210 Submarine warfare — General works 64
    V310 Salutes. Honors. Ceremonies 64
    V750 War vessels: Construction, armament, etc.
    — General works 64
**VA Navies: Organization, distribution, naval
situation** **66**
    VA10 General works 66
    VA40 Navies of the world — General works 66

VB Naval administration **69**
    VB230 Intelligence — General works 69
    VB259 Vocational guidance. The navy as a
    career. Job analysis 69
VC Naval maintenance **70**
VE Marines **70**
VF Naval ordnance **70**
    VF7 Collected works (nonserial) 70
    VF346 Naval weapons systems — General
    works 71
VG Minor services of navies **71**
    VG90 Naval aviation. Air service. Air warfare
    — General works 71
    VG95 Naval aviation. Air service. Air warfare
    — Other regions or countries, A-Z 71
VK Navigation. Merchant marine **71**
    VK15 History, conditions, etc. — General
    works 71
    VK139 Biography — Collective 72
    VK140 Biography — Individual, A-Z 72
    VK541 Seamanship — General works 72
    VK549 Science of navigation — History 73
    VK597 Marine hydrography. Hydrographic
    surveying — By region or country, A-Z 73
    VK1015 Lighthouse service — History 73
    VK1265 Shipwrecks and fires — Submarine
    disasters 73
**VM Naval architecture. Shipbuilding. Marine
engineering** **73**
    VM12 Directories 73
    VM15 History — General works 74
    VM17 History — Medieval 74
    VM140 Biography — Individual, A-Z 74
    VM145 Naval architecture (General) — General
    works, 1861- 75
    VM156 Theory of the ship. Principles of naval
    architecture — General works 75
    VM165 Study and teaching — General works ...75
    VM298 Ship models. Steamboat models —
    General works 75
    VM298.5 Shipbuilding industry. Shipyards —
    General works 75
    VM301 Shipbuilding industry. Shipyards —
    Shipbuilding companies and shipyards, A-Z ..75
    VM307 Illustrations of ships of all kinds.
    Pictorial works 75
    VM311 Special types of vessels — By
    construction or rigging, A-Z 75
    VM362 Special types of vessels — Hydrofoil
    boats 76
    VM600 Marine engineering — General works ...77
Z4-114 Books (General). Writing. Paleography **77**
    Z4 History of books and bookmaking — General
    works 77
    Z8 History of books and bookmaking — By
    region or country, A-Z 78
    Z40 Writing — General works. History 78
    Z48 Writing — Duplicating processes. Copying
    services 78
    Z105 Manuscripts. Paleography — General
    works 79
    Z112 Manuscripts. Paleography — Materials,
    instruments, etc. 79

Z116-658 Book industries and trade **79**
Z116.A2 Treatises on the modern printed book . 79
Z116.A3 Book design 79
Z116.T7513 Printing — General works 79
Z117 Printing — Bibliography 80
Z118 Printing — Collections. Series. Systematic encyclopedias, etc. 80
Z121 Printing — Museums. Exhibitions 80
Z269.3 Bookbinding — Special types of bindings, A-Z 83
Z279 Bookselling and publishing — Bibliography 83
Z282 Bookselling and publishing — Directories 83
Z282.5 Bookselling and publishing — Dictionaries. Encyclopedias 83
Z286 Bookselling and publishing — Special lines of business, A-Z 83
Z551 Copyright — General works 86
Z649 Copyright — Special topics, A-Z 87
Z657 Freedom of the press. Censorship — General works 87
Z658 Freedom of the press. Censorship — By region or country, A-Z 87
Z666-998 Libraries **88**
Z666 Library science. Information science — Bibliography 88
Z666.5 Library science. Information science — Information organization 88
Z669.7 Library science. Information science — Research 88
Z669.8 Library science. Information science — Statistical methods 88
Z673 Library science. Information science — Library associations 88
Z674 Library science. Information science — Collected works (nonserial) 88
Z675 Library science. Information science — Classes of libraries, A-Z 88
Z685 Library science. Information science — Shelving. Bookstacks 90
Z987 Private libraries. Book collecting — General works 95
Z987.5 Private libraries. Book collecting — By region or country, A-Z 95
Z988 Private libraries. Book collecting — Bibliography 95
Z989 Private libraries. Book collecting — Biography of book collectors 95
Z998 Booksellers' catalogs. Book prices — General works 96
Z1001-1065 General bibliography **96**
Z1001 Introduction to bibliography. Theory, philosophy, psychology. Bibliography. Documentation 96
Z1001.3 History of bibliography — General works 96
Z1002 Bibliography of bibliography. Books about books 96
Z1003 Choice of books. Books and reading — General works 96
Z1003.8 Biography of bibliographers — Collective 97

Z1004 Biography of bibliographers — Individual, A-Z 97
Z1006 Dictionaries. Encyclopedias 97
Z1009 Collections 98
Z1024 Special classes of books — Imaginary books. Lost books. Forgeries, etc. 98
Z1033 Special classes of books — Other special classes, A-Z 98
Z1035.A1 Best books — Book selection, reviews, etc. 98
Z1035.1 Reference books 99
Z1037.A1 Books for the young — General works 99
Z1037.A2 Books for the young — Prize books .. 99
Z1037.9 Books for the young — Reference books for children 100
Z1039 Books for other special classes, institutions, etc., A-Z 100
Z1041 Anonyms and pseudonyms — General bibliography 100
Z1201-4891 National bibliography **101**
Z1201 America — General bibliography 101
Z1206 America — Biobibliography of Americanists 101
Z1207 America — Private libraries, and booksellers' catalogs of Americana 101
Z1946 America — Saint Helena. Tristan da Cunha. Ascension Island 110
Z2000 Europe — General bibliography 110
Z2000.9 Europe — Commonwealth of Nations . 111
Z2001-2014 Europe — Great Britain and Ireland. England 111
Z2136-2137 Europe — Czechoslovakia. Czech Republic 115
Z2171-2184 Europe — France 115
Z2230-2241 Europe — Germany 115
Z2260 Europe — Mediterranean area 115
Z2281-2304 Europe — Greece 115
Z2340 Europe — Rome. Roman Empire 116
Z2341-2360.3 Europe — Italy 116
Z2691-2700 Europe — Spain and Portugal. Spain 117
Z2771 Europe — Switzerland 118
Z5052-7991 Subject bibliography **123**
Z5065 Aerospace technology — By region or country, A-Z 123
Z5071 Agriculture — General bibliography 123
Z5074 Agriculture — Special topics, A-Z 123
Z5075 Agriculture — Local, A-Z 123
Z5111 Anthropology and ethnology — General bibliography 123
Z5118 Anthropology and ethnology — Special topics, A-Z 123
Z5131 Archaeology — General bibliography 124
Z5133 Archaeology — Special topics, A-Z 124
Z5140 Archives. Records 124
Z5165 Authorship (General) 124
Z5170 Automobiles. Automobile travel. Motor vehicles — General bibliography 124
Z5301 Biography. Genealogy. Heraldry — General bibliography 124
Z5304 Biography. Genealogy. Heraldry — By class, A-Z 124

Z5052-7991 Subject bibliography *(cont.)*

Z5305 Biography. Genealogy. Heraldry —
By region or country, A-Z 124

Z5319 Biography. Genealogy. Heraldry —
Catalogs 125

Z5322 Biology — Special topics, A-Z 125

Z5351 Botany — General bibliography 125

Z5524 Chemistry 125

Z5579.5 Civilization — Medieval 125

Z5579.6 Civilization — Modern 125

Z5630-5634 Communication. Mass media 126

Z5640 Computer science. Electronic data
processing — General bibliography 126

Z5643 Computer science. Electronic data
processing — Special topics, A-Z 126

Z5691-5694 Costume 126

Z5703 Criminology — Bibliography of
bibliographies 126

Z5703.4 Criminology — Special topics, A-Z 126

Z5703.5 Criminology — By region or country,
A-Z 127

Z5710 Days. Holidays. Festivals. Birthdays —
General bibliography 127

Z5721 Deaf-mutes 127

Z5725 Death 127

Z5771 Directories — General 127

Z5776 Domestic economy. Home economics —
Special topics, A-Z 127

Z5781-5784 Drama. Theater 127

Z5811 Education — General bibliography 128

Z5813 Education — Periodicals. Societies 128

Z5814 Education — Special topics, A-Z 128

Z5815 Education — By region or country,
A-Z 129

Z5817.2 Education — Teaching aids 129

Z5818 Education — Special disciplines and
subjects, A-Z 129

Z5834 Electricity — Special topics, A-Z 130

Z5848 Encyclopedias — General 130

Z5853 Engineering — Special topics, A-Z 130

Z5861 Environment (General and human).
Human ecology — General bibliography 130

Z5863 Environment (General and human).
Human ecology — Other special topics,
A-Z 130

Z5865 Erotic literature, facetiae, curiosa, etc. —
General bibliography 130

Z5866 Erotic literature, facetiae, curiosa, etc. —
Special topics, A-Z 131

Z5883 Exhibitions 131

Z5916 Fiction — General bibliography 131

Z5917 Fiction — Special topics, A-Z 131

Z5931 Fine arts (Visual arts). The arts (General)
— General bibliography 132

Z5936 Fine arts (Visual arts). The arts (General)
— Special aspects or movements, A-Z 132

Z5937 Fine arts (Visual arts). The arts (General)
— Periodicals. Societies 132

Z5938 Fine arts (Visual arts). The arts (General)
— Biobibliography 132

Z5956 Fine arts (Visual arts). The arts (General)
— Special topics (not otherwise provided
for), A-Z 133

Z5961 Fine arts (Visual arts). The arts (General)
— By region or country, A-Z 134

Z5981-5984 Folklore 134

Z5990 Forecasting 134

Z5996.5 Gardening. Horticulture. Floriculture.
Landscape gardening and architecture —
By region or country, A-Z 135

Z6001.A1 Geography and travels. Maps.
Cartography — Bibliography of bibliography 135

Z6004 Geography and travels. Maps. Cartography
— Special topics, A-Z 135

Z6005 Geography and travels. Maps. Cartography
— Local. By region, physical feature, etc.,
A-Z 135

Z6009 Geography and travels. Maps. Cartography
— Catalogs 135

Z6031-6033 Geology. Mineralogy.
Paleontology 135

Z6121 Gymnastics. Physical education 136

Z6201.A55-S64 History —
General bibliography 136

Z6205 History — Periodicals. Societies 136

Z6207 History — Special historical events,
movements, etc., A-Z 136

Z6208 History — Special methodological topics,
A-Z 137

Z6250 Hospitality industry. Hotels 137

Z6265 Humanities 137

Z6366 Jews — General bibliography 138

Z6374 Jews — Other special topics, A-Z 138

Z6375 Jews — Catalogs 138

Z6461 International law and relations —
General bibliography 138

Z6464 International law and relations —
Special topics, A-Z 139

Z6465 International law and relations —
Foreign relations. By region or country, A-Z ... 139

Z6511 Literature — General bibliography 139

Z6514 Literature — Special subjects, A-Z 140

Z6620 Manuscripts — By region or country,
A-Z 141

Z6621 Manuscripts — Catalogs of manuscript
collections in specific libraries. By name of
library, A-Z 141

Z6653 Mathematics — Periodicals. Societies 141

Z6654 Mathematics — Special topics, A-Z 141

Z6658.I54 Medicine — General bibliography 141

Z6660.5 Medicine — Biography 141

Z6661 Medicine — By region or country, A-Z .. 141

Z6664 Medicine — Internal medicine.
Diseases and manifestations, A-Z 141

Z6671.55 Medicine — Geriatrics 142

Z6675 Medicine — Other, A-Z 142

Z6678 Metals. Metallurgy — General
bibliography 142

Z6683 Meteorology — Special topics, A-Z 143

Z6724 Military science — Special topics, A-Z ... 143

Z6725 Military science — Local, A-Z 143

Z6824 Names 143

Z6835 Naval science — Local, A-Z 143

Z6878 Occultism — Special topics, A-Z 143

Z6935 Performing arts 144

Z6940 Periodicals, newspapers, and other serials
— Journalism 144

Z6941 Periodicals, newspapers, and other serials — General bibliography 144
Z6944 Periodicals, newspapers, and other serials — Special topics, A-Z 144
Z6945 Periodicals, newspapers, and other serials — Catalogs of libraries. Union lists 144
Z7001 Philology and linguistics — General bibliography 145
Z7004 Philology and linguistics — Special topics, A-Z 145
Z7125-7128 Philosophy 145
Z7134 Photography — General bibliography 146
Z7141 Physics 146
Z7144 Physics — Special topics, A-Z 146
Z7156 Poetry — Special topics, A-Z 146
Z7161.A1 Political and social sciences — Bibliography of bibliography 146
Z7161.A15 Political and social sciences — General special 146
Z7161.A2 Political and social sciences — Theory, method, etc. 146
Z7161.C17-Y75 Political and social sciences — General bibliography 146
Z7164 Political and social sciences — Special topics, A-Z 147
Z7165 Political and social sciences — By region or country, A-Z 151
Z7201-7204 Psychology 152
Z7221 Radio — General bibliography 152
Z7224 Radio — By region or country, A-Z 152
Z7231 Railroads — Bibliography of bibliography
Z7401 Science. Natural history — General bibliography 152
Z7402 Science. Natural history — Bibliography of early works 153
Z7403 Science. Natural history — Periodicals. Societies 153
Z7404 Science. Natural history — Biobibliography 153
Z7405 Science. Natural history — Special topics, A-Z 153
Z7407 Science. Natural history — Science. By region or country, A-Z 153
Z7408 Science. Natural history — Natural history. By region or country, A-Z 153
Z7511-7515 Sports. Amusements. Recreation ... 154
Z7551-7554 Statistics 154
Z7615 Suicide 154
Z7711 Television 154
Z7721 Temperance 155
Z7751 Theology and religion — General bibliography 155
Z7753 Theology and religion — Periodicals. Directories. Yearbooks 155
Z7757 Theology and religion — By region or country, A-Z 156
Z7763 Theology and religion — Angels 156
Z7776.6 Theology and religion — Christianity and culture 157
Z7776.68 Theology and religion — Christianity and the arts 157
Z7776.7 Theology and religion — Church 157
Z7776.72 Theology and religion — Church and state. Religion and state 157

Z7782 Theology and religion — City churches . 157
Z7785 Theology and religion — Emotions 157
Z7786 Theology and religion — End of the world 157
Z7794 Theology and religion — Future life 157
Z7798 Theology and religion — Glossolalia 157
Z7799.3 Theology and religion — Holy Spirit ... 158
Z7809 Theology and religion — Liberation theology 158
Z7813 Theology and religion — Liturgy. Prayer books 158
Z7819 Theology and religion — Mysticism (Theology) 158
Z7830 Theology and religion — Reformation and Counter-Reformation 158
Z7831 Theology and religion — Religion and sociology 158
Z7836.7 Theology and religion — Revivals 159
Z7845 Theology and religion — Sects, churches, movements, heresies (Christian), A-Z 159
Z7845.1 Theology and religion — Christian unity 160
Z7849 Theology and religion — Sunday schools. Religious education in secular schools 160
Z7850 Theology and religion — Theodicy 160
Z7882 Tobacco. Smoking 160
Z7911-7914 Useful arts and applied science. Technology 160
Z7961-7964 Women 160
Z7991 Zoology — General bibliography 162
Z8015.6-8992 Personal bibliography 162
Z8015.6 A — Adams, John 162
Z8015.7 A — Adams, John Q. 162
Z8015.87 A — Addison, Joseph 163
Z8025.6 A — Alexander, Lloyd 163
Z8045 A — Arthur, King 163
Z8045.59 A — Asimov, Isaac 163
Z8047.7 A — Augustinus, Aurelius, Saint, bp. of Hippo 163
Z8048 A — Austen, Jane 163
Z8068.78 B — Balfour, Arthur 163
Z8069.2 B — Balzac, Honoré de 163
Z8086.37 B — Beckett, Samuel 163
Z8089.12 B — Benchley, Robert 163
Z8102.23 B — Blackwood, Algernon 163
Z8106 B — Boccaccio, Giovanni 163
Z8106.3 B — Boethius 163
Z8109.16 B — Boorstin, D.J. 163
Z8110.2 B — Boswell, James 164
Z8113.6 B — Bradstreet, Annie 164
Z8115.66 B — Braque, Georges 164
Z8119.2 B — Bridges, R.S. 164
Z8124.4 B — Browning, Elizabeth (Barrett) 164
Z8129.8 B — Buero Vallejo, Antonio 164
Z8131.65 B — Burchfield, Charles 164
Z8136.15 B — Burroughs, E.R. 164
Z8136.17 B — Burroughs, W.S. 164
Z8139 B — Byron, G.G.N. Byron, 6th baron 164
Z8140.62 C — Calhoun, J.C. (John Caldwell) ... 164
Z8164 C — Chaucer 164
Z8167.47 C — Chisholm, Shirley 165
Z8169.45 C — Churchill, Sir, W.L.S. 165
Z8176.45 C — Cleveland, Grover 165
Z8187 C — Columbus 165

Z8015.6-8992 Personal bibliography *(cont.)*

Z8189.7 C — Conrad, Joseph 165
Z8191.7 C — Cooper, J.F. 165
Z8196.6 C — Coward, Noel 165
Z8206.58 C — Curzon, G.N. 165
Z8212.7 D — Dalton, John 166
Z8218.7 D — Davie, Donald 166
Z8220.9 D — Dee, John 166
Z8221 D — Defoe, Daniel 166
Z8228 D — Dewey, John 166
Z8230 D — Dickens, Charles 166
Z8237 D — Donne, John 166
Z8237.9 D — Dostoevskii, F.M. 166
Z8246 D — Dürer, Albrecht 166
Z8250.3 D — Duras, Marguerite 166
Z8250.54 D — Durrell, Lawrence 167
Z8254.74 E — Eden, Anthony 167
Z8255.5 E — Edwards, Jonathan 167
Z8259 E — Eliot, George, pseud 167
Z8260.5 E — Eliot, T.S. 167
Z8308.34 F — Ford, Gerald 167
Z8309.4 F — Forsyth, P.T. 167
Z8313 F — Franklin, Benjamin 167
Z8317.15 F — Friel, Brian 167
Z8318.22 F — Fulbright, James William 167
Z8322.7 G — Gandhi, M.K. 167
Z8324.18 G — Garfield, J.A. 167
Z8324.34 G — Garland, Hamlin 167
Z8328.3 G — Gauguin, Paul 167
Z8342.5 G — Ginsberg, Allen 167
Z8369.253 G — Grenville, George 168
Z8374.6478 G — Guillaume, de Lorris 168
Z8386.2 H — Harding, W.G. 168
Z8386.5 H — Hardy, Thomas 168
Z8387.97 H — Harrison, W.H. 168
Z8388.65 H — Harte, Bret 168
Z8393 H — Hawthorne, Nathaniel 168
Z8393.6 H — Heaney, Seamus 168
Z8396.3 H — Hemingway, Ernest 168
Z8409.6 H — Hitler, Adolf 168
Z8414 H — Holbein, Hans, the younger 168
Z8423.3 H — Hughes, Langston 169
Z8428.66 H — Hurston, Z.N. 169
Z8442.65 I — Ivanov, V.I. 169
Z8443 J — Jackson, Andrew 169
Z8447 J — James, Henry 169
Z8451 J — Jeanne d'Arc, Saint 169
Z8455 J — Jesus Christ 169
Z8455.567 J — Johnson, Andrew 169
Z8455.8 J — Johnson, Samuel, 1709-1784 169
Z8456.6 J — Jonson, Ben 169
Z8460.875 K — Kavanagh, Patrick 169
Z8462.8 K — Kennedy, J.F. 170
Z8464.44 K — King, M.L. 170
Z8467.523 K — Kosinski, J.N. 170
Z8490.5 L — Lawrence, D.H. 170
Z8491.5 L — Lawrence, T.E. 170
Z8492.7 L — Le Fanu, J.S. 170
Z8505 L — Lincoln, Abraham 170
Z8511.8 L — Lispector, Clarice 170
Z8534 M — Machiavelli, Niccolò 170
Z8545.5 M — Malory, Sir Thomas 170
Z8545.8 M — Malraux, André 170
Z8547.41 M — Mann, Thomas 170

Z8548.3 M — Mao, T^se-tung 170
Z8549.8 M — March, William 171
Z8550.4 M — Marlowe, Christopher 171
Z8554.32 M — Matisse 171
Z8561.18 M — McKinley, William 171
Z8562.58 M — Melville, Herman 171
Z8563.5 M — Mencken, H.L. 171
Z8572.4 M — Michener, James A. 171
Z8578 M — Milton, John 171
Z8587.8 M — Monroe, James 171
Z8591.3 M — Montgomery of Alamein, B.L.M. 172
Z8592.6 M — Moore, George 172
Z8592.8 M — More, Sir Thomas, Saint 172
Z8610.37 N — Naipaul, V.S.
(Viviadha Surajprasad) 172
Z8614.74 N — Nasser, G.A. 172
Z8628.85 N — Nietsche, F.W. 172
Z8629.4 N — Nixon, R.M. 172
Z8641.13 O — Odets, Clifford 172
Z8644.5 O — O'Neill, E.G. 172
Z8648.43 O — Oud, J.J.P. 172
Z8662.35 P — Pasternak, B.L. 172
Z8667.8 P — Peel, Robert, Sir 172
Z8685.6 P — Piaget, Jean 172
Z8693.7 P — Pisan, Christine de 172
Z8694.5 P — Pitt, William 173
Z8699 P — Poe, E.A. 173
Z8718 P — Pushkin, A.S. 173
Z8722.3 P — Pythagoras 173
Z8730 R — Rabelais, François 173
Z8730.335 R — Radcliffe, Ann 173
Z8748.37 R — Robinson, E.A. 173
Z8757.27 R — Roosevelt, Eleanor 173
Z8763.67 R — Rowse, A.L. 173
Z8764.8 R — Rush, Benjamin 173
Z8784.43 S — Sarton, May 173
Z8802 S — Scott, Sir Walter 173
Z8809.6 S — Shaffer, Peter 174
Z8814.5 S — Shaw, G.B. 175
Z8819.125 S — Sillitoe, Alan 175
Z8822.32 S — Smith, Stevie 175
Z8830.8 S — Spenser, Edmund 175
Z8831 S — Spinoza, Benedictus de 175
Z8839.4 S — Steinbeck, John 175
Z8842.7 S — Stevens, Wallace 175
Z8847 S — Stirling-Maxwell, Sir William bart ..176
Z8854.4 S — Sun, Yat-sen 176
Z8857.6 S — Symons, Arthur 176
Z8857.88 T — Taft, W.H. 176
Z8858.5 T — Talleyrand-Périgord,
Charles Maurice de, prince de Bénévent 176
Z8862.7 T — Taylor, P.H. 176
Z8866 T — Tennyson, Alfred Tennyson, baron 176
Z8885.48 T — Trilling, Lionel 176
Z8888.9 T — Truman, Harry 176
Z8896 T — Tyler, John 176
Z8913.85 U — Updike, John 176
Z8941.7 V — Vicente, Gil 176
Z8946.82 V — Vygotskii, L.S. 176
Z8957 W — Weber, Max 177
Z8963.8 W — Wellington, A.W., Duke of 177
Z8969.2 W — Wharton, E.N. (Jones) 177
Z8971.5 W — Whitman, Walt 177
Z8975.7 W — Wilder, T.N. 177

Z8015.6-8992 Personal bibliography *(cont.)*
Z8976.424 W — Williams, Tennessee 177
Z8976.485 W — Wilson, Angus 177
Z8976.9 W — Wilson, Woodrow 177
Z8977.35 W — Windham, Donald 177
Z8978.66 W — Wirth, Louis 177
Z8979.4 W — Wittgenstein, Ludwig 177
Z8980.45 W — Wolfe, Thomas 177
Z8983.4 W — Woodson, C.G. 177
Z8984.2 W — Woolf, Virginia 178
Z8986.323 W — Wright, Richard 178
Z8989.7 X — X, Malcolm 178
Z8989.73 X — Xenophon 178
Z8992 Y — Yeats, W.B. 178

ZA Information resources (General) 178
ZA3075 Research. How to find information —
General works 178
ZA3157 Information services. Information
centers — General works 178
ZA3225 Information superhighway —
General works 178
ZA3250 Information superhighway —
By region or country, A-Z 178
Author Index to Volumes 1-10.................................... 183
Subject Guide to LC Classification Schedule 447

Introduction

ABOUT THE PROJECT:

The Best Books for Academic Libraries was created to fill a need that has been growing in collection development for undergraduate and college libraries since the late 1980's. Our editorial department organized *The Best Books Database* (designed as a resource for university libraries) by consulting the leading book review journals, bibliographies, and reference books with subject bibliographies. It was compiled based upon the bibliographic standard from the Library of Congress (LC) MARC records. Each section was arranged by Library of Congress Classification Number.

PROCESSES FOR SUBJECT SELECTION AND COMPILATION:

To create *The Best Books for Academic Libraries,* the Editor conducted a comprehensive search of prominent Subject Librarians and Subject Specialists, experts in their area(s), to participate as Subject Advisors. The editorial processes utilized by The Best Books editorial staff are as follows:

1. Subject Advisors were asked to select the best books recommended for undergraduate and college libraries. Those who volunteered selected approximately one-third from over 170,000 books in *The Best Books Database* that they felt were essential to undergraduate work in their area(s) of expertise. Each Subject Advisor made their selections from subject surveys that were arranged by LC Classification Number. They added their choices of titles that were omitted from the surveys, and updated titles to the latest editions.

2. The Best Books editorial staff tabulated the returned surveys, and added the omissions into the database, following the LC MARC record standard, to arrive at a consensus of approximately the best 80,000 books.

3. Senior Subject Advisors were selected to conduct a final review of the surveys. They added any other titles they felt were essential to undergraduate work in their area(s) of expertise.

4. The final results were tabulated to create the First Edition of the 10 Volume set – *The Best Books for Academic Libraries.*

The actual title selection was left to the Subject Advisors. Each Advisor used the bibliographic resources available to them in their subject areas to make the best possible recommendations for undergraduate and college libraries. In order to achieve results that were well rounded, two to three Subject Advisors reviewed each section.

When there were discrepancies in the LC sorting and/or the description of any titles, The Best Books editorial staff defaulted to the information available on the LC MARC records.

The intention of this project, and The Best Books editorial staff, was to include only books in this listing. However, other titles may have been included, based upon recommendations by Subject Advisors and Senior Subject Advisors. In some cases, the Advisors did select annual reviews and multi-volume sets for inclusion in this work.

The editorial department has made every attempt to list the most recent publications for each title in this work. In the interest of maintaining a current core-collection bibliographic list, our Advisors were asked to note the most recent publications available, especially with regards to series and publishers that regularly produce new editions. Books were listed as the original edition (or latest reprint) when no information of a recent publication was available.

ARRANGEMENT BY LC CLASSIFICATION SCHEDULE:

Each section of this work was arranged by Library of Congress Classification Numbers (LCCN), using the Library of Congress Classification Schedule for ready reference. For the purposes of this project, we have organized a system of varying font sizes and the incorporation of Em-dashes (—) to identify whether the subject headings herein are **primary** (Main Class), **secondary** (Sub-Class), or **tertiary** (Sub-Sub-Class) in the LC Classification Schedule outline. The primary heading is presented in 14 point Times New Roman, the secondary in 12 point, and the tertiary in 10 point. This distinction can be viewed in the examples that follow:

Primary Classification:
(14 Point Times New Roman)

P49 Addresses, essays, lectures

P49.J35 1985
Jakobson, Roman,
Verbal art, verbal sign, verbal time / Roman Jakobson; Krystyna Pomorska and Stephen Rudy, editors; with the assistance of Brent Vine. Minneapolis: University of Minnesota Press, c1985. xiv, 208 p.
84-007268 808/.00141 0816613583
Philology. Semiotics. Space and time in language.

Secondary Classification:
(12 Point Times New Roman)

P51 Study and teaching. Research — General

P51.L39 1998
Learning foreign and second languages: perspectives in research and scholarship / edited by Heidi Byrnes. New York: Modern Language Association of America, 1998. viii, 322 p.
98-039497 418/.007 087352800X
Language and languages -- Study and teaching. Second language acquisition.

Tertiary Classification:
(10 Point Times New Roman)

P92 Communication. Mass media — By region or country — Individual regions or countries, A-Z

P92.C5.C52 2000
Chinese perspectives in rhetoric and communication / edited by D. Ray Heisey. Stamford, Conn.: Ablex Pub. Corp., 2000. xx, 297 p.
99-053426 302.2/0951 1567504949
Communication and culture -- China. Rhetoric -- Political aspects -- China.

ERRORS, LACUNAE, AND OMISSIONS:

The Subject Advisors and Senior Subject Advisors were the sole source for recommending titles to include in the completed work, and no titles were intentionally added or omitted other than those that the Subject Advisors and Senior Subject Advisors recommended. There is no expressed or implied warranty or guarantee on this product.

The Best Books editorial department requests that any suggestions or errors be sent, via e-mail or regular mail, to be corrected in future editions of this project.

BEST BOOKS EDITORIAL STAFF:

This work is the ongoing product and group effort of a number of enthusiastic individuals: The Best Books editorial staff includes: Assistant Editor, Annette Wiles; Database Administrator, Richelle Tague; and Editor, Ashley Ludwig.

NOTE:

The Best Books for Academic Libraries – Volume 10 includes a Subject Guide based upon the LC Classification Schedule. The Subject Guide is derived from the Table of Contents of each volume, and includes the volume number in which each subject area can be located.

Please use the CD-ROM of *The Best Books for Academic Libraries – Volumes 1-10* to search for titles by Author, Title, Publisher, Publication Date, ISBN, LC Classification No., LC Card No. or Subject keywords.

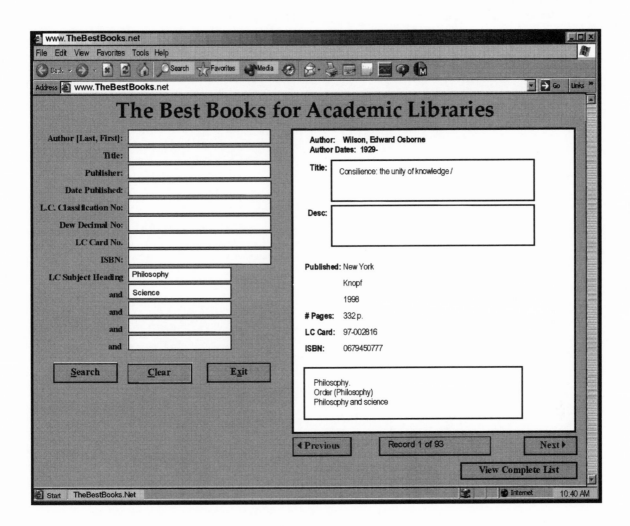

Additional CD-ROMs may be obtained at no charge by E-mailing: customerservice@thebbooks.net

DATABASE COMPARISON PROJECT:

To digitally compare your library's database to *The Best Books for Academic Libraries Database*, please see further information on our Web site: www.bestbooksfor.com.

COMPANION SERIES – *THE BEST REFERENCE BOOKS*:

For a more comprehensive listing of Reference Titles in ALL subject areas of the LC Classification Schedule (from A – General Works – through – Z – Library Science), please consult our companion series *The Best Reference Books* – 5 Volumes & CD-ROM.

Visit our Web site: www.bestbooksfor.com for more detailed information on this publication.

CONTRIBUTING ADVISORS:

This volume would not be possible without the dedicated work of our Subject Advisors and Senior Subject Advisors who donated their time, resources and knowledge towards creating this Best Books list. To them, we are truly grateful. *(Denotes Senior Subject Advisors for *Volume 10 – General Works, Military, Naval & Library Science*.)

SUBJECT ADVISORS:

Robert Behlke, *Librarian, SiTanka/Huron University - Huron Branch*
Subject Advisor for: A – General Works, U – Military Science, V – Naval Science
 Z – Library Science

Angela Camack, *Assistant Professor/Librarian, Sussex County Community College*
Subject Advisor for: A – General Works, Z – Library Science

Rebecca Johnson,* *Head, Research & Information Services, University of Iowa Libraries*
Subject Advisor for: A – General Works, Z – Library Science

Barbara Macke,* *Director of Library Services, Swedenborg Memorial Library, Urbana University*
Subject Advisor for: A – General Works, Z – Library Science

Amy Schisler, *Reference & Instructional Librarian, Chesapeake College Library, Chesapeake College*
Subject Advisor for: A – General Works, U – Military Science, V – Naval Science
 Z – Library Science

Wendy Swik, *Reference Librarian, United States Military Academy Library, West Pointe, New York**
**Any opinion of Wendy Swik's is her own, and not that of the Military Academy or the United States Government.*
Subject Advisor for: U – Military Science, V – Naval Science

Cynthia Tsick, *Social Sciences Librarian, University at Buffalo, State University of New York*
Subject Advisor for: A – General Works, Z – Library Science

Steven Vincent,* *Head of Reference, Librarian/Associate Professor, Southern Polytechnic State University, Marietta, Georgia*
Subject Advisor for: A – General Works, Z - Reference

Julienne L. Wood, *Head, Research Services, Noel Memorial Library, Louisiana State University, Shreveport, Louisiana*
Subject Advisor for: A – General Works, Z - Reference

SENIOR SUBJECT ADVISORS:

Rebecca Johnson, * *Head, Research & Information Services, University of Iowa Libraries.* Rebecca Johnson earned her Masters in Library Science from the University of Washington in Seattle. She currently is serving as the Head of the Research and Information Services Department at the University of Iowa. Previously, she has served as Team Leader for Information Services and Head of Media Services, and Reference Librarian at the University of Iowa Library. She also served as the Acting Head of the Business Library. Ms. Johnson is the subject selector for Education at the University of Iowa Library. Ms. Johnson is currently serving on: The Collection Management Committee, the InfoHawk Management Advisory Committee, the OPAC Committee, the Virtual Reference Working Group, and the NAAUG 2003 Annual Conference Program Planning Committee; she serves as Chairperson on the Public Relations Advisory Committee. Ms. Johnson belongs to many professional organizations and has delivered several presentations at the ILA/LAMA, the LAMA/COLAthe ALA, ILA/ACRL Conference, the EDUCAUSE Conference, and the Tech Connections 2 Conference. She has contributed to and written multiple articles for such publications as *Research Strategies,* and *Library Issues*.

Senior Subject Advisor for: A, Z – General Works & Library Science

Barbara M. Macke, *Director of Library Services, Swedenborg Memorial Library, Urbana University, Urbana, Ohio.* Barbara M. Macke earned her Masters Degree in French from the College of Mount St. Joseph in Cincinnati, Ohio. She has also earned her Masters of Library Science from Kent State University, and her Masters of Pubic Administration from the University of Dayton in Dayton, Ohio. Currently, Ms. Macke is serving as the Director of Library Services at Urbana University. She has worked as a Corporate Librarian at The Mead Corporation, and as a Science and Engineering Librarian at the Air Force Institute of Technology. Ms. Macke's other positions have included working as an Assistant Branch Manager and Children's Librarian at the Dayton & Montgomery County Public Library, where she has also served as Business & Science Reference Librarian and Cataloger.

Senior Subject Advisor for: A, Z – General Works & Library Science

Steven Vincent, * *Head of Reference, Librarian/Associate Professor, Southern Polytechnic State University, Marietta, Georgia.* Steven Vincent earned his Masters in Medieval Studies, and his M.S. Librarianship Degree from Western Michigan University. He is currently serving as the Head of Reference, Librarian, and Associate Professor at Southern Polytechnic State University at Marietta, Georgia. Previously, he served as a Librarian and Assistant Professor at Dickinson College in Carlisle, Pennsylvania, and as a Reference Librarian and Assistant Professor at Georgia State University. Mr. Vincent has long been a member of the American Library Association, as well as a member of Beta Phi Mu, Professional Librarian Honor Society. He has also been associated with the Atlanta Area Bibliographic Instruction Group. Steven's professional contributions include serving on the OPAC Committee for the University System Integrated Interconnected Library System, the Interlibrary Loan Subcommittee, as well as the University Center in Georgia/Atlanta Regional Consortium for Higher Education Interlibrary Loan Committee. He has contributed to workshops and seminars, and has been a presenter at the American Library Association Annual Conference, and the International Congress on Medieval Studies. He has published for *Foundations in Library and Information Science* and *Reference Services Review*.

Senior Subject Advisor for: A, Z – General Works & Library Science

AC Collections. Series. Collected works

AC1 Collections of monographs, essays, etc. — American and English — Comprehensive collections

AC1.A4 vol. 50
The editor's introduction; reader's guide; index to the first lines of poems, songs & choruses, hymns and psalms; general index; chornological index, with a photogravure frontispiece. New York, P. F. Collier & son [c1910] 470 p.
11-000513

AC1.G7
Great books of the Western World. Encyclopaedia Britannica, inc., in collaboration with the University of Chicago. [Robert Maynard Hutchins, editor in chief. Chicago] W. Benton [1952] 54 v.
52-002133   082
Literature -- Collections. Literature -- Indexes.

AC1.G72 1990 vol. 39
Kant, Immanuel, 1724-1804.
The critique of pure reason; The critique of practical reason, and other ethical treatises; The critique of judgement/ Immanuel Kant. Chicago: Encyclopaedia Britannica, Inc., c1990. xi, 613 p.
90-222483   081
Knowledge, Theory of -- Early works to 1800. Causation -- Early works to 1800. Reason -- Early works to 1800.

AC1.H5
Eliot, Charles W.,
The Harvard classics. N.Y. [c1909-10] 50 v.
82-038409

AC5 Collections of monographs, essays, etc. — American and English — Minor collections

AC5.J68
Ideas in cultural perspective. Edited by Philip P. Wiener and Aaron Noland. New Brunswick, N.J., Rutgers University Press [1962] 759 p.
62-013766   082
Idea (Philosophy) -- History. Intellectual life -- History.

AC8 Collections of monographs, essays, etc. — American and English — Collected works of individual authors

AC8.A22 1958
Adams, Henry, 1838-1918.
A Henry Adams reader. Edited and with an introd. by Elizabeth Stevenson. Garden City, N. Y., Doubleday, 1958. xviii, 381 p.
58-005929   081

AC8.B732 1975
Buckley, William F. 1925-
Execution eve, and other contemporary ballads/ William F. Buckley, Jr. New York: Putnam, [1975] 512 p.
75-017593   973.924   0399115315

AC8.H97 1956
Huxley, Aldous Leonard.
Tomorrow and tomorrow and tomorrow, and other essays. Harper, 1956.
56-008754   824.91
Essays.

AC8.R76
Russell, Bertrand, 1872-1970.
Selected papers of Bertrand Russell, selected and with a special introd. by Bertrand Russell. New York, The Modern library [c1927] 390 p.
27-023335

AC8.S662 1977
Spencer, Herbert, 1820-1903.
Essays on education and kindred subjects/ Herbert Spencer; intord. by Charles W. Eliot. New York: AMS Press, 1977. xxi, 330 p.
75-041261   081   0404146070

AC25-35 Collections of monographs, essays, etc. — Other languages — Modern languages

AC25.D4213 1987
Deleuze, Gilles.
Dialogues/ Gilles Deleuze and Claire Parnet; translated by Hugh Tomlinson and Barbara Habberjam. New York: Columbia University Press, 1987. xiii, 157 p.
87-005199   084/.1   0231066007
Deleuze, Gilles -- Interviews.

AC25.D45513
Derrida, Jacques.
Dissemination/ Jacques Derrida; translated, with an introduction and additional notes, by Barbara Johnson. Chicago: University Press, 1981. xxxiii, 366 p.
81-003359   808/.00141 19   0226143279

AC35.K64613 1995
Kracauer, Siegfried, 1889-1966.
The mass ornament: Weimar essays/ Siegfried Kracauer; translated, edited, and with an introduction by Thomas Y. Levin. Cambridge, Mass.: Harvard University Press, 1995. xi, 403 p.
94-047397   081 20   0674551621

AE Encyclopedias

AE1 History, method of use, etc.

AE1.E48 1995
Encyclopedias, atlases & dictionaries/ Marion Sader, Amy Lewis, editors; Charles A. Bunge ...[et al.], consultants. New Providence, N.J.: R.R. Bowker, c1995. xvi, 495 p.
95-006195   031   0835236692
Encyclopedias and dictionaries -- History and criticism. Atlases -- History.

AE2 Encyclopedic works — Early works — To end of middle ages (1450/1515)

AE2.H83 1991
Hugh, of St. Victor
The didascalicon of Hugh of St. Victor: a medieval guide to the arts / translated from the Latin with an introduction and notes by Jerome Taylor. New York: Columbia University Press, c1991. xii, 254 p.
91-006828   189/.4 20   0231024444
Arts, Medieval -- Early works to 1800.

AE5 Encyclopedic works — Modern encyclopedias. By language — American and English

AE5.A23 1998
Academic American encyclopedia. Danbury, Conn.: Grolier Inc., c1998. 21 v.
97-041903   031 21   0717220680
Encyclopedias and dictionaries.

AE5.A55
The Americana annual; an encyclopedia of current events. New York, Americana corporation [etc.]
23-010041   031
Encyclopedias and dictionaries.

AE5.E333 2003
Encyclopedia Americana. International ed. Danbury, Conn.: Grolier, c2003. 30 v.
2002-033910   031 21   0717201368
Encyclopedias and dictionaries.

AE5.E363 2002
The New Encyclopaedia Britannica. 15th ed. Chicago: Encyclopaedia Britannica, c2002. 32 v.
2001-089897   031 21   0852297874
Encyclopedias and dictionaries.

AE5.E399
The Encyclopaedia britannica; a dictionary of arts, sciences, literature and general information. New York, The Encyclopaedia Britannica Company, 1910-11. 29 v.
16-000592
Encyclopedias and dictionaries.

AE5.G68
Great Soviet encyclopedia. [A. M. Prokhorov, editor in chief]. New York, Macmillan [c1973-] v. <1-31 >
73-010680   037/.1
Encyclopedias and dictionaries.

AE5.O94 1985
Oxford illustrated encyclopedia/ general editor, Harry Judge; executive editor, Anthony Toyne. Oxford [England]; Oxford University Press, 1985-1993. v. <1-6, 8-9 >
85-004876   032 19   0198691297
Encyclopedias and dictionaries.

AE5.W55 2004
The World Book encyclopedia. Chicago: World Book, Inc., c2004.
2003-010760   031 21   0716601044
Encyclopedias and dictionaries. Encyclopedias and dictionaries.

AE25 Encyclopedic works — Modern encyclopedias. By language — French

AE25.E3 1996
Encyclopaedia universalis. Paris: Encyclopaedia Universalis, c1996. 23 v.
98-155834   034/.1 21
Encyclopedias and dictionaries, French.

AE25.E523
Encyclopedia; selections [by] Diderot, D'Alembert and a society of men of letters. Translated, with an introduction and notes by Nelly S. Hoyt [and] Thomas Cassirer. Indianapolis, Bobbs-Merrill [1965] 400 p.
65-026535

AE25.G64
Grand Larousse encyclopedique en dix volumes. Paris: Librairie Larousse, [1960-   ] 10 v.
60-050563
Encyclopedias and dictionaries, French. French language -- Non-fiction.

AE27 Encyclopedic works — Modern encyclopedias. By language — German

AE27.B922 1986
Brockhaus Enzyklopädie: in vierundzwanzig Bänden. 19. völlig neu bearbeitete Aufl. Mannheim: F.A. Brockhaus, c1986-<1996   > v. <1-30 >
95-213728   033/.1 20   3765311316
Encyclopedias and dictionaries, German.

AE27.G672
Brockhaus Enzyklopadie in zwanzig Banden. Siebzehnte vollig neu bearb. Aufl. des Grossen Brockhaus. Wiesbaden: Brockhaus, [1966-   ] 25 v.
66-068667   033.1   3765303224
Encyclopedias and dictionaries, German.

AE31 Encyclopedic works — Modern encyclopedias. By language — Hungarian

AE31.B75 1994
Britannica Hungarica: vilagenciklopedia/ foszerkeszto, Robert McHenry ;[vezeto szerkesztok, Arokszallasi Eva ... et al.; forditok, Almarne Illes Erzsebet ... et al.; munkatarsak, Dioszeghy Gyozone ... et al.]. Budapest: Magyar Vilag, 1994-c1998 v. 1-13
95-184148   9637815805
Encyclopedias and dictionaries, Hungarian.

AE35 Encyclopedic works — Modern encyclopedias. By language — Italian

AE35.G7 1984
Grande dizionario enciclopedico UTET/ fondato da Pietro Fedele. 4a ed. Torino: UTET, c1984-c1993. 21 v. :
87-212649   035/.1 19   8802047456
Encyclopedias and dictionaries, Italian.

AE61 Encyclopedic works — Modern encyclopedias. By language — Spanish

AE61.E6
Enciclopedia universal ilustrada europeo-americana: etimologias sanscrito, hebreo, griego, latin, arabe, lenguas indigenas americanas, etc.: versiones de la mayoria de las voces en frances, italia Madrid: Espasa-Calpe, [1907?]-c1930 70 v. in 72
32-001302   036/.1
Encyclopedias and dictionaries, Spanish.

AG Dictionaries and other general reference works

AG5-6 Dictionaries. Minor encyclopedias — Other — American and English

AG5.C26 2000
The Cambridge encyclopedia/ edited by David Crystal. 4th ed. Cambridge, UK; Cambridge University Press, 2000. vi, 1336 p.
2001-265698   032 21   0521790999
Encyclopedias and dictionaries.

AG5.C264 2000
The Cambridge factfinder/ edited by David Crystal. 4th ed. Cambridge, UK; Cambridge University Press, 2000. xx, 938 p.
2001-266311   032 21   0521794358
Encyclopedias and dictionaries.

AG5.C27 1985
The Canadian encyclopedia. Edmonton: Hurtig Publishers, c1985. 3 v.
84-243080   971/.00321   088830269X
Encyclopedias and dictionaries.

AG5.C725 2000
The Columbia encyclopedia/ edited by Paul Lagasse. New York: Columbia University Press; c2000. xiv, 3156 p.
00-027927   031   0787650153
Encyclopedias and dictionaries.

AG5.K315 1997
Kane, Joseph Nathan,
Famous first facts: a record of first happenings, discoveries, and inventions in American history/ Joseph Nathan Kane, Steven Anzovin & Janet Podell. 5th ed. New York: H.W. Wilson, 1997. xxix, 1122 p.
97-031252   031.02 21   0824209303
Encyclopedias and dictionaries.

AG5.M49 2000
Merriam-Webster's collegiate encyclopedia. Springfield, Mass.: Merriam-Webster, c2000. xiv, 1792 p.
00-062189   031   0877790175
Encyclopedias and dictionaries.

AG5.N76 1999
The Norton dictionary of modern thought/ edited by Alan Bullock and Stephen Trombley; assistant editor, Alf Lawrie. New York: W.W. Norton, 1999. xxiv, 933 p.
99-024581   032   0393046966
Encyclopedias and dictionaries.

AG5.R25 1990
The Random House encyclopedia/ James Mitchell, editor in chief; Jess Stein, editorial director. New York: Random House, c1990. 130 p.
90-038567   031   0394584503
Encyclopedias and dictionaries.

AG6.E87 2002
The Essential desk reference. New York: Oxford University Press, c2002. xvi, 815 p.
2003-268154   031 21   0195128737
Encyclopedias and dictionaries.

AG6.N49 2002
The New York Public Library desk reference. 4th ed. New York: Hyperion, 2002. xvi, 999 p.
2002-027480   031 21   0786868465
Encyclopedias and dictionaries.

AG105-106 General works, pocketbooks, receipts, etc. — Later — American and English

AG105.N9 1996
Numbers: how many, how far, how long, how much/ edited by Andrea Sutcliffe. New York: HarperPerennial, c1996. xxiv, 630 p.
95-052658   031.02   0062733621
Handbooks, vade-mecums, etc. Finance, Personal -- Handbooks, manuals, etc. Life skills -- Handbooks, manuals, etc.

AG105.W97 1995
A writer's companion/ edited by Louis D. Rubin, Jr., in association with Jerry Leath Mills. Baton Rouge: Louisiana State University Press, c1995. xiv, 1041 p.
95-000158   031.02   080711992X
Handbooks, vade-mecums, etc. Literary curiosa -- Handbooks, manuals, etc.

AG106.C425 2002
Chambers book of facts/ editor, Melanie Parry; with the assistance of Trevor Anderson and Una McGovern. Rev. ed. London: Chambers, 2002. xiii, 784 p.
2002-416330   032.02 21   0550100571
Handbooks, vade-mecums, etc.

AG243 Wonders. Curiosities. Eccentric characters, fads, etc. — 1871-

AG243.G87
Guinness world records.   [England]: Guinness World Records, Ltd., [c2000-   ]
99-047878
World records--Periodicals.

AG243.K53 1994
Visual encyclopedia of science.   New York: Kingfisher Books, 1994. 320 p.
93-043118   031.02   1856979989
Curiosities and wonders -- Juvenile literature. Curiosities and wonders.

AG250 Pictorial works (Views, events, etc.)

AG250.C65 1991
Corbeil, Jean Claude.
The Facts on File English/Spanish visual dictionary: look up the word from the picture, find the picture from the word/ Jean-Claude Corbeil, Ariane Archambault. New York: Facts on File, c1992. 924 p.
90-037183   036/.1   0816015465
Picture dictionaries, Spanish. Spanish language -- Vocabulary. Vocabulary.

AI Indexes

AI3 By language of index — English

AI3.B3 1978
Baer, Eleanora A.
Titles in series: a handbook for librarians and students/ Eleanora A. Baer. Metuchen, N.J.: Scarecrow Press, 1978. 4 v.
78-014452   011   0810810433
Indexes.

AI3.B7
British humanities index.   London, The Library Association.
63-024940   011/.34
Periodicals -- Indexes.

AI3.C32
The Catholic periodical and literature index. Haverford, Pa., Catholic Library Association.
70-649588   011
Periodicals -- Indexes. Catholic literature -- Bio-bibliography.

AI3.E752
Essay and general literature index.   New York, H.W. Wilson Co.   v.
34-014581   016
Literature -- Indexes. Essays -- Indexes. Essais (Genre littéraire) -- Index. Littérature -- Index.

AI3.H85
Humanities index.   [New York] H.W. Wilson Co.
75-648836   016.0013
Periodicals -- Indexes. Humanities -- Periodicals -- Indexes.

AI3.I48
Index to Commonwealth little magazines.   Troy, N.Y. [etc.] Whitston Pub. Co. [etc.]
66-028796   051
English periodicals -- Indexes.

AI3.I54
Index to American little magazines.   Troy, N.Y. [etc.] Whiston Pub. Co. [etc.] [n.d.]
77-097476
Periodicals -- Indexes. [from old catalog]

AI3.R48
Readers' guide to periodical literature. Minneapolis: H.W. Wilson Co., 1905- v. :
06-008232   051
Periodicals -- Indexes -- Periodicals.

AI3.R49
Social sciences & humanities index.   New York: H.W. Wilson, 1966-1974. 9 v.
17-004969
Humanities -- indexes. Periodicals -- indexes. Social Sciences -- indexes.

AI3.R496
Nineteenth Century reader's guide to periodical literature. New York: H.W. Wilson Co.,
44-005439
American periodicals -- Indexes -- Periodicals.

AI3.S62
Social sciences index.   New York, H.W. Wilson Co.
75-649443   016.3
Periodicals -- Indexes. Social sciences -- Periodicals -- Indexes. Periodicals -- indexes.

AI3.S85 1966 suppl.
Sutton, Roberta Briggs.
Speech index: an index to collections of world famous orations and speeches for various occasions: fourth edition supplement/ by Roberta Briggs Sutton and Charity Mitchell. Metuchen, N.J.: Scarecrow Press, 1972-1977. 2 v.
66-013749   016.80885   0810804980
Speeches, addresses, etc. -- Indexes.

AI21 Indexes to individual newspapers, A-Z

AI21.N45
The New York times index.   New York, New York Times Co.
13-013458   071/.47/1
Newspapers -- Indexes.

AM Museums. Collectors and collecting

AM1 Periodicals, societies, collections, etc.

AM1.M76 2001
Museums of the world/ [editor, Michael Zils]. 8th rev. and enl. ed. München: K.G. Saur, 2001. 2 v. :
2002-506840   069/.025 21   3598206070
Museums -- Directories.

AM3.6 Biography — Individual, A-Z

AM3.6.B73
Allen, Louise Anderson, 1949-
A bluestocking in Charleston: the life and career of Laura Bragg/ Louise Anderson Allen. Columbia: University of South Carolina Press, c2001. xv, 303 p.
00-011817   069/.2/092   1570033706
Bragg, Laura M. -- (Laura Mary), -- 1881-1978. Women museum directors -- South Carolina -- Charleston -- Biography. Women museum directors -- Massachusetts -- Pittsfield -- Biography. Women -- South Carolina -- Charleston -- Biography. Charleston (S.C.) -- Biography.

AM5 General works — 1801-

AM5.W66 1994
Woodhead, Peter.
Keyguide to information sources in museum studies/ Peter Woodhead and Geoffrey Stansfield. 2nd ed. London; Mansell, 1994.
93-037246   0720121515
Museums -- Management. Museums -- Information services. Museum publications -- Bibliography.

AM7 General special

AM7.D34 1994
Danilov, Victor J.
Museum careers and training: a professional guide/ Victor J. Danilov. Westport, Conn.: Greenwood Press, 1994. xi, 546 p.
93-033518   069/.023/73   031328105X
Museums -- Vocational guidance -- United States. Museums -- Employees -- Training of -- United States. Museum techniques -- Study and teaching (Higher) -- United States.

AM7.H44 1998
Hein, George E., 1932-
Learning in the museum/ George E. Hein. London; Routledge, 1998. xi, 203 p.
97-026899   069   0415097754
Museums -- Educational aspects. Constructivism (Education)

AM7.M355 1999
Maleuvre, Didier.
Museum memories: history, technology, art/ Didier Maleuvre. Stanford, Calif.: Stanford University Press, 1999. xii, 325 p.
98-035055   069/.5   0804732027
Museums -- Historiography. Historical museums -- History. Historiography -- History.

AM7.W392 1995
Weil, Stephen E.
A cabinet of curiosities: inquiries into museums and their prospects/ Stephen E. Weil. Washington: Smithsonian Institution Press, c1995. xxii, 264 p.
94-030993   069.5   1560985119
Museums -- Management. Art museums -- Management. Museum finance -- Evaluation.

AM10-13 Description and history of museums — By country — America

AM10.A2.O4
The Official museum directory. Washington, D.C.: American Association of Museums,
79-144808   069/.025/1
Museums -- North America -- Directories. Museums -- Canada -- Directories. Museums -- United States -- Directories.

AM11.C64 1998
Conn, Steven.
Museums and American intellectual life, 1876-1926/ Steven Conn. Chicago: The University of Chicago Press, c1998. 305 p.
98-016850   069/.0973   0226114929
Museums -- United States -- History.United States -- Intellectual life -- 1865-1918. United States -- Intellectual life -- 20th century. United States -- History -- 1865-1921.

AM11.D35 1996
Danilov, Victor J.
University and college museums, galleries, and related facilities: a descriptive directory/ Victor J. Danilov. Westport, Conn.: Greenwood Press, 1996. x, 692 p.
95-020544   061/.3   0313286132
Museums -- United States -- Directories. College museums -- United States -- Directories. College museums -- United States -- History.

AM11.D46 1997
Dennett, Andrea Stulman, 1958-
Weird and wonderful: the dime museum in America/ Andrea Stulman Dennett. New York: New York University Press, c1997. xiv, 200 p.
97-004880   069/.0973   081471885X
Barnum, P. T. -- (Phineas Taylor), -- 1810-1891.Curiosities and wonders -- Museums -- United States -- History. Eccentrics and eccentricity -- Museums -- United States -- History. Popular culture -- United States -- History.

AM11.M56 1992
Mermaids, mummies, and mastodons: the emergence of the American museum: [exhibition]/ edited by William T. Alderson for the Baltimore City Life Museums, Baltimore, Md. Washington, D.C.: American Association of Museums, 1992. 104 p.
92-029830   069/.0973   0931201152
Peale family. Barnum, P. T. -- (Phineas Taylor), -- 1810-1891. Museums -- United States -- History.

AM11.M8
Museums directory of the United States and Canada. Washington, American Association of Museums.
61-009712   069.0587
Museums -- United States -- Directories. Museums -- Canada -- Directories.

AM11.O76 1990
Orosz, Joel J.
Curators and culture: the museum movement in America, 1740-1870/ Joel J. Orosz. Tuscaloosa: University of Alabama Press, c1990. xii, 304 p.
89-033865   069/.0973   0817304754
Museums -- United States -- History. Museum curators -- United States -- History. Popular culture -- Museums -- United States -- History.

AM13.N5.N48 1995
New York City museum guide/ edited by Candace Ward. New York: Dover Publications, 1995. vi, 122 p.
95-014775   069/.09747/1   0486286398
Museums -- New York (State) -- New York -- Guidebooks.New York (N.Y.) -- Guidebooks.

AM40-48 Description and history of museums — By country — Europe

AM40.H83 1991
Hudson, Kenneth.
The Cambridge guide to the museums of Europe/ Kenneth Hudson and Ann Nicholls. Cambridge; Cambridge University Press, 1991. 509 p.
90-027183   069/.025/4   0521371759
Museums -- Europe -- Directories.Europe -- Guidebooks.

AM43.L6.B53 2000
Black, Barbara J., 1962-
On exhibit: Victorians and their museums/ Barbara J. Black. Charlottesville: University Press of Virginia, 2000. viii, 242 p.
99-016415   069/.09421   0813918979
Museums -- England -- London -- History -- 19th century. Literature and society -- England -- London -- History -- 19th century. Popular culture -- Great Britain -- History -- 19th century. London (England) -- Intellectual life -- 19th century. London (England) -- Civilization -- 19th century. Great Britain -- History -- Victoria, 1837-1901.

AM48.P3.K36 1996
Kaplan, Rachel.
Little-known museums in and around Paris/ by Rachel Kaplan. New York: H.N. Abrams, 1996. 216 p.
95-052781   069/.0944/36   0810926768
Museums -- France -- Paris -- Guidebooks.Paris (France) -- Guidebooks.

AM80 Description and history of museums — By country — Africa

AM80.D57 1990
Directory of museums in Africa/ Unesco-ICOM Documentation Centre; edited by Susanne Peters ... [et al.] = Repertoire des musees en Afrique/ Centre de documentation Unesco-ICOM; redige par Susan Peters ... [et al.]. London; Kegan Paul International, 1990.
90-004236   069/.025/6   0710303785
Museums -- Africa -- Directories.

AM101 Description and history of museums — Individual museums. By place, A-Z

AM101.P496.S44
Sellers, Charles Coleman, 1903-
Mr. Peale's Museum: Charles Willson Peale and the first popular museum of natural science and art/ Charles Coleman Sellers. New York: Norton, 1980. xiv, 370 p.
80-015395   069/.09748/11   0393057003
Peale, Charles Willson, -- 1741-1827. Peale family. Museum directors -- United States -- Biography.

AM151 Museology. Museum methods, technique, etc. — The collections — Exhibition

AM151.E94 1991
Exhibiting cultures: the poetics and politics of museum display/ edited by Ivan Karp and Steven D. Lavine. Washington: Smithsonian Institution Press, c1991. x, 468 p.
90-010188   069/.5   1560980206
Exhibitions -- Evaluation -- Congresses. Museum techniques -- Evaluation -- Congresses. Museums -- Public relations -- Congresses.

AM160 Museology. Museum methods, technique, etc. — Service to special groups — Handicapped

AM160.A27 1992
The Accessible museum: model programs of accessibility for disabled and older people. Washington, D.C.: American Association of Museums, c1992. 184 p.
92-029831   069/.17/0973   0931201160
Museums -- United States -- Access for the physically handicapped. Museums and the handicapped -- United States.

AS Academies and learned societies

AS2 Serial directories. Serial handbooks

AS2.W6
The World of learning. London: Allen & Unwin, [1947-]
47-030172   060.25
Learned institutions and societies -- Directories. Academies and Institutes -- directories. Societies -- directories.

AS2.5 International associations, congresses, conferences, etc. — General works

AS2.5.Y4
Encyclopedia of world problems and human potential/ edited by Union of International Associations. Munchen; K.G. Saur, [c1986-]
92-656037   050
International agencies -- Periodicals. Social problems -- Periodicals. Civilization, Modern -- 20th century -- Periodicals.

AS8 Directories and lists

AS8.A93
Awards, honors, and prizes. Detroit: Gale Research Co., [1969-]
84-643350   001.4/4 19
Awards -- United States -- Directories. Awards -- Canada -- Directories. Awards -- Directories. Awards and Prizes -- Directories. Reference Books, Medical. Prix et récompenses -- Répertoires.

AS8.B8 1960a
Buttress, F. A.
World list of abbreviations of scientific, technological and commerical organizations. London, L. Hill, 1960. 300 p.
60-002449
Abbreviations. Associations, institutions, etc. -- abbreviations.

AS8.I637 1993
International encyclopedia of learned societies and academies/ edited by Joseph C. Kiger. Westport, Conn.: Greenwood Press, 1993. xiii, 377 p.
92-035598   060/.3   0313276463
Learned institutions and societies -- Encyclopedias. Research institutes -- Encyclopedias. Associations, institutions, etc. -- Encyclopedias.

AS8.P58 1997
Pitman, L. M.
Buttress's world guide to abbreviations of organizations. 11th ed. / rev. by L.M. Pitman. London; Blackie Academic & Professional; 1149 p.
96-086429   060/.1/48 21   0751402613
Associations, institutions, etc. -- Abbreviations.

AS8.W38
Wasserman, Paul.
Awards, honors, and prizes; a directory and source book. Managing editor: Paul Wasserman; assistant editor: Janice W. McLean. Detroit, Gale Research Co., 1969. vii, 307 p.
71-084903   001.4/4
Awards -- United States. Awards -- Canada. Awards and Prizes

AS22-36 By region or country — America — United States

AS22.E53
Encyclopedia of associations. Detroit, Mich.: Gale Research Co., [c1987-]
87-640488   061/.3
Associations, institutions, etc. -- United States -- Directories. Nonprofit organizations -- United States -- Directories. Societies -- United States -- States -- Directories.

AS25.D5
Research centers directory. Detroit, Mich.: Gale Research Co., 1 v.
60-014807   001
Research -- United States -- Directories. Research -- Canada -- Directories. Learned institutions and societies -- United States -- Directories.

AS36.R332
Rand Corporation.
Index of selected publications of the Rand Corporation. [Santa Monica? Calif., Rand Corp.] 1 v.
63-001486   015.79493

AS40 By region or country — America — British North America. Canada

AS40.A86
Associations Canada: an encyclopedic directory = un répertoire encyclopédique. Toronto: Canadian Almanac & Directory Pub. Co., [c1991-]
92-641105   061.1/025 20
Associations, institutions, etc.--Canada--Directories. Societies--Canada--Directory. Organizations--Canada--Directory.

AS262 By region or country — Europe — Russia

AS262.A68.V79 1984
Vucinich, Alexander, 1914-
Empire of knowledge: the Academy of Sciences of the USSR (1917-1970)/ Alexander Vucinich. Berkeley: University of California Press, c1984. x, 484 p.
83-003484   354.470085/5   0520048717
Akademiëiia nauk SSSR -- History.

AS284 By region or country — Europe — Scandinavia

AS284.G6 v. 64, no. 7
Ellegard, Alvar.
Darwin and the general reader: the reception of Darwin's theory of evolution in the British periodical press, 1859-1872/ by Alvar Ellegard. Goteborg: [s.n.]; 1958. 394 p.
60-000366   575.0162
Darwin, Charles, -- 1809-1882. -- On the origin of species. -- cnEvolution Evolution.

AS911 Other associations, "funds," foundations, and institutions

AS911.A2.A67
Annual register of grant support. Chicago [etc.] Marquis Academic Media, Marquis Who's Who [etc.]
69-018307   001.4/4
Endowments -- Directories. Research grants -- Directories.

AS911.A2.F65
The Foundation directory. New York, Foundation Center; distributed by Columbia University Press,
60-013807   061
Endowments -- United States -- Directories. Foundations -- directories. Foundations -- periodicals.

AS911.A2.F66
The Foundation grants index. New York, Foundation Center; distributed by Columbia University Press,
72-076018   001.4/4
Endowments -- Directories. Foundations -- United States -- directories. Research Support -- directories.

AS911.P8.B74 1999
Brennan, Elizabeth A.
Who's who of Pulitzer Prize winners/ Elizabeth A. Brennan and Elizabeth C. Clarage; foreword by Seymour Topping. Phoenix, Ariz.: Oryx Press, 1999. xxii, 666 p.
98-044979   071/.3/092273   1573561118
Pulitzer Prizes. Biography -- 20th century.

AY Yearbooks. Almanacs. Directories

AY67 Almanacs — By country — United States

AY67.N5 W7
The World almanac and book of facts. New York: Press Pub. Co. (The New York World), [1923-]
04-003781   317 11
Almanacs, American. Statistics--Periodicals.

AY754 Almanacs — By country — Other countries

AY754.W5
Whitaker's almanack. London: J. Whitaker, [c1992-   ]
95-029779
Almanacs, English. Almanacs.

AZ History of scholarship and learning. The humanities

AZ103 Philosophy. Theory — Value, aims, influences etc. Addresses, essays, lectures. Pamphlets

AZ103.G75 1993
Gross, Ronald.
The independent scholar's handbook/ Ronald Gross. Berkeley, Calif.: Ten Speed Press, c1993. xviii, 301 p.
93-019276   001.2   0898155215
Learning and scholarship.

AZ103.H69 2000
Hoyrup, Jens.
Human sciences: reappraising the humanities through history and philosophy/ Jens Hoyrup. Albany, NY: State University of New York Press, c2000. xi, 448 p.
99-088563   001.3/01   0791446034
Humanities -- Philosophy. Humanities -- History. Science and the humanities.

AZ103.P44 1984
Pelikan, Jaroslav Jan, 1923-
The vindication of tradition/ Jaroslav Pelikan. New Haven: Yale University Press, c1984. x, 93 p.
84-005132   001.2   0300031548
Learning and scholarship. Tradition (Philosophy)

AZ105 Philosophy. Theory — Methods. Organization — General works

AZ105.H85 1990
Humanities and the computer: new directions/ edited by David S. Miall. Oxford [England]: Clarendon Press; 1990. x, 222 p.
89-071302   001.3/0285   0198242441
Humanities -- Data processing. Humanities -- Study and teaching (Higher) -- Data processing. Computer-assisted instruction.

AZ108 Philosophy. Theory — Methods. Organization — Symbols and their use

AZ108.B4313 1994
Becker, Udo.
The Continuum encyclopedia of symbols/ Udo Becker; translated by Lance W. Garmer. New York: Continuum, 1994. 345 p.
94-011000   302.2/2203   0826406440
Signs and symbols -- Dictionaries.

AZ108.B5313 1992
Biedermann, Hans, 1930-
Dictionary of symbolism/ Hans Biedermann; translated by James Hulbert. New York; Facts on File, c1992. x, 465 p.
91-044933   302.23   0816025932
Signs and symbols -- Dictionaries.

AZ108.W37 1996
Bruce-Mitford, Miranda.
The illustrated book of signs & symbols/ Miranda Bruce-Mitford. New York: DK Pub., Inc., 1996. 128 p.
96-014202   302.2/22   0789410001
Signs and symbols. -- sears

AZ182 Study and teaching — General works

AZ182.W56 1998
Winn, James Anderson, 1947-
The pale of words: reflections on the humanities and performance/ James Anderson Winn. New Haven: Yale University Press, c1998. xii, 143 p.
98-005743   001.3/071   0300074123
Humanities -- Study and teaching (Higher). Learning and scholarship. Humanities -- Philosophy.

AZ183 Study and teaching — By region or country, A-Z

AZ183.U5.E45 1997
Ellis, John M. 1936-
Literature lost: social agendas and the corruption of the humanities/ John M. Ellis. New Haven [Conn.]: Yale University Press, c1997. vii, 262 p.
96-037680   001.3/071/173   0300069200
Humanities -- Study and teaching (Higher) -- United States -- Evaluation. Humanities -- Political aspects -- United States. Political correctness -- United States.

AZ183.U5.W47 1997
What's happened to the humanities?/ edited by Alvin Kernan. Princeton, N.J.: Princeton University Press, c1997. viii, 267 p.
96-028325   001.3/071/173   0691011559
Humanities -- Study and teaching (Higher) -- United States. Humanities -- Philosophy. Learning and scholarship -- United States -- History.

AZ221 History — General works — 20th century

AZ221.P76 1988
Proctor, Robert E., 1945-
Education's great amnesia: reconsidering the humanities from Petrarch to Freud: with a curriculum for today's students/ Robert E. Proctor. Bloomington: Indiana University Press, c1988. xviii, 231 p.
87-046002   001.3   0253349257
Learning and scholarship -- History. Humanities -- Study and teaching -- United States. Education, Humanistic -- United States.

AZ221.W58 1996
World databases in humanities/ edited by C.J. Armstrong and R.R. Fenton. London; Bowker-Saur, c1996. xiii, 1060 p.
96-188000   025.06/0013   1857390482
Humanities -- Information services -- Directories. Humanities -- Databases -- Directories.

AZ301 History — By period — Antiquity

AZ301.P4
Pfeiffer, Rudolf, 1889-
History of classical scholarship from the beginnings to the end of the Hellenistic age. Oxford, Clarendon P., 1968. xviii, 311 p.
68-112031   001.2/0938   0198143427
Learning and scholarship -- Greece.

AZ361 History — By period — Modern

AZ361.S56 1969
Snow, C. P. 1905-
The two cultures; and, A second look: an expanded version of 'The two cultures and the scientific revolution', by C. P. Snow. London, Cambridge U.P., 1969. iv, 107 p.
70-442528   001   052109576X
Science and the humanities.

AZ505-507 By region or country — America — North America

AZ505.M28
Machlup, Fritz, 1902-
Knowledge, its creation, distribution, and economic significance/ by Fritz Machlup. Princeton, N.J.: Princeton University Press, c1980-c1984. 3 v.
80-007544   001   0691042268
Learning and scholarship -- United States. Knowledge, Theory of.

AZ507.D58 1991
Divided knowledge: across disciplines, across cultures/ edited by David Easton, Corinne S. Schelling. Newbury Park, Calif.: SagePublications, c1991. 261 p.
90-019482   001.3   0803940386
Humanities -- United States -- Congresses. Social sciences -- United States -- Congresses. Humanities -- China -- Congresses. United States -- Intellectual life -- 20th century -- Congresses. China -- Intellectual life -- 1976- -- Congresses.

AZ507.P64 1995
The politics and processes of scholarship/ edited by Joseph M. Moxley and Lagretta T. Lenker; foreword by R. Eugene Rice. Westport, Conn.: Greenwood Press, 1995. xi, 263 p.
95-016147   001.2   0313295727
Learning and scholarship -- Political aspects -- United States. Academic writing -- Political aspects -- United States. Scholarly publishing -- Political aspects -- United States.

AZ613 By region or country — Europe — Great Britain

AZ613.W4 1957
Weiss, Roberto.
Humanism in England during the fifteenth century. Oxford, Blackwell, 1957. xxiii, 202 p.
58-000673   880.7
Learning and scholarship -- Great Britain. Renaissance -- Great Britain. Humanism.

AZ999 Popular errors and delusions

AZ999.W37 1989
Ward, Philip,
A dictionary of common fallacies/ Philip Ward. Buffalo, N.Y.: Prometheus Books, 1989, c1988. 2 v.
88-032201   001.9/6/0321 19   0879755113
Errors, Popular--Dictionaries.

U Military science (General)

U11 Army lists. By region or country, A-Z

U11.P83 1991
Posen, Barry R.
Inadvertent escalation: conventional war and nuclear risks/ Barry R. Posen. Ithaca, N.Y.: Cornell University Press, 1991. xi, 280 p.
91-055055   355.02/15   0801425638
Escalation (Military science) Nuclear threshold (Strategy) Limited war. Europe -- Defenses. United States -- Military policy.

U15 Collections. Collected works — 1701- — Several authors

U15.U64 no.20-212
Kreidberg, Marvin A.
History of military mobilization in the United States Army, 1775-1945, by Marvin A. Kreidberg and Merton G. Henry. [Washington] Dept. of the Army, 1955. xvii, 721 p.
56-060717   355.2
United States -- History, Military.

U19 Addresses, essays, lectures

U19.E49
Engels, Friedrich, 1820-1895.
Engels as military critic; articles reprinted from the Volunteer Journal and the Manchester Guardian of the 1860s. With an introd. by W.H. Chaloner and W.O. Henderson. [Manchester, Eng.] Manchester University Press [c1959] 146 p.
60-004658   355.04
Military art and science Military history

U19.H75
Howard, Michael Eliot, 1922-
The theory and practice of war; essays presented to B.H. Liddell Hart on his seventieth birthday/ edited by Michael Howard. New York: F.A. Praeger, [1966, c1965] x, 376 p
66-013987   355.0008
Liddell Hart, Basil Henry, -- Sir, -- 1895-1970.Military art and science. War.

U21 War. Philosophy. Military sociology — General works — Through 1945

U21.B637 1968
Bramson, Leon,
War: studies from psychology, sociology, anthropology. Edited by Leon Bramson and George W. Goethals. New York, Basic Books [1968] 438 p.
68-024485   355.02/7/08
War.

U21.T69
Toynbee, Arnold Joseph, 1889-1975.
War and civilization, selected by Albert V. Fowler from A study of history. New York, Oxford University Press, 1950. xii, 165 p.
50-009539   355.01
Militarism.

U21.T8
Tucker, Robert W.
The just war; a study in contemporary American doctrine. Baltimore, Johns Hopkins Press [c1960] 207 p.
60-015755   355.0973
Nuclear warfare. War -- Moral and ethical aspects. United States -- Military policy.

U21.W7
Wright, Quincy, 1890-
A study of war ... by Quincy Wright. Chicago, Ill., The University of Chicago press [1942] 2 v.
42-021867   355
War. Military art and science.

U21.2 War. Philosophy. Military sociology — General works — 1946-

U21.2.G36413 2000
Gantzel, Klaus Jurgen.
Warfare since the Second World War/ Klaus Jurgen Gantzel, Torsten Schwinghammer; with an afterword by Dietrich Jung, Klaus Schlichte, and Jens Siegelberg; translated by Jonathan P.G. Bach. New Brunswick, NJ: Transaction, c2000. xxiii, 554 p.
99-043673   355/.009/045   1560003758
War -- History -- 20th century. World politics -- 1945-

U21.2.C343 1990
Carlton, Eric.
War and ideology/ Eric Carlton. Savage, Md.: Barnes & Noble Books, 1990. viii, 207 p.
91-199402   0389209457
War. War and society. War -- Psychological aspects.

U21.2.C43 1987
Ceadel, Martin.
Thinking about peace and war/ Martin Ceadel. Oxford [Oxfordshire]; Oxford University Press, 1987. 222 p.
87-005619   327.1/7   0192192000
War. Peace.

U21.2.C52 1988
Clark, Ian, 1949-
Waging war: a philosophical introduction/ Ian Clark. Oxford: Clarendon Press; 1988. 154 p.
87-030754   355/.02   0198273258
War. War -- Moral and ethical aspects.

U21.2.C54.A7613 1985
Aron, Raymond, 1905-
Clausewitz, philosopher of war/ Raymond Aron; translated by Christine Booker and Norman Stone. Englewood Cliffs, N.J.: Prentice-Hall, c1985. xi, 418 p.
84-026569   355/.02   0131363425
Clausewitz, Carl von, -- 1780-1831.War. Military art and science.

U21.2.D55 1988
Domke, William Kinkade.
War and the changing global system/ William K. Domke. New Haven: Yale University Press, c1988. ix, 209 p.
87-010577   355/.02   0300036892
War. International relations. World politics -- 1985-1995.

U21.2.D828 1987
Dunnigan, James F.
How to stop a war: the lessons of two hundred years of war and peace/ James F. Dunnigan and William Martel. New York: Doubleday, c1987. x, 298 p.
87-005278   303.6/6   0385240090
War. Military history, Modern -- 19th century. Military history, Modern -- 20th century.

U21.2.D85 1987
Dupuy, Trevor Nevitt, 1916-
Understanding war: history and a theory of combat/ T.N. Dupuy. New York: Paragon House, c1987. xxvi, 312 p.
86-025151   355/.02   0913729574
War. Combat. Combat -- Mathematical models.

U21.2.G36513 1998
Gareev, M. A.
If war comes tomorrow?: the contours of future armed conflict/ Makhmut Akhmetovich Gareev; translated by Yakov Vladimirovich Fomenko; edited and with an introduction by Jacob W. Kipp. London; Frank Cass, 1998. ix, 182 p.
97-032218   355.4/8   0714648019
World War III. Military art and science -- Forecasting. International relations.

U21.2.G3813 1975
Gaulle, Charles de, 1890-1970.
The edge of the sword/ Charles de Gaulle; translated from the French by Gerard Hopkins. Westport, Conn.: Greenwood Press, 1975, c1960. 128 p.
75-026731   355.02   0837183669
War. Leadership. France -- History, Military.

U21.2.G44 1994
Gelven, Michael.
War and existence: a philosophical inquiry/ Michael Gelven. University Park, Pa.: Pennsylvania State University Press, c1994. xiii, 271 p.
92-041697   355.02/01   0271010525
War (Philosophy)

U21.2.H627 1990
Holsti, K. J. 1935-
Peace and war: armed conflicts and international order, 1648-1989/ Kalevi J. Holsti. Cambridge; Cambridge University Press, 1991. xvii, 379 p.
90-002110   355.02   0521390486
War. World politics. Military history, Modern.

U21.2.H62723 1996
Holsti, K. J. 1935-
The state, war, and the state of war/ by K.J. Holsti. Cambridge; Cambridge University Press, 1996. xiv, 254 p.
96-003881   355.02   0521571138
War. Legitimacy of governments. Political stability.

U21.2.H83 1997
Hunt, W. Ben
Getting to war: predicting international conflict with mass media indicators/ W. Ben Hunt. Ann Arbor: University of Michigan Press, c1997. 304 p.
96-039405   355.02   0472107518
War -- Forecasting. Mass media and war. War in mass media.

U21.2.I42 1991
Ikle, Fred Charles.
Every war must end/ by Fred Charles Ikle. New York: Columbia University Press, 1991. 160 p.
91-015756   335.02   0231076894
War.

U21.2.I57 1992
The Institution of war/ edited by Robert A. Hinde. New York: St. Martin's Press, 1992. x, 253 p.
91-014437   303.6/6   0312066112
War. War and society. Disarmament.

U21.2.J627 1984
Johnson, James Turner.
Can modern war be just?/ James Turner Johnson. New Haven: Yale University Press, c1984. xi, 215 p.
84-003523   172/.42   0300031653
War -- Moral and ethical aspects. Just war doctrine.

U21.2.J6324 1999
Johnson, James Turner.
Morality & contemporary warfare/ James Turner Johnson. New Haven: Yale University Press, c1999. ix, 259 p.
98-054952   172/.42   0300078374
War -- Moral and ethical aspects. Low-intensity conflicts (Military science)

U21.2.L39 1993
Leng, Russell J.
Interstate crisis behavior, 1816-1980: realism vs. reciprocity/ Russell J. Leng. New York, NY, USA: Cambridge University Press, 1993. xvii, 259 p.
92-032370   327.1/6   0521391415
War. World politics -- 19th century. World politics -- 20th century.

U21.2.M34
Mansfield, Sue.
The gestalts of war: an inquiry into its origins and meanings as a social institution/ Sue Mansfield. New York: Dial Press, c1982. xi, 274 p.
81-012592   355/.0275   0385272197
War -- Psychological aspects.

U21.2.M346 1989
Maoz, Zeev.
Paradoxes of war: on the art of national self-entrapment/ Zeev Maoz. Boston: Unwin Hyman, 1990. xiii, 368 p.
89-032673   327.1/6   004445113X
War. International relations.

U21.2.M38 1994
McRandle, James H., 1925-
The antique drums of war/ James H. McRandle. College Station, Tex.: Texas A&M University Press, c1994. x, 219 p.
93-041325   355.02/09   0890965919
War. War and society.

U21.2.M84 1989
Mueller, John E.
Retreat from doomsday: the obsolescence of major war/ John Mueller. New York: Basic Books, c1989. viii, 327 p.
88-047899   355/.02/0904
War. World politics -- 20th century. Military history, Modern -- 20th century.

U21.2.O28 1995
O'Connell, Robert L.
Ride of the second horseman: the birth and death of war/ Robert L. O'Connell. New York: Oxford University Press, 1995. viii, 305 p.
95-009858   355.02   0195064607
War -- History. Military art and science -- History.

U21.2.O72 1989
The Origin and prevention of major wars/ edited by Robert I. Rotberg and Theodore K. Rabb; contributors, Robert Gilpin ... [et al.]. Cambridge [England]; Cambridge University Press, 1989, c1988. vi, 352 p.
88-030223   355/.02   0521370949
War. Military history, Modern.

U21.2.P47 1984
Phillips, Robert L. 1938-
War and justice/ by Robert L. Phillips. Norman: University of Oklahoma Press, 1984. xv, 159 p.
84-040278   341.6/2   0806118938
Just war doctrine. Guerrilla warfare -- Moral and ethical aspects. Deterrence (Strategy) -- Moral and ethical aspects.

U21.2.P535 1993
Pick, Daniel.
War machine: the rationalisation of slaughter in the modern age/ Daniel Pick. New Haven, Conn.: Yale University Press, 1993. 292 p.
92-044183   355.02/01   0300054173
War (Philosophy)

U21.2.P62 1973a
Discussions on war and human aggression/ ed. R. Dale Givens, Martin A. Nettleship. The Hague: Mouton; [1976] xvi, 231 p.
76-381173   355.02   0202900320
War -- Congresses.

U21.2.P6554 1990
Prisoners of war?: nation-states in the modern era/ edited by Charles S. Gochman, Alan Ned Sabrosky. Lexington, Mass.: Lexington Books, 1990. xii, 336 p.
89-013438   355.02   0669171417
War. International relations. Military history, Modern.

U21.2.S43 1989
Seabury, Paul.
War: ends and means/ Paul Seabury and Angelo Codevilla. New York: Basic Books, c1989. vi, 306 p.
88-047897   355/.02   0465090672
War. Military art and science.

U21.2.S49 1989
Shaw, R. Paul.
Genetic seeds of warfare: evolution, nationalism, and patriotism/ R. Paul Shaw and Yuwa Wong. Boston: Unwin Hyman, c1989. xii, 274 p.
88-014256   303.6/6
War. Sociobiology. Nationalism.

U21.2.S58 1991
Siverson, Randolph M.
The diffusion of war: a study of opportunity and willingness/ Randolph M. Siverson and Harvey Starr. Ann Arbor: University of Michigan Press, c1991. x, 141 p.
91-017286   355.02   0472102478
War. International relations. World politics -- 19th century.

U21.2.S68 1996
Stam, Allan C.
Win, lose, or draw: domestic politics and the crucible of war/ Allan C. Stam III. Ann Arbor: University of Michigan Press, c1996. xviii, 239 p.
96-010152   355.02   0472106821
War. Strategy. International relations.

U21.2.T465 1988
Thompson, William R.
On global war: historical-structural approaches to world politics/ William R. Thompson. Columbia, S.C.: University of South Carolina Press, c1988. xxiii, 315 p.
88-014786   355/.02   0872495620
War. International relations. Cycles.

U21.2.V34 1999
Van Evera, Stephen.
Causes of war: power and the roots of conflict/ Stephen Van Evera. Ithaca: Cornell University Press, 1999. viii, 270 p.
98-043650   355.02/7   0801432014
War. Balance of power. International relations -- Case studies.

U21.2.W38
War, strategy, and maritime power/ edited by B. Mitchell Simpson III. New Brunswick, N.J.: Rutgers University Press, c1977. x, 356 p.
77-003247   359/.009   0813508428
War. Strategy. Sea-power. United States -- Armed Forces.

U21.2.W396 1993
Welch, David A.
Justice and the genesis of war/ David A. Welch. Cambridge [England]; Cambridge University Press, 1993. xvi, 335 p.
92-043110   355.02   0521444624
War. Justice.

U21.5 War. Philosophy.
Military sociology —
Military sociology —
General works

U21.5.B4813 1998
Ben-Eliezer, Uri.
The making of Israeli militarism/ Uri Ben-Eliezer. Bloomington: Indiana University Press, c1998. xii, 278 p.
97-046020   303.6/6/095694   0253333873
Militarism -- Israel -- History. Arab-Israeli conflict. Israel -- Armed Forces -- Political activity. Israel -- Social conditions.

U21.5.D63
Doorn, Jacobus Adrianus Antonius van, 1925-
The soldier and social change: comparative studies in the history and sociology of the military/ Jacques van Doorn. Beverly Hills, Calif.: Sage Publications, c1975. xii, 189 p.
74-031573   301.5/93   0803999488
Sociology, Military. Armed Forces.

U21.5.J3
Janowitz, Morris.
The military in the political development of new nations; an essay in comparative analysis. Chicago, University of Chicago Press [1964] vii, 134 p.
64-013952   355
Armed Forces -- Political activity. Newly independent states -- Politics and government. Political development.

U21.5.J6
Johnson, John J., 1912-
The role of the military in underdeveloped countries. Princeton, N.J., Princeton University Press, 1962. viii, 427 p.
62-007406   322/.5/091724
Sociology, Military -- Congresses. Developing countries -- Armed Forces -- Political activity -- Congresses.

U21.5.L44 1990
Legitimacy and commitment in the military/ edited by Thomas C. Wyatt and Reuven Gal. New York: Greenwood Press, 1990. x, 217 p.
90-002944   306.2/7   0313268150
Sociology, Military. Morale. Military ethics.

U21.5.M47 1993
The Military family in peace and war/ Florence W. Kaslow, editor. New York: Springer Pub. Co., c1993. xvii, 277 p.
93-014560   306.2/7/0973   0826182704
Families of military personnel -- United States. Sociology, Military -- United States.

U21.5.M4985 1988
The Military: more than just a job?/ edited by Charles C. Moskos & Frank R. Wood. Washington: Pergamon-Brassey's International Defense Publishers, 1988. xiii, 305 p.
87-032850   306/.27   008034321X
Sociology, Military. Armed Forces -- Vocational guidance.

U21.5.P36
Perlmutter, Amos.
The military and politics in modern times: on professionals, praetorians, and revolutionary soldiers/ Amos Perlmutter. New Haven: Yale University Press, 1977. xix, 335 p.
76-045769   301.5/93   0300020457
Sociology, Military. Armed Forces -- Political activity.

U21.5.R32
Radine, Lawrence B.
The taming of the troops: social control in the United States Army/ Lawrence B. Radine. Westport, Conn.: Greenwood Press, 1977. xii, 276 p.
76-005262   301.5/93   083718911X
Sociology, Military. Social control.

U21.7 War. Philosophy.
Military sociology —
Military sociology —
Mathematical models.
Methodology

U21.7.R48 1978
Richardson, Lewis Fry, 1881-1953.
Arms and insecurity: a mathematical study of the causes and origins of war/ by Lewis F. Richardson; edited by Nicolas Rashevsky and Ernesto Trucco. Ann Arbor, Mich.: reprinted for Boxwood Press by University Microfilms International, 1978, c1960. xxv, 307 p.
78-027901   301.6/334/0184   0835703789
Sociology, Military -- Mathematical models. War -- Economic aspects.

U21.7.R5
Richardson, Lewis Fry, 1881-1953.
Statistics of deadly quarrels. Edited by Quincy Wright and C.C. Lienau. Pittsburgh, Boxwood Press [1960] xlvi, 373 p.
59-009487   355.01
Sociology, Military -- Mathematical models. Homicide -- Statistics. Military history -- Statistics.

U21.75 War. Philosophy.
Military sociology —
Military sociology —
Women and the military

U21.75.E55 1983b
Enloe, Cynthia H., 1938-
Does khaki become you?: the militarisation of women's lives/ Cynthia Enloe. Boston, Mass.: South End Press, c1983. vii, 262 p.
84-164990   355/.0088042   0896081834
Women and the military.

U21.75.J66 1997
Jones, David E., 1942-
Women warriors: a history/ by David E. Jones. Washington: Brassey's, c1997. xv, 279 p.
96-035003   355/.0082   157488106X
Women and the military -- History.

U21.75.S44 1992
American women and the U.S. armed forces: a guide to the records of military agencies in the National Archives relating to American women/ compiled by Charlotte Palmer Seeley; revised by Virginia C. Purdy and Robert Gruber. Washington, DC: National Archives and Records Administration, 1992. xii, 355 p.
91-040430   355/.0082   0911333908
Women and the military -- United States -- History -- Archival resources. United States -- Armed Forces -- Women -- History -- Archival resources.

U21.75.S54 1996
Sherrow, Victoria.
Women and the military: an encyclopedia/ Victoria Sherrow. Santa Barbara, Calif.: ABC-CLIO, c1996. xxii, 381 p.
96-033459   355/.0082   087436812X
Women and the military -- Encyclopedias. Women and war -- Encyclopedias.

U21.75.W665 1993
Women and the use of military force/ edited by
Ruth H. Howes, Michael R. Stevenson. Boulder:
L. Rienner Publishers, c1993. vii, 247 p.
92-046443   355/.0082   1555873294
Women and the military. Women and war.

U22 War. Philosophy.
Military sociology —
Ethics. Morale

U22.A95 1989
Axinn, Sidney.
A moral military/ Sidney Axinn. Philadelphia:
Temple University Press, 1989. xiv, 230 p.
88-029294   172/.42   0877226156
*Kant, Immanuel, -- 1724-1804 -- Ethics. Kant,
Immanuel, -- 1724-1804 -- Influence. Military
ethics. War -- Moral and ethical aspects.*

U22.B25 1988
Bailey, Sydney Dawson.
War and conscience in the nuclear age/ Sydney
D. Bailey. New York: St. Martin's Press, 1988,
c1987. xviii, 210 p.
87-018755   172/.42   0312013450
*War -- Moral and ethical aspects. War --
Religious aspects -- Christianity. War
(International law)*

U22.C5397 1997
Coates, A. J. 1940-
The ethics of war/ A.J. Coates. Manchester,
U.K.; Manchester University Press; 1997. 314 p.
97-005364   172/.42   0719040450
*War -- Moral and ethical aspects. Just war
doctrine.*

U22.D6 1944
Dollard, John, 1900-
Fear in battle, by John Dollard with the
assistance of Donald Horton. Washington, The
Infantry journal, 1944. vii, 64 p.
44-006789   [157.3] 355.12
Fear. Morale. Courage.

U22.H35 1998
Hallock, D.
Hell, healing, and resistance: veterans speak/ D.
William Hallock; foreword by Thich Nhat Hanh;
preface by Philip Berrigan. Farmington, PA:
Plough Pub. House, c1998. xix, 434 p.
98-029729   172/.42   0874869595
*War -- Moral and ethical aspects. War --
Psychological aspects. Veterans -- United States
-- Interviews.*

U22.H37 1982
Hartigan, Richard Shelly.
The forgotten victim: a history of the civilian/
Richard Shelly Hartigan. Chicago, Ill.: Precedent
Pub., 1982. xi, 173 p.
83-134732   172/.42   0913750190
*War -- Moral and ethical aspects. War
casualties. Just war doctrine.*

U22.H38 1989
Hartle, Anthony E., 1942-
Moral issues in military decision making/
Anthony E. Hartle. Lawrence, Kan.: University
Press of Kansas, c1989. 180 p.
88-033918   174/.9355   0700603972
Military ethics.

U22.H65 1989
Holmes, Robert L.
On war and morality/ Robert L. Holmes.
Princeton, N.J.: Princeton University Press,
c1989. xiii, 310 p.
88-019479   172/.42   0691077940
War -- Moral and ethical aspects.

U22.L33 1988
LaCroix, W. L. 1933-
War and international ethics: tradition and today/
W.L. LaCroix, S.J. Lanham, MD: University
Press of America, c1988. x, 305 p.
87-028053   172/.42   0819167088
*Just war doctrine. War -- Moral and ethical
aspects. International relations -- Moral and
ethical aspects.*

U22.P37
Paskins, Barrie.
The ethics of war/ Barrie Paskins & Michael
Dockrill. Minneapolis: University of Minnesota
Press, 1979. xii, 332 p.
79-010798   172/.4   0816608857
*Military ethics. War -- Moral and ethical
aspects.*

U22.R57 1978
Richardson, Frank M.
Fighting spirit: a study of psychological factors
in war/ [by] F. M. Richardson; with a foreword
by Sir Peter Hunt. London: Cooper, 1978. xv,
189 p.
78-318970   355.02/019   0850522366
Morale. Psychology, Military.

U22.S8
Studies in social psychology in World War II ...
prepared and edited under the auspices of a
special committee of the Social Science Research
Council. [Princeton, Princeton University Press,
[1949-50] 4 v.
49-002480   355.1
Soldiers -- United States. Social psychology.

U22.S953
Szunyogh, Bela, 1923-
Psychological warfare; an introduction to
ideological propaganda and the techniques of
psychological warfare. [Rev. ed., translated by
the author from his original German editions]
New York, William Frederick Press, 1955. 117 p.
55-005295
Psychological warfare.

U22.3 War. Philosophy.
Military sociology —
Military psychology

U22.3.B74 1969
Bray, Charles William, 1904-
Psychology and military proficiency; a history of
the Applied Psychology Panel of the National
Defense Research Committee, by Charles W.
Bray. New York, Greenwood Press [1969,
c1948] xviii, 242 p.
69-013837   355.2/2   0837114446
Psychology, Military.

U22.3.E37 1997
Ehrenreich, Barbara.
Blood rites: origins and history of the passions of
war/ Barbara Ehrenreich. New York:
Metropolitan Books, 1997. x, 292 p.
96-050891   355.02   0805050779
War -- Psychological aspects. War.

U22.3.G333 1988
Gabriel, Richard A.
The painful field: the psychiatric dimension of
modern war/ Richard A. Gabriel. New York:
Greenwood Press, c1988. 187 p.
87-031785   355/.001/9   0313247188
*Psychiatry, Military. War -- Psychological
aspects.*

U22.3.M63 1990
Mosse, George L. 1918-
Fallen soldiers: reshaping the memory of the
world wars/ George L. Mosse. New York:
Oxford University Press, 1990. vi, 264 p.
89-036202   303.6/6/09409041   0195062477
*War -- Psychological aspects. War and
civilization. World War, 1914-1918 -- Europe --
Psychological aspects. Europe -- Civilization --
20th century. Europe -- History, Military -- 20th
century.*

U22.3.P775 1993
The psychological effects of war and violence on
children/ edited by Lewis A. Leavitt, Nathan A.
Fox. Hillsdale, N.J.: L. Erlbaum Associates,
1993. xix, 374 p.
92-043225   305.23   0805811710
*War -- Psychological aspects -- Congresses.
Children and violence -- Congresses.*

U22.3.S43 1988
Shalit, Ben.
The psychology of conflict and combat/ Ben
Shalit. New York: Praeger, 1988. x, 205 p.
87-023729   355/.001/9   0275927539
*Combat -- Psychological aspects. Conflict
(Psychology)*

U22.3.W37
Watson, Peter.
War on the mind: the military uses and abuses of
psychology/ Peter Watson. New York: Basic
Books, c1978. 534 p.
77-075237   355/.001/9   0465090656
Psychology, Military. Psychological warfare.

U24 Dictionaries.
Encyclopedias —
General works

U24.B73 1994
Brassey's encyclopedia of military history and
biography/ executive editor Franklin D.
Margiotta; foreword by John Keegan.
Washington: Brassey's, c1994. xxx. 1197 p.
94-033551   355/.003   0028810961
*Military art and science -- Encyclopedias.
Military history -- Encyclopedias. Military
biography -- Encyclopedias.*

U24.D47 1988
The Official dictionary of military terms/
compiled by the Joint Chiefs of Staff. Cambridge
[Mass.?]: Science Information Resource Center;
c1988. ix, 478 p.
87-023694   355/.003/21   0891167927
Military art and science -- Dictionaries.

U24.D4913 1993
A dictionary of military history and the art of
war/ edited by Andre Corvisier; translated from
the French by Chris Turner. Oxford; Blackwell,
1994. xxvii, 916 p.
92-046136   355/.003   0631168486
*Military art and science -- Encyclopedias.
Military history -- Encyclopedias.*

U24.G34
Gaynor, Frank, 1911-
The new military and naval dictionary. New York, Philosophical Library [1951] viii, 295 p.
51-013233   355.03
Military art and science -- Dictionaries. Naval art and science -- Dictionaries.

U24.H38
Hayward, Philip Henry Cecil.
Jane's dictionary of military terms/ compiled by P. H. C. Hayward. London: Macdonald and Jane's, 1975. 201 p.
76-361572   355/.003   035608261X
Military art and science -- Dictionaries. Naval art and science -- Dictionaries.

U24.I58 1993
International military and defense encyclopedia/ editor-in-chief, Trevor N. Dupuy ... [et al.]. Washington: Brassey's (US), c1993. 6 v.
92-033750   355/.003   0028810112
Military art and science -- Encyclopedias.

U24.L93 1991
Luttwak, Edward.
The dictionary of modern war/ Edward Luttwak and Stuart Koehl. New York, N.Y.: HarperCollins, c1991. vi, 680 p.
90-055998   355/.003   0062700219
Military art and science -- Dictionaries.

U24.R63 1987
Robertson, David, 1946-
Guide to modern defense and strategy: a complete description of the terms, tactics, organizations and accords of today's defense/ David Robertson. Detroit, MI: Gale Research Co., c1987. xii, 324 p.
87-082651   355/.003/21   0810350432
Military art and science -- Dictionaries. Nuclear warfare -- Dictionaries.

U24.S47 1989
Shafritz, Jay M.
The Facts on File dictionary of military science/ Jay M. Shafritz, Todd J.A. Shafritz, David B. Robertson. New York: Facts on File, c1989. vi, 498 p.
88-028648   355/.003/21   0816018235
Military art and science -- Dictionaries.

U24.S7213 1993
The Soviet military encyclopedia.   Boulder: Westview, 1993. 4 v.
92-032531   355/.003   0813314321
Military art and science -- Encyclopedias.

U24.U526 1995
Dictionary of military terms/ US Department of Defense; introduction by Charles Messenger. London; Greenhill Books: 1995. 512 p.
95-013988   355/.003   1853672173
Military art and science -- Dictionaries.

U24.U56
United States.
A dictionary of United States military terms, prepared for the joint usage of the Armed Forces. Washington, Public Affairs Press [1963] viii, 316 p.
63-000942   355.03
Military art and science -- Dictionaries.

U26 Military symbols and abbreviations

U26.G88 1990
Gutzman, Philip C., 1938-
Dictionary of military, defense contractor & troop slang acronyms/ Philip C. Gutzman. Santa Barbara, Calif.: ABC-CLIO, c1990. 392 p.
89-018618   355/.00148   0874365899
Military art and science -- United States -- Abbreviations. Defense industries -- United States -- Abbreviations. Military art and science -- United States -- Acronyms. United States -- Armed Forces -- Abbreviations. United States -- Armed Forces -- Acronyms.

U27 History of military science — General works

U27.A294 1990
Addington, Larry H.
The patterns of war through the eighteenth century/ Larry H. Addington. Bloomington: Indiana University Press, c1990. xii, 161 p.
89-045190   355/.009   0253301319
Military art and science -- History. Military history.

U27.A6
Albion, Robert Greenhalgh, 1896-
Introduction to military history, by Robert Greenhalgh Albion. Maps prepared in collaboration with Girard L. McEntee. New York, The Century Co. [c1929] xv, 429 p.
29-023078
Military art and science -- History. Arms and armor -- History. United States -- History, Military.

U27.D34213 1975
Delbruck, Hans, 1848-1929.
History of the art of war within the framework of political history/ by Hans Delbruck; translated from the German by Walter J. Renfroe, Jr. Westport, Conn.: Greenwood Press, 1975-1985. 4 v.
72-000792   355/.009   083716365X
War -- History. Military art and science -- History. Naval art and science -- History.

U27.K38 1993
Keegan, John, 1934-
A history of warfare/ John Keegan. New York: Alfred A. Knopf: 1993. xvi, 432 p.
93-014884   355/.009   0394588010
Military art and science -- History.

U27.K4
Kendall, Paul Murray.
The story of land warfare. London, H. Hamilton [1957] 194 p.
58-000752
Military art and science -- History. Military history.

U27.M49 1992
Military history and the military profession/ edited by David A. Charters, Marc Milner, and J. Brent Wilson; foreword by Anne N. Foreman. Westport, Conn.: Praeger, 1992. xvi, 242 p.
92-009114   355/.009   0275940721
Military art and science -- History. Military history. Military history -- Historiography.

U27.M6 1960
Montross, Lynn, 1895-1961.
War through the ages. New York, Harper [1960] 1063 p.
60-007533   355
Military art and science -- History. Military history.

U27.O26 1989
O'Connell, Robert L.
Of arms and men: a history of war, weapons, and aggression/ Robert L. O'Connell. New York: Oxford University Press, 1989. viii, 367 p.
88-019526   355/.009   0195053591
Military art and science -- History. War.

U27.R348 1996
The Reader's companion to military history/ Robert Cowley and Geoffrey Parker, editors. Boston: Houghton Mifflin, c1996. xiv, 573 p.
96-008577   355/.009   0395669693
Military history.

U27.V27 1989
Van Creveld, Martin L.
Technology and war: from 2000 B.C. to the present/ Martin van Creveld. New York: Free Press; c1989. x, 342 p.
88-016405   355/.009   002933151X
Military art and science -- History. Military history. Technology -- History.

U27.Z6
Zook, David Hartzler, 1930-
A short history of warfare, by David H. Zook, Jr., and Robin Higham. Foreword by B. H. Liddell Hart. New York, Twayne Publishers [1966] 500 p.
65-028533   355.0009
Military art and science -- History. Military history.

U29 History of military science — Ancient — General works

U29.B73 2001
Bradford, Alfred S.
With arrow, sword, and spear: a history of warfare in the ancient world/ Alfred S. Bradford; illustrated by Pamela M. Bradford Westport, Conn.: Praeger, 2001. xviii, 312 p.
99-052982   355/.0093   0275952592
Military art and science -- History -- To 500. Military history, Ancient.

U29.G23 1990
Gabriel, Richard A.
The culture of war: invention and early development/ Richard A. Gabriel; foreword by William C. Martel. New York: Greenwood Press, 1990. xviii, 160 p.
89-026043   355/.009   0313266646
Military art and science -- History. Military history, Ancient.

U29.G233 1991
Gabriel, Richard A.
From Sumer to Rome: the military capabilities of ancient armies/ Richard A. Gabriel and Karen S. Metz. New York: Greenwood Press, 1991. xxi, 182 p.
90-020676   355/.0093   0313276455
Military art and science -- History. Military history, Ancient.

U29.G234 2001
Gabriel, Richard A.
Great captains of antiquity/ Richard A. Gabriel; forewords by Mordechai Gichon and David Jablonsky. Westport, Conn: Greenwood Press, 2000. xviii, 242 p.
00-029422   355/.0092/23   0313312850
Generals. Military art and science -- History. Military history, Ancient.

U29.K47 1999
Kern, Paul Bentley.
Ancient siege warfare/ Paul Bentley Kern. Bloomington: Indiana University Press, c1999. 419 p.
98-053763   355.4/4/093   0253335469
Siege warfare -- History. Military history, Ancient.

U29.M3 1963
McCartney, Eugene Stock, 1883-
Warfare by land and sea. New York, Cooper Square Publishers, 1963. xix, 206 p.
63-010284   355.409
Military art and science -- History. Military art and science -- Greece -- History. Military art and science -- Rome -- History.

U29.S25 1997
Santosuosso, Antonio.
Soldiers, citizens, and the symbols of war: from classical Greece to republican Rome, 500-167 B.C./ Antonio Santosuosso. Boulder, Colo.: Westview Press, 1997. x, 277 p.
97-007294   355/.0093   0813332761
Military history, Ancient. Civil-military relations -- History.

U33 History of military science — Ancient — Greek

U33.A3
Adcock, F. E. 1886-1968.
The Greek and Macedonian art of war/ by F. E. Adcock. Berkelely: University of California Press, 1962, c1957. vi, 109 p.
57-010495   355.0938
Military art and science -- History. Macedonia -- Army. Greece -- Army. Greece -- History, Military.

U33.A5
Anderson, J. K.
Military theory and practice in the age of Xenophon [by] J. K. Anderson. Berkeley, University of California Press, 1970. viii, 419 p.
74-104010   355/.00938   0520015649
Xenophon. Military art and science -- History. Greece -- History, Military.

U33.B84 1988
Bugh, Glenn Richard, 1948-
The horsemen of Athens/ Glenn Richard Bugh. Princeton, N.J.: Princeton University Press, c1988. xvii, 271 p.
88-003210   357/.1/09385   0691055300
Cavalry -- Greece -- Athens -- History. Athens (Greece) -- History, Military.

U33.C647 1981
Connolly, Peter, 1935-
Greece and Rome at war/ Peter Connolly. Englewood Cliffs, NJ: Prentice-Hall, 1981. 320 p.
81-178595   355/.00938   0133649768
Military art and science -- Greece -- History. Military art and science -- Rome -- History. Weapons, Ancient -- Greece -- History.

U33.G3513
Garlan, Yvon.
War in the ancient world: a social history/ Yvon Garlan; translated from the French by Janet Lloyd. New York: Norton, c1975. 200 p.
75-020463   355/.00938   0393055663
Military art and science -- History. Greece -- Military antiquities. Rome -- Military antiquities.

U33.H36 1989
Hanson, Victor Davis.
The Western way of war: infantry battle in classical Greece/ Victor Davis Hanson; with an introduction by John Keegan. New York: Knopf: 1989. xxiv, 244 p.
88-045779   355/.00938   0394571886
Military art and science -- Greece -- History. Infantry drill and tactics -- History.

U33.T3
Tarn, W. W. 1869-1957.
Hellenistic military & naval developments, by W. W. Tarn. Cambridge [Eng.] University press, 1930. vii, 170 p.
31-017173   355.09
Military art and science -- History. Naval art and science -- History.

U35 History of military science — Ancient — Roman

U35.B79 1994
Burns, Thomas S.
Barbarians within the gates of Rome: a study of Roman military policy and the barbarians, ca. 375-425 A.D./ Thomas S. Burns. Bloomington: Indiana University Press, c1994. xxi, 417 p.
94-012788   937/.08   0253312884
Germanic peoples -- Employment. Rome -- Army -- Recruiting, enlistment, etc. Rome -- History, Military -- 30 B.C.-476 A.D.

U35.D38 1989
Davies, Roy W.
Service in the Roman Army/ Roy W. Davies; edited by David Breeze and Valerie A. Maxfield. New York: Columbia University Press, c1989. xii, 336 p.
88-033991   355/.00937   0231069928
Rome -- Army.

U35.L8
Luttwak, Edward.
The grand strategy of the Roman Empire from the first century A.D. to the third/ Edward N. Luttwak. Baltimore: Johns Hopkins University Press, c1976. xii, 255 p.
76-017232   355.03/303/7   080181863X
Strategy. Military history, Ancient. Rome -- Army.

U35.S6
Smith, Richard Edwin.
Service in the post-Marian Roman army. [Manchester, Eng.] Manchester University Press, 1958. 76 p.
62-051276   355.0937
Rome -- Army.

U35.S648 1994
Speidel, Michael.
Riding for Caesar: the Roman emperors' horse guards/ Michael P. Speidel. Cambridge, Mass.: Harvard University Press, 1994. 223 p.
93-023539   355.3/51/0937   0674768973
Guards troops -- Rome. Rome -- Army -- Cavalry.

U35.W35 1969b
Watson, George Ronald.
The Roman soldier [by] G. R. Watson. Ithaca, N.Y., Cornell University Press [1969] 256 p.
69-011153   355.1/00937   080140519X
Soldiers -- Rome.

U35.W48 1985
Webster, Graham.
The Roman Imperial Army of the first and second centuries A.D./ Graham Webster. Totowa, N.J.: Barnes & Noble Books, 1985. xv, 343 p.
85-015696   355/.00937   0389205907
Rome -- Army. Rome -- History, Military -- 30 B.C.-476 A.D. Rome -- Military antiquities.

U37 History of military science — Medieval

U37.B44
Beeler, John.
Warfare in feudal Europe, 730-1200. Ithaca, Cornell University Press [1971] xvi, 272 p.
74-148018   355/.0094   0801406382
Military art and science -- Europe -- History. Military history, Medieval.

U37.C6513 1984
Contamine, Philippe.
War in the Middle Ages/ Philippe Contamine; translated by Michael Jones. New York, NY, USA: B. Blackwell, 1984. xvi, 387 p.
84-014647   355/.0094   0631131426
Military art and science -- Europe -- History -- Medieval, 500-1500. Europe -- History, Military.

U37.O5 1953
Oman, Charles William Chadwick, 1860-1946.
The art of war in the Middle Ages: A.D. 378-1515/ by C.W.C. Oman; rev. and ed. by John H. Beeler. Ithaca: Cornell University Press, 1968, c1953. xvi, 176 p.
53-011909   0801490626
Military art and science -- History. Military history, Medieval.

U37.O6 1959
Oman, Charles William Chadwick, 1860-1946.
A History of the art of war in the Middle Ages. New York, B. Franklin [1959] 2 v.
60-001195   355.0902
Military art and science -- History. Military history, Medieval.

U39 History of military science — Modern — General works

U39.C48
Chandler, David G.
The art of warfare in the age of Marlborough/ David Chandler. New York: Hippocrene Books, c1976. 317 p.
75-026934   355/.0094   0882543660
Military art and science -- History. Europe -- History, Military -- 1648-1789.

U39.C74
Creswell, John.
Generals and admirals; the story of amphibious command. London, Longmans, Green [1952] 192 p.
53-006373   355
Military history, Modern. Amphibious warfare.

U39.D74 1987
Duffy, Christopher, 1936-
The military experience in the age of reason/
Christopher Duffy. London; Routledge & Kegan
Paul, 1987.
87-027293 355/.0094 0710210248
*Military art and science -- Europe -- History --
18th century. Enlightenment. Military history,
Modern -- 18th century.*

U39.F8
Fuller, J. F. C. 1878-1966.
The conduct of war, 1789-1961; a study of the
impact of the French, industrial, and Russian
revolutions on war and its conduct.   New
Brunswick, N.J., Rutgers University Press, 1961.
352 p.
61-010261 355/.009
*Military art and science -- History. Military
history, Modern.*

U39.G38 1989
Gat, Azar.
The origins of military thought: from the
Enlightenment to Clausewitz/ Azar Gat. Oxford:
Clarendon Press; 1989. xii, 281 p.
88-028135 355.02/09 0198229488
*Clausewitz, Carl von, -- d1780-1831.Military
art and science -- Europe -- History -- 19th
century. War (Philosophy) -- History -- 18th
century. War (Philosophy) -- History -- 19th
century.*

U39.L38 1997
Lawrence, Philip K.
Modernity and war: the creed of absolute
violence/ Philip K. Lawrence. New York: St.
Martin's Press, 1997. viii, 206 p.
96-052561 355.02/09/04 0312174020
*Military history, Modern. War and society. Air
warfare -- Social aspects.*

U39.N67 1990
Nosworthy, Brent.
The anatomy of victory: battle tactics, 1689-
1763/ Brent Nosworthy. New York: Hippocrene
Books, c1990. xvi, 395 p.
89-035732 355.4/2/09032 0870527851
*Military art and science -- Europe -- History --
18th century. Military art and science -- Europe -
- History -- 17th century. Tactics -- History --
18th century.*

U39.O5 1937
**Oman, Charles William Chadwick, 1860-
1946.**
A history of the art of war in the sixteenth
century, by Sir Charles Oman ... with 33 maps
and 12 plates. London, Metheun [1937] xv,
784 p.
38-001590 355.0903
*Military history, Modern -- 16th century.
Military art and science -- History.*

U39.R6
Ropp, Theodore, 1911-
War in the modern world. Durham, N. C., Duke
University Press, 1959. 400 p.
60-005274 355.0903
*Military art and science -- History. Military
history, Modern.*

U39.R65
Rothenberg, Gunther Erich, 1923-
The art of warfare in the age of Napoleon/
Gunther E. Rothenberg. Bloomington: Indiana
University Press, c1978. 272 p.
77-086495 355/.0094 0253310768
*Military art and science -- History. Military
history, Modern -- 18th century. Military history,
Modern -- 19th century. Europe -- History,
Military -- 1789-1815.*

U39.T66 1990
Tools of war: instruments, ideas, and institutions
of warfare, 1445-1871/ edited by John A. Lynn.
Urbana: University of Illinois Press, c1990. xii,
262 p.
89-004887 355/.009 025201653X
*Military art and science -- History. Military
history, Modern. Technology -- History.*

U39.T87 1953
Turner, Gordon Brinkerhoff, 1915
A history of military affairs in Western society
since the eighteenth century.   New York:
Harcourt, Brace, [1953]. 776 p.
53-003995
Military art and science -- History.

U39.W37 1989
War in the world-system/ edited by Robert K.
Schaeffer. New York: Greenwood Press, 1989.
xii, 132 p.
88-035757 355/.02 031325429X
*Military history, Modern -- Congresses. War --
Congresses. History, Modern -- Congresses.*

U39.W45 1991
Weigley, Russell Frank.
The age of battles: the quest for decisive warfare
from Breitenfeld to Waterloo/ Russell F.
Weigley. Bloomington: Indiana University Press,
c1991. xviii, 579 p.
90-004757 355/.0094 0253363802
*Military art and science -- Europe -- History.
Battles -- Europe -- History. Military history,
Modern. Europe -- History, Military -- 1648-
1789.*

U42 History of military science — Modern — 20th century

U42.C55 1997
Cimbala, Stephen J.
The politics of warfare: the great powers in the
twentieth century/ Stephen J. Cimbala.
University Park, Pa.: Pennsylvania State
University Press, c1997. 245 p.
96-006450 355/.033/004 0271015977
*Military history, Modern -- 20th century.
Politics and war. World politics -- 1989-*

U42.C56 1990
Cohen, Eliot A.
Military misfortunes: the anatomy of failure in
war/ Eliot A. Cohen, John Gooch. New York:
Free Press; c1990. viii, 296 p.
89-023583 355.4/8/0904 0029060605
*Military art and science -- History -- 20th
century. Military history, Modern -- 20th
century.*

U42.C59 1990
Cordesman, Anthony H.
The lessons of modern war/ Anthony H.
Cordesman and Abraham R. Wagner. Boulder,
Colo.: Westview Press; 1990. 3 v.
89-016631 355.4/8 0813309549
*Military art and science -- History -- 20th
century. Military history, Modern -- 20th
century.*

U42.E48 1988
Emerging   doctrines   and   technologies:
implications for global and regional political-
military balances/ [edited by] Robert L.
Pfaltzgraff, Jr. ... [et al.]. Lexington, Mass.:
Lexington Books, c1988. x, 326 p.
87-045584 355/.009/04 066916755X
*Military art and science -- History -- 20th
century -- Congresses. Technology and state --
Congresses.   World   politics   --   1945-
Congresses. United States -- Military policy --
Congresses. Soviet Union -- Military policy --
Congresses.*

U42.H96 1997
Hynes, Samuel Lynn.
The soldiers' tale: bearing witness to modern
war/ Samuel Hynes. New York, N.Y., U.S.A.: A.
Lane, 1997. xvi, 318 p.
96-025842 355/.0092/2 0670865850
*Military history, Modern -- 20th century --
Sources. Soldiers -- United States -- Diaries.
Soldiers -- Great Britain -- Diaries.*

U42.J47 1989
Jessup, John E.
A chronology of conflict and resolution, 1945-
1985/ John E. Jessup. New York: Greenwood
Press, 1989. x, 942 p.
88-028974 355/.02/0904 0313243085
*Military history, Modern -- 20th century --
Chronology.   World   politics   --   1945-   --
Chronology.*

U42.M38 1988
Mearsheimer, John J.
Liddell Hart and the weight of history/ John J.
Mearsheimer. Ithaca: Cornell University Press,
1988. xi, 234 p.
88-047748 355/.009/04 080142089X
*Liddell Hart, Basil Henry, -- Sir, -- 1895-
1970.Military art and science -- History -- 20th
century.*

U42.M55 1988
Military effectiveness/ edited by Allan R. Millett
and Williamson Murray. Boston: Unwin Hyman,
[1988] v. 1
87-015284 355/.009/04 0044450532
*Military art and science -- History -- 20th
century. Military history, Modern -- 20th
century. Armed Forces -- History -- 20th century.*

U42.U53 1987
The Uncertain course: new weapons, strategies,
and mind-sets/ edited by Carl G. Jacobsen.
Oxford [Oxfordshire]; Oxford University Press,
1987. xxiii, 349 p.
86-033278 355/.02/0904 0198291159
*Military art and science -- History -- 20th
century. Weapons systems.*

U43 History of military science — By region or country, A-Z

U43.B9.B37 1992
Bartusis, Mark C.
The late Byzantine army: arms and society, 1204-1453/ Mark C. Bartusis. Philadelphia: University of Pennsylvania Press, c1992. xvii, 438 p.
92-014823   355/.009495   0812231791
   Military history, Medieval.Byzantine Empire -- Army.

U43.E95.E48 1996
Elton, Hugh.
Warfare in Roman Europe, AD 350-425/ Hugh Elton. Oxford: Clarendon Press; 1996. xv, 312 p.
95-017531   355/.00936   0198150075
   Military art and science -- Europe -- History.Europe -- History, Military. Rome -- History, Military -- 30 B.C.-476 A.D.

U43.E95.H35 1985
Hale, J. R. 1923-
War and society in Renaissance Europe, 1450-1620/ J.R. Hale. New York: St. Martin's Press, 1985. 282 p.
85-040404   306/.27/094   0312856032
   Military art and science -- Europe -- History. Sociology, Military -- Europe. Renaissance. Europe -- History, Military.

U43.E95.H36 1997
Hall, Bert S.
Weapons and warfare in renaissance Europe: gunpowder, technology, and tactics/ Bert S. Hall. Baltimore, Md.: Johns Hopkins University Press, 1997. xiii, 300 p.
96-043295   355.02/094/09024   0801855314
   Military art and science -- Europe -- History. Military weapons -- Europe -- History. Renaissance. Europe -- History, Military -- 1492-1648.

U43.E95.H68
Howard, Michael Eliot, 1922-
War in European history/ Michael Howard. London; Oxford University Press, 1976. x, 165 p.
76-372794   355/.0094   0192115642
   Military art and science -- History. War. Europe -- History, Military.

U43.E95.L86 1999
Lund, Erik A., 1964-
War for the every day: generals, knowledge, and warfare in early modern Europe, 1680-1740/ Erik A. Lund. Westport, Conn.: Greenwood Press, 1999. xii, 242 p.
99-018593   355.02/094/09032   0313310416
   Military art and science -- Europe -- History -- 17th century. Military art and science -- Europe -- History -- 18th century. Generals -- Europe -- History -- 17th century. Europe -- History, Military -- 1648-1789.

U43.E95.S76 1983
Strachan, Hew.
European armies and the conduct of war/ Hew Strachan. London; Allen & Unwin, 1983. 224 p.
83-008787   355/.0094   004940069X
   Military art and science -- Europe -- History. War. Military history, Modern.

U43.F8.G75 1989
Griffith, Paddy.
Military thought in the French army, 1815-51/ Paddy Griffith. Manchester [England]; Manchester University Press; c1989. viii, 236 p.
89-002810   355/.00944   0719028825
   Military art and science -- France -- History -- 19th century.

U43.G3.E28 2000
Echevarria, Antulio Joseph, 1959-
After Clausewitz: German military thinkers before the Great War/ Antulio J. Echevarria II. Lawrence: University Press of Kansas, c2000. ix, 346 p.
00-010228   355.02/0943/09034   0700610715
   Military art and science -- Germany -- History -- 19th century. Military art and science -- Germany -- History -- 20th century. Germany -- History, Military -- 19th century. Germany -- History, Military -- 20th century.

U43.G7.R45 1987
Reid, Brian Holden.
J.F.C. Fuller: military thinker/ Brian Holden Reid. New York: St. Martin's Press, 1987. xiii, 283 p.
87-009819   355/.0092/4   0312008287
   Fuller, J. F. C. -- (John Frederick Charles), -- 1878-1966.Military art and science -- Great Britain -- History -- 20th century. Tank warfare -- History.

U43.G7.S76 1988
Stone, Jay, 1949-
The Boer War and military reforms/ by Jay Stone and Erwin A. Schmidl. Lanham, MD: University Press of America; c1988. xi, 345 p.
87-025327   355/.00941   0819166529
   Military art and science -- Great Britain -- History -- 20th century. Military art and science -- Austria -- History -- 20th century. South African War, 1899-1902.

U43.G7.W56 1988
Winton, Harold R., 1942-
To change an army: General Sir John Burnett-Stuart and British armored doctrine, 1927-1938/ Harold R. Winton; foreword by Peter Paret. Lawrence, Kan.: University Press of Kansas, c1988. xviii, 284 p.
87-025579   358/.18/0924   0700603565
   Burnett-Stuart, John, -- Sir.Military art and science -- Great Britain -- History -- 20th century. Tank warfare -- History.

U43.R9.G3
Garthoff, Raymond L.
Soviet military doctrine; with a pref. H. A. De Weerd. Glencoe, Ill., Free Press [1953] xviii, 587 p.
53-007394   355
   Military art and science.Soviet Union -- Politics and government.

U43.T9.M87 1999
Murphey, Rhoads, 1949-
Ottoman warfare, 1500-1700/ Rhoads Murphey. New Brunswick, N.J.: Rutgers University Press, 1999. xxii, 278 p.
98-045274   355/.00956/0903   0813526841
   Military art and science -- Turkey -- History -- 16th century. Military art and science -- Turkey -- History -- 17th century. Turkey -- History, Military. Turkey -- History -- 1453-1683.

U43.U4.B37 1994
Bassford, Christopher.
Clausewitz in English: the reception of Clausewitz in Britain and America, 1815-1945/ Christopher Bassford. New York: Oxford University Press, 1994. x, 293 p.
93-019001   355.02/0941   0195083830
   Clausewitz, Carl von, -- 1780-1831 -- Influence.Military art and science -- Great Britain -- History. Military art and science -- United States -- History.

U43.U4.D43 1990
Dederer, John Morgan.
War in America to 1775: before Yankee Doodle/ John Morgan Dederer. New York: New York University Press, 1990. xvii, 323 p.
89-013520   355/.00973/09033   0814718280
   Military art and science -- United States -- History -- 18th century.United States -- History, Military -- To 1900. United States -- History -- Colonial period, ca. 1600-1775. United States -- History -- Revolution, 1775-1783.

U51 Biography — Collective

U51.W32 1976
The War lords: military commanders of the twentieth century/ edited by Sir Michael Carver. Boston: Little, Brown, c1976. xvi, 624 p.
76-014402   355.3/31/0922   0316130605
   Military biography. Military history, Modern -- 20th century.

U52-53 Biography — By region or country — United States

U52.D53 1984
Dictionary of American military biography/ Roger J. Spiller, editor, Joseph G. Dawson III, associate editor, T. Harry Williams, consulting editor. Westport, Conn.: Greenwood Press, 1984. 3 v.
83-012674   355/.0092/2   0313214336
   United States -- Armed Forces -- Biography -- Dictionaries. United States -- Biography -- Dictionaries.

U52.O5 1995
Schubert, Frank N.
On the trail of the buffalo soldier: biographies of African Americans in the U.S. Army, 1866-1917/ comp. and ed. by Frank N. Schubert. Wilmington, Del.: Scholarly Resources, 1995.
93-046408   355/.0092/273   0842024824
   Afro-American soldiers -- Biography.

U53.C48.A33
Chynoweth, Bradford Grethen, 1890-
Bellamy Park: memoirs/ by Bradford Grethen Chynoweth. Hicksville, N.Y.: Exposition Press, [1975] 301 p.
75-300646   355.3/31/0924   0682480657
   Chynoweth, Bradford Grethen, -- 1890-

U53.D38.F57 1989
Fletcher, Marvin.
America's first Black general: Benjamin O. Davis, Sr., 1880-1970/ Marvin E. Fletcher; with a foreword by Benjamin O. Davis, Jr. Lawrence, Kan.: University Press of Kansas, c1989. xix, 226 p.
88-026122   355/.008996073   0700603816
   Davis, Benjamin O., -- 1880-1970.Afro-American generals -- Biography. Generals -- United States -- Biography.

U53.E27.A34
Eardley, George C.
A letter for Josephine/ by George C. Eardley. Boston: Branden Press Publishers, c1975. 232 p.
75-009210 362.2/092/6 0828316198
Eardley, George C.Veterans -- United States -- Biography. Psychiatry, Military.

U53.F6.A3
Foulois, Benjamin Delahauf, 1879-1967.
From the Wright brothers to the astronauts; the memoirs of Benjamin D. Foulois. With C. V. Glines. New York, McGraw-Hill [1968] xi, 306 p.
68-014755 355.3/32/0924
Foulois, Benjamin Delahauf, -- 1879-1967.

U53.H5.A3
Hilleary, William M., 1840-(ca.) 19
A webfoot volunteer; the diary of William M. Hilleary, 1864-1866. Edited by Herbert B. Nelson and Preston E. Onstad, in cooperation with the Oregon Historical Society. Corvallis, Oregon State University Press [c1965] viii, 240 p.
65-065228 355.3510924
Oregon -- History -- Civil War, 1861-1865.

U53.R4.A32
Reeder, Red, 1902-
Army brat; life story of a West Pointer, by Red Reeder. New York, Meredith Press [1967] x, 240 p.
67-013910 355.1/0924
West Point. Reeder, Russell Potter.

U53.R59.A37
Roberts, Cecil E., 1919-
A soldier from Texas/ Cecil E. Roberts. Fort Worth: Branch-Smith, c1978. vi, 210 p.
78-067480 355.3/32/0924 0877061041
Roberts, Cecil E., -- 1919-Soldiers -- Texas -- Biography.Texas -- Biography.

U53.S53.C37 1989
Carlson, Paul Howard.
"Pecos Bill", a military biography of William R. Shafter/ Paul H. Carlson. College Station: Texas A&M University Press, c1989. xiii, 225 p.
88-036465 355/.0092/4 0890963487
Shafter, William Rufus, -- 1835-1906.Generals -- United States -- Biography.

U55 Biography — By region or country — Other regions or countries

U55.A45.F8 1960
Fuller, J. F. C. 1878-1966.
The generalship of Alexander the Great. New Brunswick, N.J., Rutgers University Press [1960] 336 p.
59-015620 355.48
Alexander, -- the Great, -- 356-323 B.C. -- Military leadership.Military art and science -- History. Generals -- Greece -- Biography. Greece -- History -- Macedonian expansion, 359-323 B.C. Macedonia -- Armed forces.

U55.L57.A3
Littauer, Vladimir Stanislas, 1892-
Russian Hussar by Vladimir S. Littauer; foreword by Sir Robert Bruce Lockhart. London: J.S. Allen & Co., 1965. 295 p.
66-070123
Littauer, Vladimir Stanislas, -- 1892-

U55.O26.B38 1989
Baynes, John Christopher Malcolm.
The forgotten victor: General Sir Richard O'Connor, KT, GCB, DSO, MC/ John Baynes. London; Brassey's; 1989. xiv, 320 p.
89-033821 355/.0092 0080362699
O'Connor, Richard Nugent, -- Sir, -- b. 1889.Generals -- Great Britain -- Biography.

U55.S25.A3
Sadler, Barry, 1940-
I'm a lucky one, by Barry Sadler with Tom Mahoney. New York, Macmillan [1967] 191 p.
67-015666 355/.0092/4
Sadler, Barry, -- 1940-

U55.W45.B3
Bankwitz, Philip Charles Farwell.
Maxime Weygand and civil-military relations in modern France. Cambridge, Harvard University Press, 1967. xiii, 445 p.
67-022860 944.081/0924
Weygand, Maxime, -- 1867-1965.

U101 General works — Early through 1788

U101.S932 1996
Sun-tzu, 6th cent. B.C
The complete art of war/ Sun-tzu, Sun Pin; translated, with historical introduction and commentary, by Ralph D. Sawyer; with the collaboration of Mei-chun Lee Sawyer. Boulder, Colo.: Westview Press, 1996. xv, 304 p.
96-013695 355.02 0813330858
Military art and science -- Early works to 1800.

U101.S95 1963a
Sun-tzu, 6th cent. B.C
The art of war/ Sun Tzu; translated and with an introd. by Samuel B. Griffith; with a foreword by B.H. Liddell Hart. New York: Oxford University Press, c1963. xvi, 197 p.
65-008619 355/.02 0195015401
Military art and science -- Early works to 1800.

U101.V4 1944
Vegetius Renatus, Flavius.
The military institutions of the Romans [by] Flavius Vegetius Renatus, translated from the Latin by Lieutenant John Clark, edited by Brig. Gen. Thomas R. Phillips, U. S. A. Harrisburg, Pa., The Military Service Publishing Company, [1944. 114 p.
44-051414 355
Military art and science -- Early works to 1800.

U102 General works — 1789-

U102.B985
Bush, Vannevar, 1890-1974.
Modern arms and free men: a discussion of the role of science in preserving democracy. New York, Simon and Schuster, 1949. 273 p.
49-048841 355
Military art and science. World politics -- 1945- Military weapons.

U102.C65 1984
Clausewitz, Carl von, 1780-1831.
On war/ Carl von Clausewitz; edited and translated by Michael Howard and Peter Paret; introductory essays by Peter Paret, Michael Howard, and Bernard Brodie; with a commentary by Bernard Brodie; index by Rosalie West. Princeton, N.J.: Princeton University Press, c1984. xii, 732 p.
84-003401 355 0691056579
Military art and science. War.

U102.F52 1970
Foch, Ferdinand, 1851-1929.
The principles of war. Translated by J. de Morinni. New York, AMS Press [1970] 372 p.
70-128436 355.4/3 0404024394
Military art and science.

U102.J7815
Jomini, Antoine Henri, 1779-1869.
Jomini and his Summary of the art of war; a condensed version edited, and with an introduction, by Lt. Col. J.D. Hittle ... Harrisburg [Pa.] Washington, Military Service [1947] 161 p.
47-002306 355
Military art and science.

U102.J78 1971
Jomini, Antoine Henri, 1779-1869.
The art of war. Translated from the French by G. H. Mendell and W. P. Craighill. Westport, Conn., Greenwood Press [1971] 410 p.
68-054793 355 0837150140
Military art and science.

U102.L58 1950a
Liddell Hart, Basil Henry, 1895-1970.
Defence of the West. New York, Morrow, 1950. x, 335 p.
50-010635
Military art and science.Europe -- Politics and government -- 1945-

U102.L63 1947
Liddell Hart, Basil Henry, 1895-
The revolution in warfare, by B. H. Liddell Hart. New Haven, Yale university press, c1947. x, 125 p.
47-003404 355
War. Military art and science.

U102.M68
Montgomery of Alamein, Bernard Law Montgomery, 1887-1976.
A history of warfare [by] Viscount Montgomery of Alamein. Cleveland, World Pub. Co. [1968] 584 p.
68-013718 355/.0009
Military art and science. Military history.

U102.P6713
Pokrovskii, Georgii Iosifovich.
Science and technology in contemporary war. Translated and annotated by Raymond L. Garthoff. New York, Praeger [1959] 180 p.
59-007885
Military research. Military supplies. Military art and science.

U102.R784 1989
Royle, Trevor.
A dictionary of military quotations/ compiled by Trevor Royle. New York: Simon & Schuster, 1989. xii, 210 p.
90-034034 355/.003 0132101130
Military art and science -- Quotations, maxims, etc.

U104 General special

U104.J35
Jane's weapon systems.   New York [etc.] F. Watts [etc.]
79-012909   623.4/05
Weapons systems -- Periodicals.

U104.S33
Schelling, Thomas C., 1921-
Arms and influence, by Thomas C. Schelling. New Haven, Yale University Press, 1966. viii, 293 p.
66-015744   355.0335
Military policy. World politics.

U105 Popular works

U105.P335 1989
Payne, Samuel B.
The conduct of war: an introduction to modern warfare/ Samuel B. Payne, Jr. Oxford, OX, UK; Blackwell, 1989. xiv, 309 p.
88-016652   355/.02   0631155325
Military art and science. Nuclear warfare. National security -- United States.

U155 Military planning — By region or country — Other regions or countries, A-Z

U155.G3.B83 1991
Bucholz, Arden.
Moltke, Schlieffen, and Prussian war planning/ Arden Bucholz. New York: Berg: 1991. xi, 352 p.
90-039333   355/.033543   0854966536
Schlieffen, Alfred, -- Graf von, -- 1833-1913. Moltke, Helmuth, -- Graf von, -- 1800-1891. Military planning -- Germany -- History -- 19th century. Military planning -- Germany -- History -- 20th century. Military planning -- Germany -- Prussia -- History -- 19th century.

U155.G7.P38 1989
Partridge, Michael Stephen.
Military planning for the defense of the United Kingdom, 1814-1870/ Michael Stephen Partridge. New York: Greenwood Press, 1989. viii, 240 p.
88-020637   355/.0335/41   0313268711
Military planning -- Great Britain -- History -- 19th century.Great Britain -- Defenses.

U162 Strategy — General works — 1789-

U162.C44
Chandler, David G.
Atlas of military strategy 1618-1878/ David G. Chandler; cartography by Hazel R. Watson and Richard A. Watson. Don Mills, Ont.: Collier Macmillan Canada; 1980. 208 p.
80-153960   355.4/8   0029903009
Strategy. Tactics. Military history, Modern.

U162.F89
Fryklund, Richard.
100 million lives; maximum survival in a nuclear war. New York, Macmillan [1962] 175 p.
62-012896   355.4
Strategy. Nuclear warfare.

U162.G68 1991
Grand strategies in war and peace/ edited by Paul Kennedy. New Haven: Yale University Press, c1991. x, 228 p.
90-023410   355.02/0722   0300049447
Strategy -- Case studies. Strategy -- History. National security -- Case studies. Europe -- History, Military.

U162.G69 1996
Gray, Colin S.
Explorations in strategy/ Colin S. Gray. Westport, Conn.: Greenwood Press, 1996. xx, 265 p.
95-050524   355.4   0313295107
Strategy.

U162.K49
Kingston-McCloughry, Edgar James, 1896-
Global strategy. New York, F.A. Praeger [1957] 270 p.
57-008328   355.43
Strategy.

U162.L87
Luttwak, Edward.
Strategy and politics/ Edward N. Luttwak. New Brunswick, N.J.: Transaction Books, c1980. viii, 328 p.
79-065224   355.03/3/08   0878553460
Strategy -- Addresses, essays, lectures. Military policy -- Addresses, essays, lectures. World politics -- Addresses, essays, lectures.

U162.M25 1986
Makers of modern strategy: from Machiavelli to the nuclear age/ edited by Peter Paret with the collaboration of Gordon A. Craig and Felix Gilbert. Princeton, N.J.: Princeton University Press, c1986. vii, 941 p.
85-017029   355/.02   0691092354
Strategy. Military art and science. Military history, Modern.

U162.N46 1991
Newell, Clayton R., 1942-
The framework of operational warfare/ Clayton R. Newell. London; Routledge, 1991. xiv, 186 p.
90-048001   355.02   0415050456
Operational art (Military science)

U162.S613 1975
Sokolovskii, Vasilii Danilovich, 1897-
Soviet military strategy/ V. D. Sokolovskiy; edited, with an analysis and commentary, by Harriet Fast Scott. New York: Crane, Russak, [1975] vlvii, 494 p.
73-094042   355.4/3/0947   0844803111
Strategy. War. Soviet Union -- Military policy. Soviet Union -- Armed Forces.

U162.S774
Strategic thought in the nuclear age/ editor, Laurence Martin; general editor, Hossein Amirsadeghi; contributors, Coral Bell, [et al.]. Baltimore: Johns Hopkins University Press, c1979. ix, 233 p.
79-002979   355.4/307   0801823307
Strategy -- Addresses, essays, lectures. World politics -- 1945- -- Addresses, essays, lectures.

U162.W9
Wylie, J. C. 1911-
Military strategy: a general theory of power control [by] J. C. Wylie. New Brunswick, N. J., Rutgers University Press [1967] vii, 111 p.
67-013076   355.4/3
Strategy.

U162.6 Strategy — Deterrence

U162.6.Z34 2000
Zagare, Frank C.
Perfect deterrence/ Frank C. Zagare and D. Marc Kilgour. Cambridge, UK: Cambridge University Press, c2000. xxii, 414 p.
99-088000   355.02/17   0521781744
Deterrence (Strategy)

U162.6.B66 1988
Bobbitt, Philip.
Democracy and deterrence: the history and future of nuclear strategy/ Philip Bobbitt. New York: St. Martin's Press, 1988. xii, 350 p.
86-031363   355/.0217   0312005229
Deterrence (Strategy) Nuclear warfare.

U162.6.C38 1986
Catudal, Honore Marc, 1944-
Nuclear deterrence--does it deter?/ Honore M. Catudal; foreword by Martin J. Hillenbrand. Atlantic Highlands, N.J.: Humanities Press International, Inc., 1986, c1985. 528 p.
85-030524   355/.0217   0391033905
Deterrence (Strategy) Nuclear warfare. Strategic forces. United States -- Military policy. Soviet Union -- Military policy.

U162.6.C57 1994
Cimbala, Stephen J.
Military persuasion: deterrence and provocation in crisis and war/ Stephen J. Cimbala. University Park, PA: Pennsylvania State University Press, c1994. x, 307 p.
93-001202   355.02/17   0271010053
Deterrence (Strategy) Nuclear crisis stability.

U162.6.D38 1993
Dauber, Cori Elizabeth.
Cold War analytical structures and the post post-war world: a critique of deterrence theory/ Cori Elizabeth Dauber. Westport, Conn.: Praeger, c1993. xiv, 207 p.
92-028475   355.02/17   0275944190
Deterrence (Strategy) Nuclear warfare.

U162.6.F48 1987
Finnis, John.
Nuclear deterrence, morality, and realism/ John Finnis, Joseph M. Boyle, Jr., Germain Grisez. Oxford: Clarendon Press; 1987. xv, 429 p.
86-023804   172/.42   0198247923
Deterrence (Strategy) -- Moral and ethical aspects. Nuclear warfare -- Religious aspects -- Christianity.

U162.6.G7
Green, Philip, 1932-
Deadly logic; the theory of nuclear deterrence [by] Philip Green. [Columbus] Ohio State University Press [1966] xix, 361 p.
66-023258   355.4307
Deterrence (Strategy) Nuclear warfare.

U162.6.H88 1988
Huth, Paul K., 1959-
Extended deterrence and the prevention of war/ Paul K. Huth. New Haven: Yale University Press, c1988. xi, 227 p.
88-014206   355/.0217   0300041675
Deterrence (Strategy) Military policy. International relations.

U162.6.L44 1993
Lee, Steven.
Morality, prudence, and nuclear weapons/ Steven P. Lee. Cambridge [England]; Cambridge University Press, 1993. xiv, 418 p.
92-030904 172/.422 0521382726
Deterrence (Strategy) -- Moral and ethical aspects. Nuclear weapons -- Moral and ethical aspects.

U162.6.N37 1974
Naroll, Raoul.
Military deterrence in history; a pilot cross-historical survey [by] Raoul Naroll, Vern L. Bullough [and] Frada Naroll. [Albany] State University of New York Press [1974] lxii, 416 p.
69-014647 355.03/35/09 087395047X
Deterrence (Strategy) Military history.

U162.6.P46 1989
Perspectives on deterrence/ edited by Paul C. Stern ... [et al.]; Committee on Contributions of Behavioral and Social Science to the Prevention of Nuclear War; Commission on Behavioral and Social Sciences and Education, National Research Council. New York: Oxford University Press, 1989. xiv, 343 p.
88-019606 355/.0217 0195057635
Deterrence (Strategy) -- Congresses. Nuclear warfare -- Congresses.

U162.6.S33 1984
The Security gamble: deterrence dilemmas in the nuclear age/ edited by Douglas MacLean. Totowa, N.J.: Rowman & Allanheld, 1984. xix, 170 p.
84-015080 355/.0217 0847673294
Deterrence (Strategy) Nuclear weapons. Military policy.

U163 Strategy — Miscellaneous topics (not A-Z)

U163.A7413 1981
Aron, Raymond, 1905-
The great debate: theories of nuclear strategy/ Raymond Aron; translated from the French by Ernst Pawel. Westport, Conn.: Greenwood Press, 1981, c1965. ix, 265 p.
81-000495 355.0217 0313228515
Strategy. Nuclear warfare. World politics -- 1945-

U163.B38 1982
Betts, Richard K., 1947-
Surprise attack: lessons for defense planning/ Richard K. Betts. Washington, D.C.: Brookings Institution, c1982. xii, 318 p.
82-070887 355.4/3 0815709307
Strategy. Surprise (Military science) Military history, Modern -- 20th century.

U163.C53 1998
Cimbala, Stephen J.
Coercive military strategy/ Stephen J. Cimbala. College Station: Texas A&M University Press, c1998. 229 p.
98-022791 327.1/17 0890968365
Strategy. United States -- Military policy -- Case studies.

U163.H38 2001
Harrison, Richard W., 1952-
The Russian way of war: operational art, 1904-1940/ Richard W. Harrison. Lawrence, Kan.: University Press of Kansas, c2001. xi, 351 p.
00-047775 355.4/0947/0904 070061074X
Operational art (Military science) -- History -- 20th century. Military art and science -- Russia -- History -- 20th century. Military art and science -- Soviet Union -- History Russia -- History, Military -- 20th century. Soviet Union -- History, Military.

U163.S76 1982
Strategic military deception/ edited by Donald C. Daniel, Katherine L. Herbig. New York: Pergamon Press, c1982. xiii, 378 p.
81-014364 355.4/3 0080272193
Strategy -- Addresses, essays, lectures. Deception (Military science) -- Addresses, essays, lectures.

U165 Tactics — General works — 1811-

U165.G69 1981
Griffith, Paddy.
Forward into battle: fighting tactics from Waterloo to Vietnam/ Paddy Griffith; with an introduction by John Keegan. Chichester [West Sussex]: A. Bird, 1981. 156 p.
81-215537 355.4/2/09034 0907319017
Tactics -- History -- 19th century. Tactics -- History -- 20th century. Military history, Modern -- 19th century.

U165.M495 1955a
Miksche, Ferdinand Otto, 1905-
Atomic weapons and armies. New York, Praeger [1955] 222 p.
55-007319 355.4
Tactics. Nuclear warfare Military art and science.

U167.5 Tactics — Special topics, A-Z

U167.5.R4.H4
Heilbrunn, Otto.
Warfare in the enemy's rear. With a foreword by Sir John Winthrop Hackett. New York, Praeger [c1963] 231 p.
63-020394 355.425
Guerrilla warfare. Parachute troops. Unified operations (Military science)

U168 Logistics

U168.E22
Eccles, Henry Effingham, 1898-
Logistics in the national defense. Harrisburg, Pa., Stackpole Co. [1959] 347 p.
59-011187 355.41
Logistics. United States -- Defenses.

U168.F44 1993
Feeding Mars: logistics in Western warfare from the Middle Ages to the present/ edited by John A. Lynn. Boulder, Colo.: Westview Press, 1993. xii, 326 p.
92-027652 355.4/11/09 0813317169
Logistics -- History.

U168.V36
Van Creveld, Martin L.
Supplying war: logistics from Wallenstein to Patton/ Martin Van Creveld. Cambridge; Cambridge University Press, 1977. viii, 284 p.
77-005550 355.4/1/094 052121730X
Logistics -- History. Military art and science -- History. Military history, Modern.

U200 Debarkation. Landing maneuvers

U200.V3
Vagts, Alfred, 1892-
Landing operations; strategy, psychology, tactics, politics, from antiquity to 1945 [by] Dr. Alfred Vagts. Harrisburg, Pa., Military Service Publishing Co., 1946. 831 p.
46-018796 355.422
Military history. Landing operations. Tactics.

U240 Small wars. Guerrilla warfare. Indian fighting

U240.A76 1989
Armies in low-intensity conflict: a comparative analysis/ edited by David A. Charters and Maurice Tugwell. London; Brassey's Defence Publishers, 1989. x, 272 p.
88-022219 355/.0215 0080362532
Low-intensity conflicts (Military science) Military history, Modern -- 20th century.

U240.A86
Asprey, Robert B.
War in the shadows; the guerrilla in history, by Robert B. Asprey. Garden City, N.Y., Doubleday [1975] 2 v.
72-092400 355.02/184/09 0385034709
Guerrilla warfare -- History. Vietnamese Conflict, 1961-1975.

U240.B43 1999
Beckett, I. F. W.
Encyclopedia of guerrilla warfare/ Ian F.W. Beckett. Santa Barbara, Calif.: ABC-CLIO, c1999. xxiii, 303 p.
98-055119 355.4/25 0874369290
Guerrilla warfare -- Encyclopedias. Guerrilla warfare -- Encyclopedias.

U240.B44 1999
Bell, J. Bowyer, 1931-
Dragonwars: armed struggle & the conventions of modern war/ J. Bowyer Bell. New Brunswick, N.J.: Transaction, c1999. xviii, 455 p.
99-020843 355.02 156000357X
Low-intensity conflicts (Military science) World politics -- 1989- United States -- Military policy.

U240.B53 1998
Biddiscombe, Alexander Perry, 1959-
Werwolf!: the history of the National Socialist guerrilla movement, 1944-1946/ Perry Biddiscombe. Toronto; University of Toronto Press, c1998. 455 p.
98-129905 940.54/8743 0802008623
World War, 1939-1945 -- Germany. Guerrilla warfare. Sabotage -- Germany.

U240.C8
Cross, James Eliot.
Conflict in the shadows, the nature and politics of guerrilla war. Garden City, N.Y., Doubleday, 1963. 180 p.
63-011227   355.425
Guerrilla warfare.

U240.D2813
Debray, Regis.
Revolution in the revolution? Armed struggle and political struggle in Latin America. Translated from the author's French and Spanish by Bobbye Ortiz. New York, MR Press [1967] 126 p.
67-027766   355.02/184/098
Guerrilla warfare. Guerrillas -- Latin America. Latin America -- Politics and government -- 1948-

U240.G3
Galula, David, 1919-
Counterinsurgency warfare; theory and practice. Foreword by Robert R. Bowie. New York, Praeger [1964] xiv, 143 p.
64-013387   355.425
Guerrilla warfare.

U240.G8239 1989
Guerrilla warfare and counterinsurgency: U.S.-Soviet policy in the Third World/ edited by Richard H. Shultz, Jr. ... [et al.]. Lexington, Mass.: Lexington Books, c1989. xiii, 433 p.
88-013380   355./0218   0669199346
Low-intensity conflicts (Military science)United States -- Military relations -- Developing countries. Soviet Union -- Military relations -- Developing countries. Developing countries -- Military relations -- United States.

U240.G833
Guevara, Ernesto, 1928-1967.
Guerrilla warfare [by] Che Guevara. New York, M[onthly] R[eview] Press, 1961. 127 p.
61-014052   355.425
Revolutions. Guerrilla warfare. Cuba -- History -- 1933-1959.

U240.J58 1996
Joes, Anthony James.
Guerrilla warfare: a historical, biographical, and bibliographical sourcebook/ Anthony James Joes; Robin Higham, advisory editor. Westport, Conn.: Greenwood Press, 1996. viii, 312 p.
95-052710   355.4/25/09   0313292523
Guerrilla warfare -- History. Guerrilla warfare -- Bibliography.

U240.K53 1971
Kitson, Frank.
Low intensity operations; subversion, insurgency, peace-keeping. Harrisburg, Pa.] Stackpole Books [1971] xi, 208 p.
72-162452   355.02/184   0811709574
Guerrilla warfare. Subversive activities. Insurgency.

U240.L36
Laqueur, Walter, 1921-
Guerrilla: a historical and critical study/ Walter Laqueur. Boston: Little, Brown, c1976. xii, 462 p.
76-022552   355.02/184/09   0316514691
Guerrilla warfare -- History.

U240.L68 1989
Low-intensity conflict: the pattern of warfare in the modern world/ edited by Loren B. Thompson. Lexington, Mass.: Lexington Books, c1989. xi, 207 p.
89-032014   355.62/15   0669200441
Low-intensity conflicts (Military science)

U240.M28 1966
Mao, Tse-tung, 1893-1976.
Basic tactics. Translated and with an introd. by Stuart R. Schram. Foreword by Samuel B. Griffith, II. New York, Praeger [1966] viii, 149 p.
66-018912   355.425
Guerrilla warfare.

U240.M343
Mao, Tse-tung, 1893-1976.
On guerrilla warfare. Translated and with an introd. by Samuel B. Griffith. New York, Praeger [1961] 114 p.
61-016648   355.02/18
Guerrilla warfare. Revolutions.

U240.M5 1970
Miksche, Ferdinand Otto, 1905-
Secret forces; the technique of underground movements, by F. O. Miksche. Westport, Conn., Greenwood Press [1970] 181 p.
73-110273   355.02/184   083714499X
Guerrilla warfare.

U240.O54 1990
O'Neill, Bard E.
Insurgency & terrorism: inside modern revolutionary warfare/ Bard E. O'Neill. Washington: Brassey's (US), c1990. x, 171 p.
90-036727   355.02/18/0904   0080374565
Guerrilla warfare -- History -- 20th century. Insurgency -- History -- 20th century. Terrorism -- History -- 20th century.

U240.O8
Osanka, Franklin Mark, ed.
Modern guerrilla warfare; fighting communist guerrilla movements, 1941-1961. Introd. by Samuel P. Huntington. [New York] Free Press of Glencoe [1962] 519 p.
62-011858   355.425
Guerrilla warfare. Military history, Modern -- 20th century. Communist strategy.

U240.P38 1990
Paschall, Rod, 1935-
LIC 2010: special operations & unconventional warfare in the next century/ Rob Paschall. Washington, D.C.: Brassey's, c1990. x, 166 p.
89-070807   355.02/18   0080359825
Low-intensity conflicts (Military science) Special operations (Military science)

U240.R53 1988
Rice, Edward E. 1909-
Wars of the third kind: conflict in underdeveloped countries/ Edward E. Rice. Berkeley: University of California Press, c1988. 186 p.
87-030894   909/.09724   0520062361
Low-intensity conflicts (Military science) -- History. Guerrilla warfare -- History -- 20th century. Military history, Modern -- 20th century. Developing countries -- History, Military.

U240.T56 1966a
Thompson, Robert Grainger Ker, 1916-
Defeating Communist insurgency; the lessons of Malaya and Vietnam [by] Sir Robert Thompson. New York, F. A. Praeger [1966] 171 p.
66-014507   355.425
Counterinsurgency -- Vietnam. Revolutions. Insurgency. Malaya -- History -- Malayan Emergency, 1948-1960.

U241
Counterinsurgency.
Counter-guerrilla
warfare

U241.M634 1995
Mockaitis, Thomas R., 1955-
British counterinsurgency in the post-imperial era/ Thomas R. Mockaitis. Manchester; Manchester University Press; c1995. xvi, 165 p.
94-029769   325/.341   0719039193
Counterinsurgency -- Great Britain -- History -- 20th century.Great Britain -- History, Military -- 20th century. Great Britain -- Foreign relations -- 1945-

U241.S43
Shackley, Theodore.
The third option: an American view of counterinsurgency operations/ Theodore Shackley. New York: Reader's Digest Press: c1981. xiii, 185 p.
80-026947   355./02184/0926   0070563829
Counterinsurgency -- Case studies. World politics -- 1975-1985. World politics -- 1965-1975. United States -- Military policy.

U260 Joint operations.
Combined operations

U260.B43 1993
Beaumont, Roger A.
Joint military operations: a short history/ Roger A. Beaumont. Westport, Conn.: Greenwood Press, 1993. xvii, 245 p.
92-036227   355.4/22   0313267448
Unified operations (Military science) -- History.

U262 Commando tactics

U262.K45 1989
Kelly, Ross S.
Special operations and national purpose/ by Ross S. Kelly. Lexington, Mass.: Lexington Books, c1989. xxii, 167 p.
87-046111   356/.16   0669174106
Special operations (Military science) Special forces (Military science) -- United States. Special forces (Military science) -- Europe.

U263 Atomic warfare

U263.A29 1991
After the cold war: questioning the morality of nuclear deterrence/ edited by Charles W. Kegley, Jr. and Kenneth L. Schwab. Boulder: Westview Press, 1991. xi, 276 p.
90-044539   172/.422
Nuclear warfare -- Moral and ethical aspects -- Congresses. Deterrence (Strategy) -- Moral and ethical aspects -- Congresses. World politics -- 1985-1995 -- Congresses.

U263.C483 1991
Cimbala, Stephen J.
Clausewitz and escalation: classical perspective on nuclear strategy/ Stephen J. Cimbala. London, England; F. Cass, 1991. 218 p.
91-002590   355.02/17   0714634204
Clausewitz, Carl von, -- 1780-1831. -- Vom Kriege.Nuclear warfare.

U263.C484 1990
Cimbala, Stephen J.
First strike stability: deterrence after containment/ Stephen J. Cimbala. New York: Greenwood Press, 1990. xvi, 213 p.
90-032456   355.02/17   0313274487
First strike (Nuclear strategy) Deterrence (Strategy) Nuclear crisis stability.

U263.C485 1989
Cimbala, Stephen J.
Nuclear endings: stopping war on time/ Stephen J. Cimbala. New York: Praeger, 1989. xxiii, 295 p.
88-027441   355/.0217   027593165X
Nuclear warfare -- Termination.

U263.C49 1988
Cimbala, Stephen J.
Nuclear strategizing: deterrence and reality/ Stephen J. Cimbala. New York: Praeger, 1988. x, 306 p.
87-038496   355/.0217   0275929876
Nuclear warfare. Deterrence (Strategy)

U263.C5 1987
Cimbala, Stephen J.
Nuclear war and nuclear strategy: unfinished business/ Stephen J. Cimbala. New York: Greenwood Press, 1987. xxiii, 276 p.
87-012003   355/.0217   031326015X
Nuclear warfare.

U263.C522 1989
Cimbala, Stephen J.
Strategic impasse: offense, defense, and deterrence theory and practice/ Stephen J. Cimbala. New York: Greenwood Press, 1989. xxi, 266 p.
89-002166   355.02/17   031326516X
Nuclear warfare. Deterrence (Strategy) World politics -- 1945-

U263.C75 1988
Crisis stability and nuclear war/ edited by Kurt Gottfried and Bruce G. Blair. New York: Oxford University Press, 1988. xi, 354 p.
88-012552   355/.0217   0195051467
Nuclear crisis stability.

U263.C89 1989
Cuzzort, Raymond Paul, 1926-
Using social thought: the nuclear issue and other concerns/ R.P. Cuzzort. Mountain View, Calif.: Mayfield Pub. Co., c1989. xvii, 342 p.
88-034581   355.02/17   0874848008
Nuclear warfare. Arms race -- History -- 20th century. Nuclear disarmament.

U263.E575 1985
Environmental consequences of nuclear war. Chichester; Published on behalf of the Scientific Committee on Problems of the Environment (SCOPE) of the International Council of Scientific Unions (ICSU), by J. Wiley, 1985-c1986. 2 v.
85-020114   574.5/222   0471909181
Nuclear warfare -- Environmental aspects.

U263.E58 1984
The Environmental effects of nuclear war/ edited by Julius London and Gilbert F. White. Boulder, Colo.: Westview Press, 1984. xii, 203 p.
84-019699   363.3/498   0813370140
Nuclear warfare -- Environmental aspects.

U263.E84 1989
Ethics in the nuclear age: strategy, religious studies, and the churches/ edited by Todd Whitmore. Dallas: Southern Methodist University Press, 1989. x, 240 p.
88-030568   172/.42   0870742833
Nuclear warfare -- Moral and ethical aspects. Nuclear warfare -- Religious aspects -- Christianity. Deterrence (Strategy) -- Moral and ethical aspects.

U263.F39 1988
Fateful visions: avoiding nuclear catastrophe/ edited by Joseph S. Nye, Jr., Graham T. Allison, Albert Carnesale. Cambridge, Mass.: Ballinger Pub. Co., c1988. viii, 299 p.
87-031836   355/.0217   0887302726
Nuclear warfare. Nuclear disarmament. World politics -- 1985-1995.

U263.H37 1984
Harwell, Mark A.
Nuclear winter: the human and environmental consequences of nuclear war/ Mark A. Harwell, with contributions by Joseph Berry ... [et al.]; with a foreword by Russell W. Peterson. New York: Springer-Verlag, c1984. xix, 179 p.
84-022126   355/.0217   0387960937
Nuclear warfare -- Environmental aspects. Nuclear winter.

U263.H39 1985
Hawks, doves, and owls: an agenda for avoiding nuclear war/ Graham T. Allison, Albert Carnesale, Joseph S. Nye, Jr., editors. New York: Norton, c1985. xii, 282 p.
84-029485   327.1/74   0393019950
Nuclear warfare. Nuclear disarmament.

U263.J47 1989
Jervis, Robert, 1940-
The meaning of the nuclear revolution: statecraft and the prospect of Armageddon/ Robert Jervis. Ithaca: Cornell University Press, 1989. x, 266 p.
88-043443   355/.0217   080142304X
Nuclear warfare. World politics -- 1945-

U263.K33 1984
Kahn, Herman, 1922-
Thinking about the unthinkable in the 1980s/ Herman Kahn. New York: Simon and Schuster, c1984. 250 p.
84-001432   355/.0217   0671475444
Nuclear warfare. Deterrence (Strategy)

U263.K855 1999
Kultgen, John H.
In the valley of the shadow: reflections on the morality of nuclear deterrence/ John Kultgen. New York: P. Lang, c1999. xiv, 415 p.
99-017506   172/.422   0820444731
Deterrence (Strategy) -- Moral and ethical aspects.United States -- Military policy.

U263.L39 1988
Lawrence, Philip K.
Preparing for Armageddon: a critique of Western strategy/ Philip K. Lawrence. Sussex, England: Wheatsheaf Books; 1988. xiv, 190 p.
87-032333   355/.0217   0745004539
Nuclear warfare.United States -- Military policy.

U263.L49 1988
Lewis, John Wilson, 1930-
China builds the bomb/ John Wilson Lewis and Xue Litai. Stanford, Calif.: Stanford Univeristy Press, c1988. xviii, 329 p.
87-030404   355.8/25119/0951   0804714525
Nuclear weapons -- China.China -- Military policy.

U263.L53 1990
Lifton, Robert Jay, 1926-
The genocidal mentality: Nazi holocaust and nuclear threat/ Robert Jay Lifton and Eric Markusen. New York: Basic Books, c1990. xiii, 346 p.
89-043101   355.02/17/019   0465026621
Nuclear warfare -- Psychological aspects. Genocide -- Psychological aspects. Holocaust, Jewish (1939-1945) -- Psychological aspects. United States -- Military policy.

U263.N846 1986
Nuclear winter, deterrence, and the prevention of nuclear war/ edited by Peter C. Sederberg. New York: Praeger, 1986. x, 200 p.
86-009412   355/.0217   0275921603
Nuclear warfare. Nuclear winter. Deterrence (Strategy)

U263.P77 1988
Psychoanalysis and the nuclear threat: clinical and theoretical studies/ editors, Howard B. Levine, Daniel Jacobs, Lowell J. Rubin. Hillsdale, NJ: Analytic Press: 1988. xi, 290 p.
88-026245   355/.0217/019   0881630624
Nuclear warfare -- Psychological aspects. Psychoanalysis.

U263.S378 1988
Schwartzman, David.
Games of chicken: four decades of U.S. nuclear policy/ David Schwartzman. New York, NY: Praeger, 1988. xi, 233 p.
87-029131   355/.0217/0973   0275928845
Nuclear warfare.United States -- Military policy.

U263.S53 1990
Sichol, Marcia, 1940-
The making of a nuclear peace: the task of today's just war theorists/ Marcia Sichol. Washington, D.C.: Georgetown University Press, c1990. xiv, 219 p.
89-023688   172/.422   0878404821
Ramsey, Paul -- Contributions in just war doctrine. O'Brien, William Vincent -- Contributions in just war doctrine. Walzer, Michael -- Contributions in just war doctrine. Nuclear warfare -- Moral and ethical aspects. Just war doctrine. Peace.

U263.S76 1986
Strategic nuclear targeting/ edited by Desmond Ball and Jeffrey Richelson. Ithaca, N.Y.: Cornell University Press, 1986. 367 p.
85-048195   358/.39   0801418984
Targeting (Nuclear strategy)

U263.T46 1985
Thompson, James A.
Psychological aspects of nuclear war/ James Thompson. 1st ed. Chichester; British Psychological Society and J. Wiley, ix, 127 p.
85-175840   355/.0217 19   0901715344
Nuclear warfare--Psychological aspects. Civil defense--Psychological aspects--Great Britain.

U264 Atomic weapons — General works

U264.A27 1998
The absolute weapon revisited: nuclear arms and the emerging international order/ edited by T.V. Paul, Richard J. Harknett, and James J. Wirtz. Ann Arbor: University of Michigan Press, c1998. viii, 312 p.
97-033943   327.1/747   0472108638
Nuclear weapons -- Congresses. Deterrence (Strategy) -- Congresses. World politics -- 1989- -- Congresses.

U264.B34 1995
Badash, Lawrence.
Scientists and the development of nuclear weapons: from fission to the Limited Test Ban Treaty, 1939-1963/ Lawrence Badash. Atlantic Highlands, N.J.: Humanities Press, 1995. ix, 129 p.
94-017471   355.02/17/09   0391038737
Nuclear weapons -- History. Arms race -- History.

U264.D97 1984
Dyson, Freeman J.
Weapons and hope/ by Freeman Dyson. New York: Harper & Row, c1984. viii, 340 p.
83-048343   327.1/74   006039031X
Dyson, Freeman J.Nuclear warfare. Military weapons. Arms race.

U264.M66 1987
Moore, J. D. L.
South Africa and nuclear proliferation: South Africa's nuclear capabilities and intentions in the context of international non-proliferation policies/ J.D.L. Moore. New York: St. Martin's Press, 1987. xvii, 227 p.
86-017693   355.8/25119/0968   0312746989
Nuclear weapons -- South Africa.South Africa -- Military policy.

U264.N827 1984 vol. 4
Soviet nuclear weapons/ by Thomas B. Cochran ... [et al.]. New York: Harper & Row, Ballinger Division, c1989. xviii, 433 p.
89-011156   355.8/25119/0947   0887300480
Nuclear weapons -- Soviet Union.Soviet Union -- Armed Forces -- Weapons systems.

U264.N84 1988
The Nuclear weapons world: who, how & where/ edited by Patrick Burke. Westport, Conn.: Greenwood Press, 1988. xv, 383 p.
88-030078   355/.0217   0313265909
Nuclear weapons. Military policy -- Decision making. Public officers -- Directories.

U264.O38 1983
O'Keefe, Bernard J.
Nuclear hostages/ Bernard J. O'Keefe. Boston: Houghton Mifflin, 1983. 251 p.
83-000067   355.8/25119   0395340721
O'Keefe, Bernard J.Nuclear weapons -- History. Nuclear weapons -- Testing. Nuclear disarmament.

U264.R45 1995
Reiss, Mitchell.
Bridled ambition: why countries constrain their nuclear capabilities/ Mitchell Reiss. Washington, D.C., U.S.A.: Woodrow Wilson Center Press; c1995. 346 p.
95-002646   355.02/17   0943875722
Nuclear weapons -- Government policy -- Case studies. Nuclear nonproliferation -- Case studies.

U264.S233 1995
Sagan, Scott Douglas.
The spread of nuclear weapons: a debate/ Scott D. Sagan, Kenneth N. Waltz. New York: W.W. Norton, c1995. x, 160 p.
94-024470   355.02/17   0393038106
Nuclear weapons. Arms race. Nuclear nonproliferation.

U264.S37 1990
Schwartz, William A.
The nuclear seduction: why the arms race doesn't matter--and what does/ William A. Schwartz and Charles Derber with Gordon Fellman ... [et al.]. Berkeley: University of California Press, c1990. xiii, 294 p.
89-005028   355.02/17   0520061349
Nuclear weapons. Arms race -- History -- 20th century. Nuclear warfare.

U264.S585 1989
Smith, Jeff, 1958-
Unthinking the unthinkable: nuclear weapons and western culture/ Jeff Smith. Bloomington: Indiana University Press, c1989. xvi, 190 p.
88-045458   355/.0217   025335353X
Nuclear weapons -- Social aspects -- United States. Nuclear warfare -- Social aspects -- United States. Antinuclear movement -- United States. United States -- Civilization.

U264.S636 1988
Spector, Leonard S.
The undeclared bomb/ Leonard S. Spector. Cambridge, Mass.: Ballinger Pub. Co., c1988. xix, 499 p.
88-028726   355.8/25119   088730303X
Nuclear weapons. World politics -- 1985-1995. Nuclear nonproliferation.

U264.T87 1997
Turner, Stansfield, 1923-
Caging the nuclear genie: an American challenge for global security/ Stansfield Turner. Boulder, Colo.: Westview Press, c1997. xi, 163 p.
97-019178   327.1/747   0813333288
No first use (Nuclear strategy) Security, International.

U264.U53 1992
Ungar, Sheldon.
The rise and fall of nuclearism: fear and faith as determinants of the arms race/ Sheldon Ungar. University Park, Pa.: Pennsylvania State University Press, c1992. 214 p.
91-036222   355.02/17/019   0271008407
Nuclear weapons -- Psychological aspects. Nuclear energy -- Psychological aspects. Arms race -- Psychological aspects.

U264.3 Atomic weapons — United States — General works

U264.3.H333 1994
Hacker, Barton C., 1935-
Elements of controversy: the Atomic Energy Commission and radiation safety in nuclear weapons testing, 1947-1974/ Barton C. Hacker. Berkeley: University of California Press, c1994. xxiv, 614 p.
93-041611   355.8/25119/0973   0520083237
Nuclear weapons -- United States -- Testing -- Safety measures -- History.

U264.3.H36 1990
Hamilton, Michael S.
Nuclear weapons in the university classroom: an interdisciplinary teaching reference/ Michael S. Hamilton, William A. Lindeke, John MacDougall. Lanham, Md.: University Press of America, c1990. xii, 151 p.
89-077083   327.1/74   0819177423
Nuclear weapons -- Study and teaching (Higher) Nuclear weapons -- Study and teaching (Higher) -- United States. Nuclear warfare -- Study and teaching (Higher)

U264.3.N83 1989
The Nuclear weapons complex: management for health, safety, and the environment/ Committee to Provide Interim Oversight of the DOE Nuclear Weapons Complex, Commission on Physical Sciences, Mathematics, and Resources, National Research Council. Washington, D.C.: National Academy Press, 1989. x, 146 p.
89-063691   363.1/1962345119/0973   0309041791
Nuclear weapons plants -- United States -- Safety measures. Nuclear weapons plants -- Environmental aspects -- United States. Nuclear weapons plants -- Employees -- Health and hygiene -- United States.

U264.3.R68 1990
Rosenthal, Debra.
At the heart of the bomb: the dangerous allure of weapons work/ Debra Rosenthal. Reading, Mass.: Addison-Wesley, c1990. xi, 244 p.
89-027187   172/.422   0201197944
Nuclear weapons -- Moral and ethical aspects -- United States. Nuclear weapons -- Moral and ethical aspects. Nuclear engineers -- United States -- Attitudes.

U264.3.W43 1994
Weisgall, Jonathan M., 1949-
Operation crossroads: the atomic tests at Bikini
Atoll/ Jonathan M. Weisgall. Annapolis, Md.:
Naval Institute Press, c1994. xvii, 415 p.
93-042134   363.17/99   1557509190
*Operation Crossroads, 1946. Nuclear weapons
-- Marshall Islands -- Bikini Atoll -- Testing.
Nuclear weapons -- United States.*

U264.4 Atomic weapons — United States — By region or state, A-Z

U264.4.C2.G87 1996
Gusterson, Hugh.
Nuclear rites: a weapons laboratory at the end of
the Cold War/ Hugh Gusterson. Berkeley:
University of California Press, c1996. xviii,
351 p.
96-007234   306.2/7   0520081471
*Nuclear weapons -- Research -- Social aspects
-- California -- Livermore. Antinuclear
movement -- Social aspects.*

U264.4.G73.G53 1993
Glass, Matthew, 1954-
Citizens against the MX: public languages in the
nuclear age/ Matthew Glass; foreword by Robert
N. Bellah. Urbana: University of Illinois Press,
c1993. xxii, 188 p.
91-046323   327.1/74/0979   0252019288
*Nuclear weapons -- Great Basin. Antinuclear
movement -- Great Basin. MX (Weapons system)*

U264.5 Atomic weapons — Other regions or countries, A-Z

U264.5.G7.L37 1996
Larkin, Bruce D., 1936-
Nuclear designs: Great Britain, France, and
China in the global governance of nuclear arms/
Bruce D. Larkin. New Brunswick (U.S.A.):
Transaction, c1996. 354 p.
95-023279   327.1/74   1560002395
*Nuclear weapons -- Government policy --
Great Britain. Nuclear weapons -- Government
policy -- France. Nuclear weapons --
Government policy -- China.*

U310 War games. Kriegsspiel — General works

U310.S483 1994
Shelley, Bruce.
Strike commander: the official strategy guide and
flight school/ Bruce Shelley. Rocklin, CA: Prima
Pub., c1994. xviii, 371 p.
93-086553   793.9/2/02855369   1559582030
*Computer war games. Air warfare -- Computer
simulation.*

U328 Military sports — By region or country, A-Z

U328.U5.W35 1997
Wakefield, Wanda Ellen, 1953-
Playing to win: sports and the American military,
1898-1945/ Wanda Ellen Wakefield. Albany,
NY: State University of the New York Press,
c1997. x, 216 p.
96-019224   306.2/7/0973   0791433137
*Military sports -- United States -- History.
Sociology, Military -- United States -- History.
Masculinity -- United States.*

U353 Ceremonies. Honors. Salutes — By region or country —United States

U353.B6
Boatner, Mark Mayo, 1921-
Military customs and traditions. Illustrated by
Lachlan M. Field. New York, D. McKay Co.
[1956] 176 p.
56-014010   355.1
*Military ceremonies, honors, and salutes --
United States.*

U393 Military research — By region or country — United States

U393.F64 1993
Foerstel, Herbert N.
Secret science: federal control of American
science and technology/ Herbert N. Foerstel.
Westport, Conn.: Praeger, 1993. 227 p.
92-023453   355/.07/073   0275944476
*Military research -- United States. Science and
state -- United States. Technology and state --
United States.*

U393.L385 1993
Leslie, Stuart W.
The Cold War and American science: the
military-industrial-academic complex at MIT and
Stanford/ Stuart W. Leslie. New York: Columbia
University Press, c1993. xiii, 332 p.
92-028295   355/.07/0973   0231079583
*Military research -- United States. Education,
Higher -- Political aspects -- United States.*

U408-428.5 Military education and training — By region or country — America

U408.L67
Lovell, John P., 1932-
Neither Athens nor Sparta?: The American
service academies in transition/ John P. Lovell.
Bloomington: Indiana University Press, c1979.
xviii, 362 p.
78-009509   355/.007/1173   0253129559
Military education -- United States -- History.

U408.P78 2000
Professional military education in the United
States: a historical dictionary/ edited by William
E. Simons. Westport, Conn.: Greenwood Press,
c2000. xiv, 391 p.
99-043507   355/.0071/073   0313297495
*Military education -- United States -- History -
- Encyclopedias.*

U408.3.V36 1990
Van Creveld, Martin L.
The training of officers: from military
professionalism to irrelevance/ Martin van
Creveld. New York: Free Press; c1990. ix, 134 p.
89-017214   355.3/3/07073   0029331528
*Military education -- United States.United
States -- Armed Forces -- Officers -- Education.*

U409.S9
Andrew, Rod.
Long gray lines: the Southern military school
tradition, 1839-1915/ Rod Andrew, Jr. Chapel
Hill, N.C.: University of North Carolina Press,
c2001. viii, 169 p.
00-060723   355/.0071/173   0807826103
*Military education -- Southern States -- History
-- 19th century. Military education -- Southern
States -- History -- 20th century.*

U410.L1.A7
Ambrose, Stephen E.
Duty, honor, country; a history of West Point
[by] Stephen E. Ambrose. Baltimore, Johns
Hopkins Press [1966] xv, 357 p.
66-014372   355.0071173
United States Military Academy

U410 L1.P37 1993
Pappas, George S.
To the Point: the United States Military
Academy, 1802-1902/ George S. Pappas;
foreword by Edward C. Meyer. Westport, Conn.:
Praeger, 1993. xxi, 474 p.
92-036632   355/.0071/173   0275943291
United States Military Academy -- History.

U410.P1.S54 1988
Smith, Dale O.
Cradle of valor: the intimate letters of a plebe at
West Point between the two world wars/ by Dale
O. Smith; with an introduction by John
Eisenhower. Chapel Hill, N.C.: Algonquin Books
of Chapel Hill; 1988. xx, 268 p.
87-030426   355/.007/1173   0912697806
*Smith, Dale O. -- Correspondence.Soldiers --
United States -- Biography.*

U413.C64 1995
Cohen, Eliot A.
Making do with less, or coping with Upton's
ghost/ Eliot A. Cohen. [Carlisle Barracks, Pa.]:
Strategic Studies Institute, U.S. Army War
College, [1995] v, 24 p.
95-216494   355/.00973
*Civil-military relations -- United States.
Military planning -- United States.*

U428.5.L9
Lyons, Gene Martin, 1924-
Education and military leadership; a study of the
R.O.T.C., by Gene M. Lyons [and] John W.
Masland. With a foreword by John Sloan Dickey.
Princeton, N.J., Princeton University Press, 1959.
283 p.
59-009227   355.37
*United States. Army. Reserve Officers'
Training Corps.*

U428.5.N45 2000
Neiberg, Michael.
Making citizen-soldiers: ROTC and the ideology of American military service/ Michael S. Neiberg. Cambridge, Mass.: Harvard University Press, 2000. 264 p.
99-044354   355.2/232/071173   0674543122
United States -- Armed Forces -- Officers -- Training of.

U644 Military education and training — By region or country — Asia

U644.C36.L1 1994
Li, Lincoln, 1939-
Student nationalism in China, 1924-1949/ Lincoln Li. Albany: State University of New York Press, c1994. x, 209 p.
93-006639   322.4   0791417492
Nationalism -- China -- History.

U760 Military life, manners and customs, antiquities, etc. — By period — Medieval

U760.P6
Powicke, Michael.
Military obligation in medieval England; a study in liberty and duty. Oxford, Clarendon Press, 1962. 263 p.
62-004960   355.220942
Feudalism -- Great Britain.Great Britain -- History, Military. Great Britain -- Militia.

U760.S3
Sanders, I. J.
Feudal military service in England; a study of the constitutional and military powers of the barones in medieval England. London, Oxford University Press, 1956. xv, 173 p.
56-013590
Baronetage. Feudalism -- Great Britain. Great Britain -- History, Military.

U766-773 Military life, manners and customs, antiquities, etc. — By period — Modern

U766.I73 1983
Ingraham, Larry H.
The boys in the barracks: observations on American military life/ Larry H. Ingraham; with critical commentary by Frederick J. Manning. Philadelphia: Institute for the Study of Human Issues, c1984. xxi, 242 p.
83-000250   355.1/0973   0897270487
Sociology, Military -- United States. Soldiers -- United States.

U771.W57 1990
Wirtschafter, Elise Kimerling.
From serf to Russian soldier/ Elise Kimerling Wirtschafter.   Princeton,   N.J.:   Princeton University Press, c1990. xix, 214 p.
89-010522   306.2/7/0947   0691055858
Serfdom -- Russia -- History -- 19th century.Russia -- Armed Forces -- Military life -- History -- 19th century.

U773.K4
Kennedy, Malcolm Duncan, 1895-
The military side of Japanese life, by M. D. Kennedy ... London [etc.] Constable & company. ltd., 1924. xix, 367 p.
25-009830
Japan -- Army -- Military life.

U793 Weapons of mass destruction

U793.P53 2000
Planning the unthinkable: how new powers will use nuclear, biological, and chemical weapons/ [edited by] Peter R. Lavoy, Scott D. Sagan, and James J. Wirtz. Ithaca, NY: Cornell University Press, 2000. viii, 270 p.
00-037678   358/.3   0801437768
Weapons of mass destruction. World politics -- 21st century.

U800 History of arms and armor — General works

U800.B85 1991
Bull, Stephen.
An historical guide to arms & armor/ Stephen Bull; edited by Tony North. New York: Facts on File, 1991. 224 p.
91-036681   355.8/24/09   0816026203
Military weapons -- History. Armor -- History.

U800.M64 2001
Moy, Timothy.
War machines: transforming technologies in the U.S. military, 1920-1940/ Timothy Moy. College Station: Texas A & M University Press, c2001. xiv, 218 p.
00-010344   355/.07/0973   158544104X
Military weapons -- United States -- History -- 20th century. Technology and state -- United States -- History -- 20th century.

U800.O3
Oakeshott, R. Ewart.
The archaeology of weapons; arms and armor from prehistory to the age of chivalry. Illustrated by the author. New York, Praeger [1960] 358 p.
60-011279   399
Arms and armor -- History. Military history.

U800.W4 1966
Weller, Jac.
Weapons and tactics: Hastings to Berlin/ Jac Weller. New York: St. Martin's Press, 1966. 238 p.
66-014030   356
Arms and armor. Armed Forces. Tactics.

U805 History of arms and armor — By period — Ancient

U805.S59
Snodgrass, Anthony M.
Arms and armour of the Greeks [by] A. M. Snodgrass. Ithaca, N.Y., Cornell University Press [1967] 151 p.
67-020632   399
Weapons, Ancient -- Greece. Armor, Ancient -- Greece.

U810 History of arms and armor — By period — Medieval

U810.N5 1988
Nicolle, David.
Arms and armour of the crusading era, 1050-1350/ David C. Nicolle. White Plains, N.Y.: Kraus International Publications, c1988. 2 v.
87-003566   623.4/41/09021   0527671282
Weapons. Armor, Medieval. Crusades.

U815 History of arms and armor — By period — Modern

U815.E5313 1982
The complete encyclopedia of arms & weapons/ edited by Leonid Tarassuk and Claude Blair; [translated from the Italian by Sylvia Mulcahy, Simon Pleasance, and Hugh Young]. New York: Simon and Schuster, [c1982] 544 p.
80-005922   355.8/24/03
Weapons -- Encyclopedias.

U825 History of arms and armor — Armor

U825.B55
Blair, Claude.
European armour, circa 1066 to circa 1700. London, Batsiford [1958] 248 p.
59-024447   399
Arms and armor -- History.

U883-884 History of arms and armor — Arms for throwing projectiles — By period

U883.O55
O'Neil, B. H. St. J.
Castles and cannon: a study of early artillery fortifications in England/ by B. H. ST. J. O'Neil. Oxford: Clarendon Press, 1960. xix, 121 p.
60-052201
Castles -- England. Ordnance -- History.

U884 .C3
Carman, W. Y.
A history of firearms, from earliest times to 1914. New York, St. Martin's Press [c1955] 207 p.
56-010694   623.409
Ordnance.

UA Armies: Organization, distribution, military situation

UA10 General works

UA10.B47 1982
Berghahn, Volker Rolf.
Militarism: the history of an international debate, 1861-1979/ Volker R. Berghahn. New York: St. Martin's Press, 1982. 132 p.
81-048630   355/.0213   0312532326
Militarism. Civil-military relations. Sociology, Military.

UA10.B87 1994
Burrows, William E., 1937-
Critical mass: the dangerous race for superweapons in a fragmenting world/ William E. Burrows & Robert Windrem. New York: Simon and Schuster, c1994. 573 p.
93-036604   327.1/17   0671748955
Arms race. World politics -- 1989- Nuclear weapons -- Developing countries. Developing countries -- Armed Forces -- Weapons systems.

UA10.G77 1997
Gupta, Amit, 1958-
Building an arsenal: the evolution of regional power force structures/ Amit Gupta. Westport, Conn.: Praeger, 1997. 217 p.
96-027453   355.8/2   027595787X
Arms race. Arms transfers -- India. Arms transfers -- Israel.

UA10.H36 1993
Hammond, Grant Tedrick, 1945-
Plowshares into swords: arms races in international politics, 1840-1991/ Grant T. Hammond. Columbia: University of South Carolina Press, c1993. xviii, 342 p.
93-016809   327.1/17   0872498735
Arms race -- History.

UA10.H6 1959
Howard, Michael Eliot, 1922-
Soldiers and governments; nine studies in civil-military relations. Pref. by George Fielding Eliot. Bloomington, Indiana University Press, 1959. 192 p.
59-011094   355.082
World politics. Militarism.

UA10.K53
Knorr, Klaus Eugen, 1911-
The war potential of nations.   Princeton, Princeton University Press, 1956. viii, 310 p.
56-010824   355.2
War -- Economic aspects. Armaments.

UA10.M5915 1989
The Militarization of the Western world/ edited by John R. Gillis. New Brunswick: Rutgers University Press, c1989. ix, 216 p.
88-036808   355/.0213/09   0813514495
Militarism -- History -- 19th century. Militarism -- History -- 20th century. World politics -- 19th century.

UA10.P38 1989
Payne, James L.
Why nations arm/ James L. Payne. Oxford, UK; B. Blackwell, 1989. vii, 247 p.
88-021684   355/.0213   063116524X
Military readiness. Military policy. Armed Forces. United States -- Military policy. United States -- Armed Forces.

UA10.P43 1994
Pearson, Frederic S.
The global spread of arms: political economy of international security/ Frederic S. Pearson. Boulder: Westview Press, 1994. xiii, 161 p.
94-008108   327.1/74   0813315735
Arms race. Arms transfers. Defense industries -- Social aspects.

UA10.S475 1991
Shaw, Martin.
Post-military society: militarism, demilitarization, and war at the end of the twentieth century/ Martin Shaw. Philadelphia: Temple University Press, c1991. viii, 229 p.
91-040257   355.02/13/0904   0877229406
Militarism -- History -- 20th century. War and society. World politics -- 1945-

UA10.V3 1959
Vagts, Alfred, 1892-
A history of militarism: [civilian and military. New York] Meridian Books [1959] 542 p.
59-007194   355/.0213
Militarism. Military history.

UA10.5 National security

UA10.5.B73 1988
Brams, Steven J.
Game theory and national security/ Steven J. Brams and D. Marc Kilgour. New York, NY, USA: B. Blackwell, 1988. ix, 199 p.
88-005018   355/.03/0151   1557860041
National security -- Mathematical models. War games. Game theory.

UA10.5.C665 1989
Conflict and consensus in South/North security/ edited by Caroline Thomas and Paikiasothy Saravanamuttu.   Cambridge   [England]; Cambridge University Press, 1989. ix, 204 p.
89-007210   355/.033/0048   0521372682
National security. National security -- Developing countries. World politics -- 1985-1995.

UA10.5.C85 1996
The culture of national security: norms and identity in world politics/ edited by Peter J. Katzenstein; [sponsored by the Committee on International Peace & Security of the Social Science Research Council]. New York: Columbia University Press, c1996. xv, 562 p.
96-014340   355/.03   0023110465
National security. Nationalism. Social institutions.

UA10.5.G573 1987
Global security: a review of strategic and economic issues/ edited by Barry M. Blechman and Edward N. Luttwak. Boulder, Colo.: Westview, 1987. xiv, 258 p.
87-014661   355/.03   0813304806
National security. World politics -- 1985-1995. National security -- United States.

UA10.5.K85 1994
Kupchan, Charles.
The vulnerability of empire/ Charles A. Kupchan. Ithaca: Cornell University Press, 1994. x, 527 p.
93-024323   355/.03   0801428858
National security. Military policy. Balance of power.

UA10.5.M32 1994
Mandel, Robert, 1949-
The changing face of national security: a conceptual analysis/ Robert Mandel. Westport, Conn.: Greenwood Press, 1994. xviii, 155 p.
94-017982   355/.03   0313285195
National security. World politics -- 1989-

UA10.5.M325 1999
Mandel, Robert, 1949-
Deadly transfers and the global playground: transnational security threats in a disorderly world/ Robert Mandel. Westport, Conn.: Praeger, 1999. 139 p.
98-046794   327.1/7   0275962288
National security -- International cooperation. Security, International. Subversive activities.

UA10.5.N295 1984
National security policy: the decision-making process/ edited by Robert L. Pfaltzgraff, Jr., Uri Ra'anan. Hamden, Conn.: Archon Books, 1984. xiii, 311 p.
84-002932   355/.0335   0208020039
National security -- Decision making. Military policy -- Decision making.

UA10.5.S38 1989
Security and arms control/ edited by Edward A. Kolodziej and Patrick M. Morgan. New York: Greenwood Press, 1989. 2 v.
88-007224   355/.03   0313252572
National security. Security, International. Arms control.

UA10.5.S415 1993
Security studies for the 1990s/ edited by Richard Shultz, Roy Godson, Ted Greenwood. Washington: Brassey's (US), c1993. vii, 423 p.
93-012607   355/.03/0711   0028810724
National security -- Study and teaching (Higher)

UA11 Military policy

UA11.A67 1995
Arms and technology transfers: security and economic considerations among importing and exporting states/ edited by Sverre Lodgaard and Robert L. Pfaltzgraff, Jr. New York; United Nations, 1995. xxii, 287 p.
96-154396   327.1/74   9290451033
Military policy -- Congresses. Arms transfers -- Congresses.

UA11.A84 2000
Auerswald, David P.
Disarmed democracies: domestic institutions and the use of force/ David P. Auerswald. Ann Arbor: University of Michigan Press, c2000. xii, 184 p.
99-050474 355/.03 0472111205
Military policy -- Case studies. World politics -- 1945-

UA11.B5 1962
Blackett, P. M. S. 1897-1974.
Studies of war, nuclear and conventional. New York, Hill and Wang [1962] 242 p.
62-019962 355
Military policy. Nuclear warfare. Warfare, Conventional.

UA11.B7
Brodie, Bernard, 1910-
Strategy in the missile age. Princeton, N.J., Princeton University Press, 1959. vii, 423 p.
58-006102 355.43
Military policy. Nuclear warfare. Strategy. United States -- Military policy.

UA11.B84 1987
Buzan, Barry.
An introduction to strategic studies: military technology and international relations/ Barry Buzan. New York: St. Martin's Press: 1987. xvii, 325 p.
87-013116 355/.0335 0312011776
Military policy. International relations. Military art and science -- Technological innovations.

UA11.C56 1998
Cimbala, Stephen J.
The past and future of nuclear deterrence/ Stephen J. Cimbala. Westport, Conn.: Praeger, 1998. 235 p.
97-049280 327.1/747 0275962393
Nuclear weapons -- Government policy. Deterrence (Strategy) World politics -- 1989-

UA11.F6
Foot, M. R. D. 1919-
Men in uniform; military manpower in modern industrial societies. With a foreword by Alastair Buchan. New York, Praeger for the Institute of Strategic Studies, [1961] x, 161 p.
61-010526 355.22
Military policy. Armed Forces

UA11.H3 1974
Halle, Louis Joseph, 1910-
Choice for survival [by] Louis J. Halle. Westport, Conn., Greenwood Press [1974, c1958] 147 p.
74-007539 355.02/17 083717578X
Military policy. World politics -- 1945- Nuclear warfare. United States -- Military policy.

UA11.H34
Halperin, Morton H.
Limited war in the nuclear age. New York, Wiley [1963] ix, 191 p.
63-018625 355
Limited war. Nuclear warfare.

UA11.H8
Huntington, Samuel P.
Changing patterns of military politics. [New York] Free Press of Glencoe [1962] 272 p.
61-018255 355
Military policy. World politics.

UA11.K32
Kahn, Herman, 1922-
On escalation: metaphors and scenarios. New York, Praeger [1965] xvii, 308 p.
65-018080 355/.0335
Military policy. Escalation (Military science)

UA11.K5 1960
Kingston-McCloughry, Edgar James, 1896-
Defense: policy and strategy. With a foreword by Alastair Buchan. New York, Praeger [1960] 272 p.
60-007662 355.0942
Military policy. World politics. Great Britain -- Military policy.

UA11.K6
Knorr, Klaus Eugen, 1911-
Limited strategic war. Edited by Klaus Knorr and Thornton Read. New York, Published for the Center of International Studies, Princeton University, by Praeger [1962] 258 p.
62-016380 355
Strategy. Military policy.

UA11.L3
Lapp, Ralph Eugene, 1917-
Kill and overkill; the strategy of annihilation. New York, Basic Books [1962] 197 p.
62-017243 355
Strategy. Nuclear warfare. Military policy. United States -- Military policy.

UA11.L5 1960
Liddell Hart, Basil Henry, 1895-
Deterrent or defense, a fresh look at the West's military position. New York, Praeger [1960] 257 p.
60-012092 355
Military policy. Tactics. World politics -- 1955-1965.

UA11.M46 1976
Miksche, Ferdinand Otto, 1905-
The failure of atomic strategy & a new proposal for the defence of the West/ F. O. Miksche. Westport, Conn.: Greenwood Press, 1976, c1959. 224 p.
76-027852 355.03/301/821 0837190231
Military policy. World politics -- 1945- Nuclear warfare.

UA11.S49
Slessor, John Cotesworth, 1897-
The great deterrent; a collection of lectures, articles, and broadcasts on the development of strategic policy in the nuclear age. With a foreword by Alfred M. Gruenther. New York, Praeger [1957] 321 p.
57-012232 355.43082
Military policy. World politics. Air power. Great Britain -- Military policy.

UA11.S56
Snyder, Glenn Herald.
Deterrence and defense; toward a theory of national security. Princeton, N.J., Princeton University Press, 1961. ix, 294 p.
61-012102 355
Deterrence (Strategy) Nuclear warfare. Military policy.

UA11.S8 1963
Strachey, John, 1901-1963.
On the prevention of war. New York, St. Martin's Press [1963, c1962] ix, 334 p.
63-009423 355
Military policy. World politics -- 1955-1965. Nuclear warfare.

UA11.T6 1974
Toynbee, Philip.
The fearful choice, a debate on nuclear policy conducted by Philip Toynbee with the Archbishop of Canterbury [and others] Westport, Conn., Greenwood Press [1974, c1958] 112 p.
74-011406 355.02/17 0837176778
Military policy. World politics -- 1945- Nuclear warfare.

UA12 Mutual security programs

UA12.C53 1997
Clarke, Duncan L.
Send guns and money: security assistance and U.S. foreign policy/ Duncan L. Clarke, Daniel B. O'Connor, and Jason D. Ellis. Westport, Conn.: Praeger, 1997. xiv, 211 p.
97-005885 355/.032/0973 0275959929
Security Assistance Program.United States -- Foreign relations -- 20th century.

UA12.5 Disarmament inspection. Arms control and nuclear arms control verification

UA12.5.A76 1986
Arms control verification: the technologies that make it possible/ edited by Kosta Tsipis, David W. Hafemeister, and Penny Janeway. Washington: Pergamon-Brassey's International Defense Publishers, c1986. xvi, 419 p.
86-000726 623.7/1 0080331726
Nuclear arms control -- Verification -- Congresses. Arms control -- Verification -- Congresses.

UA12.5.B34 1995
Bailey, Kathleen C.
The UN inspections in Iraq: lessons for on-site verification/ Kathleen C. Bailey. Boulder: Westview Press, c1995. vii, 151 p.
95-007621 327.1/74/09567 0813389259
Arms control -- Verification -- Iraq. Arms control -- Verification.

UA12.5.N83 1988
Nuclear weapon tests: prohibition or limitation?/ edited by Jozef Goldblat and David Cox. Oxford; Oxford University Press, 1988. xxii, 423 p.
87-025386 327.1/74 0198291205
Nuclear arms control -- Verification. Nuclear weapons -- Testing.

UA12.5.R84 1998
Rueckert, George L.
On-site inspection in theory and practice: a primer on modern arms control regimes/ George L. Rueckert. Westport, Conn.: Praeger, 1998. xv, 275 p.
97-023346 327.1/743 0275960471
Arms control -- Verification. Disarmament -- On-site inspection.

UA12.5.V464 1988
Verification and compliance: a problem-solving approach/ edited by Michael Krepon and Mary Umberger; foreword by Thomas L. Hughes. Cambridge, Mass.: Ballinger Pub. Co., c1988. xvii, 308 p.
88-014624 358/.17 0887303269
Arms control -- Verification.

UA15 Armies of the world. Armies and navies of the world

UA15.D9 1980
Dupuy, Trevor Nevitt, 1916-
The almanac of world military power/ Trevor N. Dupuy, Grace P. Hayes, John A. C. Andrews; Gay Hammerman, coordinating editor. San Rafael, Calif.: Presidio Press, c1980. xi, 418 p.
80-011844 355/.033/0047 0891410708
Armed Forces. Military readiness.

UA15.E57 1996
English, John A.
Marching through chaos: the descent of armies in theory and practice/ John A. English. Westport, Conn.: Praeger, 1996. x, 220 p.
96-029354 355.02 0275946576
Armies -- History.

UA15.5 Foreign military bases

UA15.5.H37 1989
Harkavy, Robert E.
Bases abroad: the global foreign military presence/ Robert E. Harkavy; SIPRI, Stockholm International Peace Research Institute. Oxford; Oxford University Press, 1989. xvii, 389 p.
89-009444 341.7/25 0198291310
Military bases, Foreign. Military bases, American. Military bases, Soviet.

UA17 Cost of armaments, budgets, estimates, etc.

UA17.M35 1989
McKinlay, Robert D.
Third World military expenditure: determinants and implications/ R.D. McKinlay. London; Pinter Publishers, 1989. 154 p.
88-032104 355.6/22/091724 0861877217
Developing countries -- Armed Forces -- Appropriations and expenditures.

UA18 Industrial mobilization for war and defense

UA18.U5.D67 1991
Dorwart, Jeffery M., 1944-
Eberstadt and Forrestal: a national security partnership, 1909-1949/ Jeffery M. Dorwart. College Station: Texas A&M University Press, c1991. ix, 237 p.
91-008769 355.2/6/0973 0890964696
Eberstadt, Ferdinand. Forrestal, James, -- 1892-1949. Industrial mobilization -- United States. World War, 1939-1945 -- Economic aspects. United States -- History, Military -- 20th century.

UA18.U5.U45 1988
Mobilizing U.S. industry: a vanishing option for national security?/ [edited by] John N. Ellison, Jeffrey W. Frumkin, and Timothy W. Stanley. Boulder: Westview Press, 1988. xiii, 126 p.
87-034097 355.2/6 0813375738
Industrial mobilization -- United States. Munitions -- United States. United States -- Defenses. United States -- Military policy.

UA21 By region or country — America

UA21.H39 1989
Hemispheric security and U.S. Policy in Latin America/ edited by Augusto Varas. Boulder: Westview Press, 1989. vii, 230 p.
87-014715 355/.0335/73098 0813374421
National security -- America.United States -- Military relations -- Latin America. Latin America -- Military relations -- United States.

UA22 By region or country — North America — General works

UA22.C6 1962
Conant, Melvin.
The long polar watch; Canada and the defense of North America. New York, Published for the Council on Foreign Relations by Harper, 1962. 204 p.
62-014889 355.0971
North America -- Defenses. Canada -- Military policy. United States -- Military policy.

UA23-565 By region or country — North America — United States

UA23.A274
United States defense policies in ... Washington: U.S. G.P.O.,
92-034240
United States -- Military policy -- Periodicals. United States -- Defenses -- Periodicals.

UA23.A4296
Abshire, David M.
National security: political, military, and economic strategies in the decade ahead, edited by David M. Abshire and Richard V. Allen. Introd. by Arleigh Burke. New York, Published for the Hoover Institution on War, Revolution and Peace by Praeger [1963] xxxii, 1039 p.
63-017834 355
Military policy. Economic policy. United States -- Economic policy. United States -- Military policy.

UA23.A524 1990
Adelman, Kenneth L.
The defense revolution: strategy for the brave new world/ by an arms controller and an arms builder, Kenneth L. Adelman, Norman R. Augustine. San Francisco, Calif.: ICS Press, Institute for Contemporary Studies; c1990. 239 p.
90-049904 355/.033073 1558150749
United States -- Defenses.

UA23.A593 1990
Allard, C. Kenneth 1947-
Command, control, and the common defense/ C. Kenneth Allard. New Haven: Yale University Press, c1990. xiii, 317 p.
89-025084 355.3/3041/0973 0300043600
Command and control systems -- United States.United States -- Armed Forces -- Organization. United States -- Armed Forces -- Equipment.

UA23.A66323 1996
America's armed forces: a handbook of current and future capabilities/ edited by Sam C. Sarkesian and Robert E. Connor, Jr. Westport, Conn.: Greenwood Press, 1996. x, 475 p.
95-006704 355/.033073 0313290121
National security -- United States. World politics -- 1989- United States -- Defenses.

UA23.A697
Armacost, Michael H.
The politics of weapons innovation: the Thor-Jupiter controversy, by Michael H. Armacost. New York, Columbia University Press, 1969. x, 304 p.
70-090213 355.03/35/73 0231032064
Intermediate-range ballistic missiles.United States -- Military policy.

UA23.B43 1961
Bernardo, C. Joseph, 1911-
American military policy, its development since 1775 [by] C. Joseph Bernardo and Eugene H. Bacon. Harrisburg, Pa., Military Service Division, Stackpole Co. [1961] 548 p.
61-015573 355
United States -- Military policy. United States -- History, Military.

UA23.B46
Betts, Richard K., 1947-
Soldiers, statesmen, and cold war crises/ Richard K. Betts. Cambridge: Harvard University Press, c1977. xi, 292 p.
77-008068 355.03/35/73 0674817419
United States -- Military policy. United States -- Armed Forces. United States -- Foreign relations -- 1945-1989.

UA23.B49 1992
Beyond the Soviet threat: rethinking American security policy in a new era/ edited by William Zimmerman. Ann Arbor: University of Michigan Press, c1992. xi, 223 p.
92-029848   355.033/073   0472103415
  National security -- United States.United States -- Foreign relations -- Soviet Union. Soviet Union -- Foreign relations -- United States.

UA23.B498 1993
Binkin, Martin, 1928-
Who will fight the next war?: the changing face of the American military/ Martin Binkin. Washington, D.C.: Brookings Institution, c1993. xi, 179 p.
93-009981   355/.00973/09049   0815709560
  United States -- Armed Forces -- Reorganization.

UA23.B58 1988
Boll, Michael M., 1938-
National security planning: Roosevelt through Reagan/ Michael M. Boll. Lexington, Ky.: University Press of Kentucky, c1988. xi, 271 p.
88-000043   355/.0335/73   0813116457
  National security -- United States. Military planning -- United States -- History -- 20th century. United States -- Foreign relations -- 1933-1945. United States -- Foreign relations -- 1945-1989.

UA23.B726 1996
Botti, Timothy J., 1956-
Ace in the hole: why the United States did not use nuclear weapons in the Cold War, 1945 to 1965/ Timothy J. Botti. Westport, Conn.: Greenwood Press, 1996. xi, 311 p.
95-050451   355.02/7/097309045   0313299765
  Nuclear weapons -- Government policy -- United States -- History. Deterrence (Strategy) Cold War.

UA23.B782 1992
Brement, Marshall, 1932-
Reaching out to Moscow: from confrontation to cooperation/ Marshall Brement; foreword by Claiborne Pell. New York: Praeger, 1991. ix, 191 p.
91-018920   355/.0335/73   027594073X
  United States -- Military policy. Soviet Union -- Military policy. United States -- Foreign relations -- Soviet Union.

UA23.B7845 1983
Brown, Harold, 1927-
Thinking about national security: defense and foreign policy in a dangerous world/ Harold Brown. Boulder, Colo.: Westview Press; 1983. xvi, 288 p.
82-023859   355/.033073   0865315485
  National security -- United States.

UA23.B78457 1988
Bruce-Briggs, B.
The shield of faith: a chronicle of strategic defense from zeppelins to star wars/ B. Bruce-Briggs. New York: Simon and Schuster, c1988. 464 p.
88-018394   355/.00973   0671610864
  Strategic forces -- United States -- History. Air defenses -- United States -- History. Ballistic missile defenses -- United States -- History. United States -- Defenses -- History.

UA23.B7855 1989
Builder, Carl H.
The masks of war: American military styles in strategy and analysis/ Carl H. Builder; foreword by Sam Nunn. Baltimore: Johns Hopkins University Press, c1989. xiii, 240 p.
88-013517   355/.0335/73   0801837758
  Military planning -- United States. Strategy. United States -- Military policy. United States -- Armed Forces.

UA23.B786 1988
Bundy, McGeorge.
Danger and survival: choices about the bomb in the first fifty years/ McGeorge Bundy. New York: Random House, c1988. xiii, 735 p.
88-042824   327.1/1   0394522788
  Nuclear warfare. Arms race -- History -- 20th century. United States -- Politics and government -- 1933-1945. United States -- Politics and government -- 1945-1989. United States -- Foreign relations -- 1933-1945.

UA23.B795 1993
Burton, James G., 1937-
The Pentagon wars: reformers challenge the old guard/ James G. Burton. Annapolis, Md.: Naval Institute Press, c1993. 306 p.
93-003424   355/.00973/09049   1557500819
  United States -- Armed Forces -- Reorganization. United States -- Military policy.

UA23.C24
Caraley, Demetrios.
The politics of military unification; a study of conflict and the policy process.   New York, Columbia University Press, 1966. xiii, 345 p.
66-015762   355.3
  United States -- Armed Forces -- Organization. United States -- Defenses.

UA23.C5427 1995
Cimbala, Stephen J.
Collective insecurity: U.S. defense policy and the new world disorder/ Stephen J. Cimbala. Westport, Conn.: Greenwood Press, 1995. viii, 227 p.
95-007511   355/.033573   0313296561
  Security, International. World politics -- 1989- United States -- Military policy. Russia (Federation) -- Military policy.

UA23.C5437 1995
Cimbala, Stephen J.
US military strategy and the Cold War endgame/ Stephen J. Cimbala. Ilford, Essex, England; F. Cass, 1995. viii, 271 p.
94-017487   355/.033573   0714645567
  United States -- Defenses. Europe -- Politics and government -- 1989-

UA23.C544 1993
Cimbala, Stephen J.
U.S. nuclear strategy in the new world order: backward glances, forward looks/ Stephen J. Cimbala. New York: Paragon House, 1993. xxi, 259 p.
92-010463   623.8/25119   1557785570
  Nuclear weapons -- Soviet Union.United States -- Military policy. United States -- Military relations -- Soviet Union. Soviet Union -- Military relations -- United States.

UA23.C558 1984
Clarfield, Gerard H.
Nuclear America: military and civilian nuclear power in the United States, 1940-1980/ Gerard H. Clarfield and William M. Wiecek. New York: Harper & Row, c1984. ix, 518 p.
84-047565   355/.0335/73   0060153369
  Nuclear weapons. Nuclear energy -- United States. United States -- Military policy.

UA23.C559 1989
Clarke, Duncan L.
American defense and foreign policy institutions: toward a sound foundation/ Duncan L. Clarke. New York: Harper & Row, Ballinger Division, c1989. xviii, 245 p.
89-006459   353.0089   0887302920
  National security -- United States.

UA23.C575 1989
Coffey, Joseph I.
Defense and detente: U.S. and West German perspectives on defense policy/ Joseph I. Coffey and Klaus von Schubert, with Dieter Dettke, James R. Golden and Gale Mattox. Boulder, Colo.: Westview Press, 1989.
89-030341   355/.0335/73   0813377226
  United States -- Military policy. Germany (West) -- Military policy. United States -- Military relations -- Germany (West)

UA23.C595 1989
Collective defense or strategic independence?: alternative strategies for the future/ edited by Ted Galen Carpenter. Washington, D.C.: Cato Institute; c1989. xxi, 310 p.
88-029411   355/.033/0048   0669202959
  National security -- United States. National security. World politics -- 1985-1995.

UA23.C654 1980
Congressional Quarterly, inc.
U.S. defense policy: weapons, strategy, and commitments;   [editor, John L. Moore]. Washington, D.C.: Congressional Quarterly, c1980. 89 p.
80-607772   355/.033073
  Military weapons. Military assistance, American. United States -- Military policy. United States -- Foreign relations -- 1977-1981.

UA23.C67224 1998
Craig, Campbell, 1964-
Destroying the village: Eisenhower and thermonuclear war/ Campbell Craig. New York: Columbia University Press, c1998. xiv, 216 p.
98-011023   355.02/17/097309045   0231111223
  Eisenhower, Dwight D. -- (Dwight David), -- 1890-1969.Nuclear warfare -- Government policy -- United States -- History.United States -- Politics and government -- 1953-1961.

UA23.C67374 1997
Cordesman, Anthony H.
U.S. forces in the Middle East: resources and capabilities/ Anthony H. Cordesman. Boulder, Colo.: Westview Press, 1997. xi, 145 p.
96-046615   355/.031/09730536   0813332451
  United States -- Military policy. United States -- Armed Forces -- Middle East.

UA23.D596 1996
Dockrill, Saki.
Eisenhower's new-look national security policy, 1953-61/ Saki Dockrill. Houndmills, Basingstoke, Hampshire: Macmillan Press; 1996. xvi, 400 p.
96-011588   355/.03357309045   0333656555
Eisenhower, Dwight D. -- (Dwight David), 1890-1969.Deterrence (Strategy)Europe -- Foreign relations -- United States. United States -- Politics and government -- 1953-1961. United States -- Military policy.

UA23.D69 1993
Downsizing defense/ edited by Ethan B. Kapstein. Washington, D.C.: Congressional Quarterly, c1993. xvi, 236 p.
93-005636   355/.0335/73   087187945X
Defense industries -- United States. Economic conversion -- United States. United States -- Defenses. United States -- Armed Forces -- Appropriations and expenditures.

UA23.D95 1996
Dycus, Stephen.
National defense and the environment/ Stephen Dycus. Hanover: University Press of New England, c1996. xvii, 286 p.
95-020878   363.7   0874516757
Liability for environmental damages -- United States. World politics -- 1989- United States -- Defenses -- Environmental aspects.

UA23.E89 1982
Etzold, Thomas H.
Defense or delusion?: America's military in the 1980s/ by Thomas H. Etzold. New York: Harper & Row, c1982. x, 259 p.
81-047655   355/.033073   006038011X
United States -- Military policy. United States -- Armed Forces.

UA23.F343
Fallows, James M.
National defense/ James Fallows. New York: Random House, c1981. xvii, 204 p.
80-006006   355/.033073   0394518241
United States -- Military policy. United States -- Defenses.

UA23.F37 1992
Feaver, Peter D.
Guarding the guardians: civilian control of nuclear weapons in the United States/ Peter Douglas Feaver. Ithaca, N.Y.: Cornell University Press, 1992. xviii, 261 p.
91-055544   355.02/17   0801426758
Nuclear weapons -- United States. Civil supremacy over the military -- United States. United States -- Military policy.

UA23.F39 1985
Feld, Werner J.
Congress and national defense: the politics of the unthinkable/ Werner J. Feld, John K. Wildgen. New York: Praeger, 1985. xiii, 126 p.
84-016007   355/.0335/73   0030697514
Nuclear weapons. Nuclear arms control. United States -- Military policy.

UA23.F54 1988
The Foreign and domestic dimensions of modern warfare: Vietnam, Central America, and nuclear strategy/ edited by Howard Jones. Tuscaloosa: University of Alabama Press, c1988. x, 209 p.
86-019239   355/.0335/73   0817303316
Civil-military relations -- United States -- History -- 20th century. Military history, Modern -- 20th century. United States -- Politics and government -- 1945-1989. United States -- Military policy. United States -- Foreign relations -- 1945-1989.

UA23.F84
Fulbright, James William, 1905-
The Pentagon propaganda machine [by] J. W. Fulbright. New York, Liveright [1970] vii, 166 p.
79-131268   355.03/35/73   0871405229
United States. Dept. of Defense -- Public relations.

UA23.F87
Furniss, Edgar Stephenson, 1918-
American military policy; strategic aspects of world political geography. New York, Rinehart [1957] 494 p.
57-009027   355
World politics -- 1945-United States -- Military policy. United States -- Foreign relations -- 1945-1953.

UA23.G36 1989
Gansler, Jacques S.
Affording defense/ Jacques S. Gansler. Cambridge, Mass.: MIT Press, c1989. 417 p.
88-032653   355/.335073   0262071177
United States -- Armed Forces -- Appropriations and expenditures. United States -- Armed Forces -- Procurement. United States -- Armed Forces -- Management.

UA23.G53
Gavin, James M. 1907-
War and peace in the space age. New York, Harper [1958] 304 p.
58-011396   355.4
World politics -- 1945- Military history, Modern -- 20th century. United States -- Military policy.

UA23.G554 1990
Gertcher, Frank L.
Beyond deterrence: the political economy of nuclear weapons/ Frank L. Gertcher and William J. Weida. Boulder: Westview Press, 1990. xvii, 362 p.
89-029126   355.02/17   0813304776
Nuclear weapons -- United States. Nuclear weapons -- Economic aspects -- United States. Military policy. United States -- Military policy. United States -- Armed Forces -- Appropriations and expenditures.

UA23.G58
Gilpin, Robert.
American scientists and nuclear weapons policy. Princeton, N. J., Princeton University Press, 1962. viii, 352 p.
62-011956   973.92
Scientists -- United States. Nuclear warfare -- Moral and religious aspects. United States -- Military policy.

UA23.G636 1990
Glaser, Charles L. 1954-
Analyzing strategic nuclear policy/ Charles L. Glaser. Princeton, N.J.: Princeton University Press, c1990. xii, 378 p.
90-040844   355.02/17   0691078289
Nuclear warfare. Deterrence (Strategy) United States -- Military policy.

UA23.G67 1993
Goldstein, Martin E.
Arms control and military preparedness from Truman to Bush/ Martin E. Goldstein. New York: P. Lang, c1993. viii, 275 p.
92-017958   355/.0335/730904   0820419559
Arms control -- United States -- History -- 20th century.United States -- Defenses.

UA23.G68 1963
Goldwin, Robert A., 1922-
America armed; essays on United States military policy, by Robert E. Osgood [and others] Chicago, Rand McNally [1963] 140 p.
63-011707   355.0973   0836957989
United States -- Military policy.

UA23.G77 1970
Goulding, Phil G. 1921-
Confirm or deny; informing the people on national security [by] Phil G. Goulding. New York, Harper & Row [1970] xiii, 369 p.
79-095958   659.2
Public relations -- United States.United States -- Defenses.

UA23.G7786 1988
Gray, Colin S.
The geopolitics of super power/ Colin S. Gray. Lexington, Ky.: University Press of Kentucky, c1988. 274 p.
87-025355   355/.033073   0813116279
National security -- United States. Geopolitics. Soviet Union -- Military relations -- United States. United States -- Military relations -- Soviet Union.

UA23.G785 1990
Gray, Colin S.
War, peace, and victory: strategy and statecraft for the next century/ Colin S. Gray. New York: Simon and Schuster, c1990. 442 p.
90-034592   355/.03   0671606956
Strategy. World politics -- 1945- World politics. United States -- Military policy.

UA23.G786 1993
Gray, Colin S.
Weapons don't make war: policy, strategy, and military technology/ Colin S. Gray. Lawrence, Kan.: University Press of Kansas, c1993. xi, 236 p.
92-010090   355/.0335/73   0700605592
Military doctrine -- United States -- History -- 20th century. Military art and science -- United States -- History -- 20th century. Military art and science -- History -- 20th century. United States -- Military policy. United States -- Armed Forces -- Weapons systems -- History -- 20th century.

UA23.G79 1984
Gregor, A. James 1929-
The iron triangle: a U.S. security policy for northeast Asia/ A. James Gregor, Maria Hsia Chang. Stanford, Calif.: Hoover Institution Press, Stanford University, c1984. x, 160 p.
84-000630   355/.03305   0817979212
United States -- Military relations -- Japan. United States -- Military relations -- Taiwan. United States -- Military relations -- Korea (South)

UA23.H22 1994
Haass, Richard.
Intervention: the use of American military force in the post-Cold War world/ Richard N. Haass. Washington, DC: Carnegie Endowment for International Peace, c1994. x, 258 p.
94-029672   355/.033573   0870030574
World politics -- 1989-United States -- Military policy. United States -- Military relations -- Foreign countries.

UA23.H367 1988
Hartmann, Frederick H.
Defending America's security/ Frederick H. Hartmann and Robert L. Wendzel. Washington: Pergamon-Brassey's International Defense Publishers, 1988. xii, 363 p.
87-025825   355/.033073   0080342191
National security -- United States.

UA23.H448 1988
Hendrickson, David C.
Reforming defense: the state of American civil-military relations/ David C. Hendrickson. Baltimore: Johns Hopkins University Press, c1988. xiii, 152 p.
87-017003   355/.00973   080183550X
Civil-military relations -- United States.United States -- Military policy. United States -- Armed Forces.

UA23.H45 1985
Herken, Gregg, 1947-
Counsels of war/ Gregg Herken. New York: Knopf: 1985. xvi, 409 p.
84-047876   355/.0335/73   0394527356
Nuclear weapons. Military research -- United States -- History -- 20th century. United States -- Military policy.

UA23.H46
Herring, Pendleton, 1903-
The impact of war; our American democracy under arms, by Pendleton Herring. New York, Farrar & Rinehart [c1941] ix, 306 p.
41-019543   355.0973
United States -- Politics and government. United States -- Defenses.

UA23.H53
Hitch, Charles Johnston.
The economics of defense in the nuclear age [by] Charles J. Hitch and Roland N. McKean; with contributions by Stephen Enke [and others] Cambridge, Harvard University Press, 1960. vii, 422 p.
60-010042   355
United States -- Military policy. United States -- Economic policy.

UA23.H5344 1996
Hoffman, F. G.
Decisive force: the new American way of war/ F.G. Hoffman. Westport, Conn.: Praeger, 1996. xviii, 150 p.
95-022015   355/.033073   0275953440
United States -- Military policy. United States -- Strategic aspects.

UA23.H53443 2001
Holding the line: U.S. defense alternatives for the early 21st century/ editor, Cindy Williams. Cambridge, Mass.: MIT Press, c2001. vi, 289 p.
00-050082   355/.033573   0262731401
Military planning -- United States.United States -- Military policy. United States -- Armed Forces -- Appropriations and expenditures.

UA23.H94
Huntington, Samuel P.
The common defense; strategic programs in national politics. New York, Columbia University Press, 1961. 500 p.
61-018197   355.0973
United States -- Politics and government -- 1945-1953. United States -- Military policy.

UA23.H95
Huntington, Samuel P.
The soldier and the state; the theory and politics of civil-military relations. Cambridge, Belknap Press of Harvard University Press, 1957. xiii, 534 p.
57-006349   342.73
Militarism -- United States. Civil supremacy over the military -- United States.

UA23.J3
Janowitz, Morris.
Sociology and the military establishment. Pepared for the American Sociological Society by Morris Janowitz. New York, Russell Sage Foundation, 1959. 112 p.
59-010151   355.3
Sociology.United States -- Armed Forces.

UA23.K294 1987
Kaku, Michio.
To win a nuclear war: the Pentagon's secret war plans/ by Michio Kaku and Daniel Axelrod. Boston: South End Press, c1987. xi, 357 p.
86-027974   355/.033573   0896083225
Nuclear warfare.United States -- Military policy.

UA23.K3675 1996
Kaufmann, J. E.
The sleeping giant: American Armed Forces between the wars/ J.E. Kaufmann, H.W. Kaufmann. Westport, Conn.: Praeger, 1996. xiii, 216 p.
95-043727   355/.00973/09041   0275952568
United States -- Armed Forces -- History -- 20th century. United States -- Armed Forces -- Appropriations and expenditures -- History -- 20th century.

UA23.K38
Kaufmann, William W.
Military policy and national security, edited by William W. Kaufmann [and others] Princeton, Princeton University Press, 1956. viii, 274 p.
56-013772   355
World politics -- 1945-United States -- Military policy. United States -- Foreign relations -- 1945-1953.

UA23.K3847 2001
Keeping the edge: managing defense for the future/ Ashton B. Carter and John P. White, editors. Cambridge, Mass.: MIT Press, c2001. xiii, 326 p.
00-066450   355/.033573   0262531941
National security -- United States.United States -- Military policy. United States -- Armed Forces

UA23.K49
Kissinger, Henry, 1923-
Nuclear weapons and foreign policy. Foreword by Gordon Dean. New York, Published for the Council on Foreign Relations by Harper, 1957. 455 p.
57-007801   355/.0335/73
World politics -- 1945- Nuclear warfare. United States -- Military policy. United States -- Foreign relations -- 1945-1989.

UA23.K737
Kohn, Richard H.
Eagle and sword: the Federalists and the creation of the military establishment in America, 1783-1802/ Richard H. Kohn. New York: Free Press, [1975] xx, 443 p.
74-033092   355.021/3/0973   0029175518
Militarism -- United States -- History.United States -- History -- Constitutional period, 1789-1809.

UA23.K775 1987
Kozar, Paul Michael, 1948-
The politics of deterrence: American and Soviet defense policies compared, 1960-1964/ by Paul Michael Kozar. Jefferson, N.C.: McFarland, 1987. vi, 169 p.
87-042512   355/.0335/73   0899502741
Deterrence (Strategy)United States -- Military policy. Soviet Union -- Military policy.

UA23.K777 1984
Krepon, Michael, 1946-
Strategic stalemate: nuclear weapons and arms control in American politics/ Michael Krepon. New York, NY: St. Martin's Press, 1984. xvi, 191 p.
84-013323   355/.0335/73   0312764340
Nuclear weapons. Strategic Arms Limitation Talks. World politics -- 1975-1985. United States -- Politics and government -- 1981-1989. United States -- Military policy.

UA23.L25 1988
Landau, Saul.
The dangerous doctrine: national security and U.S. foreign policy/ Saul Landau. Boulder: Westview Press, 1988. 201 p.
87-031635   355/.033073   0813375088
National security -- United States.United States -- Foreign relations -- 1945-1989.

UA23.L44 1990
Lebovic, James H.
Deadly dilemmas: deterrence in U.S. nuclear strategy/ James H. Lebovic. New York: Columbia University Press, c1990. x, 252 p.
89-025266   355/.033573   0231068441
Deterrence (Strategy) Nuclear warfare. United States -- Military policy.

UA23.L484 1990
Lepgold, Joseph.
The declining hegemon: the United States and European defense, 1960-1990/ Joseph Lepgold. New York: Greenwood Press, 1990. 225 p.
90-003132   355/.033573   0313263736
United States -- Military policy. Europe -- Defenses. United States -- Military relations -- Europe.

UA23.L493 1987
Levine, Robert A.
The arms debate and the Third World: have we learned from Vietnam?/ Robert A. Levine. Santa Monica, CA: Rand, c1987. xiii, 91 p.
88-111704   355/.0335/73   0833008757
Vietnamese Conflict, 1961-1975 -- Public opinion. Public opinion -- United States. Developing countries -- Foreign relations -- United States. United States -- Military policy. United States -- Foreign relations -- Developing countries.

UA23.L5765 1991
Lindsay, James M., 1959-
Congress and nuclear weapons/ James M. Lindsay. Baltimore: Johns Hopkins University Press, c1991. xvi, 205 p.
90-049522 355.8/25119/0973 0801841410
Nuclear warfare.United States -- Military policy.

UA23.L5768 1997
Linn, Brian McAllister.
Guardians of empire: the U.S. Army and the Pacific, 1902-1940/ Brian McAllister Linn. Chapel Hill: University of North Carolina Press, c1997. xvi, 343 p.
96-024200 355/.033073 080782321X
United States -- Military policy.

UA23.L7 1988
Lord, Carnes.
The presidency and the management of national security/ Carnes Lord. New York: Free Press; c1988. x, 207 p.
88-021248 353.0089 0029193419
National security -- United States -- Decision making. Presidents -- United States.

UA23.L73 1988
Low intensity warfare: counterinsurgency, proinsurgency, and antiterrorism in the eighties/ Michael T. Klare, Peter Kornbluh, editors. New York: Pantheon Books, c1988. vi, 250 p.
87-043008 355/.0335/73 0394555791
Low-intensity conflicts (Military science) World politics -- 1985-1995. United States -- Military policy.

UA23.L83 1990
Lucas, Michael R.
The Western Alliance after INF: redefining U.S. policy toward Europe and the Soviet Union/ Michael R. Lucas. Boulder: L. Rienner Publishers, 1990. vi, 266 p.
89-038359 355/.031/091821 1555871593
United States -- Military policy. United States -- Military relations -- Europe. Europe -- Military relations -- United States.

UA23.L95
Lyons, Gene Martin, 1924-
Schools for strategy; education and research in national security affairs [by] Gene M. Lyons [and] Louis Morton. With a foreword by John W. Masland. New York, Praeger [1965] xii, 356 p.
65-014056 355
Universities and colleges -- United States. Research -- United States. United States -- Military policy.

UA23.M273 1990
Making defense reform work/ edited by James A. Blackwell, Jr. & Barry M. Blechman; foreword by Harold Brown & James Schlesinger. Washington: Brassey's (US), c1990. xii, 278 p.
89-028852 355.3/0973 0080374492
United States -- Armed Forces -- Reorganization.

UA23.M275 1990
Mallin, Maurice A.
Tanks, fighters & ships: U.S. conventional force planning since WWII/ Maurice A. Mallin. Washington: Brassey's, c1990. xx, 275 p.
89-025307 355/.033573 0080367453
Warfare, Conventional.United States -- Military policy. United States -- History, Military -- 20th century. United States -- Armed Forces -- History -- 20th century.

UA23.M4 1990
Mazarr, Michael J., 1965-
START and the future of deterrence/ Michael J. Mazarr. New York: St. Martin's Press, 1991. viii, 257 p.
90-008881 355/.033573 0312053304
Deterrence (Strategy)United States -- Military policy. Soviet Union -- Military policy.

UA23.M43 1985
McNaugher, Thomas L.
Arms and oil: U.S. military strategy and the Persian Gulf/ Thomas L. McNaugher. Washington, D.C.: Brookings Institution, c1985. xiii, 226 p.
84-045850 355/.0335/73 0815756240
United States -- Military policy. Persian Gulf Region -- Strategic aspects.

UA23.M465 1988
Menges, Constantine Christopher.
Inside the National Security Council: the true story of the making and unmaking of Reagan's foreign policy/ Constantine C. Menges. New York: Simon and Schuster, c1988. 418 p.
88-018289 353.0089 0671649965
Menges, Constantine Christopher.National security -- United States -- Decision making.United States -- Foreign relations -- 1981- United States -- Foreign relations -- Decision making.

UA23.M565
Millis, Walter, 1899-1968,
American military thought. Indianapolis, Bobbs-Merrill [1966] liii, 554 p.
66-014831 355.033573
United States -- Military policy. United States -- History, Military.

UA23.M57
Millis, Walter, 1899-1968.
Individual freedom and the common defense. New York, Fund for the Republic [1957] 79 p.
58-000689 355
Civil rights -- United States. Internal security -- United States. United States -- Military policy.

UA23.M95 1990
Myers, David B., 1944-
New Soviet thinking and U.S. nuclear policy/ David B. Myers. Philadelphia: Temple University Press, 1990. xvii, 295 p.
90-010863 355/.033573 0877227101
National security -- United States. Nuclear warfare. United States -- Military policy. Soviet Union -- Defenses.

UA23.N248 1980
Rethinking US security policy for the 1980s: proceedings of the seventh annual National Security Affairs Conference, 21-23 July 1980/ cosponsored by the National Security Affairs Institute, National Defense University and the Office of the Principal Deputy Under Secretary of Defense for Policy. Washington, D.C.: National Defense University Press, 1980. xiv, 334 p.
81-601127 355/.033073
National Security -- United States -- Congresses.United States -- Military policy -- Congresses.

UA23.N2483 1988
National security and the U.S. Constitution: the impact of the political system/ edited by George C. Edwards III and Wallace Earl Walker. Baltimore: Johns Hopkins University Press, c1988. xii, 340 p.
88-000655 355/.033076 0801836840
National security -- United States. Civil-military relations -- United States. Constitutional history -- United States.

UA23.N65 1989
Nolan, Janne E.
Guardians of the arsenal: the politics of nuclear strategy/ Janne E. Nolan. New York: Basic Books, c1989. xiii, 320 p.
89-042524 355/.033573 0465098029
Nuclear warfare.United States -- Military policy. United States -- Politics and government -- 1945-1989.

UA23.O8
Osgood, Robert Endicott.
Limited war; the challenge to American strategy. [Chicago] University of Chicago Press [1957] xi, 315 p.
57-005275 355.43
Strategy.United States -- Foreign relations -- 20th century. United States -- Military policy.

UA23.O82 1988
Osgood, Robert Endicott.
The nuclear dilemma in American strategic thought/ Robert E. Osgood. Boulder: Westview Press, 1988. xiii, 138 p.
87-021661 355/.0335/73 0813305373
Nuclear warfare. Deterrence (Strategy) United States -- Military policy.

UA23.P265 1987
Palmer, Norman Dunbar.
Westward watch: the United States and the changing western Pacific/ Norman D. Palmer. Washington, D.C.: Pergamon-Brassey's International Defense Publishers, 1987. xv, 175 p.
86-030678 355/.00335/73 0080349579
National security -- United States.Pacific Area -- Strategic aspects. East Asia -- Strategic aspects.

UA23.P3724 2000
Paul, Septimus H.
Nuclear rivals: Anglo-American atomic relations, 1941-1952/ Septimus H. Paul. Columbus: Ohio State University Press, c2000. ix, 266 p.
00-008677   355.02/17/097309044 0814208525
Nuclear weapons -- United States. Nuclear weapons -- Great Britain. United States -- Military relations -- Great Britain. Great Britain -- Military relations -- United States.

UA23.P3747 1996
Payne, Keith B.
Deterrence in the second nuclear age/ Keith B. Payne. Lexington: University Press of Kentucky, c1996. xiv, 168 p.
96-030435 327.1/7 0813119987
Deterrence (Strategy) World politics -- 1989- United States -- Military policy.

UA23.P384 1999
Pearlman, Michael, 1944-
Warmaking and American democracy: the struggle over military strategy, 1700 to the present/ Michael D. Pearlman. Lawrence: University Press of Kansas, c1999. xi, 441 p.
98-043993 355/.033073 0700609385
Strategy. National security -- United States. United States -- Armed Forces. United States -- Military policy. United States -- History, Military.

UA23.R34 1988
Record, Jeffrey.
Beyond military reform: American defense dilemmas/ Jeffrey Record. Washington: Pergamon-Brassey's, 1988. xi, 186 p.
87-015699 355/.0332/73 0080346871
United States -- Armed Forces Reorganization. United States -- Military policy.

UA23.R6
Rockefeller Brothers Fund.
International security, the military aspect; report of panel II of the Special Studies Project. Garden City, N. Y., Doubleday, 1958. 63 p.
58-000646 355
Industrial mobilization. Foreign relations -- 1945- Security, International. United States -- Military policy. United States -- Foreign relations.

UA23.R663 1995
Roman, Peter J.
Eisenhower and the missile gap/ Peter J. Roman. Ithaca, N.Y.: Cornell University Press, 1995. x, 264 p.
95-032731 358.1/7/0973 0801427975
Nuclear weapons -- Government policy -- United States -- History. Executive power -- United States -- History. United States -- Politics and government -- 1953-1961.

UA23.R7
Roosevelt, Theodore, 1858-1919.
Fear God and take your own part, by Theodore Roosevelt. New York, George H. Doran Company [1916]
16-003624
Germans -- United States. War. World War, 1914-1918 -- United States. United States -- Defenses. United States -- Foreign relations. United States -- Politics and government -- 1913-1921.

UA23.R75
Root, Elihu, 1845-1937.
The military and colonial policy of the United States; addresses and reports by Elihu Root, collected and ed. by Robert Bacon and James Brown Scott. Cambridge, Harvard University Press; [etc., etc.] 1916. xxiv, 502 p.
17-000414
United States -- Insular possessions. United States -- Military policy. Philippines -- Politics and government -- 1898-1935.

UA23.R758 1991
Rosen, Stephen Peter, 1952-
Winning the next war: innovation and the modern military/ Stephen Peter Rosen. Ithaca: Cornell University Press, 1991. vii, 275 p.
91-055235 355/.0332/0904 0801425565
Military art and science -- United States -- Technological innovations -- History -- 20th century. Military art and science -- Great Britain -- Technological innovations -- History -- 20th century. Military art and science -- United States -- History -- 20th century. United States -- Armed Forces -- History -- 20th century. Great Britain -- Armed Forces -- History -- 20th century.

UA23.R886 1990
Russett, Bruce M.
Controlling the sword: the democratic governance of national security/ Bruce Russett. Cambridge, Mass.: Harvard University Press, 1990. x, 201 p.
89-048851 322/.5/0973
Civil-military relations -- United States. Civil-military relations. Public opinion -- United States. United States -- Military policy. United States -- Politics and government -- 1945-1989.

UA23.S275 1989
Sarkesian, Sam Charles.
U.S. national security: policymakers, processes, and politics/ Sam C. Sarkesian. Boulder: L. Rienner, 1989. xi, 217 p.
88-032394 355/.0335/73 1555870228
National security -- United States -- Decision making.

UA23.S33
Schilling, Warner Roller, 1925-
Strategy, politics, and defense budgets [by] Warner R. Schilling, Paul Y. Hammond [and] Glenn H. Snyder. New York, Columbia Univ. Press [1962] vii, 532 p.
62-017353 355
United States -- Military policy. United States -- Politics and government -- 1945-1953.

UA23.S394 1993
The Search for strategy: politics and strategic vision/ edited by Gary L. Guertner; foreword by William A. Stofft. Westport, Conn.: Greenwood Press, 1993. xxiv, 328 p.
92-035916 355/.0335/73 031328881X
Strategy. United States -- Military policy.

UA23.S47 1977
Sherry, Michael S., 1945-
Preparing for the next war: American plans for postwar defense, 1941-45/ Michael S. Sherry. New Haven: Yale University Press, 1977. x, 260 p.
76-027853 355.03/307/3 0300020317
United States -- Military policy. United States -- Armed Forces.

UA23.S5235 1988
Sloan, G. R.
Geopolitics in United States strategic policy, 1890-1987/ G.R. Sloan. New York: St. Martin's Press, 1988. xiv, 255 p.
87-037649 327.73 0312019548
Military art and science -- United States -- History -- 19th century. Military art and science -- United States -- History -- 20th century. Geopolitics -- Study and teaching -- United States -- History -- 19th century. United States -- Military policy.

UA23.S524 1984
Smoke, Richard.
National security and the nuclear dilemma: an introduction to the American experience/ Richard Smoke. Reading, Mass.: Addison-Wesley Pub. Co., c1984. xiv, 271 p.
83-017916 355/.033073 0201164205
National security -- United States. Nuclear weapons. Nuclear disarmament. United States -- Military policy. United States -- Foreign relations -- 1945-1989.

UA23.S52624 2000
Snow, Donald M., 1943-
When America fights: the uses of U.S. military force/ Donald M. Snow. Washington, D.C.: CQ Press, c2000. xiii, 221 p.
00-009486 355/.033573 1568025211
National security -- United States. World politics -- 1989- United States -- Military policy. United States -- Foreign relations -- 1993-2001.

UA23.S685 1984
Stein, Jonathan B.
From H-bomb to Star Wars: the politics of strategic decision making/ Jonathan B. Stein. Lexington, Mass.: Lexington Books, c1984. xiii, 118 p.
84-047938 355/.0335/73 0669089680
Arms race -- History -- 20th century. Hydrogen bomb. Space weapons. United States -- Military policy -- Decision making.

UA23.S687 1991
Steiner, Barry H. 1942-
Bernard Brodie and the foundations of American nuclear strategy/ Barry H. Steiner. Lawrence: University Press of Kansas, c1991. xvi, 367 p.
90-022618 355.02/17 0700604413
Brodie, Bernard, 1910-Nuclear warfare. United States -- Military policy.

UA23.S822 1990
Stoll, Richard J.
U.S. national security policy and the Soviet Union: persistent regularities and extreme contingencies/ Richard J. Stoll. Columbia, S.C.: University of South Carolina Press, c1990. xvi, 263 p.
89-022629 355/.033573 0872496988
National security -- United States. Soviet Union -- Foreign relations -- United States. United States -- Foreign relations -- 1945-1989. United States -- Foreign relations -- Soviet Union.

UA23.S82733 1997
Strategic assessment 1997: flashpoints and force structure/ [director and editor-in-chief, Hans A. Binnendijk; editor, Patrick L. Clawson]. Washington, DC: National Defense University, 1997. xvi, 300 p.
96-052237 355/.033073 1579060293
International relations. United States -- Defenses.

UA23.S8283 1990
Strategic power: USA/USSR/ edited by Carl G. Jacobsen ... [et al.]. New York: St. Martin's Press, 1990. xxiii, 519 p.
89-028848 355/.033573 0312040865
Strategy. Soviet Union -- Military policy. United States -- Military policy.

UA23.T33
Taylor, Maxwell D. 1901-1987.
The uncertain trumpet. New York, Harper [c1960] 203 p.
59-013290 355.0973
United States -- Military policy. United States -- Defenses.

UA23.T43 1995
Terriff, Terry, 1953-
The Nixon administration and the making of U.S. nuclear strategy/ Terry Terriff. Ithaca: Cornell University Press, 1995. xvi, 252 p.
94-045262 355.02/17/0973 0801430828
Nuclear weapons -- United States. Deterrence (Strategy) United States -- Politics and government -- 1969-1974. United States -- Military policy.

UA23.T57 1989
Tirman, John.
Sovereign acts: American unilateralism and global security/ John Tirman. New York: Harper & Row, Ballinger division, c1989. xv, 235 p.
89-031251 355/.0335/73 0887302998
National security -- United States. Arms control. World politics -- 1985-1995. United States -- Foreign relations -- 1989-1993.

UA23.T647 1996
Tomajczyk, Stephen F.
Dictionary of the modern United States military: over 15,000 weapons, agencies, acronyms, slang, installations, medical terms, and other lexical units of warfare/ by S. F. Tomajczyk. Jefferson, N.C.: McFarland & Co., c1996. xiii, 785 p.
95-024070 355/.00973 0786401273
Military art and science -- United States -- Dictionaries.United States -- Armed Forces -- Dictionaries.

UA23.T84 1960a
Turner, Gordon Brinkerhoff, 1915-
National security in the nuclear age; basic facts and theories. Edited by Gordon B. Turner and Richard D. Challener. New York, Praeger [1960] x, 293 p.
60-006998 355.0973
Nuclear warfare. Strategy. United States -- Military policy.

UA23.U185 1990
U.S. defense policy in an era of constrained resources/ edited by Robert L. Pfaltzgraff, Jr., Richard H. Shultz, Jr. Lexington, Mass.: Lexington Books, c1990. xxiv, 386 p.
89-036935 355.0335/73 0669213586
United States -- Military policy -- Congresses. United States -- Armed Forces -- Appropriations and expenditures -- Congresses.

UA23.U2 1994
U.S. domestic and national security agendas: into the twenty-first century/ edited by Sam C. Sarkesian and John Mead Flanagin; foreword by Richard E. Friedman. Westport, Conn.: Greenwood Press, 1994. xiv, 253 p.
93-021499 355/.033073 0313288704
National security -- United States -- Congresses.United States -- Politics and government -- 1993- -- Congresses.

UA23.U235 1988
U.S. national security policy and strategy: documents and policy proposals/ [edited by] Sam C. Sarkesian with Robert A. Vitas. New York: Greenwood Press, 1988. xxiii, 440 p.
88-010244 355/.033573 0313254826
National security -- United States.

UA23.U237 1991
U.S. national security strategy for the 1990s/ edited by Daniel J. Kaufman, David S. Clark, and Kevin P. Sheehan. Baltimore: Johns Hopkins University Press, c1991. xiv, 273 p.
90-027634 355/.033073 0801841631
National security -- United States.United States -- Military policy.

UA23.U82 2000
The use of force after the Cold War/ edited by H.W. Brands with Darren J. Pierson and Reynolds S. Kiefer. College Station, [Texas]: Texas A&M University Press, 2000. viii, 296 p
99-058775 355/.033573 0890969280
World politics -- 1989- Security, International. United States -- Military policy. United States -- Foreign relations -- 1989-

UA23.V23 2001
Van Aller, Christopher D., 1956-
The culture of defense/ Christopher D. Van Aller. Lanham: Lexington Books, c2001. viii, 187 p.
00-055653 355/.033573 0739101765
Sociology, Military -- United States. Civil-military relations -- United States. United States -- Military policy.

UA23.V293 1998
Van Tuyll, Hubert P.
America's strategic future: a blueprint for national survival in the new millennium/ Hubert P. van Tuyll. Westport, Conn.: Greenwood Press, 1998. 156 p.
98-010831 355/.033073 0313306745
National security -- United States. Political instability. World politics -- 1989- United States -- Defenses.

UA23.W364 1990
Watson, Cynthia Ann.
U.S. national security policy groups: institutional profiles/ Cynthia Watson. New York: Greenwood Press, 1990. xxviii, 289 p.
89-023381 355/.03/02573 0313257337
National security -- United States -- Societies, etc. -- Directories.United States -- Military policy -- Societies, etc. -- Directories.

UA23.W36934 1987
Wedemeyer, Albert C. 1896-
Wedemeyer on war and peace/ edited with an introduction by Keith E. Eiler; foreword by John Keegan. Stanford, Calif.: Hoover Institution, Stanford University, c1987. xxii, 245 p.
87-003847 355/.0335/73 0817986715
Strategy -- History -- 20th century. Peace. Military history, Modern -- 20th century. United States -- Military policy.

UA23.W36943 1992
Weidenbaum, Murray L.
Small wars, big defense: paying for the military after the cold war/ Murray Weidenbaum. New York: Oxford University Press, 1992. xii, 228 p.
91-025509 355.6/22/0973 0195072480
United States -- Armed Forces -- Appropriations and expenditures. United States -- Armed Forces -- Finance.

UA23.W376 1997
Wenger, Andreas.
Living with peril: Eisenhower, Kennedy, and nuclear weapons/ Andreas Wenger. Lanham, Md.: Rowman & Littlefield Publishers, c1997. xvi, 461 p.
97-002430 355.02/17/0973 0847685144
Nuclear weapons -- Government policy -- United States -- History. Nuclear crisis stability. United States -- Foreign relations -- 1961-1963. United States -- Foreign relations -- 1953-1961.

UA23.W4593 1993
Williamson, Samuel R.
The origins of U.S. nuclear strategy, 1945-1953/ Samuel R. Williamson, Jr. and Steven L. Rearden. New York: St. Martin's Press, 1993. xi, 224 p.
92-026597 355.02/17 0312089643
Nuclear warfare.United States -- Military policy.

UA23.W485 1993
Winkler, Allan M., 1945-
Life under a cloud: American anxiety about the atom/ Allan M. Winkler. New York: Oxford University Press, 1993. 282 p.
92-020013 355/.0335/73 0195078217
Nuclear weapons -- United States -- History. Nuclear engineering -- Government policy -- United States -- History. United States -- Military policy.

UA23.W486 1992
Wirls, Daniel, 1960-
Buildup: the politics of defense in the Reagan era/ Daniel Wirls. Ithaca: Cornell University Press, 1992. xi, 247 p.
91-055075 355/.0335/73 0801424429
United States -- Military policy. United States -- Armed Forces -- Appropriations and expenditures.

UA23.W63 1991
Wolpin, Miles D.
America insecure: arms transfers, global interventionism, and the erosion of national security/ by Miles D. Wolpin. Jefferson, N.C.: McFarland & Co., c1991. xii, 385 p.
90-052570 355/.033073 0899505295
National security -- United States. Military assistance, American. Arms transfers -- United States. United States -- Military relations.

UA23.Y25 1988
Yankelovich, Daniel.
Starting with the people/ Daniel Yankelovich and Sidney Harman. Boston: Houghton Mifflin, 1988. xvi, 285 p.
88-000875 355/.0335/73 039547695X
Public opinion -- United States.United States -- Military policy -- Public opinion. United States -- Economic policy -- Public opinion -- 1981-

UA23.Y28 1971
Yarmolinsky, Adam.
The military establishment; its impacts on American society. New York, Harper & Row [1971] xiv, 434 p.
73-127839 355.02/13/0973
United States -- Defenses.

UA23.15.P73 1991
Prados, John.
Keepers of the keys: a history of the National Security Council from Truman to Bush/ John Prados. New York: Morrow, c1991. 632 p.
90-026244 353.0089 0688073972
National security -- United States -- History -- 20th century.

UA23.3.A85 1997
Arkin, William M.
The U.S. military online: a directory for Internet access to the Department of Defense/ William M. Arkin. Washington: Brassey's, c1997. xiii, 240 p.
97-011163 025.06/355/00973 1574881434
Web sites -- Directories.

UA23.3.K5
Kintner, William R. 1915-
Forging a new sword, a study of the Department of Defense, by William R. Kintner in association with Joseph I. Coffey and Raymond J. Albright. New York, Harper [1958] 238 p.
58-007973　355
United States -- Military policy.

UA23.6.B67 1991
Borklund, Carl W.
U.S. defense and military fact book/ C.W. Borklund. Santa Barbara, Calif.: ABC-CLIO, c1991. x, 293 p.
90-023756　355/.033073　0874365937
United States -- Armed Forces.

UA23.6.G43
Geelhoed, E. Bruce, 1948-
Charles E. Wilson and controversy at the Pentagon, 1953 to 1957/ E. Bruce Geelhoed. Detroit: Wayne State University Press, 1979. 216 p.
79-009756　353.6/092/4　0814316352
Wilson, Charles Erwin, -- 1890-1961.United States -- Politics and government -- 1953-1961.

UA23.6.M56 1988
Mintz, Alex, 1953-
The politics of resource allocation in the U.S. Department of Defense: international crises and domestic constraints/ Alex Mintz. Boulder, Colo.: Westview Press, 1988. x, 149 p.
83-023281　355.6/22/0973　0865318093
United States -- Armed Forces -- Appropriations and expenditures -- History. Budget -- United States. United States -- Military policy.

UA23.7.P47 1989
Perry, Mark, 1950-
Four stars/ Mark Perry. Boston: Houghton Mifflin, 1989. xviii, 412 p.
88-032073　355.3/3042/0973　0395429234
United States. Joint Chiefs of Staff -- History.

UA25.A78 1959
The Army Almanac: a book of facts concerning the United States Army.　Harrisburg, PA: Stackpole, 1959. x, 797 p.
59-010070　355.0973
United States. Army.

UA25.B25 1998
Barr, Ronald J.
The progressive army: US Army command and administration, 1870-1914/ Ronald J. Barr. New York: St. Martin's Press, 1998. xi, 223 p.
98-012706　355.3/0973　0312214677
United States -- Foreign relations -- 20th century.

UA25.C6 1989
Coakley, Robert W.
The role of federal military forces in domestic disorders, 1789-1878/ by Robert W. Coakley. Washington, D.C.: Center of Military History, U.S. Army: 1989. xiii, 372 p.
88-003299　355/.00973
Riots. Insurgency -- United States. Internal security -- United States.

UA25.C73 1987
Crackel, Theodore J.
Mr. Jefferson's army: political and social reform of the military establishment, 1801-1809/ Theodore J. Crackel. New York: New York University Press, 1987. xiii, 250 p.
87-010721　355/.033573/0924　0814714072
Jefferson, Thomas, -- 1743-1826 -- Contributions in civil-military relations.Civil-military relations -- United States -- History -- 19th century.United States -- History -- 1801-1809.

UA25.G26
Gabriel, Richard A.
Crisis in command: mismanagement in the Army/ Richard A. Gabriel and Paul L. Savage. New York: Hill and Wang, 1978. xii, 242 p.
77-018689　355.3/3/0973　0809037114
Military ethics -- United States.

UA25.H67 2001
Historical dictionary of the U.S. Army/ edited by Jerold E. Brown. Westport, CT: Greenwood Press, 2000. xxi, 659 p.
00-022373　355/.00973/03　0313293228
United States. Army -- History -- Dictionaries.

UA25.H88
Huzar, Elias, 1915-
The Purse and the Sword; control of the Army by Congress through military appropriations, 1933-1950. Ithaca, N.Y., Cornell University Press, 1950. xiv, 417 p.
50-009490　355
United States. Army -- Appropriations and expenditures.

UA25.J53 1991
Jensen, Joan M.
Army surveillance in America, 1775-1980/ Joan M. Jensen. New Haven: Yale University Press, c1991. ix, 325 p.
91-004669　355.3/43/0973　0300046685
Internal security -- United States.

UA25.L28 1997
Laurie, Clayton D. 1954-
The role of federal military forces in domestic disorders, 1877-1945/ by Clayton D. Laurie and Ronald H. Cole. Washington, D.C.: Center of Military History, U.S. Army: 1997. xvi, 475 p.
94-013148　363.3/2/0973　0160489830
Riots -- United States -- History. Insurgency -- United States -- History. Internal security -- United States -- History.

UA25.M39 1990
Mazarr, Michael J., 1965-
Light forces & the future of U.S. military strategy/ Michael J. Mazarr; foreword by John Vessey. Washington: Brassey's, c1990. xi, 180 p.
90-033750　355/.033573　0080405657
United States -- Military policy.

UA25.S767 1984
Stanton, Shelby L., 1948-
Order of battle, U.S. Army, World War II/ Shelby L. Stanton. Novato, CA: Presidio, c1984. xiv, 620 p.
84-008299　355.3/0973　089141195X
United States. Army -- Organization. United States. Army -- History -- World War, 1939-1945.

UA25.U46 1990
The U.S. Army in a new security era/ edited by Sam C. Sarkesian, John Allen Williams. Boulder: Lynne Rienner Publishers, 1990. xii, 314 p.
90-008052　355/.033073　1555871917
National security -- United States.

UA25.U49 1991
The United States Army: a dictionary/ edited by Peter Tsouras, Bruce W. Watson, Susan M. Watson. New York: Garland Pub., 1991. xl, 898 p.
90-041172　355/.00973　0824053486
United States. Army -- Dictionaries.

UA25.U8
Utley, Robert Marshall, 1929-
Frontiersmen in blue; the United States Army and the Indian, 1848-1865, by Robert M. Utley. New York, Macmillan [1967] xv, 384 p.
67-019682　355.3/51/0973
Indians of North America -- Wars -- 1815-1875.West (U.S.) -- History.

UA25.W35 1984
Weigley, Russell Frank.
History of the United States Army/ Russell F. Weigley. Bloomington: Indiana University Press, c1984. vi, 730 p.
83-049010　355.3/0973　0253203236
United States -- History, Military.

UA25.W4
Weigley, Russell Frank.
Towards an American army; military thought from Washington to Marshall.　New York, Columbia University Press, 1962. xi, 297 p.
62-015388　355.0973
United States -- Military policy.

UA25.W65 1959
Worley, Marvin L.
A digest of new developments in Army weapons, tactics, organization and equipment. Harrisburg, Pa., Stackpole Co. [1959] 378 p.
59-003692
Military art and science.

UA25.W84 1983
Wright, Robert K., 1946-
The Continental Army/ by Robert K. Wright, Jr. Washington, D.C.: Center of Military History, U.S. Army: 1983. xvii, 451 p.
82-016472　355.3/0973
United States -- History -- Revolution, 1775-1783 -- Campaigns.

UA26.A2.D57 1995
Directory of U.S. military bases worldwide/ edited by William R. Evinger. Phoenix, AZ: Oryx Press, c1995. xii, 412 p.
94-038709　355.7/0973　0897748220
Military bases, American -- Directories.United States -- Armed Forces -- Facilities -- Directories.

UA26.A2.S25 2000
Sandars, C. T.
America's overseas garrisons: the leasehold empire/ C.T. Sandars. Oxford; Oxford University Press, 2000. xii, 354 p.
99-045917　355.7/0973　0198296878
Military bases, American -- History -- 20th century.United States -- Armed Forces -- Foreign countries.

UA26.A2.S67 1998
Sorenson, David S., 1943-
Shutting down the Cold War: the politics of military base closure/ David S. Sorenson. New York: St. Martin's Press, 1998. xi, 308 p.
97-045915   355.7/0973   0312210906
Military base closures -- United States.United States -- Politics and government -- 1989-

UA26.A26 1991
Directory of military bases in the U.S./ edited by William R. Evinger. Phoenix, Ariz.: Oryx Press, 1991. ix, 197 p.
90-007680   355.7/025/73   0897745310
Military bases -- United States -- Directories.United States -- Armed Forces -- Facilities -- Directories.

UA26.A45 1988
Roberts, Robert B.
Encyclopedia of historic forts: the military, pioneer, and trading posts of the United States/ Robert B. Roberts. New York: Macmillan; c1988. xviii, 894 p.
86-028494   355.7/0951   002926880X
Military bases -- United States -- Dictionaries. Fortification -- United States -- Dictionaries.

UA26.A6.M3
Mansfield, Joseph King Fenno, 1803-1862.
Mansfield on the condition of the Western forts, 1853-54. Edited and with an introduction by Robert W. Frazer. Norman, University of Oklahoma Press [1963] xxxi, 254 p.
63-018072   355.70978
Military bases -- West (U.S.)The West -- Description and travel.

UA26.A73.N54 1988
Nielson, Jonathan M.
Armed forces on a northern frontier: the military in Alaska's history, 1867-1987/ Jonathan M. Nielson; foreword by Peter Karsten. New York: Greenwood Press, 1988. xiv, 298 p.
87-031781   355/.009798   0313260303
United States -- Armed Forces -- Alaska -- History. Alaska -- History, Military.

UA26.C58.N63 1990
Noble, Dennis L.
The eagle and the dragon: the United States military in China, 1901-1937/ Dennis L. Noble. New York: Greenwood Press, 1990. xxi, 239 p.
90-003146   355.1   0313272999
United States -- Armed Forces -- China -- History -- 20th century. United States -- Armed Forces -- China -- Military life -- History -- 20th century.

UA26.F68.D63 1998
Dobak, William A., 1943-
Fort Riley and its neighbors: military money and economic growth, 1853-1895/ by William A. Dobak. Norman: University of Oklahoma Press, c1998. xvi, 241 p.
98-013474   355.7/09781/28   0806130717
Fort Riley (Kan.) -- History.

UA26.G3.H39 2001
Hawkins, John Palmer, 1946-
Army of hope, army of alienation: culture and contradiction in the American Army communities of Cold War Germany/ John P. Hawkins; foreword by Faris Kirkland. Westport, Conn.: Praeger, 2001. xix, 332 p.
00-061111   306.2/7/0973   0275967387
Sociology, Military -- Germany. Sociology, Military -- United States. Military bases, American -- Germany.

UA26.G3.N43 1987
Nelson, Daniel J.
Defenders or intruders?: the dilemmas of U.S. forces in Germany/ Daniel J. Nelson. Boulder: Westview Press, 1987. xxii, 288 p.
86-034024   355/.032/43   0813305012
United States -- Armed Forces -- Germany (West) United States -- Military relations -- Germany (West) Germany (West) -- Military relations -- United States.

UA26.G3.W55 2001
Willoughby, John, 1949-
Remaking the conquering heroes: the social and geopolitical impact of the early American occupation of Germany/ John Willoughby. New York: St. Martin's Press, 2000. xiii, 187 p.
00-062605   940.53/38   0312234007
Sociology, Military -- United States -- History -- 20th century.Germany -- History -- 1945-1955. United States -- Armed Forces -- Germany -- History -- 20th century. United States -- Military policy.

UA26.G675.T46
Thompson, Neil B., 1921-
Crazy Horse called them walk-a-heaps: the story of the foot soldier in the prairie Indian Wars/ Neil Baird Thompson. Saint Cloud, Minn.: North Star Press, c1979. vi, 150 p.
79-120364   301.6/334/0973   0878390111
Indians of North America -- Great Plains -- Wars -- 1866-1895.Great Plains -- History, Military.

UA26.H38.F47 1999
Ferguson, Kathy E.
Oh, say, can you see?: the semiotics of the military in Hawaii/ Kathy E. Ferguson and Phyllis Turnbull. Minneapolis: University of Minnesota Press, c1999. xviii, 270 p.
98-026195   355/.009969   0816629781
Sociology, Military -- Hawaii. Semiotics -- Hawaii.   Fort DeRussy (Hawaii) Hawaii -- Social life and customs. United States -- Armed Forces -- Hawaii.

UA26.N4.L66 1993
Loomis, David, 1955-
Combat zoning: military land-use planning in Nevada/ David Loomis. Reno: University of Nevada Press, c1993. xii, 144 p.
92-002838   355.7/09793   0874171873
Military bases -- Nevada -- History -- 20th century. Public lands -- Nevada -- History -- 20th century. Land use -- Nevada -- Planning -- History -- 20th century.

UA34.R36.H64 1992
Hogan, David W., 1958-
Raiders or elite infantry?: the changing role of the U.S. Army Rangers from Dieppe to Grenada/ David W. Hogan, Jr. Westport, Conn.: Greenwood Press, 1992. xxi, 272 p.
92-005422   356/.167/0973   0313268037
United States. Army -- Commando troops -- History -- 20th century.

UA34.S64.A33 1998
Adams, Thomas K.
US special operations forces in action: the challenge of unconventional warfare/ Thomas K. Adams. London; Frank Cass, 1998. xxviii, 360 p.
97-029160   355.3/43/0973   0714647950
Special forces (Military science) -- United States.United States -- History, Military.

UA34.S64.M37 1997
Marquis, Susan L. 1960-
Unconventional warfare: rebuilding U.S. special operations forces/ Susan L. Marquis. Washington, D.C.: Brookings Institution, c1997. xiii, 319 p.
96-053963   356/.16   0815754760
Special forces (Military science) -- United States.United States -- Politics and government -- 20th century.

UA42.D46
Derthick, Martha.
The National Guard in politics.   Cambridge, Harvard University Press, 1965. viii, 202 p.
65-011588   328.368
United States -- National Guard -- Political activity.

UA42.F64 1989
Fogelson, Robert M.
America's armories: architecture, society, and public order/ Robert M. Fogelson. Cambridge, Mass.: Harvard University Press, 1989. 268 p.
89-030999   355.7   0674031105
Armories -- United States. Military architecture -- United States. United States -- National Guard. United States -- Social conditions -- 1865-1918.

UA42.H5
Hill, Jim Dan, b. 1897.
The minute man in peace and war; a history of the National Guard. Foreword by George Fielding Eliot. Harrisburg, Pa., Stackpole Co. [1964] xx, 585 p.
63-022141   355.35
United States -- Militia. United States -- National Guard.

UA42.J64 1992
Johnson, Charles, 1937-
African American soldiers in the National Guard: recruitment and deployment during peacetime and war/ Charles Johnson, Jr. Westport, Conn.: Greenwood Press, 1992. xii, 218 p.
91-044510   355.3/7/08996073   0313207062
United States -- National Guard -- Afro-Americans -- History. United States -- Militia -- Afro-Americans -- History.

UA42.M33 1983
Mahon, John K.
History of the militia and the National Guard/ John K. Mahon. New York: Macmillan; c1983. vii, 374 p.
82-024902   355.3/7/0973   0029197503
United States -- Militia -- History. United States -- National Guard -- History.

UA42.R5
Riker, William H.
Soldiers of the States; the role of the National Guard in American democracy.   Washington, Public Affairs Press [1957] 129 p.
57-011749   355
United States -- National Guard. United States -- Militia.

UA264.N829 1997
Nuclear weapons in a transformed world: the challenge of virtual nuclear arsenals/ edited by Michael J. Mazarr. New York: St. Martin's Press, 1997. xii, 404 p.
96-034786   355.4/3   0312162022
Nuclear weapons. Deterrence (Strategy) World politics -- 1989-

UA565.W6.M48 1996
Meyer, Leisa D.
Creating GI Jane: sexuality and power in the Women's Army Corps during World War II/ Leisa D. Meyer. New York: Columbia University Press, c1996. x, 260 p.
96-013858 940.54/0973/082 0231101449
Sociology, Military -- United States. World War, 1939-1945 -- Women.

UA600 By region or country — North America — Canada. British America

UA600.J63 1991
Jockel, Joseph T.
Security to the north: Canada-U.S. defense relations in the 1990s/ by Joseph T. Jockel. East Lansing: Michigan State University Press, 1991. viii, 217 p.
91-052910 355/.033071 0870132938
Canada -- Defenses. Canada -- Military relations -- United States. United States -- Military relations -- Canada.

UA600.L36 1990
Langille, Howard Peter.
Changing the guard: Canada's defence in a world in transition/ Howard Peter Langille. Toronto; University of Toronto Press, c1990. xiv, 267 p.
92-185204 355/.033071 0802058701
Canada -- Military relations. Canada -- Military policy.

UA603 By region or country — North America — Mexico

UA603.D47 1997
DePalo, William A. 1941-
The Mexican National Army, 1822-1852/ William A. DePalo, Jr. College Station, Tex: Texas A&M University Press, c1997. xi, 280 p.
96-051447 355/.00972/09034 089096744X
Mexico -- Politics and government -- 1821-1861. Mexico -- History, Military.

UA606 By region or country — North America — Central America

UA606.C465 1988
The Central American security system: north-south or east-west/ edited by Peter Calvert. Cambridge [Cambridgeshire]; Cambridge University Press, 1988. x, 208 p.
88-016224 355/.0330728 0521351324
National security -- Central America. National security -- Caribbean Area.

UA612 By region or country — South America — General works

UA612.N86 1983
Nunn, Frederick M., 1937-
Yesterday's soldiers: European military professionalism in South America, 1890-1940/ Frederick M. Nunn. Lincoln: University of Nebraska Press, c1983. xiii, 365 p.
82-006961 306/.27/098 0803233051
Sociology, Military -- South America. Military art and Science -- South America -- History. Europe -- Military relations -- South America. South America -- Military relations -- Europe.

UA619 By region or country — South America — Brazil

UA619.D38 1996
Davis, Sonny B., 1948-
A brotherhood of arms: Brazil-United States military relations, 1945-1977/ Sonny B. Davis. Niwot: University Press of Colorado, c1996. xviii, 256 p.
95-042691 355/.03281 0870814184
Military assistance, American -- Brazil. Brazil -- Politics and government -- 20th century. Brazil -- Military relations -- United States. United States -- Military relations -- Brazil.

UA619.S7
Stepan, Alfred C.
The military in politics; changing patterns in Brazil. Princeton, Princeton University Press, 1971. xiii, 313 p.
73-132242 322/.5/0981 0691075379
Brazil -- Armed Forces -- Political activity.

UA646 By region or country — Europe — General works

UA646.A74 1989
Arms control and European security/ edited by Graeme P. Auton. New York: Praeger, 1989. vi, 205 p.
89-003663 355/.03304 0275931536
National security -- Europe. Arms control -- Europe.

UA646.B8 1963
Buchan, Alastair, 1918-1976.
Arms and stability in Europe; a report, by Alastair Buchan and Philip Windsor. New York, Praeger, for the Institute for Strategic Studies [c1963] x, 236 p.
63-021481
Disarmament. Europe -- Military policy.

UA646.C54 1991
Cimbala, Stephen J.
Strategy after deterrence/ Stephen J. Cimbala. New York: Praeger, 1991. xiii, 267 p.
90-039027 355/.03354 0275937410
Deterrence (Strategy) Nuclear warfare. Europe -- Military policy. United States -- Military policy.

UA646.C6813
Corvisier, Andre.
Armies and societies in Europe, 1494-1789/ Andre Corvisier; translated by Abigail T. Siddall. Bloomington: Indiana University Press, c1979. ix, 209 p.
78-062419 301.5/93/094 0253129850
Armies -- History. Sociology, Military. Europe -- History, Military -- 1492-1648. Europe -- History, Military -- 1648-1789.

UA646.C74 1987
Cowen Karp, Regina.
SDI and European security/ Regina Cowen, Peter Rajcsanyi, Vladimir Bilandzic; with an introduction by F. Stephen Larrabee. New York: Institute for East-West Security Studies; c1987. ii, 183 p.
87-035290 355/.03304 0913449075
National security -- Europe. Strategic Defense Initiative.

UA646.C97 1987
Cyr, Arthur I., 1945-
U.S. foreign policy and European security/ Arthur Cyr. New York: St. Martin's Press, 1987. vii, 156 p.
86-020379 355/.03304 0312002211
National security -- Europe.United States -- Foreign relations -- 1981-

UA646.D87 1994
Duke, Simon.
The new European security disorder/ Simon Duke. Basingstoke, Hampshire: Macmillan, in association with Antony's College, Oxford; New York: 1994. xvii, 448 p.
94-021686 355/.0334 031212371X
National security -- Europe.Europe -- Defenses. Europe -- Politics and government -- 1989-

UA646.E33 1989
Eichenberg, Richard C., 1952-
Public opinion and national security in Western Europe/ Richard C. Eichenberg. Ithaca: Cornell University Press, 1989. xvi, 293 p.
88-038906 355/.03304 080142237X
Public opinion -- Europe. National security -- Europe -- Public opinion.

UA646.E9232 1988
Europe: dimensions of peace/ edited by Bjorn Hettne. Tokyo, Japan: United Nations University; 1988. 287 p.
87-013348 327.1/7 0862327148
National security -- Europe. World politics -- 1985-1995.

UA646.E9234 1988
Europe in the Western Alliance: towards a European defence entity?/ edited by Jonathan Alford and Kenneth Hunt; foreword by Robert O'Neill. New York: St. Martin's Press, 1988. x, 246 p.
88-011328 355/.03304 0312021151
Europe -- Defenses.

UA646.E9253 1988
European security beyond the year 2000/ edited by Robert Rudney and Luc Reychler. New York: Praeger, 1988. 317 p.
87-012494 355/.03304 0275926257
Europe -- Defenses.

UA646.F45 1993
Feld, Werner J.
The future of European security and defense policy/ Werner J. Feld. Boulder: Lynne Rienner Publishers; 1993. xiv, 178 p.
92-030722 355/.03304 1555873537
National security -- Europe.Europe -- Military policy.

UA646.G38 1997
Gardner, Hall.
Dangerous crossroads: Europe, Russia, and the future of NATO/ Hall Gardner. Westport, Conn.: Praeger, 1997. xii, 279 p.
96-052629 355/.031091821 0275958574
National security -- Security, International. Russia (Federation) -- Foreign relations -- Europe. Europe -- Foreign relations -- Russia (Federation)

UA646.G59
Gooch, John.
Armies in Europe/ John Gooch. London; Routledge & Kegan Paul, 1980. x, 286 p.
79-041297 355/.0094 0710004621
Armies -- Europe -- History.

UA646.H48 1997
Heuser, Beatrice, 1961-
NATO, Britain, France, and the FRG: nuclear strategies and forces for Europe, 1949-2000/ Beatrice Heuser. New York: St. Martin's Press, 1997. xvii, 256 p.
97-001895   355.02/17/094   0312174985
Nuclear weapons -- Government policy -- Europe, Western -- History.Europe, Western -- Defenses -- History. Europe -- Politics and government -- 1945-

UA646.I37 1988
Hephaistos, Panagiotes.
Nuclear strategy and European security dilemmas: towards an autonomous European defence system?/ Panayiotis Ifestos; preface by Alfred Cahen. Aldershot [England]: Avebury, c1988. xvii, 496 p.
88-005411   355./03304   0566056410
Nuclear warfare.Europe -- Defenses.

UA646.L34 1990
Laqueur, Walter, 1921-
European security in the 1990s: deterrence and defense after the INF Treaty/ Walter Laqueur and Leon Sloss; with the assistance of Philipp Borinski; foreword by David M. Abshire. New York: Plenum Press, c1990. xv, 214 p.
89-049472   355./03304   0306434423
Nuclear weapons -- Europe.Europe -- Defenses.

UA646.M37 1996
Mandelbaum, Michael.
The dawn of peace in Europe/ Michael Mandelbaum; with a foreword by Richard C. Leone. New York: Twentieth Century Fund Press, 1996. xiv, 209 p.
96-021875   355./03304   0870783963
National security -- Europe.Russia (Federation) -- Foreign relations -- Europe. Europe -- Foreign relations -- Russia (Federation) United States -- Foreign relations -- Europe.

UA646.M73 1995
Moller, Bjorn.
Dictionary of alternative defense/ Bjorn Moller. Boulder: L. Rienner Publishers, 1995. xxxi, 553 p.
92-027347   355.4   1555873863
Offensive (Military science) -- Dictionaries. Deterrence (Strategy) -- Dictionaries. Europe -- Military policy -- Dictionaries.

UA646.R47 1988
Rethinking the nuclear weapons dilemma in Europe/ edited by P. Terrence Hopmann and Frank Barnaby; foreword by Harlan Cleveland. New York: St. Martin's Press, 1988. xvii, 374 p.
87-012914   355./0217/094   0312678045
Nuclear weapons -- Europe.Europe -- Defenses.

UA646.R896 2000
Ruane, Kevin.
The rise and fall of the European defence community: Anglo-American relations and the crisis of European defence, 1950-55/ Kevin Ruane. Houndmills, Basingstoke, Hampshire [England]: Macmillan Press; 2000. ix, 252 p.
00-027836   355/.031091821   0333913191
European cooperation.Great Britain -- Military relations -- United states. Europe, Western -- Defenses. United States -- Military relations -- Great Britain.

UA646.S643 1988
Soofer, Robert M.
Missile defenses and western European security: NATO strategy, arms control, and deterrence/ Robert M. Soofer. New York: Greenwood Press, 1988. xiv, 174 p.
88-016394   355./03304   0313263515
National security -- Europe. Strategic Defense Initiative. Anti-tactical ballistic missiles -- Europe.

UA646.U65 1988
The United States, Western Europe, and military intervention overseas/ edited by Christopher Coker. New York: St. Martin's Press, 1988. x, 190 p.
87-026111   327/.09182/1   0312016204
World politics -- 1985-1995.Europe -- Military relations -- Foreign countries. United States -- Military relations -- Foreign countries.

UA646.W28 1989
War in Europe: nuclear and conventional perspectives/ edited by Hylke Tromp. Aldershot, Hants, England; Gower, c1989. xiv, 350 p.
89-001856   355./03304   0566070227
Nuclear warfare. Warfare, Conventional. Europe -- Defenses.

UA646.W55 1988
Windass, Stan, 1930-
The crucible of peace: common security in Europe/ Stan Windass and Eric Grove; with chapters based on original work by Manfred Bartele ... [et al.]. London; Brassey's Defence Publishers, 1988. xii, 156 p.
87-036813   355./03304   0080362524
National security -- Europe.

UA646.W95 1997
Wyatt-Walter, Holly, 1968-1995.
The European Community and the security dilemma, 1979-92/ Holly Wyatt-Walter; foreword by Robert O'Neill. New York: St. Martin's Press, in association with St. Antony's College, Oxford, 1997. xiv, 339 p.
96-021864   355./03304   0333673530
National security -- Europe.Europe -- Defenses. Europe -- Politics and government -- 1945-

UA646.3-646.5 By region or country — Europe — North Atlantic Treaty Organization (NATO). Supreme Headquarters, Allied Powers, Europe (SHAPE). European Defense Community

UA646.3.B7
Buchan, Alastair, 1918-1976.
NATO in the 1960's; the implications of interdependence. With a foreword by John Slessor. New York, Praeger for the Institute for Strategic Studies, [1960] xii, 131 p.
60-010484   355
North Atlantic Treaty Organization.

UA646.3.C495 1989
Cimbala, Stephen J.
NATO strategy and nuclear escalation/ Stephen J. Cimbala. New York: St. Martin's Press, 1989. xiv, 276 p.
89-010263   355.02/17/094   0312032390
Nuclear warfare. Escalation (Military science) Strategy. Europe -- Military policy.

UA646.3.C53 1988
Clash in the north: polar summitry and NATO's northern flank/ edited by Walter Goldstein. Washington: Pergamon-Brassey's International Defense Publishers, 1988. xii, 208 p.
87-015958   355/.031/091821   0080346863
World politics -- 1985-1995 Congresses.Scandinavia -- Strategic aspects -- Congresses.

UA646.3.C62 1989
Cook, Don, 1920-
Forging the alliance: NATO 1945-1950/ Don Cook. New York: Arbor House/W. Morrow, 1989. ix, 306 p.
88-034226   355/.031/091821   1557100438
World politics -- 1945-1955.Europe -- History -- 1945-

UA646.3.D817 1995
Duffield, John S.
Power rules: the evolution of NATO's conventional force posture/ John S. Duffield. Stanford, Calif.: Stanford University Press, c1995. x, 386 p.
94-025006   355/.031/091821   0804723966
Warfare, Conventional.

UA646.3.D82 1993
Duke, Simon.
The burdensharing debate: a reassessment/ Simon Duke. New York: St. Martin's Press, 1993. xxii, 277 p.
91-033519   355/.031/091821   0312074956
United States -- Armed Forces -- Appropriations and expenditures. Europe -- Armed Forces -- Appropriations and expenditures. United States -- Military relations -- Europe.

UA646.3.G32 1992
Gates, David.
Non-offensive defence: an alternative strategy for NATO?/ David Gates. New York: St. Martin's Press, 1991. viii, 205 p.
91-025585   355/.031/091821   0312068166
Non-provocative defense (Military science) -- Europe.

UA646.3.K5
Knorr, Klaus Eugen, 1911-
NATO and American security. Princeton, N.J., Princeton University Press, 1959. 342 p.
59-013016   355
North Atlantic Treaty Organization.

UA646.3.K76 1987
Kromer, Robert Andrew, 1944-
New weapons and NATO: solutions or irritants?/ Robert Kromer. New York: Greenwood Press, 1987. vi, 185 p.
87-008649   355/.031/091821   0313255881
Precision guided munitions. Tactical nuclear weapons. Strategic Defense Initiative. Europe -- Military policy.

UA646.3.N229 1997
NATO and the quest for post-cold war security/ edited by Clay Clemens; foreword by Baroness Thatcher. New York: St. Martin's Press, 1997. xvii, 210 p.
97-003274   355/.031091821   0312176031
National security -- Europe.

UA646.3.N2425 1998
NATO enlargement: illusions and reality/ edited by Ted Galen Carpenter and Barbara Conry. Washington, DC: Cato Institute, 1998. x, 283 p.
97-052330   355/.031091821   1882577582
National security -- Europe.Russia (Federation) -- Foreign relations.

UA646.3.N24252 2001
NATO enters the 21st century/ editor Ted Galen Carpenter. London; Frank Cass, 2001. 189 p.
00-063920   355/.031091821/0905
0714650587
North Atlantic Treaty Organization.

UA646.3.N2445 1998
NATO looks East/ edited by Piotr Dutkiewicz and Robert J. Jackson. Westport, Conn.: Praeger, 1998. viii, 199 p.
98-006823   355/.031091821   0275960595
Europe, Eastern -- Military relations. National security -- Europe.

UA646.3.O8
Osgood, Robert Endicott.
NATO, the entangling alliance/ by Robert Endicott Osgood. [Chicago]: University of Chicago Press, c1962. x, 416 p.
62-008348   355
World politics -- 1945-

UA646.3.S353 1962
Schmidt, Helmut, 1918 Dec. 23-
Defense or retaliation, a German view. Translated by Edward Thomas. New York, Praeger [1962] xiii, 264 p.
62-012842
North Atlantic Treaty Organization.

UA646.3.S38 1983
Schwartz, David N., 1956-
NATO's nuclear dilemmas/ David N. Schwartz. Washington, D.C.: Brookings Institution, c1983. x, 270 p.
83-011911   355/.031/097821   0815777728
Nuclear weapons. Deterrence (Strategy) -- History -- 20th century. Cruise missiles.

UA646.3.S654 1998
Solomon, Gerald B. H., 1930-
The NATO enlargement debate, 1990-1997: the blessings of liberty/ Gerald B. Solomon. Westport, Conn.: Praeger, 1998. x, 189 p.
97-050393   355/.031091821   027596289X
North Atlantic Treaty Organization -- Europe, Eastern.

UA646.3.S794 1988
Stromseth, Jane E.
The origins of flexible response: NATO'S debate over strategy in the 1960s/ Jane E. Stromseth; foreword by Denis Healey. New York: St. Martin's Press, 1988. xiv, 274 p.
87-013117   355/.031/091821   0312011741
Europe -- Military policy.

UA646.3.Y674 1998
Yost, David S. 1948-
NATO transformed: the Alliance's new roles in international security/ David S. Yost. Washington, DC: United States Institute of Peace Press, 1998. xx, 450 p.
98-040939   355/.031091821   187837981X
Security, International.

UA646.5.U5.S55
Williams, Geoffrey Lee.
NATO and the transatlantic alliance in the 21st century: the twenty-year crisis/ Geoffrey Lee Williams and Barkley Jared Jones. New York: Palgrave, c2000. xiv, 250 p.
00-053062   355/.031091821   0333657640
Security, International. World politics -- 1989-

UA646.5.F7.B6913 2001
Bozo, Frederic.
Two strategies for Europe: De Gaulle, the United States, and the Atlantic Alliance/ Frederic Bozo; translated by Susan Emanuel. Lanham, Md.: Rowman & Littlefield, c2001. xx, 277 p.
00-040301   355/.031091821   0847695301
Gaulle, Charles de, -- 1890-1970.France -- Politics and government -- 1958- France -- Foreign relations -- 1958-1969. France -- Foreign relations -- United States.

UA646.5.S7.S63 1988
Spain's entry into NATO: conflicting political and strategic perspectives/ edited by Federico G. Gil and Joseph S. Tulchin. Boulder: Lynne Rienner Publishers, c1988. vii, 179 p.
88-004973   355/.033046   1555871178
Spain -- Military policy -- Congresses. Spain -- History -- 1975- -- Congresses.

UA646.53 By region or country — Europe — Baltic Sea region

UA646.53.S73 1999
Stability and security in the Baltic Sea region: Russian, Nordic, and European aspects/ edited by Olav F. Knudsen. Portland, Ore: Frank Cass, 1999. xiii, 287 p.
98-037435   355/.0330479   0714649325
National security -- Baltic States. National security -- Russia (Federation) Baltic States -- Relations -- Russia (Federation) Russia (Federation) -- Relations -- Baltic States. Baltic States -- Relations -- Europe.

UA646.55 By region or country — Europe — Mediterranean region

UA646.55.P76 1988
Prospects for security in the Mediterranean/ edited by Robert O'Neill. Hamden, CT: Archon Books, 1988. 245 p.
88-026005   355/.03301822   0208022333
National security -- Mediterranean Region -- Congresses.

UA646.7 By region or country — Europe — Scandinavia

UA646.7.D67 1997
Dorfer, Ingemar.
The Nordic nations in the New Western Security Regime/ Ingemar Dorfer. Washington, DC: Woodrow Wilson Center Press; 1997. xviii, 103 p.
97-008532   355/.033048   0943875838
National security -- Scandinavia.Scandinavia -- Defenses.

UA646.7.F52 1987
Fitzmaurice, John.
Security and politics in the Nordic area/ John Fitzmaurice.   Aldershot,   Hants,   England; Avebury, c1987. xi, 191 p.
87-014947   355/.033048   0566050358
Scandinavia -- Strategic aspects. Soviet Union, Northern -- Strategic aspects.

UA646.8 By region or country — Europe — Eastern Europe. Warsaw Pact Forces

UA646.8.C455 1993
Central and Eastern Europe: the challenge of transition/ edited by Regina Cowen-Karp. Stockholm, Sweden: Sipri; 1993. xiv, 322 p.
93-037946   355/.033047   0198291698
National security -- Europe, Eastern. National security -- Europe, Central. Europe, Eastern -- Politics and government -- 1989- Europe, Central -- Politics and government -- 1989-

UA646.8.M53 1992
Michta, Andrew A.
East Central Europe after the Warsaw Pact: security dilemmas in the 1990s/ Andrew A. Michta; foreword by Vojtech Mastny. New York: Greenwood Press, 1992. xv, 192 p.
91-033126   355/.033047   0313278865
National security -- Europe, Eastern. National security -- Poland. National security -- Czechoslovakia.

UA646.8.W366 1989
The Warsaw Pact and the Balkans: Moscow's southern flank/ edited by Jonathan Eyal. New York: St. Martin's Press, 1989. xvi, 246 p.
89-030604   355/.0330496   0312031513
Balkan Peninsula -- Defenses.

UA647-655 By region or country — Europe — Great Britain

UA647.B288 1995
Baylis, John, 1946-
Ambiguity and deterrence: British nuclear strategy, 1945-1964/ John Baylis. Oxford; Clarendon Press, 1995. xii, 495 p.
95-030526   355.02/17/0941   0198280122
Nuclear weapons -- Government policy -- Great Britain -- History. Deterrence (Strategy) Great Britain -- Politics and government -- 1945-1964.

UA647.B567 1995
Ball, S. J.
The bomber in British strategy: Britain's world role, 1945-1960/ S.J. Ball. Boulder: Westview Press, 1995.
95-018392   355.8/25119/0941   0813389348
Nuclear weapons -- Government policy -- Great Britain. Bombers -- Great Britain. Great Britain -- Military relations -- United States. United States -- Military relations -- Great Britain.

UA647.B575 1989
Booth, Ken.
Britain, NATO, and nuclear weapons: alternative defence versus alliance reform/ Ken Booth and John Baylis. New York: St. Martin's Press, 1989. xii, 374 p.
89-004170   355/.0335/41   031203136X
Nuclear warfare. Nuclear weapons -- Great Britain. Great Britain -- Military policy.

UA647.B85
British defence policy in a changing world/ edited by John Baylis. London: Croom Helm, c1977. 295 p.
78-301391 355.03/3041 0856643742
Great Britain -- Defenses -- Addresses, essays, lectures. Great Britain -- Military policy -- Addresses, essays, lectures. Great Britain -- Foreign relations -- 1945- -- Addresses, essays, lectures.

UA647.B857 1988
Broadbent, Ewen, 1924-
The military and government: from Macmillan to Heseltine/ Sir Ewen Broadbent; foreword by Harold Macmillan. New York: St. Martin's Press, 1988. xiii, 238 p.
87-032901 354.41066/09 0312016786
Great Britain. Ministry of Defence -- History.

UA647.F4 1989
Ferris, John Robert, 1957-
Men, money, and diplomacy: the evolution of British strategic policy, 1919-26/ John Robert Ferris. Ithaca, N.Y.: Cornell University Press, 1989. xiii, 235 p.
88-047750 355/.0335/41 0801422361
Great Britain -- Military policy. Great Britain -- Foreign relations -- 1910-1936. Great Britain -- Economic policy.

UA647.H56
Higham, Robin D. S.
The military intellectuals in Britain, 1918-1939 [by] Robin Higham. New Brunswick, N.J., Rutgers University Press [1966] xi, 267 p.
66-018872 355.0330942
Great Britain -- Military policy.

UA647.J34 1985
Jaffe, Lorna S.
The decision to disarm Germany: British policy towards postwar German disarmament, 1914-1919/ Lorna S. Jaffe. Boston: Allen & Unwin, 1985. xiii, 286 p.
84-012351 355/.0335/41 0049430343
World War, 1914-1918 -- Great Britain. World War, 1914-1918 -- Germany. Great Britain -- Military policy. Great Britain -- Military relations -- Germany. Germany -- Military relations -- Great Britain.

UA647.K43 1993
Keohane, Dan, 1961-
Labour Party defence policy since 1945/ Dan Keohane. Leicester: Leicester University Press; 1993. ix, 174 p.
92-024749 355/.0335/41 071851467X
Nuclear weapons -- Great Britain. Great Britain -- Military policy.

UA647.P35 1988
Perry, F. W.
The Commonwealth armies: manpower and organisation in two world wars/ F.W. Perry. Manchester: Manchester University Press; c1988. 250 p.
87-031519 355/.009171/241 0719025958
Armies -- Commonwealth countries -- History -- 20th century.

UA647.P68
Preston, Richard Arthur.
Canada and imperial defense; a study of the origins of the British Commonwealth's defense organization, 1867-1919 [by] Richard A. Preston. Durham, N.C., Published for the Duke University Commonwealth-Studies Center [by] Duke University Press, 1967. xxi, 576 p.
66-029550 355.03/09171/242
Great Britain -- Defenses. Canada -- Defenses.

UA647.P69 1996
Prestwich, Michael.
Armies and warfare in the Middle Ages: the English experience/ Michael Prestwich. New Haven: Yale University Press, 1996. ix, 396 p.
95-036142 355.3/0942/0902 0300064527
Military art and science -- England -- History -- Medieval, 500-1500. Great Britain -- History, Military -- 1066-1485.

UA647.S182 1995
Samuels, Martin.
Command or control?: command, training, and tactics in the British and German armies, 1888-1918/ Martin Samuels. London; Frank Cass, 1995. ix, 339 p.
95-007053 355/.033541 0714645702
Military doctrine -- Great Britain -- History -- 19th century. Military doctrine -- Great Britain -- History -- 20th century. Military doctrine -- Germany -- History -- 19th century.

UA647.S37
Shay, Robert Paul, 1947-
British rearmament in the thirties: politics and profits/ Robert Paul Shay, Jr. Princeton, N.J.: Princeton University Press, c1977. xiii, 315 p.
76-045911 355.03/3041 0691052484
Great Britain -- Defenses. Great Britain -- Politics and government -- 20th century. Great Britain -- Foreign relations -- 20th century.

UA649.B87 1988
Brodsky, G. W. Stephen, 1933-
Gentlemen of the blade: a social and literary history of the British Army since 1660/ G.W. Stephen Brodsky. New York: Greenwood Press, 1988. xxxiii, 187 p.
87-023692 355/.00941 0313260672
Sociology, Military -- Great Britain.

UA649.C75 1968
Cruickshank, Charles Greig.
Elizabeth's army, by C. G. Cruickshank. London, Oxford U.P., 1968. xii, 316 p.
70-356991 355/.00942 0198811489
Military administration.

UA649.F52 1962
Firth, C. H. 1857-1936.
Cromwell's army; a history of the English soldier during the civil wars, the Commonwealth and the Protectorate. London, Methuen; [1962] 432 p.
62-005713 942.062
Great Britain -- History, Military.

UA649.O55 1999
Oliver, Michael.
Napoleonic Army handbook: the British Army and her allies/ Michael Oliver and Richard Partridge. London: Constable, 1999. xiii, 479 p.
940.27 009477630X
Armies -- Europe -- History -- 19th century. Napoleonic Wars, 1800-1815 -- Campaigns.

UA649.S52
Sheppard, Eric William.
Red coat, an anthology of the British soldier during the last three hundred years. London, Batchworth Press 1952 245 p.
53-023806 355
Soldiers in literature.

UA649.S73
Spiers, Edward M.
The army and society, 1815-1914/ Edward M. Spiers. London; Longman, 1980. 318 p.
79-040042 301.5/93/0941 0582485657
Sociology, Military -- Great Britain.

UA649.3.D46 1987
Dennis, Peter, 1945-
The Territorial Army, 1906-1940/ Peter Dennis. Woodbridge, Suffolk: Royal Historical Society; 1987. 274 p.
87-005147 355.3/7/0941 0861932080
Great Britain. Army. Territorial Army -- History.

UA649.3.N38 1985
A Nation in arms: a social study of the British Army in the First World War/ edited by Ian F.W. Beckett and Keith Simpson. Manchester; Manchester University Press, c1985. x, 276 p.
84-025048 306/.27/0941 0719017378
Sociology, Military -- Great Britain -- History -- 20th century.

UA649.32.G3.C67 1996
Cornish, Paul.
British military planning for the defence of Germany, 1945-50/ Paul Cornish. New York: St. Martin's Press, 1996. xi, 211 p.
95-037739 943.087/5 0312129602
Military planning -- Great Britain. Great Britain -- Armed Forces -- Germany (West)

UA649.32.I4.H43 1995
Heathcote, T. A.
The military in British India: the development of British land forces in South Asia, 1600-1947/ T.A. Heathcote. Manchester; Manchester University Press; c1995. xvi, 288 p.
94-018101 954.03 0719035708
India -- History, Military. Great Britain -- History, Military.

UA649.32.I4.S73 1998
Stanley, Peter, 1956-
White mutiny: British military culture in India/ Peter Stanley. New York: New York University Press, 1998. xiv, 314 p.
97-000716 355.3/52/0941 0814780830
India -- History, Military.

UA649.32.W47.B83 1998
Buckley, Roger Norman, 1937-
The British Army in the West Indies: society and the military in the revolutionary age/ Roger Norman Buckley. Gainesville, Fla.: University Press of Florida, c1998. xx, 441 p.
98-013516 306.2/7/09729 0813016045
Garrisons, British -- West Indies -- History. Sociology, Military -- West Indies -- History. West Indies, British -- Social conditions. West Indies, British -- History, Military.

UA655 3d.B6
Bolitho, Hector, 1898-1974.
The Galloping Third; the story of the 3rd, the King's Own Hussars. [London] J. Murray [c1963] xi, 341 p.
64-001252
Great Britain. Army. 3d Dragoons (King's Own Hussars)

UA672 By region or country — Europe — Austria. Austria-Hungary

UA672.L33 1995
Lackey, Scott W.
The rebirth of the Habsburg army: Friedrich Beck and the rise of the general staff/ Scott W. Lackey. Westport, Conn.: Greenwood Press, 1995. xiii, 253 p.
95-007897   355/.009436   0313293619
Beck-Rzikowsky, Friedrich, -- Graf von, -- 1830-1906.Generals -- Austria -- Biography.Austria -- History, Military.

UA700-703 By region or country — Europe — France

UA700.A65
Ambler, John S.
The French Army in politics, 1945-1962. [Columbus] Ohio State University Press [1966] x, 427 p.
65-026274   355.00944
France -- Politics and government.

UA700.C593 1997
Cogan, Charles.
Forced to choose: France, the Atlantic Alliance, and NATO--then and now/ Charles G. Cogan. Westport, Conn.: Praeger, 1997. xii, 158 p.
96-045330   355/.033044   0275957047
France -- Foreign relations. France -- Military policy. France -- Politics and government -- 1945-1958.

UA700.C68 1994
Cox, Gary P.
The halt in the mud: French strategic planning from Waterloo to Sedan/ Gary P. Cox. Boulder: Westview Press, 1994. xii, 258 p.
93-025458   355/.0335/44   0813315360
France -- Military policy. France -- History, Military -- 19th century.

UA700.G32 1941
Gaulle, Charles de, 1890-1970.
The army of the future, by General Charles de Gaulle, foreword by Walter Millis. Philadelphia, Lippincott, 1941. 179 p.
41-051695
France -- Defenses.

UA700.K4
Kennett, Lee B.
The French armies in the Seven Years' War; a study in military organization and administration. Durham, N.C., Duke University Press, 1967. xvi, 165 p.
67-018529   355.3/1/0944
Seven Years' War, 1756-1763.

UA700.K54 1997
Kier, Elizabeth, 1958-
Imagining war: French and British military doctrine between the wars/ Elizabeth Kier. Princeton, N.J.: Princeton University Press, c1997. x, 240 p.
96-046302   355/.033544   0691011915
Military doctrine -- France. Military doctrine -- Great Britain. Political stability -- France. France -- Politics and government -- 1914-1940. Great Britain -- Politics and government -- 1910-1936.

UA700.P66 1991
Posner, Theodore Robert.
Current French security policy: the Gaullist legacy/ Theodore Robert Posner. New York: Greenwood Press, 1991. x, 171 p.
91-021195   355/.0335/44   0313279349
National security -- Europe.France -- Military relations. Europe -- Military relations. France -- Military policy.

UA700.S77 1989
Strangers and friends: the Franco-German security relationship/ edited by Robbin F. Laird. New York: St. Martin's Press, 1989. vi, 150 p.
89-033239   355/.033044   0312032420
National security -- France. National security -- Germany (West) France -- Military relations -- Germany (West) Germany (West) -- Military relations -- France.

UA702.H67 1984
Horne, Alistair.
The French Army and politics, 1870-1970/ Alistair Horne. New York: Peter Bedrick Books: c1984. xvii, 109 p.
83-013453   322/.5/0944   0911745157
France -- Politics and government -- 19th century. France -- Politics and government -- 20th century.

UA702.L2613
La Gorce, Paul Marie de.
The French Army; a military-political history. Translated by Kenneth Douglas. New York, G. Braziller [1963] 568 p.
63-010401   355.0944
France. Armée -- History.

UA702.L95 1984
Lynn, John A. 1943-
The bayonets of the Republic: motivation and tactics in the army of Revolutionary France, 1791-94/ John A. Lynn. Urbana: University of Illinois Press, c1984. xii, 356 p.
83-009093   355/.00944   0252010914
Tactics -- History -- 18th century. Military art and science -- France -- History -- 18th century.

UA702.L9523 1997
Lynn, John A. 1943-
Giant of the grand siecle: the French Army, 1610-1715/ John A. Lynn. Cambridge; Cambridge University Press, 1997. xx, 651 p.
96-022239   355/.00944/09032   0521572738
France -- History, Military -- 1610-1643. France -- History, Military -- 1643-1715.

UA702.M5 1984
Mitchell, Allan.
Victors and vanquished: the German influence on army and church in France after 1870/ by Allan Mitchell. Chapel Hill: University of North Carolina Press, c1984. xvii, 354 p.
83-025917   944.081   0807816035
Church and state -- France -- History -- 19th century.France -- Church history -- 19th century. Germany -- Relations -- France. France -- Relations -- Germany.

UA702.Q5 1968
Quimby, Robert S.
The background of Napoleonic warfare; the theory of military tactics in eighteenth-century France [by] Robert S. Quimby. New York, AMS Press [1968] viii, 385 p.
68-059257   355.4/09/033
Military art and science -- History. Tactics -- History. France -- History, Military -- 18th century.

UA702.S386 1998
Scott, Samuel F.
From Yorktown to Valmy: the transformation of the French Army in an age of revolution/ Samuel F. Scott. Niwot, Colo.: University Press of Colorado, c1998. xiii, 251 p.
98-028519   355/.00944/09033   0870815040
United States -- History -- Revolution, 1775-1783 -- Participation, French. France -- History -- Revolution, 1789-1799.

UA703.L5.O2
O'Ballance, Edgar.
The story of the French Foreign Legion. London, Faber and Faber [1961] 270 p.
62-000776   355.31
France. Armée. Légion étrangère.

UA710-719.3 By region or country — Europe — Germany

UA710.A594 1988
Abenheim, Donald, 1953-
Reforging the Iron Cross: the search for tradition in the West German armed forces/ Donald Abenheim; with a foreword by Gordon A. Craig. Princeton, N.J.: Princeton University Press, c1988. xxii, 316 p.
88-009969   322/.5/0943   0691055343
Civil-military relations -- Germany (West) -- History.Germany (West) -- Armed Forces -- History.

UA710.B494 1998
Berger, Thomas U.
Cultures of antimilitarism: national security in Germany and Japan/ Thomas U. Berger. Baltimore, Md.: The Johns Hopkins University Press, 1998. xiii, 256 p.
97-048479   355/.033043   0801858208
Militarism -- Germany -- History -- 20th century. Militarism -- Japan -- History -- 20th century. Germany -- Politics and government -- 20th century. Japan -- Defenses. Germany -- Defenses.

UA710.C54 1988
Cioc, Mark.
Pax atomica: the nuclear defense debate in West Germany during the Adenauer era/ Mark Cioc. New York: Columbia University Press, 1988. xxii, 251 p.
87-032550   355/.0217/0943   0231065906
Nuclear warfare.Germany (West) -- Military policy. Germany (West) -- Politics and government.

UA710.C55 1987
Citino, Robert Michael, 1958-
The evolution of blitzkrieg tactics: Germany defends itself against Poland, 1918-1933/ Robert M. Citino. New York: Greenwood Press, 1987. xiv, 209 p.
87-000005   355.4/22   0313256314
Germany -- Armed Forces -- History -- 20th century. Germany -- Military relations -- Poland. Poland -- Military relations -- Germany.

UA710.C67 1992
Corum, James S.
The roots of Blitzkrieg: Hans von Seeckt and German military reform/ James S. Corum. Lawrence, Kan.: University Press of Kansas, c1992. xvii, 274 p.
92-005178   355.02/0943   070060541X
Seeckt, Hans von, -- 1866-1936.Lightning war -- History. Military doctrine -- Germany -- History -- 20th century. Germany -- Armed Forces -- History -- 20th century.

UA710.L27 1996
Large, David Clay.
Germans to the front: West German rearmament in the Adenauer era/ David Clay Large. Chapel Hill: University of North Carolina Press, c1996. x, 327 p.
95-005401   355/.033043/09045   0807822353
Germany (West) -- Defenses. Germany (West) -- Politics and government. Germany (West) -- Foreign relations.

UA710.S56
Speier, Hans.
German rearmament and atomic war; the views of German military and political leaders. Evanston, Ill., Row, Peterson [1957] xi, 272 p.
57-011348   355
Germany (West) -- Military policy. Germany (West) -- Politics and government. Germany (West) -- Defenses.

UA710.U587 1990
Handbook on German military forces/ U.S. War Department; with an introduction by Stephen E. Ambrose. Baton Rouge: Louisiana State University Press, [1990] 635 p.
90-005954   355/.00943   0807116297
Germany -- Armed Forces -- Handbooks, manuals, etc. Germany -- Armed Forces -- History -- World War, 1939-1945 -- Handbooks, manuals, etc.

UA712.O5 1966
O'Neill, Robert John.
The German Army and the Nazi Party, 1933-1939 [by] Robert J. O'Neill. Foreword by Captain Sir Basil Liddell Hart. New York, J. H. Heineman [1967, c1966] 286 p.
67-011678   355.3/51/0943
Germany.   Heer   --   History. Nationalsozialistische Deutsche Arbeiter-Partei.

UA712.V256 1982
Van Creveld, Martin L.
Fighting power: German and US Army performance, 1939-1945/ Martin van Creveld. Westport, Conn.: Greenwood Press, 1982. xi, 198 p.
81-023732   355/.02   0313233330
Germany. Heer -- Evaluation. United States. Army -- Evaluation. Germany. Heer -- History -- World War, 1939-1945. Germany. Heer -- Statistics. United States. Army -- Statistics.

UA718.P9.D83 1974
Duffy, Christopher, 1936-
Army of Frederick the Great.   New York: Hippocrene Books, 1974. 272 p.
74-080439   355.3'0943   088254277X
Frederick -- II, -- King of Prussia, -- 1712-1786.

UA719.3.H6424 1998
Herspring, Dale R.
Requiem for an army: the demise of the East German military/ Dale R. Herspring. Lanham: Rowman & Littlefield Publishers, c1998. xviii, 249 p.
98-025249   355/.009431   084768718X
Germany (East) -- Military policy. Germany -- History -- Unification, 1990.

UA724 By region or country — Europe — Greece

UA724.S64 1993
Spence, I. G.
The cavalry of classical Greece: a social and military history with particular reference to Athens/ I.G. Spence. Oxford: Clarendon Press; 1993. xxxiv, 346 p.
93-000442   357/.1/0938   0198144822
Greece -- Army -- Cavalry -- History.

UA770-772 By region or country — Europe — Soviet Union

UA770.A85 1987
Asia in Soviet global strategy/ edited by Ray S. Cline, James Arnold Miller, and Roger E. Kanet. Boulder: Westview Press, 1987. viii, 193 p.
87-022477   355/.0335/47   0813374812
National security -- Soviet Union. Communist strategy. Soviet Union -- Military relations -- Pacific Area. Asia -- Military relations -- Soviet Union. Pacific Area -- Military relations -- Soviet Union.

UA770.B435 1999
Bennett, Andrew.
Condemned to repetition?: the rise, fall, and reprise   of   Soviet-Russian   military interventionism, 1973-1996/ Andrew Bennett. Cambridge, Mass: The MIT Press, c1999. xi, 387 p.
98-046251   355/.033047   0262024578
Soviet Union -- Military policy. Russia (Federation) -- Military policy. Soviet Union -- Foreign relations -- 1975-1985.

UA770.B45 1982
Berman, Robert P., 1950-
Soviet strategic forces: requirements and responses/ Robert P. Berman and John C. Baker. Washington, D.C.: Brookings Institution, c1982. xi, 171 p.
82-070889   358/.17/0947   0815709269
Strategic forces -- Soviet Union.Soviet Union -- Military policy. United States -- Military policy.

UA770.B592 1992
Bluth, Christoph.
Soviet strategic arms policy before SALT/ Christoph   Bluth.   Cambridge   [England]; Cambridge University Press, 1992. xiii, 317 p.
91-013574   358/.1754/0947   0521403723
Strategic forces -- Soviet Union -- History -- 20th century. Nuclear weapons -- Soviet Union -- History -- 20th century. Soviet Union -- Military policy.

UA770.B7
Brzezinski, Zbigniew K., 1928-
Political controls in the Soviet Army; a study based on reports by former Soviet officers, by Vyacheslav P. Artemyev [and others]. New York, Research Program on the U.S.S.R., 1954 93 p.
54-003195   355.34
Soviet Union -- Armed Forces.

UA770.C35 1991
Calingaert, Daniel.
Soviet nuclear policy under Gorbachev: a policy of disarmament/ Daniel Calingaert. New York: Praeger, 1991. x, 180 p.
90-023452   327.1/74/0947   0275937372
Nuclear disarmament -- Soviet Union.Soviet Union -- Military policy.

UA770.C37 1989
Catudal, Honore Marc, 1944-
Soviet nuclear strategy from Stalin to Gorbachev: a revolution in Soviet military and political thinking/ Honore M. Catudal; foreword by Martin J. Hillenbrand. Atlantic Highlands, NJ: Humanities Press International, 1989, c1988. 413 p.
88-013668   355/.0335/47   0391036114
Strategic forces -- Soviet Union. Nuclear warfare. Deterrence (Strategy) Soviet Union -- Military policy. United States -- Military relations -- Soviet Union. Soviet Union -- Military relations -- United States.

UA770.C56 1990
Cimbala, Stephen J.
Conflict termination in Europe: games against war/ Stephen J. Cimbala. New York: Praeger, 1990. xxiv, 268 p.
89-077107   355/.033547   0275935922
Soviet Union -- Military policy. Europe -- Defenses.

UA770.D5
Dinerstein, Herbert S. 1919-
War and the Soviet Union; nuclear weapons and the revolution in Soviet military and political thinking. New York, Praeger [1959] 268 p.
59-007696   355.450947
Nuclear warfare.Soviet Union -- Military policy.

UA770.G28 1990
Garthoff, Raymond L.
Deterrence and the revolution in Soviet military doctrine/ Raymond L. Garthoff. Washington, D.C.: Brookings Institution, c1990. x, 209 p.
90-042575   355.02/17   081573056X
Deterrence (Strategy) Nuclear warfare. Soviet Union -- Military policy. United States -- Military policy.

UA770.G29
Garthoff, Raymond L.
The Soviet image of future war. Introd. by James M. Gavin. Washington, Public Affairs Press [1959] 137 p.
59-007947   355.0947
War.Soviet Union -- Military policy.

UA770.G3
Garthoff, Raymond L.
Soviet strategy in the nuclear age/ Raymond L. Garthoff. New York: Praeger, 1958. xvi, 283 p.
58-010329   355.43
Soviet Union -- Military policy. Soviet Union -- Defenses.

UA770.G55 1992
Glantz, David M.
The military strategy of the Soviet Union: a history/ David M. Glantz. London, England; F. Cass, 1992. viii, 360 p.
91-043411   355/.0335/47   0714634352
Soviet Union -- Military policy. Soviet Union -- History, Military.

UA770.H4797 1996
Herspring, Dale R.
Russian civil-military relations/ Dale R. Herspring. Bloomington: Indiana University Press, c1996. xxiv, 230 p.
96-011635   322/.5/0947   0253332257
Civil-military relations -- Soviet Union -- History. Civil-military relations -- Russia (Federation) -- History. Soviet Union -- Politics and government -- 1917-1936. Soviet Union -- Politics and government -- 1985-1991. Russia (Federation) -- Politics and government -- 1991-

UA770.H48 1990
Herspring, Dale R. (Dale Roy)
The Soviet high command, 1967-1989: personalities and politics/ Dale R. Herspring. Princeton, N.J.: Princeton University Press, c1990. xv, 322 p.
89-035220   355/.0092/247   0691078440
Generals -- Soviet Union.Soviet Union -- Politics and government -- 1945-1991. Soviet Union -- Armed Forces -- History.

UA770.H63 1983
Holloway, David, 1943-
The Soviet Union and the arms race/ David Holloway. New Haven: Yale University Press, 1983. x, 211 p.
82-020050   355/.033047   0300029632
World politics -- 1945- Arms race -- History -- 20th century. Soviet Union -- Military policy. Soviet Union -- Defenses. Soviet Union -- Armed Forces.

UA770.H632 1994
Holloway, David, 1943-
Stalin and the bomb: the Soviet Union and atomic energy, 1939-1956/ David Holloway. New Haven: Yale University Press, 1994. xvi, 464 p.
94-008216   355.8/25119   0300060564
Atomic weapons -- Government policy -- Soviet Union -- History. Nuclear energy -- Research -- Soviet Union -- History. Science and state -- Soviet Union -- History. Soviet Union -- Foreign relations.

UA770.I55 1990
The impoverished superpower: perestroika and the Soviet military burden/ edited by Henry S. Rowen and Charles Wolf, Jr. San Francisco, Calif.: ICS Press; c1990. xiv, 372 p.
89-029818   338.4/3355/00947   1558150668
War -- Economic aspects -- Soviet Union. Perestroika. Soviet Union -- Armed Forces -- Appropriations and expenditures -- Economic aspects. Soviet Union -- Economic conditions -- 1975-1985. Soviet Union -- Politics and government -- 1985-1991.

UA770.K28
Kaplan, Stephen S.
Diplomacy of power: Soviet Armed Forces as a political instrument/ Stephen S. Kaplan, with Michel Tatu ... [et al.]. Washington, D.C.: Brookings Institution, c1981. xvi, 733 p.
80-025006   327.1/17/0947   0815748248
World politics -- 1945-Soviet Union -- Foreign relations -- 1945-1991. Soviet Union -- Military policy. Soviet Union -- Armed Forces -- History.

UA770.K6
Kolkowicz, Roman.
The Soviet military and the Communist Party. Princeton, N.J., Princeton University Press, 1967. xvi, 429 p.
67-014410   355.03/32/47
Civil supremacy over the military -- Soviet Union.Soviet Union -- Armed Forces -- Political activity.

UA770.K84 1996
Kugler, Richard L.
Enlarging NATO: the Russia factor/ Richard L. Kugler with Marianna V. Kozintseva. Santa Monica, Calif.: RAND, 1996. xxxi, 287 p.
96-025062   355/.031091821   0833023578
State, The.Russia (Federation) -- Defenses. Europe, Eastern -- Strategic aspects.

UA770.M3993 1991
MccGwire, Michael.
Perestroika and Soviet national security/ Michael MccGwire. Washington, D.C.: Brookings Institution, c1991. xi, 481 p.
90-046529   355/.033047   0815755546
National security -- Soviet Union. Perestroika. Soviet Union -- Foreign relations -- 1985-1991.

UA770.M467 1992
Menning, Bruce.
Bayonets before bullets: the Imperial Russian Army, 1861-1914/ Bruce W. Menning. Bloomington: Indiana University Press, c1992. x, 334 p.
92-008233   355.3/0947   0253337453
Military doctrine -- Russia -- History -- 19th century. Military doctrine -- Russia -- History -- 20th century. Russo-Turkish War, 1877-1878 -- Campaigns.

UA770.M754 2001
Mott, William H.
Soviet military assistance: an empirical perspective/ by William H. Mott, IV. Westport, CT: Greenwood Press, 2001. xii, 378 p.
00-064061   355/.032/0947   031331022X
Military assistance, Soviet -- History.

UA770.N48 1993
Nichols, Thomas, 1960-
The sacred cause: civil-military conflict over Soviet national security, 1917-1992/ Thomas M. Nichols. Ithaca: Cornell University Press, 1993. xiii, 259 p.
92-034543   322/.5/0947   0801427746
Civil-military relations -- Soviet Union.Soviet Union -- Armed Forces.

UA770.P666 1984
Porter, Bruce D.
The USSR in Third World conflicts: Soviet arms and diplomacy in local wars, 1945-1980/ Bruce D. Porter. Cambridge [Cambridgeshire]; Cambridge University Press, 1984. viii, 248 p.
83-026265   355/.0335/47   0521263085
Military history, Modern -- 20th century. World politics -- 1945- Developing countries -- Military relations -- Soviet Union. Soviet Union -- Military policy. Soviet Union -- Military relations -- Developing countries.

UA770.R6 1982
Rosefielde, Steven.
False science: underestimating the Soviet arms buildup: an appraisal of the CIA's direct costing effort, 1960-80/ Steven Rosefielde; foreword by Patrick Parker. New Brunswick, NJ: Transaction Books, c1982. xii, 321 p.
81-001050   355.6/22/0947   0878554270
Soviet Union -- Armed Forces -- Appropriations and expenditures.

UA770.S258 1991
Sapir, Jacques.
The Soviet military system/ Jacques Sapir; translated by David Macey. Cambridge, Mass.: Basil Blackwell, 1991. 362 p.
90-049635   0745606717
Militarism -- Soviet Union.Soviet Union -- Defenses. Soviet Union -- Military policy.

UA770.S355 1988
Scott, Harriet Fast.
Soviet military doctrine: continuity, formulation, and dissemination/ Harriet Fast Scott and William F. Scott. Boulder: Westview Press, 1988. xii, 315 p.
88-011102   355/.0335/47   0813306566
Communism -- Soviet Union. Communist strategy. Soviet Union -- Military policy.

UA770.S476 1987
Shenfield, Stephen.
The nuclear predicament: explorations in Soviet ideology/ Stephen Shenfield. [London]: Royal Institute of International Affairs; 1987. 126 p.
87-004658   355/.0335/47   0710212283
Nuclear warfare. Communism and nuclear warfare -- Soviet Union. Soviet Union -- Military policy.

UA770.S514 1988
Shultz, Richard H., 1947-
The Soviet Union and revolutionary warfare: principles, practices, and regional comparisons/ Richard H. Shultz, Jr. Stanford, Calif.: Hoover Institution Press, Stanford University, c1988. x, 283 p.
88-004536   355/.02184/0947   0817987118
Revolutions -- History -- 20th century. Military history, Modern -- 20th century. Soviet Union -- Military policy.

UA770.S6397 1999
Sokov, N. N.
Russian strategic modernization: the past and future/ Nikolai Sokov. Lanham, MD: Rowman & Littlefield Publishers, 1999. xvii, 205 p.
99-041216   355/.033547   0847694666
Strategic weapons systems -- Russia (Federation)Russia (Federation) -- Military policy.

UA770.S653 1989
Soviet-American security relations in the 1990s/ edited by Donald M. Snow. Lexington, Mass.: Lexington Books, c1989. ix, 194 p.
86-045291 355/.033/0048 0669131520
  Nuclear arms control. Nuclear crisis stability. Soviet Union -- Military relations -- United States. United States -- Military relations -- Soviet Union.

UA770.S659 1987
The Soviet defence enigma: estimating costs and burden/ edited by Carl G. Jacobsen; SIPRI, Stockholm International Peace Research Institute. Oxford; Oxford University Press, 1987. xvii, 189 p.
87-015385 355.6/22/0947 0198291183
  Budget -- Soviet Union -- Congresses.Soviet Union -- Armed Forces -- Appropriations and expenditures -- Congresses.

UA770.S6619 1989
Soviet military doctrine and western policy/ edited by Gregory Flynn. London; Routledge, 1989. xi, 418 p.
88-026537 355/.0335/47 0415004888
  Soviet Union -- Military policy. Europe -- Military policy. United States -- Military policy.

UA770.S6638 1989
Soviet military policy: an International security reader/ edited by Sean M. Lynn-Jones, Steven E. Miller, and Stephen Van Evera. Cambridge, Mass.: MIT Press, c1989. xiii, 374 p.
89-193638 355/.033547 0262121425
  Soviet Union -- Military policy.

UA770.S863 2000
Stone, David R., 1968-
Hammer and rifle: the militarization of the Soviet Union, 1926-1933/ David R. Stone. Lawrence: University Press of Kansas, c2000. vii, 287 p.
00-028314 355/.033047/09041 0700610375
  Civil-military relations -- Soviet Union.Soviet Union -- Armed Forces -- Appropriations and expenditures. Soviet Union -- Defenses. Soviet Union -- Politics and government -- 1917-1936.

UA770.V5492 1990
Von Hagen, Mark, 1954-
Soldiers in the proletarian dictatorship: the Red Army and the Soviet socialist state, 1917-1930/ Mark von Hagen. Ithaca, N.Y.: Cornell University Press, 1990. xviii, 369 p.
89-036148 322/.5/0947 0801424208
  Socialism -- Soviet Union. Civil-military relations -- Soviet Union. Soviet Union -- Politics and government -- 1917-1936.

UA770.W27 1977
Warner, Edward L.
The military in contemporary Soviet politics: an institutional analysis/ Edward L. Warner III. New York: Praeger, 1977. viii, 314 p.
77-083476 355.03/35/47 0030403464
  Soviet Union -- Military policy. Soviet Union -- Armed Forces. Soviet Union -- Politics and government -- 1953-1985.

UA770.Z54 1993
Zisk, Kimberly Marten, 1963-
Engaging the enemy: organization theory and Soviet military innovation, 1955-1991/ Kimberly Marten Zisk. Princeton, N.J.: Princeton University Press, 1993. x, 286 p.
92-033250 355.02/0947 0691069824
  Military doctrine -- Soviet Union.

UA772.B38613 1988
Benvenuti, Francesco.
The Bolsheviks and the Red Army, 1918-1922/ Francesco Benvenuti; translated from the Italian by Christopher Woodall. Cambridge [England]; Cambridge University Press, 1988. viii, 264 p.
87-027839 322/.5/0947 0521257719
  Soviet Union -- History -- Revolution, 1917-1921.

UA772.D8 1994
Dunn, Walter S. 1928-
Hitler's nemesis: the Red Army, 1930-1945/ Walter S. Dunn, Jr.; foreword by David Glantz. Westport, Conn.: Praeger, 1994. xvi, 231 p.
94-008345 940.54/1247 0275948943
  World War, 1939-1945 -- Soviet Union.

UA772.E7
Erickson, John.
The Soviet high command; a military-political history, 1918-1941. [New York] St Martin's Press, 1962. xv, 889 p.
62-006671 355
  Soviet Union -- History, Military -- 1917-Soviet Union -- Military policy.

UA772.L5 1968
Liddell Hart, Basil Henry, 1895-1970,
The Red Army: the Red Army, 1918 to 1945; the Soviet Army, 1946 to the present, edited by B. H. Liddell Hart. Gloucester, Mass., P. Smith, 1968 [c1956] xiv, 480 p.
74-002182 355/.00947
  Soviet Union -- History, Military.

UA772.R44 1996
Reese, Roger R.
Stalin's reluctant soldiers: a social history of the Red Army, 1925-1941/ Roger R. Reese. Lawrence, Kan.: University Press of Kansas, c1996. xii, 267 p.
96-004252 355/.00947/0904 0700607722
  Sociology, Military -- Soviet Union -- History -- 20th century.Soviet Union -- Politics and government -- 1917-1936. Soviet Union -- Politics and government -- 1936-1953.

UA772.S824 1998
Stoecker, Sally W.
Forging Stalin's Army: Marshal Tukhachevsky and the politics of military innovation/ Sally W. Stoecker; foreword by David Glantz. Boulder, Colo.: Westview Press, 1998. xiv, 207 p.
98-010699 355/.00947/09041 0813334101
  Tukhachevskii, M. N. -- (Mikhail Nikolaevich), -- 1893-1937.Civil-military relations -- Soviet Union -- History.Soviet Union -- Politics and government -- 1917-1936.

UA772.S86 1982
Suvorov, Viktor.
Inside the Soviet Army/ by Viktor Suvorov. London: Hamilton, 1982. viii, 296 p.
82-175848 355/.00947 0241108896
  Soviet Union. Sovetskaëiìa Armìëiìa.

UA782-787 By region or country — Europe — Spain

UA782.P3
Payne, Stanley G.
Politics and the military in modern Spain [by] Stanley G. Payne. Stanford, Calif., Stanford University Press, 1967. xiii, 574 p.
66-017564 946.08
  Spain -- Politics and government.

UA787.P69 1987
Powers, James F.
A society organized for war: the Iberian municipal militias in the central Middle Ages, 1000-1284/ James F. Powers. Berkeley: University of California Press, c1987. xii, 365 p.
86-014667 355.3/7/0946 0520056442
  Sociology, Military -- Spain. Sociology, Military -- Portugal. Military history, Medieval. Spain -- History, Military. Portugal -- History, Military. Spain -- History -- 711-1516.

UA827 By region or country — Europe — Balkan States

UA827.Y84 1988
Yugoslavia's security dilemmas: armed forces, national defence, and foreign policy/ edited by Marko Milivojevic, John B. Allcock, and Pierre Maurer. Oxford [Oxfordshire]; Berg; 1988. viii, 324 p.
87-023081 355/.0330497 0854961496
  National security -- Yugoslavia -- Congresses.Yugoslavia -- Defenses -- Congresses. Yugoslavia -- Foreign relations -- 1945- Congresses.

UA829 By region or country — Europe — Other European countries, A-Z

UA829.F5.R53 1988
Ries, Tomas, 1953-
Cold will: the defence of Finland/ Tomas Ries. London; Brassey's Defence Publishers, 1988. xiii, 394 p.
88-022213 355/.03304897 0080335926
  Finland -- Defenses. Finland -- History, Military.

UA829.I7.S25 1989
Salmon, Trevor C.
Unneutral Ireland: an ambivalent and unique security policy/ Trevor C. Salmon. Oxford: Clarendon Press; 1989. xv, 347 p.
89-003113 341.6/4/09417 0198272901
  National security -- Ireland. Neutrality -- Ireland. Nonalignment -- Ireland.

UA830 By region or country — Asia — General works

UA830.A856 1998
Asian security practice: material and ideational influences/ edited by Muthiah Alagappa. Stanford, Calif.: Stanford University Press, 1998. xvii, 851 p.
98-016563 355/.03305 0804733473
  National security -- Asia.

UA830.L4 1977
Lebra-Chapman, Joyce, 1925-
Japanese-trained armies in Southeast Asia: independence and volunteer forces in World War II/ Joyce C. Lebra. New York: Columbia University Press, 1977. iv, 226 p.
75-016116 355.3/0959 0231039956
  Military education -- Asia, Southeastern -- History.Asia, Southeastern -- Armed Forces -- History. Asia, Southeastern -- History -- Japanese occupation.

UA830.M378 1989
Mazarr, Michael J., 1965-
Missile defenses and Asian-Pacific security/
Michael J. Mazarr. New York: St. Martin's Press,
1989. xii, 226 p.
88-007805   358/.1754   0312027753
  *National security -- East Asia. National
security -- Pacific Area. Ballistic missile
defenses -- East Asia.*

UA830.M385 1987
McIntosh, Malcolm, 1953-
Arms across the Pacific: security and trade issues
across the Pacific/ Malcolm McIntosh. New
York: St. Martin's Press, 1987. x, 177 p.
87-032120   355/.0332/5   0312018681
  *East Asia -- Military relations -- United States.
Pacific Area -- Military relations -- United
States. United States -- Military relations -- East
Asia.*

UA830.M387 1989
McLaurin, R. D. 1944-1995.
The United States and the defense of the Pacific/
Ronald D. McLaurin, Chung-in Moon. Boulder,
Colo., U.S.A.: Westview Press; 1989. xiv, 353 p.
89-022626   355/.033073   0813379172
  *Pacific Area -- Defenses. United States --
Military policy.*

UA830.M532 1997
Military capacity and the risk of war: China,
India, Pakistan, and Iran/ edited by Eric Arnett.
Oxford, [Eng.]; Oxford University Press, c1997.
xiv, 367 p.
96-030040   355/.03305   0198292813
  *Arms race -- Asia -- Case studies.Asia --
Military policy -- Case studies.*

UA830.S366 1989
Security, strategy, and policy responses in the
Pacific rim/ edited by Young Whan Kihl and
Lawrence E. Grinter. Boulder, Colo.: L. Rienner
Publishers, 1989. xvi, 272 p.
88-030611   355/.03305   1555871313
  *National security -- East Asia. National
security -- Oceania. National security -- Pacific
Area.*

UA830.T58 1989
Tiwari, Chitra K., 1954-
Security in South Asia: internal and external
dimensions/ Chitra K. Tiwari. Lanham, MD:
University Press of America, c1989. xi, 317 p.
88-033700   355/.033059   0819173398
  *National security -- South Asia. World politics
-- 1945-*

UA832 By region or country — Asia — Middle East. Persian Gulf Region

UA832.A77 1992
Aronson, Shlomo, 1936-
The Politics and strategy of nuclear weapons in
the Middle East: opacity, theory, and reality,
1960-1991: an Israeli perspective/ Shlomo
Aronson with the assistance of Oded Brosh.
Albany: State University of New York Press,
c1992. xiii, 398 p.
91-046244   355/.033056   0791412075
  *Nuclear weapons -- Middle East. Nuclear
weapons -- Israel. Nuclear nonproliferation.
Israel -- Military policy. Middle East -- Military
policy.*

UA832.B37 1989
Barnaby, Frank.
The invisible bomb: the nuclear arms race in the
Middle East/ Frank Barnaby. London: I.B.
Tauris, c1989. xv, 223 p.
88-177382   355/.033056   1850430780
  *Nuclear weapons -- Middle East. Nuclear
weapons -- Israel. Nuclear weapons -- Arab
countries. Middle East -- Defenses.*

UA832.C66 1993
Cordesman, Anthony H.
After the storm: the changing military balance in
the Middle East/ Anthony H. Cordesman.
Boulder: Westview Press; 1993. xvi, 811 p.
92-039744   355/.033056   0813316928
  Middle East -- Armed Forces.

UA832.C67 1988
Cordesman, Anthony H.
The Gulf and the West: strategic relations and
military realities/ Anthony H. Cordesman.
Boulder: Westview Press; 1988. xxv, 526 p.
88-010752   355/.033053   0813307686
  *Iran-Iraq War, 1980-1988.Persian Gulf --
Strategic aspects. Persian Gulf Region --
Defenses. United States -- Military relations --
Persian Gulf Region.*

UA832.M5223 2001
The Middle East military balance, 2000-2001/
Shai Feldman and Yiftah Shapir, editors.
Cambridge, Mass.; MIT Press, c2001. 425 p.
  0262062194
  *Middle East -- Armed Forces. Middle East --
Strategic aspects.*

UA835-839.3 By region or country — Asia — China

UA835.C4466 1988
China's military modernization: international
implications/ edited by Larry M. Wortzel. New
York: Greenwood Press, 1988. xix, 204 p.
87-023657   355/.00951   0313256268
  *World politics -- 1985-1995.China -- Armed
Forces. China -- Military policy.*

UA835.C448 1984
Chinese defence policy/ edited by Gerald Segal
and William T. Tow. Urbana: University of
Illinois Press, c1984. xxii, 286 p.
83-024229   355/.033051   025201135X
  *China -- Military policy. China -- Defenses.
China -- Armed Forces.*

UA835.D45 1990
Dellios, Rosita.
Modern Chinese defence strategy: present
developments, future directions/ Rosita Dellios.
New York: St. Martin's Press, 1990. x, 256 p.
89-024359   355/.033551   0312041314
  China -- Military policy.

UA835.G5
Gittings, John.
The role of the Chinese Army. London, issued
under the auspices of the Royal Institute 1967.
xx, 331 p.
67-080303   355/.00951 19
  China. Lu Chün.

UA835.G65 2000
Goldstein, Avery, 1954-
Deterrence and security in the 21st century:
China, Britain, France, and the enduring legacy
of the nuclear revolution/ Avery Goldstein.
Stanford, Calif.: Stanford University Press,
c2000. 356 p.
00-027395   355.02/17   0804737363
  *Nuclear weapons -- China. Nuclear weapons --
Great Britain. Nuclear weapons -- France. China
-- Military policy. Great Britain -- Military
policy. France -- Military policy.*

UA835.G74 1987
Gregor, A. James 1929-
Arming the dragon: U.S. security ties with the
People's Republic of China/ A. James Gregor;
foreword by Robert F. Turner. Washington, D.C.:
Ethics and Public Policy Center; c1987. xi,
128 p.
87-024493   355/.033051   0896331199
  *National security -- China.China -- Military
relations -- United States. United States --
Military relations -- China.*

UA835.G87 1998
Gurtov, Melvin.
China's security: the new roles of the military/
Mel Gurtov, Byong-Moo Hwang. Boulder:
Lynne Rienner Publishers, 1998. x, 349 p.
97-018254   355/.033051   1555874347
  *National security -- China.China -- Military
policy. China -- Armed Forces.*

UA835.J6
Joffe, Ellis, 1934-
Party and army: professionalism and political
control in the Chinese officer corps, 1949-1964.
Cambridge, East Asian Research Center, Harvard
University, 1965. xii, 198 p.
65-029001   355.0330951
  *China (Peoples' Republic of China, 1949-) --
Armed Forces.*

UA835.L46 1988
Lin, Chong-Pin.
China's nuclear weapons strategy: tradition
within evolution/ Chong-Pin Lin. Lexington,
Mass.: Lexington Books, c1988. 272 p.
87-047761   355/.0335/51   0669167428
  Nuclear warfare.China -- Military policy.

UA835.N38 1997
Nathan, Andrew J.
The great wall and the empty fortress: China's
search for security/ by Andrew J. Nathan and
Robert S. Ross. New York: W.W. Norton, c1997.
xvii, 268 p.
97-006385   355/.033051   0393040763
  *National security -- China.China -- Foreign
relations -- 1976- Taiwan -- Foreign relations --
1945-*

UA835.R89 1989
Ryan, Mark A.
Chinese attitudes toward nuclear weapons: China
and the United States during the Korean War/
Mark A. Ryan. Armonk, N.Y.: M.E. Sharpe,
c1989. xii, 327 p.
89-004158   355/.0335/51   0873325303
  *Nuclear warfare. Korean War, 1950-1953 --
China. Korean War, 1950-1953 -- United States.
China -- Military policy. United States --
Military policy.*

UA838.C4.S54
Smith, Richard J. 1944-
Mercenaries and Mandarins: the Ever-Victorious Army in nineteenth century China/ Richard J. Smith; foreword by John K. Fairbank. Millwood, N.Y.: KTO Press, c1978. xxiii, 271 p.
78-006394   951/.03   0527839507
Taiping Rebellion, 1850-1864.

UA838.M5.T5
Ting, Li.
Militia of Communist China.   Kowloon, H. K., Union Research Institute [1954] 145 p.
55-041220
China -- History, Military. China -- Militia.

UA839.3.G4
George, Alexander L.
The Chinese Communist Army in action; the Korean War and its aftermath, by Alexander L. George. New York, Columbia University Press, 1967. xii, 255 p.
67-012659   355/.00951
Korean War, 1950-1953.

UA839.3.G7
Griffith, Samuel B.
The Chinese People's Liberation Army [by] Samuel B. Griffith, II. New York, Published for the Council on Foreign Relations by McGraw-Hill [1967] xiv, 398 p.
67-016302   355.3/1/0951
China. Chung-kuo jen min chieh fang chün.

UA839.3.H7
Hsieh, Alice Langley, 1922-1979.
Communist China's strategy in the nuclear era. Englewood Cliffs, N.J., Prentice-Hall [1962] 204 p.
62-012563   951.05
World politics -- 1945- Nuclear warfare. China -- Military policy.

UA840-842 By region or country — Asia — India

UA840.I4822 2000
India's nuclear security/ edited by Raju G.C. Thomas and Amit Gupta. Boulder: L. Rienner Publishers, c2000. vi, 325 p.
00-028261   355.02/17/0954   1555879284
Nuclear weapons -- India. National security -- India. India -- Military policy.

UA840.P47 1999
Perkovich, George,
India's nuclear bomb: the impact on global proliferation/ George Perkovich. Berkeley: University of California Press, c1999. xii, 597 p.
99-037464   355.02/17/0954 21   0520217721
Nuclear weapons--India. World politics--1989-

UA840.R67 1996
Rosen, Stephen Peter, 1952-
Societies and military power: India and its armies/ Stephen Peter Rosen. Ithaca: Cornell University Press, 1996. xiii, 280 p.
96-011014   306.2/7/0954   0801432103
Sociology, Military -- India -- History.India -- Social conditions. India -- History, Military.

UA840.S36 1987
The Security of South Asia: American and Asian perspectives/ edited by Stephen Philip Cohen. Urbana: University of Illinois Press, c1987. xiii, 290 p.
86-031784   355/.033054   0252013948
National security -- South Asia.Pakistan -- Military relations -- India. United States -- Military relations -- South Asia. South Asia -- Military relations -- United States.

UA842.C6
Cohen, Stephen P., 1936-
The Indian army; its contribution to the development of a nation [by] Stephen P. Cohen. Berkeley, University of California Press, 1971. x, 216 p.
77-111421   355.3/0954   0520016971
India (Republic). Army -- History.

UA845-847 By region or country — Asia — Japan

UA845.K376 1996
Katzenstein, Peter J.
Cultural norms and national security: police and military in postwar Japan/ Peter J. Katzenstein. Ithaca, N.Y.: Cornell University Press, c1996. xvi, 307 p.
96-006463   355/.033052   080143260X
National security -- Japan. Internal security -- Japan.

UA845.L6
Lory, Hillis, 1900-
Japan's military masters; the army in Japanese life, by Hillis Lory; foreword by Joseph C. Grew. New York, The Viking press; [1944, c1943] 203 p.
43-007705   355
Militarism.

UA845.M6
The Modern Japanese military system/ edited by James H. Buck. Beverly Hills, [Calif.]: Sage Publications, c1975. 253 p.
75-014628   355/.00952   0803905130
Japan -- Armed Forces -- Addresses, essays, lectures. Japan -- Defenses -- Addresses, essays, lectures. Japan -- Military policy -- Addresses, essays, lectures.

UA845.S327 1994
Samuels, Richard J.
"Rich nation, strong Army": national security and the technological transformation of Japan/ Richard J. Samuels. Ithaca: Cornell University Press, 1994. xiii, 455 p.
93-039156   355/.033052   0801427053
National security -- Japan. Technology and state -- Japan. Technology transfer -- Japan.

UA845.T85 1981
Tsurutani, Taketsugu.
Japanese policy and east Asian security/ Taketsugu Tsurutani. New York, N.Y.: Praeger, 1981. xi, 208 p.
81-011884   355/.033052   0030598060
National security -- Japan.East Asia -- Defenses.

UA847.H86 1995
Humphreys, Leonard A., 1924-
The way of the heavenly sword: the Japanese Army in the 1920's/ Leonard A. Humphreys. Stanford, Calif.: Stanford University Press, 1995. x, 252 p.
94-015612   355/.00952/09042   0804723753
Japan -- History -- 20th century.

UA853 By region or country — Asia — Other Asian Countries

UA853.I7.K38 1993
Katzman, Kenneth.
The warriors of Islam: Iran's Revolutionary Guard/ Kenneth Katzman. Boulder: Westview Press, 1993. vi, 192 p.
92-017902   356/.16/0955   0813378907
Iran -- History, Military.

UA853.I7.S34 1989
Schulz, Ann.
Buying security: Iran under the monarchy/ Ann Tibbitts Schulz. Boulder: Westview Press, 1989. xi, 192 p.
89-032207   338.4/3355/00955   0813376610
Iran -- Armed Forces -- Appropriations and expenditures. Iran -- Armed Forces -- Procurement. Iran -- Military policy -- Economic aspects.

UA853.I75.C65 1999
Cordesman, Anthony H.
Iraq and the war of sanctions: conventional threats and weapons of mass destruction/ Anthony H. Cordesman. Westport, Conn.: Praeger, 1999. xxiii, 684 p.
98-041447   355/.0335567   0275965287
National security -- Iraq. Weapons of mass destruction -- Iraq. Iraq -- Armed Forces -- Weapons systems. Iraq -- Military policy. Iraq -- Politics and government -- 1991-

UA853.I8.C62 1998
Cohen, Avner, 1951-
Israel and the bomb/ Avner Cohen. New York: Columbia University Press, 1998. xviii, 470 p.
98-003402   355.02/17/095694   0231104820
Nuclear weapons -- Israel.Israel -- Military policy.

UA853.I8.C67 1996
Cordesman, Anthony H.
Perilous prospects: the peace process and the Arab-Israeli military balance/ Anthony H. Cordesman. Boulder, Colo.: Westview Press, 1996. xv, 317 p.
96-007426   355/.03305694   0813329396
Israel-Arab conflicts.Israel -- Defenses. Arab countries -- Defenses.

UA853.I8.E8613 1994
Evron, Yair.
Israel's nuclear dilemma/ Yair Evron. Ithaca, N.Y.: Cornell University Press, 1994. xii, 327 p.
93-042628   327.1/74   0801430313
Nuclear weapons -- Israel. Nuclear weapons -- Middle East. Middle East -- Military policy. Israel -- Military policy.

UA853.I8.I86 1988
Israeli national security policy: political actors and perspectives/ edited by Bernard Reich and Gershon R. Kieval. New York: Greenwood Press, 1988. vi, 240 p.
87-036099   355/.0335/5694   0313261962
Israel -- Military policy. Israel -- Politics and government.

UA853.I8.L446 1997
Levy, Yagil, 1958-
Trial and error: Israel's route from war to de-escalation/ Yagil Levy. Albany: State University of New York Press, c1997. xi, 282 p.
96-042064   355/.03355694   079143429X
Social classes -- Israel. War and society -- Israel. Israel-Arab conflicts -- Social aspects. Israel -- Military policy. Israel -- Ethnic relations.

UA853.I8.N368 1993
National security and democracy in Israel/ edited by Avner Yaniv. Boulder, Co.: Lynne Rienner Publishers, c1993. xii, 257 p.
92-021085   355/.03305694   1555873243
National security -- Israel.Israel -- Military policy. Israel -- Politics and government.

UA853.I8.R67
Rothenberg, Gunther Erich, 1923-
The anatomy of the Israeli army/ Gunther E. Rothenberg. London: B. T. Batsford, 1979. 256 p.
79-321715   355/.0095694   0713419660
Israel -- Armed Forces -- History.

UA853.I8T.3513 2000
Tal, Yisrael.
National security: the Israeli experience/ Israel Tal; translated by Martin Kett. Westport, Conn.: Praeger, c2000. viii, 248 p.
99-036593   355/.03305694   027596812X
National security -- Israel. Arab-Israeli conflict. Israel -- Military policy. Israel -- History, Military.

UA853.I8.V373 1998
Van Creveld, Martin L.
The sword and the olive: a critical history of the Israeli defense force/ Martin van Creveld. New York: Public Affairs, c1998. xviii, 422 p.
98-021872   355/.0095694   1891620053
Israel -- Armed Forces -- History.

UA853.K6.H37 1990
Hayes, Peter.
Pacific powderkeg: American nuclear dilemmas in Korea/ by Peter Hayes. Lexington, Mass.: Lexington Books, c1991. xlvii, 320 p.
90-005786   355/.03305195   066924421X
Nuclear warfare.Korea (South) -- Defenses. United States -- Military policy. Korea (South) -- Military relations -- United States.

UA853.K6.M39 1995
Mazarr, Michael J., 1965-
North Korea and the bomb: a case study in nonproliferation/ Michael J. Mazarr. New York: St. Martin's Press, 1995. xi, 290 p.
94-034868   327.1/74   0312124430
Nuclear weapons -- Korea (North) Nuclear nonproliferation. United States -- Military policy. Korea (North) -- Politics and government.

UA853.N35.F37 1984b
Farwell, Byron.
The Gurkhas/ Byron Farwell. New York: Norton, c1984. 317 p.
83-011271   356/.1   0393017737
Gurkha soldiers.

UA853.P3.K37 1987
Kapur, Ashok.
Pakistan's nuclear development/ Ashok Kapur. London; Croom Helm c1987. 258 p.
87-009103   355/.0335/5491   0709931018
Nuclear weapons -- Pakistan.Pakistan -- Military policy.

UA853.P3.W57 1991
Wirsing, Robert.
Pakistan's security under Zia, 1977-1988: the policy imperatives of a peripheral Asian state/ Robert G. Wirsing. New York: St. Martin's Press, 1991. viii, 216 p.
91-014643   355/.03305491   031206067X
National security -- Pakistan.Pakistan -- Foreign relations.

UA853.P47.C66 1984
Cordesman, Anthony H.
The Gulf and the search for strategic stability: Saudi Arabia, the military balance in the Gulf, and trends in the Arab-Israeli military balance/ Anthony H. Cordesman. Boulder, Colo.: Westview Press; 1984. xxiii, 1041 p.
83-010341   355/.0330536   0865316198
Persian Gulf Region -- Strategic aspects. Arabian Peninsula -- Strategic aspects. Saudi Arabia -- Military relations -- United States.

UA853.S33.C67 1997
Cordesman, Anthony H.
Saudi Arabia: guarding the desert kingdom/ Anthony H. Cordesman. Boulder, Colo.: Westview Press, 1997. xiii, 220 p.
96-046048   355/.0330538   0813332419
Saudi Arabia -- Armed Forces. Saudi Arabia -- Strategic aspects.

UA853.V5.L63 1989
Lockhart, Greg.
Nation in arms: the origins of the People's Army of Vietnam/ Greg Lockhart. Sydney; Asian Studies Association of Australia in association with Allen & Unwin, 1989. xiv, 314 p.
89-080237   355/.009597   0043012949
Vietnam -- History -- 1858-1945. Vietnam -- History -- 1945-1975.

UA855 By region or country — Africa — General works

UA855.A74 1984
Arlinghaus, Bruce E.
Military development in Africa: the political and economic risks of arms transfers/ Bruce E. Arlinghaus. Boulder, Colo.: Westview Press, 1984. xiv, 152 p.
83-023275   355/.03306   0865314349
Arms transfers -- Africa.Africa -- Military policy. Africa -- Politics and government -- 1960-

UA855.D36 2001
Danfulani, S. A., 1952-
A source book for strategic studies in Africa/ S.A. Danfulani. Lewiston, N.Y.: Edwin Mellen Press, c2001. xxiii, 268 p.
00-046563   355/.03306   0773475451
National security -- Africa -- Study and teaching. International security -- Study and teaching. National security -- Study and teaching. Africa -- Defenses -- study and teaching.

UA855.6 By region or country — Africa — Southern Africa

UA855.6.Z37 1999
Zacarias, Agostinho.
Security and the state in Southern Africa/ Agostinho Zacarias. London; Tauris Academic Studies, c1999. xx, 275 p.
355/.033068   1860643280
International relations. National security -- Africa, Southern. National state. Africa, Southern -- Politics and government -- 1994-

UA865 By region or country — Africa — Egypt

UA865.B37 1992
Barnett, Michael N., 1960-
Confronting the costs of war: military power, state, and society in Egypt and Israel/ Michael N. Barnett. Princeton, N.J.: Princeton University Press, c1992. xiii, 378 p.
91-032121   322/.5/0962   0691078831
Civil-military relations -- Egypt -- History -- 20th century. Civil-military relations -- Israel -- History -- 20th century. Civil-military relations. Israel -- Military policy. Egypt -- Politics and government -- 1952- Israel -- Politics and government.

UA865.F26 1997
Fahmy, Khaled.
All the pasha's men: Mehmed Ali, his army, and the making of modern Egypt/ Khaled Fahmy. Cambridge; Cambridge University Press, 1997. xviii, 334 p.
96-053340   355/.00962/09034   0521560071
Muhammad Ali Basha, -- Governor of Egypt, -- 1769-1849.Nationalism -- Egypt -- History -- 19th century.

UA870-874.3 By region or country — Australia — General military situation, policy, defenses, etc.

UA870.A39 1987
Albinski, Henry Stephen.
ANZUS, the United States, and Pacific security/ by Henry S. Albinski. Lanham, MD: University Press of America; c1987. xiii, 62 p.
87-010548   355/.031/0959   0819163732
United States -- Military relations -- Australia. United States -- Military relations -- New Zealand. Australia -- Military relations -- United States.

UA870.A598 1988
ANZUS in crisis: alliance management in international affairs/ edited by Jacob Bercovitch; foreword by Robert O'Neill. New York: St. Martin's Press, 1988. xix, 267 p.
87-026856   355/.031/0959   0312012233
Australia -- Military relations -- United States. United States -- Military relations -- Australia. Australia -- Military relations -- New Zealand.

UA874.3.L36 1989
Landais-Stamp, Paul.
Rocking the boat: New Zealand, the United States, and thenuclear-free zone controversy in the 1980s/ Paul Landais-Stamp and Paul Rogers. Oxford [England]; Berg; 1989. xvi, 185 p.
89-000152   355/.0335/931   0854962794
Nuclear warships -- Government policy -- New Zealand. Nuclear weapons -- Government policy -- New Zealand. New Zealand -- Military policy. New Zealand -- Military relations -- United States. United States -- Military relations -- New Zealand.

UA874.3.M35 1988
McIntyre, W. David 1932-
New Zealand prepares for war: defence policy, 1919-39/ W. David McIntyre. Christchurch, N.Z.: University of Canterbury Press, c1988. 287 p.
88-189709   355/.033593   0908812000
New Zealand -- Military policy.

UA874.3.M38 1987
McMillan, Stuart.
Neither confirm nor deny: the nuclear ships dispute between New Zealand and the United States/ Stuart McMillan. New York: Praeger, 1987. viii, 177 p.
87-015853   327.931073   0275923525
Nuclear weapons -- United States. Nuclear weapons -- New Zealand. New Zealand -- Military relations -- United States. United States -- Military relations -- New Zealand.

UA917 Demobilization

UA917.U5.B34 1983
Ballard, Jack S.
The shock of peace: military and economic demobilization after World War II/ Jack Stokes Ballard. Washington, D.C.: University Press of America, c1983. x, 259 p.
82-024860   355.2/9/0973   081913029X
United States -- Armed Forces -- Demobilization -- History -- 20th century. United States -- Economic conditions -- 1945-

UA926 Civil defense — General works

UA926.I38
Ikle, Fred Charles.
The social impact of bomb destruction. Norman, University of Oklahoma Press [1958] xxii, 250 p.
58-011611   301.246
Disaster relief. Civil defense. Bombing, Aerial.

UA927 Civil defense — By region or country — United States

UA927.M27
Martin, Thomas Lyle.
Strategy for survival [by] Thomas L. Martin, Jr. and Donald C. Latham. Tucson, Univ. of Arizona Press, 1963. 389 p.
63-017720   355.232
Nuclear Warfare. Civil Defense. Nuclear warfare.

UA927.M33 2000
McEnaney, Laura, 1960-
Civil defense begins at home: militarization meets everyday life in the fifties/ Laura McEnaney. Princeton, N.J.: Princeton University Press, c2000. x, 213 p.
99-087365   363.3/5/097309045   0691001383
Civil defense -- United States.United States -- Politics and government -- 1945-1989.

UA927.O23 1994
Oakes, Guy.
The imaginary war: civil defense and American cold war culture/ Guy Oakes. New York: Oxford University Press, 1994. 194 p.
93-046098   363.3/5/097309045   0195090276
Civil defense -- United States -- History -- 20th century. Nuclear warfare -- History -- 20th century. Deterrence (Strategy) -- History -- 20th century. United States -- Military policy.

UA929 Civil defense — By region or country — Other regions or countries, A-Z

UA929.R9.G63
Goure, Leon.
Civil defense in the Soviet Union.   Berkeley, University of California Press, 1962. 207 p.
61-018875   355.232
Soviet Union -- Civil defense.

UA990 Military geography — General works

UA990.P67 1990
The Political geography of conflict and peace/ edited by Nurit Kliot and Stanley Waterman. London: Belhaven Press, 1991. viii, 230 p.
90-048866   327.1/1   1852931337
Military geography. Geopolitics. World politics -- 1945-

UA990.W45 1998
Winters, Harold A.
Battling the elements: weather and terrain in the conduct of war/ Harold A. Winters with Gerald E. Galloway, William J. Reynolds, and David W. Rhyne. Baltimore, Md.: Johns Hopkins University Press, c1998. ix, 317 p.
98-005983   355.4/7   080185850X
Military geography -- Case studies. Military geography.

UB Military administration

UB23-87 By region or country

UB23.D44 1991
Demchak, Chris C.
Military organizations, complex machines: modernization in the U.S. armed services/ Chris C. Demchak. Ithaca, N.Y.: Cornell University Press, 1991. xi, 202 p.
90-055731   355/.00973   0801424682
United States -- Armed Forces -- Management.

UB23.H3
Hammond, Paul Y.
Organizing for defense; the American military establishment in the twentieth century. Princeton, N.J., Princeton University Press, 1961. xi, 403 p.
61-007398   355.0973
United States -- Armed Forces -- Organization.

UB23.N43
Nelson, Otto L. 1902-1985.
National security and the General staff, by Major General Otto L. Nelson. Washington, Infantry journal press, 1946. vi, 608 p.
46-005137   355.35
Military administration.

UB23.W3
Ward, Harry M.
The Department of War, 1781-1795. [Pittsburgh] University of Pittsburgh Press [1962] 287 p.
62-011089   353.6
United States -- History, Military.

UB58 1854-1856.S94 1984
Sweetman, John.
War and administration: the significance of the Crimean War for the British Army/ John Sweetman. Edinburgh: Scottish Academic Press, 1984. 174 p.
83-220916   355/.00941   070730332X
Crimean War, 1853-1856.

UB87.T48
Thompson, I. A. A.
War and government in Habsburg Spain, 1560-1620/ by I. A. A. Thompson. London: Athlone Press; 1976. 374 p.
77-355582   355.6/0946   0485111667
Military administration -- History.Spain -- Armed Forces -- History. Spain -- History -- House of Austria, 1516-1700.

UB147 Military service as a profession

UB147.J3
Janowitz, Morris.
The professional soldier, a social and political portrait. Glencoe, Ill., Free Press [1960] 464 p.
60-007090   355.069
Soldiers -- United States. Leadership. United States -- Armed Forces -- Officers. United States -- Armed Forces -- Military life.

UB210 Command of troops. Leadership

UB210.K54
Kingston-McCloughry, Edgar James, 1896-
The direction of war; a critique of the political direction and high command in war. New York, F.A. Praeger [1955] 261 p.
55-011306   355.331
Leadership. World War, 1939-1945. Great Britain -- Military policy.

UB210.N94 1986
Nye, Roger H.
The challenge of command: reading for military excellence/ Roger H. Nye. Wayne, N.J.: Avery Pub. Group, c1986. ix, 187 p.
85-030614   355.3/3041   0895292807
Command of troops. Command of troops -- Bibliography. Military art and science -- Bibliography.

UB212 Command and control systems

UB212.B39 1989
Beam, Walter R. 1928-
Command, control, and communications systems engineering/ Walter R. Beam. New York: McGraw-Hill, c1989. xii, 339 p.
88-032564   623/.7   0070042497
Command and control systems.

UB212.B5 1985
Blair, Bruce G., 1947-
Strategic command and control: redefining the nuclear threat/ Bruce G. Blair. Washington, D.C.: Brookings Institution, c1985. xiv, 341 p.
84-073164   355.3/3041/0973   081570982X
Command and control systems -- United States. Strategic forces -- United States. United States -- Military policy.

UB220 Staffs of armies — General works

UB220.H5 1961
Hittle, J. D. 1915-
The military staff, its history and development. Harrisburg, Pa., Military Service Division, Stackpole Co. [1961, c1952] 326 p.
61-009092   355.33
Armies -- Staffs.

UB223 Staffs of armies — By region or country — United States

UB223.K67 1976
Korb, Lawrence J., 1939-
The Joint Chiefs of Staff: the first twenty-five years/ Lawrence J. Korb. Bloomington: Indiana University Press, c1976. xiii, 210 p.
75-016839   353.6   0253331692
United States. Joint Chiefs of Staff -- History.

UB225 Staffs of armies — By region or country — Other regions or countries, A-Z

UB225.R9.R53 1998
Rich, David Alan.
The Tsar's colonels: professionalism, strategy, and subversion in late Imperial Russia/ David Alan Rich. Cambridge, Mass.: Harvard University Press, 1998. xiv, 293 p.
98-019400   355/.033547/09034   0674911113
Russia -- History, Military -- 1801-1917.

UB243 Inspection. Inspectors — By region or country — United States

UB243.C56 1987
Clary, David A.
The inspectors general of the United States Army, 1777-1903/ by David A. Clary and Joseph W.A. Whitehorne. Washington, D.C.: Office of the Inspector General and Center of Military History, U.S. Army: 1987. xviii, 465 p.
86-025931   355.6/3/0973
Military inspectors general -- United States -- History.

UB250 Intelligence — General works

UB250.B87 1982
Buranelli, Vincent.
Spy/counterspy: an encyclopedia of espionage/ Vincent and Nan Buranelli. New York: McGraw-Hill, c1982. xvi, 361 p.
81-023666   327.1/2/0321   0070089159
Espionage -- Dictionaries.

UB250.C68 1988
Comparing foreign intelligence: the U.S., the USSR, the U.K., & the Third World/ edited by Roy Godson. Washington: Pergamon-Brassey's International Defense Publishers, 1988. x, 157 p.
87-032851   355.3/432/07   0080347029
Military intelligence -- Study and teaching. Intelligence service -- Study and teaching.

UB250.F3
Farago, Ladislas.
War of wits; the anatomy of espionage and intelligence. New York, Funk & Wagnalls [1954] 379 p.
54-006361   355.34
Military intelligence. World War, 1939-1945 -- Secret service.

UB250.H68 1993
House, Jonathan M. 1950-
Military intelligence, 1870-1991: a research guide/ Jonathan M. House. Westport, Conn.: Greenwood Press, 1993. xv, 165 p.
93-000226   355.3/432   0313274037
Military intelligence.

UB250.I565 1999
Intelligence, espionage and related topics: an annotated bibliography of serial, journal, and magazine scholarship, 1844-1998/ compiled by James D. Calder. Westport, CT: Greenwood Press, 1999. xxxvi, 1330 p.
99-039950   327.12   0313292906
Intelligence service -- Periodicals -- Indexes. Espionage -- Periodicals -- Indexes.

UB250.K58 1984
Knowing one's enemies: intelligence assessment before the two world wars/ edited by Ernest R. May. Princeton, N.J.: Princeton University Press, c1984. xiii, 561 p.
84-042573   327.1/2/09   0691047170
Intelligence service -- History -- 20th century. Military intelligence -- History -- 20th century.

UB250.M3
McGovern, William Montgomery, 1897-
Strategic intelligence and the shape of tomorrow. Chicago, H. Regnery Co., 1961. 191 p.
61-005909   355.43
Geopolitics. World politics -- 1955-1965. Military intelligence.

UB250.R53 1988
Richelson, Jeffrey.
Foreign intelligence organizations/ Jeffrey T. Richelson. Cambridge, Mass.: Ballinger Pub. Co., c1988. xvii, 330 p.
88-000923   327.1/2   0887301215
Intelligence service. Espionage -- United States.

UB251 Intelligence — By region or country, A-Z

UB251.G7.B75 1987
British and American approaches to intelligence/ edited by K.G. Robertson. New York: St. Martin's Press, 1987. xii, 281 p.
86-029848   355.3/432   0312005423
Military intelligence -- Great Britain -- History -- 20th century. Military intelligence -- United States -- History -- 20th century.

UB251.G7.W486 1988
West, Nigel.
The SIGINT secrets: the signals intelligence war, 1900 to today: including the persecution of Gordon Welchman/ Nigel West. New York: W. Morrow, c1988. 347 p.
88-043153   355.3/432/0941   0688076521
Military intelligence -- Great Britain -- History -- 20th century. Electronic surveillance -- Great Britain -- History.

UB251.G8 R87 1999
Russell, Frank Santi, 1965-
Information gathering in classical Greece/ Frank Santi Russell. Ann Arbor, University of Michigan Press, c1999. viii, 267 p.
99-047317   327.1238   0472110640
Military intelligence -- Greece. Greece -- History -- To 146 B.C. Greece -- History, Military.

UB251.I78.B55 1991
Black, Ian, 1953-
Israel's secret wars: a history of Israel's intelligence services/ Ian Black and Benny Morris. New York: Grove Weidenfeld, 1991. xvii, 603 p.
90-049373   355.3/432/095694   0802111599
Military intelligence -- Israel. Intelligence service -- Israel. Secret service -- Israel.

UB251.U5.B35 1982
Bamford, James.
The puzzle palace: a report on America's most secret agency/ James Bamford. Boston: Houghton Mifflin, 1982. 465 p.
82-003056   327.1/2/06073   0395312868
United States. National Security Agency.

UB251.U5.B47 1989
Berkowitz, Bruce D., 1956-
Strategic intelligence for American national security/ Bruce D. Berkowitz and Allan E. Goodman. Princeton, N.J.: Princeton University Press, c1989. xiii, 232 p.
88-029326   355.3/432/0973   069107805X
Military intelligence -- United States. National security -- United States.

UB251.U5.F73
Freedman, Lawrence.
U.S. intelligence and the Soviet strategic threat/ Lawrence Freedman. Boulder, Colo.: Westview Press, 1977. xv, 235 p.
77-007525   327/.174   0891587489
Military intelligence -- United States. Strategic forces -- Soviet Union.

UB251.U5.I55 1987
Intelligence and intelligence policy in a democratic society/ edited by Stephen J. Cimbala. Dobbs Ferry, N.Y.: Transnational Publishers, c1987. xiv, 262 p.
87-004995   327.1/2/0973   0941320448
Intelligence service -- United States.

UB251.U5.I56
Intelligence requirements for the 1980's/ edited by Roy Godson. Washington, D.C.: National Strategy Information Center, c1979-c1986 v. 1-6
79-091051   327.1/2/0973
Intelligence service -- United States.

UB251.U5.N38 2000
National insecurity: U.S. intelligence after the Cold War/ edited by Craig Eisendrath; foreword by Tom Harkin. Philadelphia: Temple University Press, 2000. viii, 241 p.
99-023807   327.1273/009/045   1566397448
Intelligence service -- United States. World politics -- 1989-

UB251.U5.T35 1991
Talbert, Roy.
Negative intelligence: the army and the American Left, 1917-1941/ Roy Talbert, Jr. Jackson, Miss.: University Press of Mississippi, c1991. xiv, 303 p.
90-023047   355.3/432/0973   0878054952
United States. Dept. of the Army. General Staff. Military Intelligence Division.

UB251.U5.T74 2001
Treverton, Gregory F.
Reshaping national intelligence for an Age of Information/ Gregory F. Treverton. New York: Cambridge University Press, 2001. xviii, 266 p.
00-068863   327.12/0973   052158096X
Intelligence service -- United States. Military intelligence -- United States. World politics -- 1989-

UB251.U5.W66 1987
Woodward, Bob.
Veil: the secret wars of the CIA, 1981-1987/ Bob Woodward. New York: Simon and Schuster, c1987. 543 p.
87-020520   327.1/2/06073   0671601172
United States. Central Intelligence Agency -- History.

UB270 Intelligence — Espionage. Spies — General works

UB270.D8
Dulles, Allen Welsh, 1893-1969.
The craft of intelligence. New York, Harper & Row [1963] viii, 277 p.
63-016507   327.1
Espionage. Spies.

UB271 Intelligence — Espionage. Spies — By region or country, A-Z

UB271.G7.R87 1991
Rusbridger, James.
The intelligence game: the illusions and delusions of international espionage/ James Rusbridger. New York: New Amsterdam, 1991.
90-040442   327.1/241   1561310085
Espionage -- Great Britain. Intelligence service -- Great Britain. Espionage, British.

UB271.I8.K37 1992
Katz, Samuel M., 1963-
Soldier spies: Israeli military intelligence/ Samuel M. Katz. Novato, CA: Presidio Press, c1992. x, 389 p.
92-004880   355.3/432/095694   089141357X
Military intelligence -- Israel -- History -- 20th century. Israel -- History, Military.

UB271.J3.S4
Seth, Ronald.
Secret servants: a history of Japanese espionage. Farrar, Straus, 1957. 1 v.
57-009106   351.74
Espionage, Japanese. Spies, Japanese.

UB271.R9.B3
Bailey, Geoffrey.
The conspirators.   New York, Harper [1960] 306 p.
60-010397   327.4704
Espionage, Soviet.

UB271.R9.F838 1987
Williams, Robert Chadwell, 1938-
Klaus Fuchs, atom spy/ Robert Chadwell Williams. Cambridge, Mass.: Harvard University Press, 1987. vi, 267 p.
87-008672   327.1/2/0924   0674505077
Fuchs, Klaus Emil Julius, -- 1911-Spies -- Soviet Union -- Biography. Spies -- Great Britain -- Biography. Spies -- United States -- Biography.

UB271.R9.G58 1987
Glees, Anthony, 1948-
The secrets of the service: a story of Soviet subversion of Western intelligence/ Anthony Glees. New York: Carroll & Graf, 1987. xvi, 447 p.
87-020862   327.1/2/0941   088184375X
Espionage, Soviet -- Great Britain -- History -- 20th century.

UB271.R9.H4 1956a
Heilbrunn, Otto.
The Soviet secret services.   London, Allen & Unwin [1956] 216 p.
56-003383   355.43
Espionage, Soviet.

UB271.R9.R66 1989
Romerstein, Herbert.
The KGB against the "main enemy": how the Soviet Intelligence Service operates against the United States/ by Herbert Romerstein, Stanislav Levchenko. Lexington, Mass.: Lexington Books, c1989. xiii, 369 p.
88-027358   327.1/2/0947   0669112283
Espionage, Soviet -- United States -- History -- 20th century.

UB271.R9.W45 1999
Weinstein, Allen.
The haunted wood: Soviet espionage in America--the Stalin era/ Allen Weinstein, Alexander Vassiliev. New York: Random House, c1999. xxviii, 402 p.
98-011801   327.1247073   0679457240
Espionage, Soviet -- United States -- History -- 20th century. Spies -- Soviet Union. Spies -- United States. United States -- History -- 1933-1945.

UB271.R92.P432 1994
Brown, Anthony Cave.
Treason in the blood: H. St. John Philby, Kim Philby, and the spy case of the century/ Anthony Cave Brown. Boston: Houghton Mifflin, 1994. 677 p.
94-026189   327.1/2/092   039563119X
Philby, Kim, -- 1912- Philby, H. St. J. B. -- (Harry St. John Bridger), -- 1885-1960. Espionage, Soviet -- Great Britain. Spies -- Great Britain -- Biography.

UB271.U5.H86 1974
Hunt, E. Howard 1918-
Undercover: memoirs of an American secret agent/ by E. Howard Hunt. [New York]: Berkley Pub. Corp.: distributed by Putnam, [1974] 338 p.
74-011602   327/.12/0924   0399114467
Hunt, E. Howard -- (Everette Howard), -- 1918-Watergate Affair, 1972-1974.

UB271.U5.M44 1991
Melton, H. Keith 1944-
OSS special weapons & equipment: spy devices of W.W. II/ H. Keith Melton; foreword by William Colby. New York: Sterling, c1991. 128 p.
90-022118   355.3/432/028   0806982381
Military intelligence -- United States -- Equipment and supplies -- Handbooks, manuals, etc. Sabotage -- United States -- Equipment and supplies -- Handbooks, manuals, etc. Espionage -- United States -- Equipment and supplies -- Handbooks, manuals, etc.

UB271.U5.O85 1988
O'Toole, G. J. A. 1936-
The encyclopedia of American intelligence and espionage: from the Revolutionary War to the present/ G.J.A. O'Toole. New York: Facts on File, c1988. xiii, 539 p.
87-030361 327.1/2/0973 0816010110
Espionage, American -- History -- Encyclopedias. Espionage -- United States -- History -- Encyclopedias.

UB271.U5.O86 1991
O'Toole, G. J. A. 1936-
Honorable treachery: a history of U.S. intelligence, espionage, and covert action from the American Revolution to the CIA/ G.J.A. O'Toole. New York: Atlantic Monthly Press, c1991. xv, 591 p.
91-013203 327.1/2/0973 087113506X
Espionage, American -- History. Espionage -- United States -- History.

UB271.U52.R66 1988
Roosevelt, Archibald, 1918-
For lust of knowing: memoirs of an intelligence officer/ Archie Roosevelt. Boston: Little, Brown, c1988. xiv, 500 p.
87-024930 327.1/2/0924 0316756008
Roosevelt, Archibald, -- 1918-Intelligence officers -- United States -- Biography.Islamic countries -- Description and travel.

UB275 Psychological warfare. Propaganda — General works

UB275.D3
Daugherty, William E.
A psychological warfare casebook. In collaboration with Morris Janowitz. Baltimore, Published for Operations Research Office, Johns Hopkins University by Johns Hopkins Press [1958] xxiii, 880 p.
58-002297 355.43
Psychological warfare.

UB276 Psychological warfare. Propaganda — By region or country — United States

UB276.S56 1994
Simpson, Christopher.
Science of coercion: communication research and psychological warfare, 1945-1960/ Christopher Simpson. New York: Oxford University Press, 1994. viii, 204 p.
93-003661 355.3/434/0973 019507193X
Psychological warfare. Communication -- Research -- United States. Cold War. United States -- Military policy.

UB323 Enlistment, recruiting, placement, promotion, discharge, etc. — By region or country — United States

UB323.A5 1970
United States.
The report of the President's Commission on an All-Volunteer Armed Force. [New York] Collier Books [1970] 218 p.
79-012775 355.2/23/0973
United States -- Armed Forces -- Recruiting, enlistment, etc.

UB323.C59 1983
Conscripts and volunteers: military requirements, social justice, and the all-volunteer force/ edited by Robert K. Fullinwider. Totowa, N.J.: Rowman & Allanheld, c1983. vi, 250 p.
83-003095 355.2/2362/0973 0847672247
Military service, Voluntary -- United States.United States -- Armed Forces -- Recruiting, enlistment, etc.

UB323.G5 1959
Ginzberg, Eli, 1911-
The ineffective soldier; lessons for management and the nation, by Eli Ginzberg [and others] With a foreword by Howard McC. Snyder. New York, Columbia University Press, 1959. 3 v.
59-007701 355.22
Psychiatry, Military -- Case studies. Soldiers -- United States. Manpower -- United States.

UB323.H46 1990
Henderson, William Darryl, 1938-
The hollow army: how the U.S. Army is oversold and undermanned/ William Darryl Henderson; foreword by Charles Moskos. New York: Greenwood Press, 1990. xvi, 166 p.
89-023286 355.6/1/0973 0313268746
Military education -- United States.

UB323.S44 1989
Segal, David R.
Recruiting for Uncle Sam: citizenship and military manpower policy/ David R. Segal. Lawrence, Kan.: University Press of Kansas, c1989. x, 221 p.
88-034461 355.2/23/0973 0700603913
Draft -- United States -- History. Sociology, Military -- United States -- History. United States -- Armed Forces -- Recruiting, enlistment, etc. -- History.

UB340 Compulsory service. Conscription and exemption — General works

UB340.M55 1982
The Military draft: selected readings on conscription/ edited by Martin Anderson, with Barbara Honegger. Stanford, Calif.: Hoover Institution Press, c1982. xvi, 668 p.
81-084641 355.2/2363 0817975810
Draft. Draft -- United States.

UB341 Compulsory service. Conscription and exemption — Conscientious objectors — General works

UB341.N49 1993
The New conscientious objection: from sacred to secular resistance/ edited by Charles C. Moskos, John Whiteclay Chambers II. New York: Oxford University Press, 1993. x, 286 p.
92-020615 355.2/24 019507954X
Conscientious objection. Draft resisters.

UB342 Compulsory service. Conscription and exemption — Conscientious objectors — By region or country, A-Z

UB342.U5.H33
Harris, David, 1946-
Coming out [by] David Harris and Joan Baez Harris. Photos. by Bob Fitch. New York, Pocket Books [1971] 1 v.
72-031613 322/.44 0671785443
Conscientious objectors -- United States -- Personal narratives.

UB342.U5.M4 1930a
Meyer, Ernest Louis, 1892-1953.
"Hey! Yellowbacks!" The war diary of a conscientious objector. Foreword by William Ellery Leonard. New York, John Day Co. [New York, J. S. Ozer, 1972, c1930] viii, 209 p.
75-143432 940.3/162
Meyer, Ernest Louis, -- 1892-1953 -- Diaries.World War, 1914-1918 -- Conscientious objectors -- United States. Conscientious objectors -- United States -- Diaries.

UB342.U5.S52
Sibley, Mulford Quickert.
Conscription of conscience; the American state and the conscientious objector, 1940-1947, by Mulford Q. Sibley and Philip E. Jacob. Ithaca, Cornell University Press, 1952. x, 580 p.
52-012673 355.22
Conscientious objectors -- United States.

UB342.U5.S83
Stapp, Andy.
Up against the brass. New York, Simon and Schuster [1970] 192 p.
71-107266 355.2/2 0671205722
Conscientious objectors -- United States -- Personal narratives.

UB343 Compulsory service. Conscription and exemption — By region or country, A-Z — United States

UB343.C483 1987
Chambers, John Whiteclay.
To raise an army: the draft comes to modern America/ John Whiteclay Chambers. New York: Free Press; c1987. xi, 386 p.
87-015150 355.2/2363/0973 0029058201
Draft -- United States -- History. World War, 1914-1918 -- United States. United States -- Armed Forces -- Recruiting, enlistment, etc. -- History.

UB343.D3
Davis, James Warren, 1935-
Little groups of neighbors; the Selective Service
System [by] James W. Davis, Jr. [and] Kenneth
M. Dolbeare. Chicago, Markham Pub. Co. [1968]
xv, 276 p.
68-009286   355.2/23
United States. Selective Service System.

UB343.F59 1993
Flynn, George Q.
The draft, 1940-1973/ George Q. Flynn.
Lawrence, Kan.: University Press of Kansas,
c1993. xiv, 376 p.
92-031081   355.2/2363/0973   070060586X
Draft -- United States -- History.

UB343.M8
Murdock, Eugene Converse.
Patriotism limited, 1862-1865; the Civil War
draft and the bounty system. Kent, Ohio] Kent
State University Press [1967] viii, 270 p.
67-064665   355.2/2
*Draft -- United States -- History. Bounties,
Military -- United States -- History.*

UB345 Compulsory service. Conscription and exemption — By region or country, A-Z — Other regions or countries, A-Z

UB345.G7.S28 1993
Scott, L. V. 1957-
Conscription and the Attlee governments: the
politics and policy of national service, 1945-
1951/ L.V. Scott. Oxford: Clarendon Press; 1993.
ix, 304 p.
93-024904   355.2/2363/094109044
0198204213
*Draft -- Great Britain -- History -- 20th
century. Great Britain -- Politics and government
-- 1945-1964.*

UB353 Universal service. Universal military training — By region or country — United States

UB353.P42 1984
Pearlman, Michael, 1944-
To make democracy safe for America: patricians
and preparedness in the Progressive Era/ Michael
Pearlman. Urbana: University of Illinois Press,
c1984. 297 p.
83-001107   355.2/2363/0973   0252010191
*Draft -- United States -- History -- 20th
century. Military education -- United States --
History -- 20th century. United States -- Politics
and government -- 20th century. United States --
Armed Forces -- Operational readiness.*

UB357-359 Provision for veterans — Employment, education, etc. — By region or country

UB357.A22
American Veterans Committee.
American   Veterans   Committee   bulletin.
Bethesda, MD: The Committee, [1991-   ]
95-017339
Veterans -- United States -- Periodicals.

UB357.B74 1985
Brende, Joel Osler.
Vietnam veterans: the road to recovery/ Joel
Osler Brende and Erwin Randolph Parson. New
York: Plenum Press, c1985. xx, 270 p.
84-026396   355.1/156/0973   0306419661
*Veterans -- United States -- Psychology.
Vietnamese Conflict, 1961-1975 -- United States.
Post-traumatic stress disorder.*

UB357.R67
Ross, Davis R. B.
Preparing for Ulysses; politics and veterans
during World War II, by Davis R. B. Ross. New
York, Columbia University Press, 1969. vi,
315 p.
78-094513   355.1/15/0973   0231032226
*Veterans -- United States. United States --
Politics and government -- 1933-1945.*

UB359.F8.W64
Woloch, Isser, 1937-
The French veteran from the Revolution to the
Restoration/ by Isser Woloch. Chapel Hill:
University of North Carolina Press, c1979. xix,
392 p.
78-026444   355.1/15/0944   0807813567
*Veterans -- France -- History -- 18th century.
Veterans -- France -- History -- 19th century.
France -- Social policy.*

UB359.G3.D5 1993
Diehl, James M.
The thanks of the fatherland: German veterans
after the Second World War/ James M. Diehl.
Chapel Hill: University of North Carolina Press,
c1993. xii, 345 p.
92-050811   362.86/0943   0807820776
Veterans -- Germany.

UB369 Provision for veterans — Medical care — By region or country

UB369.L47 1988
Lerager, Jim, 1945-
In the shadow of the cloud: photographs &
histories of America's atomic veterans/ Jim
Lerager; essays by Karl Z. Morgan, Susan D.
Lambert. Golden, Colo.: Fulcrum, c1988. 116 p.
87-033682   355.1/156/0973   1555910300
*Veterans -- Diseases -- United States. Veterans
-- United States -- Biography. Nuclear weapons
testing victims -- United States -- Biography.*

UB383 Soldiers' and sailors' homes — By region or country — United States

UB383.A5.K45 1997
Kelly, Patrick J., 1955-
Creating a national home: building the veterans'
welfare state, 1860-1900/ Patrick J. Kelly.
Cambridge, Mass.: Harvard University, 1997.
viii, 250 p.
96-040424   362.86/83/0973   0674175603
*Veterans -- Services for -- United States --
History -- 19th century. Veterans -- Government
policy -- United States -- History -- 19th century.*

UB393 Military reservations, cemeteries, etc. — By region or country — United States

UB393.A45 1989
American battle monuments: a guide to military
cemeteries and monuments maintained by the
American Battle Monuments Commission/
Elizabeth Nishiura, editor. Detroit, Mich.:
Omnigraphics, c1989. xii, 469 p.
89-061537   1558888128
*Soldiers' monuments -- Guidebooks. National
cemeteries, American -- Guidebooks. World War,
1939-1945 -- Monuments -- Guidebooks. United
States -- History, Military -- 20th century.*

UB403 Provision for soldiers' dependents: families, widows, and orphans — By region or country — United States

UB403.F47
Financial aid for veterans, military personnel,
and their dependents.   Redwood City, Calif.:
Reference Service Press, [1988-   ]
88-659116   362.8
*Military   dependents   --   Scholarships,
fellowships, etc. -- United States -- Periodicals.
Veterans -- Scholarships, fellowships, etc. --
United States -- Periodicals. Soldiers --
Scholarships, fellowships, etc. -- United States --
Periodicals.*

UB413 Officers — By region or country — United States

UB413.M68 2000
Moten, Matthew, 1960-
The Delafield Commission and the American
military profession/ Matthew Moten. College
Station: Texas A & M University Press, c2000.
xvii, 267 p.
99-053768   355/.00973/09034   0890969256
*Crimean War, 1853-1856. Armies -- Europe --
History -- 19th century.*

UB413.S54 1992
Skelton, William B., 1939-
An American profession of arms: the army
officer corps, 1784-1861/ William B. Skelton.
Lawrence, Kan.: University Press of Kansas,
c1992. xvii, 481 p.
92-010089   355.3/3/097309033   0700605606
*United States. Army -- Officers -- History --
19th century. United States. Army -- Officers --
History -- 18th century.*

UB415 Officers — By region or country — Other regions or countries, A-Z

UB415.A8.D43 1990
Deak, Istvan.
Beyond nationalism: a social and political history
of the Habsburg officer corps, 1848-1918/ Istvan
Deak. New York: Oxford University Press, 1990.
xiii, 273 p.
89-009389   306.2/7/09436   019504505X
*Sociology, Military -- Hungary. Sociology,
Military -- Austria.*

UB415.E8.P6
Pool, Ithiel de Sola, 1917-
Satellite generals; a study of military ethics in the Soviet sphere, by Ithiel de Sola Pool with the collaboration of George K. Schueller [and others] Stanford, Stanford University Press, 1956, [c1955] vi, 165 p.
54-011785
Communist parties.Soviet Union -- Armed Forces -- Officers. Europe, Eastern -- Armed Forces -- Officers. China -- Armed Forces -- Officers.

UB415.G4.D413 1965
Demeter, Karl, 1889-
The German officer-corps in society and state, 1650-1945. Translated from the German by Angus Malcolm. Introd. by Michael Howard. New York, Praeger [1965] xiv, 414 p.
65-014178   355.3320943
Germany. Heer -- Organization. Germany. Heer -- Officers.

UB416 Minorities, women, etc., in armed forces — General works

UB416.E54
Enloe, Cynthia H., 1938-
Ethnic soldiers: state security in divided societies/ Cynthia H. Enloe. Athens: University of Georgia Press, c1980. xii, 276 p.
79-005418   306/.2   0820305073
Armed Forces -- Minorities. Ethnic groups. National security.

UB416.F45 1982
Female soldiers--combatants or noncombatants?: historical and contemporary perspectives/ edited by Nancy Loring Goldman. Westport, Conn.: Greenwood Press, c1982. xix, 307 p.
81-013318   355.1/088042   0313231176
Women soldiers -- Addresses, essays, lectures. Combat -- Addresses, essays, lectures.

UB416.S65 2000
A soldier and a woman: sexual integration in the military/ edited by Gerard J. DeGroot and C.M. Peniston-Bird. New York: Pearson Education, 2000.
00-021675   355/.0082   0582414393
Women soldiers -- History.

UB418 Minorities, women, etc., in armed forces — By region or country — United States

UB418.A47.B55 1981
Blacks in the military: essential documents/ edited by Bernard C. Nalty and Morris J. MacGregor. Wilmington, Del.: Scholarly Resources, c1981. xi, 367 p.
80-054664   355.1/08996073   0842021833
Afro-American soldiers -- History -- Sources.

UB418.A47.C48 1995
Christian, Garna L.
Black soldiers in Jim Crow Texas, 1899-1917/ Garna L. Christian. College Station: Texas A&M University Press, c1995. xvi, 223 p.
94-042428   355/.008996073   0890966370
Race discrimination -- Texas -- History -- 20th century.Texas -- Race relations.

UB418.A47.M33
MacGregor, Morris J., 1931-
Integration of the Armed Forces, 1940-1965/ by Morris J. MacGregor, Jr. Washington, D.C.: Center of Military History, U.S. Army: 1981. xx, 647 p.
80-607077   355.3/3
Afro-American soldiers.United States -- Race relations.

UB418.A47.M66 1996
Moore, Brenda L., 1950-
To serve my country, to serve my race: the story of the only African American WACS stationed overseas during World War II/ Brenda L. Moore. New York: New York University Press, c1996. xv, 272 p.
95-032467   940.54/03   0814755224
World War, 1939-1945 -- Participation, Female. World War, 1939-1945 -- Afro-Americans. United States -- Armed Forces -- Women. United States -- Armed Forces -- Afro-Americans.

UB418.A47.M67 1996
Moskos, Charles C.
All that we can be: Black leadership and racial integration the Army way/ Charles C. Moskos and John Sibley Butler. New York, NY: Basic Books, c1996. xxiii, 198 p.
96-016570   355/.0089/96073   0465001084
Sociology, Military -- United States.United States -- Race relations.

UB418.G38.G35 1996
Gay rights, military wrongs: political perspectives on lesbians and gays in the military/ edited by Craig A. Rimmerman. New York: Garland Pub., 1996. xxvii, 344 p.
96-020929   355/.008/664   0815320868
United States -- Armed Forces -- Gays. United States -- Military policy. United States -- Politics and government -- 1993-

UB418.G38.G36 1994
Gays and lesbians in the military: issues, concerns, and contrasts/ Wilbur J. Scott and Sandra Carson Stanley, editors. New York: Aldine de Gruyter, c1994. xx, 278 p.
94-029004   355/.008/664   0202305406
Lesbians -- United States.United States -- Armed Forces -- Gays.

UB418.G38.H653 1991
Homosexuality and the military: a sourcebook of official, uncensored U.S. government documents. [S.l.]: Diane Pub., [between 1991 1 v.
94-121053
United States -- Armed Forces -- Gays -- Government policy.

UB418.G38.H86 1990
Humphrey, Mary Ann.
My country, my right to serve: experiences of gay men and women in the military, World War II to the present/ Mary Ann Humphrey. New York, NY: HarperCollins, c1990. xxxiii, 285 p.
89-046538   355/.008/664   0060164468
United States -- Armed Forces -- Gays.

UB418.G38.S53 1995
Shawver, Lois.
And the flag was still there: straight people, gay people, and sexuality in the U.S. military/ Lois Shawver. New York: Haworth Press, c1995. xiv, 262 p.
94-031507   355/.008/664   1560249099
Sex discrimination -- United States. Homosexuality -- United States -- Psychological aspects. United States -- Armed Forces -- Gays.

UB418.W65.B74 1997
Breuer, William B., 1923-
War and American women: heroism, deeds, and controversy/ William B. Breuer. Westport, Conn.: Praeger, 1997. viii, 255 p.
96-009013   355/.0082   0275957179
Women and the military -- United States. Women in war.

UB418.W65.F45 2000
Feinman, Ilene Rose, 1959-
Citizenship rites: feminist soldiers and feminist antimilitarists/ Ilene Rose Feinman. New York: New York University Press, c2000. xiii, 286 p.
99-006784   355/.0082/0973   0814726887
Women soldiers -- United States. Women and the military -- United States. Feminism -- United States. United States -- Armed Forces -- Women.

UB418.W65.F75 1996
Friedl, Vicki L.
Women in the United States military, 1901-1995: a research guide and annotated bibliography/ compiled by Vicki L. Friedl. Westport, Conn: Greenwood Press, 1996. xx, 251 p.
96-005253   355/.0082   031329657X
United States -- Armed Forces -- Women -- History -- 20th century. United States -- Armed Forces -- Women -- Bibliography.

UB418.W65.G46 1999
Gender camouflage: women and the U.S. military/ edited by Francine D'Amico and Laurie Weinstein. New York: New York University Press, 1999. x, 279 p.
98-040841   355/.0082/0973   0814719066
Women and the military -- United States.United States -- Armed Forces -- Women.

UB418.W65.H37 1997
Harrell, Margaret C.
New opportunities for military women: effects upon readiness, cohesion, and morale/ Margaret C. Harrell, Laura L. Miller. Santa Monica, CA: Rand, 1997. xxv, 172 p.
97-032067   355/.0082   0833025589
Morale.United States -- Armed Forces -- Operational readiness. United States -- Armed Forces -- Unit cohesion. United States -- Armed Forces -- Women.

UB418.W65.H47 1998
Herbert, Melissa S., 1956-
Camouflage isn't only for combat: gender, sexuality and women in the military/ Melissa S. Herbert. New York: New York University Press, c1998. ix, 205 p.
97-045414   355/.0082   0814735479
Sociology, Military -- United States.United States -- Armed Forces -- Women.

UB418.W65.H64 1982
Holm, Jeanne, 1921-
Women in the military: an unfinished revolution/ Jeanne Holm. Novato, CA: Presidio Press, c1982. xvii, 435 p.
82-012324   355/.0082   0891410783
United States -- Armed Forces -- Women.

UB418.W65.R63 1981
Rogan, Helen.
Mixed company: women in the modern army/ Helen Rogan. New York: Putnam, c1981. 333 p.
81-010662   355.1/088042   0399126546
United States -- Armed Forces -- Women.

UB418.W65.S56 1999
Skaine, Rosemarie.
Women at war: gender issues of Americans in combat/ by Rosemarie Skaine. Jefferson, N.C.: McFarland & Company, c1999. xii, 299 p.
98-035231   355/.0082/0973   0786405708
Women in combat -- United States. Sex discrimination in employment -- United States. United States -- Armed Forces -- Women.

UB418.W65.S75 1989
Stiehm, Judith.
Arms and the enlisted woman/ Judith Hicks Stiehm. Philadelphia: Temple University Press, 1989. 331 p.
87-033645   355/.0088042   0877225656
United States -- Armed Forces -- Women.

UB419 Minorities, women, etc., in armed forces —
By region or country —
Other regions or countries, A-Z

UB419.B46.A48 1998
Alpern, Stanley B. 1927-
Amazons of black Sparta: the women warriors of Dahomey/ Stanley B. Alpern. New York: New York University Press, c1998. xii, 280 p.
97-051832   355.3/1/082096683   0814706770
Women soldiers -- Benin -- History -- 19th century.Benin -- History, Military -- 19th century.

UB419.M6.S25 1990
Salas, Elizabeth, 1948-
Soldaderas in the Mexican military: myth and history/ Elizabeth Salas. Austin: University of Texas Press, 1990. xiii, 163 p.
89-048597   355/.0082   0292776306
Women and the military -- Mexico -- History.Mexico -- Armed Forces -- Women -- History.

UB419.S6.G78 1983
Grundy, Kenneth W.
Soldiers without politics: Blacks in the South African armed forces/ Kenneth W. Grundy. Berkeley: University of California Press, c1983. xiv, 297 p.
82-002584   322/.5/089968   0520047109
Soldiers, Black -- South Africa. Soldiers, Black -- Namibia.

UB433 Rewards, brevets, decorations, medals, etc. —
By region or country —
United States

UB433.L36 1995
Lang, George.
Medal of Honor recipients, 1863-1994/ compiled by George Lang, Raymond L. Collins, and Gerard F. White. New York: Facts on File, c1995. 2 v.
95-012529   355.1/342   0816032599
Medal of Honor.United States -- Armed Forces -- Biography.

UB775 Civil law relating to the military

UB775.M4.M3
McAlister, Lyle N.
The "fuero militar" in New Spain, 1764-1800. Gainesville, University of Florida Press, 1957. vii, 117 p.
57-010614   355.133
Military privileges and immunities -- Mexico. Jurisdiction -- Mexico. Courts-martial and courts of inquiry -- Mexico. Mexico -- History -- Spanish colony, 1540-1810.

UB800 Prisons and prisoners — General works

UB800.E53 2000
Encyclopedia of prisoners of war and internment/ Jonathan F. Vance, editor. Santa Barbara, Calif: ABC-CLIO, c2000. xviii, 408 p.
00-010129   355.1/13   1576070689
Prisoners of war -- Encyclopedias. Concentration camps -- Encyclopedias.

UB803 Prisons and prisoners — By region or country — United States

UB803.D69 1994
Doyle, Robert C.
Voices from captivity: interpreting the American POW narrative/ Robert C. Doyle. Lawrence, Kan.: University Press of Kansas, c1994. xiii, 370 p.
93-041111   813/.009358   0700606637
Prisoners of war -- United States. Prisoners' writings, American.

UB825 Military police. Gendarmes — By region or country, A-Z

UB825.U54.R33 1989
Radley, Kenneth, 1943-
Rebel watchdog: the Confederate States Army provost guard/ Kenneth Radley. Baton Rouge: Louisiana State University Press, c1989. xvii, 340 p.
88-030338   973.7/42   0807114685
United States -- History -- Civil War, 1861-1865.

UC Maintenance and transportation

UC263 Supplies and stores — By region or country — United States

UC263.F37 1997
Farrell, Theo, 1967-
Weapons without a cause: the politics of weapons acquisition in the United States/ Theo Farrell. New York, N.Y.: St. Martin's Press, 1997. xv, 230 p.
96-022369   355.8/2/0973   0312161034
United States -- Armed Forces -- Procurement. United States -- Armed Forces -- Weapons systems. United States -- Politics and government.

UC263.G74 1989
Gregory, William H.
The defense procurement mess/ William H. Gregory. Lexington, Mass.: Lexington Books, c1989. xiii, 219 p.
88-030400   355.6/212/0973   0669208078
United States -- Armed Forces -- Procurement.

UC263.H87 1988
Huston, James A. 1918-
Outposts and allies: U.S. Army logistics in the Cold War, 1945-1953/ James A. Huston. Selinsgrove: Susquehanna University Press; c1988. 349 p.
86-043218   355.4/15/0973   0941664848
World politics -- 1945-1955.

UC263.L42 1996
Lebovic, James H.
Foregone conclusions: U.S. weapons acquisition in the post-cold war transition/ James H. Lebovic. Boulder, Colo.: Westview Press, 1996. vi, 197 p.
96-016624   355.8/0973/09049   0813389852
World politics -- 1989-United States -- Armed Forces -- Weapons systems. United States -- Armed Forces -- Procurement.

UC263.M35 1991
Mayer, Kenneth R., 1960-
The political economy of defense contracting/ Kenneth R. Mayer. New Haven: Yale University Press, c1991. xviii, 232 p.
91-015358   355.6/211/0973   0300045247
Patronage, Political -- United States.United States -- Armed Forces -- Procurement.

UC263.M36 1989
McNaugher, Thomas L.
New weapons, old politics: America's military procurement muddle/ Thomas L. McNaugher. Washington, D.C.: Brookings Institution, c1989. xi, 251 p.
89-033215   355.8/2/0973   0815756267
Defense industries -- United States.United States -- Armed Forces -- Procurement.

UC263.M468 1989
Miller, Darlis A., 1939-
Soldiers and settlers: military supply in the
Southwest, 1861-1885/ Darlis A. Miller.
Albuquerque: University of New Mexico Press,
c1989. xviii, 506 p.
89-014637   355.6/212/0340979   0826311598
Southwest, New -- Economic conditions.

UC265 Supplies and stores —
By region or country —
Other regions or countries, A-Z

UC265.S65.D86 1995
Dunn, Walter S. 1928-
The Soviet economy and the Red Army, 1930-
1945/ Walter S. Dunn, Jr. Westport, Conn.:
Praeger, 1995. ix, 256 p.
95-007016   355/.033047/07049   0275948935
*Military-industrial complex -- Soviet Union --
History.Soviet Union -- History -- 1925-1953.*

UC267 Supplies and stores
— Contracts

UC267.K3
Kast, Fremont Ellsworth, 1926-
Management in the space age; an analysis of the
concept of weapon system management and its
non-military applications, by Fremont E. Kast
and James E. Rosenzweig. New York, Exposition
Press [1962] 183 p.
62-019522   355.6
*Munitions -- United States. Systems
engineering. Defense contracts -- United States.*

UC333 Transportation —
Air transportation —
By region or country

UC333.C73 1988
Crawford, William Roy, 1932-
Military space-A air opportunities around the
world: you can save thousands of authors,
William "Roy" Crawford, Lela Ann Crawford;
editor, Bryce D. Thompson. Falls Church, Va.:
Military Living Publications, c1988. xviii, 378 p.
88-001231   355.8/3/02573   0914862154
*Air travel -- Directories.United States -- Armed
Forces -- Transportation -- Directories. United
States -- Armed Forces -- Facilities --
Directories.*

UC333.T85 1985
Tunner, William H.
Over the hump/ by William H. Tunner.
Washington, D.C.: Office of Air Force History,
United States Air Force. 1985, c1964. xvii,
340 p.
86-600028   358.4/4/0973
Airlift, Military -- United States -- History.

UD Infantry

UD59 By region or country

UD59.D48 1996
DeVries, Kelly, 1956-
Infantry warfare in the early fourteenth century:
discipline, tactics, and technology/ Kelly
DeVries. Woodbridge, Suffolk, UK; Boydell
Press, 1996. 216 p.
96-012439   356/.1/09409023   0851155677
*Infantry -- History. Military art and science --
History -- Medieval, 500-1500. Infantry drill and
tactics -- History. Great Britain -- History -- 14th
century. Europe -- History -- 476-1492.*

UD160 Tactics. Maneuvers.
Drill regulations —
By region or country —
United States

UD160.J36 1994
Jamieson, Perry D.
Crossing the deadly ground: United States Army
tactics, 1865-1899/ Perry D. Jamieson.
Tuscaloosa: University of Alabama Press, c1994.
xiv, 230 p.
93-045318   356/.183   0817307605
*United States. Army. Infantry -- Drill and
tactics -- History -- 19th century.*

UD215 Tactics. Maneuvers.
Drill regulations —
By region or country — Europe

UD215.R67 1996
Ross, Steven T.
From flintlock to rifle: infantry tactics, 1740-
1866/ Steven T. Ross. London; F. Cass, c1996.
ix, 218 p.
95-014996   356/.183/09033   0714646024
*Infantry drill and tactics -- History -- 18th
century. Infantry drill and tactics -- History --
19th century. Napoleonic Wars, 1800-1815 --
Campaigns.*

UD373 Equipment —
By region or country —
United States

UD373.M33 1995
McChristian, Douglas C.
The U.S. Army in the West, 1870-1880:
uniforms, weapons, and equipment/ by Douglas
C. McChristian; foreword by John P. Langellier.
Norman: University of Oklahoma Press, c1995.
xix, 315 p.
94-048216   356/.186/097309034   0806127058
West (U.S.) -- History -- 1860-1890.

UD383-383.5 Small arms —
By region or country —
United States

UD383.H35 1994
Hallahan, William H.
Misfire: the history of how America's small arms
have failed our military/ William H. Hallahan.
New York: Scribner's, c1994. xii, 580 p.
94-001552   623.4/4/0973   0684193590
Firearms -- United States -- History.

UD383.5.A75 1991
Arms and equipment of the Confederacy/ by the
editors of Time-Life Books. Alexandria, Va.:
Time-Life Books, c1991. 312 p.
91-002278   973.7/42   0809488507
*United States -- History -- Civil War, 1861-
1865 -- Equipment and supplies.*

UE Cavalry. Armor

UE57 By region or country —
Europe — Great Britain
(General)

UE57.H37 1995
Harris, J. P.
Men, ideas, and tanks: British military thought
and armoured forces, 1903-1939/ J.P. Harris.
Manchester; Manchester University Press; 1995.
viii, 342 p.
95-021173   358/.18/094109041   071903762X
*Great Britain. Army -- Armored troops --
History.*

UE75 By region or country —
Europe — Greece

UE75.W67 1994
Worley, Leslie J.
Hippeis: the cavalry of Ancient Greece/ Leslie J.
Worley. Boulder: Westview Press, 1994. xiii,
241 p.
93-029067   357/.1/0938   0813318041
Cavalry -- Greece -- History.

UF Artillery

UF157 Tactics. Maneuvers. Drill regulations — General works

UF157.Z33 1994
Zabecki, David T.
Steel wind: Colonel Georg Bruchmuller and the birth of modern artillery/ David T. Zabecki; foreword by J.B.A. Bailey. Westport, Conn.: Praeger, 1994. xiv, 197 p.
94-007658   358/.12/092   0275947491
Bruchmuller, Georg, -- b. 1863.Artillery drill and tactics -- History -- 20th century. World War, 1914-1918 -- Artillery operations.

UF400 Field artillery — General works

UF400.D37 1994
Dastrup, Boyd L.
The field artillery: history and sourcebook/ Boyd L. Dastrup. Westport, Conn.: Greenwood Press, 1994. xii, 220 p.
93-001142   358.1/2/09   0313272646
Artillery, Field and mountain -- History.

UF500 Weapons systems — General works

UF500.B79 1994
Brzoska, Michael.
Arms and warfare: escalation, de-escalation, and negotiation/ Michael Brzoska and Frederic S. Pearson. Columbia, S.C.: University of South Carolina Press, c1994. xii, 316 p.
93-046038   327.1/74   0872499820
Arms transfers. War. Diplomatic negotiations in international disputes. Developing countries -- History, Military -- Case studies.

UF500.C42 1987
Chant, Christopher.
A compendium of armaments and military hardware/ Christpher Chant. London; Routledge & Kegan Paul, 1987. viii, 568 p.
86-031326   355.8/2/0216   0710207204
Weapons systems -- Catalogs.

UF500.G8 1995
Grossman, Mark.
Encyclopedia of the Persian Gulf War/ Mark Grossman. Santa Barbara, Calif.: ABC-CLIO, c1995. xiii, 522 p.
95-038945   956.7044/2   0874366844
Weapons systems. Persian Gulf War, 1991 -- Equipment and supplies.

UF503 Weapons systems — By region or country — United States

UF503.D43 1989
Defense technology/ edited by Asa A. Clark IV and John F. Lilley. New York: Praeger, 1989. xvi, 306 p.
88-027575   355.8/2/0973   0275930785
Munitions -- United States.United States -- Armed Forces -- Weapons systems.

UF503.J65 1998
Johnson, David E.   1950-
Fast tanks and heavy bombers: innovation in the U.S. Army, 1917-1945/ David E. Johnson. Ithaca: Cornell University Press, 1998. xii, 288 p.
98-016418   355/.07/097309041   0801434580
United States. Army -- Weapons systems -- History -- 20th century. United States. Army -- Operational readiness.

UF505 Weapons systems — By region or country — Other regions or countries, A-Z

UF505.I72.T56 1991
Timmerman, Kenneth R.
The death lobby: how the West armed Iraq/ Kenneth R. Timmerman. Boston: Houghton Mifflin, 1991. xix, 443 p.
91-028557   355/.032567   0395593050
Arms transfers -- Iraq.Iraq -- Armed Forces -- Weapons systems.

UF533-535 Ordnance and small arms — Manufacture — By region or country

UF533.E93 1988
Evangelista, Matthew, 1958-
Innovation and the arms race: how the United States and the Soviet Union develop new military technologies/ Matthew Evangelista. Ithaca: Cornell University Press, 1988. xvi, 300 p.
87-027547   355.8/2   0801421659
Defense industrie -- United States -- Technological innovations. Defense industries -- Soviet Union -- Technological innovations. Arms race -- History -- 20th century. United States -- Armed Forces -- Procurement. Soviet Union -- Armed Forces -- Procurement.

UF533.F73 1988
Franklin, H. Bruce   1934-
War stars: the superweapon and the American imagination/ H. Bruce Franklin. New York: Oxford University Press, 1988. 256 p.
87-034734   355.8/2/0973   0195052951
Military weapons -- United States -- History. Weapons systems -- United States -- History. War and society -- United States. United States -- Military policy.

UF533.M67 1988
Morris, Charles R.
Iron destinies, lost opportunities: the arms race between the U.S.A. and the U.S.S.R., 1945-1987/ Charles R. Morris. New York: Harper & Row, c1988. xiii, 544 p.
87-045650   355.8/2/0904   0060390824
Defense industries -- United States -- History -- 20th century. Defense industries -- Soviet Union -- History -- 20th century. Military weapons -- History -- 20th century.

UF535.D44.S26 1988
Sanjian, Gregory S., 1952-
Arms transfers to the Third World: probability models of superpower decisionmaking/ Gregory S. Sanjian. Boulder, Colo.: L. Rienner Publishers, 1988. vii, 111 p.
87-015642   382/.456234   1555870856
Arms transfers -- Developing countries -- Decision making -- Mathematical models. Arms transfers -- United States -- Decision making -- Mathematical models. Arms transfers -- Soviet Union -- Decision making -- Mathematical models.

UF535.G3.N48 1995
Neufeld, Michael J., 1951-
The rocket and the reich: Peenemunde and the coming of the ballistic missile era/ Michael J. Neufeld. New York: Free Press, c1995. xiii, 368 p.
94-030088   355.8/25195/094309044   0029228956
Liquid propellant rockets -- Research -- History. Ordnance -- Manufacture -- History -- 20th century. Rockets (Ordnance) -- Research -- History -- 20th century. Peenemunde (Germany) -- History.

UF535.G3.W43 1996
Wegener, Peter P., 1917-
The Peenemunde wind tunnels: a memoir/ Peter P. Wegener. New Haven: Yale University Press, c1996. x, 187 p.
95-050289   623.4/5195/0943   0300063679
Wegener, Peter P., -- 1917-Supersonic wind tunnels -- History. V-2 rocket -- History. World War, 1939-1945 -- Personal narratives, German.

UF535.I7.R44 1989
Reiser, Stewart.
The Israeli arms industry: foreign policy, arms transfers, and military doctrine of a small state/ Stewart Reiser. New York: Holmes & Meier, 1989. xiv, 252 p.
89-002205   338.4/7623/095694   0841910286
Munitions -- Israel.

UF537 Ordnance and small arms — Manufacture — By manufacturer, A-Z

UF537.A44.M38 1989
McWilliams, James P.
Armscor, South Africa's arms merchant/ by James P. McWilliams. London; Brassey's (UK); 1989. xv, 199 p.
89-033880   355.8/2/0968   0080367097
Defense industries -- South Africa.

UF537.K7.K5
Klass, Gert von, 1892-
Krupps; the story of an industrial empire. Translated from the German by James Cleugh. London, Sidgwick and Jackson [1954] 437 p.
55-004768
Krupp family.Munitions -- Germany.

UF543 Arsenals, magazines, armories, etc. — By region or country — United States

UF543.P6.F37 1994
Farley, James J., 1942-
Making arms in the Machine Age: Philadelphia's Frankford Arsenal, 1816-1870/ James J. Farley. University Park, Pa.: Pennsylvania State University Press, c1994. xv, 142 p.
93-019126   338.4/7623442/0974811
0271010002
Frankford Arsenal (Pa.) -- History Frankford (Philadelphia, Pa.) -- History.

UF700 Ordnance material (Ordnance proper) — Ammunition

UF700.H3
Hackley, F. W.
History of modern U.S. military small arms ammunition, by F. W. Hackley, W. H. Woodin [and] E. L. Scranton. Drawings by Eugene L. Scranton. Photos. by Lewis Wayne Walker. New York, Macmillan [1967]-c1978. 2 v.
67-010477   623.4/55
Ammunition.

UF767 Ordnance material (Ordnance proper) — Projectiles — Projectiles for aircraft. Bombs, etc.

UF767.B4
Beaton, Leonard.
The spread of nuclear weapons [by] Leonard Beaton and John Maddox. New York, Praeger for the Institute for Strategic Studies, [1962] 216 p.
62-020275   623.4519
Nuclear weapons.

UF767.D655 1954
Dornberger, Walter, 1895-
V-2; translated by James Cleugh and Geoffrey Halliday. Introduction by Willy Ley. New York, Viking Press, 1954. xviii, 281 p.
54-007830   *623.45 623.45432
World War, 1939-1945 -- Aerial operations, German. V-2 rocket. World War, 1939-1945 -- Germany.

UF767.K25 1960
Kahn, Herman, 1922-
On thermonuclear war.   Princeton, N.J., Princeton University Press, 1960. 651 p.
60-005751   358.39
Nuclear warfare.

UF767.L26
Lapp, Ralph Eugene, 1917-
Must we hide? Cambridge, Mass.: Addison-Wesley Press, 1949. 182 p.
49-002845
Atomic bomb.United States -- Defenses.

UF767.L3 1972
Laurence, William Leonard, 1888-
Dawn over zero; the story of the atomic bomb [by] William L. Laurence. Westport, Conn., Greenwood Press [1972, c1946] xv, 289 p.
71-153156   358/.39   0837160642
Atomic bomb.

UF767.R47
Reynolds, Earle L.
The forbidden voyage. New York, D. McKay Co. [1961] 281 p.
60-013331
Nuclear weapons -- Testing. Passive resistance to government.

UF767.S4 1971
Shepley, James R., 1917-
The hydrogen bomb: the men, the menace, the mechanism, by James R. Shepley and Clay Blair, Jr. Westport, Conn., Greenwood Press [1971, c1954] viii, 244 p.
70-136085   355.02/17   0837152356
Hydrogen bomb.United States -- Military policy.

UF767.T4
Teller, Edward, 1908-
The legacy of Hiroshima, by Edward Teller with Allen Brown. Garden City, N.Y., Doubleday, 1962. 325 p.
62-007686   341.672
Nuclear warfare Nuclear disarmament Radiation United States -- Defenses.

UF767.U6 1946
United States Strategic Bombing Survey.
The effects of atomic bombs on Hiroshima and Nagasaki. Chairman's office, 30 June 1946. Washington, U. S. Govt. print. off., 1946. v, 46 p.
46-026779   623.45
Atomic bomb. World War, 1939-1945 -- Japan -- Hiroshima-shi. World War, 1939-1945 -- Japan -- Nagasaki.

UF860 Military explosives and pyrotechnics — General works

UF860.F3
Faber, Henry Burnell, 1877-1938.
Military pyrotechnics ... by Henry B. Faber. With an historical introduction by Marvin Dana ... Washington, Govt. Print. Off., 1919. 3 v.
20-000007
Military fireworks. Fireworks.

UG23-612 Military engineering

UG23 By region or country — North America — United States

UG23.H6
Hill, Forest Garrett, 1919-
Roads, rails & waterways; the Army engineers and early transportation. Norman, University of Oklahoma Press [1957] 248 p.
57-011195   358.2
Transportation -- United States -- History. United States -- Public works.

UG128 Biography — Individual, A-Z

UG128.G76.L39 1988
Lawren, William.
The general and the bomb: a biography of General Leslie R. Groves, director of the Manhattan Project/ William Lawren. New York: Dodd, Mead, c1988. xii, 324 p.
87-026334   355.8/25119/0924   0396087612
Groves, Leslie R., -- 1896-1970.Generals -- United States -- Biography. Military engineers -- United States -- Biography. Nuclear weapons -- United States -- History.

UG401 Fortification — General works — 1801-

UG401.H66 1977
Hogg, Ian V., 1926-
Fortress: a history of military defence/ Ian V. Hogg. New York: St. Martin's Press, 1977, c1975. 160 p.
76-062774   623/.109
Fortification -- History. Military architecture -- History.

UG405 Fortification — Permanent fortification — General works

UG405.H54 1995
Higham, Robert.
Timber castles/ Robert Higham and Philip Barker. Mechanicsburg, PA: Stackpole Books, 1995. 390 p.
94-019557   355.7/094/0902   081171747X
Timber castles.

UG410 Fortification — Fortifications and defenses. By region or country — United States

UG410.C53 1990
Clary, David A.
Fortress America: the Corps of Engineers, Hampton Roads, and United States coastal defense/ David A. Clary. Charlottesville: University Press of Virginia, 1990. xii, 222 p.
89-016463 358/.22/0973 0813912385
Coast defenses -- United States -- History. Fortification -- Virginia -- Hampton Roads -- History. Fortification -- United States -- History.

UG410.M85 1981
Moore, Jamie W.
The Fortifications Board, 1816-1828, and the definition of national security/ by Jamie W. Moore. Charleston: Citadel, 1981, c1980. 33 p.
81-623581 355.7/0973
Fortification -- United States -- History -- 19th century. National security -- United States.

UG444 Attack and defense. Siege warfare — General works — 1789-

UG444.B83 1992
Bradbury, Jim.
The medieval siege/ Jim Bradbury. Woodbridge, Suffolk, UK; Boydell Press, 1992. xvi, 362 p.
92-013727 355.4/4 0851153127
Siege warfare -- History. Military art and science -- History -- Medieval, 500-1500. Military history, Medieval. Europe -- History, Military.

UG444.R64 1992
Rogers, Randall.
Latin siege warfare in the twelfth century/ R. Rogers. Oxford: Clarendon Press; 1992. xii, 292 p.
92-008978 355.4/4/091822 0198202776
Siege warfare -- History. Military history, Medieval. Mediterranean Region -- History, Military.

UG446.5 Attack and defense. Siege warfare — Tanks, armored cars, etc.

UG446.5.C54 1994
Citino, Robert Michael, 1958-
Armored forces: history and sourcebook/ Robert M. Citino. Westport, Conn.: Greenwood Press, 1994. xii, 308 p.
94-004784 358/.18/0904 0313285004
Armored vehicles, Military -- History. Tanks (Military science) -- History.

UG446.5.F78 1943
Fuller, J. F. C. 1878-1966.
Armored warfare, an annotated edition of Lectures on F. S. R. III(Operations between mechanized forces) by Major-General J. F. C. Fuller ... Foreword by Lt. Col. S. L. A. Marshall ... Harrisburg, Pa., The Military service publishing company, 1943 xix, 189 p.
43-014026 358.1
Mechanization, Military. Military art and science. Strategy.

UG446.5.O5 1960
Ogorkiewicz, Richard M.
Armor; a history of mechanized forces. New York, Praeger [1960] x, 475 p.
60-011276 623.438
Tank warfare. Motorization, Military. Arms and armor.

UG447 Attack and defense. Siege warfare — Chemical warfare. Gas and flame — General works

UG447.B73
Brown, Frederic Joseph.
Chemical warfare; a study in restraints, by Frederic J. Brown. Princeton, N.J., Princeton University Press, 1968. xix, 355 p.
68-020868 350/.895
Chemical warfare.

UG447.C76 1992
Crone, Hugh D.
Banning chemical weapons: the scientific background/ Hugh D. Crone. Cambridge [England]; Cambridge University Press, 1992. viii, 122 p.
92-008882 358/.34 052141699X
Chemical warfare. Chemical arms control.

UG447.R498 1992
Richter, Donald C., 1934-
Chemical soldiers: British gas warfare in World War I/ Donald Richter. Lawrence, Kan.: University Press of Kansas, c1992. x, 282 p.
92-012329 358/.344/0941 0700605444
Gases, Asphyxiating and poisonous -- Great Britain -- War use -- History -- 20th century. World War, 1914-1918 -- Chemical warfare. World War, 1914-1918 -- Regimental histories -- Great Britain.

UG447.T393 1998
Taylor, Eric R.
Lethal mists: an introduction to the natural and military sciences of chemical, biological warfare and terrorism/ by Eric R. Taylor. Commack, N.Y.: Nova Science Publishers, 1998. xxi, 405 p.
98-044334 358/.3 1560724595
Chemical warfare. Biological warfare. Terrorism.

UG447.8 Attack and defense. Siege warfare — Biological warfare. Bacterial warfare

UG447.8.A45 1999
Alibek, Ken.
Biohazard: the chilling true story of the largest covert biological weapons program in the world, told from the inside by the man who ran it/ Ken Alibek with Stephen Handelman. New York: Random House, c1999. xi, 319 p.
98-056454 358/.3882/0947 0375502319
Biological weapons -- Soviet Union.

UG447.8.C65 1987
Cole, Leonard A., 1933-
Clouds of secrecy: the army's germ warfare tests over populated areas/ Leonard A. Cole; foreword by Alan Cranston. Totowa, N.J.: Rowman & Littlefield, 1988. xi, 188 p.
87-012777 358/.38 0847675793
Biological weapons -- United States -- Testing. Biological weapons -- Environmental aspects -- United States.

UG447.8.C6523 1997
Cole, Leonard A., 1933-
The eleventh plague: the politics of biological and chemical warfare/ Leonard A. Cole. New York: W.H. Freeman, c1997. 284 p.
96-024094 327.1/74 0716729504
Biological warfare. Chemical warfare. Biological weapons -- Iraq.

UG447.8.E53 1998
Endicott, Stephen Lyon, 1928-
The United States and biological warfare: secrets from the early cold war and Korea/ Stephen Endicott and Edward Hagerman. Bloomington: Indiana University Press, c1998. xxi, 274 p.
98-029175 358/.38/0973 0253334721
Biological warfare -- United States. Korean War, 1950-1953 -- Biological warfare.

UG447.8.P54 1988
Piller, Charles.
Gene wars: military control over the new genetic technologies/ Charles Piller and Keith R. Yamamoto. New York: Beech Tree Books, c1988. 302 p.
87-030629 358/.38/0973 0688070507
Biological warfare. Chemical warfare. Genetic engineering industry -- Military aspects.

UG447.8.R44 1999
Regis, Edward, 1944-
The biology of doom: the history of America's secret germ warfare project / Ed Regis. New York: Henry Holt, 1999. 259 p.
99-015024 358/.38/0973 0805057641
Biological warfare -- United States.

UG460 Military architecture and building

UG460.H84 1975
Hughes, Quentin.
Military architecture/ Quentin Hughes. New York: St. Martin's Press, 1975, c1974. 256 p.
74-025217 725/.18
Military architecture -- History. Fortification -- History.

UG475 Military surveillance

UG475.J363
Jane's electro-optic systems. Coulsden, Surrey; Jane's Information Group, [c1995-   ]
96-659097 623/.042
Electrooptics -- Military applications -- Periodicals.

UG486.5 Directed-energy weapons

UG486.5.H43 1984
Hecht, Jeff.
Beam weapons: the next arms race/ Jeff Hecht.
New York: Plenum Press, c1984. xi, 363 p.
83-024713   355.8/2595   0306415461
Directed-energy weapons.

UG573 Military signaling — Signal troops. Signal corps, etc. — By region or country

UG573.R35 1996
Raines, Rebecca Robbins, 1952-
Getting the message through: a branch history of the U.S. Army Signal Corps/ by Rebecca Robbins Raines. Washington, D.C.: Center of Military History, U.S. Army, 1996. xix, 464 p.
95-002393   358/.24/0973
United States. Army -- Communication systems -- History.

UG610 Military telegraphy and telephony — Military telephony — General works

UG610.W28
Watson-Watt, Robert Alexander, 1892-1973.
The pulse of radar: the autobiography of Sir Robert Watson-Watt. New York, Dial Press, 1959. 438 p.
58-011430
Radar. Radio, Military. World War, 1939-1945 -- Technology.

UG612 Military telegraphy and telephony — Military radar — General works

UG612.R35 1988
Radar development to 1945/ edited by Russell Burns. London, United Kingdom: Peter Peregrinus on behalf of th e Institution of Electrical Engineers, c1988. 528 p.
89-165613   623/.7348/09   0863411398
Radar -- Military applications -- History. World War, 1939-1945 -- Radar.

UG626.2 Biography — Individual, A-Z

UG626.2.A335.T74 2000
Trest, Warren A.
Air Commando One: Heinie Aderholt and America's secret air wars/ Warren A. Trest. Washington: Smithsonian Institution Press, c2000. xi, 322 p.
99-053643   358.4/0092   156098807X
Aderholt, Harry C.Generals -- United States -- Biography. Special operations (Military science)

UG626.2.C48.B97 1987
Byrd, Martha, 1930-
Chennault: giving wings to the tiger/ Martha Byrd. Tuscaloosa: University of Alabama Press, c1987. xvii, 451 p.
86-019238   358.4/1332/0924   0817303227
Chennault, Claire Lee, -- 1893-1958.Generals -- United States -- Biography.

UG626.2.C7.A37
Craig, Howard A.
Sunward I've climbed: a personal narrative of peace and war/ by Howard A. Craig. El Paso: Texas Western Press, 1975. x, 171 p.
74-080106   358.4/13/310924   0874040493
Craig, Howard A.

UG626.2.C86.A35
Cunningham, Alfred Austell.
Marine flyer in France: the diary of Captain Alfred A. Cunningham, November 1917-January 1918/ edited by Graham A. Cosmas. Washington: History and Museums Division, Headquarters, U.S. 1974. vii, 43 p.
75-601057   940.4/81/73
Cunningham, Alfred Austell -- Diaries.Air pilots, Military -- United States -- Diaries. World War, 1914-1918 -- Aerial operations, American. Air pilots, Military -- France -- Diaries.

UG626.2.D37.A3 1991
Davis, Benjamin O. 1912-
Benjamin O. Davis, Jr., American: an autobiography. Washington: Smithsonian Institution Press, c1991. x, 442 p.
90-009905   358.4/0092   0874747422
Davis, Benjamin O. -- (Benjamin Oliver), -- 1912-Generals -- United States -- Biography.

UG626.2.S66.D38 1993
Davis, Richard G.
Carl A. Spaatz and the air war in Europe/ Richard G. Davis. Washington, D.C.: Center for Air Force History: 1993. xxii, 808 p.
92-014889   358.4/0092   0912799757
Spaatz, Carl, -- 1891-1974.Generals -- United States -- Biography. Aeronautics, Military -- United States -- History. World War, 1939-1945 -- Aerial operations, American.

UG628 Dictionaries. Encyclopedias

UG628.T39 1988
Taylor, Michael John Haddrick.
Encyclopedia of the world's air forces/ Michael J.H. Taylor. New York, N.Y.: Facts on File, 1988. 211 p.
88-006970   358.4/003/21   0816020043
Air forces -- Encyclopedias.

UG630 General works

UG630.B2
Baar, James, 1929-
Spacecraft and missiles of the world, 1962 [by] James Baar and William E. Howard. New York, Harcourt, Brace & World [1962] v, 117 p.
62-009434   623.4519
Rocketry. Guided missiles. Space vehicles.

UG630.B774 1999
Buckley, John (John D.)
Air power in the age of total war/ John Buckley. Bloomington, Ind.: Indiana University Press, c1999. ix, 260 p.
98-048197   358.4/009   0253335574
Air power -- History. Air warfare -- History.

UG630.E5
Emme, Eugene Morlock.
The impact of air power; national security and world politics. Princeton, N. J. Van Nostrand [1959] xiv, 914 p.
59-008654   358.4082
Air power. Military policy. World politics. United States -- Military policy.

UG630.F55 1990
Flintham, Victor.
Air wars and aircraft: a detailed record of air combat, 1945 to the present/ Victor Flintham. New York: Facts on File, c1990. 415 p.
89-023382   358.4/009   0816023565
Air warfare -- History. Military history, Modern -- 20th century.

UG630.F66 1995
Francillon, Rene J.
The Naval Institute guide to world military aviation, 1995/ Rene J. Francillon. Annapolis, Md.: Naval Institute Press, c1995. xviii, 745 p.
94-017059   358.4/009/049   1557502528
Air forces. Airplanes, Military.

UG630.G578 1962a
Golovine, Michael N., 1903-
Conflict in space; a pattern of war in a new dimension. New York, St. Martin's Press [1962] xiv, 146 p.
62-018725   355.4
Astronautics, Military. World politics -- 1955-1965.

UG630.G79 1958a
Green, William.
The air forces of the world, their history, development, and present strength [by] William Green and John Fricker. New York, Hanover House [1958] 336 p.
59-000286   358.4
Aeronautics, Military. Aeroplanes, Military.

UG630.J26
Janis, Irving Lester, 1918-
Air war and emotional stress; psychological studies of bombing and civilian defense. The Rand Corporation. New York, McGraw-Hill, 1951. ix, 280 p.
51-013330   355.23
Air warfare -- Psychological aspects. Civil defense. Civil Defense

UG630.L4
Lee, Asher.
Air power. New York, Praeger [1955] 200 p.
55-011958   358.4*
World War, 1939-1945 -- Aerial operations. Air warfare. Air power.

UG630.N44 1961
Newell, Homer Edward, 1915-
Guide to rockets, missiles, and satellites. Diagrams by Anne Marie Fauss. New York, Whittlesey House [1961] 95 p.
61-017343   623.4519
Rockets (Aeronautics) Guided missiles. Ballistics missiles.

UG630.P263
Parson, Nels A.
Missiles and the revolution in warfare. Cambridge, Harvard University Press, 1962. x, 245 p.
62-019221   623.4519
Guided missiles.

UG633 By region or country — United States — General works

UG633.A3763
United States.
Transportation and travel: [Washington] Dept. of the Army.
76-649823   358.4
United States -- Distances, etc. North America -- Distances, etc.

UG633.A3763 no. 127-101
United States.
Industrial safety accident prevention handbook. [Washington] 1970. 1 v.
70-608116   614.85
Industrial safety. Accidents -- Prevention.

UG633.A3763 no. 163-2
United States.
The veterinary technician. [Washington, For sale by the Supt. of Docs., U.S. Govt. Print, 1968. 1 v.
68-062424   614/.31
Food adulteration and inspection. Veterinary service, Military.

UG633.B418
Bergaust, Erik.
Rocket City, U.S.A.: from Huntsville, Alabama to the moon. New York: Macmillan, c1963. 216 p.
63-011780   629.4
Astronautics. Astronautics -- United States. Huntsville (Ala.)

UG633.B682 1996
Borgiasz, William S.
The Strategic Air Command: evolution and consolidation of nuclear forces, 1945-1955/ William S. Borgiasz. Westport, Conn.: Praeger, 1996. xiii, 158 p.
95-022014   358.4/2/0973   0275948617
United States. Air Force. Strategic Air Command -- History. United States. Air Force. Strategic Air Command Operational readiness.

UG633.B75 1992
Historical dictionary of the U.S. Air Force/ edited by Charles D. Bright; Robin Higham, advisory editor. New York: Greenwood Press, 1992. xix, 713 p.
91-025461   358.4/00973   0313259283
United States. Air Force -- History -- Dictionaries.

UG633.B79 1994
Builder, Carl H.
The Icarus syndrome: the role of air power theory in the evolution and fate of the U.S. Air Force/ Carl H. Builder. New Brunswick, N.J., U.S.A.: Transaction Publishers, c1994. xxii, 299 p.
93-031554   358.4/03   1560001410
Air power -- United States.

UG633.B84 1962
Burgess, Eric.
Long-range ballistic missiles. New York, Macmillan [1962, c1961] 255 p.
61-017856   623.4519
Ballistic missiles.

UG633.C14
Caidin, Martin, 1927-
Air force; a pictorial history of American airpower, by Martin Caidin, in cooperation with the U.S. Air Force. New York, Rinehart [1957] 232 p.
57-006575   358.4
Aeronautics, Military -- United States -- History. Air power -- United States -- History.

UG633.C49
Chapman, John L., 1920-
Atlas: the story of a missile. New York, Harper [c1960] 190 p.
59-013294   623.4519
Atlas (Missile)

UG633.D44
De Seversky, Alexander P. 1894-1974.
Air power: key to survival. New York, Simon and Schuster, 1950. xxiv, 376 p.
50-014963   358.4
Air warfare. Air defenses -- United States.

UG633.E85
Everest, Frank Kendall, 1920-
The fastest man alive/ by Frank K. Everest, Jr. as told to John Guenther. New York: Dutton, 1958. 252 p.
57-005998   926.2913
Aviation

UG633.G6
Goldberg, Alfred, 1918-
A history of the United States Air Force, 1907-1957, by Alfred Goldberg, editor, Wilhelmine Burch [and others] Princeton, N.J., Van Nostrand [1957] 277 p.
57-014552   358.4
United States. Air Force -- History.

UG633.H6 1971
Holley, I. B. 1919-
Ideas and weapons: exploitation of the aerial weapon by the United States durin' World War I; a study in the relationship of .echnological advance, military doctrine, and the development of weapons, by I. B. Holley, Jr. Hamden, Conn., Archon Books, 1971 [c1953] xii, 222 p.
79-122410   358.4/00973   0208010904
Aeronautics, Military -- United States. World War, 1914-1918 -- Aerial operations, American.

UG633.H8
Hubler, Richard Gibson.
SAC, the Strategic Air Command. Duell, 1958.
58-006771   358.4
U.S. Air Force. Strategic Air Command. Air warfare. United States -- Defenses.

UG633.H83
Hunter, Mel.
Strategic Air Command. Garden City, N. Y., Doubleday, c1961. 192 p.
61-007655
United States. Air Force. Strategic Air Command.

UG633.K43 1982
Kelsey, Benjamin S., d. 1981.
The dragon's teeth?: the creation of United States air power for World War II/ Benjamin S. Kelsey. Washington, D.C.: Smithsonian Institution Press, 1982. 148 p.
82-600279   358.4/00973   0874745748
United States. Army. Air Corps -- History.

UG633.K54
Klass, Philip J.
Secret sentries in space, by Philip J. Klass. New York, Random House [1971] xvi, 236 p.
77-143994   358.8   0394469720
Astronautics, Military -- United States. Astronautics, Military -- Soviet Union. Earth -- Photographs from space.

UG633.L26 2000
Lambeth, Benjamin S.
The transformation of American air power/ Benjamin S. Lambeth. Ithaca, N.Y.: Cornell University Press, 2000. xiii, 337 p.
00-009529   358.4/00973   0801438160
Air power -- United States.United States -- History, Military -- 20th century.

UG633.M325
Medaris, John B., 1902-
Countdown for decision [by] John B. Medaris, with Arthur Gordon. New York, Putnam [1960] 303 p.
60-013671   623.7
Astronautics -- United States. Astronautics, Military -- United States. United States -- Military policy.

UG633.M45.B8
Burlingame, Roger, 1889-1967.
General Billy Mitchell, champion of air defense. New York, McGraw-Hill [1952] 212 p.
52-012689
Mitchell, William, -- 1879-1936.

UG633.M45.H8
Hurley, Alfred F.
Billy Mitchell: crusader for air power, by Alfred F. Hurley. New York, F. Watts [1964] x, 180 p.
64-011917   923.573
Mitchell, William, -- 1879-1936.

UG633.R378 2000
Redmond, Kent C., 1914-
From whirlwind to MITRE: the R&D story of the SAGE air defense computer/ Kent C. Redmond and Thomas M. Smith. Cambridge, Mass.: MIT Press, 2000. vii, 535 p.
00-029228   355.4/5/0973   0262182017
SAGE (Air defense system) -- History. Military research -- United States -- History.

UG633.S68 1998
Sources of conflict in the 21st century: regional futures and U.S. strategy/ edited by Zalmay M. Khalilzad and Ian O. Lesser. Santa Monica, CA: Rand, 1998. xiii, 336 p.
97-041831   358.4/03/0973   0833025295
Air defenses -- United States. World politics -- 1989- -- Forecasting.

UG633.S77
Steinbeck, John, 1902-1968.
Bombs away; the story of a bomber team, written for the United States Army Air Forces by John Steinbeck, with 60 photographs by John Swope. New York, The Viking Press, 1942. 184 p.
42-036406   358.4
United States. Army. Air Corps.

UG633.U46 1991
Underwood, Jeffery S., 1954-
The wings of democracy: the influence of air power on the Roosevelt Administration, 1933-1941/ Jeffery S. Underwood. College Station: Texas A & M University Press, c1991. 234 p.
91-015653 358.4/13/0973 0890963886
Air power -- United States -- History.

UG633.U624 1992
United States Air Force: a dictionary/ edited by Bruce W. Watson, Susan M. Watson. New York: Garland Pub., 1992. xxx, 861 p.
91-042269 358.4/00973 082405539X
Aeronautics, Military -- United States -- Dictionaries. Aeronautics, Military -- United States -- Acronyms.

UG635 By region or country — Other regions or countries, A-Z

UG635.C2.W57
Wise, S. F. 1924-
The official history of the Royal Canadian Air Force/ S.F. Wise. [Toronto]: University of Toronto Press in co-operation with the Dept. of National Defence and the [c1980-]
81-122577 358.4/00971 0802023797
World War, 1914-1918 -- Aerial operations, Canadian. Canada. Royal Canadian Air Force -- History -- World War, 1914-1918.

UG635.G3.C68 1997
Corum, James S.
The Luftwaffe: creating the operational air war, 1918-1940/ James S. Corum. Lawrence: University Press of Kansas, c1997. ix, 378 p.
97-006943 358.4/00943 0700608362
Maneuver warfare -- History -- 20th century. Air power -- Germany -- History. Aeronautics, Military -- Germany -- History.

UG635.G3.C6823 1997
Corum, James S.
The Luftwaffe's way of war: German air force doctrine, 1911-1945/ James S. Corum & Richard R. Muller. Baltimore, Md.: The Nautical & Aviation Publishing, 1997.
97-011252 358.4/00943 187785347X
Air power -- Germany -- History. Military doctrine -- Germany -- History -- 20th century.

UG635.G3.H8
Huzel, Dieter K.
Peenemunde to Canaveral. With an introd. by Werner von Braun. Englewood Cliffs, Prentice-Hall [1962] 247 p.
62-014015 926.23
Huzel, Dieter K. World War, 1939-1945 -- Personal narratives, German. Rocketry -- History. V-2 rocket.

UG635.G7.D75 1997
Driver, Hugh, 1961-
The birth of military aviation: Britain, 1903-1914/ Hugh Driver. Suffolk, UK; Boydell Press, 1997. 356 p.
97-004456 358.4/00941 086193234X
Aeronautics, Military -- Great Britain -- History. Military-industrial complex -- Great Britain -- History.

UG635.G7.G54 1989
Gollin, A. M.
The impact of air power on the British people and their government, 1909-1914/ Alfred Gollin. Stanford, Calif.: Stanford University Press, 1989. xii, 354 p.
88-063914 358.4/03/0941 0804715912
Air power -- Great Britain -- History. Great Britain -- Military policy. Great Britain -- History, Military -- 20th century.

UG635.G7.H483 1998
Higham, Robin D. S.
Bases of air strategy: building airfields for the RAF, 1914-1945/ Robin Higham. Shrewsbury, England: Airlife, 1998. 285 p.
00-302300   358.4/17/0917124109041
1840370092
Air bases, British -- Design and construction.

UG635.G7.R63 1995
Robertson, Scot.
The development of RAF strategic bombing doctrine, 1919-1939/ Scot Robertson. Westport, Conn.: Praeger, 1995. xxix, 187 p.
94-022654 358.4/03/0941 0275949974
Bombing, Aerial -- Great Britain. Air power -- Great Britain -- History. Great Britain -- Military policy.

UG635.R9.L42
Lee, Asher.
The Soviet air and rocket forces. New York, Praeger [1959] 311 p.
59-007394 358.40947
Aeronautics, Military -- Soviet Union. Air power -- Soviet Union.

UG635.R9.S596 1978
Soviet aviation and air power: a historical view/ edited by Robin Higham and Jacob W. Kipp. London: Brassey's; 1978. xii, 328 p.
76-030815 358.4/00947 0891581162
Aeronautics, Military -- Soviet Union -- History. Aeronautics -- Soviet Union -- History. Air power -- Soviet Union.

UG700 Tactics — By region or country

UG700.H35 1989
Hallion, Richard.
Strike from the sky: the history of battlefield air attack, 1911-1945/ Richard P. Hallion. Washington: Smithsonian Institution Press, c1989. xx, 323 p.
89-032009 358.4/142 0874744520
Close air support -- History. Air interdiction -- History.

UG700.K46 1982
Kennett, Lee B.
A history of strategic bombing/ Lee Kennett. New York: Scribner, c1982. x, 222 p.
82-010673 358.4/14/09 0684177811
Bombing, Aerial -- History. World War, 1939-1945 -- Aerial operations.

UG730 Air defenses — General works

UG730.S63 1987
Space weapons and international security/ edited by Bhupendra Jasani. Oxford [Oxfordshire]; Oxford University Press, 1987. xvi, 366 p.
86-016387 358/.1754 0198291027
Ballistic missile defenses. Space weapons. Nuclear warfare.

UG730.S77 1989
Strategic air defense/ edited by Stephen J. Cimbala. Wilmington, Del.: SR Books, 1989. xix, 275 p.
88-026019 358.4/145 0842022856
Air defenses. Strategic forces.

UG740 Ballistic missile defenses — General works

UG740.B35 1984
Ballistic missile defense/ Ashton B. Carter and David N. Schwartz, editors. Washington, D.C.: Brookings Institution, c1984. xiii, 455 p.
83-024064 358.17 0815713126
Ballistic missile defenses. Ballistic missile defenses -- United States. Ballistic missile defenses -- Soviet Union.

UG740.D87 1988
Durch, William J.
The ABM Treaty and Western security/ William J. Durch. Cambridge, Mass.: Ballinger Pub. Co., c1988. xiii, 161 p.
87-026978 358/.1754 0887302645
Ballistic missile defenses. Nuclear arms control. National security -- Europe.

UG743 Ballistic missile defenses — By region or country — United States

UG743.B42 1992
Baucom, Donald R.
The origins of SDI, 1944-1983/ Donald R. Baucom. Lawrence, Kan.: University Press of Kansas, c1992. xix, 276 p.
92-005922 359.1/74/09 0700605312
Strategic Defense Initiative -- History.

UG743.C63 1988
Codevilla, Angelo, 1943-
While others build: the commonsense approach to the Strategic Defense Initiative/ Angelo Codevilla. New York: Free Press; c1988. xii, 256 p.
87-035661 358/.1754 0029056713
Strategic Defense Initiative.

UG743.D86 1997
Dunn, David H.
The politics of threat: Minuteman vulnerability in American national security policy/ David H. Dunn; foreword by Lawrence Freedman. Houndmills, Basingstoke, Hampshire: Macmillan Press; 1997. xii, 289 p.
97-013669 358.1/7/0973 0312176112
Ballistic missile defenses -- United States -- Combat survivability -- History. First strike (Nuclear strategy) Minuteman (Missile) Soviet Union -- Military policy.

UG743.L33 1989
Lakoff, Sanford A.
A shield in space?: technology, politics, and the strategic defense initiative: how the Reagan Administration set out to make nuclear weapons "impotent and obsolete" and succumbed to the fallacy o Sanford Lakoff and Herbert F. York. Berkeley: University of California Press, c1989. xv, 409 p.
89-004888   358/.1754   0520066502
Strategic Defense Initiative. Nuclear arms control.

UG743.M55 1987
Mikheev, Dmitrii, 1941-
The Soviet perspective on the Strategic Defense Initiative/ Dmitry Mikheyev. Washington: Pergamon-Brassey's International Defense Publishers, 1987. xii, 95 p.
87-002313   358/.1754/0947   0080357482
Strategic Defense Initiative.Soviet Union -- Military policy. Soviet Union -- Military relations -- United States. United States -- Military relations -- Soviet Union.

UG743.M56 1989
Milton, A. F. 1940-
Making space defense work: must the superpowers cooperate?/ A. Fenner Milton, M. Scott Davis & John A. Parmentola. Washington: Published with the cooperatiohn of the Roosevelt Center for American Policy Studies [by] Pergamon-Brassey's, 1989. xiii, 209 p.
88-017871   358/.1754   0080359809
Strategic Defense Initiative. Ballistic missile defenses. Nuclear arms control. United States -- Military relations -- Soviet Union. Soviet Union -- Military relations -- United States.

UG743.M58 2000
Mitchell, Gordon R., 1967-
Strategic deception: rhetoric, science, and politics in missile defense advocacy/ Gordon R. Mitchell. East Lansing: Michigan State University Press, c2000. xix, 390 p.
00-008705   358.1/74/097309045   0870135570
Ballistic missile defenses -- United States. Rhetoric -- Political aspects -- United States. United States -- Politics and government -- 1945-1989. United States -- Politics and government -- 1989- United States -- Armed Forces -- Appropriations and expenditures.

UG743.R44 1992
Reiss, Edward.
The strategic defense initiative/ Edward Reiss. Cambridge [England]; Cambridge University Press, 1992. xiv, 249 p.
91-029650   358.1/74/09   0521410975
Strategic Defense Initiative -- History. Arms race -- United States. United States -- Military policy.

UG743.S37 1988
SDI: technology, survivability, and software/ Congress of the United States, Office of Technology Assessment. Washington, D.C.: U.S. G.P.O.: [1988] viii, 281 p.
87-619857   358.1/754
Strategic Defense Initiative. Strategic Defense Initiative -- Data processing. Ballistic missile defenses -- Combat survivability.

UG743.S73 1987
Star Wars and European defence: implications for Europe: perceptions and assessments/ edited by Hans Gunter Brauch; foreword by Denis Healey; preface by Raymond L. Garthoff. New York: St. Martin's Press, 1987. li, 599 p.
85-019593   358/.1754   0312307861
Strategic Defense Initiative. Ballistic missile defenses -- Europe.

UG743.S735 1988
Star Wars: the economic fallout/ Council on Economic Priorities; Rosy Nimroody, senior project director; foreword by Paul C. Warnke. Cambridge, Mass.: Ballinger Pub. Co., c1988. xxiii, 234 p.
87-022463   358/.1754   0887301622
Strategic Defense Initiative -- Economic aspects.

UG743.S773 1987
The Strategic Defense Initiative: its implications for Asia and the Pacific/ edited by Jae Kyu Park and Byung-Joon Ahn. Boulder: Westview Press; 1987. xii, 274 p.
87-021605   358/.1754   0813305918
Strategic Defense Initiative -- Congresses.East Asia -- Military relations -- United States -- Congresses. Pacific Area -- Military relations -- United States -- Congresses. United States -- Military relations -- East Asia -- Congresses.

UG743.S775 1987
The Strategic defense initiative: shield or snare?/ edited by Harold Brown. Boulder: Westview Press, 1987. xii, 297 p.
87-021314   358/.1754   0813304695
Strategic Defense Initiative.

UG743.S7767 1988
Strategic defenses and arms control/ edited by Alvin M. Weinberg, Jack N. Barkenbus. New York: Paragon House Publishers, c1988. viii, 263 p.
87-002280   358/.17/0973   0887022189
Strategic Defense Initiative. Ballistic missile defenses. Civil defense.

UG743.W35 1988
Waldman, Harry.
The dictionary of SDI/ by Harry Waldman; illustrations by Douglas Holdaway. Wilmington, Del.: Scholarly Resources, 1988. x, 182 p.
87-012477   358/.1754/0321   0842022813
Strategic Defense Initiative -- Dictionaries.

UG743.W355 1987
Waller, Douglas C.
The Strategic Defense Initiative, progress and challenges: a guide to issues and references/ Douglas C. Waller, James T. Bruce, Douglas M. Cook. Claremont, Calif.: Regina Books, c1987. xi, 172 p.
87-014820   358/.1754   0941690245
Strategic Defense Initiative.

UG745 Ballistic missile defenses — By region or country — Other regions or countries, A-Z

UG745.S65.Y67 1988
Yost, David S. 1948-
Soviet ballistic missile defense and the Western alliance/ David S. Yost. Cambridge, Mass.: Harvard University Press, 1988. xii, 405 p.
88-002674   358/.1754/0947   0674826108
Ballistic missile defenses -- Soviet Union.Europe -- Military policy. Soviet Union -- Military policy. United States -- Military policy.

UG765 Aerial reconnaissance — By region or country — Other regions or countries, A-Z

UG765.I72.S63 2000
Snook, Scott A., 1958-
Friendly fire: the accidental shootdown of U.S. Black Hawks over Northern Iraq/ Scott A. Snook. Princeton, N.J.: Princeton University Press, c2000. xvii, 257 p.
99-041097   355.4/22   0691005060
Black Hawk (Military transport helicopter) -- Accidents -- Investigation. Friendly fire (Military science) -- Iraq. Organizational behavior -- Case studies.

UG834 Organization. Personnel management — Minorities, women, etc. in air forces — United States

UG834.A37.H64 2001
Homan, Lynn M.
Black knights: the story of the Tuskegee airmen/ by Lynn M. Homan and Thomas Reilly; foreword by Louis R. Purnell. Gretna, La.: Pelican Pub. Co., 2001. 336 p.
00-047850   940.54/4973   1565548280
Air pilots, Military -- United States -- History -- Pictorial works. Air pilots, Military -- Alabama -- Tuskegee -- History -- Pictorial works. Tuskegee Army Air Field (Ala.) -- Pictorial works.

UG834.A37.S36 1994
Scott, Lawrence P.
Double V: the civil rights struggle of the Tuskegee Airmen/ Lawrence P. Scott, William M. Womack, Sr. East Lansing: Michigan State University Press, 1994. 322 p.
94-020704   940.54/4973   0870133470
Air pilots, Military -- United States -- History. World War, 1939-1945 -- Participation, Afro-American. World War, 1914-1918 -- Participation, Afro-American.

UG1123-1125 Equipment and supplies — Procurement and contracts — By region or country

UG1123.B76 1991
Brown, Michael E. 1954-
Flying blind: the politics of the U.S. strategic bomber program/ Michael E. Brown. Ithaca: Cornell University Press, 1992. xvii, 358 p.
91-055064   358.4/283/00973   080142285X
Strategic bombers -- United States -- History.United States -- Military policy.

UG1125.E87.T47 1988
Tessmer, Arnold Lee.
Politics of compromise: NATO and AWACS/ Arnold Lee Tessmer. Washington, DC: National Defense University Press: 1988. xviii, 212 p.
88-017584   358.4/5
Electronic warfare aircraft -- Europe. Airborne warning and control systems.

UG1240-1243 Equipment and supplies — Operational — Airplanes

UG1240.C485 1983
Chant, Christopher.
Warplanes/ Christopher Chant. London: M. Joseph, 1983. 192 p.
84-131136   358.4/183/09   0718121805
Airplanes, Military -- History.

UG1240.F74 1999
Fredriksen, John C.
Warbirds: an illustrated guide to U.S. military aircraft, 1915-2000/ John C. Fredriksen. Santa Barbara, CA: ABC-CLIO, 1999. xiv, 363 p.
99-016624   623.7/46/0973   1576071316
Airplanes, Military -- United States. Aircraft industry -- United States.

UG1240.G74 1982
Green, William, 1927-
Observer's directory of military aircraft/ William Green, Gordon Swanborough. London: F. Warne, c1982. 256 p.
89-162462   623.7/46   0723227969
Airplanes, Military.

UG1240.H35 1984
Hallion, Richard.
Rise of the fighter aircraft, 1914-18/ Richard P. Hallion; foreword by Jay W. Hubbard. Annapolis, MD: Nautical & Aviation Pub. Co. of America, [1984] vi, 200 p.
83-026947   358.4/3/09   0933852428
Airplanes, Military -- History. Fighter planes -- History. World War, 1914-1918 -- Aerial operations.

UG1240.S532 2001
Sharpe, Mike, 1970-
Aircraft of World War II/ Mike Sharpe. Osceola, WI: MBI Pub. Co., 2000. 96 p.
00-060086   940.54/4   0760309345
Airplanes, Military. World War, 1939-1945 -- Aerial operations.

UG1242.B6.K69 1988
Kotz, Nick.
Wild blue yonder: money, politics, and the B-1 bomber/ Nick Kotz. New York: Pantheon Books, c1988. ix, 313 p.
87-043057   358.4/2   039455700X
B-1 bomber.

UG1242.F5.E873 1994
Ethell, Jeffrey L.
World War II fighting jets/ Jeffrey Ethell & Alfred Price. Annapolis, Md.: Naval Institute Press, c1994. 211 p.
94-065971   358.4/3/09044   1557509409
Jet planes, Military. Fighter planes. World War, 1939-1945 -- Aerial operations.

UG1243.K53
Knaack, Marcelle Size, 1921-
Encyclopedia of US Air Force aircraft and missile systems/ by Marcelle Size Knaack. Washington: Office of Air Force History 1978-1988 v. 1-2
77-022377   358.4/3
Guided missiles -- United States. Airplanes, Military -- United States.

UG1243.S9 1989
Swanborough, Gordon.
United States military aircraft since 1909/ Gordon Swanborough, Peter M. Bowers. Washington, D.C.: Smithsonian Institution Press, 1989. ix, 766 p.
89-060429   358.4/13/0973   0874748801
Airplanes, Military -- United States -- History.

UG1282 Equipment and supplies — Operational — Bombs

UG1282.A8.A76 2001
Arnold, Lorna.
Britain and the H-bomb/ Lorna Arnold, with Katherine Pyne; foreword by Lawrence Freedman. New York: St. Martin's Press, c2001. xiv, 273 p.
00-036898   355.8/25119/0941   0312235186
Hydrogen bomb -- Great Britain.Great Britain -- Military policy.

UG1282.A8.R46 1995
Rhodes, Richard.
Dark sun: the making of the hydrogen bomb/ Richard Rhodes. New York: Simon & Schuster, c1995. 731 p.
95-011070   623.4/5119   068480400X
Hydrogen bomb -- History.

UG1312-1315 Equipment and supplies — Operational — Missiles and rockets

UG1312.A6.W47 1999
Westrum, Ron, 1945-
Sidewinder: creative missile development at China Lake/ Ron Westrum. Annapolis, Md.: Naval Institute Press, c1999. xvi, 331 p.
99-027338   623.4/5191/0973   1557509514
Sidewinder (Missile) -- Design and construction.

UG1312.B34.M33 1990
Mackenzie, Donald A.
Inventing accuracy: an historical sociology of nuclear missile guidance/ Donald MacKenzie. Cambridge, Mass.: MIT Press, c1990. xiii, 464 p.
90-005915   358/.174   0262132583
Ballistic missiles -- United States -- Guidance systems -- History. Nuclear weapons -- United States -- History. Nuclear warfare. United States -- Military policy.

UG1312.C7.C37 1992
Carus, W. Seth.
Cruise missile proliferation in the 1990s/ W. Seth Carus; foreword by Janne E. Nolan. Westport, Conn.: Praeger, 1992. xvi, 176 p.
92-026115   358.1/754   0275945197
Cruise missiles. Arms control.

UG1312.I2 S78 2000
Stumpf, David K., 1953-
Titan II: a history of a Cold War missile program/ David K. Stumpf; with a foreword by Jay W. Kelley. Fayetteville: University of Arkansas Press, 2000. xxii, 320 p.
00-026881   358.1/754/0973   1557286019
Titan (Missile) -- History.

UG1315.A8.M67 1989
Morton, Peter.
Fire across the desert: Woomera and the Anglo-Australian Joint Project, 1946-1980/ Peter Morton. Canberra: Australian Govt. Pub. Service, 1989. xx, 575 p.
90-151251   358.1/7182/07209423   0644060689
Guided missiles -- Research -- Australia -- Woomera (S. Aust.) Rockets (Ordnance) -- Research -- Australia -- Woomera (S. Aust.)

UG1520 General works

UG1520.B76 1990
Brown, Neville.
New strategy through space/ Neville Brown. Leicester [England]; Leicester University Press, 1990. xi, 295 p.
89-029586   358.8   0718512790
Astronautics, Military. Astronautics, Military -- United States. Strategy. United States -- Military policy.

UG1520.M55 1987
The Militarisation of space/ edited by Stephen Kirby and Gordon Robson. Brighton, Sussex: Wheatsheaf Books; 1987. xiv, 253 p.
87-025064   358/.8   074500346X
Astronautics, Military.

UG1523 By region or country — United States

UG1523.G69 1991
Grabbe, Crockett L.
Space weapons and the strategic defense initiative/ Crockett L. Grabbe. Ames: Iowa State University Press, 1991. xii, 252 p.
90-028897   358/.8/0973   0813812771
Astronautics, Military -- United States. Space warfare. Strategic Defense Initiative.

UG1523.P44 1997
Peebles, Curtis.
The Corona project: America's first spy satellites/ Curtis Peebles. Annapolis, Md.: Naval Institute Press, c1997. xii, 351 p.
97-012272   327.1273   1557506884
Space surveillance -- United States -- History.

UG1523.R53 1990
Richelson, Jeffrey.
America's secret eyes in space: the U.S. keyhole spy satellite program/ Jeffrey T. Richelson. New York: Harper & Row, c1990. viii, 375 p.
89-026698   358.8/0973   0887302858
Space surveillance -- United States -- History.

UG1523.S83 1985
Stares, Paul B.
The militarization of space: U.S. policy, 1945-1984/ Paul B. Stares. Ithaca, N.Y.: Cornell University Press, 1985. 334 p.
85-047501   358.4/03/0973   0801418100
Astronautics, Military -- United States -- History. United States -- Military policy.

UG1525 By region or country — Other regions or countries, A-Z

UG1525.E85.M3497 1997
McLean, Alasdair W. M.
Europe's final frontier: the search for security through space/ Alasdair McLean and Fraser Lovie. Commack, N.Y.: Nova Science Publishers, c1997. 259 p.
97-034374   358/.8/094   1560724625
Astronautics, Military -- Europe, Western. National security -- Europe.

UG1530 Space warfare. Interplanetary warfare

UG1530.S44 1987
Seeking stability in space: anti-satellite weapons and the evolving space regime/ editors, Joseph S. Nye, Jr. and James A. Schear; contributors, Ashton B. Carter ... [et al.]. [Queenstown, Md.]: Aspen Strategy Group; c1987. xvii, 167 p.
87-021619   358/.1754   0819164216
Anti-satellite weapons -- Congresses. Space warfare -- Congresses. Arms control -- Congresses. United States -- Military policy -- Congresses.

UH Other services

UH23 Chaplains. Chaplain's assistants. Chapel managers — By region or country — United States

UH23.S56 1999
Slomovitz, Albert Isaac.
The fighting rabbis: Jewish military chaplains and American history/ Albert Isaac Slomovitz. New York: New York University Press, c1999. xiii, 171 p.
98-058003   355.3/47/0973   0814780989
Chaplains, Military -- Judaism -- History. Chaplains, Military -- United States -- History. Rabbis -- United States -- History.

UH223 Medical and sanitary service — History, statistics, etc. — By region or country

UH223.G544 1995
Gillett, Mary C.
The Army Medical Department, 1865-1917/ by Mary C. Gillett. Washington, D.C.: Center of Military History, U.S. Army: 1995. xiv, 517 p.
94-013147   355.3/45/0973
Medicine, Military -- United States -- History - - 19th century. Medicine, Military -- United States -- History -- 20th century. World War, 1914-1918 -- Medical care.

UH493-495 Medical and sanitary service — Nurses and nursing — By region or country

UH493.S27 1999
Sarnecky, Mary T.
A history of the U.S. Army Nurse Corps/ Mary T. Sarnecky. Philadelphia: University of Pennsylvania Press, c1999. xiv, 518 p.
99-012751   355.3/45   0812235029
Military nursing -- United States -- History.

UH495.G7.S86 1988
Summers, Anne, 1944-
Angels and citizens: British women as military nurses, 1854-1914/ Anne Summers. London; Routledge & Kegan Paul, 1988. xii, 371 p.
87-020522   355.3/45/0941   0710214790
Military nursing -- Great Britain -- History -- 19th century. Military nursing -- Great Britain -- History -- 20th century. Women and war -- Great Britain -- History -- 19th century.

UH500 Medical and sanitary service — Transportation. Ambulances — General works

UH500.H35 1992
Haller, John S.
Farmcarts to Fords: a history of the military ambulance, 1790-1925/ John S. Haller, Jr. Carbondale: Southern Illinois University Press, c1992. xii, 269 p.
92-003772   355.3/45   0809318172
Transport of sick and wounded -- History. Transportation, Military -- History. Ambulances -- History.

UH537 Care of sick and wounded. Relief societies — Red Cross Association — National associations. By region or country, A-Z

UH537.J3.C49 1994
Checkland, Olive.
Humanitarianism and the Emperor's Japan, 1877-1977/ Olive Checkland. New York, NY: St. Martin's Press, 1994. xxxi, 258 p.
93-026984   361.7/634/0952   0312102585
Red Cross -- Japan -- History.

UH629.3 Military hygiene and sanitation — Mental hygiene, psychiatry, etc. — By region or country

UH629.3.G5
Ginzberg, Eli, 1911-
Psychiatry and military manpower policy, a reappraisal of the experience in World War II, by Eli Ginzberg, John L. Herma, and Sol W. Ginsburg. New York, King's Crown Press, 1953. xi, 66 p.
53-012344   355.22
Military Psychiatary -- United States -- World War, 1939-1945. Military psychiatry. Soldiers -- United States -- World War, 1939-1945. United States -- Armed Forces -- Recruiting, enlistment, etc.

UH630 Protection of morals and health

UH630.B75 1996
Bristow, Nancy K., 1958-
Making men moral: social engineering during the Great War/ Nancy K. Bristow. New York: New York University Press, c1996. xxiv, 298 p.
95-032501   355.1/33   0814712207
Soldiers -- United States -- Conduct of life. Social reformers -- United States -- History -- 20th century. Military bases -- Social aspects -- United States.

UH740 Military unions. Union movements in armed forces — General works

UH740.C67 1991
Cortright, David, 1946-
Left face: soldier unions and resistance movements in modern armies/ David Cortright and Max Watts. New York: Greenwood Press, 1991. x, 282 p.
90-046702   331.89/041355/00904
0313276269
Military unions -- History -- 20th century. Armed Forces -- Management -- History -- 20th century. Armed Forces -- Political activity -- History -- 20th century.

V Naval science (General)

V23 Dictionaries and encyclopedias — General

V23.B58
Blackburn, Graham, 1940-
The Overlook illustrated dictionary of nautical terms/ Graham Blackburn. Woodstock, N.Y.: Overlook Press, 1981. 349 p.
80-039640   623.8/03/21   0879511249
Naval art and science -- Dictionaries.

V23.J36
Jane's dictionary of naval terms/ compiled by Joseph Palmer. London: Macdonald and Jane's, 1975. 342 p.
76-370529   358.4/03   035608258X
Naval art and science -- Dictionaries. Navigation -- Dictionaries.

V23.K4 1961
Kerchove, Rene de, 1883-
International maritime dictionary; an encyclopedic dictionary of useful maritime terms and phrases, together with equivalents in French and German/ by Rene de Kerchove. Princeton, N.J.: D. Van Nostrand Co., 1961. v, 1018 p.
61-016272   623.803
Naval art and science -- Dictionaries -- Polyglot. Naval art and science -- Dictionaries. Dictionaries, Polyglot.

V23.L467 1994
Lenfestey, Tom.
The Facts on File dictionary of nautical terms/ Thompson Lenfestey, with Tom Lenfestey, Jr. New York, NY: Facts on File, c1994. xiv, 541 p.
92-031490   359/.003   0816020876
Naval art and science -- Dictionaries.

V23.N63
Noel, John Vavasour, 1912-
The VNR dictionary of ships & the sea/ John V. Noel. New York: Van Nostrand Reinhold, c1981. vi, 393 p.
80-015276   359/.003/21   0442256310
Naval art and science -- Dictionaries.

V23.O96
The Oxford companion to ships & the sea/ edited by Peter Kemp; [line drawings by Peter Milne and the OUP drawing office]. London: Oxford University Press, 1976. viii, 972 p.
77-352082   387/.03   0192115537
Naval art and science -- Dictionaries. Naval history -- Dictionaries.

V23.P24 1997
Paine, Lincoln P.
Ships of the world: an historical encyclopedia/ Lincoln P. Paine; with contributions by James H. Terry and Hal Fessenden. Boston: Houghton Mifflin Co., 1997. xiv, 680 p.
97-012872   623.8/2/003   0395715563
Ships -- Encyclopedias.

V23.U64 1991
The United States Navy: a dictionary/ edited by Bruce W. Watson and Susan M. Watson. New York: Garland, 1991. xxx, 948 p.
90-020079   359/.00973   0824055381
Naval art and science -- United States -- Dictionaries. Naval art and science -- United States -- Acronyms.

V25 History and antiquities of naval science — Philosophy of history

V25.B7 1969
Brodie, Bernard, 1910-
Sea power in the machine age. New York, Greenwood Press [1969, c1943] viii, 462 p.
69-013840   359   0837114454
Sea-power. Naval art and science. Navies.

V25.C3324 1998
Cable, James, 1920-
The political influence of naval force in history/ Sir James Cable. New York: St. Martin's Press, 1998.
98-018987   359/.009   0312217544
Sea-power -- History. Sea-power -- Political aspects. Naval history, Modern.

V25.M63 1988
Modelski, George.
Seapower in global politics, 1494-1993/ George Modelski and William R. Thompson. Seattle: University of Washington Press, c1988. xii, 380 p.
87-010472   359/.009/03   0295965029
Sea-power -- History. Sea-power -- Political aspects. Warships.

V25.R48 1989
Reynolds, Clark G.
History and the sea: essays on maritime strategies/ by Clark G. Reynolds. Columbia, S.C.: University of South Carolina Press, c1989. viii, 232 p.
88-034604   359/.03   0872496147
Sea-power -- History. Naval history, Modern. Naval history.

V25.R6 1962
Roskill, Stephen Wentworth.
The strategy of sea power; its development and application. Based on the Lees-Knowles lectures delivered in the University of Cambridge, 1961. London, Collins, 1962. 287 p.
62-005641   359/.03
Sea-power. Naval strategy. Great Britain -- History, Naval.

V25.S424 1989
Seapower and strategy/ Colin S. Gray, Roger W. Barnett, editors. Annapolis, Md.: Naval Institute Press, c1989. xiv, 396 p.
89-033233   359/.03   0870215795
Sea-power. Naval strategy. Naval art and science -- History.

V25.S6
Sokol, Anthony Eugene.
Seapower in the nuclear age. Washington, Public Affairs Press [1961] 268 p.
59-015850   359.43
Sea-power. Nuclear energy. Nuclear weapons.

V25.W55 1981
Willmott, H. P.
Sea warfare: weapons, tactics and strategy/ H.P. Willmott; with an epilogue by Lord Hill-Norton. Strettington, Chichester: A. Bird, 1981. 165 p.
81-215539   359/.03   0907319025
Sea-power -- History. Naval strategy -- History. Naval tactics -- History.

V27 History and antiquities of naval science — General works

V27.B86 1998
Bruce, A. P. C.
An encyclopedia of naval history/ Anthony Bruce and William Cogar. New York: Facts on File, c1998. vii, 440 p.
97-007243   359/.003   0816026971
Naval art and science -- History -- Encyclopedias.

V27.R6 1968
Robertson, Frederick Leslie.
The evolution of naval armament. London, H. T. Storey, 1968. ix, 307 p.
72-183959   623.4/18/0903
Naval art and science -- History. Warships. Ordnance, Naval.

V39 History and antiquities of naval science — By period — Ancient history

V39.S7 1975
Starr, Chester G., 1914-
The Roman imperial navy, 31 B.C.--A.D. 324/ by Chester G. Starr, Jr. Westport, Conn.: Greenwood Press, 1975, c1941. xv, 228 p.
74-028526   359/.00937   0837179181
Rome -- Navy. Rome -- History, Naval.

V46 History and antiquities of naval science — By period — Medieval history to 1492/1600

V46.H38 1991
Haywood, John, 1956-
Dark age naval power: a re-assessment of Frankish and Anglo-Saxon seafaring activity/ John Haywood. London; Routledge, 1991. xii, 232 p.
90-024257 359/.00948/0902 0415063744
Naval art and science -- Europe, Northern -- History. Pirates -- North Sea Region -- History. Ships, Medieval -- North Sea Region -- History. Europe, Northern -- History, Naval.

V53 History and antiquities of naval science — By period — Modern history

V53.F754 2000
Friedman, Norman, 1946-
Seapower and space: from the dawn of the missile age to net-centric warfare/ Norman Friedman. London: Chatham Pub., 2000. 384 p.
00-362685 359.9/83 1861760043
Naval art and science -- History -- 20th century. Space warfare. Sea-power.

V53.K44 1989
Keegan, John, 1934-
The price of admiralty: the evolution of naval warfare/ John Keegan. New York, N.Y., U.S.A.: Viking, 1989, c1988. xii, 292 p.
88-040292 359/.009 0670814164
Naval art and science -- History -- 20th century. Naval art and science -- History -- 19th century. Naval history, Modern.

V53.S66 2001
Spector, Ronald H., 1943-
At war, at sea: sailors and naval warfare in the twentieth century/ Ronald H. Spector. New York, N.Y.: Viking, 2001. xiv, 463 p.
2001-017551 359/.009/04 0670860859
Naval art and science -- History -- 20th century. Naval history, Modern -- 20th century. Sailors -- History -- 20th century.

V55 History and antiquities of naval science — By region or country, A-Z

V55.N73.T86 1989
Tunander, Ola, 1948-
Cold water politics: the maritime strategy and geopolitics of the northern front/ Ola Tunander. London; Sage, 1989. vi, 194 p.
89-061077 327.1/16 0803982194
Sea-power -- North Atlantic Ocean. Security, International.

V55.S65.H47 1988
Herrick, Robert Waring.
Soviet naval theory and policy: Gorshkov's inheritance/ Robert Waring Herrick. Newport, R.I.: Naval War College Press; 1988. xiv, 318 p.
88-019563 359/.00947
Gorshkov, Sergei Georgievich, -- 1910-Naval strategy -- History -- 20th century. Naval art and science -- Soviet Union -- History -- 20th century.

V55.U55.W45 2001
Weir, Gary E.
An ocean in common: American naval officers, scientists, and the ocean environment/ Gary E. Weir. College Station: Texas A&M University Press, c2001. xix, 403 p.
00-011707 359/.07/0973 1585441147
Naval art and science -- United States -- History -- 20th century. Marine sciences -- United States -- History -- 20th century. Naval research -- United States -- History -- 20th century.

V62-63 Biography — By region or country — United States

V62.C662 1985
Command under sail: makers of the American naval tradition, 1775-1850/ edited by James C. Bradford. Annapolis, Md.: Naval Institute Press, c1985. xvi, 333 p.
84-029584 359/.0092/2 0870211374
United States -- History, Naval -- To 1900.

V62.U64 1989
Cogar, William B., 1949-
Dictionary of admirals of the U.S. Navy/ William B. Cogar. Annapolis, Md.: Naval Institute Press, c1989-c1991 v. 1-2
89-003339 359.3/31/092273 0870214314
Admirals -- United States -- Biography -- Dictionaries.

V63.H68.A34
Houston, Fred F., 1912-
Sam Houston's Navy/ Fred F. "Sam" Houston. New York: Grossmont Press, c1976. 135 p.
76-005597 359.3/38/0924 0913182591
Houston, Fred F., -- 1912-Sailors -- United States -- Biography.

V63.H85.M35 1986
Maloney, Linda M.
The captain from Connecticut: the life and naval times of Isaac Hull/ Linda M. Maloney. Boston: Northeastern University Press, c1986. xviii, 549 p.
85-010552 359/.0092/4 0930350790
Hull, Isaac, -- 1773-1843.Admirals -- United States -- Biography.

V63.H86.S64 1998
Spears, Sally, 1938-
Call sign Revlon: the life and death of Navy fighter pilot Kara Hultgreen/ Sally Spears. Annapolis, Md.: Naval Institute Press, c1998. xi, 306 p.
98-019084 359.9/4/092 1557508097
Hultgreen, Kara, -- 1965-1994.Women air pilots -- United States -- Biography. Air pilots, Military -- United States -- Biography.

V63.L4.A3 1970
Lederer, William J., 1912-
All the ship's at sea [by] William J. Lederer. New York, Norton [1970, c1950] 292 p.
70-095882 359.3/3/20924 039307451X
Lederer, William J., -- 1912-

V63.M57.T75 1994
Trimble, William F., 1947-
Admiral William A. Moffett, architect of naval aviation/ William F. Trimble. Washington: Smithsonian Institution Press, c1994. x, 338 p.
93-007962 359/.0092 1560983205
Moffett, William A. -- (William Adger), -- 1869-1933.Admirals -- United States -- Biography.

V63.P35.C47 1998
Christman, Albert B.
Target Hiroshima: Deak Parsons and the creation of the atomic bomb/ Al Christman. Annapolis, Md.: Naval Institute Press, c1998. xii, 305 p.
98-002553 359/.0092 1557501203
Parsons, William Sterling, -- 1901-1953.Admirals -- United States -- Biography.

V63.S38.A3 1988
Schratz, Paul R., 1915-1993.
Submarine commander: a story of World War II and Korea/ Paul R. Schratz. Lexington, Ky.: University Press of Kentucky, c1988. xii, 322 p.
88-019035 940.54/51/0924 0813116619
Schratz, Paul R., -- 1915-World War, 1939-1945 -- Personal narratives, American. Korean War, 1950-1953 -- Personal narratives, American. World War, 1939-1945 -- Naval operations -- Submarine.

V63.S68.B8 1987
Buell, Thomas B.
The quiet warrior: a biography of Admiral Raymond A. Spruance, by Thomas B. Buell. Boston, Little, Brown [1974] xviii, 486 p.
74-001181 940.54/5/0924 0316114707
Spruance, Raymond Ames, -- 1886-1969.Admirals -- United States -- Biography. World War, 1939-1945 -- Naval operations, American. World War, 1939-1945 -- Campaigns -- Pacific Ocean.

V63.V36.B87 1994
Burg, B. R. 1938-
An American seafarer in the age of sail: the erotic diaries of Philip C. Van Buskirk, 1851-1870/ B.R. Burg. New Haven: Yale University Press, c1994. xx, 218 p.
93-029923 387.5/092 0300056370
Van Buskirk, Philip C. -- (Philip Clayton), -- 1833-1903 -- Diaries.Sailors -- United States -- Diaries. Erotic literature, American.

V63.Z85.A33 1976
Zumwalt, Elmo R., 1920-
On watch: a memoir/ Elmo R. Zumwalt, Jr. New York: Quadrangle/New York Times Book Co., c1976. xv, 568 p.
75-008301 359/.03/0973 0812905202
Zumwalt, Elmo R., -- 1920-United States -- Military policy.

V64 Biography — By region or country — Other regions or countries, A-Z

V64.G3.R87 1991
Rust, Eric C., 1950-
Naval officers under Hitler: the story of Crew 34/ Eric C. Rust. New York: Praeger, 1991. xii, 229 p.
90-043918 359/.0092/243 [B] 0275937097
World War, 1939-1945 -- Naval operations, German. Soldiers -- Germany -- Biography.

V113 Seamen's handbooks — By navy — United States

V113.B552
The Bluejackets' manual. Annapolis, Md. Naval Institute, [1978-   ]
79-642868   359
United States. Navy -- Sailors' handbooks.

V163 Naval strategy — General works — 1801-

V163.B76 1977
Brodie, Bernard, 1910-
A guide to naval strategy/ by Bernard Brodie. Westport, Conn.: Greenwood Press, 1977, c1958. viii, 280 p.
77-022392   359.4/3   083719735X
Naval strategy.

V163.K64 1990
Koburger, Charles W.
Narrow seas, small navies, and fat merchantmen: naval strategies for the 1990s/ Charles W. Koburger, Jr. New York: Praeger, 1990. xxi, 157 p.
90-031579   359/.03   0275935574
Sea control. Coast defenses. States, Small.

V165 Naval strategy — General special

V165.M37 1989
Maritime strategy and the balance of power: Britain and America in the twentieth century/ edited by John B. Hattendorf and Robert S. Jordan; foreword by Robert O'Neill. New York: St. Martin's Press, 1989. xx, 373 p.
89-005885   359.4/3   0312031742
Naval strategy. Sea-power -- United States. Sea-power -- Great Britain. United States -- Military relations -- Great Britain. Great Britain -- Military relations -- United States.

V167 Naval tactics — General works

V167.F5613
Fioravanzo, Giuseppe, 1891-
A history of naval tactical thought/ Giuseppe Fioravanzo; translated by Arthur W. Holst. [Annapolis]: Naval Institute Press, c1979. x, 251 p.
78-070966   359.4/2/09   0870212710
Naval tactics -- History.

V167.R6
Robison, Samuel Shelburne, 1867-
A history of naval tactics from 1530 to 1930; the evolution of tactical maxims, by Rear Admiral S.S. Robison ... and Mary L. Robison. Annapolis, Md., The U.S. Naval Institute [1942] xxiii, 956 p.
42-016602   359.42
Naval tactics. Naval history. Naval battles.

V179 Naval logistics

V179.D9 1962
Dyer, George Carroll, 1898-
Naval logistics. Annapolis, United States Naval Institute [1962] xviii, 367 p.
62-016713
Logistics, Naval.

V182 Convoys

V182.W56 1983
Winton, John, 1931-
Convoy: the defence of sea trade, 1890-1990/ John Winton. London: M. Joseph, 1983. 378 p.
83-199609   359.3/26   0718121635
Naval convoys -- History -- 19th century. Naval convoys -- History -- 20th century.

V210 Submarine warfare — General works

V210.L4
Lewis, David D.
The fight for the sea; past, present, and future of submarine warfare in the Atlantic.   Cleveland, World Pub. Co. [1961] 350 p.
61-005991   359.4
Submarine warfare -- History. Sea-power.

V210.S692
Stafford, Edward Peary.
The far and the deep. With a foreword by Charles A. Lockwood. New York, Putnam [1967] 384 p.
67-023135   359.32/57
Submarines (Ships)

V210.W4
Weller, George, 1907-
The story of submarines.   New York, Random House [c1962] 210 p.
62-009686   359
Submarine warfare -- Juvenile literature. Submarines (Ships) -- Juvenile literature.

V310 Salutes. Honors. Ceremonies

V310.L6 1959
Lovette, Leland Pearson, 1897-
Naval customs, traditions & usage.   Annapolis, Md., United States Naval Institute [1959] xiv, 358 p.
59-011628   359.0973
Naval ceremonies, honors, and salutes -- United States. Naval art and science -- Terminology.

V394-438 Naval research — By region or country — United States

V394.A7.S37 1990
Sapolsky, Harvey M.
Science and the Navy: the history of the Office of Naval Research/ Harvey M. Sapolsky. Princeton, N.J.: Princeton University Press, c1990. xiii, 142 p.
89-048144   359./07/0973   0691078475
Science and state -- United States -- History. Federal aid to research -- United States -- History.

V415.P1.B3 1957
Banning, Kendall, 1879-1944.
Annapolis today. Rev. by A. Stuart Pitt. Annapolis, Md., United States Naval Institute [1957] 300 p.
57-009329   359.071173
Midshipmen.

V437.C73
Crump, Irving, 1887-
Our United States Coast Guard Academy. Illustrated with photos. New York, Dodd, Mead, 1961. 241 p.
61-015994   351.792
United States Coast Guard Academy.

V438.C36 1998
Campbell, R. Thomas, 1937-
Academy on the James: the Confederate naval school/ by R. Thomas Campbell. Shippensburg, Penn: Burd Street Press, 1998. xii, 283 p.
98-020355   973.7/57   1572491302
United States -- History -- Civil War, 1861-1865 -- Naval operations.

V736 Naval life, manners and customs, antiquities, etc. — By period — Modern

V736.H3
Halpern, Samuel E.
West Pac '64/ by Samuel E. Halpern. Boston: Branden Press, [1975] 236 p.
74-081874   359.3/45   0828315736
Tonkin Gulf Incidents, 1964. East Asia -- Description and travel.

V750 War vessels: Construction, armament, etc. — General works

V750.A6
Anderson, R. C. b. 1883.
Oared fighting ships, from classical times to the coming of steam. London, P. Marshall, 1962. xiv, 99 p.
64-003529   387.21
Galleys.

V750.F6
Fletcher, R. A.
Warships and their story, by R. A. Fletcher, with coloured frontispiece by Charles Dixon, R. I. and 80 full page plates. London, Cassell and company, ltd., 1911. xxii, 348 p.
12-004659
Warships. Shipbuilding.

V750.G46 1998
George, James L.
History of warships: from ancient times to the twenty-first century/ James L. George. Annapolis, MD: Naval Institute Press, c1998. xvi, 353 p.
98-003376   623.8/25/09   1557503125
Warships -- History.

V765-767 War vessels: Construction, armament, etc. — By period — Modern

V765.C663 1983
Conway's All the world's fighting ships, 1947-1982/ [editor, Robert Gardiner; contributors, Norman Friedman ... et al.]. Annapolis, Md.: Naval Institute Press, c1983. 2 v.
82-042936   359.3/25/0904   0870219235
Warships. Navies.

V765.M3
Macintyre, Donald G. F. W.
The thunder of the guns; a century of battleships. New York, W.W. Norton [1960, c1959] 352 p.
60-006276   359.32
Battleships. Naval history. Naval battles.

V767.L35 1983
Lavery, Brian.
The ship of the line/ Brian Lavery. Annapolis, Md.: Naval Institute Press, c1983-1984. 2 v.
83-043279   623.8/2/00941   0870216317
Ships of the line -- Great Britain. Ships of the line.

V799 War vessels: Construction, armament, etc. — Construction (General) — 1860-1900 (Period of armored vessels)

V799.B3 1968
Baxter, James Phinney, 1893-1975.
The introduction of the ironclad warship. [Hamden, Conn.] Archon Books, 1968 [c1933] x, 398 p.
68-016330   359.32/52/0973
Battleships. Armored vessels.

V800 War vessels: Construction, armament, etc. — Construction (General) — 1901-

V800.C66 1985
Conway's All the world's fighting ships, 1906-1921/ [editorial director, Robert Gardiner; editor, Randal Gray; contributors, Przemyslaw Budzbon ... et al.]. London: Conway Maritime Press, 1985. 439 p.
85-204543   359.3/25/09   0851772455
Warships.

V800.R38
Raven, Alan.
British battleships of World War Two: the development and technical history of the Royal Navy's battleships and battlecruisers from 1911 to 1946/ by Alan Raven and John Roberts. Annapolis: Naval Institute Press, c1976. 436 p.
76-022915   359.8/3   0870218174
Battleships -- Great Britain. Battle cruisers -- Great Britain. World War, 1939-1945 -- Naval operations, British.

V815.3 War vessels: Construction, armament, etc. — Special types — Battleships

V815.3.R44
Reilly, John C.
American battleships, 1886-1923: predreadnought design and construction/ by John C. Reilly, Jr., and Robert L. Scheina. Annapolis, Md.: Naval Institute Press, c1980. 259 p.
79-091326   359.3/252/0973   0870215248
Battleships -- United States -- History.

V820 War vessels: Construction, armament, etc. — Special types — Cruisers

V820.P73 1980
Preston, Antony, 1938-
Cruisers/ Antony Preston. Englewood Cliffs, N.J.: Prentice Hall, c1980. 191 p.
79-089592   359.8/3   0131949020
Cruisers (Warships) -- History.

V820.W49 1995
Whitley, M. J.
Cruisers of World War Two: an international encyclopedia/ M.J. Whitley. Annapolis, Md.: Naval Institute Press, c1995. 288 p.
95-070433   359.8/353/09044   1557501416
Cruisers (Warships) -- Encyclopedias. World War, 1939-1945 -- Naval operations -- Encyclopedias.

V825 War vessels: Construction, armament, etc. — Special types — Destroyers

V825.P73 1977
Preston, Antony, 1938-
Destroyers/ Antony Preston. Englewood Cliffs, N.J.: Prentice-Hall, 1977. 224 p.
77-082132   359.3/2/540904   0132021277
Destroyers (Warships) -- History. Naval history, Modern.

V857-859 War vessels: Construction, armament, etc. — Special types — Submarine boats. Submarine forces

V857.C65 1984
Compton-Hall, Richard.
Submarine boats: the beginnings of underwater warfare/ Richard Compton-Hall. New York: Arco Pub., 1984, c1983. 192 p.
83-007128   359.3/257/09   0668059249
Submarines (Ships) -- History.

V857.5.L43 1998
Leary, William M. 1934-
Under ice: Waldo Lyon and the development of the Arctic submarine/ William M. Leary. College Station, Tex.: Texas A&M University Press, 1998. xxviii, 303 p.
98-019137   359.9/3834/0973   0890968454
Nuclear submarines -- United States -- Design and construction -- History. Lyon, Waldo -- Career in naval architecture. Arctic region.

V858.P6
Polmar, Norman.
Atomic submarines. Princeton, N.J., Van Nostrand [1963] 286 p.
63-005029   359.32
Nuclear submarines -- United States.

V859.C3.F47 1995
Ferguson, Julie H., 1945-
Through a Canadian periscope: the story of the Canadian Submarine Service/ Julie H. Ferguson. Toronto; Dundurn Press, c1995. xv, 364 p.
96-126261   359.9/33/0971   1550022172
Canada. Canadian Armed Forces. Canadian Submarine Service -- History.

V859.G3.S5 1974
Showell, Jak P. Mallmann.
U-boats under the Swastika: an introduction to German submarines 1935-1945/ J. P. Mallmann Showell. New York: Arco Pub. Co., 1974, c1973. 167 p.
73-093152   940.54/51   0668034572
Submarines (Ships) World War, 1939-1945 -- Naval operations -- Submarine. World War, 1939-1945 -- Naval operations, German.

V859.S65.B74 1989
Breemer, Jan S.
Soviet submarines: design, development, and tactics/ Jan Breemer. Coulsdon, Surrey, U.K.: Jane's Information Group, 1989. 187 p.
91-202829   0710605269
Submarines (Ships) -- Soviet Union -- History -- 20th century.

V874-874.3 War vessels: Construction, armament, etc. — Special types — Aircraft carriers

V874.P6
Polmar, Norman.
Aircraft carriers; a graphic history of carrier aviation and its influence on world events, by Norman Polmar, in collaboration with Minoru Genda, Eric M. Brown [and] Robert M. Langdon. Garden City, N.Y., Doubleday, 1969. viii, 788 p.
69-012186   359.32/55
Aircraft carriers.

V874.3.M44
Melhorn, Charles M.
Two-block fox; the rise of the aircraft carrier, 1911-1929 [by] Charles M. Melhorn. Annapolis, Md., Naval Institute Press [1974] 181 p.
73-091169   359.3/2/550973   0870217089
Aircraft carriers -- History. United States -- History, Naval.

V895 War vessels: Construction, armament, etc. — Special types — Other types (not A-Z)

V895.T83 1993
Tucker, Spencer, 1937-
The Jeffersonian gunboat navy/ Spencer C. Tucker. Columbia, S.C.: University of South Carolina Press, c1993. xiii, 265 p.
92-037566   359.3/225/0973   0872498492
Gunboats -- History -- 19th century.United States -- Foreign relations -- 1801-1815. United States -- History -- War of 1812 -- Naval operations.

VA Navies: Organization, distribution, naval situation

VA10 General works

VA10.T63 1996
Todd, Daniel.
Navies and shipbuilding industries: the strained symbiosis/ Daniel Todd and Michael Lindberg. Westport, Conn.: Praeger, 1996. xvii, 197 p.
96-004848   338.4/7623825   0275953106
Navies. Shipbuilding industry.

VA40 Navies of the world — General works

VA40.A48 1990
Anthony, Ian.
The naval arms trade/ Ian Anthony. Solna, Sweden: SIPRI; 1990. x, 221 p.
89-023037   382/.4623825   019829137X
Navies. Defense industries. Sea-power.

VA40.F54 1989
Fieldhouse, Richard W.
Superpowers at sea: an assessment of the naval arms race/ Richard Fieldhouse and Shunji Taoka. Oxford; Oxford University Press, 1989. xiv, 183 p.
89-002977   359/.009/04   0198291353
Navies -- History -- 20th century. Arms race -- History -- 20th century.

VA40.M69 1987
Morris, Michael A.
Expansion of Third World navies/ Michael A. Morris. New York: St. Martin's Press, 1987. xiii, 294 p.
86-017828   359/.009172/4   031200074X
Navies -- Developing countries.

VA50-393 Naval situation, organization, etc. — By region or country — United States

VA50.D3 1971
Davis, George Theron, 1899-1944.
A Navy second to none; the development of modern American naval policy.   Westport, Conn., Greenwood Press [1971, c1940] xiii, 508 p.
77-110826   359/.03/0973   0837132266
Sea-power -- United States. Navies.

VA50.O36 1991
O'Connell, Robert L.
Sacred vessels: the cult of the battleship and the rise of the U.S. Navy/ Robert L. O'Connell. Boulder: Westview Press, 1991. xiv, 409 p.
91-024527   359/.03/09730904   0813311160
Battleships -- United States -- History -- 20th century. Sea-power -- United States -- History -- 20th century. Battleships -- History -- 20th century.

VA55.B48 1972
Bennett, Frank M. 1857-1924.
The steam navy of the United States, a history of the growth of the steam vessel of war in the U.S. Navy, and of the naval Engineer corps. Westport, Conn., Greenwood Press [1972] xi, 953 p.
70-098814   359/.00973   0837129494
Warships -- United States. Warships. Marine engineers -- United States. United States -- History, Naval -- To 1900.

VA55.C28 1990
Canney, Donald L., 1947-
The old steam navy/ Donald L. Canney. Annapolis, Md.: Naval Institute Press, c1990-1993. 2 v.
89-013675   359/.00973   0870210041
Warships -- United States -- History.

VA55.H66 1988
Hooper, Edwin Bickford.
United States naval power in a changing world/ Edwin Bickford Hooper. New York: Praeger, 1988. xvi, 294 p.
87-029942   359/.03/0973   0275927385
Sea-power -- United States -- History.United States -- History, Naval.

VA55.H69 1991
Howarth, Stephen.
To shining sea: a history of the United States Navy, 1775-1991/ Stephen Howarth. New York: Random House, c1991. xv, 620 p.
90-052889   359/.00973   0394576624
United States -- History, Naval.

VA55.M2 1968
Mahan, A. T. 1840-1914.
From sail to steam; recollections of naval life. New York, Da Capo Press, 1968 [c1907] xvi, 325 p.
68-026817   359.3/32/0924
United States. Navy -- History.

VA55.M33 2000
McBride, William M.
Technological change and the United States Navy, 1865-1945/ William M. McBride. Baltimore: Johns Hopkins University Press, c2000. xiii, 336 p.
00-009313   359/.00973/09034   0801864860
Naval art and science -- Technological innovations -- United States.

VA55.M55
Miller, Nathan, 1927-
The U.S. Navy: an illustrated history/ by Nathan Miller. New York: American Heritage Pub. Co.: [1977] 408 p.
77-024139   359/.00973   0671229842
United States. Navy -- History.

VA56.H27 2001
Hackemer, Kurt.
The U.S. Navy and the origins of the military-industrial complex, 1847-1883/ Kurt Hackemer. Annapolis, Md.: Naval Institute Press, 2001. x, 181 p.
00-053281   338.4/7359/0097309034   1557503338
Military-industrial complex -- United States -- History -- 19th century.

VA58.B283 1994
Baer, George W.
One hundred years of sea power: the U.S. Navy, 1890-1990/ George W. Baer. Stanford, Calif.: Stanford University Press, 1994. 553 p.
94-002595   359/.00973   0804722730
Sea-power -- United States -- History -- 19th century. Sea-power -- United States -- History -- 20th century. United States -- History, Naval.

VA58.C75
Coletta, Paolo Enrico, 1916-
The United States Navy and defense unification, 1947-1953/ Paolo E. Coletta. Newark: University of Delaware Press, c1981. 367 p.
79-003111   359.6/0973   087413126X
United States -- Military policy. United States -- Politics and government -- 1945-1953.

VA58.S53 1995
Shulman, Mark R.
Navalism and the emergence of American sea power, 1882-1893/ Mark Russell Shulman. Annapolis, Md.: Naval Institute Press, c1995. x, 239 p.
94-048539   359/.03/097309034   155750766X
Sea-power -- United States -- History -- 19th century.United States -- History, Naval -- To 1900. United States -- Military policy. United States -- Politics and government -- 1881-1885.

VA59.A65
Alden, John Doughty, 1921-
The American steel navy; a photographic history of the U.S. Navy from the introduction of the steel hull in 1883 to the cruise of the Great White Fleet, 1907-1909, by John D. Alden. Photographic research and editorial supervision by Ed Holm. Fifty warship profiles by Arthur D. Baker. Annapolis, Md., Naval Institute Press [1972] 396 p.
76-163111   359.3/2/50973   0870216813
United States. Navy -- Illustrations.

VA59.P283 1990
Palmer, Michael A.
Origins of the maritime strategy: the development of American naval strategy, 1945-1955/ Michael A. Palmer; sponsored by the Naval Historical Center. Annapolis, Md.: Naval Institute Press, [1990] xiv, 145 p.
90-030117   359/.03/0973   0870216678
Naval strategy. Sea-power -- United States -- History -- 20th century.

VA61.B36 1991
Bauer, K. Jack 1926-
Register of ships of the U.S. Navy, 1775-1990: major combatants/ K. Jack Bauer and Stephen S. Roberts. New York: Greenwood Press, 1991. xxiii, 350 p.
91-025241   359.3/25/0973   0313262020
Warships -- United States -- History.

VA61.S54 2001
Silverstone, Paul H.
Civil War Navies, 1854-1883/ Paul H. Silverstone. Annapolis, Md.: Naval Institute Press, c2001. xviii, 218 p.
00-048032   359.8/3/097309034   1557508941
Warships -- United States -- Lists of vessels. Warships -- Confederate States of America -- Lists of vessels. United States -- History -- Civil War, 1861-1865 -- Naval operations.

VA61.S567 2001
Silverstone, Paul H.
The sailing navy, 1775-1854/ Paul H. Silverstone. Annapolis, Md.: Naval Institute Press, c2001. xv, 101 p.
00-048198   359.8/32/097309033   1557508933
Warships -- United States -- History -- 18th century. Warships -- United States -- History -- 19th century. Navies -- United States.

VA63.M42.S54 1992
Sheehy, Edward John.
The U.S. Navy, the Mediterranean, and the cold war, 1945-1947/ Edward J. Sheehy. Westport, Conn.: Greenwood Press, 1992. 191 p.
91-033479   359/.03/09182209044   0313276153
Sea-power -- Mediterranean Region -- History -- 20th century. Sea-power -- United States -- History -- 20th century. Mediterranean Region -- History, Naval.

VA65.C7.M33
Martin, Tyrone G.
A most fortunate ship: a narrative history of "Old Ironsides"/ by Tyrone G. Martin. Chester, Conn.: Globe Pequot Press, c1980. viii, 388 p.
79-052490   359.3/225   0871060337
Constitution (Frigate)

VA65.M553.R64 1996
Rodgers, Bradley A.
Guardian of the Great Lakes: the U.S. paddle frigate Michigan/ Bradley A. Rodgers. Ann Arbor: University of Michigan Press, c1996. 214 p.
95-048841   359.3/25   0472096079
Ships, Iron and steel -- United States -- History -- 19th century. Paddle steamers -- Great Lakes -- History -- 19th century. Great Lakes -- Navigation -- History -- 19th century. United States -- History, Naval -- To 1900.

VA65.M65
Mindell, David A.
War, technology, and experience aboard the USS Monitor / David A. Mindell. Baltimore: Johns Hopkins University Press, 2000. x, 187 p.
99-038344   973.7/52   0801862493
Monitor (Ironclad) United States. Navy -- History -- Civil War, 1861-1865. United States -- History -- Civil War, 1861-1865 -- Naval operations.

VA70.W3.P4
Peck, Taylor.
Round-shot to rockets; a history of the Washington Navy Yard and U.S. Naval Gun Factory. Annapolis, United States Naval Institute, 1949. xx, 267 p.
49-011615   359.7
Naval Weapons Plant (Washington, D.C.)

VA390.H27
Hancock, Joy Bright, 1898-
Lady in the Navy; a personal reminiscence. Annapolis, Md., Naval Institute Press [1972] xi, 289 p.
76-189847   359.3/48/0924   0870213369
Hancock, Joy Bright, -- 1898-

VA393.W45
Wells, Tom Henderson, 1917-1971.
The Confederate Navy: a study in organization. University, University of Alabama Press [1971] ix, 182 p.
72-169496   359.3/0975   0817351051
Confederate States of America. Navy -- Organization.

VA400 Naval situation, organization, etc. — By region or country — Canada

VA400.R38 1982
The RCN in retrospect, 1910-1968/ edited by James A. Boutilier. Vancouver: University of British Columbia Press, c1982. xxx, 373 p.
82-181801   359/.00971   0774801522
Canada -- History, Naval.

VA454-595 Naval situation, organization, etc. — By region or country — Europe

VA454.A6 1965
Albion, Robert Greenhalgh, 1896-
Forests and sea power; the timber problem of the Royal Navy, 1652-1862. Hamden, Conn., Archon Books, 1965 [c1926] xv, 485 p.
65-024502   359.00942
Timber. Timber -- Great Britain.

VA454.B865 1989
The British navy and the use of naval power in the eighteenth century/ edited by Jeremy Black and Philip Woodfine. Atlantic Highlands, N.J.: Humanities Press International, 1989, c1988. xiii, 273 p.
88-009016   359/.00941   0391035991
Sea-power -- Great Britain -- History -- 18th century.Great Britain -- History, Naval -- 18th century.

VA454.D38 1992
Davies, J. D.
Gentlemen and tarpaulins: the officers and men of the Restoration Navy/ J.D. Davies. Oxford: Clarendon Press; 1992. xii, 270 p.
91-012205   359/.00941/09032   0198202636
Sailors -- Great Britain -- History -- 17th century.

VA454.G85 1994
Guide to British naval papers in North America/ compiled by Roger Morriss; with the assistance of Peter Bursey. London; Mansell, 1994. xxii, 418 p.
94-002456   359/.00941   0720121620
Manuscripts -- United States -- Catalogs. Manuscripts -- Canada -- Catalogs.

VA454.H67 1987
Howell, Raymond.
The Royal Navy and the slave trade/ Raymond Howell. New York: St. Martin's Press, 1987. ix, 246 p.
87-009608   326   0312008546
Slavery -- Africa, East -- History -- 19th century.

VA454.K42 1969
Kemp, Peter Kemp.
History of the Royal Navy, edited by P. K. Kemp. New York, Putnam [1969] 304 p.
76-084572   359/.00942
Great Britain. Royal Navy -- History.

VA454.L595
Lewis, Michael, 1890-1970.
The navy of Britain, a historical portrait. London, G. Allen and Unwin [1948] 660 p.
48-011154   359
Naval tactics.

VA454.L597
Lewis, Michael Arthur, 1890-
A social history of the navy, 1793-1815. London, Allen & Unwin [1960] 467 p.
60-003692
Great Britain. Royal Navy -- History -- 19th century. Great Britain. Royal Navy -- History -- 18th century.

VA454.M319
Marcus, Geoffrey Jules, 1906-
Heart of oak: a survey of British sea power in the Georgian era/ G. J. Marcus. London; Oxford University Press, 1975. xi, 308 p.
76-354759   359/.00941   0192158120
Sailors -- Great Britain. Navigation -- Great Britain -- History. Great Britain -- History, Naval.

VA454.M32
Marcus, Geoffrey Jules, 1906-
A naval history of England. Boston, Little, Brown [1962- c1961-   ] 1 v.
62-009357   942
Great Britain -- History, Naval.

VA454.M34
Marder, Arthur Jacob.
The anatomy of British sea power; a history of British naval policy in the pre-dreadnought era, 1880-1905, by Arthur J. Marder ... New York, A.A. Knopf, 1940.
40-035002   359.0942
Great Britain -- History, Naval. Great Britain -- History -- Victoria, 1837-1901.

VA454.M35
Marder, Arthur Jacob.
From the Dreadnought to Scapa Flow: the Royal Navy in the Fisher era, 1904-1919. London: Oxford Univ. Pr., 1961-1970. 5 v.
61-019563 359.0942
Fisher, John Arbuthnot Fisher, -- Baron, -- 1941-1920.World War, 1914-1918 -- Naval operations.Great Britain -- History, Naval.

VA454.M37 1981
Marder, Arthur Jacob.
Old friends, new enemies: the Royal Navy and the Imperial Japanese Navy/ by Arthur J. Marder. Oxford: Clarendon Press; 1981-1990. 2 v.
81-197393 359/.00941 0198226047
World War, 1939-1945 -- Naval operations, British. World War, 1939-1945 -- Naval operations, Japanese. World War, 1939-1945 -- Campaigns -- Pacific Area.

VA454.P24
Padfield, Peter.
Rule Britannia: the Victorian and Edwardian Navy/ Peter Padfield. London; Routledge & Kegan Paul, 1981. 246 p.
81-198788 359/.00941 0710007744
Great Britain. Royal Navy -- History -- 19th century. Great Britain. Royal Navy -- History -- 20th century.

VA454.P46 1971
Pepys, Samuel, 1633-1703.
Pepys' Memoires of the Royal Navy, 1679-1688. Edited by J. R. Tanner. New York, Haskell House, 1971. xviii, 131 p.
68-025260 359.3/0942 0838302289
Great Britain -- History, Naval -- Stuarts, 1603-1714.

VA459.S5.H36 1981
Hamill, Ian.
The strategic illusion: the Singapore strategy and the defence of Australia and New Zealand, 1919-1942/ Ian Hamill. [Singapore]: Singapore University Press, c1981. ix, 387 p.
81-941281 359.7/09595/7 997169008X
Singapore Naval Base (Singapore) -- History. Great Britain -- Colonies -- Asia -- Defenses. Great Britain -- Defenses.

VA460.A1.C6 1983
Coad, J. G.
Historic architecture of the Royal Navy: an introduction/ J.G. Coad. London: V. Gollancz, 1983. 160 p.
83-185428 623/.64/0941 0575032774
Navy-yards and naval stations -- Great Britain. Military architecture -- Great Britain -- History.

VA473.S63
Sokol, Anthony Eugene.
The Imperial and Royal Austro-Hungarian Navy [by] Anthony E. Sokol. Annapolis, U.S. Naval Institute [c1968] 172 p.
68-029133 359/.009436
Austro-Hungarian Monarchy. Kriegsmarine -- History.

VA473.S66 1989
Sondhaus, Lawrence, 1958-
The Habsburg Empire and the sea: Austrian naval policy, 1797-1866/ Lawrence Sondhaus. West Lafayette, Ind.: Purdue University Press, 1989. xvi, 326 p.
88-024028 359/.009436 0911198970
Sea-power -- Austria -- History -- 19th century.Austria -- History, Naval -- 19th century. Austria -- Military policy.

VA503.P75 1987
Pritchard, James S., 1939-
Louis XV's navy, 1748-1762: a study of organization and administration/ James Pritchard. Kingston: McGill-Queen's University Press, 1987. xiv, 285 p.
88-182466 359.3/0944 0773505709
France. Marine -- Organization -- History -- 18th century. France. Marine -- Management -- History -- 18th century.

VA513.P45 1994
Philbin, Tobias R.
The lure of Neptune: German-Soviet naval collaboration and ambitions, 1919-1941/ Tobias R. Philbin, III. Columbia, S.C.: University of South Carolina Press, c1994. xxi, 192 p.
94-003207 359/.00943/09041 0872499928
Sea-power -- Germany. Sea-power -- Soviet Union. World War, 1939-1945 -- Naval operations, German. Germany -- Military relations -- Soviet Union. Soviet Union -- Military relations -- Germany.

VA513.S52
Showell, Jak P. Mallmann.
The German Navy in World War Two: a reference guide to the Kriegsmarine, 1935-1945/ Jak P. Mallmann Showell. London: Arms and Armour Press, 1979. 224 p.
80-472380 359/.00943 0853680930
Warships -- Germany -- History. World War, 1939-1945 -- Naval operations, German.

VA513.S66 1997
Sondhaus, Lawrence, 1958-
Preparing for Weltpolitik: German sea power before the Tirpitz era/ Lawrence Sondhaus. Annapolis, Md.: Naval Institute Press, c1997. x, 326 p.
96-052043 359/.00943/09034 1557507457
Sea-power -- Germany -- History -- 19th century.

VA513.S74 1966
Steinberg, Jonathan.
Yesterday's deterrent; Tirpitz and the birth of the German battle fleet. Foreword by Commander Saunders. New York, Macmillan [1966, c1965] 240 p.
66-027011 359.00943
Tirpitz, Alfred von, -- 1849-1930.Naval history.

VA513.W255 1991
Weir, Gary E.
Building the Kaiser's navy: the Imperial Naval Office and German industry in the von Tirpitz era, 1890-1919/ Gary E. Weir. Annapolis, Md.: Naval Institute Press, c1992. xii, 289 p.
90-019529 338.4/76238225/0943 1557509298
Shipbuilding industry -- Germany -- History.

VA533.B78 1993
Bruijn, J. R.
The Dutch navy of the seventeenth and eighteenth centuries/ by Jaap R. Bruijn. Columbia, S.C.: University of South Carolina Press, c1993. xv, 258 p.
93-018700 359/.009492/0903 0872498751
United Provinces of the Netherlands. Zeemacht -- History.

VA570.H4
Herrick, Robert Waring.
Soviet naval strategy: fifty years of theory and practice. Annapolis, U.S. Naval Institute [1968] xxxiv, 197 p.
67-026080 359/.00947
Soviet Union -- History, Naval.

VA573.D33 1990
Da Cunha, Derek.
Soviet naval power in the Pacific/ Derek da Cunha. Boulder: L. Rienner Publishers, 1990. xii, 284 p.
90-008722 359/.03/0947 1555871763
Sea-power -- Soviet Union.Pacific Area -- Defenses.

VA573.F34 1971
Fairhall, David.
Russian sea power. Boston, Gambit, 1971. 286 p.
71-118209 387/.0947 0876450400
Merchant marine -- Soviet Union. Sea-power -- Soviet Union.

VA573.G6613
Gorshkov, Sergei Georgievich, 1910-
Red star rising at sea/ Sergei G. Gorshkov; translated by Theodore A. Neely, Jr. from a series of articles originally published in Morskoi sbornik; edited for publication by Herbert Preston. [Annapolis, Md.]: Naval Institute Press, c1974. 150 p.
75-304584 359/.00947 0870212449
Naval history. Sea-power.

VA573.S3
Saunders, Malcolm George
The Soviet Navy. New York, F. A. Praeger [1958] 340 p.
58-012091 359.0947
Shakespeare, William, 1564-1616 -- Authorship.

VA573.S589 1990
Soviet seapower in northern waters: facts, motivation, impact, and responses/ edited by John Kristen Skogan and Arne Olav Brundtland. New York: St. Martins Press, c1990. vi, 198 p.
90-030361 359/.03/0947 0312041799
Sea-power -- Soviet Union.North Atlantic Ocean. North Pacific Ocean.

VA583.S77 1992
Stradling, R. A.
The Armada of Flanders: Spanish maritime policy and European war, 1568-1668/ R.A. Stradling. Cambridge; Cambridge University Press, 1992. xix, 276 p.
91-009609 359/.00946/09031 0521405343
Spain -- History, Naval -- 16th century. Netherlands -- History -- Wars of Independence, 1556-1648. Balance of power.

VA595.V3.O33 1963
Ohrelius, Bengt, 1918-
Vasa, the king's ship. Translated by Maurice Michael. Philadelphia, Chilton Books [1963, c1962] 124 p.
63-001734 359.3209485
Naval history.

VA620-653 Naval situation, organization, etc. — By region or country — Asia

VA620.G84
Guide to far Eastern navies/ edited by Barry M. Blechman and Robert P. Berman. Annapolis: Naval Institute Press, c1978. xiv, 586 p.
77-087942 359/.0095 0870217976
Navies -- East Asia.

VA620.S86 1990
Superpower maritime strategy in the Pacific/
edited by Frank C. Langdon and Douglas A.
Ross. London; Routledge, 1990. xvii, 295 p.
89-049499   359/.03/091823   0415043875
*Sea-power -- Pacific Area. Sea-power -- United
States. Sea-power -- Soviet Union. Pacific Ocean
-- Strategic aspects. United States -- Military
policy. Soviet Union -- Military policy.*

VA653.E93 1997
Evans, David C.
Kaigun: strategy, tactics, and technology in the
Imperial Japanese Navy, 1887-1941/ David C.
Evans and Mark R. Peattie. Annapolis, Md.:
Naval Institute Press, c1997. xxv, 661 p.
97-011455   359/.00952   0870211927
Japan. Kaigun -- History.

VA653.H64 1983
Howarth, Stephen.
The fighting ships of the Rising Sun: the drama
of the Imperial Japanese Navy, 1895-1945/
Stephen Howarth. New York: Atheneum, 1983.
xii, 398 p.
83-045076   359/.00952   0689114028
Japan -- History, Naval.

VA653.J4513 1977b
Jentschura, Hansgeorg.
Warships of the Imperial Japanese Navy, 1869-
1945/ Hansgeorg Jentschura, Dieter Jung, and
Peter Mickel; translated by Antony Preston and J.
D. Brown. Annapolis, Md.: Naval Institute Press,
c1977. 284 p.
77-366267   623.82/5/0952   087021893X
Warships.

VA730 Naval situation, organization, etc. — By region or country — Pacific islands

VA730.N38 1993
Naval power in the Pacific: toward the year
2000/ edited by Hugh Smith and Anthony
Bergin. Boulder, Colo.: L. Rienner, 1993. xiii,
186 p.
92-046772   359/.03/099   1555873588
*Sea-power -- PacificArea.Pacific Area --
Strategic aspects.*

VB Naval administration

VB23 By region or country — North America — United States

VB23.A57
American Secretaries of the Navy/ edited by
Paolo E. Coletta. Annapolis, Md.: Naval Institute
Press, c1980. 2 v.
78-070967   353.7/092/2   0870210734
*United States. Navy -- Management -- History.
United States. Dept. of the Navy -- History.
United States. Dept. of the Navy -- Biography.*

VB23.L3
Langley, Harold D.
Social reform in the United States Navy, 1798-
1862 [by] Harold D. Langley. Urbana, University
of Illinois Press, 1967. x, 309 p.
67-010440   359/.00973
United States Navy.

VB23.P32 1968
Paullin, Charles Oscar, 1868 or 9-194
Paullin's history of naval administration, 1775-
1911: a collection of articles from the U.S. Naval
Institute Proceedings. Annapolis, U.S. Naval
Institute [1968] 485 p.
68-057010   359/.00973
United States. Navy -- History.

VB57 By region or country — Europe — Great Britain

VB57.G36
Gardiner, Leslie, 1921-
The British Admiralty. Edinburgh, Blackwood,
1968. 418 p.
68-090054   359.3/31/09   0851580017
Great Britain. Admiralty -- History.

VB205 Command of ships. Leadership — By region or country — Other regions or countries, A-Z

VB205.G7.H67
Horsfield, John.
The art of leadership in war: the Royal Navy
from the age of Nelson to the end of World War
II/ John Horsfield. Westport, Conn.: Greenwood
Press, 1980. xiv, 240 p.
79-054059   359   0313209197
Leadership. Admirals -- Great Britain.

VB230 Intelligence — General works

VB230.B8
Bucher, Lloyd M., 1927-
Bucher: my story, by Lloyd M. Bucher, with
Mark Rascovich. Garden City, N.Y., Doubleday,
1970. 447 p.
77-119919   359.3/4/320924
*Bucher, Lloyd M., -- 1927-Pueblo incident,
1968.*

VB259 Vocational guidance. The navy as a career. Job analysis

VB259.C28 1971
Calvert, James F., 1920-
The naval profession. New York, McGraw-Hill
[1971] xiv, 250 p.
71-152002   359/.0023   0070096570
United States. Navy -- Vocational guidance.

VB313 Officers — By region or country — United States

VB313.K36
Karsten, Peter.
The naval aristocracy; the golden age of
Annapolis and the emergence of modern
American navalism. New York, Free Press
[1972] xv, 462 p.
76-136609   359.3/3/20973
United States. Navy -- Officers.

VB313.M35 1991
McKee, Christopher.
A gentlemanly and honorable profession: the
creation of the U.S. naval officer corps, 1794-
1815/ Christopher McKee. Annapolis, Md.:
Naval Institute Press, c1991. xv, 600 p.
90-006232   359.3/32/0973   0870212834
*United States. Navy -- Officers -- History --
18th century. United States. Navy -- Officers --
History -- 19th century.*

VB315 Officers — By region or country — Other regions or countries, A-Z

VB315.G4.H47
Herwig, Holger H.
The German naval officer corps; a social and
political history, 1890-1918 [by] Holger H.
Herwig. Oxford, Clarendon Press, 1973. xiv,
298 p.
74-158685   359.3/3/20943   0198225172
*Germany -- Politics and government -- 1871-
1918. Germany -- Social conditions.*

VB315.G7.L4
Lewis, Michael Arthur.
England's sea-officers; the story of the naval
profession, by Michael Lewis. London, G. Allen
& Unwin [1939] 307 p.
40-010720
*Great Britain. Royal Navy -- Officers. Great
Britain. Royal Navy -- History.*

VB324 Minorities, women, etc. in navies — By region or country — United States

VB324.A47.G65 1993
The Golden Thirteen: recollections of the first
Black naval officers/ edited by Paul Stillwell,
with a foreword by Colin L. Powell. Annapolis,
Md.: Naval Institute Press, c1993. xxviii, 304 p.
92-037273   359/.008996073   1557507791
*United States. Navy -- African Americans.
United States. Navy -- Officers.*

VB324.G38.M87 1988b
Murphy, Lawrence R., 1942-
Perverts by official order: the campaign against
homosexuals by the United States Navy/
Lawrence R. Murphy. New York: Haworth Press,
c1988. xiii, 340 p.
87-033914   359/.008/6642   0866567089
*Trials (Sodomy) -- Rhode Island -- Newport --
History -- 20th century. Gays -- United States --
History -- 20th century. Newport (R.I.) --
History.*

VB324.G38.Z44 1995
Zeeland, Steven.
Sailors and sexual identity: crossing the line between "straight" and "gay" in the U.S. Navy/ Steven Zeeland. New York: Haworth Press, c1995. xxi, 296 p.
94-028996   359/.008/6642   1560248505
Sailors -- United States -- Sexual behavior. Gays -- United States -- Identity.

VB324.W65.E23 1993
Ebbert, Jean.
Crossed currents: Navy women from WWI to Tailhook/ Jean Ebbert, Marie-Beth Hall; foreword by Edward L. Beach. Washington: Brassey's (US), c1993. xx, 321 p.
92-039963   359/.0082   0028810228
United States. Navy -- Women.

VC Naval maintenance

VC263 Supplies and stores (General and personal) — By region or country — United States

VC263.C65 1972
Connery, Robert Howe, 1907-
The Navy and the industrial mobilization in World War II, by Robert H. Connery. New York, Da Capo Press, 1972 [c1951] xi, 527 p.
73-166951   940.5373   030670322X
World War, 1939-1945 -- Equipment and supplies. Industrial mobilization -- United States.

VC303 Clothing and equipment — Uniforms — By region or country

VC303.R3
Rankin, Robert H.
Uniforms of the sea service; a pictorial history. Annapolis, United States Naval Institute [1962] 324 p.
62-014382   355.14
Military uniforms.

VE Marines

VE23.H4-23.Z44 By region or country — United States. Marine Corps — General works

VE23.H4
Heinl, Robert Debs, 1916-
Soldiers of the sea; the United States Marine Corps, 1775-1962. Foreword by B. H. Liddell Hart. Annapolis, United States Naval Institute [1962] 692 p.
61-018078   359.960973
United States. Marine Corps -- History.

VE23.M54
Millett, Allan Reed.
Semper fidelis: the history of the United States Marine Corps/ Allan R. Millett. New York: Macmillan Pub. Co., c1980. xviii, 782 p.
80-001059   359.9/6/0973   0029215903
United States. Marine Corps -- History.

VE23.P28
Parker, William D.
A concise history of the United States Marine Corps, 1775-1969, by William D. Parker. Washington, Historical Division, Headquarters, U.S. Marine Corps; [for sale by the Supt. of Docs., U.S. Govt. Print. Off.] 1970 x, 143 p.
74-608606   359.9/6/0973
United States. Marine Corps -- History.

VE23.S52 1993
Shulimson, Jack.
The Marine Corps' search for a mission, 1880-1898/ Jack Shulimson. Lawrence, Kan.: University Press of Kansas, c1993. xiii, 274 p.
93-007181   359.9/6/0973   0700606084
United States. Marine Corps -- History.

VE23.Z44 1996
Zeeland, Steven.
The masculine marine: homoeroticism in the U.S. Marine Corps/ Steven Zeeland. New York: Haworth Press, c1996. xi, 203 p.
96-006803   306.76/6/088355   1560238747
Marines -- United States -- Sexual behavior. Gays -- United States -- Identity.

VE23.22 By region or country — United States. Marine Corps — Divisions. By number

VE23.22 1st.C36 1994
Cameron, Craig M., 1958-
American samurai: myth, imagination, and the conduct of battle in the First Marine Division, 1941-1951/ Craig M. Cameron. Cambridge [England]; Cambridge University Press, 1994. xiii, 297 p.
93-010530   359.9/6/09048   0521441684
War -- Psychological aspects. War -- Mythology.

VE24-25 By region or country — United States. Marine Corps — Biography

VE24.E37 1999
Ehrhart, W. D. 1948-
Ordinary lives: Platoon 1005 and the Vietman War/ W.D. Ehrhart. Philadelphia: Temple University Press, c1999. x, 334 p.
98-039963   359.9/6/092273   1566396743
Marines -- United States -- Biography. Vietnamese Conflict, 1961-1975 -- Veterans -- United States -- Biography.

VE25.B88.S36 1987
Schmidt, Hans, 1938-
Maverick Marine: General Smedley D. Butler and the contradictions of American military history/ Hans Schmidt. Lexington, Ky.: University Press of Kentucky, c1987. x, 292 p.
87-001990   359.9/6/0924   0813116198
Butler, Smedley D. -- (Smedley Darlington), -- 1881-1940. Generals -- United States -- Biography.

VE25.E45.B35 1997
Ballendorf, Dirk Anthony, 1939-
Pete Ellis: an amphibious warfare prophet, 1880-1923/ Dirk Anthony Ballendorf and Merrill Lewis Bartlett. Annapolis, Md.: Naval Institute Press, c1997. xv, 200 p.
96-043522   359.9/6/092   1557500606
Ellis, Earl H., -- d. 1923. Amphibious warfare.

VF Naval ordnance

VF7 Collected works (nonserial)

VF7.U64 no. 3624
Pearson, Frederick, 1936-
Map projection equations/ by Frederick Pearson II. Dahlgren, Va.: Naval Surface Weapons Center, 1977. ix, 329 p.
77-602944   623.4/08
Map projection.

VF57 By region or country — Europe — Great Britain

VF57.L4
Lewis, Michael, 1890-1970.
Armada guns, a comparative study of English and Spanish armaments. London, Allen & Unwin [1961] 243 p.
61-002767   623.4
Armada, 1588.

VF346 Naval weapons systems — General works

VF346.F75 1991
Friedman, Norman, 1946-
The Naval Institute guide to world naval weapons systems, 1991/92/ Norman Friedman. Annapolis, Md.: Naval Institute Press, c1991. xlii, 858 p.
90-026886   359.8/2/0202   0870212885
Weapons systems -- Handbooks, manuals, etc. Ordnance, Naval -- Handbooks, manuals, etc.

VF347 Naval weapons systems — By region or country — United States

VF347.P66 1997
Poolman, Kenneth, 1924-
The winning edge: naval technology in action, 1939-1945/ Kenneth Poolman. Annapolis, Md.: Naval Institute Press, c1997. xii, 235 p.
96-043294   359.8/0973/09045   1557506876
World War, 1939-1945 -- Naval operations.

VG Minor services of navies

VG90 Naval aviation. Air service. Air warfare — General works

VG90.L38
Layman, R. D., 1928-
To ascend from a floating base: shipboard aeronautics and aviation, 1783-1914/ R. D. Layman. Rutherford: Fairleigh Dickinson University Press, c1979. 271 p.
77-089782   358.4/009   0838620787
Naval aviation -- History.

VG93 Naval aviation. Air service. Air warfare — By region or country — United States

VG93.A79 1971
United States.
United States naval aviation, 1910-1970 [by Clarke Van Vleet, Lee M. Pearson, and Adrian O. Van Wyen. Washington] U.S. Dept. of the Navy; [for sale by the Supt. of Docs., U.S. Govt. Print. Off.] 1970 xi, 440 p.
78-612230   358.4/00973
United States. Navy -- Aviation -- Chronology.

VG93.B3
Baar, James, 1929-
Polaris! By James Baar and William E. Howard. New York, Harcourt, Brace [1960] 245 p.
60-012731   623.4519
Nuclear submarines. Polaris (Missile)

VG93.R6 1982
Robinson, Douglas Hill, 1918-
Up ship!: a history of the U.S. Navy's rigid airships 1919-1935/ by Douglas H. Robinson and Charles L. Keller. Annapolis, Md.: Naval Institute Press, c1982. xiii, 236 p.
82-006374   358.4/00973   0870217380
Airships -- History.

VG93.T8
Turnbull, Archibald Douglas.
History of United States Naval Aviation, by Archibald D. Turnbull and Clifford L. Lord. New Haven, Yale University Press, 1949. xii, 345 p.
49-011818   358.4
Aeronautics, Military -- United States.

VG95 Naval aviation. Air service. Air warfare — Other regions or countries, A-Z

VG95.G7.H5
Higham, Robin D. S.
The British rigid airship, 1908-1931; a study in weapons policy.   London, G.T. Foulis [1961] 426 p.
62-002338   629.13325
Airships -- History.

VG123 Medical service — By region or country — North America

VG123.L36 1995
Langley, Harold D.
A history of medicine in the early U.S. Navy/ Harold D. Langley. Baltimore: Johns Hopkins University Press, 1995. xix, 435 p.
94-031383   359.3/45/0973   0801848768
Medicine, Naval -- United States -- History -- 19th century. Naval Medicine -- history -- United States.

VG227-228 Medical service — Biography — Individual

VG227.P8.A3
Pugh, Herbert Lamont, 1895-
Navy surgeon.   Philadelphia, Lippincott [1959] 459 p.
59-009326   926.1
Pugh, Herbert Lamont, -- 1895-Surgeons -- Biography.

VG228.G7.C733 1982
Cree, Edward H. 1814-1901.
Naval surgeon: the voyages of Dr. Edward H. Cree, Royal Navy, as related in his private journals, 1837-1856/ illustrated by the author; edited and with an introduction by Michael Levien; [maps by Jennifer Johnson]. New York: E.P. Dutton, 1982, c1981. 275 p.
81-069225   359.3/45/0924   0525241213
Cree, Edward H. -- (Edward Hodges), -- 1814-1901 -- Diaries.Surgery, Naval -- Great Britain -- History -- 19th century. Surgeons -- Great Britain -- Diaries.

VG228.L5.R6
Roddis, Louis H. 1886-
James Lind, founder of nautical medicine.   New York, H. Schuman [c1950] xi, 177 p.
51-001222   926.1
Lind, James, -- 1716-1794.Medicine, Naval -- History.

VK Navigation. Merchant marine

VK15 History, conditions, etc. — General works

VK15.P4
Parry, J. H. 1914-
Romance of the sea/ [by J.H. Parry]; [prepared by National Geographic Book Service]. Washington, D.C.: National Geographic Society, c1981. 312 p.
80-029569   0870443461
Navigation -- History. Ships -- History. Naval art and science -- History.

VK16 History, conditions, etc. — By period — Ancient

VK16.R6413
Rouge, Jean.
Ships and fleets of the ancient Mediterranean/ by Jean Rouge; translated from the French by Susan Frazer. Middletown, Conn.: Wesleyan University Press, c1981. 228 p.
81-004927   387/.0093   0819550558
Navigation -- Mediterranean region -- History. Naval history, Ancient.

VK18 History, conditions, etc. — By period — Modern

VK18.V5 1970
Villiers, Alan John, 1903-
The way of a ship; being some account of the ultimate development of the ocean-going square-rigged sailing vessel, and the manner of her handling, her voyage-making, her personnel, her economics, he by Alan Villiers. Illustrated with the author's photos., and diagrs. and drawings by Harold A. Underhill. New York, Scribner 1970. xvii, 429 p.
70-106543   387.2/2
Sailing ships. Shipping -- History.

VK23-24 History, conditions, etc. — By region or country — North America

VK23.B88 1997
Butler, John A., 1927-
Sailing on Friday: the perilous voyage of America's merchant marine/ John A. Butler. Washington: Brassey's, c1997. xv, 287 p.
97-020850   387.5/0973   1574881248
Merchant marine -- United States -- History.

VK23.C8 1960
Cutler, Carl C., 1878-1966.
Greyhounds of the sea: the story of the American clipper ship/ by Carl C. Cutler; foreword by Charles Francis Adams. Annapolis, Md.: United States Naval Institute, c1960. 592 p.
60-016873
Clipper ships. Merchant marine -- United States.

VK23.F28 1989
Farr, James Barker, 1945-
Black odyssey: the seafaring traditions of Afro-Americans/ James Barker Farr. New York: P. Lang, c1989. 310 p.
88-036965   387.5/08996073   0820408034
Afro-American sailors -- History. Navigation -- United States -- History. United States -- History, Naval.

VK23.U18 1998
The U.S. Merchant Marine at war, 1775-1945/ edited by Bruce L. Felknor. Annapolis, Md.: Naval Institute Press, c1998. xviii, 362 p.
97-049860   387.5/0973   1557502730
Merchant marine -- United States -- History.United States -- History, Naval.

VK23.W8
Wright, E. W.
Lewis & Dryden's marine history of the Pacific Northwest; an illustrated review of the growth and development of the maritime industry, from the advent of the earliest navigators to the present time edited by E. W. Wright. Portland, Oregon: The Lewis & Dryden printing company, 1961, 1895. xxiii, 494 p.
28-001147
Merchant marine -- Northwest, Pacific.Northwest, Pacific -- History Northwest, Pacific -- Biography.

VK23.7.F85 1998
A fully accredited ocean: essays on the Great Lakes/ Victoria Brehm, editor. Ann Arbor: University of Michigan Press, c1998. 249 p.
97-025396   386/.5/0977   0472107097
Great Lakes -- Navigation -- History.

VK24.C2.D45 1990
Delgado, James P.
To California by sea: a maritime history of the California gold rush/ James P. Delgado. Columbia, S.C.: University of South Carolina Press, c1990. xiv, 237 p.
89-039117   387.5/09794   0872496732
Navigation -- California -- History -- 19th century. Shipping -- California -- History -- 19th century. California -- Gold discoveries.

VK55-57 History, conditions, etc. — By region or country — Europe

VK55.M65 1993
Mollat, Michel.
Europe and the sea/ Michel Mollat du Jourdin; translated from the French by Teresa Lavender Fagan. Oxford, UK; Blackwell, 1993. xiii, 269 p.
92-037706   623.89/094   0631172270
Navigation -- Europe -- History.

VK55.P79 1988
Pryor, John H., 1947-
Geography, technology, and war: studies in the maritime history of the Mediterranean, 649-1571/ John H. Pryor. Cambridge; Cambridge University Press, 1988. xviii, 238 p.
87-013338   387.5/091638   0521344247
Navigation -- Mediterranean Region -- History.Mediterranean Region -- History, Naval.

VK57.L55
Lloyd, Christopher, 1906-
The British seaman 1200-1860: a social survey. London, Collins, 1968. 319 p.
68-132004   359/.00942
Sailors -- Great Britain -- History.

VK57.R43 1987
Rediker, Marcus Buford.
Between the devil and the deep blue sea: merchant seamen, pirates, and the Anglo-American maritime world, 1700-1750/ Marcus Rediker. Cambridge; Cambridge University Press, 1987. xv, 322 p.
87-006304   387.5/0941   0521303427
Merchant mariners -- Great Britain -- History -- 18th century. Merchant mariners -- North America -- History -- 18th century. Navigation -- Great Britain -- History -- 18th century.

VK139 Biography — Collective

VK139.D78 1998
Druett, Joan.
Hen frigates: wives of merchant captains under sail/ Joan Druett. New York: Simon & Schuster, c1998. 274 p.
97-037624   387.5/4044   0684839687
Ship captains' spouses -- Biography.

VK140 Biography — Individual, A-Z

VK140.B53A3
Blackford, Charles Minor, 1898 or 9-
Torpedoboat sailor. Sketches by Paul Salmon. Annapolis, United States Naval Institute [1968] 156 p.
68-015771   940.4/81/73
Blackford, Charles Minor, 1898 or 9-

VK140.D46.A3 1998
Dempsey, Deborah Doane, 1949-
The captain's a woman: tales of a merchant mariner/ Deborah Doane Dempsey and Joanne Reckler Foster. Annapolis, Md.: Naval Institute Press, c1998. xi, 269 p.
97-035201   387.5/4044/092   1557501645
Dempsey, Deborah Doane, -- 1949-Women ship captains -- United States -- Biography.

VK140.S6.S6
Slocum, Victor.
Capt. Joshua Slocum.   New York, Sheridan House [1950] 384 p.
50-006422
Slocum, Joshua, -- b. 1844.Voyages and travels.

VK140.S6.T4
Teller, Walter Magnes.
The search for Captain Slocum, a biography. New York, Scribner, [1956] 258 p.
56-009879
Slocum, Joshua, -- b. 1844.

VK140.T3.A3
Tawes, Leonard S., 1853-1932.
Coasting Captain; journals of Captain Leonard S. Tawes, relating his career in Atlantic coastwise sailing craft from 1868 to 1922. Edited for the Museum by Robert H. Burgess. Newport News, Va., Mariners Museum, 1967. xix, 461 p.
67-017219   387.5/0924
Seafaring life.

VK525 Study and teaching — Individual schools — United States. By name of school, A-Z

VK525.U6.C7
Crump, Irving, 1887-
Our Merchant Marine Academy, Kings Point. Illustrated with photos. New York, Dodd, Mead, 1958. 236 p.
58-010743   387.5071173
U. S. Merchant Marine Academy, King's Point, N. Y.

VK541 Seamanship — General works

VK541.C67 1957
Cornell, Felix M.
American merchant seaman's manual, for seamen by seamen. Edited by Felix M. Cornell and Allan C. Hoffman. Cambridge, Md., Cornell Maritime Press, 1957. 834 p.
56-012402   623.8/8/0202
Merchant marine -- Handbooks, manuals, etc. Merchant mariners.

VK541.K73 1984
Knight, Austin Melvin, 1854-1927.
Knight's Modern seamanship. New York: Van Nostrand Reinhold, c1984. xi, 740 p.
82-023714   623.88   0442268637
Seamanship.

VK543 Seamanship — Sailing. Helmsmanship — General works

VK543.H5
Hiscock, Eric C.
Cruising under sail. London, Oxford University Press, 1950. xviii, 480 p.
51-009152   797.14
Sailing. Yachts and yachting.

VK549 Science of navigation — History

VK549.C63
Cotter, Charles H.
A history of nautical astronomy [by] Charles H. Cotter. London, Hollis & Carter, 1968. xii, 387 p.
68-012049   527/.09   0370004604
Nautical astronomy -- History.

VK549.T39 1971b
Taylor, E. G. R. 1879-
The haven-finding art; a history of navigation from Odysseus to Captain Cook [by] E. G. R. Taylor. With a foreword by K. St. B. Collins. Appendix by Joseph Needham. New York, American Elsevier Pub. Co., 1971. xii, 310 p.
76-151853   623.89/09   0444196080
Navigation -- History.

VK549.W3
Waters, David Watkin.
The art of navigation in England in Elizabethan and early Stuart times. With a foreword by the Earl Mountbatten of Burma. New Haven, Yale University Press, 1958. xxxix, 696 p.
58-059622   656
Navigation -- History.

VK549.W55 1992
Williams, J. E. D.
From sails to satellites: the origin and development of navigational science/ J.E.D. Williams. Oxford; Oxford University Press, 1992. ix, 310 p.
92-008456   623.89/09   0198563876
Navigation -- History.

VK555 Science of navigation — General works — 1801-

VK555.A48
American practical navigator. Washington, [etc.] Defense Mapping Agency Hydrographic Center [1802-   ]
50-046844   527
Navigation. Nautical astronomy.

VK555.D96 1985
Dutton, Benjamin, 1883-1937.
Dutton's Navigation & piloting. Annapolis, Md.: Naval Institute Press, c1985. viii, 588 p.
85-003004   623.89   0870211579
Navigation. Nautical astronomy.

VK597 Marine hydrography. Hydrographic surveying — By region or country, A-Z

VK597.U6.M36 1988
Manning, Thomas G.
U.S. Coast Survey vs. Naval Hydrographic Office: a 19th-century rivalry in science and politics/ Thomas G. Manning. Tuscaloosa: University of Alabama Press, c1988. xii, 202 p.
87-025524   526.9/9/0973   0817303901
U.S. Coast and Geodetic Survey -- History -- 19th century. United States. Hydrographic Office -- History -- 19th century.

VK597.U6.W66 1994
Woodford, Arthur M., 1940-
Charting the inland seas: a history of the U.S. Lake Survey/ Arthur M. Woodford. Detroit: Wayne State University Press, 1994. xvii, 281 p.
93-044186   526.9/0977   0814324991
Great Lakes -- Surveys.

VK1015 Lighthouse service — History

VK1015.S7
Stevenson, David Alan.
The world's lighthouses before 1820. London, Oxford University Press, 1959. xxiv, 310 p.
59-016853   627.9209
Lighthouses -- History.

VK1023-1024 Lighthouse service — By region or country — North America

VK1023.A93
Adamson, Hans Christian.
Keepers of the lights. New York, Greenberg [1955] 430 p.
55-005458   627.9
Lighthouses -- United States. Aids to navigation -- United States.

VK1023.H65
Holland, F. Ross 1927-
America's lighthouses; their illustrated history since 1716. Brattleboro, Vt., S. Greene Press [1972] x, 226 p.
74-170080   387.1/55   0828901481
Lighthouses -- United States.

VK1023.N63 1997
Noble, Dennis L.
Lighthouses & keepers: the U.S. Lighthouse Service and its legacy/ Dennis L. Noble. Annapolis, Md.: Naval Institute Press, c1997. xiv, 244 p.
97-020882   387.1/55/0973   1557506388
Lighthouses -- United States -- History.

VK1024.N38.G54 1991
Gleason, Sarah C.
Kindly lights: a history of the lighthouses of southern New England/ Sarah C. Gleason; with a foreword by John Casey. Boston, Mass.: Beacon Press, c1991. xxi, 175 p.
90-052591   387.1/55   0807051071
Lighthouses -- New England -- History.

VK1265 Shipwrecks and fires — Submarine disasters

VK1265.E75 1990
Eriksen, Viking Olver.
Sunken nuclear submarines: a threat to the environment?/ Viking Olver Eriksen. Oslo: Norwegian University Press; c1990. 176 p.
91-136814   359.9/33   8200210197
Submarine disasters. Nuclear submarines. Radioactive pollution of the sea.

VK1265.S45 1960
Shelford, W. O.
Subsunk; the story of submarine escape. With a foreword by B. W. Taylor. With 31 plates in half-tone and diagr. by the author. Garden City, N.Y., Doubleday, 1960 248 p.
60-013557   613.69
Submarine disasters. Search and rescue operations. Survival and emergency equipment.

VK1323 Saving of life and property — Lifesaving — By region or country

VK1323.N63 1994
Noble, Dennis L.
That others might live: the U.S. Life-Saving Service, 1878-1915/ Dennis L. Noble. Annapolis, Md.: Naval Institute Press, c1994. xix, 177 p.
93-037539   363.12/381/0973   1557506272
Lifesaving -- United States -- History.

VM Naval architecture. Shipbuilding. Marine engineering

VM12 Directories

VM12.A23 2000
Aak to Zumbra: a dictionary of the world's watercraft/ the Mariners' Museum; with contributions by M.H. Parry and others; illustrations by M.H. Parry. Newport News, Va.: Mariners' Museum, c2000. x, 676 p.
2001-031471   623.8/2/003   0917376463
Ships -- Dictionaries. Boats and boating -- Dictionaries.

VM15 History — General works

VM15.A22
Abell, Westcott Stile, 1877-
The shipwright's trade/ by Sir Westcott Abell. Cambridge [Eng.] University Press, 1948. xiii, 218 p.
49-014862   623.809
Shipbuilding -- Great Britain. Shipbuilding -- History.

VM15.A5
Albion, Robert Greenhalgh, 1896-
Five centuries of famous ships: from the Santa Maria to the Glomar Explorer/ Robert G. Albion; with a foreword by Benjamin Labaree. New York: McGraw-Hill, c1978. viii, 435 p.
77-004904   387.2/09/03   0070009538
Ships -- History.

VM15.A6 1963
Anderson, Romola.
The sailing-ship; six thousand years of history, by Romola & R. C. Anderson. New York, Norton [c1963] 211 p.
63-015867   623.821
Sailing ships.

VM15.C233 1971
Casson, Lionel, 1914-
Ships and seamanship in the ancient world. Princeton, N.J., Princeton University Press, 1971. xxviii, 441 p.
78-112996   623.82/1   0691035369
Ships, Ancient. Seamanship -- History.

VM15.G67 2000
Gould, Richard A.
Archaeology and the social history of ships/ Richard A. Gould. Cambridge, U.K.; Cambridge University Press, 2000. xiv, 360 p.
00-699752   930.102804   0521561035
Ships -- History. Ocean and civilization. Shipwrecks.

VM15.G72
Greenhill, Basil.
Archaeology of the boat: a new introductory study/ [by] Basil Greenhill; with chapters by J. S. Morrison and Sean McGrail; ... drawings by Eric McKee; introduced by W. F. Grimes. London: A. and C. Black, 1976. 320 p.
77-352714   623.82/1   0713616458
Boats and boating -- History. Boatbuilding -- History. Archaeology.

VM15.H33 1975
Haws, Duncan.
Ships and the sea: a chronological review/ by Duncan Haws. [New York]: Crowell, [1975] 240 p.
75-013686   387.2/09   0690009682
Ships -- History. Navigation -- History. Shipping -- History.

VM15.J613 1971
Jobe, Joseph, 1918-
The great age of sail [by] B. W. Bathe [and others] with the collaboration of Jean Merrien. Edited by Joseph Jobe. Translated by Michael Kelly. New York, Viking Press [1971, c1967] 252 p.
71-150355   623.82/2   067034835X
Sailing ships. Navigation -- History.

VM15.L213
Landstrom, Bjorn.
The ship, an illustrated history, written and illustrated by Bjorn Landstrom. [Translated by Michael Phillips] Garden City, N.Y., Doubleday [1961] 309 p.
61-014718   623.8109
Ships -- History. Naval architecture -- History.

VM17 History — Medieval

VM17.B715 1971
Brogger, Anton Wilhelm, 1884-
The Viking ships; their ancestry and evolution [by] A. W. Brogger [and] Haakon Shetelig. [English translation by Katherine John] New York, Twayne Publishers [1971] 191 p.
72-181704   623.82/1
Ships. Viking ships.

VM17.F75 1995
Friel, Ian.
The good ship: ships, shipbuilding and technology in England, 1200-1520/ Ian Friel. Baltimore: Johns Hopkins University Press, c1995. 208 p.
95-075761   623.8/2/009420902   0801852021
Ships, Medieval -- England. Shipbuilding -- England -- History.

VM17.H88 1994
Hutchinson, Gillian, 1955-
Medieval ships and shipping/ Gillian Hutchinson. Rutherford: Fairleigh Dickinson University Press, c1994. xi, 219 p.
94-019229   387.2/0941/0902   0838636284
Ships, Medieval -- Great Britain. Shipbuilding -- Great Britain -- History. Shipping -- Great Britain -- History. Great Britain -- History -- Medieval period, 1066-1485.

VM22-23 History — By region or country — North America

VM22.M54
Millar, John Fitzhugh.
American ships of the Colonial and Revolutionary periods/ John F. Millar. New York: Norton, c1978. viii, 356 p.
78-018742   623.82/2/0973   0393032221
Ships -- History -- 17th century. Ships -- History -- 18th century. North America -- History -- Colonial period, ca. 1600-1775. United States -- History -- Revolution, 1775-1783.

VM23.C53 1935a
Chapelle, Howard Irving.
The history of American sailing ships, by Howard I. Chapelle; with drawings by the author, and George C. Wales and Henry Rusk. New York, W. W. Norton & company, 1935.
35-027469   623.8220973
Sailing ships. Shipbuilding -- United States -- History. Shipping -- United States -- History.

VM23.H85 1969
Hutchins, John Greenwood Brown, 1909-
The American maritime industries and public policy, 1789-1914; an economic history, by John G. B. Hutchins. New York, Russell & Russell [1969, c1941] xxi, 627 p.
68-027065   387.5/0973
Shipbuilding -- United States -- History. Merchant marine -- United States.

VM23.S67
Society of Naval Architects and Marine Engineers (US)
Historical transactions, 1893-1943/ The Society of Naval Architects and Marine Engineers. New York, N.Y., The Society, 1945. vi, 544 p.
46-000471   623.8
Shipyards -- United States -- History. Marine engineering -- History. Shipping -- United States -- History.

VM80-83 History — By region or country — Europe

VM80.V4.L3
Lane, Frederic Chapin, 1900-
Venetian ships and shipbuilders of the Renaissance, by Frederic Chapin Lane. Baltimore, The Johns Hopkins press, 1934. ix, 285 p.
34-004368   623.809453
Shipbuilding -- Venice. Renaissance -- Italy. Ship builders. Venice -- Arsenals. Venice -- Economic conditions.

VM83.S65 1993
Smith, Roger C.
Vanguard of empire: ships of exploration in the age of Columbus/ Roger C. Smith. New York: Oxford University Press, 1993. xii, 316 p.
91-040929   623.8/22/094609024   0195073576
Ships -- Portugal -- History. Ships -- Spain -- History. Discoveries in geography -- History.

VM140 Biography — Individual, A-Z

VM140.F9.H87
Hutcheon, Wallace, 1933-
Robert Fulton, pioneer of undersea warfare/ by Wallace Hutcheon. Annapolis, Md.: Naval Institute Press, c1981. xii, 191 p.
80-081094   623.8/25/0924   0870215477
Fulton, Robert, -- 1765-1815. Naval art and science. Naval architects -- United States -- Biography.

VM140.F9.K76 1999
Kroll, Steven.
Robert Fulton: from submarine to steamboat/ by Steven Kroll; illustrated by Bill Farnsworth. New York: Holiday House, c1999. 1 v.
98-029944   623.8/24/092   0823414337
Fulton, Robert, -- 1765-1815 -- Juvenile literature. Fulton, Robert, -- 1765-1815. Inventors -- United States -- Biography -- Juvenile literature. Steamboats -- United States - History -- 19th century -- Juvenile literature. Marine engineers -- United States -- Biography -- Juvenile literature.

VM144 Naval architecture (General) — Wooden ships — General works

VM144.C28 1967
Chapelle, Howard Irving.
The search for speed under sail, 1700-1855, by Howard I. Chapelle. New York, Norton [1967] xviii, 453 p.
67-011090   623.82/03
Sailing ships. Naval architecture.

VM144.G74 1989
Greenhill, Basil.
The evolution of the wooden ship/ Basil Greenhill; illustrations by Sam Manning. New York: Facts on File, 1988. 239 p.
88-031107   623.8/207   081602121X
Ships, Wooden -- History. Shipbuilding -- History. Ships, Wooden -- History -- Pictorial works.

VM144.S73 1994
Steffy, J. Richard 1924-
Wooden ship building and the interpretation of shipwrecks/ J. Richard Steffy. College Station: Texas A&M University Press, c1994. xii, 314 p.
93-030036   623.8/207   0890965528
Ships, Wooden. Shipwrecks. Underwater archaeology.

VM145 Naval architecture (General) — General works, 1861-

VM145.H23 1949
Hardy, Alfred Cecil, 1898-
The book of the ship; an exhaustive pictorial and factual survey of world ships, shipping, and shipbuilding. London, S. Low, Marston [1949] 322 p.
49-008296   623.8
Shipping. Ships. Shipbuilding.

VM145.L57
The Lore of ships. Gothenberg, Sweden] Tre tryckare; [1963] 276 p.
63-018428
Ships. Naval architecture -- History.

VM156 Theory of the ship. Principles of naval architecture — General works

VM156.B49
Bhattacharyya, Rameswar.
Dynamics of marine vehicles/ Rameswar Bhattacharyya. New York: Wiley, c1978. x, 498 p.
78-000950   623.8/1   0471072060
Ships -- Seakeeping.

VM156.M27
Manning, George Charles, 1892-
The theory and technique of ship design; a study of the basic principles and the processes employed in the design of ships of all classes. [Cambridge] Published jointly by the Technology Press of the Massachusetts Institute of Technology and Wiley, [1956] 278 p.
56-005673   623.81
Naval architecture.

VM165 Study and teaching — General works

VM165.B4
Benford, Harry.
Your future in naval architecture, with information on marine engineering [by] Harry Benford and J. C. Mathes. New York, R. Rosen Press [1968] 156 p.
68-022156   623.8
Naval architecture -- Vocational guidance. Naval architecture -- Vocational guidance.

VM298 Ship models. Steamboat models — General works

VM298.W48 1971
Williams, Guy R.
The world of model ships and boats [by] Guy R. Williams. New York, Putnam [1971] 255 p.
74-116994   623.82/01
Ship models.

VM298.5 Shipbuilding industry. Shipyards — General works

VM298.5.T62 1991
Todd, Daniel.
Industrial dislocation: the case of global shipbuilding/ Daniel Todd. London; Routledge, 1991. xiv, 292 p.
90-008882   338.4/762382   0415042135
Shipbuilding industry. Shipbuilding industry -- Japan.

VM299.6 Shipbuilding industry. Shipyards — By region or country — United States

VM299.6.H45 1997
Heinrich, Thomas R.
Ships for the seven seas: Philadelphia shipbuilding in the age of industrial capitalism/ Thomas R. Heinrich. Baltimore: Johns Hopkins University Press, c1997. x, 290 p.
96-027104   338.4/762382/0974811   0801853877
Shipbuilding industry -- Pennsylvania -- Philadelphia -- History.

VM301 Shipbuilding industry. Shipyards — Shipbuilding companies and shipyards, A-Z

VM301.M5.F85 1992
Fukasaku, Yukiko, 1950-
Technology and industrial development in pre-war Japan: Mitsubishi Nagasaki Shipyard, 1884-1934/ Yukiko Fukasaku. London; Routledge, 1992. xviii, 189 p.
91-046065   338.4/762383/0952244   0415065526
Shipbuilding industry -- Japan -- Nagasaki-shi -- History -- 20th century. Industries -- Japan -- History -- 20th century. Technology transfer -- Japan -- History -- 20th century.

VM301.P43.S66 1999
Snow, Ralph Linwood, 1934-
A shipyard in Maine: Percy & Small and the great schooners/ Ralph Linwood Snow, Douglas K. Lee. Gardiner, Me.: Tilbury House Publishers; c1999. xvi, 391 p.
98-031176   338.7/62382/009741   088448193X
Shipyards -- Maine -- Bath -- History. Shipbuilding industry -- Maine -- Bath -- History.

VM307 Illustrations of ships of all kinds. Pictorial works

VM307.B6 1969
Bloomster, Edgar L.
Sailing and small craft down the ages. Drawings and text by Edgar L. Bloomster. Annapolis, Md., United States Naval Institute [1969] 116 p.
70-011099   623.82/2
Ships. Ships -- Pictorial works.

VM307.H3713 1968b
Hansen, Hans Jurgen, 1921-
Art and the seafarer; a historical survey of the arts and crafts of sailors and shipwrights. With contributions by Edward H. H. Archibald [and others] General editor: Hans Jurgen Hansen. Translated by James and Inge Moore. New York, Viking Press [1968] 292 p.
68-015485   725/.99
Naval architecture -- History. Carving (Art industries) -- History. Figure-heads of ships -- History.

VM311 Special types of vessels — By construction or rigging, A-Z

VM311.C3.H3
Harris, Robert B.
Modern sailing catamarans. New York, Scribner [1960] 143 p.
60-014017   623.822
Catamarans. Sailboat racing.

VM321 Special types of vessels — Small craft — General works

VM321.B3
Baay, Henry Van Lent.
Boats, boat yards, and yachtsmen. Introd. by William H. Taylor. Princeton, N. J., Van Nostrand [1961] 211 p.
61-019954　623.8231
Boatbuilding. Boats and boating -- Law and legislation -- United States. Boats and boating.

VM321.S45
Shekter, Robert J
Standard handbook of pleasure boats. New York, Crowell [1959] 341 p.
59-012497　623.8231
Boats and boating. Sailboats.

VM331 Special types of vessels — Small craft — Yachts

VM331.M36 1980
Marchaj, Czeslaw A.
Aero-hydrodynamics of sailing/ C. A. Marchaj. New York: Dodd, Mead, 1980, c1979. xv, 701 p.
79-027724　623.8/12043　0396077390
Sailboats -- Hydrodynamics. Sailboats -- Aerodynamics. Sails -- Aerodynamics.

VM341-342 Special types of vessels — Small craft — Motorboats. Launches

VM341.C63
Piloting, seamanship, and small boat handling/ Charles F. Chapman; with revisions by Elbert S. Maloney ... [et al.]. [New York]: Motor Boating & Sailing,
42-049646　623.88/2.3105
Motorboats. Seamanship. Navigation.

VM341.Z33 1985
Zadig, Ernest A., 1899-
The complete book of boating: an owner's guide to design, construction, piloting, operation, and maintenance/ Ernest A. Zadig. Englewood Cliffs, N.J.: Prentice-Hall, c1985. 640 p.
84-026407　623.8/231　0131574965
Boats and boating.

VM342.T46 1992
Thomas, David.
Basics of radio control power boat modeling/ by David Thomas; editor, Burr Angle. Waukesha, WI: Kalmbach Books, 1992. 80 p.
92-029968　623.8/20131　0890241325
Motorboats -- Models -- Radio control.

VM351 Special types of vessels — Small craft — Boats. Rowboats, small sailboats, etc.

VM351.B43
Bell, Graham, 1921-
Building your own boat. London] Methuen [c1963] xii, 180 p.
64-004905　623.82
Boatbuilding Sailboats.

VM351.B52 1968
Blanchard, Fessenden Seaver, 1888-1963.
The sailboat classes of North America; more than two hundred racers, cruisers, and catamarans in stories and pictures. Expanded and updated by Theodore A. Jones. Garden City, N.Y., Doubleday, 1968. 381 p.
68-014205　623.82/2
Sailboats. Sailboat racing.

VM351.B596 1995
Bond, Hallie E.
Boats and boating in the Adirondacks/ Hallie E. Bond; introduction by Philip G. Terrie. Syracuse, NY: Adirondack Museum: 1995. 334 p.
95-008603　797/.09747/5　0815603738
Boatbuilding -- New York (State) -- Adirondack Mountains Region -- History. Boats and boating -- New York (State) -- Adirondack Mountains Region -- History. Adirondack Mountains Region (N.Y.) -- History.

VM362 Special types of vessels — Hydrofoil boats

VM362.S56
Smith, Bernard, 1910-
The 40-knot sailboat. New York, Grosset & Dunlap [1963] xiv, 140 p.
63-018980　623.823
Sailboats. Hydrofoil boats.

VM365 Special types of vessels — Submarine boats — General works

VM365.F76 1984
Friedman, Norman, 1946-
Submarine design and development/ Norman Friedman. Annapolis, Md.: Naval Institute Press, c1984. 192 p.
83-043278　623.8/257　0870219545
Submarines (Ships)

VM365.R8
Rush, Charles W
The complete book of submarines/ [by] C. W. Rush, W. C. Chambliss and H. J. Gimpel. Cleveland: World Pub. Co., c1958. 159 p.
58-009408　623.825
Submarines (Ships) Submarine warfare.

VM365.S42
Shenton, Edward H.
Diving for science; the story of the deep submersible [by] Edward H. Shenton. New York, Norton [1972] 267 p.
74-090990　551.4/6/0028　0393063801
Oceanographic submersibles. Oceanography -- Research.

VM395 Special types of vessels — By use — Cargo ships

VM395.B38.T49 1995
Thomson, Keith Stewart.
HMS Beagle: the story of Darwin's ship/ Keith Stewart Thomson; drawings by Townsend Moore. New York: W.W. Norton, c1995. 320 p.
94-036069　910.45　0393037789
Beagle (Ship) Beagle Expedition (1831-1836)

VM453 Special types of vessels — By use — Oceanographic research ships

VM453.C67 1983
Cousteau, Jacques Yves.
Jacques Cousteau's Calypso/ by Jacques Cousteau and Alexis Sivirine. New York: H.N. Abrams, 1983. 192 p.
83-003751　551.4/6/00723　0810907887
Oceanography -- Research. Underwater exploration.

VM455 Special types of vessels — By use — Tank vessels. Oil tankers

VM455.N35 1991
National Research Council (U.S.).
Tanker spills: prevention by design/ Committee on Tank Vessel Design, Marine Board, Commission on Engineering and Technical Systems, National Research Council. Washington, D.C.: National Academy Press, 1991. xxviii, 350 p.
91-012489　623.8/245　0309043778
Tankers -- Accidents. Oil spills.

VM532-533 Means of propulsion — Special topics — Rigging, masts, spars, sails, etc.

VM532.R3 1957
Ratsey, Ernest A 1901-
Yacht sails, their care & handling, by Ernest A. Ratsey and W.H. de Fontaine. New York, Norton [1957] 263 p.
57-005499　623.86
Yachts and yachting. Sails.

VM533.B5277 2000
Budworth, Geoffrey.
The illustrated encyclopedia of knots/ Geoffrey Budworth. New York, N.Y.: Lyons Press, 2000. 159 p.
2001-265387　623.88/82　158574073X
Knots and splices -- Encyclopedias.

VM533.G49 1963
Gibson, Charles Edmund, 1916-
Handbook of knots and splices, and other work with hempen and wire ropes. New York, Emerson Books [1963] 152 p.
63-008697　623.88/82
Knots and splices.

VM533.T58 1984
Toss, Brion.
The rigger's apprentice/ Brion Toss. Camden, Me.: International Marine Pub. Co., c1984. xi, 195 p.
84-047755　623.88/82　087742165X
Knots and splices. Masts and rigging.

VM600 Marine engineering — General works

VM600.T38 1989
Taylor, D. A.,
Dictionary of marine technology/ D.A. Taylor. London; Butterworths, 1989. 244 p.
88-030419 623.8/03/21 0408021950
Marine engineering -- Dictionaries.

VM615 Marine engineering — History — General works

VM615.F63 1944
Flexner, James Thomas, 1908-
Steamboats come true: American inventors in action/ by James Thomas Flexner. New York: Viking Press, 1944. x, 406 p.
44-007758 623.8/2436
Steamboats -- History. Steam-navigation -- History. Inventors -- United States.

VM615.R85 1970b
Rowland, K. T.
Steam at sea: a history of steam navigation [by] K. T. Rowland. New York, Praeger [1970] 240 p.
77-130458 623.82/04
Steam-navigation -- History.

VM615.T9 1939
Tyler, David Budlong, 1899-
Steam conquers the Atlantic, by David Budlong Tyler. New York, D. Appleton-Century co., [1939] xv, 425 p.
39-009629 387.509
Steam-navigation. Steam-navigation -- History.

VM624 Marine engineering — By region or country — North America

VM624.M8.H4
Heckman, William L. 1869-1957.
Steamboating: sixty-five years on Missouri's rivers, the historical story of developing the waterway traffic on the rivers of the Middlewest/ by William L. Heckman, "Steamboat Bill". Kansas City [Mo.]: Burton Pub. Co., c1950. 284 p.
50-013979 386.30978
Heckman, William L. -- (William Lewis), -- 1869-1957.Steam-navigation -- Missouri.

VM728 Marine engineering — Study and teaching — By region or country

VM728.G7.P4
Penn, Geoffrey.
"Up funnel, down screw!" The story of the naval engineer. With a foreward by Sir Frank Mason. London, Hollis & Carter [1955] 184 p.
56-022581 359
Marine engineering -- History.

VM740 Marine engineering — Marine engines — Marine turbines

VM740.W6
Woodward, John B.
Marine gas turbines/ John B. Woodward. New York: Wiley, [1975] xxii, 390 p.
74-031383 623.87/23/3 0471959626
Marine gas-turbines.

VM977 Marine engineering — Diving — History

VM977.E44 1939
Ellsberg, Edward, 1891-
Men under the sea. Dodd, Mead, 1939. 1 v.
39-027859 627/.72
Ellsberg, Edward, -- 1891-Deep diving -- History. Salvage -- History.

VM983 Marine engineering — Diving — Popular works

VM983.H3 1970
Hampton, T. A.
The master diver and underwater sportsman, by T. A. Hampton. New York, Arco Pub. Co. [1970] 192 p.
79-121369 797.23 0668023538
Deep diving.

VM989 Marine engineering — Diving — Special types of diving

VM989.P53
Piccard, Jacques.
Seven miles down: the story of the bathyscaph Trieste/ [by] Jacques Piccard and Robert S. Dietz. New York: Putnam, 1961. 249 p.
60-016679 551.46078
Deep diving.

VM989.R6
Roberts, Fred M.
Basic scuba; self-contained underwater breathing apparatus. Foreword by Edgar End. [Edited by Eugene V. Connett] Princeton, N.J., Van Nostrand [1960] 386 p.
60-015136 797.23
Aqualung. Diving suits. Deep diving -- Safety measures.

Z4-114 Books (General). Writing. Paleography

Z4 History of books and bookmaking — General works

Z4.A88 1990
Avrin, Leila.
Scribes, script, and books: the book arts from antiquity to the Renaissance/ Leila Avrin; illustrations by Malla Carl and Noah Ophir. Chicago: American Library Association; 1991. xxxxii, 356 p.
89-018024 002 0838905226
Books -- History. Writing -- History. Manuscripts -- History.

Z4.K54 1998
Kilgour, Frederick G.
The evolution of the book/ Frederick G. Kilgour. New York: Oxford University Press, 1998. 179 p.
97-014430 002/.09 0195118596
Books -- History.

Z4.L5
Lehmann-Haupt, Hellmut, 1903-
The life of the book; how the book is written, published, printed, sold, and read/ Hellmut Lehmann-Haupt. With line drawings by Fritz Kredel and additional illus. London, Abelard-Schuman [1957] 240 p.
57-005138 002
Books.

Z4.L58 1995
Levarie, Norma.
The art & history of books/ by Norma Levarie; with a foreword by Nicolas Barker. New Castle, DE: Oak Knoll Press; xx, 315 p.
94-014734 002/.09 20 0712303944
Books -- History. Printing -- History. Illustration of books.

Z4.M15 1943
McMurtrie, Douglas C. 1888-1944.
The book: the story of printing & bookmaking/ by Douglas C. McMurtrie. New York: Oxford University Press, c1943. xxx, 676 p.
43-004110 002
Books. Printing -- History.

Z4.O54 1992
Olmert, Michael.
The Smithsonian book of books/ Michael Olmert. 1st ed. Washington, D.C.: Smithsonian Books, 1992. 319 p.
91-039590 002 20 089599030X
Books -- History. Book industries and trade -- History.

Z4.P99
Putnam, George Haven,
Books and their makers during the middle ages; a study of the conditions of the production and distribution of literature from the fall of the Roman empire to the close of the seventeenth century, by Geo. Haven Putnam. New York, G.P. Putnam's sons, 1896-97. 2 v.
01-020897
Books -- History -- Antiquity and middle ages. Printers. Manuscripts. Freedom of the press. Copyright.

Z4.R69 1995
Rosenblum, Joseph.
A bibliographic history of the book: an annotated guide to the literature/ by Joseph Rosenblum. Metuchen, N.J.: Scarecrow Press; 1995. xiii, 425 p.
95-005327   016.002   0810830094
Books -- History -- Bibliography. Writing -- History -- Bibliography.

Z6 History of books and bookmaking — By period — 400-1450

Z6.A96 1990
Rouse, Mary A.
Authentic witnesses: approaches to medieval texts and manuscripts/ Mary A. Rouse and Richard H. Rouse. Notre Dame, Ind.: University of Notre Dame Press, c1991. viii, 518 p.
89-040389   091   0268006229
Books -- Europe -- History -- 400-1400. Books -- Europe -- History -- 1400-1600. Manuscripts, Medieval -- History.

Z6.G44 1985
Gellrich, Jesse M.,
The idea of the book in the Middle Ages: language theory, mythology, and fiction/ Jesse M. Gellrich. Ithaca, NY: Cornell University Press, 1985. 292 p.
84-023814   002 19   0801417228
Chaucer, Geoffrey, d. 1400 -- Criticism and interpretation. Books -- Europe -- History -- 400-1400. Literature, Medieval -- History and criticism. Transmission of texts. Learning and scholarship -- Europe -- History -- Medieval, 500-1500.

Z8 History of books and bookmaking — By region or country, A-Z

Z8.G7 C36 1998
The Cambridge history of the book in Britain. Cambridge, UK; Cambridge University Press, <1998-2002> v. <3-4 >
98-004398   002/.0941 21   052166182X
Books -- Great Britain -- History.

Z8.U62.C58 1996
Celment, Richard W., 1951-
The book in America/ Richard W. Clement; with images from the Library of Congress. Golden, Colo.: Fulcrum Publishing, c1996. x, 150 p.
96-010572   002/.0974   1555912346
Books -- United States -- History.

Z40 Writing — General works. History

Z40.A5
Anderson, Donald M.
The art of written forms; the theory and practice of calligraphy [by] Donald M. Anderson. New York, Holt, Rinehart and Winston [1969] ix, 358 p.
68-021782   741   0030686253
Calligraphy.

Z40.C67 1996
Coulmas, Florian.
The Blackwell encyclopedia of writing systems/ Florian Coulmas. Oxford, OX, UK: Blackwell Publishers, c1996. xxviii, 603 p.
94-047460   411   0631194460
Writing -- Encyclopedias.

Z40.M3713 1994
Martin, Henri Jean, 1924-
The history and power of writing/ Henri-Jean Martin; translated by Lydia G. Cochrane. Chicago: University of Chicago Press, 1994. xv, 591 p.
93-026718   411/.09   0226508358
Writing -- History. Printing -- History. Books and reading -- History.

Z40.R4 1974
Reynolds, L. D.
Scribes and scholars: a guide to the transmission of Greek and Latin literature/ by L. D. Reynolds and N. G. Wilson. Oxford: Clarendon Press, 1974. x, 275 p.
75-308361   001.2   0198143710
Classical literature -- Criticism, Textual. Classical literature -- Manuscripts. Learning and scholarship -- History.

Z40.S27 1999
Sassoon, Rosemary.
Handwriting of the twentieth century/ Rosemary Sassoon. London; Routledge, 1999. 208 p.
98-048626   652/.1/0904   0415178819
Writing -- Great Britain -- History -- 20th century. Paleography, English. Penmanship -- Great Britain -- History -- 20th century.

Z40.T46 1996
Thornton, Tamara Plakins, 1957-
Handwriting in America: a cultural history/ Tamara Plakins Thornton. New Haven: Yale University Press, c1996. xiv, 248 p.
96-006282   652/.1/09   0300064772
Writing -- United States -- Psychological aspects -- History.

Z43.L86-M25 Writing — Calligraphy. Penmanship — General works

Z43.L86 2000
Lovett, Patricia.
Calligraphy & illumination: a history and practical guide/ Patricia Lovett. New York: Harry N. Abrams, 2000. 320 p.
00-031318   745.6/1   0810941198
Calligraphy. Illumination of books and manuscripts.

Z43.M25 1982
Mahoney, Dorothy.
The craft of calligraphy/ Dorothy Mahoney. New York: Taplinger Pub. Co., 1982, c1981. 128 p.
81-023238   745.6/197   0800819705
Calligraphy.

Z45 Writing — Calligraphy. Penmanship — Materials and instruments for writing (General)

Z45.T85
Tsien, Tsuen-hsuin, 1909-
Written on bamboo and silk; the beginnings of Chinese books and inscriptions. [Chicago] University of Chicago Press [1962] xiv, 233 p.
61-011897   417
Writing -- Materials and instruments. Chinese language -- Writing -- History.

Z48 Writing — Duplicating processes. Copying services

Z48.B44 1984
Bedini, Silvio A.
Thomas Jefferson and his copying machines/ Silvio A. Bedini. Charlottesville: University Press of Virginia, 1984. xvi, 239 p.
84-007288   686.4   0813910250
Jefferson, Thomas, -- 1743-1826 -- Views on copying. Jefferson, Thomas, -- 1743-1826 -- Views on machinery. Copying machines -- History. Copying processes -- History.

Z49 Writing — Typewriters. Typewriting. Keyboards. Keyboarding — Invention. History

Z49.L65 2002
Levine, Nathan.
Typing and keyboarding for everyone: 35 easy lessons to improve speed and accuracy/ Nathan Levine; Sheryl Lindsell-Roberts, editor. 12th ed. Lawrenceville, NJ: Thomson/Arco, c2002. xiii, 146 p.
2003-265436   652.3 21   0768908531
Keyboarding. Typewriting.

Z52.4 Writing — Word processing — General works

Z52.4.B65 1991
Bolter, J. David, 1951-
Writing space: the computer, hypertext, and the history of writing/ Jay David Bolter. Hillsdale, N.J.: L. Erlbaum Associates, c1991. xiii, 258 p.
90-046380   652.5   0805804277
Word processing. Hypertext systems. Electronic publishing.

Z52.4.H44 1987
Heim, Michael, 1944-
Electric language: a philosophical study of word processing/ Michael Heim. New Haven: Yale University Press, c1987. xi, 305 p.
86-028247   652/.5   0300038356
Word processing -- Philosophy. Language and languages -- Philosophy.

Z103 Writing — Cryptography — Bibliography

Z103.K28
Kahn, David, 1930-
The codebreakers; the story of secret writing. New York, Macmillan [1967] xvi, 1164 p.
63-016109   652.8
Cryptography -- History.

Z103.L46 2000
Lewand, Robert
Cryptological mathematics/ Robert Edward Lewand. Washington, DC: Mathematical Association of America, c2000. xiv, 199 p.
00-010526   0883857197
Cryptography. Crytography -- Problems, exercises, etc. Number theory.

Z103.N344 1997
Newton, David E.
Encyclopedia of cryptology/ David E. Newton. Santa Barbara, Calif.: ABC-CLIO, c1997. xi, 330 p.
97-028018   652/.8/03   0874367727
Cryptography -- Encyclopedias.

Z103.S56 1999
Singh, Simon.
The code book: the evolution of secrecy from Mary, Queen of Scots, to quantum cryptography/ Simon Singh. 1st ed. New York: Doubleday, c1999. xiii, 402 p.
99-035261   652/.8/09 21   0385495315
Cryptography -- History. Data encryption (Computer science) -- History.

Z103.W4
Weber, Ralph Edward.
United States diplomatic codes and ciphers, 1775-1938/ Ralph E. Weber. Chicago: Precedent Pub., 1979. xviii, 633 p.
78-065854   652/.8   0913750204
Cryptography -- United States -- History. Diplomatic and consular service, American -- History.

Z103.W46 1988
Welsh, Dominic.
Codes and cryptography/ Dominic Welsh. Oxford [Oxfordshire]: Clarendon Press; 1988. ix, 257 p.
87-031354   652/.8   0198532881
Ciphers. Cryptography.

Z104 Writing — Cryptography — Ciphers

Z104.T89 1990
Tunnell, James E.
Latest intelligence: an international directory of codes used by government, law enforcement, military, and surveillance agencies/ James E. Tunnell; edited by Helen L. Sanders. Blue Ridge Summit, PA: Tab Books, c1990. x, 305 p.
90-037042   652/.8   0830675310
Ciphers -- Dictionaries. Law enforcement -- Abbreviations -- Dictionaries. Intelligence service -- Abbreviations.

Z105 Manuscripts. Paleography — General works

Z105.M17 1927a
Madan, Falconer, 1851-1935.
Books in manuscript; a short introduction to their study and use. New York, Haskell House Publishers, 1968. xv, 208 p.
68-025315   091
Manuscripts.

Z107 Manuscripts. Paleography — History — General works

Z107.S74 1994
Stevick, Robert David, 1928-
The earliest Irish and English bookarts: visual and poetic forms before A.D. 1000/ Robert D. Stevick. Philadelphia: University of Pennsylvania Press, c1994. xiv, 282 p.
94-015970   745.6/7   0812232208
Manuscript design -- Ireland. Manuscript design -- Great Britain. Stichometry.

Z112 Manuscripts. Paleography — Materials, instruments, etc.

Z112.K38
Kenyon, Frederic G. 1863-1952.
Books and readers in ancient Greece and Rome. Oxford, Clarendon Press, 1951. 136 p.
52-009244
Books and reading. Manuscripts (Papyri) Parchment.

Z114 Manuscripts. Paleography — Manuals. Treatises — Special alphabets, etc.

Z114.H46 1987
Henderson, George, 1931-
From Durrow to Kells: the Insular Gospel-books, 650-800/ George Henderson. New York, N.Y.: Thames and Hudson, 1987. 224 p.
86-071619   745.6/7   0500234744
Books -- Great Britain -- History -- 400-1400. Scriptoria -- Great Britain. Manuscripts, Latin (Medieval and modern) -- Great Britain. Great Britain -- Church history -- 449-1066.

Z114.T472 1965
Thompson, Edward Maunde, 1840-1929.
An introduction to Greek and Latin palaeography. New York, B. Franklin [1965] xvi, 600 p.
74-006461   481/.7
Paleography, Latin. Paleography, Greek.

Z116-658 Book industries and trade

Z116.A2 Treatises on the modern printed book

Z116.A2.G27 1974
Gaskell, Philip.
A new introduction to bibliography/ Philip Gaskell. Oxford: Clarendon Press, 1974. xxv, 438 p.
75-330050   686.2/09   0198181507
Printing -- History. Book industries and trade -- History. Bibliography, Critical.

Z116.A2.L44 1979
Lee, Marshall, 1921-
Bookmaking: the illustrated guide to design/production/editing/ Marshall Lee. New York: Bowker, c1979. 485 p.
79-065014   686   0835210979
Book design. Book industries and trade. Editing.

Z116.A3 Book design

Z116.A3 H46 1998
Hendel, Richard.
On book design/ Richard Hendel. New Haven: Yale University Press, c1998. xii, 210 p.
98-017186   686 21   0300075707
Book design -- United States.

Z116.A3.T45 1988
Thompson, Bradbury.
The art of graphic design/ Bradbury Thompson; with contributions by noteworthy designers, critics, and art historians. New Haven: Yale University Press, 1988. xii, 218 p.
88-000210   686   0300043015
Book design. Magazine design. Graphic design (Typography)

Z116.T7513 Printing — General works

Z116.T7513 1995
Tschichold, Jan, 1902-1974.
The new typography: a handbook for modern designers/ Jan Tschichold; translated by Ruari McLean, with an introduction by Robin Kinross. Berkeley: University of California Press, c1995. xliv, 236 p.
94-020788   686.2/2   0520071468
Printing. Graphic design.

Z117 Printing — Bibliography

Z117.B59 2001
Bigmore, E. C.
A bibliography of printing: with notes and illustrations/ compiled by E.C. Bigmore and C.W.H. Wyman. 3rd ed. New Castle, Del.: Oak Knoll Press, 2001. 3 v. in 1
2001-036478   016.6862 21   1584560614
Printing -- Bibliography. Printing -- History.

Z118 Printing — Collections. Series. Systematic encyclopedias, etc.

Z118.B4 1992
Beach, Mark.
Graphically speaking: an illustrated guide to the working language of design and printing/ Mark Beach; [Spanish indexing by Marcos and Shana Galindo]. Manzanita, Or: Elk Ridge Pub.; c1992. 322 p.
92-013818   686.2   094338107X
Printing -- Dictionaries. Graphic arts -- Dictionaries. Printing -- Dictionaries -- Spanish.

Z118.B75 1983
The Bookman's glossary/ edited by Jean Peters. New York: Bowker, 1983. ix, 223 p.
83-002775   070.5/03   0835216861
Book industries and trade -- Dictionaries. Printing -- Dictionaries. Bibliography -- Dictionaries.

Z118.C58 1997
Collin, P. H.
Dictionary of printing and publishing/ P.H. Collin. 2nd ed. Teddington, Middlesex, [England]: Peter Collin, 1997. 324 p.
98-127212   686.2/03 21   0948549998
Printing -- Dictionaries. Publishers and publishing -- Dictionaries.

Z118.G29 1998
The GATF encyclopedia of graphic communications/ Richard M. Romano, editor-in-chief; Frank J. Romano, editor; Thomas M. Destree, Erika L. Kendra, associate editors; Robert J. Romano, technical illustrator. Pittsburgh: GATFPress, c1998. xxxviii, 945 p.
97-074138   686.2/03   0883621908
Printing -- United States -- Encyclopedias. Graphic arts -- United States -- Encyclopedias.

Z118.G55 1996
Glaister, Geoffrey Ashall.
Encyclopedia of the book/ by Geoffrey Ashall Glaister. 2nd ed./ with a new introduction by Donald Farren. New Castle, Del.: Oak Knoll Press, 1996. xxiii, 551 p.
96-007274   686.2/03 20   1884718140
Books--Dictionaries.

Z118.G76 1998
Groff, Pamela J.
Glossary of graphic communications/ compiled by Pamela J. Groff. Upper Saddle River, NJ: Prentice Hall PTR, c1998. 385 p.
98-019184   686.2/03   0130964107
Printing -- Dictionaries.

Z118.L96 2000
Lyons, Daniel J.
Prentice Hall graphic communications dictionary/ Daniel J. Lyons. Upper Saddle River, N.J.: Prentice Hall, 2000. xiii, 308 p.
99-034860   686.2/03   0130122262
Printing -- United States -- Dictionaries. Graphic arts -- United States -- Dictionaries.

Z121 Printing — Museums. Exhibitions

Z121.P58 1973
Art of the printed book, 1455-1955; masterpieces of typography through five centuries from the collections of the Pierpont Morgan Library. With an essay by Joseph Blumenthal. New York, 1973. xiv, 192 p.
73-082830   002/.074/01471 19   0875980414
Books -- History -- Exhibitions. Printing -- History -- Exhibitions. Book design -- History -- Exhibitions.

Z124.C47-S8 Printing — History — General works

Z124.C47 1999
Chappell, Warren,
A short history of the printed word/ Warren Chappell & Robert Bringhurst. 2nd ed., rev. and updated. Point Roberts, WA: Hartley & Marks Publishers, c1999. xx, 313 p.
98-011931   686.2/09 21   0881791547
Printing -- History.

Z124.C66 2001
Cochran, Terry, 1955-
Twilight of the literary: figures of thought in the age of print/ Terry Cochran. Cambridge, Mass.: Harvard University Press, 2001. 288 p.
00-054013   302.2/244   067400454X
Printing -- Social aspects -- History. Books -- Social aspects -- History. Written communication -- History.

Z124.E37
Eisenstein, Elizabeth L.
The printing press as an agent of change: communications and cultural transformations in early modern Europe/ Elizabeth L. Eisenstein. Cambridge [Eng.]; Cambridge University Press, 1979. 2 v.
77-091083   686.2   0521220440
Printing -- Influence. Reformation. Renaissance. Technology and civilization.

Z124.E374 1983
Eisenstein, Elizabeth L.
The printing revolution in early modern Europe/ Elizabeth L. Eisenstein. Cambridge [Cambridgeshire]; Cambridge University Press, 1983. xiv, 297 p.
83-010145   686.2/09   0521258588
Printing -- History. Technology and civilization. Europe -- Intellectual life -- History.

Z124.J64 1998
Johns, Adrian.
The nature of the book: print and knowledge in the making/ Adrian Johns. Chicago, Ill.: University of Chicago Press, 1998. xxi, 753 p.
97-047252   686.2/094   0226401219
Printing -- Social aspects -- Europe -- History. Printing -- Social aspects -- England -- History. Books -- Europe -- History. England -- Intellectual life. Europe -- Intellectual life.

Z124.S8 1996
Steinberg, S. H.
Five hundred years of printing/ S.H. Steinberg. New ed./ revised by John Trevitt. London: British Library; 1996. x, 262 p.
96-012543   686.2/09 20   071230438X
Printing -- History.

Z126 Printing — History — Origin and antecedents of printing. History of the invention

Z126.B657
Blum, Andre, 1881-
The origins of printing and engraving, by Andre Blum; translated from the French by Harry Miller Lydenberg. New York, C. Scribner's Sons, 1940. ix, 226 p.
40-027477   655.11
Printing -- History -- Origin and antecedents. Engraving -- History. Illustrated books -- 15th and 16th centuries.

Z126.Z7
Man, John,
Gutenberg: how one man remade the world with words/ John Man. New York: John Wiley & Sons, 2002. 312 p.
2002-284322   0471218235
Gutenberg, Johann, 1397?-1468. Printers -- Germany -- Biography. Printing -- History -- Origin and antecedents.

Z126.Z7.K2813 1996
Kapr, Albert.
Johann Gutenberg: the man and his invention/ Albert Kapr; translated from the German by Douglas Martin. Aldershot, England; Scolar Press, 1996. 316 p.
94-042062   686.2/092   1859281141
Gutenberg, Johann, -- 1397?-1468. Printers -- Germany -- Biography. Printing -- History -- Origin and antecedents.

Z151-208 Printing — History — By region or country

Z151.B4
Bennett, H. S. 1889-
English books & readers, 1475-1557, being a study in the history of the book trade from Caxton to the incorporation of the Stationers' Company. Cambridge [Eng.] University Press, 1952. xiii, 336 p.
52-012000   655.442
Worde, Wynkyn de, -- d. 1534? Printing -- Great Britain -- History -- Great Britain. English literature -- Translations from foreign literature -- Bibliography. Book industries and trade -- Great Britain -- History.

Z151.3.B4
Bennett, H. S. 1889-
English books & readers, 1558-1603, being a study in the history of the book trade in the reign of Elizabeth I, by H. S. Bennett. Cambridge [Eng.] University Press, 1965. xvii, 319 p.
65-008917   655.442
Printing -- Great Britain -- History -- Great Britain. Book industries and trade -- Great Britain -- History.

Z152.E5.P55 1974
Plant, Marjorie.
The English book trade: an economic history of the making and sale of books/ by Marjorie Plant. London: Allen & Unwin, 1974. 520 p.
75-307309   338.4/7/0705730942   0046550127
Book industries and trade -- England -- History. Printing -- England -- History.

Z152.L8.H3
Handover, P. M.
Printing in London: from 1476 to modern times; competitive practice and technical invention in the trade of book and Bible printing, periodical production, jobbing &c.   Cambridge, Harvard University Press, 1960. 224 p.
60-003799   655.1421
Printing -- History -- London.

Z155.R53 1994
Richardson, Brian.
Print culture in Renaissance Italy: the editor and the   vernacular   text,   1470-1600/   Brian Richardson. Cambridge [England]; Cambridge University Press, 1994. xvi, 265 p.
93-030907   686.2/0945/09024   0521420326
Printing -- Italy -- History. Early printed books -- Italy -- Venice. Early printed books -- Italy -- Florence.

Z186.C5.C3 1955
Carter, Thomas Francis, 1882-1925.
The invention of printing in China and its spread westward. Rev. by L. Carrington Goodrich. New York, Ronald Press Co. [1955] xxiv, 293 p.
55-005418   655.151
Printing -- History -- Origin and antecedents. Printing -- History -- China.

Z205.T56 1970b
Thomas, Isaiah, 1749-1831.
The history of printing in America: with a biography of printers & an account of newspapers/ by Isaiah Thomas; edited by Marcus A. McCorison from the second edition. New York: Weathervane Books: c1970. xxi, 650 p.
75-100491   686.2/0973   051717202X
Printing -- America -- History. Printing -- United States -- History. Printers -- United States -- Biography.

Z208.M18
McMurtrie, Douglas C. 1888-1944.
A history of printing in the United States; the story of the introduction of the press and of its history and influence during the pioneer period in each state of the Union, by Douglas C. McMurtrie. New York, R.R. Bowker company, [1936-]
36-018066   655.173
Printing -- History -- United States.

Z231 Printing — Printers and printing establishments — Collective biography

Z231.H83
Hudak, Leona M.,
Early American women printers and publishers, 1639-1820/ by Leona M.   Hudak. Metuchen, N.J.: Scarecrow Press, 1978. xxi, 813 p.
78-000825   686.2/092/2 B   0810811197
Women printers -- United States -- Biography. Women publishers -- United States -- Biography. Publishers and publishing -- United States -- History. Printing -- United States -- History. United States -- Imprints -- Union lists.

Z231.5 Printing — Printers and printing establishments — Classes of presses, A-Z

Z231.5.U6.P37 1989
Parsons, Paul, 1952-
Getting published: the acquisition process at university presses/ Paul Parsons. Knoxville: University of Tennessee Press, c1989. viii, 243 p.
89-031711   070.5/94   0870496115
University presses. Scholarly publishing. Authors and publishers.

Z232 Printing — Printers and printing establishments — Individual printers and establishments, A-Z

Z232.C93.G74 1988
Griffin, Clive.
The Crombergers of Seville: the history of a printing and merchant dynasty/ Clive Griffin. Oxford: Clarendon Press; 1988. x, 270 p.
86-033251   686.2/0946/86   0198158319
Cromberger family.Printing -- Spain -- Seville -- History -- 16th century. Bibliography -- Early printed books -- 16th century. Printers -- Spain -- Biography. Seville (Spain) -- Commerce -- History -- 16th century. Seville (Spain) -- Imprints.

Z232.H38 S48 2001
Sherraden, Jim.
Hatch Show Print: the history of the great American poster shop/ by Jim Sherraden, Elek Horvath, and Paul Kingsbury. San Francisco: Chronicle Books, 2001. 160 p.
00-057089   686.2/312/0976855   0811828565
Letterpress printing -- Tennessee -- Nashville -- History. Printers -- Tennessee -- Nashville -- History. Theatrical posters, American -- Tennessee -- Nashville.

Z232.H73.W54 1992
Willis, J. H. 1929-
Leonard and Virginia Woolf as publishers: the Hogarth Press, 1917-41/ J.H. Willis, Jr. Charlottesville: University Press of Virginia, 1992. xvi, 451 p.
91-041505   070.5/09421   0813913616
Woolf, Virginia, -- 1882-1941 -- Knowledge -- Publishers and publishing. Woolf, Leonard, -- 1880-1969 -- Knowledge -- Publishers and publishing. Woolf, Virginia, -- 1882-1941 -- Knowledge -- Printing. Publishers and publishing -- England -- History -- 20th century. Private presses -- England -- History -- 20th century. Printing -- England -- History -- 20th century.

Z232.J54.L69 1991
Lowry, Martin.
Nicholas Jenson and the rise of Venetian publishing in Renaissance Europe/ Martin Lowry. Oxford, UK; B. Blackwell, 1991. xvii, 286 p.
90-034919   686.2/0945/31   0631173943
Jenson, Nicolas, -- ca. 1420-1480.Printing -- Italy -- Venice -- History -- Origin and antecedents. Publishers and publishing -- Italy -- Venice -- History. Type and type-founding -- Italy -- Venice -- History. Venice (Italy) -- Intellectual life.

Z232.M87.P45 1991
Peterson, William S.
The Kelmscott Press: a history of William Morris's typographical adventure/ by William S. Peterson. Oxford [England]: Clarendon Press; c1991. xiv, 371 p.
89-003351   070.5/09426/5   0198128878
Morris, William, -- 1834-1896 -- Knowledge -- Printing.Private presses -- England -- Hammersmith (London) -- History -- 19th century. Book design -- England -- Hammersmith (London) -- History -- 19th century. Printing -- England -- Hammersmith (London) -- History -- 19th century. Hammersmith (London, England) -- Imprints -- History -- 19th century. London (England) -- Imprints -- History -- 19th century.

Z240 Printing — Incunabula. Block books — Bibliographies. Catalogs

Z240.G58 Copy 2
Goff, Frederick Richmond, 1916-
Incunabula in American libraries; a third census of fifteenth-century books recorded in North American collections, compiled and edited by Frederick R. Goff. New York, Bibliographical Society of America, 1964. lxiii, 798 p.
65-001485   016.093
Incunabula -- Bibliography -- Catalogs. Catalogs, Union -- United States. Catalogs, Union -- Canada.

Z243 Printing — Practical printing — Printing as a trade

Z243.G7.R49 1989
Reynolds, Sian.
Britannica's typesetters: women compositors in Edwardian Edinburgh/ Sian Reynolds. Edinburgh: Edinburgh University Press, c1989. viii, 170 p.
89-195114   686.2/092/2   085224634X
Women labor union members -- Scotland -- Edinburgh -- History -- 20th century. Printing industry -- Scotland -- Edinburgh -- History -- 20th century. Sex discrimination in employment -- Scotland -- Edinburgh -- History -- 20th century. Edinburgh (Scotland) -- Economic conditions.

Z244.3 Printing — Practical printing — Recipes, vest-pocket manuals, etc.

Z244.3.D47 1990
Designer's guide to print production/ edited by Nancy Aldrich-Ruenzel. New York: Watson-Guptill Publications, 1990. 159 p.
89-048706   686.2/24 20   0823013146
Printing. Graphic design (Typography)

Z244.5-244.6 Printing — Practical printing — Printing as a business

Z244.5.M42 1983
Meggs, Philip B.
A history of graphic design/ Philip B. Meggs. New York: John Wiley & Sons 1992 540 p.
82-002826   686.2/09   0442262213
Graphic design (Typography) -- History. Book design -- History.

Z244.6.S65.S84 1992
Steinberg, Mark.
Moral communities: the culture of class relations in the Russian printing industry, 1867-1907/ Mark D. Steinberg. Berkeley: University of California Press, c1992. x, 289 p.
91-039493   381/.45002/0947   0520075722
Printing industry -- Social aspects -- Russia -- History -- 19th century. Printing industry -- Social aspects -- Russia -- History -- 20th century. Industrial relations -- Russia -- History -- 19th century. Russia -- Social conditions -- 1801-1917. Russia -- Moral conditions.

Z246 Printing — Practical printing — Style. Design. Format

Z246.L86 1996
Lupton, Ellen.
Design, writing, research: writing on graphic design/ Ellen Lupton, J. Abbott Miller. New York: Kiosk, 1996. x, 211 p.
95-043396   686.2/252   1568980477
Graphic design (Typography) Graphic design (Typography) -- United States -- History -- 20th century. Commercial art -- United States -- History -- 20th century.

Z246.M43 1998
Meggs, Philip B.
A history of graphic design/ Philip B. Meggs. 3rd ed. New York: John Wiley & Sons, c1998. xiii, 510 p.
97-038055   686.2/2/09 21   0471291986
Graphic design (Typography) -- History. Book design -- History.

Z246.M44 1989
Meggs, Philip B.
Type & image: the language of graphic design/ Philip B. Meggs. New York: John Wiley & Sons 1992 208 p.
88-021108   686.2/24   0442258461
Graphic design (Typography) Type and type-founding. Graphic arts.

Z246.W63 2001
Williams, Robin,
Robin Williams design workshop/ Robin Williams + John Tollett. Berkeley, Calif.: Peachpit Press, c2001. viii, 280 p.
2001-270918   0201700883
Typesetting. Web publishing.

Z249 Printing — Practical printing — Machinery and supplies

Z249.E48 2001
Eldred, Nelson Richards.
Chemistry for the graphic arts/ by Nelson R. Eldred. Pittsburgh: GATFPress, c2001. 433 p.
00-107663   681/.6   0883622491
Printing machinery and supplies. Chemistry.

Z249.S23 1992
Saxe, Stephen O.
American iron hand presses/ by Stephen O. Saxe; wood engravings by John Depol. New Castle, Del.: Oak Knoll Books, 1992. xiv, 108 p.
91-036587   681/.62/0973   0938768352
Handpress -- United States -- History. Printing -- United States -- History. Printing-press -- History.

Z250 Printing — Practical printing — Type and type founding. Specimen books

Z250.A2.B57 1992
Blackwell, Lewis, 1958-
Twentieth-century type/ Lewis Blackwell. New York: Rizzoli, 1992. 256 p.
92-007527   686.2/24   084781596X
Type and type-founding -- History -- 20th century. Printing -- History -- 20th century.

Z250.A2.Z379 1987
Zapf, Hermann.
Hermann Zapf & his design philosophy: selected articles and lectures on calligraphy and contemporary developments in type design, with illustrations and bibliographical notes, and a complete list o introduction by Carl Zahn. Chicago: Society of Typographic Arts, c1987. 254 p.
86-063752   686.2/24   0941447006
Type and type-founding -- History -- 20th century. Calligraphy -- History -- 20th century.

Z250.W238 1990
Wallis, L. W.
Modern encyclopedia of typefaces, 1960-90/ compiled and edited by Lawrence W. Wallis. New York: Van Nostrand Reinhold, c1990. 192 p.
90-042630   686.2/24   0442308094
Type and type-founding -- Dictionaries. Printing -- Specimens -- Dictionaries.

Z253 Printing — Practical printing — Composition, typesetting, makeup. Style manuals

Z253.M483.K34 2000
Kahan, Basil Charles.
Ottmar Mergenthaler: the man and his machine: a biographical appreciation of the inventor on his centennial/ Basil Kahan; introduction by Carl Schlesinger. New Castle, Del.: Oak Knoll Press, 2000. xv, 244 p.
99-045557   070.5/092   158456007X
Mergenthaler, Ottmar, -- 1854-1899.Printers -- United States -- Biography. Inventors -- United States -- Biography. Linotype -- History -- 19th century.

Z253.M73 1970
Modern Language Association of America.
The MLA style sheet. [New York, [1970] 48 p.
78-117373   808.02   0873520025
Printing -- Style manuals. Academic writing -- Handbooks, manuals, etc.

Z253.U69 2003
The Chicago manual of style. 15th ed. Chicago: University of Chicago Press, 2003.
2003-001860   808/.027/0973 21   0226104036
Printing -- Style manuals. Authorship -- Style manuals.

Z269 Bookbinding — History. Biography of bookbinders — General works

Z269.F68 1994
Foot, Mirjam.
Studies in the history of bookbinding/ Mirjam M. Foot. Aldershot, England; Scolar Press, 1994. xv, 467 p.
93-017589   686.3/0094   0859679357
Bookbinding -- Europe -- History.

Z269.M37 1998
Marks, P. J. M.
The British Library guide to bookbinding: history and techniques/ P.J.M. Marks. Toronto; University of Toronto Press, c1998. 96 p.
98-198940   686.3/0094 21   0802081762
Bookbinding -- Europe, Western -- History.

Z269.3 Bookbinding — Special types of bindings, A-Z

Z269.3.M44.S95 1999
Szirmai, J. A.
The archaeology of medieval bookbinding/ J.A. Szirmai. Aldershot, Hants.; Ashgate, c1999. xvi, 352 p.
98-021778   686.3/009/02   0859679047
Bookbinding, Medieval.

Z269.3.O75.N59 1992
Nixon, Howard M.
The history of decorated bookbinding in England/ Howard M. Nixon and Mirjam M. Foot. Oxford [England]; Clarendon Press; 1992. xviii, 124 p.
91-011623   686.3/6   0198181825
Fine bindings -- England -- History.

Z271 Bookbinding — Handbooks. Techniques and practice of bookbinding — General works

Z271.W638 1990
Wolfe, Richard J.
Marbled paper: its history, techniques, and patterns: with special reference to the relationship of marbling to bookbinding in Europe and the Western world/ Richard J. Wolfe. Philadelphia: University of Pennsylvania Press, c1990. xvi, 245 p.
89-014614   686.3/6   0812281888
Marbled papers. Marbling (Bookbinding) Bookbinding.

Z271.Y68 1995
Young, Laura S.
Bookbinding & conservation by hand: a working guide/ Laura S. Young ; with corrections and editions by Jerilyn Glenn Davis; illustrations by Sidonie Coryn; photographs by John Hurt Whitehead III. [Rev. ed.]. New Castle, Del.: Oak Knoll Press, 1995. xiii, 273 p.
95-035094   686.3/02 20   1884718116
Bookbinding. Books -- Conservation and restoration.

Z279 Bookselling and publishing — Bibliography

Z279.L38
Lehmann-Haupt, Hellmut, 1903-
One hundred books about bookmaking; a guide to the study and appreciation of printing. New York, Greenwood 1976. 87 p.
49-011987   016.655
Bibliography -- Bibliography. Printing -- Bibliographies. Book design.

Z279.S64 1995
Speck, Bruce W.
Managing the publishing process: an annotated bibliography/ Bruce W. Speck. Westport, Conn.: Greenwood Press, 1995. ix, 350 p.
95-006289   016.381/45002/0973   031327956X
Publishers and publishing -- Bibliography.

Z280 Bookselling and publishing — History. Biography of booksellers — General works

Z280.S18 2001
Schiffrin, André.
The business of books: how international conglomerates took over publishing and changed the way we read/ André Schiffrin. London; Verso, 2001. xiv, 178 p.
2002-265885   185984362X
Schiffrin, André. Publishers and publishing -- United States -- History -- 20th century. Publishers and publishing -- United States -- Mergers -- History -- 20th Book industries and trade -- United States -- History -- 20th century. Small presses -- United States -- History -- 20th century.

Z282 Bookselling and publishing — Directories

Z282.D32 1974
De La Garza, Peter Jack.
International subscription agents; an annotated directory. Compiled by Peter J. de la Garza for the Serials and Resources Sections of the Resources and Technical Services Division, American Library Association. Chicago, American Library Association, 1974. v, 73 p.
74-002099   380.1/45/070573025   0838931537
Serials subscription agencies -- Directories.

Z282.5 Bookselling and publishing — Dictionaries. Encyclopedias

Z282.5.I58 1995
International book publishing: an encyclopedia/ edited by Philip G. Altbach, Edith S. Hoshino. New York: Garland Pub., 1995. xxvi, 736 p.
94-010027   070.503   0815307861
Publishers and publishing -- Encyclopedias.

Z286 Bookselling and publishing — Special lines of business, A-Z

Z286.A55.R67
Rostenberg, Leona.
Old & rare; thirty years in the book business [by] Leona Rostenberg and Madeleine B. Stern. New York, A. Schram [1974] 234 p.
74-008970   658.8/09/070573   0839001304
Antiquarian booksellers -- Biography. Rare books -- Bibliography -- Methodology. Rare books -- Collectors and collecting.

Z286.F45.C55 1986
Clardy, Andrea, 1943-
Words to the wise: a writer's guide to feminist and lesbian periodicals and publishers/ by Andrea Fleck Clardy. Ithaca, N.Y.: Firebrand Books, c1986. 48 p.
86-004714   070.5/025   0932379168
Feminist literature -- Publishing -- Directories. Feminism -- Periodicals -- Publishing -- Directories. Feminism -- Authorship Marketing -- Directories.

Z286.M5.M4 1982
Meckler, Alan M., 1945-
Micropublishing: a history of scholarly micropublishing in America, 1938-1980/ Alan Marshall Meckler. Westport, Conn.: Greenwood Press, 1982. xiv, 179 p.
81-006955   070.5/795/0973   031323096X
Micropublishing -- United States -- History.

Z286.P4 W53 1994
Wilkas, Lenore.
International subscription agents/ compiled by Lenore Rae Wilkas. 6th ed. Chicago: American Library Association, 1994. xxii, 410 p.
93-029753   070.5/025 20   0838906222
Serials subscription agencies -- Directories.

Z286.P46.M4
MLA directory of scholarly presses in language and literature. New York: Modern Language Association of America, [1991-   ]
93-648707   070.5/94
Philology -- Publishing -- Directories -- Periodicals. Scholarly publishing -- Directories -- Periodicals.

Z286.S37.M3
Machlup, Fritz, 1902-
Information through the printed word: the dissemination of scholarly, scientific, and intellectual knowledge/ Fritz Machlup, Kenneth Leeson, and associates. New York: Praeger Publishers, 1978-1980. 4 v.
78-019460   070.5   0030474019
Scholarly publishing. Book industries and trade. Scholarly periodicals.

Z286.S4.L33 1992
LaFollette, Marcel C. (Marcel Chotkowski)
Stealing into print: fraud, plagiarism, and misconduct in scientific publishing/ Marcel C. LaFollette. Berkeley: University of California Press, c1992. viii, 293 p.
91-041669   179/.9097   0520078314
Science publishing -- Moral and ethical aspects. Publishers and publishing -- Professional ethics. Technical writing -- Moral and ethical aspects.

Z289 Bookselling and publishing — By region or country — Developing countries

Z289.P82 1985
Publishing in the Third World: knowledge and development/ edited by Philip G. Altbach, Amadio A. Arboleda, S. Gopinathan. Portsmouth, N.H.; Mansell, Heineman, 1985. xii, 226 p.
84-027920   070.5/091724   0435080067
Publishers and publishing -- Developing countries. Book industries and trade -- Developing countries.

Z291.3-331.86 Bookselling and publishing — By region or country — Europe

Z291.3.R67 2002
Rostenberg, Leona.
From revolution to revolution: perspectives on publishing & bookselling, 1501-2001/ Leona Rostenberg & Madeleine B. Stern. 1st ed. New Castle, Del.: Oak Knoll Press, 2002. ix, 189 p.
2002-069844   070.5/094 21   1584560746
Publishers and publishing -- Europe, Western - - History. Booksellers and bookselling -- Europe, Western -- History. Publishers and publishing -- United States -- History. Booksellers and bookselling -- United States -- History.

Z291.5.I5
International literary market place.   New York, R.R. Bowker Co.
65-028326   070.5/025/4
Publishers   and   publishing--Europe--Directories.

Z305.M46.B57 1994
Bloch, R. Howard.
God's plagiarist: being an account of the fabulous industry and irregular commerce of the abbe Migne/ R. Howard Bloch. Chicago: University of Chicago Press, 1994. vii, 152 p.
93-031872   381/.45002/0944   0226059707
Migne, J.-P. -- (Jacques-Paul), -- 1800-1875.Catholic literature -- Publication and distribution -- France -- History -- 19th century. Christian literature, Early -- Publication and distribution -- France -- History -- 19th century. Plagiarism -- France -- History -- 20th century.

Z305.S45.B42 1980
Beach, Sylvia.
Shakespeare and Company/ by Sylvia Beach. Lincoln: University of Nebraska Press, 1980, c1959. xiv, 199 p.
79-026571   658.8/09/070573094436
0803260563
Beach, Sylvia -- Homes and haunts -- France -- Paris.Authors and publishers -- France -- Paris - - History -- 20th century. Literature publishing -- France -- Paris -- History -- 20th century. Booksellers and bookselling -- France -- Paris -- Biography. Paris (France) -- Intellectual life -- 20th century.

Z310.6.P37.H47 1991
Hesse, Carla Alison.
Publishing and cultural politics in revolutionary Paris, 1789-1810/ Carla Hesse. Berkeley: University of California Press, c1991. xvi, 296 p.
90-026493   070.5/094436   0520074432
Publishers and publishing -- Political aspects - - France -- Paris -- History -- 18th century. Publishers and publishing -- Political aspects -- France -- Paris -- History -- 19th century. Revolutionary literature -- Publishing -- France - - Paris -- History. France -- History -- Revolution, 1789-1799 -- Literature and the revolution. Paris (France) -- History -- 1799-1815. Paris (France) -- History -- 1789-1799.

Z315.W72.K875 1991
Kurt Wolff: a portrait in essays and letters/ edited with a foreword by Michael Ermarth; translated by Deborah Lucas Schneider. Chicago: University of Chicago Press, c1991. xxviii, 223 p.
91-016490   070.5/092   0226905519
Wolff, Kurt, -- 1887-1963. Wolff, Kurt, -- 1887-1963 -- Correspondence. Publishers and publishing -- Germany -- Correspondence. Publishers and publishing -- Germany -- Biography. Authors and publishers -- Germany -- Frankfurt am Main -- History -- 20th century.

Z325.B74 1996
The British literary book trade, 1475-1700/ edited by James K.   Bracken and Joel Silver. Detroit: Gale Research, c1996. xii, 412 p.
96-031977   016.381/45002/0942   20
0810399334
Booksellers and bookselling -- Great Britain -- Biography. Publishers and publishing -- Great Britain -- Biography. Printers -- Great Britain -- Biography. Book industries and trade -- Great Britain -- History -- Bibliography. Literature publishing -- Great Britain -- History -- Bibliography. English literature -- Early modern, 1500-1700 -- Bibliography. English literature -- Middle English, 1100-1500 -- Bibliography.

Z325.D68.S64 1996
Solomon, Harry M.
The rise of Robert Dodsley: creating the new age of print/ Harry M. Solomon. Carbondale: Southern Illinois University Press, c1996. ix, 339 p.
95-023570   070.5/092   080931651X
Dodsley, Robert, -- 1703-1764.Booksellers and bookselling -- Great Britain -- Biography. Publishers and publishing -- Great Britain -- Biography. Authors, English -- 18th century -- Biography.

Z325.D68 1988
Dodsley, Robert, 1703-1764.
The correspondence of Robert Dodsley, 1733-1764/ edited by James E. Tierney. Cambridge [Cambridgeshire]; Cambridge University Press, 1988. xxxvii, 599 p.
87-014645   070.5/092/4   0521259258
Dodsley, Robert, -- 1703-1764 -- Correspondence.Booksellers and bookselling -- Great Britain -- Correspondence. Publishers and publishing -- Great Britain -- Correspondence. Authors, English -- 18th century -- Correspondence. London (England) -- Intellectual life -- 18th century.

Z325.M385.N45 1989
Nelson, James G.
Elkin Mathews: publisher to Yeats, Joyce, Pound/ James G. Nelson. Madison, Wis.: University of Wisconsin Press, c1989. xiii, 299 p.
89-040265   070.5/092   0299122409
Mathews, Elkin -- 1851-1921. Yeats, W. B. -- (William Butler), -- 1865-1939 -- Relations with publishers. Joyce, James, -- 1882-1941 -- Relations with publishers. Publishers and publishing -- Great Britain -- Biography. Literature publishing -- Great Britain -- History. Authors and publishers -- Great Britain -- History.

Z325.M65.M37 1999
McAleer, Joseph.
Passion's fortune: the story of Mills & Boon/ Joseph McAleer. Oxford; Oxford University Press, 1999. xii, 322 p.
00-687308   070.5/0941   0198204558
Literature publishing -- Great Britain -- History -- 20th century.

Z325.N53.J64 1994
John Newbery and his books: trade and plumbcake for ever, huzza!/ edited by John Rowe Townsend. Metuchen, N.J.: Scarecrow Press, 1994. xv, 173 p.
94-023293   070.5/0941   0810829509
Newbery, John, -- 1713-1767.Children's literature -- Publishing -- Great Britain -- History -- 18th century. Children's literature, English -- History and criticism. Publishers and publishing -- Great Britain -- History -- 18th century.

Z325.S665.N45 2000
Nelson, James G.
Publisher to the decadents: Leonard Smithers in the careers of Beardsley, Wilde, Dowson/ James G. Nelson; with an appendix on Smithers and the erotic book trade by Peter Mendes and a checklist of Smithers' publications by James G. Nelson and Peter Mendes. University Park: Pennsylvania State University Press, 2000. xvi, 430 p.
99-020705   070.5/092   0271019735
Smithers, Leonard C. -- (Leonard Charles), -- 1861-1907. Beardsley, Aubrey, -- 1872-1898 -- Publishers. Wilde, Oscar, -- 1854-1900 -- Publishers. Decadence (Literary movement) -- Great Britain. Publishers and publishing -- Great Britain -- Biography. Literary publishing - - Great Britain -- History -- 19th century.

Z325.W58 F36 2002
Finkelstein, David,
The house of Blackwood: author-publisher relations in the Victorian era/ David Finkelstein. University Park, PA: Pennsylvania State University Press, c2002. viii, 199 p.
2002-000501   070.5/0941 21   0271021799
Publishers and publishing -- Great Britain -- History -- 19th century. Authors and publishers - - Great Britain -- History -- 19th century. Great Britain -- Intellectual life -- 19th century

Z326.B666 1995
The British literary book trade, 1700-1820/ edited by James K. Bracken and Joel Silver. Detroit, MI: Gale Research, c1995. xii, 366 p.
95-004825   070.5/0941   0810357151
Literature publishing -- Great Britain -- History -- 18th century. Literature publishing -- Great Britain -- History -- 19th century. Publishers and publishing -- Great Britain -- Biography -- Dictionaries.

Z326.B673 1991
British literary publishing houses, 1881-1965/ edited by Jonathan Rose and Patricia J. Anderson. Detroit: Gale Research, c1991. xi, 420 p.
91-031918   070.5/0941   0810345927
Literature publishing -- Great Britain -- History -- 20th century -- Dictionaries. Literature publishing -- Great Britain -- History -- 19th century -- Dictionaries. Publishers and publishing -- Great Britain -- Biography -- Dictionaries.

Z326.C3
Cassell's directory of publishing in Great Britain, the Commonwealth, Ireland, and South Africa. London: Cassell,
60-052232   655.442
Publishers and publishing -- Commonwealth of Nations -- Directories.

Z327.C37
Directory of publishing.   London: Cassell, [c1991-]
93-642450   070.5/025/41 19
Publishers and publishing -- Great Britain -- Directories. Book industries and trade -- Great Britain -- Directories. Publishers and publishing -- Commonwealth countries -- Directories. Book industries and trade -- Commonwealth countries -- Directories.

Z331.86.D8.P47 1998
Phillips, James W. 1916-1986.
Printing and bookselling in Dublin, 1670-1800: a bibliographical enquiry/ James W. Phillips; with a foreword by M. Pollard. Dublin; Irish Academic Press, 1998. xviii, 337 p.
95-170922   0716525801
Book industries and trade -- Ireland -- Dublin -- History -- 17th century. Book industries and trade -- Ireland -- Dublin -- History -- 18th century.

Z465.2-465.5 Bookselling and publishing — By region or country — Africa

Z465.2.Z44 1995
Zell, Hans M.
Publishing and book development in Sub-Saharan Africa: an annotated bibliography/ Hans M. Zell & Cecile Lomer. London; H. Zell Publishers, 1995. 409 p.
95-032734   016.0705/0967   1873836465
Publishers and publishing -- Africa, Sub-Saharan -- Bibliography. Book industries and trade -- Africa, Sub-Saharan -- Bibliography.

Z465.5.A48
African publishers networking directory. Oxford: African Books Collective Ltd., [1997-]
98-034302
Publishers and publishing -- Africa -- Directories. Book industries and trade -- Africa -- Directories.

Z471-479 Bookselling and publishing — By region or country — United States

Z471.J68 1991
Joyce, Donald F.
Black book publishers in the United States: a historical dictionary of the presses, 1817-1990/ Donald Franklin Joyce. New York: Greenwood Press, 1991. xiv, 256 p.
91-010528   070.5/089/96073   0313267839
Afro-American business enterprises -- History -- Dictionaries. American literature -- Afro-American authors -- Publishing -- Dictionaries. Publishers and publishing -- United States -- Dictionaries.

Z471.P47 2002
Perspectives on American book history: artifacts and commentary/ edited by Scott E. Casper, Joanne D. Chaison, and Jeffrey D. Groves. Amherst: University of Massachusetts Press; ix, 461 p.
2001-006911   002/.0973 21   1558493174
Book industries and trade -- United States -- History -- Sources. Publishers and publishing -- United States -- History -- Sources. Books and reading -- United States -- History -- Sources. Book industries and trade -- Social aspects -- United States. Publishers and publishing -- Social aspects -- United States. Books and reading -- Social aspects -- United States. United States -- Intellectual life.

Z473.A485.S64 2000
Spector, Robert, 1947-
Amazon.com: get big fast/ Robert Spector. New York: HarperBusiness, c2000. xxii, 263 p.
99-087599   380.1/45002/02854678 0066620414
Internet bookstores -- United States -- History -- 20th century. Electronic commerce -- United States -- History -- 20th century.

Z473.C25.H45 1993
Henderson, Harold, 1948-
Catalyst for controversy: Paul Carus of Open Court/ Harold Henderson. Carbondale: Southern Illinois University Press, 1993. 205 p.
92-017303   381.45002/0973   0809317974
Carus, Paul, -- 1852-1919.Religious literature -- Publication and distribution -- United States -- History. Publishers and publishing -- Illinois -- La Salle -- History. Publishers and publishing -- United States -- Biography. United States -- Intellectual life.

Z473.C45.A36 1977
Cerf, Bennett, 1898-1971.
At Random: the reminiscences of Bennett Cerf. New York: Random House, c1977. ix, 306 p.
77-001867   070.5/092/4   0394478770
Cerf, Bennett, -- 1898-1971.Publishers and publishing -- United States -- Biography.

Z473.C455.R84 1997
Ruff, Allen, 1949-
"We called each other comrade": Charles H. Kerr & Company, radical publishers/ Allen Ruff. Urbana: University of Illinois Press, c1997. xvii, 312 p.
96-010086   070.5   0252022777
Publishers and publishing -- Political aspects -- United States -- History -- 19th century. Publishers and publishing -- Political aspects -- United States -- History -- 20th century. Socialism -- United States -- History -- 19th century.

Z473.C46 B87 1997
Burlingame, Roger,
Of making many books: a hundred years of reading, writing, and publishing/ by Roger Burlingame. University Park, Pa.: Pennsylvania State University Press, 1997. xxxiv, 347 p.
96-014230   070.5 20   0271016191
Publishers and publishing -- United States -- History -- 19th century. Publishers and publishing -- United States -- History -- 20th century.

Z473.D6.A75 1991
Arner, Robert D.
Dobson's Encyclopaedia: the publisher, text, and publication of America's first Britannica, 1789-1803/ Robert D. Arner. Philadelphia: University of Pennsylvania Press, c1991. xviii, 295 p.
91-017624   381/.45002/0974811   0812230922
Dobson, Thomas, -- 1751-1823.Encyclopedias and dictionaries -- Publishing -- Pennsylvania -- Philadelphia -- History -- 18th century. Book industries and trade -- Pennsylvania -- Philadelphia -- History -- 18th century. Philadelphia (Pa.) -- Imprints -- History.

Z473.G696 1997
Graham, Katharine,
Personal history/ Katharine Graham. 1st ed. New York: A.A. Knopf, 1997. ix, 642 p.
96-049638   070.5/092 B 21   0394585852
Graham, Katharine, 1917- Publishers and publishing -- United States -- Biography. Newspaper publishing -- Washington (D.C.) -- History -- 20th century.

Z473.H4.P76 1998
Procter, Ben H.
William Randolph Hearst: the early years, 1863-1910/ Ben Procter. New York: Oxford University Press, 1998. xiv, 345 p.
97-024574   070.5/092   0195112776
Hearst, William Randolph, -- 1863-1951.Publishers and publishing -- United States -- Biography. Newspaper publishing -- United States -- History -- 19th century. Newspaper publishing -- United States -- History -- 20th century.

Z473.H4.R62 1991
Robinson, Judith, 1939-
The Hearsts: an American dynasty/ Judith Robinson. Newark, Del.: University of Delaware Press; 1991. 441 p.
89-040768   070.5/092   0874133831
Hearst, William Randolph, -- 1863-1951 -- Family. Hearst family. Newspaper publishing -- United States -- History. Publishers and publishing -- United States -- Biography.

Z473.J46.S27 1989
Sarna, Jonathan D.
JPS: the Americanization of Jewish culture, 1888-1988/ Jonathan D. Sarna. Philadelphia: Jewish Publication Society, 1989. xiii, 430 p.
88-013696   070.5/089924073   0827603185
Jewish publishing -- United States -- History. Jews -- United States -- Intellectual life.

Z473.L522 1951
Lehmann-Haupt, Hellmut, 1903-
The book in America; a history of the making and selling of books in the United States, by Hellmut Lehmann-Haupt in collaboration with Lawrence C. Wroth and Rollo G. Silver. New York, Bowker, 1951. xiv, 493 p.
51-011308   655.473
Printing -- History -- United States. Booksellers and bookselling -- United States. Publishers and publishing -- United States.

Z473.N39.B66 1989
Bonn, Thomas L.
Heavy traffic & high culture: New American Library as literary gatekeeper in the paperback revolution/ Thomas L. Bonn. Carbondale: Southern Illinois University Press, c1989. xii, 240 p.
88-018517   070.5/0973   0809314789
Literature publishing -- United States -- History -- 20th century. Paperbacks -- Publishing -- United States -- History -- 20th century. Popular literature -- Publishing -- United States -- History -- 20th century.

Z473.N44.T54 1999
Tifft, Susan E.
The trust: the private and powerful family behind the New York Times/ Susan E. Tifft, Alex S. Jones. Boston: Little, Brown, c1999. xx, 870 p.
99-018937   071/.471   0316845469
Ochs, Adolph S. -- (Adolph Simon), -- 1858-1935 -- Family. Ochs family. Sulzberger family. Newspaper publishing -- New York (State) -- New York -- History -- 20th century. Newspaper publishing -- New York (State) -- New York -- History -- 19th century.

Z473.S39 1990
Scribner, Charles, 1921-
In the company of writers: a life in publishing/ Charles Scribner, Jr.; based on the oral history by Joel R. Gardner. New York: Charles Scribner's Sons; c1990. 193 p.
90-033309   070.5/092   0684192500
Scribner, Charles, -- 1921-Authors and publishers -- United States -- History -- 20th century. Publishers and publishing -- United States -- Biography.

Z473.T4 1987
Tebbel, John William, 1912-
Between covers: The rise and transformation of book publishing in America/ John Tebbel. New York: Oxford University Press, 1987. xi, 514 p.
86-012859   070.5/0973   0195041895
Publishers and publishing -- United States -- History. Book industries and trade -- United States -- History.

Z473.U623.F78 1993
Fruge, August, 1909-
A skeptic among scholars: August Fruge on university publishing/ August Fruge. Berkeley: University of California Press, c1993. xii, 365 p.
93-013477   070.5/94   0520077334
Fruge, August, -- 1909-University presses -- California -- Berkeley -- History -- 20th century. Publishers and publishing -- California -- Berkeley -- Biography.

Z473.W36 1990
Warner, Michael, 1958-
The letters of the Republic: publication and the public sphere in eighteenth-century America/ Michael Warner. Cambridge, Mass.: Harvard University Press, 1990. xv, 205 p.
89-048644   070.5/0973   0674527852
Publishers and publishing -- United States -- History -- 18th century. Politics and literature -- United States -- History -- 18th century. Literature and society -- United States -- History -- 18th century.

Z475.A5
American booktrade directory. New York: R.R. Bowker Co.,
15-023627   655
Book industries and trade -- United States -- Directories. Book collectors -- United States -- Directories. Publishers and publishing -- United States -- Directories.

Z475.B65
Publishers directory. Detroit, Mich.: Gale Research Co., [c1984-   ]
84-645506   070.5/025/73
Publishers and publishing -- United States -- Directories. Publishers and publishing -- Canada -- Directories. Book industries and trade -- United States -- Directories.

Z479.A5852
Antiquarian, specialty, and used book sellers: a subject guide and directory. Detroit, Mich.: Omnigraphics, [c1993-   ]
98-641114   381/.45002/02573 21   1558887660
Antiquarian booksellers -- United States -- Directories. Booksellers and bookselling -- United States -- Directories.

Z479.B5 1990
Biggs, Mary.
A gift that cannot be refused: the writing and publishing of contemporary American poetry/ Mary Biggs. New York: Greenwood Press, 1990. xviii, 264 p.
89-011939   808.1   0313266735
Literature publishing -- United States -- History -- 20th century. American poetry -- 20th century -- History and criticism. Poetry -- Authorship -- History -- 20th century.

Z479.D53 1998
Dickinson, Donald C.
Dictionary of American antiquarian bookdealers/ Donald C. Dickinson. Westport, Conn.: Greenwood Press, 1998. xv, 269 p.
97-040856   381/.45002/092273   0313266751
Antiquarian booksellers -- United States -- Biography -- Dictionaries.

Z479.P53 1997
Picard, Robert G.
The newspaper publishing industry/ Robert G. Picard, Jeffrey H. Brody. Boston: Allyn and Bacon, c1997. xvi, 224 p.
96-019616   070.5/722   0205161456
Newspaper publishing -- United States. American newspapers.

Z479.S366 1996
Scholarly publishing: the electronic frontier/ edited by Robin P. Peek, Gregory B. Newby. Cambridge, Mass.: MIT Press, c1996. xxii, 363 p.
95-035556   070.5/0285   0262161575
Scholarly electronic publishing -- United States -- Data processing. Scholarly periodicals -- United States -- Data processing.

Z479.W43 1988
West, James L. W.
American authors and the literary marketplace since 1900/ James L.W. West III. Philadelphia: University of Pennsylvania Press, c1988. 172 p.
88-020620   070.5/0973   0812281144
Literature publishing -- United States -- History -- 20th century. Authors and publishers -- United States -- History -- 20th century. Authors and readers -- United States -- History -- 20th century.

Z479.W53 1989
Wilson, Raymond Jackson.
Figures of speech: American writers and the literary marketplace, from Benjamin Franklin to Emily Dickinson/ R. Jackson Wilson. New York: Knopf, 1989. xv, 295 p.
88-045338   070.5/2   0394496965
Literature publishing -- United States -- History -- 19th century. Authors and publishers -- United States -- History. Authorship -- History -- 19th century. United States -- Intellectual life.

Z483 Bookselling and publishing — By region or country — Canada

Z483.B75 1999
Brisebois, Michel.
Impressions: 250 years of printing in the lives of Canadians/ by Michel Brisebois. [Markham, Ont.?]: Fitzhenry & Whiteside; 64 p.
99-488155   1550414089
Publishers and publishing -- Canada -- History -- Exhibitions -- Catalogs. National Library of Canada -- Exhibitions -- Catalogs.

Z483.U55.J4 1989
Jeanneret, Marsh.
God and mammon: universities as publishers/ by Marsh Jeanneret. Urbana: University of Illinois Press, c1989. xi, 369 p.
89-005229   070.5/94   0252016963
University presses -- Canada -- History. Scholarly publishing -- Canada -- History. Scholarly publishing.

Z551 Copyright — General works

Z551.A68 1998
Anderson, Judy, 1946-
Plagiarism, copyright violation, and other thefts of intellectual property: an annotated bibliography with a lengthy introduction/ by Judy Anderson. Jefferson, N.C.: McFarland & Co., c1998. x, 201 p.
97-044084   016.3467304/82   0786404639
Copyright infringement -- Bibliography. Copyright infringement -- United States -- Bibliography. Intellectual property -- Bibliography.

Z642 Copyright — By region or country — United States

Z642.V35 2001
Vaidhyanathan, Siva.
Copyrights and copywrongs: the rise of intellectual property and how it threatens creativity/ Siva Vaidhyanathan. New York: New York University Press, c2001. xi, 243 p.
2001-002178   346.7304/82 21   0814788068
Copyright--Social aspects--United States. Copyright--United States--History.

Z649 Copyright — Special topics, A-Z

Z649.F35 C74 1993
Crews, Kenneth D.
Copyright, fair use, and the challenge for universities: promoting the progress of higher education/ Kenneth D. Crews. Chicago: University of Chicago Press, 1993. xiv, 247 p.
93-003839   025.1/2 20   0226120554
Photocopying -- Fair use (Copyright) -- United States. Universities and colleges -- United States.

Z657 Freedom of the press. Censorship — General works

Z657.F5 1994
Fish, Stanley Eugene.
There's no such thing as free speech, and it's a good thing, too/ Stanley Fish. New York: Oxford University Press, 1994. xii, 332 p.
93-015347   323.44/3/0973   0195080181
Freedom of speech. Freedom of speech -- United States. Academic freedom.

Z657.I525 1998
Press and speech freedoms in the world, from antiquity until 1998: a chronology/ compiled by Louis Edward Ingelhart. Westport, Conn.: Greenwood Press, 1998. viii, 307 p.
98-021823   363.3/1/09   0313308519
Censorship -- History -- Chronology. Freedom of the press -- History -- Chronology. Freedom of speech -- History -- Chronology.

Z657.J3 1988
Jansen, Sue Curry.
Censorship: the knot that binds power and knowledge/ Sue Curry Jansen. New York: Oxford University Press, 1988. 282 p.
88-004202   363.3/1   0195053257
Censorship.

Z658 Freedom of the press. Censorship — By region or country, A-Z

Z658.E85.W37 2000
The war for the public mind: political censorship in nineteenth-century Europe/ edited by Robert Justin Goldstein. Westport, Conn.: Praeger, 2000. x, 280 p.
99-046307   363.3/1   0275964612
Censorship -- Europe -- History -- 19th century. Communication in politics -- Europe -- History -- 19th century. Europe -- Politics and government -- 1789-1900.

Z658.G7.C46 1992
Censorship & the control of print: in England and France 1600-1910/ edited by Robin Myers and Michael Harris. Winchester: St Paul's Bibliographies, 1992. xii, 154 p.
93-154616   363.3/1   1873040164
Censorship -- England -- History -- Congresses. Censorship -- France -- History -- Congresses.

Z658.G7 G54 1974
Gillett, Charles Ripley,
Burned books: neglected chapters in British history and literature/ by Charles Ripley Gillett. Westport, Conn.: Greenwood Press, 1974, c1932. 2 v.
74-012951   098/.1   0837177782
Censorship -- Great Britain. Prohibited books -- Great Britain -- Bibliography. Book burning -- Great Britain.

Z658.S6.M47 1995
Merrett, Christopher Edmond.
A culture of censorship: secrecy and intellectual repression in South Africa/ Christopher Merrett. Cape Town: David Philip; 1995. xv, 296 p.
94-032888   323.44/5   0865544530
Censorship -- South Africa.

Z658.U5.B46 1987
Bennett, James R., 1932-
Control of information in the United States: an annotated bibliography/ James R. Bennett. Westport, CT: Meckler, c1987. xxiv, 587 p.
87-016475   016.3633/1/0973   0887360823
Censorship -- United States -- Bibliography. Communication policy -- United States -- Bibliography.

Z658.U5.B87 1989
Burress, Lee.
Battle of the books: literary censorship in the public schools, 1950-1985/ by Lee Burress. Metuchen, N.J.: Scarecrow Press, 1989. v, 385 p.
88-030775   098/.12/0973   0810821516
Censorship -- United States -- History -- 20th century. Children's literature -- Censorship -- United States. Young adult literature -- Censorship -- United States.

Z658.U5.C38 1997
Censorship/ consulting editors, Lawrence Amey ... [et al.]; project editor, R. Kent Rasmussen. Pasadena, Calif.: Salem Press, c1997. 3 v.
97-014245   363.3/1   0893564443
Censorship -- United States -- Encyclopedias. Censorship -- Encyclopedias.

Z658.U5.F64 1994
Foerstel, Herbert N.
Banned in the U.S.A.: a reference guide to book censorship in schools and public libraries/ Herbert N. Foerstel. Westport, Conn.: Greenwood Press, 1994. xxii, 231 p.
93-029095   025.2/13   0313285179
Censorship -- United States. Textbooks -- Censorship -- United States. Public libraries -- Censorship -- United States.

Z658.U5.F644 1997
Foerstel, Herbert N.
Free expression and censorship in America: an encyclopedia/ Herbert N. Foerstel. Westport, Conn.: Greenwood Press, 1997. ix, 260 p.
96-042157   363.3/1/0973   0313292310
Censorship -- United States -- Encyclopedias. Freedom of speech -- United States -- Encyclopedias.

Z658.U5.G37 1993
Garry, Patrick M.
An American paradox: censorship in a nation of free speech/ Patrick Garry. Westport, Conn.: Praeger, 1993. xviii, 157 p.
92-031846   363.3/1   0275945227
Censorship -- United States.

Z658.U5.H42 2001
Heins, Marjorie.
Not in front of the children: "indecency," censorship and the innocence of youth/ Marjorie Heins. New York: Hill and Wang, 2001. xiv, 402 p.
00-047274   303.3/76/0973   0374175454
Censorship -- United States -- History -- 20th century. National characteristics, American -- History -- 20th century. Obscenity (Law) -- United States. United States -- Moral conditions -- History -- 20th century.

Z658.U5.H64 1989
Hoffmann, Frank W., 1949-
Intellectual freedom and censorship: an annotated bibliography/ Frank Hoffmann. Metuchen, N.J.: Scarecrow Press, 1989. x, 244 p.
88-018811   016.3633/1/0973   0810821451
Censorship -- United States -- Bibliography. Freedom of information -- United States -- Bibliography. Libraries -- Censorship -- United States -- Bibliography.

Z658.U5.H84 1999
Hull, Mary.
Censorship in America: a reference handbook/ Mary E. Hull. Santa Barbara, Calif.: ABC-CLIO, c1999. xii, 233 p.
99-026819   363.3/1   1576070573
Censorship -- United States.

Z658.U5 K35 1999
Karolides, Nicholas J.
100 banned books: censorship histories of world literature/ Nicholas J. Karolides, Margaret Bald, and Dawn B. Sova; introduction by Ken Wachsberger. New York: Checkmark Books, 1999. xii, 420 p.
99-017140   363.3/1 21   0816040591
Censorship--United States--History--20th century. Prohibited books--United States--History--20th century. Censorship--History.

Z658.U5.K37 1998
Karolides, Nicholas J.
Literature suppressed on political grounds/ Nicholas J. Karolides; introduction by Ken Wachsberger; foreword by Robert M. O'Neil. New York, NY: Facts on File, c1998. xxi, 584 p.
97-031648   363.3/1   0816033048
Censorship -- United States -- History -- 20th century. Prohibited books -- United States -- History -- 20th century. Censorship -- History.

Z658.U5.N6 1990
Noble, William.
Bookbanning in America: who bans books?--and why?/ by William Noble. Middlebury, Vt.: P.S. Eriksson, c1990. xiv, 349 p.
90-003413   098/.1/0973   0839710801
Censorship -- United States. Prohibited books -- United States.

Z658.U5.S69 1998
Sova, Dawn B.
Literature suppressed on social grounds/ Dawn B. Sova; introduction by Ken Wachsberger; foreword by Joan Bertin. New York, NY: Facts On File, c1998. xxvii, 321 p.
97-045158   363.3/1/09   081603303X
Censorship -- United States -- History. Prohibited books -- United States -- History. Censorship -- History.

Z666-998 Libraries

Z666 Library science. Information science — Bibliography

Z666.C211
Library literature. Chicago: American Library Association, [1934-   ]
36-027468   016.02
Library science -- Indexes -- Periodicals.
Information science -- Indexes -- Periodicals.
Library Science -- indexes.

Z666.5 Library science. Information science — Information organization

Z666.5.S92 2000
Svenonius, Elaine.
The intellectual foundation of information organization/ Elaine Svenonius. Cambridge, Mass.: MIT Press, 2000. xiv, 255 p.
99-041301   025.3   0262194333
Information organization. Bibliography -- Methodology. Cataloging.

Z666.5.T39 1999
Taylor, Arlene G.,
The organization of information/ Arlene G. Taylor. Englewood, Colo.: Libraries Unlimited, 1999. xx, 280 p.
98-053625   020 21   1563084988
Information organization. Metadata.

Z668 Library science. Information science — Library education — General, and United States

Z668.R365 2000
Rehman, Sajjad ur,
Preparing the information professional: an agenda for the future/ Sajjad ur Rehman. Westport, Conn.: Greenwood Press, 2000. xi, 177 p.
99-462056   020/.71/5 21   0313306737
Library education -- United States.

Z668.5 Library science. Information science — Library education — In-service training

Z668.5.S7 2001
Staff development: a practical guide/ prepared by the Staff Development Committee, Human Resources Section, Library Administration and Management Association; coordinating editors, Elizabeth Fuseler Avery, Terry Dahlin, Deborah A. Carver. 3rd ed. Chicago: American Library Association, 2001. ix, 194 p.
00-067639   023/.8 21   0838908012
Library employees -- In-service training. Library education (Continuing education) Career development.

Z669.7 Library science. Information science — Research

Z669.7.P68 1997
Powell, Ronald R.
Basic research methods for librarians: Ronald R. Powell. 3rd ed. Greenwich, Conn.: Ablex Pub. Corp., c1997. xii, 281 p.
97-028906   020/.7/2 21   1567503381
Library science--Research--Methodology.

Z669.8 Library science. Information science — Statistical methods

Z669.8.H33 1998
Hafner, Arthur Wayne,
Descriptive statistical techniques for librarians/ Arthur W. Hafner. 2nd ed. Chicago: American Library Association, 1998. vii, 321 p.
97-019098   025/.007/23 21   0838906923
Library statistics.

Z673 Library science. Information science — Library associations

Z673.A5.A14
American Library Association.
The ALA yearbook. Chicago, American Library Association. 8 v.
76-647548   020/.622/73
Libraries -- Periodicals.

Z674 Library science. Information science — Collected works (nonserial)

Z674.A75 no. 49
Restructuring academic libraries: organizational development in the wake of technological change/ edited by Charles A. Schwartz. Chicago: Association of College and Research Libraries, 1997. xi, 289 p.
97-040243   027.7/0973 21   0838934781
Academic libraries -- United States.

Z674.A75 no. 53
People come first: user-centered academic library service/ edited by Dale S. Montanelli & Patricia F. Stenstrom. Chicago: Association of College and Research Libraries, 1999. viii, 194 p.
98-043719   027.7 21   0838979998
Academic libraries -- United States. Public services (Libraries) -- United States.

Z674.A75 no. 19
Poole's index: date and volume key [by] Marion V. Bell and Jean C. Bacon; including Muted voices from the past, by John C. Hepler. Chicago, Association of College and Reference Libraries, 1957. 61 p.
57-007157   016.05
Poole's index to periodical literature.

Z674.25 Library science. Information science — Information services. Information centers — Bibliography

Z674.25.W48 1989
Whitaker, Marian, 1961-
Bibliography of information technology: an annotated critical bibliography of English language sources since 1980/ Marian Whitaker, Ian Miles, with John Bessant, Howard Rush. Aldershot, Hants, England: E. Elgar; c1989. vi, 313 p.
88-033427   016.3/00285   1852780401
Information technology -- Bibliography.

Z675 Library science. Information science — Classes of libraries, A-Z

Z675.A2.S83
Subject directory of special libraries and information centers. Detroit, Mich.: Gale Research Co., [c1975-   ]
85-645199   026/.00025/73
Special libraries -- United States -- Directories. Special libraries -- Canada -- Directories. Information services -- United States -- Directories.

Z675.B8.B37 1994
The basic business library: core resources/ edited by Bernard S. Schlessinger; Rashelle S. Karp, associate editor. Phoenix, Ariz.: Oryx Press, 1995. viii, 371 p.
94-022809   016.0276/9   0897747399
Business libraries -- United States. Business -- Bibliography. Business libraries -- United States -- Bibliography.

Z675.B8.B87 1996
The business library and how to use it: a guide to sources and research strategies for information on business and management/ Ernest L. Maier ... [et al.]. Detroit, Mich.: Omnigraphics, c1996. vi, 329 p.
94-012700   027.6/9   0780800265
Business libraries. Library research. Business -- Research -- Methodology.

Z675.H5.T4 1993
Teaching bibliographic skills in history: a sourcebook for historians and librarians/ edited by Charles A. D'Aniello. Westport, Conn.: Greenwood Press, 1993. xviii, 385 p.
92-008833   025.5/669   0313252661
Historical libraries -- Handbooks, manuals, etc. Library orientation for history students -- Handbooks, manuals, etc. History -- Bibliography -- Methodology -- Study and teaching -- Handbooks, manuals, etc.

Z675.U5.A338 1991
Academic libraries in urban and metropolitan areas: a management handbook/ edited by Gerard B. McCabe. New York: Greenwood Press, 1992. xxv, 261 p.
91-021182   027.7/0973   031327536X
Academic libraries -- United States. Libraries and metropolitan areas.

Z678.2 Library science. Information science — Library administration and organization. Constitution — General, and United States

Z678.2.F64 1991
Foerstel, Herbert N.
Surveillance in the stacks: the FBI's library awareness program/ Herbert N. Foerstel. New York: Greenwood Press, 1991. x, 171 p.
90-038419   025.8/2   0313267154
Library science -- Political aspects -- United States. Librarians -- Professional ethics -- United States. Libraries and state -- United States.

Z678.82 Library science. Information science — Library administration and organization. Constitution — Library records

Z678.82.W54 1994
Wiegand, Shirley A.
Library records: a retention and confidentiality guide/ Shirley A. Wiegand. Westport, Conn.: Greenwood Press, 1994. xii, 243 p.
93-014465   025.6   0313284083
Library records -- United States -- Management. Government paperwork -- United States. Confidential communications -- Library records -- United States.

Z678.85 Library science. Information science — Library administration and organization. Constitution — Evaluation. Rating. Standards

Z678.85.L36
Lancaster, F. Wilfrid 1933-
The measurement and evaluation of library services/ by F. W. Lancaster, with the assistance of M. J. Joncich. Washington: Information Resources Press, c1977. xii, 395 p.
77-072081   025.1   087815017X
Libraries -- Evaluation.

Z678.9 Library science. Information science — Automation — Periodicals. Societies. Congresses

Z678.9.A4 U633 1996
The evolving virtual library: visions and case studies/ edited by Laverna M. Saunders. Medford, NJ: Information Today, 1996. viii, 153 p.
95-039544   025/.00285 20   1573870137
Libraries -- United States -- Automation -- Congresses. Online information services -- United States -- Congresses. Library information networks -- United States -- Congresses. Digital libraries -- United States -- Congresses.

Z678.9.W55 1998
Wilson, Thomas C.
The systems librarian: designing roles, defining skills/ Thomas C. Wilson. Chicago: American Library Association, 1998. ix, 199 p.
98-023105   025/.00285 20   0838907407
Libraries -- Data processing -- Management. Libraries -- United States -- Data processing -- Management.

Z678.93 Library science. Information science — Automation — Special topics, A-Z

Z678.93.D46 M39 1997
Maxymuk, John.
Using desktop publishing to create newsletters, handouts, and Web pages : a how-to-do it manual/ John Maxymuk. New York: Neal-Schuman, c1997. xi, 221 p.
97-003980   686.2/2544536/024092 21   1555702651
Libraries -- United States -- Data processing. Desktop publishing -- United States. Libraries -- United States -- Handbooks, manuals, etc. -- Data processing. Newsletters -- United States -- Data processing. Web sites -- United States.

Z679.2 Library science. Information science — Library buildings. Library architecture — By region or country, A-Z

Z679.2.U54.B74 1997
Breisch, Kenneth A.
Henry Hobson Richardson and the small public library in America: a study in typology/ Kenneth A. Breisch. Cambridge, Mass.: MIT Press, c1997. xii, 354 p.
96-043752   727/.82473   0262024160
Richardson, H. H. -- (Henry Hobson), -- 1838-1886. Library architecture -- United States -- History -- 19th century. Public libraries -- United States -- History -- 19th century. Small libraries -- United States -- History -- 19th century.

Z679.2.U54 C44 2001
Checklist of library building design considerations/ [edited by] William W. Sannwald. 4th ed. Chicago: American Library Association, c2001. vii, 183 p.
00-052164   727/.8 21   0838935060
Library architecture -- United States.

Z679.5 Library science. Information science — Library buildings. Library architecture — Planning. Furnishing

Z679.5.L45 1999
Leighton, Philip D.
Planning academic and research library buildings/ Philip D. Leighton, David C. Weber. 3rd ed. Chicago: American Library Association, 1999. xxx, 887 p.
98-046757   022/.317 21   0838907474
Library architecture -- United States. Academic libraries -- United States. Research libraries -- United States.

Z679.5.M49 1986
Metcalf, Keyes DeWitt, 1889-
Planning academic and research library buildings/ Keyes D. Metcalf. Chicago: American Library Association, 1986. xix, 630 p.
85-011207   022/.317   0838933203
Research libraries. Libraries -- Space utilization. Libraries

Z679.7 Library science. Information science — Library buildings. Library architecture — Safety measures

Z679.7.K38 2003
Kahn, Miriam
Disaster response and planning for libraries/ Miriam B. Kahn. 2nd ed. Chicago: American Library Association, 2003. xi, 152 p.
2002-008968   025.8/2 21   0838908373
Libraries -- Safety measures. Library materials -- Conservation and restoration. Libraries -- Safety measures -- Planning. Library materials -- Conservation and restoration -- Planning.

Z681.7 Library science. Information science — Trustees. Library boards, committees, etc. — By region or country, A-Z

Z681.7.U5 F75 1996
Friends of libraries sourcebook/ Sandy Dolnick, editor. 3rd ed. Chicago: American Library Association, 1996. xiii, 313 p.
96-003384   021.7 20   0838906850
Friends of the library -- United States -- Handbooks, manuals, etc.

Z682 Library science. Information science — Personnel — General works

Z682.A4995 1968
American Library Association.
Personnel organization and procedure; a manual suggested for use in college and university libraries. Chicago, American Library Association, 1968. 63 p.
68-021022   027.7
Library personnel management -- United States. Academic libraries -- United States.

Z682.P394 1989
Personnel administration in libraries/ edited by
Sheila Creth and Frederick Duda. 2nd ed. New
York: Neal-Schuman Publishers, c1989. x, 343 p.
88-033048   023 19   1555700365
Library personnel management.

Z682.2 Library science. Information science — Personnel — By region or country, A-Z

Z682.2.U5 H453 2002
McCook, Kathleen de la Peña.
Opportunities in library and information science
careers/ Kathleen de la Peña McCook, Margaret
Myers; revised by Blythe Camenson. Chicago:
VGM Career Books, c2002. viii, 152 p.
2001-026054   020/.23/73 21   0658016423
*Library science -- Vocational guidance --
United States. Information science -- Vocational
guidance -- United States.*

Z682.4 Library science. Information science — Personnel — Special groups, A-Z

Z682.4.M56 D58 2001
Diversity in libraries: academic residency
programs/ edited by Raquel V. Cogell and Cindy
A. Gruwell, foreword by E. J. Josey. Westport,
Conn.: Greenwood Press, 2001. xx, 181 p.
00-069149   023/.9 21   0313308314
*Minority librarians -- Recruiting -- United
States. Minority librarians -- In-service training
-- United States. College librarians -- Recruiting
-- United States. College librarians -- In-service
training -- United States. Interns (Library
science) -- United States. Academic libraries --
United States -- Personnel management.
Affirmative action programs -- United States.
Diversity in the workplace -- United States.*

Z682.4.M56 R44 1999
Reese, Gregory L.
Stop talking, start doing!: attracting people of
color to the library profession/ Gregory L.
Reese, Ernestine L. Hawkins. Chicago: American
Library Association, 1999. xix, 136 p.
99-018329   023/.9 21   0838907628
*Minority librarians -- Recruiting -- United
States.*

Z682.4.W65.O52 1989
On account of sex: an annotated bibliography on
the status of women in librarianship, 1982-1986/
Katharine Phenix ... [et al.] for the Committee on
the Status of Women in Librarianship, American
Library Association. Chicago: American Library
Association, 1989. xv, 136 p.
89-036547   016.02/082   0838933750
*Women in library science -- United States --
Bibliography. Women in information science --
United States -- Bibliography. Sex discrimination
against women -- United States -- Bibliography.*

Z685 Library science. Information science — Shelving. Bookstacks

Z685.P48 1999
Petroski, Henry.
The book on the bookshelf/ by Henry Petroski.
New York: Alfred A. Knopf: 1999. x, 290 p.
99-014336   022/.4/09   0375406492
*Shelving for books -- History. Shelving for
books -- Europe -- History. Bookbinding --
History.*

Z687 Library science. Information science — The collections. The books — General works

Z687.A518 1996
Guide for written collection policy statements/
Subcommittee to Revise the Guide for Written
Collection Policy Statements, Administration of
Collection Development Committee, Collection
Management and Development Section,
Association for Library Collections & Technical
Services; Joanne S. Anderson Chicago:
American Library Association, 1996. vii, 36 p.
95-053047   025.2/1 20   0838934552
*Collection development (Libraries)--Policy
statements--Standards*

Z688 Library science. Information science — The collections. The books — Special collections

Z688.A58.P67 1992
Post, Joyce A.
Gerontology and geriatrics libraries and
collections in the United States and Canada: a
history, description, and directory/ Joyce A. Post.
Westport, Conn.: Greenwood Press, 1992. xviii,
196 p.
91-046862   025.2/761267   0313284431
*Libraries -- United States -- Special collections
-- Aging. Libraries -- Canada -- Special
collections -- Aging. Libraries -- Special
collections -- Gerontology.*

Z688.G3.G54 1988
Gilmer, Lois C.
Genealogical research and resources: a guide for
library use/ by Lois C. Gilmer. Chicago:
American Library Association, 1988. ix, 70 p.
87-032534   026/.9293   0838904823
*Libraries -- Special collections -- Genealogy.
Genealogy -- Bibliography -- Methodology.
Genealogy -- Bibliography.*

Z688.S45.C67 1996
Cornog, Martha.
For sex education, see librarian: a guide to issues
and resources/ Martha Cornog and Timothy
Perper. Westport, Conn: Greenwood Press, 1996.
xxi, 403 p.
95-042445   026.6139/07   0313290229
*Libraries -- United States -- Special collections
-- Sex instruction. Libraries -- United States --
Special collections -- Family life education.
Public libraries -- Collection development --
United States.*

Z688.U53.A88 1996
Atton, Chris.
Alternative literature: a practical guide for
librarians/ Chris Atton. Aldershot, England;
Gower, c1996. xi, 202 p.
95-037319   025.2/1   0566076659
*Libraries -- United States -- Special collections
-- Underground press.*

Z688.5 Library science. Information science — The collections. The books — Processing

Z688.5.N48
New directions in technical services: trends and
sources. Chicago, IL: American Library
Association, [1997-   ]
97-657814   025 13
*Library science -- Periodicals. Technical
services (Libraries) -- Periodicals. Technical
services (Libraries) -- Management --
Periodicals. Library administration --
Periodicals.*

Z689 Library science. Information science — The collections. The books — Acquisition (selection, purchase, gifts, duplicates)

Z689.A2746 1973 no. 11
Guide to managing approval plans/ Susan Flood,
editor. Chicago: American Library Association,
1998. v, 58 p.
98-015811   025.2 21   0838934811
*Approval plans in library acquisitions --
United States.*

Z689.L49 1984
Library acquisition policies and procedures/
edited by Elizabeth Futas. 2nd ed. Phoenix,
Ariz.: Oryx Press, 1984. xxxvi, 579 p.
82-042925   025.2 19   0897740246
*Acquisitions (Libraries) Collection
development (Libraries) -- United States --
Policy statements. Academic libraries --
Collection development -- United States. Public
libraries -- Collection development -- United
States. Library surveys -- United States.*

Z689.S354 1985
Selection of library materials in the humanities,
social sciences, and sciences/ Patricia A.
McClung, editor; section editors, William Hepfer
... [et al.]. Chicago: American Library
Association, 1985. xiv, 405 p.
85-020084   025.2/1   083893305X
*Book selection. Collection development
(Libraries) Humanities -- Bibliography --
Methodology.*

Z692 Library science. Information science — The collections. The books — Special classes of materials

Z692.E43.P47 1999
Periodical acquisitions and the Internet/ Nancy Slight-Gibney, editor. New York: Haworth Press, c1999. 123 p.
98-032065   025.2/832   0789006774
Acquisition of electronic journals -- United States. Research libraries -- Acquisitions -- United States.

Z692.M3.L37 1998
Larsgaard, Mary Lynette, 1946-
Map librarianship: an introduction/ Mary Lynette Larsgaard. Englewood, Colo.: Libraries Unlimited, 1998. xxix, 487 p.
98-015451   025.2/86   1563084740
Libraries -- Special collections -- Maps. Libraries -- Special collections -- Geography.

Z692.S5.O8 1980
Osborn, Andrew Delbridge, 1902-
Serial publications, their place and treatment in libraries/ Andrew D. Osborn. Chicago: American Library Association, 1980. xxii, 486 p.
80-011686   025.17/3   0838902995
Periodicals. Serials control systems.

Z693-695.74 Library science. Information science — The collections. The books — Cataloging

Z693.W94 2000
Taylor, Arlene G.,
Wynar's introduction to cataloging and classification 9th ed./ Arlene G. Taylor; with the assistance of David P. Miller. Englewood, Colo.: Libraries Unlimited, 2000. xv, 552 p.
00-030932   025.3 21   1563088576
Cataloging. Classification--Books.

Z693.5.U6 C48 1994
Chan, Lois Mai.
Cataloging and classification: an introduction/ Lois Mai Chan. 2nd ed. New York: McGraw-Hill, c1994. xxii, 519 p.
93-022606   025.3 20   0070105065
Cataloging -- United States. Classification -- Books.

Z694.A15 C66 1989
The Conceptual foundations of descriptive cataloging/ edited by Elaine Svenonius. San Diego: Academic Press, c1989. xv, 241 p.
88-028819   025.3/2/0285 19   0126782105
Descriptive cataloging -- Data processing -- Congresses. Machine-readable bibliographic data -- Congresses. Bibliography -- Databases -- Congresses. Online library catalogs -- Congresses.

Z694.A5 1978
Anglo-American cataloguing rules/ prepared by the American Library Association ... [et al.]; edited by Michael Gorman and Paul W. Winkler. Chicago: ALA, 1978. xvii, 620 p.
78-013789   025.3/2   083893210X
Descriptive cataloging -- Rules.

Z694.15.A56 A53 1998
Anglo-American cataloguing rules/ prepared under the direction of the Joint Steering Committee for Revision of AACR, a committee of the American Library Association, the Australian Committee on Cataloguing, the British Library, the Canadian Committee on Cataloguing, the Library Associa Ottawa: Canadian Library Association; xli, 676 p.
98-008479   025.3/2 21   0838934854
Descriptive cataloging -- Rules.

Z695.A52 1949
American Library Association.
A.L.A. cataloging rules for author and title entries. Chicago, American Library Assn., 1949. xxi, 265 p.
49-009034   025.32
Descriptive cataloging -- Rules.

Z695.L695 1986
Library of Congress.
Library of Congress subject headings/ Subject Cataloging Division, Processing Services. Washington: Library of Congress, 1986. 2 v.
85-600211   025.4/9   0844405108
Cabecalhos De Assuntos -- larpcal Subject headings, Library of Congress. Subject Headings.

Z695.S43 1986
Sears, Minnie Earl, 1873-1933.
Sears list of subject headings. New York: Wilson, 1986. xl, 681 p.
86-007734   025.4/9   0824207300
Subject headings.

Z695.Z8 L524a
Library of Congress subject headings/ Subject Cataloging Division, Processing Department. Washington: Library of Congress, [1975-   ]
90-643712   025.4/9 20
Subject headings, Library of Congress.

Z695.Z8.N546 1998
National Information Center for Educational Media.
NICEM thesaurus. Albuquerque, NM: National Information Center for Educational Media, 1998. xv, 313 p.
98-072499   025.4/9
Subject headings.

Z695.1.A7 A76 1994
Art & architecture thesaurus/ Toni Petersen, director. 2nd ed. New York: Oxford University Press, 1994. 5 v.
93-030628   025.4/97 20   0195087569
Subject headings -- Art. Subject headings -- Architecture.

Z695.1.B57.B76 1995
Brown, Lorene Byron.
Subject headings for African-American materials/ Lorene Byron Brown. Englewood, Colo.: Libraries Unlimited, 1995. xvii, 118 p.
95-010847   025.4/93058/96073   1563082527
Subject headings -- Afro-Americans.

Z695.1.E3.E34 1986
Educational Resources Information Center (U.S.)
Thesaurus of ERIC descriptors/ James E. Houston, editor/lexicographer; introduction by Lynn Barnett. Phoenix, Ariz.: Oryx Press, 1986. xxvi, 588 p.
86-042555   0897741595
Subject headings -- Education.

Z695.1.E3 T49
Thesaurus of ERIC descriptors/ compiled by the Educational Research Information Center, Bureau of Research. Washington: U.S., Dept. of Health, Education and Welfare,
87-647380   025 11
Subject headings -- Education -- Periodicals.

Z695.1.E5.E5 1967
Engineers Joint Council.
Thesaurus of engineering and scientific terms; a list of engineering and related scientific terms and their relationships for use as a vocabulary reference in indexing and retrieving technical infor New York, 1967. vi, 690 p.
68-006569   025.33/6
Subject headings -- Engineering.

Z695.1.P7 T48 1994
Thesaurus of psychological index terms. 7th ed. / Alvin Walker, Jr., editor. Washington, D.C.: American Psychological Association, c1994. p. cm.
93-044714   025.4/915 20   1557982252
Subject headings -- Psychology.

Z695.66.O43 1985
Olson, Nancy B.
Cataloging of audiovisual materials: a manual based on AACR 2/ Nancy B. Olson; edited by Edward Swanson and Sheila S. Intner. 2nd ed., Rev. and expanded 2nd ed. Mankato, Minn.: Minnesota Scholarly Press, 1985. x, 306 p.
85-196488   025.3/47 19   0933474385
Cataloging of nonbook materials -- United States -- Handbooks, manuals, Cataloging of audio-visual materials -- United States -- Handbooks, Descriptive cataloging -- United States -- Rules -- Handbooks, manuals, etc.

Z695.74.D8 1973
Dunkin, Paul Shaner,
How to catalog a rare book. 2d ed., rev. Chicago, American Library Association, 1973. ix, 105 p.
72-006515   025.3/41   0838901417
Cataloging of rare books. Rare books-- Bibliography--Methodology.

Z695.9 Library science. Information science — The collections. The books — Indexing. Abstracting

Z695.9.B93 1999
Burke, Mary A., 1949-
Organizing multimedia information: principles and practice of information retrieval/ Mary A. Burke. Aldershot, Hampshire, England; Ashdale 1999. xii, 224 p.
98-036866   025.5/24   0566081717
Information retrieval. Interactive multimedia. Nonbook materials.

Z695.9.W45 1995
Wellisch, Hans H.,
Indexing from A to Z/ Hans H. Wellisch. 2nd ed., rev. and enl. New York: H.W. Wilson, 1995, c1996. xxix, 569 p. ;
95-046720   025.3 20   082420882X
Indexing.

Z695.95 Library science. Information science — The collections. The books — Alphabetizing. Filing

Z695.95.A52 1980
American Library Association
ALA filing rules/ Filing Committee, Resources and Technical Services Division, American Library Association. Chicago: ALA, 1980. 50 p.
80-022186   025.3/17   083893255X
Library filing rules. Files (Records). -- sears.

Z696 Library science. Information science — The collections. The books — Classification and notation

Z696.D52 2003
Dewey, Melvil,
Dewey decimal classification and relative index/ devised by Melvil Dewey. Ed. 22/ edited by Joan S. Mitchell, Julianne Beall, Giles Martin, Dublin, Ohio: OCLC Online Computer Library Center, 2003.
2003-050872   025.4/31 21   0910608709
Classification, Dewey decimal.

Z696.D7 S36 1998
Scott, Mona L.
Dewey decimal classification, 21st edition: a study manual and number building guide/ Mona L. Scott. Englewood, Colo.: Libraries Unlimited, 1998. ix, 198 p.
98-006948   025.4/31 21   1563085984
Classification, Dewey Decimal.

Z696.M59
Metcalfe, John Wallace, 1901-
Subject classifying and indexing of libraries and literature. New York, Scarecrow Press, 1959. xii, 347 p.
59-065011   025.4
Subject headings. Classification -- Books.

Z696.U4 C47 1999
Chan, Lois Mai.
A guide to the Library of Congress classification/ Lois Mai Chan. 5th ed. Englewood, Colo.: Libraries Unlimited, 1999. xviii, 551 p.
99-015279   025.4/33 21   1563085003
Classification, Library of Congress.

Z699-699.5 Library science. Information science — The collections. The books — Machine methods of information storage and retrieval. Mechanized bibliographic control

Z699.B3535 1993
Basch, Reva.
Secrets of the super searchers/ Reva Basch. Wilton, CT: Eight Bit Books, 1993. 235 p.
94-163207   025.5/24 20   0910965129
Electronic information resource searching -- United States. Information scientists -- United States -- Interviews.

Z699.35.E94.S68 1991
A Sourcebook on standards information: education, access, and development/ [edited by] Steven M. Spivak and Keith A. Winsell. Boston, Mass.: G.K. Hall, 1991. xiv, 451 p.
91-019207   021.6/5   0816119481
Exchange of bibliographic information -- Data processing -- Standards. Cataloging of archival material -- Data processing -- Standards. Machine-readable bibliographic data -- Standards.

Z699.35.M28 B97 1998
Byrne, Deborah J.
MARC manual: understanding and using MARC records/ Deborah J. Byrne. 2nd ed. Englewood, Colo.: Libraries Unlimited, 1998. xxiii, 263 p.
97-035961   025.3/16 21   1563081768
MARC formats -- United States -- Handbooks, manuals, etc.

Z699.5.S65.K57 1993
Knapp, Sara D.
The contemporary thesaurus of social science terms and synonyms: a guide for natural language computer searching/ compiled and edited by Sarah D. Knapp. Phoenix, Ariz.: Oryx Press, 1993. xxi, 400 p.
92-032899   025.4/93   0897745957
Social sciences -- Bibliography -- Databases. Social sciences -- Terminology. Online bibliographic searching.

Z701 Library science. Information science — The collections. The books — Physical parameters, preservation, conservation and restoration of books and other library materials

Z701.C782
Cunha, George Daniel Martin.
Conservation of library materials; a manual and bibliography on the care, repair, and restoration of library materials, by George Martin Cunha and Dorothy Grant Cunha. Metuchen, N.J., Scarecrow Press, 1971-72. 2 v.
77-163871   025.7   0810804271
Library materials -- Conservation and restoration -- Handbooks, manuals, etc. Library materials -- Conservation and restoration -- Bibliography.

Z701.L32 1992
Lavender, Kenneth.
Book repair: a how-to-do-it manual for librarians/ Kenneth Lavender, Scott Stockton. New York: Neal-Schuman Publishers, c1992. viii, 119 p.
92-008109   025.7 20   1555701035
Books -- Conservation and restoration -- Handbooks, manuals, etc. Library materials -- Conservation and restoration -- Handbooks, manuals, Bookbinding -- Repairing -- Handbooks, manuals, etc.

Z703.5 Library science. Information science — The collections. The books — Stack management. Disposition of books on shelves, etc.

Z703.5.J4 1981
Hubbard, William J.,
Stack management: a practical guide to shelving and maintaining library collections/ William J. Hubbard. Chicago: American Library Association, 1981. viii, 102 p.
80-028468   025.8/1 19   0838903193
Stack management (Libraries)

Z710 Library science. Information science — The collections. The books — Aids. Guides

Z710.L36 2000
Lane, Nancy D.
Techniques   for   student   research: a comprehensive guide to using the library/ Nancy Lane, Margaret Chisholm, Carolyn Mateer. New York: Neal-Schuman Publishers, c2000. xv, 277 p.
99-056395   025.5/24   1555703674
Library research -- United States. Report writing -- United States.

Z710.M23 1998
Mann, Thomas,
The Oxford guide to library research/ Thomas Mann. New York: Oxford University Press, 1998. xx, 316 p.
98-005888   025.5/24 21   0195123131
Library research -- United States.

Z711-711.92 Library science. Information science — The collections. The books — Reference work

Z711.A39 1994
The American Library Association guide to information access: a complete handbook and directory/ Sandy Whiteley, editor. New York: Random House, c1994. xxv, 533 p.
94-010861   025.5/24   0679430601
Library research -- United States -- Handbooks, manuals, etc. Information retrieval -- Handbooks, manuals, etc.

Z711.N65 1999
Nolan, Christopher W.
Managing the reference collection/ Christopher W. Nolan. Chicago: American Library Association, 1999. vii, 231 p.
98-037178   025.5/2/068 21   0838907482
Libraries -- United States -- Special collections -- Reference books.

Z711.W64 1999
Willis, Mark R.
Dealing with difficult people in the library/ Mark
R. Willis. Chicago: American Library
Association, 1999. ix, 195 p.
99-020426   025.5 21   0838907601
*Libraries and readers -- United States.
Communication in library science -- United
States. Public libraries -- Security measures --
United States. Public libraries -- Public relations
-- United States.*

Z711.2.B755 1998
Breivik, Patricia Senn.
Student learning in the information age/ Patricia
Senn Breivik. Phoenix, Ariz.: American Council
on Education/Oryx Press, 1998. xii, 173 p.
97-035183   027.6/2 21   1573560006
*Library orientation for college students --
United States. Information retrieval -- Study and
teaching (Higher) -- United States.*

Z711.2.Y68 1999
Young, Rosemary,
Working with faculty to design undergraduate
information literacy programs: a how-to-do-it
manual for librarians/ Rosemary M. Young and
Stephena Harmony. New York: Neal-Schuman,
c1999. x, 123 p.
98-054783   027.7/0973 21   1555703542
*Library orientation for college students --
United States. Information retrieval -- Study and
teaching (Higher) -- United States. Information
literacy -- Study and teaching (Higher) -- United
States.*

Z711.4.I57 2002
Intellectual freedom manual/ compiled by the
Office for Intellectual Freedom of the American
Library Association. 6th ed. Chicago: American
Library Association, 2002. xx, 434 p.
2001-026684   025.2/13 21   0838935192
*Libraries -- Censorship -- United States --
Handbooks, manuals, etc. Intellectual freedom --
United States -- Handbooks, manuals, etc.*

Z711.45.L57 2003
Lipow, Anne Grodzins,
The virtual reference librarian's handbook/ Anne
Grodzins Lipow. Berk[e]ley, [Calif.]: Library
Solutions Press; xxiii, 199 p.
2002-029581   025.5/2 21   155570445X
*Electronic reference services (Libraries)--
Handbooks, manuals, etc.*

Z711.45.S28 2001
Sauers, Michael P.
Using the Internet as a reference tool: a how to-
do-it manual for librarians/ Michael P. Sauers;
with contributions by Denice Adkins. New York:
Neal-Schuman Publishers, c2001. xi, 143 p.
2001-016419   025.04 21   1555704174
*Electronic reference services (Libraries)
Internet searching. Computer network resources-
-Evaluation.*

Z711.5.S27 2001
Saricks, Joyce G.
The readers' advisory guide to genre fiction/
Joyce G. Saricks. Chicago: American Library
Association, 2001. xii, 460 p.
2001-022750   025.5/4   0838908039
*Fiction in libraries -- United States. Readers'
advisory services -- United States. Reading
interests -- United States.*

Z711.9.H35 2000
Handbook of Black librarianship/ edited by E.J.
Josey and Marva L. DeLoach. 2nd ed. Lanham,
Md.: Scarecrow Press, c2000. xiii, 816 p.
99-041370   020/.896073 21   081083720X
*African Americans and libraries. African
American librarians. African Americans --
Bibliography. Libraries -- United States --
Special collections -- African Americans.*

Z711.92.G37.G37 1990
Gay and lesbian library service/ edited by Cal
Gough and Ellen Greenblatt; with a foreword by
Sanford Berman. Jefferson, N.C.: McFarland,
c1990. xxiv, 355 p.
90-052641   026.3059/0664   089950535X
*Libraries and gays. Libraries -- Special
collections -- Homosexuality. Homosexuality --
Bibliography -- Methodology.*

Z711.95 Library science. Information science — The collections. The books — Public services. Reference services

Z711.95.M58 1995
Mitchell, Eleanor,
Document delivery services: issues and answers/
by Eleanor Mitchell and Sheila A. Walters.
Medford, NJ: Learned Information, 1995. viii,
333 p.
94-183787   157387003X
*Document delivery. DOCUMENTS nasat
DELIVERY nasat INFORMATION RETRIEVAL
nasat LIBRARIES nasat*

Z712-713.5 Library science. Information science — The collections. The books — Circulation. Loans

Z712.K59 1986
Kohl, David F.,
Circulation, interlibrary loan, patron use, and
collection maintenance : a handbook for library
management/ David F. Kohl; foreword by Tom
Alford. Santa Barbara, Calif.: ABC-Clio, c1986.
xxxi, 362 p.
85-015798   025.6 20   0874364353
*Library circulation and loans -- Handbooks,
manuals, etc. Library administration --
Handbooks, manuals, etc. Interlibrary loans --
Handbooks, manuals, etc. Public services
(Libraries) -- Handbooks, manuals, etc. Library
materials -- Handbooks, manuals, etc.*

Z713.5.U6 B68 1997
Boucher, Virginia,
Interlibrary loan practices handbook/ Virginia
Boucher. 2nd ed. Chicago: American Library
Association, 1997. xii, 249 p.
96-018419   025.6/2 20   0838906672
*Interlibrary loans -- United States --
Handbooks, manuals, etc.*

Z713.5.U6 M67 2002
Morris, Leslie R.
Interlibrary loan policies directory/ Leslie R.
Morris. 7th ed. New York, NY: Neal-Schuman
Publishers, c2002. viii, 1275 p. ;
2003-389170   1555704239
*Interlibrary loans -- United States --
Directories. Interlibrary loans -- United States --
Policy statements. Interlibrary loans --
Directories. Interlibrary loans -- Policy
statements.*

Z714 Library science. Information science — The collections. The books — Charging systems

Z714.F68 1994
Fouty, Kathleen G.
Implementing an automated circulation system: a
how-to-do-it manual/ Kathleen G. Fouty. New
York: Neal-Schuman, c1994. xi, 220 p.
94-013008   025.6/0285 20   1555701752
*Charging systems (Libraries) -- Data
processing.*

Z716.3 Library science. Information science — The collections. The books — Public relations. Advertising. Publicity

Z716.3.R43 2001
Reed, Sally Gardner,
Making the case for your library: a how-to-do-it
manual/ Sally Gardner Reed. New York: Neal
Schuman Publishers, c2001. xix, 143 p.
00-061297   025.1/1 21   1555703992
*Libraries -- Public relations -- United States --
Handbooks manuals, etc. Library fund raising --
United States -- Handbooks, manuals, etc.
Library finance -- United States -- Handbooks,
manuals, etc.*

Z718.1-718.3 Library science. Information science — The collections. The books — Children's libraries. Children's departments in public libraries, etc.

Z718.1.J63 1999
Johnson, Wayne L.,
Summer reading program fun: 10 thrilling,
inspiring, wacky board games for kids/ Wayne
L. Johnson, Yvette C. Johnson. Chicago:
American Library Association, 1999. ix, 108 p.
98-045378   027.62/5 21   0838907555
*Children's libraries--Activity programs.
Reading promotion. Children--Books and
reading.*

Z718.1.S57 1992
Simpson, Martha Seif,
Summer reading clubs: complete plans for 50
theme-based library programs/ by Martha Seif
Simpson. Jefferson, N.C.: McFarland, c1992. xi,
204 p.
91-051231   027.62/5 20   0899507212
*Children's libraries--Activity programs.
Children's literature--Appreciation. Children--
Books and reading.*

Z718.2.U6.F57 1996
Fiore, Carole D.
Programming for young children: birth through age five/ Association for Library Service to Children; prepared by Carole D. Fiore with assistance from Sue McCleaf Nespeca. Chicago: American Library Association, 1996. v, 51 p.
95-050875　027.62/5　0838957579
Libraries -- Services to preschool children -- United States. Children's libraries -- Activity programs -- United States.

Z718.2.U6 F59 1998
Fiore, Carole D.
Running summer library reading programs: a how to do it manual/ Carole D. Fiore. New York: Neal-Schuman, c1998. xx, 158 p.
97-049204　027.62/5 21　1555703127
Children's libraries--Activity programs--United States. School libraries--Activity programs--United States. Children--Books and reading--United States.

Z718.3.B75 1997
Briggs, Diane.
52 programs for preschoolers: the librarian's year-round planner/ Diane Briggs. Chicago: American Library Association, 1997. vii, 217 p.
96-052415　027.62/51 21　0838907059
Storytelling--United States. Children's libraries--Activity programs--United States. Libraries and preschool children--United States.

Z718.5 Library science. Information science — The collections. The books — Library service for young people. Young people's libraries

Z718.5.K36 1998
Kan, Katharine.
Sizzling summer reading programs for young adults/ Katharine L. Kan, for the Young Adult Library Services Association. Chicago: American Library Association, 1998. x, 60 p.
97-052973　027.62/6 21　0838934803
Young adults' libraries--Activity programs--United States. Teenagers--Books and reading--United States. Reading promotion--United States.

Z720 Libraries (General) — Biography of librarians — Collective

Z720.A4.U37
American Library Association.
A.L.A. membership directory. Chicago, American Library Association.
50-003095　020.622
Libraries -- United States -- Directories. Library science -- United States -- Societies, etc. -- Directories. Library Associations -- United States -- directories.

Z720.B6.C48 1994
Chapman, Carleton B.
Order out of chaos: John Shaw Billings and America's coming of age/ Carleton B. Chapman. Boston: Boston Medical Library in the Francis A. Countway Library of Medicine; Canton, Mass.: Sole distributor, Science History Publications/USA, 1994. xvi, 420 p.
94-186079　020/.92　0881351873
Billings, John Shaw, -- 1838-1913. Billings, John Shaw, -- 1838-1913. Medical librarians -- United States -- Biography. Librarians -- United States -- biography. Libraries, Medical -- history -- United States.

Z720.D5.W54 1996
Wiegand, Wayne A., 1946-
Irrepressible reformer: a biography of Melvil Dewey/ Wayne A. Wiegand. Chicago: American Library Association, 1996. xx, 403 p.
96-001732　020/.92　083890680X
Dewey, Melvil, -- 1851-1931.Librarians -- United States -- Biography. Educators -- United States -- Biography. Social reformers -- United States -- Biography.

Z720.G89.A3 1992
Guerrier, Edith, 1870-1958.
An independent woman: the autobiography of Edith Guerrier/ edited with an introduction by Molly Matson; foreword by Polly Welts Kaufman. Amherst: University of Massachusetts Press, c1992. xxxix, 154 p.
91-018499　020/.92　087023756X
Guerrier, Edith, -- 1870-1958.Librarians -- United States -- Biography. Women social reformers -- United States -- Biography. Feminists -- United States -- Biography.

Z720.J75 E185 1992
E.J. Josey: an activist librarian/ edited by Ismail Abdullahi. Metuchen, N.J.: Scarecrow Press, 1992. xiv, 268 p.
92-024085　020/.92/273 B 20　0810825848
Josey, E. J., 1924- Librarians -- United States -- Biography.

Z720.M4.A36
Metcalf, Keyes DeWitt, 1889-
Random recollections of an anachronism: or, Seventy-five years of library work/ by Keyes DeWitt Metcalf. New York, NY: Readex Books, c1980. xviii, 401 p.
79-067213　020/.92/4　0918414024
Metcalf, Keyes DeWitt, -- 1889-Librarians -- United States -- Biography.

Z721 Libraries (General) — History and statistics — General works

Z721.E54 1994
Encyclopedia of library history/ edited by Wayne A. Wiegand and Donald G. Davis, Jr. New York: Garland Pub., 1994. xxxi, 707 p.
93-005371　020/.3　0824057872
Libraries -- History -- Encyclopedias. Library science -- History -- Encyclopedias. Information science -- History -- Encyclopedias.

Z721.H227 1995
Harris, Michael H.
History of libraries in the western world/ by Michael H. Harris. 4th ed. Metuchen, N.J.: Scarecrow Press, 1995. v, 301 p.
94-041627　027/.009 20　081082972X
Libraries -- History.

Z721.I63
World guide to libraries. Munchen; K.G. Saur, [1989-]
91-643589　027/.0025
Libraries -- Directories. Libraries -- directories.

Z721.L565 1998
Lerner, Frederick Andrew,
The story of libraries: from the invention of writing to the computer age/ Fred Lerner. New York: Continuum, 1998. 246 p.
98-022748　027/.009 21　0826411142
Libraries -- History.

Z722.5-723 Libraries (General) — History and statistics — By period

Z722.5.C3513 1990
Canfora, Luciano.
The vanished library/ Luciano Canfora; translated by Martin Ryle. Berkeley: University of California Press, 1989. ix, 205 p.
90-011087　026.932 20　0520072553
Libraries -- Egypt -- Alexandria -- History -- To 400. Civilization, Classical. Alexandria (Egypt) -- Intellectual life. Alexandria (Egypt) -- Antiquities.

Z722.5.L53 2000
The Library of Alexandria: centre of learning in the ancient world/ edited by Roy MacLeod. London; I.B. Tauris; xii, 196 p.
00-699885　027.032 21　1860644287
Libraries -- Egypt -- Alexandria -- History -- To 400. Civilization, Classical. Alexandria (Egypt) -- Intellectual life. Alexandria (Egypt) -- Antiquities. Egypt -- History -- Greco-Roman period, 332 B.C.-640 A.D.

Z723.S7313 2000
Staikos, K.
The great libraries: from antiquity to the Renaissance (3000 B.C. to A.D. 1600)/ by Konstantinos Sp. Staikos; preface by Helene Ahrweiler; translated by Timothy Cullen. New Castle, Del.: Oak Knoll Press; 2000. xvi, 563 p.
99-087263　027.04　1584560185
Libraries -- Europe -- History -- To 400. Libraries -- Europe -- History -- 400-1400. Libraries -- Europe -- History -- 1400-1600.

Z723.T47 1957
Thompson, James Westfall,
The medieval library. New York, Hafner Pub. Co., 1957. viii, 702 p.
57-007860
Libraries -- History -- 400-1400. Books -- History -- 400-1400.

Z731-733 Library reports. History. Statistics — North America — United States

Z731.A47
The Bowker annual of library and book trade information/ sponsored by the Council of National Library Associations. New York: R.R. Bowker, [c1961-]
55-012434　020/.5
Libraries -- United States -- Periodicals. Information science -- Periodicals. Library science -- Periodicals.

Z731.A53
American library directory; a classified list of libraries in the United States and Canada, with personnel and statistical data. New York, R.R. Bowker.
23-003581 021/.0025/73
Libraries -- Directories. Libraries -- United States -- Directories. Libraries -- Canada -- Directories.

Z731.A78 1993
Ash, Lee.
Subject collections: a guide to special book collections and subject emphases as reported by university, college, public, and special libraries and museums in the United States and Canada/ compiled by Lee Ash and William G. Miller, with the collaboration of Barry Scott, Kathleen Vickery, and Beverley McDonough. 7th ed., rev. and enl. New Providence, N.J.: R.R. Bowker, c1993. 2 v. (viii, 2466 p.) :
93-134319 026/.00025/7 20 0835231437
Library resources -- United States -- Directories. Library resources -- Canada -- Directories.

Z731.D527 1997
Directory of federal libraries/ edited by William R. Evinger. Phoenix, Ariz.: Oryx Press, 1997. x, 379 p.
97-005540 027.5/025/73 1573560480
Government libraries -- United States -- Directories.

Z731.D56
Directory of special libraries and information centers. Detroit, Mich.: Gale Research Co., [c1963-]
84-640165 026/.00025/73 19
Special libraries--United States--Directories. Special libraries--Canada--Directories. Information services--United States--Directories.

Z733.R9553 B85 1999
Building a scholarly communications center: modeling the Rutgers experience/ Boyd Collins ... [et al.]. Chicago: American Library Association, 1999. xiii, 161 p.
99-029859 025/.00285 21 0838907652
Libraries and electronic publishing -- New Jersey -- New Brunswick. Scholarly electronic publishing -- New Jersey -- New Brunswick. Libraries -- New Jersey -- New Brunswick -- Special collections -- Electronic.

Z733.U6.C595 2000
Conaway, James.
America's library: the story of the Library of Congress, 1800-2000/ James Conaway; foreword by James H. Billington; introduction by Edmund Morris. New Haven, CT: Yale University Press in association with the Library of Congress, 2000. xiii, 226 p.
99-058751 027.573 0300083084
National libraries -- Washington (D.C.) -- History -- 19th century. National libraries -- Washington (D.C.) -- History -- 20th century.

Z792 Library reports. History. Statistics — Europe — Great Britain

Z792.B85932.B37 1989
Barker, Nicolas.
Treasures of the British Library/ compiled by Nicolas Barker and the curatorial staff of the British Library. New York: Abrams, 1989, c1988. 272 p.
88-017683 027.541 0810916533
National libraries -- Collection development -- Great Britain. National libraries -- Great Britain -- History. Library resources -- England -- London.

Z881 Library catalogs and bulletins — By region or country — United States

Z881.N592 S35
Dictionary catalog. Boston, G. K. Hall, 1962. 9 v.
66-001573
Black race -- Bibliography -- Catalogs.

Z987 Private libraries. Book collecting — General works

Z987.B28 2002
Basbanes, Nicholas A.,
Among the gently mad: perspectives and strategies for the book hunter in the twenty-first century/ Nicholas A. Basbanes. 1st ed. New York: Henry Holt and Co., 2002. xi, 250 p.
2002-066854 002/.075 21 0805051597
Book collecting. Antiquarian booksellers. Book collecting -- Computer network resources. Antiquarian booksellers -- Computer network resources.

Z987.5 Private libraries. Book collecting — By region or country, A-Z

Z987.5.U6.D86 1997
Dunbar, Maurice, 1928-
Hooked on books: everybody's guide to book collecting/ by Maurice Dunbar; with special guest chapters by Michael J. Quigley and Dennis M. Taugher. San Mateo, Calif.: Smart's Pub. Group, c1997. xii, 214 p.
97-065549 002/.075 0965412946
Book collecting -- United States. Literature -- History and criticism.

Z988 Private libraries. Book collecting — Bibliography

Z988.M59 2000
Mizuta, Hiroshi,
Adam Smith's library: a catalogue/ [compiled and] edited with an introduction and notes by Hiroshi Mizuta. Rev. Oxford: Clarendon Press; xxiii, 290 p.
99-033443 018/.2 21 0198285906
Smith, Adam, 1723-1790 -- Library -- Catalogs. Early printed books -- England -- Bibliography -- Catalogs. Rare books -- England -- Bibliography -- Catalogs. Private libraries -- England -- Catalogs.

Z989 Private libraries. Book collecting — Biography of book collectors

Z989.H95.D53 1995
Dickinson, Donald C.
Henry E. Huntington's library of libraries/ by Donald C. Dickinson. San Marino, Calif.: Huntington Library, c1995. xvii, 286 p.
95-010396 002/.074/092 0873281535
Huntington, Henry Edwards, -- 1850-1927.Rare books -- Collectors and collecting -- United States -- History -- 20th century. Art -- Collectors and collecting -- United States -- History -- 20th century. Capitalists and financiers -- United States -- Biography.

Z989.S36.S56 1989
Sinnette, Elinor Des Verney.
Arthur Alfonso Schomburg, black bibliophile & collector: a biography/ by Elinor Des Verney Sinnette. [New York, N.Y.]: New York Public Library; 1989. xiii, 262 p.
88-029001 002/.075/0924 0814321569
Schomburg, Arthur Alfonso, -- 1874-1938.Book collectors -- United States -- Biography. Historians -- United States -- Biography. Librarians -- United States -- Biography.

Z997 Private libraries. Book collecting — History and catalogs of private libraries — Collective

Z997.J48 1989
Jefferson, Thomas,
Thomas Jefferson's library: a catalog with the entries in his own order/ edited by James Gilreath, Douglas L. Wilson. Washington: Library of Congress: vii, 149 p.
88-607928 017/.6 19 0844406341
Jefferson, Thomas, 1743-1826 -- Library -- Catalogs. Early printed books -- Virginia -- Bibliography -- Catalogs. Private libraries -- Virginia -- Catalogs. Classification -- Books.

Z998 Booksellers' catalogs. Book prices — General works

Z998.H42
Heard, J. Norman 1922-
Bookman's guide to Americana. New York, Scarecrow Press
60-007269   016.97
Books -- Prices.America -- Bibliography -- Catalogs.

Z1001-1065 General bibliography

Z1001 Introduction to bibliography. Theory, philosophy, psychology. Bibliography. Documentation

Z1001.H33 2000
Harner, James L.
On compiling an annotated bibliography/ James L. Harner. New York: Modern Language Association of America, 2000. vii, 44 p.
00-038663   010/.44   0873529790
Bibliography -- Methodology. English literature -- Bibliography -- Methodology. Abstracting.

Z1001.K86 1984
Krummel, Donald William, 1929-
Bibliographies, their aims and methods/ D.W. Krummel. London; Mansell; 1984. x, 192 p.
83-022177   011/.44   0720116872
Bibliography. Bibliography -- Methodology. Bibliography of bibliographies.

Z1001.S353
Schneider, Georg, 1876-1960.
Theory and history of bibliography. Translated by Ralph Robert Shaw. New York, Scarecrow Press [c1961] xiv, 306 p.
62-019812   010.1
Bibliography -- Methodology. Bibliography -- History.

Z1001.T255 1998
Tanselle, G. Thomas 1934-
Literature and artifacts/ G. Thomas Tanselle. Charlottesville: Bibliographical Society of the University of Virginia, 1998. xvii, 356 p.
98-025657   010/.42   1883631068
Bibliography, Critical.

Z1001.W58 1999
Proctor, William 1939-
An introduction to bibliographical and textual studies/ William Proctor Williams and Craig S. Abbott. New York: Modern Language Association of America, 1999. vi, 179 p.
99-014326   010/.42   0873522672
Bibliography, Critical. Criticism, Textual. English literature -- Criticism, Textual.

Z1001.3 History of bibliography — General works

Z1001.3.B66 1992
The Book encompassed: studies in twentieth-century bibliography/ edited by Peter Davison. Cambridge [England]; Cambridge University Press, 1992. xvi, 315 p.
91-045041   010/.42   052141878X
Bibliography -- History -- 20th century. Bibliography -- Methodology. Bibliography -- Great Britain -- History -- 20th century.

Z1002 Bibliography of bibliography. Books about books

Z1002.B28 2000
Baker, William, 1944-
Twentieth-century bibliography and textual criticism: an annotated bibliography/ compiled by William Baker and Kenneth Womack; foreword by T.H. Howard-Hill. Westport, Conn.: Greenwood Press, 2000. xix, 262 p.
00-042686   016.011   0313305374
Bibliography of bibliographies. Bibliographical literature -- Bibliography. Bibliography, Critical -- Bibliography.

Z1002.B4714 1998
Bell, Barbara L.,
An annotated guide to current national bibliographies/ by Barbara L. Bell; International Federation of Library Associations and Institutions,   IFLA Universal Bibliographic Control and International MARC Programme [and] Deutsche Bibliothek, Frankfurt am Main. 2nd completely rev. ed. München: K.G. Saur, 1998. xxvii, 487 p.
99-458714   3598113765
Bibliography, National -- Bibliography of bibliographies.

Z1002.G67 1987
Gorman, G. E.
Guide to current national bibliographies in the Third World/ G.E. Gorman and J.J. Mills. 2nd rev. ed. London; H. Zell, 1987. xx, 372 p.
88-134875   015.172/4034 20   0905450345
Developing countries -- Imprints -- Bibliography of bibliographies. Developing countries -- Imprints -- Periodicals -- Bibliography.

Z1002.S54 1996
Singerman, Robert.
American library book catalogues, 1801-1875: a national bibliography/ by Robert Singerman. Champaign, Ill.: Graduate School of Library and Information Science, University of Illinois at c1996. ix, 242 p.
96-177536   018   087845098X
Catalogs, Book -- United States -- Bibliography.

Z1003 Choice of books. Books and reading — General works

Z1003.B57 1994
Birkerts, Sven.
The Gutenberg elegies: the fate of reading in an electronic culture/ Sven Birkerts. Winchester, Mass.: Faber and Faber, 1994. x, 231 p.
94-019219   057119849X
Books and reading. Authors and readers.

Z1003.E87 1993
The Ethnography of reading/ edited by Jonathan Boyarin. Berkeley: University of California Press, c1993. vi, 285 p.
92-034690   028/.9   0520079558
Books and reading. Literature and society. Literacy.

Z1003.G45 1993
Gerrig, Richard J.
Experiencing narrative worlds: on the psychological activities of reading/ Richard J. Gerrig. New Haven: Yale University Press, c1993. xi, 273 p.
92-041688   418/.4/019   0300054343
Books and reading -- Psychological aspects. Narration (Rhetoric)

Z1003.J12 2001
Jackson, H. J.
Marginalia: readers' notes in books, 1700-2000/ H.J. Jackson. New Haven: Yale University Press, 2001. 324 p.
00-043721   028/.9/09   0300088167
Books and reading -- History. Marginalia -- History.

Z1003.M292 1996
Manguel, Alberto.
A history of reading/ by Alberto Manguel. New York: Viking, 1996. 372 p.
96-002703   028/.9   0670843024
Books and reading -- History.

Z1003.R97 2001
Ryan, Marie-Laure, 1946-
Narrative as virtual reality: immersion and interactivity in literature and electronic media/ Marie-Laure Ryan. Baltimore: Johns Hopkins University Press, 2001. xiii, 399 p.
00-008955   028/.9   0801864879
Books and reading. Interactive multimedia. Virtual reality.

Z1003.S13 1997
Saenger, Paul Henry, 1945-
Space between words: the origins of silent reading/ Paul Saenger. Stanford, Calif.: Stanford University Press, c1997. xviii, 480 p.
96-035088   028   0804726531
Books and reading -- History. Silent reading -- History.

Z1003.S3947 1989
Scholes, Robert E.
Protocols of reading/ Robert Scholes. New Haven: Yale University Press, c1989. xi, 164 p.
89-005588   028/.9   0300045131
Books and reading. Criticism.

Z1003.2-1003.3 Choice of books. Books and reading — By region or country — United States

Z1003.2.B655 1998
Books of the century: a hundred years of authors, ideas, and literature from The New York times/ edited by Charles McGrath and the staff of the Book review; illustations by Mark Summers. 1st ed. New York: Times Books, c1998. xxiv, 647 p.
98-005477   028.1/0973 21   0812929659
Books -- United States -- Reviews.

Z1003.2.K37 1982
Karetzky, Stephen, 1946-
Reading research and librarianship: a history and analysis/ Stephen Karetzky. Westport, Conn.: Greenwood Press, 1982. xxi, 385 p.
80-001715   028/.9   0313222266
Books and reading -- Research -- United States -- History. Readership surveys -- United States -- History. Library science -- Research -- United States -- History.

Z1003.2.R33 1997
Radway, Janice A.,
A feeling for books: the Book-of-the-Month Club, literary taste, and middle-class desire/ Janice A. Radway. Chapel Hill: University of North Carolina Press, c1997. xiii, 424 p.
96-052037   028/.9/0973 21   0807823570
Books and reading -- United States -- History -- 19th century. Books and reading -- United States -- History -- 20th century. Popular culture -- United States -- History -- 19th century. Popular culture -- United States -- History -- 20th century.

Z1003.3.E85 S7613 1999
A history of reading in the West/ edited by Guglielmo Cavallo and Roger Chartier; translated by Lydia G. Cochrane. Amherst: University of Massachusetts Press, 1999. viii, 478 p.
99-022447   028/.9/094 21   1558492135
Books and reading -- Europe -- History. Written communication -- Europe -- History.

Z1003.5 Choice of books. Books and reading — By region or country — Other regions or countries, A-Z

Z1003.5.E9
Amtower, Laurel.
Engaging words: the culture of reading in the later Middle Ages/ Laurel Amtower. New York: Palgrave, 2000. x, 243 p.
00-030895   028/.9   0312233833
Books and reading -- Europe -- History -- To 1500. Authors and readers -- Europe -- History -- To 1500. Libraries -- Europe -- History -- To 1500. Middle Ages.

Z1003.5.F7.A45 1991
Allen, James Smith.
In the public eye: a history of reading in modern France, 1800-1940/ James Smith Allen. Princeton, N.J.: Princeton University Press, c1991. viii, 356 p.
90-028810   028/.9/0944   0691031622
Books and reading -- France -- History -- 19th century. Books and reading -- France -- History -- 20th century. France -- Intellectual life -- 20th century. France -- Intellectual life -- 19th century.

Z1003.5.G7 A53 1998
Altick, Richard Daniel,
The English common reader: a social history of the mass reading public, 1800-1900/ by Richard D. Altick; with a foreword by Jonathan Rose. 2nd ed. Columbus: Ohio State University Press, [1998], c1957. xx, 448 p.
98-019581   028/.9/0941 21   0814207944
Books and reading -- Great Britain -- History -- 19th century.

Z1003.5.G7.C65 1996
Coleman, Joyce.
Public reading and the reading public in late medieval England and France/ Joyce Coleman. New York: Cambridge University Press, 1996. xiv, 250 p.
95-037984   028/.9/0942   0521553911
Books and reading -- England -- History. Books and reading -- France -- History. Oral tradition -- England -- History.

Z1003.5.I8.P48 1995
Petrucci, Armando.
Writers and readers in medieval Italy: studies in the history of written culture/ Armando Petrucci; edited and translated by Charles M. Radding. New Haven: Yale University Press, c1995. xiii, 257 p.
94-041633   302.2/244   0300060890
Books and reading -- Italy -- History. Written communication -- Italy -- History. Books -- Italy -- History -- 400-1400.

Z1003.5.R9.L68 2000
Lovell, Stephen, 1972-
The Russian reading revolution: print culture in the Soviet and post-Soviet eras/ Stephen Lovell. New York: St. Martin's Press, in association with the School of Slavonic and East European Studies, University of London, 2000. viii, 215 p.
99-048631   028/.9/0947   033377826X
Books and reading -- Russia (Federation) Publishers and publishing -- Russia (Federation) Books andreading -- Soviet Union.

Z1003.5.S62.M43 1983
Mehnert, Klaus, 1906-
The Russians & their favorite books/ Klaus Mehnert. Stanford, Calif.: Hoover Institution Press, Stanford University, c1983. xv, 280 p.
83-006108   028/.9/0947   0817978216
Books and reading -- Soviet Union. Popular literature -- Soviet Union -- History and criticism. Russian fiction -- 20th century -- Stories, plots, etc.

Z1003.8 Biography of bibliographers — Collective

Z1003.8.T94 1999
Twentieth-century British book collectors and bibliographers/ edited byMathew Joseph Bruccoli & Richard Layman Detroit: Gale Research, c1999. xvii, 393 p.
97-027436   010/.92/241   0787630721
Bibliographers -- Great Britain -- Biography -- Dictionaries. Book collectors -- Great Britain -- Biography -- Dictionaries. Bibliography -- Great Britain -- History -- 20th century -- Bibliography.

Z1004 Biography of bibliographers — Individual, A-Z

Z1004.A49 1997
American book collectors and bibliographers. edited by Joseph Rosenblum. Detroit: Gale Research, c1997. xix, 431 p.
97-039600   012/.092/273   078761842X
Bibliographers -- United States -- Bio-bibliography. Book collectors -- United States -- Bio-bibliography.

Z1006 Dictionaries. Encyclopedias

Z1006.A48 1983
The ALA glossary of library and information science/ Heartsill Young, editor, with the assistance of Terry Belanger ... [et al.]. Chicago: American Library Association, 1983. xvi, 245 p.
82-018512   020/.3   0838903711
Library science -- Dictionaries. Information science -- Dictionaries.

Z1006.C37 1995
Carter, John,
ABC for book collectors/ by John Carter. 7th ed./ with corrections, additions, and an introduction by Nicolas New Castle, Del.: Oak Knoll Press; 224 p.
94-029934   002/.075 20   1884718051
Bibliography--Dictionaries. Book collecting--Dictionaries. Book industries and trade--Dictionaries.

Z1006.E57 2003
Encyclopedia of library and information science. 2nd ed./ edited by Miriam A. Drake. New York: Marcel Dekker, 2003. 4 v.
2003-048938   020/.3 21   0824720806
Library science -- Encyclopedias. Information science -- Encyclopedias.

Z1006.H32 1995
Harrod's Librarians' glossary: 9,000 terms used in information management, library science, publishing, the book trades, and archive management/ compiled by Ray Prytherch. Aldershot, Hants., England: Gower; c1995. xiii, 692 p.
94-045466   020/.3   0566075334
Library science -- Dictionaries. Information science -- Dictionaries. Publishers and publishing -- Dictionaries.

Z1006.I57 2003
International encyclopedia of information and library science/ edited by John Feather and Paul Sturges. 2nd ed. New York: Routledge, 2003.
2002-032699   004/.03 21   0415259010
Information science -- Encyclopedias. Library science -- Encyclopedias.

Z1006.K39 1996
Keenan, Stella.
Concise dictionary of library and information science/ Stella Keenan. London; Bowker-Saur, c1996. x, 214 p.
96-139064   020/.3   1857390229
Library science -- Dictionaries. Information science -- Dictionaries.

Z1006.O7 1976
Orne, Jerrold,
The language of the foreign book trade: abbreviations, terms, phrases / Jerrold Orne. 3d ed. Chicago: American Library Association, 1976. x, 333 p. ;
76-011748   010/.3   0838902197
Book industries and trade -- Dictionaries -- Polyglot. Bibliography -- Dictionaries -- Polyglot. English language -- Dictionaries -- Polyglot. Bibliography -- Abbreviations.

Z1006.S595 1990
Soper, Mary Ellen.
The librarian's thesaurus/ by Mary Ellen Soper, Larry N. Osborne, Douglas L. Zweizig, with the assistance of Ronald R. Powell; edited by Mary Ellen Soper. Chicago: American Library Association, 1990. xvi, 164 p.
90-000147   020/.3 20   0838905307
Library science -- Dictionaries. Information science -- Dictionaries.

Z1006.W67 1993
World encyclopedia of library and information services/ [Robert Wedgeworth, editor]. Chicago: American Library Association, 1993. xvii, 905 p.
93-025159   020/.3
Library science -- Encyclopedias. Information science -- Encyclopedias.

Z1009 Collections

Z1009.N54 no. 17
Guide to reference sources on Africa, Asia, Latin America, and the Caribbean, Middle East and North Africa, and Russia and East Europe: selected and annotated. James R. Kennedy, Jr., general editor. Edith Ehrman, project editor. Williamsport, Pa., Bro-Dart Pub. Co., 1972. xiv, 73 p.
72-080675   011/.02   0872720233
Area studies -- Reference books -- Bibliography.

Z1019 Special classes of books — Condemned, prohibited, expurgated books — General

Z1019.H15 1978
Haight, Anne Lyon.
Banned books, 387 B.C. to 1978 A.D./ by Anne Lyon Haight. 4th ed. of Banned books, informal notes/ updated & enl. by Chandler New York: R. R. Bowker, 1978. xxv, 196 p.
78-009720   098/.1   0835210782
Prohibited books--Bibliography.

Z1019.H68 1996
Hit list: frequently challenged books for young adults/ prepared by the Intellectual Freedom Committee of the Young Adult Library Services Association; with the assistance of Merri M. Monks and Donna Reidy Pistolis. Chicago: American Library Association, 1996. viii, 92 p.
96-014418   098/.1/0973 20   0838934595
Challenged books -- United States -- Bibliography. Young adults -- Books and reading -- United States. Young adult literature -- Bibliography.

Z1024 Special classes of books — Imaginary books. Lost books. Forgeries, etc.

Z1024.C32 1983 Suppl.
Barker, Nicolas.
A sequel to An enquiry into the nature of certain nineteenth century pamphlets by John Carter and Graham Pollard: the forgeries of H. Buxton Forman & T.J. Wise re-examined/ by Nicolas Barker & John Collins. London; Scolar Press, 1983. 394 p.
82-024024   098/.3 19   0859676390
Wise, Thomas James, 1859-1937. Forman, H. Buxton (Harry Buxton), 1842-1917. Literary forgeries and mystifications.

Z1033 Special classes of books — Other special classes, A-Z

Z1033.B3.J87 1998
Justice, Keith L.
Bestseller index: all books, by author, on the lists of Publishers weekly and the New York times through 1990/ Keith L. Justice. Jefferson, N.C.: McFarland, c1998. xii, 483 p.
97-031639   016.028/9/0973   0786404221
Best sellers -- United States -- Bibliography.

Z1033.F53.F57 1989
First editions, a guide to identification: statements of selected North American, British Commonwealth, and Irish publishers on their methods of designating first editions/ edited by Edward N. Zempel and Linda A. Verkler. Peoria, Ill.: Spoon River Press, 1989. vi, 307 p.
89-183425   016.094/4   0930358082
First editions -- Handbooks, manuals, etc. Imprints (in books) -- Handbooks, manuals, etc. English imprints -- Handbooks, manuals, etc.

Z1033.M5.G8
Guide to microforms in print. Englewood, Colo. [etc.] Microcard Editions. 17 v.
61-007082   011.36
Microforms -- Catalogs. Microcards -- Catalogs.

Z1033.P52.N63 1988
Nodelman, Perry.
Words about pictures: the narrative art of children's picture books/ Perry Nodelman. Athens: University of Georgia Press, c1988. xii, 318 p.
87-038084   002   0820310360
Picture books for children. Book design. Illustrated children's books.

Z1035.A1 Best books — Book selection, reviews, etc.

Z1035.A1.B6
Book review index. Detroit, Gale Research Co.
65-009908
Books -- Reviews -- Indexes -- Periodicals.

Z1035.B545 2002
The Best Books for Academic Libraries. 1st ed. Temecula, CA : Best Books, Inc., [c2002-] 10 vols.
2002013790   011/.67 21   0722200102
Academic libraries – United States – Book lists.

Z1035.B7-W79 Best books — Lists, catalogs, etc. — 1801-

Z1035.B7
The Reader's adviser. New York, R.R. Bowker Co.
57-013277   011
Best books.

Z1035.C5 2001
Sweetland, James H.
Fundamental reference sources/ James H. Sweetland. Chicago: American Library Association, 2001. xii, 612 p.
00-024311   011/.02 0838907806
Reference books -- Bibliography.

Z1035.C69 1930
The Harvard classics, edited by Charles W. Eliot, LL. D.; fifteen minutes a day, the reading guide. New York, P. F. Collier & Son Company c1930] 95 p.
32-021478

Z1035.E78
List of books indexes in Essay and general literature index, 1900/33- New York, The H. W. Wilson company, [1934-   ]
34-018332
Literature -- Bibliography. [from old catalog] Essays -- Bibliography. [from old catalog]

Z1035.F29
Fadiman, Clifton, 1904-
The lifetime reading plan. Cleveland, World Pub. Co. [1960] 318 p.
60-005810   016.028
Best books. Books and reading.

Z1035.G63 1990
Good reading: a guide for serious readers/ Arthur Waldhorn, Olga S. Weber, Arthur Zeiger, editors. 23rd ed. New York: R.R. Bowker, c1990. xxx, 465 p.
89-017317   011/.73 20   0835227073
Best books -- United States. Books and reading -- United States.

Z1035.R263 1997
The reader's catalog: an annotated selection of more than 40,000 of the best books in print in over 300 categories/ edited by Geoffrey O'Brien. New York: Reader's Catalog, c1997. v, 1968 p.
96-042428   011/.73   0924322012
Best books.

Z1035.W79 1967
Winchell, Constance M. 1896-
Guide to reference books [by] Constance M. Winchell. Chicago, American Library Association, 1967. xx, 741 p.
66-029240   011/.02
Reference books -- Bibliography.

Z1035.1 Reference books

Z1035.1.A47 1999
Reference sources for small and medium-sized libraries/ Scott E. Kennedy, editor. 6th ed./ compiled by Reference Sources for Small and Medium-sized Chicago: American Library Association, 1999. xxii, 368 p.
98-052880   011/.02 21   0838934684
Reference books -- Bibliography. Small libraries -- United States -- Book lists.

Z1035.1.A55
American reference books annual. Littleton, Colo.: Libraries Unlimited, [c1970-   ]
75-120328   011/.02
Reference books -- Bibliography -- Periodicals.

Z1035.1.D665 1995
Dority, G. Kim, 1950-
A guide to reference books for small and medium-size libraries, 1984-1994/ G. Kim Dority. Englewood, Colo.: Libraries Unlimited, 1995. xviii, 372 p.
95-022816   016.0287   1563081032
Reference books -- Bibliography. Small libraries -- United States -- Book lists.

Z1035.1.G89 1996
Guide to reference books/ edited by Robert Balay; associate editor, Vee Friesner Carrington; with special editorial assistance by Murray S. Martin. Chicago: American Library Association, 1996. 2020 p.
95-026322   011/.02   0838906699
Reference books -- Bibliography.

Z1035.1.K35 1998
Katz, William A., 1924-
Cuneiform to computer: a history of reference sources/ Bill Katz. Lanham, Md.: Scarecrow Press, 1998. xvi, 415 p.
97-007094   028.7/09   0810832909
Reference books -- History.

Z1035.1.S43 1986
Sheehy, Eugene P. 1922-
Guide to reference books/ edited by Eugene P. Sheehy; with the assistance of Rita G. Keckeissen ... [et al.]; science, technology, and medicine compiled by Richard J. Dionne, Elizabeth E. Ferguson, Robert C. Michaelson. Chicago: American Library Association, 1986. xiv, 1560 p.
85-011208   011/.02   0838903908
Reference books -- Bibliography.

Z1035.1.T66 1991
Topical reference books/ Marion Sader, editor; Charles A. Bunge, Sharon Hogan, consultants. New Providence, N.J.: Bowker, c1991. xvii, 892 p.
91-009706   011/.02   0835230872
Reference books -- Bibliography. Reference services (Libraries)

Z1037.A1 Books for the young — General works

Z1037.A1.D678 1977
Dreyer, Sharon Spredemann.
The bookfinder: a guide to children's literature about the needs and problems of youth aged 2-15/ by Sharon Spredemann Dreyer. Circle Pines, Minn.: American Guidance Service, c1977-c1994 v. 1-5
78-105919   011/.62   0913476455
Children's literature -- Book reviews. Children -- Conduct of life -- Juvenile literature -- Book reviews. Problem solving -- Juvenile literature -- Book reviews.

Z1037.A1.G47 1997
Gillespie, John Thomas, 1928-
Characters in young adult literature/ [compiled by] John T. Gillespie, Corinne J. Naden. Detroit: Gale Research, c1997. xiv, 535 p.
97-004998   809.3/00835   0787604011
Young adult literature -- Stories, plots, etc. Characters and characteristics in literature. Young adult literature -- Book reviews.

Z1037.A1 H42 1999
Hearne, Betsy Gould.
Choosing books for children: a commonsense guide/ Betsy Hearne; with Deborah Stevenson. 3rd ed. Urbana: University of Illinois Press, c1999. xi, 229 p.
99-006144   011.62 21   0252025164
Children--Books and reading--United States. Children's literature, English--Bibliography.

Z1037.A1.J78 1997
Jones, Raymond E.
Characters in children's literature/ Raymond E. Jones. Detroit: Gale Research, c1997. xvi, 529 p.
97-004999   809.3/0083   0787604003
Children's literature -- Stories, plots, etc. Characters and characteristics in literature. Children's literature -- Book reviews.

Z1037.A2 Books for the young — Prize books

Z1037.A2 N492 2001
The Newbery & Caldecott medal books, 1986-2000: a comprehensive guide to the winners/ the Horn Book, Association for Library Service to Children. Chicago: American Library Association, 2001. viii, 368 p.
00-053430   011.62/079 21   0838935052
Newbery Medal -- Bio-bibliography. Caldecott Medal -- Bio-bibliography. Children's literature, American -- Bio-bibliography. Picture books for children -- United States -- Bio-bibliography. Children -- Books and reading -- United States.

Z1037.A2.S45 1992
Smith, Laura J.
Children's book awards international: a directory of awards and winners, from inception through 1990/ by Laura Smith. Jefferson, N.C.: McFarland & Co., c1992. xxii, 649 p.
91-050940   028.1/62/079   0899506860
Children's literature -- Awards -- Directories. Young adult literature -- Awards -- Directories. Children's literature -- Illustrations -- Awards -- Directories.

Z1037.A52-V66 Books for the young — Lists, catalogs, etc. — Modern children's books 1801-

Z1037.A52 1992
Anderson, Vicki, 1928-
Fiction index for readers 10 to 16: subject access to over 8200 books (1960-1990)/ by Vicki Anderson. Jefferson, N.C.: McFarland & Company, c1992. ix, 477 p.
91-050954   016.80883/0835   0899507034
Young adult fiction -- Stories, plots, etc. -- Indexes. Children's stories -- Stories, plots, etc. -- Indexes. Young adult fiction -- Bibliography.

Z1037.C5428 1998
Children's books from other countries/ [sponsored by] United States Board on Books for Young People; Carl M. Tomlinson, editor. Lanham, Md.: Scarecrow Press, 1998. xiii, 304 p.
97-041768   028.5/5   0810834472
Children -- United States -- Books and reading. Children's literature -- Bibliography.

Z1037.C675 1994
Colborn, Candy, 1942-
What do children read next?: a reader's guide to fiction for children/ Candy Colborn. Detroit: Gale Research, c1994. xv, 1135 p.
93-049685   016.813008/09282   0810388863
Children -- United States -- Books and reading. Children's stories, American -- Bibliography. Books and reading.

Z1037.D24 2000
Day, Frances Ann.
Lesbian and gay voices: an annotated bibliography and guide to literature for children and young adults/ Frances Ann Day; foreword by Nancy Garden. Westport, Conn.: Greenwood Press, 2000. xv, 268 p.
00-021047   016.8108/09282   0313311625
Children's literature, American -- Bibliography. Homosexuality and literature -- United States -- Bibliography. Young adult literature, American -- Bibliography.

Z1037.D35 1998
Denman-West, Margaret W., 1926-
Children's literature: a guide to information sources/ Margaret W. Denman-West. Englewood, Colo.: Libraries Unlimited, 1998. xiv, 187 p.
98-010177   016.8088/99282   1563084481
Children's literature -- Bibliography.

Z1037.H48 1994
Helbig, Alethea.
This land is our land: a guide to multicultural literature for children and young adults/ Alethea K. Helbig and Agnes Regan Perkins. Westport, Conn.: Greenwood Press, c1994. xi, 401 p.
94-016124   016.8108/09282   0313287422
Children's literature, American -- Bibliography. Ethnic groups -- United States -- Bibliography. Young adult literature, American -- Bibliography.

Z1037.H646 1996
Hirsch, E. D.
Books to build on: a grade-by-grade resource guide for parents and teachers/ edited by John Holdren and E.D. Hirsch, Jr. New York: Delta, 1996. xvi, 361 p.
96-017200   011.62 20   0385316402
Children--Books and reading--United States.

Z1037.J93 2001
Jweid, Rosann, 1933-
Building character through literature: a guide for middle school readers/ Rosann Jweid, Margaret Rizzo. Lanham, Md.: Scarecrow Press, 2001. vii, 232 p.
00-046401   809/.89283   0810839512
Best books -- Children's literature. Children's literature -- Bibliography. Middle school students -- Books and reading.

Z1037.L715 1998
Lima, Carolyn W.
A to Zoo: subject access to children's picture books/ Carolyn W. Lima, John A. Lima. 5th ed. New Providence, N.J.: R.R. Bowker, c1998. xxvii, 1398 p.
98-011920   011.62 21   0835239160
Picture books for children -- Indexes. Children's literature, English -- Indexes.

Z1037.M134 1995
McElmeel, Sharron L.
Great new nonfiction reads/ Sharron L. McElmeel. Englewood, Colo.: Libraries Unlimited, 1995. xvi, 225 p.
94-020258   028.1/62   1563082284
Children -- Books and reading. Oral reading.

Z1037.M654 1992
Miller-Lachmann, Lyn,
Our family, our friends, our world: an annotated guide to significant multicultural books for children and teenagers/ Lyn Miller-Lachmann. New Providence, N.J.: R.R. Bowker, c1992. xiii, 710 p.
91-024549   011.62 20   0835230252
Children's literature -- Bibliography. Young adult literature -- Bibliography. Pluralism (Social sciences) in literature -- Bibliography. Ethnic groups in literature -- Bibliography. Minorities in literature -- Bibliography.

Z1037.N39 2001
The new books kids like/ edited by Sharon Deeds, Catherine Chastain; prepared for Association for Library Service to Children. Chicago: American Library Association, 2001. x, 179 p.
2001-018850   011.62 21   0838935125
Children -- Books and reading -- United States -- Bibliography. Children's literature -- Bibliography.

Z1037.O24 1998
Odean, Kathleen.
Great books for boys: more than 600 books for boys 2 to 14/ Kathleen Odean. 1st ed. New York: Ballantine Books, 1998. xi, 384 p.
97-045926   028.1/6241 21   0345420837
Boys -- Books and reading.

Z1037.O25 1997
Odean, Kathleen.
Great books for girls: more than 600 books to inspire today's girls and tomorrow's women/ Kathleen Odean. 1st ed. New York: Ballantine Books, 1997. ix, 420 p.
96-044392   028.1/6242 21   034540484X
Girls -- Books and reading. Children's stories, American -- Bibliography. Children's stories, American -- Stories, plots, etc. Girls in literature -- Bibliography.

Z1037.P46 1998
Pettus, Eloise S., 1926-
Master index to more summaries of children's books, 1980-1990/ Eloise S. Pettus, with the assistance of Daniel D. Pettus, Jr. Lanham, Md.: Scarecrow Press, 1998. 2 v.
98-011254   011.62   0810832690
Children's literature -- Abstracts -- Indexes. Children's literature -- Bibliography -- Indexes. Children's literature -- Bibliography of bibliographies -- Indexes.

Z1037.R63 1992
Rollock, Barbara.
Black authors & illustrators of children's books: a biographical dictionary/ Barbara Rollock. New York, N.Y.: Garland, 1992. xviii, 234 p.
91-037402   809/.89282   082407078X
Children's literature -- Black authors -- Biography -- Dictionaries. Children's literature -- Bio-bibliography -- Dictionaries. Children's literature, American -- Afro-American authors -- Biography -- Dictionaries.

Z1037.S7575 1994
Spencer, Pam.
What do young adults read next?: a reader's guide to fiction for young adults/ Pam Spencer. Detroit: Gale Research, c1994-c1997. 2 v.
93-049806   016.813008/09283   0810388871
Young adults -- United States -- Books and reading. Young adult fiction, American -- Bibliography. Books and reading.

Z1037.V66 2000
Volz, Bridget Dealy.
Junior genreflecting: a guide to good reads and series fiction for children/ Bridget Dealy Volz, Cheryl Perkins Scheer, Lynda Blackburn Welborn. Englewood, Colo.: Libraries Unlimited, 2000. xiii, 187 p.
99-038135   016.813009/9282 21   1563085569
Children's stories -- Bibliography. Children's stories -- Themes, motives. Children's stories -- Stories, plots, etc. Children's literature in series -- Bibliography. Children -- Books and reading. Literary form.

Z1037.9 Books for the young — Reference books for children

Z1037.9.B36 1984
Baskin, Barbara Holland,
More notes from a different drummer: a guide to juvenile fiction portraying the disabled/ by Barbara H. Baskin and Karen H. Harris. New York: Bowker, 1984. xv, 495 p.
84-012283   808.06/8 19   0835218716
Children's stories -- Bibliography. People with disabilities in literature -- Bibliography. People with mental disabilities in literature -- Bibliography. Emotions in literature -- Bibliography.

Z1039 Books for other special classes, institutions, etc., A-Z

Z1039.B56.V36 1995
Valade, Roger M.
The Schomburg Center Guide to black literature from the eighteenth century to the present/ Roger M. Valade III, Denise Kasinec. Detroit: Gale Research, 1995. xxvi, 545 p.
95-036733   809/.8896   0787602892
Blacks in literature -- Bibliography. Literature -- Black authors -- Bio-bibliography. Authors, Black -- Biography -- Dictionary.

Z1039.C45 B56 2001
Biographical dictionary of literary influences: the nineteenth century, 1800-1914/ John Powell, editor; Derek W. Blakeley, associate editor; Tessa Powell, editorial assistant. Westport, Conn.: Greenwood Press, 2001. xiii, 522 p.
99-462057   028/.9/09034   031330422X
Celebrities -- Books and reading -- Europe -- History -- 19th century. Celebrities -- Books and reading -- Europe -- History -- 20th century. Celebrities -- Books and reading -- America -- History -- 19th century.

Z1039.C65 O9 1996
Outstanding books for the college bound: choices for a generation/ Young Adult Library Services Association; Marjorie Lewis, editor. Chicago: American Library Association, 1996. x, 217 p.
96-005086   011.62/5 20   0838934560
College students -- Books and reading -- United States. Best books -- United States.

Z1039.W65.H38 1996
Hayes, Kevin J.
A colonial woman's bookshelf/ Kevin J. Hayes. Knoxville: University of Tennessee Press, c1996. xv, 216 p.
95-041824   028/.9/082   0870499378
Women -- United States -- Books and reading -- History -- 17th century. Women -- United States -- Books and reading -- History -- 18th century.

Z1039.W65 R32 1984
Radway, Janice A.,
Reading the romance: women, patriarchy, and popular literature/ Janice A. Radway. Chapel Hill: University of North Carolina Press, c1984. x, 274 p.
83-023596   028/.9/024042 19   0807841250
Women -- Books and reading. Love stories -- Appreciation. Popular literature -- Appreciation. Feminism and literature. Sex role in literature. Women in literature. Patriarchy.

Z1041 Anonyms and pseudonyms — General bibliography

Z1041.R66 1998
Room, Adrian.
Dictionary of pseudonyms/ Adrian Room. Jefferson, N.C.: McFarland, c1998. viii, 404 p.
97-031640   929.4/03   078640423X
Anonyms and pseudonyms.

Z1041.T3
Taylor, Archer,
The bibliographical history of anonyma and pseudonyma, by Archer Taylor and Fredric J. Mosher. Chicago, Univ. of Chicago Press, 1951. ix, 288 p.
51-004934
Anonyms and pseudonyms. Anonyms and pseudonyms -- Bibliography.

Z1049 Anonyms and pseudonyms — By region or country — Americas

Z1049.A1.S38 1997
Scroggins, Daniel C., 1937-
20,000 Spanish American pseudonyms/ Daniel C. Scroggins. Lanham, Md.: Scarecrow Press, 1997. xxx, 1033 p.
97-018959   929.4/098   0810833646
Anonyms and pseudonyms, Latin American.

Z1065 Anonyms and pseudonyms — By region or country — Great Britain and Ireland

Z1065.A83 1987
Atkinson, Frank,
Dictionary of literary pseudonyms: a selection of popular modern writers in English/ Frank Atkinson. 4th enl. ed. London: Library Association Pub.; xi, 299 p.
86-028775   808/.03/21 19
Anonyms and pseudonyms, English. Anonyms and pseudonyms, American.

Z1065.H18 1980
Halkett, Samuel, 1814-1871.
A dictionary of anonymous and pseudonymous publications in the English language/ Halkett and Laing. Harlow: Longman, [1980-   ] v. 1
81-127850   014/.2   0582555213
Anonyms and pseudonyms, English.

Z1201-4891 National bibliography

Z1201 America — General bibliography

Z1201.A52
American book publishing record.   New York: R.R. Bowker Co., [c1968-   ]
66-019741   015.73
United States -- Imprints -- Periodicals.

Z1206 America — Biobibliography of Americanists

Z1206.M55 1995
Miller, Jay, 1947-
Writings in Indian history, 1985-1990/ compiled by Jay Miller, Colin G. Calloway, and Richard A. Sattler. Norman: University of Oklahoma Press, c1995. xiv, 216 p.
95-008776   016.973/0497   0806127597
Indians of North America -- History -- Bibliography.North America -- History -- Bibliography.

Z1207 America — Private libraries, and booksellers' catalogs of Americana

Z1207.H43 1981
Heard, J. Norman
Bookman's guide to Americana/ J. Norman Heard. 8th ed. Metuchen, N.J.: Scarecrow Press, 1981. ix, 284 p.
81-009005   016.97 19   0810814579
Out-of-print books -- Bibliography -- Catalogs. America -- Bibliography -- Catalogs.

Z1209-1210 America — American ethnology — Indians

Z1209.C57 1984
Clements, William M.,
Native American folklore, 1879-1979: an annotated bibliography/ compiled by William M. Clements, Frances M. Malpezzi. Athens, Ohio: Swallow Press, c1984. xxiii, 247 p.
83-006672   016.398/08997073   19   0804008310
Indians of North America -- Folklore -- Bibliography. Folklore -- North America -- Bibliography.

Z1209.M25 1998
Magnaghi, Russell M.
Indian slavery, labor, evangelization, and captivity in the Americas: an annotated bibliography/ Russell M. Magnaghi. Lanham, Md.: Scarecrow Press, 1998. xiii, 559 p.
97-025956   016.305897/073   0810833557
Indians -- Social conditions -- Bibliography. Indians, Treatment of -- Bibliography. Slaveholders -- America -- Bibliography.

Z1209.U5.U53 1984
United States.
American Indians: a select catalog of National Archives microfilm publications.   Washington, D.C.: National Archives Trust Fund Board, 1984. xii, 91 p.
83-013412   016.3058/97/073   0911333096
Indians of North America -- Government relations -- Manuscripts -- Microform catalogs. Indians of North America -- Government relations -- Sources -- Bibliography -- Microform catalogs. Documents on microfilm -- Catalogs.

Z1209.W52 1995
White, Phillip M.
American Indian studies: a bibliographic guide/ Phillip M. White. Englewood, Colo.: Libraries Unlimited, 1995. xi, 163 p.
94-024345   016.970004/97   1563082438
Indians of North America -- Bibliography. Indians of North America -- Reference books -- Bibliography.

Z1209.W82 Suppl.
Wolf, Carolyn E., 1941-
Indians of North and South America: a bibliography based on the collection at the Willard E. Yager Library-Museum, Hartwick College, Oneonta, N.Y.: Supplement/ by Carolyn E. Wolf and Nancy S. Chiang. Metuchen, N.J.: Scarecrow Press, 1988. viii, 654 p.
88-006055   0810821273
Indians -- Bibliography -- Catalogs.

Z1209.2.N67.H68 1991
Hoxie, Frederick E., 1947-
Native Americans: an annotated bibliography/ Frederick E. Hoxie and Harvey Markowitz. Pasadena, Calif.: Salem Press, c1991. xiii, 325 p.
91-016427   016.970004/97   0893566705
Indians of North America -- Bibliography.

Z1209.2.N67.O77 1998
Osterreich, Shelley Anne.
Native North American shamanism: an annotated bibliography/ compiled by Shelley Anne Osterreich. Westport, Conn.: Greenwood Press, 1998. xiii, 109 p.
98-028015   016.299/7   0313301689
Indians of North America -- Religion -- Bibliography. Indians of North America -- Medicine -- Bibliography. Indians of North America -- Rites and ceremonies -- Bibliography.

Z1209.2.N67 W56 2000
White, Phillip M.
Peyotism and the Native American church: an annotated bibliography/ Phillip M. White. Westport, CT: Greenwood Press, 2000. xx, 141 p.
00-042678   016.299/7   0313316260
Indians of North America -- Religion -- Bibliography. Indians of North America -- Rites and ceremonies -- Bibliography. Peyotism -- Bibliography.

Z1209.2.P4.S55 1996
Silverman, Helaine.
Ancient Peruvian art: an annotated bibliography/ Helaine Silverman. New York: G.K. Hall, 1996. xi, 275 p.
96-032694   016.7/0985/0901   0816190607
Indian art -- Peru -- Bibliography. Indians of South America -- Peru -- Antiquities -- Bibliography.

Z1209.2.U5.H54 1982
Hill, Edward E.
Guide to records in the National Archives of the United States relating to American Indians/ compiled by Edward E. Hill. Washington, D.C.: National Archives and Records Service, General Services Administration, 1981 xiii, 467 p.
81-022357   016.3231/97/073
Indians of North America -- Government relations -- Sources -- Bibliography -- Catalogs. Indians of North America -- History -- Sources -- Bibliography -- Catalogs.

Z1209.2.U5 N67 1998
Nordquist, Joan.
Native Americans: social, economic, and political aspects: a bibliography/ compiled by Joan Nordquist. Santa Cruz, CA: Reference and Research Services, 1998. 76 p.
99-196376   016.97/000497 21   0937855987
Indians of North America -- Bibliography.

Z1209.2.W47.A53 1994
Weeks, John M.
Ancient Caribbean/ John M. Weeks, Peter J. Ferbel. New York: Garland Pub., 1994. lxxi, 325 p.
93-051063   972.9/01   0815313039
Indians of the West Indies -- Bibliography. Indians of the West Indies -- Antiquities -- Bibliography. West Indies -- Antiquities -- Bibliography. Caribbean Area -- Antiquities -- Bibliography.

Z1210.D3.H66 1993
Hoover, Herbert T.
The Sioux and other Native American cultures of the Dakotas: an annotated bibliography/ compiled by Herbert T. Hoover and Karen P. Zimmerman; editorial assistant for computer operations, Christopher J. Hoover. Westport, Conn.: Greenwood Press, 1993. xx, 265 p.
93-025004   016.9783/004975   0313290938
Dakota Indians -- Bibliography. Indians of North America -- Great Plains -- Bibliography.

Z1210.E8
Crandall, Richard C.
An annotated bibliography of Inuit art/ by Richard C. Crandall and Susan M. Crandall. Jefferson, N.C.: McFarland, 2001. 458 p.
2001-030517   016.70403/9712   0786410078
Inuit art -- Bibliography.

Z1210.I7.I76 1985
Iroquois Indians: a documentary history of the diplomacy of the Six Nations and their league: guide to the microfilm collection/ Francis Jennings, editor, William N. Fenton, joint editor, Mary A. Druke, associate editor, David R. Miller, research assistant. Woodbridge, CT: Research Publications, 1985. xxi, 718 p.
85-175112   016.973/0497   0892350881
Iroquois Indians -- History -- Sources -- Microform catalogs. Indians of North America -- History -- Sources -- Microform catalogs.

Z1210.I7.J65 1996
Johansen, Bruce E. 1950-
Native American political systems and the evolution of democracy: an annotated bibliography/ compiled by Bruce E. Johansen. Westport, Conn: Greenwood Press, 1996. xv, 158 p.
96-005541   016.973/04975   0313300100
Iroquois Indians -- Politics and government -- Bibliography. Indians of North America -- Politics and government -- Bibliography. United States -- Civilization -- Indian influences -- Bibliography. United States -- Politics and government -- To 1775 -- Bibliography. United States -- Historiography -- Bibliography.

Z1210.N3.B34 1999
Bahr, Howard M.
Dine bibliography to the 1990s: a companion to the Navajo bibliography of 1969/ Howard M. Bahr. Lanham, Md.: Scarecrow Press, 1999. xxxii, 739 p.
99-010061   016.9791/004972   0810836513
Navajo Indians -- Bibliography.

Z1210.S55 N64 2001
Noe, Randolph, 1939-
The Shawnee Indians: an annotated bibliography/ Randolph Noe. Lanham, Md.: Scarecrow Press, 2001. xxxv, 721 p.
00-057378   016.974004/973   081083894X
Shawnee Indians -- Bibliography.

Z1215 America — United States — General bibliography

Z1215.P972
Books in print. New York, R.R. Bowker Co.
74-643574   015.73
Catalogs, Publishers' -- United States. Catalogs, Publishers' -- United States. Bibliography, National -- United States. United States -- Imprints -- Catalogs.

Z1215.P973
Subject guide to Books in print. New York: R.R. Bowker Co., [1957-   ]
74-643573   015.73
Catalogs, Publishers' -- United States. Catalogs, Publishers -- United States -- indexes. Literature -- United States -- bibliography. United States -- Imprints -- Catalogs.

Z1223 America — United States — Government publications

Z1223.M674 1996
Morehead, Joe,
Introduction to United States government information sources/ Joe Morehead. 5th ed. Englewood, Colo.: Libraries Unlimited, 1996. xxi, 333 p.
96-006246   015.73/053 20   1563084600
Government publications -- United States -- Handbooks, manuals, etc.

Z1223.Z7.B35 1998
Hoffmann, Frank W., 1949-
Guide to popular U.S. government publications/ Frank W. Hoffmann, Richard J. Wood. Englewood, Colo.: Libraries Unlimited, 1998. xxvi, 300 p.
98-029868   015.73/053   1563086077
Government publications -- United States -- Bibliography.

Z1223.Z7 M25 1996
Maxwell, Bruce,
How to access the federal government on the Internet, 1997/ Bruce Maxwell. Washington, D.C.: Congressional Quarterly, c1996. xxii, 455 p.
96-231280   1568021852
Government information -- United States -- Computer network resources. Internet -- United States.

Z1223.Z7.M67 1983
Morehead, Joe, 1931-
Introduction to United States public documents/ Joe Morehead. Littleton, Colo.: Libraries Unlimited, 1983. 309 p.
82-022866   015.73   0872873595
Government publications -- United States.

Z1223.Z7.R63 1996
Hardy, Gayle J., 1942-
Subject guide to U.S. government reference sources/ Gayle J. Hardy, Judith Schiek Robinson. Englewood, Colo.: Libraries Unlimited, 1996. xxi, 358 p.
96-017543   025.17/34   156308189X
Government publications -- Reference books -- Bibliography. Government publications -- United States -- Bibliography. Government publications -- United States -- Bibliography of bibliographies.

Z1223.Z7.S3 1969
Schmeckebier, Laurence Frederick, 1877-1959.
Government publications and their use [by] Laurence F. Schmeckebier [and] Roy B. Eastin. Washington, Brookings Institution [1969] viii, 502 p.
69-019694   025.17/3   0815777361
Government publications -- United States.

Z1223.Z7.S4 2001
Sears, Jean L.
Using government information sources: electronic and print/ Jean L. Sears and Marilyn K. Moody. Phoenix, Ariz..: Oryx Press, 2000. 536 p.
00-009773   015.73/053   1573562882
Government publications -- United States -- Handbooks, manuals, etc. Government publications -- United States -- Bibliography. Electronic information resources -- United States -- Handbooks, manuals, etc.

Z1223.Z7.Z88 1996
Zwirn, Jerrold.
Accessing U.S. government information: subject guide to jurisdiction of the executive and legislative branches/ compiled by Jerrold Zwirn. Westport, Conn.: Greenwood Press, 1996. xvii, 178 p.
95-038638   015.73/053   0313297657
Government publications -- United States -- Indexes. Administrative agencies -- United States -- Directories. Executive departments -- United States -- Directories.

Z1223.Z9.C65 1975
CIS US serial set index. Washington: Congressional Information Service, c1975-c1997. 14 v. in 58
75-027448   328.73   0912380268
Government publications -- United States -- Indexes.

Z1224 America — United States — Biobibliography

Z1224.C58.156
Contemporary authors. New revision ser. Detroit: Gale Research Co., [c1981-   ] 2 v.
81-640179   016.92/0073
Authors, American -- Biography -- Periodicals. United States -- Bio-bibliography -- Periodicals.

Z1225-1231 America — United States — American literature

Z1225.A1 N5
Nilon, Charles H.
Bibliography of bibliographies in American literature, by Charles H. Nilon. New York, R. R. Bowker Co., 1970. xi, 483 p.
73-103542   016.01681   0835202593
American literature -- Bibliography of bibliographies.

Z1225.B55
Blanck, Jacob, 1906-1974.
Bibliography of American literature/ compiled by Jacob Blanck for the Bibliographical Society of America. New Haven: Yale University Press, 1955-1991. 9 v.
54-005283   016.81
American literature -- Bibliography.

Z1225.B55 Index
Winship, Michael.
Bibliography of American literature: a selective index/ compiled by Michael Winship, with Philip B. Eppard and Rachel J. Howarth. Golden, Colo.: North American Press, 1995. vi, 345 p.
94-037184   016.81   1555919510
Blanck, Jacob, -- 1906-1974. -- Bibliography of American literature -- Indexes.American literature -- Bibliography -- Indexes.

Z1225.B55 Suppl.
Winship, Michael.
Epitome of Bibliography of American literature/ compiled by Michael Winship, with Philip B. Eppard and Rachel J. Howarth. Golden, Colo.: North American Press, 1995. xii, 325 p.
94-036955   016.81   1555919502
American literature -- Bibliography.

Z1225.B67 2001
Bracken, James K., 1952-
The undergraduate's companion to American writers and their web sites/ James K. Bracken, Larry G. Hinman. Englewood, Colo.: Libraries Unlimited, 2001. xiv, 309 p.
00-055848   016.8108   1563088592
American literature -- Bibliography. American literature -- Research -- Computer network resources.

Z1225.J66 1984
Jones, Steven Swann,
Folklore and literature in the United States: an annotated bibliography of studies of folklore in American literature/ Steven Swann Jones. New York: Garland Pub., 1984. xxvii, 262 p.
82-049182   016.81/09/3 19   0824091868
American literature -- History and criticism -- Bibliography. Folklore in literature -- Bibliography. Folklore -- United States -- Bibliography.

Z1225.W38 1996
Wells, Daniel A., 1943-
The literary index to American magazines, 1850-1900/ compiled by Daniel A. Wells. Westport, Conn.: Greenwood Press, 1996. xii, 441 p.
95-026447   016.8108/004   0313298408
American literature -- 19th century -- Bibliography -- Indexes. American periodicals -- Indexes.

Z1227.C58
Clark, Harry Hayden, 1901-1971.
American literature: Poe through Garland. New York, Appleton-Century-Crofts [1971] xii, 148 p.
77-137641   016.8108   0390193232
American literature -- 19th century -- Bibliography.

Z1229.E87.P43 1992
Peck, David R.
American ethnic literatures: native American, African American, Chicano/Latino, and Asian American writers and their backgrounds: an annotated bibliography/ David R. Peck. Pasadena, Calif.: Salem Press, c1992. xii, 218 p.
92-012897   016.8109/920693   0893566845
American literature -- Minority authors -- Bibliography. Hispanic Americans in literature -- Bibliography. Asian Americans in literature -- Bibliography.

Z1229.H57.Z55 1992
Zimmerman, Marc.
U.S. Latino literature: an essay and annotated bibliography/ Marc Zimmerman. Chicago, Ill.: MARCH/Abrazo Press, c1992. 156 p.
92-186823   016.8108/0868   1877636010
American literature -- Hispanic American authors -- Bibliography. Hispanic American literature (Spanish) -- Bibliography. Hispanic Americans in literature -- Bibliography.

Z1229.N39 C65 1999
The Columbia Granger's index to African-American poetry/ edited by Nicholas Frankovich and David Larzelere. New York: Columbia University Press, 1999. 302 p.
98-046181   016.811008/0896073   21   0231112343
American poetry -- African American authors -- Indexes. African Americans in literature -- Indexes.

Z1229.N39.J67 1993
A bibliographical guide to African-American women writers/ compiled by Casper LeRoy Jordan. Westport, Conn.: Greenwood Press, 1993. xix, 387 p.
93-006561   016.8108/09287/08996   0313276331
American literature -- Afro-American authors -- Bibliography. Women and literature -- United States -- Bibliography. American literature -- Women authors -- Bibliography.

Z1229.N39 M49 2002
Meyer, Adam.
Black-Jewish relations in African American and Jewish American fiction : an annotated bibliography/ Adam Meyer. Lanham, Md.: Scarecrow Press, 2002. xii, 180 p.
2001-049655   016.813009/896073   21   0810842181
American fiction -- African American authors -- Bibliography. African Americans -- Relations with Jews -- Bibliography. American fiction -- Jewish authors -- Bibliography. African Americans in literature -- Bibliography. Ethnic relations in literature -- Bibliography. Race relations in literature -- Bibliography. American fiction -- Stories, plots, etc. Jews in literature -- Bibliography.

Z1229.N39.M63 1994
Modern African American writers/ Matthew J. Bruccoli and Judith S. Baughman, series editors; foreword by Keneth Kinnamon. New York: Facts on File, c1994. xiv, 92 p.
93-008643   016.813/509896   0816029989
American fiction -- Afro-American authors -- History and criticism -- Bibliography. American fiction -- Afro-american authors -- Bibliography. Afro-Americans in literature -- Bibliography.

Z1229.N39.R53 2000
Richards, Phillip M., 1950-
Best literature by and about Blacks/ Phillip M. Richards, Neil Schlager. Detroit: Gale Group, c2000. vii, 330 p.
00-268988   016.8109/896073   0787605077
American literature -- African American authors -- Bibliography. African Americans in literature -- Bibliography. African Americans -- Bibliography.

Z1229.N39.R87
Rush, Theressa Gunnels, 1945-
Black American writers past and present: a biographical and bibliographical dictionary/ by Theressa Gunnels Rush, Carol Fairbanks Myers, Esther Spring Arata. Metuchen, N.J.: Scarecrow Press, 1975. 2 v.
74-028400   016.8108/08/96073   0810807858
American literature -- Afro-American authors -- Bio-bibliography -- Dictionaries. Afro-American authors -- Biography -- Dictionaries. Afro-Americans in literature -- Bibliography.

Z1229.N39.W55 1998
Williams, Dana A., 1972-
Contemporary African American female playwrights: an annotated bibliography/ Dana A. Williams. Westport, Conn.: Greenwood Press, 1998. xxi, 124 p.
98-017542   016.812/540809287/08996073   0313301328
American drama -- Afro-American authors -- Bibliography. Women and literature -- United States -- History -- 20th century -- Bibliography. American drama -- Afro-American authors -- History and criticism -- Bibliography.

Z1229.W8.C37 1993
Carter, Susanne.
Mothers and daughters in American short fiction: an annotated bibliography of twentieth-century women's literature/ compiled by Susanne Carter. Westport, Conn.: Greenwood Press, 1993. xx, 132 p.
93-010822   016.813/01083520431   031328511X
Short stories, American -- Women authors -- Bibliography. Women and literature -- United States -- Bibliography. Mothers and daughters in literature -- Bibliography.

Z1231.F4.G56 2000
Glitsch, Catherine.
American novel explication, 1969-1980/ compiled by Catherine Glitsch. North Haven, Conn.: Archon Books, 2000. vii, 575 p.
00-033146   016.81/813009   0208024794
American fiction -- History and criticism -- Bibliography. Canadian fiction -- History and criticism -- Bibliography.

Z1231.F4 K73 2000
Kramer, John E., 1935-
Academe in mystery and detective fiction: an annotated bibliography/ John E. Kramer with the assistance of Ron Hamm and Von Pittman. Lanham, Md.: Scarecrow Press, 2000. xiv, 426 p.
00-032230   016.813/087208   0810838419
Detective and mystery stories, American -- Bibliography. Detective and mystery stories, English -- Bibliography. Education, Higher, in literature -- Bibliography.

Z1231.A6.T66 1997
A topical index of early U.S. almanacs, 1776-1800/ compiled by Robert K. Dodge. Westport, Conn.: Greenwood Press, 1997. xv, 411 p.
97-009374   973.3   0313260494
Almanacs, American -- Indexes. United States -- History -- Revolution, 1775-1783 -- Indexes. United States -- History -- 1783-1815 -- Indexes.

Z1231.B4.L39 1998
Lawlor, William, 1951-
The beat generation: a bibliographical teaching guide/ William Lawlor. Lanham, Md.: Scarecrow Press; 1998. xv, 357 p.
98-003157   016.8109/11   0810833875
Beat generation -- Bibliography. American literature -- 20th century -- History and criticism -- Bibliography. American literature -- 20th century -- Bibliography.

Z1231.D7.A52 1995
American playwrights, 1880-1945: a research and production sourcebook/ edited by William W. Demastes. Westport, Conn.: Greenwood Press, 1995. xii, 494 p.
94-013690   016.812/409   0313286388
American drama -- 20th century -- Bio-bibliography. American drama -- 19th century -- Bio-bibliography. American drama -- 20th century -- Dictionaries.

Z1231.D7.A53 1989
American playwrights since 1945: a guide to scholarship, criticism, and performance/ edited by Philip C. Kolin. New York: Greenwood Press, c1989. xiii, 595 p.
88-010245   016.812/54/09   0313255431
American drama -- 20th century -- Bibliography. Dramatists, American -- 20th century -- Biography -- Indexes. Theater -- United States -- History -- 20th century -- Bibliography.

Z1231.D7 D38 1992
Davis, Gwenn.
Drama by women to 1900: a bibliography of American and British writers/ compiled by Gwenn Davis and Beverly A. Joyce. London, England: Mansell, 1992. xxvi, 189 p. ;
92-106664   016.812009/9287 20   0720121027
American drama -- Women authors -- Bibliography. English drama -- Women authors -- Bibliography. Women and literature -- Bibliography.

Z1231.D7.G38 1993
Gavin, Christy, 1952-
American women playwrights, 1964-1989: a research guide and annotated bibliography/ Christy Gavin. New York: Garland Pub., 1993. v, 493 p.
92-042768   016.812/54099287   082403046X
American drama -- Women authors -- History and criticism -- Bibliography. Women and literature -- United States -- History -- 20th century -- Bibliography. American drama -- 20th century -- History and criticism -- Bibliography.

Z1231.F4 A34 1996
Adelman, Irving.
The contemporary novel: a checklist of critical literature on the English language novel since 1945/ by Irving Adelman and Rita Dworkin. 2nd ed. Lanham, Md.: Scarecrow Press, 1996. xxiii, 666 p.
96-017577   016.823/91409 20   0810831031
American fiction -- 20th century -- History and criticism -- Bibliography. English fiction -- 20th century -- History and criticism -- Bibliography. English fiction -- Foreign countries -- History and criticism

Z1231.F4.B42 1996
Beam, Joan, 1947-
The Native American in long fiction: an annotated bibliography/ by Joan Beam and Barbara Branstad. Lanham, Md.: Scarecrow Press, c1996. xv, 359 p.
95-005635   016.813009/3520397   0810830167
American fiction -- Bibliography. Indians in literature -- Bibliography. American fiction -- Indian authors -- Bibliography.

Z1231.F4.D47 1999
Adamson, Lynda G.
American historical fiction: an annotated guide to novels for adults and young adults/ by Lynda G. Adamson. Phoenix, Ariz.: Oryx Press, 1999. ix, 405 p.
98-038044   016.813/08109   1573560677
Historical fiction, American -- Bibliography. Young adult fiction, American -- Bibliography. American fiction -- 20th century -- Bibliography. United States -- History -- Fiction -- Bibliography. United States -- In literature -- Bibliography.

Z1231.F4.D68 1989
Drew, Bernard A. 1950-
Heroines: a bibliography of women series characters in mystery, espionage, action, science fiction, fantasy, horror, western, romance, and juvenile novels/ Bernard A. Drew. New York: Garland Pub., 1989. 400 p.
89-034233   016.813/509352042   0824030478
American fiction -- 20th century -- Bibliography. English fiction -- 20th century -- Bibliography. Heroines in literature -- Bibliography.

Z1231.F4.G58 1998
Glitsch, Catherine.
American novel explication, 1991-1995/ compiled by Catherine Glitsch; with a foreword by Donna Gerstenberger and George Hendrick. North Haven, Conn.: Archon Books, 1998. x, 319 p.
98-027472   016.813009   0208024816
American fiction -- History and criticism -- Bibliography.

Z1231.F4.L37 1995
Larson, Randall D., 1954-
Films into books: an analytical bibliography of film novelizations, movie, and TV tie-ins/ by Randall D. Larson. Lanham, Md.: Scarecrow Press, c1995. xii, 608 p.
94-024274   016.813008   0810829282
American fiction -- Bibliography. Film novelizations -- United States -- Bibliography. Motion picture plays -- Adaptations -- Bibliography.

Z1231.F4.M65 1994
Modern women writers/ Matthew J. Bruccoli and Judith Baughman, series editors; foreword by Mary Ann Wimsatt. New York: Facts on File, c1994. xii, 100 p.
93-008642   016.813/5099287   0816030006
American fiction -- Women authors -- History and criticism -- Bibliography. Women and literature -- United States -- Bibliography. American fiction -- Women authors -- Bibliography.

Z1231.F4.S58 1995
Slide, Anthony.
The Hollywood novel: a critical guide to over 1200 works with film-related themes or characters, 1912 through 1994/ by Anthony Slide. Jefferson, N.C.: McFarland & Co., c1995. vii, 320 p.
95-015512   016.813/509357   0786400447
American fiction -- 20th century -- Bibliography. Motion picture producers and directors in literature -- Bibliography. Motion picture actors and actresses in literature -- Bibliography. Hollywood (Los Angeles, Calif.) -- In literature -- Bibliography.

Z1231.F4.W52 1988
White, Ray Lewis.
Index to Best American short stories and O. Henry prize stories/ Ray Lewis White. Boston, Mass.: G.K. Hall, c1988. 183 p.
87-028112   016.813/01/08   0816189552
Short stories, American -- Bibliography. Short stories, American -- Indexes.

Z1231.G66.F7 1990
Frank, Frederick S.
Through the pale door: a guide to and through the American gothic/ Frederick S. Frank. New York: Greenwood Press, 1990. xvii, 338 p.
90-031733   016.813/08729   0313259003
Gothic revival (Literature) -- United States -- Bibliography. Horror tales, American -- Bibliography. American literature -- Bibliography.

Z1231.P45.A44 1992
American literary magazines: the twentieth century/ edited by Edward E. Chielens. Westport, Conn.: Greenwood Press, 1992. xii, 474 p.
91-030603   016.8108/005   031323986X
American literature -- 20th century -- Periodicals -- Bibliography. American literature -- 20th century -- History and criticism. American periodicals -- History -- 20th century.

Z1231.P7.A44 1984
Alexander, Harriet Semmes, 1949-
American and British poetry: a guide to the criticism/ [compiled by] Harriet Semmes Alexander. Athens, Ohio: Swallow Press, c1984-c1996 v. 1-2
83-024114   821/.008   0804008485
American poetry -- History and criticism -- Bibliography. English poetry -- History and criticism -- Bibliography.

Z1231.P7.F45 1998
Feinstein, Sascha, 1963-
A bibliographic guide to jazz poetry/ Sascha Feinstein. Westport, Conn.: Greenwood Press, 1998. xi, 230 p.
98-010153   016.811/5080357   0313294690
American poetry -- 20th century -- History and criticism -- Bibliography. Music and literature -- Bibliography. Jazz in literature -- Bibliography.

Z1231.P7.G85 1989
Guide to American poetry explication. Boston, Mass.: G.K. Hall, c1989. 2 v.
89-002196 016.811/009 0816189196
American poetry -- 19th century -- History and criticism -- Bibliography. American poetry -- Colonial period, ca. 1600-1775 -- History and criticism -- Bibliography. American poetry -- Explication -- Bibliography.

Z1231.W8.N55 1992
Nilsen, Don Lee Fred.
Humor in American literature: a selected annotated bibliography/ Don L.F. Nilsen. New York: Garland, 1992. 580 p.
91-042821 016.817009 0824083954
American wit and humor -- History and criticism -- Bibliography. American literature -- History and criticism -- Bibliography.

Z1236-1249 America — United States — History and description

Z1236.A486
America, history and life. Santa Barbara, Calif.: Clio Press, c1975-c1989. 15 v.
84-640891 016.973/05
Dissertations, Academic -- United States -- Indexes -- Periodicals. Dissertations, Academic -- Canada -- Indexes -- Periodicals. United States -- History -- Indexes -- Periodicals. Canada -- History -- Indexes -- Periodicals. Canada -- History -- Periodicals -- Indexes -- Periodicals.

Z1236.B57 1994
Blazek, Ron.
United States history: a selective guide to information sources/ Ron Blazek and Anna H. Perrault. Englewood, Colo.: Libraries Unlimited, 1994. xxviii, 411 p.
93-041174 016.973 0872879844
Reference books -- United States -- History -- Bibliography. CD-ROM books -- United States -- Bibliography. United States -- History -- Databases -- Catalogs. United States -- History -- Bibliography.

Z1236.F77 1974
Freidel, Frank Burt.
Harvard guide to American history. Cambridge, Mass., Belknap Press of Harvard University Press, 1974. 2 v.
72-081272 016.9173/03 0674375602
United States -- History -- Bibliography.

Z1236.I73
Ireland, Norma Olin, 1907-
Index to America: life and customs/ compiled by Norma Olin Ireland. Westwood, Mass.: F.W. Faxon Co., c1976-1988. 4 v.
76-007196 016.973 0810821702
United States -- History -- Indexes.

Z1236.M47 1995
Merriam, Louise A.
United States history: a bibliography of the new writings on American history/ compiled by Louise A. Merriam and James W. Oberly. Manchester; Manchester University Press; c1995. xi, 227 p.
96-152243 016.973 0719036887
United States -- History -- Bibliography.

Z1236.P78 1987
Prucha, Francis Paul.
Handbook for research in American history: a guide to bibliographies and other reference works/ Francis Paul Prucha. Lincoln: University of Nebraska Press, c1987 xiii, 289 p.
86-030871 016.973 0803287194
Bibliography -- Bibliography -- United States. United States -- History -- Bibliography.

Z1236.R43 1997
Reader's guide to American history/ editor, Peter J. Parish. London; Fitzroy Dearborn Publishers, 1997. xxxv, 880 p.
98-101338 016.973 1884964222
United States -- History -- Bibliography. United States -- Historiography.

Z1242.A47 1996
The American Civil War: a handbook of literature and research/ Steven E. Woodworth, editor; foreword by James M. McPherson. Westport, Conn.: Greenwood Press, 1996. xiv, 754 p.
95-053132 016.9737 0313290199
United States -- History -- Civil War, 1861-1865 -- Bibliography. United States -- History -- Civil War, 1861-1865 -- Audio-visual aids -- Catalogs.

Z1242.C79 2000
Cole, Garold.
Civil War eyewitnesses: an annotated bibliography of books and articles, 1986-1996/ Garold L. Cole; foreword by James I. Robertson, Jr. Columbia: University of South Carolina Press, c2000. ix, 271 p.
99-050702 016.9737/8 1570033277
United States -- History -- Civil War, 1861-1865 -- Personal narratives -- Bibliography.

Z1242.E57 1997
Eicher, David J., 1961-
The Civil War in books: an analytical bibliography/ David J. Eicher; foreword by Gary W. Gallagher. Urbana: University Of Illinois Press, c1997. xxiii, 407 p.
96-002281 016.9737 0252022734
United States -- History -- Civil War, 1861-1865 -- Bibliography.

Z1242.8.L56 2000
Lincove, David A.
Reconstruction in the United States: an annotated bibliography/ compiled and annotated by David A. Lincove; foreword by Eric Foner. Westport, Conn.: Greenwood Press, 2000. xxv, 633 p.
99-053148 016.9738 0313291993
Reconstruction -- Bibliography. Afro-Americans -- History -- 1863-1877 -- Bibliography.

Z1244.B83 1990
Buckingham, Peter H., 1948-
Woodrow Wilson: a bibliography of his times and presidency/ compiled by Peter H. Buckingham. Wilmington, Del.: Scholarly Resources, 1990. xxxiv, 370 p.
89-010966 016.97391/3 0842022910
Wilson, Woodrow, -- 1856-1924 -- Bibliography. United States -- Politics and government -- 1913-1921 -- Bibliography.

Z1244.K95 1988
Kyvig, David E.
New day/New Deal: a bibliography of the Great American Depression, 1929-1941/ compiled by David E. Kyvig and Mary-Ann Blasio with contributions by Dawn Corley and assistance from Frank A. Caulkins ... [et al.]. New York: Greenwood Press, 1988. ix, 306 p.
87-037568 016.97391/6 0313260273
Depressions -- 1929 -- United States -- Bibliography. New Deal, 1933-1939 -- Bibliography. United States -- History -- 1919-1933 -- Bibliography. United States -- History -- 1933-1945 -- Bibliography.

Z1245.S64 1983
Smith, Myron J.
Watergate: an annotated bibliography of sources in English, 1972-1982/ by Myron J. Smith, Jr. Metuchen, N.J.: Scarecrow Press, 1983. xiii, 329 p.
83-004408 016.3641/32/0973 0810816237
Watergate Affair, 1972-1974 -- Bibliography.

Z1247.C66 1993
Conzen, Michael P.
A scholar's guide to geographical writing on the American and Canadian past/ Michael P. Conzen, Thomas A. Rumney, Graeme Wynn. Chicago: University of Chicago Press, c1993. xiii, 741 p.
92-023520 016.91173 0226115690
United States -- Historical geography -- Bibliography. Canada -- Historical geography -- Bibliography.

Z1249.K8.D38 1984
Davis, Lenwood G.
The Ku Klux Klan: a bibliography/ compiled by Lenwood G. Davis and Janet L. Sims-Wood, with the assistance of Marsha L. Moore; foreword by Earl E. Thorpe. Westport, Conn.: Greenwood Press, 1984. xv, 643 p.
83-001709 016.3224/2/0973 031322949X
Ku-Klux Klan (1866-1869) -- Bibliography. Ku Klux Klan (1915-) -- Bibliography.

Z1249.M5.D38 1985
Davis, Lenwood G.
Blacks in the American armed forces, 1776-1983: a bibliography/ compiled by Lenwood G. Davis and George Hill; forewords by Benjamin O. Davis, Jr. and Percy E. Johnston. Westport, Conn.: Greenwood Press, 1985. xv, 198 p.
84-015697 016.355/008996073 0313240922
United States -- Armed Forces -- Afro-Americans -- Bibliography.

Z1249.M5.G83 1975 Suppl. 4
A guide to the sources of United States military history. edited by Robin Higham and Donald J. Mrozek. North Haven, Conn.: Archon Books, 1998. xiii, 580 p.
98-029759 016.355/00973 0208024220
United States -- History, Military -- Bibliography.

Z1249.N3.A48
Allard, Dean C., 1933-
U.S. naval history sources in the United States/ compiled and edited by Dean C. Allard, Martha L. Crawley, Mary W. Edmison. Washington, D.C.: Naval History Division, Dept. of the Navy: for sale by the Supt. of Docs., U.S. Govt. Print. Off. 1979. vii, 235 p.
79-600070 026/.359/00973
United States -- History, Naval -- Library resources. United States -- History, Naval -- Archival resources.

Z1249.P7.M357 1987
Martin, Fenton S.
The American presidency: a bibliography/
Fenton S. Martin, Robert U. Goehlert.
Washington, D.C.: Congressional Quarterly,
c1987. xiii, 506 p.
87-000445   016.973   0871874156
Presidents -- United States -- Bibliography.

Z1249.P7.M365 1996
Martin, Fenton S.
How to research the presidency/ Fenton S.
Martin, Robert U. Goehlert. Washington:
Congressional Quarterly, c1996. x, 134 p.
96-007488   016.973   1568020295
Presidents -- United States -- Bibliography.
Presidents -- Research -- United States.

Z1249.P7.S29 1996
Sayler, James.
Presidents of the United States--their written
measure: a bibliography/ compiled by James
Sayler. Washington, D.C.: Library of Congress,
1996. ix, 216 p.
96-001758   016.973/092/2   0844409022
Presidents -- United States -- Bibliography --
Catalogs.

Z1249.S6.D8
Dumond, Dwight Lowell, 1895-
A bibliography of antislavery in America. Ann
Arbor, University of Michigan Press [1961]
119 p.
61-009306   016.326973
Slavery -- United States -- Antislavery
movements -- Bibliography. Slavery -- United
States -- Antislavery movements -- Bibliography.

Z1250-1351 America — United States — Local

Z1250.N4 1990
Neagles, James C.
The Library of Congress: a guide to genealogical
and historical research/ by James C. Neagles;
assisted by Mark C. Neagles. Salt Lake City,
Utah: Ancestry Pub., c1990. xii, 381 p.
89-018594   016.973   0916489485
United States -- History, Local -- Bibliography
-- Catalogs. United States -- Genealogy --
Bibliography -- Catalogs. United States --
History, Local -- Sources -- Bibliography --
Catalogs.

Z1251.E1.C58 1998
Clark, Suzanne M.
New England in U.S. government publications,
1789-1849: an annotated bibliography/ Suzanne
M. Clark. Westport, Conn.: Greenwood Press,
1998. xv, 598 p.
98-010085   016.974   0313281289
Government publications -- United States --
Bibliography.New England -- History -- Sources
-- Bibliography.

Z1251.E1.N452 1989
New England: a bibliography of its history/
prepared by the Committee for a New England
Bibliography; edited by Roger Parks; with a
historiographic essay by David D. Hall and Alan
Taylor. Hanover, NH: University Press of New
England, c1989. xlix, 259 p.
89-040231   016.974   0874514967
Catalogs, Union -- United States.New England
-- History -- Bibliography -- Union lists.

Z1251.E1.S57 1994
Slocum, Robert B.
New England in fiction 1787-1990: an annotated
bibliography/ Robert B. Slocum. West Cornwall,
CT: Locust Hill Press, c1994. 2 v.
93-047349   016.813008/03274   093395154X
American fiction -- New England --
Bibliography.New England -- In literature --
Bibliography.

Z1251.S7.R45 1998
Reisman, Rosemary M. Canfield.
Contemporary Southern men fiction writers: an
annotated bibliography/ Rosemary M. Canfield
Reisman and Suzanne Booker-Canfield. Lanham,
Md.: Scarecrow Press; 1998. ix, 427 p.
97-053063   016.813/540809286   0810831953
American fiction -- Southern States --
Bibliography. American fiction -- 20th century --
Bibliography. American fiction -- Male authors -
- Bibliography. Southern States -- In literature --
Bibliography.

Z1251.W5 A35 1994
The American West in the twentieth century: a
bibliography/ Richard W. Etulain, editor; with
Pat Devejian, Jon Hunner, Jacqueline Etulain
Partch. Norman: University of Oklahoma Press,
c1994. vii, 456 p.
94-016520   016.978/03 20   0806126582

Z1251.W5.K53 1995
Kich, Martin.
Western American novelists/ Martin Kich. New
York: Garland Pub., [1995-   ] v. 1
95-036470   016.813/509   0824073894
American fiction -- West (U.S.) -- History and
criticism -- Bibliography. American fiction --
20th century -- History and criticism --
Bibliography. Western stories -- History and
criticism -- Bibliography. West (U.S.) -- In
literature -- Bibliography.

Z1251.W5.W52 1989
Wilkinson, Charles F., 1941-
The American West: a narrative bibliography and
a study in regionalism/ Charles F. Wilkinson.
Niwot, Colo.: University Press of Colorado,
c1989. xiv, 144 p.
89-009044   016.978   0870812041
West (U.S.) -- Bibliography.

Z1261.G85 1989
A Guide to the history of California/ edited by
Doyce B. Nunis, Jr., and Gloria Ricci Lothrop.
New York: Greenwood Press, 1989. xii, 309 p.
88-015488   016.9794   0313249709
Archives -- California -- Directories.
Historical libraries -- California -- Directories.
California -- History -- Sources -- Bibliography.
California -- Historiography.

Z1271.S47 1993
Servies, James Albert.
A bibliography of Florida/ by James A. Servies
and Lana D. Servies. Pensacola, Fla.: J.A.
Servies and L.D. Servies, 1993-1999 v. 1-3
93-077015   016.9759   0963637002
Catalogs, Union -- United States.Florida --
Imprints -- Union lists. Florida -- Bibliography --
Union lists.

Z1277.W47 1995
Whitney, Ellen M.
Illinois history: an annotated bibliography/ Ellen
M. Whitney, compiler; Janice A. Petterchak,
editor, Sandra M. Stark, associate editor.
Wesport, Conn.: Greenwood Press, 1995. xxxiv,
603 p.
94-042122   016.9773   0313282358
Illinois -- History -- Bibliography.

Z1289.B44 1989
Beers, Henry Putney, 1907-
French and Spanish records of Louisiana: a
bibliographical guide to archive and manuscript
sources/ Henry Putney Beers. Baton Rouge:
Louisiana State University Press, c1989. x,
371 p.
88-013619   016.9763   0807114448
Spaniards -- Louisiana -- History -- Sources --
Bibliography. French -- Louisiana -- History --
Sources -- Bibliography. Louisiana -- History --
To 1803 -- Sources -- Bibliography.

Z1289.J86 2002
Jumonville, Florence M.
Louisiana history: an annotated bibliography/
compiled by Florence M. Jumonville. Westport,
Conn.: Greenwood Press, 2002. xxvi, 782 p.
2002-069625   016.9763 21   0313282404

Z1297.B43 1998
Beasecker, Robert, 1946-
Michigan in the novel, 1816-1996: an annotated
bibliography/ compiled by Robert Beasecker.
Detroit: Wayne State University Press, c1998.
382 p.
97-032194   016.813008/032774   0814327125
American fiction -- Michigan --
Bibliography.Michigan -- In literature --
Bibliography.

Z1318.N5.S54 1995
Shea, Ann M., 1933-
The Irish experience in New York City: a select
bibliography/ Ann M. Shea and Marion R. Casey.
New York: New York Irish History Roundtable,
c1995. 130 p.
95-037394   016.9747/10049162   0815681216
Irish Americans -- New York (State) -- New
York -- Bibliography.

Z1339.G84 1988
A Guide to the history of Texas/ edited by Light
Townsend Cummins and Alvin R. Bailey, Jr.
New York: Greenwood Press, 1988. xi, 307 p.
87-015021   016.9764   0313245630
Texas -- History -- Bibliography. Texas --
Historiography. Texas -- History -- Archival
resources -- Directories.

Z1351.P38 1999
Paul, Barbara Dotts.
Wisconsin history: an annotated bibliography/
compiled by Barbara Dotts Paul and Justus F.
Paul. Westport, Conn.: Greenwood Press, 1999.
xvii, 428 p.
99-014354   016.9775   0313282714
Wisconsin -- History -- Bibliography.

Z1361 America — United States — Special topics (not otherwise provided for), A-Z

Z1361.C6.H64 1995
Hoffmann, Frank W., 1949-
American popular culture: a guide to the reference literature/ Frank W. Hoffmann. Englewood, Colo.: Libraries Unlimited, 1995. xvi, 286 p.
94-029794   016.973   1563081423
Popular culture -- United States -- Bibliography. Popular culture -- Reference books -- Bibliography.

Z1361.C6.L3
Larrabee, Eric.
American panorama; essays by fifteen American critics on 350 books past and present which portray the U.S.A. in its many aspects. [New York] New York University Press, 1957. 436 p.
57-011743   016.9173
United States -- Civilization. Books -- Reviews. American literature -- Bibliography. United States -- Civilization -- Bibliography.

Z1361.E4 B89 1996
Buttlar, Lois,
Guide to information resources in ethnic museum, library, and archival collections in the United States/ compiled by Lois J. Buttlar and Lubomyr R. Wynar. Westport, Conn.: Greenwood Press, 1996. xi, 369 p.
95-039038   305.8/0025/73 20   0313298467
Ethnology -- United States -- Library resources -- Directories. Ethnology -- United States -- Archival resources -- Directories. Ethnological museums and collections -- United States -- Directories.

Z1361.E4.U58 1991
University of Minnesota.
The Immigration History Research Center: a guide to collections/ compiled and edited by Suzanna Moody and Joel Wurl; production coordinated by Judith Rosenblatt and Anne Bjorkquist Ng; foreword by Rudolph J. Vecoli. New York: Greenwood Press, 1991. xxiii, 446 p.
91-016262   016.973   0313268320
Immigrants -- United States -- History -- Sources -- Bibliography -- Catalogs. Minorities -- United States -- History -- Sources -- Bibliography -- Catalogs. United States -- Emigration and immigration -- History -- Sources -- Bibliography -- Catalogs.

Z1361.E4.W45 1990
Weinberg, Meyer, 1920-
Racism in the United States: a comprehensive classified bibliography/ compiled by Meyer Weinberg. New York: Greenwood Press, 1990. xvii, 682 p.
89-078118   016.973/04   0313273901
Racism -- United States -- Bibliography. Minorities -- United States -- Bibliography. United States -- Race relations -- Bibliography.

Z1361.I7.B54 1992
Blessing, Patrick J.
The Irish in America: a guide to the literature and the manuscript collections/ Patrick J. Blessing. Washington, D.C.: Catholic University of America Press, c1992. xi, 347 p.
90-001667   016.973/049162   0813207312
Irish Americans -- History. Irish Americans -- History -- Sources -- Bibliography.

Z1361.M4.M414 1984
Meier, Matt S.
Bibliography of Mexican American history/ compiled by Matt S. Meier. Westport, Conn.: Greenwood Press, 1984. xi, 500 p.
83-018585   016.973/046872   031323776X
Mexican Americans -- History -- Bibliography.

Z1361.N39.B52 1990
Black biography, 1790-1950: a cumulative index/ editors, Randall K. Burkett, Nancy Hall Burkett, Henry Louis Gates, Jr. Alexandria: Chadwyck-Healey, 1991. 3 v.
91-000254   920/.009296073   0898870852
Afro-Americans -- Biography -- Indexes.

Z1361.N39.B56
Blacks in America; bibliographical essays, by James M. McPherson [and others. Garden City, N.Y., Doubleday, 1971. xxii, 430 p.
70-164723   016.9173/06/96073
Afro-Americans -- History -- Bibliography.

Z1361.N39.C53 1996
Clark, Edward.
Dictionary catalog of the collection of African American literature in the Mildred F. Sawyer Library of Suffolk University/ Edward Clark. Boston, Mass.: Suffolk University, 1996. xxiii, 220 p.
95-073090   016.973/0496073
American literature -- Afro-American authors -- Bibliography -- Catalogs. Afro-Americans -- History -- Bibliography -- Catalogs. Afro-Americans -- Bibliography -- Catalogs.

Z1361.N39.D355 1986
Davis, Lenwood G.
The Black family in the United States: a revised, updated, selectively annotated bibliography/ compiled by Lenwood G. Davis. New York: Greenwood Press, 1986. x, 234 p.
86-009926   016.3068/5/08996073   0313252378
Afro-American families -- Bibliography.

Z1361.N39.G56 1995
Glover, Denise Marie.
Voices of the spirit: sources for interpreting the African American experience/ Denise M. Glover. Chicago: American Library Association, 1995. xi, 211 p.
94-029139   016.973/0496073   0838906397
Afro-Americans -- History -- Bibliography.

Z1361.N39.G67 1999
Gordon, Jacob U.
The African-American male: an annotated bibliography/ compiled by Jacob U. Gordon. Westport, Conn.: Greenwood Press, 1999. xiv, 174 p.
99-021785   016.30538/896073   0313306567
Afro-American men -- Bibliography. Afro-American boys -- Bibliography.

Z1361.N39.H37 1991
Hay, Frederick J., 1953-
African-American community studies from North America: a classified, annotated bibliography/ Fred J. Hay. New York: Garland, 1991. xxiii, 234 p.
91-008158   016.305896/073   082406643X
Afro-Americans -- Social conditions -- Bibliography. Blacks -- Canada -- Social conditions -- Bibliography.

Z1361.N39.J86 2000
Junne, George H.
Blacks in the American West and beyond--America, Canada, and Mexico: a selectively annotated bibliography/ George H. Junne, Jr. Westport, Conn.: Greenwood Press, 2000. xvi, 686 p.
00-020764   016.978/00496073   0313312087
Afro-Americans -- West (U.S.) -- History -- Bibliography. Afro-Americans -- Canada, Western -- History -- Bibliography. Afro-Americans -- Mexico -- History -- Bibliography. West (U.S.) -- History -- Bibliography. Canada, Western -- History -- Bibliography. Mexico -- History -- Bibliography.

Z1361.N39.K34 1992
The Kaiser index to Black resources, 1948-1986/ from the Schomburg Center for Research in Black Culture of the New York Public Library. Brooklyn, N.Y.: Carlson Pub., 1992. 5 v.
92-011493   016.973/0496073   0926019600
Afro-Americans -- Indexes. Blacks -- Indexes.

Z1361.N39.K45 1996
Keita, Gwendolyn Puryear.
Blacks in the United States: abstracts of the psychological and behavioral literature, 1987-1995/ editors, Gwendolyn Puryear Keita, Anne C.O. Petersen. Washington D.C.: American Psychological Association, c1996. x, 305 p.
96-036788   016.1558/496073   1557984069
Afro-Americans -- Psychology -- Bibliography.

Z1361.N39.M34 1995
Manat, G. P.
Guide to books on Black Americans/ G.P. Manat (compiler). Commack, N.Y.: Nova Science Publishers, c1995. 319 p.
94-007595   016.973/0496073   156072174X
Afro-Americans -- Bibliography.

Z1361.N39.M93 1993
Murray, Paul T.
The civil rights movement: references and resources/ Paul T. Murray. New York: G.K. Hall; c1993. xi, 265 p.
92-034223   016.3231/196073   081611837X
Afro-Americans -- Civil rights -- Bibliography. Civil rights movements -- United States -- History -- 20th century -- Bibliography. United States -- Race relations -- Bibliography.

Z1361.N39.N578 1984
Newman, Richard, 1930-
Black access: a bibliography of Afro-American bibliographies/ compiled by Richard Newman. Westport, Conn.: Greenwood Press, 1984. xxviii, 249 p.
83-008537   016.016973/0496073   0313232822
Bibliography -- Bibliography -- Afro-Americans. Afro-Americans -- Bibliography.

Z1361.N39.P59
Porter, Dorothy Burnett, 1905-
The Negro in the United States; a selected bibliography. Compiled by Dorothy B. Porter. Washington, Library of Congress; [for sale by the Supt. of Docs., U.S. Govt. Print. Off.] 1970. x, 313 p.
78-606085   016.9173/09/7496
Afro-Americans -- Bibliography. Blacks -- bibliography.

Z1361.N39 S22 1999
Sacred fire: the QBR 100 essential Black books/
[compiled and edited by] Max Rodriguez,
Angeli R. Rasbury, Carol Taylor; foreword by
Charles Johnson. New York: John Wiley, c1999.
xx, 229 p.
98-035060　016.973/0496073 21　0471243760
*African Americans -- Bibliography. American
literature -- African American authors --
Bibliography. African Americans in literature --
Bibliography. African Americans -- Books and
reading -- Bibliography.*

Z1361.N39 S53 1974
Smith, Dwight La Vern,
Afro-American history: a bibliography/ Dwight
L. Smith, editor; introduction by Benjamin
Quarles. Santa Barbara, Calif.: ABC-Clio, [1974-
1981] 2 v.
73-087155　016.973/0496073 19　0874363144
*African Americans--Bibliography. African
Americans--Periodicals--Abstracts.*

Z1361.N39 T49 2001
Thomas, Veronica G.
African American women: an annotated
bibliography/ compiled by Veronica G. Thomas,
Kisha Braithwaite, and Paula Mitchell. Westport,
Conn.: Greenwood Press, 2001. 219 p.
00-030884　016.30548/896073　031331263X
*African American women -- Bibliography.
African American women -- Social conditions --
Bibliography.*

Z1361.N39.T57 1998
Tischauser, Leslie Vincent, 1942-
Black/white relations in American history: an
annotated bibliography/ Leslie V. Tischauser.
Lanham, Md.: Scarecrow Press; 1998. xiv, 189 p.
98-003158　016.3058/00973　0810833891
*Afro-Americans -- Civil rights -- History --
Bibliography.United States -- Race relations --
Bibliography.*

Z1361.N39.W285 2000
Walters, Ronald W.
Bibliography of African American leadership: an
annotated guide/ Ronald W. Walters and Cedric
Johnson. Westport, Conn.: Greenwood Press,
2000. xvii, 279 p.
00-021554　　　　　016.3033/4/08096073
0313313148
*Afro-American leadership -- Bibliography.
Afro-Americans -- Politics and government --
Bibliography.*

Z1361.O7.B57 1995
Blake, Barbara Radke.
A guide to children's books about Asian
Americans/ Barbara Blake. Aldershot, Hants,
England: Scolar Press; c1995. xv, 215 p.
94-036078　016.973/0495　1859280145
*Asian Americans -- Juvenile literature --
Bibliography. Asian Americans -- Juvenile fiction
-- Bibliography.*

Z1361.O7.K56 1989
Kim, Hyung-chan.
Asian American studies: an annotated
bibliography and research guide/ edited by
Hyung-chan Kim. New York: Greenwood Press,
1989. x, 504 p.
89-001925　016.973/0495　0313260265
Asian Americans -- Bibliography.

Z1361.O7 N67 1996
Nordquist, Joan.
Asian Americans: social, economic, and political
aspects: a bibliography/ compiled by Joan
Nordquist. Santa Cruz, CA: Reference and
Research Services, 1996. 80 p.
97-129828　016.305895073 21　0937855820
*Asian Americans -- Social conditions --
Bibliography. Asian Americans -- Economic
conditions -- Bibliography. Asian Americans --
Politics and government -- Bibliography.*

Z1361.W45
Westmoreland, Guy T.
West Indian Americans: a research guide/ Guy T.
Westmoreland, Jr. Westport, Conn.: Greenwood
Press, 2001. xii, 143 p.
00-052109　016.97304/96972　0313297924
West Indian Americans -- Bibliography.

Z1365.A1 America — Canada. British North America — Bibliography of bibliography

Z1365.A1.I54 1994
Ingles, Ernest Boyce.
Bibliography of Canadian bibliographies/ editor
and compiler, Ernie Ingles; principal researcher
and compiler, Gordon R. Adshead; research
assistants, Donna Brockmeyer-Klebaum, Sue
Fisher, Suzanna Loeppky. Toronto: University of
Toronto Press, 1994. xliii, 1178 p.
95-114749　016.016971　0802028373
Canada -- Bibliography of bibliographies.

Z1365.B57 America — Canada. British North America — General bibliography

Z1365.B57 1996
Bond, Mary E.
Canadian reference sources: an annotated
bibliography: general reference works, history,
humanities = Ouvrages de reference canadiens:
une bibliographie annotee: ouvrages de reference
generaux, Mary E. Bond, compiler and editor;
Martine M. Caron, co-compiler. Vancouver, BC:
UBC Press, c1996. xvi, 1076 p.
96-178990　016.971　077480565X
*Canada -- Bibliography. Canada -- Reference
books -- Bibliography. Canada -- Bibliography
of bibliographies.*

Z1375-1379 America — Canada. British North America — Canadian literature

Z1375.L38 1997
Lecker, Robert, 1951-
English-Canadian literary anthologies: an
enumerative bibliography/ Robert Lecker;
associate editors, Colin Hill, Peter Lipert.
Teeswater, Ont.: Reference Press, c1997. x,
209 p.
98-164904　016.8108/0971　0919981607
*Canadian literature -- Bibliography.Canada --
Literary collections -- Bibliography.*

Z1375.W3 1972
Watters, Reginald Eyre.
A checklist of Canadian literature and
background materials, 1628-1960, in two parts:
first, a comprehensive list of the books which
constitute Canadian literature written in English;
and second, a selective list of other books by
Canadian authors whi 2d ed., rev. and enl.
[Toronto, University of Toronto Press [1972]
xxiv, 1085 p.
72-080713　013/.971　0802018661
*Canadian literature -- Bibliography. Canada --
Bibliography.*

Z1376.W65.G46 1993
Gerry, Thomas M. F., 1948-
Contemporary Canadian and U.S. women of
letters: an annotated bibliography/ Thomas M.F.
Gerry. New York: Garland, 1993. xxii, 287 p.
92-035184　016.81/08/09287　0824069897
*Canadian literature -- Women authors --
Bibliography. French-Canadian literature --
Women authors -- Bibliography. French-
Canadian literature -- 20th century --
Bibliography.*

Z1377.F8.K35 1990
Kandiuk, Mary, 1956-
French-Canadian authors: a bibliography of their
works and of English-language criticism/ by
Mary Kandiuk. Metuchen, N.J.: Scarecrow Press,
1990. xii, 222 p.
90-008944　016.8409/9714　0810823624
*French-Canadian literature -- Bibliography.
French-Canadian literature -- History and
criticism -- Bibliography.*

Z1379.L68 1988
Lougheed, W. C.
Writings on Canadian English, 1976-1987: a
selective, annotated bibliography/ W.C.
Lougheed. Kingston, Ont.: Strathy Language
Unit, Queen's University, [1988] xiii, 66 p.
89-156692　016.42/0971 20　0889115109
*English language -- Canada -- Bibliography.
Canadianisms -- Bibliography.*

Z1382 America — Canada. British North America — History and description

Z1382.C217 1994
Canadian history: a reader's guide.　Toronto;
University of Toronto Press, c1994. 2 v.
94-232675　016.971 20　0802050166
Canada -- History -- Bibliography.

Z1382.G63 1998
Gobbett, Brian, 1960-
Introducing Canada: an annotated bibliography
of Canadian history in English/ Brian Gobbett
and Robert Irwin. Lanham, Md.: Scarecrow
Press; 1998. xvi, 373 p.
98-003159　016.971　0810833832
Canada -- History -- Bibliography.

Z1411 America — Mexico — Bibliography

Z1411.P45 1993
Philip, George D. E.
Mexico/ George D.E. Philip, compiler. Rev. and
expanded ed. Oxford, England; Clio Press,
c1993. xviii, 195 p.
94-182921　016.972 20　185109198X
Mexico -- Bibliography.

Z1411.V4 1966
Veinticinco años de investigación histórica en México. Ed. especial de Historia mexicana. [1.ed. México] El Colegio de México, 1966. 674 p.
67-081896
Civilization -- History -- Bibliography. Mexico -- Imprints. Mexico -- Civilization -- History -- Bibliography.

Z1437 America — Central America — General bibliography

Z1437.G74 1988
Grieb, Kenneth J.
Central America in the nineteenth and twentieth centuries: an annotated bibliography/ Kenneth J. Grieb. Boston, Mass.: G.K. Hall, c1988. xvii, 573 p.
87-028240 016.9728 0816181306
Central America -- Bibliography.

Z1437.L46 1994
Leonard, Thomas M., 1937-
A guide to Central American collections in the United States/ Thomas M. Leonard. Westport, Conn.: Greenwood Press, 1994. x, 186 p.
94-010359 016.9728 0313286892
Manuscripts -- United States -- Facsimiles -- Archival resources -- Directories. Archival resources -- United States -- Directories. Central America -- History -- Archival resources -- Directories.

Z1502 America — West Indies — Special groups of islands, A-Z

Z1502.A58.H68 1994
Hough, Samuel J.
The Beinecke Lesser Antilles Collection at Hamilton College: a catalogue of books, manuscripts, prints, maps, and drawings, 1521-1860/ prepared by Samuel J. Hough and Penelope R.O. Hough. Gainesville: University Press of Florida, c1994. xi, 414 p.
94-004285 016.9729 0813012929
Beinecke, Walter -- Library -- Catalogs. Rare books -- New York (State) -- Clinton -- Catalogs. Manuscripts -- New York (State) -- Clinton -- Catalogs. Antilles, Lesser -- Bibliography -- Catalogs.

Z1511 America — West Indies — Cuba

Z1511.P43 1988
Perez, Louis A., 1943-
Cuba: an annotated bibliography/ compiled by Louis A. Perez, Jr. New York: Greenwood Press, 1988. xiii, 301 p.
87-028017 016.97291 0313261628
Cuba -- Bibliography.

Z1511.S8 1996
Stubbs, Jean.
Cuba/ Jean Stubbs, Lila Haines and Meic F. Haines, compilers. Oxford, England; Clio Press, c1996. xxx, 337 p.
96-223558 016.97291 21 1851090215
Cuba -- Bibliography.

Z1531 America — West Indies — Hispaniola

Z1531.H35 1991
Pratt, Frantz.
Haiti: guide to the periodical literature in English, 1800-1990/ compiled and edited by Frantz Pratt; foreword by Lambros Comitas. New York: Greenwood Press, 1991. xiv, 310 p.
91-007572 016.97294 20 0313278555
Haiti -- Bibliography.

Z1531.L39 1990
Lawless, Robert.
Haiti: a research handbook/ by Robert Lawless; with contributions from Ilona Maria Lawless ... [et al.]. New York: Garland Pub., 1990. ix, 354 p.
90-036843 016.97294 0824065433
Haiti -- Bibliography.

Z1561 America — West Indies — Other islands, A-Z

Z1561.M3.C73 1995
Crane, Janet.
Martinique/ Janet Crane, compiler. Oxford, England; Clio Press, 1995. xxxi, 140 p.
96-192593 016.97298/2 1851091513
Martinique -- Bibliography.

Z1561.S34.M6 1996
Momsen, Janet Henshall.
St Lucia/ Janet Henshall Momsen, compiler. Oxford, England; Clio Press, c1996. xxxi, 179 p.
96-191957 016.9729843 185109136X
Saint Lucia -- Bibliography.

Z1595 America — West Indies — Spanish Main. Caribbean Area

Z1595.C364 1993
Paravisini-Gebert, Lizabeth.
Caribbean women novelists: an annotated critical bibliography/ compiled by Lizabeth Paravisini-Gebert and Olga Torres-Seda; with contributions from the Dutch by Hilda van Neck-Yoder. Westport, Conn.; Greenwood Press, 1993. xv, 427 p.
92-037915 809/.89287/09729 0313283427
Caribbean fiction -- Women authors -- Bibliography. Caribbean fiction -- Women authors -- History and criticism -- Bibliography.

Z1595.F46 1992
Fenwick, M. J.
Writers of the Caribbean and Central America: a bibliography/ M.J. Fenwick. New York: Garland, 1992. 2 v.
91-035701 016.8088/99729 0824040104
Caribbean literature -- Bibliography. Central American literature -- Bibliography.

Z1595.G69 1998
Goslinga, Marian.
Caribbean literature: a bibliography/ Marian Goslinga. Lanham, Md.: Scarecrow Press, 1998. xiii, 469 p.
97-032289 016.9729 0810834529
Caribbean literature -- Bibliography.

Z1601 America — South America. Latin America — General bibliography

Z1601.L3225 1992
Latin America and the Caribbean: a critical guide to research sources/ edited by Paula H. Covington; David Block ... [et al.], associate editors. New York: Greenwood Press, 1992. xvi, 924 p.
91-034622 016.98 0313264031
Latin America -- Bibliography. Caribbean Area -- Bibliography.

Z1601.L324 1990
Latin American studies: a basic guide to sources/ Robert A. McNeil, editor, Barbara G. Valk, associate editor; [contributing editors, Carole Travis, Roger R. Macdonald, Ann E. Wade; contributors, Laurence Hallewell, et al.]. Metuchen, N.J.: Scarecrow Press, 1990. xi, 458 p.
89-034133 016.98 0810822369
Latin America -- Bibliography of bibliographies. Latin America -- Reference books -- Bibliography. Latin America -- Bibliography. Latin America -- Library resources.

Z1605 America — South America. Latin America — Periodicals

Z1605.H23
Handbook of Latin American studies. Austin [etc.] University of Texas Press [etc.]
36-032633
Latin America -- Bibliography -- Periodicals.

Z1609 America — South America. Latin America — Special topics, A-Z

Z1609.F4.B35 1992
The Latin American short story: an annotated guide to anthologies and criticism/ compiled by Daniel Balderston. Westport, Conn.: Greenwood Press, 1992. xx, 529 p.
92-007336 016.863/010898 031327360X
Short stories, Latin American -- Bibliography. Short stories, Latin American -- History and criticism -- Bibliography.

Z1609.F4.L46 1997
Leonard, Kathy S., 1952-
Index to translated short fiction by Latin American women in English language anthologies/ compiled by Kathy S. Leonard. Westport, Conn.: Greenwood Press, 1997. xiv, 120 p.
97-033141 863 0313300461
Latin American fiction -- Women authors -- Translations into English -- Indexes. Short stories, Latin American -- Translations into English -- Indexes. Latin American fiction -- 20th century -- Translations into English -- Indexes.

Z1609.L7.C35 1994
Calimano, Ivan E.
Index to Spanish language short stories in anthologies/ Ivan E. Calimano. Albuquerque, N.M.: SALALM Secretariat, General Library, University of New Mexico, c1994. 332 p.
94-200454　016.863008　091761741X
Short stories, Spanish American -- Indexes. Short stories, Spanish -- Indexes. Short stories, Hispanic American (Spanish) -- Indexes.

Z1609.L7.S6 1990
Spanish American women writers: a bio-bibliographical source book/ edited by Diane E. Marting. New York: Greenwood Press, 1990. xxvi, 645 p.
89-027283　016.8609/9287　0313251940
Spanish American literature -- Women authors -- Bio-bibliography.

Z1609.P6.S66 1998
Sonntag, Iliana L.
Twentieth-century poetry from Spanish America: an index to Spanish language and bilingual anthologies/ Iliana L. Sonntag Blay. Lanham, Md.: Scarecrow Press, 1998. xvii, 701 p.
98-019068　016.861　0810835274
Spanish American poetry -- 20th century -- Indexes. Spanish American poetry -- 20th century -- Translations into English -- Indexes.

Z1621-1911 America — South America. Latin America — By region or country

Z1621.L38 1992
Latin American military history: an annotated bibliography/ edited by David G. LaFrance and Errol D. Jones. New York: Garland, 1992. xi, 734 p.
92-012606　016.355/0098　082404634X
Latin America -- History, Military -- Bibliography.

Z1681.F73 1990
Foster, David William.
Brazilian literature: a research bibliography/ David William Foster, Walter Rela. New York: Garland Pub., 1990.
90-031766　016.86909/981　0824034422
Brazilian literature -- History and criticism -- Bibliography.

Z1731.D38 1990
Davis, Robert H. 1939-
Colombia/ Robert H. Davis, compiler. Oxford, England; Clio Press, c1990. xxi, 204 p.
90-202995　016.986　1851090932
Colombia -- Bibliography.

Z1821.W55 1995
Whigham, Thomas, 1955-
A guide to collections on Paraguay in the United States/ Thomas Whigham and Jerry W. Cooney. Westport, Conn.: Greenwood Press, 1995. xi, 114 p.
95-015449　016.9892　0313292035
Manuscripts -- United States -- Facsimiles -- Archival resources. Archival resources -- United States -- Directories. Paraguay -- History -- Archival resources -- Directories.

Z1870.3.B46 1998
Bennett, John M.
Sendero Luminoso in context: an annotated bibliography/ John M. Bennett; consulting editor, Laurence Hallewell. Lanham, Md.: Scarecrow Press, 1998. ix, 229 p.
98-008382　016.3224/2/0905　0810835592
Terrorism -- Peru -- History -- 20th century -- Bibliography. Terrorism -- Peru -- History -- 20th century -- Sources -- Bibliography. Peru -- History -- 1968-1980 -- Bibliography. Peru -- History -- 1968-1980 -- Sources -- Bibliography. Peru -- History -- 1980- -- Bibliography.

Z1870.3.S7 1995
Stern, Peter A., 1953-
Sendero Luminoso: an annotated bibliography of the Shining Path guerrilla movement, 1980-1993/ Peter A. Stern; foreword by Carlos Ivan Degregori. [New Mexico]: SALALM Secretariat, General Library, University of New Mexico, c1995. xxv, 363 p.
95-199865　0917617436
Terrorism -- Peru -- History -- 20th century -- Bibliography. Terrorism -- Peru -- History -- 20th century -- Sources -- Bibliography. Peru -- History -- 1980- -- Bibliography. Peru -- History -- 1980- -- Sources -- Bibliography.

Z1911.W33 1990
Waddell, D. A. G. 1927-
Venezuela/ D.A.G. Waddell, compiler. Oxford, England; Clio Press, c1990 xvii, 206 p.
90-158038　016.987　1851091068
Venezuela -- Bibliography.

Z1946 America — Saint Helena. Tristan da Cunha. Ascension Island

Z1946.T38 1997
Day, Alan Edwin.
St. Helena, Ascension, and Tristan da Cunha/ Alan Day, compiler. Oxford; Clio Press, c1997. xxi, 260 p.
97-180595　016.997/3　1851092722
Saint Helena -- Bibliography. Ascension Island (Atlantic Ocean) -- Bibliography. Tristan da Cunha -- Bibliography.

Z2000 Europe — General bibliography

Z2000.B8 1957
Bullock, Alan,
A select list of books on European history, 1815-1914. Edited for the Oxford Recent History Group by Alan Bullock and A. J. P. Taylor. 2d ed. Oxford, Clarendon Press, 1957. 79 p.
57-002436　016.94028
Europe -- History -- 1815-1871 -- Bibliography. Europe -- History -- 1871-1918 -- Bibliography.

Z2000.C35
Carter, Charles Howard.
The Western European powers, 1500-1700, by Charles H. Carter. London, Hodder and Stoughton [for] the Sources of History Ltd., 347 p.
74-855634　016.9402/2　0340126965
Europe -- History -- 1492-1648 -- Bibliography. Europe -- History -- 1648-1715 -- Bibliography. Europe -- History -- Sources -- Bibliography.

Z2000.C57 1987
Cook, Chris, 1945-
Sources in European political history/ Chris Cook and Geoff Pugh. New York, N.Y.: Facts on File Publications, c1987-c1991 v. 1-3
82-007365　016.9402　0816010161
Archives -- Europe -- Directories.Europe -- History -- 20th century -- Archival resources -- Directories. Europe -- Politics and government -- 20th century -- Archival resources -- Directories.

Z2000.D53 1996
Dickinson, W. Calvin
The War of the Spanish Succession, 1702-1713: a selected bibliography/ compiled by W. Calvin Dickinson and Eloise R. Hitchcock. Westport, Conn.: Greenwood Press, 1996. xvi, 140 p.
95-041984　016.9402/526　0313283028
Spanish Succession, War of, 1701-1714 -- Bibliography.

Z2000.D86 1983
Dunthorne, Hugh.
Early modern European history, c.1492-1788: a select bibliography / compiled by Hugh Dunthorne and H.M. Scott. London: Historical Association, c1983. 107 p.
84-248734　016.9402 19　0852782594
Europe -- History -- 1492-1648 -- Bibliography. Europe -- History -- 1648-1789 -- Bibliography.

Z2000.F45 1989
Ferguson, Chris D.,
Europe in transition: a select, annotated bibliography of the twelfth-century renaissance/ Chris D. Ferguson. New York: Garland, 1989. xiii, 156 p.
88-031033　016.9401/82 19　0824037227
Civilization, Medieval -- 12th century -- Bibliography. Twelfth century -- Bibliography. Europe -- History -- 476-1492 -- Bibliography.

Z2000.M395 1987
Messick, Frederic M.
Primary sources in European diplomacy, 1914-1945: a bibliography of published memoirs and diaries/ compiled by Frederic M. Messick. New York: Greenwood Press, 1987. xxii, 221 p.
87-000186　016.3274 19　031324555X
Europe -- Foreign relations -- 1871-1918 -- Sources -- Bibliography. Europe -- Foreign relations -- 1918-1945 -- Sources -- Bibliography.

Z2000.M66 2001
Moore, Reese T.
European leaders: a bibliography with indexes/ Reese T. Moore. Huntington, N.Y.: Nova Science Publishers, 2001. 388 p.
2001-270394 016.9405/092/2 21 1560728388
Political leadership -- Europe -- History -- 20th century -- Bibliography. Politicians -- Europe -- History -- 20th century -- Bibliography. Heads of state -- Europe -- History -- 20th century -- Bibliography. Government executives -- Europe -- History -- 20th century -- Bibliography. Europe -- Politics and government -- 20th century -- Bibliography.

Z2000.S7 1993
Southern European studies guide/ edited by John Loughlin. London; Bowker-Saur, c1993. xix, 233 p.
95-167009 016.94 20 0862917867
Europe, Southern -- History -- 20th century -- Bibliography. Mediterranean Region -- Civilization -- 20th century -- Historiography.

Z2000.W47 1990
Western European studies: current research trends and library resources/ editors, Eva Sartori ... [et al.]. Chicago, IL: Western European Specialists Section, 109 p.
91-191660 0838974619
Library resources -- United States. Europe -- History -- Bibliography. Europe -- History -- Library resources.

Z2000.9 Europe — Commonwealth of Nations

Z2000.9.L37 1993
Larby, Patricia M.
The Commonwealth/ Patricia M. Larby, Harry Hannam, compilers; with a foreword by Emeka Anyaoku. New Brunswick, N.J., U.S.A.: Transaction Publishers, c1993. xxxvii, 254 p.
93-009377 016.909/6971241 1560001100
Commonwealth countries -- Bibliography.

Z2001-2014 Europe — Great Britain and Ireland. England

Z2001.B75
The British national bibliography. [London] British Library, Bibliographic Services Division
51-006468 015.42
Bibliography, National -- Great Britain. Catalogs. Great Britain -- Imprints -- Periodicals.

Z2001.R33
British books in print. London, J. Whitaker;
2002-007496 015.41
Catalogs, Publishers' -- Great Britain -- Periodicals. Literature -- bibliography. Great Britain -- Imprints -- Periodicals.

Z2005.I57
International books in print. Munchen; K.G. Saur;
82-645409 018/.4
English imprints -- Bibliography -- Periodicals.

Z2010.M9
Myers, Robin.
A dictionary of literature in the English language, from Chaucer to 1940, compiled and edited by Robin Myers, for the National Book League. [1st ed.] Oxford, Pergamon Press [1970] 2 v.
68-018529 016.82 0080120792
English literature -- Bio-bibliography -- Dictionaries. American literature -- Bio-bibliography -- Dictionaries.

Z2011.A1 H68 vol. 1 1986
Howard-Hill, T. H.
Bibliography of British literary bibliographies/ T.H. Howard-Hill. 2nd ed., rev. and enl. Oxford [England]: Clarendon Press; xxv, 886 p.
86-012449 016.01682 19 0198181841
English literature -- Bibliography of bibliographies.

Z2011.A1 H68 vol. 5
Howard-Hill, T. H.
British bibliography and textual criticism: a bibliography (authors) / T.H. Howard-Hill. Oxford: Clarendon Press; viii, 488 p.
81-453060 016.0160705/73/0941 19 0198181639
English literature -- Bibliography of bibliographies. English literature -- Criticism, Textual -- Bibliography. Bibliographical literature -- Great Britain -- Bibliography. English literature -- Bibliography.

Z2011.A1 H68 vol. 6
Howard-Hill, T. H.
British literary bibliography and textual criticism, 1890-1969: an index/ T.H. Howard-Hill. Oxford: Clarendon Press; xix, 409 p.
79-040836 016.82 s 016.82 0198181809
Howard-Hill, T. H. (Trevor Howard). Index to British literary English literature -- Bibliography of bibliographies -- Indexes. English literature -- Bibliography -- Indexes.

Z2011.A1 H68 vol. 7
Howard-Hill, T. H.
British literary bibliography, 1970-1979: a bibliography/ T.H. Howard-Hill. Oxford: Clarendon Press; xix, 912 p.
91-025597 016.01682 20 0198181833
English literature -- Bibliography of bibliographies.

Z2011.A1 H68 vol. 9
Howard-Hill, T. H.
British literary bibliography, 1980-1989: a bibliography (authors)/ T.H. Howard-Hill. Oxford [England]: Clarendon Press; viii, 1062 p.
00-503642 0198186436
English literature -- Bibliography of bibliographies.

Z2011.B74 1998
Bracken, James K., 1952-
Reference works in British and American literature/ James K. Bracken. Englewood, Colo.: Libraries Unlimited, 1998. xlvii, 726 p.
98-005231 016.8209 1563085186
English literature -- Reference books -- Bibliography. American literature -- Reference books -- Bibliography. English literature -- History and criticism -- Bibliography.

Z2011.H34 2002
Harner, James L.
Literary research guide: an annotated listing of reference sources in English literary studies/ James L. Harner. 4th ed. New York: Modern Language Association of America, 2002. 802 p.
2001-059649 016.8209 21 0873529839
English literature -- History and criticism -- Bibliography. English literature -- Bibliography of bibliographies. Commonwealth literature (English) -- Bibliography. English literature -- Research -- Methodology. American literature -- Bibliography. English literature -- Bibliography.

Z2011.M69
Annual bibliography of English language and literature/ edited for the Modern Humanities Research Association by A.C. Paues. Cambridge: Bowes & Bowes, [1924-   ]
22-011861
English philology -- Bibliography -- Periodicals. English literature -- Bibliography -- Periodicals. English language -- Bibliography -- Periodicals.

Z2011.N45 1999
The Cambridge bibliography of English literature/ edited by Joanne Shattock. 3rd ed. Cambridge, [England]; Cambridge University Press, [1999-   ] v. <4 >
99-055526 016.82 21 0521391008
English literature -- Bibliography.

Z2011.O98 2002
The Oxford chronology of English literature/ edited by Michael Cox. Oxford; Oxford University Press, 2002. 2 v.
2002-510157 820/.2/02 21 0198600267
English literature -- Bibliography. English literature -- Chronology.

Z2011.W3 1965
Watson, George, 1927-
The concise Cambridge bibliography of English literature, 600-1950. Cambridge [Eng.]: University Press, 1965. 269 p.
65-014341 0521092655
English literature -- Bibliography. Chapter II.

Z2012.B925 1994
Burnley, J. D.
The language of Middle English literature/ David Burnley and Matsuji Tajima. Cambridge: D.S. Brewer, 1994. viii, 280 p.
94-006883 016.8209/001 20 0859914054
English literature -- Middle English, 1100-1500 -- Criticism, Textual English language -- Middle English, 1100-1500 -- Bibliography. Civilization, Medieval, in literature -- Bibliography.

Z2012.G83
Greenfield, Stanley B.
A bibliography of publications on Old English literature to the end of 1972: using the collections of E.E. Ericson/ Stanley B. Greenfield and Fred C. Robinson. Toronto; University of Toronto Press, c1980. xxii, 437 p.
78-004989 016.829 0802022928
English literature -- Old English, ca. 450-1100 -- History and criticism English literature -- Old English, ca. 450-1100 -- Bibliography. Civilization, Medieval, in literature -- Bibliography.

Z2012.G835 2001
Greentree, Rosemary.
The Middle English lyric and short poem/ Rosemary Greentree. Cambridge; D.S. Brewer, 2001. 570 p.
00-068885 016.821/040901 21 0859916219
English poetry -- Middle English, 1100-1500 -- Bibliography. English poetry -- Middle English, 1100-1500 -- History and criticism

Z2012.H198 1995
Hamer, R. F. S.
A manuscript index to The index of Middle English verse/ Richard Hamer. London: The British Library, 1995. 62 p.
95-170746 016.821/108 21 0712303871
Brown, Carleton, 1869-1941. Index of Middle English verse -- Indexes. English poetry -- Middle English, 1100-1500 -- Manuscripts -- Indexes. Manuscripts, English (Middle) -- Indexes.

Z2012.H23 1993
Hasenfratz, Robert J., 1957-
Beowulf scholarship: an annotated bibliography, 1979-1990/ Robert J. Hasenfratz. New York: Garland Pub., 1993. xviii, 424 p.
93-017683 016.829/3 0815300840
Epic poetry, English (Old) -- History and criticism -- Bibliography. Civilization, Medieval, in literature -- Bibliography.

Z2012.R6
Robinson, Fred C.
Old English literature; a select bibliography [by] Fred C. Robinson. [Toronto] University of Toronto Press [1970] 68 p.
76-464039 016.829 0802040268
English literature -- Old English, ca. 450-1100 -- Bibliography. Civilization, Medieval, in literature -- Bibliography.

Z2012.S53
Short, Douglas D.
Beowulf scholarship: an annotated bibliography/ Douglas D. Short. New York: Garland Pub., 1980. xvi, 353 p.
79-007924 829/.3 19 0824095308
Beowulf -- Bibliography. Epic poetry, English (Old) -- History and criticism -- Bibliography. Monsters in literature -- Bibliography. Dragons in literature -- Bibliography. Heroes in literature -- Bibliography. Scandinavia -- In literature -- Bibliography.

Z2013.B8
Buckley, Jerome Hamilton.
Victorian poets and prose writers. Compiled by Jerome H. Buckley. New York, Appleton-Century-Crofts [1966] viii, 63 p.
66-026461 016.8209008
English literature -- 19th century -- History and criticism -- Bibliography. Great Britain -- History -- Victoria, 1837-1901 -- Bibliography.

Z2013.L58 1998
Literature of the romantic period: a bibliographical guide/ edited by Michael O'Neill. Oxford: Clarendon Press; 1998. viii, 410 p.
97-033299 016.8209/007 0198711204
English literature -- 19th century -- History and criticism -- Bibliography. English literature -- 18th century -- History and criticism -- Bibliography. Romanticism -- Great Britain -- Bibliography.

Z2013.T62
Tobin, James Edward, 1905-1968.
Eighteenth century English literature and its cultural background; a bibliography [by] James E. Tobin. New York, Fordham University Press, 1939.
40-001481 016.82
English literature -- 18th century -- Bibliography.

Z2013.3.B45 1994
Beidler, Philip D.
Scriptures for a generation: what we were reading in the '60s/ Philip D. Beidler. Athens: University of Georgia Press, c1994. 254 p.
94-004172 016.8108/0054 0820316415
American literature -- 20th century -- Bibliography. Books and reading -- United States -- History -- 20th century. United States -- History -- 1961-1969 -- Sources -- Bibliography.

Z2013.5.W6.A48 1991
Alston, R. C.
A checklist of women writers, 1801-1900: fiction, verse, drama/ R.C. Alston. Boston, Mass.: G.K. Hall, c1990. ix, 517 p.
90-021780 016.8108/09287/09034
Women and literature -- Great Britain -- History -- 19th century -- Bibliography -- Catalogs. Commonwealth literature (English) -- Women authors -- Bibliography -- Catalogs. Women and literature -- Commonwealth countries -- History -- 19th century -- Bibliography -- Catalogs.

Z2013.5.W6.F83 1990
Fuderer, Laura Sue, 1944-
The female bildungsroman in English: an annotated bibliography of criticism/ Laura Sue Fuderer. New York, NY: Modern Language Association of America, 1990. 47 p.
90-039517 016.823009/9287 0873529626
English fiction -- Women authors -- History and criticism -- Bibliography. American fiction -- Women authors -- History and criticism -- Bibliography. Maturation (Psychology) in literature -- Bibliography.

Z2013.5.W6.H67 1997
Horwitz, Barbara Joan.
British women writers, 1700-1850: an annotated bibliography of their works and works about them/ Barbara J. Horwitz. Lanham, Md.: Scarecrow Press; 1997. xiv, 231 p.
97-005001 016.8208/09287 0810833158
English literature -- Women authors -- History and criticism -- Bibliography. Women and literature -- Great Britain -- History -- 18th century -- Bibliography. Women and literature -- Great Britain -- History -- 19th century -- Bibliography.

Z2013.5.W6.J33 1993
Jackson, J. R. de J.
Romantic poetry by women: a bibliography, 1770-1835/ J.R. de J. Jackson. Oxford [England]: Clarendon Press; 1993. xxx, 484 p.
92-035190 016.821/60809287 0198112394
English poetry -- Women authors -- Bibliography. Women and literature -- English-speaking countries -- Bibliography. American poetry -- Women authors -- Bibliography.

Z2014.D7.C72
Conolly, L. W.
English drama and theatre, 1800-1900/ L.W. Conolly, J.P. Wearing. Detroit: Gale Research Co., c1978. xix, 508 p.
73-016975 016.822/7/08 0810312255
English drama -- 19th century -- Bibliography. English drama -- 19th century -- History and criticism -- Bibliography. Theater -- Great Britain -- History -- Bibliography.

Z2014.D7.D68 1996
Douglas, Krystan V.
Guide to British drama explication/ Krystan V. Douglas. New York: G.K. Hall, [1996-] v. 1
95-051781 016.822009 0816173729
English drama -- History and criticism -- Bibliography.

Z2014.D7.L55
Link, Frederick M.
English drama, 1660-1800: a guide to information sources/ Frederick M. Link. Detroit: Gale Research Co., c1976. xxii, 374 p.
73-016984 016.822 0810312247
English drama -- 18th century -- History and criticism -- Bibliography. English drama -- Restoration, 1660-1700 -- History and criticism -- Bibliography. Theater -- Great Britain -- Bibliography.

Z2014.D7.M545
Mikhail, E. H.
English drama, 1900-1950: a guide to information sources/ E. H. Mikhail. Detroit: Gale Research Co., c1977. xiii, 328 p.
77-076355 016.822/9/1 0810312166
English drama -- 20th century -- Bibliography.

Z2014.F4.B6 1961
Block, Andrew, 1892-
The English novel, 1740-1850; a catalogue including prose romances, short stories, and translations of foreign fiction. London, Dawsons of Pall Mall, 1961. 349 p.
61-003325
English fiction -- Translations from foreign literature -- Bibliography. English fiction -- 18th cent -- Bibliography. English fiction -- 19th cent -- Bibliography.

Z2014.F4.H83 1994
Hubin, Allen J.
Crime fiction II: a comprehensive bibliography, 1749-1990/ Allen J. Hubin. New York: Garland Pub., 1994. 2 v.
93-041230 016.823/087208 0824068912
Detective and mystery stories -- Bibliography. Detective and mystery stories, American -- Bibliography. Detective and mystery stories -- Translations into English -- Bibliography.

Z2014.F4.L45 2000
Lesher, Linda Parent, 1947-
The best novels of the nineties: a reader's guide/ by Linda Parent Lesher. Jefferson, N.C.: McFarland, c2000. vi, 482 p.
99-044233 016.823/91409 0786407425
English fiction -- 20th century -- Bibliography. American fiction -- 20th century -- Bibliography. Commonwealth fiction (English) -- Bibliography.

Z2014.F4.L46 1997
Le Tellier, Robert Ignatius.
The English novel, 1660-1700: an annotated bibliography/ Robert Ignatius Letellier. Westport, Conn.: Greenwood Press, 1997. xxxiv, 448 p.
97-022560   016.823/408   0313303681
English fiction -- Early modern, 1500-1700 -- Bibliography. European fiction -- 17th century -- Translations into English -- Bibliography. Fiction -- Translations into English -- Bibliography.

Z2014.F4.M87 2000
Murph, Roxane C.
The English Civil War through the Restoration in fiction: an annotated bibliography, 1625-1999/ Roxane C. Murph. Westport, Conn.: Greenwood Press, 2000. viii, 349 p.
99-058883   016.8208/0358   031331425X
Historical fiction, English -- Bibliography. English fiction -- Early modern, 1500-1700 -- Bibliography. War stories, English -- Bibliography. Great Britain -- History -- Puritan Revolution, 1642-1660 -- Fiction -- Bibliography. Great Britain -- History -- Restoration, 1660-1688 -- Fiction -- Bibliography. Great Britain -- History -- Civil War, 1642-1649 -- Fiction -- Bibliography.

Z2014.F4 S64 2002
Snell, K. D. M.
The bibliography of regional fiction in Britain and Ireland, 1800-2000 / K.D.M. Snell. Hants, England; Ashgate, c2002. xi, 213 p.
2001-046422   016.823/808032   21   075460666X
English fiction -- 19th century -- Bibliography. English fiction -- 20th century -- Bibliography. English fiction -- Irish authors -- Bibliography. Regionalism in literature -- Bibliography. Great Britain -- In literature -- Bibliography. Ireland -- In literature -- Bibliography.

Z2014.F5 P26.R821
English novel explication: criticisms to 1972. Compiled by Helen H. Palmer & Anne Jane Dyson. [Hamden, Conn.] Shoe String Press, 1973. vi, 329 p.
73-000410   016.823/009   0208013229
English fiction--History and criticism--Bibliography.

Z2014.F5 P26 Suppl.
English novel explication. Hamden, Conn.: Shoe String Press, 1976-<2002 > v. <1-7 >
84-137107   016.823/009 19   0208024883
English fiction -- Explication -- Bibliography.

Z2014.G7.G67 1998
Gorlach, Manfred.
An annotated bibliography of nineteenth-century grammars of English/ Manfred Gorlach; with a foreword by Ian Michael. Amsterdam; J. Benjamins, c1998. ix, 395 p.
98-036269   016.4282/09/034   1556192568
English language -- 19th century -- Grammar - - Bibliography.

Z2014.M985.R4 1991
Recent studies in myths and literature, 1970-1990: an annotated bibliography/ compiled by Bernard Accardi ... [et al.]. New York: Greenwood Press, 1991. ix, 251 p.
91-018070   016.82/0915   0313275459
English literature -- History and criticism -- Bibliography. American literature -- History and criticism -- Bibliography. Classical literature -- History and criticism -- Bibliography.

Z2014.P7.A93
Auden, W. H. 1907-1973.
Poets of the English language, edited by W.H. Auden and Norman Holmes Pearson. New York, Viking Press, 1950. 5 v.
50-009508   821.082
English poetry. English poetry. American poetry.

Z2014.P7.M34 1991
Martinez, Nancy C.
Guide to British poetry explication/ Nancy C. Martinez and Joseph G.R. Martinez. Boston: G.K. Hall, 1991-c1995. 4 v.
90-049129   016.821009   0816189218
English poetry -- Explication -- Bibliography.

Z2014.P7.M35 1995
Mazzeno, Laurence W.
Victorian poetry: an annotated bibliography/ by Laurence W. Mazzeno. Metuchen, N.J.: Scarecrow Press; 1995. xiii, 247 p.
95-005328   016.821/8   0810830086
English poetry -- 19th century -- Bibliography.

Z2014.P7.P66 1998
Poole, Russell Gilbert.
Old English wisdom poetry/ Russell Poole. Cambridge [England]; D.S. Brewer, 1998. xi, 418 p.
98-027022   829/.1   0859915301
Didactic poetry, English (Old) -- History and criticism -- Bibliography. Learning and scholarship -- History -- Medieval, 500-1500 -- Bibliography. Anglo-Saxons -- Intellectual life -- Bibliography.

Z2014.P7.R453 1994
Reilly, Catherine W.
Late Victorian poetry, 1880-1899: an annotated biobibliography/ Catherine W. Reilly. London; Mansell, c1994. xxi, 577 p.
94-004657   016.821/808   0720120012
English poetry -- 19th century -- Bio-bibliography -- Dictionaries. Poets, English -- 19th century -- Biography -- Dictionaries.

Z2014.P7.R454 2000
Reilly, Catherine W.
Mid-Victorian poetry, 1860-1879: an annotated biobibliography/ Catherine W. Reilly. New York: Mansell, 2000. xxi, 560 p.
99-026552   820.9/008/03   0720123186
English poetry -- 19th century -- Bio-bibliography -- Dictionaries. Poets, English -- 19th century -- Biography -- Dictionaries.

Z2014.P7.R67 1999
Roberts, Adam
Romantic and Victorian long poems: a guide/ Adam Roberts. Aldershot, Hants, England; Ashgate, c1999. 223 p.
99-018600   016.821/030907   1859281567
English poetry -- 19th century -- Bibliography. Narrative poetry, English -- Bibliography. Epic poetry, English -- Bibliography.

Z2014.P795.H45
Heninger, S. K.
English prose, prose fiction, and criticism to 1660: a guide to information sources/ S.K. Heninger, Jr. Detroit: Gale Research Co., [1975] x, 255 p.
73-016980   016.082   0810312751
English prose literature -- Early modern, 1500-1700 -- Bibliography. English prose literature -- Early modern, 1500-1700 -- History and criticism -- Bibliography. English prose literature -- Middle English, 1100-1500 -- Bibliography.

Z2014.U84.S28 1988
Sargent, Lyman Tower, 1940-
British and American utopian literature, 1516-1985: an annotated, chronological bibliography/ Lyman Tower Sargent. New York: Garland, c1988. xix, 559 p.
88-002546   016.82/08/0372   0824006941
English literature -- Bibliography. Utopias -- Bibliography. American literature -- Bibliography.

Z2014.W37.O93 2000
Ouditt, Sharon, 1963-
Women writers of the First World War: an annotated bibliography/ Sharon Ouditt. London; Routledge, 2000. x, 230 p.
99-020102   016.8208/0358   0415047528
English literature -- 20th century -- Bibliography. World War, 1914-1918 -- Great Britain -- Literature and the war -- Bibliography. Women and literature -- Great Britain -- History -- 20th century -- Bibliography.

Z2014.W57.N55 1997
Nilsen, Don Lee Fred.
Humor in British literature, from the Middle Ages to the Restoration: a reference guide/ Don L.F. Nilsen. Westport, Conn.: Greenwood Press, 1997. xxiii, 226 p.
96-026190   016.827009   0313297061
English wit and humor -- History and criticism -- Bibliography. English literature -- Middle English, 1100-1500 -- History and criticism -- Bibliography. English literature -- Early modern, 1500-1700 -- History and criticism -- Bibliography.

Z2014.W57.N56 1998
Nilsen, Don Lee Fred.
Humor in eighteenth- and nineteenth-century British literature: a reference guide/ Don L.F. Nilsen. Westport, Conn.: Greenwood Press, 1998. xvii, 294 p.
98-014819   016.827009   0313297053
English wit and humor -- History and criticism -- Bibliography. English literature -- 18th century -- History and criticism -- Bibliography. English literature -- 19th century -- History and criticism -- Bibliography.

Z2014.W57.N565 2000
Nilsen, Don Lee Fred.
Humor in twentieth-century British literature: a reference guide/ Don L.F. Nilsen. Westport, Conn.: Greenwood Press, 2000. xii, 561 p.
99-054482   016.827/9109   0313294240
English wit and humor -- History and criticism -- Bibliography. English literature -- 20th century -- History and criticism -- Bibliography. Humorous stories, English -- History and criticism -- Bibliography.

Z2014.W65.B66 1989
Boos, Florence Saunders, 1943-
Bibliography of women & literature/ edited by Florence Boos with Lynn Miller. New York: Holmes & Meier, c1989. 2 v.
81-006989   016.82/09/9287   0841906939
English literature -- Women authors -- History and criticism -- Bibliography. American literature -- Women authors -- History and criticism -- Bibliography. Women in literature -- Bibliography.

Z2015 Europe — Great Britain and Ireland. England — Language. Philology

Z2015.L49
Sylvester, Louise.
Middle English word studies: a word and author index/ Louise Sylvester and Jane Roberts. Rochester, NY: D.S. Brewer, 2000. x, 322 p.
00-042921   016.427/02   0859916065
English language -- Middle English, 1100-1500 -- Lexicology -- Bibliography. English language -- Middle English, 1100-1500 -- Etymology -- Bibliography. English language -- Middle English, 1100-1500 -- Bibliography.

Z2015.R5.P57 1995
Plett, Heinrich F.
English Renaissance rhetoric and poetics: a systematic bibliography of primary and secondary sources/ by Heinrich F. Plett. Leiden; E.J. Brill, 1995. ix, 526 p.
95-034382   083/.1   9004103430
English language -- Rhetoric -- Bibliography. English poetry -- Early modern, 1500-1700 -- History and criticism -- Bibliography. Renaissance, Renaissance -- Bibliography.

Z2017-2021 Europe — Great Britain and Ireland. England — History

Z2017.B5
A Bibliography of English history to 1485: based on The sources and literature of English history from the earliest times to about 1485 by Charles Gross/ edited by Edgar B. Graves; and issued under the sponsorship of the Royal Historical Society, the American Historical Association, and the Mediaeval Academy of America. Oxford [Eng.]; Clarendon Press, 1975. xxiv, 1103 p.
76-355448   016.942   0198223919
Middle Ages -- Sources -- Bibliography. Great Britain -- History -- To 1485 -- Sources -- Bibliography.

Z2017.M87 1995
Murph, Roxane C.
The Wars of the Roses in fiction: an annotated bibliography, 1440-1994/ compiled by Roxane C. Murph. Westport, Conn.: Greenwood Press, 1995. viii, 209 p.
95-012746   016.823008/0358   0313297096
English literature -- Bibliography. English literature -- Middle English, 1100-1500 -- Bibliography. Great Britain -- History -- Wars of the Roses, 1455-1485 -- Literature and the wars -- Bibliography. Great Britain -- History -- Lancaster and York, 1399-1485 -- Historiography -- Bibliography. Great Britain -- History -- Tudors, 1485-1603 -- Historiography -- Bibliography.

Z2017.W54
Wilkinson, Bertie, 1898-
The high Middle Ages in England, 1154-1377/ Bertie Wilkinson. Cambridge; Cambridge University Press, 1978. ix, 130 p.
77-008490   016.94203   0521217326
Great Britain -- History -- Plantagenets, 1154-1399 -- Bibliography.

Z2018.P37 1951
Pargellis, Stanley McCrory, 1898-
Bibliography of British history; the eighteenth century, 1714-1789. Issued under the direction of the American Historical Association and the Royal Historical Society of Great Britain. Edited by Stanley Pargellis and D. J. Medley. Oxford, Clarendon Press, 1951. xxvi, 642 p.
51-004275   016.94207
Great Britain -- History -- 18th century -- Bibliography.

Z2018.R28 1959
Read, Conyers, 1881-
Bibliography of British history, Tudor period, 1485-1603; issued under the direction of the American Historical Association and the Royal Historical Society of Great Britain. Oxford, Clarendon Press, 1959. xxviii, 624 p.
59-003413   016.94205
Great Britain -- History -- Tudors, 1485-1603 -- Bibliography.

Z2019.H35
Hanham, H. J.
Bibliography of British history. compiled and edited by H. J. Hanham. Oxford: Clarendon Press, 1976. xxvii, 1606 p.
77-350302   016.942   0198223897
Great Britain -- History -- 19th century -- Bibliography.

Z2019.P76 1992
Propas, Sharon W., 1947-
Victorian studies: a research guide/ Sharon W. Propas. New York: Garland Pub., 1992. xxi, 334 p.
91-045048   016.941   0824058402
Great Britain -- History -- Victoria, 1837-1901 -- Bibliography. Great Britain -- Civilization -- 19th century -- Bibliography.

Z2020.H39 1996
Hazlehurst, Cameron, 1941-
A guide to the papers of British cabinet ministers, 1900-1964/ Cameron Hazlehurst, Sally Whitehead, and Christine Woodland. Cambridge; Cambridge University Press for the Royal Historical Society, 1996. viii, 417 p.
96-021151   016.3544104/0922/0904   0521587433
Cabinet officers -- Great Britain -- Archival resources. Great Britain -- Politics and government -- 20th century -- Archival resources.

Z2020.R63 1996
Robbins, Keith.
A bibliography of British history. compiled and edited by Keith Robbins. Oxford [England]: Clarendon Press; xxxix, 918 p.
96-233104   016.941 21   0198224966

Z2021.M5.H54
Higham, Robin D. S.
A guide to the sources of British military history. Edited by Robin Higham. Berkeley, University of California Press, 1971. xxi, 630 p.
74-104108   016.355/00942   0520016742
Great Britain -- History, Military -- Bibliography.

Z2024 Europe — Great Britain and Ireland. England — Local

Z2024.L8.C74 1996
Creaton, Heather.
London/ Heather Creaton, compiler. Oxford, England; Clio Press, c1996. xxxi, 165 p.
96-223555   016.9421   185109248X
London (England) -- History -- Bibliography. London (England) -- Civilization -- Bibliography.

Z2031-2043 Europe — Great Britain and Ireland. England — Ireland. Eire. Irish Free State

Z2031.L47 1987
Lester, DeeGee.
Irish research: a guide to collections in North America, Ireland, and Great Britain/ compiled by DeeGee Lester. New York: Greenwood Press, 1987. xvi, 348 p.
87-025150   016.9415/0025   0313246645
Ireland -- Library resources -- Directories. Ireland -- Archival resources -- Directories.

Z2037.M235
McKenna, Brian.
Irish literature, 1800-1875: a guide to information sources/ Brian McKenna. Detroit: Gale Research Co., c1978. xvii, 388 p.
74-011540   016.82   0810312506
English literature -- Irish authors -- Bibliography. English literature -- Irish authors -- History and criticism -- Bibliography. English literature -- 19th century -- Bibliography. Ireland -- Intellectual life -- 19th century -- Bibliography.

Z2039.W57.N55 1996
Nilsen, Don Lee Fred.
Humor in Irish literature: a reference guide/ Don L.F. Nilsen. Westport, Conn.: Greenwood Press, 1996. xvi, 225 p.
95-039489   016.8209/9415   0313295514
English literature -- Irish authors -- History and criticism -- Bibliography. Humorous stories, English -- Irish authors -- History and criticism -- Bibliography. Humorous poetry, English -- Irish authors -- History and criticism -- Bibliography. Ireland -- In literature -- Bibliography.

Z2043.N6.S5 1991
Shannon, Michael Owen.
Northern Ireland/ Michael Owen Shannon, compiler. Oxford, England; Clio Press, c1991. xxxviii, 603 p.
92-148618   016.9416   1851090320
Northern Ireland -- Bibliography.

Z2136-2137 Europe — Czechoslovakia. Czech Republic

Z2136.E36 1999
Edmondson, Vladka.
Czech Republic/ Vladka Edmondson with David Short, compilers. Oxford; CLIO Press, c1999. xxv, 430 p.
      1851093044
Czech Republic -- Bibliography.

Z2137.P68.L86 1997
Lunt, Susie.
Prague/ Susie Lunt, compiler. Oxford; Clio Press, c1997. xviii, 182 p.
97-180598   016.94371/2   1851092528
Prague (Czech Republic) -- Bibliography.

Z2171-2184 Europe — France

Z2171.C74 1947
Cabeen, David Clark, 1886-1965.
A Critical bibliography of French literature/ D.C. Cabeen, general editor. Syracuse, N.Y.: Syracuse University Press, [1947-   ]
47-003282   016.84
French literature -- Bibliography.

Z2173.F7
French XX bibliography.   New York, French Institute-Alliance Francaise, [1969-   ]
77-648803   016.8409
French literature -- 20th century -- History and criticism -- Bibliography -- Periodicals.

Z2174.D7.B43 1994
Beach, Cecilia.
French women playwrights before the twentieth century: a checklist/ compiled by Cecilia Beach. Westport, Conn.: Greenwood Press, 1994. xiv, 251 p.
94-028703   016.842008/09287   0313291748
French drama -- Women authors -- Bibliography. Women and literature -- France -- Bibliography.

Z2174.D7.B44 1996
Beach, Cecilia.
French women playwrights of the twentieth century: a checklist/ compiled by Cecilia Beach. Westport, Conn.: Greenwood Press, 1996. xi, 515 p.
95-039490   016.842/91099287   0313291756
French drama -- Women authors -- Bibliography. French drama -- 20th century -- Bibliography. Women and literature -- France -- Bibliography.

Z2174.P7.B87 1995
Burgess, Glyn S.
The Old French narrative lay: an analytical bibliography/ Glyn S. Burgess. Cambridge; D.S. Brewer, 1995. viii, 140 p.
95-021659   016.841/1   085991478X
French poetry -- To 1500 -- Bibliography. Lays -- Bibliography.

Z2175.A2.B39 1989
Bassan, Fernande.
French language and literature: an annotated bibliography/ Fernande Bassan, Donald C. Spinelli, Howard A. Sullivan. New York: Garland, 1989. xix, 365 p.
89-001186   016.44   0824047982
French philology -- Bibliography.

Z2175.A2.O8 1981
Osburn, Charles B.
Research and reference guide to French studies/ Charles B. Osburn. Metuchen, N.J.: Scarecrow Press, 1981. xxxvii, 532 p.
81-005637   016.44   0810814404
French philology -- Bibliography.

Z2179.M49 1987
Meyer, Jack Allen.
An annotated bibliography of the Napoleonic era: recent publications, 1945-1985/ compiled by Jack Allen Meyer. New York: Greenwood Press, 1987. xvii, 288 p.
87-007605   016.94405 19   0313249016
France -- History -- Consulate and First Empire, 1799-1815 -- Bibliography. Europe -- History -- 1789-1815 -- Bibliography.

Z2184.A65.B66 1994
Bonin, Hubert.
Repertoire bibliographique de l'histoire economique contemporaine de l'Aquitaine/ Hubert Bonin. Talence: Editions de la Maison des sciences de l'homme d' Aquitaine, c1994. 65 p.
94-168863   2858921954
Aquitaine (France) -- Economic conditions -- Bibliography.

Z2184.P2.B27 1989
Bailey, William G., 1947-
Americans in Paris, 1900-1930: a selected, annotated bibliography/ compiled by William G. Bailey. New York: Greenwood Press, 1989. xix, 162 p.
89-001924   016.944/360041   0313264422
Americans -- France -- Paris -- History -- 20th century -- Bibliography. Paris (France) -- Intellectual life -- 20th century -- Bibliography.

Z2184.P3.C46 1998
Chambers, Frances.
Paris/ Frances Chambers, compiler. Oxford, England; Clio Press, c1998. xviii, 138 p.
99-218231   016.94436   1851092714
Paris (France) -- Bibliography.

Z2230-2241 Europe — Germany

Z2230.C65 1997
Furness, Raymond.
A companion to twentieth-century German literature/ Raymond Furness and Malcolm Humble. 2nd ed. London; Routledge, 1997. 316 p.
97-160697   830.9/0091 21   0415150574
German literature -- 20th century -- Bio-bibliography. Austrian literature -- 20th century -- Bio-bibliography. Swiss literature (German) -- 20th century -- Bio-bibliography.

Z2233.5.W6.W65 1998
Women writers in German-speaking countries: a bio-bibliographical critical sourcebook/ edited by Elke P. Frederiksen and Elizabeth G. Ametsbichler. Westport, Conn.: Greenwood Press, 1998. xxxiii, 561 p.
97-001687   830.9/9287   0313282013
German literature -- Women authors -- Bio-bibliography. Women and literature -- Europe, German-speaking -- Bibliography. Women authors, German -- Biography.

Z2235.A2 R5 1984
Richardson, Larry L.
Introduction to library research in German studies: language, literature, and civilization/ Larry L. Richardson. Boulder, Colo.: Westview Press, 1984. xx, 227 p.
83-050976   016.943 19   0865311951
German philology -- Bibliography. German philology -- Research. Germany -- Civilization -- Bibliography. Germany -- Civilization -- Research.

Z2240.K44 1982
Kehr, Helen.
The Nazi era, 1919-1945: a select bibliography of published works from the early roots to 1980/ compiled by Helen Kehr and Janet Langmaid. London: Mansell Pub.; xvi, 621 p.
83-216788   016.943085 19   072011618X
National socialism -- Bibliography. Germany -- Politics and government -- 1918-1933 -- Bibliography. Germany -- Politics and government -- 1933-1945 -- Bibliography.

Z2241.N27.S65 1987
Snyder, Louis Leo, 1907-
The Third Reich, 1933-1945: a bibliographical guide to German national socialism/ selected, annotated, and edited by Louis L. Snyder. New York: Garland Pub., 1987. 284 p.
87-007608   016.943085   0824084632
National socialism -- Bibliography. Germany -- Politics and government -- 1933-1945 -- Bibliography.

Z2260 Europe — Mediterranean area

Z2260.F48 1996
Feuer, Bryan Avery.
Mycenaean civilization: a research guide/ Bryan Feuer. New York: Garland Pub., 1996. xl, 421 p.
94-042479   016.938/8   0815306024
Civilization, Mycenaean -- Bibliography. Mediterranean Region -- Antiquities.

Z2281-2304 Europe — Greece

Z2281.G73 2000
Greece in modern times: an annotated bibliography of works published in English in twenty-two academic disciplines during the twentieth century/ edited by Stratos E. Constantinidis. Lanham, Md.; Scarecrow Press, [c2000-   ] v. 1
99-024674   016.9495   0810836580
English imprints. Greece -- Indexes.

Z2304.E58.O87 1987
Oster, Richard.
A bibliography of ancient Ephesus/ compiled by
Richard E. Oster. [Philadelphia]: American
Theological Library Association; 1987. xxiv,
155 p.
87-012617 016.939/23 0810819961
*Ephesus (Extinct city) -- History --
Bibliography. Turkey -- Antiquities --
Bibliography. Greece -- Antiquities --
Bibliography.*

Z2340 Europe — Rome. Roman Empire

Z2340.R653 1991
Rollins, Alden M., 1946-
Rome in the fourth century A.D.: an annotated
bibliography with historical overview/ by Alden
Rollins. Jefferson, N.C.: McFarland, c1991.
xxxiii, 324 p.
91-052762 016.937/06 0899506240
*Rome -- History -- Empire, 284-476 --
Bibliography.*

Z2341-2360.3 Europe — Italy

Z2341.S66 1995
Sponza, Lucio.
Italy/ Lucio Sponza and Diego Zancani,
compilers. Oxford, England; Clio Press, c1995.
xxxi, 417 p.
96-192120 016.945 0903450445
Italy -- Bibliiography. Italy -- Bibliography.

Z2360.3.B85 1996
Bull, Martin J.
Contemporary Italy: a research guide/ Martin J.
Bull. Westport, Conn.: Greenwood Press, 1996.
xvii, 141 p.
95-039488 016.945092 0313291373
*Italy -- Politics and government -- 1945-1976 -
- Bibliography. Italy -- Politics and government -
- 1976-1994 -- Bibliography. Italy -- Economic
conditions -- 1945- -- Bibliography.*

Z2461 Europe — Benelux (Low Countries). Belgium — Luxembourg

Z2461.H87 1997
Christophory, Jul, 1939-
Luxembourg/ Jul Christophory and Emile
Thoma, compilers. Oxford, England; Clio Press,
c1997. xxxiv, 327 p.
97-188274 016.9493/5 1851092498
Luxembourg -- Bibliography.

Z2483 Europe — Eastern Europe — General works

Z2483.B89 1995
Burger, Robert H. 1947-
Eastern Europe: a bibliographic guide to English
language publications, 1986-1993/ Robert H.
Burger and Helen F. Sullivan; with the assistance
of Lisa Radloff. Englewood, Colo.: Libraries
Unlimited, 1995. xiii, 254 p.
95-033592 016.947085/4 1563080478
*English imprints.Europe, Eastern --
Bibliography.*

Z2483.G95 1994
Gyeszly, Suzanne D.
Eastern Europe: a resource guide: a selected
bibliography on social sciences and humanities/
by Suzanne D. Gyeszly. San Bernardino, Calif.:
Borgo Press, c1994. vi, 242 p.
93-003166 016.947
Europe, Eastern -- Bibliography.

Z2483.R83 1989
Russia and eastern Europe, 1789-1985: a
bibliographical guide/ compiled by Raymond
Pearson. Manchester; Manchester University
Press; c1989. xiii, 210 p.
88-025011 016.94708 0719017343
*Soviet Union -- History -- 19th century --
Bibliography. Soviet Union -- History -- 20th
century -- Bibliography. Europe, Eastern --
History -- Bibliography.*

Z2483.S554 1993
Slavic studies: a guide to bibliographies,
encyclopedias, and handbooks/ compiled and
edited by Murlin Croucher. Wilmington:
Scholarly Resources, 1993. 2 v.
92-028912 016.947 0842023747
*Europe, Eastern -- References books --
Bibliography.Slavic countries -- References
books -- Bibliography. Slavic countries --
Bibliography. Europe, Eastern -- Bibliography.*

Z2491-2511 Europe — Eastern Europe — Soviet Union. Russia

Z2491.B63 1997
Boilard, Steve D.
Reinterpreting Russia: an annotated bibliography
of books on Russia, the Soviet Union, and the
Russian Federation, 1991-1996/ Steve D.
Boilard. Lanham, Md.: Scarecrow Press; 1997.
xxii, 283 p.
96-038095 016.947 0810832984
*Russia -- Bibliography. Soviet Union --
Bibliography. Russia (Federation) --
Bibliography.*

Z2500.E17 1995
Early modern Russian writers, late seventeenth
and eighteenth centuries/ edited by Marcus C.
Levitt. Detroit: Gale Research Inc., c1995. xviii,
465 p.
95-001711 891.709/001 0810357119
*Russian literature -- To 1700 -- Bio-
bibliography. Russian literature -- 18th century -
- Bio-bibliography. Authors, Russian --
Biography -- Dictionaries.*

Z2500.K3513 1988
Kasack, Wolfgang.
Dictionary of Russian literature since 1917/
Wolfgang Kasack; translated by Maria Carlson
and Jane T. Hedges; bibliographical revision by
Rebecca Atack. New York: Columbia University
Press, 1988. xvi, 502 p.
87-020838 891.7/09/004 0231052421
*Russian literature -- 20th century -- Bio-
bibliography. Authors, Russian -- 20th century --
Biography -- Dictionaries.*

Z2500.S8 1987
Stevanovic, Bosiljka.
Free voices in Russian literature, 1950s-1980s: a
bio-bibliographical guide/ Bosiljka Stevanovic,
Vladimir Wertsman; edited by Alexander
Sumerkin. New York: Russica Publishers, 1987.
510 p.
84-061344 891.709/0044 0898300908
*Underground literature -- Soviet Union -- Bio-
bibliography.*

Z2503.P76 1990
Proffer, Carl R.
Nineteenth-century Russian literature in English:
a bibliography of criticism and translations/
compiled by Carl R. Proffer and Ronald Meyer.
Ann Arbor: Ardis, c1990. 188 p.
89-018589 891.709/003 0882339435
*Russian literature -- 19th century -- History
and criticism -- Bibliography. Russian literature
-- 19th century -- Translations into English --
Bibliography.*

Z2503.5.W6.N45 1992
Nemec Ignashev, Diane, 1951-
Women and writing in Russia and the USSR: a
bibliography of English-language sources/ Diane
M. Nemec Ignashev, Sarah Krive. New York:
Garland Pub., 1992. xiii, 328 p.
92-009246 016.891709/9287 0824036476
*Russian literature -- Women authors --
Bibliography. Russian literature -- Translations
into English -- Bibliography. Women -- Soviet
Union -- Bibliography.*

Z2506.S3 1995
Schaffner, Bradley L., 1959-
Bibliography of the Soviet Union, its
predecessors and successors/ by Bradley L.
Schaffner. Metuchen, N.J.: Scarecrow Press,
1995. xi, 569 p.
94-001673 016.947 081082860X
*Soviet Union -- Bibliography. Russia --
Bibliography. Former Soviet republics --
Bibliography.*

Z2508.R87 1997
Russian modernism: the collections of the Getty
Research Institute for the History of Art and the
Humanities, I/ introduction by Jean-Louis Cohen;
compiled and annotated by David Woodruff and
Ljiljana Grubisic. Santa Monica, CA: Getty
Research Institute for the History of Art and the
Humanities, 1997. 215 p.
96-034895 016.947/07 0892363851
*Modernism (Aesthetics) -- Bibliography.Soviet
Union -- Civilization -- Bibliography. Russia --
Civilization -- 1801-1917 -- Bibliography.*

Z2510.F73 1995
Frame, Murray.
The Russian Revolution, 1905-1921: a
bibliographic guide to works in English/
compiled by Murray Frame. Westport, Conn.:
Greenwood Press, 1995. xvi, 308 p.
95-002463 016.947084/1 031329559X
*Soviet Union -- History -- Revolution, 1917-
1921 -- Bibliography.*

Z2510.3.R57 1992
The Rise and fall of the Soviet Union: a selected
bibliography of sources in English/ edited by
Abraham J. Edelheit and Hershel Edelheit.
Westport, Conn.: Greenwood Press, 1992. xviii,
430 p.
92-024470 016.94708 0313286256
Soviet Union -- History -- Bibliography.

Z2510.3.W54 1996
Wieczynski, Joseph L., 1934-
The Gorbachev bibliography, 1985-1991: a listing of books and articles in English on perestroika in the USSR/ compiled and edited by Joseph L. Wieczynski. New York: Norman Ross Pub., c1996. x, 275 p.
95-045265   0883542757
Perestroika -- Bibliography.Soviet Union -- History -- 1985-1991 -- Bibliography.

Z2511.K55 R87 2002
Russian leaders: a bibliography with indexes/ Alexander Dragomiroff, editor. Hauppauge, N.Y.: Nova Science, c2002. viii, 168 p.
2001-059036   016.947/09/9 21   1590331648
Heads of state -- Soviet Union -- Bibliography. Presidents -- Russia (Federation) -- Bibliography. Russia -- Kings and rulers -- Bibliography. Russia -- Politics and government -- 1689-1801 -- Bibliography. Russia -- Politics and government -- 1801-1917 -- Bibliography. Soviet Union -- Politics and government -- Bibliography. Russia (Federation) -- Politics and government -- 1991- -- Bibliography.

Z2511.U5.W64 1983
Woll, Josephine.
Soviet dissident literature, a critical guide/ Josephine Woll, in collaboration with Vladimir G. Treml. Boston, Mass.: G.K. Hall, c1983. xlviii, 241 p.
83-000056   016.8917   081618626X
Russian literature -- 20th century -- Bibliography. Underground literature -- Soviet Union -- Bibliography. Exiles' writings, Russian -- Bibliography. United States -- Imprints. Europe -- Imprints.

Z2519.6 Europe — Eastern Europe — Ukraine

Z2519.6.W96 2000
Wynar, Bohdan S.
Independent Ukraine: a bibliographic guide to English-language publications, 1989-1999/ Bohdan S. Wynar. Englewood, Colo.: Ukrainian Academic Press, 2000. xiv, 552 p.
99-087124   016.9477   1563086700
Ukraine -- Bibliography.

Z2520 Europe — Eastern Europe — Finland

Z2520.B33 1993
Bako, Elemer.
Finland and the Finns: a selective bibliography/ by Elemer Bako. Washington: Library of Congress, 1993. xvi, 276 p.
93-016151   016.94897   0844407801
Finland -- Bibliography.

Z2526 Europe — Eastern Europe — Poland

Z2526.S26 1993
Sanford, George.
Poland/ George Sanford and Adriana Gozdecka-Sanford, compilers. Oxford; Clio Press, c1993. xxiii, 250 p.
93-190996   016.9438   1851091807
Poland -- Bibliography.

Z2551 Europe — Scandinavia — General bibliography

Z2551.P57 1984
Pitschmann, Louis A.
Scholars' guide to Washington, D.C., for northwest European studies/ Louis A. Pitschmann; consultants, Charles S. Fineman, Robert B. Kvavik. Washington, D.C.: Woodrow Wilson International Center for Scholars: xiv, 436 p.
84-600036   940./07/0753 19   0874747538
Archival resources -- Washington (D.C.) Library resources -- Washington (D.C.) Europe, Northern -- Library resources. Europe -- Library resources. Europe, Northern -- Archival resources. Europe -- Archival resources.

Z2556 Europe — Scandinavia — Icelandic and Old Norse

Z2556.F78
Fry, Donald K.
Norse sagas translated into English: a bibliography/ by Donald K. Fry; foreword by Paul Schach. New York, N.Y.: AMS Press, c1980. xx, 139 p.
79-008632   016.839/6/08   0404180167
Sagas -- Translations into English -- Bibliography. Old Norse literature -- Translations into English -- Bibliography.

Z2561 Europe — Scandinavia — Denmark

Z2561.M55 1987
Miller, Kenneth E., 1926 July 6-5
Denmark/ Kenneth E. Miller, compiler. Oxford, England; Clio Press, c1987. xix, 216 p.
88-149515   016.9489   1851090428
Denmark -- Bibliography.

Z2621 Europe — Scandinavia — Sweden

Z2621.S28 1987
Sather, Leland B.
Sweden/ Leland B. Sather, Alan Swanson, compilers; edited by Hans H. Wellisch. Oxford, England; Clio Press, c1987. xxiv, 370 p.
88-182988   016.9485   1851090355
Sweden -- Bibliography. Sweden -- Bibliography.

Z2691-2700 Europe — Spain and Portugal. Spain

Z2691.A1.Z85 1995
Zubatsky, David S., 1939-
Spanish, Catalan, and Galician literary authors of the eighteenth and nineteenth centuries: an annotated guide to bibliographies/ David S. Zubatsky. Metuchen, N.J.: Scarecrow Press, 1995. 156 p.
94-032155   016.01686/009033   0810829479
Catalan literature -- 16th-18th centuries -- Bibliography of bibliographies. Galician literature -- 18th century -- Bibliography of bibliographies. Spanish literature -- 18th century -- Bibliography of bibliographies.

Z2691.S54 1980
Simon Diaz, Jose.
Manual de bibliografia de la literatura espanola/ [por] Jose Simon Diaz. Madrid: Gredos, 1980. 1156 p.
81-129968   016.86   8424900235
Spanish literature -- Bibliography.

Z2694.D7.H17 2000
Harvell, Tony A., 1952-
Index to twentieth-century Spanish plays: in collections, anthologies, and periodicals/ Tony A. Harvell. Lanham, Md.: Scarecrow Press, 2000. vi, 367 p.
99-046241   016.862/6   0810837293
Spanish drama -- 20th century -- Bibliography. Anthologies -- Indexes.

Z2694.D7.R6 1998
Reynolds, John J., 1924-
Spanish Golden Age drama: an annotated bibliography of United States doctoral dissertations, 1899-1992; with a supplement of non-United States dissertations = El teatro del Siglo de Oro: bibliogr John J. Reynolds, Szilvia E. Szmuk. New York: Modern Language Association of America, 1998. vi, 573 p.
98-010630   016.862/309   0873525701
Spanish drama -- Classical period, 1500-1700 -- History and criticism -- Bibliography. Dissertations, Academic -- United States -- Bibliography.

Z2694.F4.A64 1996
Amell, Samuel.
The contemporary Spanish novel: an annotated, critical bibliography, 1936-1994/ Samuel Amell. Westport, Conn.: Greenwood Press, 1996. 273 p.
95-036085   016.863/609   0313247846
Spanish fiction -- 20th century -- History and criticism -- Bibliography.

Z2695.A2.W66 1997
Woodbridge, Hensley Charles, 1923-
Guide to reference works for the study of the Spanish language and literature and Spanish American literature/ Hensley C. Woodbridge; with three indexes by Elline Long. New York: Modern Language Association of America, 1997. xvi, 236 p.
96-035093   016.46   0873529677
Spanish philology -- Reference books -- Bibliography. Spanish philology -- Bibliography. Spanish American literature -- Reference books -- Bibliography.

Z2700.M66 1994
Monteath, Peter.
The Spanish Civil War in literature, film, and art: an international bibliography of secondary literature/ compiled by Peter Monteath. Westport, Conn.: Greenwood Press, 1994. xxx, 129 p.
94-016070   016.9737   0313292620
Spain -- History -- Civil War, 1936-1939 -- Literature and the war -- Bibliography. Spain -- History -- Civil War, 1936-1939 -- Motion pictures and the war -- Bibliography. Spain -- History -- Civil War, 1936-1939 -- Art and the war -- Bibliography.

Z2721 Europe — Spain and Portugal. Spain — Portugal

Z2721.B43
Bell, Aubrey F. G. 1882-1950.
Portuguese bibliography/ by Aubrey F. G. Bell. [Oxford]: Oxford university press, H. Milford, 1922. 381 p.
23-005763
Portuguese literature -- Bibliography.Portugal -- Bibliography.

Z2721.K86 1994
Kunoff, Hugo.
Portuguese literature from its origins to 1990: a bibliography based on the collections of Indiana University/ compiled by Hugo Kunoff. Metuchen, N.J.: Scarecrow Press, 1994. ix, 497 p.
93-049699   016.869 20   0810828448
Portuguese literature -- Bibliography -- Catalogs.

Z2771 Europe — Switzerland

Z2771.M45 1990
Meier, Heinz K., 1929-1989.
Switzerland/ Heinz K. Meier, Regula A. Meier, compilers. Oxford, England; Clio Press, c1990. xviii, 409 p.
91-121289   016.9494   1851091076
Switzerland -- Bibliography.

Z2896 Europe — Turkey and the Balkan states — Bulgaria

Z2896.C7 1989
Crampton, R. J.
Bulgaria/ Richard J. Crampton, compiler. Oxford, England; Clio Press, c1989. xxxiii, 232 p.
90-182068   016.94977   1851091041
Bulgaria -- Bibliography.

Z2956 Europe — Turkey and the Balkan states — Yugoslavia

Z2956.M38 1998
Matuliâc, Rusko.
Bibliography of sources on the region of former Yugoslavia/ Rusko Matuliâc. Boulder: East European Monographs; viii, 441 p.
98-072877   016.9497 21   0880334029
Yugoslavia -- Bibliography.

Z3001 Asia. Africa. Australia — Asia — General bibliography

Z3001.L47 1999
Library of Congress Asian collections: an illustrated guide. Washington, DC: Library of Congress, 2000. 80 p.
98-047561   026/.95/09753 21   0844409723
Library resources -- Washington (D.C.) Asia -- Library resources.

Z3008 Asia. Africa. Australia — Asia — Special topics, A-Z

Z3008.C55 1996
Lal, Vinay.
South Asian cultural studies: a bibliography/ Vinay Lal. New Delhi: Manohar, 1996. 234 p.
96-904971   016.954   8173041342
Asia, South -- Civilization -- Bibliography.

Z3008.L58.W55 1996
Williams, Mark, 1951-
Post-colonial literatures in English: Southeast Asia, New Zealand, and the Pacific, 1970-1992/ Mark Williams. New York: G.K. Hall, c1996. xxii, 370 p.
95-044859   0816173532
Oriental literature (English) -- Bibliography. Pacific Island literature (English) -- Bibliography. New Zealand literature -- 20th century -- Bibliography.

Z3013-3014 Asia. Africa. Australia — Asia — Middle East. Near East. Arab countries

Z3013.L7 1972
University of London.
Index Islamicus; a catalogue of articles on Islamic subjects in periodicals and other collective publications, compiled by J. D. Pearson, Librarian, with the assistance of Julia F. Ashton. [London] Mansell [1972, c1958] xxxvi, 897 p.
74-153350   016.9156
Islam -- Bibliography. Civilization, Islamic -- Bibliography. Middle East -- Bibliography. Africa, North -- Bibliography.

Z3013.S54 1992
Silverburg, Sanford R.
Middle East bibliography/ by Sanford R. Silverburg. Metuchen, N.J.: Scarecrow Press, 1992. xxxi, 564 p.
91-026074   016.956   0810824698
Middle East -- Bibliography.

Z3014.E85.S77 1992
Strijp, Ruud.
Cultural anthropology of the Middle East: a bibliography/ by Ruud Strijp. Leiden; Brill, 1992-1997 v. 1-2
92-000100   016.306/0956   9004096043
Ethnology -- Middle East -- Bibliography.Middle East -- Social life and customs -- Bibliography.

Z3014.H55.H85 1991
Humphreys, R. Stephen.
Islamic history: a framework for inquiry/ R. Stephen Humphreys. Princeton, N.J.: Princeton University Press, c1991. xiv, 401 p.
90-021268   016.909/097671   0691031452
Islamic Empire -- Bibliography. Islamic Empire -- Historiography.

Z3014.K85 M43 2001
Meho, Lokman I.,
Kurdish culture and society: an annotated bibliography/ compiled by Lokman I. Meho and Kelly L. Maglaughlin. Westport, CT: Greenwood Press, 2001. xv, 365 p.
00-063654   016.305891/597 21   0313315434
Kurds -- Bibliography.

Z3014.K85.M44 1997
Meho, Lokman I., 1968-
The Kurds and Kurdistan: a selective and annotated bibliography/ compiled by Lokman I. Meho. Westport, Conn.: Greenwood Press, 1997. xv, 356 p.
97-009008   016.9566/7   0313303975
Kurds -- Bibliography.Kurdistan -- Bibliography.

Z3014.L56.A52
Anderson, Margaret.
Arabic materials in English translation: a bibliography of works from the pre-Islamic period to 1977/ Margaret Anderson. Boston: G. K. Hall, c1980. viii, 249 p.
79-027708   016.909/04927   0816179549
Arabic literature -- Translations into English -- Bibliography.

Z3014.L56.M35 1998
Makar, Ragai N.
Modern Arabic literature: a bibliography/ Ragai N. Makar . Lanham, Md.: Scarecrow Press, c1998. xiii, 255 p.
98-022136   016.892708006   0810835398
Arabic literature -- 20th century -- History and criticism -- Bibliography. Arabic literature -- 20th century -- Bibliography.

Z3014.R44.B79
Bryson, Thomas A., 1931-
United States/Middle East diplomatic relations, 1784-1978: an annotated bibliography/ by Thomas A. Bryson. Metuchen, N.J.: Scarecrow Press, 1979. xiv, 205 p.
78-026754   016.32756/073   0810811979
Middle East -- Foreign relations -- United States -- Bibliography. United States -- Foreign relations -- Middle East -- Bibliography.

Z3014.R44.P66 1990
Ponko, Vincent.
Britain in the Middle East, 1921-1956: an annotated bibliography/ Vincent Ponko, Jr. New York: Garland Pub., 1990. liv, 513 p.
89-023255   016.30348/241056   0824085515
Middle East -- Relations -- Great Britain -- Bibliography. Great Britain -- Relations -- Middle East -- Bibliography.

Z3028 Asia. Africa. Australia — Asia — Arabia, Saudi Arabia

Z3028.Y39.A93 1998
Auchterlonie, Paul.
Yemen/ Paul Auchterlonie, compiler. Oxford, England; Clio Press, c1998. xxiii, 348 p.
98-137613   016.9533   1851092552
Yemen -- Bibliography.

Z3106-3108 Asia. Africa. Australia — Asia — China

Z3106.G65 Suppl. 2
Shulman, Frank Joseph, 1943-
Doctoral dissertations on China and on inner Asia, 1976-1990: an annotated bibliography of studies in western languages/ compiled and edited by Frank Joseph Shulman, with contributions by Patricia Polansky and Anna Leon Shulman. Westport, Conn.: Greenwood Press, 1998 xxviii, 1055 p.
98-029664 016.951 031329111X
Chinese -- Asia, Southeastern -- Bibliography. Chinese -- United States -- Bibliography. Dissertations, Academic -- Bibliography. Taiwan -- Bibliography. Hong Kong (China) -- Bibliography. China -- Bibliography.

Z3106.W286 1997
Wang, Richard T.
Area bibliography of China/ Richard T. Wang. Lanham, Md.: Scarecrow Press, 1997. xiii, 334 p.
97-019185 016.951 0810833506
China -- Bibliography.

Z3016.Z87 1995
Zurndorfer, Harriet Thelma.
China bibliography: a research guide to reference works about China past and present/ by Harriet T. Zurndorfer. Leiden; E.J. Brill, 1995. xiv, 380 p.
95-000203 016.951 9004102787
China -- Reference books -- Bibliography.

Z3107.T5.P55 1991
Pinfold, John.
Tibet/ John Pinfold, compiler. Oxford, England; Clio Press, c1991. xxvi, 158 p.
92-122704 016.951/5 1851091580
Tibet (China) -- Bibliography.

Z3108.A5.C37 1999
Chang, Tony H., 1951-
China during the cultural revolution, 1966-1976: a selected bibliography of English language works/ compiled by Tony H. Chang. Westport, Conn.: Greenwood Press, 1999. x, 199 p.
98-044393 016.95105 0313309051
English imprints.China -- History -- Cultural Revolution, 1966-1976 -- Bibliography.

Z3108.L5.I53 1986
The Indiana companion to traditional Chinese literature/ William H. Nienhauser, Jr., editor and compiler, Charles Hartman, associate editor for poetry, Y.W. Ma, associate editor for fiction, Stephen H. West, associate editor for drama. Bloomington: Indiana University Press, c1986-c1998. 2 v.
83-049651 895.1/09 0253329833
Chinese literature -- Bio-bibliography. Chinese literature -- History and criticism.

Z3108.L5.L67 1991
Lopez, Manuel D.
Chinese drama = Chung-kuo hsi chu: an annotated bibliography of commentary, criticism, and plays in English translation/ by Manuel D. Lopez. Metuchen, N.J.: Scarecrow Press, 1991. ix, 525 p.
91-015902 016.8951/2008 0810823470
Chinese drama -- Translations into English -- Bibliography. Chinese drama -- History and criticism -- Bibliography.

Z3116 Asia. Africa. Australia — Asia — Taiwan

Z3116.L44 1990
Lee, Wei-chin, 1956-
Taiwan/ Wei-chin Lee, compiler. Oxford, England; Clio Press, c1990. xxxiv, 247 p.
90-206517 016.95124/9 1851090916
Taiwan -- Bibliography.

Z3121 Asia. Africa. Australia — Asia — Mongolian People's Republic. Outer Mongolia

Z3121.N674 1993
Nordby, Judith.
Mongolia/ Judith Nordby, compiler. Oxford, England; Clio Press, c1993. xxix, 192 p.
93-247427 016.9517/3 1851091297
Mongolia -- Bibliography.

Z3185-3216 Asia. Africa. Australia — Asia — Indian subcontinent. South Asia

Z3185.C3
Case, Margaret H.
South Asian history, 1750-1950; a guide to periodicals, dissertations, and newspapers [by] Margaret H. Case. Princeton, N.J., Princeton University Press, 1968. xiii, 561 p.
67-021019 016.954
South Asia -- History -- Bibliography.

Z3196.L66 1998
Long, Roger D.
The founding of Pakistan: an annotated bibliography/ Roger D. Long. Lanham, Md.: Scarecrow Press; 1998. xv, 327 p.
98-030089 016.95491035 0810835576
Pakistan -- History -- Bibliography.

Z3206.D47 1995
Derbyshire, Ian.
India/ Ian D. Derbyshire, compiler. Oxford, England; Clio Press, c1995. xxx, 356 p.
96-192289 016.954 1851092005
India -- Bibliography.

Z3206.R5 1989
Riddick, John F.
Glimpses of India: an annotated bibliography of published personal writings by Englishmen, 1583-1947/ compiled by John F. Riddick. New York: Greenwood Press, 1989. xvi, 195 p.
88-037582 016.954 0313256616
India -- History -- 1526-1765 -- Bibliography. India -- History -- British occupation, 1765-1947 -- Bibliography.

Z3207.P8.T37 1995
Tatla, Darshan Singh.
Punjab/ Darshan Singh Tatla, Ian Talbot, compilers. Oxford, England; Clio Press, c1995. xlix, 323 p.
96-192648 016.954/552 1851092323
Punjab (India) -- Bibliography. Punjab (Pakistan) -- Bibliography.

Z3208.A8
Ridinger, Robert B. Marks, 1951-
The archaeology of the Indian subcontinent and Sri Lanka: a selected bibliography/ Robert B. Marks Ridinger. Westport, CT: Greenwood Press, 2001. viii, 265 p.
00-042673 016.934 0313300011
Excavations (Archaeology) -- India -- Bibliography. Excavations (Archaeology) -- Sri Lanka -- Bibliography. Excavations (Archaeology) -- South Asia -- Bibliography. India -- Antiquities -- Bibliography. South Asia -- Antiquities -- Bibliography. Sri Lanka -- Antiquities -- Bibliography.

Z3216.H47 1991
Herbert, Patricia M.
Burma/ Patricia M. Herbert, compiler. Oxford, England; Clio Press, c1991. xxiv, 327 p.
92-146756 1851090886
Burma -- Bibliography.

Z3221-3296 Asia. Africa. Australia — Asia — Southeastern Asia

Z3221.D35 1993
Dalby, Andrew, 1947-
South East Asia: a guide to reference material/ Andrew Dalby. London; Hans Zell Publishers, 1993. xiv, 302 p.
93-007674 016.959 1873836007
Asia, Southeastern -- Bibliography.

Z3221.K46 1998
Kemp, Herman C.
Bibliographies on Southeast Asia/ compiled by Herman C. Kemp. Leiden, The Netherlands: KITLV Press, 1998. xvii, 1128 p.
99-181886 9067181218
Asia, Southeastern -- Bibliography.

Z3221.S6747 1996
Southeast Asian languages and literatures: a bibliographical guide to Burmese, Cambodian, Indonesian, Javanese, Malay, Minangkabau, Thai and Vietnamese/ edited by E. Ulrich Kratz. London; I.B. Tauris, 1996. xvi, 455 p.
96-060445 016.495 1860641148
Southeast Asian literature -- Bibliography.Asia, Southeastern -- Languages -- Bibliography.

Z3226.M39 1992
Marr, David G.
Vietnam/ David G. Marr, compiler; with the assistance of Kristine Alilunas-Rodgers. Oxford, England; Clio Press, c1992. lxxviii, 393 p.
93-223446 016.9597 1851090924
Vietnam -- Bibliography.

Z3226.S56 1997
Singleton, Carl.
Vietnam studies: an annotated bibliography/ Carl Singleton. Lanham, Md.: Scarecrow Press, 1997. xx, 303 p.
97-000666 016.9597 0810833174
Vietnam -- Bibliography.

Z3228.V5.B87 1984
Burns, Richard Dean.
The wars in Vietnam, Cambodia, and Laos, 1945-1982: a bibliographic guide/ Richard Dean Burns and Milton Leitenberg. Santa Barbara, Calif.: ABC-Clio Information Services, c1984. xxxii, 290 p.
80-013246   016.959704/3   0874363101
Vietnamese Conflict, 1961-1975 -- Bibliography.Indochina -- History -- 1945- -- Bibliography. Indochina -- History, Military -- Bibliography.

Z3232.J37 1997
Jarvis, Helen.
Cambodia/ Helen Jarvis, compiler. Oxford, England; Clio Press, c1997. lxiv, 412 p.
98-128797   016.9596   1851091777
Cambodia -- Bibliography.

Z3233.C67 1991
Cordell, Helen.
Laos/ Helen Cordell, compiler. Oxford, England; Clio Press, c1991. xxxvi, 215 p.
92-146773   016.9594   1851090754
Laos -- Bibliography.

Z3236.W371986
Watts, Michael, 1918-
Thailand/ Michael Watts, compiler. Oxford: Clio, c1986. xli, 275 p.
85-046126   016.9593   1851090088
Thailand -- Bibliography.

Z3246.B76 1999
Ooi, Keat Gin, 1959-
Malaysia/ Ooi Keat Gin, compiler. Oxford, England; Clio Press, c1999. xlviii, 435 p.
1851093117
Malaysia -- Bibliography.

Z3271.L53 1996
Library of Congress.
Unveiling Indonesia: Indonesian holdings in the Library of Congress: a bibliography/ compiled by A. Kohar Rony. Washington, DC: The Library, 1996. 2 v.
95-035869   016.9598   0844408778
Indonesia -- Bibliography -- Catalogs.

Z3285.Q33 1988
Quah, Stella R.
Singapore/ Stella R. Quah, Jon S.T. Quah, compilers. Oxford, England; Clio Press, c1988. xv, 258 p.
90-156512   016.95957   1851090711
Singapore -- Bibliography.

Z3296.R53 1989
Richardson, Jim.
Philippines/ Jim Richardson, compiler. Oxford, England; Clio Press, c1989. xxx, 372 p.
90-156552   016.9599   1851090770
Philippines -- Bibliography.

Z3301-3308 Asia. Africa. Australia — Asia — Japan

Z3301.J36 1992
Japanese studies from pre-History to 1990: a bibliographical guide/ compiled by Richard Perren. Manchester; Manchester University Press: c1992. x, 172 p.
91-037386   016.952   0719024587
Japan -- Bibliography.

Z3301.M32 1994
Makino, Yasuko.
A student guide to Japanese sources in the humanities/ Yasuko Makino and Masaei Saito. Ann Arbor, Mich.: Center for Japanese Studies, University of Michigan, 1994. ix, 155 p.
93-034031   016.952   0939512645
Japan -- Bibliography. Japan -- Study and teaching -- Handbooks, manuals, etc.

Z3301.S55
Silberman, Bernard S., 1930-
Japan and Korea; a critical bibliography. Tucson, University of Arizona Press, 1962. xiv, 120 p.
62-011821   016.95
Korea -- Bibliography. Japan -- Bibliography.

Z3306.D69 1995
Dower, John W.
Japanese history and culture from ancient to modern times: seven basic bibliographies/ John W. Dower, with Timothy S. George. Princeton: Markus Wiener Publishers, 1995. xi, 459 p.
94-048170   016.952   1558760970
Japan -- History -- Bibliography.

Z3306.K86 1997
Koopmans-de Bruijn, Ria, 1955-
Area bibliography of Japan/ Ria Koopmans-de Bruijn. Lanham, Md.: Scarecrow Press, 1998. xvii, 297 p.
97-037522   016.952   0810833743
Japan -- Bibliography.

Z3308.L5.A44 1982
Algarin, Joanne P.
Japanese folk literature: a core collection and reference guide/ Joanne P. Algarin. New York: R.R. Bowker, 1982. xiv, 226 p.
82-009672   016.3982/0952   0835215164
Folk literature, Japanese -- History and criticism -- Bibliography.

Z3308.L5.M34 1989
Mamola, Claire Zebroski, 1941-
Japanese women writers in English translation: an annotated bibliography/ Claire Zebroski Mamola. New York: Garland, 1989-1992. 2 v.
89-001319   016.8956/08/09287   0824030486
Japanese literature -- Women authors -- Translations into English -- Bibliography. Women and literature -- Japan -- Bibliography.

Z3316-3317 Asia. Africa. Australia — Asia — Korea

Z3316.E36 1998
Edwards, Paul M.
The Korean War: an annotated bibliography/ compiled by Paul M. Edwards. Westport, Conn.: Greenwood Press, 1998. x, 346 p.
97-040189   016.951904/2   0313303177
Korean War, 1950-1953 -- Bibliography.

Z3317.W55 2000
Wilson, Myoung Chung.
Korean government publications: an introductory guide/ Myoung Chung Wilson. Lanham, Md.: Scarecrow Press, 2000. xi, 192 p.
99-053422   070.5/95/09519   0810837110
Government publications -- Korea (South) Government publications -- Korea (North) Government publications -- Korea.

Z3366 Asia. Africa. Australia — Asia — Iran

Z3366.G36 1989
Gardner, J. Anthony.
The Iraq-Iran war: a bibliography/ J. Anthony Gardner. Boston, Mass.: G.K. Hall, 1989, c1988. xvi, 124 p.
88-010033   016.955/054   0816189978
Iran-Iraq War, 1980-1988 -- Bibliography.

Z3366.N37 1988
Navabpour, Reza.
Iran/ Reza Navabpour, compiler. Oxford, England; Clio Press, c1988. xviii, 308 p.
88-144739   016.955   1851090363
Iran -- Bibliography.

Z3461 Asia. Africa. Australia — Asia — Armenia

Z3461.V38 1993
Vassilian, Hamo B., 1952-
The Armenians: a colossal bibliographic guide to books published in the English language/ Hamo B. Vassilian, editor. Glendale, Calif.: Armenian Reference Books Co., c1993. 206 p.
93-026487   016.95662   093153903X
Armenians -- Foreign countries -- Bibliography. English imprints. Armenia -- Bibliography.

Z3478 Asia. Africa. Australia — Asia — Israel

Z3478.J4.P87 1988
Purvis, James D.
Jerusalem, the Holy City: a bibliography/ by James D. Purvis. [St. Meinrad, Ind.]: The American Theological Library Association; 1988-1991. 2 v.
87-004758   016.95694/4   0810819996
Jerusalem -- Bibliography.

Z3483 Asia. Africa. Australia — Asia — Syria

Z3483.L4.K48 1991
Bleaney, C. H.
Lebanon/ C.H. Bleaney, compiler. Oxford, England; Clio Press, c1991. xxxi, 230 p.
92-190447   1851091505
Lebanon -- Bibliography.

Z3499 Asia. Africa. Australia — Indian Ocean region — General bibliography

Z3499.G67 1988
Gotthold, Julia J.
Indian Ocean/ Julia J. Gotthold, compiler with the assistance of Donald W. Gotthold. Oxford, England; Clio Press, c1988. xxix, 329 p.
88-141457   016.909/09824   1851090347
Indian Ocean Region -- Bibliography.

Z3501 Asia. Africa. Australia — Africa — General bibliography

Z3501.K15 1998
Kagan, Alfred.
Reference guide to Africa: a bibliography of sources/ Alfred Kagan and Yvette Scheven. Lanham, Md.: Scarecrow Press, 1998. viii, 262 p.
98-041158   016.96   0810835851
Africa -- Bibliography.

Z3501.W57
Witherell, Julian W.
The United States and Africa: guide to U.S. official documents and government-sponsored publications on Africa, 1785-1975/ compiled by Julian W. Witherell. Washington: Library of Congress: [for sale by the Supt. of Docs., U.S. Govt. Print. Off.] 1978. xix, 949 p.
78-001051   016.96   0844402613
Catalogs, Union -- United States. Government publications -- United States -- Bibliography -- Union lists. Africa -- Bibliography -- Union lists.

Z3503 Asia. Africa. Australia — Africa — Periodicals

Z3503.A34
Africa bibliography.   Manchester, England; Manchester University Press, [c1985-   ]
86-656067   016.96
Africa -- Bibliography -- Periodicals.

Z3504 Asia. Africa. Australia — Africa — Societies. Institutions

Z3504.O743.H37 1994
Harris, Gordon.
Organization of African Unity/ Gordon Harris, compiler. New Brunswick, N.J., U.S.A.: Transaction Publishers, c1994. xxxii, 139 p.
93-042579   016.34124/9   1560001534
African unity -- Bibliography.

Z3508 Asia. Africa. Australia — Africa — Special topics, A-Z

Z3508.H5.C66 1995
Cook, Chris, 1945-
The making of modern Africa: a guide to archives/ compiled by Chris Cook. New York: Facts on File, c1995. v, 218 p.
88-024397   016.96   081602071X
Africa -- History -- Archival resources -- Directories.

Z3508.L5 L562 1989
Lindfors, Bernth.
Black African literature in English, 1982-1986/ Bernth Lindfors. London; Hans Zell Publishers, 1989. xxviii, 444 p.
89-007537   820.9/896 20   0905450752
African literature (English) -- Black authors -- History and criticism Blacks -- Africa -- Intellectual life -- Bibliography. Blacks in literature -- Bibliography.

Z3508.L5.L563 1995
Lindfors, Bernth.
Black African literature in English, 1987-1991/ Bernth Lindfors. London; Hans Zell Publishers, 1995. xxxv, 682 p.
97-189537   820.9/896   1873836163
African literature (English) -- Black authors -- History and criticism -- Bibliography. Blacks -- Africa -- Intellectual life -- Bibliography. Blacks in literature -- Bibliography.

Z3508.P35.W55 1993
Williams, Michael W.
Pan-Africanism: an annotated bibliography/ Michael W. Williams. Pasadena, CA: Salem Press, 1993. ix, 142 p.
92-031354   016.3205/4/09174927
0893566748
Pan-Africanism -- Bibliography.Africa -- Politics and government -- Bibliography.

Z3509 Asia. Africa. Australia — Africa — Catalogs

Z3509.B87 2000
Burg, Barbara A.
Guide to African American and African primary sources at Harvard University/ Barbara A. Burg, Richard Newman, Elizabeth E. Sandager; with a foreword by Henry Louis Gates, Jr. Phoenix, Ariz.: Oryx Press, 2000. ix, 217 p.
00-009480   016.96   1573563390
African Americans -- History -- Sources -- Bibliography -- Catalogs. African Americans -- History -- Manuscripts -- Catalogs. Africa -- Bibliography -- Catalogs. Africa -- Manuscripts -- Catalogs. Africa -- History -- Sources -- Bibliography -- Catalogs.

Z3515 Asia. Africa. Australia — Africa — North Africa

Z3515.S57 2000
Skreslet, Paula Youngman.
Northern Africa: a guide to reference and information sources/ Paula Youngman Skreslet. Englewood, Colo.: Libraries Unlimited, 2000. xv, 405 p.
00-040543   016.961   1563086840
Africa, North -- Reference books -- Bibliography. Africa, North -- Electronic information resources. Africa, Northwest -- Reference books -- Bibliography.

Z3516 Asia. Africa. Australia — Africa — East Africa

Z3516.B55 1996
Blackhurst, Hector.
East and Northeast Africa bibliography/ Hector Blackhurst. Lanham, Md.: Scarecrow Press, c1996. xiv, 301 p.
95-040627   016.9676   0810830906
Africa, East -- Bibliography. Africa, Northeast -- Bibliography.

Z3517 Asia. Africa. Australia — Africa — Central Africa

Z3517.H37 1999
Harris, Gordon, 1946-
Central and Equatorial Africa area bibliography/ Gordon Harris. Lanham, Md.: Scarecrow Press, 1999. xli, 209 p.
98-050932   016.967   0810836068
Africa, Central -- Bibliography. Chad -- Bibliography.

Z3521 Asia. Africa. Australia — Africa — Ethiopia. Abyssinia

Z3521.M86 1995
Munro-Hay, S. C. 1947-
Ethiopia/ Stuart Munro-Hay, Richard Pankhurst, compilers. Oxford, England; Clio Press, c1995. xxxiii, 225 p.
96-192570   016.963   1851091114
Ethiopia -- Bibliography.

Z3559-3608 Asia. Africa. Australia — Africa — British Africa

Z3559.W57 1992
Wiseman, John A.
Botswana/ John A. Wiseman, compiler. Oxford, Eng.; Clio Press, c1992. xxvii, 187 p.
93-190918   016.96883   1851091718
Botswana -- Bibliography.

Z3577.D43 1995
Decalo, Samuel.
Malawi/ Samuel Decalo, compiler. Oxford, England; Clio Press, c1995. xxix, 188 p.
96-192626   016.96897
Malawi -- Bibliography.

Z3586.J36 1992
Jamison, Martin.
Idi Amin and Uganda: an annotated bibliography/ compiled by Martin Jamison. Westport, Conn.: Greenwood Press, c1992. xix, 145 p.
92-027746   016.96761   0313272735
Amin, Idi, -- 1925- -- Bibliography.Uganda -- Politics and government -- 1971-1979 -- Bibliography.

Z3597.M94 1989
Myers, Robert A.
Nigeria/ Robert A. Myers, compiler. Oxford, England; Clio Press, c1989. xxxii, 462 p.
90-156542   016.9669   1851090835
Nigeria -- Bibliography.

Z3601.A1.M9 1996
Musiker, Reuben.
South African bibliography: a survey of bibliographies and bibliographical work/ Reuben Musiker. London; Mansell, 1996. xvii, 142 p.
96-001956   016/.016968   0720122252
Bibliography, National -- South Africa.South Africa -- Bibliography of bibliographies.

Z3608.A5.S35 1996
Schoeman, Elna.
Mandela's five years of freedom: South African politics, economics and social issues, 1990-1995: a select and annotated bibliography/ compiled by Elna Schoeman, Jacqueline A. Kalley and Naomi Musiker. Johannesburg: South African Institute of International Affairs, 1996. viii, 770 p.
96-220361   016.96806   1874890625
South Africa -- Politics and government -- 1989-1994 -- Bibliography. South Africa -- Economic conditions -- 1991- -- Bibliography. South Africa -- Social conditions -- 1961- -- Bibliography.

Z3608.R3.P93 1990
Pyatt, Sherman E.
Apartheid: a selective annotated bibliography, 1979-1987/ Sherman E. Pyatt. New York: Garland Pub., 1990. xix, 169 p.
89-007710   016.3058/00968   0824076370
Apartheid -- South Africa -- Bibliography.South Africa -- Race relations -- Bibliography.

Z3631 Asia. Africa. Australia — Africa — Zaire. Congo (Democratic Republic). Belgian Congo

Z3631.W55 1995
Bastian, Dawn E. 1961-
Zaire/ Dawn Bastian Williams, Robert W. Lesh and Andrea L. Stamm. Oxford, England; Clio Press, c1995. xxxii, 268 p.
95-194520   016.96751   1851092188
Zaire -- Imprints. Zaire -- Bibliography.

Z3651 Asia. Africa. Australia — Africa — Egypt

Z3651.M34 1988
Makar, Ragai N.
Egypt/ Ragai N. Makar, compiler. Oxford, England; Clio Press, c1988. xxxi, 306 p.
88-141487   016.962   1851090398
Egypt -- Bibliography.

Z3707 Asia. Africa. Australia — Africa — French Africa

Z3707.D86 1998
Dunton, Chris.
Nigerian theatre in English: a critical bibliography/ Chris Dunton. London; Hans Zell Publishers, 1998. ix, 366 p.
97-038650   016.822008/09669
Nigerian drama (English) -- History and criticism -- Bibliography. Nigerian drama (English) -- Bibliography. Nigeria -- In literature -- Bibliography.

Z3707.Z36 1994
Zamponi, Lynda F.
Niger/ Lynda F. Zamponi, compiler. Oxford, England; Clio Press, c1994. xl, 233 p.
95-114746   016.96626   1851092048
Niger -- Bibliography.

Z3721 Asia. Africa. Australia — Africa — Rwanda

Z3721.F44 1993
Fegley, Randall, 1955-
Rwanda/ Randall Fegley, compiler. Oxford, England; Clio Press, c1993. xxxvi, 161 p.
94-159618   016.967571   1851092021
Rwanda -- Bibliography.

Z3785 Asia. Africa. Australia — Africa — Ghana

Z3785.M94 1991
Myers, Robert A.
Ghana/ Robert A. Myers, compiler. Oxford, England; Clio Press, c1991. xxvii, 436 p.
92-146703   1851091351
Ghana -- Bibliography.

Z3881 Asia. Africa. Australia — Africa — Mozambique

Z3881.D37 1987
Darch, Colin.
Mozambique/ compiler, Colin Darch, with the assistance of Calisto Pacheleke, in association with the Centro de Estudos Africanos, Universidade Eduardo Mondlane. Oxford, England; Clio Press, c1987. xxvi, 360 p.
88-144644   016.9679   1851090258
Mozambique -- Bibliography.

Z3971 Asia. Africa. Australia — Africa — Libya

Z3971.L39 1987
Lawless, Richard I.
Libya/ Richard I. Lawless, compiler. Oxford, England; Clio Press, c1987. xxi, 243 p.
88-149408   016.961/2   1851090339
Libya -- Bibliography.

Z4001 Asia. Africa. Australia — Australia. Oceania — General bibliography

Z4001.T48 1997
Thawley, John, 1953-
Australasia and South Pacific islands bibliography/ John Thawley. Lanham, Md.: Scarecrow Press, 1997. xvii, 587 p.
96-034683   016.99   0810832402
Oceania -- Bibliography. Australia -- Bibliography. Australasia -- Bibliography.

Z4011-4311 Asia. Africa. Australia — Australia. Oceania — Australia

Z4011.K46 1984
Kepars, I.
Australia/ I. Kepars, compiler. Oxford, England; Clio Press, c1984. xvii, 289 p.
84-232073   016.994   0903450836
Australia -- Bibliography.

Z4021.H66 1992
Hooton, Joy W.
Annals of Australian literature/ Joy Hooton & Harry Heseltine. Melbourne; Oxford University Press, 1992. viii, 367 p.
93-168304   016.8208/0994   0195534751
Australian literature -- Bibliography. Australian literature -- Chronology.

Z4021.L48 1996
Lever, Richard.
Post-colonial literatures in English: Australia, 1970-1992/ Richard Lever, James Wieland, and Scott Findlay. New York: G.K. Hall; c1996. xxx, 361 p.
95-044820   016.8209/994   0816173753
Australian literature -- History and criticism -- Bibliography.Australia -- In literature -- Bibliography.

Z4023.5.W6.A34 1988
Adelaide, Debra.
Australian women writers: a bibliographical guide/ Debra Adelaide. London: Pandora, 1988. xiv, 208 p.
89-140014   820.9/9287   0863581498
Australian literature -- Women authors -- Bio-bibliography. Women authors, Australian -- Biography -- Dictionaries. Women and literature -- Australia -- Bibliography.

Z4311.K46 1997
Kepars, I.
Tasmania/ I. Kepars, compiler. Oxford; Clio Press, c1997. xx, 164 p.
97-180601   016.9946   1851092730
Tasmania -- Bibliography.

Z4501-4891 Asia. Africa. Australia — Australia. Oceania — Oceania

Z4501.A87 1996
Austin, Mary C.
Literature for children and young adults about Oceania: analysis and annotated bibliography with additional readings for adults/ Mary C. Austin and Esther C. Jenkins; with the assistance of Carol A. Jenkins. Westport, Conn.: Greenwood Press, 1996. xxii, 326 p.
95-024515   016.995   0313266433
Oceania -- Juvenile literature -- Bibliography.

Z4501.S76 1999
Storie, Monique Carriveau.
Micronesia/ Monique Carriveau Storie and William L. Wuerch, compilers. Oxford, England; Clio Press, c1999. lxviii, 215 p.
   1851092897
Micronesia -- Bibliography.

Z4701.F67 1998
Forbes, David W.
Hawaiian national bibliography, 1780-1900/ compiled and annotated by David W. Forbes. Honolulu: University of Hawai'i Press, [1998-] v. 1
98-042455   016.9969   0824820428
Hawaii -- Bibliography.

Z4701.M67 1992
Morris, Nancy Jane.
Hawaii/ Nancy J. Morris and Love Dean, compilers. Oxford, England; Clio Press, c1992. xxxv, 324 p.
93-188118   016.9969
Hawaii -- Bibliography.

Z4708.E85.K57 1985
Kittelson, David J.
The Hawaiians: an annotated bibliography/ by David J. Kittelson. Honolulu: Social Science Research Institute, University of of Hawaii, 1985. xi, 384 p.
83-051207   016.9969   082480919X
Hawaiians -- Bibliography.

Z4811.M28 1988
McConnell, Fraiser, 1951-
Papua New Guinea/ Fraiser McConnell, compiler. Oxford, England; Clio Press, c1988. xxviii, 378 p.
89-103632   016.9953   1851090304
Papua New Guinea -- Bibliography.

Z4891.H83 1997
Hughes, H. G. A.
Samoa: American Samoa, Western Samoa, Samoans abroad/ H.G.A. Hughes. Oxford, England; Clio Press, c1997. lxxxix, 342 p.
96-191888   016.9961/3   1851092536
Samoan Islands -- Bibliography.

Z5052-7991 Subject bibliography

Z5052 Academies. Societies. Universities. Museums — Museums — General bibliography

Z5052.M93 1990
The Museum: a reference guide/ edited by Michael Steven Shapiro, with the assistance of Louis Ward Kemp. New York: Greenwood Press, 1990. xiv, 385 p.
89-026022   016.069   0313236860
Museums -- Bibliography. Museums -- History.

Z5065 Aerospace technology — By region or country, A-Z

Z5065.U5.G83 1994
Gubert, Betty Kaplan, 1934-
Invisible wings: an annotated bibliography on Blacks in aviation, 1916-1993/ compiled by Betty Kaplan Gubert. Westport, Conn.: Greenwood Press, 1994. xx, 274 p.
93-037180   016.6291/08996073   0313285535
Afro-Americans in aeronautics -- United States -- Bibliography. Afro-Americans in aeronautics -- United States -- History.

Z5071 Agriculture — General bibliography

Z5071.H87 1994
Hurt, R. Douglas.
The history of agricultural science and technology: an international annotated bibliography/ R. Douglas Hurt, Mary Ellen Hurt. New York: Garland Pub., 1994. xiii, 485 p.
93-028006   016.63/09   0824071824
Agriculture -- History -- Bibliography. Agriculture -- Bibliography.

Z5074 Agriculture — Special topics, A-Z

Z5074.S75.W44 1994
The spice trade: a bibliographic guide to sources of historical and economic information/ compiled by Jeanie M. Welch. Westport, Conn.: Greenwood Press, c1994. x, 188 p.
94-022863   016.3801/41383   0313291179
Spice trade -- Bibliography

Z5075 Agriculture — Local, A-Z

Z5075.G8.R64 1994
Agriculture in Britain and America, 1660-1820: an annotated bibliography of the eighteenth-century literature/ compiled by Samuel J. Rogal. Westport, Conn.: Greenwood Press, 1994. viii, 266 p.
94-012323   016.630/941   031329352X
Agriculture -- Great Britain -- Bibliography. Agriculture -- United States -- Bibliography. Agriculture -- Great Britain -- Early works to 1800 -- Bibliography.

Z5075.U5.R63 1989
Rogers, Earl M.
The American farm crisis: an annotated bibliography/ Earl M. Rogers and Susan H. Rogers. New York: Garland Pub., 1989. xii, 149 p.
89-031667   016.3381/0973   082407243X
Agriculture -- Economic aspects -- United States -- Bibliography. Farms -- United States -- Bibliography. Farms, Small -- United States -- Bibliography.

Z5111 Anthropology and ethnology — General bibliography

Z5111.K53 1991
Kibbee, Josephine Z., 1950-
Cultural anthropology: a guide to reference and information sources/ Josephine Z. Kibbee. Englewood, Colo.: Libraries Unlimited, 1991. xxi, 205 p.
91-014042   016.301   0872877396
Anthropology -- Reference books -- Bibliography. Anthropology -- Bibliography.

Z5111.W47 1994
Westerman, R. C.
Fieldwork in the library: a guide to research in anthropology and related area studies/ R.C. Westerman. Chicago: American Library Association, 1994. xvi, 357 p.
94-005684   016.301   083890632X
Anthropology -- Reference books -- Bibliography. Anthropology -- Research. Anthropology -- Bibliography.

Z5113 Anthropology and ethnology — Local — Africa

Z5113.D47 2001
Desai, Gaurav Gajanan.
Subject to colonialism: African self-fashioning and the colonial library/ by Gaurav Desai. Durham, NC: Duke University Press, c2001. xii, 197 p.
00-010753   301/.096   0822326353
Anthropology -- Africa -- Bibliography. Africa -- Colonial influence. Africans -- Ethnic identity.

Z5115 Anthropology and ethnology — Local — Asia

Z5115.K4 1962
Kennedy, Raymond, 1906-1950.
Bibliography of Indonesian peoples and cultures. Rev. and edited by Thomas W. Maretzki and H. Th. Fischer. [New Haven] Southeast Asia Studies, Yale University, by arrangement with Human Relations Area Files, 1962. xxii, 207 p.
62-020539   016.572991
Ethnology -- Indonesia -- Bibliography.

Z5118 Anthropology and ethnology — Special topics, A-Z

Z5118.A54.V37 1991
Van Willigen, John.
Anthropology in use: a source book on anthropological practice/ John van Willigen. Boulder: Westview Press, 1991. viii, 254 p.
90-025495   016.301   0813382505
Applied anthropology -- Bibliography. Applied anthropology -- History -- Chronology.

Z5118.A6.R5 1993
Ridinger, Robert B. Marks, 1951-
African archaeology: a selected bibliography/ Robert B. Marks Ridinger. New York: G.K. Hall; c1993. viii, 311 p.
92-007760   016.96   0816190860
Prehistoric peoples -- Africa -- Bibliography. Antiquities, Prehistoric -- Africa -- Bibliography. Archaeology -- Africa -- Bibliography. Africa -- Antiquities -- Bibliography.

Z5118.F58.F73
Freedman, Robert L., 1941-
Human food uses: a cross-cultural, comprehensive annotated bibliography/ compiled by Robert L. Freedman. Westport, Conn.: Greenwood Press, c1981. xxxvii, 552 p.
81-000469   016.3941   0313229015
Food habits -- Bibliography. Diet -- Bibliography.

Z5131 Archaeology — General bibliography

Z5131.H36 1994
Hand, Richard A., 1941-
A bookman's guide to archaeology: a compilation of over 7,000 books pertaining to the scientific study of prehistoric and historic people .../ Richard A. Hand. Metuchen, N.J.: Scarecrow Press, 1994. xii, 1022 p.
94-345523 016.9301 0810829460
Archaeology -- Bibliography.

Z5133 Archaeology — Special topics, A-Z

Z5133.U53.K47 1991
Kerber, Jordan E., 1957-
Coastal and maritime archaeology: a bibliography/ Jordan E. Kerber. Metuchen, N.J.: Scarecrow Press, 1991. viii, 400 p.
91-025506 016.9301/028/04 0810824655
Underwater archaeology -- Bibliography. Coastal archaeology -- Bibliography. Kitchen-middens -- Bibliography. North America -- Antiquities -- Bibliography.

Z5140 Archives. Records

Z5140.M45 1996
McIlwaine, John.
Writings on African archives/ John McIlwaine; with an essay by Anne Thurston and contributions by Pino Akotia & Justus Wamukoya. London ;[New Providence, N.J.]: Hans Zell Publishers, 1996. xviii, 279 p.
96-002089 016.02756 187383666X
Archives -- Africa -- Bibliography.

Z5165 Authorship (General)

Z5165.P83 1993
Publication peer review: an annotated bibliography/ compiled by Bruce W. Speck. Westport, Conn.: Greenwood Press, c1993. viii, 277 p.
92-042695 016.0704/1 0313288925
Editing -- Bibliography. Journalism -- Editing -- Bibliography. Peer review -- Bibliography.

Z5165.S67 1991
Speck, Bruce W.
Editing: an annotated bibliography/ Bruce W. Speck. New York: Greenwood Press, 1991. x, 295 p.
90-029290 016.808/02 0313268606
Editing -- Bibliography. Manuscript preparation (Authorship) -- Bibliography. Publishers and publishing -- Bibliography.

Z5170 Automobiles. Automobile travel. Motor vehicles — General bibliography

Z5170.C43 1994
Chao, Sheau-yueh J.
The Japanese automobile industry: an annotated bibliography/ compiled by Sheau-yueh J. Chao. Westport, Conn.: Greenwood Press, 1994. xviii, 188 p.
93-035797 016.3384/76292/0952 0313286787
Automobile industry and trade -- Japan -- Bibliography.

Z5301 Biography. Genealogy. Heraldry — General bibliography

Z5301.A82 1998
ARBA guide to biographical resources, 1986-1997/ Robert L. Wick and Terry Ann Mood, editors. Englewood, Colo.: Libraries Unlimited, 1998. xxxiv, 604 p.
98-039503 016.92 1563084538
Biography -- Dictionaries -- Bibliography.

Z5301.B96 2001
Burt, Daniel S.
The biography book: a reader's guide to nonfiction, fictional, and film biographies of more than 500 of the most fascinating individuals of all time/ Daniel S. Burt. Westport, CT: Oryx Press, 2001. vi, 629 p.
00-010116 016.92 1573562564
Biography -- Bibliography.

Z5304 Biography. Genealogy. Heraldry — By class, A-Z

Z5304.A8.F46 1996
Feminist writers/ editor, Pamela Kester-Shelton; foreword by Hortense Spillers. Detroit: St. James Press, c1996. xxiii, 641 p.
96-025679 016.30542 1558622179
Authors -- Bio-bibliography. Feminists -- Bio-bibliography. Feminism and literature -- Bio-bibliography.

Z5304.C44.R47 1992
Research guide to European historical biography, 1450-present/ [editor, James A. Moncure]. Washington, D.C.: Beacham Pub., 1992-c1993. 8 v.
92-008935 016.92004 093383330X
Celebrities -- Europe -- Biography. Celebrities -- Europe -- Biography -- Bibliography. Europe -- History -- Bio-bibliography.

Z5305 Biography. Genealogy. Heraldry — By region or country, A-Z

Z5305.G7.O94 1989
Owen, Dolores B.
Guide to genealogical resources in the British Isles/ by Dolores B. Owen. Metuchen, N.J.: Scarecrow Press, 1989. x, 399 p.
88-022574 929/.1/02541 0810821532
Great Britain -- Genealogy -- Archival resources. Great Britain -- Genealogy -- Library resources.

Z5305.U5.A74 1983
Arksey, Laura.
American diaries: an annotated bibliography of published American diaries and journals/ Laura Arksey, Nancy Pries, and Marcia Reed. Detroit, Mich.: Gale Research, c1983-c1987. 2 v.
83-008860 016.92/0073 0810318008
American diaries -- Bibliography. Autobiographies -- United States -- Bibliography. United States -- History, Local -- Sources -- Bibliography.

Z5305.U5.B56
Biography and genealogy master index. Detroit, Mich.: Gale Research Co., [c1980-   ]
81-006160
Biography -- Indexes. Biography -- indexes. Biography -- United States -- indexes. Canada -- Biography -- Indexes. United States -- Biography -- Indexes.

Z5305.U5.G66 1987
Goodfriend, Joyce D.
The published diaries and letters of American women: an annotated bibliography/ Joyce D. Goodfriend. Boston, Mass.: G.K. Hall, c1987. xiv, 230 p.
87-017908 016.920/073 0816187789
Women -- United States -- Biography -- Bibliography. American diaries -- Bibliography. United States -- Biography -- Bibliography.

Z5305.U5.S55 2000
Shivel, Gail.
New Yorker profiles, 1925-1992: a bibliography/ compiled by Gail Shivel. Lanham, Md.: University Press of America, c2000. v, 201 p.
00-036417 016.920073 076181714X
Biography -- 20th century -- Bibliography.United States -- Biography -- Bibliography.

Z5305.U5.S78 1997
Stuhr-Rommereim, Rebecca.
Autobiographies by Americans of color 1980-1994: an annotated bibliography/ by Rebecca Stuhr-Rommereim. Troy, New York: Whitston, 1997. 262 p.
96-060510 016.92 0878754660
Autobiographies -- United States -- Bibliography. Afro-Americans -- Biography -- Bibliography. Indians of North America -- Biography -- Bibliography. United States -- Biography -- Bibliography.

Z5311 Biography. Genealogy. Heraldry — Genealogy and heraldry — General bibliography. Genealogy (separately)

Z5311.P75 1998
Printed sources: a guide to published genealogical records/ edited by Kory L. Meyerink. Salt Lake City, Utah: Ancestry, c1998. xiv, 840 p. :
98-010852   016.929/373 21   0916489701
Genealogy -- Bibliography. United States -- Genealogy -- Bibliography.

Z5313 Biography. Genealogy. Heraldry — Genealogy and heraldry — By region or country, A-Z

Z5313.C2.R44 1995
Reference sources for Canadian genealogy/ compiled by Mary Bond, Reference and Information Services Division. [Ottawa]: National Library of Canada, 1995. 101 p.
96-207984   016.929/1/072071   0660164639
Canada -- Genealogy -- Bibliography -- Catalogs.

Z5313.G69.C45 1992
Colwell, Stella.
Dictionary of genealogical sources in the Public Record Office/ Stella Colwell. London: Weidenfeld and Nicolson, 1992. xvii, 206 p.
93-138987   016.941   0297831402
Great Britain -- Genealogy -- Archival sources -- Catalogs. Great Britain -- Genealogy -- Sources -- Bibliography -- Catalogs.

Z5313.L37.P56 1998
Platt, Lyman De.
Census records for Latin America and the Hispanic United States/ Lyman D. Platt. Baltimore, MD: Genealogical Pub. Co., c1998. 198 p.
97-078047   016.929/38   0806315555
Hisapnic Americans -- Genealogy -- Sources -- Bibliography -- Microform catalogs. Latin America -- Census -- Microform catalogs. United States -- Genealogy -- Sources -- Bibliography -- Microform catalogs. United States -- Census -- Microform catalogs.

Z5313.U5.F54 1981 Suppl.
Filby, P. William, 1911-
Passenger and immigration lists bibliography, 1538-1900: being a guide to published lists of arrivals in the United States and Canada. Supplement with combined index to basic volume and supplement edited by P. William Filby. Detroit, Mich.: Gale Research Co., [c1984-   ] v. 1
84-013702   016.929/373   0810316447
Ships -- Passenger lists -- Bibliography. Registers of births, etc. -- United States -- Bibliography. United States -- Genealogy -- Bibliography. United States -- Emigration and immigration -- Bibliography. United States -- History -- Sources -- Bibliography.

Z5313.U5.L37 1992
Lainhart, Ann S.
State census records/ Ann S. Lainhart. Baltimore, Md.: Genealogical Publishing, 1992. 116 p.
92-072944   016.929/373   0806313625
United States -- Census -- Bibliography -- Catalogs.

Z5313.U5.L53 1991
Library of Congress.
Genealogies cataloged by the Library of Congress since 1986: with a list of established forms of family names and a list of genealogies converted to microfilm since 1983. Washington, D.C.: Library of Congress, Cataloging Distribution Ser 1991. viii, 1349 p.
91-039573   016.9291
Genealogy -- Bibliography -- Catalogs.

Z5313.U5.U54 2000
United States.
Guide to genealogical research in the National Archives/ edited by Anne Bruner Eales and Robert M. Kvasnicka. Washington, D.C.: National Archives and Records Administration, 2000. vii, 411 p.
00-055905   016.929/1/072073   1880875241
Registers of births, etc. -- United States -- Bibliography -- Catalogs.United States -- Genealogy -- Bibliography -- Catalogs.

Z5319 Biography. Genealogy. Heraldry — Catalogs

Z5319.U53
Library of Congress.
Genealogies in the Library of Congress; a bibliography. Edited by Marion J. Kaminkow. Baltimore, Md., Magna Carta Book Co., 1972. 2 v.
74-187078   016.929/1   0910946159
United States -- Genealogy -- Bibliography -- Catalogs. Great Britain -- Genealogy -- Bibliography -- Catalogs.

Z5322 Biology — Special topics, A-Z

Z5322.E2.I85 1992
The Island Press bibliography of environmental literature/ compiled by Joseph A. Miller ... [et al.]. Washington: Island Press, c1992.
92-014099   33.7   1559631899
Ecology -- Bibliography. Environmental literature -- Bibliography. Human ecology -- Bibliography.

Z5322.E9.H39 1998
Hayward, James L., 1948-
The creation/evolution controversy: an annotated bibliography/ James L. Hayward. Lanham, Md.: Scarecrow Press; 1998. xii, 253 p.
98-003138   016.5768   0810833867
Evolution (Biology) -- Bibliography. Evolution -- Bibliography. Creationism -- Bibliography.

Z5322.E9.M38 1988
McIver, Tom, 1951-
Anti-evolution: an annotated bibliography/ by Tom McIver. Jefferson, N.C.: McFarland, c1988. xiii, 385 p.
88-042683   016.575
Evolution -- Bibliography. Creationism -- Bibliography.

Z5351 Botany — General bibliography

Z5351.D38 1996
Davis, Elisabeth B., 1932-
Guide to information sources in the botanical sciences/ Elisabeth B. Davis and Diane Schmidt. Englewood, Colo.: Libraries Unlimited, 1996. xxi, 275 p.
95-040605   016.58   1563080753
Botany -- Bibliography. Botany -- Reference books -- Bibliography. Botany -- Information services -- Directories.

Z5351.F76 2001
Frodin, D. G.
Guide to standard floras of the world: an annotated, geographically arranged systematic bibliography of the principal floras, enumerations, checklists, and chorological atlases of different areas/ David G. Frodin. 2nd ed. Cambridge, U.K.; Cambride University Press, 2001. xxiv, 1100 p.
2001-515549   016.5819 21   0521790778
Botany--Bibliography.   Phytogeography--Bibliography.   Botany--Classification--Bibliography.

Z5524 Chemistry

Z5524.A35.K74 1990
Kren, Claudia, 1929-
Alchemy in Europe: a guide to research/ Claudia Kren. New York: Garland, 1990. xiii, 130 p.
90-002899   016.54/01/12094   0824085388
Alchemy -- Europe -- History -- Bibliography.

Z5579.5 Civilization — Medieval

Z5579.5.C76 1983
Crosby, Everett Uberto,
Medieval studies: a bibliographical guide/ Everett U. Crosby, C. Julian Bishko, Robert L. Kellogg. New York: Garland Pub., 1983. xxv, 1131 p.
83-011647   016.9401 19   0824091078
Civilization, Medieval -- Bibliography. Civilization, Islamic -- Bibliography. Byzantine Empire -- Civilization -- Bibliography.

Z5579.6 Civilization — Modern

Z5579.6.C35 1990
Caldwell, Ronald J., 1943-
The era of Napoleon: a bibliography of the history of western civilization, 1799-1815/ Ronald J. Caldwell. New York: Garland Pub., 1991. 2 v.
89-037074   016.94   0824056442
Napoleonic Wars, 1800-1815 -- Bibliography. Civilization, Western -- History -- Bibliography. Europe -- History -- 1789-1815 -- Bibliography. Europe -- Civilization -- 18th century -- Bibliography. Europe -- Civilization -- 19th century -- Bibliography.

Z5579.6.M56 1995
Miller-Lachmann, Lyn, 1956-
Global voices, global visions: a core collection of multicultural books/ Lyn Miller-Lachmann. New Providence, N.J.: R.R. Bowker, c1995. xxxv, 870 p.
95-036829   016.306   0835232913
Culture -- Bibliography. Multiculturalism -- Bibliography. Civilization, Modern -- Bibliography.

Z5630-5634 Communication. Mass media

Z5630.P48 1992
Phillips, Donald E.
Human communication behavior and information processing: an interdisciplinary sourcebook/ [compiled by] Donald E. Phillips, with the assistance of Marcia K. Malott. New York: Garland Pub., 1992. xxii, 938 p.
91-037399   302.2   0824035313
Communication -- Bibliography.

Z5633.V56.S56 1988
Signorielli, Nancy.
Violence and terror in the mass media: an annotated bibliography/ compiled by Nancy Signorielli and George Gerbner. New York: Greenwood Press, 1988. xxi, 233 p.
87-029556   303.6   0313261202
Violence in mass media -- Bibliography. Terrorism in mass media -- Bibliography. Sex in mass media -- Bibliography.

Z5633.W65 L45 1999
Lent, John A.
Women and mass communications in the 1990's: an international, annotated bibliography/ compiled by John A. Lent. Westport, Conn.: Greenwood Press, 1999. ix, 510 p. ;
99-021787   016.30223/082 21   031330209X
Mass media and women -- Bibliography.

Z5634.A4.W35 1996
Walsh, Gretchen.
The media in Africa and Africa in the media: an annotated bibliography/ Gretchen Walsh; with an introductory essay by Keyan G. Tomaselli. London; H. Zell Publishers, 1996. xxv, 291 p.
96-034610   016.30223/096   1873836813
Mass media -- Africa -- Bibliography.Africa -- In mass media -- Bibliography.

Z5640 Computer science. Electronic data processing — General bibliography

Z5640.C673 1996
Cortada, James W.
A bibliographic guide to the history of computer applications, 1950-1990/ compiled by James W. Cortada. Westport, Conn.: Greenwood Press, 1996. xviii, 278 p.
95-037997   016.0053   0313298769
Computers -- History -- Bibliography. Electronic data processing -- History -- Bibliography.

Z5643 Computer science. Electronic data processing — Special topics, A-Z

Z5643.I57.C37 1993
Carande, Robert.
Information sources for virtual reality: a research guide/ Robert J. Carande. Westport, Conn.: Greenwood Press, 1993. xx, 157 p.
92-045083   016.006   0313288046
Human-computer interaction -- Bibliography. Virtual reality -- Bibliography.

Z5691-5694 Costume

Z5691.H33 2000
Haddock, Miranda Howard, 1951-
Darning the wear of time: survey and annotated bibliography of periodical literature of costume conservation, restoration, and documentation published in English, 1980-1996/ Miranda Howard Haddock. Lanham, Md.: Scarecrow Press, 2000. xi, 163 p.
99-056286   016.687/075   0810837501
Costume -- Conservation and restoration -- Periodicals -- Bibliography.

Z5691.J68 2000
Jowers, Sidney Jackson.
Theatrical costume, masks, make-up and wigs: a bibliography and iconography/ Sidney Jowers and John Cavanagh. New York: Routledge; 2000.
00-062573   792/.026   0415247748
Costume -- Bibliography. Masks -- Bibliography. Theatrical makeup -- Bibliography.

Z5691.S45 1996
Seligman, Kevin L.
Cutting for all!: the sartorial arts, related crafts, and the commercial paper pattern: a bibliographic reference guide for designers, technicians, and historians/ Kevin L. Seligman. Carbondale, [Ill.]: Southern Illinois University Press, c1996. xv, 351 p.
95-054097   016.6464   0809320053
Costume -- Bibliography. Costume design -- Bibliography. Tailoring -- Pattern design -- Bibliography.

Z5694.U5.O45 1996
Oliver, Valerie Burnham.
Fashion and costume in American popular culture: a reference guide/ Valerie Burnham Oliver. Westport, Conn.: Greenwood Press, 1996. xii, 279 p.
96-000161   016.391/00973   0313294127
Costume -- United States -- Bibliography.

Z5703 Criminology — Bibliography of bibliographies

Z5703.B67 2002
Borowitz, Albert,
Blood and ink: an international guide to fact-based crime literature / Albert Borowitz; note by Jacques Barzun; foreword by Jonathan Goodman. Kent, Ohio: Kent State University Press, c2002. xviii, 524 p.
2001-000570   016.364 21   0873387201
Crime -- Case studies -- Bibliography. Criminal investigation -- Case studies -- Bibliography. Crime writing -- Bibliography.

Z5703.4 Criminology — Special topics, A-Z

Z5703.4.C36.R3 1988
Radelet, Michael L.
Capital punishment in America: an annotated bibliography/ Michael L. Radelet, Margaret Vandiver. New York: Garland, 1988. xii, 243 p.
88-023249   016.3646/6/0973   0824016238
Capital punishment -- United States -- Bibliography.

Z5703.4.C73.N45 1997
Nelson, Bonnie R.
Criminal justice research in libraries and on the Internet/ Bonnie R. Nelson; foreword by Edward Sagarin. Westport, Conn.: Greenwood Press, 1997. xxii, 276 p.
97-016124   364/.07/22   0313300488
Criminal justice, Administration of -- Reference books. Criminal justice, Administration of -- Bibliography. Criminal justice, Administration of -- Computer network resources.

Z5703.4.C73.S36 1991
Schmalleger, Frank.
Criminal justice ethics: annotated bibliography and guide to sources/ compiled by Frank Schmalleger with the assistance of Robert McKenrick. New York: Greenwood Press, 1991. xxi, 113 p.
90-029186   174/.9364973   031326791X
Criminal justice, Administration of -- Moral and ethical aspects -- United States -- Bibliography.

Z5703.4.P75.M33 1999
McConnell, Elizabeth Huffmaster, 1949-
American prisons: an annotated bibliography/ compiled by Elizabeth Huffmaster McConnell and Laura J. Moriarty. Westport, Conn.: Greenwood Press, 1998. xi, 321 p.
98-025566   016.365/0973   0313306168
Prisons -- United States -- Bibliography. Corrections -- United States -- Bibliography. Prisoners -- United States -- Bibliography.

Z5703.4.P75.O75 1997
O'Shea, Kathleen A.
Female offenders: an annotated bibliography/ compiled by Kathleen A. O'Shea and Beverly R. Fletcher; foreword by Sister Mary Vincentia Joseph. Westport, Conn.: Greenwood Press, 1997. xiv, 264 p.
96-042163   016.3643/74   0313292280
Female offenders -- Bibliography. Women prisoners -- Bibliography.

Z5703.4.P75.V34 1999
Van Whitlock, Rodney.
Mental health services in criminal justice system settings: a selectively annotated bibliography, 1970-1997/ compiled by Rodney Van Whitlock and Bernard Lubin; foreword by Stanley L. Brodsky. Westport, CT: Greenwood Press, c1999. x, 190 p.
98-029678   016.3622/086/927   0313301867
Prisoners -- Mental health services -- Bibliography. Prisoners -- Mental health -- Bibliography.

Z5703.5 Criminology — By region or country, A-Z

Z5703.5.U5 C7 1984
Crime and punishment in America: a historical bibliography. Santa Barbara, Calif.: ABC-Clio Information Services, c1984. xii, 346 p. ;
83-012248   016.364/973 19   0874363632
Crime -- United States -- Bibliography. Violent crimes -- United States -- Bibliography. Political crimes and offenses -- United States. Criminal justice, Administration of -- United States. Punishment -- United States.

Z5703.5.U5.M67 1997
Moses, Norton H., 1935-
Lynching and vigilantism in the United States: an annotated bibliography/ compiled by Norton H. Moses. Westport, Conn.: Greenwood Press, 1997. xix, 441 p.
96-044068   016.3641/34   0313301778
Lynching -- United States -- Bibliography. Vigilantes -- United States -- Bibliography.

Z5703.5.U5.R87 2000
Russell, Katheryn K., 1961-
Race and crime: an annotated bibliography/ compiled by Katheryn K. Russell, Heather L. Pfeifer, and Judith L. Jones. Westport, Conn.: Greenwood Press, 2000. xiv, 192 p.
99-088481   016.364/089/00973   0313310335
Crime and race -- United States -- Bibliography.

Z5710 Days. Holidays. Festivals. Birthdays — General bibliography

Z5710.W67 1998
World holiday, festival, and calendar books/ edited by Tanya Gulevich. Detroit: Omnigraphics, c1998. xvii, 477 p.
97-037784   016.39426   0780800737
Holidays -- Bibliography. Festivals -- Bibliography. Calendar -- Bibliography.

Z5721 Deaf-mutes

Z5721.B87 1998
Bull, Thomas H.
On the edge of deaf culture: hearing children/deaf parents: annotated bibliography/ by Thomas Bull; [preface by Paul Preston]. Alexandria, Va.: Deaf Family Research Press, [1998] iv, 349 p.
98-072707   0966515218
Children of deaf parents -- United States -- Bibliography. Deaf parents -- United States -- Family relationships -- Bibliography.

Z5725 Death

Z5725.S67 1991
Southard, Samuel.
Death and dying: a bibliographical survey/ compiled by Samuel Southard; foreword by Therese A. Rando; G.E. Gorman, advisory editor. New York: Greenwood Press, 1991. xliv, 514 p.
91-007222   016.3069   0313264651
Thanatology -- Bibliography. Death -- Bibliography. Grief -- Bibliography.

Z5771 Directories — General

Z5771.G8
Guide to American directories. New York: B. Klein and Company, 1960-c1999.
54-004206   016.380102573
United States -- Directories -- Bibliography -- Periodicals.

Z5771.2 Directories — By region or country — United States

Z5771.2.S68 1978
Spear, Dorothea N.
Bibliography of American directories through 1860/ by Dorothea N. Spear. Westport, Conn.: Greenwood Press, 1978, c1961. 389 p.
77-028204   016.973/025   0313202516
Directories -- Bibliography.United States -- Directories -- Bibliography.

Z5776 Domestic economy. Home economics — Special topics, A-Z

Z5776.G2.C177 1998
Cagle, William R.
American books on food and drink: a bibliographical catalog of the cookbook collection housed in the Lilly Library at the University of Indiana/ William R. Cagle & Lisa Killion Stafford. New Castle, Del.: Oak Knoll Press, 1998. xviii, 794 p.
98-029889   016.6415973   1884718671
Gernon, John Talbot -- Library -- Catalogs. Gernon, John Talbot, -- Mrs. -- Library -- Catalogs. Cookery -- Bibliography -- Catalogs. Cookery -- United States -- Bibliography -- Catalogs.

Z5781-5784 Drama. Theater

Z5781.C37 1997
Carpenter, Charles A.
Modern drama: scholarship and criticism, 1981-1990: an international bibliography/ Charles A. Carpenter. Toronto; Published in association with Modern Drama, xxxvii, 632 p.
97-206771   080200914X
Drama -- 20th century -- History and criticism -- Bibliography. Drama -- 19th century -- History and criticism -- Bibliography.

Z5781.D8 1987
Drury, Francis K. W.
Drury's guide to best plays/ James M. Salem. 4th ed. Metuchen, N.J.: Scarecrow Press, 1987. viii, 480 p.
87-000380   016.80882 19   0810819805
Drama -- Bibliography. Drama -- Indexes. Drama -- Stories, plots, etc.

Z5781.H46 1995
Heniford, Lewis W., 1928-
1/2/3/4 for the show: a guide to small-cast one-act plays/ by Lewis W. Heniford. Lanham, Md.: Scarecrow Press, 1995-c1999. 2 v.
94-042180   016.80882/41   0810829851
One-act plays -- Indexes.

Z5781.K43 1990
Keller, Dean H.
Index to plays in periodicals, 1977-1987/ by Dean H. Keller. Metuchen, N.J.: Scarecrow Press, 1990. viii, 391 p.
90-008075   016.80882 20   0810822881
Drama -- Bibliography. Periodicals -- Indexes.

Z5781.O8 1988
Ottemiller, John H.
Ottemiller's index to plays in collections: an author and title index to plays appearing in collections published between 1900 and 1985. 7th ed. / revised and enlarged by Billie M. Connor and Helene G. Metuchen, N.J.: Scarecrow Press, 1988. xi, 564 p. ;
87-034160   016.80882 19   0810820811
Drama -- Indexes.

Z5781.P53
Play index. New York, H.W. Wilson Co.
64-001054
Drama -- Indexes.

Z5781.R47 1986
Research guide to biography and criticism: world drama/ edited by Walton Beacham. Washington, D.C.: Research Pub., c1986. vii, 742 p.
86-006441   016.8092 19   0933833067
Drama -- Bio-bibliography. Drama -- History and criticism -- Bibliography. Dramatists -- Biography -- Bibliography.

Z5781.S16 1984
Salem, James M.
A guide to critical reviews/ by James M. Salem. 3rd ed. Metuchen, N.J.: Scarecrow Press, 1984-<1991 > v. <1-2 >
84-001370   016.8092 19   081082387X
Theater -- New York (State) -- New York -- Reviews -- Indexes. Motion pictures -- United States -- Reviews -- Indexes.

Z5781.S55 1993
Silvester, Robert.
United States theatre: a bibliography, from the beginning to 1990/ Robert Silvester. New York: G.K. Hall; 1993. 400 p.
94-127050   016.792/0973 20   0900281030
Theater -- United States -- Bibliography. American drama -- Bibliography.

Z5781.T25 1992
Taylor, Thomas J. 1937-
American theatre history: an annotated bibliography/ Thomas J. Taylor. Pasedena, Calif.: Salem Press, c1992. xi, 162 p.
91-043961   016.792/0973   0893566721
Theater -- United States -- History -- Bibliography.

Z5784.B56.G7 1990
Gray, John, 1962-
Black theatre and performance: a pan-African bibliography/ compiled by John Gray. New York: Greenwood Press, 1990. xv, 414 p.
89-025836   016.792/089/96   0313268754
Black theater -- Africa -- Bibliography. Black theater -- Caribbean Area -- Bibliography.

Z5784.M9.B385 1993
Baskin, Ellen.
Enser's filmed books and plays: a list of books and plays from which films have been made, 1928-1991/ compiled by Ellen Baskin and Mandy Hicken. Aldershot, Hants., England; Ashgate, c1993. xiv, 970 p.
93-001536   016.8088   1857420268
Film adaptations -- Bibliography.

Z5784.M9.G72 1990
Gray, John, 1962-
Blacks in film and television: a Pan-African bibliography of films, filmmakers, and performers/ compiled by John Gray. New York: Greenwood Press, 1990. xi, 496 p.
90-003934   016.79143/096   031327486X
Motion pictures -- Africa -- Bibliography. Motion picture industry -- Africa -- Bibliography. Afro-American motion picture actors and actresses -- Bibliography.

Z5784.M9.L47 1997
Lerner, Loren R. 1948-
Canadian film and video: a bibliography and guide to the literature = Film et video canadiens: bibliographie analytique sur le cinema et la video/ Loren Lerner. Toronto; University of Toronto Press, c1997. 2 v.
97-201017   016.79143/75/0971   0802029884
Motion pictures -- Canada -- Bibliography. Video recordings -- Canada -- Bibliography. Motion pictures -- Canada -- Reviews -- Bibliography.

Z5784.M9.L54 1996
Liebman, Roy.
Silent film performers: an annotated bibliography of published, unpublished and archival sources for over 350 actors and actresses/ by Roy Liebman. Jefferson, N.C.: McFarland, c1996. vii, 383 p.
95-020915   016.79143/028/0922   0786401001
Motion picture actors and actresses -- Bibliography. Silent films -- History and criticism.

Z5784.M9.R45 1997
Reis, Brian.
Australian film: a bibliography/ Brian Reis. London; Mansell, 1997. xvii, 622 p.
96-028623   016.79143/75/0994   0720123151
Motion pictures -- Australia -- Bibliography.

Z5784.M9 W65 1987
Woll, Allen L.
Ethnic and racial images in American film and television: historical essays and bibliography/ Allen L. Woll, Randall M. Miller. New York: Garland, 1987. xv, 408 p.
84-048883   016.79143/09/093520693   19   082408733X
Minorities in motion pictures -- Bibliography. Minorities in television -- United States -- Bibliography. Motion pictures -- United States -- Bibliography. Television programs -- United States. Minorities in motion pictures. Minorities on television -- United States. Motion pictures -- United States. Television programs -- United States.

Z5811 Education — General bibliography

Z5811.B89 2000
O'Brien, Nancy P.
Education: a guide to reference and information sources/ Nancy Patricia O'Brien. 2nd ed. Englewood, Colo.: Libraries Unlimited, c2000. xv, 189 p.
99-044764   016.37 21   1563086263
Education -- Reference books -- Bibliography. Education -- Bibliography. Social sciences -- Reference books -- Bibliography. Social sciences -- Bibliography.

Z5813 Education — Periodicals. Societies

Z5813.C8
Current index to journals in education.   CIJE. Phoenix, Ariz. [etc.] Oryx Press [etc.]
80-648877   016.37/05
Education -- Periodicals -- Bibliography -- Periodicals.

Z5813.E23
The education index: a cumulative author and subject index to a selected list of educational periodicals, books, and pamphlets. New York: H.W. Wilson Co., 1932-
30-023807   016.3705
Education -- Bibliography -- Periodicals. Education -- Periodicals -- Indexes -- Periodicals.

Z5813.R4
Resources in education/ Educational Resources Information Center. Washington, D.C.: Dept. of Health, Education, and Welfare, National Institute of Education: Supt. Of Docs., U.S. G.P.O., [distributor],
75-644211   016.370/78
Education -- Research -- Bibliography -- Periodicals. Education Education -- abstracts.

Z5814 Education — Special topics, A-Z

Z5814.A24.G74 1993
Greenberg, Reva M.
Education for older adult learning: a selected, annotated bibliography/ Reva M. Greenberg. Westport, Conn.: Greenwood Press, 1993. xix, 219 p.
92-042689   016.374   0313283680
Aged -- Education -- Bibliography. Adult education -- Bibliography.

Z5814.C5.H54 1991
Higginson, Roy.
CHILDES/BIB: an annotated bibliography of child language and language disorders/ [compiled by] Roy Higginson, Brian MacWhinney. Hillsdale, N.J.: L. Erlbaum Associates, 1991. viii, 1162 p.
90-048836   016.1554/136   0805808590
Children -- Language -- Bibliography. Language acquisition -- Bibliography. Language disorders -- Bibliography.

Z5814.C52.S84 1998
Sweeney, Wilma K.
The special-needs reading list: an annotated guide to the best publications for parents and professionals/ Wilma K. Sweeney; foreword by Ann Turnbull. Bethesda, MD: Woodbine House, 1998. xvii, 314 p.
97-052803   016.3624/083   0933149743
Handicapped children -- Bibliography. Parents of handicapped children -- Books and reading. Best books.

Z5814.C88.C37 1993
Cassel, Jeris F. 1952-
Critical thinking: an annotated bibliography/ by Jeris F. Cassel and Robert J. Congleton. Metuchen, N.J.: The Scarecrow Press, 1993. x, 403 p.
92-035306   016.16   0810826356
Critical thinking -- Bibliography. Critical thinking in children -- Bibliography.

Z5814.D5.J65
Jones, Leon, 1936-
From Brown to Boston: desegregation in education, 1954-1974/ by Leon Jones. Metuchen, N.J.: Scarecrow Press, c1979. 2 v.
78-008312   016.37019/342   0810811472
School integration -- United States -- Bibliography.

Z5814.D5.S75 1994
Stitt, Beverly A., 1943-
Gender equity in education: an annotated bibliography/ Beverly A. Stitt. Carbondale: Southern Illinois University Press, c1994. vii, 168 p.
93-024315   016.37019/345   0809319373
Sex discrimination in education -- United States -- Bibliography. Sexism in education -- United States -- Bibliography. Educational equalization -- United States.

Z5814.D54 F78 2002
Fusco, Marjorie,
Distance learning for higher education: an annotated bibliography/ Marjorie Fusco and Susan E. Ketcham. Greenwood Village, Colo.: Libraries Unlimited, 2002. xi, 132 p.
2002-003184   016.3713/5 21   1563088479
Distance education -- Bibliography. University extension -- Bibliography.

Z5814.D54.M66 1995
Mood, Terry Ann, 1945-
Distance education: an annotated bibliography/ Terry Ann Mood. Englewood, Colo.: Libraries Unlimited, 1995. xi, 191 p.
94-049086   016.3713/078   1563081601
Distance education -- Bibliography.

Z5814.E59 R67 1996
Rosow, La Vergne.
Light 'n lively reads for ESL, adult, and teen readers: a thematic bibliography/ La Vergne Rosow; illustrated by the author. Englewood, Colo.: Libraries Unlimited, 1996. xxxvii, 343 p.
96-007084   016.4286/4 20   1563083655
English language -- Textbooks for foreign speakers -- Bibliography. High interest-low vocabulary books -- Bibliography. Readers -- Bibliography.

Z5814.E9.B8
Buros, Oscar Krisen, 1905-
Tests in print; a comprehensive bibliography of tests for use in education, psychology, and industry. Barbara A. Peace, editorial associate, William L. Matts, editorial assistant. Highland Park, N.J., Gryphon Press [1961] xxix, 479 p.
61-016302   016.37126
Educational tests and measurements -- Bibliography. Examinations -- Bibliography.

Z5814.I3.H56 1990
Hladczuk, John.
General issues in literacy/illiteracy: a bibliography/ compiled by John Hladczuk, William Eller, and Sharon Hladczuk. New York: Greenwood Press, 1990. xv, 420 p.
89-028646   016.374/012   0313273278
Literacy -- United States -- Bibliography.

Z5814.M86.M67 1996
Morris, Libby V.
Multiculturalism in academe: a source book/ Libby V. Morris, Sammy Parker. New York: Garland, 1996. 187 p.
95-026398   378.199/0973   0815317980
Education, Higher -- United States -- Curricula -- Bibliography. Multicultural education -- United States -- Bibliography. Minorities -- Education (Higher) -- United States -- Bibliography.

Z5814.M86 P55 2001
Pilger, Mary Anne.
Multicultural projects index: things to make and do to celebrate festivals, cultures, and holidays around the world/ Mary Anne Pilger. 3rd ed. Englewood, Colo.: Libraries Unlimited, 2001.
2001-054446   016.370117 21   1563088983
Multicultural education -- Bibliography. Multicultural education -- Activity programs -- Indexes. Festivals -- Indexes. Handicraft -- Indexes. Games -- Indexes.

Z5814.M86 1992
Nordquist, Joan.
The multicultural education debate in the university: a bibliography / compiled by Joan Nordquist. Santa Cruz, CA: Reference and Research Services, 1992. 63 p.
93-143324   016.37019/6 20   0937855480
Multicultural education -- Bibliography. Education, Higher -- Social aspects -- Bibliography.

Z5814.P8 B93
Buros, Oscar Krisen,
Educational, psychological, and personality tests of 1933/34-1936. By Oscar K. Buros. New Brunswick, N.J., School of education, Rutgers university 3 v.
36-009015
Educational tests and measurements -- Bibliography. Examinations -- Bibliography. Character tests -- Bibliography.

Z5814.P8.B932
The ... Mental measurements yearbook. Highland Park, N.J.: The Mental Measurements Yearbook, [1941-]
39-003422   016.1512
Examinations -- Bibliography. Statistics -- Bibliography. Educational tests and measurements -- Bibliography.

Z5814.R34.R45 1996
Religious higher education in the United States: a source book/ edited by Thomas C. Hunt, James C. Carper. New York: Garland Pub., 1996. xi, 635 p.
95-036782   016.377/8   0815316364
Church colleges -- United States -- Bibliography. Church and college -- United States -- Bibliography.

Z5814.T3.A97 1990
Ayers, Jerry B.
Teacher education program evaluation: an annotated bibliography and guide to research/ Jerry B. Ayers, Mary F. Berney. New York: Garland Pub., 1990. xxvii, 274 p.
90-031529   370/.71/0973   0824035372
Teachers -- Training of -- United States -- Evaluation -- Bibliography.

Z5814.U7.B75 1995
Buchanan, Anne L.
The doctor of philosophy degree: a selective, annotated bibliography/ compiled by Anne L. Buchanan and Jean-Pierre V.M. Herubel. Westport, Conn.: Greenwood Press, 1995. x, 125 p.
95-021268   016.3782/0973   0313295395
Doctor of philosophy degree -- United States -- Bibliography.

Z5814.U7.S685 1993
Sparks, Linda.
College admissions: a selected, annotated bibliography/ compiled by Linda Sparks. Westport, Conn.: Greenwood Press, 1993. x, 187 p.
92-034759   016.3781/056   0313284830
Universities and colleges -- United States -- Admission -- Bibliography.

Z5814.U7.S69 1990
Sparks, Linda.
Institutions of higher education: an international bibliography/ compiled by Linda Sparks. New York: Greenwood Press, c1990. x, 478 p.
89-029355   016.378   0313266867
Universities and colleges -- History -- Bibliography.

Z5815 Education —
By region or country, A-Z

Z5815.A69.E4 1992
El-Sanabary, Nagat.
Education in the Arab Gulf states and the Arab world: an annotated bibliographic guide/ Nagat El-Sanabary. New York: Garland Pub., 1992. xix, 572 p.
91-021261   016.37/0953   0824082494
Education -- Arabian Peninsula -- Bibliography. Education -- Arab countries -- Bibliography.

Z5815.D44.K44 1989
Kelly, Gail P.
Women's education in the Third World: an annotated bibliography/ Gail P. Kelly and Carol M. Elliott New York: Garland Pub., 1989. 478 p.
89-032058   0824086341
Women -- Education -- Developing countries -- Bibliography.

Z5815.G5 P37 1991
Parker, Franklin,
Education in England and Wales: an annotated bibliography/ Franklin Parker, Betty June Parker. New York: Garland, 1991. xcii, 531 p.
90-025455   016.37/0942 20   0824059433
Education -- England -- History -- Bibliography. Education -- Wales -- History -- Bibliography.

Z5815.H56.M53 1996
Middle level education: an annotated bibliography/ Samuel Totten ... [et al.]. Westport, Conn.: Greenwood Press, 1996. xxv, 428 p.
96-006136   016.3732/36/0973   0313290024
Middle schools -- United States -- Bibliography.

Z5815.S66.B75 1992
Brickman, William W.
Russian and Soviet education, 1731-1989: a multilingual annotated bibliography/ William W. Brickman, John T. Zepper. New York: Garland Pub., 1992. xix, 538 p.
91-045874   016.37/0947   0824090527
Education -- Russia -- History -- 18th century - - Bibliography. Education -- Russia -- History -- 19th century -- Bibliography. Education -- Russia -- History -- 20th century -- Bibliography.

Z5815.U5.O44 1993
Olevnik, Peter P.
American higher education: a guide to reference sources/ Peter P. Olevnik; with the assistance of Betty W. Chan, Sarah Hammond, and Gregory M. Toth; foreword by Philip G. Altbach. Westport, Conn.: Greenwood Press, 1993. xv, 211 p.
93-025015   016.378/73   0313277494
Education, Higher -- United States -- Bibliography.

Z5817.2 Education —
Teaching aids

Z5817.2.E45
Elementary teachers' guide to free curriculum materials. Randolph, Wis.: Educators Progress Service, [1944-]
44-052255   016.372
Teaching -- Aids and devices -- Bibliography -- Periodicals. Free material -- Catalogs -- Periodicals.

Z5818 Education —
Special disciplines and subjects, A-Z

Z5818.E5.C37 1994
Carrasquillo, Angela.
Teaching English as a second language: a resource guide/ Angela L. Carrasquillo. New York: Garland Pub., 1994. xiv, 219 p.
93-041180   016.428/007   0815308213
English language -- Study and teaching -- Foreign speakers -- Bibliography.

Z5818.E5.C64 1999
Collaborative writing: an annotated bibliography/
Bruce W. Speck ... [et al.]. Westport, Conn.:
Greenwood Press, 1999. xii, 390 p.
99-011304   016.808/042   0313305765
   *English language -- Rhetoric -- Study and
teaching -- Bibliography. Report writing -- Study
and teaching -- Bibliography. Authorship --
Collaboration -- Bibliography.*

Z5818.E5.M87 1996
Murphy, Christina, 1947-
Writing centers: an annotated bibliography/
compiled by Christina Murphy, Joe Law, and
Steve Sherwood. Westport, CT: Greenwood
Press, 1996. xiv, 287 p.
96-018521   016.808/042/07   0313298319
   *English language -- Rhetoric -- Study and
teaching -- Bibliography. English language --
Composition and exercises -- Bibliography.
Resource programs (Education) -- Management -
- Bibliography.*

Z5818.E5.R468 1990
Research in basic writing: a bibliographic
sourcebook/ edited by Michael G. Moran and
Martin J. Jacobi. New York: Greenwood Press,
1990. ix, 259 p.
89-038229   016.808/042/07   0313255644
   *English language -- Rhetoric -- Study and
teaching -- Bibliography. English language --
Grammar -- Study and teaching -- Bibliography.
Basic writing (Remedial education) --
Bibliography.*

Z5818.E5.W75 1993
Anson, Christopher M., 1954-
Writing across the curriculum: an annotated
bibliography/ compiled by Chris M. Anson, John
E. Schwiebert, and Michael M. Williamson.
Westport, Conn.: Greenwood Press, 1993. xxiv,
187 p.
93-029897   016.808/042/07   0313259607
   *English language -- Composition and exercises
-- Bibliography. Interdisciplinary approach in
education -- Bibliography. Academic writing --
Bibliography.*

Z5834 Electricity — Special topics, A-Z

Z5834.T4 S74 2000
Sterling, Christopher H.,
History of telecommunications technology: an
annotated bibliography/ Christopher H. Sterling
and George Shiers. Lanham, MD: Scarecrow
Press, 2000. xii, 333 p.
00-024823   016.621382 21   0810837811
   Telecommunication -- History -- Bibliography.

Z5848 Encyclopedias — General

Z5848.A72 1997
ARBA guide to subject encyclopedias and
dictionaries/ [edited by] Susan C. Awe.
Englewood, Colo.: Libraries Unlimited, 1997.
xxvi, 482 p.
96-044571   016.031   1563084678
   *Encyclopedias and dictionaries --
Bibliography. Encyclopedias and dictionaries --
Reviews. Encyclopedias and dictionaries --
Reviews -- Bibliography.*

Z5848.M57 1999
Mirwis, Allan,
Subject encyclopedias: user guide, review
citations, and keyword index/ Allan N. Mirwis.
Phoenix, Ariz: Oryx Press, 1999. 2 pts.
98-047465   031 21   1573562998
   *Encyclopedias and dictionaries -- Indexes.
Encyclopedias and dictionaries -- Reviews.*

Z5853 Engineering — Special topics, A-Z

Z5853.R58 R63 2002
Robotics: a bibliography with indexes/ Peter J.
Benne (editor). Hauppauge, N.Y.: Nova Science,
c2002. 232 p.
2002-728092   1590332962
   Robotics -- Bibliography.

Z5861 Environment (General and human). Human ecology — General bibliography

Z5861.B48
Bibliographic guide to the environment. Boston,
Mass.: G.K. Hall, [c1992-   ]
93-641469   016.3637 20
   *Environmental sciences -- Bibliography --
Periodicals.*

Z5861.E4 1991
Elbers, Joan S.
Changing wilderness values, 1930-1990: an
annotated bibliography/ compiled by Joan S.
Elbers. New York: Greenwood Press, c1991.
xviii, 138 p.
91-007718   016.179/1 20   0313273774
   *Environmental ethics -- Bibliography. Nature
conservation -- History -- Bibliography. Nature
conservation -- Moral and ethical aspects --
Bibliography. Wilderness areas -- Bibliography.*

Z5861.F67 1994
Fortner, Diane M.
Environmental   studies: an   annotated
bibliography/ by Diane M. Fortner. Metuchen,
N.J.: Scarecrow Press; ix, 157 p.
93-009199   016.3637 20   0810828359
   Environmental sciences -- Bibliography.

Z5861.G46
Geographic index of environmental articles.
Cincinnati, Ohio: Center for Environmental
Research Information,
94-649659   016.3637 20
   *Environmental literature -- Bibliography --
Indexes. Environmental sciences -- Bibliography
-- Indexes.*

Z5861.M45 1992
Merideth, Robert W.
The environmentalist's bookshelf: a guide to the
best books/ Robert Merideth. New York: G.K.
Hall; c1993. x, 272 p.
92-018613   016.3637   0816173591
   *Human   ecology   --   Bibliography.
Environmental protection -- Bibliography.
Environmental policy -- Bibliography.*

Z5861.N67 1991
Nordquist, Joan.
Environmental issues in the Third World: a
bibliography/ compiled   by Joan Nordquist.
Santa Cruz, CA, USA: Reference and Research
Services, 1991. 72 p.
91-229143   016.3637/009172/4   20
0937855421
   *Human ecology -- Developing countries --
Bibliography. Deforestation -- Developing
countries -- Bibliography. Pollution --
Developing   countries   --   Bibliography.
Environmental policy -- Developing countries --
Bibliography.*

Z5862.2 Environment (General and human). Human ecology — Pollution and pollution control — Special types, A-Z

Z5862.2.A26.J68 1991
Joy, Albert H.
Acid rain: a bibliography of Canadian federal
and provincial government documents/ Albert H.
Joy. Westport: Meckler, c1991. xxi, 237 p.
90-021522   016.36373/86/0971   0887365272
   *Acid rain -- Environmental aspects -- Canada -
- Bibliography. Government publications --
Canada -- Bibliography.*

Z5863 Environment (General and human). Human ecology — Other special topics, A-Z

Z5863.P6.D88 1996
Dwyer, Jim, 1949-
Earth works: recommended fiction and
nonfiction about nature and the environment for
adults and young adults/ Jim Dwyer. New York:
Neal-Schuman Publishers, c1996. xvii, 507 p.
94-036624   016.3637   1555701949
   Environmental sciences -- Bibliography.

Z5863.P6 L5
Earth decade reading list/ the Library of
Congress. [Washington, DC]: The Library,
97-648176   016.3637 21
   *Environmental sciences -- Bibliography --
Periodicals.*

Z5865 Erotic literature, facetiae, curiosa, etc. — General bibliography

Z5865.R47 2003
Research on altruism & love: an annotated
bibliography of major   studies in psychology,
sociology, evolutionary biology, and theology/
edited by Stephen G. Post ... [et al.].
Philadelphia: Templeton Foundation Press,
c2003. 292 p.
2003-001844   016.177/7 21   1932031324
   Love -- Bibliography. Altruism -- Bibliography.

Z5866 Erotic literature, facetiae, curiosa, etc. — Special topics, A-Z

Z5866.L44.G37 1993
Garber, Linda.
Lesbian sources: a bibliography of periodical articles, 1970-1990/ Linda Garber. New York: Garland, 1993. l, 680 p.
92-021941 016.30548/9664 0815307829
Lesbianism -- Bibliography. Lesbianism -- Periodicals -- Bibliography. Lesbians -- Bibliography.

Z5883 Exhibitions

Z5883.B47 1996
Bertuca, David J.
The World's Columbian Exposition: a centennial bibliographic guide/ David J. Bertuca, senior compiler, Donald K. Hartman and Susan M. Neumeister, co-compilers. Westport, Conn.: Greenwood Press, 1996. xxix, 440 p.
93-037791 907/.4773/11 0313266441
World's Columbian Exposition (1893: Chicago, Ill.) -- Bibliography.

Z5883.S63 1991
Smithsonian Institution.
The books of the fairs: materials about world's fairs, 1834-1916, in the Smithsonian Institution Libraries/ with an introductory essay by Robert W. Rydell. Chicago: American Library Association, 1992. xx, 268 p.
91-026804 016.9074 0838905560
Trade shows -- Bibliography.

Z5916 Fiction — General bibliography

Z5916.H28 1988
Hartman, Donald K.
Themes and settings in fiction: a bibliography of bibliographies/ compiled by Donald K. Hartman and Jerome Drost; foreword by Arthur Efron. New York: Greenwood Press, 1988. xv, 223 p.
88-025082 016.01680883/93 031325866X
Fiction -- Themes, motives -- Bibliography. Setting (Literature) -- Bibliography.

Z5916.W43 1995
Weaver, Bruce L.
Novel openers: first sentences of 11,000 fictional works, topically arranged with subject, keyword, author, and title indexing/ by Bruce L. Weaver. Jefferson, N.C.: McFarland & Co., c1995. ix, 986 p.
94-041653 016.80883 0786400501
Fiction -- Indexes. Openings (Rhetoric) -- Indexes. Quotations, English.

Z5916.W74
Fiction catalog. New York [etc.] H.W. Wilson Co.
09-035044 016.823
Fiction -- Indexes. Best books.

Z5917 Fiction — Special topics, A-Z

Z5917.D5 B59 1999
Bleiler, Richard.
Reference guide to mystery and detective fiction/ Richard J. Bleiler. Englewood, Colo.: Libraries Unlimited, 1999. xviii, 391 p.
99-019091 016.80883/872 21 1563083809
Detective and mystery stories -- Bibliography. Detective and mystery stories -- Reference books -- Bibliography.

Z5917.D5.G74 1997
Green, Joseph, 1920-
Sleuths, sidekicks and stooges: an annotated bibliography of detectives, their assistants and their rivals in crime, mystery and adventure fiction, 1795-1995/ Joseph Green and Jim Finch. Aldershot, Eng.: Scolar Press; c1997. 874 p.
95-049334 016.80883/872 1859281923
Detective and mystery stories -- Bibliography. Detectives in literature -- Bibliography.

Z5917.F3.A84 1995
Ashley, Michael.
The supernatural index: a listing of fantasy, supernatural, occult, weird, and horror anthologies/ Mike Ashley and William G. Contento. Westport, Conn.: Greenwood Press, 1995. xii, 933 p.
95-006290 016.80883/8738 0313240302
Fantasy fiction -- Bibliography. Supernatural in literature -- Bibliography. Horror tales -- Bibliography.

Z5917.F3.F36 1990
Fantasy literature: a reader's guide/ edited by Neil Barron. New York: Garland Pub., 1990. xxvii, 586 p.
89-023693 016.8093/8766 0824031482
Fantasy literature -- Bibliography. Fantasy literature -- History and criticism.

Z5917.F3 H47 1999
Herald, Diana Tixier.
Fluent in fantasy: a guide to reading interests/ Diana Tixier Herald. Englewood, Colo.: Libraries Unlimited, 1999. ix, 260 p.
99-010204 016.80883/8766 21 1563086557
Fantasy fiction -- Bibliography. Books and reading -- United States.

Z5917.F3.S715 1996
St. James guide to fantasy writers/ editor, David Pringle. New York: St. James Press, c1996. xvi, 711 p.
95-048783 016.8093/8766 1558622055
Fantasy literature -- Bio-bibliography. Fantasy literature -- History and criticism.

Z5917.G66 F7 1984
Frank, Frederick S.
Guide to the Gothic: an annotated bibliography of criticism/ by Frederick S. Frank. Metuchen, N.J.: Scarecrow Press, 1984. xvi, 421 p.
83-024507 016.8093/872 19 0810816695
Gothic revival (Literature) -- Bibliography. Fiction -- History and criticism -- Bibliography. Horror tales -- History and criticism -- Bibliography.

Z5917.H6.A33 1999
Adamson, Lynda G.
World historical fiction: an annotated guide to novels for adults and young adults/ by Lynda G. Adamson. Phoenix, Ariz.: Oryx Press, 1999. xiv, 719 p.
98-039981 016.80883/81 1573560669
Historical fiction -- Bibliography.

Z5917.H6 H37 1994
Hartman, Donald K.
Historical figures in fiction/ Donald K. Hartman and Gregg Sapp. Phoenix, Ariz.: Oryx Press, 1994. xii, 352 p. ;
94-015105 016.813/08108358 20
0897747186
Historical fiction, American -- Bibliography. Historical fiction, English -- Bibliography. Biographical fiction, American -- Bibliography. Biographical fiction, English -- Bibliography. Young adult fiction, American -- Bibliography. Young adult fiction, English -- Bibliography.

Z5917.H65.S72 1998
St. James guide to horror, ghost & gothic writers/ with a preface by Dennis Etchison; editor, David Pringle. Detroit, MI: St. James Press, c1998. xvi, 746 p.
98-164553 809.3/873809 1558622063
Horror tales -- Bio-bibliography. Horror tales -- History and criticism. Ghost stories -- Bio-bibliography.

Z5917.S36 B87 2003
Burgess, Michael.
Reference guide to science fiction, fantasy, and horror/ Michael Burgess, Lisa R. Bartle. 2nd ed. Westport Conn.: Libraries Unlimited, 2002. xvii, 605 p.
2002-151707 016.8093/876 21 1563085488
Science fiction -- Reference books -- Bibliography. Science fiction -- History and criticism -- Bibliography. Fantasy fiction -- Reference books -- Bibliography. Fantasy fiction -- History and criticism -- Bibliography. Horror tales -- Reference books -- Bibliography. Horror tales -- History and criticism -- Bibliography.

Z5917.S36.M24 1996
Magill's guide to science fiction and fantasy literature/ consulting editor, T.A. Shippey; project editor, A.J. Sobczak. Pasadena, Calif.: Salem Press, c1996. 4 v.
96-026261 016.80883/876 0893569062
Science fiction -- History and criticism -- Bibliography. Fantasy literature -- History and criticism -- Bibliography.

Z5917.S36.M87 1999
Murray, Terry A., 1953-
Science fiction magazine story index, 1926-1995/ by Terry A. Murray. Jefferson, N.C.: McFarland, c1999. ix, 627 p.
98-053290 016.813/08762/05 0786406917
Science fiction, American -- Periodicals -- Indexes.

Z5917.S44 H87 1997
Husband, Janet,
Sequels: an annotated guide to novels in series/ Janet Husband and Jonathan F. Husband. 3rd ed. Chicago: American Library Association, 1997. viii, 688 p. ;
96-027296 016.80883 20 0838906966
Fiction -- Bibliography. Sequels (Literature) -- Bibliography.

Z5917.S5.A43 1996
Albert, Richard N.
An annotated bibliography of jazz fiction and jazz fiction criticism/ compiled by Richard N. Albert. Westport, Conn.: Greenwood Press, 1996. xviii, 114 p.
96-008937   016.80883/9357   0313289980
Short story -- Bibliography. Jazz -- Fiction -- Bibliography. Jazz musicians -- Fiction -- Bibliography.

Z5917.S5.S56
Short story index, collections indexed 1900-1978/ edited by Juliette Yaakov. New York: H. W. Wilson Co., 1979. 349 p.
79-024887   016.808831   0824206436
Short stories -- Bibliography.

Z5917.S5.W35 1993
Walker, Warren S.
Twentieth-century short story explication. with checklists of books and journals used/ Warren S. Walker. Hamden, Conn.: Shoe String Press, 1993-1997 v. 1-3
92-022790   016.8093/1   0208023402
Short stories -- Indexes. Short stories -- Indexes.

Z5917.W33 T39 1993
Taylor, Desmond,
The novels of World War II: an annotated bibliography/ Desmond Taylor, with the assistance of Philip E. Hager. New York: Garland, 1993. 2 v.
92-035187   016.8083/9358 20   0824056841
World War, 1939-1945 -- Literature and the war -- Bibliography. Fiction -- 20th century -- Bibliography. War stories -- Bibliography.

Z5931 Fine arts (Visual arts). The arts (General) — General bibliography

Z5931.E47 1990
Ehresmann, Donald L.,
Fine arts: a bibliographic guide to basic reference works, histories, and handbooks/ Donald L. Ehresmann. 3rd ed. Englewood, Colo.: Libraries Unlimited, 1990. xvii, 373 p.
90-034857   016.7 20   0872876403
Art -- Bibliography.

Z5931.L52 1988
Lincoln, Betty Woelk,
Festschriften in art history, 1960-1975: bibliography and index/ Betty Woelk Lincoln. New York: Garland Pub., 1988. xiv, 220 p.
87-022767   016.7 19   0824084977
Art -- Bibliography. Festschriften -- Bibliography. Art -- Indexes. Festschriften -- Indexes.

Z5931.W85 1994
Writings about art/ [edited by] Carole Gold Calo. Englewood Cliffs, N.J.: Prentice Hall, c1994. viii, 367 p.
92-047106   700 20   0137617011
Art -- Bibliography.

Z5933 Fine arts (Visual arts). The arts (General) — By period — Medieval

Z5933.F75 1998
Friedman, John Block, 1934-
Medieval iconography: a research guide/ John B. Friedman and Jessica M. Wegmann. New York: Garland Pub., 1998. xxiv, 437 p.
97-042974   016.700/9/02   0815317530
Arts, Medieval -- Themes, motives -- Sources -- Bibliography.

Z5935.5 Fine arts (Visual arts). The arts (General) — By period — Modern

Z5935.5.E74 1993
Erlich, Richard D.
Clockworks: a multimedia bibliography of works useful for the study of the human/machine interface in SF/ compiled by Richard D. Erlich and Thomas P. Dunn; assisted by Edward K. Montgomery, Catherine Mills Royer, and D. Scott DeLoach. Westport, Conn.: Greenwood Press, 1993. xvi, 324 p.
93-001069   016.7   0313273057
Arts, Modern -- 20th century -- Bibliography. Science fiction -- Illustrations -- Bibliography. Conscious automata in art -- Bibliography.

Z5936 Fine arts (Visual arts). The arts (General) — Special aspects or movements, A-Z

Z5936.M34.K38 1988
Kaufmann, Thomas DaCosta.
Art and architecture in Central Europe, 1550-1620: an annotated bibliography/ Thomas DaCosta Kaufmann. Boston, Mass.: G.K. Hall, c1988. xxxvii, 316 p.
88-001816   016.7/0943   0816185948
Mannerism (Art) -- Europe, Central -- Bibliography. Mannerism (Architecture) -- Europe, Central -- Bibliography.

Z5937 Fine arts (Visual arts). The arts (General) — Periodicals. Societies

Z5937.A78
Art index. New York, H.W. Wilson.
31-007513   016.7
Art -- Periodicals -- Indexes -- Periodicals. Art -- Periodicals -- Bibliography -- Periodicals.

Z5938 Fine arts (Visual arts). The arts (General) — Biobibliography

Z5938.F73 1997
Art books: a basic bibliography of monographs on artists/ editor, Wolfgang M. Freitag. New York: Garland Pub., 1997. xxvi, 542 p.
96-028425   016.9/092/2   0824033264
Art -- Bio-bibliography. Artists -- Bibliography.

Z5938.S75 1991
Stievater, Susan M., 1939-
Biographies of creative artists: an annotated bibliography/ compiled by Susan M. Stievater. New York: Garland Pub., 1991. 210 p.
91-006744   016.7/0092/2   0824049489
Artists -- Biography -- Bibliography. Arts -- Bibliography.

Z5941 Fine arts (Visual arts). The arts (General) — Architecture — General bibliography

Z5941.A645 1994
Architectural design, architectural theory and criticism, environmental issues, human behavior, professional practice, special topics, urban design theory and history/ edited by Georgia Bizios. Chapel Hill, NC: Eno River Press, 1994. 612 p.
94-071488   016.72 20   0880242507
Architecture -- Bibliography. Architecture -- Study and teaching -- Outlines, syllabi, etc.

Z5941.A94 1997
Avery's choice: five centuries of great architectural books: one hundred years of an architectural library, 1890-1990/ Adolf K. Placzek, general editor; Angela Giral, Avery librarian. New York: G.K. Hall; xxvii, 292 p.
97-003066   016.72 21   0783815972
Architecture -- Bibliography -- Catalogs.

Z5941.S43 1999
Schimmelman, Janice Gayle.
Architectural books in early America: architectural treaties and building handbooks available in American libraries and bookstores through 1800/ Janice G. Schimmelman. 1st ed. New Castle, Del.: Oak Knoll Press, 1999. ix, 221 p.
99-026451   016.72 21   188471899X
Architecture -- History -- Bibliography. Early printed books -- United States -- 17th century -- Bibliography. Early printed books -- United States -- 18th century -- Bibliography. United States -- Imprints.

Z5941.S695 1989
Stiverson, Cynthia Zignego.
Architecture and the decorative arts: the A. Lawrence Kocher Collection of Books at the Colonial Williamsburg Foundation/ by Cynthia Zignego Stiverson; with an introduction by Lawrence Wodehouse; and a foreword by Albert Frey. West Cornwall, CT: Locust Hill Press, 1989. xli, 245 p.
88-036398   016.72 19   0933951248
Kocher, A. Lawrence (Alfred Lawrence) -- Library -- Catalogs. Architecture -- Bibliography -- Catalogs. Decorative arts -- Bibliography -- Catalogs.

Z5942 Fine arts (Visual arts). The arts (General) — Architecture — City planning, municipal improvement, etc.

Z5942.D87 1994
Duensing, Edward.
Information sources in urban and regional planning: a directory and guide to reference materials/ Edward E. Duensing. New Brunswick, N.J.: Center for Urban Policy Research, c1994. vi, 178 p.
93-026775   016.3071/2   0882851462
City planning -- Reference books -- Bibliography. City planning -- Bibliography. City planning -- United States -- Information services -- Directories.

Z5942.S464 1983
Shearer, Barbara Smith.
Periodical literature on United States cities: a bibliography and subject guide/ compiled by Barbara Smith Shearer and Benjamin F. Shearer. Westport, Conn.: Greenwood Press, c1983. xviii, 574 p.
82-024211   016.3077/64/0973   0313235112
Cities and towns -- United States -- Bibliography.

Z5943 Fine arts (Visual arts). The arts (General) — Architecture — Special topics, A-Z

Z5943.A72.A75 1997
Architecture sourcebook: a guide to resources on the practice of architecture/ edited by Kathryn M. Wayne. Detroit, MI: Omnigraphics, c1997. 417 p.
96-034505   016.72   0780800249
Architectural design -- Bibliography.

Z5944 Fine arts (Visual arts). The arts (General) — Architecture — By region or country, A-Z

Z5944.N4.L353 1996
Langmead, Donald.
Dutch modernism: architectural resources in the English language/ Donald Langmead. Westport, Conn.: Greenwood Press, 1996. x, 243 p.
96-018777   016.72/09492/0904   0313296189
Architecture, Modern -- 20th century -- Netherlands -- Bibliography. Architecture -- Netherlands -- Bibliography. English imprints.

Z5949 Fine arts (Visual arts). The arts (General) — Painting. Print media — By region or country, A-Z

Z5949.U5.P86 1996
Puniello, Francoise S.
Abstract expressionist women painters: an annotated bibliography: Elaine de Kooning, Helen Frankenthaler, Grace Hartigan, Lee Krasner, Joan Mitchell, Ethel Schwabacher/ by Francoise S. Puniello and Halina R. Rusak. Lanham, Md.: Scarecrow Press, c1996. vii, 361 p.
95-021924   016.75913/082   0810829983
Abstract expressionism -- United States -- Bibliography. Art, Modern -- 20th century -- United States -- Bibliography. Women painters -- United States -- Biography -- History and criticism -- Bibliography.

Z5956 Fine arts (Visual arts). The arts (General) — Special topics (not otherwise provided for), A-Z

Z5956.A47.R64 1998
Rodgers, Marie E.
The Harlem Renaissance: an annotated reference guide for student research/ Marie E. Rodgers. Englewood, Colo.: Libraries Unlimited, 1998. xvii, 139 p.
97-046660   016.700/89/96073007471 1563085801
Harlem Renaissance -- Bibliography. Afro-American arts -- New York (State) -- New York -- Bibliography.

Z5956.C3.L458 1996
Lent, John A.
Comic art in Africa, Asia, Australia, and Latin America: a comprehensive, international bibliography/ compiled by John A. Lent; forewords by Effat Abdel Azim, Esmail, Abu Abraham, and Ares (Aristides Estaban Hernandez Guerraro). Westport, Conn.: Greenwood Press, 1996. xxxiii, 518 p.
95-031367   016.7415   0313293430
Caricatures and cartoons -- History -- Bibliography. Wit and humor, Pictorial -- Bibliography.

Z5956.C3.S66 1998
Somers, Paul.
Editorial cartooning and caricature: a reference guide/ Paul P. Somers, Jr. Westport, Conn.: Greenwood Press, 1998. xi, 205 p.
97-026181   016.973/02/07   0313221502
Editorial cartoons -- United States -- History -- Bibliography. Editorial cartoons -- United States -- History. American wit and humor, Pictorial -- History -- Bibliography. United States -- Politics and government -- Caricatures and cartoons -- Bibliography. United States -- Politics and government -- Caricatures and cartoons.

Z5956.C6.L46 1994
Lent, John A.
Comic books and comic strips in the United States: an international bibliography/ compiled by John A. Lent; foreword by Mort Walker; introduction by Jerry Robinson. Westport, Conn.: Greenwood Press, 1994. xxvi, 596 p.
94-010852   016.7415/973   0313282110
Comic books, strips, etc. -- United States -- Bibliography.

Z5956.C6 R68 1995
Rothschild, D. Aviva.
Graphic novels: a bibliographic guide to book-length comics/ D. Aviva Rothschild. Englewood, Colo.: Libraries Unlimited, 1995. xxii, 245 p.
94-023984   016.7415 20   1563080869
Graphic novels -- Bibliography.

Z5956.C6 W45 2001
Weiner, Stephen,
The 101 best graphic novels/ by Stephen Weiner; edited by Keith R.A. DeCandido. New York: NBM, c2001. 80 p.
2001-030622   016.7415/9 21   1561632848
Graphic novels -- Bibliography. Best books -- United States.

Z5956.D3.L48 1998
Lewis, Susan A.
Interior design sourcebook: a guide to resources on the history and practice of interior design/ by Susan A. Lewis. Detroit, MI: Omnigraphics, c1998. 307 p.
97-202133   0780801989
Interior decoration -- Bibliography.

Z5956.D5.T46 1992
Thomson, Ellen Mazur.
American graphic design: a guide to the literature/ compiled by Ellen Mazur Thomson. Westport, Conn.: Greenwood Press, c1992. x, 282 p.
92-023786   016.7416/0973   0313287287
Commercial art -- United States -- Bibliography. Graphic arts -- United States -- History -- 20th century -- Bibliography. Design -- United States -- History -- 20th century -- Bibliography.

Z5956.E7.B87 1989
Burt, Eugene C., 1948-
Erotic art: an annotated bibliography with essays/ Eugene C. Burt. Boston, Mass.: G.K. Hall, c1989. xix, 396 p.
88-030709   016.7049/428   0816189579
Erotic art -- Bibliography.

Z5956.P74.M54 1999
Mieder, Wolfgang.
Proverb iconography: an international bibliography/ Wolfgang Mieder & Janet Sobieski. New York: Peter Lang, c1999. xix, 225 p.
98-052124   016.7049/493989   0820441988
Proverbs in art -- Bibliography.

Z5961 Fine arts (Visual arts). The arts (General) — By region or country, A-Z

Z5961.E8.W45 1998
Weisberg, Gabriel P.
Art nouveau: a research guide for design reform in France, Belgium, England, and the United States/ Gabriel P. Weisberg, Elizabeth K. Menon. New York: Garland Pub., 1998. xvii, 387 p.
97-036906   016.709/03/49   0824066286
Art nouveau -- Europe -- Bibliography. Art, Modern -- 19th century -- Europe -- Bibliography. Art, Modern -- 20th century -- Europe -- Bibliography.

Z5961.M58.G65 1991
Goldman, Bernard, 1922-
The ancient arts of Western and Central Asia: a guide to the literature/ Bernard Goldman. Ames: Iowa State University Press, 1991. ix, 303 p.
91-016944   016.7/0939/4   081380597X
Art, Ancient -- Middle East -- Bibliography. Art -- Middle East -- Bibliography. Art, Ancient -- Asia, Central -- Bibliography.

Z5961.U5 A515 1998
American book and magazine illustrators to 1920/ edited by Steven E. Smith, Catherine A. Hastedt, Donald H. Dyal. Detroit: Gale Research, c1998. xviii, 450 p.
97-042547   741.6/4/092273 B 21   0787618438
Illustration of books -- United States -- Bio-bibliography. Magazine illustration -- United States -- Bio-bibliography.

Z5961.U5 A73 1995
Government and art: a guide to sources in the Archives of American Art. Washington, D.C.: The Archives, 1995. 206 p.
95-079607   1880193078
Artists -- United States -- Bibliography.

Z5961.U5 A77
Arts in America: a bibliography/ Bernard Karpel, editor, Ruth W. Spiegel, editor for the publisher. Washington: Published for the Archives of American Art, 4 v.
79-015321   016.7/00973   0874745780
Arts, American -- Bibliography. Arts -- United States -- Bibliography.

Z5961.U5 B58 1991
Blum, Betty.
Art-related archival materials in the Chicago area/ Betty Blum. Washington, D.C.: Archives of American Art, Smithsonian Institution, v, 74 p.
91-072971   1880193000
Art, American -- Illinois -- Chicago Metropolitan Area -- Sources. Art -- Archival resources -- Illinois -- Chicago Metropolitan Area. Artists -- Illinois -- Chicago Metropolitan Area -- History -- Sources. Learned institutions and societies -- Illinois -- Chicago Metropolitan Area Chicago Metropolitan Area (Ill.) -- Archival resources -- Directories.

Z5961.U5 G64 1985
Goldman, Shifra M.,
Arte Chicano: a comprehensive annotated bibliography of Chicano art, 1965-1981/ compiled by Shifra M. Goldman and Tomás Ybarra-Frausto; with an introduction by the compilers. Berkeley: Chicano Studies Library Publications Unit, viii, 778 p.
85-029156   016.704/036872073   19   0918520096
Mexican American arts -- Bibliography. Ethnic arts -- United States -- Bibliography.

Z5961.U5 G85 1992
A Guide to archival sources for French-American art history in the archives of American art. Washington, D.C.: Archives of American Art, Smithsonian Institution, iv, 128 p.
92-082762   016.7/0973 20   1880193027
Art, American -- France -- History -- Sources -- Catalogs. Artists -- United States -- Biography -- Sources -- Catalogs. Art, French -- United States -- History -- Sources -- Catalogs. Artists -- France -- Biography -- Sources -- Catalogs.

Z5961.U5 K36 1994
Kalfatovic, Martin R.,
The New Deal fine arts projects: a bibliography, 1933-1992/ by Martin R. Kalfatovic. Metuchen, N.J.: Scarecrow Press, 1994. lxxii, 504 p.
93-031116   016.3530085/4 20   0810827492
Federal aid to the arts -- United States -- Bibliography. Art -- Conservation and restoration -- United States -- Bibliography. New Deal, 1933-1939.

Z5961.U5 R46 1984
Reps, John William.
Views and viewmakers of urban America: lithographs of towns and cities in the United States and Canada, notes on the artists and publishers, and a union catalog of their work, 1825-1925/ John W. Reps. Columbia: University of Missouri Press, 1984. xvi, 570 p.
83-006495   016.769/44/0973 19   0826204163
Lithography, American -- 19th century -- Union lists. Lithography, American -- 20th century -- Union lists. City and town life -- United States -- Pictorial works -- Union lists. City and town life -- Canada -- Pictorial works -- Union lists. Catalogs, Union -- North America. Lithographers -- United States -- Biography. United States -- In art -- Union lists. Canada -- In art -- Union lists.

Z5961.U5.W5
Whitehill, Walter Muir, 1905-
The arts in early American history; an essay by Walter Muir Whitehill. A bibliography by Wendell D. Garrett and Jane N. Garrett. Chapel Hill, Published for the Institute of Early American History and Culture at Williamsburg, Va., by the University of North Carolina Press [1965] xv, 170 p.
65-063132   016.70973
Art, American -- Bibliography. Art, American -- History -- Historiography.

Z5981-5984 Folklore

Z5981.B46 1993
Bennett, Gillian.
Contemporary legend: a folklore bibliography/ Gillian Bennett, Paul Smith. New York: Garland, 1993. xxv, 340 p.
93-015549   016.398/09173/2 20   0824061039
Urban folklore -- Bibliography. Legends -- Bibliography.

Z5981.S74 1992
Steinfirst, Susan.
Folklore and folklife: a guide to English-language reference sources/ Susan Steinfirst. New York: Garland Pub., 1992. 2 v.
92-013594   016.398   0815300689
Folklore -- Bibliography.

Z5983.F17.A83 1987
Ashliman, D. L.
A guide to folktales in the English language: based on the Aarne-Thompson classification system/ D.L. Ashliman. New York: Greenwood Press, 1987. xvi, 368 p.
87-015017   016.3982/012   0313259615
Tales -- Classification -- Bibliography. Tales -- Themes, motives -- Bibliography.

Z5983.F17 S67 1994
Sprug, Joseph W.,
Index to fairy tales, 1987-1992: including 310 collections of fairy tales, folktales, myths, and legends: with significant pre-1987 titles not previously indexed/ compiled by Joseph W. Sprug. Metuchen, N.J.: Scarecrow Press, 1994. xiii, 587 p. ;
93-029709   016.3982 20   0810827506
Fairy tales -- Indexes. Mythology -- Indexes. Folklore -- Indexes. Folk literature -- Indexes.

Z5984.A35 C68 1999
Coughlan, Margaret N.,
Folklore from Africa to the United States: an annotated bibliography / compiled by Margaret N. Coughlan. Detroit, MI: Omnigraphics, 1999. x, 161 p. :
99-023245   016.3982 21   0780803140
Folklore -- Africa -- Bibliography -- Catalogs. African Americans -- Folklore -- Bibliography -- Catalogs. Folklore -- West Indies -- Bibliography -- Catalogs. Folklore -- United States -- Bibliography -- Catalogs.

Z5984.A44.S95
Szwad, John F., 1936-
Afro-American folk culture: an annotated bibliography of materials from North, Central, and South America, and the West Indies/ John F. Szwad and Roger D. Abrahams, with Robert Baron ... [et al.]. Philadelphia: Institute for the Study of Human Issues, [c1978-   ]
77-016567   016.909/04/96   0915980800
Afro-Americans -- Folklore -- Bibliography. Afro-Americans -- Bibliography. Blacks -- America -- Folklore -- Bibliography.

Z5984.A75.A93 1994
Avakian, Anne M., 1906-
Armenian folklore bibliography/ Anne M. Avakian. Berkeley: University of California Press, c1994. xxvii, 212 p.
94-013033   016.398/09566/2   0520097947
Folklore -- Armenia -- Bibliography. Armenia -- Social life and customs -- Bibliography.

Z5990 Forecasting

Z5990.M39 1993
Mayne, Alan J. 1927-
Resources for the future: an international annotated bibliography for the 21st Century/ Alan J. Mayne. Westport, Conn.: Greenwood Press, 1993. ix, 351 p.
92-035820   016.30349   0313289115
Forecasting -- Bibliography.

Z5996.5 Gardening. Horticulture. Floriculture. Landscape gardening and architecture — By region or country, A-Z

Z5996.5.U6.L36 1997
Landscape architecture sourcebook: a guide to resources on the history and practice of landscape architecture in the United States/ [edited] by Diana Vogelsong. Detroit, MI: Omnigraphics, [1997-]
96-034507   016.712   0780801962
Landscape architecture -- United States -- Bibliography.

Z6001.A1 Geography and travels. Maps. Cartography — Bibliography of bibliography

Z6001.B74 1978
Brewer, James Gordon.
The literature of geography: a guide to its organisation and use/ by J. Gordon Brewer. 2d ed. London: Clive Bingley; 1978. 264 p.
78-016852   016.91   0851572804
Geography -- Bibliography. Geography -- Methodology.

Z6001.D86 1985
Dunbar, Gary S.
The history of modern geography: an annotated bibliography of selected works/ Gary S. Dunbar. New York: Garland Pub., 1985. xvi, 386 p.
83-048277   016.9 19   0824090667
Geography -- History -- Bibliography.

Z6001.G44 1985
A Geographical bibliography for American libraries/ edited by Chauncy D. Harris ... [et al.]; with assistance from Susan Fifer Canby, Phillip J. Parent, Steven S. Stettes. Washington, D.C.: Association of American Geographers, 1985. xxiii, 437 p.
85-011284   016.91   089291193X
Geography -- Bibliography.

Z6004 Geography and travels. Maps. Cartography — Special topics, A-Z

Z6004.P7.S85 1992
Sukhwal, B. L., 1929-
Political geography: a comprehensive systematic bibliography/ B.L. Sukhwal and Lilawati Sukhwal. New York: AMS Press, 1992. xx, 715 p.
91-057956   016.3201/2   0404631517
Political geography -- Bibliography.

Z6004.R38.H9 1988
Hyatt, Edward.
Keyguide to information sources in remote sensing/ Edward Hyatt. London; Mansell, 1988. xiv, 274 p.
88-004863   621.36/78072   0720118549
Remote sensing -- Bibliography. Remote sensing -- Information services.

Z6004.T6.A53 1995
Anderson, Sarah.
Anderson's Travel companion: a guide to the best non-fiction and fiction for travelling/ Sarah Anderson. Aldershot, Hants, England; Brookfield, Vt.: c1995. xxiii, 552 p.
94-024094   016.91/02/02   1859280137
Travel -- Bibliography.

Z6004.T6 T73 1993
The Traveler's reading guide: ready-made reading lists for the armchair traveler/ Maggy Simony, editor. New York: Facts on File, c1993. xv, 510 p. ;
92-008175   016.91 20   0816026483
Travel -- Bibliography.

Z6005 Geography and travels. Maps. Cartography — Local. By region, physical feature, etc., A-Z

Z6005.P7.A72
Arctic bibliography.   Montreal [etc.] McGill-Queen's University Press [etc.] 16 v.
53-061783   016.9198
Arctic regions -- Bibliography. Regions arctiques -- Bibliographie.

Z6005.P7.G47 2000
Gerald F. Fitzgerald Collection (Newberry Library)
The Gerald F. Fitzgerald Collection of polar books, maps, and art at the Newberry Library: a catalogue/ compiled by David C. White and Patrick Morris; edited by Robert W. Karrow, Jr. Chicago: Newberry Library, 2000.
00-011085   016.909/091   0911028706
Polar regions -- Bibliography -- Catalogs. Polar regions -- Maps -- Bibliography -- Catalogs. Polar regions -- In art -- Bibliography -- Catalogs.

Z6009 Geography and travels. Maps. Cartography — Catalogs

Z6009.A47
Current geographical publications/ The American Geographical Society. New York: The Society, [1938?-]
41-027154   016.91
Geography -- Bibliography -- Periodicals.

Z6011 Geography and travels. Maps. Cartography — Voyages and travels — General bibliography

Z6011.H4 1993
Heise, Jon O.
The travel book: guide to the travel guides. Metuchen, N.J.: Scarecrow Press, 1993. v, 397 p.
93-015822   016.9102/02   0810826976
Travel -- Guidebooks -- Bibliography.

Z6011.R65 1990
Robinson, Jane, 1959-
Wayward women: a guide to women travellers/ Jane Robinson. New York: Oxford University Press, c1990.
89-039701   016.9104/082   0192122614
Women travelers -- Bibliography.

Z6011.S5 1999
Smith, Harold Frederick, 1923-
American travellers abroad: a bibliography of accounts published before 1900/ Harold F. Smith. Lanham, Md.: Scarecrow Press, 1999. ix, 383 p.
98-008381   016.9104   0810835541
Voyages and travels -- Bibliography. Travelers -- United States.

Z6027 Geography and travels. Maps. Cartography — Maps and cartography — By region or country, A-Z

Z6027.C22.O68 1991
Winearls, Joan.
Mapping Upper Canada, 1780-1867: an annotated bibliography of manuscript and printed maps/ Joan Winearls. Toronto; University of Toronto Press, c1991. xli, 986 p.
92-102858   016.912713   0802027946
Ontario -- Maps -- Bibliography. Ontario -- Maps, Manuscript -- Bibliography.

Z6027.U5.L5 1989
Library of Congress.
Civil War maps: an annotated list of maps and atlases in the Library of Congress/ compiled by Richard W. Stephenson. Washington: Library of Congress, 1989. viii, 410 p.
88-600031   016.9737   0844405981
United States -- History -- Civil War, 1861-1865 -- Maps -- Bibliography -- Catalogs.

Z6028 Geography and travels. Maps. Cartography — Maps and cartography — Catalogs

Z6028.M23 1992
The Map catalog: every kind of map and chart on earth and even some above it/ Joel Makower, editor. 3rd ed., newly rev. New York: Vintage Books, c1992. 364 p. :
92-053582   912/.0294 20   0679742573
Maps -- Catalogs.

Z6031-6033 Geology. Mineralogy. Paleontology

Z6031.I55 1989
Information sources in the earth sciences/ editors, David N. Wood, Joan E. Hardy, and Anthony P. Harvey. London; Bowker-Saur, c1989. xvi, 518 p.
89-000580   016.551   0408014067
Earth sciences -- Bibliography.

Z6031.W35 1981
Ward, Dederick C.
Geologic reference sources: a subject and regional bibliography of publications and maps in the geological sciences/ by Dederick C. Ward, Marjorie W. Wheeler & Robert A. Bier, Jr. Metuchen, N.J.: Scarecrow Press, 1981. xxv, 560 p.
81-004770 016.55 0810814285
Geology -- Bibliography.

Z6033.C3.G85 1998
A guide to speleological literature of the English language: 1794-1996/ compiled and edited by Diana E. Northup ... [et al.]. Saint Louis: Cave Books, 1998. xviii, 539 p.
98-010758 016.55144/7 0939748517
Speleology -- Bibliography.

Z6033.E1 T9 1986
Tyckoson, David A.
Earthquake prediction/ by David A. Tyckoson. Phoenix, Ariz.: Oryx Press, 1986. 67 p. ;
86-002547 016.5512/2 19 0897742281
Earthquake prediction -- Bibliography.

Z6121 Gymnastics. Physical education

Z6121.A62
American Association for Health, Physical Education, and Research
Completed research in health, physical education, and recreation. [Washington] Research Council, American Association for Health, Physical Education, and Recreation.
59-015820 016.79
Health education -- Bibliography -- Periodicals. Physical education and training -- Bibliography -- Periodicals. Recreation -- Bibliography -- Periodicals.

Z6121.P85 1996
Pumroy, Eric, 1952-
Research guide to the Turner movement in the United States/ compiled by Eric L. Pumroy and Katja Rampelmann. Westport, Conn.: Greenwood Press, 1996. xxx, 358 p.
96-005846 016.796/06 0313297630
German Americans -- Societies, etc. -- Bibliography. Physical education and training -- United States -- History -- Bibliography.

Z6201.A55-S64 History — General bibliography

Z6201.A55 1995
The American Historical Association's guide to historical literature/ general editor, Mary Beth Norton; associate editor, Pamela Gerardi. New York: Oxford University Press, 1995. 2 v.
94-036720 016.9 0195057279
History -- Bibliography. Best books.

Z6201.F72 1990
Fritze, Ronald H, 1951-
Reference sources in history: an introductory guide/ Ronald H. Fritze, Brian E. Coutts, Louis A. Vyhnanek. Santa Barbara, Calif.: ABC-CLIO, c1990. xvii, 319 p.
90-045169 016.9 0874361648
History -- Bibliography.

Z6201.K38 1996
Kavanagh, Gaynor.
A bibliography for history, history curatorship, and museums/ Gaynor Kavanagh. Aldershot, Hants; Scolar Press, c1996. 221 p.
95-044268 016.9 1859282032
History -- Bibliography. Historical museums -- Bibliography. Museum techniques -- Bibliography.

Z6201.S64 1994
Slavens, Thomas P., 1928-
Sources of information for historical research/ Thomas P. Slavens. New York: Neal-Schuman, c1994. ix, 577 p.
94-008119 016.909 1555700934
History -- Bibliography.

Z6202 History — By period — Ancient

Z6202.B413
Bengtson, Hermann, 1909-
Introduction to ancient history. Translated from the 6th ed. by R. I. Frank and Frank D. Gilliard. Berkeley, University of California Press, 1970. viii, 213 p.
78-118685 016.93 0520017234
History, Ancient -- Bibliography.

Z6203 History — By period — Medieval

Z6203.I63
International medieval bibliography. [Leeds, Eng.] University of Leeds [etc.] v.
70-462591 016.914/03/1
Middle Ages -- Periodicals -- Indexes.

Z6203.I63
International medieval bibliography. [Leeds, Eng.] University of Leeds [etc.]
70-462591 016.914/03/1
Middle Ages -- Periodicals -- Indexes.

Z6203.P25 1980
Paetow, Louis John, 1880-1928.
A guide to the study of medieval history/ by Louis John Paetow; with errata compiled by Gray C. Boyce and an addendum by Lynn Thorndike; prepared under the auspices of the Mediaeval Academy of America. Millwood, N.Y.: Kraus Reprint, [1980] c1917. cxii, 643 p.
80-081364 016.9401 0527691011
Middle Ages -- Bibliography. Middle Ages -- History -- Outlines, syllabi, etc.

Z6203.P25 1980 Suppl
Boyce, Gray Cowan,
Literature of medieval history, 1930-1975: a supplement to Louis John Paetow's A guide to the study of medieval history/ compiled and edited by Gray Cowan Boyce; sponsored by the Medieval Academy of America; foreword by Paul Meyvaert. Millwood, N.Y.: Kraus International Publications, c1981. 5 v.
80-028773 016./9401 19 0527104620
Middle Ages -- Bibliography.

Z6204 History — By period — Modern

Z6204.A33 1995
Latham, A. J. H.
Africa, Asia, and South America since 1800: a bibliographical guide/ compiled by A.J.H. Latham. Manchester; Manchester University Press; c1995. xxxiii, 259 p.
93-047152 016.9098 0719018773
History, Modern -- 19th century -- Bibliography. History, Modern -- 20th century -- Bibliography. South America -- History -- Bibliography. Asia -- History -- Bibliography. Africa -- History -- Bibliography. Central America -- History -- Bibliography.

Z6204.R62
Roach, John,
A bibliography of modern history; edited by John Roach. London, Cambridge U.P., 1968. xxiv, 388 p.
67-011528 016.9402 0521071917
History, Modern -- Bibliography.

Z6205 History — Periodicals. Societies

Z6205.S73 1993
Steiner, Dale R.
Historical journals: a handbook for writers and reviewers/ by Dale R. Steiner, Casey R. Phillips. Jefferson, N.C.: McFarland & Co., c1993. xii, 274 p.
92-051090 808/.02 0899508014
History -- Periodicals -- Directories. Historiography -- Handbooks, manuals, etc. Book reviewing.

Z6207 History — Special historical events, movements, etc., A-Z

Z6207.C97 A8 1976
Atiya, Aziz Suryal,
The crusade: historiography and bibliography/ Aziz S. Atiya. Westport, Conn.: Greenwood Press, 1976, c1962. 170 p.
75-022640 016.9401/8 0837183642
Crusades -- Bibliography. Crusades -- Historiography.

Z6207.E8 E58 1990
Enser, A. G. S.
A subject bibliography of the First World War: books in English, 1914-1987/ A.G.S. Enser. Aldershot, Hants, England; Gower, c1990. xi, 412 p.
90-182882 016.9403 20 0566056194
World War, 1914-1918 -- Bibliography.

Z6207.E8.N64 1997
Noffsinger, James Philip.
World War I aviation: a bibliography of books in English, French, German, and Italian: with a price list supplement/ by James Philip Noffsinger. Lanham, Md.: Scarecrow Press, 1997. x, 609 p.
95-037995 016.9404/4 081083085X
World War, 1914-1918 -- Bibliography.

Z6207.E8 W38 1988
Wedborn, Helena.
Women in the First and Second World Wars: a checklist of the holdings of the Hoover Institution on War, Revolution, and Peace/ compiled by Helena Wedborn. [Stanford, Calif.]: Hoover Institution, Stanford University, c1988. viii, 73 p.
88-023521   016.9403/15/03042   19
0817927220
World War, 1914-1918 -- Women -- Bibliography -- Catalogs. World War, 1939-1945 -- Women -- Bibliography -- Catalogs.

Z6207.G44.T67 1991
Totten, Samuel.
First-person accounts of genocidal acts committed in the twentieth century: an annotated bibliography/ Samuel Totten. New York: Greenwood Press, 1991. lxxv, 351 p.
91-020600   016.90982   0313267138
History, Modern -- 20th century -- Bibliography. Genocide -- History -- 20th century -- Bibliography. Biography -- 20th century -- Bibliography.

Z6207.G7.H67 1995
Hopwood, Keith.
Ancient Greece and Rome: a bibliographical guide/ compiled by Keith Hopwood. Manchester [U.K.]; Manchester University Press; c1995. xiv, 450 p.
95-224070   016.938   0719024013
Civilization, Classical -- Bibliography. Civilization, Greco-Roman -- Bibliography.

Z6207.R4 B5
Bibliographie internationale de l'Humanisme et de la Renaissance. Genève, Librairie Droz.
68-002326   016.9402/1
Renaissance -- Bibliography -- Periodicals.

Z6207.W8 A34 1992
Adamczyk, Richard D.
United States Army in World War II. compiled and edited by Ricard D. Adamczyk, Morris J. MacGregor. World War II, 50th anniversary, commemorative ed. Washington, D.C.: Center of Military History, U.S. Army: ix, 173 p.
93-135094   0160378176
World War, 1939-1945 -- Campaigns -- Western Front -- Bibliography.

Z6207.W8.B36 1996
Baxter, Colin F., 1942-
The war in North Africa, 1940-1943: a selected bibliography/ Colin F. Baxter. Westport, Conn.: Greenwood Press, 1996. vii, 119 p.
95-039494   016.94054/23   0313291209
World War, 1939-1945 -- Campaigns -- Africa, North -- Bibliography.

Z6207.W8.C48 1996
Chambers, Steven D., 1955-
Political leaders and military figures of the Second World War: a bibliography/ Steven D. Chambers. Aldershot, Hants; Dartmouth, c1996. xviii, 440 p.
95-047697   016.94053/092/2   1855216469
World War, 1939-1945 -- Biography -- Bibliography. Heads of state -- Biography -- Bibliography. Military biography -- Bibliography.

Z6207.W8 E56 1990
Enser, A. G. S.
A subject bibliography of the Second World War, and aftermath: books in English, 1975-1987/ A.G.S. Enser. Aldershot, Hants, England; Gower, c1990. xii, 287 p.
90-002915   016.94053 20   0566057360
World War, 1939-1945 -- Bibliography.

Z6207.W8.R36 1998
Rasor, Eugene L., 1936-
The China-Burma-India campaign, 1931-1945: historiography and annotated bibliography/ Eugene L. Rasor. Westport, Conn.: Greenwood Press, 1998. xviii, 282 p.
97-049967   016.94054/25   0313288720
World War, 1939-1945 -- Campaigns -- China -- Bibliography. World War, 1939-1945 -- Campaigns -- China -- Historiography. World War, 1939-1945 -- Campaigns -- Burma -- Bibliography.

Z6207.W8.R37 1996
Rasor, Eugene L., 1936-
The Southwest Pacific campaign, 1941-1945: historiography and annotated bibliography/ Eugene L. Rasor. Westport, Conn.: Greenwood Press, 1996. xvi, 279 p.
96-005845   016.94054/26   0313288747
World War, 1939-1945 -- Campaigns -- South Pacific Ocean -- Bibliography. World War, 1939-1945 -- Campaigns -- South Pacific Ocean -- Historiography.

Z6207.W8 R564 1994
Rohrbach, Peter T.
The largest event: a Library of Congress resource guide for the study of World War II/ Peter T. Rohrbach. Washington: Library of Congress, 1994. vii, 137 p. :
93-016487   016.94053 20   0160431336
World War, 1939-1945 -- Library resources. Library resources -- Washington (D.C.)

Z6207.W8.S29 1989
Sbrega, John J. 1941-
The war against Japan, 1941-1945: an annotated bibliography/ John J. Sbrega. New York: Garland, 1989. xxv, 1050 p.
88-036535   016.94054/26   0824089405
World War, 1939-1945 -- Campaigns -- Pacific Area -- Bibliography. World War, 1939-1945 -- Japan -- Bibliography. World War, 1939-1945 -- United States -- Bibliography. Pacific Area -- History -- Bibliography.

Z6207.W8.S564 1991
Smith, Myron J.
Pearl Harbor, 1941: a bibliography/ Myron J. Smith, Jr. New York: Greenwood Press, 1991. xxv, 197 p.
90-049167   016.94054/26   0313281211
Pearl Harbor (Hawaii), Attack on, 1941 -- Bibliography.

Z6207.W8 S572 1990
Smith, Myron J.
World War II at sea: a bibliography of sources in English, 1974-1989 / by Myron J. Smith, Jr. Metuchen, N.J.: Scarecrow Press, 1990. ix, 304 p.
89-028213   016.94054/5 20   0810822601
World War, 1939-1945 -- Naval operations -- Bibliography.

Z6207.W8.W54 1995
Wilson, Eunice.
Dangerous sky: a resource guide to the Battle of Britain/ Eunice Wilson. Westport, Conn.: Greenwood Press, 1995. xxvii, 128 p.
94-046943   016.94054/211   0313282161
Britain, Battle of, 1940 -- Bibliography.

Z6208 History — Special methodological topics, A-Z

Z6208.H5.H47 1994
Herubel, Jean-Pierre V. M.
Annales historiography and theory: a selective and annotated bibliography/ compiled by Jean-Pierre V.M. Herubel. Westport, Conn.: Greenwood Press, 1994. ix, 173 p.
94-016073   016.9072   031329125X
Historiography -- Bibliography. History -- Philosophy -- Bibliography.

Z6208.H5.H57 1987
Historiography: an annotated bibliography of journal articles, books, and dissertations/ Susan K. Kinnell, editor; foreword by Georg G. Iggers. Santa Barbara, Calif.: ABC-Clio, c1987. 2 v.
87-014427   016.907/2   0874361680
Historiography -- Bibliography.

Z6208.O7.S54 1988
Smith, Allen.
Directory of oral history collections/ by Allen Smith. Phoenix: Oryx Press, 1988. 141 p.
87-022868   016.9072073   0897743229
Oral history -- Archival resources -- Directories. Oral history -- Library resources -- Directories.

Z6250 Hospitality industry. Hotels

Z6250.L58 1990
A Literature guide to the hospitality industry/ compiled by Philip Sawin ... [et al.]. New York: Greenwood Press, 1990. x, 99 p.
90-031740   016.64794   0313267219
Hospitality industry -- Bibliography. Hospitality industry -- Information services. Information storage and retrieval systems -- Hospitality industry.

Z6265 Humanities

Z6265.B53 2000
Blazek, Ron.
The humanities: a selective guide to information sources/ Ron Blazek and Elizabeth Aversa. Englewood, Colo.: Libraries Unlimited, 2000. xix, 603 p.
99-089831   016.0160013   1563086018
Humanities -- Bibliography of bibliographies. Humanities -- Bibliography. Humanities -- Reference books -- Bibliography.

Z6366 Jews — General bibliography

Z6366.B8 2000
Brisman, Shimeon.
A history and guide to Judaic dictionaries and concordances/ Shimeon Brisman. Hoboken, NJ: KTAV Pub. House, [2000.] v. 1
99-011033   039/.92   0881256587
Yiddish language -- Dictionaries -- Bibliography. Ladino language -- Dictionaries -- Bibliography. Hebrew language -- Dictionaries -- Bibliography.

Z6366.S39 1992
The Schocken guide to Jewish books: where to start reading about Jewish history, literature, culture, and religion/ edited by Barry W. Holtz. New York: Schocken Books, c1992. x, 357 p.
91-017760   016.909/04924   0805241086
Jews -- Bibliography. Judaism -- Bibliography. Jewish literature -- Bibliography.

Z6366.S526
Singerman, Robert.
Jewish serials of the world: a supplement to the research bibliography of secondary sources/ compiled by Robert Singerman. Westport, Conn.: Greenwood Press, 2001. xix, 422 p.
00-063653   011/.34/089924   031330663X
Jewish periodicals -- History and criticism -- Bibliography. Jews -- Periodicals -- History and criticism -- Bibliography.

Z6370 Jews — Religion — General bibliography

Z6370.S78 1990
Starkey, Edward D.
Judaism and Christianity: a guide to the reference literature/ Edward D. Starkey. Englewood, Colo.: Libraries Unlimited, 1991. xiv, 256 p.
90-046212   016.2   0872875334
Christianity -- Bibliography. Judaism -- Bibliography.

Z6372 Jews — History — General bibliography

Z6372.U55 1990
Universitah ha-Ivrit bi-Yerushalayim.
Oral history of contemporary Jewry: an annotated catalogue/ Bibliographical Center of the Institute of Contemporary Jewry, The Hebrew University of Jerusalem. New York: Garland Pub., 1990. xv, 245 p.
90-002859   016.909/04924   0824056833
Jews -- History -- 1789-1945 -- Bibliography -- Catalogs. Jews -- History -- 1945- -- Bibliography -- Catalogs. Jews -- Latin America -- History -- Bibliography -- Catalogs. Israel -- Bibliography -- Catalogs.

Z6373 Jews — History — By region or country, A-Z

Z6373.U5.K34 1995
Kaganoff, Nathan M.
Judaica Americana: an annotated bibliography of publications from 1960-1990/ Nathan M. Kaganoff; pref. by Jonathan D. Sarna. Brooklyn, N.Y.: Carlson Pub., 1995. 2 v.
95-004450   016.970004/924   0926019759
Jews -- United States -- Bibliography. Jews -- Canada -- Bibliography. Jews -- Latin America -- Bibliography. United States -- Ethnic relations -- Bibliography. Canada -- Ethnic relations -- Bibliography. Latin America -- Ethnic relations -- Bibliography.

Z6374 Jews — Other special topics, A-Z

Z6374.A56.A57 1987
Antisemitism: an annotated bibliography/ the Vidal Sassoon International Center for the Study of Antisemitism, the Hebrew University of Jerusalem; edited by Susan Sarah Cohen. New York: Garland, 1987-1994 v. 1-3
87-011842   016.3058/924   0824085329
Antisemitism -- Bibliography.

Z6374.H6 A54 1993
Annotated bibliography. Washington, DC (100 Raoul Wallenberg Place, SW, Wa   32 p.
94-149478   016.94053/18 20
Holocaust, Jewish (1939-1945) -- Bibliography. Holocaust, Jewish (1939-1945) -- Study and teaching -- United States

Z6374.H6 B58 1995
Bloomberg, Marty.
The Jewish Holocaust: an annotated guide to books in English/ by Marty Bloomberg, Buckley Barry Barrett; introduction by Jeffrey M. Elliot. 2nd ed., rev. and expanded. San Bernardino, Calif.: Borgo Press, 1995. 312 p.
94-029741   016.94053/18 20   0809514060
Holocaust, Jewish (1939-1945) -- Bibliography. English imprints.

Z6374.H6 C37 1985
Cargas, Harry J.
The Holocaust: an annotated bibliography/ Harry James Cargas. 2nd ed. Chicago: American Library Association, 1985. viii, 196 p.
85-020069   016.94053/15/03924   19
0838904335
Holocaust, Jewish (1939-1945) -- Bibliography.

Z6374.H6.E33 1986 Suppl.
Edelheit, Abraham J.
Bibliography on Holocaust literature. Abraham J. Edelheit and Hershel Edelheit. Boulder: Westview Press, 1990-c1993 v. 1-2
89-070630   016.94053/18   0813308968
Holocaust, Jewish (1939-1945) -- Bibliography.

Z6374.H6 F47 2002
Fernekes, William R.
The Oryx Holocaust sourcebook/ William R. Fernekes. Westport, CT: Oryx Press, 2002. xii, 397 p.
2001-058030   016.94053/18 21   1573562955
Holocaust, Jewish (1939-1945) -- Bibliography. Holocaust, Jewish (1939-1945) -- Audio-visual aids -- Catalogs. Holocaust, Jewish (1939-1945), in literature -- Bibliography. Holocaust, Jewish (1939-1945) -- Personal narratives -- Bibliography. Holocaust, Jewish (1939-1945) -- Study and teaching -- Bibliography.

Z6374.H6 H68 1999
Holocaust reference library: cumulative index/ Julie L. Carnagie, index coordinator. Detroit: U.X.L., c1999. 32 p.
99-160741   940.53/18 21   0787619248
Schmittroth, Linda. People of the Holocaust -- Indexes. Feldman, George. Understanding the Holocaust -- Indexes. Holocaust, Jewish (1939-1945) -- Indexes. Righteous Gentiles in the Holocaust -- Indexes. Germany -- History -- 1933-1945 -- Indexes.

Z6374.Z5.J65
Jones, A. Philip 1947-
Britain and Palestine, 1914-1948: archival sources for the history of the British Mandate/ compiled by Philip Jones. Oxford: Oxford University Press for the British Academy, c1979. x, 246 p.
80-454407   016.95694/04   0197259855
Zionism -- History -- Archival resources. Mandates -- Palestine -- Archival resources. Palestine -- History -- 1929-1948 -- Archival resources.

Z6375 Jews — Catalogs

Z6375.Y59 1998
YIVO Archives.
Guide to the YIVO Archives/ compiled and edited by Fruma Mohrer and Marek Web. Armonk, N.Y.: M.E. Sharpe, c1998. xxv, 400 p.
97-034858   026.909/04924   0765601303
YIVO Archives -- Catalogs.

Z6461 International law and relations — General bibliography

Z6461.B49 1991
Beyerly, Elizabeth.
Public international law: a guide to information sources/ Elizabeth Beyerly. London; Mansell, 1991. xviii, 331 p.
90-047238   016.341   0720120829
International law -- Bibliography.

Z6464 International law and relations — Special topics, A-Z

Z6464.M2.W36 1991
Wang, James C. F.
Ocean politics and law: an annotated bibliography/ James C.F. Wang. New York: Greenwood Press, 1991. xv, 243 p.
91-030202   016.3414/5   031327925X
Law of the sea -- Bibliography. Marine resources conservation -- Law and legislation -- Bibliography.

Z6464.N65.W55 1994
Williams, Phil, 1948-
North Atlantic Treaty Organization/ Phil Williams, compiler. New Brunswick, U.S.A.: Transaction Publishers, c1994. xxxv, 283 p.
93-042578   016.355/031/091821   1560001542
North Atlantic Treaty Organization -- Bibliography.

Z6464.Z9 M34 2000
Making peace pay: a bibliography on disarmament & conversion/ edited by Nils Petter Gleditsch ... [et al.]; with contributions by Michael Brzoska & Ron P. Smith. Claremont, Calif.: Regina Books, 2000.
00-059089   016.3384/76234   1930053037
Disarmament -- Economic aspects -- Bibliography. Economic conversion -- Bibliography. Peace -- Bibliography.

Z6465 International law and relations — Foreign relations. By region or country, A-Z

Z6465.A36.A36 1997
African international relations: an annotated bibliography. Boulder, Colo.: Westview Press, 1997. xxv, 677 p.
97-010413   327.6   0813386535
Africa -- Foreign relations -- Bibliography.

Z6465.L29 F56 1981
Finan, John J.
Latin America, international relations: a guide to information sources/ John J. Finan, John Child. Detroit, Mich: Gale Research Co., 1981. xvii, 236 p.
73-017508   016.3278 19   0810313251
Latin America -- Foreign relations -- Bibliography.

Z6465.L29 T37 1994
Tarragó, Rafael E.
Early U.S.-Hispanic relations, 1776-1860: an annotated bibliography/ by Rafael E. Tarragó. Metuchen, N.J.: Scarecrow Press, 1994. viii, 171 p.
94-008880   016.3277308 20   0810828820
Latin America -- Foreign relations -- United States -- Bibliography. United States -- Foreign relations -- Latin America -- Bibliography. Spain -- Foreign relations -- United States -- Bibliography. United States -- Foreign relations -- Spain -- Bibliography.

Z6465.L29 T7 Suppl.
Meyer, Michael C.
Supplement to A bibliography of United States-Latin American relations since 1810/ compiled and edited by Michael C. Meyer. Lincoln: University of Nebraska Press, c1979. xxvi, 193 p.
79-001243   016.32773/08   0803230516
Latin America -- Foreign relations -- United States. United States -- Foreign relations -- Latin America -- Bibliography.

Z6465.U5 A68
American foreign policy and treaty index. Bethesda, MD: Congressional Information Service, c1996-[1999]
96-647222   327.73 20
Government publications -- United States -- Periodicals. United States -- Foreign relations -- 1993- -- Indexes -- Periodicals. United States -- Foreign relations -- 1993- -- Bibliography -- Periodicals.

Z6465.U5 C24 1994
Carr, James A.,
American foreign policy during the French Revolution--Napoleonic period, 1789-1815: a bibliography/ [edited by James A. Carr]. New York: Garland Pub., 1994. x, 176 p.
94-002422   016.32773 20   0824056973
United States -- Foreign relations -- 1783-1815 -- Bibliography.

Z6465.U5.D62 1987
Doenecke, Justus D.
Anti-intervention: a bibliographical introduction to isolationism and pacifism from World War I to the early cold war/ Justus D. Doenecke. New York: Garland, 1987. xviii, 421 p.
87-008635   016.97391   0824084829
Neutrality -- United States -- Bibliography. Pacifism -- United States -- History -- 20th century -- Bibliography. United States -- Foreign relations -- 20th century -- Bibliography.

Z6465.U5 G84 2003
American foreign relations since 1600: a guide to the literature/ Robert L. Beisner, editor. 2nd ed. Santa Barbara, Calif.: ABC-CLIO, c2003. 2 v.
2003-008684   016.32773 21   1576070808
United States -- Foreign relations -- Bibliography.

Z6465.U5 K54 1983
Killen, Linda,
Versailles and after: an annotated bibliography of American foreign relations, 1919-1933/ Linda Killen, Richard L. Lael. New York: Garland Pub., 1983. xvi, 469 p.
82-049115   016.32773 19   0824092023
United States -- Foreign relations -- 20th century -- Bibliography.

Z6465.U5 K74 1995
Krewson, Margrit B.
German-American relations: a selective bibliography/ Margrit B. Krewson. Washington, D.C.: Library of Congress: 319 p.
94-047942   016.30348/273043 20
United States -- Relations -- Germany -- Bibliography -- Catalogs. Germany -- Relations -- United States -- Bibliography -- Catalogs.

Z6465.U5 L56 1988
Lincove, David A.
The Anglo-American relationship: an annotated bibliography of scholarship, 1945-1985/ compiled and annotated by David A. Lincove and Gary R. Treadway. New York: Greenwood Press, 1988. xiiii, 415 p.
88-007225   016.3034/8273/041   19 0313258546
United States -- Relations -- Great Britain -- Bibliography. Great Britain -- Relations -- United States -- Bibliography.

Z6465.U5 L84 1991
Lulat, Y. G.-M.
U.S. relations with South Africa: an annotated bibliography/ Y. G.-M. Lulat; with the assistance of R.V. Guillén... [et al.]. Boulder: Westview Press, 1991. 2 v.
86-009094   327.73068 19   0813377471
United States -- Foreign relations -- South Africa -- Bibliography. South Africa -- Foreign relations -- United States -- Bibliography.

Z6465.U5 N58 2001
Nisbet, Ada B.
British comment on the United States: a chronological bibliography, 1832-1899/ Ada B. Nisbet; edited by Elliot J. Kanter; with a foreword by Asa Briggs. Berkeley: University of California Press, c2001. xxxii, 516 p.
00-067622   016.9735 21   0520098110
National characteristics, American -- Bibliography. Public opinion -- Great Britain -- History -- 19th century -- Bibliography. United States -- Foreign public opinion, British -- Bibliography. United States -- Relations -- Great Britain -- Bibliography. Great Britain -- Relations -- United States -- Bibliography. United States -- Civilization -- 19th century -- Bibliography.

Z6465.U5 S24 1990
Saha, Santosh C.
Indo-U.S. relations, 1947-1989: a guide to information sources/ Santosh C. Saha. New York: P. Lang, c1990. xii, 213 p.
90-005936   016.32773054 20   0820413542
United States -- Foreign relations -- India -- Bibliography. India -- Foreign relations -- United States -- Bibliography.

Z6465.U5 M8
Mugridge, Ian.
United States foreign relations under Washington and Adams: a guide to the literature and sources/ Ian Mugridge. New York: Garland Pub., 1982. xi, 88 p.
78-068256   016.32773 19   0824097785
United States -- Foreign relations -- 1789-1797 -- Bibliography. United States -- Foreign relations -- 1797-1801 -- Bibliography.

Z6511 Literature — General bibliography

Z6511.H38 Suppl.
Havlice, Patricia Pate.
Index to literary biography. by Patricia Pate Havlice. Metuchen, N.J.: Scarecrow Press, 1983. 2 v.
82-025051   016.809 19   081081613X
Authors -- Biography -- Indexes.

Z6511.K4 1997
Kehler, Dorothea,
Problems in literary research: a guide to selected reference works/ Dorothea Kehler. 4th ed., rev. Lanham, Md.: Scarecrow Press, 1997. xiii, 230 p.
96-031247   026.8/072 20   0810832178
Literature -- Reference books -- Bibliography. Literature -- Research.

Z6511.M25
Magill, Frank Northen, 1907-
Magill's bibliography of literary criticism: selected sources for the study of more than 2,500 outstanding works of Western literature/ edited by Frank N. Magill, associate editors, Stephen L. Hanson, Patricia King Hanson. Englewood Cliffs, N.J.: Salem Press, c1979. 4 v.
79-063017   016.8   0893561886
Literature -- History and criticism -- Indexes.

Z6511.M2518 2001
Magill index to literature: cumulative indexes, 1984-2001/ from the editors of Salem Press. Pasadena, Calif.: The Press, 2001.
2001-031367   016.809 21   1587650932
Literature -- Indexes.

Z6511.P37 1983
Patterson, Margaret C.
Literary research guide/ Margaret C. Patterson. 2nd ed. New York: Modern Language Association of America, 1983. lxxxv, 559 p.
82-020386   016.8 19   0873521293
Literature -- Bibliography. Literature -- Reference books.

Z6511.W44 1994
Weiner, Alan R., 1938-
Literary criticism index/ by Alan R. Weiner and Spencer Means. Metuchen, N.J.: Scarecrow Press, 1994. xix, 559 p.
93-016137   016.809   0810826658
Literature -- History and criticism -- Indexes. English literature -- History and criticism -- Indexes. American literature -- History and criticism -- Indexes.

Z6514 Literature — Special subjects, A-Z

Z6514.C5.J83 1997
Bibliography of the myth of Don Juan in literary history/ edited by Jose Manuel Losada. Lewiston, N.Y.: Edwin Mellen Press, c1997. xviii, 216 p.
97-039651   016.809/93351   0773484507
Don Juan (Legendary character) in literature -- Bibliography.

Z6514.C7.A38 1996
Limb, Peter.
Bibliography of African literatures/ Peter Limb and Jean-Marie Volet. Lanham, Md.: Scarecrow Press, c1996. xxiii, 433 p.
96-000870   016.8088/9866   0810831449
Africa -- Literatures -- Bibliography. Africa -- In literature -- Bibliography.

Z6514.C7.C66 1998
The Comparative reader: a handlist of basic reading in comparative literature/ edited by John T. Kirby. New Haven, Conn.: Chancery Press, 1998.
97-050495   016.809   189065700X
Literature, Comparative -- Bibliography.

Z6514.C97.C65 1988
Cohen, Ralph, 1917-
New literary history international bibliography of literary theory and criticism/ Ralph Cohen, editor; Jeffrey M. Peck, bibliographical editor; Christopher Camuto, technical editor; Charlotte Bowen, supervisory editor. Baltimore: Johns Hopkins University Press, c1988. xix, 188 p.
88-003016   016.801/95   0801836875
Literature -- History and criticism -- Bibliography. Criticism -- History -- 20th century -- Bibliography.

Z6514.C97.F76 1988
Frost, Wendy.
Feminist literary criticism: a bibliography of journal articles, 1975-1981/ Wendy Frost, Michele Valiquette. New York: Garland Pub., 1988. xxiv, 867 p.
87-035325   016.809/89287   0824077881
Feminist literary criticism -- Bibliography. Literature, Modern -- 20th century -- History and criticism -- Bibliography.

Z6514.C97.M37 1993
Marshall, Donald G., 1943-
Contemporary critical theory: a selective bibliography/ Donald G. Marshall. New York: Modern Language Association of America, 1993. ix, 201 p.
92-033515   016.801/95   0873529642
Criticism -- Bibliography.

Z6514.C97.R36 1996
Recent work in critical theory, 1989-1995: an annotated bibliography/ compiled by William Baker and Kenneth Womack. Westport, Conn.: Greenwood Press, 1996. xvii, 585 p.
96-018346   016.801/95/0904049   0313294348
Criticism -- Bibliography.

Z6514.F35.F35 1999
Fantasy and horror: a critical and historical guide to literature, illustration, film, TV, radio, and the Internet/ edited by Neil Barron. Lanham, Md.: Scarecrow Press, 1999. xii, 816 p.
98-046564   700/.415   0810835967
Fantasy literature -- Bibliography. Fantasy literature -- History and criticism. Horror tales -- Bibliography.

Z6514.F66.K54 1995
Kiell, Norman.
Food and drink in literature: a selectively annotated bibliography/ by Norman Kiell. Lanham, Md.: Scarecrow Press, c1995. v, 361 p.
95-015427   016.809/93355   0810830302
Food in literature -- Bibliography. Beverages in literature -- Bibliography. Literature -- History and criticism -- Bibliography.

Z6514.L38
Corcos, Christine, 1953-
An international guide to law and literature studies/ Christine Alice Corcos. Buffalo, N.Y.: W.S. Hein, 2000. 2 v.
96-025036   016.809/93355   1575881160
Law in literature -- Bibliography. Law and literature -- Bibliography.

Z6514.L57.T9 1991
Twentieth-century literary movements index: a guide to 500 literary movements, groups, schools, tendencies, and trends of the twentieth century, covering more than 3,000 novelists, poets, dramatist Laurie Lanzen Harris, editor, Helene Henderson, associate editor. Detroit, Mich.: Omnigraphics, c1991. xvi, 419 p.
90-020189   016.809/91/0904   1558883061
Literary movements -- Indexes. Literature, Modern -- 20th century -- Indexes. Literature, Modern -- 20th century -- Societies, etc. -- Indexes.

Z6514.P66.K64 1981
Kolar, Carol Koehmstedt, 1931-
Plot summary index/ compiled by Carol Koehmstedt Kolar. Metuchen, N.J.: Scarecrow Press, 1981. xviii, 526 p.
80-027112   809   0810813920
Literature -- Stories, plots, etc. -- Indexes.

Z6514.P7.B43 1996
Beacham's encyclopedia of popular fiction/ edited by Kirk H. Beetz. Osprey, FL: Beacham Pub., c1996-[1998] 14 v.
96-020771   809.3   0933833385
Popular literature -- Bio-bibliography. Fiction -- 19th century -- Bio-bibliography. Fiction -- 20th century -- Bio-bibliography.

Z6514.P76.M535 1996
Mieder, Wolfgang.
Proverbs in world literature: a bibliography/ Wolfgang Mieder & George B. Bryan. New York: P. Lang, c1996. xiv, 305 p.
96-025570   016.80888/2   082043499X
Proverbs in literature -- Bibliography.

Z6514.S4.J33 1995
Jacob, Merle.
To be continued: an annotated guide to sequels/ by Merle Jacob and Hope Apple. Phoenix, Ariz.: Oryx Press, 1995. xi, 364 p.
95-003283   016.80883   0897748425
Sequels (Literature) -- Bibliography. Prose literature -- Bibliography.

Z6517 Literature — By period — Medieval

Z6517.F47
Ferguson, Mary Anne.
Bibliography of English translations from medieval sources, 1943-1967, by Mary Anne Heyward Ferguson. New York, Columbia University Press, 1974. x, 274 p.
73-007751   016.08   0231034350
Literature, Medieval -- Translations into English -- Bibliography.

Z6519 Literature — By period — Modern

Z6519.W67 1995
Wortman, William A., 1940-
A guide to serial bibliographies for modern literatures/ Wiliam A. Wortman. New York: Modern Language Association of America, 1995. xiii, 333 p.
95-033134   016.805   0873529650
Literature, Modern -- Bibliography -- Periodicals -- Bibliography.

Z6521 Literature —
Particular works (Anonymous) —
Ancient and medieval, A-Z

Z6521.R73.V37 1998
Varty, Kenneth.
The Roman de Renart: a guide to scholarly work/
Kenneth Varty. Lanham, Md.: Scarecrow Press,
1998. ix, 179 p.
97-030834   016.841/1   0810834359
*Reynard the Fox (Legendary character) --
Bibliography.*

Z6616.M69 Manuscripts —
Manuscripts of individual authors
— Individual, A-Z

Z6616.M69
Preston, Daniel, 1951-
A comprehensive catalogue of the
correspondence and papers of James Monroe/
Daniel Preston. Westport, Conn.: Greenwood
Press, 2001. 2 v.
00-061033   016.9735/4/092   0313314268
*Monroe, James, -- 1758-1831 -- Archives --
Catalogs. Monroe, James, -- 1758-1831 --
Correspondence -- Catalogs. Presidents --
United States -- Archives -- Catalogs. Presidents
-- United States -- Correspondence -- Catalogs.
United States -- Politics and government -- 1783-
1865 -- Sources -- Bibliography -- Catalogs.*

Z6620 Manuscripts —
By region or country, A-Z

Z6620.U5.I53 1988
Index to personal names in the National union
catalog of manuscript collections, 1959-1984.
Alexandria: Chadwyck-Healey, 1988. 2 v.
86-025107   011/.31/0973   0898870372
*Manuscripts -- United States -- Union lists --
Periodicals -- Indexes. Catalogs, Union -- United
States -- Periodicals -- Indexes. United States --
History -- Sources -- Bibliography -- Union lists
-- Periodicals -- Indexes.*

Z6620.U5 M6 1977
Robbins, J. Albert
American literary manuscripts: a checklist of
holdings in academic, historical, and public
libraries, museums, and authors' homes in the
United States. 2d ed. / compiled, with the
assistance of associates, by J. Albert Athens:
University of Georgia Press, c1977. liii, 387 p. ;
76-049156   016.81   0820304123
*Manuscripts, American -- United States --
Union lists. American literature -- Manuscripts --
Union lists. Catalogs, Union -- United States.*

Z6620.U5.N3
National union catalog of manuscript collections.
Washington: Library of Congress,
62-017486
*Manuscripts -- United States -- Union lists --
Periodicals. Catalogs, Union -- United States --
Periodicals. United States -- History -- Sources -
- Bibliography -- Union lists -- Periodicals.*

Z6621 Manuscripts —
Catalogs of manuscript
collections in specific
libraries.
By name of library, A-Z

Z6621.C8363.I254 1994
Fiske Icelandic Collection.
Manuscript material, correspondence, and
graphic material in the Fiske Icelandic
Collection: a descriptive catalogue/ compiled by
Dorunn Sigurdardottir. Ithaca: Cornell
University Press, 1994. xi, 291 p.
93-029520   016.94912   0801429935
*Manuscripts, Icelandic -- United States --
Catalogs.Iceland -- History -- Sources --
Bibliography -- Catalogs. Iceland -- Manuscripts
-- Catalogs.*

Z6653 Mathematics —
Periodicals. Societies

Z6653.L5 1992
Liang, Diana F.
Mathematical journals: an annotated guide/
compiled by Diana F. Liang. Metuchen, N.J.:
Scarecrow Press, 1992. x, 235 p.
92-018459   016.51/05   0810825856
Mathematics -- Periodicals -- Bibliography.

Z6654 Mathematics —
Special topics, A-Z

Z6654.C69.R63 1990
Roberts, Patricia, 1936-
Counting books are more than numbers: an
annotated action bibliography/ Patricia L.
Roberts. Hamden, Conn.: Library Professional
Publications, 1990. viii, 270 p.
89-019936   016.5135/5   0208022163
*Counting -- Bibliography. Illustrated children's
books -- Bibliography.*

Z6658.I54 Medicine —
General bibliography

Z6658.I54 1994
Introduction to reference sources in the health
sciences/ Fred W. Roper and Jo Anne Boorkman.
Chicago, Ill.: Medical Library Association;
c1994. x, 301 p.
94-010708   610/.72   0810828898
*Medicine -- Reference books -- Bibliography.
Medicine -- Bibliography. Medicine --
Information services.*

Z6660.5 Medicine —
Biography

Z6660.5.M67 1994
Morton, Leslie T.   1907-
A bibliography of medical and biomedical
biography/ Leslie T. Morton and Robert J.
Moore. Aldershot, Hants, England: Scholar
Press; c1994. xiii, 333 p.
94-008284   016.61/092   0859679810
*Medical personnel -- Great Britain --
Biography -- Bibliography. Medical personnel --
United States -- Biography -- Bibliography.
Medical scientists -- Great Britain -- Biography -
- Bibliography.*

Z6661 Medicine —
By region or country, A-Z

Z6661.N67.G73 1996
Gray, Sharon A., 1953-
Health of native people of North America: a
bibliography and guide to resources/ Sharon A.
Gray. Lanham, Md.: Scarecrow Press, 1996. x,
393 p.
96-011844   016.3621/089/97   0810831708
*Indians of North America -- Health and
hygiene -- Bibliography. Indians of North
America -- Medical care -- Bibliography.*

Z6663 Medicine —
Anatomy and physiology —
Special topics, A-Z

Z6663.N9.L5 1991
Lieberman-Nissen, Karen, 1950-
Nutrition and disease: an annotated bibliography/
Karen Lieberman-Nissen. New York: Garland
Pub., 1991. x, 180 p.
90-014114   016.6158/54   0824079779
*Chronic diseases -- Nutritional aspects --
Bibliography. Diet Therapy -- abstracts.
Nutrition -- abstracts.*

Z6664 Medicine —
Internal medicine.
Diseases and manifestations,
A-Z

Z6664.A27.M53 1993
Miletich, John J.
AIDS: a multimedia sourcebook/ compiled by
John J. Miletich; foreword by Detmar H.
Tschofen. Westport, Conn.: Greenwood Press,
1993. xx, 266 p.
93-010830   016.3621/969792   0313286698
*AIDS (Disease) -- Bibliography. AIDS
(Disease) -- Film catalogs. AIDS (Disease) --
Video catalogs.*

Z6664.A27.R87 1995
Russel, R. P.
Guide to books on AIDS/ compiled by Randall P.
Russel. New York: Nova Science Publishers,
Inc., c1995. 98 p.
94-004701   016.3621/969792   1560721790
AIDS (Disease) -- Bibliography.

Z6664.L6.W66 1997
Wood, Corinne Shear.
An annotated bibliography on leprosy/ Corinne Shear Wood. Lewiston, N.Y.: Edward Mellen Press, 1997. xxiv, 176 p.
97-042479   016.6169/98   0773484418
Leprosy -- Bibliography. Leprosy -- abstracts.

Z6664.P24
Roberto, Karen A.
Chronic pain in later life: a selectively annotated bibliography/ Karen A. Roberto and Deborah T. Gold. Westport, CT: Greenwood Press, 2001. 283 p.
00-057788   016.61897/60472   0313310998
Pain in old age -- Bibliography. Chronic pain -- Bibliography. Aged -- Diseases -- Bibliography.

Z6665.7 Medicine — Psychiatry. Psychopathology — Special topics, A-Z

Z6665.7.D46.M55 1995
Miletich, John J.
Depression: a multimedia sourcebook/ compiled by John J. Miletich; foreword by Dan G. Blazer. Westport, Conn.: Greenwood Press, 1995. xvi, 217 p.
95-004194   016.61685/27   0313293740
Depression, Mental -- Bibliography. Depressive Disorder -- bibliography.

Z6665.7.D46.M56 1997
Miletich, John J.
Depression in the elderly: a multimedia sourcebook/ John J. Miletich. Westport, Conn.: Greenwood Press, 1997. xiv, 226 p.
97-016238   016.61897/68527   0313301131
Depression in old age -- Bibliography.

Z6665.7.F35.F36 1988
Family therapy: a bibliography, 1937-1986/ compiled by Bernard Lubin ... [et al.]; foreword by Luciano L'Abate. New York: Greenwood Press, 1988. 470 p.
88-018682   016.61689/156   0313261725
Family psychotherapy -- Bibliography.

Z6671.2 Medicine — Gynecology and obstetrics — Special topics, A-Z

Z6671.2.A2.F48 1991
Fitzsimmons, Richard.
Pro-choice/pro-life: an annotated, selected bibliography (1972-1989)/ compiled by Richard Fitzsimmons and Joan P. Diana. New York: Greenwood Press, 1991. xii, 251 p.
91-012625   016.3634/6/0973   0313275793
Abortion -- United States -- Bibliography. Pro-choice movement -- United States -- Bibliography. Pro-life movement -- United States -- Bibliography.

Z6671.2.T63 W45 1994
Weiss, Wayne W.
Tobacco smoke in active and passive pollution: reports of harmful conditions and effects: index of authors and subjects/ Wayne W. Weiss. Washington, DC: Abbe Publishers Association, c1994.
94-031240   016.61686/5 20   0788303635
Smoking -- Health aspects -- Bibliography. Tobacco -- Health aspects -- Bibliography.

Z6671.52 Medicine — Pediatrics — Special topics, A-Z

Z6671.52.T47.B46 1988
Benson, Hazel B.
The dying child: an annotated bibliography/ compiled by Hazel B. Benson. New York: Greenwood Press, 1988. xxi, 270 p.
88-011008   016.1559/37   0313247080
Terminally ill children -- Psychology -- Bibliography. Children and death -- Bibliography. Terminally ill children -- Care -- Bibliography.

Z6671.55 Medicine — Geriatrics

Z6671.55.T45 1990
Teitelman, Jodi L.
Fundamentals of geriatrics for health professionals: an annotated bibliography/ compiled by Jodi L. Teitelman and Iris A. Parham. New York: Greenwood Press, 1990. viii, 247 p.
89-028653   016.61897   031326225X
Geriatrics -- Bibliography.

Z6673 Medicine — Hygiene. Public health — General bibliography

Z6673.P288 1998
Palmegiano, E. M.
Health and British magazines in the nineteenth century/ E.M. Palmegiano. Lanham, Md.: Scarecrow Press, 1998. ix, 282 p.
98-003909   016.61   0810834863
Health -- Bibliography. Health -- Press coverage -- Great Britain -- Bibliography. Medicine, Popular -- Bibliography.

Z6673.R43 2000
Consumer health information source book/ edited by Alan M. Rees. Phoenix, AZ: Oryx Press, c2000. xii, 323 p.
99-052937   016.613   1573561231
Health -- Bibliography. Medicine, Popular -- Bibliography. Health -- Information services -- Directories.

Z6673.35 Medicine — Hygiene. Public health — Aged

Z6673.35.K36 1992
Kapp, Marshall B.
Ethical aspects of health care for the elderly: an annotated bibliography/ compiled by Marshall B. Kapp. Westport, Conn.: Greenwood Press, 1992. xviii, 175 p.
92-017776   016.174/2   0313274908
Aged -- Medical care -- Moral and ethical aspects -- Bibliography.

Z6673.6 Medicine — Hygiene. Public health — By region or country, A-Z

Z6673.6.U6 H39 1997
Haynes Craig.
Ethnic minority health: a selected, annotated bibliography/ Craig Haynes. Lanham, Md.: Medical Library Association and Scarecrow Press, xv, 503 p. ;
96-046952   016.362/0973 21   0810832259
Minorities -- Health and hygiene -- United States -- Bibliography.

Z6675 Medicine — Other, A-Z

Z6675.A42.A43 1988
Allan, Barbara
Guide to information sources in alternative therapy/ Barbara Allan. Aldershot, Hants, England; Gower, c1988. viii, 216 p.
88-010530   016.6158   0566056119
Alternative medicine -- Bibliography. Alternative medicine -- Information services. Searching, Bibliographical.

Z6675.E45.M54 1990
Miletich, John J.
Police, firefighter, and paramedic stress: an annotated bibliography/ compiled by John J. Miletich. New York: Greenwood Press, 1990. xv, 224 p.
89-028649   016.1587   0313266824
Emergency medical technicians -- Job stress -- Bibliography. Police -- Job stress -- Bibliography. Fire fighters -- Job stress -- Bibliography.

Z6675.M68.G52 1996
Gibbs, Tyson.
A guide to ethnic health collections in the United States/ compiled by Tyson Gibbs. Westport, Conn.: Greenwood Press, 1996. xii, 139 p.
95-050402   016.3621/0425/0973   0313297401
Minorities -- Health and hygiene -- United States -- Library resources -- Directories. Minorities -- Health and hygiene -- United States -- Archival resources -- Directories. Ethnic Groups -- history -- United States -- directories.

Z6675.V53.H84 1990
Hughes, Marija Matich.
Computer health hazards/ Marija Matich Hughes. Washington, D.C.: Hughes Press, c1990-c1996. 3 v.
90-093371   016.36318/9   0912560053
Video display terminals -- Health aspects -- Bibliography. Electronic digital computers -- Health aspects -- Bibliography.

Z6678 Metals. Metallurgy — General bibliography

Z6678.I48 1989
Information sources in metallic materials/ editor, M.N. Patten. London [England]; Bowker-Saur, c1989. xiv, 415 p.
89-039752   016.669   0408014911
Metals -- Bibliography. Materials -- Bibliography. Metals -- Information services.

Z6683 Meteorology — Special topics, A-Z

Z6683.C5 G66 1975
Grayson, Donald K.
A bibliography of the literature on North American climates of the past 13,000 years/ Donald K. Grayson. New York: Garland Pub., 1975. 206 p.
75-005131   016.5516/9   0824099923
Paleoclimatology -- North America -- Bibliography.

Z6683.C5.P37 1995
Parker, Philip M., 1960-
Climatic effects on individual, social, and economic behavior: a physioeconomic review of research across disciplines/ Philip M. Parker. Westport, Conn.: Greenwood Press, 1995. ix, 291 p.
94-041521   016.3042/5   0313294003
Climatology -- Bibliography. Climatology -- Economic aspects -- Bibliography. Human beings -- Effect of climate on -- Bibliography.

Z6683.G46 N67 1999
Nordquist, Joan.
Global warming: a bibliography/ compiled by Joan Nordquist Santa Cruz, CA: Reference and Research Services, 1999. 64 p.
2001-267123   016.363738/74 21   1892068087
Global warming -- Bibliography.

Z6683.G74 N67 1990
Nordquist, Joan.
The greenhouse effect: a bibliography/ compiled by Joan Nordquist. Santa Cruz, CA, USA: Referenceand Research Services, 1990. 60 p.
92-126705   016.36373/87 20   0937855340
Greenhouse effect, Atmospheric -- Bibliography.

Z6724 Military science — Special topics, A-Z

Z6724.C5.C76 1997
Croddy, Eric, 1966-
Chemical and biological warfare: an annotated bibliography/ Eric Croddy. Lanham, Md.: Scarecrow Press, 1997. xxxix, 429 p.
96-037866   016.358/34   0810832712
Chemical warfare -- Bibliography. Biological warfare -- Bibliography.

Z6724.I7.C54 1996
Clements, Frank, 1942-
Israeli Secret Services/ Frank A. Clements, compiler. New Brunswick, N.J.: Transaction Publishers, c1996. xxiii, 80 p.
96-017331   016.327125694   156000228X
Intelligence service -- Israel -- Bibliography. Secret service -- Israel -- Bibliography.

Z6724.I7.D38 1996
Davies, Philip
The British secret services/ Philip H.J. Davies. New Brunswick: Transaction Publishers, c1996. xxxix, 147 p.
96-005542   327.1241/09   156000231X
Intelligence service -- Great Britain -- History -- Bibliography. Secret service -- Great Britain -- History -- Bibliography.

Z6724.I7.L69 1994
Lowenthal, Mark M.
The U.S. intelligence community: an annotated bibliography/ Mark M. Lowenthal. New York: Garland Pub., 1994. xv, 206 p.
94-010298   016.3271/273   081531423X
Intelligence service -- United States -- Bibliography.

Z6724.I7.P48 1992
Petersen, Neal H.
American intelligence, 1775-1990: a bibliographical guide/ Neal H. Petersen. Claremont, Calif.: Regina Books, 1992. 406 p.
92-016324   016.3271273/09   0941690458
Intelligence service -- United States -- History -- Bibliography.

Z6724.I7 S63
Smith, Myron J.
The secret wars, a guide to sources in English/ Myron J. Smith, Jr.; with an historical introd. by Lyman B. Kirkpatrick, Jr. Santa Barbara, Calif.: ABC-Clio, c1980-c1981. 3 v.
79-025784   016.3553/43   0874362717
Military intelligence -- Bibliography. Espionage -- Bibliography. Psychological warfare -- Bibliography. World War, 1939-1945 -- Underground movements -- Bibliography. World War, 1939-1945 -- Secret service -- Bibliography. Commando troops -- Bibliography. Guerrilla warfare -- Bibliography. Terrorism -- Bibliography.

Z6724.N37.M37 1993
McClean, Andrew.
Security, arms control, and conflict reduction in East Asia and the Pacific: a bibliography, 1980-1991/ compiled by Andrew McClean. Westport, Conn.: Greenwood Press, 1993. xx, 551 p.
93-018142   016.355/03305   0313275394
National security -- East Asia -- Bibliography. Arms control -- East Asia -- Bibliography. National security -- Pacific Area -- Bibliography.

Z6725 Military science — Local, A-Z

Z6725.E8
Crosby, Everett Uberto, 1932-
Medieval warfare: a bibliographical guide/ Everett U. Crosby. New York: Garland, 2000. xv, 215 p.
00-026506   016.355/0094/0902   081533849X
Military art and science -- Europe -- History -- To 1500 -- Bibliography. Military art and science -- Byzantine Empire -- History -- Bibliography. Military art and science -- Islamic Empire -- History -- Bibliography. Byzantine Empire -- History, Military -- Bibliography. Europe -- History, Military -- Bibliography. Islamic Empire -- History, Military -- Bibliography.

Z6725.R9.E75 1996
The Soviet Armed Forces, 1918-1992: a research guide to Soviet sources/ compiled by John Erickson and Ljubica Erickson. Westport, Conn.: Greenwood Press, 1996. xviii, 197 p.
95-041983   016.355/009470904   0313290717
Soviet Union -- Armed Forces -- History. Soviet Union -- Politics and government -- Bibliography.

Z6824 Names

Z6824.L39 1987
Lawson, Edwin D.,
Personal names and naming: an annotated bibliography/ compiled by Edwin D. Lawson. New York: Greenwood Press, 1987. xiii, 185 p.
86-031789   016.9294 19   0313238170
Names, Personal -- Bibliography.

Z6824.S4 1982
Sealock, Richard Burl,
Bibliography of place-name literature: United States and Canada/ by Richard B. Sealock, Margaret M. Sealock, and Margaret S. Powell. 3rd ed. Chicago: American Library Association, 1982. xii, 435 p.
81-022878   016.9173/01/4 19   0838903606
Names, Geographical -- United States -- Bibliography. Names, Geographical -- Canada -- Bibliography. United States -- History, Local -- Bibliography. Canada -- History, Local -- Bibliography.

Z6835 Naval science — Local, A-Z

Z6835.U5 S62
Smith, Myron J.
The American Navy, 1865-1918: a bibliography, by Myron J. Smith, Jr. Metuchen, N.J., Scarecrow Press, 1974. xiii, 372 p.
74-004230   016.359/00973   0810807203
United States -- History, Naval -- Bibliography.

Z6835.U5 S63
Smith, Myron J.
The American Navy, 1918-1941: a bibliography, by Myron J. Smith, Jr. Metuchen, N.J., Scarecrow Press, 1974. xiv, 429 p.
74-011077   016.3593/0973   0810807564
United States -- History, Naval -- Bibliography.

Z6835.U5 S6
Smith, Myron J.
The American Navy, 1789-1860: a bibliography, by Myron J. Smith, Jr. Metuchen, N.J., Scarecrow Press, 1974. xiv, 489 p.
73-018464   016.3593/0973   0810806592
United States -- History, Naval -- Bibliography.

Z6878 Occultism — Special topics, A-Z

Z6878.M3.M44 1992
Melton, J. Gordon.
Magic, witchcraft, and paganism in America: a bibliography/ by J. Gordon Melton and Isotta Poggi. New York: Garland Pub., 1992. xv, 408 p.
91-045867   016.299   0815304994
Magic -- United States -- Bibliography. Witchcraft -- United States -- Bibliography. Paganism -- United States -- Bibliography.

Z6878.P8.B37 1990
Basford, Terry K., 1947-
Near-death experiences: an annotated bibliography/ Terry K. Basford. New York: Garland, 1990. ix, 182 p.
89-078445 016.1339/013 082406349X
Near-death experiences -- Bibliography. Deathbed hallucinations -- Bibliography.

Z6878.P8.W47 1990
White, Rhea A.
Parapsychology: new sources of information, 1973-1989/ by Rhea A. White. Methuchen, N.J.: Scarecrow Press, 1990. xiv, 699 p.
90-021327 016.1338 0810823853
Parapsychology -- Bibliography.

Z6878.S8.B58 1998
Bjorling, Joel, 1952-
Consulting spirits: a bibliography/ Joel Bjorling. Westport, Conn.: Greenwood Press, 1998. x, 213 p.
97-053107 016.1339 0313302847
Spiritualism -- Bibliography.

Z6935 Performing arts

Z6935.P46
Performing arts resources. [New York] Drama Book Specialists.
75-646287 016.7902/08
Performing arts -- United States -- Library resources -- Periodicals.

Z6935.S56 1994
Simons, Linda Keir.
The performing arts: a guide to the reference literature/ Linda Keir Simons. Englewood, Colo.: Libraries Unlimited, 1994. ix, 244 p.
93-031465 016.791 0872879828
Performing arts -- Reference books -- Bibliography. Performing arts -- Bibliography.

Z6940 Periodicals, newspapers, and other serials — Journalism

Z6940.C38 1997
Cates, Jo A.
Journalism: a guide to the reference literature/ Jo A. Cates; foreword by James W. Carey. Englewood, Colo.: Libraries Unlimited, 1997. xv, 317 p.
96-048335 016.0704 1563083744
Journalism -- Reference books -- Bibliography. Journalism -- Bibliography.

Z6941 Periodicals, newspapers, and other serials — General bibliography

Z6941.B35 2000
Balay, Robert.
Early periodical indexes: bibliographies and indexes of literature published in periodicals before 1900/ Robert Balay. Lanham, Md.: Scarecrow Press, 2000. xxx, 317 p.
00-056265 011/.34 0810838680
Periodicals -- Bibliography of bibliographies. Periodicals -- Indexes -- Bibliography.

Z6941.K2 1972
Katz, William A., 1924-
Magazines for libraries; for the general reader, and school, junior college, college, and public libraries [by] Bill Katz, and Berry Gargal, science editor. New York, R. R. Bowker, 1972. xviii, 822 p.
72-006607 016.05 0835205541
Periodicals -- Bibliography.

Z6941.M23
Magazines for libraries. New York: Bowker, [1969-]
86-640971 050/.25 19
Periodicals -- Directories. Periodical selection. Periodicals -- Bibliography. Périodiques -- Répertoires. Périodiques -- Choix -- Périodiques. Périodiques -- Bibliographie -- Périodiques.

Z6941.U5
Ulrich's international periodicals directory. New York, Bowker.
32-016320 011
Periodicals -- Directories. World War, 1939-1945 -- Underground literature -- Bibliography.

Z6944 Periodicals, newspapers, and other serials — Special topics, A-Z

Z6944.N39.A37 1998
African-American newspapers and periodicals: a national bibliography/ James P. Danky, editor; Maureen E. Hady, associate editor. Cambridge, Mass.: Harvard University Press, 1998. xxxv, 740 p.
98-026099   015.73/035/08996073
0674007883
Afro-American newspapers -- Bibliography -- Union lists. Afro-American periodicals -- Bibliography -- Union lists. Afro-Americans -- Periodicals -- Bibliography -- Union lists.

Z6944.N39.H46 1995
Henritze, Barbara K.
Bibliographic checklist of African American newspapers/ Barbara K. Henritze. Baltimore, MD: Genealogical Pub. Co., c1995. xxviii, 206 p.
94-079984 071/.3 0806314575
Afro-American newspapers -- Bibliography.

Z6944.S45.G76 1996
Greenberg, Gerald S.
Tabloid journalism: an annotated bibliography of English-language sources/ Gerald S. Greenberg. Westport, Conn.: Greenwood Press, 1996. x, 187 p.
96-008942 016.30223 0313295441
Sensationalism in journalism -- Bibliography. Sensationalism in television -- Bibliography. Tabloid newspapers -- Bibliography.

Z6945 Periodicals, newspapers, and other serials — Catalogs of libraries. Union lists

Z6945.A2 P47
Periodical title abbreviations. Detroit, Mich.: Gale Research Co., [1969-]
84-640700 050/.148 19
Periodicals -- Abbreviations of titles. Abbreviations -- Abbreviations. Abbreviations -- Dictionary -- English. Periodicals -- Abbreviations. Periodicals -- Dictionary -- English. Périodiques -- Abréviations de titres -- Périodiques.

Z6945.U45 1965
Union list of serials in libraries of the United States and Canada, edited by Edna Brown Titus. New York, H. W. Wilson Co., 1965. 5 v.
65-010150 016.05
Bibliography -- Bibliography -- Periodicals. Periodicals -- Bibliography -- Union lists. Libraries -- United States.

Z6951-6953.5 Periodicals, newspapers, and other serials — By region or country — America

Z6951.A97
Gale directory of publications and broadcast media. Detroit, Mich.: Gale Research, [c1990-]
90-649034 302.23/025/73 20
American newspapers -- Directories. American periodicals -- Directories. Canadian newspapers -- Directories. Canadian periodicals -- Directories. Broadcasting -- United States -- Directories. Broadcasting -- Canada -- Directories. Newspapers -- United States -- Directory. Newspapers -- Canada -- Directory. Periodicals -- United States -- Directory.

Z6951.S35 1987
Schwarzlose, Richard Allen.
Newspapers, a reference guide/ Richard A. Schwarzlose. New York: Greenwood Press, 1987. xxxvii, 417 p.
87-000246 015.73035 0313236135
American newspapers -- History -- Bibliography. Newspaper publishing -- United States -- Bibliography.

Z6951.S54 1989
Sloan, W. David 1947-
American journalism history: an annotated bibliography/ compiled by Wm. David Sloan. New York: Greenwood Press, 1989. xv, 344 p.
88-035800 016.071/3 0313263507
Journalism -- United States -- History -- Bibliography.

Z6953.5.A1.I74 1990
Ireland, Sandra L. Jones.
Ethnic periodicals in contemporary America: an annotated guide/ compiled by Sandra L. Jones Ireland. New York: Greenwood Press, 1990. xvi, 222 p.
90-031737 016.071/3/08693 0313268177
Ethnic press -- United States -- Bibliography. American newspapers -- Foreign language press -- Bibliography. American periodicals -- Foreign language press -- Bibliography.

Z6953.5.S66
Kanellos, Nicolas.
Hispanic periodicals in the United States, origins to 1960: a brief history and comprehensive bibliography/ by Nicolas Kanellos and Helvetia Martell. Houston, TX: Arte Publico Press, 2000. 359 p.
98-028341 015.73/034/08968 1558852530
Hispanic American periodicals -- Bibliography -- Union lists. Hispanic American newspapers -- Bibliography -- Union lists. Hispanic Americans -- Periodicals -- Bibliography -- Union lists.

Z7001 Philology and linguistics — General bibliography

Z7001.D45 2000
DeMiller, Anna L.
Linguistics: a guide to the reference literature/ Anna L. DeMiller. Englewood, Colo.: Libraries Unlimited, 2000. xviii, 396 p.
99-016318 016.41 1563086190
Linguistics -- Reference books -- Bibliography. Language and languages -- Reference books -- Bibliography.

Z7001.L15
Linguistics and language behavior abstracts: LLBA. La Jolla, Calif.: Sociological Abstracts, Inc., [1985-   ]
sn 85015298 016 11
Linguistics -- Abstracts -- Periodicals. Language and languages -- Abstracts -- Periodicals. Linguistics -- abstracts. Psycholinguistics -- abstracts.

Z7001.S57 1985
Slavens, Thomas P.,
The literary adviser: selected reference sources in literature, speech, language, theater, and film/ by Thomas P. Slavens. Phoenix, Ariz.: Oryx Press, 1985. 196 p.
85-018879 016.4 19 0897742362
Philology -- References books -- Bibliography. Philology -- Bibliography. Performing arts -- References books -- Bibliography. Performing arts -- Bibliography.

Z7001.T78 1990
Troike, Rudolph C.
Bibliography of bibliographies of the languages of the world/ compiled by Rudolph C. Troike. Amsterdam; J. Benjamins Pub. Co., [1990-   ] v. <1 >
90-000426 016.01641 20 9027237433
Language and languages -- Bibliography of bibliographies.

Z7004 Philology and linguistics — Special topics, A-Z

Z7004.G7.T74 1996
Tremblay, Florent A.
Bibliotheca grammaticorum = Bibliography of grammatical writings/ Florent A. Tremblay. Lewiston [N.Y.]: E. Mellen Press, [c1996-   ] v. 1-7
95-007455 016.415 077348955X
Grammar, Comparative and general -- Bibliography.

Z7004.S4.G69 1992
Gordon, W. Terrence, 1942-
Semantics: a bibliography, 1986-1991/ by W. Terrence Gordon. Metuchen, N.J.; Scarecrow Press, 1992. ix, 280 p.
92-027597 016.401/43 0810825988
Semantics -- Bibliography.

Z7006.M64
MLA international bibliography of books and articles on the modern languages and literatures. Library ed. New York: Modern Language Association of America, [c1970-   ]
88-645059
Languages, Modern -- Bibliography. Literature -- History and criticism -- Bibliography.

Z7016 Philology and linguistics — Classical languages and literatures — General bibliography

Z7016.J4 1996
Jenkins, Fred W.
Classical studies: a guide to the reference literature/ Fred W. Jenkins. Englewood, Colo.: Libraries Unlimited, 1996. ix, 263 p.
95-052209 016.88 1563081105
Classical philology -- Reference books -- Bibliography. Civilization, Classical -- Reference books -- Bibliography. Civilization, Classical -- Bibliography.

Z7016.M35A
L'Année philologique; bibliographie critique et analytique de l'antiquité gréco-latine. Paris, Société d'édition "Les belles lettres", [1928-   ]
29-009941
Classical literature -- Bibliography -- Periodicals. Classical philology -- Bibliography -- Periodicals.

Z7031 Philology and linguistics — Romance — Bibliography of bibliography

Z7031.A1 B33
Bach, Kathryn F.
Romance linguistics and the romance languages: a bibliography of bibliographies/ by Kathryn F. Bach and Glanville Price. London: Grant & Cutler, 1977. 194 p.
78-319221 016.44 0729300552
Romance philology -- Bibliography of bibliographies.

Z7046 Philology and linguistics — Oriental — General bibliography

Z7046.C65 1975
Columbia College (Columbia University)
A guide to Oriental classics/ prepared by the staff of the Oriental Studies Program, Columbia College; and edited by Wm. Theodore De Bary and Ainslie T. Embree. New York: Columbia University Press, 1975. xi, 257 p.
74-014150 016.89 0231038917
Oriental literature -- Bibliography. Oriental literature -- Outlines, syllabi, etc.

Z7090 Philology and linguistics — Oriental — Individual languages

Z7090.P37 1993
Parameswara Aithal, K.
Veda-lakòsana, Vedic ancillary literature: a descriptive bibliography / compiled by K. Parameswara Aithal. 1st Indian ed. Delhi: Motilal Banarsidass Publishers, 1993. vi, 755 p.
93-908038 8120811208
Vedic literature -- Bibliography.

Z7116 Philology and linguistics — American Indian — General bibliography

Z7116.S55 1996
Singerman, Robert.
Indigenous languages of the Americas: a bibliography of dissertations and theses/ by Robert Singerman. Lanham, Md.: Scarecrow Press, c1996. xxix, 311 p.
95-035046 016.497 0810830329
Indians -- Languages -- Bibliography. Dissertations, Academic -- Bibliography.

Z7125-7128 Philosophy

Z7125.B34 1992
Barth, E. M.
Women philosophers: a bibliography of books through 1990/ Barth, Else M. Bowling Green, Ohio: Philosophy Documentation Center, c1992. 213 p.
92-227406 016.1/082 0912632917
Philosophy -- Bibliography. Women philosophers -- Bibliography.

Z7125.B39 1991
Bell, Albert A., 1945-
Resources in ancient philosophy: an annotated bibliography of scholarship in English, 1965-1989/ by Albert A. Bell, Jr. and James B. Allis. Metuchen, N.J.: Scarecrow Press, 1991. xvii, 799 p.
91-039912 016.18 0810825201
Philosophy, Ancient -- Bibliography. Christianity -- Philosophy -- History -- Bibliography.

Z7125.B97 1997
Bynagle, Hans E. 1946-
Philosophy: a guide to the reference literature/ Hans E. Bynagle. Englewood, Colo.: Libraries Unlimited, 1997. xii, 233 p.
96-031379 016.1 1563083760
Philosophy -- Bibliography.

Z7125.D445
De George, Richard T.
The philosopher's guide to sources, research tools, professional life, and related fields/ Richard T. De George. Lawrence: Regents Press of Kansas, c1980. x, 261 p.
79-091437 016.1 19 0700602003
Philosophy -- Bibliography. Philosophy -- Reference books -- Bibliography.

Z7125.M453 2001
Meissner, Werner.
Western philosophy in China, 1993-1997: a bibliography/ Werner Meissner. Bern; P. Lang, c2001. ix, 689 p.
2001-038846 016.181/11 21 0820456357
Philosophy -- China -- Bibliography.

Z7125.W87 1993
World philosophy: a contemporary bibliography/ edited by John R. Burr; Charlotte A. Burr, research editor. Westport, Conn.: Greenwood Press, 1993. xii, 380 p.
93-018031　016.1/09/047　0313240329
Philosophy, Modern -- 20th century -- Bibliography.

Z7127.P47 1992
The Philosopher's index thesaurus/ Richard H. Lineback, editor; Lynn Walkiewicz, assistant editor. 2nd ed. Bowling Green, Ohio: Philosophy Documentation Center, 112 p.
99-218293
Subject headings -- Philosophy. Philosophy -- Indexes -- Periodicals.

Z7128.I57 D53 1999
Daiber, Hans,
Bibliography of Islamic philosophy/ by Hans Daiber. Leiden; Brill, 1999. 2 v.
99-031637　016.181/07 21　9004113487
Philosophy, Islamic -- Bibliography. Philosophy, Islamic -- Indexes.

Z7128.P83.N38 1993
Navia, Luis E.
The presocratic philosophers: an annotated bibliography/ Luis E. Navia. New York: Garland, 1993. xxiii, 722 p.
93-016207　016.182　0824097769
Pre-Socratic philosophers -- Bibliography.

Z7128.T7.T7 1984
The Transcendentalists: a review of research and criticism/ edited by Joel Myerson. New York: Modern Language Association of America, 1984. xix, 534 p.
83-019442　016.141/3/0973　0873522605
Transcendentalism (New England) -- Bibliography.

Z7134 Photography — General bibliography

Z7134.J64 1990
Johnson, William,
Nineteenth-century photography: an annotated bibliography , 1839-1879 / William S. Johnson. Boston, Mass.: G.K. Hall, 1990. xv, 962 p.
90-004897　016.77/09/034 20　0816179581
Photography -- History -- 19th century -- Bibliography.

Z7134.K74 1999
Kreisel, Martha, 1948-
American women photographers: a selected and annotated bibliography/ Martha Kreisel. Westport, Conn.: Greenwood Press, 1999. ix, 350 p.
98-048654　016.77/082/0973　0313304785
Women photographers -- United States -- Bibliography. Photography -- United States -- History -- Bibliography.

Z7134.R66 1989
Roosens, Laurent.
History of photography: a bibliography of books/ Laurent Roosens and Luc Salu. London; Mansell, 1989-1999 v. 1-4
89-033758　016.77/09　072012008X
Photography -- History -- Bibliography.

Z7141 Physics

Z7141.S65 1996
Smith, Roger, 1953 Apr. 19-
Popular physics and astronomy: an annotated bibliography/ Roger Smith. Lanham, Md.: Scarecrow Press, 1996. 505 p.
96-003253　016.53　081083149X
Physics -- Popular works -- Bibliography. Astronomy -- Popular works -- Bibliography.

Z7141.S74 2000
Stern, David, 1956 Dec. 30-
Guide to information sources in the physical sciences/ David Stern. Englewood, Colo.: Libraries Unlimited, 2000. xxiii, 227 p.
99-045970　016.53　1563087510
Physics -- Bibliography. Reference books -- Physics -- Bibliography. Physics -- Information services -- Directories.

Z7144 Physics — Special topics, A-Z

Z7144.N8.P35 1996
Particle physics: one hundred years of discoveries: an annotated chronological bibliography/ V.V. Ezhela ... [et al.]. Woodbury, N.Y.: American Institute of Physics, c1996. viii, 328 p.
96-009558　016.5397/2　1563966425
Particles (Nuclear physics) -- History -- Bibliography.

Z7156 Poetry — Special topics, A-Z

Z7156.A1.K38 1994
Katz, William A., 1924-
The Columbia Granger's guide to poetry anthologies/ William Katz, Linda Sternberg Katz, and Esther Crain. New York: Columbia University Press, c1994. xxxiv, 440 p.
94-006482　016.80881　023110104X
Poetry -- Collections -- Bibliography. English poetry -- Bibliography.

Z7156.E6 C64
Coleman, Arthur,
Epic and romance criticism; a checklist of interpretations, 1940-1972. New York, Watermill Publishers [1973-]
73-075805　016.8091　0883700018
Epic poetry -- History and criticism -- Bibliography. Romances -- History and criticism -- Bibliography.

Z7161.A1 Political and social sciences — Bibliography of bibliography

Z7161.A1.L5 2000
Li, Tze-chung, 1927-
Social science reference sources: a practical guide/ Tze-chung Li. Westport, Conn.: Greenwood Press, 2000. xxvii, 495 p.
99-031574　016.3　0313304831
Social sciences -- Bibliography. Social sciences -- Bibliography of bibliographies. Social sciences -- Reference books -- Bibliography.

Z7161.A15 Political and social sciences — General special

Z7161.A15.H88 1995
Huttner, Harry J. M.
The multilevel design: a guide with an annotated bibliography, 1980-1993/ Harry J.M. Huttner and Pieter van den Eeden. Westport, Conn.: Greenwood Press, 1995. viii, 276 p.
94-036760　016.300/72　0313273103
Social sciences -- Research -- Bibliography. Social sciences -- Research -- Methodology -- Bibliography.

Z7161.A2 Political and social sciences — Theory, method, etc.

Z7161.A2.B76 1997
Brunk, Gregory G.
Theories of political processes: a bibliographic guide to the journal literature, 1965-1995/ compiled by Gregory G. Brunk. Westport, Conn.: Greenwood Press, 1997. xx, 251 p.
96-052498　016.320/01　0313302596
Political science literature -- Bibliography.

Z7161.C17-Y75 Political and social sciences — General bibliography

Z7161.C17
C.R.I.S.: the combined retrospective index set to journals in sociology, 1895-1974/ executive editor, Annadel N. Wile, assistant editor, Arnold Jaffe; with an introd. and user's guide by Evan I. Farber. Washington: Carrollton Press, 1978. 6 v.
78-106663　016.3　0840801947
Social sciences -- Periodicals -- Indexes. Sociology -- Periodicals -- Indexes. Anthropology -- Periodicals -- Indexes. Culture -- Periodicals -- Indexes. Social psychology -- Periodicals -- Indexes.

Z7161.H64 1986
Holler, Frederick L.
Information sources of political science/ Frederick L. Holler. 4th ed. Santa Barbara, Calif.: ABC-Clio, c1986. xvii, 417 p.
85-011279　016.32 19　0874363756
Political science -- Bibliography.

Z7161.I594
International bibliography of sociology/ prepared by the International Committee for Social Sciences Documentation in co-operation with the International Sociological Association = Bibliographie internationale de sociologie/ etablie par le Comite international pour la documentation des scienc Paris: UNESCO, 57-002949   016.301
Sociology -- Bibliography. Sociology -- Bibliography -- Periodicals.

Z7161.L578 2000
Liu, Lewis-Guodo.
Global economic growth: theories, research, studies, and annotated bibliography, 1950-1997/ Lewis-Guodo Liu and Robert Premus. Westport, Conn.: Greenwood Press, 2000. xi, 342 p.
99-053866   016.3309   0313307385
Economic history -- 1945- -- Bibliography. Economic development -- Research.

Z7161.S648 2002
The social sciences: a cross-disciplinary guide to selected sources/ general editor Nancy L. Herron. 3rd ed. Englewood, Colo.: Libraries Unlimited, 2002. xxv, 494 p.
2001-050748   016.3 21   1563089858
Social sciences -- References books -- Bibliography. Social sciences -- Bibliography.

Z7161.S65
Social sciences citation index.   Philadelphia, Institute for Scientific Information.
73-085287   016.3
Social sciences -- Indexes -- Periodicals.

Z7161.S666 1986
Sources of information in the social sciences: a guide to the literature/ William H. Webb ... [et al.]. 3rd ed. Chicago: American Library Association, 1986. x, 777 p.
84-020494   016.3 19   083890405X
Social sciences -- Bibliography.

Z7161.Y75 1990
York, Henry E.
Political science: a guide to reference and information sources/ Henry E. York. Englewood, Colo.: Libraries Unlimited, 1990. xv, 249 p.
90-041158   016.32 20   0872877949
Political science -- Reference books -- Bibliography.

Z7164 Political and social sciences — Special topics, A-Z

Z7164.A17.W27 1996
Injury prevention for young children: a research guide/ compiled by Bonnie L. Walker. Westport, Conn.: Greenwood Press, 1996. x, 182 p.
95-046143   016.6136   0313296863
Children's accidents -- Prevention -- Bibliography. Safety education -- Bibliography. Children -- Wounds and injuries -- Bibliography.

Z7164.A2 S53 1993
Simpson, Antony E.
Information-finding and the research process: a guide to sources and   methods for public administration and the policy sciences/ Antony E. Simpson. Westport, Conn.: Greenwood Press, 1993. xv, 491 p. :
92-021358   016.35 20   0313252513
Public administration -- Bibliography of bibliographies. Public administration -- United States -- Bibliography of bibliographies. Policy sciences -- Bibliography of bibliographies.

Z7164.A52.N87 1992
Nursey-Bray, Paul F.
Anarchist thinkers and thought: an annotated bibliography/ compiled and edited by Paul Nursey-Bray with the assistance of Jim Jose and Robyn Williams. New York: Greenwood Press, 1992. xix, 284 p.
91-033407   016.335/83/0922   0313275920
Anarchists -- Bibliography. Anarchism -- Bibliography.

Z7164.C45.K57 2000
Kistler, John M., 1967-
Animal rights: a subject guide, bibliography, and Internet companion/ John M. Kistler; foreword by Marc Bekoff. Westport, Conn.: Greenwood Press, 2000. xviii, 227 p.
99-088482   016.179/3   0313312311
Animal rights -- Bibliography. Animal rights -- Indexes. Animal welfare -- Bibliography.

Z7164.C5.F44 1995
Feinberg, Sandra, 1946-
Parenting: an annotated bibliography, 1965-1987/ by Sandra Feinberg, Barbara Jordan, Michele Lauer-Bader. Metuchen, N.J.: Scarecrow Press, 1995. vii, 806 p.
94-013721   016.649/1   081082664X
Parenting -- Bibliography. Child rearing -- Bibliography. Family -- Bibliography.

Z7164.C5.G68 1990
Gouke, Mary Noel.
One-parent children, the growing minority: a research guide/ Mary Noel Gouke, Arline McClarty Rollins. New York: Garland, 1990. xi, 494 p.
84-048876   306.85/6   0824085760
Children of single parents -- United States -- Bibliography. Single-parent families -- United States -- Bibliography. Children of single parents -- Education -- United States -- Bibliography.

Z7164.C5.N66 1990
Nofsinger, Mary M.
Children and adjustment to divorce: an annotated bibliography/ Mary M. Nofsinger. New York: Garland, 1990. xiii, 282 p.
89-016986   016.30689   0824042972
Children of divorced parents -- United States -- Bibliography. Divorce -- United States -- Bibliography.

Z7164.C5.S94 1992
Sutherland, Neil, 1931-
Contemporary Canadian childhood and youth: a bibliography/ compiled by Neil Sutherland, Jean Barman, and Linda L. Hale; technical consultant, W. G. Brian Owen. Westport, Conn.: Greenwood Press, 1992. ix, 492 p.
92-027766   016.30523/0971   0313285861
Children -- Canada -- Bibliography. Youth -- Canada -- Bibliography.

Z7164.C8.S33 1997
Schreiber, Mae N.
International trade sources: a research guide/ Mae N. Schreiber. New York: Garland Pub., 1997. x, 327 p.
96-030183   016.382   0815321090
International trade -- Bibliography. International business enterprises -- Bibliography. Business information services -- Handbooks, manuals, etc.

Z7164.C81.A46 1993
Alston, Jon P., 1937-
The social dimensions of international business: an annotated bibliography/ compiled by Jon P. Alston. Westport, Conn.: Greenwood Press, 1993. xx, 312 p.
92-029466   016.3888/8   0313280290
Communication in international trade -- Bibliography. Intercultural communication -- Bibliography.

Z7164.C81.B983
Business periodicals index.   New York, H.W. Wilson Co.
58-012645   016.6505
Business -- Periodicals -- Indexes. Industries -- Periodicals -- Indexes.

Z7164.C81.D16 1993
Daniells, Lorna M.
Business information sources/ Lorna M. Daniells. Berkeley: University of California Press, c1993. xix, 725 p.
92-041827   016.33   0520081803
Business -- Bibliography. Management -- Bibliography. Business -- Reference books -- Bibliography.

Z7164.C81.E93
Encyclopedia of business information sources. Detroit, Mich.: Gale Research Co., [1970-   ]
84-643366   016.33
Reference books -- Business -- Bibliography -- Periodicals. Business -- Bibliography -- Periodicals. Business information services -- Directories.

Z7164.C81.G595 1997
Goodall, Francis, 1931-
International bibliography of business history/ edited by Francis Goodall, Terry Gourvish and Steven Tolliday. London; Routledge, 1997. xvi, 668 p.
97-108068   016.3387   0415086418
Business -- History -- Bibliography. Industries -- History -- Bibliography.

Z7164.C81.V355 1996
Vandivier, Elizabeth L.
Business A to Z source finder/ Elizabeth Louise Vandivier and Kathleen Brown, editors. Annapolis, Md.: Beacon Bay Press, c1996. xxv, 590 p.
95-083030
Business -- Reference books -- Bibliography. Subject headings -- Business. Business information services -- United States -- Directories.

Z7164.C81.W67
World directory of trade and business journals. London: Euromonitor PLC, [c1996-   ]
99-034716
Business -- Periodicals -- Directories. Commerce -- Periodicals -- Directories.

Z7164.D2.V36 1997
Van Wyk, J. J., 1947-
Contemporary democracy: a bibliography of periodical literature, 1974-1994/ J.J. van Wyk, Mary C. Custy. Washington, D.C.: Congressional Quarterly, c1997. xxiii, 449 p.
96-044880   016.3209/009/049   1568022441
Democracy -- Bibliography.

Z7164.D3.P83
Population index. [Princeton, N.J., etc.] Office of Population Research, Princeton University Press,
39-010247   016.3046
Population -- Bibliography -- Periodicals. Social sciences -- Bibliography -- Periodicals. Population Control -- periodicals.

Z7164.D3.Z64 1993
Zollar, Ann Creighton.
The social correlates of infant and reproductive mortality in the United States: a reference guide/ Ann Creighton-Zollar. New York: Garland, 1993. viii, 214 p.
92-041215   304.6/4/0832   0815302215
Infants -- United States -- Mortality -- Bibliography. Mothers -- United States -- Mortality -- Bibliography. Sudden infant death syndrome -- United States -- Bibliography.

Z7164.D78.S8 1992
Substance abuse among ethnic minorities in America: a critical annotated bibliography/ Howard Rebach ... [et al.]. New York: Garland Pub., 1992. 469 p.
91-045032   016.36229/08693   0815300662
Drug abuse -- United States -- Bibliography. Alcoholism -- United States -- Bibliography. Minorities -- Drug use -- United States -- Bibliography.

Z7164.E14.B53 1995
Bibliography on forecasting and planning/ compiled by Kwok Keung (Kern) Kwong ... [et al.]. Flushing, N.Y.: Graceway Pub. Co., c1995. iv, 328 p.
94-075680   016.33/001/12   0932126162
Economic forecasting -- Bibliography. Planning -- Bibliography.

Z7164.E2.K56 1995
King, J. E.
Post Keynesian economics: an annotated bibliography/ J.E. King. Aldershot, UK; E. Elgar, 1995. 1 v.
95-019497   016.33015/6   1852788011
Keynesian economics -- Bibliography.

Z7164.E2.M43 1991
McCloskey, Deirdre N.
A bibliography of historical economics to 1980/ Donald N. McCloskey and George K. Hersh, Jr. with the assistance of John Coatsworth ... [et al.]. Cambridge [England]; Cambridge University Press, 1990. xii, 505 p.
90-045767   016.33015/42   0521403278
Historical school of economics -- Bibliography.

Z7164.E2.S39 1996
The search for economics as a science: an annotated bibliography/ [the editors of Salem Press]; Lynn Turgeon, consulting editor. Lanham, Md.: Scarecrow Press; c1996. xii, 428 p.
95-048937   016.33   0810831201
Economics -- History -- Bibliography. Economics -- Bibliography.

Z7164.F5.B76 1991
Brealey, Richard A.
A bibliography of finance/ Richard Brealey, Helen Edwards. Cambridge, Mass.: MIT Press, c1991. xli, 822 p.
90-013523   016.332   0262023199
Finance -- Bibliography.

Z7164.F5.I557 2000
International financial organizations: a bibliography/ George B. Grey (editor). Huntington, N.Y.: Nova Science Publishers, 2000. 231 p.
00-055439   016.3321/5   1560728280
Financial institutions, International -- Bibliography. Banks and banking, International -- Bibliography. International finance -- Bibliography.

Z7164.F5.J64 1993
Johnson, Mary Elizabeth.
The International Monetary Fund, 1944-1992: a research guide/ by Mary Elizabeth Johnson. New York: Garland Pub., 1993. xii, 214 p.
93-015643   016.3321/152   0815302304
International finance -- Bibliography.

Z7164.F5.W86 1995
Womack, Carol Z., 1946-
The American Stock Exchange: a guide to information resources/ Carol Z. Womack, Alice C. Littlejohn. New York: Garland Pub., 1995. 225 p.
94-042750   332.64/273   0815302231
Stock exchanges -- New York (State) -- New York -- Bibliography.

Z7164.F5.W88 1995
World Bank/ Anne C.M. Salda, compiler. New Brunswick, NJ, U.S.A. : Transaction Publishers, 1995. xxxiii, 306 p.
94-033739   016.3321/532   1560001984
World Bank -- Bibliography.

Z7164.G35.M57 1997
Mirkovich, Thomas R., 1954-
Casino gaming in the United States: a research guide/ Thomas R. Mirkovich and Allison A. Cowgill. Lanham, Md.: Scarecrow Press, 1997. xiv, 401 p.
96-031864   016.795   0810832305
Casinos -- United States -- Bibliography. Casinos -- United States -- Research -- Handbooks, manuals, etc. Gambling -- United States -- Bibliography.

Z7164.G45.D63 1992
Dobkowski, Michael N.
Genocide in our time: an annotated bibliography with analytical introductions/ by Michael N. Dobkowski and Isidor Wallimann. Ann Arbor, Mich.: Pierian Press, 1992. xvi, 183 p.
93-215834   016.3641/51   087650280X
Genocide -- History -- 20th century -- Bibliography. Crimes against humanity -- History -- 20th century -- Bibliography.

Z7164.G45.G45 1988 vol. 3
The Widening circle of genocide/ edited by Israel W. Charny; with a foreword by Irving Louis Horowitz. New Brunswick, U.S.A.: Transaction Publishers, c1994. xxvii, 375 p.
93-046257   016.364/51   1560001720
Genocide -- Bibliography.

Z7164.G7.G37 1993
Garner, Diane L.
The complete guide to citing government information resources: a manual for writers & librarians. Bethesda, MD: Congressional Information Service, c1993. xvii, 222 p.
93-016059   016.015   0886922542
Government publications -- Bibliography -- Methodology. Bibliographical citations.

Z7164.G7.G827 1996
Guide to country information in international governmental organization publications/ American Library Association, Government Documents Round Table. [Bethesda, Md.?: Congressional Information Service?], c1996. xviii, 343 p.
96-220617
International agencies -- Bibliography.

Z7164.G7.I47 1997
Information sources in official publications/ edited by Valerie J. Nurcombe. London; Bowker-Saur, c1997. xxvii, 564 p.
96-029867   011/.53   1857391519
Government publications -- Bibliography.

Z7164.G82.S74 1996
Strauss, Carol Ann, 1948-
Grandparents: an annotated bibliography on roles, rights, and relationships/ Carol Ann Strauss. Lanham, Md.: Scarecrow Press, 1996. xii, 507 p.
95-049543   016.306874/5   081083135X
Grandparents -- Bibliography. Grandparenting -- Bibliography. Grandparent and child -- Bibliography.

Z7164.H72.H46 1993
Henslin, James M.
Homelessness: an annotated bibliography/ by James M. Henslin. New York: Garland, 1993. 2 v.
92-041254   016.3625   0824041151
Homelessness -- Bibliography. Homeless persons -- Bibliography.

Z7164.H74.G55 1995
Gillon, Margaret.
Lesbians in print: a bibliography of 1,500 books with synopses/ [Gillon]. Irvine, CA: Bluestocking Books, c1995. 478 p.
95-077022   016.30676/63   1887237135
Lesbians -- Bibliography. Lesbianism -- Bibliography. Lesbians in literature -- Bibliography.

Z7164.I3.G33 1989
Gabaccia, Donna R., 1949-
Immigrant women in the United States: a selectively annotated multidisciplinary bibliography/ compiled by Donna Gabaccia. New York: Greenwood Press, 1989. xiv, 325 p.
89-017191   016.32573/082   031326452X
Women immigrants -- United States -- Bibliography.

Z7164.I3.G35 1998
Gaillard, Anne-Marie.
International migration of the highly qualified: a bibiliographic and conceptual itinerary/ by Anne Marie Gaillard and Jacques Gaillard. Staten Island, N.Y.: Center for Migration Studies, 1998. 142 p.
98-161150   1577030079
Brain drain -- Bibliography. Professional employees -- Bibliography. Emigration and immigration -- Bibliography.

Z7164.I3.H62 2001
Hofstetter, Eleanore O.
Women in global migration, 1945-2000: a comprehensive multidisciplinary bibliography/ Eleanore O. Hofstetter. Westport, Conn.: Greenwood Press, 2001. xi, 535 p.
00-068174 016.3048/082/09045 0313318107
Women immigrants -- Bibliography. Emigration and immigration -- Bibliography.

Z7164.I45.G46 1990
Ghorayshi, Parvin.
The sociology of work: a critical annotated bibliography/ Parvin Ghorayshi. New York: Garland Pub., 1990. xxvi, 214 p.
90-002840 016.3063/6 0824034384
Industrial sociology -- Bibliography. Work -- Bibliography.

Z7164.L1.I44 1998
Informal work and social change: a bibliographic survey/ edited by Shelley Feldman and Eveline Ferretti. Ithaca: ILR Press, c1998. x, 316 p.
98-011446 016.331 0801435048
Labor -- Bibliography. Informal sector (Economics) -- Bibliography. Social change -- Bibliography.

Z7164.L1.S766 1996
Stern, Robert N., 1948-
The U.S. labor movement: references and resources/ Robert N. Stern, Daniel B. Cornfield, with Theresa I. Liska and Dee Ann Warmath. New York: G.K. Hall; c1996. xvi, 356 p.
96-002160 331.88/0973 0816172773
Labor movement -- United States -- History -- Bibliography. Industrial relations -- United States -- History -- Bibliography. Labor literature -- Bibliography. United States -- Social conditions -- Bibliography.

Z7164.L1.S936 1997
Switzer, Teri R.
Telecommuters, the workforce of the twenty-first century: an annotated bibliography/ Teri R. Switzer. Lanham, Md.: Scarecrow Press, 1997. ix, 176 p.
96-023195 016.33125 0810832100
Telecommuting -- Bibliography.

Z7164.L53
Clarke, Norman F.
The recreation and entertainment industries: an information sourcebook/ by Norman F. Clarke. Jefferson, N.C.: McFarland, c2000. x, 286 p.
00-041892 016.3384/779 0786407972
Leisure industry -- United States -- Bibliography. Leisure industry -- Canada -- Bibliography. Leisure industry -- Great Britain -- Bibliography.

Z7164.L6.B46 1995
Bennett, James R., 1932-
Political prisoners and trials: a worldwide annotated bibliography, 1900 through 1993/ by James R. Bennett. Jefferson, N.C.: McFarland, c1995. viii, 363 p.
95-006232 016.3641/31/0922 0786400234
Political prisoners -- Bibliography. Human rights -- Bibliography.

Z7164.L6.W35 1994
Walters, Gregory J., 1956-
Human rights in theory and practice: a selected and annotated bibliography/ by Gregory J. Walters, with the assistance of Denice Durocher ... [et al.]. Metuchen, N.J.: Scarecrow Press; c1994. xxiv, 459 p.
95-003875 016.323 0810830108
Human rights -- Bibliography.

Z7164.M2.S73 1994
Stanton, Greta W.
Children of separation: an annotated bibliography for professionals/ by Greta W. Stanton. Metuchen, N.J.: Scarecrow Press, 1994. ix, 358 p.
93-043575 306.874 081082695X
Parent and child -- United States -- Bibliography. Family life education -- United States -- Bibliography. Children of divorced parents -- United States -- Bibliography.

Z7164.N17.D44 1990
Derivan, William J., 1951-
Prevention education: a guide to research/ William J. Derivan, Natalie Anne Silverstein. New York: Garland Pub., 1990. xix, 282 p.
89-039996 016.36229/17 0824037162
Drug abuse -- Prevention -- Study and teaching -- United States -- Bibliography. Alcoholism -- Prevention -- Study and teaching -- United States -- Bibliography.

Z7164.N3.C88 1997
Cutting across the lands: an annotated bibliography on natural resource management and community development in Indonesia, the Philippines, and Malaysia/ Eveline Ferretti, editor. Ithaca, N.Y.: Southeast Asia Program, Cornell University, 1997. 329 p.
97-175310 016.3337/0959
Natural resources -- Indonesia -- Management -- Bibliography. Natural resources -- Philippines -- Management -- Bibliography. Natural resources -- Malaysia -- Management -- Bibliography.

Z7164.O4.A37 1995
Aging well: a selected, annotated bibliography/ compiled by W. Edward Folts ... [et al.]. Westport, Conn.: Greenwood Press, 1995. x, 156 p.
95-020888 016.30526 0313287716
Aging -- Bibliography. Aged -- Bibliography. Gerontology -- Bibliography.

Z7164.O4.A55 1991
Anthropology of aging: a partially annotated bibliography/ Marjorie M. Schweitzer, general editor. New York: Greenwood Press, 1991. xvi, 338 p.
91-009707 016.30526 0313261199
Aged -- Cross-cultural studies -- Bibliography. Aging -- Cross-cultural studies -- Bibliography. Gerontology -- Bibliography.

Z7164.O4.C68 1989
Coyle, Jean M.
Women and aging: a selected, annotated bibliography/ compiled by Jean M. Coyle. New York: Greenwood Press, 1989. xxiii, 135 p.
88-028975 016.3052/6/0973 0313260214
Aged women -- United States -- Bibliography. Middle aged women -- United States -- Bibliography.

Z7164.O4.S38 1995
Schwiebert, Valerie L.
Counseling older persons: an annotated bibliography/ compiled by Valerie L. Schwiebert and Jane E. Myers. Westport, Conn.: Greenwood Press, 1995. xii, 119 p.
94-044351 016.3626/6/0973 0313292779
Aged -- Services for -- United States -- Bibliography. Aged -- Counseling of -- United States -- Bibliography.

Z7164.O4.T5 1996
Thompson, Edward H.
Men and aging: a selected, annotated bibliography/ compiled by Edward H. Thompson, Jr. Westport, Conn.: Greenwood Press, 1996. xiii, 234 p.
95-025580 016.30526 0313291063
Aged men -- Bibliography. Middle aged men -- Bibliography.

Z7164.O4.T66 1993
Topics in gerontology: selected annotated bibliographies/ edited by Thomas O. Blank. Westport, Conn.: Greenwood Press, c1993. xxxix, 212 p.
93-009311 016.6126/7 0313283370
Gerontology -- Bibliography.

Z7164.O4.W28 1995
Walker, Bonnie L.
Injury prevention for the elderly: a research guide/ compiled by Bonnie L. Walker. Westport, Conn.: Greenwood Press, 1995. xii, 311 p.
95-032989 016.3631/00846 0313296707
Aged -- Accidents -- Prevention -- Bibliography. Accidents -- Prevention -- Bibliography. Aged -- Wounds and injuries -- Bibliography.

Z7164.O7.A95 1997
Avery, Christine.
The quality management sourcebook: an international guide to materials and resources/ Christine Avery and Diane Zabel. London; Routledge, 1996. vii, 327 p.
96-008911 016.6585/62 0415108314
Total quality management -- Bibliography. Management -- Bibliography.

Z7164.O7.K35 1997
Kemper, Robert E.
Quality, TQC, TQM: a meta literature study/ Robert E. Kemper. Lanham, Md.: Scarecrow Press, 1997. xvi, 559 p.
97-016754 016.6585/62 0810833468
Total quality management -- Bibliography. Quality control -- Management -- Bibliography. Bibliographical citations -- Statistics.

Z7164.O7.W545 1997
Wilson, C. Dwayne.
Research on professional consultation and consultation for organizational change: a selectively annotated bibliography/ C. Dwayne Wilson, Bernard Lubin; foreword by William B. Eddy. Westport, Conn.: Greenwood Press, 1997. xi, 135 p.
96-042164 016.6584/06 0313280347
Organizational change -- Bibliography.

Z7164.P84.S56 2001
Slade, Joseph W.
Pornography and sexual representation: a reference guide/ Joseph W. Slade. Westport, Conn.: Greenwood Press, 2001. 3 v.
99-085695 016.3634/7 0313275688
Pornography -- United States -- Bibliography. Pornography -- United States.

Z7164.P95.P76 1992
Prostitution: a guide to sources, 1960-1990/ edited by Vern L. Bullough, Lilli Sentz; co-editors, Nancy Henry ... [et al.]. New York: Garland, 1992. 369 p.
92-005112 016.30674 0824071018
Prostitution -- Bibliography.

Z7164.P956.W33 1996
Walden, Graham R., 1954-
Polling and survey research methods, 1935-1979: an annotated bibliography/ compiled by Graham R. Walden. Westport, Conn.: Greenwood Press, 1996. xxx, 581 p.
96-033127 016.3033/8 0313277907
Public opinion polls -- Bibliography. Social surveys -- Bibliography. Public opinion -- United States -- Bibliography.

Z7164.P956 W34 1990
Walden, Graham R.,
Public opinion polls and survey research: a selective annotated bibliography of U.S. guides and studies from the 1980s/ Graham R. Walden. New York: Garland Pub., 1990. xxix, 306 p.
89-025956 016.3033/8/0723 20 0824057325
Public opinion polls -- Bibliography. Social surveys -- Bibliography. Public opinion -- United States -- Bibliography. Social surveys -- United States -- Bibliography.

Z7164.R12.W5 1992
Weinberg, Meyer, 1920-
World racism and related inhumanities: a country-by-country bibliography/ compiled by Meyer Weinberg. New York: Greenwood Press, 1992. xiii, 1048 p.
92-004094 016.3058 0313281092
Racism -- Bibliography. Human rights -- Bibliography. Discrimination -- Bibliography.

Z7164.S42.F73 1995
Frayser, Suzanne G.
Studies in human sexuality: a selected guide/ Suzanne G. Frayser, Thomas J. Whitby. Englewood, Colo.: Libraries Unlimited, 1995. xx, 737 p.
95-004259 016.3067 1563081318
Sex -- Bibliography. Sex -- Reference books -- Bibliography. Best books.

Z7164.S42.R5 1990
Ridinger, Robert B. Marks.
The homosexual and society: an annotated bibliography/ compiled by Robert B. Marks Ridinger. New York: Greenwood Press, c1990. viii, 444 p.
90-031738 016.30676/6 0313253579
Homosexuality -- Bibliography.

Z7164.S42.S42 1997
Sexuality and the elderly: a research guide/ compiled by Bonnie L. Walker. Westport, Conn.: Greenwood Press, 1997. xii, 301 p.
96-052496 016.3067/084/6 0313301336
Aged -- Sexual behavior -- Bibliography.

Z7164.S46.H37 1995
Hartel, Lynda Jones.
Sexual harassment: a selected, annotated bibliography/ Lynda Jones Hartel and Helena M. VonVille. Westport, CT: Greenwood Press, 1995. x, 158 p.
95-021267 016.30542 0313290555
Sexual harassment of women -- United States -- Bibliography. Sexual harassment of women -- Law and legislation -- United States -- Bibliography. Sexual harassment -- United States -- Bibliography.

Z7164.S6.S63 1982
Smith, John David, 1949-
Black slavery in the Americas: an interdisciplinary bibliography, 1865-1980/ compiled by John David Smith; foreword by Stanley L. Engerman. Westport, Conn.: Greenwood Press, 1982. 2 v.
82-011736 016.306/362/0973 0313231184
Slavery -- America -- Bibliography. Slavery -- United States -- Bibliography.

Z7164.S66.B83 1994
Bridging the gap: examining polarity in America/ Nancy L. Herron, Diane Zabel, editors. Englewood, Colo.: Libraries Unlimited, 1995. xv, 380 p.
94-009792 016.306/0973 1563081148
Social classes -- United States -- Bibliography.United States -- Social policy -- Bibliography. United States -- Social conditions -- Bibliography.

Z7164.S66.G38 1997
Garner, Roberta.
Social movement theory and research: an annotated bibliographical guide/ Roberta Garner and John Tenuto. Lanham, Md.: Scarecrow Press; 1997. viii, 274 p.
96-026900 016.30348/4 081083197X
Social movements -- Bibliography. Ideology -- Bibliography. Social change -- Bibliography.

Z7164.S66.J28 1992
Jackson, Rebecca.
The 1960s: an annotated bibliography of social and political movements in the United States/ Rebecca Jackson. Westport, Conn.: Greenwood Press, 1992. xv, 237 p.
92-024261 016.30348/4/0973 0313272557
Social movements -- United States -- History -- 20th century -- Bibliography.United States -- Politics and government -- 1961-1963 -- Bibliography. United States -- Politics and government -- 1963-1969 -- Bibliography. United States -- Social conditions -- 1960-1980 -- Bibliography.

Z7164.S66.L43 1994
Leaders from the 1960s: a biographical sourcebook of American activism/ edited by David DeLeon. Westport, Conn.: Greenwood Press, 1994. xxiv, 601 p.
93-031603   016.30348/4/09730922 0313274142
Social reformers -- United States -- Biography. Political activists -- United States -- Biography. Social change -- United States -- Bio-bibliography.

Z7164.S665.B37 1999
Barbuto, Domenica M., 1951-
The American settlement movement: a bibliography/ compiled by Domenica M. Barbuto. Westport, Conn.: Greenwood Press, 1999. ix, 123 p.
99-033433 016.3625/57/0973 0313307563
Social settlements -- United States -- Bibliography.

Z7164.S667 W35 2003
Walden, Graham R.,
Survey research methodology, 1990-1999: an annotated bibliography/ compiled by Graham R. Walden. Westport, CT: Greenwood Press, c2003. xx, 432 p.
2002-027118 300.723 21 0313305978
Social surveys -- Methodology -- Bibliography.

Z7164.S68.A24 1997
Aby, Stephen H., 1949-
Sociology: a guide to reference and information sources/ Stephen H. Aby. Englewood, Colo.: Libraries Unlimited, 1997. xv, 227 p.
97-026613 016.301 1563084228
Sociology -- Reference books -- Bibliography. Sociology -- Bibliography. Social sciences -- Reference books -- Bibliography.

Z7164.S68 B75 1987
Brown, Samuel R.
Finding the source in sociology and anthropology: a thesaurus-index to the reference collection/ compiled by Samuel R. Brown. New York: Greenwood Press, 1987. xv, 269 p.
86-031879 016.301 19 0313252637
Sociology -- Reference books -- Bibliography. Sociology -- Bibliography. Sociology -- Reference books -- Indexes. Sociology -- Indexes. Anthropology -- Reference books -- Bibliography. Anthropology -- Bibliography. Anthropology -- Reference books -- Indexes. Anthropology -- Indexes.

Z7164.S68 W46 1983
Wepsiec, Jan,
Sociology: an international bibliography of serial publications, 1880-1980/ Jan Wepsiec. London: Mansell Pub.; xii, 183 p.
83-217098 016.301/05 19
Sociology -- Periodicals -- Bibliography.

Z7164.T3 B33 2001
Babkina, A. M.
Terrorism: a bibliography with indexes/ A.M. Babkina, editor. 2nd ed. Huntington, N.Y.: Nova Science Publishers, c2001. 199 p.
2001-054668 016.3036/25 21 1590331044
Terrorism -- Bibliography.

Z7164.T3 G57 1986
Global terrorism: a historical bibliography/ Suzanne Robitaille Ontiveros, editor. Santa Barbara, Calif.: ABC-CLIO, c1986. xiii, 168 p.
86-003339 016.3036/25/09 19 0874364531
Terrorism -- History -- Bibliography.

Z7164.T3.L343 1991
Lakos, Amos, 1946-
Terrorism, 1980-1990: a bibliography/ Amos Lakos. Boulder: Westview Press, 1991. x, 443 p.
91-026865 016.3036/25 0813380359
Terrorism -- Bibliography.

Z7164.T3 M53
Mickolus, Edward F.
The literature of terrorism: a selectively annotated bibliography/ compiled by Edward F. Mickolus. Westport, Conn.: Greenwood Press, c1980. xii, 553 p.
80-000541 016.3036/2 0313222657
Terrorism -- Bibliography.

Z7164.T3 M54 1988
Mickolus, Edward F.
Terrorism, 1980-1987: a selectively annotated bibliography/ compiled by Edward F. Mickolus with Peter A. Flemming. New York: Greenwood Press, 1988. ix, 314 p.
87-032275 016.3036/25 19 0313262489
Terrorism -- Bibliography.

Z7164.T3.N48 1988
Newton, Michael, 1951-
Terrorism in the United States and Europe, 1800-1959: an annotated bibliography/ Michael Newton, Judy Ann Newton. New York: Garland, 1988. xi, 508 p.
88-021848   016.3036/25/094   0824057473
Terrorism -- United States -- History -- Bibliography. Terrorism -- Europe -- History -- Bibliography.

Z7164.T3.P78 1995
Prunckun, Henry W.
Shadow of death: an analytic bibliography on political violence, terrorism, and low-intensity conflict/ by Henry W. Prunckun, Jr. Lanham, Md.: Scarecrow Press, c1995. xxi, 406 p.
93-032400   016.3036/25   0810827735
Terrorism -- Bibliography. Political violence -- Bibliography. Social conflict -- Bibliography.

Z7164.T87.L36 1996
Landskroner, Ronald A.
The nonprofit manager's resource directory/ Ronald A. Landskroner. New York: Wiley, c1996. 522 p.
95-051509   016.658/048   0471148393
Nonprofit organizations -- United States -- Management -- Information services -- Directories. Nonprofit organizations -- United States -- Computer network resources -- Directories. Nonprofit organizations -- United States -- Bibliography.

Z7164.U5 A47 2001
American women: a Library of Congress guide for the study of women's history and culture in the United States/ edited by Sheridan Harvey ... [et al.]; introduction by Susan Ware. Washington: Library of Congress: xxxvi, 420 p.
2001-029547   026/.3054/0973 21   0844410489
Women--United States--History--Library resources. Women--United States--History. Women's studies--Library resources.

Z7164.U5.G438 1995
Gerhan, David R.
Bibliography of American demographic history: the literature from 1984 to 1994/ compiled by David R. Gerhan. Westport, Conn.: Greenwood Pess, 1995. xx, 339 p.
94-042117   016.3046/0973   0313266778
Demography -- United States -- History -- Bibliography.United States -- Population -- History -- Bibliography.

Z7164.U5.T46 1994
Third World resource directory, 1994-1995: an annotated guide to print and audiovisual resources from and about Africa, Asia and Pacific, Latin America and Caribbean, and the Middle East/ compiled and edited by Thomas P. Fenton and Mary J. Heffron in association with Alternative Information Center (Jerusalem) ... [et al.]. Maryknoll, N.Y.: Orbis Books, c1994. xiv, 785 p.
94-001601   016.909/09724   0883449412
Developing countries -- Directories. Developing countries -- Bibliography. Developing countries -- Audio-visual aids -- Catalogs.

Z7164.U7.B69 1989
Brown, Catherine L., 1948-
The urban South: a bibliography/ compiled by Catherine L. Brown. New York: Greenwood Press, 1989. x, 455 p.
89-002151   016.3077/6/0975   0313261547
Cities and towns -- Southern States -- Bibliography. Human settlements -- Southern States -- Bibliography.

Z7164.U7.R62 1996
Rodger, Richard.
A consolidated bibliography of urban history/ Richard Rodger. Aldershot, Hants, England: Scolar Press; c1996. xxviii, 791 p.
96-005203   016.30776/09   1859281133
Cities and towns -- History -- Bibliography. Urbanization -- History -- Bibliography.

Z7164.U8.H38 1994
Haschak, Paul G., 1948-
Utopian/dystopian literature: a bibliography of literary criticism/ by Paul G. Haschak. Metuchen, N.J.: Scarecrow Press, 1994. viii, 370 p.
93-030232   016.809/93372   0810827522
Utopias in literature -- Bibliography. Utopias -- Bibliography.

Z7164.Y8 Z95 1996
Zvirin, Stephanie.
The best years of their lives: a resource guide for teenagers in crisis/ Stephanie Zvirin. 2nd ed. Chicago: American Library Associations, 1996. xi, 154 p.
96-014446   016.30523/5 20   0838906869
Teenagers -- Juvenile literature -- Bibliography. Adolescent psychology -- Juvenile literature -- Bibliography. Children's stories -- Bibliography. Children's films -- Bibliography. Adolescence -- Bibliography. Adolescence -- Bibliography.

Z7165 Political and social sciences — By region or country, A-Z

Z7165.A67.C58 1992
Clements, Frank, 1942-
Arab regional organizations/ Frank A. Clements, compiler. New Brunswick, N.J. (U.S.A.): Transaction Publishers, c1992. xxxiii, 198 p.
92-005116   016.34124/77   1560000570
Economic assistance, Arab countries -- Societies, etc. -- Bibliography. International agencies -- Arab countries -- Bibliography. Arab countries -- Economic integration -- Societies, etc. -- Bibliography.

Z7165.E8.A4 1993
Aldcroft, Derek Howard.
Bibliography of European economic and social history/ compiled by Derek H. Aldcroft and Richard Rodger. Manchester; Manchester University Press; c1993. x, 292 p.
92-029429   016.306/094   0719034922
Europe -- Economic conditions -- Bibliography. Europe -- Social conditions -- Bibliography.

Z7165.E8.P34 1992
Paxton, John.
European communities/ John Paxton, compiler. New Brunswick, N.J.: Transaction Publishers, c1992. xxiii, 182 p.
91-041792   016.34124/22   156000052X
European Economic Community countries -- Economic policy -- Bibliography. European Economic Community countries -- Politics and government -- Bibliography.

Z7165.G8.C46 1996
Richardson, R. C.
British economic and social history: a bibliographical guide/ compiled by R.C. Richardson and W.H. Chaloner. Manchester, U.K.; Manchester University Press; c1996. xv, 271 p.
96-154274   0719036003
Great Britain -- Economic conditions -- Bibliography. Great Britain -- Social conditions -- Bibliography.

Z7165.J3.B63 1988
Boger, Karl.
Postwar industrial policy in Japan: an annotated bibliography/ by Karl Boger. Metuchen, N.J.: Scarecrow Press, 1988. ix, 208 p.
87-026535   016.338952   0810820803
Industrial policy -- Japan -- Bibliography.Japan -- Economic policy -- 1945-1989 -- Bibliography. Japan -- Economic conditions -- 1945-1989 -- Bibliography.

Z7165.S65 B37 1988
Battle, John M.
Gorbachev's reforms: an annotated bibliography of Soviet writings/ John M. Battle, Thomas D. Sherlock. Gulf Breeze, FL: Academic International Press, [1988-] v. <1 >
89-125282   016.338947/009/048 20   0875691021
Soviet Union -- Economic policy -- 1986-1991 -- Bibliography. Soviet Union -- Politics and government -- 1985-1991 -- Bibliography.

Z7165.S65 M38 1992
Manat, G. P.
Politics and economics of the Soviet Union: an annotated bibliography / edited by G.P. Manat. Commack, N.Y.: Nova Science Publishers, 1992. vii, 197 p.
92-035078   016.306/0947 20   1560720484
Soviet Union -- Social conditions -- 1970-1991 -- Bibliography. Soviet Union -- Economic conditions -- 1985-1991 -- Bibliography.

Z7165.U5.G43 1989
Gerhan, David R.
A retrospective bibliography of American demographic history from colonial times to 1983/ compiled by David R. Gerhan and Robert V. Wells. New York: Greenwood Press, 1989. xxvi, 474 p.
88-032348   016.3046/0973   0313231303
Demography -- United States -- History -- Bibliography.United States -- Population -- History -- Bibliography.

Z7165.U5.G568 1996
Goehlert, Robert, 1948-
Members of Congress: a bibliography/ Robert U. Goehlert, Fenton S. Martin, John R. Sayre. Washington, D.C.: Congressional Quarterly, c1996. ix, 507 p.
95-026756   016.32873/092/2 20   0871878658
United States. Congress -- Bio-bibliography.

Z7165.U5.G73 1984
The Great Depression: a historical bibliography. Santa Barbara, Calif.: ABC-Clio Information Services, c1984. xii, 260 p.
83-012234   016.3385/42   0874363616
Depressions -- 1929 -- United States -- Bibliography.United States -- Economic conditions -- 1918-1945 -- Bibliography. United States -- Economic policy -- 1933-1945 -- Bibliography. United States -- Social conditions -- 1933-1945 -- Bibliography.

Z7165.U5.M285 1994
Goehlert, Robert, 1948-
The United States Congress: an annotated bibliography, 1980-1993/ Robert U. Goehlert, Fenton S. Martin. Washington, D.C.: Congressional Quarterly, c1995. xxix, 640 p.
94-047925   016.32873/07   0871878100
United States. Congress -- Bibliography.

Z7165.U5 P715 1994
Pressman, Steven.
Poverty in America: an annotated bibliography/ by Steven Pressman. Metuchen, N.J.: Scarecrow Press, Inc.; xiv, 299 p. ;
93-012052   362.5/0973 20   0810828332
Poverty -- United States -- Bibliography. Poor -- United States -- Bibliography.

Z7165.U5.W27 1991
Walsh, Jim, 1951-
Vital and health statistics series: an annotated checklist and index to the publications of the "rainbow series"/ compiled by Jim Walsh and A. James Bothmer. New York: Greenwood Press, 1991. xix, 388 p.
91-018077   016.3046/0973/021   0313272603
United States -- Statistics, Vital -- Bibliography. United States -- Statistics, Medical -- Bibliography.

Z7201-7204 Psychology

Z7201.C37 1993
Caton, Hiram.
The bibliography of human behavior/ Hiram Caton, editor-in-chief; Frank K. Salter and J.M.G. van der Dennen, associate editors. Westport, Conn.: Greenwood Press, 1993. xvi, 575 p.
93-003066   016.15   0313278970
Psychology -- Bibliography. Human behavior -- Bibliography. Behavior evolution -- Bibliography.

Z7201.H52 1989
A History of American psychology in notes and news, 1883-1945: an index to journal sources/ Ludy T. Benjamin, Jr. ... [et al.]. Millwood, N.Y.: Kraus International Publications, c1989. xxiv, 591 p.
89-015251   016.15/0973/05 20   0527066265
Psychology -- United States -- History -- Sources -- Indexes. Psychology -- United States -- Periodicals -- Indexes.

Z7201.P79 1996
Psychology: an introductory bibliography/ the editors of Salem Press; consulting editor, Susan E. Beers. Lanham, Md.: Scarecrow Press; 1996. vii, 431 p.
95-048933   016.15   0810831198
Psychology -- Bibliography.

Z7203.N47a
Bibliographic guide to psychology. Boston, G.K. Hall.
76-642687   016.15
Psychology -- Bibliography -- Periodicals. Parapsychology -- Bibliography -- Periodicals. Occultism -- Bibliography -- Periodicals. Psychology -- Bibliography.

Z7204.A42.H392 1995
Hayslip, Bert.
Psychology of aging: an annotated bibliography/ compiled by Bert Hayslip, Jr., Heather L. Servaty, and Amie S. Ward. Westport, Conn.: Greenwood Press, 1995. xii, 134 p.
95-006291   016.15567   0313293767
Aging -- Psychological aspects -- Bibliography. Aged -- Psychology -- Bibliography.

Z7204.A6.R47 1996
Research on group treatment methods: a selectively annotated bibliography/ Bernard Lubin ... [et al.]; foreword by George M. Gazda. Westport, Conn.: Greenwood Press, 1996. x, 246 p.
96-023114   016.61689/152   0313283397
Group counseling -- Bibliography. Group guidance in education -- Bibliography. Group counseling for children -- Bibliography.

Z7204.I5.A29 1990
Aby, Stephen H., 1949-
The IQ debate: a selective guide to the literature/ compiled by Stephen H. Aby, with the assistance of Martha J. McNamara. New York: Greenwood Press, 1990. xvi, 228 p.
90-013986   016.1539/3   0313264406
Intelligence levels -- Bibliography.

Z7204.P8.B44 1996
Beit-Hallahmi, Benjamin.
Psychoanalytic studies of religion: a critical assessment and annotated bibliography/ Benjamin Beit-Hallahmi. Westport, Conn.: Greenwood Press, 1996. xv, 188 p.
96-018524   016.2/001/9   0313273626
Psychoanalysis and religion -- Bibliography.

Z7204.S44.S26 1994
Santrock, John W.
The authoritative guide to self-help books: based on the highly acclaimed national survey of more than 500 mental health professionals' ratings of 1,000 self-help books/ John W. Santrock, Ann M. Minnett, Barbara D. Campbell. New York: Guilford Press, c1994. xvi, 432 p.
93-040425   016.158   0898625440
Self-help techniques -- Bibliography. Life skills -- Bibliography.

Z7204.S67.C65 1996
Cole, Robert, 1939-
Propaganda in twentieth century war and politics: an annotated bibliography/ Robert Cole. Lanham, Md.: Scarecrow Press; 1996. xi, 402 p.
96-027825   016.3033/75   0810831961
Propaganda -- Bibliography.

Z7221 Radio — General bibliography

Z7221.C37 1991
Carothers, Diane Foxhill, 1927-
Radio broadcasting from 1920 to 1990: an annotated bibliography/ Diane Foxhill Carothers. New York: Garland Pub., 1991. xi, 564 p.
90-024352   016.38454/0904   0824012097
Radio broadcasting -- Bibliography.

Z7224 Radio — By region or country, A-Z

Z7224.U6.G74 1989
Greenfield, Thomas Allen, 1948-
Radio: a reference guide/ Thomas Allen Greenfield. New York: Greenwood Press, 1989. xiii, 172 p.
88-024647   016.38454   0313222762
Radio broadcasting -- United States -- Bibliography.

Z7224.U6.K7 1992
Kraeuter, David W.
Radio and television pioneers: a patent bibliography/ by David W. Kraeuter. Metuchen, N.J.: Scarecrow Press, 1992. x, 319 p.
92-008879   016.621384/027273   0810825562
Radio -- United States -- Equipment and supplies -- Patents -- Bibliography. Television -- United States -- Equipment and supplies -- Patents -- Bibliography. Inventors -- United States -- Bibliography.

Z7231 Railroads — Bibliography of bibliography

Z7231.C67
Cors, Paul B.,
Railroads/ Paul B. Cors. Littleton, Colo.: Libraries Unlimited, 1975. 152 p. ;
74-031396   016.385   0872870820
Railroads -- Bibliography.

Z7401 Science. Natural history — General bibliography

Z7401.H85 1998
Hurt, Charlie Deuel.
Information sources in science and technology/ C.D. Hurt. Englewood, Colo.: Libraries Unlimited, Inc. 1998. xvi, 346 p.
98-019547   016.5   1563085283
Science -- Reference books -- Bibliography. Technology -- Reference books -- Bibliography. Engineering -- Reference books -- Bibliography.

Z7401.M278 1994
Malinowsky, H. Robert 1933-
Reference sources in science, engineering, medicine, and agriculture/ H. Robert Malinowsky. Phoenix: Oryx, 1994. ix, 355 p.
94-016133   026.6   0897747429
Science -- Reference books -- Bibliography. Science -- Bibliography. Engineering -- Reference books -- Bibliography.

Z7401.P778 1987
Powell, Russell H.,
Core list of books and journals in science and technology/ edited by Russell H. Powell and James R. Powell, Jr. Phoenix: Oryx Press, 1987. 134 p.
87-010970   016.5 19   0897742753
Science -- Bibliography. Technology -- Bibliography. Best books.

Z7401.S3567 1995
Science and engineering conference proceedings: a guide to sources for identification and verification/ compiled by the ALA/ACRL STS Task Force on Proceedings, Committee on Bibliographic Access; edited by Barbara DeFelice. Chicago, IL: Association of College and Research Libraries, c1995. 80 p.
96-139042   0838977901
Science -- Congresses -- Bibliography. Engineering -- Congresses -- Bibliography. Conference proceedings -- Bibliography.

Z7401.S365
Science citation index. Philadelphia, Institute for Scientific Information.
63-023334   016.5
Science -- Periodicals -- Indexes -- Periodicals. Science -- Indexes -- Periodicals. Science -- Indexes.

Z7401.S573
Scientific and technical books and serials in print. New York, R.R. Bowker Co.
78-640940   016.5
Science -- Indexes. Engineering -- Indexes. Technology -- Indexes.

Z7402 Science.
Natural history —
Bibliography of early works

Z7402.B38 1990
Batschelet, Margaret.
Early American scientific and technical literature: an annotated bibliography of books, pamphlets, and broadsides/ by Margaret W. Batschelet. Metuchen, N.J.: Scarecrow Press, 1990. xii, 136 p.
90-008095   016.5 0810823187
Science -- Early works to 1800 -- Bibliography. Engineering -- Early works to 1800 -- Bibliography., United States -- Imprints -- Early works to 1800 -- Bibliography.

Z7403 Science.
Natural history —
Periodicals. Societies

Z7403.H17 1997
Handbook of Indian research journals/ ed. by H.D. Sharma. Varanasi, India: Indian Bibliographic Centre, 1997. 274 p.
97-902615   8185131139
Science -- Periodicals -- Bibliography -- Handbooks, manuals, etc. Engineering -- Periodicals -- Bibliography -- Handbooks. manuals, etc. Humanities -- Periodicals -- Bibliography -- Handbooks, manuals, etc.

Z7403.O95 1985
Owen, Dolores B.
Abstracts and indexes in science and technology: a descriptive guide / by Dolores B. Owen. 2nd ed. Metuchen, N.J.: Scarecrow Press, 1985. xv, 235 p.
84-010902   016.5 19 0810817128
Science -- Abstracts -- Periodicals -- Bibliography. Science -- Indexes -- Periodicals -- Bibliography. Technology -- Abstracts -- Periodicals -- Bibliography. Technology -- Indexes -- Periodicals -- Bibliography.

Z7403.S33
SB & F/ American Association for the Advancement of Science. Washington, DC: The Association, [c1999-   ]
2001-214543   016.5 19
Science -- Bibliography -- Periodicals. Science -- Film catalogs -- Bibliography -- Periodicals. Book Reviews -- periodicals. Motion Pictures -- periodicals. Science -- Bibliography.

Z7404 Science.
Natural history —
Biobibliography

Z7404.S64 1998
Smith, Roger, 1953 Apr. 19-
Biographies of scientists: an annotated bibliography/ Roger Smith. Lanham, Md.: Scarecrow Press; 1998. 291 p.
98-005954   016.5092/2 0810833840
Science -- Bio-bibliography. Scientists -- Biography -- Bibliography.

Z7405 Science.
Natural history —
Special topics, A-Z

Z7405.H6 I2
Isis cumulative bibliography; a bibliography of the history of science formed from Isis critical bibliographies 1-90, 1913-65. Edited by Magda Whitrow. Chairman of editorial committee: I. Bernard Cohen. [London] Mansell, in conjunction with the History of Science Society,
72-186272   016.509 0720101832
Science -- History -- Bibliography.

Z7405.H6 I2 Suppl.
Isis cumulative bibliography 1966-1975: a bibliography of the history of science formed from Isis critical bibliographies 91-100 indexing literature published from 1965 through 1974/ edited by John Neu. London: Mansell in conjunction with the History of Science Society, v. <1-2 >
80-509416   016.509 19 0720115159
Science -- History -- Bibliography.

Z7405.H6 I2 Suppl. 2
Isis cumulative bibliography 1976-1985: a bibliography of the history of science formed from Isis critical bibliographies 101-110 indexing literature published from 1975 through 1984/ edited by John Neu. Boston: G.K. Hall in conjunction with the History of Science Society, 2 v.
89-001942   016.509 19 0816190690
Science -- History -- Bibliography.

Z7405.H6.I2 1997 Suppl. 3
Isis cumulative bibliography, 1986-95: a bibliography of the history of science formed from the annual Isis current bibliographies/ edited by John Neu; computer production: Peter G. Sobol. Canton, Mass.: Published for the History of Science Society by Science History Publications/USA, [1997-   ] v. 3-4
97-018452   016.509 0881351318
Science -- History -- Bibliography.

Z7405.H6.R67 1982
Rothenberg, Marc, 1949-
The history of science and technology in the United States: a critical and selective bibliography/ Marc Rothenberg. New York: Garland Pub., 1982-1993. 2 v.
81-043355   016.50973 0824092783
Science -- United States -- History -- Bibliography. Technology -- United States -- History -- Bibliography.

Z7405.N38.S54 2000
Smith, Charles H. 1950-
Biodiversity studies: a bibliographic review/ Charles H. Smith. Lanham, Md.: Scarecrow Press, c2000. xiii, 461 p.
99-053779   016.33395/16 0810837544
Biological diversity -- Bibliography. Biological diversity conservation -- Bibliography.

Z7405.S6 S4 1992
Selin, Helaine,
Science across cultures: an annotated bibliography of books on non-western science, technology, and medicine/ Helaine Selin. New York: Garland, 1992. 431 p. ;
92-026370   016.30348/3 20 0815308396
Science -- Social aspects -- Bibliography. Technology -- Social aspects -- Bibliography. Social medicine -- Bibliography.

Z7405.W47.L45 1995
Leitch, Jay A.
Wetland economics, 1989-1993: a selected, annotated bibliography/ compiled by Jay A. Leitch and Herbert R. Ludwig, Jr. Westport, Conn.: Greenwood Press, 1995. xii, 133 p.
94-039564   016.33391/8 0313292868
Wetland conservation -- Economic aspects -- Bibliography. Wetlands -- Economic aspects -- Bibliography.

Z7407 Science.
Natural history — Science.
By region or country, A-Z

Z7407.D44 S57 1995
Shrum, Wesley,
Science, technology, and society in the Third World: an annotated bibliography/ by Wesley Shrum, Carl L. Bankston III and D. Stephen Voss. Metuchen, N.J.: Scarecrow Press, 1995. 399 p. ;
94-006256   338.9/26/091724 20 0810828715
Science and state -- Developing countries -- Bibliography. Science -- Social aspects -- Developing countries -- Bibliography. Technology and state -- Developing countries -- Bibliography. Technology -- Social aspects -- Developing countries -- Bibliography.

Z7408 Science.
Natural history —
Natural history.
By region or country, A-Z

Z7408.L29.R63 1999
Roberts, Jerry, 1956-
Rain forest bibliography: an annotated guide on over 1600 nonfiction books about Central and South American jungles/ by Jerry Roberts. Jefferson, N.C.: McFarland, c1999. vii, 312 p.
99-026061   016.33375/098 0786407174
Rain forests -- Latin America -- Bibliography.

Z7511-7515 Sports. Amusements. Recreation

Z7511.S48 1992
Shoebridge, Michele.
Information sources in sport and leisure/ Michele Shoebridge, editor. London; Bowker-Saur, c1992. xix, 345 p.
91-021637   016.796   0862919010
Sports -- Bibliography. Leisure -- Bibliography. Recreation -- Bibliography.

Z7514.B3 G36 2002
Gannes, Arthur V.
Baseball: a guide to the literature/ Arthur V. Gannes, editor. Huntington, N.Y.: Nova Science Publishers, c2002. 239 p.
2002-283568   017.796357 21   159033213X
Baseball -- Bibliography.

Z7514.B3.W35 1995
Walker, Donald E., 1941-
Baseball and American culture: a thematic bibliography of over 4,500 works/ compiled by Donald E. Walker and B. Lee Cooper. Jefferson, N.C.: McFarland & Co., 1995. xiv, 257 p.
94-048267   016.796357/0973   0786400498
Baseball -- United States -- Bibliography. Baseball -- Social aspects -- United States -- Bibliography.

Z7514.D2.B6 1994
Bopp, Mary S.
Research in dance: a guide to resources/ Mary S. Bopp; foreword by Genevieve Oswald. New York: G.K. Hall; c1994. viii, 296 p.
92-042508   016.7928   0816190658
Dance -- Bibliography. Dance -- Bibliography -- Catalogs.

Z7514.D2 C685 2001
A core collection in dance/ Mary E. Edsall, editor; compiled by Dance Librarians Committee, Association of College and Research Libraries. Chicago: The Association, 2001. xv, 242 p.
2001-027794   016.7928 21   0838981186
Dance -- Bibliography.

Z7514.D2.G48 1995
Getz, Leslie.
Dancers and choreographers: a selected bibliography/ Leslie Getz. Wakefield, R.I.: Asphodel Press, 1995. xix, 305 p.
94-012129   016.7928   1559211083
Ballet dancers -- Bibliography. Dancers -- Bibliography. Choreographers -- Bibliography.

Z7514.D2.R38 1991
Resources in sacred dance: annotated bibliography from Christian and Jewish traditions: books, booklets and pamphlets, articles and serial publications, media, and reference sources/ compiled by the Sacred Dance Guild; Kay Troxell, bibliography editor. Peterborough, N.H.: Sacred Dance Guild, c1991. 55 p.
91-187899   016.7933   0962313718
Dance -- Religious aspects -- Bibliography.

Z7514.F7.C65 1994
The College football bibliography/ compiled by Myron J. Smith, Jr. Westport, Conn.: Greenwood Press, 1994. x, 951 p.
93-001172   016.796332/63/0973   0313290261
Football -- United States -- Bibliography. College sports -- United States -- Bibliography.

Z7514.M66.J66 1992
Jones, Donald G.
Sports ethics in America: a bibliography, 1970-1990/ Donald G. Jones with Elaine L. Daly; foreword by Thomas H. Kean. New York: Greenwood Press, 1992. xvii, 291 p.
91-047538   016.175   0313277672
Sports -- Moral and ethical aspects -- United States -- Bibliography.

Z7514.O8.A27 1990
Abromowitz, Jennifer.
Women outdoors: the best 1900 books, programs & periodicals/ Jennifer Abromowitz. Williamsburg, MA (RD 1, 345c, Williamsburg 01096 J. Abromowitz, c1990. 179 p.
91-142632   016/.796/0194
Outdoor recreation for women -- Bibliography. Literature -- Women authors -- Bibliography. Outdoor life -- Bibliography.

Z7514.S72.W57 1994
Wise, Suzanne, 1946-
Social issues in contemporary sport: a resource guide/ Suzanne Wise. New York: Garland Pub., 1994. xii, 789 p.
93-029608   306.4/83   0824060466
Sports -- Sociological aspects -- Bibliography.

Z7515.L29.A73 1999
Arbena, Joseph.
Latin American sport: an annotated bibliography, 1988-1998/ compiled by Joseph L. Arbena. Westport, Conn.: Greenwood Press, 1999. xi, 244 p.
99-011260   016.796/098   0313296111
Sports -- Latin America -- Bibliography. Sports -- Latin America -- History -- Bibliography.

Z7551-7554 Statistics

Z7551.I42 1995
Instat: international statistics sources: subject guide to sources of international comparative statistics/ [edited by] Michael C. Fleming and Joseph G. Nellis. London; Routledge, 1995. 2 v.
95-119256   016.31 20   0415113598
Statistics -- Bibliography.

Z7551.S83
Statistics sources. Detroit, Mich.: Gale Research Co., [c1962-   ]
84-649356   016.31 19
Statistics -- Indexes. Statistics -- Bibliography. Statistical services. Statistics -- Bibliography. Statistics -- Directory.

Z7553.C3.C66 1996
Cook, Kevin L.
Dubester's U.S. census bibliography with SuDocs class numbers and indexes/ Kevin L. Cook. Englewood, Colo.: Libraries Unlimited, 1996. ix, 320 p.
95-043247   016.3046/2/0973   1563082950
United States -- Census -- Bibliography.

Z7553.C3.G85 1990
A Guide to Latin American and Caribbean census material: a bibliography and union list/ general editor, Carole Travis. Boston, Massachusetts: G.K. Hall, c1990. xxi, 739 p.
89-049739   016.318   0816104972
Catalogs, Union -- Great Britain.West Indies -- Census -- Bibliography -- Union lists. Latin America -- Census -- Bibliography -- Union lists.

Z7553.M43 W444 1997
Health statistics: an annotated bibliographic guide to information resources/ Frieda O. Weise, editor ... [et al.]. 2nd ed. Lanham, Md.: Medical Library Association and Scarecrow Press, x, 178 p. ;
96-044016   016.3621/0973/021   21
0810830566
Medical care -- United States -- Statistics -- Bibliography. Public health -- United States -- Statistical services -- Directories. United States -- Statistics, Medical -- Bibliography. United States -- Statistics, Vital -- Bibliography.

Z7554.U5 A46
American statistics index. Washington, Congressional Information Service.
73-082599   016.3173
Bibliography, National -- United States -- Indexes. Government Publications -- United States -- Indexes. Statistics -- United States -- Indexes. United States -- Statistics -- Bibliography -- Periodicals. United States -- Statistics -- Abstracts -- Periodicals.

Z7554.U5.G8
Guide to U.S. Government statistics. McLean, Va., Documents Index.
61-009066   016.3173
United States -- Statistics -- Bibliography. United States -- Government statistics -- Bibliography.

Z7615 Suicide

Z7615.M38 1985
McIntosh, John L.
Research on suicide: a bibliography/ compiled by John L. McIntosh. Westport, Conn.: Greenwood Press, c1985. xiii, 323 p.
84-015706   016.3622   0313239924
Suicide -- Bibliography. Suicide -- United States -- Bibliography.

Z7711 Television

Z7711.C37 1985
Cassata, Mary B.,
Television, a guide to the literature/ by Mary Cassata and Thomas Skill. Phoenix, Ariz.: Oryx Press, 1985. vii, 148 p.
83-043236   016.38455 19   0897741404
Television broadcasting -- Bibliography.

Z7711.C66 1988
Cooper, Thomas W.
Television & ethics: a bibliography/ Thomas W. Cooper, with Robert Sullivan, Christopher Weir, Peter Medaglia. Boston: G.K. Hall, c1988. xlvi, 203 p.
88-007206   174/.97914 19   0816189668
Television broadcasting -- Moral and ethical aspects -- Bibliography. Ethics -- Bibliography.

Z7711.G37 1988
Garay, Ronald.
Cable television: a reference guide to information/ Ronald Garay. New York: Greenwood Press, 1988. viii, 177 p.
87-024955   016.38455/47/0973   19
031324751X
Cable television -- United States -- Bibliography. Cable television -- United States -- Law and legislation -- Bibliography.

Z7711.G5 1991
Gibberman, Susan R., 1958-
Star trek: an annotated guide to resources on the development, the phenomenon, the people, the television series, the films, the novels, and the recordings/ by Susan R. Gibberman. Jefferson, N.C.: McFarland & Co., c1991. xii, 434 p.
91-052502   016.79145/72   0899505473
Star Trek films -- History and criticism -- Bibliography.

Z7711.S49 1997
Shiers, George.
Early television: a bibliographic guide to 1940/ compiled by George Shiers; assisted by May Shiers. New York: Garland Pub., 1997. xix, 616 p.
96-019445   621.388/009/09041
Television -- History -- Bibliography. Television broadcasting -- History -- Bibliography.

Z7711.S9 1994
Sudalnik, James E.
High definition television: an annotated multidisciplinary bibliography, 1981-1992/ compiled by James E. Sudalnik and Victoria A. Kuhl. Westport, Conn.: Greenwood Press, 1994. xv, 347 p.
93-048857   016.38455   0313281459
High definition television -- Bibliography.

Z7711.T48 1999
Television violence: a guide to the literature/ P.T. Kelly (ed.). 2nd ed. Commack, N.Y.: Nova Science Publishers, c1999. viii, 311 p.
2003-544824   016.3036 21   1560727004
Violence on television -- Bibliography.

Z7721 Temperance

Z7721.A42 1996
Alcohol in the British Isles from Roman times to 1996: an annotated bibliography/ compiled by David W. Gutzke. Westport, Conn.: Greenwood Press, 1996. xvii, 266 p.
96-001202   016.3941/3/0941   0313294208
Drinking of alcoholic beverages -- Great Britain -- History -- Bibliography. Alcoholic beverages -- Great Britain -- History -- Bibliography. Alcoholic beverage industry -- Great Britain -- History -- Bibliography.

Z7721.B45 1993
Berg, Steven L.
Jewish alcoholism and drug addiction: an annotated bibliography/ compiled by Steven L. Berg. Westport, Conn.: Greenwood Press, 1993. xviii, 160 p.
93-021634   016.3629/089924 20   031327603X
Jews -- Alcohol use -- Bibliography. Jews -- Drug use -- Bibliography. Alcoholism -- Bibliography. Drug abuse -- Bibliography.

Z7721.O83 1995
Osgood, Nancy J.
Alcoholism and aging: an annotated bibliography and review/ compiled by Nancy J. Osgood, Helen E. Wood, and Iris A. Parham. Westport, Conn.: Greenwood Press, 1995. xi, 250 p.
94-041371   016.362292/084/6   0313283982
Aged -- Alcohol use -- Bibliography. Alcoholism -- Bibliography.

Z7721.P334 1991
Page, Penny Booth, 1949-
Children of alcoholics: a sourcebook/ Penny Booth Page. New York: Garland Pub., 1991. xv, 249 p.
91-019611   016.36229/23   0824030451
Children of alcoholics -- Bibliography. Adult children of alcoholics -- Bibliography.

Z7721.W37 1986
Watts, Thomas D.
Black alcohol abuse and alcoholism: an annotated bibliography/ Thomas D. Watts, Roosevelt Wright, Jr. New York: Praeger, 1986. xix, 265 p.
85-028245   016.3622/92/08996073   19
0030057132
African Americans -- Alcohol use -- Bibliography. Alcoholism -- Treatment -- United States -- Bibliography. Alcoholism -- United States -- Prevention -- Bibliography.

Z7751 Theology and religion — General bibliography

Z7751.B595 1995
Bjorling, Joel, 1952-
Reincarnation: a bibliography/ Joel Bjorling. New York: Garland Pub., 1996. x, 184 p.
95-019357   016.2912/37   081531129X
Reincarnation -- Bibliography.

Z7751.B67 2003
Stewart, David R.
The literature of theology: a guide for students and pastors/ David R. Stewart. Rev. ed. Louisville, KY: Westminster John Knox Press, 2003.
2002-193394   016.23 21   0664223427
Theology -- Bibliography.

Z7751.D33 1988
Dawsey, James M.
A scholar's guide to academic journals in religion/ by James Dawsey. Metuchen, N.J.: Scarecrow Press, 1988. xxiii, 290 p.
88-018104   016.2/005 19   0810821354
Religion -- Periodicals -- Bibliography. Religious literature -- Authorship. Theology -- Periodicals -- Bibliography. Christian literature -- Authorship.

Z7751.G55 1996
Glaspey, Terry W.
Great books of the Christian tradition/ Terry W. Glaspey. Eugene, Or.: Harvest House Publishers, c1996. 240 p.
95-034307   016.2 20   1565073568
Christian literature -- Abstracts. Theology -- Abstracts. Best books.

Z7751.J654 1996
Johnston, William M., 1936-
Recent reference books in religion: a guide for students, scholars, researchers, buyers & readers/ William M. Johnston. Downers Grove, IL: InterVarsity Press, 1996. 318 p.
96-020804   016.2   083081440X
Religion -- Bibliography. Reference books.

Z7751.K33 1995
Kadel, Andrew.
Matrology: a bibliography of writings by Christian women from the first to the fifteenth centuries/ Andrew Kadel. New York: Continuum, 1995. 191 p.
94-030157   016.27/0082   0826406769
Christian literature -- Bibliography. Christian literature, Early -- Bibliography. Theology -- Bibliography.

Z7751.K43 1996
Kear, Lynn.
Reincarnation: a selected annotated bibliography/ Lynn Kear. Westport, Conn.: Greenwood Press, 1996. x, 327 p.
96-010546   016.1339/01/3   0313295972
Reincarnation -- Bibliography.

Z7751.K46 1992
Kepple, Robert J.
Reference works for theological research/ Robert J. Kepple and John R. Muether. 3rd ed. Lanham: University Press of America, 1991. xiv, 250 p.
91-042222   016.2 20   0819185655
Theology -- Bibliography. Religion -- Bibliography.

Z7751.M45 1992
Melton, J. Gordon.
Religious information sources: a worldwide guide/ by J. Gordon Melton and Michael A. Kôszegi. New York: Garland Pub., 1992. xxiii, 569 p.
91-047697   016.2 20   0815308590
Religion -- Bibliography. Religion -- Information services.

Z7751.R35
Religion index two: [Chicago] American Theological Library Association.
78-645074   016.2
Religion -- Indexes -- Periodicals. Theology -- Indexes -- Periodicals. Religion -- Periodicals -- Indexes -- Periodicals. Theology -- Periodicals -- Indexes -- Periodicals.

Z7753 Theology and religion — Periodicals. Directories. Yearbooks

Z7753.A5
Index to religious periodical literature. Chicago, American Theological Library Association. 13 v.
54-006085   016.2
Theology -- Periodicals -- Indexes -- Periodicals. Religion -- Periodicals -- Indexes -- Periodicals.

Z7757 Theology and religion —
By region or country, A-Z

Z7757.C6.T55 1985
Thompson, Laurence G.
Chinese religion in Western languages: a comprehensive and classified bibliography of publications in English, French, and German through 1980/ Laurence G. Thompson. Tucson, Ariz.: Published for the Association for Asian Studies by the University of Arizona Press, c1985. xlix, 302 p.
84-024010 016.2/00951 0816509263
China -- Religion -- Bibliography.

Z7757.C6.Y83 1994
Yu, David C.
Religion in postwar China: a critical analysis and annotated bibliography/ compiled by David C. Yu. Westport, Conn.: Greenwood Press, 1994. xviii, 365 p.
93-028461 016.2/00951 0313267324
China -- Religion -- Bibliography.

Z7757.S64 F46 1995
Fenton, John Y.
South Asian religions in the Americas: an annotated bibliography of immigrant religious traditions/ John Y. Fenton. Westport, Conn.: Greenwood Press, 1995. xiii, 241 p. ;
94-039769 016.294/097 20 0313278350
South Asians -- America -- Religion -- Bibliography. Immigrants -- Religious life -- America -- Bibliography. South Asia -- Religion -- Bibliography. America -- Religion -- Bibliography.

Z7757.U5.D57 1995
Discovering Latino religion: a comprehensive social science bibliography/ edited by Anthony M. Stevens-Arroyo, with Segundo Pantoja. New York: Bildner Center for Western Hemisphere Studies, c1995. 142 p.
95-011518 016.2/0089/68073 0929972139
Hispanic Americans -- Religion -- Bibliography.United States -- Religion -- Bibliography.

Z7757.U5 G6 1990
Goreham, Gary.
The rural church in America: a century of writings: a bibliography/ Gary A. Goreham. New York: Garland Pub., 1990. xiii, 272 p.
89-039156   016.2773/009173/4   20 0824034392
Rural churches -- United States -- Bibliography. United States -- Church history -- Bibliography.

Z7757.U5 M46 1985
Menendez, Albert J.
Religious conflict in America: a bibliography/ Albert J. Menendez. New York: Garland Pub., 1985. x, 130 p.
84-013779 016.2911/72/0973 19 0824089049
Church and state -- United States -- Bibliography. United States -- Religion -- Bibliography.

Z7757.U5 R45 1989
Religion and American life: resources/ edited by Anne T. Fraker. Urbana: University of Illinois Press, c1989. xiii, 236 p.
88-019933 016.2/00973 19 0252015886
United States -- Religion -- Bibliography of bibliographies.

Z7757.U5.Y68 1992
Young, Arthur P.
Religion and the American experience, 1620-1900: a bibliography of doctoral dissertations/ compiled by Arthur P. Young and E. Jens Holley; with the assistance of Annette Blum. Westport, Conn.: Greenwood Press, 1992. x, 479 p.
92-028450 016.2/00973 0313277478
Dissertations, Academic -- United States -- Bibliography.United States -- Religion -- Bibliography.

Z7757.U5.Y69 1994
Young, Arthur P.
Religion and the American experience, the twentieth century: a bibliography of doctoral disserations/ compiled by Arthur P. Young and E. Jens Holley; with the assistance of Phyllis C. Watts. Westport, Conn.: Greenwood Press, 1994. xi, 415 p.
94-036759 016.2/00973/0904 0313277486
Dissertations, Academic -- United States -- Bibliography.United States -- Religion -- Bibliography.

Z7763 Theology and religion — Angels

Z7763.A54.M37 1999
Marshall, George J., 1949-
Angels: an indexed and partially annotated bibliography of over 4300 scholarly books and articles since the 7th century B.C./ [compiled] by George J. Marshall. Jefferson, N.C.: McFarland, c1999. v, 479 p.
98-047852 016.2912/15 0786405554
Angels -- Bibliography.

Z7770 Theology and religion — Bible — General bibliography

Z7770.G66 1984
Gorman, G. E.
Theological and religious reference materials/ G.E. Gorman and Lyn Gorman; with the assistance of Donald N. Matthews and an introductory chapter by John B. Trotti. Westport, Conn.: Greenwood Press, 1984-1986 v. 1-3
83-022759 016.2 0313209243
Theology -- Bibliography.

Z7770.G77 1995
Gruber, Mayer I.
Women in the biblical world: a study guide/ by Mayer I. Gruber. [Philadelphia, Pa.]: American Theological Library Association; v. <1 >
95-035831 016.2209/082 20 0810830698
Women in the Bible -- Bibliography. Women -- Middle East -- Bibliography.

Z7770.M66 1992
Minor, Mark.
Literary-critical approaches to the Bible: an annotated bibliography/ Mark Minor. West Cornwall, CT: Locust Hill Press, 1992. xxxi, 520 p.
92-007469 016.2206/6 0933951485
Bible -- Bibliography.

Z7770.P68 1992
Powell, Mark Allan, 1953-
The Bible and modern literary criticism: a critical assessment and annotated bibliography/ compiled by Mark Allan Powell with the assistance of Cecile G. Gray and Melissa C. Curtis. New York: Greenwood Press, 1992. xv, 469 p.
91-038128 016.2206/6 0313275467
Bible as literature -- Bibliography.

Z7771 Theology and religion — Bible — Versions, A-Z

Z7771.E5 C43 1991
Chamberlin, William J.
Catalogue of English Bible translations: a classified bibliography of versions and editions including books, parts, and Old and New Testament Apocrypha and Apocryphal books/ William J. Chamberlin. New York: Greenwood Press, 1991. xliii, 898 p. ;
91-027497 016.2205/2 20 031328041X
Apocryphal books -- Bibliography.

Z7771.5 Theology and religion — Bible — Special topics, A-Z

Z7771.5.E84 B74 1997
Bretzke, James T.,
Bibliography on scripture and Christian ethics/ compiled by James T. Bretzke. Lewiston: E. Mellen Press, c1997. 364 p.
97-038505 016.241 21 088946863X
Ethics in the Bible -- Bibliography. Christian ethics -- Bibliography.

Z7772 Theology and religion — Bible — Parts

Z7772.A1 H86 1987
Hupper, William G.
An index to English periodical literature on the Old Testament and ancient Near Eastern studies/ compiled and edited by William G. Hupper. [Philadelphia]: American Theological Library Association; 8 v. ;
86-031448 016.221 19 0810819848
Middle East -- Periodicals -- Indexes.

Z7772.C1.T46 1997
Thompson, Henry O.
The book of Amos: an annotated bibliography/ Henry O. Thompson. Lanham, Md.: Scarecrow Press, 1997. xxvii, 433 p.
97-011933 016.224/8 0810832747
Bible. O.T. Amos -- Bibliography.

Z7772.D37.T48 1996
Thompson, Henry O.
The book of Jeremiah: an annotated bibliography/ Henry O. Thompson. Lanham, Md.: Scarecrow Press, 1996. xxxii, 745 p.
96-010670 016.224/2
Bible. O.T. Jeremiah -- Bibliography.

Z7772.J1.T48 1993
Thompson, Henry O.
The book of Daniel: an annotated bibliography/ Henry O. Thompson. New York: Garland Pub., 1993. xli, 547 p.
92-009349 016.224/5 0824048733
Bible. O.T. Daniel -- Bibliography.

Z7772.J2.C37 1994
Caspi, Mishael, 1932-
The book of Ruth: an annotated bibliography/ Mishael Maswari Caspi. New York: Garland Pub., 1994. xiv, 133 p.
94-021346 016.222/35 0824046323
Bible. O.T. Ruth -- Bibliography.

Z7772.L1.B4 1993
Bibliographies for biblical research. Lewiston: Mellen Biblical Press, c1993-c1999 v. 1-9, 21
93-030864 016.2262/06 077349345X
Bible. N.T. -- Criticism, interpretation, etc. -- Bibliography.

Z7772.M1 M35 2000
McKnight, Scot.
The Synoptic Gospels: an annotated bibliography/ Scot McKnight, Matthew C. Williams. Grand Rapids, Mich.: Baker Books, c2000. 126 p. ;
99-055499 016.226 21 0801022274

Z7772.P1.K54 1996
Klein, William W.
The book of Ephesians: an annotated bibliography/ William W. Klein. New York: Garland, 1996. xxiii, 312 p.
95-020253 016.227/5 0815303645
Bible N.T. Ephesians -- Bibliography.

Z7772.R1.M87 1996
Muse, Robert L.
The book of Revelation: an annotated bibliography/ Robert L. Muse. New York: Garland Publishing, 1996. xxxvi, 352 p.
95-039196 016.228 20 0824073940
Bible. N.T. Revelation -- Criticism, interpretation, etc. -- Bibliography.

Z7776.6 Theology and religion — Christianity and culture

Z7776.6.C 2002
Christianity and culture: a bibliography with indexes/ Martin S. Reed, editor. New York: Nova Science Publishers, c2002. xxix, 212 p.
2002-727181 1590333950
Christianity and culture -- Bibliography.

Z7776.68 Theology and religion — Christianity and the arts

Z7776.68.K37 1995
Kari, Daven Michael.
A bibliography of sources in Christianity and the arts/ Daven Michael Kari. Lewiston [N.Y.]: E. Mellen Press, c1995. x, 764 p.
94-009769 016.246 0773490949
Christianity and the arts -- Bibliography.

Z7776.7 Theology and religion — Church

Z7776.7.D84 1999
Dulles, Avery Robert, 1918-
The theology of the church: a bibliography/ Avery Dulles & Patrick Granfield. New York: Paulist Press, c1999. vii, 198 p.
98-045037 016.262 0809138476
Church -- Bibliography.

Z7776.72 Theology and religion — Church and state. Religion and state

Z7776.72.C48 1986
Church and state in America: a bibliographical guide/ edited by John F. Wilson. New York: Greenwood Press, 1986-c1987. 2 v.
85-031698 016.322/1/0973 031325236X
Church and state -- United States -- Bibliography.United States -- Church history -- Bibliography.

Z7776.72.O47 1998
Olson, Laura R.,
The religious dimension of political behavior: a critical analysis and annotated bibliography/ compiled by Laura R. Olson and Ted G. Jelen. Westport, Conn.: Greenwood Press, 1998. xv, 150 p.
98-028016 016.3205/5/0973 21 0313284849
Religion and politics -- United States -- Bibliography.

Z7777 Theology and religion — Church history — General bibliography

Z7777.C33
Case, Shirley Jackson, 1872-1947.
A bibliographical guide to the history of Christianity, compiled by S.J. Case, J.T. McNeill, W.W. Sweet, W. Pauck [and] M. Spinka; edited by S.J. Case. Chicago, Ill., The University of Chicago press [1931] xi, 265 p.
31-029796 016.27
Church history -- Bibliography.

Z7778 Theology and religion — Church history — Local, A-Z

Z7778.U6.B48 1990
Blumhofer, Edith Waldvogel.
Twentieth-century evangelicalism: a guide to the sources/ Edith L. Blumhofer, Joel A. Carpenter. New York: Garland Pub., 1990. xv, 384 p.
90-031842 016.2773/082 0824030400
Evangelicalism -- United States -- Bibliography. Evangelicalism -- Library resources. Evangelicalism -- Archival resources. United States -- Church history -- Bibliography.

Z7778.U6 E38 1982
Ellis, John Tracy,
A guide to American Catholic history/ John Tracy Ellis and Robert Trisco. 2nd ed., rev. and enl. Santa Barbara, Calif.: ABC-Clio, c1982. xiii, 265 p.
81-017585 016.282/73 19 0874363187
United States -- Church history -- Bibliography.

Z7782 Theology and religion — City churches

Z7782.H37 1992
Hartley, Loyde H., 1940-
Cities and churches: an international bibliography/ by Loyde H. Hartley; foreword by Martin E. Marty. Metuchen, N.J.: American Theological Library Association and Scarecrow Press, 1992. 3 v.
92-018819 016.27/009173/2 081082583X
City churches -- Bibliography. Cities and towns -- Religious aspects -- Christianity -- Bibliography. Labor movement -- Religious aspects -- Christianity -- Bibliography.

Z7785 Theology and religion — Emotions

Z7785.C67 2000
Corrigan, John, 1952-
Emotion and religion: a critical assessment and annotated bibliography/ John Corrigan, Eric Crump, and John Kloos. Westport, Conn.: Greenwood Press, 2000. x, 242 p.
00-035372 016.2/001/9 0313306001
Emotions -- Religious aspects -- Bibliography.

Z7786 Theology and religion — End of the world

Z7786.M35 1999
McIver, Tom, 1951-
The end of the world: an annotated bibliography/ by Tom McIver. Jefferson, NC: McFarland, c1999. ix, 389 p.
99-015154 016.2912/3 0786407085
End of the world -- Bibliography.

Z7794 Theology and religion — Future life

Z7794.G37 1993
Gardiner, Eileen.
Medieval visions of heaven and hell: a sourcebook/ Eileen Gardiner. New York: Garland Pub., 1993. xxxv, 257 p.
92-045794 016.2482/9 0824033485
Visions -- Bibliography. Heaven -- History of doctrines -- Middle Ages, 600-1500 -- Bibliography. Hell -- History of doctrines -- Middle Ages, 600-1500 -- Bibliography.

Z7798 Theology and religion — Glossolalia

Z7798.M54 1993
Mills, Watson E.
A bibliography of the nature and role of the Holy Spirit in twentieth-century writings/ Watson E. Mills. Lewiston, N.Y., USA: Mellen Biblical Press, c1993. xxviii, 344 p.
93-022748 016.231/3 0773423664
Gifts, Spiritual -- Bibliography. Holy Spirit -- Bibliography. Pentecostalism -- Bibliography.

Z7799.3 Theology and religion — Holy Spirit

Z7799.3.S22 1995
Schandorff, Esther Dech, 1923-
The doctrine of the Holy Spirit: a bibliography showing its chronological development/ by Esther Dech Schandorff. Lanham, Md.: Scarecrow Press, c1995. 2 v.
91-040689   016.231/3   0810825236
Holy Spirit -- Bibliography. Holy Spirit -- History of doctrines -- Bibliography.

Z7809 Theology and religion — Liberation theology

Z7809.M87 1991
Musto, Ronald G.
Liberation theologies: a research guide/ Ronald G. Musto. New York: Garland Pub., 1991. xlvii, 581 p.
90-029156   016.23/0046   0824036247
Liberation theology -- Bibliography. Feminist theology -- Bibliography.

Z7813 Theology and religion — Liturgy. Prayer books

Z7813.B5 1989
A Bibliography of Christian worship/ [edited by Bard Thompson. [Philadelphia]: American Theological Library Association; 1989. xlii, 786 p.
88-038650   016.264   0810821540
Liturgics -- Bibliography. Public worship -- Bibliography.

Z7819 Theology and religion — Mysticism (Theology)

Z7819.B68
Bowman, Mary Ann.
Western mysticism: a guide to the basic works/ compiled by Mary Ann Bowman. Chicago, Ill.: American Library Association, c1978. vi, 113 p.
78-018311   016.2914/2   0838902669
Mysticism -- Bibliography.

Z7830 Theology and religion — Reformation and Counter-Reformation

Z7830.S63 1988
Smeeton, Donald Dean, 1946-
English religion, 1500-1540: a bibliography/ by Donald Dean Smeeton. Macon, Ga.: Mercer University Press, c1988. 114 p.
88-033270   016.2742/06   0865543259
Reformation -- England -- Bibliography.England -- Church history -- 16th century -- Bibliography. Great Britain -- Church history -- 16th century -- Bibliography. Reformation -- Great Britain -- Bibliography.

Z7831 Theology and religion — Religion and sociology

Z7831.B54 1990
Blasi, Anthony J.
The sociology of religion: an organizational bibliography/ Anthony J. Blasi, Michael W. Cuneo. New York: Garland Pub., 1990. xxix, 459 p.
90-040684   016.3066   0824025849
Religion and sociology -- Bibliography. Religions -- Bibliography. Sects -- Bibliography.

Z7831.W65 1990
Wolcott, Roger T.
Church and social action: a critical assessment and bibliographical survey/ compiled by Roger T. Wolcott and Dorita F. Bolger. New York: Greenwood Press, 1990. xiv, 256 p.
89-028565   016.2911/78   0313250863
Sociology, Christian -- Bibliography. Religion and sociology -- Bibliography.

Z7833 Theology and religion — Religions (non-Christian) — General bibliography. General special bibliography

Z7833.A35 1977
Adams, Charles J.,
A reader's guide to the great religions/ edited by Charles J. Adams. 2d ed. New York: Free Press, c1977. xvii, 521 p.
76-010496   016.2   0029002400
Religions -- Bibliography.

Z7833.F57 1995
Fischer, Clare Benedicks.
Of spirituality: a feminist perspective/ by Clare B. Fischer. [Evanston, Ill.]: American Theological Library Association; 1995. xvi, 279 p.
95-005660   016.2/0082   081083006X
Women and religion -- Bibliography. Women -- Religious life -- Bibliography.

Z7833.H66 1991
Holm, Jean,
Keyguide to sources of information on world religions/ Jean Holm. Boston, Mass.: G.K. Hall, 1991. x, 259 p.
91-015873   016.291 20   081617394X
Religions -- Bibliography. Religions -- Religious books -- Bibliography. Religions -- Societies, etc. -- Directories.

Z7833.I53
International bibliography of the history of religions. Bibliographie internationale de l'histoire des religions. Leiden, E. J. Brill. 20 v.
56-019258   016.29
Religions -- Bibliography.

Z7834 Theology and religion — Religions (non-Christian) — By region or country, A-Z

Z7834.A3.G72 1989
Gray, John, 1962-
Ashe, traditional religion and healing in Sub-Saharan Africa and the diaspora: a classified international bibliography/ compiled by John Gray; foreword by Robert Farris Thompson. New York: Greenwood Press, 1989. xx, 518 p.
89-002168   016.299/6   0313265003
Blacks -- Africa, Sub-Saharan -- Religion -- Bibliography. Afro-Americans -- Religion -- Bibliography. Religion -- Africa, Sub-Saharan -- Bibliography. Africa, Sub-Saharan -- Religion -- Bibliography. America -- Religion -- Bibliography.

Z7834.A8.S82 1991
Swain, Tony.
Aboriginal religions in Australia: a bibliographical survey/ Tony Swain. New York: Greenwood Press, 1991. xv, 336 p.
91-002153   016.299/92   0313260443
Australian aborigines -- Religion -- Bibliography.Australia -- Religion -- Bibliography.

Z7834.E85 A78 1997
Arweck, Elisabeth.
New religious movements in Western Europe: an annotated bibliography / Elisabeth Arweck and Peter B. Clarke. Westport, Conn.: Greenwood Press, 1997. xliii, 380 p.
96-044066   016.291/046/094 21   0313243247
Cults -- Europe, Western -- Bibliography. Sects -- Europe, Western -- Bibliography. Europe, Western -- Religion -- 20th century -- Bibliography.

Z7834.U6 C46 1985
Choquette, Diane.
New religious movements in the United States and Canada: a critical assessment and annotated bibliography/ compiled by Diane Choquette; with an introductory essay by Robert S. Ellwood, Jr. Westport, Conn.: Greenwood Press, 1985. xi, 235 p.
85-009964   016.291/0973 19   0313237727
Cults -- United States -- Bibliography. Cults -- Canada -- Bibliography. United States -- Religion -- Bibliography. Canada -- Religion -- Bibliography.

Z7835 Theology and religion — Religions (non-Christian) — Special, A-Z

Z7835.C86.S34 1990
Saliba, John A.
Social science and the cults: an annotated bibliography/ John A. Saliba. New York: Garland Pub., 1990. xl, 694 p.
90-032106   016.3066/91   0824037197
Cults -- Periodicals -- Indexes. Sects -- Periodicals -- Indexes. Religion and sociology -- Periodicals -- Indexes.

Z7835.C86.T87 1977
Turner, Harold W.
Bibliography of new religious movements in primal societies/ Harold W. Turner. Boston: G. K. Hall, c1977-1992 v. 1-3, 6
77-004732 016.291/046 0816179271
Religion -- Bibliography. Religion -- Bibliography.

Z7835.M54.D36 1992
Daniels, Ted, 1939-
Millennialism: an international bibliography/ Ted Daniels. New York: Garland Pub., 1992. xxxiv, 657 p.
91-039298 016.2919 0824071026
Millennialism -- Bibliography. End of the world -- Bibliography.

Z7835.M6 A54 no. 9
Geddes, C. L.
Guide to reference books for Islamic studies/ C.L. Geddes. Denver, Colo.: American Institute of Islamic Studies, c1985. xiii, 429 p.
85-013558 016.909/097671 19 0933017006
Islam -- Bibliography. Civilization, Islamic -- Bibliography. Islamic countries -- Bibliography.

Z7835.M6.H23 1991
Haddad, Yvonne Yazbeck, 1935-
The contemporary Islamic revival: a critical survey and bibliography/ Yvonne Yazbeck Haddad, John Obert Voll, and John L. Esposito; with Kathleen Moore and David Sawan. New York: Greenwood Press, 1991. xiii, 230 p.
91-012618 016.297/09/045 0313247196
Islam -- 20th century -- Bibliography.

Z7835.M6.H24 1997
Haddad, Yvonne Yazbeck, 1935-
The Islamic revival since 1988: a critical survey and bibliography/ Yvonne Yazbeck Haddad and John L. Esposito with Elizabeth Hiel and Hibba Abugideiri. Westport, Conn.: Greenwood Press, 1997. xx, 295 p.
97-002733 016.297/09/045 0313304807
Islam -- 20th century -- Bibliography.

Z7835.M6.I85 1994
Israeli, Raphael.
Islam in China: a critical bibliography/ Raphael Israeli, with the assistance of Lyn Gorman. Westport, Conn.: Greenwood Press, 1994. xviii, 172 p.
93-034828 016.297/0951 0313278571
Islam -- China -- Bibliography.

Z7835.M6 W66 2002
Woodward, Claire.
Islam: background and bibliography/ Claire Woodward. Hauppauge, N.Y.: Novinka Books, c2002. 263 p.
2003-268887 159033132X
Islam -- Bibliography. Islam -- Asia -- Bibliography.

Z7835.S64.R34 1989
Rai, Priya Muhar.
Sikhism and the Sikhs: an annotated bibliography/ compiled by Priya Muhar Rai. New York: Greenwood Press, 1989. xv, 257 p.
88-038308 016.954/00882946 031326130X
Sikhism -- Bibliography.

Z7836 Theology and religion — Religions (non-Christian) — Mythology

Z7836.S54 1996
Sienkewicz, Thomas J.
World mythology: an annotated guide to collections and anthologies/ Thomas J. Sienkewicz. Lanham, Md.: Scarecrow Press; 1996. ix, 469 p.
96-010156 016.2911/3 0810831546
Mythology -- Bibliography.

Z7836.7 Theology and religion — Revivals

Z7836.7.D5 1999
Di Sabatino, David, 1966-
The Jesus people movement: an annotated bibliography and general resource/ David Di Sabatino. Westport, Conn.: Greenwood Press, 1999. xiv, 257 p.
98-039931 016.2899 0313302685
Jesus People -- Bibliography.

Z7837.7 Theology and religion — Roman Catholic Church — By region or country, A-Z

Z7837.7.G7.E44 1996
English Catholic books, 1701-1800: a bibliography/ compiled by F. Blom ... [et al.]. Aldershot, Hants, England: Scolar Press; Brooksfield, Vt.,USA: c1996. xl, 356 p.
95-036772 016.282/41 1859281486
Bibliography -- Great Britain -- Early printed books -- 18th century. Catholic literature -- Bibliography. English imprints.

Z7837.7.G7.E44 1996b
Clancy, Thomas H.
English Catholic books, 1641-1700: a bibliography/ by Thomas H. Clancy. Brookfield, Vt.: Scolar Press, 1996. xviii, 215 p.
96-012614 016.282/41 1859283292
Early printed books -- Great Britain -- 17th century -- Bibliography. Catholic literature -- Bibliography. English imprints.

Z7838 Theology and religion — Roman Catholic Church — Special topics, A-Z

Z7838.P53.C37 1990
Carlen, Claudia, 1906-
Papal pronouncements: a guide: 1740-1978/ Claudia Carlen. Ann Arbor, Mich.: Pierian Press, c1990. 2 v.
90-049617 262.9/1 0876502664
Papal documents -- Bibliography.

Z7845 Theology and religion — Sects, churches, movements, heresies (Christian), A-Z

Z7845.C48
Ayer, H. D., 1952-
The Christian and Missionary Alliance: an annotated bibliography of textual sources/ H.D. (Sandy) Ayer. Lanham, Md.: Scarecrow Press, 2001. xx, 403 p.
00-053831 016.2899 0810839954
Christian and Missionary Alliance -- Bibliography. Christian and Missionary Alliance -- Indexes.

Z7845.J45.B46 1999
Bergman, Jerry.
Jehovah's Witnesses: a comprehensive and selectively annotated bibliography/ compiled by Jerry Bergman; introduction by Joseph F. Zygmunt. Westport, Conn.: Greenwood Press, 1999. xii, 351 p.
98-037845 016.2899/2 0313305102
Jehovah's Witnesses -- Bibliography.

Z7845.L9.H83 1999
Huber, Donald L.
World Lutheranism: a select bibliography for English readers/ Donald L. Huber. Lanham, Md.: Scarecrow Press, 1999. xii, 299 p.
99-041951 016.2841 0810837269
Lutheran Church -- Bibliography.

Z7845.M8.A44 2000
Allen, James B., 1927-
Studies in Mormon history, 1830-1997: an indexed bibliography/ James B. Allen, Ronald W. Walker, and David J. Whittaker; with a topical guide to published social science literature on the Mormons [by] Armand L. Mauss and Dynette Ivie Reynolds. Urbana: University of Illinois Press, c2000. xiii, 1152 p.
99-046135 016.2893/09 0252025652
Mormon Church -- History -- Indexes. Mormon Church -- History -- Bibliography.

Z7845.O83.C78 1988
Crumb, Lawrence N.
The Oxford movement and its leaders: a bibliography of secondary and lesser primary sources/ by Lawrence N. Crumb. Metuchen, N.J.: American Theological Library Association: 1988. xxviii, 706 p.
88-010217 016.283/42 0810821419
Oxford movement -- Bibliography. Anglicans -- England -- Biography -- Bibliography. Anglican Communion -- England -- History -- 19th century -- Bibliography.

Z7845.P4.J663 1995
Jones, Charles Edwin, 1932-
The Charismatic movement: a guide to the study of Neo-Pentecostalism with emphasis on Anglo-American sources/ by Charles Edwin Jones. [Philadelphia]: American Theological Library Association; 1995. 2 v.
92-013032 016.2708/2 0810825651
Pentecostalism -- United States -- Bibliography. Pentecostalism -- Bibliography.

Z7845.S24.M69 1988
Moyles, R. G.
A bibliography of Salvation Army literature in English (1865-1987)/ R.G. Moyles. Lewiston: E. Mellen Press, c1988. viii, 209 p.
88-008964   016.267/15   0889468273
Salvation Army -- Bibliography.

Z7845.1 Theology and religion — Christian unity

Z7845.1.F34 1992
Fahey, Michael A. 1933-
Ecumenism: a bibliographical overview/ compiled by Michael A. Fahey. Westport, Conn.: Greenwood Press, 1992. xxi, 384 p.
92-028449   016.2708/2   0313251029
Ecumenical movement -- Bibliography.

Z7849 Theology and religion — Sunday schools. Religious education in secular schools

Z7849.W94 1995
Wyckoff, D. Campbell.
Religious education, 1960-1993: an annotated bibliography/ compiled by D. Campbell Wyckoff and George Brown, Jr. Westport, Conn.: Greenwood Press, 1995. xii, 325 p.
94-024125   016.268   0313284539
Christian education -- Bibliography.

Z7850 Theology and religion — Theodicy

Z7850.W48 1993
Whitney, Barry L.
Theodicy: an annotated bibliography on the problem of evil, 1960-1990/ Barry L. Whitney. New York: Garland, 1993. ix, 650 p.
92-042769   016.214   0824076389
Theodicy -- Bibliography.

Z7864 Theology and religion — Buddhism — Special modifications, schools, sects, etc.

Z7864.Y64.P69 1991
Powers, John, 1957-
The Yogacara school of Buddhism: a bibliography/ by John Powers. [Philadelphia, Pa.?]: American Theological Library Association; 1991. 257 p.
91-037139   016.2943/92   0810825023
Yogacara (Buddhism) -- Bibliography.

Z7864.Z4 G37 1991
Gardner, James L.
Zen Buddhism: a classified bibliography of Western-language publications through 1990/ by James L. Gardner. [Salt Lake City, Utah]: Wings of Fire Press, 1991. 412 p.
91-091037   016.2943/927 20   1879222035
Zen Buddhism -- Bibliography.

Z7882 Tobacco. Smoking

Z7882.R64 1999
Rogers, Pamela, 1974-
Controlled or reduced smoking: an annotated bibliography/ compiled by Pamela Rogers and Steve Baldwin. Westport, Conn.: Greenwood Press, 1999. xi, 153 p.
99-022095   016.36229/6   0313309884
Tobacco habit -- Bibliography. Smoking -- Bibliography.

Z7911-7914 Useful arts and applied science. Technology

Z7911.F5 1988
Finnegan, Robert, 1942-
Product and process: an index to the way things work/ by Robert Finnegan. Metuchen, N.J.: Scarecrow Press, 1988. xv, 238 p.
88-006691   016.6   0810821133
Technology -- Indexes. Manufacturing processes -- Indexes.

Z7913.I7
Applied science and technology index. v.1- Feb. 1913- New York [etc.] H. W. Wilson [etc.]
14-005408   016.6
Engineering -- Period -- Indexes. Industrial arts -- Period -- Indexes. Technology -- Period -- Indexes.

Z7914.B33 B56 1994
Biotechnology, commercialization, and economic aspects: January 1991 - January 1994/ Kim Guenther ... [et al.]. Beltsville, Md.: National Agricultural Library, [1994] 41 p. ;
94-190166
Biotechnology -- Economic aspects -- Bibliography. Genetic engineering -- Economic aspects -- Bibliography.

Z7914.I5.N66 1988
Noon, Patrick, 1949-
Product design management: an annotated bibliography/ Patrick Noon and Timothy Warner. Aldershot; Avebury, c1988. viii, 212 p.
88-023237   016.7452   0566054663
Design, Industrial -- Management -- Bibliography.

Z7914.M5.L35 1995
Lawal, Ibironke O.
Metalworking in Africa south of the Sahara: an annotated bibliography/ compiled by Ibironke O. Lawal. Westport, Conn.: Greenwood Press, 1995. x, 270 p.
95-007485   016.671/0967   0313293244
Metal-work -- Africa, Sub-Saharan -- Bibliography.

Z7961-7964 Women

Z7961.C37 1990
Carter, Sarah.
Women's studies: a guide to information sources/ Sarah Carter and Maureen Ritchie. London, England: Mansell; 1990. 278 p.
89-039974   016.3054   0720120586
Women's studies -- Bibliography. Women's studies -- Abstracts. Women's studies -- Periodicals.

Z7961.C38 1997
Catanese, Lynn Ann, 1957-
Women's history: a guide to sources at Hagley Museum and Library/ Lynn Ann Catanese. Westport, Conn.: Greenwood Press, 1997. viii, 338 p.
97-039753   016.3054/09   0313302707
Women -- History -- Sources -- Bibliography -- Catalogs.

Z7961.F74 1982
Frey, Linda.
Women in western European history: a select chronological, geographical, and topical bibliography/ compiled and edited by Linda Frey, Marsha Frey, and Joanne Schneider. Westport, Conn.: Greenwood Press, [c1982-] v. <1 >
81-020300   016.3054 19   0313228582
Women -- Europe -- History -- Bibliography.

Z7961.M4 1991
McCullough, Rita I.
Sources: an annotated bibliography of women's issues/ Rita I. McCullough, editor. Manchester, Conn.: KIT, 1991. xi, 320 p.
90-092201   016.3054   1879198282
Women -- Social conditions -- Bibliography.

Z7961.M85 1989
Mumford, Laura Stempel.
Women's issues: an annotated bibliography/ Laura Stempel Mumford. Pasadena, Calif.: Salem Press, c1989. vi, 163 p.
89-010831   016.30542/0973   0893566543
Women -- Bibliography. Feminism -- Bibliography. Women -- United States -- Bibliography.

Z7961.R43 1998
Reader's guide to women's studies/ editor, Eleanor B. Amico. Chicago: Fitzroy Dearborn, 1998. xxx, 732 p.
98-138939   016.3054/07   188496477X
Women's studies -- Bibliography. Women -- History -- Bibliography.

Z7961.S42 1985
Searing, Susan E.
Introduction to library research in women's studies/ Susan E. Searing. Boulder: Westview Press, 1985. xiii, 257 p.
85-003162   016.3054   0865312672
Women -- Reference books -- Bibliography. Women -- Bibliography. Women -- Research -- Methodology.

Z7961.S68 1996
South African women: a select bibliography/ compiled by Durban Women's Bibliography Group. Johannesburg: South African Institute of International Affairs, 1996. iv, 307 p.
96-220766   016.3054/0968   1874890633
Women -- South Africa -- Bibliography.

Z7961.W37 1990
Watson, G. Llewellyn.
Feminism and women's issues: an annotated bibliography and research guide/ G. Llewellyn Watson with the assistance of Janet P. Sentner. New York: Garland Pub., 1990. 2 v.
89-023327   016.30542   0824055438
Women -- Bibliography. Feminism -- Bibliography.

Z7962.W675
Women's studies index. Boston, Mass.: G.K. Hall & Co., [c1991-] 10 v.
92-660619   016.3054
Women's studies -- Periodicals -- Indexes -- Periodicals.

Z7963.A4.W54 1997
Wheeler, Helen Rippier.
Women & aging: a guide to the literature/ Helen Rippier Wheeler. Boulder, Colo.: Lynne Rienner Publishers, 1997. vii, 259 p.
96-041175   016.30526   1555876617
Aged women -- United States -- Bibliography. Middle aged women -- United States -- Bibliography. Gerontology -- United States -- Bibliography.

Z7963.A75.B32 1994
Piland, Sherry.
Women artists: an historical, contemporary, and feminist bibliography/ by Sherry Piland. Metuchen, N.J.: Scarecrow Press, 1994. xvii, 454 p.
93-027248   016.7/092/2   0810825597
Women artists -- Bibliography. Feminism and art -- Bibliography.

Z7963.A75.P84 1996
Puerto, Cecilia.
Latin American women artists, Kahlo and look who else: a selective, annotated bibliography/ Cecilia Puerto; foreword by Elizabeth Ferrer. Westport, Conn.: Greenwood Press, 1996. xiv, 237 p.
96-007150   016.7/092/28   0313289344
Women artists -- Latin America -- Bibliography. Art, Latin American -- Bibliography. Art, Modern -- 20th century -- Latin America -- Bibliography.

Z7963.B6.A27 1999
Adamson, Lynda G.
Notable women in American history: a guide to recommended biographies and autobiographies/ Lynda G. Adamson. Westport, Conn.: Greenwood Press, c1999. xiv, 450 p.
98-055350   016.92072/0973   0313295840
Women -- United States -- Biography -- Bibliography. Autobiography -- Women authors -- Bibliography. American diaries -- Women authors -- Bibliography. United States -- Biography -- Bibliography.

Z7963.B6.A28 1998
Adamson, Lynda G.
Notable women in world history: a guide to recommended biographies and autobiographies/ Lynda G. Adamson. Westport, Conn.: Greenwood Press, 1998. xiv, 401 p.
97-033136   016.92072   0313298181
Women -- Biography -- Bibliography. Autobiography -- Women authors -- Bibliography. Diaries -- Women authors -- Bibliography.

Z7963.B6.I73 Suppl.
Ireland, Norma Olin, 1907-
Index to women of the world from ancient to modern times: a supplement/ by Norma Olin Ireland. Metuchen, N.J.: Scarecrow Press, 1988. xiv, 774 p.
87-035934   016.92072   0810820927
Women -- Biography -- Indexes. Women -- Portraits -- Indexes.

Z7963.B6.K35 1997
Kanner, Barbara, 1925-
Women in context: two hundred years of British women autobiographers, a reference guide and reader/ Barbara Penny Kanner. New York: G.K. Hall, 1997. lix, 1049 p.
96-029645   016.3054/0942   081617346X
Women -- Great Britain -- Biography -- Bibliography. Women -- Great Britain -- History -- Sources -- Bibliography. Autobiography -- Women authors -- Bibliography.

Z7963.E7.A73 1999
Argos, V. P.
Sexual harassment: analyses and bibliography/ V.P. Argos and Tatiana Shohov. Commack, N.Y.: Nova Science Publishers, 1999.
99-049458   331.4/133   156072711X
Sexual harassment of women -- United States -- Bibliography. Sex discrimination in employment -- United States -- Bibliography. Sex discrimination in education -- United States -- Bibliography.

Z7963.E7.F47 1987
Ferber, Marianne A., 1923-
Women and work, paid and unpaid: a selected, annotated bibliography/ Marianne A. Ferber. New York: Garland, 1987. xvi, 408 p.
87-008652   016.3314   0824086902
Women -- Employment -- Bibliography.

Z7963.E7 G48 1994
Ghorayshi, Parvin.
Women and work in developing countries: an annotated bibliography/ compiled by Parvin Ghorayshi. Westport, Conn.: Greenwood Press, 1994. xix, 223 p. ;
93-038803   016.3314/09172/4 20   0313288348
Women -- Employment -- Developing countries -- Bibliography. Women -- Developing countries -- Economic conditions -- Bibliography.

Z7963.E7.M316 1996
Maman, Marie.
Women in agriculture: a guide to research/ Marie Maman and Thelma H. Tate. New York: Garland, c1996. x, 298 p.
95-041230   016.3314/83   0815313543
Women in agriculture -- Bibliography.

Z7963.F44.M54 1991
Miller, Connie.
Feminist research methods: an annotated bibliography/ Connie Miller, with Corinna Treitel. New York: Greenwood, 1991. 279 p.
91-003792   016.30542/072   031326029X
Feminism -- Research -- Bibliography. Women -- Research -- Bibliography.

Z7963.F44 N66 1996
Nordquist, Joan.
Feminism worldwide: a bibliography/ compiled by Joan Nordquist. Santa Cruz, CA: Reference and Research Services, 1996. 64 p.
97-129798   016.30542 21   0937855863
Feminism -- Bibliography.

Z7963.I74 K56 1997
Kimball, Michelle R.,
Muslim women throughout the world: a bibliography/ Michelle R. Kimball, Barbara R. von Schlegell. Boulder, Colo.: Lynne Rienner Publishers, c1997. ix, 309 p.
96-025718   016.30548/6971 20   1555876803
Women -- Islamic countries -- Bibliography. Muslim women Bibliography.

Z7963.J4 C36 1987
Cantor, Aviva.
The Jewish woman, 1900-1985: a bibliography/ partially annotated by Aviva Cantor with 1983-1986 citations compiled by Ora Hamelsdorf; editorial coordinator: Doris B. Gold; editorial assistant: Judith Pearl. [2nd ed.]. Fresh Meadows, N.Y.: Biblio Press, 1987. ix, 193 p.
87-070090   016.3054/089/924 19   0930395042
Jewish women -- Bibliography.

Z7963.J4 C36 1987 Suppl
Masnik, Ann S.
The Jewish woman: an annotated selected bibliography, 1986-1993: with 1994-1995 recent titles list/ compiled by Ann S. Masnik; introduction by Marcia Cohn Spiegel; Doris B. Gold, editor. New York: Biblio Press, c1996. 171 p.
95-020942   016.30548/924 20   0930395255
Jewish women -- Bibliography.

Z7963.J4 R88 1988
Ruud, Inger Marie.
Women and Judaism: a select annotated bibliography/ Inger Marie Ruud. New York: Garland, 1988. xxiv, 232 p.
87-029109   016.296/088042 19   0824086899
Women in Judaism -- Bibliography. Jewish women -- Bibliography.

Z7963.P64.C69 1997
Cox, Elizabeth, 1939-
Women in modern American politics: a bibliography, 1900-1995/ Elizabeth M. Cox. Washington, D.C.: Congressional Quarterly, c1997. xvii, 414 p.
96-038898   016.30542   156802133X
Women in politics -- United States -- History -- 20th century -- Bibliography.

Z7963.R45 B45 1995
Blevins, Carolyn DeArmond,
Women in christian history: a bibliography/ compiled and edited by Carolyn DeArmond Blevins. Macon, Ga.: Mercer University Press, 1995. viii, 114 p.
95-024835   270/.082 20   086554493X
Church history -- Bibliography. Women in Christianity -- History -- Bibliography.

Z7963.R45 J64 1995
Johnson, Dale A.,
Women and religion in Britain and Ireland: an annotated bibliography from the Reformation to 1993/ Dale A. Johnson. Lanham, Md.: Scarecrow Press, c1995. xvi, 288 p.
95-033428   016.2/0082 20   0810830639
Women and religion -- England -- History -- Bibliography. Women and religion -- Ireland -- History -- Bibliography.

Z7963.R45.W34 1999
Walsh, Mary-Paula.
Feminism and Christian tradition: an annotated bibliography and critical introduction to the literature/ Mary-Paula Walsh. Westport, Conn.: Greenwood Press, c1999. xiii, 456 p.
98-033137 016.2618/344 0313264198
Feminism -- Religious aspects -- Christianity -- Bibliography. Feminist theology -- Bibliography.

Z7963.S3.O35 1996
Ogilvie, Marilyn Bailey.
Women and science: an annotated bibliography/ Marilyn Bailey Ogilvie with Kerry Lynne Meek. New York: Garland Pub., 1996. x, 556 p.
96-021199 016.30543/5 0815309295
Women in science -- Bibliography. Women scientists -- Bibliography.

Z7963.S6.R45 1991
Remley, Mary L.
Women in sport: an annotated bibliography and resource guide, 1900-1990/ Mary L. Remley. Boston, Mass.: G.K. Hall, 1991. xi, 210 p.
90-020557 016.796/0194 0816189773
Sports for women -- Bibliography.

Z7964.A3.B84 1989
Bullwinkle, Davis.
African women, a general bibliography, 1976-1985/ compiled by Davis A. Bullwinkle. New York: Greenwood Press, 1989. xx, 334 p.
88-037379 016.3054/096 0313266077
Women -- Africa -- Bibliography.

Z7964.A3.B85 1989
Bullwinkle, Davis.
Women of northern, western, and central Africa: a bibliography, 1976-1985/ compiled by Davis A. Bullwinkle. New York: Greenwood Press, 1989. xxvii, 601 p.
89-002160 016.3054/096 0313266093
Women -- Africa -- Bibliography. Women -- Africa, North -- Bibliography. Women -- Africa, West -- Bibliography.

Z7964.A337.B84 1989
Bullwinkle, Davis.
Women of eastern and southern Africa: a bibliography, 1976-1985/ compiled by Davis A. Bullwinkle. New York: Greenwood Press, 1989. xxv, 545 p.
89-002154 016.3054/09676 0313266069
Women -- Africa, Sub-Saharan -- Bibliography. Women -- Africa, Eastern -- Bibliography. Women -- Africa, Southern -- Bibliography.

Z7964.C85.S76 2000
Stoner, K. Lynn.
Cuban and Cuban-American women: an annotated bibliography/ edited and compiled by K. Lynn Stoner, with Luis Hipolito Serrano Perez. Wilmington, Del.: Scholarly Resources, 2000. xxii, 189 p.
98-022317 016.3054/097291 0842026436
Women -- Cuba -- Bibliography. Cuban American women -- Bibliography.

Z7964.G7.H36 1996
Hannam, June, 1947-
British women's history: a bibliographical guide/ compiled by June Hannam, Ann Hughes, and Pauline Stafford. Manchester; Manchester University Press; c1996. xiv, 150 p.
95-001038 016.3054/0941 0719046521
Women -- Great Britain -- History -- Bibliography.

Z7964.J3.H82 1992
Huber, Kristina R.
Women in Japanese society: an annotated bibliography of selected English language materials/ Kristina Ruth Huber. Westport, Conn.: Greenwood Press, 1992. xviii, 484 p.
92-015371 016.30542/0952 0313252963
Women -- Japan -- History -- Bibliography. Women -- Japan -- Social conditions -- Bibliography. Women authors, Japanese -- Bibliography.

Z7964.N6.A95 1996
Azikiwe, Uche.
Women in Nigeria: an annotated bibliography/ compiled by Uche Azikiwe. Westport, Conn.: Greenwood Press, 1996. x, 144 p.
95-047167 016.3054/09669 0313299609
Women -- Nigeria -- Social conditions -- Bibliography. Women in development -- Nigeria -- Bibliography.

Z7964.S68.R88 1993
Ruthchild, Rochelle Goldberg.
Women in Russia and the Soviet Union: an annotated bibliography/ Rochelle Goldberg Ruthchild. New York: G.K. Hall; c1993. xiv, 203 p.
92-004516 016.3054/0947 0816189897
Women -- Soviet Union -- History -- Bibliography.

Z7964.U49.B53 1989
Blair, Karen J.
The history of American women's voluntary organizations, 1810-1960: a guide to sources/ Karen J. Blair. Boston, Mass.: G.K. Hall, c1989. xvii, 363 p.
88-019946 016.3054/06/073 0816186480
Women -- United States -- Societies and clubs -- History -- 19th century -- Bibliography. Women -- United States -- Societies and clubs -- History -- 20th century -- Bibliography.

Z7964.U49.H364 2000
Hardy, Lyda Mary.
Women in U.S. history: a resource guide/ Lyda Mary Hardy. Englewood, Colo.: Libraries Unlimited, 2000. xvi, 344 p.
00-055849 016.973/082 1563087693
Women -- United States -- History -- Bibliography. Women -- United States -- Historiography.

Z7964.U49.H85 1993
Huls, Mary Ellen.
United States government documents on women, 1800-1990: a comprehensive bibliography/ Mary Ellen Huls. Westport, Conn.: Greenwood Press, 1993. 2 v.
92-038990 016.3054 0313290164
Women -- United States -- History -- Sources -- Bibliography. Women -- United States -- Social conditions -- Sources -- Bibliography. Women -- Employment -- United States -- History -- Sources -- Bibliography.

Z7964.U49 N67 1995
Nordquist, Joan.
Women of color: feminist theory: a bibliography/ compiled by Joan Nordquist. Santa Cruz, CA: Reference and Research Services, 1995. 76 p. ;
96-208374 016.30542/01 21 0937855790
Minority women -- United States -- Bibliography. Feminist theory -- United States -- Bibliography. Feminist literary criticism -- United States -- Bibliography.

Z7991 Zoology — General bibliography

Z7991.B43 1994
Bell, George H., 1943-
A guide to the zoological literature: the animal kingdom/ George H. Bell and Diane B. Rhodes; illustrated by Emily R. Rhodes. Englewood, Colo.: Libraries Unlimited, 1994. xxiii, 504 p.
94-012694 016.591 1563080826
Zoology -- Bibliography.

Z7994.L3 B47 1992
Jensen, D'Anna J. B.
Information resources for reptiles, amphibians, fish, and cephalopods used in biomedical research/ D'Anna J. Berry, Michael D. Kreger, Jennifer L. Lyons-Carter. Beltsville, Md.: U.S. Dept. of Agriculture, National Agricultural iii, 87 p. :
93-205481 016.597/00724 20
Animal models in research -- Bibliography. Reptiles as laboratory animals -- Bibliography. Amphibians as laboratory animals -- Bibliography. Fish as laboratory animals -- Bibliography. Cephalopoda as laboratory animals -- Bibliography.

Z8015.6-8989 Personal bibliography

Z8015.6 A — Adams, John

Z8015.6.F46 1994
Ferling, John E.
John Adams: a bibliography/ compiled by John Ferling. Westport, Conn.: Greenwood Press, 1994. xxxi, 222 p.
93-028706 016.9734/4 0313281602
Adams, John, -- 1735-1826 -- Bibliography.United States -- Politics and government -- 1797-1801 -- Bibliography.

Z8015.7 A — Adams, John Q.

Z8015.7.P37 1993
Parsons, Lynn H.
John Quincy Adams: a bibliography/ compiled by Lynn H. Parsons. Westport, Conn.: Greenwood Press, 1993. xvii, 217 p.
92-033703 016.9735/5/092 0313281645
Adams, John Quincy, -- 1767-1848 -- Bibliography.

Z8015.87 A — Addison, Joseph

Z8015.87.K55 1994
Knight, Charles A.
Joseph Addison and Richard Steele: a reference guide, 1730-1991/ Charles A. Knight. New York: G.K. Hall; c1994. xxii, 561 p.
94-021458 016.824/5 0816189803
Addison, Joseph, -- 1672-1719 -- Bibliography. Steele, Richard, -- Sir, -- 1672-1729 -- Bibliography. English essays -- 18th century -- History and criticism -- Bibliography.

Z8025.6 A — Alexander, Lloyd

Z8025.6.J3 1991
Jacobs, James S., 1945-
Lloyd Alexander: a bio-bibliography/ James S. Jacobs and Michael O. Tunnell. New York: Greenwood Press, 1991. x, 145 p.
90-024515 813/.54 0313265860
Alexander, Lloyd -- Bibliography. Alexander, Lloyd. Authors, American -- 20th century -- Biography. Children's literature, American -- Bibliography.

Z8045 A — Arthur, King

Z8045.R45 1984
Reiss, Edmund.
Arthurian legend and literature: an annotated bibliography/ Edmund Reiss, Louis Horner Reiss, Beverly Taylor. New York: Garland, 1984- v. <1 >;
83-047612 016.809/93351 19 082409123X
Arthurian romances -- Bibliography. Knights and knighthood in literature -- Bibliography. Kings and rulers in literature -- Bibliography. Literature, Medieval -- Bibliography.

Z8045.59 A — Asimov, Isaac

Z8045.59.G74 1995
Green, Scott E.
Isaac Asimov: an annotated bibliography of the Asimov Collection at Boston University/ Scott E. Green. Westport, Conn.: Greenwood Press, 1995. xiii, 146 p.
95-022752 016.813/54 0313288968
Asimov, Isaac, -- 1920- -- Bibliography. Asimov, Isaac, -- 1920- -- Library -- Catalogs. Science fiction, American -- Bibliography.

Z8047.7 A — Augustinus, Aurelius, Saint, bp. of Hippo

Z8047.7.S47 1996
Severson, Richard James, 1955-
The confessions of Saint Augustine: an annotated bibliography of modern criticism, 1888-1995/ Richard Severson. Westport, Conn.: Greenwood Press, 1996. xiv, 149 p.
96-009465 016.2702/092 0313299951
Augustine, -- Saint, Bishop of Hippo. -- Confessiones -- Bibliography.

Z8048 A — Austen, Jane

Z8048.G54 1997
Gilson, David.
A bibliography of Jane Austen/ by David Gilson; new introduction and corrections by the author. Winchester: St Paul's Bibliographies; lxi, 877 p.
97-002148 016.823/7 21 1884718329
Austen, Jane, 1775-1817 -- Bibliography.

Z8048.R69 1996
Roth, Barry, 1942-
An annotated bibliography of Jane Austen studies, 1984-94/ Barry Roth. Athens: Ohio University Press, c1996. xxiv, 438 p.
96-017026 016.823/7 0821411675
Austen, Jane, -- 1775-1817 -- Bibliography.Women and literature -- England -- Bibliography.

Z8068.78 B — Balfour, Arthur

Z8068.78.R37 1998
Rasor, Eugene L., 1936-
Arthur James Balfour, 1848-1930: historiography and annotated bibliography/ Eugene L. Rasor. Westport, Conn.: Greenwood Press, 1998. xvi, 121 p.
98-027676 016.941082/092 0313288771
Balfour, Arthur James Balfour, -- Earl of, -- 1848-1930 -- Bibliography.Prime ministers -- Great Britain -- Biography -- Bibliography.Great Britain -- Politics and government -- 1901-1936 -- Bibliography. Great Britain -- Politics and government -- 1837-1901 -- Bibliography.

Z8069.2 B — Balzac, Honoré de

Z8069.2.W34 1990
Waggoner, Mark W.
Bibliography of Balzac criticism, 1930-1990/ Mark W. Waggoner, compiler. Encinitas, CA, U.S.A.: French Research Publications, c1990. i, 328 p.
90-080420 016.843/7
Balzac, Honore de, -- 1799-1850 -- Criticism and interpretation -- Bibliography.

Z8086.37 B — Beckett, Samuel

Z8086.37.A5 1989
Andonian, Cathleen Culotta.
Samuel Beckett: a reference guide/ Cathleen Culotta Andonian. Boston, Mass.: G.K. Hall, c1989. xxviii, 754 p.
88-024501 016.848/91409 0816185700
Beckett, Samuel, -- 1906- -- Bibliography.

Z8089.12 B — Benchley, Robert

Z8089.12.E76 1995
Ernst, Gordon E.
Robert Benchley: an annotated bibliography/ compiled by Gordon E. Ernst, Jr. Westport, Conn.: Greenwood Press, 1995. xiv, 290 p.
95-006293 016.814/52 031329321X
Benchley, Robert, -- 1889-1945 -- Bibliography.

Z8102.23 B — Blackwood, Algernon

Z8102.23.A74 1987
Ashley, Michael.
Algernon Blackwood: a bio-bibliography/ Mike Ashley; foreword by Ramsey Campbell. New York: Greenwood Press, 1987. xx, 349 p.
87-017808 016.823/912 0313251584
Blackwood, Algernon, -- 1869-1951 -- Bibliography.

Z8106 B — Boccaccio, Giovanni

Z8106.S79 1995
Stych, F. S. 1916-
Boccaccio in English: a bibliography of editions, adaptations, and criticism/ F. S. Stych. Westport, Conn.: Greenwood Press, 1995. xix, 254 p.
94-041268 016.858/109 0313289670
Boccaccio, Giovanni, -- 1313-1375 -- Bibliography.

Z8106.3 B — Boethius

Z8106.3.K38 1992
Kaylor, Noel Harold, 1946-
The medieval Consolation of philosophy: an annotated bibliography/ Noel Harold Kaylor, Jr. New York: Garland Pub., 1992. x, 262 p.
92-000459 016.189 0824055489
Boethius, -- d. 524 -- Translations -- Bibliography. Boethius, -- d. 524. -- De consolatione philosophiae -- Bibliography. Philosophy and religion -- Early works to 1800 -- Bibliography. Happiness -- Early works to 1800 -- Bibliography. Philosophy, Medieval -- Bibliography.

Z8109.16 B — Boorstin, D.J.

Z8109.16.L46 2001
Leonard, Angela M.
Daniel J. Boorstin: a comprehensive and selectively annotated bibliography/ edited and compiled by Angela Michele Leonard; foreword by Daniel J. Boorstin. Westport, Conn.: Greenwood Press, 2001. xxiii, 247 p.
00-057793 016.973/07/202 031330324X
Boorstin, Daniel J. -- (Daniel Joseph), -- 1914- -- Bibliography.

Z8110.2 B —
Boswell, James

Z8110.2.B75 1991
Brown, Anthony E.,
Boswellian studies: a bibliography/ Anthony E. Brown. 3rd ed. Edinburgh: Edinburgh University Press, c1991. xiii, 176 p.
92-164290   016.828/609 20   0748603034
Boswell, James, 1740-1795 -- Bibliography.

Z8113.6 B —
Bradstreet, Annie

Z8113.6.D65 1990
Dolle, Raymond F.
Anne Bradstreet, a reference guide/ Raymond F. Dolle. Boston, Mass.: G.K. Hall, 1990. xxviii, 145 p.
89-026888   016.811/1   0816189749
Bradstreet, Anne, -- 1612?-1672 -- Bibliography.Women and literature -- United States -- Bibliography.

Z8115.66 B —
Braque, Georges

Z8115.66.C57 1994
Clement, Russell T.
Georges Braque: a bio-bibliography/ Russell T. Clement. Westport, Conn.: Greenwood Press, 1994. xvii, 227 p.
93-045310   016.7/092   0313292353
Braque, Georges, -- 1882-1963 -- Bibliography.

Z8119.2 B — Bridges, R.S.

Z8119.2.H36 1991
Hamilton, Lee Templin, 1950-
Robert Bridges: an annotated bibliography, 1873-1988/ Lee Templin Hamilton. Newark: University of Delaware Press; c1991. 243 p.
88-040577   016.821/8   0874133645
Bridges, Robert Seymour, -- 1844-1930 -- Bibliography.

Z8124.4 B —
Browning, Elizabeth (Barrett)

Z8124.4.D66 1993
Donaldson, Sandra.
Elizabeth Barrett Browning: an annotated bibliography of the commentary and criticism, 1826-1990/ Sandra Donaldson. New York: G.K. Hall; c1993. xiv, 642 p.
92-024448   016.821/8   0816189102
Browning, Elizabeth Barrett, -- 1806-1861 -- Criticism and interpretation -- Bibliography.Women and literature -- England -- History -- 19th century -- Bibliography.

Z8129.8 B —
Buero Vallejo, Antonio

Z8129.8.F67 1988
Forys, Marsha, 1949-
Antonio Buero Vallejo and Alfonso Sastre: an annotated bibliography/ by Marsha Forys. Metuchen, N.J.: Scarecrow Press, 1988. xiii, 209 p.
87-032385   016.862/64/09   0810821001
Buero Vallejo, Antonio, -- 1916- -- Bibliography. Sastre, Alfonso, -- 1926- -- Bibliography.

Z8131.65 B —
Burchfield, Charles

Z8131.65.M35 1996
Makowski, Colleen Lahan, 1948-
Charles Burchfield: an annotated bibliography/ Colleen Lahan Makowski. Lanham, Md.: Scarecrow Press, c1996. x, 210 p.
95-026776   016.75913   0810831317
Burchfield, Charles Ephraim, -- 1893-1967 -- Bibliography.

Z8136.15 B —
Burroughs, E.R.

Z8136.15.Z48 1996
Zeuschner, Robert B., 1941-
Edgar Rice Burroughs: the exhaustive scholar's and collector's descriptive bibliography of American periodical, hardcover, paperback, and reprint editions/ by Robert B. Zeuschner; with a foreword by Philip Jose Farmer. Jefferson, N.C.: McFarland, c1996. xi, 287 p.
96-273311   016.813/52   0786401834
Burroughs, Edgar Rice, -- 1875-1950 -- Bibliography.Popular literature -- United States -- Bibliography. Fantastic fiction, American -- Bibliography. Adventure stories, American -- Bibliography.

Z8136.17 B —
Burroughs, W.S.

Z8136.17.G65 1990
Goodman, Michael B.
William S. Burroughs: a reference guide/ Michael B. Goodman with Lemuel B. Coley. New York: Garland, 1990. 270 p.
89-026026   016.813/54   0824086422
Burroughs, William S., -- 1914- -- Bibliography.Beat generation -- Bibliography.

Z8139 B —
Byron, G.G.N. Byron, 6th baron

Z8139.G66 1997
Goode, Clement Tyson, 1929-
George Gordon, Lord Byron: a comprehensive, annotated research bibliography of secondary materials in English, 1973-1994/ by Clement Tyson Goode, Jr. Lanham, Md.: Scarecrow Press, 1997. xlvii, 878 p.
96-008238   016.821/7   0810831864
Byron, George Gordon Byron, -- Baron, -- 1788-1824 -- Bibliography.

Z8140.62 C —
Calhoun, J.C. (John Caldwell)

Z8140.62.W55 1990
Wilson, Clyde Norman.
John C. Calhoun: a bibliography/ Clyde N. Wilson. Westport, CT: Meckler, c1990. ix, 172 p.
90-006508   016.9735/092   0887363024
Calhoun, John C. -- (John Caldwell), -- 1782-1850 -- Bibliography.United States -- Politics and government -- 1815-1861 -- Bibliography. South Carolina -- Politics and government -- 1775-1865 -- Bibliography.

Z8164 C — Chaucer

Z8164.B275 1988
Baird-Lange, Lorrayne Y., 1927-
A bibliography of Chaucer, 1974-1985/ Lorrayne Y. Baird-Lange and Hildegard Schnuttgen. Hamden, Conn.: Archon Books, 1988. lxxv, 344 p.
87-035157   016.821/1   0208021345
Chaucer, Geoffrey, -- d. 1400 -- Bibliography.English poetry -- Middle English, 1100-1500 -- Bibliography.

Z8164.B69 2002
Bowers, Bege K.,
Annotated Chaucer bibliography, 1986-1996/ Bege K. Bowers & Mark Allen, editors Notre Dame, Ind.: University of Notre Dame Press, c2002. xxxii, 719 p.
2002-012933   016.821/1 21   0268020167
Chaucer, Geoffrey, d. 1400 -- Bibliography.

Z8164.C37 1997
Chaucer's Miller's, Reeve's, and Cook's tales/ edited by T.L. Burton and Rosemary Greentree; annotations by David Biggs ... [et al.]. Toronto; Published in association with the University of Toronto Press, c1997. xxxvi, 287 p.
97-180935   016.821/1   0802008747
Chaucer, Geoffrey, -- d. 1400. -- Miller's tale -- Bibliography. Chaucer, Geoffrey, -- d. 1400. -- Reeve's tale -- Bibliography. Chaucer, Geoffrey, -- d. 1400. -- Cook's tale -- Bibliography. Christian pilgrims and pilgrimages in literature -- Bibliography. Tales, Medieval -- History and criticism -- Bibliography.

Z8164.C38 1998
Chaucer's Wife of Bath's prologue and tale: an
annotated bibliography, 1900 to 1995/ edited by
Peter G. Beidler and Elizabeth M. Biebel.
Toronto: University of Toronto Press; lxii,
358 p.
98-230240 016.821/1 21 0802043666
*Chaucer, Geoffrey, d. 1400. Wife of Bath's
tale -- Bibliography. Christian pilgrims and
pilgrimages in literature -- Bibliography. Tales,
Medieval -- History and criticism --
Bibliography.*

Z8164.E27 1990
Eckhardt, Caroline D.,
Chaucer's general prologue to the Canterbury
tales: an annotated bibliography, 1900 to 1982/
Caroline D. Eckhardt. Toronto; Published in
association with the University of Rochester by
University of Toronto Press, xli, 468 p.
96-114715 016.821/1 20 0802025927
*Chaucer, Geoffrey, d. 1400. Canterbury tales.
Prologue Christian pilgrims and pilgrimages in
literature -- Bibliography. English poetry --
Middle English, 1100-1500 -- Bibliography.
Civilization, Medieval, in literature --
Bibliography. Prologues and epilogues --
Bibliography.*

Z8164.L49 1986
Leyerle, John.
Chaucer, a bibliographical introduction/ John
Leyerle and Anne Quick. Toronto; University of
Toronto Press, c1986. xx, 321 p.
86-232860 016.821/1 19 0802064086
*Chaucer, Geoffrey, d. 1400 -- Bibliography.
English poetry -- Middle English, 1100-1500 --
Bibliography. Civilization, Medieval, in
literature -- Bibliography.*

Z8164.M33 1991
McAlpine, Monica E.,
Chaucer's Knight's tale: an annotated
bibliography, 1900 to 1985/ Monica E.
McAlpine. Toronto; Published in association
with the University of Rochester by University of
Toronto Press, lii, 432 p.
92-129127 016.821/1 20 0802059139
*Chaucer, Geoffrey, d. 1400. Knight's tale --
Bibliography. Knights and knighthood in
literature -- Bibliography. Tales, Medieval --
Themes, motives -- Bibliography.*

Z8164.S87 2000
Sutton, Marilyn, 1944-
Chaucer's Pardoner's prologue and tale: an
annotated bibliography, 1900 to 1995/ edited by
Marilyn Sutton. Toronto; Published in
association with the University of Toronto Press,
c2000. lii, 445 p.
00-698938 016.821/1 0802047440
*Chaucer, Geoffrey, -- d. 1400. -- Pardoner's
tale -- Bibliography.*

Z8167.47 C —
Chisholm, Shirley

Z8167.47.D83 1988
Duffy, Susan, 1951-
Shirley Chisholm: a bibliography of writings by
and about her/ compiled by Susan Duffy.
Metuchen, N.J.: Scarecrow Press, 1988. vii,
135 p.
88-002073 016.32873/092/4 0810821052
Chisholm, Shirley, -- 1924- -- Bibliography.

Z8169.45 C —
Churchill, Sir, W.L.S.

Z8169.45.A56 2002
Annotated bibliography of works about Sir
Winston S. Churchill/ Curt J. Zoller, editor.
Armonk, N.Y.: M.E. Sharpe, c2003.
2001-049602 016.941084/092 21
0765607344
*Churchill, Winston, Sir, 1874-1965 --
Bibliography. Prime ministers -- Great Britain --
Biography -- Bibliography. Great Britain --
Politics and government -- 20th century --
Bibliography.*

Z8169.45.B35 2000
Barrett, Buckley Barry, 1948-
Churchill: a concise bibliography/ Buckley Barry
Barrett. Westport, Conn.: Greenwood Press,
2000. viii, 215 p.
00-042687 016.941084/092 0313314500
*Churchill, Winston, -- Sir, -- 1874-1965 --
Bibliography.Prime ministers -- Great Britain --
Biography -- Bibliography.Great Britain --
Politics and government -- 20th century --
Bibliography.*

Z8169.45.R37 2000
Rasor, Eugene L., 1936-
Winston S. Churchill, 1874-1965: a
comprehensive historiography and annotated
bibliography/ Eugene L. Rasor. Westport, Conn.:
Greenwood Press, 2000. xxiv, 704 p.
00-030883 016.941084 0313305463
*Churchill, Winston, -- Sir, -- 1874-1965 --
Bibliography. Churchill, Winston, -- Sir, -- 1874-
1965 -- Archival resources -- Directories.
Churchill, Winston, -- Sir, -- 1874-1965 --
Manuscripts -- Union lists. Prime ministers --
Great Britain -- Biography -- Sources.Great
Britain -- Politics and government -- 20th
century -- Sources -- Union lists. Great Britain --
Politics and government -- 20th century --
Bibliography. Great Britain -- Politics and
government -- 20th century -- Archival resources
-- Directories.*

Z8176.45 C —
Cleveland, Grover

Z8176.45.M37 1988
Marszalek, John F., 1939-
Grover Cleveland: a bibliography/ John F.
Marszalek. Westport, CT: Meckler, c1988. xxxv,
268 p.
88-009096 016.9738/7/0924 0887361366
*Cleveland, Grover, -- 1837-1908 --
Bibliography.United States -- Politics and
government -- 1885-1889 -- Bibliography. United
States -- Politics and government -- 1893-1897 --
Bibliography.*

Z8187 C — Columbus

Z8187.G63 1992
The Columbus collection: a chronological list of
books and reprints in the American
Geographical Society Collection/ compiled by
Clinton R. Edwards and Damon Anderson.
Milwaukee: American Geographical Society
Collection, vi, 26 p.
92-028215 016.97001/5 20 1879281104
*Columbus, Christopher -- Bibliography --
Catalogs. America -- Discovery and exploration
-- Spanish -- Bibliography Catalogs.*

Z8187.N34 1994
Nagy, Moses M.,
Christopher Columbus in world literature: an
annotated bibliography/ Moses M. Nagy. New
York: Garland Pub., 1994. xxvi, 352 p.
93-024541 016.8088/0351 20 0815309279
*Columbus, Christopher -- In literature --
Bibliography.*

Z8187.P76 1991
Provost, Foster.
Columbus: an annotated guide to the scholarship
on his life and writings, 1750 to 1988/ by Foster
Provost. Detroit, MI: Published for the John
Carter Brown Library by Omnigraphics, Inc.,
c1991. xxxii, 225 p.
90-027572 016.97001/5 1558881573
*Columbus, Christopher --
Bibliography.America -- Discovery and
exploration -- Spanish -- Bibliography.*

Z8189.7 C —
Conrad, Joseph

Z8189.7.T38 1990
Teets, Bruce E., 1914-
Joseph Conrad: an annotated bibliography/ Bruce
Teets. New York: Garland, 1990. xix, 786 p.
88-024312 016.823/912 0824070372
Conrad, Joseph, -- 1857-1924 -- Bibliography.

Z8191.7 C — Cooper, J.F.

Z8191.7.D9 1991
Dyer, Alan Frank.
James Fenimore Cooper: an annotated
bibliography of criticism/ compiled by Alan
Frank Dyer. New York: Greenwood Press, 1991.
xvii, 293 p.
91-027084 016.813/2 0313279195
*Cooper, James Fenimore, -- 1789-1851 --
Bibliography.Historical fiction, American --
History and criticism -- Bibliography.*

Z8196.6 C — Coward, Noel

Z8196.6.C65 1993
Cole, Stephen.
Noel Coward: a bio-bibliography/ Stephen Cole.
Westport, Conn.: Greenwood Press, 1993. xvii,
319 p.
93-028704 016.822/912 0313285993
Coward, Noel, -- 1899-1973 -- Bibliography.

Z8206.58 C — Curzon, G.N.

Z8206.58.P37 1991
Parker, James G.
Lord Curzon, 1859-1925: a bibliography/ James
G. Parker. New York: Greenwood Press, 1991.
viii, 124 p.
91-009473 016.95403/55/092 031328122X
*Curzon, George Nathaniel Curzon, -- Marquis
of, -- 1859-1925 -- Bibliography.*

Z8212.7 D — Dalton, John

Z8212.7.S5 1998
Smyth, A. L.
John Dalton, 1766-1844: a bibliography of works by and about him, with an annotated list of his surviving apparatus and personal effects/ A.L. Smyth. Aldershot, Hampshire, Great Britain; Manchester Literary and Philosophical Publications in association with Ashgate, [1998] xxii, 167 p.
97-032018   016.54/092   1859284388
Dalton, John, -- 1766-1844 -- Bibliography.

Z8218.7 D — Davie, Donald

Z8218.7.W75 1991
Wright, Stuart T.
Donald Davie, a checklist of his writings, 1946-1988/ compiled by Stuart Wright. New York: Greenwood Press, 1991. x, 151 p.
90-047462   016.821/914   031327701X
Davie, Donald -- Bibliography.

Z8220.9 D — Dee, John

Z8220.9.S48 1995
Sherman, William H.
John Dee: the politics of reading and writing in the English Renaissance/ William H. Sherman. Amherst: University of Massachusetts Press, c1995. xiv, 291 p.
94-020149   001/.092   0870239406
Dee, John, -- 1527-1608 -- Library. Dee, John, -- 1527-1608 -- Books and reading. Scientists -- Great Britain. Astrologers -- Great Britain.

Z8221 D — Defoe, Daniel

Z8221.L68 1991
Lovett, Robert W.
Robinson Crusoe: a bibliographical checklist of English language editions (1719-1979)/ Robert W. Lovett assisted by Charles C. Lovett. New York: Greenwood Press, 1991. xix, 303 p.
87-028952   016.823/5   0313276951
Defoe, Daniel, -- 1661?-1731. -- Robinson Crusoe -- Bibliography.

Z8221.O94 1998
Furbank, Philip Nicholas.
A critical bibliography of Daniel Defoe/ P.N. Furbank and W.R. Owens. London; Pickering & Chatto, 1998. xxxvii, 319 p.
97-047584   016.823/5   1851963898
Defoe, Daniel, -- 1661?-1731 -- Bibliography.

Z8228 D — Dewey, John

Z8228.L48 1996
Levine, Barbara,
Works about John Dewey, 1886-1995/ compiled and edited by Barbara Levine. Carbondale: Southern Illinois University Press, c1996. x, 526 p.
95-041509   016.191 20   0809320584
Dewey, John, 1859-1952 -- Bibliography.

Z8228.T45 1962
Thomas, Milton Halsey, 1903-
John Dewey: a centennial bibliography. [Chicago] University of Chicago Press [1962] xiii, 370 p.
62-012638   012
Dewey, John, -- 1859-1952 -- Bibliography.

Z8230 D — Dickens, Charles

Z8230.C45 1989
Chittick, Kathryn, 1953-
The critical reception of Charles Dickens, 1833-1841/ Kathryn Chittick. New York: Garland Pub., 1989. xvi, 277 p.
88-033644   823/.8   0824056205
Dickens, Charles, -- 1812-1870 -- Criticism and interpretation -- Bibliography. Dickens, Charles, -- 1812-1870 -- Bibliography.

Z8230.C79 1998
Cox, Don Richard.
Charles Dickens's The mystery of Edwin Drood: an annotated bibliography/ Don Richard Cox. New York: AMS Press, c1998. xxxvi, 669 p.
97-036302   823/.8   0404614973
Dickens, Charles, -- 1812-1870. -- Mystery of Edwin Drood -- Bibliography.

Z8230.D48 2000
DeVries, Duane.
General studies of Charles Dickens and his writings and collected editions of his works: an annotated bibliography/ Duane DeVries. New York: AMS Press, [2000-   ]
99-086395   016.823/8 21   040464452X
Dickens, Charles, 1812-1870 -- Bibliography. Dickens, Charles, 1812-1870 -- Criticism and interpretation

Z8230.E5 1990
Engel, Elliot, 1948-
Pickwick papers, an annotated bibliography/ Elliot Engel. New York: Garland Pub., 1990. xxxii, 345 p.
89-071396   016.823/8   0824087666
Dickens, Charles, -- 1812-1870. -- Pickwick papers -- Bibliography.

Z8230.L58 1999
Litvack, Leon.
Charles Dickens's Dombey and son: an annotated bibliography/ Leon Litvack. New York: AMS Press, c1999. xxxv, 399 p.
99-025557   016.823/8   040461499X
Dickens, Charles, -- 1812-1870. -- Dombey and son -- Bibliography.

Z8230.L68 1990
Lougy, Robert E.
Martin Chuzzlewit, an annotated bibliography/ Robert E. Lougy. New York: Garland Pub., 1990. xxx, 290 p.
89-023263   016.823/8   0824046080
Dickens, Charles, -- 1812-1870. -- Martin Chuzzlewit -- Bibliography.

Z8237 D — Donne, John

Z8237.K38 1973
Keynes, Geoffrey,
A bibliography of Dr. John Donne, by Geoffrey Keynes. 4th ed. Oxford, Clarendon Press, 1973. x, 400 p.
73-163884   016.821/3   0198181558
Donne, John, 1572-1631 -- Bibliography.

Z8237.R63 1982
Roberts, John Richard.
John Donne, an annotated bibliography of modern criticism, 1968-1978/ John R. Roberts. Columbia: University of Missouri Press, 1982. 434 p.
82-001849   821/.3 19   0826203647
Donne, John, 1572-1631 -- Bibliography.

Z8237.S85 1993
Sullivan, Ernest W.
The influence of John Donne: his uncollected seventeenth-century printed verse/ Ernest W. Sullivan, II. Columbia: University of Missouri Press, c1993. xvii, 215 p.
93-020174   016.821/3 20   0826208924
Donne, John, 1572-1631 -- Bibliography. Early printed books -- England -- 17th century -- Bibliography. England -- Imprints.

Z8237.9 D — Dostoevskii, F.M.

Z8237.9.L4 1990
Leatherbarrow, William J.
Fedor Dostoevsky: a reference guide/ W.J. Leatherbarrow. Boston, Mass.: G.K. Hall, c1990. xxxviii, 317 p.
89-037009   016.89173/3   0816189412
Dostoyevsky, Fyodor, -- 1821-1881 -- Criticism and interpretation -- Bibliography.

Z8246 D — Dürer, Albrecht

Z8246.Z8246.H88 2000
Hutchison, Jane Campbell.
Albrecht Durer: a guide to research/ Jane Campbell Hutchison. New York: Garland, 2000. x, 408 p.
00-025906   016.76/0092   0815321147
Durer, Albrecht, -- 1471-1528 -- Criticism and interpretation -- Bibliography.

Z8250.3 D — Duras, Marguerite

Z8250.3.H37 1997
Harvey, Robert, 1951-
Marguerite Duras: a bio-bibliography/ Robert Harvey and Helene Volat. Westport, Conn.: Greenwood Press, 1997. xiv, 273 p.
96-053093   016.843/912   0313288984
Duras, Marguerite -- Bibliography.

Z8250.54 D —
Durrell, Lawrence

Z8250.54.T47 1983
Thomas, Alan G.
Lawrence Durrell, an illustrated checklist/ Alan G. Thomas, James A. Brigham. Carbondale: Southern Illinois University Press, c1983. x, 198 p.
83-006782   016.828/91209 19   080931021X
Durrell, Lawrence -- Bibliography.

Z8254.74 E —
Eden, Anthony

Z8254.74.L39 1995
Lawrance, Alan.
Anthony Eden, 1897-1977: a bibliography/ Alan Lawrance and Peter Dodd. Westport, Conn.: Greenwood Press, 1995. xlvii, 190 p.
95-007480   016.94108   0313282862
Eden, Anthony, -- Earl of Avon, -- 1897- -- Bibliography.Great Britain -- Politics and government -- 20th century -- Bibliography.

Z8255.5 E —
Edwards, Jonathan

Z8255.5.L47
Lesser, M. X.
Jonathan Edwards: a reference guide/ M. X. Lesser. Boston, Mass.: G.K. Hall, c1981. lix, 421 p.
80-028540   016.2858/092/4 19   0816178372
Edwards, Jonathan, 1703-1758 -- Bibliography.

Z8255.5.L48 1994
Lesser, M. X.
Jonathan Edwards: an annotated bibliography, 1979-1993/ compiled by M.X. Lesser. Westport, Conn.: Greenwood Press, 1994. xxxi, 189 p.
94-031540   016.2858/092   031329237X
Edwards, Jonathan, 1703-1758 -- Bibliography.

Z8259 E —
Eliot, George, pseud

Z8259.B35 2002
Baker, William,
George Eliot: a bibliographical history/ William Baker & John C. Ross. New Castle, DE: Oak Knoll Press; 2002. xxxix, 676 p.
2001-055442   016.823/8 21   0712347658
Eliot, George, 1819-1880 -- Bibliography. Women and literature -- England -- Bibliography.

Z8259.P36 1990
Pangallo, Karen L.
George Eliot: a reference guide, 1972-1987/ Karen L. Pangallo. Boston, Mass.: G.K. Hall, c1990. xviii, 300 p.
89-035908   016.823/8   0816189730
Eliot, George, -- 1819-1880 -- Bibliography.

Z8260.5 E — Eliot, T.S.

Z8260.5.M3
Martin, Mildred,
A half-century of Eliot criticism; an annotated bibliography of books and articles in English, 1916-1965.   Lewisburg, Bucknell University Press [1972] 361 p.
79-168814   016.821/9/12   0838778089
Eliot, T. S. (Thomas Stearns), 1888-1965 -- Bibliography.

Z8308.34 F — Ford, Gerald

Z8308.34.G74 1994
Greene, John Robert, 1955-
Gerald R. Ford: a bibliography/ compiled by John Robert Greene. Westport, Conn.: Greenwood Press, 1994. xxxviii, 148 p.
94-005831   016.973925/092   0313281955
Ford, Gerald R., -- 1913- -- Bibliography.

Z8309.4 F — Forsyth, P.T.

Z8309.4.B46 1993
Benedetto, Robert, 1950-
P.T. Forsyth bibliography and index/ Robert Benedetto; foreword by Donald G. Miller. Westport, Conn.: Greenwood Press, 1993. xxv, 162 p.
92-046527   016.230/58/092   0313287538
Forsyth, Peter Taylor, -- 1848-1921 -- Bibliography. Forsyth, Peter Taylor, -- 1848-1921 -- Indexes.

Z8313 F —
Franklin, Benjamin

Z8313.B89 1983
Buxbaum, Melvin H.
Benjamin Franklin: a reference guide/ Melvin H. Buxbaum. Boston, Mass.: G.K. Hall, c1983-1988. 2 v.
82-012144   016.9733/092/4   0816179859
Franklin, Benjamin, -- 1706-1790 -- Bibliography.

Z8317.15 F — Friel, Brian

Z8317.15.O27 1995
O'Brien, George, 1945-
Brian Friel: a reference guide, 1962-1992/ George O'Brien. New York: G.K. Hall; c1995. xi, 136 p.
94-030903   822/.914   0816172730
Friel, Brian -- Bibliography.Ireland -- In literature -- Bibliography.

Z8318.22 F —
Fulbright, James William

Z8318.22.A97 1995
Austin, Betty.
J. William Fulbright: a bibliography/ compiled by Betty Austin. Westport, Conn.: Greenwood Press, 1995. xx, 189 p.
94-038435   016.9739/092   0313263361
Fulbright, J. William -- (James William), -- 1905- -- Bibliography.

Z8322.7 G — Gandhi, M.K.

Z8322.7.C37 1995
Carter, April.
Mahatma Gandhi: a selected bibliography/ April Carter. Westport, Conn.: Greenwood Press, 1995. viii, 169 p.
94-046929   016.95403/5/092   031328296X
Gandhi, -- Mahatma, -- 1869-1948 -- Bibliography.

Z8322.7.P36 1995
Pandiri, Ananda M.
A comprehensive, annotated bibliography on Mahatma Gandhi/ compiled by Ananda M. Pandiri; foreword by Dennis G. Dalton. Westport, Conn.: Greenwood Press, [1995-   ] v. 1
95-018659   016.95403/5/092   0313253374
Gandhi, -- Mahatma, -- 1869-1948 -- Bibliography.

Z8324.18 G —
Garfield, J.A.

Z8324.18.R87 1997
Rupp, Robert O.
James A. Garfield: a bibliography/ compiled by Robert O. Rupp. Westport, Conn.: Greenwood Press, 1997. xxvii, 185 p.
97-033146   016.9738/4/092   0313281785
Garfield, James A. -- (James Abram), -- 1831-1881 -- Bibliography.

Z8324.34 G —
Garland, Hamlin

Z8324.34.N48 1998
Newlin, Keith.
Hamlin Garland: a bibliography, with a checklist of unpublished letters/ Keith Newlin. Troy, N.Y.: Whitston Pub. Co., 1998. 231 p.
97-061173   016.813/52   0878754970
Garland, Hamlin, -- 1860-1940 -- Bibliography. Garland, Hamlin, -- 1860-1940 -- Correspondence -- Indexes. Authors, American -- Correspondence -- Indexes.

Z8328.3 G — Gauguin, Paul

Z8328.3.C54 1991
Clement, Russell T.
Paul Gauguin: a bio-bibliography/ Russell T. Clement. New York: Greenwood Press, 1991. xxii, 324 p.
91-013903   016.7/092   0313273944
Gauguin, Paul, -- 1848-1903 -- Bibliography.

Z8342.5 G —
Ginsberg, Allen

Z8342.5.M66 1996
Morgan, Bill, 1949-
The response to Allen Ginsberg, 1926-1994: a bibliography of secondary sources/ Bill Morgan; with a foreword by Allen Ginsberg. Westport, Conn.: Greenwood Press, 1996. xv, 505 p.
95-026449   811/.54   0313295360
Ginsberg, Allen, -- 1926- -- Criticism and interpretation -- Bibliography.Beat generation -- Bibliography.

Z8342.5.M67 1995
Morgan, Bill, 1949-
The works of Allen Ginsberg, 1941-1994: a descriptive bibliography/ Bill Morgan; with a foreword by Allen Ginsberg. Westport, Conn.: Greenwood Press, 1995. xix, 456 p.
94-041266 016.811/54 0313293899
Ginsberg, Allen, -- 1926- -- Bibliography.Beat generation -- Bibliography.

Z8369.253 G — Grenville, George

Z8369.253.C67 1992
Cornish, Rory T.
George Grenville, 1712-1770: a bibliography/ Rory T. Cornish. Westport, Conn.: Greenwood Press, 1992. xxxiv, 227 p.
91-035219 016.94107/092 0313282811
Grenville, George, -- 1712-1770 -- Bibliography. Grenville, George, -- 1712-1770 -- Manuscripts -- Catalogs. Manuscripts, English -- Catalogs.Great Britain -- Politics and government -- 18th century -- Sources -- Catalogs. Great Britain -- Politics and government -- 18th century -- Bibliography.

Z8374.6478 G — Guillaume, de Lorris

Z8374.6478.A73 1993
Arden, Heather, 1943-
The Roman de la rose: an annotated bibliography/ Heather M. Arden. New York: Garland, 1993. xxx, 385 p.
93-015492 841/.1 0824057996
Guillaume, -- de Lorris, -- fl. 1230. -- Roman de la Rose -- Bibliography. Jean, -- de Meun, -- d. 1305 -- Bibliography. Civilization, Medieval, in literature -- Bibliography. Love poetry, French -- History and criticism -- Bibliography. Love poetry, French -- Bibliography.

Z8386.2 H — Harding, W.G.

Z8386.2.F74 1992
Frederick, Richard G., 1947-
Warren G. Harding: a bibliography/ compiled by Richard G. Frederick. Westport, Conn.: Greenwood Press, 1992. xxv, 386 p.
92-008211 016.97391/4/092 0313281866
Harding, Warren G. -- (Warren Gamaliel), -- 1865-1923 -- Bibliography.

Z8386.5 H — Hardy, Thomas

Z8386.5.G47
Gerber, Helmut E.,
Thomas Hardy: an annotated bibliography of writings about him. Compiled and edited by Helmut E. Gerber and W. Eugene Davis. Contributors: Richard C. Carpenter [and others] De Kalb, Northern Illinois University Press [1973-] v. <1 >
72-007514 016.823/8 0875800394
Hardy, Thomas, 1840-1928 -- Bibliography.

Z8386.5.P873 2002
Purdy, Richard Little,
Thomas Hardy: a bibliographical study/ Richard Little Purdy; with an introduction and supplement by Charles P.C. Pettit. New ed. New Castle, Del.: Oak Knoll Press; viii, 387 p.
2002-511445 016.828/8/09 0712347666
Hardy, Thomas, 1840-1928 -- Bibliography. Wessex (England) -- In literature -- Bibliography.

Z8386.5.S54 1998
Sherrick, Julie, 1963-
Thomas Hardy's major novels: an annotated bibliography/ Julie Sherrick. Lanham, Md.: Scarecrow Press; 1998. xiv, 195 p.
98-003156 016.823/8 0810833824
Hardy, Thomas, -- 1840-1928 -- Fictional works -- Bibliography.Pastoral fiction, English -- Bibliography.

Z8387.97 H — Harrison, W.H.

Z8387.97.S74 1998
Stevens, Kenneth R., 1946-
William Henry Harrison: a bibliography/ compiled by Kenneth R. Stevens. Westport, Conn.: Greenwood Press, 1998. xxv, 266 p.
98-021830 016.97358/092 031328167X
Harrison, William Henry, -- 1773-1841 -- Bibliography.

Z8388.65 H — Harte, Bret

Z8388.65.S33 1995
Scharnhorst, Gary.
Bret Harte: a bibliography/ by Gary Scharnhorst. Lanham, Md.: Scarecrow Press, c1995. xiii, 252 p.
95-038260 016.813/4 0810830671
Harte, Bret, -- 1836-1902 -- Bibliography.Western stories -- Bibliography.

Z8393 H — Hawthorne, Nathaniel

Z8393.B67 1982
Boswell, Jeanetta,
Nathaniel Hawthorne and the critics: a checklist of criticism, 1900-1978/ by Jeanetta Boswell. Metuchen, N.J.: Scarecrow Press, 1982. x, 273 p.
81-009398 813/.3 19 0810814714
Hawthorne, Nathaniel, 1804-1864 -- Criticism and interpretation

Z8393.C56
Clark, C. E. Frazer.
Nathaniel Hawthorne: a descriptive bibliography/ C. E. Frazer Clark, Jr. Pittsburgh: University of Pittsburgh Press, 1978. xxi, 478 p.
76-050885 016.818/3/03 0822933438
Hawthorne, Nathaniel, 1804-1864 -- Bibliography.

Z8393.S3 1988
Scharnhorst, Gary.
Nathaniel Hawthorne: an annotated bibliography of comment and criticism before 1900/ by Gary Scharnhorst. Metuchen, N.J.: Scarecrow Press, c1988.
88-029221 016.813/3 0810821842
Hawthorne, Nathaniel, -- 1804-1864 -- Criticism and interpretation -- Bibliography.

Z8393.6 H — Heaney, Seamus

Z8393.6.D87 1996
Durkan, Michael J.
Seamus Heaney: a reference guide/ Michael J. Durkan and Rand Brandes. New York: G.K. Hall, 1996.
96-015049 821/.914 0816173893
Heaney, Seamus -- Criticism and interpretation -- Bibliography.Northern Ireland -- In literature -- Bibliography.

Z8396.3 H — Hemingway, Ernest

Z8396.3.L37 1990
Larson, Kelli A.
Ernest Hemingway: a reference guide, 1974-1989/ Kelli A. Larson. Boston, Mass.: G.K. Hall, 1990. xxv, 318 p.
90-043750 016.813/52 0816189447
Hemingway, Ernest, -- 1899-1961 -- Bibliography.

Z8396.3.W33
Wagner-Martin, Linda.
Ernest Hemingway: a reference guide/ Linda Welshimer Wagner. Boston: G. K. Hall, c1977. xix, 363 p.
76-021821 016.813/5/2 081617976X
Hemingway, Ernest, -- 1899-1961 -- Bibliography.

Z8409.6 H — Hitler, Adolf

Z8409.6.M33 1998
Madden, Paul, 1940-
Adolf Hitler and the Nazi epoch: an annotated bibliography of English-language works on the origins, nature, and structure of the Nazi state/ Paul Madden. Lanham, Md.: Scarecrow Press; 1998. xiii, 740 p.
98-041703 016.943086 0810835584
Hitler, Adolf, -- 1889-1945 -- Bibliography.National socialism -- History -- Bibliography. Racism -- Germany -- History -- 20th century -- Bibliography. National socialism and art -- Bibliography. Germany -- Politics and government -- 1933-1945 -- Bibliography. Germany -- Social conditions -- 1933-1945 -- Bibliography.

Z8414 H — Holbein, Hans, the younger

Z8414.M53 1997
Michael, Erika, 1937-
Hans Holbein the Younger: a guide to research/ Erika Michael. New York: Garland Pub., 1997. xix, 749 p.
97-019462 016.76/0092 0815303890
Holbein, Hans, -- 1497-1543 -- Bibliography.

Z8423.3 H — Hughes, Langston

Z8423.3.M53 1990
Mikolyzk, Thomas A.
Langston Hughes: a bio-bibliography/ compiled by Thomas A. Mikolyzk. New York: Greenwood Press, 1990. xvii, 295 p.
90-003613   016.818/5209   0313268959
Hughes, Langston, -- 1902-1967 -- Bibliography.Afro-Americans -- Bibliography.

Z8428.66 H — Hurston, Z.N.

Z8428.66.D38 1997
Davis, Rose Parkman, 1947-
Zora Neale Hurston: an annotated bibliography and reference guide/ compiled by Rose Parkman Davis. Westport, Conn.: Greenwood Press, 1997. xii, 210 p.
97-037459   016.813/52   0313303878
Hurston, Zora Neale -- Bibliography.Women and literature -- Southern States -- Bibliography. Afro-Americans in literature -- Bibliography. Folklore in literature -- Bibliography.

Z8442.65 I — Ivanov, V.I.

Z8442.65.D38 1996
Davidson, Pamela.
Viacheslav Ivanov: a reference guide/ Pamela Davidson. New York: G.K. Hall, c1996. xlii, 382 p.
95-041018   016.89171/3   0816118256
Ivanov, V. I. -- (Viacheslav Ivanovich), -- 1866-1949 -- Bibliography.

Z8443 J — Jackson, Andrew

Z8443.R45 1991
Remini, Robert Vincent, 1921-
Andrew Jackson: a bibliography/ Robert V. Remini and Robert O. Rupp. Westport: Meckler, c1991. xxxi, 314 p.
90-041976   016.9735/6   0887361218
Jackson, Andrew, -- 1767-1845 -- Bibliography.United States -- Politics and government -- 1829-1837 -- Bibliography. United States -- History -- War of 1812 -- Bibliography.

Z8447 J — James, Henry

Z8447.B73 1987
Bradbury, Nicola.
An annotated critical bibliography of Henry James/ Nicola Bradbury. New York: St. Martin's Press, 1987. viii, 142 p.
86-027971   016.813/4 19   0312004818
James, Henry, 1843-1916 -- Bibliography.

Z8447.B82 1983
Budd, John,
Henry James: a bibliography of criticism, 1975-1981/ compiled by John Budd. Westport, Conn.: Greenwood Press, 1983. xx, 190 p.
82-024163   016.813/4 19   0313235155
James, Henry, 1843-1916 -- Bibliography.

Z8447.F85 1991
Funston, Judith E.
Henry James: a reference guide, 1975-1987/ Judith E. Funston. Boston, Mass.: G.K. Hall, 1991. xx, 571 p.
90-048856   016.813/4 20   0816189536
James, Henry, 1843-1916 -- Bibliography.

Z8447.M32
McColgan, Kristin Pruitt.
Henry James, 1917-1959: a reference guide/ Kristin Pruitt McColgan. Boston: G. K. Hall, c1979. 389 p.
78-027118   016.813/4   0816178518
James, Henry, 1843-1916 -- Bibliography.

Z8447.S38
Scura, Dorothy McInnis.
Henry James, 1960-1974: a reference guide/ Dorothy McInnis Scura. Boston: G. K. Hall, c1979. xxvi, 490 p.
78-027143   813/.4   081617850X
James, Henry, 1843-1916 -- Bibliography.

Z8447.T39 1982
Taylor, Linda J.
Henry James, 1866-1916, a reference guide/ Linda J. Taylor. Boston, Mass.: G.K. Hall, c1982. xxvi, 533 p.
82-000979   016.813/4 19   0816178747
James, Henry, 1843-1916 -- Bibliography.

Z8451 J — Jeanne d'Arc, Saint

Z8451.M37 1990
Margolis, Nadia, 1949-
Joan of Arc in history, literature, and film: a select, annotated bibliography/ Nadia Margolis. New York: Garland Pub., 1990. xvii, 406 p.
90-039611   016.944/026092   0824046382
Joan, -- of Arc, Saint, -- 1412-1431 -- Bibliography. Joan, -- of Arc, Saint, -- 1412-1431 -- Filmography.

Z8455 J — Jesus Christ

Z8455.H84 1988
Hultgren, Arland J.
New Testament Christology: a critical assessment and annotated bibliography/ compiled by Arland J. Hultgren; G.E. Gorman, advisory editor. New York: Greenwood Press, 1988. xiv, 485 p.
88-024645   016.232/09/015   0313251886
Jesus Christ -- History of doctrines -- Early church, ca. 30-600 -- Bibliography. Jesus Christ -- Person and offices -- Biblical teaching -- Bibliography.

Z8455.M55 1999
Mills, Watson E.
Bibliographies on the life and teachings of Jesus/ compiled by Watson E. Mills. Lewiston, N.Y.: Mellen Biblical Press, c1999-c2000 v. 1-2
99-036087   016.2329   077342458X
Jesus Christ -- Biography -- Bibliography. Jesus Christ -- Teachings -- Bibliography.

Z8455.567 J — Johnson, Andrew

Z8455.567.M33 1992
McCaslin, Richard B.
Andrew Johnson: a bibliography/ compiled by Richard B. McCaslin. Westport, Conn.: Greenwood Press, 1992. xxxii, 314 p.
92-031761   016.9735/6   0313281750
Johnson, Andrew, -- 1808-1875 -- Bibliography.

Z8455.8 J — Johnson, Samuel, 1709-1784

Z8455.8.F54 2000
Fleeman, J. D.
A bibliography of the works of Samuel Johnson: treating his published works from the beginnings to 1984/ compiled by J.D. Fleeman; prepared for publication by James McLaverty. New York: Oxford University Press, [2000-   ] v 1-2
98-051336   016.828/609   0198122691
Johnson, Samuel, -- 1709-1784 -- Bibliography.

Z8455.8.L96 2000
Lynch, Jack
A bibliography of Johnsonian studies, 1986-1998/ Jack Lynch; with a preface by Paul J. Korshin. New York: AMS Press, c2000. xvi, 147 p.
99-055818   016.828/609   0404635334
Johnson, Samuel, -- 1709-1784 -- Bibliography.

Z8456.6 J — Jonson, Ben

Z8456.6.E83 2000
Evans, Robert C.
Ben Jonson's major plays: summaries of modern monographs/ Robert C. Evans, compiler and general editor; Kimberly Barron ... [et al.], editorial team. West Cornwall, CT: Locust Hill Press, 2000. xxvii, 232 p.
00-033041   016.822/3   0933951914
Jonson, Ben, -- 1573?-1637 -- Bibliography. Jonson, Ben, -- 1573?-1637 -- Dramatic works -- Abstracts.

Z8460.875 K — Kavanagh, Patrick

Z8460.875.A55 1996
Allison, Jonathan, 1958-
Patrick Kavanagh: a reference guide/ Jonathan Allison. New York: G.K. Hall; c1996. xxviii, 218 p.
96-029255   016.821/914   0816172862
Kavanagh, Patrick, -- 1904-1967 -- Bibliography.Ireland in literature -- Bibliography.

Z8462.8 K — Kennedy, J.F.

Z8462.8.G54 1995
Giglio, James N., 1939-
John F. Kennedy: a bibliography/ compiled by James N. Giglio. Westport, Conn.: Greenwood Press, 1995. xxviii, 425 p.
95-015450 016.973922 0313281920
Kennedy, John F. -- (John Fitzgerald), -- 1917-1963 -- Bibliography.

Z8464.44 K — King, M.L.

Z8464.44.P9 1986
Pyatt, Sherman E.
Martin Luther King, Jr.: an annotated bibliography/ compiled by Sherman E. Pyatt. New York: Greenwood Press, 1986. xii, 154 p. ;
86-007593 016.3234/092/4 19 0313246351
King, Martin Luther, Jr., 1929-1968 -- Bibliography.

Z8467.523 K — Kosinski, J.N.

Z8467.523.C76 1991
Cronin, Gloria L., 1947-
Jerzy Kosinski: an annotated bibliography/ Gloria L. Cronin and Blaine H. Hall. New York: Greenwood Press, 1991. xviii, 104 p.
91-021555 016.813/54 0313274428
Kosinski, Jerzy N., -- 1933- -- Bibliography.

Z8490.5 L — Lawrence, D.H.

Z8490.5.G47 1989
Gertzman, Jay A.
A descriptive bibliography of Lady Chatterley's lover: with essays toward a publishing history of the novel/ Jay A. Gertzman. New York: Greenwood Press, 1989. xiii, 296 p.
89-017181 823/.912 0313261253
Lawrence, D. H. -- (David Herbert), -- 1885-1930. -- Lady Chatterley's lover -- Bibliography. Lawrence, D. H. -- (David Herbert), -- 1885-1930. -- Lady Chatterley's lover -- Criticism, Textual. Erotic stories, English -- Bibliography. Erotic stories -- Publishing -- History.

Z8490.5.P67 1996
Poplawski, Paul.
D.H. Lawrence: a reference companion/ Paul Poplawski; with a biography by John Worthen. Westport, Conn.: Greenwood Press, 1996. xxi, 714 p.
95-038654 016.823/912 031328637X
Lawrence, D. H. -- (David Herbert), -- 1885-1930 -- Bibliography.

Z8490.5.R6 1982
Roberts, Warren, 1916-
A bibliography of D.H. Lawrence/ Warren Roberts and Paul Poplawski. Cambridge; Cambridge University Press, 2001. xxiv, 847 p.
00-036298 016.823/912 0521391822
Lawrence, D. H. -- (David Herbert), -- 1885-1930 -- Bibliography.

Z8491.5 L — Lawrence, T.E.

Z8491.5.O27 2000
O'Brien, Philip M., 1940-
T.E. Lawrence--a bibliography/ Philip M. O'Brien. New Castle, Del.: Oak Knoll Press, 2000. x, 894 p.
00-057467 016.9404/15/092 1584560312
Lawrence, T. E. -- (Thomas Edward), -- 1888-1935 -- Bibliography.Soldiers' writings, English -- Bibliography.

Z8492.7 L — Le Fanu, J.S.

Z8492.7.C73 1995
Crawford, Gary William.
J. Sheridan Le Fanu: a bio-bibliography/ Gary William Crawford. Westport, Conn.: Greenwood Press, 1995. ix, 155 p.
94-038419 016.823/8 0313285152
Le Fanu, Joseph Sheridan, -- 1814-1873 -- Bibliography.Detective and mystery stories, English -- Bibliography. Ghost stories, English -- Bibliography.

Z8505 L — Lincoln, Abraham

Z8505.A6
Angle, Paul M. 1900-1975.
A shelf of Lincoln books; a critical, selective bibliography of Lincolniana, by Paul M. Angle. New Brunswick, Rutgers University Press, in association with the Abraham Lincoln Association of Springfield, Ill., 1946. xvii, 142 p.
46-025256 012
Lincoln, Abraham, -- 1809-1865 -- Bibliography.

Z8511.8 L — Lispector, Clarice

Z8511.8.C53 1993
Clarice Lispector: a bio-bibliography/ edited by Diane E. Marting. Westport, Conn.: Greenwood Press, 1993. xxxvi, 327 p.
93-028537 016.8693 0313278032
Lispector, Clarice -- Bibliography.

Z8534 M — Machiavelli, Niccolò

Z8534.R83 1990
Ruffo-Fiore, Silvia.
Niccolo Machiavelli: an annotated bibliography of modern criticism and scholarship/ compiled by Silvia Ruffo Fiore. New York: Greenwood Press, 1990. xiv, 810 p.
89-025602 016.32/001/1092 0313252386
Machiavelli, Niccolo, -- 1469-1527 -- Bibliography.

Z8545.5 M — Malory, Sir Thomas

Z8545.5.G35 1990
Gaines, Barry, 1942-
Sir Thomas Malory: an anecdotal bibliography of editions, 1485-1985/ Barry Gaines. New York: AMS Press, c1990. xiv, 172 p.
89-018429 016.823/2 040461440X
Malory, Thomas, -- Sir, -- 15th cent. -- Morte d'Arthur -- Bibliography.Knights and knighthood in literature -- Bibliography. Kings and rulers in literature -- Bibliography. Arthurian romances -- Bibliography.

Z8545.5.L53
Life, Page West.
Sir Thomas Malory and the Morte Darthur: a survey of scholarship and annotated bibliography/ Page West Life. Charlottesville: Published for the Bibliographical Society of the xiii, 297 p.
80-016180 016.823/2 081390868X
Malory, Thomas, Sir, 15th cent. Morte d'Arthur -- Bibliography. Malory, Thomas, Sir, 15th cent. -- Criticism and interpretation Knights and knighthood in literature -- Bibliography. Kings and rulers in literature -- Bibliography. Arthurian romances -- Bibliography.

Z8545.8 M — Malraux, André

Z8545.8.R66 1994
Romeiser, John Beals, 1948-
Andre Malraux: a reference guide, 1940-1990/ John B. Romeiser. New York: G.K. Hall & Co.; c1994. xi, 370 p.
93-046322 016.843/912 0816190712
Malraux, Andre, -- 1901-1976 -- Bibliography.

Z8547.41 M — Mann, Thomas

Z8547.41.J618
Jonas, Klaus W.
Die Thomas-Mann-Literatur. Bearb. von Klaus W. Jonas in Zusammenarbeit mit dem Thomas-Mann-Archiv Zürich. [Berlin] E. Schmidt [c1972-c1997] 3 v.
72-359004 016.833/912 19 3465028473
Mann, Thomas, 1875-1955 -- Bibliography.

Z8548.3 M — Mao, T^se-tung

Z8548.3.L38 1991
Lawrance, Alan.
Mao Zedong: a bibliography/ Alan Lawrance. New York: Greenwood Press, 1991. xxxii, 197 p.
91-008424 016.95105 0313282226
Mao, Tse-tung, -- 1893-1976 -- Bibliography.

Z8549.8 M —
March, William

Z8549.8.S55 1988
Simmonds, Roy S.
William March: an annotated checklist/ compiled by Roy S. Simmonds. Tuscaloosa: University of Alabama Press, c1988. xxiii, 191 p.
86-030786   016.813/52   0817303618
March, William, -- 1893-1954 -- Bibliography.

Z8550.4 M —
Marlowe, Christopher

Z8550.4.F75
Friedenreich, Kenneth,
Christopher Marlowe, an annotated bibliography of criticism since 1950 / Kenneth Friedenreich; foreword by Richard Levin. Metuchen, N.J.: Scarecrow Press, 1979. xiii, 150 p.
79-017646   016.822/3   0810812398
Marlowe,   Christopher,   1564-1593   -- Bibliography.

Z8554.32 M — Matisse

Z8554.32.B63 1996
Bock-Weiss, Catherine.
Henri Matisse: a guide to research/ Catherine C. Bock-Weiss. New York: Garland Pub., 1996. cii, 690 p.
96-019440   016.7/092   0815300867
Matisse, Henri, -- 1869-1954 -- Criticism and interpretation -- Bibliography.

Z8561.18 M —
McKinley, William

Z8561.18.G68 1988
Gould, Lewis L.
William McKinley: a bibliography/ Lewis L. Gould, Craig H. Roell. Westport, CT: Meckler, c1988. xvi, 238 p.
88-015531   016.9738/8/0924   0887361382
McKinley,   William,   --   1843-1901   -- Bibliography.United   States   --   Politics   and government -- 1897-1901 -- Bibliography.

Z8562.58 M —
Melville, Herman

Z8562.58.B47 1987
Bercaw, Mary K.
Melville's sources/ Mary K. Bercaw. Evanston, Ill.: Northwestern University Press, 1987. viii, 213 p.
87-005670   016.813/3 19   0810107341
Melville, Herman, 1819-1891 -- Sources -- Bibliography. Melville, Herman, 1819-1891 -- Bibliography.

Z8562.58.B67
Boswell, Jeanetta,
Herman Melville and the critics: a checklist of criticism, 1900-1978 / by Jeanetta Boswell. Metuchen, N.J.: Scarecrow Press, 1981. xi, 247 p.
80-025959   016.813/3 19   0810813858
Melville, Herman, 1819-1891 -- Bibliography.

Z8562.58.H394 1991
Hayes, Kevin J.
Checklist of Melville reviews/ revised by Kevin J. Hayes and Hershel Parker from the 1975 Checklist by Steven Mailloux and Hershel Parker. Evanston, Ill.: Northwestern University Press, 1991. xiv, 157 p.
91-040709   813/.3   0810110288
Melville,   Herman,   --   1819-1891   -- Bibliography.

Z8562.58.H52 1987
Higgins, Brian,
Herman Melville: a reference guide, 1931-1960/ Brian Higgins. Boston, Mass.: G.K. Hall, c1987. xvi, 531 p.
87-019630   016.813/3 19   0816186715
Melville, Herman, 1819-1891 -- Bibliography.

Z8562.58.H53
Higgins, Brian,
Herman Melville, an annotated bibliography/ Brian Higgins. Boston: G. K. Hall, [c1979-   ]
78-023446   016.813/3   0816178437
Melville, Herman, 1819-1891 -- Bibliography.

Z8562.58.R53
Ricks, Beatrice.
Herman Melville: a reference bibliography, 1900-1972, with selected nineteenth-century materials. Compiled by Beatrice Ricks [and] Joseph D. Adams. Boston, G. K. Hall, 1973. xxii, 532 p.
72-014197   016.813/3   0816110360
Melville, Herman, 1819-1891 -- Bibliography.

Z8563.5 M —
Mencken, H.L.

Z8563.5.S37 1998
Schrader, Richard J.
H.L. Mencken: a descriptive bibliography/ Richard J. Schrader;   with the assistance of George H. Thompson and Jack R. Sanders. Pittsburgh: University of Pittsburgh Press, c1998. xxv, 628 p.
97-040050   016.818/5209 21   0822940507
Mencken, H. L. (Henry Louis), 1880-1956 -- Bibliography.

Z8572.4 M —
Michener, James A.

Z8572.4.G76 1996
Groseclose, David A., 1942-
James A. Michener: a bibliography/ David A. Groseclose; foreword by James A. Michener. Austin, Tex.: State House Press, 1996. xviii, 315 p.
95-013090   016.813/54   1880510235
Michener, James A. -- (James Albert), -- 1907- -- Bibliography.

Z8572.4.R63 1995
Roberts, F. X., 1932-
James A. Michener: a checklist of his works, with a selected, annotated bibliography/ compiled by F.X. Roberts and C.D. Rhine. Westport, Conn.: Greenwood Press, 1995. xxii, 125 p.
94-042118   016.813/54   0313294534
Michener, James A. -- (James Albert), -- 1907- -- Bibliography.

Z8578 M — Milton, John

Z8578.H82 1996
Huckabay, Calvin.
John Milton: an annotated bibliography, 1968-1988/ compiled by Calvin Huckabay; edited by Paul J. Klemp. Pittsburgh, Pa.: Duquesne University Press, c1996. xxiv, 535 p.
95-049712   016.821/4   0820702722
Milton, John, -- 1608-1674 -- Bibliography.

Z8578.J68 1994
Jones, Edward, 1950-
Milton's sonnets: an annotated bibliography, 1900-1992/ Edward Jones. Binghamton, N.Y.: Medieval & Renaissance Texts & Studies, 1994. xii, 147 p.
94-020238   821/.4   0866981276
Milton, John, -- 1608-1674. -- Sonnets -- Bibliography.Sonnets, English -- History and criticism -- Bibliography.

Z8578.K59 1996
Klemp, P. J.
Paradise lost: an annotated bibliography/ by P.J. Klemp. Lanham, MD: The Scarecrow Press, c1996. xii, 249 p.
96-000671   016.821/4   081083152X
Milton, John, -- 1608-1674. -- Paradise lost -- Bibliography.Fall of man in literature -- Bibliography. Epic poetry, English -- Bibliography.

Z8578.S52 1984
Shawcross, John T.
Milton: a bibliography for the years 1624-1700/ compiled by John T. Shawcross. Binghamton, N.Y.: Medieval & Renaissance Texts & Studies, 1984. xiv, 452 p.
84-000653   016.821/4 19   0866980644
Milton, John, 1608-1674 -- Bibliography.

Z8578.S52 1984 Suppl
Shawcross, John T.
Milton: corrigenda/ compiled by John T. Shawcross. Binghamton, N.Y.: Medieval & Renaissance Texts & Studies, 1990. 30 p.
89-014584   016.821/4 20   0866980814
Milton, John, 1608-1674 -- Bibliography.

Z8587.8 M —
Monroe, James

Z8587.8.A46 1991
Ammon, Harry, 1917-
James Monroe: a bibliography/ Harry Ammon. Westport: Meckler, c1991. xxxi, 125 p.
90-020397   016.9735/4/092   0887361196
Monroe, James, -- 1758-1831 -- Bibliography.

Z8591.3 M —
Montgomery of Alamein, B.L.M.

Z8591.3.B39 1999
Baxter, Colin F., 1942-
Field Marshal Bernard Law Montgomery, 1887-1976: a selected bibliography/ compiled by Colin F. Baxter. Westport, Conn.: Greenwood Press, 1999. xii, 165 p.
99-033434   016.355/0092   0313291195
Montgomery of Alamein, Bernard Law Montgomery, -- Viscount, -- 1887-1976 -- Bibliography.Great Britain -- History, Military -- 20th century -- Bibliography.

Z8592.6 M —
Moore, George

Z8592.6.L36 1987
Langenfeld, Robert.
George Moore: an annotated secondary bibliography of writings about him/ Robert Langenfeld. New York: AMS Press, c1987. xii, 531 p.
84-048436   016.823/8   040461583X
Moore, George, -- 1852-1933 -- Bibliography.

Z8592.8 M —
More, Sir Thomas, Saint

Z8592.8.B67 1994
Boswell, Jackson Campbell.
Sir Thomas More in the English Renaissance: an annotated catalogue/ Jackson Campbell Boswell; introduction by Anne Lake Prescott. Binghampton, N.Y.: Medieval & Renaissance Texts & Studies, 1994. xxxiv, 362 p.
91-009356   016.94205/2/092 20   0866980946
More, Thomas, Sir, Saint, 1478-1535 -- Bibliography.

Z8592.8.G47 1998
Geritz, Albert J.
Thomas More: an annotated bibliography of criticism, 1935-1997/ compiled by Albert J. Geritz. Westport, Conn.: Greenwood Press, 1998. xvi, 428 p.
98-021331   942.05/2/092   0313293910
More, Thomas, -- Sir, Saint, -- 1478-1535 -- Bibliography.

Z8610.37 N — Naipaul, V.S. (Viviadha Surajprasad)

Z8610.37.J37 1989
Jarvis, Kelvin.
V. S. Naipaul: a selective bibliography with annotations, 1957-1987/ by Kelvin Jarvis. Metuchen, N.J.: Scarecrow Press, 1989. xvii, 205 p.
89-010057   016.823/914   0810821907
Naipaul, V. S. -- (Vidiadhar Surajprasad), -- 1932- -- Bibliography.

Z8614.74 N — Nasser, G.A.

Z8614.74.M54 1991
Mikdadi, F. H.
Gamal Abdel Nasser: a bibliography/ Faysal Mikdadi. New York: Greenwood Press, 1991. 148 p.
91-021168   016.96205/3/092   031328119X
Nasser, Gamal Abdel, -- 1918-1970 -- Bibliography.

Z8628.85 N —
Nietsche, F.W.

Z8628.85.S33 1995
Schaberg, William H.
The Nietzsche canon: a publication history and bibliography/ William H. Schaberg. Chicago: University of Chicago Press, 1995. xvi, 281 p.
95-016815   016.193   0226735753
Nietzsche, Friedrich Wilhelm, -- 1844-1900 -- Bibliography. Nietzsche, Friedrich Wilhelm, -- 1844-1900 -- Criticism, Textual.

Z8629.4 N — Nixon, R.M.

Z8629.4.C37 1988
Casper, Dale E.
Richard M. Nixon: a bibliographic exploration/ Dale E. Casper. New York: Garland Pub., 1988. ix, 221 p.
87-028064   973.924/092/4   0824084780
Nixon, Richard M. -- (Richard Milhous), -- 1913- -- Bibliography.United States -- Politics and government -- 1969-1974 -- Bibliography.

Z8641.13 O —
Odets, Clifford

Z8641.13.C66 1990
Cooperman, Robert.
Clifford Odets: an annotated bibliography, 1935-1989/ Robert Cooperman. Westport: Meckler, c1990. xiii, 147 p.
88-027299   016.812/52   0887363261
Odets, Clifford, -- 1906-1963 -- Bibliography.

Z8644.5 O — O'Neill, E.G.

Z8644.5.S63 2001
Smith, Madeline.
Eugene O'Neill: an annotated international bibliography, 1973 through 1999/ by Madeline C. Smith and Richard Eaton. Jefferson, N.C.: McFarland, c2001. vi, 242 p.
00-054806   016.812/52   0786410361
O'Neill, Eugene, -- 1888-1953 -- Bibliography.

Z8648.43 O — Oud, J.J.P.

Z8648.43.L36 1999
Langmead, Donald.
J.J.P. Oud and the international style: a bio-bibliography/ Donald Langmead. Westport, Conn.: Greenwood Press, 1999. xii, 261 p.
98-041648   720.92   031330100X
Oud, J. J. P. -- (Jacobus Johannes Pieter), -- 1890-1963 -- Bibliography. Oud, J. J. P. -- (Jacobus Johannes Pieter), -- 1890-1963 -- Library. International style (Architecture) -- Bibliography.

Z8662.35 P —
Pasternak, B.L.

Z8662.35.S46 1994
Sendich, Munir.
Boris Pasternak: a reference guide/ Munir Sendich. New York: G.K. Hall; c1994. xxi, 376 p.
93-027469   016.89171/42   0816189927
Pasternak, Boris Leonidovich, -- 1890-1960 -- Bibliography.

Z8667.8 P —
Peel, Robert, Sir

Z8667.8.C69 1996
Cowie, Leonard W.
Sir Robert Peel, 1788-1850: a bibliography/ Leonard W. Cowie. Westport, Conn.: Greenwood Press, 1996. vi, 142 p.
95-041985   016.94107/3/092   031329447X
Peel, Robert, -- Sir, -- 1788-1850 -- Bibliography.Great Britain -- Politics and government -- 19th century -- Bibliography.

Z8685.6 P — Piaget, Jean

Z8685.6.M34 1988
McLaughlin, Judith A., 1947-
Bibliography of the works of Jean Piaget in the social sciences/ compiled by Judith A. McLaughlin. Lanham, MD: University Press of America, c1988. viii, 148 p.
87-026136   016.3   0819167304
Piaget, Jean, -- 1896- -- Bibliography.Child psychology -- Bibliography. Social sciences -- Bibliography.

Z8693.7 P —
Pisan, Christine de

Z8693.7.Y45 1989
Yenal, Edith.
Christine de Pizan: a bibliography/ by Edith Yenal. Metuchen, N.J.: Scarecrow Press, 1989. xxiii, 185 p.
89-010718   016.841/2   0810822482
Christine, -- de Pisan, -- ca. 1364-ca. 1431 -- Bibliography.

Z8694.5 P — Pitt, William

Z8694.5.H37 1989
Harvey, A. D.
William Pitt the younger, 1759-1806: a bibliography/ A.D. Harvey. Westport, CT: Meckler, c1989. vi, 80 p.
89-002791 016.94107/3/0924 0887363148
Pitt, William, -- 1759-1806 -- Bibliography.Great Britain -- Politics and government -- 1760-1820 -- Bibliography.

Z8699 P — Poe, E.A.

Z8699.H94
Hyneman, Esther F.
Edgar Allan Poe: an annotated bibliography of books and articles in English, 1827-1973 [by] Esther F. Hyneman. Boston, G. K. Hall, 1974. xv, 335 p.
74-016359 016.818/3/09 0816111049
Poe, Edgar Allan, 1809-1849 -- Bibliography. Fantasy literature, American -- Bibliography.

Z8699.P48
Phillips, Leona Rasmussen.
Edgar Allan Poe: an annotated bibliography/ by Leona Rasmussen Phillips. New York: Gordon Press, 1978. 139 p.
78-006783 016.818/3/09 0849013925
Poe, Edgar Allan, 1809-1849 -- Bibliography. Fantasy literature, American -- Bibliography.

Z8699.P64 1989
Pollin, Burton Ralph.
Images of Poe's works: a comprehensive descriptive catalogue of illustrations/ compiled by Burton R. Pollin. New York: Greenwood Press, 1989. xvii, 411 p.
89-017182 016.818/309 0313265828
Poe, Edgar Allan, -- 1809-1849 -- Bibliography. Poe, Edgar Allan, -- 1809-1849 -- Film and video adaptations -- Catalogs. American fiction -- Film and video adaptations -- Catalogs.

Z8718 P — Pushkin, A.S.

Z8718.L44 1999
Leighton, Lauren G.
A bibliography of Alexander Pushkin in English: studies and translations/ compiled by Lauren G. Leighton. Lewiston: Edwin Mellen Press, c1999. xiii, 310 p.
98-053357 016.89171/3 0773481702
Pushkin, Aleksandr Sergeevich, -- 1799-1837 -- Translations into English -- Bibliography. Pushkin, Aleksandr Sergeevich, -- 1799-1837 -- Criticism and interpretation -- Bibliography.

Z8722.3 P — Pythagoras

Z8722.3.N38 1990
Navia, Luis E.
Pythagoras: an annotated bibliography/ Luis E. Navia. New York: Garland Pub., 1990. xviii, 381 p.
90-033296 016.182/2 0824043804
Pythagoras -- Bibliography.

Z8730 R — Rabelais, François

Z8730.B79 1994
Braunrot, Bruno.
Francois Rabelais: a reference guide, 1950-1990/ Bruno Braunrot. New York: G.K. Hall; c1994. xiii, 438 p.
93-048314 016.843/3 0816190798
Rabelais, Francois, -- ca. 1490-1553? -- Bibliography.

Z8730.335 R — Radcliffe, Ann

Z8730.335.R64 1996
Rogers, Deborah D., 1953-
Ann Radcliffe: a bio-bibliography/ Deborah D. Rogers. Westport, Conn.: Greenwood Press, 1996. xii, 209 p.
95-041982 016.823/6 0313283796
Radcliffe, Ann Ward, -- 1764-1823 -- Bibliography.Gothic revival (Literature) -- Great Britain -- Bibliography. Women and literature -- England -- Bibliography. Horror tales, English -- Bibliography.

Z8748.37 R — Robinson, E.A.

Z8748.37.B67 1988
Boswell, Jeanetta,
Edwin Arlington Robinson and the critics: a bibliography of secondary sources with selective annotations/ by Jeanetta Boswell. Metuchen, N.J.: Scarecrow Press, 1988. viii, 285 p.
87-032324 811/.52 19 0810820765
Robinson, Edwin Arlington, 1869-1935 -- Criticism and interpretation

Z8748.37.J68
Joyner, Nancy Carol.
Edwin Arlington Robinson: a reference guide/ Nancy Carol Joyner. Boston: G. K. Hall, c1978. xv, 223 p.
77-025280 016.811/5/2 0816178070
Robinson, Edwin Arlington, 1869-1935 -- Bibliography.

Z8748.37.L76
Lippincott, Lillian.
A bibliography of the writings and criticisms of Edwin Arlington Robinson, by Lillian Lippincott. Boston, The F.W. Faxon company [c1937] 86 p.
37-004427 012
Robinson, Edwin Arlington, -- 1869-1935 -- Bibliography.

Z8748.37.W455
White, William,
Edwin Arlington Robinson: a supplementary bibliography, by William White. [1st ed. Kent, Ohio] Kent State University Press [1971] 168 p.
70-126806 016.811/5/2 0873381076
Robinson, Edwin Arlington, 1869-1935 -- Bibliography.

Z8757.27 R — Roosevelt, Eleanor

Z8757.27.E33 1994
Edens, John A.
Eleanor Roosevelt: a comprehensive bibliography/ compiled by John A. Edens. Westport, Conn.: Greenwood Press, 1994. xvii, 506 p.
94-025906 016.973917/092 0313260508
Roosevelt, Eleanor, -- 1884-1962 -- Bibliography.

Z8763.67 R — Rowse, A.L.

Z8763.67.C38 2000
Cauveren, Sydney, 1947-
A.L. Rowse: a bibliophile's extensive bibliography/ Sydney Cauveren. Lanham, Md.: Scarecrow Press, 2000. xxxvi, 325 p.
99-015195 016.828/91209 0810836416
Rowse, A. L. -- (Alfred Leslie), -- 1903- -- Bibliography. Shakespeare, William, -- 1564-1616 -- Bibliography. English literature -- History and criticism -- Bibliography.Great Britain -- History -- Tudors, 1485-1603 -- Bibliography.

Z8764.8 R — Rush, Benjamin

Z8764.8.F69 1996
Fox, Claire G.
Benjamin Rush, M.D.: a bibliographic guide/ compiled by Claire G. Fox, Gordon L. Miller, and Jacquelyn C. Miller; foreword by Thomas A. Horrocks. Westport, Conn.: Greenwood Press, 1996. xxxvi, 216 p.
95-051766 016.973 0313298238
Rush, Benjamin, -- 1746-1813 -- Bibliography.

Z8784.43 S — Sarton, May

Z8784.43.B58
Blouin, Lenora P.
May Sarton: a bibliography/ Lenora P. Blouin. Lanham, Md.: Scarecrow Press, 2000. xxxv, 619 p.
99-087233 016.811/52 0810836874
Sarton, May, -- 1912- -- Bibliography.Women and literature -- United States -- Bibliography.

Z8802 S — Scott, Sir Walter

Z8802.R82
Rubenstein, Jill.
Sir Walter Scott: a reference guide/ Jill Rubenstein. Boston: G. K. Hall, c1978. xxiii, 344 p.
77-026785 016.828/7/09 0816178682
Scott, Walter, Sir, 1771-1832 -- Bibliography.

Z8802.T63 1998
Todd, William B.
Sir Walter Scott: a bibliographical history, 1796-1832/ William B. Todd and Ann Bowden. 1st ed. New Castle, DE: Oak Knoll Press, c1998. xx, 1071 p.
98-026869 016.828/709 21 1884718647
Scott, Walter, Sir, 1771-1832 -- Bibliography. Scotland -- In literature -- Bibliography.

Z8809.6 S — Shaffer, Peter

Z8809.6.T56 1991
Thomas, Eberle.
Peter Shaffer: an annotated bibliography/ Eberle Thomas. New York: Garland, 1991. xxviii, 270 p.
90-014052   016.822/914   0824076451
Shaffer, Peter, -- 1926- -- Bibliography.

Z8811 S — Shakespeare, William — General

Z8811.B44 1995
Bergeron, David Moore.
Shakespeare: a study and research guide/ David M. Bergeron & Geraldo U. de Sousa. Lawrence: University Press of Kansas, c1995. viii, 235 p.
94-037236   016.8223/3   0700606920
Shakespeare, William, -- 1564-1616 -- Bibliography.

Z8811.C53 1993
Champion, Larry S.
The essential Shakespeare: an annotated bibliography of major modern studies/ Larry S. Champion. New York: G.K. Hall; c1993. xviii, 568 p.
92-039078   016.8223/3   081617332X
Shakespeare, William, -- 1564-1616 -- Bibliography. Shakespeare, William, -- 1564-1616 -- Criticism and interpretation -- History -- 20th century.

Z8811.H67
Howard-Hill, T. H.
Shakespearian bibliography and textual criticism: a bibliography/ T.H. Howard-Hill. Signal Mountain, TN: Summertown, 2000.
00-027658   016.8223/3   189300905X
Shakespeare, William, -- 1564-1616 -- Bibliography of bibliographies. Shakespeare, William, -- 1564-1616 -- Criticism, Textual -- Bibliography. Shakespeare, William, -- 1564-1616 -- Bibliography.

Z8811.R68 1992
Rosenblum, Joseph.
Shakespeare: an annotated bibliography/ Joseph Rosenblum. Pasadena, Calif.: Salem Press, c1992. xi, 307 p.
92-004863   016.8223/3   0893566764
Shakespeare, William, -- 1564-1616 -- Bibliography.

Z8811.S5 1990
Shakespeare: a bibliographical guide/ edited by Stanley Wells. Oxford: Clarendon Press; 1990. vi, 431 p.
89-072129   016.8223/3   0198710364
Shakespeare, William, -- 1564-1616 -- Bibliography of bibliographies.

Z8811.S54 2003
Shakespeare: life, language, and linguistics, textual studies, and the canon: an annotated bibliography of Shakespeare studies, 1623-2000/ Michael Warren, editor. Fairview, NC: Pegasus Press, 2003.
2003-002367   016.8223/3 21   1889818348
Shakespeare, William, 1564-1616 -- Bibliography. Shakespeare, William, 1564-1616 -- Language -- Bibliography. Shakespeare, William, 1564-1616 -- Authorship -- Bibliography. Shakespeare, William, 1564-1616 -- Criticism, Textual -- Bibliography. Shakespeare, William, 1564-1616 -- Biography -- Sources -- Bibliography. Dramatists, English -- Early modern, 1500-1700 -- Biography -- Bibliography. English language -- Early modern, 1500-1700 -- Bibliography. Canon (Literature) -- Bibliography.

Z8812 S — Shakespeare, William — Individual works, A-Z

Z8812.A68 B35 1998
Bains, Y. S.
Antony and Cleopatra: an annotated bibliography/ Yashdip S. Bains. New York: Garland Pub., 1998. xxi, 527 p.
98-029860   016.8223/3 21   0815314744
Shakespeare, William, 1564-1616. Antony and Cleopatra -- Bibliography. Cleopatra, Queen of Egypt, d. 30 B.C. -- In literature -- Bibliography. Antonius, Marcus, 83?-30 B.C. -- In literature -- Bibliography. Egypt -- In literature -- Bibliography. Rome -- In literature -- Bibliography.

Z8812.A8 A8 2003
As you like it, Much ado about nothing, and Twelfth night, or, What you will: an annotated bibliography of Shakespeare studies/ edited by Marilyn L. Williamson. Fairview, N.C.: Pegasus Press, 2003.
2002-156341   018/.8223/3 21   1889818356
Shakespeare, William, 1564-1616. As you like it -- Bibliography. Shakespeare, William, 1564-1616. Much ado about nothing Shakespeare, William, 1564-1616. Twelfth night -- Bibliography.

Z8812.C9 C96 2003
Cymbeline, The winter's tale, and The tempest: an annotated bibliography of Shakespeare studies, 1864-2000/ edited by John S. Mebane. Fairview, NC: Pegasus Press, 2003.
2002-156425   822.3/3 21   1889818313
Shakespeare, William, 1564-1616. Cymbeline -- Bibliography. Shakespeare, William, 1564-1616. Winter's tale -- Bibliography. Shakespeare, William, 1564-1616. Tempest -- Bibliography.

Z8812.H2 M66 1999
Hamlet: an annotated bibliography of Shakespeare studies, 1604-1998/ Michael E. Mooney, editor. Asheville, NC: Pegasus Press, 1999. xi, 145 p.
99-049463   016.8223/3 21   1889818216
Shakespeare, William, 1564-1616. Hamlet -- Bibliography. Hamlet (Legendary character) -- Bibliography.

Z8812.K54.G57 1994
Gira, Catherine.
Henry IV, Parts 1 and 2: an annotated bibliography/ compiled by Catherine Gira, Adele Seeff. New York: Garland, 1994. xxxvii, 576 p.
94-005075   016.8223/3   0824070976
Shakespeare, William, -- 1564-1616. -- King Henry IV -- Bibliography. Henry -- IV, -- King of England, -- 1367-1413 -- In literature -- Bibliography.

Z8812.L4 B87 1996
Bushnell, Rebecca W.,
King Lear, and Macbeth, 1674-1995: an annotated bibliography of Shakespeare studies/ edited by Rebecca W. Bushnell. Binghamton, N.Y.: Medieval and Renaissance Texts & Studies, 1996.
96-027944   016.8223/3 20   0866982019
Shakespeare, William, 1564-1616. King Lear -- Bibliography. Shakespeare, William, 1564-1616. Macbeth -- Bibliography. Macbeth, King of Scotland, 11th cent. -- In literature -- Bibliography. Lear, King (Legendary character), in literature -- Bibliography. English drama (Tragedy) -- History and criticism -- Bibliography. Kings and rulers in literature -- Bibliography. Great Britain -- In literature -- Bibliography.

Z8812.O8.S64 1988
Smith, John Hazel, 1928-
Shakespeare's Othello: a bibliography/ John Hazel Smith. New York: AMS Press, c1988. xii, 337 p.
88-026211   016.8223/3   0404622968
Shakespeare, William, 1564-1616. -- Othello -- Bibliography.

Z8812.P47.M5 1987
Michael, Nancy C., 1942-
Pericles, an annotated bibliography/ Nancy C. Michael. New York: Garland, 1987. xxii, 289 p.
87-017295   016.8223/3   0824091132
Shakespeare, William, -- 1564-1616. -- Pericles -- Bibliography.

Z8812.R37 R37 2002
The rape of Lucrece, Titus Andronicus, Julius Caesar, Antony and Cleopatra, and Coriolanus: an annotated bibliography of Shakespeare studies, 1910-2000/ edited by Clifford Chalmers Huffman and John W. Velz. Fairview, NC: Pegasus Press, 2002. x, 147 p.
2002-013554   016.8223/3 21   1889818305
Shakespeare, William, 1564-1616. Rape of Lucrece -- Bibliography. Shakespeare, William, 1564-1616. Titus Andronicus -- Bibliography. Shakespeare, William, 1564-1616. Julius Caesar. Shakespeare, William, 1564-1616. Antony and Cleopatra -- Bibliography. Andronicus, Titus (Legendary character) -- Bibliography.

Z8812.R53 C36 1998
Candido, Joseph.
Richard II, Henry IV, parts I and II, and Henry V: an annotated bibliography of Shakespeare studies, 1777-1997/ edited by Joseph Candido. Asheville, NC: Pegasus Press, 1998. ix, 129 p.
98-025550   016.8223/3 21   1889818100
Shakespeare, William, 1564-1616. King Richard II -- Bibliography. Shakespeare, William, 1564-1616. King Henry IV -- Bibliography. Shakespeare, William, 1564-1616. Henry V -- Bibliography. Richard II, King of England, 1367-1400 -- In literature Henry IV, King of England, 1367-1413 -- In literature -- Bibliography. Henry V, King of England, 1387-1422 -- In literature -- Bibliography.

Z8812.T36.H37 1994
The Taming of the shrew: an annotated bibliography/ compiled by Nancy Lenz Harvey. New York: Garland Pub., 1994. xv, 310 p.
94-006493   822.3/3   0824088921
Shakespeare, William, -- 1564-1616. -- Taming of the shrew -- Bibliography.

Z8812.T55 E47 1990
Elton, William R.,
A selective annotated bibliography of Shakespeare's Timon of Athens/ co-compiled by W.R. Elton and E.A. Rauchut. Lewiston, N.Y.: E. Mellen Press, c1991. xii, 84 p.
90-019306   822.3/3 20   0889463727
Shakespeare, William, 1564-1616. Timon of Athens -- Bibliography. Timon of Athens (Legendary character) in literature -- Bibliography.

Z8813 S — Shakespeare, William — Other special topics (not A-Z)

Z8813.H83 1995
Huffman, Clifford Chalmers, 1940-
Love's labor's lost, A midsummer night's dream, and The merchant of Venice: an annotated bibliography of Shakespeare studies, 1888-1994/ edited by Clifford Chalmers Huffman. Binghamton, N.Y.: Medieval & Renaissance Texts & Studies, 1995. 74 p.
95-008285   822.3/3   0866981772
Shakespeare, William, -- 1564-1616 -- Comedies -- Bibliography. Shakespeare, William, -- 1564-1616. -- Love's labour's lost -- Bibliography. Shakespeare, William, -- 1564-1616. -- Midsummer night's dream -- Bibliography. Comedy -- Bibliography.

Z8813.K84 2001
Kujoory, Parvin.
Shakespeare and minorities: an annotated bibliography, 1970-2000/ Parvin Kujoory. Lanham, Md.: Scarecrow Press, 2001. xi, 403 p.
00-057379   016.8223/3   0810839008
Shakespeare, William, -- 1564-1616 -- Characters -- Minorities -- Bibliography. Shakespeare, William, -- 1564-1616 -- Views on minorities -- Bibliography. Minorities in literature -- Bibliography.

Z8813.S47 1999
Shakespeare and the Renaissance stage to 1616: Shakespearean stage history 1616 to 1998: an annotated bibliography of Shakespeare studies, 1576-1998/ Hugh Macrae Richmond, editor. Asheville, NC: Pegasus Press, 1999. ix, 155 p.
99-049464   016.7929/5 21   1889818224
Shakespeare, William, -- 1564-1616 -- Stage history -- To 1625 Shakespeare, William, 1564-1616 -- Dramatic production -- Bibliography. Shakespeare, William, 1564-1616 -- Stage history -- Bibliography. Theater -- England -- History -- Bibliography. Renaissance -- England -- Bibliography.

Z8813.W982 1973
Wyman, William Henry.
Bibliography of the Bacon-Shakespeare controversy, with notes and extracts. Cincinnati, P. G. Thomson, 1884. [New York, AMS Press, [1973] 124 p.
71-178379   016.8223/3   0404070655
Shakespeare, William, 1564-1616 -- Authorship -- Baconian theory

Z8814.5 S — Shaw, G.B.

Z8814.5.W4 1986
Wearing, J. P.
G.B. Shaw: an annotated bibliography of writings about him/ compiled and edited by J.P. Wearing. DeKalb, Ill.: Northern Illinois University Press, 1986-1987. 3 v.
86-008649   016.822/912   0875801250
Shaw, Bernard, -- 1856-1950 -- Bibliography.

Z8814.5.W44 1992
Weintraub, Stanley, 1929-
Bernard Shaw: a guide to research/ Stanley Weintraub. University Park, Pa.: Pennsylvania State University Press, c1992. 154 p.
91-041779   016.822/912   0271008318
Shaw, Bernard, -- 1856-1950 -- Bibliography.

Z8819.125 S — Sillitoe, Alan

Z8819.125.G47 1988
Gerard, David E.
Alan Sillitoe: a bibliography/ David Gerard. London, England: Mansell; 1988. xx, 175 p.
87-034748   016.823/914   0887361048
Sillitoe, Alan -- Bibliography.

Z8822.32 S — Smith, Stevie

Z8822.32.B37 1987
Barbera, Jack.
Stevie Smith: a bibliography/ Jack Barbera, William McBrien, Helen Bajan. Westport, Conn., U.S.A.: Meckler Pub. Corp., 1987. xvii, 183 p.
86-023738   016.828/91209   0887361013
Smith, Stevie, -- 1902-1971 -- Bibliography. Women and literature -- England -- Bibliography.

Z8830.8 S — Spenser, Edmund

Z8830.8.M33 1975
McNeir, Waldo F.
Edmund Spenser: an annotated bibliography, 1937-1972/ by Waldo F. McNeir and Foster Provost. [2d ed.] Pittsburgh: Duquesne University Press; xxxi, 490 p.
75-033311   016.821/3   039100395X
Spenser, Edmund, 1552?-1599 -- Bibliography.

Z8830.8.S58 1984
Sipple, William L.
Edmund Spenser, 1900-1936, a reference guide/ William L. Sipple, with the assistance of Bernard J. Vondersmith. Boston, MA: G.K. Hall, c1984. xxxviii, 244 p.
83-010745   821/.3 19   0816180075
Spenser, Edmund, 1552?-1599 -- Bibliography.

Z8831 S — Spinoza, Benedictus de

Z8831.B68 1991
Boucher, Wayne I.
Spinoza in English: a bibliography from the seventeenth century to the present/ by Wayne I. Boucher. Leiden; E.J. Brill, 1991. ix, 226 p.
91-024542   016.199/492 20   9004094997
Spinoza, Benedictus de, 1632-1677 -- Bibliography.

Z8839.4 S — Steinbeck, John

Z8839.4.H287 1996
Harmon, Robert B.
John Steinbeck: an annotated guide to biographical sources/ Robert B. Harmon. Lanham, MD: Scarecrow Press, c1996. xviii, 288 p.
96-005417   016.813/52 20   0810831740
Steinbeck, John, 1902-1968 -- Bibliography. Novelists, American -- 20th century -- Biography -- Bibliography.

Z8839.4.H29 1987
Harmon, Robert B.
Steinbeck bibliographies: an annotated guide/ by Robert B. Harmon. Metuchen, N.J.: Scarecrow Press, 1987. vii, 137 p.
86-033830   016.813/52 19   0810819635
Steinbeck, John, 1902-1968 -- Bibliography of bibliographies.

Z8839.4.H3
Hayashi, Tetsumaro.
John Steinbeck: a concise bibliography, 1930-65. Introd. by Warren G. French. Metuchen, N.J., Scarecrow Press, 1967. xxi, 164 p.
67-010184   016.813/5/2
Steinbeck, John, 1902-1968 -- Bibliography. Western stories -- Bibliography. California -- In literature -- Bibliography.

Z8839.4.H314 1973
Hayashi, Tetsumaro.
A new Steinbeck bibliography. Metuchen, N.J.: Scarecrow Press, 1973-<1983 > v. <1 >
73-009982   016.813/52 19   0810806479
Steinbeck, John, 1902-1968 -- Bibliography.

Z8839.4.M49 1998
Meyer, Michael J., 1943-
The Hayashi Steinbeck bibliography, 1982-1996/ Michael J. Meyer. Lanham, Md.: Scarecrow Press, 1998. xxxv, 558 p.
98-022003   016.813/52   0810834820
Steinbeck, John, -- 1902-1968 -- Bibliography.

Z8842.7 S — Stevens, Wallace

Z8842.7.S47 1994
Serio, John N., 1943-
Wallace Stevens: an annotated secondary bibliography/ John N. Serio. Pittsburgh: University of Pittsburgh Press, 1994. xiv, 435 p.
93-001005   811/.52   0822938367
Stevens, Wallace, -- 1879-1955 -- Criticism and interpretation -- Bibliography.

Z8847 S — Stirling-Maxwell, Sir William bart

Z8847.E34 1999
Edel, Leon,
A bibliography of Henry James/ Leon Edel and Dan H. Laurence. 3rd ed./ rev. with the assistance of James Rambeau. Winchester, U.K.: St. Paul's Bibliographies; 428 p.
99-031946　016.813/4 21　1873040539
James, Henry, 1843-1916 -- Bibliography.

Z8854.4 S — Sun, Yat-sen

Z8854.4.B53 1998
Bibliography of Sun Yat-sen in China's republican revolution, 1885-1925/ compiled and edited by Sidney H. Chang, Leonard H.D. Gordon; with the assistance of Elaine P. Chang, Marjorie J. Gordon. Lanham, Md.: University Press of America, c1998. xxxi, 549 p.
97-042755　016.95104/1/092　076181180X
Sun, Yat-sen, -- 1866-1925 -- Bibliography.China -- History -- 1861-1912 -- Bibliography. China -- History -- Revolution, 1911-1912 -- Bibliography. China -- History -- 1912-1928 -- Bibliography.

Z8857.6 S — Symons, Arthur

Z8857.6.A77 1990
Arthur Symons: a bibliography/ Karl Beckson ... [et al.]. Greensboro, NC: ELT Press, c1990. xii, 330 p.
89-084406　016.821/8　0944318045
Symons, Arthur, -- 1865-1945 -- Bibliography.

Z8857.88 T — Taft, W.H.

Z8857.88.C64 1989
Coletta, Paolo Enrico, 1916-
William Howard Taft: a bibliography/ Paolo E. Coletta. Westport: Meckler, c1989. xxxviii, 271 p.
89-003388　016.97391/2/092　0887361404
Taft, William H. -- (William Howard), -- 1857-1930 -- Bibliography.United States -- Politics and government -- 1909-1913 -- Bibliography.

Z8858.5 T — Talleyrand-Périgord, Charles Maurice de, prince de Bénévent

Z8858.5.D98 1996
Dwyer, Philip G.
Charles-Maurice de Talleyrand, 1754-1838: a bibliography/ compiled by Philip G. Dwyer. Westport, Conn.: Greenwood Press, 1996. xii, 218 p.
95-022753　016.94406/092　0313293546
Talleyrand-Perigord, Charles Maurice de, -- prince de Benevent, -- 1754-1838 -- Bibliography.

Z8862.7 T — Taylor, P.H.

Z8862.7.W75 1988
Wright, Stuart T.
Peter Taylor: a descriptive bibliography, 1934-87/ Stuart Wright. Charlottesville: Published for the Bibliographical Society of the University of Virginia by the University Press of Virginia, 1988. xi, 228 p.
87-032044　016.813/54　0813911680
Taylor, Peter Hillsman, -- 1917- -- Bibliography.Southern States -- In literature -- Bibliography.

Z8866 T — Tennyson, Alfred Tennyson, baron

Z8866.A53 1993
Andrew, Aletha,
An annotated bibliography and study of the contemporary criticism of Tennyson's Idylls of the king, 1859-1886/ Aletha Andrew. New York: P. Lang, c1993. viii, 243 p.
93-000469　016.821/8 20　0820420840
Tennyson, Alfred Tennyson, Baron, 1809-1892. Idylls of the king Tennyson, Alfred Tennyson, Baron, 1809-1892 -- Criticism and Arthurian romances -- Adaptations -- History and criticism -- Bibliography. Medievalism -- England -- History -- 19th century -- Bibliography. Kings and rulers in literature -- Bibliography. Middle Ages in literature -- Bibliography.

Z8866.B43 1984
Beetz, Kirk H.,
Tennyson: a bibliography, 1827-1982/ by Kirk H. Beetz. Metuchen, N.J.: Scarecrow Press, 1984. vi, 528 p.
84-001274　016.821/8 19　0810816873
Tennyson, Alfred Tennyson, Baron, 1809-1892 -- Bibliography.

Z8869.14 — T — Thatcher, Margaret

Z8869.14.M55 1993
Mikdadi, F. H.
Margaret Thatcher: a bibliography/ Faysal Mikdadi. Westport, Conn.: Greenwood Press, 1993. xii, 269 p.
92-038071　016.941085/8　0313282889
Thatcher, Margaret -- Bibliography.Great Britain -- Politics and government -- 1979-1997 -- Bibliography.

Z8885.48 T — Trilling, Lionel

Z8885.48.L43 1993
Leitch, Thomas M.
Lionel Trilling: an annotated bibliography/ Thomas M. Leitch. New York: Garland, 1993. xlvi, 626 p.
92-023192　016.818/5209　082407128X
Trilling, Lionel, -- 1905-1975 -- Bibliography.

Z8888.9 T — Truman, Harry

Z8888.9.B87 1984
Burns, Richard Dean.
Harry S. Truman: a bibliography of his times and presidency/ compiled for the Harry S. Truman Library Institute by Richard Dean Burns. Wilmington, Del.: Scholarly Resources Inc., 1984. xlviii, 297 p.
84-020223　016.973918/092/4　0842022198
Truman, Harry S., -- 1884-1972 -- Bibliography.United States -- Politics and government -- 1945-1953 -- Bibliography.

Z8896 T — Tyler, John

Z8896.M67 2001
Moser, Harold D.
John Tyler: a bibliography/ compiled by Harold D. Moser. Westport, Conn.: Greenwood Press, 2001. xxx, 293 p.
00-061034　973.5/8/092　0313281688
Tyler, John, -- 1790-1862 -- Bibliography.

Z8913.85 U — Updike, John

Z8913.85.D4 1994
De Bellis, Jack.
John Updike: a bibliography, 1967-1993/ compiled by Jack De Bellis; foreword by John Updike. Westport, Conn.: Greenwood Press, 1994. xiii, 335 p.
93-028538　016.813/54　0313288615
Updike, John -- Bibliography.

Z8941.7 V — Vicente, Gil

Z8941.7.S82 1997
Stathatos, Constantine C.
A Gil Vicente bibliography, 1975-1995: with a supplement for 1940-1975/ C.C. Stathatos. Bethlehem, Pa.: Lehigh University Press; c1997. 187 p.
97-033332　016.8692/2　0934223483
Vicente, Gil, -- ca. 1470-ca. 1536 -- Bibliography.

Z8946.82 V — Vygotskii, L.S.

Z8946.82.V94.E44 1997
Elhammoumi, Mohamed, 1956-
Socio-historicocultural psychology: Lev Semenovich Vygotsky, 1896-1934: bibliographical notes/ Mohamed Elhammoumi. Lanham, Md.: University Press of America, c1997. 225 p.
96-049101　016.15/0947　0761806482
Vygotskii, L. S. -- (Lev Semenovich), -- 1896-1934 -- Bibliography.Psychology -- Soviet Union -- History -- Bibliography.

Z8957 W — Weber, Max

Z8957.K58 1988
Kivisto, Peter, 1948-
Max Weber, a bio-bibliography/ Peter Kivisto and William H. Swatos, Jr. New York: Greenwood Press, 1988. 267 p.
88-024656   016.301/092/4   0313257949
Weber, Max, -- 1864-1920 -- Bibliography. Weber, Max, -- 1864-1920. Sociologists -- Germany -- Biography.

Z8963.8 W — Wellington, A.W., Duke of

Z8963.8.P37 1990
Partridge, Michael Stephen.
The Duke of Wellington, 1769-1852: a bibliography/ Michael S. Partridge. Westport, CT: Meckler, c1990. vii, 248 p.
90-006574   016.94107/092   0887362974
Wellington, Arthur Wellesley, -- Duke of, -- 1769-1852 -- Bibliography.

Z8969.2 W — Wharton, E.N. (Jones)

Z8969.2.G37 1990
Garrison, Stephen, 1951-
Edith Wharton: a descriptive bibliography/ Stephen Garrison. Pittsburgh, Pa.: University of Pittsburgh Press, 1990. xxiii, 514 p.
89-025034   016.813/52   0822936410
Wharton, Edith, -- 1862-1937 -- Bibliography. Women and literature -- United States -- Bibliography.

Z8971.5 W — Whitman, Walt

Z8971.5.G53 2001
Gibson, Brent.
An annotated Walt Whitman bibliography, 1976-1985/ Brent Gibson. Lewiston, N.Y.: Edwin Mellen Press, c2001. ii, 325 p.
00-046559   016.811/3   077347577X
Whitman, Walt, -- 1819-1892 -- Bibliography.

Z8971.5.B65
Boswell, Jeanetta,
Walt Whitman and the critics: a checklist of criticism, 1900-1978/ Jeanetta Boswell. Metuchen, N.J.: Scarecrow Press, 1980. xiii, 257 p.
80-020528   016.811/3 19   0810813556
Whitman, Walt, 1819-1892 -- Bibliography.

Z8971.5.G5 1981
Giantvalley, Scott,
Walt Whitman, 1838-1939: a reference guide/ Scott Giantvalley. Boston, Mass.: G.K. Hall, c1981. xxi, 465 p.
81-006538   016.811/3 19   0816178569
Whitman, Walt, 1819-1892 -- Bibliography.

Z8971.5.K85 1982
Kummings, Donald D.
Walt Whitman, 1940-1975: a reference guide/ Donald D. Kummings. Boston, Mass.: G.K. Hall, c1982. xiv, 264 p.
82-011845   016.811/3 19   081617802X
Whitman, Walt, 1819-1892 -- Bibliography.

Z8971.5.M93 1993
Myerson, Joel.
Walt Whitman: a descriptive bibliography/ Joel Myerson. Pittsburgh: University of Pittsburgh Press, 1993. xxiv, 1097 p.
92-025927   016.811/3 20   0822937395
Whitman, Walt, 1819-1892 -- Bibliography.

Z8975.7 W — Wilder, T.N.

Z8975.7.W34 1993
Walsh, Claudette.
Thornton Wilder: a reference guide, 1926-1990/ Claudette Walsh. New York: G.K. Hall; c1993. xxxv, 449 p.
91-013287   016.818/5209   0816187908
Wilder, Thornton, -- 1897-1975 -- Bibliography.

Z8976.424 W — Williams, Tennessee

Z8976.424.C73 1995
Crandall, George W., 1956-
Tennessee Williams: a descriptive bibliography/ George W. Crandall. Pittsburgh: University of Pittsburgh Press, 1995. xxiii, 673 p.
93-027928   016.812/54   0822937697
Williams, Tennessee, -- 1911-1983 -- Bibliography.

Z8976.424.G85 1991
Gunn, Drewey Wayne, 1939-
Tennessee Williams, a bibliography/ by Drewey Wayne Gunn. Metuchen, N.J.: Scarecrow Press, 1991. xxxi, 434 p.
91-034939   016.812/54   0810824957
Williams, Tennessee, -- 1911-1983 -- Bibliography.

Z8976.485 W — Wilson, Angus

Z8976.485.S7 1988
Stape, J. H.
Angus Wilson: a bibliography, 1947-1987/ J.H. Stape and Anne N. Thomas; with a foreword by Angus Wilson. London; Mansell Pub., 1988. xvi, 327 p.
87-031246   016.823/914   0720118727
Wilson, Angus -- Bibliography.

Z8976.9 W — Wilson, Woodrow

Z8976.9.M85 1997
Mulder, John M., 1946-
Woodrow Wilson: a bibliography/ compiled by John M. Mulder, Ernest M. White, and Ethel S. White. Westport, Conn: Greenwood Press, 1997. xlii, 438 p.
97-022554   016.97391/3092   0313281858
Wilson, Woodrow, -- 1856-1924 -- Bibliography.

Z8977.35 W — Windham, Donald

Z8977.35.K45 1991
Kellner, Bruce.
Donald Windham: a bio-bibliography/ Bruce Kellner; with a footnote by Donald Windham. New York: Greenwood Press, c1991. xlii, 92 p.
91-010777   016.813/54   0313268576
Windham, Donald -- Bibliography.

Z8978.66 W — Wirth, Louis

Z8978.66.S24 1987
Salerno, Roger A.
Louis Wirth: a bio-bibliography/ Roger A. Salerno. New York: Greenwood Press, 1987. ix, 143 p.
87-019631   016.301/092/4   0313254737
Wirth, Louis, -- 1897-1952. Wirth, Louis, -- 1897-1952 -- Bibliography. Sociologists -- United States -- Biography.

Z8979.4 W — Wittgenstein, Ludwig

Z8979.4.L36
Lapointe, François.
Ludwig Wittgenstein: a comprehensive bibliography/ compiled by François H. Lapointe. Westport, Conn.: Greenwood Press, 1980. ix, 297 p.
79-006565   016.192   0313221278
Wittgenstein, Ludwig, 1889-1951 -- Bibliography.

Z8980.45 W — Wolfe, Thomas

Z8980.45.B37 1996
Bassett, John Earl, 1942-
Thomas Wolfe: an annotated critical bibliography/ John E. Bassett. Lanham, Md.: Scarecrow Press, c1996. xxv, 432 p.
96-004420   016.813/52   0810831465
Wolfe, Thomas, -- 1900-1938 -- Bibliography.

Z8980.45.P47
Phillipson, John S.
Thomas Wolfe: a reference guide/ John S. Phillipson. Boston: G. K. Hall, c1977. xiii, 218 p.
76-043352   016.813/5/2   081617878X
Wolfe, Thomas, 1900-1938 -- Bibliography. Autobiographical fiction, American -- Bibliography. North Carolina -- In literature -- Bibliography.

Z8983.4 W — Woodson, C.G.

Z8983.4.S27 1985
Scally, M. Anthony.
Carter G. Woodson: a bio-bibliography/ compiled by Sister Anthony Scally. Westport, Conn.: Greenwood Press, 1985. xvii, 224 p. ;
85-010051   016.973/0496073 19   0313241856
Woodson, Carter Godwin, 1875-1950 -- Bibliography.

Z8984.2 W — Woolf, Virginia

Z8984.2.K5 1997
Kirkpatrick, B. J.
A bibliography of Virginia Woolf/ by B.J. Kirkpatrick. 4th ed./ by B.J. Kirkpatrick and Stuart N. Clarke Oxford: Clarendon Press; xiv, 472 p.
97-010213 016.823/912 21 0198183836
Woolf, Virginia, 1882-1941 -- Bibliography. Women and literature -- England -- Bibliography.

Z8984.2.R5 1984
Rice, Thomas Jackson.
Virginia Woolf: a guide to research/ Thomas Jackson Rice. New York: Garland Pub., 1984. xix, 258 p.
83-048264 016.832/912 19 0824090845
Woolf, Virginia, 1882-1941 -- Bibliography.

Z8984.2.S74 1983
Steele, Elizabeth.
Virginia Woolf's literary sources and allusions: a guide to the essays/ Elizabeth Steele. New York: Garland Pub., 1983. ix, 364 p.
82-049166 016.824/912 19 0824091698
Woolf, Virginia, 1882-1941 -- Bibliography. Woolf, Virginia, 1882-1941 -- Sources. Woolf, Virginia, 1882-1941 -- Knowledge -- Literature.

Z8984.2.S743 1987
Steele, Elizabeth.
Virginia Woolf's rediscovered essays: sources and allusions/ Elizabeth Steele. New York: Garland Pub., 1987. xv, 238 p.
86-025725 016.824/912 19 0824085272
Woolf, Virginia, 1882-1941 -- Bibliography. Woolf, Virginia, 1882-1941 -- Sources. Woolf, Virginia, 1882-1941 -- Knowledge -- Literature. Kirkpatrick, B. J. (Brownlee Jean). Bibliography of Virginia Woolf

Z8986.323 W — Wright, Richard

Z8986.323.K56 1988
Kinnamon, Keneth.
A Richard Wright bibliography: fifty years of criticism and commentary, 1933-1982/ compiled by Keneth Kinnamon with the help of Joseph Benson, Michel Fabre, and Craig Werner. New York: Greenwood Press, 1988. xi, 983 p.
87-027831 016.813/52 0313254117
Wright, Richard, -- 1908-1960 -- Bibliography.Afro-Americans in literature -- Bibliography.

Z8989.7 X — X, Malcolm

Z8989.7.J64 1986
Johnson, Timothy V.,
Malcolm X: a comprehensive annotated bibliography/ Timothy V. Johnson. New York: Garland Pub., 1986. ix, 192 p. ;
84-048401 016.297/87/0924 19 0824087909
X, Malcolm, 1925-1965 -- Bibliography.

Z8989.73 X — Xenophon

Z8989.73.M67 1988
Morrison, Donald R.
Bibliography of editions, translations, and commentary on Xenophon's Socratic writings, 1600-present/ compiled and with an introduction by Donald R. Morrison. Pittsburgh, Pa.: Mathesis Publications, 1988. xvii, 103 p.
88-001063 016.183/2 0935225021
Xenophon -- Bibliography. Socrates -- Bibliography. Philosophy, Ancient -- Bibliography.

Z8992 Y — Yeats, W.B.

Z8992.J59 1990
Jochum, K. P. S.
W. B. Yeats: a classified bibliography of criticism/ K.P.S. Jochum. 2nd ed., rev. and enl. Urbana: University of Illinois Press, c1900. xvi, 1176 p.
90-010981 016.821/8 20 0252017625
Yeats, W. B. (William Butler), 1865-1939 -- Criticism and

ZA Information resources (General)

ZA3075 Research. How to find information — General works

ZA3075.B47 2000
Berkman, Robert I.
Find it fast: how to uncover expert information on any subject online or in print/ Robert I. Berkman. 5th ed. New York, NY: HarperResource, c2000. xxiv, 372 p.
00-702906 001.4 21 0062737473
Information retrieval. Research.

ZA3075.R69 2000
Rowland, Robin.
The creative guide to research: how to find what you need-- online or offline/ by Robin Rowland. Franklin Lakes, NJ: Career Press, c2000. 284 p.
00-037882 001.4 1564144429
Information retrieval. Research.

ZA3157 Information services. Information centers — General works

ZA3157.S23 1997
St. Clair, Guy, 1940-
Total quality management in information services/ Guy St Clair. London; Bowker-Saur, c1997. ix, 261 p.
96-043536 025.52/068 1857390393
Information services -- Management. Total quality management.

ZA3225 Information superhighway — General works

ZA3225.B67 2000
Borgman, Christine L., 1951-
From Gutenberg to the global information infrastructure: access to information in the networked world/ Christine L. Borgman. Cambridge, Mass.: MIT Press, 2000. xviii, 324 p.
99-039906 025.5/24 026202473X
Information superhighway. Digital libraries. Libraries -- Special collections -- Electronic information resources.

ZA3225.G39 1996
Gay, Martin, 1950-
The new information revolution: a reference handbook/ Martin K. Gay. Santa Barbara, CA: ABC-CLIO, c1996. xv, 247 p.
96-028832 303.48/33 0874368472
Information superhighway. Information technology. Digital communications.

ZA3250 Information superhighway — By region or country, A-Z

ZA3250.U6.I58 1996
Internet dreams: archetypes, myths, and metaphors / Mark Stefik. Cambridge, Mass.: MIT Press, 1996. xxiv, 412 p.
96-028249 0262193736
Information superhighway -- United States. Internet (Computer network) -- United States.

ZA4060 Information in specific formats or media — Electronic information resources — Research. How to use electronic information resources

ZA4060.H77 1999
Houghton, Janaye Matteson
Decision points: Boolean logic for computer users and beginning online searchers/ Janaye M. Houghton and Robert S. Houghton. Englewood, Colo.: Libraries Unlimited, 1999. viii, 155 p. :
98-053624 025.04 21 1563086727
Electronic information resource searching. Computer logic. Algebra, Boolean.

ZA4060.M36 2000
Manual of online search strategies/ edited by C.J. Armstrong and Andrew Large. Brookfield, VT: Gower, 2000-2001. 3 v.
00-025154 025.5/24 0566079909
Online information resource searching -- Handbooks, manuals, etc. Online information resource searching -- United States -- Handbooks, manuals, etc.

ZA4080-4082 Information in specific formats or media — Electronic information resources — Digital libraries

ZA4080.W45 1999
The amazing Internet challenge: how leading projects use library skills to organize the Web/ [edited by] Amy Tracy Wells, Susan Calcari, Travis Koplow. Chicago: American Library Association, 1999. xii, 279 p.
99-025110   025.04   0838907660
Digital libraries -- Administration. Computer network resources.

ZA4082.U63.I555 1999
The Internet Public Library handbook/ by Joseph Janes ... [et al.]. New York: Neal Schuman Pub., c1999. x, 218 p.
98-048983   025/.00285   1555703445
Digital libraries -- United States.

ZA4150-4230 Information in specific formats or media — Electronic information resources — Computer network resources

ZA4150.D97 1997
Dyson, Esther, 1951-
Release 2.0: a design for living in the digital age/ Esther Dyson. New York: Broadway Books, c1997. viii, 307 p.
97-033983   303.48/33   0767900111
Computer networks -- Social aspects. Internet (Computer network) -- Social aspects.

ZA4150.D973 1998
Dyson, Esther,
Release 2.1: a design for living in the digital age/ Esther Dyson. 1st ed. New York: Broadway Books, c1998. 370 p.
98-034486   303.48/33 21   076790012X
Computer networks -- Social aspects. Internet - - Social aspects.

ZA4201.B688 2002
Bradley, Phil,
The advanced Internet searcher's handbook/ Phil Bradley. 2nd ed. London: Library Association Pub., 2002. xv, 256 p.
2002-483345   025.04 21   1856043800
Computer network resources. Internet (Computer network) Information retrieval.

ZA4201.B69 1999
Bradley, Phil, 1959-
Internet power searching: the advanced manual/ Phil Bradley. New York: Neal-Schuman Publishers, 1999. xv, 232 p.
98-040957   025.04   155570350X
Internet searching.

ZA4201.G35
Gale guide to Internet databases. Detroit, MI: Gale Research Inc., c1995. 1 v.
96-640602   025.04
Internet (Computer network) -- Directories. Databases -- Directories. Computer network resources -- Directories.

ZA4201.G64 2001
Gordon, Rachel Singer.
Teaching the Internet in libraries/ Rachel Singer Gordon. Chicago: American Library Association, 2001. vii, 143 p.
00-052564   025.04/071 21   0838907997
Internet searching--Study and teaching--United States. Computer network resources--Study and teaching--United States.

ZA4201.G74 1997
Grossman, Wendy, 1954-
Net.wars/ Wendy M. Grossman. New York: New York University Press, c1997. viii, 237 p.
97-021214   303.48/33   0814731031
Internet (Computer network) -- Social aspects. Electronic discussion groups -- Social aspects.

ZA4201.I56 1997
Internet culture/ edited by David Porter. New York: Routledge, 1997. xviii, 279 p.
96-036557   303.48/33   0415916836
Internet (Computer network) -- Social aspects.

ZA4201.I566 2000
The Internet handbook for writers, researchers, and journalists/ Mary McGuire ... [et al.]. New York: Guilford Press, c2000. xii, 276 p.
99-056397   025.04   1572305509
Computer network resources. Authorship -- Computer network resources.

ZA4201.K46 1998
Kennedy, Shirley Duglin.
Best bet Internet: reference and research when you don't have time to mess around/ Shirley Duglin Kennedy. Chicago: American Library Association, 1998. vii, 194 p.
97-022091   025.04   0838907121
Computer network resources.

ZA4201.M35 1999
Maloy, Timothy K.
The Internet research guide/ Timothy K. Maloy. New York: Allworth Press, c1999. x, 197 p.
98-072763   025.04   1581150121
Computer network resources.

ZA4201.M36 2002
McDermott, Irene E.,
The librarian's Internet survival guide: strategies for the high-tech reference desk/ Irene E. McDermott; edited by Barbara Quint. Medford, N.J.: Information Today, c2002. xxv, 267 p.
2002-004697   025.04 21   157387129X
Computer network resources--Directories. Web sites--Directories. Internet in library reference services.

ZA4201.M67 1999
Morville, Peter.
The Internet searcher's handbook: locating information, people & software/ Peter Morville, Louis Rosenfeld, and Joseph Janes. New York: Neal-Schuman Publishers, c1999. xxi, 172 p.
99-038213   025.04   1555703593
Internet searching.

ZA4201.W43 2002
Web of deception: misinformation on the Internet/ edited by Anne P. Mintz. Medford, N.J: CyberAge Books, c2002. xxv, 275 p.
2002-004687   025.04 21   0910965609
Internet fraud. Electronic information resource literacy. Computer network resources-- Evaluation.

ZA4226.H53 1997
Hill, Brad, 1953-
Internet directory for dummies/ by Brad Hill. Foster City, CA: IDG Books Worldwide, c1997. xxii, 407 p.
97-080406   025.04   0764502174
Web sites -- Directories.

ZA4226.H63 2001
Hock, Randolph, 1944-
The extreme searcher's guide to Web search engines: a handbook for the serious searcher/ Randolph Hock; foreword by Reva Basch. Medford, NJ: CyberAge Books, 2001. xxv, 241 p.
2001-028052   025.04   0910965471
Web search engines.

ZA4226.M35 1997
Malamud, Carl.
A world's fair for the global village/ Carl Malamud. Cambridge, Mass.: MIT Press, c1997. xix, 281 p.
97-011146   907/.4   0262133385
World Wide Web.

ZA4226.R44 1997
Reference sources on the Internet: off the shelf and onto the Web/ Karen R. Diaz, editor. New York: Haworth Press, 1997. 266 p.
97-028052   025.04   0789003589
Web sites. Electronic reference sources.

ZA4230.G57 2001
Glossbrenner, Alfred.
Search engines for the World Wide Web/ Alfred and Emily Glossbrenner. 3rd ed. Berkeley, CA: Peachpit Press, c2001. xii, 348 p.
2001-276389   025.04 21   020173401X
Web search engines. Internet searching.

ZA4450 Information in specific formats or media — Electronic information resources — Databases

ZA4450.S54 2001
Sherman, Chris.
The Invisible Web: uncovering information sources search engines can't see/ Chris Sherman and Gary Price. Medford, N.J.: CyberAge Books, c2001. xxix, 439 p.
2001-028818   025.04 21   091096551X
Online databases--Directories. Database searching. Internet searching.

ZA5055 Information from specific providers — Government information — Lists and catalogs of government information resources

ZA5055.U6.H47 1997
Herman, Edward, 1949-
Locating United States government information: a guide to sources/ by Edward Herman. Buffalo, N.Y.: W.S. Hein, 1997. xvii, 580 p.
96-051490   025.17/34   1575882035
Government information -- United States.

ZA5055.U6.R63 1998
Robinson, Judith Schiek, 1947-
Tapping the government grapevine: the user friendly guide to U.S. Government information sources/ by Judith Schiek Robinson. Phoenix, Ariz: Oryx Press, 1998. vii, 286 p.
98-020618   025.04   1573560243
Government information -- United States.

ZA5075 Information from specific providers —
Government information —
Government information in specific formats or media

ZA5075.A53 1998
Andriot, Laurie.
Internet blue pages: the guide to Federal Government web sites/ researched and compiled by Laurie Andriot. Medford, NJ: Information Today, 1998.
98-040318   025.04   0910965293
Electronic government information -- United States -- Directories. Web sites -- United States - - Directories.

ZA5075.G68
Government information on the Internet. Lanham, Md.: Bernan Press, [1997-   ]
00-214591   351 13
Electronic government information -- United States -- Directories. Internet addresses -- United States -- Directories. Web sites -- United States -- Directories.

ZA5075.H47 2001
Hernon, Peter.
U.S. government on the Web: getting the information you need/ Peter Hernon, Robert E. Dugan, John A Shuler. Englewood, Colo.: Libraries Unlimited, 2001. xxv, 405 p.
2001-029945   025.04   156308886X
Electronic government information -- United States -- Directories. Web sites -- United States - - Directories. Electronic government information -- United States.

ZA5075.M38 2001
Maxymuk, John.
Government online: one-click access to 3,400 federal and state Web sites/ John Maxymuk. New York: Neal-Schuman Publishers, 2001. xxi, 323 p.
2001-030180   025.06/35173   1555704166
Electronic government information -- United States -- Directories. Web sites -- United States - - Directories.

ZA5075.N68 1998
Notess, Greg R.
Government information on the Internet/ Greg R. Notess. Lanham, Md.: Bernan Press, c1998. xvi, 624 p.
98-045695   025.04   0890591091
Electronic government information -- United States -- Directories.

Author Index
to
Volumes 1-10

Al Aòhmad, Jal‾al. PK6561.A38A24 1982, (v3)
Al‾i, Idr‾is. PJ7812.I23D813 1998, (v3)
Ubayd Z‾ak‾an‾i, Niòz‾am al-D‾in. PK6550.U2A25 1985, (v3)
Aageson, James W. BS475.2.A155 2000, (v8)
Aalto, Alvar. NA1199.A2.A43, (v9)
  NA1455.F53.A2314 1999, (v9)
Aardema, Verna. PZ8.1.A213Wh, (v3)
Aaron, Frieda W. PJ5141.2.A27 1990, (v3)
Aaron, Henry J. HD7125.A178 1982, (v6)
  HJ4120.A62, (v6)
Aaron, Jane. PR4864.A2 1991, (v3)
Aaron, Richard Ithamar. B105.U5 A15 1967, (v8)
Aarons, Victoria. PS153.J4.A18 1996, (v3)
Aaserud, Finn. QC789.2.D4.A27 1990, (v1)
Aâsvaghoòsa. BL1416.A7 M33, (v8)
Ab‾u Zayd, Laylá. PJ7808.Z22F3713 2000, (v3)
Aballard, Pierre. B765.A23.E82 1971, (v8)
Abbas, M. A. DS796.H75.A34 1997, (v5)
Abbate, Carolyn. ML3858.A2 1991, (v9)
Abbate, Janet. TK5105.875.I57.A23 1999, (v1)
Abbott, Carl. F194.A23 1999, (v4)
  F595.A24 1993, (v4)
  F776.A22 1994, (v4)
  F884.P85 A23 2001, (v4)
Abbott, Claude Colleer. PR4525.D2.Z6, (v3)
Abbott, Edith. HD6095.A6 1969, (v6)
Abbott, Edwin Abbott. QA699.A13 1963, (v1)
Abbott, Elizabeth. F1928.A583 1988, (v4)
Abbott, Grace. HV741.A53, (v6)
Abbott, H. Porter. PR6003.E282.Z53 1996, (v3)
Abbott, John Cave. HD9000.1.F587.A23 1991, (v6)
Abbott, Keith. PS3503.R2736.Z57 1989, (v3)
Abbott, Margery Post. BX7611.A23 2003, (v8)
Abbott, Philip. E807.A68 1990, (v4)
Abbott, R. Tucker. QL411.A19 1974, (v1)
Abdel Kader, Soha. HQ1793.A67 1987, (v6)
Abdel-Rahim, Muddathir. JQ3981.S8 A42, (v7)
Abdi Ismail Samatar. HD2125.A63 1989, (v6)
Abe, Kobo. PL845.B4.H313 1980, (v3)
Abegg, Lily. CB251.A213, (v5)
Abegglen, James C. HC460.5.A516 1994, (v6)
Abel, Charles F. KF8700.A93 1994, (v7)
Abel, Donald C. BF685.A24 1989, (v2)
Abel, Emily K. R727.47.A24 2000, (v2)
Abel, Ernest L. BF209.C3.A23, (v2)
  HV5804.A23 1984, (v6)
Abel, Kerry M. E99.T56.A2 1993, (v4)
Abel, Lionel. PN1623.A35, (v3)
Abel, Reuben. B53.A23, (v8)
Abel, Richard L. BJ1533.R4 A34 1998, (v8)
  KF297.A756 1989, (v7)
  KTL2465.A93 1995, (v7)
  PN1993.5.F7.A63 1994, (v3)
  PN1993.5.F7.A64 1984, (v3)
  PN1993.5.U6.A68 1999, (v3)
Abeles, Marc. GN585.F8.A2413 1991, (v6)
Abell, George O. QB45.A16 1987, (v1)
Abell, Martha L. QA76.95.A214 1997, (v1)
  QA76.95.A22 1992, (v1)
  QA276.4.A24 1999, (v1)
  QA371.5.D37.A23 1994, (v1)
  QA371.5.D37.A24 1997, (v1)
Abell, Westcott Stile. VM15.A22, (v10)
Abella, Irving M. F1035.J5.A23 1983, (v4)
Abelman, Robert. PN1992.5.A25 1998, (v3)
Abelmann, Nancy. HN730.5.A8.A24 1996, (v6)
Abels, Richard Philip. DA59.A24 1988, (v5)
Abelson, Elaine S. HV6658.A24 1989, (v6)
Abelson, Harold. QA76.6.A255 1996, (v1)
Abelson, Raziel. BD435.A23 1988, (v8)
Abenheim, Donald. UA710.A594 1988, (v10)
Aberbach, David. PJ5010.A34 1998, (v3)
Aberbach, Joel D. JK585.A63 1990, (v7)
Aberbach, Moses. DS122.9.A23 2000, (v5)
Abercrombie, Lascelles. PN56.R7.A2, (v3)
  PR4754.A2 1964, (v3)
Abercrombie, Stanley. NK1412.N45.A24 1995, (v9)
Abercrombie, Thomas Alan. F2230.2.A9.A24 1998, (v4)
Abercromby, James. F229.A24 1991, (v4)

Abernethy, Thomas Perkins. E334.A6, (v4)
  F213.A2, (v4)
  F229.A25, (v4)
  F326.A14 1990, (v4)
Abernethy, Virginia. HB883.5.A23 1993, (v6)
Abers, Rebecca. JS2425.P67, (v7)
Aberth, John. DA245.A24 2001, (v5)
  KD610.A24 1996, (v7)
Aberth, Oliver. QA76.73.C153.A32 1998, (v1)
Abgrall, Jean-Marie. R733.A24513 2000, (v2)
Abi-Aad, Naji. DS63.1.A246 1997, (v5)
Abiteboul, S. QA76.9.D3.A26 1995, (v1)
Ablowitz, Mark J. QA331.7.A25 1997, (v1)
Abolafia, Mitchel. HG6024.3.A26 1996, (v6)
Aboubaker Alwan, Daoud. DT411.5.A34 2000, (v5)
Aboud, Frances E. BF723.P75.A24 1989, (v2)
Aboufadel, Edward. QA403.3.A34 1999, (v1)
Abra, Jock. BF64.A27 1998, (v2)
Abraham, Gerald. ML60.A215.S6, (v9)
  ML160.A27, (v9)
  ML300.A16S8 1968, (v9)
  ML300.A16S82 1970, (v9)
  ML410.S3.A56 1969, (v9)
  ML410.S54.A5, (v9)
Abraham, Henry Julian. KF8742.A72 1999, (v7)
Abraham, Karl. BF173.A3 1979, (v2)
  BF175.A25, (v2)
Abraham, Kinfe. E185.61.A17 1991, (v4)
Abraham, Margaret. HV6626.2.A27 2000, (v6)
Abraham, Ralph. QA845.A26 1982, (v1)
Abraham, Richard David. PL539.A5 1956, (v3)
Abraham, Suzanne. RC552.A5.A37 1984, (v2)
Abrahams, Cecil Anthony. PR9369.3.L3.Z58 1985, (v3)
Abrahams, Peter. PR6001.B62.T4, (v3)
  PR6001.B62.T45, (v3)
  PR6001.B62.W74 1971, (v3)
Abrahams, Roger D. E443.A26 1992, (v4)
  PE1519.A2, (v3)
Abrahamsen, Rita. HC800.A5265 2000, (v6)
Abrahamsen, Samuel. DS135.N8.A27 1990, (v5)
Abrahamson, Mark. HV700.5.A27 1998, (v6)
Abrahamsson, Hans. HC890.A57 1995, (v6)
Abram, Jan. RC438.6.W56.A27 1997, (v2)
Abramovitz, Mimi. HV699.A424 1988, (v6)
Abramowicz, Hirsz. DS135.L52.V5519313 1999, (v5)
Abramowitz, Rachel. PN1995.9.W6.A27 2000, (v3)
Abrams, Douglas Carl. F259.A27 1992, (v4)
Abrams, M. H. PE1010.E5 1957, (v3)
  PN41.A184 1993, (v3)
  PN769.R7.A2, (v3)
  PR590.A2, (v3)
Abrams, Roger I. KF3989.A93 1998, (v7)
Abramson, Glenda. PJ5026.A19 1998, (v3)
Abramson, Joanne. SF473.M33.A27 1995, (v1)
Abramson, Paul R. HQ23.A25 1995, (v6)
Abro, A. d'. QC6.A3 1950, (v1)
  QC171.A3 1952, (v1)
Abromeit, Kathleen A. ML128.S4.A27 1999, (v9)
Abromovitz, Les. HG9390.A27 1999, (v6)
Abromowitz, Jennifer. Z7514.O8.A27 1990, (v10)
Abruzzi, William S. F817.L5.A25 1993, (v4)
Abse, Dannie. PR6001.B7.A17 1977, (v3)
Abse, Joan. PR5263.A54 1981, (v3)
Abshire, David M. UA23.A4296, (v10)
Abt, Arthur F. RJ36.A2, (v2)
Abt, John J. KF373.A28.A32 1993, (v7)
Abu `Amr, Ziyad. BP63.P32.W47413 1994, (v8)
Abu Izzeddin, Nejla M. DS94.8.D8.A24 1984, (v5)
Abubakar, Ahmad. HC800.A53 1989, (v6)
Abu-Haidar, Farida. PJ6830.B3A28 1991, (v3)
AbuKhalil, Asad. DS80.9.A28 1998, (v5)
Abul-Husn, Latif. DS87.5.A29 1998, (v5)
Abu-Lughod, Ibrahim A. PJ25.P7 no.22, (v3)
Abu-Lughod, Janet L. HC41.A28 1989, (v6)
Abu-Lughod, Lila. HQ1793.A68 1993, (v6)
Abun-Nasr, Jamil M. DT194.A23 1987, (v5)
Aburish, Said K. DS110.W47.A29 1993, (v5)
Abwunza, Judith M. DT433.545.L63.A38 1997, (v5)
Aby, Stephen H. Z7164.S68.A24 1997, (v10)
  Z7204.I5.A29 1990, (v10)

Abzug, Robert H. E449.W46.A29, (v4)
Ac‾okamittiraön. PL4758.9.A29A23 1998, (v3)
Accad, Evelyne. PJ8082.A23 1990, (v3)
Accinelli, Robert. E183.8.T3.A33 1996, (v4)
Accordino, John J. HC110.D4.A58 2000, (v6)
Achebe, Chinua. PR6051.C5.A7, (v3)
  PR6051.C5.M3 1966, (v3)
  PR9387.9.A3.A83 1988, (v3)
Achenbaum, W. Andrew. HQ1064.U5.A26, (v6)
Acheson, David. QA303.A325 1997, (v1)
Acheson, Dean. D412.6.A2 1961, (v5)
  E744.A217, (v4)
  E744.A2174, (v4)
  E835.A25, (v4)
Acheson, James. PR6003.E282.Z562 1997, (v3)
Achinstein, Peter. Q174.8.A24 1991, (v1)
Achor, Amy Blount. HV4764.A24 1996, (v6)
Ackefors, Hans. SH135.A25 1994, (v1)
Acker, Ally. PN1998.2.A24 1991, (v3)
Acker, Joan. HD6061.2.U62.O72 1989, (v6)
Ackerknecht, Erwin Heinz. R131.A173, (v2)
  R131.A34 1982, (v2)
  RC438.A253, (v2)
Ackerlind, Sheila R. PQ6060.A25 1989, (v3)
Ackerman, Bruce A. KF4541.A8 1991, (v7)
Ackerman, Diane. QH75.A32 1995, (v1)
Ackerman, Evelyn Bernette. DC801.B693.A34, (v5)
Ackerman, Gretchen P. PT8900.G7.A25 1987, (v3)
Ackerman, John. PR6039.H52.Z55, (v3)
Ackerman, Peter. JC328.3.A28 1994, (v7)
Ackerman, Robert William. PE1660.A23, (v3)
Ackerman, Robert. GN21.F65.A27 1987, (v6)
Ackerman, Sandra. QP376.A23 1992, (v1)
Ackermann, Alice. JZ6368.A26 1999, (v7)
Ackermann, Robert John. B3376.W564.A64 1988, (v8)
Ackley, Clifford S. NE667.2.A25, (v9)
Ackrill, J. L. B395.A29 1997, (v8)
Ackroyd, Peter. DA334.M8.A64 1998, (v5)
  PR4146.A23 1996, (v3)
Acocella, Joan Ross. PS3505.A87.Z545 2000, (v3)
Acosta, Mercedes de. PS3501.C7.Z52, (v3)
Acosta, Oscar Zeta. CT275.A186.A25 1996, (v5)
Acquaah, George. SB318.A3 1999, (v1)
Acton, Edward. DK40.A25 1995, (v5)
  DK265.A553.A28 1990, (v5)
Acton, H. B. B809.8.A32 1957, (v8)
Acuna, Rodolfo. E184.S75.A66 1998, (v4)
  F869.L89.M5 1996, (v4)
Aczel, Amir D. QA9.A236 2000, (v1)
  QA244.A29 1996, (v1)
  QB981.A35 1999, (v1)
Ad‾un‾is. PJ7541.A2913 1990b, (v3)
  PJ7862.A519A24, (v3)
Adair, Robert Kemp. QC21.2.A28 1987, (v1)
  QC26.A23 1990, (v1)
Adam, Christopher. HD4420.8.A33 1992, (v6)
Adam, Jan. HC340.3.A56 1999, (v6)
Adam, Peter. N6868.5.N37.A34 1992, (v9)
  NA1053.G73.A83 1987, (v9)
Adamczyk, Richard D. Z6207.W8 A34 1992, (v10)
Adamec, Christine A. HV875.55.A28 2000, (v6)
Adamec, Ludwig W. BP50.A33 2001, (v8)
  DS356.A26 1996, (v5)
  DS356.A27 1997, (v5)
Adami, Christoph. Q335.A3 1998, (v1)
Adamic, Louis. HN57.A55 1976, (v6)
Adamov, Arthur. PQ2601.D323.A19 1953, (v3)
Adams, A.E. QE471.15.C3A33 1998, (v1)
Adams, Abigail. E322.1.A293, (v4)
Adams, Alice E. PN56.C49.A23 1994, (v3)
Adams, Andy. PS3501.D2152L6 2000, (v3)
Adams, Annmarie. NA1997.A32 2000, (v9)
Adams, Ansel. F862.A59 1997, (v4)
  TR140.A3.A4 1988, (v1)
  TR145.A42, (v1)
  TR654.A34, (v1)
  TR660.5.A33, (v1)
Adams, Arthur E. DK265.8.U4.A6, (v5)
Adams, Bluford. GV1811.B3.A525 1997, (v6)
Adams, Brooks. F67.A22 1962, (v4)

Adams, Bruce Friend. HV9712.A63 1996, (v6)
Adams, Carol J. HV4708.A248 1994, (v6)
 HV4708.A25 1990, (v6)
Adams, Carolyn Teich. HD6055.A3, (v6)
Adams, Charles Francis. E322.A52 1971, (v4)
 F67.A24, (v4)
Adams, Charles Hansford. PS1442.L3.A3 1990, (v3)
Adams, Charles J. Z7833.A35 1977, (v10)
Adams, Clinton. NE535.N6.A33 1991, (v9)
Adams, Colin Conrad. QA612.2.A33 1994, (v1)
Adams, David Wallace. E97.5.A35 1995, (v4)
Adams, David. MT883.A23 1999, (v9)
Adams, E. Charles. E99.P9.A24 1991, (v4)
Adams, E. M. B821.A425 1991, (v8)
 BJ37.A3, (v8)
 BJ1360.A33 1997, (v8)
Adams, Edward C. L. PS3501.D21755.A6 1987, (v3)
Adams, Edward E. T55.A35 1995, (v1)
Adams, Ephraim Douglass. E469.A25, (v4)
Adams, Frank D. LB1051.A249 2001, (v7)
Adams, George Burton. DA30.P7622 vol. 2, (v5)
Adams, H. P. B3583.A3, (v8)
Adams, Hazard. PN1031.A28, (v3)
 PR4147.A63, (v3)
 PR5904.V53.A33 1995, (v3)
 PR5907.A33 1990, (v3)
 PR6005.A77.Z58 1983, (v3)
Adams, Henry. AC8.A22 1958, (v10)
 DC20.A2 1936, (v5)
 E175.5.A2 A3 2000, (v4)
 E175.5.A712 1931, (v4)
 E302.1.A253 1967, (v4)
 E302.6.G16.A3, (v4)
 E302.6.R2.A2 1972, (v4)
 NC139.B45.A4 1990, (v9)
 PS1004.A4.D4 1982, (v3)
Adams, Ian. JA84.G7.A33 1998, (v7)
Adams, Jacob E. LB2806.15.A35 2000, (v7)
Adams, Jad. PR4613.D5, (v3)
Adams, James Eli. PR468.M38.A33 1995, (v3)
Adams, James Truslow. E169.1.H67 vol. 3, (v4)
 E175.5.A1746, (v4)
 E176.A232, (v4)
 E302.J485, (v4)
 F4.A243, (v4)
 F7.A223, (v4)
 LC5251.A63, (v7)
Adams, Jan S. F2178.S65.A3 1992, (v4)
Adams, Jane. F547.U5.A34 1994, (v4)
Adams, Jane. HF5386.A513 1979, (v6)
Adams, Jerome R. F1407.A33 1991, (v4)
Adams, John Cranford. PR2920.A38 1961, (v3)
Adams, John Quincy. E302.1.A28, (v4)
 E337.8.A2. 1970, (v4)
 E337.8.A22, (v4)
 E341.A21, (v4)
 E377.A185 1981, (v4)
 PS1005.D4 1832, (v3)
 PS1005.P6 1854, (v3)
 PS1005.W3 1972, (v3)
Adams, John. E203.A57, (v4)
 E302.A26 1977, (v4)
 E302.A262 2000, (v4)
 E302.A264, (v4)
 E302.A275, (v4)
 E322.A3 1961, (v4)
 E322.A4 1988, (v4)
 JC176.A33 2000, (v7)
Adams, Joseph Quincy. PR1260.A3, (v3)
Adams, K. Gary. ML134.M66.A5 1989, (v9)
Adams, Katherine H. PE1405.U6.A33 1993, (v3)
 PS151.A34 2001, (v3)
Adams, Kimberly VanEsveld. PR756.W65.A64 2001, (v3)
Adams, Laurie. N5300.A33 1994, (v9)
 N7480.A32 1996, (v9)
Adams, Lowell W. QH541.5.C6.A52 1994, (v1)
Adams, Marilyn Jager. LB1050.A258 1990, (v7)
Adams, Marilyn McCord. BJ1401.A435 1999, (v8)
Adams, Michael C. C. D769.A56 1994, (v5)
Adams, Nicholson B. DP48.A3 1959, (v5)

Adams, Noah. F247.N5 A33 2001, (v4)
Adams, R. J. Q. DA578.A3 1993, (v5)
Adams, Richard E. W. F1435.1.R56.A33 1999, (v4)
Adams, Richard Newbold. HN143.5.A63, (v6)
Adams, Richard. PZ10.3.A197.Wat4, (v3)
Adams, Robert Martin. CB19.A35 1983, (v5)
 PQ2441.A3, (v3)
 PR6019.O9.U515 1962, (v3)
 PR6019.O9.Z5228, (v3)
Adams, Robert McCormick. CB478.A34 1996, (v5)
Adams, Samuel Hopkins. PS3501.D317 G7, (v3)
 PS3501.D317.R4, (v3)
Adams, Stephen B. HD9697.T454.W473 1999, (v6)
Adams, Stephen. PS3054.A33 1988, (v3)
Adams, Steve. QC7.A26 2000, (v1)
Adams, Thomas K. UA34.S64.A33 1998, (v10)
Adams, Timothy Dow. PS366.A88.A33 2000, (v3)
Adams, Vincanne. DS493.9.S5.A33 1996, (v5)
Adams, Virginia Best. F868.Y6.A39, (v4)
Adams, W. M. HC59.7.A714 2001, (v6)
Adams, Walter. HD2795.A23 1991, (v6)
Adams, William Howard. E332.45.A32 1997, (v4)
Adams, William Yeudale. CC72.7.A33 1991, (v5)
Adamson, Arthur W. QD506.A3 1997, (v1)
Adamson, David L. DA722.A33 1991, (v5)
Adamson, Donald. Q143.P17.A33 1995, (v1)
Adamson, Hans Christian. VK1023.A93, (v10)
Adamson, Hugh C. BP327.A33 1998, (v8)
Adamson, Jane. PR2836.A85 1987, (v3)
Adamson, Joni. PS153.I52.A33 2001, (v3)
Adamson, Joseph. PN75.F7.A67 1993, (v3)
 PS2388.P8.A63 1997, (v3)
Adamson, Joy. QL737.C2.A38 1960, (v1)
Adamson, Joy. QL737.C2.A4, (v1)
Adamson, Lynda G. Z1231.F4.D47 1999, (v10)
 Z5917.H6.A33 1999, (v10)
 Z7963.B6.A27 1999, (v10)
 Z7963.B6.A28 1998, (v10)
Adamson, Nancy. HQ1453.A54 1988, (v6)
Adamson, Walter L. DG735.6.A33 1993, (v5)
Adamthwaite, Anthony P. DC369.A33 1995, (v5)
Adas, Michael. T15.A33 1989, (v1)
Aday, Lu Ann. RA418.5.P6.A3 2001, (v2)
Adcock, F. E. U33.A3, (v10)
Adcock, Frank Ezra. PA6246.A53, (v3)
Addams, Jane. HN64.A2 1907a, (v6)
 HV4196.C4.H7 1911, (v6)
Addams, Jane. HV4196.C4.H72, (v6)
Addington, Larry H. U27.A294 1990, (v10)
Addis, Laird. B63.A3, (v8)
Addison, James Thayer. BX5880.A33 1969, (v8)
Addison, John T. HD6483.A26 1984, (v6)
Addison, Joseph. DA498.A3 1979, (v5)
 PR3301.G8 1978, (v3)
 PR3306.A53, (v3)
Addison, Paul S. QA614.86.A23 1997, (v1)
Addison, Paul. DA566.9.C5.A63 1993, (v5)
Addiss, Stephen. ND2071.A328 1989, (v9)
 PL806.K75.Z53 2000, (v3)
Ade, George. PS1006.A6.A6 1947, (v3)
 PS1006.A6.A7 1963, (v3)
 PS1006.A6.Z53 1973, (v3)
Adebayo, Aduke. PQ3984.A28 1995, (v3)
Adelaide, Debra. Z4023.5.W6.A34 1988, (v10)
Adeleke, Tunde. E185.625.A34 1998, (v4)
Adeleye, Gabriel. PE1582.A3.A34 1999, (v3)
Adelman, Gary. PR6023.A93.R3316 1991, (v3)
Adelman, Irving. Z1231.F4 A34 1996, (v10)
Adelman, Janet. PR3065.A37 1991, (v3)
Adelman, Kenneth L. UA23.A524 1990, (v10)
Adelson, Roger. DS63.2.G7.A34 1995, (v5)
Aden, John M. PR3422.A7, (v3)
Adenauer, Konrad. DD259.7.A3.A333, (v5)
Adereth, Maxwell. PQ305.A3 1968, (v3)
Ades, Dawn. N6502.4.A3 1989, (v9)
 NC1815.A33 1984, (v9)
Adey, Lionel. PR6023.E926.Z55 1998, (v3)
Adey, Walter H. SF457.5.A32 1998, (v1)
Adger, W. Neil. HD156.A34 1994, (v6)
Adi, Hakim. DA125.N4.A35 1998, (v5)
Adickes, Sandra. HQ1439.N6.A35 1997, (v6)

Adir, Karin. PN1992.4.A2.A62 1988, (v3)
Adkin, Mark. F2056.8.A35 1989, (v4)
Adkins, A. W. H. BJ171.R4.A3, (v8)
Adkins, C. J. QC311.A3 1975, (v1)
Adkins, Lesley. BL798.A35 1996, (v8)
Adkins, Lesley. DG77.A35 1994, (v5)
Adler, Alfred. BF173.A47, (v2)
 BF173.A5 1932, (v2)
 BF173.A52 1929, (v2)
 BF833.A4, (v2)
 LB885.A3 1969, (v7)
Adler, Claire Fisher. QA473.A15, (v1)
Adler, David A. F436.C95.A4 1996, (v4)
Adler, Gerhard. BF697.A3, (v2)
Adler, Irving. QA76.A28, (v1)
Adler, Jacob. HV8675.A35 1991, (v6)
Adler, Jeffrey S. HC108.S2.A64 1991, (v6)
Adler, Mortimer Jerome. B105.L45.A3, (v8)
 B481.A3, (v8)
 B945.A2864.A35, (v8)
 BD171.A24 1984, (v8)
 BF38.A23, (v2)
 BF431.A44 1990, (v2)
 BJ1012.A29 1991, (v8)
 LA132.A3, (v7)
 LA210.A534 1982, (v7)
 LC1011.A34 1983, (v7)
 LC1035.6.A35 1984, (v7)
 PN83.A43 1972, (v3)
Adler, Patricia A. GV889.26.A33 1991, (v6)
Adler, Rachel. BM729.W6.A29 1999, (v8)
Adler, Ronald. QC173.6.A34 1975, (v1)
Adler, Samuel. MT70.A3 2002, (v9)
Adler, Stephen J. KF8972.A735 1994, (v7)
Adler-Karlsson, Gunnar. HF1411.A28, (v6)
Adlington, Robert. ML410.B605.A35 2000, (v9)
Adloff, J. P. QD601.2.A35 1993, (v1)
Adoff, Arnold. PZ8.3.A233BI 2002, (v3)
Adolphson, Mikael S. DS850.A36 2000, (v5)
Adorno, Theodor W. B3199.A33.M4813 2000, (v8)
 B3199.A33.P76 2000, (v8)
 B3199.A34.A4213 1999, (v8)
 HN16.A3313 1998, (v6)
 ML60.A26513 1999, (v9)
 PN514.A313 1991, (v3)
Adrian, Arthur A. PR4592.P34.A37 1984, (v3)
Adriani, Gotz. ND553.T7.A4 1987, (v9)
 NE650.T68.A4 1988, (v9)
Adrienne. PE2837.F7.A368 1991, (v3)
Adshead, Samuel Adrian M. DS740.4.A644 1988, (v5)
Ady, Endre. PH3202.A35A24, (v3)
Ady, Peter H. G2446.G1.A3 1965, (v6)
Aelfric. PR1502.M4 ser. B, No. 2, (v3)
Aercke, Kristiaan. PN2174.A35 1994, (v3)
Aers, David. PR311.A33, (v3)
Aeschylus. PA3827.A7.H84 1999, (v3)
Afanas§ev, Viktor Grigor§evich. B809.8.A3273 1987, (v8)
Affron, Charles. PN1995.9.A74.A35 1995, (v3)
Affron, Charles. PQ2301.A3, (v3)
Afnan, Soheil Muhsin. B751.Z7.A6, (v8)
Aftalion, Florin. HC275.A6613 1990, (v6)
Afton, Jean. E99.C53.A37 1997, (v4)
Afzal, M. Rafique. DS384.A69 2001, (v5)
Afzal-Khan, Fawzia. PR9492.2.A4 1993, (v3)
Agamben, Giorgio. BH201.A395 1999, (v8)
 JC571.A16813 1998, (v7)
Aganbegian, Abel Gezevich. HC336.26.A42 1988, (v6)
Agaoglu, Adalet. PL248.A3116.U2513 1997, (v3)
Agar, Herbert. E744.A3, (v4)
Agar, Michael. GN346.A42, (v6)
Agarwal, B. K. QC482.S6.A34, (v1)
Agashe, Shripad N. QE905.A35 1995, (v1)
Agassiz, Louis. QL351.A26 1962, (v1)
Agate, James. PR627.A6 1958, (v3)
Agbasiere, Joseph Therese. DT515.45.I33 A35 2000, (v5)

Agee, James. PS3501.G35.A17 1968, (v3)
 PS3501.G35.A6 1985, (v3)
 PS3501.G35.A6 1996, (v3)
 PS3501.G35.D43, (v3)
 PS3501.G35.P4 1934, (v3)
 PS3501.G35.Z54 1971, (v3)
Agee, Philip. JK468.I6.A75 1975b, (v7)
Ager, D. V. QE260.A37 1980, (v1)
 QE506.A34 1993, (v1)
Aggeler, Geoffrey. PR658.T7.A35 1998, (v3)
 PR6052.U638.Z53, (v3)
Agger, Ben. HM24.A38 1989, (v6)
Aglion, Raoul. D752.A36 1988, (v5)
Agnelli, Marella. SB466.I8.A35 1987, (v1)
Agnew, John A. HC103.A37 1987, (v6)
Agnon, Shmuel Yosef. PJ5053.A4.A235, (v3)
 PJ5053.A4.A26 1995, (v3)
 PJ5053.A4.B52 1967, (v3)
 PJ5053.A4.H32 1967, (v3)
 PJ5053.A4.O7, (v3)
 PJ5053.A4.S5 1966, (v3)
Agosin, Marjorie. PQ8098.1.G6.Z466 2000, (v3)
Agosta, William C. QH541.15.C44, (v1)
 QH541.15.C44.A38 1996, (v1)
 QP572.P47.A4 1992, (v1)
Agran, Edward Gale. PN4874.W52.A63 1998, (v3)
Agrasanchez, Rogelio. PN1995.9.P5A35 2001, (v3)
 PN1995.9.P5.A35 2001, (v3)
Agrawal, Arun. DS432.R13.A37 1999, (v5)
 JS7180.3.A3 A73 1999, (v7)
Agrest, Diana. NA2500.A42 1991, (v9)
Agricola, Georg. TN617.A4, (v1)
Aguero, Felipe. DP272.A35 1995, (v5)
Aguiar, Sarah Appleton. PS374.W6.A36 2001, (v3)
Aguilar, Filomeno V. DS688.N5.A34 1998, (v5)
Aguilar, Francis J. HF5387.A4 1994, (v6)
Aguilera, Luis Gabriel. F548.9.M5.A38 2000, (v4)
Aguirre, Manuel. PN3435.A38 1990, (v3)
Agulhon, Maurice. DC272.A3513 1983, (v5)
 DC335.A3813 1993, (v5)
Agus, Jacob B. DS115.95.A6, (v5)
Agutter, Paul S. QH595.A36 1990, (v1)
Agyeman, Opoku. DT512.A66 1992, (v5)
Aharoni, Yohanan. G2230.A2 1993, (v6)
Ahdieh, Robert B. KLA2110.A93 1997, (v7)
Ahearn, Edward J. PN701.A34 1996, (v3)
Ahearn, Laura M. DS493.9.M3 A54 2001, (v5)
Ahl, Diane Cole. ND623.G8.A86 1996, (v9)
Ahlburg, Marlene Sophie. SB413.H443.A4813 1993, (v1)
Ahlfors, Lars Valerian. QA331.A45 1979, (v1)
 QA333.A43, (v1)
Ahmad Khan, Sarah. HD9577.N52.A334 1994, (v6)
Ahmadjian, Vernon. QK581.A35 1993, (v1)
Ahmed, Akbar S. BP52.A35 1988, (v8)
Ahmed, Akbar S. DS385.J5.A69 1997, (v5)
Ahmed, Feroz. GN635.P27.A38 1998, (v6)
Ahmed, Ishtiaq. DS341.A38 1996, (v5)
Ahmed, Jamal Mohammed. DS42.4.M5 3, (v5)
Ahmed, Leila. HQ1784.A67 1992, (v6)
 HQ1793.Z75.A55 1999, (v6)
Ahmed, Viqar. HC440.5.A723 1984, (v6)
Ahmet Hilmi Sehbenderzade. PL248.A31723.A8313 1993, (v3)
Ahnert, Frank O. GB402.A4613 1998, (v6)
Ahnstrom, Leif. HC240.A5944 1990, (v6)
Aho, Alfred V. QA76.9.D35.A38 1983, (v1)
Aho, James Alfred. F755.A1.A46 1990, (v4)
 HM136.A324 1994, (v6)
Ahrensdorf, Peter J. B379.A87 1995, (v8)
Ahsan, Aitzaz. DS376.9.A35 1996, (v5)
Aichele, Gary Jan. KF8745.H6.A62 1989, (v7)
Aichele, George. BS521.8.A53 2001, (v8)
Aidley, David J. QH603.I54.A33 1996, (v1)
Aigotti, Ronald E. RC263.A37 1996, (v2)
Aijaz Ahmad. PN849.U43.A36 1992, (v3)
Aiken, Charles S. F215.A4 1998, (v4)
Aiken, Conrad. PR99.A46, (v3)
 PS3501.I5 A15, (v3)
 PS3501.I5.A17 1970, (v3)
 PS3501.I5.B55, (v3)

PS3501.I5.B75, (v3)
 PS3501.I5.G7 1985, (v3)
 PS3501.I5.M6, (v3)
 PS3501.I5.Z48 1978, (v3)
 PS3501.I5.Z53 1971, (v3)
Aiken, Henry David. BJ354.A42.R4, (v8)
Aiken, Lewis R. BF697.A55 1999, (v2)
Aikens, C. Melvin. GN855.J2.A36, (v6)
Aikin, Judith Popovich. PT636.A35 1982, (v3)
Ailey, Alvin. GV1785.A38.A3 1994, (v6)
Ainalov, D. V. N6250.A613 1961, (v9)
Ainsworth, G. C. (Geoffrey Clough). QK600.35.A35 2001, (v1)
Ainsworth, Katherine. F864.S417, (v4)
Ainsworth-Land, George T. BD450.A4525 1986, (v8)
Aisenberg, Nadya. LB2332.3.A38 1988, (v7)
Aistrup, Joseph A. JK2356.A37 1996, (v7)
Aitchison, Jean. P116.A38 1996, (v3)
Aitken, A. C. QA191.A5 1956, (v1)
Aitken, George Atherton. PR3316.A5.Z53, (v3)
 PR3706.A7 1968, (v3)
Aitken, Hugh G. J. TK6547.A46, (v1)
Aitken, M. J. CC75.A3 1974, (v5)
Aitken, M. J. QE508.A35 1998, (v1)
Aitmatov, Chingiz. PL65.K59.A38813, (v3)
Aj̄ ita Kaura. PK2659.A37Z46513 1998, (v3)
Ajami, Fouad. DS63.1.A35, (v5)
Ajami, Mansour. PJ7553.A36 1988, (v3)
Akarli, Engin Deniz. DS84.A35 1993, (v5)
Akbar, M. J. DS481.N35.A73 1988, (v5)
Akenside, Mark. PR3310.A5.D8 1845, (v3)
Akenson, Donald H. DA925.A36 1988, (v5)
 F1059.L4.A38 1984, (v4)
Akers, Charles W. E322.1.A38.A35, (v4)
Akhmatova, Anna Andreevna, 1889-1966.
 PG3476.A324.A234 1992, (v3)
Akhtar, Shabbir. BP163.A417 1991, (v8)
Akhund, Iqbal. DS389.22.B48 A44 2000, (v5)
Akinsha, Konstantin. N8795.3.G3.A39 1995, (v9)
Akiyama, Terukazu. ND1050.A41, (v9)
Akrigg, G. P. V. DA391.A4, (v5)
Akutagawa, Ryunosuke, 1892-1927. PL801.K8.K313 1949, (v3)
 PL801.K8.J513, (v3)
 PL898.A35.J3, (v3)
 PL898.A35.R3 1952, (v3)
Akyeampong, Emmanuel Kwaku. HV5247.G4.A49 1996, (v6)
Al Ahmad, Jalal. PK6561.A38.M813, (v3)
 PK6561.A38.N813 1988, (v3)
Al Madfai, Madiha Rashid. E183.8.J6.A4 1993, (v4)
Alain-Fournier. PQ2611.O85.G7 1933, (v3)
 PQ2611.O85 G72, (v3)
Alali, A. Odasuo. P96.T472.A43 1994, (v3)
Al-Ali, Nadje Sadig. HQ1793.A75 2000, (v6)
 PJ8212.A49 1994, (v3)
Alam, Fakrul. PR9499.3.M77.Z516 1996, (v3)
Alam, Muzaffar. DS461.8.A43 1986, (v5)
Alanbrooke, Alan Brooke. D759.A617 2001, (v5)
Alanen, Arnold R. F589.G72.A42 1987, (v4)
Alarcon, Pedro Antonio de. PQ6502.A1 1954, (v3)
 PQ6502.A24 1997, (v3)
 PQ6502.A6 1999, (v3)
Alas, Leopoldo. PQ6503.A4.A24 2000, (v3)
 PQ6503.A4A6 2000, (v3)
 PQ6503.A4.C8413 1988, (v3)
Alas, Leopoldo. PQ6503.A4.R313 1984, (v3)
Alatas, Farid. JQ776.A43 1997, (v7)
Alavi, Buzurg. PK6561.A4.C513 1989, (v3)
Alaya, Flavia. PE64.A48.A3 1999, (v3)
Alba, Victor. HD6530.9.A7213, (v6)
Albahari, Ben. QA76.73.C154, (v1)
Albanese, Catherine L. BL2525.A4 1990, (v8)
 E209.A4, (v4)
Albanese, Denise. PR438.S35.A43 1996, (v3)
Albarede, Francis. QE515.A53 1995, (v1)
Albee, Edward. PS3501.L178.A7, (v3)
 PS3501.L178.B3, (v3)
 PS3501.L178.D4, (v3)
 PS3501.L178.T5, (v3)
 PS3501.L178.W5, (v3)

PS3501.L178.Z3, (v3)
Albee, Parker Bishop. D767.99.I9.A4 1995, (v5)
 G540.A43 1999, (v6)
Albelda, Randy Pearl. HV95.A5988 1997, (v6)
Albers, Anni. NK1505.A38 2000, (v9)
Albert, Adrien. QD561.A366 1984, (v1)
Albert, Bill. D618.A42 1988, (v5)
Albert, David Z. QC39.A4 1992, (v1)
Albert, Felix. F74.L9 A4313 1991, (v4)
Albert, Michel. HC59.15.A4313 1993, (v6)
Albert, Richard N. Z5917.S5.A43 1996, (v10)
Alberti, Johanna. HQ1236.5.G7.A44 1989, (v6)
Alberti, Leon Battista. NA2515.A32 1955, (v9)
 NA2515.A3513 1988, (v9)
Alberti, Rafael. PQ6601.L2.A22 1966, (v3)
Albertini, Bianca. NA2707.S3.A4 1988, (v9)
Albertini, Luigi. D511.A574, (v5)
Albertini, Rudolf von. DS33.7.A4313 1982, (v5)
Albertoni, Ettore A. JC265.M65.A6813 1987, (v7)
Alberts, Robert C. ND237.W45.A86, (v9)
Albinski, Henry Stephen. UA870.A39 1987, (v10)
Albinski, Nan Bowman. DU110.A58 1992, (v5)
Albion, Robert Greenhalgh. E748.F68.A6, (v4)
 U27.A6, (v10)
 VA454.A6 1965, (v10)
 VM15.A5, (v10)
Albisetti, James C. LC2105.A43 1988, (v7)
Alborg, Juan Luis. PQ6032.A45 1966, (v3)
Albrecht, Don E. HD1765.A43 1990, (v6)
Albrecht, Ernest J. GV1803.A43 1995, (v6)
Albrecht-Carrie, Rene. D363.A58, (v5)
 D388.A55, (v5)
 D523.A546, (v5)
 DC369.A48, (v5)
Albright, Ann Cooper. GV1588.6.A43 1997, (v6)
Albright, Daniel. PS310.M57.A55 1997, (v3)
Albright, Peggy. TR140.T47.A72 1996, (v1)
Albrow, Martin. H61.A54 1997, (v6)
Albuquerque, Severino Joao Medeiros.
 PQ7082.D7.A44 1991, (v3)
Alburger, James R. PN1992.8.A6.A42 1999, (v3)
Albus, Anita. ND673.E9A8413 2001, (v9)
Alchon, Suzanne Austin. F3721.3.D58.A43 1991, (v4)
Alcock, Antony Evelyn. D1056.A43 2000, (v5)
 HD7801.A53 1971b, (v6)
Alcock, James E. BF1045.S33.A42 1990, (v2)
Alcock, John. QH104.5.S58.A39 1993, (v1)
Alcock, Peter. HN385.5.A43 1996, (v6)
Alcock, Rutherford. DS809.A35 1969, (v5)
Alcott, Amos Bronson. PS1012.S6 1969, (v3)
 PS1012.T3 1877, (v3)
 PS1013.A4 1938, (v3)
 PS1013.A45.H4 1969, (v3)
Alcott, Louisa May. PS1016.E43 1997, (v3)
 PS1016.S56 1988, (v3)
 PS1016.S73 1988, (v3)
 PS1016.S73 1995, (v3)
 PS1017.B4 1975, (v3)
 PS1017.L5 1983, (v3)
 PS1017.L66 1995, (v3)
 PS1017.M6 1991, (v3)
 PS1018.A425 1989, (v3)
 PS1018.A44 1987, (v3)
 PZ7.A335Li 2002, (v3)
Aldcroft, Derek Howard. HC244.A622 1995, (v6)
 Z7165.E8.A4 1993, (v10)
Alden, Dauril. BX3742.A1.A53 1996, (v8)
Alden, Douglas William. PQ2623.A216.Z56, (v3)
Alden, John Doughty. VA59.A65, (v10)
Alden, John Richard. E207.G23.A6 1969, (v4)
 E312.A58 1995, (v4)
 F213.A4, (v4)
Alden, Patricia. PR9396.9.F3.Z54 1999, (v3)
Alder, Ken. DC151.A58 1997, (v5)
Alderman, Ellen. KF4750.A43 1990, (v7)
Aldersey-Williams, Hugh. QD181.C1.A43 1995, (v1)
Alderton, David. QL666.C5.A43 1988, (v1)
 QL666.C9.A33 1991, (v1)
 QL737.C22.P44 1994, (v1)

Aldington, Richard. PR1175.A64 1958, (v3)
PR6001.L4.D4, (v3)
PR6001.L4.R6, (v3)
PR6023.A93.Z553, (v3)
Aldiss, Brian Wilson. PR830.S35.A38 1986, (v3)
PR6051.L3, (v3)
PR6051.L3.B3, (v3)
PR6051.L3.H6 1976, (v3)
Aldous, Joan M. QA166.A425 2000, (v1)
Aldred, Cyril. N5350.A586 1961, (v9)
Aldrich, Bess Streeter. PS3501.L378.A6 1959, (v3)
PS3501.L378L3 1994, (v3)
PS3501.L378 W5, (v3)
Aldrich, John Herbert. JK2261.A46 1995, (v7)
Aldrich, Mark. T55.A38 1997, (v1)
Aldrich, Richard J. D754.T4.A43 1993, (v5)
D810.S7.A482 2000, (v5)
DU50.A39 1993, (v5)
JV151.A434 1998, (v7)
JV1811.A63 1996, (v7)
Aldridge, Alan. BL60.A53 1999, (v8)
Aldridge, Alfred Owen. E183.8.C5.A658 1993, (v4)
E302.6.F8 A47 1976, (v4)
Aldridge, Susan. QH442.A43 1996, (v1)
RM301.15.A43 1998, (v2)
Aldwell, Edward. MT50.A4444 2003, (v9)
Alecson, Deborah Golden. RJ253.5.A44 1995, (v2)
Alegria, Ciro. PQ8497.A56.A6 1963, (v3)
Alegria, Claribel. PQ7539.A47.F84 1993, (v3)
PQ7539.A47.M813 1989, (v3)
Alegria, Fernando. PQ8097.A734.M313 1993, (v3)
Aleichem, Sholom. PJ5129.R2 W3, (v3)
Aleixandre, Vicente. PQ6601.L26.A23 1979, (v3)
Alekseeva, Liudmila. HN527.A4713 1985, (v6)
Alerstam, Thomas. QL698.9.A4413 1990, (v1)
Alesina, Alberto. HB3743.A45 1995, (v6)
Alex, Lynn Marie. F623.A54 2000, (v4)
Alexander of Tunis, Harold Rupert Leofric George
Alexander. D743.A57 1962a, (v5)
Alexander, Bevin. E467.1.J15.A42 1992, (v4)
Alexander, Caroline. G850 1914 .S53.A58 1998, (v6)
Alexander, Charles C. E835.A645 1975, (v4)
GV865.H6.A32 1995, (v6)
Alexander, Christine. N6797.B758.A4 1995, (v9)
Alexander, Christopher. NA9031.A38 1987, (v9)
Alexander, Claire E. HV6439.G7, (v6)
Alexander, Doris. PN871.A44 1996, (v3)
PR4589.A44 1991, (v3)
Alexander, Doris. PS3529.N5.Z555 1992, (v3)
Alexander, Edward. D804.3.A425 1994, (v5)
F128.9.J5.A48 1998, (v4)
PJ5129.S49.Z575 1990, (v3)
Alexander, Franz. RC438.A39, (v2)
Alexander, Fred. F1029.A68, (v4)
Alexander, Hanan A. BL624.A43 2001, (v8)
Alexander, Harriet Semmes. Z1231.P7.A44 1984,
(v10)
Alexander, J. J. G. ND2920.A44 1992, (v9)
Alexander, James. JN6699.A15 A43 2000, (v7)
Alexander, Janet E. TK5105.888.A376 1999, (v1)
Alexander, Jeffrey C. HM24.A4647 1988, (v6)
HM24.A4649 1989, (v6)
Alexander, John T. DK170.A58 1989, (v5)
Alexander, June Granatir. F159.P69.S642 1987, (v4)
Alexander, Karl L. LB3063.A54 1994, (v7)
Alexander, Lawrence A. KF1325.C58.A43 1988, (v7)
Alexander, Lloyd. PZ7.A3774Bn 1999, (v3)
Alexander, Martin. TD192.5.A43 1994, (v1)
Alexander, Meena. PR457.A45 1989, (v3)
Alexander, Michael Van Cleave. DA330.A43 1980,
(v5)
Alexander, Peter. PR2894.A4, (v3)
Alexander, Peter. PR6045.O72.Z537 1992, (v3)
Alexander, R. McNeill. QE862.D5.A33 1989, (v1)
Alexander, R. S. DC239.A44 1991, (v5)
Alexander, Richard D. BJ58.A43 1987, (v8)
Alexander, Robert Jackson. F2237.A44 1994, (v4)
F2326.B4.A73, (v4)
F2538.22.K8.A83 1991, (v4)
Alexander, Robin J. LB43.A44 2001, (v7)
Alexander, Ruth M. HV9105.N7.A67 1995, (v6)

Alexander, Shana. KF224.B23.A44 1988, (v7)
Alexander, Sidney. N6999.C46.A9 1978, (v9)
PS3501.L592.M5, (v3)
Alexander, Simone A. James. PR9205.4.A48 2001,
(v3)
Alexander, Victoria D. N510.A43 1996, (v9)
Alexander, William Marvin. LB1623.A43, (v7)
Alexander-Williams, John. F241.W72, (v4)
Alexandra. DK254.A5.A3 1997, (v5)
Alexandridis, Nikitas A. QA76.5.A369 1984, (v1)
Alexandrov, Vladimir E. PG3476.N3.Z56 1991, (v3)
Alexis, Jacques Stephen. PQ3949.A34.C6613 1999,
(v3)
Alexopoulos, Constantine John. QK603.A55 1979,
(v1)
Alexseev, Mikhail A. D32.A54 1997, (v5)
Alfonso X, King of Castile and Leon. PQ9191.A54.A6
1941, (v3)
Alford, C. Fred. BJ1406.A44 1997, (v8)
Alford, D. V. SB608.O7.A44 1995, (v1)
Alford, John A. PR2017.Q67.A44 1992, (v3)
Alford, William P. KNN1155.A958 1995, (v7)
Alfred, Gerald R. E99.M8.A53 1995, (v4)
Algarin, Joanne P. Z3308.L5.A44 1982, (v10)
Alger, Jeff. QA76.73.C153.A43 1998, (v1)
Algra, Keimpe. B187.S7.A54 1994, (v8)
Algren, Nelson. PS374.S5, (v3)
PS3501.I4625.A7 1947, (v3)
PS3501.L4625.M3, (v3)
PS3501.L4625.W3, (v3)
PS3501.L4625.W5, (v3)
Ali, Ahmed. PR6001.L45.T9 1966, (v3)
Ali, Asad. PJ7812.A8.A24 1991, (v3)
Ali, Azra Asghar. HQ1742.A43 2000, (v6)
Alibek, Ken. UG447.8.A45 1999, (v10)
Aliber, Robert Z. HG4538.A567 1993, (v6)
Alibhai-Brown, Yasmin. DA125.A1.A77 2001, (v5)
Alkana, Joseph. PS374.P7.A45 1997, (v3)
Alkhafaji, Abbass F. HD2746.5.A38 1990, (v6)
Al-Khalesi, Yasin M. PJ6823.K43 2001, (v3)
Al-Khalili, Jim. QC173.59.S65.A4 1999, (v1)
Alkon, Paul K. PN3433.5.A45 1994, (v3)
Allan, Barbara. QD9.A43 1994, (v1)
Z6675.A42.A43 1988, (v10)
Allan, David. DA812.A43 1993, (v5)
Allan, George. LB2322.2.A45 1997, (v7)
Allan, J. David. QH541.5.S7.A435 1995, (v1)
Allan, John A. B. RJ504.A43 1988, (v2)
Allan, Keith. PE1585.A37 1991, (v3)
Allan, Robin. PD3105.A45 1995, (v3)
PN1999.W27.A44 1999, (v3)
Allan, Sarah. B126.A44 1991, (v8)
B126.A45 1997, (v8)
Allan, Sean. PT2379.Z5.A53 1996, (v3)
Allan, Tuzyline Jita. PR888.F45.A45 1995, (v3)
Allara, Pamela. ND1329.N36.A9 1998, (v9)
Allard, C. Kenneth. UA23.A593 1990, (v10)
Allard, Dean C. Z1249.N3.A48, (v10)
Allard, Harry. PZ7.A413Mi, (v3)
Allaway, Roger. GV944.U6 A44 2001, (v6)
Allchin, Bridget. DS339.A45 1997, (v5)
DS425.A65 1968b, (v5)
Allchin, F. Raymond. DS338.A45 1995, (v5)
Allday, Jonathan. TL790.A43 2000, (v1)
Allee, Verna. HD58.82.A37 1997, (v6)
Allegre, Claude J. QE31.A4413 1992, (v1)
Allen, B. L. QM34.A39 1987, (v1)
Allen, Barry. BD171.A3855 1993, (v8)
Allen, Calvin H. DS247.O68.A59 2000, (v5)
Allen, Carolyn. PS153.L46.A45 1996, (v3)
Allen, Catherine J. F2230.2.K4.A45 1988, (v4)
Allen, Charles F. E840.8.C57.A44 1992, (v4)
Allen, Charles. DS392.N67 A45 2001, (v5)
Allen, Charlotte Vale. HQ71.A4, (v6)
Allen, Colin. BC108.A543 2001, (v8)
Allen, Craig. E836.A815 1993, (v4)
Allen, David Grayson. HF5616.U7.P752 1993, (v6)
Allen, Dennis W. PR878.S49.A43 1993, (v3)
Allen, Don Cameron. PR503.A4, (v3)
PR531.A4 1968, (v3)
PR3588.A59 1970, (v3)

Allen, Donald Merriam. PN1042.A54, (v3)
Allen, Durward Leon. SK361.A66 1962, (v1)
Allen, E. John B. GV854.4.A4 1993, (v6)
Allen, Elsa Guerdrum. Q11.P6 n.s., vol. 41, pt. 3 1969,
(v1)
Allen, Frederick Lewis. E741.A66, (v4)
E784.A63 1986, (v4)
Allen, George Edward. E748.A195.A3 1950, (v4)
Allen, Graham. PN98.I58.A45 2000, (v3)
Allen, Herman R. LB2329.5.A4, (v7)
Allen, Hervey. PS3501.L5.A25, (v3)
PS3501.L5.A59, (v3)
PS3501.L5.C5, (v3)
Allen, Irving L. PE2846.A44 1983, (v3)
Allen, J. de V. DT365.45.S93.A45 1993, (v5)
Allen, James B. Z7845.M8.A44 2000, (v10)
Allen, James Paul. G1201.E1.A4 1988, (v6)
Allen, James Smith. Z1003.5.F7.A45 1991, (v10)
Allen, Janet. LB1573.A445 2000, (v7)
Allen, John C. HN79.W2.A43 1994, (v6)
Allen, John Houghton. F391.A47, (v4)
Allen, John Logan. F592.7.A48, (v4)
Allen, Jon G. RC552.P67.A45 1995, (v2)
Allen, Larry. HC79.C3.A45 1998, (v6)
HG216.A43 1999, (v6)
Allen, Louise Anderson. AM3.6.B73, (v10)
Allen, Margaret Prosser. NA3576.A1.A45 1991, (v9)
Allen, Marvin. HQ1090.A45 1993, (v6)
Allen, Michael Patrick. QA278.2.A434 1997, (v1)
Allen, Michael. F517.A39 1990, (v4)
GV1834.A55 1998, (v6)
PN1998.3.G76.A45 1999, (v3)
PR4582.A44 1988, (v3)
Allen, Myron B. QA297.A53 1998, (v1)
Allen, P. S. CB367.A5 1963, (v5)
Allen, Paula Gunn. E98.W8.A439 1991, (v4)
Allen, Peter L. PN682.L68.A45 1992, (v3)
RA644.V4.A45 2000, (v2)
Allen, Prudence. BD450.A4725 1997, (v8)
Allen, R. T. BD450.A4727 1992, (v8)
JC585.A385 1998, (v7)
Allen, Richard F. PT7269.N5.A4, (v3)
Allen, Richard Hinckley. QB802.A4 1963, (v1)
Allen, Richard. PN1995.A376 1995, (v3)
Allen, Robert L. HN57.A57, (v6)
Allen, Robert Loring. HB119.F5.A74 1993, (v6)
HB119.S35.A64 1990, (v6)
Allen, Robert S. F196.A67, (v4)
Allen, Roger M. A. PJ7510.A43 2000, (v3)
PJ7577.A4 1995, (v3)
Allen, Roy E. HB3722.A36 1999, (v6)
Allen, Roy F. PT553.A4, (v3)
Allen, Susan Heuck. DF212.C35.A67 1999, (v5)
Allen, Terence. TA418.8.A43 1990, (v1)
Allen, Theodore. E185.A44 1994, (v4)
Allen, Thomas B. D769.2.A48 1995, (v5)
F203.4.W3 A46 2000, (v4)
Allen, W. Sidney. PA267.A4 1987, (v3)
Allen, Walter Ernest. PR821.A4 1955, (v3)
Allen, William C. F204.C2 A458 2001, (v4)
Allen, William Sheridan. DD256.5.A58, (v5)
Allende, Isabel. PQ8098.1.L54A6713 1998, (v3)
PQ8098.1.L54C313 1985, (v3)
PQ8098.1.L54R4813 2001, (v3)
PQ8098.1.L54Z465 1999, (v3)
Allensworth, Wayne, 1959-. DK510.555.A45 1998,
(v5)
Allentuch, Harriet Ray. PQ1925.A953, (v3)
Aller, Lawrence H. QB461.A568 1991, (v1)
Alley, Henry. PR4692.E8.A45 1997, (v3)
Alley, Richard B. QC884.A55 2000, (v1)
Alley, Robert S. KF4162.A94 1994, (v7)
KF4162.A944 1996, (v7)
Alleyne, Mark D. PN4784.F6.A45 1997, (v3)
Alleyne, Mervyn C. F1874.A45 1988, (v4)
Alligor, Catherine. HQ1236.5.U6.A45 2000, (v6)
Alliance for Technology Access. HV1569.5.A45 2000,
(v6)
Alligood, Kathleen T. QA614.8.A44 1997, (v1)

Allingham, Margery. PR6001.L678.B, (v3)
PR6001.L678.C7 1970, (v3)
PR6001.L678|bD42, (v3)
PR6001.L678.F6, (v3)
PR6001.L678.H5, (v3)
PR6001.L678.L66, (v3)
PR6001.L678.M58, (v3)
PR6001.L678.M97 1930, (v3)
PR6001.L678.P6, (v3)
PR6001.L678.S9 1950, (v3)
PR6001.L678.T47, (v3)
Allingham, Margery. PR6001.L678.T5, (v3)
Allinson, Gary D. DS889.A59 1997, (v5)
Allinson, Mark. HN460.5.Z9.P82 1999, (v6)
Allison, Anne. GT3415.J3.A45 1994, (v6)
Allison, David B. RC569.5.M83.A38 1998, (v2)
Allison, Henry E. B2799.F8.A44 1990, (v8)
Allison, Jenene J. PQ1963.C55.Z513 1995, (v3)
Allison, Jonathan. Z8460.875.A55 1996, (v10)
Allison, Mary Bruins. R722.32.A45.A3 1994, (v2)
Allison, Robert J. DT197.5.U6.A45 1995, (v5)
Allison, Susan. F1089.O5.A44 1976, (v4)
Alliston, April. PR858.E65.A44 1996, (v3)
Allitt, Patrick. BX4668.A1.A44 1997, (v8)
Allman, Eileen Jorge. PR678.R45.A55 1999, (v3)
Allman, Jean Marie. DT507.A45 2000, (v5)
Allman, John Morgan. QP376.A423 1999, (v1)
Allman, Paula. HB501.A553 2001, (v6)
Allmand, C. T. DA256.A4 1992, (v5)
Allmendinger, Blake. PS271.A44 1998, (v3)
Allmendinger, David F. F230.R932.A45 1990, (v4)
Allmon, Warren D. ND237.P1668, (v9)
Allott, Kenneth. PR6013.R44.Z6, (v3)
Allott, Miriam Farris. PR4168.A7 1974, (v3)
Allport, Floyd Henry. BF311.A5, (v2)
Allport, Gordon W. BF38.A38, (v2)
Allsen, Thomas T. DS22.3.A45 1987, (v5)
Allsop, Peter. ML410.C78.A8 1999, (v9)
Allsop, Peter. ML1156.A44.I8 1992, (v9)
Allsopp, Bruce. NA200.A45 1960, (v9)
Allworth, Edward. DK948.62.A45 1990, (v5)
Allyn, David. HQ18.U5.A38 2000, (v6)
Allyn, Joseph Pratt. F811.A44 1974, (v4)
Almaguer, Tomas. F870.A1.A46 1994, (v4)
Almeder, Robert F. BD161.A47 1998, (v8)
BJ1012.A45 2000, (v8)
Almeida, Anna Luiza Ozorio de. HD499.A44.A457 1995, (v6)
Almog, Oz. DS113.3.A5613 2000, (v5)
Almog, Ruth. PJ5054.A4972.M313 1993, (v3)
Almond, Barbara. PN56.P92.A47 1996, (v3)
Almond, Brenda. BD21.A38 1995, (v8)
Almquist, Sharon G. ML158.4.A46 1999, (v9)
Alnasrawi, Abbas. HC498.A667 1991, (v6)
HD9560.5.A5153 1985, (v6)
HD9576.I72.A647 1994, (v6)
Al-Nowaihi, Magda M. PJ7755.I22Z54 1993, (v3)
Alofsin, Anthony. NA737.W7.A87 1993, (v9)
Alok Rai. PR6029.R8.Z575 1988, (v3)
Alonso Pedraz, Martin. PC4667.A4, (v3)
Alonso, Ana Maria. F1261.A45 1995, (v4)
Alonso, Carlos J. PQ7082.N7.A58 1990, (v3)
Alonso, Damaso. PQ6057.A4, (v3)
PQ6077.A4, (v3)
PQ6400.J8.Z54 1966, (v3)
Alonso, Harriet Hyman. JX1965.A45 1993, (v7)
Alonso, Paula. JL2098.U6, (v7)
Alonzo, Armando C. F392.R5.A46 1998, (v4)
Alót̄ af F̄ aótimah. PK2200.A713D313 1993, (v3)
Alpatov, Mikhail Vladimirovich. N6981.A5413 1969, (v9)
Alpern, Hymen. PQ6217.A7, (v3)
Alpern, Mathew. BF292.A4, (v2)
Alpern, Stanley B. UB419.B46.A48 1998, (v10)
Alperovitz, Gar. E813.A75 1994, (v4)
HC106.8.A42 1984, (v6)
Alpers, Antony. PR6025.A57.Z557, (v3)
PR9639.3.M258.Z58, (v3)
Alpers, Edward A. HF3899.E3.A46 1975, (v6)
Alpers, Paul J. PN56.P3.A43 1996, (v3)
PR533.A65, (v3)

PR2358.A87, (v3)
Alpers, Svetlana. N6953.R4.A88 1988, (v9)
ND623.T5.A84 1994, (v9)
Alpert, Harry. H31.C7 no. 445, (v6)
Alpert, IA. L. QC16.A342, (v1)
Alpert, Jane. HN90.R3 A66 1990, (v6)
Alpert, Michael. DP257.A54 1993, (v5)
Alphey, Luke. QP625.N89A45 1997, (v1)
Alsop, Derek. PR821.A45 1999, (v3)
Alsop, Rachel. HQ1075.A435 2002, (v6)
Alsop, Susan Mary. DC707.A45, (v5)
Alspach, Russell K. PR8761.A4 1960, (v3)
Alster, Tina S. RL120.L37A45 1997, (v2)
Alston, J. B. PR9387.3.A47 1989, (v3)
Alston, Jon P. Z7164.C81.A46 1993, (v10)
Alston, R. C. Z2013.5.W6.A48 1991, (v10)
Alston, William P. BD171.A42 1996, (v8)
BD212.A47 1989, (v8)
BD214.A57 1993, (v8)
BT102.A46 1991, (v8)
Alt, Betty Sowers. DX145.A47 1995, (v5)
Alt, David D. QE79.A46 1995, (v1)
Altemeyer, Bob. HM271.A457 1988, (v6)
JC481.A48 1996, (v7)
Altenbaugh, Richard J. LC5051.A69 1990, (v7)
Alter, George. HQ1655.V47.A47 1988, (v6)
Alter, J. Cecil. PN4897.U83A6, (v3)
Alter, Joseph S. DS480.45.A782 2000, (v5)
Alter, Judith B. GV1783.A48 1994, (v6)
Alter, Nora M. PN1650.V53.A48 1996, (v3)
Alter, Robert. BS535.A57 1991, (v8)
BS1171.2.A45, (v8)
PJ5017.A4, (v3)
PN771.A69 2000, (v3)
PQ2436.A5, (v3)
PT405.A473 1991, (v3)
Alterman, Eric. E183.7.A45 1998, (v4)
Alterman, Glenn. PN2080.A447 1998, (v3)
Althaus, Horst. B2947.A67 2000, (v8)
Althusser, Louis. B785.M24.A48 1999, (v8)
B4249.L384.A69 1972, (v8)
BF109.F74.A82513 1996, (v2)
Altick, Richard Daniel. PN5130.P8.A57 1997, (v3)
PR33.A4, (v3)
PR56.A68 1993, (v3)
PR56.A7, (v3)
PR878.R4.A48 1991, (v3)
Z1003.5.G7 A53 1998, (v10)
Altintas, Yusuf. TJ1185.5.A48 2000, (v1)
Altizer, Thomas J. J. BT198.A48 1997, (v8)
Altman, Dennis. HQ16.A38 2001, (v6)
HQ76.3.U5.A4 1982, (v6)
Altman, Ida. F1391.P6, (v4)
Altman, Irwin. HQ981.A45 1996, (v6)
Altman, Joseph. BF671.A4, (v2)
Altman, Linda Jacobs. F861.3.A45 1997, (v4)
Altman, Roberta. RC262.A39 2000, (v2)
RC280.B8.A444 1996, (v2)
Altmann, Barbara K. PQ1575.Z5.A44 1998, (v3)
Altringham, John D. QL737.C5.A4 1996, (v1)
Altschiller, Donald. HV6773.52.A47 1999, (v6)
Altschule, Mark D. R145.A46 1989, (v2)
Altschuler, Bruce E. E847.2.A38 1990, (v4)
Altschuler, Glenn C. E337.5.A48 2000, (v4)
PN1992.3.U5.A47 1992, (v3)
Altschull, J. Herbert. PN4731.A389 1990, (v3)
Altshuler, Alan A. HE308.A63, (v6)
HJ9156.A64 1993, (v6)
Altshuler, Bruce. N6490.A612 1994, (v9)
Altshuler, Bruce. NB237.N6.A86 1994, (v9)
Altstadt, Audrey L. DK696.6.A48 1992, (v5)
Alvarez, A. PR541.A7 1962, (v3)
Alvarez, A. PR603.A4 1958, (v3)
Alvarez, Alex. HV6322.7.A58 2001, (v6)
Alvarez, David J. D810.C88.A48 2000, (v5)
D810.S7.A559 1997, (v5)
Alvarez, Jose E. DT324.5.A48 2001, (v5)
Alvarez, R. Michael. JK528.A64 1997, (v7)
Alvarez, Sonia E. HQ1236.5.B6.A44 1990, (v6)
Alvarez, Walter C. R154.A545.A3, (v2)
Alvarez-Borland, Isabel. PS153.C83.A58 1998, (v3)

Alvarez-Pereyre, Jacques. PR9360.9.P76.A4813 1984, (v3)
Alves, Abel A. F1230.A49 1996, (v4)
Alvesson, Mats. HD30.19.A45 1996, (v6)
Alvey, R. Gerald. GR110.K4A46 1992, (v6)
Alvord, Clarence Walworth. F212.A47, (v4)
Alwes, Karla. PR4838.W6.A45 1993, (v3)
Alwood, Edward. P96.S45.A44 1996, (v3)
Aly, Gotz. D804.3.A45813 1999, (v5)
Am̄ ir, Dayz̄ i. PJ7814.M577A8313 1994, (v3)
Amaker, Norman C. KF4757.A85 1988, (v7)
Aman, Alfred C. KF5407.A84 1992, (v7)
Amanat, Abbas. DS307.N38.A63 1997, (v5)
Amar Singh. DS485.R19 A85 2000, (v5)
Amar, Akhil Reed. KF4550.Z9.A43 1998, (v7)
KF4750.A436 1998, (v7)
KF9619.A72196 1997, (v7)
Amarasinghe, Upali. PR3424.A4, (v3)
Amato, Joseph Anthony. BJ1471.A468 1982, (v8)
RA577.D8.A48 2000, (v2)
Ambegaokar, Vinay. QC174.8.A43 1996, (v1)
Ambert, Alba N. LC3731.A65 1985, (v7)
Ambler, Charles H. DT433.57.A43 1988, (v5)
Ambler, Eric. PR6001.M48.L5, (v3)
Ambler, John S. UA700.A65, (v10)
Ambler, Scott W. QA76.64.A494 2001, (v1)
Ambroise, fl. ca. 1196. D163.A3.A52, (v5)
Ambrose, Gordon. RC495.A48 1968, (v2)
Ambrose, James E. TA658.44.A43 1999, (v1)
Ambrose, Stephen E. E836.A828 1987, (v4)
E856.A72 1988, (v4)
TF23.A48 2000, (v1)
U410.L1.A7, (v10)
Ambrosini, Richard. PR6005.O4.Z5465 1991, (v3)
Ambrosius, Lloyd E. D645.A42 1987, (v5)
Amdahl, Kenn. QC527.A58 1991, (v1)
Amelang, James S. CT25.A49 1998, (v5)
Amell, Alma. PQ6663.O554.Z56 1994, (v3)
Amell, Samuel. Z2694.F4.A64 1996, (v10)
Amenta, Edwin. HN57.A584 1998, (v6)
American Assembly. DS518.8.A856 1962, (v5)
JK851.A7, (v7)
American Association for Health, Physical Education, and Recreation. GV881.A1.A6, (v6)
Z6121.A62, (v10)
American Association for the Advancement of Science. E51.S7 no.9, (v4)
American Chemical Society. QD1.A355 no. 237, (v1)
QD1.A355 no. 241, (v1)
QD77.A54 2000, (v1)
QD474.A44 1993, (v1)
American Council on Education. LA227.3.A44a, (v7)
American Economic Association. HB34.A48, (v6)
American Home Economics Association. TS1445.A46 1974, (v1)
American Institute of Architects. NA712.A65, (v9)
NA735.D2.A4, (v9)
NA735.W3.A6, (v9)
American Institute of Physics. QC61.A5 1963, (v1)
American Library Association. Z673.A5.A14, (v10)
Z682.A4995 1968, (v10)
Z695.A52 1949, (v10)
Z695.95.A52 1980, (v10)
Z720.A4.U37, (v10)
American Museum of Natural History. E78.N78.A45 1988, (v4)
American Psychiatric Association. RC451.5.A2.A46 1994, (v2)
American Society for Testing and Materials. TA401.A653, (v1)
American Society of Photogrammetry. TA593.25.A48 1980, (v1)
American University (Washington, D.C.). DS54.A3.K43 1980, (v5)
DS70.6.S6 1979, (v5)
F1563.A63 1965, (v4)
F1563.A63 1980, (v4)
American Veterans Committee. UB357.A22, (v10)
Amerine, M. A. (Maynard Andrew). TP548.A48 1976, (v1)
Ameringer, Charles D. F1787.5.A6975 2000, (v4)

Amerson, Robert. F657.D4A48 1996, (v4)
Ames, Charles Edgar. HE2791.U55.A4, (v6)
Ames, Christopher. PN1995.9.M65.A43 1997, (v3)
Ames, Kenneth L. E168.A517 1992, (v4)
Ames, Lynda J. HV1446.N5.A54 1997, (v6)
Ames, Nancy L. LB1623.5.U6.A45 1994, (v7)
Ames, Roger T. BL1900.H824 E5 1994, (v8)
Ames, Ruth M. PR1933.R4.A43 1984, (v3)
Ames, Van Meter. B851.A48 1978, (v8)
Ames-Lewis, Francis. N6370.A58 2000, (v9)
Amico, Robert P. BD182.A45 1993, (v8)
Amiet, Pierre. N5345.A7413 1980, (v9)
Amin, Samir. HC59.A7852513 1994, (v6)
    HC59.7.A7777 1990, (v6)
Amin, Samir. HF1413.A4513 1990, (v6)
Amin, Shahid. DS486.C464.A45 1995, (v5)
Aminov, Yu A. QA643.A52, (v1)
Aminzade, Ronald. DC252.A46 1993, (v5)
Amirahmadi, Hooshang. HC473.A48 1990, (v6)
Amiran, Eyal. PR6003.E282.Z5632 1993, (v3)
Amireh, Amal. PS374.W6.A45 2000, (v3)
Amis, Kingsley. PR830.S35.A4, (v3)
    PR6001.M6.A17 1980, (v3)
    PR6001.M6.C3, (v3)
    PR6001.M6.I2, (v3)
    PR6001.M6.L8, (v3)
    PR6001.M6.M9, (v3)
    PR6001.M6.O5, (v3)
    PR6001.M6.T3, (v3)
    PR6001.M6.T5, (v3)
Amitai-Preiss, Reuven. DS19.A62 1998, (v5)
Ammer, Christine. ML82.A45, (v9)
Ammeraal, L. (Leendert). QA76.73.C153A45 1996, (v1)
Ammerman, Nancy Tatom. BX7800.F864.A45 1987, (v8)
Ammon, Harry. E372.A65 1990, (v4)
    Z8587.8.A46 1991, (v10)
Ammonius. B438.A9513 1991, (v8)
Ammons, A. R. PS3501.M6.E9 1964, (v3)
Amory, Cleveland. F73.37.A5, (v4)
Amory, Patrick. DG504.A56 1997, (v5)
Amoss, Benjamin McRae. PQ2443.A67 1992, (v3)
Amott, Teresa L. HQ1410.A46 1991, (v6)
Amrita Pritam. PK2659.A44A2 1990, (v3)
Amrita Pritam. PK2659.A44.T8, (v3)
Amsden, Alice H. HC59.7.A7784 2001, (v6)
Amsden, Charles Avery. E99.N3 A46 1991, (v4)
Amsel, Nachum. BJ1285.A53 1994, (v8)
Amselle, Jean-Loup. GN652.M25.A4713 1998, (v6)
Amsterdam, Anthony G. KF425.A48 2000, (v7)
Amstock, Joseph S. TA450.A55 1997, (v1)
Amstutz, Mark R. JZ1306.A48 1999, (v7)
Amtower, Laurel. Z1003.5.E9, (v10)
Amundsen, Roald. G585.A6.A3 1987, (v6)
    G850 1910.A5213 1976, (v6)
Amuzegar, Jahangir. HC475.A644 1993, (v6)
An, Ok-Sun. BJ69.A5 1998, (v8)
An, Tai Sung. DS557.7.A5 1998, (v5)
Anagnostopoulos, Georgios. B491.E7.A53 1994, (v8)
Anand, Mulk Raj. PR6001.N24.C6, (v3)
    PR6001.N24.P7, (v3)
Anastaplo, George. KF4528.A53 1989, (v7)
    KF4557.A53 1995, (v7)
Anastopoulos, Arthur D. RJ506.H9.A593 2001, (v2)
Anbinder, Tyler. E453.A52 1992, (v4)
Ancell, R. Manning. D736.A63 1996, (v5)
Ancheta, Angelo N. KF4757.A75.A53 1998, (v7)
Anchorage Museum of History and Art. N8214.5.U6.A53 1993, (v9)
Andaya, Barbara Watson. DS646.15.S77.A53 1993, (v5)
Andel, Jiri. QA273.25.A54 2001, (v1)
Anders, George J. TK3307.A69 1997, (v1)
Anders, George. RA413.5.U5.A55 1996, (v2)
Anders, John P. PS3505.A87.Z557 1999, (v3)
Anders, Timothy. BJ1401.A53 1994, (v8)
Andersch, Alfred. PT2601.N353.V3813 1994, (v3)
Andersen Nexo, Martin. PT8175.N4 D53, (v3)
    PT8175.N4 I513, (v3)
Andersen, Arlow W. PN4885.N6.A64 1990, (v3)

Andersen, H. C. H. C. (Hans Christian), 1805-1875.
    PT8116.E5 1980, (v3)
    PT8118.A6 1990, (v3)
    PZ8.A54Han 1978, (v3)
    PZ8.A65 F3, (v3)
Andersen, Kristi. JK2317 1928.A53 1979, (v7)
Andersen, Martin Edwin. F2848.A6 1993, (v4)
Andersen, Robin. PN1992.6.A55 1995, (v3)
Andersen, Wayne V. ND553.G27.A74 1971, (v9)
Anderson Imbert, Enrique. PQ7081.A5634, (v3)
Anderson, Amanda. PR468.W6.A53 1993, (v3)
Anderson, Anthony B. HD9769.B323.A453 1991, (v6)
Anderson, Beatrix. PF3640.A48, (v3)
Anderson, Benedict R. O'G. DS525.7.A53 1998, (v5)
Anderson, Bern. E591.A54 1977, (v4)
    G246.V3.A7 1960, (v6)
Anderson, Bonnie S. HQ1587.A53 2000, (v6)
Anderson, Carlotta R. HX843.7.L33.A53 1998, (v6)
Anderson, Celia Catlett. PR468.N6.A53 1989, (v3)
Anderson, Charles W. JC571.A498 1990, (v7)
Anderson, Christopher. PN1992.75.A49 1994, (v3)
Anderson, Clifford. BF710.A53 1995, (v2)
Anderson, D. T. QL444.C58.A53 1994, (v1)
Anderson, David D. E767.A53, (v4)
Anderson, David F. TL570.A69 2001, (v1)
Anderson, David G. E99.M6815.A53 1994, (v4)
Anderson, David L. E835.A72 1991, (v4)
    QC721.A52, (v1)
Anderson, Debra J. LB1775.2.A53 1995, (v7)
Anderson, Donald F. E761.A83, (v4)
Anderson, Donald M. Z40.A5, (v10)
Anderson, Donna K. ML410.G9134.A8 1993, (v9)
Anderson, Douglas. E302.6.F8.A57 1997, (v4)
    PS169.C65.A54 1990, (v3)
Anderson, E. Ruth. ML390.A54 1982, (v9)
Anderson, Edward F. GN635.T4.A53 1993, (v6)
Anderson, Edward F. QK495.C11, (v1)
Anderson, Elizabeth. BD232.A48 1993, (v8)
Anderson, Eugene N. GE170.A53 1996, (v6)
Anderson, Eugene Newton. D360.A5, (v5)
Anderson, Ewan W. DS44.96.A53 2000, (v5)
Anderson, Ewan W. G1046.F1 .A5 1993, (v6)
Anderson, G. M. QE515.5.T46.A53 1996, (v1)
Anderson, George Kumler. PR173.A5 1962, (v3)
Anderson, Irvine H. HD9576.S35.A72, (v6)
Anderson, J. K. U33.A5, (v10)
Anderson, Jack. GV1783.A53 1997, (v6)
Anderson, James A. QP363.3.A534 1995, (v1)
Anderson, James D. LC2802.S9.A53 1988, (v7)
Anderson, James E. HF1713.A528 1998, (v6)
Anderson, James Francis. BD190.A6 1969, (v8)
Anderson, James Maxwell. DP538.A56 2000, (v5)
Anderson, Jaynie. ND623.G5.A8913 1997, (v9)
Anderson, Jean Bradley. F262.D8.A63 1991, (v4)
Anderson, Jervis. F128.68.H3.A65 1982, (v4)
Anderson, John B. QE350.A49 1999, (v1)
Anderson, John David. TL570.A679 1997, (v1)
Anderson, John. DK857.5.A53 1997, (v5)
Anderson, Joseph. PN1995.9.A8.A5 1996, (v3)
Anderson, Judith H. PR421.A53 1996, (v3)
    PR428.B55.A52 1984, (v3)
Anderson, Judith Icke. E762.A56 1981, (v4)
Anderson, Judy. Z551.A68 1998, (v10)
Anderson, Karen L. E99.H9.A55 1990, (v4)
Anderson, Karen. E184.A1.A673 1996, (v4)
    HQ1420.A65, (v6)
Anderson, Kay. F1089.5.V22.A66 1991, (v4)
Anderson, Kevin. HX313.8.L46.A54 1995, (v6)
Anderson, Lars. GV885.4.A53 1998, (v6)
Anderson, Laurie Halse. PZ7.A54385Sp 1999, (v3)
Anderson, Lee G. SH334.A53 1986, (v1)
Anderson, Linda R. PR808.W65.A53 1997, (v3)
Anderson, Lisa M. PS338.W6.A53 1997, (v3)
Anderson, Lisa. HN784.A8.A53 1986, (v6)
Anderson, M. S. D286.A5, (v5)
    JX1635.A53 1993, (v7)
Anderson, Margaret Lavinia. JN3838.A54 2000, (v7)
Anderson, Margaret. Z3014.L56.A52, (v10)
Anderson, Margo J. HA37.U55.A53 1988, (v6)
Anderson, Marian. ML420.A6 A3 2002, (v9)
Anderson, Mark. PT2621.A26.Z5734 1992, (v3)

Anderson, Marston. PL2442.A53 1990, (v3)
Anderson, Martin. E877.A84 1990, (v4)
Anderson, Mary Desiree. PR641.A7, (v3)
Anderson, Mary M. DS727.A74 1990, (v5)
Anderson, Mary R. BH221.F8.A53 1984, (v8)
Anderson, Maxwell. PS3501.N256.A7, (v3)
    PS3501.N256.B27, (v3)
    PS3501.N256.C3 1941, (v3)
    PS3501.N256.E8 1939, (v3)
    PS3501.N256.F6, (v3)
    PS3501.N256.M35 1936, (v3)
    PS3501.N256.S75, (v3)
    PS3501.N256.T5 1926, (v3)
    PS3501.N256.Z53 1977, (v3)
Anderson, Nancy K. ND237.B585.A4 1991, (v9)
Anderson, Nancy Scott. E467.A53 1988, (v4)
Anderson, Patricia. DA533.A574 1991, (v5)
    HQ18.G7.A7 1995, (v6)
Anderson, Paul S. LB1576.A616 1988, (v7)
Anderson, Peter J. JX1395.A547 1996, (v7)
Anderson, Poul. PS3551.N378, (v3)
    PS3551.N378.B75 1971, (v3)
Anderson, R. C. V750.A6, (v10)
Anderson, Richard L. BH39.A57 1990, (v8)
Anderson, Robert A. R733.A56 2001, (v2)
Anderson, Robert Woodruff. PS3501.N34.T4 1953, (v3)
Anderson, Robert. ML410.E41.A65 1993, (v9)
Anderson, Romola. VM15.A6 1963, (v10)
Anderson, Sarah. Z6004.T6.A53 1995, (v10)
Anderson, Sean. HV6431.A537 1995, (v6)
Anderson, Sheldon R. DK4185.G3 A53 2001, (v5)
Anderson, Sherwood. E806.A652 1970, (v4)
    PS3501.N4.A6 1947, (v3)
    PS3501.N4.A6 1967, (v3)
    PS3501.N4.A6 1972, (v3)
    PS3501.N4.A6 1989, (v3)
    PS3501.N4.B4, (v3)
    PS3501.N4 D3 1960, (v3)
    PS3501.N4.H6, (v3)
    PS3501.N4.M3 1978, (v3)
    PS3501 N4.M32, (v3)
    PS3501.N4.P6 1966, (v3)
    PS3501.N4.T7 1921a, (v3)
    PS3501.N4.W48 1965, (v3)
    PS3501.N4 W5, (v3)
    PS3501.N4.W5, (v3)
    PS3501.N4.Z49, (v3)
    PS3501.N4.Z5 1969, (v3)
    PS3501.N4.Z52 1969, (v3)
    PS3501.N4.Z54, (v3)
    PS3501.N4.Z545 1972, (v3)
    NA1088.B4.A827 2000, (v9)
Anderson, Stephen J. HV413.A69 1993, (v6)
Anderson, Susan Leigh. B1607.A53 2000, (v8)
Anderson, Terry Lee. E98.E2.A53 1995, (v4)
    HC110.E5.A66163 2001, (v6)
    HC110.E5.A6663 1997, (v6)
    HD1694.A5.A75 1997, (v6)
Anderson, Thomas C. B2430.S34.A753 1993, (v8)
Anderson, Thornton. KF4541.A88 1993, (v7)
Anderson, Troyer Steele. E267.A34, (v4)
Anderson, Vicki. Z1037.A52 1992, (v10)
Anderson, Victor. BR100.A49 1998, (v8)
    HD9502.A2.A574 1993, (v6)
Anderson, Virginia DeJohn. F7.A53 1991, (v4)
Anderson, W. A. D. RB111.A5 1980, (v2)
Anderson, W. K. DA965.C7.A68 1994, (v5)
Anderson, Warren D. ML169.A66 1994, (v9)
Anderson, Wayne I. QE111.A582 1998, (v1)
Anderson, William. F291.T3.A52, (v4)
Andersson, Theodore Murdock. PT7183.A45, (v3)
Anderton, Douglas L. HB3505.B63 1997, (v6)
Ando, Clifford. DG59.A2.A64 2000, (v5)
Ando, Tadao. NA1559.A5.A4 1989, (v9)
Andolina, Valerie. RG493.5.R33A23 2001, (v2)
Andonian, Cathleen Culotta. Z8086.37.A5 1989, (v10)
Andor, Laszlo. HC240.25.H9, (v6)
Andrade, Ernest. DU627.17.W55.A7 1996, (v5)
Andrain, Charles F. JA76.A48 1995, (v7)
    JF51.A64 1994, (v7)

Andre le Chapelain. HQ461.A55 1959, **(v6)**
Andre, Rae. HQ759.A5, **(v6)**
Andre, Richard. F247.K3 A53 1995, **(v4)**
Andreach, Robert J. PS352.A53 1998, **(v3)**
Andreasen, Esben. BQ8715.4.A53 1998, **(v8)**
Andreasen, Nancy C. RC455.4.G4.A53 2001, **(v2)**
Andreescu, Titu. QA43.A52 2000, **(v1)**
Andreev-Khomiakov, Gennady. DK268.A54.A3 1997, **(v5)**
Andreikov, Todor. PN2828.A53.A3 1997, **(v3)**
Andres de San Miguel. F314.A53 2001, **(v4)**
Andres, Glenn M. N6921.F7.A387 1988, **(v9)**
Andresen, Sophia de Mello Breyner. PQ9261.A6893.A24 1986, **(v3)**
Andress, David. DC170.A53 2000, **(v5)**
Andress, Reinhard. DD286.3.A53 2000, **(v5)**
Andreu, Guillemette. DT61.A6313 1997, **(v5)**
Andrew, Aletha. Z8866.A53 1993, **(v10)**
Andrew, Anita M. DS778.M3 A74 2000, **(v5)**
Andrew, Christopher M. JK468.I6.A844 1995, **(v7)**
Andrew, James Dudley. PN1993.5.F7.A745 1995, **(v3)**
Andrew, Joe. PG3015.5.W6.A53 1988, **(v3)**
Andrew, John A. E846.A62 1998, **(v4)**
  JC573.2.U6.A53 1997, **(v7)**
Andrew, Rod. U409.S9, **(v10)**
Andrewartha, H. G. QH541.A524 1984, **(v1)**
Andrewes, Antony. DF222.A6, **(v5)**
Andrews, Alice C. HN60.A5 1995, **(v6)**
Andrews, B. G. PR9619.3.A76.Z57, **(v3)**
Andrews, Charles McLean. E188.A5745, **(v4)**
Andrews, David G. QC863.A596 2000, **(v1)**
Andrews, Deborah C. T11.A515 2001, **(v1)**
Andrews, Dee. BX8236.A53 2000, **(v8)**
Andrews, E. M. D547.A8.A53 1993, **(v5)**
Andrews, Elmer. PR6056.R5.Z57 1995, **(v3)**
Andrews, George F. F1435.3.A6.A52, **(v4)**
Andrews, George Reid. F2631.A58 1991, **(v4)**
Andrews, Gregg. F474.I23.A53 1996, **(v4)**
Andrews, Kenneth R. DA86.A74 1991, **(v5)**
Andrews, Larry C. QA351.A75 1992, **(v1)**
Andrews, Lori B. RB155.65.A53 2001, **(v2)**
Andrews, Malcolm. N8213.A53 1999, **(v9)**
Andrews, Marietta Minnigerode. F193.A52, **(v4)**
Andrews, Matthew Page. F181.A562, **(v4)**
  F184.A76, **(v4)**
Andrews, Michael Cameron. PR658.D4.A54 1989, **(v3)**
Andrews, Moya L. RF510.A53 1999, **(v2)**
Andrews, Nicholas G. DK4442.A53 1985, **(v5)**
Andrews, Oliver. NB1170.A63 1983, **(v9)**
Andrews, Robert. PN6081.A652 1993, **(v3)**
Andrews, Robert. PN6081.A656 1997, **(v3)**
Andrews, Sharon Vincz. LC311.A49 1994, **(v7)**
Andrews, Starra. PN2285.A65 1998, **(v3)**
Andrews, Stuart. DC158.8.A53 2000, **(v5)**
Andrews, Tamra. BL435.A53 1998, **(v8)**
  GR498.A53 2000, **(v6)**
Andrews, Wayne. DC146.S7.A6, **(v5)**
  NA705.A5 1978, **(v9)**
Andriâc, Ivo. PG1418.A6.N313 1977, **(v3)**
Andriano, Joseph. PS374.M544.A53 1999, **(v3)**
Andrianopoulos, Gerry Argyris. E855.A85 1991, **(v4)**
Andric, Ivo. PG1418.A6.T72 I963, **(v3)**
  PG1418.A6.V5, **(v3)**
Andrien, Kenneth J. HC202.A65 1995, **(v6)**
  HJ971.A53 1985, **(v6)**
Andriot, Laurie. ZA5075.A53 1998, **(v10)**
Andrusyshen, C. H. PG3986.E3.A5, **(v3)**
Andrusz, Gregory D. HD7345.A3.A68 1984, **(v6)**
Andrzejewski, Jerzy. PG7158.A7.P613, **(v3)**
Anfinson, Scott F. E78.M7.A55 1997, **(v4)**
Angell, James W. D659.G3.A7 1972, **(v5)**
Angelo, Bonnie. E176.3.A54 2000, **(v4)**
Angelo, Joseph A. QB500.262.A54 2000, **(v1)**
Angelou, Maya. PS3551.N464Z466 1970, **(v3)**
Angermuller, Rudolph. ML410.M9.A813 1988, **(v9)**
Angier, Natalie. QH501.A54 1995, **(v1)**
Angle, Paul M. E457.L745 1990, **(v4)**
  Z8505.A6, **(v10)**
Anglim, Christopher. KF3317.A54 1997, **(v7)**
  KF4865.A68.A54 1999, **(v7)**

Anglin, Ron. F897.C7 A54 1995, **(v4)**
Anglin, W. S. QA21.A54 1994, **(v1)**
  QA241.A53 1995, **(v1)**
Angoff, Charles. PS647.J4, **(v3)**
  PS3501.N569575.S8, **(v3)**
  PS3501.N8.W5, **(v3)**
Angresano, James. HB116.5.M9.A54 1997, **(v6)**
Angress, Werner T. DD249.A78 1972, **(v5)**
Angrosino, Michael V. HV3006.A4.A48 1998, **(v6)**
Angus, David L. LA222.A543 1999, **(v7)**
Angus, Henry Forbes. DS518.9.C3.A7, **(v5)**
Anjos, Cyro dos. PQ9697.A752.A713 1988, **(v3)**
Ankersmit, F. R. D16.8.A638 1994, **(v5)**
  JA71.A585 1996, **(v7)**
Ann, Martha. BL473.5.A66 1993, **(v8)**
Anna, Timothy E. F1232.A57, **(v4)**
  F1232.A573 1998, **(v4)**
  F1232.I853.A56 1990, **(v4)**
  F3446.A53, **(v4)**
Annan, Noel Gilroy Annan. DA566.4.A665 1991, **(v5)**
  PR5473.S6.A88 1984, **(v3)**
Annas, George J. KF3821.A75.A56 1988, **(v7)**
Annas, Julia. B398.E8.A56 1999, **(v8)**
  B837.A55 1985, **(v8)**
  BJ171.H35.A56 1993, **(v8)**
  JC71.P6.A544 1981, **(v7)**
Annenberg School of Communications (University of Pennsylvania). PN1992.16.A66 1990, **(v3)**
Annis, Sheldon. F1465.3.E2.A56 1987, **(v4)**
Annunziata, Jane. RC488.5.A56 1994, **(v2)**
Anouilh, Jean. PQ2601.N67.A69 1969, **(v3)**
  PQ2601.N67.A692 1956, **(v3)**
  PQ2601.N67.A7 1947, **(v3)**
  PQ2601.N67.B413, **(v3)**
  PQ2601.N67.P46, **(v3)**
  PQ2601.N67.P463 1967, **(v3)**
  PQ2601.N67.V63 1959, **(v3)**
  PQ2601.N67P48 1970, **(v3)**
Anreus, Alejandro. ND259.O7.A9 2001, **(v9)**
Anschutz, Richard Paul. B1607.A55 1969, **(v8)**
Anscombe, G. E. M. BC135.W52 A5 1971, **(v8)**
  BC199.I5.A5 1957a, **(v8)**
Ansell, Amy Elizabeth. E185.A496 1997, **(v4)**
Ansell-Pearson, Keith. JC233.N52.A56 1994, **(v7)**
Anselm. B765.A81.A2513 2002, **(v7)**
Anselment, Raymond A. PR438.M43.A57 1995, **(v3)**
Ansky, S. PJ5129.R3.A27 1992, **(v3)**
Ansolabehere, Stephen. JF2112.A4.A57 1995, **(v7)**
Anson, Christopher M. Z5818.E5.W75 1993, **(v10)**
Ansprenger, Franz. JV151.A5713 1989, **(v7)**
Antheil, George. ML410.A638 A3 1981, **(v9)**
Anthony, Brian. PN2287.C519.A58 1998, **(v3)**
Anthony, Ian. VA40.A48 1990, **(v10)**
Anthony, James R. ML270.2.A6 1997, **(v9)**
Anthony, Katharine Susan. E342.1.A58, **(v4)**
Anthony, Kathryn H. NA2750.A64 1991, **(v9)**
Anthony, Martin. HB135.A62 1996, **(v6)**
Anthony, Michael. PR9272.9.A5.C7 1973, **(v3)**
  PR9272.9.A5 Y43 1970, **(v3)**
Antoine, Fabrice. PC2640.A579 2000, **(v3)**
Antokoletz, Elliott. ML134.B18.A7 1988, **(v9)**
Anton, Ferdinand. F3429.3.T3.A5713 1987, **(v4)**
Anton, Thomas Julius. JK325.A75 1989, **(v7)**
Antoni, Carlo. D16.4.G3.A793, **(v5)**
Antoniades, Anthony C. NA2750.A65 1990, **(v9)**
Antonioni, Michelangelo. PN1998.3.A58.A5 1996, **(v3)**
Antonius, George. DS63.6.A46 1981, **(v5)**
Anttalainen, Tarmo. TK5105.A55 1999, **(v1)**
Antunes, Antonio Lobo. PQ9263.N77.E9713 1991, **(v3)**
  PQ9263.N77.F313 1990, **(v3)**
  PQ9263.N77A9413 1995, **(v3)**
Antwi-Boasiako, Kwabena. PR9379.9.A5.H53 1995, **(v3)**
Anunobi, Fredoline O. HC1055.A7 1992, **(v6)**
Anwar, Chairil. PL5089.A56. 1970, **(v3)**
Aoki, Haruo. PM2019.Z5.A58 1994, **(v3)**
Aoki, Masahiko. HB99.5.A63 2001, **(v6)**
Aoumiel. BF1566.A56 2000, **(v2)**
Aparicio, Frances R. ML3535.5.A63 1998, **(v9)**
Apel, Willi. ML700.A6, **(v9)**

ML880.2.A6313 1990, **(v9)**
ML3082.A64, **(v9)**
Apess, William. E78.N5.A64 1992, **(v4)**
  E99.P53.A3 1997, **(v4)**
Apfel, Roberta J. RA1242.D48.A64 1984, **(v2)**
Apollinaire, Guillaume. PQ2601.P6.P6 1947, **(v3)**
Apostol, Tom M. QA300.A573, **(v1)**
Apostolidis, Paul. BV656.A66 2000, **(v8)**
Apostolos-Cappadona, Diane. BV150.A66 1994, **(v8)**
Appel, Fredrick. JC233.N52.A66 1999, **(v7)**
Appel, Joseph Herbert. CT275.W272A7, **(v5)**
Appel, Stephen. LB1051.A619 1996, **(v7)**
Appelbaum, Eileen. HD8072.5.A66 1994, **(v6)**
Appelfeld, Aron. PJ5054.A755.A7813 1989, **(v3)**
  PN56.H55.A65 1994, **(v3)**
Apperson, Linda. PN2085.A66 1998, **(v3)**
Appiah, Anthony. DT352.4.A66 1992, **(v5)**
Appiah, Anthony. E185.615.A77 1996, **(v4)**
  HV8023.A66 1998, **(v6)**
Applbaum, Arthur Isak. BJ1031.A65 1999, **(v8)**
Apple, James M. TS178.A63 1991, **(v1)**
Apple, Max. PS3551.P56, **(v3)**
Apple, Michael W. LC89.A814 1996, **(v7)**
  LC89.A815 2000, **(v7)**
Apple, Rima D. RJ216.A65 1987, **(v2)**
Applebee, Arthur N. LB1570.A67 1996, **(v7)**
Appleby, Joyce Oldham. E163.A67 1992, **(v4)**
  E175.A67 1994, **(v4)**
  JA84.U5.A75 1984, **(v7)**
Appleby, R. Scott. BL65.S62.A66 2000, **(v8)**
Applegate, Celia. DD801.P448.A67 1990, **(v5)**
Applegate, Edd. PN4820.A66 1996, **(v3)**
  PN4888.B74.A66 1996, **(v3)**
Appleman, John Alan. JX6731.W3 A6 1971, **(v7)**
Appleman, Roy Edgar. DS918.A79 1989, **(v5)**
  DS918.A8 1990, **(v5)**
Appleton, Jay. BH301.L3 A66 1996, **(v8)**
Appleton, William Worthen. PR2434.A7, **(v3)**
Applewhite, E. J. BD443.A66 1991, **(v8)**
Applewhite, Harriet Branson. JN2775.A67 1993, **(v7)**
Appleyard, Bryan. QH442.A67 1998, **(v1)**
Appleyard, J. A. PR4484.A6, **(v3)**
Appy, Christian G. DS558.A67 1993, **(v5)**
Apraku, Kofi Konadu. HN59.2.A67 1996, **(v6)**
Aprile, Dianne. BX2525.T733, **(v8)**
ApRoberts, Ruth. PN56.B5.A67 1994, **(v3)**
  PR4024.A54 1983, **(v3)**
  PR5687.A6, **(v3)**
Apter, David Ernest. HD82.A657 1987, **(v6)**
  JC491.A58 1994, **(v7)**
Apter, David Ernest. JQ2951.A99.B843 1997, **(v7)**
Apter, T. E. HQ1059.4.A68 1995, **(v6)**
Aptheker, Bettina. HQ1154.A745 1989, **(v6)**
Aptheker, Herbert. E185.61.A62 1992, **(v4)**
  E447.A67 1983, **(v4)**
  E449.A156 1989, **(v4)**
Aquila, Philip L. D811.A646 1999, **(v5)**
Arac, Jonathan. PN94.A7 1987, **(v3)**
Arafat, K. W. DF27.P383.A73 1996, **(v5)**
Aragon. PQ2601.R2.A9, **(v3)**
Aragona, Tullia d'. BD436.D3713 1997, **(v8)**
Arai, Masami. DR572.5.A73 1991, **(v5)**
Araia, Ghelawdewos. HC845.A7 1995, **(v6)**
Arasse, Daniel. ND653.V5.A9313 1994, **(v9)**
Arat, Zehra F. JC599.D44.A73 1991, **(v7)**
Aravamudan, Srinivas. PR448.C64.A73 1999, **(v3)**
Arazi, Benjamin. TK5105.5.A7 1988, **(v1)**
Arbena, Joseph. Z7515.L29.A73 1999, **(v10)**
Arberry, A. J. PJ63.A73, **(v3)**
  PJ7655.A7 1967, **(v3)**
  PJ8453.A7, **(v3)**
  PK6406.A7, **(v3)**
  PK6449.E5.A7, **(v3)**
Arblaster, Anthony. ML1700.A7 1992, **(v9)**
Arblay, Mme. Frances (Burney) d'. PR3533.A5, **(v3)**
Arboleda, Teja. E184.A1.A747 1998, **(v4)**
Arboleya, Jesus. F1787.A6613 2000, **(v4)**
Archambeault, James. F452.A74 1999, **(v4)**
Archdeacon, Thomas J. E184.A1.A75 1983, **(v4)**
Archer, Clive. HC241.2.S743 2000, **(v6)**
Archer, Dane. HV6030.A73 1984, **(v6)**

Archer, Ian W. DA680.A74 1991, (v5)
Archer, J. S. TN870.A73 1986, (v1)
Archer, John E. HN398.E3.A73 1990, (v6)
Archer, John Michael. PR428.C64.A74 1993, (v3)
Archer, John. QL758.5.A73 1988, (v1)
Archer, Keith. JL197.N4.A73 1997, (v7)
Archer, Leonard Courtney. PN1590.N4.A7, (v3)
Archer, Margaret Scotford. BD450.A69 2000, (v8)
　HM101.A654 1988, (v6)
Archer, Michael. N6490.A669 1997, (v9)
Archer, Peter. CE73.A7, (v5)
Archer, Stanley. PR6025.A86.Z552 1993, (v3)
Archer, Stephen M. PN2287.B6.A88 1992, (v3)
Archer, W. G. PL4704.Z95.E5 1940, (v3)
Archer, William. PN1661.A8 1960, (v3)
Archibald, J. David. QE734.5.A73 1996, (v1)
Archimedes. QA31.A692, (v1)
Arcilla, Rene Vincente. LC1011.A63 1994, (v7)
Arciniegas, Germán. E135.G3.A72, (v4)
　F1408.A732, (v4)
　F1408.A735, (v4)
　F1408.3.A663, (v4)
　E125.V5 A6413 1978, (v4)
Ardagh, John. HC276.2.A72 1982, (v6)
　HC276.2.A73 1968b, (v6)
　HN445.5.A73 1995, (v6)
Arden, Heather. Z8374.6478.A73 1993, (v10)
Ardery, Julia S. NK9798.T65.A93 1998, (v9)
Ardis, Ann L. PR878.F45.A74 1990, (v3)
Arditti, Fred D. HG6024.U6.A73 1996, (v6)
Arditti, Joseph. QK495.O64.A73 1992, (v1)
　SB409.58.A73 1993, (v1)
Arditti, Rita. HV6322.3.A7.A74 1999, (v6)
Ardoin, John. ML422.F92.A85 1994, (v9)
Arebi, Saddeka. PJ8005.A87 1994, (v3)
Arendell, Terry. HQ756.A8 1995, (v6)
Arendt, Hannah. B29.A73, (v8)
　BV4639.A6513 1995, (v8)
　D16.8.A65, (v5)
　DS135.G5.V474 1997, (v5)
　JC481.A6 1966, (v7)
　JC491.A68, (v7)
　PT2546.V22.A913 1974, (v3)
Arentz, Dick. F788.5.A74 1986, (v4)
Arestis, Philip. HB76.B5 2000, (v6)
Argan, Giulio Carlo. N6410.A713, (v9)
　NA1123.B9.A8713 1993, (v9)
　NA9094.A713, (v9)
Argersinger, Jo Ann E. F189.B157.A74 1988, (v4)
Argersinger, Peter H. F595.A74 1995, (v4)
Argos, V. P. Z7963.E7.A73 1999, (v10)
Argyle, Michael. HM132.A695 1991, (v6)
　HM251.A782 1991, (v6)
Arias, Paolo Enrico. NK4645.A69, (v9)
Arias-Larreta, Abraham. PM4068.A8 1962, (v3)
Arie, Gabriel. DS135.B85.A75313 1998, (v5)
Arieti, James A. B395.A72 1991, (v8)
Arif, K. M. DS384.A786 2001, (v5)
Arif, Khalid Mahmud. DS384.A787 1995, (v5)
Arishima, Takeo. PL801.R5.A83, (v3)
Aristide, Jean-Bertrand. F1928.2.A7413 1996, (v4)
Aristophanes. PA3612.A8 1961, (v3)
Aristophanes. PA3877.A6 1980, (v3)
Aristoteles. B407.M2, (v3)
Aristotle. B407.A26 1996, (v8)
　B407.S6 1984, (v8)
　B430.A5.C5 1950, (v8)
　B430.A5 R68 2002, (v8)
　B430.A5.T4, (v8)
　B434.A5.A66, (v8)
　B434.A5.S2 1999, (v8)
　B441.A5 B37 1994, (v8)
　JC71.A41K49 1999, (v7)
　PA3405.S8.A872, (v3)
　PA3612.A8.E6 1926, (v3)
　PA3926.Z8.K53 1962, (v3)
　Q151.A7.H6, (v1)
　Q151.A72 1970, (v1)
　QL41.A719 1978, (v1)
　QL41.A7413 1862, (v1)
Ariyoshi, Koji. DU624.7.J3.A75 2000, (v5)

Ariyoshi, Sawako. PL845.R5.D62, (v3)
　PL845.R5.K613 1984, (v3)
Arkebauer, James B. HD30.28.A75 1995, (v6)
Arkell, William Joscelyn. QE681.A6 1956, (v1)
Arkes, Hadley. HC240.A832, (v6)
　KF8745.S88.A87 1994, (v7)
Arkin, Ronald C. TJ211.A75 1998, (v1)
Arkin, William M. UA23.3.A85 1997, (v10)
Arkoun, Mohammed. BP163.A69613 1994, (v8)
Arksey, Laura. Z5305.U5.A74 1983, (v10)
Arland, Marcel. PQ2601.R55.O6 1929, (v3)
Arlen, Michael J. PR6001.R7.L57 1970, (v3)
Arlen, Michael. PR6001.R7.G7 1924, (v3)
Arlett, Robert. PR888.E6.A75 1996, (v3)
Arlinghaus, Bruce E. UA855.A74 1984, (v10)
Arlington, Lewis Charles. PL2658.E5.A7 1963, (v3)
Arlinsky, Ellen. F574.G7 A77 1987, (v4)
Arlow, Jacob A. BF173.F85.A7, (v2)
Armacost, Michael H. E183.8.J3.A813 1996, (v4)
　UA23.A697, (v10)
Armarego, W.L.F. TP156.P83 P47 1996., (v1)
Armbrust, Walter. DT107.826.A76 1996, (v5)
Armes, Roy. PN1993.5.D44.A76 1987, (v3)
Armes, Roy. PN1995.A748 1994, (v3)
Armitage, David. JV1011.A75 2000, (v7)
Armitt, Lucie. PN3435.A73 2000, (v3)
Armour, Kathleen M. GV363.A76 1998, (v6)
Armour, M. A. QD64.A76 1996, (v1)
Armour, Robert A. PN1993.45.A75, (v3)
Armour, Rollin S. BP172.A736 2002, (v8)
Arms, Thomas S. D843.A668 1994, (v5)
Armson, K A. SD390.A75, (v1)
Armstrong, A. H. B171.A78 1966, (v8)
Armstrong, Anne. D815.A7, (v5)
Armstrong, Christopher. HG5160.5.A3.A76 1988, (v6)
Armstrong, D. M. B1339.A7 1988, (v8)
　BD581.A75 1983, (v8)
Armstrong, Douglas V. F1875.A7 1990, (v4)
Armstrong, Edward Allworthy. PR3081.A7 1963, (v3)
Armstrong, Elizabeth Howard. F1027.A74, (v4)
Armstrong, Gordon S. PR6003.E282.Z5634 1990, (v3)
Armstrong, J. D. JX3091.A77 1993, (v7)
　JX1995.A75 1996, (v7)
Armstrong, Jeanne. PS374.W6.A76 2000, (v3)
Armstrong, Karen. BL238.A76 2000, (v8)
　BP50.A69 2000, (v8)
　BQ882.A76 2001, (v8)
　BT98.A65 1993, (v8)
Armstrong, Lance. GV1048.A76 2000, (v6)
　GV1051.A76 A3 2000, (v6)
Armstrong, Louis. ML419.A75.A3 1999, (v9)
　ML419.A75.A7, (v9)
　ML3561.A74.S8, (v9)
Armstrong, Martin Donisthorpe. PR4156.A77, (v3)
Armstrong, Nancy. PR878.R4.A76 1999, (v3)
Armstrong, Paul B. PN98.R38.A76 1990, (v3)
Armstrong, Piers. PQ9555.A76 1999, (v3)
Armstrong, Raymond. PR6066.I53.Z594 1999, (v3)
Armstrong, Richard. PN1998.3.W56.A87 2000, (v3)
Armstrong, Tim. PR4757.P58.A76 2000, (v3)
　PS228.M63.A89 1998, (v3)
Armstrong-Hansche, Melissa. BV1534.A76 2000, (v8)
Arnason, H. Harvard. N6490.A713 1986b, (v9)
Arndt, Sven W. HF3031.A83 1987, (v6)
Arneil, Barbara. HQ1236.A76 1999, (v6)
　JC153.L87.A76 1996, (v7)
Arnell, Alvin. TA11.A7, (v1)
Arner, Robert D. Z473.D6.A76 1991, (v10)
Arnesen, Eric. HD8039.R12.U612 2001, (v6)
Arnest, Lauren Krohn. KF479.A68.A76 1998, (v7)
Arnett, Earl. F179.3.A66 1999, (v4)
Arnett, Ross H. QL464.A76 1985, (v1)
　QL473.A76, (v1)
　QL474.A76 2000, (v1)
Arnett, Willard Eugene. B945.S24.A8, (v8)
Arney, William Ray. RG526.A76 1982, (v2)
Arnhart, Larry. BJ1311.A66 1998, (v8)
Arnheim, Rudolf. N70.A69, (v9)
　N70.A693, (v9)
　N7430.A69 1982, (v9)
Arnheim, Rudolf. NA2760.A74, (v9)

Arnim, Bettina von. PT1808.A4 1959, (v3)
Arnim, Ludwig Achim. PT1809.A15.M5, (v3)
Arnold, B. H. QA266.A7, (v1)
Arnold, Barry C. QA278.7.A74 1993, (v1)
Arnold, Ben. F594.C853 A8 1999, (v4)
Arnold, Benjamin. DD114.A76 1991, (v5)
Arnold, Bruce. N6797.Y4.A76 1998, (v9)
Arnold, Corliss Richard. ML600.A76 1995, (v9)
Arnold, David. DS436.N47 1999 pt. 3, vol. 5, (v5)
Arnold, David. R606.A75 1993, (v2)
Arnold, Dean E. F3429.1.Q85.A76 1993, (v4)
Arnold, Denis. ML410.B1.A96 1984, (v9)
　ML410.B4.A75 1971b, (v9)
　ML410.M77 A8 1990, (v9)
Arnold, Dieter. NA215.A75 1999, (v9)
Arnold, Dorothea. NB1296.2.A75 1996, (v9)
Arnold, Edwin. PR4012.L3 1939, (v3)
Arnold, Elizabeth. RT86.3.A74 1999, (v2)
Arnold, Elliott. PS3501.R5933 B5, (v3)
Arnold, F. T. ML442.A7 1965, (v9)
Arnold, Guy. D883.A77 1991, (v5)
　DT21.5.A76 1999, (v5)
　HC59.7.A8335 1993, (v6)
　HC59.7.A83358 1997, (v6)
　HC60.A738 1996, (v6)
　JZ4984.5.A76 1997, (v7)
Arnold, James R. DC234.A76 1990, (v5)
　DC234.A77 1995, (v5)
Arnold, Ken. QA76.73.J38A76 2000, (v1)
Arnold, Lorna. UG1282.A8.A76 2001, (v10)
Arnold, Matthew. PR4020.A5.A4 1965, (v3)
　PR4020.A5.T7, (v3)
　PR4021.N4, (v3)
　PR4021.S8, (v3)
　PR4021.T5, (v3)
　PR4021.U45 1989, (v3)
　PR4022.E3 1932, (v3)
　PR4022.E3 1960, (v3)
　PR4023.A43 1968, (v3)
　PR4023.A44 1996, (v3)
Arnold, Michael L. QH421.A76 1997, (v1)
Arnold, Morris S. E99.Q2 A77 2000, (v4)
　F411.A788 1991, (v4)
Arnold, N. Scott. HB90.A77 1994, (v6)
Arnold, Oren. PS3501.R599.Z5, (v3)
Arnold, Philip J. F1219.1.T84.A75 1991, (v4)
Arnold, Philip P. F1219.76.R57.A75 1999, (v4)
Arnold, Thomas Walker. ND198.A7 1965, (v9)
Arnold, V. I. QA372.A6913 1983, (v1)
Arnoldi, Mary Jo. DT551.45.B35.A76 1995, (v5)
Arnot, Madeleine. LC212.9.A76 2002, (v7)
Arnot, Madeleine. LC212.93.G7.A76 1999, (v7)
Arnow, Harriette Louisa Simpson. PS3501.R64.D6, (v3)
　PS3501.R64.Z47, (v3)
Arnson, Cynthia. F1436.8.U6.A76 1989, (v4)
Arnstein, H. R. V. QP551.A693 1991, (v1)
Arnull, Anthony. KJE5461.A97 1999, (v7)
Arom, Simha. ML350.A7613 1991, (v9)
Aron, Joan B. HD9698.U54.S543 1997, (v6)
Aron, Michael. F140.A76 1994, (v4)
Aron, Nan. KF299.P8.A76 1989, (v7)
Aron, Raymond. D16.8.A725, (v5)
　D431.A7, (v5)
　D843.A683 1968, (v5)
　DC404.A7, (v5)
　HM101.A715, (v6)
　JA76.A7513 1969, (v7)
　U21.2.C54.A7613 1985, (v10)
　U163.A7413 1981, (v10)
Aron, Robert. DC397.A71343 1969, (v5)
Aron, Stephen. F454.A76 1996, (v4)
Aronica, Michele Teresa. BX810.C393.A76 1987, (v8)
Aronoff, Myron Joel. PR6062.E33.Z56 1999, (v3)
Aronowicz, Annette. PQ2631.E25.Z5312 1998, (v3)
Aronowitz, Stanley. HM24.A73 1988, (v6)
Aronowitz, Stanley. LA209.2.A76 1994, (v7)
Arons, A. B. QC30.A78 1997, (v1)
Aronson, Arnold. PN2193.E86.A88 2000, (v3)
Aronson, Robert Louis. HD6072.6.U5.A76 1991, (v6)
Aronson, Shlomo. UA832.A77 1992, (v10)

Arora, Ashish. HD62.37.A76 2002, (v6)
Arp, Jean. PQ2601.R633.O5, (v3)
Arrabal, Fernando. PQ6601.R58.P5413 1987, (v3)
Arreola, Daniel D. HT127.7.A77 1993, (v6)
Arriagada Herrera, Genaro. F3100.A73413 1988, (v4)
Arrian. DF234.A7513 1976, (v5)
Arriaza, Bernardo T. F3069.1.A74.A76 1995, (v4)
Arrington, Leonard J. BX8695.A77.A3 1998, (v8)
    BX8695.Y7.A85 1985, (v8)
    F746.A75 1994, (v4)
Arrington, Robert L. BJ1031.A77 1989, (v8)
Arrizabalaga, Jon. RC201.6.A1.A77 1997, (v2)
Arrizon, Alicia. PN2270.M48.A77 1999, (v3)
Arrom, Silvia Marina. HV63.M6, (v6)
Arron, Deborah L. KF297.A87 1991, (v7)
Arron, Deborah L. KF297.A875 1997, (v7)
Arrowsmith, William. PN241.A74, (v3)
    PN1998.3.A58.A77 1995, (v3)
Art Institute of Chicago. N530.A74 2000, (v9)
Artaud, Antonin. PQ2601.R677.A28 1976, (v3)
Arteaga, Alfred. PS153.M4.A77 1997, (v3)
Artemev, V. E. GC97.7.A7813 1996, (v6)
Arthos, John. PN511.A74, (v3)
Arthur, John A. E184.A24.A74 2000, (v4)
Arthur, John. ND1351.6.A78 1989, (v9)
Arthur, W. Brian. HD69.S5 A77 1994, (v6)
Arthur, Wallace. QH541.A725 1990, (v1)
    QH546.3.A75 1987, (v1)
Arthur, William. CS2309.A7 1990, (v5)
Artibise, Alan F. J. HN110.W5.A74, (v6)
Artmann, Benno. QA31.E9.A78 1999, (v1)
Artsimovich, L. A. QC718.A713 1965, (v1)
Artsybashev, M. PG3453.A8, (v3)
Artz, Frederick Binkerd. CB351.A56 1980, (v5)
    N6350.A7, (v9)
Aruri, Naseer Hasan. E183.8.I7.A77 1995, (v4)
Arwas, Victor. N6494.A7.A65, (v9)
Arwas, Victor. N6834.5.M8.A4 1998, (v9)
Arweck, Elisabeth. Z7834.E85 A78 1997, (v10)
Arzans de Orsua y Vela, Bartolome.
    F3351.P85.A8213 1975, (v4)
Arzelies, Henri. QC6.A713 1966, (v1)
Asad, Talal. BL50.A85 1993, (v8)
āSaik̄ īcȳ a, Bhabendra Nātha. PK1569.S24S713 1997, (v3)
Asanga. BQ3080.A2522, (v8)
Asani, Ali Sultaan Ali. PJ814.M83A84 1995, (v3)
Asante, Molefi K. E185.A79 1998, (v3)
Asante, S. K. B. HC1000.A86 1986, (v6)
Asbee, Sue. PR6029.N56.Z514 1991, (v3)
Asbell, Bernard. RG137.5.A76 1995, (v2)
Asbridge, Thomas S. DS99.A6, (v5)
Asbury, Herbert. HV5232.N3 A7, (v6)
Asch, Peter. KF1609.A87 1988, (v7)
Asch, Ronald G. D258.A83 1997, (v5)
Asch, Sholem. PJ5129.A8 A7 1943, (v3)
Asch, Sholem. PJ5129.A8.C5, (v3)
    PJ5129.A8 E33 1946, (v3)
    PJ5129.A8.G6, (v3)
    PJ5129.A8.G63, (v3)
    PJ5129.A8 M3, (v3)
    PJ5129.A8.M6713, (v3)
    PJ5129.A8.M72 1935, (v3)
    PJ5129.A8 P3, (v3)
    PJ5129.A8.P7, (v3)
    PJ5129.A8.S3, (v3)
    PJ5129.A8.S3, (v3)
    PJ5129.A8.T3, (v3)
    PJ5129.A8.W3, (v3)
Ascher, Abraham. DK254.S595, (v5)
    DK263.A9 1988, (v5)
Ascher, Marcia. F3429.3.Q6.A82 1981, (v4)
    GN476.15.A83 1991, (v6)
Ascher, William. HC85.A83 1999, (v6)
Ascherson, Neal. DK4430.A83 1982, (v5)
Aschmann, Homer. F1219.1.B3.A7 1967, (v4)
Ash, Beth Sharon. PR6005.O4.Z55245 1999, (v3)
Ash, Eric. D786.A77 1999, (v5)
Ash, Lee. Z731.A78 1993, (v10)
Ash, Major M. RK280.A74 1993, (v2)
Ash, Michael. TP9.A73 1993, (v1)

TP201.A84 1998, (v1)
TP994.A85 1993, (v1)
Ash, Rhiannon. DG286.A84 1999, (v5)
Ash, Robert B. QA162.A84 1998, (v1)
Ash, Stephen V. E487.A83 1995, (v4)
Ash, Stephen V. E531.9.A84 1988, (v4)
Ashbaugh, A. Freire. B387.A96 1988, (v8)
Ashbery, John. PS221.A84 2000, (v3)
    PS3501.S475.A86 1987, (v3)
    PS3501.S475.D6, (v3)
    PS3501.S475.S4, (v3)
    PS3501.S475.S5 1981, (v3)
Ashbourne, Alexandra. DK505.8.A84 1999, (v5)
Ashbrook, Joseph. QB51.A77 1984, (v1)
Ashbrook, William. ML410.D7.A83 1982, (v9)
Ashby, LeRoy. HV881.A78 1997, (v6)
Ashby, Warren. BJ71.A84 1997, (v8)
Ashcraft, Keith W. RD137.3.A84 1994, (v2)
Ashcroft, Bill. PN51.A86 1999, (v3)
    PR9080.A85 1989, (v3)
Ashcroft, Frances M. QP82.A75 2000, (v1)
    RB112.5.A84 2000, (v2)
Ashe, Arthur. GV583.A74 1993, (v6)
Ashe, Arthur. GV994.A7.A3 1993, (v6)
Ashe, Geoffrey. BF1786.A84 2001, (v2)
Asher, Brad. E78.W3 A84 1999, (v4)
Asher, Kenneth George. PS3509.L43.Z598 1995, (v3)
Ashford, Daisy. PR6001.S44.Y7, (v3)
Ashford, Nicholas Askounes. RB152.6.A84 1998, (v2)
Ashford, Norman. TL725.3.P5.A83 1992, (v1)
Ashkenazi, Elliott. F380.J5.A88 1988, (v4)
Ashley, Leonard R. N. DA350.A84 1988, (v5)
Ashley, Maurice. DA375.A8, (v5)
    DA396.A2.A84 1987, (v5)
    DA407.A1.A8, (v5)
    DA426.A78 1958, (v5)
    DA450.A83 1977, (v5)
    DA462.M3.A, (v5)
    Z5917.F3.A84 1995, (v10)
    Z8102.23.A74 1987, (v10)
Ashley, Robert Paul. PR1293.A8 1956, (v3)
Ashliman, D. L. Z5983.F17.A83 1987, (v10)
Ashmore, Malcolm. BD175.A85 1989, (v8)
Ashmun, Margaret Eliza. PR3671.S7.Z6, (v3)
Ashton, Dianne. F158.9.J5.A84 1997, (v4)
Ashton, Dore. ND237.G8 A82 1990, (v9)
    ND237.R725 A93 1996, (v9)
    ND553.B6.A9, (v9)
    ND553.F7.A88 1988, (v9)
    NX454.A8 1991, (v9)
    NX504.A87 1992, (v9)
Ashton, H. PQ1805.L5.A85, (v3)
Ashton, Nigel John. DS63.2.U5.A865 1996, (v5)
Ashton, Robert. DA355.A84 1984, (v5)
Ashton, Robert. DA415.A79 1994, (v5)
Ashton, Rosemary. PR4483.A85 1996, (v3)
    PR4664.A84 1990, (v3)
    PR4886.L4.Z55 1991, (v3)
Ashton, Thomas Southcliffe. HC255.A8 1964, (v6)
Ashton-Warner, Sylvia. LC3501.M3.A8, (v7)
    PR6051.S55 1959, (v3)
Ashworth, Andrew. KD7869.A84 1991, (v7)
Ashworth, G. J. G155.A1.A75 1990, (v6)
Ashworth, John. E441.A86 1995, (v4)
Ashworth, Tony. D523.A756 1980, (v5)
Ashworth, William. NA9185.A795, (v9)
Ashworth, William. QH545.W3.A68 1986, (v1)
Asimakopulos, A. HB99.7.K38.A85 1991, (v6)
Asimov, Isaac. D11.A76 1991, (v5)
    PS648.S3, (v3)
    Q125.A765 1994, (v1)
    Q141.A74 1982, (v1)
    Q162.A8 1984, (v1)
    QA141.3.A85, (v1)
    QA152.A75, (v1)
    QB44.2.A84 1980, (v1)
    QB52.A74 1991, (v1)
    QB801.6.A85 1985, (v1)
    QB843.B55A84 1977, (v1)
    QC23.A8, (v1)
    QC778.A85 1980, (v1)

QD11.A8, (v1)
QH431.A72, (v1)
Askins, Robert. QL676.57.N7.A75 2000, (v1)
Aslan, Adnan. BL51.A83 1998, (v8)
Aslin, Elizabeth. NK1175.A8, (v9)
Aslund, Anders. HC336.26.A84 1991, (v6)
    HC340.12.A84 1995, (v6)
    HD2346.P7.A85 1985, (v6)
Åslund, Anders. HC244.A813 2002, (v6)
Asmus, Peter. TK1541.A75 2001, (v1)
Asoka. PK1480.A1 1969, (v3)
Aspenson, Steven Scott. BD21.A86 1998, (v8)
Asper, Kathrin. RC553.N36.A8613 1993, (v2)
Asprey, Robert B. D530.A77 1991, (v5)
    U240.A86, (v10)
Asquith, Cynthia Mary Evelyn (Charteris).
    PR4076.A8, (v3)
Asquith, Margot. DA566.9.O8.A52 1963, (v5)
Assefa, Hizkias. F158.9.N4.A87 1988, (v4)
Assembly of Mathematical and Physical Sciences
    (U.S.). QD51.A88 1981, (v1)
Asser, John. DA153.A88 1966, (v5)
Assiter, Alison. HQ1190.A87 1996, (v6)
Association for Asian Studies. DS753.5.A84 1976, (v5)
Association of American Law Schools. KF300.A7.A8, (v7)
Assouline, Pierre. PQ2637.I53.Z5713 1997, (v3)
Astaire, Fred. GV1785.A83.A3 1979, (v6)
Astarita, Tommaso. DG848.1.A88 1992, (v5)
Aste, Tomaso. QA166.7.A78 2000, (v1)
Astell, Ann W. PA6231.C83.A88 1994, (v3)
    PR275.P64.A68 1999, (v3)
    PR1933.K6.A88 1996, (v3)
Astington, John. PN2590.C66.A88 1999, (v3)
Aston, Elaine. PN1590.W64.A88 1995, (v3)
Aston, Margaret. BX4901.2.A84 1984, (v8)
Astor, Brooke. CT275.A847.A3, (v5)
Astro, Alan. PR6003.E282.Z5637 1990, (v3)
Astrov, Margot Luise Therese Kroger. PM102.A8, (v3)
Aswell, Edward C. PS3545.O337.Z616 1988, (v3)
Atack, Margaret. DC414.A73 1999, (v5)
    PQ307.W4.A85 1989, (v3)
Atget, Eugene. DC707.A823, (v5)
Athearn, Robert G. E467.1.S55 A8 1995, (v4)
    F776.A9, (v4)
Athens, Lonnie H. HV6789.A82 1997, (v6)
Atherden, Margaret. QH137.A85 1992, (v1)
Atherton, Gertrude Franklin Horn. PS1042.B55 1923a, (v3)
    PS1042.C6 1943, (v3)
    PS1042.S64, (v3)
    PS1043.A4 1932, (v3)
Atherton, Lewis Eldon. F596.A8, (v4)
Atiya, Aziz Surval. Z6207.C97 A8 1976, (v10)
Atiyah, P. S. KD662.A86 1995, (v7)
Atkeson, Ray. F877.A797 1998, (v4)
Atkins, Annette. HQ759.96.A75 2000, (v6)
Atkins, G. Douglas. PN75.H33.A85 1990, (v3)
    PN4500.A89 1992, (v3)
Atkins, G. Pope. F1410.A79 1997, (v4)
    JZ1519.A98 2001, (v7)
Atkins, J. W. H. PN99.G7.A78, (v3)
Atkins, John Alfred. PR6013.R44.Z63 1966, (v3)
    PR6015.U9.Z56 1968, (v3)
    PR6021.O4.Z58, (v3)
    PS3515.E37.Z57, (v3)
Atkins, Jonathan M. F436.A85 1997, (v4)
Atkins, P. W. QB981.A96 1992, (v1)
    QD461.A85 1987, (v1)
    QD462.A84 1996, (v1)
    QD466.A845 1995, (v1)
Atkins, Stephen E. HV6431.A87 1992, (v6)
    QC772.A87 2000, (v1)
Atkins, Stuart Pratt. PT2177.A85 1995, (v3)
Atkinson, A. B. HC244.Z9.I514 1992, (v6)
    HJ4629.A8 1995, (v6)
Atkinson, Bernard. TP248.3.A853 1983, (v1)
Atkinson, Frank. Z1065.A83 1987, (v10)
Atkinson, John William. BF683.A8, (v2)

Atkinson, Kendall E. QA297.A84, (v1)
Atkinson, Michael. PN1995.A775 1999, (v3)
    PR4624.A37 1996, (v3)
Atkinson, Paul. GN307.7.A85 1990, (v6)
Atkinson, Paul. R133.A85 1995, (v2)
Atkinson, R. F. D16.8.A75, (v5)
Atkinson, Rick. DS79.724.U6.A887 1993, (v5)
Atkinson, William C. DP66.A9, (v5)
Atlas, Allan W. ML172.A84 1998, (v9)
Atlas, James. PS3503.E4488Z554 2002, (v3)
Atlas, Ronald M. QR66.3.A85 1997, (v1)
Atran, Scott. GN468.4.A87 1990, (v6)
Attar, Farid ud-Din. PK6451.F4.M2813 1984, (v3)
Attebery, Brian. PS374.F27.A87 1992, (v3)
Attenborough, David. QH366.2.A87 1979b, (v1)
    QK50.A77 1995, (v1)
    QL337.M26.A8 1962, (v1)
    QL698.3.A88 1998, (v1)
    QL751.A77 1990, (v1)
Attfield, Robin. BJ1012.A85 1987, (v8)
Attie, Jeanie. E628.A87 1998, (v4)
Attig, Thomas. BF575.G7.A79 1996, (v2)
Attoe, Wayne. NA9105.A87 1989, (v9)
Atton, Chris. Z688.U53.A88 1996, (v10)
Attridge, Derek. PE1505.A87 1982, (v3)
    PR535.V4.A8, (v3)
Attwell, David. PR9369.3.C58.Z635 1993, (v3)
Attwood, Lynne. HQ1418.A87 1999, (v6)
Atwood, Margaret Eleanor. PR9199.3.A8.A17 1987, (v3)
    PR9199.3.A8.H3 1986, (v3)
    PR9199.3.A8.L3, (v3)
    PR9199.3.A8.L5, (v3)
    PR9199.3.A8.Y6 1974, (v3)
Au, Susan. GV1787.A79 2002, (v6)
Au, Whitlow, W. L. QL737.C432.A92 1993, (v1)
Aubert, Jacques. PR6019.O9.Z5256513 1992, (v3)
Aubert, Jean-Jacques. HC39.A9 1994, (v6)
Aubigne, Agrippa d'. PQ1603.A82613 1989, (v3)
Aubrey, Elizabeth. ML182.A78 1996, (v9)
Aubrey, James R. PR6056.O85.Z52 1991, (v3)
Aubrey, John. DA447.A3.A8 1957, (v5)
Aubuchon, Norbert. HD58.6.A93 1997, (v6)
Auburn, Mark S. PR3684.A9, (v3)
Auchincloss, Louis. PS3501.U25.I2 1972, (v3)
    PS3501.U25.P6, (v3)
    PS3501.U25.R6, (v3)
    PS3501.U25.S9, (v3)
    PS3501.U25.Z52, (v3)
Auchter, Dorothy. PN43.A83 1998, (v3)
Auchterlonie, Paul. Z3028.Y39.A93 1998, (v10)
Auden, W. H. DS777.53.A8 1939a, (v5)
    PN56.S4.A8 1951, (v3)
    PR2976.A93 2000, (v3)
    PR6001.U4.A17 1945, (v3)
    PR6001.U4.A17 1967, (v3)
    PR6001.U4.A17 1969, (v3)
    PR6001.U4.A19 1988, (v3)
    PR6001.U4.A6 1977, (v3)
    PR6001.U4.A6 1993, (v3)
    PR6001.U4.A6 1995b, (v3)
    PR6001.U4.A62, (v3)
    PR6001.U4.A65, (v3)
    PR6001.U4.A7 1940, (v3)
    PR6001.U4.C5 1969, (v3)
    PR6001.U4.D6 1968, (v3)
    PR6001.U4.D65 1941, (v3)
    PR6001.U4.D9, (v3)
    PR6001.U4.F6, (v3)
    PR6001.U4.H6, (v3)
    PR6001.U4.L4 1969, (v3)
    PR6001.U4.L6 1936, (v3)
    PR6001.U4.N6, (v3)
    PR6001.U4.O45 1956, (v3)
    PR6001.U4.O5 1938, (v3)
    PR6001.U4.O7 1967, (v3)
    PR6001.U4.S5, (v3)
    PR6001.U4.Z47 1990, (v3)
    Z2014.P7.A93, (v10)
Audi, Robert. B105.A35 A839 1993, (v8)
Audi, Robert. B105.A35.A93 1989, (v8)

BD161.A783 2002, (v8)
BJ1012.A93 1997, (v8)
Audiberti, Jacques. PQ2601.U346.C4, (v3)
Audin, Michele. QA862.T7.A93 1996, (v1)
Audisio, Gabriel. BX4881.2.A8313 1999, (v8)
Audouze, Francoise. D70.A8313 1992, (v5)
Audretsch, David B. HD3611.A83 1989, (v6)
Audubon, John James. QL31.A9.A2 1960, (v1)
    QL31.A9.A35, (v1)
    QL674.A9 1966, (v1)
    QL681.A97 1990, (v1)
Audubon, John Woodhouse. F786.A9 1969, (v4)
Auerbach, Jerold S. E184.J5.A94 1990, (v4)
Auerbach, Jonathan. PS3523.O46.Z53 1996, (v3)
Auerbach, Nina. GR830.V3.A92 1995, (v6)
    PR469.W65.A93 1982, (v3)
    PR830.W6.A9, (v3)
    PR6007.U47.Z55 2000, (v3)
Auerbach, Paul S. RC88.9.O95A938 1999, (v2)
Auerbach, Paul. HD41.A84 1988, (v6)
Auerswald, David P. UA11.A84 2000, (v10)
Aufderheide, Arthur C. R134.8.A93 1998, (v2)
Aufderheide, Patricia. HE7781.A94 1999, (v6)
August, Eugene R. B1607.A95, (v8)
Augustine, Saint, Bishop of Hippo. BR65.A5.E53 1990, (v8)
Augustine. BR65.A6 E5 2001b, (v8)
Augustinos, Gerasimos. DR435.G8.A94 1992, (v5)
Augustithis, S.S. QE462.U4A92 1979, (v1)
Auiler, Dan. PN1998.3.H58.A84 1999, (v3)
Auletta, Ken. HV4045.A9 1999, (v6)
Aumack, Sheryl. PN1995.9.M86.A96 1990, (v3)
Aung-Thwin, Michael. DS528.4.A96 1998, (v5)
Auslander, Leora. DC33.A87 1996, (v5)
Auslander, Philip. NX504.A89 1992, (v9)
Ausonius, Decimus Magnus. PA6221.A2 1991, (v3)
Austad, Steven N. QP86.A97 1997, (v1)
Austen, Jane. PR4032.M53 1996, (v3)
    PR4034.C43 1952, (v3)
    PR4034.E58 1957, (v3)
    PR4034.L6 1963, (v3)
    PR4034.N6 1962, (v3)
    PR4034.S4, (v3)
    PR4034.P7 1962, (v3)
    PR4036.A4 1995, (v3)
    DT571.D83.A87 1999, (v5)
Austen-Leigh, James Edward. PR4036.A8 1926, (v3)
Austen-Leigh, William. PR4036.A8, (v3)
    PR4036.A86 1989, (v3)
Austerlitz, Paul. ML3465.A95 1997, (v9)
Austerman, Wayne R. HE6376.A1T417 1985, (v6)
Austin, Albert Gordon. LA2101.A8 1961, (v7)
Austin, Betty. Z8318.22.A97 1995, (v10)
Austin, David F. BD215.A97 1990, (v8)
Austin, Guy. PN1993.5.F7.A95 1996, (v3)
Austin, J. L. B1618.A8 1970, (v8)
    B1618.A83.H6, (v8)
Austin, James E. HD62.4.A88 1990, (v6)
    HD69.S8 A94 2000, (v6)
Austin, Linda Marilyn. HB103.R8.A87 1991, (v6)
Austin, Lloyd James. PQ2191.Z5.A85, (v3)
Austin, M. M. HC37.A8813 1977b, (v6)
Austin, Mary (Hunter). PS3501.U8.W6, (v3)
Austin, Mary C. Z4501.A87 1996, (v10)
Austin, Mary Hunter. F866.A9318 1997, (v4)
    PS3501.U8.A6 1987, (v3)
    PS3501.U8.O5, (v3)
    PS3501.U8.Z53 1979, (v3)
Austin-Broos, Diane J. BR1644.5.J25 A97 1997, (v8)
Ausubel, Ken. SB117.35.N6.A9 1994, (v1)
Auty, R. M. HC59.7.A923 1998, (v6)
Auyang, Sunny Y. BF311.A797 2000, (v2)
Auyero, Javier. HC177.B82, (v6)
Avakian, Anne M. Z5984.A75.A93 1994, (v10)
Avalos, Francisco. KGF150.A95 1992, (v7)
Avalos, Hector. BL65.M4 A83 1995, (v8)
Avellaneda Navas, Jose Ignacio. F2272.A84 1995, (v4)
Aveni, Anthony F. F1219.3.A85.A9, (v4)
Aveni, Anthony F. F3429.1.N3 A94 2000, (v4)
Aveni, Anthony F. QB16.A88 1997, (v1)

Averell, William Woods. E601.A85, (v4)
Averill, Gage. ML3486.H3.A94 1997, (v9)
Averill, Gerald. SK354.A93.A37 1979, (v1)
Averkieva, IUliia Pavlovna. GN2.A27 vol. 71, (v6)
Averroes. JC71.P6.A83 1974, (v7)
Averroes. JC71.P6.A95 1966a, (v7)
Avers, Charlotte J. QH366.2.A933 1989, (v1)
Avery, Charles. NB623.G465.A4 1987, (v9)
Avery, Christine. Z7164.O7.A95 1997, (v10)
Avery, Emmett Langdon. PR3368.S8.A8, (v3)
Avery, Mary W. F891.A8, (v4)
Avery, Sheldon. E185.97.P593.A95 1989, (v4)
Avery, Thomas Eugene. TR810.A9 1985, (v1)
Avi. PZ7.A953Tr 1990, (v3)
Avicenna. B751.A5 S5 1974, (v8)
Avila, Manuel. HC135.A856, (v6)
Avineri, Shlomo. DS149.A874, (v5)
Avise, John C. QH84.A95 2000, (v1)
    QH438.4.B55.A95 1994, (v1)
Avishai, Bernard. DS126.5.A914 1990, (v5)
Avrich, Paul. HX843.7.S23.A97 1991, (v6)
    HX914.A9, (v6)
    LA216.A78, (v7)
Avril, Francois. ND3147.A8813, (v9)
Avrin, Leila. Z4.A88 1990, (v10)
Awkward, Michael. PE64.A88.A3 1999, (v3)
Awoonor, Kofi. PR9379.9.A9.C65 1992, (v3)
Awoonor, Kofi. PR9379.9.A9.U5 1987, (v3)
Axelrad, Jacob. E302.6.H5.A9, (v4)
Axelrod, Alan. F591.A53 1990, (v4)
    S926.A2.A94 1993, (v1)
Axelrod, George. PS3501.X4.S4, (v3)
Axelrod, Mark. PN3355.A97 1999, (v3)
Axelrod, Steven Gould. PS3566.L27.Z517 1990, (v3)
Axford, Barrie. HF1359.A96 1995, (v6)
Axinn, Sidney. U22.A95 1989, (v10)
Axler, Sheldon Jay. QA184.A96 1996, (v1)
Axsom, Richard H. NE539.S72.A4 1983, (v9)
Axson, Stockton. E767.A95 1993, (v4)
Axtell, Horace P. E99.N5.A97 1997, (v4)
Axtell, James. E78.S65.A97 1997, (v4)
    E93.A954 1988, (v4)
    E98.F39 N37 2001, (v4)
Axton, Richard. PQ1342.E5.A9, (v3)
Ayala, Victor. RC607.A26.A97 1996, (v2)
Ayensu, Edward S. QK86.U6.A93 1978, (v1)
Ayer, A. J. B29.A94, (v8)
    B53.A9 1946, (v8)
    B804.A818 1982, (v8)
    B1618.A91 1974, (v8)
Ayer, Eleanor H. F776.3.A94 1997, (v4)
Ayer, H. D. Z7845.C48, (v10)
Ayer, Mary Farwell. F61.C71 vol. 9, (v4)
Ayers, Edward L. F215.A94 1992, (v4)
Ayers, Jerry B. Z5814.T3.A97 1990, (v10)
Ayittey, George B. N. GN645.A95 1991, (v6)
    HC800.A98 1998, (v6)
Aylesworth, Thomas G. F551.A95 1988, (v4)
Ayllon, Teodoro. RC489.B4.A9, (v2)
Ayme, Marcel. PQ2601.Y5.C5, (v3)
    PQ2601.Y5.J8 1933, (v3)
Ayres, Brenda. PR4592.W6.A97 1998, (v3)
Ayres, Clarence Edwin. CB425.A89, (v5)
Ayres, Ian. K3842.A97 1992, (v7)
Ayres, James. NA966.A98 1998, (v9)
Ayrton, Elizabeth. PR6051.Y65.S5 1964, (v3)
Ayscough, Florence Wheelock. DS721.A8, (v5)
Ayto, John. PE1580.A97 1991, (v3)
    PE1630.A98 1999, (v3)
Ayto, John. PE3721.O94 1992, (v3)
Ayubi, Nazih N. M. DS39.A94 1995, (v5)
    JC49.A928 1991, (v7)
Ayusawa, Iwao Frederick. HD6832.A97, (v6)
Azema, Jean-Pierre. D802.F8.A92313 1984, (v5)
Azevedo, Aluisio. PQ9697.A93.M813 1990, (v3)
Azevedo, Celia Maria Marinho de. E449.A99 1995, (v4)
Azevedo, Fernando de. F2510.A933 1950a, (v4)
Azevedo, Mario Joaquim. DT546.48.A97 1998, (v5)
Azicri, Max. F1788.A93 2001, (v4)
Azikiwe, Uche. Z7964.N6.A95 1996, (v10)

Aziz, Robert. BF175.5.C65.A97 1990, (v2)
Azorin. PQ6623.A816.C6, (v3)
  PQ6623.A816.D6 1940, (v3)
  PQ6623.A816.D7 1973, (v3)
Azuela, Mariano. PQ7297.A9.L6 1939, (v3)
Baabar. DS798.75.B3313 1999, (v5)
Baade, Walter. QB801.B29, (v1)
Baal-Teshuva, Jacob. ND699.C5.B33 1998, (v9)
Baar, James. UG630.B2, (v10)
  VG93.B3, (v10)
Baars, Bernard J. BF311.B227 1997, (v2)
Baars, Donald. QE79.5.B285 1995, (v1)
Baase, Sara. QA76.9.C66.B3 1997, (v1)
Baay, Henry Van Lent. VM321.B3, (v10)
Babb, Howard S. PR4037.B3 1967, (v3)
Babb, James. DS890 .T29, (v5)
Babb, Lawrence. PR658.M37.B3, (v3)
Babb, Lawrence. PR2224.B3, (v3)
Babb, Valerie Melissa. PS173.W46.B33 1998, (v3)
Babbage, Charles. QA3.B18 1989 vol. 1, (v1)
  QA29.B2.A3 1994, (v1)
  QA75.B28, (v1)
Babbitt, Irving. LC1011.B2 1986, (v7)
  PQ91.B2, (v3)
  PQ91.B2 1977, (v3)
Babbitt, Natalie. PZ7.B1135Tu, (v3)
Babbitt, Susan E. BJ1533.I58.B32 1996, (v8)
Babcock, Barbara A. E78.S7.B15 1988, (v4)
Babcock, Robert Witbeck. PR2968.B2, (v3)
Babel, I. PG3476.B2A23 2001, (v3)
Baber, Michael. HF5438.25.B243 1997, (v6)
Babin, Edith H. PE1404.B23 1999, (v3)
Babine, Alexis Vasilevich. DK265.7.B3 1988, (v5)
Babinger, Franz. DR501.B313, (v5)
Babington, Anthony. DA50.B23 1990, (v5)
Babington, Bruce. PN1995.9.B53.B3 1993, (v3)
Babkina, A. M. HV6431.B24 1998, (v6)
  KZ5675.B33 1999, (v7)
Babkina, A. M. Z7164.T3 B33 2001, (v10)
Babuts, Nicolae. PQ2191.Z5.B22 1997, (v3)
Bacchus, M. K. LA476.B33 1990, (v7)
Bacchus, Wilfred A. F2538.25.B33 1990, (v4)
Bacchus, William I. JZ1480.B33 1997, (v7)
Bacchylides. PA3943.E5 1961, (v3)
Bach, Adolf. PF3075.B25 1965, (v3)
Bach, Carl Philipp Emanuel. MT224.B132, (v9)
Bach, Eric. QA241.B1085 1996, (v1)
Bach, Friedrich Teja. N7233.B7.A4 1995, (v9)
Bach, Johann Sebastian. ML53.8.B3 C3613 2000, (v9)
Bach, Kathryn F. Z7031.A1 B33, (v10)
Bach, Rebecca Ann. PR129.A4.B33 2000, (v3)
Bach, Stanley. KF4992.B33 1988, (v7)
Bach, Steven. PN2658.D5.B3 1992, (v3)
  PS3515.A7943, (v3)
Bachchan, Harbans Rai. PK2098.B22Z464 1998, (v3)
Bache, William B. PR2995.B28 1991, (v3)
Bachman, Ben. F12.C7 B18 1985, (v4)
Bachman, David M. JQ1508.B28 1991, (v7)
Bachman, George. QA403.5.B28 2000, (v1)
Bachman, Ronet. E98.C87.B33 1992, (v4)
Bachman, Walt. KF300.Z9 B32 1995, (v7)
Bachmann, Alberto. ML800.B13 1966, (v9)
Bachmann, E. Theodore. BX8009.B33 1989, (v8)
Bachmann, Ingeborg. PT2603 A147.D7, (v3)
  PT2603.A147.D713 1987, (v3)
  PT2603.A147.M313 1990, (v3)
  PT2603.A147.S513 1988, (v3)
Bachmann, Marie-Laure. MT22.B313 1991, (v9)
Bachrach, Bernard S. D128.B34 2001, (v5)
  DC65.B33 1994, (v5)
  DC611.A606.B23 1993, (v5)
Back, Kurt W. HQ766.B143 1989, (v6)
Backer, John H. D821.G4.B3, (v5)
Backer, Thomas E. RA440.55.B33 1992, (v2)
Backhouse, Edmund Trelawny. DS735.B25 1914a, (v5)
Backhouse, Janet. ND3310.B32 1979, (v9)
Backhouse, Roger. HB75.B1363 2001, (v6)
  HB171.B135 1988, (v6)
Backscheider, Paula R. CT21.B28 1999, (v5)

PR698.P65.B33 1993, (v3)
PR3404.F653.B3 1990, (v3)
PR3406.B24 1989, (v3)
Backus, John. ML3805.B245 A3 1977, (v9)
Backus, Margot Gayle. PR8807.F25.B33 1999, (v3)
Bacon, Edmund N. NA9050.B22, (v9)
Bacon, Edward. CB311.B3, (v5)
  CC100.B3 1961, (v10)
Bacon, Francis. B1153. 1857, (v8)
  B1155.B3313 1999, (v8)
  B1168.E5 J3713 2000, (v8)
  B1190. 1975, (v8)
  B1191.K54 B33 2000, (v8)
  B1153 1996, (v8)
  PR2205.V53 1996, (v3)
Bacon, Henry. PN1998.3.V57.B34 1998, (v3)
Bacon, Jean Leslie. F548.9.E2.B33 1996, (v4)
Bacon, John. BD396.B32 1995, (v8)
Bacon, Margaret Hope. HQ1413.M68.B33, (v6)
  HV8978.G38.B33 2000, (v6)
Bacon-Smith, Camille. HQ1233.B25 1991, (v6)
Bacquart, Jean-Baptiste. N7380.B28 1998, (v9)
Badaracco, Claire. PR601.B33 1995, (v3)
Badaracco, Joseph. HD62.47.B33 1991, (v6)
  HF5387.B32 1997, (v6)
Badarayana. B132.V3.B2 1960, (v8)
Badasch, Shirley A. R697.A4, (v2)
Badash, Lawrence. U264.B34 1995, (v10)
Badawi, Muhammad Mustafa. PJ8211.B3 1988, (v3)
  PJ8211.B33 1987, (v3)
Baddeley, Alan D. QP406.B33 1982, (v1)
Baddeley, Oriana. N6502.5.B3 1989, (v9)
Baden, Nancy T. PQ9555.B29 1999, (v3)
Bader, Gershom. BM501.15.B3313 1988, (v8)
Bader, Robert Smith. F686.B33 1988, (v4)
Badger, Daniel D. NA3503.7.B32 1981, (v9)
Badger, G. M. QD331.B2, (v1)
  QD400.B25, (v1)
Badger, Reid. ML422.E87.B2 1995, (v9)
Badia, Leonard F. BX1751.2.B23 1984, (v8)
Badian, E. DF227.B3 1993, (v5)
Badie, Bertrand. JF60.B24313 2000, (v7)
Badler, Norman I. TA166.B32 1993, (v1)
Badley, Linda. PN1995.9.H6.B24 1995, (v3)
  PS374.H67.B33 1996, (v3)
Badran, Margot. HQ1793.B33 1995, (v6)
Badura-Skoda, Eva. ML410.M9.B1413 1986, (v9)
Badura-Skoda, Paul. ML410.B1.B24513 1992, (v9)
Baeck, Leo. BM535.B2, (v8)
Baecque, Antoine de. DC136.5.B3413 1997, (v5)
  PN1998.3.T78.B3413 1999, (v3)
Baehr, P. R. JA81.B243 1998, (v7)
Baer, Eleanora A. AI3.B3 1978, (v10)
Baer, George W. VA58.B283 1994, (v10)
Baer, Hans A. BR563.N4.B34 1992, (v8)
  RA418.3.U6.B34 2001, (v2)
Baer, Nancy Van Norman. PN2091.S8.B275 1991, (v3)
Baer, Werner. HC187.B147 2001, (v6)
Baerresen, Donald W. HF3230.5.B3, (v6)
Baetjer, Katharine. ND1354.4.B34 1993, (v9)
Bagby, George F. PS3511.R94.Z547 1993, (v3)
Bagby, Wesley Marvin. D753.B23 1992, (v5)
Bagchi, Amiya Kumar. HC59.7.B24 1982, (v6)
Bagchi, Prabodh Chandra. DS740.5.I5.B3 1971, (v5)
Baggott, J. E. QC174.12.B34 1992, (v1)
Bagley, Christopher. HQ72.C3.B34 1990, (v6)
Bagley, Clarence. F899.S4 B15, (v4)
Bagnall, Philip M. QB755.B24 1991, (v1)
Bagnall, Roger S. DT93.B33 1993, (v5)
  HB3661.7.A3.B33 1994, (v6)
Bagnold, Enid. PR6003.A35.C5, (v3)
  PR6003.A35.L67, (v3)
Bagozzi, Richard P. HB801.B267 2002, (v6)
Bagrow, Leo. GA201.B313 1985, (v6)
Baguley, David. DC276.5.B34 2000, (v5)
Bagwe, Anjali Narottam. HQ1745.M37.B34 1995, (v6)
Bagwell, Richard. DA935.B14 1963, (v5)
Bah, M. Alpha. DT571.F84.B34 1998, (v5)
Bahat, Dan. G2239.J4.B34 1990, (v6)
Bahcheli, Tozun. DF787.T8.B33 1990, (v5)

Bahm, Archie J. B799.B34 1995, (v8)
  PL2473.Z7.B3, (v3)
Bahn, Paul G. F3169.B34 1992, (v4)
  N5310.B34 1998, (v9)
Bahr, Diana Meyers. E99.C94.B35 1993, (v4)
Bahr, Donald M. PM2174.A2.B34 1997, (v3)
Bahr, Ehrhard. PT1982.B34 1998, (v3)
Bahr, Howard M. Z1210.N3.B34 1999, (v10)
Bahti, Timothy. PN1042.B24 1996, (v3)
Bai, Hua, 1930-. PL2895.A3465.Y813 1994, (v3)
Baierlein, Ralph. QC311.B293 1999, (v1)
Baierlein, Ralph. QC476.W38.B35 1992, (v1)
Baigell, Matthew. N6538.J4.B35 1997, (v9)
Bailar, John Christian. QD471.B23, (v1)
Bailey, Alfred Goldsworthy. F1021.B25 1969, (v4)
Bailey, Alton Edward. TP670.B28 1996, (v1)
Bailey, Anthony. ND653.R4.A73 1994, (v9)
Bailey, Beth L. D744.7.H3.B35 1992, (v5)
  HQ18.M53.B35 1999, (v6)
Bailey, Brian J. DA535.B35 1998, (v5)
Bailey, Carolyn Sherwin. PZ8.9.B16Mi 1978, (v3)
Bailey, Clinton. PJ8214.5.E5B35 1990, (v3)
Bailey, Cyril. B193.B3 1964, (v8)
Bailey, D. R. Shackleton. DG260.C5.B27 1972, (v5)
  PA6411.B28 1982, (v3)
Bailey, Don C. PL677.B3, (v3)
Bailey, Don V. R726.B25 1990, (v2)
Bailey, Donna. GV784.B35 1991, (v6)
Bailey, Douglass W. GN845.B28, (v6)
Bailey, Elizabeth E. HE9803.A4.B32 1985, (v6)
Bailey, F. G. BJ1421.B335 1991, (v8)
  GN635.I4.B345 1996, (v6)
  GN635.I4.B35 1994, (v6)
Bailey, Frankie Y. E185.86.B25 1999, (v4)
Bailey, Geoffrey. UB271.R9.B3, (v10)
Bailey, Ian L. RE91.B35 1990, (v2)
Bailey, Jackson H. DS897.T635.B35 1991, (v5)
Bailey, James Osler. PR4750.D8.B3, (v3)
  PR4753.B27, (v3)
Bailey, Kathleen C. JX1974.73.B35 1993, (v7)
  UA12.5.B34 1995, (v10)
Bailey, Kathryn. ML410.W33.B32 1998, (v9)
Bailey, L. H. QK110.B3 1949, (v1)
  SB45.B17 1925, (v1)
  SB45.B22 1976, (v1)
  SB435.B32, (v1)
Bailey, Leon. BD175.B34 1994, (v8)
Bailey, Martha J. Q141.B25 1994, (v1)
  Q141.B254 1998, (v1)
Bailey, Peter J. PN1998.3.A45.B35 2001, (v3)
Bailey, Peter. DA533.B33 1998, (v5)
  GV75.B33 1978, (v6)
Bailey, Richard W. PE1072.B33 1991, (v3)
Bailey, Richard W. PE1085.B35 1996, (v3)
Bailey, Robert G. F746.B25, (v4)
  QH540.7.B345 1998, (v1)
  QH540.7.B35 1996, (v1)
Bailey, Robert Leslie. LC3731.B34, (v7)
Bailey, Sydney Dawson. U22.B25 1988, (v10)
Bailey, Temple. PS3503.A514 H6, (v3)
Bailey, Theodore N. QL737.C23.B26 1993, (v1)
Bailey, Thomas Andrew. D592.L8.B34, (v5)
  D643.A7.B3, (v5)
  D643.A7.B3, (v5)
  E183.7.B29 1980, (v4)
Bailey, Victor. HV6548.G7.B35 1998, (v6)
Bailey, Wilford S. GV351.B34 1991, (v6)
Bailey, William G. Z2184.P2.B27 1989, (v10)
Baillie, Joanna. PR4056.A83 1999, (v3)
Baily, John. ML3758.A3.B3 1988, (v9)
Baily, Martin Neil. HC106.8.B345 1993, (v6)
Baily, Samuel L. HD6602.B3, (v6)
  JV8131.B34 1999, (v7)
Bailyn, Bernard. E203.B3, (v4)
  F67.H9805, (v4)
  JA84.U5.B3, (v7)
  JK54.B3, (v7)
Bailyn, Martin. QC311.B295 1994, (v1)
Bain, Kenneth Ray. E183.8.I7.B34, (v4)
Bain, Trevor. HD9510.5.B25 1992, (v6)

Bainbridge, Beryl. PR6052.A3195.B7 1975, (v3)
PR6052.A3195.Q5 1977, (v3)
Baines, Anthony. ML460.B14 1966a, (v9)
Baines, Anthony. ML930.B3 1963, (v9)
ML933.B33 1978, (v9)
Baines, Barbara J. PR2577.B35 1984, (v3)
Bains, William. TP248.16.B33 1998, (v1)
Bains, Y. S. Z8812.A68 B35 1998, (v10)
Bair, Deirdre. PR6003.E282.Z564 1978, (v3)
PS3527.I865.Z55 1995, (v3)
Baird, Davis. BC91.B25 1992, (v8)
Baird, Jay W. DD243.B35 1990, (v5)
Baird-Lange, Lorrayne Y. Z8164.B275 1988, (v10)
Bak, Hans. PS3505.O956.Z58 1993, (v3)
Bak, Richard. GV875.D6.B35 1991, (v6)
Bakalian, Anny P. E184.A7.B35 1992, (v4)
Bakan, Abigail B. F1886.B35 1990, (v4)
Bakan, Joel. KE4381.5.B34 1997, (v7)
Bakan, Michael B. ML345.I5.B35 1999, (v9)
Bakeless, John Edwin. F454.B724, (v4)
Baken, R. J. RC423.B28 2000, (v2)
Baker, A. C. QA184.B34 1990, (v1)
Baker, Adrienne. HQ1172.B3 1993, (v6)
Baker, Alan. BF2050.B35 2000, (v2)
Baker, Arthur Ernest. PR2892.B2 1957, (v3)
Baker, C. A. DT3219.C65.B35 1994, (v5)
DT3227.B35 1997, (v5)
HD997.Z63.B35 1993, (v6)
Baker, Carlos. PR5438.B26 1961, (v3)
PS3552.A4.F7, (v3)
PS3552.A4.L3, (v3)
Baker, David J. PR428.P6.B46 1997, (v3)
Baker, David. TL515.B23 1994, (v1)
TL781.B34, (v1)
Baker, Donald P. F231.3.W55.B35 1989, (v4)
Baker, Dorothy. PS3503.A54156.Y6, (v3)
Baker, Falcon O. HV9104.B335 1991, (v6)
Baker, Gary Lee. PT2670.O36.Z56 1999, (v3)
Baker, Geoffrey L. HF499.B26 1996, (v6)
Baker, George P. HG4028.M4.B335 1998, (v6)
Baker, Gladys L. S533.B17, (v1)
Baker, Gregory L. QA862.P4.B35 1990, (v1)
Baker, H. F. QA445.B312, (v1)
Baker, Herschel Clay. BD431.B242 1969, (v8)
Baker, Houston A. PS153.N5.B28 1991, (v3)
Baker, Hugh D. R. HQ684.A15 1979, (v6)
Baker, James Addison. E881.B35 1995, (v4)
Baker, James Volant. PR4487.I6.B2, (v3)
Baker, Jean H. E457.25.L55.B35 1987, (v4)
E748.S84.B35 1996, (v4)
JK2316.B34 1998, (v7)
Baker, Jean-Claude. GV1785.B3.B35 1993, (v6)
Baker, Jeffrey P. RJ253.5.B34 1996, (v2)
Baker, John Milnes. NA7205.B33 1994, (v9)
Baker, John Norman Leonard. G80.B3 1967, (v6)
Baker, Joseph Ellis. PR463.B27 1962, (v3)
Baker, Kenneth. N6512.5.M5.B35 1988, (v9)
Baker, Lee D. GN17.3.U6.B35 1998, (v6)
Baker, Leonard. KF8745.M3.B3, (v7)
Baker, Lynne Rudder. B105.B64 B35 2000, (v8)
BD215.B27 1987, (v8)
BD418.3.B35 1995, (v8)
Baker, Margaret L. SB409.B25 1991, (v1)
Baker, Melvin C. LB875.D5.B3 1955, (v7)
Baker, Michael John. HF5415.B277 1989, (v6)
Baker, N. V. KF5107.B34 1992, (v7)
Baker, Patrick L. F2051.B35 1994, (v4)
Baker, Patsy. PN2068.B34 1993, (v3)
Baker, Paul R. NA737.H86.B34, (v9)
Baker, Paula C. JK3495.B35 1991, (v7)
Baker, Peter. PN98.D43.B35 1995, (v3)
Baker, Raymond William. DT107.87.B35 1990, (v5)
Baker, Richard E. PN56.A24.B34 1993, (v3)
Baker, Robert Horace. QB45.B15 1971, (v1)
Baker, Robert S. PR6015.U9.B6725 1990, (v3)
Baker, Robin. T385.B348 1993, (v1)
Baker, Ronald L. F524.B34 1975, (v4)
Baker, Ross K. JK1061.B33 1989, (v7)
Baker, Wayne E. HD30.3.B364 1994, (v6)
Baker, William F. PN1992.6.B32 1998, (v3)
Baker, William J. GV571.B25 1988, (v6)

GV697.O9.B35 1986, (v6)
Baker, William. Z1002.B28 2000, (v10)
Z8259.B35 2002, (v10)
Bakhtin, M. M. B105.A35 B3413 1993, (v8)
Bakich, Michael E. QB601.B36 2000, (v1)
QB802.B35 1995, (v1)
Bako, Elemer. Z2520.B33 1993, (v10)
Bakr, Salwá. PJ7816.A466A24 1993, (v3)
Baktiari, Bahman. JQ1787.7.B35 1996, (v7)
Bal, Mieke. PN212.B313 1985, (v3)
PQ2631.R63.Z52513 1997, (v3)
Balaban, Abraham. PJ5054.O9.Z5913 1993, (v3)
Balaguru, Perumalsamy N. TA418.9.C6.B354 1992, (v1)
Balakian, Nona. PS3537.A826.Z59 1998, (v3)
Balakrishnan, R. QA166.B25 2000, (v1)
Balanchine, George. MT95.B3 1977, (v9)
Balanis, Constantine A. TK7871.6.B353 1997, (v1)
Balas, Edith. Q11.P612 vol. 216, (v1)
Balasuriya, Tissa. BX2215.2.B33 1979, (v8)
Balay, Robert. Z6941.B35 2000, (v10)
Balazs, Etienne. DS721.B213, (v8)
Balcells, Albert. DP302.C67.B3513 1995, (v5)
Bald, Margaret. BL65.C45.B35 1998, (v8)
Bald, Marjory Amelia. PR468.W6B3 1963, (v3)
Bald, R. C. PR1209.B3, (v3)
PR1263.B24, (v3)
PR2248.B35 1970, (v3)
Baldanza, Frank. PR6063.U7.Z58, (v3)
Baldassare, Mark. HN79.C23.P83 2000, (v6)
Baldassari, Anne. TR647.P512 1997, (v9)
Baldassarre, Guy A. QL696.A52.B335 1994, (v1)
Baldasty, Gerald J. PN4874.S37.B35 1999, (v3)
PN4888.C59.B34 1992, (v3)
Balderrama, Francisco E. E184.M5.B35 1995, (v4)
Balderston, Daniel. PQ7797.B635.Z623 1993, (v3)
Balderston, Katharine Canby. PR3493.P4.B3, (v3)
Baldi, Pierre. QH442.B355 2001, (v1)
Baldick, Chris. PN41.C67 1990, (v3)
PR5397.F73.B3 1987, (v3)
Baldini, Umberto. NB623.B9.B2413 1982, (v9)
Baldini, Umberto. ND2757.F5.B313 1992, (v9)
Baldino, Rachel Greene. HV5822.H4.B35 2000, (v6)
Baldock, Robert. ML418.C4.B28 1993, (v9)
Baldridge, Cates. PR830.P6.B35 1994, (v3)
Baldridge, Cates. PR6013.R44.Z6315 2000, (v3)
Baldrige, Letitia. CT275.B316.A3, (v5)
Baldry, P. E. QR46.B28, (v1)
Baldus, David C. KFG565.C2.B35 1990, (v7)
Baldwin, David. GV697.A1.B336 1996, (v6)
Baldwin, Dean R. PR6045.O72.Z542 1989, (v3)
Baldwin, Deborah J. F1234.B2 1990, (v4)
Baldwin, J. TA140.F9.B35 1996, (v1)
Baldwin, James Mark. B41.B3 1940, (v8)
Baldwin, James. E185.61.B195, (v4)
E185.61.B2 1990, (v4)
PS3503.A5527.G6, (v3)
PS3552.A45.A5, (v3)
PS3552.A45.G5, (v3)
PS3552.A45.G62, (v3)
Baldwin, John W. DC90.B35 1986, (v5)
Baldwin, Joseph G. F327.B19, (v4)
Baldwin, Leland Dewitt. E315.B25, (v4)
F159.P6.B2 1970, (v4)
Baldwin, Neil. TK140.E3.B25 1995, (v1)
Baldwin, Patricia. LB2300.B35 1995, (v7)
Baldwin, Robert E. HF3130.B35 1996, (v6)
Baldwin, Sidney. HD1765 1935.B3, (v6)
Baldwin, Stephen C. HV2508.B35 1993, (v6)
Baldwin, Thomas Whitfield. PR2903.B33, (v3)
PR2995.B33, (v3)
PR3095.B3 1961, (v3)
Baldwin, Thomas. B1647.M74.B35 1990, (v8)
Bale, John. GV351.B35 1990, (v6)
GV706.8.B35 2002, (v6)
Balee, William L. F2520.1.U7.B35 1994, (v4)
Bales, Kevin. HT867.B35 1999, (v6)
Bales, Kevin. HT867.B37 2000, (v6)
Bales, Richard A. KF3425.B27 1997, (v7)
Bales, William Leslie. DS760.9.T7.B3, (v5)
Balester, Valerie M. PE1405.U6.B34 1993, (v3)

Balfour, Alan. NA9200.B4.B35 1990, (v9)
Balfour, Michael Leonard Graham. D810.P7.G7216, (v5)
DD256.3.B27 1988, (v5)
DD257.B34 1992, (v5)
DD258.7.B35 1982, (v5)
Balfour, Sebastian. DP243.B28 1997, (v5)
Balfour-Paul, Glen. DS63.2.G7.B34 1990, (v5)
Bali, Mrinal. TL794.B34 1990, (v1)
Balibar, Etienne. B3305.M74.B21513 1995, (v8)
Balibar, Francoise. QC16.E5B3513 2001, (v1)
Balick, Michael J. GN476.73.B35 1996, (v6)
Balio, Tino. PN1993.5.U6.H55 1990 vol. 5, (v3)
Balkin, J. M. B823.3.B25 1998, (v8)
Ball, Alan M. HC335.2.B33 1987, (v6)
Ball, Douglas B. E480.5.B35 1991, (v4)
Ball, George W. D843.B25, (v5)
E183.8.I7.B35 1992, (v4)
Ball, Howard. KF228.B34 B35 2000, (v7)
KF8744.B275 1991, (v7)
KF8745.B55.B298 1996, (v7)
RC965.U7.B35 1993, (v2)
Ball, Michael. HG2040.5.U5.B35 1990, (v6)
Ball, Nicole. HC59.72.D4.B35 1988, (v6)
Ball, Philip. GB661.2.B35 2000, (v6)
QH491.B35 1999, (v1)
TA403.B2247 1997, (v1)
Ball, S. J. UA647.B567 1995, (v10)
Ball, Stuart R. TK7895.E42, (v1)
Ball, Stuart. DA566.9.B15.B34 1988, (v5)
Ball, Terence. JA81.B253 1995, (v7)
Ballance, Alton. F262.H9.B35 1989, (v4)
Ballard, Dana Harry. QP356.B345 1997, (v1)
Ballard, J. G. PR6052.A46, (v3)
Ballard, Jack S. UA917.U5.B34 1983, (v10)
Ballard, John R. DC146.B756, (v5)
Ballard, Robert D. GC65.B275 2000, (v6)
Ballendorf, Dirk Anthony. VE25.E45.B35 1997, (v10)
Ballentine, Rudolph. R733.B255 1999, (v2)
Ballentyne, D. W. G. Q123.B3 1961a, (v1)
Balliett, Whitney. ML395.B34 1986, (v9)
ML395.B36 1996, (v9)
ML3507.B35 1983, (v9)
ML3508.B34, (v9)
ML3561.J3.B24, (v9)
ML3561.J3.B244, (v9)
ML3561.J3.B25, (v9)
ML3561.J3.B255, (v9)
Balling, Robert C. QC981.8.C5.B35 1992, (v1)
Ballinger, James K. N6537.R4.B26 1989, (v9)
Ballou, Dale. LB2842.22.B35 1997, (v7)
Bally, Charles. PC2435.B3, (v3)
Balmer, Randall Herbert. BR1640.B35 2002, (v8)
BR1642.U5.B35 1989, (v8)
BX8935.B355 1993, (v8)
Balmuth, Daniel. PN5279.M63.R8733 2000, (v3)
Balmuth, Miriam. PE1133.B26, (v3)
Baloyra, Enrique A. F1488.B34 1982, (v4)
Balseiro, Jose Agustin. PQ6072.B3, (v3)
Balski, Grzegorz. PN1998.2.D55 1992, (v3)
Baltensperger, Bradley H. F666.B23 1985, (v4)
Baltsan, Hayim. PJ4833.B26 1992, (v3)
Baltzell, E. Digby. F73.3.B33 1996, (v4)
HN57.B26, (v6)
Balzac, Honore de. PQ2161.R3, (v3)
PQ2166.A3.H8, (v3)
PQ2168.B7, (v3)
Balzer, Marjorie Mandelstam. DK759.K53.B35 1999, (v5)
Balzer, Richard. GV1525.B35 1998, (v6)
Bamford, James. UB251.U5.B35 1982, (v10)
Bamforth, Nicholas. KD4103.B36 1997, (v7)
Bamman, Henry A. LB1573.B357 1973, (v7)
Bammer, Angelika. PN3401.B36 1991, (v3)
Banchoff, Thomas F. DD290.29.B34 1999, (v5)
Banchoff, Thomas. QA691.B26 1990, (v1)
Bancroft, Frederic. E384.3.B22 1966, (v4)
Bancroft, George. E178.B22 1837, (v4)

Bancroft, Hubert Howe. F796.B192, (v4)
F851.B215 v. 33, (v4)
F851.B215 vol. 18-24, (v4)
F851.B215 vol. 25, (v4)
F851.B215 vol. 26, (v4)
F851.B22, (v4)
Band, Arnold J. PJ5053.A4.Z59, (v3)
Band, Claire. DS777.53.B3, (v5)
Band, William. QC174.4.B3, (v1)
Bandeira, Manuel. PQ9697.B27.E8213 1989, (v3)
Bandelier, Adolph Francis Alphonse. E78.S7.B32, (v4)
Bandem, I Made. GV1703.I532.B34322 1995, (v6)
Bandera, Cesareo. PN49.B137 1994, (v3)
Bandura, Albert. LB1084.B357, (v7)
RC489.B4.B3, (v2)
Bandyopadhyay, Manik. PK1718.B28, (v3)
Bandyopadhyaya, Tarasankara. PK1718.B2985.G313, (v3)
Bane, Mary Jo. HQ536.B3, (v6)
Banerjee, Mukulika. DS392.N67 B36 2000, (v5)
Banerjee, Shampa. PN1993.5.I8.B27 1988, (v3)
Banerji, Arup. HF3626.B254 1997, (v6)
Banerji, H. K. PR3456.B3 1962, (v3)
Banes, Sally. GV1799.4.B35 1998, (v6)
NX511.N4.B26 1993, (v9)
Banet-Weiser, Sarah. HQ1220.U5.B36 1999, (v6)
Banfield, A. W. F. QL721.B32, (v1)
Banfield, Stephen. ML410.S6872.B3 1993, (v9)
ML2831.B35 1985, (v9)
Bang, Herman. PT8123.B3.T513 1984, (v3)
Bangerter, Lowell A. PT401.B28 1988, (v3)
PT2617.O47.Z7324, (v3)
PT2625.U8.Z567 1989, (v3)
Bangs, Carl. BX6196.B28 1985, (v8)
Bangura, Ahmed S. PL8014.W37.B36 2000, (v3)
Banham, Martin. PN2035.C27 1995, (v3)
Banham, Reyner. NA680.B25 1980, (v9)
NA9053.M43.B36, (v9)
Bank, Rosemarie K. PN2248.B36 1997, (v3)
Bank, Stephen P. BF723.S43.B36 1982, (v2)
Bank, Ted. F951.B3, (v4)
Bankier, David. DD256.5.B32 1992, (v5)
Bankowsky, Richard. PS3552.A48.G58, (v3)
Banks, Christopher P. KF8750.5.B36 1999, (v7)
Banks, F. R. DA631.B34, (v5)
Banks, Ferdinand E. HC55.B25, (v6)
Banks, Jack. PN1992.8.M87.B36 1996, (v3)
Banks, Jeri. HV2561.I483.C43 1994, (v6)
Banks, Lynne Reid. PR6003.A528.H6, (v3)
Banks, Olive. HQ1154.B268 1981, (v6)
HQ1593.B33 1993, (v6)
Banks, Olive. LA635.B3, (v7)
Banks, Robert. QA93.B358 1999, (v1)
QA93.B36 1998, (v1)
Banks, Stephen P. HM263.B323 1995, (v6)
TA1632.B35 1991, (v1)
Banks, Stuart. SF487.B182 1979, (v1)
Banks, Theodore Howard. PR3592.K6.B3 1950, (v3)
Bankston, John. RD27.35.B365B36 2002, (v2)
Bankwitz, Philip Charles Farwell. U55.W45.B3, (v10)
Banner, James M. E357.7.B3, (v4)
LB1060.B36 1999, (v7)
Banner, Lois W. HQ1413.B36.A3 1998, (v6)
Banner, Michael C. BL51.B238 1990, (v8)
Banner, Stuart. KF1070.B36 1998, (v7)
Banner-Haley, Charles Pete T. E185.615.B285 1994, (v4)
Bannerman, Helen. PZ7.B227Ls35, (v3)
Banning, Kendall. V415.P1.B3 1957, (v10)
Banning, Lance. E302.1.B2, (v4)
E342.B245 1995, (v4)
Bannister, Robert C. HM22.U6.B4717 1991, (v6)
Banno, Masataka. DS760.B3, (v5)
Bannon, John Francis. F799.B3, (v4)
Bannon, Joseph J. GV182.15.B36, (v6)
Banowetz, Joseph. MT227.B2 1985, (v9)
Banta, William F. KF3570.B36 1988, (v7)
Banting, Keith G. HC120.I5.B36 1982, (v6)
Bantjes, Adrian A. F1346.B37 1998, (v4)
Bao, Zhiming. PL1213.B36 1999, (v3)

Baptiste, Fitzroy Andre. D768.18.B39 1988, (v5)
Bar͞adah, Muòhammad. PJ7816.A6538L8313 1996, (v3)
Barabas, SuzAnne. PN1991.77.G86.B36 1990, (v3)
Barabba, Vincent P. HF5415.2.B333 1995, (v6)
Baraheni, Reza. PK6561.B35A22, (v3)
Barak, Gregg. HV4505.B37 1991, (v6)
Barak͞at, Hudá. PJ7816.A672H+, (v3)
Baraka, Imamu Amiri. PS3552.A583.A6 1991, (v3)
PS3552.A583.A6 2000, (v3)
PS3552.A583.T3 1968, (v3)
Barakat, Halim Isber. DS36.88.B36 1993, (v5)
Barakat, Huda. PJ7816.A672.H3513 1995, (v3)
Baranowski, Shelley. DD453.B37 1995, (v5)
Barany, Zoltan D. DB956.B37 1993, (v5)
Barasch, Moshe. N70.B2 1990, (v9)
Barash, Carol. PR545.W6.B37 1996, (v3)
Barash, David P. HQ806.B367 2001, (v6)
QH431.B226 2001, (v1)
QL737.R638.B37 1989, (v1)
QP34.5.B34 2000, (v1)
Barbalet, J. M. HM291.B269 1998, (v6)
Barbara, Dominick A. RC423.B3 1960, (v2)
Barbeau, Edward. QA99.B17 2000, (v1)
Barbee, David Rankin. F199.B23, (v4)
Barber, Benjamin R. JA83.B2483 1988, (v7)
JC336.B25 1998, (v7)
JK1726.B27 1998, (v7)
Barber, C. L. PR658.T7.B37 1988, (v3)
Barber, D. J. QC173.4.C65.B37 1989, (v1)
Barber, E. J. W. GN776.2.A1.B37 1990, (v6)
GN778.32.C5.B37 1999, (v6)
GN799.T43.B37 1994, (v6)
Barber, James David. JK511.B37 1992, (v7)
JK1976.B3, (v7)
Barber, James P. DT779.9.B37 1990, (v5)
Barber, Karin. PL8823.5.B33 1991, (v3)
PN2993.4.B37 2000, (v3)
Barber, Malcolm. BX4891.2.B37 2000, (v8)
CB351.B35 1992, (v5)
CR4743.B27 1994, (v5)
Barber, Michael D. BJ414.D873.B37 1998, (v8)
Barber, Paul. GR830.V3.B35 1988, (v6)
Barber, Richard W. CR4513.B33, (v5)
DA234.B37, (v5)
PR328.B3 1971, (v3)
Barber, Stanley A. S596.7.B37 1984, (v1)
Barber, William J. HC106.3.B269 1996, (v6)
Barbera, Jack. Z8822.32.B37 1987, (v10)
Barbier, Jacques A. F3091.B268, (v4)
Barbier, Patrick. ML1727.8.P2.B313 1995, (v9)
Barbosa, Valmir C. QA76.9.D5.B36 1996, (v1)
Barbour, Douglas. PR9199.3.O5.Z58 1993, (v3)
Barbour, Hugh. BX7731.2.B37 1988, (v8)
Barbour, Ian G. BL240.2.B368 1990, (v8)
BL240.2.R366 2002, (v8)
T14.B36 1970, (v1)
Barbour, J. Murray. ML3809.B234 1953, (v9)
Barbour, Julian B. QC133.B37 1989, (v1)
QC173.59.S65.B374 2000, (v1)
Barbour, Reid. PR836.B37 1993, (v3)
Barbu, Zevedei. D16.B15 1976, (v5)
Barbusse, Henri. PQ2603.A32.F4 1916, (v3)
Barbuto, Domenica M. Z7164.S665.B37 1999, (v10)
Barbuto, Richard V. E355.6.B37 2000, (v4)
Barchiesi, Alessandro. PA6537.B2813 1997, (v3)
Barcia Carballido y Zuniga, Andres Gonzalez de. F314.B243, (v4)
Barclay, David E. DD424.8.B37 1995, (v5)
Barclay, John M. G. DS135.M43.B368 1996, (v5)
Barczewski, Stephanie L. PR468.N293.B37 2000, (v3)
Bard, Allen J. QD553.B37, (v1)
TP256.B37 1994, (v1)
Bardach, Eugene. JF1601.B37 1998, (v7)
Bardach, Janusz. DK771.K67.B373 1998, (v5)
RD524.B37 1991, (v2)
Bardach, John E. QH97.B37, (v1)
Bardakjian, Kevork B. PK8505.B37 2000, (v3)
Barden, Garrett. BJ37.B27 1990, (v8)
Bardini, Thierry. QA76.17.B37 2000, (v1)

Bardo thodol. BL1411.B3.E6 1957, (v8)
Bardon, Jonathan. DA990.U46.B2254 1992, (v5)
Bardwick, Judith M. HQ1206.B23, (v6)
Barea, Arturo. PQ6613.A763Z55 1973, (v3)
Bareau, Juliet Wilson. NC287.G65, (v9)
Barenboim, Daniel. ML417.B2.A3 1992, (v9)
Barer, Burl. PR6005.H348.Z59 1993, (v3)
Barfield, Claude E. HJ275.B29, (v6)
Barfield, Owen. PN1031.B3 1964, (v3)
PR4484.B3, (v3)
Barfield, Ray E. PN1991.3.U6.B37 1996, (v3)
Bargen, Doris G. PL788.4.G43.B37 1997, (v3)
Barger, M. Susan. TR365.B37 1991, (v1)
Barger, W. K. HD1527.A14.B37 1994, (v6)
Barghoorn, Frederick Charles. DK69.B3, (v5)
Barghuthi, Murid. PJ7816.A682, (v3)
Bariand, Pierre. TS722.B3713 1992, (v1)
Barilli, Renato. BH39.B35313 1993, (v8)
PN183.B313 1989, (v3)
Baring-Gould, William Stuart. PR4624.B33, (v3)
Barish, Evelyn. PR4458.B47 1970, (v3)
Barish, Jonas A. PR2638.B27, (v3)
PR2644.B3, (v3)
Baritz, Loren. E169.1.B225, (v4)
Bar-Joseph, Uri. DS126.99.J6.B37 1987, (v5)
Bark, Dennis L. DD258.7.B37 1989, (v5)
Barkai, Avraham. HC286.3.B32513 1990, (v6)
Barkan, Elazar. GN269.B368 1992, (v6)
Barkan, Leonard. NB85.B37 1999, (v9)
Barkauskas, Violet. RT48.H38 2001, (v2)
Barke, James. PR6003.A677, (v3)
Barker, Arthur Edward. PR3588.B3, (v3)
Barker, Charles A. F184.B25 1967, (v4)
Barker, Ernest. DA110.B36, (v5)
JC73.B23 1960, (v7)
JC73.B25 1959, (v7)
JC336.B27 1967, (v7)
Barker, Eugene Campbell. F389.A936 1968, (v4)
Barker, George. PR6003.A68.D4, (v3)
Barker, Graeme. DG223.B345 1998, (v5)
Barker, James H. E99.E7.B175 1993, (v4)
Barker, Martin. PS1408.B37 1995, (v3)
Barker, Nancy Nichols. DC130.O73.B37 1989, (v5)
Barker, Nicolas. Z792.B85932.B37 1989, (v10)
Z1024.C32 1983 Suppl., (v10)
Barker, Richard Hindry. PR2716.B3, (v3)
Barker, Rocky. QH76.5.N97.B37 1993, (v1)
Barker, Roger G. BF353.B3, (v2)
Barker, Shirley. PS3503.A5684.R5, (v3)
PS3503.A5684.T6, (v3)
Barker, Thomas. HV6715.B37 2000, (v6)
Barkey, Henri J. DR435.K87.B37 1998, (v5)
Barkey, Karen. HV6453.T8.B37 1994, (v6)
Bar-Kochva, Bezalel. DS121.8.J8.B3713 1989, (v5)
Barkow, Al. GV981.B39 2000, (v6)
Barkun, Michael. E184.A1 B245 1997, (v4)
Barlas, Asma. DS341.B35 1995, (v5)
Barlet, Olivier. PN1993.5.A35.B3713 2000, (v3)
Barlow, Colin. HD9161.A2.B32 1994, (v6)
Barlow, Connie C. QH367.B35 2000, (v1)
Barlow, George W. QL638.C55, (v1)
Barlow, Harold. ML128.I65 B3 1978, (v9)
ML128.V7 B3 1976, (v9)
Barlow, Jane. PR4063.B3.I78 1970, (v3)
Barlow, Janelle. HF5415.5.B3673 2000, (v6)
Barlow, Philip L. BS500.B33 1991, (v8)
Barlow, Steven M. QP306.B28 1999, (v1)
Barlow, William. ML3521.B36 1989, (v9)
PN1991.8.A35.B37 1999, (v3)
Barlowe, Jamie. PS1868.B37 2000, (v3)
Barman, Roderick J. F2534.B366 1988, (v4)
F2536.P37.B37 1999, (v4)
Barnabe, G. QH541.5.C65, (v1)
Barnaby, Andrew Thomas. B1133.K56 B37 2002, (v8)
Barnaby, Frank. UA832.B37 1989, (v10)
Barnard, F. M. HX44.B346 1991, (v6)
JC179.R9.B37 1988, (v7)
Barnard, G. William. BV5083.B29 1997, (v8)
Barnard, Nicholas. NK1047.B37 1993, (v9)
Barnard, Rita. PS228.P67.B37 1995, (v3)
Barnard, Sylvia M. HN398.L38.B37 1990, (v6)

Barnard, T. C. DA944.4.B37, (v5)
Barnatt, Christopher. HD31.B3682 1997, (v6)
Barnes, Annette. BD439.B37 1997, (v8)
Barnes, Arthur Chapman. SB231.B3 1973, (v1)
Barnes, Bernadine Ann. ND623.B9.A69 1998a, (v9)
Barnes, Christopher J. PG3476.P27.Z56 1989, (v3)
Barnes, Djuna. PS3503.A614.A6 1962, (v3)
  PS3503.A614.A64, (v3)
  PS3503.A614.N5 1946, (v3)
  PS3503.A614.R9, (v3)
Barnes, Elizabeth. PS374.S97.B37 1997, (v3)
Barnes, Ian. E208.B36 2000, (v9)
Barnes, J. W. TN260.B27 1988, (v1)
Barnes, J. Wesley. TA340.B35 1994, (v1)
Barnes, J.W. (John Wykeham). QE36.B33 1995, (v1)
Barnes, James J. E183.8.G7.B218 1993, (v4)
Barnes, Jay. QC945.B35 1998, (v1)
  QC945.B37 2001, (v1)
Barnes, Jonathan. B188.B34 1982, (v8)
  B623.B37 1990, (v8)
Barnes, Kenneth C. F215.B29 1998, (v4)
Barnes, Margaret (Ayer). PS3503.A5722.Y4, (v3)
Barnes, Peter. PR6052.A668.A6 1981, (v3)
Barnes, Philip. HD9576.I52.B37 1995, (v6)
Barnes, R. H. DS632.L33.B37 1996, (v3)
Barnes, Ralph Mosser. T60.4.B39 1980, (v1)
Barnes, Robert D. QL362.B27 1987, (v1)
Barnes, Timothy David. DG315.B35, (v5)
  DG316.B37 1998, (v5)
Barnes, Trevor J. HF1025.B333 1996, (v6)
Barnes, Will C. F809.B27 1988, (v4)
Barnes, William R. HC106.8.B365 1998, (v6)
  JX1705.B35, (v7)
  PR4064.A2.J6, (v3)
Barnes-Svarney, Patricia L. QH45.2.B32 1999, (v1)
Barnet, Richard J. E744.B32, (v1)
Barnett, A. Doak. DS740.5.R8.B37, (v5)
  DS777.53.B32 1963, (v5)
  DS777.55.B29, (v5)
  DS777.55.B3, (v5)
  DS777.55.B322, (v5)
  HC428.N6.B37 1993, (v6)
Barnett, Alan W. ND2608.B36 1984, (v9)
Barnett, Correlli. D770.B28 1991, (v5)
Barnett, Dave. TK1001.B275 2000, (v1)
Barnett, George L. PR4863.B327, (v3)
Barnett, Harold C. HC110.P55.B37 1994, (v6)
Barnett, Lincoln Kinnear. QC6.B33 1957, (v1)
Barnett, Michael N. UA865.B37 1992, (v10)
Barnett, Randy E. K487.L5.B37 1998, (v7)
Barnett, S. QA188.B36 1990, (v1)
Barnette, W. Douglas. PQ6663.A5.Z56 1995, (v3)
Barney, Darin David. JC423.B2613 2000, (v7)
Barney, Natalie Clifford. PQ3939.B3.Z46313 1992, (v3)
Barney, Richard A. PR858.E38.B37 1999, (v3)
Barney, Stephen A. PE274.B3, (v3)
Barney, William L. E468.B319 2001, (v4)
  E468.B32 1980, (v4)
Barnhart, Bill. F546.4.K47.B37 1999, (v4)
Barnhart, David K. PE2831.B37 1997, (v3)
Barnhart, Stephen L. ML399.B38 2000, (v9)
Barnhurst, Kevin G. PN4749.B29 2001, (v3)
Barnie, John. DA185.B27 1974, (v5)
Barnitz, Albert Trovillo Siders. E83.869.B37, (v4)
Barnitz, Jacqueline. N6502.5.B36 2001, (v9)
Barnouw, Dagmar. DD239.B37 1988, (v5)
  DD257.25.B336 1996, (v5)
  DS135.G5.A753 1990, (v5)
  PN1995.2.B37 1994, (v3)
Barns, Cass G. F666.B25 1970, (v4)
Barnstone, Willis. PQ6176.B338 1993, (v3)
  PQ6176.B34, (v3)
Barnum, Barbara Stevens. RT73.B27 1999, (v2)
  RT84.5.B37 1998, (v2)
  RT85.2.B37 1996, (v2)
Barnum, P. T. GV1811.B3 A3 2000, (v6)
Barnwell, John. F273.B28 1982, (v4)
Baro, Gene. PS645.B37, (v3)
Baroja, Pio. PQ6603.A7.A9 1962, (v3)
Barolsky, Paul. NX552.Z9.M533 1990, (v9)

Baron, Jonathan. BF441.B29 1988, (v2)
Baron, Larry. HV6561.B34 1989, (v6)
Baron, Marcia. B2799.E8.B28 1995, (v8)
Bar-On, Mordechai. DS119.7.B2832 1996, (v5)
Baron, Naomi S. PE1075.B28 2000, (v3)
Baron, Salo Wittmayer. DS112.B3152, (v5)
  DS135.R9.B28 1976, (v5)
Baron, Stanley N. TK6680.5.B37 1996, (v1)
Baron-Cohen, Simon. BF444.B37 1995, (v2)
Barondes, Samuel H. RC341.B33 1993, (v2)
Barone, Tom. LA2317.F663, (v7)
Barr, Alfred Hamilton. ND553.M37.B34 1966, (v9)
Barr, Andrew. HV5292.B35 1999, (v6)
Barr, Cyrilla. ML429.C64.B37 1998, (v9)
Barr, Marleen S. PS374.P64.B37 2000, (v3)
  PS374.S35.B33 1993, (v3)
Barr, N. A. HB846.B37 1998, (v6)
Barr, Richard L. PN1851.B54 1998, (v3)
Barr, Robert D. LC4802.B37 2001, (v7)
Barr, Ronald J. UA25.B25 1998, (v10)
Barraclough, Geoffrey. D13.B33, (v5)
  DD89.B27 1966, (v5)
  DD126.B35, (v5)
Barranger, Milly S. PN2287.T16.B37 1991, (v3)
  PN2287.W4555.B37 1994, (v3)
Barratt Brown, Michael. HF3876.5.B37 1992, (v6)
Barratt, Andrew. PG3476.B78.M333 1987, (v3)
Barratt, Glynn. DU490.B37 1990, (v5)
Barrault, Jean Louis. PQ2603.A482.R313 1971b, (v3)
Barreca, Regina. PR830.H85.B37 1994, (v3)
Barrell, A. D. M. DA775.B37 2000, (v5)
Barrell, John. PR448.P6.B37 2000, (v3)
Barrell, John. PR4538.O74.B37 1991, (v3)
Barreno, Maria Isabel. PQ9264.A74.N613, (v3)
Barres, Maurice. PQ2603.A52.A6 1966, (v3)
Barreto, Amilcar Antonio. F1976.B37 1998, (v4)
Barreto, Mascarenhas. E112.B2713 1992, (v4)
Barrett, Anthony. DG282.6.B37 1996, (v5)
  DG283.B37 1990, (v5)
  NA749.R37.B37 1983, (v9)
Barrett, Buckley Barry. Z8169.45.B35 2000, (v10)
Barrett, David V. BP603.B37 2001, (v8)
Barrett, G. C. QD431.B28 1998, (v1)
Barrett, James R. HX84.F6.B37 1999, (v6)
Barrett, Jeffrey Alan. QC174.12.B364 1999, (v1)
Barrett, Laurence I. E876.B37 1983, (v4)
Barrett, Lindon. PS153.N5.B296 1999, (v3)
Barrett, Richard A. GN316.B377 1984, (v6)
Barrett, Stanley R. HN110.O5.B37 1994, (v6)
Barrett, Stephen. R730.B373 1994, (v2)
  RB152.6.B37 1998, (v2)
Barrette, Bill. NB237.H42.A4 1989, (v9)
Barrie, J. M. PR4070.F18 vol.9, (v3)
  PR4070.F29, (v3)
  PR4070.F75, (v3)
  PR4074.A3 1934, (v3)
  PR4074.L4 1954, (v3)
  PR4074.S4, (v3)
  PR4076.A4 1947, (v3)
  PZ8.B276Pet2, (v3)
  PZ8.B276P3, (v3)
Barrie, Thomas. NA4600.B37 1996, (v9)
Barrios, Richard. PN1995.9.M86.B37 1995, (v3)
Barritt, Greg J. QH604.2.B37 1991, (v1)
Barro, Robert J. HD75.B365 1997, (v6)
  HG230.3.B37 1990, (v6)
Barroll, J. Leeds. PR2983.B29 1984, (v3)
  PR3097.B37 1991, (v3)
Barron, F. L. E78.S2.B375 1997, (v4)
Barron, Hal S. HN57.B334 1997, (v6)
Barron, John M. HF5549.5.T7.B2917 1997, (v6)
Barron, Michael. NA2800.B36 1993, (v9)
Barron, W. R. J. PR321.B37 1987, (v3)
  PR2065.G31.B37, (v3)
Barros, Carolyn A. PR788.A9.B37 1998, (v3)
Barros, James. D749.5.R8.B37 1995, (v5)
Barros, Mauricio Rands. HD8290.R43.B37 1999, (v6)
Barrow, Christopher J. GF75.B37 1991, (v6)
Barrow, Clyde W. JC212.B37 2000, (v7)
  JC251.B32 1993, (v7)
Barrow, Deborah J. KF8719.B35 1996, (v7)

  KF8752 5th.B27 1988, (v7)
Barrow, G. W. S. DA176.B3 1956, (v5)
Barrow, Gordon M. QD95.B37, (v1)
  QD453.2.B373, (v1)
Barrow, John D. BD511.B34 1988, (v8)
  BH301.N3.B37 1995, (v8)
  Q175.B225 1991, (v1)
  QA36.B37 1992, (v1)
  QB981.B2798 1994, (v1)
  QB991.E94.B37 1994, (v1)
Barrow, Robin. LB85.P7.B35 1976, (v7)
Barrows, Robert G. CT275.B144, (v5)
Barrus, Clara. PS1226.B27 1968, (v3)
Barry, Ann Marie. BF241.B29 1997, (v2)
Barry, B. T. K. TN793.B37 1983, (v1)
Barry, Boubacar. DT532.25.B3713 1998, (v5)
Barry, Brian M. JC578.B37 1989 vol. 2, (v7)
Barry, E. Eldon. HD4145.B3, (v6)
Barry, James A. JZ1306.B37 1998, (v7)
Barry, John A. QA76.9.C66.B375 1991, (v1)
Barry, Kathleen. HQ117.B37 1995, (v6)
Barry, Kathleen. HQ1413.A55.B36 1988, (v6)
Barry, Mike. NK4670.7.A78.M5313 1996, (v9)
Barry, Norman P. JC571.B364 1987, (v7)
  JC571.B365 1987, (v7)
Barry, Patricia D. RC454.4.B372 2002, (v2)
Barry, Patricia S. E78.A34.B37 1991, (v4)
Barry, Peter. PR611.B37 2000, (v3)
Barry, Philip. PS3503.A648.P3 1929, (v3)
  PS3503.A648.P5 1939, (v3)
Barry, Robert Laurence. R726.B288 1994, (v2)
Barry, Terence B. DA920.B348 1987, (v5)
Barry, Tom. F1439.5.B38 1991, (v4)
  F1466.7.B37 1992, (v4)
Barsalou, Lawrence W. BF201.B37 1992, (v2)
Barsham, Diana. PR4623.B37 2000, (v3)
Barsoum, M. W. TP807.B37 1997, (v1)
Barsoux, Jean-Louis. HD38.B258 1993, (v6)
Barston, R. P. JZ1405.B37 1997, (v7)
Barstow, Jane Missner. PS151.B37 1997, (v3)
Bart, Benjamin F. PQ2246.M3.B3, (v3)
Barta, Peter I. PR6019.O9.U624 1996, (v3)
Bartee, Thomas C. QA76.5.B297 1971, (v1)
Bartels, Emily Carroll. PR2674.B37 1993, (v3)
Bartels, Larry M. JK522.B37 1988, (v7)
Bartelson, Jens. JC327.B245 1995, (v7)
Barth, E. M. Z7125.B34 1992, (v10)
Barth, Fredrik. GN635.I65.B38 1993, (v6)
Barth, Gunther Paul. E169.1.B2315 1990, (v4)
Barth, J. Robert. PR4487.L65.B37 1988, (v3)
Barth, James R. HG2491.B275 1992, (v6)
Barth, John. PS3552.A75.C5 1972, (v3)
  PS3552.A75.F4, (v3)
  PS3552.A75.G5, (v3)
  PS3552.A75.L6, (v3)
  PS3552.A75.S6 1967, (v3)
Barth, Karl. BJ1253.B3513, (v8)
  BR121.B2455 1957, (v8)
  BT65.B313, (v8)
  BT75.B283 1975, (v8)
  BT78.B3 1963, (v8)
  BV210.B333, (v8)
  BV4316.P7.B33, (v8)
  BX9410.B323, (v8)
Barth, Patte. LA219.B37 2001, (v7)
Barth, Richard P. HV1431.B37 1990, (v6)
Barth, Roland S. LA217.B38 1990, (v7)
  LA217.2.B397 2001, (v7)
Barthel, Diane L. HF5827.B37 1988, (v6)
Barthelemy, Anthony Gerard. PR678.A4.B37 1987, (v3)
Barthelme, Donald. PS3552.A76.A4, (v3)
  PS3552.A76.C5, (v3)
  PS3552.A76.C6, (v3)
  PS3552.A76.G7 1979, (v3)
  PS3552.A76.G8, (v3)
  PS3552.A76.S3, (v3)
  PS3552.A76.S63 1968, (v3)
  PS3552.A76.U5, (v3)

Barthes, Roland. NX65.B37 1982, (v9)
P85.B33.A3 1992, (v3)
PQ1905.B313 1992, (v3)
Bartholet, Elizabeth. HV875.55.B38 1993, (v6)
Bartholomew, David J. H61.B26 1982, (v6)
Bartholomew, James R. Q127.J3.B37 1989, (v1)
Bartholomew, Robert E. RC455.4.E8.B367 2000, (v2)
Bartholomew. JC121.B2813 1991, (v7)
Bartik, Timothy J. HD75.B367 1991, (v6)
Bartke, Wolfgang. DS778.A1B32 1997, (v5)
Bartkowski, Frances. PN56.A45.B37 1995, (v3)
Bartky, Ian R. QB210.U5, (v1)
Bartle, Robert Gardner. QA37.B29, (v1)
Bartlett, Anne Clark. PR275.R4.B37 1995, (v3)
Bartlett, Anthony W. BT265.2.B37 2001, (v8)
Bartlett, C. J. DA88.B37, (v5)
DA566.7.B29 1989, (v5)
Bartlett, Christopher A. HD62.4.B36 1998, (v6)
Bartlett, David L. HC300.282.B37 1997, (v6)
Bartlett, Dick. QH76.5.T4.B385 1995, (v1)
Bartlett, Eugene R. TK5105.B358 1995, (v1)
Bartlett, I. S. F761.B28, (v4)
Bartlett, John. PR2892.B34 1972, (v3)
Bartlett, Joseph W. KF1544.B37 1991, (v7)
Bartlett, M. S. QA273.B258 1966, (v1)
Bartlett, Randall. HB71.B3137 1989, (v6)
Bartlett, Richard D. QL666.O6.B3295 2000, (v1)
Bartlett, Robert. D200.B27 1993, (v5)
DA195.B28 2000, (v5)
DA209.G5.B37 1982, (v5)
Bartlett, Roger. RC1235.B37 1998, (v2)
Bartlett, Thomas. DA947.B37 1992, (v5)
Bartlett, W. B. D164.B37 2000, (v5)
Bartley, Numan V. F216.2.B36 1995, (v4)
F291.B26 1983, (v4)
JK1936.A2.B37, (v7)
Bartold, V. V. PJ709.G62 vol. 5, 1958, (v3)
Bartolini, Stefano. JN94.A979B37 2000, (v7)
Bartolome, Lilia I. LB1033.5.B37 1998, (v7)
Bartolozzi, Bruno. MT339.5.B37 1982, (v9)
Barton, Anne. PR2638.B28 1984, (v3)
PR4359.B37 1992, (v3)
Barton, Carlin A. DG78.B37 1993, (v5)
Barton, Josef J. F499.C69.I83, (v4)
Barton, Richard L. E183.8.C2.B35 1990, (v4)
Barton, William Eleazar. HV569.B3.B4, (v6)
Bartos, Rena. HC79.C6.B34 1989, (v6)
Bartoszynski, Robert. QA273.B2584 1996, (v1)
Bartov, Omer. D757.B27 1991, (v5)
Bartov, Omer. D804.348.B37 2000, (v5)
Bartra, Roger. F1210.B2513 1992, (v4)
Bartram, John. QH31.B23.A3, (v1)
Bartram, William. F213.B2893 1980, (v4)
Bartusiak, Marcia. QB791.3.B36 1993, (v1)
Bartusis, Mark C. U43.B9.B37 1992, (v10)
Baruch, Dorothy (Walter). RJ499.B3, (v2)
Barut, A. O. QC174.45.B3, (v1)
Barwise, Jon. B840.B37 1999, (v8)
Barwise, Jon. BC128.B37 1993, (v8)
Barylski, Robert V. JN6693.5.C58.B37 1998, (v7)
Barzun, Jacques. D13.B333, (v5)
D13.B334 1970, (v5)
LA226.B27, (v7)
LB1775.B36 1991, (v7)
ML410.B5.B2 1969, (v9)
PC2511.B37 1991, (v3)
Basbanes, Nicholas A. Z987.B28 2002, (v10)
Basch, Francoise. PR878.W6.B37 1974, (v3)
Basch, Paul F. QR201.S35.B37 1991, (v1)
RA441.B38 1999, (v2)
Basch, Reva. Z699.B3535 1993, (v10)
Bascom, Willard. GC211.2.B37 1980, (v6)
Bascom, William Russell. GR111.A47.B37 1992, (v6)
Baseler, Marilyn C. JV6451.B37 1998, (v7)
Basford, Terry K. Z6878.P8.B37 1990, (v10)
Basham, A. L. BL1152.3.B37 1989, (v8)
Basham, Richard Dalton. F1053.B29 1978, (v4)
Basheer, Vaikom Muhammad. PL4718.9.B33.A23, (v3)
Bashevkin, Sylvia B. HQ1236.B27 1998, (v6)
Bashford, Bruce. PR5827.L5.B37 1999, (v3)

Bashmakova, I. G. QA242.B4397 1997, (v1)
Basinger, Jeanine. PN1995.9.W6.B36 1993, (v3)
Basker, James G. PR3698.L5.B37 1988, (v3)
Baskerville, David. ML3795.B33 2001, (v9)
Baskes, Jeremy. F1219.1.O11.B29 2000, (v4)
Baskin, Barbara Holland. Z1037.9.B36 1984, (v10)
Baskin, Carol C. QK661.B37 1998, (v1)
Baskin, Ellen. PN1992.8.S4.B37 1996, (v3)
Z5784.M9.B385 1993, (v10)
Baskin, Jonathan Barron. HG4017.B37 1997, (v6)
Basler, Roy Prentice. PN49.B17 1967, (v3)
Basolo, Fred. QD171.B32 1967, (v1)
Basquiat, Jean Michel. N6537.B233.A4 1999, (v9)
Bass, Althea. E99.C5 B33 1996, (v4)
Bass, Gary Jonathan. KZ6310.B37 2000, (v7)
Bass, George Fletcher. CC77.B3, (v5)
G540.B272 1972, (v6)
Bass, Jack. F216.2.B39, (v4)
Bass, Jack. F279.O6 B37 1996, (v4)
Bass, S. Jonathan. F334.B69.N415 2001, (v4)
Bass, Thomas A. DS556.45.A43.B38 1996, (v5)
Q141.B32 1994, (v1)
Bassan, Fernande. Z2175.A2.B39 1989, (v10)
Bassan, Maurice. PS1449.C85.Z548, (v3)
Bassani, Giorgio. PQ4807.A79.C513, (v3)
Bassanini, Piero. QA377.B295 1997, (v1)
Bassard, Katherine Clay. PS153.N5.B33 1999, (v3)
Bassett, Glenn. GV995.B39 2000, (v6)
Bassett, John Earl. Z8980.45.B37 1996, (v10)
Bassford, Christopher. U43.U4.B37 1994, (v10)
Bassie-Sweet, Karen. F1435.3.P5.B37 1996, (v4)
F1435.3.S34.B87 1991, (v4)
Bassin, Mark. DK771.A3.B37 1999, (v5)
Bassler, Gerhard P. F1123.V35, (v4)
Basso, Ellen B. F2520.1.A63.B365 1987, (v4)
Basso, Hamilton. PS3503.A8423.L5, (v3)
PS3503.A8423.V5, (v3)
Basso, Keith H. E99.A6.B2295, (v4)
Basta, L. R726.B325 1996, (v2)
Bastable, Bernard. PR6052.A665.M35 1998, (v3)
Bastea, Eleni. NA9202.A8.B37 2000, (v9)
Bastian, Dawn E. Z3631.W55 1995, (v10)
Bastien, Joseph William. F3320.2.C3.B365 1987, (v4)
RA644.C26.B37 1998, (v2)
Bastin, Bruce. ML3521.B39 1986, (v9)
Bastos, Cristiana. RA644.A25.B358 1999, (v2)
Basu, Alaka Malwade. HB1050.D45.B38 1992, (v6)
Basu, Amrita. HQ1236.5.I4.B37 1992, (v6)
Basu, Aparna. HN687.S34.B37 1996, (v6)
Basu, Manoje. PK1718.B374.J3, (v3)
Basu, Srimati. HQ1236.5.I4.B375 1999, (v6)
Bataille, Georges. B3317.B41513 1992, (v8)
PQ2603.A695.C613 1988, (v3)
Bataille, Gretchen M. E98.W8.B37 1984, (v4)
Batchelor, G. K. QA911.B33, (v1)
Batchelor, John. PR5263.B37 2000, (v3)
PR6005.O4.Z557 1994, (v3)
Batchelor, Stephen. BQ704.B38 1994, (v8)
Bate, Jonathan. PR575.N3, (v3)
PR2955.O86.B38 1993, (v3)
PR5892.N2.B38 1991, (v3)
Bate, Philip. ML935.B25, (v9)
ML940.B37 1975, (v9)
ML960.B38 1978, (v9)
Bate, Walter Jackson. BH221.G7.B36, (v8)
PR3533.B33, (v3)
PR3533.B334, (v3)
PR4483.B3, (v3)
PR4836.B3, (v3)
PR4837.B34, (v3)
PR4838.S8.B, (v3)
Bateman, Alan Mara. TN263.B27, (v1)
Bateman, Bradley W. HB103.K47.B333 1996, (v6)
Bateman, Walter L. LB2331.B377 1990, (v7)
Bates, Barbara. RC309.P4.B38 1992, (v2)
Bates, Catherine. PR428.C64.B38 1992, (v3)
Bates, Daisy. F419.L7.B3, (v4)
Bates, Daniel G. DS57.B34 1983, (v5)
Bates, David R. QC806.B34 1958, (v1)
Bates, H. E. PR6003.A965.A6 1963, (v3)
PR6003.A965.B7, (v3)

PR6003.A965.C45, (v3)
PR6003.A965.C7, (v3)
PR6003.A965.C9, (v3)
PR6003.A965.D3, (v3)
PR6003.A965.D39, (v3)
PR6003.A965.D4 1957, (v3)
PR6003.A965.E5, (v3)
PR6003.A965.F3, (v3)
PR6003.A965.F31, (v3)
PR6003.A965.G6, (v3)
PR6003.A965.H68, (v3)
PR6003.A965.L6, (v3)
PR6003.A965.M9, (v3)
PR6003.A965.N3, (v3)
PR6003.A965.O3, (v3)
PR6003.A965.S32, (v3)
PR6003.A965.S6, (v3)
PR6003.A965.S8, (v3)
PR6003.A965.W3, (v3)
PR6003.A965.W43, (v3)
PR6003.A965.W6, (v3)
Bates, James Leonard. E743.B36, (v4)
Bates, L. F. QC753.B32 1961, (v1)
Bates, Marston. G515.B3, (v6)
Bates, Milton J. PS228.V5.B38 1996, (v3)
Bates, Robert H. HD82.B3257 2001, (v6)
HD2118 1981.B37, (v6)
HD9199.A2.B27 1997, (v6)
Bates, Roger G. QD561.B32 1973, (v1)
Bateson, Frederick Wilse. PR502.B3 1961, (v3)
Bateson, Mary Catherine. GN21.M36.B38 1984, (v6)
Bath, Alan Harris. D810.S7.B35 1998, (v5)
Bathie, William W. TJ778.B34 1996, (v1)
Bathrick, David. PT3707.B38 1995, (v3)
Batinski, Michael C. F67.B45.B38 1996, (v4)
Batra, N. D. PN1992.5.B36 1987, (v3)
Batra, Raveendra N. HF1455.B328 1993, (v6)
Batschelet, Margaret. Z7402.B38 1990, (v10)
Batsford, Harry. NA5461.B3 1960, (v9)
Batson, C. Daniel. BF637.H4.B39 1991, (v2)
Batt, Judy. HC270.28.B37 1988, (v6)
Battaglia, Debbora. DU740.42.B39 1990, (v5)
Battaglia, Richard A. SF65.2.B38 1998, (v1)
Battan, Louis J. QC981.B33 1985, (v1)
Batten, Charles. PR769.B3, (v4)
Battersby, Christine. BH301.C84.B37 1990, (v8)
Battersby, Martin. NK1390.B3 1988, (v9)
Battestin, Martin C. PR448.A77.B38 1974, (v3)
PR3454.J67.B3, (v3)
PR3456.B385 2000, (v3)
Battigelli, Anna. PR3605.N2.Z59 1998, (v3)
Battin, M. Pabst. BV4011.5.B38 1990, (v8)
HV6545.B26 1995, (v6)
R726.B33 1994, (v2)
Battiscombe, Georgina. PR5238.B32 1981, (v3)
Battisti, Eugenio. NA1123.B8.B3613 1981, (v9)
Battistini, Lawrence Henry. DS518.8.B34, (v5)
Battle, John M. Z7165.S65 B37 1988, (v10)
Battle, Stafford L. E185.B33 1996, (v4)
Bau, Mingchien Joshua. DS740.B36, (v5)
Baucom, Donald R. UG743.B42 1992, (v10)
Baucom, Ian. PR478.N37.B38 1999, (v3)
Baudelaire, Charles. PQ2191.F6 1936, (v3)
PQ2191.Z5.A28, (v3)
PQ2191.Z5.A42 1957, (v3)
PS2631.B3, (v3)
Baudet, E. H. P. CB251.B3813, (v5)
Baudez, Claude F. F1435.1.C7.B38 1994, (v4)
Baudin, Louis. F3429.B353, (v4)
Baudot, Georges. F1219.B3513 1995, (v4)
Baudrillard, Jean. BD236.B3813 1994, (v8)
D860.B3813 1994, (v5)
HM291.B3413 1993, (v6)
Bauer, Arnold J. HN293.B38, (v6)
Bauer, Barbara B. RC440.B353 2000, (v2)
Bauer, Brian S. F3429.3.C14.B395 1995, (v4)
Bauer, Cameron. QA152.2.B384 1998, (v1)
Bauer, Carlos. PQ6267.E5.W372 1984, (v3)
Bauer, Caroline Feller. LB1042.B38, (v7)
Bauer, Dale M. PS3545.H16.Z58 1994, (v3)
Bauer, David G. LB2336.B38 1995, (v7)

Bauer, Douglas. PN3355.B29 2000, (v3)
Bauer, Edward L. QD65.B29 1971, (v1)
Bauer, Erwin A. QL737.U55.B376 1995, (v1)
  QL737.U55.B386 1995, (v1)
  SK33.B36, (v1)
Bauer, Gretchen. HD8808.B38 1998, (v6)
Bauer, Hans. HG3204.B38 1998, (v6)
Bauer, Henry H. Q157.B24 2001, (v1)
  Q175.B25 1992, (v1)
Bauer, K. Jack. E404.B37 1993, (v4)
  E422.B26 1985, (v4)
  VA61.B36 1991, (v10)
Bauer, Wolfgang. PL2658.E8, (v3)
Bauer, Yehuda. D804.348.B39 2001, (v5)
Bauerlein, Mark. B832.B36 1997, (v8)
  PN81.B387 1997, (v3)
  PS3238.B34 1991, (v3)
Baugh, Albert Croll. PE1075.B3 1957, (v3)
  PR83.B3 1967b, (v3)
Baugh, John. PE3102.N42.B37 2000, (v3)
  PE3102.N42.B38 1983, (v3)
  PE3102.N42.B39 1999, (v3)
Baugh, Lloyd. PN1995.9.J4.B38 1997, (v3)
Baugher, Joseph F. QB54.B38 1985, (v1)
Baughman, T. H. G850 1901.D68.B38 1999, (v6)
  G870.B26 1994, (v6)
Baum, Alice S. HV4505.B378 1993, (v6)
Baum, Bruce David. JC585.B268 2000, (v7)
Baum, Howell S. HM131.B3754 1997, (v6)
Baum, Joan. PR575.S53.B38 1994, (v3)
Baum, Julius. NA5563.B39, (v9)
Baum, L. Frank. PZ7.B327Wi 1987, (v3)
Baum, Lawrence. KF8775.B38 1997, (v7)
Baum, Markus. BX8129.B68.A6913 1998, (v8)
Baum, Paull F. PR1924.B3, (v3)
Baum, Richard. DS777.55.B346, (v5)
Baum, Richard. QB605.2.B38 1997, (v1)
Baum, Willa K. D16.14.B38, (v5)
Bauman, John F. E806.B36 1988, (v4)
Bauman, R. P. QC437.B36, (v1)
Bauman, Richard A. KKE40.P64.B38 1990, (v7)
Bauman, Richard W. K201.B38 1996, (v7)
Bauman, Thomas. ML410.M9 B185 1987, (v9)
Bauman, Zygmunt. BD241.B33 1978, (v8)
  BJ319.B28 1993, (v8)
  D804.3.B377 1989, (v5)
  HM51.B364 2001, (v6)
  HM73.B29 1991, (v6)
Baumann, Gerd. QC20.7.E4.B3813 1996, (v1)
Baumann-Reynolds, Sally. DC423.B4 1995, (v5)
Baumbach, Gunter. TD883.B36313 1996, (v1)
Baumeister, Roy F. BF789.E94.B38 1997, (v2)
Baumel, Judith Tydor. DS135.G332.B3813 1997, (v5)
Baumgaertner, Jill P. PS3565.C57.Z584 1988, (v3)
Baumgartner, Frank R. JK468.P64.B38 1993, (v7)
  JK1118.B29 1998, (v7)
Baumgartner, Frederic J. D25.5.B3 1991, (v5)
  DC108.B38 1994, (v5)
  DC114.B38 1988, (v5)
Baumhart, Raymond. HF5386.B279, (v6)
Baumlin, James S. PR2248.B38 1991, (v3)
Baumol, William J. HB135.B38 1977, (v6)
  HB199.B33 1970, (v6)
  HC110.L3.B38 1989, (v6)
  HD2326.B38 1982, (v6)
  HD2731.B27 1967, (v6)
Baumrind, Diana. HV6626.52.B38 1995, (v6)
Baumslag, Naomi. RJ216.B28 1995, (v2)
Baun, Michael J. JN30.B38 1996, (v7)
Baur, John I. H. N6512.B3 1967, (v9)
Baur, Susan. RC480.8.B384 1997, (v2)
Bauschinger, Sigrid. PT123.U6.B3813 1998, (v3)
Bausell, R. Barker. Q180.55.M4.B38 1994, (v1)
Bausinger, Hermann. GR40.B3313 1990, (v6)
Baver, Sherrie L. HD3616.P92.B38 1993, (v6)
Baviskar, B. S. HD3538.B375 1995, (v6)
Bawcutt, Priscilla J. PR2269.B37 1992, (v3)
Bawden, Garth. F3430.1.M6.B38 1996, (v4)
Baxandall, Michael. N8243.S36.B38 1995, (v9)
  NB1255.G3.B39, (v9)
Baxter, Colin F. Z6207.W8.B36 1996, (v10)

Baxter, Colin F. Z8591.3.B39 1999, (v10)
Baxter, Craig. DS393.8.B39 1997, (v5)
Baxter, Edmuhnd. PR4537.B39 1990, (v3)
Baxter, James C. DS894.59.I838.B39 1994, (v5)
Baxter, James K. PR9639.3.B3.A127, (v3)
  PR9639.3.B3.A19 1982, (v3)
Baxter, James Phinney. V799.B3 1968, (v10)
Baxter, Joan. ML2080.B39 1997, (v9)
Baxter, John D. KD8024.B39 1990, (v7)
Baxter, Maurice G. E340.C6.B39 1995, (v4)
  E340.W4.B297 1984, (v4)
Bay, Edna G. JQ3376.A91 B39 1998, (v7)
Bay, Monica. KF297.Z9 B39 1990, (v7)
Bayʿ atˉ i, Abd al-Wahhˉ ab. PJ7816.A92A23 1991,
  (v3)
Bayart, Jean-François. JQ1875.A55 C63513 1999,
  (v7)
Bayat, Assef. HV4132.56.A5.B39 1997, (v6)
Bayer, Ronald. RA644.A25.B387 2000, (v2)
Bayili, Blaise. DT555.45.L94.B38 1998, (v5)
Bayle, Pierre. CT95.B33, (v5)
Bayles, Michael D. HB885.B333, (v6)
Bayley, David H. HV7921.B36 1994, (v6)
  HV8148.D4.B392, (v6)
Bayley, Harold. CB475.B3 1951, (v5)
Bayley, John. PR590.B27, (v3)
Bayley, John. PR4809.H15.B39 1992, (v3)
Bayley, Stephen. NA9355.L6, (v9)
Baylis, John. UA647.B288 1995, (v10)
Baylor, Byrd. PZ7.B3435Ev, (v3)
Bayly, C. A. DS463.B34 1996, (v5)
Bayly, M. Brian. QE601.B36 1992, (v1)
Bayly, Susan. DS484.4.B39 1989, (v5)
Baym, Nina. PS149.B38, (v3)
Baynes, John Christopher Malcolm. U55.O26.B38
  1989, (v10)
Baynton, Douglas C. HV2471.B39 1996, (v6)
Bayon, Damian. N6620.B3913 1992, (v9)
Bayor, Ronald H. E748.L23.B38 1993, (v4)
  F128.9.I6.B39, (v4)
  F294.A89.N424 1996, (v4)
Bazant, Z. P. TA656.B39 1991, (v1)
Bazaraa, M. S. T57.74.B39 1990, (v1)
Bazelon, David L. KF9223.B36 1988, (v7)
Bazin, Andre. PN1994.B3513, (v3)
Bazin, Germain. N6415.B3.B313 1968b, (v9)
Bazin, H. R489.J5, (v2)
Beabout, Gregory R. BJ1725.B33 1994, (v8)
Beach, Cecilia. Z2174.D7.B43 1994, (v10)
  Z2174.D7.B44 1996, (v10)
Beach, Cora May (Brown). F760.B36, (v4)
Beach, Frank Ambrose. QP356.B35 1961, (v1)
Beach, Joseph Warren. PR585.N3.B4 1966, (v3)
  PR4754.B4 1962, (v3)
Beach, Mark. Z118.B4 1992, (v10)
Beach, Rex. PS3503.E1135.S6, (v3)
Beach, Sylvia. Z305.S45.B42 1980, (v10)
Beagle, Peter S. PS3552.E13.F3 1978, (v3)
Beaglehole, J. C. G246.C7.B38, (v6)
Beal, John Robinson. E835.D85 B4 1974, (v4)
Beal, Merrill D. E83.877.B4, (v4)
Beale, Howard K. E757.B4 1984, (v4)
Bealey, Frank. JA61.B43 1999, (v7)
Beals, Carleton. F1215.B38, (v4)
  F1233.5.D53.B4 1971, (v4)
Beals, Ralph Leon. GN24.B4 1971, (v6)
Beam, Joan. Z1231.F4.B42 1996, (v10)
Beam, Walter R. UB212.B39 1989, (v10)
Bean, J. M. W. DA245.B43 1989, (v5)
Bean, Jonathan J. HD2346.U5.B343 1996, (v6)
Bean, Kenneth Lamont. LB1131.B323 1970, (v7)
Bean, R. HD6971.B368 1985, (v6)
Beane, James A. LB1072.B43 1990, (v7)
Bear, Firman Edward. S591.B33 1986, (v1)
Bear, H. S. QA303.B38 2001, (v1)
Beard, Charles Austin. E169.1.B282, (v4)
  E169.1.B285, (v4)
  E169.1.B33, (v4)
  E806.B434, (v4)
  HC106.3.B43, (v6)
  JK146.B5 194l, (v7)

Beard, Frances (Birkhead). F761.B36, (v4)
Beard, Geoffrey W. NA3542.B4 1983, (v9)
Beard, James. TX651.B37 1977, (v1)
Beard, Mary Ritter. E161.B42 1969, (v4)
  HQ1122.B4 1968, (v6)
Beard, Mary. BL802.B43 1998, (v8)
  PA85.H33.B43 2000, (v3)
Beard, Michael. PK6561.H43.B8334 1990, (v3)
Bearden, William O. HF5415.3.B323 1993, (v6)
Beardon, Alan F. QA333.B43 1984, (v1)
Beardsley, Aubrey. NC1115.B316, (v9)
Beardsley, John. N6494.E27.B4 1984, (v9)
  N6538.H58 B43 1987, (v9)
Beardsley, Monroe C. B790.B4, (v8)
  BC71.B3, (v8)
  BC71.B32 1966, (v8)
  BH81.B4 1966, (v8)
  BH201.B4 1981, (v8)
Bearss, Edwin C. F419.F7 B35 1979, (v4)
Beasecker, Robert. Z1297.B43 1998, (v10)
Beasley, Ina. LC2471.S73.B43 1992, (v7)
Beasley, Jerry. GV1114.3.B44 2003, (v6)
Beasley, John D. QA269.B33 1989, (v1)
Beasley, Maurine Hoffman. PN4888.W65.B45 1993,
  (v3)
Beasley, W. G. DS881.B4 1963, (v5)
Beatley, Timothy. HD205.B43 1994, (v6)
Beatley, Timothy. QH75.B43 1994, (v1)
Beaton, Cecil Walter Hardy. PR6052.E197.Q3, (v3)
Beaton, K. B. PF3460.B35 1996, (v3)
Beaton, Leonard. UF767.B4, (v10)
Beaton, Roderick. PA5165.B43 1989, (v3)
Beattie, Andrew J. QH541.15.B56, (v1)
Beattie, Ann. PS3552.E177.C4, (v3)
  PS3552.E177.S4, (v3)
Beattie, Keith. DS558.B4 1998, (v5)
Beattie, L. Elisabeth. HV6626.22.K4, (v6)
Beattie, Susan. NB467.5.N48.B42 1983, (v9)
Beatty, Arthur. PR5888.B4 1960, (v3)
Beatty, Jack. F70.C85B44 1992, (v4)
  HD30.5.B4 1998, (v6)
Beatty, Michael A. E155.B33 2001, (v4)
Beaty, Frederick L. PR6045.A97.Z6165 1992, (v3)
Beaty, Jerome. PR4167.J5.B36 1996, (v3)
Beauchamp, George A. LB1555.B42 1965, (v7)
Beaud, Michel. HC51.B38313 2001, (v6)
Beaufre, Andre. D755.1.B3813 1968, (v5)
Beaulieu, Elizabeth Ann. PS374.S58.B43 1999, (v3)
Beauman, Nicola. PR6011.O58.Z62 1994, (v3)
Beaumarchais, Jean-Pierre de. PQ41.B4 1984, (v3)
Beaumont, Francis. PR2420. 1966, (v3)
  PR2429.A12, (v3)
Beaumont, Peter. DS49.7.B36, (v5)
Beaumont, Roger A. U260.B43 1993, (v10)
Beaune, Colette. DC33.2.B413 1991, (v5)
Beauregard, David N. PR3007.B43 1995, (v3)
Beauregard, G. T. E411.B4, (v4)
Beaurline, L. A. PR2638.B4, (v3)
Beaussant, Philippe. ML410.C855.B413 1990, (v9)
Beauvoir, Simone de. BJ1063.B382, (v8)
  E169.B414 1953, (v4)
  PQ2603.E3.S3, (v3)
  PQ2603.E362.B6, (v3)
  PQ2603.E362.M6, (v3)
  PQ2603.E362.T62, (v3)
  PQ2603.E362.Z5153 1962, (v3)
  PQ2603.E362.Z523, (v3)
  PQ2603.E362.Z524, (v3)
Beavan, Colin. HV6074.B34 2001, (v6)
Beaver, Bonnie V. G. SF756.7.B43 1994, (v1)
Beaver, Frank Eugene. PN1998.3.S76.B43 1994, (v3)
  TR847.B43 1994, (v1)
Beaverbrook, Max Aitken. DA566.9.L5.B4, (v5)
Beaverbrook, Max Aitken. DA577.B34 1968, (v5)
Beavers, W. Robert. RC488.5.B3798 1990, (v2)
Beazley, Charles Raymond. G89.B38, (v6)
Becan-McBride, Kathleen. RB45.15.G37 1989 Suppl.,
  (v2)
Bechdolt, Frederick R. PS3503.E15 W5, (v3)
Becher, Anne. GE55.B43 2000, (v6)
  QH541.15.B56.B435 1998, (v1)

Becher, Paul. TP156.E6B38 2000, **(v1)**
Bechhofer, Frank. H61.B425 2000, **(v6)**
Bechler, Z. B491.N3.B43 1995, **(v8)**
  Q174.B67 vol. 127, **(v1)**
Bechtel, H. Kenneth. HV7965.B43 1995, **(v6)**
Bechtel, Helmut. SB409.B43313 1991, **(v1)**
Bechtel, William. Q175.B415 1988, **(v1)**
Bechtold, Richard L. TP343.B37 1997, **(v1)**
Beck, Aaron T. RC554.B43 1990, **(v2)**
Beck, Anatole. QA39.2.B42 2000, **(v1)**
Beck, Brenda E. F. PL4758.2.B4 1982, **(v3)**
Beck, Charlotte H. PS261.B44 2001, **(v3)**
Beck, Daisy (Woodward). CT275.B546.A3, **(v5)**
Beck, Deva. QP552.E53.B43 1987, **(v1)**
Beck, J. Murray. F1038.H82.B43 1982, **(v4)**
Beck, James H. N8560.B43 1994, **(v9)**
Beck, L. J. B1854.B4, **(v8)**
Beck, Lewis White. B2774.B4, **(v8)**
  BD573.B4, **(v8)**
Beck, Lynn G. LB2831.93.B43 1993, **(v7)**
Beck, Richard. PT7103.I7 vol. 34, **(v3)**
Beck, Robert J. E183.8.G84.B43 1993, **(v4)**
Beck, Roger B. DT1787.B43 2000, **(v5)**
Beck, Simone. TX719.B388, **(v1)**
Beck, Warren A. G1381.S1.B4 1989, **(v6)**
Becker, Allienne R. PR830.F3.B43 1992, **(v3)**
Becker, Anne E. GN671.F5.B43 1995, **(v6)**
Becker, Brian E. HD58.9.B43 2001, **(v6)**
Becker, Carl Lotus. D13.B38 1972, **(v5)**
  D16.8.B318 1966, **(v5)**
  JC599.U5.B35 1945, **(v7)**
Becker, Charles M. HC435.2.B383 1992, **(v6)**
  HC800.B42 1994, **(v6)**
Becker, E. W. TP248.27.A46.B43 1994, **(v1)**
Becker, Ernest. BD450.B39, **(v8)**
Becker, Gary Stanley. HD4903.5.U58.B4 1971, **(v6)**
Becker, Gaylene. RG133.5.B434 2000, **(v2)**
Becker, George Joseph. PN56.R3.B4, **(v3)**
  PN761.B35 1982, **(v3)**
Becker, Marvin B. DG443.B42 1981, **(v5)**
Becker, Richard. QC254.B3713 1967, **(v1)**
  QC670.B42, **(v1)**
Becker, Robert O. QP82.2.E43.B418 1990, **(v1)**
Becker, Udo. AZ108.B4313 1994, **(v10)**
Beckerman, Bernard. PN1584.B4 1990, **(v3)**
  PR3095.B4, **(v3)**
Beckerman, Michael Brim. ML410.D99 B42 2003, **(v9)**
Beckerman, Paul Ely. HG229.B379 1992, **(v6)**
Beckett, Sven. HC108.N7.B343 2001, **(v6)**
Becket, Fiona. PR6023.A93.Z5665 1997, **(v3)**
Beckett, A. H. RS403.B43 1988, **(v2)**
Beckett, I. F. W. U240.B43 1999, **(v10)**
Beckett, J. C. DA947.B4 1976, **(v5)**
  DA948.A2.B4, **(v5)**
Beckett, J. V. DA670.M64.B43 1988, **(v5)**
Beckett, Katherine. HV6791.B42 1997, **(v6)**
Beckett, S. T. TP640.B43 2000, **(v1)**
Beckett, Samuel. PQ2603.E378E5, **(v3)**
  PQ2603.E378.T5, **(v3)**
  PQ2631.R63.Z466 1957, **(v3)**
  PR6003.E282.A17, **(v3)**
  PR6003.E282.A17 1984, **(v3)**
  PR6003.E282.A6 1984, **(v3)**
  PR6003.E282.A8, **(v3)**
  PR6003.E282.C3, **(v3)**
  PR6003.E282.H3, **(v3)**
  PR6003.E282.I2 1976, **(v3)**
  PR6003.E282.K7, **(v3)**
  PR6003.E282.M64, **(v3)**
  PR6003.E282.M8 1957, **(v3)**
  PR6003.E282.W3 1959, **(v3)**
  PR6003.E282.Z495 1998, **(v3)**
Beckett, Wendy. N72.F45.B43 1988, **(v9)**
  ND50.B396 1999, **(v9)**
  ND1329.B4.B43 1997, **(v9)**
Beckford, William. PR4091.V4 1970b, **(v3)**
  PR4092.A35, **(v3)**
  PR4092.A4 1928, **(v3)**
Beckles, Hilary. F2041.B435 1990, **(v4)**
  HT1071.B44 1999, **(v6)**

Beckman, Linda Hunt. PR4886.L25, **(v3)**
Beckman, Ludvig. JC574.B4 2001, **(v7)**
Beckman, Theodore N. HF5415.1.B42 1973, **(v6)**
Beckman, William A. TH7413.B4, **(v1)**
Beckmann, George M. DS721.B38, **(v5)**
Beckner, Steven K. HB119.G74.B43 1996, **(v6)**
Beckson, Karl E. PN44.5.B334 1975, **(v3)**
  PR468.D43.B43 1992, **(v3)**
  PR5823.B34 1998, **(v3)**
Beckstead, James H. F826.B428 1991, **(v4)**
Becksvoort, Christian. NK2407.B43 1998, **(v9)**
Beckwith, Burnham P. CB161.B4, **(v5)**
Beckwith, Christopher I. DS786.B38 1987, **(v5)**
Beckwith, Francis. BJ37.B43 1998, **(v8)**
Beckwith, John. N5970.B4, **(v9)**
  N7832.B3, **(v9)**
Beckwith, T. G. (Thomas G.). TA165.B38 1993, **(v1)**
Beckwourth, James Pierson. F592.B39 1892, **(v4)**
Bécquer, Gustavo Adolfo. PQ6503.B3 1995, **(v3)**
Bed̄i, Sushama. PK2098.13.E35H313 1993, **(v3)**
Bedani, Gino. HD6709.B36 1995, **(v6)**
Bedau, Hugo Adam. HV8699.U5.B39 1987, **(v6)**
  JC328.B38, **(v7)**
Beddoe, Deirdre. HQ1593.B43 1989, **(v6)**
Beddoes, Jonathan. TS205.B299 1999, **(v1)**
Beddoes, Thomas Lovell. PR4097.A, **(v3)**
  PR4097.A27, **(v3)**
Bederson, Benjamin. QC784.B4, **(v1)**
Bedford, Kristina. PR2805.B44 1992, **(v3)**
Bedford, Sybille. PR6003.E294.F3, **(v3)**
Bedient, Calvin. PS3545.A748.Z58 1984, **(v3)**
Bedient, Philip B. GB661.2.B42 1988, **(v6)**
  TD426.B44 1994, **(v1)**
Bedini, Silvio A. Z48.B44 1984, **(v10)**
Bedrosian, Margaret. PS153.A75.B43 1991, **(v3)**
BeDuhn, Jason. BT1410.B43 2000, **(v8)**
Beebe, William. QH123.B4, **(v1)**
  QL128.B45 1951, **(v1)**
Beebee, Thomas O. PN3491.B415 1999, **(v3)**
  PR3664.C43.B44 1990, **(v3)**
Beecham, Thomas. ML422.B33 A2 1976, **(v9)**
Beecher, Jonathan. HX704.C7.B44 2001, **(v6)**
Beechert, Edward D. DU629.H7.B44 1990, **(v5)**
Beekes, R. S. P. P575.B4413 1995, **(v3)**
Beekman, E. M. PT5911.B44 1996, **(v3)**
Beeler, John F. DA88.B44 1997, **(v5)**
Beeler, John. U37.B44, **(v10)**
Beeman, Randal S. S441, **(v1)**
  F230.B43, **(v4)**
  F232.L9.B34 1984, **(v4)**
Beene, Lynn. PR861.B38 1997, **(v3)**
Beer, Ferdinand Pierre. TA350.B3552 1997, **(v1)**
  TA405.B39 2002, **(v1)**
Beer, Frances. BV5095.H55.B44 1992, **(v8)**
Beer, G. TA347.F5.B43 1992, **(v1)**
Beer, Gillian. PR5014.B4 1970, **(v3)**
Beer, John B. PR4148.P6.B4, **(v3)**
  PR5892.E5.B43, **(v3)**
Beer, Max. HB103.A2.B4 1967, **(v6)**
Beer, Samuel Hutchison. JK325.B38 1993, **(v7)**
Beer, Thomas. PS3503.E267.M7 1969, **(v3)**
  PS3503.E267.R6, **(v3)**
Beerbohm, Max. PR6003.E4.A17 1963, **(v3)**
  PR6003.E4.A17 1994, **(v3)**
  PR6003.E4.A6 1962, **(v3)**
  PR6003.E4.M3 1958, **(v3)**
  PR6003.E4.S4, **(v3)**
  PR6003.E4.Z49, **(v3)**
  PR6037.T73.Z56 1943, **(v3)**
Beere, Carole A. BF692.B38 1990, **(v2)**
  HQ1075.B44 1990, **(v6)**
Beers, Clifford Whittingham. RC439.B4 1953, **(v2)**
Beers, Henry Augustin. PR99.B35, **(v3)**
Beers, Henry Putney. Z1289.B44 1989, **(v10)**
Beetham, David. JC328.2.B43 1991, **(v7)**
Beetz, Kirk H. Z8866.B43 1984, **(v10)**
Beevor, Antony. D757.9.B418 2002, **(v5)**
  D766.7.C7.B44 1994, **(v5)**
Begam, Richard. PR6003.E282.Z5728 1996, **(v3)**
Begelman, Mitchell C. QB843.B55.B44 1996, **(v1)**
  QB857.7.B44 2000, **(v1)**

Begg, David K. H. HB172.5.B43 1982, **(v6)**
Begin, James P. HD31.B3734 1997, **(v6)**
Begin, Menachem. DS126.B375 1977, **(v5)**
Begon, Michael. QH352.B43 1981, **(v1)**
  QH541.B415 1990, **(v1)**
Behague, Gerard. ML410.V76.B44 1994, **(v9)**
Behan, Brendan. PR6003.E417.Q3 1964, **(v3)**
  PR6003.E417.Z4635 1985, **(v3)**
  PR6003.E417.Z52, **(v3)**
  PR6003.E417H6 1958, **(v3)**
  PR6003.E41H58 1963, **(v3)**
Behar, Ruth. GN346.4.B44 1996, **(v6)**
  HQ1465.M63.B44 1993, **(v6)**
Behbahani, Simin. PK6561.B5A24 1999, **(v3)**
Behl, Benoy K. ND2829.A4.B44 1998, **(v9)**
Behling, Laura L. HQ1236.5.U6.B45 2001, **(v6)**
Behlmer, George K. HQ615.B45 1998, **(v6)**
Behn, Aphra. PR3317.A15, **(v3)**
  PR3317.A6 1992, **(v3)**
  PR3317.A6 1995, **(v3)**
  PR3317.O7 1997, **(v3)**
Behrendt, John C. G850.B44 1998, **(v6)**
Behrendt, Patricia Flanagan. PR5827.S48.B44 1991, **(v3)**
Behrendt, Stephen C. PR3562.B38 1983, **(v3)**
  PR5442.R36.B44 1989, **(v3)**
Behrens, C. B. A. DC131.B4 1967, **(v5)**
Behrens-Abouseif, Doris. BH221.A65 B3413 1998, **(v8)**
Behrman, Jack N. HF1418.5.B44 1984, **(v6)**
Behrman, Martin. F379.N553.B443, **(v4)**
Behrman, S. N. PR6003.E4.Z56, **(v3)**
  PS3503.E37.C6, **(v3)**
  PS3503.E37.F6, **(v3)**
Behuniak, Susan M. KF3823.B44 1999, **(v7)**
  KF3827.E87 B44 2003, **(v7)**
Beichman, Janine. PL811.A83.Z57 1982, **(v3)**
Beidel, Deborah C. RC552.S62.B45 1998, **(v2)**
Beiderman, T. O. DT443.3.K33.B43 1997, **(v5)**
Beiderwell, Bruce John. PR5343.P68.B45 1992, **(v3)**
Beidleman, Linda H. QK150.N4 2000, **(v1)**
Beidler, Philip D. D744.55.B45 1998, **(v5)**
  PS266.A5.B45 1999, **(v3)**
  Z2013.3.B45 1994, **(v10)**
Beigbeder, Yves. K5000.B45 1999, **(v7)**
Beik, William. DC126.B45 1997, **(v5)**
Beilin, Elaine V. PR113.B45 1987, **(v3)**
Beilin, Yossi. DS132.B3413 2000, **(v5)**
Bein, Alex. DS141.B3813 1990, **(v5)**
Beinart, Haim. G1034.B413 1992, **(v6)**
Beineke, John A. LB875.K54.B44 1998, **(v7)**
Beinert, Dieter. KK2628.B45 1991, **(v7)**
Beinin, Joel. DS135.E4.B45 1998, **(v5)**
Beirne, Francis F. F189.B157 B439 1984, **(v4)**
Beiser, Arthur. QC3.B4, **(v1)**
Beiser, Frederick C. DD419.B45 1992, **(v5)**
Beit-Hallahmi, Benjamin. BL80.2.B385 1993, **(v8)**
  Z7204.P8.B44 1996, **(v10)**
Beito, David T. HJ3252.B45 1989, **(v6)**
  HS61.A17 2000, **(v6)**
Beitz, Charles R. JX1250.B4, **(v7)**
Bejan, Adrian. QC320.B44 1993, **(v1)**
  TA168.B37 2000, **(v1)**
Bejel, Emilio. PQ7389.L49.Z58 1990, **(v3)**
Belaunde, Victor Andres. F2235.B673 1967, **(v4)**
Belchem, John. HN400.R3.B45 1996, **(v6)**
Belcher, Gerald L. ND237.N43.B45 1991, **(v9)**
Belcher, Max. NA1599.L4.B4 1988, **(v9)**
Belcher, Stephen Paterson. PL8010.B44 1999, **(v3)**
Belden, Jack. DS777.53.B38 1970, **(v5)**
Belenko, Steven R. HV5810.B45 1993, **(v6)**
Belenky, Mary Field. HQ1206.B345 1997, **(v6)**
Belford, Barbara. PR5823.B346 2000, **(v3)**
Belgrad, Daniel. NX165.B35 1998, **(v9)**
Belich, James. DU420.B45 1996, **(v5)**
Beljame, A. PR441.B37 1971, **(v3)**
Belkaoui, Ahmed. HF5635.B4167, **(v6)**
  HF5686.I56.B445 1991, **(v6)**
Belkin, Samuel. BM627.B44 1979, **(v8)**
Bell, A. Craig. ML410.B8.B38 1995, **(v9)**
Bell, Adrian D. QK641.B45 1990, **(v1)**

Bell, Alan P. HQ76.B438 1981, (v6)
  HQ76.2.U5.B45, (v6)
Bell, Albert A. Z7125.B39 1991, (v10)
Bell, Andrew. JV6091.B45 1996, (v7)
Bell, Aubrey F. G. PQ6037.B35 1968, (v3)
  PQ6398.G4.B4, (v3)
  PQ9011.B4, (v3)
  PQ9212.B4, (v3)
  PQ9252.B4, (v3)
  Z2721.B43, (v10)
Bell, Augusta Grove. F443.A5.B45 1998, (v4)
Bell, Barbara L. Z1002.B4714 1998, (v10)
Bell, Caryn Cossé. F379.N59 N43 1997, (v4)
Bell, Catherine M. BL600.B46 1992, (v8)
Bell, Daniel. E169.12.B37, (v4)
  HM24.B386, (v6)
Bell, David F. PQ653.B37 1993, (v3)
  PQ2518.B45 1988, (v3)
Bell, David Scott. JN2594.2.B418 2000, (v7)
Bell, Derrick A. KF292.H325.B35 1994, (v7)
Bell, Eric Temple. QA21.B4 1945, (v1)
  QA21.B42, (v1)
  QA28.B4, (v1)
Bell, F. G. TA705.B328 1993, (v1)
Bell, G. K. A. BX6.W78.B4 1979, (v8)
Bell, George H. Z7991.B43 1994, (v10)
Bell, Gertrude Lowthian. G463.B423 1953, (v6)
Bell, Graham. VM351.B43, (v10)
Bell, Ian F. A. PS2116.W333 1993, (v3)
Bell, Ian. PR5493.B4 1993, (v3)
Bell, Ilona. PR535.L7.B45 1998, (v3)
Bell, J. Bowyer. DA959.B43 1980, (v5)
  DA963.B45 2000, (v5)
  JC328.6.B45 1998, (v7)
  U240.B44 1999, (v10)
Bell, Janice. HC340.3.B45 2001, (v6)
  ND1140.B45 1999, (v9)
Bell, Linda A. BJ1395.B45 1993, (v8)
Bell, Maureen. PR113.B46 1990, (v3)
Bell, Michael Davitt. PS374.R37.B39 1993, (v3)
Bell, Michael. PN56.S475, (v3)
  PR29.L4.B45 1988, (v3)
  PR6023.A93.Z5666 1991, (v3)
  SB413.B2.B46 2000, (v1)
Bell, P. M. H. D750.B43 1990, (v5)
  DA589.8.B45 1997, (v5)
Bell, Peter D. HN420.5.K56.B44 1984, (v6)
Bell, Peter Robert. QK45.2.B46 2000, (v1)
Bell, Peter. DA565.C4.B45 1996, (v5)
Bell, Quentin. DA685.B65.B45 1995, (v5)
Bell, Richard H. B2430.W474.B434 1998, (v8)
Bell, Richard. DS36.85.I8 no. 8, (v5)
Bell, Robert E. BL715.B445 1991, (v8)
Bell, Robert H. PR6019.O9.U6254 1991, (v3)
Bell, Robert. Q175.37.B45 1992, (v1)
Bell, Terrel Howard. E840.8.B45.A3 1988, (v4)
Bell, Wendell. CB158.B45 1996, (v5)
Bellak, Leopold. BF433.A6.B4, (v2)
  BF698.8.T5.B4 1971, (v2)
  RC514.B43, (v2)
Bellamann, Henry. PS3503.E442.K5, (v3)
Bellamy, David J. RS164.B412 1992, (v2)
Bellamy, Edward. PS1086.L6 1982, (v3)
Bellamy, Liz. PR858.C633.B45 1998, (v3)
Bellamy, Richard. HM276.B39 1992, (v6)
  JC574.B45 1999, (v7)
Bellamy, Robert V. PN1992.55.B38 1996, (v3)
Bellantoni, Lisa. B1647.M124.B45 2000, (v8)
Bellas, Ralph A. PR5238.B44 1977, (v3)
Belle, John. NA6313.N4.B45 2000, (v9)
Bellegarde-Smith, Patrick. F1924.B42 1990, (v4)
Bellesiles, Michael A. E207.A4.B44 1993, (v4)
  HV8059.B395 2000, (v4)
Bell-Gam, Ruby. DT515.22.B45 1999, (v5)
Bellico, Russell P. F127.C6.B45 1999, (v4)
Belliotti, Raymond A. JC571.B455 1995, (v7)
Bellitto, Christopher M. BX825.B45 2002, (v8)
Bellman, Geoffrey M. HD57.7.B454 1992, (v6)
Bellman, Jonathan. ML240.B37 1993, (v9)
Bellman, Richard Ernest. QA263.B36, (v1)
Bello, Andres. PC4105.B5 1941, (v3)

Bello, Walden F. HC59.7.B3873 1999, (v6)
  HC445.B45 1998, (v6)
Belloc, Hilaire. D921.B515 1927, (v5)
  DC123.9.R5.B4 1930, (v5)
  PR3581.B4 1970, (v3)
  PR6003.E45.A17 1954, (v3)
  PR6003.E45.S55 1940, (v3)
Bellour, Raymond. PN1998.3.H58.B4513 2000, (v3)
Bellow, Saul. DS107.4.B37 1976, (v5)
  PS3503.E4488.A66 1953, (v3)
  PS3503.E4488.D3 1944, (v3)
  PS3503.E4488.H38 1959, (v3)
  PS3503.E4488.H45 1964, (v3)
  PS3503.E4488.H56, (v3)
  PS3503.E4488.H8, (v3)
  PS3503.E4488.M4, (v3)
  PS3503.E4488.M6, (v3)
  PS3503.E4488.S4 1956b, (v3)
  PS3503.E4488.V5 1947, (v3)
Bellver, C. G. PQ6055.B45 2001, (v3)
Bell-Villada, Gene H. BH301.A7.B45 1996, (v8)
  PQ8180.17.A73.Z594 1990, (v3)
Bellwood, Peter S. GN871.B44 1979, (v6)
Belnap, Nuel D. BC199.Q4.B44, (v8)
Beloff, Max Beloff. D1065.G7.B45 1996, (v5)
  DA566.7.B442, (v5)
  DA566.7.B446 1984, (v5)
Beloff, Max. D273.B4, (v5)
  D415.B4, (v5)
  DS518.7.B42, (v5)
Belohlavek, John M. E384.8.B44 1985, (v4)
Belot, Raymond de. D770.B453 1951, (v5)
Belsey, Catherine. PR3069.F35.B45 2000, (v3)
Belshaw, Cyril S. HC687.F5.B4, (v6)
Belsky, Janet. BF724.55.A35.B44 1990, (v2)
Belt, Elmer. QM16.L4.B4, (v1)
Beltman, Brian W. F598.E75.B45 1996, (v4)
Beltzer, A. I. QC176.8.A3.B45 1988, (v1)
Bely, Andrey. PG3453.B84 P53 1978, (v3)
Belyea, Charles. BL1920.B46 1991, (v8)
Belz, Herman. E457.2.B38 1997, (v4)
  KF3464.B45 1991, (v7)
  KF4541.B44 1998, (v7)
Bem, Sandra L. HQ1075.B45 1993, (v6)
Bemelmans, Ludwig. PS3503.E475.A6 1955, (v3)
  PS3503.E475.D5, (v3)
  PS3503.E475.I2, (v3)
  PS3503.E475.O5, (v3)
  PS3503.E475.S8 1963, (v3)
  PZ8.3.B425Mab 1998, (v3)
Bemis, Samuel Flagg. E377.B45 1981, (v4)
Ben Rafael, Eliezer. DS113.2.B464 1991, (v5)
Benade, Arthur H. ML3805.B328 1990, (v9)
Ben-Ami, Daniel. HG3851.B427 2001, (v6)
Ben-Ami, Issachar. BM440.M8.B44 1998, (v8)
Ben-Ami, Shlomo. DP247.B39, (v5)
Ben-Amos, Ilana Krausman. HQ799.G72.E53 1994, (v6)
Benarab, Abdelkader. PQ3988.5.N6B46 1994, (v3)
Benarde, Melvin A. QC981.8.G56.B44 1992, (v1)
Benardete, Jose A. BD111.B39 1989, (v8)
Ben-Bassat, Hedda. PS374.R47.B46 2000, (v3)
Benchley, Robert. PS3503.E49.B4, (v3)
  PS3503.E49.B46, (v3)
  PS3503.E49.C5, (v3)
  PS3503.E49.I5, (v3)
Ben-Chorin, Schalom. BM620.B213 2001, (v8)
Bencivenga, Ermanno. B765.A84.B46 1993, (v8)
  B2779.B44 1987, (v8)
Bendall, A. Sarah. LF185.B46 1999, (v7)
Bendazzi, Giannalberto. NC1765.B4213 1994, (v9)
Bender, Averam Burton. F786.B45, (v4)
Bender, Barbara. GN799.A4.B46 1975b, (v6)
Bender, Claire E. PS2116.T83.B4 1988, (v3)
Bender, David A. QP771.B44 1992, (v1)
Bender, Jim. S605.5.B46 1994, (v1)
Bender, Wolfgang. ML3502.5.B4613 1991, (v9)
Bendersky, Joseph W. DD240.B35 2000, (v5)
Bendiner, Jessica. R134.B455 1990, (v2)
Bendiner, Kenneth. ND497.B73.B46 1998, (v9)
Bendix, Deanna Marohn. N6537.W4.B46 1995, (v9)

Bendix, Reinhard. HM51.B394 1970, (v6)
Bendixson, Terence. HE5611.B43 1975, (v6)
Benecke, Gerhard. DD174.B46 1982, (v5)
Benedetti, Jean. PN2062.B47 1998, (v3)
Benedetto, John. QA403.B377 1997, (v1)
Benedetto, Robert. BX9415.B46 1999, (v8)
Benedetto, Robert. Z8309.4.B46 1993, (v10)
Benedick, Richard Elliot. K3593.B46 1991, (v7)
Benedict, Carol. RC179.C6.B46 1996, (v2)
Benedict, Helen. PN4888.S49.B46 1992, (v3)
Benedict, Jeff. HV6250.4.W65.B46 1997, (v6)
Benedict, Michael Les. E666.B46 1973, (v4)
Benedict, Murray R. HD1761.B37 1966, (v6)
Benedict, Philip. BX9415.B47 2002, (v8)
  DC801.R86 B46, (v5)
Benedict, Robert P. TJ935.B46, (v1)
Benedict, Ruth. DS821.B46, (v5)
  GN6.B4, (v6)
  GN315.B4 1945, (v6)
  GN400.B4 1961, (v6)
Benedictus, David. PR6052.E45.F6 1962, (v3)
Ben-Eliezer, Uri. U21.5.B4813 1998, (v10)
Ben-Ephraim, Gavriel. PR6023.A93.Z5668 1981, (v3)
Benes, Edvard. DB217.B3.A4 1971, (v5)
Benesch, Otto. ND565.B413, (v9)
Benesch, Walter. B799.B46 1997, (v8)
Benestad, Finn. ML410.G9.B413 1988, (v9)
Benet, Stephen Vincent. E178.B43, (v4)
  PS3503.E5325.A6 1942, (v3)
  PS3503.E5325.J3 1934, (v3)
  PS3503.E5325.W4, (v3)
  PS3503.E5325.Z54 1960, (v3)
Benet, Sula. QP85.B45, (v1)
Benet, William R. PN41.B4 1965, (v3)
Benet, William Rose. PS3503.E533.G6 1935, (v3)
  PS3503.E533.S6, (v3)
Benevolo, Leonardo. NA642.B413 1971b, (v9)
Benfey, Christopher E. G. PS1449.C85.Z554 1992, (v3)
Benford, Harry. VM165.B4, (v10)
Bengelsdorf, Carollee. HX158.5.B45 1994, (v6)
Bengio, Ofra. DS79.7.B4613 1998, (v5)
Bengtson, Hermann. Z6202.B413, (v10)
Bengtsson, Frans Gunnar. PT9875.B43.R613 1954, (v3)
Ben-Gurion, David. DS125.3.B37.A5 1967, (v5)
Benhabib, Seyla. BJ1012.B45 1992, (v8)
Beniamino, Michel. PQ3809.B46 1999, (v3)
Beniston, Martin. GB501.2.B46 2000, (v6)
  QC861.2.B465 1998, (v1)
Benitez Rojo, Antonio. PN849.C3.B46 1992, (v3)
  PQ7390.B42.M313 1990, (v3)
Benjamin, Gail. LA1314.7.B46 1997, (v7)
Benjamin, Jules R. E183.8.C9.B43 1990, (v4)
Benjamin, Lois. E185.86.B3793 2000, (v4)
Benjamin, Louise Margaret. KF2814.B458 2001, (v7)
Benjamin, Martin. BJ1431.B46 1990, (v8)
Benjamin, Thomas. F1234.B465 2000, (v4)
  HC137.C47 B46 1996, (v6)
  MT55.B446 1986, (v9)
  MT55.B447, (v9)
Benjamin, Walter. PT2603.E455.P33513 1999, (v3)
  PT2603.E455.Z54813 1989, (v3)
Ben-Meir, Yehuda. JQ1825.P38.C583 1995, (v7)
Benn, Alec. HG4572.B46 2000, (v6)
Benn, Charles D. DS721.B44 2002, (v5)
Benn, Gottfried. PT2603.E46.A6 1960, (v3)
Benn, Maurice B. PT1828.B6.B37, (v3)
Benn, S. I. JC585.B378 1988, (v7)
Bennett, Alan. PR6052.E5.B4, (v3)
Bennett, Andrew. PR590.B34 1999, (v3)
  PR6003.O6757.Z515 1994, (v3)
  UA770.B435 1999, (v10)
Bennett, Andy. ML3470.B45 1999, (v9)
Bennett, Anthony J. JK611.B45 1996, (v7)

Bennett, Arnold. PR6003.E6.A65, (v3)
  PR6003.E6.B6, (v3)
  PR6003.E6.B8, (v3)
  PR6003.E6.C52, (v3)
  PR6003.E6.C56, (v3)
  PR6003.E6.E4, (v3)
  PR6003.E6.G68 1960, (v3)
  PR6003.E6.G72 1907, (v3)
  PR6003.E6.H6 1975, (v3)
  PR6003.E6.I5, (v3)
  PR6003.E6.M3, (v3)
  PR6003.E6.M3 1911, (v3)
  PR6003.E6.M5 1912, (v3)
  PR6003.E6.O4, (v3)
  PR6003.E6 P74, (v3)
  PR6003.E6 R5, (v3)
  PR6003.E6.T3 1910, (v3)
  PR6003.E6.T38, (v3)
Bennett, Barbara. PS261.B46 1998, (v3)
Bennett, Benjamin. PN1851.B38 1990, (v3)
  PT289.B38 1993, (v3)
  PT636.B4, (v3)
Bennett, Betty T. PR4897.L2.Z6 1991, (v3)
  PR5398.B46 1998, (v3)
Bennett, Bridget. PS1708.B46 1997, (v3)
Bennett, Charles E. E207.H85.B44 1991, (v4)
  F314.B39, (v4)
Bennett, Christopher. DR1246.B46 1995, (v5)
Bennett, David Harry. E183.B43 1988, (v4)
  JK2391.U5.B4, (v7)
Bennett, Deborah J. QA273.15.B46 1998, (v1)
Bennett, Edward M. D753.B45 1990, (v5)
Bennett, F. Lawrence. TA190.B36 1996, (v1)
Bennett, Fordyce R. PS1541.Z5.B435 1997, (v3)
Bennett, Frank M. VA55.B48 1972, (v4)
Bennett, George W. SH159.B38 1983, (v1)
Bennett, Gillian. Z5981.B46 1993, (v10)
Bennett, Gordon A. DS778.D34.B45, (v5)
Bennett, H. S. DA240.B4 1968, (v5)
  PR255.B43, (v3)
  Z151.B4, (v10)
  Z151.3.B4, (v10)
Bennett, Hal. PS3552.E546.I6, (v3)
Bennett, J. A. W. PR255.B45 1986, (v3)
  PR1878.B37, (v3)
  PR1886.B4, (v3)
Bennett, James R. JZ5514.B46 2001, (v7)
  Z658.U5.B46 1987, (v10)
  Z7164.L6.B46 1995, (v10)
Bennett, Jane. B931.T44 B46 1994, (v8)
Bennett, Jeffrey O. QB43.2.B45 2001, (v1)
Bennett, Jeffrey. RC86.7.B464 2002, (v2)
Bennett, Joan (Frankau). PR3327.B4, (v3)
  PR4681.B4, (v3)
Bennett, Joan. PR543.B4 1964, (v3)
Bennett, John B. LB1778.2.B46 1998, (v7)
Bennett, John Coleman. BJ1251.B43, (v8)
Bennett, John Cook. BX8645.B45 2000, (v8)
Bennett, John M. Z1870.3.B46 1998, (v10)
Bennett, John William. F597.B456 1995, (v4)
Bennett, Judith M. HD6073.L62.G723 1996, (v6)
Bennett, Julian. DG294.B46 1997, (v5)
Bennett, Lerone. E185.B43, (v4)
Bennett, Martyn. DA405.B343 2000, (v5)
  DA405.B344 2000, (v5)
  DA415.B35 1997, (v5)
Bennett, Mary. F622.B46 1990, (v4)
Bennett, Michael J. DA330.8.S55.B46 1987, (v5)
  HN58.B427 1996, (v6)
Bennett, Neville. LB1025.2.B448, (v7)
Bennett, Ralph Francis. D756.5.N6.B44 1980, (v5)
Bennett, Richard Edmond. F598.B46 1987, (v4)
Bennett, Richard. DA962.B43 1960, (v5)
Bennett, Susan. PR3100.B38 1996, (v3)
Bennett, Tony. BH41.B45, (v8)
  PN98.C6.B37 1990, (v3)
Bennett, W. Lance. HN90.P8.B46, (v6)
  PN4888.P6.B46 1996, (v3)
Bennett, William J. LC1021.B46 1984, (v7)
Bennett, William Ralph. RA569.3.B46 1994, (v2)
Bennett, William. RM222.2.B443 1982, (v2)

Bennigsen, Alexandre. DK34.M8.B46 1986, (v5)
Bennington, Geoffrey. B2430.D484.B457 2000, (v8)
  B2430.L964.B46 1988, (v8)
  PN45.B422 1994, (v8)
Bennis, Phyllis. JX1977.2.U5.B46 1995, (v7)
Bennis, Warren G. HD57.7.B4578 2002, (v6)
Bennoune, Mahfoud. HC815.B48 1988, (v6)
Benoit, William L. PN4055.U53.B46 1996, (v3)
Benowitz, June Melby. BL2525.B45 1998, (v8)
Ben-Peretz, Miriam. LB2806.15.B46 1990, (v7)
Ben-Porat, Amir. HN660.Z9.S63 1989, (v6)
Bensch, Stephen P. HC388.B3.B3 1995, (v6)
Bensel, Richard Franklin. HC105.B45 2000, (v6)
Benson, Arthur Christopher. PR4099.B5.F6 1970,
  (v3)
  PR4099.B5.R3 1926, (v3)
Benson, Bruce. HV9950.B49 1998, (v6)
Benson, Bruce. KF382.B46 1990, (v7)
Benson, C. David. PR1896.B46 1990, (v3)
Benson, E. F. DA554.B4, (v5)
Benson, Elizabeth P. E59.A7.B46 1997, (v4)
Benson, Hazel B. Z6671.52.T47.B46 1988, (v10)
Benson, Jackson J. PS3537.T316.Z59 1998, (v3)
Benson, Larry Dean. PR2045.B45, (v3)
Benson, Linda. DS731.K38.B46 1998, (v5)
  DS793.S62.B37 1990, (v5)
Benson, Lyman David. QK95.B44, (v1)
  QK97.B45 1979, (v1)
  QK495.C11.B354 1982, (v1)
Benson, Mary Sumner. H31.C7 no.405, (v6)
Benson, Michael L. KF9351.B46 1998, (v7)
Benson, Michael T. E814.B46 1997, (v4)
Benson, Michael. GV879.5.B46 1989, (v6)
Benson, Morton. PE1689.B46 1997, (v3)
  PG1376.B38 1990, (v3)
  PG1376.B4 1990, (v3)
Benstock, Bernard. PR6019.O9.U6255 1991, (v3)
Benstock, Shari. PR6019.O9.Z5259, (v3)
Benston, George J. HD2741.B39, (v6)
  HG2461.B46 1990, (v6)
Bent, Arthur Cleveland. QL681.B513, (v1)
  QL696.P56.B46 1992, (v1)
Benthall, Jonathan. HV553.B47 1993, (v6)
Bentham, Jeremy. JC223.B486 1973, (v7)
  K334.B444 2001, (v7)
Bentley, Amy. D810.W7.B45 1998, (v5)
Bentley, D. M. R. PR9190.4.B46 1994, (v3)
Bentley, E. C. PR6003.E7247.T734 1977, (v3)
Bentley, Eric. PN1851.B4 1955, (v3)
Bentley, G. E. PR4146.B377 2001, (v3)
Bentley, George R. E185.2.B4 1970, (v4)
Bentley, Gerald Eades. PN151.B54, (v3)
  PR1245.B43, (v3)
  PR2894.B4, (v3)
  PR2959.B4, (v3)
Bentley, Jerry H. DG847.17.B46 1987, (v5)
  GN345.6.B46 1993, (v6)
Bentley, K. W. QD421.B45, (v1)
Bentley, Michael. D13.B427 1999, (v5)
Bentley, Nancy. PS374.M33.B46 1995, (v3)
Bentley, Nicolas. PR4580.B46 1988, (v3)
Benton, Allen H. QH307.B32, (v1)
  QH318.5.B4 1966, (v1)
Benton, Lauren A. HD2346.S7.B46 1990, (v6)
Benton, Lisa M. F869.S38.P742 1998, (v4)
Benton, Ted. H61.15.B46 2001, (v6)
Benton, Thomas Hart. E338.B472, (v4)
  ND237.B47.A28, (v9)
  ND237.B47.A3 1968, (v9)
  ND237.B47.B3 1975, (v9)
Bentsur, Eytan. DS119.76.B49 2001, (v5)
Benvenisti, Meron. DS109.94.B4513, (v5)
  DS126.954.B46 2000, (v5)
Benvenuti, Francesco. UA772.B38613 1988, (v10)
Ben-Yehuda, Nachman. BJ1500.B47 B46 2001, (v8)
Benyei, Candace Reed. BV4392.5.B45 1998, (v8)
Benyo, Richard. GV1061.B445 2002, (v6)
Benz, Ernst. BX8748.B3913 2002, (v8)
Benz, Stephen Connely. F1464.3.B45 1996, (v4)
Benz, Wolfgang. D804.3.B45413 1999, (v5)
Ben-Zeev, Aharon. BF531.B43 2000, (v2)

Benziger, James G. PR508.R4.B4, (v3)
Ben-Zvi, Abraham. E183.8.I7.B45 1998, (v4)
Beon, Yves. D805.G3.B45613 1997, (v5)
Beranek, Leo Leroy. QC227.B4, (v1)
  TK5981.B36 1986, (v1)
Berberian, Houri. DS269.A75, (v5)
Berberian, Sterling K. QA300.B457 1994, (v1)
Bercaw, Mary K. Z8562.58.B47 1987, (v10)
Berce, Yves Marie. DC121.3.B49213 1990, (v5)
  DC121.3.B49613 1996, (v5)
Berceo, Gonzalo de. PQ6397.M513 1997, (v3)
Berch, Bettina. TR140.J64, (v1)
Berckelaers, Ferdinand Louis. ND35.B413, (v9)
  ND653.M76.B4, (v9)
Bercovici, Konrad. PS3503.E63.D8, (v3)
  PS3503.E63.S5, (v3)
  PS3503.E63.V6, (v3)
Bercovitch, Jacob. D842.B46 1997, (v5)
Bercovitch, Sacvan. PS1868.B395 1991, (v3)
Bercuson, David Jay. F1034.3.C56.B47 1993, (v4)
Berdahl, Daphne. DD289.5.B47 1999, (v5)
Berdahl, Robert M. DD419.B47 1988, (v5)
Berdan, John Milton. PR521.B4 1961, (v3)
Berdanier, Carolyn D. QP141.B52 1995, (v1)
Berdiaev, Nikolai. B4238.B43.S314 1950a, (v8)
  B4238.B43.T83 1953, (v8)
  BD118.R8.B42 1952, (v8)
  DK189.2.B4613 1979, (v5)
Berebitsky, Julie. HV875.B467 2000, (v6)
Berenbaum, M. QL467.B47 1989, (v1)
  QL467.B474 1993, (v1)
Berend, T. Ivan. DJK38.B458 1997, (v5)
  HC267.A2.B3823 1974, (v6)
  HC300.24.B44 1985, (v6)
Bérenger, Jean. DB36.3.H3 B4713 1994, (v5)
Berenson, Bernard. N7445.B546 1968, (v9)
  N8375.B46.A15, (v9)
  N8375.B46.A29, (v9)
  N8375.B46.A3, (v9)
  NA9370.R6.B43b, (v9)
  ND140.B4 1971, (v9)
Berenson, Edward. DC373.C25.B47 1992, (v5)
Berenstein, Rhona J. PN1995.9.H6.B48 1996, (v3)
Beresford, M. W. DA176.B44 1972, (v5)
Berezin, Mabel. DG571.B444 1997, (v5)
Berg, A. Scott. PN149.9.P4.B4, (v3)
Berg, Alan. TX360.5.B47 1987, (v1)
Berg, Barbara J. HQ1418.B5, (v6)
Berg, Donna Lee. PE1617.O94.B47 1993, (v3)
Berg, Francie M. RC552.O25.B47 2000, (v2)
  RJ506.E18.B47 1997, (v2)
  RJ506.E18B47 2001, (v2)
  RM222.2.B4522 1993, (v2)
Berg, Maggie. PR4167.J5.B4 1987, (v3)
Berg, Marc. R723.5.B47 1997, (v2)
Berg, Maxine. DA3.P69.B47 1996, (v5)
Berg, Maxine. HB85.B35 1980, (v6)
Berg, Richard E. QC225.15.B47, (v1)
Berg, Steven L. Z7721.B45 1993, (v10)
Bergadano, Francesco. QA76.63.B47 1996, (v1)
Bergan, Ronald. PN1998.3.E34.B47 1999, (v3)
Bergan, Ronald. PN1998.3.R46.B45 1994, (v3)
Bergaust, Erik. UG633.B418, (v10)
Bergdoll, Barry. NA956.B47 2000, (v9)
Bergeijk, Peter A. G. van. HF1413.5.B47 1994, (v6)
Bergelson, David. PJ5129.B45.A23 1996, (v3)
Bergelson, David. PJ5129.B45.O613 1999, (v3)
Bergen, Arthur R. TK1001.B44 2000, (v1)
Bergen, Bernard J. D804.3.B463 1998, (v5)
Bergen, Doris L. BR856.B398 1996, (v8)
Bergen, Doris. RJ51.D48.B47 1994, (v2)
Bergen, Raquel Kennedy. HV6561.B48 1996, (v6)
Berger, Alan L. PS153.J4.B468 1997, (v3)
Berger, Arthur Asa. P90.B413 1995, (v3)
  P91.B445 1992, (v3)
Berger, Arthur S. BF1025.B47 1991, (v2)
  BF1026.B46 1988, (v2)
  KF3823.B47 1993, (v7)
  R726.8.B467 1995, (v2)
Berger, Bennett M. HM101.B4717 1995, (v6)
Berger, Brigitte. HQ734.B56 1983, (v6)

Berger, Bruce. F787.B47 1991, (v4)
Berger, Carl. F1024.B47, (v4)
F1033.B49 1970, (v4)
Berger, David M. RC489.E46.B47 1987, (v2)
Berger, Guy. HN981.C6.B47 1992, (v6)
Berger, Harry. ND1309.B47 1999, (v9)
PQ4080.B47 2000, (v3)
PR2364.B4, (v3)
Berger, John J. SD143.B47 1998, (v1)
Berger, John. N71.B398 1980, (v9)
Berger, Josef. E173.B38, (v4)
Berger, Karl. PT2482.B45, (v4)
Berger, Karol. BH39.B393 2000, (v8)
Berger, Lisa. RC445.M4.B448 1994, (v2)
Berger, Mark T. F1418.B418 1995, (v4)
Berger, Maurice. NX512.M67.B47 1989, (v9)
Berger, Michael L. HE5623.B45, (v6)
Berger, Michael S. BM503.B47 1998, (v8)
Berger, Morroe. DS3.A2.P76 1, (v5)
Berger, Peter L. BD175.B4, (v8)
Berger, Raoul. KF4757.B42 1989, (v7)
Berger, Ronald J. HQ471.B47 1991, (v6)
Berger, Stefan. DD204.B475 1997, (v5)
Berger, Suzanne. HD1486.F8.B47, (v6)
Berger, Thomas L. PR1265.3.B4 1998, (v3)
Berger, Thomas U. UA710.B494 1998, (v10)
Berger, Thomas. PS3552.E719.L5 1964, (v3)
PS3552.E719.S6, (v3)
PS3552.E719.V5, (v3)
Bergere, Marie-Claire. DS777.B47 1998, (v5)
Bergeron, Arthur W. F334.M6.B47 1991, (v4)
Bergeron, David Moore. DA391.B46 1999, (v5)
DA391.B47 1991, (v5)
Z8811.B44 1995, (v10)
Bergeron, Louis. DC201.B4713, (v5)
NA6402.B4713 2000, (v9)
Bergeron, Paul H. E416.B47 1987, (v4)
Bergesen, Albert. PN1995.5.B44 2000, (v3)
Bergethon, P. R. QH505.B397 1990, (v1)
Berghahn, Volker Rolf. DD228.8.B38 1973b, (v5)
HC285.B395 1994, (v6)
UA10.B47 1982, (v10)
Bergin, Joseph. BX4705.L16.B47 1987, (v8)
DC123.9.R5.B44 1991, (v5)
Bergin, Thomas Goddard. CB361.B43 1987, (v5)
Berglas, Steven. RC455.4.S43.B47 1993, (v2)
Berglund, Eeva K. GE199.G3.B47 1998, (v6)
Bergman, Andrew. PN1993.5.U6.B38 1971, (v3)
Bergman, Jerry. Z7845.J45.B46 1993, (v10)
Bergman, Samuel Hugo. B803.B3813 1991, (v8)
Bergmann, Gustav. B824.6.B398, (v8)
B945.B473.N48 1991, (v8)
Bergmann, Hans. PS255.N5.B47 1995, (v3)
Bergmann, Martin S. BD436.B47 1987, (v8)
Bergmann, Merrie. BC135.B435, (v8)
Bergmann, Peter Gabriel. QC6.B453, (v1)
QC6.B454, (v1)
QC173.55.B49 1987, (v1)
Bergmann, Werner. DS146.G4.B4713 1997, (v5)
Bergmeier, H. J. P. D810.P7.G318 1997, (v5)
Bergonzi, Bernard. PR478.W67.B46 1993, (v3)
Bergquist, Charles W. F2276.5.B47, (v4)
Bergquist, Patricia R. QL371.B47 1978, (v1)
Bergquist, William H. LB2341.B476 1992, (v7)
Bergson, Abram. HC336.2.B43, (v6)
Bergson, Henri. B2430.B4.M313 1988, (v8)
B2430.B4.P362, (v8)
BD112.B42 1955, (v8)
Bergsten, C. Fred. HF1456.5.J3.R43 1993, (v6)
Bergstrom, Randolph E. KFN5311.B47 1992, (v7)
Bergua, Jose. PQ6175.B4 1958, (v3)
Berin, John J. TL570.B42 2002, (v1)
Berinstein, Paula. T21.B47 1999, (v1)
Berk, Gerald. HE2757.B47 1994, (v6)
Berkeley, Edmund. QK31.B3.B47, (v1)
QK31.C55.B4, (v1)
Berkeley, George. B1326.D36 1998, (v8)
B1331.D38 1998, (v8)
B1331.T8 1963, (v8)
Berkeley, Kathleen C. HQ1421.B47 1999, (v6)
Berkes, Niyazi. DR557.B4, (v5)

Berkhofer, Robert F. D16.B464 1995, (v5)
Berkley, George E. DS135.A92.V5214 1988, (v5)
Berkman, Robert I. ZA3075.B47 2000, (v10)
Berkman, Sylvia. PR6025.A57.Z567, (v3)
PR9639.3.M258.Z585 1971, (v3)
Berkovic, Sally. BM726.B49 1999, (v8)
Berkow, Ira. GV742.42.B47.A3 1997, (v6)
Berkowitz, Alan J. DS721.B45 2000, (v5)
Berkowitz, Bruce D. UB251.U5.B47 1989, (v10)
Berkowitz, Edward D. HD7125.B38 1991, (v6)
Berkowitz, Freda Pastor. ML113.B39 1975, (v9)
Berkowitz, N. TP343.B38 1997, (v1)
Berkowitz, N. (Norbert). TP325.B46 1994, (v1)
Berkson, Gershon. RJ506.D47.B47 1993, (v2)
Berkson, Isaac Baer. LB875.B335 1970, (v7)
Berlage, Gai. GV880.7.B47 1994, (v6)
Berlage, Hendrik Petrus. NA2750.B46 1996, (v9)
Berlak, Ann. LA637.B47 1981, (v7)
Berland, Alwyn. PS3511.A86.L5714 1992, (v3)
Berleant, Arnold. BH39.B3945 1991, (v8)
Berlekamp, Elwyn R. QA269.B39 2000, (v1)
Berley, Marc. PR508.M75, (v3)
Berlin, Edward A. ML3530.B47, (v9)
Berlin, Howard M. HG4636.B49 1990, (v6)
Berlin, Ira. E185.18.B47 1975, (v4)
Berlin, Isaiah. B29.B4465 1991, (v8)
B802.B45 1970, (v8)
D16.9.B4, (v5)
Berlin, Normand. PS3529.N5.Z567 1993, (v3)
Berliner, Joseph S. HB90.B47 1999, (v6)
Berliner, Louise. PN2287.G75.B47 1993, (v3)
Berliner, Paul. ML3506.B475 1994, (v9)
Berlinski, David. QA9.58.B47 2000, (v1)
QA303.B488 1995, (v1)
Berlioz, Hector. ML410.B5 A3 2002, (v9)
ML410.B5.A33 1997, (v9)
ML410.B5 A533 1999, (v9)
MT70.B4813 1991, (v9)
Berlitz Schools of Languages of America.
PJ4567.5.B4, (v3)
Berlow, Lawrence H. GV706.3.B47 1994, (v6)
TA15.B42 1998, (v1)
Berman Santana, Deborah. HC154.5.Z7.S343 1996,
(v6)
Berman, Aaron. E184.J5.B492 1990, (v4)
Berman, Alex. RV5.B47 2000, (v2)
Berman, Art. BH301.M54.B47 1994, (v8)
Berman, Avis. N618.B47 1990, (v9)
Berman, Boris. MT220.B515 2000, (v9)
Berman, David R. JK8216.B47 1998, (v7)
Berman, Eric. DT352.8.B47 2000, (v5)
Berman, Jeffrey. PE1404.B464 1994, (v3)
PS169.S85.B47 1999, (v3)
Berman, Joel A. RD31.3.B47 2001, (v2)
Berman, Larry. JK421.B37, (v7)
Berman, Marshall. CB425.B458 1988, (v5)
Berman, Robert P. UA770.B45 1982, (v10)
Berman, Ronald. PR3539.K65.Z58, (v3)
PS3511.I9.G823 1997, (v3)
PS3511.I9.G824 1994, (v3)
PS3511.I9.Z55774 2001, (v3)
Berman, William C. E840.8.F8.B47 1988, (v4)
Bermann, Marc. F3319.1.L8.B47 1994, (v4)
Bermant, Charles. T58.5.B47 1995, (v1)
Bermel, Albert. PN1942.B4 1982, (v3)
Bermingham, Ann. NC228.B47 2000, (v9)
Bermingham, Peter. ND1351.5.B47, (v9)
Bermudez, Jose Luis. BD450.B436 1998, (v8)
Bernac, Pierre. MT892.B4, (v9)
Bernadac, Marie-Laure. NB237.B65.B47 1995, (v9)
Bernal, Ignacio. F1219.B5162, (v4)
F1219.B51713, (v4)
F1219.1.M53.B43, (v4)
Bernal, Martin. DF78.B398 1987, (v5)
Bernanos, Georges. PQ2603.E5875E8 1971, (v3)
PQ2603.E5875.I5 1927, (v3)
PQ2603.E5875.J6 1929, (v3)
PQ2603.E5875.J7 1974, (v3)
PQ2603.E5875.S6 1926, (v3)
Bernard, H. Russell. F1221.O86.B47 1989, (v4)
GN345.B37 1988, (v6)

Bernard, Jessie Shirley. HQ518.B47 1972, (v6)
HQ1206.B374, (v6)
Bernard, John D. PR2367.P34.B4 1989, (v3)
Bernard, of Clairvaux, Saint. BX4700.B5.A413, (v8)
DB74.B43, (v5)
Bernard, Paul P. DB74.7.P47.B47 1991, (v5)
Bernard, Theos. B131.B45, (v8)
Bernardi, Adria. F549.H65.B47 1990, (v4)
Bernardi, Daniel. PN1995.9.S694.B37 1998, (v3)
Bernardin, Joseph Louis. BJ1249.B42 1998, (v8)
Bernardo, Barbara. KF320.L4 B473 1990, (v7)
Bernardo, C. Joseph. UA23.B43 1961, (v10)
Bernardoni, James. PN1993.5.U6.B39 1991, (v3)
Bernauer, James William. B2430.F724.B47 1990, (v8)
Bernays, Edward L. HM263.B394 1965, (v6)
Bernbaum, Edwin. BL447.B47 1990, (v8)
PR447.B55 1949, (v3)
PR701.B4, (v3)
Bernbaum, Ernest. PR1105.B4 1948, (v3)
Bernd, Clifford A. PT2528.Z6.B4 1966, (v3)
Berne, Eric. RC488.B43, (v2)
Berne, Samuel A. RJ506.H9B47 2002, (v2)
Berner, Brad K. E715.B47 1998, (v4)
Berner, Elizabeth Kay. QC880.4.A8.B47 1996, (v1)
Berner, Robert A. QE571.B47, (v1)
Berner, Robert L. PS153.I52.B47 1999, (v3)
Berners-Lee, Tim. TK5105.888.B46 1999, (v1)
Berney, Saffold. F326.B52 1975, (v4)
Bernhard, Thomas. PT2662.E7.E79, (v3)
PT2662.E7.W5813 1989, (v3)
PT2662.E7.Z46413 1985, (v3)
Bernhardt, Kathryn. DS755.B47 1992, (v5)
Bernhardt, Sarah. PN2638.B5.A3 1999, (v3)
Bernheimer, Charles. BH221.E853 B47 2002, (v8)
Bernier, Gerald. F1053.B49 1992, (v4)
Bernier, Olivier. DC129.B375 1987, (v5)
Bernier, Ronald M. NA1510.8.H56.B47 1997, (v9)
Bernstein, Alan E. BT836.2.B47 1993, (v8)
Bernstein, Anne E. RC451.4.W6.B469 1993, (v2)
Bernstein, Barton J. E813.B45, (v4)
Bernstein, Carl. E860.B47 1987, (v4)
Bernstein, David J. NK3049.B3.B44 1987, (v9)
Bernstein, Deborah. HD5812.2.A7.H35 2000, (v6)
Bernstein, Harry. F1418.B484, (v4)
Bernstein, Ira H. QA76.B445 1999, (v1)
Bernstein, Irving. E841.B43 1991, (v4)
E847.B45 1996, (v4)
HD8072.B365 1985, (v6)
Bernstein, Iver. F128.44.B47 1990, (v4)
Bernstein, J. M. BH151.B47 1992, (v8)
Bernstein, Jeremy. DS473.B45 2000, (v5)
Q171.B5375 2001, (v1)
QC16.B46.B47, (v1)
Bernstein, John Andrew. B3318.E9.B47 1987, (v8)
Bernstein, Leonard. ML60.B47 1965, (v9)
Bernstein, Mark F. GV958.5.I9 B47 2001, (v6)
Bernstein, Mark H. BJ1012.B47 1998, (v8)
Bernstein, Matthew. PN1998.3.W345.B47 1994, (v3)
Bernstein, Michael A. HB3717 1929.B37 1987, (v6)
Bernstein, Michael Andre. PN56.H55.B47 1994, (v3)
PT401.B47 2000, (v3)
Bernstein, Paul. HD8066.B45 1997, (v6)
Bernstein, Peter L. HD61.B466 1996, (v6)
Bernstein, Richard B. KF4555.B47 1993, (v7)
Bernstein, Richard J. B804.B46 1991b, (v8)
DS143.B55 1996, (v5)
H61.B472, (v8)
Bernstein, Richard. BQ8149.H787, (v8)
Bernstock, Judith E. ND237.M58.B47 1988, (v9)
Berofsky, Bernard. BD450.B438 1995, (v8)
BJ1451.B47 1987, (v8)
BJ1461.B47, (v8)
Berra, Tim M. QH197.B46 1998, (v1)
QH371.B47 1990, (v1)
Berres, Thomas E. E99.O5 B47 2001, (v4)
Berressem, Hanjo. PS3566.Y55.Z57 1993, (v3)
Berrett, Joshua. ML419.J62.B47 1999, (v9)
Berrey, Lester V. PE3729.A5.H4 1953, (v3)
Berrick, Jill Duerr. HV1445.B47 1995, (v6)
Berridge, Geoff. D1065.S6.B47 1992, (v5)
Berridge, Geoff. JX1662.B393 1995, (v7)

Berrigan, Daniel. BX4705.B3845.A294 1971, (v8)
Berrigan, Philip. BX4705.B3846.A3 1970, (v8)
Berrios, G. E. RC437.5.B468 1996, (v2)
Berry, Brian Joe Lobley. GA9.B53, (v6)
  HB3729.B47 1990, (v6)
  HX83.B44 1992, (v6)
Berry, Chad. HB1971.A3.B47 2000, (v6)
Berry, Christopher J. JC423.B423 1989, (v7)
Berry, Chuck. ML420.B365.A3 1987, (v9)
Berry, Edward I. PR2982.B47, (v3)
  PR3069.H85, (v3)
Berry, Ellen E. PS3537.T323.Z557 1992, (v3)
Berry, F. A. QC861.B43, (v1)
Berry, Jeffrey M. JK1118.B4, (v7)
Berry, Laura C. PR878.C5.B47 1999, (v3)
Berry, Marianne. HV699.B49 1997, (v6)
Berry, Mary Elizabeth. DS869.T6.B47 1982, (v5)
  DS897.K857.B47 1994, (v5)
Berry, Mary Frances. E185.5.B47, (v4)
  HQ778.7.U6.B49 1993, (v6)
  KF4757.B44 1999, (v7)
Berry, Michael W. TK5105.884.B47 1999, (v1)
Berry, Nicholas O. HV568.B47 1997, (v6)
Berry, Philippa. PR428.E43.B47 1989, (v3)
  PR2983.B47 1999, (v3)
Berry, Ralph. PR2983.B48 1999, (v3)
  PR3024.B47 1988, (v3)
  PR3091.B475 1993, (v3)
  PR3187.B4, (v3)
Berry, Reginald. PR3633.B47 1988, (v3)
Berry, Richard. QB88.B47 2001, (v1)
Berry, Robert C. GV583.B46 1986, (v6)
Berry, Rynn. BL65.V44.B47 1998, (v8)
Berry, Scott. DS785.B53 1995, (v5)
Berry, Wallace. MT6.B465.M9 1989, (v9)
  MT58.B34 1986, (v9)
Berryman, Jack W. RC1210.B395 1995, (v2)
Berryman, John. PR403.B4 1976, (v3)
  PR2894.B45 1999, (v3)
  PS3503.E744.A17 1989, (v3)
  PS3503.E744.B4, (v3)
  PS3503.E744.D4, (v3)
  PS3503.E744D5, (v3)
  PS3503.E744.D7 1969, (v3)
  PS3503.E744.H4 1977, (v3)
  PS3503.E744.H53, (v3)
  PS3503.E744.S4, (v3)
  PS3503.E744.S5, (v3)
  PS3503.E744.Z483 1988, (v3)
Berryman, Phillip. BR620.B48 1994, (v8)
Berstein, Serge. DC421.B4713 2000, (v5)
Bersuker, I. B. QD172.T6.B48 1996, (v1)
Berta, Annalisa. QL713.2.B47 1999, (v1)
Bertalanffy, Ludwig von. BF149.B4, (v2)
Bertaud, Jean Paul. DC151.B4313 1988, (v5)
Bertens, Johannes Willem. B831.2.B47 1995, (v8)
Berthel, Mary Wheelhouse. PN4874.G54Z7, (v3)
Berthelot, Helen W. F570.25.W55.B47 1995, (v4)
Berthoff, Rowland. E169.1.B4925 1997, (v4)
Berthoff, Warner. PS121.B52 1994, (v3)
Berthold, Margot. PN2104.B413 1991, (v3)
Berthon, Simon. GA201.B47 1991, (v6)
Berthoz, A. QP493.B47 2000, (v1)
Berthrong, John H. B127.C65.B47 1998, (v8)
  B1674.W354.B47 1998, (v8)
Bertin, Celia. PN1998.3.R46.B4713 1991, (v3)
Bertin, G. QB858.42.B47 1996, (v1)
Bertman, Stephen. E169.12.B397 1998, (v4)
Berto, Giuseppe. PQ4807.E815.M32, (v3)
Bertocci, Angelo Philip. PQ2191.Z5.B43, (v3)
Bertocci, Philip A. DC255.S5.B47, (v5)
Bertolini, John A. PR5368.T4.B4 1990, (v3)
Berton, Pierre. E355.B46 1981, (v4)
  F931.B49, (v4)
  G640.B47 1988, (v6)
Bertrand, Michael T. ML3918.R63, (v9)
Bertuca, David J. Z5883.B47 1996, (v10)
Berube, Maurice R. LB2844.53.U6.B47 1988, (v7)
Berube, Michael. PE68.U5.B48 1998, (v3)
Berve, Helmut. NA275.B413, (v9)
Berwanger, Eugene H. E415.7.B45 2002, (v4)

Besant, Walter. PR4104.A65, (v3)
  PR4106.A6 1971, (v3)
Beschloss, Michael R. E183.8.S65.B4685 1993, (v4)
Besner, Hilda F. LC192.6.B47 1995, (v7)
Bess, James L. LB2331.B48 2000, (v7)
Bessel, Richard. HN445.B47 1993, (v6)
Besser, Gretchen R. PQ2431.Z5.B47 1994, (v3)
  PQ2637.A783.Z58, (v3)
Besserman, Lawrence L. PR1933.R4.B48 1998, (v3)
Bessette, Alan. QK617.B483 1997, (v1)
Bessette, Alan. QK629.B6.B47 2000, (v1)
Bessette, Joseph M. JK1001.B47 1994, (v7)
Bessinger, J B. PE279.B4, (v3)
Bessinger, Jess B. PR1506.B47 1978, (v3)
Bessler, John D. HV8699.U5.B47 1997, (v6)
Best, Alan D. PT2647.E26.Z57, (v3)
Best, Anthony. D750.B47 1995, (v5)
Best, Charles Herbert. QP34.B5 1963, (v1)
  QP34.B54 1966, (v1)
  QP34.5.B47 1985, (v1)
Best, Gary Dean. E806.B493 1993, (v4)
  F317.M7.B46 1992, (v4)
  KF224.M35.B47 1994, (v7)
Best, Geoffrey Francis Andrew. D299.B484 1982, (v5)
  JX4508.B47 1994, (v7)
Best, Joel. HM535.B47 2001, (v6)
  HV6789.B47 1999, (v6)
Best, Judith. JK528.B44 1975, (v7)
Best, Myron G. QE461.B53 1982, (v1)
Best, Reba A. K564.C6.A125 1993, (v7)
Best, Steven. HM73.B468 1997, (v6)
  JA74.B474 1995, (v7)
Bestard-Camps, Joan. GN585.S7.B47 1990, (v6)
Besterman, Theodore. PQ2099.B42, (v3)
Bestman, Martin T. PQ3989.S46Z59, (v3)
Bestor, Arthur Eugene. LB875.B345 1985, (v7)
Bestor, Theodore C. HN730.T65.B47 1989, (v6)
Beth, Evert Willem. BC135.B45, (v8)
Beth, Loren P. KF8745.H3.B47 1992, (v7)
Bethe, Hans Albrecht. QC173.B48 1956, (v1)
Bethel, Elizabeth Rauh. F279.P66.B47, (v4)
Bethell, Tom. HB711.B477 1998, (v6)
Bethmann Hollweg, Theobald von. D515.B4665, (v5)
Bethune, Pearl Elley. F391.B57.B47 1990, (v4)
Betjeman, John. PR6003.E77.A6 1972, (v3)
  PR6003.E77Z52, (v3)
Betounes, David. QA377.B53 1998, (v1)
Betsky, Aaron. NA2543.W65.B48 1995, (v9)
Bettelheim, Adriel. HQ1064.U5.B379 2001, (v6)
Bettelheim, Bruno. HQ792.P3.B47, (v6)
  LB1050.B47 1982, (v7)
  RC504.B35 1990, (v2)
  RJ499.B48, (v2)
  RJ506.A9.B4, (v2)
Bettelyoun, Susan Bordeaux. E99.B8.B473 1998, (v4)
Betten, Neil. HN65.B47 1990, (v6)
Betteridge, Harold T. PF3640.B45 1962, (v3)
  PF3640.B45 1968, (v3)
  PF3640.B45 1977, (v3)
Betteridge, W. TN799.N6.B45 1984, (v1)
Bettey, J. H. DA576.B45, (v5)
Bettinger, Robert L. GN407.3.B48 1991, (v6)
Bettinger-Lopez, Caroline. F319.M6.B48 2000, (v4)
Bettmann, Otto. R131.B5, (v2)
Betts, Dianne C. HC137.M46.B47 1994, (v6)
Betts, Doris. PS3552.E84.B4, (v3)
Betts, Doris. PS3552.E84.R5, (v3)
Betts, John Rickards. GV583.B47, (v6)
Betts, Raymond F. H31.C7 no.604, (v6)
  JV105.B47 1975, (v7)
  JV1818.B48 1991, (v7)
Betts, Richard K. U163.B38 1982, (v10)
  UA23.B46, (v10)
Betts, Robert B. F592.7.B48 1985, (v4)
Betts, Robert Brenton. DS59.D78.B47 1988, (v5)
Beuchat, Charles. PQ295.N2.B45, (v3)
Beuf, Ann H. RJ242.B47 1989, (v2)
Beumers, Birgit. PN2728.L54.B48 1997, (v3)
Beutelspacher, Albrecht. QA471.B5613 1998, (v1)
Bevacqua, Maria. HV6561.B49 2000, (v6)

Bevan, Bernard. NA1301.B4 1939, (v9)
Bevan, Bryan. B1197.B45, (v8)
Bevan, Bryan. DA255.B48 1994, (v5)
Bevan, Clifford. ML970.B48 1978, (v9)
Bevens, William E. E553.5 1st.B48 1992, (v4)
Bever, Edward. DT31.B395 1996, (v5)
Beveridge, Albert Jeremiah. E302.6.M4 B57 1990, (v4)
Beveridge, William Henry Beveridge. HB235.G7.B4 1965, (v6)
Beversluis, John. B395.B445 2000, (v8)
Beville, Hugh Malcolm. HE8689.7.A8.B46 1985, (v6)
Bevington, David M. PR646.B4 1962, (v3)
Bevir, Mark. B822.B48 1999, (v8)
Bevis, William W. SD538.3.M4.B48 1995, (v1)
Bew, Paul. DA690.B49 1994, (v5)
  DA960.B48 1987, (v5)
  DA990.U46.B3593 1999, (v5)
Bewell, Alan. PR5888.B47 1989, (v3)
Bewick, Thomas. NE1212.B5.A45 1962, (v9)
Beyer, Edvard. PT8895.B4413 1980, (v3)
Beyer, Hans. QD251.2.B4813 1996, (v1)
Beyer, William H. QA276.25.B48 1968, (v1)
Beyerly, Elizabeth. Z6461.B49 1991, (v10)
Beyle, Marie Henri. PQ2435.R755.C2, (v3)
  PQ2435.V49 1953, (v3)
Beyme, Klaus von. JK31.B49 1987, (v7)
Bezanson, Randall P. KF4770.B49 1998, (v7)
  KF6645.B49 1994, (v7)
Bezner, Lili Corbus. TR23.B48 1999, (v1)
Bezucha, Robert J. DC733.B45 1974, (v5)
Bhacker, M. Reda. HF3765.B43 1992, (v6)
Bhaduri, Sumit. TP156.C35, (v1)
Bhagwati, Jagdish N. HC433.B47 1993, (v6)
  HF1455.B48 2000, (v6)
  HF1711.B45 1991, (v6)
Bhairappa, Es. El. PL4659.B436 P313 1994, (v3)
Bhala, Raj K. KF1001.5.B48 1994, (v7)
Bhalla, A. S. HC435.2.B449 1992, (v6)
  HF1418.7.B47 1997, (v6)
Bhana, Surendra. DT2223.E38.B47 1997, (v5)
Bharath, Ramachandran. QA76.87.B53 1994, (v1)
Bharier, Julian. HC475.B5, (v6)
Bhartrhari. PK3791.B28.S213 1967, (v3)
Bharucha, Rustom. PN2021.B53 2000, (v3)
Bhaskar, Roy. B804.B48 1989, (v8)
  B828.2.B44 1998, (v8)
  B5134.B483.P57 1994, (v8)
  BL51.B554 2000, (v8)
Bhaskarananda. BL1202.B494 2002, (v8)
Bhat, Yashoda. PR6015.U9.Z5624 1991, (v3)
Bhatt, S. R. BQ4440.B53 2000, (v8)
Bhattacharya, Nandini. PR129.I5.B49 1998, (v3)
Bhattacharya, Narendra Nath. B162.5.B483, (v8)
Bhattacharyya, Rameswar. VM156.B49, (v10)
Bhavikatti, S. S. TA350.B48 1994, (v1)
Bhote, Keki R. TS156.B563 1991, (v1)
  TS156.B563 1999, (v1)
Bhushan, Bharat. TJ1075.B47 1991, (v1)
Biagini, Eugenio F. DA560.B53 1992, (v5)
Biale, David. BM755.S295.B5, (v8)
Bialer, Seweryn. D764.B47, (v5)
Bialik, Hayyim Nahman. PJ5053.B5.A6 1999, (v3)
Bialostosky, Don H. PR5892.L5.B5 1992, (v3)
Bialystok, Franklin. F1035.J5.B525 2000, (v4)
Bianchi Bandinelli, Ranuccio. N5760.B513, (v9)
Bianchi, Robert. HD3616.E32.B53 1989, (v6)
Bianco, Anthony. F1035.J5.B53 1997, (v4)
Bianco, Carla. F159.R73.B52, (v4)
Bianco, Lucien. DS775.B513, (v5)
Bianco, Margery (Williams). PZ8.9.B47Ve, (v3)
Biancolli, Amy. ML418.K9.B53 1998, (v9)
Bianconi, Lorenzo. ML290.2.B513 1987, (v9)
Bianculli, David. PN1992.3.U5.B5 1997, (v3)
  PN1992.6.B49 1992, (v3)
Bibb, Henry. E444.B58 1969b, (v4)
Bibby, Geoffrey. CB311.B5 1973, (v5)
Biber, Barbara. LB1140.2.B523 1984, (v7)
Biberaj, Elez. JN9689.A15.B53 1998, (v7)
Bicha, Karel D. F705.B67 B52, (v4)

Bickel, Alexander M. JC328.B53, (v7)
  KF8742.A5.B5, (v7)
Bickel, Karl A. F311.B5, (v4)
Bickel, Lennard. G850 1916.B43 2000, (v6)
  G875.M33.B53 2000, (v6)
Bickerman, E. J. DS121.65.B53 1988, (v5)
Bickers, Kenneth N. HJ275.B47 1991, (v6)
Bickerton, Derek. P106.B467 1995, (v3)
  P116.B52 1990, (v3)
  P116.B54 1981, (v3)
  PM7874.G8.B5, (v3)
Bickerton, James. JL193.B49 1999, (v7)
Bickford-Smith, Vivian. DT2405.C3657.B53 1995, (v5)
Bickley, Lynn S. RC76.B37 2002, (v2)
Bicknell, Stephen. ML578.B53 1996, (v9)
Biddiscombe, Alexander Perry. U240.B53 1998, (v10)
Biddle, Livingston. NX735.B54 1988, (v9)
Biddle, Nicholas. DF721.B53 1993, (v5)
Bidelman, Patrick Kay. HQ1613.B5 1982, (v6)
Bidney, Martin. PR468.E65.B54 1997, (v3)
Bidwell, Percy Wells. S441.B5 1941, (v1)
Bidwell, R. G. S. QK711.2.B54 1979, (v1)
Bieber, Judy. F2581.B55 1999, (v4)
Bieber, Margarete. NB90.B48 1961, (v9)
  PA3201.B52 1961, (v3)
Biebuyck, Daniel P. GN645.B53 1996, (v6)
Bieder, Robert E. E78.W8.B54 1995, (v4)
Biederman, Paul. HE9803.A35.B5 1982, (v6)
Biedermann, Hans. AZ108.B5313 1992, (v10)
Biegel, David E. RC108.B54 1991, (v2)
Biegeleisen, J. I. TT273.B49, (v1)
Biek, David. QK192.B54 2000, (v1)
Biek, Leo. CC75.B47, (v5)
Biel, Andrew. QM23.2.B53 1997, (v1)
Bienen, Henry. JQ2947.A91 B53, (v7)
  JQ3519.A8 T3 1970, (v7)
Bier, Ethan. QH453.B53 2000, (v1)
Bierce, Ambrose. PS1097.A1 1946, (v3)
  PS1097.D4 1958, (v3)
  PS1097.I5 1927, (v3)
  PS1097.Z5.A3 1967, (v3)
  PS1097.Z5.A3 1998, (v3)
Bierhorst, John. PM197.E3.B48, (v3)
Bierman, Harold. HB3717 1929.B388 1998, (v6)
Biermann, Alan W. QA76.B495 1997, (v1)
Biermann, Christopher J. TS1175.B54 1996, (v1)
Biesanz, Mavis Hiltunen. F1543.B563 1999, (v4)
Biesecker, Barbara A. PN98.P67.B54 1997, (v3)
Biesold, Horst. HV2748.B5413 1999, (v6)
Biester, James. PR411.B54 1997, (v3)
Bieter, John. F755.B15, (v4)
Biggadike, E. Ralph. HD2756.U5.B53, (v6)
Biggart, Nicole Woolsey. HF5438.25.B52 1989, (v6)
Biggs, Chester M. D805.A78.B54 1995, (v5)
Biggs, Lindy. TS178.B54 1996, (v1)
Biggs, Mary. PN6084.W6.B47 1996, (v3)
  Z479.B5 1990, (v10)
Biggs, Melissa E. PN1993.5.F7.B52 1996, (v3)
Biggs, Norman. QA76.73.P2.B54 1989, (v1)
Bigham, Darrel E. F516.B54 1998, (v4)
  F534.E9.B58 1987, (v4)
Bigland, Eileen. PR4156.B53, (v3)
  PR4528.B5 1950, (v3)
Bigmore, E. C. Z117.B59 2001, (v10)
Bigsby, C. W. E. PS350.B54 2000, (v3)
Bigwood, Carol. BD311.B494 1993, (v8)
Bijker, Wiebe E. T14.5.B54 1995, (v1)
Bijlefeld, Marjolijn. HV7436.B54 1999, (v6)
Biles, Roger. E806.B496 1991, (v4)
  F215.B55 1994, (v4)
  F548.5.K44.B54 1984, (v4)
  F548.54.D34.B55 1995, (v4)
Bilger, Audrey. PR858.F45.B55 1998, (v3)
Bilgrami, Akeel. B105.I56 B55 1992, (v8)
Bilharz, Joy Ann. E99.S3.B45 1998, (v4)
Bilitewski, Bernd. TD791.B5613 1996, (v1)
Bill, James A. BP194.18.C383 2002, (v8)
  E183.8.I55.B5 1988, (v4)
  E840.8.B32.B54 1997, (v4)
Biller, Henry B. BF723.P25.B53, (v2)
Billet, Bret L. HG5993.B56 1993, (v6)

Billias, George Athan. E206.B5, (v4)
Billig, Nathan. RC451.4.A5.B5 1993, (v2)
Billinger, Robert D. DB81.B55 1991, (v5)
Billingham, J. QA927.B25 2000, (v1)
Billings, Dwight B. HC107.N8.B5, (v6)
Billings, John Shaw. RD21.B55 1970, (v2)
Billings, Marland Pratt. QE601.B5 1972, (v1)
Billingslea-Brown, Alma Jean. PS374.N4.B55 1999, (v3)
Billington, David P. TA15.B53 1996, (v1)
Billington, James H. DK32.7.B5, (v5)
Billington, Monroe Lee. E185.93.N55.B55 1991, (v4)
Billington, Ray Allen. E173.B52, (v4)
  E179.5.B625, (v4)
  F591.B55, (v4)
Billington, Ray. B121.B55 1997, (v8)
Billington, Sandra. GT3670.B45 1984, (v6)
Billips, Connie J. PN1991.77.L89.B55 1995, (v3)
Billman, Larry. GV1779.B55 1997, (v6)
Billows, Richard A. DF235.48.A57.B55 1990, (v5)
Bills, Scott L. D888.U6.B55 1990, (v5)
Billson, Janet Mancini. F74.R9.M36, (v4)
  HQ1453.B55 1995, (v6)
Billy, Andre. PQ305.B49, (v3)
  PQ2261.Z5.B53, (v3)
Bilodeau, Martin. QA278.B55 1999, (v1)
Bilotta, James D. E415.7.B53 1992, (v4)
Binder, Frederick M. F128.9.A1.B45 1995, (v4)
Binder, Frederick Moore. E437.B56 1994, (v4)
Binder, Sarah A. JK1096.B56 1997, (v7)
Binford, Leigh. F1488.3.B55 1996, (v4)
Binford, Lewis Roberts. CC165.B48 2002, (v5)
  CC173.B56 1989, (v5)
Bing, Rudolf. ML429.B52.A3, (v9)
Bingham, Millicent Todd. PS1541.Z5.B543, (v3)
Bingham, Woodbridge. DS749.2.B5, (v5)
Binion, Rudolph. PN3353.B56 1997, (v3)
Binkin, Martin. UA23.B498 1993, (v10)
Binkley, Luther John. BJ1011.B45, (v8)
Binkley, William C. F390.B588, (v4)
  JK9.B56 1999, (v7)
Binns, Ronald. PR6023.O96.Z568 1984, (v3)
Binski, Paul. DA687.W5.B56 1995, (v5)
Binswanger, Hans Christoph. PT1930.B513 1994, (v3)
Binyon, Laurence. PR6003.I75.A17 1931, (v3)
Biondich, Mark. DR1589.R33, (v5)
Biondo, Samuel J. QA76.76.E95.B57 1990, (v1)
Blow, Douglas. PN56.M3.B56 1996, (v3)
Bioy Casares, Adolfo. PQ7797.B535.A26 1992, (v3)
Bir, R. E. SB439.B49 1992, (v1)
Birch, Cyril. PL2303.B5 1963, (v3)
  PL2386.B57 1995, (v3)
  PL2658.E1.B5, (v3)
Birch, Sarah. JN6639.A5, (v7)
  PR6003.R412.Z56 1994, (v3)
Birch, Thomas William. GA9.B56 1964, (v6)
Bird, Alan. PR5827.D7.B5 1977, (v3)
Bird, Caroline. HQ1420.B5 1970, (v6)
Bird, Doni. RK60.5.T67 2003, (v2)
Bird, E. C. F. GB451.2.B55 2000, (v6)
Bird, Eric C. F. GB451.2.B58 1993, (v6)
Bird, Frederick B. HF5387.B557 1996, (v6)
Bird, Graham R. HG3891.5.B57 1989, (v6)
Bird, Graham. B945 .J24 B39 1999, (v8)
Bird, Isabella L. F782.R6 B55 1999, (v4)
Bird, J. O. TK454.B48 1997, (v1)
Bird, Junius Bouton. F3069.B53 1988, (v4)
Bird, Marion H. QA135.5.B533 1991, (v1)
Bird, Richard Miller. HJ2351.B5 1975, (v6)
  HJ4153.B57, (v6)
Bird, S. Elizabeth. PN4888.T3.B5 1992, (v3)
Bird, Tom. D805.A2.B57 1992, (v5)
Bird, William L. D743.25.B57 1998, (v5)
Birdseye, Ezekiel. E445.T3.B57 1997, (v4)
Birdwell, Michael E. PN1999.W3.B57 1999, (v3)
Birdwhistell, Ray L. BF637.C45.B57, (v2)
Bireley, Robert. JA79.B54 1990, (v7)
Birenbaum, Arnold. R690.B58 1990, (v2)
  RA413.5.U5.B495 1997, (v2)
Birge, Edward Asahel. QH434.B57 1988, (v1)

Birkeland, Peter W. S592.2.B57 1984, (v1)
Birkerts, Sven. PN771.B475 1999, (v3)
Birkerts, Sven. Z1003.B57 1994, (v10)
Birket-Smith, Kaj. CB113.D3.B513, (v5)
Birkhead, T. R. QL761.B57 2000, (v1)
Birkin, Kenneth. ML410.S93.B5 1989, (v9)
Birkner, Michael J. F144.B38.B57 1994, (v4)
Birley, Anthony Richard. DG295.B57 1997, (v5)
  DG297 .B5 2000, (v5)
Birley, Robert. PR99.B43 1975, (v3)
Birmingham, David. DP538.B57 1993, (v5)
  JV125.B57 2000, (v7)
Birmingham, George A. PR8876.H35, (v3)
Birnbaum, Pierre. DC36.9.B5713 2001, (v5)
  DS135.F9.B5713 1996, (v5)
  DS146.F8.B5713 1992, (v5)
Birney, Catherine H. E449.G88 1969, (v4)
Birney, D. Scott. QB145.B52 1990, (v1)
Birney, Hoffmann. PS3503.I76 G7, (v3)
Birney, Robert Charles. BF319.B5 1961, (v2)
  BF685.B5, (v2)
Birrell, Anne. BL1825.B57 1993, (v8)
  BL1825.B573 2000, (v8)
Birrell, Augustine. PR4115.E8 1971, (v3)
  PR4115.O52 1924a, (v3)
  PR4115.Z5.A3 1937, (v3)
Birrell, Verla Leone. NK8804.B5, (v9)
Birren, Faber. BF789.C7.B49 1961, (v2)
Birringer, Johannes H. NX212.B57 1998, (v9)
  PN2039.B57 1991, (v3)
Birth, Kevin K. GN564.T7.B57 1999, (v6)
Bisati, Muhammad. PJ7816.I76A24 1998, (v3)
Bisbee, Eleanor. DR590.B5, (v5)
Bisgrove, Richard. SB466.G7, (v1)
  SB470.J38.B57 1992, (v1)
Bishop, A. C. QE363.8.B56 1999, (v1)
Bishop, Christopher M. QA76.87.B574 1995, (v1)
  PZ7.B5245Fi 1989, (v3)
Bishop, Donald G. E183.8.R9.B5, (v4)
Bishop, Elizabeth. PQ9658.B5, (v3)
  PS3503.I785.A15 1984, (v3)
  PS3503.I785.P6, (v3)
  PS3503.I785 1983, (v3)
Bishop, George. PS2124.B52 1988, (v3)
Bishop, Hugh E. F612.L3 B5 2000, (v4)
Bishop, Jim. E457.5.B63, (v4)
  PS3503.I788 D3, (v3)
Bishop, John Lyman. PL2937.B5, (v3)
Bishop, John Peale. PS3503.I79.A16, (v3)
  PS3503.I79.A17 1948, (v3)
  PS3503.I79.A63, (v3)
  PS3503.I79.M3, (v3)
Bishop, Lloyd. PQ287.B57 1984, (v3)
Bishop, Margaret S. QE36.B5, (v1)
Bishop, Morris. B1903.B43 1968, (v8)
  PQ1677.B5, (v3)
Bishop, Nick. PR6058.U37.Z59 1991, (v3)
Bishop, O. N. QC39.B57 1984, (v1)
Bishop, Peter. DS786.B53 1989, (v5)
Bishton, Derek. BL2532.R37 B57 1986, (v8)
Biskupic, Joan. KF8742.W567 1997, (v7)
Bismarck, Otto. DD218.A2 1966, (v5)
Bismill‾aha, Abdula. PK2098.15.I85J4713 1996, (v3)
Bissell, C. C. TK5103.7.B54 1992, (v1)
Bissell, R. Ward. ND623.G364.B58 1998, (v9)
Bissell, Richard M. JK468.I6.B55 1996, (v7)
Bissinger, H. G. F158.54.R46.B57 1997, (v4)
Bisson, Lillian M. PR1933.S59.B57 1998, (v3)
Bisson, T. A. DS777.53.B5, (v5)
Biswas, A. K. TN780.B57 1994, (v1)
Biswas, Sugata. HD69.C6 B537 2002, (v6)
Bithell, Jethro. PT401.B55 1959, (v3)
Bitsch, Jorgen. DS798.B513 1963a, (v5)
Bitterli, Urs. D32.B5713 1989, (v5)
Bittner, Rüdiger. BJ1114.B5713 1989, (v8)
  B105.A35 B55 2001, (v8)
Bitton, Davis. BX8605.5.B588 1994, (v8)
Bizarro Ujpan, Ignacio. F1465.2.T9.B588 1985, (v4)
  F1465.2.T9.B59, (v4)
Bizier, Richard. F367.3.B59 1999, (v4)

Bizzarro, Salvatore. F3054.B5 1987, (v4)
Bizzarro, Tina Waldeier. NA390.W35 1992, (v9)
Bizzell, Patricia. PE1404.B585 1992, (v3)
Bjarkman, Peter C. GV863.155.B53 1994, (v6)
Bjarnhof, Karl. PT8175.B543 S782, (v3)
Bjelajac, David. ND237.A4.A64 1988, (v9)
Bjorck, Ake. QA214.B56 1996, (v1)
Björk, Christina. PR4612.B48 1993, (v3)
Bjork, Daniel W. BF109.S55.B46 1993, (v2)
Bjork, Gordon C. HC106.82.B58 1999, (v6)
Bjork, Rebecca S. PN239.P64.B56 1992, (v3)
Bjorken, James D. QC174.1.B52, (v1)
Bjorklund, David F. BF701.B57 2002, (v2)
Bjorkman, Edwin. PS3503.J6.G3, (v3)
Bjorkman, Edwin. PS3503.J6.S6 1969, (v3)
Bjorkman, Ingrid. PL8379.9.N4.M6833 1989, (v3)
Björkstén, Johan. PL1171.B5613 1994, (v3)
Björling, Anna-Lisa. ML420.B6 B48 1996, (v9)
Bjorling, Joel. Z6878.S8.B58 1998, (v10)
    Z7751.B595 1995, (v10)
Blachowicz, James. BD183.B53 1998, (v8)
Black Elk. E99.O3 B48 2000, (v4)
Black Hawk. E83.83.B53 A3 1999, (v4)
Black, Allida M. E807.1.R48.B53 1996, (v4)
Black, Barbara J. AM43.L6.B53 2000, (v10)
Black, Brian. TN872.P4, (v1)
Black, C. A. S591.B56, (v1)
Black, Charles Lund. HV8698.B47 1981, (v6)
Black, Conrad. F1053.D78.B55, (v4)
Black, Eugene Charlton. DS135.E5.B56 1988, (v5)
Black, Fischer. HB3711.B497 1987, (v6)
Black, Gregory D. PN1995.5.B48 1998, (v3)
    PN1995.5.B49 1994, (v3)
Black, Ian. UB251.I78.B55 1991, (v10)
Black, J. L. F1029.5.S65.B572 1998, (v4)
Black, Jan Knippers. HD75.B54 1999, (v6)
Black, Jeremy. D13.B54 1997, (v5)
    D214.B56 1994, (v5)
    D214.B58 1998, (v5)
    D214.B585 1998, (v5)
    DA67.B57 1999, (v5)
    DA435.B53 1991, (v5)
    DA498.B53 1985, (v5)
    E208.B6 1991, (v4)
    GA108.7.B58 1997, (v6)
Black, Joel. PN56.M85.B57 1991, (v3)
Black, John. HB61.B554 1997, (v6)
Black, Kathryn. RC181.U6.A63 1996, (v2)
Black, Maggie. HV696.F6.B53 1992, (v6)
    HV703.B53 1996, (v6)
Black, Mary E. TT848.B5 1980, (v1)
Black, Max. B29.B54, (v8)
    B29.B542 1990, (v8)
    B808.5.B53 1963, (v8)
Black, Naomi. HQ1599.E5.B57 1989, (v6)
Black, Peter E. GB980.B57 1996, (v6)
Black, Robert C. E545.B55, (v4)
Black, Stephen A. PS3529.N5.Z5676 1999, (v3)
Blackall, Eric A. PT759.B55 1983, (v3)
Blackall, Eric A. PT1984.B5, (v3)
Blackbourn, David. DD203.B59 1998, (v5)
    DD204.B5213 1984, (v5)
Blackburn, Graham. V23.B58, (v10)
Blackburn, James A. Q185.B563 2001, (v1)
Blackburn, Robert T. LB1778.2.B53 1995, (v7)
Blackburn, Robert. JN961.B58 1995, (v7)
Blackburn, Simon. BD21.B47 1999, (v8)
    BJ1311.B53 2000, (v8)
Blackburn, Stuart H. PN1979.S5.B48 1996, (v3)
Blacker, Irwin R. PS374.W4.B55, (v3)
Blackett, P. M. S. UA11.B5 1962, (v10)
Blackett, R. J. M. E449.B627 1983, (v4)
    E469.8.B66 2001, (v4)
Blackford, Charles Minor. VK140.B53A3, (v10)
Blackford, Mansel G. HC255.B59 1998, (v6)
    HD2346.U5.B56 1991, (v6)
    HD9161.U54.B143 1996, (v6)
Blackford, Susan Leigh. E605.B63 1998, (v4)
Blackhurst, Hector. Z3516.B55 1996, (v10)
Blacking, John. ML410.G75.B64 1987, (v9)
Blackman, David S. QP551.B53 1994, (v1)

Blackman, John L. HD5324.B53, (v6)
Blackman, Margaret B. E99.H2 D383 1992, (v4)
Blackman, William C. TD1040.B53 1992, (v1)
Blackmore, R. D. PR4132.L6 1943, (v3)
    PR4132.L6 1985, (v3)
Blackmore, Susan J. BF1389.A7.B53 1982, (v2)
    HM291.B535 1999, (v6)
Blackmur, R. P. PR503.B55, (v3)
    PS372.B58, (v3)
Blacksnake. E99.S3.B533 1989, (v4)
Blackstock, Charity. PR6070.O65.M6 1965, (v3)
Blackstone, Bernard. PR590.B37, (v3)
Blackwelder, Julia Kirk. HD6095.B57 1997, (v6)
Blackwelder, Richard E. PR6039.O32.Z49 1990, (v3)
Blackwell, Alice Stone. F73.5.B53 1990, (v4)
Blackwell, Lewis. Z250.A2.B57 1992, (v10)
Blackwell, Marilyn Johns. PN1998.3.B47.B63 1997, (v3)
Blackwell, Michael. DA589.8.B57 1993, (v5)
Blackwell, William L. HC333.B543, (v6)
Blackwood, Algernon. PR6003.L3.B477 1973, (v3)
Blackwood, Evelyn. DS632.M4.B53 2000, (v5)
Blades, James. ML1030.B6 1992, (v9)
Blaedel, Niels. QC16.B63.B5713 1988, (v1)
Blagg, Nigel. RJ506.S33.B58 1987, (v2)
Blahous, Charles P. HD7125.B55 2000, (v6)
Blaine, Martha Royce. E99.P3.B57 1990, (v4)
Blainey, Ann. PR4813.B55 1985, (v3)
Blair, Ann. Q125.2.B53 1997, (v1)
Blair, Anne E. E183.8.V5.B47 1995, (v4)
Blair, Bruce G. UB212.B5 1985, (v10)
Blair, Carvel Hall. F187.C5 B53, (v4)
Blair, Claude. U825.B55, (v10)
Blair, Clay. D781.B53 1996, (v5)
Blair, Diane D. JK5116.B42 1988, (v7)
Blair, Emma Helen. E78.N8.B63 1996, (v4)
Blair, Glenn Myers. LB1051.B453 1975, (v7)
Blair, Gordon P. TJ790.B577 1999, (v1)
Blair, John P. HD82.B5543 1995, (v6)
Blair, Karen J. HQ1904.B56, (v6)
    NX180.F4.B63 1994, (v9)
    Z7964.U49.B53 1989, (v10)
Blair, Roger D. KF1652.B55 1993, (v7)
Blair, Sara. PS2127.P6.B57 1996, (v3)
Blair, Timothy R. LB2157.U5.B57 1998, (v7)
Blair, William Alan. E581.B57 1998, (v4)
Blais, Andre. JF1601.B53 1997, (v7)
Blais, Madeleine. GV886.B53 1995, (v6)
Blaisdell, Thomas C. E176.1.A655, (v4)
Blaise, Clark. PS3552.B573.N8, (v3)
    QB223.B58 2000, (v1)
Blake, Andrew. ML285.5.B55 1997, (v9)
Blake, Barbara Radke. Z1361.O7.B57 1995, (v10)
Blake, Caesar R. PR6035.I34.Z65, (v3)
Blake, Casey Nelson. E169.1.B597 1990, (v4)
Blake, Judith. LC205.B57 1989, (v7)
Blake, Kathleen. PR469.W65.B57 1983, (v3)
Blake, Lillie Devereux. PS1102.B86.F48 1996, (v3)
Blake, Michael F. PN2287.C48.B58 1993, (v3)
    PN2287.C48.B59 1995, (v3)
Blake, Robert. DA564.B3.B6 1967, (v5)
Blake, Robert. DA576.B53 1985, (v5)
Blake, Robin. ND673.D9.B57 2000, (v9)
Blake, Stephen P. DS486.D3.B55 1990, (v5)
Blake, William. PR4141.E7 1982, (v3)
    PR4141.K42 1957, (v3)
    PR4141.K42 1966, (v3)
    PR4141.S5, (v3)
    PR4141.5.J64 1979, (v3)
    PR4142.F7, (v3)
    PR4142.K3, (v3)
    PR4146.A5 1968, (v3)
Blakemore, J. S. QC176.B63 1985, (v1)
Blakeslee, Ann M. QC5.3.B53 2001, (v1)
Blakeslee, Donald J. F799.B63 1995, (v4)
Blakeslee, Merritt R. PQ1543.B55 1989, (v3)
Blakeslee, Spencer. DS146.U6.B55 2000, (v5)
Blalock, Hubert M. HA29.B59 1972, (v6)
Blalock, Susan E. PS3509.L43.Z6436 1996, (v3)
Blaman, Anna. PT5878.V85.O63x 1974, (v3)
Blamires, Harry. PR3562.B53, (v3)

Blanch, Robert J. PR1972.G353.B57 1995, (v3)
Blanchard, Dallas A. HQ767.25.B53 1993, (v6)
    HQ767.5.U5.B58 1994, (v6)
Blanchard, Fessenden Seaver. VM351.B52 1968, (v10)
Blanchard, Kendall. GN454.B56 1985, (v6)
Blanchard, Margaret A. JC599.U5.B553 1992, (v7)
Blanchard, W. Scott. PN6149.S2.B53 1995, (v3)
Blanchot, Maurice. PN81.B544713 1995, (v3)
    PN710.B57413 2001, (v3)
    PQ2603.L3343.A8513 1997, (v3)
Blanck, Jacob. Z1225.B55, (v10)
Blanco, Hugo. HD556.B5513, (v6)
Bland, David. NC960.B62 1969b, (v9)
Bland, Kalman P. BM538.A7.B55 2000, (v8)
Bland, Randall Walton. KF8745.M34 B547 2001, (v7)
Bland, Sterling Lecater. PS366.A35.B6 2000, (v3)
Bland, Will. SD70.B5685 1998, (v1)
Blandford, Percy W. S674.5.B55 1976, (v1)
Blandford, Steven. PN1993.45.B49 2001, (v3)
Blaney, Joseph R. E886.2.B59 2001, (v4)
Blank, G. Kim. PR5433.B5 1988, (v3)
    PR5892.P74.B53 1995, (v3)
Blank, Stephen. DK266.5.B57 1994, (v5)
Blanke, David. HC107.A14.B553 2000, (v6)
Blankenship, Albert Breneman. HF5415.2.B555 1998, (v6)
Blankner, Frederika. PT7063.B5, (v3)
Blann, Robinson. PR4359.B53 1990, (v3)
Blanshard, Brand. BJ43.B55 1961, (v8)
Blanshard, Frances Margaret Bradshaw. N70.B55 1949, (v9)
Blasco Ibanez, Vicente. PQ6603.L2.B27 1952, (v3)
    PQ6603.L2 1964, (v3)
    PQ6603.L2 1977, (v3)
Blashfield, Jean F. F164.3.B57 2000, (v4)
    F865.B64 2001, (v4)
Blasi, Anthony J. Z7831.B54 1990, (v10)
Blasier, Cole. F1416.S65.B57 1983, (v4)
Blasier, Cole. F1418.B646, (v4)
Blaskett, D. R. TN785.B63 1990, (v1)
Blassingame, John W. E443.B55 1979, (v4)
    F379.N59 B42, (v4)
Blassingame, Wyatt. PS3503.L517.H3, (v3)
Blatner, David. QA484.B55 1997, (v1)
Blatt, Harvey. QE651.B68 1991, (v1)
Blattberg, Charles. JA71.B534 2000, (v7)
Blatter, Alfred. MT70.B56 1997, (v9)
Blatter, Christian. QA403.3.B5713 1998, (v1)
Blatter, Janet. N7417.6.B59 1981, (v9)
Blau, Eve. NA9053.B58.B55 1999, (v9)
Blau, Francine D. HQ1421.B56 2002, (v6)
Blau, Herbert. GT596.B56 1999, (v6)
    PN2039.B58 1992, (v3)
    PN2193.A8.B5 1990, (v3)
Blau, Joel. HV4505.B52 1992, (v6)
Blau, Joseph L. E184.J5.B5543, (v4)
Blau, Judith K. NX180.S6.B56 1989, (v9)
Blau, Peter Michael. HD5875.B55, (v6)
Blauert, Jens. QP469.B5413 1997, (v1)
Blaug, Mark. HB75.B664 1997, (v6)
    HB131.B56 1992, (v6)
Blaukopf, Kurt. ML3795.B6313 1992, (v9)
Blauner, Bob. E185.615.B556 1989, (v4)
Blaustein, Albert P. KF301.B5 1972, (v7)
Blaustein, Saul J. HD7096.U5.B5397 1993, (v6)
Blaut, James M. D16.9.B493 2000, (v5)
Blay, Michel. QC133.B5313 1998, (v1)
Blazek, Ron. Z1236.B57 1994, (v10)
    Z6265.B53 2000, (v10)
Blazer, Dan G. RC451.4.A5B56 1998, (v2)
Blea, Irene I. E184.M5.B56 1992, (v4)
    F790.M5.B57 1995, (v4)
Bleaney, C. H. Z3483.L4.K48 1991, (v10)
Blechschmidt, Erich. QM601.B553, (v1)
Blecker, Robert A. HF3031.B54 1992, (v6)
Bledsoe, Timothy. JS371.B54 1993, (v7)
Bledstein, Burton J. LA227.1.B53 1976, (v7)
Blee, Kathleen M. HS2330.K63.B44 1991, (v6)
Blegen, Theodore Christian. F606.B668 1975, (v4)
Blei, Norbert. F549.C56.B54 1987, (v4)

Bleiberg, German. PQ6072.B65, (v3)
Bleibtreu, Hermann K. GN60.B57, (v6)
Bleier, Ruth. QP34.5.B55 1984, (v1)
Bleikasten, Andre. PS3511.A86.Z6298 1990, (v3)
Bleiler, Everett Franklin. PS648.S3.B57 1998, (v3)
Bleiler, Richard. Z5917.D5 B59 1999, (v10)
Blessing, Patrick J. F705.B7 B55, (v4)
Blessing, Patrick J. Z1361.I7.B54 1992, (v10)
Blessington, Francis C. PR3562.B534 1988, (v3)
Blet, Pierre. D749.B4813 1999, (v5)
Blevins, Carolyn DeArmond. Z7963.R45 B45 1995, (v10)
Blevins, Robert D. TA355.B52 1990, (v1)
　TA357.B57 1984, (v1)
Blevins, Winfred. PE2970.W4.B5 1992, (v3)
Blewett, Mary H. HD8039.B72.U63 1988, (v6)
Blickle, Peter. DD182.B613, (v5)
Blier, Suzanne Preston. DT541.45.S65.B57 1987, (v5)
　N7391.65.B58 1998, (v9)
　NB1910.B57 1995, (v9)
Bliese, John Ross Edward. GE180.B57 2001, (v6)
Bligh, William. DU870.B56 1988, (v5)
Blight, David W. E449.D75.B55 1989, (v4)
　E468.9.B58 2001, (v4)
Blight, James G. E841.B57 1990, (v4)
　E841.B573 1990, (v4)
　E841.C8 1993, (v4)
Blinder, Alan S. HB171.B535 1987, (v6)
Blinder, Caroline. PS3525.I5454.Z654 2000, (v3)
Blinderman, Charles. QH302.5.B59 1990, (v1)
Bliss, Gilbert Ames. QA315.B5, (v1)
Bliss, Lee. PR2434.B55 1987, (v3)
Bliss, Michael. PN1998.3.P43.B57 1993, (v3)
　PN1998.3.S39.B65 1995, (v3)
　PN1998.3.W44.B58 2000, (v3)
　QP572.I5.B58 1982, (v1)
　R134.B55 1999, (v2)
Bliss, Robert M. E191.B57 1990, (v4)
Bliven, Bruce. F119.B69, (v4)
Blixen, Karen (Dinesen). PT8175.B545 W5 1942, (v3)
　PT8175.B545 A6, (v3)
　PT8175.B545 E352, (v3)
　PT8175.B545.S4, (v3)
Blobaum, Robert. DK4385.B57 1995, (v5)
Bloch, Chana. PR3508.B5 1985, (v3)
Bloch, Ernst. B3209.B751.J67213 1998, (v8)
　BL51.B584513, (v8)
　DD239.B713 1990, (v5)
Bloch, Felix. QC174.8.B59 1989, (v1)
Bloch, Marc Leopold Benjamin. D131.B513 1961, (v5)
　D640.B581713, (v5)
　D761.B562 1968, (v5)
　HD643.B613, (v6)
Bloch, Michael. DA580.B538 1988, (v5)
Bloch, Oscar. PC2580.B55 1968, (v3)
Bloch, R. Howard. HQ1143.B56 1991, (v6)
　PQ158.B55, (v3)
　Z305.M46.B57 1994, (v10)
Block, Adrienne Fried. ML410.B36.B56 1998, (v9)
Block, Andrew. Z2014.F4.B6 1961, (v10)
Block, B. Peter. QD149.B59 1990, (v1)
Block, Fred L. HB3730.B57 1990, (v6)
Block, Geoffrey Holden. ML134.I9.B6 1988, (v9)
　ML1711.8.N3.B56 1997, (v9)
Blocker, Joel. PJ5045.B5, (v3)
Blockson, Charles L. CS21.B55, (v5)
　E185.96.B57 1991, (v4)
Blodgett, E. D. PR9199.3.M8.Z57 1988, (v3)
Blodgett, Harriet. PR908.B56 1988, (v3)
Blodgett, Jan. PS374.C48.B58 1997, (v3)
Bloemink, Barbara J. ND237.S75.B66 1995, (v9)
Blofeld, John Eaton Calthrope. BL1923.B57, (v8)
Blomberg, Catharina. BJ971.B8 B56 1994, (v8)
Blomberg, Thomas G. HV9466.B55 2000, (v6)
Blomquist, William A. HD1694.C2.B55 1992, (v6)
Blondheim, Menahem. PN4864.B76 1994, (v3)
Blong, R. J. QE522.B6 1984, (v1)
Blood, Susan. PQ2191.Z5.B554 1997, (v3)
Bloodworth, Dennis. DS777.55.B55, (v5)
Bloom, Allan David. LA227.3.B584 1987, (v7)

Bloom, Arthur L. GB401.5.B55, (v6)
Bloom, Arthur W. PN2287.J4.B66 2000, (v3)
Bloom, Clive. PR478.P64.B58 2001, (v3)
　PS374.P63.B56 1996, (v3)
Bloom, Harold. PN81.B545 1993, (v3)
　PN83.B57 2000, (v3)
　PN1077.B55 1989, (v3)
　PR590.B39 1971, (v3)
　PR4147.B5 1970, (v3)
　PR5438.B55, (v3)
Bloom, Howard K. BD450.B526 1995, (v8)
Bloom, John. E98.G2.B56 2000, (v4)
Bloom, Jonathan. BP55.B57 2002, (v8)
　N6260.B57 1997, (v9)
　NA4670.B55 1989, (v9)
Bloom, Ken. F128.65.T5.B56 1990, (v4)
　ML128.M7.B6 1995, (v9)
　ML128.M78.B6 1996, (v9)
Bloom, Lois. LB1139.L3.B578, (v7)
Bloom, Miriam. RC641.7.S5.B56 1995, (v2)
Bloom, Paul. P118.B623 2000, (v3)
Bloom, Robert. PR6005.A77.Z63, (v3)
Bloom, Sandra L. RC569.5.C55.B56 1997, (v2)
Bloom, Stephen G. F630.J5, (v4)
Bloom, William. JX1395.B568 1990, (v7)
Bloomberg, Marty. Z6374.H6 B58 1995, (v10)
Bloomfield, David. DA990.U46.B56 1997, (v5)
Bloomfield, Leonard. PE1119.B69, (v3)
Bloomfield, Louis. QC21.2.B59 1997, (v1)
Bloomfield, Maxwell H. KF366.B5, (v7)
Bloomfield, Morton W. PR2015.B5, (v3)
Bloomfield, Victor A. QD433.B44, (v1)
Bloomster, Edgar L. VM307.B6 1969, (v10)
Blos, Joan W. PZ7.B6237Gat, (v3)
Blotner, Joseph Leo. PS3545.A748.Z59 1997, (v3)
Blouin, Lenora P. Z8784.43.B58, (v10)
Blows, Johanna M. GR366.A87.B56 1995, (v6)
Blows, William T. RT42.B576 2000, (v2)
Blue, Frederick J. E415.9.C4.B58 1987, (v4)
Blue, William R. PQ6105.B59 1996, (v3)
Bluestein, Gene. GR105.B483 1994, (v6)
　PE1582.Y5.B58 1998, (v3)
Bluestone, Barry. HC110.I5.B539 2000, (v6)
　HD5708.55.U6.B58 1982, (v6)
　HD6957.U6.B55 1992, (v6)
Bluestone, Charles D. RF225.B57 2000, (v2)
Bluestone, Daniel M. NA9127.C4.B48 1991, (v9)
Bluhm, Andreas. N8219.L5, (v9)
Blum, Andre. Z126.B657, (v10)
Blum, Ann Shelby. QL46.5.B58 1993, (v1)
Blum, Betty. Z5961.U5 B58 1991, (v10)
Blum, Bruce I. QA76.758.B78 1992, (v1)
Blum, David. ML394.B66 1999, (v9)
Blum, Jerome. D385.B58 1993, (v5)
Blum, Jerome. HN373.B55, (v6)
Blum, John Morton. E743.B6135 1980, (v4)
　E757.B65 1977, (v4)
　E767.B64, (v4)
　HJ257.B62, (v6)
Blum, Laurie. HV41.9.U5.B58 1996, (v6)
Blum, Lawrence A. BJ1031.B65 1994, (v8)
Blum, Richard H. BF209.L9.B5, (v2)
Blum, Robert M. DS518.8.B58 1982, (v5)
Blum, Susan Debra. GN495.6.B57 2000, (v6)
Blum, Virginia L. PR830.C5.B57 1995, (v3)
Blumberg, Arthur. LB2831.72.B55 1985, (v7)
Blumberg, Stanley A. QC16.T37.B57 1990, (v1)
Blume, Friedrich. ML60.B688, (v9)
　ML160.B655.R5, (v9)
　ML3100.B5913, (v9)
Blume, Helmut. F380.G3.B5313 1990, (v4)
Blume, Judy. PZ4.B65748Fo.S3552.L843, (v3)
　PZ7.B6265Ar 1990, (v3)
　PZ7.B6265Tal, (v3)
Blume, Marshall. HG4572.B67 1993, (v6)
Blumenfeld, Dennis. T57.6.B57 2001, (v1)
Blumenfeld, Jesmond. HF1613.4.Z4.A4352 1991, (v6)
Blumenfeld, Laura. BJ1490.B58 2002, (v8)
Blumenfeld, Robert. PN2071.F6.B48 1998, (v3)
Blumenfeld-Kosinski, Renate. RG761.B48 1990, (v2)
Blumenson, Martin. D763.I82.A55, (v5)

Blumenstock, David I. QC863.B55, (v1)
Blumenthal, David R. BJ1401.B58 1999, (v8)
Blumenthal, Eileen. PN2287.T28.B58 1995, (v3)
Blumenthal, W. Michael. DS135.G5.B57 1998, (v5)
Blumhofer, Edith Waldvogel. Z7778.U6.B48 1990, (v10)
Blumin, Stuart M. HN80.K5.B55 1976, (v6)
Blundell, Sue. HQ1134.B58 1995, (v6)
Blundell-Jones, Peter. NA1088.S24.B58 1995, (v9)
Blunden, Caroline. DS721.B56 1998, (v5)
Blunden, Edmund. D640.B5833 1956, (v5)
　PR5431.B5 1947, (v3)
Blunden, John. TN153.B58 1985, (v1)
Blunt, Anthony. NA1120.B55 1982, (v9)
　ND497.B6.B42, (v9)
　ND553.P8.B64, (v9)
Blunt, Wilfred Scawen. PR4149.B8 1914, (v3)
Blunt, Wilfrid. QH44.B54, (v1)
Blurton, T. Richard. N8195.A4.B58 1993, (v9)
Bluth, Christoph. UA770.B592 1992, (v10)
Blutstein, Howard I. F1503.B55, (v4)
　F1543.B66, (v4)
Bly, Robert W. HQ1090.3.B59 1990, (v6)
Bly, Robert. PS3503.L965.S5, (v3)
　PT9583.B62, (v3)
Blyden, Nemata Amelia. DT516.45.W47, (v5)
Blyth, Reginald Horace. PL729.B55, (v3)
　PL760.B55 1971, (v3)
Blythe, James M. JA82.B59 1992, (v7)
Boa, Elizabeth. PT2621.A26.Z5963 1996, (v3)
　PT2647.E26.Z58 1987, (v3)
Boag, Peter G. F882.L7.B62 1992, (v4)
Boak, Denis. PQ2625.A823.Z56 1963, (v3)
Boal, Augusto. PN2474.B63, (v3)
Boalch, Donald H. ML652.B666 1995, (v9)
Boardman, Brigid M. PR5651.B64 1988, (v3)
Boardman, Eugene Powers. DS759.B6 1972, (v5)
Boardman, John. DF251.B6 1980, (v5)
　NA225.B63 2000, (v9)
Boardman, Robert. HD9000.9.A1.B63 1986, (v6)
Boas, Franz. E99.E7.B672313 1998, (v4)
　GN6.B57 1974, (v6)
　GN8.B68, (v6)
　GN24.B6, (v6)
　GN27.B6, (v6)
　GN451.B7 1938, (v6)
Boas, Frederick S. PR646.B6, (v3)
　PR649.U6.B6, (v3)
　PR2673.B58, (v3)
Boas, George. B53.B56, (v8)
　B171.B68, (v8)
　B2430.M44.B6 1970, (v8)
　BD161.B53, (v8)
　BH39.B6, (v8)
　CB353.B6 1997, (v5)
　PS201.B6 1940a, (v3)
Boase, Alan Martin. PQ1643.B56 1970, (v3)
Boatner, Mark Mayo. U353.B6, (v10)
Boatright, John Raymond. HF5387.B63 1999, (v6)
Boatwright, Mary Taliaferro. DG295.B62 2000, (v5)
　DG295.B63 1987, (v5)
Boaz, David. JC585.B559 1997, (v7)
Boaz, Noel Thomas. GN281.B618 1997, (v6)
Bobbio, Norberto. JA79.B56 2000, (v7)
　JA83.B6413 1996, (v7)
　JA84.I8.B61913 1995, (v7)
　JC153.H66.B6313 1993, (v7)
　JC571.B56513 1996, (v7)
　JC585.B5613 1990, (v7)
Bobbitt, Philip. KF4550.B6 1991, (v7)
　U162.6.B66 1988, (v10)
Bobo, Jacqueline. PN1995.9.N4.B57 1995, (v3)
Bobo, Mike. GV956.6.B623 1998, (v6)
Bobrick, Benson. E208.B683 1997, (v4)
Bobrow, Davis B. H97.B6 1987, (v6)
Bobrow, Jerry. KF285.Z9.B6 1996, (v7)
Boccaccio, Giovanni. PR1912.B6 1980, (v3)
Boccara, Nino. QA320.B63 1990, (v1)
Bochenski, Joseph M. BC15.B643 1970, (v8)
　BC28.B58, (v8)
Bochner, Jay. PQ2605.E55.Z563, (v3)

Bochner, Ruth (Rothenberg). RC343.B59 1945, **(v2)**
Bock, Alan W. KFC632.B63 2000, **(v7)**
Bock, Kenneth Elliott. BD450.B539 1994, **(v8)**
Bocking, Richard C. F1089.F7.B63 1997, **(v4)**
Bocking, Stephen. QH540.B63 1997, **(v1)**
Bockstoce, John R. F910.5.B62 1990, **(v4)**
Bock-Weiss, Catherine. Z8554.32.B63 1996, **(v10)**
Bodanis, David. QC73.8.C6, **(v1)**
Bodansky, David. TK9145.B54 1996, **(v1)**
Bodde, Derk. DS721.B6, **(v5)**
  DS747.5.B6, **(v5)**
  DS777.55.B6, **(v5)**
  Q127.C5.B63 1991, **(v1)**
Boddy, William. PN1992.3.U5.B64 1990, **(v3)**
Bode, Barbara. F3451.A45.B63 1989, **(v4)**
Bode, Boyd Henry. LB1051.B463 1971, **(v7)**
Bode, Carl. LC6551.B6 1968, **(v7)**
Bodek, Richard. PN3307.G4.B64 1997, **(v3)**
Boden, Margaret A. BF39.5.B63 1988, **(v2)**
Bodenhamer, David J. KF4765.B63 1992, **(v7)**
  PS3503.O17 R4, **(v3)**
  PS3503.O17.S55, **(v3)**
Bodenheimer, Edgar. K237 .B6 1974, **(v7)**
Bodenheimer, Rosemarie. PR878.S62.B63 1988, **(v3)**
  PR4681.B57 1994, **(v3)**
Bodfish, Waldo. E99.E7.B675 1991, **(v4)**
Bodian, Miriam. DS135.N5.A5323 1997, **(v5)**
Bodine, A. Aubrey. F186.2.B59 1970, **(v4)**
Bodkin, Ronald G. HB172.5.B63 1991, **(v6)**
Bodnar, John E. E184.A1.B59 1985, **(v4)**
  E741.B64 1991, **(v4)**
  F159.P69.A22 1982, **(v4)**
  HN80.S78.B6, **(v6)**
Bodroghkozy, Aniko. HQ799.2.T4, **(v6)**
Boeckmann, Cathy. PS374.R34.B64 2000, **(v3)**
Boenig, Robert. PR1875.R45.B64 1995, **(v3)**
Boer, K. W. QC611.B64 1990, **(v1)**
Boer, Karin de. B3279.H49.B63313 2000, **(v8)**
Boer, Pim den. DC36.9.B6413 1998, **(v5)**
Boer, T. J. de. B741.B7 1983, **(v8)**
Boessenecker, John. F866.B64 1988, **(v4)**
Boethius, Anicius Manlius Severinus. MT5.5.B613 1989, **(v9)**
Boethius, Axel. NA300.B63 1978, **(v9)**
  NA310.B6, **(v9)**
Boethius. B659.D472 E5 1999, **(v8)**
Boewe, Charles E. F549.E3 B68 1999, **(v4)**
Boff, Leonardo. BT83.57.B59613 1987, **(v8)**
  BT202.B5313, **(v8)**
Boffa, Giuseppe. DK267.B585513 1992, **(v5)**
Bogaert, Harmen Meyndertsz van den. F122.1.B6 1988, **(v4)**
Bogan, Louise. PN511.B54, **(v3)**
  PN710.B59 1970, **(v3)**
Bogart, Barbara Allen. F882.L15.A44 1987, **(v4)**
Bogart, Leo. HF5821.B53 1996, **(v6)**
  PN4888.R37.B58 1991, **(v3)**
Bogart, Michele Helene. NB235.N5.B64 1989, **(v9)**
Bogdanor, Vernon. HC256.5.B56, **(v6)**
  JN331.B64 1995, **(v7)**
Bogdanov, A. PG3467.M29A27 1984, **(v3)**
Bogel, Fredric V. PR935.B64 2001, **(v3)**
Bogen, Don. PS3535.O39.Z586 1991, **(v3)**
Boger, Karl. Z7165.J3.B63 1988, **(v10)**
Boger, Louise Ade. NK2270.B63 1969, **(v9)**
Boggs, Marion Alexander. CT274.A43.B63 1980, **(v5)**
Boggs, Vernon. ML3475.B63 1992, **(v9)**
Bogin, Magda. PC3308.B64, **(v3)**
Bogle, Donald. PN1992.8.A34.B64 2001, **(v3)**
  PN2287.D256.B64 1997, **(v3)**
Bognar, Botond. NA1559.M8.B64 1996, **(v9)**
Bognar, Desi K. PN1990.4.B64 2000, **(v3)**
Bogue, Allan G. E175.5.T83.B64 1998, **(v4)**
Bogue, Donald Joseph. HB881.B564, **(v6)**
Bogue, Margaret Beattie. SH219.6, **(v1)**
Bogumil, Mary L. PS3573.I45677.Z58 1999, **(v3)**
Boh, Ivan. BC21.E64 B65 1993, **(v8)**
Boheemen, Christine van. PR6019.O9.Z525976 1999, **(v3)**
Bohen, Halcyone H. HQ536.B63, **(v6)**
Bohle, Robert H. LB3621.B58 1984, **(v7)**

Bohlen, Charles E. E748.B64.A38, **(v4)**
Bohlman, Philip Vilas. ML345.I8.B6 1989, **(v9)**
  ML3545.B64 1988, **(v9)**
Bohlmann, Otto. PR6005.O4.Z5635 1990, **(v3)**
Bohm, David. BH301.C84.B65 1998, **(v8)**
  QC6.B597 1957a, **(v1)**
Bohman, James. H61.B613 1991, **(v6)**
  JC423.B624 1996, **(v7)**
Bohme, Helmut. DD210.B613, **(v5)**
Bohme, Jakob. BV5080.B7.W413 1978, **(v8)**
Bohr, Niels Hendrik David. QC173.B535, **(v1)**
  QC3.B584, **(v1)**
  QC6.B598, **(v1)**
  QC6.B599 1963, **(v1)**
Bohren, Craig F. QC880.4.T5.B63 1998, **(v1)**
Boice, Robert. LB1778.2.B65 1992, **(v7)**
Boilard, Steve D. Z2491.B63 1997, **(v10)**
Boime, Albert. N332.F83.P33, **(v9)**
  N6425.N4.B6 1987, **(v9)**
  N6850.B64 1995, **(v9)**
  N8232.B57 1990, **(v9)**
  ND553.C9565.B64, **(v9)**
  ND617.5.M3.B65 1993, **(v9)**
  ND1351.5.B65 1991, **(v9)**
Bois, Guy. HN425.B6313 1992, **(v6)**
Bois, Mario. ML410.X45.B6, **(v9)**
Bois, Thomas. DS51.K7.B613, **(v5)**
Bois, Yve Alain. N6853.M33.B65 1998, **(v9)**
  NC139.K37.A4 1999, **(v9)**
Bois, Yve Alain. ND1140.B59 1990, **(v9)**
Boisdeffre, Pierre de. PQ305.B56 1968, **(v3)**
  PQ558.B6, **(v3)**
Boisseau, M. TK5105.5.B6513 1994, **(v1)**
Boisvert, Raymond D. B945.D4.B65 1998, **(v8)**
  B945.D44.B65 1988, **(v8)**
Bojer, Johan. PT8950.B6.V563, **(v3)**
Bok, Bart Jan. QB819.B735 1957, **(v1)**
  QB857.7.B64 1981, **(v1)**
Bok, Derek Curtis. HD6508.B59, **(v6)**
  HN60.B65 1996, **(v6)**
  JK468.P64B66 2001, **(v7)**
  LB2331.72.B64 1982, **(v7)**
  LC191.4.B65 1990, **(v7)**
Bok, Hilary. BJ1461.B64 1998, **(v8)**
Bok, Sissela. BD232.B595 1995, **(v8)**
  BJ1421.B64, **(v8)**
  BJ1429.5.B64 1983, **(v8)**
  HQ1687.B65 1991, **(v6)**
Bokenkotter, Thomas S. BX1795.J87.B65 1998, **(v8)**
Boker, Pamela A. PS374.G75.B65 1996, **(v3)**
Boklund, Gunnar. PR3184.D83.B6, **(v3)**
Bokovoy, Melissa K. HX550.A37.B65 1998, **(v6)**
Bol, Peter Kees. DS747.42.B64 1992, **(v5)**
Bold, Alan Norman. PR4331.B64 1990, **(v3)**
Bold, Harold Charles. QK47.B73 1987, **(v1)**
  QK566.B64 1985, **(v1)**
  QK641.B596 1987, **(v1)**
Bold, John. DA690.G83, **(v5)**
  NA997.W38.B6 1989, **(v9)**
Boldea, I. TK2411.B6 1997, **(v1)**
  TK4058.B64 1999, **(v1)**
Boldt, Menno. E78.C2.B75 1993, **(v4)**
Boles, Janet K. HQ1115.B65 1996, **(v6)**
Boles, John B. E441.B67 1983, **(v4)**
Bolger, Daniel P. E745.B57 1988, **(v4)**
Bolick, Clint. JC599.U5.B557 1988, **(v7)**
  KF4749.B55 1990, **(v7)**
Bolin, Bert. QC852.B65, **(v1)**
Bolin, Inge. F2230.2.K4.B65 1998, **(v4)**
Bolin, James Duane. F459.L6.B65 2000, **(v4)**
Bolin, Robert C. HV600 1994.C2B65 1998, **(v6)**
Bolinger, Dwight Le Merton. PE1319.B6, **(v3)**
Bolitho, Harold. DS871.5.B66, **(v5)**
Bolitho, Hector. UA655 3d.B6, **(v10)**
Bolivar, Simon. F2235.3.A13 1951a, **(v4)**
Bolkhovitinov, N. N. E183.8.R9.B613, **(v4)**
Boll, Heinrich. PT2603.O394.V4, **(v3)**
  PT2603.B632.AC7, **(v3)**
  PT2603.B632.C4, **(v3)**
  PT2603.B632.W79.E5, **(v3)**
  PT2603.O384.A6 1962, **(v3)**

  PT2603.O394.B5, **(v3)**
  PT2603.O394.B713 1976, **(v3)**
  PT2603.O394.E513, **(v3)**
  PT2603.O394.T313, **(v3)**
Boll, Michael M. UA23.B58 1988, **(v10)**
Bolland, O. Nigel. F2175.B65 1997, **(v4)**
Bolle, Kees W. BL48.B585 2002, **(v8)**
Bollen, Kenneth A. HA29.B732 1989, **(v6)**
Bollen, Math H. J. TK1010.B65 1999, **(v1)**
Bollens, Scott A. HT169.I82.J473 2000, **(v6)**
Boller, Paul F. E176.2.B65 1988, **(v4)**
Bolles, Augusta Lynn. HD6113.Z6.K553 1996, **(v6)**
Bolles, Edmund Blair. BF371.B59 1988, **(v2)**
Bolles, Richard Nelson. HF5382.7.B64, **(v6)**
Bollier, David. HB846.5.B65 2002, **(v6)**
Bolling, David M. QH76.B65 1994, **(v1)**
Bollinger, John G. TJ213.B5952 1988, **(v1)**
Bollinger, Lee C. KF4774.B65 1991, **(v7)**
Bollobas, Bela. QA320.B64 1990, **(v1)**
Bolman, Lee G. HD31.B6135 2003, **(v6)**
Bologna, Jack. HF5549.5.E43.B65 1996, **(v6)**
Bolster, Richard. PQ2152.A38Z8454 2000, **(v3)**
Bolt, Bruce A. QE509.B69 1982, **(v1)**
  QE534.2.B64 1993, **(v1)**
Bolt, John. BR115.P7 B656 2001, **(v8)**
Bolt, Robert. PR6052.O39.M3 1962, **(v3)**
Bolte, Johannes. PT921.B63, **(v3)**
Bolten, Steven E. HG4551.B485 2000, **(v6)**
Bolter, J. David. P96.T42.B59 1998, **(v3)**
  Z52.4.B65 1991, **(v10)**
Bolton, Barry. QL568.F7.B58 1994, **(v1)**
Bolton, Charles C. HC107.N83.P613 1994, **(v6)**
Bolton, H. Philip. PN2581.B64 2000, **(v3)**
Bolton, Herbert Eugene. E18.B7 1935, **(v4)**
  E125.V3.B6 1949, **(v4)**
  F389.B75 1962, **(v4)**
Bolton, S. Charles. F411.B72 1998, **(v4)**
Bolton, W. F. PR3072.B64 1992, **(v3)**
Boltzmann, Ludwig. QC175.B7213 1995, **(v1)**
Boly, John R. PR6001.U4.Z6 1991, **(v3)**
Bolyanatz, Alexander H. DU740.42.B65 2000, **(v5)**
Bombal, Maria Luisa. PQ8097.B67.A22 1995, **(v3)**
Bona, Mary Jo. PS153.I8.B66 1999, **(v3)**
Bonadeo, Alfredo. PN771.B66 1989, **(v3)**
Bonanate, Luigi. JX1395.B62613 1996, **(v7)**
Bonar, James. HB72.B65 1992, **(v6)**
Bonavia, Duccio. F3429.3.A7.B6413 1985, **(v4)**
Bond, Alma Halbert. PR6045.O72.Z5614 1989, **(v3)**
Bond, Ann. ML651.B66 1997, **(v9)**
Bond, Bradley G. F341.B76 1995, **(v4)**
Bond, Brian. D396.B63 1983, **(v5)**
Bond, David J. PQ2631.I49.Z56 1982, **(v3)**
Bond, Edward. PR6052.O5.A6 1975, **(v3)**
Bond, Hallie E. VM351.B596 1995, **(v10)**
Bond, Helen K. DS122.B66 1998, **(v5)**
Bond, James Edward. KF4558 14th.B66 1997, **(v7)**
Bond, Jon R. JK585.B52 1990, **(v7)**
Bond, Mary E. Z1365.B57 1996, **(v10)**
Bond, Michael. PZ7.B6368Be 1960, **(v3)**
Bond, Richmond Pugh. PR1365.T23.B6, **(v3)**
Bondanella, Peter E. CB245.B64 1987, **(v5)**
  PN1998.3.F45.B66 1992, **(v3)**
  PN1998.3.R67.B66 1993, **(v3)**
Bondeson, Jan. QM690.B66 2000, **(v1)**
Bondeson, Ulla. HV9276.5.B66 1994, **(v6)**
Bondi, Hermann. QC71.B63, **(v1)**
Bonds, Mark Evan. ML1255.B67 1996, **(v9)**
Bonet, Honore. PQ1551.B7.T7, **(v3)**
Bonewit-West, Kathy. R697.P45B66 1995, **(v2)**
Bonfield, Lynn A. CT274.W375.B66 1995, **(v5)**
Bongco, Mila. PN6714.B66 2000, **(v3)**
Bongie, Chris. PN849.U43.B66 1998, **(v3)**
Bonham Carter, Violet. DA566.9.B56.A3 1996, **(v5)**
Bonham-Carter, Graeme. G70.2.B66 1994, **(v6)**
Bonhoeffer, Dietrich. BJ1253.B615 1955a, **(v8)**
  BR50.B63 1990, **(v8)**
  BT83.B613 1962a, **(v8)**
  BT380.B66 1959, **(v8)**
Boniecki, Adam. BX1378.5.B67 2000, **(v8)**
Boniface, Douglas M. QA76.5.B598 1996, **(v1)**

Boniface, Saint, Archbishop of Mainz. BX4700.B7.A43 1940, **(v8)**

Bonin, Hubert. Z2184.A65.B66 1994, **(v10)**

Bonk, Kathy. HD62.6.B66 1999, **(v6)**

Bonn, Thomas L. Z473.N39.B66 1989, **(v10)**

Bonnard, Pierre. NE2349.5.B66.A4 1989, **(v9)**

Bonnefis, Philippe. PQ2607.E834.Z55913 1997, **(v3)**

Bonnefoy, Claude. PQ2617.O6.Z5413 1971, **(v3)**

Bonnell, John C. E523.6 21st.B66 1996, **(v4)**

Bonnell, Victoria E. DK266.3.B58 1997, **(v5)**

Bonner, Arthur. DS371.2.B65 1987, **(v5)**
  HN683.5.B58 1990, **(v6)**

Bonner, James Calvin. F294.M6 B63, **(v4)**

Bonner, John Tyler. QH31.B715.A3 1993, **(v1)**
  QH491.B595 2001, **(v1)**

Bonner, John. HB161.B72 1995, **(v6)**

Bonner, Thomas Neville. R210.C4.B6 1991, **(v2)**
  R692.B66 1992, **(v2)**
  R735.B66 1995, **(v2)**

Bonner, W. Nigel. QL737.C4.B67 1989, **(v1)**
  QL737.P64.B66 1990, **(v1)**
  QL737.P64.B662 1994, **(v1)**

Bonney, Richard. DC123.B66 1988, **(v5)**

Bonnicksen, Andrea L. RG135.B66 1989, **(v2)**

Bonoli, Giuliano. HV238.B66 2000, **(v6)**

Bonomi, Patricia U. F122.B65, **(v4)**
  F122.B655 1998, **(v4)**

Bonta, Juan Pablo. NA2599.5.B6613 1979b, **(v9)**

Bonta, Marcia. QH26.B66 1991, **(v1)**

Bontemps, Alex. E443.B66 2001, **(v4)**

Bontemps, Arna Wendell. E444.B67, **(v4)**

Bonvillian, Gary. LB2328.32.U6.B66 1996, **(v7)**

Bony, Jean. NA963.B66, **(v9)**

Booher, James M. RD97.B655 1995, **(v2)**

Bookbinder, Paul. DD240.B63 1996, **(v5)**

Bookchin, Murray. HN18.B635 1990, **(v6)**

Booker, Christopher B. E185.86.B635 2000, **(v4)**

Booker, M. Keith. PN1995.9.P6.B66 1999, **(v3)**
  PN3503.B619 1994, **(v3)**
  PN3503.B62 1993, **(v3)**
  PQ8498.32.A65.Z625 1994, **(v3)**
  PR888.P6.B66 1998, **(v3)**
  PR6019.O9.U6284 2000, **(v3)**
  PR6019.O9.Z52613 1995, **(v3)**
  PR6029.N56.Z55 1995, **(v3)**
  PR9344.B66 1998, **(v3)**
  PS374.S35.B66 2001, **(v3)**

Bookman, Milica Zarkovic. HC244.B695 1993, **(v6)**
  HD6056.B66 2000, **(v6)**
  JF1061.B66 1997, **(v7)**

Boole, George. BC135.B7 1940, **(v8)**
  BC51.B58 1998, **(v8)**
  BC199.M6.B65 1993, **(v8)**

Boomhower, Ray E. F526.B73 1997, **(v4)**

Boon, James A. DS647.B2.B67 1990, **(v5)**

Boone, Catherine. HC1045.B65 1992, **(v6)**

Boone, Elizabeth Hill. F1219.54.A98.B66 2000, **(v4)**

Boone, Joseph Allen. PN56.S5.B66 1997, **(v3)**
  PR830.L69.B6 1987, **(v3)**

Boone, Kristina. S494.5.C6B56 2000, **(v1)**

Boone, Margaret S. RJ60.U5.B66 1989, **(v2)**

Boone, Nathan. F454.B66.B66 1999, **(v4)**

Boone, William T. GV461.B66, **(v6)**

Boonin, David. B1248.E7 B66 1994, **(v8)**

Boor, Helmut de. PT85.B643, **(v3)**

Booraem, Hendrik. E687.B72 1988, **(v4)**
  E792.B66 1994, **(v4)**

Boorman, Howard L. DS778.A1.B6, **(v5)**

Boorse, Henry A. QC773.B66 1989, **(v1)**

Boorstin, Daniel J. B878.B6 1993, **(v8)**
  CB69.B66 1983, **(v5)**
  E169.1.B7513, **(v4)**
  E169.1.B752, **(v4)**
  E169.12.B655 1976, **(v4)**
  E188.B72, **(v4)**
  JA84.U5.B6, **(v7)**
  KD640.Z9.B66 1996, **(v7)**

Boorstin, Jon. PN1995.9.P7.B63 1990, **(v3)**

Boos, Florence Saunders. Z2014.W65.B66 1989, **(v10)**

Booth, Alan R. DT2714.B66 2000, **(v5)**

Booth, Alan. HC256.B68 2001, **(v6)**

Booth, Alison L. HD6664.B598 1995, **(v6)**

Booth, Alison. PR830.W6.B66 1992, **(v3)**

Booth, Douglas E. SD387.O43.B66 1994, **(v1)**

Booth, John A. F1439.5.B66 1989, **(v4)**

Booth, John E. PN2266.5.B66 1991, **(v3)**

Booth, John Wilkes. E457.5.B667 1997, **(v4)**

Booth, Ken. UA647.B575 1989, **(v10)**

Booth, Mark W. PR507.B63, **(v3)**

Booth, Michael R. PN2594.B58 1991, **(v3)**
  PR1271.B6, **(v3)**

Booth, Nicholas. QB501.B74 1996, **(v1)**

Booth, Philip E. PS3503.O532.A95, **(v3)**

Booth, Stephen. PR428.N65.B66 1998, **(v3)**

Booth, Wayne C. PN98.M67.B66 1988, **(v3)**

Boothby, William M. QA3.P8 vol. 63, **(v1)**

Boothroyd, G. (Geoffrey). TS17.4.B66 2002, **(v1)**

Bootle, R. P. HG229.B595 1996, **(v6)**

Bopp, Mary S. Z7514.D2.B6 1994, **(v10)**

Borchert, John R. F597.B67 1987, **(v4)**

Borchert, Wolfgang. PT2603.O725.A26, **(v3)**
  PT2603.O725A26 1971, **(v3)**
  PT2603.O725 1949, **(v3)**

Borch-Jacobsen, Mikkel. B2430.L146.B6713 1991, **(v8)**

Bordeau, Sanford P. QC507.B73 1982, **(v1)**

Bordicks, Katherine J. RB150.S5.B6 1980, **(v2)**

Bordin, Ruth Birgitta Anderson. LD7212.7 1882.B67 1993, **(v7)**

Bordley, James. R151.B58, **(v2)**

Bordman, Gerald Martin. ML410.K385.B7, **(v9)**
  ML1711.B66 1982, **(v9)**
  ML1711.B665 1985, **(v9)**
  ML1711.B67 2001, **(v9)**
  PN2256.B6 1994, **(v3)**
  PN2266.B64 1996, **(v3)**
  PN2266.3.B67 1995, **(v3)**

Bordua, David Joseph. HV7921.B6, **(v6)**

Bordwell, David. PN1993.5.H6.B63 2000, **(v3)**
  PN1993.5.U6.B655 1985, **(v3)**
  PN1995.B6174 1997, **(v3)**
  PN1998.3.E34.B67 1993, **(v3)**

Borek, David. TA409.B76 1986, **(v1)**

Borenstein, Audrey. HQ1426.B685 1983, **(v6)**

Borenstein, David G. RD771.B217B669 2001, **(v2)**

Borer, Tristan Anne. BR1450.B67 1998, **(v8)**

Boretz, Benjamin. ML55.B663 P5, **(v9)**

Borg, Carl Oscar. F786.B75, **(v4)**

Borg, Dorothy. DS740.5.U5.B6 1947a, **(v5)**

Borg, Dorothy. DS784.B65 1964, **(v5)**

Borg, Marcus J. BT303.2.B586 1994, **(v8)**

Borgerhoff, E. B. O. PQ245.B6 1968, **(v3)**

Borges, Jorge Luis. PN1064.B67 2000, **(v3)**
  PQ7761.G3.B6, **(v3)**
  PQ7797.B635.A17 1972, **(v3)**
  PQ7797.B635.A2 1978, **(v3)**
  PQ7797.B635.A2 1999, **(v3)**

Borghi, R. QD516.B6713 1998, **(v1)**

Borgiasz, William S. UG633.B682 1996, **(v10)**

Borgman, Christine L. ZA3225.B67 2000, **(v10)**

Borgmann, Albert. E169.12.B666 1992, **(v4)**

Bork, Robert H. HN59.2.B68 1996, **(v6)**

Bork, Robert H. KF5130.B59 1991, **(v7)**

Borklund, Carl W. UA23.6.B67 1991, **(v10)**

Borklund, Elmer. PS78.B56 1982, **(v3)**

Borland, Hal. PS3503.O563Z5, **(v3)**

Borman, Kathryn M. LC3731.B64 1998, **(v7)**

Bormann, F. Herbert. SB433.B64 1993, **(v1)**

Born, Daniel. PR878.G84.B67 1995, **(v3)**

Born, Max. QC6.B66 1962, **(v1)**
  QC71.B6653, **(v1)**
  QC71.B67, **(v1)**
  QC171.B63 1951, **(v1)**
  QC174.1.B64 1960, **(v1)**
  QC355.B63 1969, **(v1)**

Bornat, Richard. QA76.6.B66 1987, **(v1)**

Borneman, John. DS135.G5.A1263 1995, **(v5)**
  GN585.G4.B67 1992, **(v5)**

Bornet, Vaughn Davis. E847.B63 1983, **(v4)**

Borning, Bernard C. E175.5.B382, **(v4)**

Bornschier, Volker. HN16.B59913 1996, **(v6)**

Bornstein, Morris. HC336.23.B64 1970, **(v6)**

Borovsky, Victor. PN2727.B67 2001, **(v3)**

Borowitz, Albert. Z5703.B67 2002, **(v10)**

Borrelli, Robert L. QA371.B74 1987, **(v1)**

Borris, Kenneth. PR539.E7.B67 2000, **(v3)**

Borroff, Marie. PR2065.G31.B6, **(v3)**

Borsi, Franco. NA958.B6713 1987, **(v9)**
  NA1173.H6.B613 1991, **(v9)**

Borsody, Stephen. D443.B58, **(v5)**

Borsook, Eve. ND2756.T9.B6 1980, **(v9)**

Borst, Charlotte G. RG652.B65 1995, **(v2)**

Borstelmann, Thomas. E183.8.S6.B67 1993, **(v4)**

Borthwick, Mark. DS518.1.B64 1998, **(v5)**

Bortner, M. A. HV9104.B58 1997, **(v6)**

Borton, Hugh. DS835.B6 1970, **(v5)**

Borum, Poul. PT7671.B67, **(v3)**

Borza, Eugene N. DF261.M2.B67 1990, **(v5)**

Borzello, Frances. N71.B673 1998, **(v9)**
  N8354.B67 2000, **(v9)**

Boscagli, Maurizia. GT720.B67 1996, **(v6)**

Bose, Christine E. HD6058.B67 1985, **(v6)**

Bose, Meena. E835.B64 1998, **(v4)**

Bose, Sumantra. DS489.84.B67 1994, **(v5)**

Boserup, Ester. HB871.B587, **(v6)**
  HC59.7.B587 1990, **(v6)**

Bosher, J. F. DC148.B69 1988, **(v5)**

Bosquet, Alain. PQ3914.B6 1968, **(v3)**

Boss, Pauline. BF575.D35B67 1999, **(v2)**

Bossel, Hartmut. TA342.B67 1994, **(v1)**

Bosselmann, Peter. NA9031.B69 1998, **(v9)**

Bossier, Beverly Jo. GN480.B67 1998, **(v6)**

Bossu, M., 1720-1792. F372.B737 1962, **(v4)**

Bossuet, Jacques Benigne. D21.B745513 1976, **(v5)**

Bost, Théodore. F606.B75313, **(v4)**

Bostdorff, Denise M. E840.B66 1994, **(v4)**

Boston, Richard. PN1997.B6973.B68 1994, **(v3)**

Boston, Thomas D. HD2344.5.U62.A853 1999, **(v6)**
  HN90.S6.B67 1988, **(v6)**

Boswell, Jackson Campbell. Z8592.8.B67 1994, **(v10)**

Boswell, James. DC611.C811.B75, **(v5)**
  PR3325.A65 1951, **(v3)**
  PR3325.A8.T5, **(v3)**
  PR3325.A814 1989, **(v3)**
  PR3325.A823 1991, **(v3)**
  PR3325.A83 1966 vol. 2, **(v3)**
  PR3325.A88, **(v3)**
  PR3325.A885, **(v3)**
  PR3325.A887 1970, **(v3)**
  PR3325.A89, **(v3)**
  PR3325.A895, **(v3)**
  PR3325.A9, **(v3)**
  PR3325.A92, **(v3)**
  PR3533.B6 1970, **(v3)**

Boswell, Jeanetta. Z8393.B67 1982, **(v10)**
  Z8562.58.B67, **(v10)**
  Z8748.37.B67 1988, **(v10)**
  Z8971.5.B65, **(v10)**

Boswell, John. HQ76.3.E8.B67, **(v6)**

Boswell, Jonathan. JC328.2.B67 1990, **(v7)**

Boswell, Marshall. PS3571.P4.Z56 2001, **(v3)**

Bosworth, A. B. DF234.A773.B67, **(v5)**
  DF234.B66 1988, **(v5)**
  DF234.2.B67 1988, **(v5)**
  DF234.6.B67 1996, **(v5)**

Bosworth, Barry. HC110.S3.B67 1992, **(v6)**
  HC244.B699 1995, **(v6)**

Bosworth, Clifford Edmund. DS36.85.I8 no. 5, **(v5)**

Bosworth, R. J. B. DG568.5.B66 1983, **(v5)**
  DG571.16.B67 1998, **(v5)**

Boterbloem, Kees. DK511.K157.B68 1999, **(v5)**

Botero, Giovanni. JC158.B812 1956, **(v7)**

Botero, Rodrigo. E183.8.S7.B68 2001, **(v4)**

Bothun, Greg. QB981.B7274 1998, **(v1)**

Bothwell, Robert. E183.8.C2.B68 1992, **(v4)**

Bothwell, Robert. F1034.2.B67, **(v4)**

Botkin, Benjamin Albert. F128.B6, **(v4)**

Botkin, Daniel B. F598.B72 1999, **(v4)**
  QH31.T485, **(v1)**
  QK938.F6.B66 1993, **(v1)**

Botman, Selma. DT107.B58 1991, **(v5)**

Botsch, Robert Emil. RC965.C77.B68 1993, **(v2)**

Bott, Alexander J. KF4749.B625 1990, **(v7)**
Bott, Raoul. QA613.6.B67 1982, **(v1)**
Botta, Mario. NA1353.B67.A4 1987, **(v9)**
Botterill, George. BF38.B63 1999, **(v2)**
Bottero, Jean. DS69.5.B6813 1992, **(v5)**
Botti, Timothy J. UA23.B726 1996, **(v10)**
Bottigheimer, Karl S. DA910.B67 1982, **(v5)**
Bottigheimer, Ruth B. PT921.B67 1987, **(v3)**
Bottiglia, William F. PQ2099.B6, **(v3)**
Botting, Douglas. QL31.D87.B68 1999, **(v1)**
Botting, Fred. PN94.B67 2001, **(v3)**
  PR830.T3.B68 1996, **(v3)**
Botto, Francis. TK5105.875.I57.B64 1999, **(v1)**
Bottome, Phyllis. BF109.A4B62 1957a, **(v2)**
Bottomore, T. B. HM24.B619 1984, **(v6)**
Bottoms, Stephen J. PS3551.L25.W434 2000, **(v3)**
  PS3569.H394.Z63 1998, **(v3)**
Botwinick, Aryeh. BD215.B67 1997, **(v8)**
Botwinick, Aryeh. JF2051.B67 1990, **(v7)**
Bouce, Paul Gabriel. PR3696.B613, **(v3)**
Bouchard, Constance Brittain. CS587.B68 2001, **(v5)**
  DC33.2.B59 1998, **(v5)**
  HC277.B8.B67 1991, **(v6)**
Bouchard, Norma. PN771.B68 2000, **(v3)**
Boucher, Bruce. NA1123.P2.B68 1993, **(v9)**
Boucher, David. JC223.J662.B68 1994, **(v7)**
  JC257.C65.B68 1989, **(v7)**
Boucher, François. GT510.B6713 1987, **(v6)**
Boucher, Philip P. F1505.2.C3.B68 1992, **(v4)**
Boucher, Virginia. Z713.5.U6 B68 1997, **(v10)**
Boucher, Wayne I. Z8831.B68 1991, **(v10)**
Boucicault, Dion. PR4161.B2.A6 1984, **(v3)**
Boudreau, Gordon V. PS3048.B6 1990, **(v3)**
Boudreau, Tom. LA227.4.B67 1998, **(v7)**
Boughter, Judith A. E99.O4.B68 1998, **(v4)**
Boukreev, Anatoli. GV199.44.E85.B69 1997, **(v6)**
Boulanger, Norman. PN2091.E4.B59 1992, **(v3)**
Boulard, Garry. F379.N557.B68 1998, **(v4)**
Boulby, Mark. PT2617.E85.Z665, **(v3)**
Boulden, Jane. KZ6376.B68 2001, **(v7)**
Boulding, Elise. JZ5538.B68 2000, **(v7)**
Boulding, Kenneth Ewart. BD648.B66, **(v8)**
  CB425.B668, **(v5)**
  H83.B673, **(v6)**
  HB71.B658, **(v6)**
  HB171.5.B692 1966, **(v6)**
  HC51.B65 1972, **(v6)**
Boulding, Russell. TD878.B684 1995, **(v1)**
Boulez, Pierre. ML60.B71313 1991, **(v9)**
  ML60.B796.R43, **(v9)**
  PQ2603.O754P513 2000, **(v3)**
  PQ2603.O754.P62, **(v3)**
Bouloiseau, Marc. DC148.F7 1983 vol. 2, **(v5)**
Boulter, Clive A. QE36.B68 1989, **(v1)**
Boulton, Agnes. PS3529.N5.Z572 2000, **(v3)**
Boulton, Maureen Barry McCann. PQ151.B65 1993, **(v3)**
Boumelha, Penny. PR4169.B68 1990, **(v3)**
Bourassa, Robert. HD9685.C3.J363 1985, **(v6)**
Bourbaki, Nicolas. QA611.B65813, **(v1)**
Bourdet, Yves. HF1418.5.B68 1988, **(v6)**
Bourdier, Jean-Paul. NA1598.B68 1996, **(v9)**
Bourdieu, Pierre. PN4784.T4.B68 1998, **(v3)**
Bourdon, David. N6537.W28.B68 1989, **(v9)**
Boureau, Alain. BX958.F2.B6813 2001, **(v8)**
Bourgeois, Louise. NB237.B65.A2 1998, **(v9)**
  NB237.B65.A4 1994, **(v9)**
Bourgin, Frank. HC105.B77 1989, **(v6)**
Bourgois, Philippe I. HD8039.B232.C83 1989, **(v6)**
  HV5810.B68 1995, **(v6)**
Bourjaily, Vance Nye. PS3503.O77 C6, **(v3)**
  PS3503.O77 E5, **(v3)**
  PS3503.O77 V5, **(v3)**
Bourke, Paul. JS451.O79.W373 1995, **(v7)**
Bourke, Vernon Joseph. BD450.B64, **(v8)**
Bourke-White, Margaret. TR140.B6.A3, **(v1)**
Bourne, Edward Gaylord. E125.S7 B83 1973, **(v4)**
Bourne, Eulalia. F817.S25.B6, **(v4)**
Bourne, Kenneth. DA536.P2.B68 1982, **(v5)**
  DA550.B68 1970, **(v5)**
  E183.8.G7.B68 1967, **(v4)**

Bourque, Bruce J. E78.M2 B684 2001, **(v4)**
Bouse, Derek. TR893.5., **(v1)**
Bouson, J. Brooks. PR9199.3.A8.Z56 1993, **(v3)**
  PS3563.O8749.Z57 2000, **(v3)**
Boustani, Rafic. G1785.F3 1990, **(v6)**
Boutelle, Sara Holmes. NA737.M68.B68 1988, **(v9)**
Boutilier, Mary A. GV709.B66 1983, **(v6)**
Bouton, Cynthia A. HM283.B68 1993, **(v6)**
Bouton, Jim. GV865.B69.A3 1970, **(v6)**
Bouveresse, Jacques. BF175.4.P45.B6813 1995, **(v2)**
Bouvier, Leon F. HB3505.B67 1994, **(v6)**
Bouwsma, William James. BX9418.B715 1988, **(v8)**
  CB401.E94 2000, **(v5)**
Bouyer, Louis. BX4668.B67, **(v8)**
Bova, Ben. QC358.5.B68 1988, **(v1)**
Bove, Cheryl Browning. PR6063.U7.Z594 1993, **(v3)**
Bove, Emmanuel. PQ2603.O87.P513 1991, **(v3)**
Bovee, Warren G. PN4731.B675 1999, **(v3)**
Bovens, M. A. P. H97.B68 1996, **(v6)**
Bovis, H. Eugene. DS109.93.B68 1971, **(v5)**
Bovy, Piet H. L. HE336.R68.B68 1990, **(v6)**
Bowden, Betsy. PR1875.O73.B68 1987, **(v3)**
Bowden, Charles. F787.B69 1989, **(v4)**
Bowden, Henry Warner. BL72.B68 1993, **(v8)**
Bowden, John. BR95.B65 1991, **(v8)**
Bowden, K. F. GC150.5.B69 1983, **(v6)**
Bowden, Mark. DA3.P53.B69 1991, **(v5)**
Bowden, Muriel Amanda. PR1868.P8.B6 1954, **(v3)**
Bowden, Roger J. HB139.B69 1984, **(v6)**
Bowditch, Nathaniel H. HF3932.B69 1999, **(v6)**
Bowe, Richard. LC93.G7.B68 1992, **(v7)**
Bowen, Catherine Drinker. CS71.D77. 1970, **(v5)**
  CT21.B564, **(v5)**
  KD621.C64 B69 1990, **(v7)**
  KF8745.H6.B65 1944, **(v7)**
Bowen, David Warren. E667.B65 1989, **(v4)**
Bowen, Elizabeth. PN45.B62, **(v3)**
  PR6003.O6757.A15 1981, **(v3)**
  PR6003.O6757.A16 1950, **(v3)**
  PR6003.O6757.D4, **(v3)**
  PR6003.O6757.D45, **(v3)**
  PR6003.O6757.E3 1951, **(v3)**
  PR6003.O6757.E9 1968, **(v3)**
  PR6003.O6757.F7 1951, **(v3)**
  PR6003.O6757.H4 1949, **(v3)**
  PR6003.O6757.H6, **(v3)**
  PR6003.O6757.H6 1936, **(v3)**
  PR6003.O6757.H6 1972, **(v3)**
  PR6003.O6757.L3 1952, **(v3)**
  PR6003.O6757.T5, **(v3)**
  PR6003.O6757.T6, **(v3)**
  PR6003.O6757.W6, **(v3)**
  PR6003.O6757.Z52 1971, **(v3)**
Bowen, H. J. M. QD31.2.B68, **(v1)**
Bowen, H. V. DS471.B68 1991, **(v5)**
  JV1016.B69 1996, **(v7)**
Bowen, Howard Rothmann. LA227.3.B66, **(v7)**
Bowen, J. Donald. PC4137.B6, **(v3)**
Bowen, John. PR4588.B69 2000, **(v3)**
  PR6052.O85.B5, **(v3)**
  PR6052.O85.S8, **(v3)**
Bowen, Kurt Derek. HN400.3.A8.B69 1983, **(v6)**
Bowen, Marshall E. F849.W45.B68 1994, **(v4)**
Bowen, Thomas. F1221.S43.B69 2000, **(v4)**
Bowen, Wayne H. DD120.S7, **(v5)**
Bowen, William G. HD5724.B63, **(v6)**
  LB2351.2.B696 1998, **(v7)**
  LB2371.4.B68 1992, **(v7)**
Bowen, Zack R. PS3552.A75.Z56 1994, **(v3)**
Bower, Anne. PS374.E65.B69 1997, **(v3)**
Bower, T. G. R. BF318.B68 1989, **(v2)**
Bowers, Bege K. Z8164.B69 2002, **(v10)**
Bowers, C. A. GF27.B69 1993, **(v6)**
  LC191.B675 1987, **(v7)**
Bowers, Claude Gernade. E668.B7793, **(v4)**
Bowers, James R. KF5411.B69 1990, **(v7)**
Bowers, Jane Palatini. PS3537.T323.Z5578 1993, **(v3)**
  PS3537.T323.Z558 1991, **(v3)**
Bowers, Neal. PS3554.I32.Z57 1985, **(v3)**
Bowers,C.G. E311.B6587, **(v4)**
Bowes, Bryan G. QK642.B68 1996, **(v1)**

Bowes, Frederick Patten. F279.C45.B68 1978, **(v4)**
Bowie, Alasdair. HC441.B69 1997, **(v6)**
Bowie, Andrew. BH221.G33 B68 2003, **(v8)**
Bowie, Malcolm. PQ2631.R63.A7 1998, **(v3)**
Bowie, Theodore Robert. N6525.B6, **(v9)**
Bowker, Geoffrey C. BD175.B68 1999, **(v8)**
Bowker, Gordon. PR6023.O96.Z569 1995, **(v3)**
Bowker, John Westerdale. BS475.2.B69 1998, **(v8)**
Bowker, Lee H. HV8665.B68, **(v6)**
Bowker, Mike. DK510.764.B69 1997, **(v5)**
Bowker, Robert. DS119.7.B698 1996, **(v5)**
Bowlby, John. BF575.G7.B68 1969b, **(v2)**
  QH31.D2.B742 1991, **(v1)**
  RJ507.A77.B69 1988, **(v2)**
  CB59.B6 1963, **(v5)**
  JA83.B68, **(v7)**
  JC153.H66.B68 1969, **(v7)**
Bowler, Peter J. GE50.B68 1993, **(v6)**
  QH31.D2.B743 1991, **(v1)**
  QH361.B685 1996, **(v1)**
  QH361.B693 1988, **(v1)**
  QH428.B69 1989, **(v1)**
Bowles, Jane. PS3503.O837 1968, **(v3)**
Bowles, Joseph E. TA775.B63 1982, **(v1)**
Bowles, Paul. PS3552.O874.C64, **(v3)**
  PS3552.O874 D4, **(v3)**
  PS3552.O874.H8, **(v3)**
  PS3552.O874.L4, **(v3)**
  PS3552.O874.S48, **(v3)**
  PS3552.O874.S65, **(v3)**
  PS3552.O874 T53, **(v3)**
  PS3552.O874 U6, **(v3)**
Bowling, Barbara L. SB381.B68 2000, **(v1)**
Bowling, Kenneth R. F197.B69 1990, **(v4)**
Bowman, Barbara. PN1995.9.P7.B64 1992, **(v3)**
Bowman, Carl F. BX7815.B59 1995, **(v8)**
Bowman, D. M. J. S. QK431.B67 2000, **(v1)**
Bowman, Leslie Greene. NK1141.B64 1990, **(v9)**
Bowman, Mary Ann. Z7819.B68, **(v10)**
Bowman, Wayne D. ML3800.B79 1998, **(v9)**
Bown, Deni. SB351.H5B6464 2001, **(v1)**
Bown, Matthew Cullerne. N6988.B67 1991, **(v9)**
  ND688.B75 1998, **(v9)**
Bownas, Geoffrey. PL782.E3.B6, **(v3)**
Bowra, C. M. PN1271.B59 1967, **(v3)**
  PN1303.B67, **(v3)**
Bowring, Richard John. PL788.4.G43.B68 1988, **(v3)**
  PL811.O7.Z58, **(v3)**
Bowser, Charles W. F158.9.N4.B68 1989, **(v4)**
Bowser, Eileen. PN1993.5.U6.H55 1990 vol. 2, **(v3)**
Bowser, Pearl. PN1998.3.M494.B69 2000, **(v3)**
Bowsky, William M. DG535.B6, **(v5)**
Bowsky, William M. DG975.S5.B68 1981, **(v5)**
Boxer, C. R. DS796.M2.B59, **(v5)**
  F2528.B6 1962, **(v4)**
  JV2511.B67, **(v7)**
  JV4235.B6, **(v7)**
Boxer, Marilyn J. HQ1150.B63 2000, **(v6)**
  HQ1181.U5.B69 1998, **(v6)**
Boyajian, James C. HF3698.A78.B69 1993, **(v6)**
Boyce, Benjamin. PR3634.B65 1962, **(v3)**
Boyce, Charles. PR2892.B69 1990, **(v3)**
Boyce, David George. DA950.B69 1990, **(v5)**
  DA959.B69 1988, **(v5)**
Boyce, Gordon. HE823.B63 1995, **(v6)**
Boyce, Gray Cowan. Z6203.P25 1980 Suppl, **(v10)**
Boyce, Robert W. D. HF1533.B64 1987, **(v6)**
Boyce, William E. QA371.B773 1969, **(v1)**
Boyd, Andrew. G1035 .B6 1998, **(v6)**
Boyd, Belle. E608.B783 1968, **(v4)**
Boyd, Brian. PG3476.N3.Z59 1990, **(v3)**
  PS3527.A15.P3334 1999, **(v3)**
  PS3527.A15.Z646 1991, **(v3)**
Boyd, Carolyn P. LC93.S7.B69 1997, **(v7)**
Boyd, Claude E. SH137.4.B69 1995, **(v1)**
Boyd, Ernest Augustus. PR99.B6, **(v3)**
Boyd, James. PS3503.O885.D7, **(v3)**
Boyd, Jean Ann. ML3541.B69 1998, **(v9)**
Boyd, Loree. E99.M47.B69 1996, **(v4)**

Boyd, Malcolm. ML410.B1 B73 2000, (v9)
ML410.B13.B6 1993, (v9)
ML410.S221 B7 1987, (v9)
Boyd, Margaret Ann. TT12.B683 1999, (v1)
Boyd, Martin. PR6003.O693 W5, (v3)
Boyd, Minnie Clare. F326.B782, (v4)
Boyd, Robert T. E99.C58.B69 1996, (v4)
Boyd, Robin. NA1559.T33.B6, (v9)
Boyd, Todd. E169.04.B67 1997, (v4)
Boyd, William. LA13.B48 1975, (v7)
LB518.B66 1963, (v7)
RB111.S445 1992, (v2)
Boyden, Stephen Vickers. GF50.B67 1992, (v6)
GF50.B68 1987, (v6)
Boyd-Franklin, Nancy. RC451.5.N4.B69 1989, (v2)
Boydston, Jeanne. HD6073.H842.U625 1990, (v6)
HQ1236.5.U6.B69 1988, (v6)
Boyer, Carl B. QA303.B69, (v1)
Boyer, Ernest L. LA227.3.B678 1987, (v7)
Boyer, George R. HC254.5.B64 1990, (v6)
Boyer, Horace Clarence. ML3187.B7 1995, (v9)
Boyer, Jay. PN1998.3.L86.B69 1993, (v3)
Boyer, Jay. PN1998.3.R34.B68 1996, (v3)
Boyer, John W. DB854.B67 1995, (v5)
Boyer, M. Christine. NA9031.B72 1994, (v9)
Boyer, Paul S. BR526.B58 1992, (v8)
Boylan, Henry. CT862.B69 1998, (v5)
Boylan, Michael. QH442.B69 2001, (v1)
Boyle, Charles. T14.5.B69 1984, (v1)
Boyle, Daniel J. RC1218.C45.B69 1999, (v2)
Boyle, Deidre. PN1992.945.B68 1997, (v3)
Boyle, Francis Anthony. KZ1242.B69 1999, (v7)
Boyle, Frank. PR3728.S2, (v3)
Boyle, James. K1401.B69 1996, (v7)
Boyle, John Hunter. DS777.53.B65, (v5)
Boyle, John William. HD6670.3.B69 1988, (v6)
Boyle, Kay. PS3503.O9357 A6 1958, (v3)
PS3503.O9357 G4, (v3)
PS3503.O9357 S66, (v3)
Boyle, Kay. PS3503.O9357 T4 1946, (v3)
Boyle, Nicholas. PT2049.B53 1991, (v3)
Boyle, Peter G. E183.8.S65.B69 1993, (v4)
Boyle, Robert. BJ285.B69 1991, (v8)
PR4803.H44.Z59 1961, (v3)
QD27.B75, (v1)
Boyle, T. Coraghessan. PS3552.O932.D4, (v3)
Boyle, Thomas. PR878.S44.B69 1989, (v3)
Boyles, Deron. LC1085.2.B69 1998, (v7)
Boylestad, Robert L. TK454.B68 2000, (v1)
TK7867.B66 1999, (v1)
Boynton, Graham. DT1957.B68 1997, (v5)
Bozeman, Theodore Dwight. F7.B75 1988, (v4)
Bozo, Frederic. UA646.5.F7.B6913 2001, (v10)
Braaten, Jane. HM22.G3.H333 1991, (v6)
Brabant, Jozef M. van. HC244.B7273 1993, (v6)
HC244.B7274, (v6)
HC244.B72743 1998, (v6)
Brace, Paul. HJ9145.B73 1993, (v6)
Brack, Gene M. E183.8.M6.B72, (v4)
Bracken, Harry M. KF4772.B73 1994, (v7)
Bracken, James K. Z1225.B67 2001, (v10)
Z2011.B74 1998, (v10)
Brackenbury, John. QL496.7.B73 1992, (v1)
Brackenridge, J. Bruce. QB355.B694 1995, (v1)
Brackett, David. ML3470.B73 1995, (v9)
Brackett, Virginia. PN56.L6.B73 1999, (v3)
Brackman, Arnold C. QH31.D2B745 1980, (v1)
Brackman, Roman. DK268.S8.B69 2001, (v5)
Brackney, William H. BX6211.B73 1999, (v8)
Bracks, Lean'tin L. PS374.N4.B64 1997, (v3)
Bradbeer, J. W. QK740.B73 1988, (v1)
Bradbrook, M. C. PR423.B7 1982, (v3)
PR653.B67 1983, (v3)
PR658.T7.B7, (v3)
PR2335.B7 1965, (v3)
PR2894.B69 1978, (v3)
PR6023.O96.Z57, (v3)
PT8895.B67, (v3)
Bradburn, Norman M. HM261.B69 1988, (v6)
Bradbury, J. W. QL776.B73 1998, (v1)
Bradbury, Jim. UG444.B83 1992, (v10)

Bradbury, Malcolm. PR6003.R118.H5 1976, (v3)
PR6011.O58.Z64 1966, (v3)
PR6052.R246.R3 1983, (v3)
Bradbury, Nancy M. PR275.O72.B73 1998, (v3)
Bradbury, Nicola. Z8447.B73 1987, (v10)
Bradbury, Ray. PS3503.R167.A6 1980, (v3)
PS3503.R167.G6, (v3)
PS3503.R167.M3 1958, (v3)
PS3503.R167 S6, (v3)
Braddick, H. J. J. QC41.B7 1963, (v1)
Braddock, Theda. KF5624.B73 1995, (v7)
Braddon, M. E. PR4989.M4 A97 1979, (v3)
PR4989.M4.L2 1987, (v3)
Braddon-Mitchell, David. BD418.3.B72 1996, (v8)
Braden, Gordon. PN1181.B73 1999, (v3)
Bradford, Alfred S. U29.B73 2001, (v10)
Bradford, John. F454.B865 1993, (v4)
Bradford, Marlene. QC955.B72 2001, (v1)
Bradford, Sarah H. E444.T894, (v4)
Bradford, William. F68.B8 O73, (v4)
Bradie, Michael. BJ1298.B73 1994, (v8)
Brading, D. A. F1412.B79 1991, (v4)
Bradley, Alexander. PR5267.I8.B73 1987, (v3)
Bradley, Bill. GV884.B7.A34 1976, (v6)
Bradley, Carol June. ML111.B77 1990, (v9)
Bradley, Craig M. KF9223.B7 1993, (v7)
Bradley, David. PN2589.B73 1991, (v3)
PS3552.R226.S6, (v3)
Bradley, Denis J. M. BJ1278.5.T48.B73 1997, (v8)
Bradley, Edwin M. PN1995.9.M86.B73 1996, (v3)
Bradley, F. H. B1618.B73.E7 1914, (v8)
BD111.B8 1969, (v8)
BJ1008.B8 1962b, (v8)
Bradley, Glenn Danford. HE6375.B8 1960, (v6)
Bradley, J. F. N. DB205.B68 1971, (v5)
Bradley, James E. BR138.B69 1995, (v8)
DA480.B72 1990, (v5)
Bradley, James W. E99.O58.B7 1987, (v4)
Bradley, Jerry. PR605.M68.B73 1993, (v3)
Bradley, John R. PS2127.P8.B7 2000, (v3)
Bradley, John William. ND2890.B83, (v9)
Bradley, Mark. DS556.8.B732000, (v5)
Bradley, Omar Nelson. D756.B7, (v5)
Bradley, Patricia. E210.B73 1998, (v4)
Bradley, Peter T. F3444.B73 1990, (v4)
Bradley, Phil. ZA4201.B688 2002, (v10)
Bradley, Phil. ZA4201.B69 1999, (v10)
Bradley, Raymond S. QC884.B614 1999, (v1)
Bradley, Robert L. HD9566.B62 1996, (v6)
Bradney, Anthony. BX7748.D43, (v8)
Bradshaw, Gillian. PS3552.R235.H3, (v3)
Bradshaw, John L. QP385.5.B695 1993, (v1)
RC386.B72 1995, (v2)
Bradshaw, Leah. JC251.A74.B73 1989, (v7)
Bradshaw, Michael J. E179.5.B73 1988, (v4)
Bradu, Fabienne. PQ7133.B7 1987, (v3)
Brady, Ann P. PR4219.B7 1988, (v3)
Brady, Ben. PN1997.85.B73 1994, (v3)
Brady, Ciaran. DA935.B69 1994, (v5)
Brady, Clark A. PS3503.U687.Z58 1996, (v3)
Brady, David W. JK421.B73 1998, (v7)
Brady, Kathleen. PN2287.B16.B63 1994, (v3)
Brady, Kristin. PR4688.B73 1992, (v3)
Brady, Nyle C. S591.B79 2002, (v1)
Brady, Rose. HC340.12.B7 1999, (v6)
Brady, Thomas A. BR350.S78.B72 1997, (v8)
Braeman, John. E748.B48.B7, (v4)
KF4749.B647 1988, (v7)
Braff, Richard E. PN1999.U57.B73 1999, (v3)
Bragg, Melvyn. Q141.B777 1998, (v1)
Bragg, Rick. PN4874.B6625.A3 1997, (v3)
Bragg, Steven M. HF5686.M3.B68 1996, (v6)
Braginskiæi, S. V. HC340.12.B72 2000, (v6)
Braham, Allan. NA1046.B75, (v9)
Braham, Randolph L. DS135.H9.B74, (v5)
Brahms, Johannes. ML54.6.B82.G52 1999, (v9)
ML410.B8.A4 1997, (v9)
Brailsford, Dennis. GV706.5.B73 1990, (v6)
Brain, C. K. GN772.22.S6.B7, (v6)
Brain, Tracy. PS3566.L27.Z5827 2001, (v3)
Brainard, F. Samuel. BL51.B6487 2000, (v8)

Braine, John. PR6052.R265.F9, (v3)
PR6052.R265.L5, (v3)
PR6052.R265.R6, (v3)
PR6052.R265.V6, (v3)
Brainerd, Wesley. E523.5 50th.B73 1997, (v4)
Braithwaite, John. HV9275.B73 1989, (v6)
Braithwaite, Richard Bevan. BJ1533.F2.B7, (v8)
Braithwaite, Ronald L. RA448.5.N4.B73 2000, (v2)
Brake, Laurel. PN4759.B73 1994, (v3)
Bramall, Chris. HC427.92.B736 2000, (v6)
Bramly, Serge. N6923.L33.B7313 1991, (v9)
Brammer, Billy Lee. PS3552.R282G3 1995, (v3)
Brams, Steven J. H61.25.B7 1994, (v6)
UA10.5.B73 1988, (v10)
Bramson, Leon. U21.B637 1968, (v10)
Bramsted, Ernest Kohn. DD256.5.B674, (v5)
Bramwell, Anna. JA75.8.B73 1994, (v7)
Branch, Alan E. HE551.B52 1986, (v6)
HE567.B65, (v6)
Branch, Edward Douglas. F596.B82 1961, (v4)
Branch, Taylor. E185.61.B7914 1988, (v4)
E185.61.B7915 1998, (v4)
Brand, Laurie A. HQ1236.5.M8.B73 1998, (v6)
Brand, Max. PS3511.A87.L65 1997, (v3)
Brand, Paul W. R154.B779.A3 1993, (v2)
Brand, Stewart. BD638.B7 1999, (v8)
Brandeis, Louis Dembitz. E664.B819.A4 1971, (v4)
KF213.B68.L5 1996, (v7)
KF8745.B67.A4 1995, (v7)
Brandel, Rose. ML3740.B7, (v9)
Brander, Laurence. PR6029.R8.Z57, (v3)
Brander, Michael. SK21.B68, (v1)
Brandes, Georg Morris Cohen. PN766.B7 1975, (v3)
PR469.N3.B7, (v3)
PT8895.B75 1964, (v3)
Brandes, Stuart D. HC110.D4.B716 1997, (v6)
Brandon, George. BL2532.S3.B73 1993, (v8)
Brandon, James R. PJ433.B7, (v3)
PN1980.B63, (v3)
Brandon, Mark E. KF4541.B684 1998, (v7)
Brandon, William. F799.B813 1990, (v4)
Brands, H. W. D888.U6.B73 1989, (v5)
E183.7.B694 1998, (v4)
E183.8.I4.B73 1990, (v4)
E183.8.P6.B72 1992, (v4)
E302.6.F8.B83 2000, (v4)
E748.H412.B73 1991, (v4)
E846.B65 1995, (v4)
Brandt, Bill. TR653.B686 1999, (v1)
TR675.B65 1980, (v1)
Brandt, Conrad. DS740.5.R8.B7, (v5)
Brandt, E. N. HD9651.9.D6.B73 1997, (v6)
Brandt, Nat. F499.O2.B86 1990, (v4)
Brandt, Richard B. BJ37.B77, (v8)
BJ1012.B62 1996, (v8)
BJ1012.B63, (v8)
Brandt, Willy. DD260.8.B7413 1992, (v5)
DD857.B7.A3, (v5)
Branick, Vincent P. BS2330.2.B73 1998, (v8)
Branigan, Edward. PN1995.3.B73 1992, (v3)
Brann, Eva T. H. B105.I49 B72 1990, (v8)
BC199.N4 B73 2001, (v8)
Brannen, Daniel E. KF4550.Z9B73 2001, (v7)
Branner, H. C. PT8175.B743.A28, (v3)
Branner, Robert. NA440.B68, (v9)
Brannigan, John. PN81.B663 1998, (v3)
Branscomb, Anne W. KF2979.B67 1994, (v7)
Branscombe, Peter. ML410.M9.B76 1991, (v9)
Brant, Sebastian. PT1509.N49, (v3)
Brantley, Richard E. PR5592.R63.B73 1994, (v3)
Brantlinger, Patrick. PR469.I52.B73 1988, (v3)
PR469.P6.B65, (v3)
PR868.P68.B73 1998, (v3)
Branwhite, Tony. LB1027.55.B72 2000, (v7)
Braque, Georges. NE650.B58.H6, (v9)
Bras, Rafael L. GB661.2.B7 1990, (v6)
Brasch, Walter M. PS1813.B73 2000, (v3)
Brashear, Ronald. QB15.B67 2001, (v1)
Brasher, Brenda E. BL37.B73 2001, (v8)
Brasher, John Lawrence. BX8495.B754.B73 1994, (v8)

Braslow, Joel T. RC480.5.B725 1997, (v2)
Brass, Danny A. SF797.B73 1994, (v1)
Brasseaux, Carl A. F380.A2.B7 1992, (v4)
  F380.A2 B72 1987, (v4)
  F380.C87.B73 1994, (v4)
Braswell, Lauren. RJ496.A86.B73 1991, (v2)
Bratby, John. PR6052.R28.B73, (v3)
Bratby, John. PR6052.R285.B743, (v3)
Bratchel, M. E. DG975.L82.B73 1995, (v5)
Brathwaite, Kamau. PR9230.9.B68.A6 1973, (v3)
  PR9230.9.B68.M54 1992, (v3)
  PR9230.9.B68.M6, (v3)
  PR9230.9.B68.O8, (v3)
Bratton, William J. HV7911.B72.A3 1998, (v6)
Braudel, Fernand. D7.B7513, (v5)
  D973.A2.B7, (v5)
  DC20.5.B7313 1988, (v5)
Brauen, Martin. BQ5125.M3.B7313 1997, (v8)
Brauer, Carl M. E185.61.B7917, (v4)
Brauer, Erich. DS135.K8.B73 1993, (v5)
Braun, Barbara. N7428.5.B73 1993, (v9)
Braun, Dennis Duane. HC110.W4.B73 1991, (v6)
Braun, Dieter. DS341.B7313 1983, (v5)
Braun, Edward. PN2728.M4.B7 1995, (v3)
Braun, Hans-Joachim. HC286.B74 1990, (v6)
Braun, Hugh. NA963.B76 1968b, (v9)
Braun, Jerome. HD6955.B73 1995, (v6)
Braun, Kazimierz. PN2053.B628 2000, (v3)
  PN2859.P6.B74413 1996, (v3)
Braun, Sidney David. PQ41.B7 1971, (v3)
Braun, Stephen. QP801.A3.B73 1996, (v1)
Braun, Thom. PR4087.B7, (v3)
Braunbehrens, Volkmar. ML410.M9.B7813 1990, (v9)
  ML410.S16.B713 1992, (v9)
Braund, Kathryn E. Holland. E99.C9.B73 1993, (v4)
Braunfels, Wolfgang. NA9183.B7213 1988, (v9)
Braunmuller, A. R. PR2454.B73 1991, (v3)
Braunrot, Bruno. Z8730.B79 1994, (v10)
Braunthal, Gerard. JN3972.A979.B73 1996, (v7)
Brautigan, Richard. PS3503.R2736.A2, (v3)
  PS3503.R2736.A6 1969, (v3)
  PS3503.R2736.L6, (v3)
Braveboy-Wagner, Jacqueline Anne. F2131.B834 1989, (v4)
Braveman, Daan. KF1306.C64.B73 1989, (v7)
Braverman, Irwin M. RL100.B7 1998, (v2)
Bravman, Bill. DT433.545.T3.B73 1998, (v5)
Brawer, Moshe. G2110.B7 1994, (v6)
Brawley, Benjamin Griffith. PS1557.B7 1967, (v3)
Bray, Charles William. U22.3.B74 1969, (v10)
Bray, Charles. TP788.B73 2001, (v1)
Bray, Dennis. QH647.B73 2001, (v1)
Bray, Don E. TA417.2.B63 1997, (v1)
Bray, John. TK139.B73 1995, (v1)
Brayer, Elizabeth. TR140.E3.B73 1996, (v1)
Brazelton, T. Berry. BF720.P37.B72 1990, (v2)
Breakenridge, William M. F811.B82 1992, (v4)
Brealey, Richard A. Z7164.F5.B76 1991, (v10)
Brearton, Fran. PR8781.W68, (v3)
Breasted, James Henry. BJ132.B7 1934, (v8)
Brebner, John Alexander. PR6031.O867.Z58 1973b, (v3)
Brebner, John Bartlet. E183.8.C2.B74 1970, (v4)
  F1026.B84 1970, (v4)
  F1038.B815 1970, (v4)
Brecher, Charles. F128.52.B725 1993, (v4)
Brecher, Jeremy. HD5324.B7 1997, (v6)
  HD9539.B8.U538 1982, (v6)
Brecher, Michael. D443.B713 1988, (v5)
  D443.B7135 2000, (v5)
Brecht, Bertolt. PT2603.R397.A17 1960, (v3)
  PT2603.R397.A27, (v3)
  PT2603.R397A29, (v3)
  PT2603.R397.A29 1979, (v3)
  PT2603.R397.H3 1966, (v3)
  PT2603.R397.Z46313 1993, (v3)
Breckinridge, Scott D. JK468.I6.B74 1986, (v7)
Bredahl, A. Carl. PS3515.E37.G734 1990, (v3)
Bredbenner, Candice Lewis. KF4720.W6.B74 1998, (v7)
Bredero, Adriaan Hendrik. BR252.B7313 1994, (v8)

Bredeson, Carmen. TL796.3.B74 2000, (v1)
Bredon, Glen E. QA612.B74 1993, (v1)
Bredsdorff, Elias. PT7063.B7 1970, (v3)
  PT8119.B6532 1975, (v3)
Bredvold, Louis I. B2621.B68, (v8)
  PR448.S4.B7, (v3)
Bree, Germaine. PC2025.E8 no.45, (v3)
  PQ149.B7, (v3)
  PQ671.B7, (v3)
  PQ2605.A3734.Z555 1972, (v3)
  PQ2631.R63.A782 1969, (v3)
Bree, Linda. PR3459.F3.Z58 1996, (v3)
Breemer, Jan S. V859.S65.B74 1989, (v10)
Breen, T. H. F67.B83, (v4)
  F232.E2.B73, (v4)
  JK54.B74, (v7)
Breer, Paul E. BJ1461.B69 1989, (v8)
Breese, Gerald William. NA9040.B73, (v9)
Breeskin, Adelyn Dohme. NE539.C3.A4 1979, (v9)
Breger, Dee. QH251.B73 1994, (v1)
Breger, Irving A. QD255.B85, (v1)
Bregman, Ahron. DS119.76.B74 2000, (v5)
Brehm, John. HM261.B694 1993, (v6)
  JK768.4.B74 1997, (v7)
Breihan, Carl W. F594.J26, (v4)
Breiner, Laurence A. PR9212.B65 1998, (v3)
Breisach, Ernst. D13.B686 1983, (v5)
Breisch, Kenneth A. Z679.2.U54.B74 1997, (v10)
Breit, Harvey. PR473.B72, (v3)
Breitenberg, Mark. PR428.M37.B74 1996, (v3)
Breitmaier, E. QD476.B6713 1993, (v1)
Breitwieser, Mitchell Robert. E87.R895.B74 1991, (v4)
Breivik, Patricia Senn. Z711.2.B755 1998, (v10)
Bremen, Brian A. PS3545.I544.Z5766 1993, (v3)
Brement, Marshall. UA23.B782 1992, (v10)
Bremer, Richard G. HD1775.N2B73, (v6)
Bremner, J. Gavin. RJ134.B74 1994, (v2)
Bremner, John B. PE1116.J6.B7, (v3)
Bremner, Robert Hamlett. HV16.B74 1996, (v6)
  HV741.B77, (v6)
Brenan, Gerald. DP43.B66 1976, (v5)
Brend, Barbara. N6250.B76 1991, (v9)
Brende, Joel Osler. UB357.B74 1985, (v10)
Brendel, Alfred. ML60.B84 1990, (v9)
Brendler, Gerhard. BR325.B69513 1990, (v8)
Brendon, Piers. D727.B654 2000, (v5)
Brener, Milton E. ML1700.B79 1996, (v9)
Brengle, K. G. SB110.B685 1982, (v1)
Brenkman, John. HM101.B74 1987, (v6)
Brennan, Andrew. BC199.I4.B74 1988, (v8)
Brennan, Bernard P. B945.J24B7, (v8)
Brennan, Elizabeth A. AS911.P8.B74 1999, (v10)
Brennan, Joseph Gerard. BC108.B72 1961, (v8)
  PT2625.A44.Z543 1962, (v3)
Brennan, Maeve. PS3552.R38.C5, (v3)
Brennan, Mary C. JC573.2.U6.B74 1995, (v7)
Brennan, Richard P. QC15.B74 1997, (v1)
Brennan, Timothy J. HD9685.U5 B74 2002, (v6)
Brennan, Timothy. PR6068.U757.Z58 1989, (v3)
Brennan, Troyen A. R724.B73 1991, (v2)
Brennan, William J. KF213.B73.S47 1999, (v7)
Brenneman, James E. BS465.B74 1997, (v8)
Brenneman, Walter L. GR153.5.B74 1995, (v6)
Brenner, Charles. BF503.B73 1982, (v2)
Brenner, Clarence D. PQ1221.B7, (v3)
Brenner, Frederic. DS126.6.A2.B74 1998, (v5)
Brenner, Michael. DS135.G33.B74 1996, (v5)
Brenner, Morgan G. GV885.45.B74 1999, (v6)
Brenner, Reuven. HV6710.B74 1990, (v6)
Brenner, Robert L. QE651.B785 1988, (v1)
Brenner, Suzanne April. GN635.I65.B69 1998, (v6)
Brenner, William H. BC51.B664 1993, (v8)
Brenson, Michael. N8837.B74 2001, (v9)
Brent, Joseph. B945.P44 B74 1998, (v8)
Brentlinger, John. F1528.B74 1995, (v4)
Brereton, Geoffrey. PQ1303.B73 1973, (v3)
Bresee, Clyde. F279.C453.A227 1992, (v4)
Breslauer, S. Daniel. BM612.5.B74 1989, (v8)
Breslaw, Elaine G. F2230.2.A7.T573 1996, (v4)
Bresler, Fenton S. KD7975.B74 1988, (v7)

Breslow, Ronald. QD31.2.B75 1997, (v1)
Bressoud, David M. QA188.B73 1999, (v1)
  QA241.B788 2000, (v1)
Bretherick, L. T55.3.H3B73 1999, (v1)
Breton, Andre. PQ2603.R35.A6 1950, (v3)
  PQ2603.R35.C513 1995, (v3)
  PQ2603.R35.P3 1970, (v3)
  PQ2603.R35.P55, (v3)
  PQ2603.R35.R4, (v3)
  PQ2603.R35.V3 1955, (v3)
Breton, Raymond. F1035.A1.B7 1991, (v4)
Brett, Arlene. GV423.B74 1993, (v6)
Brett, Arlene. LC3969.5.B74 1995, (v7)
Brett, Guy. N6502.5.B74 1990, (v9)
Brett, Jeanne M. HD58.6.B74 2001, (v6)
Brett, Lewis Edward. PQ6226.B7 1935a, (v3)
Brettell, Richard R. ND553.P55.A4 1992, (v9)
Brettler, Marc Zvi. BS1197.B756 1995, (v8)
Bretton, Henry L. DD231.S83.B7, (v5)
Brettschneider, Corey Lang. JC578.B685 2001, (v7)
Bretzke, James T. Z7771.5.E84 B74 1997, (v10)
Breuer, William B. UB418.W65.B74 1997, (v10)
Brevard, Keziah Goodwyn Hopkins. F279.C7.B74 1993, (v4)
Breward, Christopher. GT511.B74 1995, (v6)
Brewer Carias, Allan-Randolph. K3175.B74 1989, (v7)
Brewer, Annie M. PN1991.8.T35.B74 1992, (v3)
Brewer, Anthony. HB501.M37.B73 1984, (v6)
Brewer, Gay. PN1998.3.M344.B74 1993, (v3)
Brewer, James Gordon. Z6001.B74 1978, (v10)
Brewer, John D. BX1766.B74 1998, (v8)
  HV8272.A2.B74 1994, (v6)
Brewer, John. DA510.B67, (v5)
Brewer, Priscilla J. GT425.U5, (v6)
Brewer, W. F326.B84 1975, (v4)
Brewer, William D. PR5438.B735 1994, (v3)
Brewington, M. V. F187.C5 B7 1956, (v4)
Brewster, Ben. PN1995.25.B74 1997, (v3)
Brewster, Charles Harvey. E513.5 10th.B74 1992, (v4)
Brewster, Dorothy. PR6045.O72.Z562, (v3)
Breyer, Chloe. BV4070.G48, (v8)
Breyer, Stephen G. KF3958.B74 1993, (v7)
Breyman, Steve. JZ5584.G3.B74 1998, (v7)
Breytenbach, Breyten. PT6592.12.R4.E5 1987, (v3)
  PT6592.12.R4Z475 1985, (v3)
Brezhneva, Luba. DK275.B73.A3 1995, (v5)
Brezianu, Andrei. DK509.37.B74 2000, (v5)
Brezonik, Patrick L. GB855.B74 1994, (v6)
Brian, Denis. CT21.B65 1994, (v5)
  QC16.E5.B737 1996, (v1)
Brick, Howard. E169.12.B6946 1998, (v4)
Bricker, David C. LB1584.B67 1989, (v7)
Brickhouse, Thomas C. B317.P68 2000, (v8)
  B365.B74 1989, (v8)
Brickman, William W. LA9.B68 1982, (v7)
  LA621.B74 1985, (v7)
  Z5815.S66.B75 1992, (v10)
Bridenbaugh, Carl. E191.B75 1955, (v4)
  F82.B73, (v4)
  F234.J3.B7, (v4)
  F2131.B84, (v4)
Bridge, F. R. DB86.B74 1990, (v5)
Bridge, Lawrence Wilford. JF515.B78, (v7)
Bridge, Susan. PN4888.T4.B75 1998, (v3)
  HQ1240.5.S65.B75 1987, (v6)
Bridges, D. S. QA300.B69 1998, (v1)
Bridges, E. M. GB401.5.B75 1990, (v6)
Bridges, Flora Wilson. BR563.N4.B67 2001, (v8)
Bridges, Robert Seymour. PR4161.B6.A6 1955, (v3)
  PR4161.B6.S5 1993, (v3)
  PR4161.B6.T4 1930, (v3)
  PR4161.B6.Z53, (v3)
Bridges, Thomas. JC585.B647 1994, (v7)
Brienzo, Gary. PS3505.A87.Z5836 1994, (v3)
Brier, Peter A. PS3519.O425.Z55 1994, (v3)
Briere, John. RC552.P67.B75 1997, (v2)
  RC569.5.C55.B75 1992, (v2)
Brietzke, Zander. PS3529.N5.Z5745 2001, (v3)
Briggs, Amy Thompson. KF287.B75 1998, (v7)

Briggs, Asa. DA530.B68, (v5)
 DA550.B75 1989, (v5)
Briggs, Asa. DA560.B84 1970, (v5)
Briggs, D. QK983.B73 1997, (v1)
Briggs, Diane. Z718.3.B75 1997, (v10)
Briggs, Emily Edson. [from old catalog]. F198.B85, (v4)
Briggs, Geoffrey. QB605.B74 1982, (v1)
Briggs, Gerald G. RJ216.B85 1997, (v2)
Briggs, Hilton Marshall. SF105.B7 1980, (v1)
Briggs, John W. F130.I8.B74, (v4)
Briggs, John. Q172.5.C45.B75 1989, (v1)
Briggs, Julia. PR4149.B4.Z59 1987, (v3)
Briggs, Kenneth A. BX1406.2.B75 1992, (v8)
Briggs, Lawrence Palmer. Q11.P6 n.s., vol.41, pt.1, (v1)
Briggs, Mark K. QH104.5.S6.B77 1996, (v1)
Briggs, Philip J. E744.B698 1991, (v4)
Briggs, Robin. DC110.B723 1998, (v5)
Briggs, Shirley A. RA1270.P4.B73 1992, (v2)
Briggs, Vernon M. HD8081.A5.B75 2001, (v6)
Brigham, E. Oran. QA403.B75 1988, (v1)
Brigham, John. KF384.B75 1996, (v7)
Brigham, Johnson. F621.B85, (v4)
Brighouse, Harry. LB1027.9.B75 2000, (v7)
Bright, Charles. HV9475.M52.M533 1996, (v6)
Bright, James Wilson. PE137.B7 1971, (v3)
Bright, Michael. PR4241.B75 1996, (v3)
Bright, William. F859.G8 1998, (v4)
Brightfield, Myron Franklin. PN81.B67, (v3)
Brightman, Carol. PS3525.A1435.Z59 1992, (v3)
Briles, Judith. R692.B745 1994, (v2)
Briley, Rebecca Luttrell. PS3511.O344.Z59 1993, (v3)
Brilliant, Richard. N7575.B75 1991, (v9)
Brillouin, Leon. QC6.B72, (v1)
Brimson, James A. HF5686.C8.B674 1991, (v6)
 HF5686.C8.B6743 1999, (v6)
Brindle, Margaret. HD31.B7417 2001, (v6)
Brink, Andre Philippus. PN3491.B75 1998, (v3)
 PT6592.12.R5.L6, (v3)
Brink, Andrew. PR888.O28.B75 1995, (v3)
Brink, C. O. PA6393.E7.B7, (v3)
Brink, Carol Ryrie. PZ7.B78Cad5, (v3)
Brink, David Owen. BJ1012.B676 1989, (v8)
Brink, J. R. PR2258.B7 1990, (v3)
Brink, Lars. QC794.6.S85.B75 1988, (v1)
Brink, Pamela J. RT81.5.B74 1994, (v2)
Brinkley, Alan. E178.1.B827 1993, (v4)
Brinkley, Alan. E806.B75 1982, (v4)
Brinkley, Douglas. E748.A15.B75 1992, (v4)
Brinkley, Roberta Florence. PR438.A7B7, (v3)
Brinkmann, Hennig. PF3105.B7, (v3)
Brinkmann, Roland. QE260.B723, (v1)
Brinkmeyer, Robert H. PS3565.C57.Z587 1989, (v3)
Brinner, Benjamin Elon. ML3838.B76 1995, (v9)
Brinnin, John Malcolm. PR6039.H52.Z6, (v3)
Brint, Michael. JA75.7.B75 1991, (v7)
Brint, Steven G. HT687.B75 1994, (v6)
Brint, Steven G. LA226.B74 1989, (v7)
Brinton, Crane. B802.B7, (v8)
 BD431.B77, (v8)
 BJ71.B69 1959, (v8)
 DC255.T3.B7, (v5)
 PR457.B7 1962, (v3)
Brion, Marcel. N6450.B52, (v9)
Brisbin, Richard A. KF8745.S33.B75 1997, (v7)
Briscoe, James R. ML134.D26.B7 1990, (v9)
Brisebois, Michel. Z483.B75 1993, (v9)
Brisk, Maria. LC3731.B684 2000, (v7)
Brisman, Shimeon. Z6366.B8 2000, (v10)
Brison, Karen J. DU740.42.B75 1992, (v5)
Brisson, Luc. B387.B7313 1995, (v8)
Bristol, Evelyn. PG3041.B67 1990, (v3)
Bristow, Geoff. TK7882.S65.B75 1984, (v1)
Bristow, Gwen. PS3503.B778, (v3)
Bristow, J. A. HC403.B75 1996, (v6)
Bristow, Joseph. PR468.H65.B75 1995, (v3)
Bristow, Nancy K. UH630.B75 1996, (v10)
British Bombing Survey Unit. D786.B718 1998, (v5)
British Library. PR1203.W67, (v3)
Britnell, R. H. DA425.B8 1997, (v5)

HF3505.B75 1993, (v6)
Brittain, Vera. D640.A2.B75 1999, (v5)
Britten, Benjamin. ML410.B853.A4 1991, (v9)
Britten, Thomas A. D570.8.I6.B75 1997, (v5)
Brittlebank, Kate. DS470.T6 B75 1997, (v5)
Britton, Andrew. PN2287.H45.B75 1995, (v3)
Britton, Celia. PQ671.B74 1992, (v3)
 PQ2637.I547.Z6 1987, (v3)
Britton, Derek. PR6023.A93.L3127 1988, (v3)
Britton, John A. F1234.B855 1995, (v4)
Brivati, Brian. DA566.9.G3.B75 1996, (v5)
Brivic, Sheldon. PR6019.O9.F563 1995, (v3)
Broad, C. D. B1618.B75.R4 1969, (v8)
Broad, Lewis. PR5366.A23 1972, (v3)
Broad, Robin. GF669.4.B75 1993, (v6)
Broadbent, Ewen. UA647.B857 1988, (v10)
Broadbent, Geoffrey. NA9053.S6.B76 1990, (v9)
Broaddus, Dorothy C. PS255.B6.B76 1999, (v3)
Broaddus, James W. PR2358.B73 1995, (v3)
Broadie, Alexander. BC34.B76 1993, (v8)
Broadwater, Jeff. E748.S84.B65 1994, (v4)
Broch, Hermann. PT2603.R64.S7, (v3)
 PT2603.R657 S541, (v3)
 PT2603.R657 T613, (v3)
Brock, Arthur John. R126.A1.B7613 1972, (v2)
Brock, Clifton. E743.B76 1985, (v4)
Brock, Dan W. R724.B753 1993, (v2)
Brock, Gerald W. HE7781.B75 1994, (v6)
Brock, Peter. JZ5560.B76 1999, (v7)
Brock, Thomas D. QH434.B76 1990, (v1)
Brock, W. H. QD11.B76 1993, (v1)
Brock, William Ranulf. HV91.B696 1988, (v6)
Brockelmann, Carl. DS38.B72, (v5)
Brockington, A. Allen. PR4231.B65 1963, (v3)
Brockington, J. L. PK2917.B76 1998, (v3)
Brockman, C. Frank. GV191.67.W5.B76 1979, (v6)
Brockman, Harold Alfred Nelson. PR4092.B7, (v3)
Brockman, Norbert C. BL580.B76 1997, (v8)
Brockman, Richard. RC337.B75 1998, (v2)
Brockman, William S. ML113.B85 1987, (v9)
Brockner, Joel. HF5548.8.B686 1988, (v6)
Brock-Sulzer, Elisabeth. PT2607.U493.Z57, (v3)
Brockunier, Samuel Hugh. F82.W718, (v4)
Brod, Harry. JC233.H46.B76 1992, (v7)
Brod, Max. PT2328.B652, (v3)
 PT2621.A26.Z62 1960, (v3)
Broda, Johanna. F1219.1.M5.B76 1988, (v4)
Brode, Douglas. PR3093.B76 2000, (v3)
Broder, Patricia Janis. N6538.A4 B7, (v9)
Broderick, Damien. PN3433.5.B76 2000, (v3)
Broderick, Francis L. E303.B85, (v4)
 E765.B76 1989, (v4)
Brodeur, Arthur Gilchrist. PR1585.B68, (v3)
Brodhead, Michael J. KF8745.B7.B76 1994, (v7)
Brodhead, Richard H. PS201.B68 1993, (v3)
Brodie, Bernard. UA11.B7, (v10)
 V25.B7 1969, (v10)
 V163.B76 1977, (v10)
Brodie, Fawn McKay. E332.B787, (v4)
 E856.B74 1981, (v4)
 G246.B8.B7, (v6)
Brodkey, Harold. PS3552.R6224.S7 1988, (v3)
Brodkin, Karen. E184.J5.B7415 1998, (v4)
Brodman, James. HV344.C37.B76 1998, (v6)
Brodo, Irwin M. QK586.5.B76 2001, (v1)
Brodsky, G. W. Stephen. UA649.B87 1988, (v10)
Brodsky, Joseph. PG3479.4.R64A25 1973, (v3)
Brodsky, Joseph. PS3552.R6229A6 2000, (v3)
Brodsky, Louis Daniel. PS3511.A86.Z6355 1990, (v3)
Brodsky, Patricia Pollock. PT2635.I65.Z6287 1988, (v3)
Brody, Baruch A. R725.5.B76 1988, (v2)
Brody, David. HD6508.B8113, (v6)
Brody, Elaine. ML2829.B76, (v9)
Brody, Howard. R724.B77 1992, (v2)
Brody, J. J. E99.M76.B766 1996, (v4)
 E99.P9.B73 1990, (v4)
 E99.P9.B732 1991, (v4)
Brody, J. Kenneth. D727.B655 1999, (v5)
Brody, Jennifer DeVere. PR468.B53.B76 1998, (v3)
Brody, Miriam. PE1404.B74 1993, (v3)

Brody, Richard A. JK518.B77 1991, (v7)
Brody, Saul Nathaniel. RC154.1.B76, (v2)
Brody, Stuart. RA644.A25.B745 1997, (v2)
Brody, Sylvia. BF723.I6.B67, (v2)
Brody, T. A. QC6.B727 1993, (v1)
Broek, David. TA409.B773 1988, (v1)
Broer, Lawrence R. PS3572.O5.Z55 1989, (v3)
Broer, Marion Ruth. QP301.B88 1979, (v1)
Broers, Michael. DG618.6.B76 1997, (v5)
Brogan, D. W. DC335.B75 1966, (v5)
 JK268.B72 1969, (v7)
Brogan, Kathleen. PS153.M56.B76 1998, (v3)
Brogden, Michael. HV6626.3.B73 2000, (v6)
Brogger, Anton Wilhelm. VM17.B715 1971, (v10)
Brohm, Jean-Marie. GV706.5.B7613, (v6)
Brokaw, Cynthia Joanne. BJ117.B76 1991, (v8)
Broker, Ignatia. E99.C6.B79 1983, (v4)
Bromberg, Joan Lisa. QC791.73.B76 1982, (v1)
 TL521.312.B76 1999, (v1)
Bromberg, Ruth. NE642.S52, (v9)
Bromberger, Sylvain. B29.B7442 1992, (v8)
Brombert, Victor H. PN761.B76 1999, (v3)
 PQ282.B75 1988, (v3)
 PQ637.I5.B7, (v3)
 PQ2304.M88.B76 1984, (v3)
Brome, Alexander. PR3326.B36.A17 1982, (v3)
Brome, Richard. PR2439.B5.E5 1983, (v3)
Bromfield, Louis. PS3503.R66.B7, (v3)
 PS3503.R66 E3, (v3)
 PS3503.R66 F3 1946, (v3)
 PS3503.R66G73, (v3)
 PS3503.R66 M48, (v3)
Bromfield, Richard. RJ504.B758 1997, (v2)
Bromley, Roger. PN1998.3.W46.B76 2001, (v3)
Bromwich, David. LC89.B745 1992, (v7)
 PR5888.B76 1998, (v3)
Brondfield, Jerry. GV939.H35B76, (v6)
Bronner, Simon J. GR55.S53.B76 1996, (v6)
Bronner, Stephen Eric. B809.3.B76 2002, (v8)
Bronowski, Jacob. BD450.B653 2002, (v8)
 CB478.B73 1978, (v5)
 NX65.B696 1978, (v9)
 Q175.B7918 1974, (v1)
Bronson, Bertrand Harris. ML3650.B82, (v9)
 PR1924.B76, (v3)
Bronson, F. H. QL739.2.B76 1989, (v1)
Bronstein, Arthur J. PE1137.B77, (v3)
Bronstein, Daniel J. B21.B7 1955, (v8)
Bronstein, Jamie L. HD1333.G7.B76 1999, (v6)
Bronstone, Adam. D1065.U5.B67 1997, (v5)
Bronte, Anne. PR4162.A2.S5 1924, (v3)
 PR4162.A54 1988, (v3)
 PR4162.T3, (v3)
Bronte, Charlotte. PR4165.A4 1971, (v3)
 PR4165.E54.B76 1996, (v3)
 PR4166.A44 1987, (v3)
 PR4166.N48 1985, (v3)
 PR4166.W5 1984, (v3)
 PR4167.L4 1933, (v3)
 PR4167.P7 1987, (v3)
 PR4167.V5, (v3)
 PR4168.A44 1995, (v3)
 PR4167.J3 1971, (v3)
Bronte, Emily. PR4172.A1 1941, (v3)
 PR4172.W8 1972, (v3)
Bronte, Patrick Branwell. PR4174.B23.A6 1990, (v3)
 PR4174.B23.H34 1993, (v3)
 PR4174.B23 1997, (v3)
Brook, Andrew. B2799.M52.B76 1994, (v8)
 BD161.B459 2000, (v8)
Brook, Timothy. DS753.B76 1998, (v5)
 DS779.32.B76 1992, (v5)
Brooke, Christopher Nugent Lawrence. DA28.1.B7 1963, (v5)
 HC258.L6.B76, (v6)
Brooke, John Hedley. BL245.B77 1991, (v8)
Brooke, John. F72.W9.B76 1989, (v4)
Brooke, L. Leslie. PZ10.3.B7593Jo, (v3)
Brooke, Rupert. PR6003.R4.Z483 1998, (v3)
 PR6003.R4.Z515 1968b, (v3)
 PR6003.R4 1946, (v3)

Brooke, Stopford Augustus. PR508.N25.B7 1920, (v3)
Brooke, Z. N. D117.B7 1969, (v5)
Brooker, Jewel Spears. PS3509.L43.W3634 1990, (v3)
PS3509.L43.Z64545 1994, (v3)
Brooker, Paul. D445.B765 1997b, (v5)
Brooker, Peter. HM101.B775 1999, (v6)
Brooker, Peter. PS255.N5.B76 1996, (v3)
Brookes, Martin. QH428.B766 2001, (v1)
Brookes, Tim. RC591.B765 1994, (v2)
Brookfield, Stephen. LB2331.B677 1995, (v7)
Brookhiser, Richard. E302.6.H2.B76 1999, (v4)
Brooking, Annie. HD53.B76 1997, (v6)
Brooklyn Museum. N6510.B75 1979, (v9)
Brookner, Anita. PR6052.R5816.D4 1981, (v3)
PR6052.R5816.F3 1985b, (v3)
PR6052.R5816.H66 1984, (v3)
PR6052.R5816.P75 1984, (v3)
Brooks De Vita, Alexis. PL8010.B76 2000, (v3)
Brooks, Barbara J. DS849.C6.B67 2000, (v5)
Brooks, Bryant B. F761.B85, (v4)
Brooks, Charles B. E356.N5.B7, (v4)
Brooks, Charles E. F127.H7.B76 1996, (v4)
Brooks, Charles R. BL1285.832.V75.B76 1989, (v8)
Brooks, Chris. NX449.7.G68.B76 1999, (v9)
Brooks, Cleanth. PN1136.B75, (v3)
PN1657.B7 1948, (v3)
PN1892.B7, (v3)
PR502.B7 1956, (v3)
PR545.H5.B7 1991, (v3)
PR1109.B676 1976, (v3)
PS29.B74.A4 1998, (v3)
PS261.B75 1995, (v3)
PS3511.A86.Z6384 1987, (v3)
Brooks, D. R. QH371.B69 1986, (v1)
Brooks, Douglas. GV481.B76 1998, (v6)
Brooks, Drex. E81.B7 1995, (v4)
Brooks, Frederick P. QA76.758.B75 1995, (v1)
Brooks, Gwendolyn. PS3503.R7244.A6 1963, (v3)
PS3503.R7244.A7 1971, (v3)
PS3503.R7244.M28 1974, (v3)
PS3503.R7244.Z524, (v3)
Brooks, H. Allen. NA1053.J4.B76 1997, (v9)
Brooks, Harold Fletcher. PR1868.P8.B7, (v3)
Brooks, John Langdon. QH31.W2.B76 1984, (v1)
Brooks, Paul. F74.C8.B79 1990, (v4)
Brooks, Peter. PN56.C67.B76 2000, (v3)
Brooks, Robert Preston. HD1775.G4.B74 1970, (v6)
Brooks, Rodney Allen. TJ211.B695 1999, (v1)
Brooks, Roy L. E185.615.B729 1996, (v4)
Brooks, Van Wyck. PS121.B7, (v3)
Brooks, Walter R. PZ7.B7994Frj 1997, (v3)
Brooks-Davies, Douglas. PR2358.B75 1977, (v3)
Brookshire, Jerry H. DA585.A8.B77 1995, (v5)
Brookshire, Robert H. RC423.B74 2003, (v2)
Broome, J. H. B2137.B7 1963, (v8)
Broome, Peter. PQ2625.I2.Z585 1977, (v3)
Broome, Richard. GN665.B76 1982, (v6)
Broonzy, Big Bill. ML420.B78.A3 1964, (v9)
Brophy, Alfred L. F704.T92 B76 2002, (v4)
Brophy, Brigid. PR6052.R583.F, (v3)
PR6052.R583.H3, (v3)
PR6052.R583.I5, (v3)
PR6052.R583.SN6, (v3)
Brophy, Elizabeth Bergen. PR858.W6.B76 1991, (v3)
PR3667.B68 1987, (v3)
Brophy, John. PR6003.R426 F76, (v3)
Brose, David S. E78.E2.B76 1985, (v4)
Brosius, J. Peter. DS666.A3.B76 1990, (v5)
Brosnan, Jim. GV865.B75.A3, (v6)
Brosseau, Mathilde. NA744.5.G67.B76 1980, (v9)
Brothwell, Don R. CC75.B73 1970, (v5)
GN780.22.G7.B76 1987, (v6)
Brottman, Mikita. PN1995.9.H6.B67 1997, (v3)
Brotton, Jerry. GA201.B75 1998, (v6)
Broude, Gwen J. GN480.B76 1994, (v6)
HQ767.84.B76 1995, (v6)
Broude, Norma. ND547.5.I4.B76 1991, (v9)
ND617.5.M3.B7 1987, (v9)
Broughton, Rhoda. PR4174.B56.B4, (v3)

Broughton, T. Alan. PS3552.R68138.F3, (v3)
Broughton, T. Robert S. DG83.5.A1.B73, (v5)
Broughton, Trev Lynn. PR788.B56.B76 1999, (v3)
Broun, Elizabeth. ND237.R8.A4 1989, (v9)
Broun, Kenneth S. KTL105.B76 2000, (v7)
Broussard, Albert S. F869.S39.N424 1993, (v4)
Brouwer, Dirk. QB351.B7 1961, (v1)
Brow, James. GN635.S72.B76 1996, (v6)
Browder, Andrew. QA300.B727 1996, (v1)
Browder, John O. HT169.A5.B76 1997, (v6)
Browder, Laura. PS228.R34.B76 1998, (v3)
Browder, Robert Paul. E183.8.R9.B7, (v4)
Brower, David Ross. QH31.B859.A3 1990, (v1)
SK601.B84, (v1)
SK601.B845, (v1)
Brower, James E. QH541.28.B76 1984, (v1)
Brower, Reuben Arthur. PR67.B7, (v3)
Brower, Robert Hopkins. PL865.B7, (v3)
Brown, Alice. JN1213.B76 1996, (v7)
Brown, Alison Leigh. PN151.B795 1995, (v3)
Brown, Andrew P. QC774.C43.B76 1997, (v1)
Brown, Anthony Cave. UB271.R92.P432 1994, (v10)
Brown, Anthony E. Z8110.2.B75 1991, (v10)
Brown, Archie. DK288.B76 1996, (v5)
Brown, Arthur. PR127.N8.B66, (v3)
Brown, Beverly A. HN79.O72.R633 1995, (v6)
Brown, Bruce Alan. ML410.M9.B819 1995, (v9)
Brown, Canter. F316.H34.B76 1997, (v4)
F317.P37.B76 1991, (v4)
F319.T2.B76 1999, (v4)
F319.T2 B765 2000, (v4)
Brown, Carleton Fairchild. PR1191.B75, (v3)
PR1203.B68, (v3)
Brown, Catherine L. Z7164.U7.B69 1989, (v10)
Brown, Chandos Michael. Q143.S56.B76 1989, (v1)
Brown, Charles Brockden. PS1130.F63, (v3)
PS1130.F77, (v3)
PS1130.O7 1962, (v3)
PS1134.W5, (v3)
Brown, Charles C. BX4827.N5.B76 1992, (v8)
Brown, Charles Henry. E717.B7, (v4)
Brown, Charles Robert. QL696.P247.B76 1996, (v1)
Brown, Christopher K. G465.B765 2000, (v6)
Brown, Christopher. ND673.D9.A4 1999a, (v9)
Brown, Claude. E185.97.B86.A3, (v4)
Brown, Clifford W. JK1991.B76 1995, (v7)
Brown, Clive. ML457.B76 1999, (v9)
Brown, Colin D. TN609.B76 1998, (v1)
Brown, Courtney. JK1965.B74 1991, (v7)
Brown, Cynthia Jane. PN144.B76 1995, (v3)
Brown, D. A. QE340.B7 1968, (v1)
Brown, D. Clayton. HD9688.U52.B76, (v6)
Brown, Daniel J. LB2844.1.V6.B76 1998, (v7)
Brown, David Alan. ND623.L5.B78 1998, (v9)
ND623.L8.A4 1997, (v9)
Brown, David E. QH102.B76 1998, (v1)
T20.B76 2002, (v1)
Brown, David J. TG300.B76 1993, (v1)
Brown, David K. LB2390.B76 1995, (v7)
Brown, David. BT28.B75 1987, (v8)
ML410.C4 B74, (v9)
ML410.M97 B75 2002, (v9)
Brown, Dee Alexander. E81.B75 1971, (v4)
F596.B864 1991, (v4)
Brown, Deming. PG3022.B68, (v3)
PG3098.4.B76 1993, (v3)
Brown, Dona. G155.U6.B76 1995, (v6)
Brown, Dorothy H. PR649.R4.B76 1999, (v3)
Brown, Dorothy M. BX2347.8.P66.B76 1997, (v8)
Brown, Edward James. PG3022.B7 1982, (v3)
Brown, Emily Clark. HD6732.B7, (v6)
Brown, Fahamisha Patricia. PS310.N4.B76 1999, (v3)
Brown, Frank Edward. NA310.B75, (v9)
Brown, Frederic Joseph. UG447.B73, (v10)
Brown, George Douglas. PR4174.B6.H6, (v3)
Brown, George Rothwell. F194.B87, (v4)
Brown, Gerald Griffiths. PQ6072.B75, (v3)
Brown, H. M. PT2603.R397.Z58113 1991, (v3)
Brown, Harold. UA23.B7845 1983, (v10)
Brown, Henry A. L. F127.A2.B67 1988, (v4)
Brown, Henry Phelps. HD6667.B76 1983, (v6)

HD7023.B78 1981, (v6)
Brown, Herbert Charles. QD181.B1.B73, (v1)
Brown, Homer Obed. PR851.B75 1997, (v3)
Brown, Howard G. DC155.B76 1995, (v5)
Brown, Howard Mayer. ML172.B86 1999, (v9)
Brown, Hunter. B945.J24.B762000, (v8)
Brown, Ian Malcolm. D530.B76 1998, (v5)
Brown, Ian. HC441.B75 1997, (v6)
Brown, Ivor John Carnegie. PE1585.B688 1945, (v3)
PR2910.B7 1960, (v3)
PR4592.S6.B7, (v3)
PR5366.B7 1965, (v3)
Brown, J. F. DJK50.B77 1988, (v5)
DJK50.B78 1991, (v5)
DJK51.B74 2001, (v5)
DJK51.B75 1994, (v5)
DR48.5.B698 1992, (v5)
DR90.B7, (v5)
Brown, James A. TS183.B76 1991, (v1)
Brown, James H. QH541.B75 1995, (v1)
Brown, James. F82.B87 1971, (v4)
TJ1185.B8234 1998, (v1)
Brown, Jane. SB457.6.B76 1989, (v1)
SB470.F37.B76 1995, (v1)
Brown, Jeffrey A. PN6725.B76 2001, (v3)
Brown, Jennifer. HV8023.B76 2000, (v6)
Brown, John A. RV9.B87, (v2)
Brown, John Russell. PR2983.B76 2001, (v3)
PR2995.B74 1996, (v3)
PR3091.B68 1981, (v3)
PR3091.B72 1999, (v3)
Brown, John Seely. HM851.B76 2000, (v6)
Brown, Jonathan C. HC175.B77, (v6)
Brown, Jonathan. ND804.B74 1991, (v9)
ND806.B76, (v9)
ND813.V4.B893 1998, (v9)
Brown, Judith M. DS481.G3.B735 1989, (v5)
Brown, Julia Prewitt. PR861.B76 1985, (v3)
PR5827.A35.B76 1997, (v3)
Brown, Kathleen M. F229.B8783 1996, (v4)
Brown, Keith M. DA800.B76 1992, (v5)
Brown, Kelly R. PN2287.L28944.B76 1999, (v3)
Brown, Kenneth Douglas. HF1534.5.J3.B76 1998, (v6)
Brown, Kenneth O. BV3798.B76 1992, (v8)
Brown, Kenny L. F705.I8 B76, (v4)
Brown, L. Carl. DS62.8.B76 1984, (v5)
Brown, Lawrence A. HC79.T4.B74 1981, (v6)
Brown, Lee Rust. PS1642.S3.B76 1997, (v3)
Brown, Les. BJ1031.B74 1987, (v8)
PN1992.18.B7 1992, (v3)
Brown, Lester Russell. HB871.B738 1994, (v6)
HB871.B74, (v6)
HC79.E5 B759 2001b, (v6)
Brown, Lloyd L. E185.97.R63.B76 1996, (v4)
Brown, Lloyd Wellesley. PR9340.B7, (v3)
Brown, Lorene Byron. Z695.1.B57.B76 1995, (v10)
Brown, Louis. D810.R33.B77 1999, (v5)
Brown, M. Leann. HC59.7.B6893 1994, (v6)
Brown, Malcolm Johnston. PR5043.B7, (v3)
Brown, Marc Tolon. PZ7.B81618Ar, (v3)
Brown, Marcia. PZ7.B8162St, (v3)
Brown, Margaret Lynn. F443.G7.W55 2000, (v4)
Brown, Margaret Wise. PZ7.B8163Go, (v3)
PZ10.3.B7656Ru5, (v3)
Brown, Mark Herbert. F737.Y4.B7, (v4)
Brown, Marshall. PR447.B75 1991, (v3)
Brown, Mary Ellen. PR5101.M3, (v3)
Brown, Mary Jane. HV6457.B76 2000, (v6)
Brown, Michael E. UG1123.B76 1991, (v10)
Brown, Michael Fobes. F3430.1.C3.B76 1991, (v4)
Brown, Michael Harold. GN281.4.B76 1990, (v6)
Brown, Michael K. HN57.B659 1999, (v6)
HV7936.D54.B76 1981, (v6)
Brown, Michelle. ND2889.B76 1994, (v9)
Brown, Milton Wolf. N5015.A8.B7, (v9)
ND212.B74, (v9)
Brown, Montague. BJ1012.B737 1996, (v8)
Brown, Nancy J. RT62.B698 2003, (v2)
Brown, Nathan J. HD1538.E3.B76 1990, (v6)
Brown, Neville. UG1520.B76 1990, (v10)

Brown, Nina W. LB1032.B74 2000, (v7)
Brown, Norman Oliver. CB19.B69 1985, (v5)
Brown, Patricia Fortini. DG675.6.B7 1996, (v5)
  N6921.V5.B75 1997, (v9)
  ND1452.I8.B76 1988, (v9)
Brown, Paul B. HF5415.1.B79 1988, (v6)
Brown, Penny. PR468.C5.B76 1993, (v3)
  PR830.W6.B76 1992, (v3)
Brown, Peter Robert Lamont. BR162.2.B76 1995, (v8)
  BR195.C45.B76 1988, (v8)
  BR1720.A9.B7 1967b, (v8)
  BX2333.B74, (v8)
Brown, Peter. PR1875.S63.B76 1991, (v3)
Brown, Phil. F127.C3.B76 1998, (v4)
Brown, Phil. RA790.6.B78 1985, (v2)
Brown, Philip C. DS894.59.I539.K343 1993, (v5)
Brown, R. Philip. B824.B76 1996, (v8)
Brown, Ralph A. E321.B84, (v4)
Brown, Raymond Edward. BS2555.3.B7633 1994, (v8)
Brown, Rexford. LC151.B77 1991, (v7)
Brown, Richard D. F64.B86 2000, (v4)
  F73.4.B89, (v4)
Brown, Richard. BR758.B76 1990, (v8)
  PR6019.O9.Z526344 1992, (v3)
Brown, Robert Alan. Q325.5.B76 1994, (v1)
Brown, Robert Craig. F1033.B87, (v4)
Brown, Robert Eldon. JK119.B7, (v7)
  JK146.B53.B7, (v7)
Brown, Robert Harold. F761.B76, (v4)
Brown, Robert J. PN1991.2.B76 1998, (v3)
Brown, Robert Leaman. F776.B67, (v4)
Brown, Robert McAfee. BR115.J8.B76, (v8)
  BX4811.B74, (v8)
Brown, Robert. BD436.B76 1987, (v8)
Brown, Roger H. HJ2368.B76 1993, (v5)
Brown, Roger Hamilton. E357.B88, (v4)
Brown, Roger Lee. HV9650.L72.F533 1996, (v6)
Brown, Rosellen. PS3552.R7, (v3)
Brown, Royal S. ML2075.B76 1994, (v9)
Brown, Samuel R. Z7164.S68 B75 1987, (v10)
Brown, Sarah Hart. KF372.B76 1998, (v7)
Brown, Sarah Jo. R853.R46.B76 1999, (v2)
Brown, Seyom. E840.B768 1994, (v4)
  E855.B76, (v4)
  JX1391.B73 1996, (v7)
Brown, Shona L. HD30.28.B7822 1998, (v6)
Brown, Stephanie. HV5132.B748 1999, (v6)
Brown, Steven C. ND237.H66948, (v9)
Brown, Stuart C. B2598.B74 1984, (v8)
Brown, Stuart Gerry. F546.S8.B72, (v4)
Brown, T. Louise. DS557.7.B76 1991, (v5)
Brown, Terence. PR5906.B76 1999, (v3)
Brown, Thomas J. HV28.D6.B75 1998, (v6)
Brown, Travis. T223.P2B77 2000, (v1)
Brown, Ursula M. E184.A1.B88 2001, (v4)
Brown, Wallace Cable. PR509.H4.B7, (v3)
Brown, Wallace. E277.B82, (v4)
Brown, Warren. DD130.B76 2001, (v5)
Brown, Wendy. JA74.B724 1995, (v7)
  JA81.B66 1988, (v7)
  PS3552.R7382.T7, (v3)
Brown, William Edward. PG3007.B7, (v3)
Brown, William Wells. PS1139.B9 C5 1969, (v3)
Browne Miller, Angela. HQ778.7.U6.B76 1990, (v6)
  LB2351.2.B76 1996, (v7)
Browne, Donald R. HE8689.4.B76 1989, (v6)
Browne, E. J. QH31.D2.B84 1995, (v1)
Browne, Edward Granville. PK6097.B7 1929, (v3)
Browne, J. Ross. F786.B87, (v4)
Browne, J. Ross. F786.B87 1950, (v4)
Browne, Martha Griffith. PS1145.B35.A95 1971, (v3)
Browne, Stephen H. E449.G865.B76 1999, (v4)
  PR3334.B4.Z57 1993, (v3)
Browne, Thomas. PR3327.A14, (v3)
  PR3327.A15, (v3)
  PR3327.A27, (v3)
  PR3327.A65 1958, (v3)
Browne, Turner. TR139.B767 1983, (v1)
Browne, William Paul. JK1118.B76 1998, (v7)
  JK5816.B76 1995, (v7)

Brownell, Morris R. PR3637.A35.B7, (v3)
Brownell, Susan. GV651.B76 1995, (v6)
Brownell, W. C. PS1145.B6.A6 1933, (v3)
Browner, Stephanie. PN73.B76 1999, (v3)
Brown-Grant, Rosalind. PQ1575.Z5B76 1999, (v3)
Browning, Barbara. GV1637.B76 1995, (v6)
Browning, Christopher R. D810.J4.B77, (v5)
Browning, Elizabeth (Barrett). PR4189.A1, (v3)
  PR4193.A2, (v3)
  PR4182.F67 1988, (v3)
  PR4185.A1 1978, (v3)
  PR4189.A1 1980, (v3)
  PR4193.A33, (v3)
  PR4193.A374 1954, (v3)
Browning, Genia K. HQ1236.5.S68.B76 1987, (v6)
Browning, Meshach. SK17.B76.A3 1972, (v1)
Browning, Reed. D292.B76 1993, (v5)
  GV865.Y58.B76 2000, (v6)
Browning, Robert. DG317.B76 1976, (v5)
  GV963.B7 1990, (v6)
  PR4200 F65, (v3)
  PR4200.F66, (v3)
  PR4202.L59 1979, (v3)
  PR4202.M6, (v3)
  PR4202.R67 1997, (v3)
  PR4203.J3 1983, (v3)
  PR4222.E8, (v3)
  PR4231.A3 1933, (v3)
  PR4231.A3 1950, (v3)
  PR4231.A38, (v3)
  PR4231.A4 1984, (v3)
  PR4231.A43 1989, (v3)
  PZ8.1.B825Pi 1993, (v3)
Browning, W. R. F. BS440.B73 1996, (v8)
Brownlee, Marina Scordilis. PQ6498.Z5.N6833 2000, (v3)
Brownlee, Richard S. E470.45.B76 1984, (v4)
Brownley, Martine Watson. PR9084.B76 2000, (v3)
Brownlow, Kevin. PN2287.P5.B76 1999, (v3)
Brownson, J. M. Jamil. GE160.E83.B76 1995, (v6)
Brownstein, Rachel M. PN2638.R3.B7 1993, (v3)
  PR830.H4.B76 1982, (v3)
Brownstone, David M. NX447.5.B76 1994, (v9)
Brox, Norbert. BR165.B712 1995, (v8)
Broyles-Gonzalez, Yolanda. PN3307.U6.B76 1994, (v3)
Brozen, Yale. HD2757.B76 1982, (v6)
Brubacher, John Seiler. LA91.B78 1969, (v7)
Brubaker, Bill. PS3523.A773.Z57 1993, (v3)
Brubaker, C. William. LB3218.A1.B78 1998, (v7)
Brucato, Thomas W. GV581.B78 2001, (v6)
Bruccoli, Matthew Joseph. PS3511.I9.T45, (v3)
  PS3529.H29.Z59, (v3)
Bruce, A. P. C. V27.B86 1998, (v10)
Bruce, Bertram C. LB1576.7.B78 1993, (v7)
Bruce, Christopher W. DA152.5.A7.B78 1999, (v5)
Bruce, David Kirkpatrick Este. D811.5.B82 1991, (v5)
Bruce, Dickson D. PS153.N5.B77 1989, (v3)
Bruce, J. Percy. B128.C54.B78 1973, (v8)
Bruce, Steve. BL2747.8.B78 2002, (v8)
  BR1642.U5.B78 1988, (v8)
  DA990.U46.B675 1994, (v5)
  DA990.U46.B678 1992, (v5)
Bruce, Willa M. HF5549.5.J63.B74 1992, (v6)
Bruce-Briggs, B. UA23.B78457 1988, (v10)
Bruce-Gardyne, Jock. DA589.7.B78 1984, (v5)
Bruce-Mitford, Miranda. AZ108.W37 1996, (v10)
Bruch, Hilde. RC552.A5.B78, (v2)
Bruchac, Joseph. PZ7.B82816Sac 2000, (v3)
Bruchey, Stuart Weems. HC51.B7, (v6)
  HC103.B78845 1990, (v6)
  HG4575.2.B78 1991, (v6)
Brucker, Gene A. DG737.26.B7 1962, (v5)
Brudney, Daniel. B3305.M74.B78 1998, (v8)
Brudny, Yitzhak M. DK274.B77 1998, (v5)
Bruegel, Martin. HC107.N72 C653 2002, (v6)
Bruegmann, Robert. NA737.H558.A4 1991, (v9)
  NA737.H558.B78 1997, (v9)
Bruer, John T. BF318.B79 1999, (v2)
Bruer, John T. LB1060.B78 1993, (v7)
Bruffee, Kenneth A. LB1032.B76 1999, (v7)

Bruford, Walter Horace. DD193.B7, (v5)
Brugel, Werner. QC457.B743, (v1)
Bruggen, Coosje van. N6537.N38.B78 1988, (v9)
Brugger, Bill. DS777.75.B78 1981, (v5)
Brugger, Robert J. F181.B85 1988, (v5)
Brugioni, Dino A. E841.B76 1991, (v4)
Bruhn, Kathleen. JL1298.A1.B78 1997, (v7)
Bruhns, Karen Olsen. F2229.B78 1994, (v4)
Bruijn, J. R. VA533.B78 1993, (v10)
Bruman, Henry J. F1219.3.A42B78 2000, (v4)
Brumberg, Joan Jacobs. HQ798.B724 1997, (v6)
Brumfield, William Craft. NA1181.B72 1993, (v9)
  NA1187.B78 1991, (v9)
Brumfitt, J. H. D15.V6.B7, (v5)
Brunas, Michael. PN1995.9.H6.B7 1990, (v3)
Brundage, James A. D157.B88, (v5)
Brundage, W. Fitzhugh. HX655.S68.B78 1996, (v6)
Brune, Lester H. E183.7.B745 1985, (v4)
Bruneau, Charles. PC2075.B69, (v3)
Bruneau, Marie-Florine. BV5095.A1.B69 1998, (v8)
Bruner, Jerome S. BF455.B75 1986, (v2)
  LB885.B79, (v7)
Brunette, Peter. PN1998.3.A58.B78 1998, (v3)
Brunhoff, Jean de. PZ7.B828428St 1984, (v3)
Brunhouse, Robert Levere. F1435.B875, (v4)
Bruni, Leonardo. DG737.A2.B813 2001, (v5)
Brunier, Serge. QB982.B7813 1999, (v1)
Brunk, Gregory G. E881.B78 1996, (v4)
  Z7161.A2.B76 1997, (v10)
Brunk, Samuel. F1234.Z37.B78 1995, (v4)
Brunner, Diane DuBose. LC196.B78 1994, (v7)
Brunner, Edward. PS310.C6.B78 2000, (v3)
Brunner, Karl. HG501.B75 1989, (v6)
Bruno, Frank Joe. RC460.B694 1993, (v2)
Bruno, Giordano. B783.D43.E6 1976, (v8)
Bruno, Leonard C. QA28.B78 1999, (v1)
  T15.B684 1997, (v1)
Brunot, Ferdinand. PC2101.B75 1969, (v3)
  PC2105.B7 1936, (v3)
Bruns, Gerald L. BD241.B78 1992, (v8)
Bruns, Roger. BV3785.S8.B75 1992, (v8)
Brunsdale, Mitzi. PR6019.O9.Z526355 1993, (v3)
  PT8950.U5.Z625 1988, (v3)
Brunsdon, Charlotte. PN1992.8.S4.B78 2000, (v3)
Brunskill, R. W. NA7328.B83 1971, (v9)
Brunsson, Nils. HD58.8.B784 1993, (v6)
Brunswik, Egon. QP355.B83 1956, (v1)
Brunt, P. A. DG271.B78 1990, (v5)
Brunton, R. DU760.B84 1989, (v5)
Brunvand, Jan Harold. GR105.B716 2000, (v6)
  GR105.34.B78 2001, (v6)
Brusca, Richard C. QL362.B924 1990, (v1)
Brush, Stephen G. Q125.B88 1988, (v1)
  QC175.S77 vol.6, (v1)
Brushwood, John Stubbs. PQ7082.N7.B7, (v3)
  PQ7197.B69, (v3)
  PQ7197.B7, (v3)
Brusse, Wendy Asbeek. HF2036.B78 1997, (v6)
Brusseau, James. B2430.D454.B78 1997, (v8)
Brustad, Kristen. PJ6123.B78 1995, (v3)
  PJ6307.B78 1997, (v3)
Brustein, William. DD253.25.B76 1996, (v5)
Bruster, Douglas. PR658.E35.B78 1992, (v3)
Bruton, Henry J. HC424.B78 1992, (v6)
Bruun, Geoffrey. DC342.8.C6.B7, (v5)
Bruyn, Severyn Ten Haut. HB501.B8453 2000, (v6)
  HG4910.B77 1987, (v6)
Bruzzi, Stella. PN1995.9.C56.B78 1997, (v3)
Bryan, Ferald Joseph. F215.B888 1994, (v4)
Bryan, George B. KF4296.B79 1993, (v7)
  PR4580.B78 1997, (v3)
  PS3529.N5.Z459 1995, (v3)
Bryan, William Frank. PR1912.A2.B, (v3)
Bryan, William Jennings. E664.B87.B8 1971, (v4)
Bryant, Arthur. D743.B73, (v5)
Bryant, C. R. S494.5.G46.B78 1992, (v1)
Bryant, E. T. ML111.B83 1985, (v9)
Bryant, Edward. GB5014.B79 1991, (v6)
  GC221.2.B78 2001, (v6)
  QC981.8.C5.B76 1997, (v1)
Bryant, Edwin. DS425.B79 2001, (v5)

Bryant, J. A. PR2638.B7, (v3)
  PR3012.B75, (v3)
  PS261.B79 1997, (v3)
Bryant, Jerry H. PS374.N4.B74 1997, (v3)
Bryant, John. PS2388.S2.B79 1993, (v3)
Bryant, Jonathan M. F292.G7.B79 1996, (v4)
Bryant, Joseph M. BJ161.B78 1996, (v8)
Bryant, Keith L. E78.S7 B78 2001, (v4)
  F700.M697, (v4)
Bryant, Kenneth E. PK1967.9.S9.Z62, (v3)
Bryant, Margaret M. PE1072.B75 1962, (v3)
Bryant, Peter. BF723.C5.B74 1974b, (v2)
Bryant, Rebecca. BD241.B785 2000, (v8)
Bryant, Victor. QA164.B82 1993, (v1)
Bryant, William Cullen. PS1150.F69 1972, (v3)
  PS1181.A4 1975, (v3)
Bryant-Bertail, Sarah. PN1851.B79 2000, (v3)
Bryce, Betty Kelly. NE508.B76 1999, (v9)
Bryce, James Bryce. F2223.B91 1929, (v4)
  JC421.B8, (v7)
  JK246.B9 1959, (v7)
Bryce, Trevor. DS66.B75 1998, (v5)
Bryden, Mary. PR6003.E282.Z57878 1998, (v3)
Brydon, Diana. PR9199.3.F52.Z58 1998, (v3)
Brydon, Lynne. HQ1870.9.B79 1989, (v6)
Bryher. PR6003.R98.Z5, (v3)
Bryk, Anthony S. LC501.B624 1993, (v7)
Brym, Robert J. DS135.R92.B78 1994, (v5)
Bryman, Alan. H62.B785 1988, (v6)
Brymer, Jack. ML945.B8 1977, (v9)
Bryner, Gary C. KF3812.Z9.B78 1993, (v7)
Brysk, Alison. E65.B78 2000, (v4)
Bryson, Conrey. F674.O59 M813 1986, (v4)
Bryson, John M. HD30.28.B79 1995, (v6)
Bryson, Joseph E. KF4124.B79 1990, (v7)
Bryson, Lois. HV31.B75 1992, (v6)
Bryson, Phillip J. HC290.78.B8 1991, (v6)
Bryson, Thomas A. DS63.2.U5.B79, (v5)
  Z3014.R44.B79, (v10)
Bryson, William E. TS320.B884 1997, (v1)
Brzezinski, Zbigniew K. D847.B7 1967, (v5)
  D860.B79 1993, (v5)
  E839.B7 1970, (v4)
  JK31.B7, (v7)
  UA770.B7, (v10)
  E840.8.B79 A36 1985, (v4)
Brzoska, Michael. UF500.B79 1994, (v10)
Bstan-dzin-rgya-mtsho. BQ7662.4.B783 2000, (v8)
  BQ7935.B774 M39 2000, (v8)
  BQ7935.B774 A93 1995, (v8)
Buber, Martin. B3213.B82.E5, (v8)
  B3213.B82 E52 2002, (v8)
  B3213.B82.E53, (v8)
  B3213.B83I213 1970, (v8)
  BJ1406.B7713, (v8)
  BL51.B82 1957, (v8)
  BM45.B8, (v8)
  BM198.B7783, (v8)
  BS580.M6.B8 1958, (v8)
  BS1192.B8, (v8)
Bubner, Rüdiger. BD241.B79 1988, (v8)
Bucciarelli, Louis L. TA174.B756 1994, (v1)
Buccini, Stefania. PQ4084.B8313 1997, (v3)
Bucco, Martin. PS3523.E94.M19 1993, (v3)
Buchan, Alastair. UA646.B8 1963, (v10)
Buchan, Alastair. UA646.3.B7, (v10)
Buchan, David. D2009.B83 1993, (v5)
Buchan, John. PR6003.U13 B5, (v3)
  PR6003.U13 G34, (v3)
  PR6003.U13 G7, (v3)
  PR6003.U13 J64, (v3)
  PR6003.U13.J64 1925, (v3)
  PR6003.U13 M5, (v3)
  PR6003.U13 M7, (v3)
  PR6003.U13 P7, (v3)
  PR6003.U13 P74, (v3)
  PR6003.U13.T5, (v3)
  PR6003.U13 W3, (v3)
Buchanan, Albert Russell. D810.N4.B82, (v5)
Buchanan, Anne L. Z5814.U7.B75 1995, (v10)
Buchanan, Christy M. HQ777.5.B796 1996, (v6)

Buchanan, Ian. B2430.D454.B83 2000, (v8)
Buchanan, James M. HB71.B7794 1989, (v6)
  HB72.B833 1994, (v6)
  HB73.B83 1991, (v6)
  HB199.B82, (v6)
  HB846.8.B79 1989, (v6)
  HJ257.2.B82 1970, (v6)
  JC423.B86, (v7)
  JC578.B83 1998, (v7)
Buchanan, James. E337.8.B9, (v4)
Buchanan, John. E382.B89 2001, (v4)
Buchanan, Joseph Ray. HD8073.B8A3 1971, (v6)
Buchanan, Keith M. DS511.B8, (v5)
Buchanan, Patrick J. E840.8.B83 A3 1990, (v4)
Buchanan, R. A. HM221.B83 1994, (v6)
Buchanan, Robert. HV2530.B83 1999, (v6)
Buchenau, Jurgen. F1436.8.M6.B83 1996, (v4)
Bucher, Charles Augustus. GV341.B86 1987, (v6)
  GV343.5.B787 2002, (v6)
Bucher, Kurt. QE475.A2B84 1994, (v1)
Bucher, Lloyd M. VB230.B8, (v10)
Buchheim, Hans. JC481.B813, (v7)
Buchholtz, C. W. F782.R59 B83 1983, (v4)
Buchholz, Todd G. HB76.B83 1989, (v6)
Buchler, Justus. B945.P44.B8 1939, (v8)
  PN1031.B85, (v3)
Buchman, Stephen L. QK926.B835 1996, (v1)
Buchmann-Moller, Frank. ML419.Y7.B75 1990, (v9)
Buchner, Georg. PT1828.B6.A26, (v3)
  PT1828.B6 1967, (v3)
  PT1828.B6 1992, (v3)
Bucholz, Arden. D214.B83 1997, (v5)
  U155.G3.B83 1991, (v10)
Bucholz, R. O. DA495.B83 1993, (v5)
Buchsbaum, Ralph Morris. QL362.B93 1987, (v1)
  QL362.B94, (v1)
Buchwald, Jed Z. QC403.B83 1989, (v1)
Buchwald, Reinhard. PT1925.B83 1983, (v3)
Buck, David D. DS796.T68.B8, (v5)
Buck, Elizabeth Bentzel. DU624.65.B83 1993, (v5)
Buck, Frank. QL61.B78 2000, (v1)
Buck, John Lossing. HD868.B8 1964, (v6)
Buck, Lucy Rebecca. E605.B89 1997, (v4)
Buck, Pearl (Sydenstricker). PS3503.U198 M6, (v3)
Buck, Pearl S. PL2415.B8 1974, (v3)
  PS3503.U198.G6, (v3)
  PS3503.U198 H5, (v3)
  PS3503.U198 L4, (v3)
  PS3503.U198 L59, (v3)
  PS3503.U198 S6, (v3)
  PS3503.U198.Z5, (v3)
  PS3503.U198.Z53 1962, (v3)
Buck, Richard. SH346.B83 1993, (v1)
Buck, Solon J. HD201.B8 1963, (v6)
  GE170.B83 1998, (v6)
  KF3775.B83 1991, (v7)
Buckingham, Marcus. HD38.2.B83 1999, (v6)
Buckingham, Peter H. HX84.O39.B83 1996, (v6)
  Z1244.B83 1990, (v10)
Buckle, Henry Thomas. CB63.B8 1964, (v5)
Buckle, Richard. GV1785.B32.B83 1988, (v6)
  GV1785.N6.B8 1971b, (v6)
  NB497.E6.B8, (v9)
Buckler, Julie A. ML1737.B83 2000, (v9)
Buckler, William Earl. PR463.B8, (v3)
  PR1301.B8, (v3)
  PR4219.B8 1985, (v3)
Buckley, Helen. E78.P7.B83 1992, (v4)
Buckley, J. F. PS217.H65.B83 1997, (v3)
Buckley, Jerome Hamilton. PR461.B75 1969, (v3)
  PR830.A8.B8, (v3)
  Z2013.B8, (v10)
Buckley, John. UG630.B774 1999, (v10)
Buckley, Mary. HN530.2.A8.B83 1993, (v6)
Buckley, Michael J. BL2747.3.B83 1987, (v8)
  LC501.B627 1998, (v7)
Buckley, Roger Norman. UA649.32.W47.B83 1998, (v10)
Buckley, Roger. DS796.H757.B83 1997, (v5)
  E183.8.J3.B78 1992, (v4)
Buckley, Vincent. PR4024.B8, (v3)

Buckley, William F. AC8.B732 1975, (v10)
  E743.5.B82, (v4)
  E748.M143.B8 1970, (v4)
  JK271.B723 1968, (v7)
  LD6309.B8 1977, (v7)
Bucklin, Steven J. E744.B827 2001, (v4)
Buck-Morss, Susan. D413.5.B83 2000, (v5)
  PT2603.E455.P334 1989, (v3)
Buckser, Andrew. BR987.M67.B83 1996, (v8)
Buckton, Oliver S. PR788.A95.B83 1998, (v3)
Bucuvalas, Tina. F316.2.B78 1994, (v4)
Budd, John. Z8447.B82 1983, (v10)
Budd, Mike. PN1992.6.B79 1999, (v3)
Budden, Julian. ML410.P89 B83 2002, (v9)
  ML410.V4 B88 1991, (v9)
Budding, E. QB135.B78 1993, (v1)
Buder, Stanley. HT161.B84 1990, (v6)
Budge, Ian. JC423.B8642 1996, (v7)
Budiansky, Stephen. GN799.A4.B83 1992, (v6)
  QH75.B823 1995, (v1)
Budick, E. Miller. PS374.F45.B83 1994, (v3)
Budick, Sanford. BH301.S7B83 2000, (v8)
Budinski, Kenneth G. TA403.B787 1999, (v1)
Budson, Richard D. RC439.5.B8, (v2)
Budworth, Geoffrey. VM533.B5277 2000, (v10)
Budyko, M. I. QC981.8.C5.B8313 1982, (v1)
Buechler, Steven M. HN13.B84 2000, (v6)
Buechner, Frederick. PS3552.U35 F5, (v3)
  PS3552.U35 L5, (v3)
  PS3552.U35 O6, (v3)
Buecker, Brad. TJ275.B827 2000, (v1)
Buehrer, Beverley Bare. PN1993.5.J3.B78 1990, (v3)
Buehrig, Edward H. E766.B92, (v4)
Buel, Joy Day. CT275.F5586.B83 1984, (v5)
Buel, Richard. E215.B84 1998, (v4)
Bueler, Lois E. PR3664.C43.B84 1994, (v3)
Buell, Lawrence. PS169.E25B84 2001, (v3)
  PS169.E25.B84 2001, (v3)
  PS3057.N3.B84 1995, (v3)
Buell, Thomas B. V63.S68.B8 1987, (v10)
Buelow, George J. MT49.B84 1986, (v9)
Buenger, Walter L. F391.B878 2001, (v4)
Bueno de Mesquita, Bruce. JX1391.B83 1992, (v7)
Bueno, Eva Paulino. PQ9601.B84 1995, (v3)
Buerger, Martin Julian. QD905.B96, (v1)
Buerger, Robert A. RS100.5.B839 1999, (v2)
Buerki, Robert A. RS100.5.B84 1994, (v2)
Buero Vallejo, Antonio. PQ6603.U4.A19 1975, (v3)
  PQ6603.U4.H613 1987, (v3)
  PQ6603.U4.M413 1987, (v3)
  PQ6603.U4.T4, (v3)
Buettner-Janusch, John. QL737.P9.B915, (v1)
Bufacchi, Vittorio. DG581.B84 1998, (v5)
Buffalo Bill. F594.C67, (v4)
Bufkin, E. C. PR6027.E855.Z6, (v3)
Buford, Kate. PN2287.L246.B84 2000, (v3)
Bugh, Glenn Richard. U33.B84 1988, (v10)
Buhle, Mari Jo. HQ1426.B82, (v6)
Buhler, Alfred. N7410.B8, (v9)
Buhler, W. K. QA29.G3.B83, (v1)
Buhler-Wilkerson, Karen. RT120.H65B84 2001, (v2)
Buhot, Jean. N7340.B653, (v9)
Builder, Carl H. UA23.B7855 1989, (v10)
  UG633.B79 1994, (v10)
Buisseret, David. DC122.B88 1984, (v5)
Buitenen, Johannes Adrianus Bernardus van.
  PK3798.S91M73 1968, (v3)
Bukatman, Scott. PS374.S35.B84 1993, (v3)
Buker, George E. E502.9.B84 1993, (v4)
  F319.J1.B89 1991, (v4)
Bukey, Evan Burr. DB99.B87 2000, (v5)
Bukharin, Nikolai Ivanovich. HB97.5.B8513 1972, (v6)
Bukowski, Douglas. F548.5.T48.B85 1998, (v4)
Bulag, Uradyn Erden. DS19.B85 1998, (v5)
Bulbeck, Chilla. HQ1823.B85 1997, (v6)
Buley, R. Carlyle. F484.3.B94 1983, (v4)
Bulgakov, Mikhail Afanas§evich. PG3476.B78M313 1992, (v3)
Bulkeley, Kelly. BF1091.B94 1999, (v2)
Bulkeley, Kelly. BL65.D67.B85 1994, (v8)

Bulkley, Barry. F194.B94, (v4)
Bull, Barry L. LC1099.3.B85 1992, (v7)
Bull, Hedley. JX1954.B79 1977, (v7)
Bull, Martin J. Z2360.3.B85 1996, (v10)
Bull, Philip. HD1251.B85 1996, (v6)
Bull, Stephen. U800.B85 1991, (v10)
Bull, Thomas H. Z5721.B87 1998, (v10)
Bull, William B. GB447.B85 1991, (v6)
Bullard, Alice. DC59.8.N5, (v5)
Bullard, Mary Ricketson. F292.C94.S733 1995, (v4)
Bullard, Monte R. DS799.816.B86 1996, (v5)
Bullen, A. H. PR421.B8 1962, (v3)
Bullert, B. J. HE8700.79.U6.B85 1997, (v6)
Bullett, Gerald William. PR4681.B8 1971, (v3)
Bullins, Ed. PS3552.U45.H8, (v3)
Bullitt, John Marshall. PR3727.B9, (v3)
Bulloch, John. DS79.72.B85 1991, (v5)
Bullock, Alan Louis Charles. DD247.H5.B85 1960, (v5)
Bullock, Alan. DD247.H5.B79 1992, (v5)
  Z2000.B8 1957, (v10)
Bullock, Charles S. JK1976.B77 1992, (v7)
Bullock, Steven C. HS523.B85 1996, (v6)
Bullough, Donald A. DC70.B84 1991, (v5)
Bullough, Geoffrey. PR508.P9.B8, (v3)
  PR2952.5.B8, (v3)
Bullough, Robert V. LC4091.B85 2001, (v7)
Bullough, Vern L. HQ12.B84, (v6)
  HQ14.B84 1982, (v6)
Bullough, Vern L. HQ77.B785 1993, (v6)
Bullwinkle, Davis. Z7964.A3.B84 1989, (v10)
  Z7964.A3.B85 1989, (v10)
  Z7964.A337.B84 1989, (v10)
Bulmer-Thomas, V. HC123.B85 1994, (v6)
  HC141.B78 1987, (v6)
Bulosan, Carlos. PR9550.9.B8.A8 1973, (v3)
Bulow, Bernhard. DD117.B8, (v5)
Bultitude, John. SB363.3.A1.B85 1983, (v1)
Bultmann, Rudolf Karl. BS2395.B83 1984, (v8)
Bumgartner, Louis E. F1438.V175.B8, (v4)
Bumiller, Kristin. JC599.U5.B837 1988, (v7)
Bumke, Joachim. DD64.B8613 1991, (v5)
Bump, Daniel. QA331.B797 1997, (v1)
Bunch, Bryan H. Q121.B86 2000, (v1)
  QC174.17.S9.B86 1989, (v1)
  T15.B73 1993, (v1)
Bunche, Ralph J. DT1058.B53.B86 1992, (v5)
  E748.B885.A25 1995, (v4)
Bunck, Julie Marie. F1788.B79 1994, (v4)
Bundy, McGeorge. UA23.B786 1988, (v10)
Bundy, William P. E855.B85 1998, (v4)
Bunge, Mario Augusto. B791.B765 2003, (v8)
  BD541.B85 1979, (v8)
Bunge, Mario Augusto. H61.B793 1996, (v6)
Bunge, William. GA9.L8 no. 1 1966, (v6)
Bunim, Miriam (Schild). ND141.B85 1970, (v9)
Bunin, Ivan Alekseevich. PG3453.B9.G613 1981, (v3)
  PG3453.B9.T43 1977, (v3)
  PG3453.B9.Z4713 1998, (v3)
Bunker, Gerald E. DS778.W3.B85, (v5)
Bunker, Matthew D. KF4772.B86 2001, (v7)
Bunn, John William. GV735.B8 1968, (v6)
Bunnell, David. HD9696.T444.C57 2000, (v6)
Bunson, Margaret. DT58.B96 1994, (v5)
Bunson, Matthew. DG270.B86 2002, (v5)
Bunting, Brian T. S591.B886, (v1)
Bunting, Eve. PZ7.B91527SI 1994, (v3)
Bunting, Josiah. PS3552.U48.L5 1972, (v3)
Bunuel, Luis. PQ6603.U56.C4713 2000, (v3)
Bunyan, John. PR3329.G1 1966, (v3)
  PR3329.H1 1980, (v3)
  PR3330.A2.W5, (v3)
Buonarroti, Michel Angelo. N6923.B9.G57, (v9)
  ND623.B9.A43, (v9)
Burakowski, Tadeusz. TS653.B87 1999, (v1)
Buranelli, Vincent. UB250.B87 1982, (v10)
Burbank, Victoria Katherine. GN663.B88 1988, (v6)
Burbidge, John W. B2901.B87 2001, (v8)
Burby, William Edward. KF570.B76 1965, (v7)
Burch, Ernest S. E99.E7.B8885 1998, (v4)
Burch, George Bosworth. B721.B8 1971, (v8)

Burch, John G. T58.6.B87 1989, (v1)
Burchard, John E. NA705.B8, (v9)
Burchfield, R. W. PE1072.B79 1985, (v3)
Burchill, Scott. JX1395.B844 1996, (v7)
Burckhardt, Jacob. D15.B8 A422 1955, (v5)
  D16.8.B812 1964, (v5)
  D21.B973, (v5)
  DG533.B85 1958, (v5)
  NA1115.B813 1985, (v9)
Burckhardt, Sigurd. PR2976.B77, (v3)
Burckhardt, Titus. NA5551.C5.B8613 1996, (v9)
Burdekin, Katharine. PR6003.U45.E5 1989, (v3)
Burden, Ernest E. NA31.B83 1998, (v9)
  NA2750.B864 1995, (v9)
Burdett, Carolyn. PR9369.2.S37.Z597 2001, (v3)
Burdette, Franklin L. JK1274.B87 1965, (v7)
Burdick, Eugene. PS3503.U68.F3 1963, (v3)
Burdick, Michael A. BX1462.2.B84 1995, (v8)
Burduck, Michael Lawrence. PS2642.F43.B87 1992, (v3)
Burdzhalov, E. N. DK265.19.B813 1987, (v5)
Burenstam Linder, Staffan. HB199.B84, (v6)
Burg, B. R. V63.V36.B87 1994, (v10)
Burg, Barbara A. Z3509.B87 2000, (v10)
Burg, David F. LA186.B87 1998, (v7)
Burg, Steven L. DR1313.7.P43.B87 1999, (v5)
Burge, David. ML707.B87 1990, (v9)
Burger, Alfred. RM300.15.B87 1986, (v2)
  RM301.15.B873 1995, (v2)
Burger, Ernst. ML410.L7.B913 1989, (v9)
Burger, Heinz Otto. PT85.B8 1971, (v3)
Burger, Julian. GN380.B87 1987, (v6)
Burger, Peter. BH301.A94.B8313 1984, (v8)
Burger, Richard L. F3429.1.C48.B86 1992, (v4)
Burger, Robert H. Z2483.B89 1995, (v10)
Burgess, Anthony. PR6052.U638.A6 1998, (v3)
  PR6052.U638.C9 1971, (v3)
  PR6052.U638.E2 1980, (v3)
  PR6052.U638.E56 1984, (v3)
  PR6052.U638.Z464 1986, (v3)
  PR6052.U638.Z465 1990, (v3)
Burgess, Eric. QB581.B87 1993, (v1)
  QB641.B819 1990, (v1)
  QB691.B87 1991, (v1)
  UG633.B84 1962, (v10)
Burgess, Glenn. JA84.G7.B83 1996, (v7)
Burgess, Glyn S. Z2174.P7.B87 1995, (v10)
Burgess, Heidi. HM136.B783 1997, (v6)
Burgess, John. QD561.B9525 1988, (v1)
Burgess, Michael. JN297.F43.B86 1995, (v7)
  Z5917.S36 B87 2003, (v10)
Burgess, Ronald. HJ2305.B87 1993, (v6)
Burgess, Susan R. KF8700.B87 1991, (v7)
Burgess, Thornton W. PZ7.B917OI 1990, (v3)
Burgess, William E. LC5805.B87 1997, (v7)
Burgett, Bruce. PS217.P64.B87 1998, (v3)
Burgoon, Judee K. BF637.C45.B86 1995, (v2)
Burgoyne, Robert. PN1997.A2133.B87 1990, (v3)
Burian, Jarka. PN2859.C9.B84 2000, (v3)
Burk, Creighton A. QE39.B85, (v1)
Burk, Kathleen. D635.B87 1985, (v5)
Burk, Robert Fredrick. GV880.B869 2001, (v6)
  GV880.B87 1994, (v6)
Burke, Bernard F. QB476.5.B87 1997, (v1)
Burke, Bernard. CR1619.B73 1969, (v5)
Burke, Carolyn. PS3523.O975.Z58 1996, (v3)
Burke, Christopher M. KF4905.B87 1999, (v7)
Burke, Colin B. HD9696.C772.B87 1994, (v6)
Burke, Edmund M. HD59.2.B87 1999, (v6)
Burke, Edmund. DA506.B85 1960, (v5)
  E211.B985, (v4)
  JC176.B8253, (v7)
  JC176.B826 1976, (v7)
Burke, Harry E. QC753.2.B85 1986, (v1)
Burke, James F. PQ6428.B87 2000, (v3)
Burke, James L. F491.3.B86 1984, (v4)
Burke, James. T15.B76 1995, (v1)
  T15.B765 1996, (v1)
Burke, John P. E183.8.V5.B87 1989, (v4)
  JK518.B87 1992, (v7)
Burke, Kenneth. B945.B773 P4 1984, (v8)

PN511.B793, (v3)
PS3503.U6134.B6, (v3)
PS3503.U6134 C6, (v3)
PS3503.U6134 T68, (v3)
PS3503.U6134.Z485 1988, (v3)
Burke, Kevin F. BX4705.E46, (v8)
Burke, Mary A. Z695.9.B93 1999, (v10)
Burke, Peter. BD175.B86 2000, (v8)
  BJ1604.C33 B87 1996, (v8)
  CB203.B87 1978, (v8)
  D16.B94 1990, (v5)
  DC128.5.B87 1992, (v5)
  DG445.B85 1999, (v5)
  HM36.B85 1993, (v6)
Burke, Phyllis. HQ75.53.B87 1993, (v6)
Burke, S. M. DS385.J5 B87 1997, (v5)
Burke, Thomas E. F129.S5.B87 1991, (v4)
Burke, Victor Lee. JN5.B87 1997, (v7)
Burke, W. Warner. HD58.8.B876 2002, (v6)
Burkert, Walter. BL610.B87 1987, (v8)
  DF78.B8513 1992, (v5)
Burkhardt, Margaret A. RT85.B766 2002, (v2)
Burkhardt, Richard W. QH31.L2.B87, (v1)
Burkhart, Charles. MT6.5.B87 1986, (v9)
Burkhart, Louise M. F1219.3.R38.B78 1989, (v4)
Burkhauser, Richard V. HD7256.U5.B87 1982, (v6)
Burkholder, J. Peter. ML410.I94.B87 1995, (v9)
Burkholder, Mark A. F1412.B96 1990, (v4)
Burki, Shahid Javed. DS382.B87 1999, (v5)
  DS382.B89 1999, (v5)
  DS384.B883 1991, (v5)
Burl, Aubrey. GN805.B866 1993, (v6)
Burl, Aubrey. GN805.B8665 1999, (v6)
Burleigh, Michael. DD256.5.B94 2000, (v5)
Burleson, Donald R. PS3523.O833.Z5654 1990, (v3)
Burley, David. F1089.P3.B87 1996, (v4)
Burling, Judith. N7340.B69, (v9)
Burling, Robbins. DS509.5.B8, (v5)
Burling, William J. PN2596.L6.B84 1993, (v3)
Burlingame, Roger. CT275.F68.B78, (v5)
  UG633.M45.B8, (v10)
  Z473.C46 B87 1997, (v10)
Burlingham, Dorothy T. RJ499.B73, (v2)
Burman, Ben Lucien. PS3503.U6245 R6, (v3)
Burmeister, Eva E. HV995.M5.L33 1949, (v6)
Burn, A. R. DF77.B9445, (v5)
Burn, William Laurence. DA550.B8, (v5)
Burnell, George M. RC455.4.L67.B87 1989, (v2)
Burner, David. E841.B84 1996, (v4)
  E842.1.B87 1984, (v4)
Burner, Eric. E185.97.M89.B87 1994, (v4)
Burnet, John. B171.B85 1950, (v8)
Burnett, Anne Pippin. PA3136.B79 1998, (v3)
Burnett, Frances Hodgson. PZ7.B934Lg 1989, (v3)
  PZ7.B934Se 1985, (v3)
Burnett, John. HD7334.A3.B87, (v6)
Burnett, Paula. PR9272.9.W3.Z55 2000, (v3)
Burnett, Robyn. F475.G3 B87 1996, (v4)
Burnett, Ron. PN1995.B86 1995, (v3)
Burnett, Stanton H. DG581.B87 1998, (v5)
Burnett, W. R. PS3503.U6258 I7, (v3)
Burney, Charles. ML159.B96 1957, (v9)
  ML423.B9.A3 1988, (v9)
Burney, Fanny. PR3316.A4.E8 1997, (v3)
Burnford, Sheila Every. PZ10.3.B935In, (v3)
Burnham, Barry C. DA145.B94 1991, (v5)
Burnham, David. HJ5018.B87 1989, (v6)
Burnham, Dorothy K. E78.Q3.B87 1992, (v4)
Burnham, Jack. NB198.B84, (v9)
Burnham, James. JC252.B8 1960, (v7)
Burnham, John C. HN57.B87 1993, (v6)
Burnham, Philip. E98.L3.B87 2000, (v4)
  E159.B92 1995, (v4)
Burnham, Robert. QB64.B85 1978, (v1)
  QB721.B79 2000, (v1)
Burniske, R. W. LB1028.43.B89 2001, (v7)
Burnley, J. D. PE1075.5.B87 1992, (v3)
  Z2012.B925 1994, (v10)
Burnley, James. TS1625.B9 1969, (v1)
Burns, Alan. QA76.73.A35.B85 1995, (v1)
Burns, Allan F. PM3968.55.E5.B87 1983, (v3)

Burns, Ben. PN4882.5.B87 1996, (v3)
Burns, Bob. GV200.4.B87 1999, (v6)
Burns, Bryan. PN1993.5.H8.B87 1996, (v3)
Burns, Christy L. PR6019.O9.Z535 2000, (v3)
Burns, Dave. F454.W18 B88 2000, (v4)
Burns, E. Bradford. F1526.25.B87 1991, (v4)
  F2521.B89 1980, (v4)
Burns, E. Jane. PQ155.W6.B87 1993, (v3)
Burns, Gene. BX1406.2.B865 1992, (v8)
Burns, Gerald. QC611.98.H54.B87 1992, (v1)
Burns, J. H. JA84.S26.B87 1996, (v7)
Burns, J. H. JC375.B87 1992, (v7)
Burns, James MacGregor. E757.B96 2001, (v4)
  E806.B94 1989, (v4)
  E807.B835, (v4)
  E842.B8 1961, (v4)
  HM141.B847 1978, (v6)
  JK1061.B8 1966, (v7)
Burns, John Horne. PS3503.U66 G3, (v3)
  PS3503.U66.L8, (v3)
Burns, Kathryn. F3611.C9.B87 1999, (v4)
Burns, Nancy. RT81.5.B86 2001, (v2)
  RT81.5.B863 1999, (v2)
Burns, Noel M. F555.B87 1985, (v4)
Burns, Richard Dean. Z3228.V5.B87 1984, (v10)
  Z8888.9.B87 1984, (v10)
Burns, Robert Homer. [from old catalog]. F761.B88,
  (v4)
Burns, Robert Ignatius. DP302.V205.B85 1984, (v5)
Burns, Robert P. KF8910.B87 1999, (v7)
Burns, Robert. PR4302.F42 1965, (v3)
  PR4331.A4 1985, (v3)
Burns, Ross. DS94.5.B87 1999, (v5)
Burns, Sarah. N6510.B87 1996, (v9)
Burns, Thomas S. U35.B79 1994, (v10)
Burns, Tom. HM22.U6.G642 1991, (v6)
Burns, W. Haywood. E185.61.B96, (v4)
Burns, Walter Noble. F819.T6 B936 1999, (v4)
Burns, Wayne. PR5216.B8, (v3)
Burnshaw, Stanley. PJ5038.B8, (v3)
Burnshaw, Stanley. PS3503.U65.A6 1990, (v3)
Buros, Oscar Krisen. BF698.5.B87, (v2)
  LB1050.46.B87, (v7)
  Z5814.E9.B8, (v10)
  Z5814.P8 B93, (v10)
Burr, Chandler. QP81.6.B87 1996, (v1)
Burr, Harold Saxton. RC346.B86, (v2)
Burrage, Henry S. E127.B96, (v4)
Burrell, Barbara C. HQ1236.5.U6.B87 1994, (v6)
Burrell, Harry. PR6019.O9.F568 1996, (v3)
Burress, Lee. Z658.U5.B87 1989, (v10)
Burrin, Philippe. D802.F8 B8613 1996, (v5)
Burritt, Elihu. PS1219.B7.Z53 1937, (v3)
Burroughs, Alan. ND205.B8 1965, (v9)
Burroughs, Catherine B. PR4056.B87 1997, (v3)
Burroughs, Charles. NA1120.B87 1990, (v9)
Burroughs, John. QH81.B963 1951, (v1)
Burroughs, Raymond Darwin. QL155.B8, (v1)
Burroughs, William James. QC879.5.B87 1990, (v1)
  QC883.2.C5.B87 1992, (v1)
Burroughs, William S. PS3552.U75.N3 1966, (v3)
Burrow, J. A. PE535.B87 1996, (v3)
  PR255.B8 1982, (v3)
Burrow, J. W. CB204.B87 2000, (v5)
Burrow, James Gordon. R15.B9, (v2)
Burrow, Rufus. BX4827.C65.B87 1994, (v8)
Burrow, T. PL4609.B8, (v3)
Burrowes, Reynold A. F2056.8.B87 1988, (v4)
Burrows, David L. ML3845.B837 1990, (v9)
Burrows, Donald. ML410.H13.B94 1994b, (v9)
  ML410.H13 B95 1991, (v9)
Burrows, Edwin G. F128.3.B95 1999, (v4)
Burrows, Paul. HB135.B87, (v6)
Burrows, Simon. PN5177.B87 2000, (v3)
Burrows, William E. QB500.262.B87 1998, (v1)
  UA10.B87 1994, (v10)
Burshtein, A. I. QC311.B95 1996, (v1)
Burstein, Andrew. E285.B88 2001, (v4)
  E332.B96 1995, (v4)
Burstein, Daniel. HE7572.U6.B87 1995, (v6)
Burstein, Janet. PS153.J4.B87 1996, (v3)

Bursten, Ben. RA1151.B935 2001, (v2)
Burstin, Barbara Stern. F159.P69.P72 1989, (v4)
Burston, Daniel. BF109.F76.B87 1991, (v2)
Burstow, Bonnie. HV6250.4.W65.B87 1992, (v6)
Bursztyn, Peter. RC1235.B87 1990, (v2)
Burt, Alfred Le Roy. F1032.B94, (v4)
Burt, Brian A. RK52.B87 1999, (v2)
Burt, Daniel S. Z5301.B96 2001, (v10)
Burt, David N. HD39.5.B875 2003, (v6)
Burt, Donald X. B655.Z7.B85 1996, (v8)
Burt, Eugene C. Z5956.E7.B87 1989, (v10)
Burt, Forrest D. PR6025.A86.Z5585 1985, (v3)
Burt, George. MT64.M65 B87 1994, (v9)
Burt, John. PS3545.A748.Z64 1988, (v3)
Burt, Martha R. HV4505.B88 1992, (v6)
Burt, Maxwell Struthers. F596.B97 1938, (v4)
  F767.P6 B8 1971, (v4)
  PS3503.U69 D4, (v3)
Burt, Robert. KF5130.B87 1992, (v7)
Burt, Robert. KF8744.B87 1988, (v7)
Burt, Vivien K. RG103.5.B87 2001, (v2)
Burt, William Henry. QL715.B8 1976, (v1)
Burtchaell, James Tunstead. BJ1249.B87 1989, (v8)
  BV648.B83 1992, (v8)
  LC383.B87 1998, (v7)
Burtness, James H. BJ1251.B87 1999, (v8)
Burton, Allen William. QP303.B87 1998, (v1)
Burton, Antoinette M. DA125.S57.B87 1998, (v5)
Burton, Audrey. DK948.83.B87 1997, (v5)
Burton, C. Emory. HC110.P6.B87 1992, (v6)
Burton, David Henry. E176.1.B935 1988, (v4)
  KF8744.B874 1998, (v7)
Burton, Humphrey. ML418.M27.B87 2001, (v9)
Burton, James G. UA23.B795 1993, (v10)
Burton, Jeffrey. KFO1705.B87 1995, (v7)
Burton, John. BP135.B79 1994, (v8)
Burton, Lloyd. KF8210.N37.B87 1991, (v7)
Burton, R. F. QP33.6.M36.B87 1994, (v1)
Burton, Richard D. E. F1874.B8 1997, (v4)
  PQ2191.Z5.B78 1991, (v3)
Burton, Robert. PR2223.A1 1932, (v3)
Burton, Robert. PR2223.A2.F38 1989, (v3)
Burton, Steven J. KF8775.B87 1995, (v7)
Burton, Virginia Lee. PZ7.B954Mi, (v3)
Burton, William C. KF156.B856 1998, (v7)
Burton, William L. E540.F6 B87 1998, (v4)
Burton-Christie, Douglas. BX2465.B87 1993, (v8)
Burtt, Edwin A. B67.B8 1954, (v8)
Buruma, Ian. D804.G4 B78 1994, (v5)
Burwick, Frederick. PN56.M536.B87 2001, (v3)
  PN1241.B87 1996, (v3)
Bury, J. B. CB67.B8 1932, (v5)
Bury, J. B. D135.B8 1963, (v5)
Bury, J. B. DG311.B98 1958, (v5)
Bury, J. P. T. DC251.B8 1989, (v5)
Bury, Karl V. TA340.B87 1999, (v1)
Busch, Andrew. JK521.B87 1997, (v7)
Busch, Briton Cooper. SH383.2.B87 1994, (v1)
Busch, Eberhard. BX4827.B3.B86313, (v8)
Busch, Frederick. PS3552.U814.D6, (v3)
  PS3552.U814.M8, (v3)
Busch, Harald. NA390.B813, (v9)
  NA440.B853, (v9)
Busch, Harris. RB121.B86, (v2)
Busch, Thomas W. B2430.S34.B87 1990, (v8)
Busek, Vratislav. DB215.5.B83, (v5)
Buser, Pierre A. QP461.B9713 1991, (v1)
Buser, Pierre A. QP475.B8413 1992, (v1)
Busette, Cedric. PQ6605.E44F3333 1994, (v3)
Bush, Barbara. E883.B87.A3 1994, (v4)
Bush, Clifford L. LB1573.B898 1979, (v7)
Bush, Clive. E169.1.B976 1991, (v4)
Bush, David M. HT391.B83 1996, (v6)
Bush, Douglas. PR431.B8 1962, (v3)
  PR502.B88, (v3)
  PR508.M9.B8 1963, (v3)
  PR508.S3.B8, (v3)
  PR4036.B8, (v3)
  PR4836.B79, (v3)
Bush, George. E840.8.B87.A3 1987, (v4)
Bush, Harold K. PS166.B87 1999, (v3)

Bush, M. L. DA339.B87 1996, (v5)
  HT867.B87 2000, (v6)
Bush, Perry. BX8116.B87 1998, (v8)
Bush, Rod. E185.61.B98 1999, (v4)
Bush, Vannevar. U102.B985, (v10)
Bush-Brown, Albert. NA737.S9.B8, (v9)
Bushell, Garvin. ML419.B89 A3 1998, (v9)
Bushman, Richard L. F67.B97 1985, (v4)
Bushnell, Brooks. PN1998.B85 1993, (v3)
Bushnell, David. F1413.B88 1988, (v4)
  F2271.B78 1993, (v4)
Bushnell, Geoffrey Hext Sutherland. E61.B95 1968b,
  (v4)
Bushnell, O. A. PS3552.U823.K3, (v3)
Bushnell, Rebecca W. LC1011.B837 1996, (v7)
  Z8812.L4 B87 1996, (v10)
Bushrui, Suheil B. PR5907.B79 1990, (v3)
Bushy, Angeline. RT120.R87, (v2)
Busoni, Ferruccio. ML410.B98.A12 1965, (v9)
Buss, David M. HQ21.B95 1994, (v6)
Buss, Robin. PN1995.9.F54.B87 1994, (v3)
Buss, Terry F. HD5708.75.U6.B87 1988, (v6)
Busse, Heribert. BP172.B8613 1997, (v8)
Bussiere, Elizabeth. KF3720.B88 1997, (v7)
Bustard, Bruce I. TR6.U6.W18 1999, (v1)
Buszynski, Leszek. DK510.764.B87 1996, (v5)
Butalia, Urvashi. DS485.P87.B87 2000, (v5)
Butcher, James Neal. BF698.8.M5.B86 1999, (v2)
  RC473.M5.B87 1990, (v2)
Butcher, Margaret (Just). NX512.3.N5.B8 1972, (v9)
Butchvarov, Panayot. BD220.B87 1998, (v8)
  BJ1012.B76 1989, (v8)
Butland, Gilbert J. F1409.2.B8, (v4)
Butler, Anne M. HQ145.A17.B88 1985, (v6)
Butler, Anne M. KF4976.A2 1995, (v7)
Butler, Brian. F534.E9.B88 2000, (v4)
Butler, Christopher. NX458.B87, (v9)
  NX542.B88 1994, (v9)
Butler, David. JN956.B8683 1997, (v7)
  TD657.B88 1999, (v1)
Butler, Deborah A. LB1631.B88 1995, (v7)
Butler, Diana Hochstedt. BX5925.B84 1995, (v8)
Butler, E. M. PN57.F3.B8, (v3)
Butler, Edgar W. HC135.B875 2001, (v6)
Butler, Edward Cuthbert. BV5075.B8 1968, (v8)
Butler, Guy. PR9864.B8, (v3)
Butler, James Newton. QD561.B985 1998, (v1)
Butler, Jeffrey. JQ1999.B63 B87, (v7)
Butler, Jerry. ML420.B899.A3 2000, (v9)
Butler, John A. VK23.B88 1997, (v10)
Butler, Jon. E184.H9.B87 1983, (v4)
Butler, Jon. E188.B97 2000, (v4)
Butler, Judith P. HQ1154.B88 1990, (v6)
Butler, Kim D. F2651.S2.B85 1998, (v4)
Butler, M. TP248.27.A53.B87 1996, (v1)
Butler, Marilyn. PR447.B8 1982, (v3)
Butler, Martin. PR678.P65.B8 1984, (v3)
Butler, Michael. PT2611.R814.Z634 1976, (v3)
  PT2611.R814.Z635 1985, (v3)
Butler, Nicholas Murray. LB875.B9 1971, (v7)
Butler, Pierce. PR6029.F3.Z594 1993, (v3)
Butler, R. J. BC6.B8, (v8)
Butler, Richard. DS79.755.B88 2000, (v5)
  HD30.23.B875 1991, (v6)
Butler, Robert William. QL696.C52.B86 1997, (v1)
Butler, Ronnie. PQ2184.H55.B87 1983, (v3)
Butler, Ruth. NB553.R7.B88 1993, (v9)
Butler, Samuel. PR3338.A64 1970, (v3)
  PR3338.A7 1967, (v3)
  PR3338.A76 1979, (v3)
  PR4349.B7.A6 1950, (v3)
  PR4349.B7.E6 1933, (v3)
  PR4349.B7.N6 1951, (v3)
  PR4349.B7.N7, (v3)
  PR4349.B7 W3, (v3)
  PR4349.B7.Z535, (v3)
  PR4349.B7.Z537, (v3)
  PR4349.B7.Z54, (v3)
Butler, Sandra. HV1444.B88 1991, (v6)
Butler, Susan. TL540.E3.B88 1997, (v1)
Butlin, N. G. HC604.B883 1994, (v6)

Butnaru, I. C. DS135.R7.B78 1992, (v5)
Butor, Michel. PQ2603.U73.M63, (v3)
  PQ2603.U73.P613 1995, (v3)
Butow, Robert J. C. D821.J3.B8 1954, (v5)
Butsch, Richard. PN1590.A9.B88 2000, (v3)
Butt, Archibald Willingham. E748.B94.A4 1971, (v4)
Butt, John Everett. PR441.B8, (v3)
  PR441.B83, (v3)
Butt, John. ML410.B1.B9 1990, (v9)
  ML410.B1.B93 1991, (v9)
  ML457.B9 1994, (v9)
Butt, John. PC4112.B88 1988, (v3)
Butterfield, Andrew. NB623.V5.B88 1997, (v9)
Butterfield, Herbert. D13.B79, (v5)
  D13.B8, (v5)
  DA1.B875 1970, (v5)
  DA505.B975 1968, (v5)
  Q125.B97 1957a, (v1)
Butterwick, Richard. DK4330.B88 1998, (v5)
Butterworth, Brian. QA141.5.B786 1999, (v1)
Buttimer, Anne. GF21.B87 1993, (v6)
Buttlar, Lois. Z1361.E4 B89 1996, (v10)
Button, James W. E185.92.B88 1989, (v4)
  HV6477.B87, (v6)
Buttress, F. A. AS8.B8 1960a, (v10)
Butts, R. Freeman. LB1584.B84 1989, (v7)
Butwin, Joseph. PJ5129.R2.Z565, (v3)
Butz, Michael R. RC488.5.B85 1997, (v2)
Butzer, Karl W. CC81.B87 1982, (v5)
  GN741.B8 1971, (v6)
Buwalda, Piet. DS135.R92.B89 1997, (v5)
Buxbaum, Melvin H. Z8313.B89 1983, (v10)
Buxton, Charles Roden. PN1111.B8, (v3)
Buxton, John. PR2343.B87 1964, (v3)
Buxton, Richard B. RC386.6.M34B895 2002, (v2)
Buytendijk, F. J. J. BF515.B83 1962, (v2)
Buzacott, Martin. PR3091.B8 1991, (v3)
Buzaglo, Meir. BC199.C55 B89 2002, (v8)
Buzan, Barry. D860.B89 1998, (v5)
  UA11.B84 1987, (v10)
Buzard, James. PR129.E85.B89 1993, (v3)
Buzzanco, Robert. DS558.B92 1999, (v5)
  DS559.62.U6.B89 1996, (v5)
Byam, L. Dale. PN2969.B93 1999, (v3)
Byars, Betsy Cromer. PZ7.B98396Su, (v3)
Byars, Jackie. PN1995.9.S47.B9 1991, (v3)
Byatt, A. S. PN3343.B93 2000, (v3)
Byatt, A. S. PR6063.U7.Z6 1994, (v3)
Bybee, Joan L. P299.G73.B93 1994, (v3)
Bybee, Keith J. KF4893.B93 1998, (v7)
Bychkova Jordan, Bella. DK781.D98, (v5)
Byerly, Alison. PR878.A74.B94 1997, (v3)
Byers, Clive. QL696.P2438.B95 1995, (v1)
Byers, Horace Robert. QC861.B9 1959, (v1)
Byers, John A. QL737.U52.B94 1997, (v1)
Byers, Walter. GV351.B94 1995, (v6)
Byg, Barton. PN1998.3.S77.B94 1995, (v3)
Bygrave, Stephen. B945.B774 B94 1993, (v8)
Byland, Bruce E. F1219.54.M59.B95 1994, (v4)
Byles, Joan Montgomery. PR605.W65.B95 1995, (v3)
Bynagle, Hans E. Z7125.B97 1997, (v10)
Bynner, Witter. PS3503.Y45.A16 1979, (v3)
  PS3503.Y45.A17 1978, (v3)
  PS3503.Y45I5 1929, (v3)
Bynum, Caroline Walker. BD373.B96 2001, (v8)
  BR253.B96 1987, (v8)
  BT741.2.B95 1990, (v8)
  BT872.B96 1995, (v8)
  BV4490.B96 1982, (v8)
Bynum, Victoria E. HQ1438.N6.B96 1992, (v6)
Bynum, W. F. R484.B95 1994, (v2)
Byock, Jesse L. HN553.B96 1988, (v6)
Byrd, Harold Eugene. HC102.5.B97.A32, (v6)
Byrd, Martha. UG626.2.C48.B97 1987, (v10)
Byrd, Max. PR449.L65.B95, (v3)
  PR449.M4.B9, (v3)
Byrd, Richard Evelyn. G585.B8.A33 1938, (v6)
Byrd, Rudolph P. PS3539.O478.Z59 1990, (v3)
Byrd, W. Michael. RA448.5.N4.B97 2000, (v2)
Byrd, William L. E185.96.B99 1999, (v4)
Byrne, D. S. H61.25.B95 1998, (v6)

HT119.B96 2001, (v6)
Byrne, Deborah J. Z699.35.M28 B97 1998, (v10)
Byrne, Eleanor. PN1999.W27.B97 1999, (v3)
Byrne, Hugh. F1488.3.B95 1996, (v4)
Byrne, John Francis. CT808.B9.A3, (v5)
Byrne, Kevin P. RC632.H83.B97 1991, (v2)
Byrne, Peter. BJ1012.B97 1999, (v8)
  HV3004.B95 2000, (v6)
Byrnes, Robert Francis. DK38.7.K53.B97 1995, (v5)
Byron, George Gordon Byron. PR4351.C5 1966, (v3)
  PR4351.M27, (v3)
  PR4352.Q4, (v3)
  PR4359.A1 1957, (v3)
  PR4381.A3.B3, (v3)
  PR4381.A3.M35 1973, (v3)
  PR4381.A3.M8, (v3)
  PR4381.A3.Q4 I950, (v3)
  PR4381.A385 1982, (v3)
  PR4383.H57 1954, (v3)
Byron, William. PQ6337.B9, (v3)
Bytheil, Duncan. HD2339.G7.B9 1978, (v6)
  HD8039.T42.G72, (v6)
Bywaters, David A. PR3427.P6.B9 1991, (v3)
Caballero, Fernan. PQ6509.G2 1930, (v3)
Cabanne, Pierre. ND553.D774.C313 1971, (v9)
Cabeen, David Clark. Z2171.C74 1947, (v10)
Cabell, James Branch. PS3505.A153.A1 1927, v.14, (v3)
  PS3505.A153.A1 1927, v.17, (v3)
  PS3505.A153.A1 1927, v.5, (v3)
  PS3505.A153.A1 1927, v.2, (v3)
  PS3505.A153.B4 1970, (v3)
  PS3505.A153 C7, (v3)
  PS3505.A153 D6, (v3)
  PS3505.A153 H5, (v3)
  PS3505.A153 J8, (v3)
  PS3505.A153.L3 1934, (v3)
  PS3505.A153.L5 1921, (v3)
  PS3505.A153.M8 1926, (v3)
  PS3505.A153.P7 1936, (v3)
  PS3505.A153.Q5 1952, (v3)
  PS3505.A153 S5, (v3)
  PS3505.A153 S55, (v3)
  PS3505.A153 S6, (v3)
  PS3505.A153 S65, (v3)
  PS3505.A153.T5 1932, (v3)
  PS3505.A153 W3, (v3)
  PS3505.A153.Z52, (v3)
  PS3505.A153.Z53 1962, (v3)
Cable, George Washington. PS1244.C74, (v3)
  PS1244.G7, (v3)
  PS1244.O6 1970, (v3)
Cable, James. V25.C3324 1998, (v10)
Cable, Lana. PR3591.C33 1995, (v3)
Cable, Mildred. DS793.G6.C3, (v5)
Cabot, Elizabeth Rogers Mason. F73.44.C333 1991, (v4)
Caccamo De Luca, Rita. HN80.M85.C313 2000, (v6)
Cachia, Pierre. PJ7538.C33 1990, (v3)
  PJ8210.C33 1989, (v3)
Cadalso, Jose. PQ6510.C3.C3 1975, (v3)
Cadava, Eduardo. PS1642.H5.C33 1997, (v3)
  TR183.C33 1997, (v1)
Cadena, Marisol de la. F3429.3.M63.C33 2000, (v4)
Cadick, John. TK152.C22 1994, (v1)
Cadmus, Paul. NC139.C32.A2 1989, (v9)
Cadogan, Jeanne K. ND623.G4.C33 2000, (v9)
Cady, Edwin Harrison. BJ1601.C2, (v8)
  PS507.C2 1969, (v3)
Cady, Jack. PS169.N35.C33 1999, (v3)
Cady, John Frank. DS518.1.C23, (v5)
  DS518.2.C3, (v5)
Cadzow, James A. TK5102.5.C24 1985, (v1)
Caenegem, R.C. van. KJC4431.C34 1995, (v7)
Caesar, Adrian. PR605.W65.C34 1993, (v3)
Caesar, Julius. DC62.C2.H2, (v5)
  DC62.C2.W36, (v5)
Caesar, Terry. PE64.C34.A3 1992, (v3)
Caferro, William. DG975.S5.C25 1998, (v5)
Caffaro, John V. RJ507.S53.C34 1998, (v2)
Caffey, David L. PS283.N6.C34 1999, (v3)

Caffrey, Margaret M. GN21.B45.C34 1989, (v6)
Cage, John. ML60.C125 1993, (v9)
Cage, John. ML60.C13.S5, (v9)
  ML410.C24.A5 1995, (v9)
Cagin, Seth. E185.93.M6.C34 1988, (v4)
Cagle, William R. Z5776.G2.C177 1998, (v10)
Cahalan, James M. PR6029.F5.Z63 1991, (v3)
  PR8718.C35 1993, (v3)
  PR8797.C34 1988, (v3)
  PR8807.W6.C35 1999, (v3)
Cahan, Abraham. PJ5129.C27.Z513, (v3)
Cahen, Claude. DR481.C3313 2001, (v5)
Cahill, Ann J. HV6558.C34 2001, (v6)
Cahill, James. ND1043.3.C3, (v9)
  ND1043.5.C34, (v9)
  ND1043.5.C35 1994, (v9)
Cahill, Lisa Sowle. BT707.7 .C35 2000, (v8)
  BT708.C283 1996, (v8)
Cahill, Marion Cotter. H31.C7 no. 380 1968, (v6)
Cahm, Caroline. HX914.7.K7.C34 1989, (v6)
Cahn, Edmond Nathaniel. KF379.C33 1981, (v7)
Cahn, Matthew Alan. GE180.C34 1995, (v6)
Cahn, R. S. QD7.C2 1979, (v1)
Cahn, Robert N. QC793.2.C34 1989, (v1)
Cahn, Victor L. PR2976.C27 1991, (v3)
  PR6066.I53.Z624 1993, (v3)
Cai, Zong-qi. PL2314.C35 1996, (v3)
Caidin, Martin. UG633.C14, (v10)
Caillet Bois, Julio. PQ7084.C3 1965, (v3)
Cain, Edward. E743.C2, (v4)
Cain, George H. KF298.C24 1994, (v7)
Cain, James M. PS3505.A3113 M5, (v3)
  PS3505.A3113 P3, (v3)
Cain, M. J. B945.F634 C35 2002, (v8)
Cain, Patricia A. KF4754.5.C35 2000, (v7)
Caine, Barbara. HQ1595.A3.C34 1992, (v6)
Caird, G. B. BS2397.C35 1994, (v8)
Cairncross, Alec. HC256.5.C257 1995, (v6)
Cairncross, Frances. HC79.E5.C27 1992, (v6)
  HD30.2.C347 2002, (v6)
  HE7631.C34 2001, (v6)
Cairney, John. PN1936.C35 2001, (v3)
Cairns, David. ML410.B5 C25 1999, (v9)
Cairns, Francis. PA6789.C26, (v3)
Cairns, John. QH501.C33 1997, (v1)
Cairo, Jimmy M. RC735.I5.R4728 1999, (v2)
Cajori, Florian. QA21.C13 1917, (v1)
  QA21.C15 1919, (v1)
  QC7.C13 1962, (v1)
Cakmak, A. S. TA330.C33 1995, (v1)
Calabrese, John. DS63.2.C5.C35 1990, (v5)
Calabrese, Michael A. PR1933.L6.C35 1994, (v3)
Calabrese, Omar. NX456.C3213 1992, (v9)
Calabro, Tony. PT2603.R397.Z58186 1990, (v3)
Calamari, John D. KF283.C34 1984, (v7)
  KF801.C26 1998, (v7)
Calasibetta, Charlotte Mankey. TT503.C34 1998, (v1)
Calasso, Roberto. PN56.M95C3513 2001, (v3)
Caldecott, Randolph. PZ8.3.C127Fo vol. 3, (v3)
Caldeira, Teresa Pires do Rio. HV6895.S3, (v6)
Calder, Alexander. N6537.C33.L56 1976, (v9)
Calder, Angus. DA587.C28 1969b, (v5)
Calder, Daniel Gillmore. PR1664.C3, (v3)
Calder, James D. HV9950.C34 1993, (v6)
Calder, Kenneth J. D611.C35, (v5)
Calder, Kent E. HF1601.C35 1993, (v6)
Calder, Lendol Glen. HG3756.U54.C35 1999, (v6)
Calderón de la Barca, Pedro. PQ6285.A1 1977b, (v3)
  PQ6287.A2 1926, (v3)
  PQ6292.V5.H6, (v3)
Calderwood, James L. PR2829.C29 1989, (v3)
  PR3069.D42.C35 1987, (v3)
Caldicott, Helen. TK9153.C34 1994, (v1)
Caldwell, Erskine. E169.C17 1941, (v4)
  PS3505.A322 G6 1934, (v3)
  PS3505.A322.J6, (v3)
  PS3505.A322 L28, (v3)
  PS3505.A322 L3, (v3)
  PS3505.A322 L6, (v3)
  PS3505.A322 M4, (v3)
  PS3505.A322 T6 1932, (v3)

PS3505.A322.T7, **(v3)**
PS3505.A322 T76, **(v3)**
PS3505.A322.Z53, **(v3)**
Caldwell, John Thornton. PN1992.6.C22 1995, **(v3)**
Caldwell, John. ML172.C28, **(v9)**
ML286.C28 1991, **(v9)**
Caldwell, Lynton Keith. HC79.E5.C333 1995, **(v6)**
KF3775.C35 1998, **(v7)**
Caldwell, Mark. BJ1853.C23 1999, **(v8)**
Caldwell, Ronald J. Z5579.6.C35 1990, **(v10)**
Caldwell, Sarah. BL1225.K3 C35 1999, **(v8)**
Calero, Luis Fernando. F2270.1.G6.C35 1997, **(v4)**
Calhoun, Charles H. HF5387.C33 1999, **(v6)**
Calhoun, Craig J. DS779.32.C35 1994, **(v5)**
JC311.C28 1998, **(v7)**
Calhoun, Daniel F. DT107.83.C25 1991, **(v5)**
Calhoun, Daniel Hovey. LA205.C16, **(v7)**
Calhoun, Frederick S. KF8794.C35 1990, **(v7)**
Calhoun, John C. E337.8.C148, **(v4)**
JK216.C17, **(v7)**
Calhoun, Laurie. BD348.C35 1997, **(v8)**
Calhoun, Richard James. PS3521.I582.Z63 1992, **(v3)**
Califano, Joseph A. E847.C32 2000, **(v4)**
HN59.C26, **(v6)**
California Coastal Commission. F859.3.C263 1987, **(v4)**
Calimano, Ivan E. Z1609.L7.C35 1994, **(v10)**
Calin, William. PQ401.C35 1987, **(v3)**
Calinescu, Matei. BH301.M54.C34 1987, **(v8)**
PN98.R38.C35 1993, **(v3)**
Calingaert, Daniel. UA770.C35 1991, **(v10)**
Calisher, Hortense. PS3505.A4.Ex, **(v3)**
PS3553.A4.A6 1975, **(v3)**
PS3553.A4.F3, **(v3)**
PS3553.A4.R3, **(v3)**
Calkin, Robert R. TP983.C33 1994, **(v1)**
Calkins, Frank. SK453.C34 1971, **(v1)**
Calkins, Robert G. N5970.C34 1979, **(v9)**
NA5453.C35 1998, **(v9)**
Callaghan, Barry. PR9199.3.C266.W39 1991, **(v3)**
Callaghan, Dympna. PR2991.C337 2000, **(v3)**
Callaghan, John. HX21.C35 2000, **(v6)**
Callaghan, Morley. PR6005.A37 L6, **(v3)**
Callahan, Daniel J. BX1920.C258, **(v8)**
Callahan, Daniel. HB3505.C35, **(v6)**
Callahan, David. E743.C233 1990, **(v4)**
E840.C335 1997, **(v4)**
Callahan, James Morton. E183.8.C2 C3 1967, **(v4)**
Callahan, James. QC173.55.C36 2000, **(v1)**
Callahan, John Francis. B187.T55.C3, **(v8)**
Callahan, Michael D. JZ4871.5.C35 1999, **(v7)**
Callan, Edward. PR6001.U4.Z633 1983, **(v3)**
PR9369.3.P37.C734 1991, **(v3)**
PR9369.3.P37.Z6 1982, **(v3)**
Callanan, Frank. DA958.H4.C35 1996, **(v5)**
DA958.P2.C35 1992, **(v5)**
Callander, Marilyn Berg. PS3505.A87.Z59 1989, **(v3)**
Callas, Maria. MT820.C17 1987, **(v9)**
Callaway, Barbara. DT515.45.H38.C35 1987, **(v5)**
HQ1810.C35 1994, **(v6)**
Callaway, Dorothy J. SB413.M34.C34 1994, **(v1)**
Callcott, Wilfrid Hardy. F1232.C142 1965, **(v4)**
F1232.S2312 1964, **(v4)**
F1418.C22 1966, **(v4)**
Calleo, David P. DD220.C34, **(v5)**
HJ2052.C35 1992, **(v6)**
Callies, David L. KFH458.C34 1994, **(v7)**
Callinicos, Alex. BD450.C23 1988, **(v8)**
Callow, John. DA450.C35 2000, **(v5)**
Callow, Philip. ND553.C33.C3 1995, **(v9)**
PR5493.C28 2001, **(v3)**
PS3231.C25 1992, **(v3)**
Callow, Simon. PN1998.3.W45.C36 1996, **(v3)**
Calloway, Colin G. E45.C34 1997, **(v4)**
E83.775.C35 1995, **(v4)**
Calloway, Paul. RC451.S65.C35 1993, **(v2)**
Calloway, Stephen. NC242.B3.C36 1998, **(v9)**
Calman, Leslie J. HQ1743.C35 1992, **(v6)**
Calmette, Joseph. DC611.B78.C263 1963, **(v5)**
Calof, Rachel. F645.J5.C353 1995, **(v4)**
Calvert, James F. VB259.C28 1971, **(v10)**

Calvert, Karin Lee Fishbeck. HQ792.U5.C35 1992, **(v6)**
Calvert, Peter. F1414.2.C23 1990, **(v4)**
Calvert, Rosalie Stier. F187.C5.C35 1991, **(v4)**
Calvert, Susan. F2843.C27 1989, **(v4)**
Calvert, William J. PR4381.C3 1962, **(v3)**
Calvet, Louis Jean. P85.B33.C2913 1995, **(v3)**
Calvin, William H. QP376.C318 1994, **(v1)**
D743.C24 1989, **(v5)**
D843.C25 1996, **(v5)**
Camacho, Jorge Abel. F2508.C18 1954, **(v4)**
Camarillo, Albert. F869.S45.C25, **(v4)**
Cambel, Ali Bulent. Q172.5.C45.C36 1993, **(v1)**
Camden, Carroll. PR442.C3, **(v3)**
Cameron, Averil. DF505.7.P7.C35 1985, **(v5)**
Cameron, Catherine M. ML3845.C36 1996, **(v9)**
Cameron, Charles M. JK586.C23 2000, **(v7)**
Cameron, Craig M. VE23.22 1st.C36 1994, **(v10)**
Cameron, Euan. BR305.2.C35 1991, **(v8)**
Cameron, Eugene N. TN23.C36 1986, **(v1)**
TN565.C43, **(v1)**
Cameron, James N. QP121.C26 1989, **(v1)**
Cameron, Jean. KF223.H86.C36 1994, **(v7)**
Cameron, Kenneth M. PN1995.9.A43.C36 1994, **(v3)**
Cameron, Kenneth Neill. PR5431.C29, **(v3)**
Cameron, Mary M. DS495.8.B456 C36 1998, **(v5)**
Cameron, Maxwell A. HF1746.C33 2000, **(v6)**
Cameron, Meribeth Elliott. DS511.C3 1960, **(v5)**
DS761.C3, **(v5)**
Cameron, Miriam. RC607.A26.C34 1993, **(v2)**
Cameron, Nigel. DS707.C36 1989, **(v5)**
DS796.H757.C36 1991, **(v5)**
Cameron, Peter J. QA162.C36 1998, **(v1)**
QA164.C346 1994, **(v1)**
Cameron, Rondo E. HC21.C33 2003, **(v6)**
Cameron, Sharon. BQ944.M47 A3 2000, **(v8)**
PS1541.Z5.C287 1992, **(v3)**
Camfield, Gregg. PS437.C36 1997, **(v3)**
Camhi, Jeffrey M. QP360.C34 1984, **(v1)**
Camic, Charles. HN398.S3.C35 1983, **(v6)**
Camille, Michael. N6310.C36 1996, **(v9)**
Camilleri, Joseph A. DU113.C34 1987, **(v5)**
HC460.5.C258 2000, **(v6)**
Caminero-Santangelo, Marta. PS374.M44.C36 1998, **(v3)**
Cammack, Paul A. JF60.C359 1997, **(v7)**
Cammann, Schuyler V. R. DS785.C15, **(v5)**
Cammisa, Anne Marie. HV95.C32 1998, **(v6)**
JK325.C27 1995, **(v7)**
Camnitzer, Luis. N6603.C26 1994, **(v9)**
Camoes, Luis de. PQ9198.A2 1973, **(v3)**
Camp, Helen C. HX84.F5.C36 1995, **(v6)**
Camp, John McK. DF275 .C28 2001, **(v5)**
Camp, L. Raymond. F82.W7.C35 1989, **(v4)**
Camp, Roderic Ai. CT552.C36 1988, **(v5)**
F1235.5.A2.C35 1995, **(v4)**
HC135.C212 1989, **(v6)**
JL1281.C34 1995, **(v7)**
JL1281.C35 1993, **(v7)**
Campagna, Anthony S. HC106.6.C287 1991, **(v6)**
HC106.7.C34 1995, **(v6)**
Campagna, Daniel S. HQ144.C35 1988, **(v6)**
Campana, Richard J. SB435.5.C26 1999, **(v1)**
Campanella, Roy. GV865.C3.A3, **(v6)**
Campany, Robert Ford. PL2629.F35.C36 1996, **(v3)**
Campbell, A. PE131.C3, **(v3)**
Campbell, Ballard C. JK421.C23 1995, **(v7)**
Campbell, Bruce. DD253.7.C36 1998, **(v5)**
Campbell, Charles Arthur. BJ1012.C3 1967, **(v8)**
Campbell, Colin. E881.B87 1991, **(v4)**
JK516.C36 1998, **(v7)**
JQ4041.C36 1993, **(v7)**
Campbell, Craig S. TD756.5.C35 1999, **(v1)**
Campbell, David A. PA3110.C25 1983, **(v3)**
Campbell, David. E840.C348 1998, **(v4)**
Campbell, Don. PN4899.W29.C36 1991, **(v3)**
Campbell, Donna M. PS374.R4.C36 1997, **(v3)**
Campbell, Douglas S. KF2750.A59.C36 1990, **(v7)**
Campbell, Edwina S. D1065.G3.C36 1989, **(v5)**
Campbell, George L. P371.C36 2000, **(v3)**
Campbell, Gordon. CR101.C3 1974, **(v5)**

Campbell, Hilbert H. PR3733.C3, **(v3)**
Campbell, Ian M. QD505.C36 1988, **(v1)**
Campbell, J. B. DG276.5.C26 1984, **(v5)**
Campbell, James B. G70.4.C23 1996, **(v6)**
Campbell, James T. BX8443.C36 1995, **(v8)**
Campbell, James. B945.D4.C36 1995, **(v8)**
Campbell, Jill. PR3458.P8.C36 1995, **(v3)**
Campbell, Joan. NK951.C35, **(v9)**
Campbell, John Charles. F210.C2 1973, **(v4)**
Campbell, John Coert. DR370.C33, **(v5)**
Campbell, John Creighton. HQ1064.J3.C36 1992, **(v6)**
Campbell, John Quincy Adams. E507.5 5th.C36 2000, **(v4)**
Campbell, John. BF467.C35 1994, **(v2)**
Campbell, Joseph. BL48.C325 1988, **(v8)**
BL303.6.C35.A3 1990, **(v8)**
BL304.C36 1988, **(v8)**
BL311.C276, **(v8)**
BL313.C28 1949, **(v8)**
Campbell, Josie P. PS3559.R8.Z6 1998, **(v3)**
Campbell, June. BQ7610.C36 2002, **(v8)**
Campbell, Keith. BD450.C244 1988, **(v8)**
Campbell, Lily Bess. PR419.R4.C3 1972, **(v3)**
Campbell, Lorne. ND1313.2.C36 1990, **(v9)**
Campbell, Lyle. PM108.C36 1997, **(v3)**
Campbell, Malcolm. F767.J8 C3, **(v4)**
Campbell, Marjorie Wilkins. F1060.C18, **(v4)**
Campbell, Matthew. PR595.W45.C36 1999, **(v3)**
Campbell, Mavis Christine. F1884.C36 1988, **(v4)**
Campbell, Mildred. DA356.C3 1968, **(v5)**
Campbell, Neil A. QH308.2.C34 2000, **(v1)**
Campbell, Neil. F596.C235 2000, **(v4)**
Campbell, Oscar James. PR2892.C3, **(v3)**
Campbell, Patricia Shehan. MT1.C22 1991, **(v9)**
MT1.C226 1995, **(v9)**
Campbell, Patrick. PR6037.A86.Z64 1999, **(v3)**
Campbell, Peter. QC757.9.C36 1994, **(v1)**
Campbell, R. E. SB732.6.C33 1989, **(v1)**
Campbell, R. H. HC257.S4 C3 1985, **(v6)**
Campbell, R. Thomas. V438.C36 1998, **(v10)**
Campbell, Randolph B. E445.T47.C35 1989, **(v4)**
F391.C27 1997, **(v4)**
Campbell, Richard. BD181.C23 1992, **(v8)**
PN4888.T4.C36 1991, **(v3)**
Campbell, Robert Wellington. HC244.C35 1991, **(v6)**
Campbell, Robert. BD445.C36 1988, **(v8)**
Campbell, Roy. PQ6613.A763.Z577 1952a, **(v3)**
Campbell, Stephen A. TK7871.85.C25 2001, **(v1)**
Campbell, Stuart L. DC276.5.C35, **(v5)**
Campbell, Susan B. RJ506.B44C36 2002, **(v2)**
Campbell, Ted. BR157.C36 1996, **(v8)**
Campbell, Terence W. RC455.2.F35.C35 1998, **(v2)**
Campbell, Thomas. PR4410.A5R6 1968, **(v3)**
Campbell, Tony. GA231.C36 1987, **(v6)**
Campbell, W. Joseph. PN4784.S4.C36 2001, **(v3)**
Campbell, Walter E. HC102.5.K457.C35 1996, **(v6)**
Campbell, William Giles. LB2369.C3 1986, **(v7)**
Campenhausen, Hans. BR1706.C313 1969, **(v8)**
Campion, Dan. PS3507.E8673.Z59 1995, **(v3)**
Campion, Frank D. R15.A55.C36 1984, **(v2)**
Campion, Jane. PN1998.3.C3545.A3 1999, **(v3)**
Campisi, Jack. E99.M4.C36 1991, **(v4)**
Campoamor, Ramon de. PQ6511.A17 1974, **(v3)**
Campos, Julieta. PQ7298.13.A398.C413 1995, **(v3)**
Campos, Paul F. KF379.C36 1998, **(v7)**
Camus, Albert. D743.9.C295 1948, **(v5)**
DC404.C3, **(v5)**
HM281.C3513 1956, **(v6)**
PQ2605.A3734.A16 1965, **(v3)**
PQ2605.A3734.A25, **(v3)**
PQ2605.A3734A6 1991, **(v3)**
PQ2605.A3734.C33 1958, **(v3)**
PQ2605.A3734.E79, **(v3)**
PQ2605.A3734E813 1989, **(v3)**
PQ2605.A3734.E8 1954, **(v3)**
PQ2605.A3734.E9, **(v3)**
PQ2605.A3734.M3 1963, **(v3)**
PQ2605.A3734.M9, **(v3)**
PQ2605.A3734.N6 1947, **(v3)**
PQ2605.A3734.P63, **(v3)**

Canaday, John. N6447.C36 1981, (v9)
  QC791.96.C36 2000, (v1)
Canavaggio, Jean. PQ6337.C2313 1990, (v3)
Canaway, W. H. PR6053.A55.H8, (v3)
Canby, Courtlandt. DS111.C36 1990, (v5)
Canby, Henry Seidel. PS88.C35 1959, (v3)
Cancian, Francesca M. HQ1075.5.U6.C36 1987, (v6)
Cancian, Frank. F1221.T9.C294 1992, (v4)
Candelaria, Michael R. BR600.C26 1990, (v8)
Candido, Antonio. PN51.C32913 1995, (v3)
Candido, Joseph. Z8812.R53 C36 1998, (v10)
Candlin, Enid Saunders. DS710.C294, (v5)
Candy, Philip C. LC5225.L42.C36 1991, (v7)
Canetti, Elias. PT2605.A58.Z46513 1982, (v3)
  PT2605.A58.Z513, (v3)
  PT2605.A58.Z51513, (v3)
  PT2605.A58.Z515 1977, (v3)
Caneva, Kenneth L. QC73.8.C6.C36 1993, (v1)
Canfield, Arthur Graves. PC13.N67 no. 37, (v3)
Canfield, J. Douglas. PR698.C6.C36 1997, (v3)
  PR698.T7.C36 2000, (v3)
  PS277.C36 2001, (v3)
Canfora, Luciano. Z722.5.C3513 1990, (v10)
Cann, John P. DT36.7.C355 1997, (v5)
Cannadine, David. DA3.T7.C36 1992, (v5)
  DA16.C28 2001, (v5)
  HN400.S6.C356 1999, (v6)
Cannell, Fenella. DS663.C35 1999, (v5)
Canney, Donald L. VA55.C28 1990, (v10)
Canning, Charlotte. PN2270.F45.C36 1996, (v3)
Cannold, Leslie. HQ767.15.C38 2000, (v6)
Cannon, Betty. RC506.C29 1991, (v2)
Cannon, John Ashton. DA40.C29 1988, (v5)
  PR3537.P6.C36 1994, (v3)
Cannon, Joseph Gurney. E664.C22.A3 1971, (v4)
Cannon, Katie G. BJ1275.C33 1988, (v8)
Cannon, Kelly. PS2127.P8.C36 1993, (v3)
Cannon, M. Hamlin. D769.A533 v.2, pt.5, (v5)
Cannon, Walter B. QP33.5.C3 1939, (v1)
Canny, Nicholas P. DA940.5.C7.C36 1982, (v5)
Canobbio, Mary M. RT90.C36 2000, (v2)
Canovan, Margaret. JC311.C337 1996, (v7)
Cantalupo, Charles. JC153.H659.C37 1991, (v7)
Cantarow, Abraham. QP514.C32 1967, (v1)
Canton, Frank M. F595.C23 1966, (v4)
Canton, Maria P. QA76.6.C36 1996, (v1)
Cantor, Aviva. Z7963.J4 C36 1987, (v10)
Cantor, Charles R. QP624.C36 1999, (v1)
Cantor, G. N. QC16.F2.C37 1996, (v1)
Cantor, Georg. QA248.C2, (v1)
Cantor, George. E185.53.A1.C36 1991, (v4)
Cantor, Norman F. CB351.C25, (v5)
  CB425.C28 1988, (v5)
  D116.C35 1991, (v5)
  D118.C3, (v5)
  KF394.C36 1997, (v7)
Cantor, Sheila. RJ506.S3.C36 1988, (v2)
Cantrell, Gregg. F213.R38.C36 1993, (v4)
  F389.A942 C36 1999, (v4)
Cantrell, Karen. KF266.C36 1990, (v7)
Cantwell, Robert. ML3551.C36 1996, (v9)
Canup, John. F7.C28 1990, (v4)
Capa, Robert. TR140.C28.A3, (v1)
Capeci, Dominic J. F474.S5.C36 1998, (v4)
  F574.D49.N4326 1991, (v4)
Capek, Karel. PG5038.C3.H63, (v3)
Capek, Karel. PG5038.C3V33 1985, (v3)
Capers, Gerald Mortimer. E415.9.D73.C28, (v4)
Capie, Forrest. HG939.C29 1985, (v6)
Capinera, John L. SB603.5, (v1)
Caplan, Arthur L. R724.C337 1997, (v2)
  R724.C338 1998, (v2)
  R724.C34 1992, (v2)
Caplan, Eric. RC443.C33 1998, (v2)
Caplan, Gerald. RJ499.A1.C3, (v2)
  RJ499.C26, (v2)
Caplan, Lincoln. KF355.N4 C37 1993, (v7)
Caplan, Nathan S. E184.I43.C37 1984, (v4)
Caplan, Paula J. LB2332.3.C37 1993, (v2)
Caplan, Russell L. KF4555.C35 1988, (v7)
Caple, Chris. CC135.C29 2000, (v5)

Caplin, William Earl. MT58.C37 1998, (v9)
Caplow, Theodore. HV91.C35 1994, (v6)
Caporaso, James A. HB74.P65.C37 1992, (v6)
  JN30.C38 2000, (v7)
Capote, Truman. HV6533.K3.C3, (v6)
  PS3505.A59.A16 1963, (v3)
  PS3505.A59.A83 1987, (v3)
  PS3505.A59.D6, (v3)
  PS3505.A59.G7 1993, (v3)
  PS3505.A59.L6 1950, (v3)
  PS3505.A59.M8, (v3)
  PS3505.A59 O9, (v3)
  PS3505.A59 T7, (v3)
  PS3505.A59.Z5 1968, (v3)
  PS3505.A59 B7 1958, (v3)
Capozzoli, Thomas. LB3013.3.C37 1999, (v7)
Capp, B. S. DA425.C24 1989, (v5)
Cappelletti, Mauro. K2110.C36 1989, (v7)
Cappelli, Peter. HD31.C3433 1999, (v6)
Cappels, Thomas M. HD30.22.C358 2000, (v6)
Capper, Arthur. HD1761.C3, (v6)
Capper, Charles. PS2506.C36 1992, (v3)
Capps, Benjamin. PS3553.A59W6 1999, (v3)
Capps, Lisa. RC552.A44.C37 1995, (v2)
Caputi, Anthony Francis. PR2696.C3, (v3)
Caputi, Mary. HQ472.U6.C36 1994, (v6)
Caputo, John D. B3279.H49.C273 1993, (v8)
  BJ1012.C316 1993, (v8)
  BL51.C325 2001, (v8)
Carabine, Deirdre. B765.J34.C33 2000, (v8)
Caracciolo-Trejo, E. PQ7087.E5.C28, (v3)
Caraley, Demetrios. UA23.C24, (v10)
Caramagno, Thomas C. PR6045.O72.Z566 1992, (v3)
Caramello, Charles. PS2127.B54.C37 1996, (v3)
Carande, Robert. Z5643.I57.C37 1993, (v10)
Carapico, Sheila. JQ1842.A91.C37 1998, (v7)
Caras, Roger A. QL100.C37, (v1)
Caratheodory, Constantin. QA360.C3 1952, (v1)
Carbaugh, Donal A. HM131.C2525 1996, (v6)
Carbone, Linda. TT705.C37, (v1)
Carbone, Peter F. LB885.R73.C37 1977, (v7)
Carbone, Teresa A. ND237.J7.A4 1999, (v9)
Carbonell Basset, Delfin. PN6491.C35 1996, (v3)
Carcopino, Jerome. DG78.C32, (v5)
Card, Claudia. BJ1531.C28 1996, (v8)
Card, Claudia. HQ75.5.C36 1995, (v6)
Card, Stuart K. QA76.9.I58C37 1983, (v1)
Cardenal, Ernesto. PQ7519.C34.C2913 1993, (v3)
  PQ7519.C34.E813 1995, (v3)
Cardoso, Fernando Henrique. HC125.C34153, (v6)
  HC187.C219 2001, (v6)
Cardoza, Anthony L. HT653.I8.C35 1997, (v6)
Cardozo, Benjamin N. K2100.C37 1949, (v7)
Cardullo, Bert. PN1994.C333 1987, (v3)
  PN1995.C3534 1999, (v3)
Cardwell, Guy. PS1342.S58.C37 1991, (v3)
Cardwell, Kenneth H. NA737.M435.C37, (v9)
Careless, J. M. S. F1032.C28, (v4)
Carello, Adrian Nicola. HC307.S69.C374 1989, (v6)
Carens, James F. PR6045.A97.Z62, (v3)
Carens, Joseph H. JC578.C43 2000, (v7)
Careri, Enrico. ML410.G26.C3 1993, (v9)
Carew, Anthony. HC240.9.L3.C37x 1987, (v6)
Carew, Thomas J. QP360.C347 2000, (v1)
Carew, Thomas. PR3339.C2 1949, (v3)
Carey, Christen Civiletto. KF300.C295 2001, (v7)
Carey, Gary. PN41.C28 1999, (v3)
Carey, George Wescott. JK155.C37 1989, (v7)
Carey, Henry Charles. HB161.C25 1965, (v6)
Carey, Henry. PR3339.C23.A17 1930, (v3)
Carey, James R. QH352.C36 1993, (v1)
Carey, John M. JK1130.C37 1996, (v7)
Carey, John. PR2248.C34, (v3)
Carey, Peter. PR9619.3.C36.O73 1988, (v3)
Carey, Philip G. QL368.A22.C66 1992, (v1)
Cargas, Harry J. Z6374.H6 C37 1985, (v10)
Cargill Thompson, W. D. J. JC141.L8.C37 1984, (v7)
Cargill, Jack. DF251.C37 1995, (v5)
Cargill, Marie. RM184.C37 1994, (v2)
Carin, Arthur A. LB1585.C28 2001, (v7)
Caristi, Dom. KF2805.C365 1992, (v7)

Carkoglu, Ali. HC415.15.C37 1998, (v6)
Carl H. Pforzheimer Library, New York. PR5431.A33,
  (v3)
Carle, Eric. PZ7.C21476Ve 1994, (v3)
Carlebach, Michael L. TR820.C357 1992, (v1)
Carlen, Claudia. Z7838.P53.C37 1990, (v10)
Carles, Emilie. DC801.B853.C2713 1991, (v5)
Carless, Jennifer. TJ807.9.U6.C37 1993, (v1)
Carleton, William. PR4416.T7 1979, (v3)
Carley, Kenneth. E83.86.C37 2001, (v4)
Carley, Michael Jabara. D748.C37 1999, (v5)
Carley, Michael. HD75.6.C368 2000, (v6)
Carlin, Deborah. PS3505.A87.Z5916 1992, (v3)
Carlin, Martha. DA685.S7.C37 1996, (v5)
Carling, Paul J. RC439.5.C37 1995, (v2)
Carlino, Andrea. QM33.4.C3613 1999, (v1)
Carlisle, Olga Andreyev. D762.O42.C37, (v5)
Carlisle, Rodney P. HE736.C37, (v6)
Carls, Stephen Douglas. HC272.5.L68.C37 1993, (v6)
Carlsen, Robert S. F1465.2.T9.C37 1997, (v4)
Carlson, A. Bruce. TK5102.5.C3 2002, (v1)
Carlson, Alvar W. F802.R4.C37 1990, (v4)
Carlson, Anton J. QP34.C25 1961, (v1)
Carlson, Bonnie E. HV8886.U5.C37 1992, (v6)
Carlson, David R. PA8045.E5.C37 1993, (v3)
Carlson, Karen J. RA778.C2163 1996, (v2)
Carlson, Lewis H. D805.U5.C29 1997, (v5)
Carlson, Marifran. HQ1533.C28 1988, (v6)
Carlson, Marvin A. PN2041.S45.C36 1990, (v3)
Carlson, Paul Howard. E78.G73.C38 1998, (v4)
  U53.S53.C37 1989, (v10)
Carlson, Richard C. CB161.C36 1994, (v5)
Carlston, Erin G. PN3401.C37 1998, (v3)
Carlton, Charles. DA396.L3.C37 1987, (v5)
  DA415.C3 1992, (v5)
Carlton, David. DA47.65.C37 2000, (v5)
Carlton, Eric. D25.5.C34 1992, (v5)
  HM141.C275 1996, (v6)
  U21.2.C343 1990, (v10)
Carlton, Peter Lynn. BF207.C28 1983, (v2)
Carlyle, A. J. JC585.C33 1980, (v7)
Carlyle, Jane Welsh. PR4419.C5.A83 1977, (v3)
  PR4419.C5.A84, (v3)
  PR4419.C5.A9 1924, (v3)
Carlyle, Thomas. DC161.C3 1934, (v5)
  PR4422.T4, (v3)
  PR4426.A2.G65 1993, (v3)
  PR4430.R4 1972, (v3)
  PR4433.A4 1970, (v3)
Carman, Bliss. PR4441.S6 1895, (v3)
Carman, Judith E. ML128.S3 C37 2001, (v9)
Carman, W. Y. U884 .C3, (v10)
Carmean, E. A. ND237.F675.A4 1989, (v9)
Carmean, Karen. PS3563.O8749.Z595 1993, (v3)
Carmer, Carl Lamson. F326.C275 2000, (v4)
  PS3505.A7265 G4, (v3)
Carmichael, Calum M. BS2615.2.C364 1996, (v8)
Carmichael, Cathie. DR1510.C37 1999, (v5)
Carmichael, Leonard. BF721.C213, (v2)
Carmichael, Stokely. E185.615.C32, (v4)
Carmo, Manfredo Perdigao do. QA381.C2813 1994,
  (v1)
  QA641.C33, (v1)
Carmody, Denise Lardner. E59.F38.C37 1993, (v4)
Carmody, James Patrick. PQ1871.C37 1993, (v3)
Carnap, Rudolf. BC135.C312, (v8)
  BC135.C316 1959, (v8)
  BC135.C323, (v8)
  BC135.C33, (v8)
  BC141.C3 1962, (v8)
  QA273.4.C37, (v1)
  QC6.C33, (v1)
Carnegie, Andrew. CT275.C3.A3, (v5)
Carnegie, Mary Elizabeth. RT83.5.C37 1995, (v2)
Carnes, Mark C. G1201.S1 .C3 1996, (v6)
Carnevale, Anthony Patrick. HF5549.5.M5.C383
  1995, (v6)
Carney, Elizabeth Donnelly. DF233.2.C37 2000, (v5)
Carney, Francis L. HV9306.J472.P383 1989, (v6)
Carney, Judith Ann. SB191.R5, (v1)
Carney, Margaret. NK4210.B5.A4 1998, (v9)

220

Carney, Raymond. PN1998.3.C384.C37 1994, (v3)
  PN1998.3.L445.C37 2000, (v3)
Carnochan, W. B. LB2361.5.C38 1993, (v7)
  PR449.F47.C3, (v3)
Carnot, Sadi. QC311.C2813 1986, (v1)
Carnovale, Norbert. ML134.G29.C37 2000, (v9)
Carnoy, Martin. HD6331.C279 2000, (v6)
  LA212.C34, (v7)
Caro, Robert A. E847.C34 1983, (v4)
Caroli, Betty Boyd. F204.W5 C27 1992, (v4)
Caron, Francois. HC273.C28 1979, (v6)
Caron, Vicki. DS135.F83.C366 1999, (v5)
Carossa, Hans. PT2605.A65 1962, (v3)
Carosso, Vincent P. HG4963.C37, (v6)
Carothers, Diane Foxhill. Z7221.C37 1991, (v10)
Carothers, N. L. QA300.C32 2000, (v1)
Carothers, Steven W. QH105.A65.C38 1991, (v1)
Carothers, Thomas. F1418.C295 1991, (v4)
Carp, E. Wayne. HV875.55.C38 1998, (v6)
Carp, Robert A. KF8700.C37 2001, (v7)
Carpelan, Bo Gustaf Bertelsson. PT9875.C35.R58 1987, (v3)
Carpenito, Lynda Juall. RT49.C38 1999, (v2)
Carpenter, Allan. F351.C33 1989, (v4)
  F591.C362 1990, (v4)
  F621.C27 1997, (v4)
Carpenter, Cecelia Svinth. E78.W3 C37 1989, (v4)
Carpenter, Charles A. Z5781.C37 1997, (v10)
Carpenter, Humphrey. ML410.B853.C37 1993, (v9)
  PN1008.5.C37 1984, (v3)
  PN1992.4.P68.C37 1998, (v3)
  PR6001.U4.Z636 1981, (v3)
  PR6045.A97.Z623 1990, (v3)
Carpenter, Jesse T. HD6515.C5.C33, (v6)
Carpenter, Kenneth J. RC627.B45.C37 2000, (v2)
  RC627.S36.C36 1986, (v2)
Carpenter, Kenneth. QE862.D5.C235 1999, (v1)
Carpenter, Rhys. NB90.C26, (v9)
Carpenter, Ronald H. PN203.C36 1995, (v3)
Carpenter, T. G. TD195.R33.C37 1994, (v1)
Carpenter, Ted Galen. PN4738.C27 1995, (v3)
Carpentier, Alejo. PQ7389.C263.A6413 1989, (v3)
  PQ7389.C263.A8913 1990, (v3)
  PQ7389.C263 1983 vol. 4, (v3)
Carper, Jean. R118.4.U6.C37 1987, (v2)
Carper, N. Gordon. D9.C37 1991, (v5)
Carr, A. D. DA715.C37 1995, (v5)
  DA716.O94.C37 1991, (v5)
Carr, Alan. RC454.C2745 2001, (v2)
  RJ503.3.C37 1999, (v2)
Carr, Albert H. Z. F1526.27.W3.C3, (v4)
Carr, Angela. NA749.B87.C37 1995, (v9)
Carr, Anne E. BT701.2.C2955 1988, (v8)
Carr, Annemarie Weyl. ND2819.C92.L974 1991, (v9)
Carr, Barry. HX113.C37 1992, (v6)
Carr, David. LB1779.C37 2000, (v7)
Carr, Duane. PS261.C37 1996, (v3)
Carr, Edward Hallett. D16.8.C33 1962, (v5)
  D359.C37 1980, (v5)
  D443.C29 1947, (v5)
  DK265.9.I5.C3 1973, (v5)
  DK266.C263, (v5)
  JX1391.C32 1956, (v7)
Carr, Ethan. SB482.A4.C37 1998, (v1)
Carr, Ian. ML419.D39 C35 1998, (v9)
Carr, James A. Z6465.U5 C24 1994, (v10)
Carr, John Dickson. PS3505.A763 C76, (v3)
Carr, Kay J. F549.B3.C37 1996, (v4)
Carr, Lois Green. F184.C29, (v4)
  HN79.M32.C37 1991, (v6)
Carr, Raymond. DP203.C3, (v5)
  DP270.C258, (v5)
  E183.8.P9.C37 1984, (v4)
Carr, Robert Kenneth. E743.5.C3, (v4)
Carr, Robert Van. PS3505.A768B5 1902, (v3)
Carr, Steven Alan. PN1993.5.U65.C37 2001, (v3)
Carr, William George. E302.6.F8.C34 1990, (v4)
Carr, William. DD247.H5.C325 1978, (v5)
Carra, Massimo. N6494.S8.C313, (v9)
Carrasquillo, Angela. Z5818.E5.C37 1994, (v10)
Carrell, Peter R. BT198.C32 1997, (v8)

Carrere d'Encausse, Helene. DK258.C3713 2000, (v5)
  DK288.C3713 1993, (v5)
Carrere, Emmanuel. PQ2663.A7678.B713 1990, (v3)
Carretta, Vincent. DA505.C36 1990, (v5)
Carrette, Jeremy R. B2430.F724.C365 1999, (v8)
Carr-Gomm, Sarah. N7740.C29 1995, (v9)
Carrias, Eugene. DC59.8.G3.C37, (v5)
Carrico, Richard L. E78.C15 C34 1987, (v4)
Carrier, David. N7476.C37 1987, (v9)
  ND553.P8.C35 1993, (v9)
  PN6710.C35 2000, (v3)
Carrier, Jeffrey L. PN2287.B17.C37 1991, (v3)
Carrier, Lois. F541.C34 1993, (v4)
Carrier, Roch. PQ3919.2.C25.D3413 1987, (v3)
Carriero, Nicholas. QA76.642.C37 1990, (v1)
Carriker, Robert C. E78.W5.S622 1995, (v4)
Carrington, Charles. DA16.C32, (v5)
Carrington, Frances C. E83.866.C3 1990, (v4)
Carrington, Paul D. KF352.C33 1999, (v7)
Carrington, Peter Alexander Rupert Carington. DA591.C36.A3 1989, (v5)
Carrithers, Gale H. PR428.H57.C37 1998, (v3)
  PR3588.C37 1994, (v3)
Carritt, E. F. BH21.C3, (v8)
  BH201.C28, (v8)
  BH201.C29 1949, (v8)
  BJ1011.C27, (v8)
  JA79.C3, (v7)
Carroll, Brendan G. ML410.K7356 C37 1997, (v9)
Carroll, Bret E. G1201.E4.C3 2000, (v6)
Carroll, Cathryn. RF292.8.C37 2002, (v2)
Carroll, David. B2430.F724.C37 1987, (v8)
Carroll, David. PR4688.C28 1992, (v3)
Carroll, Gladys Hasty. PS3505.A77533 A8, (v3)
Carroll, John Bissell. PE1691.C3, (v3)
Carroll, John J. PR3667.C3, (v3)
Carroll, John M. GV939.G7.C37 1999, (v6)
  GV939.P66.C37 1991, (v6)
Carroll, Joseph T. D754.I5.C37 1975, (v5)
Carroll, Leo. HV9304.C365 1998, (v6)
Carroll, Lewis. PR4611.A4 1993, (v3)
  PR4611.A7 2000, (v3)
  PR4611.S9 1991, (v3)
  QA95.D6, (v1)
Carroll, Mark. QH581.2.C38 1989, (v1)
Carroll, Michael C. HB119.H44.C37 1998, (v6)
Carroll, Michael P. BX1969.C37 1989, (v8)
Carroll, Noel. BH39.C376 1999, (v8)
  NX180.M3.C37 1998, (v9)
Carroll, Patrick James. F1392.B55.C37 1991, (v4)
Carroll, Paul Vincent. PR6005.A74I7, (v3)
Carroll, Peter N. DP269.47.A46.C37 1994, (v5)
  E169.12.C29 1982, (v4)
Carroll, Richard J. HC106.5.C29 1995, (v6)
Carroll, Robert Lynn. QE841.C2538 1997, (v1)
Carroll, Stephen J. HD62.4.C365 1997, (v6)
Carroll, Stuart. DC611.N894.C37 1998, (v5)
Carroll, Susan J. HQ1391.U5 C37 1994, (v6)
Carroll-Burke, Patrick. HV9650.3.C377 2000, (v6)
Carrouges, Michel. PQ2603.R35.Z65, (v3)
Carruth, Gorton. CB69.C37 1993, (v5)
  E174.5.C3 1997, (v4)
  PN1008.5.C373 1993, (v3)
Carruthers, Bruce G. HG5432.C37 1996, (v6)
Carruthers, Mary. PR2015.C3, (v3)
Carruthers, Peter. BD161.C352 1992, (v8)
  HV4708.C38 1992, (v6)
Carruthers, Susan L. DA16.C34 1995, (v5)
Carse, Adam von Ahn. ML455.C32 1964, (v9)
  ML930.C38.M9 1965, (v9)
Carsey, Thomas M. JK2447.G8 1985, (v7)
Carslaw, H. S. QC321.C28 1959, (v1)
Carson, Clayborne. E185.92.C37 1981, (v4)
Carson, D. A. BS449.C37 1998, (v8)
Carson, Donald W. E840.8.U3 C37 2001, (v4)
Carson, James Taylor. E99.C8.C33 1999, (v4)
Carson, Kit. F592.C3, (v4)
Carson, Rachel. GC21.C3 1961, (v6)
  QH31.C33.A4 1995, (v1)
  QH81.C3546 1998, (v1)
  QH91.C3, (v1)

QH92.C3 1952, (v1)
  QH545.P4.C38 1962, (v1)
Carspecken, Phil Francis. LB1028.C289 1996, (v7)
Carsten, F. L. D726.5.C35 1980, (v5)
  DD347.C3, (v5)
Carsten, Janet. GN635.M4.C39 1997, (v6)
Carstens, James R. TJ213.C293 1990, (v1)
  TK7872.T6.C38 1993, (v1)
Cartelli, Thomas. PR658.A88.C37 1991, (v3)
  PR2971.U6.C37 1999, (v3)
Carter, A. E. PQ295.D4.C3 1958, (v3)
  PQ2191.Z5.C3, (v3)
Carter, Alice A. N6536.C37 2000, (v9)
Carter, Angela. PR6053.A73.B5 1979, (v3)
  PR6053.A73.N5 1985, (v3)
  PR6053.A73.W3, (v3)
Carter, April. Z8322.7.C37 1995, (v10)
Carter, Barry E. KF1976.C37 1988, (v7)
Carter, Cecile Elkins. E99.C12.C37 1995, (v4)
Carter, Charles Howard. Z2000.C35, (v10)
Carter, Chris Allen. PS3503.U6134.Z63 1996, (v3)
Carter, D. N. G. PR6013.R35.Z63 1988, (v3)
Carter, Dan T. E185.625.C37 1996, (v4)
  E668.C28 1985, (v4)
  F330.3.W3.C37 1995, (v4)
Carter, Elliott. ML60.C22, (v9)
Carter, Erica. HC290.5.C6.C37 1997, (v6)
Carter, Gregg Lee. HV7436.C37 1997, (v6)
Carter, Hodding. F215.C26, (v4)
Carter, Hugh. HB1125.C33, (v6)
Carter, J. E. L. GN66.5.C37 1990, (v6)
Carter, James Hugh. DS797.42.H373 C37 2002, (v5)
Carter, Jimmy. E838.5.C375 1977, (v4)
  E873.A34 1982, (v4)
  E873.A38 1977, (v4)
  E873.2.C378 1994, (v4)
  SH441.C36 1988, (v1)
Carter, John Marshall. GV575.C372 1992, (v6)
Carter, John Stewart. PS3505.A7924.F8, (v3)
Carter, John. Z1006.C37 1995, (v10)
Carter, K. Holly Maze. DS518.8.C4 1989, (v5)
Carter, Marina. DT469.M445.E273 1994, (v5)
  DT469.M445.E2734 1996, (v5)
Carter, Michael W. T57.6.C367 2001, (v1)
Carter, Paul Allen. BR525.C37, (v8)
Carter, Robert Edgar. BJ970.C37 2001, (v8)
Carter, Robert Randolph. G665 1850 .C36 1998, (v6)
Carter, Sarah. HQ1459.P7.C37 1997, (v6)
  Z7961.C37 1990, (v10)
Carter, Stephen L. BL65.P7.C37 2000, (v8)
  JK736.C37 1994, (v7)
Carter, Susanne. Z1229.W8.C37 1993, (v10)
Carter, Thomas Francis. Z186.C5.C3 1955, (v10)
Carter, Tim. ML290.2.C22 1992, (v9)
  ML410.M9.C33 1987, (v9)
Carter, William C. PQ2631.R63.A7827 1992, (v3)
Carter, William. ML3508.8.N48.C3 1991, (v9)
Cartey, Wilfred G. PR9205.4.C38 1991, (v3)
Cartier-Bresson, Henri. TR650.C38, (v1)
Cartin, T. J. HD62.15.C3639 1999, (v6)
Cartledge, Paul. DF261.S8 C39 2001, (v5)
  DF261.S8.C373 1989, (v5)
Cartmell, Deborah. PR3093.C37 2000, (v3)
Cartmill, Matt. GN388.C37 1993, (v6)
Cartwright, David Edgar. GC301.2.C37 1999, (v6)
Cartwright, Frederick Fox. RD19.C38, (v2)
Cartwright, Gary. F391.2.C35 2000, (v4)
Cartwright, Kent. PR646.C37 1999, (v3)
  PR2983.C37 1991, (v3)
Cartwright, Mark. QA403.5.C37 1990, (v1)
Cartwright, Nancy. QC6.4.C3.C37 1989, (v1)
Cartwright, Richard. B29.C2785 1987, (v8)
Cartwright, Rita Cantos. KF4747.5.C37 2000, (v7)
Cartwright, W. Aubrey. N510.C3, (v9)
Carty, Mickey Dimon. F525.C37 1985, (v4)
Cartz, Louis. TA417.2.C37 1995, (v1)
Carucci, Laurence Marshall. GN671.M33.C37 1997, (v6)
Carus, W. Seth. UG1312.C7.C37 1992, (v10)
Caruso, A. Brooke. E415.2.S43.C37 1991, (v4)
Caruso, Enrico. ML420.C259.C3 1990, (v9)

Caruso, John Anthony. F212.C3, **(v4)**
Carus-Wilson, Eleanora Mary. HC12.C32, **(v6)**
Caruth, Cathy. PN81.C38 1991, **(v3)**
Caruth, Cathy. PN771.C338 1996, **(v3)**
Carvajal, Gaspar de. E125.O6 C363 1970, **(v4)**
Carvalho, Fernando J. Cardim de. HB99.7.C38 1992, **(v6)**
Carvalho, Solomon Nunes. F593.C28 1973, **(v4)**
Carver, M. O. H. DA155.C38 1998, **(v5)**
Carver, Raymond. PS3553.A7894.W5, **(v3)**
Carvounis, Chris C. HJ8899.C37 1984, **(v6)**
Carwardine, Mark. QL737.C4.C28 1995, **(v1)**
Cary, Elizabeth. PR2499.F3.T7 1993, **(v3)**
Cary, John H. E263.M4.W234, **(v4)**
Cary, Joyce. PR6005.A77 A153 1960, **(v3)**
 PR6005.A77.A37 1963, **(v3)**
 PR6005.A77 A5, **(v3)**
 PR6005.A77 C28, **(v3)**
 PR6005.A77 C3, **(v3)**
 PR6005.A77 C5, **(v3)**
 PR6005.A77 E9, **(v3)**
 PR6005.A77 F4, **(v3)**
 PR6005.A77 F5, **(v3)**
 PR6005.A77 M5 1951, **(v3)**
 PR6005.A77 M6 1946, **(v3)**
 PR6005.A77 N6, **(v3)**
 PR6005.A77 P7, **(v3)**
Cary, Noel D. JN3933.C37 1996, **(v7)**
Cary, Patrick. PR3339.C43 1978, **(v3)**
Casada, James A. G246.B8.C37 1990, **(v6)**
Casagrande, Peter J. PR4748.C33 1992, **(v3)**
Casalduero, Joaquin. PQ6325.Z5.C3, **(v3)**
Casals, Pablo. ML418.C4.A35, **(v9)**
Casanave, Suki. F32.3.C35 1999, **(v4)**
Casanova, Giacomo. D285.8.C32 1959, **(v5)**
Casanova, Jose. BL60.C375 1994, **(v8)**
Casas, Bartolome de las. F1411.C425 1974, **(v4)**
 F1411.C4275 1971, **(v4)**
Casati, Roberto. BD399.C37 1994, **(v8)**
 BD621.C35 1999, **(v8)**
Cascardi, Anthony J. B841.6.C37 1992, **(v8)**
 PQ6066.C353 1997, **(v3)**
Casdorph, Paul D. E467.C38 1992, **(v4)**
Case, Alison A. PR858.W6.C37 1999, **(v3)**
Case, James H. HB144.C37, **(v6)**
Case, Margaret H. BL1285.392.P87.C37 1999, **(v8)**
 Z3185.C3, **(v10)**
Case, Shirley Jackson. Z7777.C33, **(v10)**
Casebier, Allan. PN1995.C364 1991, **(v3)**
Caserio, Robert L. PR881.C37 1999, **(v3)**
Casey, Daniel J. PR6021.I24.Z62 1974, **(v3)**
Casey, Edward S. BD181.7.C33 2000, **(v8)**
Casey, Janet Galligani. PS3507.O743.Z549 1998, **(v3)**
Casey, Juanita. PR6053.A8.C5, **(v3)**
Casey, P. J. DA145.C37 1995, **(v5)**
Casey, T. J. TD430.C37 1997, **(v1)**
Cash, Arthur H. PR3716.C29 1975, **(v3)**
Cash, Catherine. SB409.8.S65.C37 1991, **(v1)**
Cash, Floris Loretta Barnett. E185.86.C33 2001, **(v4)**
Cash, John Daniel. DA990.U46.C36 1996, **(v5)**
Cashin, Edward J. E278.B862.C37 1989, **(v4)**
 F289.E45.C37 1994, **(v4)**
 F289.M43.C37 1992, **(v4)**
Cashin, Joan E. F213.C34 1991, **(v4)**
Cashion, Ty. F394.F636 C37 1996, **(v4)**
Cashman, Sean Dennis. E169.1.C297 1989, **(v4)**
 E661.C38 1993, **(v4)**
 E741.C27 1988, **(v4)**
Cashmore, Ernest. GV706.5.C383 2000, **(v6)**
Casillo, Robert. PS3531.O82.Z5527 1988, **(v3)**
Casimir, H. B. G. QC278.C3, **(v1)**
Caso, Alfonso. F1219.3.R38.C313, **(v4)**
Cason, Ann. HV1461.C388 2001, **(v6)**
Caspar, Max. QB36.K4.C33, **(v1)**
Caspary, William R. JC251.D48.C37 2000, **(v7)**
Casper, Dale E. Z8629.4.C37 1988, **(v10)**
 JQ1416.C37 1995, **(v7)**
Casper, Gretchen. JC421.C27 1996, **(v7)**
Casper, Leonard. PR9797.P6.C3, **(v3)**
Caspi, Mishael. Z7772.J2.C37 1994, **(v10)**
Cass, Joan. GV1588.C37 1999, **(v6)**

Cass, Joan. GV1601.C34 1993, **(v6)**
Cassady, Carolyn. PS3521.E735.Z594 1990, **(v3)**
Cassanelli, Lee V. DT402.3.C37 1982, **(v5)**
Cassar, George H. D548.C28 1985, **(v5)**
Cassaro, James P. ML134.D66.C37 2000, **(v9)**
Cassata, Mary B. Z7711.C37 1985, **(v10)**
Cassatt, Mary. N6537.C35.A4 1998, **(v9)**
Cassedy, James H. R151.C375 1991, **(v2)**
Cassedy, Steven. DS135.R9.C34 1997, **(v5)**
 PN45.C34 1990, **(v3)**
Cassel, Jeris F. Z5814.C88.C37 1993, **(v10)**
Cassell, Dana K. RC552.E18C37 2000, **(v2)**
Cassell, Eric J. R723.C42828 1991, **(v2)**
Cassell, Richard A. PR6011.O53.Z58 1962, **(v3)**
Cassen, Robert. HC60.C53 1986, **(v6)**
Casserly, Michael D. LB3249.C37, **(v7)**
Cassese, Antonio. JX4054.C32 1995, **(v7)**
 K3240.4.C36813 1990, **(v7)**
Cassiday, Julie A. KLA40.P64 C37 2000, **(v7)**
Cassidy, James G. QE22.H3, **(v1)**
Cassimatis, Louis P. DF787.U5.C37 1988, **(v5)**
Cassirer, Ernst. B775.C313 1964, **(v8)**
 B1133.C2.C353, **(v8)**
 B2797.C313, **(v8)**
 BD221.C285, **(v8)**
Cassity, Michael J. HD8085.S433.C37 1989, **(v6)**
Casson, Lionel. VM15.C233 1971, **(v10)**
Casson, Mark. HD58.7.C37 1991, **(v6)**
 HD2755.5.C392 1987, **(v6)**
Casson, Stanley. DS54.3.C25, **(v5)**
Cassutt, Michael. TL788.5.C37 1999, **(v1)**
Castagno, John. N45.C374 1991, **(v9)**
 NC961.63.C37 1989, **(v9)**
Castañeda, Carlos Eduardo. F390.C317 1976, **(v4)**
Castaneda, Carlos. E99.Y3.C3 1968, **(v4)**
Castaneda, Christopher James. HD9581.U52.A1153 1993, **(v6)**
 HD9581.U53.P363 1996, **(v6)**
Castaneda, Jorge G. F1236.C37413 2000, **(v4)**
Castel, Albert E. E467.1.P87 C3, **(v4)**
 E470.45.A53 C37 1998, **(v4)**
 E476.7.C28 1992, **(v4)**
 E508.C3 1979, **(v4)**
 E666.C23, **(v4)**
Castellanos, Rosario. PQ7297.C2596.C513 1993, **(v3)**
Castells, Manuel. HC79.I55 C373 2000, **(v6)**
 HN17.5.C354 2000, **(v6)**
Casten, Thomas R. TJ163.4.U6.C38 1998, **(v1)**
Casteras, Susan P. ND467.5.P7.C37 1990, **(v9)**
Castex, Pierre. PQ2474.Z5.C3, **(v3)**
Casti, J. L. QA29.G58, **(v1)**
 QA401.C358 1989, **(v1)**
Castiglione, Baldassarre. BJ1604.C37 1967, **(v8)**
Castile, George Pierre. E93.C35 1998, **(v4)**
Castillo, Debra A. PN98.W64.C37 1992, **(v3)**
Castle, Gregory. PR8722.M6, **(v3)**
Castle, Terry. PN56.L45.C37 1993, **(v3)**
 PR3664.C43.C37 1982, **(v3)**
 PR6005.O85.Z623 1996, **(v3)**
Castle, Timothy N. DS559.73.L28.C37 1999, **(v5)**
Castleden, Rodney. DF220.3.C37 1991, **(v5)**
 DF221.C8.C37 1990, **(v5)**
 GN776.22.G7.C36 1992, **(v6)**
Castleman, Riva. NE508.C38 1991, **(v9)**
Castner, James L. QK99.A432.C37 1998, **(v1)**
Casto, James E. F241.C36 1996, **(v4)**
Casto, William R. KF8742.C36 1995, **(v7)**
Castro, Americo. PC4127.G4.C3 1954, **(v3)**
 PQ6057.C3 1967, **(v3)**
 PQ6351.C3, **(v3)**
Castro, Eduardo Batalha Viveiros de.
 F2520.1.A77.C3713 1992, **(v4)**
Castro, Ginette. HQ1410.C3813 1990, **(v6)**
Castro, Guillen de. PQ6321.C7.M7 1913, **(v3)**
Castro, Isabel C. QL694.G2.C37 1996, **(v1)**
Castro, Jose Maria Ferrira de. PQ9261.F37 E52, **(v3)**
Castro-Klaren, Sara. PQ8498.32.A65.Z644 1990, **(v3)**
Castronovo, David. PR151.M46.C37 1987, **(v3)**
 PS3545.I6245.Z586 1984, **(v3)**
 PS3545.I6245.Z587 1998, **(v3)**
Castronovo, Russ. PS217.S55.C37 1995, **(v3)**

Catalano, Joseph S. B808.9.C38 2000, **(v8)**
Catalano, Nick. ML419.B75.C37 2000, **(v9)**
Catalano, Stephen. RJ499.C299 1990, **(v2)**
Catanese, Anthony V. JV7393.C38 1999, **(v7)**
Catanese, Lynn Ann. Z7961.C38 1997, **(v10)**
Cate, Curtis. PQ2637.A274.Z6355 1970, **(v3)**
Cate, Fred H. KF4150.C34 1998, **(v7)**
Cate, Weston A. F46.C37 1988, **(v4)**
Cates, Jo A. Z6940.C38 1997, **(v10)**
Cather, Willa. PS3505.A87.A1 1937 vol. 9, **(v3)**
 PS3505.A87 A15 1956, **(v3)**
 PS3505.A87 A15 1970, **(v3)**
 PS3505.A87.A6 1957, **(v3)**
 PS3505.A87.A8 1962, **(v3)**
 PS3505.A87 D4 1927, **(v3)**
 PS3505.A87L6 1999, **(v3)**
 PS3505.A87 L8, **(v3)**
 PS3505.A87M8 2000, **(v3)**
 PS3505.A87 M9, **(v3)**
 PS3505.A87.O2 1992, **(v3)**
 PS3505.A87.O25 1998, **(v3)**
 PS3505.A87 O44, **(v3)**
 PS3505.A87.O48 1949, **(v3)**
 PS3505.A87 O6 1922, **(v3)**
 PS3505.A87.S3 1940, **(v3)**
 PS3505.A87 S4, **(v3)**
 PS3505.A87 S6 1943, **(v3)**
 PS3505.A87.T7 1983, **(v3)**
 PS3505.A87 Y6, **(v3)**
 PS3505.A87.Z53, **(v3)**
Catholic Church. BX860.A36 1956, **(v8)**
 BX1187.A4 1969, **(v8)**
 HV8599.B7.C3813 1998, **(v6)**
Catlin, George Edward Gordon. JC257.C3 1964, **(v7)**
Catlin, George. E58.C3535, **(v4)**
 E77.C415 1989, **(v4)**
Catlin, Robert A. HT168.G37.C38 1993, **(v6)**
Caton, Carol L. M. HV4505.C37 1990, **(v6)**
Caton, Hiram. Z7201.C37 1993, **(v10)**
Caton, Steven Charles. PJ8007.2.C38 1990, **(v3)**
 PN1997.L353.C38 1999, **(v3)**
Catteau, Jacques. PG3328.Z6.C3313 1989, **(v3)**
Cattell, Raymond B. BF698.C323 vol. 1, **(v2)**
Catton, Bruce. E468.C28, **(v4)**
 E468.C3, **(v4)**
 E470.2.C36, **(v4)**
 E470.2.C37, **(v4)**
 E672.C293, **(v4)**
 E672.C295, **(v4)**
Catton, William Bruce. E458.C3, **(v4)**
Cattrall, Robert W. TP159.C46C35 1997, **(v1)**
Catty, Jocelyn. PR428.R37.C38 1999, **(v3)**
Catudal, Honore Marc. U162.6.C38 1986, **(v10)**
 UA770.C37 1989, **(v10)**
Catullus, Gaius Valerius. PA6105.S8.C26, **(v3)**
Cauchi, Francesca. B3313.A4 1998, **(v8)**
Caudill, Edward. QH360.5.C38 1997, **(v1)**
Caudill, Maureen. QA76.5.C387 1990, **(v1)**
Caufield, Catherine. HC60.C345 1996, **(v6)**
Caughey, John Walton. F865.C33, **(v4)**
Caughie, John. PN1992.65.C38 2000, **(v3)**
Caughley, Graeme. QH75.C38 1996, **(v1)**
Caulfield, Richard A. E99.E7.C38 1997, **(v4)**
Caulfield, Sueann. HQ18.B7.C38 1999, **(v6)**
Causey, Max. KF224.R8 C38 2000, **(v7)**
Caute, David. D848.C38 1988, **(v5)**
 PN1998.3.L68.C38 1994, **(v3)**
Cauveren, Sydney. Z8763.67.C38 2000, **(v10)**
Cauvin, Jacques. GN776.32.N4.C38 2000, **(v6)**
Cavaliero, Glen. PR830.C63.C38 1999, **(v3)**
 PR6031.O867.Z63, **(v3)**
 PR6045.I5.Z6 1983, **(v3)**
Cavaliero, Roderick. F2534.C38 1993, **(v4)**
Cavalli-Sforza, L. L. GN281.C385 2000, **(v6)**
 QH431.C395 1994, **(v1)**
Cavallo, Sandra. HV295.T82.C38 1995, **(v6)**
Cavanagh, Sheila T. PR2399.W7, **(v3)**
Cavanagh, Cecelia J. PQ6613.A763.Z582 1995, **(v3)**
Cavanaugh, Michael. BL255.C38 1996, **(v8)**
Cavarero, Adriana. PN212.C38 2000, **(v3)**
Cave, David. BL43.E4.C38 1993, **(v8)**

Cave, Eric M. B105.J87.C38 1998, (v8)
Cave, Richard Allen. PR2638.C35 1990, (v3)
Cave, Terence. PQ1677.C3, (v3)
Cavell, Marcia. BF175.4.P45.C38 1993, (v2)
Cavell, Stanley. B945.C271 2002, (v8)
 B945.C273.P58 1994, (v8)
 BD161.C355 1999, (v8)
Caven, Brian. DG55.S9.C38 1990, (v5)
Cavenagh, F. A. LB675.M512 1969, (v7)
Cavendish, George. PR1119.A2 no. 243, (v3)
Caves, Richard E. HD9725.C38 1990, (v6)
 NX705.5.U6.C38 2000, (v9)
Cavinder, Fred D. F526.5.C38 1985, (v4)
Caviness, Madeline Harrison. NK5344.C3.C38, (v9)
Caws, Mary Ann. DA685.B65.C39 1990, (v5)
 N6537.M67.C42 1996, (v3)
 NX543.C38 2000, (v9)
 PQ443.C28, (v3)
 PQ2605.H3345.Z633, (v3)
Cawthra, Gavin. HV8272.A3.C39 1997, (v6)
Cayleff, Susan E. GV964.Z3.C39 1995, (v6)
Cayton, Andrew R. L. F479.C34 1990, (v4)
 F491.C39 2002, (v4)
 F495.C35 1986, (v4)
 F526.C35 1996, (v4)
Cayton, Mary Kupiec. PS1642.S58.C58 1989, (v3)
Cazamian, Louis Francois. PQ103.C3, (v3)
 PR931.C3 1952, (v3)
Cazelles, Brigitte. PQ1445.P2C39 1996, (v3)
Cazenave, Odile M. PQ3984.C3913 2000, (v3)
CBE Style Manual Committee. QH304.C33 1983, (v1)
Ceadel, Martin. U21.2.C43 1987, (v10)
Ceaser, James W. E169.12.C38 1997, (v4)
 JK1968 .1992c, (v7)
Ceccarelli, Leah. QH303.6.C433 2001, (v1)
Cecil, Algernon. DB80.8.M57.C, (v5)
Cecil, David, Lord. PR99.C38, (v3)
Cecil, David. DA536.M5.C5 1954, (v5)
 PR99.C4 1961, (v3)
 PR1225.C4, (v3)
Cecil, Hugh. PR830.W65.C43 1996, (v3)
Cecil, Lamar. DD229.C4 1989, (v5)
Cecil-Fronsman, Bill. F258.C43 1992, (v4)
Cederstrom, Lorelei. PR6023.E833.Z588 1990, (v3)
Cela, Camilo Jose. DP302.L13.C4, (v5)
 PQ6605.E44.F3 1975, (v3)
 PQ6605.E44.M3313 1992, (v3)
 PQ6605.E44.V5413 1991, (v3)
Celan, Paul. PT2605.E4.A1114 1983, (v3)
 PT2605.E4.A25 1988, (v3)
 PT2605.E4.A6 1997, (v3)
 PT2605.E4.A913 1995, (v3)
Celestin, Roger. PQ145.7.A2.C45 1995, (v3)
Celichowska, Renata. GV1783.C39 2000, (v6)
Celik, Zeynep. NA957.C44 1992, (v9)
Celine, Louis-Ferdinand. PQ2607.E834.M6 1969, (v3)
 PQ2607.E834.V6 1962, (v3)
Cell, John Whitson. DA17.H3.C45 1992, (v5)
Celment, Richard W. Z8.U62.C58 1996, (v10)
Celoza, Albert F. JQ1416.C45 1997, (v7)
Cendrars, Blaise. PQ2605.E55.A6 1966, (v3)
 PQ2605.E55.H6, (v3)
Ceniza, Sherry. PS3242.W6.C46 1998, (v3)
Censer, Jack Richard. DC148.C388 2001, (v5)
 PN5176.C46 1994, (v3)
Centeno, Miguel Angel. F1236.C46 1994, (v4)
Centlivre, Susanna. PR3339.C6.A116 1982, (v3)
Ceplair, Larry. PN1993.5.U6.C4, (v3)
Ceram, C. W. CB155.M323, (v5)
 CC100.M313 1994, (v5)
Cerda, Carlos. PQ8098.13.E668.M6713 1999, (v3)
Cerf, Bennett. PN6014.00C43, (v3)
 PS647.W5.C4, (v3)
 Z473.C45.A36 1977, (v10)
Cernica, John N. TA710.C393 1995, (v1)
Cernuda, Luis. PQ6605.E7.A6 1971, (v3)
Cernuschi, Claude. NC139.P6.A4 1992, (v9)
Cerquiglini-Toulet, Jacqueline. PQ155.M52.C4713 1997, (v3)
Cerulo, Karen A. JC345.C45 1995, (v7)
 P96.V5.C47 1998, (v3)

Ceruzzi, Paul E. QA76.17.C47 1998, (v1)
Cervantes de Salazar, Francisco. F1386.C4 1970, (v4)
 PQ6323.A1 1958, (v3)
 PQ6324.A1 1971b, (v3)
 PQ6329.A2 1981, (v3)
 PQ6329.A2 1995, (v3)
 PQ6329.P4 1989, (v3)
Cessac, Catherine. ML410.C433.C4713 1995, (v9)
Cetto, Max L. NA755.C413, (v9)
Cevasco, G. A. PR6037.I8.Z575 1987, (v3)
Ch˜ubak, òS˜adiq. PK6561.C45A2 1981, (v3)
Ch˜en, Fang-cheng. DS779.23.C44145 1997, (v5)
Ch˜en, Li-fu. PL2463.Z7C513 1986, (v3)
Ch˜ien, Chung-shu. PL2461.Z6C534213 1998, (v3)
Chabal, Patrick. JQ1872.C48 1994, (v7)
Chabod, Federico. DG564.C43 1996, (v5)
 JC143.M4.C52, (v7)
Chabreck, R. H. QH104.5.G84.C48 1988, (v1)
Chabrier, Gwendolyne. PS3511.A86.Z7545 1993, (v3)
Chace, James. E881.C42 1992, (v4)
Chace, Marian. RC489.D3.C49 1975, (v2)
Chadda, Maya. DS480.84.C45 1997, (v5)
 JQ98.A91, (v7)
Chadha, Yogesh. DS481.G73.C43 1997, (v5)
Chadwick, Bruce. GV875.A1.C47 1992, (v6)
Chadwick, David. BQ988.U9.C47 1999, (v8)
Chadwick, Douglas H. QL84.2.C47 1996, (v1)
 QL737.P98.C43 1992, (v1)
Chadwick, Henry. B659.Z7.C45, (v8)
 BR165.C48 1968b, (v8)
Chadwick, John. DF220.C43, (v5)
Chadwick, Nora K. D70.C47, (v5)
Chadwick, Owen. BR145.2.C42 1996, (v8)
 BX1361.C45, (v8)
Chadwick, Whitney. N6537.B75, (v9)
Chadwick, Whitney. N8354.C48 1990, (v9)
Chadwick-Jones, J. K. HD5115.C47 1982, (v6)
Chadwick-Joshua, Jocelyn. PS1305.C45 1998, (v3)
Chae, Man-sik. PL991.13.M3.T313 1993, (v3)
Chafe, William Henry. E840.8.L68.C47 1993, (v4)
 F264.G8.C47, (v4)
 HQ1426.C45 1991, (v6)
 HQ1426.C453, (v6)
Chafee, Zechariah. JC599.U5.C48 1956, (v7)
Chafetz, Janet Saltzman. HQ21.C449 1984, (v6)
 HQ1121.C45 1986, (v6)
Chaffee, John W. DS751.3.C35 1999, (v5)
Chaffers, William. NK4215.C46 1965, (v9)
Chaffin, Tom. F1783.C44 1996, (v4)
Chai, Chu. B126.C43 1975, (v8)
 BL1829.C5, (v8)
 PL2658.E1.C5, (v3)
Chaigne, Louis. PQ2605.L2.Z6123, (v3)
Chaikin, Andrew. TL506.U6.W37315 1997, (v1)
Chaisson, Eric. QB500.268.C48 1994, (v1)
 QC173.55.C46 1988, (v1)
Chaitin, Gregory J. QA267.C48 1987, (v1)
Cha-Jua, Sundiata Keita. F549.L87 C48 2000, (v4)
Chakalov, G. Q123.C4817 1996, (v1)
Chakrabarty, Dipesh. DS435.C46 2002, (v5)
Chakravarti, Sitansu S. BL1202.C4713 1991, (v8)
Chakravarty, Sukhamoy. HC435.2.C467 1987, (v6)
Chakravarty, Sumita S. PN1993.5.I8.C48 1993, (v3)
Chalfant, William Y. F786.C42 1994, (v4)
Chaliand, Gerard. GN370.C43 1995, (v6)
Chalk, Frank Robert. HV6322.7.C44 1990, (v6)
Chall, Jeanne Sternlicht. LB1576.C418 1990, (v7)
 LB2822.8.C49 2000, (v7)
Chalmers, Alexander. PR1173.C518, (v3)
Chalmers, David John. BD418.3.C43 1996, (v8)
 BD418.3.C435 2002, (v8)
Chalmers, David Mark. E841.C46 1996, (v4)
Chalpin, Lila K. PR6037.A75.Z6, (v3)
Chamberlain, Basil Hall. DS821.C43 1971, (v5)
Chamberlain, Bobby J. PQ9697.A647.Z585 1990, (v3)
Chamberlain, Charles Joseph. QK495.G9.C5 1966, (v1)
Chamberlain, John. E743.C46 1965, (v4)
 HC106.C52 1974, (v6)
Chamberlain, Joseph W. QB603.A85.C48 1987, (v1)

Chamberlain, Joseph. DA565.C4.A32, (v5)
 RB56.C48 1995, (v2)
Chamberlain, Kathleen. E99.N3 C45 2000, (v4)
Chamberlain, Michael. DS99.D3.C48 1994, (v5)
Chamberlain, Muriel Evelyn. D217.C46 2000, (v5)
Chamberlain, Neville. D727.C5 1971, (v5)
Chamberlain, Robert Lyall. PR4513.C5, (v3)
Chamberlain, Wilt. GV884.C5.A38, (v6)
Chamberlin, J. E. PR461.C45, (v3)
Chamberlin, J. Edward. PN849.C3.C48 1993, (v3)
Chamberlin, William Henry. DK265.C43, (v5)
Chamberlin, William J. Z7771.E5 C43 1991, (v10)
Chambers, A. B. PR545.R4.C434 1992, (v3)
Chambers, Ann. TK9.C47 1996, (v1)
Chambers, David. KKH110.C87.C46 1997, (v7)
Chambers, Douglas. PR448.S69.C48 1996, (v3)
Chambers, E. K. PR99.C43 1965, (v3)
 PR291.C5 1947, (v3)
 PR2894.C44, (v3)
 PR4483.C48, (v3)
Chambers, Frances. Z2184.P3.C46 1998, (v10)
Chambers, John Whiteclay. UB343.C483 1987, (v10)
Chambers, Karen S. N8600.C484 1999, (v9)
Chambers, Liam. DA949.C48 1998, (v5)
Chambers, R. G. QC176.8.E4.C43 1990, (v1)
Chambers, R. W. PR83.C37 1967, (v3)
 PR1585.C5 1959, (v3)
 PR1788.C5 1965, (v3)
Chambers, Steven D. Z6207.W8.C48 1996, (v10)
Chambers, Whittaker. CT275.C4564.A3, (v5)
 E743.5.C45 1997, (v4)
 E743.5.C47, (v4)
Chambers, William Nisbet. E302.1.C45, (v4)
 E340.B4.C5 1970, (v4)
Chambers-Schiller, Lee Virginia. HQ800.2.C43 1984, (v6)
Chambliss, J. J. LB41.C49 1987, (v7)
Chamlee, Roy Z. E457.5.C47 1990, (v4)
Champa, Kermit Swiler. ND553.M7.A4 1999, (v9)
Champagne, Anthony. E748.R24.C48 1988, (v4)
Champagne, Duane. E99.C5.C34 1992, (v4)
Champagne, Roland A. PN75.D45.C46 1995, (v3)
 PQ79.C44 1990, (v3)
Champagne, Rosaria. PS169.I5.C43 1996, (v3)
Champdor, Albert. DS70.5.B3.C413, (v5)
Champeney, D. C. QA403.5.C47 1987, (v1)
Champion, A. G. G1812.21.E2.C4 1996, (v6)
Champion, Dean J. KF9794.C48 1991, (v7)
Champion, Larry S. PR2983.C33, (v3)
 Z8811.C53 1993, (v10)
Champlin, Edward. HN10.R7.C43 1991, (v6)
Champlin, T. S. BD450.C4715 1988, (v8)
Chan, Gerald. DS779.27.C44 1999, (v5)
Chan, Joseph Man. PN5449.H56.C47 1991, (v3)
Chan, Lois Mai. Z693.5.U6 C48 1994, (v10)
 Z696.U4 C47 1999, (v10)
Chan, Stephen. DT3077.S6.C46 1992, (v5)
Chan, Sucheng. E184.O6.C47 1991, (v4)
Chan, Wing-tsit. B125.C45, (v8)
 B126.C44, (v8)
 B128.C54.C42 1989, (v8)
Chance, Britton. QC601.C5, (v1)
Chance, John K. F1219.1.O11.C44 1989, (v4)
Chance, Joseph E. E409.5.M56.C47 1991, (v4)
Chance, Linda H. PL791.6.T73.C35 1997, (v3)
Chancellor, James D. BP605.C38 C48 2000, (v8)
Chancer, Lynn S. HQ79.C43 1992, (v6)
Chancy, Myriam J. A. PR9205.O5.C48 1997, (v3)
Chandar, Krishan. PK2200.C75, (v3)
Chandler, Alfred Dupont. HD2785.C4732 1988, (v6)
 HE2751.C45, (v6)
 HF5343.C584, (v6)
Chandler, David G. DC147.C47, (v5)
 U39.C48, (v10)
 U162.C44, (v10)
Chandler, David P. HV8599.C16.C48 1999, (v6)
Chandler, David. DR1752.C49 1999, (v5)
Chandler, Elizabeth Lathrop. PS1886.C5 1975, (v3)
Chandler, Frank Wadleigh. PQ6147.P5.C5 1961, (v3)
Chandler, Harry. TN667.C43 1998, (v1)
Chandler, James K. PR457.C39 1998, (v3)

Chandler, Lester Vernon. HB3717 1929.C47, **(v6)**
Chandler, Raymond. PS3505.H3224 R3, **(v3)**
Chandler, Richard E. PQ6033.C45, **(v3)**
Chandler, Richard Eugene. PQ6172.C48, **(v3)**
Chandler, Timothy John Lindsay. GV567.C43 2002, **(v6)**
Chandler, Yvonne J. KF242.A1.C48 1998, **(v7)**
Chandos, John. LC1390.C43 1984, **(v7)**
Chandos, Oliver Lyttelton. DA566.9.C44.A3, **(v5)**
Chandra, Sudhir. KNS516.C49 1998, **(v7)**
Chandra, Vikram. PS3553.H27165L68 1997, **(v3)**
Chandra, Vikram. PS3553.H27165R43 1995, **(v3)**
Chandrasekhar, S. QC711.C5, **(v1)**
Chandrasekhar, S. (Subrahmanyan). QA803.C48 1995, **(v1)**
Chandrasekhar, Sripati. DS777.55.C34, **(v5)**
Chandrasekharan, K. QA403.5.C48 1989, **(v1)**
Chandy, K. Mani. QA76.642.C47 1992, **(v1)**
Chaney, Margaret Stella. QP141.C5 1979, **(v1)**
Chang, Ai-ling. PS3553.H27187 R53, **(v3)**
Chang, Amos Ih Tiao. NA2500.C45, **(v9)**
Chang, Ch un. B126.C4466 1998, **(v8)**
Chang, Chieh. PL2837.C486.C4813 1989, **(v3)**
Chang, Chun-mai. B127.N4.C46 1977, **(v8)**
  DS775.C33, **(v5)**
Chang, Chun-shu. PL2698.L52.Z62 1991, **(v3)**
  PL2722.U2.Z64 1998, **(v3)**
Chang, Cyril F. RT86.7.C47 2001, **(v2)**
Chang, David W. DS796.H757.C44 1998, **(v5)**
Chang, Gordon G. HC427.92.C3375 2001, **(v6)**
Chang, Gordon H. E183.8.C6.C47 1990, **(v4)**
Chang, Hen-shui. PL2740.H413 1991, **(v3)**
Chang, Hsien-liang. PL2837.H762.N313 1988, **(v3)**
Chang, Hsin-pao. DS757.5.C45, **(v5)**
Chang, Hsu-Hsin. DS777.A567.C416 1991, **(v5)**
Chang, Hsu-tung. PL2303.C3483 1997, **(v3)**
Chang, Iris. DS796.N2.C44 1997, **(v5)**
Chang, Kai. TK5103.2.C45 2000, **(v1)**
  TK7876.C44 1994, **(v1)**
Chang, Kang-i Sun. PL2698.C4556.Z6 1991, **(v3)**
Chang, Kwang-chih. CC77.C48, **(v5)**
  DS715.C38 1986, **(v5)**
  DS723.C38, **(v5)**
  DS741.65.C53 1983, **(v5)**
  GN855.C6.C5, **(v6)**
Chang, Luke T. DS737.C4818 1982, **(v5)**
Chang, Maria Hsia. HX550.N3.C38 2001, **(v6)**
Chang, Robert S. KF4757.5.A75.C48 1999, **(v7)**
Chang, Sung-sheng. PL3031.T3C447 1993, **(v3)**
Chang, Tony H. Z3108.A5.C37 1999, **(v10)**
Chang, Valerie Nash. HV6626.22.U6.C48 1996, **(v6)**
Changeux, Jean-Pierre. BJ45.C4313 2000, **(v8)**
Chant, Christopher. UF500.C42 1987, **(v10)**
  UG1240.C485 1983, **(v10)**
Chao, Buwei Yang. CT1828.C5.A3, **(v5)**
Chao, Chung. PL2824.C5, **(v3)**
Chao, I-heng. PL2415.Z43 1995, **(v3)**
Chao, Kang. HB2114.A3.C45 1986, **(v6)**
Chao, Linda. JQ1516.C426 1998, **(v7)**
Chao, Sheau-yueh J. Z5170.C43 1994, **(v10)**
Chao, Yuen Ren. PL1071.C476, **(v3)**
Chapa, Juan Bautista. F1316.C4613 1997, **(v4)**
Chapanis, Alphonse. TA168.C42 1996, **(v1)**
Chapelle, Frank. GB1003.2.C455 1997, **(v6)**
Chapelle, Howard Irving. VM23.C53 1935a, **(v10)**
  VM144.C28 1967, **(v10)**
Chaplin, George. PN4899.H66.C43 1998, **(v3)**
Chaplin, Hamako Ito. PL537.C55, **(v3)**
Chaplin, Joyce E. E46.C48 2001, **(v4)**
  F212.C47 1993, **(v4)**
Chaplin, M. F. TP248.65.E59.C48 1990, **(v1)**
Chapman, Abraham. PS508.N3.C5 1970, **(v3)**
  PS508.N3.C53, **(v3)**
Chapman, Bill G. RE51.C48 2001, **(v2)**
Chapman, Carleton B. R724.C45 1984, **(v2)**
  Z720.B6.C48 1994, **(v10)**
Chapman, Charles Edward. F864.C46, **(v4)**
  F864.C465 1971, **(v4)**
Chapman, David L. GV545.52.S26.C43 1994, **(v6)**
Chapman, Dudley H. KF1649.C38 1991, **(v7)**
Chapman, George. PR2442.P3, **(v3)**

  PR2442.P366, **(v3)**
  PR2450.P6 1962, **(v3)**
Chapman, H. Perry. N6953.R4.C48 1990, **(v9)**
Chapman, Herrick. HD9711.F72.C53 1990, **(v6)**
Chapman, J. Harley. BL53.C42 1988, **(v8)**
Chapman, Jenny. HQ1236.C47 1993, **(v6)**
Chapman, Joan Margaret. DC280.5.H3.C5 1957, **(v5)**
Chapman, John Jay. PS1292.C3.A6 1998, **(v3)**
Chapman, John L. UG633.C49, **(v10)**
Chapman, John Stewart. PR4382.C45, **(v3)**
Chapman, John. BX4700.B3.C5 1971, **(v8)**
Chapman, Keith. HD9575.N57.C5, **(v6)**
  HD9579.C32.C45 1991, **(v6)**
Chapman, Malcolm. GN549.C3.C48 1992, **(v6)**
Chapman, Michael. PL8014.S63.C47 1996, **(v3)**
Chapman, Mike. GV1198.12.C43 1990, **(v6)**
Chapman, Paul Davis. LB1131.C447 1988, **(v7)**
Chapman, Richard E. QE28.C374 1994, **(v1)**
Chapman, Sara S. PS2127.L5.C4 1989, **(v3)**
Chapman, Sydney. QC801.3.C45, **(v1)**
Chapman, Tobias. B828.C46 1989, **(v8)**
Chapman, V. J. QK938.S27.C45 1974, **(v1)**
Chapman, Wayne K. PR5908.L5.C4 1991, **(v3)**
Chapman-Huston, Desmond. RS68.A4.C5, **(v2)**
Chappell, John D. D810.P85.U53 1997, **(v5)**
Chappell, Larry W. PN4874.W62.C43 1997, **(v3)**
Chappell, Warren. Z124.C47 1999, **(v10)**
Chappelow, Allan. PR5368.P6.C47 1971, **(v3)**
Chapple, J. A. V. PR4711.C55 1997, **(v3)**
Chapple, Janet. F722.C458 2002, **(v4)**
Chapple, Richard L. PG3328.A09.C5 1983, **(v3)**
Chapuis, Oscar. DS556.5.C47 1995, **(v5)**
Char, Rene. PQ2605.H3345.A6 1957a, **(v3)**
Charbeneau, Randall J. TC176.C43 2000, **(v1)**
Charbonneaux, Jean. N5630.C45713, **(v9)**
Chardon, Francis A. F598.C48 1997, **(v4)**
Charlebois, Lucile C. PQ6605.E44.Z625 1998, **(v3)**
Charles, Amy Marie. PR3508.C48, **(v3)**
Charles, David. B491.A27.C43 1984, **(v8)**
Charles, Jeffrey A. HS2723.C48 1993, **(v6)**
Charles, Joseph. E310.C5, **(v4)**
Charles, Philip A. QB472.C46 1995, **(v1)**
Charles, Ray. ML420.C46 A3 1992, **(v9)**
Charles, Sydney Robinson. ML134.J773 C5 1983, **(v9)**
Charles. PQ1553.C5 1973, **(v3)**
Charlesworth, M. J. R724.C455 1993, **(v2)**
Charlot, Jean. DC412.C51413 1971b, **(v5)**
  N6554.C45, **(v9)**
  PL6448.9.C5, **(v3)**
Charlot, Monica. DA555.C48 1991, **(v5)**
Charlton, Sue Ellen M. JQ24.C48 1997, **(v7)**
Charlton, William. BJ1468.5.C43 1988, **(v8)**
Charme, Stuart L. B2430.S34.C5248 1991, **(v8)**
Charmley, John. DA17.L56.C48 1987, **(v5)**
  DA585.C5.C48 1990, **(v5)**
Charnes, Linda. PR3014.C43 1993, **(v3)**
Charney, Leo. PN1995.C4475 1998, **(v3)**
Charney, Maurice. PR2982.C45, **(v3)**
  PR2987.C47, **(v3)**
  PR3069.L6.C48 2000, **(v3)**
Charnon-Deutsch, Lou. N7630.C43 2000, **(v9)**
  PQ6144.C427 1994, **(v3)**
Charns, Alexander. KF8742.C45 1992, **(v7)**
Charques, Richard Denis. DK41.C44 1956, **(v5)**
  DK260.C37 1965, **(v5)**
Charron, Jean Daniel. PC13.N67 no.34, **(v3)**
Charry, Eric S. ML3760.C38 2000, **(v9)**
Charters, Samuel Barclay. ML3508.C5 1981, **(v9)**
Chartier, Alain. PQ1557.A14, **(v3)**
Chartier, Armand B. PQ2189.B32.Z656, **(v3)**
Chartier, Roger. DC138.C4813 1991, **(v5)**
Chartkoff, Joseph L. F863.C46 1984, **(v4)**
Charvat, Petr. DS70.7.C47 1993, **(v5)**
Charvat, William. PN155.C5, **(v3)**
Chasdi, Richard J. HV6433.M5.C53 1999, **(v6)**
Chase, George Henry. NB60.C5, **(v9)**
Chase, Gilbert. ML200.C5 1987, **(v9)**
  ML315.C4 1959, **(v9)**
Chase, Karen. PR468.H63.C48 2000, **(v3)**
Chase, Malcolm. HN400.R3.C48 1988, **(v6)**

Chase, Mary Ellen. F29.B78.C453 1978, **(v4)**
  PR4754.C36 1964, **(v3)**
  PS3505.H48 E3, **(v3)**
  PS3505.H48 S5, **(v3)**
  PS3505.H48 W5, **(v3)**
Chase, Salmon P. E415.6.C48 1993, **(v4)**
  E415.9.C4.A3, **(v4)**
Chase, Stuart. BC108.C52, **(v8)**
  CB427.C48, **(v5)**
  F1215.C49, **(v4)**
  HB199.C45, **(v6)**
  HC106.4.C42 1968, **(v6)**
Chasteen, John Charles. F1410.C4397 2001, **(v4)**
Chateaubriand, Francois-Rene. DC255.C4.A43 1961a, **(v5)**
  PQ2205.A8 1973, **(v3)**
  PQ2205.N4 1932, **(v3)**
Chatellier, Louis. BV2900.C4313 1997, **(v8)**
  BX1490.C4613 1989, **(v8)**
Chatman, Seymour Benjamin. PN212.C47 1990, **(v3)**
  PS2128.C5, **(v3)**
Chatterjee, Partha. DS468.C47 1993, **(v5)**
  DS480.84.C545 1997, **(v5)**
Chatterjee, Upamanyu. PR9499.3.C4665M36 2000, **(v3)**
Chatterji, Joya. DS485.B493.C49 1994, **(v5)**
Chatters, A. W. QA251.3.C53 1998, **(v1)**
Chatterton, Lynne. SB205.M4.C48 1996, **(v1)**
Chatterton, Thomas. PR3340.A1 1990, **(v3)**
  PR3340.A2 1971, **(v3)**
Chatty, Dawn. GN635.O43.C48 1996, **(v6)**
Chaturvedi, Sanjay. G587.C48 1996, **(v6)**
Chaucer, Geoffrey. PR1850.1896, **(v3)**
  PR1851.B46 1987, **(v3)**
  PR1852.D6, **(v3)**
  PR1855.M6 1949, **(v3)**
  PR1866.R8 1983 pt. 17, **(v3)**
  PR1866.R8 1983 pt.2, **(v3)**
  PR1866.S5 1929, **(v3)**
  PR1868.W6.C5 1976, **(v3)**
  PR1870.A1.E27 1993, **(v3)**
  PR1870.A13.C6, **(v3)**
  PR1885.B7, **(v3)**
  PR1895.C57, **(v3)**
  PR1895.R6, **(v3)**
  PR1895.R65 1977, **(v3)**
Chaudhry, Kiren Aziz. HC415.33.C49 1997, **(v6)**
Chaudhuri, Nirad C. DS480.45.C46 1988, **(v5)**
Chaudhuri, Pranay. QA76.58.C43 1991, **(v1)**
Chaudhuri, Una. PN1672.9.C53 1995, **(v3)**
Chauvet, Jean-Marie. N5310.5.F7.C4713 1996, **(v9)**
Chave, Anna. ND237.R725.C5 1989, **(v9)**
Chavez, John R. F790.M5.C49 1984, **(v4)**
Chavez, Lydia. HF5549.5.A34.C484 1998, **(v6)**
Chavez, Thomas E. F800.A77.C48 1990, **(v4)**
Chawaf, Chantal. PQ2663.H379.B55, **(v3)**
  PQ2663.H379.R4, **(v3)**
Chawla, H. S. TP248.27.P55, **(v1)**
Chayefsky, Paddy. PS3505.H632.A4, **(v3)**
  PS3505.H632.G5 1962, **(v3)**
  PS3505.H632.M5, **(v3)**
  PS3505.H632.T4, **(v3)**
Chazan, Daniel. QA159.C48 2000, **(v1)**
Chazan, Robert. DS124.C43 1997, **(v5)**
  DS135.G31.C53 2000, **(v5)**
Chazin-Bennahum, Judith. GV1649.C48 1988, **(v6)**
  GV1785.T83.C53 1994, **(v6)**
Cheadle, Mary Paterson. PS3531.O82.Z554 1997, **(v3)**
Cheal, David J. HC79.P6.C44 1996, **(v6)**
Cheape, Charles W. HD9651.95.C37.C48 1995, **(v6)**
  HE310.B6.C45, **(v6)**
Checkland, Olive. UH537.J3.C49 1994, **(v10)**
Chedid, Andree. PQ2605.H4245.A19 1981, **(v3)**
Cheek, Neil H. GV14.C47, **(v6)**
Cheek, Timothy. PN5366.T45.C44 1997, **(v3)**
Cheesman, Clive. D107.6.C44 2000, **(v5)**

Cheever, John. PS3503.H6428 S8, (v3)
PS3505.H6424 E5, (v3)
PS3505.H6428.B8, (v3)
PS3505.H6428 F3, (v3)
PS3505.H6428 S6, (v3)
PS3505.H6428 W3, (v3)
PS3505.H6428.Z48 1988, (v3)
Cheever, Susan. PS3505.H6428.Z59 1984, (v3)
Chekhov, Anton Pavlovich. PG3456.A1 1965, (v3)
PG3456.A15.C66 1998, (v3)
PG3456.A15.G3 1998, (v3)
PG3456.A15 1979, (v3)
PG3456.A19.B7 1977, (v3)
PG3458.A3.K3 1975, (v3)
Chekki, Danesh A. BL1281.24.C54 1997, (v8)
Chellas, Brian F. BC199.M6.C47, (v8)
Chellen, Sydney S. R119.9.C48 2000, (v2)
Chen, An. JQ1510.C483 1999, (v7)
Chen, F. H. TA710.C5185 2000, (v1)
Chen, Feng. HC427.92.C3533 1995, (v6)
Chen, G. QA76.9.S63, (v1)
Chen, Hsueh-chao. PL2840.H784.Z47713 1991, (v3)
Chen, Jerome. DS777.2.C48 1972, (v5)
DS778.M3.C473, (v5)
DS778.M3.C474, (v5)
Chen, Jian. DS919.5.C4513 1994, (v5)
Chen, Jie. JQ1508.C462 1995, (v7)
Chen, Ke. QA76.95.C44 1999, (v1)
Chen, Kung-po. DS777.44.C5 1966, (v5)
Chen, Li-fu. DS777.5366.C4644.A3 1994, (v5)
Chen, Ming-Jer. HC427.92.C3544 2001, (v6)
Chen, Ping. PL1083.C525 1999, (v3)
Chen, Shou-jung. PL1125.E6.C47 1959b, (v3)
Chen, Shou-yi. PL2265.C45 1961, (v3)
Chen, Theodore Hsi-en. DS777.55.C395, (v5)
Chen, Tu-hsiu. DS777.15.C5.A4 1998, (v5)
Chen, Wai-Kai. TK454.2.C4253 1990, (v1)
Chen, Xiaomei. PL2393.C524 2002, (v3)
Chen, Yong. F869.S39.C515 2000, (v4)
Chen, Yu-shih. PL2409.C45 1988, (v3)
Chenevix Trench, Charles. DA68.32.G6.C46 1979, (v5)
Cheney, Patrick Gerard. PR2367.A9.C44 1993, (v3)
Cheng, Ching-wen. PL2841.C53.A27 1999, (v3)
Cheng, Chung-ying. B127.C65.C495 1990, (v8)
Cheng, Chu-yuan. DS779.32.C46 1990, (v5)
HC427.9.C52178, (v6)
Cheng, David Hong. BL1900.L35 C5439 2000, (v8)
Cheng, Francois. PQ2663.H3913, (v3)
Cheng, I-li. PL1455.C584 1984b, (v3)
Cheng, James Chester. DS759.C377 1963, (v5)
Cheng, Te-kun. DS715.C42, (v5)
Cheng, Tien-fang. DS740.5.R8.C5, (v5)
Chenier, Andre. PQ1965.A195 1978, (v3)
Chennault, Claire Lee. E745.C35.A3 1949, (v4)
Cheong, Sung-hwa. DS910.2.J3.C483 1991, (v5)
Chepesiuk, Ronald. HV5804.C47 1999, (v6)
Cheremisinoff, Nicholas P. RA1215.C483 2000, (v2)
T55.3.H3.C4857 1995, (v1)
T55.3.H3.C4859 1996, (v1)
TD191.5.C48 1993, (v1)
Cherepanov, Sergei Kirillovich. QK321.C416 1995, (v1)
Cherkovski, Neeli. PS310.B43.C44 1999, (v3)
Cherlin, Andrew J. HQ535.C415, (v6)
Cherneia, Janet Marion. F2520.1.G72.C47 1993, (v4)
Cherniavsky, Michael. DK32.C523, (v5)
Cherniss, Harold F. B395.C525 1980, (v8)
B485.C48 1962, (v8)
Chernoff, John Miller. ML3760.C48, (v9)
Chernow, Carol. LB3013.C4695 1989, (v7)
Chernow, Ron. CT275.R75.C47 1998, (v5)
Cherny, Igor V. GC10.4.R4.R39 1998, (v6)
Cherny, Julius. HV41.C4428 1992, (v6)
Cherny, Robert W. E664.B87 C47 1994, (v4)
F666.C49, (v4)
Chernyshevsky, Nikolay Gavrilovich.
PG3321.C6.C42 1989, (v3)
PG3321.C6 C5 1961, (v3)
Cheronis, Nicholas Dimitrius. QD98.C45 1965, (v1)
Cherrington, Ernest H. QB581.C44, (v1)

Cherrington, Ruth. LA1133.7.C515 1991, (v7)
Cherry, Charles L. RC450.G7.C48 1989, (v2)
Cherry, Conrad. BV4030.C46 1995, (v8)
Cherry, David. DT70.C47 1998, (v5)
Chesebrough, David B. E449.C523 1996, (v4)
Cheselka, Paul. PQ7797.B635.Z65 1987, (v3)
Cheshin, Amir. DS109.94.C49 1999, (v5)
Chesler, Mark A. LC191.C373, (v7)
Chesnais, Jean-Claude. HB887.C4813 1992, (v6)
Chesney-Lind, Meda. HV6046.C54 1997, (v6)
Chesnut, Mary Boykin Miller. E487.C5, (v4)
E487.C52 1949, (v4)
E487.C525 1984, (v4)
Chesnut, R. Andrew. BX8762.A45.B625 1997, (v8)
Chesnutt, Charles Waddell. E185.61.C548 1999, (v4)
PS1292.C6.A6 1993, (v3)
PS1292.C6 C6 1969, (v3)
PS1292.C6.M26 1997, (v3)
PS1292.C6.P38 1998, (v3)
PS1292.C6 S5, (v3)
PS1292.C6.Z47 1993, (v3)
PS1292.C6.Z48 1997, (v3)
Chess, Stella. HQ769.C437, (v6)
Chessick, Richard D. RC437.5.C48 1992, (v2)
RC475.7.C48 1993, (v2)
Chessman, G. Wallace. F124.C46, (v4)
Chester, Alfred. PS3505.H679.H38 1990, (v3)
Chester, Thomas Morris. E540.N3.C4 1989, (v4)
Chesterfield, Philip Dormer Stanhope. BJ1671.C53 1973, (v8)
Chesterman, John. KU2140.C48 1997, (v7)
Chesterton, G. K. BL48.C5 1925a, (v8)
BR121.C5 1909a, (v8)
PN511.C42, (v3)
PR4453.C4.A16 1949, (v3)
PR4453.C4.A16 1950, (v3)
PR4453.C4.A16 1955, (v3)
PR4453.C4.A16 1958, (v3)
PR4453.C4.A17 1980, (v3)
PR4453.C4.A64 1971, (v3)
PR4453.C4 F5, (v3)
PR4453.C4.F6 1962, (v3)
PR4453.C4.H4 1970, (v3)
PR4453.C4 M31, (v3)
PR4453.C4 M3 1922, (v3)
PR4453.C4.M35, (v3)
PR4453.C4.M5 1972, (v3)
PR4453.C4 N36 1978, (v3)
PR4453.C4 P3 1963, (v3)
PR4453.C4 P6, (v3)
PR4453.C4 R4, (v3)
PR4453.C4.S5 1970, (v3)
PR4453.C4.Z5 1939, (v3)
PR4453.C4 1986, (v3)
PR4588.C5 1965, (v3)
PR5493.C5 1955, (v3)
PR4588.C5, (v3)
Chestre, Thomas. PR1955.C5.L3 1960, (v3)
Chethik, Morton. RJ504.C463 2000, (v2)
Chetley, Andrew. HD9665.6.C47 1989, (v6)
Cheung, King-Kok. PS153.A84.C48 1993, (v3)
Chevalier, Haakon. PS3505.H68 F6, (v3)
Chevalier, Michel. E165.C54 1969, (v4)
Chevalley, Abel. PC2640.C54 1940, (v3)
Chevallier, Andrew. RM666.H33C522 2001, (v2)
RS164.C4437 1996, (v2)
Chevannes, Barry. BL2532.R37.C47 1994, (v8)
Chevigny, Paul. K3253.C47 1988, (v7)
PN2277.N5.C515 1991, (v3)
Chevlowe, Susan. ND237.S465.A4 1998, (v9)
Chew, Allen F. G2111.S1.C5 1970, (v6)
Chhabra, R. P. QC189.5.C55 1993, (v1)
Chi, Hsi-sheng. DS777.45.C54, (v5)
Chia, Ping-wa. PL2843.P5.F813 1991, (v3)
Chiang, Kai-shek. DS740.C5, (v5)
DS777.47.C4273 1958, (v5)
DS777.53.C4235, (v5)
Chiang, Wen-han. DS777.5.C45 1948a, (v5)
Chiang, Yee. PL1171.C58 1954, (v3)
Chiari, Joseph. PQ2344.Z5C516 1970, (v3)
Chibbett, David G. NE771.C48, (v9)

Chibnall, Marjorie. D148.C48, (v5)
Chicago, Judy. N6537.C48.A4 1985, (v9)
N7630.C49 1999, (v9)
ND237.C492.A28, (v9)
Chicherin, B. N. JA84.R9.C49213 1998, (v7)
Chichester, Francis. GV822.G5.C5 1961a, (v6)
Chick, Victoria. HB172.5.C455 1983, (v6)
Chickering, Arthur W. LB2322.2.C45 1993, (v7)
Chickering, Roger. D15.L3.C45 1993, (v5)
Chidester, David. BL2470.S6.C45 1991, (v8)
HN801.Z9.V53 1991, (v6)
Chien, Chung-shu. PL2749.C8 W45 1979, (v3)
Chien, Ning. TC175.2.C47313 1999, (v1)
Chikamatsu, Monzaemon. PL898.C5.A24, (v3)
Chikhi, Beïda. PQ3988.5.A5C48 1997, (v3)
Chilcote, Ronald H. DT613.76.C3.C54 1991, (v5)
HN290.J83.C48 1990, (v6)
JF51.C44 2000, (v7)
JF51.C453 2000, (v7)
Child, Brenda J. E99.C6.C45 1998, (v4)
Child, Greg. GV200.C44 1995, (v6)
Child, Heather. CR31.C5, (v5)
Child, Jack. F1439.5.C525 1992, (v4)
Child, Lydia Maria Francis. PS1293.A6 1997, (v3)
Childe, V. Gordon. BD181.C48, (v8)
CC75.C45 1956a, (v5)
D65.C5 1958, (v5)
DS11.C52 1953, (v5)
Childers, Erskine. PR6005.H52 R5, (v3)
Children's Defense Fund (U.S.). HV741.C5377 1994, (v6)
Children's Rights Research and Advocacy Project (Bellville, South Africa). KTL4720.C48 1992, (v7)
Childress, Diana. PR1906.5.C54 2000, (v3)
Childress, James F. R724.C477 1997, (v2)
Childs, Barton. RB155.C496 1999, (v2)
Childs, Donald J. PS3509.L43.Z64924 1997, (v3)
Childs, J. Rives. D285.8.C4.C448 1988, (v5)
Childs, John Charles Roger. D279.5.C48 1991, (v5)
Childs, Marquis William. PS3505.H774 P4, (v3)
Chilton, Bruce. BT590.J8 C45 2000, (v8)
Chilton, John. ML419.B23.C5 1987, (v9)
ML419.H35.C5 1990, (v9)
Chilton, John. ML420.J777.C55 1994, (v9)
Chin p'ing mei. PL2698.H73C513 1939, (v3)
PL2997.C26.E5 1940, (v3)
Chin, Elizabeth M. Liew Siew. HC107.C8.C47 2001, (v6)
Chin, Henk E. F2425.C48 1987, (v4)
Chinard, Gilbert. PQ145.7.A5.C5 1934, (v3)
Ching, Frank. NA31.C44 1995, (v9)
Ching, Julia. B128.C54 C465 2000, (v8)
BL1802.C548 1993, (v8)
Ching, Leo T. S. DS799.7.C484 2001, (v5)
Chinloy, Peter. KF1600.C46 1989, (v7)
Chinn, Carl. HQ1599.E5.C47 1988, (v6)
Chinn, Jeff. DK35.5.C48 1996, (v5)
Chinn, Sarah E. E185.61.C56 2000, (v4)
Chinoy, Mike. DS779.26.C47647 1999, (v5)
Chinweizu. PR9340.C48 1983, (v3)
Chion, Michel. PN1995.C4713 1999, (v3)
PN1995.7.C4714 1994, (v3)
Chiong, Jane Ayers. LC3621.C53 1998, (v7)
Chipman, Bruce L. PS374.M55.C45 1999, (v3)
Chipman, Donald E. F389.C438 2001, (v4)
F389.C44 1992, (v4)
Chipp, Herschel Browning. ND553.P5.A66 1988b, (v9)
Chiras, Daniel D. TD170.C55 1992, (v1)
Chirot, Daniel. JC495.C47 1994, (v7)
Chisholm, Anne. DA566.9.B37.C49 1993, (v5)
Chisholm, James. F767.F8.C48, (v4)
Chisholm, Roderick M. BD161.C47, (v8)
Chisholm, Shirley. E840.8.C48.A28, (v4)
Chisick, Harvey. LA691.5.C52, (v7)
Chisolm, Lawrence W. N8375.F375.C5, (v9)
Chiswick, Barry R. HD8081.A5.C473 1988, (v6)
Chitham, Edward. PR4172.W73.C48 1998, (v3)
PR4173.C45 1987, (v3)
Chitnis, Bernice. PQ2510.C47 1991, (v3)
Chittenden, Cecil Ross. F204.W5 C5, (v4)

Chittick, Kathryn. PR4582.C48 1990, **(v3)**
  Z8230.C45 1989, **(v10)**
Chittick, William C. BP189.26.I2623.C47 1998, **(v8)**
Chitty, Dennis. QL737.R666.C48 1996, **(v1)**
Chitty, Susan. PR4879.L2.Z6 1989, **(v3)**
Chitwood, Oliver Perry. E397.C48 1990, **(v4)**
Chiu Tang shu. DS741.C5 no.8, **(v5)**
Chivers, T. H. PS1294.C4 1957, **(v3)**
Chmiel, Mark. PQ2683.I32.Z63 2001, **(v3)**
Cho, George. HC445.5.C52 1990, **(v6)**
Cho, Sun. HC467.C41564 1994, **(v6)**
Cho, Tong-song. HF1414.C456 2001, **(v6)**
Cho, Z.-H. RC78.7.D53.C48 1993, **(v2)**
Choate, Ernest A. QL677.C5 1985, **(v1)**
Choay, Françoise. NA1053.J4.C5, **(v9)**
Chodorow, Nancy. HQ1206.C52 1989, **(v6)**
Choi, Jung Min. BD175.5.P65.C46 1992, **(v8)**
  JA75.7.C475 1995, **(v7)**
Choksy, Lois. MT1.C536, **(v9)**
Cholodenko, Marc. PQ2663.H575.M6713 1988, **(v3)**
Chomsky, Aviva. HD8138.5.B55.C48 1996, **(v6)**
Chomsky, Noam. DS558.C5 1993, **(v5)**
  E840.C49 1982, **(v4)**
  E881.C48 1991, **(v4)**
  KZ6374.C48 2000, **(v7)**
  LB885.C522, **(v7)**
  P106.C524 2000, **(v3)**
  P106.C544, **(v3)**
  P125.C47 1988, **(v3)**
  P291.C4, **(v3)**
  PE1133.C5, **(v3)**
Chong, Chi-yong. PL991.2.C4.A24 1994, **(v3)**
Chong, Denise. F1089.5.V22.C564 1994, **(v4)**
  HB846.5.C48 1991, **(v6)**
Chong, Edwin Kah Pin. QA402.5.C476 1996, **(v1)**
Chong, Yon-hui. PL992.2.Y6.A7313 1989, **(v3)**
Choo, Chun Wei. HD30.213.C476 2001, **(v6)**
Choper, Jesse H. KF4783.C47 1995, **(v7)**
Chopin, Kate. PS1294.C63.A6 1998, **(v3)**
  PS1294.C63.A63 2001, **(v3)**
  PS1294.C63 A9, **(v3)**
  PS1294.C63 B3 1967, **(v3)**
  PS1294.C63 1970, **(v3)**
Chopp, Rebecca S. BT83.55.C48 1989, **(v8)**
Choppin, Gregory R. QD601.2.C47 1980, **(v1)**
Chopra, Anil K. TA654.6.C466 1995, **(v1)**
Choquette, Diane. Z7834.U6 C46 1985, **(v10)**
Chorafas, Dimitris N. HG4012.C47 1995, **(v6)**
Chorley, Richard J. GA23.C46 1967, **(v6)**
  GB400.5.C45, **(v6)**
  GB401.5.C5 1985, **(v6)**
Chothia, Jean. PN2638.A64.C48 1991, **(v3)**
Chou, Chih-ping. PL1129.E5.C438 1992, **(v3)**
Chou, Ching-wen. DS777.55.C4573 1960, **(v5)**
Chou, E. Shan. PL2675.C567 1995, **(v3)**
Chou, Hsiang-kuang. DS740.C56, **(v5)**
Chou, Shu-jen. PL3000.C5.A4, **(v3)**
Chou, Tse-tsung. DS775.C5386 1960, **(v5)**
Chou, Tse-tsung. DS775.C53862, **(v5)**
Choudhury, Masudul Alam. BP173.25.C49 1998, **(v8)**
  HB126.4.C49 1992, **(v6)**
Choueiri, Youssef M. DS37.4.C46 1989, **(v5)**
  DS62.7.C46 2000, **(v5)**
Chouteau, François. F598.C55 2001, **(v4)**
Chow, Rey. DS734.97.U6.C47 1993, **(v5)**
  DS775.2.C47 1990, **(v5)**
Chowning, Margaret. F1306.C46 1999, **(v4)**
Choy, Wayson. PR9199.3.C4967, **(v3)**
Chraibi, Driss. PQ3989.C5.M4713 1989, **(v3)**
Chretien. PQ1445.E6.E5 1997, **(v3)**
  PQ1445.L3.E5 1990, **(v3)**
  PQ1445.P2 1956, **(v3)**
  PQ1447.E5.R35 1999, **(v3)**
Chrislock, Carl Henry. D570.8.C8.M63 1991, **(v5)**
Chrisman, Miriam Usher. BR355.P36.C47 1996, **(v8)**
  DC801.S577.C47 1982, **(v5)**
Christ, Henry I. CT107.C44 1987, **(v5)**
Christ, Matthew R. KL4115.A75.C48 1998, **(v7)**
Christakis, Nicholas A. RC80.C48 1999, **(v2)**
Christen, Kimberly A. GR524.C48 1998, **(v6)**
Christen, Yves. BF692.2.C4713 1990, **(v2)**

Christensen, Erwin Ottomar. N5310.C54, **(v9)**
Christensen, F. M. BD632.C48 1993, **(v8)**
  HQ471.C47 1990, **(v6)**
Christensen, George E. F572.N8 C473 1985, **(v4)**
Christensen, Gordon J. RK61.C57 2002, **(v2)**
Christensen, Jerome. PR4388.C54 1993, **(v3)**
Christensen, Thomas J. E183.8.C5.C558 1996, **(v4)**
Christian, David. HD9394.7.C48 1990, **(v6)**
Christian, Garna L. UB418.A47.C48 1995, **(v10)**
Christian, William A. B1674.W354.C5, **(v8)**
Christiano, Thomas. JC423.C567 1996, **(v7)**
Christians, Clifford G. PN4888.P6.C47 1993, **(v3)**
Christiansen, Keith. ND623.G35.C45 1982, **(v9)**
Christiansen, Rupert. DC316.C47 1994, **(v5)**
Christiansen, Sigurd. PT8950.C55 A713, **(v3)**
Christianson, Gale E. QC16.N7.C49 1984, **(v1)**
  QC981.8.G56.C48 1999, **(v1)**
Christianson, Scott. HV9466.C47 1998, **(v6)**
Christianson, Stephen G. GT4803.D6, **(v6)**
Christie, A. B. RC111.C47 1987, **(v2)**
Christie, Agatha. PR6005.H66 A7, **(v3)**
Christie, Agatha. PR6005.H66 M53, **(v3)**
  PR6005.H66 N, **(v3)**
Christie, Ian R. DA505.C48 1982, **(v5)**
Christie, Maureen. QC881.2.O9.C48 2001, **(v1)**
Christie, Nancy. HV108.C48 2000, **(v6)**
Christine, de Pisan. PQ1575.A28 1984, **(v3)**
  PQ1575.A9513 1993, **(v3)**
  PQ1575.L7513 1991, **(v3)**
Christ-Janer, Albert. NA737.S3.C5, **(v9)**
Christman, Albert B. V63.P35.C47 1998, **(v10)**
Christman, J. Richard. QC176.C47 1988, **(v1)**
Christman, John. HB701.C54 1994, **(v6)**
Christodoulou, Demetrios. HD1332.C47 1990, **(v6)**
Christoff, Peter K. DK38.C45, **(v5)**
Christoffer, V.F. TK151.C468 1998, **(v1)**
Christofferson, Thomas Rodney. JN3007.S6.C47 1991, **(v7)**
Christopher, A. J. G2566.E625.C5 1994, **(v6)**
Christopher, John. PZ7.C457Wh 2003, **(v3)**
Christopher, Martin. HF5415.C52717 1991, **(v6)**
Christopher, Milbourne. GV1543.C45 1996, **(v6)**
Christopher, Nicholas. PN1995.9.F54.C54 1997, **(v3)**
Christopher, Renny. PS228.V5.C47 1995, **(v3)**
Christopher, Warren. JZ1480.C48 1998, **(v7)**
Christophory, Jul. Z2461.H87 1997, **(v10)**
Christy, Arthur. DS518.8.C48, **(v5)**
Christy, Thomas. F593.C525, **(v4)**
Chrysler, Walter Percy. CT275.C578.A3, **(v5)**
Chryssides, George D. BP601.C47 2001, **(v8)**
  BX9750.S44.C47 1990, **(v8)**
Chu, Fang. JQ1506.C58.C58 1998, **(v7)**
Chu, Hsi. B125.C513, **(v8)**
  B128.C52.E5 1990, **(v8)**
  B128.C53 H7513 1991, **(v8)**
  GN635.C5.C4813 1991, **(v6)**
Chu, Ko-ping. HB3654.A3.C49813 1994, **(v6)**
Chu, Patricia P. PS153.A84.C485 2000, **(v3)**
Chu, Tung-tsu. DS748.H28 vol. 1, **(v5)**
Chuang-tzu. BL1900.C46.E5 1998, **(v8)**
Chubb, John E. LA217.C48 1990, **(v7)**
Chudacoff, Howard P. HQ800.3.C58 1999, **(v6)**
Chuev, Feliks Ivanovich. DK266.C47513 1993, **(v5)**
Chui, C. K. QA403.3.C48 1992, **(v1)**
Chun, Ki-Taek. BF698.5.C45, **(v2)**
Chung, Yip-wah. QC173.4.S94, **(v1)**
Church, Alonzo. BC135.C42, **(v8)**
Church, Clive H. D843.C5285 1995, **(v5)**
Church, Horace K. TA730.C48, **(v1)**
Church, Joseph. PS2132.C643.C48 1994, **(v3)**
Church, Peggy Pond. PS3501.U8.Z57 1990, **(v3)**
Church, Richard. PR6005.H8 C7, **(v3)**
  PR6005.H8 P6, **(v3)**
  PR6005.H8 P7, **(v3)**
  PR6005.H8.Z52 1957, **(v3)**
Church, Roy A. HC255.C53 1975, **(v6)**
  HD5365.M615.C48 1998, **(v6)**
Church, Thomas Dolliver. SB473.C52, **(v1)**
Church, Thomas W. HC110.P55.C48 1993, **(v6)**
Church, William Farr. DC123.9.R5.C5, **(v5)**
Churchich, Nicholas. B808.2.C48 1990, **(v8)**

Churchill, Caryl. PR6053.H786.A19 1985, **(v3)**
Churchill, Reginald Charles. PR2937.C55 1959, **(v3)**
Churchill, Ward. E98.L3.C48 1993, **(v4)**
  HV8141.C46 1988, **(v6)**
Churchill, Ward. HV8144.F43.C48 1990, **(v6)**
Churchill, Winston Leonard Spencer. D843.C53, **(v5)**
Churchill, Winston S. DA462.M3.C45 1947, **(v5)**
  PN5123.C42.C48 1996, **(v3)**
  D521.C513, **(v5)**
  D550.C4, **(v5)**
  D727.C54 1971, **(v5)**
  D743.C47, **(v5)**
  DA16.C47, **(v5)**
  DA565.C6.C6 1952, **(v5)**
  DA566.7.C53 1938a, **(v5)**
  DA566.9.C5.A375 1961, **(v5)**
  DA566.9.C5.A4 1997, **(v5)**
  DA588.C57 1951, **(v5)**
  PS1297.C75, **(v3)**
  PS1297.F3 1915, **(v3)**
  PS1297.M5 1968, **(v3)**
  PS1297.R5, **(v3)**
Churchland, Patricia Smith. QP356.C48 1992, **(v1)**
Churchland, Paul M. BD418.3.C473 1998, **(v8)**
  QP376.C496 1995, **(v1)**
Chused, Richard H. KF535.C48 1994, **(v7)**
Chute, Marchette Gaylord. PR1905.C45, **(v3)**
  PR2631.C53, **(v3)**
  PR2768.C46, **(v3)**
  PR2907.C5, **(v3)**
Chuvin, Pierre. BR128.R7.C58 1990, **(v8)**
Chyёzihevs§kyæi, Dmytro. BR932.C4513, **(v8)**
Chynoweth, Bradford Grethen. U53.C48.A33, **(v10)**
Chyzhevskyi, Dmytro. PG501.C513, **(v3)**
Ciano, Galeazzo. DG575.C52.A32, **(v5)**
Ciardi, John. PN1064.C5, **(v3)**
  PS3505.I27.A6 1984, **(v3)**
  PS3505.I27.A75, **(v3)**
  PS3505.I27.I2, **(v3)**
  PS3505.I27.I48, **(v3)**
  PS3505.I27.I5, **(v3)**
  PS3505.I27.L47, **(v3)**
  PS3505.I27.T5, **(v3)**
  PS3505.I27.Z48 1991, **(v3)**
Cibber, Colley. PR3347.A6 1973, **(v3)**
  PR3347.A8, **(v3)**
Cicero, Marcus Tullius. JC81.C613 1998, **(v7)**
  PA6297.A5 1965, **(v3)**
Cichoke, Anthony J. RM666.H33C585 2001, **(v2)**
Cichorius, Conrad. DG59.D3.C63 1988, **(v5)**
Cicourel, Aaron Victor. HV9069.C514, **(v6)**
Ciechanowski, Jan M. D765.2.W3.C48, **(v5)**
Cifelli, Edward M. PS3505.I27.Z63 1997, **(v3)**
Cigliano, Jan. F499.C675.E844 1991, **(v4)**
Cigno, Alessandro. HB851.C49 1991, **(v6)**
Cikovsky, Nicolai. N6537.H58.A4 1995, **(v9)**
  ND237.I5.C54 1993, **(v9)**
Cima, Gay Gibson. PN1590.W64.C56 1993, **(v3)**
Cimbala, Stephen J. U42.C55 1997, **(v10)**
  U162.6.C57 1994, **(v10)**
  U163.C53 1998, **(v10)**
  U263.C483 1991, **(v10)**
  U263.C484 1990, **(v10)**
  U263.C485 1989, **(v10)**
  U263.C49 1988, **(v10)**
  U263.C5 1987, **(v10)**
  U263.C522 1989, **(v10)**
  UA11.C56 1998, **(v10)**
  UA23.C5427 1995, **(v10)**
  UA23.C5437 1995, **(v10)**
  UA23.C544 1993, **(v10)**
  UA646.C54 1991, **(v10)**
  UA646.3.C495 1989, **(v10)**
  UA770.C56 1990, **(v10)**
Ciment, James. E185.C55 2001, **(v4)**
  E806.C543 2001, **(v4)**
Cinel, Dino. F869.S39.I82 1982, **(v4)**
Cini, Michelle. JN33.5.C56 1996, **(v7)**
Cioc, Mark. UA710.C54 1988, **(v10)**
Ciochon, Russell L. GN282.6.C56 1990, **(v6)**
Ciofalo, John J. ND813.G7.C56 2001, **(v9)**

Cioran, E. M. B105.S79 C5613 1995, (v8)
Cioran, E. M. BD450.C5413 1998, (v8)
Cipolla, Carlo M. HC39.C53, (v6)
  HC240.C49513 1993, (v6)
  HG243.C5 1967, (v6)
Cipra, Barry. QA303.C578 1989, (v1)
Cirasa, Robert J. PS3545.I544.Z5827 1995, (v3)
Cirillo, Renato. HB109.P3.C57 1979, (v6)
Cisneros, Sandra. PS3553.I78H6 1991, (v4)
Citino, Robert Michael. UA710.C55 1987, (v10)
  UG446.5.C54 1994, (v10)
Citron, Marcia J. ML3890.C58 1993, (v9)
Citron, Stephen. MT67.C54 1991, (v9)
Ciufolini, Ignazio. QC173.59.G44.C58 1995, (v1)
Ciuk, Andrzej. PR610.C58 1992, (v3)
Civello, Catherine A. PR6037.M43.Z59 1997, (v3)
Clack, Brian R. B3376.W564.C57 1999, (v8)
Cladis, Mark Sydney. HM22.F8.D774 1992, (v6)
Claes, Dag Harald. HD9560.6.C53 2001, (v6)
Claeys, Gregory. JC178.V2.C58 1989, (v7)
Clagett, Marshall. Q11.P612 vol. 184, etc., (v1)
Clagett, Thomas D. PN1998.3.F75.C4 1990, (v3)
Claghorn, Charles Eugene. E276.C5 1991, (v4)
Clancey, Richard W. PR5892.L5.C53 1999, (v3)
Clancey, William J. BF311.C5395 1999, (v2)
Clanchy, M. T. BX4705.A2.C57 1997, (v8)
Clancy, Flora S. F1435.3.S34.C53 1999, (v4)
Clancy, Herbert John. E685.C5, (v4)
Clancy, Kevin J. HF5415.125.C58 1994, (v6)
Clancy, Thomas H. Z7837.7.G7.E44 1996b, (v10)
Clancy, William D. ML419.H45 C53 1995, (v9)
Clandinin, D. Jean. LB1775.C598 1995, (v7)
Clanton, O. Gene. E661.C56 1991, (v4)
Clapesattle, Helen. R154.M33.C3 1954, (v2)
Clapham, Alfred William. NA390.C6, (v9)
Clapham, Andrew. KJC5132.C58 1993, (v7)
Clapham, Christopher S. JQ3752.C55 1988, (v7)
  JX1582.C55 1996, (v7)
Clapp, Elizabeth J. KF9794.C58 1998, (v7)
Clapp, Jane. NB36.C55, (v9)
Clapp, Jane. PN171.P75.C5, (v3)
Clapp, Margaret Antoinette. LB2321.C395 1968, (v7)
Clappe, Louise Amelia Knapp Smith. F865.C58 1949, (v4)
Clarac, Pierre. PQ1812.C55, (v3)
Clardy, Andrea. Z286.F45.C55 1986, (v10)
Clare, John. PR4453.C6.A16 1970, (v3)
  PR4453.C6.A6 1950, (v3)
  PR4453.C6.A6 1984, (v3)
  PR4453.C6.A6 1996, (v3)
  PR4453.C6.Z465 1996, (v3)
  PR4453.C6.Z52 1951, (v3)
  PR4453.C6.Z52 1970, (v3)
Clarendon, Edward Hyde. DA400.C6125, (v5)
Clarfield, Gerard H. E302.6.P5.C553, (v4)
Clarfield, Gerard H. UA23.C558 1984, (v10)
Clari, Robert de. D164.A3.C55 1996, (v5)
Clark, A. Kim. HE2960.C65.C54 1998, (v6)
Clark, Ailsa McGown. QL384.A8.C54 1991, (v1)
Clark, Andrew Francis. DT532.25.C55 1999, (v5)
Clark, Andrew Hill. F1047.C57, (v4)
Clark, Andrew. QE357.C53 1993, (v1)
Clark, Andy. BD418.3.C53 1997, (v8)
  GV351.G52 2000, (v6)
Clark, Ann Nolan. PZ7.C5296Se6, (v3)
  PZ7.C5296Li, (v3)
Clark, Badger. PS3505.L245S5 1935, (v3)
Clark, Barrett Harper. PN1661.C55, (v3)
Clark, Barry Stewart. HB90.C52 1998, (v6)
Clark, Beverly Lyon. PR830.E38.C53 1996, (v3)
Clark, Bruce A. KE7742.C55 1990, (v7)
Clark, Burton R. LB2322.C57 1983, (v7)
Clark, C. E. Frazer. Z8393.C56, (v10)
Clark, Cal. HC430.5.C67 1989, (v6)
Clark, Candace. BJ1475.C53 1997, (v8)
Clark, Carol. ND1839.M84.A4 1980, (v9)
Clark, Charles Badger. PS3505.L245 1936, (v3)
Clark, Charles E. F7.C6 1983, (v4)
  PN4855.C53 1994, (v3)
Clark, Charles Michael Andres. HB71.C558 1992, (v6)
Clark, Christopher M. DD229.C53 2000, (v5)

Clark, Christopher. HX656.N75.C53 1995, (v6)
Clark, Colin Whitcomb. QL751.65.M3, (v1)
Clark, Cumberland. PR3047.C6, (v3)
Clark, David. LC1036.8.G7.C53 1996, (v7)
Clark, Dennis. F158.9.I6.C545 1991, (v4)
Clark, E. Culpepper. LD73.C57 1993, (v7)
Clark, Edward. Z1361.N39.C53 1996, (v10)
Clark, G. N. D228.C52, (v5)
  DA30.C6, (v5)
Clark, Garth. NK4007.C56 1987, (v9)
  NK4210.O42.C5 1989, (v9)
Clark, George B. D570.348.C43 1999, (v5)
Clark, George L. QC481.C475, (v1)
Clark, George Rogers. E234.C55, (v4)
Clark, Gillian. HQ1127.C53 1993, (v6)
Clark, Gordon Haddon. B74.C56, (v8)
Clark, Grahame. CB301.C57, (v5)
  GN722.G7.C57 1989, (v6)
Clark, Gregory R. PE3727.S7.C57 1990, (v3)
Clark, Harry Hayden. Z1227.C58, (v10)
Clark, Ian D. GB1001.72.R34.C57 1997, (v6)
Clark, Ian. U21.2.C52 1988, (v10)
Clark, Ira. PR2707.C58 1993, (v3)
Clark, James C. E687.9.C58 1993, (v4)
Clark, James H. QD505.C57 1994, (v1)
Clark, Jerome. TL789.C555 1998, (v1)
Clark, John Bates. HB171.C59 1967, (v6)
Clark, John Owen Edward. HG151.C54 1999, (v6)
Clark, John R. HT391.C494 1996, (v6)
Clark, John R. PN56.G7.C57 1991, (v3)
Clark, Kenneth Bancroft. F128.9.N3.C65, (v4)
Clark, Kenneth. CB68.C55 1970, (v5)
  N7570.C55, (v9)
  NA610.C5 1970, (v9)
Clark, Leonard H. LB1607.C49 1976, (v7)
Clark, Mark W. D766.82.C5, (v5)
Clark, Martin P. TK5102.5.C53 1991, (v1)
Clark, Martin. DG555.C55 1996, (v5)
Clark, Mary E. CB428.C58 1989, (v5)
Clark, Mary Jo Dummer. RT98.N88 2003, (v2)
Clark, Norman H. F891.C57, (v4)
  F899.E9 C55, (v4)
Clark, Paul. PN1993.5.C4.C58 1987, (v3)
Clark, Peter. BL1571.C53 1998, (v8)
Clark, Peter. DA670.K3.C494 1977, (v5)
Clark, Ralph W. HF5387.C55 1993b, (v6)
Clark, Reginald. LC2801.C56 1983, (v7)
Clark, Robert Judson. NK1141.C55 1972, (v9)
Clark, Robert N. TJ216.C55 1996, (v1)
Clark, Robert P. DP302.B53.C55, (v5)
Clark, Robert Thomas. PT2353.C6, (v3)
Clark, Robin E. HV6626.5.C57 2001, (v6)
Clark, Roger N. QB64.C58 1988, (v1)
Clark, Ronald William. B1649.R94.C55 1976, (v8)
  QH31.D2.C57 1984, (v1)
  QP511.8.C44.C57 1985, (v1)
Clark, Stephen R. L. BJ1012.C58 1984, (v8)
Clark, Stuart. QB54.C566 2000, (v1)
  QB981.C596 1997, (v1)
Clark, Susan L. PT1535.C57 1989, (v3)
Clark, Suzanne M. Z1251.E1.C58 1998, (v10)
Clark, Suzanne. PN56.M54.C55 1991, (v3)
Clark, T. J. N6490.C584 1999, (v9)
Clark, Thomas Dionysius. E161.C57 1964, (v4)
  E179.5.C48 1969, (v4)
  F213.C26 1989, (v4)
  F451.C63 1960, (v4)
  F451.C645, (v4)
  F455.C55, (v4)
  F457.B7 C57, (v4)
  F457.K3 C6 1992, (v4)
Clark, Tim W. QL737.C25.A94 1997, (v1)
Clark, Timothy. PN98.D43.C5 1992, (v3)
Clark, Victoria. BX310.C58 2000, (v8)
Clark, W. A. V. HD7293.C583 1996, (v6)
Clark, W. Mansfield. QD281.O9.C55, (v1)
Clark, Walter Aaron. ML134.A45 C53 1998, (v9)
Clark, Walter Van Tilburg. PS3505.L376 C5, (v3)
  PS3505.L376 T7, (v3)
Clark, Wesley K. DR1313.8.C58 2001, (v5)
Clark, William F. HV1461.C53 1988, (v6)

Clark, William R. QR181.7.C624 1995, (v1)
  RB155.8.C53 1997, (v2)
Clarke, Aidan. DA941.5.C5 1966a, (v5)
Clarke, Arthur Charles. PR6005.L36 C5, (v3)
  T20.C54, (v1)
Clarke, Austin. PR6005.L312.F5, (v3)
  PR6005.L37.A17 1974, (v3)
  PR6005.L37.A19 1963, (v3)
Clarke, Brian P. F1059.7.I6.C58 1993, (v4)
Clarke, Bruce. PN56.M53.C58 1995, (v3)
Clarke, Bruce. PN5123.M345.C57 1996, (v3)
Clarke, David H. GV14.5.C55, (v6)
Clarke, David L. CC75.C535 1978, (v5)
Clarke, Deborah. PS3511.A86.Z7547 1994, (v3)
Clarke, Duncan L. UA12.C53 1997, (v10)
  UA23.C559 1989, (v10)
Clarke, Edwin. QP361.C57, (v1)
Clarke, G. M. QA279.C56 1997, (v1)
Clarke, George Robin. S591.C6 1971, (v1)
Clarke, Gerald. ML420.G253.C58 2000, (v9)
Clarke, Graham. TR15.C566 1997, (v1)
Clarke, Harold D. F1034.2.C555 2000, (v4)
Clarke, I. F. CB161.C52 1979, (v5)
Clarke, J. J. BL1920.C55 2000, (v8)
Clarke, James Freeman. PS1299.C5.A43, (v3)
Clarke, James W. HN90.V5.C56 1998, (v6)
Clarke, Jeffrey J. DS558.C58 1988, (v5)
Clarke, John Henrik. E185.97.L75.C55, (v4)
Clarke, John R. NA324.C57 1991, (v9)
Clarke, John. DA530.C5 1989, (v5)
Clarke, Kathleen. DA965.C48.A3 1991, (v5)
Clarke, Keith C. GA102.4.E4.C377 1990, (v6)
Clarke, Linda. HD9715.G73.L63 1991, (v6)
Clarke, Lindsay. PR6053.L3295.C47 1989, (v3)
Clarke, M. L. B505.C58 1968, (v8)
Clarke, Micael M. PR5642.W6.C58 1995, (v3)
Clarke, Norma. PR115.C54 1990, (v3)
Clarke, Norman F. Z7164.L53, (v10)
Clarke, P. F. DA566.C545 1997, (v5)
Clarke, Paula C. DG737.8.C57 1991, (v5)
Clarke, Peter A. DA154.8.C57 1994, (v5)
Clarke, Peter B. BL48.C5535 1993, (v8)
Clarke, Prescott. DS758.7.C63, (v5)
Clarke, Simon. HB3714.C57 1994, (v6)
Clarke, Susan E. HN49.C6.C573 1998, (v6)
Clarkin, Thomas. E93.C65 2001, (v4)
Clary, David A. UB243.C56 1987, (v10)
  UG410.C53 1990, (v10)
Clasen, Claus Peter. BX4931.2.C57, (v8)
Classen, Constance. F3429.3.R3.C53 1993, (v4)
Clastres, Helene. F2230.2.T84.C5213 1995, (v4)
Clastres, Pierre. F2679.2.G9.C5513 1998, (v4)
  GN492.C5613 1987, (v6)
Claudel, Paul. PQ2605.L2.A8 1972, (v3)
  PQ2605.L2.C5 1966, (v3)
  PQ2605.L2.P353, (v3)
  PQ2605.L2.S6 1929, (v3)
  PQ2605.L2.S62 1945, (v3)
  PQ2605.L2.T54, (v3)
  PQ2605.L2.Z52, (v3)
  PQ2605.L2.Z5312, (v3)
Clausewitz, Carl von. U102.C65 1984, (v10)
Clawson, Calvin C. QA241.C664 1996, (v1)
Clawson, Dan. JK467.C52 1998, (v7)
  JK467.C53 1992, (v7)
Clawson, James G. HD57.7.C546 2003, (v6)
Clawson, Marion. HD181.G8.C57, (v6)
  HD216.C529 1983, (v6)
  HD216.C53, (v6)
Clawson, Patrick. HV5840.A5.C58 1996, (v6)
Clay, Cassius Marcellus. E415.9.C55.A3 1969, (v4)
Clay, Diskin. B395.C57 2000, (v8)
Clay, Henry. E337.8.C55 1959, (v4)
Clay, Jason W. HC845.Z9.F33 1985, (v6)
Clay, Lucius D. DD257.C55, (v5)
Clay, Marie M. LB1139.5.L35.C53 1998, (v7)
Clay, William L. E185.96.C58 1992, (v4)
Claydon, Tony. DA452.C63 1996, (v5)
Clayton, James L. HG3701.C575 2000, (v6)
Clayton, John. F539.C55, (v4)
Clayton, Martin. ML338.C593 2000, (v9)

NC248.P64.A4 1995, **(v9)**
Clayton, Philip. BT102.S68 2000, **(v8)**
Clayton, Richard R. HV5831.K4.C53 1995, **(v6)**
Clayton, Ronnie W. E445.L8.C57 1990, **(v4)**
Cleary, Beverly. PZ7.C5792De 1983, **(v3)**
Cleary, Beverly. PZ7.C5792Ram, **(v3)**
Cleary, Edward L. JC599.L3.C58 1997, **(v7)**
Cleary, Florence Damon. LB1050.C55 1972, **(v7)**
Cleary, M. C. HD1945.C58 1989, **(v6)**
Cleary, Patricia. F73.44.C6 2000, **(v4)**
Cleary, Richard Louis . NA9070.C49 1998, **(v9)**
Cleary, Thomas F. BL1910.C63 1993, **(v8)**
Cleary, Thomas. BL325.F4.C54 2000, **(v8)**
Cleator, P. E. CN120.C55 1961, **(v5)**
Cleaver, Eldridge. E185.97.C6, **(v4)**
Cleaves, Freeman. E392.C64 1990, **(v4)**
Clebsch, Betsy. SB413.S22.C58 1997, **(v1)**
Clegg, Cyndia Susan. PN4748.G7.C48 1997, **(v3)**
Clegg, Stewart. HM131.C7393 1990, **(v6)**
Clein, Wendy. PR2065.G31.C47 1987, **(v3)**
Clej, Alina. PR4537.C57 1995, **(v3)**
Cleland, Charles E. E78.M6.C57 1992, **(v4)**
Cleland, John. PR3348.C65.M45 1963, **(v3)**
Cleland, Robert Glass. F592.C62 1950, **(v4)**
   F867.C6 1951, **(v4)**
Cleman, John. PS1246.C54 1996, **(v3)**
Clemen, Wolfgang. PR1924.C518 1968, **(v3)**
   PR2997.S7.C4813 1987, **(v3)**
   PR3072.C554 1951, **(v3)**
Clemens, Clara. PS1331.C4, **(v3)**
Clemens, Elisabeth Stephanie. JK1118.C49 1997,
   (v7)
Clemens, Martin. D767.98.C53 1998, **(v5)**
Clemens, Samuel Langhorne. PS1302.A48 1975, **(v3)**
   PS1302.N38, **(v3)**
   PS1302.W28 1971, **(v3)**
   PS1303.D8, **(v3)**
   PS1303.N37 1957, **(v3)**
   PS1305.A1 1931b, **(v3)**
   PS1322.R4, **(v3)**
   PS1322.S5 1963, **(v3)**
   PS1322.W5 1917, **(v3)**
   PS1323.L4 1946, **(v3)**
   PS1331.A3.D3 1975, **(v3)**
   PS1331.A3.H6, **(v3)**
   PS1331.A3.R57, **(v3)**
   PS1331.A3.R6, **(v3)**
   PS1331.A3 1958, **(v3)**
   PS1331.A44 1976, **(v3)**
   PS1331.A2 1959, **(v3)**
Clemens, Valdine. PR830.T3.C59 1999, **(v3)**
Clemens, Walter C. DS740.5.R8.C6, **(v5)**
   E744.C55 2000, **(v4)**
Clement, Catherine. ML2100.C613 1988, **(v9)**
Clement, Grace. BJ1475.C57 1996, **(v8)**
Clement, Peter. QL696.P246.C58 1993, **(v1)**
Clement, Priscilla Ferguson. HQ792.U5.C565 1997,
   (v6)
Clement, Russell T. Z8115.66.C57 1994, **(v10)**
   Z8328.3.C54 1991, **(v10)**
Clement, Wallace. HN17.5.C575 1994, **(v6)**
   HN110.E4.C53, **(v6)**
Clements, Barbara Evans. HQ1662.K6.C55, **(v6)**
   HX313.7.C64 1997, **(v6)**
Clements, Frank. DS36.55.C57 2001, **(v5)**
   Z6724.I7.C54 1996, **(v10)**
   Z7165.A67.C58 1992, **(v10)**
Clements, Kendrick A. E766.C44 1992, **(v4)**
   HC110.C6.C53 2000, **(v6)**
Clements, Robert John. N6923.B9.C55 1961a, **(v9)**
Clements, William M. PM218.C54 1996, **(v3)**
   Z1209.C57 1984, **(v10)**
Clemmer, Mary. F198.A512, **(v4)**
Clemmer, Richard O. E99.H7.C54 1995, **(v4)**
Clemoes, Peter. PR201.C57 1995, **(v3)**
Clendenen, Clarence Clemens. F1234.C64 1961, **(v4)**
Clendening, Logan. R131.C613 1960, **(v2)**
Clendenning, John. B945.R64 C54 1999, **(v8)**
Clendinnen, Inga. F1219.76.S64.C44 1991, **(v4)**
Clerk, Nathalie. NA743.C55 1984, **(v9)**
Clery, E. J. PR858.S85.C58 1995, **(v3)**

Cleveland Museum of Art. N7262.C59 1998, **(v9)**
Cleveland, David Arthur. SB323.C63 1991, **(v1)**
Cleveland, Les. ML3545.C54 1994, **(v9)**
Cleveland, William L. DS62.4.C53 1994, **(v5)**
Clevenot, Dominique. NA380.C5713 2000, **(v9)**
Clewell, Beatriz C. QA13.C538 1992, **(v1)**
Clewis, Beth. QH46.5.C54 1991, **(v1)**
Cliff, A. D. G1046.E51.C5 1988, **(v6)**
Clifford, Clark M. E840.8.C55.A3 1991, **(v4)**
Clifford, James Lowry. PR442.C6, **(v3)**
   PR3533.C6, **(v3)**
Clifford, Mark. HC467.C6486 1998, **(v6)**
Clifford, N. J. DS709.C634 2001, **(v5)**
Clifford, Nicholas Rowland. DS796.S29.C57 1991,
   (v5)
Clifford, Stephen P. PR6023.A93.Z62145 1998, **(v3)**
Clift, Dominique. F1053.C57 1982, **(v4)**
Clift, Dominique. F1055.B7.C5713, **(v4)**
Clift, R. QA922.C56, **(v1)**
Clifton, Larry Stephen. PR4699.F9.Z55 1993, **(v3)**
Clifton, Lucille. PS3553.L45.G4, **(v3)**
Clifton, Thomas. ML3877.C6 1983, **(v9)**
Climo, Jacob. HQ755.86.C55 1992, **(v6)**
Clinard, Marshall Barron. HV6769.C558 1990, **(v6)**
   HV6769.C56 1980, **(v6)**
Cline, Platt. F819.F57 C53 1994, **(v4)**
Cline, Sally. PR6015.A33.Z62 1998, **(v3)**
Cline, William R. HC79.A4.C55 1992, **(v6)**
   HG1496.C56, **(v6)**
Clingham, Greg. PR3533.B7.C57 1992, **(v3)**
Clinton, Bill. E884.C55 1992, **(v4)**
Clinton, Catherine. E628.C58 1995, **(v4)**
   HQ1410.C44 1984, **(v6)**
   HQ1418.C58 2000, **(v6)**
   HQ1438.A13.C58 1982, **(v6)**
   PN2598.K4.C58 2000, **(v3)**
Clinton, Robert Lowry. KF4575.C554 1989, **(v7)**
Clodfelter, Micheal. D214.C55 1991, **(v5)**
   E83.86.C56 1998, **(v4)**
Cloete, Stuart. PR6005.L8 G3, **(v3)**
   PR6005.L8 M3, **(v3)**
   PR6005.L8 R3, **(v3)**
Clogg, Richard. DF757.C56, **(v5)**
   DF802.C57 2002, **(v5)**
   DF852.C56, **(v5)**
Cloisters (Museum). NK3049.U5.N43 1976, **(v9)**
Cloke, Paul J. HN398.W45.R87 1997, **(v6)**
Cloonan, William J. PQ2680.O83.Z65 1985, **(v3)**
Clopper, Lawrence M. PR641.C58 2001, **(v3)**
   PR2017.F73.C57 1997, **(v3)**
Close, A. J. PQ6351.C66 2000, **(v3)**
Close, David. DF849.52.C56 1995, **(v5)**
   F1528.C57 1999, **(v4)**
   F1528.C58 1988, **(v4)**
Close, F. E. QC174.17.S9.C56 2000, **(v1)**
   QC791.775.C64.C56 1991, **(v1)**
   QC793.2.C56 1987, **(v1)**
Clotfelter, Charles T. HG6126.C55 1989, **(v6)**
Clottes, Jean. GN803.C5813 1998, **(v6)**
Clouard, Henri. PQ116.C6, **(v3)**
Cloud, Gary L. TA417.2.C56 1995, **(v1)**
Cloudsley-Thompson, J. L. QL116.C58 1991, **(v1)**
   QL434.35.C55 1988, **(v1)**
   QP84.C53, **(v1)**
Clough, Arthur Hugh. PR4455.A2 1869, **(v3)**
   PR4456.M8 1974, **(v3)**
   PR4456.N6, **(v3)**
   PR4456.T7, **(v3)**
   PR4458.A4 1957, **(v3)**
Clough, Marshall S. DT433.577.C58 1998, **(v5)**
Cloulas, Ivan. N6845.C5913 1998, **(v9)**
Clover, Carol J. PN1995.9.H6.C53 1992, **(v3)**
Clowse, Barbara Barksdale. PN4874.M37.C58 1998,
   (v3)
Clubb, O. Edmund. DS740.5.R8.C63, **(v5)**
Clubb, Oliver E. DS518.8.C57, **(v5)**
Clube, Victor. CB156.C56 1990, **(v5)**
Clucas, Richard A. E839.5.C57 1996, **(v4)**
Clum, John M. ML1700.C58 1999, **(v9)**
Clunas, Craig. N7340.C59 1997, **(v9)**
Clune, Henry W. F127.G2.C5, **(v4)**

Clurman, Harold. PN1861.C57, **(v3)**
Clute, John. PN3433.4.C57 1995, **(v3)**
Clutterbuck, Richard L. HV6431.C554 1990, **(v6)**
   HV9960.E86.C58 1990, **(v6)**
Clutton-Brock, Juliet. SF41.C58 1999, **(v1)**
   SF283.C63 1992, **(v1)**
Clutton-Brock, T. H. QL762.C48 1991, **(v1)**
Clyde, Paul Hibbert. DS511.C67 1971, **(v5)**
   JX1428.C6.C5, **(v7)**
Clymer, Joseph Floyd. TL23.C593, **(v1)**
Clytus, John. F1789.N3.C58, **(v4)**
Cmiel, Kenneth. HV995.C42.C553 1995, **(v6)**
   PE2809.C57 1990, **(v3)**
Coad, Emma Dent. N7108.C55 1990, **(v9)**
Coad, J. G. VA460.A1.C6 1983, **(v10)**
Coady, C. A. J. BD181.C59 1992, **(v8)**
Coakley, Davis. PR5823.C63 1994, **(v3)**
Coakley, Jay J. GV706.5.C63 2001, **(v6)**
Coakley, Robert W. UA25.C6 1989, **(v10)**
Coale, Samuel. PS1892.M47.C63 1998, **(v3)**
Coates, A. J. U22.C5397 1997, **(v10)**
Coates, David. HB501.C63 2000, **(v6)**
Coates, John. PR6003.O6757.Z613 1998, **(v3)**
Coates, Kenneth. D768.15.C62 1992, **(v5)**
   E78.Y8.C63 1991, **(v4)**
Coates, Paul. PN1993.5.G3.C64 1991, **(v3)**
Coates, Peter A. TD195.P4.C63 1991, **(v1)**
Coates, Peter. B753.I24 C58 2002, **(v8)**
Coates, Robert M. F396.C65 1986, **(v4)**
Coats, Alice M. SB404.5.C63 1970, **(v1)**
Coats, Wendell John. JC257.O244.C62 2000, **(v7)**
Coatsworth, John H. F1436.8.U6.C63 1994, **(v4)**
Cobas, Jose A. F1983.C83.C6313 1997, **(v4)**
Cobb, Buell E. ML3111.C6, **(v9)**
Cobb, Carl W. PQ6085.C56, **(v3)**
   PQ6613.A763.P7633 1983, **(v3)**
Cobb, Cathy. QD11.C59 1995, **(v1)**
Cobb, Clifford W. LB2825.C53 1992, **(v7)**
Cobb, David A. GA193.U5.C62 1986, **(v6)**
Cobb, George W. QA279.C625 1998, **(v1)**
Cobb, Irvin S. PS3505.O14 O5, **(v3)**
Cobb, James C. F347.D38.C63 1992, **(v4)**
   HC107.A13.C65 1982, **(v6)**
Cobb, Richard. DC184.C613 1987, **(v5)**
Cobban, Alan B. LA636.3.C6 1988, **(v7)**
Cobban, Alfred. B802.C6 1960a, **(v8)**
   CB411.C6 1969, **(v5)**
   DC143.C6, **(v5)**
   DC158.8.C6 1968, **(v5)**
Cobbett, Walter Willson. ML1100.C7 1963, **(v9)**
Cobbett, William. DA521.C65, **(v5)**
   PR4461.C324.A16 1923, **(v3)**
Coble, Parks M. DS777.47.C65 1991, **(v5)**
Cobley, Evelyn. PN56.W3.C63 1993, **(v3)**
Cobley, Paul. PS374.D4.C57 2000, **(v3)**
Coburn, Carol. F689.B54.C63 1992, **(v4)**
Coburn, Kathleen. PR6005.O235 G7, **(v3)**
Coburn, Robert C. BD111.C584 1990, **(v8)**
Coch, Nicholas K. GB5014.C63 1995, **(v6)**
Cochise, Ciye. E99.A6.C57, **(v4)**
Cochran, Augustus B. E839.5.C635 2001, **(v4)**
Cochran, David. PS374.P63.C63 2000, **(v3)**
Cochran, Mary E. E99.S22 J65 2000, **(v4)**
Cochran, Robert. PR6003.E282.Z594 1991, **(v3)**
Cochran, Terry. Z124.C66 2001, **(v10)**
Cochran, Thomas Childs. F149.C7, **(v4)**
   HC105.C64, **(v6)**
   HC106.C6315, **(v6)**
   HF3021.C55, **(v6)**
Cochran, William Gemmell. QA276.6.C6 1977, **(v1)**
Cochrane, Eric W. DG465.C62, **(v5)**
Cochrane, Susan. N7411.P3.C63 1997, **(v9)**
Cochrane, Willard Wesley. HD1765 1976.C6 1976,
   (v6)
Cockburn, Andrew. DS79.75.C63 1999, **(v5)**
   QH313.C74 1991, **(v1)**
Cockburn, David. BD638.C63 1997, **(v8)**
Cockcroft, James D. F1413.C66 1989, **(v4)**
   HC133.C6 1983, **(v6)**
Cockerham, William C. RA418.C655 1997, **(v2)**
Cockett, Richard. DA47.2.C59 1989, **(v5)**

Cockfield, Jamie H. D550.C62 1998, (v5)
Cockin, Katharine. PN2595.13.W65, (v3)
Cockrell, Dale. ML1711.C63 1997, (v9)
Cocks, Geoffrey. RC450.G3.C64 1998, (v2)
Cocks, Joan. JC311.C6135 2002, (v7)
Cockshut, A. O. J. PR830.L69.C6 1978, (v3)
  PR4588.C63 1962, (v3)
Cocteau, Jean. G440.G672 1958, (v6)
  PN1994.C53813 1992, (v3)
  PQ2605.O15.A19 1948, (v3)
  PQ2605.O15.A24, (v3)
  PQ2605.O15.A26, (v3)
  PQ2605.O15.J6, (v3)
  PQ2605.O15.O66 1957, (v3)
  PQ2605.O15.P3, (v3)
  PQ2605.O15.Z515, (v3)
Coddington, Dean C. RA427.C56 2001, (v2)
Code, Lorraine. HQ1190.C64 1991, (v6)
Codevilla, Angelo. JA75.7.C63 1997, (v7)
  UG743.C63 1988, (v10)
Codrescu, Andrei. DR269.6.C63 1991, (v5)
Cody, Louisa (Frederici). F594.C66, (v4)
  F594.C6703, (v4)
  F594.C6715 1954, (v4)
  F594.C674 1971, (v4)
  F594.C6745 1978, (v4)
Coe, Charles Norton. PR5893.T7.C6, (v3)
Coe, George W. F786.C65 1951, (v4)
Coe, Lewis. TK5115.C54 1993, (v1)
Coe, Michael D. F1219.C7569, (v4)
  F1219.1.V47.C63, (v4)
Coedes, George. DS511.C7713 1968, (v5)
Coers, Donald V. PS3537.T3234.M683 1991, (v3)
Coetzee, J. M. PR9358.2.W45.C64 1988, (v3)
Coffey, Amanda. LC197.C63 2000, (v7)
Coffey, Frank. TL23.C595 1996, (v1)
Coffey, Joseph I. UA23.C575 1989, (v10)
Coffey, Peter. BC71.C6 1938, (v8)
Coffey, Peter. HC241.25.U5.C56 1993, (v6)
Coffey, Timothy. QK110.C56 1993, (v1)
Coffin, Berton. MT821.C65 1987, (v9)
Coffin, David R. NA525.C35, (v9)
  NA7755.C6, (v9)
  SB457.6.C64 1994, (v1)
Coffin, Frank Morey. KF8750.C625 1994, (v7)
Coffin, Robert Peter Tristram. PS3505.O234.A17 1948, (v3)
  PS3505.O234.A7, (v3)
  PS3505.O234 J6, (v3)
Coffin, William Sloane. BX9225.C6243.A34 1977, (v8)
  HM665.C64 1999, (v6)
Coffman, Edward M. D570.C6, (v5)
Coffman, William Milo. RD701.C58, (v2)
Cofman, Judita. QA63.C64 1990, (v1)
Cogan, Charles. UA700.C593 1997, (v10)
Cogan, Robert. BC177.C64 1998, (v8)
Cogar, William B. V62.U64 1989, (v10)
Cogger, Harold G. QL663.A1.C63 1992, (v1)
Coggins, Bruce. HG181.C6515 1998, (v6)
Coggins, R. J. BS1140.2.C64 1990, (v8)
Coghlan, Brian. PT2617.O47.Z7354, (v3)
Cogley, Richard W. E78.M4.C64 1999, (v4)
Cohen, Adam S. ND3359.U82.C65 2000, (v9)
Cohen, Adam. F548.54.D34C64 2000, (v4)
Cohen, Akiba A. PN4749.S6 1990, (v3)
Cohen, Allan R. HD31.C586 1993, (v6)
Cohen, Allen. PN1998.3.H87.C65 1997, (v3)
Cohen, Ariel. DK38.C64 1996, (v5)
Cohen, Arthur Allen. BM535.C6 1971, (v8)
Cohen, Arthur M. LB2328.C55 2003, (v7)
Cohen, Asher. BM390.C62 2000, (v8)
Cohen, Avner. UA853.I8.C62 1998, (v10)
Cohen, Barbara J. QP36.M54 2000, (v1)
Cohen, Barry H. BF39.C56 2001, (v2)
Cohen, Benjamin J. HF1359.C64 1990, (v6)
Cohen, Bernard Cecil. D814.8.C54 1980, (v5)
  E813.C62, (v4)
Cohen, Daniel. HC276.2.C59813 1995, (v6)
  TX298.C58 1982, (v1)
Cohen, David B. BF341.C55 1999, (v2)
Cohen, David W. QA322.4.C64 1989, (v1)

Cohen, David. BF723.I5.C63 1990, (v2)
Cohen, Derek. PR2989.C6 1988, (v3)
  PR3024.C6 1993, (v3)
Cohen, Don. HD58.7.C6214 2001, (v6)
Cohen, Ed. PR5823.C64 1993, (v3)
Cohen, Edward E. HG237.C65 1992, (v6)
Cohen, Eliot A. U42.C56 1990, (v10)
  U413.C64 1995, (v10)
Cohen, G. A. D16.9.C56 1978b, (v5)
Cohen, Gene D. QP376.C59 1988, (v1)
Cohen, H. F. Q125.C538 1994, (v1)
Cohen, Hennig. F272.C64, (v4)
  PS2386.C64 1991, (v3)
Cohen, Herman J. DT353.5.U6, (v5)
Cohen, Howard. HV7924.C64 1991, (v6)
Cohen, Hubert I. PN1998.3.B47.C64 1993, (v3)
Cohen, I. Bernard. E302.5.C62 1995, (v4)
  Q125.C54, (v1)
  Q125.C542 1985, (v1)
  Q175.5.C62 1994, (v1)
  QA76.2.A35.C65 1999, (v1)
  QC7.C65, (v1)
  QC7.C66, (v1)
  QC16.F68.C64 1990, (v1)
  QC122.C6 1985, (v1)
Cohen, Isaac. HD9875.C63 1990, (v6)
Cohen, J. M. PN701.C57 1963, (v3)
  PR4231.C57, (v3)
Cohen, Jack. Q175.C613 1994, (v1)
Cohen, Jerry. F869.L8.C6, (v4)
Cohen, Joel E. HB1953.C64 1995, (v6)
Cohen, Jon. QR189.5.A33, (v1)
Cohen, Karl F. NC1766.5.C45.C64 1997, (v9)
Cohen, L. Jonathan. B840.C6 1963, (v8)
  BC91.C6 1989, (v8)
  BC91.C63, (v8)
Cohen, L. Jonathan. BD161.C633 1992, (v8)
Cohen, Lawrence. GN485.C64 1998, (v6)
Cohen, Lenard J. DR1309.C644 2001, (v5)
Cohen, Leonard. PR6053.O35.A17 1968, (v3)
Cohen, Lizabeth. HC110.C6 C537 2003, (v6)
Cohen, Marcel Samuel Raphael. PC2075.C58 1973, (v3)
Cohen, Margaret. PQ653.C54 1999, (v3)
Cohen, Mark Nathan. E185.615.C642 1998, (v4)
  GN799.F6.C64, (v6)
  RA418.C664 1989, (v2)
Cohen, Martin. QB806.C64 1988, (v1)
Cohen, Maxwell T. KFX2042.E58.C64 1993, (v7)
Cohen, Maynard M. D802.N7.C64 1997, (v5)
Cohen, Michael A. JQ3386.A91 C63, (v7)
Cohen, Michael D. LB2341.C56 1986, (v7)
Cohen, Michael Joseph. DS119.7.C633 1987, (v5)
  DS126.4.C645 1982, (v5)
Cohen, Michael. PR830.D4.C6 2000, (v3)
  PR868.S52.C64 1995, (v3)
Cohen, Mitchell. DS149.C627 1987, (v5)
Cohen, Monica F. PR878.D65.C64 1998, (v3)
Cohen, Morris L. KF240.C538 1989, (v7)
  KF240.C54 1985, (v7)
Cohen, Morris Raphael. B945.C53F3 1970, (v8)
  B945.C54.A3 1975, (v8)
  BC71.C63 1977, (v8)
  BC108.C67, (v8)
  K230.C63 R4, (v7)
Cohen, Morton Norton. PR4612.C588 1995, (v3)
Cohen, Myron L. GN635.T28.C63, (v6)
Cohen, Naomi Wiener. E184.J5.C619 1992, (v4)
Cohen, Norm. ML156.4.F5 C64 1994, (v9)
  ML3551.C57, (v9)
Cohen, Norman J. BM71.C64 2000, (v8)
Cohen, Norman M. BS2545.J44.C64 1988, (v8)
Cohen, Octavus Roy. PS3505.C66 A7, (v3)
Cohen, Patricia. RJ503.C635 1996, (v2)
Cohen, Paul A. CT3990.W36.C64 1974, (v5)
  DS762.C6, (v5)
Cohen, Paul S. Q105.U5.A64 1998, (v1)
Cohen, Paula Marantz. PN1998.3.H58.M27 1995, (v3)
  PN75.M24.A3 1996, (v3)
Cohen, Ralph. Z6514.C97.C65 1988, (v10)
Cohen, Richard. HF1379.C74 1989, (v6)

Cohen, Robert. F2431.J4.C64 1991, (v4)
  LA229.C62 1993, (v7)
  PT2685.E5.Z63 1993, (v3)
Cohen, Robin. JV6021.C64 1997, (v7)
Cohen, Roger. DR1313.3.C64 1998, (v5)
Cohen, Ronald D. LA285.G2.C65 1990, (v7)
Cohen, Sarah Blacher. PS3565.Z5.Z56 1994, (v3)
Cohen, Saul Bernard. DS119.65.C64 1987, (v5)
Cohen, Shaye J. D. BM176.C614 1999, (v8)
Cohen, Sheldon M. JX4511.C64 1989, (v7)
Cohen, Sherrill. HV1448.I8.C65 1992, (v6)
Cohen, Sidney. HV5035.C63 1983, (v6)
Cohen, Stan. F247.K2 C64 1987, (v4)
Cohen, Stephen D. HF3127.C64 1985, (v6)
Cohen, Stephen F. DK266.A33.C64 1985, (v5)
  DK268.B76.C63 1973, (v5)
  DK287.C64 1989, (v5)
  E183.8.R9 C56 2001, (v4)
Cohen, Stephen P. DS480.853.C634 2001, (v5)
  UA842.C6, (v10)
Cohen, Steven Martin. BM205.C62 2000, (v8)
Cohen, Thomas V. KKH38.C64 1993, (v7)
Cohen, Warren I. DS511.C786 2000, (v5)
  E768.C6, (v4)
Cohen, William A. PR878.S317.C64 1996, (v3)
Cohen, William S. E876.C63 1988, (v4)
Cohen, William. E185.6.C66 1991, (v4)
Cohen-Almagor, Raphael. K3253.C64 2001, (v7)
Cohen-Mor, Dalya. PJ7519.F37, (v3)
  PJ7519.F37C64 2001, (v3)
Cohen-Solal, Annie. B2430.S34.C5413 1987, (v8)
Cohen-Stratyner, Barbara Naomi. ML120.U5 C6 1988, (v9)
Cohen-Tannoudji, Claude. QC680.C6413 1989, (v1)
Cohler, Anne M. JC179.M753.C64 1988, (v7)
Cohler, Bertram J. RC451.4.G39.C64 2000, (v2)
Cohn, Bernard S. DS436.C65 1996, (v5)
Cohn, Deborah N. PS261.C54 1999, (v3)
Cohn, Emil. PN6071.J5 C6, (v3)
Cohn, Harvey. QA247.C63, (v1)
Cohn, Henry S. KF228.R495.C64 1991, (v7)
Cohn, Norman Rufus Colin. BL325.C7.C64 1993, (v8)
Cohn, Ruby. PR736.C54 1995, (v3)
Cohn, Ruby. PR6003.E282.Z62, (v3)
Cohn, Samuel Kline. HN475.C59 1992, (v6)
Cohn-Sherbok, Dan. B755.C54 1996, (v8)
  BM195.C64 1996, (v8)
  BM723.C64 1994, (v8)
  BR158.C645 2000, (v8)
  DS145.C574 1997, (v5)
Cohn-Sherbok, Lavinia. BR1700.2.C64 1998, (v8)
Cohodas, Nadine. E748.T58.C64 1993, (v4)
Cohodas, Nadine. ML405.C64 2000, (v9)
Coit, Margaret L. E340.C15.C63, (v4)
Coke, Van Deren. N72.P5.C6 1972, (v9)
  N6535.T3.C6, (v9)
Coker, Richard J. RC309.N7.C64 2000, (v2)
Colamery, S. N. KF4755.5.C65 1998, (v7)
Colander, David C. HB131.C65 1996, (v6)
Colas, Dominique. JC336.C8313 1997, (v7)
Colberg, Sheri R. RC660.C4746 2001, (v2)
Colbert, Evelyn S. DS518.1.C587, (v5)
Colbert, Judy. F179.3.C65 2001, (v4)
Colborn, Candy. Z1037.C675 1994, (v10)
Colborn, Theo. RA1224.2.C65 1997, (v2)
Colby, Anne. BJ1408.5.C65 1987, (v8)
Colby, Robert Alan. PR5638.C6, (v3)
Colcord, Charles Francis. F700.C6.A3, (v4)
Coldstream, J. N. DF220.C58 1977, (v5)
Cole, Allan Burnett. DS507.C63, (v5)
Cole, Arthur Charles. E415.7.C69 1971, (v4)
Cole, Bill. ML419.C645.C6, (v9)
Cole, Brock. PZ7.C67342Go 1987, (v3)
Cole, Bruce. N7477.C645 1999, (v9)
Cole, Charles Chester. F499.C757 C57 2001, (v4)
Cole, Charles Woolsey. HC275.C64, (v6)
Cole, Cyrenus. F621.C68, (v4)
Cole, David Chamberlin. HG187.I5.C65 1996, (v6)
  HN787.Z9.C625 1997, (v6)
Cole, David. HV9950.C58 1999, (v6)
  PN2061.C59 1992, (v3)

Cole, Donald B. E382.C69 1993, (v4)
　E387.C65 1984, (v4)
　F38.C6 1970, (v4)
Cole, Douglas. E78.N78.C632 1990, (v4)
　GN21.B56.C65 1999, (v6)
　PR2674.C59 1995, (v3)
Cole, Garold. Z1242.C79 2000, (v10)
Cole, Gregory K. PQ6055.C55 2000, (v3)
Cole, Hubert. DC373.L35.C6, (v5)
Cole, Hugh M. D769.A533 vol. 3, pt. 1, (v5)
Cole, J. P. HD82.C5714, (v6)
Cole, Joshua. HB3593.C614 2000, (v6)
Cole, Larry. HQ796.C635, (v6)
Cole, Leonard A. UG447.8.C65 1987, (v10)
　UG447.8.C6523 1997, (v10)
Cole, Luella. LA13.C7, (v7)
Cole, Mary Hill. DA356.C56 1999, (v5)
Cole, Michael. ML655.C63 1998, (v9)
Cole, Phyllis. F8.C67 1998, (v4)
Cole, Robert. D810.P7.G7238 1990, (v5)
Cole, Robert. DA3.T36.C65 1993, (v5)
　Z7204.S67.C65 1996, (v10)
Cole, Sally J. E78.C6.C6 1990, (v4)
Cole, Simon A. HV6074.C557 2001, (v6)
Cole, Stephen. Z8196.6.C65 1993, (v10)
Cole, Susan Letzler. PN2071.R45.C64 1992, (v3)
Cole, Sylvia. PN43.C58 2000, (v3)
Cole, Thomas R. F394.H89.N426 1997, (v4)
　HQ1064.U5.C526 1991, (v6)
Cole, Thomas. PA401.C65 1991, (v3)
Cole, Toby. PN1661.C56, (v3)
Cole, Wayne S. E748.N9 C6 1980, (v4)
Cole, Wayne S. E806.C594 1983, (v4)
Colebrook, Claire. PN81.C69 1997, (v3)
Colegate, Isabel. BJ1499.S65 C65 2002, (v8)
　PR6053.O414.S5 1981, (v3)
Coleman, Ann Raney Thomas. CT275.C684.A3, (v5)
Coleman, Arthur. Z7156.E6 C64, (v10)
Coleman, Clive. HV6025.C582 2000, (v6)
Coleman, D. C. DA378.B3.C6 1963, (v5)
　HC254.4.C64, (v6)
　HC255.C623 1992, (v6)
Coleman, Daniel A. GE195.C65 1994, (v6)
Coleman, Daniel. PR9188.2.M44.C65 1998, (v3)
Coleman, Deirdre. PR4480.F73.C65 1988, (v3)
Coleman, Dorothy Gabe. PQ1643.C57 1987, (v3)
Coleman, Earle Jerome. BL65.A4.C65 1998, (v8)
Coleman, J. Winston. F455.C64 1995, (v4)
Coleman, James William. PS3573.J26.Z6 1989, (v3)
Coleman, Janet. PR275.D53.C6 1981, (v3)
Coleman, Jeanine G. HV891.C63 1999, (v6)
Coleman, Joyce. Z1003.5.G7.C65 1996, (v10)
Coleman, Kathleen. PQ401.C65 1993, (v3)
Coleman, Kenneth. F290.C55, (v4)
Coleman, Mary DeLorse. JK4668.C65 1993, (v7)
Coleman, Michael C. E97.5.C64 1993, (v4)
Coleman, Ray. ML421.C28.C6 1994, (v9)
Coleman, Satis N. (Satis Narrona) CC205.C6 1971b,
　(v5)
Coleman, William D. F1053.2.C65 1984, (v4)
Coleman, William D. HG173.C665 1996, (v6)
Coleman, William S. E. E83.89.C66 2000, (v4)
Coleridge, Hartley. PR4467.A2.G7 1972, (v3)
Coleridge, Samuel Taylor. BS480.C6 1957, (v8)
　PR2976.C54 1969, (v3)
　PR4470.F69, (v3)
　PR4470.F69 vol. 5, (v3)
　PR4471.C4, (v3)
　PR4472.M67 1991, (v3)
　PR4472.R5 1950, (v3)
　PR4483.A39 1957, (v3)
　PR4483.A428, (v3)
Coles, Bryony. CC77.W48.C65 1989, (v5)
Coles, Gerald. LB1050.C574 1998, (v7)
Coles, Robert. BF723.M54.C63 1997, (v2)
　BL625.5.C64 1990, (v8)
　HQ759.64.C65 1997, (v6)
　HQ1412.C638 1980, (v6)
　HQ1412.C64 1978, (v6)
　HV91.C62 1993, (v6)
　PS3565.C57.Z63, (v3)

Colescott, Warrington. NE538.M33.C65 1999, (v9)
Coletta, Paolo Enrico. E664.B87.C55, (v4)
　E761.C64, (v4)
　VA58.C75, (v10)
　Z8857.88.C64 1989, (v10)
Colette, Sidonie Gabrielle. PQ2605.O28.V313 1955,
　(v3)
　PQ2605.O28 A27, (v3)
　PQ2605.O28.C48 1933p, (v3)
　PQ2605.O28.C5 1946, (v3)
　PQ2605.O28.M3 1922, (v3)
　PQ2605.O28.M32 1972, (v3)
　PQ2605.O28.S392 1960, (v3)
Colgrave, Bertram. BX4700.C8.C6, (v8)
Colie, Rosalie Littell. PR2819.C6, (v3)
Colignon, Richard A. HD9685.U7.T333 1997, (v6)
Colin, Amy D. PT2605.E4.Z594 1991, (v3)
Colish, Marcia L. CB351.C54 1997, (v5)
Colker, Ruth. KF3455.Z9.C65 1998, (v7)
　KF3771.C65 1992, (v7)
　KF4749.C64 1996, (v7)
Collatz, L. QA371.C68213 1986, (v1)
Collcutt, Martin. BQ9294.4.J3 C64, (v8)
　DS821.C62 1988, (v5)
Collecott, Diana. PS3507.O726.Z615 1999, (v3)
Colletta, John Philip. CS49.C63 1989, (v5)
Collette, Carolyn P. PR1875.P79, (v3)
Colley, Ann C. PR468.N64.C65 1998, (v3)
　PR4879.L2.Z62 1993, (v3)
Colley, John Scott. PR2821.C65 1992, (v3)
Colley, Linda. DA485.C65 1992, (v5)
Collier, Christopher. E302.6.S5 C6, (v4)
Collier, Gary. BF341.C57 1994, (v2)
Collier, James Lincoln. BJ1535.S4.C65 1991, (v8)
　ML422.G65.C6 1989, (v9)
　ML3508.C62 1993, (v9)
Collier, John. E58.C6, (v4)
　GN347.C64 1986, (v6)
　PR6005.O36 H5, (v3)
Collier, Ken. JC479.C66 1997, (v7)
Collier, Peter. E747.C64, (v4)
Collier, Peter. PQ2631.R63.Z54598413 1989, (v3)
Collier, Richard. RC150.4.C64 1996, (v2)
Collier, Simon. F1410.C7, (v4)
　F3093.C65 1996, (v4)
Colligan, Robert C. BF698.8.M5.C65 1992, (v2)
Collignon, Stefan. HG925.C655 1994, (v6)
Collin, Hamish A. SB123.6.C65 1998, (v1)
Collin, P. H. HF1002.C59 1990, (v6)
　Z118.C58 1997, (v10)
Collin, Richard H. E756.C76 1990, (v4)
　E757.C65 1985, (v4)
Collinge, William J. BX945.2.C65 1997, (v8)
Collinge, William. R733.C65 1996, (v2)
Collingham, H. A. C. DC266.5.C68 1988, (v5)
Collingridge, David. T14.5.C64 1980, (v1)
Collings, Peter J. QD923.C638 2002, (v1)
Collingwood, R. G. B1618.C73.E86 2000, (v8)
　B1618.C73.S6 1982, (v8)
　D13.C6, (v5)
　DA145.C57 1969, (v5)
Collini, Stefan. DA550.C62 1991, (v5)
　PR4024.C64 1988, (v3)
Collins, Alan. JZ1720.C65 2000, (v7)
Collins, Arthur W. B2779.C54 1999, (v8)
Collins, Catherine Fisher. HV9469.C65 1997, (v6)
Collins, Donald E. F335.N4.C65 1998, (v4)
Collins, Douglas. PQ2637.A82.Z597, (v3)
Collins, George Roseborough. NA1313.G3.C63 1983,
　(v9)
Collins, H. M. T14.5.C645 1998, (v1)
Collins, Howard Stuart. PR2477.C6, (v3)
Collins, Hubert E. F697.C73 1998, (v4)
Collins, Irene. RA038.C53.C64 1993, (v3)
Collins, J. A. TA460.C63 1993, (v1)
Collins, James B. DC110.C575 1995, (v5)
Collins, James Daniel. B791.C582, (v8)
Collins, Jane Lou. F2230.2.A9.C65 1988, (v4)
Collins, John M. E745.C63 1991, (v4)
Collins, Joseph. HC192.C575 1995, (v6)
　HD1817.C64 1982, (v6)

Collins, Lewis. F451.C73 1979, (v4)
Collins, Marva. LA2317.C62.A35 1982, (v7)
Collins, Michael L. E757.C655 1989, (v4)
Collins, Michael. NK1396.P66.C65 1989, (v9)
　PR6053.O4263.M36 1993, (v3)
　TL789.8.U5.C59 1988, (v1)
Collins, P. M. QD325.C66 1995, (v1)
Collins, Philip Arthur William. PR4592.C7.C6, (v3)
　PR4592.E4.C62, (v3)
Collins, Randall. BD175.C565 1998, (v8)
Collins, Richard. HE8700.4.C65 1990, (v6)
Collins, Robert M. HB99.7.C63, (v6)
　HC110.W4.C65 2000, (v6)
Collins, Robert O. DT17.C65 2001, (v5)
Collins, Roger. DC73.C65 1998, (v5)
　DP99.C58 1989, (v5)
Collins, Ronald K. L. KF4772.Z9.C65 1996, (v7)
Collins, Stephen L. DA320.C65 1989, (v5)
Collins, T. H. TK7825.C63 1989, (v1)
Collins, Tony. GV945.9.G7.C65 1998, (v6)
Collins, Wilkie. PR4494.A7, (v3)
　PR4494.I56 1999, (v3)
　PR4494.M6, (v3)
　PR4494.N6, (v3)
　PR4494.P66, (v3)
　PR4494.W6 1969, (v3)
　PR4496.A4 1999, (v3)
Collins, William. PR3350.A2 1979, (v3)
Collinson, J. D. QE472.C64 1982, (v1)
Collis, Maurice. DS757.5.C6 2002, (v5)
Collischan, Judy. NB1220.C65 2000, (v9)
Collodi, Carlo. PZ8.C7Ad 1996, (v3)
Colman, Andrew M. BF31.C65 2001, (v2)
Colman, David. HC59.7.C595 1994, (v6)
　HD1417.C63 1989, (v6)
Colman, E. A. M. PR2976.C57, (v3)
Colman, William G. JS348.C65 1989, (v7)
Colmer, John. PR4483.C57, (v3)
Colmer, John. PR6011.O58.Z647, (v3)
Cologne-Brookes, Gavin. PS3569.T9.Z6244 1995,
　(v3)
Colomb, Gregory G. PR559.M63.C6 1992, (v3)
Colombat, Andre. PN1995.9.H53.C66 1993, (v3)
Colon, A. R. RJ36.C65 1999, (v2)
Colon, Fernando. E111.C737, (v4)
Coltman, Rodney R. B3248.G34.C64 1998, (v8)
Colton, Elizabeth O. E840.8.J35.C65 1989, (v4)
Colton, Harold Sellers. E99.H7 C6 1959, (v4)
Colton, Joel G. DC373.B5.C6, (v5)
Colton, Ray Charles. E470.9.C7, (v4)
Colton, Timothy J. JS6082.C65 1995, (v7)
Coltrane, Scott. HQ503.C65 1996, (v6)
Colum, Mary (Maguire). PR6019.O9.Z527, (v3)
Colum, Padraic. PR6005.O38.A6 1985, (v3)
　PR8851 C47 1948, (v3)
Columbia College (Columbia University).
　CB245.C362, (v5)
　Z7046.C65 1975, (v10)
　PR2890.C64 1962, (v3)
Columbus, Christopher. E118.C725 1989a, (v4)
Colvin, A. Vonnie. GV443.C59 2000, (v6)
Colvin, Howard Montagu. NA961.C6 1999, (v9)
　NA996.C6 1978, (v9)
　NA6120.C65 1991, (v9)
Colvin, Mark. HV6035.C65 2000, (v6)
Colwell, Anne. PS3503.I785.Z6 1997, (v3)
Colwell, Stella. Z5313.G69.C45 1992, (v10)
Colyar, Margaret R. RT82.8.C64 1999, (v2)
Comaroff, Jean. DT1058.T78.C66 1991, (v5)
Comba, Peter. QD480.C66 1995, (v1)
Combalia Dexeus, Victoria. N7113.T3.C63 1990, (v9)
Combs, Allan. BD595.C65 2001, (v8)
Combs, Cindy C. HV6431.C6472 1997, (v6)
Combs, James E. E877.2.C66 1993, (v4)
　JC423.C6493 1996, (v7)
Combs, Jerald A. E183.7.C655 1983, (v4)
　E314.C6, (v4)
Combs, Richard E. PN524.C57 1993, (v3)
Combs-Orme, Terri. HV699.C535 1990, (v6)
Comensoli, Viviana. PR658.D65.C66 1997, (v3)

Comer, Douglas. TK5105.5.C5897 1999, (v1)
  TK5105.875.I57C65 2000, (v1)
Comerio, Mary C. HV555.U6.C64 1998, (v6)
Cometti, Elizabeth. F241.C7, (v4)
Comfort, Alex. BD111.C624 1984, (v8)
  PR6005.O388.D3 1962, (v3)
  PR6005.O388 P6, (v3)
Comfort, Nathaniel C. QH429.2.M38 (v1)
Comings, Lydia Jane Newcomb. F332.B2C7, (v4)
Comins, Neil F. QB44.2.C65 2001, (v1)
Commager, Henry Steele. E169.1.C673, (v4)
  E203.C69 1967, (v4)
  E464.C6, (v4)
  JC599.U5.C59, (v7)
Commager, Steele. PA6411.C59, (v3)
Comment, Bernard. ND2880.C6613 2000, (v9)
Commins, David Dean. BP63.S95 C66 1990, (v8)
  DS94.9.C66 1996, (v5)
Commission of Inquiry into the Black Panthers and
  the Police. HV8148.C42.C65 1973, (v6)
Committee for Economic Development.
  HD60.5.U5.C66, (v6)
Common, Michael S. HD75.6.C6454 1995, (v6)
Commoner, Barry. HD9502.A2.C643 1976, (v6)
Comnena, Anna. DF605.C6 1967a, (v5)
Como, James T. PR6023.E926.Z6413 1998, (v3)
Comotti, Giovanni. ML169.C6513 1989, (v9)
Compagnon, Antoine. PQ2631.R63.A784413 1992,
  (v3)
Compton, Arthur Holly. QC773.A1.C65, (v1)
Compton, Beulah Roberts. HV37.C62 1999, (v6)
Compton, Robert R. QE45.C63 1985, (v1)
  QE45.C65, (v1)
Compton, Robert W. JQ1499.A91 C65 2000, (v7)
Compton-Burnett, I. PR6005.O389.M6 1948, (v3)
  PR6005.O3895 B8, (v3)
  PR6005.O3895 D38, (v3)
  PR6005.O3895 D6 1971, (v3)
  PR6005.O3895.E42, (v3)
  PR6005.O3895 G6, (v3)
  PR6005.O3895 M3, (v3)
  PR6005.O3895 M4, (v3)
  PR6005.O3895.M54 1990, (v3)
  PR6005.O3895 M6, (v3)
  PR6005.O3895 P34, (v3)
  PR6005.O3895 T9, (v3)
  PR6005.O3895 B7 1956, (v3)
  PR6005.O3895 D3, (v3)
  PR6005.O3895 F3, (v3)
  PR6005.O3895 F36, (v3)
  PR6005.O3895 H68 1951, (v3)
Compton-Hall, Richard. V857.C65 1984, (v10)
Comrie, Bernard. PG2074.C6 1996, (v3)
Comstock, Gary David. HV6250.4.H66.C66 1991, (v6)
Comstock, Gary. S494.5.B563, (v1)
Comstock, Helen. NK805.C65 1965, (v9)
  NK2406.C58, (v9)
Comstock, John Henry. QL457.1.C7 1948, (v1)
  QL463.C71 1940, (v1)
Comyns, Alan E. TP155.7.C66 1993, (v1)
Comyns, Alan E. TP155.7.C664 1999, (v1)
Conable, Barber B. KF6369.C66 1989, (v7)
Conaghan, Catherine M. HD3616.E23.C65 1988, (v6)
Conant, Howard. N85.C6, (v9)
Conant, James Bryant. CT275.C757.A3, (v5)
  LA209.2.C6 1969, (v7)
  LB695.J4.C6, (v7)
  LB1715.C617 1963, (v7)
  Q171.C76225 1952, (v1)
  Q181.C56 1951, (v1)
  QD14.C77, (v1)
Conant, Kenneth John. NA365.C6 1973, (v9)
Conant, Melvin. UA22.C6 1962, (v10)
Conard, Henry Shoemaker. QK533.84.N67.C66 1979,
  (v1)
Conard, Robert C. PT2603.O394.Z597 1991, (v3)
Conaway, Charles F. TN870.C58 1999, (v1)
Conaway, James. Z733.U6.C595 2000, (v10)
Concina, Ennio. NA1121.V4.C65613 1998, (v9)
Conde, H. Victor. K3239.3.C66 1999, (v7)
Condit, Carl W. NA712.C65 (v9)

Condit, Carl W. NA735.C4.C6 1964, (v9)
Condit, Celeste Michelle. QH438.7.C65 1999, (v1)
Condon, Edward Uhler. QC21.C7 1967, (v1)
  QC174.2.C6, (v1)
  QC454.C64, (v1)
Condon, Richard G. E99.E7.C7284 1996, (v4)
Condon, Richard. PS3553.O487.M36 1959, (v3)
Condon, Robert J. GV697.A1.C67 1990, (v6)
  GV697.A1.C68 1991, (v6)
Condoor, Sridhar S. TA171.C5875 2002, (v1)
Condori Mamani, Gregorio. F2230.2.K4.C66313 1996,
  (v4)
Condren, Conal. B1247.C66 2000, (v8)
Cone, John Frederick. ML420.P32.C66 1993, (v9)
Cone, Joseph. GB1198.C66 1991, (v6)
Confer, Robert G. RC963.A3C66 1999, (v2)
Confino, Alon. DD801.W765.C66 1997, (v5)
Conforti, Joseph A. BX7260.E3.C64 1995, (v8)
Confucius. B128.C7.L5 1943, (v8)
  PL2471.R47 1971, (v3)
  PL2478.L328 1998, (v3)
  PL2478.L33 1997, (v3)
  PL2478.L513 1997, (v3)
  PL2478.L7 1968, (v3)
  PL2478.L8 1999, (v3)
  PL2997.L82 1956, (v3)
  PL2997.L82 1962, (v3)
Conger, Syndy M. PR5841.W8.Z654 1994, (v3)
Congressional Quarterly, inc. E859.C62 1973, (v4)
  UA23.C654 1980, (v10)
Congreve, William. PR3361.S8, (v3)
  PR3362.D3 1967, (v3)
Conigliaro, Vincenzo. RC489.D74.C66 1997, (v2)
Conisbee, Philip. ND546.C66, (v9)
  ND553.L28.A4 1996, (v9)
  ND1353.4.C66 1996, (v9)
Conkin, Paul Keith. BL245.C66 1998, (v8)
  BR516.5.C65 1997, (v8)
  BV3774.K4 C65 1991, (v8)
  E847.C53 1986, (v4)
Conklin, Alice L. JQ3360.C69 1997, (v7)
Conlan, Timothy J. JK325.C617 1998, (v7)
Conley, Brenda Edgerton. LC46.4.C66 2002, (v7)
Conley, Carolyn. HV9960.G72.K463 1991, (v6)
Conley, Dalton. E185.8.C77 1999, (v4)
  HQ792.U5.C66 2000, (v6)
Conley, Tom. GA863.5.A1.C66 1996, (v6)
  PN1995.C63 1990, (v3)
Conlon, Lawrence. QA614.3.C66 1993, (v1)
Conn, Edwin. PN241.C6, (v3)
Conn, Peter J. PS3503.U198.Z624 1996, (v3)
Conn, Steven. AM11.C64 1998, (v10)
Connah, Graham. DU106.C66 1988, (v5)
Connaughton, R. M. D842.C64 1992, (v5)
Connell, D. W. TD193.B37 1997, (v1)
Connell, Evan S. PS3553.O5.M5, (v3)
Connell, Maria Bryan Harford. F290.C66 1996, (v4)
Connelley, William Elsey. F594.H622, (v4)
Connell-Smith, Gordon. F1418.C8132, (v4)
Connelly, Elizabeth Russell. F67.W79 C66 2001, (v4)
Connelly, Marc. PS3505.O4814.G7 1930, (v3)
Connelly, Marie Katheryn. PN1998.3.S39.C66 1993,
  (v3)
Connelly, Owen. DC203.9.C647 1987, (v5)
Connelly, Thomas Lawrence. E176.1.A626 1991, (v4)
Connely, Willard. NA737.S9.C6, (v9)
Conner, Clifford D. DC146.M3.C57 1997, (v5)
Conner, Daniel Ellis. F780.C75, (v4)
  F786.W33, (v4)
Conner, Karen Ann. HV1461.C666 1999, (v6)
Conner, Lester I. PR5906.A23 1998, (v3)
Conner, Paul W. E302.6.F8.C72, (v4)
Conner, Randy P. BL795.H6.C65 1997, (v8)
Conner-Sax, Kiersten. TK5105.875.I57.C658 1999,
  (v1)
Connery, Christopher Leigh. PL2262.C75 1998, (v3)
Connery, Robert Howe. VC263.C65 1972, (v10)
Conniff, Michael L. E183.8.P2 C65 2001, (v4)
Connolly, Cyril. NA8450.C58, (v9)
  PR6005.O393.C6 1946, (v3)
  PR6005.O393 R6 1968, (v3)

Connolly, Deborah R. HV4506.O76.C66 2000, (v6)
Connolly, James J. F73.5.C745 1998, (v4)
Connolly, Joseph. DA965.C74.A3 1996, (v5)
Connolly, Paula T. PR6025.I65.W646 1995, (v3)
Connolly, Peter. U33.C647 1981, (v10)
Connolly, Roy. PN2602.B42, (v3)
Connolly, S. J. DA947.C66 1992, (v5)
Connolly, Thomas Edmund. PR5514.C6 1965, (v3)
  PR6019.O9.P644, (v3)
  PS3511.A86.Z759 1988, (v3)
Connolly, William E. JA83.C636 1988, (v7)
Connor, Celeste. N6512.5.S75, (v9)
Connor, Kimberly Rae. BT83.57.C68 2000, (v8)
  PS153.N5.C64 1994, (v3)
Connor, Seymour V. E404.C8, (v4)
Connor, Steven. PN98.P67.C66 1989, (v3)
Connor, Walker. JC311.C644 1994, (v7)
Connor, Walter D. HN380.Z9.S638, (v6)
Connor, Walter. HD8526.5.C594 1991, (v6)
Connors, Joseph. NA5620.O7.C66 1980, (v9)
Connors, Robert J. PE1405.U6.C664 1997, (v3)
Conolly, L. W. Z2014.D7.C72, (v10)
Conot, Robert E. JX5437.8.C66 1983, (v7)
Conover, Ted. HV9475.N72.S563 2000, (v6)
Conquest, Robert. DK254.K52.C66 1989, (v5)
  DK268.S8.C65 1991, (v5)
  DK274.C62, (v5)
  DK274.C63, (v5)
Conrad, Alfred H. HC53.C57, (v6)
Conrad, Bryce. PS3545.I544.I533 1990, (v3)
Conrad, David Eugene. HD1478.U6.C6, (v6)
Conrad, Geoffrey W. F1219.73.C66 1984, (v4)
Conrad, Jessie George. PR6005.O4.Z578 1935, (v3)
Conrad, Joseph. PR6005.O4.A83 1963, (v3)
  PR6005.O4 C4 1923, (v3)
  PR6005.O4.H4 1989, (v3)
  PR6005.O4 L67, (v3)
  PR6005.O4 N5 1951, (v3)
  PR6005.O4.N5638 1979, (v3)
  PR6005.O4 N6 1951, (v3)
  PR6005.O4.P7 1971, (v3)
  PR6005.O4 P83, (v3)
  PR6005.O4 R4 1920, (v3)
  PR6005.O4 R6 1950, (v3)
  PR6005.O4 R67, (v3)
  PR6005.O4.S4 1989, (v3)
  PR6005.O4 V5 1932, (v3)
  PR6005.O4.Z48 1983, (v3)
  PR6005.O4.Z54, (v3)
Conrads, Margaret C. ND237.H7.A4 2001, (v9)
Conran, Patricia Cannon. LB2817.C69 1989, (v7)
Conron, Brandon. PR6005.A37.Z6, (v3)
Conron, John. NX503.7.C66 2000, (v9)
Conroy, David W. F67.C756 1995, (v4)
Conroy, Glenn C. QL737.P9.C66 1990, (v1)
Conroy, Jack. PS3505.O53.W67 2000, (v3)
Conroy, Mary Schaeffer. RS67.S65.C66 1994, (v2)
Conroy, Peter V. PQ2012.C66 1992, (v3)
Conroy, W. J. F59.B9.C66 1990, (v4)
Consolmagno, Guy. QB36.C76.A3 2000, (v1)
  QB63.C69 2000, (v1)
Constable, Giles. BX2590.C66 1996, (v8)
Constable, Henry. PR2235.5.A17 1960, (v3)
Constable, Pamela. F3100.C64 1991, (v4)
Constantelos, Demetrios J. BX320.2.C66 1982, (v8)
Constantine, David. PT2359.H2.C56 1988, (v3)
Constantine, Stephen. HC259.C73 1984, (v6)
Constantinidis, Stratos E. PN2053.C62 1993, (v3)
Constantz, George. QH104.5.A6.C65 1994, (v1)
Contamine, Philippe. U37.C6513 1984, (v10)
Conteh-Morgan, Earl. HC60.C6534 1990, (v6)
Contenau, G. DS75.S6.C63, (v5)
Conterio, Karen. RC552.S4.C66 1998, (v2)
Conversi, Daniele. DP302.B55.C66 1997, (v5)
Conversino, Mark J. D790.C657 1997, (v5)
Conway, Cecelia. ML3556.C667 1995, (v9)
Conway, David. BD555.C57 2000, (v8)
  JC574.C66 1995, (v7)
Conway, Hazel. SB484.G7.C59 1991, (v1)
Conway, Moncure Daniel. JC178.V2.C7 1970, (v7)
Conway, Stephen. DA510.C73 2000, (v5)

Conze, Edward. BQ336.C66x 1983, **(v8)**
Conzen, Michael P. Z1247.C66 1993, **(v10)**
Coogan, Tim Pat. DA959.C68 1993, **(v5)**
 DA963.C64, **(v5)**
 DA965.D4 C66 1995, **(v5)**
Cook, A. H. QR151.C58 1958, **(v1)**
Cook, Adrian. F128.44.C76, **(v4)**
Cook, Albert S. PR1508.C5 1970, **(v3)**
Cook, Albert Spaulding. PN81.C75 1993, **(v3)**
 PN4151.C67 1995, **(v3)**
Cook, Alexandra Parma. KKT174.N64.C66 1991, **(v7)**
Cook, Alice Hanson. HD6197.C66, **(v6)**
Cook, Ann Jennalie. PR3069.M3.C66 1991, **(v3)**
Cook, Blanche Wiesen. E807.1.R48.C66 1992, **(v4)**
Cook, Brian J. KF3812.C66 1988, **(v7)**
Cook, Bruce. HQ799.7.C66 1971, **(v6)**
Cook, Chris. D419.C58 1997, **(v5)**
 D843.N62 1998, **(v5)**
 DA498.C66 1988, **(v5)**
 DA566.2.C67 1993, **(v5)**
 E174.C66 1998, **(v4)**
 JN12.C643 2001, **(v7)**
 Z2000.C57 1987, **(v10)**
 Z3508.H5.C66 1995, **(v10)**
Cook, Christopher D. K. QK358.C67 1996, **(v1)**
Cook, Constance Ewing. LC173.C66 1998, **(v7)**
Cook, David A. PN1993.5.A1.C65 1981, **(v3)**
 PN1993.5.U6.H55 1990 vol. 9, **(v3)**
Cook, David B. QC174.26.W28.C657 1988, **(v1)**
Cook, David. PR9381.9.N45.Z562 1983, **(v3)**
Cook, Don. UA646.3.C62 1989, **(v10)**
Cook, Eleanor. PN1042.C586 1998, **(v3)**
 PS3537.T4753.Z6229 1988, **(v3)**
Cook, G. C. RC962.G7.C66 1992, **(v2)**
Cook, Garrett W. F1465.2.Q5.C66 2000, **(v4)**
Cook, Harold John. R489.G79.C66 1994, **(v2)**
Cook, Haruko Taya. D811.A2.C62 1992, **(v5)**
Cook, Ian. JC223.M66.C66 1998, **(v7)**
Cook, James Gordon. TS1540.C639 1968, **(v1)**
Cook, James H. F594.C76 1992, **(v4)**
Cook, James L. QC94.C67 1990, **(v1)**
Cook, John W. B3376.W564.C65 2000, **(v8)**
 BJ52.C66 1999, **(v8)**
Cook, Jonathan A. PS2384.C63.C66 1996, **(v3)**
Cook, Kevin L. Z7553.C3.C66 1996, **(v10)**
Cook, M. A. BJ1291.C66 2000, **(v8)**
 BP130.4.C66 2000, **(v8)**
Cook, Nicholas. ML3845.C67 1990, **(v9)**
 MT6.C775 M88 1998, **(v9)**
Cook, Noble David. E59.D58.C66 1998, **(v4)**
Cook, Patrick J. PN694.E6.C66 1996, **(v3)**
Cook, Philip L. BX7415.C66 1996, **(v8)**
Cook, Ramsay. F1027.C76, **(v4)**
 F1033.D2.C6, **(v4)**
Cook, Richard I. PR3545.M6.Z6, **(v3)**
Cook, Richard. ML156.4.J3 C67 2002, **(v9)**
Cook, Robert Davis. TA347.F5.C665 1995, **(v1)**
Cook, Sherburne Friend. E78.C15.C698 1976, **(v4)**
 HB3531.C6 1978, **(v6)**
Cook, Sylvia Jenkins. PS3505.A322.Z534 1991, **(v3)**
Cook, Timothy E. PN4738.C66 1998, **(v3)**
Cook, Warren L. F851.5.C83, **(v4)**
Cook-Deegan, Robert M. QH445.2.C66 1994, **(v1)**
Cooke, Alan. F1090.5.C67, **(v4)**
Cooke, Alistair. E743.5.H55.C6 1952, **(v4)**
Cooke, D. J. QA76.9.M35.C66 1984, **(v1)**
Cooke, Deryck. MT92.M14.C66, **(v9)**
Cooke, James J. D570.3 82nd.C66 1999, **(v5)**
 D606.C66 1996, **(v5)**
Cooke, John Daniel. PR461.C6, **(v3)**
Cooke, John Esten. E605.C77 1959, **(v4)**
 PS1382.V5, **(v3)**
Cooke, Miriam. HQ1170.C75 2001, **(v6)**
 PJ8078.C66 1996, **(v3)**
 PN3448.W3.C66 1996, **(v3)**
Cooke, Nathalie. PR9199.3.A8.Z57 1998, **(v3)**
Cooke, Robert. RC271.N46, **(v2)**
Cooke, Ronald U. GB611.C66 1993, **(v6)**
Cookson, Catharine. KF4783.C665 2001, **(v7)**
Cookson, J. E. DA68.C66 1997, **(v5)**
Cookson, John T. TD192.5.C66 1995, **(v1)**

Coolidge, Calvin. E792.A32 1984, **(v4)**
Coolidge, Dane. F591.C78, **(v4)**
Coolidge, Grace. E99.A7C66 1984, **(v4)**
Coolidge, Olivia E. F27.K32.C66 1999, **(v4)**
 PS3553.O572C34 1991, **(v3)**
Cooling, B. Franklin. E472.97.C66 1997, **(v4)**
Coomaraswamy, Ananda Kentish. N7445.C78 1956, **(v9)**
Coombes, Kevin Robert. QA303.5.C65.C66 1998, **(v1)**
Coombs, H. C. GN666.C657 1994, **(v4)**
Coombs, Philip Hall. LA132.C64 1985, **(v7)**
Cooney, Barbara. PZ7.C783 Mi 1982, **(v3)**
Cooney, Mark. HM291.C652 1998, **(v6)**
Coontz, Stephanie. HQ535.C643 1992, **(v6)**
Coop, Richard H. GV979.P75.C66 1993, **(v6)**
Cooper Alarcon, Daniel. F1216.5.C69 1997, **(v4)**
Cooper Union for the Advancement of Science and
 Art. NA2440.N47.M873 1971, **(v9)**
Cooper, Alan. PS3568.O855.Z62 1996, **(v3)**
 QA76.9.H85C673 1999, **(v1)**
Cooper, Allan D. DT1625.C66 1990, **(v5)**
Cooper, Andre R. GE123.C64 1996, **(v6)**
Cooper, Andrew Fenton. F1034.2.C66 1993, **(v4)**
 HD1927.C66 1989, **(v6)**
Cooper, Andrew. GV706.4.C67 1998, **(v6)**
Cooper, Ann. TX353.C623 2000, **(v1)**
Cooper, Anna J. F1923.C7213 1988, **(v4)**
Cooper, Arthur R. V. PL2671.C6, **(v3)**
Cooper, Barbara MacGowan. DT547.45.H38.C66 1997, **(v5)**
Cooper, Barry. JC263.V632.C65 1999, **(v7)**
Cooper, Brenda. PR9344.C66 1998, **(v3)**
Cooper, Carolyn. F1874.C66 1995, **(v4)**
 RT41.C7787 2001, **(v2)**
Cooper, Charles William. PN1655.C6, **(v3)**
Cooper, Darius. PN1998.3.R4.C66 2000, **(v3)**
Cooper, David Edward. B819.C62 1990, **(v8)**
 BD21.C656 1996, **(v8)**
 BJ1012.C669 1993, **(v8)**
Cooper, Duff. DA566.9.C64.A3, **(v5)**
Cooper, Emmanuel. NK3780.C663 1999, **(v9)**
Cooper, Frederick. HD8776.C66 1996, **(v6)**
Cooper, Gabriele von Natzmer. PT2621.A26.Z6635 1991, **(v3)**
Cooper, Gail. LB1044.87.C67 1999, **(v7)**
Cooper, Geoffrey M. QH581.2.C66 2000, **(v1)**
Cooper, Grosvenor. MT42.C642, **(v9)**
Cooper, Helen M. PR4194.C66 1988, **(v3)**
Cooper, Helen. PR1874.C65 1984, **(v3)**
Cooper, Ilay. NA1501.C58 1998, **(v9)**
Cooper, James Fenimore. BJ352.C66 1999, **(v8)**
 BX7148.M4.C66 1999, **(v8)**
 PS1400.F69, **(v3)**
 PS1402.N4, **(v3)**
 PS1405.B7 1963, **(v3)**
 PS1405.C7 1962, **(v3)**
 PS1406.A1, **(v3)**
 PS1407.H7 1961, **(v3)**
 PS1410.P43 1952, **(v3)**
 PS1412.A1 1968, **(v3)**
 PS1414.A1 1988, **(v3)**
 PS1416.A1 1987, **(v3)**
 PS1417.S7 1960, **(v3)**
 PS1431.A3 1960, **(v3)**
 PS1431.A3 1971b, **(v3)**
Cooper, John M. BJ161.C66 1999, **(v8)**
Cooper, John Michael. ML134.M53 C6 2001, **(v9)**
Cooper, John Milton. E176.1.C7919 1983, **(v4)**
 E756.C78 1990, **(v4)**
Cooper, John Rex. PR3757.W6.C633, **(v3)**
Cooper, John Xiros. PS3509.L43.F642 1995, **(v3)**
Cooper, Leo. DS135.P6.C655 2000, **(v5)**
Cooper, Madison. PS3505.O64.S5 1952, **(v3)**
Cooper, Martin. ML270.4.C7, **(v9)**
Cooper, Pamela. GV1065.2.C66 1998, **(v6)**
Cooper, Phillip J. KF5425.C66 1988, **(v7)**
 KF8742.C66 1995, **(v7)**
Cooper, Stephen. PS3511.A594.Z62 2000, **(v3)**
Cooper, Susan. PZ7.C7878Gt3, **(v3)**
Cooper, Thomas W. Z7711.C66 1988, **(v10)**
Cooper, William J. E467.1.D26.C66 2000, **(v4)**

 F213.C69, **(v4)**
 H31.J6 ser. 86, no. 1, **(v6)**
Cooper, William. PR6015.O28 S3 1961, **(v3)**
Cooperman, Robert. Z8641.13.C66 1990, **(v10)**
Coote, Stephen. DA447.P4.C66 2001, **(v5)**
Cooter, Robert. K487.E3.C667 2000, **(v7)**
Coover, Robert. PS3553.O633.P8, **(v3)**
Cope, David. ML197.C757 2001, **(v9)**
 MT56.C69 2001, **(v9)**
Cope, Esther S. DA395.C66 1987, **(v5)**
Cope, Jack. PT6510.C65 1982, **(v3)**
Cope, Jackson I. PR3562.C63, **(v3)**
Copeau, Jacques. PN2638.C74.C36 1990, **(v3)**
Copeland, Dale C. D511.C626 2000, **(v5)**
Copeland, David A. E187.C78 2000, **(v4)**
 PN4861.C74 1997, **(v3)**
Copeland, E. Luther. BX6462.7.C67 1995, **(v8)**
Copeland, L.O. (Lawrence O.). SB117.C73 2001, **(v1)**
Copeland, Rebecca L. PL726.6.C67 2000, **(v3)**
 PL726.6.C67 2000, **(v3)**
 PL840.N58.Z58 1992, **(v3)**
Copeland, Richard W. QA11.C673, **(v1)**
Copeland, Robert Allen. QP601.C753 2000, **(v1)**
Copeland, Tom. KF221.M8.C67 1993, **(v7)**
Copernicus, Nicolaus. QB41.C84 1939a, **(v1)**
Copi, Irving M. BC108.C69 1986, **(v8)**
 BC135.C58 1979, **(v8)**
Copland, Aaron. ML63.C48, **(v9)**
 ML197.C76 1968, **(v9)**
 ML410.C756 A3 1989, **(v9)**
 ML3853.C7, **(v9)**
Copland, Ian. DS480.45.C69 1997, **(v5)**
Copleston, Frederick Charles. B765.T54 C64 1976, **(v8)**
Copp, J. T. D807.C2.C66 1990, **(v5)**
Coppa, Frank J. BX1386.C58 1998, **(v8)**
Coppard, A. E. PR6005.O55 A15, **(v3)**
Coppard, Brenda M. RD559.C68 2001, **(v2)**
Copper, John Franklin. DS798.96.C67 2000, **(v5)**
 DS799.C67 1990, **(v5)**
 JC599.C6.C69 1997, **(v5)**
 JQ1539.A15.C665 1998, **(v7)**
Copperud, Roy H. PE1460.C648, **(v3)**
Coppin, Clayton A. KF1900.C67 1999, **(v7)**
Copsey, Nigel. DA566.7.C64 1999, **(v5)**
Coquery-Vidrovitch, Catherine. HQ1787.C6613 1997, **(v6)**
Coquet, Michele. N7391.65.C66613 1998, **(v9)**
Corballis, Michael C. QP385.5.C67 1991, **(v1)**
Corbeil, Jean Claude. AG250.C65 1991, **(v10)**
 PL1455.C675 1988, **(v3)**
Corbeill, Anthony. DG82.C67 1996, **(v5)**
Corber, Robert J. PN1998.3.H58.C67 1993, **(v3)**
Corbet, G. B. QL708.C67 1991, **(v1)**
Corbet, Philip S. QL520.C67 1999, **(v1)**
Corbet, Richard. PR3369.C2 1955, **(v3)**
Corbett, James. DC33.7.C597 1994, **(v5)**
Corbett, Mary Jean. PR788.W65.C6 1992, **(v3)**
 PR8807.P64, **(v3)**
Corbett, Michael. BL2525.C68 1999, **(v8)**
Corbett, P. Scott. D753.8.C67 1987, **(v5)**
Corbett, Richard. JN36.C69 1998, **(v7)**
Corbiere, Tristan. PQ2211.C32.A814, **(v3)**
 PQ2211.C32.A8 1953, **(v3)**
Corbin, Alain. DC33.5.C6713 1998, **(v5)**
 DC280.5.M67.C6713 1992, **(v5)**
 HN425.C6713 1995, **(v6)**
 HQ194.C6513 1990, **(v6)**
Corbin, Annalies. F598.C67 2000, **(v4)**
Corbin, John. KF240.C63 1989, **(v7)**
Corbin, Juliet M. RC108.C67 1988, **(v2)**
Corbridge, Stuart. DS480.84.C783 2000, **(v5)**
Corcoran, Mike. GV965.C664 1999, **(v6)**
Corcoran, Neil. PR8753.C665 1997, **(v3)**
Corcos, Christine. Z6514.L38, **(v10)**
Cordasco, Francesco. LA14.C72 1976, **(v7)**
Cordell, Alexander. PR6053.O65.R3, **(v3)**
Cordell, Dennis D. HB2126.4.A3.C67 1996, **(v6)**
Cordell, Helen. Z3233.C67 1991, **(v10)**
Cordell, Linda S. E78.S7.C67 1984, **(v4)**

Corden, W. M. HG3881.C674 1986, **(v6)**
Cordesman, Anthony H. DS79.7.C67 1997, **(v5)**
  DS247.A13.C67 1997, **(v5)**
  DS247.K88.C67 1997, **(v5)**
  U42.C59 1990, **(v10)**
  UA23.C67374 1997, **(v10)**
  UA832.C66 1993, **(v10)**
  UA832.C67 1988, **(v10)**
  UA853.I7.C63 1997, **(v10)**
  UA853.I75.C65 1999, **(v10)**
  UA853.I8.C67 1996, **(v10)**
  UA853.P47.C66 1984, **(v10)**
  UA853.S33.C67 1997, **(v10)**
Cordier, Mary Hurlbut. LB2837.C66 1992, **(v7)**
Cordingly, David. G540.C685 2001, **(v6)**
Cordle, Daniel. PN55.C67 2000, **(v3)**
Cordle, Thomas. PQ2613.I2.Z6153 1993, **(v3)**
Cordovero, Moses ben Jacob. BM525.C65413 1994, **(v8)**
Cordovez, Diego. DS371.2.C67 1995, **(v5)**
Cordry, Harold V. PE2815.C67 1998, **(v3)**
Core, H.A. SD536.C67 1979, **(v1)**
Core. F247.M7 C67, **(v4)**
Corea, Gena. QP251.C78 1985, **(v1)**
Coreil, Jeannine. RA418.C673 2001, **(v2)**
Coren, Michael. PR4453.C4.Z5876 1990, **(v3)**
  PR5776.C58 1993, **(v3)**
Coren, Stanley. BF233.C59 1994, **(v2)**
  QP425.C62 1996, **(v1)**
  QP495.C67, **(v1)**
  SF433.C67 1994, **(v1)**
Corey, Elizabeth. F656.C67 1990, **(v4)**
Corey, Mary F. PN4900.N35.C67 1999, **(v3)**
Corey, Melinda. PN1998.C65 1992, **(v3)**
Corey, Michael Anthony. BL263.C774 1993, **(v8)**
  BL263.C776 2000, **(v8)**
Corkin, Stanley. PS374.R37.C67 1996, **(v3)**
Corle, Edwin. F786.C8 1941, **(v4)**
  F817.G52.C6, **(v4)**
Corlew, Edward Ewing. F436.C78 1981, **(v4)**
Corley, T. A. B. DC280.C6, **(v5)**
Cormack, Michael J. PN1995.9.P6.C67 1994, **(v3)**
Cormack, William S. DC153.C66 1995, **(v5)**
Corman, Roger. PN1998.3.C68.A3 1990, **(v3)**
Cormier, Robert. PZ7.C81634Ch 1988, **(v3)**
Corn, Alfred. PE1505.C67 1997, **(v3)**
Corn, Wanda M. N6512.C597 1999, **(v9)**
Cornbleth, Catherine. LB2806.15.C69 1990, **(v7)**
Cornblit, Oscar. F3351.O7.C67 1995, **(v4)**
Cornebise, Alfred E. PN4888.M54.C67 1993, **(v3)**
Corneille, Pierre. PQ1745.E5.C3 1975, **(v3)**
  PQ1745.E5.L3, **(v3)**
  PQ1745.E5.L6 1957, **(v3)**
  PQ1749.E5.C44 1987, **(v3)**
Cornelius, Janet Duitsman. E443.C7 1991, **(v4)**
  E449.C82 1999, **(v4)**
Cornell, Drucilla. HQ1101.C64 1998, **(v6)**
Cornell, Felix M. VK541.C67 1957, **(v10)**
Cornell, Saul. E310.C79 1999, **(v4)**
Cornell, Tim. DG77.C597 1982, **(v5)**
Cornell, Vincent J. BP188.8.M6.C67 1998, **(v8)**
Cornfeld, Gaalyahu. BS621.C6415 1976, **(v8)**
Cornford, Daniel A. HD6515.L92.H853 1987, **(v6)**
Cornford, Francis Macdonald. B171.C7, **(v8)**
  B188.C6 1957, **(v8)**
  B1618.C763.U5, **(v8)**
Cornforth, Maurice Campbell. B809.8.C68, **(v8)**
Corngold, Stanley. PT75.C67 1998, **(v3)**
Corngold, Stanley. PT2621.A26.Z664 1988, **(v3)**
Corning Museum of Glass. NK5102.C65, **(v9)**
Cornish, Dudley Taylor. E540.N3.C77 1966, **(v4)**
Cornish, Edward. CB158.C67, **(v5)**
Cornish, Paul. UA649.32.G3.C67 1996, **(v10)**
Cornish, Rory T. Z8369.253.C67 1992, **(v10)**
Cornish-Bowden, Athel. QP601.C756, **(v1)**
Cornog, Evan. E176.1.C793 2000, **(v4)**
  E340.C65.C74 1998, **(v4)**
Cornog, Martha. Z688.S45.C67 1996, **(v10)**
Corns, Thomas N. PR435.C67 1992, **(v3)**
  PR3592.P7.C67 1998, **(v3)**
Cornwall, Mark. D639.P7.A93 2000, **(v5)**

Cornwell, Ethel F. PR161.C6, **(v3)**
Corp, Ronald. MT875.C68 1987, **(v9)**
Corrales, Javier. HC175.C6684 2002, **(v6)**
Correa, Carlos Maria. K1401.C679 1999, **(v7)**
Correa, Hector. HD4854.C6, **(v6)**
Corrigan, John. Z7785.C67 2000, **(v10)**
Corrigan, Lesa Carnes. PS3545.A748.Z657 1999, **(v3)**
Corrigan, Timothy. PN1993.5.G3.C67 1994, **(v3)**
  PN1993.5.U6.C64 1991, **(v3)**
Corrin, Chris. HQ1610.5.C67 1994, **(v6)**
Cors, Paul B. Z7231.C67, **(v10)**
Corsini, Raymond J. BF31.C72 1999, **(v2)**
  BF56.C65, **(v2)**
Corso, Gregory. PS3505.O763.A6 1989, **(v3)**
Cort, John E. BL1356.C67 2001, **(v8)**
Cortada, James W. HD62.15.C668 1995, **(v6)**
  HD9696.C62.C47 1987, **(v6)**
  HD9801.U542.C67 1993, **(v6)**
  HF5548.2.C675 1996, **(v6)**
  QA76.17.C67 1996, **(v1)**
  TK7885.A5.C67 1993, **(v1)**
  Z5640.C673 1996, **(v10)**
Cortes, Hernan. F1230.C833 1945, **(v4)**
Cortes, Hernando. F1230.C856 1977, **(v4)**
Cortes, Juan B. HV6025.C65, **(v6)**
Cortese, Anthony Joseph Paul. BJ1031.C67 1990, **(v8)**
Corthell, Ronald. PR2248.C65 1997, **(v3)**
Corti, Lillian. PN57.M37.C67 1998, **(v3)**
Cortner, H. GE300.C66 1999, **(v6)**
Cortner, Richard C. E748.L86.C67 1996, **(v4)**
  F417.P45.C67 1988, **(v4)**
  KF228.H43 C67 2001, **(v7)**
Cortright, David. HF1413.5.C67 2000, **(v6)**
Cortright, David. UH740.C67 1991, **(v10)**
Corum, James S. UA710.C67 1992, **(v10)**
  UG635.G3.C68 1997, **(v10)**
  UG635.G3.C6823 1997, **(v10)**
Corvisier, Andre. UA646.C6813, **(v10)**
Corwin, Edward Samuel. KF4575.C67 1994, **(v7)**
Corwin, Elizabeth J. RB113.C785 1996, **(v2)**
Corwin, Phillip. DR1313.3.C67 1999, **(v5)**
  DS371.3.C67 2003, **(v5)**
Cosculluela, Victor. HV6545.C67 1995, **(v6)**
Cose, Ellis. E184.A1.C654 1992, **(v4)**
Cosell, Howard. GV719.C67.A32 1973, **(v6)**
Coser, Rose Laub. HM131.C74775 1991, **(v6)**
Cosgrove, Denis E. DG975.V38.C67 1993, **(v5)**
  G71.5.C68 2001, **(v6)**
Cosgrove, Michael. HC106.5.C685 1996, **(v6)**
Cosic, Dobrica. PG1418.C63.V713, **(v3)**
Coss, Peter R. DA690.C75.C56 1991, **(v5)**
Cossa, Ralph A. E183.8.S645.C67 1999, **(v4)**
Cosslett, V. E. QC447.C63 1950, **(v1)**
Costa, Marie. HQ767.5.U5.C67 1991, **(v6)**
Costa, Richard Hauer. PR6023.O96.Z59, **(v3)**
  PS3562.U7.Z63 1992, **(v3)**
Costain, Anne N. HQ1236.5.U6.C67 1992, **(v6)**
Costansó, Miguel. F864.C7713 2000, **(v4)**
Costanzo, Angelo. E444.C67 1987, **(v4)**
Costello, Elaine. HV2475.C66 1997, **(v6)**
Costello, Harry Todd. BD241.C65, **(v8)**
Costello, John. D582.J8.C63 1977, **(v5)**
  D750.C67 1991, **(v5)**
  D767.C67 1982, **(v5)**
Costello, Lawrence F. LB1044.7.C7 1965, **(v7)**
Costello, Paul. D13.C674 1993, **(v5)**
Costello, Peter. PQ2469.Z5.C66 1978, **(v3)**
  PR8753.C67 1977, **(v3)**
Costin, Lela B. HV741.C665 1996, **(v6)**
Costlow, Jane T. PG3443.C66 1990, **(v3)**
Cosulich, Bernice. F819.T9 C6, **(v4)**
Cot, Richard N. F279.C453 P7453 2000, **(v4)**
Cote, Charlotte. HQ1413.B76.C68 1988, **(v6)**
Cote, Jane McL. DA958.P24.C67 1991, **(v5)**
Cothern, C. Richard. GE145.C68 1995, **(v6)**
Cothey, A. L. BH39.C67 1990, **(v8)**
Cotman, John Walton. F2056.63.C9.C6 1993, **(v4)**
Cotran, Ramzi S. RB111.R62 1999, **(v2)**
Cott, Nancy F. HQ536.C757 2000, **(v6)**
  HQ1418.C67 1997, **(v6)**

HQ1420.C67 1987, **(v6)**
Cottam, Martha L. F1418.C845 1994, **(v4)**
  JC311.C66 2001, **(v7)**
Cottell, Philip G. HF5657.C687 1990, **(v6)**
Cotter, Charles H. VK549.C63, **(v10)**
Cotter, John L. F158.39.C68 1992, **(v4)**
Cotterell, Arthur. BL303.C67 1989, **(v8)**
Cotterell, Arthur. DS511.C82 1994, **(v5)**
Cotterill, R.S. E78.S65 C6, **(v4)**
Cotterill, Rodney. QA76.87.C685 1998, **(v1)**
  QC173.3.C66 1985, **(v1)**
  KD640.C67 1992, **(v7)**
Cottle, Basil. CS2505.C67, **(v5)**
Cottle, Thomas J. BF468.C6, **(v2)**
  HD5708.C68 2001, **(v6)**
  HV9104.C59 1977, **(v6)**
Cottom, Daniel. PR778.A38.C68 1985, **(v3)**
Cotton, F. Albert. QD461.C65 1990, **(v1)**
Cotton, James Harry. B945.R64.C6, **(v8)**
Cotton, John. BX7260.C79.A4 2001, **(v8)**
Cotton, Nancy. PR635.W62.C6 1980, **(v3)**
Cotton, William R. QC921.6.D95.C67 1989, **(v1)**
  QC981.C72 1995, **(v1)**
Cottrell, Alan Howard. TN665.C69 1967b, **(v1)**
Cottrell, Leonard. CB311.C85, **(v5)**
  DS747.5.C6, **(v5)**
Cottrell, Robert C. JC599.U5B353 2000, **(v7)**
  PN4874.S69.C67 1992, **(v3)**
Cottrell, Tony. PN1861.C68 1991, **(v3)**
Cottret, Bernard. BX9418.C5913 2000, **(v8)**
  DA125.H84.C66 1991, **(v5)**
Couch, Arthur. PR1285.O9, **(v3)**
Couch, Carl J. HM258.C678 1996, **(v6)**
Couch, Jim F. HC106.3.C748 1998, **(v6)**
Couch, Leon W. TK5101C69 2001, **(v1)**
Coughlan, Margaret N. Z5984.A35 C68 1999, **(v10)**
Coughlin, Edward V. PQ6503.A52.Z6 1988, **(v3)**
Coughlin, Teresa A. HD7102.U4.C638 1994, **(v6)**
Coulborn, Rushton. JC111.C6 1965, **(v7)**
Coulby, David. LB1564.E85, **(v7)**
Coulmas, Florian. Z40.C67 1996, **(v10)**
Coulson, Andrew J. LA212.C68 1999, **(v7)**
Coulson, Andrew. HC885.C68 1982, **(v6)**
Coulson, Charles Alfred. QD469.C74 1979, **(v1)**
Coulson, Noel J. D199.3.I8.2, **(v5)**
Coulson, Robert N. SB761.C68 1984, **(v1)**
Coulter, Charles Russell. BL473.C67 2000, **(v8)**
Coulter, Jeff. BD175.C68 1989, **(v8)**
Coulton, G. G. D127.C6 1930, **(v5)**
  DA185.C87 1968, **(v5)**
Coulton, J. J. NA270.C65 1977, **(v9)**
Council, Norman. PR3069.H6.C6 1973, **(v3)**
Counihan, Carole. GT2850.C68 1999, **(v6)**
Counter, S. Allen. E99.E7.C747 1991, **(v4)**
Countryman, Edward. E169.1.C792 1996, **(v4)**
  E263.N6 C68 1989, **(v4)**
Countryman, Ruth S. GT615.C68 1997, **(v6)**
Couprie, Dirk L. B208.Z7 C68 2003, **(v8)**
Courant, Richard. QA37.C675, **(v1)**
  QA303.C838, **(v1)**
  QA303.S845, **(v1)**
Courbage, Youssef. BP172.C6413 1997, **(v8)**
Courbin, Paul. CC165.C6613 1988, **(v5)**
Courcelle, Pierre Paul. PA3081.C753 1969, **(v3)**
Cournot, A. A. HB74.M3.C653 1960, **(v6)**
Coursen, Herbert R. PR2823.C67 1997, **(v3)**
  PR2987.C68 1997, **(v3)**
  PR3091.C68 1992, **(v3)**
  PR3093.C68 1993, **(v3)**
  PR3100.C68 1999, **(v3)**
Coursey, Oscar William. F594.H623, **(v4)**
Court, Jamie. RA413.5.U5.C68 1999, **(v2)**
Courthion, Pierre. ND553.S5.C643 1988, **(v9)**
Courtine-Denamy, Sylvie. B3332.S674 C6813 2000, **(v8)**
Courtney, C. P. DA506.B9.C65, **(v5)**
Courtney, Thomas H. TA405.C859 2000, **(v1)**
Courtney, Winifred F. PR4863.C6 1982, **(v3)**
Courtney-Clarke, Margaret. N7398.C68 1990, **(v9)**
Courtwright, David T. HV4997.C68 2001, **(v6)**
Cousens, Roger. SB611.C67 1995, **(v1)**

Cousin, Geraldine. PR2818.C68 1994, **(v3)**
Cousineau, Diane. PR119.C74 1997, **(v3)**
Cousineau, Guy. QA76.62.C68 1998, **(v1)**
Cousineau, Thomas. PQ2603.E378.Z6 1999, **(v3)**
Cousteau, Jacques Yves. QH91.C628, **(v1)**
   QH91.C66, **(v1)**
   QH91.15.C652, **(v1)**
   QH541.5.C7.C613, **(v1)**
   VM453.C67 1983, **(v10)**
Coutin, Susan Bibler. BV4466.C63 1993, **(v8)**
Coutinho, Afranio. PQ9511.C6313, **(v3)**
Coutinho, S. C. QA241.C69513 1999, **(v1)**
Couto, Maria. PR6013.R44.Z63188 1988, **(v3)**
Couto, Richard A. F443.H4.C68 1993, **(v4)**
Couto, Richard A. HN59.2.C68 1999, **(v6)**
Covarrubias Horozco, Sebastian de. PC4620.C7
   1943, **(v3)**
Covarrubias, Miguel. E98.A7.C63, **(v4)**
   F1219.3.A7.C58, **(v4)**
   F1219.3.A7.C6, **(v4)**
   F1359.C6 1976, **(v4)**
Covell, Charles. KZ2322.C68 1998, **(v7)**
Covello, Vincent T. RA427.3.C68 1993, **(v2)**
Coveney, Peter. PR151.C5.C6, **(v3)**
Cover, Robert M. KF213.C63 1993, **(v7)**
Coverdale, John F. DP219.2.C68 1984, **(v5)**
Covici, Pascal. PS430.C68 1997, **(v3)**
Covington, James W. E99.S28.C73 1993, **(v4)**
Covington, Martin V. LB1065.C65 1992, **(v7)**
Cowan, David. PJ6307.C6, **(v3)**
Cowan, Edward J. DA803.7.A3.C68, **(v5)**
Cowan, Geoffrey. KF224.D28.C68 1993, **(v7)**
Cowan, J. A. QP531.C68 1997, **(v1)**
Cowan, James C. PR6023.A93.Z62317 1990, **(v3)**
Cowan, Nelson. BF444.C68 1995, **(v2)**
Cowan, Ruth Schwartz. T14.5.C69 1997, **(v1)**
   TX23.C64 1983, **(v1)**
Cowan, Sam. TK7868.D5.C68 1985, **(v1)**
Coward, Barry. DA375.C74 1980, **(v5)**
Coward, Harold G. BJ122.C7 1989, **(v8)**
Coward, Joan Wells. F454.C68, **(v4)**
Coward, John M. PN4888.I52.C68 1999, **(v3)**
Coward, L. Andrew. QP376.C68 1990, **(v1)**
Coward, Noel Pierce. PR6005.O85 S7, **(v3)**
Coward, Noel. PR6005.O85 P6, **(v3)**
   PR6005.O85.S58, **(v3)**
   PR6005.O85.T6, **(v3)**
   PR6005.O85.Z5 1937, **(v3)**
   PR6005.O85.Z52, **(v3)**
Cowart, David. PN771.C647 1993, **(v3)**
   PS3566.Y55.Z6, **(v3)**
Cowdrey, Albert E. D807.U6.C685 1994, **(v5)**
Cowell, Frank A. HJ2348.6.C68 1990, **(v6)**
Cowell, Henry. ML60.C85 1996, **(v9)**
Cowen Karp, Regina. UA646.C74 1987, **(v10)**
Cowen, David L. RS61.C69 1988, **(v2)**
Cowen, Richard. QE711.2.C68 1995, **(v1)**
Cowen, Tyler. NX634.C68 1998, **(v9)**
Cowger, Thomas W. E98.T77.C68 1999, **(v4)**
Cowhey, Peter F. HD9560.6.C68 1985, **(v6)**
Cowie, Elizabeth. PN1995.9.W6.C68 1997, **(v3)**
Cowie, Isaac. F1060.9.C87 1993, **(v4)**
Cowie, Jefferson R. HD9696.A3.U5334 1999, **(v6)**
Cowie, Leonard W. Z8667.8.C69 1996, **(v10)**
Cowing, Cedric B. HG4910.C66, **(v6)**
Cowles, Lois A. Fort. HV687.C68 2000, **(v6)**
Cowles, Michael. BF39.C67 1989, **(v2)**
Cowles, Virginia. CS71.A85. 1979, **(v5)**
Cowley, Abraham. PR3370.A5.C35 1989, **(v3)**
   PR3372.C5 1973, **(v3)**
Cowley, John. GT4229.T7.C69 1996, **(v6)**
Cowley, Malcolm. HQ1061.C663 1980, **(v6)**
   PS3505.O956.B6 1968, **(v3)**
   PS3505.O956.Z464 1980, **(v3)**
Cowley, W. H. LA226.C8 1991, **(v7)**
Cowling, Elizabeth. N6758.C68 1990, **(v9)**
Cowling, T. G. QC809.M3.C65, **(v1)**
Cowlishaw, Gillian. HN850.N49.C68 1988, **(v6)**
Cowper, William. PR3380.A2 1980, **(v3)**
   PR3383.A3.K5 1979, **(v3)**
   PR3383.A3.V3, **(v3)**

PR3383.A44 1989, **(v3)**
Cox, Andrew W. HC256.C65 1997, **(v6)**
Cox, Brian. PN2598.C38.A3 1991, **(v3)**
Cox, C. B. PR6005.O4.Z585 1974, **(v3)**
   PR6039.H52.Z615, **(v3)**
   QH84.C65 1980, **(v1)**
Cox, C. Philip. QA276.12.C69 1987, **(v1)**
Cox, Carole B. HV1461.C74 1993, **(v6)**
Cox, David A. QA564.C688 1992, **(v1)**
   QA564.C6883 1998, **(v1)**
Cox, David. DK68.7.G3.C69 1996, **(v5)**
Cox, Don Richard. Z8230.C79 1998, **(v10)**
Cox, Earl. QA76.9.S88C72 1999, **(v1)**
Cox, Elizabeth. Z7963.P64.C69 1997, **(v10)**
Cox, Gary P. UA700.C68 1994, **(v10)**
Cox, Gary W. JF1001.C69 1997, **(v7)**
   JK1429.C69 1993, **(v7)**
Cox, Gary. PG3325.P73.C68 1990, **(v3)**
Cox, George W. SB990.5.U6.C68 1999, **(v1)**
Cox, Harvey Gallagher. BJ1251.F55 C6, **(v8)**
   BR127.C66 1988, **(v8)**
   BX4705.B545.C69 1988, **(v8)**
Cox, Isaac Joslin. F301.C87 1967, **(v4)**
Cox, James L. F341.C68 1995, **(v4)**
Cox, Jeffrey N. PR8477.C69 1998, **(v3)**
Cox, John D. PR3017.C68 1989, **(v3)**
Cox, John K. DR1965.C69 2002, **(v5)**
Cox, LaWanda C. Fenlason. E457.2.C84 1994, **(v4)**
Cox, Lindsay. DU423.P63.C69 1993, **(v5)**
Cox, Michael. E840.C69 1995, **(v4)**
Cox, P. A. QD31.2.C682 1995, **(v1)**
   QD6.C875 1989, **(v1)**
Cox, Peter Alfred. SB413.R47.C628 1993, **(v1)**
Cox, Ralph Merritt. PQ6538.M5.Z62, **(v3)**
Cox, Richard Howard. JC153.L87C6, **(v7)**
Cox, Ronald W. HF1456.5.C4.C69 1994, **(v6)**
Coxall, W. N. DA589.7.C69 1998, **(v5)**
Coxe, Louis Osborne. PS2384.B6.C6 1962, **(v3)**
Coye, Dale F. PR3081.C87 1998, **(v3)**
Coyle, J. D. QD708.2.C69 1986, **(v1)**
Coyle, Jean M. Z7164.O4.C68 1989, **(v10)**
Coyle, Michael. PS3531.O82.Z565 1995, **(v3)**
Coyne, Gary S. QD53.C69 1992, **(v1)**
   QD53.C69 1997, **(v1)**
Coyner, David H. F592.C88 1995, **(v4)**
Cozarinsky, Edgardo. PQ7797.B635.Z663813 1988,
   (v3)
Cozzens, James Gould. PS3503.O99.S8 1967, **(v3)**
   PS3505.O99 A, **(v3)**
   PS3505.O99 B9 1998, **(v3)**
   PS3505.O99 C3, **(v3)**
   PS3505.O99 G8, **(v3)**
   PS3505.O99 J8, **(v3)**
   PS3505.O99.L3, **(v3)**
   PS3505.O99 M4, **(v3)**
   PS3505.O99 S6 1929, **(v3)**
Cozzens, Peter. E467.1.P76.C68 2000, **(v4)**
   E474.77.C69 1990, **(v4)**
   E475.81.C78 1992, **(v4)**
Crabb, Cecil Van Meter. JK585.C73 2000, **(v7)**
Crabbe, George. PR4510.A5.C3 1972, **(v3)**
   PR4511.P6 1986, **(v3)**
   PR4513.C7 1947, **(v3)**
Crabtree, John. F3448.2.C73 1992, **(v4)**
Crabtree, Phillip. ML113.C68 1993, **(v9)**
Crabtree, Robert H. QD411.8.T73, **(v1)**
Crackel, Theodore J. UA25.C73 1987, **(v10)**
Craddock, Patricia B. DG206.G5.C7 1989, **(v5)**
Craft, Anna. LB1062.C73 2000, **(v7)**
Craft, Robert. ML410.S932.C8 1994, **(v9)**
Craft, William. PR2343.C73 1994, **(v3)**
Craft-Fairchild, Catherine. PR858.W6.C73 1993, **(v3)**
Crafton, Donald. PN1993.5.U6.H55 1990 vol. 4, **(v3)**
Crafts, N. F. R. HC254.5.C73 1985, **(v6)**
Cragg, Claudia. HF3820.5.Z5.C7 1993, **(v6)**
Cragg, Kenneth. BR1067.A7 C74 1991, **(v8)**
Craib, Ian. HM22.G8.G5434 1991, **(v6)**
   RC506.C73 1990, **(v2)**
Craig, Albert M. DS895.C5.C7, **(v5)**
Craig, Barbara Hinkson. HQ767.5.U5.C73 1993, **(v6)**
Craig, Cairns. PR8603.C73 1999, **(v3)**

Craig, Campbell. UA23.C67224 1998, **(v10)**
Craig, D. H. PR2285.C7 1985, **(v3)**
Craig, David. MT956.C7 1987, **(v9)**
Craig, Douglas B. JK2317. 1993, **(v7)**
   PN1991.3.U6.C73 2000, **(v3)**
Craig, Edward. B791.C73 1987, **(v8)**
Craig, Edwin C. TK7878.7.C72 1993, **(v1)**
Craig, Gerald M. F1058.C68, **(v4)**
Craig, Gordon Alexander. DD220.C72 1978b, **(v5)**
   DD259.C7 1982, **(v5)**
   PT289.C7313 1995, **(v3)**
Craig, Hardin. PR85.C68, **(v3)**
   PR421.C67 1950, **(v3)**
   PR641.C7, **(v3)**
   PR3071.C7, **(v3)**
Craig, Howard A. UG626.2.C7.A37, **(v10)**
Craig, Lee A. HC240.C68 2000, **(v6)**
   HC241.C73 1997, **(v6)**
   NA4205.C7, **(v9)**
Craig, Mary. DK4382.C73 1987, **(v5)**
Craig, Maurice James. NA982.C72 1983, **(v9)**
Craig, P. P. K3150.C7 1990, **(v7)**
Craig, Robert H. BR115.P7.C689 1992, **(v8)**
Craig, Roy R. TA405.C89 2000, **(v1)**
Craig, Steve. GV17.C73 2002, **(v6)**
Craige, Betty Jean. QH31.O27, **(v1)**
Craigie, William A. PE2116.C7, **(v3)**
   PT7181.C7 1913a, **(v3)**
Craik, D. J. QC753.2.C73 1995, **(v1)**
Crain, Caleb. PS173.M36.C7 2001, **(v3)**
Crain, Edward E. NA791.C73 1994, **(v9)**
Craine, Debra. GV1585.C78 2000, **(v6)**
Crainer, Stuart. HD30.23.C73 1999, **(v6)**
Crainer, Stuart. HD30.3.C725 1998, **(v6)**
Crais, Clifton C. DT1787.C73 1992, **(v5)**
Cralle, Trevor. GV840.S8 C66 2001, **(v6)**
Cramer, Clayton E. E185.18.C73 1997, **(v4)**
Cramer, Friedrich. Q172.5.C45.C713 1993, **(v1)**
Cramer, Jeffrey S. PS3511.R94.Z6115 1996, **(v3)**
Crampton, C. Gregory. E99.Z9.C7, **(v4)**
Crampton, R. J. DR67.C72 1997, **(v5)**
   DR67.C73 1987, **(v5)**
   Z2896.C7 1989, **(v10)**
Cranch, Christopher Pearse. PS1449.C8.Z5 1969,
   (v3)
Crandall, David P. DT1558.H56, **(v5)**
Crandall, George W. Z8976.424.C73 1995, **(v10)**
Crandall, Richard C. E99.E7.C754 2000, **(v4)**
   Z1210.E8, **(v10)**
Crandell, Gina. SB470.5.C73 1993, **(v1)**
Crandon-Malamud, Libbet. F2230.2.A9.C73 1991,
   (v4)
Crane, Conrad C. D790.C69 1993, **(v5)**
Crane, Diana. N72.S6.C73 1987, **(v9)**
Crane, Elaine Forman. F89.N5 C8 1992, **(v4)**
   HQ1438.N35.C73 1998, **(v6)**
Crane, Eva. SF523.C856 1990, **(v1)**
   SF524.C738 1999, **(v1)**
Crane, Hart. PS3505.R272. 1968, **(v3)**
   PS3505.R272.Z48 1997, **(v3)**
   PS3505.R272.Z54 1974, **(v3)**
Crane, Janet. Z1561.M3.C73 1995, **(v10)**
Crane, John O. DB2188.7.C73 1991, **(v5)**
Crane, Jonathan Lake. PN1995.9.H6.C72 1994, **(v3)**
Crane, Milton. PR3087.C7, **(v3)**
Crane, Ralph J. PR830.I6.C73 1992, **(v3)**
Crane, Ronald Salmon. PN81.C8, **(v3)**
Crane, Stephen. PS1449.C85 A15 1967, **(v3)**
   PS1449.C85 A153 1963, **(v3)**
   PS1449.C85 M3, **(v3)**
   PS1449.C85 R3, **(v3)**
   PS1449.C85.S9, **(v3)**
   PS1449.C85.Z48 1988, **(v3)**
   PS1449.C85.Z5, **(v3)**
   PS1449.C85.Z53, **(v3)**
   PS1449.C85.Z54, **(v3)**
Crane, Susan A. DD86.C73 2000, **(v5)**
Crane, Susan. PR1875.R65.C73 1994, **(v3)**
Crane, Walter. PZ8.C8496Be 1982, **(v3)**
Cranin, A. Norman. RK667.I45C7 1999, **(v2)**

Crankshaw, Edward. DB71.C7 1970, **(v5)**
  DB85.C7 1983, **(v5)**
  DD218.C7, **(v5)**
  DK189.C66 1976, **(v5)**
  DK274.C69, **(v5)**
  PR6005.O4.Z59 1963, **(v3)**
Cranmer-Byng, L. PL2658.E3.C7 1978, **(v3)**
Cranor, Carl F. KF3958.C73 1993, **(v7)**
Cranston, Maurice William. PQ2637.A82.Z63 1962, **(v3)**
Cranston, S. L. BP585.B6.C73 1993, **(v8)**
Crapol, Edward P. E664.B6 C83 2000, **(v4)**
Crary, Jonathan. N7430.5.C7 1990, **(v9)**
Craske, Matthew. N6756.C73 1997, **(v9)**
Craske, Michelle Genevieve. RC531.C727 1999, **(v2)**
Craton, Michael. F1656.C72 1992, **(v4)**
Cratty, Bryant J. BF295.C72, **(v2)**
  LB1029.G3.C7 1985, **(v7)**
Craven, Avery Odelle. E338.C92 1957, **(v4)**
  F213.C75, **(v4)**
Craven, David. ND259.R5.C66 1997, **(v9)**
Craven, Kenneth. PR3724.T33.C7 1992, **(v3)**
Craven, Thomas. N6450.C7 1940, **(v9)**
  ND1170.C7 1958, **(v9)**
  NE950.C7, **(v9)**
Craven, Wayne. N6505.C7 1994, **(v9)**
Craven, Wesley Frank. F212.C7, **(v4)**
Cravens, Thomas E. QB529.C7 1997, **(v1)**
Cravey, Altha J. HD6073.O332.M4954 1998, **(v6)**
Craw, R. C. QH84.C678 1999, **(v1)**
Crawford, Donald R. TL671.2.C7 1981, **(v1)**
Crawford, Dorothy H. QR364.C73 2000, **(v1)**
Crawford, Elizabeth. JN979.C73 2001, **(v7)**
Crawford, F. Marion. PS1456.A45, **(v3)**
  PS1456.K3, **(v3)**
Crawford, Fred D. D568.4.L45.A633 1998, **(v5)**
  PR605.W65.C7 1988, **(v3)**
Crawford, Gary William. Z8492.7.C73 1995, **(v10)**
Crawford, Harriet E. W. DS247.B23.C729 1998, **(v5)**
Crawford, James Pyle Wickersham. PQ6104.C7 1937, **(v3)**
Crawford, Lewis F. F636.C89, **(v4)**
Crawford, Lucy. F41.44.C89 1999, **(v4)**
Crawford, Mark. E404.C93 1999, **(v4)**
  QH76.C73 1999, **(v1)**
Crawford, Mary. HQ1206.U49 2000, **(v6)**
Crawford, Michael H. DF12.C7 1983, **(v5)**
Crawford, Richard. ML200.C68 1993, **(v9)**
Crawford, Richard. ML200.C69 2001, **(v9)**
Crawford, Robert M. A. JZ1307.C73 2000, **(v7)**
Crawford, T. Hugh. PS3545.I544.Z5835 1993, **(v3)**
Crawford, Tad. KF390.A96.C734 1998, **(v7)**
Crawford, Thomas. PR4338.C77, **(v3)**
Crawford, William Rex. F1408.3.C7 1961, **(v4)**
Crawford, William Roy. UC333.C73 1988, **(v10)**
Crawford, William. TR330.C68, **(v1)**
Cray, Ed. E745.M37.C73 1990, **(v4)**
Craycraft, Kenneth R. KF4783.C73 1999, **(v7)**
Creamer, Robert W. GV865.R8 C73 1992, **(v6)**
Crease, Robert P. QC789.2.U62.B763 1999, **(v1)**
Creaton, Heather. Z2024.L8.C74 1996, **(v10)**
Crecelius, Kathryn J. PQ2417.C74 1987, **(v3)**
Cree, Edward H. VG228.G7.C733 1982, **(v10)**
Creeber, Glen. PR6066.O77.Z62 1998, **(v3)**
Creech, James. PS2384.P53.C74 1993, **(v3)**
Creech, Sharon. PZ7.C8615Wal 1994, **(v3)**
Creed, Robert Payson. PR1588.C7 1990, **(v3)**
Creegan, Charles L. B3376.W564.C74 1989, **(v8)**
Creel, Herrlee Glessner. B126.C67, **(v8)**
  B126.C7 1975, **(v8)**
  B128.C8.C65 1972, **(v8)**
  DS723.C7 1954, **(v5)**
Creel, Margaret Washington. E445.S7.C74 1988, **(v4)**
Creeley, Robert. PS3505.R43.G6, **(v3)**
Creese, Mary R. S. Q141.C69 1998, **(v1)**
Creeth, Edmund. PR1262.C68, **(v3)**
Creigh, Dorothy Weyer. F666.C83, **(v4)**
Creighton, Donald Grant. F1026.C74 1958, **(v4)**
  F1033.M126.C7 1965, **(v4)**
Creighton, Joanne V. PR6054.R25.Z63 1985, **(v3)**
Creighton, John. DA141.C74 2000, **(v5)**

Creighton, Sarah Hammond. GE310.C74 1998, **(v6)**
Creighton, Thomas E. QH506.C74 1999, **(v1)**
Crellin, J. K. RS164.B324.C74 1990, **(v2)**
  RS164.C83 1997, **(v2)**
Cremer, Lothar. NA2800.C713 1982, **(v9)**
Cremin, Lawrence Arthur. LA212.C73, **(v7)**
  LA216.C73 1988, **(v7)**
Cremony, John Carey. E99.A6 C7 1983, **(v4)**
Crenshaw, James L. LA47.C74 1998, **(v7)**
Crenson, Matthew A. JK686.C74, **(v7)**
Crepeau, Richard C. F319.M5.C74 1988, **(v4)**
Crerar, Duff. D639.C38.C74 1995, **(v5)**
Crespi, Irving. HM261.C695 1997, **(v6)**
Cressey, George Babcock. DS49.7.C7, **(v5)**
  DS710.C73, **(v5)**
Cressman, Luther Sheeleigh. CC115.C74.A3 1988, **(v5)**
Cressman, Robert. D767.99.W3.C74 1995, **(v5)**
  D773.C74 2000, **(v5)**
Cressy, David. DA320.C94 1997, **(v5)**
  F7.C93 1987, **(v4)**
Creswell, John. U39.C74, **(v10)**
Creswell, William H. LB3409.U5 C69 1993, **(v7)**
Crevecoeur. E163.C873, **(v4)**
Crevier, Daniel. Q335.C66 1993, **(v1)**
Crew, David F. HV275.C74 1998, **(v6)**
Crewe, Ivor. JN956.C74 1991, **(v7)**
  JN1129.S58.C74 1995, **(v7)**
Crews, Donald. PZ7.C8682Fr, **(v3)**
Crews, Frederick C. PN56.P92.C7, **(v3)**
  PR6011.O58.Z65 1962, **(v3)**
  PR6025.I65.W65, **(v3)**
Crews, Gordon A. LB3013.3.C74 1997, **(v7)**
Crews, Harry. PS3553.R46.F4, **(v3)**
Crews, Kenneth D. Z649.F35 C74 1993, **(v10)**
Crews, Mickey. BX7032.C662 1990, **(v8)**
Crews, Phillip. QD272.S6.C74 1998, **(v1)**
Cribb, Joe. CJ59.C75 1990, **(v5)**
Cribb, R. B. G2401.S1, **(v6)**
Crichton, Michael. N6537.J6.A4 1977, **(v9)**
Crick, Bernard R. CD1048.U5.C7, **(v5)**
  PR6029.R8.Z627 1980, **(v3)**
Crick, Francis. QH31.C85.A3 1988, **(v1)**
  QH331.C9, **(v1)**
Crimmins, James E. B1574.B34.C75 1990, **(v8)**
Crimmins, Mark. BD215.C825 1992, **(v8)**
Cripps, Thomas. PN1995.9.S6.C73 1997, **(v3)**
Crisp, Brian F. JL3831.C74 2000, **(v7)**
Crisp, C. G. PN1993.5.F7.C78 1993, **(v3)**
Crispin, Edmund. PR6025.O46 L6, **(v3)**
  PR6025.O46 S9, **(v3)**
Critchlow, Donald T. HD9710.U54.S834 1996, **(v6)**
Critchlow, James. DK948.86.C75 1991, **(v5)**
Crites, Stephen. B2949.R3.C73 1998, **(v8)**
Crittenden, Jack. JC571.C698 1992, **(v7)**
Critto, Adolfo. BJ1470.C75 1999, **(v8)**
Croall, Hazel. HV6768.C76 1992, **(v6)**
Croall, Jonathan. PN2598.G45.C76 2001, **(v3)**
Croce, Benedetto. B3614.C74.A5, **(v8)**
  D13.C682 1970, **(v5)**
  D16.9.C7613 1966, **(v5)**
  D359.C73, **(v5)**
  N69.C813, **(v9)**
  PN49.C69 1990, **(v3)**
Crochemore, Maxime. QA76.9.T48.C76 1994, **(v1)**
Crockatt, Richard. E183.8.S65.C75 1995, **(v4)**
Crocker, Lester G. B2016.C68 1966, **(v8)**
Crocker, Matthew H. F73.44.C9 1999, **(v4)**
Crocker, Richard L. ML430.5.C76, **(v9)**
  ML3082.C73 2000, **(v9)**
Crockett, Bryan. PR658.R43.C76 1995, **(v3)**
Crockett, Davy. F436.C9395 1834, **(v4)**
Crockett, James Underwood. SB453.C778, **(v1)**
Crockett, Lawrence J. SB612.A2.C72, **(v1)**
Crockett, Roger A. PT2607.U493.Z59 1998, **(v3)**
Croddy, Eric. Z6724.C5.C76 1997, **(v10)**
Croft, Robert W. PS3570.Y45.Z633 1998, **(v3)**
Crofts, Daniel W. E459.C92 1989, **(v4)**
Crofts, Daniel W. F232.S7.C76 1992, **(v4)**
Croissant, Michael P. DK699.N34.C76 1998, **(v5)**
Croizier, Ralph C. DS724.C7 1970, **(v5)**

Croly, Herbert David. HN64.C89 1965, **(v6)**
Crombie, A. C. Q125.C68 1961, **(v1)**
  Q127.E8.C76 1994, **(v1)**
Crombie, I. M. B395.C72, **(v8)**
Cromer, Mark. RA965.6.C76 1997, **(v2)**
Crompton, Frank. HV8749.G7.C76 1997, **(v6)**
Cromwell, Peter R. QA491.C76 1997, **(v1)**
Cronbach, Lee J. BF176.C76 1990, **(v2)**
Crone, Hugh D. UG447.C76 1992, **(v10)**
Crone, Rainer. N6999.M34.C7 1991, **(v9)**
Cronin, A. J. PR6005.R68.A65, **(v3)**
Cronin, Anthony. PR6029.N56.Z64 1998, **(v3)**
Cronin, Gloria L. PS3503.E4488.Z619 2001, **(v3)**
  Z8467.523.C76 1991, **(v10)**
Cronin, Helena. QL761.C76 1991, **(v1)**
Cronin, Kieran. BJ1275.C76 1992, **(v8)**
Cronin, Nigel J. QC661.C76 1995, **(v1)**
Cronin, Thomas E. JF493.U6.C76 1989, **(v7)**
  JK516.C73 1998, **(v7)**
  JK7816.C76 1993, **(v7)**
Cronin, Vincent. DC203.C9 1972, **(v5)**
Cronk, J.K. QK938.M3C76 2001, **(v1)**
Cronon, William. F548.4.C85 1991, **(v4)**
Cronquist, Arthur. QK495.A1.C76, **(v1)**
  QK495.A56.C7, **(v1)**
Crook, D. P. E469.C76, **(v4)**
Crook, J. Mordaunt. NA975.C7 1987, **(v9)**
Crook, Keith. PR3727.C79 1998, **(v3)**
Crook, Malcolm. JN2959.C76 1996, **(v7)**
Crook, Tim. PN1991.65.C66 1999, **(v3)**
Crook, W. H. E661.C94, **(v4)**
Crooks, James B. F319.J1.C76 1991, **(v4)**
Cropper, William H. QC174.1.C7, **(v1)**
Cros, Charles. PQ2211.C65 1970, **(v3)**
Crosby, Alfred W. D202.C76 1997, **(v5)**
Crosby, Donald A. B828.3.C76 1988, **(v8)**
  BD581.C76 2002, **(v8)**
Crosby, Donald G. RA1226.C76 1998, **(v2)**
Crosby, Everett Uberto. Z5579.5.C76 1983, **(v10)**
  Z6725.E8, **(v10)**
Crosby, Janice C. PS374.F27.C76 2000, **(v3)**
Crosby, Travis L. DA563.4.C76 1997, **(v5)**
Crosland, Margaret. PQ149.C7, **(v3)**
  PQ2605.O15.Z66 1956, **(v3)**
Crosman, Robert. PR3562.C68, **(v3)**
Cross, Anthony Glenn. DK34.B7.C76 1997, **(v5)**
Cross, Barbara M. HQ1412.C7, **(v6)**
Cross, David A. ND1329.R65.C76 2000, **(v9)**
Cross, Frank B. KF3803.C3.C76 1989, **(v7)**
Cross, Frank Moore. BS1171.2.C77 1998, **(v8)**
Cross, Gary S. GV14.45.C76 1990, **(v6)**
  HC110.C6 C76 2000, **(v6)**
Cross, James Eliot. U240.C8, **(v10)**
Cross, Jonathan. ML410.B605.C76 2000, **(v9)**
  ML410.S932.C87 1998, **(v9)**
Cross, K. Patricia. LC5219.C744, **(v7)**
Cross, Mary. PS2128.C76 1992, **(v3)**
Cross, Tom Peete. PB1421.C76 1969, **(v3)**
Cross, Toni M. DS51.A6, **(v5)**
Cross, Wilbur. HF1001.C68 1995, **(v6)**
Crossan, John Dominic. BT301.2.C76 1991, **(v8)**
  BT301.2.C77 1994, **(v8)**
  BT306.C76 1983, **(v8)**
  BT431.5.C76 1995, **(v8)**
Crosset, Todd W. GV966.C76 1995, **(v6)**
Crossick, Geoffrey. HT690.E73.C7613 1995, **(v6)**
Crossley, David W. DA90.C93 1990, **(v5)**
Crossley, Pamela Kyle. DS731.M35.C76 1990, **(v5)**
  DS754.17.C76 1999, **(v5)**
Crossman, Virginia. DA950.C76 1996, **(v5)**
Crosswhite, James. BC177.C765 1996, **(v8)**
Croswell, Ken. QB820.C76 1997, **(v1)**
Crotty, William J. JK521.C76 1985, **(v7)**
Crouch, Ben M. HV9475.T4.C76 1989, **(v6)**
Crouch, Colin. HN373.5.C78 1999, **(v6)**
Crouch, Harold A. JQ712.C76 1996, **(v7)**
Crouch, Margaret A. HQ1237.C76 2001, **(v6)**
Crouse, William Harry. TL152.C692, **(v1)**
Crouzel, Henri. BR1720.O7.C7613 1989, **(v8)**
Crouzet, Francois. HC240.C763 2001, **(v6)**
  HC255.C7313 1982, **(v6)**

Crow, Garrett E. QK117.C84 2000, (v1)
Crow, John Armstrong. DP48.C8 1975, (v5)
  F1216.C7, (v4)
Crow, Thomas E. N6846.5.N4.C76 1995, (v9)
Crowder, Michael. DT791.C76 1988, (v5)
Crowe, David. DX241.C76 1995, (v5)
Crowe, Michael J. QB54.C76 1986, (v1)
Crowe, Norman. NA2542.35.C77 1995, (v9)
Crowell, Aron. F914.T49.C76 1997, (v4)
Crowell, Norton B. PR4043.C7, (v3)
  PR4242.P4.C7, (v3)
Crowl, Daniel A. TP150.S24C76 2002, (v1)
  TP155.5.C76 1990, (v1)
Crowl, Samuel. PR3093.C76 1992, (v3)
Crowley, Brian Lee. JC571.C73 1987, (v7)
Crowley, F. K. DU115.2.F67, (v5)
Crowley, John E. GT481.U6, (v6)
Crowley, John William. PS2033.C74 1999, (v3)
Crowley, Joseph M. QC571.C76 1986, (v1)
Crowley, Leonard V. RB112.C76 2001, (v2)
Crowley, Sharon. PE1405.U6.C76 1998, (v3)
Crowley, Walt. F899.S45.C76 1995, (v4)
Crowther, J. G. B1198.C7, (v8)
Crozier, Andrew J. JV2018.C76 1988, (v7)
Crozier, Brian. D842.C7 1963, (v5)
Crozier, Brian. DS778.C55.C7, (v5)
Cruickshank, Charles Greig. D767.C75 1983, (v5)
  UA649.C75 1968, (v10)
Cruickshank, Dan. DA485.C78 1990, (v5)
Cruickshank, John. PQ103.C7, (v3)
Cruikshank, Jeffrey L. N8835.C78 1988, (v9)
Cruikshank, Julie. E99.T92.C78 1990, (v4)
Cruikshank, Margaret. HQ76.8.U5.C78 1992, (v6)
Cruise, James. PR858.C25.C78 1999, (v3)
Crum, Alison. MT338.C93 1989, (v9)
Crum, Steven J. E99.S4.C78 1994, (v4)
Crumb, Lawrence N. Z7845.O83.C78 1988, (v10)
Crumbine, Samuel Jay. R154.C83.A3, (v2)
Crumbley, Paul. PS1541.Z5.C75 1997, (v3)
Crummell, Alexander. E185.97.C87.A25 1992, (v4)
Crump, Andy. GE10.C78 1993, (v6)
Crump, Charles G. D113.5.C7 1943, (v5)
Crump, Galbraith M. PR3562.C7, (v3)
Crump, Irving. V437.C73, (v10)
Crump, Irving. VK525.U6.C7, (v10)
Crump. J. I. DS747.2.C725 1998, (v5)
Crunden, Robert Morse. E169.1.C8358 1994, (v4)
  E661.C945 1982, (v4)
  NX503.7.C78 1993, (v9)
  NX504.C78 2000, (v9)
Cruse, Amy. PR461.C7, (v3)
Cruse, Harold. E185.82.C74, (v4)
Crusius, Timothy W. BD241.C76 1991, (v8)
Cruttwell, Charles Robert Mowbray Fraser. D521.C7
  1936, (v5)
Cruttwell, Patrick. PS3553.R75.M3 1962, (v3)
Cruz, Anne J. PQ6147.P5.C78 1999, (v3)
Crystal, David. PE1072.C68 1995, (v3)
  PE2751.C79 1997, (v3)
Csaba, Laszlo. HC243.5.C7513 1990, (v6)
Csanadi, Maria. DB956.C7913 1997, (v5)
Csikszentmihalyi, Mihaly. BF575.H27.C848 1997, (v2)
  BF701.C676 1993, (v2)
Cua, A. S. BJ117.C83 1998, (v8)
Cuadra, Angel. PQ7389.C84.A6 1994, (v3)
Cuadra, Pablo Antonio. PQ7519.C8.A28 1988, (v3)
Cuban, Larry. LA216.C82 1984, (v7)
  LB1028.3.C8 1986, (v7)
Cubberley, Ellwood Patterson. LA205.C82 1970, (v7)
Cubitt, Gerald S. QH186.C83 1992, (v1)
Cubitt, Sean. PN1992.935.C84 1990, (v3)
  PN1992.935.C85 1993, (v3)
Cudahy, Brian J. HE5784.N5.C84 1990, (v6)
  TF725.N5.C8, (v1)
Cuddon, J. A. PN41.C83 1998, (v3)
  PR6053.U3.A3, (v3)
Cuddy, Lois A. PS3509.L43.Z658 2000, (v3)
Cuero, Delfina. E99.D5 C84 1991, (v4)
Cuevas, Bryan J. BQ4490.K373 C83 2002, (v8)
Cuevas, Tomasa. HV9742.5.C84.A313 1998, (v6)
Cuff, Dana. NA1996.C84 1991, (v9)

Cuff, David J. TJ163.25.U6.C83 1986, (v1)
Cuffaro, Harriet K. LB1139.23.C84 1995, (v7)
Culbertson, Evelyn Davis. ML410.F228.C8 1992, (v9)
Culbertson, Margaret. NA7207.C85 1994, (v9)
  NA7235.T4.C85 1999, (v9)
Culbertson, Philip Leroy. BT375.2.C85 1995, (v8)
Culhane, John. GV1803.C85 1990, (v6)
Cullather, Nick. F1466.5.A688.C85 1999, (v4)
Cullen, Countee. PS3505.U287.B6 1929, (v3)
  PS3505.U287.C65 1927, (v3)
Cullen, Daniel E. JC179.R9.C85 1993, (v7)
Cullen, Dolores L. PR1875.A44.C85 2000, (v3)
Cullen, Jim. E161.C85 1996, (v4)
Cullen, L. M. HF3508.G3.C8, (v6)
Cullen, Patrick. PR2359.C8, (v3)
Cullen-DuPont, Kathryn. HQ1410.C85 2000, (v6)
Culler, A. Dwight. PR4024.C8, (v3)
  PR5588.C8, (v3)
Culler, Jonathan D. PN98.D43.C8 1982, (v3)
  PN98.S7.C8, (v3)
Cullick, Jonathan S. PS3545.A748.Z662 2000, (v3)
Cullingford, Elizabeth. PR5908.L65.C85 1993, (v3)
Cullmann, Oscar. BV6.C8413 1978, (v8)
Culpitt, Ian. HV31.C85 1992, (v6)
Culver, John C. E748.W23 C85 2000, (v4)
Cumberland, Charles C. F1234.C976, (v4)
Cumbler, John T. HD8085.L963.C85, (v6)
Cumings, Bruce. DS518.8.C76 1999, (v5)
  DS917.C86 1997, (v5)
Cumming, Elizabeth Wells Randall. F826.C96.A34,
  (v4)
Cumming, Kate. E625.C58 1998, (v4)
Cumming, William Patterson. GA405.C8, (v6)
Cummings, Abbott Lowell. NA730.M4.C85, (v9)
Cummings, E. E. D570.9.C82 1970, (v5)
  PS3505.U334.A16 1965, (v3)
  PS3505.U334.A17 1991, (v3)
  PS3505.U334.N5, (v3)
  PS3505.U334.Z53, (v3)
Cummings, Paul. N6512.C854 1994, (v9)
  N6536.C8, (v9)
Cummings, Ronald G. HB846.5.C86 1986, (v6)
Cummings, Scott. F394.F7.C86 1998, (v4)
Cummings, Sherwood. PS1342.S3.C86 1988, (v3)
Cummins, Elizabeth. PS3562.E42.Z6 1990, (v3)
Cummins, Eric. HV9475.C3.C83 1994, (v6)
Cummins, John G. SK183.C86 1988, (v1)
Cummins, Maria S. PS1474.C5.L3 1988, (v3)
Cumpiano, William R. ML1015.G9.C85 1987, (v9)
Cuneo, Pia F. N6888.B6957 C86 1998, (v9)
Cunha, Celso Ferreira da. PC5067.3.C8 1976, (v3)
Cunha, Euclydes da. F2537.C9752, (v4)
Cunha, George Daniel Martin. Z701.C782, (v10)
Cunico, Robert L. QP519.9.H53.C86 1998, (v1)
Cunliffe, Barry W. DA670.W48.C86 1993, (v5)
  GN780.22.G7.C86 1991, (v6)
  HF377.C86 1988, (v6)
Cunliffe, John William. PR461.C83 1963, (v3)
Cunliffe, Marcus Falkner. E301.C85, (v4)
Cunliffe, Marcus. E301.C86, (v4)
  E312.C88, (v4)
Cunliffe, W. Gordon. PT2613.R338.Z6, (v3)
Cunningham, Alfred Austell. UG406.2.C86.A35, (v10)
Cunningham, Andrew. D231.C86 2000, (v5)
Cunningham, Anne S. NA8360.C86 2000, (v9)
Cunningham, Bernadette. DA908.7.K43, (v5)
Cunningham, Eldon L. NE508.C86 1992, (v9)
Cunningham, Frank R. PN1998.3.L86.C8 1991, (v3)
Cunningham, Graham. BL41.C86 1999, (v8)
Cunningham, J. Barton. H62.C813 1993, (v6)
Cunningham, J. V. PS3505.U435.A16 1976, (v3)
Cunningham, John T. F137.C94, (v4)
Cunningham, Keith. E78.S7.C84 1992, (v4)
Cunningham, Lawrence J. DU645.C86 1992, (v5)
Cunningham, Lawrence. BX4662.C86 1980, (v8)
  BX4705.M542.C86 1999, (v8)
Cunningham, Merle. SF61.A3 2001, (v1)
Cunningham, Michael J. DA990.U46.C86 1991, (v5)
Cunningham, Noble E. E176.1.C97 1991, (v4)
  E310.C86 2000, (v4)
  E332.C95 1987, (v4)

E371.C86 1996, (v4)
Cunningham, Philip J. PL696.C86 1995, (v3)
Cunningham, Richard B. BX5199.L53.C8, (v8)
Cunningham, Robert. HN766.A8.C86 1993, (v6)
  ML134.R12.C86 2001, (v9)
Cunningham, Valentine. PR478.S57.C86 1988, (v3)
Cunningham, Valentine. PR878.D57.C8, (v3)
Cunnington, C. Willett. GT730.C86 1968, (v6)
Cuomo, S. QA22.C86 2000, (v1)
Cupach, William R. HM132.C86 1994, (v6)
Cuppage, Francis E. RC627.S36.C87 1994, (v2)
Curie, Eve. QD22.C8.C85 1937, (v1)
Curl, James Stevens. NA997.R6.C87 1983, (v9)
Curley, Daniel. PS3553.U65.L6, (v3)
Curley, E. M. B1878.S55.C87, (v8)
Curley, Michael J. DA140.G49.C87 1994, (v5)
Curley, Thomas M. KD621.C48.C87 1998, (v7)
Curme, George Oliver. PE1105.C77, (v3)
  PE1105.G7 vol. 2, (v3)
  PE1105.G7 vol. 3, (v3)
Curnow, Allen. PR9657.C8, (v3)
Curnutt, Kirk. PS374.S5.C85 1997, (v3)
Curran, Charles E. BJ1249.C8173 1996, (v8)
  BJ1249.C83 1988, (v8)
  BX1753.C86 1982, (v8)
Curran, Daniel. PN1993.5.U6.C87 1998, (v3)
Curran, David K. HV6546.C87 1987, (v6)
Curran, Jim. GV199.44.P18.C87 1995, (v6)
Curren, Randall R. LB85.A7, (v7)
Current, Richard Nelson. E668.C985 1988, (v4)
  F209.5.C87 1983, (v4)
  F581.C87, (v4)
  GV1785.F8.C87 1997, (v6)
Current-Garcia, Eugene. PS648.S5.A55 1952, (v3)
Currie, Bob. HC440.P6.C87 2000, (v6)
Currie, David P. KF4541.C834 1997, (v7)
  KF4550.C873 1990, (v7)
Currie, Elliott. HV9104.C85 1992, (v6)
Currie, J. M. HD1510.C87, (v6)
Currie, Mark. PN212.C87 1998, (v3)
Currie, Philip J. QE862.D5.C862 1997, (v1)
Currie, W. Scott. TK5105.7.C87 1988, (v1)
Curry, Anne. DC96.C87 1993, (v5)
Curry, Constance. F347.S9.C87 1995, (v4)
Curry, David Park. N6537.W4.A4 1984, (v9)
Curry, Jane Kathleen. PN2291.C87 1994, (v3)
Curry, Jane. PS1949.H5.Z6 1996, (v3)
Curry, Leonard P. JS319.C87 1997, (v7)
Curry, Renee R. PS173.W46.C87 2000, (v3)
Curry, Richard Orr. E536.C8, (v4)
Curry, Roy Watson. DS518.8.C8 1968, (v5)
Curry, Walter Clyde. PR1933.S3.C8 1960, (v3)
Curson, Jon. QL696.P2438.C87 1994b, (v1)
Curti, Lidia. PN3401.C87 1998, (v3)
Curti, Merle Eugene. E169.1.C87 1982, (v4)
  E169.1.C877, (v4)
Curtin, Deane W. GE42.C87 1999, (v6)
Curtin, Mary Ellen. HV8929.A22.C87 2000, (v6)
Curtin, Michael. PN1992.8.D6.C87 1995, (v3)
Curtin, Philip D. HC503.W4 C87, (v6)
  HN223.C8 1968, (v6)
  RC961.C87 1989, (v2)
  RC971.C87 1998, (v2)
Curtis, Christopher Paul. PZ7.C94137Bu 1999, (v3)
  PZ7.C94137Wat 1995, (v3)
Curtis, Edward E. E267.C95 1969, (v4)
Curtis, Edward S. E77.C97, (v4)
Curtis, George William. PS1485.A1 1969, (v3)
  PS1493.A3 1971, (v3)
Curtis, James C. E386.C93, (v4)
Curtis, James L. R695.C86 1971, (v2)
Curtis, James. TR820.5.C87 1989, (v1)
Curtis, Jean Louis. PQ2605.U55.F6, (v3)
Curtis, Kimberley. JC251.A74.C87 1999, (v7)
Curtis, Michael Kent. KF4772.C87 2000, (v7)
Curtis, Nancy C. E159.C95 1996, (v4)
Curtis, Philip C. ND237.C884.A4 1999, (v9)
Curtis, Stanley James. LA631.C8 1971, (v7)
Curtis, Susan. ML410.J75.C87 1994, (v9)
Curtis, Susan. PN2270.A35.C87 1998, (v3)

Curtis, William J. R. NA680.C87 1996, (v9)
  NA1510.D67.C87 1988, (v9)
Curtius, Ernst Robert. PN674.C82, (v3)
Curtler, Hugh Mercer. BJ1012.C87 1993, (v8)
  PN98.P67.C88 1997, (v3)
Curwen, E. Cecil. S419.C82, (v1)
Curwood, James Oliver. PS3505.U92 A4, (v3)
  PS3505.U92 N64 1926, (v3)
  PS3505.U92 V4, (v3)
Curzon, Robert. DS48.C97x 1983, (v5)
Cusack, Odean. RM931.A65.C88 1984, (v2)
Cuscuna, Michael. ML156.4.J3.C87 2001, (v9)
Cushing, Frank Hamilton. E99.Z9.C88 1990, (v4)
Cushing, Harvey. R489.O7.C8 1940, (v2)
Cushing, Steven. TL509.C87 1994, (v1)
Cushman, Karen. PZ7.C962Cat 1994, (v3)
  PZ7.C962Mi 1995, (v3)
Cushman, Philip. RC443.C84 1995, (v2)
Cusine, Douglas J. KD3415.C87 1988, (v7)
Cussler, E. L. TP149.C85 2001, (v1)
  TP156.D47.C878 1997, (v1)
Cust, Richard. HJ1012.C87 1987, (v6)
Custen, George Frederick. PN1995.9.B55.C87 1992,
  (v3)
Custer, Elizabeth Bacon. E467.1.C99 C78 1996, (v4)
  F594.C983 1994, (v4)
Custer, George Armstrong. F594.C97 1969, (v4)
Cutler, Brian L. KF9672.C87 1995, (v7)
Cutler, Carl C. VK23.C8 1960, (v10)
Cutler, Charles L. PE3102.I55.C88 1994, (v3)
Cutler, Evan Karl. HV1431.C88 1994, (v6)
Cutler, G. Ripley. D630.C8.A36, (v5)
Cutler, Irving. F548.9.J5.C87 1996, (v4)
Cutler, John. TL671.6.C88 1999, (v1)
Cutler, William W. LC225.33.G7P36 1993, (v7)
Cutlip, Michael B. TP168.C88 1999, (v1)
Cutrer, Thomas W. F391.M128.C87 1993, (v4)
Cutright, Paul Russell. E757.C985 1985, (v4)
Cutter, Donald C. F851.5.C93 1991, (v4)
Cutter, Donald C. F864.C95 1990, (v4)
Cutting-Gray, Joanne. PR3316.A4.Z586 1992, (v3)
Cuvalo, Ante. DR1675.5.C88 1997, (v5)
Cuyas, Arturo. PC4640.C8 1972, (v3)
Cuyler, Louise Elvira. ML1255.C9 1995, (v9)
Cuzzort, Raymond Paul. U263.C89 1989, (v10)
Cvetkovich, Ann. PR878.F45.C85 1992, (v3)
Cybriwsky, Roman A. DS896.35.C93 1998, (v5)
Cynewulf. PR1647.A3.G7, (v3)
Cyr, Arthur I. E840.C9 1999, (v4)
  UA646.C97 1987, (v10)
Cyr, Mary. ML457.C9 1992, (v9)
Cyrano de Bergerac. PQ1793.A1 1977, (v3)
  PQ1793.A2.E5 1965, (v3)
Cyriax, Oliver. HV6017.C97 1996, (v6)
Cysarz, Herbert. PT1165.C87 1964, (v3)
Cytryn, Leon. RJ506.D4.C97 1996, (v2)
Czech, Danuta. D805.P7.C8713 1989, (v5)
Czerniakow, Adam. DS135.P62.W2613 (v5)
Czernis, Loretta. F1027.C94 1994, (v4)
Czigany, Lorant. PH3012.C94 1984, (v3)
Cziko, Gary. HM1033.C95 2000, (v6)
Czitrom, Daniel J. HN90.M3.C96 1982, (v6)
Da Cunha, Derek. VA573.D33 1990, (v10)
Da Graca, John V. JF37.D3 1985, (v7)
Da Ponte, Lorenzo. ML423.D15 A3 2000, (v9)
Daalder, Ivo H. DR2087.D33 2000, (v5)
Dabbs, Thomas. PR2674.D33 1991, (v3)
Dabney, Virginius. E332.2.D3 1990, (v4)
Dabrowski, Magdalena. N6999.R62.A4 1998, (v9)
Dacal Moure, Ramon. F1619.2.T3.D33 1996, (v4)
D'Acci, Julie. PN1992.77.C24.D33 1994, (v3)
Dacey, John S. BF713.D33 1994, (v2)
Daddario, Gina. GV742.3.D33 1998, (v6)
Dadlez, E M. PN49.D23 1997, (v3)
Dadrian, Vahakn N. DS195.5.D337 1998, (v5)
Daemmrich, Horst S. PT2361.Z5.D28 1973, (v3)
Daffa`, `Ali `Abd Allah. QA23.D33 1977, (v1)
Dagan, Avigdor. PJ5054.D2195.L4813 1989, (v3)
Dagher, Carole. DS87.54.D34 2000, (v5)
D'Agostino, Annette M. PN2287.L5.D34 1994, (v3)
D'Agostino, Anthony. DK288.D34 1998, (v5)

Dahl, Henry S. K52.S6 D33 1999, (v7)
Dahl, Jens. E99.E7.D32 2000, (v4)
Dahl, Karin L. LB1576.D12 1998, (v7)
Dahl, Linda. ML417.W515.D34 1999, (v9)
Dahl, Nils Alstrup. BT198.D25 1991, (v8)
Dahl, Per F. QC611.92.D34 1992, (v1)
Dahl, Per F. QC793.5.E62.D34 1997, (v1)
Dahl, Roald. PR6054.A35 A153, (v3)
  PZ7.D1515Ch, (v3)
Dahl, Robert Alan. JC423.D2478 1989, (v7)
  JC423.D2497 1998, (v7)
  JC423.D25, (v7)
  JK31.D33 1981, (v7)
Dahlberg, Arthur. HB501.D3, (v6)
Dahlberg, Edward. PR473.D22, (v3)
Dahlhaus, Carl. ML60.D158 1987, (v9)
  ML196.D2513 1989, (v9)
  ML410.B4.D213 1991, (v9)
  ML410.W13.D153, (v9)
  ML3797.D2313 1983, (v9)
  ML3811.D3913 1990, (v9)
  ML3845.D2913 1982, (v9)
  ML3854.D3413 1989, (v9)
Dahlstrom, W. Grant. RC469.D3, (v2)
Dahmus, Joseph Henry. CB351.D24 1984, (v5)
Dahrendorf, Ralf. H67.L9.D33 1995, (v6)
Dahrendorf, Ralf. HM51.D25, (v6)
Dai, Zhen. PL2474.Z7T313 1990, (v3)
Daiber, Franklin C. QL114.D34, (v1)
Daiber, Hans. Z7128.I57 D53 1999, (v10)
Daiches, David. PR83.D29 1970, (v3)
  PR83.D3 1938, (v3)
  PR99.D25, (v3)
  PR471.D3, (v3)
  PR601.D25, (v3)
  PR1175.D2, (v3)
  PR4331.D25 1967, (v3)
  PR5496.D3, (v3)
  PR6045.O72.Z58, (v3)
Daileader, Celia R. PR658.W6.D35 1998, (v3)
Dailey, Nancy. HQ1063.2.U6.D35 1998, (v6)
Dainotto, Roberto M. PR878.P525.D35 2000, (v3)
Daix, Pierre. N6853.P5.D2613 1994, (v9)
Dakers, Caroline. N72.S6.D34 1999, (v9)
Dakin, Nick. SF457.1.D35 1992, (v1)
Dakin, Theodora P. R692.D34 1992, (v2)
Dal Co, Francesco. NA737.G44.D35 1998, (v9)
Dalal-Clayton, D. Barry. S411.D245 1985, (v1)
Dalby, Andrew. D371.D35 1998, (v5)
Dalby, Andrew. TX406.D35 2000, (v1)
  Z3221.D35 1993, (v10)
Dalby, Liza Crihfield. GT1560.D35 1993, (v6)
Dalby, Simon. E872.D35 1990, (v4)
Dale, Alan S. PN1995.9.C55.D35 2000, (v3)
Dale, Alzina Stone. PR4453.C4.Z588 1982, (v3)
Dale, Delbert A. MT440.D34 1985, (v9)
Dale, Edward Everett. F596.D25 1965, (v4)
  F596.D26, (v4)
  F694.D128, (v4)
Dale, Peter Allan. PR468.S34.D35 1989, (v3)
Dale, Stephen Frederic. HF3788.E83.D35 1994, (v6)
Daleiden, Joseph L. BJ57.D35 1998, (v8)
Dales, Richard C. CB351.D27 1992, (v5)
Daleski, H. M. PR4757.L65.D35 1997, (v3)
  PR6023.A93.Z6235, (v3)
Daley, Daryl J. RA652.2.M3.D34 1999, (v2)
Dalfiume, Richard M. E185.63.D3, (v4)
Dalgarno, Emily. PR6045.O72.Z5815 2001, (v3)
Dali, Salvador. ND813.D3.A4 2000, (v9)
  ND813.D3.D4413, (v9)
Dalin, Per. LB2805.D14 1993, (v7)
Dallas, Roland. DS154.55.D32 1999, (v5)
Dallas, Sandra. F777.D28 1986, (v4)
  F784.D4 D27, (v4)
Dalle Vacche, Angela. PN1993.5.I88.D35 1991, (v3)
  PN1995.25.D36 1996, (v3)
Dallek, Matthew. F866.2.D35 2000, (v4)
Dallek, Robert. E806.D33, (v4)
  E847.D25 1991, (v4)
  E847.D26 1998, (v4)
  E877.D34 1999, (v4)

Dallimore, William. QK495.C75.D3 1967, (v1)
Dallin, Alexander. DK63.3.D32, (v5)
  DK274.D28, (v5)
Dallin, David J. DK63.3.D33, (v5)
  DS518.7.D3 1971, (v5)
Dallman, Peter R. QK938.M45.D35 1998, (v1)
Dallmayr, Fred R. BD175.5.M84 D33 1998, (v8)
  BD175.5.M84.D35 1996, (v8)
Dally, Ann G. HQ759.D248 1983, (v6)
Dally, James W. TA407.D32 1991, (v1)
Dalmage, Heather M. HQ1031.D34 2000, (v6)
DalMolin, Eliane Francoise. PQ2191.Z5.D23 2000,
  (v3)
Dalrymple, G. Brent. QE508.D28 1991, (v1)
Dalrymple, Larry. E78.C15.D18 2000, (v4)
Dalsimer, Adele. PR6029.B65.Z64 1989, (v3)
Dalton, David. MT280.D34 1988, (v9)
Dalton, Dennis. DS481.G3.D215 1993, (v5)
Dalton, Paul. DA670.Y4.D35 1994, (v5)
D'Altroy, Terence N. F3429.3.P65.D35 1992, (v4)
Dalven, Richard. QC176.D24, (v1)
Daly, Ann. GV1785.D8.D35 1995, (v9)
Daly, Augustin. PS1499.D85.A6 1984, (v3)
Daly, Brenda O. PS3565.A8.Z635 1996, (v3)
Daly, Herman E. HD75.6.D35 1994, (v6)
Daly, Jonathan W. HV8224.D29 1998, (v6)
Daly, Kathleen. HV9956.N48.D35 1994, (v6)
Daly, M. W. DT156.6.D35 1997, (v5)
  DT156.7.D35 1990, (v5)
Daly, Martin. DU880.D35 1999, (v5)
Daly, Mary. BV639.W7.D28, (v8)
  HQ1154.D314 1984, (v6)
  HQ1154.D3 1985, (v6)
  HQ1394.D28 1985, (v6)
Daly, Nicholas. PR878.P68.D35 1999, (v3)
Daly, Saralyn R. PR9639.3.M258.Z635 1965, (v3)
Dalzell, Robert F. E312.5.D24 1998, (v4)
  HD9858.L9.D35 1987, (v6)
Dalziel, Margaret. PR871.D3, (v3)
Damanpour, Faramarz. HG2491.D36 1990, (v6)
Damas, David. DU568.P55.D35 1994, (v5)
Damaz, Paul F. NA702.D3, (v9)
D'Ambrosio, Vinnie-Marie. PS3509.L43.Z66186 1989,
  (v3)
Damerell, Reginald G. LB1811.D35 1985, (v7)
Dames, Nicholas. PR868.A49, (v3)
D'Amico, Diane. PR5238.D35 1999, (v3)
D'Amico, Jack. PR658.M87.D36 1991, (v3)
  PR3069.I8, (v3)
D'Amico, Robert. B804.D28 1998, (v8)
Damodaran, Vinita. DS485.B51.D26 1992, (v5)
Damon, Frederick H. DU740.42.D36 1990, (v5)
Damon, S. Foster. PR4146.A24 1988, (v3)
Damon-Moore, Helen. PN4879.D36 1994, (v3)
Damp, Dennis V. HE6499.D18 2000, (v6)
Dampier, William Cecil Dampier. Q125.D17 1966, (v1)
Damrosch, Leopold. PR858.P8.D3 1985, (v3)
  PR3634.D36 1987, (v3)
Dams, Bernd H. NA8450.D35 1995, (v9)
Dana, Julian. F865.S948 1972, (v4)
Dana, Leo Paul. HC415.15.D36 2000, (v6)
Dana, Richard Henry. E415.9.D15.A15, (v4)
  G540.D2 2001, (v4)
Danahay, Martin A. PR778.A9.D34 1993, (v3)
Danbom, David B. E179.D25 1995, (v4)
Danby, John F. PR2819.D33, (v3)
Dance, Stanley. ML385.D26, (v9)
Danchin, Sebastian. ML420.K473.D36 1998, (v9)
Dancy, Jonathan. BJ1012.D263 1993, (v8)
Dandekar, Vinayak Mahadev. HC435.2.D2927 1994,
  (v6)
Dandeker, Christopher. HN49.P6.D36 1990, (v6)
Dandin. PK3794.D4.D3, (v3)
D'Andrade, Roy G. GN502.D36 1995, (v6)
Dane, Barbara O. RC455.4.L67.D36 1992, (v2)
Dane, Clemence. PR6001.S5.B7, (v3)
  PR6001.S5.L4, (v3)
  PR6001.S5.R4, (v3)
Dane, Joseph A. PR1939.D36 1998, (v3)
Danel, Adam D. B785.M24.D36 1997, (v8)
Danese, Tracy E. F316.B19.D36 2000, (v4)

Daneshvar, Simin. PK6561.D262.A25 1989, (v3)
  PK6561.D263.S213 1990, (v3)
Danesi, Marcel. GV1493.D334 1997, (v6)
  GV1493.D337 2002, (v6)
  P87.5.D36 2000, (v3)
Danford, John W. B1499.R4.D35 1990, (v8)
Danforth, Loring M. DR2173.D36 1995, (v5)
Danfulani, S. A. UA855.D36 2001, (v10)
Dangarembga, Tsitsi. PR9390.9.D36.N47 1989, (v3)
Dangerfield, George. DA576.D3 1997, (v5)
  DA962.D27, (v5)
  E338.D3, (v4)
  E371.D3 1986, (v4)
Dangerfield, Stanley. SF422.D28 1974, (v1)
Dangler, Jamie Faricellia. HD6073.E372.U653 1994, (v6)
Dangor, Achmat. PR9369.3.D26.K33 1999, (v3)
Danhof, Clarence H. S441.D3, (v1)
Daniel, Elton L. DS272.D36 2001, (v5)
Daniel, Glyn Edmund. CC100.D27 1975, (v5)
  GN720.D32 1988, (v6)
Daniel, Malcolm R. TR680.D25 1998, (v1)
Daniel, Norman. CB353.D26, (v5)
Daniel, Oliver. ML422.S76 D3 1982, (v9)
Daniel, Pete. F216.2.D36 2000, (v4)
Daniel, Samuel. PR2241.A14 1963, (v3)
Daniel, Thomas M. RC310.D36 2000, (v2)
  RC311.D25 1997, (v2)
Daniel, W. W. HD8391.D3535 1987, (v6)
Daniel, Yvonne. GV1796.R8 D36 1995, (v6)
Daniell, Jere R. F37.D25 1981, (v4)
  F37.D26, (v4)
Daniells, Lorna M. Z7164.C81.D16 1993, (v10)
Daniels, Arlene Kaplan. HV40.42.D36 1988, (v6)
Daniels, Charlotte. PQ648.D27 2000, (v3)
Daniels, Cynthia R. KF481.D36 1993, (v7)
Daniels, David. ML128.O5 D3 1996, (v9)
Daniels, Douglas Henry. F869.S39.N43, (v4)
  ML419.Y7 D36 2002, (v9)
Daniels, F. J. PL537.D3, (v3)
Daniels, George H. Q127.U6.D33, (v1)
Daniels, Harvey. PE2808.D3 1983, (v3)
Daniels, Josephus. E766.D3 1974, (v4)
Daniels, Marilyn. HV2474.D25 2001, (v6)
Daniels, Mark Ross. JK468.P64.D36 1997, (v7)
Daniels, Pamela. HQ755.83.D36 1982, (v6)
Daniels, Raymond Bryant. GB406.D26 1992, (v6)
Daniels, Rebecca. PN2053.D36 1996, (v3)
Daniels, Robert Vincent. DK265.D27, (v5)
Daniels, Roger. E173.C15 vol. 71, 1977.870.J3, (v4)
  E184.A1.D26 1990, (v4)
  E184.O6.D36 1988, (v4)
Daniels, Stephen. N8214.5.G7.D36 1993, (v9)
  SB470.R4.D35 1999, (v1)
Daniels, Ted. Z7835.M54.D36 1992, (v10)
Danielson, Dennis Richard. PR3562.D28 1982, (v3)
Danielson, Michael N. GV706.35.D36 1997, (v6)
  HT169.57.U62.S63 1995, (v6)
  JK325.D27, (v7)
Danilov, Victor J. AM7.D34 1994, (v10)
  AM11.D35 1996, (v10)
  Q105.U5.D36 1990, (v1)
Danishvar, Simin. PK6561.D263.S213 1992, (v3)
Danko-McGhee, Katharina. LB1139.5.A78, (v7)
Danley, John R. HD60.D26 1994, (v6)
Danly, Robert Lyons. PL808.I4.Z63, (v3)
Dann, Kevin T. BF495.D36 1998, (v2)
Dannen, Fredric. ML3790.D32 1990, (v9)
Dannenfeldt, Karl H. CB361.D27, (v5)
Dannenmaier, William D. DS921.6.D36 1999, (v5)
Danow, David K. P85.B22.D3 1991, (v3)
  PN3352.C37.D36 1995, (v3)
Danson, Lawrence. PR5824.D36 1997, (v3)
Dantanus, Ulf. PR6056.R5.Z65 1985, (v3)
Danto, Arthur Coleman. BD21.D36 1989, (v8)
  BH39.D349 1998, (v8)
  BH39.D35 1986, (v8)
  BH39.D36, (v8)
Dantzer, Robert. RC49.D2613 1993, (v2)
Danzger, Murray Herbert. BM205.D27 1989, (v8)
Danziger, Kurt. BF181.D27 1990, (v2)

Danziger, Paula. PZ7.D2394Di 1982, (v3)
Darby, Barbara. PR3316.A4.Z6424 1997, (v3)
Darby, H. C. DA13.D3, (v5)
  DA610.D23, (v5)
  DA640.D27, (v5)
Darby, Ron. TP155.5.D28 2001, (v1)
Darby, William. ML2075.D33 1990, (v9)
  PN1998.D285 1991, (v3)
  PN1998.3.F65.D37 1996, (v3)
Darbyshire, A. E. PE1421.D3, (v3)
Darch, Colin. Z3881.D37 1987, (v10)
D'Arcy, Martin Cyril. BD215.D3 1958, (v8)
D'Ardenne, Patricia. BF637.C6D35 1999, (v2)
Darder, Antonia. LC1099.3.D37 1991, (v7)
Dardess, John W. DS753.2.D37 2002, (v5)
  HN740.T55.D37 1996, (v6)
Dargahi-Noubary, G.R. QE539.2.S34D38 1999, (v1)
Dargan, Amanda. HT206.D327 1990, (v6)
Darío, Rubén. PQ7519.D3.A17 1942, (v3)
Darity, William A. HD4903.5.U58.D37 1998, (v6)
Dark, Eleanor. PR9619.3.D37 N6, (v3)
  PR9619.3.D37 T5 1941, (v3)
Dark, K. R. DA145.D36 1997, (v5)
  E840.D36 1996, (v4)
Darley, Gillian. NA997.S7.D37 1999, (v9)
Darling, David J. QH327.D37 2001, (v1)
Darling, R. W. R. QA641.D23 1994, (v1)
Darling, Robert. PR9619.3.H65.Z58 1997, (v3)
Darling, Sharon S. NA3507.D37 1989, (v9)
Darlington, Philip Jackson. QL101.D3, (v1)
Darnell, A. C. HB139.D358 1994, (v6)
Darnell, Regna. GN17.3.N7, (v6)
  GN21.S27.D37 1990, (v6)
Darnton, Robert. DC133.3.D37 1982, (v5)
  DC158.8.D37 1990, (v5)
  DD289.D27 1991, (v5)
  PQ265.D367 1995, (v3)
  PQ265.D37 1995, (v3)
Darroch, Sandra Jobson. DA566.9.M63.D37 1975, (v5)
Darrow, Clarence. CT275.D2374.A3 1957, (v5)
  KF213.D3.W4, (v7)
Darrow, Margaret H. D639.W7.D38 2000, (v5)
  DC801.M76.D37 1989, (v5)
Darsey, James Francis. PN4055.U53.D37 1997, (v3)
Darst, David H. PQ6279.B6.D3, (v3)
  PQ6399.Z5.D37 1987, (v3)
Darst, Paul W. GV365.P36 2001, (v6)
Darst, Robert G. TD170.D37 2001, (v1)
Dart, Gregory. PR129.F8.D37 1998, (v3)
Dart, Rufus. F196.D26, (v4)
Dart, Thurston. ML430.5.D3 1967, (v9)
Darton, Eric. NA6233.N5.W673 1999, (v9)
Darvill, T. C. GN805.D26 1996, (v6)
Darwīsh, Maòhmūd. PJ7820.A7A2 2000, (v3)
Darwall, Stephen L. BJ1012.D325 1997, (v8)
Darwin, Charles Galton. CB160.D3 1953a, (v5)
Darwin, Charles. QE565.D2 1962, (v1)
  QH11.D2 1839a, (v1)
  QH31.D2.A16, (v1)
  QH31.D2.A37, (v1)
  QH31.D2.A4 1985, (v1)
  QH365.A1 1958, (v1)
  QH365.A1 1977, (v1)
  QH365.A1 1988, (v1)
  QH365.O2, (v1)
  QH365.O2 1859a, (v1)
  QH365.V2.D37 1998, (v1)
  QH365.Z9.D37 1996, (v1)
  QP401.D3 1965, (v1)
Darwish, Mahmud. PJ7694.E3.D37 1984, (v3)
  PJ7820.A7.A27, (v3)
Dary, David. PN4894.D37 1998, (v3)
Das, Ashok. QC776.D37 1994, (v1)
Das, Braja M. TA710.D264 2002, (v1)
  TA775.D227 1999, (v1)
Das, G. K. PR6011.O58.Z652 (v3)
Das, Pankaj K. TA1677.D37 1991, (v1)
Das, Shukavak. BL1175.T47, (v8)
Dasenbrock, Reed Way. PN49.D265 2001, (v3)
  PN49.D265 2001, (v3)

Dasgupta, Ajit Kumar. HB126.I4.D365 1993, (v6)
Dasgupta, Partha. HC59.72.P6.D37 1993, (v6)
  HD75.6.D367 2001, (v6)
Dasgupta, Sathi Sengupta. E184.E2.D37 1989, (v4)
DasGupta, Sayantani. GR305.5.B4.D27 1995, (v6)
Dasgupta, Subrata. T49.5.D38 1994, (v1)
Dasgupta, Surendranath. B132.Y6.D27 1973, (v8)
Dash, Irene G. PR2991.D26 1996, (v3)
Dash, J. Michael. PN849.C3.D36 1998, (v3)
Dash, Mike. SB425, (v1)
Dashefsky, H. Steve. GE10.D37 1993, (v6)
Dashti, `Alī. PK6525.D313 1971b, (v3)
Dashwood, Hevina S. HC910.M357 1998, (v6)
Dastrup, Boyd L. UF400.D37 1994, (v10)
Dastur, Françoise. B3279.H49.D33 1998, (v8)
Dathorne, O. R. G95.D38 1994, (v6)
  PL8010.D37, (v3)
  PN56.R16.D38 2001, (v3)
Datta, Pradip Kumar. DS422.C64.D39 1999, (v5)
Datta, Venita. DC33.6.D28 1999, (v5)
Dattilo, John. GV183.5.D37 2002, (v6)
Dauben, Joseph Warren. QA248.D27, (v1)
Daubenmire, Rexford F. QK101.D26, (v1)
Dauber, Cori Elizabeth. U162.6.D38 1993, (v10)
Daudet, Alphonse. PQ2216.P4 1934a, (v3)
Daudet, Alphonse. PQ2216.T4 1911, (v3)
Daugherty, Ray. HV5279.D38 1998, (v6)
Daugherty, William E. UB275.D3, (v10)
D'Aulaire, Ingri. PZ8.1.A86In, (v3)
Daum, E. PG2271.D313 1974b, (v3)
Daumal, Rene. PQ2607.A86.T813 1995, (v3)
Daumas, Maurice. T15.D2613, (v1)
Daunton, M. J. HC254.5.D23 1995, (v6)
Dauster, Frank N. PQ7171.D38 1987, (v3)
Dauzat, Albert. PC2711.D3, (v3)
Dave, Har¯indra. PK1859.D3616A813 1996, (v3)
Davenport, Horace Willard. QP93.D38 1974, (v1)
Davenport, J. QH653.D38 1991, (v1)
Davenport, Marcia. PS3507.A66515 O3, (v3)
Davenport, T. R. H. DT1787.D38 2000, (v5)
Davenport, Thomas H. HC79.I55.D37 1993, (v6)
  HD30.213.D38 2000, (v6)
Davenport, W. A. PR1874.D38 1998, (v3)
Davenport-Hines, R. P. T. HD9667.9.G53.D38 1992, (v6)
Daverio, John. ML410.S4.D38 1997, (v9)
Davey, B. A. QA171.5.D38 1990, (v1)
Davey, B. J. HV6950.L56.D38 1994, (v6)
Davey, Peter. NA966.D37 1980, (v9)
Daviau, P. M. Michele. DS111.9.D38 1993, (v5)
David, A. Rosalie. DT76.D38 1992, (v5)
David, Alfred. PR1924.D3 1976, (v3)
David, Charles Philippe. E183.8.I55.D38 1993, (v4)
David, Deirdre. PR468.I49.D38 1995, (v3)
  PR469.F44.D38 1987, (v3)
David, F. N. QA273.D29 1962, (v1)
David, Guy. QA614.86.D38 1997, (v1)
David, H. A. QA276.15.D39 2000, (v1)
David, Jay. E169.12.A35, (v4)
David, Martin Heidenhain. HJ4653.C3.D33, (v6)
David, Neil. E99.H7.D36 1993, (v4)
David, Robert G. G630.G7, (v6)
David, Solomon D. RD728.D38.A34, (v2)
Davidian, H. H. SB413.R47.D258 1982, (v1)
Davidoff, Jules B. QP441.D38 1991, (v1)
Davidov, Judith Fryer. TR23.D38 1998, (v1)
Davidson, Alan. TX349.D36 1999, (v1)
Davidson, Alastair. JQ4083.D38 1997, (v7)
  KU1760.D38 1991, (v7)
Davidson, Andrew Parks. HC835.D38 1996, (v6)
Davidson, Audrey. BF723.F28.D38 1952, (v2)
Davidson, B. LeRoy. SB413.L48.D38 2000, (v1)
Davidson, Bruce. F128.67.O5.D3, (v4)
Davidson, Chandler. F394.H8.D33, (v4)
Davidson, Clarissa Start. BX8080.N48.D3, (v8)
Davidson, Clifford. PN2587.D38 1996, (v3)
Davidson, Donald. B105.A35 D37 2001, (v8)
  PS3507.A666.A6 1966, (v3)
  PS3507.A666.Z554, (v3)
Davidson, Eric A. HC79.E5 D345 2000, (v6)
Davidson, Eugene. DD247.H5.D384 1996, (v5)

Davidson, Graham. PR4484.D38 1990, **(v3)**
Davidson, Hilda Roderick Ellis. PT7162.D4.D3 1943, **(v3)**
Davidson, James Wightman. DU819.A2.D3, **(v5)**
Davidson, Jane Ilene. PN3171.D29 1996, **(v3)**
Davidson, John. HD8081.M6.D38 1981, **(v6)**
  PR4525.D5.A17 1961, **(v3)**
  PR4525.D5.A6 1995, **(v3)**
Davidson, Jonathan R. T. RM666.H33.D378 2000, **(v2)**
Davidson, Keay. QB36.S15.D38 1999, **(v1)**
Davidson, Lawrence. BP60.D38 1998, **(v8)**
Davidson, Linda Kay. BV5067.D38 1993, **(v8)**
Davidson, Miriam. HN120.N64, **(v6)**
Davidson, Neil. DA809.D38 2000, **(v5)**
Davidson, Osha Gray. HN59.2.D35 1996, **(v6)**
  QH95.8.D38 1998, **(v1)**
Davidson, Pamela. Z8442.65.D38 1996, **(v10)**
Davidson, Scott. KDZ578.I5.D38 1997, **(v7)**
Davidson, Thomas. LA75.D24 1969b, **(v7)**
  LA75.D25 1969, **(v7)**
  LB518.D3 1970, **(v7)**
Davie, Donald. PR611.D38 1989b, **(v3)**
  PR6007.A667.N4, **(v3)**
Davies, A. C. (Arthur Cyril). TS227.D22 1992, **(v1)**
Davies, Andrew. HE7645.D38 1994, **(v6)**
Davies, Anthony. PR3093.D38 1988, **(v3)**
Davies, B. QA614.8.D38 1999, **(v1)**
Davies, Brian. B765.T54.D35 1992, **(v8)**
Davies, Catherine. PQ7378.D38 1997, **(v3)**
Davies, Cecil W. PN2654.D36 2000, **(v3)**
Davies, Christie. PN6149.E83.D39 1990, **(v3)**
Davies, Douglas James. BX8643.S25, **(v8)**
Davies, E. T. JC137.H7.D3, **(v7)**
Davies, Gareth. HV91.D3524 1996, **(v6)**
Davies, Geoffrey F. QE509.4.D38 1999, **(v1)**
Davies, Godfrey. DA390.D3 1959, **(v5)**
  DA425.D39 1969, **(v5)**
Davies, Hunter. PR5881.D34 1980, **(v3)**
Davies, Ioan. HD6857.D3, **(v6)**
Davies, J. Clarence. TD180.D39 1998, **(v1)**
Davies, J. D. VA454.D38 1992, **(v10)**
Davies, James A. PR6039.H52.Z6225 1998, **(v3)**
Davies, John Booth. ML3830.D28 1978b, **(v9)**
Davies, John Kenyon. DF214.D37 1993, **(v5)**
Davies, John. LB1043.D38 1996, **(v7)**
Davies, Kevin. QH445.2.D37 2001, **(v1)**
Davies, Laurence. ML410.F82 D29 1977, **(v9)**
Davies, Martin. BC71.D25 1981, **(v8)**
Davies, N. B. QL696.C83, **(v1)**
Davies, Nigel. F1219.D2783, **(v4)**
  F1219.73.D38 1987, **(v4)**
  F3429.3.P65.D38 1995, **(v4)**
Davies, Norman. D57.D28 1996, **(v5)**
  DA30.D355 1999, **(v5)**
  DK4140.D38 1982, **(v5)**
  DK4140.D385 2001, **(v5)**
Davies, P. C. W. QB54.D38 1995, **(v1)**
  QB982.D38 1994, **(v1)**
  QC174.12.D365 1986, **(v1)**
  QC793.3.B5.D38, **(v1)**
  QH325.D345 1999, **(v1)**
Davies, Paul Sheldon. QH375.D36 2001, **(v1)**
Davies, Paul. PN751.D38 1998, **(v3)**
Davies, Peter Jonathan. D802.F8.D32 2001, **(v5)**
Davies, Peter. PE1574.D3, **(v3)**
Davies, Philip. Z6724.I7.D38 1996, **(v10)**
Davies, R. E. G. HE9785.D38 1995, **(v6)**
Davies, R. R. DA715.D37 1987, **(v5)**
  DA716.G5.D5 1995, **(v5)**
Davies, R. W. DK266.D28 1997, **(v5)**
Davies, Reginald Trevor. DP162.D3, **(v5)**
Davies, Richard O. F499.C177.D38 1998, **(v4)**
  GV717.D38 2001, **(v6)**
Davies, Robertson. PR9199.3.D3.M3, **(v3)**
  PR9199.3.D3.W6 1976, **(v3)**
Davies, Roy W. U35.D38 1989, **(v10)**
Davies, Stevie. PR3562.D36 1983, **(v3)**
  PR3588.D3 1991, **(v3)**
Davies, W. H. PR6007.A8.A17 1965, **(v3)**
  PR6007.A8 Z52, **(v3)**

Davies, Wendy. HN438.B73.D38 1988, **(v6)**
Davin, Anna. HV752.L7.D39 1996, **(v6)**
Davis, A. R. PL2658.E3.D3 1962, **(v3)**
Davis, Allen Freeman. HV4194.A3.D3 1967, **(v6)**
Davis, Angela Yvonne. E185.86.D383 1981, **(v4)**
  E185.97.D23.A32, **(v4)**
  ML3521.D355 1998, **(v9)**
Davis, Audrey B. R856.A5.D38, **(v2)**
Davis, Belinda. D538.5.B47.D38 2000, **(v5)**
Davis, Benjamin O. UG626.2.D37.A3 1991, **(v10)**
Davis, Bertram Hylton. PR29.P4.D39 1989, **(v3)**
Davis, Brian L. E183.8.L75.D38 1990, **(v4)**
Davis, Burke. E467.1.L4.D3 1956, **(v4)**
  E467.1.S9 D3 1988, **(v4)**
Davis, Charles L. HD8368.D38 1989, **(v6)**
Davis, Charles R. JF1351.D38 1996, **(v7)**
Davis, Clark. PS2387.D39 1995, **(v3)**
Davis, Clyde Brion. PS3507.A7137 G7, **(v3)**
  PS3507.A7137A7, **(v3)**
Davis, Colin. PQ2683.I32.Z655 1994, **(v3)**
Davis, Cortney. RA564.85.D38 2001, **(v2)**
Davis, Cynthia J. PS147.D38 1996, **(v3)**
Davis, Cynthia J. PS217.M44.D38 2000, **(v3)**
Davis, Daniel J. TH9446.H38.D38 1991, **(v1)**
Davis, Darrell William. PN1993.5.J3.D38 1996, **(v3)**
Davis, Dena S. RG133.5.D38 2001, **(v2)**
Davis, Derek. KF4783.D38 1991, **(v7)**
  KF4783.D385 2000, **(v7)**
Davis, Diane E. HT384.M62.M483 1994, **(v6)**
Davis, Douglas. NA6695.D38 1990, **(v9)**
Davis, Douglas. NX458.D38 1977, **(v9)**
Davis, Earle Rosco. PR4588.D3, **(v3)**
Davis, Edward L. BL1802.D38 2001, **(v8)**
Davis, Edwin Adams. F369.D24, **(v4)**
Davis, Elisabeth B. Z5351.D38 1996, **(v10)**
  PQ6089.D38 2000, **(v3)**
Davis, Francis. ML385.D29 1990, **(v9)**
  ML394.D36 1996, **(v9)**
  ML3521.D36 1995, **(v9)**
Davis, Frank Marshall. PS3507.A727.T48 1938, **(v3)**
Davis, Gary A. LC3993.9.D38 1989, **(v7)**
Davis, George Theron. VA50.D3 1971, **(v10)**
Davis, George. HF5500.3.U54.D38 1982, **(v6)**
Davis, Grady Scott. B105.W3.D38 1992, **(v8)**
Davis, Gwenn. Z1231.D7 D38 1992, **(v10)**
Davis, H. L. PS3507.A7327 B4, **(v3)**
  PS3507.A7327 H6, **(v3)**
  PS3507.A7327 T4, **(v3)**
  PS3507.A7327 W5, **(v3)**
Davis, Harold E. F289.D24, **(v4)**
  F1415.D34, **(v4)**
Davis, Herbert John. PR3727.D29 1964, **(v3)**
Davis, Howard. TH153.D374 1999, **(v1)**
Davis, J. Frank. PS3507.A7343 R6, **(v3)**
Davis, J. Madison. PR2892.D33 1995, **(v3)**
  PR6056.R27.Z666 1989, **(v3)**
Davis, James C. D221.V4.D3 1970, **(v5)**
Davis, James Edward. F545.D38 1998, **(v4)**
Davis, James Kirkpatrick. DS559.62.U6.D38 1997, **(v5)**
Davis, James R. LB2361.5.D38 1995, **(v7)**
Davis, James W. JF2085.D38 1998, **(v7)**
  JK516.D39 1992, **(v7)**
  JK522.D28 1997, **(v7)**
  JZ1253.D38 2000, **(v7)**
Davis, James Warren. UB343.D3, **(v10)**
Davis, Jane. PS173.W46.D38 2000, **(v3)**
Davis, Janet M. GV1803.D38 2002, **(v6)**
Davis, Jefferson. E467.1.D2596, **(v4)**
  E487.C746 1966, **(v4)**
  E487.D263 1990, **(v4)**
  E664.D28.A4, **(v4)**
Davis, Joel. QP376.D38 1997, **(v1)**
Davis, John C. QE48.8.D38 1986, **(v1)**
Davis, John Emmeus. HT123.D39 1991, **(v6)**
Davis, Joseph Stancliffe. HC57.D36 1975, **(v6)**
Davis, Julian L. QA927.D32 2000, **(v1)**
Davis, Karen. SF487.D27 1996, **(v1)**
Davis, Kenneth Sydney. E807.D34 1993, **(v4)**
Davis, Leith. PR448.N38.D38 1998, **(v3)**
Davis, Lenwood G. Z1249.K8.D38 1984, **(v10)**

  Z1249.M5.D38 1985, **(v10)**
  Z1361.N39.D355 1986, **(v10)**
Davis, Leonard. HV640.5.V5.D38 1991, **(v6)**
Davis, Linda H. PS1449.C85.Z5793 1998, **(v3)**
Davis, Marsha Jane. QA331.3.D38 1998, **(v1)**
Davis, Martin, 1928-. QA9.615.D38 1982, **(v1)**
  QA76.17.D38 2000, **(v1)**
Davis, Mary Elizabeth (Moragne). PS1514.D95.Z5, **(v3)**
Davis, Mary Kemp. PS374.S725.D38 1999, **(v3)**
Davis, Michael C. KNR171 .D38 1990, **(v7)**
Davis, Michael D. KF8745.M34 D38 1994, **(v7)**
Davis, Michael. JC71.A7.D35 1996, **(v7)**
Davis, Mike. HC79.F3.D38 2001, **(v6)**
Davis, Miles. ML419.D39.A3 1990, **(v9)**
Davis, Nanette J. HQ796.D335 1999, **(v6)**
Davis, Natalie Zemon. DC33.D33, **(v5)**
  GT3041.F8, **(v6)**
  PN1995.9.S557.D38 2000, **(v3)**
  PQ613.D38 1987, **(v3)**
Davis, Nathaniel. F3100.D36 1985, **(v4)**
Davis, Paul B. PR4572.C7.D38 1990, **(v3)**
  PR4580.D38 1998, **(v3)**
Davis, Paul K. D25.A2.D38 1996, **(v5)**
  D25.9.D38 1998, **(v5)**
  D568.5.D38 1994, **(v5)**
Davis, Philip J. QA8.6.D39 1986, **(v1)**
  QA567.D38 1993, **(v1)**
  PR3534.D34 1989, **(v3)**
Davis, R. O. TA705.D3 1996, **(v1)**
Davis, Ralph. HC240.D32, **(v6)**
Davis, Rebecca Harding. PS1517.L5 1985, **(v3)**
Davis, Reuben. F341.D27 1972, **(v4)**
Davis, Richard Beale. F212.D28, **(v4)**
  PR2338.D3 1955, **(v3)**
Davis, Richard G. UG626.2.S66.D38 1993, **(v10)**
Davis, Richard H. NB1912.H55.D38 1997, **(v9)**
Davis, Richard Harding. PS1522.S57 1999, **(v3)**
  PS1523.A43 1974, **(v3)**
Davis, Richard L. DS751.D38 1996, **(v5)**
  HV6626.2.D39 1998, **(v6)**
Davis, Richard P. DA990.U46.D38 1994, **(v5)**
Davis, Richard. JK1764.D38 1999, **(v7)**
  MT820.D27 1994, **(v9)**
  PN4888.P6.D38 1991, **(v3)**
Davis, Robert C. DG675.6.D38 1994, **(v5)**
Davis, Robert H. F2254.D38 1993, **(v4)**
  Z1731.D38 1990, **(v10)**
Davis, Robert Leigh. PS3242.M43.D38 1997, **(v3)**
Davis, Robert Murray. PR6045.A97.B734 1990, **(v3)**
  PR6045.A97.Z634 1989, **(v3)**
  PR6045.A97.Z64 1981, **(v3)**
Davis, Rod. BL2490.D37 1998, **(v8)**
Davis, Ronald L. PN1993.5.U65.D34 1993, **(v3)**
  PN1998.3.F65.D38 1995, **(v3)**
  PN2287.W454.D38 1998, **(v3)**
Davis, Rose Parkman. Z8428.66.D38 1997, **(v10)**
Davis, Sam. NA7540.D38 1995, **(v9)**
Davis, Scott C. F234.R59.N43 1988, **(v4)**
Davis, Sonny B. UA619.D38 1996, **(v10)**
Davis, Stanley M. HC79.W4.D377 2000, **(v6)**
Davis, Stephen M. DT779.952.D38 1987, **(v5)**
Davis, Steven J. HD5717.5.U6.D38 1996, **(v6)**
Davis, Sue. KF8745.R44.D38 1989, **(v7)**
Davis, T. Neil. GB641.D39 2001, **(v6)**
  QC971.D38 1992, **(v1)**
Davis, Thadious M. PS3523.A7225.Z63 1994, **(v3)**
Davis, Townsend. E185.61.D36 1998, **(v4)**
Davis, Tracy C. PN2594.D34 1991, **(v3)**
  PN2599.5.E25D38 2000, **(v3)**
  PR5368.S6.D38 1994, **(v3)**
Davis, Troy D. DA964.U6.D39 1998, **(v5)**
Davis, Wade. BL2530.H3 D38 1985, **(v8)**
Davis, Walter R. PR2229.D38 1987, **(v3)**
Davis, William E. E415.9.B79.D38 1974, **(v4)**
  E467.D3 2001, **(v4)**
  E473.2.D36, **(v4)**
  E487.D276 1996, **(v4)**
  E564.5 1st.D38 1993, **(v4)**
  F390.D276 1998, **(v4)**

Davis, William Columbus. F2217.D38 1995, (v4)
Davis, William Stearns. CB355.D3, (v5)
  DR441.D2, (v5)
Davis, Winston Bradley. BL2203.D37 1992, (v8)
Davis-Floyd, Robbie. R733.D38 1998, (v2)
Davison, Andrew. BL2747.8.D28 1998, (v8)
Davison, Gary Marvin. DS799.4.D38 1998, (v5)
Davison, Judith A. KF2910.D3D38 2000, (v7)
Davison, Peter Hobley. PR6029.R8.Z6279 1996, (v3)
Davison, Roderic H. DR569.D3, (v5)
Davison, W. Phillips. DD881.D3, (v5)
Davoust, Emmanuel. QB54.D3913 1991, (v1)
Daw, Kurt. PN2061.D38 1997, (v3)
  PN2080.D38 1998, (v3)
Dawes, Clinton J. QK931.D38 1998, (v1)
Dawes, Greg. PQ7512.D38 1993, (v3)
Dawes, Robyn M. RC480.5.D38 1994, (v2)
Dawick, John. PR5183.D39 1993, (v3)
Dawidoff, Robert. E302.6.R2.D28 1979, (v4)
Dawidowicz, Lucy S. D810.J4.D33, (v5)
  DS135.E9.A13 1967, (v5)
  DS135.R93.V523 1989, (v5)
Dawisha, Karen. DJK45.S65.D38 1988, (v5)
  DK293.D38 1994, (v5)
Dawkins, Cecil. PS3554.A943.Q5 1963, (v3)
Dawkins, Marian Stamp. QL785.25.D39 1993, (v1)
Dawkins, Marvin P. GV981.D39 2000, (v6)
Dawkins, Richard. Q175.D33 1998, (v1)
  QH375.D376 1996, (v1)
  QH375.D38 1982, (v1)
  QH375.D38 1999, (v1)
  QH430.D39 1995, (v1)
  QH437.D38 1989, (v1)
Dawley, Alan. E743.D345 1991, (v4)
Dawsey, James M. Z7751.D33 1988, (v10)
Dawson, Anthony B. PR2807.D35 1995, (v3)
  PR3095.D38 2001, (v3)
Dawson, Barry. NA1526.D39 1994, (v9)
Dawson, Carl. PR461.D35, (v3)
Dawson, Christopher. DS6.D3, (v5)
Dawson, Elmer Yale. QK571.D35 1978, (v1)
Dawson, J. L. PS3509.L43.Z459 1995, (v3)
Dawson, John A. HF5415.D38, (v6)
Dawson, John Philip. KJC3673.D39 1999, (v7)
Dawson, Michael C. E185.615.D39 1994, (v4)
Dawson, Mildred Agnes. LB1573.D34 1963, (v7)
Dawson, Raymond Stanley. DS721.D357, (v5)
Dawson, Robert MacGregor. F1033.K53.D3, (v4)
Dawson, Sarah Morgan. E565.D27 1972, (v4)
  E605.D28 1991, (v4)
Dawson, Terence J. QL737.M35.D39 1995, (v1)
Dawson, Thomas H. QP105.D38 1991, (v1)
Day Lewis, C. PR6007.A95.A17 1992, (v3)
Day, A. Colin. BS432.D34 1992, (v8)
Day, A. Grove. PR9619.3.D25.Z65 1976, (v3)
Day, Aidan. PR457.D38 1996, (v3)
Day, Alan Edwin. Z1946.T38 1997, (v10)
Day, Albert M. SK361.D28 1959, (v1)
Day, Clarence. PS3507.A858.B4, (v3)
  PS3507.A858.L5 1961, (v3)
  PS3507.A858.T5 1936, (v3)
Day, David A. TH900.D38 1991, (v1)
Day, David. D748.D38 1989, (v5)
  D767.8.D39 1991, (v5)
  PR6039.O32.Z634 1991, (v3)
Day, Dorothy. BX4668.D3.A33 1952, (v8)
  HN37.C3 D358 1992, (v6)
Day, Douglas. PR6013.R35.Z67, (v3)
Day, Frances Ann. Z1037.D24 2000, (v10)
Day, George S. HF5415.13.D367 1999, (v6)
Day, Holliday T. NB212.D39 2000, (v9)
Day, John A. QC863.D285, (v1)
Day, Ken W. TA439.D39 1999, (v1)
Day, Malcolm M. PR3736.T7.Z64 1982, (v3)
Day, Richard J. F. F1035.A1.D39 2000, (v4)
Day, Robert W. TA654.6.D39 2002, (v1)
Day, Timothy. ML1055.D37 2000, (v9)
Dayan, Daniel. PN4784.T4.D38 1992, (v3)
Dayan, Joan. F1916.D39 1995, (v4)
Dayan, Moshe. DS110.5.D313 1966a, (v5)
  DS126.6.D3.A35, (v5)

Daydi-Tolson, Santiago. PQ6085.D37 1983, (v3)
Dayton, Cornelia Hughes. KFC3691.W6.D39 1995,
  (v7)
Dazai, Osamu. PL825.A8 N6, (v3)
  PL825.A8 S513, (v3)
D'Cruze, Shani. HV6250.4.W65.D4 1998, (v6)
De Almeida, Hermione. PR4838.M4.D4 1991, (v3)
De Bary, William Theodore. B127.N4.D397 1991, (v8)
  B127.N4.D399 1989, (v8)
  B127.N4 D4, (v8)
  BL1852.D43 1991, (v8)
  DS509.3.D43 1988, (v5)
  DS721.D37 1999, (v5)
  JC599.A78.D4 1998, (v7)
  JQ1508.H7883.D4 1993, (v7)
De Beer, Gavin. QH31.D2.D4, (v1)
De Bellis, Jack. PS3571.P4.Z459 2000, (v3)
  Z8913.85.D4 1994, (v10)
De Benedictis, Matthew M. B765.B74.D4, (v8)
De Bolla, Peter. BH301.S7.D4 1989, (v8)
De Bruhl, Marshall. F390.H84.D4 1993, (v4)
De Bruyn, Frans. PR3334.B4.Z63 1996, (v3)
De Camp, L. Sprague. PR830.F3.D4, (v3)
De Charms, Desiree. ML128.S3.D37, (v9)
De Chasca, Edmund. PQ6373.D4, (v3)
De Conde, Alexander. E333.D42, (v4)
De Costa, Elena. PN2309.D4 1991, (v3)
De Duve, Christian. QH325.D4 1990, (v1)
  QH325.D42 1995, (v1)
De Forest, John William. PS1525.D5 M5 1955, (v3)
De George, Richard T. BJ1012.D4, (v8)
  LB2335.7.D4 1997, (v7)
  Z7125.D445, (v10)
De Grand, Alexander J. DG575.G5.D4, (v5)
De Grazia, Alfred. JK1846.D4 1951, (v7)
  JK2493.D4, (v7)
De Grazia, Victoria. HQ1638.D4 1991, (v6)
De Groot, Gerard J. D521.D35 2000, (v5)
  DA69.3.H3, (v5)
De Hass, Wills. [from old catalog]. F517.D32, (v4)
De Janvry, Alain. HD1790.5.Z8.D4 1981, (v6)
De Jongh, Nicholas. PN1861.D43 1991, (v3)
De Kruif, Paul. QR31.A1.D4 1932d, (v1)
De La Garza, Peter Jack. Z282.D32 1974, (v10)
De la Mare, Walter. PR4612.D4 1932, (v3)
De la Mare, Walter. PR6007.E3.A17 1970, (v3)
  PR6007.E3 A6 1950, (v3)
  PR6007.E3.B4, (v3)
  PR6007.E3 B43, (v3)
  PR6007.E3.C6 1925, (v3)
  PR6007.E3 M4, (v3)
  PR6007.E3.P4 1961, (v3)
De La Pedraja Toman, Rene. HE745.D39 1994, (v6)
De la Roche, Mazo. PR6007.E34 F5, (v3)
  PR6007.E34 J3, (v3)
  PR6007.E34 M3, (v3)
  PR6007.E34 W48, (v3)
  PR6007.E34 Y6, (v3)
De Laguna, Frederica. F912.Y9, (v4)
De Laubenfels, David J. QK63.D44, (v1)
De Leon, Arnoldo. F395.M5.D43 1983, (v4)
  F395.M5 D4 1997, (v4)
  F596.2.D4 2002, (v4)
De Leon, David. HN65.D339 1988, (v6)
De Levie, Robert. QD75.4.S8, (v1)
De Lisle, Harold F. QL666.L29.D4 1996, (v1)
De Looze, Laurence. PN3448.A8.D45 1997, (v3)
De Madariaga, Isabel. DK171.D44 1990, (v5)
  DK171.D45, (v5)
De Mallet Burgess, Thomas. MT956.D4 2000, (v9)
De Man, Paul. PN75.D45.A25 1989, (v3)
  PN603.D39 1993, (v3)
De Maria, Robert. PS3554.E455.C3, (v3)
De Marinis, Marco. PN2041.S45.D413 1993, (v3)
De Marly, Diana. GT603.D4 1990, (v6)
  TT504.D45, (v1)
De Mendelssohn, Peter. PT2625.A44.Z5446, (v3)
De Meneses, Filipe Ribeiro. DP269.D35 2001, (v5)
De Mente, Boye. F1210.D38 1996, (v4)
De Micheli, Giovanni. TK7874.65.D4 1994, (v1)
De Mijolla, Elizabeth. PN452.D38 1994, (v3)

De Mille, Agnes. GV1785.G7.D4 1992, (v6)
De Montmollin, Olivier. F1435.1.R67.D39 1995, (v4)
De Morgan, William Frend. PR6007.E5 O43 1920, (v3)
De Mowbray, Stephen. DK266.D39 1990, (v5)
De Murias, Ramon. HE9777.7.D4 1989, (v6)
De Nevers, Noel. QC145.2.D42 1991, (v1)
De Onis, Jose. F1418.D45, (v4)
De Paola, Tomie. PZ8.1.D43St, (v3)
De Quille, Dan. PS1525.D35.D5 1988, (v3)
De Quincey, Thomas. PR4531.M3 1889, (v3)
  PR4532.S8, (v3)
  PR4532.T3, (v3)
  PR4534.C6 1950, (v3)
  PR4534.E4, (v3)
De Santillana, Giorgio. Q125.D34, (v1)
  QB36.G2.D4 1955, (v1)
De Santis, Vincent P. H31.J6 ser. 77, no. 1, (v6)
De Selincourt, Aubrey. B72.D4, (v8)
  DF214.D4 1963, (v5)
  PN1031.D398 1976, (v3)
De Selincourt, Ernest. PR453.D4 1964, (v3)
  PR5849.D4, (v3)
De Seversky, Alexander P. UG633.D44, (v10)
De Silva, Clarence W. TA355.D384 2000, (v1)
De Silva, K. M. DS480.853.D384 1995, (v5)
  DS489.83.J3.D4 1988, (v5)
  DS489.84.D4 1998, (v5)
De Silva, Padmasiri. BQ4570.E23.D35 1998, (v8)
De Sola, Ralph. HV6025.D43 1988, (v6)
De Somogyi, Nick. PR3069.M5.D4 1998, (v3)
De Sousa, Ronald. B815.D4 1987, (v8)
De Ste. Croix, G. E. M. (Geoffrey Ernest Maurice).
  DF91.D4, (v5)
De Vane, William Clyde. PR4231.D45 1955, (v3)
De Vany, Arthur S. HD9581.U5.D43 1995, (v6)
De Vecchi, Pierluigi. ND623.B9.D453 1996, (v9)
De Ville, Kenneth Allen. KF2905.3.D4 1990, (v7)
De Villiers, Marq. DT763.5.D4 1988, (v5)
De Vitis, A. A. PR6013.R44.Z632 1986, (v3)
De Voto, Bernard Augustine. E179.5.D4, (v4)
  F592.D36 1947a, (v4)
  F592.D38 2000, (v4)
  PS3507.E867.C5, (v3)
  PS3507.E867.C7, (v3)
  PS3507.E867.E2, (v3)
  PS3507.E867.H65, (v3)
  PS3507.E867.M5 1940, (v3)
  PS3507.E867.Z53 1975, (v3)
De Vries, Barend A. HG3881.5.W57.D4 1987, (v6)
De Vries, Jan. HC240.D48 1976, (v6)
De Vries, Louis. T9.D47, (v1)
De Vries, Margaret Garritsen. HG3890.D4 1987, (v6)
De Vries, Peter. PS3507.E8673 T8, (v3)
  PS3507.E8673 W5, (v3)
De Waal, Cornelis. B945.M464 D48 2002, (v8)
De Weever, Jacqueline. PR1903.D4 1987, (v3)
De Weydenthal, Jan B. DK4442.D4 1983, (v5)
De Wolf, David A. QC760.D33 2001, (v1)
De Zuane, John. TD365.D4897 1997, (v1)
De, Sushil Kumar. PK871.D42, (v3)
  PK2916.D4, (v3)
Deac, Wilfred P. DS554.8.D397 1997, (v5)
Deacon, Terrence William. QP399.D43 1997, (v1)
Deak, Frantisek. PN2634.D43 1993, (v3)
Deak, Gloria-Gilda. F128.3.D38 2000, (v4)
  N8214.5.U6.D43 1988, (v9)
Deak, Istvan. DB937.D42, (v5)
Deak, Istvan. UB415.A8.D43 1990, (v10)
Deakin, F. W. D802.Y8.D4, (v5)
Deakin, Motley F. PR6045.E8.Z63, (v3)
Deal, Michael. F1221.T8.D43 1998, (v4)
Dean, Anne. PS3563.A4345.Z66 1990, (v3)
  PS3573.I458.Z63 1994, (v3)
Dean, D. M. KD4230.D43 1996, (v7)
Dean, Joan Fitzpatrick. PR6058.A678.Z65 1990, (v3)
Dean, Jodi. HQ1206.D357 1996, (v6)
Dean, John R. QD63.E88.D43 1998, (v1)
Dean, John W. E860.D38, (v4)
Dean, Kenneth. BL1802.D43 1998, (v8)
Dean, Leonard Fellows. PR2976.D4 1967, (v3)
Dean, Sharon L. PS3363.D43 1995, (v3)

Dean, Vera (Micheles). CB253.D4, (v5)
Dean, Warren. HC188.S3.D4, (v6)
  SB291.H4.D43 1987, (v1)
  SD418.3.B6.D43 1995, (v1)
Dean, William D. BL2525.D43 1994, (v8)
  BR115.H5.D4 1988, (v8)
Dean, Winton. ML410.B62 D35 1975, (v9)
  ML410.H13.D37 1987, (v9)
  ML1700.D4 1990, (v9)
Deane, Herbert Andrew. JC257.L4.D4 1972, (v7)
Deane, Marjorie. HG1811.D423 1994, (v6)
Deane, Phyllis. HC254.5.D3 1979, (v6)
DeAngelis, D. L. QH344.D43 1992, (v1)
Dear, M. J. HV4028.D43 1987, (v6)
Dear, Peter Robert. Q127.E8, (v1)
Dearborn, Mary V. PS3525.A4152.Z635 1999, (v3)
  PS3525.I5454.Z6595 1991, (v3)
Dearden, Philip. GF511.D43 1998, (v6)
Deardorff, Donald L. GV704.D42 2000, (v6)
Deasey, Denison. LB1140.D37 1978, (v7)
Deaver, Jeffery. KF283.D4 1992, (v7)
DeBach, Paul. SB933.3.D43 1991, (v1)
DeBauche, Leslie Midkiff. D522.23.D43 1997, (v5)
DeBenedetti, Charles. JX1961.U6.D42, (v7)
Debicki, Andrew Peter. PQ6085.D398 1994, (v3)
Debnath, Lokenath. QA322.4.D43 1990, (v1)
Debo, Angie. E78.I5 D4 1966, (v4)
  E99.A6 G324 1976, (v4)
  F694.D4 1998, (v4)
  F700.D4, (v4)
DeBoer, Clara Merritt. E449.D267 1994, (v4)
DeBoer, George E. Q183.3.A1.D4 1991, (v1)
DeBonis, Steven. DS556.45.A43.D43 1995, (v5)
Debray, Regis. U240.D2813, (v10)
Debre, P. Q143.P2.D3313 1998, (v1)
Debreczeny, Paul. PG3358.F5.D4 1983, (v3)
Debroey, Steven. DT1756.D4213 1989, (v5)
Debs, Eugene V. HX84.D3.A4 1995, (v6)
Debus, Allen G. Q125.2.D4, (v1)
Debussy, Claude. ML410.D28.A333, (v9)
  ML410.D28.A42 1987, (v9)
Decalo, Samuel. DT546.457.D4 1997, (v5)
  DT547.5.D4 1997, (v5)
  JQ1873.5.C58 D43 1998, (v7)
  Z3577.D43 1995, (v10)
DeCaro, Louis A. BP223.Z8.L5733339 1998, (v8)
DeCarvalho, Roy Jose. BF204.D4 1991, (v2)
Decher, Reiner. TK2896.D43 1997, (v1)
Decker, Jeffrey Louis. BJ1611.D36 1997, (v8)
Decker, Scott H. HV6439.U7.S723 1996, (v6)
Decker, William Merrill. PS417.D43 1998, (v3)
Decker, Wolfgang. GV573.D4213 1990, (v6)
Declercq, Dominik. PL2409.D43 1998, (v3)
DeConde, Alexander. E176.1.D42 2000, (v4)
  E311.D4, (v4)
  HV7436.D43 2001, (v6)
DeCordova, Richard. PN1995.62.D43 1990, (v3)
DeCorse, Christopher R. DT512.9.E46, (v5)
DeCoster, Cyrus Cole. PQ6573.Z5.D4, (v3)
DeCredico, Mary A. F273.C54.D43 1995, (v4)
Decter, Jacqueline. ND699.R6.D43 1989, (v9)
Dederer, John Morgan. U43.U4.D43 1990, (v10)
Dedijer, Vladimir. DB89.F7.D4, (v5)
  DR359.T5.D4, (v5)
Dedrick, Jason. HD9696.2.E182.D43 1998, (v6)
Deeb, Mary Jane. DT197.5.L75.D44 1989, (v5)
Deedy, John G. BX1406.2.D42 1987, (v8)
Deegan, Heather. DT1757.D44 2001, (v5)
Deegan, Mary Jo. HM22.U6.A34 1988, (v6)
  HN59.2.D44 1989, (v6)
Deery, June. PR6015.U9.Z5967 1996, (v3)
Dees, Morris. KF373.D43.A3 1991, (v7)
Deese, David A. JX1417.D42 1994, (v7)
Deetz, James. F6.D43, (v4)
  F68.D4 2000, (v4)
  F234.F56.D43 1993, (v4)
Deffaa, Chip. ML395.D44 1990, (v9)
  ML400.D4 1996, (v9)
  ML3506.D43 1989, (v9)
  ML3506.D433 1993, (v9)
Defoe, Daniel. PR3403.A1, (v3)

PR3404.F6 1946, (v3)
DeFrancis, John. PL1111.D36 1963, (v3)
  PL1171.D38 1984, (v3)
  PL1171.D4, (v3)
DeFreitas, Gregory. HD8081.H7.D44 1991, (v6)
Degas, Edgar. N6853.D33.A4 1999, (v9)
Degen, A. Allan. QL739.8.D44 1997, (v1)
Degen, Robert A. HG501.D44 1987, (v6)
Degh, Linda. GR105.D44 1994, (v6)
Degler, Carl N. HM106.D37 1991, (v6)
Deglin, Judith Hopfer. RM301.12.D44 2000, (v2)
DeGlopper, Donald R. HN749.L8.D44 1995, (v6)
Degner, Lesley F. R723.5.D44 1987, (v2)
DeGraaf, Richard M. QL681.D43 1995, (v1)
DeGrandpre, Richard J. RJ506.H9.D476 1999, (v2)
DeGrazia, David. HV4708.D44 1996, (v6)
DeGregorio, Christine A. JK1319.D44 1997, (v7)
DeGregorio, William A. E176.1.D43 1994, (v4)
Dehaene, Stanislas. QA141.D44 1997, (v1)
Dehejia, Vidya. N8195.A3.W384 1999, (v9)
Dehgan, Bijan. SB407.3.T73.D45 1998, (v1)
Deigh, John. BF47.D45 1996, (v2)
Deighton, Anne. DA47.2.D47 1990, (v5)
Deivert, Bert. PN1998.A1.D36 1996, (v3)
Dejnozka, Edward L. LB15.D37 1991, (v7)
DeJong, David H. E97.D45 1993, (v4)
Dejours, Pierre. QP121.D36 1981, (v1)
Dekker, Thomas. PR2490.A1 1979b, (v3)
Dekmejian, R. Hrair. BP63.A4.D45 1985, (v8)
DeKoven, Marianne. PR888.M63.D45 1991, (v3)
Del Caro, Adrian. PT2605.E4.Z596 1997, (v3)
Del Mar, Norman. ML410.S93 D4 1986, (v9)
  ML1200.D45, (v9)
Del Vecchio, Deborah. PN2598.C94.D4 1992, (v3)
Delacampagne, Christian. B804.D3713 1999, (v8)
Delahunty, Andrew. PE1580.D45 2001, (v3)
Delamar, Gloria T. PR507.D45 1987, (v3)
  PS1018.D45 1990, (v3)
Delamont, Sara. LC191.D445 1989, (v7)
DeLamotte, Eugenia C. PR868.T3.D45 1990, (v3)
  PS3563.A7223.Z63 1998, (v3)
DeLancey, Mark. DT564.D45 1989, (v5)
Deland, Margaret Wade (Campbell). PS1532.D63, (v3)
Delaney, C. F. G. QC795.5.D45 1992, (v1)
Delaney, Carol Lowery. GR450.D45 1992, (v6)
Delaney, David. KF4755.D45 1998, (v7)
Delaney, Frank. PR6019.O9.U638 1982, (v3)
Delaney, Julie. G70.212.D45 1999, (v6)
Delaney, Paul. PR6069.T6.Z64 1990, (v3)
Delaney, Shelagh. PR6007.E327.L5 1961, (v3)
  PR6007.E327.S9 1963, (v3)
  PR6007.E327.T3 1959, (v3)
Delanty, Gerard. H61.D3377 1999, (v6)
Delany, Martin Robison. PS3507.E36 B6, (v3)
Delany, Paul. PR6003.R4.Z63 1987, (v3)
Delany, Samuel R. PR6054.E4.E55, (v3)
  PS3554.E437.B28 1976, (v3)
  PS3554.E437.D5 1977, (v3)
Delany, Sheila. PR1840.B5.L443 1998, (v3)
  PR1882.D45 1994, (v3)
Delaporte, Francois. RC133.F9.P33 1986, (v2)
  RC210.D4513 1991, (v2)
Delaporte, Louis. DS69.D5, (v5)
Delasara, Jan. PN1992.77.X22, (v3)
DeLaura, David J. PR785.D4, (v3)
Delaware Federal Writers' Project. F164.F45 1955, (v4)
Delay, Jean. PQ2613.I2.Z618, (v3)
Delbanco, Andrew. BX9322.D45 1989, (v8)
  PS25.D45 1997, (v3)
Delbo, Charlotte. D805.P7.D41613 1995, (v5)
Delbruck, Hans. U27.D34213 1975, (v10)
Delcourt, Hazel R. QE720.D45 1991, (v1)
Deledalle, Gerard. B945.P44 D434 2000, (v8)
DeLeon, Peter. H97.D45 1988, (v6)
Deleuze, Gilles. AC25.D4213 1987, (v10)
  B2430.D453.Q4713 1994, (v8)
Delevoy, Robert L. N6465.S9.D4413, (v9)
DelFattore, Joan. LB3045.7.D45 1992, (v7)
Delgado, James P. G525.D38 1996, (v6)

G640.D45 1999, (v6)
  VK24.C2.D45 1990, (v10)
Delgado, Richard. E185.615.D44 1996, (v4)
  HN65.D37 1994, (v6)
  KF4772.D45 1997, (v7)
Delgado-Gaitan, Concha. HQ783.D44 1991, (v6)
DelGaudio, Sybil. PN1998.3.V66.D4 1993, (v3)
Delibes, Miguel. PQ6607.E45.C513 1988, (v3)
Delius, Frederick. ML410.D35 A4 1983, (v9)
Dell, Floyd. PS3507.E49 B7, (v3)
  PS3507.E49 M6, (v3)
Dellamora, Richard. PR468.H65.D45 1990, (v3)
Dellenbaugh, Frederick Samuel [from old catalog].
  F788.D35, (v4)
Dellheim, Charles. HC256.6.D448 1995, (v6)
Delli Carpini, Michael X. JK1764.D453 1996, (v7)
Dellinger, David T. HN90.R3.D47, (v6)
Dellios, Rosita. UA835.D45 1990, (v10)
Delmas, Philippe. JC330.2.D4513 1997, (v7)
Delo, David Michael. F591.D354 1992, (v4)
DeLoach, Charlene. RD798.D4, (v2)
DeLoach, Charles. PR2892.D37 1988, (v3)
Deloney, Thomas. PR2244.D2 A12, (v3)
  PR2244.D2 1912, (v3)
DeLong, Thomas A. PN1991.4.A2.D46 1996, (v3)
Deloria, Ella Cara. E99.D1.D3913 1994, (v4)
Deloria, Ella Cara. E99.O3.D4513 1993, (v4)
Deloria, Philip Joseph. E98.P99.D45 1998, (v4)
Deloria, Vine. E93.D36 1988, (v4)
  E98.F6 D35 1997, (v4)
  E98.T77.D44 1984, (v4)
  E99.Y25.D45 1999, (v4)
Delpar, Helen. E183.8.M6.D45 1992, (v4)
Delsemme, A. H. QB981.D4313 1998, (v1)
DeLuca, Anthony R. DK288.D45 1998, (v5)
DeLuca, Kevin Michael. GE195.D45 1999, (v6)
DeLuca, Tom. JK1764.D47 1995, (v7)
Delville, Michel. PS309.P67.D45 1998, (v3)
Demaine, Jack. LC191.D527x 1981, (v7)
Demand, Nancy H. DF85.D46 1990, (v5)
Demaray, John G. PR2833.D46 1998, (v3)
  PR3562.D44, (v3)
Demaree, Robert W. MT85.D36 1995, (v9)
DeMaria, Robert. PR3537.B6.D45 1997, (v3)
Demarquez, Suzanne. ML410.F215 D43 1983, (v9)
DeMarr, Mary Jean. PS3561.I496.Z64 1999, (v3)
Demars, Stanford E. F868.Y6.D44 1991, (v4)
Demastes, William W. PR625.D46 1998, (v3)
  PS3529.D46.Z67 1991, (v3)
Demb, Ada. HD2745.D45 1992, (v6)
Dember, William N. BF241.D4, (v2)
Dembo, L. S. PL2478.F63.D4, (v3)
Demchak, Chris C. UB23.D44 1991, (v10)
Demerec, M. QL537.D75.D4 1965, (v1)
Demers, David P. PN4888.O85.D46 1996, (v3)
Demers, Patricia. PR990.D46 1993, (v3)
  PR3605.M6.D46 1996, (v3)
  PR6039.R32.Z6 1991, (v3)
Demeter, Karl. UB415.G4.D413 1965, (v10)
Demetz, Peter. PT405.D4, (v3)
  PT2603.R397.Z587, (v3)
D'Emilio, John. HQ18.U5.D45 1988, (v6)
  HQ76.8.U5.D45 1983, (v6)
DeMiller, Anna L. Z7001.D45 2000, (v10)
Demorest, Jean-Jacques. PQ243.D38, (v3)
Demos, John. E162.D4 1972, (v4)
  HQ535.D42 1986, (v6)
DeMott, Benjamin. HN90.S6.D46 1990, (v6)
DeMott, Robert J. PS3537.T3234.Z627 1996, (v3)
Dempsey, Deborah Doane. VK140.D46.A3 1998, (v10)
Dempsey, Michael W. DS36.7.D45 1983, (v5)
Dempsey, Paul Stephen. HE206.2.D46 1989, (v6)
Dempsey, Stanley. HD9506.U63C64 1986, (v6)
Demski, Joel S. HF5657.4.D46 1994, (v6)
Den Tandt, Christophe. PS374.C5.D46 1998, (v3)
Denby, Edwin. GV1599.D393 1998, (v6)
Dendle, Brian J. PQ6629.A5.Z665 1995, (v3)
Deng, Francis Mading. PR9408.S83.D44 1989, (v3)
Deng, Ming-Dao. BL1940.K93 D435 1993, (v8)
Deng, Peng. LC54.C6.D46 1997, (v7)
Denham, James M. HV6793.F6.D46 1997, (v6)

Denham, John. PR3409.D2 1969, (v3)
Denis, Claude. KE237.T47.D46 1997, (v7)
Denisoff, R. Serge. ML3795.D34, (v9)
  PN1995.9.M86.D45 1990, (v3)
Denison, Daniel R. HD58.7.D46 1990, (v6)
Denison, Edward Fulton. HC106.3.D3667, (v6)
Denitch, Bogdan Denis. D860.D46 1992, (v5)
Denker, Alfred. B3279.H49.D455 2000, (v8)
Denman, Clarence Phillips. F326.D36 1971, (v4)
Denman-West, Margaret W. Z1037.D35 1998, (v10)
Dennen, William H. TN145.D46 1989, (v1)
Dennes, William Ray. B828.2.D4 1960, (v8)
Dennett, Andrea Stulman. AM11.D46 1997, (v10)
Dennett, Daniel Clement. B105.I56 D46 1987, (v8)
  B105.I56 D464 1996, (v8)
  BD418.3.D46 1998, (v8)
  BJ1461.D426 1984, (v8)
Dennett, Tyler. DS518.8.D55 1941, (v5)
Denney, Robert E. E468.3.D44 1992, (v4)
Dennie, Joseph. PS1534.D6.L3 1943, (v3)
Dennis, Lawrence J. LB885.C662.D45 1989, (v7)
Dennis, Mike. DD283.D46 1988, (v5)
  DD286.4.D46 2000, (v5)
  HN460.5.A8.D46 1993, (v6)
Dennis, Peter. D829.E2.D46 1987, (v5)
  DS597.D46 1996, (v5)
  UA649.3.D46 1987, (v10)
Dennis, Roger L. H. QL562.4.D46 1993, (v1)
Dennis, William Herbert. TN615.D4 1964, (v1)
Denniston, Dorothy Hamer. PS3563.A7223.Z64 1995, (v3)
Denniston, J. D. PA351.D4 1954, (v3)
Denniston, Robin. D810.C88.D46 1997, (v5)
Denny, Frederick Mathewson. BP161.2.D46 1994, (v8)
Denny, Sidney G. E99.M6815 D45 1997, (v4)
DeNoon, Christopher. NC1807.U5.D46 1987, (v9)
Denoon, Donald. DU28.3.D46 2000, (v5)
Densmore, Frances. E99.C6 D38 1979, (v4)
Dent, David W. F1418.D458 1999, (v4)
Dent, Edward Joseph. ML410.S22.D2 1960, (v9)
  ML1704.D46, (v9)
Dent, H. C. LA631.D385 1977b, (v7)
Dent, N. J. H. JC179.R9.D36 1989, (v7)
Dent, Richard J. E78.M3.D45 1995, (v4)
Dentith, Simon. PN6149.P3.D43 2000, (v3)
Denton, Frank. PN4867.D43 1993, (v3)
Denton, James A. HX84.R43.D45 1997, (v6)
Denton, Kirk A. PL2302.D45 1998, (v3)
Denton, Michael. BD541.D46 1998, (v8)
Denton, Sally. F849.L35 D46 2002, (v4)
Denyer, Nicholas. B187.T7.D39 1990, (v8)
Denzin, Norman K. HV5279.D43 1993, (v6)
  PN1995.9.A45.D46 1991, (v3)
Deol, Harnik. DS485.P87.D44 2000, (v5)
DePalo, William A. UA603.D47 1997, (v10)
DePaul, Michael R. BJ319.D47 1993, (v8)
DePauw, Karen P. GV709.3.D47 1995, (v6)
Depew, David J. QH361.D46 1995, (v1)
Deppa, Joan. PN4784.D57.D46 1994, (v3)
Der Derian, James. JF1525.I6.D47 1992, (v7)
Der Nister. PJ5129.K27.M513 1987, (v3)
Derber, Milton. HD5660.U5.D44, (v6)
  HD6508.D44 1972, (v6)
Derby, George Horatio. PS1535.R49 1990, (v3)
Derbyshire, Ian. Z3206.D47 1995, (v10)
Derbyshire, J. Denis. JF51.D467 1996, (v7)
Derian, Jean-Claude. T21.D4713 1990, (v1)
Derickson, Alan. RC733.D44 1998, (v2)
Deringil, Selim. DR477.D44 1989, (v5)
Derivan, William J. Z7164.N17.D44 1990, (v10)
Derleth, August William. F587.W8.D4, (v4)
  PS3507.E69 R4, (v3)
  PS3507.E69 W5, (v3)
DeRosa, David F. HG3877.D47 2001, (v6)
DeRosa, Marshall L. KF4558 9th.D47 1996, (v7)
  KFZ9002.D47 1991, (v7)
DeRose, Laurie Fields. HC79.P6.D47 1998, (v6)
DeRosia, Victoria R. HV6089.D47 1998, (v6)
Derounian-Stodola, Kathryn Zabelle. E85.D47 1993, (v4)

Derr, Mark. F311.D47 1998, (v4)
Derrick, Scott S. PS374.H63.D47 1997, (v3)
Derrida, Jacques. AC25.D45513, (v10)
  B53.D4613 1982, (v8)
  B809.6.D46 1997, (v8)
  B2430.D483.D6613 1995, (v8)
  B2430.D483.P6613 1997, (v8)
  B2430.L484.D4513 1999, (v8)
  BD181.7.D4713 1996, (v8)
  BD444.D46513 1993, (v8)
  BH39.D4513 1987, (v8)
  P304.D4713 1991, (v3)
  PN98.D43.D44 1991, (v3)
Derry, Gregory Neil. Q158.5.D47 1999, (v1)
Derry, John W. DA505.D47 2001, (v5)
  DA522.L8.D47 1976, (v5)
Derry, T. K. DL46.D43, (v5)
  DL448.D4, (v5)
  DL506.D47, (v5)
Dershowitz, Alan M. HV6431.D473 2002, (v6)
Derthick, Martha. HJ275.D47, (v6)
  UA42.D46, (v10)
Dervan, Peter A. RC280.B8.D425 2001, (v2)
Des Chene, Dennis. QP21.D378 2001, (v1)
Des Granges, Charles Marc. PQ1181.D4, (v3)
Desai, Anita. PR9499.3.D465B38 2000, (v3)
  PR9499.3.D465D52 2000, (v3)
  PR9499.3.D465J68 1995, (v3)
Desai, Gaurav Gajanan. Z5113.D47 2001, (v10)
Desai, Padma. HC336.26.D47 1989, (v6)
DeSalvo, Louise A. PR6045.O72.Z613 1989, (v3)
Desborough, V. R. d'A. DF220.D44 1972, (v5)
Descargues, Pierre. N3350.D4, (v9)
Descartes, René. B1837.C67 1988, (v8)
  B1837.S55 1958, (v8)
  Q155.D433, (v1)
  B1848.E5 C73 1998b, (v8)
Desch, Michael C. F1418.D467 1993, (v4)
  JF195.D47 1999, (v7)
Descola, Philippe. F2230.2.J58.D4713 1996, (v4)
  F3430.1.A25.D4713 1994, (v4)
Desens, Marliss C. PR658.D43.D47 1994, (v3)
De-Shalit, Avner. GE170.D465 2000, (v6)
DeShell, Jeffrey. PS2642.F43.D47 1997, (v3)
DeSimone, Livio D. HC79.E5.D4637 1997, (v6)
Deskis, Susan E. PR1587.P75.D47 1996, (v3)
Desmangles, Leslie Gerald. BL2530.H3.D48 1992, (v8)
Desmet, Christy. PR2989.D47 1992, (v3)
Desmond, Adrian J. Q143.H956.D47 1997, (v1)
Desmond, Ray. QK73.G72R6928 1995, (v1)
Desnos, Robert. PQ2607.E75.A6, (v3)
Despain, Don G. QK195.D47 1990, (v1)
Desqulure, Lilas. PQ3949.2.D445.C4813 1998, (v3)
Dessalles, Pierre. F2081.D4813 1996, (v4)
Dessen, Alan C. PR658.S59.D47 1999, (v3)
  PR2638.D47, (v3)
  PR2835.D47 1989, (v3)
  PR3091.D47 1995, (v3)
Desser, David. PN1998.2.D47 1993, (v3)
Dessler, Andrew Emory. QC879.7.D47 2000, (v1)
D'Este, Carlo. D766.D47 1990, (v5)
Desveaux, James A. JL108.D47 1995, (v7)
Dethier, V. G. QL495.D4, (v1)
  QL533.D4, (v1)
Dethloff, Henry C. HD9066.U45.D48 1988, (v6)
Detienne, Marcel. DF78.D4613, (v5)
Detrez, Raymond. DR65.D48 1997, (v5)
Detroit Institute of Arts. ND205.D298 1991, (v9)
Detter, Thomas. PS1536.D47.N45 1996, (v3)
Detweiler, Robert. PN98.R44.D4 1989, (v3)
  PS374.R47.D48 1996, (v3)
Detwiler, Bruce. JC233.N52.D48 1990, (v7)
Detzer, David. E471.1.D48 2001, (v4)
Deuel, Leo. CC76.A3.D4, (v5)
  DS56.D4, (v5)
Deursen, Arie Theodorus van. HN513.D4813 1991, (v6)
Deutsch, Babette. PN44.5.D4 1969, (v3)
  PS3507.E84.A17 1969, (v3)
  PS3507.E84.C6, (v3)

Deutsch, Charles. HV5132.D43, (v6)
Deutsch, Eliot. B132.V3.D542, (v8)
Deutsch, Francine. HQ755.8.D489 1999, (v6)
Deutsch, Harold C. DC201.D4, (v5)
Deutsch, Karl Wolfgang. JA73.D55 1966, (v7)
Deutsch, Otto Erich. ML410.S3.D52, (v9)
Deutsch, Sarah. F785.M5.D48 1987, (v4)
  HQ1439.B7.D48 2000, (v6)
Deutsch, W. J. GB855.D48 1997, (v6)
Deutscher, Irwin. HM291.D467 1993, (v6)
Deutscher, Isaac. DK254.T6.D4, (v5)
  DK254.T6.D415, (v5)
  DK254.T6.D42, (v5)
  DK268.S8.D48 1967, (v5)
DeValeria, Dennis. GV865.W33.D38 1996, (v6)
Devane, Richard S. B824.D4 1976, (v8)
Devaney, Kathleen. LB1029.O6.D48, (v7)
Devaney, M. J. B831.2.D48 1997, (v8)
Deveaux, Monique. JC574.D478 2000, (v7)
DeVeaux, Scott Knowles. ML3506.D48 1997, (v9)
DeVenney, David P. ML128.M78.D48 1998, (v9)
Devens, Carol. E78.G7.D48 1992, (v4)
Deveny, Thomas G. PN1993.5.S7.D48 1993, (v3)
  PN1993.5.S7.D49 1999, (v3)
Dever, Carolyn. PR878.M69.D48 1998, (v3)
Dever, William G. BS1180.D66 2001, (v8)
Deverell, William Francis. HE2771.C2.D48 1994, (v6)
Devereux, Owen F. TN690.D47 1983, (v1)
Devettere, Raymond J. R724.D48 1995, (v2)
Devine, Jeremy M. DS557.73.D48 1995, (v5)
Devine, John. LB3013.3.D48 1996, (v7)
Devine, P. J. HD82.D45 1988, (v6)
Devine, Philip E. BD175.5.M84 D48 1996, (v8)
  BJ1012.D455 2000, (v8)
Devine, T. M. DA760.D48 1999, (v5)
  DA880.H6.D37 1994, (v5)
Devine, Theresa J. HD4901.D49 1991, (v6)
Devins, Neal E. KF3771.D48 1996, (v7)
DeVitis, Joseph L. BJ1611.2.D45 1996, (v8)
Devitt, Michael. B835.D48 1991, (v8)
Devkota, Laxmi Prasad. PK2598.D37.A27, (v3)
Devlin, Keith J. QA93.D457 1994, (v1)
  QA93.D4578 1998, (v1)
  QA93.D458 1998, (v1)
Devlin, Kimberly J. PR6019.O9.F578 1991, (v3)
Devore, Wynetta. HV3176.D46 1996, (v6)
DeVorkin, David H. TL789.8.U5.D48 1992, (v1)
Devoto, Giacomo. PC1075.D3913, (v3)
  PC1625.D4, (v3)
DeVries, Duane. Z8230.D48 2000, (v10)
DeVries, Kelly. DA161.D48 1999, (v5)
  UD59.D48 1996, (v10)
Dew, Charles B. E459.D4 2001, (v4)
Dew, Edward M. F2425.2.D49 1994, (v4)
Dewald, Jonathan. DC121.7.D48 1993, (v5)
Dewart, Gilbert. G875.D49.A3 1989, (v6)
Dewdney, A. K. Q172.5.E77.B48 1997, (v1)
  QA76.D45 1989, (v1)
  QA93.D49 1993, (v1)
Dewdney, John C. DR417.D48 1971, (v5)
D'Ewes, Simonds. DA397.D43 1970, (v5)
Dewey, Donald. HB201.D48, (v6)
  HD2795.D485 1990, (v6)
  PN2287.S68.D48 1996, (v3)
Dewey, George. E714.6.D51.A3 1971, (v4)
Dewey, Godfrey. PE1143.D4, (v3)
Dewey, John. B945.D41.B4, (v8)
  B945.D41 G68 1994, (v8)
  B945.D41.H53 1998, (v8)
  B945.D41 1967, (v8)
  B945.D41 1976, (v8)
  B945.D41 1981, (v8)
  B945.D43.I5, (v8)
  B945.D43.P5, (v8)
  B945.D43 P7 1975, (v8)
  B945.D44.A43, (v8)
  B2741.D5, (v8)
  BC50.D42, (v8)
  BC50.D43, (v8)
  BD161.D4, (v8)
  BF57.D4 1930, (v2)

BJ1025.D5 1957, (v8)
BJ1025.D53 1960, (v8)
BL48.D4, (v8)
HM276.D4, (v6)
JC423.D524, (v7)
LB875.D35, (v7)
LB875.D39 1969, (v7)
LB875.D3943, (v7)
LB875.D3947, (v7)
LB875.D4 1915, (v7)
LB875.D48 1970, (v7)
Dewey, Melvil. Z696.D52 2003, (v10)
Dewey, Patrick R. PN6714.D49 1991, (v3)
Dewhurst, C. Kurt. NK805.D48 1979, (v9)
DeWiel, Boris. JC421.D48 2000, (v7)
DeWitt, Howard A. ML420.B365.D5 1985, (v9)
  ML420.P96.D49 1993, (v9)
Dewlen, Al. PS3554.E93B66 2002, (v3)
Dews, Peter. B841.4.D49 1987, (v8)
Deyermond, A. D. PQ6428.D4 1975, (v3)
DeYoung, Terri. PJ7862.A93.D49 1997, (v3)
Dhada, Mustafah. DT613.78.D47 1993, (v5)
Dhar, P. N. DS480.852.D49 2000, (v5)
Dhillon, B. S. TS173.D48, (v1)
Dhruvarajan, Vanaja. HQ1743.D38 1989, (v6)
Dhuoda. BJ1550.D48513 1991, (v8)
Di Donato, Pietro. PS3507.I37 C5 1939, (v3)
Di Leonardo, Micaela. GN33.D5 1998, (v6)
Di Lorenzo, Marjorie Schaub. RB45.15.D525 2001, (v2)
Di Palma, Giuseppe. JC423.D54 1990, (v7)
Di Renzo, Anthony. PS3565.C57.Z646 1993, (v3)
Di Sabatino, David. Z7836.7.D5 1999, (v10)
Di Tella, Torcuato S. JL966.D513 1990, (v7)
Diacon, Todd A. F2537.D52 1991, (v4)
Diamond, Barbara J. LC1099.3.D53 1995, (v7)
Diamond, Dermot. QD39.3.S7.D53 1997, (v1)
Diamond, Edwin. JK528.D53 1995, (v7)
Diamond, Etan. BM229.T67, (v8)
Diamond, Harold J. ML128.A7.D5 1991, (v9)
Diamond, Irene. HQ1233.D5 1994, (v6)
Diamond, Jared M. HM206.D48 1997, (v6)
Diamond, Jonathan. RC564.D535 2000, (v2)
Diamond, Malcolm Luria. B3213.B84.D48, (v8)
Diamond, Marian Cleeves. QM455.D49 1988, (v1)
Diamond, Michael. KF3775.Z9.D53 1996, (v7)
Diamond, Richard. RK61.D52 2000, (v2)
Diamond, Robert E. PE135.D5 1970, (v3)
Diamond, Sara. BR1642.U5.D52 1998, (v8)
Diamond, Sigmund. HV6285.D53 1992, (v6)
DiAntonio, Robert E. PQ9603.D5 1989, (v3)
Dias, Maria Odila Leite da Silva. HV1448.B72.S26413 1995, (v6)
Diawara, Manthia. E184.A24.D53 1998, (v4)
  PN1993.5.A35.D5 1992, (v3)
Diaz Espino, Ovidio. HE537.D5 2001, (v6)
Diaz Polanco, Hector. E59.G6.D5213 1997, (v4)
Diaz, Carlos. LC1090.D53 1999, (v7)
Diaz, Maria Elena. HT1079.E4, (v6)
Diaz, Nancy Gray. PQ7082.N7.D48 1988, (v3)
Diaz-Briquets, Sergio. HB1379.D52 1983, (v6)
Diaz-Cotto, Juanita. HV9475.N6.D53 1996, (v6)
Diaz-Plaja, Guillermo. PQ6070.D5 1953, (v3)
  PQ6073.M6.D5 1979, (v3)
  PQ6032.D4913, (v3)
Diaz-Stevens, Ana Maria. BR563.H57.D53 1998, (v8)
DiBattista, Maria. PN1995.9.W6.D53 2001, (v3)
Dibble, Jeremy. ML410.P173.D5 1992, (v9)
Dibblin, Jane. DU710.D53 1989, (v5)
Dicaire, David. ML400.D53 1999, (v9)
DiCenso, James. BF175.4.R44.D53 1999, (v2)
Dichter, Harry. ML112.D53 1977, (v9)
Dick, Everett Newfon. F396.D5, (v4)
  F591.D54, (v4)
  F591.D544, (v4)
  F591.D545, (v4)
  HD216.D5, (v6)
Dick, Philip K. PS3554.I3.M36x, (v3)
  PS3554.I3.T48 1979, (v3)
Dick, Steven J. QB54.D475 1998, (v1)
Dickason, Olive Patricia. E78.C2 D459 2002, (v4)

Dicke, Robert H. QC174.D5, (v1)
Dicken Garcia, Hazel. F454.D53 1991, (v4)
Dickens, A. G. BR375.D52 1968, (v8)
Dickens, Charles. PR4550.F37, (v3)
  PR4552.1994, (v3)
  PR4553.C6 1975, (v3)
  PR4553.S58 1978, (v3)
  PR4553.Z3 1969, (v3)
  PR4556.A2 F67, (v3)
  PR4558.A2 P3 1934, (v3)
  PR4559.A1 1957, (v3)
  PR4560.A1 1961, (v3)
  PR4563.A1 1951, (v3)
  PR4564.A1 1972, (v3)
  PR4565.A1 1950, (v3)
  PR4566.A1 1951, (v3)
  PR4567.A1, (v3)
  PR4568.A1 1960, (v3)
  PR4570.A1 1957, (v3)
  PR4570.A2.S57 1994, (v3)
  PR4571.A1 1958, (v3)
  PR4572.A83.S58 1996, (v3)
  PR4572.C68 1976, (v3)
  PR4572.M37 1981, (v3)
  PR4572.S6 1960, (v3)
  PR4572.U54 1987, (v3)
  PR4581.A3.H6, (v3)
Dickenson, Donna. PQ2412.D5 1988, (v3)
  PS2506.D45 1993, (v3)
Dickerson, Debra J. PN4874.D435, (v3)
Dickerson, Donna Lee. KF4774.D53 1996, (v7)
Dickerson, Gary E. PN1995.9.B28.D5 1991, (v3)
Dickerson, James. DS559.62.U6.D53 1999, (v5)
Dickerson, M. O. E78.N79.D53 1992, (v4)
Dickerson, O. M. E215.1.D53 1974, (v4)
Dickerson, Vanessa D. PR878.S85.D53 1996, (v3)
Dickey, James. PS3554.I32.A17 1992, (v3)
  PS3554.I32.D4, (v3)
  PS3554.I32.D7, (v3)
  PS3554.I32.E9 1970, (v3)
  PS3554.I32.H4, (v3)
  PS3554.I32.S85 1996, (v3)
  PS3554.I32.T6 1993, (v3)
  PS3554.I32.Z48 1999, (v3)
Dickey, Sara. PN1993.5.I8.D5 1993, (v3)
Dickey, William. PS3507.I28.I5, (v3)
Dickhut, Harold W. HF5383.D47 1981, (v6)
Dickie, George. BH39.D48, (v8)
  BH39.D493 1988, (v8)
  BH39.D494 1996, (v8)
Dickie, George. BH181.D53 1996, (v8)
Dickie, Margaret. PS151.D53 1997, (v3)
Dickinson, Donald C. Z479.D53 1998, (v10)
  Z989.H95.D53 1995, (v10)
Dickinson, Edward Ross. HV763.D53 1996, (v6)
Dickinson, Emily. PS1541.A1 1955, (v3)
  PS1541.A133, (v3)
  PS1541.A6 1993, (v3)
  PS1541.A6 1995, (v3)
  PS1541.Z5.A45 1998, (v3)
  PS1541.Z55 1958, (v3)
Dickinson, Eric. TP453.C65.D53 1992, (v1)
Dickinson, Frederick R. D621.J3.D53 1999, (v5)
Dickinson, H. T. DA480.D53 1995, (v5)
Dickinson, Matthew J. JK518.D54 1997, (v7)
Dickinson, O. T. P. K. DF220.D49 1994, (v5)
Dickinson, Peter. PZ7.D562Ro 2001, (v3)
Dickinson, W. Calvin. Z2000.D53 1996, (v10)
Dickison, William C. QK641.D53 2000, (v1)
Dicklitch, Susan. HC870.D53 1998, (v6)
Dick-Read, Grantly. RG661.D5 1956, (v2)
Dickson, Bruce J. JQ1510.D53 1997, (v7)
Dickson, D. Bruce. GN772.22.E854.D53 1990, (v6)
Dickson, L. L. PR6013.O35.Z615 1990, (v3)
Dickson, Lovat. PR5776.D5, (v3)
Dickson, Paul. E741.D5 1999, (v4)
  GV862.3.D53 1999, (v6)
  GV863.A1.D53 1994, (v6)
Dickson-Carr, Darryl. PS374.N4.D53 2001, (v3)
Dickstein, Morris. PS78.D5 1992, (v3)
Diderot, Denis. PQ1979.A25 1991, (v3)

PQ1979.A62.E5 1993, (v3)
PQ1979.A65E5 1999, (v3)
PQ1979.A66 1950, (v3)
PQ1979.A76, (v3)
PQ1979.A8 1938, (v3)
PQ1979.A82.V613 1972, (v3)
Didi-Huberman, Georges. ND623.F5.D5313 1995, (v9)
Didion, Joan. F319.M6.D49 1987, (v4)
  PS3554.I33.B6, (v3)
  PS3554.I33.P5, (v3)
Diebold, Francis X. HB3711.D54 1999, (v6)
Diefendorf, Barbara B. DC719.D54 1991, (v5)
Diehl, Charles. DF531.D42, (v5)
Diehl, James M. UB359.G3.D5 1993, (v10)
Diehl, Paul F. JX1981.P7.D46 1993, (v7)
Diem, Max. QD96.V53.D54 1993, (v1)
Diener, Edward. H62.D53, (v6)
Dienstag, Eleanor Foa. CT275.D463.A34 1976, (v5)
Dierckx, Paul. QA297.6.D54 1993, (v1)
Dies, Martin. E743.5.D52, (v4)
Diestel, Reinhard. QA166.D51413 1997, (v1)
Diethe, Carol. B3311.D54 1999, (v8)
Dietrich, Craig. DS777.55.D52 1986, (v5)
Dietrich, Donald J. BX1536.D54 1988, (v8)
Dietrich, Julia. E743.D495 1996, (v4)
Dietrich, Kurt. ML399.D54 1995, (v9)
Dietrich, Richard F. PR721.D54 1989, (v3)
  PR5368.F5.D54 1996, (v3)
Dietrich, Richard Vincent. QE363.2.D52 1990, (v1)
Dietrich, William. F853.D54 1996, (v4)
Dietschy, Marcel. ML410.D28.D5513 1990, (v9)
Dietz, Henry A. HN350.L5.D54 1998, (v6)
Dietze, Gottfried. JK155.D5, (v7)
Diez Echarri, Emiliano. PQ6032.D54, (v3)
Diez Medrano, Juan. DP302.B53.D54 1995, (v5)
Diffie, Bailey W. F1410.D5 1967, (v4)
Diffie, Whitfield. KF9670.D54 1998, (v7)
Diffley, P. B. PC1064.B46.D5 1988, (v3)
Digby, Anne. R729.5.G4.D54 1999, (v2)
Digby-Junger, Richard. PN4874.L56.D54 1996, (v3)
Digeon, Aurelien. PR3457.D513 1962, (v3)
Digeser, Elizabeth DePalma. BR65.L26.D54 2000, (v8)
Digeser, Peter. JA79.D54 2001, (v7)
Diggins, John P. E169.1.D495 1994, (v4)
  E175.9.D54 2000, (v4)
  H59.W4.D54 1996, (v6)
Diggle, Peter. QA278.D545 1994, (v1)
Diggs, Nancy Brown. E184.J3.D52 1998, (v4)
DiGiovanna, Augustine Gaspar. QP86.D54 2000, (v1)
Digre, Brian Kenneth. D651.A4.D54 1990, (v5)
Dijk, Kees van. DS524.8.E85.D55 1998, (v5)
  DS644.4.D45 2001, (v5)
Dijk, Teun Adrianus van. HM291.D4962 1993, (v6)
Dijkstra, Bram. HQ1122.D55 1996, (v6)
Dika, Vera. PN1995.9.H6.D48 1990, (v3)
Dill, Vicky Schreiber. LB3013.3. D55 1998, (v7)
Dillard, Angela D. E184.A1.D46 2001, (v4)
Dillard, Annie. QH81.D56 1974, (v1)
Dillard, Dudley D. HC21.D5, (v6)
Dillard, J. L. PE3102.N4.D5, (v3)
Dillehay, Tom D. E58.D538 2000, (v4)
Dillenberger, Jane. N6537.W28.D56 1998, (v9)
Diller, Daniel C. E176.1.D55 1989, (v4)
Diller, Jerry V. RC339.52.F733.D55 1990, (v2)
Dillery, John. DF229.D55 1995, (v5)
Dillingham, Rick. E99.A16.D55 1992, (v4)
Dillingham, William B. PS2387.D525 1986, (v3)
  PS2387.D53, (v3)
Dillon, Bert. PR2045.D5, (v3)
Dillon, George L. PE1404.D54 1991, (v3)
Dillon, Janette. PR646.D55 1998, (v3)
  PR658.S47.D55 2000, (v3)
Dillon, Merton Lynn. E446.D54, (v4)
  E449.L889.D5, (v4)
Dillon, Patrick M. QA76.575.D548 1998, (v1)
Dillon, Richard H. F865.S93 D54 1981, (v4)
Dillon, Robert T. QL430.4.D55 2000, (v1)
Dilman, çilham. BJ1460.D55 1999, (v8)
Dilman, Ilham. BD436.D54 1998, (v8)
  BF199.D52 1988, (v2)

Dilsaver, Lary M. F868.S4.D55 1990, (v4)
Dilthey, Wilhelm. D16.8.D49 1962, (v5)
  PT287.D6 1929, (v3)
Dilts, David A. KF3409.P77.D55 1988, (v7)
  KF5390.D55 1992, (v7)
Dilworth, Leah. E78.S7.D525 1996, (v4)
Dimbleby, Jonathan. DS119.7.D54 1980, (v5)
Dimitrijevic, Dimitrije. HG226.3.D56 1991, (v6)
Dimock, George. PA4167.D56 1989, (v3)
Dimond, Paul R. KF4575.D56 1989, (v7)
Dimsdale, Thomas Josiah. F731.D584, (v4)
Din, Gilbert C. E445.L8.D56 1999, (v4)
  F372.B78.D54 1993, (v4)
  F379.N557.D56 1996, (v4)
  F380.C22.D56 1988, (v4)
Dinan, Desmond. HC241.2.D476 1999, (v6)
Dincauze, Dena Ferran. CC81.D56 2000, (v5)
Dine, Jim. NE539.D5.A4 1977, (v9)
Diner, Hasia R. E184.I6.D56 1983, (v4)
  F128.9.J5 D56 2000, (v4)
Diner, Steven J. E661.D56 1998, (v4)
Dinerstein, Herbert S. UA770.D5, (v10)
Dinesen, Isak. PT8175.B545.Z5313 1981, (v3)
Dingman, Roger. D777.5.A92.D56 1997, (v5)
Dinkin, Robert J. JK1965.D54 1982, (v7)
Dinneen, Mark. PQ9691.N59.D5 1996, (v3)
Dinnerstein, Leonard. DS146.U6.D555 1994, (v5)
Dinshaw, Carolyn. PR1933.S35.D56 1989, (v3)
Dinsmoor, William Bell. NA270.D5 1975b, (v9)
Dintrone, Charles V. PN1992.9.D56 1996, (v3)
Diop, David. PQ3989.2.D56.H3, (v3)
Diouf, Sylviane. E443.D56 1998, (v4)
DiPasquale, Theresa M. PR2248.D5 1999, (v3)
Dipchand, Cecil R. HG187.C6.D56 1994, (v6)
DiPego, Gerald. PS3554.I63.W5, (v3)
Dipert, Randall R. BH39.D555 1993, (v8)
Dippel, John Van Houten. DS135.G3315.D57 1996,
  (v5)
Dippie, Brian W. N6537.R4.D57 2001, (v9)
Dippie, Brian W. N8835.D57 1990, (v9)
Dipple, Elizabeth. PR6063.U7.Z64, (v3)
Dirac, P. A. M. QC21.2.D57 1995, (v1)
  QC71.D55, (v1)
  QC174.3.D5 1958, (v1)
Dircks, Phyllis T. PR3469.D56 1985, (v3)
Dirks, Nicholas B. DS422.C3 D58 2001, (v5)
Dirksen, Everett McKinley. E748.D557.A3 1998, (v4)
Dirlik, Arif. DS734.7.D57, (v5)
Dirr, Michael. SB435.5.D556 1997, (v1)
  SB435.5.D57 1990, (v1)
Disch, Thomas M. PN3433.5.D57 1998, (v3)
  PS3554.I8.T5x, (v3)
DiSessa, Andrea A. LB1028.43.D57 2000, (v7)
DiSilvestro, Roger L. QH76.D58 1993, (v1)
Disney, Doris Miles. PS3507.I75, (v3)
Dispenza, Joseph. ND237.F6728.D57 1999, (v9)
Disraeli, Benjamin. PR4084.C6, (v3)
  PR4084.L6, (v3)
  PR4084.S95, (v3)
  PR4084.T3 1970, (v3)
Disraeli, Isaac. PR99.D55 1871, (v3)
Dissanayake, Ellen. BH39.D56 1992, (v8)
  N71.D57 1988, (v9)
  NX180.S6.D58 2000, (v9)
Dissanayake, Wimal. PR9272.9.N32.Z66 1993, (v3)
Ditchek, Stuart H. RJ47.D55 2001, (v2)
Ditmars, Raymond Lee. QL641.D6 1933, (v1)
  QL651.D6 1936, (v1)
  QL666.O6.D54, (v1)
Ditsky, John. PS3537.T3234.Z6278 2000, (v3)
Dittmar, Helga. HM211.D58 1992, (v6)
Dittmer, Lowell. DK68.7.C5.D58 1992, (v5)
  DS777.75.D57 1987, (v5)
  DS778.L49.D57, (v5)
Diubaldo, Richard J. F1090.5.D58, (v4)
Divine, Robert A. D753.D56, (v5)
  E745.D58 2000, (v4)
  E807.D57, (v4)
  E835.D535 1993, (v4)
  E835.D54, (v4)
  E841.C84 1988, (v4)

E846.J64 1987, (v4)
Dix, Neville J. QK604.2.E26.D59 1995, (v1)
Dixit, Avinash K. HD30.28.D59 1991, (v6)
Dixon, A. F. G. QL596.C65.D58 2000, (v1)
Dixon, Bernard. QR56.D59 1976, (v1)
  QR56.D594 1994, (v1)
Dixon, C. J. HC445.D59 1999, (v6)
Dixon, Chris. E185.18.D59 2000, (v4)
Dixon, E. James. E61.D59 1993, (v4)
Dixon, Franklin W. PZ7.D644To 1991, (v3)
Dixon, John A. QH77.D44.D59 1990, (v1)
Dixon, Joy. BP573.F46 D59 2001, (v8)
Dixon, R. O. D. QK898.N6.D59 1986, (v1)
Dixon, Robert C. (Robert Clyde). TK5102.5.D55 1994,
  (v1)
Dixon, Robert M. W. ML156.4.B6.D59 1997, (v9)
  PE3601.D5 1990, (v3)
Dixon, Robert. PR830.A38.D58 1995, (v3)
Dixon, Roger. NA967.D59, (v9)
Dixon, Suzanne. HQ511.D59 1991, (v6)
Dixon, Wheeler W. PN1994.D545 2000, (v3)
  PN1995.D52 1998, (v3)
  PN1995.9.A8.D58 1995, (v3)
  PN1995.9.E96.D55 1997, (v3)
  PN1998.3.F58.D5 1991, (v3)
  PN1998.3.G63.D55 1997, (v3)
Dixon-Kennedy, Mike. BL930.D58 1998, (v8)
Dixson, Miriam. HQ1822.D58 1999, (v6)
Djata, Sundiata A. DT551.9.S44.D53 1997, (v5)
Djebar, Assia. PQ3989.2.D57A813 1993, (v3)
Djilas, Milovan. PG1419.14.I43.M6, (v3)
D'Lugo, Carol Clark. PQ7203.D5 1997, (v3)
D'Lugo, Marvin. PN1998.3.S28.D57 1991, (v3)
Dluhosch, Barbara. HG3882.D58 1996, (v6)
Dmytryk, Edward. PN1998.3.D6.A3 1996, (v3)
Dmytryshyn, Basil. DK3.D55 1974, (v5)
Dobak, William A. UA26.F68.D63 1998, (v10)
Dobb, Maurice Herbert. HB171.D7 1972, (v6)
  HC335.D63 1966a, (v6)
Dobbie, Elliott Van Kirk. PR1502.D6, (v3)
Dobbs, Dan B. KF1250.D59 2001, (v7)
Dobbs, David. SH221.5.M35, (v1)
Dobbs-Weinstein, Idit. B759.M34 D62 1995, (v8)
Dobby, Ernest Henry George. DS10.D59 1967, (v5)
  DS508.2.D6 1973, (v5)
Dobel, J. Patrick. JA79.D56 1989, (v7)
Doberer, Kurt Karl. QD13.D62, (v1)
Dobie, J. Frank. F387.D63, (v4)
  F391.D63, (v4)
  F786.D633 1978, (v4)
Dobkin de Rios, Marlene. GN472.4.D625 1984, (v6)
Dobkin, Bethami A. PN4784.T4.D6 1992, (v3)
Dobkin, David S. QL683.R63.D63 1994, (v1)
Dobkowski, Michael N. Z7164.G45.D63 1992, (v10)
Doblin, Alfred. PT2607.O35.B5 1977, (v3)
  PT2607.O35.Z468 1991, (v3)
  PT2607.O35.Z4685 1992, (v3)
Dobranski, Stephen B. PR3586.D63 1999, (v3)
Dobratz, Betty A. E184.A1 D63 2000, (v4)
Dobree, Bonamy. D285.1.D6, (v5)
  PR691.D6, (v3)
  PR698.T7.D6, (v3)
  PR1266.D58, (v3)
  PR4857.D6 1967, (v3)
Dobrin, Milton B. (Milton Burnett). TN269.D6 1988,
  (v1)
Dobroszycki, Lucjan. DS135.P6.D62, (v5)
  PN5355.P6.D613 1994, (v3)
Dobrynin, Anatoliy Fedorovich. DK275.D63.A3 1995,
  (v5)
Dobson, Alan P. E183.8.G7.D63 1995, (v4)
Dobson, Andrew. B2430.S34.D63 1993, (v8)
  JA75.8.D63 1995, (v7)
  JC271.O74.D63 1989, (v7)
Dobson, Austin. PR4606.A1 1923, (v3)
  PR4606.A1 1970, (v3)
Dobson, E. J. PE1137.D58 1968, (v3)
  PR1810.D6, (v3)
Dobson, Joanne. PS1541.Z5.D57 1989, (v3)
Dobson, John Frederic. LA71.D6 1963, (v7)
Dobson, John M. E661.7.D62, (v4)

E713.D63 1988, (v4)
Dobson, Michael. PR2968.D6 1992, (v3)
Dobson, Narda. F1446.D56 1973, (v4)
Dobyns, Henry F. F3431.D6, (v4)
Dobzhansky, Theodosius Grigorievich. QH366.D6
  1951, (v1)
  QH368.D6, (v1)
Docherty, J. C. DU90.D63 1999, (v5)
  HD4839.D58 1996, (v6)
  HX17.D63 1997, (v6)
Docherty, Thomas. PN98.P64.D64 1990, (v3)
  PN98.S6.D62 1996, (v3)
Dockrell, Julie. LC4704.D63 1993, (v7)
Dockrill, M. L. DA47.1.D63 1999, (v5)
Dockrill, Saki. D1065.G7.D63 1991, (v5)
  UA23.D596 1996, (v10)
Dockstader, Frederick J. E98.A7 D57 1974, (v4)
  E98.T35 D62 1993, (v4)
Docter, Richard F. HQ77.D63 1988, (v6)
Doctor, Ronald M. RC535.D63 2000, (v2)
Doctorow, E. L. PS3554.O3.B6, (v3)
  PS3554.O3.L5 1984, (v3)
  PS3554.O3.R3x, (v3)
  PS3554.O3.Z465 1999, (v3)
Dodd, A. H. HC257.W3.D6 1971, (v6)
Dodd, Christopher. GV791.D63 1992, (v6)
Dodd, Elizabeth Caroline. PS151.D63 1992, (v3)
Dodd, Robert T. QB755.D63 1986, (v1)
Dodd, W. J. PT2621.A26.Z6766 1992, (v3)
Dodd, William Edward. E467.1.D26.D8 1966, (v4)
Dodds, Jerrilynn Denise. NA1303.D63 1989, (v9)
Dodds, Sherril. GV1779.D63 2001, (v6)
Doder, Dusko. DR370.D62, (v5)
Doderer, Heimito von. PT2607.O3.S7, (v3)
Dodge, Charles. ML1092.D54 1997, (v9)
Dodge, Mary Mapes. PZ7.D664Han 1902, (v3)
Dodgen, Randall A. DS793.Y45 D63 2001, (v5)
Dodgson, Charles Lutwidge. PR4611.A17 1960, (v3)
Dodsley, Robert. Z325.D68 1988, (v10)
Dodson, Michael. F1528.D63 1990, (v4)
Dodson, Peter. QE862.O65.D64 1996, (v1)
Dodwell, C. R. N5970.D64 1993, (v9)
  N6763.D62 1982, (v9)
Dodwell, P. C. BF311.D568 2000, (v2)
Doe, Paula. PL785.4.Z5.D6 1982, (v3)
D'Oench, Ellen. NE642.S6.D64 1999, (v9)
Doenecke, Justus D. D769.1.D64 1997, (v5)
  E686.D63, (v4)
  E806.D628 2000, (v4)
  Z6465.U5.D62 1987, (v10)
Doenges, Marilynn E. RT49.D64 2002, (v2)
Doerries, Reinhard R. DA965.C3.D64 2000, (v5)
Doets, Kees. QA76.63.D64 1994, (v1)
Doezema, Marianne. ND237.B45.D6 1991, (v9)
Dohar, William J. DA670.H4.D64 1995, (v5)
Doherty, J. E. DA910.D66 1990, (v5)
Doherty, M. A. D810.P7.G726 2000, (v5)
Doherty, Richard. D754.I5.D64 1999, (v5)
Doherty, Thomas Patrick. D743.23.D63 1993, (v5)
  PN1995.62.D65 1999, (v3)
Dohla, Johann Conrad. E268.D6413 1990, (v4)
Dohner, Janet Vorwald. SF105.275.U6D65 2001, (v1)
Doi, Takeo. PL812.A8.Z613, (v3)
Dolan, Frederick Michael. E169.1.D65 1994, (v4)
Dolan, J. R. CS2505.D65 1972, (v5)
Dolan, John. PR509.O24.D65 1999, (v3)
Dolan, Josephine A. RT31.D64 1983, (v2)
Dolatyar, Mostafa. HD1698.M53.D65 1999, (v6)
Dolbow, Sandra W. PQ41.D65 1986, (v3)
Dole, John M. SB405.D58 1999, (v1)
Dolgin, Janet L. KF3830.D65 1997, (v7)
Doll, Ronald C. LB2806.15.D65 1986, (v7)
Doll, William E. LB1570.D616 1993, (v7)
Dollar, David. HF1414.D65 1993, (v6)
Dollard, John. F215.D65 1957, (v4)
  U22.D6 1944, (v10)
Dolle, Raymond F. Z8113.6.D65 1990, (v10)
Dollenmayer, David B. PT2607.O35.Z66 1988, (v3)
Dollimore, Jonathan. BD444.D42 1998, (v8)
Dollinger, Marc. E184.36.P64.D65 2000, (v4)
Dolmetsch, Mabel. ML424.D65.D57 1980, (v9)

Dolvers, Horst. PR468.F32.D64 1997, **(v3)**
Domb, Risa. PJ5030.E94.D66 1995, **(v3)**
Dombhart, John Martin. F332.W3 D6, **(v4)**
Dombroski, Robert S. PC1064.G7.D66 1989, **(v3)**
Dombrowski, Daniel A. B945.H354.D65 1988, **(v8)**
 B1618.C57, **(v8)**
 BX4700.J7.D56 1992, **(v8)**
 JC574.D63 2001, **(v7)**
Dombrowski, John. F1463.D65, **(v4)**
Dombrowski, Paul M. T10.5.D66 2000, **(v1)**
Dombrowski, Peter. HG2569.D65 1996, **(v6)**
Domenach, Jean-Luc. DS793.H5.D6513 1995, **(v5)**
Domenico, Roy Palmer. DG572.D56 1991, **(v5)**
Domhoff, G. William. HN58.D575, **(v6)**
 HN58.D58, **(v6)**
 HN90.E4.D648 1990, **(v6)**
 HN90.E4 D652 1998, **(v6)**
Dominguez, Frank. PQ6412.M6.D66 1988, **(v3)**
Dominguez, Jorge I. F1412.D67, **(v4)**
 F1788.D59 1989, **(v4)**
 JL1292.D66 1996, **(v7)**
Dominice, Pierre. LB1029.B55 D64 2000, **(v7)**
Dominick, Raymond H. HC290.5.E5.D66 1992, **(v6)**
Dominik, Mark. PR2958.M53.D66 1988, **(v3)**
Domke, William Kinkade. U21.2.D55 1988, **(v10)**
Domnarski, William. KF255.D66 1996, **(v7)**
Domosh, Mona. HT168.N5.D66 1996, **(v6)**
Donagan, Alan. B105.A35.D66 1987, **(v8)**
 BJ1012.D57, **(v8)**
Donahue, Debra L. KF5505.A68.D66 1998, **(v7)**
Donahue, Hugh Carter. KF2812.D66 1989, **(v7)**
Donahue, John D. HD3850.D66 1989, **(v6)**
Donahue, M. Patricia. RT31.D66 1996, **(v2)**
Donahue, Neil H. PT735.D66 1993, **(v3)**
Donahue, Thomas John. PQ6601.R58.Z64, **(v3)**
Donald, David Herbert. E338.D58 1978, **(v4)**
 E415.9.S9.D6, **(v4)**
 E415.9.S9.D62 1970, **(v4)**
 E457.D66 1995, **(v4)**
 E457.8.D69, **(v4)**
 E468.D65, **(v4)**
Donald, Janet Gail. LB2341.D66 1997, **(v7)**
Donald, Leland. E78.N78.D63 1997, **(v4)**
Donald, Merlin. BF311.D57 2001, **(v2)**
Donald, Peter. DA803.3.D66 1990, **(v5)**
Donald, Stephanie. PN1993.5.C4.D66 2000, **(v3)**
Donaldson, Bruce K. TL671.6.D56 1993, **(v1)**
Donaldson, Gary. E815.D66 1999, **(v4)**
Donaldson, Gordon A. LB2822.82.D65 2001, **(v7)**
Donaldson, Gordon. DA755.D57, **(v5)**
 DA787.A1.D59, **(v5)**
Donaldson, Margaret C. LB1115.D59 1979, **(v7)**
Donaldson, Peter J. HB884.5.D66 1990, **(v6)**
Donaldson, Robert H. DK266.45.D66 1998, **(v5)**
Donaldson, Sandra. Z8124.4.D66 1993, **(v10)**
Donaldson, Scott. PS3515.E37.Z58574 1999, **(v3)**
 PS3525.A27.Z63 1992, **(v3)**
Donaldson, Susan Van D'Elden. PS377.D66 1998, **(v3)**
Donaldson, Terence L. BS2651.D66 1997, **(v8)**
Donaldson, Thomas. HD2755.5.D65 1989, **(v6)**
Donato, Eugenio. PQ2249.D56 1992, **(v3)**
Donato, Ruben. LC2683.D66 1997, **(v7)**
Donawerth, Jane. PS374.S35.D66 1997, **(v3)**
Doner, Richard F. HD9710.A7852.D66 1991, **(v6)**
Doniger, Wendy. BL304.D54 1998, **(v8)**
 BL304.D55 1988, **(v8)**
 BL325.S42.D65 1999, **(v8)**
Donington, Robert. ML460.D63 1982, **(v9)**
 ML1700.D66, **(v9)**
 ML1700.D665 1990, **(v9)**
 ML1700.D67, **(v9)**
Donker, Marjorie. PR2997.P7.D66 1992, **(v3)**
Donleavy, J. P. PS3507.O686.G56, **(v3)**
Donn, Linda. BF173.F85.D6 1988, **(v2)**
Donnan, Elizabeth. E441.D66, **(v4)**
Donnan, Hastings. GN491.7.D66 1999, **(v6)**
Donne, John. BV245.D65, **(v8)**
 PR2245.A5, **(v3)**
 PR2245.A5.C6, **(v3)**
 PR2246.C37 1990, **(v3)**

PR2246.G26 1978, **(v3)**
PR2246.G27, **(v3)**
PR2247.A5 1963, **(v3)**
PR2247.P3 1980, **(v3)**
Donnelly, Dorothy F. HX806.D66 1998, **(v6)**
Donnelly, Ignatius. PS1545.D55 C3 1960, **(v3)**
Donnelly, Jack. JC571.D74 1985, **(v7)**
 JC571.D75 1989, **(v7)**
 JZ1307.D66 2000, **(v7)**
Donnelly, Marian C. NA1201.D66 1992, **(v9)**
Donnelly, William M. DS919.D658 2001, **(v5)**
Donner, Frank J. HV8138.D66 1990, **(v6)**
Donner, Fred McGraw. DS38.1.D66, **(v5)**
Donner, Wendy. B1607.D58 1991, **(v8)**
Donnet, Pierre-Antoine. DS786.D6613 1994, **(v5)**
Donno, Elizabeth Story. PR1207.D58 1963, **(v3)**
Donoghue, Denis. PR21.D66 1998, **(v3)**
 PR508.R4.D66 2001, **(v3)**
 PR736.D6, **(v3)**
 PR3727.D6, **(v3)**
 PS3509.L43.Z668 2000, **(v3)**
Donoghue, Frank. PR448.B67.D66 1996, **(v3)**
Donohue, William A. JC599.U5.D66 1985, **(v7)**
Donoso, Jose. PQ8097.D617.D4713 1988, **(v3)**
 PQ8097.D617.O2, **(v3)**
Donovan, Arthur. QD22.L4.D58 1993, **(v1)**
Donovan, Denis M. RJ504.D65 1990, **(v2)**
Donovan, John. PZ7.D7228II, **(v3)**
Donovan, Josephine. PN3401.D66 1999, **(v3)**
Donovan, Robert J. E813.D63 1996, **(v4)**
 PN4888.T4.D66 1992, **(v3)**
Doob, Leonard William. PL8013.E5.D65, **(v3)**
Doody, Margaret Anne. PN3355.D66 1996, **(v3)**
 PR3316.A4.Z63 1988, **(v3)**
Dooley, Brian. E840.8.K4.D66 1996, **(v4)**
Dooley, Deborah Anne. PE1404.D66 1995, **(v3)**
Dooley, Patrick Kiaran. PS1449.C85.Z5795 1993, **(v3)**
Dooley, Thomas A. RA390.U5.D583, **(v2)**
Doolittle, James. PQ2474.Z5.D67, **(v3)**
Doolittle, William Emery. F1219.3.I77.D66 1989, **(v4)**
Doorn, Jacobus Adrianus Antonius van. U21.5.D63, **(v10)**
Dor, Mosheh. PJ5054.D6.O913 1989, **(v3)**
Doran, J. E. CC75.D63, **(v5)**
Doran, Kevin. BD450.D65 1989, **(v8)**
Doran, Madeleine. PR3072.D6, **(v3)**
Doran, Michael Scott. DT107.82.D67 1999, **(v5)**
Doran, Susan. BR756.D65 1994, **(v8)**
Dordick, Gwendolyn A. HV4506.N6.D67 1997, **(v6)**
Dore, Clement. BJ1031.D67 1990, **(v8)**
Dore, M. H. I. HB3714.D67 1993, **(v6)**
Dore, Ronald Philip. HC462.9.D663 1987, **(v6)**
 HD70.J3 D67 2000, **(v6)**
 LC1047.J3.D67 1989, **(v7)**
Doremus, R. H. TP857.D67 1994, **(v1)**
Doreski, Carole. PS153.N5.D597 1998, **(v3)**
 PS3503.I785.Z635 1993, **(v3)**
Doreski, William. PS310.M57.D67 1995, **(v3)**
Dorf, Philip. SB63.B3.D6, **(v1)**
Dorf, Richard C. TJ216.D67 1986, **(v1)**
 TK454.D67 2001, **(v1)**
Dorfer, Ingemar. UA646.7.D67 1997, **(v10)**
Dorff, Elliot N. BM538.H43.D68 1998, **(v8)**
Dorfman, Ariel. PQ7082.N7.D67 1991, **(v3)**
 PQ8098.14.O7.M613 1990, **(v3)**
 PQ8098.14.O7.M9 1990, **(v3)**
 PQ8098.14.O7.P3713 1988, **(v3)**
Dorfman, Gerald Allen. HD8383.D67 1983, **(v6)**
 HD8383.T74.D66, **(v6)**
Dorian, A. F. Q123.D673 1981, **(v1)**
Dorian, Frederick. ML430.5.D66.H5, **(v9)**
Doriani, Beth Maclay. PS1541.Z5.D64 1996, **(v3)**
Dority, G. Kim. Z1035.1.D665 1995, **(v10)**
Dorkenoo, Efua. GN484.D64 1994, **(v6)**
Dorling, Daniel. G1812.21.E1.D6 1995, **(v6)**
Dormael, Armand van. HG205 1944.D67 1978, **(v6)**
Dorman, Peter. HD7262.D58 1996, **(v6)**
Dormandy, Thomas. RC311.D67 2000, **(v2)**
Dormer, Peter. NK1390.D67 1990, **(v9)**
Dorn, Frank. D767.6.D58 1971, **(v5)**

Dorn, Harold. Q125.D65 1991, **(v1)**
Dornberger, Walter. UF767.D655 1954, **(v10)**
Dornbusch, Rudiger. HG3821.D69 1988, **(v6)**
 HJ8899.D67 1989, **(v6)**
Dornfeld, Barry. PN1992.8.D6.D69 1998, **(v3)**
Dorondo, D. R. DD801.B42.D68 1992, **(v5)**
Doronila, Amando. HC453.D67 1992, **(v6)**
Dorr, Rheta Louise (Childe). JK1899.A6.D6 1970, **(v7)**
Dorra, Henri. N6505.D65, **(v9)**
Dorrance, Ward Allison. PS3507.O7373 W5, **(v3)**
Dorrien, Gary J. JA84.U5.D67 1993, **(v7)**
Dorsch, Nina G. LB2805.D67 1998, **(v7)**
Dorsett, Lyle W. F474.K2D6, **(v4)**
Dorson, Richard Mercer. GR340.D66, **(v6)**
Dorst, John Darwin. F159.C33.D67 1989, **(v4)**
Dorwart, Jeffery M. F142.C2.D67 1992, **(v4)**
 UA18.U5.D67 1991, **(v10)**
Dos Passos, John Roderigo. G463.D66, **(v6)**
Dos Passos, John. E169.D68, **(v4)**
 E302.1.D6, **(v4)**
 PS3507.O743.A6 1988, **(v3)**
 PS3507.O743 B5, **(v3)**
 PS3507.O743 C4, **(v3)**
 PS3507.O743 C5, **(v3)**
 PS3507.O743 D5 1952, **(v3)**
 PS3507.O743 F6, **(v3)**
 PS3507.O743 G7, **(v3)**
 PS3507.O743 G73, **(v3)**
 PS3507.O743.M3 1963, **(v3)**
 PS3507.O743 M5, **(v3)**
 PS3507.O743.M6, **(v3)**
 PS3507.O743 N5, **(v3)**
 PS3507.O743 N8, **(v3)**
 PS3507.O743 S65 1939, **(v3)**
 PS3507.O743.S77 1990, **(v3)**
 PS3507.O743.T47 1970, **(v3)**
 PS3507.O743 T5, **(v3)**
 PS3507.O743.U5 1937, **(v3)**
 PS3507.O743.Z487 1989, **(v3)**
 PS3507.O743.Z49, **(v3)**
 PS3507.O743.Z53 1973, **(v3)**
Dosal, Paul J. HD9259.B3.G834 1993, **(v6)**
Dosick, Wayne D. BJ1631.D66 1995, **(v8)**
Doss, Erika Lee. N8835.D67 1995, **(v9)**
 ND237.B47.D67 1991, **(v9)**
Dossey, Barbara Montgomery. RT37.N5.D67 2000, **(v2)**
 RT42.H65 2000, **(v2)**
Dostoevskii, Fedor Mikhailovich. PG3326.A15 1946, **(v3)**
 PG3326.A16.B7, **(v3)**
Dostoyevsky, Fyodor. PG3325.U5.E5, **(v3)**
 PG3325.Z3.E5, **(v3)**
 PG3326.A16M3 1997, **(v3)**
 PG3326.B6, **(v3)**
 PG3326.B7.G3 1990, **(v3)**
 PG3326.Z4 1982, **(v3)**
 PG3326.Z4 2001, **(v3)**
Dote, Yasuhiko. TK7881.15.D68 1998, **(v1)**
Doten, Alfred. F865.D67 1973, **(v4)**
Dothan, Trude Krakauer. DS90.D613 1982, **(v5)**
Doty, Alexander. PN1995.9.H55.D68 2000, **(v3)**
Doty, William G. BF692.5.D67 1993, **(v2)**
 BL304.D58 2000, **(v8)**
Double, Richard. B74.D68 1999, **(v8)**
 BJ1461.D67 1991, **(v8)**
 BJ1468.5.D68 1996, **(v8)**
Doubler, Michael D. D761.D64 1994, **(v5)**
Douchant, Mike. GV885.7.D68 1995, **(v6)**
Douchet, Jean. PN1993.5.F7.D6813 1998, **(v3)**
Dougherty, Carol. PA4167.D68, **(v3)**
Dougherty, David M. PQ1109.D63, **(v3)**
Dougherty, James E. JX1395.D67 1981, **(v7)**
Dougherty, James. PS3242.C56.D68 1993, **(v3)**
Dougherty, Keith L. JK316.D68 2001, **(v7)**
Dougherty, Richard. PS3554.O82.D9, **(v3)**
Doughty, Harold. KF266.D68 1999, **(v7)**
 R735.A4.D68 1999, **(v2)**
Doughty, Oswald. PR4483.D6 1981, **(v3)**
Dougill, John. PR8489.O93.D68 1998, **(v3)**

Douglas, A. E. QH548.D68 1994, **(v1)**
Douglas, Aileen. PR3698.B57.D68 1995, **(v3)**
Douglas, Alfred Bruce. PR4613.D4 1919, **(v3)**
  PR5823.D58 1940, **(v3)**
  PR6007.O86.Z5 1970, **(v3)**
Douglas, Allen. DC373.V3.D68 1992, **(v5)**
Douglas, Bodie Eugene. QD475.D65 1983, **(v1)**
Douglas, Emily (Taft). HQ764.S3.D66, **(v6)**
Douglas, George H. PN4877.D67 1991, **(v3)**
  TF23.D67 1992, **(v1)**
Douglas, J. Yellowlees. PN3377.5.C57.D68 2000, **(v3)**
Douglas, Jack D. HV6545.D6, **(v6)**
Douglas, Krystan V. Z2014.D7.D68 1996, **(v10)**
Douglas, Lloyd C. PS3507.O7573 R6, **(v3)**
Douglas, Marjory Stoneman. F317.E9.D6, **(v4)**
Douglas, Mary Tev. GN494.D6 1966a, **(v6)**
Douglas, Mary. BH39.D68 1996, **(v8)**
  BL48.D67 1970b, **(v8)**
  GN448.D68 1982, **(v6)**
Douglas, Norman. PR6007.O88 I3, **(v3)**
  PR6007.O88 S6, **(v3)**
Douglas, R. M. HV8023.D68 1999, **(v6)**
Douglas, Roy. D743.2.D69 1990, **(v5)**
  D748.D68 1981, **(v5)**
Douglas, Stephen Arnold. E415.9.D73.A4, **(v4)**
Douglas, William O. DS49.5.D62, **(v5)**
  E457.2.D7, **(v4)**
  F851.7.D68 1990, **(v4)**
  KF8745.D6.A28, **(v7)**
  KF8745.D6 A43 2000, **(v7)**
Douglass, Carrie B. DP52.D68 1997, **(v5)**
Douglass, Elisha P. JK2413.D6, **(v7)**
Douglass, Fenner. ML574.D69 1995, **(v9)**
Douglass, Frederick. E449.D733, **(v4)**
  E449.D736, **(v4)**
  E449.D738 1968, **(v4)**
  E449.D744 1962, **(v4)**
  E449.D749 1989, **(v4)**
Douglass, Harl Roy. LB1628.D67 1964, **(v7)**
Doumas, Christos. DF221.T38.D68 1983, **(v5)**
Doumato, Eleanor Abdella. HQ1730.D68 2000, **(v6)**
Douville, Judith A. RA1242.T6.D68 1990, **(v2)**
Douzinas, Costas. JC571.D77 2000, **(v7)**
Dove, George N. PN3448.D4.D68 1997, **(v3)**
Dove, Richard. PT2642.O65.Z63 1990, **(v3)**
Dovell, Junius Elmore. F311.D68, **(v4)**
Dover, Cedric. N6538.N5.D6 1960, **(v9)**
Dover, G. A. QH366.2.D67 2000, **(v1)**
Dover, Kenneth James. HQ76.3.G8.D68 1978, **(v6)**
  PA373.D6, **(v3)**
Doverspike, Dennis. HF5549.5.A34.D68 1999, **(v6)**
Dovlatov, Sergei. PG3479.6.O85.C513 1990, **(v3)**
Dovring, Folke. HD1415.D68 1988, **(v6)**
Dovring, Karin. PE2751.D68 1997, **(v3)**
Dow Chemical Company. QD1.A355 no. 6, etc., **(v1)**
Dow, Bonnie J. PN1992.8.W65.D69 1996, **(v3)**
Dow, J. C. R. HG939.5.D68 1988, **(v6)**
Dow, Peter B. LC89.D68 1991, **(v7)**
Dow, Sheila C. HB131.D69 2002, **(v6)**
  HB172.5.D69 1996, **(v6)**
Dowd, Douglas Fitzgerald. HB119.V4.D65, **(v6)**
  HB501.D68 2000, **(v6)**
  HC79.W3.D69 1989, **(v6)**
  HC103.D753 1993, **(v6)**
  HC106.8.D68 1997, **(v6)**
Dowd, Gregory Evans. E77.D694 1992, **(v4)**
Dowd, Kevin. HG1685.D68 1996, **(v6)**
  HG1811.D68 1989, **(v6)**
Dowd, Nancy E. HQ759.915.D69 1997, **(v6)**
Dowden, Ken. BL689.D68 2000, **(v8)**
Dowden, Stephen D. PT2621.A26.S3975 1995, **(v3)**
  PT2662.E7.Z65 1991, **(v3)**
Dowdey, Clifford. E476.5.D6 1960, **(v4)**
Dower, John W. Z3306.D69 1995, **(v10)**
Dowling, Colette. HQ1206.D683 2000, **(v6)**
Dowling, David. PR6045.O72.M735 1991, **(v3)**
Dowling, Linda C. PR468.A33.D69 1996, **(v3)**
  PR468.H65.D68 1994, **(v3)**
Downer, Alan Seymour. PR625.D55, **(v3)**
Downes, David Anthony. PR4803.H44.Z62, **(v3)**
  PR4803.H44.Z623 1990, **(v3)**

Downes, Edward. MT125.D68 1981, **(v9)**
Downes, Jeremy M. PN56.E65.D69 1997, **(v3)**
Downes, Kerry. NA997.H3.D6 1980, **(v9)**
  NA997.V3.D68, **(v9)**
  NA997.W8.D59 1982, **(v9)**
Downes, Larry. HD30.2.D68 1998, **(v6)**
Downes, Randolph C. F486.O526 vol. 3, **(v4)**
Downey, Glanville. DR729.D6, **(v5)**
  DS99.A6.D6, **(v5)**
Downey, Paul. RX71.D69 1997, **(v2)**
Downey, Roger. E78.W3.D69 2000, **(v4)**
Downey, Susan B. DS57.D68 1988, **(v5)**
Downing, David C. PR6023.E926.Z642 1992, **(v3)**
Downing, Douglas. QA303.D77 1982, **(v1)**
Downing, Taylor. PN1997.O4193.D68 1992, **(v3)**
Downs, Anthony. HE355.3.C64.D69 1992, **(v6)**
  HN90.C6.D68, **(v6)**
Downs, Brian Westerdale. PT8890.D6 1972, **(v3)**
Downs, Charles. DP681.D68 1989, **(v5)**
Downs, David. PN2061.D68 1995, **(v3)**
Downs, Donald Alexander. KF9444.D69 1989, **(v7)**
Downs, Jacques M. HF3840.C36.D69 1997, **(v6)**
Downs, Norton. D113.5.D6, **(v5)**
Downs, Robert Bingham. LB627.D68, **(v7)**
  LB638.D68, **(v7)**
Dowson, Ernest Christopher. PR4613.D5.A17 1970, **(v3)**
Dowswell, Christopher R. SB191.M2.D685 1996, **(v1)**
Doxey, Margaret P. JX1246.D69 1987, **(v7)**
Doyle, Arthur Conan. PR4620.A2 1937, **(v3)**
  PR4621.B47 2001, **(v3)**
  PR4621.M6, **(v3)**
  PR4622.P6, **(v3)**
  PR4622.P76 1976, **(v3)**
  PR4623.A4 1924, **(v3)**
Doyle, Billy H. PN1998.2.D688 1999, **(v3)**
  PN1998.2.D69 1995, **(v3)**
  PN2285.D68 1999, **(v3)**
Doyle, Charles. PR6001.L4.Z59 1989, **(v3)**
Doyle, Christine. PS1018.D69 2000, **(v3)**
Doyle, Don Harrison. F444.N257.D69 1985, **(v4)**
  F549.J2.D68, **(v4)**
  HT123.S6.D69 1990, **(v6)**
Doyle, Jack. HD9006.D65 1985, **(v6)**
Doyle, Kevin. GE60.D69 1999, **(v6)**
Doyle, Paul A. PR6045.A97.Z682 1988, **(v3)**
Doyle, Peter. QE651.D64 1994, **(v1)**
  QE770.D69 1996, **(v1)**
Doyle, Robert C. E181.D69 1997, **(v4)**
  UB803.D69 1994, **(v10)**
Doyle, Rodger Pirnie. G1200.D6 1994, **(v6)**
Doyle, William. DC147.8.D69, **(v5)**
  DC148.D69 1989, **(v5)**
Doyno, Victor. PS1305.D69 1991, **(v3)**
Dozer, Donald Marquand. F181.D65, **(v4)**
Draaisma, D. BF371.D6813 2000, **(v2)**
Drabble, Margaret. PR149.L35.D7 1979, **(v3)**
  PR6003.E6.Z715 1974, **(v3)**
  PR6045.I577.Z63 1996, **(v3)**
  PR6054.R25.I25, **(v3)**
  PR6054.R25.J4, **(v3)**
  PR6054.R25.M5, **(v3)**
  PR6054.R25.M5 1980, **(v3)**
  PR6054.R25.N4, **(v3)**
  PR6054.R25.R4, **(v3)**
  PR6054.R25.S, **(v3)**
  PR6054.R25.W3, **(v3)**
Drabkin, William. ML410.B42.D8 1991, **(v9)**
Drache, Hiram M. F642.R3 D7, **(v4)**
Drachler, Jacob. PL8013.E5.D68, **(v3)**
Drachman, Edward R. E840.D73 1997, **(v4)**
Drago, Edmund L. F274.D7 1998, **(v4)**
Drago, Raymond J. TJ184.D7 1988, **(v1)**
Dragoo, Jason L. RC1210.D73 1993, **(v2)**
Draitser, Emil. DK510.33.D73 1998, **(v5)**
Drake, C. J. M. HV6431.D73 1998, **(v6)**
Drake, Daniel. F455.D73 1999, **(v4)**
Drake, Durant. BD21.D7 1968, **(v8)**
Drake, Ellen T. QE22.H76.D74 1996, **(v1)**
Drake, Frances. QC981.8.G56.D73 2000, **(v1)**
Drake, Francis. G420.D7A3 1969, **(v6)**

Drake, Frank D. QB54.D72 1992, **(v1)**
Drake, James David. E83.67.D74 1999, **(v4)**
Drake, James W. RC684.E4, **(v2)**
Drake, Paul W. HD8259.S65.D7 1996, **(v6)**
Drake, Richard B. F106.D73 2001, **(v4)**
Drake, St. Clair. CB195.D72 1987, **(v5)**
Drake, Stillman. QB36.G2.D688, **(v1)**
Drake, Thomas Edward. E441.D75 1965, **(v4)**
Drake, Willie Avon. HF5549.5.A34.D73 1996, **(v6)**
Drakeman, Donald L. KF4865.D73 1991, **(v7)**
Drame, Kandioura. PQ3989.2.B45.Z64 1990, **(v3)**
Dramstad, Wenche E. SB472.3.D73 1996, **(v1)**
Draper, Allison Stark. F69.R43 D73 2001, **(v4)**
Draper, Elaine. RB155.6.D73 1991, **(v2)**
Draper, Hal. JC474.D734 1987, **(v7)**
Draper, Ronald P. PR601.D67 1999, **(v3)**
  PR6023.A93.Z624, **(v3)**
  PR6023.A93.Z6245 1970b, **(v3)**
Draper, Theodore. E210.D73 1996, **(v4)**
Dray, William H. D16.8.D69, **(v5)**
  D16.8.D7, **(v5)**
Drayton, Michael. PR2255.A5.B8 1953, **(v3)**
Drayton, Richard Harry. DA470.D73 2000, **(v5)**
Draz, Mohammad Abd Allah. BP130.D73 2000, **(v8)**
Drea, Edward J. D767.D66 1991, **(v5)**
Drees, Ludwig. DF261.O5.D713 1968, **(v5)**
Dreger, Alice Domurat. RC883.D695 1998, **(v2)**
Dreifort, John E. DS518.2.D74 1991, **(v5)**
Dreiser, Theodore. PS3507.R55.A15 1956, **(v3)**
  PS3507.R55.A16 1988, **(v3)**
  PS3507.R55.A6 1996, **(v3)**
  PS3507.R55 A8 1948, **(v3)**
  PS3507.R55 B8, **(v3)**
  PS3507.R55.C45, **(v3)**
  PS3507.R55 D73 1970, **(v3)**
  PS3507.R55 F5 1967, **(v3)**
  PS3507.R55 F7, **(v3)**
  PS3507.R55 S8, **(v3)**
  PS3507.R55 T5 1925, **(v3)**
  PS3507.R55.T9 1998, **(v3)**
  PS3507.R55.Z476 1991, **(v3)**
  PS3507.R55.Z54 1959, **(v3)**
Drell, Sidney D. QC773.3.U5.D74 1993, **(v1)**
Dresang, Eliza T. PN1009.5.T43.D74 1999, **(v3)**
Drescher, John. F260.D74 2000, **(v4)**
Drescher, Tim. ND2638.S26 D74 1991, **(v9)**
Dresden, S. PN56.H55.D7413 1995, **(v3)**
Dressler, Alan Michael. QB991.G73.D74 1994, **(v1)**
Dretske, Fred I. BD418.3.D74 1995, **(v8)**
  BF38.D675 1988, **(v2)**
Drew, Bernard A. Z1231.F4.D68 1989, **(v10)**
Drew, David E. QA13.D74 1996, **(v1)**
Drew, Elizabeth A. PR821.D7 1964, **(v3)**
  E860.D73, **(v4)**
  E868.D73, **(v4)**
  E885.D74 1996, **(v4)**
  E886.D74 1994, **(v4)**
Drew, John. PR129.I5.D74 1987, **(v3)**
Drew, Philip. NA4160.D73 1979, **(v9)**
  PR4231.D75, **(v3)**
Drewal, Henry John. N7399.N52.Y68 1989, **(v9)**
Drewe, Sheryle Bergmann. GV342.D74 2001, **(v6)**
Drews, Arthur. BT303.2.D753 1998, **(v8)**
Drews, Robert. DF220.D73 1988, **(v5)**
  GN778.3.A1.D74 1993, **(v6)**
Drexler, Arthur. NA737.N4.A4 1982, **(v9)**
  NA1088.M65.D7, **(v9)**
Drexler, K. Eric. T45.D74 1991, **(v1)**
  T47.D74 1986, **(v1)**
  T174.7.D74 1992, **(v1)**
Dreybrodt, Wolfgang. GB600.D75 1988, **(v6)**
Dreyer, Edward L. DS775.4.D74 1995, **(v5)**
Dreyer, J. L. E. QB15.D77 1953, **(v1)**
Dreyer, Lynette. HN801.Z9.E436 1989, **(v6)**
Dreyer, Sharon Spredemann. Z1037.A1.D678 1977, **(v10)**
Dreyfus, Laurence. ML410.B1 D63 1996, **(v9)**
Dreyfuss, Henry. TS149.D678 1967, **(v1)**
Driankov, Dimiter. TJ217.5.D75 1996, **(v1)**
Dries, Angelyn. BV2240.N7.D75 1998, **(v8)**
Driesen, David M. HC110.E5 D74 2003, **(v6)**

Drieu La Rochelle, Pierre. PQ2607.R56.F42E5 1965, **(v3)**

Driggs, Sarah Shields. F234.R58.D75 2001, **(v4)**

Drinan, Joanne. TD430.D764 2001, **(v1)**

Drinker, Elizabeth Sandwith. F158.9.F89.D75 1991, **(v4)**

Drinkwater, J. F. DC62.D69 1983, **(v5)**

Drinkwater, John. PR6007.R5.A19 1968, **(v3)**
PR6007.R5.Z52 1970, **(v3)**
PR6007.R5.Z5 I93la, **(v3)**

Drinkwater, Michael. HD2131.Z8.D75 1991, **(v6)**

Drinnon, Richard. E98.P99.D74, **(v4)**

Dripps, R. D. NA2500.D75 1997, **(v9)**

Driscoll, C. J. SB123.D75 1990, **(v4)**

Driscoll, John Paul. N6537.K43.A4 1985, **(v9)**

Driskel, Michael Paul. NA6165.D75 1993, **(v9)**

Driskell, David C. N6538.N5.D74, **(v9)**

Driskell, Judy A. TX361.A8.D75 2000, **(v1)**

Driver, Ciaran. HD5713.2.D75 1987, **(v6)**

Driver, Felix. G70.D75 2001, **(v6)**

Driver, Hugh. UG635.G7.D75 1997, **(v10)**

Driver, Stephen. JN1129.L32.D75 1998, **(v7)**

Drlica, Karl. QH442.2.D75 1997, **(v1)**
RB155.D76 1994, **(v2)**

Droge, Arthur J. HV6543.D76 1991, **(v6)**

Droste-Hulshoff, Annette von. PT1848.A1 1963, **(v3)**
PT1848.A1 1994, **(v3)**

Drowatzky, John N. RC1235.D76 1996, **(v2)**

Droz, Jacques. D383.D7, **(v5)**

Drozdek, Adam. QA76.73.C153D76 2001, **(v1)**

Drucker, Dan. KF3771.A7.D8 1990, **(v7)**

Drucker, H. M. B823.5.D78, **(v8)**

Drucker, Johanna. N7433.3.D78 1995, **(v9)**

Drucker, Peter Ferdinand. H59.D75.A33 1979, **(v6)**
HC59.D69 1969b, **(v6)**
HC59.15.D78 1993, **(v6)**
HD30.27.D78 1999, **(v6)**
HD31.D77337 1995, **(v6)**
HD31.D77339 2002, **(v6)**
HD31.D7742 1998, **(v6)**
HD62.6.D78 1990, **(v6)**
HD82.D7, **(v6)**
HD2346.U5.D78 1985, **(v6)**
HD2731.D7 1972, **(v6)**

Druett, Joan. RC986.D78 2000, **(v2)**
VK139.D78 1998, **(v10)**

Drug Abuse Council (Washington, D.C.).
HV5825.D772 1980, **(v6)**

Drukman, Mason. E748.M76.D78 1997, **(v4)**

Druks, Herbert. E183.8.I7.D78 2001, **(v4)**

Drum, Jean. PN1998.3.D74.D78 2000, **(v3)**

Drummond, Ian M. KF6668.U55.D78 1989, **(v7)**

Drummond, William. PR2260.A5K3. 1968, **(v3)**

Drummy, Michael F. BT695.5.D78 2000, **(v8)**

Drury, Allen. PS3554.R8.A3, **(v3)**
PS3554.R8.S5, **(v3)**

Drury, Francis K. W. Z5781.D8 1987, **(v10)**

Drury, John. ND1432.E85.D78 1999, **(v9)**
PN1021.D78 1995, **(v3)**

Drury, Nevill. BF1407.D78 1992, **(v2)**

Drury, Richard Toshiyuki. HC415.25.Z7.W4725 1992, **(v6)**

Drury, S. A. G70.4.D78 1990, **(v6)**
QB632.D78 1999, **(v1)**

Drury, Shadia B. JC251.D78 1997, **(v7)**
JC273.K57.D78 1994, **(v7)**

Drury, W. H. QH541.D77 1998, **(v1)**

Drury, Wells. F849.V8.D73 1984, **(v4)**

Dry, Avis M. BF109.J8.D7, **(v2)**

Dryden, Charles W. D790.D78 1997, **(v5)**

Dryden, Deborah M. TT851.D79 1993, **(v1)**

Dryden, John. PR3410.F50, **(v3)**
PR3412.K5, **(v3)**
PR3413.W3, **(v3)**
PR3417.A1 1961, **(v3)**

Dryfoos, Joy G. HV1431.D79 1990, **(v6)**
LB3409.U5.D79 1994, **(v7)**

Drysdale, Peter. HF1583.D79 1988, **(v6)**

Drysdale, Robert G. TH1199.D78 1994, **(v1)**

Dryzek, John S. JC423.D725 2000, **(v7)**

Dshalalow, Jewgeni H. QA300.D74 2001, **(v1)**

Du Bellay, Joachim. PC2079.D8 1948, **(v3)**
PQ1668.R4, **(v3)**

Du Boff, Richard B. HC110.S3.D8 1989, **(v6)**

Du Bois, W. E. B. E185.5.D817 1969, **(v4)**
E185.5.D8 1969, **(v4)**
E185.5.D84, **(v4)**
E185.97.D73.A25 1982, **(v4)**
E185.97.D73.A26, **(v4)**
E185.97.D73.A3, **(v4)**
E185.97.D73 A322 2000, **(v4)**
E185.97.D73.A4 1973, **(v4)**
E185.97.D73 D8, **(v4)**
E441.D81 1969, **(v4)**
E668.D83, **(v4)**

Du Boulay, F. R. H. DD156.D83 1983, **(v5)**

Du Maurier, Daphne. PR4174.B2.D8 1961, **(v3)**
PR6007.U47 R4, **(v3)**
PR6007.U47 T45, **(v3)**

Du Maurier, George. PR4634.M3, **(v3)**
PR4634.P4, **(v3)**

Du Pont de Nemours, Pierre Samuel.
DC131.9.D85.A3413 1984, **(v5)**

Du Preez, Wilhelmus Petrus. JA74.5.D8 1980, **(v7)**

Du Prey, Pierre de la Ruffiniere. NA997.S7.D85 1982, **(v9)**

Du Puy, David. SB409.8.C95.D8 1988, **(v1)**

Du Toit, Brian M. DT429.5.A47.D88 1998, **(v5)**
F2881.D8 1995, **(v4)**

Du Toit, P. van der P. JQ2760.A91.D8 1995, **(v7)**

Du Vall, Nell. TX15.D8 1988, **(v1)**

Du, Dingzhu. QA267.7.D8 2000, **(v1)**

Du, Phuoc Long. HV6439.U5.D8 1996, **(v6)**

Duara, Prasenjit. DS734.7.D83 1995, **(v5)**
HN740.Z9.C633 1988, **(v6)**

Duban, James. PS2127.E8.D83 2001, **(v3)**

Dubbey, J. M. QA27.G7.D8, **(v1)**

Dube, Marcel. PQ3919.2.D76.B4, **(v3)**

Dube, Saurabh. DS432.S359.D834 1998, **(v5)**

Dubin, Lois C. DS135.I85.T735 1999, **(v5)**

Dubin, Michael J. JK1967.D77 1998, **(v7)**

Dubin, Steven C. NX735.D79 1992, **(v9)**

Dubinsky, David. HD6509.D8.A33, **(v6)**

Dubnov, Simon. DS117.D7213, **(v5)**

DuBoff, Leonard D. KF4290.A68.D8 1996, **(v7)**

Dubofsky, Melvyn. HD8066.D76 2000, **(v6)**
HD8072.D846 1985, **(v6)**

DuBois, Ellen Carol. HQ1423.D8 1999, **(v6)**

Dubois, Philip L. KF4881.D83 1998, **(v7)**

Dubos, Rene J. HM206.D87, **(v6)**
Q125.D814, **(v1)**

DuBose, John Witherspoon. F326.D797, **(v4)**

Dubost, Thierry. PS3529.N5.Z6285 1997, **(v3)**

Dubrow, Heather. PR535.L7.D83 1995, **(v3)**

Duby, Georges. DC33.2.D7513 1991, **(v5)**
DC90.D813 1990, **(v5)**
HD1917.D813, **(v6)**
HN11.D78 1977b, **(v6)**
HN425.D78313, **(v6)**
HQ623.D8313 1983, **(v6)**
N5970.D8313, **(v9)**
NB170.D813 1990, **(v9)**

Ducasse, Isidore Lucien. PQ2220.D723.C53 1965, **(v3)**

Duchen, Claire. HQ1613.D8 1986, **(v6)**

Duchene, Francois. D413.M56.D73 1994, **(v5)**

Duchovnay, Gerald. PN2287.B48.D83 1999, **(v3)**

DuCille, Ann. E185.615.D78 1996, **(v4)**

Duck, Steve. HM132.D828 1991, **(v6)**

Duckett, Eleanor Shipley. LB125.A4.D8 1965, **(v7)**

Duckett, Kenneth W. CD950.D8, **(v5)**

Duckles, Vincent H. ML113.D83 1997, **(v9)**

Ducklin, Keith. PN2071.F4.D837 2001, **(v3)**

Duckworth, George Eckel. PA6069.D8, **(v3)**
PA6165.D8, **(v3)**

Dudden, Arthur Power. DU30.D83 1992, **(v5)**

Dudden, Faye E. HD6072.2.U5.D82 1983, **(v6)**
PN1590.W64.D84 1994, **(v3)**

Dudek, Gregory. TJ211.415.D83 2000, **(v1)**

Duderstadt, James J. GV351.D83 2000, **(v6)**
TK1078.D83, **(v1)**

Dudley, Darle W. TJ184.D784 1984, **(v1)**

Dudley, Mark E. KF228.B76.D83 1994b, **(v7)**

Dudley, Robert. QL496.7.D83 2000, **(v1)**

Dudley, Underwood. QA99.D83 1992, **(v1)**

Dudziak, Mary L. E185.61.D85 2000, **(v4)**

Duellman, William Edward. QL667.D84 1986, **(v1)**

Duensing, Edward. Z5942.D87 1994, **(v10)**

Duff, Antony. HV8693.D85 2001, **(v6)**

Duff, David. PR5442.L5.D84 1994, **(v3)**

Duffield, Holley Gene. BX9765.D84 2000, **(v8)**

Duffield, John S. DD290.25.D84 1998, **(v5)**
UA646.3.D817 1995, **(v10)**

Duffin, Henry Charles. PR6007.E3.Z64 1970, **(v3)**
PR6025.O645.Z64, **(v3)**

Duffin, Jacalyn. R464.L36.D84 1993, **(v2)**
R507.L25.D84 1998, **(v2)**

Duffus, R. L. F786.D85 1930b, **(v4)**

Duffy, Christopher. DK52.5.D83, **(v5)**
U39.D74 1987, **(v10)**
UA718.P9.D83 1974, **(v10)**

Duffy, Dean G. TA330.D84 1998, **(v1)**

Duffy, Eamon. BR742.D84 1992, **(v8)**

Duffy, John. RA445.D84 1990, **(v2)**
RA650.5.D8 1972, **(v2)**

Duffy, Joseph. TJ211.D84 1996, **(v1)**

Duffy, Maureen. PR3317.Z5.D8, **(v3)**

Duffy, Michael. F1621.D84 1987, **(v4)**

Duffy, Robert J. HD9698.U5.D76 1997, **(v6)**

Duffy, Susan. PS338.S74.D84 1996, **(v3)**
Z8167.47.D83 1988, **(v10)**

Dugatkin, Lee Alan. QL751.D746 1997, **(v1)**
QL751.D7465 2000, **(v1)**
QL775.D84 1999, **(v1)**

Dugaw, Dianne. PR3474.D84 2001, **(v3)**

Duggal, Kartar Singh. PK2659.D8.A6 1973, **(v3)**
PK2659.D8I3813 1992, **(v3)**

Duggan, Alfred Leo. PR6007.U358 E4, **(v3)**
PR6007.U358 W5, **(v3)**

Duggan, Christopher. HV6453.I83.M327 1989, **(v6)**

Duggan, Joseph J. PQ6380.D8 1989, **(v3)**

Duhamel, Georges. PQ1165.D8 1946, **(v3)**
PQ2607.U53.C5 1918, **(v3)**

Duignan, Peter. CB245.D76 1992, **(v5)**
D1065.U5.D86 1994, **(v5)**
E441.D83, **(v4)**

Duiker, William J. DS550.D8 1994, **(v5)**
DS556.8.D83 1996, **(v5)**
DS740.5.V5 D85 1986, **(v5)**

Duina, Francesco G. KJE971.5.D85 1999, **(v7)**

Duis, Perry. HN80.C5.D85 1998, **(v6)**

Dujardin, Edouard. PQ2220.D8.A278 1991, **(v3)**

Duke University. F1029.D8 1981, **(v4)**

Duke, Daniel Linden. LB2840.2.D85 1984, **(v7)**

Duke, James A. GN564.P4.D85 1994, **(v6)**
QK99.A1D83 2001, **(v1)**
SB401.A4D84 2001, **(v1)**

Duke, Martin. R131.D79 1991, **(v2)**

Duke, P. G. E78.A34.D84 1991, **(v4)**

Duke, Simon. UA646.D87 1994, **(v10)**
UA646.3.D82 1993, **(v10)**

Dukes, Paul. DK40.D84, **(v5)**
DK113.2.D84, **(v5)**

Dukkipati, Rao V. TL243.D85 2000, **(v1)**

Dukore, Bernard Frank. PN1621.D8, **(v3)**
PN1998.3.P43.D85 1999, **(v3)**
PR5368.S75.D85 2000, **(v3)**

Dulaney, W. Marvin. HV8138.D85 1996, **(v6)**

Dulberger, Judith A. HV995.A32.A533 1996, **(v6)**

Duley, W. W. TA1695.D845 1996, **(v1)**

Dull, Jonathan R. E249.D859 1985, **(v4)**

Dulles, Allen Welsh. D810.S7.D78 1996, **(v5)**
UB270.D8, **(v10)**

Dulles, Avery Robert. Z7776.7.D84 1999, **(v10)**

Dulles, Foster Rhea. E161.D852 1965, **(v4)**
E661.7.D8, **(v4)**
E744.D8, **(v4)**

Dulles, John Foster. E744.D85 1957, **(v4)**

Dulles, John W. F. F2538.22.L3.D85 1991, **(v4)**

Dulmen, Richard van. DD65.D8513 1992, **(v5)**
KK754.D8513 1991, **(v7)**

Dumarcay, Jacques. DS523.2.D86 1991, **(v5)**

Dumas, Alexandre. DK26.D8 1961, (v5)
PQ2228.E6 1953b, (v3)
PQ2229.V6.E5 1998, (v3)
Dumbrell, John. E183.8.G7.D86 2001, (v4)
E872.D859 1996, (v4)
E872.D86 1995, (v4)
Dumesnil, Rene. PQ2353.D8 1947, (v3)
Dumett, Raymond E. HD9536.G5.D86 1998, (v6)
Dumm, Thomas L. JC261.F68.D85 1996, (v7)
Dummett, Michael A. E. B29.D85, (v8)
B808.5.D86 1994, (v8)
BC51.D85 1991, (v8)
JF1001.D84 1997, (v7)
Dumond, Dwight Lowell. E440.5.D89 1964, (v4)
E441.D84, (v4)
Z1249.S6.D8, (v10)
Dumont, Herve. PN1998.3.D49.D86 1994, (v3)
Dumont, René. HC502.D8413 1966, (v6)
Dumoulin, Heinrich. BQ4015.D8413 1994, (v8)
BQ9262.3.D85513 1988, (v8)
Dumper, Michael. DS109.94.D86 1996, (v5)
Dun Karm. PJ7820.U4A22, (v3)
Dunaway, David King. ML420.S445.D8, (v9)
PR6015.U9.Z599 1989, (v3)
Dunayer, Joan. HV4708.D86 2001, (v6)
Dunbabin, T. J. DG55.M3.D8 1968, (v5)
Dunbar, Gary S. Z6001.D86 1985, (v10)
Dunbar, Janet. PR5366.D8, (v3)
Dunbar, Leslie. JC571.D918 1991, (v7)
Dunbar, Maurice. Z987.5.U6.D86 1997, (v10)
Dunbar, Pamela. PR9639.3.M258.Z6354 1997, (v3)
Dunbar, Paul Laurence. PS1556.A1 1993, (v3)
PS1556.L55 1903, (v3)
Dunbar, William. PR2265.A5.K5 1979, (v3)
PR2266.K5, (v3)
Dunbar, Willis Frederick. F566.D84 1995, (v4)
Dunbar-Nelson, Alice Moore. PS3507.U6228.Z465
1984, (v3)
Duncan, A. A. M. DA760.E3 vol. 1, (v5)
Duncan, Acheson J. TS156.D83 1986, (v1)
Duncan, Alastair B. PQ2637.I547.Z643 1994, (v3)
N6537.T5.A4 1989, (v9)
NK1382.M63.D86 1998, (v9)
Duncan, Andrew. G1019.D863 2000, (v6)
Duncan, Carol. N72.S6.D775 1993, (v9)
Duncan, Charles. PS1292.C6.Z69 1998, (v3)
Duncan, Christopher M. JA84.U5.D85 1995, (v7)
Duncan, Cynthia M. HC110.P6.D86 1999, (v6)
Duncan, David Ewing. R153.D86 1996, (v2)
Duncan, David. PR6007.U52 M3, (v3)
Duncan, Jane. PR6054.U46.M9 1967, (v3)
Duncan, Joseph Ellis. PR581.D8, (v3)
Duncan, Michael. N6537.T67.D86 1997, (v9)
Duncan, Otis Dudley. F548.9.N3 D8, (v4)
Duncan, Peter J. S. DK49.D86 2000, (v5)
Duncan, Richard R. E581.D86 1998, (v4)
Duncan, Robert Edward. PS3507.U629.C3, (v3)
PS3507.U629.O6, (v3)
Duncan, Roger F. F19.D86 1992, (v4)
Duncan, Ronald J. F2269.1.L18, (v4)
Duncan, Russell. F291.B93.D86 1994, (v4)
Duncan, T. Michael. TP155.D74 1998, (v1)
Duncan, W. Raymond. D888.S65.D855 1990, (v5)
Duncan-Clark, Samuel John. JK2387.D8 1972, (v7)
Duncan-Jones, Katherine. PR2343.D86 1991, (v3)
Duncan-Jones, Richard. HC39.D886 1990, (v6)
Dunch, Ryan. BR1287.D86 2001, (v8)
Dundas, Paul. BL1351.2.D86 1992, (v8)
Duneier, Mitchell. F548.9.N4.D86 1992, (v4)
Dungan, Myles. D547.I6.D86 1997, (v5)
D640.A2.D86 1995, (v5)
Dunham, Barrows. B72.D7, (v8)
Dunham, Kelli S. RT73.D79 2001, (v2)
Dunham, William. QA29.E8.D86 1999, (v1)
Dunitz, Jack D. QD945.D84 1979, (v1)
Dunitz, Robin J. N8243.S65 D85 1993, (v9)
Dunkelman, Mark H. E475.53.D86 1999, (v4)
Dunkerley, James. F1438.D86 1988, (v4)
Dunkerton, Jill. ND170.D86 1999, (v9)
Dunkin, Paul Shaner. Z695.74.D8 1973, (v10)
Dunkling, Leslie. CS2367.D83 1984, (v5)

PE1582.A3.D8 1990, (v3)
Dunlap, Patricia Riley. F596.D78 1995, (v4)
Dunlap, Thomas R. QH545.P4.D86, (v1)
Dunlap, W. Crawford. QC611.D85, (v1)
Dunlap, William. PS1561.A3 1969, (v3)
Dunlay, Thomas W. E83.866.D86 1982, (v4)
F592.C33, (v4)
Dunleavy, Janet Egleson. DA965.H9.D88 1991, (v5)
Dunlop, Charles E. M. BF311.D84 1993, (v2)
Dunlop, David J. QE431.6.M3D86 1997, (v1)
Dunlop, Ian. N6447.D86, (v9)
Dunlop, John B. DK288.D865 1993, (v5)
DK511.C37.D86 1998, (v5)
Dunmore, John. DU19.D78 1991, (v5)
Dunn, Charles W. JC573.2.U6.D85 1996, (v7)
Dunn, D. Elwood. DT631.D95 2001, (v5)
Dunn, Dana. BF76.5.D864 1999, (v2)
Dunn, David H. UG743.D86 1997, (v10)
Dunn, Dennis J. E183.8.S65.D86 1998, (v4)
Dunn, Durwood. F444.C26.D86 1988, (v4)
Dunn, Esther Cloudman. PR1263.D8 1950, (v3)
PR2638.D8 1963, (v3)
Dunn, G. QA275.D86 1989, (v1)
Dunn, James D. G. BS2651.D84 1998, (v8)
Dunn, John. JA66.D85 2000, (v7)
JA74.D86 1996, (v7)
Dunn, Judy. BF723.S43.D85 1990, (v2)
BF723.S6.D86 1988, (v2)
Dunn, Marvin. F319.M6.D86 1997, (v4)
Dunn, Peter Carroll. TK7816.D86 2000, (v1)
Dunn, Peter N. PQ6147.P5.D8, (v3)
PQ6147.P5.D82 1993, (v3)
PQ6428.D8, (v3)
Dunn, Richard J. PR4567.D85 1993, (v3)
Dunn, Richard S. F67.W7957, (v4)
Dunn, Rita Stafford. LC3731.D85 1995, (v7)
Dunn, Thomas Alexander. PR2706.D8, (v3)
Dunn, Timothy J. F787.D46 1996, (v4)
Dunn, Walter S. F482.D86 1998, (v4)
UA772.D8 1994, (v10)
UC265.S65.D86 1995, (v10)
Dunn, William N. H61.D882, (v6)
Dunn, William Parmly. PR3327.D8 1950, (v3)
Dunnage, Jonathan. HV8215.B65.D86 1997, (v6)
Dunne, Andrew P. JZ1305.D86 1996, (v7)
Dunne, Gerald T. KF8745.B55.D86, (v7)
KFM7878.D86 1993, (v7)
Dunne, Michael. PS1891.D86 1995, (v3)
Dunnell, Robert C. CC78.D85, (v5)
Dunnell, Ruth W. BQ640.D86 1996, (v8)
Dunnett, Peter J. S. HE8700.4.D86 1990, (v6)
Dunnigan, James F. D767.9.D86 1998, (v5)
U21.2.D828 1987, (v10)
Dunning, Chester S. L. DK111.D86 2001, (v5)
Dunning, Eric. GV706.5.D85 1999, (v6)
Dunning, Jennifer. GV1785.A38 D85 1996, (v6)
Dunning, John H. HG4538.D823 1987, (v6)
Dunning, John. PN1991.3.U6.D8, (v3)
Dunning, Thomas Patrick. PR2015.D8 1975, (v3)
Dunning, William Archibald. JA81.D7 1972, (v7)
Dunning, William V. ND1475.D86 1991, (v9)
Dunning-Davies, J. QC311.D86 1996, (v1)
Dunphy, Richard. DA963.D86 1995, (v5)
Dunsby, Jonathan. ML410.S283.D83 1992, (v9)
MT6.D92.M9 1988, (v9)
Dunseath, T. K. PR2358.D8, (v3)
Dunsmore, Roger. PM157.D85 1997, (v3)
Dunster, Julian A. HC15.D86 1996, (v6)
Dunthorn, David J. DA47.8.D86 2000, (v5)
Dunthorne, Hugh. Z2000.D86 1983, (v10)
Dunton, Chris. Z3707.D86 1998, (v10)
Dupont, Florence. DG78.D8713 1993, (v5)
Dupont, Jacques. ND140.D85, (v9)
ND180.D8 1951a, (v9)
DuPont, Robert L. RC564.29.D87 1997, (v2)
Dupre, John. Q172.5.C45.D87 1993, (v1)
Dupré, John. BD450.D87 2001, (v8)
Dupree, A. Hunter. QK31.G8D8 1988, (v1)
DuPree, Sherry Sherrod. BX8762.5.D87 1996, (v8)
Dupuy, Alex. F1928.2.D86 1997, (v4)
Dupuy, Edward J. PS3566.E6912.Z66 1996, (v3)

Dupuy, Jean Pierre. BF311.D84513 2000, (v2)
Dupuy, R. Ernest. D25.D86 1993, (v5)
Dupuy, Trevor Nevitt. U21.2.D85 1987, (v10)
UA15.D9 1980, (v10)
Duquette, Jerold J. KF3989.D87 1999, (v7)
Duquette, Michel. HC187.D865 1999, (v6)
Duran, Jane. HQ1190.D87 1991, (v6)
Duran, Victor M. PQ7082.N7.D87 1994, (v3)
Durand, Arthur A. D805.P7.D87 1988, (v5)
Durand, Jorge. ND1432.M46.D87 1995, (v9)
Durand, Maurice M. PL4378.D813 1985, (v3)
Durant, Robert F. HD243.N5.D87 1992, (v6)
Durant, Will. B72.D8 1949, (v8)
D15.D87.A33, (v5)
Duranti, Alessandro. GN671.S2.D87 1994, (v6)
Duras, Marguerite. PQ2607.U8245.A626 1984, (v3)
PQ2607.U8245.A63, (v3)
PQ2607.U8245.D413 1984, (v3)
Durbach, Errol. PT8861.D87 1991, (v3)
Durbin, Kathie. SD428.T6.D87 1999, (v1)
Durch, William J. UG740.D87 1988, (v10)
Durden, Robert Franklin. E415.9.P53.D8, (v4)
HV98.N82.D853 1998, (v6)
Durell, Clement V. QC6.D85 1960, (v1)
Durer, Albrecht. NE654.D9.B63, (v9)
NE1205.D9.A3 1963, (v9)
NE1205.D9.K5, (v9)
Durham, David L. F859.D87 1998, (v4)
Durham, Jennifer L. HV6787.D87 1996, (v6)
Durham, Michael S. F789.D87 1997, (v4)
Durham, Walter T. F865.D94 1997, (v4)
Durham, William H. GN360.D87 1991, (v6)
Duri, Abd al-Aziz. DS63.6.D8713 1987, (v5)
During, Jean. ML344.D86 1991, (v9)
During, Simon. GV1543.D87 2002, (v6)
Durix, Jean-Pierre. PN56.M24.D87 1998, (v3)
Durkan, Michael J. Z8393.6.D87 1996, (v10)
Durkheim, Emile. GN480.D843 1963, (v6)
GN490.D813 1963, (v6)
HM24.D962 1938, (v6)
JC179.M8.D83, (v7)
Durkin, Dolores. LB1181.D8, (v7)
Durling, Dwight Leonard. PR509.D5.D8 1964, (v3)
Durnil, Gordon K. GE160.G75.D87 1995, (v6)
Durning, Alan Thein. GF75.D88 1992, (v6)
HQ2044.U62.N674 1996, (v6)
Durning-Lawrence, Edwin. PR2944.D8 1910, (v3)
Durocher, Leo Ernest. GV865.D83.A36, (v6)
Durr, Alfred. ML410.B13 2000, (v9)
Durr, Karl. B659.Z7.D8 1980, (v8)
Durrant, John D. QP461.D87 1984, (v1)
Durrell, Gerald Malcolm. QH151.D8 1956a, (v1)
Durrell, Lawrence. PR591.D8, (v3)
PR6007.U76.A17 1980, (v3)
PR6007.U76.A6 1960, (v3)
PR6007.U76 B3, (v3)
PR6007.U76 B53 1960, (v3)
PR6007.U76 C5, (v3)
PR6007.U76 C5, (v3)
PR6007.U76 D3, (v3)
PR6007.U76 E8, (v3)
PR6007.U76 J8, (v3)
PR6007.U76 M6 1959, (v3)
PR6007.U76 N8 1971, (v3)
PR6007.U76.T8, (v3)
PR6007.U76.Z53, (v3)
Durrenberger, Robert W. G1525.D8 1972, (v6)
Durrenmatt, Friedrich. PT2607.U493.A19 1964, (v3)
PT2607.U493.A24 1965, (v3)
PT2607.U493.A9413 1988, (v3)
PT2607.U493.B43, (v3)
PT2607.U493.V4, (v3)
Durrett, Richard. QA274.D87 1999, (v1)
Dusinberre, Juliet. PR6045.O72.Z626 1997, (v3)
Dusinberre, William. E445.S7.D87 1996, (v4)
Duston, Thomas E. TD794.5.D85 1993, (v1)
Dutourd, Jean. PQ2607.U865.A88 1952, (v3)
Dutta, Shanta. PR4757.W6.D87 2000, (v3)
Dutton, Benjamin. VK555.D96 1985, (v10)
Dutton, Bertha Pauline. E78.S7.D79, (v4)

Dutton, David. DA566.9.E28.D88 1997, (v5)
Dutton, Donald G. RC569.5.F3.D87 1998, (v2)
Dutton, Michael Robert. HV8260.A2.D87 1992, (v6)
Dutton, Paul Edward. DC73.D88 1994, (v5)
Dutton, Richard. PR2631.D8 1983, (v3)
  PR2642.L5.D88 1996, (v3)
  PR2894.D88 1989, (v3)
Duus, Peter. DS882.D88 1995, (v5)
Duval, Edwin M. PQ1694.P63.D88 1991, (v3)
Duvall, John N. PS3511.A86.Z78218 1990, (v3)
Duvoisin, Roger. PZ10.3.D96Pe4, (v3)
Duyfhuizen, Bernard. PN212.D89 1992, (v3)
Duyvendak, Jan Willem. HN425.5.D89 1995, (v6)
Dvorak, Max. N6310.D813, (v9)
Dvorkin, Elizabeth. KF272.D8, (v7)
Dvornik, Francis. D147.D84, (v5)
  DR36.D9, (v5)
Dwight, Timothy. F8.D9952, (v4)
Dworetz, Steven M. JC153.L87.D86 1990, (v7)
Dwork, Deborah. D804.3.D86 1991, (v5)
Dworkin, Andrea. HQ1172.D85 2000, (v6)
Dworkin, R. M. JC575.D86 2000, (v7)
  KF4552.D96 1996, (v7)
  KF9315.D85 1993, (v7)
Dworkin, Roger B. KF3821.D87 1996, (v7)
Dwyer, Augusta. F787.D98 1994, (v4)
Dwyer, Jim. Z5863.P6.D88 1996, (v10)
Dwyer, Peter D. DU740.42.D89 1990, (v5)
Dwyer, Philip G. Z8858.5.D98 1996, (v10)
Dwyer, Rachel. PR9499.3.D99, (v3)
Dwyer, Richard A. PS1525.D35.D8 1990, (v3)
Dwyer, T. Ryle. DA965.D4.D868 1991, (v5)
Dwyre, Diana. JK1991.D99 2001, (v7)
Dy, Felipe Gonzales. PL6057.D9 1991, (v3)
Dyal, Donald H. E715.D93 1996, (v4)
Dyck, Ian. DA522.C5.D93 1992, (v5)
Dycus, Stephen. UA23.D95 1996, (v10)
Dye, Alan. HD9114.C89.D79 1998, (v6)
Dye, Bob. DU627.17.A46.D84 1997, (v5)
Dye, Eva Emery. PS3507.Y312.C6 1936, (v3)
Dye, Pete. GV964.D94.A3 1995, (v6)
Dye, Thomas R. HN90.E4 D93 2002, (v6)
  JK325.D94 1990, (v7)
Dyer, Alan Frank. Z8191.7.D9 1991, (v10)
Dyer, Betsey Dexter. QH371.D93 1993, (v1)
Dyer, Colin L. HB3593.D9 1978, (v6)
Dyer, George Carroll. V179.D9 1962, (v10)
Dyer, Hugh C. JZ1306.D94 1997, (v7)
Dyer, Joel. HV9950.D94 2000, (v6)
Dyer, Joyce. PS1294.C63.A64336 1993, (v3)
Dyer, Thomas G. E757.D9, (v4)
  F294.A857.D94 1999, (v4)
Dyer-Witheford, Nick. HC79.H53.D94 1999, (v6)
Dykes, Vivian. D750.D95 1990, (v5)
Dykstra, Robert R. HD9433.U5.K215, (v6)
Dym, Clive L. TA645.D95 1997, (v1)
Dyreson, Mark. GV706.35.D97 1998, (v6)
Dyson, A. E. PR502.D9 1976b, (v3)
Dyson, Esther. ZA4150.D97 1997, (v10)
  ZA4150.D973 1998, (v10)
Dyson, Freeman J. Q158.5.D97 1992, (v1)
  U264.D97 1984, (v10)
Dyson, George. Q335.D97 1997, (v1)
Dyson, James. T15.D87 2001, (v1)
Dyson, Michael Eric. E185.97.K5.D97 2000, (v4)
Dyson, Stephen L. DE60.D97 1998, (v5)
  DG59.A2.D97 1985, (v5)
  DG231.D95 1991, (v5)
Dziewanowski, M. K. DK4382.D9, (v5)
Dzimba, John. DT2996.D95 1998, (v5)
Dziuban, Stanley W. D769.A533 vol. 8, pt. 4, (v5)
Eades, Lindsay Michie. DT1757.E33 1994, (v5)
Eagle, Adam Fortunate. E78.C15 E16 2002, (v4)
  E99.D1.E15 1992, (v4)
Eagle, Dorothy. PR109.E18 1981, (v3)
Eagles, Robin. DA485.E18 2000, (v5)
Eagleton, Terry. BH151.E2 1990, (v8)
  DA950.1.E24 1999, (v5)
  PR3664.C43.E2 1982, (v3)
  PR8714.E28 1998, (v3)
Eagly, Alice Hendrickson. BF327.E19 1993, (v2)

Eakin, Paul John. CT25.E25 1999, (v5)
Eames, Arthur Johnson. QK643.A5.E2, (v1)
Eamon, William. Q125.E34 1994, (v1)
Eardley, A. J. QE33.E28 1942, (v1)
  QE71.E17 1962, (v1)
Eardley, George C. U53.E27.A34, (v10)
Earhart, Amelia. TL540.E3.A3 1977, (v1)
Earl, James Whitby. PR1585.E37 1994, (v3)
Earle, Jason. LB2806.E27 1999, (v7)
Earle, Neil. PS3503.A923.W593 1993, (v3)
Earle, Peter. DA448.9.E17 1978, (v5)
Earle, Ralph. RC560.S43.E23 1995, (v2)
Earle, Swepson. F187.C5 E23, (v4)
Earls, Irene. N6370.E27 1987, (v9)
Early, Eleanor. [from old catalog]. F199.E17, (v4)
Early, Frances H. D570.1.E27 1997, (v5)
Early, John D. DS666.A3.E37 1998, (v5)
Earman, John. QC173.59.S65.E17 1989, (v1)
Earney, Fillmore C. F. TN264.E37 1990, (v1)
Earp, Josephine Sarah Marcus. F786.E175, (v4)
Earp, Lawrence Marshburn. ML134.G956.E3 1995, (v9)
Easter, Gerald. JN6531.E27 2000, (v7)
Easterbrook, Gregg. GE195.E18 1995, (v6)
Easterlin, Nancy. PR5892.R4.E27 1996, (v3)
Easterlin, Richard A. HB3505.E247, (v6)
Easterly, William Russell. HC59.72.P6.E17 2001, (v6)
Eastlake, Charles L. NA988.E17 1872a, (v9)
Eastlake, Charles Lock, Sir. ND50.E2 1960, (v9)
Eastlake, William. PS3555.A7.C3 1965, (v3)
Eastman, Byron D. HB135.E27 1984, (v6)
Eastman, Carol M. E99.H2.E27 1991, (v4)
Eastman, Charles Alexander. E90.E14 E14 1925, (v4)
  E99.D1 E183 1990, (v4)
Eastman, Jacqueline Fisher. PS3503.E475.Z65 1996, (v3)
Eastman, Lloyd E. DS777.47.E24, (v5)
  HN733.E25 1988, (v6)
Eastman, Yvette Szekely. PS3507.R55.Z62 1995, (v3)
Easton, Alison. PS1892.S9.E27 1996, (v3)
Easton, Malcolm. DC715.E2 1965, (v5)
Easton, Robert Olney. PS3509.A9 H3, (v3)
Easton, Stewart Copinger. B765.B24.E28 1970, (v8)
Eaton, Clement. E340.C6.E2, (v4)
Eaton, Frank. F700.E22 A36 1979, (v4)
Eaton, John L. QL562.E28 1988, (v1)
Eaton, Leonard K. NA710.E24, (v9)
Eaton, Marcia Muelder. BH39.E26 1989, (v8)
  BH39.E265 2001, (v8)
Eaton, Richard Maxwell. DS485.B46.E16 1993, (v5)
Eaton, Susan E. LC214.523.B67, (v7)
Eatwell, Roger. JC481.E23 1996, (v7)
Eaves, T. C. Duncan. PR3666.E2, (v3)
Eayrs, James George. F1034.E17, (v4)
Eban, Abba Solomon. DS126.6.E2.A32, (v5)
Ebbert, Jean. VB324.W65.E23 1993, (v10)
Ebbinghaus, Hermann. LB1063.E213 1964, (v7)
Ebel, Roland H. F1415.E24 1991, (v4)
Ebeling, Walter. S441.E23, (v1)
Ebenstein, Alan O. HB103.H3.E23 2001, (v6)
Eber, Christine Engla. F1221.T9.E24 1995, (v4)
Eberhard, Wolfram. BJ117.E2, (v8)
  DS721.E32613 1986, (v5)
  DS730.E17 1982, (v5)
Eberle, Suzanne Girard. TX361.A8E39 2000, (v1)
Eberlein, Harold Donaldson. F127.H8.E18 1990, (v4)
  NA707.E23, (v9)
Ebersole, Gary L. E85.E24 1995, (v4)
Eberstadt, Nick. HC470.2.E25 1999, (v6)
  HC710.P6 E24 1988, (v6)
Ebert, John David. Q125.E362 1999, (v1)
Ebert, Teresa L. HQ1190.E24 1996, (v6)
Ebert-Schifferer, S. ND1390.E2313 1998, (v9)
Eble, Connie C. PE3727.S8.E255 1996, (v3)
Eble, Kenneth Eugene. LB2331.E328 1988, (v7)
Ebrey, Patricia Buckley. DS706.E37 1996, (v5)
  DS721.E336 1991, (v5)
  HQ684.A25 1993, (v6)
Ebright, Malcolm. KFN4055.E27 1994, (v7)
Eby, Carl P. PS3515.E37.Z5858 1999, (v3)
Eby, Edwin Harold. PS3245.E2, (v3)

Eby, Frederick. LB7.E3 1971, (v7)
Eccles, Henry Effingham. U168.E22, (v10)
Eccles, John C. QP331.E3, (v1)
  QP361.E3, (v1)
  QP376.E258 1989, (v1)
  QP376.E265, (v1)
  QP376.E27 1977, (v1)
Eccles, Mark. PR2673.E4 1967, (v3)
  PR2916.E25, (v3)
Eccles, Peter J. QA9.54.E23 1997, (v1)
Eccles, W. J. E18.82.E25 1972, (v4)
  F1030.E3, (v4)
  F1030.E312, (v4)
Echard, William E. DC277.E27 1983, (v5)
Echeruo, Michael J. C. PR6005.A77.Z647 1979, (v3)
Echevarria, Antulio Joseph. U43.G3.E28 2000, (v10)
Echeverri-Gent, John. HC440.P6.E243 1993, (v6)
Echols, Alice. HQ1421.E25 1989, (v6)
  ML420.J77.E25 1999, (v9)
Echols, Anne. CT3220.A56 1992, (v5)
Echols, Gordon. NA730.T5.E26 2000, (v9)
Echols, Harrison. QH506.E246 2001, (v1)
Echols, John M. PL5076.E25, (v3)
Echtermeyer, Ernst Theodor. PT1155.E4 1966, (v3)
Eck, Diana L. BL1205.E25 1998, (v8)
  BL2525.E35 2001, (v8)
Eck, Paul. SB386.B7.E26 1988, (v1)
Eckardt, Jo-Jacqueline. PT2399.E25 1993, (v3)
Eckart, Peter. TL799.M6, (v1)
Eckersley, Robyn. JA75.8.E26 1992, (v7)
Eckert, Allan W. F517.E25 1995, (v4)
  F545.E24 1988, (v4)
Eckert, Michael. Q125.E36313 1990, (v1)
Eckhardt, Caroline D. Z8164.E27 1990, (v10)
Eckhardt, Celia Morris. HQ1413.D2.E25 1984, (v6)
Eckhardt, Homer D. TJ175.E32 1998, (v1)
Eckhardt, Joseph P. PN1998.3.L82.E34 1997, (v3)
Eckhart, Meister. BV5080.E45.E43 1958a, (v8)
Eckley, Grace. PR6065.B7.Z65, (v3)
Eckley, Robert S. HD9680.U52.E25 1991, (v6)
Eckstein, Alexander. HC427.9.E28, (v6)
Eckstein, Barbara J. PN3401.E25 1990, (v3)
Eckstein, Max A. LB3060.28.E25 1993, (v7)
Eckstein, Rick. HD9698.U52.E25 1997, (v6)
Eckstein, Susan. HX158.5.E35 1994, (v6)
Eco, Umberto. BH39.E29213 1989, (v8)
  P99.E28, (v3)
  P99.E3, (v3)
  PN98.S46.E25 1992, (v3)
  PN241.E28 2001, (v3)
Edbury, P. W. D181.G56.E33 1997, (v5)
  DS54.6.E33 1991, (v5)
Eddington, Arthur Stanley. QB981.E3, (v1)
  QC6.E33, (v1)
  QC6.E35, (v1)
  QC6.E37 1958, (v1)
  QC6.E4 1929, (v1)
Eddins, Dwight. PR5907.E3, (v3)
Eddison, Sydney. SB413.D3.E33 1992, (v1)
Edds, Margaret. F231.3.W55.E33 1990, (v4)
Eddy, Clyde. F788.E25, (v4)
Eddy, William Alfred. PR3724.G8.E4 1963, (v3)
Edel, Leon. PR408.P83.E3 1982, (v3)
  Z8847.E34 1999, (v10)
Edelheit, Abraham J. Z6374.H6.E33 1986 Suppl., (v10)
Edelman, Charles. PR3069.M5, (v3)
Edelman, John W. HD8073.E33.A3, (v6)
Edelman, Marc. HD1339.C8.E33 1999, (v6)
  HD1471.C82.G84 1992, (v6)
Edelman, Murray J. N8236.P5.E3 1995, (v9)
Edelman, Robert. GV623.E27 1993, (v6)
  HN530.U5.E34 1987, (v6)
Edelman, Shimon. BF241.E28 1999, (v2)
Edelman, Marshall. BF175.E29 1984, (v2)
Edelson, Paula. GV697.A1 E28 2002, (v6)
Edelstein, Ludwig. CB155.E26, (v5)
Edelstein, Michael R. QC913.2.R3.E35 1998, (v1)
Eden, Anthony. DA566.9.E28.A36, (v5)
Edens, John A. Z8757.27.E33 1994, (v10)
Edensor, Tim. DS486.A3.E34 1998, (v5)

Eder, Donna. LC208.4.E33 1995, (v7)
Edey, Marion (Armstrong). PS3509.D43.E3x, (v3)
Edgar, Kathleen J. F869.M653 D34 2000, (v4)
  F869.M665 E24 2000, (v4)
  F869.S22E34 2000, (v4)
Edgar, Stacey L. QA76.9.M65.E34 1997, (v1)
Edgar, Walter B. F269.E34 1998, (v4)
Edgar, William J. BC38.E33 1989, (v8)
Edgecombe, Rodney Stenning. PR595.R4.E34 1996, (v3)
  PR6037.P29.Z64 1990, (v3)
Edgell, Derek. LB2862.E35 1998, (v7)
Edgell, Stephen. HB119.V4.E34 2001, (v6)
Edgerton, Harold Eugene. TR593.E34 1987, (v1)
Edgerton, Mary Wright. F731.E33 1976, (v4)
Edgerton, Robert B. DK214.E34 1999, (v5)
Edgerton, Samuel Y. N7430.5.E34 1991, (v9)
Edgeworth, Maria. PR4644.C3 1964, (v3)
Edgley, Alison. P85.C47.E34 2000, (v3)
Edie, Carlene J. HC154.E34 1990, (v6)
Edie, James M. B4201.E3, (v8)
Edin, Kathryn. HQ759.915.E34 1997, (v6)
Edinger, Lewis Joachim. JN3971.A58.E35 1998, (v7)
Edington, Carol. PR2296.L6.Z677 1994, (v3)
Edley, Christopher F. KF4755.5.E33 1996, (v7)
  KF5425.E35 1990, (v7)
Edman, Irwin. B945.E33.P5, (v8)
Edmonds, Anthony O. DS558.E29 1998, (v5)
Edmonds, Beverly C. HQ789.E35 1996, (v6)
Edmonds, Robin. D749.E36 1991, (v5)
Edmonds, W. D. DC195.L9.E36 1990, (v5)
Edmonds, Walter Dumaux. PS3509.D564 D7, (v3)
Edmondson, Belinda. PR9205.5.E36 1999, (v3)
Edmondson, Vladka. Z2136.E36 1999, (v10)
Edmunds, John C. HC79.W4.E35 2001, (v6)
Edmunds, Marilyn W. RM301.28.E33 2002, (v2)
Edmunds, R. David. E99.F7.E35 1993, (v4)
  E99.P8.E35, (v4)
Edmunds, Susan. PS3507.O726.Z63 1994, (v3)
Edmundson, William A. JC497.E35 1998, (v7)
Edney, Matthew H. GA1131.E36 1997, (v6)
Educational Resources Information Center (U.S.).
  Z695.1.E3.E34 1986, (v10)
Edwards, A. W. F. QA241.E37 1987, (v1)
Edwards, Alexander. SB421.E3 158, (v1)
Edwards, Allen Jack. RC521.E43 1994, (v2)
Edwards, Allen. ML410.C3293.E3, (v9)
Edwards, B. C. RD768.E39 1999, (v2)
Edwards, Brian. PN56.P53.E38 1996, (v3)
Edwards, Clive. TS880.E39 1994, (v1)
Edwards, David B. DS358.E38 1996, (v5)
  DS371.2.E38 2002, (v5)
Edwards, David Lawrence. BR145.2.E26 1997, (v8)
Edwards, Derek. LB1033.E33 1987, (v7)
Edwards, Douglas R. BR185.E38 1996, (v8)
Edwards, Duane. PR6023.A93.R3337 1990, (v3)
Edwards, E. D. PL3277.E1.E35, (v3)
Edwards, Elwyn Hartley. SF285.E345 2000, (v1)
Edwards, Ernest Preston. QL687.A1.E39 1998, (v1)
Edwards, Franklin R. HG2491.E39 1996, (v6)
Edwards, Fred L. DS559.5.E28 2000, (v5)
Edwards, George C. JK585.E32 1989, (v7)
Edwards, Gerry. QK882.E295 1983, (v1)
Edwards, Holly. NX503.7.E355 2000, (v9)
Edwards, Honeyboy. ML420.E28.A3 1997, (v9)
Edwards, J. S. S. HF5686.C7.E34 1987, (v6)
Edwards, John. DP164.E39 2000, (v5)
  DS135.E81.E38 1988, (v5)
Edwards, Jonathan. B870.A5 1972, (v8)
  BJ1520.E3, (v8)
Edwards, Jorge. F3101.E33.A3413 1993, (v4)
Edwards, June. LC89.E38 1998, (v7)
Edwards, Karen L. PR3562.E39 1999, (v3)
Edwards, Keith. QA76.54.E52 1993, (v1)
Edwards, Laura F. HQ1438.S63.E35 1997, (v6)
Edwards, Lee. E748.G64.E38 1995, (v4)
Edwards, Madaline Selima. CT275.E357 1996, (v5)
Edwards, Margaret J. A. RT50.5.E36 2002, (v2)
Edwards, Mike. PR4169.E39 1999, (v3)
Edwards, Nancy. DA930.E38 1990, (v5)
Edwards, P. G. DS559.62.A8.E38 1997, (v5)

Edwards, Paul M. DS918.E39 2000, (v5)
  Z3316.E36 1998, (v10)
Edwards, Philip R. QR82.E6.E3 1972, (v1)
Edwards, Philip. PR428.O24.E39 1997, (v3)
Edwards, R. E. QA404.E25 1979, (v1)
Edwards, Ralph. LC90.M4.E39 1998, (v7)
Edwards, Richard. HD6971.8.E38 1993, (v6)
  TN265.E33 1986, (v1)
Edwards, Susan S. M. HV6626.E28 1989, (v6)
Edwards, Thomas R. PR3634.E3, (v3)
Edwardson, Barbara M. RC925.5.E39 1994, (v2)
Efland, Arthur. N105.E35 1990, (v9)
Efron, John M. GN547.E34 1994, (v6)
  R694.E376 2001, (v2)
Egan, Ferol. E415.9.F8.E33, (v4)
  F865.E35 1984, (v4)
  F869.S353.B684 1998, (v4)
Egan, Jack. DU178.E37 1999, (v5)
Egan, Jim. PS191.E37 1999, (v3)
Egan, Ken. PS377.E35 1997, (v3)
Egan, Kieran. LB1117.E38 1988, (v7)
Egan, Ronald C. PL2683.Z5.E3 1984, (v3)
Egerton, Douglas R. F230.E37 1993, (v4)
Eggan, Fred. E98.S7.E4, (v4)
Eggeling, Hans F. PF3640.E38, (v3)
Eggenberger, David. CR113.E35 1964, (v5)
Eggert, Katherine. PR428.F45.E44 2000, (v3)
Eggertsson, Thrainn. HB171.T48 1990, (v6)
Eggins, Brian R. R857.B54.E35 1996, (v2)
Eggleston, Edward. PS1582.C5 1966, (v3)
  PS1582.E5 1872, (v3)
  PS1582.H6, (v3)
  PS1582.H62 1984, (v3)
Egmond, Florike. D16.E32 1997, (v5)
Egnal, Marc. E210.E27 1988, (v4)
Egnal, Marc. HC107.A115.E37 1996, (v6)
Egoff, Sheila A. PR830.F3.E43 1988, (v3)
Egret, Jean. DC138.E3613, (v5)
Egusa, Shuzo. SH171.E4313 1992, (v1)
Ehler, Sidney Z. BV630.AI.E33 1954, (v8)
Ehlers, Ernest G. QE431.2.E38, (v1)
Ehlers, Henry J. LB7.E45 1981, (v7)
Ehlers, Jurgen. QE696.E2813 1996, (v1)
Ehre, Milton. PG3337.G6.Z633, (v3)
Ehrenberg, John. JC474.E37 1992, (v7)
Ehrenberg, Margaret R. GN799.W66.E47 1989, (v6)
Ehrenberg, Ralph E. GA193.U5.E37 1987, (v6)
Ehrenberg, Victor. DF77.E35 1973, (v5)
  JC73.E353 1969, (v7)
  PA3416.Z5.H5 1955, (v3)
Ehrenburg, Il'i<BE>a Grigor'evich. PN517.E4, (v3)
Ehrenfeld, David W. B821.E35, (v8)
Ehrenfeld, David. GF21.E47 1993, (v6)
Ehrenpreis, Irvin. PR442.E38 1980, (v3)
  PR3726.E37, (v3)
Ehrenreich, Barbara. HD4918.E375 2001, (v6)
  HQ1426.E38, (v6)
  U22.3.E37 1997, (v10)
Ehrenreich, John. HV91.E38 1985, (v6)
Ehrenstein, G. W. TA455.P58, (v1)
Ehrenzweig, Anton. N71.E5 1967, (v9)
Ehresmann, Donald L. Z5931.E47 1990, (v10)
Ehret, Christopher. DT365.65.E37 1998, (v5)
Ehrhart, W. D. VE24.E37 1999, (v10)
Ehrismann, Gustav. PT175.E49 1932, (v3)
Ehrlich, Cyril. ML652.E4 1990, (v9)
Ehrlich, Eugene H. PE1137.E52 1984, (v3)
  PS141.E74 1982, (v3)
Ehrlich, Jacob W. KF373.E35.A32, (v7)
Ehrlich, Paul R. GE195.E37 1996, (v6)
  GF75.E4 1991, (v6)
  GN281.4.E374 2000, (v6)
  HB871.E35 1972, (v6)
  HB875.E35 1971, (v6)
  QH366.E47, (v1)
  QL676.55.E38 1992, (v1)
  QL681.E37 1988, (v1)
Ehrlich, Robert. Q171.E374 2001, (v1)
  QC33.E54 1990, (v1)
  QC33.E55 1997, (v1)
  QC75.E37 1994, (v1)

Ehrlich, Walter. F474.S29.J53 1997, (v4)
Ehrlichman, John. E855.E35 1982, (v4)
Ehrman, Bart D. BS2325.E47 1993, (v8)
  BS2330.2.E36 2000, (v8)
Ehrman, John. E744.E36 1995, (v4)
Eich, Christoph. PQ6613.A763.Z62, (v3)
Eichenbaum, Luise. HQ1206.E43 1988, (v6)
Eichenberg, Richard C. UA646.E33 1989, (v10)
Eichendorff, Joseph. PT1856.A116 1985, (v3)
  PT1856.A1 1957, (v3)
Eichengreen, Barry J. HG3881.E346 1990, (v6)
Eicher, David J. Z1242.E57 1997, (v10)
Eichler, Geo. R. F774.E37, (v4)
Eichler, Margrit. H62.E453 1988, (v6)
Eichler, Ned. HG2151.E34 1989, (v6)
Eichner, Alfred S. HD9105.E4, (v6)
Eickelman, Dale F. DS35.69.E37 1996, (v5)
Eidintas, A. DK505.74.E38 1998, (v5)
Eiesland, Nancy L. BL2527.D33.E35 2000, (v8)
Eigen, Lewis D. PN6084.P6.E54 1993, (v3)
Eigner, Edwin M. PR4592.P45.E34 1989, (v3)
Eiguren, J. PH5035.E4, (v3)
Eilenberg, Susan. PR5886.E45 1992, (v3)
Eiler, Keith E. D769.E55 1997, (v5)
Eilon, Daniel. PR3728.S2.E37 1991, (v3)
Einar Olafur Sveinsson. PT7269.N5.E313, (v3)
Einarsson, Stefan. PT7103.I7 vol. 32-33, (v3)
  PT7150.E4, (v3)
Einhard, ca. 770-840. DC73.32.T8 1960, (v5)
Einhorn, Lois J. PM217.E37 2000, (v3)
Einsele, Gerhard. QE571.E36 1992, (v1)
Einstein, Albert. QC6.E43 1956, (v1)
  QC7.E5 1961, (v1)
  QC16.E5.A3 1970, (v1)
  QC16.E5.A33, (v1)
  QC16.E5.A4 1992, (v1)
  QC16.E5.A4513, (v1)
  QC173.55.E384513 2001, (v1)
  QC183.E53 1956, (v1)
Einstein, Daniel. PN1992.8.D6.E56 1997, (v3)
Einstein, Lewis. D413.E36.A3, (v5)
  E277.E56 1970, (v4)
Einzig, Paul. HG3811.E35 1970, (v6)
Eisaguirre, Lynne. HF5549.5.A34.E39 1999, (v6)
  KF4758.E36 1993, (v7)
Eisberg, Robert Martin. QC173.E358, (v1)
Eisele, Albert. E748.H945.E5, (v4)
Eiseley, Loren C. BD435.E38, (v8)
  QH81.E6, (v1)
  QH361.E35, (v1)
  QH368.E38, (v1)
Eisenach, Eldon J. BL2525.E415 2000, (v8)
  E743.E26 1994, (v4)
Eisenberg, Carolyn Woods. E183.8.G3.E35 1996, (v4)
Eisenberg, Ellen. F145.J5.E38 1995, (v4)
Eisenberg, Joyce. BM50.E47 2001, (v8)
Eisenberg, Laura Zittrain. DS119.7.E353 1998, (v5)
Eisenberg, Marvin. ND623.L77.E35 1989, (v9)
Eisenberg, Mickey S. RC87.9.E37 1997, (v2)
Eisenbud, David. QA251.3.E38 1995, (v1)
Eisenbud, Merril. TD196.R3.E597 1997, (v1)
Eisenhart, Luther Pfahler. QA3.P7 3 1940, (v1)
Eisenhower, Dwight David. D743.E35 1990, (v5)
  E742.5.E37 1970, (v4)
  E742.5.E372 1998, (v4)
  E835.E47, (v4)
  E836.A3155 1981, (v4)
  E836.A44, (v4)
  E745.E35.A48, (v4)
Eisenhower, John S. D. D756.5.A7.E4, (v5)
  E405.E37 1989, (v4)
Eisenman, Stephen. N6450.E39 1994, (v9)
Eisenson, Jon. RJ496.A6.E57 1984, (v2)
Eisenstadt, S. N. CB205.E37 1987, (v5)
Eisenstein, Elizabeth L. Z124.E37, (v10)
  Z124.E374 1983, (v10)
Eisenstein, Hester. HQ1823.E47 1991, (v6)
Eisenstein, Sergei. PN1998.3.E34.A3 1995, (v3)
Eisenstein, Zillah R. KF4758.E38 1988, (v7)
Eiser, Christine. RJ380.E37 1990, (v2)
Eisinger, Peter K. HC110.I53.E56 1988, (v6)

HV696.F6.E47 1998, (v6)
Eisler, Colin T. N6888.D8.E57 1991, (v9)
Eisler, Ronald. TD196.C45E38 2000, (v1)
Eisner, Elliot W. LB1570.E4254 2002, (v7)
Eisner, Howard. TA168.E38 1997, (v1)
Eisner, Robert. HC106.8.E45 1994, (v6)
Eisnitz, Gail A. TS1963.E37 1997, (v1)
Eitington, Julius E. HD31.E477 1997, (v6)
Eitner, Lorenz. N6425.N4.E35, (v9)
Eitner, Lorenz. ND553.G45.E317 1983, (v9)
Ekberg, Carl J. F474.S135 E38 2002, (v4)
  F474.S33 E43 1996, (v4)
  F544.E38 1998, (v4)
Ekedahl, Carolyn McGiffert. DK290.3.S54.E38 1997, (v5)
Ekeland, I. QA273.E4313 1993, (v1)
  QA614.58.E3413 1988, (v1)
Ekelund, Robert B. HB91.E42 1997, (v6)
Ekiert, Grzegorz. HX240.7.A6.E44 1996, (v6)
Ekirch, A. Roger. HC107.N8.E37, (v6)
Ekirch, Arthur Alphonse. GF503.E46, (v6)
  JK31.E5, (v7)
Eklof, Ben. DK288.E35 1989, (v5)
Ekserdjian, David. N6923.C638.E39 1997, (v9)
Eksteins, Modris. DK502.74.E39 1999, (v5)
Ekstrom, Ruth B. LA222.E39 1988, (v7)
El Guindi, Fadwa. GT2112.E5 1999, (v6)
Elad, Ami. PJ8190.E42 1999, (v3)
El-Agraa, A. M. HF1418.5.E4 1989, (v6)
Elam, Harry Justin. PN3307.U6.E4 1997, (v3)
El-Ashker, Ahmed Abdel-Fattah. HG3368.A6.E4 1987, (v6)
Elashmawi, Farid. HD62.4.E423 2001, (v6)
Elaydi, Saber. QA431.E43 1996, (v1)
Elazar, Daniel Judah. BL65.P7.E43 1995 vol. 4, (v8)
  E183.E43 1994, (v4)
  F1035.J5.E43 1989, (v4)
  JC355.E384 1991, (v7)
  JK6116.E43 1999, (v7)
Elberg, Yehudah. PJ5129.E534.K313 1997, (v3)
  PJ5129.E534.O913 1997, (v3)
Elbers, Joan S. Z5861.E4 1991, (v10)
Elbogen, Ismar. BM660.E513 1993, (v8)
Elcock, H. J. D644.E5 1972, (v5)
Elder, Bruce. PN1993.5.C2.E42 1989, (v3)
Elder, John P. RA441.5.E43 2001, (v2)
Elderfield, John. N6494.F3.E42, (v9)
  N6853.M33.A4 1992, (v9)
Eldersveld, Samuel James. JS78.E43 1995, (v7)
Eldred, Nelson Richards. Z249.E48 2001, (v10)
Eldredge, Charles C. ND237.O5.E43 1991, (v9)
Eldredge, Niles. GN281.E4 1982, (v6)
  QE711.2.E47 1991, (v1)
  QH75.E58 1998, (v1)
  QH366.2.E52 1989, (v1)
  QH366.2.E535 1999, (v1)
  QH371.E44 1985, (v1)
Eldridge, Larry D. KF4772.E39 1994, (v7)
Eldridge, Michael. B945.D44.E43 1998, (v8)
Eldridge, Philip J. JQ762.E44 1995, (v7)
Elections Research Center (Governmental Affairs Institute). JK524.G6, (v7)
Elegant, Robert S. DS778.A1.E4, (v5)
El-Enany, Rasheed. PJ7846.A46.Z597 1993, (v3)
Eley, Geoff. DD210.E48 1986, (v5)
  DD228.5.E45, (v5)
Elfenbein, Andrew. PR448.H65.E44 1999, (v3)
  PR468.R65.E44 1995, (v3)
Elfstrom, Gerard. JA71.E4 1997, (v7)
Elgar, Edward. ML410.E41.A4 1990, (v9)
Elhammoumi, Mohamed. Z8946.82.V94.E44 1997, (v10)
Elia, Irene. QP259.E45 1988, (v1)
Eliade, Mircea. BD701.E383 1959, (v8)
  BL41.E5, (v8)
  BL48.E3813, (v8)
  BL48.E413, (v8)
  BL50.E46, (v8)
  BL74.E4 1967, (v8)
  BL80.E513, (v8)
  BL603.E45 1985, (v8)

Eliæson, Sven. HM511.E45 2002, (v6)
Elias, John L. LB17.E4 1995, (v7)
Elias, Norbert. BD638.E42 1992, (v8)
  CB83.E413 1994, (v6)
  HM26.E43 1998, (v6)
  HM136.E4613 1991, (v6)
Elias, Robert. HV6250.3.U5.E46 1993, (v6)
Elias, Scott A. QE831.E45 1993, (v1)
Elias, Thomas S. QK481.E38, (v1)
Eliasoph, Nina. JK1764.E45 1998, (v7)
Eliel, Ernest Ludwig. QD481.E525 1994, (v1)
Eliens, Anton. QA76.64.E428 1995, (v1)
Elikann, Peter T. HV7431.E38 1996, (v6)
  HV9104.E438 1999, (v6)
Eling, Kim. DC423.E44 1999, (v5)
Eliot, Charles W. AC1.H5, (v10)
Eliot, Charles William. LD2175. 1869b, (v7)
Eliot, George. PR4650.F70, (v3)
  PR4653.W53 1981, (v3)
  PR4656.A1, (v3)
  PR4658.L4, (v3)
  PR4659.E7 1963, (v3)
  PR4662.A1 1991, (v3)
  PR4662.A2 H67, (v3)
  PR4664.A1 1963, (v3)
  PR4668.A2.B76 1993, (v3)
  PR4670.A1 1961, (v3)
  PR4681.A35 1998, (v3)
  PR4681.A4 1954, (v3)
  PR4681.A4 1985, (v3)
Eliot, John. BF469.E42 1987, (v2)
Eliot, T. S. HN37.A6.E45 1940, (v6)
  PN511.E43 1970, (v3)
  PN511.E435, (v3)
  PN1031.E47, (v3)
  PS3509.L43.A17 1963, (v3)
  PS3509.L43.A19 1962, (v3)
  PS3509.L43.C6, (v3)
  PS3509.L43.C69 1954, (v3)
  PS3509.L43.E4; (v3)
  PS3509.L43.F3 1939, (v3)
  PS3509.L43.M8 1935, (v3)
  PS3509.L43.T6, (v3)
  PS3509.L43.W385 1998, (v3)
  PS3509.L43F6, (v3)
  PS3509.L43O55 1939, (v3)
Eliraz, Israel. PJ5054.E488.V513 1987, (v3)
Elizabeth I, Queen of England, 1533-1603.
  DA350.A25 2000, (v5)
El-Kikhia, Mansour O. DT236.E45 1997, (v5)
Elkin, Judith Laikin. F1419.J4.E43, (v4)
  F1419.J4.E44 1998, (v4)
Elkind, David. BF723.S75.E44 1981, (v2)
Elkind, David. LB775.P49.E44, (v7)
Elkins, Andrew. PS3573.R5358.Z67 1991, (v3)
Elkins, James. BF241.E45 1996, (v2)
  BH39.E54 1998, (v8)
  N346.A1, (v9)
  N7480.E44 1997, (v9)
  NC750.E44 1994, (v9)
  ND1135.E44 1999, (v9)
Elkins, Stanley M. E310.E45 1993, (v4)
  E441.E44 1976, (v4)
Elkins, T. H. DD866.E44 1988, (v5)
Ellanna, Linda J. E99.T185.E55 1992, (v4)
Elledge, Paul. PR4382.E36 2000, (v3)
Elledge, Scott. PR74.E4, (v3)
Ellegard, Alvar. AS284.G6 v. 64, no. 7, (v10)
Elleh, Nnamdi. NA1580.E44 1997, (v9)
Elleman, Bruce A. DS740.5.J3 E44 2002, (v5)
  DS755.2.E46 2001, (v5)
Ellen, Ingrid Gould. HD7288.72.U5.E45 2000, (v6)
Ellenberger, Allan R. PN1998.2.E448 2001, (v3)
Ellenberger, Wilhelm. NC780.E62 1956, (v9)
Eller, Cynthia. BL625.7.E45 1993, (v8)
  D810.C82.E45 1991, (v5)
Eller, Ronald D. HC107.A127.E4 1982, (v6)
Ellerby, Janet Mason. PS366.A88.E44 2001, (v3)
Elliker, Calvin. ML134.F6.E4 1988, (v9)
Ellingson, Terry Jay. GN33.E44 2001, (v6)
Elliot, James. QB603.R55.E44 1984, (v1)

Elliott, Alan J. A. BL1950.S5 E4 1990, (v8)
Elliott, Anthony. B831.2.E55 1996, (v8)
  ML420.L38.E45 1999, (v9)
Elliott, Bruce S. F1035.I6.E45 1988, (v4)
Elliott, Cecil D. TH18.E45 1992, (v1)
Elliott, Clark A. Q125.E45 1996, (v1)
Elliott, David J. TK7874.E495 1986, (v1)
Elliott, Douglas B. QK99.N67.E44, (v1)
Elliott, Emory. PS193.E4 1982, (v3)
Elliott, George P. PS3555.L58.D38, (v3)
Elliott, John Huxtable. CB401.E43, (v5)
  DP171.E4 1964, (v5)
Elliott, Lorraine M. GE170.E47 1998, (v6)
  KWX705.E43 1994, (v7)
Elliott, Marianne. BX1504.U57 E44 2001, (v8)
  DA948.6.T6.E45 1989, (v5)
Elliott, Mark C. DS731.M35, (v5)
Elliott, Ralph Warren Victor. PD2013.E4, (v3)
  PD2013.E4 1989, (v3)
Elliott, Sumner Locke. PR9619.3.E44.F3 1990, (v3)
Elliott, Sydney. DA990.U46.E44 1999, (v5)
Ellis, Albert. BF632.E55 2001, (v2)
  RC489.R3.E427 1996, (v2)
  RC489.R3.E437 1990, (v2)
Ellis, Alexander John. PR1901.A3 2d ser. vol. 1, 4, 5, 11, 25, (v3)
Ellis, B. D. B105.E65.E45 2001, (v8)
  BD215.E43 1979, (v8)
Ellis, Charles M. B905.E4 1842a, (v8)
Ellis, David. CT21.E414 2000, (v5)
Ellis, Frank. HD1417.E45 1992, (v6)
  P92.R9.E45 1998, (v3)
Ellis, George Francis Rayner. QC173.65.E45 1988, (v1)
Ellis, Harold A. DC36.98.B58.E44 1988, (v5)
Ellis, Havelock. D429.E5 1951, (v5)
  DP48.E5 1937, (v5)
  PR6009.L8.D3 1923a, (v3)
Ellis, Jack C. PN1998.3.G75.E44 2000, (v3)
Ellis, Jack D. R505.E44 1990, (v2)
Ellis, Janice Rider. RT82.E45 2001, (v2)
Ellis, John H. RA644.Y4.E44 1992, (v2)
Ellis, John M. AZ183.U5.E45 1997, (v10)
  PN98.D43.E45 1989, (v3)
Ellis, John R. DF233.E4, (v5)
Ellis, John Tracy. Z7778.U6 E38 1982, (v10)
Ellis, John. D743.E43 1990, (v5)
  D744.E45 1993, (v5)
Ellis, Joseph J. E302.5.E45 2000, (v4)
  E321.E45 1993, (v4)
Ellis, Kate Ferguson. PR830.T3.E53 1989, (v3)
Ellis, Lee. HV6558.E45 1989, (v6)
Ellis, Lewis Ethan. E784.E4, (v4)
  E791.E5, (v4)
Ellis, Marc H. BL65.V55.E55 1997, (v8)
  BM645.H6.E43 1990, (v8)
Ellis, Peter Berresford. BL900.E45 1992, (v8)
  DG225.C44.E44 1998, (v5)
Ellis, Rafaela. JK468.I6.E44 1988, (v7)
Ellis, Richard. GC9.E38 2000, (v6)
  GC87.2.A86.E45 1996, (v6)
  HN90.R3.E55 1998, (v6)
  QL638.9.E44, (v1)
Ellis, Robert Richmond. PQ2637.A82.Z67 1988, (v3)
Ellis, Stephen. DT636.5.E45 1999, (v5)
  JQ1998.C64 E45 1991, (v7)
Ellis, Steve. PS3509.L43.F6445 1991, (v3)
Ellis, Steven G. DA315.E54 1995, (v5)
  DA935.E58 1985, (v5)
Ellis, Virginia Ridley. PR4803.H44.Z625 1991, (v3)
Ellis, William Donohue. F499.C657E43, (v4)
Ellis, William E. F457.K3.E45 2000, (v4)
Ellis, Willis Davis. BF203.E48, (v2)
Ellis-Fermor, Una Mary. PN1623.E6 1964, (v3)
Ellison, Curtis W. ML3524.E4 1995, (v9)
Ellison, Harlan. PS3555.L62.D4, (v3)
  PS3555.L62.S77 1977, (v3)
Ellison, John W. BS425.E4 1984, (v8)
Ellison, Peter Thorpe. QP251.E43 2001, (v1)
Ellison, Ralph. PS3555.L625.G6 1986, (v3)
  PS3555.L625.I5 1952, (v3)

Ellmann, Richard. PE1010.E5 1959, **(v3)**
　PR5823.E38 1988, **(v3)**
　PR5824.E4, **(v3)**
　PR6019.O9.U64 1972b, **(v3)**
　PR6019.O9.Z5332 1982, **(v3)**
Ellmann, Stephen. KTL2020.E45 1992, **(v7)**
Ellrodt, Robert. PR545.M4.E43 2000, **(v3)**
Ellsberg, Edward. VM977.E44 1939, **(v10)**
Ellsworth, Scott. F704.T92.E44, **(v4)**
Ellul, Jacques. HM263.E413, **(v6)**
Ellwood, B. B. QE77.E45 1996, **(v1)**
Ellyard, David. QB63.E39 1993, **(v1)**
Elm, Demus. E99.O45 E45 2000, **(v4)**
Elm, Mostafa. HD9576.I62.E46 1992, **(v6)**
Elman, Benjamin A. B5233.C6 E45 1990, **(v8)**
Elman, Robert. QH26.E44, **(v1)**
Elmendorf, Mary L. HQ1465.C5.E45 1976, **(v6)**
Elmendorf, William W. E99.T98.E43 1993, **(v4)**
Elmer, Jonathan. PS2637.4.U6.E46 1995, **(v3)**
Elmore, Richard F. LB2805.E46 1990, **(v7)**
Elms, Alan C. BF39.4.E46 1994, **(v2)**
Elovitz, Mark H. F334.B6 E46, **(v4)**
Elsaesser Valarino, Evelyn. BF1045.N4.E57 1997, **(v2)**
Elsaesser, Thomas. PN1993.5.G3.E58 2000, **(v3)**
El-Sanabary, Nagat. Z5815.A69.E4 1992, **(v10)**
Elsass, Peter. F2319.2.M6.E37 1992, **(v4)**
Elsbree, Willard H. DS518.1.E44, **(v5)**
Else, Gerald Frank. PN1040.A7.E6 1978, **(v3)**
Elsen, Albert Edward. N5303.E45 1981, **(v9)**
　NB458.E45, **(v9)**
　NC248.R58.E4, **(v9)**
El-Shamy, Hasan M. GR268.A73.E4 1995, **(v6)**
El-Shazly, Nadia El-Sayed. DS318.85.E4 1998, **(v5)**
Elshtain, Jean Bethke. BT701.2.E47 2000, **(v8)**
　HQ1236.E47 1993, **(v6)**
　JA74.5.E46 1986, **(v7)**
　JK31.E57 1995, **(v7)**
　JZ1306.E44 1998, **(v7)**
Elsky, Martin. PE1081.E45 1989, **(v3)**
Elsner, James B. QC945.E46 1999, **(v1)**
Elsom, John. PN2189.E45 1992, **(v3)**
Elson Roessler, Shirley. DC158.8.E57 1996, **(v5)**
Elster, Charles Harrington. PE1137.E56 1999, **(v3)**
Elster, Jon. HB523.E45 1992, **(v6)**
　JN96.A58.E57 1998, **(v7)**
Elstun, Esther N. PT2603.E27.Z63 1983, **(v3)**
Elsworth, J. D. PG3453.B84.Z634 1983, **(v3)**
Elting, John Robert. DC152.E44 1988, **(v5)**
Eltis, David. HT1048.E47 2000, **(v6)**
Elton, Charles S. QH541.E398 2001, **(v1)**
　QH541.E4 2000, **(v1)**
Elton, G. R. DA118.E48 1992, **(v5)**
　DA315.E6 1974, **(v5)**
　DA332.E496, **(v5)**
　DA332.E497 1977, **(v5)**
Elton, Hugh. DG59.A2.E44 1996, **(v5)**
　U43.E95.E48 1996, **(v10)**
Elton, William R. Z8812.T55 E47 1990, **(v10)**
Elton, William. BH41.E4, **(v8)**
Eluard, Paul. PQ2609.L75.C56 1946, **(v3)**
Elwell-Sutton, L. P. PK6235.E5, **(v3)**
Ely, James W. KF562.E54 1992, **(v7)**
　KF8745.F8.E44 1995, **(v7)**
Ely, John Hart. KF5060.E58 1993, **(v7)**
Ely, Melvin Patrick. PN1991.77.A6.E49 1991, **(v3)**
Ely, Richard Theodore. HB119.E5.A3 1977, **(v6)**
Elyot, Thomas. JC393.B3.E5 1967, **(v7)**
Elytes, Odysseas. PA5610.E43.A25 1981, **(v3)**
Emanuel, Ezekiel J. R724.E5 1991, **(v2)**
Ember, Carol R. GN345.7.E53 2001, **(v6)**
Embry, Jessie L. HQ994.E52 1987, **(v6)**
Emch-Dériaz, Antoinette Suzanne. R566.T57.E43 1992, **(v2)**
Emdad-ul Haq, M. HV5840.S64.E45 2000, **(v6)**
Emden, Cecil Stuart. PR3618.P2.E4, **(v3)**
Emecheta, Buchi. PR9387.9.E36.G88 1990, **(v3)**
Emerson, Caryl. ML410.M97 E42 1999, **(v9)**
　PG2947.B3.E49 1997, **(v3)**
Emerson, Edward Waldo. PS3053.E45, **(v3)**
Emerson, Everett H. PS1331.E48 2000, **(v3)**

Emerson, Ken. ML410.F78.E46 1997, **(v9)**
Emerson, Michael O. BT734.2.E48 2000, **(v8)**
Emerson, Michael. D2009.E49 1998, **(v5)**
Emerson, Nathaniel Bright. PL6448.E6 1965, **(v3)**
Emerson, Ralph Waldo. PN37.E45 1979, **(v3)**
　PS1600.F71, **(v3)**
　PS1602.V28, **(v3)**
　PS1602,W5 1966, **(v3)**
　PS1603.P55 1990, **(v3)**
　PS1613.A1 1836, **(v3)**
　PS1631.A3.G5, **(v3)**
　PS1631.A34N6 1971, **(v3)**
　PS1631.A35.C3, **(v3)**
　PS1631.A35G7 1971, **(v3)**
　PS1631.A37 1990, **(v3)**
　PS1631.A4 1997, **(v3)**
Emerson, Sheila. PR5264.E46 1993, **(v3)**
Emerson, Thomas Irwin. KF373.E47.A3 1991, **(v7)**
Emerton, J. H. QL457.1.E53 1961, **(v1)**
Emery, Clark Mixon. PR6039.H52.Z63, **(v3)**
Emery, Edwin. E173.E5, **(v4)**
Emery, Irene. TS1449.E42 1980, **(v1)**
Emery, K. O. GC89.E54 1991, **(v6)**
Emery, Lynne Fauley. GV1624.7.A34 E43 1988, **(v6)**
　GV1624.7.N4.E44 1972, **(v6)**
Emery, Mary Lou. PR6035.H96.Z64 1990, **(v3)**
Emery, Michael C. PN4874.E7.A3 1995, **(v3)**
Emery, Robert E. RJ507.D59E44 1999, **(v2)**
Emery, Robert F. HG1270.5.E47 1991, **(v6)**
Emig, Rainer. PR6001.U4.Z67 1999, **(v3)**
Emiliani, Cesare. QB631.E55 1992, **(v1)**
Emilio, Luis F. E513.5 54th.E43 1995, **(v4)**
Emin, Gevorg. PK8548.E5.D313 1988, **(v3)**
Emler, Nicholas. HV9145.E45 1995, **(v6)**
Emme, Eugene Morlock. UG630.E5, **(v10)**
Emmeche, Claus. QH324.2.E4613 1994, **(v1)**
Emmel, Hildegard. PT741.E5413 1984, **(v3)**
Emmerich, Andre. F1219.3.A7.E48, **(v4)**
Emmet, Alan. SB466.U65.N4825 1996, **(v1)**
Emmet, Dorothy Mary. BD372.E55 1991, **(v8)**
Emmitt, Robert. E83.879.E5 2000, **(v4)**
Emmons, David M. F739.B8.E48 1989, **(v4)**
Emmons, Della Florence Gould. PS3509.M5 L4 1965, **(v3)**
Emmons, George Thornton. E99.T6.E46 1991, **(v4)**
Emmons, Robert D. SB433.E44 2000, **(v1)**
Emmons, Shirlee. ML420.M352.E4 1990, **(v9)**
　MT892.E54, **(v9)**
　MT892.E55 1998, **(v9)**
Emmons, Terence. F869.S39.R94 1997, **(v4)**
Empereur, James L. BV5053.E474 1998, **(v8)**
Empson, William. PE1585.E6, **(v3)**
　PR149.P3.E6 1974, **(v3)**
　PR2664.E47 1987, **(v3)**
Emsley, Clive. HV8196.A2.E47 1991, **(v6)**
Emsley, Clive. HV8203.E47 1999, **(v6)**
Emsley, John. QD466.E48 1998, **(v1)**
　QD466.E48 1998, **(v1)**
　RA1213.E47 1994, **(v2)**
　RA1258.E48 1999, **(v2)**
Enchi, Fumiko. PL826.N3.N313 2000, **(v3)**
Endacott, G. B. DS796.H7.E48, **(v5)**
Endelman, Todd M. DS135.E5.E49 1990, **(v5)**
Ender, Evelyne. PS2127.P8.E53 1995, **(v3)**
Enders, Jody. PN1751.E49 1998, **(v3)**
　PN1751.E5 1992, **(v3)**
Endicott, Stephen Lyon. UG447.8.E53 1998, **(v10)**
Endo, Shusaku. PL849.N4.C413 1980, **(v3)**
Endore, S. Guy. PS3555.N3.K5, **(v3)**
　PS3555.N4 V6, **(v3)**
Engel, Arthur. QA76.95.E54 1993, **(v1)**
Engel, Barbara Alpern. HQ1662.E54 1994, **(v6)**
　HQ1663.E53 1983, **(v6)**
Engel, David. DS135.P6.E53 1993, **(v5)**
Engel, Elliot. Z8230.E5 1990, **(v10)**
Engel, James F. HF5415.E65 1983, **(v6)**
Engel, Monroe. PR4588.E5, **(v3)**
Engel, William E. PR428.D4.E54 1995, **(v3)**
Engelhardt, H. Tristram. R725.56.E54 2000, **(v2)**
Engelhardt, Tom. E169.04.E64 1995, **(v4)**
Engelhardt, Wolfgang. SK353.E513, **(v1)**

Engell, James. PR442.E47 1999, **(v3)**
Engelman, Ralph. HE8689.8.E53 1996, **(v6)**
Engelmann, Larry. GV994.L4.E54 1988, **(v6)**
Engeln-Mullges, Gisela. QA297.E56213 1996, **(v1)**
Engels, Dagmar. HQ1744.B4.E64 1996, **(v6)**
Engels, Freidrich. HB501.M5.E48, **(v6)**
　B2973.E5 1934a, **(v8)**
　D16.9.E57 1979, **(v5)**
　DD182.E52 1967, **(v5)**
　U19.E49, **(v10)**
Engeman, Thomas S. KF4515.E53 1988, **(v7)**
Engemann, Joseph G. QL362.H4 1981, **(v1)**
Engen, Glenn F. TK7874.6.E54 1992, **(v1)**
Engholm, Christopher. HF5389.E53 1991, **(v6)**
Engineer, Asgharali. DS422.C64 E55 1995, **(v5)**
Engineers Joint Council. Z695.1.E5.E5 1967, **(v10)**
England, Eugene. PS3104.T5.Z64 1990, **(v3)**
England, J. B. A. QC786.E54, **(v1)**
England, Paula. HD6061.2.U6.E54 1992, **(v6)**
Englander, Irv. QA76.5.E566 1996, **(v1)**
Engle, Paul. PS3509.N44 A49, **(v3)**
Englebert, Pierre. HC800.E543 2000, **(v6)**
Englefield, Dermot J. T. DA28.4.E54 1995, **(v5)**
English Institute. PN75.F7.E5, **(v3)**
　PN80.5.E5, **(v3)**
　PR509.L8.E5, **(v3)**
English, Fenwick W. LB2806.15.E54 2000, **(v7)**
English, James F. PR937.E54 1994, **(v3)**
English, John A. UA15.E57 1996, **(v10)**
English, Richard. DA963.E53 1994, **(v5)**
　DA965.O553.E54 1998, **(v5)**
Enheduanna. PJ4083.E54 2000, **(v3)**
Enloe, Cynthia H. HQ1233.E55 1993, **(v6)**
　U21.75.E55 1983b, **(v10)**
　UB416.E54, **(v10)**
Ennin. DS707.E512, **(v5)**
Ennis, Philip H. ML3534.E55 1992, **(v9)**
Eno, Robert. B127.C65.E56 1990, **(v8)**
Enos, Richard Leo. KJA190.E56 1988, **(v7)**
Enos, Sandra. HV9471.E5 2001, **(v6)**
Enright, D. J. PN99.G7.E5, **(v3)**
　PR6009.N6.L3 1953, **(v3)**
Enríquez, Laura J. HD1333.N5 E569 1997, **(v6)**
Ensel, Remco. GN649.M65.E57 1999, **(v6)**
Enser, A. G. S. Z6207.E8 E58 1990, **(v10)**
　Z6207.W8 E56 1990, **(v10)**
Enslow, Sam. F2270.1.A7.E44 1990, **(v4)**
Ensminger, M. Eugene. SF375.E57 1986, **(v1)**
　SF207.E5 1997, **(v1)**
Ensminger, Robert F. NA8230.E5 1992, **(v9)**
Enteman, Willard F. HD31.E654 1993, **(v6)**
Enterline, Lynn. PN56.B62.E58 2000, **(v3)**
　PR428.M4.E58 1995, **(v3)**
Entine, Jon. GV706.32.E57 2000, **(v6)**
Entman, Robert M. P94.5.A372.U55 2000, **(v3)**
Entwisle, Doris R. LA303.B3.E58 1997, **(v7)**
　LB1511.E57 1982, **(v7)**
Entwistle, William J. PC4075.E5 1962, **(v3)**
　PG45.E6 1964, **(v3)**
Enzensberger, Hans Magnus. PT1825.Z5.E5 1961, **(v3)**
　PT2609.N9.A24 1982, **(v3)**
Eosze, Laszlo. ML410.K732.E582, **(v9)**
Ephron, Beulah (Kanter). BF456.R2.E65, **(v2)**
Epictetus. B561.M52 E5 1995, **(v8)**
Epicurus. B570.E5 I582 1994, **(v8)**
　B570.E5.S8, **(v8)**
Epperly, Elizabeth R. PR5688.S8.E66 1989, **(v3)**
Epps, Bradley S. PQ6613.O79.Z58 1996, **(v3)**
Epps, Willie J. KF292.H34 E67 1996, **(v7)**
Epstein, A. L. GN495.6.E67, **(v6)**
Epstein, Barbara Leslie. HN90.R3.E67 1991, **(v6)**
Epstein, Cynthia Fuchs. HQ1075.5.U6.E67 1988, **(v6)**
　KF299.W6 E65 1993, **(v7)**
Epstein, Daniel Mark. ML420.C63.E67 1999, **(v9)**
Epstein, David F. JK155.E64 1984, **(v7)**
Epstein, David. MT58.E67, **(v9)**
Epstein, Dena J. Polacheck. ML3556.E8, **(v9)**
Epstein, Eliot. TD796.5.E67 1997, **(v1)**
Epstein, Julia. PR3316.A4.Z6415 1989, **(v3)**

Epstein, Lee. KF8742.E67 1992, (v7)
  KF8742.E68 1993, (v7)
Epstein, Maram. PL2436.E67 2001, (v3)
Epstein, Marc J. HD30.255.E67 1996, (v6)
  KF2920.3.E63 1993, (v7)
Epstein, Richard Allen. KF380.E67 1998, (v7)
  KF385.E67 1995, (v7)
  KF3464.E64 1992, (v7)
Epstein, Richard L. BC71.E57 1994, (v8)
  BC181.E67 2001, (v8)
Epstein, Robert M. DC234.8.E67 1994, (v5)
Epstein, Steven. DG637.E67 1996, (v5)
  HT1191.E67 2001, (v6)
  RA644.A25.E68 1996, (v2)
Eraly, Abraham. DS461.E72 1997, (v5)
Erasmus, Desiderius. BT810.E63, (v8)
  BV4509.L2.E833, (v8)
  PA8502.E5.T5 1978, (v3)
Erb, Cynthia Marie. PN1997.K437.E72 1998, (v3)
Erb, Uwe. Q179.E64 2001, (v1)
Ercilla y Zuniga, Alonso de. PQ6389.A2 1956, (v3)
Erdelyi, Matthew Hugh. BF173.E646 1985, (v2)
Erdem, Y. Hakan. HT1238.E73 1996, (v6)
Erdinast-Vulcan, Daphna. PR6005.O4.Z67 1991, (v3)
  PR6005.O4.Z675 1999, (v3)
Erdman, David V. PR61.E7, (v3)
  PR4147.E7 1969, (v3)
Erdmann, Carl. D157.E713, (v5)
Erdmans, Mary Patrice. F548.9.P7.E73 1998, (v4)
Erdos, Paul. QA171.5.E73 1989, (v1)
Erdrich, Louise. PZ7.E72554Bi 2000b, (v3)
Erenberg, Lewis A. F128.5.E65, (v4)
  ML3518.E74 1998, (v9)
Erenburg, Ilia. D764.E352 1964, (v5)
Erfani, Julie A. JL1224.E74 1995, (v7)
Ergang, Robert Reinhold. DD76.E7 1966, (v5)
Eribon, Didier. B2430.F724.E7513 1991, (v8)
Ericksen, J. L. TA403.6.E74 1991, (v1)
Erickson, Carolly. CB351.E76, (v5)
  DA332.E74 1997, (v5)
  DA347.E74 1998, (v5)
  DA355.E74 1997, (v5)
  DA814.A5.E7 1989, (v5)
  DC137.1.E77 1991, (v5)
Erickson, Darlene Williams. PS3525.O5616.Z66 1992, (v3)
Erickson, Glenn W. BC199.P2.E75 1998, (v8)
Erickson, H. Lynn. LB1570.E74 2001, (v7)
  LB2806.15.E75 1998, (v7)
Erickson, Hal. PN1992.55.E67 1989, (v3)
  PN1992.8.A59.E74 1995, (v3)
  PN1995.9.B28.E7 1992, (v3)
Erickson, John D. BP89.E75 1998, (v8)
  PQ3984.E27, (v3)
Erickson, John. D764.E74 1975b vol. 1, (v5)
  UA772.E7, (v10)
Erickson, Jon. GB581.E75 1996, (v6)
Erickson, Jon. QE33.E75 1993, (v1)
Erickson, Kenneth A. F892.E75 1994, (v4)
Erickson, Lee. PR451.E75 1996, (v3)
Erickson, Martin J. QA164.E74 1996, (v1)
Erickson, Paul D. E877.2.E64 1985, (v4)
Erickson, Wayne. PR2358.E75 1996, (v3)
Erickson, Winston P. E99.P25 E75 1994, (v4)
Ericson, Joan E. PL829.A8.Z63 1997, (v3)
Ericson, Margaret D. ML128.W7.E75 1995, (v9)
Ericson, Richard Victor. HV7921.E75 1997, (v6)
  PN4914.C74.E75 1991, (v3)
Erie, Steven P. E184.I6.E75 1988, (v4)
Eriksen, Viking Olver. VK1265.E75 1990, (v10)
Erikson, Erik H. BF697.E7, (v2)
  BF713.E73 1997, (v2)
Erikson, Robert S. HN90.P8.E76 1993, (v6)
Erisman, H. Michael. F1787.5.E75 2000, (v4)
  F2183.E75 1992, (v4)
Erkkila, Betsy. PS3242.P64.E74 1989, (v3)
Erlich, Richard D. Z5935.5.E74 1993, (v10)
Erlich, Victor. PG3022.E74 1994, (v3)
Erlikh, Hagai. DS63.2.E7.E75 1994, (v5)
Erlmann, Veit. ML350.E77 1991, (v9)
  ML3760.E76 1995, (v9)

Erman, Adolf. PJ1481.E7, (v3)
  PJ1943.E72 1966, (v3)
Ermatinger, Emil. PT537.E7 1925, (v3)
Ermolaev, Herman. PG2948.E7, (v3)
  PG3026.C45.E76 1997, (v3)
  PG3476.S52.T57, (v3)
Ernest, John. PS153.N5.E76 1995, (v3)
Ernst, Alice Henson. PS3509.R445H5 1935, (v3)
Ernst, Carl H. QL666.C5.E76 1994, (v1)
  QL666.C5.E77 1989, (v1)
  QL666.O6.E77 1992, (v1)
Ernst, Daniel R. KF3431.E76 1995, (v7)
Ernst, Dennis J. RB45.15.E76 2001, (v2)
Ernst, Earle. PL772.E7, (v3)
Ernst, Gordon E. Z8089.12.E76 1995, (v10)
Ernst, Robert. GV333.M3.E76 1990, (v6)
Erny, Pierre. GN645.E7613 1981, (v6)
Erricker, Clive. BL42.E75 2000, (v8)
Errington, Jane. HQ1459.O57.E77 1995, (v6)
Errington, R. M. DF261.M2.E7713 1990, (v5)
Errington, Shelly. GN635.I65.E76 1989, (v6)
Erskine, John. PS3509.R5.P7, (v3)
Erspamer, Peter R. PT149.J4.E78 1997, (v3)
Ertas, Atila. TA174.E78 1993, (v1)
Ertman, Thomas. JN5.E77 1997, (v7)
Ertz, Susan. PS3509.R6.P6, (v3)
Ervin, Sam J. E860.E78, (v4)
Ervine, St. John Greer. PR5366.E7 1956, (v3)
Erwin, Allen A. F786.S58 E7, (v4)
Esau, Katherine. QK671.E8 1965, (v1)
Escher, M. C. N6953.E82, (v9)
Eschle, Catherine. JC423.E68 2001, (v7)
Eschmeyer, William N. QL623.4.E83 1983, (v1)
Escobar, Arturo. HD75.E73 1994, (v6)
Escobar, Edward J. HV8148.L55.E73 1999, (v6)
Escott, Paul D. HN79.N8E83 1985, (v4)
Esdaile, Charles J. DP208.E82 1988, (v5)
Eskew, Glenn T. F334.B69.N435 1997, (v4)
Eskildsen, Stephen. BL1923.E84 1998, (v8)
Eskridge, William N. KF538.E85 1996, (v7)
Esman, Milton J. D842.E83 1994, (v5)
  JK468.P64.E75 2000, (v7)
Esmein, Jean. DS777.55.E813, (v5)
Espagnat, Bernard d'. QC6.4.R42.E8713 1989, (v1)
Espana, Rafael de. PN1993.5.S7.E83 1994, (v3)
Espina, Noni. ML128.S3.E8, (v9)
Esping-Andersen, Gosta. HB846.E78 1990, (v6)
Espinosa y Tello, Josef. F851.5.V68 1990, (v4)
Espiritu, Yen Le. F869.S22.E9 1995, (v4)
Esposito, John L. BL80.2.E76 2002, (v8)
  BP60.E84 1999, (v8)
  BP63.A4 M533 1998, (v8)
  BP70.E86 2001, (v8)
  JC49.E76 1996, (v7)
Espriu, Salvador. PC3941.E84.A23 1989, (v3)
Espy, Willard R. PE1519.E87 2001, (v3)
Esquenazi-Mayo, Roberto. PN4937.P4.E84 1993, (v3)
Esrock, Ellen J. PN56.V54.E85 1994, (v3)
Essah, Patience. E445.D3 E87 1996, (v4)
Essary, Jesse Frederick. F199.E78, (v4)
Essif, Les. PN1861.E77 2001, (v3)
Esslin, Martin. PQ2601.R677.Z636 1977, (v3)
  PR6003.E282.Z64, (v3)
Esslin, Martin. PT2603.R397.Z6 1971b, (v3)
Estell, Kenneth. E185.96.E88 1994, (v4)
Estes, Eleanor. PZ7.E749Gi 2000, (v3)
  PZ7.E749Hu10, (v3)
Estes, Mary Ellen Zator. RT48.H425 2002, (v2)
Estes, Richard J. HN17.5.E82 1988, (v6)
Estes, Richard. ND237.E75.A4 1978, (v9)
  QL731.A1.E84 1990, (v1)
Esthus, Raymond A. DS517.7.E88 1988, (v5)
Estrin, Barbara L. PR535.L7.E88 1994, (v3)
Estroff, Sue E. RC439.5.E84, (v2)
Estruch, Juan. BX819.3.O68.E7413 1995, (v8)
Etchemendy, John. BC135.E83 1990, (v8)
Etcheson, Nicole. F484.3.E83 1996, (v4)
Etheil, Jeffrey L. UG1242.F5.E873 1994, (v10)
Ethem T. Turkdogan Symposium. TN730.E77 1994, (v1)
Etherege, George. PR3432.A13 1971, (v3)

  PR3432.A133 1982, (v3)
  PR3432.A69 1963, (v3)
Etheridge, David. TH7654.E84 1996, (v1)
Etheridge, Elizabeth W. RA650.5.E84 1991, (v2)
Etherington, Dan M. HD9198.C5.E85 1993, (v6)
Etherton, Michael. PR8789.E8 1989, (v3)
  PR9343.E86 1982, (v3)
ëTiSvetaeva, Marina. PG3476.T75A26 1987, (v3)
Etlin, Richard A. NA737.W7.E84 1994, (v9)
  NA1118.E86 1990, (v9)
Ettema, James S. PN4781.E88 1998, (v3)
Etter, D. M. TA345.E547 1997, (v1)
Etter, Don D. F784.D4 E88, (v4)
Etter, Patricia A. F786.E88 1998, (v4)
Ettorre, E. M. RC564.5.W65.E77 1992, (v2)
Etulain, Richard W. PS374.W4.E93 1999, (v3)
Etzioni, Amitai. HM35.E89 1988, (v6)
  HM216.E85 1996, (v6)
  HN90.C6.E88 1993, (v6)
  JC596.2.U5.E79 1999, (v7)
Etzkowitz, Henry. Q130.E85 2000, (v1)
Etzold, Thomas H. UA23.E89 1982, (v10)
Euba, Femi. PN1590.B53.E93 1989, (v3)
Eubank, Keith. D749.E82 1985, (v5)
  DC342.8.C32.E8, (v5)
Euben, J. Peter. JC73.E93 1997, (v7)
Eulau, Heinz. JA71.E9 1996, (v7)
Euler, Leonhard. QA295.E8413 1988, (v1)
Euler, Leonhard. QA302.E8513 2000, (v1)
Euraque, Dario A. F1508.E87 1996, (v4)
Euripides. PA3975.A2 2000, (v3)
Eusden, John Dykstra. DA390.E8, (v5)
Evangelista, Anita. BF1411.E82 1991, (v2)
Evangelista, Matthew. D860.E93 1999, (v5)
  UF533.E93 1988, (v10)
Evangelou, V. P. TD878.E93 1998, (v1)
Evans, Alfred John. PR2937.E85 1956, (v3)
Evans, Anna Margaret. F1058.M8.E93 1992, (v4)
Evans, Anthony M. TN260.E93 1997, (v1)
Evans, Arthur B. PQ2469.Z5.E88 1988, (v3)
Evans, Arthur R. PQ2256.F5Z65, (v3)
Evans, Arthur S. F319.B6.E83 1990, (v4)
Evans, Arthur. DF221.C8.E75, (v5)
Evans, Augusta J. PS3332.B48 1992, (v3)
  PS3332.M33 1992, (v3)
  PS3332.S3, (v3)
Evans, Bergen. PE1460.E9, (v3)
Evans, Bertrand. PR2981.E9, (v3)
Evans, Brendan. DA566.7.E93 1996, (v5)
Evans, Brendan. LC5256.G7.E92 1987, (v7)
Evans, C. Lawrence. JK1239.E93 1991, (v7)
Evans, C. Stephen. BT205.E83 1996, (v8)
Evans, Charles F. H. PN1998.A3.E92, (v3)
Evans, Colin. PR6055.V3.H4, (v3)
Evans, D. Fennell. QD549.E93 1999, (v1)
Evans, David C. VA653.E93 1997, (v10)
Evans, David S. HG3755.8.U6.E94 1999, (v6)
Evans, David. E476.7.E93 1996, (v4)
  ML3521.E9 1982, (v9)
Evans, Donald D. BL624.E93 1993, (v8)
Evans, Donald. R853.H8.E87 1996, (v2)
Evans, Dylan. BF531.E79 2001, (v2)
Evans, Eli N. F220.J5.E82 1973, (v4)
Evans, Eric J. HC255.E89 2001, (v6)
Evans, Evan David. DA720.E79, (v5)
Evans, G. R. B721.E86 1993, (v8)
  BJ1401.E77 1982, (v8)
  BV600.2.E94 1994, (v8)
Evans, Gary R. HJ2051.E93 1997, (v6)
Evans, Graham. JA61.E85 1990, (v7)
Evans, Grant. HN700.4.A8.E9 1990, (v6)
Evans, H. David. HF1008.E83 1989, (v6)
Evans, Ivan Thomas. DT1798.E83 1997, (v5)
Evans, J. A. S. D56.52.H45.E93 1991, (v5)
Evans, J. Martin. PR3562.E89 1996, (v3)
  PR3588.E9 1998, (v3)
Evans, James. KF242.A1.E94 1995, (v7)
Evans, James. QB16.E93 1998, (v1)
Evans, Joan. NA5544.E8, (v9)
Evans, John G. CC81.E93 1978, (v5)
Evans, John Henry. F826.E96, (v4)

Evans, John L. DK771.A3.E83 1999, (v5)
Evans, John. SB419.E795 1994, (v1)
Evans, Joyce A. PN1995.9.W3.E82 1998, (v3)
Evans, Ken (Kenneth W.). TJ1189.E85 2001, (v1)
Evans, L. T. HB871.E92 1998, (v6)
Evans, L. T. SB106.O74.E93 1993, (v1)
    KJC9400.5.T67.E95 1998, (v7)
Evans, Mark Llewellyn. D771.E95 1999, (v5)
Evans, Martha Noel. PQ149.E83 1987, (v3)
Evans, Mary. CT21.E83 1999, (v5)
    HQ1190.E92 1997, (v6)
Evans, Maurice. PR521.E9, (v3)
Evans, Peter William. PN1998.3.B86.F55 1995, (v3)
Evans, Peter. ML410.B853.E9 1979, (v9)
Evans, Poppy. NC999.E825 1999, (v9)
Evans, R. J. DA550.E9 1968b, (v5)
Evans, Richard I. BF109.R63.E9 1975, (v2)
    RC339.52.L34.E9 1976, (v2)
Evans, Richard J. D16.8.E847 1999, (v5)
    DD256.5.E92 1989, (v5)
    HN458.H3.E95 1987, (v6)
    HQ1154.E8 1977, (v6)
    HQ1236.5.E85.E82 1987, (v6)
    HV6974.E95 1998, (v6)
    HV8699.G3.E93 1996, (v6)
Evans, Robert C. PR2642.B6.E93 1995, (v3)
    PR2642.H5.E93 1994, (v3)
    PS374.S5.E93 1997, (v3)
    Z8456.6.E83 2000, (v10)
Evans, Robert John Weston. DB65.E9, (v5)
Evans, Robert O. PR6013.R44.Z633, (v3)
Evans, Rowland. E847.E9, (v4)
    E855.E9, (v4)
Evans, Sara M. HQ1410.E83 1989, (v6)
Evans, Sara. HQ1426.E9 1979, (v6)
Evans, Scott D. PR3537.P5.E73 1999, (v3)
Evans, Stephen Hadley. HJ6645.E8, (v6)
Evans, Stephen S. DA59.E94 1997, (v5)
Evans, Steven Ross. E99.N5.M34 1996, (v4)
Evans, Terry. F548.37.E93 1998, (v4)
Evans, Tony. K3240.E95 1996, (v7)
Evans, W. Howard. QH601.E823 1989, (v1)
Evans, Walker. E169.E8613 1991, (v4)
    TR647.E9 2000, (v1)
    TR654.E918 1991, (v1)
Evans, William McKee. F262.C2E9 1995, (v4)
Evans-Pritchard, E. E. GN651.E9, (v6)
Evans-Pritchard, Edward Evan. GN475.8.E9 1963, (v6)
Evanzz, Karl. BP223.Z8.E434 1999, (v8)
Evarts, Jeremiah. E99.C5.E88 1981, (v4)
Evdokimova, Svetlana. PG3358.H45.E94 1999, (v3)
Eve, Raymond A. BS651.E94 1990, (v8)
Evelyn, John. DA447.E9.A44, (v5)
Evenhuis, Anthony John. PQ2538.E92 1998, (v3)
Evensen, Bruce J. DS126.4.E86 1992, (v5)
Evenson, Debra. KGN327.E93 1994, (v7)
Everest, Frank Kendall. UG633.E85, (v10)
Everest, Kelvin. PR571.E94 1990, (v3)
Everett, Anna. PN1995.9.N4.E94 2001, (v3)
Everett, Dianna. E99.C5.E89 1990, (v4)
Everett, Dorothy. PR255.E9, (v3)
Everett, Paul. ML410.V82 E84 1996, (v9)
Everett, Thomas H. SB317.58.E94, (v1)
Everhart, W. Harry. SH328.R69 1981, (v1)
Everhart, William C. SB482.A4.E95 1983, (v1)
Everitt, Brian. QA273.E84 1999, (v1)
    QA276.15.E84 1998, (v1)
Everitt, David. PN1992.4.H55, (v3)
Evers, Alf. F129.W85.E94 1987, (v4)
Evers, Frederick T. LC1032.E84 1998, (v7)
Evers, Myrlie B. E185.97.E94.E9, (v4)
Everson Museum of Art. NK4005.E94 1989, (v9)
Everson, William K. PN1993.5.U6.E9, (v3)
Everson, William. PS3509.V65.A17 1997 vol. 1, (v3)
Everstine, Diana Sullivan. RJ507.S49.E94 1989, (v2)
Everton, Macduff. F1435.E89 1991, (v4)
Evett, Ian. RA1057.5.E945 1998, (v2)
Eviota, Elizabeth U. HD6060.65.P6.E95 1992, (v6)
Evron, Boas. DS149.E9313 1995, (v5)
Evron, Yair. DS87.53.E87 1987, (v5)

UA853.I8.E8613 1994, (v10)
Ewald, Janet. DT156.3.E93 1990, (v5)
Ewald, Johann von. E268.E9213, (v4)
Ewans, Martin. DS356.E95 2002, (v5)
Ewell, Judith. E183.8.V3.E9 1996, (v4)
    F2325.E93 1984, (v4)
Ewen, Charles Robin. F319.T14.E94 1998, (v4)
Ewen, Stuart. HM263.E849 1996, (v6)
Ewert, A. PC2073.E8 1961, (v3)
Ewert, Alan W. GV191.6.E85 1989, (v6)
Ewick, Patricia. K487.C8.E94 1998, (v7)
Ewing, A. C. B29.E9 1968, (v8)
    B823.E8 1974, (v8)
    BJ1011.E84, (v8)
Ewing, Charles Patrick. HV9067.H6.E95 1990, (v6)
Ewing, Galen Wood. QD75.E9 1960, (v1)
Ewing, K. D. DA576.E95 2000, (v5)
    KD4080.E95 1990, (v7)
    KE4646.E96 1992, (v7)
Ewing, Preston. F549.C2.E85 1996, (v4)
Ewing, Steve. D790.E95 1997, (v5)
Exner, Judith Katherine Campbell. CT275.E97.A35, (v5)
Exum, J. Cheryl. PN1995.9.B53.E88 1996, (v3)
Eyck, Erich. DD237.E913, (v5)
Eye, Alexander von. HA31.3.E94 1998, (v6)
Eyer, Diane E. HQ759.48.E94 1996, (v6)
Eyerman, Ron. HN17.5.E99 1991, (v6)
Eyler, Jonathan. F572.M9 E94 1986, (v4)
Eyman, Scott. PN1995.7.E96 1997, (v3)
    PN1998.3.L83.E95 1993, (v3)
Eyo, Ekpo. N7399.N5.E94 1980, (v9)
Eyre-Todd, George. PR8655.E87 1971, (v3)
Eyre-Todd, George. PR8655.E9 1971, (v3)
Eyring, Henry. QD453.E9, (v1)
Eysenck, H. J. BF173.E9, (v2)
    BF412.E97 1995, (v2)
    BF431.B97 1998, (v2)
    BF698.E97 1970, (v2)
    BF698.9.B5.E9, (v2)
    RC530.E9, (v2)
Eysenck, Michael W. BF121.E95 1994, (v2)
Eyzaguirre, Jaime. F3094.O3555, (v4)
Ezekiel, Nissim. PR9499.3.E9A6 1992, (v3)
Ezekiel, Raphael S. E574.D49.N438 1984, (v4)
Ezell, Margaret J. M. PR111.E94 1993, (v3)
    PR438.S63.E94 1999, (v3)
Ezergailis, Andrew. DS135.L3.E94 1996, (v5)
Ezra, Elizabeth. JV1835.E97 2000, (v7)
    PN1998.A3.M4138 2000, (v3)
Ezrahi, Sidra DeKoven. PN842.E87 2000, (v3)
Ezrahi, Yaron. JA80.E97 1990, (v7)
Fār ābī. B753.F32 E5 2001, (v8)
    B753.F33 A25 2001, (v8)
Faarlund, Jan Terje. PD2621.F33 1997, (v3)
Faas, Ekbert. PR595.P85.F34 1988, (v3)
Fabel, Robin F. A. E93.F23 2000, (v4)
Fabend, Firth Haring. BX9498.D87, (v8)
    F127.R6.H37 1991, (v4)
Faber, Daniel J. HC141.Z9.E54 1993, (v6)
Faber, Eli. F2191.J4.F33 1998, (v4)
Faber, Henry Burnell. UF860.F3, (v10)
Faber, K. (Kurt). TP248.65.E59F73 2000, (v1)
Faber, M. D. BF1566.F27 1993, (v2)
Faber, Nancy W. PS3556.A32.S8, (v3)
Faber, Richard. DA559.7.F29 1987, (v5)
Faber, Roger J. BD553.F25 1986, (v8)
Faber, Scott. TC530.F32 1996, (v1)
Faber, T. E. QC151.F33 1995, (v1)
Fabian, Ann. E337.5.F33 2000, (v4)
Fabian, Ann. HV6715.F33 1990, (v6)
Fabian, Johannes. DT650.L8.F32 1990, (v5)
    GN654.F35 1998, (v6)
Fabian, Stephen Michael. F2520.1.B75.F34 1992, (v4)
Fabozzi, Frank J. HG4651.F28 1989, (v6)
Fabre, Michel. PS153.N5.F34 1991, (v3)
Fabre, Michel. PS3545.R815.Z65128 1990, (v3)
Fabricant, Carole. PR3728.S46.F3 1982, (v3)
Fabricant, Michael. HV91.F3 1992, (v6)
Fabrycky, W. J. HD69.D4.F3, (v6)

Fabun, Don. CB427.F25, (v5)
Facciola, Stephen. SB175.F332 1998, (v1)
Fackenheim, Emil L. BS1186.F36 1990, (v8)
Fackre, Gabriel J. BT30.U6.F33 1982, (v8)
Fadala, Sam. GV1185.F33 1999, (v6)
Faderman, Lillian. HQ75.5.F33 1981b, (v6)
    HQ75.6.U5.F35 1999, (v6)
Fadiman, Clifton. PS3511.A33.A6 1955, (v3)
    PS3511.A33.A84 1957, (v3)
    Z1035.F29, (v10)
Fadiman, Jeffrey. DT433.545.M47.F34 1993, (v5)
Faery, Rebecca Blevins. PS173.I6.F34 1999, (v3)
Fagan, Brian M. E58.F28 1991, (v4)
    E61.F34 1987, (v4)
    GC296.8.E4.F34 1999, (v6)
    QC989.A1, (v1)
Fagen, Richard R. F1439.5.F34 1987, (v4)
Fager, Charles. F334.S4.F34, (v4)
Fagg, Lawrence W. BD638.F33 2002, (v8)
Fagin, Claire M. RT89.F34 2000, (v2)
Fagothey, Austin. BJ1025.F18 1989, (v8)
Faherty, William Barnaby. F474.S253.S523 1987, (v4)
Fahey, David M. HV5006.F33 1996, (v6)
Fahey, James J. D767.F3 1974, (v5)
Fahey, Michael A. Z7845.1.F34 1992, (v10)
Fahim, Shadia S. PR6023.E833.Z64 1994, (v3)
Fahmy, Khaled. UA865.F26 1997, (v10)
Fahn, James. HC441.Z9 E538 2003, (v6)
Fahs, Alice. PS217.C58.F34 2001, (v3)
Faigley, Lester. PE1404.F35 1992, (v3)
Faigman, David L. K487.S3.F35 1999, (v7)
Faille, Christopher C. KF8748.F28 1995, (v7)
Fain, Benjamin. QC680.F313 1969, (v1)
Fain, Gordon L. QP363.F35 1999, (v1)
Fairbank, John King. DS511.F28 1989, (v5)
    DS721.F26, (v5)
    DS734.9.F3.A33 1982, (v5)
    DS735.F27 1998, (v5)
    DS735.F28 1989, (v5)
    DS735.F3 1983, (v5)
    DS740.4.F26, (v5)
    E183.8.C5.F28, (v4)
Fairbanks, Evelyn. F614.S4.F19 1990, (v4)
Fairbanks, Jo. RA425.F25 1998, (v2)
Fairbanks, Robert B. F394.D2157.F35 1998, (v4)
    HD7288.78.U52.C54 1988, (v6)
Fairbridge, Rhodes Whitmore. GB10.F3, (v6)
    QE5.F33, (v1)
Fairbrother, Trevor J. ND237.S3.F334 2000, (v9)
Fairchild, Hoxie Neale. PR457.F3 1965, (v3)
    PR508.R4.F3, (v3)
Fairclough, Adam. E185.61.F17 1987, (v4)
    E185.93.L6.F35 1995, (v4)
    LC212.2.F35 2001, (v7)
Fairclough, Ellen Louks. F1034.3.F35.A3 1995, (v4)
Fairfield, Paul. JC574.F35 2000, (v7)
Fairfield-Sonn, James W. HD62.15.F35 2001, (v6)
Fairhall, David. VA573.F34 1971, (v10)
Fairhead, James. GF746.2.F35 1996, (v6)
Fairholm, Gilbert W. HD57.7.F348 1997, (v6)
Fairley, Barker. PT1925.F3, (v3)
    PT2049.F33, (v3)
    PT2451.Z5.F3, (v3)
Fairtile, Linda Beard. ML134.P94.F35 1999, (v9)
Fairweather, Eugene Rathbone. B734.F3, (v8)
Fajans, Jane. DU740.42.F35 1997, (v5)
Fakhry, Majid. B741.F265 1997, (v8)
    BJ1291.F28 1991, (v8)
Faksh, Mahmud A. BP63.A65.F35 1997, (v8)
Falasca-Zamponi, Simonetta. DG571.F2 1997, (v5)
Falco, Kristine L. RC281.W65.F35 1998, (v2)
Falco, Raphael. PR658.T7.F29 2000, (v3)
Falcoff, Mark. F3100.F32 1989, (v4)
Falconer, Ian. PZ7.F1865Om 2001, (v3)
Fales, Evan. BD541.F35 1990, (v8)
Falicov, Celia Jaes. RC451.5.H57F35 1998, (v2)
    RC451.5.H57.F35 1998, (v2)
Falk, Gerhard. RA395.A3.F337 1999, (v2)
Falk, Quentin. PN2598.H66.F35 1993, (v3)

Falk, Richard A. JC585.F35 2000, (v7)
    JX1954.F248 1991, (v7)
    JX1954.F249 1995, (v7)
    JX4471.F2, (v7)
Falk, Thomas H. PT2605.A58.Z685 1993, (v3)
Falkner, Gerda. HN373.5.F35 1998, (v6)
Falkowski, James E. KDZ480.F35 1992, (v7)
Falla, Ricardo. F1466.5.F3513 1994, (v4)
Faller, Kathleen Coulborn. RJ507.S49.F35 1988, (v2)
Fallis, Richard. PR8750.F34, (v3)
Fallon, Brian. DA959.1.F355 1998, (v5)
Fallon, Gabriel. PR6029.C33.Z63 1965, (v3)
Fallon, Richard H. KF8742.F35 2001, (v7)
Fallon, Robert Thomas. PR3592.P64.F33 1995, (v3)
    PR3592.P64.F35 1993, (v3)
Fallon, Stephen M. PR3592.P5.F35 1991, (v3)
Fallows, James M. DS504.5.F35 1994, (v5)
    HC108.S725F3, (v6)
    UA23.F343, (v10)
Falls, Cyril. DA937.F3 1970, (v5)
Falola, Toyin. BL2470.N5.F35 1998, (v8)
    DT30.5.F35 2001, (v5)
Falsetto, Mario. PN1998.3.K83.F35 1994, (v3)
Falvo, Donna R. RC108.F35 1999, (v2)
Fancher, Robert T. RC437.5.F335 1995, (v2)
Fanchi, John R. QA37.2.F35 1997, (v1)
Fanning, Charles. PS3507.U6755.Z63, (v3)
Fanning, Connell. HB99.7.F364 1998, (v6)
Fanshawe, Andy. GV199.44.H55.F36 1996, (v6)
Fanshel, David. HV743.N49.L694 1992, (v6)
    HV881.F36, (v6)
Fant, Clyde E. BS475.3.F36 2001, (v8)
Fante, John. PS3511.A594 D3, (v3)
Fantham, Elaine. PA6003.F36 1996, (v3)
Faòs¯iòh, ism¯a¯il. PK6561.F266S813 1985, (v3)
Faour, Muhammad. DS63.1.F34 1993, (v5)
Faqir, Fadia. PR9570.J653.F356 1997, (v3)
Farabi. B753.F33.P53, (v8)
Farace, Joe. TR267.F35 1996, (v1)
Faraday, Michael. QC71.F3 1960, (v1)
    QC503.F21 1965, (v1)
Faragher, John Mack. F454.B66.F37 1992, (v4)
    F547.S94.F37 1986, (v4)
    HQ553.F37, (v6)
Farago, Ladislas. E745.P3.F3 1966, (v4)
    UB250.F3, (v10)
Farah, Caesar E. BP161.2.F3 2000, (v8)
Faralla, Dana. PS3556.A65 C45, (v3)
Farber, Barry A. LB2840.2.F37 1991, (v7)
Farber, Bernard. HV3006.A4.F33, (v6)
Farber, Daniel A. K370.F37 1997, (v7)
Farber, David R. F548.52.F37 1988, (v4)
Farber, Eduard. QD11.F34 1969, (v1)
    QD21.F35, (v1)
    QD21.F37 1963, (v1)
Farber, Paul Lawrence. BJ1298.F37 1994, (v8)
    QH15.F27 2000, (v1)
Farber, Samuel. DK266.F37 1990, (v5)
    F1787.5.F37, (v4)
Farber, Seth. RC437.5.F35 1993, (v2)
Farber, Sharon Klayman. RC552.S4.F36 2000, (v2)
Farcau, Bruce W. F2688.5.F37 1996, (v4)
Fardon, Richard. BL2480.C45 1991, (v8)
    GN21.D68.F37 1999, (v6)
Farge, Arlette. DC133.4.F3713 1995, (v5)
    DC715.F3713 1993, (v5)
Fargnoli, A. Nicholas. PR6019.O9.Z533376 1995, (v3)
Fargo, Lucile Foster. F899.S7F3 1957, (v4)
Farias, Victor. B3279.H49.F3413 1989, (v8)
Farid, Abdel Majid. DT107.83.F374 1994, (v5)
Farin, Gerald E. QA462.F26 1998, (v1)
Faringer, Gunilla L. PN4748.S58.F37 1991, (v3)
Faris, James C. E99.N3.F38 1990, (v4)
    E99.N3.F384 1996, (v4)
Farish, Thomas Edwin. F811.F23, (v4)
Farjeon, Eleanor. PR6011.A67Z52, (v3)
Farkas, Daniel. QA76.76.O63.F37 1988, (v1)
Farkas, George. LC3731.F37 1996, (v7)
Farley, James Aloysius. E806.F255 1984, (v4)
Farley, James J. UF543.P6.F37 1994, (v10)
Farley, Reynolds. HC108.D6.F37 2000, (v6)

Farley, Reynolds. HN58.F37 1996, (v6)
Farley, Walter. PZ10.3.F22Bl, (v3)
Farley-Hills, David. PR651.F35 1988, (v3)
    PR2976.F28 1990, (v3)
    PR3669.R2.F34 1978, (v3)
Farmer, Brett. PN1995.9.H55.F37 2000, (v3)
Farmer, Edward L. DS753.F37 1994, (v5)
Farmer, Henry George. ML1300.F33 1970, (v9)
Farmer, James. E185.97.F37.A35 1985, (v4)
Farmer, Kenneth C. HN530.Z9.E434 1992, (v6)
Farmer, Philip Jose. PS3556.A72.L6, (v3)
Farmer, Sarah Bennett. D804.G4.F2913 1998, (v5)
Farmer, William Reuben. BM176.F37 1956, (v8)
Farnell, Brenda M. E98.S5.F37 1995, (v4)
Farneth, David. ML410.W395.F37 1999, (v9)
Farnham, Barbara. E183.8.G3.F37 1997, (v4)
Farnham, Willard. PR2983.F35, (v3)
Farnham-Diggory, Sylvia. LB1060.F36 1990, (v7)
Farnsworth, E. Allan. K840.F37 1998, (v7)
    KF387.F3 1996, (v7)
Farnsworth, Martha. F686.F37.A37 1986, (v4)
Farnsworth, Robert M. PN4874.S5715.F37 1996, (v3)
Faroqhi, Suraiya. DR432.F2313 2000, (v5)
Farquhar, Francis Peloubet. F868.S5F18, (v4)
Farquhar, George. PR3435.A1 1930, (v3)
    PR3435.A5.K44 1988, (v3)
Farquhar, Mary Ann. PL2449.F37 1999, (v3)
Farquharson, A. S. L. DG297.F3 1975, (v5)
Farr, Anthony. JC261.S372.F37 1998, (v7)
Farr, James Barker. VK23.F28 1989, (v10)
Farr, Judith. PS1541.Z5.F27 1992, (v3)
Farr, William E. F731.F37, (v4)
Farrar, Cynthia. JC75.D36.F37 1988, (v7)
Farrar, Geraldine. ML420.F27 A2 1970b, (v9)
Farrar, John Laird. QK110.F3 1995, (v1)
Farrar, Marjorie Milbank. DC393.M55.F37 1990, (v5)
Farrar, Ronald T. PN4874.W634.F67 1998, (v3)
Farred, Grant. PR9355.2.F37 2000, (v3)
Farrell, Amy Erdman. PN4900.M77.F37 1998, (v3)
Farrell, David M. JF1001.F35 2001, (v7)
Farrell, Edwin William. LA229.F36 1990, (v7)
Farrell, Eileen. ML420.F275.A3 1999, (v9)
Farrell, Gerry. ML338.F37 1997, (v9)
Farrell, James T. PN49.F3, (v3)
    PS3511.A738 A15 1956, (v3)
    PS3511.A738 B4, (v3)
    PS3511.A738 D4, (v3)
    PS3511.A738 E4, (v3)
    PS3511.A738 F3, (v3)
    PS3511.A738 J9, (v3)
    PS3511.A738 M9, (v3)
    PS3511.A738 O4, (v3)
    PS3511.A738 S5, (v3)
    PS3511.A738 S8, (v3)
Farrell, John Philip. PR469.P6.F3, (v3)
Farrell, Joseph. PA2061.F395 2001, (v3)
    PA6804.G4.F37 1991, (v3)
Farrell, Kirby. PR3069.D42.F37 1989, (v3)
Farrell, Michael P. HQ1059.5.U5.F37 1981, (v6)
Farrell, Michele Longino. PQ1925.F37 1991, (v3)
Farrell, Sean. DA990.U46.F345 2000, (v5)
Farrell, Theo. UC263.F37 1997, (v10)
Farrell, Thomas B. P301.F37 1993, (v3)
Farrer, Austin Marsden. BJ1461.F3 1960, (v8)
Farrer, Reginald John. DS793.K2.F3, (v5)
Farrington, Benjamin. B485.F3 1969, (v8)
Farris, William Wayne. DS838.5.F37 1992, (v5)
    DS855.F37 1998, (v5)
Farriss, Nancy M. F1435.F28 1984, (v4)
Farrukhzad, Furugh. PK6561.F264.A24 1982, (v3)
Farsoun, Samih K. DS119.7.F336 1997, (v5)
Farwell, Byron. UA853.N35.F37 1984b, (v10)
Farwell, Marilyn R. PS153.L46.F37 1996, (v3)
Fasching, Darrell J. BJ1188.F37 1993, (v8)
Fash, William Leonard. F1435.C7.F37 1991, (v4)
Fasman, Mark J. ML128.W5.F3 1990, (v9)
Fass, Paula S. LA217.F38 1989, (v7)
Fass, Simon M. HC153.F37 1988, (v6)
Fassbinder, Rainer Werner. PN1998.3.F37.A3 1992, (v3)
Fassett, Norman C. QK105.F3 1957, (v1)

Fast, Howard. PS3511.A784 A5, (v3)
    PS3511.A784 A6, (v3)
    PS3511.A784 C6, (v3)
    PS3511.A784 F7, (v3)
    PS3511.A784 P3, (v3)
Fast, Robin Riley. PS310.I52.F37 1999, (v3)
Fast, Timothy. G1201.E1.G5 1995, (v6)
Fastovsky, David E. QE862.D5.F38 1996, (v1)
Fatout, Paul. PS1331.F3, (v3)
Faubion, James D. DF920.F38 1993, (v5)
Faugeras, Olivier. TA1632.F38 1993, (v1)
Faulhaber, Gerald R. HE8846.A55.F38 1987, (v6)
Faulk, Odie B. F786.F337, (v4)
    F811.F26, (v4)
Faulkner, Harold Underwood. HC103.F3 1976, (v6)
Faulkner, Jim. PS3511.A86.Z78285 1996, (v3)
Faulkner, Rupert. NE1325.A5.A4 2001, (v9)
Faulkner, Virginia. F666.F3, (v4)
Faulkner, William. PS3511.A86.A6 1987, (v3)
    PS3511.A86 A62 1951, (v3)
    PS3511.A86 A8 1957, (v3)
    PS3511.A86 B5, (v3)
    PS3511.A86 C64 1950, (v3)
    PS3511.A86 F3, (v3)
    PS3511.A86 F38, (v3)
    PS3511.A86 I5, (v3)
    PS3511.A86 K55, (v3)
    PS3511.A86 L54 1950, (v3)
    PS3511.A86 M3, (v3)
    PS3511.A86.M3 1924, (v3)
    PS3511.A86.M36 1976, (v3)
    PS3511.A86 M6, (v3)
    PS3511.A86 N4, (v3)
    PS3511.A86.N6, (v3)
    PS3511.A86 P9, (v3)
    PS3511.A86 R4, (v3)
    PS3511.A86.R4 1951, (v3)
    PS3511.A86 S3 1931, (v3)
    PS3511.A86 S37, (v3)
    PS3511.A86 S59 1970, (v3)
    PS3511.A86 S65 1946, (v3)
    PS3511.A86 T6, (v3)
    PS3511.A86.W5 1984, (v3)
    PS3511.A86.Z546 1976, (v3)
Faunce, Sarah. ND553.C9.F28 1993, (v9)
Faúndez, Julio. HX198.F38 1988, (v6)
Faure, Bernard. BQ4570.S48.F3813 1998, (v8)
    BQ9262.9.C5.F37813 1997, (v8)
Faure, Christine. HQ1236.5.F8.F3813 1991, (v6)
Faure, Edgar. DS777.55.F373, (v5)
Faure, Gunter. QE501.4.N9.F38 1986, (v1)
    QE515.F28 1991, (v1)
Fauriol, Georges A. F1466.5.F38 1988, (v4)
Fauset, Jessie Redmon. PS3511.A864 T47, (v3)
Fausett, David. G560.F25 1993, (v6)
Fausold, Martin L. E664.P62.F3, (v4)
Fausold, Martin L. E801.F25 1985, (v4)
Fausset, Hugh l'Anson. PN511.F32 1967, (v3)
Faust, Betty Bernice. F1435.3.A37.F38 1998, (v4)
Faust, Drew Gilpin. E628.F35 1996, (v4)
    F213.F25 1992, (v4)
    F273.H25.F38 1982, (v4)
Faust, John R. DS779.27.F38 1995, (v5)
Fausto-Sterling, Anne. HQ1075.F39 2000, (v6)
    QP81.5 F38 1992, (v1)
Faux, Marian. HQ767.5.U5.F38 1990, (v6)
    KF228.R59.F38 1988, (v7)
Favell, Adrian. JV7933.F38 1998, (v7)
Favez, Jean-Claude. D804.6.F3813 1999, (v5)
Favier, Jean. HF3495.F3813 1998, (v6)
Favor, J. Martin. PS153.N5.F38 1999, (v3)
Favret, Mary A. PR911.F38 1993, (v3)
Fawcett, Don Wayne. QH581.F3, (v1)
Fawcett, Melissa Jayne. E99.M83 T364 2000, (v4)
Fawkner, Harald William. PR2981.5.F39 1992, (v3)
Fawtier, Robert. DC82.F313, (v5)
Fax, Elton C. N6538.N5.F29, (v9)
Fay, Brian. H61.F355 1996, (v6)
Fay, Elizabeth A. PR468.F46.F39 1998, (v3)
Fay, John Foster. TL716.F35 1976, (v1)
Fay, Laurel E. ML410.S53.F39 2000, (v9)

Fay, Marie-Therese. DA990.U46.F39 1999, **(v5)**
Fay, Peter Ward. D767.63.F39 1993, **(v5)**
  DS757.5.F39, **(v5)**
Feagin, Joe R. E185.615.F39 2001, **(v4)**
  E185.86.F43 1994, **(v4)**
Feagin, Susan L. PN98.R38.F43 1996, **(v3)**
Fearing, Kenneth. PS3511.E115.A6 1983, **(v3)**
  PS3511.E115 B5, **(v3)**
Fearn-Banks, Kathleen. HD59.F37 2002, **(v6)**
Fearnley-Whittingstall, Jane. SB413.I84.F43 1991, **(v1)**
  SB413.P4F425 1999, **(v1)**
Fearnow, Mark. PS351.F44 1997, **(v3)**
Feather, Carl E. F217.A65.F43 1998, **(v4)**
Feather, Leonard G. ML102.J3.F39 1999, **(v9)**
Featherstone, Mike. HM101.F35 1995, **(v6)**
Feaver, Peter D. UA23.F37 1992, **(v10)**
February, V. A. PM7831.F44 1988, **(v3)**
Febvre, Lucien Paul Victor. DC33.3.F4 1977, **(v5)**
  PQ1697.R4.E3 1982, **(v3)**
Feck, Luke. F499.C543 F43 1987, **(v4)**
Fedak, Janos. NA6139.F4 1990, **(v9)**
Fedden, Robin. DS94.F4 1955, **(v5)**
Feder, Elaine. RC489.A7.F43, **(v2)**
Federal Writers' Project (N.C.). F259.F44 1955, **(v4)**
Federal Writer's Project (R.I.). F79.F38, **(v4)**
Federal Writers' Project (S.C.). F269.W7, **(v4)**
Federal Writers' Project of the Works Progress Administration. F866.2.F4 1954, **(v4)**
Federal Writer's Project. F539.3.F4 1973, **(v4)**
  E444.F26, **(v4)**
  F2.3.F42 1973, **(v4)**
  F25.F44, **(v4)**
  F39.F43 1974, **(v4)**
  F47.3.F42 1973, **(v4)**
  F215.F4 1972, **(v4)**
  F436.F45 1949, **(v4)**
  F666.F46 1947, **(v4)**
  F731.F44 1949, **(v4)**
  F874.3.F4 1972, **(v4)**
Federal Writers' Project. Iowa. F621.F45 1949, **(v4)**
Federbusch, Simon. DS102.9.F4 1959a, **(v5)**
Federici, Carla. PC1128.F43 1986, **(v3)**
Federico, Annette. PR4505.F43 2000, **(v3)**
Federn, Karl. D16.8.M294.F4 1971, **(v5)**
Federspiel, Howard M. BP63.I5 F43 1995, **(v8)**
Fedorko, Kathy A. PS3545.H16.Z647 1995, **(v3)**
Feduccia, Alan. QL677.3.F43 1999, **(v1)**
Fee, Chester Anders. E90.J8 F3, **(v4)**
Fee, Margery. PE3235.F44 1997, **(v3)**
Feeley, Malcolm. KF9730.F44 1998, **(v7)**
Feeley-Harnik, Gillian. DT469.M277.S355 1991, **(v5)**
Feelings, Muriel L. PL8701.F4, **(v3)**
Feenberg, Andrew. HM221.F384 1995, **(v6)**
Feeney, Don J. RC552.R44.F44 1999, **(v2)**
Feeney, Judith. BF575.A86.F44 1996, **(v2)**
Fegley, Randall. Z3721.F44 1993, **(v10)**
Feher, Ferenc. DC178.F44 1987, **(v5)**
Fehler, Timothy G. HV280.E45.F44 1999, **(v6)**
Fehrenbach, Heide. PN1993.5.G3.F35 1995, **(v3)**
Fehring, Gunter P. D125.F4413 1992, **(v5)**
Fehrman, Carl Abraham Daniel. PN1116.F413, **(v3)**
Feibleman, James Kern. B398.R4.F4, **(v8)**
  B945.F24.A36 1983, **(v8)**
  PN1922.F4 1962, **(v3)**
Feifel, Herman. BD444.F415, **(v8)**
Feigen, Richard L. N8660.F383.A2 2000, **(v9)**
Feigenbaum, A. V. (Armand Vallin). TS156.F44 1991, **(v1)**
Feigl, Fritz. QD81.F453 1972, **(v1)**
  QD271.F3513 1966, **(v1)**
Feigon, Lee. DS777.15.C5.F44 1983, **(v5)**
  DS785.F34 1996, **(v5)**
Feijoo, Benito Jeronimo. PQ6523.F3.T4 1923, **(v3)**
Feil, Arnold. ML410.S3.F3313 1988, **(v9)**
Feil, D. K. GN671.N5.F45 1987, **(v6)**
Feiler, Gil. HF1610.Z4.I825 1998, **(v6)**
Feiling, Keith Grahame. DA585.C5.F44 1970, **(v5)**
Fein, David A. PQ1553.C5.F44 1983, **(v3)**
Fein, Leonard J. E184.J5.F373 1988, **(v4)**
Fein, Melvyn L. HM216.F38 1997, **(v6)**

Feinberg, Joel. BJ21.F4, **(v8)**
  BJ1012.F42 1992, **(v8)**
  BJ1451.F43, **(v8)**
Feinberg, Leslie. HQ77.9.F45 1996, **(v6)**
Feinberg, Richard E. HC336.26.F45 1990, **(v4)**
Feinberg, Richard. GN671.S6.F46 1988, **(v6)**
Feinberg, Sandra. Z7164.C5.F44 1995, **(v10)**
Feinberg, Walter. LC191.F4 1998, **(v7)**
Feinberg, Walter. LC212.2.F45 1998, **(v7)**
Feingold, Henry L. D804.3.F45 1995, **(v5)**
Feingold, Richard. PR579.P3.F4 1978, **(v3)**
Feingold, S. Norman. LB2338.F4, **(v7)**
Feininger, Andreas. TR146.F43, **(v1)**
Feinman, Ilene Rose. UB418.W65.F45 2000, **(v10)**
Feinstein, Elaine. PG3350.F45 1999, **(v3)**
Feinstein, John. GV884.K58 F44 1986, **(v6)**
  GV970.F45 1995, **(v6)**
Feinstein, Karen. QD272.S6.F45 1995, **(v1)**
Feinstein, Sascha. PS310.J39.F45 1997, **(v3)**
  Z1231.P7.F45 1998, **(v10)**
Feis, Herbert. D734.B4 1945ad, **(v5)**
  D748.F4, **(v5)**
  D753.F4, **(v5)**
  D767.2.F4 1966, **(v5)**
  HC60.F35, **(v6)**
Feitlowitz, Marguerite. F2849.2.F37 1998, **(v4)**
Felber, Lynette. PR888.C92.F45 1996, **(v3)**
Feld, Barry C. HV9104.F44 1993, **(v6)**
Feld, Jacob. TH441.F43 1997, **(v1)**
Feld, Steven. DU740.42.F44 1990, **(v5)**
Feld, Werner J. UA23.F39 1985, **(v10)**
  UA646.F45 1993, **(v10)**
Feldberg, Georgina D. RC310.5.F45 1995, **(v2)**
Feldherr, Andrew. DG207.L583.F45 1998, **(v5)**
Feldman, Alan. LB1583.3.N48 2000, **(v7)**
Feldman, Allen. HN400.V5.F45 1991, **(v6)**
Feldman, Daniel L. KF4550.F45 1990, **(v6)**
Feldman, Fred. BD444.F44 1992, **(v8)**
Feldman, Gerald D. HC286.2.F4, **(v6)**
Feldman, Glenn. F326.W55.F45 1995, **(v4)**
  HS2330.K63.F44 1999, **(v6)**
Feldman, Leonard C. QD506.F39 1986, **(v1)**
Feldman, Louis H. BM534.F45 1993, **(v8)**
Feldman, Martha S. HM131.F388 1995, **(v6)**
Feldman, Ofer. JQ1665.F45 1999, **(v7)**
Feldman, Ofer. PN5404.F45 1993, **(v3)**
Feldman, Stephen M. KF379.F45 2000, **(v7)**
Feldmeyer, Gerhard G. NA1068.F36 1993, **(v9)**
Felheim, Marvin. PN6120.2.F44 1951, **(v3)**
Felice, William. JC571.F425 1996, **(v7)**
Felkay, Andrew. DB957.F47 1989, **(v5)**
Felknor, Peter S. QC955.5.U6.F45 1992, **(v1)**
Fell, Robin. TC540.F45 1992, **(v1)**
Felleman, Susan. PN1993.3.L4678.F46 1997, **(v3)**
Feller, Daniel. E338.F45 1995, **(v4)**
Fellman, Michael. E467.1.S55.F45 1995, **(v4)**
  E470.45.F36 1989, **(v4)**
Fellowes, Edmund Horace. ML2631.F45 1972, **(v9)**
  ML2631.F46 1948, **(v9)**
  ML3131.F3 1969, **(v9)**
Fellows, Jay. PR5137.F4 1991, **(v3)**
Fellows, Otis. PQ1131.F4, **(v3)**
  PQ1979.F44, **(v3)**
Felman, Shoshana. PN56.P92.F45 1991, **(v3)**
Felsenstein, Frank. PR151.J5.F44 1995, **(v3)**
Felson, Nancy. PA4170.P46.F45 1994, **(v3)**
Felstiner, John. PQ8097.N4A763, **(v3)**
  PR6003.E4.Z66, **(v3)**
  PT2605.E4.Z599 1995, **(v3)**
Felter, Harvey Wickes. RV401.F4, **(v2)**
Feltes, N. N. PR878.C25.F44 1993, **(v3)**
Felton, Keith Spencer. PN4193.P6.F45 1995, **(v3)**
Feltwell, John. QL541.5.F44 1993, **(v1)**
Felty, Harold G. F547.H17.F437 1987, **(v4)**
Femia, Joseph V. JC474.F46 1993, **(v7)**
Fenby, Jonathan. HC276.2.F44 1999, **(v6)**
Fenchel, Tom. QH518.5.F46 1995, **(v1)**
Fendrich, James Max. F319.T14.F46 1993, **(v4)**
Feng, Chi-tsai. DS778.7.F462513 1991, **(v5)**
Feng, Menglong. PL3277.E3.F4, **(v3)**
  PL2698.F4.K7813 2000, **(v3)**

Feng, Yu-lan. B126.F42 1948, **(v8)**
  B126.F43, **(v8)**
  B5234.F44.A3713 2000, **(v8)**
Fenlon, Iain. ML2633.F46 1988, **(v9)**
Fenn, Courtenay Hughes. PL1455.F4 1942, **(v3)**
Fenn, Richard K. BT78.F36 2001, **(v8)**
Fenna, Donald. QC82.F43 1998, **(v1)**
Fennell, Desmond. DA959.1.F43 1993, **(v5)**
Fenno, Richard F. E840.8.D66.F46 1991, **(v4)**
  JK1074.F4, **(v7)**
  JK1161.F46 1991, **(v7)**
  JK1319.F43 2000, **(v7)**
  JK1323 1978.F46, **(v7)**
  JK2281.F46 1996, **(v7)**
Fenollosa, Ernest Francisco. PL887.F45 1959, **(v3)**
Fenrick, Maureen H. QA248.F46 1991, **(v1)**
Fenton, Carroll Lane. QE21.F4 1952, **(v1)**
Fenton, Charles A. PL2658.E8.F4, **(v3)**
Fenton, John Y. Z7757.S64 F46 1995, **(v10)**
Fenton, William Nelson. E99.I7.F453 1998, **(v4)**
Fentress, James. HV6453.I83.M3415 2000, **(v6)**
Fenwick, M. J. Z1595.F46 1992, **(v10)**
Feofanov, IUrii Vasilevich. KLA40.P64.F46 1996, **(v7)**
Fer, Briony. N6494.R4.F47 1993, **(v9)**
Ferber, Abby L. E184.A1.F46 1998, **(v4)**
Ferber, Edna. PS3511.E46 G5, **(v3)**
  PS3511.E46 G7, **(v3)**
  PS3511.E46.O5, **(v3)**
  PS3511.E46 S48, **(v3)**
  PS3511.E46 S6, **(v3)**
Ferber, Gene. HF1002.F43 1993, **(v6)**
Ferber, Marianne A. Z7963.E7.F47 1987, **(v10)**
Ferber, Michael. PN56.S9.F47 1999, **(v3)**
Fergus, Jan S. PR4036.F47 1991, **(v3)**
Ferguson, Ann Arnett. LC2771.F47 2000, **(v7)**
Ferguson, Arthur B. CR4529.G7.F4, **(v5)**
  DA314.F47, **(v5)**
Ferguson, Bruce K. TD657.F47 1998, **(v1)**
Ferguson, C. E. HB98.2.F47, **(v6)**
Ferguson, Chris D. Z2000.F45 1989, **(v10)**
Ferguson, Eugene S. TA145.F37 1992, **(v1)**
Ferguson, George Andrew. HA29.F4 1971, **(v6)**
Ferguson, George Wells. N7830.F37 1959, **(v9)**
Ferguson, Harvie. BD331.F428 1989, **(v8)**
Ferguson, James Milton. HJ8119.F4, **(v6)**
Ferguson, James. F1928.F47 1987, **(v4)**
  HD2132.Z8.F47 1990, **(v6)**
Ferguson, John. BJ101.F4, **(v8)**
  CB68.F4, **(v8)**
Ferguson, Julie H. V859.C3.F47 1995, **(v10)**
Ferguson, Kathy E. UA26.H38.F47 1999, **(v10)**
Ferguson, Kitty. BL240.2.F45 1995, **(v8)**
Ferguson, Mary Anne. Z6517.F47, **(v10)**
Ferguson, Moira. PR408.S57.F47 1992, **(v3)**
  PR555.W6.F47 1995, **(v3)**
  PR5841.W8.Z67 1984, **(v3)**
  PR9275.A583.K5644 1994, **(v3)**
Ferguson, Niall. HG1552.A1.F46 1998, **(v6)**
Ferguson, R. Brian. F2520.1.Y3.F47 1995, **(v4)**
Ferguson, Robert. G545.F44 1979, **(v6)**
  P94.5.M55.F47 1998, **(v3)**
  PS3525.I5454.Z675 1991, **(v3)**
Ferguson, T. Reed. F292.G58.C684 1994, **(v4)**
Ferguson, Wallace Klippert. CB361.F373, **(v5)**
  D202.F4, **(v5)**
Ferguson, William Scott. DF285.F4 1969, **(v5)**
  HJ219.F4, **(v6)**
Ferguson, Yale H. JC11.F45 1996, **(v7)**
Fergusson, David. BJ1275.F47 1998, **(v8)**
Fergusson, Erna. E78.N65 F42 1988, **(v4)**
  F786.F49, **(v4)**
Fergusson, Francis. PR2976.F42, **(v3)**
Fergusson, James. NA1501.F4 1910, **(v9)**
Fergusson, Peter. NA5463.F4 1984, **(v9)**
Ferkiss, Victor C. GF21.F47 1993, **(v6)**
Ferling, John E. E302.5.F46 2000, **(v4)**
  E312.F47 1988, **(v4)**
  E322.F47 1992, **(v4)**
  Z8015.6.F46 1994, **(v10)**

Ferlinghetti, Lawrence. PS3511.E557.H4 1960, **(v3)**
  PS3511.E557.P5, **(v3)**
  PS3511.E557.S8, **(v3)**
  PS3511.E557.U5 1963, **(v3)**
Ferlita, Ernest. PR4803.H44.Z6264 1990, **(v3)**
Ferm, Vergilius Ture Anselm. BJ63.F4, **(v8)**
Fermi, Enrico. QC173.F397, **(v1)**
  QC174.F44, **(v1)**
Fermi, Laura. QC774.F4.F4, **(v1)**
Fern, Alan Maxwell. NE539.B3.A4 1984, **(v9)**
Fern, Fanny. PS2523.P9 F3, **(v3)**
Fernandes, Florestan. F2659.N4.F413, **(v4)**
Fernandez Castro, Maria Cruz. GN778.22.S72.F45 1995, **(v6)**
Fernandez de Lizardi, Jose Joaquin. PQ7297.F37.P3 1933, **(v3)**
Fernandez Retamar, Roberto. F1408.3.F398 1989, **(v4)**
Fernandez, Damian J. JL1010.F47 2000, **(v7)**
Fernandez, John P. HF5500.3.U54.F474 1981, **(v6)**
  HF5549.5.D39.F47 1990, **(v6)**
Fernandez, Ramon. PN513.F43, **(v3)**
  PQ1852.F413, **(v3)**
Fernandez, Ronald. F1954.F47 1998, **(v4)**
  F2178.U6.F49 1994, **(v4)**
Fernandez-Armesto, Felipe. DA360.F43 1988, **(v5)**
  DE94.F47 1987, **(v5)**
  DP302.C42.F47 1982, **(v5)**
Fernandez-Morera, Dario. LA226.F47 1996, **(v7)**
Fernando, M. Daniel. RA644.A25.F47 1993, **(v2)**
Fernando, Suman. RC455.4.E8F468 2002, **(v2)**
  RC455.4.E8.F47 1988, **(v2)**
Ferncase, Richard K. PN1993.5.U6.F44 1996, **(v3)**
Fernekes, William R. Z6374.H6 F47 2002, **(v10)**
Fernett, Gene. PN1993.5.U6.F45 1988, **(v3)**
Fernie, E. C. NA963.F4 1983, **(v9)**
Fernlund, Kevin J. E76.45.H65, **(v4)**
Ferns, John. PR6037.T73.Z65 1988, **(v3)**
Ferns, P. N. QL690.B65.F47 1992, **(v1)**
Feros, Antonio. DP183.F47 2000, **(v5)**
Ferracane, Jack L. RK652.5.F47 2001, **(v2)**
Ferrante, Joan M. PN682.W6.F39 1997, **(v3)**
  PN682.W6.F4 1985, **(v3)**
Ferraris, Maurizio. BD241.F4213 1996, **(v8)**
Ferre, Felipe. NA1053.G8.F4713 1988, **(v9)**
Ferre, Frederick. BD111.F29 1996, **(v8)**
  BD161.F39 1998, **(v8)**
Ferre. B824.6.F45, **(v8)**
Ferree, Myra Marx. HQ1426.F475 1994, **(v6)**
Ferreiro, Emilia. LB1140.5.L3.F4713 1982, **(v7)**
Ferrell, Jeff. GT3913.C62.D473 1993, **(v6)**
Ferrell, Robert H. D619.F34 1985, **(v5)**
  E744.F47 1975, **(v4)**
  E791.F47 1998, **(v4)**
  E801.F4 1969, **(v4)**
  E807.F4 1998, **(v4)**
  E812.F47 1994, **(v4)**
  E814.F46 1994, **(v4)**
Ferrell, William K. PN1995.3.F47 2000, **(v3)**
Ferrer, Daniel. PR6045.O72.Z628 1990, **(v3)**
Ferretti, Silvia. BH221.G34.W37413 1989, **(v8)**
Ferriday, Peter. NA967.F4 1964, **(v9)**
Ferrier, Grace Bacon. LA2317.F46.A3 1986, **(v7)**
Ferri-Pisani, Camille. E167.F383, **(v4)**
Ferris, David. ML410.S4.F47 2000, **(v9)**
Ferris, Ina. PR5341.F47 1991, **(v3)**
  PR5638.F47 1983, **(v3)**
Ferris, John Robert. UA647.F4 1989, **(v10)**
Ferris, Kathleen. PR6019.O9.Z533378 1995, **(v3)**
Ferris, Paul. PR6039.H52.Z637 2000, **(v3)**
Ferris, Timothy. Q125.F425 1988, **(v1)**
Ferry, Anne. PN1059.T5.F47 1996, **(v3)**
  PR3562.F4, **(v3)**
Ferry, David. PR5888.F4, **(v3)**
Ferry, Luc. D16.8.F45213 1990, **(v5)**
Ferry, Luc. GF21.F4813 1995, **(v6)**
Ferster, Judith. PR275.D53.F47 1996, **(v3)**
Ferziger, Joel H. QA911.F434 1996, **(v1)**
  TA335.F47 1998, **(v1)**
Feshbach, Murray. RA566.5.S65.F47 1992, **(v2)**
Feske, Victor. DA1.F45 1996, **(v5)**

Fessler, Susanna. PL829.A8.Z64 1998, **(v3)**
Fest, Joachim C. DD247.H5.F4713, **(v5)**
Festle, Mary Jo. GV709.F37 1996, **(v6)**
Fetler, Andrew. PS3556.E84, **(v3)**
Fetrow, Alan G. PN1993.5.U6.F457 1999, **(v3)**
  PN1993.5.U6.F46 1991, **(v3)**
Fetter, C. W. GB1003.2.F47 2001, **(v6)**
Fetzer, James H. BF311.F423 2001, **(v2)**
Fetzer, Joel S. JV6455.F47 2000, **(v7)**
Feuchtwang, Stephan. BL1802.F48 1992, **(v8)**
Feuchtwanger, E. J. DA560.F48 1985, **(v5)**
  DA564.B3.F48 2000, **(v5)**
  DD240.F46 1993, **(v5)**
Feuer, Bryan Avery. Z2260.F48 1996, **(v10)**
Feuer, Jane. PN1992.6.F44 1995, **(v3)**
Feuer, Lewis Samuel. B3998.F43, **(v8)**
  Q125.F43 1991, **(v1)**
Feuerbach, Ludwig. B2971.G7.E52, **(v8)**
Feuerman, Francine. R733.F48 1997, **(v2)**
Feuerstein, Georg. B132.Y6.F46 1990, **(v8)**
  BL1238.52.F47 1997, **(v8)**
Feuerwerker, Albert. DS734.F4, **(v5)**
Feuerwerker, Yi-tsi Mei. PL2419.P39.F48 1998, **(v3)**
  PL2747.P5.Z65 1982, **(v3)**
Feydeau, Georges. PQ2611.E86.A28, **(v3)**
Feyerabend, Paul K. B3240.F483.C66 1999, **(v8)**
Feyereisen, Pierre. BF637.N66.F47 1991, **(v2)**
Feynman, Richard Phillips. Q175.5.F52 1998, **(v1)**
  QC3.F4513 2000, **(v1)**
  QC16.F49.A3 1988, **(v1)**
  QC16.F49.A37 1985, **(v1)**
  QC21.2.F49 1989, **(v1)**
  QC21.2.F52 1995, **(v1)**
  QC23.F47, **(v1)**
  QC28.F4 1965, **(v1)**
  QC793.28.F49 1987, **(v1)**
  QC793.3.S9.F49 1997, **(v1)**
Ffolliott, Peter F. HC85.F44 2001, **(v6)**
Fforde, Adam. HC444.F458 1996, **(v6)**
  HD1492.V5.F47 1989, **(v6)**
Fforde, John. HG2994.F46 1991, **(v6)**
Fiala, John L. SB413.C644.F53 1994, **(v1)**
Fialka, John J. HD38.7.F5 1997, **(v6)**
Fibonacci, Leonardo. QA32.F4813 1987, **(v1)**
Ficher, Miguel. ML105.F53 2002, **(v9)**
Fichte, Johann Gottlieb. B2808. 1988, **(v8)**
  B2844.B52.E5 1987, **(v8)**
Fichtenau, Heinrich. BT1319.F5313 1998, **(v8)**
Fichtner, Paula S. DB35.F53 1999, **(v5)**
Fick, Carolyn E. F1923.F5 1990, **(v4)**
Ficken, Robert E. F891.F49 1988, **(v4)**
  HD9757.W2R443, **(v6)**
  PN4874.W6934.F53 1995, **(v3)**
Fido, Martin. PR5823.F47, **(v3)**
Fiedler, Leslie A. PN511.F5, **(v3)**
  PS3556.I34.A153 1962, **(v3)**
  PS3556.I34.S4, **(v3)**
Field, Elinor Whitney. PN1009.A1.F45, **(v3)**
Field, Eugene. PS1665.A2 1910, **(v3)**
Field, George Wallis. PT2617.E85.Z693, **(v3)**
Field, Kate. PS1669.F2.Z48 1996, **(v3)**
Field, Martha A. KF480.F54 1999, **(v7)**
  KF540.F53 1988, **(v7)**
Field, Norma. DS822.5.F54 1997, **(v5)**
Field, Peter S. F69.F48 1998, **(v4)**
Field, Phyllis F. E185.93.N56.F54 1982, **(v4)**
Field, Rachel. PS3511.I25 A65, **(v3)**
Field, Rachel. PZ8.9.F442Hi, **(v3)**
Field, Richard S. NE508.F54 1987, **(v9)**
Field, Shelly. PN1580.F5 1992, **(v3)**
Field, Tiffany. RM721.F54 2000, **(v2)**
Fieldhouse, D. K. HC800.F543 1994, **(v6)**
  JV105.F519 1981, **(v7)**
  JV105.F52x 1984, **(v7)**
Fieldhouse, Richard W. VA40.F54 1989, **(v10)**
Fielding, Henry. PR3451.M5 1972, **(v3)**
  PR3452.G65 1987, **(v3)**
  PR3454.C5, **(v3)**
  PR3454.J6 1951, **(v3)**
  PR3454.J67 1971, **(v3)**
  PR3454.J7 1963, **(v3)**

  PR3454.T6 1970c, **(v3)**
Fielding, Mantle. N6536.F5 1965, **(v9)**
Fielding, Penny. PR8601.F54 1996, **(v3)**
Fielding, R. Kent. F826.F49 1993, **(v4)**
Fielding, Sarah. PR3459.F3 A3 1969, **(v3)**
  PR3459.F3.A7 1998, **(v3)**
Fields, Armond. PN2287.F44.F54 1993, **(v3)**
  PN2287.F65.F54 1999, **(v3)**
  PN2287.R83.F54 1999, **(v3)**
Fields, Barbara Jeanne. E445.M3.F54 1985, **(v4)**
Fields, Karl J. HD70.K6.F54 1995, **(v6)**
Fieleke, Norman S. HF1359.F54 1988, **(v6)**
Fiell, Charlotte. TS171.4.F54 2000, **(v1)**
Fienup-Riordan, Ann. E99.E7.F46 1990, **(v4)**
  E99.E7.F464 2000, **(v4)**
Fierce, Milfred C. E185.625.F54 1993, **(v4)**
Fiero, Bill. QE79.F54 1986, **(v1)**
Fieser, Louis Frederick. QD243.F5, **(v1)**
  QD251.F44, **(v1)**
  QD251.F5 1956, **(v1)**
  QD261.F5 1998, **(v1)**
  QD405.F44, **(v1)**
Fife, Graeme. GV1049.2.T68 F54 2001, **(v6)**
Fifer, Elizabeth. PS3537.T323.Z589 1992, **(v3)**
Fifer, J. Valerie. F2217.F54 1991, **(v4)**
Fiffer, Steve. QE862.S3.F54 2000, **(v1)**
Fifield, Christopher. ML410.B87.F53 1988, **(v9)**
Fifield, Russell H. DS518.1.F47, **(v5)**
  DS518.8.F48, **(v5)**
  DS793.S4.F5, **(v5)**
Figal, Gunter. B3240.F493.F8713 1998, **(v8)**
Figert, Anne E. RG165.F526 1996, **(v2)**
Figes, Eva. PR6056.I46.N4 1985, **(v3)**
  PR6056.I46.T74 1991, **(v3)**
Figes, Orlando. DK260.F54 1997, **(v5)**
Figg, Kristen Mossler. PQ1461.F8.Z66 1994, **(v3)**
Figgis, B. N. QD475.F54 2000, **(v1)**
Figueira, Thomas J. DF227.F54 1991, **(v5)**
Filbert, Preston. F474.S18 F55 2001, **(v4)**
Filby, P. William. Z5313.U5.F54 1981 Suppl., **(v10)**
Fildes, Valerie A. RJ216.F5 1986, **(v2)**
Filene, Benjamin. ML3551.F55 2000, **(v9)**
Filene, Peter G. E183.8.R9.F5, **(v4)**
  R726.F45 1998, **(v2)**
Filichia, Peter. GV875.A1.F45 1993, **(v6)**
Filler, Louis. E99.C5 F5 1977, **(v4)**
Filler, Susan Melanie. ML134.M34.F54 1989, **(v9)**
Fillmore, Peter A. QA326.F55 1996, **(v1)**
Filmer-Davies, Kath. PR6023.E926.Z6466 1993, **(v3)**
Filoramo, Giovanni. BT1390.F5513 1990, **(v8)**
Filreis, Alan. PS3537.T4753.Z636 1991, **(v3)**
Filson, John. F454.F48 1784, **(v4)**
Finaldi, Gabriele. ND616.5.B3.F56 1997, **(v9)**
Finan, John J. Z6465.L29 F56 1981, **(v10)**
Finch, Alison. PQ149.F66 2000, **(v3)**
Finch, Caleb Ellicott. QP85.F47 1990, **(v1)**
Finch, Christopher. PN1982.H46.F56 1993, **(v3)**
Finch, Henry Le Roy. B2430.W474.F54 1999, **(v8)**
Finch, M. H. J. HC232.F56 1982, **(v6)**
Finckenauer, James O. HV6446.F56 1998, **(v6)**
Findlay, Alexander. QD15.F45 1948, **(v1)**
Findlay, Alison. PR658.F45.F56 1999, **(v3)**
  PR658.I43.F56 1994, **(v3)**
Findlay, James F. E185.61.F47 1993, **(v4)**
Findlay, Mark. HV6025.F46 1998, **(v6)**
Findly, Ellison Banks. DS461.9.N8 F56 1993, **(v5)**
Fine, Ben. HB801.F52 2002, **(v6)**
Fine, David M. PS374.L57.F56 2000, **(v3)**
Fine, Elsa Honig. N43.F56 1978, **(v9)**
Fine, Melinda. LC311.F47 1995, **(v7)**
Fine, Michelle. LC146.7.N7.F56 1991, **(v7)**
Fine, Reuben. RC451.4.M45.F56 1988, **(v2)**
Fine, Richard. PS3505.A3113.Z66 1992, **(v3)**
Fine, Ruth. N6537.M37.A4 1990, **(v9)**
  N6537.O39.A4 2000, **(v9)**
  NE539.F68.A4 1993, **(v9)**
Fine, Sidney. E178.6.F523 1976, **(v4)**
  KFM4611.F56 2000, **(v7)**
Finegan, Edward. PE1098.F5, **(v3)**
Finegan, Jack. BS637.2.F5 1998, **(v8)**
Finello, Dominick L. PQ6351.F56 1994, **(v3)**

Fineman, Daniel. DS586.F56 1997, **(v5)**
Finer, S. E. JF195.M48.F5, **(v7)**
Finerty, John F. E83.866.F52 1994, **(v4)**
Finger, John R. E99.C5.F55 1991, **(v4)**
Finger, Matthias. LC5251.F56 2001, **(v7)**
Finger, Stanley. QP353.F548 2000, **(v1)**
Fink, Arthur E. HV40.F5 1968, **(v6)**
Fink, Carole. D15.B596.F56 1989, **(v5)**
Fink, Dale Borman. GV183.6.F56 2000, **(v6)**
Fink, Daniel. F127.G2.F56 1987, **(v4)**
Fink, Karl J. Q143.G53.F56 1991, **(v1)**
Fink, Leon. E169.1.F525 1997, **(v4)**
Fink, Lois Marie. N6510.F57 1990, **(v9)**
Fink, Steven. PS3054.F48 1992, **(v4)**
Fink, Zera Silver. JA84.G7.F5 1962, **(v7)**
Finke, Laurie. PR113.F56 1999, **(v3)**
Finke, Roger. BR515.F56 1992, **(v8)**
Fink-Eitel, Hinrich. B2430.F724.F5713 1992, **(v8)**
Finkel, Donald L. LB14.7.F56 1995, **(v7)**
Finkel, Norman J. BJ1533.F2 F56 2001, **(v8)**
   KF9242.F53 1988, **(v7)**
Finkelpearl, Philip J. PR2434.F53 1990, **(v3)**
   PR2697.F5, **(v3)**
Finkelstein, David Michael. E183.8.T3.F56 1993, **(v4)**
Finkelstein, David. Z325.W58 F36 2002, **(v10)**
Finkelstein, Joanne. GT525.F556 1998, **(v6)**
Finkelstein, Louis. DS102.4.F5 1960, **(v5)**
Finkelstein, Monte S. DG869.2.F56 1998, **(v5)**
Finkelstein, Norman. PS153.J4.F56 2001, **(v3)**
Finkin, Matthew W. LB2335.7.F55 1996, **(v7)**
Finkler, Kaja. GN480.2.F56 2000, **(v6)**
Finlay, Ian. DA880.H7.F5, **(v6)**
Finlay, John L. F1027.F5, **(v4)**
Finlayson, Geoffrey B. A. M. HV245.F56 1994, **(v6)**
Finlayson-Pitts, Barbara J. QC879.6.F56 1986, **(v1)**
   QC879.6.F57 2000, **(v1)**
Finler, Joel W. PN1998.3.H58.F55 1992, **(v3)**
Finley, Don. RA644.R3.F54 1998, **(v2)**
Finley, Karen. PN6231.P3.F56 1996, **(v3)**
Finley, M. I. DE8.F55 1986, **(v5)**
   DF77.F53 1970, **(v5)**
   HC31.F5x 1985, **(v6)**
   HC37.F56, **(v6)**
   PA4037.F48 1978, **(v3)**
Finley, Randy. F411.F445 1996, **(v4)**
Finn, Geraldine. B831.2.F56 1996, **(v8)**
Finn, Janet L. HD9539.C7.U539 1998, **(v6)**
Finn, John E. K5256.F56 1991, **(v7)**
Finn, Patrick J. LC5051.F56 1999, **(v7)**
Finn, Thomas M. BL805.F56 1997, **(v8)**
Finnan, Christine R. LB1029.A22 F56 2000, **(v7)**
Finnegan, Robert. Z7911.F5 1988, **(v10)**
Finnegan, Ruth H. PL8010.F5, **(v3)**
Finnegan, William. HV1431.F56 1998, **(v6)**
Finnemore, Martha. JX1395.F485 1996, **(v7)**
Finney, Charles G. DS775.F5, **(v5)**
Finney, Gail. PN56.5.W64.F5 1989, **(v3)**
Finnis, John. U162.6.F48 1987, **(v10)**
Finson, Jon W. ML3477.F55 1994, **(v9)**
Finston, H. L. QD477.F56 1982, **(v1)**
Fioravanzo, Giuseppe. V167.F5613, **(v10)**
Fiore, Carole D. Z718.2.U6.F57 1996, **(v10)**
   Z718.2.U6 F59 1998, **(v10)**
Fiore, Peter Amadeus. PR2248.F5, **(v3)**
   PR3562.F47, **(v3)**
Fiore, Robert L. PQ6409.F56 1984, **(v3)**
Fiorina, Morris P. JK1071.F55, **(v7)**
Firbank, Ronald. PR6011.I7 F5, **(v3)**
   PR6011.I7 1961, **(v3)**
Firchow, Peter Edgerly. PR6015.U9.B674 1984, **(v3)**
   PR6015.U9.Z63 1972, **(v3)**
Firda, Richard Arthur. PT2635.E68.I67 1993, **(v3)**
   PT2668.A5.Z635 1993, **(v3)**
Firdawsi. PK6456.A12.R82 1987, **(v3)**
Firdawsi. PK6456.A13, **(v3)**
Fire, John. E99.T34.F57, **(v4)**
Fireman, Bert M. F811.F57 1982, **(v4)**
Firestone, Reuven. BP182.F5 1999, **(v8)**
Firestone, Robert. RC569.F57 1997, **(v2)**
Firestone, Ross. ML422.G65.F6 1992, **(v9)**
Firmage, Edwin Brown. KF4869.M6.F57 1988, **(v7)**

Firmin-Sellers, Kathryn. KRX986.F57 1996, **(v7)**
Firor, John. QC861.2.F57 1990, **(v1)**
Firro, Kais. DS113.72.F57 1999, **(v5)**
First, Ruth. PR9369.2.S37.Z64 1980, **(v3)**
Firth, C. H. UA649.F52 1962, **(v10)**
Firth, Edith G. F1059.5.T68.F5, **(v4)**
Firth, Frank E. SH201.F56 1969, **(v1)**
Firth, Raymond William. GN24.F5 1956, **(v6)**
   GN400.F53 1969, **(v6)**
   GN470.H35 1996, **(v6)**
   GN473.F5 1967, **(v6)**
Fisch, Harold. PN3352.B53.F57 1998, **(v3)**
   PR408.B53.F57 1999, **(v3)**
Fisch, Menachem. BM538.S3.F57 1997, **(v8)**
Fischbeck, Helmut J. QC61.F58 1982, **(v1)**
Fischel, Jack. D804.3.F58 1998, **(v5)**
Fischel, William A. KF5698.F573 1995, **(v7)**
Fischer, Bernd Jurgen. D802.A38.F57 1999, **(v5)**
Fischer, Beth A. E876.F569 1997, **(v4)**
Fischer, Clare Benedicks. Z7833.F57 1995, **(v10)**
Fischer, Daniel. QB500.268.F5813 1996, **(v1)**
Fischer, David Hackett. E169.1.F539 1989 vol. 1, **(v4)**
   F69.R43 F57 1994, **(v4)**
Fischer, Dennis. PN1995.9.H6.F5 1991, **(v3)**
   PN1995.9.S26.F54 2000, **(v3)**
Fischer, Ernst Peter. QH31.D434.F573 1988, **(v1)**
Fischer, Fritz. DD228.5.F5513, **(v5)**
   HC60.5.F57 1998, **(v6)**
Fischer, Gayle V. GT610.F57 2001, **(v6)**
Fischer, John Martin. BJ1451.F57 1998, **(v8)**
   BJ1461.F49 1994, **(v8)**
Fischer, Klaus P. DD256.5.F55 1995, **(v5)**
   DS146.G4.F57 1998, **(v5)**
Fischer, Louis. DK254.L4.F53, **(v5)**
Fischer, Lucy. PN1995.9.W6.F565 1996, **(v3)**
Fischer, Mary Ellen. DR267.5.C4.F567 1989, **(v5)**
Fischer, Michael. PN81.F545 1985, **(v3)**
Fischer, Thomas C. KJE949.F49 1995, **(v7)**
Fischer, Wolfdietrich. PJ6303.F3513 2002, **(v3)**
Fischer-Dieskau, Dietrich. ML420.F51.A3 1989, **(v9)**
   PT1160.E6.F5 1977, **(v3)**
Fischer-Lichte, Erika. PN2041.S45.F5713 1992, **(v3)**
Fischl, Richard Michael. KF283.F57 1999, **(v7)**
Fischman, Dennis K. HX550.J4.F57 1991, **(v6)**
Fischman, Gustavo. LB1719.A7, **(v7)**
Fiscus, Ronald Jerry. KF4755.5.F57 1992, **(v7)**
Fiset, Louis. D769.8.A6.F49 1997, **(v5)**
Fish, Charles. S555.V5.F57 1998, **(v1)**
Fish, Joe. F1488.3.F57 1988, **(v4)**
Fish, M. Steven. JN6598.A1.F57 1995, **(v7)**
Fish, Peter J. TK7867.5.F56 1993, **(v1)**
Fish, Stanley Eugene. B105.P7.F57 1999, **(v8)**
   PN441.F44 1989, **(v3)**
   PN741.F5, **(v3)**
   PR2348.F5, **(v3)**
   PR3507.T43.F57, **(v3)**
   PR3588.F57 2001, **(v3)**
   Z657.F5 1994, **(v10)**
Fishbein, Bette K. KK6254.F57 1994, **(v7)**
Fishbein, Morris. R119.F55 1972, **(v2)**
   R154.F65.A3, **(v2)**
Fishel, Edwin C. E608.F57 1996, **(v4)**
Fisher, Alan W. DK511.C7 F497, **(v5)**
Fisher, Alec. BC177.F57 1988, **(v8)**
Fisher, Barbara C. RC394.A85.F57 1998, **(v2)**
Fisher, Charles Alfred. DS508.2.F5 1966, **(v5)**
Fisher, David E. QH325.F47 1998, **(v1)**
Fisher, Donald M. GV989.F56 2002, **(v6)**
Fisher, Donald. H62.A1.F57 1993, **(v6)**
Fisher, Dorothy Canfield. PS3511.I7416.A6 1996, **(v3)**
   PS3511.I7416.B45 1997, **(v3)**
   PS3511.I7416 B7, **(v3)**
   PS3511.I7416 H3, **(v3)**
   PS3511.I7416 S4, **(v3)**
   PS3511.I7416.Z48 1993, **(v3)**
Fisher, Franklin M. HD2326.F55 1991, **(v6)**
Fisher, Harry. DP269.47.A46.F58 1998, **(v5)**
Fisher, Helen E. GN479.7.F57 1999, **(v6)**
   HQ728.F454 1992, **(v6)**
Fisher, James F. DS493.9.S5.F57 1990, **(v5)**
   DS495.592.A34 F57 1997, **(v5)**

Fisher, James L. LB2341.F497 1996, **(v7)**
Fisher, James T. R722.32.D66.F57 1997, **(v2)**
Fisher, Jo. HQ1236.5.S63.F57 1993, **(v6)**
Fisher, John H. PE524.7.F7 1996, **(v3)**
   PR1924.F57 1992, **(v3)**
   PR1986.F5, **(v3)**
Fisher, John. DS63.2.G7.F496 1999, **(v5)**
Fisher, Lois H. PR109.F5, **(v3)**
Fisher, Louis. JK305.F53 2000, **(v7)**
   KF4550.F57 1988, **(v7)**
   KF4565.F57 1991, **(v7)**
   KF5060.F57 1995, **(v7)**
Fisher, Noel C. E531.F57 1997, **(v4)**
Fisher, Peter Francis. PR4147.F5, **(v3)**
Fisher, Peter S. PT772.F57 1991, **(v3)**
Fisher, Philip. N6512.F57 1991, **(v9)**
Fisher, Raymond Henry. G296.B4.F57, **(v6)**
Fisher, Robin. E78.B9.F57, **(v4)**
Fisher, Roger. JX4473.F57 1994, **(v7)**
Fisher, Ronald J. JZ6045.F57 1997, **(v7)**
Fisher, Rudolph. PS3511.I7436.A6 1987, **(v3)**
   PS3511.I7436.Z78 1987, **(v3)**
Fisher, Seymour. BF173.F85.F55, **(v2)**
   BF692.F53 1989, **(v2)**
   QP356.F5, **(v1)**
Fisher, Sue. RG103.7.F57 1986, **(v2)**
Fisher, Vardis. PS3511.I744 C49, **(v3)**
   PS3511.I744 D3, **(v3)**
   PS3511.I744 I5, **(v3)**
   PS3511.I744 L6, **(v3)**
   PS3511.I744 M6, **(v3)**
Fisher, W. B. DP17.F5 1966, **(v5)**
Fisher, William F. DS493.9.T45 F57 2001, **(v5)**
Fisher, William H. F2520.1.X5, **(v4)**
Fishgall, Gary. PN2287.L246.F57 1995, **(v3)**
   PN2287.S68.F57 1997, **(v3)**
Fishkin, James S. JC423.F63 1991, **(v7)**
   JK1764.F53 1995, **(v7)**
Fishkin, Shelley Fisher. PS1305.F57 1993, **(v3)**
Fishman, H. Charles. RJ503.F57 1988, **(v2)**
Fishman, Jack. QC995.F55 1994, **(v1)**
Fishman, Joshua A. PJ5111.5.B5.F57 1987, **(v3)**
Fishman, Robert M. HD6763.5.F57 1990, **(v6)**
Fishman, Sarah. D810.W7.F57 1991, **(v5)**
Fishman, Stephen M. LB875.D5.F57 1998, **(v7)**
Fishman, Sylvia Barack. HQ1172.F57 1993, **(v6)**
Fishman, William J. DS135.E5.F5 1975, **(v5)**
Fishwick, Marshall William. E169.12.F64, **(v4)**
Fisk, Elizabeth Chester. F731.F53 1989, **(v4)**
Fiske Icelandic Collection. Z6621.C8363.I254 1994, **(v10)**
Fiske, John. CB151.F574 1989, **(v5)**
   E169.04.F574 1994, **(v4)**
   PN1992.6.F57 1987, **(v3)**
Fiske, Robert Hartwell. PE1460.F47 1996, **(v3)**
Fiss, Owen M. JC591.F57 1996, **(v7)**
   KF4772.F57 1996, **(v7)**
Fister, Barbara. PN849.U43.F58 1995, **(v3)**
Fitch, John Samuel. JL956.C58.F57 1998, **(v7)**
Fitchen, Janet M. HN79.N4.F58 1991, **(v6)**
Fitchen, John. NA440.F5 1981, **(v9)**
Fite, Emerson David. E440.F54 1967, **(v4)**
Fite, Gilbert Courtland. HD8039.F32.U64, **(v6)**
Fite, Warner. BJ1011 .F57 1957, **(v8)**
Fitts, Donald D. QD462.F55 1999, **(v1)**
Fitts, Dudley. PQ7084.F5 1947, **(v3)**
Fitz Gibbon, Constantine. PR6039.H52.Z643 1965, **(v3)**
Fitz, Earl E. PN843.F58 1991, **(v3)**
Fitzell, Philip B. HF5429.6.E9.F58 1992, **(v6)**
Fitz-enz, Jac. HF5548.32.F57 2001, **(v6)**
Fitzgerald, A. E. (Arthur Eugene). TK2181.F5 1990, **(v1)**
Fitzgerald, C. P. DS721.F55 1954, **(v5)**
   DS749.3.F5 1971, **(v5)**
Fitzgerald, Daniel. F679.3.F57 1994, **(v4)**
FitzGerald, Edward. PR4701.R5, **(v3)**

Fitzgerald, F. Scott. PS3511.I9 A6 1951a, (v3)
PS3511.I9.A6 1989, (v3)
PS3511.I9.A6 2001, (v3)
PS3511.I9 A65, (v3)
PS3511.I9 B3 1960, (v3)
PS3511.I9 B4, (v3)
PS3511.I9.C7 1956, (v3)
PS3511.I9.F54 2000, (v3)
PS3511.I9.G7 1991, (v3)
PS3511.I9 L38 1941, (v3)
PS3511.I9.L68 1993, (v3)
PS3511.I9.N6 1978, (v3)
PS3511.I9.P3 1995, (v3)
PS3511.I9.T3, (v3)
PS3511.I9 T4 1951, (v3)
PS3511.I9.T48 1995, (v3)
PS3511.I9.T75 2000, (v3)
PS3511.I9.V4 1976, (v3)
PS3511.I9.Z464 1996, (v3)
PS3511.I9.Z48 1994, (v3)
PS3511.I9.Z53 1980, (v3)
PS3511.I9.Z55, (v3)
PS3511.I9.Z554, (v3)
PS3511.I9.Z556 1973, (v3)
FitzGerald, Frances. E175.85.F57, (v4)
Fitzgerald, John. DS776.6.F58 1996, (v5)
Fitzgerald, Keith A. JV6483.F58 1996, (v7)
Fitzgerald, M. Desmond. HG6024.A3.F58 1988, (v6)
Fitzgerald, Michael W. E185.2.F54 1989, (v4)
Fitzgerald, Penelope. PR6056.I86.B66, (v3)
PR6056.I86.O3, (v3)
Fitzgerald, Sarah. QL82.F58 1989, (v1)
S930.F57 1990, (v1)
Fitzgerald, Stephen. DS732.F56, (v5)
Fitzgerald, Terrence D. QL561.L3.F58 1995, (v1)
FitzGerald, Thomas E. BX735.F57 1995, (v8)
Fitzgerald, Thomas K. GN512.F57 1993, (v6)
Fitzgerald, Zelda. PS3511.I9234 1991, (v3)
Fitzgibbons, Athol. HB103.S6.F58 1995, (v6)
Fitzhugh, George. E449.F555 1960, (v4)
Fitzhugh, Louise. PZ7.F5768Har, (v3)
Fitzlyon, April. ML420.M2 F6 1987, (v9)
Fitzmaurice, John. DB99.2.F58 1990, (v5)
JN96.A58.F57 1998, (v7)
UA646.7.F52 1987, (v10)
Fitzmaurice-Kelly, James. PQ6176.O8 1940, (v3)
Fitzpatrick, Brendan. DA940.F59 1989, (v5)
Fitzpatrick, Lilian Linder. F664.F55 1960, (v4)
Fitzpatrick, Patrick J. QC944.F58 1999, (v1)
Fitzpatrick, Sheila. DK265.F48 1982, (v5)
HD1492.S65 F58 1994, (v6)
HN523.F57 1999, (v6)
Fitzpatrick, Tony. GF504.M53.F58 1993, (v6)
Fitzsimmons, Allan K. QH76.F58 1999, (v1)
Fitzsimmons, Michael P. DC165.F57 1994, (v6)
Fitzsimmons, Richard. Z6671.2.A2.F48 1991, (v10)
Fiume, Eugene L. QA76.F54 1995, (v1)
Fixico, Donald Lee. E93.F515 1998, (v4)
E98.U72 F57 2000, (v4)
Fjellman, Stephen M. GV1853.3.F62.W344 1992, (v6)
Flaceliere, Robert. DF78.F5513 1965, (v5)
Flack, Marjorie. PZ7.F593St 2000, (v3)
Flacks, Richard. JK1764.F57 1988, (v7)
Flage, Daniel E. B1499.M47.F55 1990, (v8)
Flake, Gary William. QA76.6.F557 1998, (v1)
Flam, Gila. ML3776.F62 1992, (v9)
Flam, Jack D. ND237.R7254.F63 1998, (v9)
ND553.M37.A64 1993, (v9)
Flamhaft, Ziva. DS119.7.F595 1996, (v5)
Flamini, Roland. PN1998.3.T467.F63 1994, (v3)
Flamm, Kenneth. HD9696.S43.U466 1996, (v6)
Flamming, Douglas. HD9884.U64.C764 1992, (v6)
Flanagan, Laurence. DA920.F57 1992, (v5)
GN806.5.F53 1998, (v6)
Flanagan, Mike. F591.F53 1995, (v4)
Flanagan, Owen J. B808.9.F57 1992, (v8)
BD450.F535 2002, (v8)
BJ45.F53 1991, (v8)
Flanagan, Thomas. E92.F52 2000, (v4)
Flanagan, William G. HT151.F52 1993, (v6)
Flanders, Harley. QA76.73.P2.F55 1996, (v1)

Flandrin, Jean Louis. HQ31.F65413 1991, (v6)
HQ623.F5513, (v6)
Flanner, Janet. DC34.F6, (v5)
Flanner, Janet. DC737.F55, (v5)
Flannery, Kathryn T. PR751.F58 1995, (v3)
Flannery, Kent V. F3430.1.W35.F53 1989, (v4)
Flannery, Michael A. RV76.L56.F53 1998, (v2)
Flannery, Raymond B. RC569.5.V55.F56 1997, (v2)
Flannery, Tim F. QH102.F63 2001, (v1)
Flapan, Simha. DS126.4.F57 1987, (v5)
Flathman, Richard E. JC153.H66.F53 1993, (v7)
JC571.F523 1992, (v7)
Flattau, Edward. GE197.F55 1998, (v6)
Flatter, Richard. PR2807.F57 1949, (v3)
PR2995.F5 1948, (v3)
Flatto, Edwin. RG661.5.F56 1998, (v2)
Flaubert, Gustave. PQ2246.A25 1991, (v3)
PQ2246.A26 1991, (v3)
PQ2246.B7 1979, (v3)
PQ2246.M2.E5 1957b, (v3)
PQ2246.T4.E5 1981, (v3)
PQ2246.T4 1938 Rosenwald Coll, (v3)
Flaumenhaft, Harvey. JA84.U5.F59 1992, (v7)
Flavell, John H. BF431.F47, (v2)
Flavell, Linda. PE1571.F57 1999, (v3)
Flavin, Christopher. TJ163.2.F58 1994, (v1)
Flavin, Martin. PS3511.L36 J6, (v3)
Flayhart, William H. DC227.F57 1992, (v5)
Fleagle, John G. QL737.P9.F57 1999, (v1)
Fleagle, Robert Guthrie. GE180.F54 1994, (v6)
Fleche, Anne. PS338.R42.F58 1997, (v3)
Fleck, Steven J. GV505.F58 1987, (v6)
Fleeman, J. D. Z8455.8.F54 2000, (v10)
Fleer, Jack D. JK4116.F58 1994, (v7)
Fleet, Kate. HF3868.Z7.E854 1999, (v6)
Flegg, Jim. QH88.F58 1993, (v1)
Fleischacker, Samuel. BJ1031.F56 1994, (v8)
JC181.K4.F58 1999, (v7)
Fleischer, Alan B. RL721.F56 2000, (v2)
Fleischer, Doris Zames. HV1553.F58 2001, (v6)
Fleischhauer, Carl. ML3520.F6 2001, (v9)
Fleischer, Jennifer. E444.F577 1996, (v4)
Fleischner, Thomas Lowe. QH105.U8.F58 1999, (v1)
Fleisher, Mark S. HV9106.K2.F58 1998, (v6)
Fleisher, Michael L. DT433.545.K87, (v5)
Fleisher, Robert Jay. ML390.F59 1997, (v9)
Fleishman, Avrom. PN1995.F55 1991, (v3)
PR51.U5.F54 1998, (v3)
PR6045.O72.Z63 1975, (v3)
Fleishman, Lazar. PG3476.P27.Z6788 1990, (v3)
Fleming, Denise. PZ8.3.F6378In 1991, (v3)
Fleming, Donald. E169.1.F6, (v4)
R154.W32.F5, (v2)
Fleming, Gerald. D810.J4.F5413 1984, (v5)
Fleming, James Rodger. QC857.U6.F54 1990, (v1)
QC981.8.C5.F45 1998, (v1)
Fleming, John G. KF1250.F55 1988, (v7)
Fleming, John V. PR1896.F86 1990, (v3)
Fleming, Kevin. F165.F57 1984, (v4)
Fleming, Macklin. KF315.F58 1997, (v7)
Fleming, Peter. DS771.F55 1959a, (v5)
DS785.F56 1961a, (v5)
HQ615.F64 2001, (v6)
Fleming, Robert E. PS3515.E37.Z5936 1994, (v3)
Fleming, Robin. DA197.F57 1991, (v5)
Fleming, Stuart James. CC78.F54 1977, (v5)
Fleming, Walter L. F326.F71 1978, (v4)
Flemings, Merton C. TN690.F59, (v1)
Flemming, John Stanton. HG229.F624, (v6)
Flemming, Roy B. KF9223.F43 1992, (v7)
Flender, Harold. D810.J4.F55, (v5)
Fleras, Augie. DU420.F555 1999, (v5)
Flesch, Carl F. ML418.F81.F6 1990, (v9)
Flesch, Rudolf Franz. LB1573.F552 1981, (v7)
Flesch, William. PR428.G45.F58 1992, (v3)
Fletcher, Alice C. E51.U55 27th, (v4)
Fletcher, Angus John Stewart. PN56.A5.F5, (v3)
Fletcher, Angus. PR2358.F58, (v3)
PR3557.F5 1972, (v3)
Fletcher, Anthony. HQ1075.5.E5.F54 1995, (v6)
Fletcher, Banister. NA200.F63 1961, (v9)

Fletcher, Ben. RC49.F58 1991, (v2)
Fletcher, Colin. GV199.6.F532 2002, (v6)
Fletcher, Ebenezer. E275.F62 1970, (v4)
Fletcher, Frank W. GB1001.7.F57 1997, (v6)
Fletcher, George P. BJ1533.L8.F54 1993, (v8)
E457.2.F57 2001, (v4)
KF224.G63.F54 1988, (v7)
KF9763.F58 1995, (v7)
Fletcher, Giles. PR2271.A2.B6 1968, (v3)
Fletcher, Harris Francis. PR3581.F5, (v3)
PR3594.F5 1970, (v3)
Fletcher, Ian. NC242.B3.F55 1987, (v9)
Fletcher, John Gould. F411.F5, (v4)
Fletcher, John. PR2870.A2.W35 1989, (v3)
Fletcher, Joyce K. TA157.F54 1999, (v1)
Fletcher, Marvin. U53.D38.F57 1989, (v10)
Fletcher, Neville H. QC921.5.F55, (v1)
Fletcher, Nina. KD2968.N8.F56 1995, (v7)
Fletcher, Peri L. JV7409.Z6.N364 1999, (v7)
Fletcher, Peter. MT1.F53 1987, (v9)
Fletcher, Philip. QE515.5.T46.F57 1993, (v1)
Fletcher, R. A. DA145.2.F55 1989, (v5)
V750.F6, (v10)
Fletcher, Robert H. F732.F56 1999, (v4)
Fletcher, Roland. CC72.4.F54 1995, (v5)
Fletcher, Scott. LC191.4.F54 2000, (v7)
Fletcher, Valerie J. N6502.57.M63.F57 1992, (v9)
N6853.G5.A4 1988, (v9)
Flew, Antony. B1626.F573.P48 1998, (v8)
Flew, Antony. BD421.F54 2000, (v8)
Flexner, Abraham. R745.F57 1972, (v2)
Flexner, James Thomas. E175.5.F549.A3 1996, (v4)
E236.F75 1991, (v4)
E312.F556 1984, (v4)
E312.2.F6, (v4)
E312.29.F55, (v4)
E312.29.F56, (v4)
ND207.F55 1967, (v9)
VM615.F63 1944, (v10)
Flexner, Simon. R154.W32.F6, (v2)
Flexner, Stuart Berg. PE2846.S59 1997, (v3)
Fliege, Norbert. TK5103.7.F58 1994, (v1)
Fliegel, Frederick C. S494.5.I5.F65 1993, (v1)
Flieger, Verlyn. PR6039.O32.Z646 1997, (v3)
Flinn, Anthony. PS310.M57.F58 1997, (v3)
Flinn, Denny Martin. ML1711.F57 1997, (v9)
Flinn, Michael W. HB3581.F54, (v6)
Flint, Christopher. PR858.F29.F58 1998, (v3)
Flint, Mary Louise. SB993.3.F59 1998, (v1)
Flint, Richard Foster. QE696.F54, (v1)
QE696.F553, (v1)
Flintham, Victor. UG630.F55 1990, (v10)
Fliter, John A. KF9731.A7, (v7)
Flitterman-Lewis, Sandy. PN1995.9.W6.F6 1996, (v3)
Flood, Charles Bracelen. DD247.H5.F54 1989, (v5)
Flood, Curt. GV865.F45.A3, (v6)
Flood, Josephine. GN666.F58 1997, (v6)
Flood, Patrick James, 1939-. K3240.4.F547 1998, (v7)
Flood, Renee S. E99.D1.L773 1995, (v4)
Flora, Snowden Dwight. QC929.H1.F4, (v1)
Florence, Namulundah. LB885.H662.F56 1998, (v7)
Flores, A. PQ6469.F6, (v3)
Flores, Angel. PQ1170.E6.F5 1962, (v3)
PQ6267.E1.F5, (v3)
PQ6267.E2 1961, (v3)
PQ6341.B47.F6, (v3)
PQ7083.F55, (v3)
PT1308.F55, (v3)
PT2621.A26.Z69, (v3)
Flores, Juan. E184.P85.F58 2000, (v4)
Flores, Richard R. PN3211.S27.F66 1995, (v3)
Florinsky, Michael T. D1060.F55, (v5)
Florkin, Marcel. QD415.F54, (v1)
Florman, Samuel C. T14.F56, (v1)
TA157.F57 1994, (v1)
Floros, Constantin. ML410.M23.F5513 1993, (v9)
Floud, J. E. LA631.F6 1973, (v7)
Flournoy, Don M. PN4784.T4.F57 1992, (v3)
Flower, Harriet I. DG103.F56 1996, (v5)
Flower, Michael A. DE9.T54.F56 1994, (v5)
Flowers, Charles. Q125.F592 1998, (v1)

Flowers, Edward B. HD9685.U5.F59 1998, (v6)
Flowers, James R. PN6714.F565 2000, (v3)
Flowers, Ronald B. HV6250.4.W65.F55 1994, (v6)
HV6626.2.F56 2000, (v6)
HV6789.F58 1989, (v6)
KF4865.F57 1994, (v7)
Floyd, Samuel A. ML128.B45.F6 1983, (v9)
ML3556.F65 1995, (v9)
Flueckiger, Joyce Burkhalter. GR305.5.C46.F58 1996, (v6)
Fluehr-Lobban, Carolyn. BP64.A4 N6423 1994, (v8)
Flugel, J. C. BF95.F5 1964, (v2)
BF173.F58 1947, (v2)
Flynn, Charles L. F291.F58 1983, (v4)
Flynn, Eileen P. R724.F59 1997, (v2)
Flynn, George Q. UB343.F59 1993, (v10)
Flynn, James T. LA837.F59 1988, (v7)
Flynn, John Thomas. DS518.8.F57, (v5)
Flynn, M. K. DP203.F58 1999, (v5)
Flynn, Michael J. QA76.9.A73.F58 1995, (v1)
Flynn, Peter. F2538.2.F55, (v4)
Flynn, Tom. NB1930.F59 1998, (v9)
Flynt, J. Wayne. HC107.A13.F66, (v6)
HN79.A133.C64 1989, (v6)
Flyvbjerg, Bent. H61.F6144 2001, (v6)
Foa, Anna. DS124.F6213 2000, (v5)
Foakes, R. A. PR2965.F6 1993, (v3)
Foch, Ferdinand. U102.F52 1970, (v10)
Focillon, Henri. BH202.F63 1948, (v8)
Focillon, Henri. N6280.F613 1969, (v9)
Foden, Charles R. RC86.8.F64 1993, (v2)
Foderaro, Anthony Harolde. QC721.F66, (v1)
Fodor, Jerry A. B818.F66 1992, (v8)
BD418.3.F627 2000, (v8)
BD418.3.F63 1990, (v8)
BF38.F63 1987, (v2)
Foelix, Rainer F. QL458.4.F6313 1996, (v1)
Foerstel, Herbert N. P96.C42.U654 1998, (v3)
U393.F64 1993, (v10)
Z658.U5.F64 1994, (v10)
Z658.U5.F644 1997, (v10)
Z678.2.F64 1991, (v10)
Foerstel, Karen. HQ1391.U5.F64 1996, (v6)
JK1012.F57 1999, (v7)
Foerster, Donald Madison. PN1303.F6, (v3)
Fogel, Joshua A. DS709.F64 1996, (v5)
Fogel, Robert William. E449.F65 1984, (v4)
HC103.F58, (v6)
JC575.F64 2000, (v7)
Fogel, Stanley. PS3552.A75.Z625 1990, (v3)
Fogelin, Robert J. B1334.F64 2001, (v8)
Fogelman, Betsy. R601.F64 1993, (v2)
Fogelquist, Donald F. PQ6619.I4.Z615, (v3)
Fogelson, Nancy. G626.F65 1992, (v6)
Fogelson, Robert M. UA42.F64 1989, (v10)
Fogg, G. E. G860.F64 1992, (v6)
Fogg, Martyn J. TL795.7.F64 1995, (v1)
Fogle, Richard Harter. PR4484.F6, (v3)
PR4837.F56, (v3)
Fogleman, Aaron Spencer. E184.G3.F724 1996, (v4)
Foglesong, David S. DK265.42.U5.F64 1995, (v5)
Folb, Edith A. PE3102.N42.F6, (v3)
Folbre, Nancy. HB72.F637 2001, (v6)
Foldes, Stephan. QA155.F65 1994, (v1)
Foldy, Michael S. PR5823.F65 1997, (v3)
Foley, Douglas E. F395.M5.F65 1990, (v4)
F629.T36.F65 1995, (v4)
Foley, Helene P. PA3136.F65 2001, (v3)
Foley, James D. T385.F63, (v1)
Foley, John Miles. D16.14.F65 1988, (v5)
GR72.F62 1991, (v6)
GR72.3.F65 1995, (v6)
PN56.E65.F65 1990, (v3)
Foley, Martha. PS648.S5.T86 1982, (v3)
Foley, Michael. JN406.F65 1993, (v7)
K3165.F65 1989, (v7)
Foley, Neil. F395.A1.F65 1997, (v4)
Foley, Richard. BD161.F565 2001, (v8)
BD161.F57 1987, (v8)
BD161.F58 1993, (v8)
Foley, Robert. GN281.F64 1987, (v6)

GN281.F66 1995, (v6)
Foley, Stephen Merriam. PR2404.F57 1990, (v3)
Foley, William E. F466.F64 1989, (v4)
F474.S253 A24 2000, (v4)
Folgarait, Leonard. ND2644.F63 1998, (v9)
Folkenflik, Robert. PR3537.B54.F64, (v3)
Follett, Richard R. HV9960.G72.E544 2001, (v6)
Föllmi, Olivier. BQ400.H542 F65 2002, (v8)
Folly, Martin H. DA47.65.F65 2000, (v5)
Folsom, Ed. PS3242.A54.F65 1994, (v3)
Folsom, Franklin. E99.P9 F64 1996, (v4)
Foltz, Ramon D. KF3114.8.E54.F65 1988, (v7)
Foltz, Richard. DS340.F65 1998, (v5)
Fonda, Luciano. QC174.5.F6, (v1)
Fone, Byrne R. S. HQ76.25.F7 2001, (v6)
Foner, Eric. E179.F69 1998, (v4)
E185.96.F64 1993, (v4)
E436.F6 1970, (v4)
E668.F66 1988, (v4)
Foner, Philip Sheldon. E449.F68 1983, (v4)
F1418.F676 1988, (v4)
HD6079.2.U5.F65 1979, (v6)
HD6508.F57 1975, (v6)
LC2801.F57 1984, (v7)
Fones-Wolf, Elizabeth A. HB95.F66 1994, (v6)
Fong, Chan Onn. HC445.5.F66 1989, (v6)
Fong, Grace S. PL2687.W83.Z64 1987, (v3)
Fong, Wen. ND1045.F66 2001, (v9)
Fonseca, Isabel. DX115.F66 1995, (v5)
Fonseca, James W. G1201.E68.F6 1993, (v6)
Fonstad, Clifton G. TK7874.F645 1994, (v1)
Font, Mauricio. HD9199.B8.S217 1990, (v6)
Fontaine, Gerard D. PC2168.F6, (v3)
Fontaine, Karen Lee. RT42.F64 2000, (v2)
Fontana i Lazaro, Josep. D13.5.E85.F66 1995, (v5)
Fontana, Andrea. HQ1061.F65, (v6)
Fontane, Theodor. PT1863.A1 1976, (v3)
PT1863.A15 1982, (v3)
PT1863.A7 E5 1979, (v3)
PT1863.E313 1995, (v3)
Fontein, Jan. NB1026.F6 1990, (v9)
Fontenrose, Joseph Eddy. DF261.D35.F6, (v5)
Food and Agriculture Organization of the United Nations. HD1421.P76, (v6)
Fools Crow, Frank. E99.O3.F664, (v4)
Foonberg, Jay G. KF300.F66 1999, (v7)
Foot, M. R. D. UA11.F6, (v10)
Foot, Michael. DA585.B38.F62, (v5)
Foot, Mirjam. Z269.F68 1994, (v10)
Foot, Philippa. BJ21.F6, (v8)
BJ1012.F57 1978, (v8)
Foot, Rosemary. K3240.F66 2000, (v7)
Foote, Cheryl J. F801.F56 1990, (v4)
Foote, Geoffrey. JN1129.L32.F64 1997, (v7)
Foote, Henry S. E415.7.F68 1968, (v4)
Foote, Henry Wilder. ML3111.F6.T4 1961, (v9)
Foote, Horton. PS3511.O344.T7 1993, (v3)
Foote, Joe S. HE8700.76.U6.F66 1990, (v6)
Foote, Kenneth E. E159.F68 1997, (v4)
Foote, Richard H. QL537.T42.F66 1993, (v1)
Foote, Shelby. E468.F7, (v4)
PS3511.O348 S5 1952, (v3)
Foote, Stephanie. PS217.R44.F66 2001, (v3)
Footitt, Hilary. D761.F65 1988, (v5)
Footlick, Jerrold K. LB2342.8.F66 1997, (v7)
Footner, Hulbert. F186.F65 1967, (v4)
Footner, Hulbert. F187.E2F6 1979, (v4)
Foran, John. HN670.2.A8.F67 1993, (v6)
Forbath, William E. HD6510.F67 1991, (v6)
Forbes, A. S. C. F870.M6 F65, (v4)
Forbes, David W. Z4701.F67 1998, (v10)
Forbes, Ernest R. F1035.8.F59, (v4)
Forbes, Esther. PS3511.O35 G4, (v3)
PS3511.O35 P3, (v3)
PS3511.O37 M5, (v3)
PS3511.O37 R3, (v3)
PS3511.O37 R8, (v3)
PZ7.F749Jo 10, (v3)
Forbes, Gerald. F704.G9 F7, (v4)
Forbes, Geraldine Hancock. DS436.N47 1987 pt. 4, vol. 2.Q1742, (v5)

Forbes, H. D. GN496.F67 1997, (v6)
Forbes, Jack D. E59.M66 F67 1993, (v4)
E78.S7 F6 1994, (v4)
E99.Y94.F59, (v4)
Forbes, Neil. HF1533.Z4, (v6)
Ford, Alice. QL31.A9.F63 1988, (v1)
Ford, Andrew. ML390.F69 1993, (v9)
Ford, Betty. E867.F66 1978, (v4)
Ford, Brian J. Q222.F67 1993, (v1)
Ford, Brian J. QH204.F65 1985, (v1)
Ford, Caroline C. DC611.F498.F67 1993, (v5)
Ford, Charles V. BF637.D42.F67 1996, (v2)
Ford, Daniel. D790.F584 1991, (v5)
Ford, Derek. GB600.F66 1989, (v6)
Ford, Donna Y. LC3993.9.F66 1996, (v7)
Ford, E. D. QH541.2.F66 2000, (v1)
Ford, Edward R. NA2840.F67 1990, (v9)
Ford, Ford Madox. D395.F67 1988, (v5)
PR6005.O4.Z72 1965, (v3)
PR6011.O53.A17 1936, (v3)
PR6011.O53 F5 1963, (v3)
PR6011.O53.G6, (v3)
PR6011.O53 N6, (v3)
PR6011.O53 P3, (v3)
Ford, Franklin L. D308.F65 1970, (v5)
DD901.S87.F6, (v5)
Ford, Gerald R. E176.1.F75 1987, (v4)
E839.5.F67, (v4)
E866.F67 1987, (v4)
Ford, J. D. M. PC4715.F6 1911, (v3)
Ford, Jane M. PR408.F36.F67 1998, (v3)
Ford, Jesse Hill. PS3556.O7.L5, (v3)
PS3556.O7.R3, (v3)
Ford, John. PR2522.E5 1957, (v3)
PR2524.T5 1995, (v3)
Ford, Lacy K. F273.F68 1988, (v4)
Ford, Larry. NA705.F67 1994, (v9)
Ford, Lewis S. B1674.W354F68 2000, (v8)
Ford, Marcus Peter. B945.J24 F67 1982, (v8)
Ford, Mark. PQ2635.O96168, (v3)
Ford, Norman Robert. PS3556.O71.B5, (v3)
Ford, S. Dennis. BJ1251.F67 1990, (v8)
Ford, Thomas R. HB885.F58, (v6)
Ford, Thomas. F545.F7 1995, (v4)
Forde, Steven. DF230.A4.F67 1989, (v5)
Fordham, Benjamin O. E813.F55 1998, (v4)
Fordin, Hugh. ML423.H24.F7, (v9)
Forell, George Wolfgang. BR53.F6, (v8)
Foreman, Amanda. DA522.D5.F68 2000, (v5)
Foreman, Christopher H. JK585.F68 1988, (v7)
Foreman, Grant. E78.I5 F8 1953, (v4)
E90.S47 F6, (v4)
F694.F67, (v4)
F700.F67, (v4)
F704.G5 F6 1936, (v4)
Foreman-Peck, James. HC54.F565 1983, (v6)
Forer, Lois G. KF475.F67 1991, (v7)
Foresta, Ronald A. QH77.A53.F67 1991, (v1)
Forester, Cecil Scott. PR6011.O56 A3, (v3)
PR6011.O56 C28, (v3)
PR6011.O56 C65, (v3)
PR6011.O56 F5 1939, (v3)
PR6011.O56 G6, (v3)
PR6011.O56 H6, (v3)
PR6011.O56 H65, (v3)
PR6011.O56 L5, (v3)
PR6011.O56 L6, (v3)
PR6011.O56 M5, (v3)
PR6011.O56 S51, (v3)
Forester, John. HE5736.F67 1983, (v6)
Forester, Tom. QA76.9.M65.F67 1994, (v1)
Forest-Hill, Lynn. PR641.F67 2000, (v3)
Forêt, Philippe. DS796.C49 F67 2000, (v5)
Forgacs, David. DG441.F67 1990, (v5)
Foriska, Terry J. LB3060.83.F67 1998, (v7)
Forker, Charles R. PR2976.F58 1990, (v3)
Forman, Milos. PN1998.3.F66.A3 1994, (v3)
Forman, Richard T. T. GE170.F57 1995, (v6)
QH541.F67 1986, (v1)
Forman, Seth. E185.61.F7216 1998, (v4)

Fornara, Charles W. DE8.F67 1983, (v5)
  DF277.F68 1990, (v5)
Forrest, Alan I. DC151.F6713 1989, (v5)
  DC151.F68 1990, (v5)
  DC195.A625.F67 1996, (v5)
  DC195.B6.F67, (v5)
  HV265.F64 1981, (v6)
Forrest, Andrew. DP269.F62 2000, (v5)
Forrest, Derek William. RC497.F67 2000, (v2)
Forrest, Earle Robert. F786.F72, (v4)
Forrest, John. F265.A1.F67 1988, (v4)
Forrest, Joshua. JQ3543.5.R43.F67 1998, (v7)
Forrest, Peter. BL200.F65 1996, (v8)
Forrest, R. A. D. PL1075.F6 1948, (v3)
  PL1075.F6 1948, (v3)
Forrest, Suzanne. F805.S75.F67 1989, (v4)
Forrest, Tom. HD2928.F67 1994, (v6)
Forrester, Duncan B. BR115.J8.F67 1997, (v8)
Forrester, James W. BC145.F67 1989, (v8)
Forrester, Kevin. TA749.F67 2001, (v1)
Forry, Steven Earl. PR5397.F73.F67 1990, (v3)
Forsas-Scott, Helena. PT9315.F67 1997, (v3)
Forse, James H. PN2589.F67 1993, (v3)
Forshaw, Joseph Michael. QL696.P7F63 1981, (v1)
Forshee, Jill. DS632.S89, (v5)
Forshey, Gerald Eugene. PN1995.9.R4.F67 1992, (v3)
Forster, Bruce A. TD195.5.F67 1993, (v1)
Forster, E. M. CT788.T566.F6, (v5)
  PR6011.O58.P5 1962, (v3)
  PR6011.O58.A6 1947, (v3)
  PR6011.O58.A6 1971, (v3)
  PR6011.O58 C4 1976, (v3)
  PR6011.O58 E8, (v3)
  PR6011.O58.H6 1997, (v3)
  PR6011.O58 L6, (v3)
  PR6011.O58 M3, (v3)
  PR6011.O58.T8 1951, (v3)
  PR6011.O58 W5, (v3)
  PR6011.O58.Z48 1983, (v3)
  PR6011.O58R6, (v3)
  PR6045.O72.Z64, (v3)
Forster, Keith. DS793.C268 F67 1990, (v5)
Forster, Michael N. B2949.S54.F67 1989, (v8)
Forster, Peter G. DT429.F67 1999, (v5)
Forster, Robert. CT1017.D46.F67, (v5)
Forsyth, Adrian. QH471.F69 1986, (v1)
Forsyth, Andrew Russell. QA371.F72, (v1)
Forsyth, Ian. LB1044.87.F67 1998, (v7)
Forsyth, Phyllis Young. DF221.T38.F67 1997, (v5)
Forsythe, David P. JC571.F634 1983, (v7)
  K3240.4.F677 1993, (v7)
  K3240.4.F68 1988, (v7)
  K3240.4.F683 1991, (v7)
Forte, Allen. ML3477.F67 1995, (v9)
  MT6.F642.I6 1982, (v9)
  MT50.F713.T7 1979, (v9)
Forter, Greg. PS374.D4.F67 2000, (v3)
Fortescue, William. PQ2326.F58 1983, (v3)
Fortey, Richard A. QE711.2.F66 1991, (v1)
  QE821.F67 2000, (v1)
Forthofer, Ron N. R853.S7.I59 1995, (v2)
Fortner, Diane M. Z5861.F67 1994, (v10)
Fortner, Robert S. PN4784.R2.F67 1994, (v3)
Fortune, Dion. DA690.G45, (v5)
Forys, Marsha. Z8129.8.F67 1988, (v10)
Foscue, Virginia O. F324.F67 1989, (v4)
Foshay, Arthur Wellesley. LB2806.15.F66 2000, (v7)
Foshay, Ella M. ND210.F65 1990, (v9)
Fosnot, Catherine Twomey. LB1715.F64 1989, (v7)
Foss, Phillip O. HD241.F6 1969, (v6)
Fossett, Mark Alan. HN79.A13.F67 1997, (v6)
Fossey, Dian. QL737.P96.F67 1983, (v1)
Foster, Adriance S. QK641.F6 1974, (v1)
Foster, Brian. PE1095.F6 1968, (v3)
Foster, Catherine. JX1965.F67 1989, (v7)
Foster, Charles Richard. LB2846.F58 1971, (v7)
Foster, Christopher D. HD3616.G73.F67 1992, (v6)
Foster, David R. PS3053.F66 1999, (v4)
Foster, David William. F3001.2.F65 1998, (v4)
  PC4410.F68 1999, (v3)
  PN1993.5.A7.F6 1992, (v3)

PQ6090.F6, (v3)
PQ7081.F628 1994, (v3)
PQ7703.F6, (v3)
Z1681.F73 1990, (v10)
Foster, Dennis A. PS169.S84.F67 1997, (v3)
Foster, Dennis L. HF5429.23.F673 1989, (v6)
Foster, Don H. HV8599.S6.F67 1987, (v6)
Foster, Donald H. ML134.R14.F7 1989, (v9)
Foster, Edward E. PR1875.P5.F67 1999, (v3)
Foster, George McClelland. CB478.F6, (v5)
  E51.S4 no. 6, (v4)
  F1221.T3.F67 1973, (v4)
  F1408.3.F6, (v4)
Foster, George. HF5681.B2.F64 1986, (v6)
Foster, Gwendolyn Audrey. BJ1853.F62 2000, (v8)
  PN1995.9.C333.F67 1999, (v3)
  PN1998.2.F67 1995, (v3)
  PN1998.2.F672 1997, (v3)
Foster, H. Schuyler. E744.F7698 1983, (v4)
Foster, John T. F316.F695 1999, (v4)
Foster, John. B828.45.F67 2000, (v8)
  BD418.3.F67 1991, (v8)
Foster, Joseph S. F153.B88.F67 1994, (v4)
Foster, Kathryn Ann. JS426.F67 1997, (v7)
Foster, Lynn V. F1436.F68 2000, (v4)
Foster, Maxwell E. PR2807.F64 1998, (v3)
Foster, Michael Beresford. JC71.P6.F6 1965, (v7)
Foster, Morris W. E99.C85.F67 1991, (v4)
Foster, R. F. DA938.F67 1988, (v5)
  PR5906.F66 1997, (v3)
Foster, Richard Jackson. PN94.F6, (v3)
Foster, Robert John. DU740.42.F67 1995, (v5)
Foster, Robert. PR6039.O32.Z49 1978, (v3)
Foster, Shirley. PR830.G57.F67 1995, (v3)
  PR878.W6.F67 1985, (v3)
Foster, Stephen William. F262.A7.F67 1988, (v4)
Foster, Stephen. F7.F758 1991, (v4)
  F7.F76 1971, (v4)
Foster, Steven. QK99.U6.F68 1999, (v1)
  RM666.H33.T94 1999, (v2)
Foster, Susan Leigh. GV1649.F67 1996, (v6)
Foster, Thomas C. PR6056.O85.Z665 1994, (v3)
Foster, William Z. JK2391.C5.F58 1968, (v7)
Foth, H. D. S591.F68 1980, (v1)
  S596.7.F68 1997, (v1)
Fotion, N. BJ1431.F68 1992, (v8)
Foucault, Michel. B2430.F722.E5 1997, (v8)
  HV8666.F6813 1977, (v6)
  PQ2603.L3343.Z65 1987, (v3)
Foucher, A. BL1470.F623, (v8)
Foulke, Robert. PN56.T7.F68 1997, (v3)
Foulkes, David. BF1071.F73, (v2)
Foulkes, Julia L. GV1623.F68 2002, (v6)
Foulkes, Richard. PN2594.F68 1991, (v3)
Foulois, Benjamin Delahauf. U53.F6.A3, (v10)
Fountain, Charles. GV742.42.R53 F68 1993, (v6)
Fourquin, Guy. HC41.F6913 1976b, (v6)
Foust, James C. HE8698.F68 2000, (v6)
Fouty, Kathleen G. Z714.F68 1994, (v10)
Fowden, Garth. DF531.F69 1993, (v5)
Foweraker, Joe. JC571.F637 1997, (v7)
Fowkes, Ben. DK33.F68 1997, (v5)
Fowkes, Katherine A. PN1995.9.S8.F68 1998, (v3)
Fowkes, Neville D. QA401.F68 1994, (v1)
Fowler, Alastair. PR83.F65 1987, (v3)
Fowler, Cary. SB175.F68 1990, (v1)
Fowler, David C. PR275.B5.F68 1984, (v3)
Fowler, Don D. GN17.3.S67F68 2000, (v6)
Fowler, Doreen. PS3511.A86.Z783248 1997, (v3)
Fowler, Edward. PL747.63.A85.F6 1988, (v3)
Fowler, Gene. PS3511.O93.S3, (v3)
Fowler, Ira. QM23.2.F68 1984, (v1)
Fowler, Jacob. F592.F78 1970, (v4)
Fowler, Jeaneane D. BL1153.5.F68 1997, (v8)
Fowler, Kenneth Alan. D128.F68 2001, (v5)
Fowler, Linda L. JK1021.F68 1989, (v7)
  JK1764.F68 1993, (v7)
Fowler, Loretta. E99.A7.F68 1982, (v4)
  E99.A87.F69 1987, (v4)
Fowler, Robert Booth. JA84.U5.F683 1991, (v7)
  JK1899.C3 F69 1986, (v7)

Fowler, T. Kenneth. QC791.73.F69 1997, (v1)
Fowler, Virginia C. PS3557.I55.Z66 1992, (v3)
Fowler, Wilfred. PR6056.O84, (v3)
Fowler, Will. F1232.T696.F69 2000, (v4)
Fowler, William M. E271.F68, (v4)
  E591.F77 2001, (v4)
Fowler, William R. F1485.2.P5.F68 1989, (v4)
Fowles, Jib. HF5805.F69 1996, (v6)
Fowles, John. PR6056.O85.C6 1963, (v3)
  PR6056.O85.D3 1977, (v3)
  PR6056.O85.E3 1974, (v3)
  PR6056.O85.F7 1979, (v3)
  PR6056.O85.M28 1985, (v3)
  PR6056.O85.M3 1978, (v3)
  PR6056.O85.M35 1982, (v3)
  PR6056.O85.P6 1973, (v3)
  PR6056.O85.W6 1998, (v3)
  PR6056.O85.Z474 1983, (v3)
Fowlie, Wallace. BH301.S75.F6 1960, (v8)
  PN99.F8.F6, (v3)
  PQ556.F6, (v3)
  PQ1184.F6, (v3)
  PQ2220.D723.Z654, (v3)
  PQ2613.I2.Z6275, (v3)
  PS3563.O8746.Z66 1994, (v3)
Fox, Alice. PR6045.O72.Z643 1990, (v3)
Fox, Alistair. PR129.I8.F68 1997, (v3)
Fox, Anthony. PF3112.F69 1990, (v3)
Fox, Claire G. Z8764.8.F69 1996, (v10)
Fox, Daniel M. HB119.P35.F6, (v6)
  R134.F69 1990, (v2)
  RA395.G6.F68 1986, (v2)
Fox, Dian. PQ6485.F69 1991, (v3)
Fox, Elaine. R726.F69 1999, (v2)
Fox, Francis S. F157.N7, (v4)
Fox, Grace Estelle. DS740.5.G5 F6 1940, (v5)
Fox, John Howard. PC2075.F6 1969, (v3)
Fox, Jonathan. HD9014.M62.F69 1993, (v6)
Fox, Julian. PN1998.3.A45.F68 1996, (v3)
Fox, L. QA372.F69 1987, (v1)
Fox, Michael W. QH332.F68 2001, (v1)
  SF51.F69 1996, (v1)
  SF406.F69 1986, (v1)
  TP248.6.F687 1999, (v1)
Fox, Nicols. RA601.5.F68 1997, (v2)
Fox, Paul. BR420.P7.F6 1971, (v8)
Fox, Paula. PZ7.F838SI 1988, (v3)
Fox, Renee C. RD120.7.F68 1992, (v2)
Fox, Richard A. E83.876.F6 1993, (v4)
Fox, Richard Gabriel. HN683.F69 1989, (v6)
Fox, Richard L. P96.C742.U63 2001, (v3)
Fox, Richard Wightman. BX7260.B31.F68 1999, (v8)
Fox, Robert. D973.F69 1993, (v5)
Fox, Robin. GN487.F7 1993, (v6)
Fox, Ronald W. KF299.P8 F69 1995, (v7)
Fox, Roy F. LB1044.8.F69 1996, (v7)
Fox, Sandi. NK9112.F698 1990, (v9)
Fox, Stephen C. D769.8.A6.F66 1990, (v5)
Fox, Stephen R. QH76.F69, (v1)
Fox, Stephen. D805.U5.F69 2000, (v5)
Fox, Thomas C. PT3723.F68 1993, (v3)
Fox, William L. F789.F69 2000, (v4)
  HS765.F69 1997, (v6)
Fox-Genovese, Elizabeth. HQ1438.A13.F69 1988, (v6)
Foxley, Alejandro. HC165.F675 1983, (v6)
Fox-Lockert, Lucia. PQ6055.F6, (v3)
Foxon, David F. PR3637.B58.F69 1990, (v3)
Foyer, Christine H. QK882.F64 1984, (v1)
Fracasso, Evelyn E. PS3545.H16.Z648 1994, (v3)
Fraden, Jacob. TA165.F72 1993, (v1)
Fradenburg, Louise Olga. DA784.5.F74 1991, (v5)
Frader, Laura Levine. HD1536.F8.F66 1991, (v6)
Fradin, Dennis B. F184.F73 1990, (v4)
  F681.3.F73 1995, (v4)
  F826.3.F69 1993, (v4)
Fradkin, Philip L. F861.F75 1995, (v4)
Fradkin, Robert A. ML109.F73 1996, (v9)
Frady, Marshall. E185.97.J25.F73 1996, (v4)
Fragola, Anthony N. PN1998.3.R59.F73 1992, (v3)
Fraiman, Susan. PR830.W6.F73 1993, (v3)

Fraioli, Deborah A. DC104.F73 2000, (v5)
Fraisse, Paul. BF182.F7423, (v2)
Frakes, Lawrence A. QC884.F69 1992, (v1)
Fraleigh, Sondra Horton. GV1783.2.B87.F73 1999, (v6)
Fram, Edward. DS135.P6.F676 1997, (v5)
Frame, Donald Murdoch. PQ1643.F72, (v3)
Frame, Janet. PR9639.3.F7.D3 1972, (v3)
Frame, Janet. PR9639.3.F7.F3 1982, (v3)
  PR9639.3.F7.I58x 1970, (v3)
  PR9639.3.F7.O94 1982, (v3)
  PR9639.3.F7.S5 1963, (v3)
  PR9639.3.F7.Z463 1984, (v3)
  PR9639.3.F7.Z464 1985, (v3)
  PR9639.3.F7.Z477 1982, (v3)
Frame, John. SB203.F735 1998, (v1)
Frame, Murray. Z2510.F73 1995, (v10)
Frampton, Kenneth. NA500.F75 1992, (v9)
  NA642.F7 1983, (v9)
  NA1605.S4.A4 1992, (v9)
Francaviglia, Richard V. F386.F68 1998, (v4)
  HT167.F73 1996, (v6)
France, Anatole. PQ2254.C7.E5 2000, (v3)
  PQ2254.D5 1912, (v3)
  PQ2254.J3 1895, (v3)
  PQ2254.L4 1902, (v3)
  PQ2254.Z3S8, (v3)
France, John. D160.F73 1999, (v5)
France, Peter. HC687.F5 F72, (v6)
Franceschina, John Charles. PR635.H65.F73 1997, (v3)
Francese, Joseph. PN771.F68 1997, (v3)
Francillon, Rene J. UG630.F66 1995, (v10)
Francione, Gary L. HV4764.F73 1996, (v6)
Francis, Becky. LC212.9. F73 2000, (v7)
Francis, Bettina Magnus. QH545.A1.F72 1994, (v1)
Francis, Claude. PQ2605.O28.Z66475 1999, (v3)
Francis, de Sales, Saint. BX2179.F8.I54 1992, (v8)
Francis, Lesley Lee. PS3511.R94.Z6527 1994, (v3)
Francis, Wayne L. JK2495.F73 1989, (v7)
Franciscono, Marcel. N6888.K55.F7 1991, (v9)
Franck, Irene M. GV571.F73 2001, (v6)
  HQ769.F717 1996, (v6)
  R690.F713 1989, (v2)
Franck, Matthew J. KF8748.F647 1996, (v7)
Franck, Thomas M. JK573 1979.F7, (v7)
  JX1245.F73 1995, (v7)
  JX4044.F68 1990, (v7)
  KF4651.F73 1992, (v7)
Francke, Kuno. PT91.F8 1969, (v3)
  PT1113.F7, (v3)
  PT1113.F72, (v3)
Francke, Lizzie. PN1995.9.W6.F675 1994, (v3)
Franscks, Penelope. HD3628.J33.F73 1992, (v6)
Franco, Jean. PQ7081.F643 1973, (v3)
Franco, Jere Bishop. D810.I5.F73 1999, (v5)
Franco, Paul. JC257.O244.F73 1990, (v7)
Franda, Marcus F. HD2072.F68, (v6)
Frank, Andre Gunder. HC187.F733 1971, (v6)
Frank, Anne. D810.J4.F715, (v5)
  PT5834.F68.A53, (v3)
Frank, Barbara E. DT474.6.M36.F73 1998, (v5)
Frank, Francine Harriet Wattman. PE1460.F64 1989, (v3)
Frank, Frederick S. Z1231.G66.F7 1990, (v10)
  Z5917.G66 F7 1984, (v10)
Frank, Frederick S. and Anthony Magistrale. PS2630.P58 1997, (v3)
Frank, Howard A. HJ9147.F7 1993, (v6)
Frank, Isaiah. HD2755.5.F734, (v6)
Frank, John Paul. KF8742.F7 1991, (v7)
Frank, Joseph. DA405.F7, (v5)
  PG3012.F7 1990, (v3)
  PG3328.F678 2002, (v3)
  PG3328.F73 1986, (v3)
  PN771.F7, (v3)
Frank, Katherine. PR4173.F7 1990, (v3)
Frank, Larry. E99.P9 F69 1990, (v4)
Frank, Nancy. KF1418.F73 1988, (v7)
Frank, Norman. QL645.F73 1995, (v1)
Frank, Philipp. Q175.F782, (v1)

Frank, Richard B. D767.98.F73 1990, (v5)
Frank, Robert Gregg. QP21.F76, (v1)
Frank, Ronald Edward. HE8700.7.A8.F69 1982, (v6)
Frank, Ross. HC107.N6.F73 2000, (v6)
Frank, Rusty E. GV1785.A1.F69 1990, (v6)
Frank, Stephen. HV9960.R9.F7 1999, (v6)
Frank, Steven J. KF283.F73 1997, (v7)
Frank, Waldo David. PS3511.R258 D4, (v3)
  PS3511.R258 I7, (v3)
Frankel, Charles. B934.F7, (v8)
  QB603.G46.F73 1996, (v1)
  QE506.F7313 1999, (v1)
Frankel, Ernst G. GC1085.F75 1995, (v6)
Frankel, Felice. QC173.4.S94.F73 1997, (v1)
Frankel, Jonathan. DS135.S95.F728 1997, (v5)
Frankel, Max. PN4874.F615.T56 1999, (v3)
Frankel, Nicholas. PR5827.B58, (v3)
Frankel, Noralee. E185.93.M6.F73 1999, (v4)
Frankel, O. H. QK86.A1.F73 1995, (v1)
Frankfort, Henri. BL325.K5 F7 1978, (v8)
Frankfurter, Felix. JK271.F75, (v7)
Frankfurter, Felix. KF8745.F7P505, (v7)
Frank-Kamenetskii, D. A. QC718.F713, (v1)
Frank-Kamenetskii, M. D. QP624.F6913 1993, (v1)
Frankland, Graham. PN56.P92.F66 2000, (v3)
Franklin, Alexander. PR1260.F7, (v3)
Franklin, Allan. QC6.F673 1993, (v1)
Franklin, Benjamin. E302.F82 1959, (v4)
  E302.6.F7.A2 1986a, (v4)
  E302.6.F75.A12, (v4)
  PS749.A6 2000, (v3)
  QC516.F85 1941, (v1)
Franklin, Buck Colbert. KF373.F745.A3 1997, (v7)
Franklin, Caroline. PR4381.F7 2000, (v3)
  PR4392.H47.F7 1992, (v3)
Franklin, Daniel P. HJ2051.F73 1993, (v6)
  JK339.F73 1991, (v7)
Franklin, David Byrd. DA786.F73 1995, (v5)
Franklin, David. N6923.R597.F73 1994, (v9)
Franklin, Donna L. E185.86.F68 1997, (v4)
Franklin, Gene F. TJ223.M53F73 1998, (v1)
Franklin, H. Bruce. DS559.62.U6.F73 2000, (v5)
  UF533.F73 1988, (v10)
Franklin, J. Jeffrey. PR868.R4.F73 1999, (v3)
Franklin, Jimmie Lewis. E185.93.O4 F73 1982, (v4)
  F334.B653.A774 1989, (v4)
Franklin, John Hope. E447.F7 1999, (v4)
  E453.F8 1995, (v4)
  E668.F7 1994, (v4)
  F213.F76, (v4)
Franklin, Marc A. KF8719.F7, (v7)
Franklin, Peter. ML410.M23 F69 1997, (v9)
  ML410.M23 F7 1991, (v9)
Franklin, Stephen T. B1674.W354.F7 1990, (v8)
Franklyn, Julian. CR13.F7 1970, (v5)
Franko, Patrice M. HC125.F682 1999, (v6)
Franks, Don. PN2270.A93.F68 1996, (v3)
Franks, Felix. QD169.W3, (v1)
Franks, Jill. PR6023.A93.Z6289 1994, (v3)
Fransman, Martin. HC59.72.T4.F7 1986, (v6)
Frantz, Donald. PM2343.F7 1989, (v3)
Frantz, Joe Bertram. F596.F75, (v4)
Frantzen, Allen J. PR179.H66.F73 1998, (v3)
  PR1896.F7 1993, (v3)
Frantzich, Stephen E. HE8700.79.U6.F73 1996, (v6)
Franz, Uli. DS778.T39.F7313 1988, (v5)
Franzen, Trisha. HQ75.6.U5.F73 1996, (v6)
Franzese, Robert J. HD87.F715 2002, (v6)
Frappier, Jean. PQ1448.F713, (v3)
Frappier-Mazur, Lucienne. PQ2063.S3.F7313 1996, (v3)
Frascari, Marco. NA2500.F73 1990, (v9)
Fraser, Cary. F2131.F73 1994, (v4)
Fraser, D. A. QC611.F72 1986, (v1)
Fraser, David. DA69.3.A55.F7, (v5)
Fraser, G. S. PR471.F72 1965, (v3)
  PR6007.U76.Z65 1968b, (v3)
Fraser, Gertrude Jacinta. RG950.F7 1998, (v2)
Fraser, Gordon. QB991.B54.S45 1995, (v1)
  QC173.3.F73 2000, (v1)
  QC793.27.F7 1997, (v1)

Fraser, Hilary. PR468.A76.F73 1992, (v3)
Fraser, J. T. BD638.F68 1999, (v8)
  BD638.F69 1987, (v8)
  BD638.F7, (v8)
  QB209.F7 1982, (v1)
Fraser, James Howard. HF5843.F73 1991, (v6)
Fraser, James. NC998.6.J3.F73 1996, (v9)
Fraser, Nancy. JC578.F696 1997, (v7)
Fraser, Neil. PN2091.E4.F73 1999, (v3)
Fraser, P. M. DF234.2.F73 1996, (v5)
  DT73.A4 F7, (v5)
Fraser, Robert. PR9080.F73 2000, (v3)
Fraser, Robert. PR9379.9.A7.Z65, (v3)
Fraser, Russell A. PR502.F73 1999, (v3)
  PR2894.F66 1991, (v3)
  PR2903.F7 1988, (v3)
Fraser, Valerie. NA702.5.F73 2000, (v9)
  NA913.F73 1990, (v9)
Fraser, Walter J. F279.C457.F69 1989, (v4)
Fraser, Wayne. PR9188.F7 1991, (v3)
Frasier, David K. HV6245.F74 1996, (v6)
Frasier, David K. PN1998.3.M49.F7 1990, (v3)
Frawley, Maria H. PR4163.F73 1994, (v3)
Frayser, Suzanne G. GN484.3.F73 1985, (v6)
  Z7164.S42.F73 1995, (v10)
Frazer, Heather T. D810.C82.F73 1996, (v5)
Frazer, James George. BL310.F715 1936, (v8)
  BL310.F72 1951, (v8)
Frazer, John Francis Deryk. QP251.F7, (v1)
Frazer, Tim. K3856.F73 1988, (v7)
Frazier, Adrian Woods. PN2602.D82.A25 1990, (v3)
  PR5043.F57 2000, (v3)
Frazier, Claude Albee. RC965.M5.F73 1992, (v2)
Frazier, Kendrick. E99.P9 F74 1999, (v4)
Frazier, William J. QE651.F75 1987, (v1)
Freccero, Carla. PQ1697.F38.F7 1991, (v3)
Fredendall, Lawrence D. HD38.5.F738 2001, (v6)
Frederic, Harold. PS1705.A2 1977 vol. 1, (v3)
  PS1707.D3 1960, (v3)
Frederick, David C. KF8752 9th.F74 1994, (v7)
Frederick, Richard G. Z8386.2.F74 1992, (v10)
Frederick, William Crittenden. HD58.7.F735 1995, (v6)
Frederickson, Kari A. F216.2.F74 2001, (v4)
Fredman, Norman. RC488.5.F73 1987, (v2)
Fredricks, Nancy. PS2388.P6.F74 1995, (v3)
Fredriksen, John C. UG1240.F74 1999, (v10)
Freeberg, Ernest. HV1624.B7.F74 2001, (v6)
Freeborn, Richard. PG2951.F7, (v3)
Freed, Eugenie R. PR4148.W6.F74 1994, (v3)
Freed, Lynn. PR9369.3.F68.H6 1999, (v3)
Freed, Melvyn N. LB1028.27.U6 F74 2002, (v7)
  RC81.F865 1994, (v2)
Freedberg, David. N71.F65 1989, (v9)
Freedberg, S. J. ND615.F66 1971, (v9)
  ND615.F67, (v9)
Freedman, Alan. QA76.15.F732 1996, (v1)
Freedman, Benjamin. R725.5.F75 2000, (v2)
Freedman, Carl Howard. PN3433.5.F74 2000, (v3)
Freedman, David A. BF719.F74 1997, (v2)
Freedman, David Noel. BS1285.2.F74 2000, (v8)
Freedman, Estelle B. HV8978.V35.F74 1996, (v6)
  HV9466.F73, (v6)
Freedman, James O. LC1011.F72 1996, (v7)
Freedman, Jean R. D760.L7.F74 1999, (v5)
Freedman, Jonathan. E184.35.F74 2000, (v4)
Freedman, Jonathan. PS2127.A35.F74 1990, (v3)
Freedman, Lawrence. F3031.5.F74 1988, (v4)
  F3031.5.F75 1991, (v4)
  UB251.U5.F73, (v10)
Freedman, Leonard. ND1143.F69, (v9)
Freedman, Martin. KF3790.F74 1993, (v7)
Freedman, Paul H. PN682.P35.F74 1999, (v3)
Freedman, Richard. ML410.L3 F74 2000, (v9)
Freedman, Robert L. Z5118.F58.F73, (v10)
Freedman, Robert Owen. DS63.2.S65.F72 1991, (v5)
Freedman, Ronald. HB881.F76, (v6)
Freedman, Samuel G. LD7501.N525.F74 1990, (v7)

Freedman, Warren. KF3771.F74 1991, (v7)
KF3941.F74 1989, (v7)
KF4772.F74 1988, (v7)
KF9223.4.F74 1989, (v7)
Freedman, William. GV865.A1.F72 1998, (v6)
Freehling, William W. E384.3.F7, (v4)
E468.9.F84 1990, (v4)
E487.F83 2001, (v4)
Freeland, Chrystia. HC336.27.F744 2000, (v6)
Freeland, Cynthia A. PN1995.9.H6.F755 2000, (v3)
Freeland, Richard M. E813.F74 1985, (v4)
Freeland, Robert F. HD9710.U54.G397 2001, (v6)
Freeman, A. Myrick. HC79.E5.F7, (v6)
Freeman, Bud. ML419.F74 1989, (v9)
Freeman, Derek. GN671.S2.F73 1983, (v6)
Freeman, Douglas Southall. E312.F82, (v4)
E467.1.L4 F83, (v4)
E470.2.F7 1997, (v4)
Freeman, James M. E184.V53.F74 1989, (v4)
Freeman, Joan. QC16.F713.A3 1991, (v1)
Freeman, Judi. ND553.P5.A4 1994, (v9)
Freeman, Julia B. RM300.F72 1997, (v2)
Freeman, Laurence. BT202.F695 2000, (v8)
Freeman, Mark Philip. N71.F655 1993, (v9)
Freeman, Marsha. TL873.F74 2000, (v1)
Freeman, Mary Eleanor Wilkins. PS1710.A2 1971, (v3)
PS1711.R45 1997, (v3)
PS1712.N48 1920, (v3)
Freeman, Michael J. DD256.5.F73354 1987, (v5)
Freeman, Philip. DA931.F74 2001, (v5)
Freeman, Richard B. HD6278.U5.F73 1976, (v6)
Freeman, Roger L. TK5101.F6595 1999, (v1)
TK5102.5.F68 2002, (v1)
TK5103.F68 1996, (v1)
Freeman, Rosemary. PR2358.F7, (v3)
Freeman, Walter J. QP409.F73 2001, (v1)
Freeman, William Hardin. GV211.F73 2001, (v6)
Freeman, William. PR19.F7, (v3)
Freeman-Grenville, G. S. P. CE59.F7 1977, (v5)
G2446.S1.F73 1991, (v6)
Freemon, Frank R. E621.F84 1998, (v4)
Frega, Donnalee. PR3664.C43.F74 1998, (v3)
Frege, Gottlob. BC135.F6813 1964, (v8)
BC135.F7 1980, (v8)
QA3.F732513 1984, (v1)
QA9.F7514 1968, (v1)
Fregoso, Rosa Linda. PN1995.9.M49.F74 1993, (v3)
Frei, Hans W. BR118.F75 1992, (v8)
Frei, Norbert. DD256.5.F7335713 1993, (v5)
Freidel, Frank Burt. E715.F7, (v4)
E807.F75 1990, (v4)
F204.W5.W65 1994, (v4)
Z1236.F77 1974, (v10)
Freifeld, Alice. DB933.F74 2000, (v5)
Freije, Matthew R. RA644.L23.F74 1996, (v2)
Freilich, Morris. GN325.F7, (v6)
Freire, Paulo. LB880.F73.L43 1989, (v7)
LB880.F73.P76413 1998, (v7)
LB880.F732.P432 1994, (v7)
LC71.F7413 1997, (v7)
LC149.F76 1985, (v7)
Fremantle, Anne Jackson. B720.F7 1970, (v8)
Fremon, David K. F548.52.F74 1988, (v4)
Fremont, Jessie Benton. E415.9.F79.F74 1993, (v4)
E517.6.F87, (v4)
Fremont, John Charles. F592.F852, (v4)
F592.F8647, (v4)
E415.9.F8 F8 2001, (v4)
Fremont, Lily. F819.P9.F74 1997, (v4)
French, Benjamin B. E338.F74 1989, (v4)
French, David. D759.F76 2000, (v5)
DA576.F74 1995, (v5)
French, Hilary F. HC79.E5.F723 2000, (v6)
French, Joseph Lewis. PL3277.E3.F8, (v3)
French, Joseph Milton. PR3581.F7, (v3)
PR3581.F72, (v3)
French, Joyce N. LC4704.87.F74 1995, (v7)
French, Lois Angelina (Meredith). HV689.F7, (v6)
French, Lorely. PT811.F74 1996, (v3)
French, Marilyn. HQ1154.F744 1992, (v6)

French, Michael. HC106.5.F727 1997, (v6)
French, Peter A. BJ1490.F74 2001, (v8)
HD60.F74 1984, (v6)
PN1995.9.W4.F69 1997, (v3)
French, R. K. QP26.H3.F74 1994, (v1)
French, Rebecca Redwood. KNQ8708.F74 1995, (v7)
French, Robert Dudley. PR1905.F7 1947, (v3)
French, William E. HN120.S6.F74 1996, (v6)
Frend, W. H. C. BR132.F74 1996, (v8)
Freneau, Philip Morin. PS755.A2 1963, (v3)
Frere, Sheppard Sunderland. DA145.F8 1987, (v5)
Freris, Andrew F. HG187.H85.F74 1991, (v6)
Frese, Dolores Warwick. PR1875.T48.F74 1991, (v3)
Freshney, R. Ian. QH585.2.F74 2000, (v1)
Freston, Paul. BR1642.A357, (v8)
Freuchen, Peter. G743.F67, (v6)
Freud, Anna. BF173.F6173 1946, (v2)
BF721.F692, (v2)
Freud, Anna. BF721.F692 vol. 2, (v2)
Freud, Sigmund. BF109.F74.A25 1995, (v2)
BF109.F74.A4 1993b, (v2)
BF173.F625, (v2)
BF173.F6253, (v2)
BF173.F6255, (v2)
BF173.F626, (v2)
BF173.F6265 1986, (v2)
BF173.F627 1957a, (v2)
BF173.F62913 1970, (v2)
BF173.F62943, (v2)
BF173.F64 1936a, (v2)
BF173.F645 1961, (v2)
BF173.F65 1970, (v2)
BF173.F662 1975, (v2)
BF173.F673, (v2)
BF173.F678, (v2)
BF173.F682 1930, (v2)
BF173.F7 1966, (v2)
BF173.F76, (v2)
BF173.F825, (v2)
BF173.F85.A3 1952, (v2)
BF173.F85.A4 1985, (v2)
BF175.F77513 1990, (v2)
BF1078.F693, (v2)
BF1078.F72 1950, (v2)
BF1078.F773, (v2)
BL53.F67 1962, (v8)
BS580.M6.F7 1939, (v8)
ND623.L58.F88 1955, (v9)
RC343.F75, (v2)
RC506.F69713, (v2)
Freudenthal, Gad. B491.S8.F74 1995, (v8)
Freund, L. B. TA409.F77 1990, (v1)
Frevert, Ute. HQ1627.F69713 1989, (v6)
Frey, Charles H. PR2976.F664 1999, (v3)
Frey, Hans-Jost. PQ431.F7413 1996, (v3)
Frey, John Andrew. PQ2292.F73 1999, (v3)
Frey, Linda. KZ4078.F74 1999, (v7)
Frey, Linda. Z7961.F74 1982, (v10)
Frey, Richard L. GV1243.F85 1956, (v6)
Frey, Sylvia R. BR563.N4.F74 1998, (v8)
Freyd, Jennifer J. RJ506.C48.F74 1996, (v2)
Freymond, Jacques. DD801.S13.F74, (v5)
Freyre, Gilberto. F2510.F7519, (v4)
F2510.F7522 1956, (v4)
F2510.F754163 1970, (v4)
F2510.F7563, (v4)
Frick, Paul J. RJ506.C65.F75 1998, (v2)
Fricke, Thomas E. DS493.9.T35 F75 1994, (v5)
Frickhinger, Karl Albert. QE851.F89213 1995, (v1)
Friday, Chris. HD6515.C27.F75 1994, (v6)
Friday, Karl F. DS838.5.F75 1992, (v5)
Friday, Nancy. HQ1206.F72 1997, (v6)
Fridlund, Alan J. QP327.F75 1994, (v1)
Fried, Albert. E807.F77 1999, (v4)
Fried, Amy. E876.F78 1997, (v4)
Fried, Charles. BJ1012.F74, (v8)
Fried, Marc. HD8085.B63.F75, (v6)
Fried, Martha Nemes. GN473.F68 1980, (v6)
Fried, Michael. N6490.F727 1998, (v9)
ND553.C9.F74 1990, (v9)
ND553.M3.F75 1996, (v9)

Fried, Morton H. HN680.C55.F7 1969, (v6)
Fried, Richard M. E743.5.F67 1990, (v4)
Friedan, Betty. HQ1413.F75.A34 1976, (v6)
Friedberg, Aaron L. JC330.F74 2000, (v7)
Friedberg, Anne. PN1995.F743 1993, (v3)
Friedberg, Errol C. QH467.F748 1997, (v1)
Friedberg, Fred. RB150.F37.F753 1998, (v2)
Friedberg, Maurice. PN241.5.R8.F75 1997, (v3)
Friedberg, Ruth C. MT220.F83 1993, (v9)
Friedel, Helmut. ND237.H667.F7513 1998, (v9)
Friedel, Robert D. T19.F75 1994, (v1)
Friedelbaum, Stanley H. KF8748.F78 1994, (v7)
Frieden, Bernard J. HT175.F75 1989, (v6)
Frieden, Ken. PJ5129.A2.Z6725 1995, (v3)
Friedenreich, Kenneth. Z8550.4.F75, (v10)
Friedenthal, Jack H. KF8840.F72 1999, (v7)
Friederich, Werner Paul. PN871.F7, (v3)
Friedl, Vicki L. UB418.W65.F75 1996, (v10)
Friedlander, Albert H. D804.3.F74 1994, (v5)
Friedlander, Henry. DD256.5.F739 1995, (v5)
Friedlander, Judith. DS135.F83.F75 1990, (v5)
Friedlander, Max J. ND588.C8.A4 1978, (v9)
Friedlander, Michael W. QC485.F75 2000, (v1)
QC485.F75 1989, (v1)
Friedman, Alan F. RC473.M5.F75 1989, (v2)
Friedman, Albert B. PR507.F85 1961, (v3)
Friedman, Benjamin M. HJ257.2.F75 1988, (v6)
Friedman, Bruce Jay. PS3556.R5.A6, (v3)
Friedman, Daniel. HB131.F75 1994, (v6)
Friedman, David D. HB171.F767 1996, (v6)
HB171.F768 2000, (v6)
Friedman, David F. PN1998.3.F77.A3 1990, (v3)
Friedman, David. NA9053.N4.F75 1988, (v9)
Friedman, Edward. HN733.5.F75 1991, (v6)
Friedman, Gerald M. QE471.F73 1992, (v1)
Friedman, Isaiah. DS125.5.F73 1973b, (v5)
DS126.F76 2000, (v5)
Friedman, John Block. Z5933.F75 1998, (v10)
Friedman, Jonathan C. DS135.G4.F664 1998, (v5)
Friedman, Lawrence Jacob. E449.F86 1982, (v4)
RC445.K3.T626 1990, (v2)
Friedman, Lawrence Meir. KF352.F7 1985, (v7)
KF387.F74 1998, (v7)
KF9223.F75 1993, (v7)
Friedman, Lawrence S. PN1998.3.S39.F75 1997, (v3)
PR6013.O35.Z63 1993, (v3)
PS3565.Z5.Z65 1991, (v3)
Friedman, Leon. E185.61.F857, (v4)
Friedman, Marilyn. BD175.5.P65.F75 1995, (v8)
Friedman, Marilyn. BJ1533.F8.F75 1993, (v8)
Friedman, Maurice S. B3213.B84.F726 1991, (v8)
PN49.F665 1999, (v3)
PN761.F68, (v3)
Friedman, Meyer. R145.F75 1998, (v2)
Friedman, Michael. B808.5.F76 2000, (v8)
Friedman, Milton. HB119.A3.F75 1998, (v6)
HG538.F866, (v6)
Friedman, Murray. E185.61.F858 1995, (v4)
Friedman, Norman. V53.F754 2000, (v10)
VF346.F75 1991, (v10)
VM365.F76 1984, (v10)
Friedman, Raymond A. HD6971.5.F75 1994, (v6)
Friedman, Reena Sigman. HV983.F75 1994, (v6)
Friedman, Saul S. E185.S443.F75 1998, (v4)
Friedman, Susan Stanford. HQ1190.F77 1998, (v6)
PS3507.O726.Z65 1990, (v3)
Friedman, Susan W. D15.B596.F75 1996, (v5)
Friedman, William F. PR2937.F7, (v3)
Friedman, William J. BF468.F75 1990, (v2)
Friedman-Kasaba, Kathie. F128.9.A1.F75 1996, (v4)
Friedmann, Herbert. ND1432.E85.F74 1980, (v9)
Friedrich, Carl J. CB401.F7, (v5)
D246.F74 1952, (v5)
JC131.F7, (v7)
JK116.F7, (v7)
Friedrich, Hugo. PQ1643.F6913 1991, (v3)
Friedrich, Otto. DD219.M7.F75 1995, (v5)
ML417.G68.F7 1989, (v9)
Friedrich, Walter L. QE523.S27.F65 2000, (v1)
Friedrichs, David O. HV6768.F75 1996, (v6)

263

Friedwald, Will. ML420.S565 F78 1995, (v9)
ML3508.F74 1990, (v9)
Friel, Ian. VM17.F75 1995, (v10)
Friend, Julius Weis. DC423.F748 1998, (v5)
Frier, Bruce W. KJA2612.F75 1989, (v7)
Frier, John P. TK4399.F2.F74, (v1)
Fries, Heinrich. BX8.2.F6813 1985, (v8)
Frieseke, Frederick C. ND237.F75 (v9)
Friesel, Evyatar. G1030.F6513 1990, (v6)
Friesen, Gerald. F1062.F74 1984, (v4)
Frigon, Normand L. T57.37.F75 1997, (v1)
Frigyesi, Judit. ML410.B26 F75 1997, (v9)
Friis Johansen, K. B115.D36.F7513 1998, (v8)
Friis, Henning Kristian. DL30.F75 1950, (v5)
Friman, H. Richard. HV5801.F75 1996, (v6)
Frings, Theodor. PD700.F7, (v3)
Frisch, Hillel. DS119.7.F75 1998, (v5)
Frisch, Karl von. QL568.A6.F62 1971, (v1)
QL568.A6.F643, (v1)
Frisch, Max. PT2611.R814.A19 1974, (v3)
PT2611.R814H6x 1977, (v3)
PT2611.R814 M4613 1980, (v3)
PT2611.R814.T43, (v3)
Frisch, Michael H. F74.S8.F7 1972, (v4)
Frisch, Otto Robert. QC783.F7, (v1)
Frisch, Teresa Grace. N6310.F7, (v9)
Frisch, Walter. ML410.B8.F75 1996, (v9)
Frith, Simon. ML3534.F75 1988, (v9)
Frith, Simon. ML3790.F74, (v9)
Fritz, James S. (James Sherwood). QD101.2.F74
1987, (v1)
Fritz, Jean. PS858.W8.F7, (v3)
Fritze, Ronald H. E61.F75 1993, (v4)
G151.F75 1998, (v6)
Z6201.F72 1990, (v10)
Fritzer, Penelope Joan. PR4038.C6.F75 1997, (v3)
Fritzsche, Peter. DD238.F74 1998, (v5)
PN5219.B59.F75 1996, (v3)
Frobisher, Martin. QR41.F84 1968, (v1)
Frodin, D. G. Z5351.F76 2001, (v10)
Frodsham, J. D. DS740.4.F7185, (v5)
PL2665.H7.Z65, (v3)
Froehle, Bryan. BX1406.2.F74 2000, (v8)
Froelicher, Victor F. RC683.5.E94, (v2)
Frohn, Robert C. QH541.15.L35.F76 1998, (v1)
Frohnen, Bruce. JC176.B83.F76 1993, (v7)
Frohock, Fred M. R733.F79 1992, (v2)
RJ253.5.F76 1986, (v2)
Frohock, W. M. PQ2625.A716.Z65, (v3)
Frohock, Wilbur Merrill. PQ671.F7 1967a, (v3)
Froissart, Jean. D113.F77 1968, (v5)
Froman, Lewis A. BD438.F76 1992, (v8)
Frome, Michael. PN4888.E65.F76 1998, (v3)
SB482.A4.F76 1991, (v1)
Froment Meurice, Marc. PN49.F7313 1995, (v3)
Fromentin, Eugene. PQ2256.F5.D6 1972, (v3)
Fromkin, David. E744.F865 1995, (v4)
Fromm, Erich. BD450.F78 1968, (v8)
BD450.F7825, (v8)
BF173.F866413 1992, (v2)
BF204.F756 1994, (v2)
BF1078.F84, (v2)
BJ45.F7, (v8)
HM271.F74, (v6)
Fromm, Erika. RC495.F74 1997, (v2)
Fromm, Gary. HE193.F75, (v6)
Fromm, Gloria G. PR6035.I34.Z68, (v3)
Frost, Alan. DU172.P58.F76 1987, (v5)
Frost, David. F334.E84.F76 1995, (v4)
Frost, Frank J. DF77.F75 1980, (v5)
Frost, Ginger Suzanne. KD754.F76 1995, (v7)
Frost, Jack. F73.7.F76 2000, (v4)
Frost, Mervyn. JX1255.F76 1996, (v7)
Frost, Robert L. HD9685.F84.E52 1991, (v6)
Frost, Robert. PS3511.R94.A16 1966, (v3)
PS3511.R94.A6 1982, (v3)
PS3511.R94.I5, (v3)
PS3511.R94.M26, (v3)
PS3511.R94.M3, (v3)
PS3511.R94.N4 1924, (v3)
Frost, Wendy. Z6514.C97.F76 1988, (v10)

Frost, William. PR3424.F74 1988, (v3)
Frost-Knappman, Elizabeth. HQ1410.F76 1994, (v6)
K58.F76 1998, (v7)
KF220.F76 1997, (v7)
Froude, James Anthony. PR4433.F73 1970, (v3)
PR4433.F74 1970, (v3)
PR4433.F742 1979, (v3)
Froula, Christine. PR6019.O9.Z5334415 1996, (v3)
Frug, Gerald E. HT167.F78 1999, (v6)
Frug, Mary Joe. K349.F78 1992, (v7)
Fruge, August. Z473.U623.F78 1993, (v10)
Fruman, Norman. PR4484.F7, (v3)
HC103.F9 2000, (v6)
HC106.8.F78 1998, (v6)
Frushell, Richard C. PR2364.F73 1999, (v3)
Frutkin, Susan. PQ3949.C44.Z67 1973, (v3)
Fruzzetti, Lina. GN397.7.S73.F78 1990, (v6)
Fry, Brian R. JF1341.F78 1989, (v7)
Fry, C. H. QL696.C72.F79 1992, (v1)
Fry, Christopher. PR6011.R9.C8 1965, (v3)
PR6011.R9.D3, (v3)
PR6011.R9.F5 1958, (v3)
PR6011.R9.L2 1950, (v3)
PR6011.R9.S6, (v3)
PR6011.R9.T5 1949, (v3)
PR6011.R9.V4, (v3)
Fry, Dennis Butler. QP306.F8 1979, (v1)
Fry, Donald K. PR1585.F7, (v3)
Z2556.F78, (v10)
Fry, Edward F. N6537.S616.A4 1982, (v9)
Fry, Iris. QH325.F78 2000, (v1)
Fry, Michael. DA821.F79 1987, (v5)
Fry, Paul H. PR502.F78 1995, (v3)
Fry, Sara T. RT85.V4 2000, (v2)
Fryd, Vivien Green. N6535.W3.F78 1992, (v9)
Fryde, E. B. DA235.F79 1996, (v5)
Frye, David L. F1219.1.S22.F79 1996, (v4)
Frye, Northrop. F1021.2.F79 1982, (v4)
PN56.B5.F7, (v3)
PN56.R6.F7, (v3)
PN203.F7, (v3)
PN751.F7, (v3)
PR447.F7, (v3)
PR503.F7, (v3)
PR2981.F68 1983, (v3)
PR4146.F7, (v3)
PR4147.F7 1969, (v3)
Frye, Roland Mushat. PR2807.F79 1984, (v3)
PR3011.F7, (v3)
PR3562.F7 1972, (v3)
PR3592.A66.F78, (v3)
Frye, Timothy. HF5415.12.R9, (v6)
Fryer, Sarah Beebe. PS3511.I9.Z624 1988, (v3)
Fryklund, Richard. U162.F89, (v10)
Fryxell, Fritiof. F767.T29 F8, (v4)
Fryxell, John M. QL751.F878 1998, (v1)
Fu, Lo-shu. DS754.2.F8, (v5)
Fu, Poshek. DS796.S257.F8 1993, (v5)
Fuchida, Mitsuo. D774.M5.F812, (v5)
Fuchs, Adalbert. RE48.F8, (v2)
Fuchs, Anne. PN2986.J62.M374 1990, (v3)
Fuchs, Elinor. PN2193.E86.F83 1996, (v3)
Fuchs, Esther. BS1199.W7, (v8)
Fuchs, Hans U. QC311.F83 1996, (v1)
Fuchs, Jacob. PR3630.I53.F84 1989, (v3)
Fuchs, Lawrence H. BM627.F83 2000, (v8)
Fuchs, Stephan. BD175.F834 1992, (v8)
Fuderer, Laura Sue. Z2013.5.W6.F83 1990, (v10)
Fuegi, John. PT2603.R397.Z61928 1994, (v3)
Fuegi, John. PT2603.R397.Z6193, (v3)
Fuente, Angel de la. HB137.F83 2000, (v6)
Fuentes, Carlos. F1256.F8413 1996, (v4)
PQ7297.F793.M8, (v3)
PQ7297.F793.T413 1976, (v3)
Fuentes, Patricia de. F1230.F9, (v4)
Fugard, Athol. PR9369.3.F8.B4 1964, (v3)
PR9369.3.F8.L4 1981, (v3)
PR9369.3.F8.S5 1976, (v3)
PR9369.3.F8.S8, (v3)
Fugate, Bryan I. D764.F845 1997, (v5)
Fugita, Stephen. E184.J3.F78 1991, (v4)

Fuguitt, Glenn Victor. HB2385.F836 1989, (v6)
Fuhrmann, Horst. DD141.F8313 1986, (v5)
Fuhrmann, Manfred. DG260.C5.F8413 1992, (v5)
Fujii, James A. PL777.55.F85 1993, (v3)
Fujimura, Joan H. RC268.415.F84 1996, (v2)
Fujisawa, Chikao. B136.F83 1971, (v8)
Fujitani, Takashi. DS881.9.F847 1996, (v5)
Fujiwara Michitsuna no haha. PL789.F8.K313, (v3)
Fukasaku, Yukiko. VM301.M5.F85 1992, (v10)
Fukuda, Arihiro. DA413.F85 1997, (v5)
Fukuoka, Yasunori. DS832.7.K6.F817 2000, (v5)
Fukutake, Tadashi. HN727.F813 1972, (v6)
Fukuyama, Francis. HB72.F85 1995, (v6)
Fulbright, J. William. E744.F866, (v4)
E744.F9, (v4)
Fulbright, James William. UA23.F84, (v10)
Fulbrook, Mary. DD240.F85 1992, (v5)
Fulbrook, Mary. DD283.F85 1995, (v5)
Fuld, James J. ML113.F8 2000, (v9)
Fulford, Glenn. QA401.F94 1997, (v1)
Fulford, Tim. PR457.F85 1999, (v3)
Fulford, Tim. PR4487.R4.F85 1991, (v3)
Fulghum, Robert. BD431.F85 1988, (v8)
Fullbrook, Kate. PQ2603.E362.Z684 1994, (v3)
Fuller, C. J. BL1150.F85 1992, (v8)
Fuller, Errol. QL696.C42.F85 1999, (v1)
Fuller, George W. F851.F96 1976, (v4)
Fuller, J. F. C. D25.F935, (v5)
E672.F962 1991, (v4)
U39.F8, (v10)
U55.A45.F8 1960, (v10)
UG446.5.F78 1943, (v10)
Fuller, John. PN1514.F8, (v3)
PR6001.U4.Z69 1970, (v3)
PR6001.U4.Z694 1998, (v3)
Fuller, Kathryn H. PN1993.5.U6.F77 1996, (v3)
Fuller, Linda K. PN1992.77.C68.F84 1992, (v3)
Fuller, Linda. HD5660.C9.F85 1992, (v6)
HD8455.F85 1999, (v6)
Fuller, Lon L. K150.F84 1976, (v7)
Fuller, Margaret. D919.F963 1992, (v5)
F551.F86 1991, (v4)
PS2501.W3, (v3)
PS2502.S68 1992, (v3)
PS2506.A4 2001, (v3)
Fuller, Michael Anthony. PL1128.F85 1999, (v3)
Fuller, R. Buckminster. GA9.F85 1992, (v6)
Fuller, Robert C. TP557.F85 1996, (v1)
Fuller, Roy Broadbent. PR6011.U55.F3, (v3)
Fuller, Steve. BD175.F85 2002, (v8)
Q175.F927 2000, (v1)
Q175.5.F845 2000, (v1)
Fuller, Wayne Edison. HE6371.F84, (v6)
LB1567.F85 1994, (v7)
Fullerton, Brian. DL11.F84, (v5)
Fullerton, Mark D. N5630.F85 2000, (v9)
Fulmer, Robert M. HD30.4.F84 2001, (v6)
Fulmer, William E. HD6490.O72.U64 1982, (v6)
Fulton, A. R. PN1994.F83 1960, (v3)
Fulton, Ann. B944.E94 F85 1999, (v8)
Fulton, Joe B. PS1308.F85 2000, (v3)
Fulton, John F. QP31.F8 1955, (v1)
R154.C96.F8, (v2)
Fulton, John Farquhar. RD529.F85, (v2)
Fulton, William. QA612.F85 1995, (v1)
Fumerton, Richard A. BJ1012.F85 1990, (v8)
Fung, Edmund S. K. JQ1516.F86 2000, (v7)
Funigiello, Philip J. HF1413.5.F86 1988, (v6)
Funk, Arthur Layton. D762.S68.F86 1992, (v5)
Funston, Judith E. Z8447.F85 1991, (v10)
Fuoss, Donald E. GV346.F86, (v6)
Furbank, Philip Nicholas. PQ1979.F85 1992, (v3)
Z8221.O94 1998, (v10)
Furbish, David Jon. QE517.5.F87 1997, (v1)
Furci, Carmelo. JL2698.C5 F87 1984, (v7)
Furdell, Elizabeth Lane. DA437.W4.F87 1998, (v5)
Furedi, Frank. HB849.41.F87 1997, (v6)
HT1521.F84 1998, (v6)

Furet, Francois. DC138.F813, (v5)
  DC148.F8713 1992, (v5)
  HX40.F86513 1999, (v6)
Furia, Philip. ML423.G334.F87 1996, (v9)
Furley, David J. BD495.F87 1987, (v6)
Furlong, Monica. BV5077.E85.F87 1996, (v8)
Furlong, Patrick J. DT1924.F87 1991, (v5)
Furlough, Ellen. HD3334.F87 1991, (v6)
Furman, Andrew. PS153.J4.F86 2000, (v3)
  PS153.J4.F87 1997, (v3)
Furman, Erna. BF723.P4.F87 1992, (v2)
Furman, Frida Kerner. HQ1064.U5.F84 1997, (v6)
Furman, Jan. PS3563.O8749.Z65 1996, (v3)
Furman, Necah Stewart. QC792.8.U6.S264 1990, (v1)
Furnas, J. C. PR5493.F8, (v3)
Furness, Raymond. Z2230.C65 1997, (v10)
Furnham, Adrian. HD4905.F87 1990, (v6)
Furnish, Victor Paul. BS2675.2.F87 1999, (v8)
Furniss, Edgar Stephenson. UA23.F87, (v10)
Furon, Raymond. QE320.F813, (v1)
Furphy, Joseph. PR6011.U9 S9, (v3)
Furr, A. Keith. QD51.C73 2000, (v1)
Furst, Lilian R. PN98.R4.F87 1995, (v3)
  PQ2496.F87 1990, (v3)
Furstenberg, Frank F. HQ777.5.F87 1991, (v6)
Furtado, Celso. HC125.F78, (v6)
Furui, Yoshikichi. PL850.R74.A26 1997, (v3)
Furukawa, Yasu. QD381.F87 1998, (v1)
Fury, David. PN1995.9.T3.F87 1994, (v3)
Fusco, Marjorie. Z5814.D54 F78 2002, (v10)
Fusfeld, Herbert I. T175.F87 1994, (v1)
Fussell, Edwin S. PS2127.F7.F8 1990, (v3)
Fussell, Paul. D810.P7.U365 1989, (v5)
  PR478.E8.F8, (v3)
Fustel de Coulanges. JC51.F95 1980, (v7)
Futrell, Alison. GV35.F88 1997, (v6)
Futterman, Marilyn Suriani. PN1949.S7.F87 1992,
  (v3)
Fux, Johann Joseph. MT40.F83 1965, (v9)
Fyfe, John William. RV41.F8, (v2)
Fysh, Peter. DC369.F97 1998, (v5)
Gaard, Greta Claire. GE197.G33 1998, (v6)
Gabaccia, Donna R. DG453.G33 2000, (v5)
  Z7164.I3.G33 1989, (v10)
Gabba, Emilio. DG233.G33 1991, (v5)
Gabba, Emilio. DG254.G3132, (v5)
Gabbard, Carl. GV443.G15 1987, (v6)
Gabbard, Krin. ML2075.G33 1996, (v9)
Gabbedy, J. P. DU370.G33 1988, (v5)
Gabel, Stewart. RJ503.5.G33 1986, (v2)
Gabin, Nancy Felice. HD6079.2.U5.G33 1990, (v6)
Gabler, Edwin. HD5325.T252 1883, (v6)
Gabler, Neal. PN1995.9.S6.G23 1998, (v3)
Gabler-Hover, Janet. PS374.H27.G33 2000, (v3)
Gablik, Suzi. ND673.M35.G3 1970, (v9)
Gabor, Andrea. HD70.U5.G33 1999, (v6)
  HQ759.G3 1995, (v6)
Gabor, Dennis. T173.8.G3 1970, (v1)
Gabor, Thomas. HV6080.G28 1994, (v6)
Gabriel, H. Paul. HQ772.G24 1990, (v6)
Gabriel, J. Philip. PL838.H57.Z63 1999, (v3)
Gabriel, John. P94.5.M552.U634 1998, (v3)
Gabriel, Richard A. RC971.G33 1992, (v2)
  U22.3.G333 1988, (v10)
  U29.G23 1990, (v10)
  U29.G233 1991, (v10)
  U29.G234 2001, (v10)
  UA25.G26, (v10)
Gabriel, Yiannis. HD58.7.G334 2000, (v6)
Gabrieli, Francesco. DS38.G243 1961a, (v5)
Gadamer, Hans Georg. B29.G17 1982, (v8)
  B187.5.G3313 1998, (v8)
  B381.G3313 1991, (v8)
  B398.E8 G2913 1986, (v8)
  B3248.G33.H47 1999, (v8)
  B3248.G343.L6313 1998, (v8)
  BD241.G313 1989, (v8)
Gadd, Laurence. QL100.G28, (v1)
Gaddis, John Lewis. E183.8.S65.G33 1987, (v4)
  E183.8.S65 G34 1990, (v4)
  E183.8.S65.G345 1992, (v4)

E744.G24 1982, (v4)
E744.G25 2000, (v4)
Gaddis, William. PS3557.A28.R4 1955, (v3)
Gaddy, Clifford G. HC79.D4.G33 1996, (v6)
Gadon, Elinor W. BL473.5.G33 1989, (v3)
Gaeffke, Hans Peter Theodor. PK2038.G28, (v3)
Gaff, Alan D. E506.5 19th.G34 1996, (v4)
Gaff, Jerry G. LC985.G34 1991, (v7)
Gaffaney, Timothy J. HV95.G32 2000, (v6)
Gaffikin, Frank. DA990.U46.G32 1990, (v5)
Gaffurius, Franchinus. MT5.5.G2613 1993, (v9)
Gage, John D. QH91.8.B4.G34 1990, (v1)
Gage, N. L. LB1025.2.G29, (v7)
Gager, John B. BM535.G33 1983, (v8)
  BS2655.J4 G34 2000, (v8)
Gagiano, Annie. PR9340.5.G34 2000, (v3)
Gagliardo, John G. DD175.G34 1991, (v5)
Gagne, Cole. ML390.S6682 1993, (v9)
Gagne, Laurie Brands. BT83.55.G34 2000, (v8)
Gagne, Patricia. HV6626.2.G34 1998, (v6)
Gahart, Betty L. RM170.G33 2000, (v2)
Gahn, Bessie Wilmarth (Brown). F197.G25 1969, (v4)
Gailey, Christine Ward. GN671.T5.G35 1987, (v6)
Gailey, Harry A. D767.99.B68.G35 1991, (v5)
Gaillard, Anne-Marie. Z7164.I3.G35 1998, (v10)
Gaines, Barry. Z8545.5.G35 1990, (v10)
Gaines, Ernest J. PS3557.A33.B56 1976, (v3)
  PS3557.A355.A8, (v3)
Gaines, Kevin Kelly. E185.86.G35 1996, (v4)
Gaines, Thomas A. LB3223.3.G35 1991, (v7)
Gainor, J. Ellen. PR5368.W6.G3 1991, (v3)
Gais, Thomas. KF4920.G35 1996, (v7)
Gaita, Raimond. BJ1401.G35 1990, (v8)
Gaither, Carl C. QA273.G3124 1996, (v1)
Gaitskell, Hugh. D843.G26, (v5)
Gaius. KJA882.A34.A4 1988, (v7)
Gajowski, Evelyn. PR2983.G35 1991, (v3)
Gal, Allon. DS125.3.B37.G3513 1991, (v5)
Galamian, Ivan. MT260.G34 1985, (v9)
Galanter, Marc. KF300.G35 1991, (v7)
Galanti, Geri-Ann. RT86.54.G35 1997, (v2)
Galarza, Ernesto. HD6515.A292.C33, (v6)
Galassi, Peter. N6450.G23, (v9)
  ND553.C8.G245 1991, (v9)
  TR647.C36 1987, (v1)
Galasso, Francis S. TS695.G35 1991, (v1)
Galbraith, James K. HD4975.G28 1998, (v6)
Galbraith, John Kenneth. E183.8.I4.G3 1988, (v4)
  HB75.G27, (v6)
  HB75.G274 1987, (v6)
  HB119.G33 A25 2001, (v6)
  HB119.G33.A34, (v6)
  HB846.G35 1996, (v6)
  HC79.P6.G34, (v6)
  HC106.5.G32 1984, (v6)
  HC106.6.G344, (v6)
  HC106.6.G35 1978, (v6)
  HC106.8.G3394 1992, (v6)
  HD82.G2 1964a, (v6)
  HG4528.G35 1993, (v6)
Galbraith, John S. F1060.8.G3, (v4)
Galbraith, Stuart. PN1993.5.J3.G35 1996, (v3)
Galbraith, V. H. DA190.D7.G28, (v5)
Galbreath, C. B. F491.G13, (v4)
Galdorisi, George. KZA1146.U6.G35 1997, (v7)
Gale Research Company. PE1693.G3 1970, (v3)
  PN771.G27, (v3)
Gale, Bradley T. HF5415.157.G34 1994, (v6)
Gale, Fredric G. K290.G35 1994, (v7)
Gale, Richard M. B945.J24.G35 1999, (v8)
Gale, Robert L. E426.G147 1993, (v4)
  PS1880.G3 1991, (v3)
  PS2122.G35 1989, (v3)
  PS2133.A3 1999, (v3)
  PS2386.G3 1995, (v3)
  PS3511.I9.Z6247 1998, (v3)
  PS3515.A4347.Z459 2000, (v3)
Gale, Xin Liu. PE1404.G35 1996, (v3)
Gale, Zona. PS3513.A34 M5, (v3)
  PS3513.A34 Y4 1927, (v3)
Galeano, Eduardo H. GV942.5.G35 1998, (v6)

PQ8520.17.A4.L513 1991, (v3)
Galef, David. PR888.C47.G3 1993, (v3)
Galenson, Walter. HD6508.G275 1996, (v6)
Galeotti, Anna E. HM1271.G35 2002, (v6)
Galeotti, Mark. DS371.2.G3447 1995, (v5)
Galie, Peter J. KFN5681.G35 1996, (v7)
Galilei, Galileo. QB36.G2.A233, (v1)
  QB36.G2.A25 1957, (v1)
  QB41.G1356, (v1)
  QB41.G136 1953, (v1)
  QB41.G173 1997, (v1)
  QC123.G1153, (v1)
  QC123.G13 1991, (v1)
Galinsky, Karl. DG279.G17 1996, (v5)
Galkin, Elliott W. ML457.G3 1988, (v9)
Gall, Gilbert J. KF373.P65.G35 1999, (v7)
Gallagher, Catherine. PN81.G237 2000, (v3)
  PR113.G35 1994, (v3)
Gallagher, Gary W. E467.1.L4.G3 1998, (v4)
Gallagher, Jean. D640.A2.G35 1998, (v5)
Gallagher, John. HQ76.8.U5.G355 1996, (v6)
Gallagher, Matthew P. DK273.G3, (v5)
Gallagher, Sally K. HV1465.G36 1994, (v6)
Gallagher, Shaun. LB14.7.G35 1992, (v7)
Gallagher, Susan E. JC176.S63.G35 1998, (v7)
Gallagher, Susan V. PR9369.3.C58.Z66 1991, (v3)
Gallagher, Tag. PN1998.3.R67.G36 1998, (v3)
Gallagher, Tom. DP675.G34 1983, (v5)
  DR268.G35 1995, (v5)
Gallagher, Winifred. BF353.G355 1993, (v2)
Gallaher, John G. DC226.6.P362.G35 1993, (v5)
Galland, Leo. R733.G35 1997, (v2)
Gallant, Stephen I. QA76.87.G35 1993, (v1)
Gallant, Thomas W. DF105.G35 1991a, (v5)
Gallas, Karen. LB1139.L3.G34 1994, (v7)
Gallati, Barbara Dayer. ND237.C48.G36 1995, (v9)
Gallatin, Albert. E302.G16 1960, (v4)
Gallay, Alan. F289.B888.G35 1989, (v4)
Galle, Fred C. SB413.H7.G34 1997, (v1)
Gallegos, Romulo. PQ8549.G24 1958, (v3)
Gallicchio, Marc S. DS518.8.G33 1988, (v5)
  E185.61.G166 2000, (v4)
Gallick, Edward C. HD9581.U5.G23 1993, (v6)
Gallico, Paul. PS3513.A4 C58, (v3)
  PS3513.A4 F8, (v3)
  PS3513.A4 S6 1941, (v3)
  PS3513.A4 T7, (v3)
Galligan, Edward L. PN81.G24 1998, (v3)
Galliou, Patrick. DC611.B854.G35 1991, (v5)
Gallman, J. Matthew. F158.9.I6.G35 2000, (v4)
Gallo, Carmenza. HJ915.G35 1991, (v6)
Gallo, F. Alberto. ML290.2.G313 1995, (v9)
Gallo, Robert C. QR359.72.G35.A3 1991, (v1)
Gallois, Andre. BD236.G35 1998, (v8)
Gallop, Jane. PN98.W64.G34 1992, (v3)
Gallop, Rodney. DC611.B313.G3 1970, (v5)
Galloway, George B. JK1316.G2, (v7)
Galloway, J. H. HD9100.5.G29 1989, (v6)
Galloway, William Albert. F499.C4 G3, (v4)
Gallup, Alec. HN90.P8.G29 1999, (v6)
Gallup, Donald Clifford. PS3529.N5.Z6455 1998, (v3)
Galperin, William H. PR5888.G25 1989, (v3)
Galpin, Francis W. ML460.G14.T35 1976, (v9)
Galston, Miriam. B753.F34 G35 1990, (v8)
Galsworthy, John. PR6013.A5.A17 1934, (v3)
  PR6013.A5.A19 1928, (v3)
  PR6013.A5 C3 1923, (v3)
  PR6013.A5 C64, (v3)
  PR6013.A5 F5, (v3)
  PR6013.A5 F54, (v3)
  PR6013.A5 F56 1922, (v3)
  PR6013.A5 F7, (v3)
  PR6013.A5 F74 1915, (v3)
  PR6013.A5 G3 1967, (v3)
  PR6013.A5 J6, (v3)
  PR6013.A5 M3, (v3)
  PR6013.A5 M53 1929b, (v3)
  PR6013.A5 M69, (v3)
  PR6013.A5 O56 1930, (v3)
  PR6013.A5 O9 1933, (v3)
  PR6013.A5.R4 1924, (v3)

Galsworthy, John. (cont.)
  PR6013.A5 S3, (v3)
Galt, John. PR4708.G2 L3, (v3)
Galula, David. U240.G3, (v10)
Galvez, Manuel. PQ7797.G25.G3, (v3)
Galvin, Mary E. PS153.L46.G35 1999, (v3)
Galvin, Peter R. G535.G28 1999, (v6)
Gamber, Wendy. HD6054.4.U6.G355 1997, (v6)
Gamble, Andrew. HC256.6.G35 1994, (v6)
Gamble, Clive. GN740.G36 1994, (v6)
Gamble, Clive. GN772.2.A1.G38 1999, (v6)
Gamble, Harry Y. BR67.2.G35 1995, (v8)
Gamboa, Erasmo. HD1527.A19.G36 1990, (v6)
Gambone, Michael D. E183.8.N5.G36 1997, (v4)
Game, Ann. HM24.G284 1991, (v6)
Gamer, Michael. PR448.G6.G36 2000, (v3)
Gamm, Gerald H. F75.A1.G36 1999, (v4)
Gamow, George. Q162.G23 1988, (v1)
  QB521.G26, (v1)
  QC7.G26, (v1)
  QC171.G29, (v1)
  QC171.G3, (v1)
Gamqrelicze, T amaz. P572.G3613 1995, (v3)
Gamson, Joshua. PN1992.8.T3.G35 1998, (v3)
Gamson, William A. HN90.P8.G36 1992, (v6)
Gamwell, Lynn. RC443.G35 1995, (v2)
Gander, Eric. JC251.R59.G35 1998, (v7)
Gandhi, Rajmohan. DS436.G36 1999, (v5)
Gandhi. B133.G4.A3, (v8)
Gandolfo, Anita. PS153.C3.G36 1992, (v3)
Gandy, Oscar H. P94.5.M55.G36 1998, (v3)
Gane, Mike. HM22.F8.B383 1991, (v6)
Gangadean, Ashok K. BD331.G273 1998, (v8)
Gangi, William. KF4552.G36 1995, (v7)
Ganguly, Sumit. DS385.9.G36 1994, (v5)
  DS450.P18 G36 2001, (v5)
  DS485.K27.G37 1997, (v5)
Ganguly, Suranjan. PN1998.3.R4.G36 2000, (v3)
Ganim, Asad. DS113.7.G38 2001, (v5)
Ganivet, Angel. DP52.G29, (v5)
Ganly, John. HF5415.124.F7 1994, (v6)
Gann, Kyle. ML200.5.G36 1997, (v9)
Gann, Lewis H. DT1945.G35 1990, (v5)
Gannes, Arthur V. Z7514.B3 G36 2002, (v10)
Gannon, Linda. RG161.G35 1985, (v2)
Gannon, Michael. D781.G36 1990, (v5)
Gans, Chaim. JC328.3.G35 1992, (v7)
Gans, Eric Lawrence. BD450.G317 1990, (v8)
Gans, Herbert J. HC110.P6.G36 1995, (v6)
  HN80.L4.G3, (v6)
  JC571.G28 1988, (v7)
Ganshof, François Louis. JC111.G3213 1996, (v7)
Gansler, Jacques S. UA23.G36 1989, (v10)
Ganson, Eve. PS3513.A57D4 1928, (v3)
Gantenbein, James Watson. F1418.G2, (v4)
Gantzel, Klaus Jurgen. U21.2.G36413 2000, (v10)
Ganzl, Kurt. ML102.M88.G3 2001, (v9)
  ML1700.G322 1997, (v9)
Gao, Chunchang. E185.2.G36 2000, (v4)
Gao, Xingjian. PL2869.O128A24 2000, (v3)
  PL2869.O128L5613 2000, (v3)
Gao, Xiongya. PS3503.U198.Z68 2000, (v3)
Gapinski, James H. HC412.G34 1999, (v6)
Gaposchkin, Cecilia Helena Payne. QB801.G24, (v1)
  QB801.G25, (v1)
Gara, Larry. E432.G37 1991, (v4)
  E450.G22 1996, (v4)
Garafola, Lynn. GV1786.B355.G37 1989, (v6)
Garard, Charles. PR6056.O85.Z68 1991, (v3)
Garaudy, Roger. B809.8.G29913 1970b, (v8)
Garay, Ronald. Z7711.G37 1988, (v10)
Garb, Howard N. RC455.2.D42.G37 1998, (v2)
Garb, Tamar. N72.F45.G37 1994, (v9)
Garbarino, James. BF723.C57.G37 1989, (v2)
Garber, Daniel. B1875.G33 2001, (v8)
Garber, Linda. Z5866.L44.G37 1993, (v10)
Garber, Marjorie B. PR2989.G3, (v3)
  PR3069.D67.G3, (v3)
Garber, Nicholas J. TE145.G35 2002, (v1)
Garbowsky, Maryanne M. PS1541.Z5.G37 1989, (v3)
Garbuny, Max. QC401.G36, (v1)

Garceau, Dee. F767.S9.G36 1997, (v4)
Garceau, Oliver. R15.A55.G3 1961, (v2)
Garcés, Francisco Tomas Hermenegildo. F786.G21, (v4)
Garcia Canclini, Nestor. F1414.2.G36513 1995, (v4)
Garcia Gutierrez, Antonio. PQ6523.G2835.T7 1984, (v3)
Garcia Lorca, Federico. PQ6613.A763.A17 1988 vol. 1, (v3)
  PQ6613.A763.A213 1988, (v3)
  PQ6613.A763.A226 1987, (v3)
  PQ6613.A763.A257 1937, (v3)
  PQ6613.A763.A258 1980, (v3)
  PQ6613.A763.A275, (v3)
  PQ6613.A763.A6 1989, (v3)
  PQ6613.A763A225 2001, (v3)
  PQ6613.A763 1997, (v3)
Garcia Mainar, Luis M. PN1998.3.K83.G37 1999, (v3)
Garcia Marquez, Gabriel. F3100.G37513 1987, (v4)
  PQ8180.17.A73.G413 1990, (v3)
  PQ8180.17.A73A27 1984, (v3)
  PQ8180.17.A73A813 1997, (v3)
  PQ8180.17.A73C513 1998, (v3)
  PQ8180.17.A73C6813 1983, (v3)
Garcia Pinto, Magdalena. PQ7081.G3613 1991, (v3)
Garcia, Alfredo. KF9625.Z9.G37 1992, (v7)
Garcia, Eugene E. LC2669.G37 2001, (v7)
Garcia, G. G. HG2562.L6.G37 1988, (v6)
Garcia, Juan R. F358.2.M5.G37 1996, (v4)
Garcia, Maria Cristina. F320.C97.G37 1996, (v4)
Garcia, Mario T. F394.E4.G36, (v4)
  HD8073.C67.G37 1994, (v6)
Garcia, Nasario. PS283.N6.G37 2000, (v3)
Garcia-Marquez, Vicente. GV1785.M35.G37 1995, (v6)
Garcia-Perez, Gladys Marel. F1787.5.G37 1998, (v4)
Gard, Roger. PR4037.G37 1992, (v3)
Gard, Wayne. F591.G215, (v4)
  F596.G3, (v4)
Gardaphe, Fred L. PS153.I8.G37 1996, (v3)
Gardella, Robert Paul. HD9198.C52.F854 1994, (v6)
Gärdenfors, Peter. Q335.G358 2000, (v1)
  B820.3.G37 1988, (v8)
Gardiner, A. QA43.G345 1997, (v1)
  QA43.G346 1997, (v1)
Gardiner, Alan Henderson. PJ1135.G3 1957, (v3)
Gardiner, Eileen. Z7794.G37 1993, (v10)
Gardiner, H. Norman. BF511.G3 1970, (v2)
Gardiner, Leslie. VB57.G36, (v10)
Gardiner, William C. QD501.G323, (v1)
Gardner, Albert Ten Eyck. NB210.G3 1968, (v9)
  ND237.H7.G3, (v9)
Gardner, Averil. PR6045.I577.Z67 1985, (v3)
Gardner, Carol Brooks. HQ1237.5.U6.G37 1995, (v6)
Gardner, E. Clinton. BJ1275.G35 1995, (v8)
Gardner, Hall. UA646.G38 1997, (v10)
Gardner, Helen Louise. PN85.G33, (v3)
  PR2248.G25, (v3)
Gardner, Helen. N5300.G25 1980, (v9)
Gardner, Howard. B841.4.G37 1981, (v8)
  BF408.G33 1993, (v2)
  BF412.G27 1997, (v2)
  BF432.3.G378 1999, (v2)
  LB885.G37.W45 1999, (v7)
  LB1060.G357 1993, (v7)
  LB1062.G36 1991, (v7)
Gardner, Isabella. PS3513.A6335.A17 1990, (v3)
Gardner, J. Anthony. Z3366.G36 1989, (v10)
Gardner, J. W. TK7872.T6.G37 1994, (v1)
Gardner, James L. Z7864.Z4 G37 1991, (v10)
Gardner, Jared. PS208.G37 1998, (v3)
Gardner, John William. JC330.3.G37 1990, (v7)
Gardner, John. PR201.G37, (v3)
  PS3557.A712.N55 1981, (v3)
  PS3557.A712.O28, (v3)
  PS3557.A712.S8, (v3)
Gardner, Joseph Lawrence. E757.G29, (v4)
Gardner, Katy. HN690.6.A8.G37 1995, (v6)
Gardner, Lloyd C. D749.G37 1993, (v5)
  E744.G3425 1984, (v4)
Gardner, Martin. B29.G253 1983, (v8)

Q173.G34 2000, (v1)
QA95.G24, (v1)
QA95.G255 1997, (v1)
QA95.G3, (v1)
QA95.G32, (v1)
QA95.G3325 1996, (v1)
QC173.G34 1979, (v1)
Gardner, Philip. PR6001.M6.Z67 (v3)
  PR6011.O58.Z657, (v3)
Gardner, Sheldon. BF108.A92.G37 1992, (v2)
Gardner, Stanley. PR4144.S63.G37 1998, (v3)
Gardner, W. J. R. D770.G37 1999, (v5)
Garebian, Keith. PR5368.S75.G37 1993, (v3)
Gareev, M. A. U21.2.G36513 1998, (v10)
Garfield, James A. E470.G2, (v4)
  E660.G217, (v4)
Garfield, Simon. TP140.P46, (v1)
Garfield, Viola Edmundson. PM101.A5 vol. 18, (v3)
Garfinkle, Adam M. DS126.5.G357 1997, (v5)
Garfinkle, Norton. E459.G33, (v4)
Garfinkle, Robert A. QB65.G37 1994, (v1)
Gargan, Edward T. CB63.T68.G3, (v5)
Garian, Yvon. U33.G3513, (v10)
Garland, Carl W. QD457.G37 2002, (v1)
Garland, Hamlin. E78.W5.G37 1976, (v4)
  PS1732.B7, (v3)
  PS1732.M3 1970, (v3)
  PS1732.P73 1969, (v3)
  PS1732.R6 1969, (v3)
  PS1732.T48 1916, (v3)
  PS1732.T68, (v3)
  PS1733.A38 1974, (v3)
  PS1733.A42, (v3)
  PS1733.A425 1928, (v3)
  PS1733.A47 1931, (v3)
  PS1733.A47 1995, (v3)
  PS1733.A483 1934, (v3)
  PS1733.A483 1934, (v3)
Garland, Henry B. PT41.G3 1997, (v3)
  PT1863.Z7.G34, (v3)
  PT2406.G3 1963, (v3)
  PT2482.G3, (v3)
Garland, J. D. TK260.G37 1998, (v1)
Garland, Lynda. DF572.8.E5.G37 1999, (v5)
Garland, Robert. DF78.G28 1990, (v5)
  DF287.P4.G37 1987, (v5)
Garlinski, Jozef. D802.P62.W3369 1991, (v5)
Garman, Bryan K. ML3477.G36 2000, (v9)
Garner, Bryan A. KF156.G367 1995, (v7)
  PE2827.G37 1998, (v3)
Garner, Diane L. Z7164.G7.G37 1993, (v10)
Garner, Richard L. HC134.G37 1993, (v6)
Garner, Richard. BJ1031.G376 1994, (v8)
Garner, Roberta. Z7164.S66.G38 1997, (v10)
Garner, Ross. PR3743.G3, (v3)
Garner, Stanton B. PN2039.G37 1994, (v3)
Garner, Stanton. PS2384.B3.G37 1993, (v3)
Garner, William Robert. F864.G236, (v4)
Garnett, David. PR6013.A66 B4, (v3)
  PR6013.A66Z52 1954, (v3)
Garnett, Robert Reginald. PR6045.A97.Z687 1990, (v3)
Garnier, Rowan. QA9.54.G367 1996, (v1)
Garnier, Tony. NA2707.G37.A4 1951, (v9)
Garnsey, Peter. DG276.G36 1987, (v5)
Garofalo, Charles. JF1525.E8.G37 1999, (v7)
Garrard, John Gordon. PG3337.L46.G3 1982, (v3)
Garrard, Mary D. ND623.G364.G368 2001, (v9)
Garrard, Mary D. ND623.G364.G37 1989, (v9)
Garraty, John Arthur. HD5706.G33 1978, (v6)
Garraway, Michael O. QK601.G27 1984, (v1)
Garret, Maxwell R. GV1147.G36 1994, (v6)
Garrett, Alfred Benjamin. Q125.G38, (v1)
Garrett, Catherine. RC552.A5.G375 1998, (v2)
Garrett, Charles Geoffrey Blythe. QC753.G36, (v1)
Garrett, Charles. F128.5.G25, (v4)
Garrett, Donald E. TN919.G3 1995, (v1)
Garrett, George P. PS3557.A72.D4, (v3)
  PS3557.A72.M3x, (v3)

Garrett, Laurie. RA441.G37 2001, (v2)
  RA644.A25G386 1996, (v2)
  RA651.G37 1994, (v2)
Garrett, Marc A. E508.G37 1996, (v4)
Garrett, Mark. HE206.2.G37 1996, (v6)
Garrett, Stephen A. D744.4.G35 1996, (v5)
  D786.G36 1993, (v5)
Garrett, Valery M. GT1555.G36 1994, (v6)
Garrick, David. PR3465.A5.P4 1980, (v3)
Garrick, James G. RD97.G373 1999, (v2)
Garrison, Fielding H. R131.G3 1929, (v2)
Garrison, George Pierce. E338.G35 1969, (v4)
Garrison, J. Ritchie. F72.F8.G37 1991, (v4)
Garrison, Myrtle. F864.G24, (v4)
Garrison, Sharon Hatten. HG4026.G37 1988, (v6)
Garrison, Stephen. Z8969.2.G37 1990, (v10)
Garrison, William Lloyd. E449.G245, (v4)
Garrison, William T. RJ380.G37 1989, (v2)
Garrisson, Janine. DC33.3.G36 1995, (v5)
Garro, Elena. PQ7297.G3585.A28 1997, (v3)
Garrow, David J. E185.97.K5.G37 1981, (v4)
  JK1929.A2.G37, (v7)
  KF3771.G37 1994, (v7)
Garry, Patrick M. JA84.U5.G29 1992, (v7)
  KF4774.G373 1994, (v7)
  Z658.U5.G37 1993, (v10)
Garside, W. R. HD5765.A6.G367 1990, (v6)
Gart, Alan. HG181.G358 1989, (v6)
  HG181.G367 1988, (v6)
Garten, Helen A. KF974.G369 2001, (v7)
Garthoff, Raymond L. DS740.5.R8.G3, (v5)
  E183.8.S65.G38 1994, (v4)
  U43.R9.G3, (v10)
  UA770.G28 1990, (v10)
  UA770.G29, (v10)
  UA770.G3, (v10)
Gartner, Leslie P. QM695.F32G37 1999, (v1)
Gartner, Lloyd P. DS124.G37 2001, (v5)
Gartner, Richard B. RC569.5.A28.G37 1999, (v2)
Garton Ash, Timothy. D2009.G37 1999, (v5)
  DD290.25.G37 1993, (v5)
  DJK50.G35 1990, (v5)
Garubo, Raymond C. LB2806.4.G37 1998, (v7)
Garver, Eugene. JC143.M3946.G37 1987, (v7)
Garver, John W. DS740.5.S65.G37 1988, (v5)
  E183.8.C5.G38 1997, (v4)
Garvey, Ellen Gruber. PS374.S5.G34 1996, (v3)
Garvin, Alexander. NA9105.G37 1996, (v9)
Garvin, David A. HD58.82.G37 2000, (v6)
Garvin, Tom. DA951.G37 1988, (v5)
  DA963.G37 1996, (v5)
Gary, Romain. PQ2613.A58.R213, (v3)
Gary, Romain. PQ2613.A58.R3, (v3)
  PQ2613.A58.Z47413 1961, (v3)
Garza-Falcon, Leticia. PS153.M4.G37 1998, (v3)
Gasche, Rodolphe. PN75.D45.G37 1998, (v3)
Gaschnitz, K. Michael. GV581.G37 1997, (v6)
Gascoigne, Bamber. DA27.5.G37 1993, (v5)
Gascoigne, George. PR2277.A25 1969, (v3)
Gascoigne, John. DA690.C2.G37 1989, (v5)
Gash, Norman. DA522.L7.G37 1984, (v5)
  DA535.G37, (v5)
  DA536.P3.G3, (v5)
  DA559.7.G35, (v5)
Gasiorowicz, Stephen. QC721.G353, (v1)
Gaskell, Elizabeth Cleghorn. PR4710.C7 1934, (v3)
  PR4710.M21 1911, (v3)
  PR4710.M37 1970, (v3)
  PR4710.N6 1927, (v3)
  PR4710.N67, (v3)
  PR4710.W5 1969, (v3)
  PR4711.A4 2000, (v3)
Gaskell, Philip. DA890.M87.G3, (v5)
  PN701.G37 1999, (v3)
  PR6019.O9.U645 1989, (v3)
  Z116.A2.G27 1974, (v10)
Gaskell, Ronald. PN1851.G25, (v3)
Gaskill, Malcolm. HV6949.E5.G37 2000, (v6)
Gaspar de Alba, Alicia. N6538.M4 G37 1998, (v9)
Gasparrini, Claudia. TN411.G37 1993, (v1)
Gasperetti, David Wayne. PG3095.G37 1998, (v3)

Gass, Patrick. F592.5.G2 1904, (v4)
Gass, William H. PN45.5.G355 1996, (v3)
  PS3557.A845 I5 1968, (v3)
  PS3557.A845.O5, (v3)
  PT2635.I65.Z72 1999, (v3)
Gassier, Pierre. ND813.G7.G324, (v9)
Gassmann, Günther. BX8007.G37 2001, (v8)
Gassner, John. PN1655.G3, (v3)
  PN1851.G3, (v3)
Gasster, Michael. DS773.G35, (v5)
Gaster, Theodor Herzl. BL96.G3 1961, (v8)
Gastil, Raymond D. E169.02.G32, (v4)
Gaston, Anne-Marie. GV1796.B4.G38 1996, (v6)
Gaston, Georg. PR6013.R44.Z6334 1984, (v3)
Gaston, Patricia Sullivan. PR5341.G33 1991, (v3)
Gaston, Paul M. F209.G3, (v4)
Gastrow, Shelagh. DT1774.G37 1990, (v5)
Gastwirth, Joseph L. KF8968.75.G37 1988, (v7)
Gat, Azar. U39.G38 1989, (v10)
Gat, Moshe. DA47.9.I8.G38 1996, (v5)
  DS135.I7.G37 1997, (v5)
Gatchel, Theodore Dodge. F199.G26, (v4)
Gates, Bill. HD30.37.G38 1999, (v6)
Gates, Bruce C. QD505.G38 1991, (v1)
Gates, David Murray. QH545.T4.G38 1993, (v1)
Gates, David. UA646.3.G32 1992, (v10)
Gates, Grace Hooten. F334.A6.G37, (v4)
Gates, Henry Louis. E185.86.G374 1997, (v4)
  PS153.N5.G28 1988, (v3)
Gates, Hill. DS799.812.G38 1987, (v5)
Gates, Joanne E. PS2719.R4.Z65 1994, (v3)
Gates, John Boatner. KF8742.G285 1991, (v7)
Gates, Lillian F. F1032.M14.G38 1988, (v4)
  HD319.O5.G37, (v6)
Gates, Paul Wallace. HC105.6.G3, (v6)
  HD211.K2G3, (v6)
Gates, Robert Allan. PS438.G37 1999, (v3)
Gatewood, Willard B. E185.86.G38 1990, (v4)
Gathorne-Hardy, Geoffrey Malcolm. D720.G3 1950, (v5)
Gati, Charles. DJK45.S65.G37 1990, (v5)
Gatrell, Anthony C. RA792.G38 2002, (v2)
Gatrell, Simon. PR4757.P6.G37 1993, (v3)
Gatrell, V. A. C. HV8699.G8.G38 1994, (v6)
Gatta, John. PS217.M35.G38 1997, (v3)
Gatten, Jeffrey N. ML128.R6.G37 1995, (v9)
Gatti, Paolo L. TA654.G34 1999, (v1)
Gattiker, Urs E. HD45.G36 1990, (v6)
Gatto, John Taylor. LA217.2.G39 2000, (v7)
Gaubatz, Kathlyn Taylor. HV9950.G38 1995, (v6)
Gaubatz, Piper Rae. HT384.C6.G38 1996, (v6)
Gauchet, Marcel. RC439.G2813 1999, (v2)
Gauci, Perry. JS3425.G744.G38 1996, (v7)
Gaudi, Antoni. NA1313.G3.J4, (v9)
Gaudi, Antoni. NA1313.G3.M273, (v9)
Gauguin, Paul. ND553.G27.A4813 1978, (v9)
Gauld, Alan. BF1125.G38 1992, (v2)
Gaull, Marilyn. PR590.G38 1988, (v3)
Gaulle, Charles de. D843.G2813 1971b, (v5)
  DC373.G3.A25, (v5)
  U21.2.G3813 1975, (v10)
  UA700.G32 1941, (v10)
Gauna, Max. PQ639.G38 1992, (v3)
Gaunt, Peter. DA426.G38 1996, (v5)
Gaunt, Philip. PN4785.G38 1992, (v3)
Gaunt, William. ND467.G3 1966, (v9)
Gauntlett, David. PN1992.55.G38 1999, (v3)
Gaus, Gerald F. BD232.G38 1990, (v8)
  JA71.G28 2000, (v7)
Gauthier, David P. BJ21.G38, (v8)
Gautier, Theophile. PQ2258.E4 1927, (v3)
  PQ2258.G4, (v3)
Gavaghan, Helen. TL796.G38 1998, (v1)
Gavin, Christy. Z1231.D7.G38 1993, (v10)
Gavin, James M. UA23.G53, (v10)
Gavin, Lettie. D639.W7.G38 1997, (v5)
Gavin, Robin Farwell. NK835.N5 G38 1994, (v9)
Gavins, Raymond. F234.R53.H363, (v4)
Gavora, Jessica. GV709.18.U6 G38 2002, (v6)
Gaxotte, Pierre. DD404.G32 1942, (v5)
Gay, John. PR3473.A1 1975, (v3)

  PR3473.A4 1983, (v3)
  PR3474.B8, (v3)
Gay, Kathlyn. GT2853.U5.G39 1996, (v6)
  HX830.G39 1999, (v6)
  QH541.5.R27G39 2001, (v1)
  RA778.G39 2002, (v2)
Gay, L. R. LB3051.G34, (v7)
Gay, Martin. ZA3225.G39 1996, (v10)
Gay, Penny. PR2991.G38 1994, (v3)
Gay, Peter. BF109.F74.G39 1988, (v2)
  D6.G35, (v5)
  DD239.G38, (v5)
  PQ2131.G3, (v3)
Gay, Ruth. DS135.G3.G32 1992, (v5)
  F128.9.J5.G39 1996, (v4)
Gay, William. JN6692.G39 1996, (v7)
Gaylord, Edwin Henry. TA635.G3 1979, (v1)
Gaynor, Alan K. LB2805.G338 1998, (v7)
Gaynor, Frank. U24.G34, (v10)
Gaythwaite, John. TC1645.G39, (v1)
Gazzaniga, Michael S. QP360.G38, (v1)
Geach, P. T. BC50.G4 1956, (v8)
  BC71.G34 1980, (v8)
Geanakoplos, Deno John. DF635.G4, (v5)
Gear, C. William. QA372.G4, (v1)
Gearson, John P. S. DA566.9.M33.G4 1998, (v5)
Geary, David C. QP81.5.G43 1998, (v1)
Geary, Dick. HD8376.G4 1981, (v6)
Geary, James W. E491.G42 1991, (v4)
Geary, Patrick, J. DC65.G43 1988, (v5)
Gebby, Margaret Dow. F499.B4.G43 1990, (v4)
Gebhard, David. NA730.I8.G43 1993, (v9)
  NA737.S625.G43 1993, (v9)
Gedalge, Andre. MT59.G4.T75, (v9)
Geddes, Barbara. JL958.G44 1994, (v7)
Geddes, C. L. Z7835.M6 A54 no. 9, (v10)
Geddes, K. O. QA155.7.E4.G43 1992, (v1)
Geddes, Patrick. NA9030.G4 1968b, (v9)
Gedicks, Al. E99.C6.G44 1993, (v4)
Gedicks, Frederick Mark. KF4865.G43 1995, (v7)
Gedmin, Jeffrey. DD289.G44 1992, (v5)
Gedo, John E. RC503.G433 1999, (v2)
Gee, Henry. QE721.2.S7.G44 1999, (v1)
Gee, Henry. QL607.5.G44 1996, (v1)
Geehr, Richard S. DB844.L8.G44 1990, (v5)
Geelhoed, E. Bruce. UA23.6.G43, (v10)
Geer, J. P. van de. QA278.G433 1993, (v1)
Geertz, Armin W. E99.H7.G446 1994, (v4)
Geertz, Clifford. GN307.7.G44 1988, (v6)
  GN315.G36, (v6)
  HN710.M6.G4 1975, (v6)
Gehl, Jurgen. DB48.G4 1963, (v5)
Gehlbach, Stephen H. R118.6.G43 2002, (v2)
Gehring, Wes D. PN1995.9.C55.G427 1997, (v3)
Gehry, Frank O. NA737.G44.A4 1985, (v9)
Geier, Gabriele. HV696.F6.G3813 1995, (v6)
Geiger, George Raymond. B945.D44.G4, (v8)
Geiger, H. Kent. HQ637.G37, (v6)
Geiger, Randall L. TK7874.G43 1990, (v1)
Geiger, Reed G. HE443.G45 1994, (v6)
Geiringer, Karl. ML410.B8 G42 1982, (v9)
  ML410.H4 G4 1982, (v9)
Geis, Gilbert. HV6635.G35 1977, (v6)
  KD371.W56.G45 1997, (v7)
  KF220.G45 1998, (v7)
Geis, Michael L. P95.55.G38 1995, (v3)
Geisler, Norman L. BT1102.G42 1999, (v8)
Geiss, Imanuel. D505.G2713 1968, (v5)
Geisst, Charles R. HG4910.G44 1992, (v6)
Geist, Johann Friedrich. NA6218.G4313 1983, (v9)
Geiter, Mary K. F152.2.G42 2000, (v4)
Gelb, Joyce. HQ1236.G45 1989, (v6)
Gelbaum, Bernard R. QA300.G42 1995, (v1)
Gelber, Yoav. DS119.7.G389 1997, (v5)
Gelbspan, Ross. QC981.8.G56.G45 1998, (v1)
Gelder, G. J. H. van. PJ7519.F6G35 2000, (v3)
Gelderen, C. J. van. SB413.M365.G45 1999, (v1)
Gelderen, Martin van. DH186.5.G37 1992, (v5)
Gelderman, Carol W. E176.1.G35 1997, (v4)
Geldzahler, Henry. ND212.G36, (v9)
Gelfand, I. M. QA533.G45 2001, (v1)

Gelfand, Stanley A. RF290.E73 2001, (v2)
Gelis, Jacques. GT2465.F8.G44 1991, (v6)
Gell, Alfred. GN670.G35 1993, (v6)
Gella, Aleksander. HN380.Z9.S6434 1989, (v6)
Gelles, Edith Belle. E322.1.A38.G44 1998, (v4)
   E322.1.A38.G45 1995, (v4)
Gelles, Richard J. HQ536.G44 1974, (v6)
Gellhorn, Ernst. QP361.G43, (v1)
Gellhorn, Martha. PS3513.E46.Z475, (v3)
Gelling, Margaret. DA670.M64.G45 1992, (v5)
Gellman, Estelle S. LB3051.G365 1995, (v7)
Gell-Mann, Murray. QC774.G45.A3 1994, (v1)
Gellner, Ernest. BP173.25.G44, (v8)
   D16.8.G413 1989, (v5)
   HM24.G425 1992, (v5)
   JA76.G38 1987, (v7)
   JC336.G45 1994, (v7)
Gellrich, Jesse M. PR275.O72.G45 1995, (v3)
   Z6.G44 1985, (v10)
Gellrich, Michelle. PN1892.G38 1988, (v3)
Gelm, Richard J. BX1407.P63.G45 1994, (v8)
Gelman, Charles. DS135.R93.K7954 1989, (v5)
Gelman, Sheldon. RC514.G44 1999, (v2)
Gelpi, Albert. PR6007.A95.Z68 1998, (v3)
Gelven, Michael. U21.2.G44 1994, (v10)
Gelvin, James L. DS98.G45 1998, (v5)
Gelzer, Matthias. DG83.3.G413 1969b, (v5)
Gemelli, Ralph J. BF721.G4652 1996, (v2)
Gemie, Sharif. LC2092.G46 1995, (v7)
Gemmett, Robert J. PR4092.G4, (v3)
Genet, Jean. PQ2613.E53.M53, (v3)
   PQ2613.E53 N62 1963, (v3)
   PQ2613.E53.P33 1962, (v3)
Genette, Gerard. BH202.G4713 1999, (v8)
   PQ2631.R63.A791713, (v3)
Genini, Ronald. PN2287.B178.G46 1996, (v3)
Gennaro, Rocco J. BJ1469.G46 2002, (v8)
Gennep, Arnold van. GN473.G513 1960a, (v6)
Gennes, Pierre-Gilles de. QC171.2.G4613 1996, (v1)
Genovese, Eugene D. E441.G4, (v4)
   E441.G42 1989, (v4)
   E449.G3724 1998, (v4)
   E449.G3725 1991, (v4)
   F209.5.G46 1994, (v4)
Genovese, Michael A. JK516.G49 2001, (v7)
Genscher, Hans Dietrich. DD260.65.G47.A3 1998, (v5)
Gensler, Harry J. BC135.G39 1990, (v8)
   BJ1012.G44 1996, (v8)
Gentile, Emilio. DG571.G3913 1996, (v5)
Gentili, Bruno. PA3093.G4613 1988, (v3)
Gentles, I. J. DA405.G46 1991, (v5)
Gentry, Curt. HV7911.H6.G46 1991, (v6)
Gentry, Roger L. QL737.P63.G45 1998, (v1)
Gentzler, J. Mason. DS721.G37, (v5)
Genz, Henning. QC6.G35913 1999, (v1)
Geoghegan, Patrick M. DA949.5.G46 1999, (v5)
George Philip & Son. G1021.G417 2000, (v6)
George Washington university, Washington, D.C. F1412.G46, (v4)
George, Albert Joseph. PQ287.G4, (v3)
George, Alexander L. JK511.G46 1998, (v7)
   JK570.G46, (v7)
   UA839.3.G4, (v10)
George, Alexandra. D805.G3.G45 1998, (v5)
   DK908.867.G46 2001, (v5)
George, Carol V. R. BX9543.P4.G46 1993, (v8)
George, Christopher T. E360.G46 2000, (v4)
George, J. David. QL121.G4, (v1)
George, James L. V750.G46 1998, (v10)
George, K. M. PL4718.G37 1968, (v3)
George, M. Dorothy. HN398.L7 G4 1985, (v6)
George, Margaret. HQ1599.E5.G36 1988, (v6)
George, Robert P. K5284.G46 1993, (v7)
George, Sara. PR6057.E55.J68 1999, (v3)
George, Stefan Anton. PT2613.E47.A25 1974, (v3)
   PT2613.E47 1982, (v3)
   PT2613.E47 1984, (v3)
George, Stephen. HD62.15.G463 1994, (v6)
George, Susanne K. F761.S77 1992, (v4)
Georgescu, Vlad. DR217.G4613 1990, (v5)

Georgescu-Roegen, Nicholas. HB171.G43, (v6)
Georgia. F287.G27 1982, (v4)
Georgieva, Valentina. DR2175.5.G46 1998, (v5)
Geraghty, Christine. PN1992.8.S4.G45 1991, (v3)
   PN1993.5.G7.G47 2000, (v3)
Geraghty, Tony. DA914.G47 2000, (v5)
Gerald F. Fitzgerald Collection (Newberry Library). Z6005.P7.G47 2000, (v10)
Gerald, Michael C. PR6005.H66.Z653 1993, (v3)
Gerami, Shahin. HQ1170.G45 1996, (v6)
Gerard, Albert S. PL8010.G39 1981, (v3)
   PL8010.G4, (v3)
Gerard, Charley. ML394.M86 2001, (v9)
Gerard, Charley. ML3508.G47 1998, (v9)
Gerard, David E. Z8819.125.G47 1988, (v10)
Gerassi, John. F1414.G4, (v4)
Gerber, David A. F129.B89.A24 1989, (v4)
Gerber, Douglas E. PA4274.O5.G47 1982, (v3)
Gerber, Haim. HN656.G47 1987, (v6)
Gerber, Hans U. HG8782.G4713 1995, (v6)
Gerber, Helmut E. Z8386.5.G47, (v10)
Gerber, Jane S. DS135.S7.G47 1992, (v5)
Gerber, Richard. PR888.U7.G4 1955, (v3)
   RZ401.G35 2001, (v2)
Gerber, Rudolph Joseph. HV9950.G47 1999, (v6)
   KF297.G47 1989, (v7)
Gerber, Scott Douglas. KF4550.G46 1995, (v7)
Gerber, Scott Douglas. KF8745.T48.G47 1999, (v7)
Gerdts, William H. ND210.5.I4.G474 1984, (v9)
   ND210.5.I4.G476 1991, (v9)
   ND212.G47 1990, (v9)
   ND237.A4.A4 1979, (v9)
   ND551.G5.G47 1993, (v9)
   ND1441.5.G47 1988, (v9)
   ND1839.S33 A4 2001, (v9)
Gerdy, John R. GV351.G47 1997, (v6)
Gere, Charlotte. NK1443.A1.G47 1994, (v9)
   NK2043.G45 1989, (v9)
Geremek, Bronislaw. D21.5.G4713 1996, (v5)
   HC240.9.P6.G4713 1994, (v6)
   HN440.M26.G4713 1987, (v6)
Geretsegger, Heinz. NA1011.5.W3.G413 1979, (v9)
Gergen, Kenneth J. BF697.G39 1991, (v2)
Gergen, Mary M. BF201.4.G47 2001, (v2)
Gerhan, David R. Z7164.U5.G438 1995, (v10)
   Z7165.U5.G43 1989, (v10)
Gerhard, Anselm. ML1727.8.P2.G3813 1998, (v9)
Gerhard, Dietrich. CB203.G47, (v5)
Gerhard, Jane F. HQ1421.G47 2001, (v6)
Gerhardt, Mia Irene. PJ7737.G4, (v3)
Gerhardt, Michael J. JK731.G47 2000, (v7)
Gerhart, Mary. PN771.G47 1992, (v3)
Gerin, Winifred. PR4168.G4, (v3)
   PR4173.G4, (v3)
   PR4174.B2.G4, (v3)
   PR4711.G4, (v3)
   PR5227.R7.G47 1981, (v3)
Geritz, Albert J. Z8592.8.G47 1998, (v10)
Gerlach, Michael L. HD69.S8.G47 1992, (v6)
Gerlach, Wolfgang. DS146.G4.G4813 2000, (v5)
Gerli, E. Michael. PQ6356.G47 1995, (v3)
Germain, Carel B. HV43.G47 1996, (v6)
Germain, Martha Hawkes. LB1775.2.G47 1998, (v7)
Germain, Sylvie. PQ2667.E6845.L513 1993, (v3)
German, Randall M. TN697.I7.G47 1998, (v1)
Germany, Lisa. NA737.H295.G4 1991, (v9)
Germond, Jack. JK526 1980.G47, (v7)
Gerner, Deborah J. DS119.7.G425 1991, (v5)
Gernet, Jacques. BQ638.G4713 1995, (v8)
   DS721.G413 1962b, (v5)
Gernet, Louis. DF78.G5313, (v5)
Gernsheim, Helmut. TR15.G37 1969, (v1)
   TR15.G37 1982 vol. 2, (v1)
   TR140.D3.G47 1968, (v1)
Geroch, Robert. QC173.6.G47, (v1)
Gerontological Society. QP187.G386, (v1)
Gerrard, John. GB406.G498 1992, (v6)
   S591.G44 2000, (v1)
Gerrig, Richard J. Z1003.G45 1993, (v10)
Gerring, John. JK2261.G47 1998, (v7)
Gerrish, B. A. BX9422.2.G47, (v8)

Gerry, Thomas M. F. Z1376.W65.G46 1993, (v10)
Gerschenkron, Alexander. HC240.G465, (v6)
Gershenfeld, Neil A. QA401.G47 1999, (v1)
   TK5103.G45 2000, (v1)
Gershman, Herbert S. PQ661.G4, (v3)
Gershman, Michael. GV879.5.G47 1993, (v6)
Gershoni, I. DT107.82.G43 1995, (v5)
Gershoni, Yekutiel. DT14.G47 1997, (v5)
Gershovich, Moshe. DT316.G47 1999, (v5)
Gershuny, Jonathan. HM548.G47 2000, (v6)
Gerson, Kathleen. HQ1420.G4 1985, (v6)
Gerson, Lloyd P. B398.G6 G47 1994, (v8)
Gerson, Mark. LD7501.J6785.G47 1997, (v7)
Gerstäcker, Friedrich. F411.5.G47 1991, (v4)
Gerstell, Richard. SH351.S5.G47 1998, (v1)
Gerstenberger, Erhard. BS1192.6.Y34 1996, (v8)
Gerstenfeld, Sheldon L. SF994.2.A1.G47, (v1)
Gerstle, Gary. E741.G475 2001, (v4)
Gerstmann, Evan. KF4754.5.G47 1999, (v7)
Gert, Bernard. BJ1012.G45 1998, (v8)
Gertcher, Frank L. UA23.G554 1990, (v10)
Gerteis, Louis S. F474.S257 G47 2001, (v4)
Gertsch, Willis John. QL458.4.G47 1979, (v1)
Gertzel, Cherry J. JQ2811.G47 1984, (v7)
Gertzman, Jay A. Z8490.5.G47 1989, (v10)
Gervais, David. PR478.N37.G47 1993, (v3)
Gerzina, Gretchen. ND497.C375.G47 1989, (v9)
Gesell, Arnold. BF721.G5, (v2)
   BF723.I6.G42, (v2)
   RJ131.G46 1947, (v2)
   RJ131.G47, (v2)
Gesler, Wilbert M. RA792.G486 2001, (v2)
Gess, Denise. F589.P48 G78 2002, (v4)
Getis, Victoria. KFX1248.G48 2000, (v7)
Getman, Julius G. LA227.4.G48 1992, (v7)
Getz, Faye Marie. R487.G47 1998, (v2)
Getz, Leslie. Z7514.D2.G48 1995, (v10)
Getz, Lynne Marie. LC2674.N6.G48 1997, (v7)
Geuens, Jean Pierre. PN1995.9.P7.G437 2000, (v3)
Gewehr, Wesley Marsh. DR36.G4, (v5)
Gewertz, Deborah B. DU740.42.G47 1991, (v5)
Gewirth, Alan. BJ1012.G47, (v8)
   BJ1470.G48 1998, (v8)
   JC571.G437 1996, (v7)
Geyh, Mebus A. QE508.G443 1990, (v1)
Gezari, Janet. PR4169.G49 1992, (v3)
Gh⁻iǒt̄ an⁻ī, Jam⁻al. PJ7826.H5Z2313 1988, (v3)
Ghadbian, Najib. BP63.A4.A7247 1997, (v8)
Ghai, Yash P. KNR171.G49 1997, (v7)
Ghanim, Fathi. PJ7826.H276.R33, (v3)
Ghanoonparvar, M. R. PK6415.G47 1984, (v3)
   PK6424.C58G48 1993, (v3)
Ghaus, Abdul Samad. DS357.5.G42 1988, (v5)
Ghazoul, Ferial Jabouri. PJ7737.G53 1996, (v3)
Gheissari, Ali. DS266.G44 1998, (v5)
Ghelderode, Michel de. PQ2613.H17.A19 1950, (v3)
Gheng, T. C. E. (T. C. Edwin). TS157.4.C44 1996, (v1)
Ghilarducci, Teresa. HD7105.35.U6.G45 1992, (v6)
Ghirardo, Diane Yvonne. NA682.P67.G49 1996, (v9)
Ghiselin, Michael T. QH360.5.G48 1997, (v1)
Ghorayshi, Parvin. Z7164.I45.G46 1990, (v10)
   Z7963.E7 G48 1994, (v10)
Ghose, Aurobindo. B5134.G42 G46 1998, (v8)
Ghose, Sudhindra Nath. PR9499.3.G534 A65 1949, (v3)
   PR9499.3.G534F, (v3)
   PR9499.3.G534V, (v3)
Ghose, Zulfikar. PR2983.G47 1993, (v3)
Ghosh, Amitav. PR9499.3.G536C35 1996, (v3)
   PR9499.3.G536S53 1989, (v3)
Ghosh, Jyotish Chandra. PK1701.G5 1976, (v3)
Ghosh, Sumit. TK7885.7.G46 2000, (v1)
Ghulam Sarwar (Ghulam Sarwar Yousof). PN2860.G48 1994, (v3)
Giacometti, Alberto. NE650.G5.L8, (v9)
Giamo, Benedict. PS3521.E735, (v3)
   PS3561.E428.I74 1996, (v3)
Gianakaris, C. J. PR6037.H23.Z65 1992, (v3)

Gianaris, Nicholas V. HB501.G443 1996, (v6)
  HC241.2.G52 1994, (v6)
  HC295.G5 1988, (v6)
  HC295.G52 1984, (v6)
  HF1746.G53 1998, (v6)
Giannone, Richard. PS3565.C57.Z679 1999, (v3)
  PS3565.C57.Z6794 2000, (v3)
Gianos, Phillip L. PN1995.9.P6.G53 1998, (v3)
Gianturco, Paola. TT127.G53 2000, (v1)
Giantvalley, Scott. Z8971.5.G5 1981, (v10)
Gibaldi, Joseph. LB2369.G53 2003, (v7)
Gibb, H. A. R. DS38.G485, (v5)
  PJ7510.G5 1963, (v3)
Gibb, T. C. QC491.G52, (v1)
Gibbard, Allan. BJ1012.G53 1990, (v8)
Gibberd, Frederick. NA961.G5 1953, (v9)
Gibberman, Susan R. Z7711.G5 1991, (v10)
Gibbins, Peter. QC174.12.G52 1987, (v1)
Gibbon, Edward. PR3476.A16 1972, (v3)
Gibbon, Guy E. CC72.4.G53 1984, (v5)
Gibboney, Richard A. LA210.G49 1994, (v7)
Gibbons, Andrew S. LB1028.5.G487 1998, (v7)
Gibbons, Brian. PR658.C6.G5 1968b, (v3)
Gibbons, John H. Q127.U6.G43 1997, (v1)
Gibbons, Robert D. TD426.G52 1994, (v1)
Gibbons, Stella. PR6013.I24 C6 1964, (v3)
Gibbs, A. C. PR2064.G5 1966, (v3)
Gibbs, A. M. PR5366.A238 2001, (v3)
Gibbs, Brian H. D849.G53 1993, (v5)
Gibbs, Christopher Howard. ML410.S3 G53 2000, (v9)
Gibbs, David N. DT658.G53 1991, (v5)
Gibbs, David. QL696.C63, (v1)
Gibbs, Henry. PR6013.I254 F56, (v3)
Gibbs, Jewelle Taylor. KF220.G53 1996, (v7)
  RJ507.M54.G53 1989, (v2)
Gibbs, Lois Marie. RA1242.D55.G53 1995, (v2)
Gibbs, Tyson. Z6675.M68.G52 1996, (v10)
Gibbs-Smith, Charles Harvard. TL515.G495 1974, (v1)
Gibert, Stephen P. E744.G49 1977, (v4)
Giblin, James Leonard. HD2128.5.G5 1992, (v6)
Gibran, Daniel K. F3031.5.G53 1998, (v4)
Gibran, Kahlil. PJ7826.I2.A233 1951, (v3)
  PJ7826.I2A713 1998, (v3)
  PJ7826.I2.Z54, (v3)
  PS3513.I25.P7 1923, (v3)
Gibson, Althea. GV994.G5.A3, (v6)
Gibson, Ann Eden. N6512.5.A25.G53 1997, (v9)
Gibson, Arrell Morgan. DU30.G53 1993, (v5)
  F694.G523, (v4)
Gibson, Arthur C. QK495.C11.G5 1986, (v1)
Gibson, Brent. Z8971.5.G53 2001, (v10)
Gibson, Charles Edmund. VM533.G49 1963, (v10)
Gibson, Charles. E18.82.G5, (v4)
  F1219.1.M53.G5, (v4)
  JL3400.G5 1969, (v7)
Gibson, Christopher G. QA565.G5 1998, (v1)
Gibson, Clark C. QH77.A35.G525 1999, (v1)
Gibson, David. RC571.G5, (v2)
Gibson, H N. PR2937.G5, (v3)
Gibson, H. B. BF724.85.L64, (v2)
  RC495.G464 1991, (v2)
Gibson, Ian. PQ6613.A763Z6477 1985, (v3)
Gibson, James R. F907.G52, (v4)
Gibson, James. PR4753.G45 1996, (v3)
Gibson, John G. ML980.G53 1998, (v9)
Gibson, John S. DA813.G53 1988, (v5)
  K3239.3.G53 1996, (v7)
Gibson, Jon L. E99.P84 G5 2001, (v4)
Gibson, Margaret A. LC3745.M56 1991, (v7)
Gibson, Mary Ellis. PS3531.O82.Z6345 1995, (v3)
Gibson, Michael. ND553.G27 G53 1993, (v9)
Gibson, Paul J. G70.4.G52 2000, (v6)
Gibson, Roger F. B945.Q54.G5 1982, (v8)
Gibson, Rosalind S. RC621.G52 1990, (v2)
Gibson, W. Walker. PE1421.G5, (v3)
  PN1064.G5, (v3)
Gibson, Walter Murray. DU627.17.G5.A3, (v5)
Gibson, Walter S. ND673.B73.G47 1977b, (v9)
  ND1359.2.G5 1989, (v9)

NE954.3.N4.G53 2000, (v9)
Gibson, Wendy. HQ1613.G53 1989, (v6)
Gicovate, Bernard. PQ6392.G5, (v3)
Giddens, Anthony. D16.9.G47, (v5)
  HM19.G532, (v6)
  HM24.G446, (v6)
  HM131.G397 1990, (v6)
  JC573.G53 1994, (v7)
  JZ1318.G53 2000, (v7)
Giddins, Gary. ML385.G53 1998, (v9)
  ML420.C93.G53 2001, (v9)
  ML3507.G5 1985, (v9)
  ML3507.G52, (v9)
Gide, André. PQ2613.I2.A26, (v3)
  PQ2613.I2.A77 1952, (v3)
  PQ2613.I2.F3 1967, (v3)
  PQ2613.I2 I482 1948, (v3)
  PQ2613.I2.I7 1947, (v3)
  PQ2613.I2.N72, (v3)
  PQ2613.I2.P33 1953a, (v3)
  PQ2613.I2.P43, (v3)
  PQ2613.I2.P6 1907, (v3)
  PQ2613.I2.P73, (v3)
  PQ2613.I2.P7363, (v3)
  PQ2613.I2.R4, (v3)
  PQ2613.I2.S9 1954, (v3)
  PQ2613.I2.V6 1929, (v3)
  PQ2613.I2.Z48513 1983, (v3)
  PQ2613.I2.Z564, (v3)
  PQ2613.I2I48 1974, (v3)
Gidley, M. E77.5.G53 1998, (v4)
Giedion, S. NA203.G5 1962, (v9)
Gielgud, John. PR3091.G54 1992, (v3)
Gienapp, William E. JK2357. 1852, (v7)
Gienow-Hecht, Jessica C. E. PN5219.M793.N484 1999, (v3)
Gier, Nicholas F. BL51.G625 2000, (v8)
Gierke, Otto Friedrich von. JA82.G4 1958, (v7)
  JC156.A5.G52, (v7)
Giersch, Herbert. HC286.G54 1992, (v6)
Gierzynski, Anthony. JK1991.G53 1992, (v7)
Gies, Frances. DC103.G47 1981, (v5)
  HN398.E45.G54 1990, (v6)
  HQ513.G53 1987, (v6)
  HQ1143.G53 1978, (v6)
Giesberg, Judith Ann. E628.G54 2000, (v4)
Giffard, Sydney. DS881.9.G54 1994, (v5)
Gifford, Denis. PN1997.85.G54 1991, (v3)
  PN6726.G54 1990, (v3)
Gifford, Don. PR6019.O9.U647 1988, (v3)
  PR6019.O9.Z5335 1982, (v3)
Gifford, Paul M. ML1041.G54 2001, (v9)
Gifford, Paul. BR1430.G54 1998, (v8)
Giglio, Ernest D. PN1995.9.P6.G56 2000, (v3)
Giglio, James N. E841.G54 1991, (v4)
  Z8462.8.G54 1995, (v10)
Giglio, Virginia. ML3557.G53 1994, (v9)
Gijsen, Marnix. PT6430.G67 K5513, (v3)
Gikandi, Simon. PL8010.6.G55 1987, (v3)
  PR9205.4.G55 1992, (v3)
  PR9387.9.A3.Z68 1991, (v3)
Gil, Victor M. S. QD461.G52 2000, (v1)
Gilbar, Gad G. HB3633.3.A3.G55 1997, (v6)
Gilberg, Trond. HX550.N3.G53 1990, (v6)
Gilbert, A. C. CT275.G3917.A3 1954, (v5)
Gilbert, Alan D. BR755.G54, (v8)
Gilbert, Alan. HD7287.82.M62.M494 1993, (v6)
  JC571.G515 1990, (v7)
  JZ1242.B54 1999, (v7)
Gilbert, Bentley B. DA566.9.L5.G56 1987, (v5)
Gilbert, Charles E. TD223.G46 1992, (v1)
Gilbert, Charles. HJ257.G54, (v6)
Gilbert, Clinton W. E747.G46, (v4)
Gilbert, Creighton. ND623.C26.G53 1995, (v9)
Gilbert, Daniel R. HF5387.G55 1996, (v6)
Gilbert, Dennis L. JL1619.A52 G55 1988, (v7)
Gilbert, Douglas. PN1967.G5, (v3)
Gilbert, Elliot L. PR4856.G5, (v3)
Gilbert, Felix. D16.8.G532 1990, (v5)
  E310.7.G5, (v4)
Gilbert, G. M. D804.G42.G5, (v5)

Gilbert, George Thomas. QA43.G54 1993, (v1)
Gilbert, Helen, 1956-. PR9611.5.G55 1998, (v3)
Gilbert, Jack Glenn. PR3753.G5, (v3)
Gilbert, James Burkhart. BL245.G55 1997, (v8)
  E169.12.G54 1981b, (v4)
  F545.G43 1991, (v4)
Gilbert, Jeremy. ML3406.G55 1999, (v9)
Gilbert, Joan. E99.C5 G33 1996, (v4)
Gilbert, Katharine (Everett). BH81.G5 1953, (v8)
Gilbert, Margaret. HM24.G479 1989, (v6)
Gilbert, Mark. DG555.G53 1999, (v5)
  JN5451.G48 1995, (v7)
Gilbert, Martin. D755.7.G55 1995, (v5)
  DA47.2.G5 1963a, (v5)
  DA566.9.C5.G463 1982, (v5)
  DS109.925.G54 1985, (v5)
  DS109.93.G55 1996, (v5)
  G1030.G48 1990, (v6)
  G1797.21.E29.G58 1982, (v6)
  G2111.S1.G52 1993, (v6)
  G2236.S1.G52 1993, (v6)
Gilbert, Micheal Francis. PR6013.I3335 C64, (v3)
Gilbert, Miriam. PR2822.G5 1993, (v3)
Gilbert, Neal Ward. BD241.G48 1960, (v8)
Gilbert, Paul. BD436.G55 1991, (v8)
  JF1061.G49 2000, (v7)
  RC454.4.G54 1992, (v2)
Gilbert, Rob. LC1390.G55 1998, (v7)
Gilbert, Robert E. E176.1.G55 1998, (v4)
Gilbert, Sandra M. PR115.G5, (v3)
  PR116.G5 1988, (v3)
Gilbert, Stephen G. QM602.G55 1989, (v1)
Gilbert, W. S. PR4713.A4 1982, (v3)
  PR4713.B3 1970, (v3)
Gilchrist, J. D. (James Duncan). TN665.G48 1989, (v1)
Gilchrist, John Thomas. DC141.G5 1971, (v5)
Gilchrist, Roberta. CC72.4.G55 1999, (v5)
Gildea, Robert. D358.G55 1987, (v5)
Gilder, George F. HB501.G46, (v6)
Giles, Donald T. D805.J3.G54 1994, (v5)
Giles, Edward. BX953.G5, (v8)
Giles, Fiona. PR9608.G56 1998, (v3)
Giles, Herbert Allen. DS735.G5, (v5)
Giles, James Richard. PS374.N29.G55 1995, (v3)
  PS374.V58.G55 2000, (v3)
  PS3501.L4625.Z68 1989, (v3)
Giles, Judy. HQ1593.G55 1995, (v6)
Giles, Lancelot. DS772.G54 1970, (v5)
Giles, Paul. PS159.G8.G5 2001, (v3)
Giles, Paul. PS159.G8G5 2001, (v3)
Giles-Sims, Jean. HV6626.G54 1983, (v6)
Gilfoyle, Timothy J. HQ146.N7.G55 1992, (v6)
Gilkes, Cheryl. BR563.N4.G54 2001, (v8)
Gilkes, Michael. PR9214.G5, (v3)
Gilkey, Langdon Brown. BX4827.N5.G55 2001, (v8)
Gill, Anton. D805.A2.G49 1988, (v5)
  N5220.G886 G55 2002, (v9)
Gill, Brendan. PS3513.I468.Z52, (v3)
Gill, Christopher. B171.G55 1995, (v8)
Gill, Diane L. GV706.4.G55 1986, (v6)
Gill, Gillian. BX6995.G49 1998, (v8)
  PR6005.H66.Z655 1990, (v3)
Gill, Glenda Eloise. PN2286.G55 2000, (v3)
Gill, Graeme J. JC421.G545 2000, (v7)
  JN6695.G55 2000, (v7)
Gill, Ian. F1089.Q3.G55 1997, (v4)
Gill, Jerry H. BD183.G55 1993, (v8)
Gill, Lesley. HC183.E4 G54 2000, (v6)
  HD1870.S25.G54 1987, (v6)
Gill, Merton Max. BF173.G496 1994, (v2)
Gill, Philip E. QA402.5.G54 1981, (v1)
Gill, Robin. BJ1275.G55 1999, (v8)
Gill, Sam D. E98.R3.G46 1992, (v4)
  E98.R3.G49 1983, (v4)
  GN470.G5, (v6)
Gill, Stephen Charles. PR5881.G55 1989, (v3)
  PR5887.3.G55 1998, (v3)
Gill, Stephen. HF1359.G55 1988, (v6)
Gillan, Garth. BD435.G46 1998, (v8)
Gillaspie, Jon A. ML128.W5.G52 1998, (v9)

Gillenkirk, Jeff. F869.L67.G55 1987, (v4)
Giller, Pinchas. BM525.A59.G55 2001, (v8)
Gillespie, Alexander. K3585.4.G55 1997, (v7)
Gillespie, Angus K. NA6233.N5.W674 1999, (v9)
Gillespie, C. Richard. PN2293.S4.G5 1991, (v3)
Gillespie, Charles. JL3698.A1 G5 1991, (v7)
Gillespie, Cynthia K. KF9246.G55 1989, (v7)
Gillespie, David C. PG3098.4.G56 1996, (v3)
Gillespie, Dizzy. ML419.G54.A3, (v9)
Gillespie, James R. SF61.G5 1995, (v1)
Gillespie, John H. QH455.G56 1991, (v1)
   QH455.G565 1998, (v1)
Gillespie, John Thomas. Z1037.A1.G47 1997, (v10)
Gillespie, Michael Allen. B828.3.G55 1995, (v8)
Gillespie, Michael Patrick. PR5827.A63.G55 1996,
   (v3)
   PR6019.O9.U6522 2000, (v3)
Gillespie, Michele. HD2346.U52G44 2000, (v6)
Gillespie, Neal C. QH31.D2.G55, (v1)
Gillespie, Richard. HD30.42.U5.G55 1991, (v6)
Gillespie, Susan D. F1219.73.G55 1989, (v4)
Gillespie, Thomas D. TL243.G548 1992, (v1)
Gillett, Charles Ripley. Z658.G7 G54 1974, (v10)
Gillett, James B. F391.G473 1976, (v4)
Gillett, Mary C. UH223.G544 1995, (v10)
Gillett, Paula. ND467.5.V52.G55 1990, (v9)
Gillette, Howard. HN80.W3.G55 1995, (v4)
Gillette, Maris Boyd. HC430.C6.G56 2000, (v6)
Gilley, Bruce. DS779.29.C477.G55 1998, (v5)
   HC428.T23, (v6)
Gilliam, Bryan Randolph. ML410.S93.G53 1999, (v9)
Gilliard, Charles. DQ55.G513 1978, (v5)
Gilliatt, Penelope. PN6147.G5 1990, (v3)
Gillick, Muriel R. RC952.G54 1994, (v2)
Gillies, Alexander. PT2353.G5, (v3)
Gillies, David. JC599.A78.G55 1996, (v7)
Gillies, Donald. BC141.G55 2000, (v8)
   DA566.9.C525.G55 1999, (v5)
   Q174.8.G55 1993, (v1)
   Q335.G54 1996, (v1)
Gillies, James. TK5105.888.G544 2000, (v1)
Gillies, Mary Ann. PR478.M6.G55 1996, (v3)
Gillieson, David S. GB601.G5 1996, (v6)
Gilligan, Carol. HQ1206.G58 1993, (v6)
Gillilan, David M. TC423.6.G55 1997, (v1)
Gilliland, Hap. E97.G55 1999, (v4)
Gilliland, Marion Spjut. F319.M39.G55 1989, (v4)
Gillin, Donald G. DS778.Y4.G6, (v5)
Gillingham, John. DA207.G48 1979, (v5)
Gillis, Chester. BX1406.2.G45 1999, (v8)
Gillis, John R. HQ613.G55 1985, (v6)
Gillis, William R. F865.G48 1970, (v4)
Gillison, Gillian. GR385.P36.G55 1993, (v6)
Gillispie, Charles Coulston. Q125.G49, (v1)
Gillman, Howard. KF5399.G55 1993, (v7)
Gillman, Neil. BM610.G53 2000, (v8)
Gillman, Susan Kay. PS1342.D64.G55 1989, (v3)
Gillmeister, Heiner. GV1002.95.E85.G5613 1997, (v6)
Gillmor, Alan M. ML410.S196.G54 1988, (v9)
Gillmor, Donald M. KF1266.G55 1992, (v7)
Gillmor, Frances. F786.G46, (v4)
Gilloch, Graeme. PT2603.E455.Z674 1996, (v3)
Gillon, Adam. PR6005.O4.Z7264 1994, (v3)
Gillon, Margaret. Z7164.H74.G55 1995, (v10)
Gillon, Steven M. E743.G45 1987, (v4)
   E840.8.M66.G55 1992, (v4)
   HV57.G56 2000, (v6)
Gilluly, James. QE26.G5 1968, (v1)
Gilman, Carolyn. E99.H6.G55 1987, (v4)
Gilman, Charlotte Perkins. HQ1426.G45 1970, (v6)
   PS1744.G57.A6 1996, (v3)
   PS1744.G57.A6 1999, (v3)
   PS1744.G57.B46 1994, (v3)
   PS1744.G57.U56 1997, (v3)
   PS1744.G57.W5 1997, (v3)
   PS1744.G57.Y45 1998b, (v3)
   PS1744.G57.Z463 1998, (v3)
   PS1744.G57.Z465 1994, (v3)
   PS1744.G57.Z48 1995, (v3)
Gilman, Margaret. PQ401.G5, (v3)
Gilman, Richard. PG3458.Z8.G5 1995, (v3)

Gilman, Sander L. BF109.F74.G55 1993, (v2)
   DS135.A9.G55 1998, (v5)
   RC438.G54 1988, (v2)
   RD118.5.G55 1998, (v2)
Gilman, Stephen. PQ6428.G53, (v3)
Gilman, Theodore J. HT178.J3.G55 2001, (v6)
Gilmartin, Christina K. HX546.G54 1995, (v6)
Gilmartin, David. DS485.P2.G54 1988, (v5)
Gilmartin, Kevin. PN5117.G55 1996, (v3)
Gilmartin, Pat. HV6558.G55 1994, (v6)
Gilmartin, Sophie. PR868.G354.G55 1998, (v3)
Gilmer, Lois C. Z688.G3.G54 1988, (v10)
Gilmore, Alec. BS455.G55 2000, (v8)
Gilmore, Allison B. D810.P7.U5 1998, (v5)
Gilmore, Bob. ML410.P176 G55 1998, (v9)
Gilmore, David D. GT4262.A55.G55 1998, (v6)
Gilmore, Glenda Elizabeth. E185.93.N6.G55 1996,
   (v4)
Gilmore, Grant. KF352.A2.G5, (v7)
Gilmore, Leigh. PN98.W64.G55 1994, (v3)
Gilmore, Melvin R. E99.M682 G55 1991, (v4)
Gilmore, Michael T. PN1995.9.S6.G56 1998, (v3)
Gilmore, Robert K. F472.O9.G55 1984, (v4)
Gilmore, Robert. QA387.G54, (v1)
   QC792.4.G55 2001, (v1)
Gilmour, David. DP272.G545 1985, (v5)
Gilmour, John B. JK2265.G55 1995, (v7)
Gilmour, John. DP271.F7.G56 1999, (v5)
   ND588.K464.G55 1990, (v9)
Gilmour, Robin. PR878.C64.G5, (v3)
Gilpin, Alan. K3584.6.G55 2000, (v7)
Gilpin, Alec Richard. F566.G5, (v4)
Gilpin, Robert. HF1359.G5515 2000, (v6)
   HF1359.G5516 2001, (v6)
   HF1455.G5, (v6)
   UA23.G58, (v9)
Gilroy, Paul. CB235.G55 1993, (v5)
Gilsenan, Michael. DS89.A42.G55 1996, (v5)
Gilson, David. Z8048.G54 1997, (v10)
Gilson, Etienne. B52.G5, (v8)
   B655.Z7.G52, (v8)
   B721.G5714 1991, (v8)
   B765.T54.G47, (v8)
   B765.T54 G5 1971, (v8)
   BH201.G55, (v8)
   ND1150.G5 1957, (v9)
Gimbel, John. DD257.2.G5, (v5)
Gimbutas, Marija Alseikaite. GN803.G57 1999, (v6)
Gimpel, James G. JK2261.G56 1996, (v7)
Gimpel, Jean. NA4830.G5313 1983, (v9)
Ginat, Rami. HX443.A6.G56 1997, (v6)
Gindikin, S. G. QC7.G5613 1988, (v1)
Gindin, James Jack. PR861.G5, (v3)
   PR881.G5, (v3)
Ginell, Cary. ML3541.G56 1994, (v9)
Gines, Montserrat. PS261.G56 2000, (v3)
Ginger, Ann Fagan. KF373.K48.G56 1993, (v7)
Ginger, John. F549.D3.G56 1985, (v4)
Ginger, Ray. F548.5.G45 1986, (v4)
Gingerich, Owen. Q125.G495 1989, (v1)
   QB15.G563 1993, (v1)
Ginsberg, Allen. PS3513.I74.A17 1984, (v3)
   PS3513.I74.A6 1970, (v3)
   PS3513.I74.D42 1999, (v3)
   PS3513.I74.F3, (v3)
   PS3513.I74.H6 1959, (v3)
   PS3513.I74.R4 1963, (v3)
   PS3513.I74.Z516, (v3)
   PS3513.I74.Z543, (v3)
Ginsberg, Leon H. HV91.G47 1983, (v6)
Ginsberg, Roy H. KJE5105.G56 1989, (v7)
Ginsborg, Paul. DG678.55.G56, (v5)
Ginsburg, Evelyn Harris. LB3013.4.G55 1990, (v7)
Ginsburg, Herbert. BF723.C5.G56 1988, (v2)
Ginsburg, Michal Peled. PR868.S615.G56 1996, (v3)
Ginzberg, Eli. RA981.A2.G495 1996, (v2)
   RA981.A2.G56 2000, (v2)
   UB323.G5 1959, (v10)
   UH629.3.G5, (v10)
Ginzberg, Lori D. HQ1418.G56 1990, (v6)
Ginzburg, Carlo. BR877.F74.G5613, (v8)

Ginzburg, Evgeniia Semenovna. DK268.G47.A3413
   1981, (v5)
   DK268.3.G513, (v5)
Ginzburg, Lidiia. PN56.P93.G513 1991, (v3)
Gioello, Debbie Ann. TT494.G56, (v1)
Gioia, Ted. ML3506.G54 1997, (v9)
   ML3508.7.C28.G5 1992, (v9)
Giono, Jean. PQ2613.I57.C3 1929, (v3)
   PQ2613.I57.H9, (v3)
   PQ2613.I57 H92 1953, (v3)
Giovanni, Nikki. PS3557.I55.Z47 1994, (v3)
Gipe, Paul. TJ820.G56 1995, (v1)
Gippius, Vasilii Vasilevich. PG3335.G4913, (v3)
Gira, Catherine. Z8812.K54.G57 1994, (v10)
Giraldus Cambrensis. PR1119.A2 no. 107, (v3)
Girard, Marcel. PQ305.G5 1968b, (v3)
Girard, René. PR2976.G5 1991, (v3)
   BL600.G5413, (v8)
Girardi, Michele. ML410.P89.G5713 2000, (v9)
Giraud, Marcel. F372.G513, (v4)
Giraud, Raymond Dorner. PQ2249.G5, (v3)
Giraudoux, Jean. PQ2613.I74.F6 1955, (v3)
   PQ2613.I74.G8 1935, (v3)
   PQ2613.I74.P693 1958a, (v3)
   PQ2613.I74.S4 1922, (v3)
   PQ2613.I74.T43, (v3)
Giray-Saul, Eren. GR350.32.D98.G57 1996, (v6)
Girdlestone, Cuthbert Morton. MT130.M8.G62 1964,
   (v9)
Girgus, Sam B. PN1993.5.U6.G497 1998, (v3)
   PN1998.3.A45.G57 1993, (v3)
Girling, J. L. S. CB245.G55 1993, (v5)
Girouard, Mark. HT133.G57 1990, (v6)
   NA630.G57, (v9)
   NA961.G55 1992, (v9)
   NA997.S6.G5 1983, (v9)
   NA7562.G5 1979, (v9)
Giroux, Henry A. LA212.G48, (v7)
   LA217.G57 1988, (v7)
   LC196.G573 1997, (v7)
   PN1999.W27.G57 1999, (v3)
Girshick, Lori B. HV9475.N82.B534 1999, (v6)
Gisevius, Hans Bernd. DD256.5.G52, (v5)
Gish, Robert. E175.5.F4.G57 1996, (v4)
   PS277.G57 1996, (v3)
Gisler, Margaret. F524.3.G573 2000, (v4)
Gissing, George. PR4716.A6 1970, (v3)
   PR4716.B6 1978, (v3)
   PR4716.E6 1977, (v3)
   PR4716.I5 1976, (v3)
   PR4716.N37 1974, (v3)
   PR4716.N4 1958, (v3)
   PR4716.P7 1982, (v3)
   PR4716.U5 1976, (v3)
   PR4716.V4 1968, (v3)
   PR4716.W4 1977, (v3)
   PR4717.A3 1970, (v3)
   PR4717.A33, (v3)
   PR4717.A35 1961, (v3)
   PR4717.D4 1971, (v3)
Gitelman, Howard M. HD6490.C612.U65 1988, (v6)
Gitelman, Zvi Y. DS135.R9.G444 1988, (v5)
Gitlin, Todd. E184.A1.G48 1995, (v4)
   E841.G57 1987, (v4)
Gitlitz, David M. DS135.S7.G58 1996, (v5)
Gittell, Ross J. HT175.G56 1992, (v6)
Gitter, Elisabeth. HV1624.B7G57 2001, (v6)
Gittes, Katharine S. PR1875.S75.G58 1991, (v3)
Gittings, John. DS740.5.R8.G5, (v5)
   UA835.G5, (v10)
Gittings, Robert. PR4739.H774.Z67, (v3)
   PR4753.G49 1978, (v3)
   PR4753.G55 1975, (v3)
   PR5398.G58 1991, (v3)
   PR5849.G5 1985, (v3)
Gittins, Diana. HB995.G55 1982, (v6)
Giulianotti, Richard. GV943.9.S64.G576 1999, (v6)
Giustozzi, Antonio. DS371.2.G59 1999, (v5)
Given, David R. QK86.A1.G54 1994, (v1)
Given, James Buchanan. JN2433.L36.A44 1990, (v7)
Givens, Douglas R. GN21.K5.G58 1992, (v6)

Givens, Terryl. BX8645.5.G58 1997, **(v8)**
Givner, Joan. PR9199.3.D42.Z68 1989, **(v3)**
Givoni, Baruch. TH7687.5.G54 1994, **(v1)**
Giziowski, Richard J. D804.G4.G54 1996, **(v5)**
Gjelsvik, Tore. D802.N7.G5413 1979, **(v5)**
Gjerde, Jon. F358.G58 1997, **(v4)**
    F358.2.S2.G54 1985, **(v4)**
Gjerset, Knut. DL338.G5, **(v5)**
Gjerset, Knut. DL449.G5 1969, **(v5)**
Gjertsen, Derek. Q125.G54 1984, **(v1)**
Gjording, Chris N. F1565.G8.G65 1991, **(v4)**
Gladden, James N. KF5646.B68.G55 1990, **(v7)**
Gladden, Washington. F70.G54, **(v4)**
Gladdish, Ken. JN5801.G53 1991, **(v7)**
Gladkov, Fedor. PG3476.G53 T83 1960, **(v3)**
Gladney, Dru C. DS731.M87.G53 1991, **(v5)**
Gladsky, Thomas S. PS159.P7.G53 1992, **(v3)**
Gladwin, Thomas N. HD69.I7.G54, **(v6)**
Glaeser, Bernhard. HC79.E5.G57 1995, **(v6)**
Glaessner, Gert-Joachim. DD290.25.G57 1992, **(v5)**
Glaessner, Martin F. QE770.G54 1984, **(v1)**
Glaister, Geoffrey Ashall. Z118.G55 1996, **(v10)**
Glancy, Ruth F. PR4571.G43 1991, **(v3)**
Glantz, David M. D764.G556 1998, **(v5)**
    D764.G557 1995, **(v5)**
    D764.G5575 1999, **(v5)**
    D764.7.D6.G53 1990, **(v5)**
    D810.S7.G552 1990, **(v5)**
    UA770.G55 1992, **(v10)**
Glantz, Michael H. GC296.8.E4.G53 2001, **(v6)**
Glantz, Stanton A. KFC417.T6.G58 2000, **(v7)**
Glanville, Brian. PR6013.L35.R5, **(v3)**
    PR6057.L28.D5, **(v3)**
Glanville, Philippa. NK7143.G55 1990, **(v9)**
Glanz, James. S624.A1.G58 1995, **(v1)**
Glanz, Rudolf. E184.J5.G493, **(v4)**
Glaser, Barney G. BF789.D4.G5, **(v2)**
Glaser, Bert. RE661.D3G56 2001, **(v2)**
Glaser, Charles L. UA23.G636 1990, **(v10)**
Glaser, Clive. HV6439.S62, **(v6)**
Glaser, Daniel. HV8978.M34.G53 1995, **(v6)**
Glaser, Hugo. RD27.G553 1962, **(v2)**
Glaser, James M. JK2683.G58 1996, **(v7)**
Glaser, Roland. QH505.G5413 2001, **(v1)**
Glaser, William A. HD7101.G54 1991, **(v6)**
Glasgow, Edward James. F786.G57 1993, **(v4)**
Glasgow, Ellen Anderson Gholson. PS3513.L34 A15, **(v3)**
    PS3513.L34 V4 1935, **(v3)**
    PS3513.L34.Z5 1954, **(v3)**
    PS3513.L34.Z53, **(v3)**
Glasheen, Adaline. PR6019.O9.F59 1977, **(v3)**
Glashow, Sheldon L. QC776.G59 1991, **(v1)**
Glaspell, Susan. PS3513.L35.A7 1930, **(v3)**
Glaspell, Susan. PS3513.L35.P6 1920, **(v3)**
Glaspey, Terry W. Z7751.G55 1996, **(v10)**
Glass, Beaumont. ML420.L33.G6 1988, **(v9)**
Glass, Bentley. QH361.G55, **(v1)**
Glass, James M. D804.3.G587 1997, **(v5)**
Glass, Leon. QH527.G595 1988, **(v1)**
Glass, Matthew. U264.4.G73.G53 1993, **(v10)**
Glass, Philip. ML410.G398.A3 1987, **(v9)**
Glass, Willie Elmore. CT275.G47.A35, **(v5)**
Glasser, Bradley Louis. HC415.15.G58 2001, **(v6)**
Glasser, Ira. KF4749.G53 1991, **(v7)**
Glasser, Irene. HV4493.G53 1994, **(v6)**
Glasser, Leah Blatt. PS1713.G58 1996, **(v3)**
Glasser, Ronald J. R149.G53 1997, **(v2)**
Glasser, Ruth. ML3481.G53 1995, **(v9)**
Glasser, William. PN70.G53 1994, **(v3)**
Glassey, Robert. QA76.73.C15.G57 1993, **(v1)**
Glassie, Henry H. GN406.G53 1999, **(v6)**
    NK607.G5 1989, **(v9)**
    NK1051.6.B3.G53 1997, **(v9)**
    PR8793.F6.G6, **(v3)**
Glassman, Deborah N. PQ2607.U8245.Z68 1991, **(v3)**
Glassman, Jonathon. DT365.65.G57 1995, **(v5)**
Glassner, Andrew S. T385.G578 1999, **(v1)**
Glassner, Barry. HV5824.Y68.G55 1987, **(v6)**
Glasstone, Samuel. QC311.G55, **(v1)**
    QC776.G6 1967, **(v1)**

QD453.G53 1960, **(v1)**
Glatstein, Jacob. PJ5129.G535.K513 1992, **(v3)**
Glatthaar, Joseph T. E540.N3.G53 1990, **(v4)**
Glazebrook, G. P. de T. F1059.5.T6857.G55, **(v4)**
Glazebrook, Trish. B3279.H49.G57 2000, **(v8)**
Glazener, Nancy. PN4877.G49 1997, **(v3)**
Glazer, Amihai. HC106.82.G55 2001, **(v6)**
Glazer, Myron. JK468.W54.G55 1989, **(v7)**
Glazer, Nathan. HN59.G57 1988, **(v6)**
    JK2391.C5.G55, **(v7)**
Glazer, Penina Migdal. GE55.G54 1998, **(v6)**
Glazier, Jack. E184.353.G53 1998, **(v4)**
Gleaser, C. M. F567.G58 2000, **(v4)**
Gleason, Abbott. D445.G54 1995, **(v5)**
Gleason, Elisabeth G. DG678.24.C66.G54 1993, **(v5)**
Gleason, Gregory. JQ1070.G54 1997, **(v7)**
Gleason, Harold. MT182.G55 1988, **(v9)**
Gleason, Henry A. PE1111.G575, **(v3)**
    PE1135.G59 1961, **(v3)**
    QK117.G49 1991, **(v1)**
Gleason, John B. BR754.C6.G57 1989, **(v8)**
Gleason, Philip. BX1406.2.G58 1987, **(v8)**
    LC501.G56 1995, **(v7)**
Gleason, Sarah C. VK1024.N38.G54 1991, **(v10)**
Gleason, William A. PS217.L44.G58 1999, **(v3)**
Gleckner, Robert F. PR146.G5 1970, **(v3)**
    PR3503.G48 1997, **(v3)**
    PR4147.G55, **(v3)**
    PR4388.G57, **(v3)**
Gledhill, D. QK96.G54 1989, **(v1)**
Gledhill, John. GN492.G55 1994, **(v6)**
    HN120.M53.G58 1995, **(v6)**
Glees, Anthony. JN3971.A58.G723294 1996, **(v7)**
    UB271.R9.G58 1987, **(v10)**
Gleick, James. QC16.F49.G54 1992, **(v1)**
Glenday, Michael K. PS3525.A4152.Z655 1995, **(v3)**
Glendinning, James. F392.B54 G58 1995, **(v4)**
Glendinning, Miles. NA975.G56 1996, **(v9)**
Glendinning, Nigel. ND813.G7.G53, **(v9)**
    PQ6069.G6, **(v3)**
Glendinning, Victoria. PR3726.G57 1999, **(v3)**
    PR5686.G58 1993, **(v3)**
    PR6037.A35.Z68 1983, **(v3)**
    PR6037.I8.Z59 1981, **(v3)**
    PR6045.E8.Z65 1987, **(v3)**
Glendon, Mary Ann. K3238.31948.G58 2001, **(v7)**
    KF297.G58 1994, **(v7)**
Glenn, Charles Leslie. HV95.G54 2000, **(v6)**
    LA622.G54 1995, **(v7)**
    LC3745.G54 1996, **(v7)**
Glenn, H. Patrick. K559.G545 2000, **(v7)**
Glenn, John. DK859.56.G57 1999, **(v5)**
Glenn, Kathleen Mary. PQ6623.A816.Z597, **(v3)**
Glenn, Leigh. KF9763.G58 1997, **(v7)**
Glenn, Russell W. DS558.G6 2000, **(v5)**
Glenn, Susan A. PN1590.W64.G59 2000, **(v3)**
Glennon, Michael J. JK529.G58 1992, **(v7)**
    KF4651.G59 1990, **(v7)**
Gless, Darryl J. PR2824.G5, **(v3)**
Glick, Bernard R. TP248.2.G58 1998, **(v1)**
Glick, Henry Robert. KF3827.E87.Z954 1992, **(v7)**
Glick, Thomas F. DP99.G46 1995, **(v5)**
    DP99.G47, **(v5)**
Glicksberg, Charles Irving. PN771.G56, **(v3)**
Glicksman, Abraham M. QA265.G55, **(v1)**
Glickstein, Jonathan A. HD8070.G58 1991, **(v6)**
Glied, Sherry. RA395.A3G54 1997, **(v2)**
Gliessman, Stephen R. S589.7, **(v1)**
Glines, Carroll V. G585.B3.G58 1999, **(v6)**
Glinsky, Albert. ML429.T43, **(v9)**
Gliserman, Martin J. PR830.B63.G58 1996, **(v3)**
Glissant, Edouard. F2081.G5313 1989, **(v4)**
    PS3511.A86.Z7833513 1999, **(v3)**
Glitsch, Catherine. Z1231.F4.G56 2000, **(v10)**
    Z1231.F4.G58 1998, **(v10)**
Glob, P. V. GN780.D4.G53 1969b, **(v6)**
Gloppen, Siri. KTL2070.G59 1997, **(v7)**
Glossbrenner, Alfred. ZA4230.G57 2001, **(v10)**
Glover, David. PR6037.T617.Z67 1996, **(v3)**
Glover, Denise Marie. Z1361.N39.G56 1995, **(v10)**
Glover, T. R. D59.G6 1979, **(v5)**

Glowka, Arthur Wayne. PR1951.G57 1991, **(v3)**
Gluck, Jay. PL782.E8.G6, **(v3)**
Glueck, Sheldon. HV9094.B7.G6, **(v6)**
    HV9094.B7.G63, **(v6)**
Glusker, Jenny Pickworth. QD945.G58 1985, **(v1)**
    QD945.G583 1994, **(v1)**
Glusker, Susannah Joel. PN4973.B74.G5 1998, **(v3)**
Glymour, Clark N. B74.G59 1992, **(v8)**
Glyn Jones, Kenneth. QB851.J6 1990, **(v1)**
Glynn, Jerry. QA76.95.G552 2000, **(v1)**
Glynn, Kevin. PN1992.8.R43.G59 2000, **(v3)**
Gneuss, Helmut. PE65.G58 1996, **(v3)**
Gobbett, Brian. Z1382.G63 1998, **(v10)**
Gobetti, Piero. JN5450.G6313 2000, **(v7)**
Goble, Alan. PN1997.85.G64 2000, **(v3)**
Goble, Andrew Edmund. DS863.G63 1996, **(v5)**
Goble, Danney. F699.G6, **(v4)**
Goble, Frank G. BF698.G56 1970, **(v2)**
Gocek, Fatma Muge. HN656.5.A8.G63 1996, **(v6)**
Goda, Norman J. W. D757.G56 1998, **(v5)**
Godbout, Jacques. PQ3919.2.G55.H5713 1988, **(v3)**
Goddard, George W. TR140.G6.A3, **(v1)**
Goddard, Robert Hutchings. TL781.85.G6.A34, **(v1)**
Godden, Malcolm. PR2015.G64 1990, **(v3)**
Godden, Richard. PS3511.A86.Z7834 1997, **(v3)**
Godden, Rumer. PR6013.O2 B3, **(v3)**
    PR6013.O2 E6, **(v3)**
    PR6013.O2 I65 1969, **(v3)**
Gode, Alexander. PT1160.E5G6, **(v3)**
Godfray, H. C. J. QL496.G59 1994, **(v1)**
Godfrey, Sheldon J. F1035.J5.G53 1995, **(v4)**
Godineau, Dominique. DC731.G6313 1998, **(v5)**
Godish, Thad. RA577.5.G63 1995, **(v2)**
    TD883.G57 1997, **(v1)**
    TD883.17, **(v1)**
Godlove, Terry F. BL51.G69 1989, **(v8)**
Godman, Peter. DG737.55.G63 1998, **(v5)**
Godoy, Ricardo A. F3320.2.J84.G63 1990, **(v4)**
Godson, Roy. JK468.I6.G62 1995, **(v7)**
Godwin, E. W. NA997.G6.A4 1999, **(v9)**
Godwin, Gail. PS3557.O315.D7, **(v3)**
Godwin, John L. F264.W7.G64 2000, **(v4)**
Godwin, Mike. KF4772.G63 1998, **(v7)**
Godwin, Peter. DT2988.G64 1993, **(v5)**
Godwin, R. Kenneth. JK1118.G63 1988, **(v7)**
Godwin, William. HB701.G45 1969, **(v6)**
    PR4722.C2, **(v3)**
    PR5841.W8.Z7 1969, **(v3)**
Goebbels, Joseph. DD247.G6.A25 1970, **(v5)**
    DD247.G6.A2913 1983, **(v5)**
Goehlert, Robert. KF240.G63 1989, **(v7)**
    Z7165.U5.G568 1996, **(v10)**
    Z7165.U5.M285 1994, **(v10)**
Goehr, Lydia. ML3800.G576 1992, **(v9)**
Goemans, H. E. D613.G62 2000, **(v5)**
Goertzel, Ted George. Q143.P25.G64 1995, **(v1)**
Goethe, Johann Wolfgang von. PT1891.C85 1985b, **(v3)**
    PT2026.A1.C83 1983, **(v3)**
    PT2026.A1.C83 1983 vol. 9, **(v3)**
    PT2026.A2.M3, **(v3)**
    PT2026.A2.U4, **(v3)**
    PT2026.A3.L85 1999, **(v3)**
    PT2026.F2.F3313 2000, **(v3)**
    PT2026.F2.G77 1992, **(v3)**
    PT2027.A2.W4, **(v3)**
    PT2027.C5.O8 1971, **(v3)**
    PT2027.L4.H4, **(v3)**
    PT2027.W3H813 1990, **(v3)**
    PT2027.W3.M6, **(v3)**
Goetz, Hans-Werner. CB361.G6213 1993, **(v5)**
Goetzfridt, Nicholas J. GN440.I53 1992, **(v6)**
    PN849.O26.I53 1995, **(v3)**
Goetzmann, William H. F591.G62, **(v4)**
Goff, Brian L. HC110.W4.G58 1999, **(v6)**
Goff, Frederick Richmond. Z240.G58 Copy 2, **(v10)**
Goff, James B. ML3187.G64 2002, **(v9)**
Goff, Janet Emily. PL735.G58 1991, **(v3)**
Goff, M. Lee. RA1063.45.G64 2000, **(v2)**
Goffart, Walter A. D121.G64 1989, **(v5)**
    DG319.G63, **(v5)**

Goffen, Rona. ND623.B39.G64 1989, (v9)
ND623.G6.G58 1988, (v9)
Goffen, Rona. ND623.T7.G56 1997, (v9)
Goffman, Daniel. DR435.B74.G64 1998, (v5)
HF3756.5.Z7.M6284 1990, (v6)
Goffman, Erving. HM131.G55, (v6)
Goffman, Ethan. PS173.N4.G64 2000, (v3)
Gofman, John W. RC268.55.G63 1990, (v2)
Goforth, Frances S. LB1583.8.G64 1994, (v7)
Goggin, Jacqueline Anne. E175.5.W65.G64 1993, (v4)
Goggin, James E. RC503.G63 2001, (v2)
Goggin, Malcolm L. RJ102.G64 1987, (v2)
Gogh, Vincent van. ND653.G7.A26 1959, (v9)
ND653.G7.A43 1946, (v9)
Gogol, Nikolaæi Vasilevich. PG3333.A15 1985, (v3)
PG3333.M4 1985, (v3)
PG3333.M42 1965, (v3)
GoGwilt, Christopher Lloyd. PR878.P6.G64 2000, (v3)
PR6005.O4.Z7275 1995, (v3)
Goheen, Miriam. DT571.N74.G64 1996, (v5)
Going, Allen Johnston. F326.G65 1992, (v4)
Goitein, S. D. DS119.G58, (v5)
Golan, Galia. DB215.5.G5, (v5)
DS63.2.S65.G648 1990, (v5)
Golan, Jonathan S. QA184.G6313 1995, (v1)
Golan, Naomi. RC451.4.M54.G65 1986, (v2)
Golani, Moti. DS110.5.G634 1998, (v5)
Golant, Stephen M. HD7287.92.U54.G63 1992, (v6)
HQ1064.U6.I28 1984, (v6)
Golany, Gideon. NA7448.G6 1992, (v9)
Golb, Norman. BM487.G65 1995, (v8)
DS135.F85.N675 1998, (v5)
Golczewski, James A. RA776.75.G646 1998, (v2)
Gold, Alice Ross. LA186.G59, (v7)
Gold, Ann Grodzins. GR305.5.R3.G65 1992, (v6)
Gold, Hazel. PQ6555.Z5.G65 1993, (v3)
Gold, Herbert. PS3557.O34.F3, (v3)
PS3557.O34.S3, (v3)
Gold, Ivan. PS3557.O35.N5 1963, (v3)
Gold, Mark S. RC568.C6.G653 1993, (v2)
Gold, Martin. HV9105.M5.G65 1992, (v6)
LC45.4.G64 1984, (v7)
Gold, Mary Jayne. D809.F7.G57, (v5)
Gold, Maxwell Benjamin. PR3726.G6, (v3)
Gold, Penny Schine. HQ1147.F7.G65 1985, (v6)
Gold, Thomas. QB209.G56, (v1)
TN870.5.G66 1999, (v1)
Goldberg, Alfred. UG633.G6, (v10)
Goldberg, Anatol. PG3476.E5.Z687 1984, (v3)
Goldberg, Ann. RC450.G4.G64 1999, (v2)
Goldberg, Bruce. LA212.G64 1996, (v7)
Goldberg, Carl. RC455.4.S53.G65 1991, (v2)
RC509.8.G65 2000, (v2)
Goldberg, David Joseph. E784.G65 1999, (v4)
Goldberg, Edward L. N7483.B28.G6 1988, (v9)
Goldberg, Elkhonon. QP382.F7, (v1)
Goldberg, Harriet. GR230.G57 1998, (v6)
Goldberg, Harvey E. DS135.L44.G65 1990, (v5)
Goldberg, Harvey. DC342.8.J4.G63, (v5)
Goldberg, Jonathan. PR113.G65 1997, (v3)
PR428.H66.G6 1992, (v3)
PS3505.A87.Z647 2001, (v3)
Goldberg, Kathy E. QM101.G63 1982, (v1)
Goldberg, Myla. PS3557.O35819, (v3)
Goldberg, Nancy Sloan. PQ637.W35.G65 1999, (v3)
Goldberg, Robert Alan. E748.G64.G65 1995, (v4)
Golden, Eve. PN2287.H24.G65 1991, (v3)
PN2287.H42.G65 2000, (v3)
Golden, James Reed. HC110.I55.G65 1994, (v6)
Golden, Joanne Marie. PN1009.A1.G566 1990, (v3)
Golden, Leon. PN1040.A53.G65 1992, (v3)
Golden, Marissa Martino. JK723.E9.G65 2000, (v7)
Golden, Mark. GV573.G65 1998, (v6)
HQ792.G73.G65 1990, (v6)
Golden, Morris. PR3503.G57, (v3)
PR3667.G6, (v3)
Golden, Olivia Ann. HV699.G64 1992, (v6)
Golden, Renny. HV1448.S2.G65 1991, (v6)
Goldenberg, Robert. BS1199.G63.G65 1998, (v8)

Goldenberg, Suzanne. DK509.G65 1994, (v5)
Goldensohn, Lorrie. PS3503.I785.Z67 1992, (v3)
Goldfarb, Jeffrey C. DK4440.G64 1982, (v5)
Goldfarb, Ronald L. KF8725.G65 1998, (v7)
Goldfield, David R. E185.61.G584 1990, (v4)
Goldfinger, Eliot. NC760.G67 1991, (v9)
Goldgar, Bertrand A. PR448.P6.G6, (v3)
Goldgeier, James M. DK266.45.G65 1994, (v5)
Goldhagen, Daniel Jonah. D804.3.G648 1996, (v5)
Goldin, Claudia Dale. HD6095.G65 1990, (v6)
Goldin, Judah. BM514.G65 1988, (v8)
Goldin, Paul Rakita. B128.H7.G64 1999, (v8)
Golding, Brian. DA197.G65 1994, (v5)
Golding, John. N6494.M64.G65 1994, (v9)
ND196.C8.G6 1968, (v9)
ND553.B86.A4 1997, (v9)
Golding, Martin P. LC72.2.G64 2000, (v7)
Golding, Sue. JC265.G68.G65 1992, (v7)
Golding, William. PR6013.C35.P3 1985, (v3)
PR6013.O35.B7 1969, (v3)
PR6013.O35.C5 1987, (v3)
PR6013.O35.D3, (v3)
PR6013.O35.F7, (v3)
PR6013.O35.H6 1966, (v3)
PR6013.O35.I5 1962, (v3)
PR6013.O35.L6 1997, (v3)
PR6013.O35.M6 1982, (v3)
PR6013.O35.P9 1967, (v3)
PR6013.O35.R5 1980, (v3)
PR6013.O4.S64, (v3)
Goldleaf, Steven. PS3529.H29.Z69 1999, (v3)
Goldman, Alan H. BD161.G64 1988, (v8)
BH39.G5815 1995, (v8)
BJ1031.G65 1988, (v8)
Goldman, Albert Harry. ML420.P96.G66, (v9)
Goldman, Alvin I. B945.G593.L52 1991, (v8)
BD175.G64 1999, (v8)
BD212.G65 2002, (v8)
Goldman, Anne E. HQ1186.U6.G65 1996, (v6)
Goldman, Bernard. Z5961.M58.G65 1991, (v10)
Goldman, Dorothy. PR478.W65.G65 1995, (v3)
Goldman, Eric Frederick. E661.G58, (v4)
E813.G6 1966, (v4)
Goldman, Harvey. BV4740.G65 1988, (v8)
JC263.W42.G65 1992, (v7)
Goldman, Herbert G. ML420.J74.G6 1988, (v9)
Goldman, Irving. DU510.G58 1970, (v5)
Goldman, Lawrence. LC5325.O92.G654 1995, (v7)
Goldman, Marshall I. DK288.G59 1991, (v5)
HC335.G565, (v6)
Goldman, Martin. QC16.M4.G65 1983, (v1)
Goldman, Merle. DS777.55.G67, (v5)
DS777.6.G64, (v5)
Goldman, Michael. PN1631.G59 2000, (v3)
Goldman, Minton F. DB2848.G65 1999, (v5)
DJK51.G654 1997, (v5)
Goldman, Ralph Morris. KZ5625.G65 1997, (v7)
Goldman, Richard Franko. ML1300.G65, (v9)
Goldman, Sheldon. KF8776.G65 1997, (v7)
Goldman, Shifra M. N6501.G64 1994, (v9)
Z5961.U5.G64 1985, (v10)
Goldman, Stan. PS2384.C53.G65 1993, (v3)
Goldman, Wendy Z. KLA540.G65 1993, (v7)
Goldovsky, Boris. ML1700.G738.B7, (v9)
Goldowsky, Seebert J. RD27.35.P38.G65 1988, (v2)
Goldscheider, Calvin. HN660.A8.G65 1996, (v6)
Goldscheider, Frances K. HQ536.G65 1991, (v6)
Goldschmidt, Arthur. DS62.G64 1983, (v5)
DT97.G65 1999, (v5)
Goldschmidt, Bertrand. QC773.G6413 1990, (v1)
Goldsmith, Donald. QB820.G65 1997, (v1)
Goldsmith, Donald. QB981.G594 1995, (v1)
Goldsmith, Emanuel S. PJ5113.G66, (v3)
Goldsmith, John A. E747.G63 1993, (v4)
Goldsmith, Oliver. PR3481.D6 1927, (v3)
PR3481.F7, (v3)
PR3482.H5, (v3)
PR3487.E9 1968, (v3)
Goldsmith, Peter David. ML429.A83.G65 1998, (v9)
Goldsmith, Robert Hillis. PR2992.F6.G6, (v3)
Goldsmith, William W. HV4045.G65 1992, (v6)

Goldsteen, Raymond L. HN80.G65.G65 1991, (v6)
Goldstein, Avery. UA835.G65 2000, (v10)
Goldstein, Avram. RC564.G66 2001, (v2)
Goldstein, Brian. RC428.8.G65 2000, (v2)
Goldstein, Herman. HV9950.G65 1990b, (v6)
Goldstein, Joel K. JK609.5.G64 1982, (v7)
Goldstein, Joseph. KF8742.G65 1992, (v7)
Goldstein, Judith. HF1455.G65 1993, (v6)
Goldstein, Kenneth M. JK1118.G634 1999, (v7)
Goldstein, Kurt. RC343.G56513 1995, (v2)
Goldstein, Laurence. B804.G59 1990, (v8)
Goldstein, Leslie Friedman. KF478.A4.G65 1994, (v7)
Goldstein, Lisa S. LB1139.25.G65 1997, (v7)
Goldstein, Martin E. UA23.G67 1993, (v10)
Goldstein, Martin. QC318.E57.G65 1993, (v1)
Goldstein, Melvyn C. DS786.G635 1989, (v5)
DS786.G636 1997, (v5)
GN635.C5.G65 1990, (v6)
Goldstein, Myrna Chandler. RA418.G56 2001, (v2)
Goldstein, Philip. PN98.C6.G6 1990, (v3)
Goldstein, Robert D. KF3771.G65 1988, (v7)
Goldstein, Robert J. SF457.G648 2000, (v1)
Goldstein, Robert Justin. CR113.G57 1995, (v5)
KF224.J64, (v7)
Goldstein, Ronald E. RK54.G64 1998, (v2)
Goldstein, Sam. LB3013.G63 1995, (v7)
RJ506.H9.G652 1998, (v2)
Goldstein, Warren Jay. GV863.A1.G66 1989, (v6)
Goldston, R. J. QC718.G63 1995, (v1)
Goldstone, Jack A. D210.G58 1991, (v5)
Goldsworthy, Adrian Keith. DG242.G65 2000, (v5)
Goldsworthy, Andy. NB497.G64, (v9)
Goldsworthy, Vesna. PR129.B35.G65 1998, (v3)
Goldthorpe, J. E. HN16.G65 1996, (v6)
Goldthorpe, John H. HN400.S6.G64 1987, (v6)
Goldwater, Barry M. E748.G64.A37, (v4)
F811.G6 1940, (v4)
JK271.G668, (v7)
Goldwhite, Harold. QD181.P1.G67, (v1)
Goldwin, Robert A. KF4541.G65 1997, (v7)
KF4749.A2.G65 1990, (v7)
UA23.G68 1963, (v10)
Goldziher, Ignac. BP161.G5713, (v8)
Gole, Nilufer. HQ1726.7.G65 1996, (v6)
Golemba, Beverly E. CT3203.G57 1992, (v5)
Golenbock, Peter. GV1029.9.S74.G65 1993, (v6)
Goll, Yvan. PT2613.O474 1960, (v3)
Gollaher, David. HV28.D6.G65 1995, (v6)
Gollan, Robin. HD8848.G6 1967, (v6)
Golley, Frank B. QH540.8.G64 1993, (v1)
Gollin, A. M. UG635.G7.G54 1989, (v10)
Gollin, Rita K. PS1892.A66.G65 1991, (v3)
Golob, Richard. TJ808.3.G65 1993, (v1)
Golomb, Jacob. B105.A8.G65 1995, (v8)
Golomb, Solomon W. QA166.75.G65 1994, (v1)
Golombek, Lisa. NA5991.G6 1988, (v9)
Golovine, Michael N. UG630.G578 1962a, (v10)
Golovnev, A. V. DK34.N4.G65 1999, (v5)
Golsan, Richard Joseph. DC397.G59 2000, (v5)
Golub, Edward S. QR181.G66 1991, (v1)
R133.G656 1994, (v2)
Golub, Gene H. QA76.58.G64 1993, (v1)
Golub, L. QB521.G65 2001, (v1)
Golub, Spencer. PN1655.G66 1999, (v3)
PN2724.G56 1994, (v3)
Gomara, Francisco Lopez de. F1230.C9216, (v4)
Gombosi, Tamas I. QC861.2.G64 1998, (v1)
Gombrich, Ernst Hans Josef. N5300.G643 1984, (v9)
Gomersall, Meg. HQ1229.G66 1997, (v6)
Gomery, Douglas. PN1993.5.U6.G59 1992, (v3)
Gomes, Leonard. HF1008.G65 1987, (v6)
Gomes, Mercio Pereira. F2519.3.G6.G6613 2000, (v4)
Gomes-Casseres, Benjamin. HD69.S8.G66 1996, (v6)
Gomez de Avellaneda y Arteaga, Gertrudis. PQ6524.S313 1993, (v3)
Gomez de la Serna, Ramon. PQ6613.O4.T6813 1989, (v3)
PQ6641.A47.Z63, (v3)
Gomez M., Alejandro. JC421.M57 1999, (v7)
Gomez, Edmund Terence. HC445.5.G65 1999, (v6)
Gomez, Joan. RC451.4.M45.G66 1991, (v2)

Gomez, Michael Angelo. DT549.9.B68.G66 1992, (v5)
E185.18.G18 1998, (v4)
Gomez-Pena, Guillermo. NX512.G66, (v9)
Gomez-Quinones, Juan. E184.M5.G634 1990, (v4)
F790.M5.G65 1994, (v4)
Gommans, Jos J. L. DS442.3.G68 2002, (v5)
DS331.A12 G66 2001, (v5)
Gompers, Samuel. HD8073.G6.A3 1984, (v6)
Goncharov, Ivan Aleksandrovich. PG3337.G6.O122 1967, (v3)
Goncharov, S. N. DS740.5.S65.G66 1993, (v5)
Goncourt, Edmond de. PQ2261.Z5.A2, (v3)
Gondwe, Derrick K. HB98.2.G65 1992, (v6)
Góngora y Argote, Luis de. PQ6394.A1 2000, (v3)
PQ6394.A16 1986b, (v3)
Gongora, Mario. F1410.G75, (v4)
Gonnaud, Maurice. PS1642.S58.G66 1987, (v3)
Gonzales, Manuel G. E184.M5.G638 1999, (v4)
Gonzalez Mandri, Flora Maria. PQ8097.D617.Z63 1995, (v3)
Gonzalez Pena, Carlos. PQ7111.G62 1968, (v3)
Gonzalez, Alexander G. PR8727.G66 1997, (v3)
Gonzalez, Anibal. PQ7082.N7.G66 1993, (v3)
Gonzalez, Francisco J. B398.D5.G66 1998, (v8)
González, Justo L. BR145.2.G65 1996, (v8)
Gonzalez, Mario. E99.T34.G65 1999, (v4)
Gonzalez, Mike. PQ7082.P7.G66 1992, (v3)
Gonzalez, N. V. M. PR9550.9.G66 S4 1975, (v3)
Gonzalez, Nancie L. Solien. F1505.2.C3.G63 1988, (v4)
Gonzalez-Arias, Francisca. PQ6629.A7.Z68 1992, (v3)
González-Wippler, Migene. BL2532.S3 G66, (v8)
Gooch, Brad. PS3529.H28.Z687 1993, (v3)
Gooch, Bryan N. S. ML134.5.S52.G6 1991, (v9)
Gooch, G. P. D13.G7 1959, (v5)
D15.G64.A3, (v5)
D397.G58 1969, (v5)
D511.G592, (v5)
DC280.4.G6, (v5)
DD5.G66 1969, (v5)
PT111.G6, (v3)
Gooch, John. DG484.G66 1989, (v5)
UA646.G59, (v10)
Gooch, Paul W. B317.G66 1996, (v8)
Good Housekeeping Institute (New York, N.Y.). TX715.G624 1955, (v1)
Good, Edwin M. ML652.G6 2001, (v9)
Good, Harry Gehman. LA13.G6 1960, (v7)
LA209.G58 1973, (v7)
Good, Howard. PN4871.G66 1993, (v3)
Good, Thomas L. LB2806.36.G66 2000, (v7)
Goodale, Jane C. DU740.42.G66 1995, (v5)
GN671.N5.G66 1996, (v6)
Goodall, Francis. Z7164.C81.G595 1997, (v10)
Goodall, Jane. QL31.G58, (v1)
QL737.P96.G585 1986, (v1)
Goodare, Julian. DA785.G665 1999, (v5)
Goodby, John. PR8771.G66 2000, (v3)
Goodchild, Peter. QC16.O62.G66 1981, (v1)
Goode, Clement Tyson. Z8139.G66 1997, (v10)
Goode, G. Brown. Q105.U5.G66 1991, (v1)
Goode, Judith Granich. F158.9.A1.G66 1994, (v4)
Goode, Richard B. HJ1620.G66 1984, (v6)
HJ4652.G6 1976, (v6)
Goode, Stephen W. QA371.G644 1991, (v1)
Goode, William Josiah. HQ814.G62 1993, (v6)
Goodenough, Florence Laura. BF721.G64, (v2)
Goodenough, John B. QD171.G65, (v1)
Goodenough, Ursula. QH331.G624 1998, (v1)
Gooderson, Ian. D785.G58 1998, (v5)
Goodey, Brian. F640.G65, (v4)
Goodfellow, Samuel Huston. DC650.5.G66 1998, (v5)
Goodfellow, William D. ML128.P63.G65 1995, (v9)
ML128.P63 G65 1995 Suppl., (v9)
Goodfriend, Joyce D. F122.G643 1991, (v4)
Z5305.U5.G66 1987, (v10)
Goodhart, Sandor. PN81.G628 1996, (v3)
Goodheart, Eugene. PN81.G636 1997, (v3)
Goodheart, Eugene. PR6023.A93.Z6297, (v3)
Goodin, Robert E. B843.G66 1995, (v8)

HM216.G564 1988, (v6)
JA79.G643 1992, (v7)
Gooding, James Henry. E513.5 54th .G66 1991, (v4)
Goodkin, Richard E. PQ1907.G66 1991, (v3)
PQ2631.R63.A7928 1991, (v3)
Goodlad, John I. LA210.G626 1997, (v7)
LA217.G654 1984, (v7)
LB1715.G53 1990, (v7)
Goodman, Allegra. PS3557.O5829.K3 1999, (v3)
Goodman, Aviel. RC560.S43.G66 1998, (v2)
Goodman, Bryna. DS796.S25.G66 1995, (v5)
Goodman, David C. DP81.5.G6 1997, (v5)
Goodman, David S. G. DS793.S8 G66 1986, (v5)
HN740.T34, (v6)
Goodman, David. DT1974.G66 1999, (v5)
Goodman, Dena. PQ618.G66 1994, (v3)
Goodman, Felicitas D. BF1389.A7.G66 1990, (v2)
Goodman, Jack. E806.G65, (v4)
Goodman, Jennifer R. PR149.A79.G66 1988, (v3)
PR651.G66 1990, (v3)
Goodman, John B. HG2980.5.A7.G66 1992, (v6)
Goodman, Jordan. HC240.G564 1988, (v6)
Goodman, Jordan. RC271.P27G66 2001, (v2)
Goodman, Kenneth S. BF456.R2.G63, (v7)
Goodman, Lenn Evan. B751.Z7 G66 1992, (v8)
B755.G66 1999, (v8)
BM645.H85.G66 1998, (v8)
BP190.5.T78 G66 2002, (v8)
Goodman, Libby. LC3965.G58 1990, (v7)
Goodman, Lizbeth. PN2595.13.W65.G66 1993, (v3)
Goodman, Louis Wolf. HD2755.5.G66 1987, (v6)
Goodman, Marshall R. HD3616.U47.G67 1987, (v6)
Goodman, Martin. DS110.G2.G66 1983, (v5)
Goodman, Melvin A. D888.S65.G66 1991, (v5)
Goodman, Michael Z. Z8136.17.G65 1990, (v10)
Goodman, Nan. PS217.A25.G66 1998, (v3)
Goodman, Nelson. B29.G619 1984, (v8)
B829.5.G6 1966, (v8)
BC181.G58 1965, (v8)
BD241.G65 1988, (v8)
BD331.G65, (v8)
Goodman, Paul S. HD45.G58 1990, (v6)
Goodman, Paul. E449.G67 1998, (v4)
LB2321.G63, (v7)
PS3513.O527.L67 1962, (v3)
PS3513.O527 M3, (v3)
Goodman, Percival. NA9030.G6, (v9)
Goodman, Peter W. ML410.G695 G66 2000, (v9)
Goodman, Richard E. TA706.G644 1993, (v1)
Goodman, Richard M. RJ50.G65 1983, (v2)
Goodman, Robert B. TJ219.G66 1997, (v1)
Goodman, Sandra. QP772.A8.G66 1991, (v1)
Goodman, Susan E. F68.G63 1999, (v4)
Goodman, Susan. PS3513.L34.Z668 1998, (v3)
PS3545.H16.Z653 1990, (v3)
PS3545.H16.Z654 1994, (v3)
Goodman, Walter. F128.52.G66, (v4)
Goodnow, Jacqueline J. HQ1075.5.A8.G66 1994, (v6)
Goodrich, Chauncey A. PR901.G6 1963, (v3)
Goodrich, Chris. KF272.G66 1991, (v7)
Goodrich, Frances. PS3513.O53515.D5 1956, (v3)
Goodrich, Jonathan N. HD9711.75.U62.G66 1989, (v6)
Goodrich, L. Carrington. DS735.G58 1969, (v5)
Goodrich, Lloyd. N6537.E3.G6 1982, (v9)
Goodrich, Marcus. PS3513.O5352 D4, (v3)
Goodrich, Samuel G. PS1755.A6 1967, (v3)
Goodrich, Th. E470.45.G66 1995, (v4)
E474.97.G66 1991, (v4)
F685.G66 1998, (v4)
Goodridge, John. PR555.R87.G66 1995, (v3)
Goodrum, Charles A. HF5813.U6.G64 1990, (v6)
Goodsell, David S. QH581.2.G66 1993, (v1)
QP514.2.G66 1996, (v1)
Goodsell, Don. TL9.G64 1995, (v1)
Goodsell, Willystine. LC1752.G6 1970, (v7)
Goodson, A. C. PR4487.L33.G66 1988, (v3)
Goodson, Larry P. DS371.3.G66 2001, (v5)
Goodstein, Anita Shafer. F444.N257.G66 1989, (v4)
Goodstein, David L. QB603.M6.G66 1996, (v1)
Goodwin, Albert. DA520.G6 1979, (v5)

Goodwin, Andrew. PN1992.8.M87.G66 1992, (v3)
Goodwin, Brian C. QH366.2.G655 1994, (v1)
Goodwin, Bridget. D810.C38.G66 1998, (v5)
Goodwin, C. James. BF105.G66 1999, (v2)
Goodwin, Doris Kearns. CT274.F58.G66 1991, (v5)
E807.G66 1994, (v4)
E847.G64 1991, (v4)
Goodwin, H. Eugene. PN4888.E8.G66 1994, (v3)
Goodwin, James. PN1998.3.E34.G66 1993, (v3)
PN1998.3.K87.G66 1994, (v3)
Goodwin, Joanne L. HV699.4.C48.G66 1997, (v6)
Goodwin, Mark. BS2398.G66 2001, (v8)
Goodwin, Philip Lippincott. NA850.G6, (v9)
Goodwin, Richard N. E881.G66 1992, (v4)
Goodwin, William Lawrence. LB1115.G635, (v7)
Goodwyn, Frank. F392.K47.G66 1993, (v4)
Goodwyn, Janet. PS3545.H16.Z655 1990, (v3)
Goodwyn, Lawrence. E661.G67, (v4)
HD8537.N783.G66 1991, (v6)
Goody, Jack. GN476.73.G66 1993, (v6)
GT2772.A2.G66 1990, (v6)
Goodyear, Frank Henry. N6512.5.P45.G6, (v9)
Goonetilleke, D. C. R. A. PR129.S64.G66 1988, (v3)
PR6068.U757.Z625 1998, (v3)
Goossen, Rachel Waltner. D810.C82.G66 1997, (v5)
Goossens, Leon. MT360.G66, (v9)
Gopal, Christopher. HD38.5.G67 1992, (v6)
Gopaul-McNicol, Sharon-Ann. LC3731.G68 1998, (v7)
Goralski, Walter. TK5103.2.G67 1996, (v1)
Gorbachev, Mikhail Sergeevich. DK49.G6713 2000, (v5)
DK289.G675 1987, (v5)
DK290.3.G67.A3 1996, (v5)
Gordan, John Dozier. PR6005.O4.Z728 1963, (v3)
Gordiejew, Paul Benjamin. DS135.Y8.G67 1999, (v5)
Gordimer, Nadine. PR9369.3.G6.A6 1971, (v3)
PR9369.3.G6.C65 1975, (v3)
PR9369.3.G6.O3, (v3)
PR9369.3.G6.Z467 1988, (v3)
Gordis, Robert. BM520.5.G67 1990, (v8)
Gordon, A. D. D. DS480.4.G67 1995, (v5)
Gordon, Albert Isaac. HQ1031.G6, (v6)
Gordon, Andrew. HD8728.G65 1990, (v6)
Gordon, April A. HQ1240.5.A35.G67 1996, (v6)
Gordon, Bernard K. DS518.1.G6, (v5)
HF1456.5.A64.G67 1990, (v6)
Gordon, Bernard. PN1998.3.G662.A3 1999, (v3)
Gordon, Bertram M. D802.F8.G67, (v5)
Gordon, Beverly. HV544.G67 1998, (v6)
Gordon, Caroline. PS3513.O5765.A6 1981, (v3)
PS3513.O5765 F6, (v3)
PS3513.O5765 G3, (v3)
PS3513.O5765 M3, (v3)
PS3513.O5765 O4 1963, (v3)
PS3513.O5765 P4 1969, (v3)
PS3513.O5765 S7, (v3)
PS3513.O5765 W6 1971, (v3)
PS3513.O5765.Z49 1999, (v3)
PS3513.O5765.Z497 1984, (v3)
Gordon, Colin. HC106.3.G625 1994, (v6)
Gordon, Cyrus Herzl. BS635.G73 1997, (v8)
Gordon, Daniel. DC33.4.G62 1994, (v5)
Gordon, David C. DS80.G67 1983, (v5)
Gordon, David J. PR5368.C56.G67 1990, (v3)
Gordon, David J. PR6063.U7.Z663 1995, (v3)
Gordon, Deborah. QL568.F7.G64 1999, (v1)
Gordon, Donald E. NX550.A1.G63 1987, (v9)
Gordon, Edmund I. PJ4075.G6, (v3)
Gordon, Edmund Tayloe. F1536.B58.G67 1998, (v4)
Gordon, Edmund W. LC213.2.G65 1999, (v7)
Gordon, Edward E. HF5549.5.T7.G547 1994, (v6)
LC41.G58 1990, (v7)
Gordon, Felicia. HQ1615.A3.G67 1996, (v6)
Gordon, Fon Louise. E185.93.A8 G67 1995, (v4)
Gordon, G. A. H. D582.J8.G68 1996, (v5)
Gordon, Gary D. TK5104.G67 1993, (v1)
Gordon, Gregory. PN4841.U66.G67 1990, (v3)
Gordon, Hayim. B2430.S34.G63 1995, (v8)
PJ7846.A46.Z65 1990, (v3)
Gordon, Jacob U. E185.615.G666 2000, (v4)
Z1361.N39.G67 1999, (v10)

Gordon, Jill. B395.G455 1999, **(v8)**
Gordon, Joel. DT107.83.G67 1991, **(v5)**
Gordon, John D. RC889.G665 2002, **(v2)**
Gordon, Lesley J. E467.1.P57.G67 1998, **(v4)**
Gordon, Lewis R. B944.A37.G67 2000, **(v8)**
Gordon, Lincoln. F2538.2.G76 2001, **(v4)**
Gordon, Linda. HQ766.5.U5.G67, **(v6)**
Gordon, Lois G. E169.1.G664 1999, **(v4)**
  E169.1.G665 1987, **(v4)**
  PR6003.E282.Z6666 1996, **(v3)**
Gordon, Lyndall. PR4168.G65 1995, **(v3)**
  PS2123.G67 1999, **(v3)**
  PS3509.L43.Z6794 1999, **(v3)**
Gordon, Malcolm S. QH366.2.G657 1995, **(v1)**
  QP33.G65 1982, **(v1)**
Gordon, Matthew J. PE3101.M5G67 2001, **(v3)**
Gordon, Michael A. F128.9.I6.G67 1993, **(v4)**
Gordon, Milton Myron. HN57.G6, **(v6)**
Gordon, Nancy D. GB1205.G65 1992, **(v6)**
Gordon, Paul. BH301.T7.G67 2001, **(v8)**
Gordon, Peter. HQ1945.G67 2001, **(v6)**
Gordon, Philip H. DC417.G67 1995, **(v5)**
  DC420.G67 1993, **(v5)**
Gordon, Rachel Singer. ZA4201.G64 2001, **(v10)**
Gordon, Rae Beth. PN1969.C34G67 2001, **(v3)**
  PQ283.G67 1992, **(v3)**
Gordon, Richard A. RC552.A5.G67 1990, **(v2)**
Gordon, Richard L. HD9502.A2.G67, **(v6)**
Gordon, Robert B. T21.G67 1994, **(v1)**
  TN704.N5.G67 1996, **(v1)**
Gordon, Robert J. DT1558.H45.G67 1997, **(v5)**
Gordon, Robert M. B815.G67 1987, **(v8)**
Gordon, Sara L. HG3891.G67 1995, **(v6)**
Gordon, Scott. H51.G67 1991, **(v6)**
  JF229.G67 1999, **(v7)**
Gordon, Stewart. ML700.G65 1996, **(v9)**
Gordon, Suzanne. HQ1426.G657 1991, **(v6)**
Gordon, Thomas T. T339.G67 2000, **(v1)**
Gordon, Thomas. LB3013.G66, **(v7)**
  R727.3.G63 1995, **(v2)**
Gordon, Virginia N. LB2343.G64 1984, **(v7)**
Gordon, W. Terrence. Z7004.S4.G69 1992, **(v10)**
Gordon-McCutchan, R. C. E99.T2.G67 1991, **(v4)**
Gordon-Reed, Annette. E332.2.G67 1997, **(v4)**
Gordon-Wise, Barbara Ann. PN57.G85.G67 1991, **(v3)**
Gordus, Jeanne P. HD5708.5.G67 1981, **(v6)**
Gore, Albert. GE170.G67 1992, **(v6)**
Gore, Chris. PN1993.4.G67 1999, **(v3)**
Gore, Pelham. HF5626.G67 1992, **(v6)**
Gore, Robert H. F296.G67 1992, **(v4)**
Goreau, Angeline. PR3317.Z5.G6, **(v3)**
Goreham, Gary. Z7757.U5 G6 1990, **(v10)**
Goren, Charles Henry. GV1282.3.G6532 1971, **(v6)**
Gorer, Geoffrey. PQ2063.S3.G6 1978, **(v3)**
Gores, Steven J. PR858.S615.G67 2000, **(v3)**
Gorges, Arthur. PR2279.G5 1953, **(v3)**
Gorham, Deborah. PR6003.R385.Z67 1996, **(v3)**
Gorkin, Michael. HQ1728.5.G67 1996, **(v6)**
Gorky, Maksim. PG3463.A15 1959, **(v3)**
  PG3463.A19 1959, **(v3)**
  PG3463.A19 1978, **(v3)**
Gorlach, Manfred. PE821.G613 1991, **(v3)**
  Z2014.G7.G67 1998, **(v10)**
Gorlitz, Walter. DD247.P38.G613 1964, **(v5)**
Gorman, G. E. Z1002.G67 1987, **(v10)**
  Z7770.G66 1984, **(v10)**
Gorman, Joseph Bruce. E748.K314.G6, **(v4)**
Gorman, Linda M. RC440.G659 2002, **(v2)**
Gorman, M. L. QL737.I57.G67 1990, **(v1)**
Gorman, Martha. GC1085.G67 1993, **(v6)**
Gorman, Robert F. HV640.G66 1994, **(v6)**
  JC571.G655 1997, **(v7)**
  KZ4968.G67 2001, **(v7)**
Gormley, William T. JK421.G645 1989, **(v7)**
Gormly, James L. D445.G57 1990, **(v5)**
Gorn, Elliott J. GV1125.G67 1986, **(v6)**
  HD8073.J6.G67 2001, **(v6)**
Gorni, Yosef. DS119.7.G4313 1987, **(v5)**
Gornick, Vivian. HQ1154.G63, **(v6)**
Gorovitz, Samuel. R725.5.G67 1991, **(v2)**

Gorra, Michael Edward. PR888.I6.G67 1997, **(v3)**
Gorriti Ellenbogen, Gustavo. F3448.2.G6713 1999, **(v4)**
Gorshkov, Sergei Georgievich. VA573.G6613, **(v10)**
Gorski, William T. PR5908.O25.G67 1996, **(v3)**
Gorsky, Susan Rubinow. PR115.G67 1992, **(v3)**
Gorsuch, Anne E. HX313.G666 2000, **(v5)**
Gorzalka, Ann. F760.G67 1998, **(v4)**
Goscilo, Helena. PG3476.T58.Z67 1996, **(v3)**
Gose, Elliott B. PR888.F3.G67 1988, **(v3)**
Gose, Peter. F3429.3.S6.G63 1994, **(v4)**
Goslee, David. PR5589.G6 1989, **(v3)**
Goslee, Nancy Moore. PR5343.P63.G66 1988, **(v3)**
Gosling, Francis G. RC552.N5.G67 1987, **(v2)**
Gosling, J. C. B. BJ1461.G67 1990, **(v8)**
  BJ1481.G636 1982, **(v8)**
Goslinga, Marian. Z1595.G69 1998, **(v10)**
Gosnell, Harold Foote. F548.9.N3.G67, **(v4)**
Gosner, Kevin. F1221.T8.G67 1992, **(v4)**
Goss, Glenda Dawn. ML134.S49 G67 1998, **(v9)**
  ML385.G7 1995, **(v9)**
Goss, R. O. HE571.G67, **(v6)**
Gossen, Gary H. F1221.T9.G67, **(v4)**
Gossman, Lionel. PQ1860.G6, **(v3)**
Gossman, Patricia A. DS480.45.G675 1999, **(v5)**
Gossy, Mary S. PQ6066.G68 1989, **(v3)**
Gosudarstvennaia Tretiakovskaia galereia.
  ND681.M6 1979a, **(v9)**
Gosw̄am̄i, M̄amaòni Raçyachama.
  PK1569.G578D3613 1993, **(v3)**
Goswami, Amit. Q162.G67 1983, **(v1)**
Goswami, Jaideva C. TK5102.9.G69 1999, **(v1)**
Goswami, Usha. LB1139.R4, **(v7)**
Gotch, A.F. (Arthur Frederick). QL9.G67 1996, **(v1)**
Gotelli, Nicholas J. QH352.G67 1995, **(v1)**
  QH541.15.N84.G67 1996, **(v1)**
Gotham, Kevin Fox. HC108.K2 G68 2002, **(v6)**
Goto, Junichi. HD5710.7.G68 1990, **(v6)**
Gotshalk, Dilman Walter. B945.G63.S8, **(v8)**
  BD232.G63, **(v8)**
Gotshalk, Richard. B131.G635 1998, **(v8)**
Gott, J. Richard. QC173.59.S65, **(v1)**
Gottesman, Irving I. RC514.G673 1991, **(v2)**
Gottfredson, Michael R. HV6018.G68 1990, **(v6)**
Gottfried, Alex. F548.5.C38, **(v4)**
Gottfried, Amy S. PS374.V58.G68 1998, **(v3)**
Gottfried, Kurt. QC793.2.G68 1984, **(v1)**
Gottfried, Leon Albert. PR4024.G6 1963, **(v3)**
Gottfried, Paul. JC479.G67 1998, **(v7)**
Gottfried, Robert R. BT695.5.G68 1995, **(v8)**
Gottfried, Roy K. PR6019.O9.P6444 2000, **(v3)**
  PR6019.O9.U65324 1995, **(v3)**
Gottfried, von Strassburg, 13th cent. PT1525.A423 1988, **(v3)**
Gotthold, Julia Z. Z3499.G67 1988, **(v10)**
Gottlieb, Alma. DT545.45.B45.O26 1992, **(v5)**
Gottlieb, Anthony. B72.G68 2000, **(v8)**
Gottlieb, Gilbert. QH438.5.G68 1992, **(v1)**
Gottlieb, Robert. GE180.G68 1993, **(v6)**
  GE197.G67 2001, **(v6)**
Gottlieb, Roger S. JA74.G68 1987, **(v7)**
Gottman, John Mordechai. HQ734.G7137 1994, **(v6)**
Gottmann, Jean. JC319.G66, **(v7)**
Gottschalk, Charles M. TJ163.3.G68 1995, **(v1)**
Gottschalk, Louis Moreau. ML410.G68.A3 1979, **(v9)**
Gottschalk, Louis Reichenthal. DC146.L2.G59, **(v5)**
  DC146.L2.G6, **(v5)**
Gottschalk, Peter. DS430.G66 2000, **(v5)**
Gottschild, Brenda Dixon. PN1590.B53.G68 1996, **(v3)**
Goubert, Pierre. DC129.G613 1970b, **(v5)**
Goudeket, Maurice. PQ2605.O28.Z673 1972, **(v3)**
Goudge, Thomas A. B945.P44.G68 1969, **(v8)**
Goudie, Andrew. GB436.G7.G69 1990, **(v6)**
Goudie, Andrew. GF75.G68 1982, **(v6)**
Gougeon, Len. PS1642.S56.G68 1990, **(v3)**
Gough, Barry M. F851.5.G68, **(v4)**
  F1026.G69 1999, **(v4)**
  F1060.7.M1783.G68 1997, **(v4)**
  F3031.G68 1992, **(v4)**
Gough, Ian. HC256.5.G68, **(v6)**

Gough, J. W. JC153.G68, **(v7)**
  JC336.G6 1957, **(v7)**
Gough, Kathleen, 1925-. HC438.T47.G68 1989, **(v6)**
Gough, Robert. F586.G68 1997, **(v4)**
Gouinlock, James. BJ1012.G665 1993, **(v8)**
Gouke, Mary Noel. Z7164.C5.G68 1990, **(v10)**
Goulbourne, Harry. DA125.A1.G6 1991, **(v5)**
Gould, Andrew. JN94.A58 G68 1999, **(v7)**
Gould, Carol C. JC423.G67 1988, **(v7)**
Gould, Cecil Hilton Monk. ND623.P255.G68 1994, **(v9)**
Gould, D. E. DL976.3.G68 1997, **(v5)**
Gould, Eliga H. DA510.G68 2000, **(v5)**
Gould, Evlyn. PQ543.G6 1989, **(v3)**
  PQ2362.C33.G68 1996, **(v3)**
Gould, Frederick L. TK5105.G68 1997, **(v1)**
Gould, Glenn. ML60.G68 1984, **(v9)**
Gould, James L. QL761.G68 1989, **(v1)**
Gould, Jay M. RA569.E55 1996, **(v2)**
Gould, Jeffrey L. F1525.3.C84.G68 1998, **(v4)**
  HD1531.N5.G68 1990, **(v6)**
Gould, John A. RJ399.A6.G68 1993, **(v2)**
Gould, John. B398.E8.G6 1972, **(v8)**
Gould, Laura L. SF449.C34.G68 1996, **(v1)**
Gould, Lewis L. E661.G675 2001, **(v4)**
  E711.G68, **(v4)**
  E756.G62 1991, **(v4)**
  E756.G63 1996, **(v4)**
  F761.G6, **(v4)**
  Z8561.18.G68 1988, **(v10)**
Gould, Milton S. KF373.G64.A35, **(v7)**
Gould, Peter C. DA550.G68 1988, **(v5)**
Gould, Phillip L. TA660.S5.G644 1999, **(v1)**
Gould, Richard A. CC75.G66 1990, **(v5)**
  CC79.E85.G68, **(v5)**
Gould, Richard A. VM15.G67 2000, **(v10)**
Gould, Stephen Jay. BL240.2.G68 1999, **(v8)**
  QE770.G67 1989, **(v1)**
  QH45.5.G68 1991, **(v1)**
  QH45.5.G7 1993, **(v1)**
  QH81.G673 1985, **(v1)**
  QH361.G65 1977, **(v1)**
  QH361.G66 1980, **(v1)**
  QH366.2.G66 1983, **(v1)**
  QH366.2.G663 2002, **(v1)**
  QH371.G68, **(v1)**
Gould, Timothy. B945.C274.G68 1998, **(v8)**
Gould, Todd. GV1033.5.G65 G68 2002, **(v6)**
Gould, Tony. RC180.9.G68 1995, **(v2)**
Gould, Wilbur A. SB349.G68 1991, **(v1)**
Gould, William B. KF3372.G68 2000, **(v7)**
Goulding, Michael. QH77.A53.G68 1996, **(v1)**
Goulding, Phil G. UA23.G77 1970, **(v10)**
Gouldner, Alvin Ward. HM24.G65, **(v6)**
Goulet, Robert. PR6057.O9.V5, **(v3)**
Goulter, Christina J. M. D790.G665 1995, **(v5)**
Goulty, George A. QH75.G645 1991, **(v1)**
Gouma-Peterson, Thalia. N6537.S34.G68 1999, **(v9)**
Gounard, Jean-Francois. PS153.N5.G6813 1992, **(v3)**
Goure, Leon. UA929.R9.G63, **(v10)**
Gourevitch, Philip. DT450.435.G68 1998, **(v5)**
Gourgouris, Stathis. JC311.G657 1996, **(v7)**
Gourmont, Remy de. PC2073.G6 1955, **(v3)**
Gourse, Leslie. ML420.C63 G7 1991, **(v9)**
Gouwens, Kenneth. DG812.12.G68 1998, **(v5)**
Gouyet, Jean-Francois. QC20.7.F73.G6813 1996, **(v1)**
Gove, H. E. QC454.A25.G68 1999, **(v1)**
Gove, Samuel Kimball. JK5716.G66 1996, **(v7)**
Govenar, Alan B. E444.G68 2000, **(v4)**
Gover, C. Jane. TR23.G68 1988, **(v1)**
Govier, Trudy. BJ1476.G685 2002, **(v8)**
Govrin, Yosef. DS119.8.S65.G6813 1998, **(v5)**
Gow, James. DR1313.7.D58.G69 1997, **(v5)**
  DR1360.G68 2000, **(v5)**
Gow, Peter. F3429.1.U78.G68 1991, **(v4)**
Gowa, Joanne S. HG3903.G68 1983, **(v6)**
Gowdy, John M. HC79.E5.G6848 1995, **(v6)**
Gower, John. PA8520.G74.P633, **(v3)**
  PR1980. 1968, **(v3)**
  PR1984.C6 1963, **(v3)**
Gowing, Lawrence. ND553.C33.A4 1988, **(v9)**

Gowland, D. A. HC241.25.G7.G675 1999, **(v6)**
Goy, Richard J. NA7594.G6 1989, **(v9)**
Goya, Francisco. N7113.G68.A4 1989, **(v9)**
Goyen, William. PS3513.O97 H6, **(v3)**
  PS3513.O97 I5 1955, **(v3)**
Goytisolo, Juan. PQ6613.O79.A25 1987, **(v3)**
  PQ6613.O79.C813 1994, **(v3)**
  PQ6613.O79.Z46413 1990, **(v3)**
Gozansky, Sue. GV1015.5.C63 G69 2001, **(v6)**
Grˆciˆc, Joseph. BJ55.G73 2000, **(v8)**
Grabar, Andre. N6250.G6713, **(v9)**
  ND140.G683, **(v9)**
  ND140.G7, **(v9)**
  ND142.G7, **(v9)**
Grabar, Oleg. DS109.916.G73 1996, **(v5)**
  NA5997.5.I84.G73 1990, **(v9)**
Grabau, Warren. E475.27.G79 2000, **(v4)**
Grabbe, Christian Dietrich. PT2253.G3.A6 1964, **(v3)**
Grabbe, Crockett L. UG1523.G69 1991, **(v10)**
Graber, Mark A. KF4772.G73 1991, **(v7)**
Grabois, Aryeh. CB353.G7, **(v5)**
Grace, Nancy McCampbell. PN56.M316.G73 1995, **(v3)**
Grachev, A. S. DK290.3.G67.G7313 1995, **(v5)**
Gracia, Jorge J. E. B51.4.G72 1992, **(v8)**
Gracian y Morales, Baltasar. PQ6398.G3.C7 1971, **(v3)**
Gracy, David B. F389.A92.G73 1987, **(v4)**
Grade, Chaim. PJ5129.G68.T713x, **(v3)**
Gradenwitz, Peter. ML345.I5.G73 1996, **(v9)**
  ML410.B566.G713 1987, **(v9)**
Gradman, Barry. PR4838.M47.G7, **(v3)**
Gradwohl, David M. F629.B98 G73 1984, **(v4)**
Gradwohl, Judith. SD414.T76.G73 1988, **(v1)**
Grady, Hugh. PR2969.G7 1991, **(v3)**
Graebner, Norman A. E179.5.G7 1983, **(v4)**
  E744.G69 1977, **(v4)**
Graebner, William. E169.1.G698 1990, **(v4)**
  HM291.G659 1987, **(v6)**
Graedel, T. E. TL240.G73 1998, **(v1)**
Graef, Ortwin de. PN75.D45.G74 1995, **(v3)**
Graf, Alfred Byrd. SB407.G7 1982, **(v1)**
  SB407.G72 1992, **(v1)**
Graf, Miller. G640.G7 1992, **(v6)**
Graff, Harvey J. HN57.G64 1995, **(v6)**
Graffenried, Michael von. DT295.6.G73 1998, **(v5)**
Grafton, Anthony. CB361.G69 1991, **(v5)**
  E121.G7 1992, **(v4)**
  NA1123.A5.G73 2000, **(v9)**
Gragg, Larry Dale. F74.S1.P34 1990, **(v4)**
Graham Scott, Peter. PN1992.4.G72.A3 2000, **(v3)**
Graham, A. C. B126.G72 1990, **(v8)**
  B128.C364 G73 1992, **(v8)**
  PL2658.E3.G7 1977, **(v3)**
Graham, Bruce Desmond. JQ298.B5.G73 1990, **(v7)**
Graham, Carol. JL3498.A6 G7 1992, **(v7)**
Graham, Cole Blease. JK4216.G73 1994, **(v7)**
Graham, Dominick. D546.G47 1999, **(v5)**
Graham, Edward M. HG4910.G74 1991, **(v6)**
Graham, Elizabeth A. F1445.G727 1994, **(v4)**
Graham, Frank. QH75.G68, **(v1)**
Graham, Gordon. BV4639.G67 1990, **(v8)**
Graham, Harvey. RG51.F55 1950, **(v2)**
Graham, Helen. R733.G724 1999, **(v2)**
Graham, Hugh Davis. JC599.U5.G685 1990, **(v7)**
  LA227.4.G73 1997, **(v7)**
Graham, John D. RC268.6.G73 1988, **(v2)**
Graham, John T. D16.8.G6985 1997, **(v5)**
Graham, John W. HD30.28.G697 1994, **(v6)**
Graham, Judith S. F7.G73 2000, **(v4)**
Graham, Katharine. Z473.G696 1997, **(v10)**
Graham, Kenneth. PS2123.G73 1996, **(v3)**
Graham, Laura R. F2520.1.A4.G73 1995, **(v4)**
Graham, Laurie. F159.P657.G73 1998, **(v4)**
Graham, Linda E. QK566.G735 2000, **(v1)**
Graham, Lisa Jane. DC133.4.G73 2000, **(v5)**
Graham, Loren R. Q127.S696.G729 1993, **(v1)**
  Q175.5.G73 1998, **(v1)**
Graham, Otis L. E743.G7, **(v4)**
Graham, Patricia Albjerg. L13.A417, **(v7)**
Graham, Peter W. PR4359.G7 1990, **(v3)**

Graham, Peter W. PR4388.G65 1998, **(v3)**
Graham, Richard C. QD39.3.S7.G73 1993, **(v1)**
Graham, Richard. JL2481.G73 1990, **(v7)**
Graham, Robin Lee. G530.G599713 1972, **(v6)**
Graham, Roger. F1034.M46.G7, **(v4)**
  F1058.F85.G73 1990, **(v4)**
Graham, Ronald L. QA39.2.G733 1994, **(v1)**
Graham, Ronnie. ML3502.5.G7 1988, **(v9)**
Graham, Sara Hunter. JK1896.G693 1996, **(v7)**
Graham, Sheilah. PS3513.R219 L38, **(v3)**
Graham, Stephen. DK106.G7 1968, **(v5)**
  PG3286.G7, **(v3)**
Graham, Wendy. PS2127.S48.G72 1999, **(v3)**
Graham-Brown, Sarah. DS79.75.G734 1999, **(v5)**
  HQ1726.5.G73 1988, **(v6)**
Graham-Smith, Francis. QB43.2.G72 1988, **(v1)**
Grahn, Judy. GN484.38.G73 1993, **(v6)**
Graig, Laurene A. RA411.G68 1999, **(v2)**
Grainger, John D. DS82.G73 1992, **(v5)**
  DS96.2.G72 1990, **(v5)**
Grainger, John J. TK3001.G73 1994, **(v1)**
Grajeda-Higley, Leilani. RM300.G717 2000, **(v2)**
Grambs, David. PE1591.G67 1993, **(v3)**
Grammont, Maurice. PC2509.G7 1967, **(v3)**
Grams, Martin. PN1991.9.G73 2000, **(v3)**
Gran, Peter. D359.7.G73 1996, **(v5)**
Granatstein, J. L. F1033.K53.G73, **(v4)**
  F1034.G68, **(v4)**
  F1034.2.G72 1972, **(v4)**
Grandazzi, Alexandre. DG65.G7313 1997, **(v5)**
Grandin, Greg. F1465.2.Q5.G73 2000, **(v4)**
Grandin, Temple. RC553.A88.G74 1995, **(v2)**
Grandy, Richard E. BC135.G7, **(v8)**
Grane, Leif. B765.A24 G73 1970b, **(v8)**
Granet, Marcel. DS721.G788, **(v5)**
  PL2466.Z9.L6413, **(v3)**
Granet, Roger. RC535.G724 1998, **(v2)**
Granfield, Robert. KF292.H328 G73 1992, **(v7)**
Grange, Joseph. BD581.G55 1997, **(v8)**
Granger, Edith. PN1022.G7 1986, **(v3)**
Granit, Ragnar. QP376.G69, **(v1)**
Granlund, Gosta H. TA1634.G73 1995, **(v1)**
Grano, J. G. GB23.G6813 1997, **(v6)**
Grano, Joseph D. KF9664.G73 1993, **(v7)**
Granqvist, Raoul. PR129.U5.G68 1995, **(v3)**
Grant, Alexander. DA783.G72 1984, **(v5)**
Grant, Barry Keith. PN1998.3.W57.G73 1991, **(v3)**
Grant, Brian W. BT707.7.G73 2000, **(v8)**
Grant, Campbell. E98.P23.G73 1983, **(v4)**
  E99.C815 G7, **(v4)**
Grant, Daniel. N8600.G69 1994, **(v9)**
Grant, Elliott Mansfield. PQ1222.G7, **(v3)**
  PQ1223.G7, **(v3)**
  PQ2504.G733, **(v3)**
Grant, Eugene Lodewick. TA177.4.G7 1990, **(v1)**
Grant, Francis James. CR23.G8 1976, **(v5)**
Grant, Gerald. LA222.G69 1988, **(v7)**
  LB1775.2.G73 1999, **(v7)**
Grant, I. F. DA880.H6.G64 1987, **(v5)**
  HC257.S4.G7 1976, **(v6)**
Grant, Judith. HQ1190.G7 1993, **(v6)**
Grant, Julia Dent. E672.1.G73 A3 1988, **(v4)**
Grant, Julia. HQ759.G75 1998, **(v6)**
Grant, Kimberly, 1961-. F73.18.B655, **(v4)**
Grant, Mary Hetherington. PS2018.G73 1994, **(v3)**
Grant, Michael Johnston. HD1476.U5 G7 2002, **(v6)**
Grant, Michael. D59.G6878, **(v5)**
  DF214.G78 1988, **(v5)**
  DF555.G73 1998, **(v5)**
  DG292.G73 1994, **(v5)**
  DG298.G73 1996, **(v5)**
  HN10.G7.G73 1992, **(v6)**
  PA31.G7, **(v3)**
Grant, Nancy. F217.T3.G73 1990, **(v4)**
Grant, Nicole J. HD9995.C64.A234 1992, **(v6)**
Grant, Patrick. B828.5.G73 1996, **(v8)**
  PR8891.N67.G73 1999, **(v3)**
Grant, Richard B. PQ2261.Z5.G7, **(v3)**
Grant, Robert M. HD30.28.G716 2003, **(v6)**
Grant, Ruth Weissbourd. JA79.G683 1997, **(v7)**
Grant, S. G. LB1576.G7263 1998, **(v7)**

Grant, Shelagh D. F1090.5.G76 1988, **(v4)**
Grant, Ulysses S. E660.G756 1967, **(v4)**
  E672.G7619 1969, **(v4)**
Grant, Verne. QH368.5.G7 1981, **(v1)**
Grantham, Dewey W. F215.G737 1988, **(v4)**
  F216.G73 1983, **(v4)**
Granville-Barker, Harley. PR2976.G673, **(v3)**
Grapard, Allan G. BL2225.N32 K423 1992, **(v8)**
Gras, Norman Scott Brien. S419.G8 1940, **(v1)**
Grass, Gunter. DD259.4.G653, **(v5)**
  PT2613.G769.H8.E5, **(v3)**
  PT2613.G769.K15.E5, **(v3)**
  PT2613.G769.T4, **(v3)**
  PT2613.R338.B55, **(v3)**
  PT2613.R338.B83, **(v3)**
  PT2613.R338.K3 1967, **(v3)**
  PT2613.R338.O413, **(v3)**
  PT2613.R338.T713, **(v3)**
Grasselli, Margaret Morgan. N6853.W38.A4 1984, **(v9)**
Grasso, Christopher. F97.G73 1999, **(v4)**
Grattan-Guinness, I. QA21.G695 1998, **(v1)**
  QA248.G684 2000, **(v1)**
Gratton, Chris. GV181.3.G73 2000, **(v6)**
Grau, Shirley Ann. PS3557.R283.B58, **(v3)**
  PS3557.R283.C6, **(v3)**
  PS3557.R283.E9, **(v3)**
  PS3557.R283.H3, **(v3)**
  PS3557.R283.H6, **(v3)**
  PS3557.R283.K4, **(v3)**
Graubard, Stephen Richards. DA531.2.G7, **(v5)**
  E882.2.G73 1991, **(v4)**
Graustein, Jeannette E. QH31.N8.G7, **(v1)**
Grauwe, Paul de. HG3815.G72 1989, **(v6)**
Grave, Floyd K. ML134.H272.G74 1990, **(v9)**
Graver, Suzanne. PR4692.S58.G7 1984, **(v3)**
Graves, Carson. TR591.G73 1997, **(v1)**
Graves, Frank Pierrepont. LA96.G7, **(v7)**
  LA2301.G7 1971, **(v7)**
Graves, John William. E185.93.A8 G73 1990, **(v4)**
Graves, Joseph L. GN269.G73 2001, **(v6)**
Graves, Karen. LC1759.S8.G73 1998, **(v7)**
Graves, Laura. E99.N3.K324 1998, **(v4)**
Graves, R. B. PN2091.E4.G73 1999, **(v3)**
Graves, Richard Perceval. PR6013.R35.Z7173 1995, **(v3)**
  PR6013.R35.Z718 1990, **(v3)**
Graves, Richard. PR3499.G77 S6 1926, **(v3)**
Graves, Robert. BL225.G75 1958, **(v8)**
Graves, Robert. BL781.G65 1957, **(v8)**
  BT309.G68, **(v8)**
  PR6013.R35.A17 1966, **(v3)**
  PR6013.R35.A17 1977, **(v3)**
  PR6013.R35 C6, **(v3)**
  PR6013.R35 G6, **(v3)**
  PR6013.R35 H4, **(v3)**
  PR6013.R35 I2, **(v3)**
  PR6013.R35 W5, **(v3)**
Graves-Brown, P. GN406.G73 2000, **(v6)**
Gravil, Richard. PS159.E5.G73 2000, **(v3)**
Gray, Alfred. QA371.5.D37.G74 1997, **(v1)**
Gray, Andrew. F3430.1.M38.G75 1996 vol. 2, **(v4)**
  F3430.1.M38.G75 1996 vol. 3, **(v4)**
Gray, Asa. QK117.G75 1950, **(v1)**
Gray, Basil. ND980.G72 1977, **(v9)**
Gray, Bradford H. RA410.53.G73 1991, **(v2)**
Gray, Christine Rauchfuss. PS3535.I3374.Z68 1999, **(v3)**
Gray, Colin S. U162.G69 1996, **(v10)**
  UA23.G7786 1988, **(v10)**
  UA23.G785 1990, **(v10)**
  UA23.G786 1993, **(v10)**
Gray, Donald H. TA710.G6286 1996, **(v1)**
Gray, Gary G. QL82.G73 1993, **(v1)**
Gray, Harry B. QD37.G64 1995, **(v1)**
Gray, Henry. QM23.G7 1959, **(v1)**
  QM23.2.G73 1985, **(v1)**
Gray, Jack. DS755.G72 1990, **(v5)**
Gray, James Henry. CT310.G728.A3, **(v5)**
  F1033.B47.G73 1991, **(v4)**

Gray, James P. HV5825.G6954 2001, **(v6)**
　HD9433.U4.G7, **(v6)**
Gray, Jeffrey Alan. BF575.F2.G73 1987, **(v2)**
Gray, John Chipman. K230.G73.N38 1997, **(v7)**
Gray, John S. E83.876.B79.G73 1991, **(v4)**
Gray, John. HB101.H39 G73 1998, **(v6)**
　JC574.G73 2000, **(v7)**
　JC585.G7365 1993, **(v7)**
　ML120.A35.G7 1991, **(v9)**
　ML128.B45.G7 1988, **(v9)**
　ML128.J3.G7 1991, **(v9)**
　Z5784.B56.G7 1990, **(v10)**
　Z5784.M9.G72 1990, **(v10)**
　Z7834.A3.G72 1989, **(v10)**
Gray, L. C. HD1773.A5.G73 1973, **(v6)**
Gray, Margaret E. PQ2631.R63.A795 1992, **(v3)**
Gray, N. F. TD257.G72 1994, **(v1)**
Gray, Peter. DA950.7.G72 1999, **(v5)**
Gray, Richard J. PS3511.A86.Z784127 1994, **(v3)**
Gray, Richard. BV3520.G72 1991, **(v8)**
Gray, Rob. HF5686.C7.G568 1993, **(v6)**
Gray, Rockwell. PQ6627.R8.Z68 1989, **(v3)**
Gray, Ronald D. PT2177.G7, **(v3)**
　PT2621.A26.Z746, **(v3)**
Gray, S. J. HD2755.5.G73 1990, **(v6)**
Gray, Sharon A. Z6661.N67.G73 1996, **(v10)**
Gray, Stephen. PR9354.3.G7, **(v3)**
Gray, Susan E. F566.G788 1996, **(v4)**
Gray, Thomas. PR3500.A2 1966, **(v3)**
　PR3500.A5.P6 1937d, **(v3)**
　PR3501.C47, **(v3)**
　PR3503.A3 1971, **(v3)**
Graybill, Lyn S. BR1450.G73 1995, **(v8)**
Grayling, A. C. BC71.G7 1997, **(v8)**
　BJ1360.G72 2003, **(v8)**
Graymont, Barbara. E99.I7.G67, **(v4)**
Grayson, Benson Lee. E426.G7, **(v4)**
Grayson, Donald K. QE697.G8 1993, **(v1)**
　Z6683.C5 G66 1975, **(v10)**
Grayson, George W. F1236.G76 1988, **(v4)**
Grayson, Richard S. DA566.9.C43.G73 1997, **(v5)**
Grayson, William J. F273.G66 1990, **(v4)**
Graziano, Anthony M. RJ505.B4.G723 1984, **(v2)**
Graziano, Loretta. HG226.3.G72 1987, **(v6)**
Grazulis, T. P. QC955.G74 2001, **(v1)**
Great Britain. Foreign Office. DD257.4.G75, **(v5)**
Greatbatch, Wilson. RC684.P3, **(v2)**
Greaves, Bettina Bien. HB101.V66.G7 1993, **(v6)**
Greaves, C. Desmond. DA965.C7.G7 1971, **(v5)**
Greaves, M. F. RC268.48.G74 2000, **(v2)**
Greaves, Richard L. DA448.G7 1992, **(v5)**
　DA448.G75 1986, **(v5)**
　DA448.G754 1990, **(v5)**
　DA995.D75.G74 1998, **(v5)**
Grebanier, Bernard D. N. PR2825.G67, **(v3)**
　PR3112.G73, **(v3)**
Greek, C. Ray. HV4915.G73 2000, **(v6)**
Greeley, Andrew M. BX1754.G697 2000, **(v8)**
Greeley, Horace. E415.9.G8.G83 1971, **(v4)**
　F593.G79 1999, **(v4)**
Green, Andrew. RA395.D44.G74 1992, **(v2)**
Green, Andy. LC71.G76 1997, **(v7)**
Green, Archie. GR105.G94 1993, **(v6)**
Green, Barbara B. DK61.G74 1994, **(v5)**
Green, Ben. E185.97.M79 G74 1999, **(v4)**
Green, Carl R. F865.G74 2000, **(v4)**
　KF8700.Z9.G74 1990, **(v7)**
Green, Charles. F128.9.N3.G74 1989, **(v4)**
Green, Constance McLaughlin. TS1570.W4.G7, **(v1)**
Green, D. J. TA455.C43.G738 1998, **(v1)**
Green, David R. HC258.L6.G73 1995, **(v6)**
Green, December. HV6250.4.W65.G74 1999, **(v6)**
Green, Dennis Howard. PD75.G74 1998, **(v3)**
Green, Elizabeth A. H. MT85.G785 1997, **(v9)**
Green, Ely. E185.97.G795A3 1970, **(v4)**
Green, Frederick Charles. PQ2043.G75 1970, **(v3)**
Green, Geoffrey. PS3527.A15.Z724 1988, **(v3)**
Green, Gerald. PS3513.R4493 L3, **(v3)**
Green, Hannah. BX4700.F37, **(v8)**
Green, Henry. PR6013.R416 B55, **(v3)**
　PR6013.R416 C38 1943, **(v3)**

PR6013.R416 C6, **(v3)**
PR6013.R416 D6 1952, **(v3)**
PR6013.R416 L5, **(v3)**
PR6013.R416 N6, **(v3)**
PR6013.R416 P3 1970, **(v3)**
Green, J. QL445.G7, **(v1)**
Green, J. R. PA3201.G73 1995, **(v3)**
Green, J. Ronald. PN1998.3.M494.G74 2000, **(v3)**
Green, James H. (James Harry). TK5102.3.U6G74
　2000, **(v1)**
Green, Jeffrey. DA125.A1.G69 1998, **(v5)**
Green, John Alfred. LB628.G7 1969, **(v7)**
Green, Jonathan D. ML134.B1.G74 2000, **(v9)**
Green, Jonathon. PE1689.G73 1987, **(v3)**
Green, Joseph. Z5917.D5.G74 1997, **(v10)**
Green, Judith A. DA195.G74 1997, **(v5)**
Green, Julien. PQ2613.R3.A65 1927, **(v3)**
　PQ2613.R3.L4 1929, **(v3)**
　PQ2613.R3.M57, **(v3)**
　PQ2613.R3.Z49 1988, **(v3)**
　PQ2613.R3.Z5, **(v3)**
Green, Katherine Sobba. PR858.C69.G74 1991, **(v3)**
Green, Leslie. JC571.G77 1988, **(v7)**
Green, Lewis. F912.B7.G79 1982, **(v4)**
Green, Martin Burgess. PN3448.A3.G73 1991, **(v3)**
　PR3403.Z5.G7 1990, **(v3)**
Green, Martin. PR2848.G76 1993, **(v3)**
Green, Matthew. PR3505.G27.S7 1936, **(v3)**
Green, Michael D. E99.C9.G74 1982, **(v4)**
Green, Otis Howard. PQ6059.G7, **(v3)**
Green, Paul. PS3513.R452 D6, **(v3)**
　PS3513.R452.W37 1993, **(v3)**
　PS3513.R452 W5 1970, **(v3)**
　PS3513.R452.Z48 1994, **(v3)**
Green, Peter. CB311.G69, **(v5)**
　DE59.G74 1989, **(v5)**
　DE86.G738 1990, **(v5)**
　DF234.G68 1974, **(v5)**
　PR4727.G7, **(v3)**
Green, Philip. JC575.G76 1999, **(v7)**
　PN1995.9.W6.G74 1998, **(v3)**
　U162.6.G7, **(v10)**
Green, Richard Firth. PR275.L35.G74 1999, **(v3)**
Green, Richard. KF9325.G74 1992, **(v7)**
Green, Roger Lancelyn. PR4076.G7 1961, **(v3)**
Green, Ronald Michael. B4377.G715 1992, **(v8)**
　BJ47.G74 1988, **(v8)**
Green, Roy. HG220.A2.G68 1992, **(v6)**
Green, Scott E. Z8045.59.G74 1995, **(v10)**
Green, Stanley. ML1711.G74 1980, **(v9)**
Green, Thomas F. LC268.G667 1999, **(v7)**
Green, Vivian Hubert Howard. D228.G74 1964, **(v5)**
Green, William A. D16.G78 1993, **(v5)**
　HC157.B8.G74, **(v6)**
Green, William H. PR6039.O32.H6 1995, **(v3)**
Green, William. PR2826.G7 1962, **(v3)**
　UG630.G79 1958a, **(v10)**
　UG1240.G74 1982, **(v10)**
Greenawalt, Kent. KF4772.G738 1995, **(v7)**
　KF4772.G74 1989, **(v7)**
Greenaway, Peter. PN1997.P777 1991, **(v3)**
Greenbaum, Fred. E743.G738 2000, **(v4)**
Greenbaum, Susan D. F319.T2 G69 2002, **(v4)**
Greenberg, Blu. BM729.W6.G73, **(v8)**
Greenberg, Cheryl Lynn. F128.68.H3.G74 1991, **(v4)**
Greenberg, Clement. N72.G68, **(v9)**
Greenberg, Dolores. HE2236.G73, **(v6)**
Greenberg, Ellen. KF8742.Z9.G728 1997, **(v7)**
Greenberg, Gary. RC569.5.C63.G74 1994, **(v2)**
Greenberg, Gerald S. Z6944.S45.G76 1996, **(v10)**
Greenberg, Hank. GV865.G68.A3 1989, **(v6)**
Greenberg, Herbert J. PR6001.U4.Z7, **(v3)**
Greenberg, Ira A. RC489.P7.G72, **(v2)**
Greenberg, James B. F1221.C47.G72 1989, **(v4)**
Greenberg, Joanne. PS3557.R3784S56 1986, **(v3)**
Greenberg, Joseph Harold. PL8005.G7 1966, **(v3)**
　PM101.I5 vol. 29, no. 1, pt. 2, **(v3)**
Greenberg, Kenneth J. E213.G793 1996, **(v4)**
Greenberg, Mark T. HV2469.S63.G74 1993, **(v6)**
Greenberg, Michael R. HN57.G695 1999, **(v6)**
Greenberg, Mike. HT167.G75 1995, **(v6)**

Greenberg, Reva M. Z5814.A24.G74 1993, **(v10)**
Greenberg, Robert. B2779.G74 2001, **(v8)**
Greenberg, Samuel. PS3513.R4582.P6, **(v3)**
Greenblatt, Stephen. PR2807.G69 2001, **(v3)**
　PR2976.G737 1988, **(v3)**
Greene, A. C. F391.2.G66 1998, **(v4)**
Greene, B. QC794.6.S85.G75 1999, **(v1)**
Greene, David Herbert. PR5533.G7, **(v3)**
Greene, Donald Johnson. PR3533.G74, **(v3)**
　PR3537.P6.G7, **(v3)**
Greene, Douglas G. PS3505.A763.Z67 1995, **(v3)**
Greene, E. J. H. PQ2003.Z5.G75, **(v3)**
Greene, Felix. DS711.G7, **(v5)**
Greene, Gayle. PR888.F45.G7 1991, **(v3)**
　PR6023.E833.Z68 1994, **(v3)**
　R489.S78, **(v2)**
Greene, Graham. F1215.G82 1978, **(v4)**
　PR6013.R44 A15 1973, **(v3)**
　PR6013.R44 A153 1963, **(v3)**
　PR6013.R44.A16 1969, **(v3)**
　PR6013.R44 B8, **(v3)**
　PR6013.R44 C5, **(v3)**
　PR6013.R44.C55 1961, **(v3)**
　PR6013.R44 C6 1939, **(v3)**
　PR6013.R44 E5, **(v3)**
　PR6013.R44 G8 1947, **(v3)**
　PR6013.R44 H4 1956, **(v3)**
　PR6013.R44 H6, **(v3)**
　PR6013.R44 H8 1978, **(v3)**
　PR6013.R44 I9 1962, **(v3)**
　PR6013.R44.L5 1954, **(v3)**
　PR6013.R44 L67
090　PR6013.R44 L67 1989, **(v3)**
　PR6013.R44 M29, **(v3)**
　PR6013.R44.M5 1943, **(v3)**
　PR6013.R44.O9 1981, **(v3)**
　PR6013.R44.P58, **(v3)**
　PR6013.R44 P6, **(v3)**
　PR6013.R44 Q5 1956, **(v3)**
　PR6013.R44 S7 1932, **(v3)**
　PR6013.R44.T4 1985, **(v3)**
　PR6013.R44 T6, **(v3)**
　PR6013.R44 T7, **(v3)**
　PR6013.R44 T75 1971, **(v3)**
　PR6013.R44 T8, **(v3)**
　PR6013.R44.Z5 1962, **(v3)**
　PR6013.R44.Z52, **(v3)**
　PR6013.R44.Z54 1980, **(v3)**
Greene, Helen Taylor. HV6023.G74 2000, **(v6)**
Greene, Jack P. E162.G85 1993, **(v4)**
　HN50.G74 1988, **(v6)**
Greene, Janet C. TX601.H54 1991, **(v1)**
Greene, Jeffrey P. NK2406.G74 1996, **(v9)**
Greene, Jerome A. E83.876.M55.G74 1992, **(v4)**
　E83.877.G74 2000, **(v4)**
Greene, John C. PN2602.D8.G7 1993, **(v3)**
Greene, John Robert. E855.G7 1992, **(v4)**
　E865.G74 1995, **(v4)**
　Z8308.34.G74 1994, **(v10)**
Greene, Kathanne W. KF3464.G73 1989, **(v7)**
Greene, Lorenzo Johnston. E185.93.M7 G73 1993,
　(v4)
Greene, Maxine. B819.G67, **(v8)**
　LA205.G72 1988, **(v7)**
　LA217.2.G74 1995, **(v7)**
　LB45.G68, **(v7)**
Greene, Melissa Fay. F294.A89.J536 1996, **(v4)**
　HN79.G42.M354 1991, **(v6)**
Greene, Molly. DF901.C83.G74 2000, **(v5)**
Greene, Mott T. BL435.G74 1992, **(v8)**
Greene, Naomi. PN1998.3.P367.G74 1990, **(v3)**
Greene, Nathanael. DC389.G68, **(v5)**
Greene, Norman Nathaniel. B2430.S34.G7, **(v8)**
Greene, Richard Leighton. PR1195.C2.G7 1977, **(v3)**
Greene, Richard. ML410.H748 G74 1995, **(v9)**
Greene, Robert Everist. QA331.7.G75 1997, **(v1)**
Greene, Robert Michael. KF300.Z9 G74 1992, **(v7)**
Greene, Robert. B52.G74 1999, **(v8)**
Greene, Theodore P. D644.G7, **(v5)**
Greene, Thurston. KF4548.5.G74 1991, **(v7)**
Greene, Victor R. E184.P7.G73, **(v4)**

Greene, Warwick. D570.9.G7 1971, (v5)
Greene, William H. HB139.G74 2003, (v6)
Greene-McCreight, Kathryn. BT83.55.G73 2000, (v8)
Greenfeld, Howard. N6537.S5.G74 1998, (v9)
Greenfeld, Liah. JC311.G715 1992, (v7)
Greenfield, Jeanette. CC135.G74 1996, (v9)
Greenfield, Kent Roberts. D743.G666, (v5)
  D769.A533 vol. 1, pt. 1, (v5)
Greenfield, Stanley B. PR173.G7, (v3)
  Z2012.G83, (v10)
Greenfield, Susan. BF515.G74 2000, (v2)
  QP411.G69 1995, (v1)
Greenfield, Thomas Allen. Z7224.U6.G74 1989, (v10)
Greenhalgh, Susan. RB127.G745 2001, (v2)
Greenhill, Basil. VM15.G72, (v10)
  VM144.G74 1989, (v10)
Greenhill, Pauline. F1059.7.E53.G74 1994), (v4)
Greenhut, Melvin L. KF1649.G75 1989, (v7)
Greenidge, A. H. J. DG254.G8 1960, (v5)
Greenland, D. J. SB191.R5.G724 1997, (v1)
Greenlaw, Jean-Pierre. NA1591.6.S82.S284 1995, (v9)
Greenleaf, Robert K. HM141.G687 1998, (v6)
Greenlee, John. SB431.7.G74 1992, (v1)
Greenler, Robert. QC975.2.G73, (v1)
Green-Lewis, Jennifer. TR15.G69 1996, (v1)
Greenslet, Ferris. CS71.L915. 1946, (v5)
Greenspan, Ezra. PS3237.4.U6.G74 1990, (v3)
Greenspan, Henry. D804.195.G74 1998, (v5)
Greenspan, Patricia S. BJ1471.5.G74 1995, (v8)
Greenspan, Stanley I. BF311.G714 1997, (v2)
  RC489.D46.G74 1997, (v2)
  RJ503.G74 1991, (v2)
Greenstein, Carol Horn. QA9.G698, (v1)
Greenstein, Daniel I. D16.12.G74 1994, (v5)
Greenstein, Jack Matthew. ND623.M3.G7 1992, (v9)
Greenstein, Jesse P. QD305.A7.G85, (v1)
Greenstein, Michael. PR9188.2.J48.G74 1989, (v3)
Greenstone, J. David. E302.1.G84 1993, (v4)
Greentree, Rosemary. Z2012.G835 2001, (v10)
Greenwald, Elissa. PS374.R34.G7 1989, (v3)
Greenwald, Howard P. RC262.G736 1992, (v2)
Greenway, John L. PT7048.G7, (v3)
Greenwood, F. Murray. KEQ189.G74 1993, (v7)
Greenwood, Justin. JN36.G74 1997, (v7)
Greenwood, N.N. (Norman Neill). QD466.G74 1997, (v1)
Greenwood, Val D. CS47.G79 2000, (v5)
Greer, Germaine. HQ1413.G74.A3 1987, (v6)
Greer, Germaine. ND38.G73 1979, (v9)
Greer, Margaret Rich. PQ6312.G74 1991, (v3)
  PQ6498.Z5.G74 2000, (v3)
Greever, William S. F591.G79, (v4)
Greg, W. W. PR509.P3G7 1959, (v3)
Gregg, John. TK7888.4.G74 1998, (v1)
Gregg, Josiah. F786.G797, (v4)
Gregg, Pauline. HC256.5.G73 1969, (v6)
  HN385.G7 1982, (v6)
Gregg, Robert W. E840.G73, (v4)
Gregg, Veronica Marie. PR6035.H96.W535 1995, (v3)
Gregor, A. James. DS775.7.G74 2000, (v5)
  UA23.G79 1984, (v10)
  UA835.G74 1987, (v10)
Gregory, Brad S. BR307.G74 1999, (v8)
Gregory, Cedric Errol. TN15.G44 2001, (v1)
Gregory, Chris. PN1995.5.S694.G73 1999, (v3)
Gregory, Derek. G70.G72 1994, (v6)
Gregory, Desmond. DP302.B28.G74 1990, (v5)
  DP702.M18.G74 1988, (v5)
Gregory, Eileen. PS3507.O726.Z675 1997, (v3)
Gregory, Horace. PR99.G6847, (v3)
  PS3513.R558.A6 1964, (v3)
  PS3513.R558.C5 1930, (v3)
  PS3513.R558.Z5, (v3)
Gregory, James Noble. HB1985.C2G74 1989, (v6)
Gregory, Jane. Q175.5.G744 1998, (v1)
Gregory, K. J. GB11.G739 2000, (v6)
Gregory, Lady. PR4728.G5.A19 1975, (v3)
  PR4728.G5.I7 1971, (v3)
  PR4728.G5.S4 1970, (v3)
  PR4728.G5.T4 1971, (v3)

PR4728.G5.Z53 1946, (v3)
PR4728.G5.Z534 1976, (v3)
Gregory, Paul R. HC334.5.G74 1994, (v6)
  HC335.G723 1998, (v6)
Gregory, R. L. BF38.G67, (v2)
Gregory, Robert G. DT429.5.S68.G74 1993, (v5)
Gregory, Robin. ML955.G7 1969b, (v9)
Gregory, Ross. E169.G845 1989, (v4)
Gregory, Ruth W. GT3930.G74 1983, (v6)
Gregory, Sheila T. LC2781.G74 1995, (v7)
Gregory, Steven. F128.68.C65.G74 1998, (v4)
Gregory, Thaumaturgus, Saint. BR60.F3.G74 1998, (v8)
Gregory, William H. UC263.G74 1989, (v10)
Gregson, Ian. PR508.M35.G74 1999, (v3)
Greider, William. HC106.8.G73 1982, (v6)
Greif, Geoffrey L. HQ759.G76 1988, (v6)
Greiff, Louis K. PR6023.A93.Z63113 2001, (v3)
Greil, Arthur L. HQ734.G743 1991, (v6)
Grenard, Steve. QL666.C9.H26 1991, (v1)
Grenberg, Bruce L. PS2388.Q5.G7 1989, (v3)
Grene, David. PR3034.G74 1988, (v3)
Grene, Marjorie Glicksman. B485.G595, (v8)
  B819.G68 1959, (v8)
  BD161.G74 1966a, (v8)
Grene, Nicholas. PR2983.G74 1991, (v3)
  PR8795.P64.G74 1999, (v3)
Grenham, John. CS483.G74 1999b, (v5)
Grenke, Arthur. F1064.5.W7.G74 1991, (v4)
Grenkevich, Leonid D. D802.S75.G74 1999, (v5)
Grennan, Eamon. PR8771.G74 1998, (v3)
Grenville, J. A. S. D421.G65 1984, (v5)
  KZ64.G74 2000, (v7)
Grese, Robert E. SB470.J4.G74 1992, (v1)
Gretlund, Jan Nordby. PS3545.E6.Z686 1994, (v3)
Greven, Philip J. F74.A6.G7, (v4)
  HQ770.4.G74 1990, (v6)
Greville, Fulke. PR2215.A4 1968, (v3)
Grevisse, Maurice. PC2112.G84 1980, (v3)
Grew, Raymond. LA693.G74 1992, (v7)
Grewal, Gurleen. PS3563.O8749.Z655 1998, (v3)
Grey, Alex. N6537.G718.A4 1998, (v9)
Grey, Gene W. SB436.G72 1996, (v1)
Grey, George. BL2615.G7 1956, (v8)
Grey, Loren. BF175.5.A33G74 1998, (v2)
Grey, Thomas C. PS3537.T4753.Z654 1991, (v3)
Grey, Zane. PS3513.R6545C3 1982, (v3)
  PS3513.R6545.G46 1994, (v3)
  PS3513.R6545.R5 1994, (v3)
Greyson, Richard I. QK653.G75 1994, (v1)
Grey-Wilson, C. SB413.C6.G74 2000, (v1)
Gribbin, John R. QB44.2.G752 1998, (v1)
  QB44.2.G753, (v1)
  QB44.2.G758 1997, (v1)
  QB450.G75 2000, (v1)
  QB843.B55.G75 1992, (v1)
  QC173.98.G75 1984, (v1)
  QC793.2.G747 1998, (v1)
  QC912.3.G75 1990, (v1)
Gribble, C. D. QE369.O6.G74 1993, (v1)
Gribetz, Judah. DS114.G68 1993, (v5)
Gribin, Anthony J. ML3527.G75 1992, (v9)
Gribkov, A. I. E841.G675 1994, (v4)
Gridley, Mark C. ML3506.G74 2003, (v9)
Gridley, Roy E. PR4238.G67, (v3)
Grieb, Kenneth J. Z1437.G74 1988, (v10)
Grieder, Jerome B. DS754.14.G74, (v5)
Grieder, Terence. E59.A7.G74, (v4)
Grieg, Edvard. ML410.G9.A25 2001, (v9)
Grier, Katherine C. E166.G83 1988, (v4)
Grierson, Alice Kirk. F594.G765 1989, (v4)
Grierson, Edward. DA16.G736, (v5)
Grierson, Herbert John Clifford. PR502.G76 1946, (v3)
  PR1209.G7, (v3)
Grierson, Ian. RE51.G75 2000, (v2)
Gries, David. QA39.2.G7473 1993, (v1)
Grieve, Thomas F. PS3531.O82.Z64115 1997, (v3)
Griffen, William B. E99.A6.G754 1988, (v4)
Griffin, Alice Sylvia (Venezky). PR658.P27.G7, (v3)
Griffin, Alice. PS3515.E343.Z69 1999, (v3)

PS3525.I5156.Z675 1996, (v3)
Griffin, Attrices Dean. R859.7.D36.G75 1999, (v2)
Griffin, Clive. Z232.C93.G74 1988, (v10)
Griffin, David Ray. BD418.3.G75 1998, (v8)
  BT28.G754 1989, (v8)
Griffin, Donald R. QL785.G715 2001, (v1)
  QL785.G72 1981, (v1)
Griffin, Dustin H. PN6149.S2.G75 1994, (v3)
Griffin, Farah Jasmine. PS374.N4.G75 1995, (v3)
Griffin, Gabriele. PN810.W66.G75 1993, (v3)
Griffin, Gwyn. PR6057.R5.S5, (v3)
Griffin, James Bennett. E53.G7, (v4)
Griffin, James. BD232.G667 1996, (v8)
  BJ1012.G75 1986, (v8)
Griffin, John C. RM725.G75 1998, (v2)
Griffin, John Ignatius. HD5324.G7 1968, (v6)
Griffin, John R. BX5199.K3.G75 1987, (v8)
Griffin, Keith B. HC59.7.G747 1999, (v6)
  HC59.7.G749 1987, (v6)
  HD75.G74 2000, (v6)
Griffin, Michael. DS371.2.G74 2001, (v5)
Griffin, Pat. GV708.8.G75 1998, (v6)
Griffin, Robert S. GV709.2.G75 1998, (v6)
  LC4691.G76 1988, (v7)
Griffin, Stephen M. KF4550.G74 1996, (v7)
Griffin, Susan M. PS2127.P8.G7 1991, (v3)
Griffin-Pierce, Trudy. E78.S7 G76 2000, (v4)
Griffith, Barbara S. HD8055.C75.G75 1988, (v6)
Griffith, Clark. PS1338.G75 1998, (v3)
Griffith, Elisabeth. HQ1413.S67.G74 1984, (v6)
Griffith, Ernest Stacey. JK516.G73, (v7)
Griffith, Ivelaw L. HV5840.C315.G75 1997, (v6)
Griffith, James John. PN1997.85.G66 1997, (v3)
Griffith, John W. PR6005.O4.Z736 1995, (v3)
  PS3545.H5187.C534 1993, (v3)
Griffith, Paddy. E470.G82 1989, (v4)
  U43.F8.G75 1989, (v10)
  U165.G69 1981, (v10)
Griffith, R. Marie. BR1644.5.U6.G75 1997, (v8)
Griffith, Robert. E748.M143.G7, (v4)
Griffith, Samuel B. UA839.3.G7, (v10)
Griffith, Thomas E. D767.G75 1998, (v5)
Griffith. PR3505.G43.D45 1997, (v3)
Griffiths, Anne M. O. DT2458.K84.G75 1997, (v5)
Griffiths, Antony. NE400.G74 1996, (v9)
Griffiths, David. ML394.G84 1998, (v9)
Griffiths, Ieuan Ll. DT30.5.G74 1995, (v5)
Griffiths, Mark. SB403.2.G75 1994, (v1)
Griffiths, Martin. JZ1305.G75 1999, (v7)
Griffiths, Mel. F781.3.G74 1983, (v4)
Griffiths, Nicholas. F3429.3.R3.G74 1996, (v4)
Griffiths, Paul. ML197.G76 1995, (v9)
  ML410.B26.G7 1984, (v9)
  ML410.M595.G7 1985, (v9)
  ML410.S932.G76 1993, (v9)
  ML1160.G74 1983, (v9)
  PR6057.R515.M97 1990, (v3)
Griffiths, Percival Joseph. HD9198.I42.G75, (v6)
Griffiths, Ralph Alan. DA715.G75 1994, (v5)
Griffler, Keith P. HD6490.R22.U647 1995, (v6)
Grigg, David B. HD1415.G684 1992, (v6)
  S439.G788, (v1)
Grigg, John. DA566.9.L5.G78 1978b, (v5)
Grigg, Richard. BT102.G747 1995, (v8)
Grillo, Evelio. E184.C97.G73 2000, (v4)
Grillo, R. D. JC330.G75 1998, (v7)
Grillparzer, Franz. PT2256.A1 1986, (v3)
Grim, Patrick. B54.G75 1998, (v8)
Grimal, Henri. D445.G7313 1978, (v5)
Grimaldi, David A. QE391.A5.G76 1996, (v1)
Grimes, John A. B131.G67 1989, (v8)
Grimes, Michael D. HM22.U5.G76 1997, (v6)
  HN90.S6.G75 1991, (v6)
Grimes, Robert R. ML3554.G75 1996, (v9)
Grimes, Ronald L. BL600.G74 1995, (v8)
Grimes, William W. HC462.9.G74 2001, (v6)
Grimke, Sarah Moore. HQ1423.G79 1988, (v6)
Grimm, Jacob. PD101.G72 1967, (v3)
  PZ8.G882.Ho32, (v3)
Grimmelshausen, Hans Jakob Christoph von. PT1731.A6 1967, (v3)

Grimsditch, Herbert Borthwick. PR4757.E5.G7 1962, (v3)
Grimshaw, James A. PS3545.A748.Z677 2001, (v3)
Grimshaw, Polly. E91.G75 1991, (v4)
Grimshaw, Rex W. TP810.5.G75 1971, (v1)
Grimshaw, William J. F548.9.N4.G73 1992, (v4)
Grimsley, Mark. E487.G78 1995, (v4)
Grimson, William Eric Leifur. TA1632.G735 1990, (v1)
Grimsted, David. E415.7.G75 1998, (v4)
Grimwade, Nigel. HF1379.G75 1989, (v6)
Grinberg, Arkady. TK5105.5.G74 1997, (v1)
Grinde, Donald A. E98.T77.G75 1991, (v4)
Grindle, Merilee Serrill. JS2061.G73 2000, (v7)
Grindon, Leger. PN1995.9.H5.G75 1994, (v3)
Gringauz, Alex. RS403.G76 1997, (v2)
Grinker, Roy Richard. DS917.444.G75 1998, (v5)
  DT650.E34.G75 1994, (v5)
Grinnell, Joseph. F909.G86 1983, (v4)
Grinnell-Milne, Duncan William. DC373.G3.G67 1962, (v5)
Grinspoon, David Harry. QB621.G75 1997, (v1)
Griscom, Richard. ML128.R31 G75 2003, (v9)
Griskey, Richard G. TP1087.G75 1995, (v1)
Grist, Leighton. PN1998.3.S39.G75 2000, (v3)
Griswold del Castillo, Richard. E184.M5.G74 1996, (v4)
  E408.G75 1990, (v4)
  F790.M5 G75 1984, (v4)
  HD6509.C48.G75 1995, (v6)
Griswold, Alfred Whitney. DS518.8.G75 1962, (v5)
  LC1011.G75 1962, (v7)
Griswold, Charles L. B1545.Z7.G74 1999, (v8)
Griswold, Erwin N. KF373.G745 A3 1992, (v7)
Griswold, Robert L. HQ756.G78 1993, (v6)
Gritsch, Eric W. BX8065.2.G74, (v8)
Groarke, Leo. B525.G66 1990, (v8)
Grob, Gerald N. RA790.6.G76 1991, (v2)
  RC443.G747 1994, (v2)
Grobman, Arnold B. LB2328.4.G76 1988, (v7)
Groce, W. Todd. E579.G76 1999, (v4)
Grodal, Torben Kragh. PN1995.G6887 1997, (v3)
Grodecki, Louis. NA480.G7613 1985, (v9)
Grodin, Joseph R. KF373.G75.A3 1989, (v7)
Grodner, Michele. RM216.G946 2000, (v2)
Grodzins, Dean. BX9869.P3 G76 2002, (v8)
Groenewegen, Peter D. HB98.2.G76 1995, (v6)
Groetsch, C. W. QA371.G73 1999, (v1)
Grof, Stanislav. RC480.5.G76 1988, (v2)
Groff, Pamela J. Z118.G76 1998, (v10)
Grofman, Bernard. KF4893.G76 1992, (v7)
Grogan, F. James. RS51.G85 2001, (v2)
Grogan, Sarah. BF697.5.B63.G76 1999, (v2)
Grogin, R. C. E183.8.S65.G756 2001, (v4)
Grondin, Jean. BD241.G69513 1994, (v8)
Gronke, Paul. JK1967.G76 2000, (v7)
Gronlund, Norman Edward. LB3051.G74 1990, (v7)
Gronroos, Christian. HD9980.5.G776 1990, (v6)
Groom, Bernard. PR508.G76 (v3)
Groom, Gloria Lynn. ND553.V9.G76 1993, (v9)
  NK1449.A1.G76 2001, (v9)
Gropius, Walter. NA680.G7 1965, (v9)
  NA680.G73, (v9)
  NA9030.G7, (v9)
Gropman, Donald. GV865.J29 G76 1999, (v6)
Grosberg, A. IU. QD381.G755 1997, (v1)
Grose, Peter. E748.D865.G76 1994, (v4)
Groseclose, Barbara S. N6507.G76 2000, (v9)
Groseclose, David A. Z8572.4.G76 1996, (v10)
Gross, Ariela Julie. KF482.G76 2000, (v7)
Gross, David. BF378.S65, (v2)
  CB358.G76 1992, (v5)
Gross, Donald. T57.9.G76 1998, (v1)
Gross, Ernie. BR149.G66 1990, (v8)
  E174.5.G76 2001, (v4)
Gross, Francis L. BX4700.T4.G76 1993, (v8)
Gross, Gloria Sybil. PR3537.P8.G7 1992, (v3)
Gross, Harvey Seymour. PE1505.G7 1996, (v3)
Gross, Jan Tomasz. DK4410.G76, (v5)
  DK4415.G76 2002, (v5)
  DS135.P62 J444 2001, (v5)

Gross, John J. PR2825.G76 1992, (v3)
Gross, Jonathan David. PR4392.P64, (v3)
Gross, Kenneth. PR3072.G76 2001, (v3)
Gross, M. Grant. GC16.G7 1987, (v6)
Gross, Martin L. RC437.5.G75 1971, (v1)
Gross, Michael L. JA79.G73 1997, (v7)
Gross, Michael. QH546.G7613 1998, (v1)
  TJ163.G7613 1999, (v1)
Gross, Patricia A. LB2806.15.G68 1997, (v7)
Gross, Rita M. BQ4570.S6.G76 1998, (v8)
Gross, Robert A. F74.C8 G76 2001, (v4)
Gross, Ronald. AZ103.G75 1993, (v10)
Gross, Samuel R. HV8699.U5.G76 1989, (v6)
Gross, Thomas. QA76.8.I93.G76 1998, (v1)
Grossberg, Lawrence. E169.04.G757 1992, (v4)
Grosse, Robert E. HG3915.5.G76 1994, (v6)
Grosse, W. Jack. KF3775.G76 1992, (v7)
Grosser, Morton. QB691.G7, (v1)
Grossman, Barbara Wallace. PN2287.B69.G76 1991, (v3)
Grossman, David. PJ5054.G728.A9713 1989, (v3)
Grossman, James R. F548.9.N4.G76 1989, (v4)
Grossman, James. PS1431.G77 1949, (v3)
Grossman, Mark. D727.G2.G745 2000, (v5)
  E176.G89 2000, (v4)
  E185.61.G895 1993, (v4)
  GE197.G76 1994, (v6)
  HV8694.G76 1998, (v6)
  KF8203.36.G76 1996, (v7)
  UF500.G8 1995, (v10)
Grossman, Marshall. PR545.S44.G76 1998, (v3)
Grossman, Nathaniel. QB351.G69 1996, (v1)
Grossman, Peter Z. HE5903.A55.G76 1987, (v6)
Grossman, Wendy. ZA4201.G74 1997, (v10)
Grossmith, George. PR6013.R795 D5 1969, (v3)
Grossvogel, David I. PN1995.9.M46.G76 2000, (v3)
Grosvenor, Edwin S. TK6143.B4.G76 1997, (v1)
Grosz, George. N6888.G742.G4613, (v9)
Grote, David. PE1704.G76 1992, (v3)
Groth, A. Nicholas. HV6558.G76, (v6)
Groth-Kimball, Irmgard. F1219.3.A7.G713, (v4)
Grotpeter, John J. DT3037.G76 1998, (v5)
Grotta, Daniel. TA1509.G76 1998, (v1)
Grouchy, Jean de. RB44.G7613 1984, (v2)
Groueff, Stéphane. DR89.G76 1987, (v5)
Group, David. RM334.G76 2001, (v2)
Grousset, Rene. DS735.G7, (v5)
Grout, Donald Jay. ML160.G872 2001, (v9)
  ML1700.G83 2003, (v9)
Grove, A P. PT6560.G7, (v3)
Grove, A. T. QH150.G76 2001, (v1)
Grove, Nancy. NB237.N6.A4 1989, (v9)
  NB439.M3.A4 1991, (v9)
Grover, Dorothy. BC171.G76 1992, (v8)
Grover, Kathryn. F129.G3.G76 1994, (v4)
Groves, Donald G. GC9.G76, (v6)
Groves, Julian McAllister. R853.A53.G76 1997, (v2)
Groves, Leslie R. QC773.A1.G7, (v1)
Groze, Victor K. HV875.55.G76 1996, (v6)
Grubb, Davis. PS3513.R865.N55 1977, (v3)
Grubb, James S. DG975.V7.G78 1988, (v5)
Gruber, Helmut. HN418.V5.G78 1991, (v6)
Gruber, Mayer I. Z7770.G77 1995, (v10)
Gruber, William E. PN1689.G78 1994, (v3)
Grubgeld, Elizabeth. PR5044.G78 1994, (v3)
Grubrich-Simitis, Ilse. BF109.F74.G7813 1996, (v2)
Grudin, Michaela Paasche. PR1933.S73.G78 1996, (v3)
Gruen, Erich S. DG77.G78 1992, (v5)
  DG241.2.G78 1984, (v5)
Gruenbaum, Ellen. GN484.G78 2001, (v6)
Gruening, Ernest. F904.G7 1968, (v4)
Gruesser, John Cullen. PS159.A35.G78 2000, (v3)
Gruetzner, Howard. RC523.G78 2001, (v2)
Grugel, Jean. DP270.G78 1997, (v5)
  F2183.G78 1995, (v4)
Gruhn, George. ML1015.G9.G76 1993, (v9)
  ML1015.G9.G763 1994, (v9)
Gruhn, William Theodore. LB1623.G7 1971, (v7)
Gruman-Trinkner, Carrie T. RD525.G78 2001, (v2)
Grumberg, Jean-Claude. PQ2667.R73.A6 1993, (v3)

Grumet, Madeleine R. LB2837.G78 1988, (v7)
Grumet, Robert Steven. E78.E2.G78 1995, (v4)
Grunbaum, Adolf. BF173.G76 1984, (v2)
Grunder, Garel A. DS685.G75, (v5)
Grundy, George Beardoe. DF225.G88 1969, (v5)
Grundy, Kenneth W. UB419.S6.G78 1983, (v10)
Gruner, Charles R. BF575.L3.G78 1997, (v2)
Grunfeld, Frederic V. DS135.G33.G8, (v5)
  NB553.R7.G78 1987, (v9)
Grunig, Larissa A. HD59.G78 2001, (v6)
Grupen, Claus. QC787.C6.G78 1996, (v1)
Gruzalski, Bart. B133.G4 G78 2001, (v8)
Gruzinski, Serge. F1219.3.C85.G7813 1993, (v4)
  F1219.3.R38.G7813 1989, (v4)
  F1219.76.P35.G7813 1992, (v4)
Gualtieri, Elena. PR6045.O72.Z67 1999, (v3)
Guardini, Romano. PT2359.H2.G8 1955, (v3)
Guare, John. ND1329.C54.A4 1995a, (v9)
Guarino-Ghezzi, Susan. HV9104.G83 1996, (v6)
Guattari, Felix. GF21.G8313 2000, (v6)
Gubar, Susan. NX652.A37.G83 1997, (v9)
Gubert, Betty Kaplan. Z5065.U5.G83 1994, (v10)
Gubrium, Jaber F. H62.G82 1997, (v6)
Gucht, Karel de. D2009.G83 1991, (v5)
Gudeman, Stephen. HD1825.L67.G8, (v6)
Guderian, Heinz. D757.G813 1952, (v5)
Gudmundur Halfdanarson. DL338.G82 1997, (v5)
Gudykunst, William B. E184.O6.G84 2001, (v4)
Gue, Benjamin F. F621.G92, (v4)
Gueguen, Yves. QE431.5.G8413 1994, (v1)
Guehenno, Jean-Marie. D860.G8413 1995, (v5)
Guelke, Adrian. HV6431.G79 1995, (v6)
Guelzo, Allen C. BX6065.G84 1994, (v8)
Guenter, Scot M. CR113.G83 1990, (v5)
Guerard, Albert J. PR4754.G78, (v3)
  PR6005.O4.Z737, (v3)
  PS3513.U353 B9, (v3)
  PS3513.U353 E9, (v3)
Guerard, Albert Leon. B945.G83.B6, (v8)
  PM8008.G75 1922, (v3)
Guerin, Wilfred L. PN81.G8 1979, (v3)
Guerin-Gonzales, Camille. HD1527.C2.G84 1994, (v6)
Guerlac, Suzanne. PQ283.G84 1990, (v3)
  PQ305.G78 1997, (v3)
Guernsey, Charles Arthur. [from old catalog]. F761.G93, (v4)
Guernsey, Thomas F. KF4210.G84 1993, (v7)
Guerrero, Ed. PN1995.9.N4.G84 1993, (v3)
Guerrier, Edith. Z720.G89.A3 1992, (v10)
Guest, David. PS374.L34.G84 1997, (v3)
Guest, Harriet. PR448.W65.G84 2000, (v3)
  PR3687.S7.Z69 1989, (v3)
Guest, Harry. PL782.E3.G8, (v3)
Guest, Ivor Forbes. GV1650.P3.G8, (v6)
Guest, John S. DS48.2.G86 1991, (v5)
Guevara, Ernesto. F1787.5.G8253 1996, (v4)
  U240.G833, (v10)
Guggenheim, Marguerite. N5220.G886.A36 1979, (v9)
Guggenheimer, Heinrich W. CS3010.G84 1992, (v5)
Guha, Sumit. DS485.M348.G84 1999, (v5)
Guibbory, Achsah. PR438.R45.G85 1998, (v3)
Guibernau i Berdun, M. Montserrat. JC311.G783 1999, (v7)
Guibert, J. de. BX3703.G813, (v8)
Guicciardini, Francesco. DG539.G813 1984, (v5)
  DG737.5.G813 1970, (v5)
Guicciardini, Niccolo. QA303.G94 1989, (v1)
Guicharnaud, Jacques. PQ556.G8, (v3)
Guignebert, Charles. BM176.G82, (v8)
Guilbert, John M. QE390.G85 1986, (v1)
Guilcher, Andre. GB461.G85 1988, (v6)
Guilds, John Caldwell. PS2853.G84 1992, (v3)
Guiley, Rosemary. BF1091.G84 1993, (v2)
  BF1407.G85 1991, (v2)
  BF1566.G85 1999, (v2)
  BL477.G87 1996, (v8)
  G1106.E627.G8 1994, (v6)
Guillain, Robert. DS777.55.G823, (v5)

Guillaume. PQ1483.G3.E4 1992, (v3)
  PQ1483.G5.A6813 1988, (v3)
  PQ1483.G5.A6813 1988b, (v3)
  PQ1483.G5.A703 1988, (v3)
Guillebaud, C. W. HN445.G85 1971, (v6)
Guillebaud, John. RG136.G765 1985, (v2)
Guillemin, Jeanne. E99.M6.G54, (v4)
  RJ253.5.G85 1986, (v2)
Guillen, Claudio. PN865.G8513 1993, (v3)
Guillen, Jorge. PQ6077.G8, (v3)
  PQ6613.U5.G78, (v3)
Guillen, Michael. QC24.5.G85 1995, (v1)
Guillet de Monthoux, Pierre. HD30.5.G85 1993, (v6)
Guillet, Edwin Clarence. F1032.G89 1968, (v4)
  F1058.G87 1963, (v4)
Guilmartin, John Francis. E865.G85 1995, (v4)
Guimaraes, Fernando Andresen. DT1428.G85 1998, (v5)
Guinagh, Kevin. PE1670.G8 1983, (v3)
Guindon, Hubert. F1053.G85 1988, (v4)
Guiney, Louise Imogen. PS1767.H3 1927, (v3)
  PS1768.A45 1926, (v3)
Guiney, Patrick R. E513.5 9th.G85 1998, (v4)
Guinier, Andre. QC176.G8513 1989, (v1)
Guinier, Lani. KF287.G85 1997, (v7)
Guinn, Matthew. PS261.G84 2000, (v3)
Guinnane, Timothy. HB3589.G84 1997, (v6)
Guinther, John. KF8972.G85 1988, (v7)
Guiraldes, Ricardo. PQ7797.G75.D613 1995, (v3)
Guiton, Margaret. PQ1808.G8, (v3)
Gulbranssen, Trygve. PT8950.G79 B52 1937, (v3)
Gulick, John. DS57.G84, (v5)
Gullan, Harold I. E815.G85 1998, (v4)
Gullberg, Jan. QA36.G86 1997, (v1)
Gulliford, Andrew. E98.M34 G85 2000, (v4)
Gulliksen, Harold. BF176.G85 1987, (v2)
Gulliver, P. H. DA995.T46.G85 1995, (v5)
Gumerman, George J. E78.A7.G964 1984, (v4)
Gummere, Richard M. E162.G88, (v4)
Gump, James O. E99.D1.G86 1994, (v4)
Gundell, Glenn. PN137.G8, (v3)
Gundersen, Adolf G. HC110.E5.G86 1995, (v6)
Gundersen, Joan R. E276.G86 1996, (v4)
Gundle, Stephen. JN5657.C63 G86 2000, (v7)
Gundolf, Friedrich. PT2051.G8 1925, (v3)
Guneratne, Arjun. DS493.9.T47 G85 2002, (v5)
Gunew, Sneja Marina. PR9608.2.M55.G86 1994, (v3)
Gunn, Daniel. PN98.P75.G86 1988, (v3)
Gunn, Drewey Wayne. Z8976.424.G85 1991, (v10)
Gunn, Edward M. PL2412.G86 1991, (v3)
  PL2412.G86 1991, (v3)
  PL3032.S48.G8, (v3)
Gunn, Geoffrey C. KZ4997.5.I5.G86 1997, (v7)
Gunn, S. J. DA325.G86 1995, (v5)
Gunn, Simon. DA110.G86 2000, (v5)
Gunn, T. Jeremy. KF4865.G86 1992, (v7)
Gunn, Thom. PR6013.U65.A6 1979, (v3)
Gunnar Karlsson. DL338.H849 2000, (v5)
Gunnarsson, Torsten. ND1361.5.G87 1998, (v9)
Gunnell, John G. JA71.G88 1998, (v7)
Gunning, Jennifer. KD3415.G86 1993, (v7)
Gunning, Sandra. PS173.N4.G86 1996, (v3)
Gunning, Tom. PN1998.3.G76.G8 1991, (v3)
  PN1998.3.L36.G86 2000, (v3)
Gunsberg, Maggie. PQ4136.G86 1997, (v3)
Gunson, Phil. F2183.G86 1991, (v4)
  F2237.G86 1989, (v4)
Gunter, Barrie. HC260.C6.G86 1998, (v6)
Gunter, Carl A. QA76.7.G86 1992, (v1)
Gunther, John J. JS344.F4.G86 1990, (v7)
Gunther, John. CT275.G855.G8 1971, (v5)
  D1058.G8 1962, (v5)
Gunther-Canada, Wendy. JC176.W65 G86 2001, (v7)
Gunzberg, Lynn M. PQ4055.J48.G86 1992, (v3)
Guo, Rongxing. HC427.92.G86 1998, (v6)
Guo, Sujian. JQ1510.G86 2000, (v7)
Gup, Benton E. HG3881.5.I58.G867 1998, (v6)
Gupta, Amit. UA10.G77 1997, (v10)
Gupta, Chandra Bhan. PN2881.G86 1991, (v3)
Gupta, Dipankar. DS422.C3 I57 2000, (v5)
Gupta, Kajal K. TA347.F5G87 2000, (v1)

Gupta, Kanhaya L. HD5852.G87 1989, (v6)
Gupta, Sumitra. HV393.G87 1989, (v6)
Gura, Philip F. F7.G87 1984, (v4)
  ML1015.B3.G87 1999, (v9)
Guralnick, Elissa S. PN1991.65.G87 1996, (v3)
Guralnick, Peter. ML420.P96.G87 1994, (v9)
  ML3521.G9 1986, (v9)
Gurevich, Aron IAkovlevich. CB353.G8713 1988, (v5)
Gurevitch, Jessica. QK901.G96 2002, (v1)
Gurian, Michael. LC212.92.G87 2001, (v7)
Gurko, Leo. PR6005.O4.Z7417, (v3)
Gurney, Kevin. QA76.87.G87 1997, (v1)
Gurney, Peter. HD3325.A4.G87 1996, (v6)
Gurr, Andrew. PR3095.G869 1996, (v3)
Gurr, Nadine. HV6431.G87 2000, (v6)
Gurr, Ted Robert. HM281.G82, (v6)
Gurtov, Melvin. JZ1305.G87 1999, (v7)
  UA835.G87 1998, (v10)
Guschov, Stephen D. GV875.C65.G87 1998, (v6)
Gusfield, Joseph R. HV5292.G77 1996, (v6)
Guss, David M. F2319.2.Y4.G87 1989, (v4)
  HN363.5.G87 2000, (v6)
Gussow, Joan Dye. S441.G87 1991, (v1)
Gussow, Zachary. RA644.L3.G878 1989, (v2)
Gustafson, Alrik. PT7083.G8 1969, (v3)
  PT9263.G8 1961, (v3)
Gustafson, James M. BJ1251.G8765 1996, (v8)
Gustafson, Ralph. PR9251.G864, (v3)
Gustafson, Sandra M. PN4055.U5.G87 2000, (v3)
Gustafson, Thane. HC340.12.G87 1999, (v6)
  HD9502.S652.G87 1989, (v6)
Gustaitis, Rasa. RJ253.5.G87 1986, (v2)
Gusterson, Hugh. U264.4.C2.G87 1996, (v10)
Guter, Robert P. NA7235.N5.G87 1992, (v9)
Gutfreund, H. QP601.3.G88 1995, (v1)
Guth, Alan H. QB991.I54.G88 1997, (v1)
Gutheim, Frederick Albert. NA705.G8, (v9)
Guthke, Karl Siegfried. PT2616.Z9.G79 1980, (v3)
Guthrie, Helen Andrews. TX354.G8 1983, (v1)
Guthrie, Kenneth Sylvan. B243.G88 1987, (v8)
Guthrie, Patricia. F277.B3.G88 1996, (v4)
Guthrie, Stewart. BL215.G88 1993, (v8)
Guthrie, W. K. C. B171.G84, (v8)
Guthrie, Woody. ML429.G95.A3 1976, (v9)
  PS3513.U9.A6 1975, (v3)
Gutierrez Najera, Manuel. PQ7297.G8.A15 1958, (v3)
Gutierrez, C. Paige. GR111.F73.G85 1992, (v6)
Gutierrez, David. E184.M5.G86 1995, (v4)
Gutierrez, Donald. PS3535.E923.Z74 1996, (v3)
Gutierrez, Gustavo. F1411.G97913 1993, (v4)
  HN39.L3.G8413 1983, (v6)
Gutierrez, Jose Angel. F394.C83.G88 1998, (v4)
Gutman, Herbert George. HD8072.G97 1987, (v6)
  HD8072.G98 1976, (v6)
Gutman, Judith Mara. TR140.H52.G8, (v1)
Gutman, Robert W. ML410.M9 G96 1999, (v9)
Gutmann, Amy. JC423.G925 1996, (v7)
Gutmann, Caroline. RG76.L35G8813 2001, (v2)
Guttenplan, Samuel D. BD418.3.G88 2000, (v8)
Gutteridge, Thomas G. HF5549.5.C35.G88 1993, (v6)
Guttery, Ben R. HE9882.A35.G88 1998, (v6)
Gutting, Gary. B2421.G88 2001, (v8)
Guttmann, Allen. E169.1.G97, (v4)
  GV583.G87 1988, (v6)
  GV655.G88 2001, (v6)
  GV706.5.G87, (v6)
  GV709.G85 1991, (v6)
  GV715.G88 1986, (v6)
  GV721.5.G85 2002, (v6)
Gutwirth, Madelyn. DC158.8.G88 1992, (v5)
  PQ2431.Z5.G87, (v3)
Gutzman, Philip C. U26.G88 1990, (v10)
Guy, J. A. DA315.G89 1988, (v5)
Guy, J. A. DA334.M8.G88 2000, (v5)
Guy, Josephine M. PR878.S62.G89 1996, (v3)
Guyatt, Nicholas. DS119.76.G89 1998, (v5)
Guymon, Gary L. GB848.G89 1994, (v6)
Guynn, William Howard. PN1995.9.D6.G89 1990, (v3)
Guyomarch, Alain. DC424.G89 1998, (v5)
Guyot, Dorothy. HV8141.G89 1991, (v6)

Guy-Sheftall, Beverly. E185.86.B543 1990 vol. 11, (v4)
Guyton, Bill. GB2425.C2.G89 1998, (v6)
Guzman, Daniel de. PQ7297.F793.Z67, (v3)
Guzman, Martin Luis. F1234.G9745 1969, (v4)
Guzzo, Richard A. HD57.G88 1983, (v6)
Gvosdev, Nikolas K. DK67.7.G28.G88 2000, (v5)
Gwilliam, Tassie. PR3667.G93 1993, (v3)
Gwin, Minrose. PS3511.A86.Z78418 1990, (v3)
Gwyn, Richard J. F1034.3.T7.G9, (v4)
Gwynn, Aubrey. LA81.G8 1966, (v7)
Gwynne-Thomas, E. H. E176.1.G89 1989, (v4)
Gyekye, Kwame. DT352.4.G94 1997, (v5)
Gyeszly, Suzanne D. Z2483.G95 1994, (v10)
Gygax, Franziska. PS3537.T323.Z63 1998, (v3)
Gyory, Andrew. E184.C5.G9 1998, (v4)
H. D. (Hilda Doolittle), 1886-1961. PS3507.O726.B5 1960, (v3)
  PS3507.O726.A6 1983, (v3)
  PS3507.O726.A93 1992, (v3)
  PS3507.O726.B8, (v3)
  PS3507.O726.H44 1972, (v3)
  PS3507.O726.T74 1973, (v3)
  PS3507.O726.Z464 1998, (v3)
  PS3507.O726.Z494 1997, (v3)
Haac, Oscar A. PQ2003.Z5.H3, (v3)
Haack, Susan. BC71.H15, (v8)
  BD175.H28 1998, (v8)
Haag, Pamela. HQ32.H3 1999, (v6)
Haan, C. T. GB656.2.S7.H3, (v6)
Haan, Hilde de. NA2335.H34 1988, (v9)
Haar, B. J. ter. BQ8672.H23 1999, (v8)
Haar, Charles Monroe. KF5740.Z9.H3 1996, (v7)
Haarsager, Sandra. F899.S453.L364 1994, (v4)
Haas, Charles N. TD1060.H33 1995, (v1)
Haas, Christopher. DT154.A4.H36 1997, (v5)
Haas, Edward F. F379.N553 M63, (v4)
Haas, Ernst B. D860.H33 1997, (v5)
  JX1995.H24 1990, (v7)
Haas, Garland A. E873.H3 1992, (v4)
Haas, Lisbeth. F869.S395.H33 1995, (v4)
Haas, Michael. DU624.6.H33 1992, (v5)
  JA74.H23 1992, (v7)
Haass, Richard. JF1351.H2 1999, (v7)
  UA23.H22 1994, (v10)
Habakkuk, H. J. T19.H23, (v1)
Habeeb, William Mark. JX4473.H33 1988, (v7)
Habegger, Alfred. B921.J24 H23 1994, (v8)
Habegger, Jerryll. NK2395.H34 1989, (v9)
Haber, Carole. HQ1064.U5.H183 1993, (v6)
Haber, Joram Graf. BJ1476.H33 1991, (v8)
Haber, Judith Deborah. PR539.P3.H33 1994, (v3)
Haber, Samuel. HT687.H26 1991, (v6)
Haberer, Erich. DS135.R9.H23 1995, (v5)
Habermas, Jurgen. B831.5.H33 1998, (v8)
  B3258.H323.P5513 1987, (v8)
  HC54.H213 1975, (v6)
  HM24.H2713 1989, (v6)
  JA68.H2313 1998, (v7)
Haberski, Raymond J. PN1995.H213 2001, (v3)
Haberstroh, Patricia Boyle. PR8733.H33 1996, (v3)
Habib, Rafey. PS3509.L43.Z68148 1999, (v3)
Habicht, Christian. DF285.H313 1997, (v5)
Habig, Marion Alphonse. BX4700.F6 H27 1977, (v8)
Habington, William. PR3505.H3, (v3)
Haboucha, Reginetta. GR98.H225 1992, (v6)
Hachette, Dominique. HD4098.H3313 1993, (v6)
Hachiya, Michihiko. D767.25.H6.H3, (v5)
Hachten, William A. PN4784.F6.H3 1996, (v3)
  PN4855.H24 1998, (v3)
  PN5450.H26 1993, (v3)
Hackemer, Kurt. VA56.H27 2001, (v10)
Hacker, Andrew. E185.615.H23 1995, (v4)
  HC110.I5.H27 1997, (v6)
Hacker, Barton C. U264.3.H333 1994, (v10)
Hacker, Jonathan. PN1998.2.H33 1991, (v3)
Hacker, P. M. S. B3376.W564.H244 1999, (v8)
Hackett, Cecil Arthur. PQ1183.H3 1964, (v3)
Hackett, Robert A. PN4784.O24.H33 1998, (v3)
Hackey, Robert B. RA981.A2.H27 1998, (v2)

Hacking, Ian. BC141.H33 2001, (v8)
    BD175.H29 1999, (v8)
    BD595.H33 1990, (v8)
    RC553.F83.H33 1998, (v2)
    RC569.5.M8.H33 1995, (v2)
Hackley, F. W. UF700.H3, (v10)
Hackney, Sheldon. F326.H14, (v4)
Hacohen, Malachi Haim. B1649.P64.H33 2000, (v8)
Hacsi, Timothy A. HV983.H33 1997, (v6)
Hadaller, David. PS3569.T9.Z73 1996, (v3)
Hadar, Leon T. DS63.2.U5.H34 1992, (v5)
Hadas, Moses. B528.H3, (v8)
    B778.H3, (v8)
    PA3001.H3, (v3)
Hadda, Janet. PJ5129.S49.Z695 1997, (v3)
Haddad, Yvonne Yazbeck. Z7835.M6.H23 1991, (v10)
    Z7835.M6.H24 1997, (v10)
Hadden, Sally E. E443.H33 2001, (v4)
Haddock, Miranda Howard. Z5691.H33 2000, (v10)
Haddox, John H. B1019.V34 H3, (v8)
Hadfield, Andrew. PR418.P65.H33 1994, (v3)
    PR2363.H23 1997, (v3)
Hadfield, Charles. HE526.H33 1986, (v6)
Hadgraft, Cecil. PR9576.H3 1963, (v3)
Hadjor, Kofi Buenor. D883.H33 1992, (v5)
Hadley, D. M. DA158.H34 2000, (v5)
Hadley, Elaine. PR728.M4.H33 1995, (v3)
Hadot, Pierre. B105.S66.H3313 1995, (v8)
    B172.H33513 2002, (v8)
    B583.H3313 1998, (v8)
    B693.Z7 H2813 1993, (v8)
Haeberlin, Hermann Karl. E78.P8.H13, (v4)
Haefner, James W. QH323.5.H325 1996, (v1)
Haeger, Knut. RD19.H34, (v2)
Haesaerts, Paul. ND673.E6.H313, (v9)
Hafen, Le Roy Reuben. F761.H24, (v4)
Haffner, Sebastian. DD247.H5.H26513, (v5)
Haffner, Katie. DD857.A2.H34 1995, (v8)
Haftmann, Werner. ND195.H323 1965, (v9)
Hagan, John. DS559.8.D7.H33 2001, (v5)
    HV6025.H274 1989, (v6)
    KE332.W6.H34 1995, (v7)
Hagan, Kenneth J. E182.H16 1991, (v4)
Hagan, Susannah. NA2542.36.H34 2001, (v9)
Hagan, William Thomas. E93.H227 1997, (v4)
    E99.C85 H26 1990, (v4)
    E99.C85 P3838 1993, (v4)
Hage, George Sigurd. PN4897.M59H3, (v3)
Hage, Per. GN663.H37 1996, (v6)
Hagedorn, Hermann. E757.H142, (v4)
Hagedorn, John. HV742.W5.H34 1995, (v6)
Hagen, Jon B. TK6560.H34 1996, (v1)
Hagen, Susan K. PQ1483.G4.H3 1990, (v3)
Hager, Bengt Nils Richard. GV1786.B315.H3413 1990, (v6)
Hager, Dorothy. F635.H34 1967, (v4)
Hager, George. HJ2051.H325 1997, (v6)
Hagerman, Edward. E491.H16 1988, (v4)
Haggard, Stephan. HC59.7.H275 1990, (v6)
    JC423.H29 1995, (v7)
Haggard, William. PR6053.L38.A7, (v3)
Hagger, Mark S. DA175.H34 2001, (v5)
Haggerty, Gary. ML128.P63.H34 1995, (v9)
Haggerty, George E. PR830.T3.H25 1989, (v3)
    PR858.W6.H34 1998, (v3)
Haggerty, Kevin D. HV6806.H35 2001, (v6)
Haggett, Peter. G70.H22 1990, (v6)
    GF50.H33 1977, (v6)
    RA792.5.H34 2000, (v2)
Haghayeghi, Mehrdad. DK859.5.H34 1995, (v5)
Hagopian, Frances. JL2481.H34 1996, (v7)
Hagstrom, Robert G. GV1029.9.S74 H34 1998, (v6)
    HG4521.H227 2001, (v6)
Hagstrum, Jean H. PN56.M28.H34 1992, (v3)
    PR409.L67.H3, (v3)
    PR445.H3, (v3)
    PR3537 C7H3)

Hague, Angela. PR6063.U7.Z67 1984, (v3)
Hague, Harlan. F864.L32.H34 1990, (v4)
Hagy, James William. F279.C4.H34 1993, (v4)
Hahamovitch, Cindy. HD1527.A9.H34 1997, (v6)
Hahm, Sung Deuk. JQ1725.H345 1997, (v7)
Hahn, Alexander. QA303.H154 1998, (v1)
Hahn, Emily. DS778.A1.H3 1943, (v5)
Hahn, Gerald J. QA276.H22 1991, (v1)
Hahn, Lewis Edwin. B809.14.H34 2001, (v8)
Hahn, Liang-shin. QA255.H34 1994, (v1)
Hahn, Reynaldo. MT820.H1413 1990, (v9)
Hahn, Roger. Q46.A15.H33, (v1)
Hahn, Stephen. B2430.D484 H34 2002, (v8)
Hahn, Steven. F290.H33 1983, (v4)
Hahner, June Edith. F2537.H34, (v4)
Haidu, Peter. PQ1522.H33 1993, (v3)
Haig, Stirling. PQ653.H35 1987, (v3)
Haigh, Christopher. DA315.H28 1993, (v5)
Haigh, John. QA273.15.H35 1999, (v1)
Haight, Anne Lyon. Z1019.H15 1978, (v10)
Haight, Gordon Sherman. PR1285.H27, (v3)
Haight, M. R. BC108.H18 1999, (v8)
Haight, Roger. BT202.H24 1999, (v8)
Haiken, Elizabeth. RD119.H35 1997, (v2)
Hail, William James. DS759.H15, (v5)
Haile Selassie. DT387.7.H2513 1976, (v5)
Hailey, Elizabeth Forsythe. PS3558.A327W67 1998, (v3)
Hailwood, Simon A. JC571.N683.H325 1996, (v7)
Haiman, Franklyn Saul. KF4772.H343 1993, (v7)
Haine, W. Scott. DC35.H35 2000, (v5)
Haines, Aubrey L. F722.H17 1996, (v4)
Haines, Catharine M.C. Q141.H2167 2001, (v1)
Haines, Duane E. QM451.H18 2000, (v1)
Haines, Gerald K. HV8144.F43.H35 1993, (v6)
Haines, Herbert H. E185.615.H25 1988, (v4)
Haines, Simon. PR5438.H33 1997, (v3)
Haines-Eitzen, Kim. BR67.2.H35 2000, (v8)
Haining, Robert P. HA30.6.H35 1990, (v6)
Hainstock, Elizabeth G. LB775.M8.H26 1986, (v7)
Hair, Donald S. PR4244.H35 1999, (v3)
    PR5594.H35 1991, (v3)
Hair, William Ivy. E748.L86 H25 1991, (v4)
    F375.H16, (v4)
    F379.N553.C424, (v4)
Hairer, E. QA300.H352 1996, (v1)
Haj, Samira. DS79.H27 1997, (v5)
Hajdu, David. ML410.S9325.H35 1996, (v9)
Haji, Ishtiyaque. BJ1461.H26 1998, (v8)
Hake, Sabine. PN1995.H215 1993, (v3)
Hake, Sabine. PN1998.3.L83.H35 1992, (v3)
Haken, H. QC355.2.H33, (v1)
Hakim, Tawfiq. PJ7828.K52.A24 1998, (v3)
    PJ7828.K52.A25 1973, (v3)
    PJ7828.K52.Y283, (v3)
    PJ7828.K52.Y33 1989, (v3)
Hakutani, Yoshinobu. PS3545.R815.Z666 1996, (v3)
Halberstam, David. E169.02.H34 1993, (v4)
    E185.61.H195 1998, (v4)
    E881.H34 2001, (v4)
    GV878.4.H35 1994, (v6)
    GV884.J67.H35 2000, (v6)
Halberstam, Judith. PR830.T3.H27 1995, (v3)
Halberstam-Rubin, Anna. PJ5129.R2.Z66 1989, (v3)
Halbert, Debora J. KF2979.H35 1999, (v7)
Halbert, Henry S. E83.813.H15 1995, (v4)
Halbert, Michael. HF5415.H178, (v6)
Halbreich, Harry. ML410.H79.H313 1999, (v9)
Halbrook, Stephen P. D757.S9.H35 1998, (v5)
    KF3941.Z95.H35 1989, (v7)
    KF4749.H34 1998, (v7)
Hald, Anders. QA276.15.H35 1998, (v1)
Haldane, R. B. Haldane. B1645.H4.H8 1970b, (v8)
Haldeman, H. R. E855.H35 1994, (v4)
Haldon, John F. DF571.H35 1990, (v5)
Hale, Austin. PL3551.H34 1982, (v3)
Hale, Charles A. F1233.5.H35 1989, (v4)
Hale, Dorothy J. PN3365.H33 1998, (v3)
Hale, Edward Everett. PS1772.M26, (v3)
    PS1773.A4 1970, (v3)
Hale, Francis J. TL791.H35 1994, (v1)

Hale, Grace Elizabeth. F215.H18 1998, (v4)
Hale, J. R. CB367.H35 1994, (v5)
    DG737.42.H34, (v5)
    N6370.H25 1990, (v9)
    U43.E95.H35 1985, (v10)
Hale, Janet Campbell. E99.S63.H35 1993, (v4)
Hale, John K. PR3594.H35 1997, (v3)
Hale, Mason E. QK583.H35 1983, (v1)
    QK587.H25 1979, (v1)
Hale, Nancy. PS3515.A273 P3, (v3)
    PS3515.A273.Z5, (v3)
Hale, Oron J. D395.H24 1971, (v5)
Hale, Sondra. HQ1236.5.S73.H35 1996, (v6)
Hale, Susan. PS1774.H25.Z5 1919, (v3)
Hale, Thomas A. DT532.27.M63.H35 1990, (v5)
Hale, William Harlan. E415.9.G8.H17, (v4)
Hale, William M. DR474.H35 2000, (v5)
Halecki, Oskar. DK4140.H3413 1992, (v5)
Halem, Lynne Carol. HQ834.H33, (v6)
Hales, E. E. Y. BX1261.H3, (v8)
Hales, Peter B. QC773.3.U5.H35 1997, (v1)
Halevy, Elie. B1571.H33 1955, (v8)
Haley, Alex. E185.97.H24.A33, (v4)
Haley, David. PR3427.P6.H34 1997, (v3)
Haley, J. Evetts. F391.H16 1967, (v4)
    F596.G66 1949, (v4)
Haley, James Evetts. F391.M66 H3, (v4)
Haley, Kenneth Harold Dobson. DA407.S5.H3, (v5)
Halfin, Igal. DK266.A33.H35 2000, (v5)
Haliburton, Thomas Chandler. PR4735.H25 S33, (v3)
Halifax, George Savile. DA447.H2.A2 1989, (v5)
Halio, Jay L. PR2831.H28 1998, (v3)
Halisi, C. R. D. DT1928.H35 1999, (v5)
Halivni, David. BS1225.2.H32 1997, (v8)
Halkett, Samuel. Z1065.H18 1980, (v10)
Halkin, Leon-E. PA8518.H3313 1993, (v3)
Halkin, Simon. PJ5017.H3 1970, (v3)
Hall, A. Rupert. Q125.H28 1983, (v1)
    QC16.N7.H35 1992, (v1)
    QC353.H35 1993, (v1)
Hall, Anthony L. HC188.A5.H35 1997, (v6)
Hall, Bert S. U43.E95.H36 1997, (v10)
Hall, Bruce Edward. F128.68.C47.H35 1998, (v4)
Hall, Carl W. Q40.H35 2000, (v1)
    TP369.H36, (v1)
Hall, Carrie M. RM725.H33 1998, (v2)
Hall, Catherine. JN955.H25 2000, (v7)
Hall, Cecil Edwin. QC373.E4.H3 1966, (v1)
Hall, Charles J. ML200.H15 1996, (v9)
Hall, Christopher D. DC226.6.P362.H34 1992, (v5)
Hall, Clayton Colman. F184.H19, (v4)
Hall, Cordelia. QA76.95.H35 2000, (v1)
Hall, D. G. E. DS511.H15 1968, (v5)
Hall, D. J. F1033.S59.H254, (v4)
Hall, D. O. (David Oakley). QK882.H19 1999, (v1)
Hall, David L. B126.H255 1998, (v8)
    B128.C8.H35 1987, (v8)
Hall, David Locke. KF5060.H35 1991, (v7)
Hall, Donald E. ML3805.H153 2002, (v9)
    PR878.F45.H35 1996, (v3)
Hall, Donald. PS3515.A3152.W4 1982, (v3)
Hall, Douglas John. BT96.2.H34 1995, (v8)
Hall, Douglas Kent. F797.H35 1990, (v4)
Hall, E. Raymond. QL715.H15 1981, (v1)
Hall, Edith. PA3136.H35 1989, (v3)
Hall, Edward Twitchell. GN21.H24.A3 1992, (v6)
    HD31.H229 1990, (v6)
Hall, Edwin Presley. RD27.35.H34.A33, (v2)
Hall, Edwin. ND673.E9.W44 1994, (v9)
Hall, Everett Wesley. BD232.H25, (v8)
    BD232.H26 1952, (v8)
Hall, Francis. DS809.H18 1992, (v5)
Hall, Fred. ML410.B868.H35 1996, (v9)
Hall, G. Stanley. LB875.H18, (v7)
Hall, George M. T59.5.H27 1995, (v1)
Hall, Granville Davisson. F226.H17 2000, (v4)
Hall, Gwendolyn Midlo. E185.93.L6 H16 1992, (v4)
Hall, H. Lark. PS29.P3.H24 1994, (v3)
Hall, James. N7740.H35 1994, (v9)
    PR881.H3, (v3)
    PR5907.H3, (v3)

Hall, Joan Lord. PR2829.H35 1999, **(v3)**
Hall, John A. HF5415.153.H36 1991, **(v6)**
  HN59.2.H34 1999, **(v6)**
  JC325.H25 1994, **(v7)**
  JC585.H175 1988, **(v7)**
Hall, John C. RL74.S25 2000, **(v2)**
Hall, John R. BL65.V55.H33 2000, **(v8)**
Hall, John Richard Clark. PE279.H3 1961, **(v3)**
Hall, John Whitney. DS806.H25, **(v5)**
Hall, Jonathan M. DF135.H33 1997, **(v5)**
Hall, Joseph. PE537.H3 1920, **(v3)**
  PR2283.H7.A17 1971, **(v3)**
Hall, Judith G. QM28.H23 1989, **(v1)**
Hall, Julia. LC4069.3.H35 2001, **(v7)**
Hall, Kenneth E. PN1998.3.W655.H36 1999, **(v3)**
Hall, Kermit. KF352.A7.H35 1991, **(v7)**
  KF352.H35 1989, **(v7)**
Hall, Kim F. PR428.R35.H35 1995, **(v3)**
Hall, Lee. N6537.A43.H35 1990, **(v9)**
Hall, Leslie. E263.G3, **(v4)**
Hall, Linda B. F1234.O2.H34, **(v4)**
Hall, Louis Brewer. QB721.H25 1990, **(v1)**
Hall, Marcia B. ND170.H3 1991, **(v9)**
Hall, Marie Boas. Q41.L85.H35 1984, **(v1)**
Hall, Mark A. HG9396.H322 1994, **(v6)**
Hall, Max. PN171.F7.B3 1960, **(v3)**
Hall, Maximilian. K1066.H35 1994, **(v7)**
Hall, Michael G. F67.M468.H35 1988, **(v4)**
Hall, N. A. T. HT1119.V6.H36 1992, **(v6)**
Hall, N. John. PR5686.H26 1991, **(v3)**
Hall, Radclyffe. PR6015.A33 W45, **(v3)**
  PR6015.A33.Z494 1997, **(v3)**
Hall, Randal L. HV28.P67, **(v6)**
Hall, Rex. TL789.8.S652, **(v1)**
Hall, Richard Seymour. DS340.H35 1998, **(v5)**
Hall, Richard. E628.H35 1993, **(v4)**
Hall, Robert Anderson. PC21.H3, **(v3)**
  PC1105.H3 1948, **(v3)**
Hall, Robert Ernest. HB3711.H263 1991, **(v6)**
Hall, Robert L. E98.R3.H16 1997, **(v4)**
Hall, Robert T. BJ319.H25 1987, **(v8)**
Hall, Sam. G606.H35 1987, **(v6)**
Hall, Sharlot Mabridth. F811.H17, **(v4)**
Hall, Stephen H. TK7888.3.H315 2000, **(v1)**
Hall, Stephen K. TP187.H35 1994, **(v1)**
Hall, Susan G. F497.H5 H18 2000, **(v4)**
Hall, Susan. LC311.H33 2000, **(v7)**
Hall, Thomas D. HN79.A165.H35 1989, **(v6)**
Hall, Thomas E. HB3711.H265 1990, **(v6)**
  HB3717 1929 .H325 1998, **(v6)**
Hall, Thomas Steele. QP21.H34 1969, **(v1)**
Hall, Timothy D. BR520.H323 1994, **(v8)**
Hall, Timothy. KF4783.H35 1998, **(v7)**
Hall, Van Beck. F69.H3, **(v4)**
Hall, Vernon. PN86.H3, **(v3)**
Hall, Wayne E. PN5150.D83.H35 1999, **(v3)**
Hallahan, William H. UD383.H35 1994, **(v10)**
Hallak, Jacques. LC98.H35 1990, **(v7)**
Hallam, Arthur Henry. PR4735.H4.Z53 1981, **(v3)**
Hallberg, Peter. PT7170.H313, **(v3)**
  PT7181.H313, **(v3)**
Halle, David. N72.S6.H32 1993, **(v9)**
Halle, Louis Joseph. JA76.H35, **(v7)**
  UA11.H3 1974, **(v10)**
Halleck, Fitz-Greene. PS1780.S2 1869, **(v3)**
Haller, John S. R152.H354, **(v2)**
  RV8.T47, **(v2)**
  RV61.H35 1994, **(v2)**
  UH500.H35 1992, **(v10)**
Haller, William. DA400.H3 1964, **(v5)**
Hallett, Brien. KF5060.H355 1998, **(v7)**
Hallett, Charles A. PR2995.H26 1991, **(v3)**
Hallett, Cynthia Whitney. PS374.S5.H35 1999, **(v3)**
Hallett, Garth. BJ1278.P73.H35 1998, **(v8)**
Hallett, Richard William. PG3476.B2Z68 1973, **(v3)**
Hallgarten, George Wolfgang Felix. JC495.H243, **(v7)**
Halliburton, David. PN81.H24 1997, **(v3)**
Halliday, David. QC21.2.H355 1986, **(v1)**
Halliday, F. E. PR2976.H24 1958, **(v3)**
Halliday, Fred. D2003.H35 2001, **(v5)**
  DS63.H282 1996, **(v5)**

Halliday, Jon. HC462.7.H25 1975, **(v6)**
Halliday, Mark. PS3537.T4753.Z655 1991, **(v3)**
Halliday, Paul D. JN191.H34 1998, **(v7)**
Hallinan, Joseph T. HV9469.H25 2001, **(v6)**
Hallion, Richard. UG700.H35 1989, **(v10)**
  UG1240.H35 1984, **(v10)**
Hallissy, Margaret. PR1874.H27 1995, **(v3)**
  PR1928.W64.H35 1993, **(v3)**
Halliwell, Brian. SB421.H34 1992, **(v1)**
Hallock, D. U22.H35 1998, **(v10)**
Hallock, John W. M. PS1783.H35 2000, **(v3)**
Halls, W. D. DC397.H32 1995, **(v5)**
  PQ2625.A6.H25, **(v3)**
Hallsworth, A. G. HC240.9.C6.H34 1992, **(v6)**
Hallwas, John E. HV5090.I3.H35 1998, **(v6)**
Halm, Ben B. PN1631.H27 1995, **(v3)**
Halmos, Paul R. QA9.H293 1998, **(v1)**
  QA184.5.H35 1995, **(v1)**
  QA261.H33 1958, **(v1)**
Halperin Donghi, Tulio. F2845.H33, **(v4)**
Halperin, Charles J. DK90.H28 1985, **(v5)**
Halperin, Joan U. NX640.5.F46.H35 1988, **(v9)**
Halperin, John. PR871.H3 1974, **(v3)**
  PR4036.H24 1984, **(v3)**
Halperin, Maurice. F1788.H27, **(v4)**
Halperin, Michael. HD2746.5.H357 1992, **(v6)**
Halperin, Morton H. UA11.H34, **(v10)**
Halperin, Rhoda H. HN80.C55.H35 1998, **(v6)**
Halperin, Samuel William. D14.H3, **(v5)**
  DG799.H3 1968, **(v5)**
Halperin, Samuel. DS149.H337, **(v5)**
Halpern, Ben. DS149.H344 1998, **(v5)**
Halpern, Martin. HD6515.A82.I574 1988, **(v6)**
Halpern, Paul G. D580.H34 1994, **(v5)**
  D580.H35 1987, **(v5)**
Halpern, Paul. BC181.H34 2000, **(v8)**
  QB461.H24 1992, **(v1)**
Halpern, Richard. PR2969.H35 1997, **(v3)**
Halpern, Samuel E. V736.H3, **(v10)**
Halpern, Stephen C. KF4755.H35 1995, **(v7)**
Halpern, Sydney A. RJ42.U5.H36 1988, **(v2)**
Halpern, Thomas. KF4558 2nd.H35 1996, **(v7)**
Halpert, Herbert. GR113.5.N54.H35 1996, **(v6)**
Halphen, Louis. D20.P37 vol. 5, 2d set, **(v5)**
  DC70.H313, **(v5)**
  DC73.H29 1995, **(v5)**
Halporn, James W. PA186.H25, **(v3)**
Halprin, Anna. GV1785.H267.A3 1995, **(v6)**
  RM931.D35.H34 2000, **(v2)**
Halsall, A. W. PQ2301.H448 1998, **(v3)**
Halsall, Guy. DC801.M65.H36 1995, **(v5)**
Halsband, Robert. DA501.H47.H34 1974, **(v5)**
Halsband, Robert. DA501.M7.H3, **(v5)**
Halsey, Margaret. CT275.H28743.A36, **(v5)**
Halsey, William Frederick. E746.H3.A3, **(v4)**
Halstead, Bruce W. QL100.H3 1995, **(v1)**
Halstead, Jill. ML82.H35 1997, **(v9)**
Halstead, Ward Campbell. QP385.H3, **(v1)**
Halter, Marilyn. E184.A1.H214 2000, **(v4)**
Haltof, Marek. PN1998.3.W44.H36 1996, **(v3)**
Halzen, F. QC793.5.Q2522.H34 1984, **(v1)**
Hamalian, Leo. PN3373.H275, **(v3)**
Hamalian, Linda. PS3535.E923.Z69 1991, **(v3)**
Hamann, Carl H. QD553.H29 1998, **(v1)**
Hambleton, Ronald. PR6007.E34.Z64, **(v3)**
Hamblin, William Kenneth. QE28.2.H35 1998, **(v1)**
Hambrey, M. J. GB2403.2.H35 1994, **(v6)**
  GB2403.2.H36 1992, **(v6)**
Hambrick-Stowe, Charles E. BX7260.F47.H35 1996, **(v8)**
Hamburg, David A. HQ536.H318 1992, **(v6)**
Hamburger, Jeffrey F. ND3380.4.R65.H36 1990, **(v9)**
Hamburger, Joseph. DA3.M3.H27, **(v5)**
  JC223.M66.H363 1999, **(v7)**
Hamburger, Michael. PT117.4.H3, **(v3)**
  PT343.H3, **(v3)**
  PT3734.H3 1973, **(v3)**
Hamby, Alonzo L. E813.H26, **(v4)**
Hamel, Réginald. PQ3904.H3, **(v3)**
  PQ3900.2.H36 1989, **(v3)**
Hamer, D. A. E159.H19 1998, **(v4)**

HT361.H35 1990, **(v6)**
Hamer, Frank. TT919.5.H35 1997, **(v1)**
Hamer, Jennifer. E185.86.H28 2001, **(v4)**
Hamer, R. F. S. Z2012.H198 1995, **(v10)**
Hamermesh, Daniel S. HD5706.H36 1993, **(v6)**
  HD7096.U5.H275, **(v6)**
Hamerow, Theodore S. D445.H32 1990, **(v5)**
  DD210.H25, **(v5)**
  HC240.H314 1983, **(v6)**
Hameso, Seyoum Y. DT30.5.H34 1997, **(v5)**
Hamid, Mohsin. PS3558.A12M68 2000, **(v3)**
Hamill, Hugh M. F1232.H6243, **(v4)**
Hamill, Ian. VA459.S5.H36 1981, **(v10)**
Hamill, James F. GN502.H34 1990, **(v6)**
Hamill, Lee B. LC4031.H355 2002, **(v7)**
Hamill, Pete. ND259.R5.H28 1999, **(v9)**
Hamill, Sam. PL727.H36 1989, **(v3)**
Hamilton, A. C. PR2358.H28, **(v3)**
Hamilton, A. G. QA184.H36 1987, **(v1)**
Hamilton, Alexander. E302.H2 1961, **(v4)**
Hamilton, Alice. R154.H238.A34 1985, **(v2)**
Hamilton, Bernard. DA64.4.H36 2000, **(v5)**
Hamilton, Betty. R121.H232 1987, **(v2)**
Hamilton, C. I. DA88.H36 1993, **(v5)**
Hamilton, C. Mark. NA717.H36 1995, **(v9)**
Hamilton, Carolyn. DT1768.Z95.H36 1998, **(v5)**
Hamilton, Charles D. DF231.4.H35, **(v5)**
  DF232.A33.H36 1991, **(v5)**
Hamilton, Charles V. E748.P86.H35 1991, **(v4)**
Hamilton, David E. HD1761.H355 1991, **(v6)**
Hamilton, Dona C. E185.615.H277 1997, **(v4)**
Hamilton, Donna B. PR3017.H36 1992, **(v3)**
Hamilton, George Heard. N6450.H29, **(v9)**
  N6981.H34 1975, **(v9)**
Hamilton, Holman. E423.H2, **(v4)**
Hamilton, James. PN1992.8.V55.H36 1998, **(v3)**
Hamilton, John Arnott. NA370.H3 1956, **(v9)**
Hamilton, John Maxwell. PN4731.H28 1996, **(v3)**
Hamilton, K. G. PR541.H3, **(v3)**
Hamilton, Kristie. PS368.H35 1998, **(v3)**
Hamilton, Lee Templin. Z8119.2.H36 1991, **(v10)**
Hamilton, Mary. F347.M6.H36 1992, **(v4)**
Hamilton, Michael S. U264.3.H36 1990, **(v10)**
Hamilton, Neil A. E169.02.H3515 1997, **(v4)**
  HC102.5.A2.H36 1999, **(v6)**
  HN90.R3.H355 1996, **(v6)**
Hamilton, Neil W. LC72.2.H36 1995, **(v7)**
Hamilton, Nigel. DA69.3.M56.H355 1983, **(v5)**
  PT2625.A43.Z647 1979, **(v3)**
Hamilton, Peter J. F334.M6 H18 1976, **(v4)**
Hamilton, Peter Joseph. F334.M6 H2, **(v4)**
Hamilton, Richard F. D13.H282 1996, **(v5)**
  HD8435.H3, **(v6)**
  HN380.Z9.S64365 1991, **(v6)**
Hamilton, Russell G. PQ9900.H3, **(v3)**
Hamilton, Sarah. F3721.1.H33.H35 1998, **(v4)**
Hamilton, Scott. PS3531.O82.Z6413 1992, **(v3)**
Hamilton, V. Lee. K5064.H36 1992, **(v7)**
Hamilton, Virginia Van der Veer. F326.H26, **(v4)**
  F330.3.H55.H36 1987, **(v4)**
Hamilton, W. T. F591.H23 1960, **(v4)**
Hamlin, Huybertie Pruyn. F129.A353.H35 1990, **(v4)**
Hamlin, Talbot. NA707.H32, **(v9)**
Hamlin, William M. PR129.A4.H36 1995, **(v3)**
Hamlyn, D. W. B52.H25 1992, **(v8)**
Hamm, Charles. ML200.H17 1983, **(v9)**
  ML410.B499.H36 1997, **(v9)**
  ML3477.H35, **(v9)**
  ML3503.S6.H35 1988, **(v9)**
Hamm, Mark S. HV6432.H365 1997, **(v6)**
  HV6439.U5.H34 1993, **(v6)**
  HV9471.H29 1995, **(v6)**
Hamm, Richard F. KF3919.H35 1995, **(v7)**
Hamm, Thomas D. BX7637.H35 1988, **(v8)**
Hammacher, Abraham Marie. ND653.G7.H255 1982, **(v9)**
Hammack, David C. F128.47.H2 1982, **(v4)**
Hammer, Martin. N6999.G2.H36 2000, **(v9)**
Hammer, Olav. BL51.H3 2001, **(v8)**
Hammer, Paul E. J. DA358.E8.H28 1999, **(v5)**
Hammer, Tad Bentley. PN1993.4.H28 1991, **(v3)**

Hammergren, Linn A. KG495.H36 1998, (v7)
Hammersley, Martyn. GN345.H36 1991, (v6)
Hammett, Dashiell. PS3515.A4347, (v3)
   PS3515.A4347 C6, (v3)
   PS3515.A4347 M3 1972, (v3)
   PS3515.A4347 N6 1965, (v3)
Hammett, Louis P. QD476.H33 1970, (v1)
Hamming, R. W. QA273.H3544 1991, (v1)
Hammond Incorporated. G1021 .H2662 1996, (v6)
   G1021 .H2665 1997, (v6)
Hammond, Allen L. HC59.15.H33 1998, (v6)
Hammond, C. QD905.2 H355 2001, (v1)
   QD905.2.H36 1990, (v1)
Hammond, George Peter. E125.V3.H4, (v4)
Hammond, Grant Tedrick. UA10.H36 1993, (v10)
Hammond, J. R. PR5776.H36 1991, (v3)
   PR5776.H375 2001, (v3)
   PR5777.H294 1992, (v3)
   PR6029.R8.Z663 1982, (v3)
   PR6029.R8.Z677 2000, (v3)
Hammond, James Henry. F273.H24 1988, (v4)
Hammond, Kenneth R. R834.H3, (v2)
Hammond, Lansing Van der Heyden. PR3714.S53H3 1970, (v3)
Hammond, Mason. HT114.H35, (v6)
   JC51.H33, (v7)
Hammond, N. G. L. DF214.H28 1986, (v5)
   DF233.8.P59.H35 1994, (v5)
   DF261.M2.H35 1989, (v5)
Hammond, Norman. F1435.H35 1982, (v4)
Hammond, Paul Y. E847.2.H36 1992, (v4)
   UB23.H3, (v10)
Hammond, Paul. PR120.G39.H35 1996, (v3)
   PR3423.H36 1991, (v3)
Hammond, Phillip E. BL2525.H36 2000, (v8)
   BR515.H334 1992, (v8)
   BR516.H2 1998, (v8)
   BR526.H25 1992, (v8)
Hammond, Robert. G70.3.H35 1978, (v6)
Hammond, Susan Webb. JK1108.H36 1998, (v7)
Hammond, William M. DS559.46.H37 1996, (v5)
   DS559.46.H38 1998, (v5)
Hammonds, Evelynn Maxine. RA644.D6.H36 1999, (v2)
Hammontree, Patsy Guy. PN2287.T33.H26 1998, (v3)
Hammoudi, Abdellah. JQ3949.A15.H3613 1997, (v7)
Hamnett, Brian R. F1233.J9.H36 1994, (v4)
   HF3239.O3.H35 1971, (v6)
Hamouda, O. F. HB103.H47.H36 1993, (v6)
Hampden, John. PR1272.H32 1954, (v3)
Hampel, Clifford A. QD5.H34 1982, (v1)
   QD466.H295, (v1)
Hampshire, Stuart. BJ1461.H27, (v8)
   JA79.H264 1989, (v7)
Hampson, Fen Osler. JX1952.H28 1996, (v7)
Hampson, Margaret Daphne. BL458.H35 1996, (v8)
   BX8063.7.C3, (v8)
Hampson, Norman. CB411.H38 1968, (v5)
   DC146.D2.H35 1978, (v5)
   DC146.S135.H36 1991, (v5)
   DC148.H26, (v5)
   DC165.H35 1988, (v5)
Hampson, R. G. PR6005.O4.Z74187 1992, (v3)
Hampton, Benjamin B. PN1993.5.A1H25 1970, (v3)
Hampton, Bill R. LB2822.H29, (v7)
Hampton, Henry. E185.61.H224 1990, (v4)
Hampton, Lionel. ML419.H26.A3 1989, (v9)
Hampton, Mary N. E183.8.G3.H24 1996, (v4)
Hampton, O. W. DU744.35.D32.H35 1999, (v5)
Hampton, T. A. VM983.H3 1970, (v10)
Hamrock, Bernard J. TJ1063.H35 1994, (v1)
Hamsun, Knut. PT8950.H3 L33 1980b, (v3)
   PT8950.H3 M32 1921, (v3)
   PT8950.H3 M92, (v3)
   PT8950.H3 P32 1956, (v3)
Hamsun, Knut. PT8950.H3 S82 1967, (v3)
   PT8950.H3 U593 1975, (v3)
Han, Fei. PL2662.H3.A28, (v3)
Han, Henry Hyunwook. F1402.H28 1987, (v4)
Han, Suyin. PR6015.A6474.A653 1956, (v3)
Han, Ying. PL2997.H172 1952, (v3)

Han, Yu-shan. DS734.7.H3, (v5)
Hanan, Patrick. PL2417.H3, (v3)
   PL2698.L52.Z65 1988, (v3)
Hanawalt, Barbara. HQ792.G7.H27 1993, (v6)
Hanaway, Joseph. R749.M42.H36 1996, (v2)
Hance, William Adams. HC502.H33 1967, (v6)
Hanchard, Michael George. F2659.A1.H36 1994, (v4)
Hanchett, Thomas W. F264.C4.H28 1998, (v4)
Hancock, David. HF3520.L65.H36 1995, (v6)
Hancock, Eleanor. D757.H297 1991, (v5)
Hancock, Graham. HC845.Z9.F343 1985, (v6)
Hancock, James F. SB385.H34 1999, (v1)
Hancock, Joy Bright. VA390.H27, (v10)
Hancock, Lyn. E99.E9 H35 1995, (v4)
Hancock, Mary Elizabeth. DS432.T3.H33 1999, (v5)
Hancocks, David. QL76.H35 2001, (v1)
Hand, Richard A. Z5131.H36 1994, (v10)
Handel, Ruth D. LC152.N58.H36 1999, (v7)
Handke, Peter. PT2668.A5.K813, (v3)
   PT2668.A5.L5 1979, (v3)
   PT2668.A5.L53, (v3)
   PT2668.A5.S773, (v3)
Handler, Joel F. HV95.H259 1991, (v6)
   HV95.H264 1997, (v6)
   K370.H36 1990, (v7)
Handler, Richard. F234.W7.H27 1997, (v4)
   F1053.2.H36 1988, (v4)
   PR4038.P6.H36 1990, (v3)
Handley, George B. PS374.S58.H36 2000, (v3)
   PS374.S58H36 2000, (v3)
Handley, Graham. PR4037.H27 1992, (v3)
Handlin, Lilian. E340.B2.H36 1984, (v4)
Handlin, Oscar. E161.H3, (v4)
   E169.1.H265 1966, (v4)
   E175.9.H35, (v4)
   E178.H24, (v4)
   E183.H32 1986, (v4)
   E184.A1.H27, (v4)
   E457.H238 1980, (v4)
   E748.S63.H16, (v4)
   F73.9.A1.H3 1959, (v4)
   HC107.M4.H23 1969, (v6)
   HQ796.H256, (v6)
Handover, P. M. Z152.L8.H3, (v10)
Hands, Elizabeth S. TX551.H274 2000, (v1)
Hands, Timothy. PR4754.H229 1995, (v3)
Handy, Charles B. HD58.8.H3618 1994, (v6)
Handy, D. Antoinette. ML402.H36 1995, (v9)
Handy, Jim. F1466.5.H29 1994, (v4)
Handy, W. C. ML410.H18.A3 1985, (v9)
Hane, Mikiso. DS850.H36 1991, (v5)
Hanegraaff, Wouter J. BP605.N48.H36 1998, (v8)
Hanes, William Travis. DT82.5.G7.H36 1995, (v5)
Haney, Patrick Jude. E840.H36 1997, (v4)
Haney-Lopez, Ian. KF4755.H36 1996, (v7)
Hanfling, Oswald. B3376.W564.H295 1989, (v8)
Hanfmann, George Maxim Anossov. N5740.H3, (v9)
Hanford, James Holly. PR3588.H2 1970, (v3)
Hanger, Kimberly S. F379.N59.N44 1997, (v4)
Hanham, H. J. Z2019.H35, (v10)
Hanhimaki, Jussi M. DL59.U6.H36 1997, (v5)
Hanioglu, M. Sukru. DR572.5.H37 1995, (v5)
Hankamer, Paul. PT238.H3, (v3)
Hanke, Ken. PN1995.9.H6.H36 1991, (v3)
Hanke, Lewis. F1411.H33 1970, (v4)
Hanke, Udo. GV365.5.G3.H3613 1993, (v6)
Hankey, Maurice Pascal Alers Hankey, Baron. D546.H43, (v5)
Hankin, Jo Ann. HG4027.7.H356 1998, (v6)
Hankins, John Erskine. PR2358.H29 (v3)
Hankins, Thomas L. Q125.H355 1985, (v1)
Hankinson, R. J. B187.C38 H36 1998, (v8)
   B525.H26 1995, (v8)
Hanks, Patrick. CS2385.H27 1988, (v5)
Hanley, Gerald. PR6058.A59 J6, (v3)
Hanley, James. PR6015.A474 C55, (v3)
   PR6015.A474 S4, (v3)
Hanley, Keith. PR5892.H5, (v3)
Hanley, Lynne. PR888.W37.H36 1991, (v3)
Hanley, Nick. HC79.E5.H3295 1993, (v6)
Hanley, Susan B. GN635.J2.H35 1997, (v6)

Hanlon, David L. DU500.H35 1998, (v5)
   DU568.P7.H36 1988, (v5)
Hanlon, Gregory. DG483.5.H36 1998, (v5)
   DG540.H36 2000, (v5)
Hanlon, Joseph F. TS195.H35 1998, (v1)
Hanlon, Roger T. QL430.2.H37 1996, (v1)
Hanna, Alfred Jackson. F317.O4.H3, (v4)
   F1233.H2, (v4)
Hanna, J. Ray. QA379.H36, (v1)
Hanna, Judith Lynne. GV1589.H35 1999, (v6)
   GV1595.H33 1988, (v6)
Hanna, Martha. D639.P88.F743 1996, (v5)
Hanna, Owen T. TP184.H36 1995, (v1)
Hanna, Thomas. B2430.B43.H33, (v8)
Hanna, William S. F152.H37, (v4)
Hannabuss, Keith. QC174.12.H364 1997, (v1)
Hannaford, Robert V. BJ319.H276 1993, (v8)
Hannam, June. JF851.H28 2000, (v7)
   Z7964.G7.H36 1996, (v10)
Hannan, Michael T. HD58.8.H363 1989, (v6)
Hannay, Margaret P. PR2329.P2.Z69 1990, (v3)
Hanne, Michael. PN3499.H28 1994, (v3)
Hanners, John. PN2245.H36 1993, (v3)
Hannesson, Rognvaldur. HD9560.5.H26 1998, (v6)
Hanning, Robert W. PN682.I5.H3 1977, (v3)
Hannon, Bruce M. QA76.9.C65.H35 1994, (v1)
Hannon, Peter. LC156.G7, (v7)
Hannoosh, Michele. ND553.D33.H36 1995, (v9)
Hannoosh, Michele. PQ2323.L8.M634 1989, (v3)
Hannsberry, Karen Burroughs. PN1995.9.W6.H26 1998, (v3)
Hannum, Hurst. JX4054.H34 1990, (v7)
Hanrahan, Stephanie J. GV363.H28 2000, (v6)
Hanrieder, Wolfram F. DD258.8.H37 1989, (v5)
Hans, James S. BD232.H296 1989, (v8)
Hansberry, Lorraine. PS3515.A515.R3, (v3)
Hanscombe, Gillian E. PR6035.I34.Z72 1983, (v3)
Hansell, Michael H. QL675.H34 2000, (v1)
Hansen, Bent. HC830.H36 1991, (v6)
Hansen, Birthe. DS63.1.H365 2001, (v5)
Hansen, Chad. B126.H277 1992, (v8)
Hansen, Charles M. QD543.H258 2000, (v1)
Hansen, David T. LB1775.2.H35 1995, (v7)
Hansen, Debra Gold. E449.H25 1993, (v4)
Hansen, Elaine Tuttle. PR1928.W64.H36 1991, (v3)
   PS374.M547.H36 1997, (v3)
Hansen, Hans Jurgen. VM307.H3713 1968b, (v10)
Hansen, Harry. PS273.H3 1923, (v3)
Hansen, Karen Tranberg. GN657.R4.H36 1996, (v6)
   GT1589.Z33, (v6)
Hansen, Klaus J. BX8635.2.H36, (v8)
Hansen, Martin Alfred. PT8175.H33 L613, (v3)
   PT8175.H33 L82, (v3)
Hansen, Miriam. PN1995.75.H36 1991, (v3)
Hansen, Mogens Herman. JC79.A8.H33 1991, (v7)
Hansen, Niles M. HT392.H35, (v6)
Hansen, Phillip Birger. JC251.A74 H38 1993, (v7)
Hansen, Randall. JV7633.H35 2000, (v7)
Hansen, Richard. SB434.H29513 1993, (v1)
Hansen, Robert C. TK7871.67.M53.H36 1998, (v1)
Hansen, Thomas Blom. BL1215.P65 H36 1999, (v8)
Hansen, Thomas S. PS2642.G43.H36 1995, (v3)
Hansen, Valerie. BL1802.H35 1990, (v8)
   DS735.H25 2000, (v5)
   KNN858.H36 1995, (v7)
Hansford, Charles. PS767.H2.P6 1961, (v3)
Hanslick, Eduard. ML60.H2043, (v9)
Hanslick, Eduard. ML3847.H3 1957, (v9)
Hanson, Clare. PR888.F45.H36 2000, (v3)
Hanson, David J. HV5035.H25 1995, (v6)
Hanson, F. Allan. BF697.5.S43.H365 1993, (v2)
Hanson, Jim M. D860.H365 1996, (v5)
Hanson, John H. DT532.3.H36 1991, (v5)
   DT532.3.T35.H36 1996, (v5)
Hanson, Joseph Mills. F597.M364H36 2003, (v4)
Hanson, K. C. BS2545.S55.H37 1998, (v8)
Hanson, Kenneth. BM723.H33 1998, (v8)
Hanson, Lawrence. ND553.G27.H33 1955, (v9)
   ND653.G7H275, (v9)
   PQ2464.H3, (v3)
   PR4168.H25 1967, (v3)

Hanson, Nancy Edmonds. F644.F2H357 1987, **(v4)**
Hanson, Paul R. DC195.C2.H36 1989, **(v5)**
Hanson, Robert M. QD461.H263 1995, **(v1)**
Hanson, Sandra L. Q130.H365 1996, **(v1)**
Hanson, Victor Davis. HD133.H36 1995, **(v6)**
  HD1476.U5 H28 1996, **(v6)**
  PA78.U6.H36 1998, **(v3)**
  S441.H28 2000, **(v1)**
  U33.H36 1989, **(v10)**
Hanssen, Beatrice. PT2603.E455.H36 1998, **(v3)**
  PT2603.E455H36 1998, **(v3)**
Hanyan, Craig. F123.C645.H23 1996, **(v4)**
Hapgood, Fred. T171.M49.H37 1993, **(v1)**
Hapgood, Robert. PR2976.H29 1988, **(v3)**
Happe, Francesca. RC553.A88.H36 1995, **(v2)**
Haq, Mahbub ul. HC59.7.H35, **(v6)**
Haramundanis, Katherine. T11.H28 1998, **(v1)**
Harari, Josue V. PQ261.H37 1987, **(v3)**
Haraszti, Emil. ML410.B26.H2, **(v9)**
Haraway, Donna Jeanne. GN365.9.H37 1991, **(v6)**
  HQ1190.H37 1997, **(v6)**
Harbage, Alfred. PR2976.H32, **(v3)**
  PR3007.H3, **(v3)**
  PR3091.H36, **(v3)**
  PR3091.H37, **(v3)**
Harbaugh, William Henry. E757.H28 1975b, **(v4)**
Harbeck, Karen Marie. LC192.6.H37 1997, **(v7)**
Harber, Clive. LC95.A2.H37 1997, **(v7)**
Harbison, James P. QC688.H37 1998, **(v1)**
Harbison, Peter. N6784.H35 1999, **(v9)**
Harbottle, Thomas Benfield. D25.A2.H2 1981, **(v5)**
Harbour, Frances Vryling. JZ1480.H37 1999, **(v7)**
Harbury, Jennifer. F1466.5.H3 1994, **(v4)**
Harcleroad, Fred F. LB2329.5.H327 1987, **(v7)**
Harclerode, Peter. HV6431.H363 2000, **(v6)**
Hardach, Gerd. HC56.H3713, **(v6)**
Hardach, Karl. HC286.H3613, **(v6)**
Hardcastle, Valerie Gray. BD418.3.H37 1996, **(v8)**
Hardeman, Hilde. DK35.5.H37 1994, **(v5)**
Harden, Edgar F. PR5638.H34 1998, **(v3)**
Harden, O. Elizabeth McWhorter. PR4647.H26 1984, **(v3)**
Harden, Victoria Angela. RA11.D6.H37 1986, **(v2)**
  RC182.R6.H37 1990, **(v2)**
Hardenberg, Friedrich. PT2291.H22 1964, **(v3)**
Hardesty, Donald L. F868.T2.H27 1997, **(v4)**
Hardesty, Von. D792.S65.H37 1982, **(v5)**
Hardie, William Francis Ross. B491.E7.H3 1980, **(v8)**
Hardin, C. L. B105.C455.H37 1988, **(v8)**
Hardin, Charles M. KF4565.A75.H37 1989, **(v7)**
Hardin, Garrett James. HQ766.7.H35 1993, **(v6)**
Hardin, John Wesley. F391.H26 1961, **(v4)**
Hardin, Richard F. PN56.P3.H37 2000, **(v3)**
  PR428.P6.H34 1992, **(v3)**
Hardin, Russell. BJ1012.H285 1988, **(v8)**
  BJ1500.T78 H37 2002, **(v8)**
  JC423.H345 1999, **(v7)**
Hardin, Stephen L. F390.H29 1994, **(v4)**
Harding, Alan. DA225.H37 1993, **(v5)**
Harding, Anne S. R133.H36 2000, **(v2)**
Harding, Anthony John. PR468.A72.H37 1995, **(v3)**
Harding, Bertita Leonarz. F1233.H28, **(v4)**
Harding, Davis Philoon. PR3562.H34, **(v3)**
Harding, Denys Clement Wyatt. PR4037.H29 1998, **(v3)**
Harding, Harry. HC427.92.H37 1987, **(v6)**
Harding, James. ML410.M41.H4 1971, **(v9)**
Harding, Les. HE6182.H34 1998, **(v6)**
Harding, Mildred Davis. PR4515.C7.H37 1996, **(v3)**
Harding, Neil. HX311.5.H37 1996, **(v6)**
Harding, Rebecca. HB171.5.H3253 1997, **(v6)**
Harding, Richard. DA85.H37 1995, **(v5)**
  F2272.5.H29 1990, **(v4)**
  RC1135.H37 1989, **(v2)**
Harding, Susan Friend. BT82.2.H36 2000, **(v8)**
Harding, Walter Roy. B931.T44 H37, **(v8)**
Harding, Wendy. PS3563.O8749.Z66 1994, **(v3)**
Hardison, O. B. PN1040.A5.H3, **(v3)**
  PR70.H3, **(v3)**
  PR535.V4.H37 1989, **(v3)**
Hardman, Charlotte. DS493.9.R34 H37 2000, **(v5)**

Hardman, John. DC137.H37 1993, **(v5)**
  DC146.R6 H27 1999, **(v5)**
Hardt, Michael. JC359.H279 2000, **(v7)**
Hardwick, Susan Wiley. F855.2.R9.H37 1993, **(v4)**
Hardwig, John. R725.5.H37 2000, **(v2)**
Hardy, Alfred Cecil. VM145.H23 1949, **(v10)**
Hardy, Anne. RA643.7.G7.H37 1993, **(v2)**
Hardy, Christine. BF463.M4.H37 1998, **(v2)**
Hardy, Emma Lavinia Gifford. PR4739.H77.Z5 1961, **(v3)**
Hardy, Florence Emily. PR4753.H3 1928, **(v3)**
Hardy, G. H. QA7.H3 1967, **(v1)**
Hardy, Gayle J. JC599.U5.H273 1993, **(v7)**
  Z1223.Z7.R63 1996, **(v10)**
Hardy, Grant. DS741.3.S683 H37 1999, **(v5)**
Hardy, J. P. PR3534.H3, **(v3)**
Hardy, John. F334.S4 H2 1978, **(v4)**
Hardy, Lew. GV706.4.H373 1996, **(v6)**
Hardy, Lyda Mary. Z7964.U49.H364 2000, **(v10)**
Hardy, Phil. PN1995.9.W4.H37 1994, **(v3)**
Hardy, Thomas. PR4741.F61, **(v3)**
  PR4741.H9 1982, **(v3)**
  PR4742.D35 1992, **(v3)**
  PR4746.A1 1978, **(v3)**
  PR4748.A1 1951, **(v3)**
  PR4748.A2.R57 1998, **(v3)**
  PR4749.A1 1952, **(v3)**
  PR4750.D7 1965, **(v3)**
  PR4750.G7, **(v3)**
  PR4750.H35 1951, **(v3)**
  PR4750.L36 1975, **(v3)**
  PR4750.M3 1977, **(v3)**
  PR4750.P3, **(v3)**
  PR4750.T84 1998, **(v3)**
  PR4750.U5 1974, **(v3)**
  PR4750.W45, **(v3)**
  PR4750.W6, **(v3)**
  PR4753.A28 1985, **(v3)**
  PR4753.A4 1978, **(v3)**
  PR4753.A4 1989, **(v3)**
Hare, F. Kenneth. QC981.H3, **(v1)**
Hare, J. E. BJ1275.H24 1996, **(v8)**
Hare, Lloyd Custer Mayhew. E449.M96, **(v4)**
Hare, R. M. BJ1012.H3, **(v8)**
  BJ1012.H31352 1997, **(v8)**
  BJ1025.H3, **(v8)**
Hare, William. LB41.H285, **(v7)**
Haren, Michael. B721.H34 1992, **(v8)**
Harer, John B. KF4770.Z9.H3 1992, **(v7)**
Hareven, Shulamith. PJ5054.H292.A2 1992, **(v3)**
Hargis, Jeffrey W. BR160.3.H37 1999, **(v8)**
Hargrave, Catherine Perry. GV1233.H3 1966, **(v6)**
Hargrave, Frank. TK5102.H37 2001, **(v1)**
Hargreaves, Alec G. JV7925.H375 1995, **(v7)**
Hargreaves, Andy. LB1775.H284 1994, **(v7)**
Hargreaves, David J. ML3830.H23 1986, **(v9)**
Hargreaves, J. K. QC879.H278 1992, **(v1)**
Hargreaves, Margaret Barnwell. LC5159.3.U6.H37 1991, **(v7)**
Hargreaves, Mary W. M. E376.H24 1985, **(v4)**
  SB110.H37 1993, **(v1)**
Hargreaves, Reginald. DS517.3 .H3, **(v5)**
Hargreaves-Mawdsley, W. N. LB2389.H26 1978, **(v7)**
Hargrove, Erwin C. E873.H36 1988, **(v4)**
Hargrove, Hondon B. E540.N3.H35 1988, **(v4)**
Hariharan, P. QC411.H35 1992, **(v1)**
Harik, Iliya F. HC830.H37 1987, **(v6)**
Haring, Bernhard. BJ1249.H36, **(v8)**
  BX1758.2.H32, **(v8)**
Haring, Clarence Henry. F1410.H25, **(v4)**
Haring, Hermann. BX4705.K76.H3713 1998, **(v8)**
Haring, Lee. GR357.H38 1992, **(v6)**
Harington, Donald. F415.H37 1986, **(v4)**
Harington, John. PR2284.N4 1962, **(v3)**
Harkabi, Yehoshafat. DS126.5.H357213 1988, **(v5)**
Harkavy, Robert E. UA15.5.H37 1989, **(v10)**
Harkins, William Edward. PG2940.H3 1971, **(v3)**
Harkness, Georgia Elma. BJ101.H35, **(v8)**
Harkness, Mabel G. SB408.H36 1993, **(v1)**
Harkness, Marguerite. PR6019.O9.P6447 1990, **(v3)**
Harkrider, Jack. PN4797.H35 1997, **(v3)**

Harl, Kenneth W. CJ843.H35 1996, **(v5)**
  CJ969.H37 1987, **(v5)**
Harlan, David. E175.H37 1997, **(v4)**
Harlan, Edgar Rubey. F621.H28, **(v4)**
Harlan, Jack R. GN799.A4.H37 1995, **(v6)**
Harlan, Jacob Wright. F861.6.H37 1996, **(v4)**
Harlan, Judith. HQ1410.H365 1998, **(v6)**
Harlan, Louis R. E185.97.W4.H373 1983, **(v4)**
Harland, David M. QB661.H37 2000, **(v1)**
Harland, Richard. PN81.H2843 1999, **(v3)**
Harle, Vilho. HM271.H297 1998, **(v6)**
Harley, John Brian. GA405.5.H37, **(v6)**
Harley, John. ML410.B996.H37 1997, **(v9)**
Harline, Craig E. BX4705.H7645, **(v8)**
Harlow, Barbara. PN51.H373 1996, **(v3)**
  PN51.H375 1987, **(v3)**
  PN494.H37 1992, **(v3)**
Harlow, Harry Frederick. BF671.H37, **(v2)**
Harlow, Neal. F864.H295 1982, **(v4)**
Harlow, Ralph Volney. E302.6.A2.H2, **(v4)**
Harman, Barbara Leah. PR878.P6.H37 1998, **(v3)**
Harman, Gilbert. BJ1012.H316 1996, **(v8)**
  BJ1012.H317, **(v8)**
Harmer, Catherine M. BX1746.H37 1995, **(v8)**
Harmer, Florence Elizabeth. CD105.H3, **(v5)**
Harmer, H. J. P. JN1129.L32.L32H32 1999, **(v7)**
Harmon, Alexandra. E78.W3.H37 1999, **(v4)**
Harmon, Christopher C. HV6431.H365 2000, **(v6)**
Harmon, David Andrew. F294.A89.N443 1996, **(v4)**
Harmon, Robert B. Z8839.4.H287 1996, **(v10)**
  Z8839.4.H29 1987, **(v10)**
Harms, Jeanne McLain. LB1044.9.P49.H37 1996, **(v7)**
Harms, Thelma. LB3011.5.H37 1998, **(v7)**
Harner, James L. Z1001.H33 2000, **(v10)**
  Z2011.H34 2002, **(v10)**
Harnett, Bertram. KF297.H33 1984, **(v7)**
Harney, Nicholas De Maria. F1059.5.T689.I84 1998, **(v4)**
Harnish, Robert M. BF311.H339 2001, **(v2)**
Harnoncourt, Nikolaus. ML60.H33713 1989, **(v9)**
  ML457.H313 1988, **(v9)**
Harnwell, G. P. QC518.H27 1949, **(v1)**
Haroian-Guerin, Gil. PR830.H4.H37 1996, **(v3)**
Harold, Franklin M. QH510.H37 1986, **(v1)**
Haroon, Mohammed. ML120.I5.H37 1991, **(v9)**
Harootunian, Harry D. DS822.4.H36 2000, **(v5)**
Haroutunian-Gordon, Sophie. LB1027.H339 1991, **(v7)**
Harp, Gillis J. E169.1.H2725 1994, **(v4)**
Harpaz, Amos. QC173.6.H37 1992, **(v1)**
Harper, Christopher. PN4784.E5.H36 1998, **(v3)**
Harper, David. RA644.H32.H37 1999, **(v2)**
Harper, Donna Sullivan. PS3515.U274.Z645 1995, **(v3)**
Harper, George McLean. PR5881.H3 1960, **(v3)**
Harper, George Mills. PR4148.P5.H3, **(v3)**
  PR5907.H32, **(v3)**
Harper, John L. QK911.H35, **(v1)**
Harper, John Lamberton. D1065.U5.H275 1994, **(v5)**
Harper, Lila Marz. PR788.T72.H37 2001, **(v3)**
Harper, Marjory. DA774.5.H37 1998, **(v5)**
Harper, R. Eugene. F153.H37 1991, **(v4)**
Harper, Sue. PN1993.5.G7.H35 1994, **(v3)**
Harper, Susan Billington. BX7066.5.Z8.A934 2000, **(v8)**
Harper, William Rainey. PJ4567.H33 1921, **(v3)**
Harpham, Geoffrey Galt. BJ46.H37 1999, **(v8)**
  PR6005.O4.Z74188 1996, **(v3)**
Harpsfield, Nicholas. PR1119.A2 no.186, **(v3)**
Harpstead, Milo I. S591.H28 2001, **(v1)**
Harr, John Ensor. CT274.R59.H37 1988, **(v5)**
Harr, Jonathan. KF228.A7 H37 1996, **(v7)**
Harraway, Clare. PR2673.H34 2000, **(v3)**
Harre, Rom. B72.H317 2000, **(v8)**
Harrell, David Edwin. BX7077.Z8.H354 2000, **(v8)**
Harrell, David. PS3505.A87.P7 1992, **(v3)**
Harrell, Margaret C. UB418.W65.H37 1997, **(v10)**
Harrer, Heinrich. DS785.H273 1954, **(v5)**
Harries, Jill. DG312.5.S5.H37 1994, **(v5)**
  KJA2700.H37 1999, **(v7)**

Harries, Karsten. BD348.H37 2001, (v8)
  NA2500.H375 1997, (v9)
  NA5573.H37 1983, (v9)
Harries, Martin. B3305.M74.H333 2000, (v8)
Harries, Meirion. D570.A46 1997, (v5)
Harrigan, Stephen. PS3558.A626A88 1986, (v3)
Harriger, Katy J. (Katy Jean). KF4568.H37 1992, (v7)
Harriman, W. Averell. D753.H28, (v5)
Harring, Sidney L. KE7709.H37 1998, (v7)
Harrington, C. Lee. PN1992.8.S4.H37 1995, (v3)
Harrington, Gary. PS3511.A86.Z78456 1990, (v3)
Harrington, John P. PR6003.E282.Z6678 1991, (v3)
Harrington, Michael. CB425.H24, (v5)
  H59.H36.A3 1988, (v6)
  HC59.7.H353, (v6)
  HC110.P6.H37 1984, (v6)
  HN58.H245 1981, (v6)
Harrington, Mona. KF299.W6 H36 1995, (v7)
Harrington, Nicki. RT82.H37 1996, (v2)
Harrington, Philip S. QB541.H35 1997, (v1)
Harris, Albert Josiah. LB1050.53.H37 1985, (v7)
Harris, Ann G. QE77.H36 1997, (v1)
Harris, Ann Sutherland. N6350.H35 1976, (v9)
Harris, Arthur Travers. D786.H318 1995, (v5)
Harris, Brice. PR1266.H3, (v3)
Harris, Chauncy Dennison. H31.C514 no. 179, etc., (v6)
Harris, Christopher. KF3958.H368 1994, (v7)
Harris, Cyril M. TD892.H37 1979, (v1)
Harris, David A. HV8141.H298 2002, (v6)
Harris, David Golightly. F277.S7.H37 1990, (v4)
Harris, David. F869.S343.H37 1993, (v4)
  UB342.U5.H33, (v10)
Harris, Diana K. HQ1061.H338 1988, (v6)
Harris, Elizabeth H. QK569.C486.H37 1989, (v1)
Harris, Ellen T. ML410.P93.H3 1987, (v9)
Harris, Enriqueta. ND813.V4.H37 1982, (v9)
Harris, Errol E. B3998.H275 1992, (v8)
  BD638.H277 1988, (v8)
  BD701.H37 1991, (v8)
Harris, Forest Klaire. QC535.H35, (v1)
Harris, Frank. PR4759.H37 B6 1963, (v3)
  PR4759.H37.Z5 1991, (v3)
  PR5823.H3 1959, (v3)
Harris, Fred R. JK1161.H26 1993, (v7)
Harris, Geoff. JA84.E9.H37 1990, (v7)
Harris, George Lawrence. DS70.6.H3, (v5)
Harris, George W. BJ1533.R42.H37 1997, (v8)
Harris, George Washington. PS1799.H87.S8 1966, (v3)
Harris, Gordon. Z3504.O743.H37 1994, (v10)
  Z3517.H37 1999, (v10)
Harris, Harold Arthur. GV573.H3, (v6)
Harris, Henry. QH577.H37 1999, (v1)
Harris, Irving B. HV741.H338 1996, (v6)
Harris, J. QA40.S76 1998, (v1)
Harris, J. P. UE57.H37 1995, (v10)
Harris, J. William. F215.H29 2001, (v4)
Harris, James F. BD221.H37 1992, (v8)
Harris, James G. QK9.H37 1994, (v1)
Harris, Jane Gary. PG3476.M355.Z7 1988, (v3)
Harris, Janice Hubbard. PR808.D58.H37 1996, (v3)
Harris, Jocelyn. PR4038.L5.H37 1989, (v3)
Harris, Joe. QA564.H24 1992, (v1)
Harris, Joel Chandler. PZ7.H242.Co, (v3)
Harris, John M. QA165.H37 2000, (v1)
Harris, John W. QP91.H3 1963, (v1)
Harris, John. LB1139.L3.H277 1990, (v7)
  NA970.H34 1994, (v9)
  RG133.5.H38 1992, (v2)
Harris, Jose. HN385.H33 1993, (v6)
Harris, Joseph E. DT387.8.H36 1994, (v5)
  HN793.Z9.E44 1987, (v6)
Harris, Katherine. F782.S7.H37 1993, (v4)
Harris, Kathleen Mullan. HQ759.4.H387 1997, (v6)
Harris, LaDonna. E99.C85 H284 2000, (v4)
Harris, Larry D. QH75.H37 1984, (v1)
Harris, Marshall Dees. HD194.H3 1970, (v6)
Harris, Marvin. GN320.H328, (v6)
  GN320.H33, (v6)
  GN357.H39 1999, (v6)

  GN358.H37, (v6)
  HN59.H27, (v6)
Harris, Max. PN2049.H26 1993, (v3)
Harris, Maxine. HV4493.H37 1991, (v6)
Harris, Michael H. Z721.H227 1995, (v10)
Harris, Michael T. PR9084.H27 1992, (v3)
Harris, Michael W. ML3187.H37 1992, (v9)
Harris, Nigel G. E. BJ1725.H35 1996, (v8)
Harris, P. M. G. HB851.H286 2001, (v6)
Harris, Paul. KF9244.5.H37 1997, (v7)
Harris, Philip R. HD62.4.H37 2000, (v6)
  TL795.7.H37 1991, (v1)
Harris, Phyllis Braudy. HV1461.H39 1997, (v6)
Harris, R. W. DA447.C6.H37 1983, (v5)
Harris, Richard A. KF5407.H37 1989, (v7)
Harris, Richard E. E185.93.A7 H37 1983, (v4)
Harris, Richard Wilson. SB435.H317 1999, (v1)
Harris, Richard. HT352.C22.T674 1996, (v6)
Harris, Robert B. VM311.C3.H3, (v10)
Harris, Robin Sutton. LA417.5.H37, (v7)
Harris, Roy. P211.H3515 2000, (v3)
Harris, Seymour Edwin. HJ257.H33, (v6)
Harris, Sheldon H. DS777.533.B55 H37 2002, (v5)
Harris, Sheldon. ML102.B6.H3, (v9)
Harris, Stephen L. QE535.2.U6.H37 1990, (v1)
Harris, Stephen M. DK215.H27 1999, (v5)
Harris, Susan K. PS1332.H375 1996, (v3)
Harris, Thomas Anthony. RC480.5.H32, (v2)
Harris, Tim. DA445.H24 1987, (v5)
Harris, Tom. QH545.S45.H37 1991, (v1)
Harris, Townsend. E183.8.J3.H3 1959, (v4)
Harris, Trevor A. Le V. PQ2357.H37 1990, (v3)
Harris, Trudier. PS3563.O8749.Z67 1991, (v3)
Harris, Wendell V. PN41.H36 1992, (v3)
  PN81.H2847 1996, (v3)
  PR861.H35, (v3)
  PR4458.H3, (v3)
Harris, Wendy. HD62.5.H37374 1999, (v6)
Harris, William C. E668.H37 1997, (v4)
  F259.H72.H37 1987, (v4)
  F341.H298, (v4)
  F341.H3, (v4)
Harris, William F. KF4550.H375 1992, (v7)
Harris, William V. DG231.3.H3, (v5)
Harris, William W. DS87.H3723 1997, (v5)
Harris, Wilson. PR9320.9.H3.A8, (v3)
  PR9320.9.H3.D3, (v3)
  PR9320.9.H3.T7, (v3)
Harrison, Albert A. TL1500.H37 2001, (v1)
Harrison, Antony H. PR595.H5.H37 1998, (v3)
  PR5517.M42.H3 1988, (v3)
Harrison, Benjamin. E660.H294 1893, (v4)
Harrison, Bernard. ML410.H4.H314 1998, (v9)
  ML410.H4.H315 1997, (v9)
  PN45.H384 1991, (v3)
Harrison, Beverly Wildung. HQ767.3.H37 1983, (v6)
  HQ1221.H27 1985, (v6)
Harrison, Brian Howard. DA530.H446 1982, (v5)
Harrison, Charles. N6494.P7.H37 1993, (v9)
Harrison, Christopher. DT530.5.M88.H37 1988, (v5)
Harrison, Cynthia Ellen. HQ1236.5.U6.H37 1988, (v6)
Harrison, Daphne Duval. ML3521.H38 1988, (v9)
Harrison, Edward Robert. QB981.H32 2000, (v1)
Harrison, G. B. PR651.H3, (v3)
  PR2907.H3 1958, (v3)
Harrison, Gary Lee. PR5892.P64.H37 1994, (v3)
Harrison, Gordon A. D769.A533 vol. 3, pt. 2, (v5)
Harrison, Henrietta. DS776.6.H37 2000, (v5)
Harrison, James. PR6068.U757.Z63 1992, (v3)
Harrison, Jane Ellen. BH91.H32 1969, (v8)
  BL785.H4 1955, (v8)
Harrison, John E. RC394.S93, (v2)
Harrison, Kathryn. KDZ697.H37 1994, (v7)
Harrison, Lowell Hayes. E509.H37, (v4)
  F451.H315 1997, (v4)
  F455.H37 1992, (v4)
Harrison, Mark. HC335.6.H36 1996, (v6)
Harrison, Nancy Rebecca. PR6035.H96.Z66 1988, (v3)
Harrison, Patricia Greenwood. JK1896.H37 2000, (v7)
Harrison, Paul R. B317.H37 1994, (v8)

Harrison, Paul. HB849.415.H374 2000, (v6)
Harrison, Regina. PM6308.6.H37 1989, (v3)
Harrison, Richard W. U163.H38 2001, (v10)
Harrison, Robert Pogue. PN56.F64.H37 1992, (v3)
Harrison, Ross. JC421.H28 1993, (v7)
Harrison, Selig S. DS33.4.U6.H35, (v5)
Harrison, Suzan. PS3545.E6.Z695 1997, (v3)
Harrison, Thomas J. BH201.H29 1996, (v8)
Harrison, Thomas. D58.H7, (v5)
Harrison, Victoria. PS3503.I785.Z69 1993, (v3)
Harrison, William Henry. E337.8.H37 1975, (v4)
Harrison-Pepper, Sally. PN3209.H37 1990, (v3)
Harriss, G. L. HJ1005.H37, (v6)
Harrod, Howard L. E78.G73.H355 1995, (v4)
Harrod, Roy Forbes. HB34.H25 1972, (v6)
  HB3711.H32 1965, (v6)
Harrold, Stanley. E449.H297 1995, (v4)
  E449.H298 2001, (v4)
Harrop, Jeffrey. HC240.H3516 2000, (v6)
Harrop, John. PN2061.H328 1992, (v3)
Harsch, Donna. JN3970.S6.H37 1993, (v7)
Harsh, Joseph L. E487.H34 1998, (v4)
Hart, Albert Bushnell. F64.H322, (v4)
Hart, Betty. LB1139.L3.H279 1995, (v7)
Hart, Christopher W. L. HD62.15.H37 1992, (v6)
Hart, Clive. PR6019.O9.F593, (v3)
  PR6019.O9.U6542, (v3)
Hart, Dianne Walta. F869.L89.N53 1997, (v4)
  F1528.H36 1990, (v4)
Hart, Donn Vorhis. GN671.P5.H37, (v6)
Hart, Francis Russell. PR8597.H37, (v3)
Hart, Gail Kathleen. PT671.H37 1996, (v3)
  PT2374.Z5.H28 1989, (v3)
Hart, Gillian Patricia. HC905.Z7 K8343 2002, (v6)
Hart, H. L. A. K237.H3 1994, (v7)
Hart, Henry Hersch. PL3277.E3.H33 1954, (v3)
  PQ9212.H3, (v3)
Hart, Henry. PS3523.O89.Z684 1995, (v3)
  PS3554.I32.Z695 2000, (v3)
Hart, J. W. QK757.H37 1988, (v1)
  QK771.H36 1990, (v1)
Hart, James David. F859.H33 1987, (v4)
  PS21.H3 1995, (v3)
Hart, James S. KD6850.H355 1991, (v7)
Hart, John Fraser. GF127.H38 1998, (v6)
  S441.H2954 1991, (v1)
Hart, John. GV199.6.H37, (v6)
Hart, Jonathan Locke. PR2982.H37 1991, (v3)
Hart, Kevin. PR3537.E25.H37 1999, (v3)
Hart, Kylo-Patrick R. PN1995.9.A435.H37 2000, (v3)
Hart, Lynda. HQ79.H36 1998, (v6)
  PN1995.9.L48.H27 1994, (v3)
Hart, M. G. GB401.5.H37 1986, (v6)
Hart, Michael. HF1766.H388 1994, (v6)
Hart, Mitchell Bryan. DS140.H37 2000, (v5)
Hart, Moss. PS3515.A7943.Z52, (v3)
Hart, Parker T. E183.8.S25.H37 1998, (v4)
Hart, Patricia. PQ8098.1.L54Z69 1989, (v3)
Hart, Peter. DA960.H36 1998, (v5)
Hart, Philip. ML422.R38 H37 1994, (v9)
Hart, R. D756.5.N6.H345 2001, (v5)
Hart, Robert A. HD4928.N6.H37 1984, (v6)
Hart, Roderick P. PN4055.U53.P6428 2000, (v3)
Hart, W. D. B812.H37 1988, (v8)
Hart, William D. BL51.H336 2000, (v8)
Hartcup, Guy. D810.S2.H37 2000, (v5)
Harte, Bret. PS1822.L5 1947, (v3)
  PS1829.T3, (v3)
  PS1833.A5 1973, (v3)
Hartel, Lynda Jones. Z7164.S46.H37 1995, (v10)
Harter, Carol C. PS3554.O3.Z69 1990, (v3)
Harter, Deborah A. PN3435.H37 1996, (v3)
Harter, H. Leon. QA278.7.H36 1996, (v1)
Hartfield-Mendez, Vialla. PQ6635.A32.Z712 1996, (v3)
Hartford, William F. F74.H73.H37 1990, (v4)
Harth, Erich. QP360.H34 1993, (v1)
  QP376.H292 1990, (v1)
  QP411.H37, (v1)
Harth, John Phillip. PR3724.T33.H3, (v3)
Harth, Phillip. PR3427.P6.H37 1993, (v3)
Hartigan, John. F574.D49 A1 1999, (v4)

Hartigan, Richard Shelly. U22.H37 1982, (v10)
Hart-Landsberg, Martin. E183.8.K6.H388 1998, (v4)
Hartle, Anthony E. U22.H38 1989, (v10)
Hartley, John. PN1992.6.H367 1999, (v3)
Hartley, L. P. PR6015.A6723 F3, (v3)
  PR6015.A6723 G6, (v3)
  PR6015.A6723 P4, (v3)
  PR6015.A6723 S5, (v3)
  PR6015.A6723 M85, (v3)
  PR6015.H255, (v3)
Hartley, Loyde H. Z7782.H37 1992, (v10)
Hartley, Stephen J. QA76.73.J38.H375 1998, (v1)
Hartley, T. E. DA356.H37 1992, (v5)
Hartlyn, Jonathan. F1938.55.H37 1998, (v4)
  JL2811.H37 1988, (v7)
Hartman, Ann. HV699.H35 1983, (v6)
Hartman, Donald K. Z5916.H28 1988, (v10)
  Z5917.H6 H37 1994, (v10)
Hartman, Geoffrey H. PN94.H34, (v3)
  PN94.H344 1997, (v3)
  PN94.H35 1991, (v3)
  PN710.H32, (v3)
  PR4803.H44.Z647, (v3)
  PR5888.H37, (v3)
Hartman, Keith. BR115.H6.H38 1996, (v8)
Hartman, Saidiya V. E443.H37 1997, (v4)
Hartmann, Eduard von. B3273.P53.E7 1972, (v8)
Hartmann, Ernest. BF1099.N53.H37 1984, (v2)
Hartmann, Frederick H. E744.H37 1994, (v4)
  UA23.H367 1988, (v10)
Hartmann, Nicolai. BD331.H334, (v8)
Hartmann, Paul. HN690.Z9.M325 1989, (v6)
Hartmann, Robert Trowbridge. E865.H37, (v4)
Hartmann, Susan M. HQ1236.5.U6.H38 1989, (v6)
Hartmann, von Aue, 12th cent. PT1534.E8 1987, (v3)
  PT1534.I3 1979, (v3)
Hartmann, William M. BF251.H35 1997, (v2)
Hartnett, Koula Svokos. PS3511.I9234.Z69 1990, (v3)
Hartog, Hendrik. KF510.H37 2000, (v7)
Hartog, Leo de. DS22.H3413 1989, (v5)
Hartree, Douglas R. QC174.5.H35, (v1)
Hartshorn, Peter. PR6019.O9.Z578 1997, (v3)
Hartshorne, Charles. B945.H354.A3 1990, (v8)
  BD573.H29, (v8)
Hartshorne, Richard. G70.H32, (v6)
Hartshorne, Robin. QA451.H37 2000, (v1)
Hartsock, John C. PS366.R44.H37 2000, (v3)
Hartsock, Ralph. ML134.L86.H4 1991, (v9)
Hartwig, Joan. PR2976.H364, (v3)
Harty, Kevin J. PN1995.9.M52.H37 1999, (v3)
Haruf, Kent. PS3558.A716T5 1984, (v3)
Harutyunyan, Artem. PK8548.H346.L4 1994, (v3)
Harvard University. LA210.H4 1945a, (v7)
  N526.A84 1996, (v9)
Harvell, Tony A. Z2694.D7.H17 2000, (v10)
Harvey, A. D. DA65.H37 1992, (v5)
  Z8694.5.H37 1989, (v10)
Harvey, Brian. QA76.H3475 1994, (v1)
  TL789.8.R9.H37 1996, (v1)
Harvey, Charles. HC930.H37 1990, (v6)
Harvey, Daniel Cobb. F1048.H34 1970, (v4)
Harvey, David L. HN79.A14.H37 1993, (v6)
Harvey, David. CB428.H38 1989, (v5)
  HB501.H3597 1982, (v6)
  HM216.H26 1996, (v6)
Harvey, Eleanor Jones. ND1351.5.H27 1998, (v9)
Harvey, Elizabeth. HV1441.G3.H37 1993, (v6)
Harvey, J. R. PR149.C67.H37 1995, (v3)
Harvey, Jerry B. HD58.7.H376 1988, (v6)
Harvey, John Hooper. NA350.H26 1972b, (v9)
Harvey, Karen D. E76.6.H364 1995, (v4)
Harvey, L. P. DP102.H34 1990, (v5)
Harvey, Margaret. BR745.H37 1993, (v8)
Harvey, Neil. F1236.H37 1998, (v4)
Harvey, P. D. A. G1815.H36 1993, (v6)
  GA221.H37 1991, (v6)
  GA304.R5.H37 1996, (v6)
Harvey, Paul. BX6241.H37 1997, (v8)
Harvey, Peter. BJ1289.H37 2000, (v8)
Harvey, Robert C. PN6710.H35 1994, (v3)

Harvey, Robert. PQ2637.A82.Z726 1991, (v3)
  Z8250.3.H37 1997, (v10)
Harvey, Sally Peltier. PS3505.A87.Z66 1994, (v3)
Harvey, W. J. PR4688.H28, (v3)
Harvey, William. QM21.H313, (v1)
Harvie, Charles. HC444.H37 1997, (v6)
  HC467.H3675 2002, (v6)
Harwell, George C. PE1408.H393, (v3)
Harwell, Mark A. U263.H37 1984, (v10)
Harwit, Martin. D767.25.H6.H348 1996, (v5)
Harwood, Britton J. PR2017.B44.H37 1992, (v3)
Harwood, Gregory W. ML134.V47.H37 1998, (v9)
Harwood, Sarah. PN1995.9.F35.H37 1997, (v3)
Harwood-Gordon, Sharon. PQ1789.H36 1989, (v3)
Hasan, Mubashir. DS384.H37 2000, (v5)
Hasan, Mushirul. DS479.L36 1997, (v5)
Hasan, Syed E. TD1064.H37 1996, (v1)
Hasan, Zoya. DS485.U64.H38 1998, (v5)
Hasbrouck, Alfred. F2235.H34 1969, (v4)
Haschak, Paul G. Z7164.U8.H38 1994, (v10)
Hasek, Jaroslav. PG5038.H28 O72, (v3)
  PG5038.H28 O73 1974, (v3)
Haseler, Stephen. DA566.4.H39 1996, (v5)
Haselkorn, Avigdor. DS79.744.C46.H37 1999, (v5)
Hasenfratz, Robert J. Z2012.H23 1993, (v10)
Hashmi, Taj ul-Islam. HQ1745.6.H375 2000, (v6)
Haskell, Ann S. PR1120.H36, (v3)
Haskell, Barbara. N6512.H355 1999, (v9)
  NX504.H36 1984, (v9)
Haskell, Francis. D5.H25 1993, (v5)
  N4395.H37 2000, (v9)
  N6916.H37 1980, (v9)
Haskell, Guy H. DS135.B8.H37 1994, (v5)
Haskell, John. JF494.H37 2001, (v7)
Haskell, Paul G. KF306.H29 1998, (v7)
Haskell, Thomas L. E175.H38 1998, (v4)
Hasker, William. BD418.3.H375 1999, (v8)
Haskett, Robert Stephen. F1221.N3.H37 1991, (v4)
Haskins, Charles Homer. CB351.H3 1958, (v5)
  LA177.H3 1976, (v7)
Haskins, James. ML420.M388.H4 1987, (v9)
Haslam, S. Alexander. HD58.7.H385 2000, (v6)
Haslett, Beth. HD6054.H37 1991, (v6)
Haslett, Moyra. PN98.C6.H33 1999, (v3)
Haslip-Viera, Gabriel. HV6815.M4.H37 1999, (v6)
Hass, Aaron. D804.3.H374 1990, (v5)
Hass, Robert. PN1271.H35 1984, (v3)
Hassam, Andrew. DU113.5.G7, (v5)
  PR888.D52.H37 1993, (v3)
Hassanein, Neva. S494.5.A65.H37 1999, (v1)
Hassani, Sadri. QC20.H392 2000, (v1)
Hasse, John Edward. ML410.E44.H37 1993, (v9)
Hassell, Ulrich von. DD247.H33.A315, (v5)
Hassen, Mohammed. DT390.G2.H38 1990, (v5)
Hassig, Ross. F1219.76.C35.H372001, (v4)
  F1219.76.P75.H37 1988, (v4)
Hassrick, Peter H. N6537.R88.H37 1989, (v9)
Hassrick, Royal B. E99.D1.H3, (v4)
Hastings, Daniel. TL1489.H37 1996, (v1)
Hastings, Scott E. F55.H37 1990, (v4)
Hastings, Selina. PR6045.A97.Z689 1994, (v3)
Hastorf, Christine Ann. F3429.1.J37.H37 1993, (v4)
Hastrup, Kirsten. GN33.H34 1995, (v4)
Hasty, Will. PT1535.H37 1996, (v3)
Haswell, Janis Tedesco. PR5908.W6.H37 1997, (v3)
Haswell, Richard H. PE1404.H39 1991, (v3)
Hatab, Lawrence J. B3279.H285 2000, (v8)
Hatch, Elvin. HN930.5.C36.H38 1991, (v6)
Hatch, James Vernon. PS3507.O364.Z64 1993, (v3)
Hatch, Mary Jo. HD58.7.H4 1997, (v6)
Hatch, Nathan O. BR525.H37 1989, (v8)
Hatch, Thom. F390.H33 1999, (v4)
Hatch, Walter. HF1602.15.A74.H38 1996, (v6)
Hatchard, John. KTZ262.H37 1993, (v7)
Hatcher, John. HB3585.H37 1977, (v6)
  PR6003.I75.Z68 1995, (v3)
Hatcher, O. Latham. PR2910.H35, (v3)
Hatfield, Gary C. BF469.H34 1990, (v2)
Hatfield, Glenn W. PR3458.L3.H3, (v3)
Hatfield, Henry Caraway. PT313.H3, (v3)
  PT2625.A44.Z596, (v3)

Hatfield, Shelley Ann Bowen. F1219.3.G6.H37 1998, (v4)
Hathaway, Heather. PS3525.A24785.Z69 1999, (v3)
Hathaway, Robert M. E183.8.G7.H36 1990, (v4)
Hatley, M. Thomas. E99.C5.H28 1993, (v4)
Hatry, Harry P. HD62.15.H38 1999, (v6)
Hatt, Sue. HD6135.H377 1997, (v6)
Hatton, Ragnhild Marie. CB401.H3 1969b, (v5)
  DA501.A2.H4, (v5)
Hatton, T. J. JV6217.H37 1998, (v7)
Hatzfeld, Adolphe. PC2625.H4 1920, (v3)
Hatzfeld, Helmut Anthony. PQ142.H3, (v3)
Haubenstock, Susan H. N6505.H35 1994, (v9)
Haubrich, William S. R123.H29 1997, (v2)
Haude, Sigrun. BX4933.G3, (v8)
Hauerwas, Stanley. BJ1012.H347 1997, (v8)
  BJ1241.H38, (v8)
  BJ1251.H325, (v8)
  BJ1251.H326 2001, (v8)
Haug, Walter. PT179.H3813 1997, (v3)
Haugeland, John. BD418.3.H38 1998, (v8)
Haugen, Einar Ingvald, . ML418.B9 H38 1992, (v9)
  PD1545.H3, (v3)
  PD2615.H3 1969, (v3)
  PT9150.R55Z59 1983, (v3)
Haugerud, Angelique. JQ2947.A2.H38 1995, (v7)
Haugh, Robert F. PR6057.O63.Z7, (v3)
Haught, John F. BT712.H38 2000, (v8)
Hauke, Kathleen A. PN4874.P595.H38 1998, (v3)
Haule, James M. PR6045.O72.Z695 1991, (v3)
Haupt, Randy L. QA402.5.H387 1998, (v1)
Hauptli, Bruce W. BD212.H38 1995, (v8)
Hauptman, Laurence M. E78.N7.H36 1988, (v4)
  E98.P99.H38 1995, (v4)
  E99.I7.H33, (v4)
  E99.I7.H335 1993, (v4)
  E540.I3.H38 1995, (v4)
Hauptmann, Gerhart. PT2616.A1 1962, (v3)
  PT2616.Z3.L4, (v3)
  PT2616.Z3 1951, (v3)
Haury, Emil W. F813.V4.H3, (v4)
Haus, Leah A. HF1721.H347 1991, (v6)
Hauser, Arnold. NX180.S6.H3413 1982, (v9)
Hauser, Gerard A. P301.5.P67.H38 1999, (v3)
Hauser, Marc D. QL776.H38 1996, (v1)
  QL785.H359 2000, (v1)
Hauser, Thomas. GV1133.H34 2000, (v6)
Hausman, Daniel M. HB71.H4 1992, (v6)
  HB72.H355 1996, (v6)
Hausmann, Klaus. QL366.H3613 1996, (v1)
Hausmann, Manfred R. TA710.H34 1990, (v1)
Hauss, Charles. DC417.H38 1991, (v5)
  JX1391.H38 1996, (v7)
Havard, Robert. PQ6187.H38 1988, (v3)
Havel, James T. JK528.H38 1996, (v7)
Havel, Václav. DB2238.H38.A5 1997, (v5)
  DB2241.H38.A513 1990, (v5)
  DB2241.H38.A5 1991b, (v5)
  PG5039.18.A9A2 1993, (v3)
Havelock, Christine Mitchell. NB163.V62.C575 1995, (v9)
Havelock, Eric Alfred. PA273.H27 1982, (v3)
Haveman, Robert H. HD7256.U5.H39 1984, (v6)
Havens, Raymond Dexter. PR3588.H3 1961, (v3)
Havens, Thomas R. H. D767.2.H29 1978, (v5)
Haver, William Wendell. RC607.A26.H38 1996, (v2)
Haverkamp Begemann, Egbert. ND653.R4.A7 1982, (v9)
Haverkamp, Anselm. PT2359.H2.H34813 1996, (v3)
Haverstock, Nathan A. PN4874.P25.H38 1996, (v3)
Havighurst, Walter. F479.H28, (v4)
  F491.H4, (v4)
  F491.H4 2001, (v4)
  F516.H28 1970, (v4)
Haviland, Beverly. PS2127.H5.H38 1997, (v3)
Havir, Linda Marie. HV1468.M6.H38 1995, (v6)
Havlice, Patricia Pate. ML128.S3 H4, (v9)
  ML128.S3 H4 Suppl. 1, (v9)
  ML128.S3 H4 Suppl. 2, (v9)
  Z6511.H38 Suppl., (v10)
Hawass, Zahi A. DT73.B33, (v5)

Hawcroft, David M. QP519.9.E434.H39 1996, (v1)
Hawes, Clement. PR448.E57.H39 1996, (v3)
Hawes, Elizabeth. NA7860.H34 1993, (v9)
Hawes, William. PN1992.3.U5.H385 2001, (v3)
Hawke, Constance S. KF390.5.C6 H39 2001, (v7)
Hawke, David Freeman. T21.H39 1988, (v1)
Hawken, Paul. HD60.H393 1993, (v6)
Hawkes, David. PN81.H298 1996, (v3)
Hawkes, Jacquetta Hopkins, 1910-. CB311.H35 1993, (v5)
    CC115.W58.H38 1982, (v5)
Hawkes, John. PS3558.A82 B5, (v3)
    PS3558.A82 D4, (v3)
    PS3558.A82 T7, (v3)
Hawkes, Lory. QA76.9.H85, (v1)
Hawkes, Nena. GV697.A1.H367 2000, (v6)
Hawkes, Nigel. QA76.5.H442 1972, (v1)
Hawkesworth, Celia. PG1404.9.W65.H39 2000, (v3)
Hawkin, David J. BS2615.5.H38 1996, (v8)
Hawking, S. W. QB981.H377 1988, (v1)
    QC173.59.S65.H4 1996, (v1)
Hawkins, Anne Hunsaker. RJ387.A25.H39 2000, (v2)
Hawkins, Bruce R. F832.G7.H38 1990, (v4)
Hawkins, Denis John Bernard. B721.H36 1947, (v8)
Hawkins, Gerald S. DA142.H3, (v5)
Hawkins, Gordon. HQ471.H387 1988, (v6)
Hawkins, Hugh. LA226.H355 1992, (v7)
    LD2628.3.H3, (v7)
Hawkins, John. ML159.H39 1963, (v9)
    PR3533.H3 1961, (v3)
Hawkins, Michael. QB981.H3775 1997, (v1)
Hawkins, Mike. HM106.H38 1997, (v6)
Hawley, John Stratton. PK1967.9.S9.Z68 1984, (v3)
Hawley, R. Scott. QH431.H353 1999, (v1)
Haworth, Paul Leland. JK526 1876.H43 1979, (v7)
Haws, Duncan. VM15.H33 1975, (v10)
Hawthorn, Audrey. E99.K9.H3 1979, (v4)
Hawthorn, Geoffrey. D16.9.H39 1991, (v5)
Hawthorn, Jeremy. PN44.5.H37 2000, (v3)
Hawthorne, Douglas B. TL789.85.A1.H38 1992, (v1)
Hawthorne, Nathaniel. E432.H38 1970, (v4)
    PS1850.F37, (v3)
    PS1850.F63, (v3)
    PS1850.F63 v.4, (v3)
    PS1852.A7, (v3)
    PS1855.A1 1978, (v3)
    PS1856.A1 1954, (v3)
    PS1861.A1 1924, (v3)
    PS1865.A2.W43 1989, (v3)
    PS1868.A1 1978, (v3)
    PZ8.1.H318.Ta62, (v3)
Hawthorne, Peter. RD598.H4 1968, (v2)
Hawton, Hector. B803.H33 1952, (v8)
Hay, Denys. D104.H27 1968, (v5)
    DG533.H39 1977, (v5)
Hay, Eloise (Knapp). PR6005.O4.Z743, (v3)
Hay, Frederick J. Z1361.N39.H37 1991, (v10)
Hay, James G. QP303.H389, (v1)
Hay, John. E457.H39 1998, (v4)
    E664.H41.A4 2000, (v4)
    E664.H41.A3 1997, (v4)
    PS1900.A2 1970, (v3)
Hay, Malcolm. PR6052.O5.Z677 1980, (v3)
Hay, Peter. PN1999.M4.H3 1991, (v3)
Hay, Samuel A. PN2270.A35.H39 1994, (v3)
Hay, Stephen. PN1998.3.T377.H39 2000, (v3)
Hay, William Walter. TF200.H38 1982, (v1)
Haya de la Torre, Victor Raul. F3448.H2912, (v4)
Hayakawa, S. I. B820.H3, (v8)
    PE1585.H36 1964, (v3)
Hayao, Kenji. JQ1641.H42 1993, (v7)
Hayashi, Brian Masaru. F869.L89.J32 1995, (v4)
Hayashi, Chikio. DS821.H375 1997, (v5)
Hayashi, Tetsumaro. Z8839.4.H3, (v10)
    Z8839.4.H314 1973, (v10)
Haydar Mirza. DS19.H3613 1972, (v5)
Hayden, Dolores. F869.L857.H39 1995, (v4)
    HQ1426.H33, (v6)
Hayden, John O. PR5341.H35 1970, (v3)
Haydn, Hiram Collins. PN44.H38, (v3)

PN3373.H34, (v3)
PR1125.H35, (v3)
Haydon, Benjamin Robert. D497.H4A37, (v5)
Haydon, Leslie M. T10.5.H39 1995, (v1)
Hayek, Friedrich A. von. BF233.H35, (v2)
    HB34.H3 1972, (v6)
    HB97.5.H36 1967, (v6)
    HB3711.H365, (v6)
    HG221.H346 1984, (v6)
    HG229.H3 1967, (v6)
    JC585.H293 1982, (v7)
Hayek, Lee-Ann C. QH352.H39 1997, (v1)
Hayes, Carlton Joseph Huntley. CB245.H35, (v5)
Hayes, Derek. F851.H38 1999, (v4)
Hayes, Francis C. PQ6469.H3, (v3)
Hayes, Herbert Kendall. SB123.H43 1955, (v1)
Hayes, Joanne Lamb. TX715.H3937 2000, (v1)
Hayes, John T. NC242.G3.A4 1970, (v9)
    ND497.G2.H383 1982, (v9)
    NE2047.6.G34.H39 1972, (v9)
Hayes, Kevin J. GR41.3.H39 1997, (v6)
    PS2388.F64.H39 1999, (v3)
    Z1039.W65.H38 1996, (v10)
    Z8562.58.H394 1991, (v10)
Hayes, Michael T. JF529.H39, (v7)
Hayes, Paul M. DA530.H447 1975b, (v5)
    DL529.Q5.H38 1972, (v5)
Hayes, Peter. UA853.K6.H37 1990, (v10)
Hayes, Robert H. HD9725.H38 1988, (v6)
Hayes, Rutherford Birchard. E682.H48, (v4)
Hayes-Bautista, David E. F870.S75.H38 1988, (v4)
Hayhoe, Ruth. LA1133.H388 1996, (v7)
Hayles, N. Katherine. PN771.H35 1990, (v3)
Hayman, Richard. GN805.H39 1997, (v6)
Hayman, Robert L. KF480.H37 1998, (v7)
Hayman, Ronald. BF109.J8 H39 2001, (v2)
    PQ2631.R63.Z6185 1990, (v3)
    PT2603.R397.Z6667 1984, (v3)
Haymes, Edward. PT204.H38 1996, (v3)
Hayne, M. B. DC369.H36 1993, (v5)
Hayne, Paul Hamilton. PS1905.A2 1882, (v3)
    PS1908.A4.M4 1970, (v3)
Hayner, Don. F548.67.A1H38 1988, (v4)
Hayner, Priscilla B. JC571.H39 2002, (v7)
Haynes Craig. Z6673.6.U6 H39 1997, (v10)
Haynes, Alan. DA358.S2.H35 1989, (v5)
Haynes, Bruce. ML128.O2.H55 1991, (v9)
    ML3807.H39 2002, (v9)
Haynes, Douglas E. HN690.S97.H38 1991, (v6)
Haynes, Gary. QE882.P8.H39 1991, (v1)
Haynes, George Henry. JK1161.H28 1960, (v7)
Haynes, Jeffrey. BL65.P7.H38 1994, (v8)
    JF60.H37 1998, (v7)
Haynes, John Earl. F606.H28 1984, (v4)
Haynes, Jonathan. PR2642.S58.H39 1992, (v3)
Haynes, Robert V. F394.H8.H39, (v4)
Haynes, Sam W. F390.H34 1990, (v4)
Haynie, Donald T. QP517.T48, (v1)
Hays, J. N. RA649.H29 1998, (v2)
Hays, Peter L. PS3515.E37.Z6145 1990, (v3)
Hays, Samuel P. GE180.H392 2000, (v6)
Hays, Sharon. HQ759.H37 1996, (v6)
Hayslip, Bert. Z7204.A42.H392 1995, (v10)
Hayt, William Hart. TK454.H4 2002, (v1)
Haythornthwaite, Philip J. DC151.H32 1990, (v5)
Hayward, Charles Harold. TT185.H3915 1972, (v1)
Hayward, Jack Ernest Shalom. JN2451.H38 1991, (v7)
Hayward, James L. Z5322.E9.H39 1998, (v10)
Hayward, Joel S. A. D764.H374 1998, (v5)
Hayward, Mary Ellen. NA7238.B3.H38 1999, (v9)
Hayward, Philip Henry Cecil. U24.H38, (v10)
Hayward, Susan. PN1993.45.H36 1996, (v3)
Haywood, C. Robert. F686.H38 1991, (v4)
Haywood, Eliza Fowler. PR3506.H94.I5 1999, (v3)
Haywood, John A. PJ6307.H36 1962, (v3)
Haywood, John. DL65.H39 2000, (v5)
    V46.H38 1991, (v10)
Haywood, Richard Mowbray. HE3138.H385 1998, (v6)
Haywood, Trevor. HM221.H395 1995, (v6)
Hazama, Hiroshi. HD8724.H39 1997, (v6)

Hazard, Harry W. PJ25.P7 vol. 12, 1954, (v3)
Hazard, Mary E. DA320.H286 2000, (v5)
Hazard, Paul. D273.5.H32 1953a, (v5)
Hazareesingh, Sudhir. DC277.H39 1998, (v5)
    JN2451.H39 1994, (v7)
Hazel, John. DE7.H39 2000, (v5)
Hazel, John. DG203.H39 2001, (v5)
Hazell, P. B. R. HD2075.N56.H39 1991, (v6)
Hazeltine, Barrett. T49.5.H4 1999, (v1)
Hazen, Craig James. BL245.H36 2000, (v8)
Hazen, Edith P. PN1022.H39 1994, (v3)
Hazen, Robert M. TP873.5.D5.H39 1999, (v1)
Hazlehurst, Cameron. Z2020.H39 1996, (v10)
Hazlitt, Margaret. PR4769.H9.Z5, (v3)
Hazlitt, William. PR99.H35 1969, (v3)
    PR4771.B6, (v3)
Hazon, Mario. PC1640.H35 1963, (v3)
Hazzard, Shirley. PR6058.A99.E9 1966, (v3)
He, Liyi. PL2861.E26.Z473 1993, (v3)
Head, Barclay Vincent. CJ335.H45 1967, (v5)
Head, Bessie. PR9369.3.H4Z468 1990, (v3)
Head, Dominic. PR9369.3.C58.Z68 1997, (v3)
    PR9369.3.G6.Z685 1994, (v3)
Head, K. H. TA710.5.H4 1994, (v1)
Head, Lesley. GF801.H36 2000, (v6)
Headington, Christopher. ML1700.H42 1987, (v9)
Headlam, David John. ML410.B47.H43 1996, (v9)
Headland, Robert. G860.H36 1989, (v6)
Headley, Bernard D. HV6534.A7.H43 1998, (v6)
Headley, John M. B785.C24 H43 1997, (v8)
Headley, Robert K. PN1993.5.U79.H43 1999, (v3)
Headrick, Daniel R. JC359.H39 1988, (v7)
Heal, Felicity. BJ2021.H42 1990, (v8)
Heald, Morrell. HD60.5.U5.H4, (v6)
Heale, M. J. E183.H43 1990, (v4)
    E743.5.H39 1998, (v4)
Healey, Christopher J. DU740.42.H42 1990, (v5)
Healey, Denis. DA591.H38.A3 1990, (v5)
Healey, Dorothy. HX84.H43.A3 1990, (v6)
Healy, David. F2178.U6.H43 1988, (v4)
    RM332.H42 1997, (v2)
Healy, Kathleen. BR128.H5.H42 1990, (v8)
Heaney, Seamus. PR503.H38 1995, (v3)
    PR6058.E2.F5 1979, (v3)
    PR6058.E2.S9 1984, (v3)
Heap, Shaun Hargreaves. H61.25.H4 1995, (v6)
Heard, J. Norman. E76.2.H43 1987, (v4)
    Z998.H42, (v10)
    Z1207.H43 1981, (v10)
Hearder, Harry. DG467.L67 1980 vol. 6, (v5)
Hearn, Charles R. E169.1.H32, (v4)
Hearn, Chester G. E467.1.B87.H43 1997, (v4)
    E467.1.F23.H544 1998, (v4)
    E472.88.H43 1995, (v4)
    E596.H43 1992, (v4)
    F249.H2.H47 1996, (v4)
    F334.M6.H43 1993, (v4)
Hearn, Frank. HN90.M6.H38 1997, (v6)
Hearn, Lafcadio. PS1916.G6, (v3)
    PS1917.C4 1969, (v3)
    PS1917.J3, (v3)
Hearn, M. F. NB175.H39, (v9)
Hearne, Betsy Gould. Z1037.A1 H42 1999, (v10)
Hearne, John. PS3558.E258.A8, (v3)
Hearnshaw, J. B. QB815.H43 1996, (v1)
Hearon, Shelby. PS3558.E256 A8 1968, (v3)
Heartz, Daniel. ML410.M9.H2 1992, (v9)
Heat Moon, William Least. F687.C35.H44 1991, (v4)
Heater, Derek Benjamin. E767.1.H43 1994, (v4)
    JC362.H34 1996, (v7)
Heath, Dwight B. GT2884.H4 2000, (v6)
Heath, Helen Truesdell. DA447.P4.H4, (v5)
Heath, Jeffrey M. PR6045.A97.Z69 1982, (v3)
Heath, Jim F. HC106.6.H35, (v6)
Heath, Robert L. HD30.3.H4 1994, (v6)
    HD59.5.H4 1988, (v6)
Heath, Thomas Little. QA22.H4, (v1)
Heath, William Webster. PR6003.O6757.Z67, (v3)
Heathcote, T. A. UA649.32.I4.H43 1995, (v10)
Heather, P. J. D137.H425 1996, (v5)
Heathorn, Stephen J. LC93.G7 H42 1999, (v7)

Heath-Stubbs, John Francis Alexander.
  PR595.R6.H4 1950, **(v3)**
  PR6015.E24.B43 1962, **(v3)**
Heaton, Donald D. SB354.8.H43 1997, **(v1)**
Heaton, Ruth M. QA13.H43 2000, **(v1)**
Heavens, O. S. QC358.H43 1991, **(v1)**
Heawood, Edward. G97.H4, **(v6)**
Hebard, Grace Raymond. F591.H4 1990, **(v4)**
  F591.H44, **(v4)**
Hebblethwaite, Brian. BJ1401.H4 1976, **(v8)**
Hebda, Toni. RT50.5.H43 2001, **(v2)**
Hebel, John William. PR1125.H4, **(v3)**
Heber, Reginald. DS412.H443 1971, **(v5)**
Heberer, Thomas. DS730.H4213 1989, **(v5)**
Hebert, Ernest. PS3558.E277.D6, **(v3)**
Hecht, Ann. TT848.H39 1990, **(v1)**
Hecht, Anthony. PR6001.U4.Z73 1993, **(v3)**
Hecht, Ben. KMK41.G75.H4 1997, **(v7)**
  PS3515.E18 F56, **(v3)**
  PS3515.E18 G3, **(v3)**
  PS3515.E18.L4, **(v3)**
  PS3515.E18.Z5, **(v3)**
Hecht, Harry G. QD39.3.M3.H43 1990, **(v1)**
Hecht, Jeff. TA1800.H42 1999, **(v1)**
  UG486.5.H43 1984, **(v10)**
Hecht, Tobias. HV887.B82.N674 1998, **(v6)**
Hechter, Michael. JC311.H383 2000, **(v7)**
Hecht-Nielsen, Robert. QA76.5.H4442 1990, **(v1)**
Heck, A. QA155.7.E4.H43 1993, **(v1)**
Heck, Shirley F. LB1775.H42 1984, **(v7)**
Heckel, Robert V. RJ506.H65.H43 2001, **(v2)**
Heckman, William L. VM624.M8.H4, **(v10)**
Heckscher, Charles C. HD8072.5.H42 1988, **(v6)**
Heckscher, Morrison H. NK1403.5.H4 1992, **(v9)**
Hedblad, Alan. PN451.M37 Suppl. 1998, **(v3)**
Hedeen, Robert A. QL430.6.H43 1986, **(v1)**
Hedge, David. JK2408.H44 1998, **(v7)**
Hedges, Inez. PN1995.H398 1991, **(v3)**
Hedges, William R. R725.5.H44 1999, **(v2)**
Hedican, Edward J. E78.C2.H37 1995, **(v4)**
Hedin, Sven Anders. DS8.H43 1935, **(v5)**
  DS710.H58 1938, **(v5)**
  DS785.H4 1934, **(v5)**
  DS793.G6.H413, **(v5)**
Hedlund, Stefan. HD1993.H43 1984, **(v6)**
Hedren, Paul L. F769.F6.H43 1988, **(v4)**
Hedrick, Joan D. PS2956.H43 1994, **(v3)**
Hedrick, Ulysses Prentiss. SB83.H4, **(v1)**
Hee, Kees Max van. TA168.H44 1994, **(v1)**
Heel, A. C. S. van. QC355.H533 1968, **(v1)**
Heeney, Brian. BX5182.3.H43 1988, **(v8)**
Heer, David M. E184.M5.H376 1990, **(v4)**
  HB881.H38, **(v6)**
  JV6483.H395 1996, **(v7)**
Heer, Friedrich. DD89.H3513 1968, **(v5)**
Heffer, Simon. ML410.V3.D4.H37 2001, **(v9)**
  PR4433.H44 1995, **(v3)**
Heffernan, Carol Falvo. PR1933.M4.H44 1995, **(v3)**
Heffernan, Nancy Coffey. F44.K2.H44 1993, **(v4)**
Heffernan, Richard. JN1129.L32H393 2000, **(v7)**
Heffernan, Thomas J. PR275.R4.H44 1988, **(v3)**
Heflin, Ruth J. PS153.I52.H44 2000, **(v3)**
Hefling, Stephen E. ML437.H43 1993, **(v9)**
Hefner, Robert W. BP63.I5 H44 2000, **(v8)**
Hegel, Georg Wilhelm Friedrich. B2908.E5.L6, **(v8)**
  B2942.A313, **(v8)**
  B2942.E5.H288 1991, **(v8)**
  B2949.H5P54 1956, **(v8)**
  D16.8.H462, **(v5)**
Hegel, Robert E. PL2415.H44 1998, **(v3)**
  PL2436.H4, **(v3)**
Hegeman, Susan. PS228.M63.H44 1999, **(v3)**
Heggenhougen, Kris. RA564.H45 1997, **(v2)**
Hegland, Kenney F. KF273.H4 2000, **(v7)**
Hegner, Robert William. QL366.H43 1968, **(v1)**
Hehn, Anton H. TJ840.H44 1993, **(v1)**
Heidar, Knut. JN7461.H45 2001, **(v7)**
Heide, Fritz. QB755.H43, **(v1)**
Heide, Kathleen M. HV6542.H45 1992, **(v6)**
  HV9067.H6.H44 1999, **(v6)**
Heide, Margaret J. PN1992.77.T558.H45 1995, **(v3)**

Heidegger, Martin. B2799.M5.H43, **(v8)**
  B3279.H48.B44513 1999, **(v8)**
  B3279.H48.F7313 1967, **(v8)**
  B3279.H48.G7713 1994, **(v8)**
  B3279.H48.S43 1996, **(v8)**
  B3279.H48.W413 1998, **(v8)**
  B3279.H48V63, **(v8)**
  BD23.H412, **(v8)**
  BD111.H42 2000, **(v8)**
  BD236.H413 1969, **(v8)**
  BD331.H4313, **(v8)**
  PN1031.H38, **(v3)**
Heidel, Alexander. PJ3771.G6.H4, **(v3)**
Heidenheimer, Arnold J. HN65.H4 1990, **(v6)**
Heidenreich, Rosmarin Elfriede. PR9192.5.H44 1989,
  (v3)
Heidensohn, Frances. HV6025.H36 1989, **(v6)**
  HV8023.H48 1992, **(v6)**
Heider, Karl G. PN1993.5.I84.H45 1991, **(v3)**
Heidsieck, Arnold. PT2621.A26.Z746225 1994, **(v3)**
Heifetz, Ronald A. HM141.H385 1994, **(v6)**
Heikkila, Eric John. HT321.H388 2000, **(v6)**
Heil, John. RD97.H45 1993, **(v2)**
Heilbron, J. L. QB29.H33 1999, **(v1)**
  QC16.P6.H45 1986, **(v1)**
  QC789.2.U62.L384 1989, **(v1)**
Heilbroner, Robert L. CB428.H44 1974, **(v5)**
  E744.H45, **(v4)**
  HB75.H375 1996, **(v6)**
  HB76.H4 1999, **(v6)**
  HB87.H35 1995, **(v6)**
  HB171.5.H39 1972, **(v6)**
  HB501.H395 1993, **(v6)**
  HB501.H397 1976, **(v6)**
  HB501.H398 1985, **(v6)**
  HC51.H44 2001, **(v6)**
  HD82.H388, **(v6)**
  HJ8119.H43 1989, **(v6)**
Heilbronner, Oded. DD801.B64.H3813 1998, **(v5)**
Heilbrun, Carolyn G. HQ1206.H43 1979, **(v6)**
Heilbrunn, Otto. U167.5.R4.H4, **(v10)**
  UB271.R9.H4 1956a, **(v10)**
Heilbut, Anthony. ML3187.H44 1985, **(v9)**
Heilig, Peggy. JS395.H44 1984, **(v7)**
Heilke, Thomas W. B3317.H38 1998, **(v8)**
Heilman, Arthur W. LB1573.H325 1986, **(v7)**
  LB1573.3.H44 1985, **(v7)**
Heilman, Robert Bechtold. PN1892.H38, **(v3)**
  PN6014.H45, **(v3)**
  PR2829.H4, **(v3)**
Heilman, Samuel C. BM712.H45 2001, **(v8)**
  E184.J5.H5345 1995, **(v4)**
Heilmann, Ann. PR878.F45.H45 2000, **(v3)**
Heim, Michael. Z52.4.H44 1987, **(v10)**
Heims, Steve J. H62.5.U5.H45 1991, **(v6)**
  QA28.H44, **(v1)**
Heimsoeth, Heinz. B738.M47.H4513 1994, **(v8)**
Hein, George E. AM7.H44 1998, **(v10)**
Hein, Jeremy. HV640.5.I5.H44 1995, **(v6)**
  HV640.5.I5.H46 1993, **(v6)**
Heine, Heinrich. PT2301.A1 1973b, **(v3)**
  PT2316.A3.H4 1982, **(v3)**
  PT2316.A4.A76 1995, **(v3)**
  PT2316.A4.U5 1957, **(v3)**
  PT2316.D4.S3, **(v3)**
Heine, Irwin M. HE894.H45 1989, **(v6)**
Heine, Jorge. F1981.M4.C644 1993, **(v4)**
Heineman, Helen. PR5699.T3.Z714 1984, **(v3)**
Heineman, Kenneth J. E839.5.H45 1998, **(v4)**
  LA229.H39 2001, **(v7)**
Heineman, Toni Vaughn. RJ507.A29.H45 1998, **(v2)**
Heinemann, Margot. PR2718.P87.H44, **(v3)**
Heinemann, Margot. PR6058.E38.A3 1961, **(v3)**
Heinemann, Ronald L. E748.B95.H45 1996, **(v4)**
Heinl, Robert Debs. VE23.H4, **(v10)**
Heinrich, Bernd. QL495.H38 1993, **(v1)**
Heinrich, Thomas R. VM299.6.H45 1997, **(v10)**
Heinrich. PT1537.H35.K713 1989, **(v3)**
Heinrichs, Ann. F526.3.H45 2000, **(v4)**
Heinrichs, Katherine. PR1912.A3.H45 1990, **(v3)**
Heinrichs, R. Walter. RC514.H434 2001, **(v2)**

Heinrichs, Waldo H. D753.H38 1988, **(v5)**
  E748.G835.H4, **(v4)**
Heins, Marjorie. Z658.U5.H42 2001, **(v10)**
Heinselman, Miron L. QH105.M55.H43 1996, **(v1)**
Heintze, James R. ML120.U5.H46 1990, **(v9)**
Heinze, Richard. PA6825.H413 1993, **(v3)**
Heiple, Daniel L. PQ6392.H45 1994, **(v3)**
Heirich, Max. RA395.A3.H44 1998, **(v2)**
Heise, Jon O. Z6011.H4 1993, **(v10)**
Heiseler, Bernt von. PT2482.H383 1963, **(v3)**
Heisenberg, Werner. QC6.H34613 1974, **(v1)**
  QC173.H3854, **(v1)**
  QC173.H38613 1971, **(v1)**
  QC174.1.H4 1950, **(v1)**
Heiserman, Arthur Ray. PR2348.H4, **(v3)**
Heisig, James W. BL53.H378, **(v8)**
Heiskanen, Weikko A. QC815.H4, **(v1)**
Heiskell, Hugh Brown. F593.H45 1998, **(v4)**
Heisman, John W. GV951.H45 2000, **(v6)**
Heisner, Beverly. PN1995.9.A74.H46 1997, **(v3)**
Heitler, Walter. QC174.2.H4 1956, **(v1)**
  QC475.H43 1954, **(v1)**
Heizer, Donna K. PT169.H45 1996, **(v3)**
Heizer, Robert Fleming. CC75.H44, **(v5)**
  CC75.H445 1975, **(v5)**
Hejmadi, Padma. PR9499.3.P4.Z47 1999, **(v3)**
Hekman, Susan J. HQ1206.H45 1990, **(v6)**
Helander, Brock. ML102.R6.H5 1996, **(v9)**
Helbig, Alethea. PR9084.H45 1992, **(v3)**
  PS374.C454.H45 1993, **(v3)**
  Z1037.H48 1994, **(v10)**
Helbling, Mark Irving. PS153.N5.H38 1999, **(v3)**
Helbling, Robert E. PT2379.Z5.H4 1975, **(v3)**
Held, Colbert C. DS44.H418 2000, **(v5)**
Held, David. HM24.H457, **(v6)**
  JC421.H44 1996, **(v7)**
  JC423.H466 1995, **(v7)**
Held, Gilbert. TK5105.8.I24.H45 1994, **(v1)**
Held, Joseph. DJK50.H43 1994, **(v5)**
Held, Julius Samuel. N6415.B3.H4, **(v9)**
  N6973.R9.H44 1982, **(v9)**
Heldman, Robert K. HE7631.H453 1994, **(v6)**
Helfer, Ray E. HV741.H4, **(v6)**
Helfgot, Daniel. MT892.H44 1993, **(v9)**
Helgesen, Geir. JQ1729.A15.H45 1998, **(v7)**
Helias, Pierre Jakez. DC611.B9173.H4413, **(v5)**
Heliodorus. PA3998.H2.E5 1976, **(v3)**
Helleiner, Gerald K. HF1413.H45 1990, **(v6)**
Hellenbrand, Harold. E332.2.H45 1990, **(v4)**
Heller, Agnes. BJ1012.H45 1988, **(v8)**
  BJ1012.H46 1990, **(v8)**
  HM73.H38 1990, **(v6)**
Heller, Erich. B3317.H43 1988, **(v8)**
  PT343.H47 1957, **(v3)**
  PT343.H47 1975, **(v3)**
  PT2625.A44.Z613 1958, **(v3)**
Heller, Henry. DC111.H45 1991, **(v5)**
  HC280.T4.H45 1996, **(v6)**
Heller, Jan Cristian. QH447.H45 1996, **(v1)**
Heller, Janet Ruth. PN1707.H45 1990, **(v3)**
Heller, Joseph. PS3558.E476.C3 1961, **(v3)**
  PS3558.E476.G6 1979, **(v3)**
  PS3558.E476.S6, **(v3)**
Heller, Karl. ML410.V82 H4413 1997, **(v9)**
Heller, Mark. DS119.7.H3855 1983, **(v5)**
Heller, Nancy. N8354.H45 1987, **(v9)**
Heller, Peter. RJ504.2.H4513 1990, **(v2)**
Heller, Reinhold. ND553.T7.H39 1997, **(v9)**
  ND773.M8.H43 1984, **(v9)**
Heller, Ruth. PE1241.H43 1992, **(v3)**
Heller, Steven. NC1883.U6.H45 1995, **(v9)**
Heller, Tamar. PR4497.H4 1992, **(v3)**
Hellige, Joseph B. QP385.5.H45 1993, **(v1)**
Hellinger, Daniel. F2326.H36 1991, **(v4)**
Hellison, Donald R. GV342.27.H45 2003, **(v6)**
Hellman, Hal. Q125.H5574 1998, **(v1)**
Hellman, Hal. R133.H455 2001, **(v2)**
Hellman, Judith Adler. HQ1638.H45x 1987, **(v6)**

Hellman, Lillian. PS3515.E343.A6 1972, (v3)
  PS3515.E343.A85, (v3)
  PS3515.E343.T5, (v3)
  PS3515.E343.T6, (v3)
  PS3515.E343.Z498, (v3)
  PS3515.E343.Z499, (v3)
  PS3515.E343.Z5, (v3)
Hellmann, Donald C. DS518.45.H44, (v5)
Hellmann, John. E842.1.H44 1997, (v4)
Hellweg, Susan A. JK524.H396 1992, (v7)
Helm, June. E99.A86 H45 2000, (v4)
  E99.T4.H45 1994, (v4)
Helm, P. J. D228.H4 1964, (v5)
Helm, Paul. BD215.H439 1994, (v8)
  BL51.H455 2000, (v8)
Helmer, John. HV5825.H43, (v6)
Helmer, Olaf. CB158.H415 1983, (v5)
Helmholtz, Hermann von. ML3820.H42 1954, (v9)
  Q174.8.H45 1995, (v1)
Helmreich, Ernst Christian. DR46.3.H4 1969, (v5)
Helmreich, Stefan. QH324.2.H45 1998, (v1)
Helmreich, William B. F144.N69.J54 1998, (v4)
Helms, Lorraine Rae. PR655.H45 1997, (v3)
Helms, Mary W. F1565.1.C6.H45 1995, (v4)
  F1565.1.C6.H47 2000, (v4)
  GN366.H44 1988, (v6)
Helpern, Milton. RA1025.H4.A3 1977, (v2)
Helphand, Kenneth I. F776.H48 1991, (v4)
Helpman, Elhanan. HF1379.H45 1989, (v6)
Helsing, Jeffrey W. DS558.H443 2000, (v5)
Helsinger, Elizabeth K. PR468.R87.H45 1997, (v3)
Helson, Harry. BF335.H4, (v2)
Helvarg, David. GC1020.H45 2001, (v6)
Hemans, Felicia Dorothea Browne. PR4780.A4 2000, (v3)
Hemingway, Albert. D767.99.I9.H38 1988, (v5)
Hemingway, Ernest. GV1107.H4 1999, (v6)
  PS3515.E37.A15 1969, (v3)
  PS3515.E37.A15 1987, (v3)
  PS3515.E37.A6 1985, (v3)
  PS3515.E37 F37 1929, (v3)
  PS3515.E37.G37 1986, (v3)
  PS3515.E37.G7 1935, (v3)
  PS3515.E37 I8, (v3)
  PS3515.E37 M4, (v3)
  PS3515.E37 N5, (v3)
  PS3515.E37 O4, (v3)
  PS3515.E37 S8, (v3)
  PS3515.E37 T6, (v3)
  PS3515.E37.W5, (v3)
  PS3515.E37.Z464 1985, (v3)
  PS3515.E37.Z475 1964, (v3)
  PS3515.E37.Z492 1996, (v3)
  PS3515.E37.Z53 1981, (v3)
Hemingway, Gregory H. PS3515.E37.Z617, (v3)
Hemingway, Mary Welsh. PS3515.E37.Z6175, (v3)
Hemleben, Ch. QL368.F6.H46 1989, (v1)
Hemlow, Joyce. PR3316.A4.Z647, (v3)
Hemmer, Christopher M. DS63.2.U5.H46 2000, (v5)
Hemmer, Helmut. SF41.H4613 1989, (v1)
Hemmerly, Thomas E. QK122.3.H46 1999, (v1)
Hemming, John. F2519.H45, (v4)
  F2519.1.A6.H43 1987, (v4)
  F3429.H38 1982, (v4)
Hemminger, Jane M. TX911.3.S24.H46 1999, (v1)
Hemmings, F. W. J. DC33.5.H46 1987, (v5)
  PN2044.F7.H46 1994, (v3)
  PN2634.H39 1993, (v3)
  PQ2528.H4 1966, (v3)
  PQ2528.H44 1977b, (v3)
Hemmons, Willa Mae. E185.86.H46 1996, (v4)
Hempel, Carl Gustav. B945.H451 2001, (v8)
Hempel, Lamont C. HC79.E5.H457 1996, (v6)
Hempleman, H. V. RC1015.H45, (v2)
Hen, Yitzak. DC64.H46 1995, (v5)
Henaff, Marcel. GN21.L4.H4613 1998, (v6)
Henbest, Nigel. QB857.7.H46 1994, (v1)
Henck, Fred W. HE8846.A55.H46 1988, (v6)
Hendel, Charles William. B1498.H4 1983, (v8)
  B2798.H43, (v8)
Hendel, Richard. Z116.A3 H46 1998, (v10)

Hendershot, Cynthia. PR830.T3.H39 1998, (v3)
Hendershot, Heather. PN1992.8.C46.H46 1999, (v3)
Henderson, Aileen Kilgore. D811.5.H429, (v5)
Henderson, Alice Corbin. BX3653.U6 H3 1998, (v8)
Henderson, Andrew. QK495.P17.H44 1995, (v1)
Henderson, Bernard W. DG270.H45, (v5)
Henderson, C. J. PN1995.9.S26.H38 2001, (v3)
Henderson, Diana E. PR535.L7.H46 1995, (v3)
Henderson, G. F. R. E467.1.J15 H55 1988, (v4)
  E470.H55, (v4)
Henderson, George L. PS283.C2.H46 1999, (v3)
Henderson, George. HF5549.5.M5.H46 1994, (v6)
  HV3176.H46 1994, (v6)
  Z114.H46 1987, (v10)
Henderson, Harold Gould. PL768.H3.H4, (v3)
Henderson, Harold P. F291.A7.H46 1991, (v4)
Henderson, Harold. Z473.C25.H45 1993, (v10)
Henderson, Harry. HV6431.H43 2001, (v6)
  KF1263.C65.H46 1999, (v7)
  KF3941.H46 2000, (v7)
  KF9227.C2 F53 2000, (v7)
  TK9146.H45 2000, (v1)
Henderson, Heather. PR788.A9.H4 1989, (v3)
Henderson, Isabel. DA774.H4, (v5)
Henderson, James D. F2276.5.H46 2001, (v4)
Henderson, Jeffrey. PA3166.H4, (v3)
Henderson, John B. PL2461.Z7H46 1991, (v3)
Henderson, Karla A. GV181.55.H45 2002, (v6)
Henderson, Linda Dalrymple. N6853.D8.A64 1998, (v9)
Henderson, Loy W. E748.H412 A36 1986, (v4)
Henderson, Mary C. PN2096.M5.H464 2001, (v3)
  PN2221.H38 1996, (v3)
Henderson, Nevile. D750.H4, (v5)
Henderson, Peter V. N. F1235.5.B36.H46 1999, (v4)
Henderson, Robert W. GV861.H4 2001, (v6)
Henderson, W. O. HC285.H442, (v6)
Henderson, William Darryl. UB323.H46 1990, (v10)
Henderson, William. DS518.8.H4, (v5)
Hendler, Glenn. PS217.E47.H46 2001, (v3)
Hendley, Brian Patrick. LA126.H42 1986, (v7)
Hendricks, Barbara E. GV425.H46 2001, (v6)
Hendricks, Bonnie L. SF291.H37 1995, (v1)
Hendricks, Janet Wall. F3722.1.J5.T854 1993, (v4)
Hendricks, Walter Anton. HA33.H4, (v6)
Hendricks, Wanda A. F550.N4.H46 1998, (v4)
Hendrickson, Carol Elaine. F1465.2.C3.H46 1995, (v4)
Hendrickson, David C. UA23.H448 1988, (v10)
Hendrickson, Robert. PE2751.H46 2001, (v3)
  PE2835.H46 2000, (v3)
  PE2926.H46 1993, (v3)
  PE2970.A6.H46 1996, (v3)
Hendrix, James E. QA76.73.S58.H45 1988, (v1)
Hendry, A. W. TH2243.H46 2000, (v1)
Hendry, Joy. GV1853.4.J3, (v6)
Heneghan, Tom. DD290.29.H46 2000, (v5)
Henehan, Marie T. JZ1480.H46 2000, (v7)
Hengel, Martin. BS2555.2.H46 2000, (v8)
Henggeler, Paul R. E847.2.H46 1991, (v4)
Henggeler, Scott W. RC488.5.H47 1990, (v2)
  RJ387.A25.H46 1992, (v2)
Heng-tang-tui-shih. PL2658.E3.S83 1940, (v3)
  PL2658.E3.S83 1944, (v3)
Henham, Ralph J. KD8406.H45 1996, (v7)
Henlford, Lewis W. Z5781.H46 1995, (v10)
Henig, Gerald S. E468.9.H5 2001, (v4)
Henig, Jeffrey R. LB1027.9.H46 1994, (v7)
Henige, David P. E59.P75.H45 1998, (v4)
  E112.H46 1991, (v4)
Heninger, S. K. QC855.H5, (v1)
  Z2014.P795.H45, (v10)
Henissart, Paul. PS3558.E4958.M3, (v3)
Henke, Robert. PR2981.5.H46 1997, (v3)
Henke, Suzette A. PS366.A88.H46 1998, (v3)
Henkel, Friedrich-Wilhelm. SF515.5.G43.H4613 1995, (v1)
Henken, Elissa R. DA716.G5.H46 1996, (v5)
Henkes, Robert. N6538.H58.H46 1999, (v9)
  ND212.H46 1991, (v9)
Henkin, Leo Justin. PR878.E9.H4 1963, (v3)

Henkin, Louis. JX1395.H45 1979, (v7)
  KF4651.H45 1996, (v7)
  KF4749.H46 1990, (v7)
Henkle, Roger B. PR468.C65.H4, (v3)
Henle, Mary. BF203.H43, (v2)
Henle, Michael. QA473.H46 1997, (v1)
Henle, Paul. BC135.H35, (v8)
Henley, Andrew. HB238.H46 1990, (v6)
Henley, Beth. PS3558.E4962.D4 1991, (v3)
Henley, Ernest J. TS173.H47 1981, (v1)
Henley, William Ernest. PR4783.A1 1970, (v3)
Hennel, Jacek W. QC762.H39 1993, (v1)
Henneman, John Bell. DC97.C54.H46 1996, (v5)
Hennen, John. F241.H54 1996, (v4)
Hennessee, Judith Adler. HQ1413.F75.H456 1999, (v6)
Hennessey, Thomas J. ML3508.H46 1994, (v9)
Hennessey, Thomas. DA962.H46 1998, (v5)
  DA990.U46.H43 1997, (v5)
  DA990.U46.H435 2001, (v5)
Hennessy, C. A. M. F1410.H45 1978, (v4)
Hennessy, Michael A. DS558.H448 1997, (v5)
Hennessy, Peter. DA588.H46 1994, (v5)
Henning, Sylvie Debevec. PR6003.E282.Z674 1988, (v3)
Henningham, Stephen. DU17.H46 1995, (v5)
Henricks, Robert G. PL2677.H3.A244 1990, (v3)
Henriksen, Margot A. E169.12.H49 1997, (v4)
Henrion, Claudia. QA27.5.H46 1997, (v1)
Henriot, Christian. DS796.S257.H4613 1993, (v5)
  HQ250.S52.H4613 2001, (v6)
Henriquez Urena, Max. PQ7081.H357, (v3)
  PQ7371.H38, (v3)
Henriquez Urena, Pedro. F1408.3.H4513, (v4)
  PC4505.H4 1933, (v3)
Henritze, Barbara K. Z6944.N39.H46 1995, (v10)
Henry, Albert. PQ2643.A26.Z64, (v3)
Henry, Charles P. E185.615.H365 1990, (v4)
  E748.B885.H46 1999, (v4)
Henry, Donald O. GN776.32.M628.H45 1989, (v6)
  GN855.J67.H46 1995, (v6)
Henry, Francoise. N6784.H4213 1965b, (v9)
Henry, Granville C. BC108.H36 1993, (v8)
Henry, Jane L. RF293.8. H463 2002, (v2)
Henry, Jay C. NA730.T5.H46 1993, (v9)
Henry, John F. HB119.C5.H46 1995, (v6)
Henry, John. Q125.H5587 2001, (v1)
Henry, Jules. HQ728.H395, (v6)
Henry, Laurie. PN3355.H46 1995, (v3)
Henry, Laurin L. E743.H4, (v4)
Henry, Madeleine Mary. DF228.A8.H46 1995, (v5)
Henry, Nora. PN1998.3.V67.H46 2001, (v3)
Henry, Paget. B1028.P34 2000, (v8)
Henry, Richard. PN3329.H46 1996, (v3)
Henryson, Robert. PR1990.H4.A17 1981, (v3)
  PR1990.H4.A6 1963, (v3)
  PR1990.H4 1958, (v3)
Hensel, Chase. E99.E7.H467 1996, (v4)
Henslee, William D. KF299.E57 M46 1990, (v7)
Henslin, James M. Z7164.H72.H46 1993, (v10)
Henson, Eithne. PR3537.L5.H46 1992, (v3)
Hentschel, Klaus. QB462.65.H4613 1997, (v1)
Henze, Paul B. DT381.H465 2000, (v5)
Henzold, G. TS172.H46 1995, (v1)
Hepburn, James G. PR6003.E6.Z763, (v3)
Heper, Metin. DR436.H47 1994, (v5)
Hephaistos, Panagiotes. UA646.I37 1988, (v10)
Hepher, Balfour. SH156.H47 1988, (v1)
Hepler, Allison L. RC963.6.W65, (v2)
Hepokoski, James A. ML410.S54 H4 1993, (v9)
  ML410.V4 H46 1983, (v9)
  ML410.V4 H48 1987, (v9)
Heppenheimer, T. A. HE9803.A3.H47 1995, (v6)
  TL515.H455 2001, (v1)
  TL789.8.U5.H49 1997, (v1)
Heppenstall, Rayner. PR6015.E56.B5, (v3)
  PR6015.E56 B53 1940, (v3)
  PR6015.E56 C6 1968, (v3)
  PR6015.E56 G7, (v3)
  PR6015.E56 W6, (v3)

Heraclitus. B223.K48, (v8)
Herald, Diana Tixier. Z5917.F3 H47 1999, (v10)
Herb, Michael. JQ1840.H47 1999, (v7)
Herber, Harold L. LB1050.H437 1978, (v7)
Herber, Mark D. CS414.H47 1997, (v5)
Herberg, Will. BL2525.H47 1983, (v8)
Herbert, George. PR3507.A33 1941, (v3)
Herbert, George. PR3507.AI 1927, (v3)
Herbert, James D. ND548.5.F3.H4 1992, (v9)
Herbert, Melissa S. UB418.W65.H47 1998, (v10)
Herbert, Nick. B808.9.H47 1993, (v8)
Herbert, Patricia M. Z3216.H47 1991, (v10)
Herbert, Robert L. N6490.H45, (v9)
   N6853.S48, (v9)
   ND553.M7.H43 1994, (v9)
   ND553.S5.A4 1991, (v9)
   NK27.H47 2000, (v9)
Herbert, Rosemary. PN3448.D4.H37 1999, (v3)
Herbert, Ulrich. HD8450.H43213 1997, (v6)
Herberts, Kurt. ND1260.H463 1958, (v9)
Herbig, Paul A. HC465.T4.H47 1995, (v6)
Herbst, Edward. ML3758.I53.H47 1997, (v9)
Herbst, Jeffrey Ira. HC1060.H47 1993, (v6)
   JQ1875.H47 2000, (v7)
   JQ2922.H47 1990, (v7)
Herbst, Josephine. PS3515.E596.R6 1984, (v3)
Herbst, Jurgen. LA222.H386 1996, (v7)
   LB1715.H395 1989, (v7)
Herbst, L. J. TK7874.H418 1996, (v1)
Herbst, Philip. E184.A1.H466 1997, (v4)
Herbst, Susan. HN90.P8.H47 1993, (v6)
Herdan, Innes. PL2303.H45 1992, (v3)
Herdeck, Donald E. PL8010.H38, (v3)
Herdegen, Lance J. E493.5.I72.H47 1997, (v4)
Herder, Johann Gottfried. BL51.H4695 1993, (v8)
   PT2351.A1 1985, (v3)
   PT2351.A1 1985, (v3)
   PT2352.Z2 1991, (v3)
Herding, Klaus. ND553.C9.H47 1991, (v9)
Herdman, John. PN3500.H47 1990, (v3)
Herdt, Gilbert H. GN484.35.H47 1997, (v6)
   HQ76.2.U5.H47 1993, (v6)
Herf, Jeffrey. DD238.H45 1984, (v5)
Hergesheimer, Joseph. PS3515.E628 B7, (v3)
   PS3515.E628 C9 1922, (v3)
   PS3515.E628 J3 1946, (v3)
   PS3515.E628 L55, (v3)
   PS3515.E628 M6 1919, (v3)
Herget, James E. KF380.H47 1990, (v7)
Heriat, Philippe. PQ2615.E66.E5 1972, (v3)
Herissone, Rebecca. ML3800.H43 2000, (v9)
Heritage, J. QR41.2.H46 1996, (v1)
Heriteau, Jacqueline. SB406.93.U6.H47 1992, (v1)
   SB407.H493 1990, (v1)
Heritier, Jean. DC119.8.H44 1959, (v5)
Herken, Gregg. UA23.H45 1985, (v10)
Herland, Leo. QA5.H42, (v1)
Herlihy, David. CB351.H4, (v5)
   DG975.P65.H4, (v5)
   HC308.F6.H4713 1985, (v6)
Herman, A. L. BL1212.72.H47 1991, (v8)
   HN18.H399 1999, (v6)
Herman, Arthur. CB245.H429 1997, (v5)
   E748.M143.H47 2000, (v4)
Herman, Edward. ZA5055.U6.H47 1997, (v10)
Herman, Gerald. D522.5.H43 1991, (v5)
Herman, Jerry John. LB3218.A1 H47 1995, (v7)
Herman, Jiri. QA218.H4713 2000, (v1)
Herman, John. DA47.1.H47 1998, (v5)
Herman, Michael. JF1525.I6.H47 1996, (v7)
Herman, Vimala. PN1631.H47 1995, (v3)
Hermand, Jost. PT731.H4713 1992, (v3)
Hermann, Janet Sharp. F341.D25.H47 1990, (v4)
   F349.D38.H47, (v4)
Hermanowicz, Joseph C. Q147.H47 1998, (v1)
Hernandez, Eugenio. QA403.3.H47 1996, (v1)
Hernandez, Jose M. E183.8.C9.H47 1993, (v4)
Hernandez, Jose. PQ7797.H3.M3 1967, (v3)
Herndon, Ruth Wallis. HN79.A11.H47 2001, (v6)
Herndon, William Henry. E457.H575 1983, (v4)
Hernon, Joseph M. E183.H46 1997, (v4)

Hernon, Peter. ZA5075.H47 2001, (v10)
Hero, Alfred O. F369.H47 1995, (v4)
Hero, Rodney E. E184.A1.H469 1998, (v4)
Herodotus. D58.H46 1949, (v5)
Herr, Richard. DC138.T6344.H4, (v5)
   HD779.J34.H47 1989, (v6)
Herr, Sharon M. RM302.H47 2000, (v2)
Herrera-Sobek, Maria. ML3558.H47 1993, (v9)
Herrick, C. Judson. QP376.H4 1963, (v1)
Herrick, Marvin Theodore. PN1902.H4, (v3)
   PQ4149.H4 1970, (v3)
Herrick, Robert Waring. V55.S65.H47 1988, (v10)
   VA570.H4, (v10)
Herrick, Robert. PR3510.A5.M3, (v3)
   PR3510.A5.P3, (v3)
   PR3510.A5.P3 1968, (v3)
   PS1922.C4 1970, (v3)
   PS1922.C5, (v3)
   PS1922.C6, (v3)
   PS1922.O5 1913, (v3)
   PS1922.W4, (v3)
Herrigel, Eugen. BL1493.H413 1964, (v8)
Herring, Eric. D843.H439 1995, (v5)
Herring, George C. DS558.H454 1994, (v5)
Herring, Hubert Clinton. F1410.H47 1968, (v4)
Herring, Joseph B. E78.K16 H47 1990, (v4)
Herring, Pendleton. UA23.H46, (v10)
Herring, Phillip F. PS3503.A614.Z68 1995, (v3)
Herrington, Joan. PS3573.I45677.Z68 1998, (v3)
Herrmann, Dorothy. HV1624.K4.H47 1998, (v6)
Herrmann, Luke. NE642.T9.H47 1990, (v9)
Herrnson, Paul S. JK2265.H475 1988, (v7)
Herrnstein, Richard J. BF431.H398 1994, (v2)
Herron, Jerry. F574.D45.H47 1993, (v4)
Herron, Jim. F596.H4 1969, (v4)
Hersey, George L. N8241.5.H47 1996, (v9)
Hersey, John. D767.25.H6.H4 1946c, (v5)
   E813.H45, (v4)
   PS3515.E7715.B5 1944, (v3)
   PS3515.E7715 S5, (v3)
   PS3515.E7715 W3 1967, (v3)
   PS3515.E7715 W37, (v3)
Hersey. PS3515.E7715 M3, (v3)
Hersh, Blanche Glassman. HQ1423.H47, (v6)
Hersh, Reuben. QA8.4.H47 1997, (v1)
Hershenson, Maurice. BF469.H45 1999, (v2)
Hershfield, Joanne. PN2318.D4, (v3)
Hershman, D. Jablow. BF423.H474 1998, (v2)
Hershock, Peter D. BQ4570.I55.H47 1999, (v8)
Herspring, Dale R. UA719.3.H6424 1998, (v10)
   UA770.H4797 1996, (v10)
   UA770.H48 1990, (v10)
Herstein, Robert Edwin. E806.H48 1989, (v4)
Hertog, Susan. PS3523.I516.Z69 1999, (v3)
Hertsbert, Richard W. TA417.6.H46 1996, (v1)
Hertsog, Hanah. HQ1236.5.I75.H46 1999, (v6)
Hertz, Aleksander. DS135.P6.H413 1988, (v5)
Hertz, Noreena. HD60.H47 2001, (v6)
Hertzberg, Arthur. DS135.F82.H4, (v5)
Hertzberg, Arthur. DS149.H4376, (v5)
Hertzberg, Steven. F294.A89.J54, (v4)
Hertzke, Allen D. E880.H47 1992, (v4)
Hertzler, Arthur E. R154.H39.A3 1970, (v2)
Hertzog, Mark. HQ76.3.U5.H49 1996, (v6)
Herubel, Jean-Pierre V. M. Z6208.H5.H47 1994, (v10)
Herwig, Holger H. D507.H47 1982, (v5)
   D531.H464 1997, (v5)
   VB315.G4.H47, (v10)
Herwig, Rob. SB419.H557413 1985, (v1)
Herwitz, Daniel Alan. N71.H45 1993, (v9)
Herz, Judith Scherer. PR6011.O58.P3744 1992, (v3)
   PR6011.O58.Z684 1988, (v3)
Herzberger, David K. PQ6144.H47 1995, (v3)
Herzel, Leo. KF1477.H48 1990, (v7)
Herzen, Aleksandr. D387.H413, (v5)
   DK209.6.H4.A32, (v5)
   DK209.6.H4.A33, (v5)
Herzenberg, Stephen. HD5724.H43 1998, (v6)
Herzfeld, Michael. DF951.R4.H47 1991, (v5)
   GN345.H47 2001, (v6)
Herzog, Chaim. DS119.2.H47 1982, (v5)

DS128.1.H467 1975, (v5)
Herzog, Don. JC328.2.H47 1989, (v7)
Herzog, Lawrence A. NA2543.S6.H48 1999, (v9)
Herzog, Peter J. JQ1681.H68 1993, (v7)
Herzog, Tobey C. PS3565.B75.Z69 1997, (v3)
Heschel, Abraham Joshua. BL51.H476, (v8)
   BM560.H46, (v8)
Heschel, Susannah. BM755.G4.H47 1998, (v8)
Hesiod. PA3405.S8.H44, (v3)
   PA4010.E5.O6 1959, (v3)
Heskin, Allan David. HM131.H399 1991, (v6)
Heslep, Robert D. LB885.H45.P48 1997, (v7)
   LC311.H47 1995, (v7)
Hess, Carol A. ML410.F215 H47 2001, (v9)
Hess, David J. RC268.5.H47 1997, (v2)
Hess, Earl J. E468.9.H57 1988, (v4)
   E468.9.H58 1997, (v4)
Hess, Gary R. E183.8.V5 H44 1998, (v4)
Hess, Peter N. HB1108.H48 1988, (v6)
Hess, Stephen. JK552.H47 2002, (v7)
Hess, Stephen. PN4784.F6.H47 1996, (v3)
Hesse, Carla Alison. Z310.6.P37.H47 1991, (v10)
Hesse, Fritz. DD247.H5.H369, (v5)
Hesse, Hermann. PT2617.E85A26 1992, (v3)
   PT2617.E85.A28, (v3)
   PT2617.E85.A287 1995, (v3)
   PT2617.E85 G52 1969, (v3)
   PT2617.E85 G53 1990, (v3)
   PT2617.E85 K553, (v3)
   PT2617.E85 M7, (v3)
   PT2617.E85 N413 1969, (v3)
   PT2617.E85 P42 1969, (v3)
   PT2617.E85.S52, (v3)
   PT2617.E85.S7, (v3)
   PT2617.E85.Z53 1954, (v3)
   PT2617.E85.Z54513, (v3)
Hesse, Karen. PZ7.H4364Ou 1997, (v3)
Hesse, M. G. PQ3919.R74.Z659 1984, (v3)
Hesse-Biber, Sharlene Janice. BF697.5.B63.H47 1996, (v2)
Hesseltine, William Best. E456.H43, (v4)
   E467.H58 1970, (v4)
   E615.H37 1998, (v4)
   F209.H48 1960, (v4)
Hesse-Wartegg, Ernst von. F354.H5813 1990, (v4)
Hession, Jane King. NA737.R294.R36 1999, (v9)
Hessler, Peter. DS796.F855 H47 2001, (v5)
Hester, Joseph P. BJ63.H47 1996, (v8)
Heston, Leonard L. RC460.H47 1991, (v2)
Hetherington, Stephen Cade. BD161.H45 1996, (v8)
   BD201.H48 1991, (v8)
Hettle, Wallace. F214.H48 2001, (v4)
Heusch, Luc de. GN478.H4713 1981, (v6)
Heuser, Beatrice. UA646.H48 1997, (v10)
Heusken, Henry C. J. DS809.H523 1964, (v5)
Heusler, Andreas. PT1589.H38x 1982, (v3)
Heussenstamm, George. MT35.H55 1987, (v9)
Heuterman, Thomas H. F897.Y2.H48 1995, (v4)
Heuvelmans, Bernard. QL88.3.H4813 1995, (v1)
Heuving, Jeanne. PS3525.O5616.Z683 1992, (v3)
Hevia, James Louis. DS740.5.G5.H48 1995, (v5)
Hewett, Edgar Lee. E78.S7 H5 1968, (v4)
Hewett, Edward A. HC336.25.H48 1988, (v6)
Hewett, Waterman Thomas. PF3117.H63 1933, (v3)
Hewison, Robert. PR478.W67.H4 1977, (v3)
Hewitson, Gillian J. HQ1381.H48 1999, (v6)
Hewitt, Andrew. PN56.H57.H49 1996, (v3)
Hewitt, Leah Dianne. PQ629.H49 1990, (v3)
Hewitt, Mark A. NA7238.P25, (v9)
   NA7561.H4 1990, (v9)
Hewitt, Martin. HN398.M27.H48 1996, (v6)
Hewitt, Nancy A. HQ1439.R62 H48 2001, (v6)
Hewlett, Barry S. DT546.345.A35.H48 1991, (v5)
Hewlett, Dorothy. PR4193.H4 1972, (v3)
Hewlett, Maurice Henry. PR4787.L3 1968, (v3)
   PR4787.Q4, (v3)
Hewlett, Nick. JN2594.H49 1998, (v7)
Hewlett, Richard G. HD9698.U52.H55 1989 vol. 3, (v6)
Hexham, Irving. BL31.H498 1993, (v8)
Hey, Anthony J. G. QC174.12.H48 1987, (v1)
Heyck, Thomas William. DA533.H48 1982, (v5)

Heyd, David. R724.H49 1992, (v2)
Heyde, Ludwig. BD573.H4513 1999, (v8)
Heydebrand, Wolf V. KF8754.H45 1990, (v7)
Heydenreich, Ludwig Heinrich. NA1115.H49 1996, (v9)
  T40.L46.H49, (v1)
Heyer, Anna Harriet. ML113.H52 1980, (v9)
Heyer, Paul. G530.T6.H49 1995, (v6)
Heyerdahl, Thor. G530.H46.H463 1950, (v6)
Heyman, Barbara B. ML410.B23.H5 1992, (v9)
Heyman, Therese Thau. NC1807.U5.H49 1998, (v9)
  TR820.5.H5 1994, (v1)
Heymann, Daniel. HG229.H49 1995, (v6)
Heymann, H. G. HF5686.C8.H48 1990, (v6)
Heymann, Philip B. HV6432.H49 1998, (v6)
  JK261.H49 1987, (v7)
Heyns, Michiel. PR868.S32.H49 1994, (v3)
Heyrman, Christine Leigh. BR535.H47 1997, (v8)
Heyward, Carter. BR124.H49 1999, (v8)
Heyward, DuBose. PS3515.E98 M3 1929, (v3)
  PS3515.E98 P6 1953, (v3)
Heyward, Vivian H. GV436.H48 2002, (v6)
  QP33.5.H49 1996, (v1)
Heywood, Andrew. JA71.H49 1992, (v7)
Heywood, John B. TJ755.H45 1988, (v1)
Heywood, Leslie. GV1061.15.H49.A3 1998, (v6)
  PN771.H43 1996, (v6)
Heywood, Linda Marinda. DT1373.H49 2000, (v5)
Heywood, Paul. JN8111.H49 1995, (v7)
Heywood, Thomas. PR2574.W8 1961, (v3)
Heyworth, Peter. ML422.K67 H53 1996, (v9)
Hezel, Francis X. DU565.H49 1983, (v5)
Hiam, Alexander. HF5415.13.H47 1992, (v6)
Hibbard, G. R. PR2326.N3.Z68, (v3)
Hibbard, Howard. NB60.H5, (v9)
  ND623.C26.H44 1983, (v9)
Hibbard, Scott W. DS35.74.H53 1997, (v5)
Hibbeler, R. C. TA350.H48 1998, (v1)
Hibbeler, R. C. TA645.H47 1999, (v1)
Hibbert, Christopher. DA87.1.N4.H53 1994, (v5)
  DA415.H53 1993, (v5)
  DA506.A2.H53 1998, (v5)
  DA538.A1 H53 1975, (v5)
  DA554.H5 2000, (v5)
  DA564.B3.H52 1978b, (v5)
Hibbett, Howard. PL740.H5 1970, (v3)
Hibbing, John R. JK1041.H53 1995, (v7)
Hibbs, Douglas A. HB3743.H52 1987, (v6)
Hibbs, Thomas S. PN1995.9.N55.H53 1999, (v3)
Hick, John. BL48.H45 1989, (v8)
Hick, John. BL51.H494, (v8)
Hickey, Dennis. DT38.7.H5 1993, (v5)
Hickey, Donald R. E354.H53 1989, (v4)
Hickey, Gerald Cannon. GN635.V5.H53 1993, (v6)
Hickey, Michael. QK10.H53 2000, (v1)
Hickey, William. CT788.H5.A53 1962, (v5)
Hickman, Ian. TK7867.H53 1990, (v1)
Hickman, John. F3081.H48 1998, (v4)
Hickok, Ralph. GV567.H518 2002, (v6)
Hicks, Douglas A. BJ1275.H49 2000, (v8)
Hicks, George L. D810.C698.H53 1995, (v5)
  HC455.H53, (v6)
Hicks, Granville. PR461.H5 1969, (v3)
  PS214.H5 1935, (v3)
Hicks, John Donald. E784.H5, (v4)
  JK2372.H5 1961, (v7)
  HB171.H6343, (v6)
  HC26.H5, (v6)
  HD4909.H5 1963, (v6)
  HG221.H633 1989, (v6)
Hicks, Karen M. HD9995.C64.A2344 1994, (v6)
Hicks, M. A. DA177.H53 1991, (v5)
Hicks, Michael. ML3534.H53 1999, (v9)
Hicks, Philip Stephen. DA1.H53 1996, (v5)
Hickson, Joyce. RJ502.S6.H53 1996, (v2)
Hidʹayat, ŏSˉadiq. PK6561.H4B813 1997, (v3)
  PK6561.H43.H313, (v3)
Hiddleston, J. A. PQ2191.Z5.H54 1999, (v3)
Hiebert, Erwin N. QC73.H55, (v1)
Hiebert, Murray. HD57.7.H525 2001, (v6)
Hiesinger, Kathryn B. NK1390.H44 1993, (v9)

Hiesinger, Ulrich W. ND210.5.I4.H53 1991, (v9)
Hietala, Thomas R. GV1131.H64 2002, (v6)
Higashi, Sumiko. PN1998.3.D39.H54 1994, (v3)
Higbie, Robert. PR4588.H48 1998, (v3)
Higginbotham, A. Leon. KF4757.H535 1996, (v7)
Higginbotham, Don. E209.H54 1988, (v4)
Higgins, Antony. F1231.H54 2000, (v4)
Higgins, Benjamin Howard. HC59.7.H45 1979, (v6)
Higgins, Brian. Z8562.58.H52 1987, (v10)
  Z8562.58.H53, (v10)
Higgins, George V. PS3558.I356.C5, (v3)
Higgins, Iain Macleod. G370.M2.H3634 1997, (v6)
Higgins, Lynn A. PN1995.9.H5 1996, (v3)
Higgins, Michael Denis. QE271.H54 1996, (v1)
Higgins, Michael James. HN170.B37.H54 1992, (v6)
Higgins, Paul C. HV2395.H53, (v6)
Higgins, Trumbull. D568.3.H5, (v5)
Higginson, Roy. Z5814.C5.H54 1991, (v10)
Higginson, Thomas Wentworth. E185.18.H54 2000, (v4)
  E492.94 33rd.H53 2000, (v4)
Higgs, Catherine. DT1927.J34.H54 1997, (v5)
Higgs, Laquita M. DA690.C7.H54 1998, (v5)
Higgs, Robert. E185.8.H6, (v4)
Higham, Charles. DS523.H55 1996, (v5)
Higham, John. E175.H654, (v4)
  E184.A1.H49 1984, (v4)
  E184.A1.H5, (v4)
Higham, N. J. DA150.G483.H54 1994, (v5)
  DA152.H53 1995, (v5)
  DA152.H533 1997, (v5)
Higham, Robert. UG405.H54 1995, (v10)
Higham, Robin D. S. UA647.H56, (v10)
  UG635.G7.H483 1998, (v10)
  VG95.G7.H5, (v10)
  Z2021.M5.H54, (v10)
Highet, Gilbert. PA6047.H5, (v3)
  PN511.H485, (v3)
  PN883.H5 1957, (v3)
  PR99.H47, (v3)
  PR99.H48, (v3)
Highsmith, Carol M. E159.H65 1994, (v4)
  F203.7.P4.H54 1988, (v4)
Hight, Eleanor M. TR140.M584.H54 1995, (v1)
Highton, Jake. PN4897.N45.H54 1990, (v3)
Hightower, James Robert. PL2308.H54 1998, (v3)
  PL2909.H5 1953, (v3)
Highwater, Jamake. HQ76.25.H54 1997, (v6)
  N6538.A4 H5 1980, (v9)
  ND238.A4 H53, (v9)
Higonnet, Anne. N7640.H54 1998, (v9)
  ND553.M88.H5 1990, (v9)
  ND553.M88.H53 1992, (v9)
Higonnet, Patrice L. R. DC178.H54 1998, (v5)
  E210.H64 1988, (v4)
Higson, Andrew. PN1993.5.G7.H54 1995, (v3)
Hijab, Nadia. HQ1784.H54 1988, (v6)
Hijiya-Kirschnereit, Irmela. PL747.67.A85.H5513 1996, (v3)
Hilberg, Raul. D810.J4.H5 1985b, (v5)
Hilberseimer, Ludwig. NA1088.M65.H5, (v9)
Hilbert, David. BC135.H514, (v8)
  QA201.H716 1993, (v1)
  QA685.H515, (v1)
Hildebidle, John. PR8753.H57 1989, (v3)
Hildebrand, Ann Meinzen. PQ2603.R9453.Z69 1991, (v3)
Hildebrand, George C. HN700.C32.H54, (v6)
Hildebrand, George Herbert. HC305.H47, (v6)
Hildebrand, George. HB3730.H54 1992, (v6)
Hildebrand, Klaus. DD221.H5713 1989, (v5)
Hildebrandt, Stefan. BH301.N3.H555 1996, (v8)
Hildegard. BX4700.H5 A4 1994, (v8)
Hildemann, W. H. QR184.H54, (v1)
Hilden, Patricia. E90.H55.A3 1995, (v4)
Hiley, David R. B837.H55 1988, (v8)
Hiley, David. ML3082.H54 1993, (v9)
Hilfer, Anthony Channell. PN3448.D4.H55 1990, (v3)
Hilfiker, David. R729.5.G4H55 1998, (v2)
Hilgard, Ernest Ropiequet. LB1051.H52 1966, (v7)
Hilgard, Josephine (Rohrs). BF1156.S83.H53, (v2)

Hilgeman, Sherri Lynn. E78.I53 H56 2000, (v4)
Hilger, Gustav. DD241.R8.H5 1953, (v5)
Hill, Archibald A. PE1105.H5, (v3)
Hill, Brad. ZA4226.H53 1997, (v10)
Hill, Brian W. DA480.H45 1996, (v5)
Hill, C. P. DA337.H55 1988b, (v5)
Hill, Charles E. BT819.5.H55 2001, (v8)
Hill, Charles G. PQ2637.A82.Z733 1992, (v3)
Hill, Christopher R. GV721.5.H54 1996, (v6)
Hill, Christopher S. BD214.H54 1991, (v8)
Hill, Christopher. DA375.H5, (v5)
  DA375.H54 1985, (v5)
  DA380.H47, (v5)
  DA380.H48, (v5)
  DA380.H5, (v5)
  DA380.H52 1964, (v5)
  DA405.H49 1984, (v5)
  DA426.H49 1970b, (v5)
  DA586.H48 1991, (v5)
  HC254.H55 1968, (v6)
  PR3331.H55 1989, (v3)
  PR3592.P64.H5 1978, (v3)
Hill, Constance Valis. GV1785.A1.V35 2000, (v6)
Hill, David. ND497.T8.H56 1993, (v9)
Hill, Denise. KF1355.Z9.H55 2000, (v7)
Hill, Derek. NA380.H5 1967, (v9)
Hill, Edward E. Z1209.2.U5.H54 1982, (v10)
Hill, Errol. PR3105.H54 1984, (v3)
Hill, Forest Garrett. UG23.H6, (v10)
Hill, Gary L. KF240.H534 1998, (v7)
Hill, Geoffrey. PR6015.I4735B7 1981, (v3)
  PR6015.I4735.S6 1975, (v3)
Hill, George Francis. DF209.5.H65 1951, (v5)
Hill, George H. PN1992.8.A34.H55 1990, (v3)
Hill, George Robert. ML113.H55 1997, (v9)
Hill, Gerald N. KF156.H55 1995, (v7)
Hill, Grace Livingston. PS3515.I486 O27, (v3)
Hill, Hal. HC447.H55 2000, (v6)
Hill, Jacqueline R. DA995.D75.H55 1997, (v5)
Hill, James Michael. DA784.3.M33.H55 1993, (v5)
Hill, Janice. TL798.M4.H55 1991, (v1)
Hill, Jim Dan. UA42.H5, (v10)
Hill, John L. TX392.H528 1996, (v1)
Hill, John M. PR179.W37.H55 2000, (v3)
  PR1875.P5.H55 1991, (v3)
Hill, John. PN1993.5.G7.H549 1999, (v3)
Hill, Jonathan David. F2270.2.C87.H55 1993, (v4)
Hill, Kenneth L. E183.8.S65.H55 1993, (v4)
Hill, Kevin A. JK1764.H55 1998, (v7)
Hill, Kim Quaile. JK2408.H54 1994, (v7)
Hill, Kim. F2679.2.G9.H55 1996, (v4)
Hill, L. M. KD621.C34.H55 1988, (v7)
Hill, Leslie. PR6003.E282.Z6794 1990, (v3)
Hill, Lowell D. KF1724.G7.H55 1990, (v7)
Hill, Lynda Marion. PS3515.U789.Z715 1996, (v3)
Hill, Lynn. GV199.92.H52 A3 2002, (v6)
Hill, Malcolm R. HC340.12.Z9.A445 1997, (v6)
Hill, Mark D. (Mark Donald). QA76.9.H73H55 2000, (v1)
Hill, Marquita K. TD174.H55 1997, (v1)
Hill, Martin J. D. HN793.K58.H37 1991, (v6)
Hill, Mary Armfield. HQ1413.G54.H54, (v6)
Hill, Michael J. HD7165.H55 1990, (v6)
Hill, Ned C. HG4028.W65.H54 1995, (v6)
Hill, Patricia Evridge. F394.D2157.H35 1996, (v4)
Hill, Peter. ML410.S932 H55 2000, (v9)
Hill, R. TJ163.2.H53 1995, (v1)
Hill, R. Carter. HB139.H548 2001, (v6)
Hill, Richard Leslie. F1233.H65 1995, (v4)
Hill, Robert Dickson. QC778.H5, (v1)
Hill, Robert M. F1465.2.Q5.H55 1987, (v4)
Hill, Roland. D15.A25.H487 2000, (v5)
Hill, Samuel S. BR535.H5 1999, (v8)
  E872.H54 1982, (v4)
Hill, Susan. PR6058.I45.B54x, (v3)
  PR6058.I45.I56, (v3)
Hill, Thomas English. BJ319.H5, (v8)
  BJ1011.H48, (v8)
Hill, W. W. E99.T35.H5 1982, (v4)
Hill, William Henry. ML424.S8.H62 1963, (v9)
Hilleary, William M. U53.H5.A3, (v10)

Hillegas, Mark Robert. PR5777.H5, (v3)
Hillel, Daniel. HD1698.M53.H55 1994, (v6)
  S591.H62 1991, (v1)
  S592.3.H53, (v1)
  S592.3.H535 1998, (v1)
  S592.3.H55, (v1)
  S594.H563, (v1)
Hillenbrand, Carole. DS38.6.H55 2000, (v5)
Hiller, Ilo. QL737.U55.H54 1996, (v1)
Hillerbrand, Hans Joachim. BR302.8.H55 2000, (v8)
  BR305.2.H5 1964, (v8)
Hillerman, Tony. F787.H54 1987, (v4)
  PS3558.I45.B53, (v3)
Hillert, Mats. QD503.H554 1998, (v1)
Hillgarth, J. N. DP171.5.H54 2000, (v5)
Hilliard, David. E185.97.H55.A3 1993, (v4)
Hilliard, Robert L. PN1990.6.U5.H48 1992, (v3)
Hilliard, Sam Bowers. G1281.J1.H5 1984, (v6)
Hillier, Bevis. NX180.S6.H5 1983, (v9)
Hillier, S. M. R601.H5 1983, (v2)
Hillis, W. Daniel. QA76.5.H4918 1998, (v1)
Hillman, Richard S. F1938.H55 1992, (v4)
  JL3881.H55 1994, (v7)
Hillman, Richard. PR658.S79.H55 1997, (v3)
  PR2981.5.H55 1993, (v3)
Hill-Miller, Katherine. PR5398.H5 1995, (v3)
Hills, Paul. N6921.V5.H56 1999, (v9)
Hills, Richard Leslie. TJ461.H57 1989, (v1)
  TJ823.H55 1994, (v1)
Hillstrom, Kevin. DS557.73.H55 1998, (v5)
  HD62.7.H553 2002, (v6)
Hillyar, Anna. DK219.3.H55 2000, (v5)
Hilmar, Ernst. ML410.S3.H5613 1988, (v9)
Hilmes, Michele. PN1990.6.U5.H5 1990, (v3)
Hilmes, Michele. PN1991.3.U6.H56 1997, (v3)
Hilsman, Roger. DS79.72.H56 1992, (v5)
  E841.H55 1996, (v4)
Hilton, George Woodman. G530.E18.H55 1995, (v6)
Hilton, James. PR6015.I53 G6, (v3)
  PR6015.I53 L6 1957, (v3)
  PR6015.I53 R3, (v3)
Hilton, R. H. HD594.H54, (v6)
  HT115.H55 1992, (v6)
Hilton, Stanley E. F2523.5.S65.H55 1991, (v4)
Hilton, Timothy. PR4836.H58 1971, (v3)
  PR5263.H5 1985, (v3)
Hilts, Philip J. QC16.W56.H54 1982, (v1)
Himanen, Pekka. QA76.9.M65, (v1)
Himbara, David. HC865.H56 1994, (v6)
Himes, Chester B. PS3515.I713.A6 1991, (v3)
  PS3515.I713.P58 1993, (v3)
  PS3515.I713.Y47 1998, (v3)
Himmel, Kelly F. E99.K23.H53 1999, (v4)
Himmel, Richard. PS3515.I7147, (v3)
Himmelblau, David Mautner. TP151.H5 1996, (v1)
Himmelfarb, Gertrude. D15.A25.H5 1952a, (v5)
  DA533.H55, (v5)
  HN59.2.H56 1995, (v6)
  HV4086.A3.H54 1991, (v6)
  HV4086.A3.H55 1985, (v6)
Himmelstein, Hal. PN1992.3.U5.H55 1994, (v3)
Himmelstein, Jerome L. JA84.U5.H55 1990, (v7)
Himmerich y Valencia, Robert. F1230.H56 1991, (v4)
Hinchliffe, Alan. QD455.3.C64.H46 1999, (v1)
Hinchliffe, Arnold P. PR6066.I53.Z675 1981, (v3)
Hinckley, Robert H. F826.H66.A34, (v4)
Hind, Arthur Mayger. NE400.H66 1963, (v9)
  NE1030.H55 1963, (v9)
Hinde, Robert A. BL48.H475 1999, (v8)
Hinde, Wendy. DA950.3.H54 1992, (v5)
Hindemith, Paul. ML410.H685.A4 1995, (v9)
  ML3800.H55, (v9)
  MT35.H6, (v9)
  MT40.H523, (v9)
Hinderaker, Eric. F517.H55 1997, (v4)
Hindle, Steve. DA315.H46 2000, (v5)
Hindley, A. PC2891.H56 2000, (v3)
Hindman, Elizabeth Blanks. KF4774.H56 1997, (v7)
Hinds, Harold E. PN6790.M48.H56 1992, (v3)
Hinds, Lynn Boyd. D1053.H525 1991, (v5)
Hinds, Mary Hancock. ML134.5.P73 H56 2001, (v9)

Hindus, Milton. PQ2631.R63.Z624, (v3)
Hine, Darlene Clark. E185.86.H68 1998, (v4)
  RT83.5.H56 1989, (v2)
Hine, Robert V. F591.H663 1984, (v4)
  F591.H67, (v4)
  RE36.H56.A3 1993, (v2)
Hines, Jerome. ML420.H452.A3, (v9)
  ML1460.H46 1982, (v9)
Hines, Thomas S. NA737.N4.H5 1982, (v9)
  PS3511.A86.Z7876 1996, (v3)
Hines, W. D. KD532.A1.H56 1990, (v7)
Hiney, Tom. PS3505.H3224.Z67 1997, (v3)
Hing, Bill Ong. E184.A1.H54 1997, (v4)
  KF4817.H56 1999, (v7)
Hingley, Ronald. PG3012.H5, (v3)
  PG3022.H5 1979, (v3)
Hinitz, Blythe Simone Farb. LB1139.5.S64.H56 1992, (v7)
Hinkle, James. PS3511.A86.U537 1995, (v3)
Hinkley, Daniel J. SB434.H56 1999, (v1)
Hinman, C. Wiley. S613.H67 1992, (v1)
Hinman, Robert B. PR3373.H5, (v3)
Hinnant, Charles H. PR3537.L5.H56 1994, (v3)
  PR3537.P5.H56 1988, (v3)
Hinshaw, David. E802.H65, (v4)
Hinsley, F. H. JX1944.H5 1967, (v7)
Hinson, Glenn. BR563.N4.H56 2000, (v8)
Hinson, Maurice. ML128.C4.H5, (v9)
  ML128.P3 H5 2000, (v9)
  ML128.P3 H53 1993, (v9)
  ML128.P3 H534 1998, (v9)
  ML128.P3.H536 1990, (v9)
  ML128.P3.H54 1987, (v9)
Hinterding, Erik. NE2054.5.R4.A4 2000, (v9)
Hintikka, Jaakko. B3376.W564 H56 2000, (v8)
  QA8.4.H56 1996, (v1)
Hinton, Laura. PR830.S45.H56 1999, (v3)
Hinton, Leanne. PM501.C2.H56 1996, (v3)
Hinton, Richard J. F811.H672, (v4)
Hinton, William. DS777.55.H553, (v5)
Hintz, Martin. F566.3.H56 1998, (v4)
  F606.3.H54 2000, (v4)
  F636.3.H56 2000, (v4)
Hiorns, Frederick R. NA9090.H54 1958, (v9)
Hipkiss, Robert A. PS3521.E735.Z67, (v3)
Hippel, Eric von. HC79.T4.H56 1988, (v6)
Hipple, Walter John. BH221.G72.H5, (v8)
Hirabayashi, Lane Ryo. D769.8.A6.H58 1999, (v5)
  F1221.Z3.H57 1993, (v4)
Hirai, Masako. PR888.S52.H57 1998, (v3)
Hirano, Kyoko. PN1993.5.J3.H57 1992, (v3)
Hirano, Umeyo. PL782.E5.H5, (v3)
Hiraoka, Kimitake. PL833.I7 S52, (v3)
Hiro, Dilip. DS43.H57 1996, (v5)
Hirrel, Leo P. BX7252.N5.H57 1998, (v8)
Hirsch, Abraham. HB119.F84.H57 1990, (v6)
Hirsch, Adam Jay. HV9304.H57 1992, (v6)
Hirsch, Arthur Henry. F280.H8.H6 1962, (v4)
Hirsch, David H. PN98.D43.H57 1991, (v3)
Hirsch, E. D. E169.1.H614 2002, (v4)
  PN81.H49, (v3)
  Z1037.H646 1996, (v10)
Hirsch, Edward. PN1042.H48 1999, (v3)
Hirsch, Eli. BD390.H57 1993, (v8)
Hirsch, Eric L. HD8079.C4.H57 1990, (v6)
Hirsch, Foster. ML429.P78.H6 1989, (v9)
  PN2285.H56 1998, (v3)
Hirsch, H. N. KF8745.F7.H57, (v7)
Hirsch, John L. DT516.826.H57 2001, (v5)
Hirsch, Morris W. QA3.P8 vol. 60, (v1)
Hirsch, Philip. HN700.55.Z9.C634 1990, (v6)
Hirsch, Robert. TR15.H557 2000, (v1)
Hirsch, Susan F. KSK541.H57 1998, (v7)
Hirschberger, Johannes. B82.H5613 1976b, (v8)
Hirschfeld, Christian Cajus Lorenz. SB454.3.P45, (v1)
Hirschfelder, Arlene B. E77.H59 1993, (v4)
  E98.P99 H57 1999, (v4)
  E98.R3.H73 1992, (v4)
  E98.R3 H73 2000, (v4)
  HV5760.H57 1999, (v6)

Hirschkop, Ken. PN75.B25.H57 1999, (v3)
Hirschman, Albert O. HD82.H489 1995, (v6)
  HF1411.H5 1980, (v6)
Hirschmann, Nancy J. JC329.5.H57 1992, (v7)
Hirsh, John C. PE64.A59.H67 1988, (v3)
Hirsh, Richard F. HD9685.U5.H568 1999, (v6)
  HD9685.U5.H57 1989, (v6)
Hirshberg, Jehoash. ML345.P3.H57 1995, (v9)
Hirst, Derek. DA390.H57 1986, (v5)
Hirst, Francis Wrigley. D651.G5.H5 1968, (v5)
Hirst, Michael. NC257.B8.H57 1988, (v9)
Hirst, Paul Q. HF1359.H575 1999, (v6)
Hischak, Thomas S. ML102.M88.H59 1995, (v9)
  PN1995.9.M86.H57 2001, (v3)
  PN2266.H53 1997, (v3)
  PN2277.N5.H57 2000, (v3)
Hiscock, Eric C. VK543.H5, (v10)
Hiscock, Walter George. PR3433.E5.Z7, (v3)
Hiscocks, Richard. DD259.7.A3.H5, (v5)
Hiscoe, Helen B. F217.A65.H57 1991, (v4)
Hise, Greg. HT394.L67.H57 1997, (v6)
Hiskett, M. BP64.A1 H57 1994, (v8)
Hislop, Codman. F127.M55.H57, (v4)
Hiss, Alger. E743.5.H54 1957, (v4)
  E743.5.H544 1988, (v4)
Historical Evaluation and Research Organization. DS798.H57 1970, (v5)
Hitakonanulaxk. E99.D2.H73 1994, (v4)
Hitch, Charles Johnston. UA23.H53, (v10)
Hitchcock, David. T210.H58 2000, (v1)
Hitchcock, Ethan Allen. E78.I5 H57 1996, (v4)
Hitchcock, H. Wiley. ML200.H58 2000, (v9)
Hitchcock, Henry Russell. NA500.H5, (v9)
  NA642.H57, (v9)
  NA680.H5 1966, (v9)
  NA702.H5, (v9)
  NA737.W7.H5 1973, (v9)
  NA967.H55, (v9)
  NA1065.H57, (v9)
Hitchcock, John L. BL53.H557 1991, (v8)
Hitchcock, Michael. DS647.S952.B554 1996, (v5)
Hitchcock, William I. DC404.H53 1998, (v5)
Hitchins, Keith. DB739.H57, (v5)
  DR241.H575 1996, (v5)
  DR250.H58 1994, (v5)
Hite, Katherine. JA74.5.H58 2000, (v7)
Hitler, Adolf. DD247.H5.A33 1940, (v5)
  DD247.H5.A57513 1990, (v5)
  DD247.H5.A664553, (v5)
  DD247.H5.A685 1953a, (v5)
Hitt, Jim. PN1995.9.W4.H48 1990, (v3)
Hitti, Philip Khuri. DS37.7.H58 1970, (v5)
Hittle, J. D. UB220.H5 1961, (v10)
Hix, Simon. JN30.H5 1999, (v7)
Hixon, Donald L. ML134.M533 H59 2000, (v9)
Hixson, Richard F. KF2750.A59.H58 1989, (v7)
Hixson, Walter L. E748.K37.H58 1989, (v4)
Hixson, William F. HC106.3.H544 1991, (v6)
  HG501.H53 1993, (v6)
Hjelte, George. GV182.H56, (v6)
Hla Myint, U. HC412.H55 1972, (v6)
Hla Myint. HB171.H646 1965, (v6)
Hladczuk, John. Z5814.I3.H56 1990, (v10)
Hlihor, Constantin. D766.4.H55 2000, (v5)
Hlophe, Stephen S. HN835.Z9.S65, (v6)
Ho, Sam P. S. HC430.5.H6, (v6)
Ho, Wendy. PS153.A84.H6 1999, (v3)
Ho, Yong. PL1241.H56 1993, (v3)
Hoadley, R. Bruce. TT180.H59 2000, (v1)
Hoag, John D. NA380.H58 1977, (v9)
Hoagland, Alison K. NA730.A4.H63 1993, (v9)
Hoagland, Mahlon B. QP511.8.H63.A3 1990, (v1)
Hoagwood, Terence Allan. PR457.H63 1996, (v3)
  PR4809.H15.H56 1995, (v3)
Hoar, William Stewart. QP33.H6 1983, (v1)
Hoare, James. DS795.3.H63 2000, (v5)
  DS916.H62 1999, (v5)
Hobart, Angela. DS647.B2.H58 1996, (v5)
Hobart, Henry. F572.K43.H6 1991, (v4)
Hobart, Michael E. QA76.9.C66.H63 1998, (v1)
Hobbelink, Henk. S494.5.B563.H63 1989, (v1)

Hobbes, Thomas. JC153.H633, **(v7)**
  JC153.H65 1996b, **(v7)**
Hobbs, James B. PE2833.H63 1999, **(v3)**
Hobbs, Joseph J. DT72.B4.H6 1989, **(v5)**
Hobbs, Peter Victor. QC861.2.H63 1995, **(v1)**
Hobbs, Philip C. D. TA1750.H63 2000, **(v1)**
Hobbs, Richard. ND553.R35.H6, **(v9)**
Hobbs, Robert Carleton. ND212.5.A25.H63 1981, **(v9)**
  ND237.A85.H6 2001, **(v9)**
  ND237.K677.H63 1993, **(v9)**
Hobbs, Sandy. HD6231.H63 1999, **(v6)**
Hobbs, Susan. N6537.D4464.A4 1996, **(v9)**
Hobbs, Thomas Hubbard. F334.A8.H62, **(v4)**
Hobden, Stephen. JZ1251.H63 1998, **(v7)**
Hoberman, J. HX40.H5673 1998, **(v6)**
Hoberman, John M. GV583.H6 1997, **(v6)**
Hoberman, Louisa Schell. HF3235.H63 1991, **(v6)**
Hoberman, Michael. GR110.M4H63 2000, **(v6)**
Hoberman, Ruth. PR888.H5.H63 1997, **(v3)**
Hobfoll, Stevan E. BF575.S75.H623 1998, **(v2)**
Hobhouse, L. T. HM276.H7 1980, **(v6)**
Hobhouse, Leonard Trelawney. BJ1311.H6 1951, **(v8)**
Hobsbaum, Philip. PR502.H55 1979, **(v3)**
Hobsbawm, E. J. D16.8.H626 1997b, **(v5)**
  D299.H6 1969, **(v5)**
  D358.H56 1975b, **(v5)**
  D359.7.H63 1987, **(v5)**
  D421.H582 1994, **(v5)**
Hobson, Charles F. KF8745.M3.H63 1996, **(v7)**
Hobson, Christopher Z. PR4148.H63, **(v3)**
  PR4148.P6.H63 1999, **(v3)**
Hobson, Fred C. F220.A1.H63 1999, **(v4)**
Hobson, J. A. HB99.3.H6 1968, **(v6)**
Hobson, J. Allan. QP411.H63 1994, **(v1)**
  QP426.H63 1988, **(v1)**
  RC454.4.H625 2001, **(v2)**
Hobson, Wes. GV1060.73.H63 2001, **(v6)**
Hoch, Charles. HV4045.H63 1989, **(v6)**
Hochachka, Peter W. QP82.H63 1984, **(v1)**
Hochhuth, Rolf. PT2668.O3.S8, **(v3)**
  PT2668.O3.S813, **(v3)**
Hochman, Barbara. PS374.R37.H64 2001, **(v3)**
  PS2473.H6 1988, **(v3)**
Hochman, Baruch. PR4592.O76.H63 1999, **(v3)**
Hochman, Elaine S. N332.G33.B4455 1997, **(v9)**
Hochman, Jhan. PN1995.9.N38.H63 1998, **(v3)**
Hochman, Jiri. DK267.H596 1984, **(v5)**
Hochman, Stanley. E838.6.H62, **(v4)**
Hochschild, Adam. DK267.H597 1994, **(v5)**
  DT655.H63 1998, **(v5)**
Höchsmann, Hyun. BL1900.C576 H63 2001, **(v8)**
Hock, Randolph. ZA4226.H63 2001, **(v10)**
Hocking, Jenny. KU110.M87.H63 1997, **(v7)**
Hocking, M. B. TP155.H58 1998, **(v1)**
Hockings, Paul. DS432.B25.H62 1999, **(v5)**
Hockney, David. N6797.H57.A4 1988a, **(v9)**
Hocutt, Max. BJ1311.H64 2000, **(v8)**
Hodapp, Robert M. RJ137.H63 1998, **(v2)**
Hodd, Michael. HC800.H633 1991, **(v6)**
Hodder, Ian. GN776.2.A1.H63 1990, **(v6)**
Hodder-Williams, Richard. JQ1872.H63 1984, **(v7)**
Hodel-Hoenes, Sigrid. DT73.T3.H5813 2000, **(v5)**
Hodes, Martha Elizabeth. HQ1075.5.U6.H63 1997, **(v6)**
Hodgdon, Barbara. PR2971.U6.H64 1998, **(v3)**
  PR2982.H56 1991, **(v3)**
Hodge, A. Trevor. DC801.M37.H63 1999, **(v5)**
Hodge, Bob. P35.5.C6H63 1998, **(v3)**
  PR25.H64 1990, **(v3)**
Hodge, Errol. HE8697.45.A8.H63 1995, **(v6)**
Hodge, Merle. PR9272.9.H6.C7 1981, **(v3)**
Hodge, Paul W. QB755.H63 1994, **(v1)**
Hodges, Andrew. QA29.T8H63 2000, **(v1)**
Hodges, C. Walter. PR2920.H6 1968, **(v3)**
  PR3095.H59 1999, **(v3)**
Hodges, Donald Clark. F2849.H6 1988, **(v4)**
  F2849.2.H63 1991, **(v4)**
  HX851.H63 1995, **(v6)**
Hodges, Gabrielle Ashford. DP264.F7 H63 2002, **(v5)**
Hodges, Graham Russell. F128.9.N3.H63 1999, **(v4)**
  F142.M7.H66 1997, **(v4)**

Hodges, Luther Hartwell. F260.H63, **(v4)**
Hodges, Michael P. B3376.W564.H63 2000, **(v8)**
Hodges, Richard. DA152.H59 1989, **(v5)**
Hodges, William F. RJ507.D59H63 1991, **(v2)**
Hodgetts, Richard M. HD62.15.H623 1998, **(v6)**
Hodgkin, Thomas. DA30.P762 vol. 1, **(v5)**
Hodgkins, Christopher. PR3508.H64 1993, **(v3)**
Hodgson, Godfrey. E748.S883.H63 1990, **(v4)**
Hodgson, Godfrey. JC573.2.U6.H63 1996, **(v7)**
Hodgson, James D. HD58.6.H63 2000, **(v6)**
Hodgson, Peter John. ML134.B85.H63 1996, **(v9)**
Hodgson, William Hope. PR6015.O253 N5 1976, **(v3)**
Hodkinson, Yvonne. PR9188.H63 1991, **(v3)**
Hoebel, E. Adamson. E99.C53.H6 1978, **(v4)**
Hoecker-Drysdale, Susan. HM22.G8.M344 1992, **(v6)**
Hoedemaker, L. A. BT83.7.H64 1998, **(v8)**
Hoefte, Rosemarijn. HD4875.S75.H64 1998, **(v6)**
Hoehling, A. A. E473.2.H57, **(v4)**
Hoel, Paul Gerhard. QA276.H57 1984, **(v1)**
Hoel, Sigurd. PT8950.H58.T713 1991, **(v3)**
Hoeller, Hildegard. PS3545.H16.Z664 2000, **(v3)**
Hoelscher, Steven D. F589.N5.H64 1998, **(v4)**
Hoen, Herman Willem. HC244.H565 1998, **(v6)**
Hoensch, Jorg K. DB945.H5613 1988, **(v5)**
Hoermann, Roland. PT1809.Z5.H63 1984, **(v3)**
Hoernle, Reinhold Friedrich Alfred. B4695.H63 S8, **(v8)**
Hoerr, John P. LD2120.H64 1997, **(v7)**
Hoerth, Alfred J. BS621.H56 1998, **(v8)**
Hoeveler, Diane Long. PR585.A49.H6 1990, **(v3)**
Hoeveler, J. David. JA84.U5.H63 1990, **(v7)**
Hoff, Joan. KF4758.H64 1990, **(v7)**
Hoffa, James R. HD6515.T3.H6, **(v6)**
Hoffbeck, Steven R. SB198, **(v1)**
Hoffe, Otfried. JC578.H6313 1995, **(v7)**
Hoffecker, Carol E. F164.H62, **(v4)**
Hoffer, Peter Charles. KF361.H63 1992, **(v7)**
  KF399.H59 1990, **(v7)**
  KFM2478.8.W5.H64 1996, **(v7)**
  KFM2478.8.W5.H645 1997, **(v7)**
Hoffert, Robert W. JK131.H64 1992, **(v7)**
Hoffert, Sylvia D. HQ1236.5.U6.H64 1995, **(v6)**
Hoffman, Alice M. D811.H648 1990, **(v5)**
Hoffman, Andrew J. HD30.255.H638 2000, **(v6)**
Hoffman, Anne Golomb. PJ5053.A4.Z614 1991, **(v3)**
Hoffman, Antoni. QE721.H64 1989, **(v1)**
Hoffman, Arthur W. PR3424.H6 1962, **(v3)**
Hoffman, Beatrix Rebecca. HG9396.H638 2001, **(v6)**
Hoffman, Betty N. F104.H3.H64 2001, **(v4)**
Hoffman, Bob. GV546.H6, **(v6)**
Hoffman, Bruce. HV6431.H626 1998, **(v6)**
Hoffman, Charlene. LC2781.H64 1992, **(v7)**
Hoffman, Charles Anthony. R154.H62.A33, **(v2)**
Hoffman, Daniel N. KF4550.H63 1997, **(v7)**
Hoffman, Daniel. D790.H64 2000, **(v5)**
Hoffman, Edward. BF109.M33.H63 1988, **(v2)**
Hoffman, F. G. UA23.H5344 1996, **(v10)**
Hoffman, Frederick John. PN49.H6 1957, **(v3)**
  PR6003.E282.Z68, **(v3)**
  PR6023.A93.Z6315, **(v3)**
Hoffman, John. JC327.G417 2001, **(v7)**
Hoffman, Lawrence A. BM705.H63 1996, **(v8)**
Hoffman, Malvina. NB1140.H6, **(v9)**
Hoffman, Michael A. GN865.E3.H63 1979, **(v6)**
Hoffman, Miles. ML108.H64 1997, **(v9)**
Hoffman, Paul E. F212.H64 1990, **(v4)**
  F314.H75 2002, **(v4)**
Hoffman, Paul. QA7.H72 1988, **(v1)**
  QA29.E68.H64 1998, **(v1)**
Hoffman, Philip T. HD1943.H64 1996, **(v6)**
Hoffman, Piotr. B844.H65 1989, **(v8)**
Hoffman, Robert Louis. DC354.H63, **(v5)**
Hoffman, Ronald. HC107.M3.H63, **(v6)**
Hoffman, Valerie J. BP188.8.E3.H64 1995, **(v8)**
Hoffmann, Ary A. QH456.H64 1991, **(v1)**
  QH546.H63 1997, **(v1)**
Hoffmann, Banesh. LB3051.H68, **(v7)**
Hoffmann, Charles G. F292.B85.A753 1988, **(v4)**
Hoffmann, Charles. HC105.H8 1970, **(v6)**
Hoffmann, E. T. A. PT2360.A1 1924, **(v3)**
  PT2360.A1 1985, **(v3)**

  PT2360.A3, **(v3)**
  PT2360.T48, **(v3)**
Hoffmann, Edmond de. QD96.M3.H6413 1996, **(v1)**
Hoffmann, Frank W. ML128.R6.H6, **(v9)**
  Z658.U5.H64 1989, **(v10)**
  Z1223.Z7.B35 1998, **(v10)**
  Z1361.C6.H64 1995, **(v10)**
Hoffmann, Henryk. PN1998.2.H625 2000, **(v3)**
Hoffmann, Hilmar. PN1995.9.N36.H6413 1996, **(v3)**
Hoffmann, Joyce. PN4874.W517.H64 1995, **(v3)**
Hoffmann, Leon-Francois. PQ3948.5.H2.H64 1984, **(v3)**
Hoffmann, Peter. DD247.S342.H6413 1995, **(v5)**
  DD256.3.H59513 1988, **(v5)**
Hoffmann, Roald. QD37.H612 1995, **(v1)**
Hofheinz, Thomas C. PR6019.O9.F59352 1995, **(v3)**
Hofman, Andre A. HC125.H645 1999, **(v6)**
Hofmann, Karl Heinrich. QA387.H636 1998, **(v1)**
Hofmann, Werner. ND588.F75.H629 2000, **(v9)**
Hofmann, Werner. TS1890.H69313 1989, **(v1)**
Hofmannsthal, Hugo von. PT2617.O47.A16 1950, **(v3)**
  PT2617.O47.A19 1953, **(v3)**
  PT2617.O47.A233, **(v3)**
  PT2617.O47.A24, **(v3)**
Hofrenning, Daniel J. B. BL2525.H65 1995, **(v8)**
Hofstadter, Douglas R. QA9.8.H63, **(v1)**
Hofstadter, Richard. E169.1.H74, **(v4)**
  E175.45.H6, **(v4)**
  E178.H728, **(v4)**
  E179.H8 1970, **(v4)**
  E179.5.H62, **(v4)**
  E183.H67 1973, **(v4)**
  E743.H63, **(v4)**
  E743.H632, **(v4)**
  JK2260.H73, **(v7)**
Hofstede, Geert H. HM258.H574 1991, **(v6)**
Hofstetter, Eleanore O. Z7164.I3.H62 2001, **(v10)**
Hogan, Ben. GV965.H59, **(v6)**
Hogan, David W. UA34.R36.H64 1992, **(v10)**
Hogan, Linda. BD581.H573 1995, **(v8)**
  BT83.55.H64 1995, **(v8)**
Hogan, Michael J. HC240.H614 1987, **(v6)**
Hogan, Patrick Colm. PN98.P64.H64 1990, **(v3)**
  PR6019.O9.Z587 1995, **(v3)**
  PR9080.H64 2000, **(v3)**
Hogan, Rex. QA76.9.D26.H64 1990, **(v1)**
Hogan, Richard. HN79.C6.H64 1990, **(v6)**
Hogan, Robert Goode. PR8789.H62, **(v3)**
  PR8789.H62 vol. 6, **(v3)**
Hogan, Roseann Reinemuth. F450.H64 1992, **(v4)**
Hogan, Steve. HQ75.H63 1998, **(v6)**
Hogan, W. P. HG3897.H63 1982, **(v6)**
Hogan, William Ransom. F390.H6, **(v4)**
Hoganson, Kristin L. E721.H69 1998, **(v4)**
Hogarth, William. NE642.H6.A4 1970, **(v9)**
Hogben, Lancelot Thomas. QA21.H729 1961, **(v1)**
  QA36.H6 1951, **(v1)**
Hoge, Dean R. BR526.H64 1994, **(v8)**
Hogeland, Lisa Maria. PS374.F45.H64 1998, **(v3)**
Hogg, Ian V. D25.A2.H64 1995, **(v5)**
  UG401.H66 1977, **(v10)**
Hogg, James. PR4791.A4 1970, **(v3)**
  PR4791.P7 1969, **(v3)**
Hoggan, Daniel H. GB656.2.E43.H64 1989, **(v6)**
Hogler, Raymond L. KF3369.H64 1992, **(v7)**
Hogrefe, Jeffrey. N6537.O39.H64 1992, **(v9)**
Hogue, Charles Leonard. QL476.5.H64 1993, **(v1)**
Hogue, W. Lawrence. PS153.M56.H64 1996, **(v3)**
Hogwood, Christopher. ML410.H13.H57 1985, **(v9)**
Hoh, LaVahn G. GV1803.H64 1990, **(v6)**
Hohenberg, John. DS126.5.H58 1998, **(v5)**
  E888.H65 1997, **(v4)**
  PN4784.F6.H6 1995, **(v3)**
Hohne, Heinz. DD253.6.H613 1970, **(v5)**
Hoidal, Oddvar K. DL529.Q5.H6513 1989, **(v5)**
Hoig, Stan. E99.C5.H7 1998, **(v4)**
  E99.K5 K535 2000, **(v4)**
  F704.F69, **(v4)**
Hoisington, William A. DT324.H54 1984, **(v5)**
Hoke, Jacob. E475.5.H72 1959, **(v4)**
Holberton, Paul. NA1123.P2.A66, **(v9)**

Holbl, Gunther. DT92.H6513 2001, **(v5)**
Holbrook, David. PR635.W6.H65 1989, **(v3)**
  PR4592.W6.H63 1993, **(v3)**
  PR6023.A93.Z6316 1991, **(v3)**
  PR6023.E926.Z675 1991, **(v3)**
Holbrook, Morris B. PN1992.8.Q5.H65 1993, **(v3)**
Holbrook, Thomas M. JK524.H65 1996, **(v7)**
Holbrooke, Richard C. DR1313.7.D58.H65 1998, **(v5)**
Holcombe, Charles. DS514.H65 2001, **(v5)**
Holcombe, Lee. KD760.H64 1983, **(v7)**
Holcombe, Randall G. HB135.H63 1989, **(v6)**
Holcombe, Susan. HC440.8.Z9.P6155 1995, **(v6)**
Holdaway, Simon. HV8195.A2.H65 1996, **(v6)**
Holden, Alan. QD921.H58 1982, **(v1)**
Holden, Andrew. G155.A1.H64 2000, **(v6)**
Holden, Barry. JC423.H7444 1988, **(v7)**
Holden, G. TS1928.H65 2000, **(v1)**
Holden, George W. BF723.P25.H65 1997, **(v2)**
Holden, J. H. W. SB123.3.H65 1993, **(v1)**
Holden, Lynn. GN471.4.H65 2000, **(v6)**
Holden, Martin. QE392.H65 1991, **(v1)**
Holden, Philip. PR6025.A86.Z613 1996, **(v3)**
Holden, William Curry. F391.H78 1998, **(v4)**
Holder, Alan. PE1505.H58 1995, **(v3)**
Holder, Harold D. HV5035.H65 1998, **(v6)**
Holderlin, Friedrich. PT2359.H2.A6 1967, **(v3)**
  PT2359.H2.A6 1988, **(v3)**
  PT2359.H2 1975, **(v3)**
Holderness, Graham. PR2832.H65 1989, **(v3)**
Holderness-Roddam, Jane. SF294.2.H65 1988, **(v1)**
Holdheim, William W. PQ2211.C24.H6 1961, **(v3)**
Holdridge, Jefferson. PR5907, **(v3)**
Holdridge, John H. E183.8.C6.H65 1997, **(v4)**
Holdstock, Robert. PR6058.O442.M9 1984, **(v3)**
Holdstock, T. Len. BF108.A3.H65 2000, **(v2)**
Holian, Timothy J. D769.8.F7.G47 1996, **(v5)**
Holiday, Billie. ML420.H58.A3 1984, **(v9)**
Holl, Adolf. BT123.H6513 1998, **(v8)**
Holl, Jack M. QC789.2.U62.A754 1997, **(v1)**
Holl, Karl. BR307.H643, **(v8)**
Holladay, William Lee. PJ4833.H6, **(v3)**
Hollan, Douglas Wood. DS632.T7.H65 1994, **(v5)**
Holland, C.H. (Charles Hepworth). QB209.H57 1999, **(v1)**
Holland, Charles Donald. TP149.H64 1989, **(v1)**
Holland, Clive. G606.H66 1994, **(v6)**
Holland, Dorothy C. LC1756.H65 1990, **(v7)**
Holland, F. Ross. F128.63.H65 1993, **(v4)**
  VK1023.H65, **(v10)**
Holland, Heidi. JQ1998.A4 H65 1990, **(v7)**
Holland, Heinrich D. QC879.6.H63 1984, **(v1)**
Holland, Israel Irving. SD373.H65 1997, **(v1)**
Holland, James. ML1030.H64 1981, **(v9)**
Holland, John H. QA401.H527 1998, **(v1)**
Holland, Nancy J. BJ1418.5.H65 1998, **(v8)**
Holland, Norman Norwood. PN56.P92.H6, **(v3)**
  PR3432.H6, **(v3)**
Holland, Patrick. PR808.T72.H65 1998, **(v3)**
Holland, Peter. PR3106.H65 1997, **(v3)**
Holland, W. L. DS518.1.H6, **(v5)**
Hollander, Anne. N8217.C63.H64 1978, **(v9)**
Hollander, Paul. E839.H65 1995, **(v4)**
Hollander, Robert. PQ4335.H63 2001, **(v3)**
Hollander, Stanley C. HF5415.127.H65 1992, **(v6)**
Hollandsworth, James G. E540.N3.H65 1995, **(v4)**
  F379.N557.H65 2001, **(v4)**
  RC514.H59 1990, **(v2)**
Holldobler, Bert. QL568.F7.H57 1990, **(v1)**
Holldobler, Bert. QL568.F7.H575 1994, **(v1)**
Holledge, Julie. PN1590.W64.H65 2000, **(v3)**
Holleman, Warren Lee. JC585.H755 1987, **(v7)**
Hollenbach, David. BJ1249.H578 2002, **(v8)**
Hollenberg, Donna Krolik. PS3507.O726.Z74 1991, **(v3)**
Holler, Clyde. E99.O3.H65 1995, **(v4)**
Holler, Frederick L. Z7161.H64 1986, **(v10)**
Holleran, Michael. F73.37.H5 1998, **(v4)**
Hollerman, Leon. HF1601.H6, **(v6)**
Holley, Donald. HD210.M55.H64, **(v6)**
Holley, I. B. UG633.H6 1971, **(v10)**
Holli, Melvin G. F548.54.W36.H65 1989, **(v4)**

Holliday, Carl. PJ307.H6, **(v3)**
Holliday, Keith. QB43.2.H65 1999, **(v1)**
Holliday, Paul. SB728.H65 1998, **(v1)**
Holliday, R. QP86.H65 1995, **(v1)**
Hollinger, David A. B945.C54 H64, **(v8)**
Hollinger, Mannfred A. RM300.H65 2003, **(v2)**
Hollinger, Robert. JC574.H64 1996, **(v7)**
Hollings, Robert L. KF2900.A1.P76 1997, **(v7)**
Hollingsworth, Keith. PR868.C7.H6, **(v3)**
Hollingsworth, Sandra. LB1576.H627 1994, **(v7)**
Hollingsworth, Thomas Henry. HB881.H625, **(v6)**
Hollington, Michael. PT2613.R338.Z67, **(v3)**
Hollingworth, Harry Levi. BF47.H6, **(v2)**
Hollis, Martin. BC177.H65 1987, **(v8)**
Hollis, Richard. NC998.H65 1994, **(v9)**
Hollon, W. Eugene. F786.H6, **(v4)**
Holloran, Peter C. HV885.B7.H65 1989, **(v6)**
Hollos, Marida. DT515.45.I35.H65 1989, **(v5)**
Holloway, David. UA770.H63 1983, **(v10)**
  UA770.H632 1994, **(v10)**
Holloway, John H. QD162.H6, **(v1)**
Holloway, John. PR502.H58, **(v3)**
  PR2983.H6 1963, **(v3)**
Holloway, Joseph E. PE3102.N4.H65 1993, **(v3)**
Holloway, Karla F. C. PS153.N5.H65 1992, **(v3)**
Holloway, R. Ross. DG63.H57 1994, **(v5)**
Holloway, Thomas H. HV8185.R5.H65 1993, **(v6)**
Holly, Carol. PS2123.H63 1995, **(v3)**
Holly, David C. HE630.C4.H65 1991, **(v6)**
Holly, Michael Ann. N7483.P3.H64 1984, **(v9)**
Holm, Bill. TR849.C87.H64 1980, **(v1)**
Holm, Jean. Z7833.H66 1991, **(v10)**
Holm, Jeanne. UB418.W65.H64 1982, **(v10)**
Holm, Soren. R724.H59 1997, **(v2)**
Holman, J. Alan. QE862.O6.H65 2000, **(v1)**
  QE867.H63 1998, **(v1)**
  QE867.H65 1995, **(v1)**
Holman, J. K. ML410.W22.H65 1996, **(v9)**
Holman, Peter. ML410.P93.H63 1994, **(v9)**
Holman, Peter. ML756.H64 1993, **(v9)**
Holmberg, Arthur. PN2287.W494.H65 1996, **(v3)**
Holmberg, David H. DS493.9.T35.H65 1989, **(v5)**
Holmes, Anne. PQ2323.L8.Z67 1993, **(v3)**
Holmes, Brian. LA133.H64, **(v7)**
Holmes, David L. RC553.A88H64 1997, **(v2)**
Holmes, Diana. PQ149.H65 1996, **(v3)**
Holmes, Douglas R. D2009.H65 2000, **(v5)**
Holmes, Gwendolyn. TD191.5.H65 1993, **(v1)**
Holmes, John Clellon. PS3558.O3594.G6 1977, **(v3)**
Holmes, John Wendell. F1034.2.H63, **(v4)**
Holmes, Larry E. LA831.8.H65 1991, **(v7)**
Holmes, Linda Goetz. D805.J3 H58 2001, **(v5)**
Holmes, Louis A. F666.R7, **(v4)**
Holmes, Marjorie. CT275.H645515.A38, **(v5)**
Holmes, Martin. HC256.6.H545 1989, **(v6)**
Holmes, Megan. ND623.L7.H65 1999, **(v9)**
Holmes, Oliver W. B4568.O74.H63, **(v8)**
Holmes, Oliver Wendell. E601.H73 2000, **(v4)**
  K588.H65 1881, **(v7)**
  KF213.H6.N68 1995, **(v7)**
  KF8745.H6.A434 1994, **(v7)**
  PS1950.F72, **(v3)**
  PS1960.A1 1961, **(v3)**
Holmes, Richard. PR4483.H57 1990, **(v3)**
Holmes, Robert L. U22.H65 1989, **(v10)**
Holmes, Ronald M. HV6529.H644 1994, **(v6)**
Holmes, Stephen R. BX7260.E3.H59, **(v8)**
Holmes, Stephen. JC229.C8.H64 1984, **(v7)**
Holmes-Siedle, A. G. QC475.H59 1993, **(v1)**
Holmgren, Noel H. QK117.H65 1998, **(v1)**
Holmgren, Richard A. QA614.8.H65 1994, **(v1)**
Holmquist, June Drenning. F607.H6 1972, **(v4)**
Holmstrom, Lynda Lytle. HQ535.H58, **(v6)**
Holoman, D. Kern. ML410.B5.H58 1989, **(v9)**
  MT125.H62 1992, **(v9)**
Holroyd, Michael. PR5366.H56 1998, **(v3)**
  PR6037.T73.Z69 1968, **(v3)**
  PR6037.T73.Z693 1995, **(v3)**
Holst, Arthur W. SB409.8.C36.H65 1999, **(v1)**
Holsti, K. J. U21.2.H627 1990, **(v10)**
  U21.2.H62723 1996, **(v10)**

Holsti, Ole R. E840.H592 1996, **(v4)**
Holstun, James. PR435.H65 2000, **(v3)**
Holst-Warhaft, Gail. GT3390.H65 2000, **(v6)**
Holt, Charles A. QC631.H72, **(v1)**
Holt, Charles Michael. TK151.H67 1995, **(v1)**
Holt, Daniel M. E621.H76 1994, **(v4)**
Holt, David. E568.5 16th.H65 1995, **(v4)**
Holt, Edwin B. BJ45.H7, **(v8)**
Holt, Elizabeth Basye (Gilmore). N5303.H762, **(v9)**
  N6450.H62 1980, **(v9)**
Holt, Frank Lee. DS374.B28.H66 1999, **(v5)**
Holt, John Caldwell. LB885.H6394 1972, **(v7)**
  LB885.H64 1970, **(v7)**
  LB1060.H64 1983, **(v7)**
  LB1060.H66 1989, **(v7)**
  LB3063.H627 1995, **(v7)**
Holt, Mack P. DC111.3.H65 1995, **(v5)**
Holt, Marilyn Irvin. HV985.H65 1992, **(v6)**
Holt, Marion Peter. PQ6115.H65, **(v3)**
Holt, Michael F. E415.7.H74, **(v4)**
  E415.7.H75 1991, **(v4)**
  JK2331.H63 1999, **(v7)**
Holt, P. M. DS63.H62 1966a, **(v5)**
Holt, Rackham. S417.C3.H6 1963, **(v1)**
Holt, Richard. GV605.H65 1989, **(v6)**
Holt, Robert R. BF173.H737 1989, **(v2)**
Holt, Ronald L. E99.P2.H65 1992, **(v4)**
Holt, Sharon Ann. F262.G85.H66 2000, **(v4)**
Holte, James Craig. BV4930.H65 1992, **(v8)**
Holthusen, Hans Egon. PT1187.H63, **(v3)**
  PT2635.I65.Z7425 1952, **(v3)**
Holton, Gerald James. Q175.H7748 1993, **(v1)**
Holton, James R. QC880.H65 1979, **(v1)**
Holton, Milne. PG1595.E3.H65 1988, **(v3)**
Holtzman, Linda. P94.5.M552.U646 2000, **(v3)**
Holtzman, Neil A. RB155.H59 1989, **(v2)**
Holum, Kenneth G. DG322.H64 1982, **(v5)**
Holy, Ladislav. DB2238.7.H65 1996, **(v5)**
  DT155.2.B47.H65 1991, **(v5)**
Holyoak, Keith James. BD190.H65 1995, **(v8)**
Holzbock, Werner G. TJ211.H65 1986, **(v1)**
Holzer, Burghild Nina. PN4390.H65 1994, **(v3)**
Holzknecht, Karl Julius. PR2894.H6, **(v3)**
Holzman, Franklyn D. HF3496.5.H62 1987, **(v6)**
Holzman, Lois. LC46.4.H65 1997, **(v7)**
Homan, Lynn M. UG834.A37.H64 2001, **(v10)**
Homan, Sidney. PR6003.E282.Z6844 1992, **(v3)**
  PR6066.I53.O434 1993, **(v3)**
Homans, Margaret. DA533.H74 1998, **(v5)**
Homberger, Eric. F128.3.H65 1994, **(v4)**
  F128.44.H755 1994, **(v4)**
  HX84.R4.H66 1990, **(v6)**
Hombs, Mary Ellen. HV95.H554 1996, **(v6)**
  HV4505.H647 1990, **(v6)**
Homburg, Cornelia. ND550.H66 2001, **(v9)**
Homer, William Innes. N6537.E3.H65 1992, **(v9)**
  ND237.R8.H66 1989, **(v9)**
Homer, Winslow. ND237.H7.A4 1990b, **(v9)**
Homer. PA4025.A2.F5, **(v3)**
  PA4025.A5.M36 1990, **(v3)**
Homer-Dixon, Thomas F. HM846.H663 2000, **(v6)**
Homerin, Th. Emil. PJ7755.I18.Z68 1994, **(v3)**
Homerus. PR3621.B82 vol. 7-8, **(v3)**
Homo, Leon Pol. JC83.H74 1962, **(v7)**
Homolka, Walter. BM538.P3.H6613 1994, **(v8)**
Homsher, Deborah. HV7436.H65 2001, **(v6)**
Homuth, Donald. ML128.V5.H66 1994, **(v9)**
Homza, Lu Ann. BX1584.H66 2000, **(v8)**
Honan, Park. PR2894.H65 1998, **(v3)**
  PR4036.H66 1988, **(v3)**
Honda, Katsuichi. DS777.5316.N36 H6613 1999, **(v5)**
Honderich, Ted. B1646.H764, **(v8)**
  BJ1461.H57 2002, **(v8)**
Hondros, John Louis. D802.G8.H66 1983, **(v5)**
Hone, Ralph E. PR6037.A95.Z73, **(v3)**
Hones, Donald F. LC3731.H635 1999, **(v7)**
Honey, Martha. G156.5.E26.H66 1999, **(v6)**
Honey, Michael K. HD6519.M45.H66 1993, **(v6)**
  HD8081.A65.H66 1999, **(v6)**
Honeycombe, R. W. K. TA460.H57 1984, **(v1)**
  TN693.I7.H65 1996, **(v1)**

Honeycutt, James M. BF575.I5H66 2001, (v2)
Honeygold, Derek. HG3821.H63 1989, (v6)
Honeygosky, Stephen R. PR3592.R4.H66 1993, (v3)
Honeyman, Katrina. HQ1599.E5.K37 2000, (v6)
Hong, Junhao. PN1992.3.C6.H66 1998, (v3)
Hong, Nathaniel J. B4375.K54 2000, (v8)
Honig, Bonnie. JA71.H62 1993, (v7)
Honig, Emily. DS796.S29.H66 1992, (v5)
   HQ1767.H65 1988, (v6)
Honigmann, E. A. J. PR2976.H58 1989, (v3)
   PR2983.H63, (v3)
Honigsberg, Peter Jan. F376.H66 2000, (v4)
Honigsheim, Paul. H59.W4.H65 2000, (v6)
Honneth, Axel. HM136.H59813 1995, (v6)
Honnighausen, Lothar. PR468.S9.H66 1988, (v3)
   PS3511.A86.Z829 1997, (v3)
Honolka, Kurt. ML423.S346.H613 1990, (v9)
Honore, Tony. KD662.H66 1995, (v7)
   KJA420.H66 1998, (v7)
Honour, Hugh. N5300.H68 1999, (v9)
Honsberger, Ross. QA7.H773 1991, (v1)
Honsberger, Ross. QA43.H63 1996, (v1)
   QA43.H633 1997, (v1)
   QA241.H63, (v1)
   QA471.H76 1995, (v1)
Hood, Clifton. TF847.N5.H66 1993, (v1)
Hood, Thomas. PR4798.A44 1972, (v3)
Hood, William. ND623.F5.H66 1993, (v9)
Hoogbergen, Wim S. M. F2423.H66 1990, (v4)
Hoogenboom, Ari Arthur. E681.H69 1988, (v4)
   E682.H78 1995, (v4)
Hoogland, John L. QL737.R68.H65 1995, (v1)
Hoogland, Renee C. PN56.L45.H66 1997, (v3)
   PR6003.O6757.Z672 1994, (v3)
Hooijmans, Pieter W. TK5103.59.H66 1994, (v1)
Hook, J. N. CS2487.H66 1982, (v5)
   PE1591.H66 1990, (v3)
Hook, Jonathan B. E99.A4.H66 1997, (v4)
Hook, Sidney. B945.D44.H47 1971, (v8)
   B945.H68 1971, (v8)
   B3305.M74.H6 1994, (v8)
   H61.H68, (v6)
   HB501.M5.H6, (v6)
Hook, Steven W. E744.S8 2000, (v4)
Hooker, Brad. BJ1031.H755 2000, (v8)
Hooker, J. T. DF220.H65, (v5)
Hooker, Virginia Matheson. PL5134.H66 2000, (v3)
Hooks, Bell. E185.615.H645 1995, (v4)
   E185.86.H73 1984, (v4)
   E185.86.H734 1992, (v4)
   HN90.S6.H66 2000, (v6)
   LC196.H66 1994, (v7)
Hookway, Christopher. B945.P44 H67 2000, (v8)
Hoole, William Stanley. PS1999.H25.Z6, (v3)
Hoon, Elizabeth Evelynola. HJ6891.H65, (v6)
Hooper, David. GV1445.H616 1992, (v6)
Hooper, Edwin Bickford. VA55.H66 1988, (v10)
Hooper, Osman Castle. PN4897.O33H6, (v3)
Hoopes, Donelson F. ND1839.E2.H6, (v9)
Hoopes, James. BF108.U5.H66 1989, (v2)
   JC574.2.U6.H66 1998, (v7)
Hoopes, Townsend. JZ4986.H66 1997, (v7)
Hoople, Robin P. PS2116.T83.H66 1997, (v3)
   PS2124.H647 2000, (v3)
Hooton, Earnest Albert. GN24.H7, (v6)
   HV6035.H65 1969, (v6)
Hooton, Joy W. Z4021.H66 1992, (v10)
Hoover, Dwight W. PN1995.9.D6.H64 1992, (v3)
Hoover, Herbert T. Z1210.D3.H66 1993, (v10)
Hoover, Herbert. D637.H6 1959, (v5)
   D643.A7.H7, (v5)
   D743.9.H68, (v5)
   E767.H78 1992, (v4)
   E801.H64 1971, (v4)
   E802.A3 1986, (v4)
   E802.A35 1979, (v4)
   E802.H7, (v4)
   HC106.3.H6149 1972, (v6)
Hoover, Irwin Hood. E716.1.H78, (v4)
Hoover, Kevin D. HB172.5.H66 1988, (v6)
Hoover, Stewart M. BV656.3.H66 1988, (v8)

Hopcroft, Rosemary L. HD1333.E85 H66 1999, (v6)
Hope, Augustine. QC494.2.H67 1990, (v1)
Hope, Jeremy. HD30.335.H67 1997, (v6)
Hope, Kempe R. HC59.7.H655 1996, (v6)
   HC930.H67 1997, (v6)
Hope, Nicholas. BX4844.H66 1995, (v8)
Hope, T. E. PC2582.I8.H6 1971b, (v3)
Hope, W. H. St. John (William Henry St. John).
   CR1612.H7 1953, (v6)
Hope, W. Martin. F259.H83 1997, (v4)
Hope, Warren. PR2937.H66 1992, (v3)
Hopf, Ted. JX1391.H65 1994, (v7)
Hopkin, Stephen P. QL449.6.H67 1992, (v1)
Hopkins, Andrea. PR365.H57 1990, (v3)
Hopkins, Bruce R. KF1389.5.H66 1991, (v7)
Hopkins, David. N6512.H657 2000, (v9)
Hopkins, Donald R. RC183.1.H66 2002, (v2)
Hopkins, Dwight N. BT82.7.H663 2000, (v8)
Hopkins, Edward Washburn. BJ122.H6 1968, (v8)
Hopkins, Gerald. TK5103.75.H67 1995, (v1)
Hopkins, Gerard Manley. PR4803.H44.A12 1959, (v3)
   PR4803.H44.A16 1959, (v3)
   PR4803.H44.A17 1989, (v3)
   PR4803.H44.A6 1986, (v3)
   PR4803.H44.A6 1989, (v3)
   PR4803.H44.A6 1991, (v3)
   PR4803.H44.Z48 1990, (v3)
Hopkins, Harry Lloyd. HV91.H6, (v6)
Hopkins, James K. DP269.47.B7.H66 1998, (v5)
Hopkins, June. HV28.H66.H66 1999, (v6)
Hopkins, Kevin R. HF5549.5.M3.H66 1991, (v6)
Hopkins, Lisa. PR2527.H66 1994, (v3)
   PR2673.H59 2000, (v3)
   PR3069.M32.H66 1998, (v3)
Hopkins, MaryCarol. E184.K45.H66 1996, (v4)
Hopkins, W. Wat. KF213.B73.H66 1991, (v7)
   KF1266.H64 1989, (v7)
Hopkinson, Michael. DA963.H63 1988, (v5)
Hopp, Glenn. PN1998.H66 1999, (v3)
Hoppen, K. Theodore. DA560.H58 1998, (v5)
   DA950.H68 1984, (v5)
Hoppensteadt, F. C. QP363.3.H67 1997, (v1)
Hopper, Edward. ND237.H75.A4 1980, (v9)
   ND237.H75.G6 1971, (v9)
   NE539.H65.A4 1979, (v9)
Hopper, Isaac T. F158.9.N4.H67 1994, (v4)
Hoppin, Richard H. ML172.H8, (v9)
Hoppit, Julian. HG3769.G73.E54 1987, (v6)
Hopwood, Keith. Z6207.G7.H67 1995, (v10)
Horace. PA6164.H713, (v3)
   PA6394.A54 1999, (v3)
   PA6394.S48 1983, (v3)
Horan, Patrick N. PR5827.M64.H67 1997, (v3)
Horatius Flaccus, Quintus. PA6156.H6.A4, (v3)
Hordeski, Michael F. TK7887.5.H668 1995, (v1)
Horenstein, Mark N. TK7874.H675 1996, (v1)
Horgan, A. D. PR3537.L33.H67 1994, (v3)
Horgan, John. DA965.R63.H67 1997, (v5)
   Q175.H794 1996, (v1)
   RC343.H636 1999, (v2)
Horgan, Paul. E123.H65, (v4)
   F392.R5 H65 1991, (v4)
   F790.A1 H6, (v4)
   PS3515.O6583 E9, (v3)
Horiguchi, Sutemi. SB466.J3.K6 1963, (v1)
Horio, Teruhisa. LA1311.H66 1988, (v7)
Horisch, Jochen. PN56.M547.H6713 2000, (v3)
Horle, Craig W. KD4102.Q3.H67 1988, (v7)
Horlick, Allan Stanley. LA205.H57 1994, (v7)
Horn, Barbara Lee. PN2287.S6793.H67 1993, (v3)
   PS3515.E343.Z72 1998, (v3)
Horn, Bernard. PJ5054.Y42.Z54 1997, (v3)
Horn, David Bayne. DA47.H6, (v5)
Horn, David. ML120.U5.H7 Suppl. 1, (v9)
   ML120.U5 H7, (v9)
Horn, Delton T. TK7816.H69 1994, (v1)
Horn, Gerd-Rainer. HX238.H67 1996, (v6)
Horn, James P. P. F187.C5.H66 1994, (v4)
Horn, Jason Gary. PS1342.P74.H67 1996, (v3)
Horn, Margo. RJ501.A2.H67 1989, (v2)
Horn, Michiel. F1035.D8.H67 1992, (v4)

Horn, Murray J. JF1411.H67 1995, (v7)
Horn, Pamela. HD1534.H59, (v6)
   HN398.E5.H68 1987, (v6)
Horn, Rebecca. F1219.1.M5.H67 1997, (v4)
Horn, Stanley Fitzgerald. E668.H78 1969b, (v4)
Hornback, Bert G. PR4662.H67 1988, (v3)
Hornblower, Simon. DF227.H67 1983, (v5)
   DF229.T6.H65 1991, (v5)
   DF229.T6.H67 1987, (v5)
Hornblum, Allen M. R853.H8.H67 1998, (v2)
Hornby, Richard. PN2061.H645 1992, (v3)
Horne, Aaron. ML128.W5.H62 1996, (v9)
   ML128.W5.H65 1990, (v9)
Horne, Alistair. D545.V3.H6, (v5)
   DA566.9.M33.H6 1989, (v5)
   UA702.H67 1984, (v10)
Horne, Esther Burnett. E99.S4.H67 1998, (v4)
Horne, Gerald. F869.L89.N4 1995, (v4)
   HX84.D28.H67 1993, (v6)
   PN1993.5.U65.H67 2001, (v3)
Horne, James. QP426.H67 1988, (v1)
Horne, John N. HD6687.H67 1990, (v6)
Horne, Lena. ML420.H65 A3 1986, (v9)
Horner, Avril. PR6007.U47.Z67 1998, (v3)
Horner, Harlan Hoyt. E457.2.H79, (v4)
Horner, Helmut. D805.A2.H67 1991, (v5)
Horner, Shari. PR179.W65, (v3)
   PR179.W65H67 2001, (v3)
Horney, Karen. BF173.H7625, (v2)
   BF173.U55 2000, (v2)
   RC343.H65, (v2)
   RC509.H67 1987, (v2)
Hornsby, Alton. E185.H64 1991, (v4)
Hornsby, Joseph Allen. PR1933.L38.H67 1988, (v3)
Hornung, Clarence Pearson. NK805.H67, (v9)
Hornung, E. W. PR6015.O687 R3, (v3)
Hornung, Erik. B141.H6713 1992, (v8)
   BL2443.H6613 1999, (v8)
Horobin, Richard W. QH613.H67 1988, (v1)
Horonjeff, Robert. TL725.3.P5H6 1994, (v1)
Horowitz, Dan. JQ1825.P3.H68 1989, (v7)
Horowitz, Daniel. HC110.C6.H58 1985, (v6)
   HM22.U6.P274 1994, (v6)
Horowitz, David A. E743.H679 1997, (v4)
Horowitz, Donald L. HV6474.H67 2001, (v6)
Horowitz, Edward. PJ4567.H66 1967, (v3)
Horowitz, Helen Lefkowitz. LC1756.H67 1984, (v7)
Horowitz, Irving Louis. BD175.H65, (v8)
   HD82.H618, (v6)
   JA76.H66 1999, (v7)
   JX5418.H68 1997, (v7)
Horowitz, Mardi Jon. RC455.4.S87H67 2002, (v2)
   RC552.P67.H67 1997, (v2)
Horowitz, Maryanne Cline. B105.S43.H67 1998, (v8)
Horowitz, Sara R. PN56.3.J4.H67 1997, (v3)
Horrigan, Brian. F614.S4 H76 1996, (v4)
Horrocks, Roger. HQ1090.H67 1995, (v6)
   HQ1090.H68 1994, (v6)
Horrox, Rosemary. DA260.H65 1989, (v5)
Horse Capture, George P. E78.G73 H66 1989, (v4)
Horsfield, John. VB205.G7.H67, (v10)
Horsky, Charles A. KF300.H65 1981, (v7)
Horsley, Lee. PS374.D4.H65 2001, (v3)
Horsley, Richard A. DS110.G2.H619 1996, (v5)
Horsman, E. A. PR871.H67 1990, (v3)
Horsman, Reginald. RD27.35.B42.H67 1996, (v2)
Horster, Marita. ND623.C47.H67, (v9)
Hortmann, Wilhelm. PR3108.H67 1998, (v3)
Horton, Andrew. PN1993.5.R9.H63 1992, (v3)
   PN1996.H67 1994, (v3)
   PN1998.3.A53.H67 1997, (v3)
Horton, Donald J. F1053.L3699.H67 1992, (v4)
Horton, George Moses. PS1999.H473.A6 1997, (v3)
Horton, James Oliver. E185.H643 2001, (v4)
   F73.9.N4.H67 1979, (v4)
Horton, Mark. DT429.5.S94, (v5)
Horton, Susan R. PR9369.2.S37.Z67 1995, (v3)
Horton, Tom. F187.C5 H67 1989, (v4)
Horton, William F. QP82.2.E43.H67 1995, (v1)
Horvitz, Deborah M. PS374.W6.H68 2000, (v3)
Horwin, Michael. PN1995.9.P7.H67 1990, (v3)

Horwitz, Barbara Joan. Z2013.5.W6.H67 1997, (v10)
Horwitz, Lester V. E475.18 H69 1999, (v4)
Horwitz, Morton J. KF380.H67 1992, (v7)
 KF8742.H67 1998, (v7)
Horwitz, Richard P. F29.W9.H67, (v4)
Hoschek, Josef. T385.H69613 1993b, (v1)
Hoshizaki, Barbara Joe. SB429, (v1)
Hosinski, Thomas E. B1674.W354.H67 1993, (v8)
Hosking, Geoffrey A. DK40.H66 2001, (v5)
 DK49.H68 1997, (v5)
 DK266 .H58 1993, (v5)
 DK286.5.H67 1992, (v5)
 DK288.H67 1990, (v5)
Hoskins, Robert. PR6013.R44.Z63348 1991, (v3)
Hoskins, W. G. DA600.H6 1970, (v5)
Hosler, Dorothy. F1219.3.M52.H676 1994, (v4)
Hosley, William N. TS533.62.C65.H67 1996, (v1)
Hosokawa, Bill. PN4899.D45P62, (v3)
Hospers, John. B808.5.H6 1997, (v8)
 BJ1025.H66, (v8)
Hospital, Janette Turner. PR9619.3.H674.D57 1987, (v3)
Hostetler, John Andrew. E184.M45 H63 1993, (v4)
Hostetler, Laura. GN635.C5.H67 2001, (v6)
Hostler, Charles Warren. DS26.H6 1993, (v5)
Hoston, Germaine A. DS775.7.H67 1994, (v5)
Hottinger, Arnold. DS62.H8233, (v5)
Hou, Fu-wu. DS777.57.H6, (v5)
Houaiss, Antonio. PC5333.H6, (v3)
Houck, Carter. NK9104.H68 1991, (v9)
Houck, Davis W. JA85.2.U6.H68 2001, (v7)
Hough, Emerson. F596.H69 1970, (v4)
Hough, Graham Goulden. PR6023.A93.Z6318 1957, (v3)
Hough, Jack Luin. QE78.H65, (v1)
Hough, Jerry F. DK266.H59 1988, (v5)
 DK274.H68, (v5)
 HC340.12.H68 2001, (v6)
Hough, Michael. GF90.H68 1990, (v6)
Hough, Richard Alexander. D581.H56 1983, (v5)
 D756.5.B7.H67 1989, (v5)
 DA89.1.M59.H68, (v5)
Hough, Samuel J. Z1502.A58.H68 1994, (v10)
Houghton, Henry G. QC861.2.H68 1985, (v1)
Houghton, Janaye Matteson. ZA4060.H77 1999, (v10)
Houghton, John Theodore. QC981.8.G56.H68 1997, (v1)
Houghton, Norris. PN2287.H68.A3 1990, (v3)
Houghton, Walter Edwards. DA533.H85, (v5)
 PR1223.H6 1968, (v3)
Houglum, Peggy A. RD97.H68 2000, (v2)
Hougron, Jean. PQ2615.O67.T4 1973, (v3)
Houk, Rose. F868.M65 H68 2000, (v4)
Houlahan, Micheal. ML134.K64.H68 1998, (v9)
Houlbrooke, Ralph A. GT3244.A2.H68 1998, (v6)
Houlden, Brian Thomas. HD30.28.H69 1990, (v6)
Houle, Cyril Orvin. LC5251.H69 1992, (v7)
Houlgate, Laurence D. KF505.H68 1988, (v7)
Hoult, Norah. PR6015.O784 H6, (v3)
Hounshell, David A. TS149.H68 1984, (v1)
Houppert, Joseph W. PR2303.H6, (v3)
Hourani, Albert Habib. DS37.7.H67 1991, (v5)
Hourani, George Fadlo. PJ25.P7 vol. 13, (v3)
House, Adrian. BX4700.F6.H595 2001, (v8)
House, J. E. QC174.12.H67 1998, (v1)
House, John. ND553.R45.A73 1997, (v9)
House, Jonathan M. UB250.H68 1993, (v10)
House, Peter William. H97.H67 1991, (v6)
 H97.H68 1988, (v6)
Household, Geoffrey. PR6015.O7885 T47 1963, (v3)
Houseman, Susan N. HD9525.E8.H68 1991, (v6)
Housley, Norman. D202.H68 1992, (v5)
Housman, A. E. PR4809.H15.A6 1961, (v3)
 PR4809.H15.A6 1972, (v3)
 PR4809.H15.A68 1922, (v3)
 PR4809.H15.A7 1946, (v3)
Housman, Laurence. PR4809.H18 T7, (v3)
 PR4809.H18.V55 1935, (v3)
Houston, Brant. PN4784.E5.H68 1996, (v3)
Houston, Cecil J. F1035.I6.H68 1990, (v4)
Houston, Christopher. DS59.K86.H68 2001, (v5)

Houston, Fred F. V63.H68.A34, (v10)
Houston, J. M. GB178.H6 1967, (v6)
Houston, John Porter. PQ2387.R5.Z692, (v3)
 PR6019.O9.U657 1989, (v3)
Houston, Penelope. PN1993.4.H68 1994, (v3)
Houston, R. A. RC553.A88.H67 2000, (v2)
Houston, Sam. F390.H833 1995, (v4)
Houston, Stephen D. F1435.3.P6.H67 1989, (v4)
Hout, Michael. HN400.3.Z9.S654 1989, (v6)
Hout, Wil. HB199.H647 1993, (v6)
Houthakker, Hendrik S. HC110.C6.H6 1970, (v6)
Houwink, R. QC171.H75, (v1)
Hovdenakk, Per. N7193.C5.A4 1982, (v9)
Hovell, Mark. DA559.7.H7 1967, (v5)
Hovey, Richard. PS2007.A6 1969, (v3)
Hoveyda, Fereydoun. P91.H66 2000, (v3)
Hoving, Thomas. N6537.N36.A4 2000, (v9)
Hovland, Michael A. ML128.V7.H67 1986, (v9)
Howard, Christopher. HJ2381.H684 1997, (v6)
Howard, David A. E125.N9.H68 1997, (v4)
Howard, Deborah. NA1121.V4 H69 2000, (v9)
Howard, Donald Roy. PR1874.H65, (v3)
 PR1905.H58 1987, (v3)
 PR2065.G31.H6, (v3)
Howard, Donald S. HV95.H6 1943, (v6)
Howard, Douglas A. DR441.H69 2001, (v5)
Howard, Gene L. F334.C68.H68 1984, (v4)
Howard, James Henri. E99.C8.H66 1990, (v4)
Howard, James. PN1998.3.K83.H68 1999, (v3)
Howard, Jeremy. N6757.5.A78.H68 1996, (v9)
Howard, John R. KF4757.H69 1999, (v7)
Howard, John Tasker. ML410.F78 H6 1962, (v9)
Howard, Joseph Kinsey. F731.H86 1959, (v4)
Howard, Judith A. HM251.H72 1997, (v6)
Howard, Michael Charles. HB97.5.H659 1989, (v6)
Howard, Michael Eliot. D431.H68 1991, (v5)
 U19.H75, (v10)
 U43.E95.H68, (v10)
 UA10.H6 1959, (v10)
Howard, O. O. E83.866.H84 1972, (v4)
Howard, Peter. BJ10.M6 H567 1962, (v8)
Howard, Peter. BJ10.M6.H63 1951b, (v8)
Howard, Philip A. F1789.N3.H68 1998, (v4)
Howard, Philip K. KF384.H69 1994, (v7)
Howard, Roger. G525.H827 1999, (v6)
Howard, Thomas Frederick. HE356.C2.H68 1998, (v6)
Howard, Thomas. PR6045.I5.Z77 1983, (v3)
Howard, Victor B. E449.H8494 1990, (v4)
 E459.H8 1990, (v4)
Howard, Warren S. E449.H8495, (v4)
Howard-Hill, T. H. Z2011.A1 H68 vol. 1 1986, (v10)
 Z2011.A1 H68 vol. 5, (v10)
 Z2011.A1 H68 vol. 6, (v10)
 Z2011.A1 H68 vol. 7, (v10)
 Z2011.A1 H68 vol. 9, (v10)
 Z8811.H67, (v10)
Howarth, Mike. LA632.H59 1990, (v7)
Howarth, Stephen. VA505.H69 1991, (v10)
Howarth, Stephen. VA653.H64 1983, (v10)
Howatson, M. C. PA31.H69 1989, (v3)
Howe, Christopher. HF3824.H68 1996, (v6)
Howe, Daniel Walker. E169.1.H76 1997, (v4)
Howe, Dianne Shelden. GV1783.H67 1996, (v6)
Howe, E. W. PS2014.H5 S7, (v3)
 PS2014.H5.Z5 1929, (v3)
 PS2014.H5.Z5 1974, (v3)
Howe, Elizabeth. PN2592.H65 1992, (v3)
Howe, Henry F. QH541.H65 1988, (v1)
Howe, Irving. F128.9.J5.H6, (v4)
 HD6515.A8.H6, (v6)
 JK2391.C5.H68, (v7)
 PJ5191.E3.H6, (v3)
 PN501 H65, (v3)
Howe, James. F1565.2.C8.H694 1998, (v4)
Howe, Julia Ward. PS2506.H6 1970, (v3)
Howe, Lawrence. PS1342.F53.H69 1998, (v3)
Howe, Margot C. RM735.H68 2001, (v2)
Howe, Mark De Wolfe. KF8745.H6.H67, (v7)
Howe, Marvine. BP190.5.S35.H69 2000, (v8)
Howe, Michael J. A. BF426.H78 1989, (v2)
 BF723.A25.H69 1999, (v2)

Howe, Stephen. DA18.H714 1993, (v5)
Howe, Stephen. DA963.H69 2000, (v5)
Howell, Benjamin F. QE534.2.H68 1990, (v1)
Howell, Joel D. RA975.5.D47.H68 1995, (v2)
Howell, Joseph T. HC108.W3.H68 1973, (v6)
Howell, Margaret. DA228.E44.H69 1998, (v5)
Howell, Mark D. GV1029.9.S74.H68 1997, (v6)
Howell, Nancy. GN34.3.F53.H68 1990, (v6)
Howell, Raymond. VA454.H67 1987, (v10)
Howell, Stephen H. QK731.H68 1998, (v1)
Howell, Steve B. QB127.4.H69 2000, (v1)
Howell, Wilbur Samuel. BC38.H6 1961, (v8)
Howells, Christina. B2430.D484.H69 1998, (v8)
 PQ2637.A82.Z7368 1988, (v3)
Howells, Coral Ann. PR858.T3.H6, (v3)
 PR6035.H96.Z69 1991, (v3)
 PR9199.3.A8.Z695 1996, (v3)
 PR9199.3.M8.Z7 1998, (v3)
Howells, Gwyneth Parry. QH545.A17.H69 1988, (v1)
Howells, W. W. QH368.H64, (v1)
Howells, William Dean. PS2020.F68 vol. 5, (v3)
 PS2020.F68 vol. 6, (v3)
 PS2020.F68 vol. 16, (v3)
 PS2020.F68 vol. 20, (v3)
 PS2020.F68 vol. 26, (v3)
 PS2020.F68 vol. 29, (v3)
 PS2020.F68 vol. 32, (v3)
 PS2025.D6 1969, (v3)
 PS2025.F4, (v3)
 PS2025.I5 1951, (v3)
 PS2025.L4 1916, (v3)
 PS2025.R5 1951, (v3)
 PS2025.S5 1962, (v3)
 PS2025.T7 1996, (v3)
 PS2030.C33 2000, (v3)
Hower, Ralph Merle. HF5465.U6.M27, (v6)
Howes, Chris. TR605.H69 1990, (v1)
Howes, Kelly King. PN56.4.H69 1993, (v3)
 PN56.4.H7 1995, (v3)
Howes, Laura L. PR1933.G37.H69 1997, (v3)
Howes, Marjorie Elizabeth. PR5908.P6.H69 1996, (v3)
Howie, Crawford. ML410.B88 H69 2002, (v9)
Howland, Douglas. DS821.5.C5.H68 1996, (v5)
Howland, Jacob. B395.H85 1998, (v8)
Howlett, Kathy M. PR3093.H69 2000, (v3)
Howlett, Michael. H97.H69 1995, (v6)
 HC113.H68 1999, (v6)
Howorth, Henry H. DS19.H862, (v5)
Howse, Derek. QB36.M378.H69 1989, (v1)
 QB223.H75, (v1)
Howse, Justin. RC1220.D35.H68 1988, (v2)
Howson, Colin. BC135.H68 1997, (v8)
Howson, Colin. Q175.H87 1993, (v1)
Howson, Susan. HG939.5.H648 1993, (v6)
 HG939.5.H65, (v6)
Hoxie, Frederick E. E99.C92 H69 1995, (v4)
 Z1209.2.N67.H68 1991, (v10)
Hoy, James F. F595.2.H68 1987, (v4)
Hoy, Paula. HC60.H69 1998, (v6)
Hoy, Suellen M. RA780.H69 1995, (v2)
Hoy, Terry. JA71.H68 2000, (v7)
Hoyle, Fred. BD523.H67, (v8)
 QB43.2.H69, (v1)
 QB44.H86 1955a, (v1)
 QB51.H8 1960, (v1)
 QB460.72.H69.A3 1994, (v1)
 QB981.H754 2000, (v1)
Hoyle, Russ. GE80.H69 1993, (v6)
Hoyles, John. PN771.H69 1991, (v3)
Hoyrup, Jens. AZ103.H69 2000, (v10)
Hoyt, Edwin Palmer. D756.3.H68 1988, (v5)
 DS774.H62 1989, (v5)
Hoyt, Katherine. F1528.H69 1997, (v4)
Hoyt, Robert S. CB351.H6 1966, (v5)
Hrabal, Bohumil. PG5039.18.R2.O813 1981, (v3)
Hrebenar, Ronald J. JQ1698.A1.H74 2000, (v7)
Hrushevskyi, Mykhailo. DK508.5.H683 1970, (v5)
Hsia, Chih-tsing. PL2415.H8, (v3)
 PL2442.H8 1971, (v3)
 PL2442.H8 1999, (v3)
Hsiang, Wu Yi. QA303.H747 1995, (v1)

Hsiao, Chun. PL2765.I2 V5, (v3)
Hsiao, Kung-chuan. DS763.K3.H75, (v5)
Hsiao, Li-hung. PL2862.I3177.C4813 2000, (v3)
Hsiao-hsiao-sheng. PL2698.H73.C4713 1993, (v3)
Hsiau, A-chin. PL3031.T32H725 2000, (v3)
Hsieh, Alice Langley. UA839.3.H7, (v10)
Hsieh, Chiao-min. G2305.H84 1995, (v6)
Hsieh, Daniel. PL2309.C48.H74 1996, (v3)
Hsing shih heng yen. PL2998.H8.G5 1947, (v3)
Hsing, Chun. PN1995.9.A77.H75 1998, (v3)
Hsiung, David C. HN79.T22.E35 1997, (v6)
Hsiung, James Chieh. JZ1305.H75 1997, (v7)
Hsu, Cho-yun. DS747.H79 1988, (v5)
Hsu, Cho-yun. HN673.H75, (v6)
Hsu, Francis L. K. DS721.H685 1970, (v5)
  DS721.H687, (v5)
  DS721.H69, (v5)
Hsu, John C. HF1604.H78 1990, (v6)
Hsu, Kai-yu. PL2658.E3.H8, (v3)
Hsu, Kenneth J. QE285.H7813 1995, (v1)
Hsu, Madeline Yuan-yin. E184.O6.H78 2000, (v4)
Hsueh, Chun-tu. DS778.H85.H7, (v5)
Hsun-tzu. B128.H66.E5 1988, (v8)
Hu, Ch'ang-tu. LA1131.H78 1974, (v7)
Hu, Chang-tu. DS706.H8, (v5)
Hu, David Y. DS734.7.H824 1992, (v5)
Hu, David. QA76.6.H79 1989, (v1)
Hu, Shih. B126.H8 1963, (v8)
Huang, Chin-hsing. B5234.L485 H83 1995, (v8)
Huang, Hongquan. PL2553.H83 1988, (v3)
Huang, Hsiu-chi. B128.L83.H8 1944, (v8)
Huang, Jichi. PL2658.E3H86 1977, (v3)
Huang, Jing. JQ1519.A5 H8725 2000, (v7)
Huang, Junjie. B128.M324 H83 2001, (v8)
Huang, Kerson. QC174.45.H82 1998, (v1)
Huang, Martin W. PL2437.H828 2001, (v3)
  PL2437.H83 1995, (v3)
Huang, Mei. PR830.C527.H8 1990, (v3)
Huang, Siu-chi. B127.N4 H86 1999, (v8)
Huang, Yen-kai. [from old catalog]. PL1497.H9 1967, (v3)
Huband, Mark. BP60.H8 1998, (v8)
Hubbard, B. A. F. B382.H82 1982, (v8)
Hubbard, Barbara Burke. QA403.3.H83 1998, (v1)
Hubbard, Charles M. E488.H83 1998, (v4)
Hubbard, Elbert. PS2041.A2 1959, (v3)
Hubbard, Frank. ML651.H83, (v9)
Hubbard, John H. QA303.H79 1999, (v1)
Hubbard, Ruth. QP81.5.H83 1990, (v1)
  RB155.H8 1999, (v2)
Hubbard, William J. Z703.5.J4 1981, (v10)
Hubbartt, William S. KF3455.H83 1998, (v7)
Hubbell, Ken. F417.A67 H83 1990, (v4)
Hubbell, Sue. QL463.H89 1993, (v1)
Huber, Donald L. Z7845.L9.H83 1999, (v10)
Huber, Jeffrey T. RC607.A26.H8955 2000, (v2)
  RC607.A26.H896 1996, (v2)
Huber, Kristina R. Z7964.J3.H82 1992, (v10)
Huber, Richard M. BJ1611.H824, (v8)
Huber, Thomas M. DS894.79.Y349.C4637, (v5)
  HC462.95.H84 1994, (v6)
Huber, Thomas Patrick. GB10.H82 1988, (v6)
Huber, Wolfgang. BT736.15.H8313 1996, (v8)
Hubert, Henri. BL570.H813, (v8)
Hubert, Henry A. PE68.C3.H83 1994, (v3)
Hubert, Jean. N6245.H813, (v9)
  N7832.H813 1969, (v9)
Hubert, Judd David. PQ1860.H8 1971, (v3)
  PR2995.H84 1991, (v3)
Hubert, Marie Louise. B1901.P44.H8, (v8)
Hubert, Renee Riese. NC963.S87.H8 1988, (v9)
Hubin, Allen J. Z2014.F4.H83 1994, (v10)
Hubler, Clark. QE621.5.N7.H83 1995, (v1)
Hubler, Edward. PR2848.H8, (v3)
Hubler, Richard Gibson. UG633.H8, (v10)
Huch, Ricarda Octavia. PT361.H8 1951, (v3)
  PT2617.U28.A15, (v3)
Huck, Charlotte S. LB1575.5.U5.H79 1987, (v3)
Huckabay, Calvin. Z8578.H82 1996, (v10)
Hucke, Matt. F547.C7H84 1999, (v4)
Hucker, Charles O. DS721.H724, (v5)

DS753.H829, (v5)
DS753.H83, (v5)
Huckfeldt, R. Robert. JS1459.S43.A84 1995, (v7)
Hudak, Leona M. Z231.H83, (v10)
Huddleston, Mark W. JK681.H83 1996, (v7)
Huddleston, Sisley. DC397.H83, (v5)
Hudler, George W. QK603.H79 1998, (v1)
Hudlicky, Milos. QD281.O9.H83 1990, (v1)
Hudnut-Beumler, James David. BR526.H83 1994, (v8)
Hudson, Benjamin T. DA777.H83 1994, (v5)
Hudson, Charles M. E99.C24.P374 1990, (v4)
Hudson, Christopher G. HV4505.H854 1998, (v6)
Hudson, Christopher. PR6058.U313.W44 1987, (v3)
Hudson, D. Dennis. BV3255.T3, (v8)
Hudson, D. L. R859.7.A78.H84 2000, (v2)
Hudson, David M. KF4891.H83 1998, (v7)
Hudson, Deal Wyatt. BJ1481.H83 1996, (v8)
Hudson, Derek. PR4612.H8 1977, (v3)
Hudson, Geoffrey Francis. DS740.5.R8.H78, (v5)
Hudson, Glenda A. PR4038.P8.H83 1992, (v3)
Hudson, Heather E. TK5104.H83 1990, (v1)
Hudson, Hugh D. NA1188.H84 1994, (v9)
Hudson, John B. QC173.4.S94.H84 1991, (v1)
Hudson, John C. F351.H858 1994, (v4)
Hudson, John. DA195.H83 1994, (v5)
  KD671.H83 1996, (v7)
  QD11.H84 1992, (v1)
Hudson, Kenneth. AM40.H83 1991, (v10)
Hudson, Liam. BF692.5.H83 1992, (v2)
Hudson, Marc. PR1585.H84 1990, (v3)
Hudson, Michael C. DS62.4.H82, (v5)
Hudson, Miles. PN4784.W37.H83 1998, (v3)
Hudson, Nicholas. P211.H83 1994, (v3)
  PR3537.P5.H84 1988, (v3)
Hudson, Raymond. HB241.H83 2001, (v6)
Hudson, Richard. ML457.H83 1994, (v9)
Hudson, Stephen. PR6015.H869 T7, (v3)
Hudson, W. D. BJ21.H8, (v8)
Hudson, W. H. PR6015.U23 C7 1968, (v3)
  PR6015.U23 G7 1943, (v3)
  PR6015.U23 T3 1939, (v3)
Huebner, Kenneth H. TA347.F5.H83 1995, (v1)
Huebner, Steven. ML410.G7.H8 1990, (v9)
Huelsman, Lawrence P. TK7872.F5.H797 1993, (v1)
Huer, Jon. BH39.H787 1987, (v8)
Huer, Jon. HC467.H76 1989, (v6)
Huerta, Jorge A. PS153.M4.H84 2000, (v3)
Huet, Michel. GV1705.H8313 1995, (v6)
Huettich, H. G. PT3721.H8, (v3)
Huey, Robert N. PL792.K9.Z69 1989, (v3)
Hufbauer, Gary Clyde. HF3211.H83 1993, (v6)
Huff, Archie Vernon. F279.G79.H84 1995, (v4)
Huff, C. Ronald. KF9765.H84 1996, (v7)
Huff, Darrell. BC141.H83 1959, (v8)
Huff, Toby E. Q127.A5.H84 1993, (v1)
Huff, W. G. HC445.8.H84 1994, (v6)
Huffaker, Robert. PR6056.O85.Z69 1980, (v3)
Huffington, Arianna Stassinopoulos. N6853.P5.S74 1988, (v9)
Huffman, Clifford Chalmers. Z8813.H83 1995, (v10)
Huffman, James L. PN5404.H78 1997, (v3)
Huffman, Joseph P. DA47.2.H84 2000, (v5)
Huffman, Karen. BF121.H78 2002, (v2)
Huffman, Thomas R. GE198.W6.H84 1994, (v6)
Hufford, Larry. F1436.8.U6.U54 1984 Suppl., (v4)
Hufstader, Jonathan. PR8761.H84 1999, (v3)
Hufton, Olwen H. HC278.B3.H8, (v6)
Huggett, Richard J. GF23.M35.H85 1993, (v6)
Huggins, Martha Knisely. HV8160.A2.H84 998, (v6)
Huggins, Nathan Irvin. E449.D75.H83, (v4)
  NX512.3.N5.H8, (v9)
Hugh, of St. Victor. AE2.H83 1991, (v10)
Hughes, Angela. ML418.F814.H84 1998, (v9)
Hughes, Barry. H61.4.H828 1993, (v6)
Hughes, Christopher. DQ17.H8 1975, (v5)
Hughes, Clair. PS2117.C58, (v3)
Hughes, Derek. PR3317.Z5 H84 2001, (v3)
  PR3427.H4.H8 1981, (v3)
Hughes, E. R. B126.H84 1954, (v8)
  PL2997.C2.Z68, (v3)

Hughes, Edward J. PQ295.M37, (v3)
Hughes, Emmet John. E835.H8 1963, (v4)
Hughes, Emmy. F444.R9.H76, (v4)
Hughes, G. E. BC199.M6 H85 1996, (v8)
Hughes, Glenn. B3354.V884.H84 1993, (v8)
Hughes, H. G. A. Z4891.H83 1997, (v10)
Hughes, H. Stuart. D15.H88.A3 1990, (v5)
  D424.H83 1987, (v5)
  DC365.H8, (v5)
  DG577.5.H83 1979, (v5)
Hughes, Howard. CT275.H6678.A3, (v5)
Hughes, James W. HD7293.H826 1987, (v6)
Hughes, Jan N. LB1060.2.H84 1988, (v7)
Hughes, Jim. TR140.S627.H84 1989, (v1)
Hughes, John G. QA76.9.D3.H844 1988, (v1)
Hughes, Jonathan R. T. HC103.H76 1991, (v6)
Hughes, Judith M. BF109.F74.H845 1994, (v2)
Hughes, Kathryn. PR4681.H84 1999, (v3)
Hughes, Langston. E185.5.N276.H8, (v4)
  PL8013.E5.H8, (v3)
  PR9799.H8, (v3)
  PS3515.U274.A19 1963, (v3)
  PS3515.U274.A6 1995, (v3)
  PS3515.U274.A8, (v3)
  PS3515.U274.G6 1973, (v3)
  PS3515.U274 L3, (v3)
  PS3515.U274 T3, (v3)
  PS3515.U274 W35, (v3)
  PS3515.U274.W4 1926, (v3)
  PS3515.U274.Z5 1963, (v3)
  PS3515.U274.Z58, (v3)
  PS3515.U274.Z598 2001, (v3)
  PS3515.U274 2001, (v3)
Hughes, Leo. PR698.F35.H77, (v3)
Hughes, Linda K. PR468.P37.H84 1991, (v3)
  PR4711.H84 1999, (v3)
Hughes, Lindsey. DK131.H84 1998, (v5)
Hughes, Lora Wood. CT275.M668.A3, (v5)
Hughes, Marija Matich. Z6675.V53.H84 1990, (v10)
Hughes, Michael. DD175.H84 1992, (v5)
Hughes, Nathaniel Cheairs. E477.7.H84 1996, (v4)
  PS2488.H75 1998, (v3)
Hughes, Neil C. HC427.9.H868 2002, (v6)
Hughes, Norman F. QE721.H84 1989, (v1)
Hughes, Philip. BX825.H8, (v8)
Hughes, Quentin. UG460.H84 1975, (v10)
Hughes, R. N. QL430.4.H85 1986, (v1)
Hughes, R. S. PS3537.T3234.Z7146 1987, (v3)
Hughes, Richard Arthur Warren. PN37.H84 1984, (v3)
  PR6015.U35 F6, (v3)
  PR6015.U35 I5, (v3)
  PR6015.U35 W6, (v3)
Hughes, Richard T. BX7075.H84 1996, (v8)
Hughes, Robert. N6447.H83 1981, (v9)
  N6505.H84 1997, (v9)
Hughes, Ted. PR6015.U36.E2, (v3)
  PR6058.U37.A6 1982, (v3)
  PR6058.U37.C3 1978, (v3)
  PR6058.U37.C67 1971, (v3)
  PR6058.U37.G3 1977, (v3)
  PR6058.U37.S37 1975, (v3)
  PR6058.U37.W63 1991, (v3)
Hughes, Thomas Aloysius. LB375.L6.H8 1969, (v7)
Hughes, Thomas Parke. T21.H82 1989, (v1)
Hughes, Thomas Patrick. BP40.H8 1982, (v8)
Hughes, William. PR6037.T617.Z68 2000, (v3)
Hughes, Winifred. PR878.S44.H8, (v3)
Hughes-Warrington, Marnie. D13.H75 2000, (v5)
Hugill, Peter J. HC21.H84 1993, (v6)
  HN80.C36.H84 1995, (v6)
Hugo, Graeme. HB3675.H84 1986, (v6)
Hugo, Leon. PR5366.H84 1998, (v3)
Hugo, Victor. PQ2283.P24 2001, (v3)
  PQ2283.P24 2002, (v3)
  PQ2285.C89 1935, (v3)
  PQ2285.H8 2002, (v3)
  PQ2285.L2 1950, (v3)
  PQ2286.A38 1997, (v3)
  PQ2288.A345 2002, (v3)
  PQ2289.O4 1980, (v3)

Huh, Kyung Mo. HF3828.S64.H8, (v6)
Huhndorf, Shari M. E98.P99 H85 2001, (v4)
Huizenga, John R. QC791.775.C64.H85 1992, (v1)
Huizinga, Johan. D7.H823, (v5)
  DC33.2.H83 1985, (v5)
Hula, Kevin W. JK1118.H85 1999, (v7)
Hulbert, Archer Butler. E159.H94 vol. 9.E394.O4, (v4)
  F593.H96 1931a, (v4)
Hull, David L. QH360.5.H86 2001, (v1)
Hull, Derek. TA418.9.C6.H85 1996, (v1)
Hull, Mary. Z658.U5.H84 1999, (v10)
Hull, Richard W. HG5851.A3.H85 1990, (v6)
Hulme, Derek C. ML134.S485 H8 2002, (v9)
Hulme, Kathryn. PS3515.U374 N8, (v3)
Hulme, Keri. PR9639.3.H75.B6 1985, (v3)
Hulnick, Arthur S. JK468.I6.H85 1999, (v7)
Huls, Mary Ellen. Z7964.U49.H85 1993, (v10)
Hulse, Clark. NX450.5.H8 1990, (v6)
Hulse, Clark. PR539.E64.H8, (v3)
Hulse, James W. F841.H8 1990, (v4)
Hulsey, Byron C. E748.D557.H85 2000, (v4)
Hulsker, Jan. ND653.G7.H79413 1990, (v9)
Hulsman, John C. E885.H85 1997, (v4)
Hultgren, Arland J. BT24.H85 1994, (v8)
  BT375.2.H78 2000, (v8)
  Z8455.H84 1988, (v10)
Hults, Linda C. NE400.H79 1996, (v9)
Human Kinetics (Organization). GV443.H77 1999,
  (v6)
Humayun Kabir. LB880.H85, (v7)
Humboldt, Alexander von. F1211.H924, (v4)
  F2216.H928, (v4)
Hume, David. B1455.A5 1975, (v8)
  B1485. 1978, (v8)
  B1497.A25, (v8)
  BJ1005.H8 1957, (v8)
  BL51.H963 1976, (v8)
  DA30.H92 1975, (v5)
Hume, Janice. E169.1.H94 2000, (v4)
Hume, John. DA990.U46.H854 1996, (v5)
Hume, Kathryn. PS374.F24.H86 2000, (v3)
Hume, Robert D. PR691.H8, (v3)
  PR708.C6.H8 1983, (v3)
  PR3458.D7.H8 1988, (v3)
Hume-Rothery, William. TN690.H95 1963, (v1)
Humes, Harold Louis. PS3558.U43.M4, (v3)
Humes, James C. J81.C92 1992, (v7)
Humfrey, Peter. ND621.V5.H77 1995, (v9)
Humm, Harold Judson. QK569.C96.H85, (v1)
Humm, Maggie. HQ1115.H86 1995, (v6)
  PN1995.9.W6.H86 1997, (v3)
Humma, John B. PR6023.A93.Z631923 1990, (v3)
Hummel, Richard. SK14.3.H86 1994, (v1)
Hummel, Rolf E. TA401.6.A1.H86 1998, (v1)
Hummert, Paul A. PR5368.P6.H93, (v3)
Humpherys, Anne. PR4989.M48.Z687 1984, (v3)
Humphrey, Carol Sue. PN4855.H57 1994 no. 2, (v3)
  PN4891.H86 1992, (v3)
Humphrey, Caroline. BL2370.S5.H85 1996, (v8)
  HC340.12.H86 2002, (v6)
Humphrey, David C. LD1249.H85, (v7)
Humphrey, Doris. GV1782.5.H85 1978, (v6)
Humphrey, Hubert H. E748.H945 A3 1991, (v4)
  E838.5.H855 1978, (v4)
Humphrey, James Harry. GV346.H86 2002, (v6)
  GV347.H86 2000, (v6)
Humphrey, John P. K3240.4.H855 1989, (v7)
Humphrey, John. HD6060.65.B6.H86 1987, (v6)
Humphrey, Mary Ann. UB418.G38.H86 1990, (v10)
Humphrey, William. PS3558.U464, (v3)
Humphreys, J. F. QA177.H85 1996, (v1)
Humphreys, L. R. SB199.H84 1997, (v1)
Humphreys, Leonard A. UA847.H86 1995, (v10)
Humphreys, Margaret. RC211.S85H85 1999, (v2)
Humphreys, Paul. BD541.H78 1989, (v8)
Humphreys, R. Stephen. Z3014.H55.H85 1991, (v10)
Humphreys, Robert. HV245.H88 1995, (v6)
  HV4545.A3.H85 1999, (v6)
Humphreys, W. J. QC861.H8 1964, (v1)
Humphries, C.J. (Christopher John). QK306.H885
  2000, (v1)

Humphries, Charles W. F1058.W47.H86 1985, (v4)
Humphries, Christopher John. QH83.H86 1999, (v1)
Humphries, John. ML955.H86 2000, (v9)
Humpston, Giles. TS610.H85 1993, (v1)
Hundert, E. J. HM22.G8.M334 1994, (v6)
Hundert, Edward M. BD161.H86 1995, (v8)
Hundley, Norris. HD1694.C2.H83 1992, (v6)
Hunefeldt, Christine. HT1148.L56.H87 1994, (v6)
Huneidi, Sahar. DA47.9.I77.H86 2001, (v5)
Huneker, James. PS2044.H4 M4 1969, (v3)
Hung, William. PL2675.H87 1969, (v3)
Hunker, Henry L. F499.C757.H86 2000, (v4)
Hunninger, Benjamin. PN1737.H8 1961, (v3)
Hunt, Alan. KJC6066.S85.H86 1996, (v7)
Hunt, Albert. PN2598.B69.H86 1995, (v3)
Hunt, Andrew E. DS559.62.U6.H86 1999, (v5)
Hunt, Charles Butler. GB121.H79, (v6)
  GB121.H8, (v6)
Hunt, Darnell M. PN4888.T4.H855 1999, (v3)
  PN4888.T4.H86 1997, (v3)
Hunt, Diana. HD75.H86 1989, (v6)
Hunt, Donnell. S675.H83 2001, (v1)
Hunt, E. Howard. UB271.U5.H86 1974, (v10)
Hunt, E. K. HB75.H77 2002, (v6)
Hunt, Edgar. ML935.H85, (v9)
Hunt, Edwin S. HF416.H86 1994, (v6)
Hunt, Garry E. QB681.H86 1989, (v1)
Hunt, Herbert James. PQ2178.H8 1969, (v3)
Hunt, Herbert. F891.H94, (v4)
Hunt, John Dixon. SB457.6.H865 1992, (v1)
Hunt, Joseph McVicker. BF21.H8, (v2)
Hunt, Leigh. PR4813.A3 1949, (v3)
Hunt, Leigh. PR4813.A44 1998, (v3)
Hunt, Lester H. B3319.E9.H85 1990, (v8)
Hunt, Lynn Avery. DC148.H86 1992, (v5)
  DC158.8.H86 1984, (v5)
  DC195.T8.H86, (v5)
Hunt, Margaret R. HT690.G7.H85 1996, (v6)
Hunt, Maurice. PR2981.5.H8 1990, (v3)
  PR3069.W67.H86 1995, (v3)
Hunt, Michael H. DS775.8.H86 1996, (v5)
  E744.H885 1996, (v4)
Hunt, Nancy Rose. GT2465.C74.H85 1999, (v6)
Hunt, Paul. K1700.H86 1996, (v7)
Hunt, Peter. PN1009.A1.H76 1991, (v3)
  PR990.H86 1994, (v3)
  PR6035.A63.Z65 1991, (v3)
Hunt, Richard N. JC233.M299.H85 vol. 2, (v7)
Hunt, Roy E. TA705.H86 1984, (v1)
Hunt, V. Daniel. QC611.92.H86 1989, (v1)
  TK1541.H86, (v1)
Hunt, W. Ben. U21.2.H83 1997, (v10)
Hunter Blair, Peter. DA135.B59, (v5)
  DA152.2.H86 1977, (v5)
Hunter, Alastair G. BS1430.2.H85 1999, (v8)
Hunter, Alvah Folsom. E595.N33.H86 1987, (v4)
Hunter, Chris. SH157.8.H86 1991, (v1)
Hunter, Dard. TS1090.H816 1978, (v1)
Hunter, Diana. RJ506.H9H86 1995, (v2)
Hunter, G. K. PR2303.H8 1962, (v3)
Hunter, Graeme K. QP514.2.H86 2002, (v1)
Hunter, Holland. HC335.3.H86 1992, (v6)
Hunter, J. Paul. PR858.S615.H8 1990, (v3)
  PR3457.H8, (v3)
Hunter, James Davison. E169.12.H77 1991, (v4)
Hunter, Jim. PR6058.U535.E3 1963, (v3)
  PR6058.U535.P53, (v3)
Hunter, Kathryn Montgomery. R737.H78 1991, (v2)
Hunter, Louis C. HD1694.A5.H76, (v6)
Hunter, Mary Kathleen. ML1723.8.V6.H86 1999, (v9)
Hunter, Mel. UG633.H83, (v10)
Hunter, Michael Cyril William. Q41.L85.H95 1982,
  (v1)
Hunter, Neale. DS777.55.H83, (v5)
Hunter, R. H. F. QL959.H96 1995, (v1)
Hunter, Richard Alfred. RC438.H84, (v2)
Hunter, Richard J. HC340.3.H86 1998, (v6)
Hunter, Robert Grams. PR2983.H8, (v3)
Hunter, Robert. HV31.H9 1965, (v6)
Hunter, Sam. N6537.R57.H8 1989, (v9)
  NB237.N6.H86, (v9)

Hunter, Shelagh. PR4984.M5.Z67 1996, (v3)
Hunter, Shireen. DK509.H88 1994, (v5)
  DK859.5.H86 1996, (v5)
Hunter, Wendy. JL2420.C58.H86 1997, (v7)
Huntington, John. PR535.S6.H86 2001, (v3)
Huntington, Samuel P. UA11.H8, (v10)
  UA23.H94, (v10)
  UA23.H95, (v10)
Huntley, E. D. PS3561.I52.Z695 2001, (v3)
Huntley, Frank Livingstone. PR3327.H8, (v3)
Huntsman, Judith. GN671.T46.H86 1996, (v6)
Huntzicker, William. PN4855.H57 1994 no. 3, (v3)
Huot, Marie Claire. DS779.23.H8613 2000, (v5)
Huot, Sylvia. PQ211.H86 1987, (v3)
Hupchick, Dennis P. DR36.H87 2002, (v5)
  G2081.S1 .H8 1996, (v6)
Huppe, Bernard Felix. PR182.H8, (v3)
  PR1585.H86 1984, (v3)
  PR1863.H8, (v3)
Hupper, William G. Z7772.A1 H86 1987, (v10)
Huq, M. M. HC1060.H87 1989, (v6)
Hura, Gurdeep S. TK5105.5.H865 2001, (v1)
Hurewitz, J. C. DS42.H87 1975, (v5)
Hurford, Peter. MT180.H94 1988, (v9)
Hurka, Thomas. BJ171.V55 H87 2001, (v8)
  BJ1533.P36.H87 1993, (v8)
Hurlburt, Laurance P. ND2608.H84 1989, (v9)
Hurlbut, Cornelius Searle. QE365.H845 1998, (v1)
Hurley, Alfred F. UG633.M45.H8, (v10)
Hurley, Andrew. HC108.G3.H87 1995, (v6)
  HC110.C6.H87 2001, (v6)
Hurley, Mark J. DA990.U46.H87 1990, (v5)
Hurley, Neil P. PN1998.3.H58.H87 1993, (v3)
Hurley, S. L. B808.9.H87 1998, (v8)
  BJ1419.H87 1989, (v8)
  BJ1451.H87 2003, (v8)
Hurlimann, Martin. NA5543.H8 1961, (v9)
Hursh, David W. LB1584.H87 2000, (v7)
Hurst, Jack. E467.1.F72.H87 1993, (v4)
Hurst, James Willard. KF352.H8 2001, (v7)
  KF352.H82 2000, (v7)
Hurst, Mary Jane. PS169.L36.H8 1990, (v3)
Hurst, Steven. E183.8.V5.H87 1996, (v4)
Hurston, Zora Neale. PS3515.U787.S94 1997, (v3)
  PS3515.U789.A6 1979, (v3)
  PS3515.U789.Z5 1971, (v3)
Hurt, Charlie Deuel. Z7401.H85 1998, (v10)
Hurt, James. PR1533.H8, (v3)
Hurt, R. Douglas. E98.A3.H87 1987, (v4)
  E445.M67.H87 1992, (v4)
  F466.B68.H87 1998, (v4)
  S441.H918 1994, (v1)
  S441.H919 1996, (v1)
  S441.H92, (v1)
  Z5071.H87 1994, (v10)
Hurtado, Aida. HQ1421.H87 1996, (v6)
Hurtado, Albert L. F864.H897 1999, (v4)
Hurwit, Jeffrey M. DF287.A2.H87 1999, (v5)
Hurwitz, Leon. KF4770.A59 H87 1985, (v7)
Husain, Ishrat. HC440.5.H747 1999, (v6)
Husain, Syed Arshad. RJ499.H87 1991, (v2)
  RJ506.A58.H87 1992, (v2)
Husband, Janet. Z5917.S44 H87 1997, (v10)
Husband, M. F. A. PR5331.H8 1962, (v3)
Husch, Bertram. SD555.H8 1982, (v1)
Huse, Norbert. N6921.V5.H8713 1990, (v9)
Husher, Helen. F55.H87 1999, (v4)
Hussain, J. DS382.H8 1997, (v5)
Hussainmiya, B. A. DS650.6.H87 1995, (v5)
Hussein, Lutfi. PJ6818.H87 1993, (v3)
Husserl, Edmund. B3279.H972i, (v8)
Hussey, Christopher. NA7620.H8, (v9)
Hussey, Harry. DS763.T8.H8, (v5)
  DS778.H89.A3, (v5)
Hussey, Mark. PR6045.O72.Z729 1995, (v3)
Hussey, S. S. PE1101.H94 1995, (v3)
Huston, Hollis. PN2039.H87 1992, (v3)
Huston, James A. UC263.H87 1988, (v10)
Huston, James L. HB3717 1857.H87 1987, (v6)
  HC110.I5.H87 1998, (v6)
Huston, Reeve. HD211.N2.H87 2000, (v6)

Hutcheon, Linda. ML1700.H87 1996, **(v9)**
Hutcheon, Wallace. VM140.F9.H87, **(v10)**
Hutcheson, Richard G. BR516.H78 1988, **(v8)**
Hutchings, Arthur. ML3131.H88, **(v9)**
  MT130.M8.H8 1950, **(v9)**
Hutchings, Kimberly. JZ1242.H88 1999, **(v7)**
Hutchings, Peter. PN1995.9.H6.H835 1993, **(v3)**
Hutchings, Raymond. DR927.H88 1996, **(v5)**
Hutchings, Robert L. D1065.U5.H88 1997, **(v5)**
Hutchings, Stephen C. PG3096.M35.H88 1997, **(v3)**
Hutchings, William. PR6069.T65.Z69 1988, **(v3)**
Hutchins, John Greenwood Brown. VM23.H85 1969, **(v10)**
Hutchins, Maude Phelps (McVeigh). PS3515.U8457 D5, **(v3)**
  PS3515.U8457 D5, **(v3)**
Hutchins, Robert Maynard. LA209.2.H87 1964, **(v7)**
  LB875.H96 1972, **(v7)**
  LB2325.H77, **(v7)**
Hutchinson, Allan C. KE4381.5.H88 1995, **(v7)**
Hutchinson, Bill. HV6322.3.S2.H87 1998, **(v6)**
Hutchinson, Earl Ofari. HV9950.H87 1996, **(v6)**
  HX86.O35 1995, **(v6)**
Hutchinson, F. E. PR3743.H8, **(v3)**
Hutchinson, G. Evelyn. QH81.H898, **(v1)**
  QH98.H82, **(v1)**
Hutchinson, George. PS153.N5.H86 1995, **(v3)**
Hutchinson, Gillian. VM17.H88 1994, **(v10)**
Hutchinson, John F. HV568.H87 1996, **(v6)**
Hutchinson, John. DA925.H88 1987, **(v5)**
Hutchinson, Lucy. PR3517.H85O74 2001, **(v3)**
Hutchinson, Peter. PT2617.E948.Z68 1992, **(v3)**
Hutchinson, R. C. PR6015.U76 E4, **(v3)**
Hutchinson, Thomas. F67.H985, **(v4)**
Hutchison, Charles S. QE433.H87, **(v1)**
Hutchison, David. GE70.H8 1998, **(v6)**
Hutchison, Jane Campbell. N6888.D8.H88 1990, **(v9)**
  Z8246.Z8246.H88 2000, **(v10)**
Hutchison, Kevin Don. DS79.72.H88 1995, **(v5)**
Hutchison, T. W. HB71.H799 1977, **(v6)**
  HB83.H8 1988, **(v6)**
Hutchisson, James M. PS3523.E94.Z58 1996, **(v3)**
Huters, Theodore. PL2749.C8.Z69 1982, **(v3)**
Huth, Michael. QA76.9.L63.H88 2000, **(v1)**
Huth, Paul K. U162.6.H88 1988, **(v10)**
Hutson, James H. E249.H87, **(v4)**
  F152.H86, **(v4)**
Huttner, Harry J. M. Z7161.A15.H88 1995, **(v10)**
Hutton, Frankie. PN4882.5.H87 1993, **(v3)**
Hutton, Patrick H. D13.H87 1993, **(v5)**
Hutton, Ronald. BF1581.H88 1999, **(v2)**
  DA320.H87 1994, **(v5)**
  DA446.H93 1989, **(v5)**
Huxley, Aldous Leonard. AC8.H97 1956, **(v10)**
Huxley, Aldous. BF1101.H8, **(v2)**
  BL51.H98, **(v8)**
  DC123.9.L5.H8 1959, **(v5)**
  PR6015.U9.A16 1959, **(v3)**
  PR6015.U9.A17 1971, **(v3)**
  PR6015.U9 A635, **(v3)**
  PR6015.U9.A77 1983, **(v3)**
  PR6015.U9.A8 1971, **(v3)**
  PR6015.U9.A82 1957, **(v3)**
  PR6015.U9 A84 1948, **(v3)**
  PR6015.U9 B65 1974, **(v3)**
  PR6015.U9 B7 1930, **(v3)**
  PR6015.U9 C6, **(v3)**
  PR6015.U9 C7 1922a, **(v3)**
  PR6015.U9.E84 1936, **(v3)**
  PR6015.U9 G4, **(v3)**
  PR6015.U9 I8, **(v3)**
  PR6015.U9 L5, **(v3)**
  PR6015.U9 L58, **(v3)**
  PR6015.U9.M8 1970, **(v3)**
  PR6015.U9.O4 1936, **(v3)**
  PR6015.U9.O5 1971, **(v3)**
  PR6015.U9 P6, **(v3)**
  PR6015.U9.T45 1970, **(v3)**
  PR6015.U9.T5 1925, **(v3)**
  PR6015.U9 T55, **(v3)**
  PR6015.U9.T8 1929, **(v3)**

  PR6015.U9.Z53 1970, **(v3)**
  RE925.H8, **(v2)**
  RM666.P48.H9, **(v2)**
Huxley, Julian. CB425.H86 1962, **(v5)**
  QH311.H9, **(v1)**
  QH311.H916, **(v1)**
  QH311.H918 1957a, **(v1)**
  QH366.H85 1943, **(v1)**
  QH367.H96, **(v1)**
  QH431.H89, **(v1)**
Huxley, Thomas Henry. BJ1311.H8 1971, **(v8)**
  Q171.H902, **(v1)**
Huxsoll, Jean F. RS380.H88 1994, **(v2)**
Huxtable, Ada Louise. NA735.N5.H8, **(v9)**
  NA6230.H89 1984, **(v9)**
Huyghe, Rene. N2030.H8 1960, **(v9)**
  N5970.H813, **(v9)**
  N6350.H813, **(v9)**
Huyler, Jerome. JC153.L87.H89 1995, **(v7)**
Huysmans, J.-K. PQ2309.H4.Z48 1989, **(v3)**
Huysmans, Joris Karl. PQ2309.H4.A6213 1930, **(v3)**
Huzar, Elias. UA25.H88, **(v10)**
Huzel, Dieter K. UG635.G3.H8, **(v10)**
Hviding, Edvard. DU850.H95 1996, **(v5)**
Hwang, Kai. TK7888.3.H9, **(v1)**
Hwang, Sun-won. PL991.29.S9.A24 1989, **(v3)**
Hyam, R. QK96.P35 1995, **(v1)**
Hyams, Edward Solomon. S419.H9, **(v1)**
Hyams, Joe. E882.2.H93 1991, **(v4)**
Hyatt, A. M. J. F1028.C87.H93 1987, **(v4)**
Hyatt, Edward. Z6004.R38.H9 1988, **(v10)**
Hyclak, Thomas. HD4975.H929 2000, **(v6)**
Hyde, Alan. K564.H8.H93 1997, **(v7)**
Hyde, Anne Farrar. F591.H99 1990, **(v4)**
Hyde, George E. E99.O3 H9 1976, **(v4)**
  E99.P3 H93 1974, **(v4)**
Hyde, H. Montgomery. F1233.H9, **(v4)**
  PR5823.H88, **(v3)**
Hyde, Michael J. BJ1471.H93 2001, **(v8)**
Hyde, Samuel C. F377.F6.H94 1996, **(v4)**
Hyde, William De Witt. B505.H75, **(v8)**
Hyder, Clyde Kenneth. PE64.K5.H9, **(v3)**
Hyers, M. Conrad. BQ4570.H85.H9 1989, **(v8)**
Hyink, Bernard L. JK8716.H95 2000, **(v7)**
Hyland, Francis P. HV6431.H95 1991, **(v6)**
Hyland, Peter. PR3095.H95 1996, **(v3)**
  PS3503.E4488.Z7 1992, **(v3)**
Hyland, William. ML3477.H95 1995, **(v9)**
Hyman, Colette A. PN3307.U6.H96 1997, **(v3)**
Hyman, Eric. HD75.6.H95 1988, **(v6)**
Hyman, Harold Melvin. F394.G2.H96 1990, **(v4)**
Hyman, Herbert Hiram. H62.5.U5.H96 1991, **(v6)**
  HQ1058.5.U5.H95 1983, **(v6)**
Hyman, Irwin A. LB3012.2.H96 1990, **(v7)**
Hyman, Jane Wegscheider. RC552.S4.H95 1999, **(v2)**
Hyman, Libbie Henrietta. QL362.H9, **(v1)**
Hyman, Meryl. DS143.H96 1998, **(v5)**
Hyman, Michael R. F215.H93 1990, **(v4)**
Hyman, Paula. DS135.F8.H96 1998, **(v5)**
  DS148.H93 1995, **(v5)**
Hyman, Ray. BF1042.H96 1989, **(v2)**
Hyman, Stanley Edgar. PN94.H9, **(v3)**
  PN771.H9, **(v3)**
Hyman, Steven E. RC341.H96 1993, **(v2)**
Hymes, Dell H. PM483.5.H9 1981, **(v3)**
Hymes, Robert P. BL65.C8 H95 2002, **(v8)**
Hynds, Susan. LB1632.H95 1997, **(v7)**
Hyneman, Esther F. Z8699.H94, **(v10)**
Hynes, H. Patricia. QH545.P4.H96 1989, **(v1)**
Hynes, Samuel Lynn. D523.H96 1991, **(v5)**
  PR479.P6.H9 1977, **(v3)**
  PR4754.H9, **(v3)**
  PR6029.R8.N5346 1971, **(v3)**
  U42.H96 1997, **(v10)**
Hyppolite, Jean. D16.8.H913 1996, **(v5)**
Hyslop, John. F3429.3.A65.H97 1990, **(v4)**
Hyslop, Lois Boe. PQ2191.Z5.H9, **(v3)**
Hytier, Jean. PQ2643.A26.Z6513, **(v3)**
Hyun, Peter. DU624.7.K67.H983 1995, **(v5)**
Iaccino, James F. PN1995.9.S26.I23 1998, **(v3)**
  QP385.5.I23 1993, **(v1)**

Iacovetta, Franca. F1059.5.T689.I85 1992, **(v4)**
IAmpolskii, M. B. PN1995.I1813 1998, **(v3)**
Iankova, Elena A. HC244.I24 2002, **(v6)**
Iannone, A. Pablo. B41.I26 2001, **(v8)**
Iatrides, John O. DF849.I2, **(v5)**
Ibach, H. QC176.I2313 1990, **(v1)**
Ibarra Grasso, Dick Edgar. F2821.I2 1991, **(v4)**
Ibarra, Jorge. HN203.I23 1998, **(v6)**
Iber, Jorge. F835.S75.I24 2000, **(v4)**
Ibn Batuta. G490.I2 1929, **(v6)**
Ibn Gabirol. PJ5050.I3, **(v3)**
Ibn Hisham, Abd al-Malik. BP75.I25 1997, **(v8)**
Ibn Khaldun. D16.7.I24, **(v5)**
Ibn Khaldun. D16.7.I2413 1969, **(v5)**
Ibn Said, Ali ibn Musa. PJ7694.E3.I2, **(v3)**
Ibn Zabara, Joseph ben Meir. PJ5050.J6.S45, **(v3)**
Ibrāhīm, Sun Allāh. PJ7838.B7173L313 2001, **(v3)**
  PJ7838.B7173L313 2001, **(v3)**
Ibsen, Henrik. PT8852.E5.M3, **(v3)**
  PT8854.F5 1978, **(v3)**
  PT8854.L4, **(v3)**
  PT8860.A35 1990, **(v3)**
Icher, Francois. NA4830.I2713 1998, **(v9)**
Ickes, Anna Wilmarth. F786.I34, **(v4)**
Ickes, Harold L. E748.I28.A3 1985, **(v4)**
Idel, Moshe. BM198.I32 1995, **(v8)**
Idelsohn, A. Z. ML3776.I3 1967, **(v9)**
Idema, W. L. PL2271.I3413 1997, **(v3)**
Idinopulos, Thomas A. DS125.I35 1998, **(v5)**
Ienaga, Saburo. DS834.9.I35, **(v5)**
Ietto-Gillies, Grazia. HD2755.5.I38 1992, **(v6)**
Iezzoni, Lynette. RC150.5.A2.I494 2000, **(v2)**
Ifrah, Georges. QA76.17.I2713 2000, **(v1)**
  QA141.I3713 2000, **(v1)**
Igarashi, Yoshikuni. DS822.5.I33 2000, **(v5)**
Iger, Arthur L. ML3477.I44 1998, **(v9)**
Iggers, Georg G. D13.2.I3413 1997, **(v5)**
  DD86.I34 1983, **(v5)**
Iggers, Jeremy. PN4756.I34 1998, **(v3)**
Ignatius, of Loyola, Saint. BX2179.L7.E5 1978, **(v8)**
Ignatow, David. PS3517.G53.A6 1970, **(v3)**
  PS3517.G53.Z525, **(v3)**
Ihara, Saikaku. PL898.I35 K62, **(v3)**
  PL898.I35 N52, **(v3)**
Ihde, Aaron John. QD11.I44 1984, **(v1)**
Ihimaera, Witi Tame. PR9639.3.I5.T3, **(v3)**
IJsseling, Samuel. PN179.I513, **(v3)**
Ikard, Robert W. F444.C72.I39 1997, **(v4)**
Ikels, Charlotte. HC428.C34.I38 1996, **(v6)**
Ikenberry, G. John. D363.I46 2001, **(v5)**
  HD9566.I525 1988, **(v6)**
Ikle, Fred Charles. U21.2.I42 1991, **(v10)**
Ikle, Fred Charles. UA926.I38, **(v10)**
Ilan, Amitzur. DS126.92.I425 1996, **(v5)**
Ilankovatikal. PL4758.9.I4.C538513 1992, **(v3)**
Ilarione. F1211.I4213 2000, **(v4)**
Ilie, Paul. PC13.N67 no. 78, **(v3)**
  PQ6073.I4, **(v3)**
Iliffe, John. HC800.Z9.P625 1987, **(v6)**
Illich, Ivan. LA210.I4 1971, **(v7)**
Illick, Joseph E. F152.I44, **(v4)**
Illuminating Engineering Society of North America.
  TK4161.I46 1981, **(v1)**
Imamura, Keiji. DS855.I45 1996, **(v5)**
Imber, Mark. GE160.D44.I43 1994, **(v6)**
Imbert, Dorothee. SB470.55.F8.I43 1993, **(v1)**
Imbo, Samuel Oluoch. B5305.I43 1998, **(v8)**
Imhoff, Edgar A. F549.M98 I45 1993, **(v4)**
Imig, Douglas R. HC110.P6.I45 1996, **(v6)**
Imlay, Elizabeth. PR4167.J5.I45 1989, **(v3)**
Immerman, Richard H. E748.D868.I46 1999, **(v4)**
Immerso, Michael. F144.N66 L55 1997, **(v4)**
Imms, Augustus Daniel. QL463.I57 1977, **(v1)**
Imperato, Pascal James. DT434.R75.I47 1998, **(v5)**
  RA431.I46 1985, **(v2)**
Inaba, Darryl. RM332.I43 1997, **(v2)**
Inalcik, Halil. DR486.I5 1973b, **(v5)**
Inamdar, Subhash C. BP75.I53 2001, **(v8)**
Inbody, Tyron. BT732.7.I55 1997, **(v8)**
Ince, E. L. QA372.I6 1956, **(v1)**

Ince, W. N. PQ2643.A26.Z653, (v3)
Inchausti, Robert. BX4705.M542.I53 1998, (v8)
Inchbald, Elizabeth. PR3518.A6 1987, (v3)
Inden, Ronald B. DS435.8.I47 1990, (v5)
Independent Commission on International Development Issues. HF1411.I368 1980, (v6)
Inder Singh, Anita. DS480.82.I44 1987, (v5)
Indy, Vincent d'. ML410.F82.I63 1965, (v9)
Infomap, Inc. G1201.E2.I5 1982, (v6)
Ingalls, Robert P. F124.I53, (v4)
F319.T2.I64 1988, (v4)
Ingard, K. Uno. QC157.I54 1988, (v1)
Ingarden, Roman. BJ1453.I49 1983, (v8)
PN45.I513, (v3)
Inge, M. Thomas. PN6725.I54 1990, (v3)
Inge, William Ralph. BJ1251.I54 1970, (v8)
BL625.I5 1948, (v8)
Inge, William. PS3517.N265.B8, (v3)
PS3517.N265.D3, (v3)
PS3517.N265.F6, (v3)
PS3517.N265.L6, (v3)
PS3517.N265.N3, (v3)
PS3517.N265.P5 1962, (v3)
Ingebretsen, Ed. PS374.H67.I54 1996, (v3)
Ingersent, K. A. HD1918.I53 1999, (v6)
Ingersoll, Christopher D. GV361.I652 2001, (v6)
Ingersoll, Earl G. PR6019.O9.D8745 1996, (v3)
Ingersoll, John G. TL228.I54 1996, (v1)
Ingersoll, Thomas N. F379.N557.I54 1999, (v4)
Ingham, A. E. QA246.I6 1990, (v1)
Ingham, Kenneth. JQ1879.A15 I54 1990, (v7)
Ingham, Patricia. PR4592.W6.I54 1992, (v3)
Ingle, H. Larry. BX7795.F7.I54 1994, (v8)
Ingle, Stephen. PR6029.R8.Z7116 1993, (v3)
Inglehart, Marita Rosch. BF637.L53.I5413 1991, (v2)
Inglehart, Ronald. E40.I54 1996, (v4)
HM73.I544 1998, (v6)
Ingles, Ernest Boyce. Z1365.A1.I54 1994, (v10)
Inglis, Laura Lyn. B29.I54 2000, (v8)
Ingman, Heather. PR888.M69.I54 1998, (v3)
Ingraham, Holly. CS2305.I54 1996, (v5)
Ingraham, Larry H. U766.I73 1983, (v10)
Ingraham, Patricia W. JK681.I53 1995, (v7)
Ingram, Allan. PR6023.A93.Z63194 1990, (v3)
Ingram, David. JF1061.I54 2000, (v7)
Ingram, Edward. DS63.2.G7.I56 1992, (v5)
Ingram, Richard T. LB2341.I5325 1993, (v7)
Ingram, William. PN2596.L6.I54 1992, (v3)
PR3595.I55, (v3)
Ingrao, Charles W. DB36.3.H3.I54 1994, (v5)
DD801.H57.I54 1987, (v5)
Ingres, Jean-Auguste-Dominique. ND1329.I53.A4 1999, (v9)
Inhelder, Barbel. BF721.I473, (v2)
Inkeles, Alex. DK276.I5, (v5)
Inkster, Ian. T18.I55 1991, (v1)
Inman, D. J. TA355.I519 2001, (v1)
Inman, Henry. F786.I587, (v4)
Innaurato, Albert. PS3559.N46.A19 1978, (v3)
Innes, C. D. PR736.I5 1991, (v3)
Innes, Catherine Lynette. PR8752.I54 1993, (v3)
PR9387.9.A3.Z7 1990, (v3)
Innes, Clive. SB421.I56 1995, (v1)
Innes, Matthew. DD801.R76.I56 2000, (v5)
Innes, Paul. PR2848.I56 1997, (v3)
Inness, Sherrie A. P94.5.W65.I56 1999, (v3)
PS228.L47.I56 1997, (v3)
Innis, Harold Adams. F1060.I58 1956, (v4)
Inoguchi, Rikihei. D792.J3.I513 1958, (v5)
Inoguchi, Takashi. D860.I55 2001, (v5)
Inoue, Kyoko. KNX2201.I56 1991, (v7)
Inouye, Charles Shiro. PL809.Z9.Z7396 1998, (v3)
Inscoe, John C. E524.I54 2000, (v4)
Insdorf, Annette. PN1998.3.T78.I57 1994, (v3)
Inskip, Donald Percival. PQ2613.I74.Z65, (v3)
Insoll, Timothy. DS36.855.I47 1999, (v5)
Institute of Electrical and Electronics Engineers. TK9.I35 1996, (v1)
Institute of Medicine (U.S.). QP86.I56 1991, (v1)
RA564.8.I57 1990, (v2)
RA644.V4.I495 1997, (v2)

RA644.6.I58 1991, (v2)
RC564.I544 1997, (v2)
International Council for Physical Fitness Research. GV481.I58 1988, (v6)
International Military Tribunal. D804 G42.I55, (v5)
International Repertory of Music Literature (Organization). ML1.I83, (v9)
International Union of Geological Sciences. QE651.I57 1976, (v1)
International Union of Pure and Applied Chemistry. QD7.I543, (v1)
Inverso, MaryBeth. PN1861.I58 1990, (v3)
Inwood, Brad. B528.I59 1985, (v8)
Inwood, M. J. B2901.I58 1992, (v8)
B3279.H48.Z44 1999, (v8)
Ioanid, Radu. DS135.R7.I6513 2000, (v5)
Ioannides, Christos P. DS54.95.N67I55 1991, (v5)
Ionazzi, Daniel A. PN2085.I5 1992, (v3)
Ionesco, Eugène. PQ2617.O6.J613 1968b, (v3)
PQ2617.O6.N613, (v3)
PQ2617.O6A19 1954, (v3)
PQ2617.O6R5 1960a, (v3)
Ionescu, Ghita. DR267.I65, (v5)
Iorga, Nicolae. DR217.I77 1970, (v5)
Ippolito, Dennis S. HJ2051.I66 1990, (v6)
HJ2052.I77, (v6)
Irace, Kathleen O. PR3071.I73 1994, (v3)
Iram, Yaacov. LA1441.I73 1998, (v7)
Irani, Manuchehr. PK6561.I64.S513 1990, (v3)
Ireland, Ken. PN3383.N35.I74 2001, (v3)
Ireland, Norma Olin. Z1236.I73, (v10)
Ireland, Norma Olin. Z7963.B6.I73 Suppl., (v10)
Ireland, Sandra L. Jones. Z6953.5.A1.I74 1990, (v10)
Ireland, Tom. F801.2.I74 1991, (v4)
Ireson, Carol J. DS555.45.M5.I74 1996, (v5)
Irigaray, Luce. B3279.H49.I7513 1999, (v8)
Irish, Mary. SB317.A2.I75 2000, (v1)
Iriye, Akira. DS518.8.I73, (v5)
Iriye, Akira. E183.8.J3.I74, (v4)
Irlam, Shaun. PR555.E6.I73 1999, (v3)
Irons, Edward D. HG1615.7.M5.I76 1985, (v6)
Irons, Janet Christine. HD5325.T42 1934.I76 2000, (v6)
Irons, Peter H. KF4748.I76 1988, (v7)
KF8742.I76 1999, (v7)
KF8748.I76 1994, (v7)
Irschick, Eugene F. DS484.7.I77 1994, (v5)
Irvin, Dale T. BR145.3.I78 2001, (v8)
Irvine, Demar. ML410.M41.I8 1994, (v9)
Irvine, J. M. QC173.I73, (v1)
Irvine, Janice M. HQ60.I79 1990, (v6)
Irvine, Jill A. DR1302.I78 1993, (v5)
Irvine, Leslie. RC569.5.C63.I78 1999, (v2)
Irvine, Lorna. PR9199.3.L33.Z72 1995, (v3)
Irvine, William. QH31.D2.I7 1959, (v1)
Irving, Clifford. CT275.H6678.I78, (v5)
Irving, Helen. JQ4081.I79 1997, (v7)
Irving, John. PS3559.R8.T48, (v3)
Irving, Katrina. HQ1419.I75 2000, (v6)
Irving, Washington. E123.I728 1986, (v4)
F122.1.I835 1959, (v4)
F592.I73 1986, (v4)
F592.I75, (v4)
F697.I743 1956, (v4)
PS2052.O6, (v3)
PS2053.P6, (v3)
PS2060.A1 1983, (v3)
PS2066.A1 1929, (v3)
PS2081.A3 1969, (v3)
PS2081.A4 1978, (v3)
Irwin, Douglas A. HF1713.I78 1996, (v6)
HF1756.I68 2002, (v6)
Irwin, Geoffrey. GN871.I78 1992, (v6)
Irwin, H. J. BF1031.I79 1999, (v2)
Irwin, Judith Westphal. LB2805.I7 1996, (v7)
Irwin, Lee. E78.G73.I76 1994, (v4)
Irwin, Manley Rutherford. HE7781.I694 1989, (v6)
Irwin, Michael. PR868.D39.I7, (v3)
PR4757.L3.I79 1999, (v3)
Irwin, Richard Gregg. PL2997.S633.I7, (v3)
Irwin, Robert. PJ7737.I78 1995, (v3)

Irwin, Steven M. T21.I76 1993, (v1)
Irwin, Terence. B171.I77 1989, (v8)
B485.I74 1988, (v8)
Irwin, William. F127.N8.I79 1996, (v4)
Isaac, Jeffrey C. JC330.I84 1987, (v7)
Isaac, Rael Jean. RC439.5.I78 1990, (v2)
Isaac, Rhys. F229.I8 1982, (v4)
Isaac, Susan. QK604.I73 1991, (v1)
Isaacs, Anita. F3738.I83 1993, (v4)
Isaacs, Arnold R. DS557.7.I82 1983, (v5)
Isaacs, Arnold R. DS558.I84 1997, (v5)
Isaacs, Harold Robert. DS721.I8, (v5)
DS774.I7 1961, (v5)
PL2658.E8.I8, (v3)
Isaacs, Reginald R. NA1088.G85.I79 1991, (v9)
Isaacson, Eugene. QA297.I8 1994, (v1)
Isaaks, Edward H. QE33.2.M3.I83 1989, (v1)
Isailovic, Jordan. TK6685.I83 1987, (v1)
Isaksson, Hans. PT9875.G95.Z74 1978, (v3)
Isasi-Diaz, Ada Maria. BR563.H57.I82 1993, (v8)
Isbister, John. HB501.I665 2001, (v6)
JV6455.5.I73 1996, (v7)
Ise, John. F687.O7 I84 1996, (v4)
Isely, Duane. QK26.I75 1994, (v1)
Iseminger, Gary. BC6.I8, (v8)
Isenberg, Michael T. GV1132.S95.I84 1988, (v6)
Isenberg, Nancy. HQ1236.5.U6.I83 1998, (v6)
Iser, Wolfgang. PN83.I813, (v3)
PR3714.T73.I84 1988, (v3)
Isern, Thomas D. SB189.73.I74 1990, (v1)
Isernhagen, Hartwig. PS153.I52.I84 1999, (v3)
Iserson, Kenneth V. QP87.I83 1993, (v1)
Isfandiyari, Halah. HQ1735.2.I75 1997, (v6)
Ishai, Yael. JQ1825.P359.I84 1991, (v7)
Isherwood, Christopher. F2223.I8 1949, (v4)
PR6017.S2.S25 1937, (v3)
PR6017.S5 A4, (v3)
PR6017.S5 B4 1954, (v3)
PR6017.S5 D6, (v3)
PR6017.S5.L5 1947, (v3)
PR6017.S5 M45, (v3)
PR6017.S5.P73 1987, (v3)
PR6017.S5.W67 1999, (v3)
PR6017.S5.Z498, (v3)
PR6017.S5.Z514 1980, (v3)
Isherwood, Robert M. DC729.I84 1986, (v5)
Ishida, Hiroshi. HN730.Z9.S654 1992, (v6)
Ishiguro, Kazuo. PR6059.S5.R46 1989, (v3)
Ishihara, Kenji. TA710.I73 1996, (v1)
Ishikawa, Jun. PL830.S5.A6 1998, (v3)
Ishikawa, Takuboku. PL809.S5.K313 1977, (v3)
Ishimoto, Yasuhiro. NA1557.K9.I83 1960, (v9)
Isichei, Elizabeth Allo. BR1360.I75 1995, (v8)
Islam, Nurul. HF1590.5.I84, (v6)
Ismael, Jacqueline S. HN669.A8.I82, (v6)
Ismay, Hastings Lionel Ismay. DA69.3.I8.A3, (v5)
Isozaki, Arata. NA1559.I79.A4 1998, (v9)
Israel, John. DS740.2.I8, (v5)
Israel, John. LG51.K85.I77 1998, (v7)
Israel, Jonathan Irvine. B802.I87 2001, (v8)
D231.I55 1997, (v5)
F1231.I83, (v4)
HF3614.I87 1989, (v6)
Israeli, Raphael. Z7835.M6.I85 1994, (v10)
Israeloff, Roberta. RC464.I87.A3 1990, (v2)
Isralowitz, Richard. HV5825.I85 1998, (v6)
Issari, Mohammad Ali. PN1993.5.I846.I87 1989, (v3)
Issawi, Charles Philip. HC415.15.I84 1982, (v6)
Isser, Edward R. PN1879.H65.I86 1997, (v3)
Isserlin, B. S. J. DS121.I87 1998, (v5)
Itaya, Kikuo. PL830.T35.T413 1983, (v3)
Ito, Ken Kenneth. PL839.A7.Z695 1991, (v3)
Ito, Kiyosi. QA273.I822513 1984, (v1)
Ito, Makoto. HB97.5.I823 1988, (v6)
HC462.5.I86 2000, (v6)
Ito, Teiji. SB458.I833 1984, (v1)
Itoh, Hiroshi. KNX1587.I86 1989, (v7)
Itzigsohn, Jose. HD2346.C8.I89 2000, (v6)
Itzkoff, Seymour W. BF431.5.U6.I87 1994, (v2)
Itzkowitz, Gary. HM24.I799 1996, (v6)
Iudicello, Suzanne. SH334.I84 1999, (v1)

Ivanhoe, P. J. BJ117.I8 1993, (v8)
Ivanhoe, P. J. BJ117.I83 2002, (v8)
Ivanoff, Andre Marie. HV11.I93 1994, (v6)
Ivers, Gregg. E184.J5.I92 1995, (v4)
  KF4783.I94 1992, (v7)
Iversen, Edwin S. SH138.I93 1976, (v1)
  SH380.62.U6.I94 1993, (v1)
Iversen, Margaret. N7483.R54.I83 1993, (v9)
Iverson, Peter. E77.I94 1998, (v4)
Iverson, Peter. E99.Y5.M6534 1982, (v4)
Iverson, Timothy J. HV741.I94 1990, (v6)
Ives, Colta Feller. N6853.T6.A4 1996, (v9)
Ives, Joseph Christmas. F788.I9, (v4)
Ivey, Paul Eli. NA5210.I83 1999, (v9)
Ivins, William Mills. NE430.I85 1969, (v9)
Ivison, Duncan. JC585.I93 1997, (v7)
Ivry, Benjamin. ML410.R23.I97 2000, (v9)
Ivry, Richard B. QP385.5.I886 1998, (v1)
Iwao, Sumiko. HQ1762.I925 1993, (v6)
Iwasaki, Yozan T. PL887.I77, (v3)
Iwu, Maurice M. RS164.I84 1993, (v2)
Iyam, David Uru. DT515.45.B5.I93 1995, (v5)
Iyengar, Shanto. PN4888.I93 1991, (v3)
Iyob, Ruth. DT397.I96 1995, (v5)
Izenour, George C. NA6821.I94, (v9)
Izod, John. PN1993.5.U6.I97 1988, (v3)
Izod, John. PN1998.3.R635.I96 1992, (v3)
Izutsu, Toshihiko. BH221.J3 I95, (v3)
J˘am¯ı. PK6490.Y8E5 1980, (v3)
J˘aòhiòz. PJ7745.J3A26 1969b, (v3)
Jabbur, Jibrail Sulayman. DS36.9.B4.J3313 1995, (v5)
Jaber, Hala. DS119.7.J224 1997, (v5)
Jabes, Edmond. PQ2619.A112.E3813 1984, (v3)
  PQ2619.A112.L5513 1987, (v3)
Jablon, Madelyn. PS374.N4.J33 1997, (v3)
Jablonski, Edward. ML410.B499 J33 1999, (v9)
  ML410.G288.J3 1996, (v9)
  ML423.L3 J3 1996, (v9)
Jablonsky, Thomas J. F548.5.J32 1993, (v4)
Jabra, Jabra Ibrahim. PJ7840.A322.B3413 2000, (v3)
  PJ7840.A322.Z46813 1995, (v3)
Jack, Belinda Elizabeth. PQ2412.J33 2000, (v3)
  PQ3980.J33 1996, (v3)
Jack, Dana Crowley. RC537.J26 1991, (v2)
Jack, Ian Robert James. PR565.L3.J3, (v3)
  PR4238.J3, (v3)
Jack, Rand. KF306.J33 1989, (v7)
Jacka, Tamara. HQ1767.J33 1997, (v6)
Jackall, Robert. HF5813.U6.J33 2000, (v6)
Jackaway, Gwenyth L. PN4815.J27 1995, (v3)
Jackendoff, Ray S. BF444.J33 1987, (v2)
  BF444.J333 1992, (v2)
Jackman, John S. E564.5 1st.J33 1990, (v4)
Jackman, Mary R. HN90.S6.J3 1983, (v6)
Jacknin, Jeanette. RL85.J33 2001, (v2)
Jackson, A. T. TP248.24.J33 1991, (v1)
Jackson, Allan Stuart. PN2596.L7.S736 1993, (v3)
Jackson, Alvin. DA952.S28.J33 1995, (v5)
Jackson, Andrew. E302.J35 1980, (v4)
  E337.8.J3, (v4)
Jackson, Andrew. E382.J115, (v4)
Jackson, Barbara Ward. GF41.J3, (v6)
Jackson, Beverly. CR6020.A2.J33 1999, (v5)
Jackson, Bruce. GR45.5.J33 1987, (v6)
Jackson, Byron M. JK468.P64.J33 1999, (v7)
Jackson, Carlton. D772.R62.J33 1997, (v5)
  PN1998.3.R578.J3 1994, (v3)
  PN2287.M165.J3 1990, (v3)
Jackson, Christine E. N40.J33 1999, (v9)
Jackson, Cynthia L. LC2741.J33 2001, (v7)
Jackson, Donald W. KF4764.J33 1992, (v7)
Jackson, Donald Wilson. KJC5132.J32 1997, (v7)
Jackson, Frank. B808.5.J33 1998, (v8)
  BC199.C56.J33 1987, (v8)
  BC199.C56 J34 1998, (v8)
Jackson, George D. HD585.J29, (v6)
Jackson, George Pullen. ML3551.J2 1965, (v9)
Jackson, Gordon. PN5474.J33 1993, (v3)
Jackson, H. J. Z1003.J12 2001, (v10)
Jackson, Helen Hunt. PS2108.A44 1998, (v3)

Jackson, J. R. de J. Z2013.5.W6.J33 1993, (v10)
Jackson, Jack. F389.J25 1986, (v4)
Jackson, James. R154.J315.J2 1972, (v2)
Jackson, John A. ML429.F75.J3 1991, (v9)
Jackson, John Howard. K4602.2.J33 1989, (v7)
Jackson, Joy J. F377.M6.J33 1993, (v4)
  F379.N557.J3, (v4)
Jackson, Julian. DC396.J335 1988, (v5)
Jackson, Julian. DC397.J18 2001, (v5)
Jackson, Kathi. D807.U5.J33 2000, (v5)
Jackson, Leonard Cecil. QC278.J3 1962, (v1)
Jackson, Leonard. PN98.S7.J33 1991, (v3)
Jackson, Louise A. HV6570.4.G7.J32 2000, (v6)
Jackson, Mark. KD7967.J33 1996, (v7)
Jackson, Michael. DU125.W3.J33 1995, (v5)
Jackson, Myles W. QC450.5.J33 2000, (v1)
Jackson, P. M. HD38.4.J32 1983, (v6)
Jackson, Pamela Irving. HV8138.J33 1989, (v6)
Jackson, Patrick. DA565.D4.J33 1994, (v5)
Jackson, Paul. ML1711.8.N3 M434 1992, (v9)
  ML1711.8.N3 M4343 1997, (v9)
Jackson, Peter A. DS459.J27 1999, (v5)
Jackson, Phil. GV884.J32, (v6)
Jackson, Philip W. B945.D4.J33 1998, (v8)
  LC268.J33 1993, (v7)
Jackson, Ralph. R138.5.J33 1988, (v2)
Jackson, Rebecca. Z7164.S66.J28 1992, (v10)
Jackson, Richard L. PQ7081.J264, (v3)
Jackson, Robert H. E59.E75.J33 1999, (v4)
  E78.C15.J318 1995, (v4)
Jackson, Robert Max. HQ1236.J33 1998, (v6)
Jackson, Roland John. ML128.P235.J3 1988, (v9)
Jackson, Shirley. PS3519.A392 B5, (v3)
Jackson, Shirley. PS3519.A392 H3 1962, (v3)
  PS3519.A392 L6, (v3)
  PS3519.A392.R3 1957, (v3)
  PS3519.A392 S8, (v3)
  PS3519.A392.Z5 1953, (v3)
Jackson, Susan A. GV706.4.J33 1999, (v6)
Jackson, Susan K. PQ2043.J33 1991, (v3)
Jackson, Thomas Graham. NA440.J3, (v9)
Jackson, Ulys. R154.J33.A33, (v2)
Jackson, W. A. Douglas. DS740.5.R8.J3 1968, (v5)
Jackson, W. G. F. DP302.G38.J19 1987, (v5)
Jackson, W. T. H. PN671.J3 1960, (v3)
Jackson, Walter A. HN57.J246 1990, (v6)
Jackson, William J. E521.J33 2000, (v4)
Jackson, William Keith. DU420.J24 1996, (v5)
Jackson-Laufer, Guida M. PN56.E65.J33 1996b, (v3)
Jacob, Bill. QA184.J333 1995, (v1)
Jacob, Daniel J. QC879.6.J33 1999, (v1)
Jacob, Evelyn. LB1032.J33 1999, (v7)
Jacob, Francois. QH429.2.J33.A313 1988, (v1)
  QH506.J3313 1998, (v1)
Jacob, Heinrich Eduard. CB151.J34 1970, (v5)
Jacob, Herbert. KF535.J33 1988, (v7)
Jacob, James R. Q125.2.J33 1998, (v1)
Jacob, Jeffrey. HT381.J33 1997, (v6)
Jacob, Judith M. PL4328.J33 1996, (v3)
Jacob, Max. PQ2619.A17.A225 1992, (v3)
  PQ2619.A17.C6 1945, (v3)
  PQ2619.A17.D4, (v3)
Jacob, Merle. Z6514.S4.J33 1995, (v10)
Jacobi, Jolande (Szekacs). BF173.J85.J32 1968, (v2)
Jacobs, Arthur. ML410.S95.J28 1984, (v9)
Jacobs, David C. JK467.J33 1999, (v7)
Jacobs, Diane. PN1998.3.S78.J3 1992, (v3)
Jacobs, Edward H. PR858.T3.J33 2000, (v3)
Jacobs, Fredrika Herman. N72.F45.J33 1997, (v9)
Jacobs, Harriet A. E444.J17 1973b, (v4)
Jacobs, J. A. QE509.J27 1992, (v1)
Jacobs, Jack Lester. HX550.J4.J33 1991, (v6)
Jacobs, James B. KF224.M2.J33 1994, (v7)
Jacobs, James S. Z8025.6.J3 1991, (v10)
Jacobs, Janet Liebman. HV6570.7.J33 1994, (v6)
Jacobs, Jerry A. HD6060.J33 1989, (v6)
Jacobs, John Arthur. QE501.J25 1973, (v1)
Jacobs, Karen. PN56.M54.J33 2001, (v3)
Jacobs, Lawrence R. JK468.P64.J36 2000, (v7)
Jacobs, Lea. PN1995.62.J3 1991, (v3)
Jacobs, Louis. BM50.J28 1995, (v8)

Jacobs, Michael. HD75.6.J33 1991, (v6)
Jacobs, Naomi. PN3335.J27 1990, (v3)
Jacobs, O. L. R. QA402.3.J29 1993, (v1)
Jacobs, Philip Walker. TR140.U426, (v1)
Jacobs, Ron. HN90.R3.J33 1997, (v6)
Jacobs, Ronald N. P94.5.A372.U557 2000, (v3)
Jacobs, Wilbur R. E175.5.P28.J3 1991, (v4)
  F591.J33 1994, (v4)
Jacobsen, Hans Adolf. D743.J313 1965, (v5)
Jacobsen, Hugh Newell. NA737.J3.A4 1988, (v9)
Jacobsen, J. P. PT8140.M3 E5 1975, (v3)
  PT8140.N5.E5 1990, (v3)
  PT8140.N52 1967, (v3)
Jacobsohn, Gary J. K3165.J33 1993, (v7)
Jacobson, David. GN307.7.J33 1991, (v6)
  JF801.J34 1996, (v7)
Jacobson, Matthew Frye. E661.J34 2000, (v4)
  JV6477.J33 1995, (v7)
Jacobson, Nolan Pliny. B162.J32 1988, (v8)
Jacobson-Hardy, Michael. HV9471.J32 1999, (v6)
Jacobstein, J. Myron. KF240.J32 1998, (v7)
Jacobus, John M. NA737.J6.J3, (v9)
Jacobus, Mary. PN511.J13 1999, (v3)
  PR5869.L93.J3, (v3)
Jacoby, Daniel. HD8066.J33 1998, (v6)
Jacoby, Karl. SB486.S65, (v1)
Jacoby, Sanford H. HC106.5.J33 1997, (v6)
Jacoby, Tamar. F128.9.N4.J34 1998, (v4)
Jacoby, Wade. JN3971.A58.J33 2000, (v7)
Jacques, Edwin E. DR941.J33 1995, (v5)
Jacques, Francis. BD450.J2413 1991, (v8)
Jacques, Kathryn. DS394.73.J4 33 1999, (v5)
Jacquette, Dale. B3376.W564.J33 1998, (v8)
Jacquot, Raymond G. TJ216.J29, (v1)
  TJ223.M53J34 1995, (v1)
Jaeger, C. Stephen. LA95.J34 1994, (v7)
Jaeger, Edmund Carroll. F867.J232 1965, (v4)
  QH13.J3 1960, (v1)
Jaeger, Mary. DG241.J34 1997, (v5)
Jaeger, Werner Wilhelm. B778.J3, (v8)
Jaenen, Cornelius J. E92.J33 1976, (v4)
Jaffa, Harry V. E459.J34 2000, (v4)
  KF4550.J35 1994, (v7)
Jaffe, A. J. E98.A84.J34 1992, (v4)
Jaffe, Audrey. PR878.C25.J34 2000, (v3)
Jaffe, Bernard. QC16.M56.J3, (v1)
  QD21.J3 1976, (v1)
Jaffe, Eliezer David. HV800.I8.J33 1982, (v6)
Jaffe, Frederick S. HQ767.5.U5.J33, (v6)
Jaffe, Hans H. QD95.J24, (v1)
Jaffe, Irma B. ND237.S685.J3, (v9)
Jaffe, Jacqueline A. PR4624.J28 1987, (v3)
Jaffe, Lorna S. UA647.J34 1985, (v10)
Jaffe, Mark. QE707.C63.J34 2000, (v1)
Jaffe, Richard C. TK5102.9.J34 2000, (v1)
Jagchid, Sechin. DS793.M7.J32, (v5)
Jager, Eric. PN56.F29.J34 1993, (v3)
  PN56.H374.J34 2000, (v3)
Jager, Ronald. BC6.J3, (v8)
Jaggar, Alison M. HQ1206.J33 1983, (v6)
Jaggard, Edwin. DA670.C8.J27 1999, (v5)
Jahangir. DS461.5.J28813 1999, (v5)
Jaher, Frederic Cople. HC103.J3, (v6)
Jahn, Hubertus. D639.P7.R85 1995, (v5)
Jahn, Janheinz. PL8010.J313 1969, (v3)
Jahnke, E. QA55.J3 1960, (v1)
Jahoda, Gloria. E93.J2, (v4)
Jahoda, Gustav. GN495.8.J34 1999, (v6)
  GN502.J325 1993, (v6)
Jaimoukha, Amjad M. DK34.C57, (v5)
Jain, H. K. QH430.J35 1999, (v1)
Jain, Raj. QA76.9.E94.J32 1991, (v1)
Jakab, Peter L. TL670.5.J35 1990, (v1)
Jaki, Stanley L. BD511.J35 1989, (v8)
Jakle, John A. F517.J28, (v4)
  TX909.J35 1996, (v1)
  TX945.J35 1999, (v1)
Jakobsen, Janet R. HQ1190.J356 1998, (v6)
Jakobson, Max. DK459.5.J33, (v5)
  DL1066.5.J35 1998, (v5)
Jakobson, Roman. P49.J35 1985, (v3)

Jaksic, Ivan. B1046.J35 1989, **(v8)**
Jalal al-Din Rumi. PK6481.M8.E52 1963, **(v3)**
 PK6481.M8.E52 1990, **(v3)**
 PK6481.M8.E52 1991, **(v3)**
Jalal, Ayesha. DS341.J34 1995, **(v5)**
Jalland, Patricia. GT3243.A2.J35 1996, **(v6)**
Jam ̄alz ̄adah, Muòhammad Al ̄i. PK6561.J3S3513
 1983, **(v3)**
James George Wharton. F811.J28, **(v4)**
James I, King of England, 1566-1625. DA391.J35
 1984, **(v5)**
James II, King of England, 1633-1701. D274.J3.A3,
 (v5)
James, Alice. CT275.J29.A3 1964, **(v5)**
James, Bill. GV863.A1 J36 2001, **(v6)**
James, Brian. PR9617.32.J3 1963, **(v3)**
James, C. L. R. PR9272.9.J35.A6 1992, **(v3)**
James, David E. PN1993.5.U6.J27 1989, **(v3)**
James, David Gwilym. B1131.J3, **(v8)**
 PR457.J3, **(v3)**
 PR4024.J25, **(v3)**
James, Edward. DC64.J36 1988, **(v5)**
 DC65.J35 1982, **(v5)**
James, Francis Godwin. DA940.J36 1995, **(v5)**
 DA947.J35, **(v5)**
James, Gary. F384.3.J36 2000, **(v4)**
James, Glenn. QA5.J32 1976, **(v1)**
James, Harold. DD76.J36 1989, **(v5)**
 HF1359.J36 2001, **(v6)**
 HG3058.D4, **(v6)**
James, Harry Clebourne. PS3519.A455 R4, **(v3)**
James, Heather. PR2836.J36 1997, **(v3)**
James, Henry. DA630.J27 1969, **(v5)**
 DC735.J3, **(v5)**
 DG428.J3 1959, **(v5)**
 PR463.J2 1968, **(v3)**
 PS121.J3, **(v3)**
 PS2111.E4, **(v3)**
 PS2112.A3 1984, **(v3)**
 PS2112.E3, **(v3)**
 PS2112.E3 1962, **(v3)**
 PS2112.F3, **(v3)**
 PS2112.F47, **(v3)**
 PS2112.R35, **(v3)**
 PS2116.A5 1930, **(v3)**
 PS2116.A55 1978, **(v3)**
 PS2116.A9 1949, **(v3)**
 PS2116.B74 1956, **(v3)**
 PS2116.C6 1962, **(v3)**
 PS2116.E8, **(v3)**
 PS2116.G6 1932, **(v3)**
 PS2116.I9 1917, **(v3)**
 PS2116.L66, **(v3)**
 PS2116.M2 1883, **(v3)**
 PS2116.O75, **(v3)**
 PS2116.P6 1975, **(v3)**
 PS2116.P7, **(v3)**
 PS2116.R6 1960, **(v3)**
 PS2116.S4, **(v3)**
 PS2116.T7, **(v3)**
 PS2116.T8 1930, **(v3)**
 PS2116.W27, **(v3)**
 PS2116.W4 1947, **(v3)**
 PS2116.W5, **(v3)**
 PS2120.T4 1971, **(v3)**
 PS2123.A3 1987, **(v3)**
 PS2123.A46 1993, **(v3)**
 PS2123.A47 1979, **(v3)**
 PS2123.A48 1990, **(v3)**
 PS2123.A4 1999, **(v3)**
James, I. M. QA611.J33 1984, **(v1)**
James, J. F. QC20.7.F67.J36 1995, **(v1)**
James, James Alton. E207.C5 J3 1970b, **(v4)**
James, Joy. E184.A1.J27 1996, **(v4)**
James, Judith Giblin. PS3525.A1772.Z69 1995, **(v3)**
James, Laurie. PS2506.J35 1990, **(v3)**
James, Louis. PR9205.J36 1999, **(v3)**
James, Marquis. F390.H84J36 1988, **(v4)**
James, Max H. PR3069.F35.J3 1989, **(v3)**
James, Oliver. HV9145.A5.J35 1995, **(v6)**
James, P. D. PR6060.A467, **(v3)**
 PR6060.A467.B, **(v3)**
 PR6060.A467.T3 1986, **(v3)**
James, Patricia. HB863.M23.J35 1979, **(v6)**
James, Peter. CC165.J35 1993, **(v5)**
 T16.J36 1994, **(v1)**
James, Preston Everett. G80.J34 1981, **(v6)**
James, Robert Rhodes. D568.3.J3 1965a, **(v5)**
James, Scott Curtis. JK2316.J36 2000, **(v7)**
James, Simon R. HJ2305.J328 1998, **(v6)**
James, Susan E. DA333.P3.J36 1999, **(v5)**
James, Sydney V. F82.J35, **(v4)**
James, T. G. H. DT61.J35 1984, **(v5)**
James, Thomas. D769.8.A6.J345 1987, **(v5)**
James, Thurston. PN2091.S8.J35 1992, **(v3)**
James, Valentine Udoh. HC800.Z65.J35 1991, **(v6)**
James, William H. HV5824.E85.J36 1996, **(v6)**
James, William. B804.J2 1977, **(v8)**
 B832.J2 1955, **(v8)**
 B832.J2 1978, **(v8)**
 B945.J21.P4 1962, **(v8)**
 B945.J21 1984, **(v8)**
 B945.J21 2000, **(v8)**
 B945.J23.E66, **(v8)**
 B945.J23 M47 2002, **(v8)**
 BF121.J2 1981, **(v2)**
 BL50.J35 1982, **(v8)**
 BL53.J36 2002, **(v8)**
 LB1051.J34 1958, **(v7)**
James, Wilmot Godfrey. HD8039.M732.S646 1992,
 (v6)
James. PR2002.K5 1939, **(v3)**
Jameson, E. W. QP251.J27 1988, **(v1)**
Jameson, Fredric. PN94.J364 2000, **(v3)**
 PN98.P67.J3 1991, **(v3)**
 PN1995.J34 1990, **(v3)**
 PN1995.9.G39.J3 1992, **(v3)**
 PQ2637.A82.Z75, **(v3)**
 PT2603.R397.Z71265 1998, **(v3)**
Jameson, John R. F392.B53.J37 1996, **(v4)**
Jameson, Michael H. DF901.A69.J35 1994, **(v5)**
Jameux, Dominique. ML410.B773.J313 1990, **(v9)**
Jamieson, Barrie G. M. QL618.J36 1991, **(v1)**
Jamieson, Kathleen Hall. JK524.J36 1984, **(v7)**
Jamieson, Lynn. BF575.I5.J36 1998, **(v2)**
Jamieson, Perry D. UD160.J36 1994, **(v10)**
Jamieson, Ross W. F3791.C9.J36 2000, **(v4)**
Jamison, Kay R. RC516.J36 1993, **(v2)**
Jamison, Martin. Z3586.J36 1992, **(v10)**
Jammer, Max. QC6.J3 1969, **(v1)**
 QC16.E5.J36 1999, **(v1)**
 QC173.J28, **(v1)**
 QC173.98.J35, **(v1)**
 QC174.1.J26, **(v1)**
Jamrozik, Adam. HN850.Z9.S6446 1991, **(v6)**
Janaway, Christopher. B3148.J36 1989, **(v8)**
Jancar-Webster, Barbara. HQ1715.5.J36 1990, **(v6)**
Jancovich, Mark. PN1995.9.H6.J36 1992, **(v3)**
 PN1995.9.H6.J37 1996, **(v3)**
 PS78.J35 1993, **(v3)**
Jandora, John Walter. DS37.8.J36 1997, **(v5)**
Janes, Craig R. F870.S17.J36 1990, **(v4)**
Janes, Regina. PQ8180.17.A73.C5325 1991, **(v3)**
Janetzky, Kurt. ML955.J313 1988, **(v9)**
Janeway, Elizabeth. HQ1154.J3, **(v6)**
Janeway, Michael. PN4888.P6.J36 1999, **(v3)**
Janicaud, Dominique. B2430.J283.P8513 1994, **(v8)**
Janik, Allan. B3376.W564.J364 2001, **(v8)**
Janis, Harriet (Grossman). N6490.J3 1967, **(v9)**
Janis, Irving Lester. BF441.J3, **(v2)**
 UG630.J26, **(v10)**
Janken, Kenneth Robert. E175.5.L64.J36 1993, **(v4)**
Janko, Susan. HV6626.52.J36 1994, **(v6)**
Jankovic, Vladimir. QC857.G77, **(v1)**
Jankowiak, William R. DS796.H84.J36 1993, **(v5)**
Jankowski, Gene F. PN1992.3.U5.J36 1995, **(v3)**
Jankowski, Katherine A. HV2530.J35 1997, **(v6)**
JanMohamed, Abdul R. PR9344.J36 1983, **(v3)**
Jannuzi, F. Tomasson. HD1333.I4.J36 1994, **(v6)**
Janos, Andrew C. JN96.A58J36 2000, **(v7)**
Janosik, Ellen Hastings. RC488.J36 1982, **(v2)**
Janosik, Robert J. KF4546.A1.J36 1991, **(v7)**
Janoski, Thomas. HB846.J36 1994, **(v6)**
 HD5724.J36 1990, **(v6)**
Janov, Arthur. RC480.5.J28 1970, **(v2)**
Janowitz, Anne F. PR585.H5.J36 1998, **(v3)**
Janowitz, Morris. JK526 1952.J3, **(v7)**
 U21.5.J3, **(v10)**
 UA23.J3, **(v10)**
 UB147.J3, **(v10)**
Jansen, Katherine Ludwig. BS2485.J36 2000, **(v8)**
Jansen, Marius B. DS777.J3, **(v5)**
 DS871.J35 2000, **(v5)**
 DS881.3.J28 1971, **(v5)**
Jansen, Sue Curry. Z657.J3 1988, **(v10)**
Janson, Anthony F. ND237.W624.J36 1989, **(v9)**
Janson, H. W. N5300.J3 1986b, **(v9)**
 N5301.J3, **(v9)**
 NB197.3.J36 1985, **(v9)**
Jansson, Bruce S. HV95.J355 2001, **(v6)**
Jantz, Harold Stein. PT1925.J345, **(v3)**
Jantzen, Grace. BV5083.J36 1995, **(v8)**
Jantzen, Hans. NA453.J23, **(v9)**
Janvier, Thomas Allibone. PS2129.J5.S2, **(v3)**
Janz, Denis. HX536.J28 1998, **(v6)**
Janzen, John M. DT450.435.J36 2000, **(v5)**
 GR358.J36 1992, **(v6)**
Janzen, William. F1035.A1.J36 1990, **(v4)**
Jaques, Mary J. F391.J36 1989, **(v4)**
Jaques-Dalcroze, Emile. MT22.A74 1972, **(v9)**
Jaramillo, Alvaro. QL696.P2475.J27 1999, **(v1)**
Jarausch, Konrad Hugo. D16.17.J37 1991, **(v5)**
 DD290.25.J37 1994, **(v5)**
Jardin, Andre. DC36.98.T63.J3713 1988, **(v5)**
Jardine, Lisa. CB361.J34 2000, **(v5)**
Jargowsky, Paul A. HN90.C6.J37 1996, **(v6)**
Jarlett, Franklin. PN2287.R88.J37 1990, **(v3)**
Jarman, Derek. PN1998.3.J3.A3 1993, **(v3)**
Jarman, Douglas. ML410.B47.J28 1991, **(v9)**
 ML410.B47.J3 1989, **(v9)**
 ML410.B47.J33, **(v9)**
 ML410.W395.J37 1982, **(v9)**
Jarnow, Jeannette A. HD9940.U4.J3 1987, **(v6)**
Jarolimek, John. LB1584.J3 1986, **(v7)**
Jaros, Dean. TL539.J37 1993, **(v1)**
Jarraway, David R. PS3537.T4753.Z667 1993, **(v3)**
Jarrell, Howard R. HG4636.J37 1989, **(v6)**
Jarrell, Randall. PS3519.A86.A16 1969, **(v3)**
 PS3519.A86.A17 1969, **(v3)**
 PS3519.A86.A6 1990, **(v3)**
 PS3519.A86.K5 1980, **(v3)**
 PS3519.A86.P5, **(v3)**
 PS3519.A86.S3, **(v3)**
 PS3519.A86.W6, **(v3)**
Jarrett, Derek. DA485.J37, **(v5)**
Jarrett, William S. GV721.5.J37 1990, **(v6)**
Jarry, Alfred. PQ2619.A65.T6 1968, **(v3)**
Jarvie, I. C. PN1993.5.U6.J3 1992, **(v3)**
Jarvis, Edward. F74.C8.J33 1993, **(v4)**
Jarvis, Helen. Z3232.J37 1997, **(v10)**
Jarvis, Kelvin. Z8610.37.J37 1989, **(v10)**
Jarvis, Matt. GV706.4.J37 1999, **(v6)**
Jarvis, Paul. QA76.73.C15.J38 1994, **(v1)**
Jarvis, Peter. LC5211.J37 1989, **(v7)**
 PN1992.75.J36 1998, **(v3)**
Jarvis, Robin. PR408.W35.J37 1997, **(v3)**
Jary, David. HM17.J37 1991, **(v6)**
Jascalevich, Alejandro A. BF701.J3 1926a, **(v2)**
Jaschok, Maria. HQ281.J37 1988, **(v6)**
Jasen, David A. ML390.J26 1998, **(v9)**
Jashemski, Wilhelmina Mary Feemster.
 DG70.P7.J29, **(v5)**
Jaskoski, Helen. PS3569.I44.Z75 1998, **(v3)**
Jason, Philip K. PS3527.I865.Z73 1993, **(v3)**
Jasper, James M. JV6450.J37 2000, **(v7)**
Jaspers, Karl. B3279.J33.P533 1968, **(v8)**
 B3279.J33.V453, **(v8)**
 B3279.J33P513, **(v8)**
 B3316.J313, **(v8)**
 B3318.R4.J33, **(v8)**
 BD23.J313 1951a, **(v8)**
 BL51.J353, **(v8)**
 D13.J314 1953a, **(v5)**

Jaspers, Karl. (cont.)
D829.G3.J315, (v5)
D843.J3714, (v5)
Jaspers, Karls. LB2321.J32, (v7)
Jastram, Roy W. HG307.E5.J37, (v6)
Jastrow, Robert. QP376.J36, (v1)
Jastrzebski, Zbigniew D. TA403.J35 1987, (v1)
Jaszi, Oazkar. DB91.J3 1961, (v5)
Jauch, Josef M. QC174.1.J27 1973, (v1)
Jauregui, Jose Antonio. QP401.J3813 1995, (v1)
Jaworski, Leon. KF373.J38.A33, (v7)
Jay, Elisabeth. PR5114.J39 1995, (v3)
Jay, Gregory S. PS25.J37 1997, (v3)
Jay, Jennifer W. DS751.J38 1991, (v5)
Jay, John. E302.J423 1971, (v4)
Jay, Karla. PQ3939.B3.Z72 1988, (v3)
Jay, Martin. P325.J34 1998, (v3)
Jay, Paul. PS25.J395 1997, (v3)
Jay, Peter. HC79.W4.J39 2000, (v6)
Jay, Stewart. KF8775.J39 1997, (v7)
Jayadeva. PK3794.J3.G53 1977b, (v3)
Jayakar, Pupul. DS481.G23.J38 1992, (v5)
Jaynes, Richard A. SB413.K3.J38 1997, (v1)
Jayyusi, Salma Khadra. PJ7561.J33, (v3)
Jazairy, Idriss. HN981.C6.S73 1992, (v6)
Jeal, Tim. DA68.32.B2.J43 1990, (v5)
Jean Paul. PT2455.A13.C37 1991, (v3)
Jean, Clinton M. GN645.J42 1991, (v6)
Jean, Roger V. QK649.J44 1994, (v1)
Jean, Yves. QD461.J4313 1993, (v1)
Jeanneret, Marsh. Z483.U55.J4 1989, (v10)
Jeanneret-Gris, Charles Edouard. NA1053.J4.A48, (v9)
NA1053.J4.A49, (v9)
NA2520.J4 1970, (v9)
Jeannin, Pierre. HF493.J413, (v6)
Jeans, James Hopwood. QB500.J4 1944, (v1)
QC6.J383, (v1)
QC175.J43 1925, (v1)
QC518.J43 1925, (v1)
Jeans, Peter D. PE1583.J43 1993b, (v3)
Jeansonne, Glen. HQ1904.J43 1996, (v6)
Jech, Thomas J. QA3.P8 vol. 79, (v1)
Jeffares, A. Norman. PR1248.J4, (v3)
PR5906.J42 1996, (v3)
PR5907.J39 1984, (v3)
PR5908.D7.J4, (v3)
PR8711.J4 1982, (v3)
PR8714.J43 1996, (v3)
Jefferies, Matthew. NA6403.G3.J44 1995, (v9)
Jefferies, Richard. PR4823.A3 1968, (v3)
Jeffers, Robinson. PS3519.E27.A17 1988, (v3)
PS3519.E27.A6 1987, (v3)
PS3519.E27.Z53, (v3)
Jefferson, Ann. PQ2443.J44 1988, (v3)
PQ2637.A783.Z72 2000, (v3)
Jefferson, Thomas. E302.J442, (v4)
E302.J442 1975, (v4)
E302.J454, (v4)
E302.J4564 1969, (v4)
E302.J472, (v4)
E332.J464 1970, (v4)
E332.88.M33 1995, (v4)
E332.9.A8 1959, (v4)
JC176.J4 1955, (v7)
JC423.J4 1969, (v7)
KF4982.J43 1993a, (v7)
KF4982.J44 1988, (v7)
LB695.J36 1961, (v7)
S451.V8.J4 1976, (v1)
Z997.J48 1989, (v10)
Jeffery, L. H. CN362.J44 1990, (v5)
Jeffery, Patricia. HQ1742.J44 1989, (v6)
Jefferys, Kevin. D759.J44 1990, (v5)
DA589.7.J44 1997, (v5)
Jeffords, Susan. PN1995.9.M46.J44 1993, (v3)
Jeffrey, Charles. QH83.J43 1977, (v1)
QK95.J43 1982, (v1)
Jeffrey, George A. QD461.J44 1997, (v1)
QP517.H93.J44 1991, (v1)
Jeffrey, Julie Roy. E449.J46 1998, (v4)

HQ1438.W45.J43 1979, (v6)
Jeffrey, Richard C. BC71.J38 1981, (v8)
BC141.J44 1992, (v8)
Jeffrey, Thomas E. F258.J44 1989, (v4)
Jeffreys, Harold. QE501.J4 1976, (v1)
Jeffreys-Jones, Rhodri. DS558.J44 1999, (v5)
E744.J35 1995, (v4)
Jeffries, Edward. F574.D453.J44 1996, (v4)
Jeffries, Ian. HC704.J34 1990, (v6)
Jeffries, John Calvin. KF8745.P69.J44 1994, (v7)
Jeffries, John W. F100.J43, (v4)
Jejeebhoy, Shireen J. LC2607.J45 1995, (v7)
Jelavich, Barbara. DB80.J38 1987, (v5)
DK66.J4 1974, (v5)
DR36.J37 1983, (v5)
DR38.3.S65.J45 1991, (v5)
Jelavich, Charles. DJK4.S93 vol. 8, (v5)
DK67.4.J4, (v5)
Jelavich, Peter. PN1968.G3.J45 1993, (v3)
Jelen, Ted G. BV4327.J45 1993, (v8)
Jellicoe, Geoffrey Alan. NA9030.J45 1961, (v9)
Jellison, Charles A. E207.A4 J4 1974, (v4)
Jember, Gregory K. PE279.J4, (v3)
Jena, A. K. TA407.J39 1992, (v1)
Jencks, Charles. NA680.J457, (v9)
NA682.P67.J4 1990, (v9)
NX456.5.P66.J46 1987, (v9)
Jencks, Christopher. HV4505.J46 1994, (v6)
Jenkin, Penelope M. QP187.J4, (v1)
Jenkins, Annibel. PR3671.R5.J4, (v3)
Jenkins, Anthony. PR734.S5.J46 1991, (v3)
Jenkins, Brian. DC58.J46 1991, (v5)
Jenkins, D. T. HD9901.5.J46 1982, (v6)
Jenkins, Dilwyn. F3409.5.J45 1989, (v4)
Jenkins, Edward Sidney. Q141.J46 1996, (v1)
Jenkins, Elizabeth. PR6060.E518 B7, (v3)
Jenkins, Everett. BP50.J46 1999, (v8)
E185.18.J46 1996, (v4)
E185.2.J46 1998, (v4)
Jenkins, Francis A. QC355.J4 1957, (v1)
QC355.2.J46 1976, (v1)
Jenkins, Fred W. Z7016.J4 1996, (v10)
Jenkins, Geraint H. DA714.H58 1981 vol. 4, (v5)
Jenkins, Greg. PN1997.85.J46 1997, (v3)
Jenkins, Henry. PN1995.9.C55.J46 1992, (v3)
Jenkins, John J. B1294.J46 1983, (v8)
B1498.U53 1992, (v8)
Jenkins, Mary Zuazua. SB466.U6J45 1998, (v1)
Jenkins, McKay. PS261.J46 1999, (v3)
Jenkins, Peter. DA591.T47.J46 1988, (v5)
Jenkins, Philip. BL2525.J46 2000, (v8)
BS2851.J46 2001, (v8)
BX1912.9.J46 1996, (v8)
F160.A1.J46 1997, (v4)
HN400.M6.J46 1992, (v6)
HV5825.J46 1999, (v6)
Jenkins, Rob. JQ281.J46 1999, (v7)
Jenkins, Ronald Scott. PN1955.J46 1988, (v3)
Jenkins, Roy. DA563.4.J45 1997, (v5)
DA566.9.C5 J46 2001, (v5)
DA566.9.O7.J42, (v5)
Jenkins, Roy. DA591.J46.A3 1991, (v5)
Jenkins, Ruth Y. PR878.W6.J46 1995, (v3)
Jenkins, T. A. DA550.J45 1994, (v5)
DA563.5.J46 1988, (v5)
JN543.J45 1996, (v7)
Jenkins, Virginia Scott. SB433.J46 1994, (v1)
Jenkins, Walter S. ML410.B36 J46 1994, (v9)
Jenkins, Wilbert L. F279.C49.N427 1998, (v4)
Jenkins, William D. HS2330.K63.J44 1990, (v6)
Jenks, William Furness. QE230.J4, (v1)
Jenkyns, Richard. N6767.5.V52.J46 1992, (v9)
Jenness, Valerie. HQ125.U6.J46 1993, (v6)
HV6250.3.U5.J45 1997, (v6)
Jennings, D. H. QK601.J46 1995, (v1)
Jennings, Francis. E93.J44 1984, (v4)
E210.J43 2000, (v4)
E302.6.F8.J45 1996, (v4)
Jennings, James. HV4045.J46 1994, (v6)
Jennings, Jeremy. HD6684.J46 1990, (v6)
Jennings, John F. LB3060.83.J46 1998, (v7)

Jennings, John M. HV5840.A74.J45 1997, (v6)
Jennings, Kenneth M. GV880.15.J46 1990, (v6)
Jennings, Lawrence C. DC273.6.J46, (v5)
HT1178.J46 2000, (v6)
Jennings, Ronald C. DS54.7.J46 1993, (v5)
Jenny, Hans. S591.J4, (v1)
Jensen, Arthur Robert. BF432.A1.J46, (v2)
BF433.G45.J46 1998, (v2)
Jensen, Clayne R. GV191.4.J46 1985, (v6)
Jensen, D'Anna J. B. Z7994.L3 B47 1992, (v10)
Jensen, Deborah (MacLurg). RT31.J4 1969, (v2)
Jensen, Eric Frederick. ML410.S4 J45 2001, (v9)
Jensen, J. Vernon. QH31.H9.J46 1991, (v1)
Jensen, Joan M. UA25.J53 1991, (v10)
Jensen, Joli. ML3524.J46 1998, (v9)
Jensen, Larry R. F1779.J46 1988, (v4)
Jensen, Leif. HV4010.J46 1989, (v6)
Jensen, Mead Leroy. TN260.B3 1979, (v1)
Jensen, Merrill. E195.J4, (v4)
E303.J45 1950, (v4)
Jensen, Neal F. SB123.J46 1988, (v1)
Jensen, Peter R. TK5102.2.J46 2000, (v1)
Jensen, Richard E. E83.89.J46 1991, (v4)
Jensen, Richard J. F354.J4, (v4)
Jensen, Ronald J. E669.J46, (v4)
Jensen, William B. QD477.J46, (v1)
Jentschura, Hansgeorg. VA653.J4513 1977b, (v10)
Jeppesen, Knud. ML3003.J362 1970, (v9)
MT55.J45.K63, (v9)
Jeremiah, David. NA7328.J44 2000, (v9)
Jeremy, David J. HD9855.J47, (v6)
Jermyn, Jim. SB459, (v1)
Jernigan, E. Jay. PN4874.W525.J47 1997, (v3)
Jerome, Jerome K. PR4825.J3 T48, (v3)
Jerome, Judson. LA226.J47, (v7)
Jervis, Robert. HM131.J44 1997, (v6)
JX1291.J47, (v7)
U263.J47 1989, (v10)
Jespersen, Otto. PE1105.J4 1964, (v3)
Jesse, Rosalie Cruise. RJ507.A42.J47 1989, (v2)
Jessee, W. Scott. DC611.A607, (v5)
Jessop, Ralph. PR4437.P5.J47 1997, (v3)
Jessup, Deborah Hitchcock. KF3816.R4.J47 1991, (v7)
Jessup, John E. D842.J47 1998, (v5)
U42.J47 1989, (v10)
Jestice, Phyllis G. BL980.I7 J47 2000, (v8)
Jesus, Carolina Maria de. F2651.S253.J47413 1999, (v4)
F2659.N4.J4213 1997, (v4)
F2659.N4.J47 1998, (v4)
Jett, Dennis C. JZ6374.J48 2000, (v7)
Jevons, William Stanley. HB171.J57 1965, (v6)
HG221.J46 1964, (v6)
Jewell, Keala Jane. PQ4088.L46 1992, (v3)
Jewett, Sarah Orne. PS2131.M67 1996, (v3)
PS2132.U5, (v3)
PS2132.W6 1962, (v3)
PS2133.A3 1967, (v3)
Jewish Theological Seminary of America. BJ1533.S3.I5 1972, (v8)
Jezer, Marty. HN90.R3.J49 1992, (v6)
Jhabvala, Ruth Prawer. PR9499.3.J5.E8 1958, (v3)
PR9499.3.J5.H6 1960, (v3)
PR9499.3.J5.H68, (v3)
Jhally, Sut. PN1992.77.C68.J4 1992, (v3)
Jhingran, Saral. BJ122.J55 1989, (v8)
Jia, Dao. PL2677.C42, (v3)
Jian, Sanqiang. DS779.27.J53 1996, (v5)
Jigs-med-glin-pa Ran-byun-rdo-rje. BQ966.I32965.A3 1998, (v8)
Jiji, Latif Menashi. QC320.J55 1998, (v1)
Jiles, David. QC753.2.J55 1990, (v1)
Jillson, Calvin C. KF4520.J55 1988, (v7)
Jimenez, Juan Ramon. PQ6619.I4.A22 1987, (v3)
PQ6619.I4.P6 1958, (v3)
PQ6619.I4.S613 1996, (v3)
PQ6619.I4.T5413 1988, (v3)
PQ6619.I4A26, (v3)
Jimenez, Luz. F1391.M55.J5 1972, (v4)
Jimenez-Fajardo, Salvador. PQ2637.I547.Z76, (v3)

Jimerson, Randall C. E468.9.J55 1988, (v4)
Jin, Ha. PS3560.I6.F3 1996, (v3)
　PS3560.I6.O24 1996, (v3)
Jin, Qiu. DS778.7.J56 1999, (v5)
Jing, Jun. HN740.K365.J56 1996, (v6)
Jiobu, Robert M. E184.A1.J49 1990, (v4)
　F870.A1.J56 1988, (v4)
Jirásek, Jan E. RG613.J56 2001, (v2)
Jirat-Wasiutynski, Vojtech. ND553.G27.J58 2000,
　(v9)
Joachim, Harold H. B1868.R43.J6, (v8)
　BD161.J6 1969, (v8)
Joad, C. E. M. B1646.J73.R4 1936a, (v8)
　BJ1406.J6, (v8)
Joannou, Maroula. PR808.W65.J63 1995, (v3)
Jobe, Joseph. VM15.J613 1971, (v10)
Jobe, Ron. LB1573.J538 1999, (v7)
Jobert, Barthelemy. ND553.D33.J5713 1998, (v9)
Jochelson, Waldemar. E99.A34 J63 2002, (v4)
Jochens, Jenny. PT7162.W6.J6 1996, (v3)
Jochum, K. P. S. Z8992.J59 1990, (v10)
Jockel, Joseph T. UA600.J63 1991, (v10)
Jodidio, Philip. NA1313.C35.J62 1998, (v9)
Joel, Lucille A. RT82.K43 2002, (v2)
Joes, Anthony James. E181.J64 2000, (v4)
　U240.J58 1996, (v10)
Joffe, Ellis. UA835.J6, (v10)
Jogerst, Michael A. JN679.J64 1993, (v7)
Johannes, John R. JK1071.J63 1984, (v7)
Johannesson, Eric O. PT8175.B545.Z73, (v3)
Johanningsmeier, Charles. PN4864.J64 1997, (v3)
Johanningsmeier, Edward P. HX84.F6.J65 1994, (v6)
Johannsen, Robert Walter. E404.J64 1985, (v4)
　E415.7.J685 1991, (v4)
Johansen, Bruce E. E89.J69 1997, (v4)
　E98.L3.J65 2000, (v4)
　Z1210.I7.J65 1996, (v10)
Johansen, Dorothy O. F852.J67 1967, (v4)
Johansen, Julian. BP189.7.S5.J64 1996, (v8)
Johanson, Donald C. GN50.6.J64.A3 1989, (v6)
　GN281.J57 1996, (v6)
John of the Cross. BV5080.J64213 1989, (v8)
　PQ6400.J8 1959, (v3)
John, Angela V. PS2719.R4.Z73 1995, (v3)
John, Elizabeth Ann Harper. E78.S7 J64 1996, (v4)
John, Eric. DA152.J65 1996, (v5)
John, Juliet. PR4592.V54, (v3)
John, of Salisbury, Bishop of Chartres. JC121.J5813
　1990, (v7)
John, Richard R. HE6185.U5.J634 1995, (v6)
Johns, Adrian. Z124.J64 1998, (v10)
Johns, Anthony H. PL5080.5.J64, (v3)
Johns, Edward Alistair. HN385.5.J6 1979, (v6)
Johns, Elizabeth. ND1451.5.J64 1991, (v9)
Johns, Jasper. N6537.J6.K6, (v9)
Johns, Michael. F1386.3.J6 1997, (v4)
Johns, Timothy. GN476.73.J64 1990, (v6)
Johnsen, Egil Borre. LB3045.J64 1993, (v7)
Johnsgard, Paul A. QH105.N2.J64 1995, (v1)
　QL696.F3.J6 1990, (v1)
　QL696.G27.J64 1999, (v1)
　QL696.G27.J65 1988, (v1)
　QL696.P4745.J64 1993, (v1)
　QL696.S8.J64 1988, (v1)
　QL698.3.J68 1997, (v1)
Johnson, A. H. B1674.W354.J6 1962, (v8)
Johnson, Abby Arthur. PS153.N5.J6, (v3)
Johnson, Allan G. HQ1075.J64 1997, (v6)
Johnson, Allen S. DA501.G73.J64 1997, (v5)
Johnson, Alvin Saunders. PS3519.O168.B3, (v3)
Johnson, Andrew. E415.6.J65 1967, (v4)
　SF140.L58.J64 1991, (v1)
Johnson, Arthur T. GV880.J64 1993, (v6)
Johnson, Barbara. PN98.W64.J64 1998, (v3)
Johnson, Ben F. F411.J64 2000, (v4)
Johnson, Betty M. RT84.5.J637 2001, (v2)
Johnson, C. G. QL496.J6, (v1)
Johnson, Carol. JQ4029.P64, (v7)
Johnson, Chalmers A. DS777.53.J58 1965, (v5)
　E840.J63 2000, (v4)
　HD3616.J33.J643 1982, (v6)

Johnson, Charles Richard. PS3560.O3733.F3, (v3)
Johnson, Charles. UA42.J64 1992, (v10)
Johnson, Christopher. HC256.6.J63 1993, (v6)
Johnson, Claudia Alta (Taylor) "Lady Bird". E848.J6,
　(v4)
Johnson, Claudia L. PR858.W6.J64 1995, (v3)
　PR4038.P6.J64 1988, (v3)
Johnson, Clifton. LA206.J6 1963, (v7)
Johnson, D. Gale. HD1415.J6 1990, (v6)
Johnson, Dale A. Z7963.R45 J64 1995, (v10)
Johnson, David Alan. F593.J59 1992, (v4)
Johnson, David E. UF503.J65 1998, (v10)
Johnson, David R. PS3535.I429.Z74 2001, (v3)
Johnson, David. B1499.M5.J64 1999, (v8)
Johnson, Donald Bruce. JK2255.J64 1978, (v7)
Johnson, Donald Leslie. NA737.W7.J6 1990, (v9)
Johnson, Douglas L. GE140.J64 1995, (v6)
Johnson, Douglas L. H31.C514 no. 118, (v6)
Johnson, Douglas W. J. DC255.G8.J6, (v5)
Johnson, E. D. H. PR593.J6 1963, (v3)
Johnson, Earl. HV741.J63 1999, (v6)
Johnson, Edgar. PR5332.J6, (v3)
Johnson, Edward A. QK110.J64 1992, (v1)
Johnson, Elizabeth A. BT972.J57 1998, (v8)
Johnson, Elizabeth S. HB99.7.J64 1978, (v6)
　HQ1064.U5.J64, (v6)
Johnson, Elmer Hubert. HV9813.J64 1996, (v6)
Johnson, Eric A. D804.G4.J55 1999, (v5)
　HV6973.J64 1995, (v6)
Johnson, Gary L. TK1541.J64 1985, (v1)
Johnson, George Lloyd. F277.P3.J64 1997, (v4)
Johnson, George. BL240.2.J547 1995, (v8)
Johnson, Grace G. RS57.J64 1986, (v2)
Johnson, Graham. ML54.6.J76, (v9)
Johnson, Greg. PS3565.A8.Z485 1998, (v3)
Johnson, Harmer. E59.A7.J64 1992, (v4)
Johnson, Harry G. HG221.J663, (v6)
Johnson, Haynes Bonner. E876.J64 1992, (v4)
Johnson, Herbert Alan. KF8745.M3.J63 1997, (v7)
Johnson, Hillary. RB150.F37.J64 1996, (v2)
Johnson, Huey D. GE195.J64 1995, (v6)
Johnson, Hugh. TP548.J632 1998, (v1)
Johnson, Ida M. HV6558.J64 1997, (v6)
Johnson, J. David. HD30.213.J64 1996, (v6)
Johnson, J. K. F1056.8.J64 1989, (v4)
Johnson, J. Stewart. NK1404.J65 2000, (v9)
Johnson, J. Wilfred. ML156.7.F594 J64 2001, (v9)
Johnson, James H. ML270.J64 1995, (v9)
Johnson, James Turner. BT736.2.J64 1997, (v8)
　U21.J627 1984, (v10)
　U21.2.J6324 1999, (v10)
Johnson, James W. F810.J64 2002, (v4)
Johnson, James Weldon. PS3519.O2625.A6 1995,
　(v3)
　PS3519.O2625.Z463 1973, (v3)
Johnson, James William. PR441.J6, (v3)
Johnson, Janis Tyler. HQ71.J58 1992, (v6)
Johnson, Jeffrey Allan. QD18.G3.J64 1990, (v1)
Johnson, John J. F1418.J753 1990, (v4)
　U21.5.J6, (v10)
Johnson, John W. KF385.A4.J64 1992, (v7)
Johnson, Joseph. E99.M83.J657 1998, (v4)
Johnson, Josephine Winslow. PS3519.O2633 N6,
　(v3)
Johnson, Julie Greer. PQ7081.J54 1983, (v3)
Johnson, Karen Ann. LA2311.J63 2000, (v7)
Johnson, Keith. LB1578.J63 1996, (v7)
Johnson, Keith. MT418.J64 2002, (v9)
Johnson, Laurie M. B1248.M36.J64 1993, (v8)
Johnson, Lawrence E. BD171.J59 1992, (v8)
　GF80.J64 1991, (v6)
Johnson, Lee. ND553.D33.A4 1981, (v9)
Johnson, Leland. QC789.2.U62.O257 1994, (v1)
Johnson, Lemuel A. PN56.3.N4.J6 1971, (v3)
Johnson, Leonard W. PQ211.J64 1990, (v3)
Johnson, Linda Cooke. DS796.S257 J614 1995, (v5)
Johnson, Loch K. JK468.I6.J63 1989, (v7)
Johnson, Loch K. JK468.I6.J66 1996, (v7)
Johnson, Lyndon B. DS557.4.J64 1997, (v5)
　E846.J56 1978, (v4)
　E846.J58, (v4)

Johnson, Lynn Staley. PR2359.J65 1990, (v3)
Johnson, Marilynn S. F869.O2.J64 1993, (v4)
Johnson, Mark H. BF242.J64 1991, (v2)
Johnson, Mark. B105.M4 J64 1987, (v8)
Johnson, Mark. BJ1031.J644 1993, (v8)
Johnson, Mary Elizabeth. Z7164.F5.J64 1993, (v10)
Johnson, Maurice O. PR3457.J6, (v3)
Johnson, Michael P. F290.J65, (v4)
Johnson, Michael. E76.2.J64 1994, (v4)
Johnson, Miriam M. HQ759.J645 1988, (v6)
Johnson, Nan. PE1068.U5.J64 1991, (v3)
Johnson, Nevil. JA71.J58 1989, (v7)
Johnson, Orval G. BF722.J643, (v2)
Johnson, Pamela Hansford. PQ2631.R63.A774, (v3)
　PR6019.O3938 N5, (v3)
　PR6019.O3938 U5, (v3)
Johnson, Patricia Altenbernd. B3279.H49 J34 2000,
　(v8)
Johnson, Paul. D203.J64 2000, (v5)
　D421.J64 1983, (v5)
Johnson, Pauline. HQ1190.J64 1994, (v6)
Johnson, Peter. JA79.J63 1992, (v7)
Johnson, Philip. NA680.J63, (v9)
　NA682.D43.J6 1988, (v9)
Johnson, Phillip E. QH366.2.J65 1991, (v1)
Johnson, Phillip. KDZ670.J64 1996, (v7)
Johnson, Pierre-Marc. KDZ670.J64 1996, (v7)
Johnson, Ralph W. F264.D37, (v4)
Johnson, Richard E. HV9069.J57, (v6)
Johnson, Richard R. F73.4.J67 1991, (v4)
Johnson, Robert David. E748.G898.J64 1998, (v4)
Johnson, Roberta Ann. HD60.5.U5 J664 2003, (v6)
Johnson, Rolf M. BD436.J64 2001, (v8)
Johnson, Rolf. F672.P5 J64 2000, (v4)
Johnson, Samuel. DA880.H4.J6 1970, (v5)
　PE1620.J6 1755, (v3)
　PE1620.J6 1979, (v3)
　PR1365.I43 1932, (v3)
　PR3521.Y3 1958, (v3)
　PR3522.B3 1968, (v3)
　PR3522.G73 1984, (v3)
　PR3522.H3 1935, (v3)
　PR3529.A14 H2 1971, (v3)
　PR3533.A2 1952, (v3)
　PR3533.A4 1992, (v3)
Johnson, Sherry E. BF575.G7.J625 1987, (v2)
Johnson, Stanley. HB884.5.J64 1987, (v6)
Johnson, Stephen. F868.C45.J65 1993, (v4)
Johnson, Steven L. KF8201.A1 J63 2000, (v7)
Johnson, Steven. Q325.J65 2001, (v1)
Johnson, Susan Lee. F865.J675 2000, (v4)
Johnson, Susan Moore. LB1775.J546 1990, (v7)
　LB2831.72.J65 1996, (v7)
Johnson, Timothy D. E403.1.S4.J65 1998, (v4)
Johnson, Timothy V. Z8989.7.J64 1986, (v10)
Johnson, Tom Loftin. F496.J69 1970, (v4)
Johnson, Troy R. E78.C15.J612 1996, (v4)
Johnson, Una E. NE508.J63, (v9)
Johnson, Uwe. PT2619.O56.D7 1967, (v3)
　PT2619.O56.M82, (v3)
　PT2619.O56M8, (v3)
　PT2670.O36.J3213 1975, (v3)
Johnson, Vida T. PN1998.3.T36.J64 1994, (v3)
Johnson, W. R. PA6480.J64 1987, (v3)
Johnson, Walter. F379.N59.N4 1999, (v4)
　PN4874.W52J65, (v3)
Johnson, Wanda Yvonne. HV6546.J645 1999, (v6)
Johnson, Wayne L. Z718.1.J63 1999, (v10)
Johnson, Wendell Stacy. PR4024.J6, (v3)
Johnson, Whittington Bernard. E185.8.J753 1993,
　(v4)
　F294.S2.J64 1996, (v4)
Johnson, William C. HF5415.13.J587 1996, (v6)
Johnson, William Clarence. PR2360.A53.J64 1990,
　(v3)
Johnson, William Stacy. BX4827.B3.J64 1997, (v8)
Johnson, William. E185.97.J697.A3 1968, (v4)
　Z7134.J64 1990, (v10)
Johnsonbaugh, Richard. QA76.73.C15.J655 1997,
　(v1)

Johnson, Charles. UA42.J64 1992, (v10)

Johnson-Cartee, Karen S. JF2112.A4.J63 1991, **(v7)**
  JK2281.J639 1997, **(v7)**
  JK2281.J64 1997, **(v7)**
Johnson-Laird, P. N. BC71.J53 1991, **(v8)**
Johnson-Odim, Cheryl. HQ1815.5.Z75.R355 1997, **(v6)**
Johnston, Alastair I. DS753.J64 1995, **(v5)**
Johnston, Brian. PT8895.J588 1989, **(v3)**
Johnston, Carla B. P94.J638 2000, **(v3)**
Johnston, Carol Ann. PS3545.E6.Z73 1997, **(v3)**
Johnston, David. JC571.J57 1994, **(v7)**
  KJA2421.J64 1988, **(v7)**
Johnston, Denis William. PN2306.T6.J64 1991, **(v3)**
Johnston, Denis. PR3726.J6, **(v3)**
Johnston, Francine R. LB2844.1.V6.J65 1998, **(v7)**
Johnston, Henry Phelps. E280.H2 J74, **(v4)**
Johnston, Jennifer. PR6060.O394.C5 1982, **(v3)**
  PR6060.O394.G3, **(v3)**
  PR6060.O394.H6 1974, **(v3)**
  PR6060.O394.O4 1980, **(v3)**
  PR6060.O394.S5 1978, **(v3)**
Johnston, Jill. N6537.J6.J64 1996, **(v9)**
Johnston, John. PS374.M43.J64 1998, **(v3)**
Johnston, Judith. PR4821.J6.Z57 1997, **(v3)**
Johnston, Kenneth R. PR5882.J65 1998, **(v3)**
Johnston, Marilyn. LB2331.53.J64 1997, **(v7)**
Johnston, Mark D. B765.L84.J64 1987, **(v8)**
Johnston, Mark. D767.8.J62 1996, **(v5)**
Johnston, Paul. BJ1012.J64 1989, **(v8)**
Johnston, Sona. ND1316.5.J65 1999, **(v9)**
Johnston, Susan. PR868.D65, **(v3)**
Johnston, Victor S. BF511.J65 1999, **(v2)**
Johnston, William I. RC607.A26.J654 1995, **(v2)**
Johnston, William M. Z7751.J654 1996, **(v10)**
Johnstone, John Keith. PR471.J6 1954a, **(v3)**
Johnstone, Peggy Fitzhugh. PR4692.P74.J64 1994, **(v3)**
Joiner, Brian L. HD62.15.J65 1994, **(v6)**
Jok, Jok Madut. HT1381.J65 2001, **(v6)**
Joll, James. DC337.J6, **(v5)**
Jolliffe, John Edward Austin. DA122.J8.J6 1962, **(v5)**
Jolly, Alison. GN281.J6 1999, **(v6)**
Jolly, Rosemary Jane. PT6525.J65 1996, **(v3)**
Jolly, Roslyn. PS2127.H5.J64 1993, **(v3)**
Jolowicz, Herbert Felix. JC85.L3.J6, **(v7)**
Jomini, Antoine Henri. U102.J7815, **(v10)**
  U102.J78 1971, **(v10)**
Jomo K. S. HC445.5.J65 1990, **(v6)**
Jonas, Frank H. F591.J619, **(v4)**
  F591.J62, **(v4)**
Jonas, Gerald. GV1594.J66 1992, **(v6)**
Jonas, Hans. BD431.J48, **(v8)**
  BJ1453.J6613 1984, **(v8)**
Jonas, Klaus W. Z8547.41.J686, **(v10)**
Jonas, Manfred. E183.8.G3.J66 1984, **(v4)**
Jonas, Raymond Anthony. BX2157.J57 2000, **(v8)**
Jonas, Susanne. F1466.5.J66 1991, **(v4)**
  F1466.7.J66 2000, **(v4)**
Jonassen, Niels. QC571.J65 1998, **(v1)**
Jones, A. H. M. DF85.J615, **(v5)**
  DF85.J6 1971, **(v5)**
  DG209.J652, **(v5)**
  DG311.J6 1964, **(v5)**
  DG311.J62 1966a, **(v5)**
  HC39.J65 1974, **(v6)**
Jones, A. Philip. Z6374.Z5.J65, **(v10)**
Jones, A. W. QB107.J66 2000, **(v1)**
Jones, Adrienne Lash. E185.86.B543 1990 vol. 12, **(v4)**
Jones, Alan V. TN343.J66 1992, **(v1)**
Jones, Aled. PN5117.J66 1996, **(v3)**
  PN5154.J66 1993, **(v3)**
Jones, Alice Hanson. HC104.J67, **(v6)**
Jones, Alison. GR35.J664 1995, **(v6)**
Jones, Allen Keith. DS392.S58 J66 2002, **(v5)**
Jones, Ann Rosalind. GT135.J66 2000, **(v6)**
Jones, Arthur J. LB1027.5.J6 1970, **(v7)**
Jones, Barri. G1812.21.S2.J6 1990, **(v6)**
Jones, Barrie William. QB501.J65 1999, **(v1)**
Jones, Barry O. HD6331.2.A8.J66 1982, **(v6)**
Jones, Bessie. ML420.J75.A3 1983, **(v9)**

Jones, Bruce. GV1029.J68 1998, **(v6)**
Jones, Charles A. JZ1305.J66 1998, **(v7)**
Jones, Charles Colcock. GR111.A47J69 2000, **(v6)**
Jones, Charles Edwin. Z7845.P4.J663 1995, **(v10)**
Jones, Charles O. JK516.J64 1998, **(v7)**
Jones, Chris. GV199.44.N67 J66 1997, **(v6)**
Jones, Colin. DC33.J66 1994, **(v5)**
Jones, D. S. QC670.J63 1964, **(v1)**
Jones, D. W. DA460.J66 1988, **(v5)**
Jones, David E. U21.75.J66 1997, **(v10)**
Jones, David H. D804.3.J66 1999, **(v5)**
Jones, David J. V. HN398.W26.J624 1989, **(v6)**
Jones, David L. SB317.P3.J66 1995, **(v1)**
  SB413.C88.J65 1993, **(v1)**
Jones, David Michael. PR6019.O53.I6 1962, **(v3)**
Jones, David Seth. HD1641.I73.J66 1995, **(v6)**
Jones, Donald G. Z7514.M66.J66 1992, **(v10)**
Jones, Dorothy Richardson. PR5295.J6 1992, **(v3)**
Jones, Dorothy V. E93.J63 1982, **(v4)**
Jones, E. L. HC681.J66 1993, **(v6)**
Jones, E. Michael. PN3435.J66 2000, **(v3)**
Jones, Edmund David. PR67.J6 1922, **(v3)**
Jones, Edward Trostle. PR6015.A6723.Z72 1978, **(v3)**
Jones, Edward. Z8578.J68 1994, **(v10)**
Jones, Eldred D. PR9387.9.S6.Z7 1983, **(v3)**
Jones, Emrys. HT330.J66 1989, **(v6)**
Jones, Ernest. BF173.F85.J6, **(v2)**
Jones, Evan. F614.F7 J6 2001, **(v4)**
Jones, Francis Clifford. DS796.S2.J64, **(v5)**
Jones, G. William. PN1995.9.N4.J66 1991, **(v3)**
Jones, Gareth A. Q360.J68 2000, **(v1)**
  QA331.J66 1987, **(v1)**
Jones, Gareth Elwyn. DA714.J585 1984, **(v5)**
Jones, Gavin Roger. PS217.D53.J66 1999, **(v3)**
Jones, Gavin W. DS523.4.M35.J66 1994, **(v5)**
Jones, Gayl. PS3560.O483.W45X, **(v3)**
Jones, George Fenwick. F295.G3.J66 1992, **(v4)**
Jones, Grant D. F1435.J76 1989, **(v4)**
  F1465.2.I87.J65 1998, **(v4)**
Jones, Gwyn. DL31.J6, **(v5)**
Jones, Gwyn. PR6019.O593 S4 1974, **(v3)**
Jones, Gwyn. PT7262.E5.J6, **(v3)**
Jones, Harry Stuart Vedder. PR2363.J6, **(v3)**
Jones, Helen. HQ1391.G7.J66 2000, **(v6)**
Jones, Henry Arthur. PR4827.A4 1982, **(v3)**
Jones, Howard Mumford. B821.J627, **(v8)**
  BJ1481.J65, **(v8)**
  E169.1.J6435 1971, **(v4)**
  JC591.J64 1949, **(v7)**
  LB885.J6 1969, **(v7)**
  PS121.J6, **(v3)**
  Q111.J58, **(v1)**
Jones, Howard. B573.J57 1989, **(v8)**
  E398.J66, **(v4)**
  E813.J63 1989, **(v4)**
  HV525.J66 1989, **(v6)**
Jones, Ian Shore. HE308.J65 1977, **(v6)**
Jones, J. Benton. QK867.J64 1998, **(v1)**
  SB349.J65 1999, **(v1)**
Jones, J. Gwynfor. DA715.J635 1994, **(v5)**
Jones, J. R. DA435.J66, **(v5)**
Jones, Jacqueline. E185.8.J767 1998, **(v4)**
  LC2802.G4.J66 1980, **(v7)**
Jones, James Earl. PN2287.J589.A3 1993, **(v3)**
Jones, James H. HQ18.32.K56.J65 1997, **(v6)**
Jones, James William. BF175.4.R44.J65 1991, **(v2)**
  F7.J66, **(v4)**
Jones, James. PS3560.O49.P5, **(v3)**
  PS3560.O49.S6, **(v3)**
  PS3560.O49.T4 1962, **(v3)**
Jones, Jerry W. D589.U6.J65 1998, **(v5)**
Jones, John Paul. E207.J7.A34, **(v4)**
Jones, Joseph Jay. PR4349.B7.Z82, **(v3)**
  PR9632.2.J6 1983, **(v3)**
Jones, Joseph L. TJ211.415.J65 1999, **(v1)**
Jones, Judith A. BD311.J66 1998, **(v8)**
Jones, Katharine M. PS374.S5.J6, **(v3)**
Jones, Kathleen W. RJ501.A2.J64 1999, **(v2)**
Jones, Kathleen. HN383.5.J66 1991, **(v6)**
  RA790.7.G7.J658 1993, **(v2)**
Jones, Kenneth Lyons. RG627.5.S57 1997, **(v2)**

Jones, Kent Albert. HF1414.5.J66 1994, **(v6)**
Jones, Leon. Z5814.D5.J65, **(v10)**
Jones, LeRoi. PS3552.A583.D8, **(v3)**
Jones, Lesley. RF291.J63 1987, **(v2)**
Jones, Lois Swan. N59.J66 1999, **(v9)**
  N85.J64, **(v9)**
Jones, Major J. BT102.J647 1987, **(v8)**
Jones, Marc Edmund. B945.M54.J6 1948a, **(v8)**
Jones, Margaret C. PS151.J65 1993, **(v3)**
Jones, Margaret E. W. PQ6144.J64 1985, **(v3)**
Jones, Mark W. GV1589.J65 1999, **(v6)**
Jones, Marnie. F499.T6.J66 1998, **(v4)**
Jones, Matthew. D766.J66 1996, **(v5)**
Jones, Michael E. DA145.J665 1996, **(v5)**
Jones, Michael K. DA330.8.R5.J66 1992, **(v5)**
Jones, Michael. DC611.B854.J66 1988, **(v5)**
Jones, Mother. HD8073.J6A3 1990, **(v6)**
Jones, Neville. D602.J66, **(v5)**
Jones, Norman L. DA355.J65 1993, **(v5)**
Jones, Norman. TA654.J66 1989, **(v1)**
Jones, Oakah L. F799.J75, **(v4)**
  F1231.J68 1988, **(v4)**
Jones, Owen Bennett. DS382.J66 2002, **(v5)**
Jones, P. M. DC163.J64 1988, **(v5)**
Jones, P. V. PA4167.J66 1988, **(v3)**
Jones, Percy Mansell. PQ45.J6, **(v3)**
  PQ442.J6, **(v3)**
Jones, Phyllis Maud. PR67.J65, **(v3)**
Jones, Preston. PS3560.O5244T4 1976, **(v3)**
Jones, Prudence. BL689.J66 1995, **(v8)**
Jones, R. V. D810.C88.J66 1978, **(v5)**
Jones, Raymond E. PR9193.9.J66 2000, **(v3)**
  Z1037.A1.J78 1997, **(v10)**
Jones, Richard E. QP251.J636 1991, **(v1)**
Jones, Richard Foster. PE1073.J6, **(v3)**
Jones, Robert B. PS3539.O478.Z69 1993, **(v3)**
Jones, Robert C. PR2982.J66 1991, **(v3)**
Jones, Robert Emmet. PQ558.J6, **(v3)**
Jones, Robert Emmet. PQ2260.G36.Z66, **(v3)**
Jones, Robert M. TA418.9.C6.J59 1999, **(v1)**
Jones, Robert W. PR448.A77.J66 1998, **(v3)**
Jones, Robin. QA76.73.L23.J66 1990, **(v1)**
Jones, Rufus Matthew. E184.F89.J7 1962, **(v4)**
Jones, Samuel B. QK95.J63 1986, **(v1)**
Jones, Sondra. KF223.L85.J66 2002, **(v7)**
Jones, Stephen. ML3746.J66 1995, **(v9)**
Jones, Stephen. PN1995.9.M6J66 2000, **(v3)**
Jones, Steve. QH375.J66 1999, **(v1)**
Jones, Steven E. PR936.J66 2000, **(v3)**
  PR5442.H62.J66 1994, **(v3)**
Jones, Steven Swann. Z1225.J66 1984, **(v10)**
Jones, Stuart. HC905.J66 1992, **(v6)**
Jones, Terry L. E565.4.J65 1987, **(v4)**
Jones, Terry. PR1868.K63.J6 1985, **(v3)**
Jones, Tom Bard. F2223.J67 1968, **(v4)**
  PJ4075.J6, **(v3)**
Jones, Vernon F. LB3013.J66 1986, **(v7)**
Jones, Virgil Carrington. E591.J6, **(v4)**
Jones, W. Gareth. PG3317.N6.Z67 1984, **(v3)**
Jones, W. T. B72.J65, **(v8)**
Jones, Whitney R. D. DA300.J66 2000, **(v5)**
Jones, William David. HX273.J66 1999, **(v6)**
Jones, William Henry. E185.93.D6 J7 1970, **(v4)**
Jones, William Powell. PR3503 J6 1966, **(v3)**
  PR3503.J6, **(v3)**
  PR6019.O9.Z647, **(v3)**
Jones-Correa, Michael. F130.S75.J66 1998, **(v4)**
Jonge, Marinus de. BT198.J643 1998, **(v8)**
Jonke, Gert. PT2670.O5.G413 1994, **(v3)**
Jonscher, C. T58.5.J66 1999, **(v1)**
Jonsen, Albert R. BJ1441.J66 1988, **(v8)**
Jonson, Ben. PR2601.H4, **(v3)**
  PR2601.W5 1981, **(v3)**
  PR2602.A3 1979, **(v3)**
  PR2602.O86 1997, **(v3)**
  PR2603.R4, **(v3)**
  PR2605.A1, **(v3)**
  PR2606.A16 1968, **(v3)**
  PR2613.A145, **(v3)**
  PR2622.A143, **(v3)**

PR2625.A2 1982, (v3)
Jonsson, Lars. QL690.A1.J6513 1992, (v1)
Jonza, Nancylee Novell. PS3513.O5765.Z72 1995, (v3)
Joos, Martin. PE1271.J6 1968, (v3)
Joos, Martin. PE1421.J65 1967, (v3)
Jopplen, Rudiger. G420.C62.J66 1985, (v6)
Joravsky, David. BF108.S65.J67 1989, (v2)
Jordan, Barbara Charline. E840.8.J62.A33, (v4)
Jordan, Barry. PN1993.5.S7.J6 1998, (v3)
Jordan, D. W. QA300.J82 1997, (v1)
Jordan, David C. F1788.J62 1993, (v4)
Jordan, David P. DC137.08.J68, (v5)
  DC146.R6.J67 1985, (v5)
  DG311.G6.J67, (v5)
Jordan, David William. F184.J67 1987, (v4)
Jordan, Donald A. DS740.5.J3.J67 1991, (v5)
Jordan, Heather Bryant. PR6003.O6757.Z674 1992, (v3)
Jordan, Jim M. N6888.K55.J67 1984, (v9)
Jordan, Karl. DD147.5.H5.J6713 1986, (v5)
Jordan, Manuel. DT1308.C67.J67 1998, (v5)
Jordan, Michael. BL473.J67 1993, (v8)
Jordan, Pat. GV865.J67.A34, (v6)
Jordan, Richard N. SD412.J67 1994, (v1)
Jordan, Rita. LC4717.J67 1995, (v7)
Jordan, Robert B. QD502.J67 1998, (v1)
Jordan, Robert Furneaux. NA950.J6 1961, (v9)
Jordan, Thomas Edward. DA950.7.J67 1997, (v5)
  HQ792.G7.J67 1987, (v6)
Jordan, Thomas F. QC174.12.J67 1986, (v1)
Jordan, W. K. DA345.J59, (v5)
  DA345.J6, (v5)
Jordan, Weymouth Tyree. F326.J67, (v4)
Jordan, William C. D202.8.J67 1996, (v5)
Jordan, William G. PN4882.5.J67 2001, (v3)
Jordan, William. B178.J67 1990, (v8)
Jordan, Winthrop D. E185.J69, (v4)
  E446.J67, (v4)
  F347.A2.J67 1993, (v4)
Jordan-Bychkov, Terry G. F157.D4.J67 1989, (v4)
  F391.J69, (v4)
  F395.G3 J6 1966, (v4)
  F590.7.J67 1997, (v4)
  GF41.J67 1982, (v6)
  SF196.N7.J67 1993, (v1)
Jordens, J. T. F. BL1255.D3.J67, (v8)
  DS481.G3.J7184 1998, (v5)
Jorge, Lidia. PQ9272.O69.C6713 1995, (v3)
Jorgensen, Beth Ellen. PQ7297.P63.Z73 1994, (v3)
Jorgensen, Elizabeth Watkins. HB119.V4.J67 1999, (v6)
Jorgensen, Estelle Ruth. MT1.J676 1997, (v9)
Jorgensen, Joseph G. E99.E7.J634 1990, (v4)
Jorgensen, Owen. MT165.J667 1991, (v9)
Jorgensen, Theodore P. QC26.J67 1993, (v1)
Jorgenson, Dale Weldeau. HC110.I52.J668 1995, (v6)
Jorgenson, Theodore. PT8363.J6, (v3)
Jorm, A. F. RC523.J67 1987, (v2)
Jose, Nicholas. PR437.J67 1984, (v3)
Joseph, Bertram Leon. PR2807.J68, (v3)
Joseph, Gerhard. PR5588.J598 1992, (v3)
Joseph, Gloria I. HQ1426.J67 1986, (v6)
Joseph, H. W. B. BC71.J7 1916, (v8)
  JC71.P6.J59 1948, (v7)
Joseph, Janice. HV9104.J67 1995, (v6)
Joseph, Joseph S. DS54.9.J68 1997, (v5)
Joseph, Roger. DT313.3.R53.J67 1987, (v6)
Josephson, Matthew. E743.J65 1979, (v4)
Josephson, Susan G. N6494.P66.J67 1996, (v9)
Josephy, Alvin M. E58.J6 1991, (v4)
  E99.N5 J62 1997, (v4)
Joshi, A. W. QC174.17.G7.J67 1982, (v1)
Joshi, S. T. PR6007.U6.Z726 1995, (v3)
  PS374.H67.J67 2001, (v3)
  PS3505.A763.Z75 1990, (v3)
Josipovici, Gabriel. PN56.T77.J67 1999, (v3)
Josselson, Ruthellen. HM132.J675 1992, (v6)
  HQ1206.J67 1987, (v6)
  HQ1206.J673 1996, (v6)
Josselyn, Amos Piatt. F593.J67.A33, (v4)

Josselyn, Irene Milliken. BF721.J6, (v2)
Jost, Jurgen. QA333.J8513 1997, (v1)
Josuttis, Nicolai M. QA76.73.C153J69, (v1)
Joubert, Jean. PQ2670.O9.A6 1988, (v3)
Joughin, Louis. LB2332.J68 1969, (v7)
Joukowsky, Martha. CC76.J68, (v5)
Jourda, Pierre. PQ1275.J68, (v3)
Jouvenel, Bertrand de. BC181.J6613, (v8)
Jouvet, Michel. QP426.J68313 1999, (v1)
Jovanovic, Miroslav N. HF1418.5.J68 1992, (v6)
Jovellanos, Gaspar de. PQ6532.J7A124 1984, (v3)
Jowdy, John. GV903.J69 2002, (v6)
Jowers, Sidney Jackson. Z5691.J68 2000, (v10)
Jowett, Garth. PN1993.5.U6.J67, (v3)
  PN1995.9.C45.C373 1996, (v3)
Jowitt, Deborah. GV1601.J68 1988, (v6)
Joy, Albert H. Z5862.2.A26.J68 1991, (v10)
Joyce, Barry Alan. GN663.J69 2001, (v6)
Joyce, Bruce R. LB1555.J6, (v7)
Joyce, Christopher. RS164.J69 1994, (v2)
Joyce, Donald F. Z471.J68 1991, (v10)
Joyce, Elisabeth W. PS3525.O5616.Z685 1998, (v3)
Joyce, James. PR6019.O9.A17 1937, (v3)
  PR6019.O9.A6 1947, (v3)
  PR6019.O9.A6 1959, (v3)
  PR6019.O9.C5 1954, (v3)
  PR6019.O9.D43 1994, (v3)
  PR6019.O9 D8, (v3)
  PR6019.O9.D8 1993d, (v3)
  PR6019.O9.E9 1951, (v3)
  PR6019.O9 F5 1939b, (v3)
  PR6019.O9 F5 1961, (v3)
  PR6019.O9 F5 1963, (v3)
  PR6019.O9.P63 1993c, (v3)
  PR6019.O9.U4 1986, (v3)
  PR6019.O9.Z483 1987, (v3)
  PR6019.O9.Z52, (v3)
Joyce, Joseph P. HD2731.J69 1988, (v6)
Joyce, Michael. PN56.T37.J69 1995, (v3)
  PN3377.C57.J69 2000, (v3)
Joyce, Miriam. DS247.K88.J69 1998, (v5)
Joyce, Patrick. HC255.J69 1980b, (v6)
Joyce, Patrick. HN388.E53.J69 1990, (v6)
Joyce, Rosemary A. F1434.2.S63, (v4)
  F1435.1.C42.J69 1991, (v4)
Joyce, Stanislaus. PR6019.O9.Z649, (v3)
Joyner, Charles W. F279.A43.J69 1984, (v4)
Joyner, Christopher C. KWX70.J694 1998, (v7)
Joyner, Nancy Carol. Z8748.37.J68, (v10)
Joyner, Tim. G420.M2.J69 1992, (v6)
Jrade, Cathy Login. PQ7081.J73 1998, (v3)
Ju, Ching-hua. NA1543.5.J813 1998, (v9)
Juan de la Cruz. PQ6400.J8.A17 1968, (v3)
Juan Manuel. PQ6401.A1 1953, (v3)
Juan, Jorge. F3444.J8213, (v4)
Juana Ines de la Cruz. PQ7296.J6.D5813 1998, (v3)
Juarrero, Alicia. B105.A35 J83 1999, (v8)
Judah, Tim. DR1230.S45.J83 1997, (v5)
  DR2087.J83 2000, (v5)
Judd, Deane Brewster. QC495.J79 1975, (v1)
Judd, Denis. DA16.J88 1997, (v5)
Judd, Elizabeth. HG4910.J84 1990, (v6)
Judd, J. Stephen. QA76.5.J83 1990, (v1)
Judge, Harry George. LA634.J82 1984, (v7)
Judge, Joan. PN5369.S483.S545 1996, (v3)
Judovitz, Dalia. N6853.D8.J83 1995, (v9)
Judson, Horace Freeland. QH506.J83 1996, (v1)
  QP624.J82, (v1)
Judson, Katharine Berry. E78.N78 J83 1997, (v4)
Judson, Lyman Spicer. QP306.J83, (v1)
Judson, Pieter M. DB85.J8 1996, (v5)
Judson, William V. DK265.7.J83 1998, (v5)
Judt, Tony. DC33.7.J83 1998, (v5)
  DC33.7.J84 1992, (v5)
Juergensmeyer, Mark. BL65.V55.J84 2000, (v8)
Juhasz, Suzanne. PS1541.Z5.J78 1993, (v3)
Juhasz, Suzanne. PS1541.Z5.J8 1983, (v3)
Jules-Rosette, Bennetta. PQ3981.J85 1998, (v3)
Julian, Hubert Fauntleroy. CT275.J97.A3, (v5)
Julian, of Norwich. BV4831.J8 1978, (v8)
Juliana. PR1652.A3.S7 1972, (v3)

Juliani, Richard N. F158.68.L58.J84 1998, (v4)
Juliano, Annette L. DS793.N6 J85 2001, (v5)
Juliano, Bienvenido O. QP144.R53.J85 1993, (v1)
Julien, Catherine J. F3429.J85 2000, (v4)
Julien, Eileen. PQ3984.J85 1992, (v3)
Julien, Robert M. RM300.J85 1988, (v2)
Julier, Guy. NK1390.J85 1993, (v9)
Jullian, Philippe. DC752.M7.J8413, (v5)
  PR5823.J813 1969, (v3)
Jumars, Peter A. QH541.5.S3.J85 1993, (v1)
Jumonville, Florence M. Z1289.J86 2002, (v10)
Jumonville, Neil. F128.52.J86 1990, (v4)
Jump, John Davies. PR4023.J8, (v3)
Jung, C. G. BF173.J6623 1983, (v2)
  BF173.J67, (v2)
  BF173.J74 1950, (v2)
  BF173.J8 1963, (v2)
  BL53.J8, (v8)
  BL313.J83 1963, (v8)
  BL1238.56.K86.J86 1996, (v8)
Jung, Courtney Elizabeth. JQ1981.J85 2000, (v7)
Junge, Ewald. CJ67.J86 1984, (v5)
Jungk, Robert. QC773.J813, (v1)
Jungnickel, Christa. Q11.P612 vol. 220, (v1)
  QC7.J86 1986, (v1)
  QD22.C4.J86 1999, (v1)
Juniper, Tony. QL696.P7.J86 1998, (v1)
Junker, Patricia A. ND237.C88.A4 1998, (v9)
Junne, George H. Z1361.N39.J86 2000, (v10)
Junod, Dominique-D. HV568.J86 1996, (v6)
Juo, Pei-Show. R121.J86 1996, (v2)
Jupp, Victor. HV6024.5.J87 1989, (v6)
Jura, Jean-Jacques. PN1999.B36.J87 1998, (v3)
Jurafsky, Dan. P98.J87 2000, (v3)
Jurich, Marilyn. PN56.5.T74.J87 1998, (v3)
Jurinski, James. KF6289.J87 2000, (v7)
  LC111.J87 1998, (v7)
Jurkevich, Gayana. PQ6623.A816.Z64 1999, (v3)
  PQ6639.N3.Z745 1991, (v3)
Jusczyk, Peter W. BF720.S67.J87 1997, (v2)
Jusdanis, Gregory. JC311J87 2001, (v7)
Jussen, Bernhard. BV1478.J89 2000, (v8)
Jusserand, J. J. PR93.J82 1969, (v3)
Jussim, Estelle. TR660.J87 1985, (v1)
Just, Peter. DS632.D68, (v5)
Juster, Susan. BX6239.J87 1994, (v8)
Justesen, Benjamin R. E664.W593, (v4)
Justice, Donald Rodney. PS3519.U825.A17 1979, (v3)
  PS3519.U825N5, (v3)
Justice, Keith L. Z1033.B3.J87 1998, (v10)
Justman, Stewart. BF38.J87 1998, (v2)
  JC585.M75.J87 1990, (v7)
  PR931.J87 1999, (v3)
Jutikkala, Eino. DL1032.J8713 1962, (v5)
Juvenal. PA6447.E5.R8 1991, (v3)
Juvenalis, Decimus Junius. PA6446.A2 1967, (v3)
Juviler, Peter H. JC599.F6.J88 1998, (v7)
Juvinall, Robert C. TJ230.J88 2000, (v7)
Jweid, Rosann. Z1037.J93 2001, (v10)
K., Nora. B105.C45.K1513 2000, (v8)
K̄alid ̄asa. PK3795.A6E6 1997, (v3)
Kaariainen, Kimmo. BX493.K33 1998, (v8)
Kabir. PK2095.K3.A25 1961, (v3)
  PK2095.K3.B4913 1983, (v3)
Kabisama, H. W. TK1005.K32 1993, (v1)
Kadare, Ismail. PG9621.K3G513 1990, (v3)
  PG9621.K3L8513 2002, (v3)
  PG9621.K3T7513 2000, (v3)
Kadel, Andrew. Z7751.K33 1995, (v10)
Kadish, Alon. HB103.A2.K24 1989, (v6)
Kadish, Doris Y. PQ653.K3 1991, (v3)
Kadison, Lars. QA471.K224 1996, (v1)
Kadlec, Robert H. TD755.K33 1996, (v1)
Kadushin, Alfred. HV41.K22, (v6)
  HV43.K26 1997, (v6)
  HV741.K26 1980, (v6)
Kaempfer, Engelbert. DS835.K2 1971, (v5)
Kaempfer, William H. HF1413.5.K34 1992, (v6)
Kaeo, Peter Young. DU627.17.K28.A44, (v5)
Kaes, Anton. PN1993.5.G3.K2913 1989, (v3)

Kaestle, Carl F. LA215.K33 1983, (v7)
   LC151.K32 1991, (v7)
Kafadar, Cemal. DR486.K34 1995, (v5)
Kafai, Yasmin B. LB1028.66.K34 1995, (v7)
Kafesoglu, Ibrahim. DS27.K28 1988, (v5)
Kafka, Franz. PT2621.A26 A24 1971, (v3)
   PT2621.A26 A6 1952, (v3)
   PT2621.A26 A82, (v3)
   PT2621.A26 B32, (v3)
   PT2621.A26B34, (v3)
   PT2621.A26.D4, (v3)
   PT2621.A26.H6, (v3)
   PT2621.A26.P4, (v3)
   PT2621.A26 P74, (v3)
   PT2621.A26.S33 1998, (v3)
   PT2621.A26 S3513 1954, (v3)
   PT2621.A26.Z5, (v3)
   PT2621.A26.Z53 1958, (v3)
   PT2621.A26.Z53913 1982, (v3)
   PT2621.A26.Z5513 1954, (v3)
   PT2621.A26.Z625, (v3)
   PT2621.A26 1947, (v3)
Kafka, Phillipa. PS153.A84.K34 1997, (v3)
   PS153.H56.K34 2000, (v3)
   PS153.M4.K34 2000, (v3)
Kagan, Alfred. Z3501.K15 1998, (v10)
Kagan, B. A. GC190.5.K34 1995, (v6)
Kagan, Donald. DF229.2.K3, (v5)
   DF229.37.K34 1987, (v5)
   JC73.K28, (v7)
Kagan, Jerome. BF38.K23 1998, (v2)
   BF721.K158 1984, (v2)
   BF723.T53.K34 1994, (v2)
Kagan, Norman. PN1998.3.S76.K35 1995, (v3)
Kagan, Richard L. HT127.5.K34 2000, (v6)
Kagan, Richard. HV699.K35 1996, (v6)
Kagan, Sharon Lynn. HV95.K278 1993, (v6)
Kagan, Shelly. BJ1012.K244 1998, (v8)
Kaganoff, Nathan M. Z6373.U5.K34 1995, (v10)
Kagen, Sergius. ML128.V7.K3 1968, (v9)
Kahan, Arcadius. HC334.5.K34 1989, (v6)
Kahan, Basil Charles. Z253.M483.K34 2000, (v10)
Kahan, Jeffrey. PR2950.K35 1998, (v3)
Kahane, Howard. BC175.K25 1988, (v8)
   BJ1031.K23 1995, (v8)
Kahane, Leo H. QA278.2.K34 2001, (v1)
Kahin, Audrey. E183.8.I5.K34 1995, (v4)
Kahlenberg, Richard D. KF373.K34 A3 1999, (v7)
Kahler, Heinz. N5760.K313, (v9)
   NA5870.A9.K33, (v9)
Kahlo, Frida. ND259.K33.A2 1995, (v9)
Kahn, Ada P. RC437.K34 1993, (v2)
   RG121.K218 1990, (v2)
Kahn, Alfred J. HN18.K22, (v6)
   HN18.K23, (v6)
Kahn, Charles H. B395.K24 1996, (v8)
Kahn, David. D810.C88.K34 1991, (v5)
   D810.S7.K25, (v5)
   PN2053.K34 1995, (v3)
   Z103.K28, (v10)
Kahn, Douglas. NX650.S68.K25 1999, (v9)
Kahn, Harold L. DS754.4.C5.K3, (v5)
Kahn, Herman. CB160.K3 1967, (v5)
   U263.K33 1984, (v10)
   UA11.K32, (v10)
   UF767.K25 1960, (v10)
Kahn, Jonathan. HJ2051.K34 1997, (v6)
Kahn, Kenneth B. TS170 K34 2001, (v1)
Kahn, Lothar. PT169.K34 1993, (v3)
Kahn, Louis I. NA737.K32.A2 1991, (v9)
Kahn, Miriam. Z679.7.K38 2003, (v10)
Kahn, Paul W. KF380.K34 1997, (v7)
   PR2819.K34 2000, (v3)
Kahn, Roger. GV875.B7.K3 1972, (v6)
Kahn, Sholom Jacob. PJ5059.E1.K3, (v3)
Kahn, Susan Martha. KMK1527.K34 2000, (v7)
Kahn, Victoria Ann. PN173.K33 1994, (v3)
Kahn, Wolf. NC139.K27, (v9)
Kahnweiler, Daniel Henry. ND813.G75.K313 1969b, (v9)
Kahrl, William L. HD4464.L7K33 1982, (v6)

Kaiko, Takeshi. PL855.A32.N313x, (v3)
Kain, Philip J. JC233.M299.K35 1993, (v7)
Kain, R. J. P. GA109.5.K35 1992, (v6)
Kain, Richard Morgan. DA995.D75.K3, (v5)
   PR6019.O9.U67, (v3)
Kainz, Howard P. BC199.P2.K35 1988, (v8)
Kaiser, Charles. HQ76.3.U52.N486 1997, (v6)
Kaiser, David E. D217.K32 1990, (v5)
Kaiser, Geoffrey. KF299.P8.K35 1987, (v7)
Kaiser, Gerald. QA403.3.K35 1994, (v1)
Kaiser, Robert John. JN6520.R43.K37 1994, (v7)
Kaiser, Rolf. PR1505.K313 1971, (v3)
Kakac, S. TJ263.K25 1998, (v1)
Kakar, M. Hasan. DS371.2.K35 1995, (v5)
Kakar, Sudhir. DS422.C64 K35 1996, (v5)
Kakar, Suman. HV6626.2.K35 1998, (v6)
Kaku, Michio. QC21.2.K3 1995, (v1)
   UA23.K294 1987, (v10)
Kalaidjian, Walter B. NX180.S6.K32 1993, (v9)
Kalamkarov, Alexander L. TA418.9.C6.K34 1992, (v1)
Kalb, Jonathan. PR6003.E282.Z7538 1989, (v3)
   PT2673.U29.Z725 1998, (v3)
Kalb, Marvin L. E840.8.K58.K34, (v4)
   E856.K345 1994, (v4)
Kaldor, Mary. D1053.K35 1990, (v5)
Kaldor, Nicholas. HB171.K28 1980, (v6)
   HB171.K2852 1981, (v6)
   HB171.K286 1989, (v6)
Kale, Steven D. DC340.K26 1992, (v5)
Kalecki, Michal. HD74.5.K35 1986, (v6)
Kaler, James B. QB145.K33 1996, (v1)
   QB801.K25 1992, (v1)
   QB857.K35 1997, (v1)
   QB871.K33 1989, (v1)
Kaleta, Kenneth C. PN1998.3.L96.K35 1993, (v3)
Kalfatovic, Martin R. Z5961.U5 K36 1994, (v10)
Kalfus, Melvin. SB470.O5.K35 1990, (v1)
Kalicharan, Noel. QA76.73.C15.K35 1994, (v1)
Kalichman, Seth C. RC607.A26K356 1998, (v2)
Kalidasa. PK3795.E5 1984, (v3)
   PK3796.M6.N3, (v3)
Kallberg, Jeffrey. ML410.C54.K16 1996, (v9)
Kallen, Horace Meyer. BH81.K3, (v8)
Kalley, Jacqueline A. DT1147.K35 1999, (v5)
   KTL2558.K35 2001, (v7)
Kallina, Edmund F. F316.23.K57.K35 1993, (v4)
Kallir, Jane. N6811.5.S34.A4 1994, (v9)
Kallir, Jane. ND237.M78.A4 2001, (v9)
Kallis, Aristotle A. DG571.K34 2000, (v5)
Kalman, Dan. QA401.K24 1997, (v1)
Kalman, Laura. KF292.Y314 K35 2001, (v7)
   KF4552.K35 1996, (v7)
   KF8745.F65.K35 1990, (v7)
Kalnein, Wend von. NA1046.K35 1995, (v9)
Kaloudis, George Stergiou. JN5147.K35 2000, (v7)
Kalupahana, David J. BQ4090.K36 1992, (v8)
Kalven, Harry. KF4772.K35 1988, (v7)
Kalyvas, Stathis N. JN94.A979.K35 1996, (v7)
Kamarck, Andrew M. HC695.K25, (v6)
Kamber, Richard. B2430.S34 K337 2000, (v8)
Kamen, Charles Samuel. HD2058.5.K36 1991, (v6)
Kamen, Edward W. TK5102.9.K35 1997, (v1)
Kamen, Henry Arthur Francis. BX1735.K312 1998, (v8)
   D106.K36 2000, (v5)
   D281.5.K36 1969, (v5)
   DP66.K3 1973b, (v5)
   DP178.K36 1997, (v5)
   DP186.K35, (v5)
   DP194.K3613 2001, (v5)
   HN373.K293 2000, (v6)
Kamenetsky, Christa. PD63.K36 1992, (v3)
Kamenka, Eugene. B3305.M74.K3 1972, (v8)
Kamens, Edward. PL728.K236 1997, (v3)
Kamerman, Sheila B. HD6065.5.U6.K35 1983, (v6)
Kamiânski, Andrzej Sulima. DK4185.R9 K35 1993, (v5)
Kamien, Morton I. HC79.T4.K3, (v6)
Kamin, Leon J. BF431.K3646, (v2)
Kaminer, Wendy. BF632.K36 1993, (v2)
   KF4758.K35 1990, (v7)

Kaminkow, Marion J. F179.3.K36 1996, (v4)
Kaminsky, Amy K. PN98.W64.K36 1993, (v3)
Kaminsky, Howard. DB208.K3, (v5)
Kamm, Antony. PR106.K35 1997, (v3)
Kamm, F. M. HQ767.15.K36 1992, (v1)
Kammen, Carol. E180.K25 2000, (v4)
Kammen, Michael G. E169.1.K294 1991, (v4)
   F122.K27, (v4)
   KF4541.K35 1988, (v7)
   N6537.G9.K36 1999, (v9)
   N7483.S38.K36 1996, (v9)
Kamminga, Menno T. K3240.4.K26 1992, (v7)
Kampar. PL4758.9.K27.R35213 1989, (v3)
Kampelman, Max M. HD8055.C75.K32 1971, (v6)
Kamphoefner, Walter D. F475.G3.K354 1987, (v4)
Kamps, Ivo. PR678.H5.K36 1996, (v3)
Kamra, Sukeshi. DS480.842.K355 2002, (v5)
Kamuf, Peggy. PN81.K338 1997, (v3)
   PQ645.K3, (v3)
Kan, Katharine. Z718.5.K36 1998, (v10)
Kan, Pao. GR335.K3313 1996, (v6)
Kan, Sergei. E99.T6.K339 1999, (v4)
Kanafʿānʾī, Ghassʿan. PJ7842.A5R513 1998, (v3)
Kandall, Stephen R. HV5824.W6.K35 1996, (v6)
Kandinsky, Wassily. N7454.K3 1982, (v9)
   ND699.K3.A4 1979, (v9)
Kandiuk, Mary. Z1377.F8.K35 1990, (v10)
Kane, Francis. JC330.15.K36 1998, (v7)
Kane, George. PR311.K36 1979, (v3)
   PR313.K3 1989, (v3)
Kane, Harnett Thomas. F375.K16, (v4)
Kane, Joseph Nathan. AG5.K315 1997, (v10)
Kane, Leslie. PS3563.A4345.Z79 1999, (v3)
Kane, Patricia E. NK2715.K36 1976, (v9)
Kane, Paul. ND249.K3.H3, (v9)
   PR9610.2.K36 1996, (v3)
Kane, Paula M. F73.9.C3.K36 1994, (v4)
Kane, Penny. PR878.D65.K36 1995, (v3)
Kane, Robert. BJ1012.K274 1993, (v8)
Kanellos, Nicolas. PN2270.H57.K36 1990, (v3)
   Z6953.5.S66, (v10)
Kanfer, Stefan. F127.C3.K36 1989, (v4)
Kanfer, Stefan. PN2287.M53.K36 2000, (v3)
Kang, Etsuko Hae-jin. DS849.K8.K34 1997, (v5)
Kang-hsi. DS754.4.C53.A33 1974, (v5)
Kanigel, Robert. QA29.R3.K36 1991, (v1)
Kanin, Fay (Mitchell). PS3521.A448.G6, (v3)
Kanin, Garson. PS3521.A45.B6, (v3)
   PS3521.A45.G5, (v3)
Kanipe, Jeff. QB44.2.K35 1999, (v1)
Kaniss, Phyllis C. PN4749.K35 1991, (v3)
   PN4899.P5.K36 1995, (v3)
Kaniuk, Yoram. PJ5054.K326.A8913 1988, (v3)
Kaniuk, Yoram. PJ5054.K326.B5813 1989, (v3)
Kann, Kenneth. F869.P4.K36 1993, (v4)
Kann, Mark E. JK54.K26 1998, (v7)
Kann, Robert A. DB86.K3 1964, (v5)
   DJK4.S93 vol. 6, (v5)
Kanner, Barbara. Z7963.B6.K35 1997, (v10)
Kano, Takayoshi. QL737.P96.K27 1992, (v1)
Kant, Immanuel. AC1.G72 1990 vol. 39, (v10)
   B2758 .B5, (v8)
   B2758.F7, (v8)
   B2758.1992, (v8)
   B2766.E6.G7 1998, (v8)
   B2766.E6.P3 1967, (v8)
   B2773.E5.B4, (v8)
   B2791.E5.G7 1960a, (v8)
   B2799.H7.B43, (v8)
   BC63.K3 1972, (v8)
   BH183.K313 1960, (v8)
   LB675.K18513 1971, (v7)
Kanter, Donald L. HD70.U5.K36 1989, (v6)
Kanter, Rosabeth Moss. H31.S67 no. 9, (v6)
   HC79.I55.K358 2001, (v6)
Kantha, Sachi Sri. QC16.E5.K36 1996, (v1)
Kantor, J. R. BF44.K3, (v2)

Kantor, MacKinlay. PS3521.A47 A65, (v3)
 PS3521.A47.G7, (v3)
 PS3521.A47 I35, (v3)
 PS3521.A47 L6, (v3)
 PS3521.A47 S65, (v3)
Kantor, Tadeusz. PN2859.P6.K36 1993, (v3)
Kantorski, Vincent. ML128.I64.K36 1997, (v9)
Kantra, Robert A. PR931.K3 1984, (v3)
Kantrowitz, Stephen David. E664.T57.K36 2000, (v4)
Kany, Charles Emil. PC4821.K27, (v3)
 PC4821.K3 1951, (v3)
 PC4822.K3, (v3)
Kao, Shang-chuan. HC427.92.K383 1996, (v6)
Kapchan, Deborah A. HF3882.K37 1996, (v6)
Kaplan, Abraham. H61.K24, (v6)
Kaplan, Alice Yaeger. D802.F8.B6985 2000, (v5)
Kaplan, Barbara Beigun. R489.B693.K37 1993, (v2)
Kaplan, Bernard. BF149.K37, (v2)
Kaplan, Caren. PN56.T7.K37 1996, (v3)
Kaplan, Carter. PN6149.S2.K36 2000, (v3)
Kaplan, Cora. PR119.K37 1986, (v3)
Kaplan, Daniel. QA845.K36 1995, (v1)
Kaplan, Deborah. RF4036.K3 1992, (v3)
Kaplan, Edward S. HG2525.K36 1999, (v6)
Kaplan, Fred. PR4581.K27, (v3)
 PR4581.K28 1988, (v3)
 PS2123.K36 1992, (v3)
Kaplan, Harold Morris. QP306.K3 1971, (v1)
Kaplan, Helen Singer. RC556.K33, (v2)
Kaplan, Herbert H. DK434.K33 1972, (v5)
Kaplan, Jacob J. HG3881.K28 1989, (v6)
Kaplan, John. HV5822.H4.K36 1983, (v6)
Kaplan, Jonathan Michael. RB155.K36 2000, (v2)
Kaplan, Karel. DB2222.K37x 1987b, (v5)
Kaplan, Lawrence S. E744.K177 1999, (v4)
Kaplan, Louis. N6822.5.M63.K36 1995, (v9)
Kaplan, M. Lindsay. PR428.L53.K37 1997, (v3)
Kaplan, Marion A. DS135.G33.K292 1991, (v5)
Kaplan, Martha. GN671.F5.K37 1995, (v6)
Kaplan, Max. NX180.S6.K36 1989, (v9)
Kaplan, Rachel. AM48.P3.K36 1996, (v10)
Kaplan, Robert M. RA395.A3.K35 1993, (v2)
Kaplan, Robert S. HD30.28.K3544 2001, (v6)
Kaplan, Robert. QA141.K36 2000, (v1)
Kaplan, S. A. QB801.K2813 1983, (v1)
Kaplan, Stephen S. UA770.K28, (v10)
Kaplan, Steven L. DC160.K36 1995, (v5)
 HD9058.B743.F85 1996, (v6)
Kaplan, Steven M. TK9.K37 1996, (v1)
Kaplan, Steven. DS135.E75.K35 1992, (v5)
Kaplan, Temma. HN590.B3.K37 1992, (v6)
Kaplar, Richard T. PN4888.E8.K37 1995, (v3)
Kapleau, Philip. BD444.K34 1989, (v8)
Kaplin, William A. KF4550.K36 1992, (v7)
Kaplowitz, Donna Rich. HF1500.5.U5.K36 1998, (v6)
Kapoor, L. D. RS165.O6.K37 1995, (v2)
Kapoun, Robert W. E98.C8.K36 1992, (v4)
Kapp, Marshall B. KF3608.A4.A125 1988, (v7)
 Z6673.35.K36 1992, (v10)
Kappes, Marcianne. PS3531.O9723.Z74 1994, (v3)
Kappraff, Jay. QA447.K37 1990, (v1)
Kapr, Albert. Z126.Z7.K2813 1996, (v10)
Kapsis, Robert E. PN1998.3.H58.K36 1992, (v3)
Kapstein, Ethan B. HC79.D4.K37 1992, (v6)
Kapstein, Matthew. BQ7576.K37 2000, (v8)
Kaptur, Marcy. E747.K37 1996, (v4)
Kapur, Ashok. UA853.P3.K37 1987, (v10)
Kapur, Ratna. KNS516.K36 1996, (v7)
Kapur, Sudarshan. E185.61.K344 1992, (v4)
Karabell, Zachary. E813.K37 1999, (v4)
 E815.K37 2000, (v4)
 LA227.4.K37 1998, (v7)
Karakasidou, Anastasia N. DF901.A75.K37 1997, (v5)
Karam, Azza M. HQ1793.K37 1998, (v6)
Karamanski, Theodore J. HD9944.U46.A193 1983, (v6)
Karamzin, Nikolai Mikhailovich. PG3314.A25, (v3)
Karandikar, Govind Vinayak. PK2418.K318A24 1998, (v3)
Karasu, Bilge. PL248.K33.G4313 1994, (v3)
Karatani, Kojin. PL726.6.K2813 1993, (v3)

Karch, Steven B. QP801.C68.K369 1998, (v1)
Karcher, Carolyn L. HQ1413.C45.K37 1994, (v6)
Karetnikova, Inga. PN1998.3.E34.K37 1991, (v3)
Kari, Daven Michael. Z7776.68.K37 1995, (v10)
Karier, Clarence J. LA205.K3 1986, (v7)
Karimi-Hakkak, Ahmad. PK6418.K37 1995, (v3)
Karimov, I. A. DK948.8657.K3747 1998, (v5)
Kark, Ruth. DS110.J3.K3713 1990, (v5)
Karl, Barry Dean. E741.K33 1983, (v4)
Karl, Frederick Robert. PR881.K25 1972, (v3)
 PR4681.K37 1995, (v3)
 PR6005.O4.Z759, (v3)
 PR6005.O4.Z76, (v3)
 PR6037.N58.Z7, (v3)
 PT2621.A26.Z7619 1991, (v3)
Karlen, Arno. PS3561.A61.W5, (v3)
Karlgren, Bernhard. PL1073.K3, (v3)
Karlin, Daniel. PR4242.H34.K37 1993, (v3)
Karlin, Fred. ML2075.K37 1994, (v9)
Karlinsky, Simon. PG3476.T75Z743 1985, (v3)
Karloff, Howard. T57.74.K37 1991, (v1)
Karma-gliçn-pa. BQ4490.K3713 1993, (v8)
Karmel, Paul R. TK7876.K35 1997, (v1)
Karnes, Frances A. KF4209.5.K369 2000, (v7)
Karnes, Thomas L. F593.G48K3, (v4)
 F1438.K26, (v4)
Karny, Yo'av. DK511.C2.K27 2000, (v5)
Karol, K. S. DS777.55.K32413 1974, (v5)
Karolides, Nicholas J. Z658.U5 K35 1999, (v10)
 Z658.U5.K37 1998, (v10)
Karp, Abraham J. BM205.K38 1998, (v8)
Karp, David Allen. RC537.K367 1996, (v2)
Karp, Rashelle S. PN1627.K37 1990, (v3)
Karpat, Kemal H. DR572 .K28 2001, (v5)
Karras, Alan L. F187.C5.K37 1992, (v4)
Karras, Ruth Mazo. HT1211.K37 1988, (v6)
Karsh, Efraim. DS115.5.K37 2000, (v5)
Karsh, Yousuf. TR680.K3, (v1)
Karski, Jan. DK4402.K37 1985, (v5)
Karson, Robin S. SB470.S65.K37 1989, (v1)
Karst, Kenneth L. KF4700.K37 1989, (v7)
 KF4750.K37 1993, (v7)
Karsten, Eileen. PN1995.9.B55.K37 1993, (v3)
Karsten, Peter. KF4575.K37 1997, (v7)
 VB313.K36, (v10)
Karta (Firm). G2205.K33 1988, (v6)
Kartesz, John T. QK110.K37 1994, (v1)
Kartsev, Vladimir Petrovich. DK510.766.Z48.K37 1995, (v5)
Karwatka, Dennis. T21.K55 1996, (v1)
Kasaba, Resat. HC492.K37 1988, (v6)
Kasabov, Nikola K. QA76.76.E95.K375 1996, (v1)
Kasack, Wolfgang. Z2500.K3513 1988, (v10)
Kaschak, Ellyn. HQ1206.K37 1992, (v6)
Kase, Francis Joseph. K1500.A51 K38, (v7)
Kasfir, Sidney Littlefield. N7380.K36 2000, (v9)
Kashani, Javad H. RJ507.F35.K37 1998, (v2)
Kashap, S. Paul. B3999.F8.K37 1987, (v8)
Kashner, Sam. ML417.L64.K37 1994, (v9)
Kasinitz, Philip. F128.9.W54.K37 1992, (v4)
Kaske, Carol V. PR2367.R4.K37 1999, (v3)
Kasler, Dirk. HM22.G3.W446813 1988, (v6)
Kasravi, Ahmad. BP163.K3813 1990, (v8)
Kass, Ilana. DS119.7.K2996 1997, (v5)
Kass, Leon. QH442.2.K37 1998, (v1)
Kass, Ray. N6537.G688.A4 1983, (v9)
Kassin, Saul M. KF8972.K37 1988, (v7)
Kassis, Hanna E. BP133.K37 1983, (v8)
Kasson, John F. F129.C75.K37 1978, (v4)
Kasson, Joy S. GV1821.B8.K37 2000, (v6)
 NB1210.M3.K3 1990, (v9)
Kassow, Samuel D. LA838.7.K37 1989, (v7)
Kast, Fremont Ellsworth. UC267.K3, (v10)
Kast, Verena. RC480.K28513 1992, (v2)
Kastan, David Scott. PR3014.K37 1999, (v3)
Kastely, James L. B52.7.K37 1997, (v8)
Kaster, Robert A. PA53.K37 1988, (v3)
Kasun, Jacqueline R. HB883.5.K37 1988, (v6)
Kasza, Gregory James. JC481.K34 1995, (v7)
Kat̄o, Sh̄uichi. N7350.K3513, (v9)

Kataev, Valentin. PG3476.K4V713 1995, (v3)
Katcher, Philip R. N. E468.K24 1992, (v4)
Katchmer, George A. PN2285.K34 1991, (v3)
Kateb, George. JC571.K344 1992, (v7)
Kater, Michael H. ML275.5.K38 1997, (v9)
 ML390.K198 2000, (v9)
 ML3509.G3.K37 1992, (v9)
Kates, Gary. DC158.8.K38 1985, (v5)
Kates, Susan. PE1405.U6.K38 2001, (v3)
Katok, A. B. QA614.8.K38 1995, (v1)
Katouzian, Homa. DS298.K38 2000, (v5)
Katra, William H. F2846.3.K38 1996, (v4)
 F2849.2.K38 1988, (v4)
Kats, Yosef. DS126.K38 1998, (v5)
Katsh, M. Ethan. K87.K38 1995, (v7)
Kattenburg, Paul M. E183.8.V5.K36, (v4)
Kattsoff, Louis Osgood. BD331.K3 1967, (v8)
Kattwinkel, Susan. PS549.N5.K38 1998, (v3)
Katz, Barbara. QL696.G84.K385 1993, (v1)
Katz, Barry M. D810.S7.K33 1989, (v5)
Katz, Bernard. QP356.3.K3, (v1)
Katz, D. Mark. TR140.G35.K38 1991, (v1)
Katz, David. BF80.5.K32, (v2)
 BF203.K313, (v2)
 BF275.K3713 1989, (v2)
Katz, Donald La Verne. TN880.K38 1990, (v1)
Katz, Dovid. PJ5151.K38 1987, (v3)
Katz, Elihu. HE8689.95.K37, (v6)
Katz, Ephraim. PN1993.45.K34 1994, (v3)
Katz, Fred E. BJ1401.K38 1993, (v8)
Katz, Jack. BF531.K38 1999, (v2)
Katz, Jacob. BM376.H8.K3813 1998, (v8)
 DS112.K373, (v5)
 DS145.K354, (v5)
Katz, Jonathan. HQ76.3.U5.K37 1976, (v6)
Katz, Joseph. B693.Z7.K3, (v8)
Katz, Linda Sobel. GE1.K38 1993, (v6)
Katz, Michael B. HV91.K349 1986, (v6)
 LA212.K275 1987, (v7)
Katz, Michael Jay. QP517.B48.K37 1988, (v1)
Katz, Nathan. DS135.I6.K38 2000, (v5)
Katz, Paul R. BL1812.G63 K37 1995, (v8)
 BL1941.5.J84 K37 1999, (v8)
Katz, Peter. NA2542.4.K38 1994, (v9)
Katz, Raul Luciano. HD9696.A3.D446 1988, (v6)
Katz, Richard. HC462.95.K388 2003, (v6)
 HF1601.K29 1998, (v6)
Katz, Samuel M. UB271.I8.K37 1992, (v10)
Katz, Sandra L. PS3511.R94.Z7575 1988, (v3)
Katz, Steven T. D804.3.K378 1994, (v5)
Katz, Tamar. PR888.M63.K38 2000, (v3)
Katz, William A. Z1035.1.K35 1998, (v10)
 Z6941.K2 1972, (v10)
 Z7156.A1.K38 1994, (v10)
Katzan, Harry. QA76.5.K374 1975, (v1)
Katzen, Sid. TJ223.P76, (v1)
Katzenbach, Jon R. HD66.K384 1993, (v6)
Katzenstein, Peter J. UA845.K376 1996, (v10)
Katzman, David M. F574.D49 N448, (v4)
 HD6072.2.U5.K37, (v6)
Katzman, Kenneth. UA853.I7.K38 1993, (v10)
Katzmann, Robert A. KF8700.K37 1997, (v7)
Katzner, Kenneth. PG2640.K34 1984, (v3)
Kauffman, Christopher J. HS1538.K65, (v6)
Kauffman, Erle. E312.17.K29, (v4)
Kauffman, Linda S. PN3448.E6.K38 1992, (v3)
Kauffman, Stuart A. QH325.K388 1995, (v1)
Kaufman, Andrew L. KF8745.C3.K38 1998, (v7)
Kaufman, Bruce E. HD8066.K38 1993, (v6)
Kaufman, Burton Ira. E872.K38 1993, (v4)
 HF1455.K282 1982, (v6)
Kaufman, Edy. F3100.K4 1988, (v4)
Kaufman, George S. PS3521.A727.S5 1942a, (v3)
Kaufman, Gershen. RC455.4.S53.K38 1989, (v2)
Kaufman, Jonathan. E185.615.K33 1988, (v4)
Kaufman, Kenn. QL681.K36 2000, (v1)
Kaufman, Natalie Hevener. K3240.4.K36 1990, (v7)
Kaufman, Peter Iver. BR195.A89.K38 1996, (v8)
Kaufman, Sharon R. R153.K24 1993, (v2)
Kaufman, Wallace. GE195.K38 1994, (v6)
Kaufmann, A. HD20.5.K313 1968, (v6)

Kaufmann, David. PR868.E37.K38 1995, (v3)
Kaufmann, Emil. NA590.K3 1966, (v9)
Kaufmann, Fritz. PT2625.A44.Z732 1973, (v3)
Kaufmann, J. E. UA23.K3675 1996, (v10)
Kaufmann, Ralph James. PR653.K3, (v3)
PR2439.B5.Z75 1961, (v3)
PR5366.K28, (v3)
Kaufmann, Thomas DaCosta. N6754.K38 1995, (v9)
Z5936.M34.K38 1988, (v10)
Kaufmann, Vincent. PQ611.K3814 1994, (v3)
Kaufmann, Walter Arnold. B819.K32, (v8)
B2948.K3, (v8)
Kaufmann, Walter. ML108.K37 1990, (v9)
Kaufmann, William J. QA76.88.K38 1993, (v1)
Kaufmann, William W. F1416.G7.K3, (v4)
UA23.K38, (v10)
Kaufman-Osborn, Timothy V. T14.K26 1997, (v1)
Kaunda, Kenneth D. HN803.Z9.V54 1981, (v6)
Kausler, Donald H. HQ1064.U5.K39 2001, (v6)
Kautsky, Karl. DK265.K33 1964, (v5)
Kauvar, Elaine M. PS3565.Z5.Z67 1993, (v3)
Kavale, Kenneth A. LC4705.K38 1995, (v7)
Kavan, Anna. PR6009.D63 A8 1980, (v3)
PR6009.D63 J8 1975, (v3)
PR6009.D63 W47, (v3)
Kavanagh, Dennis. DA591.T47.K38 1987, (v5)
Kavanagh, Gaynor. Z6201.K38 1996, (v10)
Kavanagh, Patrick. PR6021.A74 T3, (v3)
Kavanagh, Peter. PR8783.K3, (v3)
Kavanagh, Thomas M. PQ648.K38 1993, (v3)
Kavanagh, Thomas W. E99.C85.K39 1996, (v4)
Kavenik, Frances M. PR708.S46.K38 1995, (v3)
Kawabata, Yasunari. PL832.A9 L3, (v3)
PL832.A9 T453 1968, (v3)
PL832.A9 U813, (v3)
PL832.A9 Y32, (v3)
PL832.A9 Y813 1956, (v3)
PL832.A9 Y82 1969, (v3)
Kawakami, Barbara F. GT617.H3.K39 1993, (v6)
Kawakami, Kiyoshi Karl. DS784.K3, (v5)
Kawamura, Noriko. D610.K39 2000, (v5)
Kawamura, Susumu. TH4538.K39 1991, (v1)
Kawash, Samira. PS153.N5.K38 1997, (v3)
Kay, Dennis. PR2894.K34 1992, (v3)
Kay, Jane Holtz. HE5623.K36 1997, (v6)
Kay, Lily E. QH450.2.K39 2000, (v1)
Kay, Margarita Artschwager. RS172.W4.K38 1996, (v2)
Kay, Marvin L. Michael. E445.N8.K39 1995, (v4)
Kay, Melvyn. TC160.K38 1998, (v1)
Kayal, Philip M. HQ76.2.U5.K39 1993, (v6)
Kayali, Hasan. DS63.2.T8.K39 1997, (v5)
Kaye, Dalia Dassa. DS119.76.K354 2001, (v5)
Kaye, Frances W. PS3505.A87.Z684 1993, (v3)
Kaye, Harvey L. D13.K315 1992, (v5)
HC26.K39 1984, (v6)
Kaye, Lenard W. HV1461.K39 1990, (v6)
Kaye, Nick. PN2037.K35 1994, (v3)
Kaye, Sharon M. B655.Z7 K29 2001, (v8)
Kaylor, Noel Harold. Z8106.3.K38 1992, (v10)
Kayman, Martin A. PR830.D4.K39 1992, (v3)
Kayser, Karen. HQ734.K353 1993, (v6)
Kayser, Wolfgang Johannes. N8217.G8.K33, (v9)
Kazantzakis, Nikos. PA5610.K39.O33, (v3)
Kazin, Alfred. PN75.K3.A3, (v3)
PN511.K25, (v3)
Keach, William. PR5444.K4 1984, (v3)
Kealey, Edward J. R141.K4, (v2)
Kean, Beverly Whitney. N5276.2.S5.K4 1983, (v9)
Keane, Molly. PR6021.E33.G6 1981, (v3)
PR6021.E33.T5 1984, (v3)
Keane, Patrick J. PR5908.I52.K43 1987, (v3)
Keane, Webb. DS632.A52.K43 1997, (v5)
Kear, Lynn. Z7751.K43 1996, (v10)
Kearney, Christopher A. RJ506.S33.K42 2001, (v2)
Kearney, Hugh F. Q125.K42, (v1)
Kearney, Richard. B804.K363 1994, (v8)
Kearns, George. PS3531.O82.C2858 1989, (v3)
Kearns, John T. B945.K393.R43 1996, (v8)
Kearns, Sheila M. PR4476.K43 1995, (v3)
Kearns, William. ML410.P163 K4 1990, (v9)

Keast, William R. PR543.K4 1971, (v3)
Keates, Jonathan. ML410.H13.K33 1985, (v9)
ML410.P93.K4 1996, (v9)
Keating, AnaLouise. PS151.K43 1996, (v3)
Keating, Anne B. LB2331.K43 1999, (v7)
Keaton, Eleanor. PN2287.K4.K43 2001, (v3)
Keats, John. PR4830.F51, (v3)
PR4831.S75 1978, (v3)
PR4832.C66 1990, (v3)
PR4836.A45 1970, (v3)
PR4836.A5776, (v3)
PR4836.A58, (v3)
Keaveney, Arthur. DG260.L8.K43 1992, (v5)
Kebbede, Girma. HC845.K43 1992, (v6)
Keck, Leander E. BT303.2.K435 2000, (v8)
Keck, Margaret E. JF529.K43 1998, (v7)
Keddie, Nikki R. DS298.K39 1999, (v5)
Keddy, Paul A. QH541.5.M3, (v1)
Kedourie, Elie. DS63.2.G7.K38 1978, (v5)
JQ1758.A2.K4 1992, (v7)
Kedward, H. R. D802.F8.K4, (v5)
D802.F8.S675 1993, (v5)
Kee, Howard Clark. BS2407.K37 1983, (v8)
BV598.K425 1995, (v8)
Kee, Joyce LeFever. RM301.K44 2003, (v2)
Keeble, Curtis. DA47.65.K44 1990, (v5)
Keefe, James W. LB1031.K383 2000, (v7)
Keefe, Simon P. ML410.M9 K25 2001, (v9)
Keefe, Terry. PQ2603.E362.Z75 1983, (v3)
Keefer, Janice Kulyk. PR9199.3.G26.Z74 1989, (v3)
Keegan, John. D25.K43 1976, (v5)
D521.K345 1999, (v5)
D736.K43 1978, (v5)
D743.42.K42 1996, (v5)
E46.5.K44 1996, (v4)
U27.K38 1993, (v10)
V53.K44 1989, (v10)
Keegan, Timothy J. DT1756.K44 1996, (v5)
HN801.A8.K44 1988, (v6)
Keegan, Warren J. HF1009.5.K39 1984, (v6)
Keegan, William F. F1655.K44 1992, (v4)
Keehn, J. D. BF105.K44 1996, (v2)
Keele, Alan Frank. PT2613.R338.Z687 1988, (v3)
Keeler, Robert F. PN4899.N42.N525 1990, (v3)
Keeler, Ward. PN1979.S5.K444 1992, (v3)
Keeling, David J. F3001.K44 1996, (v4)
HC175.K44 1997, (v6)
Keeling, Ralph. HD69.P75.G564 1996, (v6)
Keeling, Richard. ML128.F75.K44 1997, (v9)
ML3557.K43 1992, (v9)
Keen, A. Myra (Angeline Myra). QL415.P3K43 1974, (v1)
QL415.P3K43 1974, (v1)
Keen, Alan. PR2903.K4, (v3)
Keen, Benjamin. F1219.K43, (v4)
Keen, Benjamin. F1408.3.K44, (v4)
Keen, David. HC835.Z9.F3476 1994, (v6)
Keen, Ernest. BF105.K45 2001, (v2)
RC483.K44 1998, (v2)
RM315.K44 2000, (v2)
Keen, Lisa. KF228.E94.K44 1998, (v7)
Keen, Maurice Hugh. CR4513.K44 1984, (v5)
Keen, Mike Forrest. HM22.U5.K44 1999, (v6)
Keen, Peter G. W. HD30.23.K35, (v6)
HF5548.2.K395 1991, (v6)
Keenan, Stella. Z1006.K39 1996, (v10)
Keene, Donald. DS821.K33, (v5)
PL713.K43.A3413 1979, (v3)
PL726.1.K44 1988, (v3)
PL726.115.K44 1993, (v3)
PL726.35.K4, (v3)
PL726.55.K39 1984, (v3)
PL727.5.K38, (v3)
PL738.K4, (v3)
PL741.1.K44 1989, (v3)
PL855.KI4 1955, (v3)
PL882.K4, (v3)
PL882.K43, (v3)
PL890.K4, (v3)
Keene, Raymond D. GV1317.K44 1991, (v6)
Keener, John F. PS374.H5.K44 2001, (v3)

Keeney, Elizabeth. QK46.5.B66.K44 1992, (v1)
Keep, John L. H. DK267.K38 1995, (v5)
Keesing, Felix Maxwell. GN670.K43 1980, (v6)
Keeton, Morris T. LB2381.K43, (v7)
Keevil, John J. RC986.K36, (v2)
Kegley, Jacquelyn Ann K. B945.R64.K44 1997, (v8)
Kehler, Dorothea. Z5511.K4 1997, (v10)
Kehoe, Alice Beck. BL2370.S5 K43 2000, (v8)
Kehoe, Dennis P. HD139.A36.K439 1997, (v6)
Kehoe, Terence. HC107.A14.K45 1997, (v6)
Kehr, Helen. Z2240.K44 1982, (v10)
Keiger, John F. V. DC341.K44 1983, (v5)
DC385.K45 1997, (v5)
Keightley, David N. DS744.K43 2000, (v5)
DS744.K44, (v5)
Keijzer, Fred A. BF311.K45 2001, (v2)
Keil, Charles. ML3556.K43, (v9)
Keillor, Steven J. F595.P48.K45 1987, (v4)
Keim, Nancy. LB1031.5.K45 1993, (v7)
Keir, Robert Malcolm. E178.5.P2 vol. 5, (v4)
Keiser, Elizabeth B. PR1964.K45 1997, (v3)
Keiser, John H. HN79.I3K44, (v6)
Keiser, Richard A. JK1764.K45 1997, (v7)
Keister, Lisa A. HC110.I5.K38 2000, (v6)
Keita, Gwendolyn Puryear. Z1361.N39.K45 1996, (v10)
Keita, Maghan. E185.K38 2000, (v4)
Keith, Arthur Berriedale. BL1150.K43 1971, (v8)
PK2931.K4, (v3)
Keith, Caroline H. E748.T93.K45 1991, (v4)
Keith, Elmer. SK17.K45.A33 1979, (v1)
Keith, Herbert F. F127.A2.K4, (v4)
Keith, Lawrence H. TD193.K45 1991, (v1)
Keith, Michael C. PN1991.8.I53.K45 1995, (v3)
Keith, Nelson W. HC154.K45 1992, (v6)
Keith, W. J. PR9198.2.O5.K45 1992, (v3)
Keithley, Joseph F. QC535.K45 1999, (v1)
Kekes, John. B53.K38, (v8)
BD435.K37 2000, (v8)
BJ1012.K4 1988, (v8)
BJ1031.K24 1993, (v8)
JC573.K44 1998, (v7)
Kelbaugh, Doug. HT169.57.U62.S45 1997, (v6)
Kelen, Leslie G. F835.A1.K45 1996, (v4)
Kellas, James G. JC311.K43 1991, (v7)
Kellehear, Allan. BF1045.N4.K45 1996, (v2)
Kellenberger, James. BJ1188.K44 1989, (v8)
HM132.K4 1995, (v6)
Keller, Catherine. BD450.K368 1986, (v8)
Keller, Dean H. Z5781.K43 1990, (v10)
Keller, Edmond J. DT387.95.K45 1988, (v5)
Keller, Edward A. QE38.K45 2000, (v1)
QE511.4.K45 1996, (v1)
Keller, Evelyn Fox. QH428.K448 2000, (v1)
QH428.K45 1995, (v1)
Keller, Gary D. PN1995.9.H47.K46 1997, (v3)
PN1995.9.L37.K46 1994, (v3)
Keller, Gottfried. PT2374.A1 1985, (v3)
PT2374.A2 1982, (v3)
Keller, Harald. TA11.K45 1994, (v1)
TA11.K45 1994, (v1)
Keller, Max. PN2091.E4.K45 1999, (v3)
Keller, Morton. E661.K27, (v4)
HN57.K38 1994, (v6)
NC1429.N3.K4, (v9)
Keller, Nora Okja. PS3561.E38574C66 1997, (v3)
Keller, Pierre. B2799.S37.K45 1998, (v8)
Keller, William W. E743.5.K35 1989, (v4)
HD9743.A2.K45 1995, (v6)
Kellert, Stephen R. GE140.K47 1997, (v6)
GF21.K47 1996, (v6)
Kelley, Alice van Buren. PR6045.O72.T676 1987, (v3)
PR6045.O72.Z75, (v3)
Kelley, D. Lynn. QA276.K254 1999, (v1)
Kelley, David H. F1435.3.P6.K44, (v4)
Kelley, David. BC177.K38 1998, (v8)
Kelley, Donald R. D16.8.K37 1998, (v5)
DC33.3.K44, (v5)
Kelley, Earl Clarence. LB1025.K32 1970, (v7)
Kelley, Maurice. PR3592.R4.K4, (v3)
Kelley, Robin D. G. E185.61.K356 1994, (v4)

Kelley, Stanley. JK524.K34 1983, (v7)
Kelley, Theresa M. PR5892.A34.K44 1988, (v3)
Kelley, Wyn. PS2388.C52.K45 1996, (v3)
Kellie, Luna. F666.K45 1992, (v4)
Kelliher, Daniel Roy. HN740.Z9.C6388 1992, (v6)
Kelling, George L. HV8141.K45 1996, (v6)
Kellman, Philip J. BF720.P47.K45 1998, (v2)
Kellman, Steven G. PN171.M93, (v3)
Kellner, Bruce. Z8977.35.K45 1991, (v10)
Kellner, Douglas. PN4888.T4.K45 1992, (v3)
Kellner, Leon. PR3071.K4 1925, (v3)
Kellner, Menachem Marc. B759.M34.K44 1991, (v8)
Kellogg, Charles Flint. E185.5.N276.K4, (v4)
Kellogg, Louise Phelps. F482.K29, (v4)
    F584.K27 1968, (v4)
Kellogg, Susan. KDZ480.K45 1995, (v7)
Kellough, Gail. KE8920.K45 1996, (v7)
Kellum, Jo. SB434.7.K45 2001, (v1)
Kelly, Aileen. DK189.2.K45 1998, (v5)
Kelly, Alfred Hinsey. JK31.K4 1955, (v7)
Kelly, Amy Ruth. DA209.E6.K45 1950, (v5)
Kelly, Ann Cline. PR3728.L33.K45 1988, (v3)
Kelly, Barbara M. NA7571.K44 1993, (v9)
Kelly, Catriona. PG2997.K45 1994, (v3)
Kelly, Charles. F826.G654, (v4)
    F832.G7K45 1996, (v4)
Kelly, Christine A. HM881.K45 2001, (v6)
Kelly, David F. R725.56.K44 1991, (v2)
Kelly, Deirdre M. LC5551.K44 1993, (v7)
Kelly, Douglas. PQ201.K46 1993, (v3)
Kelly, Errol G. TN500.K44 1982, (v1)
Kelly, Fanny Wiggins. E99.D1 K46 1990, (v4)
Kelly, Franklin. ND237.C52.K45 1988, (v9)
Kelly, Gail P. Z5815.D44.K44 1989, (v10)
Kelly, Gary. PR851.K4, (v3)
Kelly, George Armstrong. JA84.F8.K45 1992, (v7)
Kelly, Ian. DS796.H757.K45 1986, (v5)
Kelly, J. M. K215.E53.K45 1992, (v7)
Kelly, J. N. D. BR1720.C5.K45 1995, (v8)
Kelly, Joan. HQ1154.K38 1984, (v6)
Kelly, John Dunham. DU600.K38 1991, (v5)
Kelly, John R. GV14.45.K447 2000, (v6)
Kelly, Joseph. PR6019.O9.Z6696 1998, (v3)
Kelly, Joyce. F1219.K44, (v4)
Kelly, Katherine E. PR6069.T6.Z73 1991, (v3)
Kelly, Kathleen Coyne. PN682.V56.K45 2000, (v3)
Kelly, Liz. HV6561.K45 1988, (v6)
Kelly, Lucie Young. RT82.K4 1999, (v2)
Kelly, Luther S. F594.K35 1973, (v4)
Kelly, Mary Pat. PN1998.3.S39.K45 1991, (v3)
Kelly, Michael J. KF300.K45 1994, (v7)
Kelly, Patrick J. UB383.A5.K45 1997, (v10)
Kelly, Petra Karin. JA75.8.K464 1994, (v7)
Kelly, R. Gordon. PS374.D4.K45 1998, (v3)
Kelly, Raymond C. GN497.K45 2000, (v6)
Kelly, Richard Michael. PR6013.R44.Z6345 1984, (v3)
    PR6013.R44.Z6346 1992, (v3)
Kelly, Rita Mae. HD6060.5.U52.A65 1991, (v6)
    HQ1236.K45, (v6)
Kelly, Robert Glynn. PS3561.E45.L3, (v3)
Kelly, Robert J. HV6446.K43 2000, (v6)
Kelly, Robert L. GN388.K44 1995, (v6)
Kelly, Ross S. U262.K45 1989, (v10)
Kelly, S. Graham. QA935.K38 1993, (v1)
Kelly, Saul. D1058.K35 2000, (v5)
Kelly, Thomas J. TL795.K45 2001, (v1)
Kelman, Herbert C. H62.K416, (v6)
Kelman, Mark. K230.K43.G85 1987, (v7)
    KF4215.K45 1997, (v7)
Kelsall, M. M. E332.2.K45 1999, (v4)
    PR408.C65.K45 1993, (v3)
Kelsay, Isabel Thompson. E99.I7.B784 1984, (v4)
Kelsen, Hans. JA37.C3 vol.2,no.1, (v7)
    K252.K45 1999, (v7)
    KZ4991.K45 2000, (v7)
Kelsey, Benjamin S. UG633.K43 1982, (v10)
Kelsey, Harry. DA86.22.D7.K45 1998, (v5)
Kelsey, Michael. F325.K45 1995, (v4)
Kelsey, W. Michael. PL787.K63.K4 1982, (v3)
Kelso, J. A. Scott. QP360.K454 1995, (v1)
Kelso, Robert Wilson. HV98.M39 K4 1969, (v6)

Kelton, Elmer. PS3561.E3975 T5, (v3)
Kemble, Edward C. PN4897.C2K4, (v3)
Kemble, Edwin C. QC174.1.K45 1958, (v1)
Kemble, Fanny. E445.G3 K46 1992, (v4)
    F290.K332 1961, (v4)
Kemenade, Willem van. DS706.K464 1997, (v5)
Kemeny, John G. QA39.K35 1966, (v1)
    QA76.73.B3.K46 1987, (v1)
Kemerer, Frank R. KF373.J87.K46 1991, (v7)
Kemmerer, Kathleen Nulton. PR3537.F44.K46 1998, (v3)
Kemmis, Daniel. JK2687.K46 1990, (v7)
Kemp, Charles. RT87.T45K45 1999, (v2)
Kemp, David D. GE10.K45 1998, (v6)
Kemp, Geoffrey. DS63.1.K44 1997, (v5)
Kemp, Herman C. Z3221.K46 1998, (v10)
Kemp, Martin. ND1475.K46 1990, (v9)
Kemp, Peter Kemp. VA454.K42 1969, (v10)
Kemp, Thomas Jay. CS21.K46 1997, (v5)
    CS49.K4 2001, (v5)
Kempe, Margery. PR2007.K4.A199 1998, (v3)
Kemper, Edward J. F474.H5.K46 1998, (v4)
Kemper, Robert E. Z7164.O7.K35 1997, (v10)
Kemple, James J. HD5715.2.K45 1993, (v6)
Kemple, Thomas M. HX39.5.K388 1995, (v6)
Kempton, Willett. GE150.K46 1995, (v6)
Kendall, Alan. ML410.R8.K43 1992, (v9)
    ML423.B52.K4, (v9)
Kendall, Bonnie L. RK60.K44 2001, (v2)
Kendall, Leon T. HG2151.K4 1977, (v6)
Kendall, Marion D. QR181.7.K46 1998, (v1)
Kendall, Paul Murray. U27.K4, (v10)
Kendall, Richard. N6853.D33.K46 1993, (v9)
    ND653.G7.A4 1998, (v9)
Kendle, John. DA960.K46 1992, (v5)
Kendrew, W. G. QC981.K4 1961, (v1)
Kendrick, John W. HD56.K46, (v6)
Kendrick, Laura. NK3610.K46 1999, (v9)
    PC3304.K46 1988, (v3)
Kendrick, Robert L. ML290.8.M4 K46 1996, (v9)
Keneally, Thomas. PR9619.3.K46.G6 1976, (v3)
Kenez, Peter. DK265.2.K453, (v5)
Kenez, Peter. PN1993.5.R9.K39 1992, (v3)
Keniry, Julian. LB3223.3.K45 1995, (v7)
Keniston, Kenneth. HQ799.7.K45, (v6)
    HQ799.7.K46, (v6)
Kennamer, John Robert. F332.J2 K3 1993, (v4)
Kennan, George Frost. D511.K34 1984, (v5)
    D840.K4, (v5)
    DK63.3.K38, (v5)
    E183.8.R9.K4, (v4)
    E183.8.S65.K44 1996, (v4)
    E744.K3 1984, (v4)
    E748.K374.A3 1968, (v4)
    E835.K4 1966, (v4)
    E865.K46, (v4)
Kennan, George. DK755.K342x, (v5)
Kennan, Kent Wheeler. MT55.K53 1999, (v9)
    MT70.K37 2002, (v9)
Kennard, E. H. QC175.K45, (v1)
Kenneally, James Joseph. BX1407.W65.K43 1990, (v8)
Kenneally, Michael. PR6029.C33.Z658 1988, (v3)
Kennedy, Andrew K. PR6003.E282.Z754 1989, (v3)
Kennedy, Charles Stuart. JX1706.K46 1990, (v7)
Kennedy, Charles W. PR1508.K36, (v3)
    PR1508.K38, (v3)
Kennedy, D. E. DA415.K44 2000, (v5)
Kennedy, David M. E173.O94 vol. 9.801, (v4)
    HQ764.S3.K45, (v6)
Kennedy, Dennis. PR3100.K46 1993, (v3)
Kennedy, Donald. LA227.4.K465 1997, (v7)
Kennedy, Emmet. DC158.8.K46 1989, (v5)
Kennedy, Gavin. DA87.1.B6.K46 1989, (v5)
    HB135.K47 1982, (v6)
Kennedy, George Alexander. P301.K45 1998, (v3)
    PA3265.K4, (v3)
Kennedy, Hugh. DP102.K46 1996, (v5)
Kennedy, J. Gerald. PS144.P37.K46 1993, (v3)
Kennedy, James F. Q337.3.K45 2001, (v1)
Kennedy, John Charles. HN110.L3.K45 1995, (v6)

Kennedy, John F. DA578.K4 1962, (v5)
    E176.K4 1993, (v4)
    E835.K48, (v4)
    E838.5.K42 1991, (v4)
    E841.K43, (v4)
    J82.D9 1988, (v7)
Kennedy, John Pendleton. PS2162.S9 1929, (v3)
    PS2162.S93 1986, (v3)
Kennedy, Kenneth A. R. GN58.S64.K46 2000, (v6)
Kennedy, Kieran Anthony. HC257.I6.K39 1975, (v6)
Kennedy, Liam. HT221.K46 2000, (v6)
    PS3569.O6547.Z75 1995, (v3)
Kennedy, Malcolm Duncan. U773.K4, (v10)
Kennedy, Michael L. DC178.K45 2000, (v5)
Kennedy, Michael. ML100.K35 1994, (v9)
    ML410.B853 K45 2001, (v9)
    ML410.S93.K46 1999, (v9)
    ML410.V3 K4 1980, (v9)
    ML410.W292.K4 1989, (v9)
    ML422.B79.K4 1987, (v9)
Kennedy, Paul M. CB161.K44 1994, (v5)
    D210.K46 1987, (v5)
    DA47.2.K44, (v5)
Kennedy, Paul T. HC800.K46 1988, (v6)
Kennedy, Peter. HB139.K45 2003, (v6)
    HB172.5.K457 2000, (v6)
Kennedy, Raymond. Z5115.K4 1962, (v10)
Kennedy, Richard S. PR4222.A73.K46 1993, (v3)
    PS3505.U334.Z713 1994, (v3)
Kennedy, Robert F. E183.8.R9.K42, (v4)
Kennedy, Shirley Duglin. ZA4201.K46 1998, (v10)
Kennedy, Stetson. E185.2.K33 1995, (v4)
Kennedy, Susan Estabrook. HQ1410.K45, (v6)
Kennedy, Thomas E. PS3554.U265.Z74 1988, (v3)
Kennedy, W. HJ2610.K4, (v6)
Kennedy, William Francis. H31.C2 vol. 17, (v6)
Kennedy, William P. HC255.K45 1987, (v6)
Kennedy-Pipe, Caroline. D1065.S65.K46 1995, (v5)
    DK266.45.K46 1998, (v5)
Kennelly, Brendan. PR6061.E6.C7, (v3)
Kenner, Charles L. E185.925.K394 1999, (v4)
Kenner, Hugh. PR478.M6.K4 1988, (v3)
    PR6003.E282.Z76 1968, (v3)
    PR6019.O9.U672, (v3)
    PR6019.O9.U6723, (v3)
    PR6023.E97.Z7, (v3)
    PR8750.K46 1983, (v3)
Kennes, Walter. HC59.7.K386 2000, (v6)
Kennett, James P. QE39.K46, (v1)
Kennett, Lee B. D600.K46 1991, (v5)
    UA700.K4, (v10)
    UG700.K46 1982, (v10)
Kenney, Catherine McGehee. PR6037.A95.Z74 1990, (v3)
Kenney, Charles. F71.22.D85.K46 1988, (v4)
Kenney, Edwin J. PR6003.O6757.Z675, (v3)
Kenney, William Howland. ML3477.K46 1999, (v9)
    ML3508.8.C5.K46 1993, (v9)
Kennington, Donald. ML128.J3.K45 1980, (v9)
Kennish, Michael J. QH541.5.E8.K47 1991, (v1)
Kenny, Anthony John Patrick. B72.K44 1998, (v8)
    B491.E7.K47, (v8)
    B765.T54.K44 1998, (v8)
Kenny, Kevin. HV6452.P4.M64 1998, (v6)
Kenny, Virginia C. PR448.C68.K4 1984, (v3)
Kenrick, Donald. DX115.K46 1998, (v5)
Kenrick, Paul. QK980.K44 1997, (v1)
Kens, Paul. KF228.L63.K463 1998, (v7)
Kent, A. E. JC599.C6.K46 1993, (v7)
Kent, Anthony. QC278.K46 1993, (v1)
Kent, Christopher. ML134.E613 K46 1993, (v9)
Kent, D. V. NX701.2.M43, (v9)
Kent, Deborah. F94.3.K46 1990, (v4)
Kent, George E. PS3503.R7244.Z73 1990, (v3)
Kent, George. HB1323.C5.K46 1990, (v6)
Kent, John. D476.2.K46 1992, (v5)
Kent, Neil. N7006.K4 1987, (v9)
Kent, Noel J. E711.K46 2000, (v4)
Kent, Roland G. PE1582.L3.K4 1963, (v3)
Kent, Susan Kingsley. HQ1075.5.G7.K46 1993, (v6)
Kent, Thomas H. RB111.K45 1998, (v2)

Kentgens-Craig, Margret. N332.G33.B447513 1999, (v9)

Kenworthy, Eldon. F1418.K46 1995, (v4)

Kenyon, Cecelia M. JK116.K4, (v7)

Kenyon, Frederic G. Z112.K38, (v10)

Kenyon, J. P. DA375.K4 1977, (v5)
DA415.K45 1988, (v5)
DA448.K45 1972, (v5)

Kenyon, Kathleen Mary. DS109.K39, (v5)

Keogh, Dermot. DA959.K463 1994, (v5)

Keohane, Dan. UA647.K43 1993, (v10)

Keown, Damien. BJ1289.K44 1992, (v8)

Kepars, I. Z4011.K46 1984, (v10)
Z4311.K46 1997, (v10)

Kepel, Gilles. BL238.K4613 1994, (v8)
BP65.G7.K4713 1997, (v8)

Kepes, Gyorgy. N72.S3.K5, (v9)
N76.K4, (v9)
N6490.K4, (v9)
N7428.K4, (v9)
N7430.K47, (v9)

Kepler, Angela Kay. DU624.65.K46 1998, (v5)

Kepler, Johannes. QB3.K3313 1992, (v1)

Kepnes, Steven. B5802.P67.K46 1998, (v8)

Keppel, Ben. E185.61.K39 1995, (v4)

Keppie, L. J. F. CN510.K46 1991, (v5)

Kepple, Robert J. Z7751.K46 1992, (v10)

Keppler, Michael. HG5993.K46 1997, (v6)

Ker, David I. PR9344.K47 1997, (v3)

Ker, I. T. BX1747.K47 1990, (v8)

Ker, W. P. PR255.K4 1932, (v3)
PR255.K4 1969, (v3)

Kerasote, Ted. SK14.K47 1993, (v1)

Kerber, August. LA209.2.K43 1968, (v7)

Kerber, Jordan E. Z5133.U53.K47 1991, (v10)

Kerber, Linda K. HQ1236.5.U6.K47 1998, (v6)
HQ1418.K47 1986, (v6)

Kerby, Robert Lee. E470.9.K42, (v4)

Kerchove, Rene de. V23.K4 1961, (v10)

Keren, Michael. JQ1825.P32.K47 1995, (v7)

Kerensky, Oleg. PR736.K4 1979, (v3)

Kerlow, Isaac Victor. T385.K47 1994, (v1)

Kerman, Joseph. ML1263.K47 1999, (v9)
ML2631.K47, (v9)
ML3797.K47 1985, (v9)
ML3858.K4 1988, (v9)
MT6.K365 2000, (v9)
MT145.B425.K47 1982, (v9)

Kermode, Frank. PR473.K4, (v3)
PR3072.K47 2000, (v3)

Kern, Edith. PQ2637.A82.Z76, (v3)

Kern, Kathi. HQ1413.S67K47 2001, (v6)

Kern, Martin. DS747.9.C47 K47 2000, (v5)

Kern, Paul Bentley. U29.K47 1999, (v10)

Kern, Robert W. DP48.K45 1995, (v5)

Kernan, Alvin B. PR3034.K47, (v3)

Kernberg, Otto F. BF175.5.L68.K47 1995, (v2)

Kernfeld, Barry Dean. ML3506.K47 1995, (v9)

Kern-Foxworth, Marilyn. HF5813.U6.K47 1994, (v6)

Kernohan, Andrew William. JC574.K47 1998, (v7)

Kerns, Thomas A. RA566.K465 2001, (v2)

Kerouac, Jack. PS3521.E735 B5, (v3)
PS3521.E735 D5, (v3)
PS3521.E735.D6, (v3)
PS3521.E735.H4 1977, (v3)
PS3521.E735.L6, (v3)
PS3521.E735.O534 1957, (v3)
PS3521.E735 S8, (v3)
PS3521.E735 T6, (v3)
PS3521.E735 V5, (v3)
PS3521.E735.Z48 1999, (v3)

Kerr, Andrea Moore. HQ1413.S73.K47 1992, (v6)

Kerr, Charles. F451.K46, (v4)

Kerr, Clark. HD21.K45 1964, (v6)
LA227.3.K45 1991, (v7)
LB2325.K43 2001, (v7)

Kerr, David. PN2969.K47 1995, (v3)

Kerr, Donal. DA955.K47 1994, (v5)

Kerr, Donald Gordon Grady. G1116.S1.K4 1975, (v6)

Kerr, Douglas. PR6029.W4.Z69 1993, (v3)

Kerr, Fergus. B56.K47 1997, (v8)

Kerr, Graham. TX725.N4.K43 1969, (v1)

Kerr, Jeffrey B. QM557.K47 1999, (v1)

Kerr, K. Austin. HE2751.K47, (v6)

Kerr, Walter. CB425.K45, (v5)

Kerridge, Roy. DA125.A1.K44 1983, (v5)

Kerrigan, John. PN56.R48.K47 1996, (v3)

Kerr-Ritchie, Jeffrey R. F235.N4.K47 1999, (v4)

Kersaudy, Francois. D750.K47 1982, (v5)

Kersbergen, Kees van. HN373.5.K47 1995, (v6)

Kerschen, Lois. PN6426.K47 1998, (v3)

Kershaw, Baz. PN1643.K47 1999, (v3)
PN2595.3.K47 1992, (v3)

Kershaw, Diana R. QL45.2.K47 1983, (v1)

Kershaw, Greet. DT433.577.K47 1996, (v5)

Kershaw, Ian. DD247.H5.K46 2001, (v5)
DD256.5.K46513 1987, (v5)
DD256.5.K47 1985, (v5)
HN460.P8.K47 1983, (v6)

Kerslake, R. T. D766.84.K47 1997, (v5)

Kersten, Krystyna. DK4410.K4713 1991, (v5)

Kersten, Rikki. JQ1681.K47 1996, (v7)

Kertesz, Stephen Denis. D376.U6.K4, (v5)

Kerttula, Anna M. DK759.C45, (v5)

Kertzer, David I. DS135.I9.M595 1997, (v5)
GN492.3.K47 1988, (v6)
JN5657.C63.K47 1996, (v7)

Kerwin, C. M. KF5411.K47 1994, (v7)

Kesey, Ken. PS3561.E667.O5x, (v3)
PS3561.E667.S6, (v3)

Keshavarz, Fatemeh. PK6482.K46 1998, (v3)

Kessler, Carol Farley. PS1744.G57.Z73 1995, (v3)

Kessler, Donna J. F592.7.S123.K47 1996, (v4)

Kessler, Harry. DD231.R3.K43 1969, (v5)

Kessler, Herbert L. BR115.A8.K47 2000, (v8)
N7952.R6.K48 2000, (v9)

Kessler, Lawrence D. DS754.4.C53.K47, (v5)

Kessler, Rachael. LB1072.K48 2000, (v7)

Kessler-Harris, Alice. HD6095.K449 1982, (v6)
HD6095.K45, (v6)

Kessner, Thomas. E748.L23.K47 1989, (v4)
F128.9.I8.K47, (v4)

Kesteloot, Lilyan. PQ3897.K3913 1991, (v3)

Kesten, Seymour R. HX654.K46 1993, (v6)

Kestenberg, Judith S. RC451.4.H62.K47 1996, (v2)

Kesting, Jurgen. ML420.C18.K513 1993, (v9)

Kestner, Joseph A. PR888.D4.K47 2000, (v3)

Ketcham, Ralph Louis. E169.1.K417, (v4)
E342.K46 1971, (v4)

Ketchum, Richard M. E806.K5 1989, (v4)

Kete, Mary Louise. PS217.M67.K48 2000, (v3)

Ketelaar, James Edward. BQ693.K48 1990, (v8)

Ketner, Joseph D. ND1839.D85.K48 1993, (v9)

Kett, Joseph F. R151.K47, (v2)

Kettell, Brian. HG4027.5.K47 1981, (v6)

Ketterer, David. PR9192.6.S34.K4 1992, (v3)

Kettl, Donald F. HD3888.K48 1993, (v6)

Kettler, David. HM22.G3.M3253 1995, (v6)

Ketton-Cremer, Robert Wyndham. DA483.W2.K4 1966, (v5)
PR3503.K4 1955, (v3)

Keve, Paul W. HV9466.K48 1991, (v6)

Kevles, Bettyann. RC78.7.D53.K48 1997, (v2)

Keyder, Caglar. HC492.K497 1987, (v6)

Keyes, C. D. B808.9.K49 1999, (v8)

Keyes, Frances Parkinson. F199.K46, (v4)

Keyes, Jessica. HD30.3.K49 1993, (v6)

Keyes, Ken. BJ1581.2.K45 1986, (v8)

Keyes, Roger S. NE1321.8.K487 1989, (v9)

Keyfitz, Nathan. HB881.K48, (v6)

Keyishian, Harry. PR6001.R7.Z68, (v3)

Keyman, Emin Fuat. JZ1251.K49 1997, (v7)

Keymer, Tom. PR3664.C43.K49 1992, (v3)

Keynes, Edward. KF4575.K49 1989, (v7)
KF4765.K49 1996, (v7)

Keynes, Geoffrey. N6797.B57.K4 1971, (v9)
Z8237.K38 1973, (v10)

Keynes, John Maynard. BC141.K4 1979, (v8)
D641.K4, (v5)
HB171.K44, (v6)
HB171.K45, (v6)
HC57.K4 1988, (v6)

HC57.K45, (v6)

HG221.K45, (v6)

Keyser, Elizabeth Lennox. PS1018.K48 1993, (v3)

Keyser, Lester J. PN1998.3.S39.K49 1992, (v3)

Keyso, Ruth Ann. HQ1764.O44, (v6)

Keyssar, Alexander. JK1846.K48 2000, (v7)

Keyssar, Helene. PN1998.3.A48K49 1991, (v3)

Kh̲u̲r̲i̲, I̲ly̲ a̲s. PJ7842.H823M3513 1996, (v3)

Khadduri, Majid. DS79.K43 1960, (v5)
DS79.65.K49, (v5)
DS79.72.K397 1997, (v5)

Khademian, Anne M. KF1444.K47 1992, (v7)

Khal̄ ifah, Saòhar. PJ7842.H2938S913 1989, (v3)

Khaldei, Evgenii. D764.K454 1997, (v5)

Khalid, Adeeb. BP63.A34.K54 1998, (v8)

Khalidi, Rashid. DS113.7.K53 1997, (v5)

Khalidi, Tarif. DS36.85.K4 1985, (v5)

Khalidi, Tarif. DS38.16.K445 1994, (v5)

Khan, Jahan Dad. DS385.K498 A3 1999, (v5)

Khan, Nosheen. PR478.W65.K48 1988, (v3)

Khan, Riaz M. DS371.2.K48 1991, (v5)

Khan, Shahrukh Rafi. HG3881.5.W57.K48 1999, (v6)

Khan, Sharharyar M. DS485.B5.K456 2000, (v5)

Khan-Magomedov, S.O. NA1188.K4713 1987, (v9)

Khansari, Mehdi. SB458.5.K48 19987, (v1)

Kharbanda, Om Prakash. HD4482.K47 1990, (v6)

Khashan, Hilal. DS39.K43 2000, (v5)

Khatchadourian, Haig. HV6431.K43 1998, (v6)

Khawlie, M. R. HD9506.A59.K48 1990, (v6)

Khazanov, Anatoly M. DK33.K4527 1995, (v5)

Khinchin, Aleksandr IAkovlevich. QC175.K52, (v1)

Khisty, C. Jotin. TA1145.K48 1990, (v1)

Khlebnikov, Velimir. PG3476.K485.A23 1987, (v3)

Khouri, Mounah Abdallah. PJ7695.E3.K48, (v3)

Khoury, Elias. PJ7842.H823.J3413 1989, (v3)

Khoury, Philip S. DS98.K46 1987, (v5)

Khrushchev, Nikita Sergeevich. DK275.K5.A326, (v5)
DK275.K5.A36, (v5)

Khrushchev, Sergei. DK275.K5.K4874213 2000, (v5)

Khuòdayr̄ i, Bat̄ ul. PJ7842.H68513 2001, (v3)

Ki, Tsurayuki. PL788.3.Z5.A313 1976, (v3)

Kibbee, Josephine Z. Z5111.K53 1991, (v10)

Kiberd, Declan. PR8714.K54 2001, (v3)

Kibler, M. Alison. PN1968.U5.K53 1999, (v3)

Kibria, Nazli. E184.V53.K53 1993, (v4)

Kich, Martin. Z1251.W5.K53 1995, (v10)

Kidane Mengisteab. HD1333.E8.K53 1990, (v6)

Kidd, Colin. DA759.K53 1993, (v5)

Kidd, Michael. PQ6102.K53 1999, (v3)

Kidder, Alfred Vincent. E78.S7 K5 2000, (v4)

Kidder, Tracy. TK7885.4.K53, (v1)

Kideckel, David A. HN650.O48.K53 1993, (v6)

Kidger, Mark R. QB805.K525 1999, (v1)

Kidson, Ruth. RM184.K526 2000, (v2)

Kidwell, Clara Sue. E98.R3 K53 2001, (v4)

Kidwell, Claudia Brush. TT497.K44, (v1)

Kidwell, Peggy Aldrich. QA76.5.K47 1994, (v1)

Kiefer, Frederick. PR658.W7.K54 1996, (v3)

Kiefer, Geraldine W. TR140.S7.K53 1991, (v1)

Kiefer, Monica Mary. PN1009.A1.K5, (v3)

Kiel, R. Andrew. E743.5.K48 2000, (v4)

Kiell, Norman. Z6514.F66.K54 1995, (v10)

Kiely, Benedict. PR6021.I24.N6 1985, (v3)
PR6021.I24.S8 1980, (v3)

Kiely, Robert. PR858.R73.K5, (v3)
PR5497.K5, (v3)

Kier, Elizabeth. UA700.K54 1997, (v10)

Kieran, John. GV23.K5 1977, (v4)

Kierkegaard, Søren, 1813-1855. PT8131.G9.T63413 1978, (v3)
PT8142.A6 1990, (v3)
B4351.A34.K5, (v8)
B4372.E5.A8, (v8)
B4372.E5 2000, (v8)
B4373.O42.E5 1989, (v8)
B4373.S83.E55 1967, (v8)
BL51.K48713 1985, (v8)
BT715.K5313 1941, (v8)
BV4836.K4813 1989, (v8)
BR100.K52 1941, (v8)
PT8142.E57.E5 1987, (v3)

Kiernan, Frances. PS3525.A1435.Z69 2000, (v3)
Kiernan, Kevin S. PR1585.K5 1981, (v3)
Kiernan, Pauline. PR2986.K54 1996, (v3)
  PR3106.K53 1999, (v3)
Kiernander, Adrian. PN2638.M445.K54 1993, (v3)
Kierner, Cynthia A. F122.K54 1992, (v4)
  HQ1391.U5.K55 1998, (v6)
Kieschnick, John. BQ6160.C6 K54 1997, (v8)
Kiesling, Eugenia C. D761.K54 1996, (v5)
Kieval, Hillel J. DS135.C95.K54 2000, (v5)
  DS135.C96.B638 1988, (v5)
Kilbourn, William. F1032.M148, (v4)
Kilbourne, Jean. HF5823.K363 1999, (v6)
Kilbride, Philip Leroy. HV887.K4.K55 2000, (v6)
Kilby, Peter. HB601.K53, (v6)
Kilcup, Karen L. PS3511.R94.Z7618 1998, (v3)
Kile, Orville Merton. HD1485.A45.K5, (v6)
Kilgour, Frederick G. Z4.K56 2000, (v10)
Kilgour, Maggie. PR830.T3.K5 1995, (v3)
Kilham, Christopher. R733.K54 2000, (v2)
Killen, Linda. Z6465.U5 K54 1983, (v10)
Killham, Ken. QH541.5.S6.K54 1994, (v1)
Killingsworth, M. Jimmie. PS3238.K43 1993, (v3)
  PS3242.B58.K55 1989, (v3)
Killingsworth, Mark R. HD6061.2.U6.K56 1990, (v6)
Killoran, Helen. PS3545.H16.Z687 1996, (v3)
Killoren, John J. E78.W5.K55 1994, (v4)
Kilmer, Joyce. PS3521.I38.T7 1914, (v3)
Kilmer, Paulette D. BJ1611.2.K55 1996, (v8)
Kilminster, Richard. HM19.K48 1998, (v6)
Kilner, John Frederic. R724.K54 1990, (v2)
Kilpatrick, Alan. E99.C5.K45 1997, (v4)
Kilpatrick, Hilary. PJ8212.K54, (v3)
Kilpatrick, Jacquelyn. PN1995.9.I48.K56 1999, (v3)
Kilpatrick, William Heard. LB875.K44, (v7)
Kilson, Marion. E184.A1.K45 2001, (v4)
Kim, Byoung-lo Philo. HC467.K45 1992, (v6)
Kim, Chewon. NK1073.5.K52, (v9)
Kim, Claire Jean. F128.9.N4.K56 2000, (v4)
Kim, Elaine H. E184.K6.E27 1996, (v4)
Kim, Hyung-chan. Z1361.O7.K56 1989, (v10)
Kim, Illsoo. F128.9.K6.K55, (v4)
Kim, Jaegwon. BD418.3.K53 1998, (v8)
  BD418.3.K54 1996, (v8)
Kim, Richard E. PS3561.I415.M3, (v3)
Kim, Shoon Kyung. QD455.3.G75.K56 1999, (v1)
Kim, Steven H. QA76.73.P76.K46 1991, (v1)
Kim, Sunhyuk. JQ1729.A15 S58 2000, (v7)
Kim, Won. QA76.9.D3.K54 1990, (v1)
Kimball, Bob. HF5438.25.K546 1994, (v6)
Kimball, Bruce A. LC1011.K56 1986, (v7)
Kimball, Charles. BJ1406.K56 2002, (v8)
Kimball, Fiske. ND1145.K5 1948, (v9)
Kimball, Geoffrey D. PM1571.Z5.K55 1994, (v3)
Kimball, Jean. PR6019.O9.U6726 1997, (v3)
Kimball, Michelle R. Z7963.I74 K56 1997, (v10)
Kimball, Penn. PN4899.W29.T45 1994, (v3)
Kimball, Roger. B791.K535 2002, (v8)
Kimball, Stanley Buchholz. F591.K48 1988, (v4)
Kimball, Warren F. E807.K48 1991, (v4)
Kimbell, David R. B. ML410.B44 K56 1998, (v9)
  ML1733.K55 1990, (v9)
Kimbrell, Andrew. HQ1090.3.K55 1995, (v6)
Kimbrough, Robert. PR3069.S45.K5 1990, (v3)
Kimche, David. DS119.7.K49256 1991, (v5)
Kimmel, Allan J. BF76.4.K55 1996, (v2)
Kimmel, Douglas C. BF724.5.K55, (v2)
Kimmel, Michael S. HM281.K47 1990, (v6)
Kimmel, William Breyfogel. BT10.K5, (v8)
Kimmelman, Michael. N71.K56 1998, (v9)
Kimmerling, Baruch. DS119.7.K4943 1993, (v5)
Kimmey, John Lansing. PS2127.E46.K5 1990, (v3)
Kimmich, Christoph M. DD901.D283.K5, (v5)
Kimmins, J. P. SD387.E58.K57 1992, (v1)
Kimura, Hiroshi. DK68.7.J3 K56 2000, (v5)
Kimura, Motoo. QH371.K53 1983, (v1)
Kincaid, Harold. H62.K515 1996, (v6)
Kincaid, James R. HV6570.K545 1998, (v6)
Kincheloe, Joe L. LC1045.K545 1998, (v7)
Kindelan, Nancy Anne. PN2053.K534 1996, (v3)
Kinder, Marsha. PN1993.5.S7.K5 1993, (v3)

Kinderman, William. ML410.B4.K56 1995, (v9)
Kindermann, Gottfried Karl. DB97.K5513 1988, (v5)
Kindleberger, Charles Poor. HB71.K48 1989, (v6)
  HB97.K57 1990, (v6)
  HB3717 1929.K55 1986, (v6)
  HC51.K49 1996, (v6)
  HC276.K55 1964, (v6)
  HF1411.K5 1968, (v6)
Kindlon, Daniel J. HQ775.K56 1999, (v6)
Kindscher, Kelly. E78.G73.K56 1992, (v4)
Kinealy, Christine. HC260.5.K564 1994, (v6)
King, Adele. PQ673.K56 1989, (v3)
King, Alex. D663.K56 1998, (v5)
King, Alexander. CT275.K49.A3, (v5)
King, Andrew. PR2358.K47 2000, (v3)
King, Anthony D. NA7570.K56 1984, (v9)
King, Anthony Stephen. HC241.25.G7.K5, (v6)
King, Anthony. DC63.K56 1990, (v5)
King, Barbara J. GN281.4.K48 1994, (v6)
King, Basil. PS3556.E3 S5, (v3)
King, Bruce Alvin. PR431.K48 1982, (v3)
  PR9080.K5, (v3)
  PR9080.K53 1980, (v3)
  PR9272.9.N32.Z749 1993, (v3)
  PR9490.5.K5 1987, (v3)
King, Bruce. PR9272.9.W3.Z72 2000, (v3)
King, Charles L. PQ6635.E65.Z7, (v3)
King, Charles R. RJ102.K46 1993, (v2)
King, Charles. DK509.54 .K56 2000, (v5)
King, Coretta Scott. E185.97.K5.K5, (v4)
King, David B. CB245.K544 1988, (v5)
King, David C. F128.47.K49 2000, (v4)
  JK1029.K56 1997, (v7)
King, David N. NA997.A4.K55 1991, (v9)
King, Debra Walker. PS153.N5.K44 1998, (v3)
King, Dennis. E840.8.L33.K55 1989, (v4)
King, Desmond S. JK723.A34.K56 1995, (v7)
  JV6483.K54 2000, (v7)
King, Edmund James. LA132.K55 1979, (v7)
King, Edward Louis. QD501.K7514 1964b, (v1)
King, Frank Marion. F786.K56 1946, (v4)
King, Gary. H61.K5437 1994, (v6)
  JK516.K46 1988, (v7)
King, Grace Elizabeth. PS2177.B3 1968, (v3)
  PS2178.A4 1971, (v3)
King, H. Roger. F72.C3 K58 1994, (v4)
King, Henry C. QB88.K5 1979, (v1)
King, Henry. PR3539.K65 1965, (v3)
King, J. C. H. E77.K56 1999, (v4)
King, J. E. HB103.A3.K485 1988, (v6)
  Z7164.E2.K56 1995, (v10)
King, James C. QH401.K55, (v1)
King, James. PR4146.K56 1991, (v3)
King, Jere Clemens. D650.M5.K5, (v5)
King, John Kerry. DS518.1.K5, (v5)
King, John N. PR2367.R4.K56 1990, (v3)
  PR3562.K45 2000, (v3)
King, John. PN1993.5.L3.K45 1990, (v3)
  QK50.K46 1997, (v1)
  QK711.2.K57, (v1)
King, Joseph A. F868.N5. K56 1992, (v4)
King, K. N. QA76.73.C15.K49 1996, (v1)
  QA76.73.J38, (v1)
King, L. W. DS71.K5 1969, (v5)
King, Larry L. E185.61.K524 1971, (v4)
  PS3561.I48A8, (v3)
King, Larry. PN1991.4.K45.A3 1990, (v3)
King, Lawrence P. HC244.K485 2001, (v6)
King, Leslie J. G74.K47, (v6)
King, Lester S. R151.K56 1991, (v2)
  RB151.K5, (v2)
King, Lester Snow. R148.K5, (v2)
King, Margaret L. DG677.99.M37.K56 1994, (v5)
  HQ1148.K56 1991, (v6)
King, Martin Luther. BX6449.K56.A3, (v8)
  E185.61.K54, (v4)
  E185.615.K5, (v4)
  E185.97.K5.A2 1992, (v4)
King, Max. QH380.K56 1993, (v1)
King, Michael. PR9639.3.F7, (v3)
King, Neville J. RJ506.P38.K56 1988, (v2)

King, Paul G. BR115.E3.K45 1999, (v8)
King, R. Barry. TD192.5.K56 1998, (v1)
King, R. Bruce. QD151.2.K5 1995, (v1)
King, Richard. B131.K49 1999, (v8)
King, Roma G. PR4238.K5, (v3)
King, Ronald Frederick. HV696.F6.K56 2000, (v6)
King, Ross. NA5621.F7, (v9)
King, Stephen. PS3561.I483.S3 1975, (v3)
King, Steven. HC254.5.K535 2001, (v6)
King, Stewart R. F1911.K56 2001, (v4)
King, T. J. PR3095.K5 1991, (v3)
King, Thomas. PR9199.3.K4422.M43 1990, (v3)
King, W. D. PR4622.W33.K56 1993, (v3)
King, William Richard. HF5415.1.K5, (v6)
King, Wilma. E441.K59 1995, (v4)
King, Woodie. PS647.N35, (v3)
Kingdon, Jonathan. QL84.6.A1.K56 1989, (v1)
Kingdon, Robert McCune. DC118.K56 1988, (v5)
Kingery, W. D. TP807.K52 1975, (v1)
Kingfisher, Catherine Pelissier. HV1445.K57 1996,
  (v6)
King-Hele, Desmond. PR5431.K5, (v3)
  PR5438.K5 1971, (v3)
Kingma, Bruce R. HD47.4.K56 2001, (v6)
Kingman, J. F. C. QA274.42.K56 1993, (v1)
Kingsbury, John M. F786.K575 1996, (v4)
Kingseed, Cole C. E836.K55 1995, (v4)
Kingsley, Charles. PR4842.A4, (v3)
  PR4842.W3 1995, (v3)
Kingsley, Henry. PR4845.K5 R3 1967, (v3)
Kingsley, Peter. B235.P24.K56 1999, (v8)
Kingston, Jeff. DS889.K546 2001, (v5)
Kingston, Maxine Hong. CT275.K5764.A33 1976, (v5)
Kingston, Paul W. HN90.S6.K56 2000, (v6)
Kingston-McCloughry, Edgar James. U162.K49,
  (v10)
  UA11.K5 1960, (v10)
  UB210.K54, (v10)
Kingwell, Mark. JC578.K56 1995, (v7)
Kinkead-Weekes, Mark. PR6023.A93.Z6379 1996, (v3)
Kinkley, Jeffrey C. PL2443.K55 2000, (v3)
  PL2801.N18.Z73 1987, (v3)
Kinnaird, John. PR4773.K5, (v3)
Kinnamon, Keneth. Z8986.323.K56 1988, (v10)
Kinnard, Roy. PN1995.9.H6.K46 1995, (v3)
Kinnear, Karen L. HV6439.U7.K55 1996, (v6)
  HV6570.K55 1995, (v6)
Kinnell, Galway. PS3521.I582.A6 1993, (v3)
Kinney, Arthur F. PS3511.A86.G6349 1996, (v3)
Kinney, Clare Regan. PR509.N3.K56 1992, (v3)
Kinney, Jill. HV699.3.W2.K56 1991, (v6)
Kinney, Katherine. PS228.V5.K56 2000, (v3)
Kinoshita, Junji. PL832.I5.K313, (v3)
Kinsbruner, Jay. F1983.B55.K56 1996, (v4)
Kinsella, Sharon. PN6790.J3.K56 2000, (v3)
Kinsey, Alfred C. HQ18.U5.K5, (v6)
Kinsey, Joni. ND237.M715.K56 1992, (v9)
Kinsey, L. Christine. QA611.K47 1993, (v1)
Kinshasa, Kwando Mbiassi. E185.K49 1988, (v4)
Kinsky, Georg. ML89.K55, (v9)
Kinsley, James. PR1181.K55 1969, (v3)
  PR8561.K5, (v3)
Kinsman, Blair. GC211.K5, (v6)
Kintner, William R. UA23.3.K5, (v10)
Kintz, Linda. BR1642.U5.K56 1997, (v8)
Kintz, Linda. PN1861.K48 1992, (v3)
Kinzer, Bruce L. DA950.K56 2001, (v5)
Kip, Arthur F. QC523.K5, (v1)
Kip, Lawrence. E83.84.K57 1999, (v4)
Kipfer, Barbara Ann. CC70.K56 2000, (v5)
  PE1591.K54 1992, (v3)
Kipling, Rudyard. PR4850.F70, (v3)
  PR4852.B4, (v3)
  PR4852.I45 1963, (v3)
  PR4852.J32, (v3)
  PR4852.J37, (v3)
  PR4852.M39 1953, (v3)
  PR4854.C3 1959, (v3)
  PR4854.K4 1990, (v3)
  PR4854.L5 1899, (v3)
  PR4856.A34 1988, (v3)

Kipling, Rudyard. *(cont)*
PR4856.A4 1990, **(v3)**
PZ7.K632.JW2, **(v3)**
Kipnis, Aaron R. HQ1090.K57 1991, **(v6)**
Kipnis, David. T14.5.K57 1990, **(v1)**
Kippen, James. ML1038.T3 K36 1988, **(v9)**
Kippenhahn, Rudolf. QB521.K6313 1994, **(v1)**
QB806.K5313 1983, **(v1)**
Kirby, D. G. DK459.K57 1979, **(v5)**
DK502.7.K57 1995, **(v5)**
DL78.K57 1990, **(v5)**
Kirby, David K. PS2386.K57 1993, **(v3)**
Kirby, F. E. ML700.K45 1995, **(v9)**
Kirby, James E. BX8382.2.A4.K57 1996, **(v8)**
Kirby, John B. E185.6.K548, **(v4)**
NA1553.K58, **(v9)**
Kirby, John T. PQ4088.K57 2000, **(v3)**
PQ4088.K57 2000, **(v3)**
Kirby, Stuart. DS518.45.K59 1995, **(v5)**
Kirby-Smith, H. T. PN1356.K54 1999, **(v3)**
PS2772.L3.K57 1997, **(v3)**
Kirch, Patrick Vinton. DU624.65.K56 1992, **(v5)**
GN670.K56 1984, **(v6)**
GN871.K57 1997, **(v6)**
GN871.K575 2000, **(v6)**
Kirchhoff, Frederick. PR5087.M36.K57 1990, **(v3)**
PR5264.K57 1984, **(v3)**
Kirilov, Nikolai. PG1145.E8.K5, **(v3)**
Kirisci, Kemal. DR435.K87.K57 1997, **(v5)**
Kirk, Donald. DS686.614.K57 1998, **(v5)**
Kirk, Elise K. ML1711.K56 2001, **(v9)**
Kirk, G. S. B188.K5 1983, **(v8)**
Kirk, John M. BR645.C9.K57 1989, **(v8)**
BX1442.2.K57 1992, **(v8)**
Kirk, John T. O. QK882.K53 1994, **(v1)**
Kirk, Mary Wallace. F334.T94 K57, **(v4)**
Kirk, Neville. HD8388.K57 1994, **(v6)**
Kirk, Russell. JA81.K55, **(v7)**
Kirk, Ruth. F889.3.K57, **(v4)**
Kirk, Tim. HD8410.K57 1996, **(v6)**
Kirkby, Diane Elizabeth. HD6079.2.U5.K57 1991, **(v6)**
TX950.59.A8.K57 1997, **(v1)**
Kirk-Duggan, Cheryl A. BT736.15.K57 2001, **(v8)**
Kirkeby, Willy. PD2691.K49 1989, **(v3)**
Kirkendall, Richard Stewart. F621.W183.K56 1993,
(v4)
HD1761.K5, **(v6)**
Kirker, Harold. NA730.C2.K5, **(v9)**
Kirkham, Michael. PR6013.R35.Z73, **(v3)**
Kirkham, Pat. NK1412.E18.K57 1995, **(v9)**
Kirkham, Richard L. BC171.K55 1992, **(v8)**
Kirkow, Peter. JN6693.5.R43.K57 1998, **(v7)**
Kirkpatrick, B. J. Z8984.2.K5 1997, **(v10)**
Kirkpatrick, C. H. HD3616.D44.K57 1984, **(v6)**
Kirkpatrick, David W. LB2825.K58 1990, **(v7)**
Kirkpatrick, F. A. F1411.K57 1967, **(v4)**
Kirkpatrick, Frank G. BJ1251.K52 2001, **(v8)**
Kirkpatrick, Jeane J. DK288.K57 1991, **(v5)**
E838.5.K57 1988, **(v4)**
HQ1391.U5.K57, **(v6)**
Kirkpatrick, Ralph. ML410.S221 K5 1983, **(v9)**
Kirkpatrick, Robin. PQ4050.E5.K57 1995, **(v3)**
Kirkpatrick, Susan. PQ6048.W6.K5 1989, **(v3)**
Kirkwood, Burton. F1226.K57 2000, **(v4)**
Kirkwood, T. B. L. QP86.K52 1999, **(v1)**
Kirp, David L. LC214.2.K57 1982, **(v7)**
Kirp, David L. RJ387.A25.K57 1989, **(v2)**
Kirsch, Arthur C. PR2983.K497 1990, **(v3)**
Kirsch, George B. GV863.A1.K57 1989, **(v6)**
Kirschbaum, Leo. PR2989.K5, **(v3)**
Kirschbaum, Stanislav J. DB2744.K57 1999, **(v5)**
DB2763.K57 1995, **(v5)**
Kirschten, Robert. PS3501.M6.Z83 1998, **(v3)**
PS3554.I32.Z75 1988, **(v3)**
Kirsh, Andrea. ND1635.K57 2000, **(v9)**
Kirtland, Joseph. QA155.5.K, **(v1)**
Kirwan, A. D., Jr. QC311.K57 2000, **(v1)**
Kirwan, Albert Dennis. E340.C9.K5, **(v4)**
F341.K5 1964, **(v4)**
Kirwan, Frances Clare. QA565.K57 1992, **(v1)**
Kirzner, Israel M. HB98.K57, **(v6)**

HB101.V66 K57 2001, **(v6)**
HB615.K58 1989, **(v6)**
Kis, Danilo. PG1419.21.I8.G713 1980, **(v3)**
Kisacanin, Branislav. QA164.K57 1998, **(v1)**
Kisch, Guido. DS135.G31.K58, **(v5)**
Kiser, Lisa J. PR1933.K6.K57 1991, **(v3)**
Kishima, Takako. JQ1681.K54 1991, **(v7)**
Kisliuk, Michelle Robin. DT546.345.A35.K57 1998,
(v5)
Kissel, Howard. PN2287.M618.K57 1993, **(v3)**
Kissel, Susan S. PS374.H47.K57 1996, **(v3)**
Kisseloff, Jeff. PN1992.3.U5.K52 1995, **(v3)**
Kissick, William L. RA410.53.K55 1994, **(v2)**
Kissinger, Henry Alfred. E855.K57, **(v4)**
Kissinger, Henry. D383.K5 1957a, **(v5)**
D845.K5, **(v5)**
E835.K5, **(v4)**
E840.8.K58.A3 1999, **(v4)**
E840.8.K58.A38, **(v4)**
UA23.K49, **(v10)**
Kissman, Kris. HV699.K58 1993, **(v6)**
Kister, Kenneth F. PE1611.K57 1992, **(v3)**
Kistler, John M. Z7164.C45.K57 2000, **(v10)**
Kistler, Mark Oliver. PT643.K5, **(v3)**
Kitagawa, Joseph Mitsuo. BL2202.K49 1987, **(v8)**
Kitch, Sally. HQ800.15.K58 1989, **(v6)**
Kitchen, John. BX4682.K58 1998, **(v8)**
Kitchen, Martin. D727.K516 1988, **(v5)**
D757.K5 1995, **(v5)**
Kitchener, Andrew. QL737.C23.K58 1991, **(v1)**
Kitchener, Richard F. BD161.K53 1986, **(v8)**
Kitcher, Patricia. BF311.K57 1990, **(v2)**
Kitcher, Philip. GN365.9.K58 1985, **(v6)**
QH431.K54 1996, **(v1)**
Kitching, G. N. HX541.K54 1994, **(v6)**
Kite, Elizabeth Sarah. F195.K62, **(v4)**
Kitschelt, Herbert. JN94.A979.K569 1995, **(v7)**
JN94.A979.K57 1994, **(v7)**
JN6371.A42.K58 1990, **(v7)**
Kitson Clark, G. S. R. DA533.K55, **(v5)**
Kitson, Frank. U240.K53 1971, **(v10)**
Kitt, Eartha. ML420.K5.A32, **(v9)**
Kittel, Charles. QC171.K5 1962, **(v1)**
QC175.K58, **(v1)**
QC176.K5 1986, **(v1)**
Kittel, Ellen E. HJ1199.F55.K58 1991, **(v6)**
Kittelson, David J. Z4708.E85.K57 1985, **(v10)**
Kittler, Friedrich A. P96.T42.K5713 1999, **(v3)**
Kittredge, George Lyman. PR2065.G31.K5 1960, **(v3)**
Kitts, Thomas M. PS1106.K58 1994, **(v3)**
Kitzen, Michael L. S. E335.K57 1993, **(v4)**
Kitzhaber, Albert Raymond. PE1068.U5.K5 1963, **(v3)**
Kitzinger, Ernst. N5963.K5 1969, **(v9)**
Kivisto, Peter. Z8957.K58 1988, **(v10)**
Kivy, Peter. BH39.K575 1997, **(v8)**
ML390.K595 2001, **(v9)**
ML457.K58 1995, **(v9)**
ML3845.K58, **(v9)**
ML3845.K583 1993, **(v9)**
ML3845.K585 1990, **(v9)**
ML3845.K59 1984, **(v9)**
ML3858.K53 1988, **(v9)**
Kiyosawa, Kiyoshi. D811.5.K54313 1999, **(v5)**
Klahr, David. Q180.55.D57, **(v1)**
Klaiber, Jeffrey L. F1414.2.K5313 1998, **(v4)**
Klaic, Dragan. PN1650.F88.K58 1991, **(v3)**
Klaidman, Stephen. PN4784.M4.K55 1991, **(v3)**
RC685.C6.K53 2000, **(v2)**
Klain, Daniel A. QA273.5.K47 1997, **(v1)**
Klekowski, Edward J. QK981.K54 1988, **(v1)**
Klamer, Arjo. HB74.8.K57 1990, **(v6)**
Klammer, Martin. PS3242.S56.K53 1995, **(v3)**
Klarsfeld, Serge. DS135.F83.K43313 1996, **(v5)**
Klasner, Lily. F802.L7.K55 1972, **(v4)**
Klass, Donald L. TP339.K54 1998, **(v1)**
Klass, Gert von. UF537.K7.K5, **(v10)**
Klass, Morton. BL256.K57 1995, **(v8)**
Klass, Philip J. UG633.K54, **(v10)**
Klatell, David A. GV742.3.K53 1988, **(v6)**
Klaus, Alisa. RJ102.K5 1993, **(v2)**
Klausen, Jytte. HC240.K53 1998, **(v6)**
Klausner, Joseph. PJ5017.K513 1972, **(v3)**

Klausner, Neal W. BD21.K55, **(v8)**
Klaver, Elizabeth. PN1992.65.K59 2000, **(v3)**
Klawans, Harold L. RC1236.N47.K53 1996, **(v2)**
Kleck, Gary. HN90.V5.K56 1991, **(v6)**
Kleckner, Simone-Marie. KZ6009.K58 1985, **(v7)**
Klee, Paul. N6490.K553 1966, **(v9)**
NC703.K58 1952, **(v9)**
Klee, Robert. Q175.K548 1997, **(v1)**
Klee, Victor. QA466.K63 1991, **(v1)**
Kleeman, Terry F. BL1942.85.W45 K56 1994, **(v8)**
Kleg, Milton. E184.A1.K49 1993, **(v4)**
Klehr, Harvey. E743.5.K55 1996, **(v4)**
Kleijwegt, Marc. DE61.Y68.K55 1991, **(v5)**
Kleiman, Mark. HV5822.M3.K53 1989, **(v6)**
Klein, Alan M. GV863.29.A1.D655 1991, **(v6)**
Klein, Barry T. E76.2.K58 1986, **(v4)**
Klein, Bernhard. GA793.5.K57 2001, **(v6)**
Klein, Carole. F128.68.G77.K43 1987, **(v4)**
Klein, Cornelis. QE372.K54 1999, **(v1)**
Klein, Dennis A. PQ6613.A763.Z7347 1991, **(v3)**
Klein, Donald W. DS778.A1.K55 1971, **(v5)**
Klein, Ernest. PJ4833.K54 1987, **(v3)**
Klein, Ethel. HQ1426.K58 1984, **(v6)**
Klein, Felix. QA466.K64 1956, **(v1)**
Klein, George Stuart. BF173.K47, **(v2)**
Klein, H. Arthur. QC88.K58, **(v1)**
Klein, Herbert S. F3321.K54 1982, **(v4)**
HD489.L3.K57 1993, **(v6)**
HT1322.K54 1999, **(v6)**
Klein, Joe. ML429.G95.K6, **(v9)**
Klein, Josephine. RJ502.5.K57 1987, **(v2)**
Klein, Julie Thompson. BD255.K538 1996, **(v8)**
BD255.K54 1990, **(v8)**
Klein, Kathleen Gregory. PR830.D4.K58 1988, **(v3)**
Klein, Kerwin Lee. E179.5.K53 1997, **(v4)**
Klein, Lisa M. PR2343.K56 1998, **(v3)**
Klein, Maury. HB3717 1929.K588 2001, **(v6)**
TF23.K54 1994, **(v1)**
TF25.U5.K53 1987, **(v1)**
Klein, Melanie. RC509.K64, **(v2)**
Klein, Melanie. RJ504.2.K4413 1984, **(v2)**
Klein, Menachem. DS109.95.K55 2001, **(v5)**
Klein, Rachel N. F272.K56 1990, **(v4)**
Klein, Randall S. BF175.5.O24.K44 1990, **(v2)**
Klein, Richard G. GN281.K55 1989, **(v6)**
Klein, Sandra Jacoby. RC607.A26.K5753 1998, **(v2)**
Klein, Scott W. PR6019.O9.Z676 1994, **(v3)**
Klein, William W. Z7772.P1.K54 1996, **(v10)**
Klein, Maury. HN57.K55 1993, **(v6)**
Kleinbard, David. PT2635.I65.Z753 1993, **(v3)**
Kleinberg, Robert. HC427.92.K55 1990, **(v6)**
Kleinberg, S. J. HC108.P7.K64 1989, **(v6)**
Kleine-Ahlbrandt, W. Laird. D645.K54 1995, **(v5)**
Kleiner, Diana E. E. NB115.K57 1992, **(v9)**
Kleinfeld, Erwin. QA188.K58 1997, **(v1)**
Kleinfeld, Margaret. QA184.K585 1996, **(v1)**
Kleinfelder, Karen L. N6853.P5.K58 1993, **(v9)**
Kleinman, Arthur. GN296.K566 1995, **(v6)**
Kleinman, Hyman H. PR6039 H52Z74, **(v3)**
Kleinman, Mark L. E748.W23.K58 2000, **(v4)**
Kleinschmidt, Harald. JZ1242.K58 2000, **(v7)**
Kleinstreuer, C. QA911.K57 1997, **(v1)**
Kleist, Heinrich von. PT1327.K58 1993, **(v3)**
PT2378.A1 1961, **(v3)**
PT2378.A15 E5, **(v3)**
PT2378.A2.E5 1982, **(v3)**
PT2378.A2.E5 1988, **(v3)**
Kleitman, Nathaniel. QP425.K53 1963, **(v1)**
Klekowski, Edward J. QK981.K54 1988, **(v1)**
Klement, Frank L. E458.8.K673 1984, **(v4)**
E458.8.K68 1999, **(v4)**
E537.9.K54 1997, **(v4)**
Klemke, Lloyd W. HV6658.K54 1992, **(v6)**
Klemp, P. J. Z8578.K59 1996, **(v10)**
Klemperer, Victor. DS135.G3315.K54513 1998, **(v5)**
Klenk, Virginia. BC135.K53 2002, **(v8)**
Klepper, Robert K. PN1995.75.K57 1999, **(v3)**
Kleppner, Paul. F548.52.W36.K54 1985, **(v4)**
JK1965.K53, **(v4)**
Klessinger, Martin. QD476.K53 1995, **(v1)**
Klevar, Harvey L. PS3505.A322.Z69 1993, **(v3)**

Kley, Roland. JC273.H382.K54 1994, (v7)
Klibbe, Lawrence Hadfield. PQ6554.P3.Z7, (v3)
Kliebard, Herbert M. LB1570.K585 1987, (v7)
Klieman, Aaron S. DS119.6.K54 1990, (v5)
Klier, Betje Black. F374.P38, (v4)
Kliewer, Christopher. LC4631.K55 1998, (v7)
Kliger, David S. QC441.K55 1990, (v1)
Kligman, Gail. HB3631.K58 1998, (v6)
Kliman, Bernice W. PR2807.K57 1988, (v3)
   PR2823.K58 1992, (v3)
Klinck, Carl Frederick. PR9111.K4, (v3)
   PR9184.3.K5 1976, (v3)
Kline, George Louis. B1674.W354.K5, (v8)
Kline, James E. TS1105.K665 1991, (v1)
Kline, Morris. QA21.K52, (v1)
   QA37.K62, (v1)
Kline, Paul. BF698.4.K56 1983b, (v2)
Kline, Stephen. HQ784.T4.K57 1993, (v6)
Kline, T. Jefferson. PN1993.5.F7.K57 1992, (v3)
Kline, Victoria. PN1022.K55 1992, (v3)
Klingberg, Frank Wysor. E173.C15 vol.50, (v4)
Klingender, F. D. N7660.K55 1971, (v9)
Klingensmith, Samuel John. NA7740.K55 1993, (v9)
Klingenstein, Susanne. E184.37.A15 1998, (v4)
Klinger, Barbara. PN1998.3.S57.K55 1994, (v3)
Klinger, Eric. BF778.K56 1977, (v2)
Klinghoffer, Arthur Jay. DT450.435.K55 1998, (v5)
   HD9575.R82.K57, (v6)
Klinkowitz, Jerome. PS3572.O5.Z748 1998, (v3)
   PT2668.A5.Z75 1983, (v3)
Klintworth, Gary. HC430.5.K57 1995, (v6)
Klir, George J. QA248.K487 1995, (v1)
Klitzman, Robert. RA644.P93.K57 1998, (v2)
   RC607.A26.K5755 1997, (v2)
Kliuchevskii, V. O. DK114.K573, (v5)
Kliuchevskii, Vasilii Osipovich. DK131.K553, (v5)
Klobucka, Anna. PQ1799.G795, (v3)
Kloczowski, Jerzy. BR952.K58132000, (v8)
Kloepfer, Deborah Kelly. PR6035.H96.Z76 1989, (v3)
Klopfer, Bruno. BF698.8.R5.K56, (v2)
Kloppenberg, James T. JC574.2.U6.K58 1998, (v7)
Kloppenborg, John S. BS2555.2.K567 2000, (v8)
Klopstock, Friedrich Gottlieb. PT2381.A3 1962, (v3)
Klosko, George. JC329.5.K57 1991, (v7)
   JC574.K56 2000, (v7)
Kloss, William. N6505.K56 1992, (v9)
Klostermaier, Klaus K. BL1202.K56 1994, (v8)
Klotman, Phyllis Rauch. PN1995.9.N4.K58 1997, (v3)
Klots, Alexander Barrett. QL542.K55, (v1)
Klotter, James C. F456.G64 K57, (v4)
Klotz, Heinrich. NA680.K5713 1988, (v9)
   NA1123.B8.K5513 1990, (v9)
Klotz, Irving M. QD501.K7557, (v1)
   QP517.L54.K57 1997, (v1)
Klotz, Irving Myron. QD504.K55 1994, (v1)
Kluckhohn, Clyde. BF698.K58 1953, (v2)
   E99.N3 K54 1974, (v4)
Kluckhohn, Paul. PT361.K5 1953, (v3)
Kluger, Garry Michael. PN2080.K58 1997, (v3)
Kluger, Richard. KF4155.K55 1976, (v7)
Klumpke, Anna. ND553.B6.K613 1997, (v9)
Klunder, Willard Carl. E340.C3.K57 1996, (v4)
Klyza, Christopher McGrory. F49.K59 1999, (v4)
Kmiec, Douglas W. KF5107.K57 1992, (v7)
Knaack, Marcelle Size. UG1243.K53, (v10)
Knaplund, Paul. DA563.4.K5 1966, (v5)
Knapp, Anthony W. QA387.K58 1986, (v1)
Knapp, Bettina Liebowitz. BL325.F4.K53 1997, (v8)
   PN56.G27.K58 2000, (v3)
   PQ556.K55 1995, (v3)
   PQ2122.K63 2000, (v3)
   PQ2538.K64, (v3)
   PR4168.K6 1991, (v3)
Knapp, Gerhard Peter. BF109.F76.K59 1989, (v2)
Knapp, Jeffrey. PR129.A4.K58 1992, (v3)
Knapp, Laurence F. PN1998.3.E325.K63 1996, (v3)
Knapp, Lewis M. PR3696.K5, (v3)
Knapp, Mona. PR6023.E833.Z735 1984, (v3)
Knapp, Peggy Ann. HB62.K57 2000, (v6)
Knapp, Robert S. PR2976.K57 1989, (v3)
Knapp, Sara D. Z699.5.S65.K57 1993, (v10)

Knapton, Ernest John. DC216.1.K55, (v5)
Knauft, Bruce M. GN671.N5.K64 1993, (v6)
Knaut, Andrew L. E99.P9.K59 1995, (v4)
Kneale, W. C. BC15.K55, (v8)
Knecht, R. J. DC110.K64 2001, (v5)
   DC111.3.K55 2000, (v5)
   DC113.K58, (v5)
   DC119.8.K64 1998, (v5)
   DC123.9.R5 K54 1991, (v5)
Knee, Stuart E. BX6931.K54 1994, (v8)
Kneese, Allen V. HC79.E5.K578 1984, (v6)
Knellwolf, Christa. PR3637.W6.K6 1998, (v3)
Knepper, George W. F491.K63 1997, (v4)
Knestrick, Walter. NE539.G74, (v9)
Kneubuhl, Victoria N. PS3561.N418H39 2002, (v3)
Knies, Earl A. PR4169.K6, (v3)
Kniffen, Fred Bowerman. E78.L8.K59 1987, (v4)
Knight, Alfred H. KF385.A4 K58 1998, (v7)
Knight, Amy W. DK268.B384.K58 1993, (v5)
   DK268.K5 K58 1999, (v5)
   HV8224.K57 1988, (v6)
   HV8227.2.A3.K59 1996, (v6)
Knight, Andrew. TA345.K63 2000, (v1)
Knight, Austin Melvin. VK541.K73 1984, (v10)
Knight, Charles A. Z8015.87.K55 1994, (v10)
Knight, Chris. GN484.38.K58 1991, (v6)
Knight, David M. QD11.K53 1992, (v1)
Knight, Edgar Wallace. LA201.K6 1970, (v7)
Knight, Ellen E. ML410.L798 K6 1992, (v9)
Knight, Frances. BX5055.2.K55 1995, (v8)
Knight, Frank Hyneman. HB171.K62 1969, (v6)
Knight, George Wilson. PN49.K6 1962, (v3)
   PR625.K58, (v3)
   PR2976.K64, (v3)
   PR2983.K59 1977, (v3)
   PR4382.K54 1957, (v3)
Knight, Julia. PN1993.5.G3.K58 1992, (v3)
Knight, Keith. QA276.K565 2000, (v1)
Knight, Nick. B809.82.C5 K65 1996, (v8)
Knight, R.C. PQ1779.K65 1991b, (v3)
Knight, Stephen Thomas. PR2129.K58 1994, (v3)
Knights, Ben. PR888.M45.K58 1999, (v3)
Knights, Mark. DA448.K62 1994, (v5)
Knights, Peter R. F73.25.K55 1991, (v4)
Knights, Vanessa. PQ6663.O554.Z75 1999, (v3)
Knobel, Dale T. E183.K645 1996, (v4)
Knobel, Roger. QA927.K693 2000, (v1)
Knobloch, Frieda. S441.K57 1996, (v1)
Knock, Thomas J. E767.1.K56 1992, (v4)
Knoepflmacher, U. C. PR990.K58 1998, (v3)
   PR4681.K6, (v3)
Knohl, Israel. BM487.K63 2000, (v8)
Knoke, David. HD69.S8 K58 2001, (v6)
Knoper, Randall K. PS1342.P45.K57 1995, (v3)
Knopf, Robert. PN2287.K4.K67 1999, (v3)
Knopp, Guido. DD243.K5613 2000, (v5)
Knopp, Konrad. QA295.K72, (v1)
Knoppers, Laura Lunger. DA427.K66 2000, (v5)
   PR3592.P64.K57 1994, (v3)
Knorr, Klaus Eugen. UA10.K53, (v10)
   UA11.K6, (v10)
   UA646.3.K5, (v10)
Knott, Kim. BL1202.K564 2000, (v8)
Knott, Stephen F. JK468.I6.K56 1996, (v7)
Knottenbelt, E. M. PE1.C66 n. s., vol. 77, (v3)
Knowland, A. S. PR1263.K6, (v3)
Knowles, David. BV5077.G7.K58, (v8)
   BX2592.K58 1963, (v8)
   DA536.M15.K5, (v5)
Knowles, John. G464.K62, (v6)
   PS3561.N68.S4, (v3)
Knowles, Mark. GV1794.K67 2002, (v6)
Knowles, Norman James. F1058.K58 1997, (v4)
Knowles, Owen. PR6005.O4.Z7617 1989, (v3)
Knowles, Ronald. PR3724.G8.K66 1996, (v3)
   PR6066.I53.Z714 1995, (v3)
Knowles, Sebastian D. G. PR6019.O9.U6728 2001, (v3)
Knowlton, Robert Almy. PS3561.N685.C6 1961, (v3)
Knowlton, Steven R. PN4756.K687 1997, (v3)

Knox, Alan Boyd. LC5215.K635 1993, (v7)
Knox, D. Edward. DA47.9.I77.K58, (v5)
Knox, Edward C. PQ1803.K5 1974, (v3)
Knox, G. A. QH95.58.K58 1994, (v1)
   QH541.5.S35, (v1)
Knox, George L. F535.N4.K554, (v4)
Knox, George W. HV6439.U5.K663 1994, (v6)
Knox, George. N6923.P457.A4 1983, (v9)
Knox, MacGregor. DG571.K63 2000, (v5)
   PA4417.K55, (v3)
Knox, Ronald Arbuthnott. PR99.K6, (v3)
Knox, William E. LB2424.K58 1993, (v7)
Knudson, Duane V. QP303.K59 1997, (v1)
Knupfer, Peter B. E302.1.K58 1991, (v4)
Knuth, Donald Ervin. QA76.5.K57, (v1)
Knutsen, Torbjørn L. JZ1305.K59 1997, (v7)
Knutson, Harold C. PQ1860.K53 1988, (v3)
Kobayashi, Shoshichi. QA641.K6, (v1)
Kobayashi, Takiji. PL782.E8.K6, (v3)
Kobkua Suwannathat-Pian. DS578.32.P55.K63 1995,
   (v5)
Kobler, J. F. PR9639.3.M258.Z74 1990, (v3)
Koblitz, Ann Hibner. QA29.K67.K6 1983, (v1)
Koblitz, Neal. QA268.K585 1998, (v1)
Koburger, Charles W. V163.K64 1990, (v10)
Kocandrle, Mirek. ML156.4.R6.K64 1988, (v9)
Koch, Adrienne. E175.9.K6, (v4)
   E332.2.K63 1986, (v4)
Koch, Christof. QP357.5.K63 1998, (v1)
Koch, Etta. F392.B53 K63 1999, (v4)
Koch, H. W. KK9430.A65.K63 1989, (v7)
Koch, Jean. R154.G827.K63 1997, (v2)
Koch, Richard. HV891.K58 1976, (v6)
Koch, Tom. HV1461.K63 1993, (v6)
   PN4784.E53.K63 1991, (v3)
   QA76.55.K63 1996, (v1)
Kochan, Lionel. DS140.K598 1990, (v5)
Kochavi, Arieh J. D803.K63 1998, (v5)
Kocher, Paul Harold. PR2673.K6 1962, (v3)
Kochka, Mary Murray. [from old catalog]. F194.K76,
   (v4)
Kochman, Thomas. E185.625.K6, (v4)
Kocis, Robert. JC143.M4.K596 1998, (v7)
Kocka, Jürgen. HN460.S6.K613 1984, (v6)
   HC285.K659 1999, (v6)
Kockler, Norbert. TA345.K653 1994, (v1)
Kocks, Dorothee E. PS374.L28.K63 2000, (v3)
Koditschek, Theodore. HN400.S6.K63 1990, (v6)
Koechner, Walter. TA1705.K63 1999, (v1)
Koehler, Stanley. PS3545.I544.Z614 1998, (v3)
Koehn, Daryl. BJ1395.K64 1998, (v8)
Koehn, Nancy F. HB615.K64 2001, (v6)
Koelb, Clayton. PN50.K64 1998, (v3)
   PT2621.A26.Z7644 1989, (v3)
Koelble, Thomas A. HX249.K64 1991, (v6)
Koen, Avraam. B572.K64 1995, (v8)
Koenig, Harold George. BL65.A46.K64 1995, (v8)
   BL65.M4 K646 2001, (v8)
Koenig, Herbert A. TA330.K64 1998, (v1)
Koenigsberger, H. G. D228.K6 1971, (v5)
Koenker, Diane. HD5395.K64 1989, (v6)
Koepsell, David R. K1401.K64 2000, (v7)
Koerner, David. QB54.K54 2000, (v1)
Koerner, Joseph Leo. ND588.F75.K64 1990, (v9)
Koestenbaum, Peter. HF5351.K584 1987, (v6)
Koestenbaum, Wayne. ML429.K74.A3 1993, (v9)
Koestler, Arthur. B1646.K77.I55, (v8)
   CB427.K6 1961, (v5)
   PR6021.O4 A6, (v3)
   PR6021.O4.A7 1969, (v3)
   PR6021.O4 D3, (v3)
   PR6021.O4.G47 1968, (v3)
   PR6021.O4 G5, (v3)
   PR6021.O4 T5 1967, (v3)
   PR6021.O4.T7 1970, (v3)
   PR6021.O4.Y6, (v3)
   PR6021.O4.Z469 1984, (v3)
   PR6021.O4.Z5 1970, (v3)
   PR6021.O4.Z53 1970, (v3)
Kofalk, Harriet. QL31.B24.K63 1989, (v1)

Kofman, Sarah. B317.K6413 1998, (v8)
    B823.3.K613 1999, (v8)
Kofsky, Frank. E183.8.S65.K63 1993, (v4)
Koggel, Christine M. HM146.K64 1998, (v6)
Kogler, Hans-Herbert. BD241.K6413 1996, (v8)
Kohak, Erazim V. BD581.K54 1984, (v8)
    GE42.K64813 2000, (v6)
Kohen, J. L. GF801.K65 1995, (v6)
Kohl, Benjamin G. DG975.P15.K64 1998, (v5)
Kohl, David F. Z712.K59 1986, (v10)
Kohl, Herbert R. LA2317.K64.A33 1984, (v7)
    LB1025.2.K62, (v7)
    LB1050.K6 1973, (v7)
Kohl, Lawrence Frederick. JK2260.K64 1989, (v7)
Kohlein, Fritz. SB413.G3.K64 1991, (v1)
Kohlenberger, John R. BS425.K645 1991, (v8)
Kohler, Eric Louis. HF5621.K6 1983, (v6)
Kohler, Joachim. DD247.H5.K73 2000, (v5)
Kohler, Robert E. Q180.55.M4.K63 1994, (v1)
Kohler, Wolfgang. BD232.K6 1966, (v8)
Kohlhoff, Dean. D810.A53.K64 1995, (v5)
Kohlstedt, Sally Gregory. Q11.K66 1999, (v1)
Kohn, Alfie. LB3011.K64 1996, (v7)
Kohn, George C. D9.K63 1990, (v5)
    D25.A2.K63 1999, (v5)
Kohn, Hans. D7.K73, (v5)
    JC311.K567, (v7)
Kohn, Howard. F187.P9.K64 1998, (v4)
Kohn, James P. HD7654.K63 1996, (v6)
Kohn, Livia. BL1900.H7965.K64 1991, (v8)
    BL1910.K64 1993, (v8)
Kohn, Livia. BL1930.K58 1998, (v8)
Kohn, Richard H. UA223.K737, (v10)
Kohn, Robert Rothenberg. QP86.K58 1978, (v1)
Koht, Halvdan. PT7181.K6, (v3)
Kohut, Heinz. RC438.6.K64.A4 1994, (v2)
Kohut, Thomas August. DD229.K54 1991, (v5)
Koistinen, Paul A. C. HC110.D4.K638 1996, (v6)
    HC110.D4.K643 1997, (v6)
Koivisto, Mauno. DL1141.6.K65.A3 1997, (v5)
Kojeve, Alexandre. B2929.K613, (v8)
Kokeritz, Helge. PR3081.K57, (v3)
Kokoschka, Oskar. PT2621.O664.E79 1998, (v3)
Kokusai Bunka Shinkokai. PL717.K6 1970, (v3)
Kolakowski, Leszek. B3279.H94.K64, (v8)
Kolankiewicz, George. DK4442.K635 1988, (v5)
Kolar, Carol Koehmstedt. Z6514.P66.K64 1981, (v10)
Kolata, Alan L. F3319.1.T55.K64 1993, (v4)
Kolata, Gina Bari. RC150.4.K64 1999, (v2)
Kolb, Albert. DS509.3.K6313 1971, (v5)
Kolb, Edward W. QB981.K689 1996, (v1)
Kolb, Jocelyne. PN603.K65 1995, (v3)
Kolbrener, William. PR3588.K65 1997, (v3)
Kolin, Philip C. PS3545.I5365.S824 2000, (v3)
Kolinsky, Martin. DS63.2.G7.K65 1999, (v5)
Kolinsky, Martin. DS126.K65 1993, (v5)
Koliodimos, Dimitris. PN1993.5.G75.K65 1999, (v3)
Kolker, Robert Phillip. PN1998.3.W46.K64 1993, (v3)
Kolkey, Jonathan Martin. JA84.U5.K54 1983, (v7)
Kolko, Gabriel. E744.K65, (v4)
Kolkowicz, Roman. UA770.K6, (v10)
Kollander, Patricia. DD224.K65 1995, (v5)
Kollek, Teddy. DS109.15.K65 1990, (v5)
Koller, John M. B121.K56 1985, (v8)
Kollman, Ken. JK1118.K65 1998, (v7)
Kolm, Serge-Christophe. JC578.K68 1996, (v7)
Kolmar, Gertrud. PT2605.H54.A24 1997, (v3)
Kolneder, Walter. ML410.W33.K63, (v9)
    ML800.K6413 1998, (v9)
Kolodko, Grzegorz W. HC244.K6315 2000, (v6)
    HC340.3.K656363 2000, (v6)
Kolodny, Annette. E179.5.K64 1984, (v4)
    LA227.4.K65 1998, (v7)
    PS88.K65, (v3)
Kolp, John Gilman. F229.K75 1998, (v4)
Kolsto, Pal. DK510.36.K65 1995, (v5)
Kolthoff, I. M. QD75.2.K64 1978, (v1)
    QD111.K642, (v1)
Kolve, V. A. PR643.C7.K6, (v3)
    PR1875.A44.K64 1984, (v3)
Komar, Kathleen L. PT2635.I65.D8627 1987, (v3)

Komar, Paul D. GB451.2.K65 1998, (v6)
Komarovsky, Mirra. HQ728.K64, (v6)
Kominz, Laurence Richard. PL790.S63.K6 1995, (v3)
Komiya, Ryutaro. HC462.K63 1990, (v6)
Kommers, Donald P. KK4446.7.K66 1989, (v7)
Kondepudi, D. K. QC311.K66 1998, (v1)
Kondoleon, Christine. N5865.A75, (v9)
Konefsky, Samuel Joseph. KF8748.K65 1974, (v7)
Koner, Pauline. GV1785.K596.A3 1989, (v6)
Konig, Karl. RC504.K6613 1995, (v2)
Konigsberg, Ira. PN1993.45.K66 1997, (v3)
    PR3667.K6, (v3)
Konigsburg, E. L. PZ7.K8352Fr 1988, (v3)
Konishi, Jinichi. PL716.K64813 1984, (v3)
Konjaku monogatari. PL890.K6 1959, (v3)
Konn, Tania. HF54.52.C36, (v6)
Konneh, Augustine. DT630.5.M34.K65 1996, (v5)
Kono, Juliet S. PS3561.O515T77 1995, (v3)
Kono, Taeko. PL855.O44.A25 1996, (v3)
Kononenko, Natalie O. ML399.K65 1998, (v9)
Konopinski, Emil Jan. QC20.K66, (v1)
Konorski, Jerzy. QP376.K65, (v1)
Kon-sprul Blo-gros-mtha-yas. BJ1289.K6513 1998, (v8)
    KF358.K66 1998, (v7)
    KF4749.K633 2001, (v7)
Konyndyk, Kenneth. BC199.M6.K66 1986, (v8)
Koocher, Gerald P. RC281.C4.K64, (v2)
    RJ499.K64 1990, (v2)
Koon, Helene. PN2285.K73 1994, (v3)
    PR3105.K66 1989, (v3)
Koop, Allen V. D805.U6.K57 1988, (v5)
Koopmann, Georg. HD9560.5.K685 1989, (v6)
Koopmans-de Bruijn, Ria. Z3306.K86 1997, (v10)
Koos, Earl Lomon. HV43.K64, (v6)
Koos, Leonard Vincent. LB2328.K62 1970, (v7)
Koot, Gerard M. HB103.A2.K65 1987, (v6)
Kooyman, Brian P. GN799.T6.K66 2000, (v6)
Kooyman, Gerald L. QP82.2.U45.K66 1989, (v1)
Kopelson, Kevin. GV1785.N6.K66 1997, (v6)
    ML700.K56 1996, (v9)
Kopinak, Kathryn. HD9734.M42.K67 1996, (v6)
Kopka, Deborah L. LB3013.3.K68 1997, (v7)
Koppel, Gene. PR4038.R4.K67 1988, (v3)
Koppes, Clayton R. TL568.J47.K66 1982, (v1)
Koppett, Leonard. GV863.A1.K66 1998, (v6)
Kops, Bernard. PR6061.O6.F57, (v3)
Kopstein, Jeffrey. HC290.78.K66 1997, (v6)
Korb, Lawrence J. UB223.K67 1976, (v10)
Korbel, Josef. DB215.K588, (v5)
    DB215.5.K68, (v5)
Korda, Michael. RC280.P7.K67 1996, (v2)
Koreman, Megan. D802.F8.K65 1999, (v5)
Koren, Leonard. BH221.J3 K67 1994, (v8)
Korenman, Joan Smolin. HQ1180.K67 1997, (v6)
Koreny, Fritz. ND1954.D8.K5713 1988, (v9)
Korey, William. JC571.K595 1998, (v7)
Korey, William. KJC5132.K67 1993, (v7)
Koritz, Amy. PR478.D35.K67 1995, (v3)
Korn, Granino Arthur. QA37.K74, (v1)
Korn, Jessica. JK305.K67 1996, (v7)
Kornai, Janos. HC244.K66913 1995, (v6)
    HC300.282.K6713 1990, (v6)
    HX73.K6715 1992, (v6)
Kornberg, Arthur. HD9999.B443.U647 1995, (v6)
    QP511.8.K68.A3 1989, (v1)
Kornberg, Jacques. DS151.H4.K68 1993, (v5)
Kornblith, Hilary. BD161.K62 2002, (v8)
Kornbluh, Mark Lawrence. JK1965.K67 2000, (v7)
Kornbluh, Peter. E183.8.N5.K67 1987, (v4)
Kornblum, William. HD8039.I52.U56, (v6)
Kornegay, Chris. QA5.K692 1999, (v1)
Korner, Christian. QK937.K67 1999, (v1)
Korner, T. W. QA403.5.K67 1988, (v1)
Kornick, Rebecca Hodell. MT955.K82 1990, (v9)
Kornilov, A. A. DK189.K7 1970, (v5)
Kornilovich, K. N6981.K573, (v9)
Kornstein, Daniel. PR3028.K67 1994, (v3)

Kornweibel, Theodore. E185.61.K59 1998, (v4)
Korobkin, Laura Hanft. PS374.A34.K67 1998, (v3)
Korosenyi, Andras. JN2067.K6813 1999, (v7)
Kôròsòn ̄ar ̄avu, Guònòd ̄epalli Veçnkaòta. PL4780.9.K749K5513 1997, (v3)
Korovkin, Tanya. HD1491.P4.K67 1990, (v6)
Korp, Maureen. E73.K67 1990, (v4)
Korsch, Dietrich. QC383.K67 1991, (v1)
Korsmeyer, Carolyn. B105.F66 K67 1999, (v8)
Kort, Carol. PS147.K67 2000, (v3)
Kort, Michael. DK246.K64 1985, (v5)
    E744.K696 1998, (v4)
Kort, Wesley A. BS537.K67 1988, (v8)
Korte, George. G70.212.K67 2001, (v6)
Korver, Ton. HD5724.K64 1990, (v6)
Korwin, Yala H. N7525.K67, (v9)
Korytova-Magstadt, Stepanka. F596.3.B67.K67 1993, (v4)
Kosambi, D. D. DS425.K576 2002, (v5)
Koseki, Shoichi. KNX2101.K6713 1997, (v7)
Koselleck, Reinhart. JA83.K6613 1988, (v7)
Koshar, Rudy. DD67.K67 1998, (v5)
    DD222.K67 2000, (v5)
Koshiro, Yukiko. E183.8.J3.K67 1999, (v4)
Kosian, R. D. GB451.2.K6813 2000, (v6)
Kosinski, Dorothy M. N72.P5.K67 1999, (v9)
    N6797.M5 A4 2001, (v9)
Kosinski, Jerzy N. PS3561.O8.B55X, (v3)
    PS3561.O8.C6, (v3)
    PS3561.O8.H4 1988, (v3)
    PS3561.O8.P3, (v3)
    PS3561.O8.S76, (v3)
Kosko, Bart. BC108.K59 1993, (v8)
Koskoff, David E. E748.K376.K67, (v4)
Koslow, Arnold. BC135.K67 1992, (v8)
Koslowski, Barbara. Q175.32.R45.K67 1996, (v1)
Koslowski, Rey. JV7590.K67 2000, (v7)
Koss, Stephen E. DA565.M78.K66, (v5)
    DA566.9.H27.K6, (v5)
    DA566.9.O7.K67 1976b, (v5)
Kossak, Steven. ND1337.I5.K68 1997, (v9)
Kossmann, E. H. DH620.K67, (v5)
Kosso, Peter. Q175.K8648 1992, (v1)
Kosta, Barbara. PT735.K68 1994, (v3)
Kostelanetz, Richard. ML410.C24.K68 1988, (v9)
    N7454.M6.K6 1970, (v9)
Kostenevich, A. G. N6847.K67 1999, (v9)
    ND547.K683 1995, (v9)
Kostka, Stefan M. MT50.K85 2000, (v9)
Kosto, Adam J. HN590.C36, (v6)
Kostof, Spiro. NA200.K65 1995, (v9)
    NA705.K64 1987, (v9)
Kosuge, Koji. QD921.K676613 1994, (v1)
Koszarski, Richard. PN1993.5.U6.H55 1990 vol. 3, (v3)
Kotenev, Anatol M. DS774.K6, (v5)
Kothari, Sunil. GV1796.K38.K68 1989, (v6)
Kotkin, Joel. HT123.K67 2000, (v6)
Kotkin, Stephen. DK651.M159.K675 1995, (v5)
    DK651.M159.K68 1991, (v5)
Kotler, Philip. HD75.K697 1997, (v6)
    HF5415.122.K68 1989, (v6)
Kotlikoff, Laurence J. HB843.K68 1989, (v6)
Kotlowitz, Alex. F574.S26.K68 1998, (v4)
Kottak, Conrad Phillip. DT469.M264.K67 1980, (v5)
    PN1992.6.K67 1990, (v3)
Kotter, John P. HD57.7.K67 1988, (v6)
    HD58.8.K645 2002, (v6)
Kotz, David M. HC336.26.K668 1997, (v6)
Kotz, Mary Lynn. N6537.R27.K67 1990, (v9)
Kotz, Nick. UG1242.B6.K69 1988, (v10)
Kotzwinkle, William. PS3561.O85.D6x, (v3)
Kourouma, Ahmadou. PQ3989.2.K58.M6613 1993, (v3)
Kourvetaris, George A. DF717.K68 1987, (v5)
Kouzes, James M. HD57.7.K68 2002, (v6)
Kovach, Bill. PN4888.P6.K68 1999, (v3)
Kovach, Robert L. GB5014.K68 1995, (v6)
Kovel, Joel. E743.5.K68 1994, (v4)
Kovetz, Attay. QC670.K694 1990, (v1)
Kovinick, Phil. N8214.5.U6.K68 1998, (v9)

314

Kowaleski-Wallace, Elizabeth. HC260.C6.K69 1997, (v6)
Kowalewski, David. BD581.K597 2000, (v8)
Kowalewski, Mark R. BX2347.8.A52.K683 1994, (v8)
Kowallis, Jon Eugene. PL2754.S5.Z69625 1996, (v3)
Kowalski, Theodore J. LB3218.A1 K638 2002, (v7)
Koyama, Junji. QE534.2.K695 1997, (v1)
Koyre, Alexandre. BD511.K67, (v8)
Kozar, Paul Michael. UA23.K775 1987, (v10)
Kozhamthadam, Job. QB355.3.K69 1994, (v1)
Kozinn, Allan. ML418.E48.K7 1990, (v9)
Kozioff, Sarah. PN1995.9.D49.K69 2000, (v3)
Kozloski, Lillian D. TL1550.K68 1994, (v1)
Kozlowski, Lynn T. RC567.K65 2001, (v2)
Kozlowski, Rob. PN2071.C58.K69 2000, (v3)
Kozlowski, T. T. QK711.2.K72 1997, (v1)
Kozol, Jonathan. HQ792.U5.K69 2000, (v6)
    LA217.K688, (v7)
    LA486.K69, (v7)
    LB1029.F7.K6 1982, (v7)
    LC151.K68 1985, (v7)
Kozulin, Alex. BF108.S65.K68 1984, (v2)
Kraay, Colin M. CJ401.K72, (v5)
Kracauer, Siegfried. AC35.K64613 1995, (v10)
    PN1993.5.G3.K7 1959, (v3)
Kraditor, Aileen S. E449.K7, (v4)
Kraemer, David Charles. BM501.K72 1990, (v8)
    BM504.2.K688 1996, (v8)
Kraeuter, David W. Z7224.U6.K7 1992, (v10)
Kraft, Elizabeth. PR858.H85.K73 1992, (v3)
    PR3716.K73 1996, (v3)
Kraft, Victoria Marie. KF4651.K73 1991, (v7)
Kragh, Helge. QB981.K73 1996, (v1)
    QC7.K7 1999, (v1)
    QC16.D57.K73 1990, (v1)
Krainer, Robert E. HB3722.K73 1992, (v6)
Krajcinovic, Ivana. RA413.7.M55.K73 1997, (v2)
Krajicek, David J. PN4888.C8.K73 1998, (v3)
Krakauer, Jon. GV199.44.E85.K725 1997, (v6)
Krakowiak, Sacha. QA76.76.O63.K73l3 1988, (v1)
Krakowski, Shmuel. D810.J4.K68413 1984, (v5)
Kramer, Dale. PR4754.K7, (v3)
Kramer, Heinz. DR576.K73 2000, (v5)
Kramer, Jack. GV994.K7.A34 1979, (v6)
Kramer, Jane S. HV1461.K68 1991, (v6)
Kramer, Jerry. GV956.G7.K7, (v6)
Kramer, John E. Z1231.F4 K73 2000, (v10)
Kramer, Jonathan D. ML3850.K72 1988, (v9)
    MT125.K72 1988, (v9)
Kramer, Lawrence. ML3849.K7 1984, (v9)
    ML3880.K7 1990, (v9)
Kramer, Lloyd S. DC146.L2.K73 1996, (v5)
Kramer, Matthew H. JC153.H66.K725 1997, (v7)
Kramer, Michael P. PE2807.K73 1991, (v3)
Kramer, Peter D. RC483.5.F55.K7 1993, (v2)
Kramer, Rita. HV9104.K68 1988, (v6)
Kramer, Samuel Noah. DS72.K7 1981, (v5)
    DS72.K73, (v5)
Kramer, T. D. DS135.H9.K73 2000, (v5)
Krammer, Arnold. D769.8.A6.K73 1997, (v5)
Kramnick, Isaac. BR516.K66 1996, (v8)
    DA501.B6.K7 1968, (v5)
    JA84.G7.K73 1990, (v7)
    JC257.L4.K73 1993, (v7)
Kramnick, Jonathan Brody. PR421.K73 1998, (v3)
Krampner, Jon. PN1992.4.C64.K73 1997, (v3)
Kramrisch, Stella. NA6002.K72 1976, (v9)
    NB1007.S67.K7, (v9)
Krane, Dale. JK4616.K73 1992, (v7)
    KF5305.Z95, (v7)
Kranidis, Rita S. HQ1593.K73 1999, (v6)
Krantz, Grover S. QL89.2.S2.K73 1992, (v1)
Krantz, Steven G. QA42.K73 1997, (v1)
    QA63.K73 1997, (v1)
    QA331.5.K713 1991, (v1)
    QA331.7.K744 1999, (v1)
Kranz, Rachel. HQ76.8.U5.K73 2000, (v6)
Kranzberg, Melvin. T15.K7, (v1)
Kranzler, David. F1497.J48, (v4)
Krapohl, Robert H. BV3773.K73 1999, (v8)
Krapp, George Philip. PR767.K7 1963, (v3)

Krasilovsky, M. William. ML3790.S5 2003, (v9)
Krasker, Tommy. ML128.M78.K7 1988, (v9)
Krass, Allan S. KZ5624.K73 1997, (v7)
Kratoska, Paul H. DS596.6.K73 1997, (v5)
Kraus, Hans-Joachim. BM656.K713, (v8)
Kraus, Jody S. JC153.H66.K73 1993, (v7)
Kraus, Karl. PT2621.R27, (v3)
    PT2621.R27.A235 1977, (v3)
Kraus, Michael. CB411.K7 1961, (v5)
    E169.1.K688 1964, (v4)
Kraus, Richard Curt. NK3634.A2.K73 1991, (v9)
Krause, Chester L. CJ1755.K72, (v5)
Krause, Corinne Azen. HQ1439.P58.K73 1991, (v6)
Krause, David J. F572.K43.K73 1992, (v4)
Krause, David. PR6029.C33.Z678 1976, (v3)
Krause, Elliott A. HT687.K68 1996, (v6)
Krause, Shari Stamford. TL553.5.K73 1996, (v1)
Krauss, Beatrice H. DU624.65.K72 1993, (v5)
Krauss, Bob. DU22.K776 1988, (v5)
Krauss, Ellis S. PN5407.T4, (v3)
Krauss, Lawrence Maxwell. QB500.K64 1997, (v1)
    QB500.K65 1995, (v1)
    QB791.3.K73 1989, (v1)
    QC21.2.K73 1993, (v1)
Krauss, Rosalind E. N6490.K727 1985, (v9)
Kraut, Alan M. RA448.5.I44.K73 1994, (v2)
Krautheimer, Richard. DG63.K7 1983, (v5)
    DG811.K7, (v5)
    NA4817.K7 1986, (v9)
Kravitt, Edward F. ML2829.K7 1996, (v9)
Kravitz, Walter. JK9.K73 2001, (v7)
Kraybill, Donald B. BX8128.E36.K73 1995, (v8)
Kraynak, Robert P. DA400.H63.K73 1990, (v5)
Krebs, Charles J. QH541.28.K74 1985, (v1)
Krebs, Harald. MT92.S24.K7 1999, (v9)
Krebs, Robert E. Q158.5.K74 2001, (v1)
    Q172.5.E77.K74 1999, (v1)
    QD466.K69 1998, (v1)
Krech, Shepard. E98.P5 K74 1999, (v4)
    F187.T2.S894, (v4)
Kreher, Donald L. QA164.K73 1999, (v1)
Kreidberg, Marvin A. U15.U64 no.20-212, (v10)
Kreiger, Barbara. BV3202.M55.D58 1999, (v8)
Kreilkamp, Vera. PR8807.C68.K74 1998, (v3)
Kreimeier, Klaus. PN1999.U35.K713 1996, (v3)
Kreisel, Martha. Z7134.K74 1999, (v10)
Kreis-Schinck, Annette. PR3317.Z5.K74 2001, (v3)
Kreissman, Bernard. PR3664.P4.K7 1960, (v3)
Kreith, Frank. TJ810.K73, (v1)
Kreitner, Kenneth. ML1311.7.P4 K73 1990, (v9)
Krejci, Jaroslav. DB2188.7.K73 1996, (v5)
    DS12.K74 1990, (v5)
Krell, David Farrell. B2430.D484.K74 2000, (v8)
Kremer, Gary R. E664.T88.K74 1991, (v4)
Kremer, John M. D. GV706.4.K74 1994, (v6)
Kremer, S. Lillian. PN56.H55.K74 1999, (v3)
Kremers, Edward. RS61.K73 1976, (v2)
Kreml, William P. JA74.5.K72 1991, (v7)
    KF4541.K66 1997, (v7)
Kren, Claudia. Z5524.A35.K74 1990, (v10)
Krenn, Michael L. F1436.8.U6.K74 1996, (v4)
    HF1456.5.L3.K74 1990, (v6)
Krenz, Jerrold H. TK7816.K73 2000, (v1)
Krepon, Michael. UA23.K777 1984, (v10)
Kreps, Gary L. R118.K73 1984, (v2)
Kress, George. HF5415.2.K748 1994, (v6)
Kress, Stephen W. QL677.5.K73, (v1)
Kreusler, Abraham. PB38.R8.K7, (v3)
Kreutz, Barbara M. DG827.K74 1992, (v5)
Kreutzer, Wolfgang. QA76.6.K735 1990, (v1)
Krewson, Margrit B. Z6465.U5 K74 1995, (v10)
Kreyche, Gerald F. F591.K75 1989, (v4)
Kreyling, Michael. PS3545.E6.Z752 1999, (v3)
Kricher, John C. QH102.K75 1988, (v1)
    QH106.5.K75 1997, (v1)
Krieg, Joann P. PS3231.A2 1998, (v3)
    PS3233.K75 2000, (v3)
    RA650.5.K75 1992, (v2)
Krieger, Joel. E876.K75 1986, (v4)
Krieger, Leonard. D13.K7 1989, (v5)
    D15.R3.K74, (v5)

    DD112.K82, (v5)
Krieger, Martin H. QC29.K75 1992, (v1)
Krieger, Murray. PN85.K67 1988, (v3)
    PN1031.K7, (v3)
    PN1126.K75 1991, (v3)
Krieger, Susan. H35.K68 1991, (v6)
Kriger, Norma J. DT2988.K75 1992, (v5)
Krikler, Jeremy. HD1538.S6.K75 1993, (v6)
Krikorian, Betty Linn. KF1083.K752, (v7)
Krimsky, Sheldon. S494.5.B563.K75 1996, (v1)
Kringlen, Einar. RC512.K7, (v2)
Krinitzsky, E. L. TA658.44.K75 1993, (v1)
Kripalani, Krishna. PK1725.K7, (v3)
Kriplen, Nancy. GV994.D39 K75 1999, (v6)
Krishnan, Rajam. PL4758.9.K7C813 1995, (v3)
Krishnaswamy, Revathi. DS479.K75 1998, (v5)
Kristal, Efrain. PQ8498.32.A65.Z697 1998, (v3)
Kristeller, Paul Oskar. B775.K73, (v8)
    B778.K74 1961, (v8)
Kristensen, Tom. PT8175.K78 H32, (v3)
Kristeva, Julia. JC251.A74 K7513 2001, (v7)
Kristeva, Julia. P121.K7413 1989, (v3)
Kristiansen, Kristian. GN778.2.A1.K75 1998, (v6)
Kristol, Irving. JC573.2.U6.K75 1995, (v7)
Kristy, Davida. GV721.2.C68.K75 1995, (v6)
Kritzeck, James. PJ409.K7, (v3)
Kritzer, Amelia Howe. PR6053.H786.Z75 1991, (v3)
Kritzer, Herbert M. KF8700.K77 1990, (v7)
    KF9084.K75 1991, (v7)
Krock, Arthur. E743.K7, (v4)
Kroeber, A. L. CB19.K686 1963, (v5)
    CB59.K7 1962a, (v5)
    E51.C15 vol. 38, (v4)
    E51.H337 vol. 47, no. 1, (v4)
    E78.C15.K78 1976, (v4)
    F3429.1.N3.K76 1998, (v4)
    GN6.K7, (v6)
    GN24.K7 1948, (v6)
    PN603.K76 1988, (v3)
Kroeber, Theodora. E98.F6.K82, (v4)
    E99.Y23 K76 1976, (v4)
Kroeger, Brooke. PN4874.C59.K76 1994, (v3)
Kroemer, K.H.E. QP309.G7313 1997, (v1)
Kroen, Sheryl. DC256.8.K76 2000, (v5)
Kroes, Rob. E169.04.K755 1996, (v4)
    F739.A48.K76 1992, (v4)
Krog, Carl E. E802.H38 1984, (v4)
Kroger, Jane. BF724.3.I3.K76 1989, (v2)
Krogness, Mary Mercer. LC4085.K76 1995, (v7)
Krogsgaard, Michael. ML156.7.D97.K67 1991, (v9)
Krohn, Bill. PN1998.3.H58.K76 2000, (v3)
Krohn, Claus-Dieter. LD3837.K7613 1993, (v7)
Krohn, Lauren. KF1607.5.K76 1995, (v7)
Kroll, Steven. VM140.F9.K76 1999, (v10)
Kroll-Smith, J. Stephen. RB152.K76 1997, (v2)
Kromer, John. HT175.K76 2000, (v6)
Kromer, Robert Andrew. UA646.3.K76 1987, (v10)
Kronenberg, Kenneth. F472.M7.K76 1998, (v4)
Kronenberger, Louis. PR631.K7, (v3)
    PR3522.K7, (v3)
Kronenberger, Louis. PR5366.K7, (v3)
Kronenfeld, Jennie J. RA395.A3.K757 1997, (v2)
Kronenfeld, Judy. PR2819.K76 1998, (v3)
Kronish, Amy. PN1993.5.I86.K76 1996, (v3)
Krook, Dorothea. BJ71.K75, (v8)
Kropotkin, Petr Alekseevich. HM131.K92 1972c, (v6)
Krout, John Allen. E178.5.P2 vol.15, (v4)
Kroyanker, David. NA1478.J4.K767 1994, (v9)
Krstic, Radivoj V. QM557.K79 1991, (v1)
Krueger, Anne O. HC59.7.K75 1992, (v6)
    HF1413.K73 1995, (v6)
    HF1456.5.D44.K78 1993, (v6)
Krueger, Christine L. PR868.W6.K78 1992, (v3)
Krueger, Roberta L. PQ155.W6.K85 1993, (v3)
Kruft, Hanno-Walter. NA2500.K7513 1994, (v9)
Kruger, Loren. PN2582.N3.K78 1992, (v3)
    PR9361.2.K78 1999, (v3)
Kruger, Steven F. PN671.K7 1992, (v3)
    PS169.A42.K78 1996, (v3)

Krugman, Paul R. HB99.7.K77 1994, (v6)
HB199.K75 1996, (v6)
HB3716.K76 1999, (v6)
HC106.8.K78 1990, (v6)
HF1025.K75 1991, (v6)
HJ2381.K77 2001, (v6)
Krukowski, Lucian. BH39.K69 1987, (v8)
BH191.K78 1992, (v8)
Kruman, Marc W. JK2484.K78 1997, (v7)
Krummel, Donald William. ML112.K765 1992, (v9)
ML120.U5.K78 1987, (v9)
Z1001.K86 1984, (v10)
Krupat, Arnold. E89.5.K78 1985, (v4)
Krupnik, I. I. GF891.K7813 1993, (v6)
Kruse, Robert Leroy. QA76.6.K77 1984, (v1)
Krutch, Joseph Wood. B804.K68, (v8)
CB425.K75, (v5)
F788.K9, (v4)
F1246.K7, (v4)
PR3533.K7, (v3)
Krutnik, Frank. PN1995.9.F54.K78 1991, (v3)
PN2287.L435.K78 2000, (v3)
Kruty, Paul Samuel. NA6212.K78 1998, (v9)
Krutz, Gary. TJ1480.K73 1984, (v1)
Krutz, Glen S. KF4945.K78 2001, (v7)
Krutz, Ronald L. QA76.5.K77, (v1)
Krynine, Dimitri Pavlovitch. TN260.K8, (v1)
Kryzanek, Michael J. F1418.K77 1992, (v4)
F1938.55.K77 1988, (v4)
Krzanowski, W. J. QA278.K73 1988, (v1)
Kselman, Thomas A. GT3249.A2.K74 1993, (v6)
Kuan, Han-ching. PL2689.A27, (v3)
Kubackova, Ludmila. QA279.K83 1992, (v1)
Kuberski, Philip. PS3531.O82.Z7146 1992, (v3)
Kubicek, Paul. JN6635.K8 1999, (v7)
Kubik, Gerhard. ML3521.K83 1999, (v9)
Kubik, Jan. HD8537.N783.K83 1994, (v6)
Kubizek, August. DD247.H5.K813 1955, (v5)
Kubler, George. E51.S4 no. 14, (v4)
E59.A7.K8 1984, (v4)
E59.A7.K82 1991, (v4)
N7104.K8, (v9)
NA753.K8, (v9)
Kubler-Ross, Elisabeth. BF789.D4.K8, (v2)
RC607.A26.K83 1987, (v2)
Kubly, Herbert. PS3561.U2.W5, (v3)
Kucer, Stephen B. LB1576.K83 2001, (v7)
Kuczewski, Mark G. R724.K82 1997, (v2)
Kudish, Michael. QK177.K83 1992, (v1)
Kudlick, Catherine Jean. RC133.F9.P334 1996, (v2)
Kudszus, Winfried. PN1031.K82 1995, (v3)
Kuebrich, David. PS3242.R4.K84 1989, (v3)
Kuehl, Warren F. E744.K77 1997, (v4)
Kuehn, Manfred. B2797.K86 2001, (v8)
Kuehn, Robert E. PR6015.U9.Z745, (v3)
Kuehn, Thomas. KKH5601.15.K84 1991, (v7)
Kuenne, Robert E. HC110.I5.K76 1993, (v6)
Kuester, Martin. PR9192.6.H5.K84 1992, (v3)
Kugel, Rebecca. E99.C6 K84 1998, (v4)
Kugler, Richard L. UA770.K84 1996, (v10)
Kuhl, Stefan. HQ755.5.U5.K84 1994, (v6)
Kuhlman, Edward. LB14.7.K84 1994, (v7)
Kuhlman, Erika A. D639.P77.K84 1997, (v5)
Kuhn, Cynthia. RM316.K84 1998, (v2)
Kuhn, Merrily A. RM666.H33K84 2000, (v2)
Kuhn, Philip A. DS754.17.K8413 2002, (v5)
DS755.K77, (v5)
JQ1508.K84 1990, (v7)
Kuhn, Thomas S. Q175.K95, (v1)
QB41.C815.K8, (v1)
Kuhn, William M. JN341.K85 1996, (v7)
Kuhne, Dave. PS159.A38.K84 1999, (v3)
Kuhnel, Ernst. N6260.K7783 1966, (v9)
Kuhns, David F. PN2654.K85 1997, (v3)
Kuhns, Richard Francis. N72.P74.K8 1983, (v9)
Kuhn-Schnyder, Emil. QE761.K8413 1986, (v1)
Kuin, Roger. PR539.S7.K85 1998, (v3)
Kuipers, Joel Corneal. DS632.W48.K84 1998, (v5)
Kuisel, Richard F. DC59.8.U6.K85 1993, (v5)
HC276.K94, (v6)
Kuitenbrouwer, M. DJ261.K8413 1990, (v5)

Kujoory, Parvin. Z8813.K84 2001, (v10)
Kukathas, Chandran. JC578.R383.K85 1990, (v7)
Kukla, André. BF38.K84 2001, (v2)
Kuklick, Bruce. B851.K85 2001, (v8)
B935.K84, (v8)
D821.G4.K85, (v5)
E176.1.K84 1988, (v4)
Kuklick, Henrika. GN308.3.G7.K85 1991, (v6)
Kula, Witold. QC83.K813 1986, (v1)
Kularatna, Nihal. TK7881.15.K84 1999, (v1)
Kuletz, Valerie. E78.N4.K85 1998, (v4)
Kulick, Don. GN671.N5.K85 1992, (v6)
Kulikoff, Allan. HC104.K85 2000, (v6)
HC105.K87 1992, (v6)
Kull, Steven. DK288.K85 1992, (v5)
E840.K85 1999, (v4)
Kulp, Daniel Harrison. DS721.K85, (v5)
Kulski, Wladyslaw Wszebor. DK268.3.K86 1963, (v5)
Kultermann, Udo. NA1590.K813, (v9)
Kultgen, John H. BJ1533.R42 K85 1995, (v8)
BJ1725.K84 1988, (v8)
U263.K855 1999, (v10)
Kumagai, Fumie. HN723.5.K756 1996, (v6)
Kumar, Deepak. Q127.I4.K86 1995, (v1)
Kumar, H. D. QH541.15.B56.K86 1999, (v1)
Kumar, Nita. GN21.K86.A3 1992, (v6)
Kumar, P. Pratap. BL1225.L3.K86 1997, (v8)
Kumar, Udaya. PR6019.O9.U6735 1991, (v3)
Kumin, Maxine. PS3521.U638.D4x, (v3)
Kummings, Donald D. Z8971.5.K85 1982, (v10)
Kuna, Franz. PT2621.A26.Z7666 1974, (v3)
Kuncewiczowa, Maria Szczepanska. PG7445.E8.K8, (v3)
Kunda, Ziva. BF323.S63K86 1999, (v2)
Kundahl, George G. E546.7.K86 2000, (v4)
Kundera, Milan. PG5039.21.U6.K613 1980, (v3)
PG5039.21.U6.N413 1984, (v3)
PG5039.21.U6.V33, (v3)
Küng, Hans. B2949.R3.K8313 1987, (v8)
BL535.K8613 1984, (v8)
BT77.K79 1994, (v8)
BT78.K8613 1988, (v8)
BX945.3.K86 2001, (v8)
BX1746.K7913 1990, (v8)
BJ1125.K8713 1998, (v8)
Kung, K o-ch ang. PL2309.F8K8613 1997, (v3)
Kung, Shang-jen. PL2717.U47.T313 1976, (v3)
Kunhardt, Philip B. E457.K94 1992, (v4)
Kuniholm, Bruce Robellet. DS63.K86, (v5)
Kunitz, Stanley. PN451.K8, (v3)
PR105.K9, (v3)
PR451.K8 1936, (v3)
PS21.K8, (v3)
PS3521.U7.P6, (v3)
Kunkel, H. O. HV4757.K86 2000, (v6)
Kunkel, Thomas. PN4874.R65.K86 1995, (v3)
Kunnukuttan, Matamp. PL4718.9.K8547B4713 1996, (v3)
Kunoff, Hugo. Z2721.K86 1994, (v10)
Kunstler, Charles. DC133.3.K8, (v5)
Kunstler, William Moses. KF373.K8 A35 1996, (v7)
Kunz, Diane B. HF1456.5.Z4.E855 1991, (v6)
Kunze, Bonnelyn Young. BX7795.F75.K86 1994, (v8)
Kunzel, Regina G. HV700.5.K86 1993, (v6)
Kuo chia ti tu chi pien tsuan wei yuan hui (China). G2306.G1 .K813 1994, (v9)
Kuo li ku kung po wu yuan. N3750.T32.A66 1996, (v9)
N3750.T32.A87 1996, (v9)
Kuo, Benjamin C. TJ213.K8354 1995, (v1)
TJ216.K812 1980, (v1)
Kuo, Pin-chia. DS757.5.K8, (v5)
DS777.55.K75, (v5)
Kuo, Tai-Chün. DS734.97.U6 K86 1986, (v5)
Kupchan, Charles. UA10.5.K85 1994, (v10)
Kuper, Adam. GN25.K87 1994, (v6)
Kuper, Adam. GN308.K87 1988, (v6)
GN325.K89 1999, (v6)
GN357.K87 1999, (v6)
GN656.K86 1982, (v6)
Kuper, Jenny. KZ6515.K87 1997, (v7)

Kuper, Leo. JX5418.K86 1981, (v7)
Kupers, Terry Allen. RC489.T45.K87 1988, (v2)
Kupfer, Joseph H. PN1995.5.K87 1999, (v3)
Küpper, Heinz. PF5991.K83 1982, (v3)
Kupper, Susan J. CS2389.K87 1990, (v5)
Kupperman, Joel. B121.K85 2001, (v8)
B121.K86 1999, (v8)
BJ1521.K87 1991, (v8)
Kupperman, Karen Ordahl. E59.F53.K86 2000, (v4)
Kuramoto, Kazuko. DS731.J3.K87 1999, (v5)
Kuran, Timur. HM259.K87 1995, (v6)
Kurenberg, Joachim von. DD228.K812 1954, (v5)
Kurian, George Thomas. D847.K82 1990, (v5)
E38.K87 1990, (v4)
HA36.K87 1997, (v6)
HT108.5.K87 1994, (v6)
Kurihara, Sadako. PL855.U66.A26 1994, (v3)
Kuritz, Paul. PN2061.K7868 1997, (v3)
Kurke, Leslie. DF222.2.K87 1999, (v5)
Kurlansky, Mark. PN6071.C66.K87 1997, (v3)
Kurokawa, Kisho. NA2543.S6.K87 1991, (v9)
HC335.4.K87 1988, (v6)
Kurski, Jaroslaw. DK4452.W34.K8713 1993, (v5)
Kurten, Bjorn. QE35.K97613 1986, (v1)
QE881.K796 1988, (v1)
Kurtz, Barbara Ellen. PQ6317.R4.K87 1991, (v3)
Kurtz, Carl. QH105.I8.K87 1996, (v1)
Kurtz, Carmen. PQ6620.U7.D4, (v3)
Kurtz, Donn M. KF354.L6.K87 1997, (v7)
Kurtz, Edwin Bernard. TK3221.K83 1986, (v1)
Kurtz, Howard. PN1992.8.T3.K87 1997, (v3)
Kurtz, Maurice. PN2638.C74.K84 1999, (v3)
Kurtz, Max. TA332.K87 1991, (v1)
Kurtz, Michael L. F376.3.L67.K87 1990, (v4)
Kurtz, Paul. B837.K87 1992, (v8)
Kurtz, Paul. B934.K8 1966, (v8)
Kurz, Raymond A. KF242.A1.K87 1996, (v7)
Kurz, Rudolf Friedrich. E51.U6 no. 115, (v4)
Kurzweil, Edith. BF173.K83 1989, (v2)
Kurzweil, Ray. Q335.K87 1990, (v1)
Q335.K88 1999, (v1)
Kurzydlowski, Krzysztof J. TA403.6.Q36 1995, (v1)
Kusch, Robert. PS3535.O39.Z655 1999, (v3)
Kushigian, Nancy. PR6023.A93.Z6395 1990, (v3)
Kushin, Nathan. CT275.K897.A3, (v5)
Kushner, Harvey W. HV6432.K87 1998, (v6)
Kushner, Howard I. HV6548.U5.K87 1989, (v6)
Kushner, Marilyn S. ND237.R754.A4 1990, (v9)
Kusin, Vladimir V. DB215.5.K87, (v5)
Kusmer, Kenneth L. F499.C69.N34, (v4)
Kuspit, Donald B. N6490.K86 1993, (v9)
N6490.K87 1988, (v9)
ND237.E7.K87 2000, (v9)
Kusse, Bruce. QC20.K82 1998, (v1)
Kussmaul, Ann. HC254.5.K87 1989, (v6)
Kutchins, Laurie. PS3561.U793.B48 1992, (v3)
Kutenplon, Deborah. PS153.N5.K88 1996, (v3)
Kuttner, Robert. HC106.82.K87 1997, (v6)
Kutulas, Judy. E169.1.K835 1995, (v4)
Kutzer, M. Daphne. PR830.I54.K88 2000, (v3)
PR830.I54K88 2000, (v3)
Kutzner, Patricia L. HD9000.5.K883 1991, (v6)
Kuyk, Dirk. PS3511.A86.A6745 1990, (v3)
Kuzio, Taras. DK508.84.K89 1994, (v5)
Kuznets, Lois R. PN56.M53.K89 1994, (v3)
Kuznetsov, Anatoly. PG3478.N34.B313 1970, (v3)
Kvanvig, Jonathan L. BJ1531.K72 1991, (v8)
Kwakye, Benjamin. PR9379.9.K87.C57 1998, (v3)
Kwan, C. H. HC412.K895 2001, (v6)
Kwan, Daniel Y. K. DS777.488.T45.K83 1997, (v5)
Kwanten, Luc. DS786.K93, (v5)
Kwiatkowski, Lynn M. DS666.I15.K85 1998, (v5)
Kwon, Young W. TA347.F5K86 2000, (v1)
Kwon, Yung-Hee K. PL787.R943.K86 1994, (v3)
Kwong, Charles Yim-tze. PL2665.T3.K96 1994, (v3)
Kwong, Peter. F128.68.C47.K96 1987, (v4)
Kyburg, Henry Ely. BC141.K9, (v8)
Kyel, T. E. CT2508.K94, (v5)
Kyle, Donald G. GV21.K95 1993, (v6)
HQ1073.5.R66.K95 1998, (v6)

Kyle, Richard G. BT876.K95 1998, (v8)
Kymlicka, Will. HM276.K96 1989, (v6)
  JF1061.K96 1995, (v7)
Kythe, Prem K. QA374.K97 1997, (v1)
Kyvig, David E. E180.5.N98 2000, (v4)
  KF4555.K98 1996, (v7)
  Z1244.K95 1988, (v10)
La Barre, Weston. E98.R3 L3 1989, (v4)
La Belle, Jenijoy. PN56.M537.L3 1988, (v3)
La Botz, Dan. F1236.L32 1995, (v4)
La Due, William J. BX955.2.L35 1999, (v8)
La Farge, Christopher. PS3523.A266 S8, (v3)
La Farge, Oliver. E77.L24, (v4)
  PS3523.A2663 A4, (v3)
  PS3523.A2663 E5, (v3)
  PS3523.A2663 L3, (v3)
La Fayette. PQ1805.L5.A6 1963, (v3)
La Flesche, Francis. E99.O8.L18 1995, (v4)
La Follette, Belle Case. E664.L16 L13 1971, (v4)
La Fond, John Q. KF3828.D87 1992, (v7)
La Fontaine, J. S. HQ71.L24 1990, (v6)
  HV6626.54.G7.L3 1998, (v6)
La Fontaine, Jean de. PQ1808.A2 1961, (v3)
  PQ1811.E3.M6 1964, (v3)
La Gorce, Paul Marie de. UA702.L2613, (v10)
La Grange, Henry-Louis de. ML410.M23.L3413 1995, (v9)
La Londe, William S. TA159.L3 1984, (v1)
La Motta, Jake. GV1132.L3 A3 1997, (v6)
La Rochefoucauld, Francois. PQ1815.A72 1959, (v3)
La Vere, David. E78.S65 L3 2000, (v4)
Laaksonen, Pirjo. HF5415.32.L33 1994, (v6)
Laba, Roman. HD8537.N783.L33 1991, (v6)
Laband, John. DT1875.L33 1992, (v5)
Labanyi, Jo. PQ6144.L23 2000, (v3)
  PQ6144.L33 1989, (v3)
Labaree, Benjamin Woods. F67.L34, (v4)
  F74.N55 L3 1975, (v4)
Labaree, David F. LA210.L33 1997, (v7)
Labaree, Robert V. KF1611.L32 2000, (v7)
Labbe, Armand J. F2270.1.G57.L33 1998, (v4)
Labbe, Jacqueline M. PR576.L7, (v3)
LaBelle, Maurice Marc. PQ2619.A65.Z72, (v3)
LaBerge, David. QP405.L33 1995, (v1)
Laborit, Emmanuelle. PN2638.L22.A313 1998, (v3)
Labounsky, Ann. ML410.L2487 L33 2000, (v9)
LaBrecque, Ron. KF224.L33.L33 1988, (v7)
Labrie, Ross. PS153.C3.L33 1997, (v3)
Labunski, Richard E. KF4555.L33 2000, (v7)
LaCapra, Dominick. B2430.S34.L24, (v8)
  D13.L26 1985, (v5)
  D804.348.L33 1998, (v5)
  DC36.9.L24 2000, (v5)
Lacaze, Yvon. DC396.L22513 1995, (v5)
LaCerra, Charles. E807.L22 1997, (v4)
Lacey, A. R. B41.L32 1986, (v8)
Lacey, A. R. B53.L29 1982, (v8)
Lacey, Richard. TX353.L23 1994, (v1)
Lacey, Robert. DA358.E8.L3, (v5)
Lacey, Stephen. PR739.R37.L33 1995, (v3)
Lach, Donald F. CB203.L32, (v5)
Lachin, John M. RA409.L33 2000, (v2)
Lack, David Lambert. QL696.P2.L27 1968, (v1)
  QL751.L3, (v1)
Lack, Paul D. F390.L194 1992, (v4)
Lackey, Scott W. UA672.L33 1995, (v10)
Lackmann, Ronald W. PN1991.3.U6.L29 2000, (v3)
  PN1991.3.U6.L32 1996, (v3)
Laclos, Choderlos de. PQ1993.L22.L53 1961, (v3)
  PQ1993.L22.L53 1952, (v3)
  PQ1993.L22 1959, (v3)
Lacocque, Andre. BS511.2.L24 1998, (v8)
Lacouture, Jean. DC373.B5.L3313 1982, (v5)
  DC373.G3.L2513, (v5)
  DC407.M4.L3213 1984, (v5)
  DC420.L313 1990, (v5)
  PQ2625.A716.Z686813 1975, (v3)
Lacovara, Peter. DT60.L33 1997, (v5)
LaCroix, W. L. U22.L33 1988, (v10)
Lacy, Bill. NA2700.L26 1991, (v9)
Lacy, Norris J. PN685.L3 1988, (v3)

Lacy, Stephen. PN4888.F6.L34 1993, (v3)
Lacy, Terry G. DL326.L33 1998, (v5)
Ladd, Helen F. HJ9145.L32 1989, (v6)
Laden, Anthony Simon. JC574.L33 2001, (v7)
Ladimer, Bethany. PQ149.L27 1999, (v3)
Ladino, Robyn Duff. LC214.2.L33 1996, (v7)
LaDow, Beth. F737.B63, (v4)
Ladson-Billings, Gloria. LC2717.L32 2001, (v7)
Laessoe, Jorgen. DS73.2.L313, (v5)
Laessoe, Thomas. QK617.L248 1998, (v1)
LaFargue, Michael. BL1900.L35 L32 1994, (v8)
LaFave, Wayne R. KF9619.L34 2000, (v7)
Lafaye, Jacques. F1210.L313, (v4)
Lafayette, Marie Joseph Paul Yves Roch Gilbert Du Motier, marquis de, 1757-1834. E207.L2.A4 1977, (v4)
LaFeber, Walter. E183.7.L27 1989, (v4)
  E661.7.L2 1998, (v4)
  F1436.8.U6.L33 1983, (v4)
Lafferty, R. A. PS3562.A28.P37 1975, (v3)
LaFleur, William R. PL726.33.B8.L34 1983, (v3)
LaFollette, Marcel C. (Marcel Chotkowski). Z286.S4.L33 1992, (v10)
Lafontaine, Oskar. DD290.33.L34, (v5)
Lafore, Laurence Davis. D741.L26, (v5)
Laforet, Andrea Lynne. F1089.5.S75.L34 1998, (v4)
Laforet, Carmen. PQ6621.A38.N3 1958, (v3)
Laforgue, Jules. PQ2323.L134, (v3)
  PQ2323.L8.A17 1965, (v3)
LaFrance, David G. F1326.L3 1989, (v4)
LaFree, Gary D. HV6789.L34 1998, (v6)
Lagemann, Ellen Condliffe. HV97.C3.L34 1989, (v6)
  L13.C433.L34 1983, (v7)
  LB1028.25.U6.L33 2000, (v7)
Lagerkvist, Par. PT9875.L2 B32, (v3)
  PT9875.L2 D42, (v3)
  PT9875.L2 H42, (v3)
  PT9875.L2 M3, (v3)
  PT9875.L2 P52, (v3)
  PT9875.L2 S482, (v3)
Lagerkvist, Ulf. QP624.L34 1998, (v1)
Lagerlof, Margaretha Rossholm. NB91.A7.L27 2000, (v9)
Lagerlof, Selma. PT9767.G6.E5 1959, (v3)
  PT9767.J4 1970, (v3)
Lagerquist, L. DeAne. F358.2.S2.L34 1991, (v4)
Lago, Mary. PR6011.O58.Z74 1995, (v3)
Lagos, Maria L. F3319.1.T56.L34 1994, (v4)
Lagrou, Pieter. D809.E8.L44 1999, (v5)
Laguerre, Michel S. BL2490.L26 1989, (v8)
  BL2490.L27, (v8)
  E184.H27.L34 1998, (v4)
  F869.S39.O65 1999, (v4)
  F1926.L27 1993, (v4)
  HN80.S4.L34 1994, (v6)
Laham, Nicholas. RA395.A3.L339 1996, (v2)
Lahee, Frederic H. QE28.L2 1961, (v1)
Lahr, John. PR6065.R7.Z77, (v3)
Lai, Chuen-yan David. F1035.C5.L18 1988, (v4)
Lai, Tse-han. DS799.823.L35 1991, (v5)
Laidler, David E. W. HG221.L243 1990, (v6)
  HG229.L2, (v6)
  HG230.3.L34 1982, (v6)
Laidler, Keith James. Q125.L25 1998, (v1)
  QD452.L35 1993, (v1)
Laing, Ellen Johnston. N7345.L35 1988, (v9)
Laing, Lloyd Robert. DA140.L33 1979b, (v5)
Lainhart, Ann S. Z5313.U5.L37 1992, (v10)
Laird, Charlton Grant. PE1075.5.L3, (v3)
  PE1591.L27, (v3)
Laird, Holly A. PR115.L33 2000, (v3)
Laird, Paul R. ML134.B512 L35 2002, (v9)
Laird, Robbin F. DK67.5.G3.L25 1991, (v5)
Laird, Ron. GV1071.L35 2000, (v6)
Laird, Sam. HF1430.L34 1990, (v6)
Laistner, M. L. W. CB351.L26, (v5)
Laitinen, Herbert A. QD101.2.L34 1975, (v1)
Lake, Peter. BX5071.L34 1988, (v8)
Lake, Stuart N. F786.E12, (v4)
Laker, Anthony. GV342.27.L25 2000, (v6)
Laker, Kenneth R. TK7874.L26 1994, (v1)

Lakes, Roderic S. TA418.2.L35 1999, (v1)
Lakeway, Ruth C. ML2533.L25 1989, (v9)
Lakin, Martin. RC455.2.E8.L35 1988, (v2)
Lakoff, George. BD418.3.L35 1999, (v8)
  HN90.M6.L35 1996, (v6)
  PN228.M4.L27 1989, (v3)
Lakoff, Robin Tolmach. P40.45.U5.L35 2000, (v3)
Lakoff, Sanford A. JC423.L295 1996, (v7)
Lakoff, Sanford A. UG743.L33 1989, (v10)
Lakos, Amos. Z7164.T3.L343 1991, (v10)
Lakòsmi. PL4758.9.T37O7813 1992, (v3)
Lakritz, Andrew M. PS310.M57.L35 1996, (v3)
Lakshminarayana, B. TJ267.L35 1996, (v1)
Lal, Deepak. HC13.L35 1998, (v6)
  HC434.L35 1988, (v6)
Lal, R. S625.T76.L35 1990, (v1)
Lal, Vinay. Z3008.C55 1996, (v10)
LaLande, Jeffrey M. F880.L34 1987, (v4)
Lall, Arthur S. PS3562.A4.H6, (v3)
  PS3562.A4.S4, (v3)
Lalla, Barbara. PR9265.4.L35 1996, (v3)
Lalli, Carol M. QH91.L35 1997, (v1)
Lally, Kevin. PN1998.3.W56.L36 1996, (v3)
Lalou, Rene, 1889-. PQ296.L3 1953, (v3)
Lalou, Rene. PQ671.L35 1969, (v3)
  PQ2603.A52.Z828, (v3)
Lam, Joseph Sui Ching. BL1812.R57 L35 1998, (v8)
Lam, Maivan. K3247.L36 2000, (v7)
Lam, Truong Buu. DS556.8.L25 2000, (v5)
Lamar, Howard Roberts. F786.L27 2000, (v4)
Lamarque, Peter. PN45.L316 1994, (v3)
  PN3383.P64.L29 1996, (v3)
Lamb, Charles. PR99.L27 1970, (v3)
  PR4860.A2 1935, (v3)
  PR4860.A2 1971, (v3)
  PR4860.A4B7, (v3)
Lamb, G. L. QA374.L32 1995, (v1)
Lamb, H. H. QC981.L27, (v1)
  QC981.L277 1995, (v1)
  QC981.4.L36 1988, (v1)
Lamb, Jonathan. PR756.T72.L36 2001, (v3)
  PR3716.L28 1989, (v3)
Lamb, Richard. D741.L29 1991, (v5)
Lamb, Robert. HJ9145.L35, (v6)
Lamb, Sharon. HM291.L235 1996, (v6)
Lambers, H. QK717.L35 1998, (v1)
Lambert Colomeda, Lorelei Anne. RA448.5.I5.L36 1998, (v2)
Lambert, Eddie. ML410.E44.L33 1999, (v9)
Lambert, Gavin. PN2287.N29.L36 1997, (v3)
Lambert, John. DT2250.L35 1995, (v5)
Lambert, Joseph B. CC75.L297 1997, (v5)
Lambert, Malcolm. BT1319.L35 2002, (v8)
Lambert, of Ardres, b. ca. 1140. DC801.A677, (v5)
Lambert, Philip. ML410.I94.L36 1997, (v9)
Lambert, S. D. DF275.L36 1993, (v5)
Lambert, W. G. PJ3941.L26, (v3)
Lambertini, M. QH84.5.L3613 2000, (v1)
Lambeth, Benjamin S. UG633.L26 2000, (v10)
Lambourne, Lionel. ND467.L36 1996, (v9)
Lambton, Ann Katharine Swynford. [from old catalog]. PK6235.L35 1960, (v3)
Lamfalussy, Alexandre. HB3711.L24 2000, (v6)
Laming, D. R. J. BF317.L3 1968, (v2)
  QP435.L34 1997, (v1)
Lamis, Alexander P. F216.2.L35 1984, (v4)
Lamm, Martin. BX8748.L3613 2000, (v8)
  PT9816.L27213, (v9)
Lamm, Maurice. BM712.L3 2000, (v8)
Lammers, William W. HQ1064.U5.L29 1983, (v6)
Lamming, George. PR6023.A518.P5, (v3)
  PR6023.A518.S4, (v3)
  PR6023.A518.W3, (v3)
  PR9230.9.L25.I5 1991, (v3)
  PR9230.9.L25.Z466 1992, (v3)
Lamont, Corliss. B821.L3 1949a, (v8)
  BT921.L167 1965, (v8)
Lamont, Lansing. E183.8.C2.L27 1994, (v4)
Lamont, Thomas Stilwell. HG2463.L28.L3, (v6)
Lamoreaux, Naomi R. HD2785.L36 1985, (v6)
Lamos, Colleen. PS3509.L43.Z69174 1998, (v3)

Lampe, John R. DR1246.L36 1996, (v5)
Lampe, Kenneth F. RA1250.L27 1985, (v2)
Lampert, Evgenii. DK219.3.L3, (v5)
Lampi, Paul. NA9245.N4.L3, (v9)
Lamport, F. J. PT643.L34 1990, (v3)
Lamprecht, Sterling Power. B72.L3, (v8)
Lampton, David M. E183.8.C5.L26 2001, (v4)
Lamson, Peggy. JC599.U5.L28, (v7)
Lana, Robert E. HM251.L242 1991, (v6)
Lancaster, F. Wilfrid. Z678.85.L36, (v10)
Lancaster, Henry Carrington. PQ526.L32, (v3)
   PQ536.L3, (v3)
Lancaster, Jane F. E99.S28.L35 1994, (v4)
Lancaster, Kelvin. HB801.L233 1991, (v6)
Lancaster, Nicholas. GB632.L36 1995, (v6)
Lancaster, Paul. PS2673.R15.Z75 1992, (v3)
Lancaster, Roger N. BR625.N5.L35 1988, (v8)
Lancaster, William. HF5465.G73.L36 1995, (v6)
Lancel, Serge. DG249.L3513 1998, (v5)
Lanctot, Gustave. E263.C2.L34, (v4)
Land, Aubrey C. F184.L34, (v4)
Land, Stephen K. DA345.L36 1977, (v5)
   PR6011.O58.Z78 1990, (v3)
Landa, Louis A. PR3726.L3, (v3)
Landais-Stamp, Paul. UA874.3.L36 1989, (v10)
Landau, David. NE441.5.R44.L35 1994, (v9)
Landau, Diana. F622.L36 1998, (v4)
Landau, Ellen G. ND237.P73.L36 1989, (v9)
Landau, Jacob M. DS35.7.L36 1989, (v5)
Landau, L. D. QA931.L283 1986, (v1)
   QC21.L2713 1967, (v1)
   QC173.L2463 1959, (v1)
   QC174.12.L3513 1977, (v1)
   QC174.8.L3613 1979, (v1)
   QC175.L32 1969, (v1)
   QC518.L313, (v1)
   QC665.E4.L3713 1975, (v1)
   QC670.L313 1962, (v1)
Landau, Rubin H. QC20.82.L36 1997, (v1)
Landau, Sarah Bradford. NA6232.L36 1996, (v9)
Landau, Saul. UA23.L25 1988, (v10)
Landauer, Susan. ND235.S27.L36 1996, (v9)
Landauer, Thomas K. QA76.5.L3226 1995, (v1)
Lande, Nathaniel. PN4784.W37.L36 1995, (v3)
Landeira, Ricardo. PQ6144.L36 1985, (v3)
Lander, Ernest McPherson. F274.L32 1970, (v4)
Landes, David S. HC240.Z9.W45 1998, (v6)
   TS542.L24 2000, (v1)
Landes, Joan B. HQ1391.F7.L36 1988, (v6)
Landes, Kenneth K. TN870.L25 1959, (v1)
Landesman, Charles. B105.U5.L35, (v8)
   BD161.L32 1989, (v8)
Landgren, Signe. HD9743.S62.L36 1989, (v6)
Landis, James McCauley. JK421.L33, (v7)
Landman, Janet. BF575.R33.L36 1993, (v2)
Landon, Brooks. PN1995.9.S26.L36 1992, (v3)
   PN3433.8.L36 1997, (v3)
Landon, Donald D. KF297.L355 1990, (v7)
Landon, Fred. F554.L3, (v4)
   F1058.L3 1970, (v4)
Landon, H. C. Robbins. ML410.B4.L287, (v9)
   ML410.H4.L257, (v9)
   ML410.H4.L265 1988, (v9)
   ML410.M9.L236 1988, (v9)
   ML410.M9.L239 1991, (v9)
   ML410.M9.L245 1989, (v9)
Landor, Walter Savage. PR4870.A2 1969, (v3)
   PR4871.C47 1978, (v3)
Landow, George P. PN81.L28 1992, (v3)
   PR5264.L3, (v3)
Landowska, Wanda. ML417.L26.A33, (v9)
Landrine, Hope. E185.625.L36 1996, (v4)
Landrum, Gene N. HC29.L36 1993, (v6)
Landrum, Larry N. PS374.D4.L34 1999, (v3)
Landry, Donna. PR555.W6.L36 1990, (v3)
Landry, Hilton. PR2848.L3, (v3)
Landry, Lorraine Y. JC233.M299 L36 2000, (v7)
Landsberg, Brian K. KF4755.L36 1997, (v7)
Landsberg, Helmut Erich. QC981.7.U7.L36, (v1)
Landsberg, Peter Theodore. QC23.L324 2000, (v1)
Landsberger, Henry A. HD320.5.L3, (v6)

Landsbergis, Vytautas. DK505.85.L36, (v5)
Landskroner, Ronald A. Z7164.T87.L36 1996, (v10)
Landsman, Ned C. F145.S3.L36 1985, (v4)
Landstrom, Bjorn. VM15.L213, (v10)
Landy, Marc Karnis. TD171.L36 1990, (v1)
Landy, Marcia. PN1993.5.G7.L36 1991, (v3)
   PN1993.5.I88.L38 2000, (v3)
   PN1995.9.H5.L36 1996, (v3)
Lane Fox, Robin. BS480.L347 1992, (v8)
Lane, Ann J. E443.E42.L3, (v4)
   PS1744.G57.Z74 1990, (v3)
Lane, Barbara Miller. NA1067.5.N38, (v9)
   NA1068.L3, (v9)
Lane, Christina. PN1998.2.L35 2000, (v3)
Lane, Christopher. PR468.H65.L36 1995, (v3)
   PR468.M38.L36 1999, (v3)
Lane, David Stuart. DK288.L36 1990, (v5)
   HC336.L29 1985, (v6)
   HN530.2.Z9.E454 1999, (v6)
   HX40.L248 1996, (v6)
Lane, Edward William. DT53.L36 2000, (v5)
Lane, Frederic Chapin. H31.J6 ser.62, no.1, (v6)
   VM80.V4.L3, (v10)
Lane, Harlan L. HV2367.L36 1984, (v6)
   HV2380.L27 1996, (v6)
Lane, James B. F534.G2 L36 1978, (v4)
Lane, Jan-Erik. HD87.L374 2002, (v6)
Lane, Kris E. E18.75.L36 1998, (v4)
Lane, M. S. B317.L34 2001, (v8)
Lane, Maggie. PR4038.F66.L36 1995, (v3)
Lane, Mills. NA720.L36 1993, (v9)
Lane, Nancy D. Z710.L36 2000, (v10)
Lane, Richard. NE1321.8.L36 1978, (v9)
Lane, Robert Edwards. HB72.L364 2000, (v6)
Lane, Robert Wheeler. LB3012.2.L36 1995, (v7)
Lane, Roger. F158.9.N4.L36 1991, (v4)
Lane, Ruth. JA71.L24 1997, (v7)
Lane, Tony. D810.T8.L36 1990, (v5)
Lane, Wheaton Joshua. CT275.V23.L3, (v5)
Lang, Berel. BJ44.L36 1991, (v8)
   D804.3.L357 1999, (v5)
   D810.J4.L267 1990, (v5)
Lang, Bernhard. BV5.L36 1997, (v8)
Lang, Daniel. QC782.L3, (v1)
Lang, David Marshall. DK511.G4.L3, (v5)
   PG3317.R3.Z72 1977, (v3)
   PJ307.L3 1971b, (v3)
Lang, Frederick K. PR6019.O9.U6742 1993, (v3)
Lang, George. UB433.L36 1995, (v10)
Lang, Harry G. HV2373.L36 1995, (v6)
Lang, Helen S. Q151.A8.L36 1992, (v1)
Lang, James. HN290.Z9.C647 1988, (v6)
   SB191.R5.L37 1996, (v1)
Lang, Jon T. NA1504.L36 1997, (v9)
   NA2542.35.L36 1994, (v9)
Lang, Kenneth R. QB521.4.L36 1995, (v1)
Lang, Michael H. HD7293.L27 1989, (v6)
Lang, Olga. PL2780.F4.Z82, (v3)
Lang, Paul Henry. ML89.L15, (v9)
   ML160.L25 1997, (v9)
Lang, Sabine. E98.S48.L3613 1998, (v4)
Lang, Serge. QA7.L28 1985, (v1)
   QA7.L286 1999, (v1)
   QA152.2.L36 1987, (v1)
   QA300.L27, (v1)
   QA300.L273, (v1)
Lang, Theodore F. E536.L27, (v4)
Lang, Thomas A. RA409.L357 1997, (v2)
Lang, Timothy. DA375.L35 1995, (v5)
Lang, William L. F891.M545.L36 1996, (v4)
Langan, Thomas. B53.L333 1991, (v8)
Langbauer, Laurie. PR878.P68.L36 1999, (v3)
Langbaum, Robert Woodrow. PR4754.L36 1995, (v3)
   PT8175.B545.Z75, (v3)
Langdale, Abram Barnett. PR2275.L3 1968, (v3)
Langdon, George D. F68.L25, (v4)
Langdon, Helen. ND623.C26.L36 1999, (v9)
Langdon, Philip. HT352.U6.L36 1994, (v6)
Lange, Charles H. E57.B36.L36 1996, (v4)
Lange, Kenneth. QH438.4.M33.L36 1997, (v1)
Lange, Thomas. HC286.8.L33 1998, (v6)

Lange, Victor. PT311.L26 1982, (v3)
   PT395.L3 1967, (v3)
   PT2178.L3, (v3)
Lange, Walter Henry. HF5694.L36 1988, (v6)
Langenfeld, Robert. Z8592.6.L36 1987, (v10)
Langenfelt, Gosta. HD5166.L35, (v6)
Langer, Ellen J. BF632.5.L36 1983, (v2)
Langer, Erick Detlef. HC183.C48.L36 1989, (v6)
Langer, Glenn A. RB113.L322 1999, (v2)
Langer, Lawrence L. D804.3.L36 1991, (v5)
   PN56.H55.L29 1998, (v3)
Langer, Susanne Katherina (Knauth).
   B945.L273.P45, (v8)
   N70.L28, (v9)
   BF161.L28, (v2)
   N79.L2, (v9)
Langer, William L. D21.L27 1972, (v5)
   D385.L36 1969, (v5)
   D397.L282 1951, (v5)
Langeraar, W. GA359.L36 1984, (v6)
Langevin, Gilbert. PQ3919.2.L24.A26 1987, (v3)
Langford, J. Oscar. F392.B54.L36 1973, (v4)
Langford, Jeffrey Alan. ML134.B5.L3 1989, (v9)
Langford, Michael John. TR150.L364 1982, (v1)
Langford, Nathaniel Pitt. F722.L28 1972, (v4)
Langford, Paul. DA118.L33 2000, (v5)
   DA480.L27 1991, (v5)
Langguth, A. J. DG254.L36 1994, (v5)
   DS558.L36 2000, (v5)
   PR6025.U675.Z76, (v3)
Langholm, Odd Inge. HB79.L36 1992, (v6)
Langille, Howard Peter. UA600.L36 1990, (v10)
Langlais, Jacques. F1055.J5.L3613 1991, (v4)
Langland, William. PR2010.K3, (v3)
   PR2010.K3 1988 vol. 1, (v3)
   PR2010.K3 1988 vol.3, (v3)
   PR2010.P4 1979, (v3)
   PR2011.B7 1975, (v3)
   PR2013.E38 1996, (v3)
Langley, Billy C. TH7687.7.L373 1995, (v1)
Langley, Harold D. VB23.L3, (v10)
   VG123.L36 1995, (v10)
Langley, Lester D. E18.82.L36 1996, (v4)
   F1418.L27 1989, (v4)
   F1440.A54.L36 1995, (v4)
   F2178.U6.L34 1983, (v4)
Langley, Stephen. PN2291.L29 1990, (v3)
Langley, T. R. PR438.P65.L36 2001, (v3)
Langley, Winston. JC571.L2747 1999, (v7)
Langman, Jan. QM601.L35 1995, (v1)
Langman, Larry. PN1995.75.L37 1998, (v3)
   PN1995.9.D4.L35 1995, (v3)
   PN1995.9.D4.L36 1994, (v3)
   PN1995.9.G3.L36 1995, (v3)
   PN1995.9.J6.L35 1997, (v3)
   PN1995.9.W4.L33 1992, (v3)
   PN1998.2.L36 2000, (v3)
Langman, Rodney E. QR182.2.E94.L36 1989, (v1)
Langmead, Donald. Z5944.N4.L353 1996, (v10)
   Z8648.43.L36 1999, (v10)
Langmuir, Erika. N33.L353 2000, (v9)
Langmuir, Gavin I. DS145.L32 1990, (v5)
Langmuir, Robert V. QC521.L25, (v1)
Langsam, Walter Consuelo. D735.L3, (v5)
Langston, Thomas S. JK518.L35 1992, (v7)
Langstroth, Lovell. QH105.C2, (v1)
Langum, David J. KF373.K8.L36 1999, (v7)
   KF9449.L36 1994, (v7)
Langwill, Lyndesay Graham. ML950.L29, (v9)
Lanham, Richard A. PE1445.A2.L3 1991, (v3)
   PN88.L3, (v3)
Lanier, Sidney. PS2202.A5, (v3)
   PS2205.F47, (v3)
Lanigan, Esther F. PS3501.U8.Z88 1989, (v3)
Lanker, Brian. D810.L36 2000, (v5)
Lankevich, George J. F128.3.L355 1998, (v4)
Lankshear, Colin. LB1028.43.L369 2000, (v7)
Lankton, Larry D. HD9539.C7.U548 1991, (v6)
Lanning, John Tate. F289.L35, (v4)
Lanoue, David J. JK524.L36 1991, (v7)
Lansbury, Coral. PR4711.L29 1984, (v3)

Lansdown, Richard. PR4392.D7.L3 1992, (v3)
Lansing, John Stephen. GN635.I65.L35 1991, (v6)
Lansing, Robert. D619.L347 1970, (v5)
  D644.L3 1971, (v5)
Lanson, Gustave. PQ2099.L313, (v3)
Lant, Antonia. PN1995.9.W6.L36 1991, (v3)
Lanters, Jose. PR8815.L36 2000, (v3)
Lantos, John D. R723.L35 1997, (v2)
Lantz, K. A. PG3337.L5.Z7495, (v3)
Lanza, Michael L. KF5670.L36 1990, (v7)
Lanza, Sheri R. HF54.56.L364 2001, (v6)
Lanzinger, Klaus. PS159.E85.L36 1989, (v3)
Lao, She. PL2804.C5.A26 1999, (v3)
  PL2804.C5 L613 1979, (v3)
Lao-tzu. BL1900.L26.E5 2000, (v8)
Laozi. BL1900.L26 E513 1999, (v8)
Lapan, Maureen T. LB1060.L36 1995, (v7)
Lape, Noreen Groover. PS271.L37 2000, (v3)
  PS271.L37 2000, (v3)
Lapesa, Rafael. PC4075.L3 1981, (v3)
Lapham, Robert. D802.P52.L896 1996, (v5)
Lapidus, Gail Warshofsky. HQ1663.L33, (v6)
Lapiner, Alan C. F2230.1.A7.L36, (v4)
Lapointe, François. Z8979.4.L36, (v10)
Lapp, Benjamin. DD801.S352.L36 1997, (v5)
Lapp, Ralph Eugene. UA11.L3, (v10)
  UF767.L26, (v10)
Lappé, Frances Moore. GE42.L364 2002, (v6)
Lappe, Marc. QP88.5.L37 1996, (v1)
  RB152.L37 1995, (v2)
  RM267.L36, (v2)
Lapsley, Hilary. GN21.M36 L36 1999, (v6)
Lapsley, Robert. PN1994.L332 1988, (v3)
Laqueur, Walter. D419.L36 1974, (v5)
  D810.J4.L278 1980b, (v5)
  D1051.L28 1992, (v5)
  D1058.L25, (v5)
  DD239.L3 1974b, (v5)
  DK267.L36 1990, (v5)
  DK286.L37 1990, (v5)
  DS135.G3315.L37 2001, (v5)
  DS149.L315, (v5)
  JC481.L34 1996, (v7)
  U240.L36, (v10)
  UA646.L34 1990, (v10)
Larabee, Ann. HV553.L38 2000, (v6)
Larby, Patricia M. Z2000.9.L37 1993, (v10)
Larcher, W. QK901.L3513 1980, (v1)
Lardas, John. PS228.B6.L37 2001, (v3)
Lardner, Ring. PS3523.A7.A6 1946, (v3)
  PS3523.A7.A6 1995, (v3)
  PS3523.A7 H6, (v3)
  PS3523.A7 L6, (v3)
  PS3523.A7 Y6, (v3)
Lardy, Nicholas R. HC427.92.L37 1994, (v6)
  HD2098.L37 1983, (v6)
Large, David Clay. D720.L34 1990, (v5)
  DD860.L37 2000, (v5)
  DD901.M83.L36 1997, (v5)
  UA710.L27 1996, (v10)
Larina, Anna. DK268.B76.N4913 1993, (v5)
Larkcom, Joy. SB321.L344 1997, (v1)
Larkin, Bruce D. U264.5.G7.L37 1996, (v10)
Larkin, Emmet J. DA957.9.L36 1990, (v5)
  HD8393.L3.L3, (v6)
Larkin, John A. HD9116.P61.L37 1993, (v6)
Larkin, Maurice. DC369.L27 1988, (v5)
Larkin, Oliver W. N6505.L37 1960, (v9)
  ND237.M75.L3, (v9)
Larkin, Philip. PR1225.L3, (v3)
  PR6023.A66.H5 1974, (v3)
  PR6023.A66.R4 1984, (v3)
  PR6062.AU64.B5, (v3)
Larkin, Robert P. G67.L37 1993, (v6)
Larkin, Thomas Oliver. F864.L29 1970, (v4)
Larmore, Charles E. BJ1012.L34 1987, (v8)
Laroche, Maximilien. PQ3919.2.D76.Z76, (v3)
Laroque, Francois. PR3069.M3.L3713 1991, (v3)
Larpenteur, Charles. F598.L332 1989, (v4)
Larra, Mariano Jose de. PQ6533.A84 1929, (v3)
  PQ6533.A84 1989b, (v3)

Larrabee, Eric. Z1361.C6.L3, (v10)
Larrain, Jorge. F1408.3.L246 2000, (v4)
Larsen, Clark Spencer. CC77.B8.L37 1997, (v5)
  CC77.B8.L375 2000, (v5)
Larsen, Jack Lenor. NK8998.L3.A2 1998, (v9)
Larsen, Jakob Aall Ottesen. JC75.F3.L3, (v7)
Larsen, James Arthur. QH106.L283 1989, (v1)
Larsen, Jens Peter. ML195.L13 1988, (v9)
Larsen, Lawrence Harold. F474.K253.P465 1997, (v4)
  HT384.U52.A135 1990, (v6)
Larsen, Neil. BH301.M54.L37 1990, (v8)
  F1414.2.L28 1995, (v4)
Larsen, Nella. PS3523.A7225.A6 1992, (v3)
  PS3523.A7225 P3, (v3)
  PS3523.A7225 Q5, (v3)
Larsen, Rebecca. E856.L37 1991, (v4)
Larsen, Sonja. KF240.L27 1997, (v7)
Larsgaard, Mary Lynette. GA125.L37 1984, (v6)
  Z692.M3.L37 1998, (v10)
Larson, Brooke. HD1870.C62.L37 1988, (v6)
Larson, Carole. F796.L27 1993, (v4)
Larson, Charles R. PS3539.O478.Z73 1993, (v3)
Larson, Deborah Aldrich. PR2248.L35 1989, (v3)
Larson, Deborah Welch. E183.8.S65.L358 1997, (v4)
Larson, Donald R. PQ6490.H7.L3, (v3)
Larson, Douglas W. QH541.5.C62.L27 2000, (v1)
Larson, Edward J. HQ755.5.U5.L37 1995, (v6)
  QH366.2.L375 2001, (v1)
Larson, Erik. F394.G2.L37 1999, (v4)
Larson, George A. NA735.C4.L37 1993, (v9)
Larson, Gerald James. BL2003.L37 1995, (v8)
Larson, James L. QH21.E853.L37 1994, (v1)
Larson, Jill. PR878.E67, (v3)
Larson, John Lauritz. HC105.L26 2001, (v6)
Larson, Kelli A. Z8396.3.L37 1990, (v10)
Larson, Magali Sarfatti. NA1996.L37 1993, (v9)
Larson, Pier Martin. DT469.M277.M475 2000, (v5)
Larson, Randall D. Z1231.F4.L37 1995, (v10)
Larson, Reed. HQ799.15.L37 1994, (v6)
Larson, Robert W. E99.O3.R374 1997, (v4)
Larson, Ron. QH105.F6.L37 1995, (v1)
Larson, Sidner J. PS153.I52.L37 2000, (v3)
Larson, Stephanie Greco. PN4738.L35 1992, (v3)
Larson, T. A. F761.L3 1978, (v4)
Larson, Wendy. PL2277.L35 1991, (v3)
LaRue, C. Steven. ML410.H13.L23 1995, (v9)
LaRue, Jan. MT6.L146 G8 1992, (v9)
LaRue, Lewis H. KF4552.L37 1995, (v7)
Larzelere, Alex. DS558.7.L37 1997, (v5)
LaSalle, Mick. PN1995.9.W6.L37 2000, (v3)
Lasater, Martin L. DS35.2.L37 1996, (v5)
  E183.8.T3.L36 1995, (v4)
Lasch, Christopher. HN15.5.L37, (v6)
  HN64.L29, (v6)
  HN65.L33 1978, (v6)
  HN90.P57.L37 1995, (v6)
  HQ518.L27, (v6)
Laseau, Paul. NA737.W7.L37 1991, (v9)
Lash, Jeffrey N. E467.1.J74.L37 1991, (v4)
Lash, Joseph P. D753.L27 1976, (v5)
  D839.7.H3.L3, (v5)
  E806.L32 1988, (v4)
  E807.1.R48.L355 1981, (v4)
  E807.1.R574, (v4)
Lash, Scott. HM73.L35 1990, (v6)
Lashley, Felissa R. RB155.L37 1998, (v2)
Laski, Harold Joseph. CB151.L36 1972, (v5)
  HB501.M5.L3 1933, (v6)
  JC257.L3 1938, (v7)
  JC257.L37, (v7)
  JC327.L3 1968, (v7)
  JC327.L35 1968, (v7)
  JC423.L35 1933a, (v7)
  JC585.L3 1972, (v7)
  JK516.L3 1972, (v7)
Laskier, Michael M. DS135.A25.L36 1994, (v5)
Laskin, David. PS255.N5.L37 2000, (v3)
Lasky, Kathryn. TT175.L37, (v1)
Lasky, Melvin J. DB957.L3 1970, (v5)
  PN4783.L37 2000, (v3)
Lasky, Victor. E873.L37, (v4)

LaSpina, James Andrew. LB3045.5.L37 1998, (v7)
Lass, Abraham Harold. PN43.L37 1987, (v3)
Lassaigne, Jacques. ND450.L3, (v9)
  ND665.L33, (v9)
Lasser, J. K. HF5351.L352 1968, (v6)
Lasser, William. KF8742.L38 1988, (v7)
Lassey, Marie L. RA393.L328 1997, (v2)
Lassieur, Allison. E77.4.L37 1998, (v4)
Lassiter, Sybil M. RA418.5.T73.L37 1995, (v2)
Lassner, Jacob. DS35.65.L37 2000, (v5)
Lassus, Bernard. SB472.L375 1998, (v1)
Lasswell, Harold Dwight. JA73.L28 1979, (v7)
  JA73.L3 1950, (v7)
  JC251.L27, (v7)
  JC599.U5.L35 1971, (v7)
Laster, James. ML128.C54.L4 1996, (v9)
Latash, Mark L. QP301.L36 1993, (v1)
  QP301.L364 1998, (v1)
Latham, A. J. H. HC59.7.L322 1978, (v6)
  Z6204.A33 1995, (v10)
Latham, Earl. CT275.R75.L3, (v5)
  E767.L3, (v4)
Latham, J. E. M. HX51.L494 1999, (v6)
Latham, Robert. D843.L287 1997, (v5)
Lather, Patricia Ann. RC607.A26.L377 1997, (v2)
Lathi, B. P. (Bhagwandas Pannalal). TK5101.L333
  1998, (v1)
Lathrop, George. F761.L35, (v4)
Latimer, Louise Payson. F194.L352, (v4)
Latimer, Wendell M. QD151.L3 1951, (v1)
  QD561.L35 1952, (v1)
Latner, Richard B. E381.L37, (v4)
Latour, Bruno. QR22.F8.L3813 1988, (v1)
Latourette, Kenneth Scott. BR145.L28, (v8)
  BV3415.L35 1967, (v8)
  DS511.L3 1964, (v5)
  DS518.8.L28, (v5)
  DS706.L3 1964, (v5)
Latrobe, Benjamin Henry. NA2707.L37.A4 1994, (v9)
Lattas, Andrew. GN671.N5.L35 1998, (v6)
Lattimore, Owen. DS518.1.L315 1949, (v5)
  DS706.5.L3 1951, (v5)
  DS783.7.L3 1969, (v5)
  DS786.L3 1962, (v5)
  DS793.M7.L3, (v5)
  DS793.M7.L33 1955a, (v5)
  DS793.S62.L3 1950, (v5)
  DS798.L3, (v5)
  E748.L34.A3 1990, (v4)
Lattimore, Richmond Alexander. PA3133.L3, (v3)
  PA3545.L3, (v3)
Latzer, Barry. KF9227.C2.L38 1998, (v7)
Lau, Beth. PR4838.B6.L38 1991, (v3)
Lauber, Daniel. HF5383.F37, (v6)
Lauck, John H. D804.S65.L38 1988, (v5)
Lauck, Jon. HD1773.A3.L38 2000, (v6)
Laue, Thomas. QD291.L35 1998, (v1)
Lauer, Quentin. B2936.Z7.L37, (v8)
Laufer, Gabriel. TA367.5.L39 1996, (v1)
Laufer, Romain. JF2112.P8.L3813 1990, (v7)
Lauffer, Armand. HV91.L35 1987, (v6)
Laughlin, John C. H. BS621.L37 2000, (v8)
Laughton, Bruce. N6853.D3.L39 1996, (v9)
Launay, Robert. DT545.45.D85.L37 1992, (v5)
Laune, Seigniora Russell. F786.L33 1974, (v4)
Launius, Roger D. BX8678.S6.L38 1988, (v8)
  E403.1.D6.L39 1997, (v4)
  QB500.262.L38 1998, (v1)
Lauren, Paul Gordon. JC571.L285 1998, (v7)
Laurence, Margaret. PR9199.3.L33.B5 1970, (v3)
  PR9199.3.L33.F5 1969, (v3)
  PR9199.3.L33.J4, (v3)
  PR9199.3.L33.T6, (v3)
  PR9199.3.L339.D5, (v3)
Laurence, Patricia Ondek. PR6045.O72.Z7728 1991,
  (v3)
Laurence, William Leonard. UF767.L3 1972, (v10)
Laurens, Henry. E302.L32 1968, (v4)
Laurents, Arthur. PS3523.A827.I5 1961, (v3)
  PS3523.A827.Z469 2000, (v3)
Lauret, Maria. PS3573.A425.Z77 1999, (v3)

Laurie, Bruce. HD8085.P53.L38, **(v6)**
Laurie, Clayton D. D810.P7.U395 1996, **(v5)**
  UA25.L28 1997, **(v10)**
Laurie, Simon Somerville. LA31.L38 1970, **(v7)**
Lauring, Palle. DL148.L353 1968, **(v5)**
Laursen, John Christian. B837.L38 1992, **(v8)**
Laussat, Pierre Clément de, 1756-1835. F374.L2613 1977, **(v4)**
Laut, Agnes C. F591.L38, **(v4)**
Lauter, Estella. NX180.F4.L38 1984, **(v9)**
Lauter, Paul. E175.8.L39 2001, **(v4)**
Lauwerier, H. A. QA614.86.L3813 1991, **(v1)**
Lauwers, Judith. RJ216.L354 2000, **(v2)**
Laux, Jeanne Kirk. HD4005.L38 1988, **(v6)**
LaValley, Albert J. PR4434.L3, **(v3)**
Lavdas, Kostas A. HC241.25.G8.L39 1997, **(v6)**
Lavender, Abraham D. F127.C3.L38 1995, **(v4)**
Lavender, David Sievert. F592.7.L38 1988, **(v4)**
  F781.L3 1977, **(v4)**
  F782.A7 L3 1968, **(v4)**
Lavender, Kenneth. Z701.L32 1992, **(v10)**
Lavery, Brian. V767.L35 1983, **(v10)**
Lavie, P. QP425.L3713 1996, **(v1)**
Lavigne, Marie. HC244.L3749 1995, **(v6)**
Lavin, Audrey A. P. PR6011.O58.Z79 1995, **(v3)**
Lavin, David E. LD3835.L375 1996, **(v7)**
Lavin, Deborah. DA17.C87.L38 1995, **(v5)**
Lavin, Irving. N72.H58.L38 1993, **(v9)**
Lavin, Marilyn Aronberg. ND2755.L38 1990, **(v9)**
Lavin, Mary. PR6023.A914 A6 1985, **(v3)**
  PR6023.A914 I5 1969, **(v3)**
  PS3523.A914 A6 1971, **(v3)**
  PS3523.A914 G74, **(v3)**
Lavin, Michael R. HA201.1990ar, **(v6)**
Lavine, Jay B. RE51.L28 2001, **(v2)**
Lavine, Shaughan. QA8.4.L38 1994, **(v1)**
Lavrin, Asuncion. HQ1532.L38 1995, **(v6)**
Law, Alma H. PN2728.M4.L38 1996, **(v3)**
Law, Charles J. LC1045.L33 1994, **(v7)**
Law, Christopher M. G155.A1.L377 1993, **(v6)**
Law, Graham. PR878.P78.L39 2000, **(v3)**
Lawal, Ibironke O. Z7914.M5.L35 1995, **(v10)**
Lawler, Edward E. HD5650.L354 1992, **(v6)**
Lawler, James R. PQ2387.R5.Z6954 1992, **(v3)**
  PQ2643.A26.C656, **(v3)**
Lawler, Jennifer. GV709.L38 2002, **(v6)**
Lawler, Peter Augustine. B944.P67.L38 1999, **(v8)**
  JC229.T8.L39 1993, **(v7)**
Lawler, Peter. JX1904.5.L39 1995, **(v7)**
Lawler, Sylvia D. QP98.L38 1972, **(v1)**
Lawless, Richard I. Z3971.L39 1987, **(v10)**
Lawless, Robert. Z1531.L39 1990, **(v10)**
Lawlis, Merritt E. PR1293.L3, **(v3)**
Lawlor, John. PR6023.E926.Z768 1998, **(v3)**
Lawlor, Mary. PS374.W4.L39 2000, **(v3)**
Lawlor, William. Z1231.B4.L39 1998, **(v10)**
Lawrance, Alan. Z8254.74.L39 1995, **(v10)**
  Z8548.3.L38 1991, **(v10)**
Lawrence, William. UG128.G76.L39 1988, **(v10)**
Lawrence, A. W. NA270.L36 1996, **(v9)**
Lawrence, Amy. PN1995.9.W6.L38 1991, **(v3)**
  PN1998.3.G73.L38 1997, **(v3)**
Lawrence, C. H. BX2820.L38 1994, **(v8)**
Lawrence, D. H. PR6023.A37 1954, **(v3)**
  PR6023.A93 A15 1965, **(v3)**
  PR6023.A93 A153 1955, **(v3)**
  PR6023.A93.A16 1956, **(v3)**
  PR6023.A93.A17 1948, **(v3)**
  PR6023.A93.A17 1977, **(v3)**
  PR6023.A93.A6 1947, **(v3)**
  PR6023.A93.A6 1952, **(v3)**
  PR6023.A93.A6 1969, **(v3)**
  PR6023.A93.B6 (Rare bk. Coll.), **(v3)**
  PR6023.A93 B6 1972, **(v3)**
  PR6023.A93 J6, **(v3)**
  PR6023.A93.K3 1923, **(v3)**
  PR6023.A93.L2 1959, **(v3)**
  PR6023.A93.L4 1933, **(v3)**
  PR6023.A93.L6, **(v3)**
  PR6023.A93.P53 1998, **(v3)**
  PR6023.A93 P55, **(v3)**

PR6023.A93 R3 1927, **(v3)**
PR6023.A93.S4, **(v3)**
PR6023.A93 S65 1962, **(v3)**
PR6023.A93 T34, **(v3)**
PR6023.A93.T7 1960, **(v3)**
PR6023.A93 V5, **(v3)**
PR6023.A93.W, **(v3)**
PR6023.A93 W35 1966, **(v3)**
PR6023.A93.W63 1998, **(v3)**
PR6023.A93 W65, **(v3)**
PR6023.A93.Z5315, **(v3)**
PR6023.A93.Z5354 1976, **(v3)**
PR6023.L43.A13, **(v3)**
Lawrence, David G. JK524.L37 1996, **(v7)**
Lawrence, David Peter. BL1281.1547.L38 1999, **(v8)**
Lawrence, Frederick M. KF9345.L39 1999, **(v7)**
Lawrence, Frieda von Richthofen. PR6023.A934.Z52 1964, **(v3)**
Lawrence, George Hill Mathewson. QK93.L38, **(v1)**
Lawrence, Jerome. PS3523.A934.A6 1995, **(v3)**
Lawrence, Jon. DA560.L29 1998, **(v5)**
Lawrence, Madelaine. RB150.C6.L39 1997, **(v2)**
Lawrence, Mary Chipman. G545.L27, **(v6)**
Lawrence, Paul R. GV351.L38 1987, **(v6)**
Lawrence, Peter A. HD70.E8 L39 2000, **(v6)**
Lawrence, Philip K. U39.L38 1997, **(v10)**
  U263.L39 1988, **(v10)**
Lawrence, R. D. QL737.C22.L34 1986, **(v1)**
Lawrence, Regina G. P94.5.P64L38 2000, **(v3)**
  P94.5.P64.L38 2000, **(v3)**
Lawrence, Susan C. R488.L8.L38 1996, **(v2)**
Lawrence, Susan E. KF336.L35 1990, **(v7)**
Lawrence, T. E. D568.4.L4 1966, **(v5)**
  D568.4.L45.A43, **(v5)**
Lawrence, William Witherle. PN681.L3 1962, **(v3)**
  PR2981.L3 1960, **(v3)**
Lawrence-Lightfoot, Sara. BJ1533.R42.L39 1999, **(v8)**
Laws, Kenneth. QP310.D35.L39 1984, **(v1)**
Lawson, Annette. HQ809.3.G7.L39 1988, **(v6)**
Lawson, Colin. ML457.L39 1999, **(v9)**
  ML945.L39 2000, **(v9)**
Lawson, Donna. RJ216.L36, **(v2)**
Lawson, Edwin D. Z6824.L39 1987, **(v10)**
Lawson, Gary. HV5825.L38 2001, **(v6)**
Lawson, Henry. PR6023.A94 A15 1966, **(v3)**
Lawson, Jacqueline Elaine. PR858.D65.L38 1993, **(v3)**
Lawson, John Howard. PN1661.L3 1960, **(v3)**
Lawson, Lewis A. B4377.L35, **(v8)**
  PS3566.E6912.Z74 1988, **(v3)**
  PS3566.E6912.Z766 1996, **(v3)**
Lawson, Linda. PN4738.L36 1993, **(v3)**
Lawson, Richard H. PT2621.A26.Z7674 1987, **(v3)**
Lawson, Rowena M. HD9450.5.L38 1984, **(v6)**
Lawson, Stephanie. JC423.L373 1996, **(v7)**
Lawson, Steven F. E185.61.L38 1991b, **(v3)**
Lawson-Peebles, Robert. PS195.L35.L38 1988, **(v3)**
Lawton, Anna. PN1993.5.R9.L36 1992, **(v3)**
Lawton, Barbara Perry. SB413.I8L39 1998, **(v1)**
Lawton, H. W. PN1631.L33 1972, **(v3)**
Lax, Roger. ML128.S3 L4 1989, **(v9)**
Laxalt, Robert. E184.B15.L3 1986, **(v4)**
Laxer, Gordon. HG5152.L39 1989, **(v6)**
Lay, M. G. TA1015.L39 1992, **(v1)**
Lay, Shawn. HS2330.K63.L33 1995, **(v6)**
Lay, Thorne. QE534.2.M62 1995, **(v1)**
Layamon. PR2023.A2.A34 1992, **(v3)**
Layamon. PR2023.A2.B9613 1989, **(v3)**
Laybourn, Keith. DA578.L33 1990, **(v5)**
Layman, Charles S. BJ1251.L34 1991, **(v8)**
Layman, Nancy S. KF4155.L39 1994, **(v7)**
Layman, R. D. VG90.L38, **(v10)**
Layoun, Mary N. PN3503.L376 1990, **(v3)**
Layton, Robert. N72.S6.L39 1981, **(v9)**
Layton, Thomas N. F868.M5.L39 1997, **(v4)**
Lazard, Madeleine. PQ521.L3, **(v3)**
Lazarus, Edward. E99.D1 L37 1999, **(v4)**
  KF8742.L39 1998, **(v7)**
Lazarus, John. MT95.L5 1990, **(v9)**
Lazarus, Neil. PR9379.9.A7.Z75 1990, **(v3)**

Lazarus, Richard S. BF335.L35, **(v2)**
  BF561.L38 1994, **(v2)**
  BF575.S75.L315 1999, **(v2)**
Lazarus-Black, Mindie. KGK43.L39 1994, **(v7)**
Lazear, Edward P. HB523.L39 1988, **(v6)**
Lazell, James D. QL169.L39 1989, **(v1)**
Lazerow, Jama. HD6338.2.U5.L39 1995, **(v6)**
Lazerson, Marvin. LA304.L38, **(v7)**
Lazonick, William. HB95.L39 1991, **(v6)**
Lazzaro, Claudia. SB457.85.L39 1990, **(v1)**
Le Brocquy, Sybil. PR3726.L37, **(v3)**
Le Corbusier. NA1053.J4.A2 1997, **(v9)**
  NA2560.L413 1981, **(v9)**
  NA9090.J413 1929a, **(v9)**
Le Goff, Jacques. PQ155.M27.L413 1988, **(v3)**
Le Guerer, Annick. QP458.L4413 1992, **(v1)**
Le Guin, Magnolia Wynn. F292.H73.L4 1990, **(v4)**
Le Guin, Ursula K. PS3562.E42.D5, **(v3)**
  PS3562.E42.L4 1980, **(v3)**
  PS3562.E42.W55, **(v3)**
Le May, Alan. PS3523.E517 S4, **(v3)**
Le May, G. H. L. DT1768.A57.L4 1995, **(v5)**
Le May, Reginald. DS511.L4, **(v5)**
Le Navenec, Carole-Lynne. RC521.L4 1996, **(v2)**
Le Prestre, Philippe G. HG3881.5.W57.L4 1989, **(v6)**
Le Roy Ladurie, Emmanuel. DC36.9.L37213 1979, **(v5)**
  DC36.9.L37213 1981, **(v5)**
  DC106.L3513 1994, **(v5)**
  DC121.L4713 1996, **(v5)**
  DC126.L4613 2001, **(v5)**
  DC801.M753.L4713 1978b, **(v5)**
  DC801.R75.L4713, **(v5)**
Le Sage, Laurent. PQ671.L45, **(v3)**
Le Strange, G. DS44.9.L6 1966, **(v5)**
Le Tellier, Robert Ignatius. Z2014.F4.L46 1997, **(v10)**
Le Tissier, Tony. D757.9.B4.L44 1999, **(v5)**
Le Wita, Beatrix. DC34.L413 1994, **(v5)**
Le, Luu. PL4378.9.L356.T4713 1997, **(v3)**
Lea, F. A. B3317.L37, **(v8)**
Lea, Tom. F596.L45 1957a, **(v4)**
  PS3523.E1142W6 2002, **(v3)**
  PS3523.E15 B7, **(v3)**
  PS3523.E3 W6, **(v3)**
Leab, Daniel J. F159.P653.C85 2000, **(v4)**
Leabhart, Thomas. PN1986.A2.L44 1989, **(v3)**
Leach, Dan. F392.J6.L43 1998, **(v4)**
Leach, David. QH443.L43 1996, **(v1)**
Leach, Edmund Ronald. GN316.L4 1982, **(v6)**
  GN362.L42, **(v6)**
Leach, Penelope. RJ131.L37 1983, **(v2)**
Leaf, Munro. BJ1631.L452, **(v8)**
Leahy, James E. KF4749.L413 1999, **(v7)**
  KF4749.L4 1992, **(v7)**
  KF4770.L4 1991, **(v7)**
  KF8744.L43 1996, **(v7)**
Leahy, Michael P. T. HV4708.L43 1991, **(v6)**
Leahy, William D. D769.L4, **(v5)**
Leak, Andrew N. PQ2637.A82.Z76629 1989, **(v3)**
Leakey, L. S. B. GN772.A35.L4, **(v6)**
  QH367.L4 1953, **(v1)**
Leakey, Mary D. GN21.L372.A33 1984, **(v6)**
Leaman, Oliver. B121.L43 2000, **(v8)**
  B741.L42 2001, **(v8)**
  B741.L43 2002, **(v8)**
  B749.Z7 L43 1998, **(v8)**
  BJ1401.L35 1995, **(v8)**
Leaming, Barbara. PN2287.H45.L43 1995, **(v3)**
Leaming, Hugo Prosper. E450.L39 1995, **(v4)**
Leamon, James S. E263.M4.L3 1993, **(v4)**
Lean, Mary. HN49.C6.L43 1995, **(v6)**
Leap, Terry L. KF4240.L43 1993, **(v7)**
Leap, William. PE3102.I55.L4 1993, **(v3)**
  PE3727.G39.L43 1996, **(v3)**
Lear, Edward. PR4879.L2.N47 1947, **(v3)**
Lear, Jonathan. B491.L8.L38 1980, **(v8)**
  BF175.4.P45.L42 2000, **(v2)**
Leary, John. DS595.2.S3.L43 1995, **(v5)**
Leary, Lewis Gaston. PS682.L4, **(v3)**
Leary, Mark R. BF575.A6.L387 1995, **(v2)**
Leary, William Gordon. PR2976.L38, **(v3)**

Leary, William M. V857.5.L43 1998, (v10)
Lease, Benjamin. PS1541.Z5.L36 1990, (v3)
Leask, Nigel. PR129.A78.L4 1992, (v3)
Leask, Nigel. PR4487.I6.L4 1988, (v3)
Leaska, Mitchell Alexander. PR6045.O72.Z7729 1998, (v3)
    PR6045.O72.Z773, (v3)
Leather, S. R. QL463.L43 1993, (v1)
Leatherbarrow, David. NA2540.5.L43 1993, (v9)
Leatherbarrow, William J. Z8237.9.L4 1990, (v10)
Leautaud, Paul. PQ2623.E14.Z517, (v3)
Leavell, Linda. PS3525.O5616.Z686 1995, (v3)
Leavis, F. R. LC31.L4 1977, (v7)
    PR601.L4, (v3)
    PR4588.L36 1971, (v3)
    PR6023.A93.Z65 1956, (v3)
Leavitt, Judith Walzer. RA644.T8.L43 1996, (v2)
    RG518.U5.L4 1986, (v2)
LeBar, Frank M. DS509.5.L4, (v5)
Lebedoff, David. KF228.E98.L43 1997, (v7)
Leberg, Eric. HV6570.2.L42 1997, (v6)
Lebergott, Stanley. HC110.C6.L393 1993, (v6)
Lebesgue, Henri Leon. QA312.L43 1966, (v1)
LeBlanc, Robin M. HQ1236.5.J3.L43 1999, (v6)
LeBlanc, Steven A. E99.P9.L42 1999, (v4)
LeBor, Adam. DD256.7.L43 2001, (v5)
Lebot, Vincent. GN663.L43 1992, (v6)
Lebovic, James H. UA23.L44 1990, (v10)
    UC263.L42 1996, (v10)
Lebovich, William L. NA4431.A47 1984, (v9)
Lebovics, Herman. DC33.7.L43 1992, (v5)
    DD238.L43, (v5)
Lebow, Eileen F. D570.65.L43 1998, (v5)
Lebow, Richard Ned. D849.L425 1994, (v5)
Lebowitz, Naomi. PT8895.L37 1990, (v3)
Lebra, Takie Sugiyama. DS821.L346, (v5)
    HQ1763.L4 1984, (v6)
Lebra-Chapman, Joyce. UA830.L4 1977, (v10)
Lebsock, Suzanne. HQ1423.L39 1984, (v6)
    HQ1438.V5L43 1987, (v6)
Lebwohl, Mark. RL100.L43 1995, (v2)
Lech, Raymond B. DS921.L43 2000, (v5)
Lechner, Carl B. F157.E6 L43 1994, (v4)
Lechte, John. B804.L37 1994, (v8)
Lecker, Robert. Z1375.L38 1997, (v10)
Lecky, William Edward Hartpole. DA480.L462, (v5)
LeClair, Mark S. HD2757.5.L43 2000, (v6)
Leclerc, Ivor. B1674.W354.L38 1961, (v8)
Leclercq, Jean. BX2470.L413 1982, (v8)
LeCompte, Mary Lou. GV1834.55.W47.L43 1993, (v6)
Lecourt, Dominique. B2421.L3713 2001, (v8)
Ledbetter, David. ML497.2.L4 1987, (v9)
Ledbetter, Mark. PR888.B63.L43 1996, (v3)
Leddy, Susan. RT41.L53 1998, (v2)
Leder, Sharon. PS1541.Z5.L37 1987, (v3)
Lederer, William J. E744.L42, (v4)
    PS3562.E3.U55, (v3)
    V63.L4.A3 1970, (v10)
Lederhendler, Eli. DS135.R9.L33 1989, (v5)
Lederman, Leon M. QB43.2.L43 1989, (v1)
    QC793.5.B62.L43 1993, (v1)
LeDonne, John P. DK127.L43 1991, (v5)
Lee, A. D. DG312.L44 1993, (v5)
Lee, Alfred McClung. HM51.L352 1988, (v6)
Lee, Alison. PR6053.A73.Z75 1997, (v3)
Lee, Alvin A. PR1585.L44 1998, (v3)
Lee, Anthony K. QL737.M3.L44 1985, (v1)
Lee, Asher. UG630.L4, (v10)
    UG635.R9.L42, (v10)
Lee, Bob. F659.F675.L43 1991, (v4)
Lee, C. C. KF3775.A68 L44 1997, (v7)
Lee, Chae-Jin. DS740.5.K6.L44 1996, (v5)
    DS778.C593.L44 1994, (v5)
Lee, Chana Kai. E185.97.H35.L44 1999, (v4)
Lee, Charles A. TK7876.L436 1994, (v1)
Lee, Daniel B. BX8129.O43, (v8)
Lee, Daniel E. JC578.L44 1996, (v7)
Lee, Donald C. BJ1012.L43 1992, (v8)
Lee, Dwight Erwin. D453.L43, (v5)
Lee, Dwight R. HD87.L44 1993, (v6)
Lee, Gaylen D. E99.M86.L44 1998, (v4)

Lee, Gregory B. DS779.23.L4 1996, (v5)
Lee, H. P. KPG2070.L44 1995, (v7)
Lee, Harper. PS3537.E58.T6 1960, (v3)
Lee, Hermione. PR6045.O72.Z774 1997, (v3)
Lee, Hong Yung. JQ1519.A5.L35 1991, (v7)
Lee, Hyangjin. PN1993.5.K6.L44 2000, (v3)
Lee, Jean Butenhoff. F187.C4.L44 1994, (v4)
Lee, John Doyle. F826.L4715 1984, (v4)
Lee, John F. QC311.5.L4, (v1)
Lee, Johnathan Murray. LB1555.L422, (v7)
Lee, Jonathan Scott. PN98.P75.L38 1990, (v3)
Lee, Joseph. DA963.L44 1989, (v5)
Lee, Josephine D. PS338.A74.L44 1997, (v3)
Lee, Kenneth B. DS907.18.L44 1997, (v5)
Lee, Kenneth K. JV6483.L43 1998, (v7)
Lee, Leo Ou-fan. DS796.S25.L43 1999, (v5)
    PL2277.L4 1973, (v3)
Lee, Mabel Barbee. F784.C8 L4 1984, (v4)
Lee, Marshall. Z116.A2.L44 1979, (v10)
Lee, Martin A. JC481.L43 1997, (v7)
Lee, Maurice. DA391.L43 1990, (v5)
Lee, Maurice. DA803.15.L43, (v5)
Lee, Nathaniel. PR3540.A1 1954, (v3)
Lee, Peter H. PL961.23.Y63.L4, (v3)
    PL976.L4, (v3)
    PL980.6.L44, (v3)
    PL984.E3.L4 1974, (v3)
Lee, R. Alton. KF3400.A32.A165 1990, (v7)
Lee, Rachel C. PS153.A84.L44 1999, (v3)
Lee, Rensselaer W. HV6433.F6.L44 1998, (v6)
Lee, Robert E. E470.L48 1957, (v4)
Lee, Robert Edward. QK566.L44 1999, (v1)
Lee, Ronald R. RC489.S43.L43 1991, (v2)
Lee, Sander H. PN1998.3.A45.L44 1997, (v3)
Lee, Sherman E. N7336.L43 1982, (v9)
    N7352.L43 1983, (v9)
Lee, Sidney. PR129.F8.L4 1968, (v3)
Lee, Simon. ND553.D25.L44 1999, (v9)
Lee, Sonia. PQ3989.C27.Z75 1984, (v3)
Lee, Stephen J. D723.L43 1987, (v5)
    D727.L37 2000, (v5)
Lee, Steven Hugh. DS33.3.L44 1995, (v5)
Lee, Steven. U162.6.L44 1993, (v10)
Lee, Sunggyu. TP360.L46 1996, (v1)
Lee, Wayne C. F666.L44 1988, (v4)
Lee, Wayne. TL793.L3137 1995, (v1)
Lee, Wei-chin. Z3116.L44 1990, (v10)
Lee, Wendy Lynne. B809.8.L4734 2001, (v8)
Lee, Yong S. KF5337.L42 1992, (v7)
Leech, Clifford. PR2514.L4, (v3)
    PR2673.L36, (v3)
Leech, Geoffrey N. PE1128.L45, (v3)
Leech-Wilkinson, Daniel. ML410.G966.L3 1990, (v9)
Leed, Eric J. D523.L443, (v5)
    G151.L44 1991, (v6)
Leed, Richard L. PG2112.L36 1981, (v3)
Leedham-Green, E. S. LF109.L44 1996, (v7)
Leedy, Paul D. Q180.55.M4L43 2001, (v1)
Leeming, David Adams. BL325.F4 L44 1994, (v8)
    BL1005.L46 2001, (v8)
    PN56.A5.L44 1996, (v3)
    PR6037.P47.Z76 1999, (v3)
Leeming, Frank. DS706.7.L44 1993, (v5)
Lees, Gene. ML394.L39 1994, (v9)
    ML394.L4 1988, (v9)
    ML3477.L43 1987, (v9)
    ML3507.L47 1991, (v9)
Lees, Lorraine M. E183.8.Y8.L44 1997, (v4)
Leeson, Richard M. PS3517.N265.Z74 1994, (v3)
Leeson, Robert. HB98.3.L435 2000, (v6)
Lee-Treweek, Geraldine. H62.L419 2000, (v6)
Leeuw, G. van der. N72.L413, (v9)
Leeuwen, Thomas A. P. van. NA9053.S4.L44 1988, (v9)
Lefebvre, Georges. DC148.L413, (v5)
    DC163.L413 1973, (v5)
Lefebvre, Henri. BD431.L36513 1991, (v8)
    BD621.L4813 1991, (v8)
Lefever, Ernest W. E744.L429 1999, (v4)
Lefever, Harry G. F1556.T67.L44 1992, (v4)
Leff, Carol Skalnik. DB2238.7.L44 1996, (v5)

Leff, Gordon. B721.L4 1960, (v8)
Leffler, John E. QD471.L5 1993, (v1)
Leffler, Melvyn P. E813.L45 1991, (v4)
Leffler, Phyllis K. D16.163.L44 1989, (v5)
Lefkowitz, Bernard. HV6568.G54.L43 1997, (v6)
Lefkowitz, Mary R. PA4276.L425 1991, (v3)
Lefley, Harriet P. RC439.5.L44 1996, (v2)
LeFlore, Ron. GV865.L37.A33 1978, (v6)
Lefort, Claude. PN51.L37513 2000, (v3)
Lefranc, Norbert. QL696.P248.L43 1997, (v1)
Lefschetz, Solomon. QA371.L36 1977, (v1)
Leftwich, Joseph. PJ5191.E1.L43, (v3)
Leger, Alexis Saint-Leger. PQ2623.E386.C43, (v3)
    PQ2623.E386.E92, (v3)
Leggatt, Alexander. PR631.L44 1998, (v3)
    PR651.L44 1988, (v3)
    PR658.C6.L43 1999, (v3)
    PR2819.L4 1988, (v3)
Legge, James. PL2461.R43 1970, (v3)
Legget, Robert Ferguson. F1054.O9.L43, (v4)
    TA705.L4 1988, (v1)
Legler, Dixie. NA7218.L44 1999, (v9)
Legouis, Emile. PR93.L43 1957, (v3)
Legouis, Pierre. PR2248.L4 1962, (v3)
Lehan, Richard Daniel. PN56.C55.L44 1998, (v3)
Lehane, M. J. QL494.L34 1991, (v1)
Lehman, Cheryl R. HF5657.L394 1992, (v6)
Lehman, Daniel W. PN4867.L43 1997, (v3)
Lehman, David. PS255.N5.L45 1998, (v3)
Lehman, Hugh. BJ52.5.L48 1995, (v8)
Lehman, John F. KF5060.L44 1992, (v7)
Lehman, Peter. PN1995.9.M46.L45 1993, (v3)
Lehmann, A. G. PQ2391.Z5.L25, (v3)
Lehmann, David. BR1644.L44 1996, (v8)
Lehmann, John. PR6023.E4.Z519 1979, (v3)
Lehmann, Karl. E332.2.L4 1985, (v4)
Lehmann, Paul Louis. BJ1241.L4, (v8)
Lehmann, Rosamond. PR6023.E42 D8, (v3)
    PR6023.E42 E2, (v3)
    PR6023.E42 I5, (v3)
    PR6023.E42 W4, (v3)
Lehmann, Scott. HD216.L44 1995, (v6)
Lehmann-Haupt, Hellmut. Z4.L5, (v10)
    Z279.L38, (v10)
    Z473.L522 1951, (v10)
Lehman-Wilzig, Sam N. JQ1825.P359.L44 1990, (v7)
    JQ1825.P359.L46 1992, (v7)
Lehmberg, Stanford E. BX5173.L44 1996, (v8)
Lehner, Philip N. QL751.L398 1996, (v1)
Lehnert, Martin. PR1505.L4, (v3)
Lehning, James R. DC34.L5 1995, (v5)
Lehrer, Adrienne. B840.L4, (v8)
Lehrer, Keith. BD161.L368 1990, (v8)
    BD418.3.L44 1990, (v8)
    BJ1461.L4, (v8)
Leibenstein, Harvey. HD2326.L45 1987, (v6)
Leiber, Fritz. PS3523.E4583 O8, (v3)
Leibman, Nina C. PN1992.8.F33.L45 1995, (v3)
Leibovitz, Annie. TR681.W6.L34 1999, (v1)
Leibovitz, Clement. D727.L385 1998, (v5)
Leiby, James. HV91.L37, (v6)
Leicester, Henry Marshall. QP511.L44, (v1)
Leichter, Howard M. RA427.8.L45 1991, (v2)
Leick, Gwendolyn. BL1060.L44 1991, (v8)
    DS62.2.L45 1999, (v5)
    NA212.L45 1988, (v9)
Leider, Emily Wortis. PS1043.L4 1991, (v3)
Leiderman, Leonardo. HG1210.L46 1993, (v6)
Leidholdt, Alexander. LC214.22.V8.L45 1997, (v7)
Leifer, Eric Matheson. GV583.L45 1995, (v6)
Leigh, David J. BL71.5.L45 2000, (v8)
Leigh, Julia. PR9619.3.L4417, (v3)
Leigh, Nigel. PS3525.A4152.Z735 1990, (v3)
Leighten, Patricia Dee. N6853.P5.L38 1989, (v9)
Leighton, Angela. PR595.W6.L45 1992, (v3)
Leighton, C. D. A. DA948.A2.L38 1993, (v5)
Leighton, Hudson. F604.L45 1998, (v4)
Leighton, Lauren G. PN241.L37 1991, (v3)
    Z8718.L44 1999, (v10)
Leighton, Marian Kirsch. D849.L45 1989, (v5)
Leighton, Philip D. Z679.5.L45 1999, (v10)

Leinen, Stephen H. HV8138.L353 1993, (v6)
Leinsdorf, Erich. ML422.L38.A3, (v9)
  MT75.L44, (v9)
Leinwand, Theodore B. PR658.E35.L45 1999, (v3)
Leipold, L. Edmond. RD598.L38, (v2)
Leiris, Michel. PQ2623.E424.Z5 1973, (v3)
Leisinger, Klaus M. HB849.53.L44 2002, (v6)
Leiss, William. JC253.M34.L45 1989, (v7)
Leistyna, Pepi. LC196.L45 1998, (v7)
Leitch, Jay A. Z7405.W47.L45 1995, (v10)
Leitch, Thomas M. Z8885.48.L43 1993, (v10)
Leitch, Vincent B. PS78.L4 1988, (v3)
Leiter, Samuel L. PN2205.L44 1994, (v3)
  PN2277.N5.L365 1992, (v3)
  PN2570.L45 1991, (v3)
  PN2597.L45 1991, (v3)
  PN2924.5.K3.L44 1997, (v3)
Leith, Dick. PE1075.L44 1983, (v3)
Leja, Michael. ND212.5.A25.L45 1993, (v9)
Leland, Charles Godfrey. PS2243.A4 1968, (v3)
Lellinger, David B. QK524.5.L45 1985, (v1)
Leloudis, James L. LA340.L45 1996, (v7)
Lem, Stanislaw. PG7158.L39D9213 2000, (v3)
  PG7158.L39.S613 1987, (v3)
Lemaitre, Georges Edouard. PQ305.L4 1947, (v3)
  PQ2625.A95.Z73 1968, (v3)
Lemaître, Henri. PQ41.L45 1994, (v3)
Lemann, Nicholas. E185.6.L36 1991, (v4)
Lemarchand, Rene. DT450.64.L46 1994, (v5)
LeMaster, Carolyn Gray. F420.J5 L46 1994, (v4)
Lembcke, Jerry. DS559.73.U6.L46 1998, (v5)
Lembede, Anton Muziwakhe. DT1927.L46.A2 1996, (v5)
Lembke, Janet. QH548.L46 1999, (v1)
Lemco, Jonathan. F1436.8.C2.L46 1991, (v4)
  JL246.S8.L45 1994, (v7)
Lemire, Beverly. HD9940.G82.E545 1997, (v6)
Lemke, Sieglinde. NX542.L46 1998, (v9)
Lemke-Santangelo, Gretchen. F868.S156.L45 1996, (v4)
Lemma, Alessandra. RC454.L456 1996, (v2)
Lemmermeyer, Franz. QA241.L56 2000, (v1)
Lemon, Alaina. DX241.K46 2000, (v5)
Lemon, Harvey Brace. QC23.L4 1946, (v1)
Lemonick, Michael D. QB981.L36 1993, (v1)
Lemons, Don S. QC20.7.C3.L46 1997, (v1)
Lemons, J. Stanley. HQ1426.L45, (v6)
Lemos, Ramon M. BD111.L43 1988, (v8)
  BD232.L398 1995, (v8)
Lenau, Nicolaus. PT2393.A1 1989, (v3)
Lenburg, Jeff. NC1766.U5.L46 1999, (v9)
Lenczowski, George. DS62.8.L46 1980, (v5)
  DS63.2.U5.L43 1990, (v5)
Lenczowski, John. E840.L42 1982, (v4)
Lender, Mark Edward. HV5292.L4 1982, (v6)
Lendon, J. E. JC83.L464 1997, (v7)
Lenfestey, Tom. V23.L467 1994, (v10)
Leng, Russell J. U21.2.L39 1993, (v10)
Leng, Shao Chuan. DS777.L4 1976, (v5)
L'Engle, Madeleine. PS3523.E55.Z5, (v3)
  PS3523.E55.Z52 1974, (v3)
  PZ7.L5385Wr 2002, (v3)
Lenin, Vladimir Ilich. DK254.L3.A254 1973, (v5)
  HB97.5.L318 1989, (v6)
  HB501.L332 1970, (v6)
  HB501.L372 1970, (v6)
Lenk, John D. TK7868.P6.L455 1994, (v1)
  TK7868.P6.L456 1995, (v1)
  TK7887.6.L46 1997, (v1)
Lenman, Bruce. DA66.L46 2001, (v5)
  DA67.L46 2001, (v5)
Lennan, Richard. BX4705.R287.L46 1995, (v8)
Lenneberg, Eric H. P132.L4, (v3)
Lennig, Arthur. PN1998.3.V67.L46 2000, (v3)
Lennon, Colm. DA935.L46 1995, (v5)
Lennon, J. John. G155.A1.L434 2000, (v6)
Lennon, Nigey. PS1334.L47 1990, (v3)
Lennox, Charlotte. PR3541.L27 F4, (v3)
Lennox, James G. QH331.L528 2001, (v1)
Lensing, George S. PS3537.T4753.Z67454 2001, (v3)
Lenski, Branko Alan. PG583.L4, (v3)

Lent, John A. Z5633.W65 L45 1999, (v10)
  Z5956.C3.L458 1996, (v10)
  Z5956.C6.L46 1994, (v10)
Lentin, Ronit. D804.195.L46 2000, (v5)
Lentricchia, Frank. PN94.L43, (v3)
Lentz, Harris M. GV1196.A1.L45 1997, (v6)
  HV6278.L45 1988, (v6)
  PN1992.8.W4.L46 1997, (v3)
  PN1995.9.S26.L46 1994 Suppl., (v3)
  PN1995.9.S26.L46 2001, (v3)
  PN1995.9.W4.L383 1996, (v3)
Lenz, Allen J. HF3004. 1992, (v6)
Lenz, Siegfried. PT2623.E583.D413, (v3)
LeoGrande, William M. F1436.8.U6.L453 1998, (v4)
Leon Portilla, Miguel. F1219.3.P5.L43, (v4)
  F1219.73.L4513 1992, (v4)
  F1220.L4613 1990, (v4)
  F1230.L383, (v4)
Leon, Harry J. DS135.I85.R64, (v5)
Leon, Ruth. PN2277.N5.L377 1991, (v3)
Leonard, Angela M. Z8109.16.L46 2001, (v10)
Leonard, Arthur S. KF9325.A7.L46 1993, (v7)
Leonard, David K. HC800.L465 2003, (v6)
Leonard, Garry Martin. PR6019.O9.Z694 1998, (v3)
Leonard, Irving Albert. F1210.L4, (v4)
  F1411.L57 1964, (v4)
Leonard, Karen Isaksen. F870.P36.L46 1992, (v4)
Leonard, Kathy S. Z1609.F4.L46 1997, (v10)
Leonard, Laurence B. RJ496.L46 1998, (v2)
Leonard, Olen E. F3308.L4, (v4)
Leonard, Peggy C. R123.L46 2001, (v2)
Leonard, Stephen J. F781.L4 1993, (v4)
Leonard, Stephen T. HM24.L447 1990, (v6)
Leonard, Thomas M. F1436.8.U6.L45 1991, (v4)
  Z1437.L46 1994, (v10)
Leonardo da Vinci. QM21.L49, (v1)
  NC1055.L5.P58, (v9)
  ND623.L5.A15 1970b, (v9)
  ND1130.L47213 1989, (v9)
Leonardo. Q143.L5.A3 1989, (v1)
Leong, Sow-Theng. DS731.H3.L46 1997, (v5)
Leonov, V. N. D772.3.L47 1993, (v5)
Leontidou, Lila. HT384.G8.L46 1990, (v6)
Leontief, Wassily W. HC60.L443, (v6)
Leopold, A. Carl. QK731.L4, (v1)
  QK731.L44 1975, (v1)
Leopold, A. Starker. SK367.L4, (v1)
  SK473.L4, (v1)
Leopold, Aldo. QH81.L56, (v1)
  SK361.L38, (v1)
Leopold, Donald Joseph. QK115.L43 1998, (v1)
Leopold, Luna Bergere. GB55.L4, (v6)
  GB671.L43 1997, (v6)
  GB1215.L42 1994, (v6)
Leopold, Richard William. E664.R7.L4, (v4)
Leopold, Silke. ML410.M77.L513 1999, (v9)
LePage-Lees, Pamela. LC4091.L47 1997, (v7)
Lepak, Keith John. DK4440.L47 1988, (v5)
Lepgold, Joseph. UA23.L484 1990, (v10)
Lepley, Ray. BD232.L42 1970, (v8)
LePore, Ernest. BC108.L44 2000, (v8)
Lepore, Monica. GV837.4.L47 1998, (v6)
Lepowsky, Maria Alexandra. DU740.42.L47 1993, (v5)
Leppert, Richard D. N72.S6.L46 1996, (v9)
Leppmann, Wolfgang. PT2635.I65.Z782313 1984, (v3)
Lepschy, Anna Laura. PC1087.L46 1977, (v3)
Lerager, Jim. UB369.L47 1988, (v10)
Lerdahl, Fred. MT6.L36.G4 1983, (v9)
Lerer, Seth. PR418.P65.L47 1997, (v3)
  PR1924.L38 1993, (v3)
Lermack, Paul. KF285.L47 1997, (v7)
Lerman, Katharine Anne. DD231.B8.L47 1990, (v5)
Lerner, Alan Jay. ML423.L3.A3 1978b, (v9)
Lerner, Allan W. JA74.5.L47 1990, (v7)
Lerner, Barron H. RC280.B8L375 2001, (v2)
Lerner, Eric J. QB991.B54.L47 1991, (v1)
Lerner, Frederick Andrew. Z721.L565 1998, (v10)
Lerner, Gerda. E449.G89, (v4)
  HQ1121.L47 1986 vol. 2, (v6)
  HQ1426.L47, (v6)
Lerner, Jacqueline V. HQ759.48.L47 1991, (v6)

Lerner, Janet W. LC4704.L48 1985, (v7)
Lerner, Laurence. PR468.D42.L47 1997, (v3)
Lerner, Loren R. Z5784.M9.L47 1997, (v10)
Lerner, Marcia. QA39.3.L47 2001, (v1)
Lerner, Max. LB885.L422, (v7)
Lerner, Michael G. PQ2472.Z8.L44, (v3)
Lerner, Monroe. RA445.L45, (v2)
Lerner, Natan. BL65.H78.L47 2000, (v8)
Lerner, Paul M. RC473.R6.L468 1998, (v2)
Lerner, Ralph. JA82.L4 1972, (v7)
Lerner, Richard M. GN365.9.L47 1992, (v6)
Lerner, Robert. HN90.E4.L47 1996, (v6)
Lerner, Steve. GE150.L47 1997, (v6)
Lerner, Vladimir S. T58.6.L45 2000, (v1)
Lernout, Geert. PT2359.H2.L44 1994, (v3)
Lerski, Jerzy J. DK4123.L47 1996, (v5)
Lery, Jean de. F2511.L655 1990, (v4)
Lesch, Ann Mosely. DS126.L37, (v5)
Lesch, David W. E183.8.S95.L47 1992, (v4)
Leser, Esther H. PT2625.A44.Z7357 1989, (v3)
LeSeur, Geta J. PS374.N4.L47 1995, (v3)
Lesher, Linda Parent. Z2014.F4.L45 2000, (v10)
Leskov, N. S. PG3337.L5 A25 1961, (v3)
  PG3337.L5 T3 1977, (v3)
Leslie, Charles M. F1221.Z3.L4, (v4)
Leslie, Kent Anderson. F292.H3.L47 1995, (v4)
Leslie, Marina. HX806.L47 1998, (v6)
Leslie, R. F. DK437.L48 1969, (v5)
  PR1490.L4 1961, (v3)
Leslie, Stuart W. U393.L385 1993, (v10)
Leslie, Winsome J. DT658.L46 1993, (v5)
Lesnik-Oberstein, Karin. PN1009.A1.L475 1994, (v3)
Lesnikowski, Wojciech G. NA1048.L47 1990, (v9)
Lesourne, Jacques. HX240.7.A6.L4713 1991, (v6)
Lesser, Ian O. HC110.S8.L47 1989, (v6)
Lesser, Jeff. F2659.A1.L47 1999, (v4)
Lesser, M. X. Z8255.5.L47, (v10)
  Z8255.5.L48 1994, (v10)
Lesser, Wendy. PN2598.D22.L47 1997, (v3)
Lessing, Doris May. PR6023.E833 A4, (v3)
  PR6023.E833 C5, (v3)
  PR6023.E833.D59 1983, (v3)
  PR6023.E833 G6, (v3)
  PR6023.E833.G66 1985, (v3)
  PR6023.E833.G7 1976, (v3)
  PR6023.E833 H3, (v3)
  PR6023.E833 M25 1963, (v3)
  PR6023.E833 M3, (v3)
  PR6023.E833 M32, (v3)
  PR6023.E833.M34 1982, (v3)
  PR6023.E833 M4, (v3)
  PR6023.E833.P55, (v3)
  PR6023.E833 P76, (v3)
  PR6023.E833 R5, (v3)
  PR6023.E833 S48, (v3)
  PR6023.E833.S57 1981, (v3)
  PR6023.E833 S8, (v3)
  PR6023.E833.Z5, (v3)
  PR6023.E833.Z52 1974, (v3)
  PR6069.O42.D5 1983, (v3)
Lessnoff, Michael H. JA83.L39 1999, (v7)
Lester, DeeGee. Z2031.L47 1987, (v10)
Lester, James P. GE180.L47 2001, (v6)
Lester, James. ML417.T2.L47 1994, (v9)
Lester, Joel. ML430.L46 1992, (v9)
  MT42.L48 1986, (v9)
Lester, John. PR6005.O4.Z766 1988, (v3)
Lester, Neal A. PS3569.H3324.Z77 1995, (v3)
Lester, Richard K. HC110.I52.L47 1998, (v6)
Lestienne, Remy. BC141.L4713 1998, (v8)
Lestringant, Frank. GA13.L4713 1994, (v6)
LeSueur, Stephen C. F466.L47 1987, (v4)
Lesure, Francois. ML85.L4813, (v9)
Lesurf, J. C. G. T58.5.L48 1995, (v1)
Leszczynski, Nancy A. SB472.45.L47 1997, (v1)
Letcher, John Seymour. D767.3.L48 1998, (v5)
LeTendre, Gerald K. LB1135.L47 2000, (v7)
Lett, Denise Potrzeba. HT690.K8.L48 1998, (v5)
Lettis, Richard. PR4592.L5.L48 1990, (v3)
Letts, Malcolm Henry Ikin. PR2054.L4 1949, (v3)

Letwin, Oliver. BJ1012.L47 1987, (v8)
Leuchtenburg, William Edward. E743.L49 1993, (v4)
  E806.L474 1995, (v4)
  E806.L475, (v4)
  KF8742.L48 1995, (v7)
Leuschner, William A. SD373.L45 1984, (v1)
Leuthold, David A. F470.L48 1994, (v4)
Leuthold, Steven. E59.A32.L48 1998, (v4)
Leuzinger, Elsy. N7380.L363, (v9)
Lev, Peter. PN1993.5.E8.L48 1993, (v3)
Lev, Peter. PN1993.5.U6.L44 2000, (v3)
Levack, Brian P. DA375.L48 1987, (v5)
Levander, Caroline Field. PS374.W6.L48 1998, (v3)
Levant, Oscar. ML417.L64.A35, (v9)
Levarie, Norma. Z4.L58 1995, (v10)
LeVay, Simon. HQ76.2.U5.L46 1995, (v6)
  HQ76.25.L497 1996, (v6)
  QP360.L4926 1993, (v1)
Levenback, Karen L. PR6045.O72.Z778 1999, (v3)
Levene, Ricardo. F2831.L653 1963, (v4)
Levenson, Claude B. BQ5115.C5 L4813 1996, (v8)
Levenson, Joseph Richmond. DS721.L538, (v5)
Levenson, Michael H. PR888.C47.L48 1991, (v3)
Levenstein, Harvey A. GT2853.U5.L47 1993, (v6)
Lever, Evelyne. DC137.1.L4813 2000, (v5)
Lever, J. W. PR539.S7.L4, (v3)
  PR678.P65.L48 1971, (v3)
Lever, Richard. Z4021.L48 1996, (v10)
Levere, Trevor Harvey. QD18.E85.L48 1994, (v1)
Leverich, Lyle. PS3545.I5365.Z736 1995, (v3)
Leverington, David. QB136.L48 2000, (v1)
Leverton, Roy. QL555.G7, (v1)
Levertov, Denise. PR6023.E88.P6, (v3)
  PS3562.E8876.A17 1979, (v3)
  PS3562.E8876.A6 1983, (v3)
  PS3562.E8876.A6 1987, (v3)
  PS3562.E8876.J3, (v3)
Levesque, Catherine. NE954.3.N4.L48 1994, (v9)
Levesque, Rene. F1053.2.L5813, (v4)
Levett, Paul N. QR89.5.L48 1990, (v1)
Levey, Michael. PR5136.L4, (v3)
Levey, Zach. DS119.6.L49 1997, (v5)
Levi, Albert William. N105.L48 1991, (v9)
  PN45.L435, (v3)
Levi, Anthony. DC123.9.R5.L48 2000, (v5)
Levi, Daniel. HD66.L468 2001, (v6)
Levi, Darrell E. F1887.M29.L48 1990, (v4)
Levi, Edward Hirsch. KF425.L48x 1972, (v7)
Levi, Howard. QA681.L4, (v1)
Levi, Isaac. BD215.L45 1991, (v8)
Levi, Leo. QC371.L48, (v1)
Levi, Margaret. HJ2250.L48 1988, (v6)
Levi, Peter. DF77.L43, (v5)
  PR4879.L2.Z73 1995, (v3)
  PR5581.L48 1993, (v3)
Levi, Werner. BV639.P6.L48 1989, (v8)
  DS740.63.L48, (v5)
Leviant, Curt. PJ5059.E1.L4, (v3)
Leviatin, David. F128.9.J5.L47 1989, (v4)
Levich, Eugene William. DS793.K6.L48 1993, (v5)
Levich, Marvin. BH21.L4, (v8)
Levick, Barbara. DG284.L47 1990, (v5)
Levin, Amy K. PR868.S52.L48 1992, (v3)
Levin, Carole. DA355.L458 1994, (v5)
Levin, Daniel Lessard. KF4552.L476 1999, (v7)
  B828.3.L39 1988, (v8)
  B846.L48 1999, (v8)
Levin, David. F67.M43L48, (v4)
Levin, Elaine. NK4005.L48 1988, (v9)
Levin, Gail. N6537.H6.L48 1995, (v9)
Levin, Gail. ND212.5.S9.L48 1978, (v9)
Levin, Harold L. (Harold Leonard). QE770.L485 1999, (v1)
  QE28.3.L48 1996, (v1)
Levin, Harry. PN511.L36, (v3)
  PN771.L47 1982, (v3)
  PQ637.R4.L4, (v3)
  PR2807.L39, (v3)
  PR6019.O9.Z7 1960, (v3)
  PS1888.L4, (v3)
Levin, Harvey Joshua. HE8700.8.L48, (v6)

Levin, Irina. PN2062.L48 1992, (v3)
Levin, Itamar. D810.C8.L4813 2001, (v5)
Levin, Meyer. DS125.3.L4.A3, (v5)
  PS3523.E7994 C6, (v3)
  PS3523.E7994 F3, (v3)
  PS3523.E7994 S4, (v3)
Levin, Michael E. GN269.L49 1997, (v6)
Levin, Michael. JC421.L48 1992, (v7)
Levin, Murray Burton. LC5131.L44 1998, (v7)
Levin, Nora. DS135.R92.L48 1988, (v5)
Levin, Norman Gordon. E768.L62 1970, (v4)
Levin, Richard A. PR2992.T74, (v3)
Levin, Richard Louis. PR651.L48, (v3)
  PR658.P6.L4, (v3)
Levin, Theodore Craig. ML3758.A783.L48 1996, (v9)
Levinas, Emmanuel. B2430.L483 D5413 2000, (v8)
  B3279.H94.L395 1998, (v8)
  BD331.L45813 1998, (v8)
Levine, Alan J. D790.L484 1992, (v5)
  D805.L49 2000, (v5)
  TL788.5.L47 1994, (v1)
Levine, Andrew. JC328.2.L48 1993, (v7)
Levine, Arthur. LA229.L423 1998, (v7)
Levine, Barbara. Z8228.L48 1996, (v10)
Levine, Bruce C. E184.G3.L5 1992, (v4)
Levine, Daniel. HV28.A35.L47, (v6)
Levine, Daniel. CB351.L44 2001, (v5)
  HC258.W47.L48 1991, (v6)
Levine, Frances. E99.P9.L465 1999, (v4)
Levine, George Lewis. PR868.R4.L48, (v3)
  PR878.S34.L4 1988, (v3)
Levine, Gustav. BF181.L48 1994, (v2)
Levine, Hillel. D804.66.S84.L48 1996, (v5)
  DS146.P6.L48 1991, (v5)
Levine, Joseph M. PR438.A53.L48 1999, (v3)
Levine, Laura. PR658.S42.L48 1994, (v3)
Levine, Lawrence W. E169.1.L536 1988, (v4)
  E169.1.L5372 1996, (v4)
  E169.1.L5374 1993, (v4)
  GR103.L48, (v6)
Levine, Lee I. BM653.L38 2000, (v8)
Levine, Madeline. HQ784.M3.L48 1996, (v6)
Levine, Mark. MT239.L46 1989, (v9)
Levine, Martin. HD6279.L48 1988, (v6)
Levine, Marvin J. HD8653.5.L48 1997, (v6)
Levine, Nancy E. DS493.9.N92.L48 1988, (v5)
Levine, Nathan. Z49.L65 2002, (v10)
Levine, Paul. PS3554.O3.Z78 1985, (v3)
Levine, Peter. BJ42.L48 1998, (v8)
Levine, Rhonda F. HC106.3.L398 1988, (v6)
Levine, Robert A. UA23.L493 1987, (v10)
Levine, Robert M. F319.M6.L48 2000, (v4)
  F1413.L66 1989, (v4)
  F1419.A1.L48, (v4)
  F1763.L65 1990, (v4)
  F1789.J4.L48 1993, (v4)
  F2521.L49 1999, (v4)
  F2537.L472 1997, (v4)
  F2537.L475 1992, (v4)
  F2538.L48 1998, (v4)
  F2659.N4.L48 1995, (v4)
Levine, Robert S. PS366.A35.L48 1997, (v3)
Levine, Susan. LB1756.L4 1995, (v7)
Levine, Suzanne Jill. PQ7798.26.U4 Z772 2000, (v3)
Levinger, Matthew Bernard. DD347.L45 2000, (v5)
Levins Morales, Aurora. PN6071.W7.M67 1998, (v3)
Levinson, David. BL80.2.L463 1996, (v8)
  BL80.2.L464 2000, (v8)
  GN325.L46 1998, (v6)
  GN496.L48 1994, (v6)
Levinson, Harry. HD58.9.L48 2002, (v6)
Levinson, Henry S. B945.S24 L48 1992, (v8)
Levinson, Jerrold. BH39.L495 1996, (v8)
  ML3845.L47 1997, (v9)
Levinson, Marc. HB87.L45 1988, (v6)
Levinson, Paul. P90.L413 1999, (v3)
Levinson, Peter J. ML419.J36.L48 1999, (v9)
Levinson, Ronald Bartlett. B395.L38, (v8)
Levinson, Sanford. KF4552.L48 1988, (v7)
Levinton, Jeffrey S. QH91.L427 1995, (v1)
Levin-Waldman, Oren M. HD4918.L447 2001, (v6)

Levi-Setti, Riccardo. QC721.L64, (v1)
  QE821.L46 1993, (v1)
Levi-Strauss, Claude. E59.R38.L6313 1988, (v4)
  E78.N78.L4513 1982, (v4)
  E98.F6.L57718 1995, (v4)
  F2515.L48913 1995, (v4)
  F2519.3.R3.L4813 1969, (v4)
  F2520.L4813 1974, (v4)
  GN21.L4.A513 1991, (v6)
  GN362.L4813, (v6)
  GN451.L3813, (v6)
  NX165.L4513 1997, (v9)
Levit, Fred. PR4595.L4 1990, (v3)
Levit, Nancy. KF475.L48 1998, (v7)
Levitchi, Leon. PC779.L4 1973, (v3)
Levitine, George. N6847.5.P68.L48, (v9)
Levitt, Ian. HV249.S5.L48 1988, (v6)
Levitt, Morton. BF173.F85.L4 1971, (v2)
  PR6019.O9.Z7115 2000, (v3)
Levy, Alan Howard. NX735.L48 1997, (v9)
Levy, Amy. PR4886.L25.A6 1993, (v3)
Levy, Andre. PL2266.L48 2000, (v3)
Levy, Anita. PR778.W65.L49 1991, (v3)
Levy, Barry. F157.D4.L48 1988, (v4)
Levy, Beryl Harold. KD640.L48 1990, (v7)
Levy, Bill. PN1998.3.F65.L48 1998, (v3)
Levy, David Benjamin. ML410.B42.L48 1995, (v9)
Levy, David H. QB35.L48 2001, (v1)
  QB36.B63.L48 1993, (v1)
  QB61.L47 1997, (v1)
  QB454.2.S48, (v1)
  QB721.4.L48 1994, (v1)
  QB723.S56.L48 1995, (v1)
Levy, Dore Jesse. PL2309.N47.L48 1988, (v3)
Levy, Emanuel. PN1995.9.E96.L43 1999, (v3)
Levy, Frank. HC110.I5.L47 1998, (v6)
Levy, Hermann. HD2859.L4 1966, (v6)
Levy, Jerrold E. E99.N3.L623 1998, (v4)
Levy, Jo Ann. F865.L67 1990, (v4)
Levy, John M. HB172.L48 1995, (v6)
Levy, Jonah D. HC276.L46 1999, (v6)
Levy, Judith. PR9272.9.N32.Z758 1995, (v3)
Levy, Kenneth. ML3082.L44 1998, (v9)
Levy, Leonard Williams. JC591.L2 1963, (v7)
  KF4550.L48 1988, (v7)
  KF4749.L484 1989, (v7)
  KF4749.L488 1999, (v7)
  KF4783.L48 1994, (v7)
  KF9747.L48 1996, (v7)
Levy, Matthys. TH441.L48 1992, (v1)
Levy, Peter B. HN90.R3.L495 1994, (v6)
Levy, Pierre. QA76.9.H85.L49 1998, (v1)
Levy, Reuben. PK6406.L4, (v3)
Levy, Richard C. T339.L38 1990, (v1)
Levy, Robert. DR267.5.P38, (v5)
Levy, Shimon. PN1650.B3, (v3)
Levy, Steven. QA76.6.L469 2001, (v1)
  QA76.8.M3.L487 1994, (v1)
  QA76.9.A25L49 2001, (v1)
Levy, Yagil. UA853.I8.L446 1997, (v10)
Levy, Zeev. BJ1491.L48 1989, (v8)
Lewald, Fanny. PT2423.L3.Z4513 1992, (v3)
Lewald, H. Ernest. PQ7797.M225.Z73, (v3)
Lewalski, Barbara Kiefer. PR113.L53 1993, (v3)
  PR3581.L45 2001, (v3)
Lewand, Robert. Z103.L46 2000, (v10)
Lewell, John. PL747.55.L48 1993, (v3)
Lewellen, Ted C. HC59.7.L4172 1995, (v6)
Lewenson, Sandra. RT4.L49 1996, (v2)
Lewes, Darby. PR830.U7.L4 1995, (v3)
Lewes, Kenneth. RC558.L49 1988, (v2)
Lewiecki-Wilson, Cynthia. PR6023.A93.Z6556 1994, (v3)
Lewin, Abraham. DS135.P62.W314 1988, (v5)
Lewin, Benjamin. QH430.L487 2000, (v1)
Lewin, Ellen. HQ75.53.L49 1993, (v6)
Lewin, Esther. PE3721.L45 1988, (v3)
Lewin, Leif. DL658.8.L4513 1988, (v5)
Lewin, Moshe. DK286.L48 1988, (v5)
Lewin, Ralph A. QK565.L4, (v1)
Lewin, Roger A. RC480.8.L49 1996, (v2)

Lewin, Roger. GN281.L487 1987, (v6)
Lewin, Ronald. D810.C88.L48, (v5)
Lewin, Samuel. PJ5129.L47.B4913, (v3)
Lewin-Epstein, Noah. HC415.25.L48 1993, (v6)
Lewington, Anna. SD383.L48 1999, (v1)
Lewinsohn, Richard. QL85.L414 1954a, (v1)
Lewis, Adrian R. D756.5.N6 L435 2001, (v5)
Lewis, Alan E. BT468.L49 2001, (v8)
Lewis, Allan. PN1861.L4 1971, (v3)
Lewis, Anne Gillespie. F604.3.L5 1999, (v4)
Lewis, Anthony. KF228.G53L49 1989, (v7)
  KF1266.L48 1991, (v7)
Lewis, Archibald Ross. CB353.L48 1988, (v5)
Lewis, Arnold. NA735.C4.L49 1997, (v9)
Lewis, Benjamin Roland. PR2893.L47 1969, (v3)
Lewis, Bernard. DR583.L48 2002, (v5)
  DR726.L4, (v5)
  DS63.2.E8.L48 1982, (v5)
Lewis, C. S. BJ1401.L4, (v8)
  BR85.L484, (v8)
  BR123.L482, (v8)
  BR123.L484 1952, (v8)
  BR125.L67 1982, (v8)
  BV4515.L37 1959, (v8)
  PN85.L48, (v3)
  PN671.L4, (v3)
  PR99.L4 1972, (v3)
  PR411.L4, (v3)
  PR3562.L4, (v3)
  PR6023.E926.O5 1982, (v3)
  PR6023.E926 P4, (v3)
  PR6023.E926.T5, (v3)
  PZ8.L48.Li2, (v3)
Lewis, Catherine C. LB1140.25.J3.L48 1995, (v7)
Lewis, Charles A. QK46.5.H85.L48 1996, (v1)
Lewis, Charles Lee. E467.1.F23 L48 1980, (v4)
Lewis, Charles. JK1118.L47 1998, (v7)
Lewis, Clarence Irving. B945.L451G6, (v8)
  BD161.L38 1956, (v8)
  BD181.L47, (v8)
Lewis, Clive Staples. BJ1251.L4 1943a, (v8)
Lewis, Cynthia. PR2993.A58.L48 1997, (v3)
Lewis, David D. V210.L4, (v10)
Lewis, David H. GV859.L48 1997, (v6)
Lewis, David L. NX511.N4.L48 1981, (v9)
Lewis, David Rich. E78.W5.L48 1994, (v4)
Lewis, David. HD62.6.L49 2001, (v6)
Lewis, Earl. F234.N8.L48 1990, (v4)
Lewis, Eugene. JF1411.L48, (v7)
Lewis, Faye Cashatt. F656.L4, (v4)
Lewis, Geoffrey L. PL115.L47 1999, (v3)
  PL123.L39, (v3)
Lewis, Gilbert Newton. QC311.L4 1961, (v1)
Lewis, Gladys S. PS2954.U6.L49 1994, (v3)
Lewis, Gordon K. F2169.L48 1983, (v4)
Lewis, Grace Ross. TP200.L49 1999, (v1)
Lewis, Harold W. TJ213.L433 1997, (v1)
Lewis, Harry R. QA267.L49, (v1)
Lewis, Helen Block. RC454.L48 1981, (v2)
Lewis, Herbert S. DS113.8.Y4.L49 1989, (v5)
Lewis, Hywel David. B840.L46, (v8)
Lewis, Ivor. PE3502.I64.L49 1991, (v3)
Lewis, J. G. E. QL449.5.L48, (v1)
Lewis, James E. E183.8.S7.L48 1998, (v4)
Lewis, James P. HD69.P75 L488 2002, (v6)
Lewis, James R. BF1091.L53 1995, (v2)
  BF1655.L485 1994, (v2)
  BL72.L48 1999, (v8)
  BL477.L45 1996, (v8)
  BL2525.L486 1998, (v8)
Lewis, Jane. HQ1599.E5.L49 1984, (v6)
  HV249.E89.L48 1991, (v6)
Lewis, Jayne Elizabeth. DA787.A1.L62 1998, (v5)
  PR448.F34.L49 1996, (v3)
Lewis, Jessica H. QP90.4.L48 1996, (v1)
Lewis, Jill. HD8419.S82.L49 1991, (v6)
Lewis, Johanna Miller. F262.R8.L44 1995, (v4)
Lewis, John Lowell. GV1796.C145.L48 1992, (v6)
Lewis, John S. QB501.L497 1995, (v1)
  QB721.L419 2000, (v1)
Lewis, John Wilson. U263.L49 1988, (v10)

Lewis, John. B809.8.L48 1955, (v8)
Lewis, Jon. PN1995.9.Y6.L49 1992, (v3)
  PN1998.3.C69.L48 1995, (v3)
Lewis, Justin. HM1236.L48 2001, (v6)
  PN1992.6.L49 1991, (v3)
Lewis, Linda M. PR4197.R4.L49 1998, (v3)
Lewis, Lloyd. E467.1.S55.L48 1958, (v4)
Lewis, M. G. PR4887.M7 1952, (v3)
  PR4887.M7 1973, (v3)
Lewis, Mark Edward. HN740.Z9.V55 1990, (v6)
  PL2280.L48 1999, (v3)
Lewis, Martin W. G71.5.L48 1997, (v6)
  GF852.P6.L48 1992, (v6)
  HC79.E5.L48 1992, (v6)
Lewis, Marvin A. PQ7623.B57.L4 1996, (v3)
Lewis, Meriwether. F592.4 2002b, (v4)
Lewis, Michael Arthur. VA454.L597, (v10)
  VB315.G7.L4, (v10)
Lewis, Michael. BF714.L48 1997, (v2)
  DS894.59.T698, (v5)
  VA454.L595, (v10)
  VF57.L4, (v10)
Lewis, Naphtali. DG13.L4, (v5)
Lewis, Norman. LB1050.5.L4 1978, (v7)
Lewis, Oscar. F860.L44, (v4)
  F1391.T3.L4, (v4)
  HE2752.L48 1981, (v6)
  HN203.5.L48 1977, (v6)
  HQ562.L39, (v6)
  HQ562.L43, (v6)
Lewis, Paul H. F2688.L49 1993, (v4)
Lewis, Paul M. F892.L48 1989, (v4)
Lewis, Pericles. PN3503.L39 2000, (v3)
Lewis, Peter Elfed. PR3458.D7.L49 1987, (v3)
Lewis, Peter M. HE8675.L49 1990, (v6)
Lewis, Peter. SB413.C2.L48 1998, (v1)
Lewis, Rand C. DD262.L48 1991, (v5)
Lewis, Randolph. PN1998.3.D3846.L48 2000, (v3)
Lewis, Richard D. HD62.4.L49 2000, (v6)
Lewis, Richard J. T55.3.H3.L494 2000, (v1)
Lewis, Richard S. G860.L9, (v6)
Lewis, Robert A. RA1193.L48 1996, (v2)
Lewis, Robert Alan. S411.L39 2002, (v1)
Lewis, Robert. HC118.M6.L49 2000, (v6)
Lewis, Ronald J. TS165.L48 1995, (v1)
Lewis, Ronald L. E445.M3.L48, (v4)
  HC107.W5.L39 1998, (v6)
Lewis, Roy. PC2511.L4 1982, (v3)
Lewis, Rupert. F2380.6.R63.L49 1998, (v4)
Lewis, Samella S. N6538.N5.L39, (v9)
  N6538.N5.L4, (v9)
Lewis, Saunders. PB2298.L49.P7, (v3)
Lewis, Sinclair. PS3523.E94 A6, (v3)
  PS3523.E94.A6 1997, (v3)
  PS3523.E94.A65 1933, (v3)
  PS3523.E94.A7, (v3)
  PS3523.E94.C3 1945, (v3)
  PS3523.E94.D6, (v3)
  PS3523.E94.E4, (v3)
  PS3523.E94 F7, (v3)
  PS3523.E94 G5, (v3)
  PS3523.E94 G6, (v3)
  PS3523.E94 I9, (v3)
  PS3523.E94 K5, (v3)
  PS3523.E94.M3, (v3)
  PS3523.E94 M3, (v3)
  PS3523.E94 M33, (v3)
  PS3523.E94 M35, (v3)
  PS3523.E94 O9 1951, (v3)
  PS3523.E94 P7, (v3)
  PS3523.E94.S75, (v3)
  PS3523.E94 T73, (v3)
  PS3523.E94 W67, (v3)
  PS3523.E94.Z53 1952, (v3)
Lewis, Stephen R. HC905.L49 1990, (v6)
Lewis, Susan A. Z5956.D3.L48 1998, (v10)
Lewis, Terrance L. DA578.L45 1990, (v5)
Lewis, Thomas A. E312.2.L48 1993, (v4)
Lewis, Thomas H. E99.O3.L49 1990, (v4)
Lewis, W. David. HD9519.S68.L49 1994, (v6)

Lewis, W. S. PR3757.W2.Z73, (v3)
Lewis, Walter Hepworth. RS164.L475, (v2)
Lewis, Ward B. PT2647.E26.Z727 1996, (v3)
Lewis, Wyndham. BD638.L4 1957, (v8)
  PN710.L44 1976, (v3)
  PR6023.E97.B6 1967b, (v3)
  PR6023.E97 C5, (v3)
  PR6023.E97.C5 1928, (v3)
  PR6023.E97 H8, (v3)
  PR6023.E97 R4, (v3)
  PR6023.E97 R6, (v3)
Lewisohn, Ludwig. PS3523.E96 A8, (v3)
  PS3523.E96 C3, (v3)
  PS3523.E96 D6, (v3)
  PS3523.E96 I8, (v3)
  PS3523.E96 S8, (v3)
  PS3523.E96.Z55, (v3)
Lewison, Jeremy. NE539.M23.A4 1992, (v9)
Lewontin, Richard C. QH455.L48, (v1)
  QH506.L443 2000, (v1)
Lewy, Guenter. D804.5.G85.L49 2000, (v5)
Ley, David. HT178.C2.L49 1996, (v6)
Ley, Willy. QB15.L4, (v1)
Leyburn, James Graham. E184.S4.L5, (v4)
Leyda, Jay. ML410.M97.L5 1970, (v9)
Leyden, W. von. JC571.L524 1982, (v7)
Leyerle, John. Z8164.L49 1986, (v10)
Leymarie, Jean. ND547.L54 1969, (v9)
  ND644.L42, (v9)
  ND1265.L52, (v9)
Leys, Colin. HC517.K4.L49, (v6)
  HC800.C628 1996, (v6)
Leys, Ruth. RC552.T7.L49 2000, (v2)
Leys, Wayne A. R. BC55.L4, (v8)
Leyser, Henrietta. HQ1147.G7.L49 1995, (v6)
Leyster, Judith. ND653.L73.A4 1993, (v9)
Lhamon, W. T. PN1969.M5.L53 1998, (v3)
Li, Ao. PL2877.A6, (v3)
Li, C. Y. PS3562.I12.F5, (v3)
Li, Cheng. HX518.L4, (v6)
Li, Chenyang. B127.C65.L495 1999, (v8)
Li, Chi. DS730.L5 1967, (v5)
  DS796.A55.L5, (v5)
Li, Chieh-jen. PL2877.C528.T3, (v3)
Li, Chien-nung. DS755.L4313 1956, (v5)
Li, Chih-Ch'ang. DS707.L5, (v5)
Li, Ching-chao. PL2682.A27 1979, (v3)
Li, Chin-Yang. PS3523.E3158.M3x, (v3)
Li, CongHua. HC430.C6.L48 1999, (v6)
Li, David Leiwei. PS153.A84.L5 1998, (v3)
Li, Hsing-tao. PL2997.L44 H8, (v3)
Li, Ju-chen. PL2718.I15 C5 1965, (v3)
Li, Jun. DS741.65.L514 1996, (v5)
Li, Lincoln. DS777.53.L4634, (v5)
  U644.C36.L1 1994, (v10)
Li, Po. PL2997.L5.A26 1965, (v3)
Li, Tieh-cheng. DS785.L5 1960, (v5)
Li, Tsun-pao. PL2877.T74.K3413 1990, (v3)
Li, Tze-chung. Z7161.A1.L5 2000, (v10)
Li, Wai-yee. PL2275.L68L5 1993, (v3)
Li, Yen. QA27.C5.L4713 1987, (v1)
Li, Yen-hui Audrey. PL1231.5.L5 1990, (v3)
Li, Yuan-Hui. QE515.L385 2000, (v1)
Li, Zhisui. DS778.M3 L5164 1994, (v5)
Liang, Chi-chao. DS721.L5483, (v5)
Liang, Diana F. Z6653.L5 1992, (v10)
Liang, Hsi-huey. HV8194.A2.L53 1992, (v6)
Liang, Ssu-cheng. NA1540.L536 1984, (v9)
Liang, Xiaosheng. PL2878.A5974, (v3)
Liao, Kai-lung. DS777.53.L484, (v5)
Liao, Kang. PS3503.U198.Z6984 1997, (v3)
Libai, A. TA660.S5.L457 1998, (v1)
Libbey, James K. HF1456.5.S624.L53 1989, (v6)
Libby, Ronald T. HD9036.L53 1992, (v6)
  KU1006.5 .L53 1989, (v7)
Libby, Willard F. QC798.D3.L5 1955, (v1)
Libman, Lillian. ML410.S932.L44, (v9)

Library of Congress. DS734.U65, (v5)
 F195.L66 1989, (v4)
 Z695.L695 1986, (v10)
 Z3271.L53 1996, (v10)
 Z5313.U5.L53 1991, (v10)
 Z5319.U53, (v10)
 Z6027.U5.L5 1989, (v10)
Lichatowich, Jim. SH348.L53 1999, (v1)
Lichine, Alexis. TP546.L5 1979, (v1)
Licht, Fred. ND813.G7.L564 1983, (v9)
Licht, Walter. HC105.L53 1995, (v6)
Lichten, Frances. NK835.P4.L5 1963, (v9)
Lichtenberg, Peter A. RC451.4.N87.L53 1994, (v2)
Lichtenstadter, Ilse. PJ7528.L5 1976, (v3)
Lichtenstein, Diane Marilyn. PS153.J4.L5 1992, (v3)
Lichtenstein, Nelson. HD6509.R4.L53 1995, (v6)
Lichtenstein, Peter M. HC427.92.L524 1991, (v6)
Lichter, S. Robert. PN1992.6.L53 1994, (v3)
Lichterman, Paul. JK1764.L53 1996, (v7)
Lichtheim, George. B809.8.L499, (v8)
 CB205.L53 2000, (v5)
 D1051.L5 1963, (v5)
Lichtheim, Miriam. PJ1943.L5, (v3)
Lichtman, Allan J. JK524.L53 1990, (v7)
Lickorish, W. B. Raymond. QA612.2.L53 1997, (v1)
Liddell Hart, Basil Henry. D521.L48 1963, (v5)
 D568.4.L45.L52 1936, (v5)
 D743.L514 1971, (v5)
 D757.L5 1948a, (v5)
 U102.L58 1950a, (v10)
 U102.L63 1947, (v10)
 UA11.L5 1960, (v10)
 UA772.L5 1968, (v10)
Liddell, Henry George. PA445.E5.L6 1925, (v3)
Liddell, Robert. DR722.L5, (v5)
Liddle, Andrew R. QB981.L534 1999, (v1)
Liddy, G. Gordon. E860.L53, (v4)
Lide, David R. TP247.5.L53 1995, (v1)
Lidell, Lucy. RA780.5.L53 2001, (v2)
Lidoff, Joan. PR9619.3.S75.Z7 1982, (v3)
Lidz, Theodore. RC455.4.F3.L53 1992, (v2)
Lieb, Elliott H. QA300.L54 1997, (v1)
Lieb, Fred. GV863.A1.L5 1977, (v6)
Lieb, Michael. PR3562.L52, (v3)
 PR3588.L46 1989, (v3)
 PR3592.V56.L54 1994, (v3)
Lieb, Sandra R. ML420.R274.L5, (v9)
Liebau, Friedrich. QD181.S6.L614 1985, (v1)
Liebeck, M. W. QA8.4.L47 2000, (v1)
Liebenberg, A. C. TG340.L54 1992, (v1)
Lieber, Edvard. N6537.D43.L53 2000, (v9)
Lieber, Lillian Rosanoff. BC135.L5 1960, (v8)
Lieber, Michael D. GN671.C3.L54 1994, (v6)
Lieberman, Benjamin David. JS5431.L53 1998, (v7)
Lieberman, Bruce S. QE721.2.P24, (v1)
Lieberman, David. KD612.L54 1989, (v7)
Lieberman, Joseph I. F101.B3 L5, (v4)
Lieberman, Myron. LA217.L542 1989, (v7)
Lieberman, Myron. LA217.2.L54 1993, (v7)
Lieberman, Phil L. RC591.L54 1999, (v2)
Lieberman, Philip. QP399.L535 2000, (v1)
Lieberman, Richard K. ML424.S76.L54 1995, (v9)
Lieberman, Robbie. HX83.L54 2000, (v6)
 ML3795.L44 1989, (v9)
Lieberman, Sally Taylor. PL2443.L54 1998, (v3)
Lieberman, Sima. HC385.L463 1995, (v6)
 HF1411.L533 1988, (v6)
Lieberman-Nissen, Karen. Z6663.N9.L5 1991, (v10)
Liebersohn, Harry. HM22.G2.L53 1988, (v6)
Lieberson, Stanley. CS2367.L54 2000, (v5)
Lieberthal, Kenneth. DS777.75.L557 1995, (v5)
 DS796.T5 L53, (v5)
Liebes, Sidney. QH367.L525 1998, (v1)
Liebes, Yehuda. BM530.L457 1993, (v8)
Liebeschuetz, J. H. W. G. DF543.L53 1990, (v5)
Liebich, Andre. DK265.9.M45.L54 1997, (v5)
Liebig, James E. HF5387.L54 1990, (v6)
Lieblich, Amia. PJ5053.B34.Z7613 1997, (v3)
Liebling, A. J. F376.L6.L5 1970, (v4)
Liebling, Jerome. F607.L54 1997, (v4)
Liebman, Charles S. BM565.L54 1990, (v8)

DS112.L65 1983, (v5)
Liebman, Herbert. PR6069.T65.Z73 1996, (v3)
Liebman, Matt. SB611.5.L54 2001, (v1)
Liebman, Roy. PN1998.2.L52 1998, (v3)
Liebman, Roy. Z5784.M9.L54 1996, (v10)
Liebmann, George W. JS113.L54 1995, (v7)
 JS211.L54 2000, (v7)
Liebovich, Louis. E802.L52 1994, (v4)
 E839.5.L495 2001, (v4)
Liebow, Elliot. HV4506.W2.L54 1993, (v6)
Liebowitz, S. J. HD9696.63.U64.M5364 1999, (v6)
Lieder, Michael. KF8208.L54 1997, (v7)
Liehm, Mira. PN1993.5.E8.L5, (v3)
Lien, Carsten. F897.O5.L54 1991, (v4)
Lienesch, Michael. JC599.U5.L48 1988, (v7)
Lienhard, John H. T14.5.L52 2000, (v1)
Lieske, Ewald. QL621.58.L54 1996, (v1)
Liess, Andreas. ML410.O65.L57 1966a, (v9)
Liestol, Knut. PT7269.A4.L5, (v3)
Lieven, Anatol. DK502.7.L54 1993, (v5)
 DK508.57.R9.L54 1999, (v5)
 DK511.C37.L54 1998, (v5)
Lieven, D. C. B. DK40.L55 2001, (v5)
 DK253.L54 1989, (v5)
 DK258.L46 1994, (v5)
Liew, K. S. DS778.S8.L5 1971b, (v5)
Life, Page West. Z8545.5.L53, (v10)
Lifton, Betty Jean. LB775.K6272.L53 1988, (v7)
Lifton, Robert Jay. BF697.5.S65.L53 1993, (v2)
 D767.25.H6.L4, (v5)
 DS777.55.L457, (v5)
 U263.L53 1990, (v10)
Light, Jonathan Fraser. GV862.3.L54 1997, (v6)
Light, Paul Charles. HD62.6.L543 2002, (v6)
 HJ9801.L54 1993, (v6)
 JK411.L54 1997, (v7)
Lightbown, R. W. ND623.B7.L53 1978b, (v9)
 ND623.P548.L54 1992, (v9)
Lightfoot, Cynthia. HQ796.L444 1997, (v6)
Lightfoot, Sara Lawrence. E185.96.L54 1994, (v4)
Lightman, Alan P. QB15.L54 1992, (v1)
 QB981.L54 1990, (v1)
Lightman, Marjorie. HQ1136.L54 2000, (v6)
Likaka, Osumaka. HD8039.C662.Z285 1997, (v6)
Likens, Gene E. QH105.N4.L55 1995, (v1)
Likhachev, Dmitrii Sergeevich. DK268.L46.A3 2000, (v5)
Lilie, Ralph-Johannes. DF547.L37.L5413 1993, (v5)
Lilienfeld, Jane. PR888.A4.L55 1999, (v3)
Lilienthal, Meta. CT275.L44.A3, (v5)
Lilja, David J. QA76.9.E94L54 2000, (v1)
Liller, William. QB63.L55 1985, (v1)
 QB64.L55 1992, (v1)
 QB461.L52, (v1)
 G1201.F7 .L5 1998, (v6)
Lillo, George. PR3541.L5 1979, (v3)
Lilly, Mark. PN56.H57.L55 1993, (v3)
Lim, Walter S. H. PR428.I54.L56 1998, (v3)
Lima, Carolyn W. Z1037.L715 1998, (v10)
Lima, Luiz Costa. PN45.L47513 1996, (v3)
Lima, Robert. PQ6613.A763.Z737, (v3)
 PQ6641.A47.Z734 1988, (v3)
Liman, Arthur L. KF373.L496.A3 1998, (v7)
Limb, Peter. Z6514.C7.A38 1996, (v10)
Limbaugh, Ronald H. SF426.2.L56 1996, (v1)
Limon, John. PN1969.C65, (v3)
Limon, Jose Eduardo. F395.M5.L56 1994, (v4)
Limon, Jose. GV1785.L515.A3 1998, (v6)
Lin, Ann Chih. HV9304.L56 2000, (v6)
Lin, Chong-Pin. UA835.L46 1988, (v10)
Lin, E. C. C. QH434.L56 1984, (v1)
Lin, Jing. DS778.7.L57 1991, (v5)
Lin, Nan. DS779.32.L56 1992, (v5)
Lin, T. Y. TA683.9.L5 1981, (v1)
Lin, Yi-min. HC427.92.L55 2001, (v6)
Lin, Yutang. BD431.L42 1940, (v8)
 DS795.L52, (v5)
 PJ409.L5 1955, (v3)
 PL3277.E1.L47, (v3)
Lincoln, Abraham. E457.2.L753 1998, (v4)
 E457.4.L77, (v4)

E457.4.L776 1993, (v4)
E457.92. 1955, (v4)
E457.92. 1980b, (v4)
E457.92 1990, (v4)
E457.92. 1990a, (v4)
E457.92 1999, (v4)
E457.99.S49 1980, (v4)
Lincoln, Andrew. PR4144.F683.L56 1995, (v3)
Lincoln, Betty Woelk. Z5931.L52 1988, (v10)
Lincoln, Bruce. GN479.L56 1989, (v6)
Lincoln, Edward J. HF1601.L55 1993, (v6)
Lincoln, Evelyn. NE659.L56 2000, (v9)
Lincoln, Kenneth. E78.N75 L56 1997, (v4)
 E98.H77.L56 1993, (v4)
 PS310.I52.L56 2000, (v3)
Lincoln, Roger J. QH13.L56 1987, (v1)
 QH540.4.L56 1998, (v1)
Lincoln, W. Bruce. DK210.L56, (v5)
 DK220.L56 1990, (v5)
 DK240.L56 1983, (v5)
 DK262.L53 1986, (v5)
 DK761.L56 1994, (v5)
Lincove, David A. Z1242.8.L56 2000, (v10)
 Z6465.U5 L56 1988, (v10)
Lind, David. QC26.L56 1997, (v1)
Lind, John. RJ423.L56, (v2)
Lindberg, Carter. BR305.2.L486 1996, (v8)
Lindberg, David C. Q124.95.L55 1992, (v1)
Lindberg, Richard. HV8148.C4.L55 1991, (v6)
Lindbergh, Anne (Morrow). PS3523.I516.U5, (v3)
 BD435.L52 1955a, (v8)
 PS3523.I516.Z516, (v3)
 PS3523.I516.Z52, (v3)
 PS3523.I516.Z528, (v3)
Lindblom, Charles Edward. HB501.L512 2001, (v6)
 HN28.L56 1990, (v6)
 JK271.L52 1980, (v7)
Lindee, M. Susan. RA1231.R2.L497 1994, (v2)
Lindeman, Fredrik Otto. P589.L513 1997, (v3)
Lindemann, Barbara. KF3467.L56 1992, (v7)
Lindemann, Gottfried. N6861.L513, (v9)
Lindemann, Mary. HV280.H3.L56 1990, (v6)
Linden, Robin Ruth. E184.J5.L668 1993, (v4)
Linden, Stanton J. PR428.A44.L56 1996, (v3)
Lindenmeyer, Kriste. HV741.L525 1997, (v6)
Lindenmeyr, Adele. HV313.L55 1996, (v6)
Linden-Ward, Blanche. F73.61.M8.L56 1989, (v4)
Linder, Leslie. PR6031.O72.Z63, (v3)
Linderman, Frank Bird. E98.F6 L69 2001, (v4)
Lindert, Peter H. HB915.L56, (v6)
Lindey, Christine. N6988.L56 1990, (v9)
Lindfors, Bernth. Z3508.L5 L562 1989, (v10)
 Z3508.L5.L563 1995, (v10)
Lindgren, Astrid. PZ7.L6585Pi, (v3)
Lindgren, H. Elaine. F636.L56 1996, (v4)
Lindgren, James Michael. F5.L73 1995, (v4)
 F227.L55 1993, (v4)
Lindgren, Waldemar. TN263.L7 1933, (v1)
Lindholm, Charles. HM141.L553 1990, (v6)
Lindholt, Lone. KQC572.L56 1997, (v7)
Lindio-McGovern, Ligaya. HQ1757.L55 1997, (v6)
Lindley, Arthur. PR658.S5.L56 1996, (v3)
Lindley, D. V. QA276.25.L56 1995, (v1)
Lindley, David. QC794.6.G7.L55 1993, (v1)
Lindley, Keith. DA415.L48 1997, (v5)
Lindley, Susan Hill. BL2525.L55 1996, (v8)
Lindop, Grevel. PR4536.L5 1981, (v3)
Lindow, John. BL860.L56 2001, (v8)
Lindroth, Colette. PS3505.R895.Z76 1995, (v3)
Lindsay, A. D. HB501.M37.L5, (v6)
Lindsay, David. PS3523.T565 V6, (v3)
Lindsay, Hamish. TL789.8.U6, (v1)
Lindsay, Howard. PS3523.I575.S65 1946, (v3)
Lindsay, Jack. ND553.C33.L5 1969b, (v9)
 PR5013.L5, (v3)
Lindsay, James M. UA23.L5765 1991, (v10)
Lindsay, James Martin. PT2625.A44.Z744, (v3)
Lindsay, Jennifer. ML1251.I53 L56 1992, (v9)
Lindsay, Maurice. PR8511.L5, (v3)
Lindsay, Michael. DS777.53.L573, (v5)
 DS777.55.L46, (v5)

Lindsay, Robert Bruce. QC6.L42 1957, (v1)
  QC6.L425, (v1)
  QC225.7.L56, (v1)
Lindsay, Vachel. PS3523.I58.A17 1984, (v3)
  PS3523.I58.A6 1963, (v3)
Lindsey, Duncan. HV741.L527 1994, (v6)
Lindsey, Mary P. RC569.95.L56 1989, (v2)
Lindsey, Mary. F234.A3 L5, (v4)
Lindskold, Jane M. PS3576.E43.Z76 1993, (v3)
Lindstrom, Naomi. PQ7081.L49 1998, (v3)
  PQ7634.J48.L56 1989, (v3)
  PQ7797.B635.Z7735 1990, (v3)
Lindy, Jacob D. RC552.P67.L56 1988, (v2)
Linebarger, Paul Myron Anthony. DS774.L48, (v5)
  DS775.L48, (v5)
  DS777.L49 1936, (v5)
  PS3523.I63 B4 1975a, (v3)
Linebarger, Paul Myron Wentworth. DS777.L5 1969, (v5)
Linehan, Thomas P. DA685.E1.L56 1996, (v5)
  JN1129.C62.L56 2000, (v7)
Lines, Clifford John. HC254.5.L72 1990, (v6)
Lines, Malcolm E. QA93.L553 1994, (v1)
Lines, William J. GF801.L55 1991, (v6)
Linfield, Michael. KF4749.L56 1990, (v7)
Linford, Laurance D. E99.N3.L645 2000, (v4)
Ling, Huping. E184.C5.L6 1998, (v4)
Ling, Jinqi. PS153.A84.L56 1998, (v3)
Ling, Roger. DG70.P7.L55 1997, (v5)
Lingayah, Sam. HV470.5.L56 1996, (v6)
Lingeman, Richard R. E806.L568 1970, (v4)
Linger, Daniel Touro. HN290.S32.L56 1992, (v6)
Ling-hu, Te-fen. DS741.L56 no.6, (v5)
Lingis, Alphonso. BC199.C5.L56 1998, (v8)
  BD223.L56 1989, (v8)
Link, Arthur Stanley. E741.L55 1967, (v4)
  E743.L56 1983, (v4)
  E766.L5 1989, (v4)
  E767.L64, (v4)
  E768.L66 1974, (v4)
  F208.2.L5, (v4)
Link, E. Perry. PL2303.L543 2000, (v3)
  PL2303.L543 2000, (v3)
  PL2442.L5, (v3)
Link, Eugene P. HD6338.2.U5.L55 1984, (v6)
  R152.L56 1992, (v2)
Link, Frederick M. Z2014.D7.L55, (v10)
Link, John F. ML134.C19 L56 2000, (v9)
Link, William A. F215.L56 1992, (v4)
Links, J. G. ND623.C2.L49 1982b, (v9)
Linn, Brian McAllister. DS682.A2 1989, (v5)
  UA23.L5768 1997, (v10)
Linn, James Weber. HV28.A35.L5, (v6)
Linn, Karen. ML1015.B3.L5 1991, (v9)
Linn, Marcia C. LB1585.3.L56 2000, (v7)
Linneman, Robert E. HF5415.13.L538 1995, (v6)
Linney, Romulus. PS3562.I55.A6 1992, (v3)
  PS3562.I55.A6 1993, (v3)
Linsky, Arnold S. HN90.V5.L55 1995, (v6)
Linsky, Leonard. BC199.M64.L54, (v8)
Linsley Hood, John. TK7874.L55 1993, (v1)
Linsley, Ray K. TC145.L55 1979, (v1)
Linton, Ralph. E98.C9.L6, (v4)
  N7410.L5, (v9)
Lintott, A. W. DG211.L5, (v5)
Linville, Susan E. PN1993.5.G3.L56 1998, (v3)
Linz, Juan J. JC480.L59 2000, (v7)
Lipham, James M. LB2831.92.L57 1985, (v7)
Lipkin, Robert Justin. KF4575.L47 2000, (v7)
Lipking, Lawrence I. PR3533.L56 1998, (v3)
Lipkowitz, Myron A. RC585.N38 2001, (v2)
Lipman, Jean. ND210.5.P7.L56 1942, (v9)
Lipman, Matthew. B52.L559 1988, (v8)
Lipman, Pauline. LB2806.L54 1998, (v7)
Lipman, V. D. DS135.E5.L46 1990, (v5)
Lipnack, Jessica. HD66.2.L56 2000, (v6)
Lipner, Julius. BL1202.L56 1994, (v8)
Lipovetsky, Gilles. GT596.L5713 1994, (v6)
Lipow, Anne Grodzins. Z711.45.L57 2003, (v10)
Lippard, Lucy R. N6512.L57 1990, (v9)
  N6537.5.L5 1990, (v9)

N7428.L56 1983, (v9)
  NX600.S9.L5, (v9)
Lippi, Filippino. NC257.L56.A4 1997, (v9)
Lippincott, Benjamin Evans. JC423.L57 1964, (v7)
Lippincott, Lillian. Z8748.37.L76, (v10)
Lippit, Victor D. HC427.L486 1987, (v6)
Lippke, Richard L. HF5387.L56 1995, (v6)
Lippman, Edward A. ML169.L68, (v9)
Lippman, Stanley B. QA76.73.C153L577 2000, (v1)
Lippmann, Walter. BJ47.L5 1934, (v8)
  E744.L56 1972, (v4)
  E766.L57, (v4)
  E835.L52, (v4)
  HB199.L5, (v6)
  HC106.3.L53, (v6)
  HN64.L53 1985, (v6)
  JC251.L48, (v7)
Lippy, Charles H. BL2525.L566 1996, (v8)
  BL2525.L567 2000, (v8)
  BR500.L54 1992, (v8)
  BX6666.L56 1989, (v8)
Lipschutz, Mark R. DT352.6.L56 1987, (v5)
Lipschutz, Ronnie D. D860.L55 2000, (v5)
  GE195.L57 1996, (v6)
Lipscomb, Mance. ML420.L67.A3 1993, (v9)
Lipset, David. DU740.42.L565 1997, (v5)
Lipset, Seymour Martin. BF755.A5.R525, (v2)
  E169.1.L5447 1996, (v4)
  E169.1.L545 1989, (v4)
  E169.1.L546, (v4)
  E183.L56 1978, (v4)
Lipsey, Roger. N8248.S77.L56 1988, (v9)
Lipsitz, George. E184.A1.L56 1998, (v4)
  HD8072.5.L56 1994, (v6)
Lipsitz, Joan. LB1623.L56 1984, (v7)
Lipsky, Dorothy Kerzner. LC1201.L56 1997, (v7)
Lipsky, Michael. HV41.L53, (v6)
Lipstadt, Deborah E. D804.35.L57 1993, (v5)
Liptak, Dolores Ann. BX1407.I45.L57 1989, (v8)
Lipton, Helene L. HV5824.A33.L56 1988, (v6)
Lipton, Kathryn L. S411.L55 1995, (v1)
Lipton, Michael. HC79.P6.L56 1977b, (v6)
Liptzin, Solomon. PJ5120.L55, (v3)
LiPuma, Edward. DU740.42.L57 1988, (v5)
Lisagor, Nancy. KF355.N4.L57 1988, (v7)
Lisboa, Maria Manuel. PQ9697.M18.Z6965 1996, (v3)
Lischer, Richard. BV4208.U6.L57 1995, (v8)
Liscombe, R. W. NA737.M5.L58 1994, (v9)
  NA997.W48.L57, (v9)
Lisio, Donald J. E802.L56 1985, (v4)
Liska, George. D443.L4964 1998, (v5)
  D443.L4966 1999, (v5)
Lisman, C. David. LC220.5.L57 1998, (v7)
Liss, Peggy K. HF3211.L57 1983, (v6)
Liss, Sheldon B. F1438.L74 1991, (v4)
  F1787.L57 1987, (v4)
Lissner, Ivar. CB301.L513, (v5)
Lister, Florence Cline. F819.T99.C55 1989, (v4)
Liszt, Franz. ML410.C54.L738, (v9)
Liszt, Franz. ML410.L7.A4 1998, (v9)
Litfin, A. Duane. PN4121.L56 1992, (v3)
Litfin, Karen. QC879.7.L58 1994, (v1)
Litman, Todd. TK2511.L54 1995, (v1)
Litowitz, Douglas E. K230.L4482.P67 1997, (v7)
Littauer, Vladimir Stanislas. U55.L57.A3, (v10)
Littell, Franklin Hamlin. G1046.E4.L5 1976, (v6)
Little, Charles E. SB762.L58 1995, (v1)
Little, Colin. QH95.7.L57 1996, (v1)
  QH371.L58 1990, (v1)
Little, Daniel. H61.L58 1990, (v6)
Little, David. BJ1188.L57 1978, (v8)
Little, Elbert Luther. QK481.L49 1980, (v1)
Little, J. I. F1054.E13.L57 1997, (v4)
  F1054.S254.L57 1991, (v4)
  F1054.5.W56.L58 1991, (v4)
Little, J. M. R727.3.L565 1995, (v2)
Little, John Buckner. F332.B9L7 1971, (v4)
Little, Judy. PR888.W6.L58 1996, (v3)
  PR4837.L56, (v3)
Little, Lawrence S. BX8443.L58 2000, (v8)
Little, M. Ruth. GT3210.N8.L57 1998, (v6)

Little, Meredith. ML410.B13 L52 2001, (v9)
Little, Stephen. N8199.T3, (v9)
Little, William. PE1625.L53 1973, (v3)
Littlefield, Daniel C. E445.S7 L57 1991, (v4)
Littlefield, Daniel F. E99.C55 L57, (v4)
  E99.C9.L57, (v4)
Littlefield, Larry J. SB741.R8.L39, (v1)
Littleton, A. C. HF5605.L5 1981, (v6)
Littlewood, Thomas B. KF228.G74.L58 1988, (v7)
Littmann, Mark. QB541.L69 1991, (v1)
Litvack, Leon. Z8230.L58 1999, (v10)
Litvak, Joseph. PN3331.L58 1997, (v3)
Litwack, Leon F. E185.2.L57 1979, (v4)
  E185.6.L58 1998, (v4)
Litwak, Robert. KZ6374.L58 2000, (v7)
Litz, A. Walton. PR4037.L57, (v3)
  PR6019.O9.U675 1961, (v3)
Litzinger, Boyd. PR4231.L58 1970, (v3)
Litzinger, Ralph A. DS731.Y3, (v5)
Liu, Alan P. L. JQ1516.L54 1996, (v7)
Liu, Alan. PR5892.H5.L5 1989, (v3)
Liu, Bao-Lin. QB579.L58 1992, (v1)
Liu, E. PL2999.L5.A74, (v3)
Liu, F. F. DS738.L5, (v5)
Liu, Henry. TA654.5.L58 1991, (v1)
Liu, Hsieh. PL2806.L513, (v3)
Liu, Hsin-ju. HF3788.C6.L58 1988, (v6)
Liu, James J. Y. PL1279.L496 1988, (v3)
  PL2307.L57 1962, (v3)
  PL2307.L572 1982, (v3)
  PL2343.L5, (v3)
Liu, John. QA41.L58 1999, (v1)
Liu, Kang. BH39.L5595 2000, (v8)
Liu, KeShun. SB205.S7L585 1997, (v1)
Liu, Laurence G. NA1540.L57 1989, (v9)
Liu, Lewis-Guodo. HF54.56.L58 1998, (v6)
  Z7161.L578 2000, (v10)
Liu, Lydia He. PL2302.L534 1995, (v3)
Liu, Shu-hsien. B127.C65.L59 1998, (v8)
Liu, Ta-chung. HC427.9.L599 1965, (v6)
Liu, Tsai-hsing. HC427.9.L599213 1988, (v6)
Liu, Wu-chi. B128.C8.L58 1979, (v8)
  PL2265.L5, (v3)
Liu, Xiaogan. BL1900.C576 L5863 1994, (v8)
Liu, Xiaoyuan. D754.C5.L58 1996, (v5)
Liu, Xin. HN740.S54, (v6)
Liu, Yiqing. DS748.2.L492513 2002, (v5)
Liulevicius, Vejas G. D551.L58 2000, (v5)
Liungman, Carl G. BL603.L5413 1991, (v8)
Lively, Adam. PS173.N4.L58 2000, (v3)
Lively, Donald E. KF4549.L58 1999, (v7)
  KF4550.L58 1992, (v7)
  KF4755.L57 1992, (v7)
Livermore, H. V. DP538.L72, (v5)
Livermore, Shaw. E338.L5 1972, (v4)
Livesey, Anthony. G1037.L55 1994, (v6)
Livezeanu, Irina. DR264.L58 1995, (v5)
Livezey, William Edmund. E182.M242.L58 1981, (v4)
Livi Bacci, Massimo. HB871.L56513 2000, (v6)
  HB3581.L58 1990, (v6)
Livingston, Alan. NC997.L54 1992, (v9)
Livingston, Eric. PR601.L58 1995, (v3)
Livingston, James D. QC757.L58 1996, (v1)
  TK7871.L58 1999, (v1)
Livingston, James. E169.1.L58 1994, (v4)
Livingston, Jane. N6538.N5.L58 1982, (v9)
Livingston, John A. GF75.L59 1994, (v6)
Livingston, Lili Cockerille. GV1785.A1.L526 1997, (v6)
Livingston, M. Stanley. QC721.L725, (v1)
Livingston, Steven. HV6431.L578 1994, (v6)
Livingstone, David N. G69.S49.L58 1987, (v6)
  G80.L54 1993, (v6)
Livingstone, J. M. HD2755.5.L59 1989, (v6)
Livingstone, Marco. N6494.P6.L58 1990, (v9)
Livio, Mario. QB981.L57 2000, (v1)
Livo, Norma J. LB1042.L545 1991, (v7)
Livy. DG250.L58213, (v5)
Llanes, Lilian. NA7274.L5913 1999, (v9)
Llewellyn Smith, Virginia. PS2124.L54 1994, (v3)
Llewellyn, D. T. TN730.L53 1998, (v1)

Llewellyn, Karl N. KF273.L55 1951, (v7)
Llewellyn, Richard. PR6023.L47 H6 1940, (v3)
Llewellyn-Jones, Rosie. DS470.M3 L55 1992, (v5)
Lloyd Evans, Barbara. PR4168.L56 1982, (v3)
Lloyd Evans, Gareth. PR2976.E9 1978b, (v3)
    PR2976.L57 1982, (v3)
Lloyd George, David. D546.L5 1933, (v5)
    D644.L55 1972, (v5)
Lloyd, Brian. HX83.L56 1997, (v6)
Lloyd, Christopher. DC225.L55 1973, (v5)
    VK57.L55, (v10)
Lloyd, Craig. E802.L6, (v4)
Lloyd, Cynthia B. HD6095.L558, (v6)
Lloyd, Dan Edward. BF311.L59 1989, (v2)
Lloyd, David. PR8753.L56 1993, (v3)
Lloyd, Donald J. PE1105.L58, (v3)
Lloyd, Llewelyn S. ML3809.L55 1979, (v9)
Lloyd, Norman. PN2287.L53.A3 1990, (v3)
Lloyd, Peter E. HF1025.L584 1977, (v6)
Lloyd, Rosemary. PN56.J43.L56 1995, (v3)
    PQ283.L58 1992, (v3)
    PQ2344.Z5.L56 1999, (v3)
Lloyd, S. A. JC153.H659.L56 1992, (v7)
Lloyd, S. D. DA225.L56 1988, (v5)
Lloyd, Seton. DS68.L57, (v5)
    DS70.L48 1980b, (v5)
    N5345.L55 1961a, (v9)
Lloyd, Tom. PR868.R4.L58 1997, (v3)
Lloyd, Trevor Owen. DA300.L58 1984, (v5)
Lloyd, William Bross. DQ70.L55 1980, (v5)
Lo, Hsiang-lin. DS796.H7.L593, (v5)
Lo, Jack. T223.U3L6 2001, (v1)
Lo, Kuan-chung. PL2690.S3 E53, (v3)
    PL2690.S3.E53 1976, (v3)
Loades, D. M. DA86.L6 2000, (v5)
    DA315.L578 1997, (v5)
    DA340.L5794 1992, (v5)
    DA345.1.N6.L63 1996, (v5)
    DA347.L579 1989, (v5)
    DA347.L58 1979, (v5)
Loasby, Brian J. HB133.L6 1999, (v6)
Lobanov-Rostovsky, Andrei. DK197.L6 1954, (v5)
    DK197.L6 1968, (v5)
Lobban, Christopher S. QK570.2.L64 1994, (v1)
Lochnan, Katharine Jordan. NE2012.W45.L6 1984,
    (v9)
Lochrie, Karma. PR275.W6.L63 1999, (v3)
Lochrie, Karma. PR2007.K4.Z77 1991, (v3)
Lock, F. P. PR3339.C6.L6 1979, (v3)
Lock, G. S. H. GB2403.2.L63 1990, (v6)
    TJ260.L59 1994, (v1)
Lock, Graham. ML390.L79 1999, (v9)
Lock, Peter. DF609.L63 1995, (v5)
Lock, Shmuel. HV9950.L63 1999, (v6)
Lockard, Craig A. ML3502.A785.L6 1998, (v9)
Lockard, Duane. TN805.A5.L63 1998, (v1)
Locke, David M. Q225.5.L63 1992, (v1)
Locke, Edwin A. BF503.L63 1990, (v2)
Locke, Frederick W. PQ1475.L6, (v3)
Locke, Hubert G. BT93.L63 2000, (v8)
Locke, John. B1253. 1990, (v8)
    BR120.L62, (v8)
    JC153.L79 1947, (v7)
    JC153.L8 1967a, (v7)
    JC153.L85 2002, (v7)
    LB475.L6A2 1968, (v7)
    LB475.L6.S65 1988, (v7)
Locke, Karen D. HD30.4.L63 2001, (v6)
Locke, Nancy. ND553.M3.L63 2001, (v9)
Locke, Richard M. HC305.L64 1995, (v6)
Locke, Robert R. DC340.L6, (v5)
Locke-Elliott, Sumner. PR9619.3.E44.C3x, (v3)
Lockerd, Benjamin G. PS3509.L43.Z6933 1998, (v3)
Lockeretz, William. S540.A2.L63 1993, (v1)
Lockert, Lacy. PQ563.L6, (v3)
Lockhart, Greg. UA853.V5.L63 1989, (v10)
Lockhart, James. F1219.76.H57.L63 1991, (v4)
    F1221.N3.L63 1992, (v4)
    F1411.L792 1983, (v4)
Lockhart, Paul Douglas. D263.L63 1996, (v5)
Lockhart, Robert Hamilton Bruce. DK265.7.L6, (v5)

Lockheed, Marlaine E. LC2608.L63 1991, (v7)
Lockie, Andrew. RX73.L59 2001, (v2)
Lockley, M. G. QE845.L625 1995, (v1)
    QE845.L626 1999, (v1)
Lockley, Timothy James. F290.L63 2001, (v4)
Lockridge, Kenneth A. F74.D3.L83 1970, (v4)
Lockridge, Laurence S. PN603.L63 1989, (v3)
    PS3523.O246.Z74 1994, (v3)
Lockridge, Ross. PS3562.O274 R3, (v3)
Lockspeiser, Edward. ML410.D28.L8 1980, (v9)
Lockwood, E. H. QA483.L62, (v1)
Lockwood, Frank C. F810.L82, (v4)
    F811.L75, (v4)
Lockwood, Lewis. ML410.B4.L595 1992, (v9)
Lockwood, M. J. PR6023.A93.Z658 1987, (v3)
Lockwood, Victoria S. HN939.5.T34.L625 1992, (v6)
Lockyer, Judith. PS3511.A86.Z879 1991, (v3)
Lockyer, Roger. DA391.1.B9.L63 1981, (v5)
Lodder, Christina. N6988.5.C64.L63 1983, (v9)
Lodge, David. PR6013.R44.Z645, (v3)
Lodge, Henry Cabot. E748.L8.A37, (v4)
    E835.L57 1976, (v4)
Lodge, R. Anthony. PC2075.L75 1993, (v3)
Lodge, Rupert Clendon. B398.A4.L6, (v8)
    LB85.P7.L6 1970, (v7)
Lodge, Thomas. PR2297.A1 1963, (v3)
Lodish, Leonard M. HD62.5.L63 2001, (v6)
Loeb, Louis E. B801.L63, (v8)
Loeffelholz, Mary. PS1541.Z5.L596 1991, (v3)
Loehlin, John C. BF432.A1.L6, (v2)
Loescher, Gil. HV640.L62 1993, (v6)
Loesser, Arthur. ML650.L64 1990, (v9)
Loevenberg, Alfred. ML102.O6.L6 1978, (v9)
Loevenberg, Frank M. HV530.L6 1988, (v6)
Loewenberg, Jacob. B2929.L6, (v8)
Loewenberg, Peter. D16.16.L64 1983, (v5)
    D16.16.L65 1995, (v5)
Loewenstein, Andrea Freud. PR151.J5.L64 1993, (v3)
Loewy, Erich H. BJ1031.L59 1997, (v8)
    BJ1409.L64 1991, (v8)
    R724.L63 1986, (v2)
Loewy, Raymond. TS140.L63.A34 1979, (v1)
Loflin, Christine. PR9344.L64 1998, (v3)
Loftin, John D. E99.H7.L64 1991, (v4)
Loftis, John Clyde. PR693.L6, (v3)
    PR695.L6, (v3)
    PR714.P6.L6, (v3)
Loftness, Robert L. TJ163.235.L64 1984, (v1)
Logan, F. Donald. BX2592.L64 1996, (v8)
    DL65.L63 1983, (v5)
Logan, John R. HQ755.86.L64 1996, (v6)
Logan, Mary Simmerson (Cunningham). F194.L82,
    (v4)
Logan, Michael F. HT371.L64 1995, (v6)
Logan, Peter Melville. PR778.H95.L64 1997, (v3)
Logan, Rayford Whittingham. E185.61.L64 1965, (v4)
    E185.61.L65, (v4)
Logan, Shirley W. E185.86.L57 1999, (v4)
Logan, William Stewart. DS559.93.H36, (v5)
Logan, William. PS323.5.L645 1999, (v3)
Loggins, Vernon. CS71.H4 1951, (v5)
Logsdon, Joseph. E415.9.W395.L6, (v4)
Logstrup, K. E. BJ78.D3.L613 1997, (v8)
Logue, Barbara. R726.L6 1993, (v2)
Logue, Cal M. F291.T3.L64 1989, (v4)
Logue, Larry M. F834.S15.L64 1988, (v4)
Loimeier, Roman. BP64.N6.L65 1997, (v8)
Lojasiewicz, Stanislaw. QA331.L7913 1988, (v1)
Lomask, Milton. E302.6.B9.L7 1979, (v4)
Lomatuway'ma, Michael. E99.H7.L65 1993, (v4)
Lomawaima, K. Tsianina. E97.6.C4.L65 1994, (v4)
Lomax, Alan. ML410.M82 L6 2001, (v9)
    ML3521.L64 1993, (v9)
    ML3545.L63, (v9)
Lomax, John Avery. ML429.L68.A3 1947, (v9)
Lomax, Richard G. QA276.12.L66 1998, (v1)
    QA276.12.L67 2001, (v1)
Lomax, William. DB957.L6, (v5)

Lombardi, John V. F2321.L58 1982, (v4)
Lomborg, Bjørn. GE149.L65 2001, (v6)
Lomnitz, Cinna. QE538.8.L66 1994, (v1)
Lomnitz, Larissa Adler de. JL698.A1, (v7)
LoMonaco, Martha Schmoyer. PN2275.P4.L67 1992,
    (v3)
Lomont, John S. QA343.L68 2001, (v1)
Lomperis, Timothy J. DS558.L64 1996, (v5)
London, April. PR858.W6.L66 1999, (v3)
London, Barbara. TR145.L66 1998, (v1)
London, Bette Lynn. PR111.L66 1999, (v3)
London, Charmian. PS3523.O46Z7, (v3)
London, Jack. PS3523.O46 A6 1945, (v3)
    PS3523.O46.A6 1979, (v3)
    PS3523.O46.A6 1990, (v3)
    PS3523.O46.A6 1993, (v3)
    PS3523.O46.A6 1994, (v3)
    PS3523.O46 B6, (v3)
    PS3523.O46 B8 1910, (v3)
    PS3523.O46C3 1980, (v3)
    PS3523.O46 C5, (v3)
    PS3523.O46 C7 1963, (v3)
    PS3523.O46 C8, (v3)
    PS3523.O46 D3 1963, (v3)
    PS3523.O46 I7 1957, (v3)
    PS3523.O46.Mx, (v3)
    PS3523.O46.S5 1904, (v3)
    PS3523.O46.S6 1992, (v3)
    PS3523.O46 S65, (v3)
    PS3523.O46 S9 1963, (v3)
    PS3523.O46W5 1907, (v3)
    PS3523.O46.Z53, (v3)
London, Louise. DS135.E5.L66 2000, (v5)
London, Manuel. HF5381.L6558 1998, (v6)
Londre, Felicia Hardison. PN2219.5.L66 1998, (v3)
    PR6069.T6.Z75, (v3)
Lone, Stewart. DS765.L66 1994, (v5)
Loney, Norman W. TP155.2.M36, (v1)
Long, Carolyn Morrow. GR105.L58 2001, (v6)
Long, Carolyn Nestor. KF228.O74 L66 2000, (v7)
Long, David E. DS204.L65 1997, (v5)
Long, David. JX1395.L63 1996, (v7)
Long, Edward Le Roy. BJ1231.L66 1982, (v8)
Long, Helen C. NA7328.L66 1993, (v9)
Long, James W. DK34.G3.L66 1988, (v5)
Long, Jeff. F390.L63 1990, (v4)
Long, Kenneth R. ML3131.L6, (v9)
Long, Kim. D11.5.L64 1992, (v5)
    QL696.A558.L66 1997, (v1)
Long, Priscilla. HD8039.M62.U6444 1989, (v6)
Long, Ralph Bernard. PE1105.L66 1961, (v3)
Long, Richard A. GV1624.7.A34.L66 1989, (v6)
Long, Robert Emmet. PN1998.3.B47.L66 1994, (v3)
    PN1999.M38.L6 1991, (v3)
    PS3539.H94.Z76 1988, (v3)
Long, Roger D. Z3196.L66 1998, (v10)
Long, Rose-Carol Washton. ND699.K3.L66, (v9)
Long, Simon. DS799.816.L66 1990, (v5)
Longacre, Doris Janzen. TX715.L822 2000, (v1)
Longair, M. S. QC20.L66 1984, (v1)
Longair, M. S. QC485.8.O7.L66, (v1)
Longenbach, James. PS325.L66 1997, (v3)
    PS3537.T4753.Z6764 1991, (v3)
Longenecker, Stephen L. F334.S4.L66 1987, (v4)
Longfellow, Fanny Appleton. PS2281.L54, (v3)
Longfellow, Henry Wadsworth. PS2252.S37, (v3)
    PS2281.A3.H5, (v3)
Longfield, Bradley J. BX8937.L65 1991, (v8)
Longford, Elizabeth (Harman) Pakenham.
    DA68.12.W4.L62, (v5)
    PR4381.L6, (v3)
Longford, Frank Pakenham. D412.7.L66 1973b, (v5)
    DA965.D4.L6 1971, (v5)
Longhurst, Brian. BD175.L66 1989, (v8)
Longhurst, John Edward. DS135.S71.L815, (v5)
Longinus. PA4229.L4 1964, (v3)
Longley, Kyle. E183.8.C8.L66 1997, (v4)
Longley, Lawrence D. JK1111.L65 1989, (v7)
Longmore, Donald. RD130.L64 1968, (v2)
Longmore, Paul K. E312.17.L84 1988, (v4)
Longrigg, Roger. PR6062.O516.S9 1957, (v3)

Longrigg, Stephen Hemsley. DS70.6.L6, (v5)
Longshore, David. QC944.L66 1998, (v1)
Longstreet, James. E470.L85 1969, (v4)
Longstreth, Richard W. HF5429.5.L7.L663 1999, (v6)
Longworth, Philip. DK118.L66 1984, (v5)
Longyard, William H. TL539.L57 1994, (v1)
Longyear, Rey M. ML196.L65 1988, (v9)
Lonnroth, Lars. PT7269.N5.L6, (v3)
Lonsdale, Hugh Cecil Lowther. F1060.9.L66 1989, (v4)
Lonsdale, Sarah. DS822.5 .L65 2001, (v5)
Looby, Christopher. PS193.L66 1996, (v3)
Look Lai, Walton. HD8039.S86.W475 1993, (v6)
Loomie, Albert J. DP86.G7.L6, (v5)
Loomis, David. UA26.N4.L66 1993, (v10)
Loomis, Frederic Brewster. QE375.L6, (v1)
Loomis, John A. NA6602.A76.L66 1999, (v9)
Loomis, John B. HD221.L66 2002, (v6)
Loomis, Laura Alandis (Hibbard). PR321.L6 1969, (v3)
Loomis, R. S. S589.7.L66 1992, (v1)
Loomis, Roger Sherman. PN57.A6.L6, (v3)
    PR1120.L6, (v3)
Loomis, William F. QH371.L65 1988, (v1)
Looney, Robert E. HC440.5.L66 1997, (v6)
Loos, Anita. PS3523.O557 G4 1963, (v3)
Loose, Gerhard. PT2619.U43.Z66, (v3)
Looser, Devoney. DA1.L66 2000, (v5)
Lopach, James J. E78.M9 L67 1998, (v4)
Lopata, Helena Znaniecka. HQ1058.L64 1996, (v6)
    HQ1420.L66, (v6)
Lopate, Carol. R692.L65, (v2)
LoPatin, Nancy D. JN543.L66 1999, (v7)
Lopez, Alfred J. PN98.P62.L67 2001, (v3)
Lopez, Barry Holstun. PS3562.O67.R5, (v3)
Lopez, Daniel. PN1998.L63 1993, (v3)
Lopez, Donald S. BQ4012.L65 2001, (v8)
    BQ7604.L66 1998, (v8)
Lopez, Gerald P. KF390.5.P78.L66 1992, (v7)
Lopez, Manuel D. Z3108.L5.L67 1991, (v10)
Lopez, Nancy. GV964.L67.A33, (v6)
Lopez-Alves, Fernando. JL1860.L66 2000, (v7)
Lopez-Rey, Jose. ND813.V4.L627 1968b, (v9)
Lopez-Stafford, Gloria. F394.E4.L67 1996, (v4)
Lorand, Sandor. RC506.L58, (v2)
Lorange, Peter. HD2755.5.L67 1992, (v6)
Loraux, Nicole. JC75.C5L6713 2000, (v7)
Lorcin, Patricia M. E. DT298.K2.L57 1995, (v5)
Lord, Albert Bates. GR72.L66 1991, (v6)
    PN1303.L62, (v3)
    PN1341.L67 1995, (v3)
Lord, Carnes. UA23.L7 1988, (v10)
Lord, Charles R. T10.7.L67 2000, (v1)
Lord, George de Forest. PR3546.L6, (v3)
Lord, Israel Shipman Pelton. F597.L86 1995, (v4)
Lord, Robert Howard. DK434.L7 1969, (v5)
Lord, Walter. F390.L66 1987, (v4)
    G530.T6.L6, (v6)
Lorde, Audre. PS3562.O75.A17 1997, (v3)
    PS3562.O75.M37 1993, (v3)
Lorelli, John A. D769.45.L67 1995, (v5)
Lorence, James J. E748.B645.L67 1994, (v4)
    PN1997.S14.L67 1999, (v3)
Lorentz, H. A. QC721.L88, (v1)
Lorentz, Pare. PN1998.3.L67.A3 1992, (v3)
Lorenz, Albert. GR940.L67 1999, (v6)
Lorenz, Richard. TR140.C78.L67 1993, (v1)
Lorey, David E. F787.L67 1999, (v4)
Lorimer, Rowland. HM258.L674 1994, (v6)
Lorin, Harold. QA76.6.L639, (v1)
Loring, John. NK7398.F37, (v9)
Lorriman, John. HD70.J3.L67 1994, (v6)
Lorwin, Lewis Levitzki. HD8055.A5.L6 1972, (v6)
Lory, Hillis. UA845.L6, (v10)
Los Angeles County Museum of Art. F1219.3.A7.L6 1989, (v4)
    N6505.L6 1991, (v9)
    NK4008.L67 1990, (v9)
Los, Maria. HN537.5.L67 2000, (v6)
Loshitzky, Yosefa. PN1998.3.G63.L67 1995, (v3)
Losonsky, Michael. B801.L67 2001, (v8)

Loss, Archie K. PR6025.A86.O56 1990, (v3)
Losse, Deborah N. PQ643.L67 1994, (v3)
Lotchin, Roger W. F869.S3.L82, (v4)
    HD9743.U7.C25 1992, (v6)
Lote, Christopher J. QP249.L67 2000, (v1)
Loth, David Goldsmith. KF8745.M3.L6 1949, (v7)
Loth, Wilfried. DD286.5.L6713 1998, (v5)
Lothe, Jakob. PR6005.O4.Z7664 1989, (v3)
Loti, Pierre. PQ2472.M2 1893, (v3)
Lott, Eric J. B132.V3.L62 1980, (v8)
Lott, Eric. ML1711.L67 1993, (v9)
Lotte, Fernand. PQ2159.C72.L6, (v3)
Lottman, Herbert R. DC342.8.P4.L67 1985, (v5)
    PQ2605.A3734Z698, (v3)
    PQ2605.A3734.Z698, (v3)
Lotz, Roy. PN4888.C8.L67 1991, (v3)
Lotz, Wolfgang. NA1115.L666 1995, (v9)
Loubere, J. A. E. PQ2637.I547.Z79, (v3)
Loud, G. A. DG867.215.R64, (v5)
Loud, Pat. CT275.L69244.A36, (v5)
Loud, Patricia Cummings. NA6695.L68 1989, (v9)
Louda, Jiri. CR1605.L68 1991, (v5)
Louden, Robert B. BJ1012.L67 1992, (v8)
Loudon, Irvine. RG516.L68 1992, (v2)
Loue, Sana. HV6626.L677 2001, (v6)
    RA448.4.L68 1999, (v2)
Lougee, Carolyn C. HQ1616.L68, (v6)
Lough, John. JA84.F8.L65 1982, (v7)
    PQ146.L66, (v3)
Lougheed, W. C. Z1379.L68 1988, (v10)
Loughery, John. HQ76.2.U5.L68 1998, (v6)
    ND237.S57.L68 1995, (v9)
Loughlin, James. DA990.U46.L687 1998, (v5)
Lougy, Robert E. Z8230.L68 1990, (v10)
Louis, Margot Kathleen. PR5517.R4.L68 1990, (v3)
Louis-Frederic. NA6001.L613, (v9)
Loukaitou-Sideris, Anastasia. HT167.5.C2.L68 1998, (v6)
Lounsberry, Clement A. F636.L892, (v4)
Lounsberry, Clement Augustus. F636.L89, (v4)
Lounsbury, Carl. NA4473.C48, (v9)
Lounsbury, Floyd G. PM2073.L6 1976, (v3)
Loureiro, Angel G. PQ6137.L68 2000, (v3)
Loustaunau, Martha O. GN296.L68 1997, (v6)
Louthan, Doniphan. PR2248.L6 1951, (v3)
Louvish, Simon. PN1997.I7573.L68 1994, (v3)
Louw, Eric. QA76.76.C68.L68 1992, (v1)
Loux, Ann Kimble. HV875.55.L68 1997, (v6)
Loux, Michael J. BD131.L83 2001, (v8)
Louys, Pierre. PQ2623.O8.A27, (v3)
    PQ2623.O8.C5 1932, (v3)
    PQ2623.O8.P6, (v3)
Love, Glen A. PS3523.E94.B297 1993, (v3)
Love, Jean O. PR6045.O72.Z812, (v3)
Love, John A. QL737.C25.L68 1992, (v1)
Love, Joseph LeRoy. HC405.L68 1996, (v6)
Love, Nat. F594.L89. 1968, (v4)
Love, Rosaleen. QH197.L68 2001, (v1)
Love, Spencie. RD27.35.D74.L68 1996, (v2)
Lovecraft, H. P. PS3523.O833.Z48 2000, (v3)
    PS3523.O833.Z543 1975, (v3)
Lovejoy, Arthur O. B945.L583 R48 1996, (v8)
    CB53.L58, (v5)
Lovejoy, David S. F82.L68, (v4)
Lovelace, Ada King, Countess of. QA29.L72A4, (v1)
Lovelace, Richard. PR3542.L2 1925, (v3)
Loveland, Anne C. BR1644.5.U6.L68 1996, (v8)
Lovell, Bernard. QB51.L6, (v1)
Lovell, Ernest James. PR4392.N3.L6 1966, (v3)
Lovell, Jim. TL789.8U6A5488 1994, (v1)
Lovell, John P. U408.L67, (v10)
Lovell, Mary S. G246.B8.L68 1998, (v6)
Lovell, Stephen. Z1003.5.R9.L68 2000, (v10)
Loveman, Brian. F3081.L68, (v4)
    HD505.L68 1975, (v6)
Loveman, Brian. JL952.L68 1993, (v7)
Lovenduski, Joni. HQ1236.5.G7.L68 1993, (v6)
Loveridge, Mark. PR448.F34.L68 1998, (v3)
Lovesey, Oliver. PR9381.9.N45.Z76 2000, (v3)
Lovett, Bobby L. F444.N29.N45 1999, (v4)

Lovett, Charles C. GV1065.L69 1997, (v6)
    PR4611.A73.L68 1990, (v3)
Lovett, Clara Maria. DG552.5.L68, (v5)
    DG552.8.C25.L68, (v5)
Lovett, John R. E98.A7 L68 1998, (v4)
Lovett, Patricia. Z43.L86 2000, (v10)
Lovett, Robert Morss. PR55.L6.A3, (v3)
    PR821.L7, (v3)
Lovett, Robert W. Z8221.L68 1991, (v10)
Lovette, Leland Pearson. V310.L6 1959, (v10)
Lovin, Robin W. BX4827.N5.L68 1995, (v8)
Loving, Jerome. PS201.L64 1993, (v3)
    PS3231.L68 1999, (v3)
Lovinger, Paul W. PE1464.L68 2000, (v3)
Lovoll, Odd Sverre. E184.S2.L686 1998, (v4)
Low, Alfred D. DS740.5.S65.L68 1987, (v5)
Low, Ann Marie. F636.L92 1984, (v4)
Low, Anthony. PR535.L7.L68 1993, (v3)
Low, Bobbi S. GN281.4.L68 2000, (v6)
Low, D. A. DA16.L8684 1990, (v5)
Low, Donald A. PR4338.L6, (v3)
Low, Setha M. F1410.L69 2000, (v4)
Lowden, Pamela. JC599.C5.L69 1996, (v7)
Lowe, Barrett. F651.B367, (v4)
Lowe, Benjamin. GV706.L59, (v6)
Lowe, Christopher. DA880.P25.L69 1998, (v5)
Lowe, Denise. PN1992.8.W65.L69 1999, (v3)
Lowe, E. J. BD418.3.L69 2000, (v8)
    BD450.L65 1996, (v8)
Lowe, James A. F767.O94 L69 1999, (v4)
Lowe, James. PS3501.G35.Z77 1994, (v3)
Lowe, Janet. HD9697.A3.U588 2001, (v6)
Lowe, Lisa. PQ143.O75.L6 1992, (v3)
Lowe, N. J. PA3014.N37, (v3)
Lowe, Peter. DS518.4.L675 1981, (v5)
    DS518.4.L676 1997, (v5)
Lowe, Richard G. F231.L68 1991, (v4)
Lowe, Rodney. HD8390.L68 1986, (v6)
    HN383.5.L69 1999, (v6)
Lowe, Sarah M. TR647.M554.L69 1995, (v1)
Lowe, Stephen R. GV583.L696 1995, (v6)
    GV964.H3.L69 2000, (v6)
Lowe, Walter James. BR118.L69 1993, (v8)
Lowe, William T. LB1530.L6, (v7)
Lowe-Evans, Mary. PR5397.F73.L68 1993, (v3)
Lowell, Amy. PS3523.O88.A6 1928, (v3)
    PS3523.O88.C3 1918, (v3)
    PS3523.O88.E2 1926, (v3)
    PS3523.O88.W5 1925, (v3)
Lowell, James Russell. PS2302.C5, (v3)
    PS2302.C53, (v3)
    PS2305.S5, (v3)
Lowell, Robert. PS3523.O89.A17 1976, (v3)
    PS3523.O89.A6 1969, (v3)
    PS3523.O89.D39 1977, (v3)
    PS3523.O89.F6, (v3)
    PS3523.O89.L5, (v3)
    PS3523.O89.L6, (v3)
    PS3523.O89.M5, (v3)
    PS3523.O89.N4, (v3)
    PS3523.O89.O4 1968, (v3)
Lowen, Rebecca S. LD3030.L68 1997, (v7)
Lowen, Tirzah. PR2802.L69 1990, (v3)
Lowenberg, Anton David. DT1757.L685 1998, (v5)
Lowenberg, Carlton. ML134.5.D5 L7 1992, (v9)
Lowenstein, Jerome. R727.3.L68 1997, (v2)
    RC630.L68 1992, (v2)
Lowenstein, Roger. HG172.B84.L69 1995, (v6)
    HG4930.L69 2000, (v6)
Lowenstein, Steven M. DS135.G4.B46725 1994, (v5)
    F128.9.J5.L69 1989, (v4)
Lowenthal, Cynthia. DA501.M7.L68 1994, (v5)
Lowenthal, David. E415.9.M185.L6 2000, (v4)
    KF4770.L68 1997, (v7)
Lowenthal, Leo. HM22.U6.L698 1987, (v6)
    PN51.L58 1970, (v3)
    PN511.L69, (v3)
Lowenthal, Marjorie Fiske. BF724.55.A35.L68 1990, (v2)
Lowenthal, Mark M. Z6724.I7.L69 1994, (v10)

Lower, Arthur Reginald Marsden. DS518.9.C3.L6 1973, (v5)
  F1021.L67, (v4)
  F1026.L75 1947, (v4)
Lower, Cheryl Bray. PN1998.3.M35.B73 2001, (v3)
Lower, J. Arthur. DS511.L68, (v5)
Lower, Richard Coke. E748.J73.L68 1993, (v4)
Lowes, John Livingston. PN1031.L8, (v3)
  PR1924.L63 1944, (v3)
  PR4484.L6 1964, (v3)
Lowes, Mark Douglas. PN4914.S65.L69 1999, (v3)
Lowi, Theodore J. HM276.L57 1979, (v6)
Lowinsky, Edward E. ML160.L83 1989, (v9)
Lowitt, Richard. E748.N65 L6 1980, (v4)
  E748.N65.L62, (v4)
  HC107.A17.L68 1984, (v6)
Lowman, Charles Leroy. QP301.L68, (v1)
Lowney, John. PS3545.I544.Z62 1997, (v3)
Lowrie, Michele. PA6411.L69 1997, (v3)
Lowry, Bates. N7425.L88, (v9)
  NA510.L6, (v9)
Lowry, Bullitt. D641.L68 1996, (v5)
Lowry, Malcolm. PR6023.O96 D3, (v3)
  PR6023.O96 H4, (v3)
  PR6023.O96 U4 1962, (v3)
  PR6023.O96 U5, (v3)
Lowry, Martin. Z232.J54.L69 1991, (v10)
Lowry, Richard S. PS1336.L68 1996, (v3)
Lowry, Richard. QA273.L685 1989, (v1)
Lowry, S. Todd. HB108.A2.L68 1987, (v6)
Lowry, Terry. E536.9.L69 2000, (v4)
Lowry, Thomas H. QD476.L68 1987, (v1)
Lowry, William R. HC110.P55.L68 1991, (v6)
  SB421.L72 1998, (v1)
  SB482.A4.L68 1994, (v1)
Lowy, Michael. BT83.57.L69 1996, (v8)
Loyer, Francois. NA1050.L6713 1988, (v9)
  NA9094.8.L6913 1983, (v9)
Loza, Steven Joseph. ML419.P82.L6 1999, (v9)
  ML3558.L69 1992, (v9)
Lozano, Beverly. HD2336.U5.L69 1989, (v6)
Lozovsky, Natalia. G89.L68 2000, (v6)
Lu, Chi. PL2997.L67.A75, (v3)
Lu, Hanchao. DS796.S25.L8 1999, (v5)
Lu, Hsiao-peng. DS734.7.L8 1994, (v5)
Lu, Hsun. PL2415.C513 1973, (v3)
  PL2754.S5.A25 1990, (v3)
  PL2754.S5.A29 1973, (v3)
  PL2754.S5.A294 1981, (v3)
Lu, L. TN698.L85 1998, (v1)
Lu, Ning. JZ1730.L8 1997, (v7)
  TA1637.L8 1997, (v1)
Lu, Tonglin. PL2443.L8 1995, (v3)
Lü, Tung-pin. BL1923.L78 1991, (v8)
Lu, Xiaobo. JQ1509.5.C6 L8 2000, (v7)
Lu, Xun. PL2658.E8L8 1983, (v3)
Lu, Yu. PL2997.L72.Y6, (v3)
Luard, Evan. D217.L82 1991, (v5)
  H85.L83 1990, (v6)
  HM36.5.L8 1987, (v6)
Luard, Evan. JX1391.L83 1990, (v7)
Luban, David. KF306.L83 1988, (v7)
Lubarsky, Sandra B. BM535.L76 1990, (v8)
Lubbe, J. C. A. van der. QA76.9.A25.L83 1998, (v1)
Lubbock, Francis Richard. F386.L92 1969, (v4)
Lubbock, Percy. PR6023.U22.A6 1957, (v3)
Lubet, Steven. KF384.Z9, (v7)
Lubin, David M. ND210.L83 1994, (v9)
Lublin, David. JK1341.L83 1997, (v7)
Lubove, Roy. HV91.L8, (v6)
Lubow, Arthur. PS1523.L8 1992, (v3)
Lucan. PA6479.E5.G7 1957, (v3)
Lucas, Angela M. HQ1147.G7.L82 1983, (v6)
Lucas, Christopher J. LB1715.L73 1997, (v7)
Lucas, Henry Stephen. CB53.L8 1953, (v5)
Lucas, Henry Stephen. CB359.L8 1960, (v5)
Lucas, J. R. BD638.L83 1989, (v8)
Lucas, James Sidney. D766.9.L83 1982b, (v5)
Lucas, John A. GV721.6.L83 1992, (v6)
Lucas, John. DA578.L77 1999, (v5)
  PR508.N2.L8 1990, (v3)

Lucas, Marion Brunson. E185.93.K3 L83 1992, (v4)
Lucas, Michael R. UA23.L83 1990, (v10)
Lucas, Oliver W. R. SB475.9.F67.L83 1990, (v1)
Lucas, Robert E. HB3711.L83, (v6)
  HD75.L824 2002, (v6)
Lucas, Rose. PR9608.L83 1996, (v3)
Lucas, Samuel Roundfield. LC191.4.L85 1999, (v7)
Lucassen, Leo. DX145.L83 1998, (v5)
Luce, Gay Gaer. QP425.L82, (v1)
Luce, John Victor. B171.L83 1992, (v8)
Luce, R. Duncan. BF39.L79 1963, (v2)
  BF39.L83, (v2)
Lucero, Helen R. F805.S75.L83 1999, (v4)
Lucey, Michael. PQ2613.I2Z6534 1995, (v3)
Luciak, Ilja A. HC146.L83 1995, (v6)
Luciano, Lynne. BF697.5.B63L83 2001, (v2)
Lucic, Karen. ND237.S47.L82 1997, (v9)
Lucie-Smith, Edward. DC103.L96 1977, (v5)
  N6489.L83 1999, (v9)
  N6490.L792 1997, (v9)
  N6502.5.L83 1993, (v9)
  N7429.4.L83 1994, (v9)
  NB198.L83 1987, (v9)
  NK600.L8 1984, (v9)
  NK2270.L82 1979, (v9)
Luckenbill, Daniel David. DS68.L8 1968, (v5)
Lucker, Andrew M. JC251.K49, (v7)
Luckhardt, C. Grant. BC177.L83 1994, (v8)
Luckingham, Bradford. F819.P57.L83 1989, (v4)
Luckmann, Joan. RT23.L83 1999, (v2)
Lucky, R.W. Q360.L84 1989, (v1)
Luckyj, Christina. PR3188.T4.L83 1989, (v3)
Luckyj, George Stephen Nestor. PG3916.2.L83 1992, (v3)
Luconi, Stefano. F158.9.I8.L83 2001, (v4)
Lucotte, Gerard. QH442.2.L8313 1993, (v1)
Lucy, Niall. PN94.L83 1997, (v3)
Lucy, William H. HT352.U6.L83 2000, (v6)
Ludden, David E. DS436.N47 1999 pt.4, vol.4, (v5)
Luddy, Maria. HV541.L83 1995, (v6)
Ludema, K. C. TJ1075.L82 1996, (v1)
Ludeman, Lonnie C. TK5102.5.L83 1986, (v1)
Ludendorff, Erich. D531.L7713 1971, (v5)
Luderer, Bernd. HB135.L83 2002, (v6)
Ludlow, N. Piers. KJE4443.41972.A3.L83 1997, (v7)
Ludlow, Peter. QA76.9.C66.L84 1996, (v1)
Ludlum, David McWilliams. QC857.U6.H56 no.1, (v1)
  QC857.U6.H56 no. 2, (v1)
  QC857.U6.H56 no. 4, (v1)
Ludman, Joan. N6537.P63.A4 2001, (v9)
Ludmerer, Kenneth M. R745.L843 1999, (v2)
Ludowyk, E. F. C. PR2894.L8, (v3)
Ludtke, Melissa. HQ759.45.L83 1997, (v6)
Ludwig, Arnold M. BF423.L83 1995, (v2)
Ludwig, Jack Barry. PS3523.U38.Co, (v3)
Ludwig, Theodore M. BL80.2.L83 2001, (v8)
Ludwikowski, Rett R. JN6766.L84 1991, (v7)
Ludwikowski, Rett R. KJC4445.L83 1996, (v7)
Luebke, David Martin. DD801.B64.L84 1997, (v5)
Luebke, Frederick C. F666.L83 1995, (v4)
  F2659.G3.L84 1987, (v4)
Luecking, D. H. QA331.L818 1984, (v1)
Luening, Otto. ML410.L947.A3, (v9)
Lufrano, Richard John. HF3834.L84 1997, (v6)
Luft, David S. PT2625.U8.Z795, (v3)
Luftig, Victor. PR468.M36.L85 1993, (v3)
Lugalla, Joe. HT384.T34.L84 1995, (v6)
Luger, Michael I. HC110.R4.L84 1991, (v6)
  KF5730.L84 2000, (v7)
Luginbuhl, Christian B. QB64.L84 1990, (v1)
Lugones, Leopoldo. PQ7797.L85 1948, (v3)
Luhan, Mabel Dodge. CT275.L838.A3 1999, (v5)
  CT275.L838.A4 1996, (v5)
Luhmann, Niklas. BH39.L8313 2000, (v8)
  HM256.L8413 1993, (v6)
Luhrmann, T. M. RC336.L78 2000, (v2)
Lui, Hsin-ju. HD9926.E92.L85 1996, (v6)
Luijpen, W. B829.5.L8132, (v8)
Luis, William. PS153.C27.L85 1997, (v3)
Lukacher, Maryline. PQ653.L84 1994, (v3)

Lukacher, Ned. PR3069.C56.L84 1994, (v3)
Lukacs, Gyorgy. HX40.L7913 1991, (v6)
Lukacs, John A. D1055.L8, (v5)
Lukacs, John. D421.L85 1993, (v5)
  D759.L84 1991, (v5)
  D840.L8 1966, (v5)
Lukacs, Paul. TP557.L87 2000, (v1)
Lukacs, Yehuda. DS119.8.J67.L85 1997, (v5)
Lukas, J. Anthony. E860.L84 1999, (v4)
  F73.9.A1.L85 1985, (v4)
Luke, Carmen. LA721.4.L84 1989, (v7)
Luke, Harry. DR440 .L8 1955, (v5)
Luker, Kristin. HQ767.5.U5.L84 1984, (v6)
Luker, Ralph. E185.61.L84 1997, (v4)
  E185.61.L85 1991, (v4)
Lukes, Igor. DB2078.G3.L85 1996, (v5)
Lukes, Steven. BJ1390.L79 1988, (v8)
  HM22.F8.D845 1972, (v6)
Lukic, Reneo. DJK51.L85 1996, (v5)
Lukin, Alexander. JN6699.A15 L85 2000, (v7)
Lukitz, Liora. DS79.L85 1995, (v5)
Lukowski, Jerzy. DK4314.5.L84 1991, (v5)
Lulat, Y. G.-M. Z6465.U5 L84 1991, (v10)
Lule, Jack. PN4759.L85 2001, (v3)
Lumiansky, R. M. PR1874.L8, (v3)
  PR2045.L8, (v3)
Lumley, John L. (John Leask). TJ755.L94 1999, (v1)
Lumley, Robert. DG577.5.L86 1990, (v5)
Lummis, C. Douglas. JC421.L86 1996, (v7)
Lummis, Charles Fletcher. E83.88.L85 1979, (v4)
  F786.L935, (v4)
Lumsdaine, David Halloran. HC60.L86 1993, (v6)
Lumsdaine, Joycelyn Pang. NE539.D44.A4 1987, (v9)
Lund, Erik A. U43.E95.L86 1999, (v10)
Lund, Helen S. DF235.48.L97.L86 1992, (v5)
Lund, Michael S. JX4473.L86 1996, (v7)
Lundahl, Mats. HD2126.L86 1990, (v6)
Lundberg, Erik. HC54.L85, (v6)
Lundeen, Kathleen. PR4148.P5, (v3)
Lundestad, Geir. D843.L8413 1999, (v5)
Lundin, Roger. PS1541.Z5.L86 1998, (v3)
Lungo, Mario. F1488.3.L8713 1996, (v4)
Lunn, Mary. QA807.L95 1991, (v1)
Lunsford, Andrea A. PE1112.L86 1989, (v3)
Lunt, Susie. DB2711.L86 2000, (v5)
  Z2137.P68.L86 1997, (v10)
Luntley, Michael. B105.T54.L86 1999, (v8)
Luo, Zhaohui. QA76.L79 1994, (v1)
Lupack, Alan. PS169.A9.L86 1999, (v3)
Lupack, Barbara Tepa. PS374.M44.L87 1995, (v3)
Lupher, Mark. HN740.Z9.P65 1996, (v6)
Lupia, Arthur. JA76.L86 1998, (v7)
Luppino, Grace A. KF505.Z9L87 2002, (v7)
Lupton, Ellen. NC1002.L47.L87 1996, (v9)
  Z246.L86 1996, (v10)
Luraghi, Raimondo. E596.L8713 1996, (v4)
Luria, Maxwell. PR1187.L8, (v3)
Lurie, Adolph G. HG4028.B2.L87 1984, (v6)
Lurie, Edward. QH31.A2.L8, (v1)
Lurie, Jonathan. KF7667.L87 1992, (v7)
Lurie, Nancy Oestreich. E78.W8 L87 2002, (v4)
Lurieiia, Aleksandr Romanovich. QP383.L87 1980, (v1)
Lury, Celia. HC79.C6.L87 1996, (v6)
Lusardi, James P. PR2819.L8 1990, (v3)
Luscombe, D. E. B721.L87 1997, (v8)
Lusebrink, Hans-Jurgen. DC167.5.L8713 1997, (v5)
Lusky, Louis. KF8748.L83 1993, (v7)
Lust, Annette. PN1942.L87 2000, (v3)
Lustick, Ian. JX4088.L87 1993, (v7)
Lustig, Nora. HC135.L87 1998, (v6)
Lustig, T. J. PS2127.O25.L87 1994, (v3)
Lutes, Della (Thompson). PS3523.U62 G3, (v3)
Luther, Martin. BJ1460.L8 1957a, (v8)
  BR331.E5.W6, (v8)
  BR331.E5 1989a, (v8)
Lutholtz, M. William. HS2330.K63.L87 1991, (v6)
Lutkehaus, Nancy. DU740.42.L88 1995, (v5)
Lutterbie, John Harry. PN1851.L88 1997, (v3)
Luttge, Ulrich. QK936.L88 1997, (v1)
Luttrell, Barbara. DC146.M7.L95 1990, (v5)

Luttwak, Edward. HF1455.L88 1993, (v6)
U24.L93 1991, (v10)
U35.L8, (v10)
U162.L87, (v10)
Lutz, Alma. LA2317.W5.L82 1964, (v7)
Lutz, Carroll A. RM217.L88 2001, (v2)
Lutz, Catherine. GN671.C3.L87 1988, (v6)
Lutz, Christopher. HB3539.A83.L87 1994, (v6)
Lutz, Donald S. JA84.U5.L88 1992, (v7)
KF4541.L87 1988, (v7)
Lutz, Friedrich A. HB501.L93 1969, (v6)
HB539.L813, (v6)
Lutz, Norma Jean. F67.M4738 2001, (v4)
Lutz, Ralph Haswell. DD228.8.L8 1969, (v5)
Lutz, William. PE2832.L88 1994, (v3)
Lutze, Peter C. PN1998.3.K598.L88 1998, (v3)
Lutzker, Marilyn. LB2369.L83 1988, (v7)
Lux, David Stephan. Q46.L89 1989, (v1)
Luxenberg, Stan. HF5429.235.U5.L88 1985, (v6)
Luxon, Thomas H. PR3332.L89 1995, (v3)
Luza, Radomir. DB99.L89 (v5)
Lyas, Colin. BH39.L95 1997, (v8)
Lycan, William G. BD215.L92 1988, (v8)
Lydall, Harold. HC407.L95 1989, (v6)
Lydgate, John. PR1119.E5 no.107, (v3)
PR2034.L9 1961, (v3)
Lydon, Mary. PQ45.L93 1995, (v3)
Lyell, William A. PL2754.S5.Z759, (v3)
Lyftogt, Kenneth. F629.C3.L94 1993, (v4)
Lykken, David Thoreson. RC555.L95 1995, (v2)
Lyly, John. PR2300.A2 1997, (v3)
Lyly, John. PR2659.L9.A12 1988, (v3)
Lyman, Stanford M. E184.A1.L95 1994, (v4)
HM73.L95 1997, (v6)
Lyman, Stanley David. E99.O3.L96 1991, (v4)
Lyman, Warren J. QD271.L95 1990, (v1)
Lynch, Andrew. PR2047.L96 1997, (v3)
Lynch, David K. QC355.2.L96 1995, (v1)
Lynch, Deidre. PR858.C47.L94 1998, (v3)
Lynch, Edward A. BT83.57.L95 1991, (v8)
JL969.A45 L96 1993, (v7)
Lynch, J. M. QH541.15.M64.L95 1998, (v1)
Lynch, Jack. Z8455.8.L96 2000, (v10)
Lynch, James Jeremiah. PE1068.U5.L93, (v3)
Lynch, Jerry. GV711.L96 2001, (v6)
Lynch, John Roy. F341.L97.A3, (v4)
Lynch, John. DP182.L96 1992, (v5)
F1412.L94 1992, (v4)
F1412.L96 1973, (v4)
F3011.T28.L94 1998, (v4)
JL950.L9 1969, (v7)
Lynch, Joseph H. BV1478.L96 1986, (v8)
Lynch, Joseph M. KF4510.L96 1999, (v7)
Lynch, Kathryn L. PN690.D73.L96 1988, (v3)
Lynch, Kevin. CB155.L95, (v5)
NA9085.L96.A4 1990, (v9)
NA9108.L9, (v9)
Lynch, Lawrence W. PQ2063.S3.L9 1984, (v3)
Lynch, Michael P. BD171.L87 1998, (v8)
Lynch, Michael. E876.L96 1996, (v4)
Lynch, Nancy A. (Nancy Ann.). QA76.9.A43L96 1997, (v1)
Lynch, Patrick J. TK5105.888.L96 1999, (v1)
Lynch, Richard Chigley. ML19.L9 1994, (v9)
Lynch, Stephen J. PR2952.L96 1998, (v3)
Lynd, Robert Staughton. HN57.L8 1929, (v6)
HN57.L84, (v6)
Lynd, Staughton. E302.1.L9, (v4)
HN90.R3.L93 1997, (v6)
Lynes, Barbara Buhler. ND237.O5.L96 1989, (v9)
Lynn, Conrad J. KF373.L96 A3 1993, (v7)
Lynn, Edward S. HJ9777.A3.L95 1983, (v6)
Lynn, John A. UA702.L95 1984, (v10)
UA702.L9523 1997, (v10)
Lynn, Kenneth Schuyler. PN2287.C5.L94 1997, (v3)
Lynn, Laurence E. JF1338.A3.U56 1996, (v7)
Lynn, Loretta. ML420.L947.A3, (v9)
Lynn, Martha Drexler. NK4210.S367.A4 1993, (v9)
Lynn, Martin. HD9490.5.P343.A3585 1997, (v6)
Lynn, Steven. PR3537.T4.L96 1992, (v3)
Lynn, Susan. HQ1236.5.U6.L96 1992, (v6)

Lynton, E. A. QC612.S8.L9 1969, (v1)
Lynton, Norbert. N6490.L93 1980b, (v9)
Lyon, Danny. E185.615.L96 1992, (v4)
Lyon, David. TK7882.E2.L96 1994, (v1)
Lyon, Eugene. F314.L98 1976, (v4)
Lyon, Henry C. E523.5 34th.L96 1999, (v4)
Lyon, J. G. QH104.L95 1993, (v1)
Lyon, James K. PT2603.R397.Z74593, (v3)
Lyon, Janet. PN51.L936 1999, (v3)
Lyon, Jeff. RB155.8.L96 1995, (v2)
RJ253.5.L96 1985, (v2)
Lyon, John. PR2825.L96 1988, (v3)
Lyon, Leverett S. HC106.3.L9, (v6)
Lyon, Peyton V. F1034.2.L93, (v4)
Lyon, William S. E98.M4.L96 1996, (v4)
E98.M4.L98 1998, (v4)
Lyons, Albert S. R131.L95, (v2)
Lyons, Bridget Gellert. PR411.L9, (v3)
Lyons, Charles R. PT8868.L96 1990, (v3)
Lyons, Charles. PN1995.62.L96 1997, (v3)
Lyons, Daniel J. Z118.L96 2000, (v10)
Lyons, David. BJ55.L95 1984, (v8)
Lyons, Eugene. E802.L82 1989, (v4)
Lyons, F. S. L. DA951.L94 1971b, (v5)
DA958.P2.L89, (v5)
DA958.P2.L9, (v5)
Lyons, Gene Martin. U428.5.L9, (v10)
UA3.L95, (v10)
Lyons, Joseph. BF698.3.L94 1987, (v2)
Lyons, Leonard. ML394.L97 1989, (v9)
Lyons, Louis. QA39.2.L97 1995, (v1)
Lyons, M. C. PJ7580.L86 1995, (v3)
Lyons, Martyn. DC186.L9, (v5)
DC201.L96 1994, (v5)
Lyons, Nathan. TR185.L9, (v1)
Lyons, Paul. HN59.L96 1996, (v6)
Lyons, Phyllis I. PL825.A8.Z74117 1985, (v3)
Lyons, Sherrie Lynne. QH31.H9.L96 1999, (v1)
Lyons, William E. B105.I56 L86 1995, (v8)
Lyons, William. HV7936.C83.L86 1999, (v6)
Lyotard, Jean Francois. B3279.H49.L9613 1990, (v8)
Lyra, Carmen. PQ7489.L9, (v3)
Lytle, Andrew Nelson. PS3523.Y88 N6, (v3)
Lytton, Edward Bulwer Lytton. PR4905.A2 P8, (v3)
PR4919.A1 1961, (v3)
M̄ agh̄ uòt, Muòhammad. PJ7846.A43A24 1991, (v3)
M̄ inah, òHann̄ a. PJ7846.I48F73 1993, (v3)
M̄ ir, M̄ ir Taq̄ i. PK2198.M49A24 1997, (v3)
Ma, L. Eve Armentrout. E29.C5.M3 1990, (v4)
Ma, Sheng-mei. E184.O6.M22 2000, (v4)
PS153.A84.M3 1998, (v3)
Ma, Van Khang. PL4378.9.M25, (v3)
Maag, Karin. LA179.M22 1995, (v7)
Maas, Michael. DF572.M34 1991, (v5)
Maas, Stephen A. TK6560.M22 1998, (v1)
Maass, Walter B. D763.N4.M3 1970, (v5)
Mabberley, D. J. QK11.M29 1997, (v1)
Mabee, Carleton. E185.97.T8.M32 1993, (v4)
Mabro, Robert. HC535.M17, (v6)
Mac Lane, Saunders. QA266.M254, (v1)
Mac Liammoir, Micheal. PR5823.M3, (v3)
MacArthur, Douglas. E745.M3.A2 1965, (v4)
MacArthur, E. Mairi. DA880.I7.M14 1990, (v5)
MacArthur, Robert H. QH85.M3, (v1)
Macartney, C. A. D651.H7.M15, (v5)
Macartney, Carlile Aylmer. DB80.M3 1969, (v5)
Macartney, George Macartney. DS708.M14, (v5)
Macaulay, James. NA966.M32, (v9)
Macaulay, Rose. PR6025.A16 S5, (v3)
PR6025.A16 T6, (v3)
Macaulay, Rose. PR6025.A16 W6, (v3)
Macaulay, Rose. PR6025.A16.Z54, (v3)
Macaulay, Thomas Babington Macaulay. DA3.M3.A4 1974, (v5)
DA435.M14 1953, (v5)
DA536.M15.A35, (v5)
Macauley, Melissa Ann. KNQ1572.M33 1998, (v7)
MacAvoy, Paul W. KF2130.M33 2000, (v7)
MacBride, Maud Gonne. DA958.M25.A4 1993, (v5)
Macbride, Thomas Huston. F621.M14, (v4)
MacCaffrey, Isabel Gamble. PR2358.M3, (v3)

PR3562.M18, (v3)
MacCaffrey, Wallace T. DA355.M25 1992, (v5)
DA355.M26, (v5)
DA355.M27, (v5)
MacCann, Donnarae. PS173.N4.M33 1998, (v3)
MacCary, W. Thomas. PR2807.M28 1998, (v3)
MacClancy, Jeremy. DP302.N33, (v5)
Maccoby, Eleanor E. BF692.M274, (v2)
BF692.2.M33 1998, (v2)
HQ835.C2.M33 1992, (v6)
MacCormack, Sabine. DG124.M33, (v5)
F3429.3.R3.M28 1991, (v4)
MacCulloch, Diarmaid. DA317.8.C8.M34 1996, (v5)
MacCurdy, Raymond R. PQ6218.M3, (v3)
MacCurtain, Margaret. DA935.M22, (v5)
MacDonagh, Oliver. DA950.M18 1977, (v5)
DA950.22.M228 1989, (v5)
DA950.22.M23 1988, (v5)
Macdonald, Andrew. PS374.I49M33 2000, (v3)
PS374.I49.M33 2000, (v3)
MacDonald, Betty Bard. CT275.M43.A43, (v5)
MacDonald, Bonney. PS2120.I83.M3 1990, (v3)
MacDonald, Charles Brown. D756.M27, (v5)
MacDonald, Dennis Ronald. BS2585.5.M33 2000, (v8)
Macdonald, Douglas J. E744.M215 1992, (v4)
MacDonald, Edgar E. PS3505.A153.Z65 1993, (v3)
MacDonald, Erik. PN2193.E86.M33 1993, (v3)
MacDonald, George F. E99.H2.M3 1996, (v4)
Macdonald, George. PR4966.L4, (v3)
Macdonald, Gordon Andrew. QE349.H3M32 1983, (v1)
Macdonald, Hugh. ML410.B5 M13 2000, (v9)
ML410.S5988 M2, (v9)
MacDonald, J. Fred. PN1991.3.U6.M3, (v3)
MacDonald, John D. PS3563.A28 D44, (v3)
MacDonald, Kevin B. DS145.M14 1998, (v5)
MacDonald, Malcolm. ML410.B8.M113 1990, (v9)
ML410.S283 M15, (v9)
MacDonald, Michael. HV6548.G8.E55 1990, (v6)
RC438.M27, (v2)
Macdonald, Myra. P94.5.W65.M3 1995, (v3)
MacDonald, Norbert. F899.S457.M33 1987, (v4)
MacDonald, R. H. PN4784.B75.M24 1994, (v3)
MacDonald, Robert H. PR468.I49.M33 1994, (v3)
MacDonald, Scott B. HC125.M23 1997, (v6)
HV5840.A5.M33 1989, (v6)
MacDonald, Scott. PN1995.9.E96.M33 1993, (v3)
Macdonald, Sharon. DA880.S6.M26 1997, (v5)
MacDonald, William Lloyd. NA310.M2, (v9)
NA360.M3, (v9)
MacDonald, William. E381.M22 1971, (v4)
Macdonell, Arthur Anthony. PK666.M3, (v3)
PK2903.M35, (v3)
MacDonogh, Giles. DD247.T766.M33 1992, (v5)
MacDougall, David. GN347.M33 1998, (v6)
MacDougall, Hugh A. DA135.M15 1982, (v5)
Macdougall, Norman. DA784.5.M23 1989, (v5)
Mace, Gordon. E18.85.M27 1999, (v4)
Mace, John. PJ6307.M232 1996, (v3)
Mace, Nancy A. PR3458.L5.M33 1996, (v3)
MacEachren, Alan M. GA105.3.M32 1995, (v6)
Macesich, George. HC244.M224 1991, (v6)
HG230.3.M32 1992, (v6)
MacEwan, Arthur. HJ8899.M33 1990, (v6)
Macey, David A. J. HD1992.M19 1987, (v6)
Macey, David. B2430.F724.M327 1993, (v8)
MacFadden, Bruce J. QE882.U6.M27 1992, (v1)
MacFadyen, David Ward. PG3479.4.R64Z769 2000, (v3)
Macfadyen, J. Tevere. HD1476.U5.M32 1984, (v6)
Macfarlane, Alan. HB3585.M33 1997, (v6)
Macfarlane, Alan. HQ615.M33 1986, (v6)
Macfarlane, L. J. JC571.M2132 1985, (v7)
MacFarquhar, Roderick. DS777.57.M3, (v5)
DS777.75.M32 1974, (v5)
MacGillivray, J. A. DF212.E82.M33 2000, (v5)
MacGorman, D. R. QC961.M18 1998, (v1)
MacGregor, Graham. QP535.N2.M33 1998, (v1)
MacGregor, John M. RC455.4.A77.M33 1989, (v2)
MacGregor, Morris J. UB418.A47.M33, (v10)
MacGregor, Neil. N8050.M29 2000, (v9)

Machado de Assis. PQ9697.M18 E713 2000, (v3)
  PQ9697 M18 M413, (v3)
Machado, Antonio. PQ6623.A3.A23, (v3)
  PQ6623.A3.A24, (v3)
  PQ6623.A3.A245 1978, (v3)
Machado, Manuel. PQ6623.A34.A17 1974, (v3)
Machann, Clinton. PR788.A9.M33 1994, (v3)
  PR4023.M28 1998, (v3)
Machen, Arthur. PR6025.A245.A6, (v3)
  PR6025.A245.T52, (v3)
Machiavelli, Niccolò. DG737.A2.M4 1960, (v5)
  DG738.14.M2.A4 1996, (v5)
  JC143.M16313 1996, (v7)
  JC143.M38 1992, (v7)
Machin, G. I. T. BR759.M27 1987, (v8)
  DA550.M28 2001, (v5)
Machle, Edward J. B128.H74 M33 1993, (v8)
Machlis, Joseph. MT90.M23 2003b, (v9)
Machlup, Fritz. AZ505.M28, (v10)
  Z286.S37.M3, (v10)
Macht, Joel. LC4031.M22 1998, (v7)
Macinnes, Allan I. DA803.3.M33 1991, (v5)
Macinnes, Colin. PR6063.A239.L6, (v3)
Macinnes, Gordon. E185.615.M22 1995, (v4)
MacInnis, Donald E. BL1802.M29 1989, (v8)
Macintyre, Alasdair C. BJ37.M23 1990, (v8)
  BJ71.M3 1998, (v8)
  BJ1012.M325 1984, (v8)
  BJ1012.M326 1999, (v8)
Macintyre, Donald G. F. W. V765.M3, (v10)
MacIver, Robert M. BJ1481.M16, (v8)
Mack Smith, Denis. DG552.M25 1989, (v5)
  DG552.M26, (v5)
  DG552.5.M3, (v5)
  DG552.8.C3.M17 1985, (v5)
  DG554.M3 1985, (v5)
  DG571.M22, (v5)
  DG575.M8.M223 1982, (v5)
Mack, Arien. BF241.M26 1998, (v2)
Mack, Burton L. BS2361.2.M13 1995, (v8)
Mack, John E. D568.4.L45.M28, (v5)
Mack, Kibibi Voloria C. F279.O6.M33 1999, (v4)
Mack, Maynard. PR2983.M326 1993, (v3)
  PR3633.M27 1985, (v3)
  PR3633.M3, (v3)
Mack, Phyllis. BX7748.W64.M33 1992, (v8)
Mack, Robert L. PR3503.M24 2000, (v3)
MacKay, Angus. DP99.M23 1977, (v5)
MacKay, Donald MacCrimmon. QP355.2.M33 1990, (v1)
Mackay, Douglas. F1060.M14, (v4)
Mackay, Ruddock F. DA89.1.F5.M3, (v5)
MacKay, William. RD27.7.M33, (v2)
MacKaye, Percy. PS2359.M42.Z8 1968, (v3)
MacKendrick, Paul Lachlan. B553.M33 1989, (v8)
Mackenney, Richard. D220.M33 1993, (v5)
Mackenzie, Compton. PR6025.A2526 S5, (v3)
  PR6025.A2526.Z5, (v3)
MacKenzie, Craig. PR9369.3.H4.Z77 1999, (v3)
MacKenzie, David S. SB432.M336 1997, (v1)
Mackenzie, Donald A. UG1312.B34.M33 1990, (v10)
Mackenzie, G. Calvin. JK271.M13 1996, (v7)
Mackenzie, Henry. PR3543.M2.M13 1987, (v3)
Mackenzie, Hettie Millicent (Hughes). LB675.H4.M3 1971, (v7)
MacKenzie, John M. NX650.E85.M33 1995, (v9)
Mackenzie, Mary Margaret. B398.E8.M3 1981, (v8)
Mackenzie, Molly. DF923.M35 1992, (v5)
MacKenzie, Norman H. PR4803.H44.Z716, (v3)
MacKenzie, Norman Ian. DC238.M32 1982, (v5)
  PR5776.M3 1973, (v3)
Mackenzie, S. P. DA69.M33 1995, (v5)
MacKenzie, W. S. QE434.M33 1994, (v1)
Mackerras, Colin. DS706.M24 2001, (v5)
  DS706.M245 2000, (v5)
  DS730.M336 1994, (v5)
  DS730.M338 1995, (v5)
  DS731.U4.M33 1973, (v5)
  ML1751.C4.M32 1997, (v9)
MacKerron, Conrad B. HC695.Z65 M33 1993, (v6)
Mackesy, Piers. DA522.P6.M33 1984, (v5)

E208.M14, (v4)
Mackey, Eva. F1035.A1.M33 1999, (v4)
Mackey, James Patrick. BJ1275.M34 1994, (v8)
  BT28.M247 1987, (v8)
Mackey, Peter Francis. PR6019.O9.U6817 1999, (v3)
MacKichan, Margaret A. F672.S17 M33 1992, (v4)
Mackie, Erin Skye. PR925.M26 1997, (v3)
Mackie, J. L. B1294.M18, (v8)
  B1499.E8.H855, (v8)
  BJ37.M24, (v8)
Mackie, Richard. F1060.8.S56.M33 1997, (v4)
Mackiewicz, Andrea. HD59.2.M33 1993, (v6)
MacKillop, I. D. PR55.L43.M32 1997, (v3)
MacKinnon, Catharine A. HQ1236.M34 1989, (v6)
  KF4772.M33 1993, (v7)
MacKinnon, Kenneth. PN1998.3.D4.M33 1990, (v3)
MacKinnon, Laurel T. QP301.M159 1999, (v1)
MacKinnon, Laurie K. RC569.5.C55.M33 1998, (v2)
MacKinnon, Stephen R. DS777.533.P825.U65 1987, (v5)
Mackintosh, Charles Rennie. NA997.M3.A4 1980, (v9)
Macklin, Ruth. R724.M16135 1993, (v2)
Mackrell, Alice. TT509.M33 1997, (v1)
MacLachlan, Alastair. DA403.M33 1996, (v5)
MacLachlan, Colin M. F1231.M32, (v4)
  F1234.F663.M33 1991, (v4)
  JV4062.M32 1988, (v7)
MacLachlan, Patricia. PZ7.M2225Sar 1985, (v3)
MacLaran, Andrew. DA995.D75.M22 1993, (v5)
Maclean, Anne. B843.M23 1993, (v8)
MacLean, Nancy. HS2330.K63.M225 1994, (v6)
Maclean, Norman. SD421.32.M9.M33 1992, (v1)
MacLeish, Archibald. E169.M16, (v4)
  PS3525.A27.A17 1985, (v3)
  PS3525.A27.A6 1933, (v3)
  PS3525.A27.C6 1934, (v3)
  PS3525.A27.C69, (v3)
  PS3525.A27.F7 1933, (v3)
  PS3525.A27.H25 1928, (v3)
  PS3525.A27.J2 1958, (v3)
  PS3525.A27.P3 1935, (v3)
  PS3525.A27.P8 1936a, (v3)
  PS3525.A27.S3, (v3)
  PS3525.A27.S72, (v3)
  PS3525.A27.T47, (v3)
  PS3525.A27.W5, (v3)
  PS3531.O82.P53, (v3)
MacLennan, Hugh. PR6025.A2594.R4 1967, (v3)
MacLeod, Bruce A. ML3795.M14 1993, (v9)
Macleod, Dianne Sachko. N72.S6.M23 1996, (v9)
MacLeod, Don. KF242.A1.M3 1995, (v7)
MacLeod, Glen G. PS3537.T4753.Z6775 1993, (v3)
MacMaster, Neil. DC34.5.A4.M33 1997, (v5)
  DP269.8.R3.M34 1990, (v5)
Macmillan, Harold. DA566.9.M33.A27 1971b, (v5)
  DA566.9.M33.A28 1969, (v5)
  DA574.A1.M33 1975b, (v5)
Macmillan, Malcolm. RC387.5.G34, (v2)
MacMullen, Edith Nye. LA2317.B18.M33 1990, (v7)
MacMullen, Ramsay. BR170.M33 1997, (v8)
  DG89.M13, (v5)
  DG270.M33 1988, (v5)
  DG273.M33 2000, (v5)
  DG306.M3, (v5)
MacMurraugh-Kavanagh, M. K. PR6037.H23.Z76 1998, (v3)
MacMurray, John Van Antwerp. DS518.M2 1991, (v5)
MacNair, Harley Farnsworth. DS721.M3, (v5)
  DS774.M35, (v5)
MacNally, Ralph C. QH541.M225 1995, (v1)
Macnamara, Daniel George. E513.5 9th.M33 2000, (v4)
MacNeice, Louis. PR6025.A316.A17 1949, (v3)
  PR6025.A316.A17 1967, (v3)
  PR6025.A316.C5 1944, (v3)
  PR6025.A316.D3, (v3)
MacNeil, Heather. CD986.5.M33 1992, (v9)
MacNeil, Robert. HE8697.P6.M3, (v6)
MacNeill, Jim. HD75.6.M33 1991, (v6)
MacNeish, Richard S. GN799.A4.M34 1991, (v6)
MacNiven, Ian S. PR6007.U76.Z74 1998, (v3)

MacNutt, W. Stewart. F1043.M29, (v4)
Macomber, Roger S. QD96.N8.M3 1998, (v1)
Maconie, Robin. ML410.S858.M3 1990, (v9)
Macpherson, C. B. JC153.M2, (v7)
  JC423.M159, (v7)
Macpherson, James. LA2106.7.M22 1983, (v7)
  PR3544.A1 1970, (v3)
Macquarrie, John. BJ63.M3, (v8)
  BL72.M33 1996, (v8)
  BT198.M295 1990, (v8)
MacQueen, Bruce D. PA4229.L9.M28 1990, (v3)
Macqueen, J. G. DS66.M23 1975, (v5)
MacQueen, John. PR8650.M3, (v3)
Macqueen, Norrie. DT36.5.M33 1997, (v5)
Macrae, Alasdair D. F. PR5906.M276 1995, (v3)
MacRae, Cathi Dunn. PS374.F27.M33 1998, (v3)
Macrae, Janet. RT85.2.M33 2001, (v2)
MacRaild, Donald M. HD8390.M175 2000, (v6)
Macrakis, Kristie. Q180.G4.M3 1993, (v1)
Macrina, Francis L. Q180.5.M67M33 2000, (v1)
MacRitchie, Finlay. QD506.M26 1990, (v1)
Macrobius, Ambrosius Aurelius Theodosius. PA6498.E6.D3, (v3)
MacSween, Morag. RC552.A5.M33 1993, (v2)
Macura, Paul. Q123.M182 1999, (v1)
MacWillson, Alastair C. HV6431.M335 1991, (v6)
Madan, Falconer. Z105.M17 1927a, (v10)
Madan, P. L. GA1131.3.M34 1997, (v6)
Madariaga, Salvador de. F1410.M25 1947a, (v4)
  F1414.M28, (v4)
  F2235.3.M163, (v4)
Maddala, G. S. HB139.M355 1983, (v6)
Madden, David. PS3563.A339.B4, (v3)
Madden, Etta M. PS153.S54.M33 1998, (v3)
Madden, Paul. Z8409.6.M33 1998, (v10)
Maddern, Philippa C. HN400.Z9.V56 1992, (v6)
Maddex, Jack P. F231.M2, (v4)
Maddex, Robert L. JC571.M3243 2000, (v7)
  K3157.E5.M33 1995, (v7)
Maddicott, John Robert. DA228.M7.M33 1994, (v5)
Maddison, Angus. HC21.M285 2001, (v6)
  HC54.M255 1995, (v6)
  HC187.M2823 1992, (v6)
Maddock, Richard C. HF5822.M33 1996, (v6)
Maddox, Brenda. PR6019.O9.Z7184 1988, (v3)
  PR6023.A93.Z6758 1994, (v3)
Maddox, Donald. PQ1448.M33 1991, (v3)
Maddox, John Royden. Q180.55.D57.M33 1998, (v1)
Maddox, Lucy. PS173.I6.M3 1991, (v3)
Maddox, Robert James. D767.25.H6.M23 1995, (v5)
Maddy-Weitzman, Bruce. DS63.M23 1993, (v5)
Madeleva, Sister M[ary]. PR99.M32, (v3)
Madeley, John. HF4055.M33 1993, (v6)
Madelung, Wilferd. DS38.1.M336 1997, (v5)
Madge, Steve. QL696.A52.M33 1988, (v1)
  QL696.P2367.M34 1994, (v1)
Madigan, Patrick. B485.M24 1991, (v8)
Madison, Charles Allan. PJ5120.M2, (v3)
Madison, Dolley. E342.1.M18 1971, (v4)
Madison, Gary Brent. BD241.M25 1988, (v8)
Madison, James H. F526.H55 vol. 5, (v4)
  F526.M22 1986, (v4)
Madison, James. E302.M192 1981, (v4)
Madriz, Esther. HV6250.4.W65.M325 1997, (v6)
Madsen, Axel. HC102.5.A76.M33 2001, (v6)
Madsen, Borge Gedso. PT9816.M28, (v3)
Madsen, Brigham D. F826.C74.M33 1990, (v4)
Madsen, Chris. D771.M29 1998, (v5)
Madsen, Deborah L. PS153.M4.M33 2000, (v3)
Madsen, Richard. BJ966.M3 1984, (v8)
  BX1665.M29 1998, (v8)
Madsen, Roy P. PN1994.M3226 1990, (v3)
Maduakor, Obi. PR9387.9.S6.Z77 1987, (v3)
Maeda, John. QA76.6.M336 1999, (v1)
Maeder, Beverly. PS3537.T4753.Z6776 1999, (v3)
Maehr, Martin L. LB2822.82.M33 1996, (v7)
Maeroff, Gene I. LB2840.M28 1988, (v7)
Maes, Francis. ML300.M1313 2002, (v9)
Maeterlinck, Maurice. PQ2625.A506 1967, (v3)
Maffi, Mario. F128.9.A1.M34 1995, (v4)
Maga, Timothy P. KZ1181.M34 2001, (v7)

Magalaner, Marvin. PR6019.O9.Z72, (v3)
PR6019.O9 Z7192, (v3)
Magalini, Sergio I. RC69.M33 1997, (v2)
Magdalino, Paul. DF607.M34 1993, (v5)
Magder, Ted. PN1993.5.C2.M24 1993, (v3)
Magdoff, Fred. S592.8.M34 1992, (v1)
Magee, Bryan. B804.M257 1979, (v8)
B1647.M186.A3 1998, (v8)
B3148.M27 1983, (v8)
Magee, Dennis W. QK121.M34 1999, (v1)
Magennis, Hugh. PR203.M24 1996, (v3)
Maggin, Donald L. ML419.G48.M34 1996, (v9)
Maggio, Rosalie. PE1460.M26 1991, (v3)
PE1689.M23 1987, (v3)
Maggiotto, Michael A. JK2295.A13 M34 2000, (v7)
Magid, Alvin. F2119.M34 1988, (v4)
Magie, William Francis. QC3.M26, (v1)
Magill, Frank Northen. PN41.M26 1958a, (v3)
PN44.M3 1990, (v3)
PN44.M32, (v3)
PN44.M34 1977, (v3)
Z6511.M25, (v10)
Maginnis, Hayden B. J. ND613.M25 1997, (v9)
ND621.S6.M34 2001, (v9)
Magistrale, Tony. PS374.D4.M26 1999, (v3)
Maglischo, Ernest W. GV838.67.T73 M33 2003, (v6)
GV838.67.T73.M34 1982, (v6)
Magnaghi, Russell M. E16.M34 1998, (v4)
Z1209.M25 1998, (v10)
Magnarella, Paul J. DS51.S94.M3, (v5)
KTD454.M34 2000, (v7)
Magner, Lois N. R131.M179 1992, (v2)
Magness, Jodi. BM175.Q6 M34 2002, (v8)
Magnus, Philip Montefiore. DA68.32.K6.M3 1968, (v5)
Magnus, Ralph H. DS371.2.M28 1998, (v5)
Magnus, Shulamit S. DS135.G4.C684 1997, (v5)
Magnuson, Landis K. PN2266.3.M35 1995, (v3)
Magnuson, Paul. PR590.M22 1998, (v3)
Magnusson, Lars. HC375.M25 2000, (v6)
Magoc, Chris J. F722.M23 1999, (v4)
Magocsi, Paul R. DB2742.R8.M3413 1993, (v5)
DK508.51.M34 1996, (v5)
G2081.S1.M3 1993, (v6)
Magoffin, Susan Shelby. F786.M22 1962, (v4)
Magone, Jose M. JN8605.M34 1997, (v7)
Magoun, Francis Peabody. PR1941.M3, (v3)
Magoun, Horace Winchell. QP376.M28 1963, (v1)
Magritte, Rene. ND673.M35.A4 1998, (v9)
Magruder, Jeb Stuart. E840.8.M345.A32, (v4)
Maguire, G. E. D752.M34 1995, (v5)
Maguire, Jack. BQ9294.4.U6, (v8)
Maguire, Keith. DS799.816.M33 1998, (v5)
Maguire, Laurie E. PR3071.M28 1996, (v3)
Maguire, Nancy Klein. PR698.K58.M3 1992, (v3)
Maguire, Peter H. K5301.M34 2001, (v7)
Mah, Harold. B3305.M74.M326 1987, (v8)
Mah āsvet a Deb ī. PK1718.B48A22 1997, (v3)
Mahaffey, Vicki. PR8750.M34 1998, (v3)
Mahajan, Virendra N. QC671.M36 1998, (v1)
Mahan, A. T. E182.M24, (v4)
E354.M23, (v4)
VA55.M2 1968, (v10)
Mahan, Bruce E. F616.I67 no. 14, (v4)
Mahan, Harold E. E175.5.L67.M34 1996, (v4)
Mahan, Jeffrey H. PS3525.I486.Z77 1990, (v3)
Mahanty, Gopinath. PK2579.M288D313 1995, (v3)
Maharatna, Arup. HC439.M35 1996, (v6)
Mahdi, Muhsin. D116.7.I3.M43 1964, (v5)
PJ7737.M32 1995, (v3)
Maher, Jane. HV2534.S76.M35 1996, (v6)
Maher, Lisa. HV5824.W6.M345 1997, (v6)
Maher, Vanessa. HQ1816.M62.M3, (v6)
Maheshwari, Shriram. JS7010.M35 2000, (v7)
Maheu, Marlene M. R119.95.M344 2001, (v2)
Mahfouz, Naguib. PJ7846.A46.R513 1992, (v3)
Mahfuz, Najib. PJ7846.A46.G6, (v3)
Mahiri, Jabari. LC2717.M35 1998, (v7)
Mahl, Thomas E. D810.S7.M254 1998, (v5)
Mahler, Margaret S. RJ499.M234, (v2)
Mahler, Sarah J. HN90.M26.M34 1995, (v6)

Mahmood, Cynthia Keppley. DS485.P88.M25 1997, (v5)
Mahmud, S. F. DS38.M24 1960, (v5)
Mahmutcehajic, Rusmir. DR1673.M3413 2000, (v5)
DR1752.M33313 2000, (v5)
Mahon, James E. HG3891.M34 1996, (v6)
Mahon, John K. UA42.M33 1983, (v10)
Mahoney, Daniel J. DC420.M325 1996, (v5)
Mahoney, Dorothy. Z43.M25 1982, (v10)
Mahoney, John L. PR5887.3.M34 2001, (v3)
Mahoney, John. BJ1249.M1644 1987, (v8)
Mahoney, Michael J. BF637.B4.M32, (v2)
BF637.C4.M29 1991, (v2)
Mahoney, Timothy R. HT123.5.M53.M34 1989, (v6)
Mahony, Christina Hunt. PR8753.M34 1998, (v3)
Mahony, Patrick. RC532.M34 1996, (v2)
Mahony, Rhona. HQ755.8.M34 1995, (v6)
Mahony, Robert. PR3728.I67.M34 1995, (v3)
Mahony, William K. BL1112.7.M35 1998, (v8)
Mahood, Linda. HV9147.S4.M34 1995, (v6)
Mahowald, Mary Briody. RB155.M3135 2000, (v2)
Mahrer, Alvin R. BF204.M34, (v2)
Maia Neto, Jose Raimundo. PQ9697.M18.Z7153 1994, (v3)
Maida, Patricia D. PS2733.M35 1989, (v3)
Maier, Charles S. D804.3.M35 1988, (v5)
Maier, Henry W. BF721.M196 1969, (v2)
Maier, Joseph. F1414.2.M25, (v4)
Maier, Karl. DT352.8.M35 1998, (v5)
Maier, Pauline. E210.M27 1974, (v4)
E221.M24 1997, (v4)
E302.5.M23 1980, (v4)
Maihafer, Harry J. E672.M126 1998, (v4)
Mailer, Norman. GV1132.A44 M35 1997, (v6)
PS3525.A4152 A7, (v3)
PS3525.A4152 B3, (v3)
PS3525.A4152.D4, (v3)
PS3525.A4152 D4, (v3)
PS3525.A4152.E84, (v3)
PS3525.A4152.E9, (v3)
PS3525.A4152.N34 1948, (v3)
PS3525.A4152.P5 1982, (v3)
PS3525.A4152 W5, (v3)
PS3525.A4152.Z52 1959, (v3)
PS3525.I5454.A6 1976, (v3)
Mailloux, Peter Alden. PT2621.A26.Z7696 1989, (v3)
Mailloux, Steven. PN81.M38 1989, (v3)
PN98.R38.M3 1982, (v3)
Main, Gloria L. HC107.M3.M23 1982, (v6)
Main, Iain G. QC136.M34 1984, (v1)
Main, Jackson Turner. JK116.M2, (v7)
JK2506.M3, (v7)
Mainardi, Patricia. N6850.M35 1993, (v9)
Maine, Henry Sumner. JC21.M2 1883, (v7)
Maine, Margo. RJ506.E18.M35 1991, (v2)
Maines, Rachel P. HQ29.M35 1998, (v6)
Mainstone, R. J. NA5870.A9.M28 1988, (v9)
Mainwaring, Marion. PN4874.F774, (v3)
Mainwaring, Scott. JL2498.A1.M35 1999, (v7)
Maiolo, Joseph A. DA47.2.M19 1998, (v5)
Mair, George Herbert. PR401.M2 1960, (v3)
Mair, Lucy Philip. GN645.M26, (v6)
Mair, Lucy Philip. GN658.M34 1977, (v6)
Mair, Peter. JN50.M35 1997, (v7)
Maisels, Charles Keith. CB311.M27 1999, (v5)
DS57.M37 1990, (v5)
Maistre, Joseph Marie. PQ2053.A3.M3513 1996, (v3)
Maitland, A. QC446.2.M34, (v1)
Maitland, Leslie. NA744.5.N45.M35 1984, (v9)
Maitland, Peter S. SH327.7.M35 1997, (v1)
Maitra, Priyatosh. HC59.72.C3.M355 1996, (v6)
Maiuri, Amedeo. ND120.M25, (v9)
Maizell, Robert E. QD8.5.M34 1998, (v1)
Maizels, John. N7432.5.A78.M34 1996, (v9)
Maizlish, Stephen E. F495.M34 1983, (v4)
Maja-Pearce, Adewale. PR9387.4.M3 1992, (v3)
Majewski, John D. HE2771.P4, (v6)
Major, Charles. PS2359.M648 B4 1984, (v3)
PS2359.M648 W5, (v3)
Major, Clarence. PE3727.N4.M3, (v3)
Major, Devorah. PS3563.A3915.O7 1995, (v3)

Major, F. G. QB107.M35 1998, (v1)
Major, J. Russell. DC111.5.M3 1994, (v5)
Major, Mabel. PS277.M3 1972, (v3)
Major, Patrick. JN3971.A98.K6536 1997, (v7)
Major, Ralph Hermon. R131.M26, (v2)
Majors, Alexander. F596.M19 1989, (v4)
Majors, William R. F436.B86.M34 1982, (v4)
Makar, Ragai N. Z3014.L56.M35 1998, (v10)
Z3651.M34 1988, (v10)
Makarushka, Irena S. M. PS1642.R4.M35 1994, (v3)
Makdisi, Saree. PR468.I49.M35 1998, (v3)
Makdisi, Ussama Samir. DS84.M35 2000, (v5)
Makeham, John. B126.M34 1994, (v8)
Makela, Maria Martha. N6867.5.M83.M35 1990, (v9)
Makhijani, Arjun. QC879.7.M34 1995, (v1)
Maki, John M. DS503.M28 1962, (v5)
Maki, Wilbur R. HT321.M23 2000, (v6)
Makin, John H. HG3891.5.M34 1984, (v6)
HJ241.M36 1994, (v6)
Makino, Seiichi. PL533.M25 1989, (v3)
Makino, Yasuko. Z3301.M32 1994, (v10)
Makinson, Larry. JK1991.M26 1992, (v7)
Makovsky, David. DS119.7.M253 1996, (v5)
Makowski, Colleen Lahan. Z8131.65.M35 1996, (v10)
Makowsky, Veronica A. PS3513.L35.Z75 1993, (v3)
PS3513.O5765.Z74 1989, (v3)
Makuchi. PR9372.9.M34.Y68 1999, (v3)
Makus, Ingrid. HQ1236.M343 1996, (v6)
Malamed, Stanley F. RK510.M33 1997, (v2)
Malamud Goti, Jaime E. HV5840.B6.M35 1992, (v6)
Malamud, Bernard. PS3563.A4.A8, (v3)
PS3563.A4.D8 1979, (v3)
PS3563.A4.F5, (v3)
PS3563.A4.I3 1963, (v3)
PS3563.A4.M3 1958b, (v3)
PS3563.A4.M34x, (v3)
PS3563.A4.N3 1952, (v3)
PS3563.A4.T4, (v3)
PS3563.A4.T9, (v3)
Malamud, Carl. ZA4226.M35 1997, (v10)
Malamud, Randy. PS3509.L43.Z715 1992, (v3)
Malan, Marais. RD598.M17, (v2)
Maland, David. D247.M23 1979, (v5)
Malbin, Michael J. JK1083.M34, (v7)
Malchow, Howard L. PR868.T3.M25 1996, (v3)
Malcolm, Cheryl Alexander. PR6035.H96.Z79 1996, (v3)
Malcolm, Noel. DR1685 .M35 1994, (v5)
DR2082 .M35 1998, (v5)
ML410.E55.M27 1990, (v9)
Malcolm, Norman. B3376.W564.M2 1958, (v8)
BD161.M28, (v8)
BD161.M283, (v8)
Malcolm, W. M. QK537.M35 2000, (v1)
Malcolmson, Cristina. PR3508.M29 1999, (v3)
Maldifassi, Jose O. HD9743.B682.M35 1994, (v6)
Male, Emile. N7949.A1.M3313 1986, (v9)
N7949.M313 1958, (v9)
Malecki, Edward J. HC79.T4.M346 1991, (v6)
Maleuvre, Didier. AM7.M355 1999, (v10)
Maley, Willy. PR2367.I67.M35 1997, (v3)
Malherbe, Francois de. PQ1819.A6 1968, (v3)
Malhotra, Inder. DS481.G23.M314 1991, (v5)
Mali, Joseph. B3581.P73.M35 1992, (v8)
Malia, Martin E. DK32.M18 1999, (v5)
DK209.6.H4.M3, (v5)
Malik, Iftikhar Haider. DS341.3.U6.M35 1990, (v5)
DS384.M2718 1997, (v5)
Malik, Jamal. BP63.P2.M348 1996, (v8)
Malin, David. QB121.M34 1993, (v1)
QB816.M34 1984, (v1)
Malin, James Claude. GF504.W35.M34 1984, (v6)
Malin, Jo. PS366.A88.M35 2000, (v3)
Malin, Shimon. QC174.12.M34 2001, (v1)
Malinowitz, Harriet. PE1405.U6.M34 1995, (v3)
Malinowski, Bronislaw. GN8.M286, (v6)
GN27.M34, (v6)
GN645.M3 1961, (v6)
Malinowsky, H. Robert. Z7401.M278 1994, (v10)
Malins, Edward Greenway. PR5906.M296 1974, (v3)
Malizia, Emil E. HD75.M25 1999, (v6)

Malkiel, Burton Gordon. HG4521.M284 1996, (v6)
Malkin, Irad. DF85.M35 1994, (v5)
Malkin, Jeanette R. PN1861.M278 1999, (v3)
Malkki, Liisa H. DT443.3.H88.M35 1995, (v5)
Malkmus, Lizbeth. PN1993.5.A65.M3 1991, (v3)
Mallabarmaòna, Advaita. PK1718.M2476T513 1993, (v3)
Mallarmé, Stéphane. PQ2344.A1 1926, (v3)
　PQ2344.A13 1951, (v3)
　PQ2344.Z5.A4 1988, (v3)
　PQ2344.A128 1998, (v3)
Mallea, Eduardo. PQ7797.M225.F5 1942, (v3)
Mallea-Olaetxe, J. F870.B15 M35 2000, (v4)
Mallet-Joris, Francoise. PQ2625.A7124.J4, (v3)
Mallett, Michael Edward. DG537.M34 1974, (v5)
Mallett, Robert. DG571.M255 1998, (v5)
Malley, Robert. DT295.5.M34 1996, (v5)
Mallgrave, Harry Francis. NA1353.S45.M36 1996, (v9)
Mallick, Ross. HC437.W44.M35 1993, (v6)
　HX392.5.M35 1994, (v6)
Mallin, Eric Scott. PR2910.M32 1995, (v3)
Mallin, Maurice A. UA23.M275 1990, (v10)
Mallinson, Vernon. PQ3814.M25, (v3)
Mallon, Florencia E. F1231.5.M34 1995, (v4)
Mallon, Gerald P. HV1449.M35 1998, (v6)
Mallory, J. P. GN293.M34 2000, (v6)
Mallory, James. F332.T14.M35 1997, (v4)
Malloy, James M. F3326.M25, (v4)
　F3326.M26 1988, (v4)
Mally, Lynn. PN3169.S65.M27 2000, (v3)
Malm, William P. ML330.M3 1996, (v9)
　ML340.M33, (v9)
Malmgren, Carl Darryl. PN3433.5.M35 1991, (v3)
Malmquist, Carl P. RC569.5.H65.M35 1996, (v2)
Malmstrom, Vincent Herschel. F1219.3.C2.M25 1997, (v4)
Maines, Raino. GE170.M35 1995, (v6)
Malnig, Julie. GV1746.M28 1992, (v6)
Maloba, Wunyabari O. DT433.577.M35 1993, (v5)
Malof, Joseph. PE1505.M3 1970, (v3)
Malone, Ann Patton. E445.L8.M35 1992, (v4)
Malone, Bill C. ML3524.M34 2002, (v9)
　ML3524.M344 2002, (v9)
　ML3551.M26 1993, (v9)
Malone, David. E748.C228.M35 1989, (v4)
Malone, Dumas. E332.M25, (v4)
　JK128.M3, (v7)
Malone, Jacqui. GV1624.7.A34.M35 1996, (v6)
Malone, John Williams. GV849.M34 1998, (v6)
Malone, Kemp. PR1924.M25, (v3)
Malone, Michael P. F595.M3 1989, (v4)
　F731.M339 1991, (v4)
　F731.M35, (v4)
　F746.M3, (v4)
Maloney, Linda M. V63.H85.M35 1986, (v10)
Maloof, Judy. F1787.5.M34 1999, (v4)
Malory, Thomas. PR2041.V5 1954, (v3)
Malotki, Ekkehart. E99.P9 M225 2000, (v4)
Malouf, David. PR9619.3.M265.H3 1984, (v3)
Maloy, Otis C. SB731.M364 1993, (v1)
Maloy, Timothy K. ZA4201.M35 1999, (v10)
Malozemoff, Andrew. DS515.M28 1977, (v5)
Malpas, J. E. B105.P53.M35 1999, (v6)
Malphrus, Benjamin K. QB475.A25.M35 1996, (v1)
Malraux, Andre. PQ2625.A716.A73 1968, (v3)
　PQ2625.A716.E7 1937, (v3)
　PQ2625.A716.V6 1930, (v3)
Maltby, Richard. PN1993.5.U6.M2296 1995, (v3)
Maltese, John Anthony. JK518.M35 1994, (v7)
　KF8742.M26 1995, (v7)
Malthus, T. R. HB401.M19 1969, (v6)
　HB861.E7 1976, (v6)
Malti-Douglas, Fedwa. PJ7519.W66M34 1992, (v3)
Maltz, Earl M. KF4550.M26 1994, (v7)
　KF4757.M29 1990, (v7)
Maltzman, Forrest. KF8748.M285 2000, (v7)
Maluccio, Anthony N. HV741.M344 1986, (v6)
Malvasi, Mark G. PS261.M28 1997, (v3)
Mamalakis, Markos. HC192.M29, (v6)
Maman, Marie. Z7963.E7.M316 1996, (v10)
Mamber, P. A. PM7895.P3.M28 1983, (v3)

Mamduòh, Aliyah. PJ7846.A543H33 1996, (v3)
Mamdani, Mahmood. DT450.435.M35 2001, (v5)
Mamet, David. PS3563.A4345.A8 1977, (v3)
　PS3563.A4345.R4, (v3)
　PS3563.A4345.S4 1978, (v3)
Mamola, Claire Zebroski. Z3308.L5.M34 1989, (v10)
Man, John. Z126.Z7, (v10)
Manahan, Stanley E. QD31.2.M35 1994, (v1)
　TS161.M353 1999, (v1)
Manaster, Jane. QL666.L25.M345 1997, (v1)
Manat, G. P. Z1361.N39.M34 1995, (v10)
　Z7165.S65 M38 1992, (v10)
Mancall, Mark. DS754.18.M36 1984, (v5)
Mancall, Peter C. E98.L7.M28 1995, (v4)
　HC107.A12.M26 1991, (v6)
Manchen-Helfen, Otto. D141.M33, (v5)
Manchester, William Raymond. CB369.M36 1992, (v5)
　D840.M23 1989, (v5)
　DA566.9.C5.M26 1983, (v5)
　E806.M34, (v4)
Manchuelle, Francois. DT549.45.S66.M35 1997, (v5)
Mancini, Matthew J. DC36.98.T63.M36 1994, (v5)
　HV8929.S92.M36 1996, (v6)
Mandel, Ernest. HB97.5.M2713 1969, (v6)
　JC474.M325 1991, (v7)
Mandel, Jerome. PR1874.M345 1992, (v3)
Mandel, Neville J. DS119.7.M263, (v5)
Mandel, Robert. UA10.5.M32 1994, (v10)
　UA10.5.M325 1999, (v10)
Mandel, Siegfried. PT405.M33, (v3)
Mandelbaum, David Goodman. HQ1075.5.I4.M36 1988, (v6)
Mandelbaum, Maurice. D16.9.M26, (v5)
Mandelbaum, Michael. D363.M29 1988, (v5)
　UA646.M37 1996, (v10)
Mandelbaum, Seymour J. HM756.M36 2000, (v6)
Mandelbrot, Benoit B. QA447.M3613, (v1)
Mandell, Daniel R. E78.M4 M32 1996, (v4)
Mandell, Richard D. GV722 1936.M3, (v6)
　GV722 1972.M35 1991, (v6)
Mandelshtam, Nadezhda. PG3476.M355Z8313, (v3)
Mandelshtam, Osip. PG3476.M355.A27, (v3)
Mander, Jerry. E98.S67.M36 1991, (v4)
Mandeville, Bernard. BJ1520.M4 1988, (v8)
Mandic, Danilo P. Q325.5.M36 2001, (v1)
Mandle, Jay R. E185.92.M36, (v4)
Mandle, Joan D. HQ1181.U5.M37 2000, (v6)
Mandle, Jon. JC574.M36 2000, (v7)
Mandler, Michael. HB201.M2985 1999, (v6)
Mandrell, James. PN57.D7.M33 1992, (v3)
Manegold, Catherine S. KF228.C53.M36 2000, (v7)
Manent, Pierre. JC229.T8.M3213 1996, (v7)
Maner, Martin. PR3537.B54.M36 1988, (v3)
Manes, Christopher. HC79.E5.M353 1990, (v6)
Maney, Ardith. HV696.F6.M35 1989, (v6)
Manfred, Frederick Feikema. PS3525.A52233 W3, (v3)
Manfull, Helen. PN2053.M357 1996, (v3)
Mangan, J. A. GV346.M36, (v6)
　LA631.7.M364 1998, (v7)
Mangan, John. HD4903.M36 2000, (v6)
Manganaro, Marc. PN51.M267 1992, (v3)
Manganelli, Raymond L. HD58.8.M257 1994, (v6)
Manganiello, Dominic. PS3509.L43.Z72 1989, (v3)
Mangano, Joseph J. RA569.M36 1999, (v2)
Manger, Leif O. DT155.2.N82.M36 1994, (v5)
Manger, William. F1402.M3, (v4)
Mangerich, Agnes Jensen. D807.U6.M357 1999, (v5)
Mangione, Jerre Gerlando. E175.4.W9.M3, (v4)
Mango, Andrew. DR590.M35, (v5)
　DR592.K4 M36 2000, (v5)
　DR603.M36 1994, (v5)
Mango, Cyril A. DF521.M36 1980, (v5)
Mangold, Peter. D443.M289 1998, (v5)
Manguel, Alberto. GR650.M36 2000, (v6)
　Z1003.M292 1996, (v10)
Mangum, Bryant. PS3511.I9.Z684 1991, (v3)
Mangum, Teresa. PR4728.G112.Z78 1998, (v3)
Manhart, Warren. SB363.3.A1M36 1995, (v1)
Manheim, Marvin L. HE199.9.M34, (v6)

Manheimer, Ronald J. LC5251.M287 1995, (v7)
Manifold, Gay. PQ2419.M3 1985, (v3)
Maniguet, Xavier. GV200.5.M3513 1994, (v6)
Manin, Bernard. JF1051.M2513 1997, (v7)
Manion, Melanie. JQ1512.Z2.M36 1993, (v7)
Mank, Gregory W. PN1995.9.W6.M354 1999, (v3)
　PN1995.9.W6.M355 1999, (v3)
Manke, Mary Phillips. LB1033.M2123 1997, (v7)
Mankiewicz, Frank. HE8700.8.M36 1978, (v6)
Manko, Howard H. TT267.M26 1979, (v1)
Manley, John. GN805.M36 1989, (v6)
Manley, Lawrence. PR421.M27 1995, (v3)
Manley, Walter W. HF5387.M335 1990, (v6)
Manlove, C. N. PR21.M28 1989, (v3)
　PR149.F35.M36 1999, (v3)
　PR830.F3.M28 1983, (v3)
　PR6023.E926.C536 1993, (v3)
Manlowe, Jennifer L. BV4596.A25.M36 1995, (v8)
Manly, John Matthews. PR1261.M3, (v3)
　PR1874.M35, (v3)
Mann, Alfred K. Q127.U5, (v1)
Mann, Alfred. ML410.H13.M36 1996, (v9)
　ML430.M28 1987, (v9)
　ML448.M25 1987, (v9)
Mann, Barbara A. E99.I69 M35 2000, (v4)
Mann, Catherine L. HF5548.32.M36 2000, (v6)
Mann, Coramae Richey. HV6046.M36 1984, (v6)
　HV9950.M26 1993, (v6)
Mann, David. PR635.W6.M36 1996, (v3)
Mann, E. A. DS486.A485.M36 1992, (v5)
Mann, Georg. PS3563.A5357.D6, (v3)
Mann, Golo. DD203.M2713, (v5)
Mann, Henrietta. E99.C53.M35 1997, (v4)
Mann, Horace. LB695.M235, (v7)
　LB695.M27, (v7)
Mann, J. RM301.25.M36 1999, (v2)
Mann, Mary Tyler Peabody. PS2359.M6914, (v3)
Mann, Michael. HB195.M225 1988, (v6)
Mann, Ralph. F869.G76M3 1982, (v4)
Mann, Robert. DS558.M34 2001, (v5)
Mann, Ronald A. QA852.M36, (v1)
Mann, Thomas. PT343.M28, (v3)
　PT2625.A44A16 1993, (v3)
　PT2625.A44.A23, (v3)
　PT2625.A44.A24, (v3)
　PT2625.A44.B513 1983, (v3)
　PT2625.A44 B82 1924, (v3)
　PT2625.A44 C6 1955, (v3)
　PT2625.A44.D63, (v3)
　PT2625.A44.D688 1961, (v3)
　PT2625.A44 J62 1948, (v3)
　PT2625.A44 L62, (v3)
　PT2625.A44 S82, (v3)
　PT2625.A44.T613 1998, (v3)
　PT2625.A44 V413, (v3)
　PT2625.A44 Z3 1952, (v3)
　PT2625.A44.Z46613 1982, (v3)
　PT2625.A44.Z485 1998, (v3)
　PT2625.A44.Z5 1960, (v3)
　PT2625.A44.Z523, (v3)
　PT2625.A44 1960, (v3)
　Z710.M23 1998, (v10)
Mann, William M. QL31.M26.A3 1948, (v1)
Mann, William. MT100.M76.M3, (v9)
　MT100.S84 M3 1966, (v9)
Manna, Anthony L. LB1587.A3.M36 1992, (v7)
Mannering, Fred L. TE147.M28 1998, (v1)
Manners, William. E757.M34, (v4)
Mannheim, Karl. BD175.M31513 1986, (v8)
　HN15.M263 1967, (v6)
Mannikka, Eleanor. DS554.98.A5.M36 1996, (v5)
Manning, Christel. BT704.M355 1999, (v8)
Manning, Christopher D. P98.5.S83M36 1999, (v3)
Manning, Diane. LA2315.T4.M36 1990, (v7)
Manning, Frederic. PR6025.A49 M5 1977, (v3)
Manning, George Charles. VM156.M27, (v10)
Manning, Michael. R726.M315 1998, (v2)
Manning, Patrick. DT532.5.M36 1988, (v5)
Manning, Peter J. PR590.M23 1990, (v3)
Manning, Richard. QH104.M37 1995, (v1)
Manning, Rita C. BJ1031.M29 1992, (v8)

Manning, Robert A. DS518.7.M34 1988, (v5)
Manning, Robert D. HG3755.8.U6.M36 2000, (v6)
Manning, Robert E. GV191.6.M314 1999, (v6)
Manning, Roger B. DA315.M36 1988, (v5)
Manning, Susan. GV1785.W5.M36 1993, (v6)
Manning, Thomas G. VK597.U6.M36 1988, (v10)
Mannion, Antoinette M. GE149.M37 1999, (v6)
Manns, James W. BH39.M385 1998, (v8)
Mano, M. Morris. TK7888.3.M343 2002, (v1)
Manor, James. DS489.83.B3.M36 1989, (v5)
Manòto, Sa ̄adat òHasan. PK2199.H338A23 1997, (v3)
Mansbach, Steven A. N6758.M352 1999, (v9)
   N6820.5.N93.M36 1991, (v9)
Mansbridge, Jane J. HQ1236.5.U6.M37 1986, (v6)
Mansbridge, Michael. NA997.N3.A4 1991, (v9)
Mansel, Philip. DC33.5.M34 1988, (v5)
Mansergh, Nicholas. D397.M28, (v5)
   DA963.M28 1991, (v5)
Mansfield, Edward D. HF1379.M36 1994, (v6)
Mansfield, Harvey Claflin. JC143.M4.M355 1996, (v7)
   JK21.M26 1991, (v7)
Mansfield, Joseph King Fenno. UA26.A6.M3, (v10)
Mansfield, Katherine. PR6025.A57.A4 1929, (v3)
   PR6025.A57.S35 1940, (v3)
   PR6025.A57 S5 1937, (v3)
   PR6025.A57.Z5 1954, (v3)
   PR6025.A57.Z556 1951, (v3)
   PR9639.3.M258.Z48 1984, (v3)
Mansfield, Nick. PN56.M32.M36 1997, (v3)
Mansfield, Peter. DS37.7.M33 1976, (v5)
   DS62.4.M36 1991, (v5)
   DS62.8.M348 1973b, (v5)
Mansfield, Sue. U21.2.M34, (v10)
Mansion, J. E. PC2112.M313 1971, (v3)
Mansoor, Peter R. D769.M34 1999, (v5)
Manthey-Zorn, Otto. B3317.M29, (v8)
Manton, Catherine. HQ1410.M355 1999, (v6)
Mantyla, Martti. T385.M363 1988, (v1)
Manucy, Albert C. F319.S2.M34 1997, (v4)
Manuel, Frank Edward. B1911.M3, (v8)
   BT93.M35 1992, (v8)
   D15.N4.M3, (v5)
   D286.M33, (v5)
Manuel, Peter Lamarche. ML3470.M33 1988, (v9)
   ML3565.M36 1995, (v9)
Manutchehr-Danai, Mohsen. QE392.M29 2000, (v1)
Manvell, Roger. PR3518.Z5.M36 1987, (v3)
Manville, Philip Brook. JC75.C5.M36 1990, (v7)
Manwell, Reginald D. QL366.M3 1968, (v1)
Manz, Beatrice Forbes. DS23.M28 1989, (v5)
Manz, Beatriz. F1465.3.G6.M36 1988, (v4)
Manzetti, Luigi. JL2081.M36 1993, (v7)
Manzini, Ezio. TS171.M3713 1989, (v1)
Manzione, Carol Kazmierczak. HV1150.L8.C486 1995, (v6)
Manzione, Joseph. E99.D1.S6123 1990, (v4)
Manzo, Kathryn A. JC311.M345 1996, (v7)
Mao, Douglas. PN56.M54.M36 1998, (v3)
Mao, Tse-tung. B5234.M35.M3413 1990, (v8)
   DS778.M3.A4295 (v5)
   DS778.M3.A515, (v5)
   DS778.M3.A516, (v5)
   DS778.M3.A538 1969, (v5)
   HN740.H78.M3613 1990, (v6)
   U240.M28 1966, (v10)
   U240.M343, (v10)
Mao, Tun. PL2801.N2.T9213, (v3)
Maòhf ̄uòz, Naj ̄ib. PJ7846.A46A25 1991, (v3)
   PJ7846.A46A6913 1984, (v3)
   PJ7846.A46A913 1995, (v3)
   PJ7846.A46C35 2001, (v3)
   PJ7846.A46H5413 1988, (v3)
   PJ7846.A46L513 1989, (v3)
   PJ7846.A46M2813 1994, (v3)
   PJ7846.A46S413 1986, (v3)
   PJ7846.A46S9613 1995, (v3)
   PJ7846.A46T513 1993, (v3)
   PJ7846.A46Z4813 1992, (v3)
Maor, Eli. QA9.M316 1991, (v1)
   QA247.5.M33 1994, (v1)

Maoz, Moshe. DS95.6.I75.M36 1995, (v5)
Maoz, Zeev. U21.2.M346 1989, (v10)
Maple, Frank F. HV43.M285 1998, (v6)
Mapp, Edward. PN1590.B53.M3 1990, (v3)
Marable, Manning. E185.61.M32 1991, (v4)
   E185.615.M2783 1998, (v4)
Marah, John Karefah. LA1501.M34 1989, (v7)
Maraini, Dacia. PQ2246.M3.M3713 1998, (v3)
Maramba, Asuncion David. PL5543.D38, (v3)
Marani, Pietro C. ND623.L5.M32413 2000, (v9)
Maraniss, David. E886.M29 1995, (v4)
Maraniss, James E. PQ6312.M3, (v3)
Marantz, Sylvia S. NC965.M34 1992, (v9)
Mararike, C. G. HN802.Z9.C648 1995, (v6)
Maravall, Jose Maria. JN96.A58.M37 1997, (v7)
Marback, Richard. B395.M275 1999, (v8)
Marble, Allan Everett. R463.N8.M37 1993, (v2)
Marc, David. PN1992.3.U5.M26 1984, (v3)
   PN1992.3.U5.M264 1992, (v3)
   PN1992.6.M366 1995, (v3)
   PN1992.8.C66.M35 1997, (v3)
Marcel, Gabriel. B2430.M253.A93, (v8)
   B2430.M253.E85 1965, (v8)
March, Ivan. ML156.9.G73 1999, (v9)
March, James G. JC249.M37 1989, (v7)
March, John. PS3505.A87.Z73 1993, (v3)
March, William. PS3505.A53157.A6 1956, (v3)
Marchaj, Czeslaw A. VM331.M36 1980, (v10)
Marchalonis, Shirley. PS2223.M37 1989, (v3)
Marchand, C. Roland. JX1961.U6.M37, (v7)
Marchand, Leslie Alexis. PR4381.M33, (v3)
   PR4381.M3317, (v3)
   PR4381.M332, (v3)
Marchand, Roland. HF5813.U6.M26 1985, (v6)
Marchand, Suzanne L. DD193.5 .M37 1996, (v5)
Marchetti, Gina. PN1995.9.A78.M37 1993, (v3)
Marchionini, Gary. QA76.9.H85.M38 1995, (v1)
Marchitello, Howard. PR438.S35.M37 1997, (v3)
Marckwardt, Albert Henry. PE123.M3 1972, (v3)
Marco, Guy A. ML120.U5.M133 1996, (v9)
   ML120.U5 M135 1996, (v9)
   ML128.O4 M28 2001, (v9)
Marcombe, David. DA690.R44.M37 1993, (v5)
Marconi, Joe. HD69.B7.M373 2000, (v6)
Marconi, Joe. HF5415.122.M367 1997, (v6)
Marcus Aurelius. B580.H53 M3713 2002, (v8)
Marcus, Alan I. RA1270.F4.M37 1994, (v2)
   T21.M372 1999, (v1)
Marcus, Alan R. E99.E7.M285 1995, (v4)
Marcus, Daniel A. QA164.M345 1998, (v1)
Marcus, Geoffrey Jules. VA454.M319, (v10)
   VA454.M32, (v10)
Marcus, Greil. CB428.M356 1989, (v5)
   E169.04.M365 1995, (v4)
   ML420.D98.M16 1997, (v9)
Marcus, Harold G. DT381.M33 1994, (v5)
Marcus, Jacob Rader. E184.J5.M237 1989, (v4)
   HQ1172.M37, (v6)
Marcus, Jane. PR6045.O72.Z8147 1987, (v3)
Marcus, Joyce. F1219.3.W94.M37 1992, (v4)
Marcus, Leah S. PR2976.M39 1988, (v3)
Marcus, Marvin. PL811.O7.Z768 1993, (v3)
Marcus, Millicent Joy. PN1993.5.I88.M278 1993, (v3)
Marcus, Mordecai. PS3511.R94.Z785 1991, (v3)
Marcus, Robert D. JK2320.A7 1880, (v7)
Marcus, Stanley E. NB237.S567.M27 1983, (v9)
Marcuse, Herbert. B945.M298 1998 vol. 1, (v8)
   B945.M2983 S86 1972, (v8)
   HM101.M268, (v6)
Marcuse, Michael J. PR56.M37 1990, (v3)
Marcuse, Peter M. R130.M346 1996, (v2)
Marcy, Randolph Barnes. F593.M33, (v4)
Marder, Arthur Jacob. VA454.M34, (v10)
   VA454.M35, (v10)
   VA454.M37 1981, (v10)
Marder, Herbert. PR6045.O72.Z8152 2000, (v3)
Marder, Louis. PR2965.M3, (v3)
Maré, Gerhard. JQ1998.I54 M375 1993, (v7)
Maré, Margaret Laura. PT2434.Z5.M33, (v3)
Marechera, Dambudzo. PR9390.9.M3.C46 1992, (v3)
Marenbon, John. B765.A24 M37 1997, (v8)

Marentes, Luis A. F1234.V3, (v4)
Margalit, Avishai. JC336.M35 1996, (v7)
Margary, Ivan Donald. DA145.M34, (v5)
Margavio, Anthony V. SH380.62.U6.M37 1996, (v1)
Margenau, Henry. QA37.M33 1956, (v1)
   QC6.M3514, (v1)
Margerison, Kenneth. DC150.M32 1998, (v5)
Margo, Robert A. LC66.5.S68.M37 1990, (v7)
Margolian, Howard. D803.M365 2000, (v5)
   D804.G4.M3225 1998, (v5)
Margolick, David. K184.M367 1995, (v7)
   PR2983.M338 1992, (v3)
Margolin, Victor. N6494.M64.M36 1997, (v9)
Margoliouth, Herschel Maurice. PR5883.M3 1966, (v3)
Margolis, Diane Rothbard. BF697.M32 1998, (v2)
Margolis, Joseph. B29.M3673 1984, (v8)
   B804.M284 1995, (v8)
   BD221.M33 1991, (v8)
   BH39.M394 1978, (v8)
   BJ21.M28, (v8)
   BJ1031.M312 1996, (v8)
   D16.9.M276 1993, (v5)
   N7445.2.M26 1999, (v9)
Margolis, Maxine L. F128.9.B68.M37 1994, (v4)
Margolis, Michael. HM851.M37 2000, (v6)
Margolis, Nadia. Z8451.M37 1990, (v10)
Margolis, Richard J. HV1461.M36 1990, (v6)
Margolis, Sheldon. KF273.M35 1993, (v7)
Margulies, Donald. PS3563.A653.A6 1995, (v3)
Margulies, Ivone. PN1998.3.A435.M37 1996, (v3)
Margulies, Sheldon. KF273.M35 1993, (v7)
Margulis, Alexander. PN6505.S5.M34 2000, (v3)
Margulis, Lynn. HQ12.M35 1991, (v6)
   QH83.M36 1998, (v1)
   QH311.M37 1997, (v1)
   QH325.M298 1995, (v1)
   QH366.2.M36, (v1)
   QH371.M28 1986, (v1)
   QH481.M27 1986, (v1)
   QH548.M35 1998, (v1)
Mariani, Giorgio. PS1449.C85.Z735 1992, (v3)
Mariani, Paul L. PR4803.H44.Z717, (v3)
   PS3503.E744.Z79 1990, (v3)
   PS3505.R272.Z753 1999, (v3)
Mariano, Nicky. N8375.B46.M3 1966a, (v9)
Mariategui, Jose Carlos. F3408.M3313, (v4)
Marichal, Carlos. HJ8514.5.M357 1989, (v6)
Marien, Mary Warner. TR187.M37 1997, (v1)
Marietta, Don E. B162.9.M34 1998, (v8)
Maril, Robert Lee. F392.R5 M37 1989, (v4)
Marilley, Suzanne M. JK1896.M37 1996, (v7)
Marin, John. ND237.M24.G7, (v9)
Marincola, John. D56.M37 1997, (v5)
Marine Biological Association of the United Kingdom. GC1311.M37, (v6)
Marinetti, Filippo Tommaso. NX600.F8.M37 1972, (v9)
Marini, Stephen A. BR520.M36 1982, (v8)
Marino, Adrian. PN81.M47313 1996, (v3)
Marino, Andy. D809.U5.M37 1999, (v5)
Marion, David E. KF8745.B68.M37 1997, (v7)
Marion, Donald J. PN1993.5.C4.M37 1997, (v3)
Marion, Jean-Luc. B3279.H49.M27413 1998, (v8)
Marion, Nancy E. HV7921.M37 1994, (v6)
Mariscal, George. PQ6424.Z5.M28 1991, (v3)
Maritain, Jacques. B792.M33, (v8)
   B1875.M342, (v8)
   B2430.M33.R32, (v8)
   BD22.M37 1989, (v8)
   BD162.M273 1959, (v8)
   BJ72.M313, (v8)
   BT102.M3, (v8)
   D16.8.M286 1973, (v5)
   LB775.M3566, (v7)
Marius, Richard. DA334.M8.M275 1984, (v5)
Marivaux, Pierre Carlet de Chamblain de. PQ2003.A136, (v3)
   PQ2003.V5 1934, (v3)
Mark, James E. QD196.M37 1992, (v1)
Mark, Joan T. E57.F54.M37 1988, (v4)
Mark, Margaret. HF5415.15.M334 2001, (v6)

Mark, Michael L. MT3.U5.M32 1996, (v9)
Mark, Robert. NA2760.M365 1990, (v9)
Mark, Samuel. DT60.M36 1998, (v5)
Markakis, John. DT367.75.M37 1987, (v5)
Markandaya, Kamala. PR6063.A642.T85x, (v3)
Marke, Julius J. KF1.M3 1984, (v7)
Markel, Michael H. T10.5.M34 2001, (v1)
Markell, Edward K. RC119.M3 1999, (v2)
Marken, Mitchell W. DP44.M27 1994, (v5)
Marker, Chris. PN1997.J444 1992, (v3)
Marker, Frederick J. PT7082.M3, (v3)
Markert, Jenny. F737.G5.M37 1993, (v4)
Markevitch, Dimitry. ML128.V5.M28 1989, (v9)
Markham, Ian S. BJ1275.M365 1994, (v8)
Markman, Peter T. F1219.3.M4.M36 1989, (v4)
Markos, Donald W. PS3545.I544.Z6265 1994, (v3)
Markov, Vladimir. PG3065.F8.M33, (v3)
Markovits, Andrei S. DD290.29.M37 1997, (v5)
Markovits, Andrei S. GV706.5.M363 2001, (v6)
Markovits, Richard S. KF4749.M37 1998, (v7)
Markowitz, Fran. F128.9.J5.M27 1993, (v4)
Marks, Carole. E185.8.M22 1989, (v4)
Marks, Deborah. HV1568.2.M37 1999, (v6)
Marks, Frederick W. E756.M37, (v4)
  E835.M328 1993, (v4)
Marks, John. B2430.D454.M35 1998, (v8)
Marks, Jonathan. GN62.8.M37 1995, (v6)
Marks, Laura U. PN1993.5.D44.M37 1999, (v3)
Marks, Lynne Sorrel. F1057.M27 1996, (v4)
Marks, Martin Miller. ML2075.M242 1997, (v9)
Marks, P. J. M. Z269.M37 1998, (v10)
Marks, Paula Mitchell. F819.T6.M37 1989, (v4)
Marks, Richard Lee. F2936.M335 1991, (v4)
Marks, Sally. D644.M37 1976, (v5)
Marks, Steven G. DK766.M36 1991, (v5)
Marks, Thomas A. DS586.M37 1995, (v5)
  DS799.82.W346.M37 1996, (v5)
Markun, Leo. BJ71.M35, (v8)
Markus, John. TK454.M29 1988, (v1)
Markus, John. TK7804.M354 1994, (v1)
Markus, Kurt. F596.M25 1985, (v4)
Markus, R. A. BR219.M37 1990, (v8)
Markusen, Eric. HV6322.7.M37 1995, (v6)
Markwick, Roger D. DK38.M2725 2001, (v5)
Marley, David. E18.75.M374 1998, (v4)
Marlin, Emily. HV5133.M37 1987, (v6)
Marling, Karal Ann. D767.99.I9.M28 1991, (v5)
  E169.02.M3534 1994, (v4)
  E312.17.M3 1988, (v4)
Marlow, James E. PR4592.T5.M37 1993, (v3)
Marlowe, Christopher. PR2661.B7 1970, (v3)
  PR2661.G5 1987 vol. 2, (v3)
  PR2662.M22, (v3)
  PR2662.R5 1963, (v3)
  PR2664.A, (v3)
  PR2664.A1 1928, (v3)
  PR2665.A1 1967, (v3)
Marmier, Pierre. QC776.M3, (v1)
Marmol, Jose. PQ7797.M27.A7 1955, (v3)
Marmor, Theodore R. HN59.2.M374 1990, (v6)
Marmullaku, Ramadan. DR701.S5.M3213 1975, (v5)
Marnef, Guido. BR828.A4.M37 1996, (v8)
Marolda, Edward J. DS79.744.N38, (v5)
Marov, Mikhail IAkovlevich. QB621.M37 1998, (v1)
Marowitz, Charles. PN2061.M234 1998, (v3)
Marowitz, Charles. PR2965.M35 1991, (v3)
Marples, David R. DK265.M3153 2000, (v5)
  DK507.73.M37 1996, (v5)
  HC337.U5.M28 1991, (v6)
  TK1362.S65.M37 1988, (v1)
Marquand, C. TJ265.M317 1994, (v1)
Marquand, David. DA566.9.M25.M37, (v5)
Marquand, John P. PS3525.A6695 B2, (v3)
  PS3525.A6695 H2, (v3)
  PS3525.A6695 L2, (v3)
  PS3525.A6695 L3 1940, (v3)
  PS3525.A6695.L5 1957, (v3)
  PS3525.A6695 P6, (v3)
  PS3525.A6695 S5, (v3)
  PS3525.A6695 S7, (v3)
  PS3525.A6695.T55 1954, (v3)

PS3525.A6695 W5, (v3)
PS3525.A6695 W6, (v3)
Marquard, Odo. B29.M36774 1989, (v8)
Marquart, Frank. HD6509.M37.A33, (v6)
Marquart, James W. HV8699.U5.M35 1994, (v6)
Marques, Antonio Henrique R. de Oliveira.
  DP532.3.M3413, (v5)
  DP538.M37, (v5)
Marquez, Benjamin. E184.M5.M357 1993, (v4)
Marquis, Alice Goldfarb. PN2293.E35.M27 1995, (v3)
Marquis, Don, 1878-1937. PS3525.A67.O4 1937, (v3)
  PS3525.A67.A6 1946, (v3)
  PS3525.A67.L5 1950, (v3)
Marquis, Susan L. UA34.S64.M37 1997, (v10)
Marquis, Vivienne. SF271.M247 1985, (v1)
Marqusee, Mike. GV1132.A44.M37 1999, (v6)
Marr, David G. Z3226.M39 1992, (v10)
Marr, David. PR9619.3.W5.Z76 1991, (v3)
Marr, Phebe. DS79.65.M33 1985, (v5)
Marra, Ben. E98.P86.M37 1996, (v4)
Marra, Michele. BH221.J3.M36 1999, (v8)
Marrelli, T. M. RA645.35.M37 2001, (v2)
  RT50.M37 2000, (v2)
Marrese, Michelle Lamarche. HQ1662.M367 2002, (v6)
Marriner-Tomey, Ann. RT89.3.M37 2000, (v2)
Marriott, Alice Lee. E98.P8.M28, (v4)
Marriott, Kim. QA76.63.M37 1998, (v1)
Marris, Robin Lapthorn. HD20.4.M33 1964, (v6)
Marrone, Claire. PQ149.M29 2000, (v3)
Marrone, Gaetana. PN1998.3.C4.M37 2000, (v3)
Marrou, Henri Irenee. LA31.M32, (v7)
Marrus, Michael Robert. D804.3.M37 1987, (v5)
  DS135.F83.M3813, (v5)
Marryat, Frederick. E165.M372, (v4)
  PR4977.M7 1990, (v3)
Mars, P. TK5102.9.M374 1996, (v1)
Marschark, Marc. HV2391.M26 1997, (v6)
Marsden, George M. BT82.2.M39 1991, (v8)
  LA226.M34 1994, (v7)
Marsden, Peter. DS371.2.M373 2002, (v5)
Marsh, Alec. PS3531.O82.Z746 1998, (v3)
Marsh, Charles. F347.L3, (v4)
Marsh, Christopher. BR756.M45 1998, (v8)
Marsh, David. DA589.7.M37 1999, (v5)
  HD8391.M33 1992, (v6)
Marsh, George Perkins. GF31.M35 1965, (v6)
Marsh, J. B. T. ML400.M34 1969, (v9)
Marsh, Jan. PR5238.M37 1995, (v3)
Marsh, Margaret S. RC889.M368 1996, (v2)
Marsh, Nicholas. PR6023.A93.Z6777 2000, (v3)
Marsh, Peter T. DA565.C4.M35 1994, (v5)
Marsh, Robert Mortimer. DS754.M37, (v5)
  HN749.T35.M37 1996, (v6)
Marsh, Rosalind J. PG2975.M34 1995, (v3)
Marshak, Laura E. HV1568.M277 1999, (v6)
Marshall, Adre. PS2127.P8.M37 1998, (v3)
Marshall, Alex. HT166.M259 2000, (v6)
Marshall, Alfred. HB98.2.M37, (v6)
  HB171.M354, (v6)
  HD2326.M3 1970, (v6)
Marshall, Catherine. H62.M277 1989, (v6)
Marshall, Charles F. D810.S7.M274 1998, (v5)
Marshall, Cynthia. PR2981.5.M37 1991, (v3)
Marshall, Donald G. Z6514.C97.M37 1993, (v10)
Marshall, Edison. SK17.M34.A3, (v1)
Marshall, Gail. PN2582.W65.M37 1998, (v3)
Marshall, Geoffrey. PR691.M37, (v3)
Marshall, George C. D570.9.M37 1976, (v5)
Marshall, George J. Z7763.A54.M37 1999, (v10)
Marshall, George O. PR5588.M3, (v3)
Marshall, Helen E. RT37.N87.M37, (v2)
Marshall, Herbert. PN2287.A457.M37 1993, (v3)
Marshall, Howard W. NA730.N32.P376 1995, (v9)
Marshall, Ian. PS286.A6.M37 1998, (v3)
Marshall, James M. F586.M78.M37 1986, (v4)
Marshall, John R. RC552.S62.M37 1994, (v2)
Marshall, John. E302.M365, (v4)
Marshall, Judi. HF5500.2.M248 1984, (v6)
Marshall, Louise H. QP353.M367 1998, (v1)
Marshall, Paule. PS3563.A7223.C5 1984, (v3)

Marshall, Peter H. F1788.M256 1987, (v4)
Marshall, Richard. N6608.B276.A4 1992, (v9)
Marshall, Robert Lewis. ML410.B13.M28 1989, (v9)
Marshall, Robert. F909.M373, (v4)
Marshall, Rosalind Kay. BX9223.M37 2000, (v8)
Marshall, S. J. PL2464.Z7M37 2001, (v3)
Marshall, S. L. A. D15.M34.A32, (v5)
  D743.9.M287, (v5)
Marshall, Suzanne. F456.M37 1994, (v4)
Marshall, Thomas R. KF8748.M287 1989, (v7)
Marshall, Thurgood. KF8745.M34 A4 2001, (v7)
Marshall, W. Gerald. PR3777.M37 1993, (v3)
Marshall, William Harvey. PR4381.M334, (v3)
  PR4388.M3, (v3)
Marston, John. PR2691.W6, (v3)
Marston, John. PR2694.A52 1991, (v3)
Marston, Nicholas. ML410.B42.M25 1995, (v9)
Marston, R. M. TK7871.99.M44.M26 1995, (v1)
  TK7881.15.M37 1997, (v1)
Marszalek, John F. E467.1.S55.M34 1993, (v4)
  Z8176.45.M37 1988, (v10)
Martel, Leon. D753.2.R9.M37, (v5)
Martell, Bill. GV1195.M327 1993, (v6)
Marten, Harry. PS3501.I5.Z748 1988, (v3)
Marten, James Alan. E468.9.M125 1998, (v4)
  E532.9.M37 1990, (v4)
Martens, Rainer. GV711.M355 1997, (v6)
Marti, Donald B. HD1485.N39.M37 1991, (v6)
Marti, James. R733.M38 1998, (v2)
Marti, Kevin. PR1972.G353.M37 1991, (v3)
Martial. PA6502.B35 1993, (v3)
Martienssen, Rex Distin. NA270.M34 1964, (v9)
Martin Du Gard, Roger. PQ2613.I2.Z65462, (v3)
Martin Gaite, Carmen. GT2762.A2.M37 1991, (v6)
Martin, A. Lynn. HV5438.M37 2001, (v6)
  RC178.A1.M37 1996, (v2)
Martin, Albro. HE2751.M35 1992, (v6)
Martin, Alexander M. DK194.M3 1997, (v5)
Martin, Augustine. PR8714.M37 1996, (v3)
Martin, Benjamin. HD8584.M28 1990, (v6)
Martin, Bessie. E551.M25 2003, (v4)
Martin, Bill. HX542.M31785 1996, (v6)
Martin, Brian G. DS796.S257.M36 1996, (v5)
Martin, Burns. PR3657.M3 1973, (v3)
Martin, Calvin. E78.C2.M33, (v4)
Martin, Calvin. E98.P5.M36 1999, (v4)
Martin, Carmela. HC385.M27213 1999, (v6)
Martin, Carol A. PR4688.M38 1994, (v3)
Martin, Carol J. GV1623.M37 1994, (v6)
Martin, Catherine Gimelli. PR3562.M287 1998, (v3)
Martin, Cathie J. HJ4653.C7.M334 1991, (v6)
Martin, Charles. PA6276.M37 1992, (v3)
Martin, Cheryl English. F1391.C447.M37 1996, (v4)
Martin, Claude. PQ2613.I2.Z654615, (v3)
Martin, Constance R. QP187.M3458 1995, (v1)
Martin, Daniel R. RC440.9.M37 1989, (v2)
Martin, David E. GV1065.17.T73.M37 1997, (v6)
Martin, David. BX4832.5.M37 1990, (v8)
  D754.Y9.M37 1990, (v8)
Martin, Edwin M. D802.J3.M37, (v5)
Martin, Emily. GN296.5.U6.M37 1994, (v6)
Martin, F. David. NB1137.M37, (v9)
Martin, Fenton S. JK1108.M349 1996, (v7)
  KF8741.A1.M36 1992, (v7)
  KF8741.A1.M37 1990, (v7)
  Z1249.P7.M357 1987, (v10)
  Z1249.P7.M365 1996, (v10)
Martin, Francis. BT83.55.M27 1994, (v8)
Martin, Frederick N. RF290.M34 2002, (v2)
Martin, Gary J. GN476.73.M37 1995, (v6)
Martin, Gay N. F367.3.M37 1996, (v4)
Martin, Glen T. B828.3.M27 1989, (v8)
Martin, Graham Dunstan. PQ1184.M28 1971, (v3)
Martin, Gus. HV6431.M367 2003, (v6)
Martin, Harold C. PN3365.S79 1959, (v3)
Martin, Harold H. F294.A857.M37 1987, (v4)
Martin, Henri Jean. Z40.M3713 1994, (v10)
Martin, Jacqueline. PN2071.S65.M37 1990, (v3)
Martin, James Alfred. BL65.A4.M35 1990, (v8)
Martin, James Kirby. E278.A7.M37 1997, (v4)

Martin, James. HD30.2122.M37 1996, **(v6)**
　JC265.G68.M37 1998, **(v7)**
　LB2341.M2894 1997, **(v7)**
　QL666.L23.M365 1992, **(v1)**
Martin, Janet M. KF4136.A32.A165 1994, **(v7)**
Martin, Joel W. E98.R3 M333 2001, **(v4)**
Martin, John D. HD47.3.M37 2000, **(v6)**
Martin, John Rupert. N6415.B3.M37 1977b, **(v9)**
Martin, Joseph Plumb. E275.M38 1995, **(v4)**
Martin, Kenneth W. TK7874.65.M37 2000, **(v1)**
Martin, Len D. PN1999.C57.M37 1991, **(v3)**
Martin, Lisa L. HF1413.5.M37 1992, **(v6)**
Martin, Mart. HQ1236.M347 2000, **(v6)**
　HQ1236.5.U6.M3778 1999, **(v6)**
Martin, Mary. ML420.M332.A3, **(v9)**
Martin, Michael. BL2747.3.M3313 1990, **(v8)**
Martin, Mildred. Z8260.5.M3, **(v10)**
Martin, Nicholas. BH221.G32.M37 1996, **(v8)**
Martin, Paul Sidney. E61.M36, **(v4)**
Martin, Peter J. ML3795.M188 1995, **(v9)**
Martin, Peter. PR3325.M37 2000, **(v3)**
Martin, Philip W. PR4388.M35 1982, **(v3)**
Martin, R. D. QL737.P9.M32 1990, **(v1)**
Martin, R. M. B831.5.M3, **(v8)**
　B840.M36 1958a, **(v8)**
Martin, Ralph G. DA565.C6.M3, **(v5)**
Martin, Rex. K258.M37 1993, **(v7)**
Martin, Richard. PN1995.9.F54.M37 1997, **(v3)**
Martin, Robert Bernard. PR4803.H44.Z71727 1991,
　(v3)
　PR5581.M3 1980, **(v3)**
Martin, Robert K. PS310.H66.M3 1998, **(v3)**
Martin, Ronald E. PS169.K45.M37 1991, **(v3)**
Martin, Sandy Dwayne. BV2521.M37 1989, **(v8)**
Martin, Scott C. F138.M37 1995, **(v4)**
Martin, Shannon E. PN4855.M325 1998, **(v3)**
Martin, Susan Ehrlich. HV9950.M3 1996, **(v6)**
Martin, Thomas Lyle. UA927.M27, **(v10)**
Martin, Thomas Wesley. F335.F8 M33 1949, **(v4)**
Martin, Thomas. F375.M37, **(v4)**
Martin, Tovah. SB419.M32 1988, **(v1)**
Martin, Tyrone G. VA65.C7.M33, **(v10)**
Martin, Vanessa. DS318.84.K48, **(v5)**
Martin, W. PF640.M37 1998, **(v3)**
　PF640.M38 1986, **(v3)**
Martin, W. R. PS2124.M295 1994, **(v3)**
Martin, Waldo E. E449.D75.M37 1984, **(v4)**
Martin, William Oliver. BD111.M3, **(v8)**
　BD241.M3, **(v8)**
Martindale, Charles. PR3037.M37 1990, **(v3)**
Martindale, Kathleen. PS153.L46.M37 1997, **(v3)**
Martindale, Meredith. ND237.P375.A4 1990, **(v9)**
Martine, Brian J. B105.D47 M37 1992, **(v8)**
Martine, James J. PS3525.I5156.C735 1993, **(v3)**
Martineau, Belinda. SB123.57.M37 2001, **(v1)**
Martineau, Harriet. E165.M379, **(v4)**
　PR4984.M5.A6 1994, **(v3)**
Martineau, Henri. PQ2441.M19 1951, **(v3)**
Martinelli, Phylis Cancilla. F819.S37.M27 1989, **(v4)**
Martines, Lauro. DG494.M37 1979, **(v5)**
　DG737.55.M3, **(v5)**
Martinez Amador, Emilio Maria. PC4640.M3 1958,
　(v3)
Martinez Bengoa, Javier. HC192.M34 1996, **(v6)**
Martinez Bonati, Felix. PQ6353.M369 1992, **(v3)**
Martinez Cuenca, Alejandro. F1528.22.M35.A3 1992,
　(v4)
Martinez de Castillo, Sandra Luz. RT42.M246 1999,
　(v2)
Martinez, Elena M. PQ7081.M3617 1996, **(v3)**
Martinez, Elizabeth Sutherland. E184.A1.M313 1998,
　(v4)
Martinez, Luis. DT295.6.M3713 2000, **(v5)**
Martinez, Michael E. LB1060.M337 2000, **(v7)**
Martinez, Nancy C. Z2014.P7.M34 1991, **(v10)**
Martinez, Oscar J. F786.M42 1988, **(v4)**
　F790.M5.M37 2001, **(v4)**
Marting, Diane E. PQ7082.N7.M354 2001, **(v3)**
Martini, Fritz. PT85.M3 1984, **(v3)**
　PT391.M3 1981, **(v3)**
Martinich, Aloysius. B1246.M38 1999, **(v8)**

Martino, Joseph Paul. Q180.U5.M326 1992, **(v1)**
Martino, Pierre. PQ145.7.E2M3 1971, **(v3)**
　PQ438.M3, **(v3)**
Martinon, Philippe. PC2105.M3, **(v3)**
Martins, Wilson. PQ9555.M313 1970, **(v3)**
Martinson, Steven D. PT2492.M36 1996, **(v3)**
Martinussen, John. HC59.7.M326 1997, **(v6)**
　JS7180.3.A3 M37 1995, **(v7)**
Martis, Kenneth C. G1201.F7.M3 1993, **(v6)**
　G1201.F9.M26 1989, **(v6)**
　G1201.F9.M3 1982, **(v6)**
　G1281.F8.M3 1994, **(v6)**
Marton, Andrew. PN1998.3.M37.A3 1991, **(v3)**
Martos, Joseph. BX2200.M355, **(v8)**
Marty, Martin E. BR515.M324 1984, **(v8)**
　BR526.M35, **(v8)**
　BX8080.B645.M3, **(v8)**
　JK1764.M37 1997, **(v7)**
Marty, Myron A. NA2127.S66.M37 1999, **(v9)**
Martyn, Barrie. ML410.R12.M17 1990, **(v9)**
Martz, Louis Lohr. PR533.M37 1991, **(v3)**
　PR2322.M35 1990, **(v3)**
　PR3581.M28, **(v3)**
　PR3588.M376, **(v3)**
Martzolff, Clement L. F492.M38, **(v4)**
Maruyama, Kaoru. PL833.A7.A6 1990, **(v3)**
Marvel, William. E467.1.B8.M37 1991, **(v4)**
　E591.M3 1996, **(v4)**
　E612.A5.M44 1994, **(v4)**
Marvell, Andrew. PR3546.A1 1974, **(v3)**
　PR3546.A6 1990, **(v3)**
Marven, Craig. TK5102.9.M38 1996, **(v1)**
Marvin, Clara. ML134.P2 M37 2001, **(v9)**
Marwick, Arthur. DA566.4.M357 1968, **(v5)**
　DA577.M37, **(v5)**
Marx, Adolf Bernhard. MT6.M313 1997, **(v9)**
Marx, Anthony W. DT1757.M38 1991, **(v5)**
　HT1521.M283 1998, **(v6)**
Marx, Elisabeth. HD58.7.M3747 1999, **(v6)**
Marx, Karl. B2923.Z7.M313 1970, **(v8)**
　BL2775.M3983 1964, **(v8)**
　D363.M37 1974b, **(v5)**
　DC274.M35, **(v5)**
　DC312.M3 1940, **(v5)**
　E469.8.M374, **(v4)**
　HB97.5.M3313 1971b, **(v6)**
　HB301.M4, **(v6)**
　HB501.M3393, **(v6)**
　HB501.M367T6 1942, **(v6)**
　HB863.M253 1971, **(v6)**
　HM57.M33 1964, **(v6)**
Marx, Leo. E169.1.M35 2000, **(v4)**
Marx-Scouras, Danielle. PN5190.T44.M37 1996, **(v3)**
Mary Crow Dog. E99.D1.M425 1990, **(v4)**
Marzan, Julio. PQ7439.P24.Z76 1995, **(v3)**
Marzolf, Marion. PN4864.M37 1991, **(v3)**
Marzulla, Nancie G. KF5599.M3 1997, **(v7)**
Masamune, Hakucho. PL811.A8.B5 1934, **(v3)**
Masaoka, Shiki. PL811.A83.A28 1997, **(v3)**
Masaryk, T. G. DK32.M4 1955, **(v5)**
Maschio, Thomas. DU740.42.M373 1994, **(v5)**
Maschke, Karen J. KF3467.M37 1989, **(v7)**
Mascia-Lees, Frances E. HQ1190.M376 2000, **(v6)**
Masefield, John. PR6025.A77S3 1916, **(v3)**
　PR6025.A77 B5, **(v3)**
　PR6025.A77 C3, **(v3)**
　PR6025.A77 O3 1926, **(v3)**
　PR6025.A77.Z487 1985, **(v3)**
Mashaw, Jerry L. KF2212.M37 1990, **(v7)**
　KF4930.M37 1997, **(v7)**
Masih, Joseph R. DK687.5.M37 1999, **(v5)**
Maskell, Brian H. HD9725.M367 1991, **(v6)**
Masland, Richard L. RJ499.M3, **(v2)**
Maslen, Elizabeth. PR888.P6, **(v3)**
Maslen, R. W. PR839.S65.M38 1997, **(v3)**
Maslon, Laurence. PN2277.W22.A7336 1990, **(v3)**
Maslow, Abraham H. BD232.M34, **(v8)**
　BF199.M3, **(v2)**
　BF683.M37 1970, **(v2)**
　BF698.M338 1968, **(v2)**
　BL53.M38, **(v8)**

　HF5548.8.M3754 1998, **(v6)**
Masnik, Ann S. Z7963.J4 C36 1987 Suppl, **(v10)**
Mason, Alpheus Thomas. KF8745.S8.M3 1968, **(v7)**
　KF8745.T27.M3 1983, **(v7)**
Mason, Bim. PN3203.M37 1992, **(v3)**
Mason, David S. DJK50.M38 1992, **(v5)**
Mason, Eudo Colecestra. PT1925.M32 1967, **(v3)**
Mason, George. E302.M38 1970, **(v4)**
Mason, Germaine. PQ119.M3, **(v3)**
Mason, H. A. PR418.H8.M3 1960, **(v3)**
Mason, Haydn Trevor. PQ2122.M3 1975b, **(v3)**
Mason, John R. TK2831.M37 1993, **(v1)**
Mason, Katrina R. QC773.3.U5.M29 1995, **(v1)**
Mason, Laura. ML3621.R48.M37 1996, **(v9)**
Mason, Mary Ann. KF547.M368 1999, **(v7)**
　KF547.M37 1994, **(v7)**
Mason, Michael. D883.M39 1997, **(v5)**
Mason, Michael. HQ18.G7.M28 1994, **(v6)**
Mason, Owen K. GB5010.M37 1997, **(v6)**
Mason, Penelope E. N7350.M26 1993, **(v9)**
Mason, Richard. BC50.M36 2000, **(v8)**
Mason, Robert J. G1201.G3.M3 1990, **(v6)**
Mason, Robert L. QA279.M373 1989, **(v1)**
Mason, Robin. LC1090.M36 1998, **(v7)**
Mason, Stephen Finney. QH325.M32 1990, **(v1)**
Mason, T. J. QD801.M374 1999, **(v1)**
Mason, Tony. GV944.S64.M27 1995, **(v6)**
Masquelier, Adeline Marie. BL2480.M32, **(v8)**
Mass, Jeffrey P. DS859.M25, **(v5)**
Mass, Wendy. PS490.M37 2000, **(v3)**
Massa, Werner. QD945.M37713 2000, **(v1)**
Massaro, John. KF8776.M335 1990, **(v7)**
Masschaele, James. HF3515.M37 1997, **(v6)**
Massengale, Jean Montague. ND553.F7.M38 1993,
　(v9)
Massey, A.G. QD151.2.M37 2000, **(v1)**
Massey, Anne. PN1993.5.A1.M37 2000, **(v3)**
Massey, Calvin R. KF4558 9th.M37 1995, **(v7)**
Massey, Douglas S. E185.61.M373 1993, **(v4)**
Massey, Gerald J. BC135.M35, **(v8)**
Massey, Patrick. HC665.M38 1995, **(v6)**
Massey, William S. QA612.M37 1977, **(v1)**
Massie, Henry N. RJ506.P69.M37 1984, **(v2)**
Massie, Robert K. DK131.M28, **(v5)**
Massie, Robert. E183.8.S6.M28 1997, **(v4)**
Massinger, Philip. PR2701.5.M3 1976, **(v3)**
Masson, VeNeta. RT98.M28 2001, **(v2)**
Mast, Gerald. ML1711.M39 1987, **(v9)**
　PN1993.5.A1.M39 1986b, **(v3)**
Mast, Robert H. HV98.H3.M37 1996, **(v6)**
Mastanduno, Michael. HF1414.5.M27 1992, **(v6)**
Masten, Jeffrey. PR658.T4.M37 1997, **(v3)**
Masters, Anthony. PN2592.M2 1992, **(v3)**
Masters, Colin J. QH603.P47.M37 1995, **(v1)**
Masters, Edgar Lee. PS3525.A83.A6 1925, **(v3)**
　PS3525.A83.F3 1929, **(v3)**
　PS3525.A83.G7 1916, **(v3)**
　PS3525.A83.I44 1941, **(v3)**
　PS3525.A83.I6 1935, **(v3)**
　PS3525.A83.L5 1930, **(v3)**
　PS3525.A83.N4 1937, **(v3)**
　PS3525.A83.S5 1991, **(v3)**
　PS3525.A83.Z5 1969, **(v3)**
Masters, John. PS3525.A8314 B5, **(v3)**
　PS3525.A8314 T6, **(v3)**
　PS3525.A8314.Z5, **(v3)**
Masters, Marick Francis. HD42.M38 2002, **(v6)**
Masters, Roger D. B53.M36 1993, **(v8)**
　JA80.M37 1989, **(v7)**
Masters, William H. HQ21.M46157 1985, **(v6)**
　QP251.M35, **(v1)**
　RC556.M37, **(v2)**
Masterson, Daniel M. F3448.M34 1991, **(v4)**
Masterson, James F. RC553.N36.M369 1993, **(v2)**
Masterson, William H. E302.6.B6.M3, **(v4)**
Mastny, Vojtech. DB215.3.M38, **(v5)**
　DK267.M3567 1996, **(v5)**
Masuda, Wataru. DS822.2.M355 2000, **(v5)**
Masumoto, David Mas. F869.D29.M37 1987, **(v4)**
Masur, Gerhard. CB417.M36, **(v5)**
　F2235.3.M39 1969, **(v4)**

Masur, Louis P. E381.M37 2001, (v4)
  HV8699.U5.M36 1989, (v6)
Maswood, Syed Javed. HF3826.5.M37 1989, (v6)
Matar, Sami. TP692.3.M38 2001, (v1)
Matarasso, Pauline Maud. DC36.7.M38 2001, (v5)
Matchinske, Megan. PR113.M37 1998, (v3)
Mate, Gabor. RJ506.H9.M42326 1999, (v2)
Matelski, Marilyn J. PN1992.8.S4.M27 1988, (v3)
  PN1992.8.S4.M273 1998, (v3)
  PN4888.E8.M38 1991, (v3)
Materer, Timothy. PR6023.E97.Z74, (v3)
Mates, Benson. B21.C25 vol. 26, (v8)
Mates, Benson. BC135.M37 1972, (v8)
Mather, Alexander S. SD373.M344 1990, (v1)
Mather, Cotton. F67.M4213, (v4)
Mather, Cotton. F67.M4215, (v4)
Mather, Jennie P. QH585.2.M38 1998, (v1)
Mather, John Russell. QC858.T48.M38 1996, (v1)
  QC981.M43, (v1)
Matheson, Peter. BR305.2.M35 2001, (v8)
Matheson, Richard. PS3563.A8355.B5 1976, (v3)
Matheson, Terry. BF2050.M36 1998, (v2)
Mathew, W. M. F230.R932.M38 1988, (v4)
Mathews, Donald G. HQ1236.5.U6.M38 1990, (v6)
Mathews, Donald K. GV436.M37 1978, (v6)
Mathews, Freya. BD111.M45 1991, (v8)
Mathews, Jay. LC4941.M38 1998, (v7)
Mathews, John Joseph. HD9570.M3M3 1992, (v6)
  PS3525.A8477.S8 1979, (v3)
Mathews, Max V. MT41.M38, (v9)
Mathews, Mitford McLeod. PE1574.M27, (v3)
Mathews, Nancy Mowll. NE539.C3.A4 1989, (v9)
Mathews, Nieves. B1197.M47 1996, (v8)
Mathews, Richard. PN56.F34.M38 1997, (v3)
Mathews, Thomas F. N6250.M33 1998, (v9)
  N7832.M36 1993, (v9)
  NA5870.I7.M3, (v9)
Mathews, Timothy. DC33.6.M33 2000, (v5)
Mathias, Roland. PR8951.M37 1987, (v3)
Mathiesen, Thomas. HV8705.M38 1990, (v6)
Mathieu, Jean. QA913.M39 2000, (v1)
Mathieu, Pierre-Louis. NX600.S95.M3813 1990, (v9)
Mathur, Anuradha. N6537.M3943, (v9)
Mathy, Jean-Philippe. DC33.7.M285 2000, (v5)
Matilasevich, IU. V. QA242.M4213 1993, (v1)
Matisse, Henri. ND553.M37.A35 1995, (v9)
Matkin, Gary W. LC5251.M36 1997, (v7)
Matlak, Richard E. PR5883.M34 1997, (v3)
Matlaw, Myron. PN1851.M36, (v3)
Matlock, Jack F. DK288.M386 1995, (v5)
Matlock, Jann. PQ653.M36 1994, (v3)
Matloff, Gregory L. TL795.3, (v1)
Matovina, Timothy M. F394.S2.M39 1995, (v4)
Matray, James Irving. DS889.M345767 2001, (v5)
Matson, Floyd W. HV1788.M52 1990, (v6)
Matson, N. F544.M43 2001, (v4)
Matson, R. G. E99.N78.M37 1995, (v4)
  E99.P9.M3575 1991, (v4)
Matsumoto, David Ricky. DS830.M345 1996, (v5)
Matsumoto, Valerie J. F869.C815.M38 1993, (v4)
Matsuo, Basho. PL794.4.A24 1998, (v3)
  PL794.4.A29, (v3)
  PL794.4.O5.E52 1974, (v3)
Matsusaka, Yoshihisa Tak. DS849.C6.M32 2001, (v5)
Matta, Roberto da. GT4233.A2.M38 1991, (v6)
Mattar, Philip. DS125.3.H79.M37 1988, (v5)
Matte, James Allan. HV8078.M36 1996, (v6)
Matteo. GV1673.M35 1990, (v6)
Mattfeld, Julius. ML128.V7 M4 1971, (v9)
Matthelj, Robert M. M. QA372.M388 1996, (v1)
Matthew, Robert. PL747.57.S3.M37 1989, (v3)
Matthews, Anne. QL84.22.G7.M37 1992, (v1)
Matthews, Bonnye L. RB152.M37 1992, (v2)
Matthews, Brander. PQ541.M3 1881, (v3)
Matthews, Christopher. E842.1.M38 1996, (v4)
Matthews, Donald Henry. BT82.7.M38 1998, (v8)
Matthews, Elizabeth W. KF368.L52.M37 1991, (v7)
Matthews, Glenna. HQ1391.U5.M38 1992, (v6)
  HQ1410.M38 1987, (v6)
Matthews, J. H. PQ671.M38, (v3)
Matthews, Jean V. HQ1236.5.U6.M3845 1997, (v6)

Matthews, John D. SD392.M38 1989, (v1)
Matthews, John Pengwerne. PR9469.M3 1962, (v3)
Matthews, John. DG316.7.M38 1989, (v5)
  DG319.M37, (v5)
Matthews, L. R. QP121.M378 1996, (v1)
Matthews, Mervyn. HN530.Z9.E45, (v6)
  LA831.82.M33 1982, (v7)
Matthews, Nicole. PN1995.9.C55.M384 2000, (v3)
Matthews, P. H. P146.M36 2001, (v3)
Matthews, Patrick. HV5822.C3, (v6)
Matthews, Sallie Reynolds. F391.M453 1982, (v4)
Matthews, Steven. PR8771.M38 1999, (v3)
  PR8781.P64.M38 1997, (v3)
Matthews, W. K. PH671.E5.M3, (v3)
Matthews, William. PE1961.M3, (v3)
  PR2049.M3 1966, (v3)
Matthiessen, F. O. PS121.M3, (v3)
Matthiessen, Peter. F2224.M35, (v4)
  PS3525.A9.R3, (v3)
  SK361.M36, (v1)
Mattingly, Carol. HV5229.M37 1998, (v6)
Mattingly, Garrett. DA333.A6.M3 1942, (v5)
  DA360.M3, (v5)
Mattis, Daniel Charles. QC753.M34, (v1)
Mattison, Christopher. QL666.O6.E53 1995, (v1)
  QL668.E2.M33 1987, (v1)
Mattison, Robert Saltonstall. ND237.H3434.M38 1990, (v9)
Matto de Turner, Clorinda. PQ8497.M3.A913 1996, (v3)
Mattson, Catherine M. G1200.M355 1990, (v6)
Mattson, Kevin. JK1764.M384 1998, (v7)
Mattson, Mark T. G1200.M4 1996, (v6)
  G1201.E2.M3 1992, (v6)
Mattusch, Carol C. NB135.M38 1996, (v9)
  NB140.M38 1988, (v9)
Matuliâc, Rusko. Z2956.M38 1998, (v10)
Maturi, Richard J. PN2287.R74.M38 1999, (v3)
Maturin, Charles Robert. PR4987.M7 M4, (v3)
Matusky, Patricia Ann. ML1751.M4.M35 1993, (v9)
Matusow, Allen J. HC106.6.M383 1998, (v6)
Matute, Ana Maria. PQ6623.A89.F5, (v3)
  PQ6623.A89.H5 1960, (v3)
Matystik, Walter F. GE180.M38 1999, (v6)
Matz, David. DG241.2.M38 1997, (v5)
  GV17.M38 1991, (v6)
Mau, Hermann. DD256.5.M383 1968, (v5)
Mauceri, Philip. JL3431.M38 1996, (v7)
Maud, Ralph. PS3529.L655.Z482 1996, (v3)
Maude, R. B. SB732.8.M38 1996, (v1)
Maugham, W. Somerset. PR6025.A86.A17 1926, (v3)
  PR6025.A86.A19 1952, (v3)
  PR6025.A86.A82 1928, (v3)
  PR6025.A86.C3 1950, (v3)
  PR6025.A86 C38 1948, (v3)
  PR6025.A86 C5 1967, (v3)
  PR6025.A86.E5, (v3)
  PR6025.A86 M3, (v3)
  PR6025.A86 M47 1955, (v3)
  PR6025.A86.M66 1935, (v3)
  PR6025.A86 N3 1932, (v3)
  PR6025.A86 O5 1930, (v3)
  PR6025.A86 P28, (v3)
  PR6025.A86.R3 1944, (v3)
  PR6025.A86.S8 1954, (v3)
  PR6025.A86 T48 1937, (v3)
  PR6025.A86 T5, (v3)
  PR6025.A86.T63, (v3)
  PR6025.A86.V3 1969, (v3)
  PR6025.A86.W7 1970, (v3)
  PR6025.A86A6 1950, (v3)
  PR6025.A86 A6, (v3)
Maul, George A. GC10.4.R4.M38 1985, (v6)
Mauldin, Barbara. F1219.3.M4.M39 1999, (v4)
Mauldin, Bill. D745.2.M34 1968, (v5)
  E169.M426, (v4)
  NC1429.M428.A2 1971, (v9)
Maule, Harry E. PS374.W4.M38, (v3)
Maulitz, Russell Charles. RB25.M36 1987, (v2)
Maund, K. L. DA715.M33 1991, (v5)
Maunder, C. R. F. ML549.M38 1998, (v9)

Mauner, George L. ND553.M3.A4 2000, (v9)
Maung, Mya. HC422.M382 1998, (v6)
Maung, Mya. HN670.7.A8.M38 1991, (v6)
Maupassant, Guy de. PQ2349.A2 1945, (v3)
  PQ2349.A2 1987, (v3)
  PQ2349.A4.E53, (v3)
  PQ2349.C82 1973, (v3)
  PQ2349.V513 1978, (v3)
Maurel, Sylvie. PR6035.H96.Z794 1998, (v3)
Maurer, Brian A. QH541.M384 1999, (v1)
Maurer, Friedrich. PD71.P33 Bd.17, T.1-, (v3)
Maurer, Warren R. PT2616.Z9.M36 1982, (v3)
Maurlac, Francois. PQ635.M3, (v3)
  PQ2625.A93 A6 1968, (v3)
  PQ2625.A93.B3 1922, (v3)
  PQ2625.A93.D4 1925, (v3)
  PQ2625.A93.N6, (v3)
Maurice, Catherine. RJ506.A9.M39 1993, (v2)
Maurin, Krzysztof. QA641.M35 1997, (v1)
Mauro, Tony. KF4549.M334 2000, (v7)
Maurois, Andre. DC39.M372 1957, (v5)
  PQ2178.M333 1966, (v3)
  PQ2230.M32, (v3)
  PQ2230.M3313 1971, (v3)
  PQ2293.M353 1956a, (v3)
  PQ2412.M313 1953a, (v3)
  PQ2625.A95.M74, (v3)
  PQ2625.A95.S5 1918, (v3)
  PQ2625.A95.Z53, (v3)
  PQ2631.R63.Z782, (v3)
  PQ2631.R63.Z7822, (v3)
  PR4581.M46 1967, (v3)
  PR5431.M32 1952, (v3)
  QR31.F5.M353, (v1)
Maus, Katharine Eisaman. PR658.P48.M38 1995, (v3)
Mauskopf, Seymour H. BF1028.M38, (v2)
Mautner, Thomas. B41.M38 1996, (v8)
Maveety, Nancy. KF4905.M28 1991, (v7)
Maverick, Lewis A. DS740.2.M4, (v5)
Mawby, R. I. HV6250.25.M38 1994, (v6)
Mawdsley, Evan. JN6549.E9M39 2000, (v7)
Mawhiney, Anne-Marie. E92.M39 1994, (v4)
Mawsilili, Ahmad. BP60.M36 1999, (v8)
  BP173.7.M38 1999, (v8)
Mawson, Christopher Orlando Sylvester. PE1670.M3 1975, (v3)
Maxford, Howard. PN1995.9.H6.M3245 1997, (v3)
Maxon, Robert M. DT433.215.M39 2000, (v5)
Maxson, Cheryl Lee. HV9104.M28 1997, (v6)
Maxwell, Baldwin. PR2875.M3, (v3)
Maxwell, Bruce. JK1764.M39 2000, (v7)
  RA773.6.M39 1998, (v2)
  Z1223.Z7 M25 1996, (v10)
Maxwell, D. E. S. PR8789.M39 1984, (v3)
Maxwell, David. BR1367.H94.M39 1999, (v8)
Maxwell, E. A. QA556.M15, (v1)
Maxwell, Grant L. ML700.M39 1993, (v9)
Maxwell, James Clerk. QA846.M39, (v1)
  QA846.M39 2002, (v1)
  QC310.2.M39 1995, (v1)
  QC665.E4.M38 1982, (v1)
Maxwell, Kenneth E. QP251.M417 1994, (v1)
Maxwell, Kenneth. DP272.M39 1994, (v5)
Maxwell, Nicholas. Q175.M4116 1998, (v1)
Maxwell, Richard. PR4592.L58.M38 1992, (v3)
Maxwell, Robert A. RS420.M38 1990, (v2)
Maxwell, T. T. TP343.M295 1995, (v1)
Maxwell, Thomas R. F1059.5.T689.F85 1977, (v4)
Maxwell, William J. PS153.N5.M269 1999, (v3)
Maxwell, William. PS3525.A9464 F6, (v3)
  PS3525.A9464 O43, (v3)
  PS3525.A9464 T5, (v3)
Maxymuk, John. Z678.93.D46 M39 1997, (v10)
  ZA5075.M38 2001, (v10)
May, Brian. PR6011.O58.Z8226 1997, (v3)
May, Charles E. PN3373.M36 1995, (v3)
May, Christopher N. KF4575.M39 1989, (v7)
  KF5065.M39 1998, (v7)
May, Elaine Tyler. HQ535.M386 1995, (v6)

May, Ernest R. D619.M383, (v5)
　D802.F8.M34 2000, (v5)
　E371.M38, (v4)
　E661.M34, (v4)
　E661.7.M3 1991, (v4)
　JK558.M3 1960, (v7)
May, Gary. E748.V564.M39, (v4)
May, Glenn Anthony. DS676.8.B66.M39 1996, (v5)
　DS688.B3.M39 1991, (v5)
May, Henry Farnham. E163.M39, (v4)
May, Jill P. PN1009.A1.M38 1995, (v3)
May, John. DA709.M38 1994, (v5)
May, Larry. BJ1451.M36 1992, (v8)
　BJ1725.M35 1996, (v8)
May, Lary. PN1995.9.S6.M343 2000, (v3)
May, Rollo. BF692.M34, (v2)
　BL600.M35, (v8)
　RC489.M96.M39 1990, (v2)
May, Stephen. F781.3.M39 1987, (v4)
　PS3513.R6545.Z8 1997, (v3)
May, Steven W. PR535.C69.M3 1991, (v3)
May, Todd. B831.3.M332 2001, (v8)
　BJ703.D44.M38 1995, (v8)
May, William D. QA276.M375 2000, (v1)
May, William F. R724.M285 1991, (v2)
Mayakovsky, Vladimir. PG3476.M3.A24 1975, (v3)
Mayall, David. DX211.M39 1988, (v3)
Mayall, R. Newton. QB121.M39, (v1)
Maybin, Harry B. TK5103.12.M39 1995, (v1)
Mayekiso, Mzwanele. HN801.A95.M39 1996, (v6)
Mayer, Adrian C. DU600.M34, (v1)
Mayer, Ann Elizabeth. PR6039.H52.Z772 1995, (v3)
Mayer, Arno J. DC183.5.M35 2000, (v5)
Mayer, Bernard S. BF637.I48M39 2000, (v2)
Mayer, David N. E332.2.M38 1994, (v4)
Mayer, David. PN1985.M3, (v3)
Mayer, Frank A. DA589.7.M39 1991, (v5)
Mayer, Frederick. HF1746.M338 1998, (v6)
　LA11.M35 1973, (v7)
　LA210.M36, (v7)
Mayer, Hans. PT105.M3, (v3)
Mayer, Harold M. F548.3.M37, (v4)
Mayer, Henry. E302.6.H5 M35 2001, (v4)
Mayer, Jane. E876.M38 1988, (v4)
　KF8745.T48.M39 1994, (v7)
Mayer, Joseph Edward. QC174.8.M37 1977, (v1)
Mayer, Kenneth R. KF5053.M39 2001, (v7)
　UC263.M35 1991, (v10)
Mayer, Lawrence C. JF51.M444 1989, (v7)
Mayer, Martin. HG2491.M342 1997, (v6)
　HG4928.5.M39 1992, (v6)
　KF297.M3 1980, (v7)
Mayer, Melanie J. F1095.K5.M29 1989, (v4)
Mayer, Ralph. N33.M37 1992, (v9)
Mayer, Ralph. ND1500.M3 1982, (v9)
Mayer, Robert. PR858.H5.M39 1997, (v3)
Mayer, Susan E. HQ792.U5.M39 1997, (v6)
Mayer, Thomas F. DA317.8.P6, (v5)
Mayer, Thomas. HB131.M39 1993, (v6)
　HG540.M39 1981, (v6)
Mayer, William G. JK2316.M29 1996, (v7)
Mayerfeld, Jamie. BJ1409.M28 1999, (v8)
Mayers, David Allan. E183.8.S65.M373 1995, (v4)
　E661.7.M32 1998, (v4)
　E748.K374.M39 1988, (v4)
Mayfield, Craig K. KF283.M39, (v7)
Mayhall, C. Wayne. B945.C164 M39 2002, (v8)
Mayhew, David R. JK1021.M39 2000, (v7)
　JK2261.M36 1991, (v7)
Mayhew, Jonathan. PQ6073.S45.M39 1994, (v3)
Mayhew, Robert J. DA600.M295 2000, (v5)
Mayhew, Susan. G63.M39 1997, (v6)
Maynard, Herman Bryant. HD30.27.M355 1993, (v6)
Maynard, Joyce. CT275.M46518.A34, (v5)
Maynard, Kimberly A. HV553.M39 1999, (v6)
Mayne, A. J. C. HV4028.M38 1993, (v6)
Mayne, Alan J. Z5990.M39 1993, (v10)
Mayne, Judith. PN1995.9.A8.M28 1993, (v3)
Mayo, Bernard. E206.M3, (v4)
Mayo, Charles W. R154.M33.A3, (v2)
Mayo, Elton. HD6971.M39 1977, (v6)

Mayo, Marjorie. HM776.M39 2000, (v6)
Mayo, Mike. PN1998.M319 2001, (v3)
Mayo, Robert Donald. PR851.M37, (v3)
Mayor, Adrienne. QE705.G8.M39 2000, (v1)
Mayor, Archer H. HD9760.B83.M39 1988, (v6)
Mayr, Ernst. QH305.M26 1982, (v1)
　QH366.2.M3933 2001, (v1)
　QH371.M33, (v1)
　QH371.M33 1988, (v1)
　QL351.M28, (v1)
　QL351.M29 1991, (v1)
Mayr, Helmut. QE711.2.M3913 1992, (v1)
Mays, Glen P. RA445.M36 2000, (v2)
Mays, Terry M. E209.M36 1999, (v4)
Maza, Sarah C. HD8039.D52.F85 1983, (v6)
Mazari, Sherbaz Khan. DS385.M39 A3 1999, (v5)
Mazarr, Michael J. DS79.72.M384 1993, (v5)
　UA25.M4 1990, (v10)
　UA25.M39 1990, (v10)
　UA830.M378 1989, (v10)
　UA853.K6.M39 1995, (v10)
Mazda, Xerxes. TK5102.M34 1999, (v1)
Maze, J. R. PR6045.O72.Z8153 1997, (v3)
Mazel, David. PS169.E25.M39 2000, (v3)
Mazian, Florence. HV6322.7.M39 1990, (v6)
Mazier, Jacques. HC54.M3513 1999, (v6)
Mazlish, Bruce. H85.M394 1998, (v6)
　HM19.M39 1989, (v6)
Mazour, Anatole Gregory. DK41.M39 1962, (v5)
Mazower, Mark. D424.M39 1999, (v5)
Mazumdar, Pauline M. H. QR182.M39 1995, (v1)
Mazur, Eric Michael. BL2525.M39 1999, (v8)
Mazurs, Edward G. QD467.M35 1974, (v1)
Mazzeno, Laurence W. Z2014.P7.M35 1995, (v10)
Mazzeo, Joseph Anthony. CB411.M3, (v5)
Mazzini, Giuseppe. DG552.8.M292, (v5)
Mbalia, Doreatha D. PS3563.O8749.Z77 1991, (v3)
Mbeki, Govan. HC905.M39 1991, (v6)
Mbiti, John S. BL205.M34 1970, (v8)
　BL2400.M383 1991, (v8)
　BL2462.5.M36 1990, (v8)
Mc Court, John. PR6019.O9.Z7275 2000, (v3)
Mc Craw, David R. PL2327.M4 1990, (v3)
McAdam, Doug. E185.93.M6.M28 1988, (v4)
McAdams, A. James. DD257.M26 1993, (v5)
　DD290.29.M49 2001, (v5)
McAdams, Benton. E616.R6, (v4)
McAdoo, William Gibbs. E748.M14.M2 1971, (v4)
McAffee, Thomas B. KF4749.M39 2000, (v7)
McAleavy, Henry. DS773.M28, (v5)
McAleer, Joseph. Z325.M65.M37 1999, (v10)
McAleer, Kevin. CR4595.G3.M35 1994, (v5)
McAlester, Virginia. NA7205.M35 1984, (v9)
McAlester, Virginia. NA7205.M36 1994, (v9)
McAlindon, T. PR2983.M37 1991, (v3)
McAlister, Lyle N. E123.M38 1984, (v4)
　UB775.M4.M3, (v10)
McAllester Jones, Mary. PN55.M34 1991, (v3)
McAllister, Robert. E467.1.M17 A4 1998, (v4)
McAllister, Ward. CT275.M23.A3 1975, (v5)
McAlpine, Monica E. Z8164.M33 1991, (v10)
McAnany, Patricia Ann. F1435.3.K57.M33 1995, (v4)
McAndrew, John. NA1121.V4.M32, (v9)
McArdle, William D. QP301.M1149 2000, (v1)
McAuley, Alastair. HC340.I5.M2, (v6)
McAuley, Gay. PN2091.S8.M383 1999, (v3)
McAuley, Mary. DK288.M42 1992, (v5)
McAuliffe, Dennis. E99.O8.B656 1994, (v4)
McBeath, Gerald A. HC430.5.M38 1998, (v6)
McBeth, B. S. F2325.M39 2001, (v4)
McBeth, Kate C. E99.N5 M2 1993, (v4)
McBride, Bunny. E99.P5.S755 1995, (v4)
McBride, Glynn. HD1491.U5.M37 1986, (v6)
McBride, Ian. DA948.5.M38 1998, (v5)
McBride, Joseph. PN1998.3.S65.M32 1997, (v3)
McBride, Katharine Winters. PS3505.U334.Z76 1989, (v3)
McBride, William Leon. JC261.S372.M35 1991, (v7)
McBride, William M. VA55.M33 2000, (v10)
McBrien, J. Lynn. LB15.M32 1997, (v7)
McBrien, William. ML410.P7844.M33 1998, (v9)

McBurney, William H. PR1297.M3, (v3)
McCabe, James Dabney. F198.M12, (v4)
McCabe, John. ML410.R233 M33 1998, (v9)
McCabe, Marsha. F74.N5.M37 1996, (v4)
McCabe, R. K. HF5657.M34 1993, (v6)
McCabe, Richard A. PR658.I47.M38 1993, (v3)
McCabe, Susan. PS3503.I785.Z77 1994, (v3)
McCabe, Terry. PN2053.M393 2001, (v3)
McCabe, Warren L. (Warren Lee). TP155.7.M3 2001, (v1)
McCaffery, Ellen. BF1701.M2 1970, (v2)
McCaffery, Margo. RT87.P35M325 1999, (v2)
McCaffery, Robert Paul. F44.M2.M38 1997, (v4)
McCaffrey, Anne. PZ7.M122834Dr3, (v3)
McCaffrey, Donald W. PN1995.75.M33 1999, (v3)
　PN1995.9.C55.M39 1992, (v3)
McCaffrey, James M. E409.2.M35 1992, (v4)
McCagg, William O. DS135.A9.M34 1989, (v5)
McCain, Ted D. E. LB1028.43.M364 2001, (v7)
McCall, Cathal. DA990.U46.M432 1999, (v5)
McCall, Catherine. BD450.M345 1990, (v8)
McCall, Dan. PS2127.L5.M38 1999, (v3)
　PS2384.B28.M3 1989, (v3)
McCall, Douglas L. PN2599.5.T54.M37 1991, (v3)
McCall, Henrietta. BL1620.M36 1990, (v8)
McCall, John C. DT515.45.I33.M39 2000, (v5)
McCall, Storrs. BD511.M18 1994, (v8)
McCalla, Douglas. HC117.O6.M28 1993, (v6)
McCalla, Robert B. E183.8.S65.M374 1992, (v4)
McCalley, Russell W. HF5415.129.M38 1992, (v6)
McCally, David. GE155.E84.M34 1999, (v6)
McCalman, Iain. HN400.R3.M34 1988, (v6)
McCanles, Michael. PR2642.P63.M38 1992, (v3)
McCann, Franklin Thresher. E127.M15 1969, (v4)
McCann, Graham. PN1998.2.M4 1993, (v3)
　PN2287.A53.M3 1990, (v3)
　PN2287.G675.M33 1996, (v3)
McCann, Janet. PS3537.T4753.Z6777 1995, (v3)
McCann, Michael W. KF3464.M338 1994, (v7)
McCann, Sean. PS374.D4.M38 2000, (v3)
McCants, Anne E. C. HV1210.A52.B86 1997, (v6)
McCarraher, Eugene. BR526.M27 2000, (v8)
McCarthy, Anna. PN1992.6.M377 2001, (v3)
McCarthy, B. Eugene. PR3503.M43 1997, (v3)
　PR3776.M3 1979, (v3)
McCarthy, Charles Hallan. E456.M23, (v4)
McCarthy, Desmond F. PS374.D57.M38 1997, (v3)
McCarthy, George E. B3305.M74.M3915 1990, (v8)
McCarthy, J. M. QA841.M33 1990, (v1)
McCarthy, J. Thomas. KF2976.4.M38 1991, (v7)
McCarthy, John A. PT2569.M3, (v3)
McCarthy, Justin. DR27.M87.M33 1995, (v5)
McCarthy, Kathleen D. N72.F45.M34 1991, (v9)
McCarthy, Leo. JZ1242.M38 1998, (v7)
McCarthy, Margaret William. ML417.F286.M43 1995, (v9)
McCarthy, Mary. DG734.2.M36 1959, (v5)
　PS3525.A1435.A16 1970, (v3)
　PS3525.A1435.C3 1950, (v3)
　PS3525.A1435 C5, (v3)
　PS3525.A1435 G62, (v3)
　PS3525.A1435 G7, (v3)
　PS3525.A1435.Z55 1981, (v3)
McCarthy, Michael J. NA966.5.G66.M33 1987, (v9)
McCarthy, Michael R. DA90.M28 1988, (v5)
McCarthy, Mike. DU106.M38 2000, (v5)
McCarthy, Patrick A. PR6019.O9.U6835 1990, (v3)
McCarthy, Paul. PS2388.M45.M38 1990, (v3)
McCarthy, Terence. PR2045.M36 1988, (v3)
McCarthy, Thomas A. B809.3.M33 1991, (v8)
McCarthy, Thomas J. PR457.M4 1997, (v3)
McCarthy, Todd. PN1998.3.H38.M33 1997, (v3)
McCartin, Joseph Anthony. HD8072.M189 1997, (v6)
McCartney, Eugene Stock. U29.M3 1963, (v10)
McCarty, Clifford. ML128.M7.M3 2000, (v9)
McCarty, Marilu Hurt. HB87.W3613 2001, (v6)
McCash, William B. F290.C67.M37 1983, (v4)
McCaskie, T. C. DT507.M34 1995, (v5)

McCaslin, Richard B. E524.M38 1997, **(v4)**
 E577.9.M38 1994, **(v4)**
 F394.G15.M33 1994, **(v4)**
 Z8455.567.M33 1992, **(v10)**
McCauley, Deborah Vansau. BR535.M38 1995, **(v8)**
McCauley, Martin. DK266.M354, **(v5)**
McCawley, William. E99.G15.M34 1996, **(v4)**
McCay, Mary A. QH31.C33.M34 1993, **(v1)**
MccGwire, Michael. UA770.M3993 1991, **(v10)**
McChesney, Fred S. HV6301.M33 1997, **(v6)**
McChristian, Douglas C. UD373.M33 1995, **(v10)**
McClain, Charles J. KF4757.5.C47.M37 1994, **(v7)**
McClain, Paula Denice. E184.A1 M347 2002, **(v4)**
McClamrock, Ronald Albert. BD418.3.M36 1995, **(v8)**
McClane, A. J. SH411.M18 1974, **(v1)**
McClary, Susan. ML82.M38 1990, **(v9)**
 ML410.B62.M25 1992, **(v9)**
McClaurin, Irma. HQ1470.5.M33 1996, **(v6)**
McClean, Andrew. Z6724.N37.M37 1993, **(v10)**
McCleary, John. QA641.M38 1994, **(v1)**
McClellan, Aubrey Lester. QD571.M27, **(v1)**
McClellan, B. Edward. LC311.M38 1999, **(v7)**
McClellan, Edwin. PL812.A8.Z78, **(v1)**
McClellan, George Brinton. E467.1.M2.A4 1989, **(v4)**
McClellan, James E. Q10.M38 1985, **(v1)**
McClellan, Keith. GV954.M37 1998, **(v6)**
McClelland, Charles E. LA727.M32, **(v7)**
McClelland, Grigor. D809.G3.M33 1997, **(v5)**
McClelland, Peter D. HB523.M37 1990, **(v6)**
McClenon, James. BF1040.M326 1984, **(v2)**
McCline, John. E514.5 13th.M38 1998, **(v4)**
McClintock, Anne. DA16.M37 1995, **(v5)**
McClintock, James H. F811.M12, **(v4)**
 F820.M8 M35 1985, **(v4)**
McClinton, Calvin A. PN2287.C293.M33 2000, **(v3)**
McCloskey, Deirdre N. HB71.M38 1998, **(v6)**
 HQ77.8.M39.A3 1999, **(v6)**
 Z7164.E2.M43 1991, **(v10)**
McCloskey, Robert Green. JA84.U5.M35, **(v7)**
McClosky, Herbert. HN90.P8.M4 1984, **(v6)**
McClung, David. QC929.A8.M39 1993, **(v1)**
McClure, Bud A. HM131.M3767 1998, **(v6)**
McClure, Grace. F781.B37 M33 1985, **(v4)**
McClure, Kirstie Morna. JC153.L87.M385 1996, **(v7)**
McClymond, Michael James. BX7260.E3.M33 1998, **(v8)**
McCole, John. PT2603.E455.Z7335 1993, **(v3)**
McColgan, Kristin Pruitt. Z8447.M32, **(v10)**
McColley, Diane Kelsey. PR3562.M19 1993, **(v3)**
 PR3562.M34 1983, **(v3)**
McColm, I. J. TP788.M38 1993, **(v1)**
McComas, Alan J. QP321.M3376 1996, **(v1)**
McComb, W. D. QA913.M43 1990, **(v1)**
McCombs, Maxwell E. HN90.P8.M43 1991, **(v6)**
McConkey, James. PR6011.O58.Z82, **(v3)**
McConkey, Kenneth. ND467.5.I46.M38 1989, **(v9)**
McConnell, Brian. QB54.M23 2001, **(v1)**
McConnell, Elizabeth Huffmaster. Z5703.4.P75.M33 1999, **(v10)**
McConnell, Fraiser. Z4811.M28 1988, **(v10)**
McConnell, Frank D. PR5777.M3 1981, **(v3)**
McConnell, Louise. PR2892.M33 2000, **(v3)**
McConnell, Michael N. F517.M14 1992, **(v4)**
McConnell, Roland C. F189.B16 M665 2000, **(v4)**
McConnell, Stuart Charles. E462.1.A7.M34 1992, **(v4)**
McConnell, William John. F746.M123 1984, **(v4)**
McConnell, Winder. PT1589.M37 1984, **(v3)**
McCooey, David. PR9606.2.M37 1996, **(v3)**
McCook, Kathleen de la Peña. Z682.2.U5 H453 2002, **(v10)**
McCord, Edward Allen. DS777.36.M33 1993, **(v5)**
McCord, Louisa Susanna Cheves. F213.M35 1995, **(v4)**
McCorduck, Pamela. NC242.C46.M34 1990, **(v9)**
McCormac, Eugene Irving. E417.M12 1965, **(v4)**
McCormack, Arthur. HB881.M2553, **(v6)**
McCormack, Gavan. DS778.C5.M3, **(v5)**
McCormack, Kathleen. PR4692.D78.M38 1999, **(v3)**
McCormick, Barrett L. JQ1502.M34 1990, **(v7)**
McCormick, Charles H. F159.P657.M38 1997, **(v4)**
McCormick, Donald. PN56.E7.M34 1992, **(v3)**

PN3448.S66.M3 1990, **(v3)**
McCormick, E. H. PR9606.M3, **(v3)**
McCormick, John P. JC263.S34.M385 1997, **(v7)**
McCormick, John. PN1978.E85.M38 1998, **(v3)**
McCormick, Kathleen. PE1404.M39 1994, **(v3)**
McCormick, Marjorie. PR830.M69.M37 1991, **(v3)**
McCormick, Michael E. TK1081.M39, **(v1)**
McCormick, Naomi B. HQ29.M46 1994, **(v6)**
McCormick, Peter. BH181.M36 1990, **(v8)**
McCormick, Richard L. F124.M14, **(v4)**
McCormick, Richard Patrick. E310.M44, **(v4)**
McCormick, Richard W. NX180.F4.M37 1991, **(v9)**
McCormick, Theresa Mickey. LC212.82.M33 1994, **(v7)**
McCormick, Thomas J. E744.M416 1995, **(v4)**
 NA1053.C58.M38 1990, **(v9)**
McCormick, Virginia E. F499.W92 M384 1998, **(v4)**
McCormick, William Symington. PR1874.M3, **(v3)**
McCormmach, Russell. QC7.M35, **(v1)**
McCoy, Bob. R730.M44 2000, **(v2)**
McCoy, Donald R. E814.M38 1984, **(v4)**
McCoy, Drew R. E342.M33 1989, **(v4)**
McCoy, Esther. NA730.C2.M3 1975, **(v9)**
McCoy, Judy. ML128.R28.M3 1992, **(v9)**
McCoy, Ralph E. K3255.A12.M3 1993, **(v7)**
McCoy, Richard C. PR428.C45.M34 1989, **(v3)**
McCracken, Bane. GV363.M33 2001, **(v6)**
McCracken, Harold. ND237.C35.M3 1959, **(v9)**
McCracken, Peggy. PQ207.M33 1998, **(v3)**
McCracken, Scott. PN56.P55.M39 1998, **(v3)**
McCrae, Robert R. BF637.C5.M36 1990, **(v2)**
McCrary, Peyton. F374.M32, **(v4)**
McCrary, William Carlton. PC13.N67 no. 62, **(v3)**
McCraw, Thomas K. HC106.82.M39 2000, **(v6)**
McCrea, Brian. PR3458.P6.M3 1981, **(v3)**
McCready, Sam. PR5906.M44 1997, **(v3)**
McCrillis, Neal R. JN1129.C7.M38 1998, **(v7)**
McCrone, David. HN398.S3 M38 2001, **(v6)**
 JC311.M392 1998, **(v7)**
McCrossen, Alexis. BV111.M35 2000, **(v8)**
McCrum, Michael. DG286.M3 1990, **(v5)**
McCrum, Robert. RC388.5.M28 1998, **(v2)**
McCue, Margi Laird. HQ809.3.U5.M385 1995, **(v6)**
McCullagh, C. Behan. D13.M363 1984, **(v5)**
McCullers, Carson. PS3525.A177.S69, **(v3)**
 PS3525.A1772 B3, **(v3)**
 PS3525.A1772 C6, **(v3)**
 PS3525.A1772.H4 1940, **(v3)**
 PS3525.A1772.M5 1951, **(v3)**
 PS3525.A1772.M6 1971, **(v3)**
 PS3525.A1772.R4 1941, **(v3)**
 PS3525.A1772.Z74 1999, **(v3)**
McCulloch, Gregory. BC199.N3.M33 1989, **(v8)**
McCulloch, Susan. ND1101.M37 1999, **(v9)**
McCullough, David G. E757.M45, **(v4)**
 E814.M26 1992, **(v4)**
 F159.J7 M16 1987, **(v4)**
 F1569.C2.M33, **(v4)**
McCullough, Kate. PS374.W6.M29 1999, **(v3)**
McCullough, Malcolm. QA76.9.C65.M393 1996, **(v1)**
McCullough, Rita I. Z7961.M4 1991, **(v10)**
McCumber, John. B936.W55 2000, **(v8)**
 B3279.H49.M3754 1999, **(v8)**
McCune, Evelyn. N7360.M31, **(v9)**
McCunn, Ruthanne Lum. E184.C5 M195 1996, **(v4)**
McCurdy, Charles W. KFN5145.M33 2001, **(v7)**
McCurdy, Howard E. TL789.8.U5M338 1997, **(v1)**
McCurry, Stephanie. F273.M48 1995, **(v4)**
McCutchan, Ann. ML419.M69.M3 1994, **(v9)**
McCutcheon, Marc. PE1591.M415 2000, **(v3)**
McCutcheon, Marc. PE1591.M416 1995, **(v3)**
McCutcheon, Russell T. BL41.M35 1997, **(v8)**
McDaniel, Bruce A. HB615.M3732 2002, **(v6)**
McDaniel, George W. F182.M32 1982, **(v4)**
McDaniel, Tim. DK510.762.M4 1996, **(v5)**
McDaniel, Tim. HD8526.M385 1988, **(v6)**
McDaniels, Carl. HF5381.M39625 1989, **(v6)**
McDannell, Colleen. BR515.M35 1995, **(v8)**
McDermott, Gerald R. BT1180.M34 2000, **(v8)**
McDermott, Irene E. ZA4201.M36 2002, **(v10)**
McDermott, John Francis. ND237.B59.M3, **(v9)**

McDermott, John. PR6001.M6.Z78 1989, **(v3)**
McDonagh, Josephine. PR4537.M37 1994, **(v3)**
McDonald, Christie. PQ2631.R63.A834 1992, **(v3)**
McDonald, David J. HD8073.M2.A3, **(v6)**
McDonald, Forrest. E302.6.H2.M32 1979, **(v4)**
 E311.M12, **(v4)**
 E331.M32, **(v4)**
 JK146.M27, **(v7)**
 JK511.M34 1994, **(v7)**
McDonald, Helen B. RC558.M43 1990, **(v2)**
McDonald, Joyce. PS3505.A87.Z737 1998, **(v3)**
McDonald, Keiko I. PL747.55.M36 2000, **(v3)**
 PN1993.5.J3.M36 1994, **(v3)**
McDonald, M. B. SB117.M36 1997, **(v1)**
McDonald, Malcolm. HF5415.13.M3691832 1997, **(v6)**
McDonald, Michael J. HD211.T2M35 1982, **(v6)**
McDonald, Peter. PR6025.A316.Z79 1991, **(v3)**
McDonald, Robert A. J. F1089.5.V22.M43 1996, **(v4)**
McDonald, Roderick A. HT1096.M4 1993, **(v6)**
McDonald, Ronald H. JL969.A45 M37 1989, **(v7)**
McDonald, Russ. PR2958.J6.M35 1988, **(v3)**
McDonald, T. David. T27.C5.M33 1989, **(v1)**
McDonnell, Janet A. E98.L3.M43 1991, **(v4)**
McDonough, Carla J. PS338.M46.M33 1997, **(v3)**
McDonough, Edwin J. PS3529.N5.Z693 1991, **(v3)**
McDonough, Frank. DA47.2.M26 1998, **(v5)**
McDonough, James L. E476.7.M34 1987, **(v4)**
McDonough, Peter. JN8210.M39 1998, **(v7)**
McDorman, Kathryne Slate. PR9639.3.M27.Z79 1991, **(v3)**
McDougal, Dennis. PN2287.W4525.M34 1998, **(v3)**
McDougall, Bonnie S. PL2303.M43 1997, **(v3)**
McDougall, Harold A. F189.B19.N45 1993, **(v4)**
McDougall, Walter A. TL789.8.U5.M34 1985, **(v1)**
McDowell, Banks. BJ352.M39 2000, **(v8)**
McDowell, Frederick P. W. PR6011.O58.Z822 1982, **(v3)**
McDowell, Gary L. KF8700.M37 1988, **(v7)**
McDowell, John Henry. BD418.3.M37 1994, **(v8)**
McDowell, Josh. BS1225.2.M33 1993, **(v8)**
McDowell, Paula. PR8476.M38 1998, **(v3)**
McDowell, R. B. DA947.M198, **(v5)**
McDowell, Sally Campbell Preston. BX9225.M39.A4 2000, **(v8)**
McEachran, F. PT2353.M2, **(v3)**
McElheran, Brock. MT85.M125 1989, **(v9)**
McElhinny, M. W. QE501.4.P35.M35 2000, **(v1)**
McElligott, Anthony. DD901.H28.M42 1998, **(v5)**
McElmeel, Sharron L. Z1037.M134 1995, **(v10)**
McElroy, Bernard. PN56.G7.M36 1989, **(v3)**
McElroy, Guy C. N6538.N5.M35 1989, **(v9)**
 N8232.M44 1990, **(v9)**
McElroy, John Harmon. E169.1.M156 1999, **(v4)**
 E169.1.M157 1989, **(v4)**
McElroy, Robert McNutt. F451.M14, **(v4)**
McElroy, Robert W. JX1417.M37 1992, **(v7)**
McElvaine, Robert S. F125.3.C86.M34 1988, **(v4)**
 HQ1075.M386 2001, **(v6)**
McEnaney, Laura. UA927.M33 2000, **(v10)**
McEvedy, Colin. HB851.M32, **(v6)**
McEvilley, Thomas. B165.M22 2002, **(v8)**
McEvoy, Sean. PR2976.M34 2000, **(v3)**
McEvoy-Levy, Siobhan. E881.M39 2001, **(v4)**
McEwan, Barbara. E332.M42 1991, **(v4)**
 LB3013.M383 2000, **(v7)**
McEwan, Neil. PR6013.R44.Z653 1988, **(v3)**
McFadden, David W. E183.8.S65.M378 1993, **(v4)**
McFadden, George. BH301.C7.M38, **(v8)**
 PR3427.P6.M3, **(v3)**
McFadden, Johnjoe. QH366.2.M396 2001, **(v1)**
McFadden, Margaret. HQ1154.M3965 1999, **(v6)**
McFague, Sallie. BR115.E3.M315 2001, **(v8)**
McFalls, Laurence H. HX280.5.A6.M4 1995, **(v6)**
McFarland, E. W. DA815.M38 1990, **(v5)**
 DA947.M23 1994, **(v5)**
McFarland, Gerald W. E661.M14, **(v4)**
McFarland, Philip James. E210.M15 1998, **(v4)**
McFarland, Stephen Lee. D785.M39 1991, **(v5)**
McFarland, Thomas. PQ2057.A2.M28 1995, **(v3)**
 PR5888.M39 1992, **(v3)**

McFarland-Icke, Bronwyn Rebekah. RC440.M325 1999, **(v2)**
McFarlane, Anthony. F2272.M4 1993, **(v4)**
McFarlane, Brian. PN1993.5.A8.M36 1992, **(v3)**
McFarlane, Deborah R. HQ766.5.U5.M436 2001, **(v6)**
McFarlane, James Walter. PT8363.M3, **(v3)**
McFaul, John M. HG2471.M3, **(v6)**
McFeat, Tom. E78.N78.M3 1967, **(v4)**
McFee, Graham. GV1588.3.M37 1992, **(v6)**
McFeely, Mary Drake. TX649.A1, **(v1)**
McFeely, William S. E449.D75.M374 1991, **(v4)**
McFerson, Hazel M. F970.M39 1997, **(v4)**
McGahey, Robert. PN1035.M34 1994, **(v3)**
McGann, Jerome J. PR585.S46.M35 1996, **(v3)**
  PR5247.M37 2000, **(v3)**
McGarrell, Edmund F. HV9104.M33 1988, **(v6)**
McGeary, M. Nelson. E664.P62 M2 1979, **(v4)**
McGee, Mark Thomas. PN1995.9.M86.M4 1990, **(v3)**
  PN1999.A6.M35 1995, **(v3)**
McGee, Marty. ML106.U4 B66 2000, **(v9)**
  TK7881.4.M47 2001, **(v1)**
McGee, Patrick. PR6019.O9.U68358 2001, **(v3)**
McGee, R. Jon. F1221.L2.M4 1990, **(v4)**
McGee, Robert W. HF1713.M37 1994, **(v6)**
McGee, Thomas D. QC271.M384 1988, **(v1)**
McGehee, O. Carruth. QA300.M275 2000, **(v1)**
McGerr, Rosemarie Potz. PR1931.M38 1998, **(v3)**
McGervey, John D. QA273.M46 1986, **(v1)**
  QC174.12.M378 1995, **(v1)**
McGhee, George Crews. DD259.4.M36 1989, **(v5)**
  E183.8.T8.M33 1990, **(v4)**
McGhee, Richard D. PN2287.W454.M35 1990, **(v3)**
McGill, Ralph. F215.M16 1963, **(v4)**
McGilligan, Patrick. PN1590.B5.M35 1997, **(v3)**
  PN1998.3.L36.M38 1997, **(v3)**
McGillis, Roderick. PN1009.A1.M234 1996, **(v3)**
McGillivray, Alice V. JK524.M33 2001, **(v7)**
McGinn, Bernard. BT985.M29 1994, **(v8)**
McGinn, Bernard. BV5075.M37 1994, **(v8)**
McGinn, Colin. B804.M355 2001, **(v8)**
  BC71.M36 2000, **(v8)**
  BF161.M45 1991, **(v2)**
  BJ46.M34 1997, **(v8)**
McGinn, Marie. BD201.M37 1989, **(v8)**
McGinn, Thomas A. KJA3468.P76.M39 1998, **(v7)**
McGinniss, Joe. E851.M3, **(v4)**
McGinty, Alice B. F869.M655 M34 2000, **(v4)**
McGladdery, Christine. DA783.7.M38 1990, **(v5)**
McGlathery, James M. PN3437.M34 1991, **(v3)**
McGlew, James F. JC75.D4.M38 1993, **(v7)**
McGlothlen, Ronald L. E748.A15.M3 1993, **(v4)**
McGoodwin, James R. SH328.M39 1990, **(v1)**
McGovern, Barbara. PR3765.W57.Z77 1992, **(v3)**
McGovern, Dan. E99.C19.M33 1995, **(v4)**
McGovern, George S. E840.8.M34.A33, **(v4)**
  HD1761.M27, **(v6)**
McGovern, Stephen J. HT177.S38.M34 1998, **(v6)**
McGovern, William Montgomery. DS785.M28, **(v5)**
  UB250.M3, **(v10)**
McGowan, Christopher. QE707.A2, **(v1)**
  QL799.M38 1994, **(v1)**
McGowan, John. PN98.P67.M37 1991, **(v3)**
McGowan, Margaret M. DC33.3.M39 2000, **(v5)**
McGowan, Richard. HV6715.M4 1994, **(v6)**
McGowan, Todd. PS374.P7.M37 2001, **(v3)**
McGrady, Donald. PQ6272.Z5.M25, **(v3)**
McGrath, Alister E. BL240.2.M413 1999, **(v8)**
  BS186.M33 2001, **(v8)**
  BT26.M37 1988, **(v8)**
  BX9418.M29 1990, **(v8)**
McGrath, Dennis. LB2328.15.U6.M39 1991, **(v7)**
McGrath, Elizabeth Z. BJ1012.M318 1994, **(v8)**
McGrath, F. C. PR6056.R5.Z825 1999, **(v3)**
McGrath, John T. F314.M19 2000, **(v4)**
McGrath, Thomas. PS3525.A24234.T45 1988, **(v3)**
McGrayne, Sharon Bertsch. Q141.B42 1993, **(v1)**
  Q141.M358 1998b, **(v1)**
McGreevy, John T. E185.912.M38 1996, **(v4)**
McGregor, C. M. QA37.2.M43 1994, **(v1)**
McGregor, R. S. PK2037.M32, **(v3)**
McGregor, Robert Kuhn. PR6037.A95.Z78 2000, **(v3)**

PS3057.N3.M28 1997, **(v3)**
McGrew, Timothy J. BD161.M387 1995, **(v8)**
McGucken, William. QH104.5.E73.M35 2000, **(v1)**
McGuigan, Patrick B. KF8742.M33 1990, **(v7)**
McGuire, J. E. B1299.N34 M37 1995, **(v8)**
McGuire, James W. F2849.M393 1997, **(v4)**
McGuire, Kevin T. KF8742.M34 1993, **(v7)**
McGuire, Phillip. D810.N4.M38 1983, **(v5)**
  KF373.H38.M35 1988, **(v7)**
McGuire, William. HN65.M38 1993, **(v6)**
McHale, John. CB161.M3, **(v5)**
  NA737.F8.M2, **(v9)**
McHarg, Ian L. HC110.E5.M33, **(v6)**
McHose, Allen Irvine. MT50.M153, **(v9)**
McHugh, Kathleen Anne. PN1995.9.W6.M38 1999, **(v3)**
McHugh, Roland. PR6019.O9.F59357 1991, **(v3)**
  PR6019.O9.F5936, **(v3)**
McHughen, Alan. TP248.65.F66, **(v1)**
McIlroy, John. HD6664.M37 1988, **(v6)**
McIlwaine, John. Z5140.M45 1996, **(v10)**
McIlwaine, Shields. PS173.P7.M3 1970, **(v3)**
McInerney, Daniel John. E449.M474 1994, **(v4)**
McInerney, Peter K. BD638.M38 1990, **(v8)**
McInerny, Ralph M. BJ255.T5.M35 1992, **(v8)**
McIntosh, C. Alison. HB3581.M37 1983, **(v6)**
McIntosh, Carey. PR769.M38 1998, **(v3)**
McIntosh, Elaine N. GT2853.U5.M39 1995, **(v6)**
McIntosh, Elizabeth P. D810.S7.M375 1998, **(v5)**
McIntosh, James. PS1541.Z5.M22 2000, **(v3)**
McIntosh, Jane. DS425.M34 2002, **(v5)**
McIntosh, John L. Z7615.M38 1985, **(v10)**
McIntosh, Malcolm. UA830.M385 1987, **(v10)**
McIntosh, Marjorie Keniston. DA685.H28.M39 1991, **(v5)**
  HN398.E5.M38 1998, **(v6)**
McIntosh, Roderick J. GN652.M25.M35 1998, **(v6)**
McIntosh, Wayne V. KF8775.M36 1997, **(v7)**
McIntosh, Wm. Alex. GT2855.M35 1996, **(v6)**
McIntyre, Ian. PR4331.M445 1995, **(v3)**
McIntyre, Lee C. B63.M45 1996, **(v8)**
McIntyre, W. David. UA874.3.M35 1988, **(v10)**
McIver, Colin. HF5415.M2583 1987, **(v6)**
McIver, Tom. Z5322.E9.M38 1988, **(v10)**
  Z7786.M35 1999, **(v10)**
McIvor, Arthur. HD8390.M365 2001, **(v6)**
McJannet, Linda. PR658.S59.M38 1999, **(v3)**
McJimsey, George T. E806.M46 2000, **(v4)**
McKay, Claude. PS3525.A24785.A6 1973, **(v3)**
  PS3525.A24785 B3, **(v3)**
  PS3525.A24785.Z5 1970, **(v3)**
McKay, David H. JN15.M37 1996, **(v7)**
McKay, Derek. D273.5.M36 1983, **(v5)**
McKay, Donald C. E183.8.F8.M3, **(v4)**
McKay, Elizabeth Norman. ML410.S3.M34 1996, **(v9)**
McKay, Ernest A. F128.44.M46 1990, **(v4)**
McKay, Floyd J. F881.S68.M38 1998, **(v4)**
McKean, Henry P. QA567.2.E44.M38 1997, **(v1)**
McKean, Lise. BL1215.P65 M35 1996, **(v8)**
McKean, Robert B. DK568.M35 1990, **(v5)**
McKee, Christopher. VB313.M35 1991, **(v10)**
McKee, James B. HT1581.M35 1993, **(v6)**
McKee, Jeffrey Kevin. GN281.M396 2000, **(v6)**
McKee, Patricia. PR868.S62.M35 1997, **(v3)**
  PS374.R32.M38 1999, **(v3)**
McKee, Sally. DF901.C83, **(v5)**
McKee, Thomas Hudson. JK2255.M2 1971, **(v7)**
McKeen, William. ML420.D98.M25 1993, **(v9)**
  PN4874.T444.M35 1991, **(v3)**
McKeever Furst, Jill Leslie. F1219.76.R45.M4 1995, **(v4)**
McKeever, Robert J. KF8742.M35 1993, **(v7)**
McKelway, St. Clair. PS3525.A2556.E3, **(v3)**
McKendrick, Melveena. PQ6105.M24 1989, **(v3)**
  PQ6490.H5M3 2000, **(v3)**
McKendrick, Neil. HC257.E5.M37 1982, **(v6)**
McKenna, Brian. Z2037.M235, **(v10)**
McKenna, Patrick J. HD66.M3946 2002, **(v6)**
McKenna, Richard. PS3525.A254.S3, **(v3)**
McKenna, Ted. TS9.M43 1997, **(v1)**
McKenna, Teresa. PS153.M4.M55 1997, **(v3)**

McKenna, Thomas M. DS689.C67.M35 1998, **(v5)**
McKenney, Ruth. PS3525.A25573 A2, **(v3)**
McKenney, Ruth. PS3525.A25573I5 1992, **(v3)**
McKenny, Gerald P. R724.M2922 1997, **(v2)**
McKenry, Leda M. RM301.H33 2001, **(v2)**
McKenzie, Steven L. BS580.D3.M37 2000, **(v8)**
McKeown, Adam. DS732.M39 2001, **(v5)**
McKeown, Thomas. RB151.M28 1988, **(v2)**
McKercher, B. J. C. DA565.H75.M35 1989, **(v5)**
McKernan, Luke. PN5124.M68.M35 1992, **(v3)**
McKhann, Charles F. R726.M355 1999, **(v2)**
McKibbin, Ross. HN400.S6.M39 1998, **(v6)**
McKie, Douglas. QD22.L4.M32 1952, **(v1)**
McKillop, A. B. F1021.M346, **(v4)**
McKim, Robert. BL51.M226 2001, **(v8)**
McKim-Smith, Gridley. ND813.V4.M35 1988, **(v9)**
McKinlay, Robert D. UA17.M35 1989, **(v10)**
McKinley, Archibald C. F292.M15.J68 1991, **(v4)**
McKinley, Georgia. PS3563.A3175.M5, **(v3)**
McKinley, William. E660.M17, **(v4)**
McKinnell, Robert Gilmore. QH442.2.M32 1985, **(v1)**
  RC261.M436 1998, **(v2)**
McKinney, Tim. E472.17.M37 1993, **(v4)**
McKinnon, Malcolm. DU421.M35 1993, **(v5)**
McKinnon, Sharon M. HF5657.4.M38 1992, **(v6)**
McKinnon, William T. PR6025.A316.Z8, **(v3)**
McKinven, John A. PN2599.5.T54.M38 1998, **(v3)**
McKirahan, Richard D. B441.M525 1992, **(v8)**
McKisack, May. DA225.M34 1959, **(v5)**
McKissack, Pat. PZ7.M478693Go 2001, **(v3)**
McKitrick, Eric L. E668.M156 1988, **(v4)**
McKnight, Brian E. HV8260.A2.M35 1992, **(v6)**
McKnight, Gerald. E185.97.K5.M38 1998, **(v4)**
McKnight, Gerald. ML410.L78.M3 1984, **(v9)**
McKnight, Jean Sinclair. KF1.H68 1997, **(v7)**
McKnight, Natalie. PR878.M69.M35 1996, **(v3)**
McKnight, Scot. Z7772.M1 M35 2000, **(v10)**
McKnight, Stephen A. CB203.M35 1989, **(v5)**
McKown, Delos Banning. BS651.M3976 1993, **(v8)**
McKusick, James C. PR468.N3.M38 2000, **(v3)**
McKusick, Marshall Bassford. E78.I6.M284 1991, **(v4)**
McLachlan, James M. B819.M39 1992, **(v8)**
McLafferty, Fred W. QC454.M3.M39 1993, **(v1)**
McLanahan, Sara. HQ777.4.M39 1994, **(v6)**
McLane, Joan Brooks. LB1139.L3.M3348 1990, **(v7)**
McLaren, Angus. HQ766.M35 1991, **(v6)**
McLaren, Deborah. G155.A1.M388 1998, **(v6)**
McLaren, John D. PN771.M44 1993, **(v3)**
Mclaren, John D. PR9609.6.M375 1996, **(v3)**
McLaren, Peter. LC191.4.M38 1989, **(v7)**
  LC196.M35 1994, **(v7)**
  LC196.5.U6.M35 1997, **(v7)**
McLarty, Margaret C. R836.M3, **(v2)**
McLaughlin, Andrew Cunningham. JK54.M3 1972, **(v7)**
McLaughlin, Judith A. Z8685.6.M34 1988, **(v10)**
McLaughlin, M. L. PQ4075.M45 1995, **(v3)**
McLaughlin, Marie L. E99.M435 M37 1990, **(v4)**
McLaughlin, Megan. BX2170.D5 M375 1994, **(v8)**
McLaughlin, Thomas. PS25.M4 1997, **(v3)**
McLaughlin, Vance. HV8148.S452.M35 1992, **(v6)**
McLaurin, Melton Alonza. KF223.C43.M34 1991, **(v7)**
McLaurin, R. D. UA830.M387 1989, **(v10)**
McLean, Alasdair W. M. UG1525.E85.M3497 1997, **(v10)**
McLean, Donald. PR6025.A275.Ro, **(v3)**
McLean, J. W. HD57.7.M396 1992, **(v6)**
McLean, Lorraine Arnal. PN2287.D523.M39 1999, **(v3)**
McLean, Mervyn. ML360.M28 1999, **(v9)**
  ML3770.M35 1996, **(v9)**
McLendon, Jacquelyn Y. PS3511.A864.Z77 1995, **(v3)**
McLeod, Glenda. PN682.W6.M37 1991, **(v3)**
McLeod, Hugh. BL690.M38 1981, **(v8)**
  BR477.M34 1996, **(v8)**
  BR759.M37 1996, **(v8)**
McLeod, W. H. BL2018.M319 1989, **(v8)**
  BL2018.M38 1995, **(v8)**
  DS485.P3.M39 1989, **(v5)**
McLerran, Jennifer. PN56.O4.M34 1991, **(v3)**

McLeskey, James. LC1201.M39 2000, **(v7)**
McLindon, Michael P. HG4523.M35 1997, **(v6)**
McLoone, Martin. PN1993.5.I85.M34 2000, **(v3)**
McLoskey, Lansing D. ML120.D3.M35 1998, **(v9)**
McLoughlin, John. F880.M1684 1973, **(v4)**
McLoughlin, William Gerald. E99.C5.J625 1990, **(v4)**
   E99.C5.M43 1994, **(v4)**
   F79.M32, **(v4)**
McLuhan, Marshall. P90.M25775 1988, **(v3)**
   P90.M26, **(v3)**
McLuhan, T. C. E98.C9 M24 1971, **(v4)**
McLynn, F. J. DA814.A5.M37 1988, **(v5)**
   HV6949.E5.M35 1989, **(v6)**
McMahon, Christopher. HM271.M39 1994, **(v6)**
McMahon, Joseph H. PQ2613.E53.Z77, **(v3)**
McMahon, Margaret. SB91.P56 2002, **(v1)**
McMahon, Robert J. E183.8.I4.M36 1994, **(v4)**
McMahon, Robert. PR3562.M36 1998, **(v3)**
McMahon, Walter W. LC65.M35 1999, **(v7)**
McManis, Douglas R. HC107.A11.M17, **(v6)**
McManners, John. DC158.2.M3, **(v5)**
McManus, Edgar J. KF9223.M38 1993, **(v7)**
McManus, John C. D769.2.M36 1998, **(v5)**
McManus, Michael J. F586.M33 1998, **(v4)**
McMaster, Marvin C. QD79.C454.M36 1994, **(v1)**
McMaster, Rowland. PR5614.M36 1991, **(v3)**
McMenamin, Michael. HD9282.U4.M25, **(v6)**
McMicking, Thomas. F1060.8.M39 1981, **(v4)**
McMillan, Alan D. E78.C2 M36 1995, **(v4)**
McMillan, Carol. HQ1206.M37 1982, **(v6)**
McMillan, Della E. HD1018.Z63.M33 1995, **(v6)**
McMillan, Dougald. PR6003.E282.Z776 1988, **(v3)**
McMillan, Stuart. UA874.3.M38 1987, **(v10)**
McMillen, Donald Hugh. DS793.S62.M24 1979, **(v5)**
McMillen, Margot Ford. CT3260.M36 2002, **(v5)**
McMillen, Neil R. E185.93.M6.M33 1989, **(v4)**
McMillin, Scott. PN2599.5.T54.M39 1998, **(v3)**
McMillin, T. S. PS1638.M38 2000, **(v3)**
McMinn, Joseph. PR3726.M35 1990, **(v3)**
McMinn, R. M. H. QM25.M23, **(v1)**
McMullan, James. PN2099.U6.M36 1998, **(v3)**
McMullen, Conley K. QK473.G2.M37 1999, **(v1)**
McMullen, Joanne Halleran. PS3565.C57.Z784 1996, **(v3)**
McMullen, Roy. ND553.D3.M38 1984, **(v4)**
McMurray, Christine. RA441.M43 2001, **(v2)**
McMurry, Linda O. S417.C3.M3, **(v1)**
McMurry, Richard M. E545.M37 1989, **(v4)**
McMurry, Sally Ann. NA8208.5.M36 1988, **(v9)**
McMurtrie, Douglas C. Z4.M15 1943, **(v10)**
   Z208.M18, **(v10)**
McMurtry, Jo. PR2808.M38 1998, **(v3)**
   PR2910.M35 1989, **(v3)**
McNair, Brian. JA85.M36 1995, **(v7)**
McNair, Harold Monroe. QD79.C45.M425 1998, **(v1)**
McNairn, Barbara. CC115.C45.M38, **(v5)**
McNall, Scott G. F686.M4 1988, **(v4)**
McNally, David. HB94.M37 1988, **(v6)**
McNally, Michael David. E99.C6 M35 2000, **(v4)**
McNally, Richard J. RC535.M396 1994, **(v2)**
McNally, Tom. SH456.M36 1993b, **(v1)**
McNamara, Dennis L. HD2908.M36 1990, **(v6)**
   HF3830.5.M39 1996, **(v6)**
McNamara, Ken. QH395.M36 1997, **(v1)**
McNamara, Patrick H. BX932.M36 1992, **(v8)**
McNamara, Robert S. DS558.M439 1999, **(v5)**
   JZ5538.M36 2001, **(v7)**
McNaugher, Thomas L. UA23.M43 1985, **(v10)**
   UC263.M36 1989, **(v10)**
McNaught, Kenneth William Kirkpatrick.
   F1034.W6.M23, **(v4)**
McNaughton, David. BJ1012.M42 1988, **(v8)**
McNaughton, Howard Douglas. PR9631.2.M27, **(v3)**
McNaughton, S. LB1050.M38 1987, **(v7)**
McNee, Lisa. PL8785.5.M35 2000, **(v3)**
McNeil, Frank. F1439.5.M42 1988, **(v4)**
McNeil, W. K. F417.O9.M36 1995, **(v4)**
McNeill, John Robert. GF13.M39 2000, **(v6)**
McNeill, William Hardy. CB69.M33, **(v5)**
   D21.3.M29 1995, **(v5)**
   D21.3.M3, **(v5)**

DA3.T68.M37 1989, **(v5)**
   HC295.M2, **(v6)**
   HN650.5.A8.M33, **(v6)**
McNeilly, Donald P. F411.M144 2000, **(v4)**
McNeir, Waldo F. PR423.M3, **(v3)**
McNeir, Waldo F. Z8830.8.M33 1975, **(v10)**
McNerney, Kathleen. PQ8180.17.A73.Z724 1989, **(v3)**
McNickle, Chris. F128.5.M39 1992, **(v4)**
McNickle, D'Arcy. E58.M18, **(v4)**
McNiff, Shaun. N71.M35 1998, **(v9)**
McNitt, Frank. E98.C7.M25, **(v4)**
McNulty, Paul J. HD4901.M22, **(v6)**
McNutt, Randy. F489.3.M37 1996, **(v4)**
McPartland, Joseph F. TK3271.M35 1999, **(v1)**
McPartland, Marian. ML3507.M38 2003, **(v9)**
McPeck, John E. LB885.M35.T43 1990, **(v7)**
McPhail, Clark. HM281.M39 1991, **(v6)**
McPharlin, Paul. PN1978.U6.M22 1969, **(v3)**
McPhee, Colin. ML345.B3 M25 1976, **(v9)**
McPhee, John A. F591.M39 1988, **(v4)**
   F910.M29 1977, **(v4)**
   QE79.M28 1981, **(v1)**
McPhee, Peter. JN2536.M37 1992, **(v7)**
McPherran, Mark L. B318.R45.M38 1996, **(v8)**
McPherson, Barry D. GV706.5.M37 1989, **(v6)**
McPherson, David C. PR3069.I8.M28 1990, **(v3)**
McPherson, Harry. E846.M33 1995, **(v4)**
McPherson, James Alan. PS3563.A325.E4 1977, **(v3)**
McPherson, James M. E185.61.M18 1995, **(v4)**
   E468.M23, **(v4)**
   E492.3.M38 1997, **(v4)**
McPherson, Karen S. PN3401.M27 1994, **(v3)**
McPherson, Michael S. LB2342.M375 1993, **(v7)**
McPherson, Natalie. HD78.M38 1994, **(v6)**
McPhilemy, Sean. DA990.U46.M458 1998, **(v5)**
McQuain, Jeff. PE2839.M38 1999, **(v3)**
McQuarrie, Donald A. QD453.2.M394 1997, **(v1)**
McQueen, Clyde. BR563.N4.M37 2000, **(v8)**
McQuillan, D. Aidan. F690.A1.M37 1990, **(v4)**
McRae, Barry. ML419.G54.M4 1988, **(v9)**
McRae, Edward A. SB413.L7.M39 1998, **(v1)**
McRandle, James H. U21.2.M38 1994, **(v10)**
McReynolds, Edwin C. F694.M16, **(v4)**
   F694.M17 1971, **(v4)**
McRoberts, Kenneth. HN110.Q4.M32, **(v6)**
McRoy, Ruth G. HV875.55.M39 1988, **(v6)**
   RJ507.A36.M37 1988, **(v2)**
McRuer, Robert. PS153.G38.M38 1997, **(v3)**
McShane, Clay. HE5623.M35 1994, **(v6)**
McShea, Robert J. BJ1031.M354 1990, **(v8)**
McSheffrey, Shannon. BX4901.2.M37 1995, **(v8)**
McShine, Kynaston. N6487.N4.M85 1984, **(v9)**
McSorley, Harry J. BJ1460.L85.M23, **(v8)**
McSween, Harry Y. QB755.M465 1999, **(v1)**
McSweeney, Bill. JZ1251.M37 1999, **(v7)**
McSweeney, Kerry. PR595.L7.M38 1998, **(v3)**
   PR4662.M39 1984, **(v3)**
McTeague, James. PN2078.U6.M37 1993, **(v3)**
McTighe, James. F776.M42 1989, **(v4)**
McTyre, Ruthann Boles. ML128.V7.M45 1998, **(v9)**
McVaugh, M. R. R557.A7.M38 1993, **(v2)**
McVay, Gordon. PG3476.E8.Z774, **(v3)**
McVeigh, Brian J. JQ1631.M4 1998, **(v7)**
McWade, Patricia. LB2337.4.M34 1996, **(v7)**
McWhiney, Grady. F213.M38 1988, **(v4)**
McWhirter, Darien A. HF5549.5.A34.M38 1996, **(v6)**
   KF1262.M45 1992, **(v7)**
McWhirter, David Bruce. PS2127.L65.M39 1989, **(v3)**
McWhorter, Diane. F334.B69.N449 2001, **(v4)**
McWhorter, John H. PE2808.8.M39 1998, **(v3)**
   PM7834.C37.M38 2000, **(v3)**
McWilliams, Carey. F786.M215 1968, **(v4)**
McWilliams, James P. UF537.A44.M38 1989, **(v10)**
McWilliams, John C. E841.M37 2000, **(v4)**
McWilliams, John P. PS1408.M37 1995, **(v3)**
McWilliams, Tennant S. E661.7.M34 1988, **(v4)**
Mda, Zakes. PN2969.M42 1993, **(v3)**
Mead, Christopher Curtis. NA6840.F72.P379 1991, **(v9)**
Mead, Frank Spencer. BL2525.M425 1995, **(v8)**
Mead, George Herbert. B945.M461.R4, **(v8)**

Mead, Harold. PR6063.E19.B7, **(v3)**
Mead, Margaret. E169.1.M5 1999, **(v4)**
   GN21.M36.A35 1979, **(v6)**
   GN21.M36.A4 1977, **(v6)**
   GN33.M4, **(v6)**
   GN405.M4 1961, **(v6)**
   GN671.N5.M4 1953, **(v6)**
   HQ21.M464, **(v6)**
   LC191.M52, **(v7)**
Meade, Marion. PN2287.K4.M43 1995, **(v3)**
Meade, Robert C. HV6433.I82.R436 1990, **(v6)**
Meadow, Rosalyn M. RC552.E18.M43 1996, **(v2)**
Meadows, Michael. PN5514.A83, **(v3)**
Meadows, Thomas Taylor. DS759.M48 1953, **(v5)**
Meagher, John C. PR3091.M43 1997, **(v3)**
Meagher, Margaret Mary. QH105.W6.M435 1998, **(v1)**
Meagher, Timothy J. F74.W9.M38 2001, **(v4)**
Meany, Edmond S. F889.M485 1968, **(v4)**
Mearsheimer, John J. U42.M38 1988, **(v10)**
Measures, Howard. CR3515.M4 1970, **(v5)**
Mebane, John S. PR658.O3.M43 1989, **(v3)**
Mecham, J. Lloyd. F1418.M373, **(v4)**
   F1418.M374, **(v4)**
Mecham, John Lloyd. BR600.M4 1966, **(v8)**
Mechanic, David. LB1083.M4, **(v7)**
Mechikoff, Robert A. GV211.M43 2002, **(v6)**
Meckel, Richard A. RJ102.M43 1990, **(v2)**
Meckier, Jerome. PR878.R4.M4 1987, **(v3)**
   PR4581.M48 1990, **(v3)**
Meckler, Alan M. Z286.M5.M4 1982, **(v10)**
Medaris, John B. UG633.M325, **(v10)**
Medawar, P. B. Q175.M433 1984, **(v1)**
Medding, Peter. JQ1825.P3.A443 1990, **(v7)**
Medhurst, Kenneth. BX5056.M43 1988, **(v8)**
Medina, Joyce. ND547.5.I4.M37 1995, **(v9)**
Medina, Vicente. JC336.M39 1990, **(v7)**
Medley, Margaret. NK4165.M39 1976b, **(v9)**
Medlik, S. G155.A1.M397 1993, **(v6)**
Medlin, William K. LA21.M4, **(v7)**
Medoff, Rafael. DS149.M375 2000, **(v5)**
   DS149.5.U6M33 1997, **(v5)**
   E184.36.P64.M44 2001, **(v4)**
Medvedev, F. A. QA331.5.M413 1991, **(v1)**
Medvedev, Roy Aleksandrovich. DK265.M375, **(v5)**
   DK267.M41413, **(v5)**
   DK274.M3513, **(v5)**
Medvedev, Zhores A. QH431.M3613, **(v1)**
Medwick, Cathleen. BX4700.T4.M38 1999, **(v8)**
Medwid, Linda M. DE9.A1, **(v5)**
Mee, Charles L. E786.M23, **(v4)**
Meeker, Ezra. F891.M485, **(v4)**
Meeks, Dimitri. BL2450.G6.M4413 1996, **(v8)**
Meeks, John E. RJ503.M44, **(v2)**
Meeks, Wayne A. BJ1212.M43 1993, **(v8)**
   BR166.M44 1983, **(v8)**
Meerloo, Joost Abraham Maurits. BF633.M4, **(v2)**
Meerschaert, Mark M. QA401.M48 1993, **(v1)**
Meese, Elizabeth A. PN98.W64.M44 1990, **(v3)**
Meethan, Kevin. G155.A1.M399 2001, **(v6)**
Meeuse, Bastiaan. QK926.M418 1984, **(v1)**
Megargee, Geoffrey P. D757.G339 2000, **(v5)**
Megarry, Tim. GN281.M444 1995, **(v6)**
Meggs, Philip B. Z244.5.M42 1983, **(v10)**
   Z246.M43 1998, **(v10)**
   Z246.M44 1989, **(v10)**
Meggyesy, Dave. GV939.M4.A3, **(v6)**
Megill, Allan. BH301.M54.M44 1985, **(v8)**
Megivern, James J. K5104.M44 1997, **(v7)**
Mehan, Hugh. LB1027.M376, **(v7)**
Mehl, Margaret. DS834.7.M43 1998, **(v5)**
Mehler, Jacques. BF719.M4413 1994, **(v2)**
Mehlman, Jeffrey. PT2603.E455.Z734 1993, **(v3)**
Mehmet, Ozay. BP63.T8.M44 1990, **(v8)**
   HC445.5.Z9 I51834 1986, **(v6)**
Mehnert, Klaus. DS740.5.R8.M373, **(v5)**
Mehnert, Klaus. Z1003.5.S62.M43 1983, **(v10)**
Meho, Lokman I. Z3014.K85 M43 2001, **(v10)**
   Z3014.K85.M44 1997, **(v10)**
Mehra, Jagdish. QC16.F49.M45 1994, **(v1)**
Mehrez, Samia. PJ8212.M44 1994, **(v3)**
Mehrling, Perry. HG539.M44 1997, **(v6)**

Mehrotra, Asha. TK5103.483.M45 1997, (v1)
Mehta, Dipaka. DS432.M84.M44 1997, (v5)
Mehta, Gita. PS3563.E344R58 1993, (v3)
Mehta, J. L. B29.M453 1985, (v8)
Mehta, Ved. B1111.M4, (v8)
    PN149.9.S53.Z77 1998, (v3)
Mei, Chiang C. TA330.M43 1995, (v1)
Meier, August. E185.6.M5 1988, (v4)
    F574.D49.N46, (v4)
Meier, Christian. DG261.M3713 1995, (v5)
    JC73.M3913 1990, (v7)
Meier, Daniel R. LB1140.5.L3.M45 2000, (v7)
Meier, Gerald M. HD75.M44 1984, (v6)
Meier, Heinz K. Z2771.M45 1990, (v10)
Meier, Kenneth J. HG8535.M44 1988, (v6)
    LC212.2.M45 1989, (v7)
    LC2670.M45 1991, (v7)
Meier, Matt S. E184.M5.M458 2000, (v4)
    E184.S75.M435 1997, (v4)
    Z1361.M4.M414 1984, (v10)
Meier, Regula A. DB886.M45 1993, (v5)
Meier, Richard. NA737.M44.A4 1984, (v9)
Meier, Scott T. BF176.M45 1994, (v2)
Meiggs, Russell. DF227.M44 1979, (v5)
    DG70.O8.M4 1973, (v5)
Meigs, Cornelia. PN1009.A1.M4 1969, (v3)
Meigs, Mark. D570.1.M45 1997, (v5)
Meijer, Fik. HF373.M45 1992, (v6)
Meijer, Reinder P. PT5061.M4 1978b, (v3)
Meikle, Denis. PN1999.H3.M45 1996, (v3)
Meikle, Jeffrey L. TP1117.M45 1995, (v1)
Meikle, Scott. HB77.M45 1995, (v6)
Meilaender, Gilbert. BJ1251.M487 1991, (v8)
    BJ1251.M49 1987, (v8)
Meillet, A. PD101.M413 1970, (v3)
Meilman, Patricia. ND623.T7.A65 2000, (v9)
Meindl, Dieter. PS374.G78.M45 1996, (v3)
Meine, Curt. QH31.L618.M45 1988, (v1)
Meinecke, Friedrich. D16.8.M4613 1972b, (v5)
    DD197.M413, (v5)
Meiners, Phyllis A. E98.F3.M45 1998, (v4)
Meinesz, Alexandre. QK569.C37.M4513 1999, (v1)
Meinig, D. W. F386.M35, (v4)
    F853.M4 1995, (v4)
Meir, Avinoam. DS110.N4.M38 1997, (v5)
Meir, Golda. DS126.6.M42.A37 1975, (v5)
Meisami, Julie Scott. PK6416.M45 1987, (v3)
Meisel, Martin. PR5367.M38, (v3)
Meisel, Perry. PR478.M6.M4 1987, (v3)
Meisenhelder, Susan Edwards. PR5892.R36.M4
    1988, (v3)
    PS3515.U789.Z785 1999, (v3)
Meisner, Maurice J. DS777.55.M455 1986, (v5)
Meiss, Millard. ND2755.M4, (v9)
Meissner, Collin. PS2127.P6.M45 1999, (v3)
Meissner, W. W. BF173.M3593 2000, (v2)
    BX4700.L7.M54 1992, (v8)
Meissner, Werner. Z7125.M453 2001, (v10)
Meister, Dick. HD6515.A29.M44, (v6)
Meister, Jeanne C. HF5549.5.T7.M423 1994, (v6)
Meital, Yoram. DT82.5.I7.M45 1997, (v5)
Meites, Samuel. RB40.M32 1989, (v2)
Meixner, John Albert. PR6011.O53.Z76, (v3)
Mekhitarian, Arpag. ND75.M4, (v9)
Melamed, Daniel R. ML134.B1.M45 1998, (v9)
Melanchthon, Philipp. BR336.A33. 1962, (v8)
Melanson, Philip H. E185.97.K5.M39 1989, (v4)
Melanson, Richard A. E840.M43 2000, (v4)
Melba, Nellie. ML420.M35.M41, (v9)
Melby, Ernest Oscar. LB875.M345, (v7)
Melchior, Paul J. QC809.E2.M48 1983, (v1)
Melchiori, Giorgio. PR3014.M45 1994, (v3)
Melden, A. I. BJ1461.M4, (v8)
Meldolesi, Luca. HB119.H57.M45 1995, (v6)
Mele, Alfred R. B105.A35.M44 1992, (v8)
Mele, Alfred R. BJ1533.D49.M45 1995, (v8)
Meléndez Valdés, Juan. PQ6538.M5A17 1991, (v3)
Melendez, Edgardo. JL1056.M45 1988, (v7)
Meletinskii, E. M. PN56.M94.M4413 1998, (v3)
Meletis, Chris D. RM302.N38 2001, (v2)
Melhorn, Charles M. V874.3.M44, (v10)

Melko, Matthew. HN79.O3.M45 1994, (v6)
Mellars, Paul. GN285.M45 1996, (v6)
Mellen, Joan. PS3515.E343.Z775 1996, (v3)
Mellencamp, Patricia. PN1992.6.M44 1992, (v3)
    PN1995.9.E96.M45 1990, (v3)
    PN1995.9.W6.M46 1995, (v3)
Meller, Patricio. HC192.M4553 2000, (v6)
Meller, Susan. NK9500.M45 1991, (v9)
Mellers, Wilfrid Howard. ML410.G75.M4 1992, (v9)
    ML410.P787.M44 1993, (v9)
Mellersh, H. E. L. D11.M39 1999, (v5)
Melleuish, Gregory. DU107.M4 1995, (v5)
Melley, Timothy. PS374.C594.M45 2000, (v3)
Mellnik, Stephen M. D767.4.M4, (v5)
Mello, Jeffrey A. KF3470.M45 1995, (v7)
Mello, Michael. KF9227.C2.M38 1996, (v7)
    KF9227.C2.M383 1997, (v7)
Mellon, M. G. QD8.5.M44 1982, (v1)
Mellon, Thomas. HC102.5.M377.A3 1994, (v6)
Melloni, June L. RG45.M45 2000, (v2)
Mellor, Anne Kostelanetz. PR468.F46.M45 1992, (v3)
    PR468.P57.M45 2000, (v3)
    PR5398.M4 1988, (v3)
Mellor, G. L. GC150.5.M45 1996, (v6)
Mellor, Roy E. H. JC319.M56 1989, (v7)
Mellow, James R. PS3515.E37.Z74176 1992, (v3)
Melman, Billie. DS61.7.A1.M45 1992, (v5)
Melmoth, William. PR3548.M7.L46, (v3)
Melnick, Daniel C. PN3499.M45 1994, (v3)
Melnick, Jeffrey Paul. ML3477.M45 1999, (v9)
Melnick, R. Shep. KF3720.M45 1994, (v7)
Melnick, Ralph. PS3523.E7994.Z76 1997, (v3)
    PS3523.E96.Z76 1998, (v3)
Melnyk, Steven A. TS155.6.M45 1991, (v1)
Melograno, Vincent. GV365.M45 1996, (v6)
Melone, Albert P. JN9607.M45 1998, (v7)
    KF4575.M4 1988, (v7)
Melosh, Barbara. NX504.M44 1991, (v9)
Melosi, Martin V. D742.U5.M44, (v5)
Melot, Michel. NE647.6.I4.M4413 1996, (v9)
Melton J. Gordon. BL2525.M45 1992, (v8)
Melton, Buckner F. E302.6.B9 M45 2004, (v4)
    E334.M45 2001, (v4)
    KF4961.B58.M45 1998, (v7)
Melton, H. Keith. UB271.U5.M44 1991, (v10)
Melton, J. Gordon. BL2525.M449 1999, (v8)
    BV656.M45 1997, (v8)
    Z6878.M3.M44 1992, (v10)
    Z7751.M45 1992, (v10)
Melton, James Van Horn. LC135.G32.P785 1988, (v7)
Melton, Judith M. D808.M45 1998, (v5)
Melton, Reginald F. LB1570.M388, (v7)
Meltsner, Michael. KF9227.C2.M4, (v7)
Meltz, Eva Stolar. F548.9.J5.M45 2000, (v4)
Meltzer, Ellen. D848.M45 1995, (v5)
Meltzer, Francoise. PN166.M45 1994, (v3)
Meltzer, Herbert L. QP376.M525, (v1)
Meltzer, Milton. HD8072.M328 1991, (v6)
Melville, Herman. PS2380.F222, (v3)
    PS2380.F68, (v3)
    PS2382.L4, (v3)
    PS2382.S5 1942, (v3)
    PS2384.B3 1963, (v3)
    PS2384.B54 1962, (v3)
    PS2384.C6 1954, (v3)
    PS2384.I7 1925, (v3)
    PS2384.M6 1950, (v3)
    PS2384.O4 1924, (v3)
    PS2384.T9 1959, (v3)
    PS2384.W5 1956, (v3)
    PS2386.A57, (v3)
    PS2386.M4 1948, (v3)
Melville, Tom. GV917.M45 1993, (v6)
    GV928.U6 M45 1998, (v6)
Melvin, Patricia Mooney. HN90.C6.M45 1987, (v6)
Melvoin, Richard I. F74.D4.M4 1989, (v4)
Melzer, Sondra. PS3531.A5855.Z78 1997, (v3)
Mena, Juan de. PQ6413.M2.T7 1943, (v3)
Menashri, David. DS318.825.M476 2001, (v5)
Menchaca, Martha. F869.S53.M46 1995, (v4)
Mencius. PL2478.P5 1970, (v3)

Mencken, H. L. BJ71.M5 1977, (v8)
    E742.M4, (v4)
    HQ1221.M25 1931, (v6)
    JC423.M45 1977, (v7)
    ML60.M499 1975, (v9)
    PE2808.M43, (v3)
    PS121.M4, (v3)
    PS3525.E43.A16 1961, (v3)
    PS3525.E43.A6 1949, (v3)
    PS3525.E43.A6 1968, (v3)
    PS3525.E43.A6 1990, (v3)
    PS3525.E43.A75 1965, (v3)
    PS3525.E43.B3, (v3)
    PS3525.E43.B6 1920, (v3)
    PS3525.E43 C4, (v3)
    PS3525.E43.D34 1947, (v3)
    PS3525.E43.M4, (v3)
    PS3525.E43.P86 1927, (v3)
    PS3525.E43.Z463 1989, (v3)
    PS3525.E43.Z4634 1988, (v3)
    PS3525.E43.Z464 1987, (v3)
    PS3525.E43.Z4663 1996, (v3)
    PS3525.E43.Z47 1987, (v3)
    PS3525.E43.Z475 1994, (v3)
    PS3525.E43.Z48 1981, (v3)
    PS3525.E43.Z497 2001, (v3)
Mendel, Gregor. QH423.M5313 1965a, (v1)
    QK982.M4613 1993, (v1)
Mendelberg, Tali. E185.615.M46 2001, (v4)
Mendel-Reyes, Meta. JK1764.M46 1995, (v7)
Mendelsohn, Oliver. DS422.C3.M39 1998, (v5)
Mendelson, Edward. PR6001.U4.Z7585 1999, (v3)
Mendelson, Elliott. QA9.M4 1979, (v1)
Mendelson, Jack H. HV5292.M4 1985, (v6)
Mendelssohn, Kurt. QC278.M43 1966a, (v1)
Mender, Donald. RC343.M44 1994, (v2)
Mender, Mona. MT35.M56 1991, (v9)
Mendes-Flohr, Paul R. DS113.M424 1990, (v5)
Mendes-France, Pierre. DC397.M413, (v5)
Mendez Rodenas, Adriana. F1799.H3.M4736 1998,
    (v4)
Mendoza-Lopez, Margarita. PQ7189.M4 1987, (v3)
Mendus, Susan. JC571.M425 1989, (v7)
Menen, Aubrey. PR6025.E5 S48, (v3)
Menendez Alarcon, Antonio V. PN1992.3.D65.M46
    1992, (v3)
Menendez Pidal, Ramon. DP52.M4 1950a, (v5)
    PC4095.M4, (v3)
    PC4101.M4 1977, (v3)
    PQ6088.M375 1974, (v3)
Menendez, Albert J. BR1642.U5.M46 1996, (v8)
    Z7757.U5 M46 1985, (v10)
Menezes, A. J. QA76.9.A25.M463 1997, (v1)
Meng, Chiao. PL2677.M4.A24 1996, (v3)
Menges, Constantine Christopher. UA23.M465 1988,
    (v10)
Menjivar, Cecilia. F869.S39.S155 2000, (v4)
Menke-Eggers, Christoph. B3199.A34.M4413 1998,
    (v8)
Mennell, Robert L. KF755.Z9.M38 1994, (v7)
Mennell, Stephen. CB18.E44.M46 1989, (v5)
Menning, Bruce. UA770.M467 1992, (v10)
Menninger, Karl A. BF173.M36 1945, (v2)
    BF692.M4, (v2)
    RC438.6.M46.A4 1995, (v2)
    RC454.M38 1977, (v2)
Menninghaus, Winfried. PN754.M4613 1999, (v3)
Mennis, Edmund A. HB171.M523 1999, (v6)
Menocal, Maria Rosa. PN682.A67.M46 1987, (v3)
Menon, Dilip M. DS485.K48.M46 1994, (v5)
Menon, Ritu. DS480.842.M46 1998, (v5)
Mensch, James R. B831.2.M46 1996, (v8)
Mensh, Elaine. PS1305.M46 2000, (v3)
Menta, Ed. PN2287.S354.M46 1995, (v3)
Mentzer, Raymond A. DC801.C287.M46 1994, (v5)
Menuhin, Yehudi. ML418.M27.A3 1997, (v9)
    ML418.M27.D8 1992, (v9)
Menz, Henner. N2280.M413, (v9)
Menzel, Donald Howard. PE1475.M4, (v3)
    QB521.M4 1959, (v1)
Menzel, Paul T. RA395.A3.M46 1990, (v2)

Menzel, Peter. TJ211.M45 2000, **(v1)**
Menzel, Sewall H. HV5825.M377 1996, **(v6)**
Mepham, John. PR6045.O72.Z8163 1992, **(v3)**
Mera, H. P. TT848.M47 1987, **(v1)**
Meral, Jean. PS159.F5.M4713 1989, **(v3)**
Mercatante, Anthony S. BL303.M45 1988, **(v8)**
    BL2428.M47 1995, **(v8)**
Mercer, Asa Shinn. F761.M557, **(v4)**
Mercer, Bill. E98.A7.M475 1997, **(v4)**
Mercer, H. HD3616.G72.M47 1995, **(v6)**
Mercer, Jonathan. JX1391.M437 1996, **(v7)**
Mercer-Taylor, Peter Jameson. ML410.M5.M66 2000, **(v9)**
Merchant, Carolyn. GF504.N45.M47 1989, **(v6)**
    Q130.M47 1980, **(v1)**
Mercier, Richard. ML410.P32.M47 1998, **(v9)**
Mercier, Vivian. PR6003.E282.Z7813, **(v3)**
    PR8753.M47 1994, **(v3)**
Merdinger, J. E. BR190.M47 1997, **(v8)**
Meredith, David. HC603.D97 1999, **(v6)**
Meredith, George. PR5000.F09, **(v3)**
    PR5002.A1.I94 1998, **(v3)**
    PR5006.D5 1930, **(v3)**
    PR5006.E3 1979, **(v3)**
    PR5006.O7 1950, **(v3)**
    PR5007.A1 1978, **(v3)**
    PR5013.A3, **(v3)**
    PR5013.A4 1997, **(v3)**
Meredith, Howard L. E78.G73.M45 1995, **(v4)**
Meredith, James H. PS228.W37.M47 1999, **(v3)**
Meredith, James. LD3412.9.M4.A3, **(v7)**
Meredith, Roy. E415.8.M4, **(v4)**
Mergen, Bernard. HQ782.M47 1982, **(v6)**
Merideth, Robert W. Z5861.M45 1992, **(v10)**
Merimee, Prosper. PQ2362.C6 1960, **(v3)**
    PQ2362.C6 1963, **(v3)**
Merk, Frederick. E416.M4, **(v4)**
Merkl, Peter H. DD289.M47 1993, **(v5)**
Merkley, Paul Charles. DS150.5.M47 1998, **(v5)**
Merkur, Daniel. RC553.H3.M47 1998, **(v2)**
Merlan, Philip. B517.M4, **(v8)**
Merleau-Ponty, Maurice. B2430.M3763.T49 1991, **(v8)**
    B2430.M378.E5 1964, **(v8)**
    B2430.M379.S43, **(v8)**
    B2430.M379.V513, **(v8)**
Merman, Ethel. ML420.M39.A32, **(v9)**
Mermin, Dorothy. PR4193.M43 1989, **(v3)**
Mernissi, Fatima. BP135.8.W67 M4713 1991, **(v8)**
    BP163.M4713 1992, **(v8)**
    HQ1170.M46 1987, **(v6)**
Mero, Laszlo. QA269.M457 1998, **(v1)**
Meron, Theodor. K3240.4.M484 1989, **(v7)**
    PR3069.M5.M47 1998, **(v3)**
Merrell, Floyd. B105.S55.M47 1998, **(v8)**
    B945.P44.M465 1997, **(v8)**
Merrell, James Hart. E99.C24.I53 1989, **(v4)**
Merrell, Kenneth W. RJ506.D4M47 2001, **(v2)**
Merrett, Christopher Edmond. Z658.S6.M47 1995, **(v10)**
Merrett, Stephen. HD1691.M47 1997, **(v6)**
Merriam, Charles Edward. JA84.U5.M5 1969b, **(v7)**
Merriam, Louise A. Z1236.M47 1995, **(v10)**
Merrick, Jeffrey. DC138.M46 1990, **(v5)**
Merrick, Leonard. PR6025.E7 W67 1920, **(v3)**
Merridale, Catherine. GT3256.2.A2, **(v6)**
Merrill, Christopher. GV943.M475 1993, **(v6)**
Merrill, Deborah M. HQ1063.6.M47 1997, **(v6)**
Merrill, Hugh. PN4900.E8.M47 1995, **(v3)**
Merrill, James Ingram. PS3525.E6.D, **(v3)**
    PS3525.E6645.S4 1958, **(v3)**
Merrill, John Calhoun. PN4749.M47 2001, **(v3)**
    PN4756.M385 1994, **(v3)**
Merrill, Linda. KD379.W47.M47 1992, **(v7)**
Merrill, Lisa. PN2287.C8.M47 1999, **(v3)**
Merrill, Peter. HD62.15.M47 1997, **(v6)**
Merrill, Robert. ML420.M42.A3, **(v9)**
    PR2047.M47 1987, **(v3)**
Merrill, Ronald T. QC816.M47 1996, **(v1)**
Merrill, Walter McIntosh. E449.G2557, **(v4)**
Merrill, William L. F1221.T25.M47 1988, **(v4)**
Merrim, Stephanie. PQ7296.J6.Z697 1999, **(v3)**

Merriman, A. D. TN609.M475, **(v1)**
Merriman, Brigid O'Shea. BX4705.D283.M477 1994, **(v8)**
Merriman, David. HJ9157.M47 1987, **(v6)**
Merriman, John M. DC272.5.M42, **(v5)**
Merriman, Roger Bigelow. DR506.M4, **(v5)**
Merritt, Greg. PN1995.9.P7.M428 2000, **(v3)**
Merritt, Helen. NE1322.M48 2000, **(v9)**
Merritt, Richard L. DD259.5.M47 1995, **(v5)**
Merrow, Susan D. GE195.M47 1992, **(v6)**
Merry, John A. TL512.M37 1998, **(v1)**
Merry, Robert W. PN4874.A43.M47 1996, **(v3)**
Merry, Sally Engle. KF379.M47 1990, **(v7)**
Merryman, Molly. D810.W7.M44 1997, **(v5)**
Mertens, Donna M. LB1028.M3966 1998, **(v7)**
Mertes, Kate. DA185.M47 1988, **(v5)**
Merton, Robert King. HM24.M472, **(v6)**
Merton, Thomas. BX2350.M535, **(v8)**
    PS3525.E7174.A6 1962, **(v3)**
    PS3525.E7174.E4, **(v3)**
    PS3525.E7174.Z485 1997, **(v3)**
    PS3525.E7174.Z49 1978, **(v3)**
    PS3525.E7174.Z49 2001, **(v3)**
Mertz, Leslie A. QH307.2.M47 2000, **(v1)**
Mervin, David. E881.M47 1996, **(v4)**
Merwick, Donna. F129.A357.M47 1990, **(v4)**
Merwin, W. S. PS3563.E75F56 1998, **(v3)**
Meryman, Richard. ND237.W93.M4 1996, **(v9)**
Merzbacher, Eugen. QC174.1.M36 1970, **(v1)**
Merzkirch, Wolfgang. TA357.M47 1987, **(v1)**
Mesa-Lago, Carmelo. HC152.5.M47, **(v6)**
    HC192.M47 2000, **(v6)**
    HD7130.5.M44 1989, **(v6)**
Mesa-Lago, Carmelo. HD7130.5.M445 1994, **(v6)**
Mesarovic, Mihajlo D. HC59.M458 1974, **(v6)**
Meschke, Michael. PN1871.M45 1992, **(v3)**
Mesibov, Gary B. RC553.A88M675 2001, **(v2)**
    RJ506.A9.M48 1997, **(v2)**
Meskill, John Thomas. DS736.5.M47 1965, **(v5)**
Mesnet, Marie Beatrice. PR6013.R44.Z654, **(v3)**
Messenger, Charles. G1038.M37 1989, **(v6)**
Messenger, Troy. BX8476.O2.M47 1999, **(v8)**
Messer, Thomas M. ND699.K3.M47 1997, **(v9)**
Messer-Kruse, Timothy. HX11.I5.M43 1998, **(v6)**
Messerly, John G. BF109.P5.M47 1996, **(v2)**
Messiaen, Olivier. ML410.M595.A3 1994, **(v9)**
Messick, Frederic M. Z2000.M395 1987, **(v10)**
Messing, Karen. RC963.6.W65.M47 1998, **(v2)**
Messinger, Gary S. D639.P7.G775 1992, **(v5)**
Messinger, Lisa Mintz. N6537.O39.M477 2001, **(v9)**
Messinger, Thane Josef. KF297.Z9 M45 2000, **(v7)**
Messner, Michael A. GV706.32.M47 2003, **(v6)**
    GV706.4.M47 1992, **(v6)**
    GV706.5.M47 1994, **(v6)**
    HQ1090.3.M475 1997, **(v6)**
Mesta, Perle (Skirvin). CT275.M498.A3, **(v5)**
Mester, Terri A. PR478.D35.M47 1997, **(v3)**
Mestrovic, Stjepan Gabriel. HM73.M478 1994, **(v6)**
    HM73.M479 1993, **(v6)**
    HN380.7.A8.M47 1993, **(v6)**
    HN613.5.M47 1993, **(v6)**
Met, Philippe. PQ443.M47 1999, **(v3)**
Metcalf, George R. KF5740.M48 1988, **(v7)**
    LC214.2.M46 1983, **(v7)**
Metcalf, Keyes DeWitt. Z679.5.M49 1986, **(v10)**
    Z720.M4.A36, **(v10)**
Metcalf, Michael. QA76.73.F16.M47 1996, **(v1)**
Metcalf, Peter. GN486.M48 1991, **(v6)**
Metcalf, Robert Lee. SB931.M47 1993, **(v1)**
Metcalf, Thomas R. NA1502.M46 1989, **(v9)**
Metcalfe, C. R. QK643.M7M4, **(v1)**
    QK671 M4, **(v1)**
Metcalfe, Charles Russell. QK495.A12M47 1979, **(v1)**
Metcalfe, John Wallace. Z696.M59, **(v10)**
Metellus, Jean. PQ2673.E7244.F3513 1995, **(v3)**
Metoyer, Cynthia Chavez. HQ1487.M48 2000, **(v6)**
Métraux, Alfred. BL2490.M453 1959a, **(v8)**
Metraux, Daniel Alfred. BP605.O88.M48 2000, **(v8)**
Metropolitan Museum of Art (New York, N.Y.).
    N611.L43.M46 1987, **(v9)**
    NB210.M48 1999, **(v9)**

    ND205.N373 1980, **(v9)**
    ND669.F5.M47 1998, **(v9)**
    NK7983.22.N48 1980, **(v9)**
    TR646.U6.N484, **(v1)**
Mettam, Roger. DC126.M43 1988, **(v5)**
Mettenheim, Kurt von. JL2492.M47 1995, **(v7)**
Metter, Ellen. PN146.M47 1995, **(v3)**
    PN146.M47 1999, **(v3)**
Metz, Allan. KDZ944.A12.M48 1996, **(v7)**
Metz, G. Harold. PR2835.M48 1996, **(v3)**
Metzger, Melanie. HV2042.M37 1999, **(v6)**
Metzger, Robert P. E877.2.M48 1989, **(v4)**
Mews, C. J. PA8201.A9.M49 1999, **(v3)**
Meyendorff, John. BX290.M413, **(v8)**
Meyer, Adam. Z1229.N39 M49 2002, **(v10)**
Meyer, Adolf. BF109.M49.A4 1990, **(v2)**
Meyer, Agnes Elizabeth Ernst. CT275.M5124.A3, **(v5)**
Meyer, Annette E. HJ2051.M49 1989, **(v6)**
Meyer, C. D. QA188.M495 2000, **(v1)**
Meyer, Conrad Ferdinand. PT2432.A15 1976, **(v3)**
Meyer, David R. DS796.H757.M48 2000, **(v5)**
Meyer, Duane Gilbert. F466.M578 1982, **(v4)**
Meyer, Eric. RZ440.M476 2001, **(v2)**
Meyer, Ernest Louis. UB342.U5.M4 1930a, **(v10)**
Meyer, Esther da Costa. NA2707.S28.M48 1995, **(v9)**
Meyer, Eugene L. F181.M47 2000, **(v4)**
Meyer, Eugene. TH9446.H38M48 1989, **(v1)**
Meyer, Harold Diedrich. GV171.M43 1969, **(v6)**
Meyer, Harvey Kessler. F1502.M56 1994, **(v4)**
Meyer, Henry Cord. D447.M4, **(v5)**
Meyer, Henry Joseph. HV741.M4, **(v6)**
Meyer, Jack Allen. Z2179.M49 1987, **(v10)**
Meyer, Janet L. PN1998.3.P655.M48 1998, **(v3)**
Meyer, Jeffrey F. BL1812.P45.M49 1991, **(v8)**
    BL2527.W18 M49 2001, **(v8)**
Meyer, John P. HF5549.5.M63.M49 1997, **(v6)**
Meyer, Laure. N7398.M4913 1992, **(v9)**
Meyer, Leisa D. UA565.W6.M48 1996, **(v10)**
Meyer, Leonard B. ML430.5.M5 1989, **(v9)**
    ML3800.M63, **(v9)**
    ML3800.M633, **(v9)**
Meyer, Lysle E. DT352.7.M49 1992, **(v5)**
Meyer, Mary Keysor. CS5.W5 1990, **(v5)**
Meyer, Melissa L. E99.C6 M46 1999, **(v4)**
Meyer, Michael A. BM197.M48 1988, **(v8)**
    DS115.5.M48, **(v5)**
    DS143.M39 1990, **(v5)**
Meyer, Michael C. F1226.M54, **(v4)**
    F1234.H87.M48, **(v4)**
    F1234.O73.M4, **(v4)**
    Z6465.L29 T7 Suppl., **(v10)**
Meyer, Michael D. HE305.M49 1984, **(v6)**
Meyer, Michael J. Z8839.4.M49 1998, **(v10)**
Meyer, Michael Leverson. PT8890.M47, **(v3)**
Meyer, Roy Willard. E99.M2.M48, **(v4)**
    E99.S22 M4 1993, **(v4)**
Meyer, Rudolph X. TL795.M48 1999, **(v1)**
Meyer, Stefan G. PJ7577.M49 2001, **(v3)**
Meyer, Susan. PR878.R34.M49 1996, **(v3)**
Meyer, William B. QC983.M455 2000, **(v1)**
Meyer-Arendt, Jurgen R. QC357.2.M48, **(v1)**
Meyerbeer, Giacomo. ML410.M61.A3 1999, **(v9)**
    ML410.M61.A4 1989, **(v9)**
Meyering, Sheryl L. PS3505.A87.Z7425 1994, **(v3)**
Meyerowitz, Rael. PS27.M49 1995, **(v3)**
Meyers, Diana T. BJ1395.M48 1994, **(v8)**
Meyers, Jeffrey. PR6005.O4.Z778 1991, **(v3)**
    PR6023.A93.Z679 1982, **(v3)**
    PS2631.M48 1992, **(v3)**
    PS3511.R94.Z788 1996, **(v3)**
    PS3545.I6245.Z76 1995, **(v3)**
Meyers, Marc A. TA460.M466 1984, **(v1)**
Meyers, Valerie. PR6029.R8.Z73725 1991, **(v3)**
Meyers, William K. F1266.M49 1994, **(v4)**
Meyerson, Emile. BD162.M43 1962, **(v8)**
Meyerson, Julia. F2230.2.K4.M47 1990, **(v4)**
Meyerson, Martin. NA9030.M48, **(v9)**
Meynell, Alice Christiana (Thompson).
    PR5021.M3.A67 1970, **(v3)**
    PR5021.M3.A723 1970, **(v3)**

Meynell, Hugo Anthony. B831.2.M48 1999, **(v8)**
Meyrowitz, Joshua. HM258.M49 1985, **(v6)**
Mezerik, A. G. D839.3.I56 vol.4, no.43, **(v5)**
Mezey, Paul G. QD461.M583 1993, **(v1)**
Mezey, Susan Gluck. KF3649.M49 1988, **(v7)**
 KF3735.M492000, **(v7)**
Mezirow, Jack. LB1059.M49 2000, **(v7)**
Mezu, Sebastian Okechukwu. PQ3989.S47.Z79 1973b, **(v3)**
Miall, Andrew D. QE471.2.M53 1996, **(v1)**
 QE615.M3 2000, **(v1)**
Miall, Hugh. JX4473.M48 1992, **(v7)**
Miano, Giovanni. TK7872.T74, **(v1)**
Micale, Mark S. RC532.M53 1995, **(v2)**
Micaud, Charles Antoine, 1910-. DC396.M5 1964, **(v5)**
Michael, Erika. Z8414.M53 1997, **(v10)**
Michael, Franz H. DS753.M5 1965, **(v5)**
 DS759.M57, **(v5)**
Michael, Magali Cornier. PR888.I45.M53 1996, **(v3)**
Michael, Nancy C. Z8812.P47.M5 1987, **(v10)**
Michael, Paul. PN1993.5.U6.M53, **(v3)**
Michaelis, David. ND237.W94.M53 1998, **(v9)**
Michaelis, H. PC5333.M58 1955, **(v3)**
 PC5333.N6 1958, **(v3)**
Michaelis, John Udell. LB1584.M43 1992, **(v7)**
Michaels, Ed. HD38.2.M53 2001, **(v6)**
Michaels, Walter Benn. E169.1.M6 1995, **(v4)**
Michalewicz, Zbigniew. QA63.M53 2000, **(v1)**
Michalski, L. QC271.M483 1991, **(v1)**
Michal-Smith, Harold. RJ499.M46, **(v2)**
Michaud, Guy. PQ287.M5, **(v3)**
 PQ2344.Z5.M483, **(v3)**
Michaux, Henri. PQ2625.I2.A6 1968, **(v3)**
Michaux, Henry. DS9.M443, **(v5)**
Michel, Henri. DC397.M53, **(v5)**
Michel, Laurence Anthony. PN1892.M5, **(v3)**
Michel, Sonya. HQ778.63.M52 1999, **(v6)**
Michelet, Jules. DC161.M51532, **(v5)**
Michell, George. DS436.N47 1987 pt. 1, vol. 7, **(v5)**
 N8195.A4.M53 2000, **(v9)**
Michell, Joel. BF39.M545 1999, **(v2)**
Michelman, Irving S. HB501.M632 1994, **(v6)**
Michelson, Bruce. PS430.M48 2000, **(v3)**
 PS1342.A54.M53 1995, **(v3)**
Michelson, Paul E. DR244.M54 1998, **(v5)**
Michener, Anna J. HV6626.52.M54 1998, **(v6)**
Michener, Charles Duncan. QL566.M53 2000, **(v1)**
 QL569.M5, **(v1)**
Michener, James A. DP43.M45, **(v5)**
 NE1310.M48, **(v9)**
 PS3525.I19 B7, **(v3)**
 PS3525.I19 C4, **(v3)**
 PS3525.I19 F5, **(v3)**
 PS3525.I19 H3, **(v3)**
 PS3525.I19 S3, **(v3)**
 PS3525.I19 S6, **(v3)**
Michie, Allen. PR3667.M53 1999, **(v3)**
Michie, Jonathan. HD4906.M43 1987, **(v6)**
Michigan State University. PN6725.M53 1993, **(v3)**
Michnik, Adam. DK4442.M53 1985, **(v5)**
 DK4449.M53 1998, **(v5)**
Michno, Gregory. E83.876.M5 1997, **(v4)**
Michta, Andrew A. DK4436.M55 1990, **(v5)**
 UA646.8.M53 1992, **(v10)**
Mickel, Emanuel J. PQ1495.M5, **(v3)**
Mickelsen, William C. ML430.M5, **(v9)**
Mickelson, Sig. HE8700.76.U6.M54 1989, **(v6)**
Mickens, Ronald E. QA431.M426 1987, **(v1)**
Mickiewicz, Adam. PG7158.M5.A26 1975, **(v3)**
 PG7158.M5P312 1992, **(v3)**
Micklewicz, Ellen Propper. PN1992.6.M48 1999, **(v3)**
Mickle, Isaac. F144.C2.M52, **(v4)**
Mickolus, Edward F. HV6431.M499 1997, **(v6)**
 Z7164.T3 M53, **(v10)**
 Z7164.T3 M54 1988, **(v10)**
Micucci, Joseph A. RJ503.M495 1998, **(v2)**
Middlebrook, Diane Wood. PS3537.E915.Z775 1991, **(v3)**
Middlekauff, Robert. E206.M484, **(v4)**
 E302.6.F8.M644 1996, **(v4)**
 F67.M4865, **(v4)**

Middleton, Arthur Pierce. F187.C5 M5 1984, **(v4)**
Middleton, Drew. D787.M5 1960a, **(v5)**
 D811.5.M44, **(v5)**
Middleton, Gerard V. QA808.M49 1994, **(v1)**
 QE33.2.S82M53 2000, **(v1)**
Middleton, John. DT429.5.S94.M54 1992, **(v5)**
Middleton, Peter. PR478.H57, **(v3)**
Middleton, Roger. HB103.A2.M53 1998, **(v6)**
 HC256.3.M418 1985, **(v6)**
Middleton, Stephen. KF4757.M48 1993, **(v7)**
Middleton, Thomas. PR2315.M5.G5 1937, **(v3)**
 PR2711.B8, **(v3)**
 PR2712.M8 1975, **(v3)**
Middleton, Victor T. C. G155.A1.M4753 1998, **(v6)**
Middleton, W. E. Knowles. QC271.M5, **(v1)**
Middleton, William D. TF23.M52 1999, **(v1)**
Midelfort, H. C. Erik. RC450.G3.M53 1994, **(v2)**
Midgley, Mary. BJ1012.M5 1984, **(v8)**
 BJ1012.M52, **(v8)**
 BJ1401.M52 1984, **(v8)**
 BJ1408.5.M52 1991, **(v8)**
Midkiff, Pat. TT270.M53 1978, **(v1)**
Mieder, Wolfgang. Z5956.P74.M54 1999, **(v10)**
 Z6514.P76.M535 1996, **(v10)**
Mielczarek, Eugenie V. QP535.F4, **(v1)**
Mielnik, Edward M. TS205.M52 1991, **(v1)**
Miermont, Jacques. RC488.5.M53313 1995, **(v2)**
Mierop, Caroline. NA6230.M513 1995, **(v9)**
Miers, Earl Schenck. E475.27.M64, **(v4)**
Mierzejewski, Alfred C. HC286.4.M45 1988, **(v6)**
 HE3080.D4.M535 1999, **(v6)**
Mies van der Rohe, Ludwig. NA1088.M65.P3, **(v9)**
Miesfeld, Roger L. QH442.M5425 1999, **(v1)**
Miethe, Terance D. HV6018.M54 1994, **(v6)**
Migdalski, Edward C. QL615.M49, **(v1)**
 SH462.M5, **(v1)**
Mighall, Robert. PR878.T3.M54 1999, **(v3)**
Migliorini, Bruno. PC1075.M513x 1984, **(v3)**
Mignolo, Walter. F1409.7.M56 1995, **(v4)**
Mignon, Molly Raymond. CC70.M45 1993, **(v5)**
Mignot, Claude. NA957.M5313 1984, **(v9)**
Mihailovich, Vasa D. PG501.M518, **(v3)**
Mihesuah, Devon A. E97.6.C35.M54 1993, **(v4)**
Mikalson, Jon D. PA3136.M54 1991, **(v3)**
Mikdadi, F. H. Z8614.74.M54 1991, **(v10)**
 Z8869.14.M55 1993, **(v10)**
Mikhail, E. H. Z2014.D7.M545, **(v10)**
Mikhail, Mona. PJ8212.M55 1992, **(v3)**
Mikheev, Dmitrii. UG743.M55 1987, **(v10)**
Mikics, David. PR2367.E8.M55 1994, **(v3)**
Miklowitz, Paul S. B2948.M48 1998, **(v8)**
Mikolyzk, Thomas A. Z8423.3.M53 1990, **(v10)**
Miksche, Ferdinand Otto. U165.M495 1955a, **(v10)**
 U240.M5 1970, **(v10)**
 UA11.M46 1976, **(v10)**
Mikus, Joseph A. DB679.M513 1963, **(v5)**
Milakovich, Michael E. HD31.M435 1995, **(v6)**
Milani, Farzaneh. PK6413.5.W65.M5 1992, **(v3)**
Milanich, Jerald T. E78.F6.M545 1994, **(v4)**
 E78.F6.M55, **(v4)**
 E78.F6.M557 1992, **(v4)**
Milanovic, Petar T. GB843.M5413 1981, **(v6)**
Milbank, Alison. PR595.D36.M55 1998, **(v3)**
Milbrath, Constance. N351.M54 1998, **(v9)**
Milbrath, Lester W. HC79.E5.M47 1984, **(v6)**
Milbrath, Lester W. JF2051.M48, **(v7)**
Milbrath, Susan. F1435.3.C14.M55 1999, **(v4)**
Milburn, G. J. QA76.889.M55 1998, **(v1)**
Milburn, Michael A. JA74.5.M55 1996, **(v7)**
Milburn, Michael Peter. R733.M535 2001, **(v2)**
Milburn, R. L. P. N7832.M47 1988, **(v9)**
Mileck, Joseph. PT2617.E85.Z833, **(v3)**
Miles, Agnes. RC451.4.W6.M55 1988, **(v2)**
Miles, Gary B. DG207.L583.M5 1995, **(v5)**
Miles, James A. R. DS779.32.M54 1996, **(v5)**
Miles, Jennifer A. TN870.5.M493 1989, **(v1)**
Miles, Josephine. PR468.N3.M5 1965, **(v3)**
 PR502.M48, **(v3)**
Miles, Margaret Ruth. PN1995.9.R4.M56 1996, **(v3)**
Miles, Nelson Appleton. E83.866.M64 1992, **(v4)**
Miles, Robert. PR5204.M55 1995, **(v3)**

Miles, Rosalind. PR2638.M55 1990, **(v3)**
Miles, William F. S. DT515.45.H38.M55 1994, **(v5)**
 DU760.M55 1998, **(v5)**
Miletich, John J. Z6664.A27.M53 1993, **(v10)**
 Z6665.7.D46.M55 1995, **(v10)**
 Z6665.7.D46.M56 1997, **(v10)**
 Z6675.E45.M54 1990, **(v10)**
Mileur, Jean-Pierre. PR4484.M5 1982, **(v3)**
Miley, William M. R726.7.M55 1999, **(v2)**
Milford, Nancy. PS3511.I9234.Z8 1970, **(v3)**
Milfull, Inge B. BX1999.85.A3.D876 1996, **(v8)**
Milgrom, Lionel R. QD441.M55 1997, **(v1)**
Milhaud, Darius. ML410.M674.A32 1970, **(v9)**
Miliaras, Barbara A. PR6023.A93.Z68137 1987, **(v3)**
Miliband, Ralph. HB501.M655 1989, **(v6)**
 JC474.M52, **(v7)**
Milkis, Sidney M. JK511.M55 1990, **(v7)**
 JK2261.M53 1999, **(v7)**
Milkman, Paul. PN4899.N42.P485 1997, **(v3)**
Milkman, Ruth. HD8039.A82.U653 1997, **(v6)**
Milkovich, Barbara A. F614.V7 M55 2000, **(v4)**
Mill, John Stuart. B1574.B34.M5 1951, **(v8)**
 B1602.A2 1963, **(v8)**
 B1606.A2 1961, **(v8)**
 BC91.M6 1930, **(v8)**
 BL51.M62 1969, **(v8)**
 HB161.M6 1965, **(v6)**
 HB161.M645 1968, **(v6)**
 JA41.M5, **(v7)**
 JC423.M6 1962, **(v7)**
 JC585.M6 2002, **(v7)**
 JC585.M74 1983, **(v7)**
 JC585.M77, **(v7)**
 LB675.M517, **(v7)**
Millar, Fergus. DG254.2.M55 1998, **(v5)**
Millar, James R. HC335.M495 1990, **(v6)**
Millar, John Fitzhugh. VM22.M54, **(v10)**
Millard, F. DK4449.M55 1994, **(v5)**
Millard, Kenneth. PS379.M47 2000, **(v3)**
Millay, Edna St. Vincent. PS3525.I495.A17 1956, **(v3)**
 PS3525.I495.A6 1988, **(v3)**
 PS3525.I495.A6 1998, **(v3)**
 PS3525.I495.C6 1937, **(v3)**
 PS3525.I495.F4, **(v3)**
 PS3525.I495.K5 1927, **(v3)**
 PS3525.I495.L3 1921, **(v3)**
 PS3525.I495.M3 1940, **(v3)**
 PS3525.I495.S4 1950, **(v3)**
 PS3525.I495.T5 1926, **(v3)**
 PS3525.I495.Z53 1972, **(v3)**
 PS3525.I495 1943, **(v3)**
 PS3525.I 495F3 1931, **(v3)**
 PS3525.I 495M5 1954, **(v3)**
Millen, Charles W. RV81.M64, **(v2)**
Millen, James Knox. BF271.M5, **(v2)**
Miller Frank, Felicia. PQ283.M53 1995, **(v3)**
Miller, Alan S. GF80.M53 1990, **(v6)**
Miller, Angela L. ND1351.5.M53 1993, **(v9)**
Miller, Arthur G. HM291.M49 1986, **(v6)**
Miller, Arthur I. QC680.M55 1994, **(v1)**
Miller, Arthur Selwyn. KF224.F69.M55 1988, **(v7)**
Miller, Arthur. PS3525.I5156.A19 1957, **(v3)**
 PS3525.I5156.A66 1968, **(v3)**
 PS3525.I5156.A7, **(v3)**
 PS3525.I5156.C7 1953, **(v3)**
 PS3525.I5156.D4, **(v3)**
 PS3525.I5156 F6, **(v3)**
 PS3525.I5156.I17 1967, **(v3)**
 PS3525.I5156.M5 1961, **(v3)**
 PS3525.I5156.T5, **(v3)**
 PS3525.I5156.V5 1977, **(v3)**
 PS3525.I5156.Z477 1987, **(v3)**
Miller, Audrey. QD251.2.M53 1992, **(v1)**
Miller, Bertha E. Mahony. NC965.M59, **(v9)**
Miller, Blair. PN1995.9.C55.M53 1995, **(v3)**
Miller, Carol Poh. F499.C657 M55 1997, **(v4)**
Miller, Caroline Pafford. PS3525.I517 L3, **(v3)**
Miller, Casey. PN218.M5 1988, **(v3)**
Miller, Christopher L. PQ145.7.A35M55 1985, **(v3)**
Miller, Connie. Z7963.F44.M54 1991, **(v10)**
Miller, Crane S. F861.M55 2000, **(v4)**

Miller, D. A. PR878.P59.M55 1988, **(v3)**
Miller, D. Quentin. PS3571.P4.Z783 2001, **(v3)**
Miller, Daniel. CC72.4.M55 1987, **(v5)**
Miller, Darlis A. PS1469.C3.Z75 1993, **(v3)**
  UC263.M468 1989, **(v10)**
Miller, David M. BL1226.85.M54, **(v8)**
  PR3588.M47, **(v3)**
Miller, David. HB90.M54 1989, **(v6)**
  JC311.M475 1995, **(v7)**
  JF801.M55 2000, **(v7)**
Miller, Dean A. PN56.E65.M55 2000, **(v3)**
Miller, Derek. RJ503.M55 1983, **(v2)**
Miller, Donald E. BR826.M554 1997, **(v8)**
Miller, Dorothy C. HV95.M49 1990, **(v6)**
Miller, Douglas T. E169.02.M485, **(v4)**
  F123.M6, **(v4)**
Miller, Dusty. RC569.5.S45.M54 1994, **(v2)**
Miller, E. Willard. TD223.M53 1992, **(v1)**
  TJ163.235.M55 1993, **(v1)**
Miller, Edward A. E492.94 29th .M55 1998, **(v4)**
Miller, Edwin Haviland. PR428.A8.M5, **(v3)**
  PS1881.M48 1991, **(v3)**
  PS3222.S63.M55 1989, **(v3)**
Miller, Eugene E. PS3545.R815.Z77 1990, **(v3)**
Miller, Floyd John. E448.M56, **(v4)**
Miller, Francis Pickens. F231.M58, **(v4)**
Miller, Fred Dycus. JC71.A7.M55 1995, **(v7)**
Miller, Fredric. F158.37.M56 1988, **(v4)**
Miller, G. Wayne. RD598.M523 2000, **(v2)**
Miller, Henry I. RA401.A3.M55 2000, **(v2)**
Miller, Henry. PQ2387.R5.Z712 1956, **(v3)**
  PR6023.A93.Z6814, **(v3)**
  PS3525.I5454.B5, **(v3)**
  PS3525.I5454.B6 1963, **(v3)**
  PS3525.I5454.C6 1939, **(v3)**
  PS3525.I5454.J8, **(v3)**
  PS3525.I5454.N4 1964, **(v3)**
  PS3525.I5454.S75 1962, **(v3)**
  PS3525.I5454.S8, **(v3)**
  PS3525.I5454.T5, **(v3)**
  PS3525.I5454.T7 1961, **(v3)**
  PS3525.I5454.T8 1962, **(v3)**
  PS3525.I5454.Z518, **(v3)**
  PS3525.I5454.Z52 1969, **(v3)**
  PS3525.I5454.Z524, **(v3)**
  PS3525.I5454.Z54, **(v3)**
  PS3525.I5454.Z544, **(v3)**
  PS3525.I5454.Z57, **(v3)**
Miller, Irwin. HG9396.M55 1996, **(v6)**
  TS156.M517 1995, **(v1)**
Miller, J. Hillis. NX640.M55 1992, **(v9)**
  PN81.M527 1999, **(v3)**
  PN212.M55 1998, **(v3)**
  PN3355.M48 1992, **(v3)**
  PR469.R4.M5, **(v3)**
  PR601.M5, **(v3)**
  PR4754.M5, **(v3)**
Miller, J. R. E92.M55 1989, **(v4)**
  E96.5.M55 1996, **(v4)**
  F1027.M57, **(v4)**
Miller, James Clifford. HJ2051.M52 1994, **(v6)**
Miller, James M. QD79.C4.M55 1988, **(v1)**
Miller, Janet L. LB1775.M615 1990, **(v7)**
Miller, Jay. Z1206.M55 1995, **(v10)**
Miller, Jerome G. HV9950.M55 1996, **(v6)**
Miller, Jerry. HD38.7.M55 2000, **(v6)**
Miller, Joaquin. PS2395.A2 1923, **(v3)**
  PS2398.A2 1930, **(v3)**
Miller, John Chester. E187.O7.M5, **(v4)**
  E302.6.A2.M56 1960, **(v4)**
  E332.2.M54 1991, **(v4)**
Miller, John E. F586.L3.M54 1982, **(v4)**
  PS3545.I342.Z77 1994, **(v3)**
Miller, John W. BT590.P9.M55 1997, **(v8)**
Miller, John William. B29.M533 1978, **(v8)**
Miller, John. D769.A533 vol. 2, pt. 3, **(v5)**
Miller, Jonathan. N8224.M6.M54 1998, **(v9)**
  QH31.D2.M54 1982, **(v1)**
Miller, Joseph. F812.M5, **(v4)**
Miller, Judith A. HD9042.7.N67.M64 1998, **(v6)**
Miller, Judith Fitzgerald. RT120.C45M55 2000, **(v2)**

Miller, Kenneth E. Z2561.M55 1987, **(v10)**
Miller, Kenton. SD414.T76.M55 1991, **(v1)**
Miller, L. Scott. LC3731.M54 1995, **(v7)**
Miller, Lawrence. PR6003.E282.Z7814 1992, **(v3)**
Miller, Leta E. ML410.H2066.M55 1998, **(v9)**
Miller, Lynn F. N6512.M518, **(v9)**
Miller, Margaret Christina. DF227.5.M56 1997, **(v5)**
Miller, Mark C. KF299.L4.M55 1995, **(v7)**
Miller, Martin A. BF175.M485 1998, **(v2)**
Miller, Mary Ellen. F1435.3.A7.M55 1999, **(v4)**
  F1435.3.R3.M55 1993, **(v4)**
Miller, Mary Jane. PN1992.65.M54 1996, **(v3)**
Miller, Maureen C. BR874.M55 2000, **(v8)**
Miller, Merle. E847.M54 1980, **(v4)**
Miller, Mervyn. NA997.U59.M55 1992, **(v9)**
Miller, Michael Barry. DC369.M525 1994, **(v5)**
Miller, Nancy K. PN98.W64.M55 1991, **(v3)**
  PQ149.M54 1988, **(v3)**
Miller, Naomi J. PR2399.W7.Z76 1996, **(v3)**
Miller, Nathan. D770.M49 1995, **(v5)**
  E757.M67 1992, **(v4)**
  VA55.M55, **(v10)**
Miller, Neil. HQ76.25.M55 1992, **(v6)**
Miller, Nicholas John. DR1524.S47.M55 1997, **(v5)**
Miller, Nicola. F1416.S65.M55 1989, **(v4)**
Miller, Nina. PS255.N5.M55 1999, **(v3)**
Miller, Norman P. GV171.M55, **(v6)**
Miller, Pavla. HM104.M55 1998, **(v6)**
Miller, Penny M. JK5316.M55 1994, **(v7)**
Miller, Perry. B905.M5, **(v8)**
  E169.1.M628, **(v4)**
  E169.1.M635, **(v4)**
  F7.M54, **(v4)**
  F7.M56 1954, **(v4)**
  F82.W788, **(v4)**
  PS682.M5, **(v3)**
Miller, Peter N. DA480.M627 1994, **(v5)**
  DC121.8.P4, **(v5)**
Miller, Philip Lieson. ML54.6.M5 R5 1973, **(v9)**
Miller, R. Craig. NK1390.M54 1990, **(v9)**
Miller, R. H. PR56.M54 1995, **(v3)**
  PR6013.R44.Z655 1990, **(v3)**
Miller, Raymond W. S591.M733 2001, **(v1)**
Miller, Richard Brian. B105.W3.M55 1991, **(v8)**
Miller, Richard E. LA227.4.M555 1998, **(v7)**
Miller, Richard Lawrence. KK928.M55 1995, **(v7)**
Miller, Richard W. BJ1012.M54 1992, **(v8)**
Miller, Richard. HF1416.M55 1995, **(v6)**
  MT121.S38.M55 1999, **(v9)**
  MT820.M599 1996, **(v9)**
  MT820.M5995 2000, **(v9)**
  MT820.M6 1993, **(v9)**
  MT823.M55, **(v9)**
  MT823.M55 1997, **(v9)**
  MT825.M646 1986, **(v9)**
Miller, Robert H. KF283.M55 2000, **(v7)**
Miller, Robert Keith. PR5824.M5 1982, **(v3)**
Miller, Robert Moats. BX6495.F68.M54 1985, **(v8)**
Miller, Robert Ryal. F864.A484.M55 1998, **(v4)**
Miller, Robert W. SB436.M55 1997, **(v1)**
Miller, Ronald E. QA402.5.M553 1999, **(v1)**
Miller, Ronnie. DS79.724.A8.M55 1994, **(v5)**
Miller, Rory. DS149.5.G4, **(v5)**
Miller, Rowland S. BF575.E53.M55 1996, **(v2)**
Miller, Roy Andrew. PL523.M493, **(v3)**
  PL525.M49, **(v3)**
  PL529.M46, **(v3)**
  PL537.M5, **(v3)**
Miller, Russell. TR690.M55 1998, **(v1)**
Miller, Stephen Paul. E855.M56 1999, **(v4)**
Miller, Stuart Creighton. DS679.M59 1982, **(v5)**
Miller, Susan L. HV7936.C83.M6 1999, **(v6)**
Miller, Susan. PE1404.M554 1989, **(v3)**
  PE1405.U6.M54 1998, **(v3)**
Miller, Timothy. HQ971.M55 1999, **(v6)**
Miller, Toby. GV706.2.M55 2001, **(v6)**
Miller, Tyrus. PR888.M63.M55 1999, **(v3)**
Miller, Vivien M. L. HV9475.F6.M55 2000, **(v6)**
Miller, Walter James. PQ2469.D33.M5 1978, **(v3)**
Miller, Walter M. PS3563.I423.C3 1969, **(v3)**
Miller, Warren E. JK1976.M55 1996, **(v7)**

Miller, Warren. PS3525.I5, **(v3)**
Miller, Wayne. F548.9.N4M55 2000, **(v4)**
Miller, Wilbur R. HJ5021.M55 1991, **(v6)**
Miller, William Christopher. SF609.M5 1972b, **(v1)**
Miller, William Lee. E342.M55 1992, **(v4)**
Miller, William Lockley. JN96.A91.M55 1998, **(v7)**
  JN231.M55 1996, **(v7)**
Miller, William R. BF637.C4M55 2001, **(v2)**
Miller, Zane L. HT177.C53.M55 1998, **(v6)**
Miller-Lachmann, Lyn. Z1037.M654 1992, **(v10)**
  Z5579.6.M56 1995, **(v10)**
Millero, Frank J. GC111.2.M55 1991, **(v6)**
Millett, Allan Reed. VE23.M54, **(v10)**
Millett, John David. LC173.M54 1984, **(v7)**
Millett, Kate. HQ1154.M5, **(v6)**
  HQ1413.M54.M55 1995, **(v6)**
Millett, Martin. DA145.M5 1990, **(v5)**
Millgate, Michael. PR4753.M54 1982, **(v3)**
  PR4754.M54 1971b, **(v3)**
Millgram, Abraham Ezra. PJ5059.E3.M5 1962, **(v3)**
Millican, Edward. JK155.M55 1990, **(v7)**
Millichap, J. Gordon. RA591.M54 1995, **(v2)**
Millier, Brett Candlish. PS3503.I785.Z78 1993, **(v3)**
Milligan, Barry. PR468.O6.M55 1995, **(v3)**
Millikan, Robert Andrews. QC721.M68 1963, **(v1)**
Milliken, Roger. HD9759.B37M54 1983, **(v6)**
Milling, Jane. PN2039.M518 2001, **(v3)**
Millington, Barry. ML410.W1 M58 1999, **(v9)**
Millington, Richard H. PS1892.S58.M55 1991, **(v3)**
Millington, Thomas. F2235.M63 1996, **(v4)**
Millis, Walter. UA23.M565, **(v10)**
  UA23.M57, **(v10)**
Millon, Henry A. NA590.M5, **(v9)**
Mills, A. D. DA645.M55 1991, **(v5)**
Mills, Antonia Curtze. E99.W56.M55 1994, **(v4)**
Mills, Bruce. PS1293.Z5.M55 1994, **(v3)**
Mills, C. Wright. E169.1.M64, **(v4)**
  HD6508.M583 1971, **(v6)**
  HM27.M5 1964, **(v6)**
  HM479.M55.A3 2000, **(v6)**
Mills, Charles W. E185.615.M54 1998, **(v4)**
Mills, D. E. PL790.U4.M5, **(v3)**
Mills, Daniel Quinn. HD9696.C64.I4858 1988, **(v6)**
Mills, Enos Abijah. F782.R59 M5, **(v4)**
Mills, Eric. F187.C5.M55 1996, **(v4)**
Mills, Howard. PR5163.M5, **(v3)**
Mills, John A. BF199.M485 1998, **(v2)**
Mills, Kenneth. F2230.2.K4.M56 1997, **(v4)**
Mills, Margaret Ann. GR302.7.H47.M54 1991, **(v6)**
Mills, Randy Keith. DS921.6.M55 2000, **(v5)**
Mills, Sara. PR788.T72.M5 1991, **(v3)**
Mills, Stephanie. QH541.15.R45.M55 1995, **(v1)**
Mills, Watson E. Z7798.M54 1993, **(v10)**
  Z8455.M55 1999, **(v10)**
Millward, James A. DS793.S62.M535 1998, **(v5)**
Milne, A. A. PR6025.I65.Z5 1939, **(v3)**
Milne, A. J. M. JA79.M55 1998, **(v7)**
Milne, Alan Alexander. PZ7.M64Wi2, **(v3)**
Milne, Christopher. PR6025.I65.Z79 1998, **(v3)**
Milne, Lorus Johnson. QP431.M5, **(v1)**
Milne, William Edmund. QA371.M57 1970, **(v1)**
Milner, Anthony Crothers. DS596.6.M55 1995, **(v5)**
Milner, Helen V. HF1713.M56 1988, **(v6)**
Milner, Henry. HV31.M55 1994, **(v6)**
Milner, John. DC325.M55 2000, **(v5)**
  N6850.M48 1988, **(v9)**
Milner, Marc. D779.C2.M55 1985, **(v5)**
Milner, Murray. HM136.M52 1993, **(v6)**
Milner, Peter M. BF161.M5 1999, **(v2)**
Milner, Richard. GN281.M53 1990, **(v6)**
Milner-Gulland, R. R. DK32.M62 1998, **(v5)**
  DK32.M626 1997, **(v5)**
Milnes, Gerald. ML3551.7.W4.M55 1999, **(v9)**
Milofsky, Carl. LB3013.6.M55 1989, **(v7)**
Milonni, Peter W. QC688.M55 1988, **(v1)**
Milosz, Czeslaw. DK411.M5, **(v5)**
  PG7012.M48 1983, **(v3)**
  PG7158.M553A2 2001, **(v3)**
  PG7158.M553.Z22, **(v3)**
  PN1081.M5 1983, **(v3)**
Milroy, James. PE1101.M55 1992, **(v3)**

Milsom, John. TN269.M53 1996, (v1)
Milson, Menahem. PJ7846.A46.Z7125 1998, (v3)
Milstein, Linda Breiner. RA965.3.M55 1994, (v2)
Milton, A. F. UG743.M56 1989, (v10)
Milton, Anthony. BR756.M55 1995, (v8)
Milton, John. PR3550.F31, (v3)
 PR3551.B76, (v3)
 PR3551.C3 1972, (v3)
 PR3551.S4, (v3)
 PR3552.D3 1958, (v3)
 PR3558.A1 1961, (v3)
 PR3560. 1975, (v3)
 PR3563. 1752, (v3)
 PR3566. 1957, (v3)
Milton, Joyce. TL540.L5.M52 1993, (v1)
Milward, Alan S. HC58.M53 1977, (v6)
 HC240.M645 1977b, (v6)
 HC241.2.M487 2000, (v6)
Milward, Bob. HB97.5.M5525 2000, (v6)
Min, Pyong Gap. F128.9.K6.M56 1996, (v4)
Minahan, James. D21.3.M55 2000, (v5)
 D860.M55 1998, (v5)
 D860.M56 1996, (v5)
Minahan, John A. PR4838.M74.M56 1992, (v3)
Minasian, Stanley M. QL737.C4.M66 1984, (v1)
Minc, Alain. HC241.M5313 1992, (v6)
Minchom, Martin. HN320.Q57.M56 1994, (v6)
Mincoff, Marco. PR2981.5.M56 1993, (v3)
Minda, Gary. KF380.M56 1995, (v7)
Minda, Gary. KF3431.Z9.M56 1999, (v7)
Mindell, David A. VA65.M65, (v10)
Minden, Karen. R602.M56 1994, (v2)
Mindich, David T. Z. PN4888.O25.M56 1998, (v3)
Miner, Earl Roy. PL726.1.M495 1985, (v3)
 PL732.R4.M5, (v3)
 PL733.2.M5, (v3)
 PN56.N16.M56 1996, (v3)
 PR129.J3M5, (v3)
 PR541.M5, (v3)
 PR693.M5 1966, (v3)
 PR3424.M53, (v3)
Miner, H. Craig. F686.M56 1986, (v4)
Miners, Norman. DS796.H757.M56 1987, (v5)
Mines, Mattison. DS432.K17.M56 1984, (v5)
 DS484.4.M57 1994, (v5)
Mingay, G. E. HN398.E5.M57 1990, (v6)
Mingst, Karen A. JX1977.M54 1995, (v7)
Mink, Gwendolyn. HV699.M525 1995, (v6)
 HV700.5.M56 1998, (v6)
Minkler, Meredith. HV5825.M58 1993, (v6)
Minnaert, M. G. J. QC358.5.M5613 1993, (v1)
Minne-Seve, Viviane. N6843.M5613 2000, (v9)
Minnick, Sylvia Sun. F869.S8.M56 1988, (v4)
Minnick, Wendell L. JF1525.I6.M56 1992, (v7)
Minnis, A. J. PR1924.M47 1995, (v3)
Mino, Yutaka. NK4166.T95.M56, (v9)
Minogue, Kenneth R. JA66.M55 1995, (v7)
Minogue, Valerie. PQ2637.A783.Z766 1981, (v3)
Minois, Georges. RC569.M55 1998, (v2)
Minor, Mark. Z7770.M66 1992, (v10)
Minor, Mary Alice D. RT87.T72M56 1999, (v2)
Minor, Vernon Hyde. N380.M556 1994, (v9)
Minot, Stephen. PS3563.I475, (v3)
Minoux, Michel. QA402.5.M5613 1986, (v1)
Minow, Martha. K627.M56 1990, (v7)
Minow, Newton N. KF2840.M56 1995, (v7)
Minowitz, Peter. HB72.M53 1993, (v6)
Minrath, William R. HF5691.M562 1967, (v6)
Minshull, G. N. HC241.2.M49 1978, (v6)
Minter, William. DT1436.M56 1994, (v5)
Minton, Henry L. BF109.T39.M56 1988, (v2)
Minton, Sandra Cerny. GV452.M56 1989, (v6)
 GV1782.5.M56 1997, (v6)
Minton, Sherman A. QL666.O6.M66 1980, (v1)
Mints, Lloyd W. HG2986.M5, (v6)
Mintz, Alan L. PJ5029.M45 1989, (v3)
 PR4662.M5, (v3)
Mintz, Alex. UA23.6.M56 1988, (v10)
Mintz, Jerome R. F128.9.J5.M46 1992, (v4)
Mintz, Joel A. GE180.M56 1995, (v6)
Mintz, Max M. E235.M56 1999, (v4)

 E241.S2.M56 1990, (v4)
Mintz, Ruth Finer. PJ5059.E3.M53, (v3)
Mintz, Steven. HN57.M56 1995, (v6)
Mintzberg, Henry. HD30.28.M56 1994, (v6)
Minuchin, Salvador. RC488.5.M56, (v2)
 RC552.A5.M56, (v2)
Mir, Mustansir. BP133.M57 1987, (v8)
Miracle, Andrew W. GV346.M57 1994, (v6)
Miramontes, Ofelia B. LC3731.M566 1997, (v7)
Miranda, Carlos R. F2689.M54 1990, (v4)
Miranda, M. L. F850.S75.M57 1997, (v4)
Miranda, Roger. F1528.M57 1993, (v4)
Miranti, Paul J. HF5616.U5.M54 1990, (v6)
Mirel, Jeffrey. LC5133.D48.M57 1993, (v7)
Mirelman, Victor A. F3001.9.J5.M58 1990, (v4)
Mir-Hosseini, Ziba. HQ1735.2.M55 1999, (v6)
 K675.M57 1993, (v7)
Miringoff, Marque-Luisa. RB155.M56 1991, (v2)
Mirkovich, Thomas R. Z7164.G35.M57 1997, (v10)
Miro, Gabriel. PQ6623.I7.L5 1938, (v3)
Miroff, Bruce. E841.M54 1979, (v4)
Mirollo, James V. PN605.M3.M57 1984, (v3)
Miron, Jeffrey A. HB3711.M49 1996, (v6)
Mirowski, Philip. HB74.P49.M57 1989, (v6)
Mirrer, Louise. PQ6060.M57 1996, (v3)
Mirsky, Jeannette. E27.M5 1970, (v4)
Miruka, Simon Okumba. PL8014.K4.M57 1994, (v3)
Mirwis, Allan. Z5848.M57 1999, (v10)
Misak, C. J. BD212.5.M57 1995, (v8)
Miscamble, Wilson D. E748.K374.M57 1992, (v4)
Misch, Carl E. RK667.I45C66 1999, (v2)
Mish, Charles Carroll. PR1295.M5, (v3)
Mishan, E. J. HB846.2.M55 1988, (v6)
Mishima, Yukio. BJ971.B8.Y333313, (v8)
 PL755.65.M5, (v3)
 PL833.I7.A24 1989, (v3)
 PL833.I7 A4 1973, (v3)
 PL833.I7 H3, (v3)
 PL833.I7 K32, (v3)
 PL833.I7 K5, (v3)
 PL833.I7.T313, (v3)
 PL833.I7 T4513 1975, (v3)
Mishkin, Tracy. PS153.N5.M57 1998, (v3)
Mishler, Paul C. HX81.M57 1999, (v6)
Mishra, Ganeswar. PK2579.M4914S2713 1996, (v3)
Mishra, Rammurti S. B132.Y6.M5, (v8)
Mishra, Vijay. PR830.T3.M53 1994, (v3)
Misiunas, Romuald J. DK511.B3.M57 1983, (v5)
Miskimin, Harry A. HG976.M49 1984, (v6)
Mistral, Gabriela. PQ8097.G6.A6 1971, (v3)
Mistry, Rohinton. PR9199.3.M494F56 1996, (v3)
 PR9199.3.M494T35 1997, (v3)
Misztal, Barbara A. HM126.M57 1996, (v6)
Mitcham, Carl. T14.M56 1994, (v1)
Mitcham, Samuel W. D756.5.N6.M496 1997, (v5)
 D787.M56 1988, (v5)
Mitchell, Allan. UA702.M5 1984, (v10)
Mitchell, Andrew W. QH104.A1.M58 1990, (v1)
Mitchell, B. R. HA1107.M5 2003, (v6)
 HA4675.M552 2003, (v6)
Mitchell, Basil. BT40.M5, (v8)
Mitchell, Brian Christopher. F74.L9 M64 1988, (v4)
Mitchell, Bruce M. LC1099.M583 1996, (v7)
 LC1099.3.M59 2000, (v7)
Mitchell, D. C. LB1050.M56 1982, (v7)
Mitchell, David J. BX3706.2.M57 1981, (v8)
Mitchell, Deborah R. RG491.M68 2001, (v2)
Mitchell, Domhnall. PS1541.Z5.M58 2000, (v3)
Mitchell, Donald W. BQ266.M48 2002, (v8)
Mitchell, Donald. ML410.M23.M48 1986, (v9)
Mitchell, Eleanor. Z711.95.M58 1995, (v10)
Mitchell, Frank. E99.N3.M64 1978, (v4)
Mitchell, George T. R154.M648.A3 1994, (v2)
Mitchell, Gordon R. UG743.M58 2000, (v10)
Mitchell, Greg. E856.M57 1998, (v4)
 F866.M65 1992, (v4)
Mitchell, Harvey. DC36.98.T63.M57 1996, (v5)
Mitchell, James Leslie. PR6025.I833 S35, (v3)
Mitchell, John C. QA76.7.M57 1996, (v1)
Mitchell, John Donald. F786.M69, (v4)
Mitchell, John G. LB2805.M555 1990, (v7)

Mitchell, John Hanson. F74.L77 M57 1997, (v4)
 QH104.5.N58.M58 1985, (v1)
Mitchell, Judith. PR878.F45.M57 1994, (v3)
Mitchell, Juliet. HQ1154.M53 1972, (v6)
Mitchell, L. G. DA536.M5.M58 1997, (v5)
Mitchell, Margaret. PS3525.I972.G6 1936, (v3)
 PS3525.I972.Z53 1976, (v3)
Mitchell, Mary. F202.G3 M48 1986, (v4)
Mitchell, Marybelle. E99.E7.M663 1996, (v4)
Mitchell, Melanie. QH441.2.M55 1996, (v1)
Mitchell, Neil J. JK467.M57 1997, (v7)
Mitchell, P. M. PT7663.M5, (v3)
Mitchell, Reid. E492.3.M58 1988, (v4)
 GT4211.N4.M57 1995, (v6)
Mitchell, Richard E. KJA2930.M58 1990, (v7)
Mitchell, Richard H. HV6321.J3.M57 1996, (v6)
Mitchell, Richard Scott. QE423.M58 1985, (v1)
Mitchell, Robert Cameron. HB846.5.M58 1989, (v6)
Mitchell, Rose. E99.N3 M66 2001, (v4)
Mitchell, Rosemary. DA1.M58 2000, (v5)
Mitchell, S. Weir. PS2414.H8, (v3)
Mitchell, Sally. PR468.G5.M58 1995, (v3)
Mitchell, Samuel. LB1591.5.U6, (v7)
Mitchell, Susan. HC110.C6 M544 2001, (v6)
 HC110.C6 M545 2003, (v6)
 HN90.P8.M58 1998, (v6)
Mitchell, Theodore R. HD1485.N35.M58 1987, (v6)
Mitchell, Theresa. PN2071.M6.M55 1998, (v3)
Mitchell, Thomas N. DG260.C53.M57, (v5)
 DG260.C53.M58 1991, (v5)
Mitchell, Thomas R. PS1892.F45.M57 1998, (v3)
Mitchell, Timothy. GV1108.5.M58 1991, (v6)
Mitchell, W. J. Thomas. NX170.M58 1994, (v9)
Mitchell, Wesley Clair. HG604.M68 1960, (v6)
Mitchell, William C. HB846.8.M57 1994, (v6)
Mitchell, William J. ML55.M49, (v9)
 NA2750.M58 1990, (v9)
 TK5105.5.M57 1995, (v1)
Mitchell, William P. F3429.1.Q56.M58 1991, (v4)
Mitchell, William. D606.M5, (v5)
Mitchison, Naomi. PR6025.I86 C67, (v3)
 PR6025.I86.T6, (v3)
Mitchison, Rosalind. DA760.M58 2002, (v5)
 DA800.M56 1983, (v5)
Mitford, Nancy. PE1449.M5 1956, (v3)
 PQ2103.D7.M5 1957a, (v3)
 PR6025.I88.T25 1987, (v3)
 PR6025.I88.W3 1962, (v3)
 PR6025.I88.Z48 1993, (v3)
Mithen, Steven J. GN281.4.M57 1996, (v6)
Mitler, Louis. PL213.M46 1988, (v3)
Mitman, Gregg. PN1995.9.A5.M58 1999, (v3)
Mitra, Narendran̄atha. PK1718.M498A27 1998, (v3)
Mitra, Subrata Kumar. HN690.Z9.E464 1992, (v6)
Mitroff, Ian I. HF1131.M58 1993, (v6)
Mitry, Jean. PN1995.M54513 1997, (v3)
 PN1995.M54813 2000, (v3)
Mitsch, William J. QH104.M57 2000, (v1)
Mittelman, James H. HC59.7.M5337 1988, (v6)
 HC59.7.M5338 1997, (v6)
Mittelman, Jerome S. RK61.M75 2001, (v2)
Mitten, Richard. DB99.2.M58 1992, (v5)
Mitter, Sara S. HQ1745.B65.M58 1991, (v6)
Mitton, Jeffry B. QH371.M68 1997, (v1)
Mitzman, Arthur. DC36.98.M5.M54 1990, (v5)
Miura, Akira. PL679.M58 1983, (v3)
Mixon, Wayne. PS3505.A322.Z75 1995, (v3)
Mixter, Keith E. ML113.M59 1996, (v9)
Miyagawa, Makio. HF1413.5.M59 1992, (v6)
Miyake, Akiko. PS3531.O82.C2864 1991, (v3)
Miyamori, Asataro. PL884.M58 1932, (v3)
 PL884.M585, (v3)
Miyanaga, Kuniko. HM136.M59 1991, (v6)
Miyoshi, Masao. PL747.55.M5, (v3)
Mizejewski, Linda. PN2287.Z5.M58 1999, (v3)
 PR6017.S5.Z78 1992, (v3)
Mizener, Arthur. PR6011.O53.Z78, (v3)
Mizruchi, Mark S. JK467.M59 1992, (v7)
Mizruchi, Susan L. PS169.S23.M59 1998, (v3)
Mizuta, Hiroshi. Z988.M59 2000, (v10)
Mladenovic, Milorad. QC773.M54 1998, (v1)

Mo, Ti. B128.M7.E5, (v8)
Moane, Geraldine. HQ1122.M62 1999, (v6)
Moberg, Vilhelm. DL648.M62 1972, (v5)
PT9875.M5 D52, (v3)
PT9875.M5 I62, (v3)
PT9875.M5 L3, (v3)
Mock, John Allan. DS897.S2.M63 1999, (v5)
Mockaitis, Thomas R. U241.M634 1995, (v10)
Moddelmog, Debra. PN3503.M52 1993, (v3)
PS3515.E37.Z7424 1999, (v3)
Modell, John. F869.L89.J35, (v4)
Modell, Judith Schachter. F159.H7.M63 1998, (v4)
GN21.B45.M63 1983, (v6)
Modelski, George. V25.M63 1988, (v10)
Modern Language Association of America.
Z253.M73 1970, (v10)
Modest, M. F. QC320.M63 1993, (v1)
Modiano, Patrick. PQ2673.O3.R8, (v3)
Modigliani, Franco. HB171.M557, (v6)
Modler, Karl W. PQ2605.A3734Z72154 2000, (v3)
Modleski, Tania. PN1995.9.W6.M55 1991, (v3)
PS152.M63 1998, (v3)
Moe, Terry M. LB2828.8.M64 2001, (v7)
Moehring, Eugene P. F849.L35.M64 1989, (v4)
Moeller, D. W. RA565.M64 1997, (v2)
Moeller, Susan D. PN4888.D57.M64 1998, (v3)
Moeller, Therald. QD151.2.M63 1982, (v1)
Moen, Matthew C. BR115.P7.M5444 1992, (v8)
BR1642.U5.M64 1989, (v8)
Moerman, Daniel E. E98.B7.M66 1998, (v4)
Moffat, Donald W. TS184.M63 1991, (v1)
Moffatt, Michael. LD4756.M62 1989, (v7)
Moffett, George D. HB871.M57 1994, (v6)
Moffett, Samuel H. BR1065.M63 1992, (v8)
Moffitt, John F. E59.P89.M63 1996, (v4)
Moffitt, Michael. HG3881.M575 1983, (v6)
Mofid, Kamran. HC480.D4.M64 1990, (v6)
Mofolo, Thomas. PL8689.9.M57C513 1981, (v3)
Moggridge, D. E. HB103.K47.M563 1992, (v6)
Moghadam, Valentine M. HD6181.9.M644 1998, (v6)
HQ1726.5.M64 1993, (v6)
Mogie, Michael. QK826.M64 1992, (v1)
Moglen, Helene. PR858.F45, (v3)
PR858.F45M64 2001, (v3)
Mohanty, Chandra Talpade. HQ1870.9.M64 2003, (v6)
Mohanty, Jitendranath. B131.M54.M64 2000, (v8)
Mohd. Taib Osman. PL5130.M58, (v3)
Mohen, Jean-Pierre. GN790.M7413 1990, (v6)
Mohl, Ruth. PN51.M6, (v3)
PN511.M43 1962, (v3)
Mohlenbrock, Robert H. QK86.U6.M63 1983, (v1)
QK525.5.I4.M6 1999, (v1)
Moholy-Nagy, Laszlo. N7430.M62, (v9)
Moholy-Nagy, Sibyl. N6838.M6.M6 1969, (v9)
NA203.M6 1976, (v9)
NA9090.M58, (v9)
Mohr, Lillian Holmen. HD8073.P38.M63, (v6)
Mohr, Merilyn Simonds. GV1201.M67 1997, (v6)
Mohrman, Susan Albers. LB2806.35.M64 1994, (v7)
Mohs, Mayo. PS648.S3.M55 1971, (v4)
Mohun, Arwen. HD9999.L383.U634 1999, (v6)
Moi, Toril. PQ2603.E362.Z855 1994, (v3)
Moir, Alfred. ND1329.D93.A4 1994, (v9)
Moise, Edwin E. DS557.8.T6.M65 1996, (v5)
Mojares, Resil B. PL5542.M64 1983, (v3)
Mojtabai, A. G. PS3563.O374.S75, (v3)
Mok, Ka-Ho. HC427.92.M635 1999, (v6)
JQ1516.M65 1998, (v7)
Moked, Gabriel. B1349.M35.M65 1988, (v8)
Mokler, Alfred James. F591.M72, (v4)
F767.N2 M7, (v4)
Mokyr, Joel. HC79.T4.M648 1990, (v6)
HC260.5.M64 1983, (v6)
Moldenhauer, Hans. ML410.W33.M55 1979, (v9)
Mole, Gary D. PN771.M63 1997, (v3)
Molenaar, Dee. GV199.42.W22R345 1979, (v6)
Moler, Kenneth L. PR4034.P72.M64 1989, (v3)
Molesworth, Charles. PS3525.O5616.Z697 1990, (v3)
PS3569.N88.Z78 1983, (v3)
Molière. PQ1825.E5.F68, (v3)
PQ1832.E3.E58, (v3)
PQ1825.E5W583 2000b, (v3)
PQ1852.A2 1967, (v3)
Molina, Tirso de. PQ6434.A2 1946, (v3)
PQ6434.B8 1969, (v3)
Moline, Jon. B398.K7.M64, (v8)
Moliterno, James E. KF272.M64 1991, (v7)
Moll, Richard. KF300.Z9 M57 1990, (v7)
Mollat, Michel. VK55.M65 1993, (v10)
Molle, Willem. HC241.2.M58 2001, (v6)
Mollenhoff, Clark R. QA76.2.A75.M65 1988, (v1)
Mollenhoff, David V. NA6880.5.U62.M335 1999, (v9)
Mollenkopf, John H. F128.55.M65 1992, (v4)
G1254.N4E1.M6 1993, (v6)
Mollenkott, Virginia R. BS544.M64 1983, (v8)
Moller, Bjorn. UA646.M73 1995, (v10)
Moller, C. QC6.M52, (v1)
Moller, J. Orstrom. JC362.M55 2000, (v7)
Mollin, Richard A. QA241.M598 1998, (v1)
QA247.M63 1999, (v1)
QA247.M65 1995, (v1)
QA268.M65 2000, (v1)
Molnár, Miklós. DB925.1.M6413 2001, (v5)
Molodowsky, Kadia. PJ5129.M7.A25 1999, (v3)
Molt, Cynthia Marylee. PN1997.G59.M6 1990, (v3)
Molt, Mary. TX820.M57 2001, (v1)
Moltke, Helmuth James. DD247.M6.A413 1990, (v5)
Moltmann, Jurgen. BR115.W6.M45413 1999, (v8)
BT111.2.M613 1981, (v8)
BT821.2.M6313 1967b, (v8)
BX4827.M6, (v8)
Molyneux, Maxine. HQ1460.5.M64 2001, (v6)
Momaday, N. Scott. E99.K5.M64, (v4)
PS3563.O47.A78 1989, (v3)
PS3563.O47.G6 1976, (v3)
PS3563.O47.Z464 1989, (v3)
PS3563.O47.Z52, (v3)
Momeyer, Richard W. BD444.M65 1988, (v8)
Momigliano, Arnaldo. DF78.M6, (v5)
DG284.M62 1962, (v5)
PA3043.M6, (v3)
Mommaers, Paul. BV5095.J3.M63 1995, (v8)
Mommsen, Hans. DD237.M5713 1996, (v5)
Mommsen, Theodor Ernst. D7.M77, (v5)
Mommsen, Wolfgang J. DD220.M5613 1995, (v5)
JC263.W42.M66 1989, (v7)
JC359.M5813, (v7)
Momsen, Janet Henshall. Z1561.S34.M6 1996, (v10)
Monaco, James. PN1993.5.F7.M6, (v3)
PN1994.M59 1981, (v3)
Monaco, Richard. PS3563.O515.P38 1977, (v3)
Monaco, Thomas J. SB611.M58 2001, (v1)
Monagan, John S. KF8745.H6.M66 1988, (v7)
Monaghan, Frank. E302.6.J4.M6, (v4)
Monaghan, Jay. E467.1.C99.M65, (v4)
Monaghan, John. F1221.M7.M66 1995, (v4)
Monahan, John F. QA276.4.M65 2001, (v1)
Monahan, Patrick. KE4270.M66 1991, (v7)
KE4270.Z82.M66 1990, (v7)
Monahon, Cynthia. RJ506.P66M366 1997, (v2)
Monamy, Vaughan. HV4915.M65 2000, (v6)
Monberg, Torben. DU850.M66 1991, (v5)
Mondor, Henri. PQ2344.Z5.M6 1943, (v3)
Monet, Claude. ND553.M7.A4 1978, (v9)
Monet, Jacques. F1027.M66, (v4)
Money, John. QP278.M66 1988, (v1)
RC556.M665 1994, (v2)
Moneyhon, Carl H. E532.M66 1998, (v4)
E553.M66 2002, (v4)
F411.M74 1997, (v4)
Monga, Celestin. JQ1879.A15.M6613 1996, (v7)
Mongaæit, A. L. CC105.R9 M613 1970, (v5)
Mongillo, John F. GE10.M66 2000, (v6)
Monies, Finn. NA1218.M613, (v9)
Monk, Leland. PR888.F35.M66 1993, (v3)
Monk, Samuel Holt. BH301.S7.M6 1960, (v8)
Monkman, Betty C. NK2438.W37, (v9)
Monleon, Jose B. PN56.F34.M59 1990, (v3)
Monmonier, Mark S. GA108.7.M66 1993, (v6)
QC878.M59 1999, (v1)
Monnet, Jean. D413.M56.A3313 1978b, (v5)
Monnett, John H. E99.C53 M65 2001, (v4)
Monod, Paul Kleber. BR115.K55.M66 1999, (v8)
DA813.M86 1989, (v5)
Monoson, Susan Sara. JC75.D36.M65 2000, (v7)
Monrad, Kasper. ND717.5.R65.M66 1993, (v9)
Monro, Isabel Stevenson. ND45.M6, (v9)
ND205.M57, (v9)
Monroe, Elizabeth. DS63.2.G7.M6 1981, (v5)
Monroe, J. P. JK2261.M57 2001, (v7)
Monroe, James. E302.M74 1969, (v4)
E372.A3, (v4)
JC212.M75 1987, (v7)
Monroe, Kristen R. BJ1474.M74 1996, (v8)
Monroe, Walter Scott. LA128.M6 1969, (v7)
Monroe, William Frank. PS228.A6.M66 1998, (v3)
Monroy, Douglas. F867.M69 1990, (v4)
Monsarrat, Nicholas. PR6025.O36 C7, (v3)
Monshipouri, Mahmood. JC599.M53.M66 1998, (v7)
JF60.M66 1995, (v7)
Monsivais, Carlos. F1234.M779 1997, (v4)
Monsma, Stephen V. BV630.2.M595 1997, (v8)
KF4865.M66 1993, (v7)
KF4865.M664 1996, (v7)
Monson, Ingrid T. ML3506.M64 1996, (v9)
Montag, Warren. PR3728.R4.M66 1994, (v3)
Montagnier, Luc. QR201.A37.M6613 2000, (v1)
Montagu, Ashley. BD421.M58, (v8)
BD431.M69, (v8)
BF698.M63, (v2)
CB63.T68M6, (v5)
GN24.M58 1969, (v6)
GN666.M58 1974, (v6)
HQ12.M57, (v6)
LB885.M6, (v7)
Montagu, Jennifer. NB620.M66 1989, (v9)
NB623.A44.M66 1985, (v9)
Montagu, Jeremy. ML465.M65, (v9)
Montagu, John Drogo. D25.A2.M66 2000, (v5)
Montagu, Mary Wortley. PR3604.A6 1977, (v3)
Montague, Charles Edward. PR6025.O4 F5 1970, (v3)
Montague, John. PR8851.M6 1976, (v3)
Montague, William Pepperell. BD161.M7 1928, (v8)
Montaigne, Michel de. PQ1642.E5.F6 1931a, (v3)
PQ1643.A22, (v3)
Montanaro, Tony. PN2071.G4.M66 1995, (v3)
Montaner, Carlos Alberto. F1788.M66 2001, (v4)
Montano, Mary Caroline. NX510.N43, (v9)
Montauk, Richard. KF285.M66 2001, (v7)
Monteath, Peter. PN56.W3.M66 1994, (v3)
Z2700.M66 1994, (v10)
Montefiore, Alan. BJ1011.M69, (v8)
Monteiro, George. PQ9261.P417.Z782 2000, (v3)
PS159.P8.M66 1996, (v3)
PS1449.C85.Z745 2000, (v3)
PS3511.R94.Z793 1988, (v3)
Monteith, Sharon. PS261.M65 2000, (v3)
Montejano, David. F395.M5 M66 1987, (v4)
Montejo, Victor. F1465.2.J3.M65 1991, (v4)
Montenbruck, Oliver. QB51.3.E43, (v1)
Monter, E. William. BR735.M66 1984, (v8)
Montero, Rosa. PQ6663.O554C7613 1991, (v3)
Monterroso, Augusto. PQ7297.M62.A613 1995, (v3)
Montesquieu, Charles de Secondat. JC179.M6813
1977, (v7)
JC179.M74, (v7)
PQ2011.L5.E37, (v3)
Montessori, Maria. LB775.M7 1962, (v7)
LB775.M7613 1964a, (v7)
LB775.M785 1966, (v7)
LB775.M7863, (v7)
Monteverdi, Claudio. ML410.M77.A4 1995, (v9)
Montgomery of Alamein, Bernard Law Montgomery.
U102.M68, (v10)
Montgomery, David. HD8072.M74, (v6)
Montgomery, Diane. LC3997.G7.M65 1996, (v7)
Montgomery, Florence M. TS1767.M66 1984, (v1)
Montgomery, John Dickey. HN981.C6.M66 1988, (v6)
Montgomery, Marion. PR575.A34.M66 1997, (v3)
Montgomery, Maureen E. PS3545.H16.Z747 1998,
(v3)

Montgomery, Robert Bruce. PR6025.O46 B87 1949, **(v3)**
  PR6025.O46 H64, **(v3)**
Montgomery, Robert L. BV2063.M626 1999, **(v8)**
Montgomery, Scott L. Q124.M66 2000, **(v1)**
  QB581.M6475 1999, **(v1)**
Montgomery, Stephen L. QA76.9.D3.M649 1994, **(v1)**
Montgomery, Sy. QL26.M66 1991, **(v1)**
Montgomery, Thomas. PQ6058.M66 1998, **(v3)**
Montherlant, Henry de. PQ2625.O45.A28 1961, **(v3)**
  PQ2625.O45.J4 1973, **(v3)**
  PQ2625.On45.R3 1951, **(v3)**
Montias, John Michael. ND653.V5.M65 1989, **(v9)**
Montrose, Louis Adrian. PR3095.M66 1996, **(v3)**
Montrose, Mark I. TK7868.P7.M65 1999, **(v1)**
Montross, Lynn. E303.M82, **(v4)**
  U27.M6 1960, **(v10)**
Montserrat, Dominic. DT87.4.M64 2000, **(v5)**
Mood, Alexander McFarlane. LB2322.M66, **(v7)**
Mood, Terry Ann. Z5814.D54.M66 1995, **(v10)**
Moodie, Susanna. PR9199.2.M65.Z49 1993, **(v3)**
Moodie, T. Dunbar. HD8039.M732.S655 1994, **(v6)**
Moody, Anne. E185.97.M65.A3, **(v4)**
Moody, Bill. ML3506.M66 1993, **(v9)**
Moody, Christopher J. QD476.M66 1992, **(v1)**
Moody, Ernest A. BC171.M65, **(v8)**
Moody, Fred. QA76.9.H85.M67 1999, **(v1)**
Moody, John. HD2785.M64 1968, **(v6)**
Moody, Joycelyn. BR1690.M59 2001, **(v8)**
Moody, Peter R. DS779.26.M66 1983, **(v5)**
Moody, T. W. DA958.D2.M66 1981, **(v5)**
Moody, William Vaughn. PR85.M615 1956, **(v3)**
  PS2425.A2 1969, **(v3)**
  PS2426.L6, **(v3)**
  PS2428.A4 1969, **(v3)**
Moody-Adams, Michele M. BJ52.M66 1997, **(v8)**
Moog, Clodomir Vianna. PQ9516.M613 1970, **(v3)**
Moogk, Peter N. F1030.M793 2000, **(v4)**
Mooij, Marieke K. de. HF5415.127.M66 1998, **(v6)**
Mook, Delo E. QC173.55.M66 1987, **(v1)**
Mookerjee, R. N. PS3537.I85.Z8 1988, **(v3)**
Moon, Bucklin. PS3525.O51 W5, **(v3)**
Moon, Elaine Latzman. F574.D49.N476 1994, **(v4)**
Moon, J. Donald. HM276.M56 1993, **(v6)**
Moon, Marilyn. HV1461.M66 1996, **(v6)**
Moon, Okpyo. HC463.K346 M66 1989, **(v6)**
Moon, Samuel. F817.M6.G686 1992, **(v4)**
Moon, Spencer. PN1998.2.M66 1997, **(v3)**
Moondance, Wolf. BF1623.M43W65 2001, **(v2)**
Mooney, Christopher F. KF380.M66 1990, **(v7)**
Mooney, Douglas D. QA401.M63 1998, **(v1)**
Mooney, James. E98.R3.M6 1973b, **(v4)**
Mooney, Jayne. HV6626.M665 2000, **(v6)**
Mooneyham, Laura G. PR4038.E3.M66 1988, **(v3)**
Moorcock, Michael. PR6063.O59, **(v3)**
  PR6063.O59.B9 1981, **(v3)**
Moore, A. W. BD411.M59 1990, **(v8)**
Moore, Alex. LC3736.G6.M66 1999, **(v7)**
Moore, Allan F. ML421.B4.M66 1997, **(v9)**
Moore, Arthur Keister. F454.M65, **(v4)**
  PR354.M6, **(v3)**
Moore, Barrington. HN15.M775 1993, **(v6)**
Moore, Brenda L. UB418.A47.M66 1996, **(v10)**
Moore, Brian. PR9199.3.M617 A7, **(v3)**
  PR9199.3.M617.L6, **(v3)**
  PR9199.3.M617.L8, **(v3)**
Moore, Catherine L. PS3563.O59.B48 1977, **(v3)**
Moore, Charles Willard. NA2765.M66, **(v9)**
  SB472.M64 1988, **(v1)**
Moore, Charles. F479.M66 1996, **(v4)**
Moore, Clarence B. E78.A28 M66 1996, **(v4)**
Moore, D. QK601.M648 1998, **(v1)**
Moore, David S. (David Scott). QH438.5.M66 2002, **(v1)**
Moore, Deborah Dash. F128.9.J5.M66, **(v4)**
  F319.M6.M824 1994, **(v4)**
Moore, Donald J. BM755.H37.M66 1989, **(v8)**
Moore, Doris Langley-Levy. PR4381.M67 1961, **(v3)**
Moore, Edward. PR3605.M3.F6 1995, **(v3)**
Moore, Emmett Burris. TD1030.M66 2000, **(v1)**
Moore, F. Michael. PN2071.I47.M66 1994, **(v3)**

Moore, F. Richard. MT723.M6 1990, **(v9)**
Moore, G. E. B1647.M73.C6 1962, **(v8)**
  B1647.M73.P4 1959, **(v8)**
  BJ1011.M7 1966, **(v8)**
Moore, Gareth. BX1795.S48.M66 2000, **(v8)**
Moore, George William. GB601.M58 1997, **(v6)**
Moore, George. PR5042.B4 1969, **(v3)**
  PR5042.B7 1929, **(v3)**
  PR5042.B7 1929, **(v3)**
  PR5042.C6 1971, **(v3)**
  PR5042.E8 1942, **(v3)**
  PR5042.H, **(v3)**
  PR5042.H3 1976, **(v3)**
  PR5042.S8 1928, **(v3)**
Moore, Gerald. ML410.S4.M65, **(v9)**
  ML417.M85.A3 1979, **(v9)**
  MT68.M6 1984, **(v9)**
  PL8010.M6, **(v3)**
  PL8010.M63 1980b, **(v3)**
  PL8013.E5.M6, **(v3)**
Moore, Glover. E373.M77, **(v4)**
Moore, Harriet Lucy. DS518.7.M66, **(v5)**
Moore, Harry R. LA209.2.M66, **(v7)**
Moore, Harry Thornton. PR6007.U76.Z75, **(v3)**
  PR6023.A93.Z687, **(v3)**
Moore, Helen H. QL737.R632.M66 1996, **(v1)**
Moore, Henrietta L. GN479.7.M66 1988, **(v6)**
Moore, Henry. NB497.M6.A35 1967, **(v9)**
Moore, Henry. NB497.M6.F52, **(v9)**
Moore, J. D. L. U264.M66 1987, **(v10)**
Moore, Jacqueline M. E185.93.D6.M66 1999, **(v4)**
Moore, James Gregory. F868.S5.M66 2000, **(v4)**
Moore, Jamie W. UG410.M85 1981, **(v10)**
Moore, Jerrold Northrop. ML410.E41 M65 1984, **(v9)**
Moore, Jerry D. F2230.1.A5.M66 1996, **(v4)**
Moore, Jesse Thomas. E185.61.M784, **(v4)**
Moore, Joan W. F790.M5.M6, **(v4)**
Moore, John Alexander. QH331.M59 1993, **(v1)**
Moore, John H. E99.C53.M82 1987, **(v4)**
  E99.C53.M95 1996, **(v4)**
Moore, John Hammond. F279.C7.M67 1993, **(v4)**
Moore, John Leo. E183.M78 1993, **(v4)**
Moore, John Noell. PS490.M66 1997, **(v3)**
Moore, John Robert. PR3406.M58, **(v3)**
Moore, John. PE1585.M6 1962, **(v3)**
Moore, Judith. PR769.M66 1994, **(v3)**
Moore, Katen. RC263.M574 2001, **(v2)**
Moore, Kathleen Dean. KF9695.M66 1989, **(v7)**
Moore, Kathleen M. KF4755.M66 1995, **(v7)**
Moore, Leonard Joseph. HS2330.K63 M66 1991, **(v6)**
Moore, Lillian. GV1595.M6, **(v6)**
Moore, Margaret B. PS1884.M66 1998, **(v3)**
Moore, Margaret. JC571.M775 1993, **(v7)**
Moore, Marianne. PS3525.O5616.A17 1967, **(v3)**
  PS3525.O5616.A6 1935, **(v3)**
  PS3525.O5616.L5, **(v3)**
  PS3525.O5616.M3, **(v3)**
  PS3525.O5616.N4, **(v3)**
  PS3525.O5616.O2, **(v3)**
  PS3525.O5616.O3 1924, **(v3)**
  PS3525.O5616.P7, **(v3)**
  PS3525.O5616.W5 1941, **(v3)**
Moore, Mark Harrison. JF1525.E8.M66 1995, **(v7)**
Moore, Mary B. PN1514.M58 2000, **(v3)**
Moore, Michael C. R723.M617 1983, **(v2)**
Moore, Michael S. K5018.M665 1997, **(v7)**
Moore, Patrick. QB44.M5425, **(v1)**
  QB63.M63 2000, **(v1)**
  QB63.M66 2001, **(v1)**
  QB64.M623 2000, **(v1)**
  QB500.22.M66 1992, **(v1)**
  QB501.M687 1983, **(v1)**
  QB601.M68 1962a, **(v1)**
  QB621.M6, **(v1)**
  QB801.M64 1989, **(v1)**
Moore, Peter D. GB621.M66, **(v6)**
Moore, R. I. D201.M66 2000, **(v5)**
  HN380.P6.M66 1987, **(v6)**
Moore, R. J. DS341.3.G7.M66 1987, **(v5)**
Moore, R. Laurence. BL2525.M67 1994, **(v8)**
Moore, Rachel O. PN1995.M569 1999, **(v3)**

Moore, Raymond Cecil. QE770.M6, **(v1)**
Moore, Reese T. Z2000.M66 2001, **(v10)**
Moore, Richard B. F2131.M66 1988, **(v4)**
Moore, Robert C. PN4748.Z33.M66 1992, **(v3)**
Moore, Robert Etheridge. ND497.H7.M6 1969, **(v9)**
Moore, Robin. ML3486.C8.M66 1997, **(v9)**
Moore, Roy L. KF2750.M66 1994, **(v7)**
Moore, Sally Falk. GN308.3.A35.M66 1994, **(v6)**
Moore, Samuel. PE1133.M7 1969, **(v3)**
Moore, Sara. D645.M66 1994, **(v5)**
Moore, Shirley Ann Wilson. F869.R5.M66 2000, **(v4)**
Moore, Stephen D. BS2555.5.M66 1989, **(v8)**
Moore, Thomas Geoffrey. HC427.92.M665 2002, **(v6)**
Moore, Thomas. PR5050.F79 1979, **(v3)**
  PR5054.L4 1930, **(v3)**
Moore, Walter John. QC16.S265.M66 1989, **(v1)**
Moore, Wayne D. KF4552.M66 1996, **(v7)**
Moore, Will Grayburn. PQ241.M64, **(v3)**
  PQ526.M6, **(v3)**
  PQ1860.M6 1968, **(v3)**
Moore-Gilbert, B. J. JV51.M65 1997, **(v7)**
Moorehead, Alan. G246.C7.M6 1966a, **(v6)**
  QL336.M6 1960, **(v1)**
Moorehead, Caroline. HV580.S9.M66 1999, **(v6)**
Moorhouse, H. F. GV1029.3.M59 1991, **(v6)**
Moorman, Charles. PN685.M6, **(v3)**
Moorman, Donald R. F826.M66 1992, **(v4)**
Moorman, Frederic William. PR3513.M6 1962, **(v3)**
Moorman, Lewis Jefferson. R154.M734.A3, **(v2)**
Moorman, Mary Trevelyan. PR5881.M6, **(v3)**
Moortgat, Anton. N5370.M6613, **(v9)**
Moos, Stanislaus von. NA1053.J4.M613, **(v9)**
Moosa, Matti. PJ7846.A46.Z713 1994, **(v3)**
Moote, A. Lloyd. DC123.8.M66 1989, **(v5)**
Mora, Carl J. PN1993.5.M4.M6 1982, **(v3)**
Moraes, Dom F. PR6063.O67Z75 1992, **(v3)**
Moraes, F. R. DS777.55.M6, **(v5)**
  DS786.M6, **(v5)**
Morag, Shelomo. PJ3027.M66, **(v3)**
Morain, Thomas J. HN80.J44.M67 1988, **(v6)**
Morales, Edmundo. F2230.1.D65.M67 1995, **(v4)**
Morales, Mario Roberto. PQ7499.2.M65.S4613 1999, **(v3)**
Morales, Waltraud Q. F3321.M75 1992, **(v4)**
Moramarco, Fred S. PS325.M67 1998, **(v3)**
Moran, Daniel. PN5213.C67.M6 1990, **(v3)**
Moran, Dermot. B829.5.M647 2000, **(v8)**
Moran, Emilio F. GF51.M58 1982, **(v6)**
  GF532.A4.M6713 1993, **(v6)**
Moran, Gabriel. BJ1451.M649 1996, **(v8)**
Moran, Jeffrey P. HQ57.5.A3.M66 2000, **(v6)**
Moran, Karen. LB1575.5.U5.M67 1999, **(v7)**
Moran, Mary H. DT630.5.G6.M67 1990, **(v5)**
Moran, Mary Hurley. PR6054.R25.Z76 1983, **(v3)**
  PR6062.I89.Z77 1993, **(v3)**
Moran, P. A. P. QA273.M75, **(v1)**
Moran, Sean Farrell. DA965.P4.M67 1994, **(v5)**
Moran, Thomas. N6537.M6443.A4 1996, **(v9)**
Morange, Michel. QH447.M6713 2001, **(v1)**
  QH506.M7213 1998, **(v1)**
Morantz-Sanchez, Regina Markell. R692.M64 2000, **(v2)**
Morash, Chris. DA950.7.M67 1995, **(v5)**
Moravcsik, Andrew. JN15.M567 1998, **(v7)**
Moravcsik, J. M. E. B395.M79 1992, **(v8)**
Moravec, Hans P. TJ211.M655 1999, **(v1)**
Moravia, Alberto. PQ4829.O62 A82, **(v3)**
  PQ4829.O62 C653, **(v3)**
Morawska, Ewa T. F159.J7.M83 1985, **(v4)**
  F159.J7.M835 1996, **(v4)**
Morawski, Stefan. BH39.M618, **(v8)**
Moraze, Charles. DC369.M593, **(v5)**
  HC53.M613 1967, **(v6)**
Morby, John E. CS27.M67 1989, **(v5)**
Mordden, Ethan. ML410.R6315.M7 1992, **(v9)**
  ML1705.M67, **(v9)**
More, Ellen Singer. R692.M645 1999, **(v2)**
More, Paul Elmer. PR99.M75, **(v3)**
  PS2431.P3 1972, **(v3)**
More, Thomas. HX810.5.E54 2001, **(v6)**
  PR2322.A4 1961, **(v3)**

Moreas, Jean. PQ2367.M3 1923, (v3)
Morehead, Joe. Z1223.M674 1996, (v10)
  Z1223.Z7.M67 1983, (v10)
Morehouse, Barbara J. GF504.A6.M67 1996, (v6)
Morehouse, Maggi M. D810.N4.M67 2000, (v5)
Morehouse, Sarah McCally. JK2447.M67 1998, (v7)
Morel, Francois. GB855.M67 1993, (v6)
Morello, Karen Berger. KF299.W6 M67 1988, (v7)
Moreman, T. R. DS392.N67.M67 1998, (v5)
Moreno, Dario. F1436.8.U6.M66 1990, (v4)
  F1439.5.M67 1994, (v4)
Moreno, Jonathan D. R724.M677 1995, (v2)
  R853.H8.M66 1999, (v2)
Moreno, Paul D. KF3464.M665 1997, (v7)
Moreo, Dominic W. LA209.M66 1996, (v7)
Moreto, Agustín. PQ6416.D4 1999, (v3)
Moretti, Franco. G1797.21.E65.M6 1999, (v6)
Morey, Ann-Janine. PS166.M67 1992, (v3)
Morey, Carl. ML120.C2.M67 1997, (v9)
Morey, Charles Rufus. N5970.M6, (v9)
Morey, James H. PR275.B5.M67 2000, (v3)
Morford, Mark P. O. BL723.M67 2003, (v8)
Morgan, Al. PS3563.O78.M5, (v3)
Morgan, Ann Haven. QL47.M6, (v1)
Morgan, Austen. DA591.W5.M67 1992, (v5)
  DA965.C7.M67 1988, (v5)
Morgan, Bill. Z8342.5.M66 1996, (v10)
  Z8342.5.M67 1995, (v10)
Morgan, Catherine. DF261.D35.M57 1990, (v5)
Morgan, Charles Hill. N6923.B9.M59, (v9)
Morgan, Charles. PR6025.O645 B7, (v3)
  PR6025.O645 E5, (v3)
  PR6025.O645 F6, (v3)
  PR6025.O645.R4 1945, (v3)
  PR6025.O645 S7, (v3)
  PR6025.O645 V6, (v3)
Morgan, Charlotte Elizabeth. PR841.M6 1963, (v3)
Morgan, Clifford Thomas. QP355.M6 1965, (v1)
Morgan, Conway Lloyd. NA1053.N68.M67 1998, (v9)
Morgan, David R. JK7116.M67 1991, (v7)
Morgan, David T. E302.6.F8.M85 1996, (v4)
Morgan, Douglas. BX6154.M624 2001, (v8)
Morgan, Edmund Sears. E208.M85, (v4)
  E215.2.M58 1963, (v4)
  E302.6.F8 M86 2002, (v4)
  E322.M85, (v4)
  E445.V8.M67 1975, (v4)
  F7.M8 1966, (v4)
  F67.W798, (v4)
  F82.W789, (v4)
  JF1059.G7.M67 1988, (v7)
Morgan, Elizabeth. RD27.35.M65.A33, (v2)
Morgan, Frank. QA95.M58 2000, (v1)
  QA611.M674 1992, (v1)
Morgan, Gareth. HD31.M628 1997, (v6)
Morgan, George Allen. B3317.M65, (v8)
Morgan, Gwendolyn A. PR317.N28.M67 1993, (v3)
Morgan, H. Wayne. E168.M84, (v4)
  E711.6.M7, (v4)
  ND237.C8.M67 1994, (v9)
Morgan, Harry. LB1060.M674 1997, (v7)
  LC2741.M67 1995, (v7)
Morgan, Iwan W. E839.5.M64 1994, (v4)
Morgan, Janet P. DA585.M6.M67 1991, (v5)
Morgan, Joseph G. E183.8.V5.M58 1997, (v4)
Morgan, Judith. PS3513.E2.Z785 1995, (v3)
Morgan, Kenneth O. DA588.M637 1984, (v5)
  DA592.M67 1990, (v5)
  DA714.H58 1981 vol. 6, (v5)
  DA722.M617 1995, (v5)
Morgan, Lael. F908.M67 1998, (v4)
Morgan, Lewis Henry. E78.W5 M6 1993, (v4)
  E98.D9.M65 1965, (v4)
  JC21.M84 1964, (v7)
Morgan, Marjorie. DA533.M75 2001, (v5)
Morgan, Michael L. BM565.M63 2001, (v8)
Morgan, Murray Cromwell. F899.S457 M67 1982, (v4)
Morgan, Nicholas H. PR4592.R36.M67 1992, (v3)
Morgan, Nigel J. ND3128.M67, (v9)
Morgan, Philip D. F232.C43.M67 1998, (v4)
Morgan, Philip. DA670.L19.C5 3rd ser. vol. 34, (v5)

DG571.M6422 1995, (v5)
Morgan, Prys. PR3765.W535.Z68, (v3)
Morgan, R. P. C. S623.M68, (v1)
Morgan, Robert C. N6512.5.C64.M67 1994, (v9)
Morgan, Robert J. BV4811.M578 1998, (v8)
  E396.M6 1974, (v4)
  KF4541.M675 1988, (v7)
Morgan, Robert P. ML197.M675 1990, (v9)
Morgan, Ronald B. HF5549.5.S38.M67 1996, (v6)
Morgan, Ronald R. LB1060.M677 1998, (v7)
Morgan, Rosemarie. PR4757.W6.M67 1988, (v3)
Morgan, Susan. PR868.H4.M67 1989, (v3)
Morgan, Ted. E45.M67 1993, (v4)
  F591.M865 1995, (v4)
Morgan, W. B. HD1417.M68 1978, (v6)
Morgan, William John. GV706.M6 1994, (v6)
Morgan, William N. E78.S7.M756 1994, (v4)
Morganstern, Anne McGee. NB1820.M72 2000, (v9)
Morgenthau, Hans Joachim. E744.M68, (v4)
  JX1391.M6 1985, (v7)
Mori, Jennifer. DA522.P6.M65 1997, (v5)
Mori, Masaki. PN56.E65.M675 1997, (v3)
Mori, Ogai. PL811.O7.G313 1995, (v3)
  PL811.O7 G33, (v3)
Móricz, Zsigmond. PH3291.M5L413 1995, (v3)
Morike, Eduard Friedrich. PT2434.A1 1967, (v3)
  PT2434.A23, (v3)
Morillo, Stephen. DA60.M67 1994, (v5)
Morin, Ann Miller. E747.M73 1995, (v4)
Morin, Relman. DS518.8.M7, (v5)
Morisawa, Marie. GB1203.2.M67 1985, (v6)
Morison, Elting Elmore. T21.M7 1975, (v1)
Morison, James. F865.M8 1977, (v4)
Morison, Samuel Eliot. D743.M74, (v5)
  D773.M6, (v5)
  D773.M62, (v5)
  E101.M85, (v4)
  E111.M86 1942a, (v4)
  E111.M863, (v4)
  E112.M84, (v4)
  E178.M855, (v4)
  E178.6.M83, (v4)
  E203.M86 1965, (v4)
  E340.O8.M8 1969, (v4)
  F7.M82 1956, (v4)
  F27.M9 M6, (v4)
  F67.M6, (v4)
  F73.5.M6, (v4)
  JC599.U5.M68, (v7)
  LD2151.M65, (v7)
Moriyasu, K. QC793.3.F5.M67 1983, (v1)
Morley, Christopher. PS3525.O71.G4, (v3)
  PS3525.O71 H3, (v3)
  PS3525.O71 K5, (v3)
  PS3525.O71 M28, (v3)
  PS3525.O71 P3 1955, (v3)
  PS3525.O71.P5 1920, (v3)
  PS3525.O71.S7 1917, (v3)
  PS3525.O71 W4 1922, (v3)
Morley, David. HM1206.M67 2000, (v6)
Morley, James William. D558.M6 1957, (v5)
Morley, Neville. HC39.M67 1996, (v6)
Morley, Patricia A. PR9199.3.L33.Z79 1981, (v3)
Morley, Patrick. PN1991.3.G7.M67 2001, (v3)
Morley, Sylvanus Griswold. F1435.M75 1983, (v4)
Morley, Thomas. MT6.M86 1953, (v9)
Morlino, Leonardo. JN94.A91.M67 1998, (v7)
Mormino, Gary Ross. F474.S29 I86 2002, (v4)
Mornet, Daniel. PQ261.M6, (v3)
Moro, Ruben O. F3031.5.M6713 1989, (v4)
Morone, Joseph G. TK1343.M67 1989, (v1)
Moroni Bracamonte, Jose Angel. F1488.3.M67 1995, (v4)
Morony, Michael G. DS76.M67 1984, (v5)
Morowitz, Harold J. QH505.M62 1991, (v1)
  QM601.M768 1992, (v1)
Morphet, Richard. N6494.A66, (v9)
Morphy, Howard. DU125.M8.M65 1991, (v4)
Morray, J. P. DC423.M672 1997, (v5)
Morreall, John. BL85.M72 1999, (v8)
Morrell, William Parker. TN420.M7, (v1)

Morrice, David. JA71.M67 1996, (v7)
Morrill, Richard L. GF95.M67 1988, (v6)
Morris, Aldon D. E185.61.M845 1984, (v4)
Morris, Ann Axtell. F786.M86, (v4)
Morris, Anne E. KD811.M67 1995, (v7)
Morris, Benny. DS119.7.M656 1993, (v5)
  HV640.5.A6.M67 1987, (v6)
Morris, Bonnie J. BM729.W6.M67 1998, (v8)
Morris, Brian. GN345.M67 1991, (v6)
Morris, C. B. PQ6073.S9.M6, (v3)
  PQ6085.M64, (v3)
  PQ6613.A763.Z7772 1997, (v3)
Morris, Celia. F391.4.R53.M67 1992, (v4)
  HQ1237.5.U6.M67 1994, (v6)
Morris, Charles G. BF121.M598 1998, (v2)
Morris, Charles R. UF533.M67 1988, (v10)
Morris, Charles William. B840.M6 1955, (v8)
Morris, Christopher W. JC11.M67 1998, (v7)
Morris, Christopher. F347.W29.M67 1995, (v4)
Morris, Clay Louise. F179.M67, (v4)
Morris, Colin. BR270.M64 1989, (v8)
Morris, Daniel. PS3545.I544.Z656 1995, (v3)
Morris, David B. PR3634.M67 1984, (v3)
  RA418.M68 1998, (v2)
  RB127.M67 1991, (v2)
  RB127.M67 1991, (v2)
Morris, David. HD30.28.M6479 1996, (v6)
Morris, Desmond. BF701.M6 1969, (v2)
Morris, Edmund. E757.M883 2001, (v4)
Morris, Edwin T. SB457.55.M66 1983, (v1)
Morris, G. S. Don. GV443.M66 1999, (v6)
Morris, Gareth. MT340.M73 1991, (v9)
Morris, Herbert. BJ1451.M65, (v8)
Morris, Ian. DE61.B87.M67 1992, (v5)
  DF78 .M635 1999, (v5)
  DF101.M67 1987, (v5)
Morris, Irvine Ernest. TG260.M812, (v1)
Morris, Ivan I. DS834.M64, (v5)
  PL782.E8 M6, (v3)
Morris, James. GV199.44.E85.M66 2000, (v6)
Morris, Jan. D849.M72, (v5)
Morris, John Miller. F391.M637 M67 2001, (v4)
  F392.L62.M67 1997, (v4)
Morris, John Wesley. G73.M62, (v6)
Morris, Kenneth Earl. E873.M67 1996, (v4)
Morris, Leslie R. Z713.5.U6 M67 2002, (v10)
Morris, Libby V. Z5814.M86.M67 1996, (v10)
Morris, Linda. PS3174.W45.Z78 1992, (v3)
Morris, Margaret. E263.N5.M8 1969, (v4)
Morris, Marilyn. DA520.M67 1998, (v5)
Morris, Michael A. VA40.M69 1987, (v10)
Morris, Michael H. HB615.M674 1998, (v6)
Morris, Michael P. E78.S65.M67 1999, (v4)
Morris, Michael. BD111.M67 1992, (v8)
Morris, Morris David. HC59.7.M592 1979, (v6)
Morris, Nancy Jane. Z4701.M67 1992, (v10)
Morris, Nancy. F1975.M67 1995, (v4)
Morris, Norval. HV9304.M67 1990, (v6)
  K5077.M67 1998, (v7)
Morris, Pam. PR4592.S58.M67 1990, (v3)
Morris, Peter. QA269.M66 1994, (v1)
Morris, Randall C. BD372.M67 1990, (v8)
Morris, Richard Brandon. E173.M92 1980, (v4)
  E173.M93 1973, (v4)
  E249.M68 1965, (v4)
Morris, Richard. QH366.2.M683 2001, (v1)
Morris, Robert K. PR888.T5.M6, (v3)
Morris, Robert. E302.M82 1973, (v4)
Morris, Rosalind C. E78.N78.M665 1994, (v4)
Morris, Roy. PS3232.M67 2000, (v3)
Morris, S. Brent. QA165.M594 1998, (v1)
Morris, Thomas D. KF482.M67 1996, (v7)
Morris, Timothy. PS374.B37.M35 1997, (v3)
Morris, Van Cleve. LB885.M67 P45 1994, (v7)
Morris, Virginia B. PR878.W6.M67 1990, (v3)
Morris, Walter F. F1435.M765 1987, (v4)
Morris, William N. BF521.M67 1989, (v2)
Morris, William. PE1580.M6 1977, (v3)
  PR5072.B7, (v3)
  PR5083.A4 1984, (v3)
Morris, Willie. CT275.M59444.A3, (v5)

Morris, Wright. PS3525.O7475 C3, (v3)
  PS3525.O7475 F54, (v3)
  PS3525.O7475 H4, (v3)
  PS3525.O7475 H6, (v3)
  PS3525.O7475 H8, (v3)
  PS3525.O7475 L5, (v3)
  PS3525.O7475 L6, (v3)
  PS3525.O7475 M3 1974, (v3)
  PS3525.O7475 M35, (v3)
  PS3525.O7475 M9, (v3)
  PS3525.O7475 R4, (v3)
  PS3525.O7475Z476 1982, (v3)
Morris-Hale, Walter. JC330.2.M67 1996, (v7)
Morrison, Ann M. HD38.2.M67 1992, (v6)
Morrison, Chaplain W. E416.M6, (v4)
Morrison, Craig. ML3535.M67 1996, (v9)
Morrison, Dane Anthony. E99.A35.M64 1995, (v4)
Morrison, Donald R. Z8989.73.M67 1988, (v10)
Morrison, George H. QD117.M6, (v1)
Morrison, Hugh. NA707.M63, (v9)
  NA737.S9.M6, (v9)
Morrison, Jack G. D805.G3.M6143 2000, (v5)
Morrison, James. PN1993.5.U6.M656 1998, (v3)
Morrison, John W. PL747.55.M67 1975, (v3)
Morrison, Karl Frederick. BH131.M67 1990, (v8)
Morrison, Michael A. E415.7.M88 1997, (v4)
Morrison, Paul. PS3531.O82.Z7542 1996, (v3)
Morrison, Philip. QB981.M865 1982, (v1)
Morrison, Ralph. TK7836.M65 1995, (v1)
Morrison, Reg. QH457.M67 1999, (v1)
Morrison, Robert D. KF3775.A68.M67 2000, (v7)
Morrison, Robert Thornton. QD251.2.M67 1992, (v1)
Morrison, Susan Signe. BX2320.5.G7, (v3)
Morrison, Terri. HF1416.M78 1997, (v6)
Morrison, Theodore. LC6301.C5.M67, (v7)
Morrison, Theodore. PS3563.O8748.S8, (v3)
Morrison, Toni. PS173.N4.M67 1992, (v3)
  PS3563.O8749.B4 1987, (v3)
  PS3563.O8749.B54, (v3)
  PS3563.O8749.S6 1987, (v3)
  PS3563.O8749 S9, (v3)
Morrison, William R. HD8109.N672.M67 1994, (v6)
Morrison, William. PN2277.N5.M58 1999, (v3)
Morriss, Peter. BD438.M63 1987, (v8)
Morriss, Roger. DA88.1.C58.M67 1997, (v5)
Morrissette, Bruce. PQ2635.O117.Z7613, (v3)
Morrissey, Katherine G. F852.M67 1997, (v4)
Morrisson, Mark S. PR478.M6.M67 2001, (v3)
Morris-Suzuki, Tessa. HB126.J2.M67 1989, (v6)
  T27.A3.M67 1994, (v1)
Morrow, John Howard. D600.M565 1993, (v5)
  D604.M64 1982, (v5)
Morrow, John. PR4487.P6.M67 1990, (v3)
Morrow, Raymond Allen. HM24.M622 1994, (v6)
Morse, David. PR408.S64.M67 1989, (v3)
  PR448.V57.M67 1999, (v3)
  PR461.M64 1993, (v3)
Morse, Douglass H. QL696.P2618.M67 1989, (v1)
Morse, Hosea Ballou. DS511.M88 1967, (v5)
  DS740.4.M6, (v5)
Morse, Josiah Mitchell. PR6019.O9Z73, (v3)
Morse, Philip McCord. QC16.M66.A34, (v1)
  QC20.M6, (v1)
  QC225.M67 1968, (v1)
Morse, William Charles. LB1051.M72 1962, (v7)
Morsink, Johannes. K3238.31948.M67 1999, (v7)
Morson, Gary Saul. PN212.M67 1994, (v3)
Mort, Frank. HF5415.33.G7.M67 1996, (v6)
Mort, J. TR1045.M67 1989, (v1)
Mortensen, C. David. P90.M66 1997, (v3)
Mortensen, Preben. BH39.M6227 1997, (v8)
Mortimer, Anthony Robert. PR2845.M67 2000, (v3)
Mortimer, Ernest. B1903.M63 1978, (v8)
Mortimer, Gail L. PS3545.E6.Z78 1994, (v3)
Mortimer, Halina. BC99.P65.M6713 1988, (v8)
Mortimer, Penelope. PR6063.O815.H3 1985, (v3)
Mortimer, Robert G. QD455.3.M3M67 1999, (v1)
Mortimore, Peter. LB2822.75.M67 1998, (v7)
Morton, David. TK7881.4.M66 2000, (v1)
Morton, F. L. KE4381.5.M67 2000, (v7)
Morton, Helen. GN671.T5.M67 1996, (v6)

Morton, Ian. RS51.M67 1999, (v2)
Morton, J. Sterling. F666.M89, (v4)
Morton, Jacqueline. PE1099.M67, (v3)
Morton, John Edward. QL403.M67 1967, (v1)
Morton, Leslie T. R133.M717 1997, (v2)
  Z6660.5.M67 1994, (v10)
Morton, Mark Steven. TX349.M67 1996, (v1)
Morton, Maurice. TS1890.M68, (v1)
Morton, Peter. UG1315.A8.M67 1989, (v10)
Morton, Richard Allen. F546.D92.M67 1997, (v4)
Morton, Timothy. PR408.S665, (v3)
  PR5442.B58.M67 1994, (v3)
Morton, W. L. F1029.M6 1972b, (v4)
  F1032.M88, (v4)
  F1063.M88 1967, (v4)
Morus, Iwan Rhys. QC527.5.M67 1998, (v1)
Moruzzi, Norma Claire. JC251.A74 M66 2000, (v7)
Morville, Peter. TK5105.875.I57.M668 1996, (v1)
  ZA4201.M67 1999, (v10)
Mosby, Dewey F. N6537.T35.A4 1991, (v9)
Mosca, Gaetano. JC265.M62, (v7)
Moschella, David C. HD9696.C63.U52628 1997, (v6)
Moschis, George P. HF5415.13.M677 1994, (v6)
Moscow, Warren. JK2319.N56.M66, (v7)
Moseley, F. QE36.M67 1979, (v1)
Moseley, James G. F67.W79.M67 1992, (v4)
Moseley, Michael Edward. F3429.M848 1992, (v4)
Moser, Antonio. BJ1249.M713 1990, (v8)
Moser, Caroline O. N. HN150.Z9.V545 2001, (v6)
  HV4028.M68 1996, (v6)
Moser, Charles A. PG1001.M67, (v3)
Moser, Harold D. Z8896.M67 2001, (v10)
Moser, Joann. NE2245.U54.M67 1997, (v9)
Moser, John E. E183.8.G7.M74 1999, (v4)
Moser, Paul K. BD161.M848 1989, (v8)
  BD161.M8485 1998, (v8)
  BD220.M67 1993, (v8)
Moser, Richard R. DS559.62.U6.M67 1996, (v5)
Moser, Robert G. JN6699.A5 M67 2001, (v7)
Moser, Stephanie. GN746.M67 1998, (v6)
Moser, Thomas C. PR6005.O4.Z784 1966, (v3)
  PR6011.O53.Z795, (v3)
Moses ben Maimon. BM545.A45T9 1972, (v8)
Moses, Cathy. PS374.P6.M67 2000, (v3)
Moses, Claire Goldberg. HQ1615.M67 1984, (v6)
Moses, Gavriel. PN3503.M627 1995, (v3)
Moses, Greg. E185.97.K5.M65 1997, (v4)
Moses, L. G. GV1833.M67 1996, (v6)
Moses, Michael Valdez. PR830.C84.M67 1995, (v3)
Moses, Norton H. Z5703.5.U5.M67 1994, (v10)
Moses, Russell Leigh. E183.8.I55.M67 1996, (v4)
Moses, Wilson Jeremiah. E185.625.M66 1998, (v4)
  E185.625.M67, (v4)
Moses. ND237.M78.A22, (v9)
Mosher, Frederick C. JK691.M65, (v7)
Mosher, Steven W. DS740.4.M67 2000, (v5)
Moskal, Jeanne. PR4148.E8.M67 1994, (v3)
Moskin, J. Robert. D743.M75 1996, (v5)
Moskoff, William. HC336.26.M69 1993, (v6)
  HD5796.M67 1984, (v6)
  HD9015.S652.M67 1990, (v6)
Moskos, Charles C. UB418.A47.M67 1996, (v10)
Moskow, Michael H. HD8008.M6, (v6)
Moskowitz, Eva S. HN64.M872 2001, (v6)
Mosler, David. DU122.A5.M68 1998, (v5)
Mosler, David. JZ1480.M67 2000, (v7)
Mosley, Albert G. KF3464.M67 1996, (v7)
Mosley, Leonard. DD247.M67 1982, (v5)
Mosley, Nicholas. DA574.M6.M67 1991, (v5)
Mosley, Oswald. DA574.M6.A35 1972, (v5)
Mosley, Paul. HG3881.5.W57.M68 1991, (v6)
Mosley, Philip. PN1993.5.B4.M67 2001, (v3)
Moss, D. J. DA536.A88.M67 1990, (v5)
Moss, David. HN490.V5.M67 1989, (v6)
Moss, Joyce. PQ7081.M625 1999, (v3)
Moss, Kay. GR108.M67 1998, (v6)
Moss, Leonard. PN1892.M67 2000, (v3)
Moss, Ralph W. QP511.8.S94.M67 1988, (v1)
Moss, Richard J. GV979.S63, (v6)
  PE64.W5.M68 1984, (v3)
Moss, Sanford A. QH84.2.M67 1988, (v1)

Moss, Scott J. HB172.5.M683 1984, (v6)
Moss, Sidney Phil. PR4592.A54.M67 1984, (v3)
Moss, Walter. DK40.M67 1997, (v5)
Mossberger, Karen. HD257.5.M67 2000, (v6)
Mosse, Fernand. PE535.M62, (v3)
Mosse, George L. HQ18.E8.M67 1985, (v6)
  JC481.M63 1999, (v7)
  U22.3.M63 1990, (v10)
Mosse, Werner Eugen. DK189.M68 1992, (v5)
  DK220.M6 1992, (v5)
  DS135.G33.M63 1987, (v5)
  DS135.G5.A155 1989, (v5)
Mossiker, Frances. PQ1925.M64 1985, (v3)
Mossner, Ernest Campbell. B1497.M65 1980, (v8)
Mossop, D. J. PQ2191.F63.M6, (v3)
Mosteghanemi, Ahlem. PJ7846.O88D4813 2000, (v3)
Mostow, Joshua S. PL728.5.O4.M64 1995, (v3)
Motavalli, Jim. TL221.15.M68 2000, (v1)
Mote, Frederick W., 1922-. DS750.64.M67 1999, (v5)
Mote, Victor L. DK761.M68 1998, (v5)
Moten, A. Rashid. JC49.M67 1996, (v7)
Moten, Matthew. UB413.M68 2000, (v10)
Motes, Martin R. SB409.8.V36.M67 1997, (v1)
Motherwell, Robert. ND237.M852.A35 1992, (v9)
Motion, Andrew. PR4836.M67 1998, (v3)
Motion, Andrew. PR6063.O842.W35 2000, (v3)
Motley, Constance Baker. KF373.M64.A34 1998, (v7)
Motley, Willard. PS3525.O88 K5, (v3)
Mott, N. F. QC174.2.M6 1952, (v1)
  QC721.M88 1965, (v1)
Mott, Robert L. PN1991.8.S69.M68 1993, (v3)
  TA357.M67 2000, (v1)
Mott, Wesley T. BV4208.U6.M68 1989, (v8)
Mott, William H. UA770.M754 2001, (v10)
Motte, Warren F. PN81.M675 1995, (v3)
Motz, Lloyd. QA21.M846 1993, (v1)
  QB43.M55, (v1)
  QB43.2.M674 1989, (v1)
  QC21.2.M65 1989, (v1)
Mouat, Jeremy. F1089.5.R67.M68 1995, (v4)
Moubayed, Sami M. DS98.2.M68 2000, (v5)
Moulakis, Athanasios. LC1011.M76 1993, (v7)
Moule, A. C. DS733.M6 1957a, (v5)
Moulin, Annie. HD1536.F8.M6813 1991, (v6)
Moulson, A. J. TK7871.15.C4.M68 1990, (v1)
Moulsworth, Martha. PR2323.M67.M9 1993, (v3)
Moulton, Candy Vyvey. F761.M68 1995, (v4)
Moulton, Charles Wells. PR83.M73 1966, (v3)
Moulton, Ian Frederick. PR428.S48.M68 2000, (v3)
Mounfield, Peter R. TK1078.M68 1990, (v1)
Mount, David W. QH441.2.M68 2001, (v1)
Mount, Eric. BJ1725.M68 1990, (v8)
Mount, Jeffrey F. GB1225.C3.M68 1995, (v6)
Mountain Wolf Woman. E90.M6.A3, (v4)
Mountbatten of Burma, Louis Mountbatten.
  D767.M67.A3 1988, (v5)
Mourad, Samiha. TK7867.M697 2000, (v1)
Moure, Nancy Dustin Wall. N6530.C2 M68 1998, (v9)
Mourgues, Odette de. PQ1815.M68, (v3)
Mouritzen, Hans. JZ1251.M68 1998, (v7)
Mourning Dove. E99.S21.M68 1990, (v4)
  PS3525.O872.C6 1981, (v3)
Mouroulis, Pantazis. QC381.M68 1997, (v1)
Mousavi, Sayed Askar. DS354.6.H3.M68 1997, (v5)
Mousley, Andy. PR651.M83 2000, (v3)
Mousnier, Roland. D247.M6813 1970, (v5)
Moussalli, Ahmad S. BP80.Q86.M68 1992, (v8)
Moussis, Nicolas. HC240.M754 1995, (v6)
Moustakas, Clark E. BD260.M68 1990, (v8)
  RC489.E93.M68 1994, (v2)
Mouzelis, Nicos P. HM24.M685 1995, (v6)
Mowat, Farley. D811.M684 1992, (v5)
  QL84.24.M69 1984, (v1)
Mower, A. Glenn. K3240.4.M678 1991, (v7)
Mowery, David C. HC110.T4.M68 1989, (v6)
Mowl, Tim. NA966.M68 1995, (v9)
Mowrey, Peter C. PN1993.9.M68 1994, (v3)
Mowry, George Edwin. E756.M85, (v4)
  E757.M9, (v4)
Moxey, Keith P. F. NE958.3.G3.M68 1989, (v9)

QL638.9.M67 1984, (v1)

Moy, James S. PS159.C5.M69 1993, **(v3)**
Moy, Patricia. P95.82.U5.M69 2000, **(v3)**
Moy, Timothy. U800.M64 2001, **(v10)**
Moya, Jose C. F3001.9.S7.M6 1998, **(v4)**
Moyer, Albert E. QC16.H37.M69 1997, **(v1)**
Moyer, Wayne. HD1761.M68 1990, **(v6)**
Moylan, Tom. PN3433.6.M69 2000, **(v3)**
Moyle, James Henry. F826.M795 1975, **(v4)**
Moyles, R. G. Z7845.S24.M69 1988, **(v10)**
Moynahan, Brian. DK254.R3.M69 1997, **(v5)**
Moynahan, Julian. PR6023.A93.Z689 1963, **(v3)**
PR8752.M69 1995, **(v3)**
Moynihan, Daniel P. E744.M79 1990, **(v4)**
HC110.P63.M6, **(v6)**
HN28.M69 1996, **(v6)**
JK468.S4.M68 1998, **(v7)**
Moynihan, Donald T. RD27.35.M68.A33, **(v2)**
Moynihan, Ruth Barnes. HQ1413.D86.M69 1983, **(v6)**
Mozart, Leopold. MT262.M93 1951, **(v9)**
Mozart, Wolfgang Amadeus. ML49.M83 M42 1991, **(v9)**
ML410.M9 A187 1990, **(v9)**
ML410.M9 A4 2000, **(v9)**
Mozier, Jeanne. F239.3.M69 1999, **(v4)**
Mozley, James Frederic. BR350.T8.M6, **(v8)**
Mozumder, A. QD636.M69 1999, **(v1)**
Mozur, Joseph P. PL44.9.A36.Z78 1995, **(v3)**
Mphahlele, Ezekiel. PL8013.E5.M64, **(v3)**
PR9369.3.M67.R4 1988, **(v3)**
PR9369.3.M67.Z466 1971, **(v3)**
Mroczkowski, Robert S. TK3521.M76 1998, **(v1)**
Mrozek, Donald J. GV583.M76 1983, **(v6)**
Mrozowski, Stephen A. F74.L9 M76 1996, **(v4)**
Mruk, Christopher J. BF697.5.S46.M78 1995, **(v2)**
Mubarak, Jamil Abdalla. HC850.M83 1996, **(v6)**
Mucciaroni, Gary. HD5724.M78 1990, **(v6)**
Muchnic, Helen. PB13.S6 vol. 20, no. 3-4, **(v3)**
Muckle, James Y. LA832.M83 1990, **(v7)**
Mudde, Cas. JN5981.M83 2000, **(v7)**
Mudge, Bradford Keyes. PR830.P73.M83 2000, **(v3)**
PR4489.C2.Z78 1989, **(v3)**
Mudge, Lewis Seymour. BJ1241.M83 1998, **(v8)**
Mudimbe, V. Y. PQ3989.2.M77.E2513 1993, **(v3)**
Mudrick, Marvin. PR4037.M8, **(v3)**
PR6005.O4.Z7842 1966, **(v3)**
Mueggler, Erik. DS793.Y8 M83 2001, **(v5)**
Muego, Benjamin N. DS686.5.M84 1988, **(v5)**
Muehrcke, Phillip. GA105.3.M83 1986, **(v6)**
Muehsam, Gerd. N7425.M88, **(v9)**
Mueller, Charles F. HD5717.M83, **(v6)**
Mueller, Frederick O. RD97.M84 1996, **(v2)**
Mueller, John E. DS79.724.U6.M84 1994, **(v5)**
U21.2.M84 1989, **(v10)**
Mueller, Milton. HE8819.M84 1993, **(v6)**
Mueller, Reinhold C. HG1040.V46.M84 1997, **(v6)**
Mueller, Werner A. PT1589.M8 1962, **(v3)**
Mueller, William Randolph. PR2248.M8, **(v3)**
Muellner, Leonard Charles. PA3015.A58.M84 1996, **(v3)**
Muenger, Elizabeth A. DA957.M8 1991, **(v5)**
Muggeridge, Malcolm. PR4349.B7.Z85 1937, **(v3)**
Mugglestone, Lynda. PE1074.7.M84 1995, **(v3)**
Mughni, Haya. HQ1734.M84, **(v6)**
Mugny, Gabriel. HM291.M772513 1991, **(v6)**
Mugridge, Ian. Z6465.U5 M8, **(v10)**
Muhammad Haji Salleh. PL5139.M777.B49 1995, **(v3)**
Muhammad, En. Pi. PL4718.9.M72E94 1997, **(v3)**
Muhlberger, Detlef. DD256.5.M75 1990, **(v5)**
Mui, Ada C. HV1465.M84 1998, **(v6)**
Muir, Edward. DG975.U3.M85 1993, **(v5)**
Muir, Edwin. PN1136.M8, **(v3)**
PR99.M85, **(v3)**
PR6025.U6.A17 1965, **(v3)**
Muir, John Kenneth. PN1998.3.C38.M85 2000, **(v3)**
PN1998.3.C72.M85 1998, **(v3)**
Muir, John. F594.M95, **(v4)**
F866.M95 1961, **(v4)**
F868.S5.M9 1972, **(v4)**
F868.Y6.M915, **(v4)**
QH31.M9.M85 1996, **(v1)**
Muir, Kenneth. PR424.M8, **(v3)**

PR2403.M8, **(v3)**
PR2848.M8 1979, **(v3)**
PR2890.M8, **(v3)**
PR2952.M84 1978, **(v3)**
PR2976.M754, **(v3)**
PR2976.M76 1937, **(v3)**
PR2981.M774, **(v3)**
Muir, Lynette R. PN1880.M85 1995, **(v3)**
Muir, Rory. DC151.M9 1998, **(v5)**
DC232.M85 1996, **(v5)**
Muir, William Ker. E877.M85 1992, **(v4)**
Muirden, James. QB88.M85 1985, **(v1)**
Muirhead, John H. B29.M88 1979, **(v8)**
B832.M85, **(v8)**
Muirhead, L. Russell. DL607.M75, **(v5)**
Mukaidono, Masao. QA9.64.M86 2001, **(v1)**
Mukherjee, Meenakshi. PR4037.M85 1991, **(v3)**
PR9489.6.M85 2000, **(v3)**
Mukherjee, Pranab. HC435.2.M825 1984, **(v6)**
Mukhopadhyay, Sirshendu. PK1730.29.U463G513 1996, **(v3)**
Mukonoweshuro, Eliphas G. HN833.Z9.S66 1991, **(v6)**
Mulder, John M. E767.M75, **(v4)**
Z8976.9.M85 1997, **(v10)**
Mulder, Marcel. TP159.M4M85 1996, **(v1)**
Muldoon, James. F1411.S6973.M85 1994, **(v4)**
JC359.M86 1999, **(v7)**
Muldoon, Mark. B2430.R554 M85 2002, **(v8)**
Muldoon, Paul. PR8714.U367.T6 2000, **(v3)**
Mulford, Charles W. HF5681.P8.M85 1996, **(v6)**
Mulhauser, Ruth E. PQ1705.S5.Z8, **(v3)**
Mulholland, Marc. DA990.U46.M78 1999, **(v5)**
Mulisch, Harry. PT5860.M85A6313 1985, **(v3)**
Mulkay, M. J. RG133.5.M846 1997, **(v2)**
Mullahy, Patrick. BF173.M82, **(v2)**
Mullen, Bill. PS285.C47.M85 1999, **(v3)**
Mullen, Laura. HV5745.M85 1997, **(v6)**
Mullen, Patrick B. GR108.M85 1991, **(v6)**
Mullen, Paul E. HV6594.M85 2000, **(v6)**
Muller, Georg P. HA155.M85 1988, **(v6)**
Muller, Gilbert H. PS374.I48.M85 1999, **(v3)**
Muller, Gustav Emil. B945.M82A3, **(v8)**
Muller, Heiner. PT2673.U29.A28 1984, **(v3)**
Muller, Herbert Joseph. CB57.M9, **(v5)**
CB245.M8, **(v5)**
CB428.M854, **(v5)**
Muller, Herta. PT2673.U29234.H4713 1998, **(v3)**
Muller, Ingo. KK3655.M8513 1991, **(v7)**
Muller, J. M. QA331.M866 1997, **(v1)**
Muller, Jan-Werner. DD256.6.M85 2000, **(v5)**
Muller, Jeffrey M. ND673.R9.M766 1989, **(v9)**
Muller, Jerry Z. HB103.S6 M83 1995, **(v6)**
HM22.G3.F458 1987, **(v6)**
Muller, Nathan J. TK5105.5.M85696 1999, **(v1)**
Muller, Peter. KF4298.M85 1991, **(v7)**
Muller, R. QE698.M85 2000, **(v1)**
Muller, Rolf-Dieter. D764.M825 1997, **(v5)**
Muller-Hill, Benno. D804.G4.M7713 1988, **(v5)**
Mullett, Michael A. CB353.M83 1987, **(v5)**
Mulligan, Timothy. D781.M85 1999, **(v5)**
D802.S75.M85 1988, **(v5)**
Mulliken, Ruth K. RJ506.M4.M84 1983, **(v2)**
Mullin, Donald C. NA6821.M83, **(v9)**
Mullin, Michael. PN2596.S82.S86 Suppl., **(v3)**
Mullins, Carolyn J. H91.M8, **(v6)**
Mullins, Mark. BR1307.M85 1998, **(v3)**
Mullins, Michael G. SB388.M85 1991, **(v1)**
Mullins, Paul R. F189.A6.N46 1999, **(v4)**
Mulqueen, Maggie. HQ1206.M83 1992, **(v6)**
Mulryan, John. PR3592.M96.M85 1996, **(v3)**
Multatuli. PT5829.M3.E3 1982, **(v3)**
Multhauf, Robert P. QD14.M97 1967a, **(v1)**
Mulvaney, Kieran. G580.M85 2001, **(v6)**
Mulvaney, Rebekah Michele. BL2532.R37.M84 1990, **(v8)**
Mulvey, Charles. HD6483.M78, **(v6)**
Mulvey, Laura. PN1997.C51173.M85 1992, **(v3)**
Mulvihill, James. PR5164.M85 1987, **(v3)**
Mumby, Dennis K. HD30.3.M86 1988, **(v6)**
Mumey, Nolie. F593.B17, **(v4)**

F767.T29 M8, **(v4)**
Mumford, Kevin J. F548.9.N4.M86 1997, **(v4)**
Mumford, Laura Stempel. PN1992.8.S4.M86 1995, **(v3)**
Z7961.M85 1989, **(v10)**
Mumford, Lewis. BD431.M897, **(v8)**
CB53.M8 1973, **(v5)**
CB53.M82, **(v5)**
CB425.M79, **(v5)**
CB478.M78, **(v5)**
CT275.M73.M8, **(v5)**
CT275.M734.A35, **(v5)**
E169.1.M943 1957, **(v4)**
NA705.M78 1967, **(v9)**
NA710.M8 1972, **(v9)**
Mumtaz, Khawar. HQ1236.5.P18.M86 1987, **(v6)**
Mun¯if, Abd al-Raòhm¯an. PJ7850.U514M8413 1989, **(v3)**
PJ7850.U514S76 1996, **(v3)**
Munby, Jonathan. PN1995.9.G3.M86 1999, **(v3)**
Munch, Charles. ML422.M9 A32 1978, **(v9)**
Munch, Edvard. N7073.M8.T6413 2001, **(v9)**
NE2415.M8.L5, **(v9)**
Munck, Gerardo L. JL2031.M78 1998, **(v7)**
Munck, Ronaldo. F2217.M96 1989, **(v4)**
HD8400.B42.M86 1987, **(v6)**
Muncy, Robyn. HV741.M82 1991, **(v6)**
Munday, Anthony. PR2324.Z4 1963, **(v3)**
Mundy, Barbara E. GA481.M86 1996, **(v6)**
Mungall, Elizabeth Cary. SK241.M86 1994, **(v1)**
Mungazi, Dickson A. DT2979.T63.M86 1999, **(v5)**
DT2984.S65.M86 1998, **(v5)**
E185.2.M86 2001, **(v4)**
HN800.A8.M86 1989, **(v6)**
LA1591.M85 1991, **(v7)**
LA1591.M856 1992, **(v7)**
LB41.M967 1993, **(v7)**
Munger, Susan H. HF5718.M83 1993, **(v6)**
Mungo, Paul. HV6773.M86 1992, **(v6)**
Mungo, Raymond. CT275.M755.A3 1970, **(v5)**
Munich, Adrienne. DA554.M86 1996, **(v5)**
Munif, Abd al-Rahman. PJ7850.U514.U3513 1991, **(v3)**
Munitz, Milton Karl. BD331.M87 1990, **(v8)**
BD511.M8 1981, **(v8)**
QB981.M9, **(v1)**
Munk, Linda. PS186.M86 1997, **(v3)**
Munneke, Gary A. KF266.M86 1990, **(v7)**
KF297.M8619 2002, **(v7)**
KF297.M86 2004, **(v7)**
KF297.M862 2002, **(v7)**
Munns, Jessica. PR3613.M86 1995, **(v3)**
Munoz, Braulio. PQ8498.32.A65.Z77 2000, **(v3)**
Munro, Alice. PR9199.3.M8.B4x 1979, **(v3)**
PR9199.3.M8.M66 1983, **(v3)**
PR9199.3.M8.S6, **(v3)**
Munro, Barbara Hazard. RT81.5.M86 2001, **(v2)**
Munro, Dana Gardner. F1410.M95 1960, **(v4)**
F1428.M95 1967, **(v4)**
Munro, Donald J. BD450.M863 1988, **(v8)**
Munro, Eleanor C. N6512.M78, **(v9)**
Munro, H. H. PR6025.U675. 1971, **(v3)**
PR6025.U675 A6, **(v3)**
Munro, N. BL2370.A5.M8 1963, **(v8)**
Munro, Pamela. PM801.Z5.M85 1994, **(v3)**
Munro, Roderick H. HG8053.M86 1995, **(v6)**
Munro, Thomas. BH39.M83, **(v8)**
N7425.M9 1967, **(v9)**
Munro-Hay, S. C. Z3521.M86 1995, **(v10)**
Munro-Kua, Anne. JQ1062.A91.M85 1996, **(v7)**
Munslow, Alun. D13.M86 2000, **(v5)**
Munson, Carlton E. RC455.2.C4.M86 2001, **(v2)**
Munson, Lynne. NX705.5.U6.M86 2000, **(v9)**
Munson, Wayne. PN1990.9.T34.M86 1993, **(v3)**
Munsterberg, Hugo. NK3780.M86 1998, **(v9)**
Muoria, Henry. PN5499.K4.M86 1994, **(v3)**
Mura, Toshio. TA347.F5.M87 1992, **(v1)**
Murakami, Haruki. PL856.U673.H5713 1989, **(v3)**
PL856.U673.S4513 1991, **(v3)**
Muramatsu, Takashi. QH607.M87 1990, **(v1)**

Murasaki Shikibu. PL788.4.G4.E5 1976, **(v3)**
  PL788.4.Z5.A3513 1982, **(v3)**
  PL898.M8 G3, **(v3)**
Murase, Miyeko. N7352.M84 2000, **(v9)**
Muraskin, William A. RA644.H4.M87 1995, **(v2)**
Murata, Sachiko. BP161.2.M78 1994, **(v8)**
Muratorio, Bianca. F3721.1.N3.M8613 1991, **(v4)**
Muravchik, Joshua. E840.M873 1996, **(v4)**
Murayama, Milton. PS3563.U723A79 1988, **(v3)**
Murchison, Kenneth M. KF9219.M85 1994, **(v7)**
Murdin, Paul. QB843.S95.M87 1985, **(v1)**
Murdoch, Brian. PN688.M87 1996, **(v3)**
  PT183.M85 1983, **(v3)**
Murdoch, Dugald. QC16.B63.M87 1987, **(v1)**
Murdoch, Iris. B72.M87 1993, **(v8)**
  B398.A4.M87, **(v8)**
  B2430.S34.M8, **(v8)**
  PR6063.U7, **(v3)**
  PR6063.U7.A3 1971b, **(v3)**
  PR6063.U7.B4, **(v3)**
  PR6063.U7.F3 1970b, **(v3)**
  PR6063.U7.G6 1986, **(v3)**
  PR6063.U7.M8X, **(v3)**
  PR6063.U7.N5, **(v3)**
  PR6063.U7.N8 1981, **(v3)**
  PR6063.U7.P44 1983, **(v3)**
  PR6063.U7.S2 1974b, **(v3)**
  PR6063.U7.S3 1957, **(v3)**
  PR6063.U7.S4 1961b, **(v3)**
  PR6063.U7.T5 1974, **(v3)**
  PR6063.U7.U48 1964, **(v3)**
  PR6063.U7.U53, **(v3)**
  PR6063.U7.W67, **(v3)**
Murdoch, Norman H. BX9715.M87 1994, **(v8)**
Murdock, Eugene Converse. GV863.A1.M87 1991, **(v6)**
  PS3014.T3.C336 1984, **(v3)**
  UB343.M8, **(v10)**
Murdock, George Peter. DS509.5.M8, **(v5)**
  GN400.M78, **(v6)**
Murdock, Steven H. HB3505.M868 1995, **(v6)**
Mure, G. R. G. B485.M8 1964, **(v8)**
Murfin, Ross C. PN44.5.M86 1997, **(v3)**
  PR6023.A93.S6835 1987, **(v3)**
Murfree, Mary Noailles. PS2454.I5 1968, **(v3)**
  PS2454.P7, **(v3)**
Murie, Olaus Johan. QL768.M87 1975, **(v1)**
Murillo, L. A. PQ6352.M87 1988, **(v3)**
Muriuki, Godfrey. DT433.542.M85, **(v5)**
Murph, Roxane C. Z2014.F4.M87 2000, **(v10)**
  Z2017.M87 1995, **(v10)**
Murphey, Rhoads. U43.T9.M87 1999, **(v10)**
Murphy, Arthur D. HN120.O29.M87 1991, **(v6)**
Murphy, Arthur Edward. BD161.M88, **(v8)**
Murphy, Arthur. PR3605.M9.A66 1963, **(v3)**
Murphy, Brenda. PS3545.I5365.Z78 1992, **(v3)**
Murphy, Bruce Allen. KF8744.M87, **(v7)**
  KF8745.F65.M87 1988, **(v7)**
Murphy, Bruce. PN3448.D4.M87 1999, **(v3)**
Murphy, Christina. Z5818.E5.M87 1996, **(v10)**
Murphy, Cullen. BS680.W7.M87 1998, **(v8)**
Murphy, Daniel. PN49.M86 1997, **(v3)**
  PQ6601.L26.D436 2001, **(v3)**
Murphy, David E. E183.8.S65.M86 1997, **(v4)**
Murphy, David. PN5124.P6.M87 1990, **(v3)**
Murphy, Donn B. PN2287.H35.M87 1993, **(v3)**
Murphy, Emma. HC820.M87 1999, **(v6)**
Murphy, James Frederick. BJ1498.M87 1981, **(v8)**
Murphy, James H. PR8807.S63.M87 1997, **(v3)**
Murphy, James Jerome. PN173.M8, **(v3)**
  PN185.M8, **(v3)**
Murphy, Jeffrie G. B2799.E8.M85 1970, **(v8)**
  BJ21.M83, **(v8)**
  BJ1012.M88 1982, **(v8)**
  BJ1476.M87 1988, **(v8)**
Murphy, John C. QL666.O63.M87 1997, **(v1)**
Murphy, John Francis. HV6431.M87 1989, **(v6)**
Murphy, John W. HM26.M87 1989, **(v6)**
  HV29.2.M87 1991, **(v6)**
Murphy, John. TP1177.M87 1998, **(v1)**
Murphy, Joseph M. BL2490.M87 1994, **(v8)**

BL2532.S3 M87 1988, **(v8)**
Murphy, Kevin D. NA1053.V7.M87 2000, **(v9)**
Murphy, Kevin R. HF5549.5.R3.M863 1995, **(v6)**
Murphy, Lawrence R. VB324.G38.M87 1988b, **(v10)**
Murphy, Lucy Eldersveld. E99.W7 M87 2000, **(v4)**
Murphy, Madonna M. LC311.M87 1998, **(v7)**
Murphy, Marjorie. LB2844.53.U6.M87 1990, **(v7)**
Murphy, Martin F. HD8039.S86.D647 1991, **(v6)**
Murphy, Mary. F739.B8.M87 1997, **(v4)**
Murphy, Nancey C. BD511.M85 1996, **(v8)**
Murphy, Neville Richard. JC71.P357.M8, **(v7)**
Murphy, Patrick D. PN48.M87 2000, **(v3)**
  PS3569.N88.Z79 1992, **(v3)**
Murphy, Paul L. JC599.U5.M83, **(v7)**
Murphy, Philip. JN231.M87 1995, **(v7)**
Murphy, Raymond. HM206.M95 1997, **(v6)**
Murphy, Robert. PN1993.5.G7.M88 1992, **(v3)**
Murphy, Sara Alderman. LC212.523.L58.M87 1997, **(v7)**
Murphy, Sean D. KZ6369.M87 1996, **(v7)**
Murphy, Stephen. PN86.M87 1997, **(v3)**
Murphy, Teresa Anne. HD8083.A11.M87 1992, **(v6)**
Murphy, William Michael. PR5906.M87 1995, **(v3)**
Murphy-O'Connor, J. BS2506.M855 1996, **(v8)**
Murray, Albert. PS3563.U764.T7x, **(v3)**
Murray, Andrew Wood. QH605.M95 1993, **(v1)**
Murray, Christopher. PR8789.M87 1997, **(v3)**
Murray, David. E78.E2 M87 2000, **(v4)**
  PM218.M8 1990, **(v3)**
  PN4784.T3.M87 2001, **(v3)**
Murray, G. T. TA403.M84 1993, **(v1)**
Murray, Gail Schmunk. PS490.M85 1998, **(v3)**
Murray, Geoffrey. HC427.92.M87 1998, **(v6)**
Murray, Gilbert. PA3105.M85 1960, **(v3)**
Murray, Jack. PN3352.P7.M87 1991, **(v3)**
Murray, James Augustus Henry. PE1625.N53 1933, **(v3)**
Murray, Judith Sargent. PS808.M8.A6 1995, **(v3)**
  PS808.M8.G5 1992, **(v3)**
Murray, Katharine Maud Elisabeth. PE64.M8.M78, **(v3)**
Murray, Margaret Alice. PJ1945.M8, **(v3)**
Murray, Martin J. HC442.M87, **(v6)**
Murray, Michael L. HV95.M87 1997, **(v6)**
Murray, Michael. ML396.M87 1998, **(v9)**
  ML416.S33.M9 1994, **(v9)**
Murray, Nicholas. PR3546.M87 2000, **(v3)**
Murray, Oswyn. DF77.M82 1993, **(v5)**
Murray, Paul T. Z1361.N39.M93 1993, **(v10)**
Murray, Paul. PS3509.L43.F6627 1989, **(v3)**
  PS3509.L43.F6627 1989, **(v3)**
Murray, Peter. N7830.M87 1996, **(v9)**
  NA1115.M8, **(v9)**
Murray, Raymond LeRoy. TD898.M87 1994, **(v1)**
  TK9145.M87 2001, **(v1)**
Murray, Robert K. E743.5.M8, **(v4)**
  E786.M8 1969, **(v4)**
  E786.M83, **(v4)**
Murray, Ruth Beckmann. RT48.M8 2001, **(v2)**
Murray, Scott W. DA565.M75.M87 2000, **(v5)**
Murray, Shoon Kathleen. E840.M88 1996, **(v4)**
Murray, Stephen O. HQ76.3.N67.M87 1996, **(v6)**
Murray, Stuart. PR9629.6.M87 1998, **(v3)**
Murray, Terry A. Z5917.S36.M87 1999, **(v10)**
Murray, Thomas H. TP248.16M87 2000, **(v1)**
Murray, W. J. GV942.5.M87 1994, **(v6)**
  GV942.5.M88 1996, **(v6)**
Murray, Williamson. D727.M87 1984, **(v5)**
  D767.98.M87 2000, **(v5)**
Murrell, G. D. G. DK288.M88 1997, **(v5)**
Murrell, John Norman. QD541.M9 1994, **(v1)**
Murrin, Michael. PN56.E65.M87 1994, **(v3)**
Murry, John Middleton. BD436.M8, **(v8)**
  PN203.M8 1960, **(v3)**
  PN511.M838, **(v3)**
  PN710.M84 1968, **(v3)**
  PN710.M84 1968b, **(v3)**
  PR3726.M8 1955, **(v3)**
  PR4836.M8 1978, **(v3)**
  PR6025.U8.Z5 1936, **(v3)**
Murstein, Bernard I. BF433.A6.M82, **(v2)**

Musacchio, George. PR3562.M78 1991, **(v3)**
Musacchio, Jacqueline Marie. GT2465.I8.M87 1999, **(v6)**
Muscatine, Charles. PR1912.A3.M8, **(v3)**
Musciano, Chuck. QA76.76.H94M875 2000, **(v1)**
Muscio, Giuliana. PN1995.9.N47.M87 1997, **(v3)**
Muse, Robert L. Z7772.R1.M87 1996, **(v10)**
Museum of Modern Art (New York, N.Y.).
  N620.M9.A57 1999, **(v9)**
  N620.M9.A72 2000, **(v9)**
  N6447.M88 1992, **(v9)**
  N6490.N374 1968, **(v9)**
  N6490.N38, **(v9)**
  N6512.N4 1969, **(v9)**
  N6868.N38 1957, **(v9)**
  NA968.N4 1969, **(v9)**
  NB553.A7.A4 1980, **(v9)**
  NC1806.8.M87 1988, **(v9)**
  ND553.V9.N4 1969, **(v9)**
  ND813.G75.N4, **(v9)**
  TR140.L3.N4, **(v1)**
  TR645.N72.M876 1995, **(v1)**
Musgrave, Alan. BD161.M89 1992, **(v8)**
Musgrave, Michael. ML410.B8.M86 1996, **(v9)**
  ML410.B8.M865 2000, **(v9)**
Musgrave, Peter. HC240.M793 1999, **(v6)**
Musgrave, Richard Abel. HJ141.M79, **(v6)**
  HJ141.M796 1986, **(v6)**
  HJ275.M8, **(v6)**
Musgrave, Thomas D. KZ4024.M87 1997, **(v7)**
Musgrove, Frank. DA670.N73.M87 1990, **(v5)**
Mushaben, Joyce Marie. DD290.29.M87 1998, **(v5)**
Mushanokoji, Saneatsu. PL887.H5, **(v3)**
Mushkat, Jerome. F128.44.W8713 1990, **(v4)**
  KF368.V35.M87 1997, **(v7)**
Mushkat, Miron. HC470.3.M87 1990, **(v6)**
Musicant, Ivan. F2178.U6.M87 1990, **(v4)**
Musick, Judith S. HQ759.4.M87 1993, **(v6)**
Musiker, Naomi. DT2405.J6557.M87 1999, **(v5)**
Musiker, Reuben. Z3601.A1.M9 1996, **(v10)**
Musil, Robert. PT2625.U8, **(v3)**
  PT2625.U8.A25 1990, **(v3)**
  PT2625.U8.M3 1968, **(v3)**
Muskie, Edmund S. E840.8.M85.A34, **(v4)**
Muslin, Hyman L. E847.2.M87 1991, **(v4)**
Muso Soseki. PL2694.M87.A26 1989, **(v3)**
Musolf, Karen J. DA574.A8.M87 1999, **(v5)**
Musrey, Alfred G. HC498.M75, **(v6)**
Mussen, Paul Henry. HQ783.M83, **(v6)**
Musser, Charles O. E507.5 29th.M87 1995, **(v4)**
Musser, Charles. PN1993.5.U6.H55 1990 vol. 1, **(v3)**
  PN1998.3.H69.M87 1991, **(v3)**
  PN1998.3.P67.M87 1991, **(v3)**
Musset, Alfred de. PQ2369.C6 1973, **(v3)**
Musset, Lucien. D135.M8813, **(v5)**
Mussolini, Benito. DG571.M764 1968, **(v5)**
  DG575.M8.A2 1970, **(v5)**
Mussolini, Rachele. DG575.M8.M835313 1974, **(v5)**
Mustafa, Fawzia. PR9272.9.N32.Z78 1995, **(v3)**
Mustazza, Leonard. ML420.S565.M9 1998, **(v9)**
  PS3572.O5.Z79 1990, **(v3)**
Musto, Ronald G. Z7809.M87 1991, **(v10)**
Musurillo, Herbert. BR1603.A1 M87, **(v8)**
Mutahaba, G. R. JQ2945.A5 M88 1989, **(v7)**
Mutch, Robert E. KF4920.M88 1988, **(v7)**
Muthesius, Hermann. NA7328.M8713, **(v9)**
Muybridge, Eadweard. QP301.M83 1957, **(v1)**
  QP301.M85 1955, **(v1)**
Muzny, Charles C. F704.O41.M89 1989, **(v4)**
Muzzey, David Saville. E664.B6 M8 1963, **(v4)**
Mwereria, G. K. HC800.M86 1990, **(v6)**
Myant, M. R. DB2218.7.M9 1981, **(v5)**
  HD4215.7.M93 1993, **(v6)**
Myer, Valerie Grosvenor. PR6054.R25.Z75 1991, **(v3)**
Myerly, Scott Hughes. DA68.M94 1996, **(v5)**
Myers, A. R. DA30.P4 vol. 4, **(v5)**
  DA680.M9, **(v5)**
Myers, David B. UA23.M95 1990, **(v10)**
Myers, David G. HN90.M6.M94 2000, **(v6)**
  RF290.M84 2000, **(v2)**
Myers, Doris T. PR6023.E926.Z798 1994, **(v3)**

Myers, Douglas G. TK5102.5.M89 1990, (v1)
Myers, Drew. QD506.M93 1999, (v1)
Myers, Greg. HF5823.M93 1998, (v6)
Myers, Jack Elliott. PN1042.M94 1989, (v3)
Myers, John G. HF5415.2.M945, (v6)
Myers, L. H. PN6071.S412 S7, (v3)
  PS3525.Y44 O7, (v3)
Myers, Lois E. F391.M94 1991, (v4)
Myers, Margaret G. HJ241.M93, (v6)
Myers, Martha A. HV9475.S65.M94 1998, (v6)
Myers, Norma. DA125.N4.M94 1996, (v5)
Myers, Norman. GE40.M94 1994, (v6)
Myers, Robert A. Z3597.M94 1989, (v10)
  Z3785.M94 1991, (v10)
Myers, Robert G. HV804.M94 1992, (v6)
Myers, Robert John. DS916.M94 2001, (v5)
  E840.M94 1999, (v4)
Myers, Robert M. PS1708.M94 1995, (v3)
Myers, Robert Manson. F290.M9, (v4)
Myers, Robin. Z2010.M9, (v10)
Myers, Sylvia Harcstark. PR448.W65.M94 1990, (v3)
Myers, Walter Dean. PZ7.M992Mon 1999, (v3)
Myerson, Joel. Z8971.5.M93 1993, (v10)
Myklebust, Helmer R. RF291.M9, (v2)
Myles, Brenda. RC553.A88.M97 1998, (v2)
Mylne, Vivienne. PQ648.M9, (v3)
Mylonas, George E. DF221.M9.M93, (v5)
  DF261.E4.M88, (v5)
Myrdal, Alva Reimer. HB3617.M82 1945, (v6)
Myrdal, Gunnar. E185.6.M95 1944h, (v4)
  HB75.M953 1953, (v6)
  HB871.M9, (v6)
  HC59.7.M926, (v6)
  HC412.M9 1968b, (v6)
Myrdal, Jan. DS777.55.M913, (v5)
Myrer, Anton. PS3563.Y74.V5x, (v3)
Myres, J. N. L. DA152.M97 1986, (v5)
Myres, Sandra L. HQ1410.M96 1982, (v6)
Myrsiades, Linda S. PN2664.M97 1999, (v3)
Naber, Gregory L. QC20.7.T65.N33 1997, (v1)
Nabhan, Gary Paul. E99.P25 N32 1982, (v4)
Nabokov, Vladimir Vladimirovich. PG3476.N3 P613, (v3)
  PG3476.N3 S613, (v3)
  PG3476.N3 Z243, (v3)
  PG3476.N3Z476 1999, (v3)
  PS3527.A15L6 1991, (v3)
  PS3527.A15.S7, (v3)
Nachmani, Amikam. DS119.8.T9.N33 1987, (v5)
Nachmias, Nitza. DS119.2.N33 1988, (v5)
Nachtmann, Otto. QC793.2.N3313 1990, (v1)
Nachtrieb, Norman Harry. QD95.N28, (v1)
Nacos, Brigitte Lebens. E839.5.N33 1990, (v4)
Nadal, Octave. PQ1785.L6.N3, (v3)
Naddaff, Sandra. PJ7737.N34 1991, (v3)
Nadeau, Maurice. BH301.S75.N33, (v8)
  PQ306.N3, (v3)
  PQ671.N313 1969, (v3)
Nadeau, Remi A. D749.N33 1990, (v5)
Nadeau, Robert. QC174.12.N32 1999, (v1)
Nadel, Alan. E169.12.N324 1995, (v4)
  PN1995.9.S6.N33 1997, (v3)
  PS3555.L625.I5358 1988, (v3)
Nadel, Ira Bruce. PR6019.O9.Z746 1989, (v3)
Nadel, Stanley. F128.9.G3.N3313 1990, (v4)
Nadelhaft, Ruth L. PR6005.O4.Z78437 1991, (v3)
Nadell, Pamela Susan. BM750.N33 1988, (v8)
Nader, Helen. DP60.M4.N3, (v5)
Nader, Ralph. KF299.I5.N33 1996, (v7)
  TL242.N3 1972, (v1)
  TL553.5.N25 1994, (v1)
Nadler, Steven M. B3997.N33 1999, (v8)
Naess, Arne. B3279.H49.N33, (v8)
Naess, Harald. PT8950.H3.Z745 1984, (v3)
Naffine, Ngaire. HV6030.N33 1996, (v6)
Naficy, Hamid. PN1992.8.E84.N34 1993, (v3)
Nafte, Myriam. GN69.8.N33 2000, (v6)
Nafziger, E. Wayne. HC438.V57.N34, (v6)
  HC800.Z9 I5136 1988, (v6)
  HJ8826.N34 1993, (v6)
Nagai, Althea K. HV91.N23 1994, (v6)

Nagashima, Hiroyuki. Q172.5.C45.N3413 1999, (v1)
Nagel, Ernest. BC50.N23, (v8)
  QA9.N3, (v1)
Nagel, James. PS374.S5.N34 2001, (v3)
Nagel, Joane. E98.E85.N34 1996, (v4)
Nagel, Paul C. CS71.A2. 1983, (v5)
  E322.1.A38.N34 1987, (v4)
  E377.N34 1997, (v4)
  F466.N3, (v4)
  JK311.N2, (v7)
Nagel, Robert F. KF4575.N34 1989, (v7)
  KF5130.N34 1994, (v7)
Nagel, Stuart S. H97.N335 1988, (v6)
Nagel, Thomas. B945.N333 O74 1995, (v8)
  BD431.N32, (v8)
Nagele, Rainer. PT129.N34 1987, (v3)
  PT2603.E455Z79 1991, (v3)
Nagibin, ëliUriæi Markovich. PG3476.N34A2 1986, (v3)
Nagler, A. M. PR3091.N313, (v3)
Nagrin, Daniel. GV1588.3.N34 2001, (v6)
  GV1595.N35 1997, (v6)
  GV1786.W67 N34 1993, (v6)
Nagtegaal, Lucas Wilhelmus. DS642.N3413 1996, (v5)
Nagy, Gregory. PA3015.R4.N34 1990, (v3)
  PA4276.N34 1990, (v3)
Nagy, Marilyn. BF175.4.P45.N34 1990, (v2)
Nagy, Moses M. Z8187.N34 1994, (v10)
Nagy-Talavera, Nicholas M. DB955.N37, (v5)
Nahal, Chaman Lal. PR9499.3.N25.A9x 1975, (v3)
Nahaylo, Bohdan. DK33.N26 1990, (v5)
Nahin, Paul J. QA255.N34 1998, (v1)
  QA273.N29 2000, (v1)
  TK6550.N16 2001, (v1)
Nahm, Andrew C. DS909.N34 1993, (v5)
Nahm, Milton Charles. BH201.N32 1978, (v8)
Nahon, Marco. D805.P7.N3413 1989, (v5)
Naidu, Prabhakar S. QA280.N34 1996, (v1)
Naifeh, Steven W. ND237.P73 N34 1989, (v9)
Naim, Abd Allah Ahmad. K408 .N255 1990, (v7)
Naiman, Eric. DK266.N22 1997, (v5)
Naimark, Norman M. DD285.N35 1995, (v5)
  GN575.N15 2001, (v6)
Naipaul, Shiva. PR6064.A33.F5 1971, (v3)
Naipaul, V. S. PR6027.A29.I5 1973x, (v3)
  PR6064.A378.H62, (v3)
  PR9272.9.N32.B4x 1979, (v3)
  PR9272.9.N32E5 1987, (v3)
  PR9272.9.N32.G8 1975, (v3)
  PR9272.9.N32H55 2001, (v3)
  PR9272.9.N32.M7 1964, (v3)
  PR9272.9.N32W39 1994, (v3)
  PR9272.9.N32.Z48 2000, (v3)
Nair, Gwyneth. DA690.H702.N35 1988, (v5)
Nair, Supriya. PR9230.9.L25.Z79 1996, (v3)
Nairn, A. E. M. QC884.N3, (v1)
Nairn, Tom. JC311.N245 1997, (v7)
Naisbitt, John. HC79.I55.N34 1994, (v6)
  HC412.N2433 1996, (v6)
Najder, Zdzislaw. PR6005.O4.Z78439 1997, (v3)
  PR6005.O4.Z7844313 1983, (v3)
Najera-Ramirez, Olga. F1219.1.J63.N35 1997, (v4)
Najib Ullah. PJ807.N3, (v3)
Najmabadi, Afsaneh. HD1333.I7.N34 1987, (v6)
Nakamoto, Kazuo. QD96.I5.N33 1997, (v1)
Nakamura, Hajime. B799.N29 1986, (v8)
  DS12.N35 1964, (v5)
Nakamura, Yoshihiko. TJ211.N34 1991, (v1)
Nakano, Makiko. DS897.K85.N3313 1995, (v5)
Nakano, Minoru. JQ1629.P64.N3513 1996, (v7)
Nakash, Yitzhak. DS70.8.S55.N35 1994, (v5)
Nakos, George. QA184.N34 1998, (v1)
Nalbantian, Suzanne. PR756.A9.N35 1994, (v3)
Nalivkin, D. V. QE276.N2813 1973b, (v1)
Namath, Joe Willie. GV939.N28.A3, (v6)
Namias, June. E85.N34 1993, (v4)
Namier, Julia. D15.N3.N35 1971, (v5)
Namier, Lewis Bernstein. D210.N32, (v5)
  D387.N3 1964, (v5)
  D720.N3 1963, (v5)

  D748.N3, (v5)
  DA480.N3 1970, (v5)
Namkoong, Gene. SD399.5.N355 1988, (v1)
Nammalvar. PL4758.9.N3155.A27, (v3)
Nan, Huai-chin. BQ9262.9.C5 N39 1995, (v8)
Nance, Joseph Milton. F390.N3, (v4)
Nancy, Jean-Luc. B2430.N363.E8713 2000, (v8)
  BD311.N36 1993, (v8)
  BH39.N2713 1996, (v8)
Nanda, B. R. DS479.N352 1998, (v5)
  DS481.G3 N3395 2002, (v5)
  DS481.N35 N285 1995, (v5)
Nanda, Serena. HQ449.N36 1989, (v6)
Nandy, Ashis. DS475.N354 1998, (v5)
Napier, A. David. GN452.5.N37 1992, (v6)
Napier, Kristine M. RA1242.T6.N34 1996, (v2)
Napier, Susan Jolliffe. NC1766.J3.N37 2001, (v9)
Napoleon I, Emperor of the French, 1769-1821. DC213.H6, (v5)
  DC214.H4 1969, (v5)
Naquin, Susan. DS754.N4 1987, (v5)
Naquin, Susan. DS795.3.N36 2000, (v5)
Narayan, R. K. PR9499.3.N3 F5, (v3)
  PR9499.3.N3 G7 1953, (v3)
  PR9499.3.N3G74 1994, (v3)
  PR9499.3.N3 M35, (v3)
  PR9499.3.N3 S9, (v3)
  PR9499.3.N3T69 1999, (v3)
  PR9499.3.N3 V4, (v3)
  PR9499.3.N3 W3, (v3)
Narayanan, R. S. TA174.N35 2000, (v1)
Nardi, Bonnie A. QA76.9.E53.N37 1993, (v1)
Nardi, Marcia. PS3527.A5.Z468 1994, (v3)
Nardin, Jane. PR5688.E8.N37 1996, (v3)
  PR5688.W6.N37 1989, (v3)
Nardinelli, Clark. HD6250.G7.N28 1990, (v6)
Naregal, Veena. DS463.N37 2001, (v5)
Nariman, Heidi Noel. PN1992.8.S4.N37 1993, (v3)
Narlikar, Jayant Vishnu. QB331.N37 1982, (v1)
  QB801.N29 1995, (v1)
Naroll, Raoul. U162.6.N37 1974, (v10)
Narrett, David E. KFN5200.N37 1992, (v7)
Narveson, Jan. JC571.N28 1988, (v7)
Narwekar, Sanjit. PN1998.2.N37 1994, (v3)
Nascimento, Abdias do. F2659.N4.N36 1992, (v4)
Nasgaard, Roald. ND588.R48.A4 1988b, (v9)
Nash, Dennison. G155.A1.N37 1996, (v6)
Nash, Elizabeth. PN2205.N35 1991, (v3)
Nash, Ernest. NA310.N28 1968, (v9)
Nash, Gary B. E445.P3.N37 1991, (v4)
  E446.N37 1990, (v4)
  F152.N25, (v4)
  F158.9.N4.N37 1988, (v4)
  LB1582.U6.N37 1997, (v7)
Nash, George H. E743.N37, (v4)
Nash, Gerald D. F591.N37 1991, (v4)
  F595.N37 1977, (v4)
  F595.2.N37 2001, (v4)
  HC107.A17.N37 1985, (v4)
Nash, Jay Robert. F591.N38 1992, (v4)
Nash, Kate. JA76.N32 1999, (v7)
Nash, Mary. DP269.8.W7.N38 1995, (v5)
Nash, Ogden. PS3527.A637.A6 1975, (v3)
  PS3527.A637.E85, (v3)
  PS3527.A637.F3, (v3)
  PS3527.A637.P73, (v3)
  PS3527.A637.Y6, (v3)
Nash, Philip. E835.N37 1997, (v4)
Nash, Robert J. BJ66.N37 2002, (v8)
  LC111.N25 1999, (v7)
  LC311.N27 1997, (v7)
Nash, Roderick. E169.1.N37 1982, (v4)
  GF80.N36 1989, (v6)
Nash, Thomas. PR2326.N3.P5 1970, (v3)
  PR2721.M, (v3)
  PR2722.W4 1965, (v3)
Nash, Walter. PE1585.N37 1993, (v3)
  PN187.N37 1989, (v3)
Nasmyth, Peter. DK672.9.N38 1998, (v5)
Nasr, Seyyed Hossein. B745.C6.N3 1993, (v8)
  Q125.N17, (v1)

Nasr, Seyyed Vali Reza. BP80.M34.N37 1996, (v8)
JQ559.A54.N37 1994, (v7)
Nassaar, Christopher S. PR5824.N27 1974, (v3)
Nassau, Jason John. QB145.N3 1948, (v1)
Nassau, Kurt. QC495.N35 1983, (v1)
Nasson, Bill. DT1896.N37 1990, (v5)
Nasstrom, Kathryn L. HQ1438.G4.N37 2000, (v6)
Natanson, Maurice Alexander. PN49.N35 1998, (v3)
Nathan, Andrew J. DS779.26.N38 1990, (v5)
DS779.26.N383 1997, (v5)
UA835.N38 1997, (v10)
Nathan, George Jean. PS3527.A72.A6 1952, (v3)
Nathan, N. M. L. BJ1461.N37 1992, (v8)
Nathan, Peter E. RC480.515.N38 1999, (v2)
Nathan, Peter Wilfred. QP361.N37 1988, (v1)
Nathan, Richard P. HJ2051.N167 1987, (v6)
Nathan, Robert. PS3527.A74 P6, (v3)
PS3527.A74 W5, (v3)
Nathanielsz, P. W. RJ91.N235 1999, (v2)
Nathanson, Paul. PN1997.W593.N38 1991, (v3)
Nathanson, Stephen. JC329.N325 1993, (v7)
Nathanson, Tenney. PS3238.N38 1992, (v3)
National Consortium for Physical Education and
Recreation. GV445.N38 1995, (v6)
National Council of Teachers of Mathematics.
QA1.N3 26, (v1)
National Fire Protection Association. TK260.N47B,
(v1)
National Information Center for Educational Media.
Z695.Z8.N546 1998, (v10)
National Museum of American Art (U.S.). N857.A617
1995, (v9)
NK805.N35 1990, (v9)
National Museum of India. F3429.3.G5 N38 1999, (v4)
National Museum of Women in the Arts (U.S.).
N8354.N38 2000, (v9)
National Research Council (U.S.). HV6626.52.N38
1993, (v6)
JS422.N39 1999, (v7)
LB1140.23.N38 2001, (v7)
QC981.8.C5.N35 1990, (v1)
RA408.A3.N37 1988, (v2)
RA1199.N375 1984, (v2)
RC108.N38 1989, (v2)
S481.N38 1993, (v1)
SH351.T8.N37 1992, (v1)
TL1499.N38 1995, (v1)
TX551.N38, (v1)
VM455.N35 1991, (v10)
National Task Force on African-American Men and
Boys. E185.86.N368 1996, (v4)
Natoli, Joseph P. PN1995.N36 2001, (v3)
Natoli, Joseph. PN1995.9.S6.N38 1998, (v3)
Natriello, Gary. LC4091.N39 1990, (v7)
Natsios, Andrew S. HC470.2.Z9 F36 2001, (v6)
HV553.N37 1997, (v6)
Natsume, Soseki. PL812.A8.K5713 1988, (v3)
PL812.A8 K613 1957, (v3)
PL812.A8 M413, (v3)
PL812.A8 S5813 1978, (v3)
Nattiez, Jean Jacques. PQ2631.R63.A85213 1989,
(v3)
Nattrass, Brian F. HD30.255.N388 1999, (v6)
Natwar-Singh, K. PK2978.E5.N3, (v3)
Naum, Gellu. PC840.24.A8.Z3513 1995, (v3)
Naumann, Francis M. N6535.N5.N32 1996, (v9)
N6853.D8.N39 1999, (v9)
Navabpour, Reza. Z3366.N37 1988, (v10)
Navarette, Susan J. PR878.T3.N38 1998, (v3)
Navarrete, Ignacio Enrique. PQ6066.N38 1994, (v3)
Navarro Tomas, Tomas. PC4137.N4 1990, (v3)
PC4511.N3, (v3)
Navarro, Armando. F394.C83.N37 1998, (v4)
F395.M5.N39 1995, (v4)
Naveh, Eyal J. E661.N38 1990, (v4)
Navia, Luis E. B293.A34, (v8)
B305.D44.N38 1998, (v8)
BD21.N38 1999, (v8)
Z7128.P83.N38 1993, (v10)
Z8722.3.N38 1990, (v10)
Navlakha, Suren. HN690.Z9.E466 1989, (v6)
Navrotsky, Alexandra. QC171.2.N38 1994, (v1)

Nawang Gehlek. BQ4485.N39 2001, (v8)
Nayar, Alok. TA459.N39 1997, (v1)
Nayder, Lillian. PR4497.N39 1997, (v3)
Nayfeh, Ali Hasan. QA371.N32, (v1)
QA845.N39 1994, (v1)
Naylor, Gloria. PS3564.A895.L5 1985, (v3)
Naylor, Gloria. PS3564.A895.W6 1982, (v3)
Naylor, Phillip Chiviges. DT283.7.N39 1994, (v5)
DT287.5.F8, (v5)
Naylor, Robert A. F1529.M9.N39 1989, (v4)
Naylor, Thomas H. D849.N39 1991, (v5)
Nazarea, Virginia D. HN720.Z9.C66417 1995, (v6)
Nazzal, Nafez. DS102.8.N397 1997, (v5)
Nead, Lynda. DA683.N425 2000, (v5)
Neagles, James C. Z1250.N4 1990, (v10)
Neal, Frank. DA125.I7.N43 1998, (v5)
DA690.L8.N43 1988, (v5)
Neal, Fred Warner. DR370.N4, (v5)
Neal, Larry. HC241.N4 1998, (v6)
HG5432.N43 1990, (v6)
Neal, Patrick. JC574.N4 1997, (v7)
Neal, Steve. E748.W7.N43 1984, (v4)
Neale, Stephen. PN1993.5.U6.N43 2000, (v3)
Neaman, Judith S. PE1449.N34 1983, (v3)
Neary, John. PS3571.P4.Z785 1992, (v3)
Neary, Peter. F1123.N45 1989, (v4)
Neatby, Hilda. F1032.N34, (v4)
Nebehay, Christian Michael. NC245.S34.N4313 1989,
(v9)
Nebenzahl, Kenneth. G1036.N4 1990, (v6)
G1201.S3.N4 1974, (v6)
Neblette, C. B. TR145.N4 1977, (v1)
Necker, Claire. SF442.N4, (v1)
Nectoux, Jean Michel. ML410.F27.N413 1991, (v9)
Nedelsky, Jennifer. KF562.N43 1990, (v7)
Nederman, Cary J. HM1271.N44 1999, (v6)
Nederveen Pieterse, Jan. NX653.A35.N4313 1992, (v9)
Needham, Anuradha Dingwaney. PR120.M55.N44
2000, (v3)
Needham, H. A. PN99.G7.N4, (v3)
Needham, Joseph. DS721.N39, (v5)
DS721.N392, (v5)
Neel, James V. RB155.N44 1994, (v2)
Neel, Jasper P. PE1405.U6.N44 1994, (v3)
Neeley, G. Steven. KF3827.E87.N44 1994, (v7)
Neely, John. TN665.N3 2000, (v1)
Neely, Mark E. E457.N49 1993, (v4)
E457.2.N46 1991, (v4)
E487.N44 1999, (v4)
Neely, Sylvia. DC146.L2.N44 1991, (v5)
Nef, John Ulric. CB478.N4, (v5)
Neff, Emery Edward. PR4433.N4 1926, (v3)
Neff, Stephen C. HF1713.N35 1990, (v6)
Negandhi, Anant R. HD70.I4.N43 1975, (v6)
Negash, Tekeste. DT388.35.N44 2000, (v5)
Negrey, Cynthia. HD5110.2.U5.N44 1993, (v6)
Negri Zamagni, Vera. HC305.N35913 1993, (v6)
Negroponte, Nicholas. TK5103.7.N43 1995, (v1)
Negus, Keith. ML3470.N44 1997, (v9)
ML3790.N4 1999, (v9)
Negwer, Martin. RS154.N428 2001, (v2)
Nehamas, Alexander. BJ1595.N37 1998, (v8)
Neher, Clark D. JQ96.A91.N44 1995, (v7)
Nehring, Neil. ML3534.N44 1997, (v9)
Neiberg, Michael. U428.5.N45 2000, (v10)
Neider, Charles. F591.N4, (v4)
Neier, Aryeh. K5301.N45 1998, (v7)
Neihardt, John Gneisenau. F598.N39 1997, (v4)
PS3527.E35S6 1915, (v3)
Neill, Catherine A. RJ426.C64N45 2001, (v2)
Neill, Edward. PR4754.N39 1999, (v3)
Neill, Michael. PR658.P65.N45 2000, (v3)
Neils, Jenifer. DF123.N45 1992, (v5)
Neilson, Alasdair H. QH545.W3.N45 2000, (v1)
Neilson, Jim. PS228.V5.N45 1998, (v3)
Neilson, Keith. DA47.65.N45 1995, (v5)
Neiman, Susan. BJ1401.N45 2002, (v8)
Nekrich, A. M. DD120.S65.N45 1997, (v5)
Nel, Etienne Louis. HT395.S62.E375 1999, (v6)
Nelken, Halina. DS135.P63.N46 1999, (v5)
Nelkin, Dorothy. HE9797.5.U52 B66, (v6)

QH430.N46 1995, (v1)
RA427.5.N45 1989, (v2)
Nelkin, Norton. BD418.3.N45 1996, (v8)
Nelli, Humbert S. F548.9.I8.N4, (v4)
Nellis, J. G. HD30.22.N45 1997, (v6)
Nellist, John G. TK5105.5.N45 1999, (v1)
Nelson, Alan H. PN2596.C3.N45 1994, (v3)
Nelson, Benjamin. BF173.F85.N37, (v2)
Nelson, Bonnie R. Z5703.4.C73.N45 1997, (v10)
Nelson, Bruce. HD6515.S4.N45 1988, (v6)
HD8081.A65.N45 2001, (v6)
Nelson, Cary. LB2324.N45 1999, (v7)
Nelson, Claudia. PN5124.P4.N45 1995, (v3)
Nelson, Daniel J. UA26.G3.N43 1987, (v10)
Nelson, Daniel. HD2356.U5.N44 1995, (v6)
HD8083.M53.N45 1995, (v6)
Nelson, David M. GV955.N44 1994, (v6)
F1435.3.E72.N45 1999, (v4)
Nelson, Glen. HF5679.N445 1994, (v6)
Nelson, Hilde Lindemann. R724.N43 1995, (v2)
Nelson, J. C. C. TK7871.58.O6.N454 1995, (v1)
Nelson, James G. Z325.M385.N45 1989, (v10)
Z325.S665.N45 2000, (v10)
Nelson, Joel I. HC106.8.N453 1995, (v6)
Nelson, John D. TA711.5.N5 1992, (v1)
Nelson, John K. BL2220.N45 2000, (v8)
BL2225.N2552.S883 1996, (v8)
Nelson, Joseph S. QL618.N4 1994, (v1)
Nelson, Keith L. E183.8.S65.N45 1995, (v4)
Nelson, Lawrence J. F341.J64.N45 1999, (v4)
Nelson, Lowry. PN1356.N4, (v3)
Nelson, Lynn Hankinson. B945.Q54 N45 2000, (v8)
Nelson, Mariah Burton. GV709.N44 1991, (v6)
Nelson, Michael. HE8697.8.N45 1997, (v6)
Nelson, Otto L. UB23.N43, (v10)
Nelson, Paul David. DA67.1.G76.N45 1996, (v5)
E207.W35 N34 1985, (v4)
F257.T79.N45 1990, (v4)
F1032.D67.N45 2000, (v4)
Nelson, Paula. F656.N455 1996, (v4)
Nelson, Richard Alan. HM263.N44 1996, (v6)
Nelson, Richard R. HB71.N44 1982, (v6)
Nelson, Robert H. HB72.N45 2001, (v6)
Nelson, Robert James. PS3505.A87.Z745 1988, (v3)
Nelson, Robert L. KF300.N45 1988, (v7)
Nelson, Robin. PN1992.6.N47 1997, (v3)
Nelson, Sarah M. CC72.4.N45 1997, (v5)
Nelson, Scott Reynolds. F216.N45 1999, (v4)
Nelson, T. G. A. PR858.C5.N45 1995, (v3)
Nelson, William Edward. KF4575.N45 2000, (v7)
KF4757.N45 1988, (v7)
Nelson, William Javier. E183.8.D65.N45 1990, (v4)
Nelson, William. PR2364.N38, (v3)
PR2364.N4, (v3)
Nem aòde, Bh alacandra. PK2418.N37K613 1997,
(v3)
Nemec Ignashev, Diane. Z2503.5.W6.N45 1992, (v10)
Nemerov, Alexander. ND237.P29.N46 2001, (v9)
Nemerov, Howard. PN1031.N44, (v3)
PN1136.N43, (v3)
PS3527.E5.A17 1960, (v3)
PS3527.E5.A17 1977, (v3)
PS3527.E5 C6, (v3)
PS3527.E5 H6, (v3)
PS3527.E5.I5, (v3)
PS3527.E5.M5, (v3)
PS3527.E5.S8, (v3)
Nemiroff, Robert. PS3515.A515.Z8, (v3)
Nemo, John. PR6021.A74.Z79, (v3)
Nenner, Howard. KD4456.S8.N46 1995, (v7)
Nenno, Mary K. HT123.N36 1996, (v6)
Nepaulsingh, Colbert I. PQ6066.N46 1995, (v3)
Nequatewa, Edmund. E99.H7.N45 1993, (v4)
Nerlich, Graham. BD232.N47 1989, (v8)
BD632.N4 1994, (v8)
Neruda, Jan. PG5038.N45 P62, (v3)

Neruda, Pablo. PQ8097.N4.A22 1988, (v3)
  PQ8097.N4.A6 1961, (v3)
  PQ8097.N4.A6 1969, (v3)
  PQ8097.N4.C1713 1990, (v3)
  PQ8097.N4.C613 1990, (v3)
  PQ8097.N4.L513 1991, (v3)
  PQ8097.N4.M3413 1988, (v3)
  PQ8097.N4.P5213 1987, (v3)
Nerval, Gerard de. PQ2260.G36.C5 1973, (v3)
  PQ2260.G36 1952, (v3)
Nervo, Amado. PQ7297.N5.A17 1964, (v3)
Nesiah, Devanesan. E184.A1.N37 1997, (v4)
Ness, Immanuel. JK1118.N47 2000, (v7)
Ness, Richard. PN1998.3.R84.N47 1996, (v3)
Nesse, Randolph M. R723.N387 1994, (v2)
Nesse, William D. QE363.2.N48 2000, (v1)
Nester, William R. E83.76.N47 2000, (v4)
  E183.8.J3.N366 1996, (v4)
  F592.C263.N47 1999, (v4)
  HC462.9.N397 1990, (v6)
  HD3616.U46.N38 1998, (v6)
  HF1452.5.J3.N47 1993, (v6)
Netanyahu, Binyamin. HV6431.N48 1995, (v6)
Nethercot, Arthur Hobart. PR4480.C52.N4 1978, (v3)
Netravali, Arun N. TK5103.7.N47 1995, (v1)
Nettel, Stephen, 1938-. QC157.N48 1995, (v1)
Nettels, Elsa. PS374.S46.N48 1997, (v3)
Netting, Robert McC. GN407.4.N48 1993, (v6)
Nettl, Bruno. ML3545.N285 1990, (v9)
  ML3551.N47 1976, (v9)
  ML3557.N38 1989, (v9)
  ML3798.N47 1983, (v9)
Nettl, J. P. DD257.4.N44, (v5)
Nettle, Daniel. P40.5.L33.N48 2000, (v3)
Netton, Ian Richard. B745.K53.N48 1992, (v8)
  B745.K53.N485 1996, (v8)
  B746.N47 1982, (v8)
  BP40.N48 1992, (v8)
Netzley, Patricia D. G465.N47 2001, (v6)
  PN56.S65.N48 1999, (v3)
  TR858.N48 2000, (v1)
Neubauer, John. PN761.N48 1992, (v3)
Neuberger, Richard L. F852.N54 1989, (v4)
Neuenschwander, Ed. NA1193.N45 1954a, (v9)
Neufeld, Mark A. JX1391.N477 1995, (v7)
Neufeld, Michael J. UF535.G3.N48 1995, (v10)
Neuffer, M. Gerald. SB191.M2.N39 1997, (v1)
Neugarten, Bernice Levin. HQ1061.N65, (v6)
Neugeboren, Bernard. HV31.N47 1996, (v6)
Neugeboren, Jay. RC439.5.N46 1999, (v2)
Neuhart, John. NK1535.E25.N48 1989, (v9)
Neuman, Johanna. PN4784.B75.N48 1996, (v3)
Neuman, W. Russell. PN5648.N38 1992, (v3)
Neumann, Erich. BF175.4.F45.N48 1994, (v2)
  BF311.N488, (v2)
  NB497.M6.N43, (v9)
Neumann, Frederick. ML457.N46 1993, (v9)
Neumann, Klaus. DD20.N48 2000, (v5)
Neumann, P. M. QA183.N48 1994, (v1)
Neumann, Roderick P. SB484.T3.N48 1998, (v1)
Neumann, Sigmund. JF2011.N4, (v7)
Neumeyer, David. ML410.H685 N5 1986, (v9)
Neurath, Hans. QD431.N453, (v1)
Neuse, Richard. PR1875.A44.N4 1991, (v3)
Neuse, Steven M. E748.L7.N48 1996, (v4)
Neusner, Jacob. BM177.N474 1988, (v8)
  BM496.5.N4826 1989, (v8)
Neustadt, Kathy. GT2956.U6N48 1992, (v6)
Neustadt, Richard E. E183.8.G7.N47 1970, (v4)
  JK516.N4 1990, (v7)
Neutra, Richard Joseph. NA737.N4.A2 1989, (v9)
Neuzil, Mark. P96.E572.U66 1996, (v3)
Nevadomsky, Joseph-john. DS503.C35 no. 6, (v5)
Nevaer, Louis E. V. HF3230.5.Z7.U55 1996, (v6)
Neve, Brian. PN1995.9.S6.N46 1992, (v3)
Nevett, Lisa C. DF99.N48 1999, (v5)
Neville, Richard C. TK2960.N48 1995, (v1)
  BD581.N48 1989, (v8)
  BJ1012.N48 1987, (v8)
  BL1852.N48 2000, (v8)
  BT65.N48 1991, (v8)

Nevin, Thomas R. B2430.W474.N48 1991, (v8)
  PT2619.U43.Z73 1996, (v3)
Nevins, Allan. D13.N367 1975, (v5)
  E173.C58 vol. 31, (v4)
  E178.4.N47, (v4)
  E303.N52 1969, (v4)
  E415.7.N38, (v4)
  E458.N45, (v4)
  E468.N428 1992, (v4)
  E468.N43, (v4)
  E697.N46 1989, (v4)
  LB2329.5.N38 1962, (v7)
Nevo, Ruth. PR545.P6.N38, (v3)
  PR2981.5.N48 1987, (v3)
New York University Institute of Philosophy.
  BJ1461.N4 1957, (v8)
New York. N6494.C8.N4 1966, (v9)
  NA680.N44, (v9)
  NA1550.N4, (v9)
New Zealand. G9250 1976.N4, (v6)
New, Melvyn. PR3714.T73.N44 1994, (v3)
New, William H. PR9639.3.M258.Z854 1999, (v3)
Newberg, Paula R. KPL3409.N49 1995, (v7)
Newberry, Benjamin H. RC49.N493 1991, (v2)
Newbery, David M. G. HD2763.N45 1999, (v6)
  HF1428.N485, (v6)
Newbould, Brian. ML410.S3.N48 1997, (v9)
Newbould, Ian. DA539.N48 1990, (v5)
Newburn, Tim. KD7975.N49 1991, (v7)
Newbury, C. W. DU870.N48, (v5)
Newbury, Catharine. JQ3567.A2.N48 1988, (v7)
Newby, Eric. G80.N43 1975, (v6)
Newby, Hayes A. RF290.N47 1992, (v2)
Newby, I. A. E185.61.N475, (v4)
  E185.93.S7 N4 1973, (v4)
  HN79.A13.N48 1989, (v6)
Newby, P. H. PR6027.E855 B3, (v3)
  PR6027.E855 G8, (v3)
  PR6027.E855 K5, (v3)
  PR6027.E855 P5, (v3)
  PR6027.E855 R45, (v3)
  PR6027.E855 R47, (v3)
  PR6027.E855 Y6, (v3)
Newcastle, Margaret Cavendish. PR3605.N2.A6 1999,
  (v3)
  PR3605.N2.S63 1997, (v3)
Newcomb, Charles King. PS2459.N348.A6, (v3)
Newcomb, Lawrence. QK118.N42, (v1)
Newcomb, Michael D. HV5824.Y68.N49 1988, (v6)
Newcomb, Mildred. PR4588.N39 1989, (v3)
Newcomb, William W. E78.T4 N4, (v4)
Newell, Clayton R. DS79.72.N48 1998, (v5)
  E472.17.N49 1996, (v4)
  U162.N46 1991, (v10)
Newell, Dianne. KEB529.5.H8.N48 1993, (v7)
Newell, Frederick Haynes. F199.N47, (v4)
Newell, Frederick. HF5415.1265.N495 2000, (v6)
Newell, Homer Edward. UG630.N44 1961, (v10)
Newell, Margaret Ellen. HC107.A11 N46 1998, (v6)
Newey, Glen. JC574.N49 2001, (v7)
Newhall, Beaumont. TR15.N47 1964, (v1)
  TR365.N4 1976, (v1)
Newhall, David S. DC342.8.C6.N43 1991, (v5)
Newhall, John B. [from old catalog]. F621.N53, (v4)
Newhouse, Edward. PS3527.E8643 M3 1951, (v3)
Newhouse, John. D2009.N5 1997, (v5)
Newhouse, Joseph P. RA410.53.N52 1993, (v2)
Newhouse, Victoria. NA6695.N49 1998, (v9)
Newitt, M. D. D. DT3341.N48 1995, (v5)
Newlands, Anne. N6540.N49 2000, (v9)
Newlin, George. PR4553.N48 1996, (v3)
  PR4589.N48 1996, (v3)
Newlin, Keith. Z8324.34.N48 1998, (v10)
Newman, Arnold. F312.N48 1988, (v4)
  TR681.A7.N48, (v1)
Newman, Barbara. BX4700.H5.N48 1987, (v8)
Newman, Barnett. N6537.N48.A4 1978, (v9)
Newman, Bob. GV200.5.N486 1996, (v6)
Newman, Edward. JZ5008.N49 1998, (v7)
Newman, Ernest. ML410.G5.N3 1967, (v9)
  ML410.W8.N5 1966, (v9)

  MT100.W2 N53 1991, (v9)
Newman, Frances. PS3527.E883.Z5 1929, (v3)
Newman, Frank. LA227.3.N46 1985, (v7)
Newman, James L. GF701.N48 1995, (v6)
Newman, James Roy. QA3.N48, (v1)
Newman, John Henry. BX4705.N5.A15, (v8)
  BX4705.N5.A3 1968, (v8)
Newman, Judie. PR9084.N49 1995, (v3)
Newman, Karen. PR658.W6.N48 1991, (v3)
Newman, Katherine S. HN90.S6.N47 1993, (v6)
  HN90.S65 N48 1989, (v6)
  HV4045.N48 1999, (v6)
Newman, Louis E. BJ1285.N49 1998, (v8)
Newman, Louise Michele. HQ1410.N475 1998, (v6)
Newman, P. R. DA912.N485 1991, (v5)
Newman, Peter Charles. F1034.D5.N4, (v4)
  F1060.N48 1988 vol. 2, (v4)
Newman, Richard. E185.N59 1996, (v4)
  Z1361.N39.N578 1984, (v10)
Newman, Robert D. PN98.R38.N48 1993, (v3)
Newman, Robert P. E748.L34.N48 1992, (v4)
  PS3515.E343.Z8 1989, (v3)
Newman, Roger K. KF8745.B55.N49 1994, (v7)
Newman, Roxana Ma. PL8233.N49 1990, (v3)
Newman, Simon. TL716.N39 1994, (v1)
Newman, William M. BR515.N49 2000, (v8)
Newman, William S. ML410.B4.N45 1988, (v9)
  ML1156.N42 1983, (v9)
  ML1156.N43 1983, (v9)
  ML1156.N44 1983, (v9)
  ML1156.N4S63, (v9)
  MT220.N5 1984, (v9)
Newmark, Maxim. PQ6006.N4, (v3)
Newmyer, R. Kent. KF8745.S83.N48 1985, (v7)
Newsinger, John. PR6029.R8.Z7374 1999, (v3)
Newsom, David D. JX1417.N49 1996, (v7)
  JX1706.N535 1988, (v7)
Newsome, David. DA550.N49 1997, (v5)
Newson, Linda A. F3721.3.P76.N49 1995, (v4)
Newstrom, Harvey. QP141.N48 1993, (v1)
Newstrom, John W. HD38.N42 1990, (v6)
Newton, Adam Zachary. PN49.N52 1995, (v3)
Newton, Adolph W. D773.N495 1999, (v5)
Newton, Candelas. PQ6613.A763.Z7775 1995, (v3)
Newton, D. B. PS3527.E9178 C76, (v3)
Newton, David E. Q175.5.N49 1999, (v1)
  QD31.2.N49 1999, (v1)
  Z103.N344 1997, (v10)
Newton, Douglas J. DA47.2.N49 1997, (v5)
Newton, Douglas P. LB1025.3.N495 2000, (v7)
Newton, Harry. TK5102.N49 2001, (v1)
Newton, Huey P. E185.97.N48.A37, (v4)
Newton, Ian. QL677.4.N48 1998, (v1)
Newton, Isaac. QA35.N5647, (v1)
Newton, Isaac. QA803.A45 1969, (v1)
  QC3.N52, (v1)
  QC353.N52 1984, (v1)
  QC353.N57 1952, (v1)
Newton, Jack. QB64.N49 1988, (v1)
Newton, Judith Lowder. PR830.W62.N4, (v3)
Newton, Michael T. JN8210.N48 1997, (v7)
Newton, Michael. HV6245.N49 2000, (v6)
  Z7164.T3.N48 1988, (v10)
Newton, Roger G. QC6.N485 2000, (v1)
  QC6.4.R42.N49 1997, (v1)
  QC21.2.N53 1993, (v1)
  QC721.N4755, (v1)
Newton, Ronald C. F2848.N4 1992, (v4)
Newton, Scott. DA586.N49 1996, (v5)
Newton, Wesley Phillips. D769.85.A21, (v5)
Ney, Ronald E. TD196.O73.N49 1995, (v1)
Neziroglu, Fugen A. RC533.N49 1997, (v2)
Nfah-Abbenyi, Juliana Makuchi. PL8010.N467 1997,
  (v3)
Ng, Larry K. Y. HB885.N5 1965, (v6)
Ng, Mau-sang. PL2443.N45 1988, (v3)
Ng, Wai-ming. PL2464.Z7.N46 2000, (v3)
Ngate, Jonathan. PQ3984.N46 1988, (v3)
Ngaugai wa Thiong o. PL8010.N48 1986, (v3)
Ngcobo, Lauretta G. PR9369.3.N4.A8 1991, (v3)
Ngugi wa Thiong'o. PL8010.N485 1993, (v3)

Nguyen, Hung T. QA76.87.N497 2000, (v1)
Nguyen, Khac Vien. DS560.3.N4513, (v5)
Nguyen, Ngoc Bich. PL4382.E3.N4 1975, (v3)
Nguyen, Quoc Tri. HC59.7.N44 1989, (v6)
Nhat Hanh. GR313.N4813 1993, (v6)
Niblett, William Roy. LB880.N463 1970, (v7)
Niblock, Tim. JZ6373.N53 2001, (v7)
Nice, David C. HE2791.A563.N53 1998, (v6)
  JK325.N53 1987, (v7)
  JK2431.N53 1994, (v7)
Nichiren. BQ8349.N573 E5 1990, (v8)
Nicholas II, Emperor of Russia, 1868-1918.
  DK258.N458 1999, (v5)
Nicholas, David. HT115.N53 1997, (v6)
Nicholas, Sian. D810.P7.G765 1996, (v5)
Nicholas, Warwick L. QL391.N4.N5 1984, (v1)
Nicholas. B765.N53 D63 1981, (v8)
Nicholls, Anthony James. HC286.5.N474 1994, (v6)
  JN3971.A58.N53 1997, (v7)
Nicholls, David. DA565.D6.N53 1995, (v5)
  DD247.H5.N53 2000, (v5)
  F1921.N58, (v4)
  ML200.5.N55 1990, (v9)
  PN1998.3.T78.N53 1993, (v3)
  PS153.N5N53 2000, (v3)
Nicholls, John G. LB1065.N53 1989, (v7)
Nicholls, Mark. DA392.N53 1991, (v5)
Nicholls, Peter. PN56.M54.N53 1995, (v3)
Nichols, Ashton. PR585.E85.N53 1987, (v3)
  PR5892.P64.N53 1998, (v3)
Nichols, Bill. PN1995.9.D6.N538 1994, (v3)
  PN1995.9.D6.N54 1991, (v3)
Nichols, Carol Susan. QC173.454.N53 1995, (v1)
Nichols, Geraldine Cleary. PQ6615.E57.Z86, (v3)
Nichols, Kenneth. F499.A3 N52, (v4)
Nichols, Marie Hochmuth. PN175.N5, (v3)
Nichols, Mary P. JC71.A7.N49 1992, (v7)
  PN1998.3.A45.N53 1998, (v3)
Nichols, Michael P. BF323.L5.N53 1995, (v2)
Nichols, Robert. DS392.2.P47 N53 2001, (v5)
Nichols, Roger L. E77.N554 1998, (v4)
Nichols, Roger. ML410.R23 N53 1988, (v9)
Nichols, Roy F. JK2260.N5, (v7)
  JK2317. 1850, (v7)
Nichols, Thomas Low. E166.N625 1968, (v4)
Nichols, Thomas. UA770.N48 1993, (v10)
Nicholsen, Shierry Weber. B3199.A34.N53 1997, (v8)
Nicholson, Colin. PR448.C34.N53 1994, (v3)
Nicholson, Graeme. B380.N53 1999, (v8)
Nicholson, Kathleen Dukeley. ND497.T8.N5 1990, (v9)
Nicholson, Reynold Alleyne. PJ827.N5 1969, (v3)
  PJ7510.N5 1969, (v3)
Nicholson, Stuart. ML410.E44.N53 1999, (v9)
  ML420.H58.N53 1995, (v9)
Nickell, Louis G. SB128.N52, (v1)
Nickerson, Catherine Ross. PS374.D4.N532 1999, (v3)
Nickerson, Warren Sears. E78.N5.N53 1994, (v4)
Nicklaus, Jack. GV964.N5.A3, (v6)
  GV965.N494, (v6)
Nickson, R. Andrew. JS2061.2.N53 1995, (v7)
Nicol, Donald MacGillivray. DF547.I8.N53 1988, (v5)
  DF633.3.N53 1994, (v5)
Nicol, J. A. Colin. QL121.N5 1967a, (v1)
Nicola, Pier Carlo. HB135.N52 2000, (v6)
Nicolaides, Roy A. QA76.95.N53 1996, (v1)
Nicolay, Helen. E467.1.N5.N5 1971, (v4)
  F194.N64, (v4)
Nicole, Robert. DU870.N53 2001, (v5)
Nicolet, Claude. G86.N5313 1990, (v6)
Nicoll, Allardyce. PN1631.N4 1966, (v3)
  PR625.N5, (v3)
  PR658.M3.N5 1963, (v3)
  PR2976.N5, (v3)
  PR2983.N5 1973, (v3)
Nicolle, David. U810.N5 1988, (v10)
Nicolosi, Joseph. RC558.N52 1993, (v2)
Nicolosi, Lucille. RC423.N52 1996, (v2)
Nicolson, Colin. F137.B47 N53 2001, (v4)
Nicolson, Harold George. D644.N36 1965, (v5)

DC249.N5 1946, (v5)
Nicolson, Iain. QB43.2.N53 1999, (v1)
Nicolson, Marjorie Hope. PR545.S3.N5 1960, (v3)
  PR3588.N5, (v3)
Nicolson, Nigel. PR6037.A35.Z8, (v3)
Nie, Norman H. JK1764.N54 1996, (v7)
Niebel, Benjamin W. T60.7.N54 1982, (v1)
Niebuhr, Gary Warren. PN3448.D4.N54 1993, (v3)
Niebuhr, H. Richard. BJ1251.N52 1963, (v8)
  BL221.N52, (v8)
  BR85.N615 1996, (v8)
  BT771.2.N54 1989, (v8)
Niebuhr, Reinhold. BJ1251.N5, (v8)
  BR123.N53, (v8)
  BT701.N5213 1996, (v8)
  D16.9.N5, (v5)
  E169.1.N67, (v4)
  E175.9.N5, (v4)
  E744.N53, (v4)
  JA38.N5, (v7)
Niebylski, Dianna C. PN1161.N54 1993, (v3)
Niehans, Jürg. HG221.N66, (v6)
  HG3821.N595 1984, (v6)
  HB75.N54 1990, (v6)
Nielsen, Alan. PS2434.M43.P336 1991, (v3)
Nielsen, Claus. QH367.5.N53 2001, (v1)
Nielsen, Jakob. QA76.76.H94.N54 1990, (v1)
  QA76.76.H94.N543 1995, (v1)
Nielsen, Kai. B945.N533.O6 1995, (v8)
  B945.R524.N54 1991, (v8)
  BJ1390.N465 1989, (v8)
Nielsen, Michael A. QA76.889.N54 2000, (v1)
Nielsen, Niels Christian. BL238.N54 1993, (v8)
Nielsen, Stevan L. RC489.R3.N54 2001, (v2)
Nielson, Jonathan M. UA26.A73.N54 1988, (v10)
Nieman, Donald G. E185.61.N5 1991, (v4)
Niemeyer, E. Victor. JL1215 1917.N53, (v7)
Niemeyer, Oscar. NA859.N5.P29, (v9)
  NA859.N5.P3, (v9)
Niemi, Richard G. JA88.U6.N54 1998, (v7)
Niemira, Michael P. HB3743.N53 1994, (v6)
Niepoth, E. William. GV181.4.N53 1983, (v6)
Niess, Frank. F1418.N4813 1990, (v4)
Niethammer, Carolyn J. E99.N3 W385 2001, (v4)
Nietzsche, Friedrich Wilhelm. B187.5.N5413 2001, (v8)
  B188.N513, (v8)
  B3312.E52.K3, (v8)
  B3312.E52.W67, (v8)
  B3313.A43 E5 1999, (v8)
  B3313.J43 E5 2002, (v8)
  B3313.M52.E5 1984, (v8)
Nieuwenhuys, R. QM455.N48 1988, (v1)
Nieuwenhuys, Robert. PT5911.N513 1982, (v3)
Nievo, Ippolito. PQ4720.N7 C613 1974, (v3)
Niewyk, Donald L. D804.3.N54 2000, (v5)
Niezen, Ronald. E78.C2.N55 2000, (v4)
Nigg, Walter. BX2432.N513, (v8)
Nightingale, Andrea Wilson. B395.N54 1996, (v8)
Nightingale, Benedict. PR736.N5 1982, (v3)
Nightingale, Florence. RT40.N5 1992, (v2)
Nightingale, Peggy. PR9272.9.N32.Z79 1987, (v3)
Nigrin, Albert. QA76.87.N5 1993, (v1)
Nigro, August J. D785.G3, (v5)
  PR408.T72.N54 2000, (v3)
Nijenhuis, Albert. QA164.N54 1978, (v1)
Nijhout, H. Frederik. QL495.N54 1994, (v1)
Nijman, Jan. D843.N52 1993, (v5)
Niklas, Karl J. QK793.N55 1992, (v1)
Nikolajeva, Maria. PN1009.A1.N56 2001, (v3)
  PN1009.5.T55.N55 2000, (v3)
Niles, John D. GR72.3.N56 1999, (v6)
  PR1585.N54 1983, (v3)
Nill, Kimball R. TP248.16.F54 1998, (v1)
Nilles, Jack M. HD2336.3.N55 1998, (v6)
Nilon, Charles H. Z1225.A1 N5, (v10)
Nilsen, Aileen Pace. PS438.N55 2000, (v3)
Nilsen, Don Lee Fred. Z1231.W8.N55 1992, (v10)
  Z2014.W57.N55 1997, (v10)
  Z2014.W57.N56 1998, (v10)
  Z2014.W57.N565 2000, (v10)

Z2039.W57.N55 1996, (v10)
Nilson, Herman. B2430.F724.N55 1998, (v8)
Nilsson, Annika. QC879.7.N55 1996, (v1)
  QC912.3.N55 1992, (v1)
Nilsson, Martin P. PA4037.N57 1968, (v3)
Nin, Anais. PS3527.I865.A6 1975, (v3)
  PS3527.I865 L3, (v3)
  PS3527.I865 S6, (v3)
  PS3527.I865.U6 1995, (v3)
  PS3527.I865 W5, (v3)
  PS3527.I865.Z49 1987, (v3)
  PS3527.I865.Z495 1998, (v3)
  PS3527.I865.Z5, (v3)
  PS3527.I865.Z53 1968, (v3)
Nininger, Harvey Harlow. QB755.N52, (v1)
Ninio, Jacques. BF491.N5613 2001, (v2)
Ninkovich, Frank A. DD257.25.N55 1988, (v5)
  E744.N544 2001, (v4)
  E744.N545 1999, (v4)
Nino, Carlos Santiago. JC423.N54 1996, (v7)
  JC585.N574 1991, (v7)
  KHA3003.N56 1996, (v7)
Ninomiya, Takamichi. PL782.E3.N48 1957b, (v3)
Nippel, Wilfried. HV8212.N56 1995, (v6)
Nipperdey, Thomas. DD203.N5513 1996, (v5)
Nirenberg, David. D164.N57 1996, (v5)
Nirk, Endel. PH631.N4813 1987, (v3)
Nisan, Mordechai. DS119.7.N6 1992, (v5)
Nisbet, Ada B. Z6465.U5 N58 2001, (v10)
Nisbet, E. G. GF75.N566 1991, (v6)
Nisbet, Robert A. HM19.N53, (v6)
  HM101.N574 1980, (v6)
Nishiguchi, Toshihiro. HD2385.J3.N57 1994, (v6)
Nishijima, K. QC174.45.N57, (v1)
Nissen, Axel. PS1833.N57 2000, (v3)
Nist, John A. PE1075.N5, (v3)
Nitze, Paul H. E748.N49.A3 1989, (v4)
Niven, John. E340.C15.N58 1988, (v4)
  E387.N58 1983, (v4)
  E415.9.C4.N58 1995, (v4)
  E467.1.W46.N58, (v4)
Niven, Penelope. PS3537.A618.Z785 1991, (v3)
Niven, William John. DD257.25.N58 2001, (v5)
Nivison, David S. BL1840.N56 1996, (v8)
Nivola, Pietro S. HF1455.N58 1993, (v6)
Nixon, H. C. F210.N5. 1971, (v4)
Nixon, Howard M. Z269.3.O75.N59 1992, (v10)
Nixon, Lucille M. PL889.U52.N5, (v3)
Nixon, Richard M. D445.N58 1990, (v5)
  E743.N58 1990, (v4)
  E835.N54, (v4)
  E838.5.N52 1988, (v4)
  E840.N57 1990, (v4)
  E856.A3.N59 1990, (v4)
  E856.A35 1990, (v4)
  E860.N57 1974d, (v4)
  E881.N59 1992, (v4)
  E885.N59 1994, (v4)
Nizer, Louis. KF220.N5, (v7)
  KF373.N56.A37, (v7)
Njala. PT7269.N4.E52, (v3)
Nkosi, Lewis. PL8010.N55, (v3)
Noailles, Anna Elisabeth de Brancovan.
  PQ2627.O17.A6 1976, (v3)
Noakes, Jeremy. DD256.5.N59 1975, (v5)
Nobel, Park S. QK495.A26.N63 1988, (v1)
Noble, Allen George. NA703.N6 1984, (v9)
  NA8230.N63 1995, (v9)
Noble, Bruce J. QP303.N55 1996, (v1)
Noble, Charles. HV95.N53 1997, (v6)
Noble, Colin. LC1390.N63 2000, (v7)
Noble, David F. BR115.T42.N63 1997, (v8)
Noble, Dennis L. UA26.C58.N63 1990, (v10)
  VK1023.N63 1997, (v10)
  VK1323.N63 1994, (v10)
Noble, Gregory W. HC460.5.N63 1998, (v6)
Noble, Stuart Grayson. LA205.N6 1970, (v7)
Noble, William. GN281.4.N63 1996, (v6)
Noble, William. Z658.U5.N6 1990, (v10)
Nobles, Gregory H. F72.H3 N63 1983, (v4)
Nobles, Melissa. HT1523.N63 2000, (v6)

Noblit, George W. LC311.N56 1996, (v7)
Nochimson, Martha. PN1992.8.S4.N63 1992, (v3)
  PN1998.3.L96.N63 1997, (v3)
Nochlin, Linda. N72.F45.N64 1988, (v9)
  N72.S6.N63 1989, (v9)
  N6537.F735, (v9)
  ND1460.W65.N63 1999, (v9)
Noddings, Nel. BJ1401.N63 1989, (v8)
  BJ1475.N62 1984, (v8)
Nodelman, Perry. Z1033.P52.N63 1988, (v10)
Noe, Randolph. Z1210.S55 N64 2001, (v10)
Noegel, Scott B. BM645.P67 N64 2002, (v8)
Noel, John Vavasour. V23.N63, (v10)
Noelle, Christine. DS363.N64 1997, (v5)
Noffsinger, James Philip. Z6207.E8.N64 1997, (v10)
Nofsinger, Mary M. Z7164.C5.N66 1990, (v10)
Nogales, Patti D. B840.N64 1999, (v8)
Noggle, Anne. D792.S65.N64 1994, (v5)
Noggle, Burl. E785.N6 1962, (v4)
Noguchi, Yone. PR9515.9.N64.A6 1990, (v3)
Noice, Tony. PN2058.N65 1997, (v3)
Nokes, David. PR3474.N64 1995, (v3)
  PR4036.N65 1997, (v3)
Nolan, Alan T. E467.1.L4.N66 1991, (v4)
Nolan, Barbara. PR1896.N64 1992, (v3)
Nolan, Cathal J. JZ1160.N65 2002, (v7)
Nolan, Christopher W. Z711.N65 1999, (v10)
Nolan, Dick. E467.1.B87.N65 1991, (v4)
Nolan, Emer. PR6019.O9.Z755 1995, (v3)
Nolan, Frederick W. F786.N62 1998, (v4)
  ML423.H32.N6 1994, (v9)
Nolan, James F. LB1777.2.N64 2000, (v7)
Nolan, James L. JA75.7.N65 1998, (v7)
  KF3890.N65 2001, (v7)
Nolan, James. PS3242.A34.N64 1994, (v3)
Nolan, Janne E. UA23.N65 1989, (v10)
Nolan, Mary Lee. BX2320.5.E85.N65 1989, (v8)
Nolan, Peter. HC427.92.N64 2001, (v6)
  HD1492.C5.N65 1988, (v6)
Nolan, Tom. PS3525.I486.Z79 1999, (v3)
Noland, Carrie. PQ433.N65 1999, (v3)
Noland, Marcus. HC467.N658 2000, (v6)
Nolan-Haley, Jacqueline M. KF9084.Z9 N65 1992,
  (v7)
Nold, Robert. SB413.P37.N65 1999, (v1)
Nolen, Claude H. E185.6.N83 2001, (v4)
Nolen, William A. RD27.35.N64.A3 1990, (v2)
  RD598.N512 1976, (v2)
Nolen-Hoeksema, Susan. RC537.N65 1990, (v2)
Noll, A. Michael. TK5101.N782 2001, (v1)
Noll, Mark A. BV3773.N65 2001, (v8)
Noll, Richard. BF371.N55 1994, (v2)
  RC514.N63 2000, (v2)
Nollen, Scott Allen. PN2287.K25.N6 1991, (v3)
Nolutshungu, Sam C. DT546.48.N65 1996, (v5)
Noon, Patrick J. ND497.B63.A4 1991, (v9)
Noon, Patrick. Z7914.I5.N66 1988, (v10)
Noon, Randall. TA219.F67, (v1)
Noonan, Harold W. B3245.F24.N66 2001, (v8)
  BD450.N635 1989, (v8)
Noonan, John Thomas. BR516.N59 1998, (v8)
  E446.N63, (v4)
  HQ766.3.N6, (v6)
Noonan, Melvin A. RK51.5.N66 1999, (v2)
Nooteboom, Cees. PT5881.24.O55.R613 1983, (v3)
Norall, Frank. F598.V44.N67 1988, (v4)
Norbrook, David. PR545.H5.N67 1999, (v3)
Norbye, Jan P. TL227.N67 1975, (v1)
Nord, Deborah Epstein. PR878.W6.N67 1995, (v3)
Nord, Philip G. DC340.N67 1995, (v5)
Nord, Warren A. LC111.N67 1995, (v7)
Nordahl, Per. F548.9.S23.N67 1994, (v4)
Nordby, Judith. Z3121.N674 1993, (v10)
Nordell, John R. DS553.3.D5.N67 1995, (v5)
Norden, Deborah L. F2849.2.N67 1996, (v4)
Norden, Martin F. PN1995.9.H34.N67 1994, (v3)
Nordenfalk, Carl Adam Johan. ND2940.N67, (v9)
Nordhaus, William D. QC981.8.C5.N66 1994, (v1)
Nordhoff, Charles. PS3527.O437 B6, (v3)
  PS3527.O437 M8 1932, (v3)
  PS3527.O437 P5, (v3)

Nordin, Dennis S. E748.M63.N67 1997, (v4)
Nordland, Gerald. ND237.D465.N67 1987, (v9)
Nordlinger, Eric A. E840.N65 1995, (v4)
Nordlinger, Eric A. JF1820.N67, (v7)
Nordquist, Joan. Z1209.2.U5 N67 1998, (v10)
  Z1361.O7 N67 1996, (v10)
  Z5814.M86 1992, (v10)
  Z5861.N67 1991, (v10)
  Z6683.G46 N67 1999, (v10)
  Z6683.G74 N67 1990, (v10)
  Z7963.F44 N66 1996, (v10)
  Z7964.U49 N67 1995, (v10)
Nordstrom, Byron J. DL46.N7 2000, (v5)
Nordstrom, Karl F. HT391.N58 2000, (v6)
Norgate, Kate. DA205.N838 1969b, (v5)
Norgren, Jill. KF4755.N67 1988, (v7)
Norich, Anita. PJ5129.S5.Z79 1991, (v3)
Noriega, Chon A. PN1995.9.M49.N69 2000, (v3)
Norland, Howard B. PR646.N67 1995, (v3)
Norling, Bernard. D802.P52.L8965 1999, (v5)
Norman, Albert. D770.N6, (v5)
Norman, Donald A. HC79.H53.N67 1998, (v6)
  TS171.4.N67 1988, (v1)
Norman, Edward R. BR744.N67, (v8)
Norman, Geraldine. N3350.N67 1998, (v9)
  ND190.N57 1977b, (v9)
Norman, Jerry. PL1075.N67 1988, (v3)
Norman, Larry F. PQ1860.N67 1999, (v3)
Norman, R. O. C. QD262.N6 1978, (v1)
Norman, Richard. B809.7.N67 1980, (v8)
Norman, Sylva. PR5438.N6, (v3)
Normano, J. F. HC165.N62 1973, (v6)
Norrander, Barbara. JK526. 1988I, (v7)
Norrgard, Lee E. HV6695.N67 1998, (v6)
Norrie, Kenneth McK. K2000.N67 1991, (v7)
Norris, Christopher. B809.3.N67 1994, (v8)
  B831.2.N66 1993, (v8)
  B831.2.N68 1992, (v8)
  PN98.D43.N6 1982, (v3)
Norris, David A. DR24.5.N67 1999, (v5)
Norris, Frank. PS2471.A1931, (v3)
  PS2471.H35, (v3)
  PS2472.M35, (v3)
  PS2472.M6 1898, (v3)
  PS2472.O3, (v3)
  PS2472.P5 1956, (v3)
  PS2472.V3 1914, (v3)
  PS2473.A45 1956, (v3)
Norris, Geoffrey. ML410.R12.N67 1994, (v9)
Norris, H. T. DR23.N67 1993, (v5)
Norris, J. R. QA274.7.N67 1997, (v1)
Norris, James D. HF5813.U6.N67 1990, (v6)
Norris, Kathleen Thompson. PS3527.O5 M6, (v3)
Norris, Margot. PN56.W3.N67 2000, (v3)
Norris, Nigel. LB2822.75.N67 1990, (v7)
Norris, Pamela. BS580.E85.N67 1999, (v8)
Norris, Pippa. JA85.N67 2000, (v7)
  JN558.N67 1995, (v7)
Norris, Robert M. QE89.N67 1990, (v1)
Norstog, Knut. QK494.N67 1997, (v1)
North, Douglass Cecil. HB99.5.N67 1990, (v6)
  HC103.N63 1968b, (v6)
  HC240.N66, (v6)
North, E. Lee. F247.A15 N68 1998, (v4)
North, John David. DA142.N67 1997, (v5)
North, Michael. PR478.M6.N67 1999, (v3)
North, Percy. ND237.G82.N67 1995, (v9)
North, Robert Carver. DS740.5.R8.N6 1963, (v5)
North, Stephen M. PE1404.N67 1987, (v3)
North, Wheeler J. QK569.L2N67 1971, (v1)
Northam, John. PT8897.D7.N6 1971, (v3)
Northcott, D. G. QA611.N65, (v1)
Northcutt, Wayne. DC33.7.N63 1996, (v5)
  DC423.N67 1992, (v5)
Northen, Helen. HV31.N67, (v6)
Northern, Jerry L. RF291.5.C45N67 2001, (v2)
Northrop, F. S. C. BC71.N6, (v8)
  CB19.N59 1971, (v5)
  CB19.N6, (v5)
Northrop, Robert B. TK7870.N66 1997, (v1)
Northrup, Christiane. RG186.N67 2001, (v2)

Northrup, David. HD8811.Z8.K586 1988, (v6)
Northup, George Tyler. PQ6037.N6 1960, (v3)
Northup, Solomon. E444.N87 1968, (v4)
Norton, Anne. JA74.5.N67 1988, (v7)
  JA84.U5.N58 1993, (v7)
Norton, Arthur P. QB65.N7 1989, (v1)
Norton, Bryan G. HC110.E5.N67 1991, (v6)
Norton, David L. BJ1431.N67 1996, (v8)
  BJ1470.N68, (v8)
  JA79.N67 1991, (v7)
Norton, David. BS585.N67 2000, (v8)
Norton, Hugh Stanton. HC106.3.N59 1985, (v6)
Norton, M. P. TA365.N67 1989, (v1)
Norton, Mary Beth. HQ1075.5.U6.N67 1996, (v6)
  HQ1418.N67 1996, (v6)
Norton, Robert Edward. BJ311.N67 1995, (v8)
Norton, Robert L. TJ230.N63 1999, (v1)
Norway, Nevil Shute. PR6027.O54 O5, (v3)
  PR6027.O54 R6, (v3)
Norwich, John Julius. DF553.N67 1989, (v5)
  PR2982.N67 2000, (v3)
Norwich, Kenneth H. BF311.N68 1993, (v2)
Noss, Luther. ML410.H685 N7 1989, (v9)
Noss, Reed F. QH76.N67 1994, (v1)
Nostrand, Richard L. F805.M5.N67 1992, (v4)
Nosworthy, Brent. U39.N67 1990, (v10)
Notess, Greg R. ZA5075.N68 1998, (v10)
Notter, Harley. E767.N67 1965, (v4)
Noun, Louise R. JK1911.I8 N6, (v7)
Novack, Cynthia Jean. GV1781.2.N68 1990, (v6)
Novak, Arne. PG5001.N6313, (v3)
Novak, Barbara. ND210.N68 1969, (v9)
  ND1351.5.N68, (v9)
Novak, David. BM520.6.N69 1998, (v8)
Novak, Joseph Donald. LB1051.N68, (v7)
Novak, Maximillian E. PR3406.N68 2001, (v3)
  PR3408.R45.N6, (v3)
Novak, Michael. B851.N6, (v8)
  HB72.N684 2001, (v6)
Novak, William J. KF366.N68 1996, (v7)
Novalis. PT2291.A1 1923, (v3)
  PT2291.A1 1977, (v3)
  PT2291.H6.E55 1984, (v3)
Novarr, David. CT21.N68 1986, (v5)
Nove, Alec. HC335.N68 1992, (v6)
Novick, Peter. D804.45.U55.N68 1999, (v5)
Novick, Sheldon M. KF8745.H6.N69 1989, (v7)
Novitz, David. PN49.N64 1987, (v3)
Novotny, Vladimir. TD420.N69 1994, (v1)
Nowak, John E. KF4550.N6 2000, (v7)
Nowak, Ronald M. QL703.W222 1999, (v1)
Nowell, Charles E. G286.M2.N6, (v6)
Nowell, Gregory P. HD9560.5.N67 1994, (v6)
Nowlan, Kevin B. DA959.1.N68 1970, (v5)
Nowlan, Robert A. PN1994.9.N69 1994, (v3)
  PN1995.9.C36.N696 1993, (v3)
  PN1998.N784 2001, (v3)
Nowotny, Helga. QC611.98.H54.N69 1997, (v1)
Noyes, Alfred. PR6027.O8.W3 1971, (v3)
  PR6027.O8.Z5, (v3)
  PR 6027.O8 1950, (v3)
Noyes, George Rapall. PG3245.N6 1961, (v3)
Nozick, Robert. B945.N683 S63 1997, (v8)
  BC177.N69 1993, (v8)
  JC571.N68, (v7)
Ntantala, Phyllis. DT1949.N75.A3 1993, (v5)
Ntoumanis, Nikos. GV558.N86 2001, (v6)
Nucci, Larry P. LC268.N83 2001, (v7)
Nuechterlein, Donald Edwin. E881.N84 2001, (v4)
Nugent, Elizabeth M. PR1293.N8, (v3)
Nugent, Robert. PQ2609.L75.Z78, (v3)
Nugent, Walter T. K. F591.N84 1999, (v4)
Nuland, Sherwin B. QP38.N894 1997, (v1)
  R133.N77 2000, (v2)
  R134.N85 1988, (v2)
Nunez, Benjamin. DT352.4.N86 1995, (v5)
Nunez, Benjamin. F1408.3.N86, (v4)
Nunley, John W. GN419.5.N85 1999, (v6)
Nunn, Frederick M. F1414.2.N83 1992, (v4)
  UA612.N86 1983, (v10)
Nunn, William Curtis. F391.N965, (v4)

Nunney, M.J. (Malcolm James). TL240.N8597 1998, **(v1)**

Nuovo, Gerard J. RB43.8.P64N86 1997, **(v2)**

Nurmi, Raimo. HD31.N86 1997, **(v6)**

Nursey-Bray, Paul F. Z7164.A52.N87 1992, **(v10)**

Nuseibeh, Hazem Zaki. DS38.N8, **(v5)**

Nussbaum, Felicity. PR449.W65.N87 1984, **(v3)**
  PR756.W65.N87 1995, **(v3)**

Nussbaum, Martha Craven. BJ46.N87 1990, **(v8)**
  BJ192.N87 2001, **(v8)**
  HQ1240.N87 2000, **(v6)**
  LC1011.N87 1997, **(v7)**
  PN51.N78 1995, **(v3)**

Nute, Grace Lee. F552.N8, **(v4)**

Nute, Kevin. NA737.W7.N88 1993, **(v9)**

Nutini, Hugo G. F1221.N3.N87 1993, **(v4)**
  F1221.N3.N895 1988, **(v4)**
  HT653.M6.N88 1995, **(v6)**

Nutt, Paul C. HD30.23.N883 2002, **(v6)**

Nuttall, A. D. PN1892.N88 1996, **(v3)**
  PR408.G56.N88 1998, **(v3)**
  PR2834.N88 1989, **(v3)**

Nwaubani, Ebere. DT476.2.N88 2001, **(v5)**

Nwomonoh, Jonathan. LC191.8.A4.N86 1998, **(v7)**

Nyanatiloka. BQ130.N9 1983, **(v8)**

Nybakken, James Willard. QH91.N9 2001, **(v1)**

Nyberg, Amy Kiste. PN6725.N953 1998, **(v3)**

Nye, Andrea. B1873.N93 1999, **(v8)**

Nye, Andrea. BC57.N94 1990, **(v8)**
  HQ1190.N93 1995, **(v6)**

Nye, David E. HD9685.U5.N94 1990, **(v6)**
  T14.5.N93 1994, **(v1)**

Nye, Edgar Wilson. PS2482.A3 1971, **(v3)**

Nye, Joseph S. E840.N94 1990, **(v4)**

Nye, Robert A. BJ1533.H8.N84 1993, **(v8)**

Nye, Roger H. UB210.N94 1986, **(v10)**

Nye, Russel Blaine. E175.5.B186 1972, **(v4)**

Nye, Wilbur Sturtevant. F694.N95, **(v4)**

Nygren, Carolyn. KF273.N97 1997, **(v7)**

Nylan, Michael. PL2462.Z6N95 2001, **(v3)**

Nyland, Ralph D. SD373.N96 1996, **(v1)**

Nylander, Jane C. F8.N95 1993, **(v4)**

Nyquist, Richard A. QC457.N927 1997, **(v1)**
  QD96.I5.N96 2001, **(v1)**

Nyrop, Richard F. DR417.R54 1980, **(v5)**

Nyvall, Robert F. SB731.N94 1999, **(v1)**

Ó Broin, León. DA954.O24 1971b, **(v5)**
  DA962.O27 1971, **(v5)**

O Ciosain, Niall. DA947.3.O29 1997, **(v5)**

O Drisceoil, Donal. D799.I73.O37 1996, **(v5)**

O Grada, Cormac. DA950.7.O366 1999, **(v5)**
  HC260.5.O435 1994, **(v6)**

O Suilleabhain, Sean. PB1383.O7 1966, **(v3)**

O Tuathail, Gearoid. JC319.O29 1996, **(v7)**

Oakeley, Hilda Diana. BJ161.A2.O3 1969, **(v8)**

Oakes, David A. PS374.G68.O18 2000, **(v3)**

Oakes, Elizabeth H. Q141.O25 2001, **(v1)**

Oakes, Guy. UA927.O23 1994, **(v10)**

Oakes, James. E441.O19 1990, **(v4)**

Oakes, Jeannie. LB3061.O22 1985, **(v7)**

Oakes, Len. BL633.O24 1997, **(v8)**

Oakes, Maud. F1465.2.M3.O3 1969, **(v4)**

Oakeshott, Michael Joseph. BD181.O3, **(v8)**
  BJ1581.2.O2, **(v8)**
  BL65.P7.O34 1993, **(v8)**
  JA71.O23 1996, **(v7)**
  JA79.O18 1993, **(v7)**
  LB41.O177 1989, **(v7)**

Oakeshott, R. Ewart. U800.O3, **(v10)**

Oakley, Ann. HQ1154.O18 1981, **(v6)**
  HQ1597.O15 1975, **(v6)**

Oakley, Justin. BJ1473.O24 1991, **(v8)**

Oakley, Kenneth Page. CC75.O15, **(v5)**

Oates, John F. QL84.6.A358.O28 1999, **(v1)**

Oates, Joyce Carol. GV1133.O2 1987, **(v6)**
  PS3565.A8.A75 1979, **(v3)**
  PS3565.A8.C5, **(v3)**
  PS3565.A8.C7, **(v3)**
  PS3565.A8.E9, **(v3)**
  PS3565.A8.G3 1967, **(v3)**
  PS3565.A8.H8, **(v3)**

PS3565.A8.N5X, **(v3)**
  PS3565.A8.S6 1978, **(v3)**
  PS3565.A8.T5, **(v3)**
  PS3565.A8.T7, **(v3)**
  PS3565.A8.W5, **(v3)**

Oates, Stephen B. E185.97.K5.O18 1982, **(v4)**
  E451.O17 1984, **(v4)**
  E457.O16 1984, **(v4)**
  E457.O17 1994, **(v4)**
  E621.O24 1994, **(v4)**

Oates, Wallace E. HJ192.O18, **(v6)**

Oates, Whitney Jennings. B491.W6.O2, **(v8)**

Obaldia, Claire de. PN4500.D35 1995, **(v3)**

O'Ballance, Edgar. DS59.K86.O23 1996, **(v5)**
  DS87.5.O14 1998, **(v5)**
  DS119.75.O22 1998, **(v5)**
  DS318.825.O23 1997, **(v5)**
  UA703.L5.O2, **(v10)**

Ober, Josiah. DF275.O33 1998, **(v5)**
  JC75.D36.O24 1996, **(v7)**

Oberai, A. S. HB884.O253 1993, **(v6)**

Oberdiek, Hans. BJ1431.O24 2001, **(v8)**

Oberdorfer, Don. DS922.2.O25 1997, **(v5)**

Oberg, James E. TL799.M3.O23 1982, **(v1)**

Oberhaus, Dorothy Huff. PS1541.Z5.O24 1994, **(v3)**

Oberhettinger, Fritz. QA404.O213 1990, **(v1)**

Oberhuber, Konrad. ND553.P8.O24 1988, **(v9)**

Oberman, Heiko Augustinus. BM535.O2413 1984, **(v8)**
  BR325.O2713 1989, **(v8)**

Oberschall, Anthony. HN17.5.O24 1992, **(v6)**

Obeyesekere, Gananath. BQ4485.O24 2002, **(v8)**
  DU626.O28 1992, **(v5)**

Obeyesekere, Ranjini. PN2960.S72.O23 1999, **(v3)**

Oblinger, Diana. LC1085.2.O35 1998, **(v7)**

Obojski, Robert. GV875.A1 O26, **(v6)**

Obolensky, Dimitri. DF552.O25 1971b, **(v5)**
  PG3230.5.O2, **(v3)**
  PG3237.E5.O2 1976, **(v3)**

O'Brian, Patrick. QH31.B19.O27 1993, **(v1)**

O'Brien, Anthony. PR9359.6.O27 2001, **(v3)**

O'Brien, D. P. HB103.J66.O27 1993, **(v6)**

O'Brien, David J. E184.C3.O2, **(v4)**

O'Brien, David M. KNX2472.O27 1996, **(v7)**

O'Brien, Dennis. LA228.O37 1998, **(v7)**

O'Brien, Eugene J. TG325.6.O27 1999, **(v1)**

O'Brien, Flann. PR6029.N56 B413 1974, **(v3)**
  PR6029.N56.F55 1978, **(v3)**

O'Brien, Geoffrey. PN1995.O17 1993, **(v3)**

O'Brien, George. PR6056.R5.Z84 1990, **(v3)**
  Z8317.15.O27 1995, **(v3)**

O'Brien, Gerard. DA948.4.O25 1987, **(v5)**

O'Brien, Jean M. E78.M4.O27 1997, **(v4)**

O'Brien, John Maxwell. DF234.O27 1992, **(v5)**

O'Brien, John. CT275.O24 A3 2001, **(v5)**

O'Brien, Justin. PQ2613.I2.Z6568, **(v3)**

O'Brien, L. Stephen. RC552.P67.O27 1998, **(v2)**

O'Brien, Lawrence J. RA395.A3.O28 1999, **(v2)**

O'Brien, Mary Elizabeth. RT85.2.O37 2002, **(v2)**

O'Brien, Mary. HQ1206.O24, **(v6)**

O'Brien, Michael J. E76.45.F67.O37 1998, **(v4)**
  E78.M8.O37 1996, **(v4)**
  E78.M8.O38 1998, **(v4)**

O'Brien, Michael. E840.8.H287.O37 1995, **(v4)**

O'Brien, Nancy P. Z5811.B89 2000, **(v10)**

O'Brien, Pat. D627.G3.O3, **(v5)**

O'Brien, Patricia. HV9304.O145 2001, **(v6)**

O'Brien, Philip M. Z8491.5.O27 2000, **(v10)**

O'Brien, Ronald F. GV837.O17 2003, **(v6)**

O'Brien, Steven. E176.O27 1991, **(v4)**

O'Brien, Thomas F. HD2810.5.O18 1996, **(v6)**
  HG5160.5.A3.O27 1999, **(v6)**

O'Brien, Tim. PS3565.B75.G6 1978, **(v3)**
  PS3565.B75.T48 1990, **(v3)**

O'Brien, William Arctander. PT2291.Z5.O27 1995, **(v3)**

O'Cadiz, Maria Pilar. LC92.B8.O32 1998, **(v7)**

O'Callaghan, Joseph F. DP96.O25, **(v5)**

Ocampo, Victoria. PQ7797.O295.A613 1999, **(v3)**

O'Casey, Sean. PR6029.C33.A19 1949-52, **(v3)**
  PR6029.C33.A19 1954, **(v3)**

PR6029.C33.A6 1968, **(v3)**
  PR6029.C33.B4, **(v3)**

O'Cathaoir, Brendan. DA952.D55.O25 1990, **(v5)**

Ochoa, Carlos M. SB211.P8.O24 1990, **(v1)**

Ochoa, Enrique. HD9014.M62.O24 2000, **(v6)**

Ochoa, George. Q125.O24 1995, **(v1)**

Ochs, Stephen J. F379.N557.O25 2000, **(v4)**

Ochse, Orpha Caroline. ML624.O25 1994, **(v9)**

Ochshorn, Kathleen G. PS3563.A4.Z82 1990, **(v3)**

Ochsner, Jeffrey Karl. NA737.R5.A4 1982, **(v9)**

Ockendon, Hilary. QA929.O25 1995, **(v1)**

Ockershausen, Jane. F192.3.O26 2000, **(v4)**

O'Collins, Gerald. BR95.O25 1991, **(v8)**
  BT202.O313 1995, **(v8)**

Ocone, Lynn. SB457.O24 1990, **(v1)**

O'Connell, David. PQ2607.E834.Z795, **(v3)**

O'Connell, Joanna. PQ7297.C2596.Z76 1995, **(v3)**

O'Connell, Marvin Richard. D228.O26 1974, **(v5)**

O'Connell, Mary. PS3571.P4.Z8 1996, **(v3)**

O'Connell, Michael. PN2590.R35.O28 2000, **(v3)**
  PR2224.O36 1986, **(v3)**

O'Connell, P. J. PN1998.3.D73.O25 1992, **(v3)**

O'Connell, Robert J. B398.M4.O26 1997, **(v8)**

O'Connell, Robert L. U21.2.O28 1995, **(v10)**
  U27.O26 1989, **(v10)**
  VA50.O36 1991, **(v10)**

O'Connell, Shaun. PS255.N5.O36 1995, **(v3)**

O'Connor, Alice. HC110.P6.O33 2001, **(v6)**

O'Connor, Colin. DG28.O36 1993, **(v5)**

O'Connor, D. J. LB775.O33 1957, **(v7)**

O'Connor, David E. HB71.O26 2000, **(v6)**

O'Connor, David. BT102.O29 1998, **(v8)**

O'Connor, Edwin. PS3529.C6.L3, **(v3)**
  PS3565.C55.E3 1961, **(v3)**

O'Connor, Flannery. PS3529.C7625 1971, **(v3)**
  PS3565.C57.G6 1977, **(v3)**
  PS3565.C57.V54 1960, **(v3)**
  PS3565.C57.W5 1962b, **(v3)**
  PS3565.C57.Z48 1979, **(v3)**
  PS3565.C57 1988, **(v3)**

O'Connor, Francis V. N8838.O25, **(v9)**

O'Connor, Frank, [pseud.]. PR6029.D58 D6, **(v3)**
  PB1424.O39, **(v3)**
  PR6029.D58.A15 1981, **(v3)**

O'Connor, Garry. PR6029.C33.Z7823 1988, **(v3)**

O'Connor, Harvey. TN140.G8.O25, **(v1)**

O'Connor, Jack. SK40.O28, **(v1)**

O'Connor, Jacqueline. PS3545.I5365.Z795 1997, **(v3)**

O'Connor, Kevin J. RJ505.P6O26 2000, **(v2)**

O'Connor, Mallory McCane. E78.S65.O36 1995, **(v4)**

O'Connor, Philip F. PS3565.C64.S4, **(v3)**

O'Connor, Raymond Gish. D816.O24 1971, **(v5)**
  E182.O26 1994, **(v4)**

O'Connor, Richard. CT275.G6.O27, **(v5)**

O'Connor, T. P. CC79.5.A5.O36 2000, **(v5)**

O'Connor, Thomas Austin. PQ6317.M84.O26 1988, **(v3)**

O'Connor, Thomas H. BX1417.B6 O36 1998, **(v8)**
  F73.3.O26 2001, **(v4)**
  F73.44.O25 1997, **(v4)**
  F73.9.I6.O28 1995, **(v4)**

O'Connor, Timothy Edward. DK254.C57.O36 1988, **(v5)**

O'Connor, William Van. PN99.U52.O3, **(v3)**
  PR471.O3, **(v3)**

Oda, Makoto. PL858.D3.H5713 1990, **(v3)**

òDa¯ if, Rash¯id. PJ7820.A46F87 2000, **(v3)**

O'Day, Alan. DA957.O24 1998, **(v5)**

Odean, Kathleen. Z1037.O24 1998, **(v10)**
  Z1037.O25 1997, **(v10)**

Oded, Arye. DS63.2.A357.O34 1987, **(v5)**

O'Dell, Cary. PN1992.8.W65.O34 1997, **(v3)**

Odell, John S. HG3881.O27 1982, **(v6)**

Odell, Peter R. HC125.O33 1978, **(v6)**

O'Dell, S. Jack. B1649.R94 O34 2000, **(v8)**

O'Dell, Scott. PZ7.O237ls 1990, **(v3)**

O'Dell, T. H. QC754.2.M34.O32 1981, **(v1)**
  TK7878.4.O34 1991, **(v1)**

Odem, Mary E. HQ27.5.O34 1995, **(v6)**

Oden, Howard W. HD58.7.O324 1997, **(v6)**

Odenwald, Neil G. SB435.5.O34 1996, **(v1)**

Odenwald, Sten F. QB52.O34 1998, **(v1)**
Oderberg, David S. BD236.O27 1993, **(v8)**
  BJ1012.O34 2000, **(v8)**
  BJ1031.O34 2000, **(v8)**
Oderman, Stuart. PN2287.A68.O33 1994, **(v3)**
  PN2287.G55.O34 2000, **(v3)**
Odets, Clifford. PS3529.D46.B5 1949, **(v3)**
  PS3529.D46.C6, **(v3)**
  PS3529.D46.S5 1939, **(v3)**
  PS3529.D46.Z477 1988, **(v3)**
Odner, Knut. DL442.L3.O35 1992, **(v5)**
Odom, Keith C. PR6013.R416.Z78, **(v3)**
Odom, Richard B. RL71.O33 2000, **(v2)**
Odom, William E. D883.O36 1992, **(v5)**
  DK54.O36 1998, **(v5)**
O'Donnell, Brennan. PR5897.O36 1995, **(v3)**
O'Donnell, James Joseph. P96.T42.O36 1998, **(v3)**
O'Donnell, L. A. HD6508.5.O36 1997, **(v6)**
O'Donnell, Patrick K. D769.347.O36 2001, **(v5)**
O'Donnell, Patrick. PS374.P35.O36 2000, **(v3)**
O'Donnell, R. M. HB103.K47.O36 1989, **(v6)**
O'Donnell, Thomas J. PR6023.A937.Z83, **(v3)**
O'Donoghue, Michael. TS752.O3 1988, **(v1)**
O'Donohue, William T. BF199.O39 2001, **(v2)**
O'Donovan, Michael. PB1306.O3 1968, **(v3)**
  PR6029.D58 A6, **(v3)**
  PR6029.D58 M6, **(v3)**
  PR6029.D58 S4, **(v3)**
  PR6029.D58.Z47 1969, **(v3)**
  PR6029.D58.Z52, **(v3)**
O'Donovan, Michael. PR8876.O35, **(v3)**
O'Dowd, Michael J. RG51.O36 1994, **(v2)**
Odum, Eugene Pleasants. QH541.O312 1983, **(v1)**
Odum, Howard T. QA76.9.C65, **(v1)**
Oe, Kenzaburo. PL858.E14.P4 1969x, **(v3)**
  PL858.E14.T4, **(v3)**
Oehser, Paul Henry. Q11.S8.O4, **(v1)**
Oelschlaeger, Max. GF21.O34 1991, **(v6)**
Oertel, Robert. ND613.O3213, **(v9)**
O'Faolain, Julia. PR6065.F3.W6, **(v3)**
O'Faolain, Sean. PR888.H4.O3 1957, **(v3)**
  PR6029.F3 C6 1972, **(v3)**
  PR6029.F3 F5, **(v3)**
  PR6029.F3 F6 1976, **(v3)**
  PR6029.F3 I2 1961, **(v3)**
  PR6029.F3 N4, **(v3)**
  PR6029.F3 T3, **(v3)**
O'Farrell, Clare. B2430.F724.O43 1989, **(v8)**
O'Farrell, Mary Ann. PR868.B58.O34 1997, **(v3)**
O'Farrell, Patrick James. DA938.O37 1971, **(v5)**
  DA950.O37, **(v5)**
Ofcansky, Thomas P. DT444.O33 1997, **(v5)**
Offe, Claus. HN380.7.A8.O38 1997, **(v6)**
  JC11.O33 1996, **(v7)**
Offer, Avner. D635.O38 1989, **(v5)**
Officer, Charles B. G608.O33 2001, **(v6)**
  QB631.O34 1993, **(v1)**
  QE721.2.E97.O36 1996, **(v1)**
Officer, James E. F820.S75.O33 1987, **(v4)**
Officer, Lawrence H. HG297.O35 1996, **(v6)**
Offner, John L. E723.O44 1992, **(v4)**
Offord, Derek. PG2361.O37 1996, **(v3)**
Offutt, William M. KF4869.Q83.O37 1995, **(v7)**
O'Flaherty, Liam. PR6029.F5 A16 1956, **(v3)**
  PR6029.F5 I5, **(v3)**
O'Flaherty, Wendy Doniger. BJ1401.O35, **(v8)**
Ofrat, Gideon. N7277.O378 1998, **(v9)**
Ofstad, Harald. BJ1461.O35, **(v8)**
O'Gara, Gordon Carpenter. E182.O34 1969, **(v4)**
Ogata, Katsuhiko. TJ213.O28 2001, **(v1)**
Ogata, Sadako N. DS783.7.O4 1984, **(v5)**
Ogbaa, Kalu. PR9387.9.A3.T5365 1999, **(v3)**
  PR9387.9.A3.Z846 1992, **(v3)**
Ogbomo, Onaiwu W. DT515.45.O88.O33 1997, **(v5)**
Ogborn, Miles. DA682.O33 1998, **(v5)**
Ogden, August Raymond. E743.5.O34 1984, **(v4)**
Ogden, C. K. BH201.O5 1948, **(v8)**
Ogden, Henry Vining Seton. BH301.L3.O3, **(v8)**
Ogden, Tom. GV1815.O33 1993, **(v6)**
Ogede, Ode. PL8274.5.O35 1997, **(v3)**
Ogg, David. D246.O4 1971, **(v5)**

DA445.O5 1979, **(v5)**
Ogg, Frederic Austin. E173.C56 vol. 19, **(v4)**
  E178.5.P2 vol.8, **(v4)**
Ogilvie, Marilyn Bailey. Q141.O34 1986, **(v1)**
  Z7963.S3.O35 1996, **(v10)**
Ogilvy, C. Stanley. QA95.O34 1972, **(v1)**
Ogilvy, J. D. A. PR1585.O37 1983, **(v3)**
Oglethorpe, James Edward. F289.O3625 1994, **(v4)**
Ogorkiewicz, Richard M. UG446.5.O5 1960, **(v10)**
O'Gorman, Frank. DA480.O38 1997, **(v5)**
O'Gorman, James F. NA710.O35 1991, **(v9)**
  NA737.R5.O36 1987, **(v9)**
O'Grady, John P. PS163.O18 1993, **(v3)**
O'Grady, P. J. TS155.8.O35 1988, **(v1)**
Ogren, Kathy J. ML3508.O37 1989, **(v9)**
Ogrizek, Dore. DL10.O373, **(v5)**
Ogude, James. PR9381.9.N45.Z82 1999, **(v3)**
òHab̄ ib̄ i, Im̄ il. PJ7828.B53W313 1982, **(v3)**
Ohadike, Don C. DT474.6.I35.O33 1994, **(v5)**
  DT515.7.O36 1991, **(v5)**
O'Halloran, Sharyn. HF1455.O37 1994, **(v6)**
O'Halpin, Eunan. DA964.A2.O39 1999, **(v5)**
O'Hanlon, John F. TJ940.O37 1989, **(v1)**
òHaqq̄ ī, Yaòhyá. PJ7827.Q7D513 1999, **(v3)**
O'Hara, Frank Hurburt. PN1655.O5, **(v3)**
O'Hara, Frank. PS3529.H28.A6 1977, **(v3)**
O'Hara, Frederick M. HC106.8.O47 2000, **(v6)**
O'Hara, Georgina. GT507.O53 1998, **(v6)**
O'Hara, John. PS3529.H29 A6, **(v3)**
  PS3529.H29 A6 1956, **(v3)**
  PS3529.H29 A8, **(v3)**
  PS3529.H29 B5, **(v3)**
  PS3529.H29 B8 1935, **(v3)**
  PS3529.H29 C3, **(v3)**
  PS3529.H29.E4, **(v3)**
  PS3529.H29 E8, **(v3)**
  PS3529.H29 F28, **(v3)**
  PS3529.H29 F7, **(v3)**
  PS3529.H29 G6, **(v3)**
  PS3529.H29 H3, **(v3)**
  PS3529.H29 O9, **(v3)**
  PS3529.H29 P35, **(v3)**
  PS3529.H29 R3 1949, **(v3)**
  PS3529.H29 S4, **(v3)**
  PS3529.H29 T4, **(v3)**
  PS3529.H29.Z48 1978, **(v3)**
O'Hara, Mary L. BD450.O376 1997, **(v8)**
O'Hara, Patrick D. HD30.28.O35 1995, **(v6)**
O'Hear, Ann. HT1394.I43.O34 1997, **(v6)**
O'Hear, Anthony. BD418.3.O34 1997, **(v8)**
O'Heffernan, Patrick. E872.O37 1991, **(v4)**
Ohl, John Kennedy. D810.L64.O36 1994, **(v5)**
Ohles, Frederik. LA2311.O55 1997, **(v7)**
Ohlin, Bertil Gotthard. HF81.O5 1967, **(v6)**
Ohly, Friedrich. PN56.G8.O3713 1992, **(v3)**
Ohmae, Kenichi, 1943-. HF1418.7.O45 1995, **(v6)**
Ohnuki-Tierney, Emiko. DS830.O33 1993, **(v5)**
Ohrelius, Bengt. VA595.V3.O33 1963, **(v10)**
Ohrnberger, D. QK495.G74.O355 1999, **(v1)**
òHusayn, òT̄ ah̄ a. PJ7864.A35D39 1997, **(v3)**
  PJ7864.A35D813, **(v3)**
Oi, Jean Chun. HC427.92.O35 1999, **(v6)**
Oinas, Felix J. PH610.O35 1979, **(v3)**
Ojaide, Tanure. PL8010.4.O36 1996, **(v3)**
Okamoto, Shumpei. DS517.13.O37, **(v5)**
O'Kane, Bernard. NA1486.K5.O43 1987, **(v9)**
O'Kane, Rosemary H. T. JC491.O44 1991, **(v7)**
Okbazghi Yohannes. DT395.3.O38 1991, **(v5)**
Oke, T. R. QC981.7.M5.O34 1978, **(v1)**
O'Keefe, Bernard J. U264.O38 1983, **(v10)**
O'Keefe, Deborah. PS374.G55.O44 2000, **(v3)**
O'Keefe, Mark. BJ1249.O37 1995, **(v8)**
O'Keefe, Richard R. PS1642.A62.O38 1995, **(v3)**
O'Keeffe, John. PR3605.O3.A77 1977, **(v3)**
O'Kelly, Eve. ML990.R4.O5 1990, **(v9)**
O'Kelly, Michael J. GN806.5.O38 1989, **(v6)**
Okenfuss, Max J. LA831.5.O39 1995, **(v7)**
Okihiro, Gary Y. D753.8.O38 1999, **(v5)**
  D769.8.A6.O36 1996, **(v5)**
  DU624.7.J3.O38 1991, **(v5)**
  E175.9.O38 2001, **(v4)**

E184.O6.O38 1994, **(v4)**
Okimoto, Daniel I. HC465.H53.O35 1989, **(v6)**
Okin, Susan Moller. HQ1206.O38 1992, **(v6)**
  HQ1426.O85 1989, **(v6)**
Okonski, Walter. D765.O56 1997, **(v5)**
Okpewho, Isidore. GR350.O37 1992, **(v6)**
  GR351.32.I34.O56 1998, **(v6)**
Okumiya, Masatake. D792.J3.O38, **(v5)**
Okun, Arthur M. HB90.O38 1975, **(v6)**
  HB172.5.O38, **(v6)**
  HC106.6.O46, **(v6)**
  HG538.O5, **(v6)**
Olafson, Frederick A. BD418.3.O42 1995, **(v8)**
Olasky, Marvin N. E195.O43 1995, **(v4)**
  PN4801.O4 1991, **(v3)**
Olcen, Mehmet Arif. D627.R8.O43 1995, **(v5)**
Olcott, Martha Brill. DK859.5.O43 1996, **(v5)**
  DK908.6 .O43 1995, **(v5)**
Old, R. W. QH442.O42 1994, **(v1)**
Oldenbourg, Zoe. PQ2629.L4.P5, **(v3)**
Oldenburg, S. S. DK262.O413, **(v5)**
Oldenburg, Veena Talwar. DS486.L9.O42 1984, **(v5)**
Oldenski, Thomas. LC196.5.U6.O53 1997, **(v7)**
Olderr, Steven. CB475.O37 1992, **(v5)**
  PR830.D4.O43 1987, **(v3)**
Oldfather, Penny. LB1060.O43 1999, **(v7)**
Oldfield, Adrian. JC329.5.O43 1990, **(v7)**
Oldfield, Duane Murray. BR526.O57 1996, **(v8)**
Oldfield, Homer R. QA76.17.O45 1996, **(v1)**
Oldham, Gabriella. PN2287.K4.O48 1996, **(v3)**
Oldham, K. Michael. HF5616.E8.O43 1987, **(v6)**
Oldroyd, George. ML448.O4 1986, **(v9)**
Olds, Sally B. RG951.O43 2000, **(v2)**
Olds, Sarah E. F847.W3.O47, **(v4)**
Oldstone-Moore, Jennifer. BL1853.O44 2002, **(v8)**
O'Leary, Brendan. DA990.U46.O52 1993, **(v5)**
O'Leary, Cecilia Elizabeth. E661.O46 1999, **(v4)**
O'Leary, Daniel Florencio. F2235.O4, **(v4)**
O'Leary, De Lacy. B741.O4 1939, **(v8)**
  DS38.O38, **(v5)**
O'Leary, Rosemary. KF3775.O45 1993, **(v7)**
Oleksiw, Susan. PR888.D4.O4 1988, **(v3)**
Olere, David. D805.5.A96.O54 1998, **(v5)**
Olesen, Asta. DS361.O43 1995, **(v5)**
Olesha, IUrii Karlovich. PG3476.O37 A22, **(v3)**
  PG3476.O37.Z23, **(v3)**
Olesko, Kathryn Mary. QC47.G3.O43 1991, **(v1)**
Oleszek, Walter J. JK1096.O43 1996, **(v7)**
Olevnik, Peter P. Z5815.U5.O44 1993, **(v10)**
Olgyay, Victor. NA2540.O44, **(v9)**
Olien, Roger M. HD9565.O647 1990, **(v6)**
Olin, Laurie. SB470.55.G7.O44 2000, **(v1)**
Oliner, Pearl M. BJ1474.O39 1995, **(v8)**
Olins, Wally. HD59.2.O39 1990, **(v6)**
Oliphant, (Margaret), Mrs. PR5114.A3 1974, **(v3)**
Oliphant, Dave. ML3508.7.T4.O45 1996, **(v9)**
Oliphant. PR5113.B4 1970, **(v3)**
Olitzky, Kerry M. BM205.O45 1996, **(v8)**
  BM660.O43 2000, **(v8)**
Oliver, Douglas L. DU870.O43, **(v5)**
  GN662.O46 1989, **(v6)**
Oliver, Edward James. PR5143.O4, **(v3)**
Oliver, Kelly. B828.45.O55 2001, **(v8)**
Oliver, Kendrick. KZ5680.21963.O43 1998, **(v7)**
Oliver, Laurence J. PS2373.O43 1992, **(v3)**
Oliver, Mary. PE1505.O35 1994, **(v3)**
Oliver, Michael. UA649.O55 1999, **(v10)**
Oliver, Paul. ML3521.O42 1990, **(v9)**
Oliver, Peter. F1058.F466.O43, **(v4)**
  HV9509.O5.O54 1998, **(v6)**
Oliver, Phil. B945.J24.O55 2001, **(v8)**
Oliver, Robert Tarbell. DS915.2.O45 1993, **(v5)**
Oliver, Roland Anthony. DT19.7.O45.A3 1997, **(v5)**
  GN780.4.A1.O44, **(v6)**
Oliver, Valerie Burnham. Z5694.U5.O45 1996, **(v10)**
Oliver, William Irvin. PQ7087.E5.O4, **(v3)**
Olivera, Ruth R. F1210.O54 1991, **(v4)**
Oliveri, Ernest J. HJ8519.O42 1992, **(v6)**
Oliverio, Annamarie. HV6431.O55 1998, **(v6)**
Oliviero, Jeffrey. PN1998.O55 1991, **(v3)**
Olkowski, William. SB950.O35 1991, **(v1)**

Ollapally, Deepa Mary. D888.U6.O43 1993, **(v5)**
Ollard, Richard Lawrence. DA447.C6.O45 1988, **(v5)**
　PR3618.P2.O5 1975, **(v3)**
Ollier, Claude. PQ2675.L398.D4413 1989, **(v3)**
Ollier, Cliff. GB406.O44, **(v6)**
　QE501.4.P3.O45 1991, **(v1)**
　QE521.O43 1988, **(v1)**
Olmert, Michael. Z4.O54 1992, **(v10)**
Olmstead, A. T. DS121.O4 1931, **(v5)**
Olmstead, Andrea. ML410.S473 O4 1985, **(v9)**
　MT4.N5.J846 1999, **(v9)**
Olmstead, Earl P. E99.D2.Z456 1991, **(v4)**
　E99.D2 Z457 1997, **(v4)**
Olmstead, Judith V. DT380.4.G19.O55 1997, **(v5)**
Olmsted, Barney. HD5109.2.U5.O46 1994, **(v6)**
Olmsted, Frederick Law. F213.O53 1953, **(v4)**
　F391.O512 1978, **(v4)**
Olmsted, Kathryn S. JK468.I6.O45 1996, **(v7)**
Olney, James. PR5908.P5.O45, **(v3)**
O'Looney, John. HV95.O44 1996, **(v6)**
Olowofoyeku, Abimbola A. K2146.O45 1993, **(v7)**
Olrik, Axel. GR72.O5613 1992, **(v6)**
Olschki, Leonardo. DG441.O48, **(v5)**
　DS6.O373, **(v5)**
Olsen, Alexandra Hennessey. PR1984.C63.O47 1990, **(v3)**
Olsen, Christopher J. F341.O47 2000, **(v4)**
Olsen, Dale A. ML3575.V3 O47 1996, **(v9)**
Olsen, Jack. E185.97.P73 O47 2000, **(v4)**
Olsen, Kirstin. HQ1121.O47 1994, **(v6)**
Olsen, Lance. PS3527.A15.L6347 1995, **(v3)**
Olsen, Wallace C. HD1415.O47 1991, **(v6)**
Olson, Carl. BL43.E4.O47 1992, **(v8)**
　BQ9268.6.O46 2000, **(v8)**
Olson, Charles. PS3529.L655.A17 1987, **(v3)**
　PS3529.L655.A6 1997, **(v3)**
　PS3529.L655.N38 1989, **(v3)**
　PS3529.L655.Z48 2000, **(v3)**
Olson, Edwin E. HD58.8.O47 2001, **(v6)**
Olson, Eric T. BD450.O46 1997, **(v8)**
Olson, Gerald W. S592.14.O36 1984, **(v1)**
Olson, Glending. PN47.O58 1982, **(v3)**
Olson, Gregory Allen. E183.8.V5.O45 1995, **(v4)**
Olson, James C. F666.O48 1966, **(v4)**
Olson, James Stuart. DS730.O47 1998, **(v5)**
　E169.12.O44 2000, **(v4)**
　E184.C97.O46 1995, **(v4)**
　E784.O44 1988, **(v4)**
　F1434.O45 1991, **(v4)**
　GN645.O47 1996, **(v6)**
　HC102.O57 1992, **(v6)**
　RC262.O47 1989, **(v2)**
Olson, Kent C. KF240.O365 1999, **(v7)**
Olson, Kirby. PR931.O47 2001, **(v3)**
Olson, Laura R. Z7776.72.O47 1998, **(v10)**
Olson, Lester C. CR69.U6.O38 1991, **(v5)**
Olson, Mancur. HD87.O47 2000, **(v6)**
Olson, Nancy B. Z695.66.O43 1985, **(v10)**
Olson, Paul A. LA93.O47 1995, **(v7)**
Olson, Richard. H51.O57 1993, **(v6)**
Olson, Robert W. DR435.K87.O45 1998, **(v5)**
　DS63.2.T8.O47 2001, **(v5)**
Olson, Sherry H. F189.B157 O43 1997, **(v4)**
Olson, Sigurd F. F1060.A2.O4, **(v4)**
Olson, Walter K. KF3457.O44 1991, **(v7)**
Olssen, Mark. LB880.F682.O47 1999, **(v7)**
Olweus, Dan. LB1124.O48 1993, **(v7)**
Olyan, Saul M. BS1199.S59, **(v8)**
Olyanova, Nadya. BF891.O59, **(v2)**
Olzak, Susan. E184.A1.O455 1992, **(v4)**
Omae, Kenichi. HC79.I55.O45 2000, **(v6)**
　HF1418.5.O46 1990, **(v6)**
O'Mahony, Patrick. DA908.O46 1998, **(v5)**
O'Malley, Frank Ward. F199.O54, **(v4)**
O'Malley, Padraig. DA959.O5 1983, **(v5)**
Oman, Charles William Chadwick. U37.O5 1953, **(v10)**
　U37.O6 1959, **(v10)**
　U39.O5 1937, **(v10)**
Omar Khayyam. PK6513.A1 1997, **(v3)**
　PK6516.A1 1952, **(v3)**

PK6516.S25 1991, **(v3)**
O'Meara, Thomas F. BX4700.T6.O44 1997, **(v8)**
Omissi, David E. DA89.5.O47 1990, **(v5)**
Ommundsen, Wenche. PN3335.O48 1993, **(v3)**
Omotoso, Kole. PR9387.9.A3.Z855 1996, **(v3)**
Omoyajowo, J. Akinyele. BX6600.C373.O46 1982, **(v8)**
O'Nan, Stewart. F104.H3.O5 2000, **(v4)**
Onassis, Jacqueline Kennedy. CT275.O552.A36, **(v5)**
Ondaatje, Michael. PR9199.3.O5A84 2000, **(v3)**
　PR9199.3.O5C5 1991, **(v3)**
　PR9199.3.O5.C6, **(v3)**
　PR9199.3.O5E54 1992, **(v3)**
　PR9199.3.O5.T5 1979, **(v3)**
O'Neal, William Bainter. LD5678.3.O5, **(v7)**
O'Neale, Sondra A. PS767.H15.Z75 1993, **(v3)**
O'Neil, B. H. St. J. U883.O55, **(v10)**
O'Neil, James L. JC75.D36.O54 1995, **(v7)**
O'Neil, Robert M. LC72.2.O54 1997, **(v7)**
O'Neill, Bard E. U240.O54 1996, **(v6)**
O'Neill, Brian Juan. HN600.F66.O5413 1987, **(v6)**
O'Neill, Edward Hayes. CT34.U6.O5, **(v5)**
O'Neill, Edward L. QC383.O5, **(v1)**
O'Neill, Eugene. PS3529.N5.A6 1933, **(v3)**
　PS3529.N5.A6 1950, **(v3)**
　PS3529.N5.A6 1964, **(v3)**
　PS3529.N5.A6 1972, **(v3)**
　PS3529.N5.A6 1988, **(v3)**
　PS3529.N5.E5 1937, **(v3)**
　PS3529.N5.I3 1946, **(v3)**
　PS3529.N5.L6 1989, **(v3)**
　PS3529.N5.L62 1940, **(v3)**
　PS3529.N5.M68 1952, **(v3)**
　PS3529.N5.M736 1988, **(v3)**
　PS3529.N5.M75 1931b, **(v3)**
　PS3529.N5.S7 1928g (Rare Bk Coll), **(v3)**
　PS3529.N5.T6 1957, **(v3)**
　PS3529.N5.U5 1988, **(v3)**
　PS3529.N5.Z48 1988, **(v3)**
　PS3529.N5.Z495 1987, **(v3)**
　PS3529.N5 1988, **(v3)**
O'Neill, Gerard K. TL795.7.O53 2000, **(v1)**
O'Neill, Hugh B. DS705.O63 1987, **(v5)**
O'Neill, John. HM73.O55 1994, **(v6)**
　P90.O5 1989, **(v3)**
O'Neill, Kate. TD1030.O72 2000, **(v1)**
O'Neill, Kevin M. QL563.O53 2001, **(v1)**
O'Neill, Michael. PR5438.O5 1989, **(v3)**
O'Neill, Onora. B105.J87.O54 1996, **(v8)**
O'Neill, Onora. BJ1533.J9 O64 2000, **(v8)**
O'Neill, P. A. TJ990.O815 1993, **(v1)**
O'Neill, Patricia. PR4237.3.O54 1995, **(v3)**
O'Neill, Philip. PR4498.W6.O54 1988, **(v3)**
O'Neill, Robert John. UA712.O5 1966, **(v10)**
O'Neill, William L. D769.O64 1993, **(v5)**
Onetti, Juan Carlos. PQ8519.O59.G66 1990, **(v3)**
Onians, John. N5610.O5 1999, **(v9)**
Onians, Richard Broxton. B72.O5 1954, **(v8)**
Onimode, Bade. HC800.O55 1988, **(v6)**
Onions, Oliver. PR6065.N45 I55 1968, **(v3)**
Onkvisit, Sak. HF5415.155.O55 1989, **(v6)**
O'Nolan, Brian. PR6029.N56 A8 1966, **(v3)**
Onslow, Barbara. PN5124.W58.O59 2000, **(v3)**
Onuf, Peter S. E332.2.J48 1993, **(v4)**
Ooi, Keat Gin. DS597.37.O65 1999, **(v5)**
　Z3246.B76 1999, **(v10)**
Ooka, Makoto. PL727.5.O49 1991, **(v3)**
Ooka, Shohei. PL898.O5.N6 1969, **(v3)**
Oommen, T. K. HN683.5.C59 1990, **(v6)**
　JC311.O65 1997, **(v7)**
Oosting, Henry John. QK901.O6 1956, **(v1)**
Opello, Walter C. DP556.O64 1991, **(v5)**
Ophir, Adi. JC71.P6.O64 1990, **(v7)**
Opie, Iona Archibald. GV1215.O65 1985, **(v6)**
　PZ8.3.O6.Ox, **(v3)**
Opie, John. S616.U6.O65 2000, **(v1)**
Opland, Jeff. PR203.O6, **(v3)**
Oppelt, Norman T. E97.55.O67 1990, **(v4)**
　E99.P9.O6 1991, **(v4)**
Oppenheim, A. Leo. DS69.5.O6 1977, **(v5)**
Oppenheim, Frank M. B945.R64 O657 1987, **(v8)**

Oppenheim, Lois Hecht. F3100.O66 1993, **(v4)**
Oppenheim, Michael D. B5800.O77 1997, **(v8)**
Oppenheimer, J. Robert. Q171.O6, **(v1)**
　QC780.O6, **(v1)**
Oppenheimer, Michael. QC912.3.O66 1990, **(v1)**
Oppenheimer, Paul. BJ1401.O66 1996, **(v8)**
Optical Society of America. QC495.O6, **(v1)**
Oraa, Jaime. K3240.4.O73 1992, **(v7)**
Orams, Mark. G155.A1.O65 1999, **(v6)**
Oravec, Jo Ann. QA76.9.H85.O73 1996, **(v1)**
Orbach, Israel. RJ506.S9.O73 1988, **(v2)**
Orczy, Emmuska Orczy. PR6029.R25 O43, **(v3)**
Orde, Anne. DA16.O74 1996, **(v5)**
Ordonez, Elizabeth J. PQ6055.O7 1991, **(v3)**
Oregon State University. G1466.G3.O7 1985, **(v6)**
O'Reilly, Charles A. HD70.U5.O69 2000, **(v6)**
O'Reilly, Kenneth. E185.615.O74 1989, **(v4)**
Orel, Harold. PR75.O73 1984, **(v3)**
Orel, Vitezslav. QH31.M45.O67 1994, **(v1)**
Orellana, Sandra L. F1465.1.P335.O74 1995, **(v4)**
Orem, Dorothea E. RT84.5.O73 2001, **(v2)**
Oremland, Jerome D. BF408.O74 1997, **(v2)**
　ND623.B9.O74 1989, **(v9)**
Orenstein, Claudia. PN3305.O74 1998, **(v3)**
Orenstein, Mitchell A. HC340.3.O73 2001, **(v6)**
Orfalea, Gregory. D756.5.A7.O74 1997, **(v5)**
Orfield, Gary. F294.A89.N45 1991, **(v4)**
　LC212.62.O72 1996, **(v7)**
　LC214.5.O73, **(v7)**
Orfield, Lester B. KJ690.O74 2001, **(v7)**
Organ, Troy Wilson. B131.O73, **(v8)**
　BD450.O72 1987, **(v8)**
Orgel, Stephen. PR3095.O74 1996, **(v3)**
Oriard, Michael. GV950.O73 2001, **(v6)**
　GV950.O75 1993, **(v6)**
O'Riordan, William D. RJ370.O74 1983, **(v2)**
Orkin, Michael. QA273.15.O75 1999, **(v1)**
Orians, F. Barbara. HV4915.O75 1993, **(v6)**
Orledge, Robert. ML410.S196.O74 1990, **(v9)**
Orlin, Lena Cowen. DA320.O74 1994, **(v5)**
Orlova, Aleksandra Anatolevna. ML410.G46.O813 1988, **(v9)**
Orlove, Benjamin S. F128.9.J5.O75 1995, **(v4)**
Orlow, Dietrich. DD253.25.O7, **(v5)**
　DD453.O76 1991, **(v5)**
Orme, John David. E840.O76 1989, **(v4)**
Orme, Nicholas. LA631.3.O737 1989, **(v7)**
Orme, William A. HF1746.O75 1993, **(v6)**
Ormond, Richard. ND237.S3.A4 1998, **(v9)**
　ND237.S3.O7 1970b, **(v9)**
Ormrod, W. M. DA233.O74 1990, **(v5)**
Ormsby, Margaret A. F1088.O7, **(v4)**
Ormsby, Waterman Lilly. F593.O7 1991, **(v4)**
Orne, Jerrold. Z1006.O7 1976, **(v10)**
Ornstein, Robert E. QP376.O76 1984, **(v1)**
Ornstein, Robert. PR658.T7.O7, **(v3)**
　PR1263.O72, **(v3)**
Orosz, Joel J. AM11.O76 1990, **(v10)**
O'Rourke, James L. PR4837.O75 1998, **(v3)**
O'Rourke, Joseph. QA448.D38.O76 1998, **(v1)**
Orr, Bill. HG3881.O772 1992, **(v6)**
Orr, Clyde. QC863.O7, **(v1)**
Orr, Elaine Neil. PS374.W6.O77 1997, **(v3)**
Orr, Eleanor Wilson. PE3102.N42.O77 1987, **(v3)**
Orr, Leonard. PN98.S6.O77 1991, **(v3)**
Orr, Linda. DC147.8.O77 1990, **(v5)**
Orr, Robert M. HC60.O78 1990, **(v6)**
Orrell, John. NA6840.G7.O76 1988, **(v9)**
Orren, Karen. KF894.O77 1991, **(v7)**
Orsenna, Erik. PQ2675.R7.E9713 1991, **(v3)**
Orser, Charles E. CC77.H5.O78 1996, **(v5)**
　F270.O77 1988, **(v4)**
Orser, W. Edward. F189.B16.E266 1994, **(v4)**
Ortakovski, Vladimir. DR24.O77 2000, **(v5)**
Ortega y Gasset, José. B4568.O73.Q4313 1961, **(v8)**
　BH205.O713 1968, **(v8)**
　D16.8.O72 1961, **(v5)**
　PQ6627.R8.M43, **(v3)**
　CB103.O713 1993, **(v6)**
Ortega, James M. QA297.O778 1999, **(v1)**
Ortiz de Montellano, B. F1219.76.M43.O78 1990, **(v4)**

Ortiz, David. PN5317.P6.O78 2000, (v3)
Ortiz, Flora Ida. LB3218.A1 O78 1993, (v7)
Ortiz, Valerie Malenfer. DS503.S77 vol. 22, (v5)
Ortloff, H. Stuart (Henry Stuart). SB472.O7 1975, (v1)
Ortner, Robert. HC106.8.O78 1990, (v6)
Ortner, Sherry B. BL2032.S45.O77, (v8)
    GV199.44.E85.O78 1999, (v6)
Orton, Joe. PR6065.R7.A19 1977, (v3)
Orum, Anthony M. F394.A957.O78 1987, (v4)
Orvell, Miles. E169.1.O783 1989, (v4)
Orwell, George. D743.O76 1986, (v5)
    PR6029.R8.A6 1968, (v3)
    PR6029.R8.A6 1985, (v3)
    PR6029.R8 A65 1954, (v3)
    PR6029.R8 B8, (v3)
    PR6029.R8 C55 1960, (v3)
    PR6029.R8 C6, (v3)
    PR6029.R8.I6 1940, (v3)
    PR6029.R8 K4, (v3)
    PR6029.R8.N49 1949, (v3)
    PR6029.R8 N52 1963, (v3)
    PR6029.R8.N647 1984, (v3)
    PR6029.R8.S9 1953, (v3)
òS‾aliòn, al-òTayyib. PJ7862.A564B313 1996, (v3)
Osagie, Iyunolu Folayan. E447.O73 2000, (v4)
Osam‾ana, âSaokata. PK1718.O8J313 1993, (v3)
Osanka, Franklin Mark. U240.O8, (v10)
Osaragi, Jiro. PL835.S3 T32, (v3)
    PL898.O8.K52, (v3)
Osborn, Andrew Delbridge. Z692.S5.O8 1980, (v10)
Osborn, Carolyn. PS3565.S348.H6x, (v3)
Osborn, Chase S. PS2267.O8, (v3)
Osborn, James Marshall. DA358.S5.O8 1972, (v5)
    PR3423.O7 1965, (v3)
Osborn, William C. HD9827.M2O8, (v6)
Osborne, Harold. BH39.O8 1953, (v8)
Osborne, John Walter. DA522.C5.O8, (v5)
Osborne, John. PR6029.S39.E6 1958a, (v3)
    PR6029.S39.P5 1966, (v3)
    PR6029.S39.S8, (v3)
    PR6029.S39.W6 1961, (v3)
    PR6065.S18.I5 1965, (v3)
    PR6065.S18.L8 1962, (v3)
    PR6065.S18.W47 1973, (v3)
Osborne, Laurie E. PR2837.O83 1996, (v3)
Osborne, Patrick L. QH84.5.O82 2000, (v1)
Osborne, Richard. ML410.R8 O9 2001, (v9)
    ML422.K22.O83 2000, (v9)
Osborne, Robert A. PN1993.5.U6.O78 1989, (v3)
    PN1993.92.O82 1999, (v3)
Osborough, W. N. KDK1930.D9.O82 1996, (v7)
Osburn, Charles B. Z2175.A2.O8 1981, (v10)
Osen, James L. JA84.F8.O84 1995, (v7)
Oser, Lee. PS3509.L43.Z7975 1998, (v3)
Osgood, Charles Egerton. B840.O7, (v8)
Osgood, Charles Grosvenor. PR83.O7 1952, (v3)
    PR2362.O7 1963, (v3)
Osgood, Nancy J. Z7721.O83 1995, (v10)
Osgood, Robert Endicott. UA23.O8, (v10)
    UA23.O82 1988, (v10)
    UA646.3.O8, (v10)
O'Shaughnessy, Andrew Jackson. F2131.O74 2000, (v4)
O'Shaughnessy, John. HF5415.32.O74 1992, (v6)
O'Shea, Kathleen A. HV9466.O74 1999, (v6)
    Z5703.4.P75.O75 1997, (v10)
Oshima, Nagisa. PN1993.5.J3.O794 1991, (v3)
Oshinsky, David M. HV9475.M72.M576 1996, (v6)
Osiel, Mark. KZ1168.5.O83 1997, (v7)
Osio, Antonio Maria. F864.O85 1996, (v4)
Osler, William. RC46.O8 1967, (v2)
Osmanczyk, Edmund Jan. JX1977.O8213 1990, (v7)
Osmond, Jonathan. DD801.R682.O86 1993, (v5)
Osmond-Smith, David. ML410.B4968.O55 1990, (v9)
Osofsky, Gilbert. F128.9.N3.O73, (v4)
Osorio, Ruben. F1234.V63, (v4)
Ospovat, Dov. QH31.D2.O74, (v1)
Ossenkop, David. ML134.W75.O87 1988, (v9)
Osswald, Tim A. TA455.P58.O68 1996, (v1)
Osten, Gert von der. N6925.O813 1969, (v9)
Oster, Judith. PS3511.R94.Z857 1992, (v3)

Oster, Richard. Z2304.E58.O87 1987, (v10)
Osterfeld, David. HC59.7.O835 1992, (v6)
Osterman, Paul. HF5549.2.U5.O77 1988, (v6)
Osterreich, Shelley Anne. Z1209.2.N67.O77 1998,
    (v10)
Osterud, Nancy Grey. HQ1438.N57.O88 1991, (v6)
Osthaus, Carl R. PN4893.O88 1994, (v3)
Ostler, Jeffrey. F621.O88 1993, (v4)
Ostriker, Alicia. PS147.O8 1986, (v3)
    PS3565.S84.G7 1989, (v3)
Ostroff, Jeff. HF5415.1.O87 1989, (v6)
Ostrogorski, Georgije. DF552.5.O8153 1969, (v5)
Ostrom, Vincent. JC423.O8 1997, (v7)
Ostrovsky, Aleksandr Nikolaevich. PG3337.O8.A23,
    (v3)
Ostrovsky, Erika. PQ2607.E834.Z8, (v3)
    PQ2683.I8.Z8 1991, (v3)
Ostrow, Rona. HF5415.O76 1988, (v6)
Ostrowski, Donald G. DK90.O86 1998, (v5)
Ostwald, Martin. PA430.N6.O8, (v3)
Ostwald, Peter F. GV1785.N6.O88 1990, (v6)
Ostwalt, Conrad Eugene. F264.L68.O88 1998, (v4)
O'Sullivan, Arthur. HJ4191.O85 1995, (v6)
O'Sullivan, Patrick J. HB73.O78 1987, (v6)
Oswalt, Wendell H. E99.E7.O786 1990, (v4)
    E99.E7 O79 1999, (v4)
Ota, Hirotaro. NA1550.O813, (v9)
Otero, Miguel Antonio. F801.O88 1987, (v4)
Otieno, Wambui Waiyaki. DT433.582.O75.A3 1998,
    (v5)
Otis, Carol L. RC1218.W65.O68 2000, (v2)
Otis, Laura. PN55.O87 1999, (v3)
O'Toole, Fintan. PR3683.O86 1998, (v3)
O'Toole, G. J. A. UB271.U5.O85 1988, (v10)
    UB271.U5.O86 1991, (v10)
O'Toole, Michael. N7565.O87 1994, (v9)
Ott, Attiat F. HJ2005.O88 1993, (v6)
Ott, David H. DS119.7.O88 1980, (v5)
Ottaway, Patrick. DA90.O86 1992, (v5)
Otte, Daniel. QL508.A2.O88, (v1)
Otte, Max. DD290.3.O89 2000, (v5)
Ottemiller, John H. Z5781.O8 1988, (v10)
Otten, Karl. PT1334.O83 1977, (v3)
Ottenberg, Simon. DT515.45.I33.O88 1989, (v5)
Otter, Samuel. PS2388.B57.O88 1999, (v3)
Otteson, James R. HB501.O824 2002, (v6)
Ottman, Robert W. MT50.O923 2000, (v9)
    MT50.O924 1998, (v9)
    MT870.O86 2001, (v9)
Otto I, Bishop of Freising, d. 1158. D17.O85, (v5)
Otto, Beatrice K. GT3670.O77 2001, (v6)
Otto, Henry John. LB875.O83 1969, (v7)
Otto, John Solomon. F212.O88 1989, (v4)
Otto, Matthias. QD75.4.S8.O88 1999, (v1)
Otto, Stella. SB355.O78 1993, (v1)
Ottonello, Giulio. QE515.O8813 1997, (v1)
Ottoson, David. QP361.O874 1983, (v1)
Otway, Thomas. PR3610.A5.G5 1968, (v3)
    PR3612.O7 1976, (v3)
Ouditt, Sharon. Z2014.W37.O93 2000, (v10)
Oudshoorn, Nelly. QP572.S4.O83 1994, (v1)
Ouellette, Fernand. ML410.V27.O83, (v9)
Ousby, Ian. PR85.O97 1996, (v3)
Ousby, Ian. PR868.D4.O9, (v3)
Outcault, Richard Felton. PN6727.O98.Y45 1995, (v3)
Outhwaite, R. B. KD755.O93 1995, (v7)
Outhwaite, William. H61.O895 1987, (v6)
    H61.O9 1976, (v6)
Outwater, Alice B. GB701.O88 1996, (v6)
Ou-yang, Hsiu. PL2683.A6 1989, (v3)
Oved, Iaacov. BX8129.B63.O94 1996, (v8)
Ovendale, Ritchie. DS63.2.G7.O93 1996, (v5)
Overholt, Thomas W. BS661.O94 1996, (v8)
Overmyer, Daniel L. BL1802.O93 1996, (v8)
Overmyer, James. GV865.M325 O94 1998, (v6)
Overstreet, Deborah Wilson. PS374.V55.O94 1998,
    (v3)
Overton, Bill. PN3352.A38.O84 1996, (v3)
Overton, Mark. HD1930.E5.O93 1996, (v6)
Overton, Richard Cleghorn. HE2791.C643.O79, (v6)
Overy, R. J. D741.O85 1990, (v5)

    D743.O94 1996, (v5)
    D764.O94 1997, (v5)
    D785.O9, (v5)
Ovid. PA6105.S8.O89, (v3)
    PA6522.F2.N34 1995, (v3)
    PA6522.H4.H56 1991, (v3)
Oviedo y Banos, Jose de. F2322.O9613 1987, (v4)
Oweis, Issa S. TD795.7.O93 1990, (v1)
Owen, Barbara. MT189.O94 1997, (v9)
Owen, Bobbi. PN2096.A1.O94 1991, (v3)
Owen, Charles A. PR1874.O93, (v3)
Owen, David. GV964.W66 O94 2001, (v6)
    LB2353.57.O94 1985, (v7)
Owen, Dolores B. Z5305.G7.O94 1989, (v10)
    Z7403.O95 1985, (v10)
Owen, Harold. MT55.O97 1992, (v9)
    PR6029.W4.Z8, (v3)
Owen, John D. HD5124.O94 1989, (v6)
Owen, John M. E183.7.O94 1997, (v4)
Owen, Oliver S. S938.O87 1998, (v1)
Owen, Rob. PN1992.6.O93 1997, (v3)
Owen, Roger C. E77.2.O93, (v4)
Owen, Roger. HC415.15.O935 1998, (v6)
Owen, Stephen. PL2291.O84 1996, (v3)
    PL2321.O94, (v3)
    PL2321.O95, (v3)
Owen, Susan J. PR698.H5094 1996, (v3)
Owen, Thomas C. HC335.O83 1995, (v6)
Owen, Thomas McAdory. F326.O93, (v4)
Owen, Wilfred. HE305.O9, (v6)
    HE355.O848 1966, (v6)
    PR6029.W4.P6 1949, (v3)
    PR6029.W4.Z54 1967, (v3)
Owens, David. BD541.O84 1992, (v8)
Owens, Harry P. HE566.P3.O84 1990, (v6)
Owens, Jesse. E185.61.O93, (v4)
Owens, Jessie Ann. ML430.O94 1997, (v9)
Owens, Owen D. QH76.5.P4.O93 1993, (v1)
Owens, William A. F392.L36O9 1989b, (v4)
Owensby, Brian Philip. HT690.B7.O95 1999, (v6)
Owensby, Jacob. D16.8.O94 1994, (v5)
Owings, Alison. D811.5.O885 1993, (v5)
Owings, Marvin Alpheus. PR321.O9, (v3)
Ownby, David. HS310.O86 1996, (v6)
Ownby, Ted. F215.O87 1990, (v4)
Owoahene-Acheampong, Stephen.
    DT510.43.A53.O93 1998, (v5)
Owomoyela, Oyekan. GR351.32.Y56.O86 1997, (v6)
Owram, Doug. F1060.9.O94, (v4)
    HN103.5.O93 1996, (v6)
Owsley, Frank Lawrence. E355.1.N5.O97, (v4)
    E488.O85 1959, (v4)
    F213.O94, (v4)
    F296.O94 1997, (v4)
Owst, Gerald Robert. PR275.O8 1961, (v3)
Oxendine, Joseph B. BF295.O9, (v2)
    E98.G2.O94 1988, (v4)
Oxenhandler, Neal. PQ305.O94 1996, (v3)
Oxley, Deborah. HV8950.A8.O95 1996, (v6)
Oyama, Susan. QH507.O93 2000, (v1)
Oyewole, A. DT515.15.O94, (v5)
Oyono, Ferdinand. PQ3989.O9.C513 1989, (v3)
    PQ3989.O9 V5 1970, (v3)
Oyster, Clyde W. QP475.O97 1999, (v1)
Oz, Amos. PJ5054.O9M513 1972, (v3)
Ozaki, Robert S. HD5660.J3.O95 1991, (v6)
Ozbay, Hitay. TJ216.O97 2000, (v1)
Ozenfant, Amedee. N7438.O82 1952, (v9)
Ozick, Cynthia. PS3565.Z5C3 1995, (v3)
Ozieblo Rajkowska, Barbara. PS3513.L35.Z78 2000,
    (v3)
Ozinga, James R. BJ1474.O85 1999, (v8)
    HX626.O95 1995, (v6)
Ozkirimli, Umut. JC311.O93 1999, (v7)
Ozment, Steven E. BR270.O9, (v8)
    HQ611.O968 2001, (v6)
    HQ611.O97 1983, (v6)
Ozouf, Mona. DC159.O9613 1988, (v5)
    PQ149.O9613 1997, (v3)
Ozsvath, Zsuzsanna. PH3321.R27, (v3)
Pa, Chin. PL2780.F4 C513 1978, (v3)

Paar, Jack. PN1992.4.P3.A33, (v3)
Paarlberg, Don. S494.5.I5, (v1)
Paasi, Anssi. JC319.P32 1996, (v7)
Pacatus Drepanius, Latinus. DG330.P3313 1987, (v5)
Pace, Richard. F2651.G98.P3 1998, (v4)
Pacelle, Richard L. KF8742.P3 1991, (v7)
Pacey, Arnold. T14.P28 1999, (v1)
   T15.P353 1990, (v1)
Pach, Chester J. E835.P26 1991, (v4)
Pach, Janos. QA167.P33 1995, (v1)
Pacheco, Jose Emilio. PQ7298.26.A25.A27 1987, (v3)
   PQ7298.26.A25.A6813 1993, (v3)
Pachmuss, Temira. PG3213.P3, (v3)
Pachter, Henry Maximilian. DD228.P33, (v5)
Pack, Janet Rothenberg. HB3505.P33 2002, (v6)
Pack, Spencer J. HB501.P125 1991, (v6)
Packard, Francis R. R151.P12 1963, (v2)
Packard, Jerome Lee. PL1230.P34 2000, (v3)
Packard, Jerrold M. D749.P33 1992, (v5)
Packard, Robert T. NA705.P3 1995, (v9)
Packard, Sidney Raymond. CB354.6.P32, (v5)
Packard, William. PN44.5.P3 1989, (v3)
Packe, Michael St. John. B1606.P3, (v8)
Packer, Cathy Lee. KF7680.P33 1989, (v7)
Packer, Lona Mosk. PR5236.R9.A38, (v3)
Packer, Nancy Huddleston. PS3566.A318.S6, (v3)
Paddock, Lisa. KF8742.P32 1996, (v7)
Padfield, Peter. VA454.P24, (v10)
Padhi, Bibhu. BL2001.2.P22 1990, (v8)
Padilla, Elena. F128.9.P8.P3, (v4)
Padilla, Genaro M. E184.M5.P28 1993, (v4)
Padmanabhan, T. QB981.P243 1998, (v1)
Padover, Saul Kussiel. E302.P3, (v4)
Pae, Sung M. HC467.P22 1992, (v6)
Paesler, Michael A. QH212.N43.P34 1996, (v1)
Paetow, Louis John. Z6203.P25 1980, (v10)
Paffard, Mark. PR4857.P24 1989, (v3)
Pagan, A. R. HB139.P34 1999, (v6)
Pagana, Kathleen Deska. RB38.2.P34 2002, (v2)
Pagano, Michael A. HT175.P32 1995, (v6)
Pagden, Anthony. CB203.P3 1993, (v5)
   D135.P33 2001, (v5)
   DP75.P34 1990, (v5)
   JC359.P278 1995, (v7)
Page, Benjamin I. HC110.P6.P328 2000, (v6)
   HN90.P8.P34 1991, (v6)
   JK524.P33, (v7)
Page, Caroline. DS559.8.P65.P34 1996, (v5)
Page, Christopher. ML270.2.P22 1993, (v9)
   ML497.2.P33 1990, (v9)
Page, F. C. PR5143.P3, (v3)
Page, Frederick. PR5143.P3 1970, (v3)
Page, Joseph A. F2510.P34 1995, (v4)
Page, Judith W. PR5892.F45.P34 1994, (v3)
Page, Lawrence M. QL627.P34 1991, (v1)
Page, Max. HT168.N5.P34 1999, (v6)
Page, Norman. PR4387.P34 1988, (v3)
   PR4588.P33 1984, (v3)
   PR4754.P3, (v3)
   PR4809.H15.P33 1983, (v3)
   PR5823.P34 1991, (v3)
   PR6001.U4.Z765 1998, (v3)
Page, Penny Booth. Z7721.P334 1991, (v10)
Page, Philip. PS374.N4.P34 1999, (v3)
Page, R. I. DL65.P26 1995, (v5)
   PD2014.P34 1995, (v3)
Page, Reba Neukom. LB3061.8.P34 1991, (v7)
Page, Rosewell. PS2516.P3 1969, (v3)
Page, Sheila. HC59.7.P283 1999, (v6)
Page, Talbot. HF1052.P33, (v6)
Page, Thomas Nelson. E312.5.P13 1932, (v4)
   F206.P13 1969, (v4)
   PS2514.I5 1969, (v3)
Pagedas, Constantine A. E183.8.F8.P34 2000, (v4)
Pagell, Ruth A. HF54.5.P33 1994, (v6)
Pagels, Elaine H. BS2545.S36.P34 1988, (v8)
Paglia, Camille. PN751.P34 1990, (v3)
Pagnol, Marcel. PQ2631.A26.C4 1937, (v3)
Pahel, Kenneth. BJ21.P33, (v8)
Pahl, Jon. E162.P135 1992, (v4)
Pahlavan, Kaveh. TK5103.2.P34 1995, (v1)

Pahlen, Kurt. MT110.P3313 1990, (v9)
Pahl-Wostl, Claudia. QH541.P33 1995, (v1)
Pahre, Robert. HC59.15.P33 1999, (v6)
Pai, Chu-i. PL2674.A28 2000, (v3)
Pai, Hyung Il. DS903.P35 2000, (v5)
Paidar, Parvin. HQ1236.5.I7.P35 1995, (v6)
Paige, Leroy. GV865.P3.A3 1992, (v6)
Paik, Nam June. N7369.P35.A4 1993, (v9)
Paine, Albert Bigelow. PS1300.F22 1922 vol. 30-
   33.S1331, (v3)
Paine, Lincoln P. V23.P24 1997, (v10)
Paine, Thomas. E211.P1455 1975, (v4)
   JC177.A5 1953, (v7)
   JC177.B3 1969, (v7)
Painter, Charlotte. PS3566.A346.C6, (v3)
Painter, Franklin Verzelius Newton. LB7.P2 1970,
   (v7)
Painter, James. F1466.5.P35 1987, (v4)
Painter, Robert. E98.A7.P27 1998, (v4)
Pais, Abraham. QC16.P24.A3 1997, (v1)
   QC773.P35 1991, (v1)
Paisley, Clifton. F317.R43.P35 1989, (v4)
Pak, Chong-dong. HC430.Z6.P35 1997, (v6)
Pak, Mog-wol. PL992.62.Y6.A25 1990, (v3)
Pak, Wan-so. PL992.62.W34.S54 1999, (v3)
Pakenham, Thomas. DA949.P3 1970, (v5)
Pal, Izzud-Din. HC440.5.P3638 1999, (v6)
Pal, Pratapaditya. NB1000.P34, (v9)
Palacio Valdes, Armando. PQ6629.A5.A23 1993, (v3)
Palais, James B. BL1842.P33 1996, (v8)
Palan, Ronen. HF1359.P338 1996, (v6)
Palazzolo, Daniel J. JK1411.P35 1992, (v7)
Palda, Kristian S. HF5415.P233, (v6)
Paldiel, Mordecai. D804.65.P35 2000, (v5)
Paletz, David L. HE8689.7.P6.P35 1998, (v6)
Palevsky, Mary. QC773.3.U5.P53 2000, (v1)
Paley, Grace. PS3566.A46.E5, (v3)
   PS3566.A46.L5 1973, (v3)
Paley, Julia. HN293.5.P34 2001, (v6)
Paley, Morton D. PR585.A66.P35 1999, (v3)
   PR4147.P3, (v3)
   PR4483.P35 1999, (v3)
Paley, Vivian Gussin. LB1140.3.P35 1990, (v7)
   LB1140.3.P356 1995, (v7)
   LB1195.P18 1984, (v7)
Paley, William S. HE8689.8.P34, (v6)
Palfrey, Simon. PR2981.5.P34 1997, (v3)
Palisca, Claude V. ML193.P34 1991, (v9)
   ML290.2.P34 1985, (v9)
Palka, Joel W. F1434.H57 2000, (v4)
Palko, Zsuzsanna. GR154.7.K39.P35 1996, (v6)
Palladio, Andrea. NA2515.P253 1997, (v9)
Pallas-Areny, Ramon. TK7874.P345 1999, (v1)
Palley, Thomas I. HC106.8.P345 1998, (v6)
Palling, Bruce. DS414.P26 1992a, (v5)
Pallister, Janis L. PN1993.5.C2.P27 1995, (v3)
   PN1998.2.P28 1997, (v3)
Pallone, Nathaniel J. KF9750.5.P35 1990, (v7)
Pallottino, Massimo. DG221.P34513 1990, (v5)
   DG223.P283 1975, (v5)
Palma, Robert J. TX158.P24 1995, (v1)
Palmatier, Robert A. PE1583.P33 1995, (v3)
   PE1689.P27 1989, (v3)
   TX349.P353 2000, (v1)
Palmegiano, E. M. Z6673.P288 1998, (v10)
Palmer, Alan Warwick. DK191.P348, (v5)
   DR36.P3 1970b, (v5)
   DR486.P35 1993, (v5)
Palmer, Ben W. E302.6.M4.P25, (v4)
Palmer, Bertha Rachel. F636.P17, (v4)
Palmer, Bryan D. HM646.P35 2000, (v6)
Palmer, Christopher M. TD426.P35 1991, (v1)
Palmer, Christopher. ML2075.P28 1990, (v9)
Palmer, Clare. GE42.P35 1997, (v6)
Palmer, Frederick. D570.P32, (v5)
   E181.P512 1970, (v4)
Palmer, George Herbert. BJ1474.P3, (v8)
Palmer, John A. PR6005.O4.Z7848, (v3)
Palmer, John Anderson. B395.P166 1999, (v8)
Palmer, John D. QL121.P343 1995, (v1)
Palmer, John. PR691.P3 1962, (v3)

Palmer, Larry I. KF3821.P35 1989, (v7)
   KF3827.E87.P35 2000, (v7)
Palmer, Larry. ML651.P3 1989, (v9)
Palmer, Leonard Robert. DF220.P3 1965, (v5)
Palmer, Louis J. HV8694.P35 2001, (v6)
Palmer, Louis J. KF9725.P35 1998, (v7)
Palmer, Michael A. VA59.P283 1990, (v10)
Palmer, Monte. JQ3831.P35 1988, (v7)
Palmer, Norman Dunbar. UA23.P265 1987, (v10)
Palmer, R. Barton. PN1995.9.F54.P36 1994, (v3)
Palmer, R. R. D209.P26 1984, (v5)
   D295.P3, (v5)
   D769.A533 vol. 1, pt. 2, (v5)
Palmer, R. R. DC177.P3 1970, (v5)
Palmer, Richard H. PN1707.P27 1988, (v3)
   PR739.H5.P35 1998, (v3)
Palmer, Robert C. KD610.P35 1993, (v7)
Palmer, Roy. ML285.P18 1988, (v9)
Palmer, Tim. QH76.P355 1994, (v1)
   QH76.P36 1993, (v1)
Palmer, William J. PN1995.9.S6.P33 1993, (v3)
Palmer, William. DA935.P35 1994, (v5)
Palmieri, Patricia Ann. LD7212.2.P35 1995, (v7)
Palmore, Erdman Ballagh. HQ1064.U5.P26, (v6)
   QP86.P3, (v1)
Palmowski, Jan. DD901.F78.P35 1999, (v5)
Palmquist, Bonnie Beatson. F606.6.P35 1999, (v4)
Paloczi Horvath, Gyorgy. DS778.M3.P28 1963, (v5)
Palsson, Hermann. PT7262.E5.P3, (v3)
Palter, Robert. Q175.P33, (v1)
Paltock, Robert. PR3615.P5.L5, (v3)
Paludan, Ann. DS734.P285 1998, (v5)
Palumbi, Stephen R. QH371.P25 2001, (v1)
Palumbo-DeSimone, Christine. PS374.W6.P35 2000,
   (v3)
Palumbo-Liu, David. E184.O6.P26 1999, (v4)
Pammer, William J. HJ9145.P35 1990, (v6)
Pampel, Fred C. HV37.P28 1998, (v6)
Pamuk, Orhan. PL248.P34.W4713 1991, (v3)
Pan, David. BH301.E9.P36 2001, (v8)
Pan, Ku. DS748.P3 1974, (v5)
Pan, Lynn. DS732.P36 1990, (v5)
PanAfrican Association for Prehistory and Related
   Studies. GN861.P36 1996, (v6)
Panaiotov, Todor. HC59.72.E5.P36 1993, (v6)
Panaiotov, Todor. SD247.P68 1992, (v1)
Panayi, Panikos. DA125.G4.P36 1990, (v5)
   DD74.P27 2000, (v5)
   JV7685.G47.P35 1995, (v7)
Pandey, Rajyashree. PL791.2.Z5.P36 1998, (v3)
Pandiri, Ananda M. Z8322.7.P36 1995, (v10)
Pandit, Sneh. BH221.I53.P33 1977, (v8)
Pandolfini, Bruce. GV1445.P2579 1992, (v6)
Panek, LeRoy. PR888.S65.P36, (v3)
Pang, Hildegard Delgado. F1219.3.A7.P26 1992, (v4)
Pang, Tao. QC20.7.E4.P36 1997, (v1)
Pangallo, Karen L. Z8259.P36 1990, (v10)
Pangle, Thomas L. JC153.L87.P36 1988, (v7)
   JC423.P249 1991, (v7)
Panikkar, K. M. DS777.55.P3, (v5)
   DS485.M35.P22 1989, (v5)
Panish, Jon. ML3849.P27 1997, (v9)
Panitch, Leo. HC260.W24.P35, (v6)
Pankhurst, Richard. DT381.P39 1998, (v5)
   HC591.A3.P24, (v6)
Pankratz, Tom M. TD9.P36 2001, (v1)
Pannenberg, Wolfhart. BT80.P3413 1983, (v8)
Pano, Nicholas C. DR701.S86.P3, (v5)
Panofsky, Dora. N7760.P29 1962, (v9)
Panofsky, Erwin. N6370.P3 1962, (v9)
   N7445.P22, (v9)
   N7445.2.P36 1995, (v9)
   NA440.P23 1957, (v9)
   NC750.P2313 1991, (v9)
   ND588.D9.P28 1955, (v9)
   ND623.T7.P32 1969, (v9)
Panourgia, E. Neni K. GN585.G85.P35 1995, (v6)
Panova, Vera Fedorovna. PG3476.P255.K72, (v3)
Pantojas-Garcia, Emilio. HC154.5.P36 1990, (v6)
Panton, Kenneth J. DA34.P36 1997, (v5)
Pao, Yoh-Han. TK7882.P3.P36 1989, (v1)

Paoletti, John T. N6915.P26 1997, (v9)
Pap, Arthur. B808.5.P3, (v8)
Papadaki, Stamo. NA859.N5.P27, (v9)
Papadakis, Elim. GE195.P36 1998, (v6)
  HD58.8.P35 1996, (v6)
Papadimitriou, Christos H. QA267.7.P36 1994, (v1)
Papanastasiou, Tasos C. TA357.P33 1994, (v1)
Papandreou, Andreas George. DF852.P34, (v5)
Papenfuse, Eric Robert. E302.6.H29.P36 1997, (v4)
Paper, Jordan D. BL458.P36 1997, (v8)
  BL1802.P37 1995, (v8)
  E98.T6.P36 1988, (v4)
Paperno, Irina. HV6548.R9.P36 1997, (v6)
Papert, Seymour. LB1028.5.P325 1993, (v7)
Papke, David Ray. KF379.P37 1998, (v7)
Papke, Mary E. PS3513.L35.Z83 1993, (v3)
Pappas, George S. U410 L1.P37 1993, (v10)
Pappas, George Sotiros. B1348.P36 2000, (v8)
Pappas, Takis Spyros. JN5185.A1.P37 1999, (v7)
Pappe, Ilan. DS126.93.G7.P36 1988, (v5)
Paquette, Radnor Joseph. TA1145.P34 1982, (v1)
Paquette, Robert L. F1783.P25 1988, (v4)
Paradis, James G. Q223.P33 1991, (v1)
Paradis, James M. E492.94 6th.P37 1998, (v4)
Parakilas, James. ML460.P34 1992, (v9)
  ML650.P37 1999, (v9)
Parameswara Aithal, K. Z7090.P37 1993, (v10)
Parascandola, John. RM62.A24.P37 1992, (v2)
Parasuraman, S. HC440.E44.P37 1999, (v10)
Paratiyar. PL4758.9.S8437.K3313, (v3)
Paravisini-Gebert, Lizabeth. PR9250.9.A44.Z83 1996, (v3)
  Z1595.C364 1993, (v10)
Pardailhe-Galabrun, Annik. GT298.P37.P3713 1991, (v6)
Pardeck, John T. RJ507.A36.P37 1998, (v2)
Pardes, Ilana. BS1225.5.P37 2000, (v8)
Pardo Bazan, Emilia. PQ6629.A7.A24 1993, (v3)
  PQ6629.A7.P313 1992, (v3)
  PQ6629.A7.T7513 1999, (v3)
  PQ6629.A7 1973, (v3)
Pardo, Mary S. HN80.M66.P37 1998, (v6)
Pardo-Maurer, R. F1528.P32 1990, (v4)
Pardridge, William M. RM315.P365 2001, (v2)
Parducci, Allen. BF575.H27.P37 1995, (v2)
Pare, Ambroise. RD34.P27 1960, (v2)
Paredes, Americo. PQ7297.A1.C63, (v3)
Parekh, Bhikhu C. DS481.G3 P3465 1997, (v5)
  HM1271.P37 2000, (v6)
Parelli, R. J. KF2910.R33.P37 1994, (v7)
Parenti, Michael. E876.P37 1989, (v4)
Paret, Peter. DD422.C5.P33, (v5)
Paret, Peter. N6868.5.B3.P37, (v9)
Pareto, Vilfredo. HB177.P2913, (v6)
  HM59.P1813, (v6)
Parfitt, George A. E. PR2248.P26 1989, (v3)
Pargament, Kenneth I. BL53.P228 1997, (v8)
Pargellis, Stanley McCrory. Z2018.P37 1951, (v10)
Parikh, Sunita. HT1523.P27 1997, (v6)
Paringer, William Andrew. LB875.D5.P37 1990, (v7)
Parini, Jay. PS3511.R94.Z868 1999, (v3)
Paris, Arthur E. BX8770.A4.P37 1982, (v8)
Paris, Bernard J. PN56.P93.P38 1997, (v3)
Paris, Bernard J. PR2982.P37 1991, (v3)
Paris, David C. LA217.2.P38 1995, (v7)
Paris, F. TA347.B69.P34 1997, (v1)
Paris, Yvette. PN2287.P237.A3 1990, (v3)
Parish, James Robert. PN1995.9.H55.P37 1993, (v3)
  PN1995.9.M86.P37 1992, (v3)
  PN1995.9.P49.P37 1995, (v3)
  PN1995.9.P68.P37 1991, (v3)
  PN2285.P333 1991, (v3)
Parish, Peter J. E441.P367 1989, (v4)
Parish, R. V. QD95.P25 1990, (v1)
Parish, Steven M. DS493.9.N4.P36 1996, (v5)
Parish, William L. HQ684.P37, (v6)
Park, Chris C. GF895.P37 1992, (v6)
Park, Clara Claiborne. RC454.4.P37, (v2)
Park, David Allen. QC352.P34 1997, (v1)
Park, James William. F1418.P357 1995, (v4)
Park, Linda Sue. PZ7.P22115Si 2001, (v3)

Park, R. D. SF61.P37 1970, (v1)
Park, Robert Ezra. HM51.P312, (v6)
Park, Robert L. Q172.5.P77P37 2002, (v1)
  Q175.52.U5.P37 2000, (v1)
Park, Se Hark. HD75.6.P375 1998, (v6)
Park, Yeon Hwan. GV1114.9.P36 1997, (v6)
Parke, Catherine Neal. PR3537.B54.P37 1991, (v3)
Parke, H. W. DF123.P37, (v5)
Parker, Alexander Augustine. PQ6312.P37 1988, (v3)
Parker, Barry R. QB43.2.P33 1996, (v1)
  QB82.U62.M387 1994, (v1)
  QB209.P35 1991, (v1)
  QC173.7.P36 1986, (v1)
Parker, Blanford. PR561.P37 1998, (v3)
Parker, Coralie. HJ2425.A2P3 1928a, (v6)
Parker, D. S. HT690.P4.P37 1998, (v6)
Parker, David. PN98.M67.P37 1994, (v3)
Parker, DeWitt Henry. BD232.P27, (v8)
Parker, Donald Dean. E175.7.P3, (v4)
Parker, Donn B. HV6773.C65.P37 1983, (v6)
Parker, Dorothy R. PS3525.A2844.Z83 1992, (v3)
Parker, Dorothy. PS3531.A5855.A17 1944, (v3)
Parker, Frank S. QP519.9.S6.P37 1983, (v1)
Parker, Franklin. HV28.P4 P29 1995, (v6)
  Z5815.G5 P37 1991, (v10)
Parker, G. F. PR2975.J643.P37 1989, (v3)
Parker, Geoffrey. DH186.5.P283, (v5)
  DP179.P39 1998, (v5)
Parker, Glenn M. HD66.P348 2001, (v6)
Parker, Glenn R. JK1331.P37 1992, (v7)
Parker, Hershel. PS2384.B7.P37 1990, (v3)
Parker, Ian. P302.8.P37 1991, (v3)
Parker, J. Carlyle. CS65.P37, (v5)
Parker, James G. Z8206.58.P37 1991, (v10)
Parker, Jo Alyson. PR3458.A9.P37 1998, (v3)
Parker, John. DT512.9.A3, (v5)
Parker, Julia. HV541.P37 1998, (v6)
Parker, Linda S. E98.L3.P37 1989, (v4)
Parker, Mark Louis. PR468.P37.P37 2000, (v3)
Parker, Noel. D16.9.P2654 1999, (v5)
Parker, Patricia. PR2997.P8.P37 1996, (v3)
Parker, Pauline. PR2358.P35, (v3)
Parker, Peter. KTL42.S38.P37 1998, (v7)
Parker, Philip M. BL85.P325 1997, (v8)
  GN495.4.P37 1997, (v6)
  Z6683.C5.P37 1995, (v10)
Parker, Robert Dale. PS3503.I785.Z83 1988, (v3)
Parker, Rozsika. N8354.P37 1981, (v9)
Parker, Sharon. T60.8.P39 1998, (v1)
Parker, Steve. R130.5.P369 1998, (v2)
Parker, Sue Taylor. BF311.P31363 1999, (v2)
Parker, Thomas William. CR4755.G7.P3 1963, (v5)
Parker, Watson. F657.B6P32 2003, (v4)
Parker, William D. VE23.P28, (v10)
Parker, William Nelson. HC51.P37 1984, (v6)
Parker, William Riley. PR3581.P27, (v3)
Parker-Hale, Mary Ann. ML134.H16.P37 1988, (v9)
Parkes, Adam. PR888.C4.P37 1996, (v3)
Parkes, James William. DS123.P35 1949a, (v5)
Parkhill, Forbes. F784.D4 P3 1957, (v4)
Parkhill, Thomas. E98.R3.P245 1997, (v4)
Parkin, Alan J. BF201.P37 2000, (v2)
  BF371.P277 1993, (v2)
Parkin, Robert E. TJ211.4.P37 1991, (v1)
Parkin, Tim G. HB853.R66.P37 1992, (v6)
Parkin-Gounelas, Ruth. PR830.W6.P37 1991, (v3)
Parkinson, Alan F. DA990.U46.P355 1998, (v5)
Parkinson, Brian. BF311.P31367 1995, (v2)
Parkinson, Thomas Francis. PR5907.P29, (v3)
  PR5907.P3 1971, (v3)
Parkinson-Bailey, John J. NA971.M3, (v9)
Parkman, Francis. E175.5.P205, (v4)
  F592.P284 2002, (v4)
Parkman, Patricia. F1487.5.P37 1988, (v4)
Parks, Edd Winfield. PN99.U52.P3 1978, (v3)
Parks, Gordon. PS3566.A73.L4 1964, (v3)
Parks, John G. PS3554.O3.Z8 1991, (v3)
Parks, Richard S. ML410.D28.P24 1989, (v9)
Parks, Robert H. HG4572.P33 1998, (v6)
Parks, Robert J. HE2771.M5.P37, (v6)
Parks, Sharon Daloz. BL42.P37 2000, (v8)

Parlej, Piotr. PN56.R7.P37 1997, (v3)
Parlett, David Sidney. GV1233.P37 1991, (v6)
  GV1312.P37 1999, (v6)
Parmelee, David Freeland. QL695.2.P368 1992, (v1)
Parmenter, Barbara M. PJ8190.P3P37 1994, (v3)
Parmet, Harriet L. PS310.H64.P37 2001, (v3)
Parmet, Robert D. HD8081.A5.P37, (v6)
Parnell, Thomas. PR3616.A17 1989, (v3)
Parr, E. A. TJ213.P314 1996, (v1)
Parr, Elizabeth. RD120.7.P365 2001, (v2)
Parra, Teresa de la. PQ8549.P35.I413 1993, (v3)
Parris, Guichard. E185.5.N33.P3, (v4)
Parrish, Michael E. E784.P37 1992, (v4)
Parrish, Nancy C. PS267.H65.P37 1998, (v3)
Parrish, Paul A. PR3386.P3 1980, (v3)
Parrish, Stephen Maxfield. PR4023.A3.P3, (v3)
  PR5907.P26, (v3)
Parrish, William Earl. F466.P27 1992, (v4)
Parrot, Andre. N5370.P333, (v9)
  N5370.P343, (v9)
Parrott, Bruce. HC340.T4.P29 1983, (v6)
Parrott, Les. BF637.C6.P275 1997, (v2)
Parrott, Thomas Marc. PR461.P3, (v3)
  PR2894.P3 1955, (v3)
  PR2981.03 1962, (v3)
Parry, Adam. PA27.P257 1989, (v3)
Parry, Alan. RC489.S74.P37 1994, (v2)
Parry, Ellwood. N6537.C593 P37 1988, (v9)
Parry, Geraint. JN1121.P377 1992, (v7)
Parry, J. H. F1410.P3 1966, (v4)
  G80.P36 1981, (v6)
  JV61.P3 1961, (v7)
  VK15.P4, (v10)
Parry, J. P. DA550.P28 1993, (v5)
Parry, Linda. NK8898.M67.P37 1983, (v9)
Parry, Pamela Jeffcott. N6490.P3234, (v9)
Parry, William T. BC71.P377 1991, (v8)
Parsa, Misagh. JC491.P36 2000, (v7)
Parsipur, Shahrnush. PK6561.P247.Z3613 1998, (v3)
Parson, Nels A. UG630.P263, (v10)
Parsons, D. W. H97.P373 1995, (v6)
  PN4888.C59.P37 1990, (v3)
Parsons, Deborah L. PN56.5.F53P37 2000, (v3)
Parsons, Elsie Worthington Clews. E99.T35 P37 1994, (v4)
Parsons, John Carmi. DA229.P37 1995, (v5)
Parsons, Laila. DS113.72.P37 2000, (v5)
Parsons, Lee Allen. F1219.3.A7.P29 1988, (v4)
Parsons, Lynn H. Z8015.7.P37 1993, (v10)
Parsons, M. L. QC981.8.G56.P39 1995, (v1)
Parsons, Michael D. LC173.P37 1997, (v7)
Parsons, Neil. DA125.N4.P37 1998, (v5)
Parsons, Paul. Z231.5.U6.P37 1989, (v10)
Parsons, Schuyler Livingston. CT275.P3875.A3, (v5)
Parsons, Stanley B. G1201.F7.P3 1978, (v6)
  G1201.F7.P353 1990, (v6)
Parsons, Susan Frank. BJ1278.F45 P37 1996, (v8)
Parsons, Talcott. BF698.P256, (v2)
Parsons, Talcott. HM51.P37, (v6)
Parsons, William Barclay. BF175.4.R44.P37 1999, (v2)
Partch, Harry. ML410.P176.A3 1991, (v9)
Partch, Harry. ML1400.P3 1974, (v9)
Partington, J. R. QD11.P28, (v1)
Partner, Peter. DG797.P37 1972b, (v5)
  DG812.P37, (v5)
Partner, Simon. HD9696.A3.J39317 1999, (v6)
Partnow, Elaine. PN471.P37 1998, (v3)
Parton, Anthony. NX556.Z9.L376 1993, (v9)
Partridge, A. C. PR508.L3.P3, (v3)
Partridge, Eric. PE27.P3 1980, (v3)
  PR2892.P27 1991, (v3)
Partridge, Lloyd D. QP355.2.P37 1993, (v1)
Partridge, Michael Stephen. U155.G7.P38 1989, (v10)
  Z8963.8.P37 1990, (v10)
Pas, Julian F. BL1923.P37 1998, (v8)
Pasachoff, Jay M. QB64.P37 2000, (v1)
Pascal, Blaise. B1900.E5.C3, (v8)
  B1901.P42 E5 1986, (v8)
  QC143.P33 1937, (v1)

Pascal, Roy. PT238.P3, **(v3)**
  PT317.P38 1967, **(v3)**
  PT741.P3 1956, **(v3)**
Pascarella, Ernest T. LA229.P34 1991, **(v7)**
Paschall, Rod. U240.P38 1990, **(v10)**
Pasco, Allan H. DC33.4.P385 1997, **(v5)**
  PQ637.N37.P37 1987, **(v3)**
Pascoe, Peggy. HV1446.A17.P37 1990, **(v6)**
Pasek, Jan Chryzostom. DK4312.P3.A3513, **(v5)**
Paskins, Barrie. U22.P37, **(v10)**
Pasnau, Robert. B765.T53 S8166 2002, **(v8)**
Passage, Charles E. PT1682.W6.E56, **(v3)**
  PT2492.P3, **(v3)**
Passant, Ernest James. DD232.P35, **(v5)**
Passerin d'Entreves, Alessandro. JA82.P32, **(v7)**
Passerini, Luisa. DA110.P34 1999, **(v3)**
Passmore, Kevin. DC801.L967.P37 1997, **(v5)**
Passty, Jeanette N. PR6025.A16.Z86 1988, **(v3)**
Pasternack, Carol Braun. PR203.P37 1995, **(v3)**
Pasternak, Boris Leonidovich. PG3476.P27.A26, **(v3)**
  PG3476.P27D63 1991b, **(v3)**
Pasternak, Burton. DS793.M7.P3625 1993, **(v5)**
Pasternak, Charles A. QP514.2.P374 1998, **(v1)**
Pasto, Daniel J. QD476.P35, **(v1)**
Pastor, Robert A. E183.8.N5.P37 1987, **(v4)**
Pasuk Phongpaichit. HC445.P39 2002, **(v6)**
Pasztory, Esther. F1219.1.T27.P37 1997, **(v4)**
  F1219.76.A78.P37 1983, **(v4)**
Patai, Daphne. LC212.86.P37 1998, **(v7)**
Patai, Raphael. DS57.P3 1962, **(v5)**
  DS109.86.P39.A3 1992, **(v5)**
Patai, Saul. QD305.H7.P3, **(v1)**
  QD305.I6.P3, **(v1)**
  QD412.S6.P37 1989, **(v1)**
Patch, Howard Rollin. PN687.H37.P37 1970, **(v3)**
Patch, William L. DD247.B7.P38 1998, **(v5)**
Patchen, Kenneth. PS3531.A764.A6 1957, **(v3)**
  PS3531.A764.A6 1968, **(v3)**
  PS3531.A764 M4, **(v3)**
  PS3531.A764.S5, **(v3)**
Pateman, Carole. HQ1206.P35 1988, **(v6)**
  JC328.P27, **(v7)**
Pater, Walter. NX450.5.P37 1980, **(v9)**
  PR5134.M31, **(v3)**
  PR5134.M3 1985, **(v3)**
  PR5136.A43 1970, **(v3)**
Paterek, Josephine. E98.C8.P37 1994, **(v4)**
Paternosto, Cesar. F3429.3.S39.P3813 1996, **(v4)**
Paterson, John. DA684.P293 1996, **(v5)**
Paterson, Katherine. PZ7.P273Jac 1980, **(v3)**
Paterson, Linda M. PC3308.P33 1993, **(v3)**
Paterson, Matthew. GE170.P38 2000, **(v6)**
Paterson, Thomas G. E183.8.C9.P36 1994, **(v4)**
  E744.P3118 1988, **(v4)**
  E744.P312 1992, **(v4)**
Patey, Douglas Lane. PR6045.A97.Z7494 1998, **(v3)**
Patin, Thomas. N71.P32 1997, **(v9)**
Patman, Robert G. DT367.63.S65.P38 1990, **(v5)**
Patman ap aōn, N ila. PL4758.9.P218T313 1997, **(v3)**
Patnaik, Pradyot. TD193.P38 1997, **(v1)**
Paton, Alan. PR9369.3.P37.D4 1961, **(v3)**
  PR9369.3.P37.K6 1975b, **(v3)**
Paton, T. R. S592.2.P373 1995, **(v1)**
Patraka, Vivian. PN56.H55.P37 1999, **(v3)**
Patrick, Dale R. TK2000.P35 1997, **(v1)**
  TK3001.P37 1999, **(v1)**
Patrick, Graham L. RS403.P38 2001, **(v2)**
Patrick, Jean L. S. E342.1.M2, **(v4)**
Patrick, Ludmilla A. PG3242.P3, **(v3)**
Patrick, Steven R. TJ163.3.P38 1993, **(v1)**
Patt, Beatrice P. (Shapiro). PQ6603.A7.Z63, **(v3)**
  PQ6174.P35, **(v3)**
Patten, Chris. DS796.H757.P39 1998, **(v5)**
Patterson, Annabel M. DA130.P34 1994, **(v5)**
  PR3546.P3, **(v3)**
Patterson, Austin M. QD5.P3 1991, **(v1)**
Patterson, Beverly Bush. ML3160.P28 1995, **(v9)**
Patterson, Bradley H. JK518.P37 1988, **(v7)**
Patterson, C. Perry. E332.P32, **(v4)**
Patterson, Catherine F. JS3265.P37 1999, **(v7)**

Patterson, Christine P. F437.P38 1996, **(v4)**
Patterson, Cynthia. HQ662.5.A25 1998, **(v6)**
Patterson, Daniel W. ML3178.S5.P4, **(v9)**
Patterson, David. D804.195.P37 1998, **(v5)**
  PJ5049.R8.P3, **(v3)**
  PN56.H55.P38 1992, **(v3)**
Patterson, James T. E741.P377, **(v4)**
  E748.T2.P37, **(v4)**
  HN59.P39 2000, **(v6)**
  JK325.P36, **(v7)**
Patterson, Kelly D. JK2261.P318 1996, **(v7)**
Patterson, Lee. PR1933.H57.P38 1991, **(v3)**
Patterson, Margaret C. Z6511.P37 1983, **(v10)**
Patterson, Michael. PN2652.P38 1990, **(v3)**
Patterson, Thomas E. HJK524.P38 1993, **(v7)**
  JK526 1976.P37, **(v7)**
Patterson, Walter C. TK9360.P38 1984, **(v1)**
Patterson, Wayne. DU624.7.K67.P37 1988, **(v5)**
Patteson, Richard F. PR9214.P37 1998, **(v3)**
Patti, Charles H. HF5823.P3528 1991, **(v6)**
Pattillo, Donald M. TL521.P38 1998, **(v1)**
Pattison, George. BT84.P37 1999, **(v8)**
Pattison, Walter Thomas. PQ6555.Z5.P28, **(v3)**
Patton, Adell. R652.P38 1996, **(v2)**
Patton, George S. D743.P3, **(v5)**
Patton, Mark. GN588.P37 1996, **(v6)**
Patton, Venetria K. PS374.N4.P38 2000, **(v3)**
Patton-Hulce, Vicki. KF3775.A68.P38 1995, **(v7)**
Pauka, Kirstin. PN2904.5.R35.P38 1998, **(v3)**
Pauketat, Timothy R. E78.I3.P38 1994, **(v4)**
Paul, Anne. F3429.1.P25.P38 1990, **(v4)**
Paul, Barbara Dotts. Z1351.P38 1999, **(v10)**
Paul, Diane B. QH431.P34 1998, **(v1)**
Paul, Ellen Frankel. KF3467.P38 1988, **(v7)**
Paul, Gregory S. QE862.D5.P38 1988, **(v1)**
Paul, Rhea. RJ496.L35P38 2001, **(v2)**
Paul, Rodman W. F591.P3 2001, **(v4)**
  F595.P27 1988, **(v4)**
  F865.P25, **(v4)**
  F865.P26, **(v4)**
Paul, Septimus H. UA23.P3724 2000, **(v10)**
Paul, William. PN1995.9.H6.P35 1994, **(v3)**
Paulding, James Kirke. PS2527.K6, **(v3)**
  PS2527.K6 1988, **(v3)**
Pauley, Garth E. E176.1.P3946 2001, **(v4)**
Paulhan, Jean. PQ139.P27, **(v3)**
Pauling, Linus. Q143.P25, **(v1)**
  Q143.P25.A3 1995, **(v1)**
  QC174.1.P38, **(v1)**
  QD31.2.P38 1975, **(v1)**
  QD469.P38 1960, **(v1)**
  RM666.A79.P3, **(v2)**
Paullin, Charles Oscar. VB23.P32 1968, **(v10)**
Paulos, John Allen. BC71.P38 2000, **(v8)**
  QA276.P285 1998, **(v1)**
Paulson, Arthur C. JK528.P38 2000, **(v7)**
Paulson, Ronald. BH221.G72.P38 1989, **(v8)**
  N6797.H6.P38 1991, **(v9)**
  PR858.A74.P38 1996, **(v3)**
  PR3456.P38 2000, **(v3)**
  PR3457.P3, **(v3)**
Paulson, Ross Evans. JC599.U5.P38 1997, **(v7)**
Paulson, William R. PQ283.P3 1987, **(v3)**
Paulsson, Martin. F144.A8.P28 1994, **(v4)**
Paulston, Christina Bratt. PE1128.A2.P34, **(v3)**
Pauly, Louis W. HG3881.P34 1997, **(v6)**
Pauly, Mark V. HG9396.P38 1997, **(v6)**
Pauly, Philip J. QH305.2.U6, **(v1)**
Pauly, Rebecca M. PN1993.5.F7.P35 1993, **(v3)**
Pauly, Reinhard G. ML195.P38 2000, **(v9)**
Paunovic, Milan. TS670.P29 1998, **(v1)**
Pausanias. DF27.P4 1913, **(v5)**
Pava, Moses L. HD60.P33 1995, **(v6)**
Pavao, Joyce Maguire. HV875.P38 1998, **(v6)**
Pavese, Cesare. PQ4835.A846 A6 1968, **(v3)**
Pavie, Theodore. PQ2380.P44.T35 1998, **(v3)**
Pavis, Patrice. PN1643.P3813 1992, **(v3)**
Pavis, Patrice. PN2035.P2913 1998, **(v3)**
Pavkovic, Aleksandar. DR1282.P37 1997, **(v5)**
Pavlov, Ivan Petrovich. QP381.P4, **(v1)**
Pawel, Ernst. PT2621.A26.Z8155 1984, **(v3)**

Pawley, Martin. CB428.P4, **(v5)**
Pawluch, Dorothy. RJ47.7.P38 1996, **(v2)**
Paxton, Frederick S. GT3242.P39 1990, **(v6)**
Paxton, John. DK14.P39 2001, **(v5)**
  DK36.P39 1993, **(v5)**
  Z7165.E8.P34 1992, **(v10)**
Paxton, Nancy L. DS479.P42 1999, **(v5)**
  PR4692.F45.P39 1991, **(v3)**
Paxton, Robert O. DC397.P37, **(v5)**
Payne, Charles M. E185.93.M6.P39 1995, **(v4)**
  LC5131.P39 1984, **(v7)**
Payne, Christiana. ND1354.4.P39 1993, **(v9)**
Payne, Darwin Reid. PN2091.S8.P349 1994, **(v3)**
Payne, Elizabeth Anne. HD6079.2.U5.P38 1988, **(v6)**
Payne, James L. HJ2381.P39 1993, **(v6)**
  HJ7537.P39 1991, **(v6)**
  HV91.P38 1998, **(v6)**
  UA10.P38 1989, **(v10)**
Payne, Judith A. PQ7082.N7.P37 1993, **(v3)**
Payne, Keith B. UA23.P3747 1996, **(v10)**
Payne, Leigh A. F1414.2.P355 2000, **(v4)**
Payne, Neil F. SK355.P39 1994, **(v1)**
Payne, Philip. PT2625.U8.M415 1988, **(v3)**
Payne, Richard J. D888.S6.P39 1992, **(v5)**
  E184.A1.P36 1998, **(v4)**
Payne, Robert O. PR1924.P35, **(v3)**
Payne, Robert. DS778.M3.P32 1961, **(v5)**
Payne, Robert. PN56.P6.P3 1960, **(v3)**
Payne, Rodger M. BV4930.P38 1998, **(v8)**
Payne, Samuel B. U105.P335 1989, **(v10)**
Payne, Stanley G. BX1583.P29 1984, **(v8)**
  DP243.P39 1999, **(v5)**
  DP257.P34, **(v5)**
  JC481.P375 1995, **(v7)**
  UA782.P3, **(v10)**
Payson, Steven. HB171.5.P34 2000, **(v6)**
  HF5415.157.P39 1994, **(v6)**
Paz Salinas, Maria Emilia. D753.P35 1997, **(v5)**
Paz, D. G. BR759.P388 1992, **(v8)**
Paz, Octavio. F1210.P313, **(v4)**
  PN1031.P3513, **(v3)**
  PQ7297.P285.E2, **(v3)**
  PQ7299.E3B4, **(v3)**
Peabody, Marian Lawrence. CT275.P488.A3, **(v5)**
Peabody, Sue. DC133.4.P43 1996, **(v5)**
Peacey, J. G. TN713.P42 1979, **(v1)**
Peach, Linden. PR6045.O72.Z8575 1999, **(v3)**
  PR6053.A73.Z83 1998, **(v3)**
  PS3563.O8749Z827 2000, **(v3)**
Peacock, D. Keith. PN2595.P43 1999, **(v3)**
  PR6066.I53.Z735 1997, **(v3)**
Peacock, Thomas Love. PR5160.A2 1947, **(v3)**
  PR5160.A2 1967, **(v3)**
Peacocke, Christopher. BD181.P43 1992, **(v8)**
Peake, Mervyn Laurence. PR6031.E183 T5 vol. 1, **(v3)**
  PR6031.E183 T5 vol. 2, **(v3)**
  PR6031.E183 T5 vol. 3, **(v3)**
Peake, Tom H. RA564.8.P4 1998, **(v2)**
Pearce, E. A. QC982.P43, **(v1)**
Pearce, Frank. HM22.F8.D869 1989, **(v6)**
Pearce, George F. F319.P4.P36 2000, **(v4)**
Pearce, John Ed. F456.P42 1987, **(v4)**
Pearce, Joseph. PG3488.O4.O4 Z833 2001, **(v3)**
Pearce, Lynne. PR119.P43 1997, **(v3)**
Pearce, R. D. DA585.A8.P43 1997, **(v5)**
Peare, Catherine Owens. F152.2.P34, **(v4)**
Pearl, Judea. BD541.P43 2000, **(v8)**
Pearl, Richard Maxwell. TN270.P4 1973, **(v1)**
Pearlman, E. PR2982.P43 1992, **(v3)**
Pearlman, Michael. UA23.P384 1999, **(v10)**
  UB353.P42 1984, **(v10)**
Pearlman, Mickey. PS3565.L82.Z84 1991, **(v3)**
Pearlstein, Elinor L. N7336.P43 1993, **(v9)**
Pearlstein, Richard M. HV6431.P43 1991, **(v6)**
Pears, David Francis. B1489.P43 1990, **(v8)**
Pearsall, Deborah M. CC79.5.P5 P43 2000, **(v5)**
Pearsall, Derek Albert. PR502.R58 vol. 1, **(v3)**
  PR1905.P43 1992, **(v3)**
Pearson, Charles E. F371.P43 1995, **(v4)**
Pearson, Frederic S. UA10.P43 1994, **(v10)**
Pearson, Frederick. VF7.U64 no. 3624, **(v10)**

Pearson, Hesketh. PR3533.P34, (v3)
    PR4581.P35, (v3)
    PR5332.P4 1954, (v3)
    PR5823.P4, (v3)
Pearson, Hugh. F294.B35.P43 2000, (v4)
Pearson, John H. PS2127.T4.P43 1997, (v3)
Pearson, M. N. DT432.P43 1998, (v5)
Pearson, Margaret M. HC427.92.P39 1997, (v6)
    HG5782.P43 1991, (v6)
Pearson, Paul David. NA1455.F53.A255, (v9)
Pearson, Roberta E. PN1995.75.P43 1992, (v3)
Pearson, Roger. PQ2344.Z5.P43 1996, (v3)
Pease, Allison. PR478.E76, (v3)
Pease, William Henry. KF368.P44.P43 1995, (v7)
Peattie, Elia (Wilkinson). PS3531.E255 M6 1969, (v3)
Peattie, Lisa Redfield. HN370.C5.P4, (v6)
Peattie, Mark R. DU500.P43 1988, (v5)
Peavy, Linda S. F596.P4 1998, (v4)
    F614.L58.F477 1990, (v4)
Peccei, Aurelio. CB161.P35 1981, (v5)
    CB478.P4, (v5)
Peceny, Mark. E744.P33 1999, (v4)
Pechman, Joseph A. HJ257.2.P4 1983, (v6)
    HJ2322.A3.P42 1985, (v6)
Pechter, Edward. PR2829.P43 1999, (v3)
    PR2970.P43 1995, (v3)
Peck, David R. Z1229.E87.P43 1992, (v10)
Peck, Demaree C. PS3505.A87.Z756 1995, (v3)
Peck, Donna. F839.3.M29 1999, (v4)
Peck, Graham. DS777.53.P37, (v5)
Peck, Gunther. HD4875.N7.P43 2000, (v6)
Peck, H. Daniel. PS3054.P4 1990, (v3)
Peck, Jamie. HD5707.P425 1996, (v6)
Peck, Jamie. HV95.P43 2001, (v6)
Peck, John. PR468.W37.P43 1998, (v3)
    PR830.S4.P43 2001, (v3)
Peck, Linda Levy. DA390.P43 1990, (v5)
Peck, Louis F. PR4888.P4, (v3)
Peck, Richard. PR9362.5.P43 1997, (v3)
    PZ7.P338Yh 2000, (v3)
Peck, Robert S. KF4749.P38 1991, (v7)
Peck, Russell A. PR1905.Z99.P43 1988, (v3)
Peck, Taylor. VA70.W3.P4, (v10)
Peckenpaugh, Nancy J. RM216.P67 1999, (v2)
Pecker, Jean Claude. QB15.P38 2001, (v1)
Peckham, Howard Henry. E230.P35, (v4)
    E230.P36, (v4)
Peckham, Morse. B803.P4, (v8)
    PN751.P43 1995, (v3)
Pecora, Norma Odom. HF6161.C33.P43 1998, (v6)
Pecora, Vincent P. PN56.H557.P43 1997, (v3)
Pederson, Jane Marie. HN79.W6.P43 1992, (v6)
Pederson, Lucille M. RC280.B8.P34 1995, (v2)
Pedley, John Griffiths. DF130.P44 1993, (v5)
    DG70.P3.P42 1990, (v5)
Pedro IV, King of Aragon, 1319?-1387. DP124.8.P413 1991, (v5)
Pedrycz, Witold. QA248.5.P38 1998, (v1)
Peebles, Curtis. QB651.P44 2000, (v1)
    TL789.3.P44 1994, (v1)
    UG1523.P44 1997, (v10)
Peebles, Gavin. HC445.8.P44 1996, (v6)
Peebles, P. J. E. QC174.12.P4 1992, (v1)
Peel, J. D. Y. BV3625.N5, (v8)
Peel, Robert. BX6943.P4, (v8)
    BX6950.P44 1988, (v8)
Peele, George. PR2731.P345, (v3)
Peerenboom, R. P. B126.P38 1993, (v8)
Peers, E. Allison. BV5077.S7.P52, (v8)
    DP66.P4 1956, (v5)
    PQ6065.P43 1976, (v3)
    PQ6070.P4 1940a, (v3)
    PQ6176.P245 1968, (v3)
Peers, Laura L. E99.C6.P43 1994, (v4)
Peery, Nelson. E185.97.P44.A3 1994, (v4)
Peet, Richard. HB97.5.P335 1991, (v6)
Peffer, George Anthony. F869.S39.C56 1999, (v4)
Pegram, Thomas R. HV5292.P44 1998, (v6)
    JK5774.5.P44 1992, (v7)
Peguy, Charles Pierre. PQ2631.E25.M7 1936, (v3)
Pei, Mario. PE1571.P45, (v3)

Pei, Mario. PM8008.P4, (v3)
Peierls, Rudolf Ernst. QC71.P38 1997, (v1)
Peiffer, Katrina Schimmoeller. PS163.P45 2000, (v3)
Peikoff, Leonard. B945.R234 P44 1991, (v8)
Peim, Nick. LB1631.P38 1993, (v7)
Peirce, Charles S. B945.P43.C5 1968, (v8)
    B945.P44.A3 1998, (v8)
Peirce, Neal R. F721.P45 1972, (v4)
    F851.P4 1972, (v4)
Peiss, Kathy Lee. F124.P38 1986, (v4)
Peitgen, Heinz-Otto. QA447.P45 1986, (v1)
    QA614.86.P43 1992, (v1)
Peixoto, Jose Pinto. QC981.P434 1991, (v1)
Pelcovits, Nathan A. DS740.5.G5.P4 1969, (v5)
Pelczar, Michael J. QR41.2.P4 1986, (v1)
Peleg, Ilan. JC599.W47.P45 1995, (v7)
Peletz, Michael G. GN635.M4.P45 1988, (v6)
Pelikan, Jaroslav Jan. AZ103.P44 1984, (v10)
    BL245.P45 1993, (v8)
    BT21.2.P42, (v8)
    BT198.P44 1985, (v8)
    BT610.P45 1996, (v8)
    BX1765.2.P4, (v8)
    DG312.P38 1987, (v5)
    LB2321.P383 1992, (v7)
    PT1925.P36 1995, (v3)
Pelinka, Anton. DK4435.J37.P454 1998, (v5)
Pelinka, Anton. JN2026.P44 1998, (v7)
Pellegrino, Charles R. QB981.P44 1983, (v1)
Pellegrino, Edmund D. R723.P38, (v2)
    R723.P3813, (v2)
    R724.P34 1993, (v2)
    R725.5.P45 1988, (v2)
    R725.56.P45513 1997, (v2)
Pelli, Cesar. NA737.P39.A4 1990, (v9)
Pelling, Henry. DA592.P45 1997, (v5)
Pellowski, Anne. LB1042.P43 1984b, (v7)
Pells, Richard H. D1065.U5.P388 1997, (v5)
Pelton, Gordon E. TK7882.S65.P48 1993, (v1)
Pelton, Leroy H. HV741.P445 1989, (v6)
Peltz, Rakhmiel. F158.9.J5.P45 1998, (v4)
Peltzman, Barbara R. LB1139.23.P45 1998, (v7)
Pelupessy, Wim. HD1333.S2.P45 1997, (v6)
Pelzer, Linda Claycomb. PS3511.I9.Z812 2000, (v3)
Pemberton, William E. E877.P46 1997, (v4)
Pemble, John. DA533.P455 1987, (v5)
Pempel, T. J. HC462.9.P4 1982, (v6)
Pena, Devon Gerardo. HD8119.M49.P46 1997, (v6)
Peña, José Enrique de la. F390.P34313 1997, (v4)
Pena, Manuel H. ML3481.P44 1999, (v9)
Pena, Milagros. BX1484.2.P46 1995, (v8)
Pender, Nola J. RT67.P56 2002, (v2)
Pendergast, Richard J. BD511.P38, (v8)
Pendergrast, Mark. RC455.2.F35.P46 1995, (v2)
Pendleton, Robert. PR6013.R44.Z6578 1996, (v3)
Pendleton, Thomas A. PS3511.I9.G868 1993, (v3)
Pendleton, Wade C. DT1680.P46 1996, (v5)
Pendse, Shripad Narayan. PK2418.P4.G313x, (v3)
Penelhum, Terence. BL51.P3449 1995, (v8)
Penelis, George G. TA658.44.P46 1997, (v1)
Penelope, Julia. PE1074.75.P46 1990, (v3)
Penfield, Wilder. QP376.P39, (v1)
    QP383.P46 1967, (v1)
    QP385.P38, (v1)
    RD529.P4, (v2)
Penkala, Maria. DS511.P45 1966a, (v5)
Penlington, Norman. F1033.P4, (v4)
Penn, C. W. QR63.P455 1990, (v1)
Penn, Geoffrey. VM728.G7.P4, (v10)
Penn, James R. G141.P43 1997, (v6)
Penn, William. F152.2.P3956 1981, (v4)
Penney, David W. E98.A7.A77 1992, (v4)
Penniman, Clara. HJ4655.A1.P43, (v6)
Pennington, Kenneth. K3334.P46 1993, (v7)
Pennington, Michael. PR2837.P39 2000, (v3)
Pennock, Robert T. QH366.2.P428 1999, (v1)
Penny, Nicholas. NB1202.P46 1993, (v9)
Penny, Ralph J. PC4101.P46 1991, (v3)
Pennycook, Alastair. PE2751.P47 1998, (v3)
Pennycuick, C. J. QH513.P46 1992, (v1)
Penrose, Roger. Q335.P415 1989, (v1)

Penrose, Roland. NB553.P45.P42 (v9)
Pensky, Max. PT2603.E455.Z796 1993, (v3)
Penslar, Derek Jonathan. DS135.E83.P46 2001, (v5)
    DS149.P424 1991, (v5)
Penton, M. James. BX8526.P46 1985, (v8)
Pentony, DeVere Edwin. LD729.C975.P4, (v7)
Penuel, Arnold M. PQ8180.17.A73.Z827 1994, (v3)
Penvenne, Jeanne. HD8798.Z8.M325 1995, (v6)
Peou, Sorpong. DS554.8.P443 1999, (v5)
Pepper, Art. ML419.P48 A3 2000, (v9)
Pepper, Stephen Coburn. BD111.P38 1966, (v8)
    BH201.P4 1970, (v8)
    BH201.P42, (v8)
Pepper, Suzanne. LA1131.82.P47 1996, (v7)
Peppiatt, Michael. ND497.B16.P46 1997, (v9)
Pepys, Samuel. DA447.P4.A4 1970, (v5)
    VA454.P46 1971, (v10)
Pera, Marcello. QP341.P4713 1992, (v1)
Peralta-Ramos, Monica. HC175.P42 1991, (v6)
Perces, Marjorie B. GV1783.P46 1992, (v6)
Perceval, John. RC463.P4 1974, (v2)
Percival, Donald B. QA280.P47 2000, (v1)
Percival, Florence. PR1882.P47 1998, (v3)
Percival, Ian. QA614.8.P47 1982, (v1)
Percy, Stephen L. HV1553.P46 1989, (v6)
Percy, Thomas. PR29.P4.A4 1944, (v3)
Percy, Walker. PS3566.E59.L3, (v3)
    PS3566.E6912.L3, (v3)
    PS3566.E6912.M6, (v3)
Perdue, Theda. E99.C5.P3934 1998, (v4)
Pereboom, Maarten L. DA47.1.P47 1995, (v5)
Perec, Georges. PQ2676.E67.V513 1987, (v3)
Pereira, A. HD9560.4.P37 1987, (v6)
Pereira, Anthony W. HD6614.A29.P47 1997, (v6)
Pereira, Jose. NA4670.P47 1994, (v9)
Pereira, Kim. PS3573.I45677.Z83 1995, (v3)
Pereira, Luiz Carlos Bresser. HC125.P4379 1996, (v6)
    HC165.P46 1993, (v6)
    HC187.P392213 1984, (v6)
    HG835.P4413 1987, (v6)
Perelman, Chaïm. BC177.P395, (v8)
Perelman, Michael. HB99.7.K38.P46 1989, (v6)
    HB3711.P377 1999, (v6)
    HC103.P417 2002, (v6)
    HM221.P44 1998, (v6)
Perelman, S. J. PS3531.E6544.B4 1963, (v3)
    PS3531.E6544.P4, (v3)
    PS3531.E6544.R5, (v3)
    PS3531.E6544.R6, (v3)
Perera, Nihal. HN670.8.A8.P454 1998, (v6)
Perera, Victor. F1221.L2.P47 1982, (v4)
Peres, Shimon. DS126.6.P47.A5 1998, (v5)
Peressini, Anthony L. QA402.5.P42 1988, (v1)
Peretti, Burton W. ML3508.P45 1992, (v9)
Peretz, Don. JQ1830.A58.P47 1997, (v7)
Peretz, Isaac Leib. PJ5129.P4 A6 1958, (v3)
    PJ5129.P4 B66, (v3)
Perez de Ayala, Ramon. PQ6629.E64.B4 1939, (v3)
Perez Firmat, Gustavo. E184.C97.P47 1994, (v4)
Perez Galdos, Benito. PQ6555.F613 1989, (v3)
    PQ6555.F7.E5 1986, (v3)
    PQ6555.V6 1993, (v3)
Perez Gomez, Alberto. NA956.P413 1983, (v9)
Perez y Gonzalez, Maria. E184.P85.P47 2000, (v4)
Perez, Douglas Werner. HV8141.P36 1994, (v6)
Perez, Gilberto. PN1995.P397 1998, (v3)
Perez, Janet. PQ6055.P4 1988, (v3)
    PQ6055.P5 1996, (v3)
Perez, Janet. PQ6605.E44.Z783 2000, (v3)
Perez, Louis A. E715.P45 1998, (v4)
    F1776.P46 1988, (v4)
    F1785.P47 1983, (v4)
    HD1531.C9.P47 1989, (v6)
    Z1511.P43 1988, (v10)
    E183.8.C9 P465 1997, (v4)
Perez, Ramon. F1221.Z3.P44 1999, (v4)
Perez-Lopez, Jorge F. HC152.5.P47 1987, (v6)
    HD2346.C84.P47 1995, (v6)
Perez-Ramos, Antonio. B1198.P44 1988, (v8)
Perez-Torres, Rafael. PS153.M4.P47 1995, (v3)

Perinbam, B. Marie. DT551.45.M36.P47 1997, (v5)
Peritz, Rudolph J. R. KF1649.P47 1996, (v7)
Perkin, Harold James. HN398.E5.P47 1981, (v6)
  HN400.S6.P47 1989, (v6)
Perkin, Joan. HQ1599.E5.P47 1995, (v6)
Perkin, Joan. KD758.P37 1989, (v7)
Perkins, Bradford. E357.P64, (v4)
  E357.P66, (v4)
  E358.P4, (v4)
Perkins, David N. BF431.P365 1995, (v2)
Perkins, David. PR1139.P4, (v3)
  PR5888.P46, (v3)
  PR5892.P5.P4, (v3)
Perkins, Dexter. F2171.P4, (v4)
  JX1425.P385 1966, (v7)
Perkins, Dorothy. DS705.P47 1999, (v5)
Perkins, Edwin J. HC104.P47, (v6)
Perkins, Elizabeth A. F517.P46 1998, (v4)
Perkins, Eric John. QH95.9.P47, (v1)
Perkins, Frances. E807.P4, (v4)
Perkins, Howard Cecil. E440.5.P45, (v4)
Perkins, John H. SB191.W5.P42 1997, (v1)
Perkins, Leeman L. ML172.P47 1999, (v9)
Perkins, Moreland. PR4034.S43.P47 1998, (v3)
Perkinson, Henry J. LA132.P39 1984, (v7)
  LA205.P45, (v7)
  LA209.P422 1977, (v7)
Perko, Lawrence. QA372.P47 1991, (v1)
Perkovich, George. UA840.P47 1999, (v10)
Perkowitz, S. QC355.2.P48 1996, (v1)
Perl, William R. D810.J4.P477 1979, (v5)
Perle, George. ML410.B47.P48, (v9)
  ML410.P2925.A3 1990, (v9)
  MT40.P45 1991, (v9)
Perlès, Catherine. GN776.22.G8 P47 2001, (v6)
Perlin, John. SD418.P47 1989, (v1)
Perlin, Michael L. KF480.P474 2000, (v7)
Perlingieri, Ilya Sandra. ND623.A5395.P4 1992, (v9)
Perlis, Sam. QA263.P4, (v1)
Perlman, Janice E. HN290.R47.P47, (v6)
Perlman, Mark. HB75.P453 1998, (v6)
Perlman, Richard. HD6061.P47 1994, (v6)
Perlman, Selig. HD4841.P4, (v6)
Perlmann, Joel. LC3733.P76.P47 1988, (v7)
Perlmutter, Amos. U21.5.P36, (v10)
Perloff, Marjorie. PN49.P413 1996, (v3)
Perloff, Nancy Lynn. ML410.S196.P47 1991, (v9)
Perloff, Richard M. BF637.P4.P39 1993, (v2)
  JA85.2.U6.P47 1998, (v7)
  RA644.A25.P43 2001, (v2)
Perlstein, Rick. E748.G64.P37 2001, (v4)
Permaloff, Anne. F330.P47 1995, (v4)
Perman, Michael. F216.P47 1984, (v4)
Pernanen, Kai. HV5053.P45 1991, (v6)
Pernick, Martin S. RD80.3.P47 1985, (v2)
Pernoud, Regine. D158.P413 1963, (v5)
Peron, Eva. F2849.P313 1978, (v4)
Perpener, John O. GV1785.A1 P47 2001, (v6)
Perraton, H. D. LC5808.D48.P47 2000, (v7)
Perrault, Charles. PQ1877.A25 1977, (v3)
  PZ8.P426.Fai12, (v3)
Perreault, Jeanne Martha. PS151.P47 1995, (v3)
Perret, Geoffrey. E745.M3.P42 1996, (v4)
  E806.P466 1985, (v4)
  E836.P47 1999, (v4)
Perret, Jacques. PQ2631.E367.B3, (v3)
Perrie, Maureen. GR203.R88.P47 1987, (v6)
Perrin, Annie Elliott. F499.G44.P47 1999, (v4)
Perrin, Norman. BS2330.2.P46 1982, (v8)
Perrine, Doug. QL638.9.P437 1999, (v1)
Perritt, Henry H. KF390.5.C6 P47 2001, (v7)
Perrone, Charles A. PQ9571.P47 1996, (v3)
Perrot, Philippe. GT871.P3913 1994, (v6)
Perrot, Pierre. QC310.3.P4713 1998, (v1)
Perruchot, Henri. PQ2625.O45.Z85, (v3)
Perry, Anne Griffin. RT51.P365 1994, (v2)
Perry, Barbara A. KF8742.P336 1991, (v7)
Perry, Barbara. HV6773.52.P47 2001, (v6)
Perry, Charles R. HD6515.M615.P47 1984, (v6)
Perry, Charles. PS3566.E7.P6, (v3)
Perry, David A. QK938.F6.P46 1994, (v1)

Perry, Edward Delavan. PK666.P5 1936, (v3)
Perry, Elisabeth Israels. F124.M885.P47 1987, (v4)
Perry, Elizabeth J. DS740.2.P47, (v5)
  DS761.2.P47 2002, (v5)
Perry, F. W. UA647.P35 1988, (v10)
Perry, Gillian. ND548.P39 1995, (v9)
Perry, H. W. KF8742.P3365 1991, (v7)
Perry, Helen Swick. RC339.52.S87P37, (v2)
Perry, Henry Ten Eyck. PR698.C6.P4 1962, (v3)
Perry, James M. E609.P47 2000, (v4)
Perry, James R. F229.P47 1990, (v4)
Perry, John Curtis. HF3043.P48 1994, (v6)
Perry, John. BD161.P43 2001, (v8)
Perry, Lewis. E165.P47 1993, (v4)
Perry, Mark. UA23.7.P47 1989, (v10)
Perry, Marvin. CB18.T65.P47 1982, (v5)
Perry, Matthew Calbraith. DS809.P456 1967, (v5)
  DS881.8.P4, (v5)
Perry, Michael J. BL65.H78.P47 1998, (v8)
  JK468.E7.P47 1991, (v7)
  KF4552.P47 1988, (v7)
  KF4575.P47 1994, (v7)
Perry, Nellie M. F392.P168.P47 2000, (v4)
Perry, Ralph Barton. B804.P3 1955, (v8)
  BD232.P45 1950, (v8)
Perry, Thomas Sergeant. PS2554.P16.A8 1971, (v3)
Perse, Saint-John. PQ2623.E386.E4 1956, (v3)
Pershing, John J. D570.P44 1931, (v5)
Persico, Joseph E. JX5437.8.P37 1994, (v7)
Persius. PA6555.E5.M4, (v3)
Persky, Joseph. HC107.A13.P48 1992, (v6)
  HC108.C4 P47 2000, (v6)
Persons, Stow. BL2760.P4, (v8)
Persons, Stow. E169.1.P476, (v4)
Persoon, James. PR610.P43 1999, (v3)
Pertman, Adam. HV875.55.P47 2000, (v6)
Pertschuk, Michael. KF8742.P337 1989, (v7)
Pertusati, Linda. E99.M8.P46 1997, (v4)
Pescatello, Ann M. HQ1166.P47 1976, (v6)
  ML423.S498.P5 1992, (v9)
Pesch, Ludwig. ML338.P423 1999, (v9)
Peshkin, Alan. LC562.P47 1986, (v7)
Pesic, Peter. Q175.P3865 2000, (v1)
Peskin, Allan. E687.P47 1999, (v4)
Peskine, Christian. QA564.P47 1996, (v1)
Pessen, Edward. E338.P4 1985, (v4)
Pessis, Jacques. PN1968.F8.P4713 1990, (v3)
Pessoa, Fernando. PQ9261.P417.A6 1971b, (v3)
  PQ9261.P417.Z462 1991, (v3)
Pestana, Carla Gardina. BR555.M4 P47 1991, (v8)
Peszke, Michael Alfred. D765.2.W3.P47 1995, (v5)
Petech, Luciano. DS785.45, (v5)
Peteet, Julie Marie. DS80.55.P34.P47 1991, (v5)
Peter, Frances Dallam. E601.P48 2000, (v4)
Peter, John. NA680.P374, (v9)
Peterkin, Julia Mood. PS3531.E77 B6, (v3)
  PS3531.E77 C6, (v3)
  PS3531.E77 S25, (v3)
Peters, Alan H. HD1393.5.P484 2002, (v6)
Peters, B. Guy. JF1351.P393 1996, (v7)
Peters, Catherine. PR4496.P48 1993, (v3)
Peters, Cynthia. HV2471.P38 2000, (v6)
Peters, Daniel. PS3566.E7548.B6, (v3)
Peters, Emrys L. DT238.C8.P47 1990, (v5)
Peters, F. E. BM157.P47 1982, (v8)
  BP75.P4 1994, (v8)
  BP187.3.P475 1994, (v8)
  DS109.916.P48 1993, (v5)
Peters, H. F. PT2635.I65.Z825, (v3)
Peters, Harry Twyford. NE2415.C7.P43, (v9)
Peters, Herman Jacob. LB1027.5.P422 1974, (v7)
Peters, John G. PR6005.O4.Z784947 2001, (v3)
Peters, John Marshall. LC5215.P436 1991, (v7)
Peters, Julie Stone. PR3368.B58.P4 1990, (v3)
Peters, Kenneth E. TN271.P4.P463 1993, (v1)
Peters, Lisa N. ND237.T85.P48 1999, (v9)
Peters, Margot. PR4168.P38, (v3)
  PR5366.P45 1980, (v3)
Peters, Michael. LC196.P48 1996, (v7)
Peters, Raymond Harry. TS1449.P45, (v1)
Peters, Robert. PR5514.P4, (v3)

Peters, Ronald M. JK1411.P48 1990, (v7)
Peters, Rudolph. BP182.P48 1996, (v8)
Peters, Sally. PR5366.P46 1996, (v3)
Peters, Sarah Whitaker. N6537.O39.P48 1991, (v9)
Peters, Shawn Francis. BX8525.P48 2000, (v8)
Peters, Thomas J. HD70.U5.P425 1985, (v6)
Peters, Virginia Bergman. E99.M2.P47 2000, (v4)
Petersen, Andrew. NA380.P43 1996, (v9)
Petersen, Carolyn Collins. QB500.268.P48 1995, (v1)
Petersen, David. QL737.C27.P425 1995, (v1)
  SK14.3, (v1)
Petersen, Donna J. RA425.P38 2001, (v2)
Petersen, Julie K. TK5102.P48 1999, (v1)
Petersen, Karen. N40.P45 1976, (v9)
Petersen, Neal H. Z6724.I7.P48 1992, (v10)
Petersen, Norman R. BS2361.2.P47, (v8)
Petersen, Tore T. DS63.2.U5.P48 2000, (v5)
Petersen, William John. F621.P55, (v4)
Petersen, William. HB851.P46 1975, (v6)
  HB863.P47, (v6)
Peterson, A. D. C. DS508.P43 1957, (v5)
Peterson, Anna Lisa. BJ1012.P454 2001, (v8)
  BX1446.2.P47 1997, (v8)
Peterson, Bernard L. PN2270.A35.P48 1997, (v3)
  PN2286.P46 2001, (v3)
  PS153.N5.P44 1990, (v3)
Peterson, Carla L. PS153.N5.P443 1995, (v3)
Peterson, D. J. HC340.P55.P47 1993, (v6)
Peterson, Dale. QL737.P96.P47 1993, (v1)
Peterson, Donald A. BS2585.2.P48 2000, (v8)
Peterson, Dwight N. BS2585.2.P48 2000, (v8)
Peterson, Edward Norman. D757.P48 1990, (v5)
  DD285.P48 1999, (v5)
  DD257.4.P43, (v5)
Peterson, Ivars. QA273.15.P48 1998, (v1)
  QB351.P48 1993, (v1)
Peterson, James C. QH438.7.P485 2001, (v1)
Peterson, Jane T. PS338.W6.P48 1997, (v3)
Peterson, John Alton. E83.867.P47 1998, (v4)
Peterson, Lee. QK98.5.U6.P47, (v1)
Peterson, Levi S. F826.B877.P48 1988, (v4)
Peterson, Linda H. PR788.W65.P47 1999, (v3)
Peterson, Mark A. BX9355.M4.P48 1997, (v8)
  JK585.P48 1990, (v7)
Peterson, Merrill D. E332.P45 1987, (v4)
  E339.P47 1987, (v4)
  E457.2.P484 1994, (v4)
Peterson, Nadezhda L. PG3098.F34.P48 1997, (v3)
Peterson, Nancy J. PS153.M56.P48 2001, (v3)
Peterson, Nancy L. HQ800.4.U6.P47 1981, (v6)
Peterson, Norma Lois. E391.P48 1989, (v4)
Peterson, Peter G. HJ2052.P48 1988, (v6)
  HQ1061.P388 1999, (v6)
Peterson, Richard F. PR6023.A914.Z83, (v3)
  PS169.B36.P48 2001, (v3)
Peterson, Richard T. B65.P43 1996, (v8)
Peterson, Roger Tory. QH102.P38, (v1)
  QL683.W4.P4 1990, (v1)
Peterson, Scott. DT407.4.P48 2000, (v5)
Peterson, Susan. E99.S213 M377 1989, (v4)
  NK3930.P4 2000b, (v9)
Peterson, William S. Z232.M87.P45 1991, (v10)
Petesch, Donald A. PS153.N5.P45 1989, (v3)
Petesch, Natalie L. M. PS3566.E772.A3, (v3)
Pethick, Derek. F851.5.P47, (v4)
  F1089.N8.P47 1980, (v4)
Petit, Susan. PQ2680.O83.Z84 1991, (v3)
Petitfils, Pierre. PQ2387.R5.Z754513 1987, (v3)
Petot, Jean-Michel. RJ504.2.P4613 1991, (v2)
Petraglia, Joseph. LB1062.P42 1998, (v7)
Petras, James F. F1414.2.P398 1992, (v4)
  F1418.P52 1990, (v4)
  HC192.P48 1994, (v6)
Petrement, Simone. B2430.W474.P4613, (v8)
  BT1390.P4513 1990, (v8)
Petrides, George A. QK482.P43, (v1)
Petrie, Duncan J. PN1993.5.G7.P47 2000, (v3)
Petrikovsky, Boris M. RG525.P437 2001, (v2)
Petrin, Ronald Arthur. F75.F85.P48 1990, (v4)

Petrinovich, Lewis F. BJ1311.P48 1995, (v8)
  HV4708.P48 1999, (v6)
  R724.P436 1996, (v2)
Petro, Nicolai N. JN6581.P47 1995, (v7)
Petrone, Karen. GT4856.A2, (v6)
Petrone, Penny. PM238.P4 1990, (v3)
Petronius Arbiter. PA6558.E5.W3 1996, (v3)
Petropoulos, Jonathan. N6868.5.N37.P4823 2000, (v9)
Petropulos, John Anthony. DF823.P4, (v5)
Petroski, Henry. T212.P465 1992, (v1)
  TA174.P473 1994, (v1)
  TG23.P47 1995, (v1)
  Z685.P48 1999, (v10)
Petrovich, Michael Boro. D377.5.S65.P47 1985, (v5)
Petrow, Richard. D802.D4.P45, (v5)
Petrucci, Armando. Z1003.5.I8.P48 1995, (v10)
Petruso, Thomas F. PN3341.P47 1991, (v3)
Petry, Ann Lane. PS3531.E933.S75 1985, (v3)
Petry, Carl F. DT96.7.P48 1993, (v5)
Petterssen, Sverre. QC861.P4 1969, (v1)
  QC995.P52, (v1)
Pettet, E. C. PR3742.S43.P4, (v3)
Petteys, Chris. N43.P47 1985, (v9)
Pettifer, Adrian. DA660.P48 1995, (v5)
Pettijohn, F. J. QE471.P46 1975, (v1)
  QE471.2.P47 1987, (v1)
Pettinger, Peter. ML417.E9.P53 1998, (v9)
Pettis, Joyce Owens. PS3563.A7223.Z83 1995, (v3)
Pettit, Philip. JC421.P49 1997, (v7)
Pettus, Eloise S. Z1037.P46 1998, (v10)
Petulla, Joseph M. HC103.7.P48 1988, (v6)
Petyt, M. TA356.P47 1990, (v1)
Petzinger, Thomas. HD31.P394 1999, (v6)
Peucker, Brigitte. PN1995.25.P48 1995, (v3)
Peursen, Cornelis Anthonie van. B829.5.P393 1972, (v8)
Pevsner, Nikolaus. N6350.P4 1968b, (v9)
  NA950.P4 1960, (v9)
  NA5461.P48 1985, (v9)
Peyer, Bernd. PS153.I52.P49 1997, (v3)
Peyre, Henri. PN86.P44, (v3)
  PN871.P4, (v3)
  PQ439.P413, (v3)
  PQ671.P47 1967, (v3)
Peyrefitte, Alain. DA47.9.C5.P4913 1992, (v5)
Peyton, A. J. TK7874.P459 1993, (v1)
Pezzoli, Keith. HT243.M62.M487 1998, (v6)
Pezzullo, Lawrence. F1528.P49 1993, (v4)
Pfaff, Daniel W. PN4874.P8.P47 1991, (v3)
Pfaff, Donald W. QP251.P467 1999, (v1)
Pfammatter, Ulrich. T69.P45313 2000, (v1)
Pfanz, Harry W. E475.53.P475 1993, (v4)
Pfeffer, J. Alan. PE1582.G24.P49 1994, (v3)
Pfeffer, Leo. KF4783.P46 1984, (v7)
Pfeffer, Paula F. E185.97.R27.P44 1990, (v4)
Pfefferkorn, Ignaz. F1346.P353, (v4)
Pfefferkorn, Kristin. PT2291.Z5.P4 1988, (v3)
Pfeifer, Rolf. Q335.P46 1999, (v1)
Pfeiffer, Bruce Brooks. NA2707.W74.A4 1990, (v9)
Pfeiffer, Paul E. QA273.P423 1990, (v1)
Pfeiffer, Rudolf. AZ301.P4, (v10)
Pfeil, Fred. PN51.P46 1990, (v3)
Pfeil, W. (Wolfgang). QP551.P42 1998, (v1)
Pfiffner, James P. JK511.P47 1994, (v7)
Pfister, Joel. PS1892.P74.P45 1992, (v3)
  PS3529.N5.Z7742 1995, (v3)
Pfitzer, Gregory M. E175.P48 1991, (v4)
Pflanze, Otto. DD218.P44 1990, (v5)
Pflieger, Pat. PS3553.L3914.Z88 1991, (v3)
Pflug, Melissa A. E99.O9.P45 1998, (v4)
Phadnis, Urmila. DS341.P53 2001, (v5)
Phaedrus. PA6564.E5.W5 1992, (v3)
Phan, Boi Chau. DS556.83.P46.A3 1997, (v5)
Pharand, Michel W. PR5368.F7, (v3)
Phares, Walid. DS87.P5 1995, (v5)
Pharr, Susan J. JC599.J3.P47 1990, (v7)
Phayer, Michael. BX1378.P49 2000, (v8)
Phelan, Craig. HD8073.G7.P54 1989, (v6)
  HD8073.M5.P48 1994, (v6)
Phelan, James. PR830.C47.P47 1989, (v3)

Phelan, Peggy. NX650.P6.P47 1993, (v9)
Phelps, Edmund S. HJ257.P45 1965, (v6)
Phelps, Glenn A. E312.29.P44 1993, (v4)
Phelps, William Dane. F851.5.P49 1997, (v4)
Phelps, William Lyon. PR4238.P55, (v3)
Phelts, Marsha Dean. F319.A45.P47 1997, (v4)
Phenix, Philip Henry. BD431.P5, (v8)
Philander, S. George. QC981.8.G56.P48 1998, (v1)
Philbin, Tobias R. VA513.P45 1994, (v10)
Philip, Alan Butt. DA722.P47, (v5)
Philip, George D. E. Z1411.P45 1993, (v10)
Philip, James A. B243.P45, (v8)
Philip, Neil. BL311.P46 1999, (v8)
  PZ8.P54Ar 1994, (v3)
Philippi, Nancy S. HV609.P45 1996, (v6)
Philips, Ambrose. PR3619.P2.A17 1969, (v3)
Philips, Michael. BJ1012.P455 1994, (v8)
Philipson, Robert. D1056.2.B55, (v5)
Phillips, Anne. HQ1190.P46 1993, (v6)
  HQ1236.P49 1991, (v6)
Phillips, Catherine. PR4161.B6.Z82 1992, (v3)
Phillips, Charles L. TJ223.M56P47 1995, (v1)
Phillips, Charles. KZ1160.P48 2001, (v7)
Phillips, Christopher. BD31.P56 2001, (v8)
  E467.1.L9 P48 1996, (v4)
  E469.J33 P47 2000, (v4)
  F189.B19.N47 1997, (v4)
Phillips, D. Z. BD21.P44 1996, (v8)
Phillips, David Graham. PS3531.H5 S8, (v3)
Phillips, Donald E. Z5630.P48 1992, (v10)
Phillips, Duncan. N858.P4.A87 1999, (v9)
Phillips, Edward N. ML134.F29.P55 2000, (v9)
Phillips, Elizabeth. PS1541.Z5.P46 1988, (v3)
Phillips, G. M. QA99.P48 2000, (v1)
Phillips, Gene D. PN1998.2.P54 1998, (v3)
  PN1998.2.P55 1990, (v3)
  PR6005.O4.Z78496 1995, (v3)
  PS3505.H3224.Z836 2000, (v3)
Phillips, George Harwood. E78.C15.P46 1997, (v4)
  E78.C15.P47 1993, (v4)
Phillips, Helen. PR1874.P48 1999, (v3)
Phillips, J. R. S. G89.P48 1988, (v6)
Phillips, James W. Z331.86.D8.P47 1998, (v10)
Phillips, Jayne Anne. PS3566.H479.M3 1984, (v3)
Phillips, John. B809.3.P49 2000, (v8)
Phillips, Jonathan. D183.P45 1996, (v5)
Phillips, Kathy J. PN3503.P47 1990, (v3)
  PR6045.O72.Z859 1994, (v3)
Phillips, Kenneth J. H. QB521.P45 1992, (v1)
Phillips, Kevin P. E209.P48 1999, (v4)
  JK2357 1969.P53, (v7)
Phillips, Leona Rasmussen. Z8699.P48, (v10)
Phillips, Leonard E. SB436.P45 1993, (v1)
Phillips, Lisa. N6512.H355 1999 Suppl., (v9)
Phillips, Mark. DG738.14.P37.P45 1987, (v5)
  PN1992.8.S35.P48 1996, (v3)
Phillips, Michael K. QL737.C22.P5 1996, (v1)
Phillips, Michael. PR4144.S63, (v3)
Phillips, Patricia. Q130.P53 1990, (v1)
Phillips, Peggy A. DC417.P55 1993, (v5)
Phillips, Robert L. PS3511.O348.Z83 1992, (v3)
  U21.2.P47 1984, (v10)
Phillips, Ulrich Bonnell. E441.P549 1966, (v4)
  F209.P56, (v4)
Phillips, William D. E111.P67 1991, (v4)
Phillips-Matz, Mary Jane. CT275.K26.M3, (v5)
  ML410.V4.P43 1993, (v9)
Phillipson, John S. Z8980.45.P47, (v10)
Phillpotts, Bertha Surtees. PT7063.P5, (v3)
Philo. B689.A4.E5 1981, (v8)
Philoponus, John. B415.A5.C48 1991, (v8)
Philp, Richard B. RA565.P48 1995, (v2)
Philpott, Daniel. JZ4034.P48 2001, (v7)
Philpott, Thomas Lee. F548.9.N4.P48 1978, (v4)
Philpott, William James. D544.P49 1996, (v5)
Phim, Toni Samantha. GV1703.C3.P55 1999, (v6)
Phipps, Clarence B. TJ1051.P55 1997, (v1)
Phipps, William E. BP75.P45 1996, (v8)
Phrantzes, Georgios. DF645.P4813, (v5)
Phythian, Mark. HV6321.I693.P48 1997, (v6)
Piaf, Edith. ML420.P52.A3 1990, (v9)

Piaget, Jean. B841.4.P513, (v8)
  BF431.P48272, (v2)
  BF721.P43, (v2)
  BF721.P452 1951, (v2)
  BF721.P473, (v2)
  BF721.P4813, (v2)
  BF721.P5, (v2)
  BF723.C5.P494, (v2)
  BF723.C5.P5, (v2)
  BF723.D7.P513 1967, (v2)
  LB1139.G4.P53, (v7)
  LB1139.L3 P5 1997, (v7)
Pianka, Eric R. QL31.P57.A3 1994, (v1)
Piatt, Bill. KF3466.P55 1993, (v7)
  KF4767.P53 1990, (v7)
Piatt, Sarah M. B. PS2581.A4 2001, (v3)
Piazza, Tom. ML156.4.J3 P53 1995, (v9)
Picanço, Luciano C. PQ3948.5.M37P53 2000, (v3)
Picard, Robert G. PN4784.T45.P5 1993, (v3)
  Z479.P53 1997, (v10)
Picard, Rosalind W. QA76.9.H85.P53 1997, (v1)
Picasso, Pablo. N6853.P5.A4 1997, (v9)
  ND553.P5.A4 1998, (v9)
  PQ6629.I23.A23 1989 fol., (v3)
Piccard, Jacques. VM989.P53, (v10)
Pichanick, Valerie Kossew. PR4984.M5.Z78 1980, (v3)
Pick, Daniel. PN56.M52.P54 2000, (v3)
Pick, Daniel. U21.2.P535 1993, (v10)
Pick, Hella. DB99.2.P47 2000, (v5)
Pick, James B. G1545.P5 1989, (v6)
Pick, Zuzana M. PN1995.9.S6.P5 1993, (v3)
Pickard-Cambridge, Arthur Wallace. PA3201.P5 1968, (v3)
Pickel, Andreas. HC290.782.P53 1997, (v6)
Picken, Stuart D. B. BL2216.1.P53 2002, (v8)
  BL2220.P47 1994, (v8)
Pickering, Andrew. QC793.16.P53 1984, (v1)
Pickering, David. GR35.P53 1999, (v6)
Pickering, Jeffrey. DS33.4.G7.P53 1998, (v5)
Pickering, Michael. D16.166.P53 1997, (v5)
Pickett, Albert James. F326.P6 1975, (v4)
Pickett, Terry H. JC311.P47 1996, (v7)
Pickett, William B. E816.P53 2000, (v4)
Pickford, Nigel. G1046.P57.P5 1994, (v6)
Pickle, Linda Schelbitzki. F358.2.G3.P53 1996, (v4)
Pickover, Clifford A. Q147.P53 1998, (v1)
  Q175.P523 1997, (v1)
  QA9.P515 1995, (v1)
  QA76.P465 1991, (v1)
  QA95.P53 2001, (v1)
Pickstone, John V. Q125.P595 2001, (v1)
Pickus, David. DK4185.G3 P54 2001, (v5)
Pico della Mirandola, Giovanni Francesco. PA8555.P6.D4, (v3)
Picon, Antoine. NA1046.5.N4.P513 1991, (v9)
Picon, Jacinto Octavio. PQ6629.I3.D813 2000, (v3)
Picon-Salas, Mariano. F1408.3.P5213 1962, (v4)
Picot, Edward. PR605.L27.P53 1997, (v3)
Piderit, John J. HB72.P53 1993, (v6)
Piedmont-Palladino, Susan. NA737.J47.P54 1997, (v9)
Piekalkiewicz, Jaroslaw. JC481.P463 1995, (v7)
Piel, Gerard. HM206.P54 1992, (v6)
Pielke, Roger A. QC945.P64 1997, (v1)
Pielou, E. C. GB661.2.P54 1998, (v6)
  QC73.P54 2001, (v1)
  QE721.2.P24.P54 1991, (v1)
Piening, Christopher. D1058.P54 1997, (v5)
Pieper, Josef. BD215.P513 1975, (v8)
Pierce, Benjamin C. QA76.9.M35.P54 1991, (v1)
Pierce, David. PR5906.P54 1995, (v3)
Pierce, Jennifer L. KF300.P53 1995, (v7)
Pierce, John J. PN3433.5.P54 1994, (v3)
Pierce, John Robinson. Q360.P5, (v1)
Pierce, Richard A. DK858.P5, (v5)
Pierce, Roy. JN2959.P54 1995, (v7)
Pierik, R. L. M. SB123.6.P4813 1987, (v1)
Pieroth, Doris Hinson. GV722 1932.P54 1996, (v6)
Pierpaoli, Paul G. DS919.P54 1999, (v5)
Pierpont, Claudia Roth. PS151.P54 2000, (v3)

Piersen, William Dillon. E169.1.P553 1993, **(v4)**
  E185.P49 1996, **(v4)**
  E185.917.P54 1988, **(v4)**
Pierson, Christopher. HX73.P54 1995, **(v6)**
  JC325.P48 1991, **(v7)**
Pierson, Donald. F2651.C72.P53 1973, **(v4)**
Pierson, Paul. HN59.2.P52 1994, **(v6)**
Pierson, William Harvey. N6505.P55, **(v9)**
  NA705.P5, **(v9)**
Pierzynski, Gary M. TD878.P54 2000, **(v1)**
Pietilä, Hilkka. HQ1240.P54 1994, **(v6)**
Pifer, Ellen. PS374.C45.P54 2000, **(v3)**
Piff, Mike. QA76.9.M35.P55 1991, **(v1)**
Piganiol, Andre. D20.P37 t.3, 1967, **(v3)**
Piggott, Joan R. DS855.P54 1997, **(v5)**
Piggott, Stuart. CB301.P5 1961, **(v5)**
  CC75.P5, **(v5)**
  GT5280.P54 1992, **(v6)**
Piglia, Ricardo. PQ7798.26.I4.N613 1995, **(v3)**
Pignatti, Terisio. ND623.G5.P5613 1999, **(v9)**
Pigou, A. C. HD5706.P47 1968, **(v6)**
  HF2046.P65 1968, **(v6)**
Piirto, Jane. BF408.P87 1992, **(v2)**
Pikarsky, Milton. HE308.P44, **(v6)**
Pike, David L. PN56.H38.P55 1997, **(v3)**
Pike, David Wingeate. D805.M38.P55 2000, **(v5)**
Pike, Fredrick B. F1414.P54, **(v4)**
  F1418.P553 1995, **(v4)**
  JL952.P5, **(v7)**
Pike, James Shepherd. F274.P632, **(v4)**
Pike, Ruth. DS135.S75.S455 2000, **(v5)**
  HN590.S4.P54, **(v6)**
Pike, Zebulon Montgomery. F592.P638 1972, **(v4)**
Piket, Vincent. PS3501.U25.Z83 1990, **(v3)**
Pikirayi, Innocent. DT2942.P55 2001, **(v5)**
Piland, Sherry. Z7963.A75.B32 1994, **(v1)**
Pilardi, Jo-Ann. B2430.B344.P55 1999, **(v8)**
Pilbeam, Pamela M. DC252.P53 1995, **(v5)**
Pilch, John J. BS2555.6.H4.P55 2000, **(v8)**
Pilcher, Jeffrey M. PN2318.C3, **(v3)**
Pile, John F. NK1390.P53 1990, **(v9)**
  NK2110.P55 1988, **(v9)**
Pilger, Mary Anne. Q182.3.P55 1996, **(v1)**
  Z5814.M86 P55 2001, **(v10)**
Pilipp, Frank. PT2685.A48.Z82 1991, **(v3)**
Pilkey, Walter D. TA407.2.P55 1994, **(v1)**
Pilkington, Ace G. PR3093.P55 1991, **(v3)**
Pilkington, Colin. JN900.P55 1997, **(v7)**
Pilkington, Hilary. HQ799.R9.P495 1994, **(v6)**
Pillai, Vijayan K. HQ766.P542 1999, **(v6)**
Pillar, Paul R. HV6431.P56 2001, **(v6)**
Pillari, Vimala. RJ507.A29.P55 1991, **(v2)**
Pillement, Georges. PQ1223.P5, **(v3)**
Piller, Charles. UG447.8.P54 1988, **(v10)**
Pilling, John. PR6003.E282.Z7869 1997, **(v3)**
Pilling, M. J. QD502.P54 1995, **(v1)**
Pillsbury, Richard. G1201.J1 .P5 1996, **(v6)**
  TX360.U6.P55 1998, **(v1)**
Pillsbury, Samuel H. K5172.P55 1998, **(v7)**
Pilniak, Boris. PG3476.V6.V6, **(v3)**
Pilsudski, Bronislaw. PL481.O85.P55 1987, **(v3)**
Pilsudski, Jozef. DK440.5.P5.A42, **(v5)**
Pimlott, John. G1038.P55 1995, **(v6)**
Pimm, David. QA11.P586 1995, **(v1)**
Pimm, Stuart L. QH541.P558 1991, **(v1)**
Pina Chan, Roman. F1219.8.O56.P5613 1989, **(v4)**
Pina-Cabral, João de. DS796.M2 P55 2002, **(v5)**
Pinault, David. BP192.7.I4.P56 1992, **(v8)**
  PJ7737.P56 1992, **(v3)**
Pincas, Stephane. SB466.F82.V47613 1996, **(v1)**
Pinch, Adela. PR448.E46.P56 1996, **(v3)**
Pincherle, Marc. ML410.C78.P52 1979, **(v9)**
Pinchin, Calvin. BD21.P485 1989, **(v8)**
Pinchon, Edgcumb. F1234.V698, **(v4)**
Pinchot, Amos. JK2387.P5, **(v7)**
Pinchot, Gifford. E664.P62 A3 1998, **(v4)**
  HC106.P6, **(v6)**
  HD38.4.P56 1993, **(v6)**
Pinchuk, Ben-Cion. DS135.P6.P49 1991, **(v5)**
Pinciss, G. M. PR658.R43.P56 2000, **(v3)**
Pinckney, Eliza Lucas. F272.P6416, **(v4)**

Pincus, Steven C. A. DA425.P56 1996, **(v5)**
Pindar. PA3411.H3.P5 1970, **(v3)**
Pindarus. PA3405.S8.P5 1935, **(v3)**
Pinder, George Francis. GB656.2.M33.P56, **(v6)**
Pinderhughes, Howard. HV9106.N6.P56 1997, **(v6)**
Pindyck, Robert S. HB3730.P56 1998, **(v6)**
Pine, L. G. CR191.P55 1970b, **(v5)**
Pine, Richard. PR5823.P63 1995, **(v3)**
Pine, Richard. PR6056.R5.Z86 1990, **(v3)**
Pinedo, Isabel Cristina. PN1995.9.H6.P46 1997, **(v3)**
Pinero, Arthur Wing. PR5180.A2 1967, **(v3)**
  PR5181. 1985, **(v3)**
  PR5182.T8 1995, **(v3)**
Pines, Yuri. DS741.65.P55 2002, **(v5)**
Pinfold, John. Z3107.T5.P55 1991, **(v10)**
Pingaud, Bernard. PQ305.P5, **(v3)**
Pinget, Robert. PQ2631.I638.A23 1966, **(v3)**
  PQ2631.I638.F313 1980, **(v3)**
  PQ2631.I638.P3x 1978, **(v3)**
Ping-Robbins, Nancy R. ML134.J75.P56 1998, **(v9)**
Pinion, F. B. PR4752.P5, **(v3)**
  PR5581.P47 1990, **(v3)**
  PR5581.P5 1984, **(v3)**
  PR5887.P56 1988, **(v3)**
Pink, Thomas. BJ1461.P55 1996, **(v8)**
Pinkard, Terry P. B2947.P56 2000, **(v8)**
  B2949.D5.P56 1988, **(v8)**
Pinker, Steven. P106.P477 1999, **(v3)**
  QP360.5.P56 1997, **(v1)**
Pinkney, Alphonso. E185.8.P56 1984, **(v4)**
Pinkney, David H. DC261.P56, **(v5)**
  DC733.P59, **(v5)**
Pinkney, Robert. JQ3036.P56 1997, **(v7)**
Pinkus, Allan. QA404.P56 1997, **(v1)**
Pinkus, Benjamin. DS135.R92.P56 1984, **(v5)**
Pinney, Thomas. TP557.P56 1989, **(v1)**
Pino, Julio Cesar. HC189.R4.P56 1997, **(v4)**
Pinsker, Sanford. PS153.J4.P56 1992, **(v3)**
Pinsky, Robert. PS3566.I54.E9, **(v3)**
Pinter, Harold. PR6031.I525.B5, **(v3)**
  PR6066.I53.A19 1961b, **(v3)**
  PR6066.I53.A19 1962, **(v3)**
  PR6066.I53.D8 1990, **(v3)**
  PR6066.I53 1977, **(v3)**
Pinto, Fernao Mendes. DS7.P5513 1989, **(v5)**
Pinto, Vivian de Sola. PR3717.S15.Z8, **(v3)**
  PR4147.P5, **(v3)**
Piontelli, Alessandra. BF723.T9P56 2002, **(v2)**
Piott, Steven L. F466.F65.P56 1997, **(v4)**
Piozzi, Hester Lynch. PR3619.P5.A2, **(v3)**
  PR3619.P5.A827 1977, **(v3)**
  PR3619.P5.Z48 1989, **(v3)**
Piper, H. W. PR4487.S95.P56 1987, **(v3)**
Piper, J. Richard. JC573.2.U6.P57 1997, **(v7)**
Piper, William Bowman. PR448.P5.P56 1999, **(v3)**
Pipes, Daniel. D21.3.P55 1997, **(v5)**
  DS63.P5 1990, **(v5)**
  PR6068.U757.S27355 1990, **(v3)**
Pipes, Richard. DK32.7.P49, **(v5)**
  DK40.P47 1974b, **(v5)**
  DK254.S597.P5, **(v5)**
  DK254.S597 P52, **(v5)**
  DK265.P474 1990, **(v5)**
  DK265 .P4742 1995, **(v5)**
  DK266.P53 1964, **(v5)**
  JC605.P56 1999, **(v7)**
Pipkin, Donald L. QA76.9.A25.P56 1997, **(v1)**
Pippett, Aileen. PR6045.O72Z86, **(v3)**
Pippin, Robert B. B803.P57 1999, **(v8)**
  B823.P55 1997, **(v8)**
  PS2127.E8.P57 2000, **(v8)**
Pirazzoli-t'Serstevens, Michele. DS748.P5713 1982, **(v5)**
Pirenne, Henri. D20.P37 1931, **(v5)**
  D121.P52 1968, **(v5)**
Pirenne, Jacques. D20.P513, **(v5)**
Piro, Timothy J. HC415.26.P57 1998, **(v6)**
Pirone, Pascal Pompey. SB603.5.P57 1978, **(v1)**
Pirounakis, Nicholas G. HC295.P55 1997, **(v6)**
Pirsson, Louis V. QE431.P68 1947, **(v1)**

Pisani, Donald J. HD1695.W4.P57 1996, **(v6)**
  HD1739.C2.P57 1984, **(v6)**
Pisciotta, Alexander W. HV9304.P57 1994, **(v6)**
Piskulich, John Patrick. HD8005.6.U5.P57 1992, **(v6)**
Pissarro, Joachim. ND553.M7.A4 1997, **(v9)**
  ND553.P55.P488 1993, **(v9)**
Pistolese, Clifford. HG4638.P57 1989, **(v6)**
Piston, Walter. MT50.P665 1987, **(v9)**
  MT55.P67, **(v9)**
  MT70.P56, **(v9)**
Piston, William Garrett. E467.1.L55.P57 1987, **(v4)**
  E472.23.P57 2000, **(v4)**
Pistorius, Philippus Villiers. B693.Z7.P5, **(v8)**
Piszkiewicz, Dennis. TL540.R38.P57 1997, **(v1)**
  TL781.85.V6.P57 1998, **(v1)**
Pitch, Anthony. E356.W3.P49 1998, **(v4)**
Pitcher, George. B3376.W564.P5, **(v8)**
Pitcher, Seymour Maitland. PR2411.F37.P5, **(v3)**
Pite, Ralph. PR457.P58 1994, **(v3)**
Pitkin, Hanna Fenichel. JC143.M4.P57 1984, **(v7)**
  JC251.A74.P57 1998, **(v7)**
Pitman, L. M. AS8.P58 1997, **(v10)**
Pitre, Merline. F391.W575.P58 1999, **(v4)**
Pitschmann, Louis A. Z2551.P57 1984, **(v10)**
Pitsula, James M. F1072.P58 1990, **(v4)**
Pitt, Leonard. F869.L84.P58 1997, **(v4)**
Pittman, Avril. DD258.85.S6.P58 1992, **(v5)**
Pittock, Murray. DA485.P54 1997, **(v5)**
  DA758.3.S8.P58 1991, **(v5)**
Pitt-Rivers, Julian Alfred. HN380.M4.P5, **(v6)**
Pitts, Michael R. PN1993.5.U65.P55 1997, **(v3)**
Pitts, Robert Franklin. QP249.P57 1974, **(v1)**
Pitts, Vincent J. DC112.B6.P58 1993, **(v5)**
  DC130.M8, **(v5)**
Pivcevic, Edo. BD373.P58 1990, **(v8)**
Piver, M. Steven. RC280.O8.P576 1996, **(v2)**
Pizarro, Pedro. F3442.P78 1972, **(v4)**
Pizer, Donald. PS159.F5.P59 1996, **(v3)**
Pizzato, Mark. PN1631.P58 1998, **(v3)**
Placksin, Sally. ML3508.P58 1982, **(v9)**
Plain, Gill. PR888.W66.P53 1996, **(v3)**
Plaine, Henry L. CB358.P53 1962, **(v5)**
Plait, Philip C. QB44.3.P58 2002, **(v1)**
Plakans, Andrejs. DK504.37.P58 1997, **(v5)**
Plaks, Andrew H. PL2436.P53 1987, **(v3)**
Plamondon, Martin. G1417.L4P5 2000, **(v6)**
Planck, Max. Q171.P7, **(v1)**
  Q175.P57, **(v1)**
  QC6.P625, **(v1)**
  QC311.P72 1945, **(v1)**
  QC331.P73 1959, **(v1)**
Plane, Ann Marie. E78.N5.P53 2000, **(v4)**
Planhol, Xavier de. DC20.5.P5813 1993, **(v5)**
Plank, Geoffrey Gilbert. F1038.P59 2001, **(v4)**
Plank, Steven Eric. ML3000.P53 1994, **(v9)**
Plano, Jack C. JK9.P55 1985, **(v7)**
Plant, Deborah G. PS3515.U789.Z82 1995, **(v3)**
Plant, Marjorie. Z152.E5.P55 1974, **(v10)**
Plant, Sadie. HV5801.P595 2000, **(v6)**
Plantinga, Alvin. BD161.P57 1993, **(v8)**
  BD161.P58 1993, **(v8)**
  BT1102.P57 2000, **(v8)**
Plantinga, Leon. ML196.P6 1984, **(v9)**
  ML410.B42.P6 1999, **(v9)**
  ML410.C64.P5, **(v9)**
  ML410.S4.P6, **(v9)**
Plas, Jeanne M. HD5660.U5.P53 1996, **(v6)**
Plaskow, Judith. BM729.W6 P55 1990, **(v8)**
Plass, Paul. DG205.P53 1988, **(v5)**
Plath, Sylvia. PS3566.L27.A17 1981, **(v3)**
  PS3566.L27.A7 1966, **(v3)**
Platizky, Roger S. PR5592.P74.P57 1989, **(v3)**
Platner, Samuel Ball. DG16.P685, **(v5)**

Plato. B316.P8 1963, **(v8)**
B358.A44 1984 vol. 2.385, **(v8)**
B358.C57, **(v8)**
B358.N54 1999, **(v8)**
B371.A5.I78, **(v8)**
B379.A2.B8, **(v8)**
B379.A5 G34 1993, **(v8)**
B380.A5 H3, **(v8)**
B381.A5.T35, **(v8)**
B382.A5 T39 1996, **(v8)**
B384.A5 1990, **(v8)**
B385.A5.C63 1993, **(v8)**
B385.A5.G68 1989, **(v8)**
B386.A5.C6, **(v8)**
B391.E8.M6 1962, **(v8)**
JC71.P2213 1987, **(v7)**
JC71.P2633 1980, **(v7)**
JC71.P35 1993, **(v7)**
JC71.P6.P525 1993, **(v7)**
PA4279.A2 1917, **(v3)**
Platonov, Andreæi Platonovich. PG3476.P543K613 1994, **(v3)**
PG3476.P543 F5, **(v3)**
Platonov, S. F. DK106.P5513, **(v5)**
DK109.P513, **(v5)**
Platt, Anthony M. HM22.U6.F736 1991, **(v6)**
Platt, Colin. RC179.G7.P56 1996, **(v2)**
Platt, D. C. M. HF1533.P58, **(v6)**
HG5422.P56 1984, **(v6)**
Platt, Jerome J. RC568.C6.P53 1997, **(v2)**
RC568.H4.P55 1986, **(v2)**
Platt, John Rader. BD450.P57 1970, **(v8)**
Platt, John Talbot. PE2751.P57 1984, **(v3)**
Platt, Kevin M. F. PG2987.S58.P58 1997, **(v3)**
Platt, Lyman De. CS2745.P55 1996, **(v5)**
Z5313.L37.P56 1998, **(v10)**
Platt, Washington. CB197.P6, **(v5)**
Platts, John Thompson. PK1986.P4 1960, **(v3)**
Platts, Mark de Bretton. BJ1012.P633 1991, **(v8)**
Platzker, David. NE400.P58 2000, **(v9)**
Plauger, P. J. QA76.73.C15.P56 1996, **(v1)**
Plaut, Joshua Eli. DS135.G7.P56 1996, **(v5)**
Plax, Julie Anne. ND553.W3 P65 2000, **(v9)**
Pleasants, Julian M. F259.P64 1990, **(v4)**
Pleck, Elizabeth Hafkin. GT4986.A1.P54 2000, **(v6)**
Pleck, Joseph H. HQ536.P59 1985, **(v6)**
Pleij, Herman. CB353.P5413 2001, **(v5)**
Pleins, J. David. BS1199.S6.P54 2001, **(v8)**
Plekhanov, Georgii Valentinovich. DK32.7.P512 1967, **(v5)**
Plenty Coups. E99.C92 P552 2003, **(v4)**
Plenzdorf, Ulrich. PT2676.L39.N413x, **(v3)**
Pletcher, David M. E179.5.P57, **(v4)**
HE2818.P59 1972, **(v6)**
Pletcher, Larry. F64.6.P54 1999, **(v4)**
Plett, Heinrich F. Z2015.R5.P57 1995, **(v10)**
Plimpton, George A. PR1905.P55, **(v3)**
PR2903.P6, **(v3)**
Pliny. QH41.P713 1961, **(v1)**
Plischke, Elmer. JZ1480.A4 1999, **(v7)**
Plomin, Robert. QH457.P57 1990, **(v1)**
Plotinus. B693.E59 E5 1992, **(v8)**
PA3612.P683, **(v3)**
Plotke, David. JK2316.P56 1996, **(v7)**
Plotkin, H.C. BD161.P6 1994, **(v8)**
Plotnik, Arthur. PN162.P55 1982, **(v3)**
SB435.5.P58 2000, **(v1)**
Plough, Alonzo L. RA645.R35.P55 1986, **(v2)**
Plowden, David. E169.04.P57 1994, **(v4)**
Plucknett, Theodore Frank Thomas. KD671.P58 2001, **(v7)**
Pluhar, Evelyn B. HV4708.P67 1995, **(v6)**
Plumb, J. H. DA110.P58, **(v5)**
DA480.P55 1975, **(v5)**
DA480.P56 1979, **(v5)**
DA501.W2.P52, **(v5)**
Plumbe, John. [from old catalog]. F621.P73, **(v4)**
Plummer, Brenda Gayle. E183.8.H2.P55 1992, **(v4)**
E185.6.P68 1996, **(v4)**
F1926.P68 1988, **(v4)**
Plumridge, Andrew. TH1301.P55 1993, **(v1)**

Plunkett, Dudley. LB41.P67 1990, **(v7)**
Plutchik, Robert. RC489.E45.P58 2000, **(v2)**
Pluvier, Jan M. DS518.P55, **(v5)**
Pluvier, Jan M. G2361.S1.H5 1995, **(v6)**
Poague, Leland A. PN1998.3.C36.P63 1994, **(v3)**
Pochmann, Henry A. B905.P6 1970, **(v8)**
E169.1.P596, **(v4)**
Pocius, Gerald L. HN110.C35.P63 1991, **(v6)**
Pocock, Gordon. PQ1723.P6, **(v3)**
Pocock, Rowland F. HD9696.R363.G747 1988, **(v6)**
Pocock, Tom. DA87.1.N4 P57 1988, **(v5)**
Podet, Allen Howard. DS126.4.P57 1986, **(v5)**
Podgorecki, Adam. HN537.5.P532 1994, **(v6)**
LB2322.2.P64 1997, **(v7)**
Podhoretz, Norman. PS29.P63.A3 1999, **(v3)**
Podhorsky, M. TJ263.P63 1998, **(v1)**
Podolny, Walter. TG405.P6 1986, **(v1)**
Podro, Michael. N71.P64 1998, **(v9)**
N380.P53 1982, **(v9)**
Poe, Edgar Allan. PS2600.F38, **(v3)**
PS2600.F66, **(v3)**
PS2601.Q5, **(v3)**
PS2611.P7 1923, **(v3)**
PS2612.A12, **(v3)**
PS2618.N3 1960, **(v3)**
PS2619.A1 1981, **(v3)**
PS2631.A33 1966, **(v3)**
Poe, Marshall. D34.R9, **(v5)**
Poeschke, Joachim. NB623.D7.P59213 1993, **(v9)**
Poesse, Walter. PQ6431.R8.Z83 1973, **(v3)**
Pogany, Istvan S. DS36.2.P64 1987, **(v5)**
Pogge, Thomas Winfried Menko. JC578.R383.P64 1989, **(v7)**
Poggi, Christine. N6494.C6.P6 1992, **(v9)**
Poggi, Gianfranco. JC325.P58 1990, **(v7)**
Poggioli, Renato. NX456.P613, **(v9)**
Pohanish, Richard P. RA1226.P64 1997, **(v2)**
T55.3.H3.P64 1996, **(v1)**
Pohl, Frances K. N6537.S5.P64 1989, **(v9)**
Pohlman, H. L. KF4770.P64 1991, **(v7)**
Poinar, George O. QE742.P65 1992, **(v1)**
QE742.P66 1994, **(v1)**
Poincare, Henri. Q175.P8 1946, **(v1)**
QB351.P7513 1993, **(v1)**
Poirier, Louis. PQ2603.R35.Z8, **(v3)**
Poirier, Richard. PS88.P6, **(v3)**
Poisson, Camille L. PN3178.P7.P65 1994, **(v3)**
Poitras, Guy E. F1418.P66 1990, **(v4)**
HC95.P64 2001, **(v6)**
Poizat, Bruno. QA9.7.P65 2000, **(v1)**
Pokrant, Marvin. DS79.744.N38.P645 1999, **(v5)**
Pokrovskii, Georgii Iosifovich. U102.P6713, **(v10)**
Pol Pot. KNM41.P65, **(v7)**
Pol, Louis G. HB849.41.P633 1997, **(v6)**
RA407.P65 2001, **(v2)**
Polacheck, Hilda Satt. F548.9.J5.P65 1989, **(v4)**
Polachek, James M. DS757.55.P65 1991, **(v5)**
Polak, Fred. CB158.P6213 1973, **(v5)**
Polakow, Valerie. HQ759.45.P66 1993, **(v6)**
Polano, Sergio. NA1153.B4.A4 1988, **(v9)**
Polanyi, Karl. HC53.P6 1957, **(v6)**
Polanyi, Michael. B945.P583 S63 1997, **(v8)**
Polcari, Stephen. NX504.P65 1991, **(v9)**
Pole, David. BC181.P58, **(v8)**
Pole, J. R. JK54.P6, **(v7)**
Polednak, Anthony P. GN296.P65 1989, **(v6)**
Polette, Nancy. LC3993.2.P63 1982, **(v7)**
Polhemus, Robert M. PR868.C63.P6, **(v3)**
PR868.L69.P65 1990, **(v3)**
Poliakoff, Michael. GV17.P65 1987, **(v6)**
Polier, Justine Wise. KFN6195.P65 1989, **(v7)**
Poling, Bruce E. TP242.P62 2001, **(v1)**
Poling-Kempes, Lesley. F786.P84 1989, **(v4)**
Polit, Denise F. RT81.5.P64 1999, **(v2)**
Politzer, Heinrich. PT2621.A26Z817 1966, **(v3)**
Polizzotto, Lorenzo. DG737.97.P58 1994, **(v5)**
Polk, Dora. F864.P67 1991, **(v4)**
Polk, James K. E416.P77 1952, **(v4)**
E417.A4 1969, **(v4)**
Polk, Keith. ML499.2.P64 1992, **(v9)**
Polk, Kenneth. HV6535.A82.V536 1994, **(v6)**

Polk, Noel. PS3511.A86.Z94635 1996, **(v3)**
Polk, William Roe. DS84.P6 1963, **(v5)**
DS123. P68, **(v5)**
Polkinhorn, Harry. PC4829.S6.P65 1986, **(v3)**
Pollack, Barbara. GV1785.L515.P65 1993, **(v6)**
Pollack, Burton R. RK58.P65 2002, **(v2)**
Pollack, David. PL747.65.P65 1992, **(v3)**
Pollack, Howard. ML390.P745 1992, **(v9)**
ML410.C756.P6 1999, **(v9)**
Pollack, Norman. HB501.P638 1990, **(v6)**
JK2372.P6 1962, **(v7)**
Pollack, Robert. R726.5.P63 1999, **(v2)**
Pollack, Sheldon David. HJ2362.P65 1996, **(v6)**
Pollak, G. D. QL737.C5.P65 1989, **(v1)**
Pollak, Mark. GV583.P655 1998, **(v6)**
Pollak, Michael. DS135.C5.P6, **(v5)**
Pollak, Robert A. HB225.P62 1989, **(v6)**
Pollak, Vivian R. PS1541.Z5.P59 1988, **(v3)**
PS3242.S47, **(v3)**
Pollan, Michael. QK46.5.H85, **(v1)**
Pollard, A. J. DA260.P65 1991, **(v5)**
Pollard, Alfred W. PR1260.P7 1927, **(v3)**
Pollard, Arthur. PR5687.P57, **(v3)**
Pollard, Helen Perlstein. F1219.8.T37.P65 1993, **(v4)**
Pollard, Hugh M. LA123.P6 1957, **(v7)**
Pollard, Miranda. DC397.P595 1998, **(v5)**
Pollard, Sidney. HC240.P596, **(v6)**
HC256.P62 1983, **(v6)**
Pollatschek, Henriette. DS135.C95.P65 1999, **(v5)**
Pollens, Stewart. ML655.P64 1995, **(v9)**
Pollet, Maurice. PR2348.P613, **(v3)**
Pollin, Burton Ralph. Z8699.P64 1989, **(v10)**
Pollio, Howard R. BF204.5.P65 1997, **(v2)**
Pollitzer, Anita. N6537.O39.P65 1988, **(v9)**
Pollock, Bruce. ML128.R6.P65 1997, **(v9)**
Pollock, Frederick. K588.P65 2000a, **(v7)**
Pollock, Griselda. N72.F45.P64 1988, **(v9)**
ND237.C3.P65 1998, **(v9)**
Pollock, John Charles. BV3785.G69.P597 1979, **(v8)**
DA522.W6.P64 1978, **(v5)**
Pollock, John L. B820.P58 1984, **(v8)**
BC135.P683 1990, **(v8)**
BC177.P599 1995, **(v8)**
BD161.P7245 1999, **(v8)**
Pollock, Linda A. HQ767.87.P64 1983, **(v6)**
Pollock, Nancy J. GN670.P59 1992, **(v6)**
Polloczek, Dieter. PR830.L43.P65 1999, **(v3)**
Polmar, Norman. D743.5.P57 1996, **(v5)**
JF1525.I6.P65 1997, **(v7)**
V858.P6, **(v10)**
V874.P6, **(v10)**
Poloma, Margaret M. BX6198.A74.P65 1989, **(v8)**
Polowetzky, Michael. PR119.P65 1996, **(v3)**
Pols, Edward. BD418.3.P65 1998, **(v8)**
Polsky, Milton E. PN2071.I5.P65 1997, **(v3)**
Polster, Miriam. HQ1206.P58 1992, **(v6)**
Polt, Richard F. H. B3279.H49.P65 1999, **(v8)**
Polvinen, Tuomo. DL1065.5.B62.P6413 1995, **(v5)**
Poly, Jean-Pierre. DC82.P6513 1990, **(v5)**
Polya, George. QA9.P57, **(v1)**
QA11.P6 1957, **(v1)**
QA164.8.P6513 1987, **(v1)**
Polyanin, A. D. QA372.P725 1995, **(v1)**
Polybius. D58.P7 1967, **(v5)**
Pombo. F3326.P5713 1997, **(v4)**
Pomerance, Bernard. PR6066.O48.E4 1979, **(v3)**
Pomeranz, Kenneth. HC428.S52.P66 1993, **(v6)**
Pomeroy, Earl S. F851.P57 1992, **(v4)**
Pomeroy, Sarah B. HQ1134.P64, **(v6)**
HQ1137.E3.P65 1984, **(v6)**
Pomfret, Richard W. T. HC420.3.P76 1995, **(v6)**
HF1411.P5915 1988, **(v6)**
HF1418.7.P66 1997, **(v6)**
Pommier, Jean. PQ1904.P78, **(v3)**
Pompa, Leon. B3581.P74.P65, **(v8)**
Pomper, Gerald M. JK2261.P674 1992, **(v7)**
Pond, Caroline M. QP751.P645 1998, **(v1)**
Ponder, Stephen. E176.1.P816 1999, **(v4)**
Poneman, Daniel. F2849.P64 1987, **(v4)**
Ponge, Francis. PQ2631.O643.R3, **(v3)**
Poniatowska, Elena. F1386.3.P6513 1995, **(v4)**

Ponko, Vincent. Z3014.R44.P66 1990, **(v10)**
Pont, Sally. GV939.A1 P63 2001, **(v6)**
Pontin, A. J. QH546.3.P66 1982, **(v1)**
Ponting, Clive. D421.P66 1999, **(v5)**
Poo, Mu-chou. BL1802.P65 1998, **(v8)**
Pool, Ithiel de Sola. H61.3.P66 2000, **(v6)**
  JC362.P6, **(v7)**
  UB415.E8.P6, **(v10)**
Pool, Robert. QP81.5.P66 1994, **(v1)**
  T45.P66 1997, **(v1)**
Poole, Adrian. PR2805.P6 1988, **(v3)**
Poole, Austin Lane. DA130.P65 1958, **(v5)**
Poole, David L. Q335.P657 1997, **(v1)**
Poole, Deborah. GN347.P66 1997, **(v6)**
Poole, Ernest. F452.P75, **(v4)**
  PS3531.O53 H3 1957, **(v3)**
  PS3531.O53 H5 1917, **(v3)**
Poole, Harry H. TJ211.P65 1989, **(v1)**
Poole, Joyce. QL31.P68.A3 1996, **(v1)**
Poole, Kristen. BX9334.2.P66 2000, **(v8)**
Poole, Ross. BJ301.P66 1991, **(v8)**
Poole, Russell Gilbert. Z2014.P7.P66 1998, **(v10)**
Poole, Scott. NA1455.F5.P66 1992, **(v9)**
Poole, Stafford. BT660.G8.P66 1995, **(v8)**
Poole, Steve. DA530.P66 2000, **(v5)**
Pooley, Robert C. PE1065.P55, **(v3)**
Poolman, Kenneth. VF347.P66 1997, **(v10)**
Poor, Belinda. R726.8.P65 2001, **(v2)**
Poor, Harold L. PT2642.U4.Z8, **(v3)**
Poos, Lawrence R. DA670.E7.P66 1991, **(v5)**
Poovey, Mary. DA533.P66 1995, **(v5)**
  HQ1075.5.G7.P66 1988, **(v3)**
  PR469.W65.P66 1984, **(v3)**
Popa, Vasko. PG1419.26.O48A26 1997, **(v3)**
Pope, Alexander. PR3620.B82 v.3, pt.1, **(v3)**
  PR3620.B82 vol. 4, 1953, **(v3)**
  PR3620.B82 vol.5 1963, **(v3)**
  PR3620.E71, **(v3)**
  PR3621.B82, vol. 2 1954, **(v3)**
  PR3621.B82 vol.1, **(v3)**
  PR3621.B82 vol.3, pt.2, **(v3)**
  PR3621.B83, **(v3)**
  PR3622.M3 1984, **(v3)**
  PR3629.A2.L6 1998, **(v3)**
  PR3633.A4 2000, **(v3)**
Pope, Arthur Upham. NA1480.P6, **(v9)**
Pope, Daniel. HF5821.P64 1983, **(v6)**
Pope, Elizabeth Marie. PR3565.P6 1962, **(v3)**
Pope, Jacqueline. HV99.N59.P66 1989, **(v6)**
Pope, John Collins. PR1588.P6, **(v3)**
Pope, Kenneth S. RC569.5.A28.P67 1996, **(v2)**
Pope, Mildred Katharine. PC2075.P6 1952, **(v3)**
Pope, Norris. PR4592.R4.P65 1978, **(v3)**
Pope, Randolph D. PQ6613.O79.Z834 1995, **(v3)**
Pope, Robert. DA722.P66 1998, **(v5)**
Pope, S. W. GV706.34.P67 1997, **(v6)**
Pope, Stephen. DC151.P67 1999, **(v5)**
Pope, Thomas H. F277.N5 P66, **(v4)**
Pope-Hennessy, James. PR5493.P6 1975, **(v3)**
  PR5686.P63 1971b, **(v3)**
Pope-Hennessy, John Wyndham. NB623.R72.P66 1980, **(v9)**
  ND623.R2.P677, **(v9)**
Pope-Hennessy, Una (Birch). PR4581.P6 1946, **(v3)**
Popenoe, David. HQ756.P65 1996, **(v6)**
Popkewitz, Thomas S. LB1570.P6 1982, **(v7)**
  LC191.4.P66 1991, **(v7)**
Popkin, Richard Henry. B779.P65 2003, **(v8)**
Popkin, Samuel L. HD1513.V5.P66, **(v6)**
  JK524.P64 1991, **(v7)**
Popkin, William D. KF425.P67 1999, **(v7)**
Poplawski, Paul. PR6023.A93.Z785 1993, **(v3)**
  Z8490.5.P67 1996, **(v10)**
Pople, Anthony. ML410.B47.P6 1991, **(v9)**
  ML410.M595.P58 1998, **(v9)**
Popovic, Alexandre. DS76.4.P6613 1998, **(v5)**
Poppe, N. N. PL1.P65 1983, **(v3)**
Popper, Frank. N72.E53.P66 1993, **(v9)**
Popper, Karl Raimund. B63.P6 1950, **(v8)**
  B187.5.P66 1998, **(v8)**
  B1649.P633.A9413 1992, **(v8)**

BD241.P65 1962, **(v8)**
  D16.8.P57 1964, **(v5)**
  Q175.P863, **(v1)**
Popper, Micha. BF637.L4, **(v2)**
Poppino, Rollie E. F2521.P58 1973, **(v4)**
Popplestone, John A. BF108.U5P67 1994, **(v2)**
Popplewell, Richard J. DS480.3.P66 1995, **(v5)**
Porada, Edith. N5390.P613, **(v9)**
Porarinsson, Sigurdur. GB478.58.S513 1967, **(v6)**
Porcella, Yvonne. TT699.P67 1998, **(v1)**
Porch, Douglas. D361.P64 2000, **(v5)**
Porksen, Uwe. P324.P613 1988, **(v3)**
Porphyrios, Demetri. NA260.P67 1992, **(v9)**
Porritt, Vernon L. DS597.37.P67 1997, **(v5)**
Porshnev, B. F. D271.R8.P67 1995, **(v5)**
Porsild, Charlene L. F1095.K5.P67 1998, **(v4)**
Port, M. H. NA4287.L6.P67 1995, **(v9)**
Portal, Jane. N7360.P67 2000, **(v9)**
Portelli, Alessandro. D16.14.P67 1990, **(v5)**
Porteous, Andrew. GE10.P67 1996, **(v6)**
Porter, Bernard. DA16.P67, **(v5)**
Porter, Bruce D. UA770.P666 1984, **(v10)**
Porter, C. L. QK95.P6 1967, **(v1)**
Porter, David L. GV697.A1.P576 1993, **(v6)**
Porter, David. QA431.P67 1990, **(v1)**
Porter, Dean A. ND212.5.T34.P67 1999, **(v9)**
  ND237.H584.P67 1991, **(v9)**
Porter, Deborah Lynn. BL1825.P37 1996, **(v8)**
Porter, Dennis. PN56.T7.P6 1991, **(v3)**
Porter, Dorothy Burnett. Z1361.N39.P59, **(v10)**
Porter, Doug. HN793.C63.P67 1991, **(v6)**
Porter, Edgar A. LB2285.C55.P67 1990, **(v7)**
  R604.H37.P67 1997, **(v2)**
Porter, Fairfield. ND237.E15.P6, **(v9)**
Porter, Gareth. HC79.E5.P669 1991, **(v6)**
Porter, Glenn. HF5415.1.P55, **(v6)**
Porter, J. R. BS635.2.P67 1998, **(v8)**
Porter, James I. B3313.G43.P67 2000, **(v8)**
  B3318.C56 P67 2000, **(v8)**
Porter, Jean. BJ1190.P67 1995, **(v8)**
Porter, Jean. BJ1217.P67 1990, **(v8)**
Porter, Jonathan. DS796.M2.P67 1996, **(v5)**
Porter, Joseph Ashby. PR2831.P67 1988, **(v3)**
Porter, Katherine Anne. PS3531.O752 A15 1965, **(v3)**
  PS3531.O752.A6 1991, **(v3)**
  PS3531.O752.A6 1993, **(v3)**
  PS3531.O752.D3, **(v3)**
  PS3531.O752 F5, **(v3)**
  PS3531.O752.H3 1934, **(v3)**
  PS3531.O752 L4, **(v3)**
  PS3531.O752 S5 1963, **(v3)**
  PS3531.O752.Z48 1990, **(v3)**
Porter, Kenneth Wiggins. E99.S28.P67 1996, **(v4)**
Porter, Kirk Harold. JK1846.P82 1969, **(v7)**
  JK2255.P6 1970, **(v7)**
Porter, Laurence M. PQ439.P7 1990, **(v3)**
  PQ2301.P67 1999, **(v3)**
Porter, Lewis. ML419.C645 P65 1998, **(v9)**
Porter, Michael E. HD41.P668 1985, **(v6)**
  HD41.P67 1980, **(v6)**
  HD3611.P654 1990, **(v6)**
  HF1414.P67 1998, **(v6)**
Porter, Neil A. QC15.P67 1998, **(v1)**
Porter, Norman. DA990.U46.P66 1996, **(v5)**
Porter, Richard C. HE5611.P67 1999, **(v6)**
Porter, Roger B. HC106.7.P67, **(v6)**
Porter, Roy. B1302.E65 P67 2000, **(v8)**
  DA677.P67 1995, **(v5)**
  HQ18.G7.P67 1995, **(v6)**
  R131.P59 1998, **(v2)**
  RC464.A1.P67 1988, **(v2)**
  RC629.P67 1998, **(v2)**
Porter, Theodore M. Q175.5.P67 1995, **(v1)**
Porter, Valerie. SF198.P67 1992, **(v1)**
  SF395.P59 1993, **(v1)**
Porter, William Sidney,. PS2649.P5 A6 1945a, **(v3)**
  PS2649.P5 1953, **(v3)**
Porterfield, Amanda. BX9354.2.P67 1992, **(v8)**
  HQ1426.P67, **(v6)**
Porterfield, Nolan. ML423.L635.P67 1996, **(v9)**
Porterfield, Sally F. PR3065.P67 1994, **(v3)**

Portes, Alejandro. F319.M6.P68 1993, **(v4)**
Porteus, Stanley D. (Stanley David). PR6031.O658 R4 1949, **(v3)**
Portinaro, Pierluigi. GA401.P67 1987, **(v6)**
Portmann, John. BJ1409.P67 2000, **(v8)**
Portner, Hal. LB1731.4.P67 1998, **(v7)**
Portoghesi, Paolo. NA682.P67.P6713 1982, **(v9)**
Portuges, Catherine. PN1998.3.M47.P67 1993, **(v3)**
Portz, John. HD5708.55.U6.P67 1990, **(v6)**
Posada Carbo, Eduardo. F2281.A79.P67 1996, **(v4)**
Posada, Jose Guadalupe. NE546.P6.B47 1972, **(v9)**
Posen, Barry R. U11.P83 1991, **(v10)**
Posin, Daniel Q. QD22.M43.P67, **(v1)**
Posner, David Matthew. PN721.P67 1999, **(v3)**
Posner, Donald. ND553.W3.P66 1984b, **(v9)**
Posner, Eric A. K370.P67 2000, **(v7)**
Posner, Ernst. CD996.P67, **(v5)**
  CD3050.P67, **(v5)**
Posner, Gerald L. E185.97.K5.P67 1998, **(v4)**
Posner, Michael I. QP360.5.P67 1994, **(v1)**
Posner, Richard A. BJ55.P67 1997, **(v8)**
  HQ16.P67 1992, **(v6)**
  JC578.P67, **(v7)**
  K230.P665.P76 1990, **(v7)**
  KF379.P67 1996, **(v7)**
  KF5076.C57.P67 1999, **(v7)**
  KF8700.P67 1996, **(v7)**
  KF8745.C3.P64 1990, **(v7)**
Posner, Theodore Robert. UA700.P66 1991, **(v10)**
Posnock, Ross. PS153.N5.P68 1998, **(v3)**
Pospielovsky, Dimitry. BX492.P67 1984, **(v8)**
Post, Chandler Rathfon. ND801.P85, **(v9)**
Post, Emily. BJ1853.P6 1969b, **(v8)**
Post, Gaines. DA578.P65 1993, **(v5)**
Post, Jonathan F. S. PR541.P67 1999, **(v3)**
Post, Joyce A. Z688.A58.P67 1992, **(v10)**
Post, Lauren C. F380.A2.P67 1974, **(v4)**
Post, Melville Davisson. PS3531.O76427 U52 1977, **(v3)**
Post, Peggy. BJ1853.P6 1997, **(v8)**
Post, Robert C. GV1029.P675 1994, **(v6)**
Post, Robert. KF4552.P67 1995, **(v7)**
Post, Stephen Garrard. RC523.P67 1995, **(v2)**
  R724.P665 1993, **(v2)**
Postel, Sandra. S618.P67 1999, **(v1)**
Postgate, J. N. DS69.5.P64 1992, **(v5)**
Postgate, J. R. QR100.9.P67 1994, **(v1)**
Postgate, Raymond William. D351.P86 1969, **(v5)**
Post-Lauria, Sheila. PS2388.T4.P67 1996, **(v3)**
Postman, Neil. CB430.P637 1999, **(v5)**
  LA217.P6, **(v7)**
  LA217.2.P67 1995, **(v7)**
Poston, Jonathan H. NA735.C35.P67 1997, **(v9)**
Postrel, Virginia I. HN25.P67 1998, **(v6)**
Posusney, Marsha Pripstein. HD8786.P67 1997, **(v6)**
Potholm, Christian P. JQ1872.P67 1988, **(v7)**
  JQ2721.A2 P68, **(v7)**
Potkay, Adam. BJ1481.P56 2000, **(v8)**
Potkay, Monica Brzezinski. PR113.P68 1997, **(v3)**
Pott-Buter, Hettie. HD6162.P68 1993, **(v6)**
Potter, Beatrix. PR6031.O72.Z48 1989, **(v3)**
  PZ7.P85Co 1982, **(v3)**
Potter, Claire Bond. HV8144.F43.P67 1998, **(v6)**
Potter, D. S. BF1768.P67 1994, **(v2)**
Potter, David Morris. E169.1.P6, **(v4)**
  F215.P66, **(v4)**
Potter, David. DC95.6.P68 1995, **(v5)**
Potter, David. DC611.P588.P68 1993, **(v5)**
Potter, E. B. E746.B87.P68 1990, **(v4)**
Potter, Edward E. HD5724.P58 1995, **(v6)**
Potter, Harry. HV8699.G8.P67 1993, **(v6)**
Potter, Keith. ML390.P759 1999, **(v9)**
Potter, Michael D. QA248.P68 1990, **(v1)**
Potter, Pamela Maxine. ML3797.P67 1998, **(v9)**
Potter, Parker B. F189.A647.P68 1994, **(v4)**
Potter, Patricia Ann. RT41.P844 2001, **(v2)**
Potter, Russell A. ML3531.P68 1995, **(v9)**
Potter, Sulamith Heins. HN733.5.P68 1990, **(v6)**
Potter, T. W. DA145.P67 1992, **(v5)**
Potter, Tiffany. PR3458.L49.P68 1999, **(v3)**
Potter, W. James. P96.V5.P68 1999, **(v3)**

Potterfield, Peter. GV199.42.A42.F676 1996, (v6)
Pottier, Johan. DT963.42.P68 1988, (v5)
Pottier, Johan. GN407.P67 1999, (v6)
Pottle, Frederick Albert. PR3325.P62, (v3)
Potts, Cassandra. BX2613.P68 1997, (v8)
Potts, Daniel T. DS57.P67 1997, (v5)
Potts, Donna L. PS3527.E5.Z8 1994, (v3)
Potts, Louis W. E302.6.L38.P67, (v4)
Potts, Lydia. HD6300.P6813 1990, (v6)
Potts, Richard. GN281.4.P65 1996, (v6)
   GN772.42.T34.P67 1988, (v6)
Potts, Stephen W. PS3511.I9.Z825 1993, (v3)
Potts, Willard. PR6019.O9.Z78236 2000, (v3)
Pouchelle, Marie-Christine. RD27.3.F8.P6813 1990,
   (v2)
Pouchert, Charles J. QD96.N8.P68 1983, (v1)
Pough, Frederick H. QE367.2.P68 1976, (v1)
Poulet, Georges. PQ282.P843, (v3)
Poulton, Diana. ML410.D808 P7 1982, (v9)
Poulton, Hugh. DR2185.P68 1995, (v5)
Poulton, M. L. TL210.P637 1994, (v1)
Pound, Ezra. NB553.G35.P6 1970, (v9)
   PJ1945.P6, (v3)
   PN511.P633 1966, (v3)
   PS3531.O82.A17 1976, (v3)
   PS3531.O82.A6 1949, (v3)
   PS3531.O82.C24 1972, (v3)
   PS3531.O82.C8 1938, (v3)
   PS3531.O82.C8 1952, (v3)
   PS3531.O82.H6 1976, (v3)
   PS3531.O82.M33 1996, (v3)
   PS3531.O82.Z4895 1984, (v3)
   PS3531.O82.Z4986 1991, (v3)
   PS3531.O82.Z53, (v3)
   PS3531.O82.Z533, (v3)
   PS3531.O82.Z535, (v3)
   PS3531.O82.I6 1930, (v3)
Pound, Louise. PN1376.P6 1962, (v3)
Pound, Roscoe. K230.P67.J87 2000, (v7)
   KF394.P613 1995, (v7)
Pounds, Norman John Greville. D21.5.P634, (v5)
   DA660.P68 1990, (v5)
   G141.P6, (v6)
   GT76.P67 1989, (v6)
Pousse, Michel. PR9499.3.N3.Z82 1995, (v3)
Poveda, Tony G. HV6769.P67 1994, (v6)
Povey, John. PR9369.3.C35.Z85, (v3)
Povinelli, Elizabeth A. GN667.N6.P68 1993, (v6)
Powaski, Ronald E. E744.P68 1991, (v4)
Powe, L. A. Scot. KF4774.P69 1991, (v7)
   KF8742.P68 2000, (v7)
Powell, Adam Clayton. E748.P86.A3, (v4)
Powell, Anthony. DA93.A8.P68, (v5)
   PR6031.O74 A33 1963, (v3)
   PR6031.O74 A9, (v3)
   PR6031.O74 B6, (v3)
   PR6031.O74 C3, (v3)
   PR6031.O74 D3, (v3)
   PR6031.O74 D32, (v3)
   PR6031.O74 D34, (v3)
   PR6031.O74 F7, (v3)
   PR6031.O74 K5, (v3)
   PR6031.O74 M5, (v3)
   PR6031.O74 S6, (v3)
   PR6031.O74 V3 1964, (v3)
   PR6031.O74 V4, (v3)
   PR6031.O74 W48, (v3)
   PR6031.O74.Z516 1977, (v3)
   PR6031.O74.Z52 1978, (v3)
Powell, Anton. DF82.P64 1988, (v5)
Powell, Arthur G. LC58.4.P68 1996, (v7)
Powell, Brian. PL811.A9.Z85 1990, (v3)
Powell, David A. PQ2419.P65 2001, (v3)
Powell, David. HD8390.P79 1992, (v6)
Powell, Dawn. PS3531.O936 G6, (v3)
   PS3531.O936.Z47 1995, (v3)
   PS3531.O936.Z48 1999, (v3)
Powell, Earl A. ND237.C6.A4 1990, (v9)
Powell, J. M. DU96.5.P69 1988, (v5)
Powell, James Lawrence. QE506.P735 1998, (v1)
Powell, Jefferson. KF5406.A62 1999, (v7)

Powell, Jocelyn. PR691.P68 1984, (v3)
Powell, John Benjamin. DS775.P67 1976, (v5)
Powell, John Wesley. F788.P886 1987, (v4)
Powell, Josh. RC607.A26.P686 1996, (v2)
Powell, Ken. NA2793.P69 1999, (v9)
Powell, Kerry. PR5827.D7.P6 1990, (v3)
Powell, Lawrence Clark. F811.P73, (v4)
Powell, Lawrence N. DS135.P63.L3996 2000, (v5)
   HD1471.U5.P68, (v6)
Powell, Mark Allan. Z7770.P68 1992, (v10)
Powell, Michael J. KF334.N4.A8454 1988, (v7)
Powell, Ralph L. DS761.P69 1972, (v5)
Powell, Richard J. N6538.N5.P68 1999, (v9)
   ND237.J73.P69 1991, (v9)
Powell, Robert. NA1525.8.Y43 P69 1999, (v9)
Powell, Ronald R. Z669.7.P68 1997, (v10)
Powell, Russell H. Z7401.P778 1987, (v10)
Powell, Timothy B. PS153.M56.P69 2000, (v3)
Powell, Trevor J. RC531.P69 1990, (v2)
Powelson, John P. HB72.P65 1998, (v6)
Power, Edward J. LA11.P65 1991, (v7)
   LB14.7.P68 1995, (v7)
   LC405.P69 1995, (v7)
Power, Eileen Edna. HQ1143.P68 1997, (v6)
Power, F. Clark. LC311.P69 1989, (v7)
Power, J. Tracy. E470.2.P69 1998, (v4)
Power, Jonathan. JC571.P68, (v7)
Power, Margaret. GN365.9.P68 1991, (v6)
Power, T. P. DA990.T5.P69 1993, (v5)
Power, Thomas M. HB171.P697 1996, (v6)
Powers, Bernard Edward. F279.C49.N4 1994, (v4)
Powers, James F. UA787.P69 1987, (v10)
Powers, John. BQ7604.P69 1995, (v8)
   Z7864.Y64.P69 1991, (v10)
Powers, Martin Joseph. NB1880.C6.P68 1991, (v9)
Powers, Meredith A. PN56.5.W64.P69 1991, (v3)
Powers, Richard Gid. E743.5.P65 1995, (v4)
Powers, Ron. PS1332.P68 1999, (v3)
Powers, Stephen. PN1995.9.S6.P67 1996, (v3)
Powers, Thomas. QC16.H35.P69 1993, (v1)
Powers-Beck, Jeffrey P. PR431.P69 1998, (v3)
Powicke, Frederick James. B1133.C2 P6 1971, (v8)
Powicke, Michael. U760.P6, (v10)
Powledge, Fred. E185.61.P75 1990, (v4)
Powys, John Cowper. BJ1481.P6 1974, (v8)
   PR6031.O867.C6 1971, (v3)
   PR6031.O867 G4 1955, (v3)
   PR6031.O867.P67 1994, (v3)
   PR6031.O867 W6, (v3)
   PR6031.O867.Z5 1968, (v3)
Powys, Llewelyn. PR6031.O87 A85 1930, (v3)
Powys, Theodore Francis. PR6031.O873 M5, (v3)
   PR6031.O873 M58, (v3)
   PR6031.O873 U52, (v3)
Poyer, Lin. D767.99 M53, (v5)
   DU568.N44.P69 1993, (v5)
Poznanski, Kazimierz. HC340.3.P699 1996, (v6)
Poznansky, Alexander. ML134.C42 P69 2002, (v9)
   ML410.C4 P85 1991, (v9)
   ML410.C4.P856 1996, (v9)
Pozrikidis, C. QA297.P69 1998, (v1)
Prabhakara, F. S. TK4035.F3.P73 1995, (v1)
Prado Salmon, Gary. F3326.P7213 1990, (v4)
Prado, C. G. B2430.F724.P73 1995, (v8)
Prados, John. D810.C88.P73 1995, (v5)
   JK468.I6.P72, (v7)
   UA23.15.P73 1991, (v10)
Prag, John. GN74.P73 1997, (v6)
Prager, Ellen J. QE534.2.P73 2000, (v1)
Prager, Jan C. TD196.C45.P73 1995, (v1)
Prager, Karen Jean. BF575.I5.P73 1995, (v2)
Prahlad, Sw. Anand. PN6426.P73 1996, (v3)
Prakash, Gyan. DS463.P67 1999, (v5)
Prakash, Om. DS436.N47 1987 pt. 2, vol. 5, (v5)
Prance, Ghillean T. QK649.P7 1985, (v1)
Prange, Gordon William. D767.92.P7215 1988, (v5)
   D774.M5.P7 1982, (v5)
Prankerd, T. A. J. QP91.P79 1961, (v1)
Prantzos, Nikos. QB500.262.P7313 2000, (v1)
Prasad, Kedar N. RC271.V58P73 2001, (v2)
Prasad, Rajendra. S633.P83 1997, (v1)

Prashad, Vijay. DS422.C3.P728 2000, (v5)
Prasifka, David W. TD353.P7 1994, (v1)
Prater, Donald A. PT2625.A44.Z7658 1995, (v3)
Prather, H. Leon. F264.W7.P72 1984, (v4)
Prather, Marla. N6537.C33.A4 1998, (v9)
   ND237.D334.A4 1994, (v9)
Prather, Patricia Smith. F391.H79.P73 1993, (v4)
Pratt, Alice Day. F881.P93 P73 1993, (v4)
Pratt, Annis. PR508.A66.P73 1994, (v3)
Pratt, Annis. PR830.W62.P7, (v3)
Pratt, Dale J. PQ6073.S33, (v3)
Pratt, Fletcher. PS3531.R23 W4, (v3)
Pratt, Frantz. Z1531.H35 1991, (v10)
Pratt, James Bissett. BD331.P7 1970, (v8)
Pratt, Linda Ray. PR4024.P73 2000, (v3)
Pratt, Louisa Barnes. BX8695.P68.A3 1998, (v8)
Pratt, Ray. ML3470.P7 1990, (v9)
Pratt, Richard. JK9316.P73 2000, (v7)
Pratt, Walter F. KF8742.P73 1999, (v7)
Pratt, William. PS324.P73 1996, (v3)
Pratte, Paul Alfred. PN4841.A1.P73 1995, (v3)
Prawer, Siegbert Salomon. PR5642.J48.P73 1991,
   (v3)
   PT2340.P7, (v3)
Praz, Mario. PR129.I8.P7, (v3)
Prazak, Milos. BC71.P7 1972, (v8)
Prazmowska, Anita. D742.E852, (v5)
   D750.P68 1995, (v5)
Prazniak, Roxann. HD1537.C5.P73 1999, (v6)
Prebish, Charles S. BQ130.P74 1993, (v8)
   BQ732.P736 1999, (v8)
Prechel, Harland N. HD2356.U5.P73 2000, (v6)
Pred, Allan Richard. HC105.P94, (v6)
Predko, Michael. TJ223.P76P73 1999, (v1)
Preeg, Ernest H. HF1721.P7324 1995, (v6)
   HF1756.P68 1998, (v6)
Prelinger, Elizabeth. N6888.K62.A4 1992, (v9)
Prelovsek, Damjan. NA1455.S563.P643613 1997, (v9)
Premacanda. PK2098.S7 G613, (v3)
Premchand, A. HJ7390.P74 2000, (v6)
Prendergast, John. HV551.5.S83.P74 1997, (v6)
Prendergast, Mark J. ML197.P76 2000, (v9)
Prendergast, Roy M. ML2075.P73 1991, (v9)
Prendeville, Brendan. ND196.R4, (v9)
Prentice, Geoffrey. TP255.P74 1991, (v1)
Prentice, Penelope. PR6066.I53.Z75 1994, (v3)
Prentice, Richard. DA655.P74 1993, (v5)
Prentis, Barbara. PR115.P74 1987, (v3)
Prentiss, Karen Pechilis. BL1214.32.B53, (v8)
Presberg, Charles D. PQ6353.P72 2001, (v3)
Prescott, G. W. (Gerald Webber). QK571.P67 1962,
   (v1)
Prescott, H. F. M. PR6031.R47 M3, (v3)
Prescott, Laurence E. PQ8180.1.R77.Z85 2000, (v3)
Prescott, Philander. F606.P74 1966, (v4)
Prescott, William Hickling. DP162.P8 1962a, (v5)
   PS2657.A3 1970, (v3)
   PS2657.A32, (v3)
Presley, Delma Eugene. PS3545.I5365.G5365 1990,
   (v3)
Presner, Lewis A. HF1359.P74 1991, (v6)
Presniakov, A. E. DK210.P713, (v5)
Press, Andrea Lee. HQ1233.P74 1991, (v6)
Press, Bill. BJ1421.P74 2001, (v8)
Press, John. PN1031.P72, (v3)
   PR601.P69 1963, (v3)
   PR6025.A316.Z9, (v3)
Press, Robert M. DT353.P74 1999, (v5)
Presser, Stephen B. KF4550.P68 1991, (v7)
Pressing, Jeff. ML1092.P68 1992, (v9)
Pressley, Michael. LB1573.P72 2002, (v7)
Pressman, Steven. HB76.P74 1999, (v6)
   Z7165.U5 P715 1994, (v10)
Prest, John M. HC258.C85.P7, (v6)
   QK73.E85.P73 1981, (v1)
Preston, Antony. V820.P73 1980, (v10)
   V825.P73 1977, (v10)
Preston, Christine. F799.P94 1998, (v4)
Preston, Claire. PS3545.H16.Z77 1999, (v3)
Preston, Daniel. Z6616.M69, (v10)
Preston, Dickson J. E449.D75.P74, (v4)

Preston, Howard L. HC108.A75.P73, (v6)
Preston, Ivan L. KF1614.P74 1994, (v7)
Preston, Laurence W. DS485.M348.P74 1989, (v5)
Preston, Lee E. HD60.P73, (v6)
Preston, Paul. DP270.S624 1976b, (v5)
Preston, Richard Arthur. UA647.P68, (v10)
Preston, Richard. QB44.2.P74 1996, (v1)
Preston, Samuel H. HB1323.C52.U655 1991, (v6)
Preston, Thomas A. R726.8.P73 2000, (v2)
Preston, Thomas. E840.P74 2001, (v4)
Preston, William. E743.5.P7, (v4)
Preston-Dunlop, Valerie Monthland. GV1585.P74 1995, (v6)
  GV1785.L2 P74 1998, (v6)
Preston-Mafham, Ken. QH195.M2.P74 1991, (v1)
  QL506.P74 1991, (v1)
Preston-Mafham, Rod. QL364.2.P74 1993, (v1)
  QL737.P9.P66 1992, (v1)
Prestwich, Michael. DA229.P72 1988, (v5)
  UA647.P69 1996, (v10)
Preti, Consuelo. B945.F634 P74 2001, (v8)
  B945.K794 P74 2003, (v8)
Prettyman, Barrett. KF9227.C2 P74, (v7)
Pretzel, Oliver. QA268.P74 1992, (v1)
Preus, James S. BL41.P69 1987, (v8)
Preuss, Charles. F592.P713, (v4)
Preuss, Ulrich Klaus. JF1051.P7213 1995, (v7)
Prevelakes, Panteles. PA5610.K39.Z8, (v3)
Prevert, Jacques. PQ2631.R387.P3, (v3)
Previts, Gary John. HF5616.U5.P72, (v6)
Prevost, Jean. PQ2443.P7 1951, (v3)
Prevost, Robert. BD555.P87 1990, (v8)
Prevost. PQ2021.M3 1978, (v3)
Prevots, Naima. PN3209.P74 1990, (v3)
Preziosi, Donald. N380.P68 1989, (v9)
Price Herndl, Diane. PS374.W6.P74 1993, (v3)
Price, Alan. PS3545.H16.Z78 1996, (v3)
Price, Catherine. E99.O3.P75 1996, (v4)
Price, Charles C. QD381.P68, (v1)
Price, David H. G1046.E1.P7 1989, (v6)
Price, David P. T. K3611.T7, (v7)
Price, David W. D16.8.P737 1999, (v5)
Price, Diana. PR2937.P75 2001, (v3)
Price, Don C. DS773.P7, (v5)
Price, Ernest Batson. DS783.7.P7 1933, (v5)
Price, Eva Jane. DS771.P75 1989, (v5)
Price, Fred W. QB601.P67 2000, (v1)
Price, H. H. BD215.P7, (v8)
Price, H. Marcus. KF8210.A57.P75 1991, (v7)
Price, Huw. BD638.P73 1996, (v8)
Price, J. L. DJ401.H6.P75 1994, (v5)
Price, Jody. PR5827.P6.P75 1996, (v3)
Price, Leah. PR851.P74 2000, (v3)
Price, Leah. PR851.P74 2000, (v3)
Price, Michael E. PS266.G4.P75 2000, (v3)
Price, Neville J. QE511.4.P74 2000, (v1)
  QE601.P694 1990, (v1)
Price, Pamela G. DS485.M28.P74 1996, (v5)
Price, Raymond. E856.P74, (v4)
Price, Richard. E211.P9692, (v4)
  F2084.8.P75 1998, (v4)
  F2431.N3.P73 1983, (v4)
  F2431.S27.A457 1990, (v4)
Price, Robert M. BT303.2.P75 2000, (v8)
  DT1963.P75 1991, (v5)
Price, Robert. S417.C45.P7, (v1)
Price, Roger. HN425.P75 1987, (v6)
Price, Theodore. PN1998.3.H58.P75 1992, (v3)
Prichard, Harold Arthur. BD161.P75, (v8)
  BJ1451.P7, (v8)
Prickett, Stephen. BS535.P75 1996, (v8)
  PR129.F8.P7 1989, (v3)
  PR468.F35.P7, (v3)
Prideaux, Tom. ND237.W6.P7, (v9)
Pridgen, Allen. PS3566.E6912.Z8315 2000, (v3)
Prieberg, Fred K. ML422.F92.P7513 1994, (v9)
Priest, John M. E476.52.P75 1995, (v4)
Priest, Stephen. BD418.3.P75 1991, (v8)
Priest, W. Curtiss. KF3300.P75 1988, (v7)
Priestley, H. A. QA308.P75 1997, (v1)
Priestley, J. B. DA630.P7 1984, (v5)

F786.P95 1955a, (v4)
PN701.P7, (v3)
PR4581.P67 1962, (v3)
PR6031.R6 A66, (v3)
PR6031.R6 F47 1951, (v3)
PR6031.R6 G6, (v3)
PR6031.R6 I5, (v3)
PR6031.R6 L4, (v3)
PR6031.R6 S47, (v3)
PR6031.R6 T445 1962, (v3)
PR6031.R6.Z468, (v3)
PR6031.R6.Z52, (v3)
Priestley, M. J. N. TG300.P64 1996, (v1)
Priestman, Martin. PN3448.D4.P75 1990, (v3)
Prigogine, I. Q175.P8822 1984, (v1)
Prilleltensky, Isaac. BF76.4.P75 1994, (v2)
Primack, Richard B. . QH75.P7525 2000, (v1)
Primeau, Ronald. PS366.T73.P75 1996, (v3)
Primm, James Neal. F474.S257 P75 1998, (v4)
Primorac, Igor. HV8675.P75 1989, (v6)
Prince, Henry. E83.835.P875 1998, (v4)
Prince, Stephen. PN1993.5.U6.H55 1990 vol. 10, (v3)
  PN1998.3.K87.P75 1991, (v3)
  PN1998.3.P43.P75 1998, (v3)
Prindl, Andreas R. HG3324.P74 1981, (v6)
Prindle, David F. PN1993.5.U6.P76 1993, (v3)
Pring, George W. KF4780.P75 1996, (v7)
Pringle, David. PN56.4.P75 1996, (v3)
Prins, Harald E. L. E99.M6.P75 1996, (v4)
Prins, Yopie. PR129.S25.P75 1999, (v3)
Prior, A. N. BC199.M6 P7 2003, (v8)
Prior, Arthur N. BC108.P8 1962, (v8)
  BC135.P775, (v8)
  BC135.P78, (v8)
  BJ37.P7, (v8)
Prior, Matthew. PR3640.A25.W7 1971, (v3)
Prior, Moody Erasmus. PR2982.P7, (v3)
Prior, Robin. D530.P75 1991, (v5)
Prior, Robin. D542.Y72.P75 1996, (v5)
Prior, William J. BJ161.P72 1990, (v8)
Prishvin, Mikhail Mikhailovich. QH81.P8613, (v1)
Pritchard, James Bennett. DS56.P7, (v5)
Pritchard, James S. DC52.P75 1995, (v5)
  VA503.P75 1987, (v10)
Pritchard, John Paul. PN99.U5.P69, (v3)
Pritchard, Michael S. LC268.P72 1996, (v7)
Pritchard, William H. PS3571.P4.Z83 2000, (v3)
Pritchett, C. Herman. JK1561.P7, (v7)
Pritchett, V. S. DA677.P7 1962a, (v5)
  PR6031.R7 A15, (v3)
  PR6031.R7.A6 1985b, (v3)
  PR6031.R7 B6, (v3)
  PR6031.R7 W48 1961, (v3)
Pritchett, William L. SD390.P74 1987, (v1)
Prittie, Terence. DD259.P74 1979, (v5)
  DD259.7.B7.P74 1974b, (v5)
Pritzker, Barry. E77.P89 1998, (v4)
Prizel, Ilya. F1416.S65.P75 1990, (v4)
Probst, Gerhard F. PN2658.P5.P76 1991, (v3)
Probyn, Clive T. PR851.P76 1987, (v3)
Probyn, Elspeth. HQ1206.P745 1993, (v6)
Prochaska, Bernadette. PS3566.E6912.L3637 1992, (v3)
Prochaska, David. DT299.B6.P76 1990, (v5)
Prochnow, Herbert Victor. BJ2121.P74 1972, (v8)
Procida, Mary A. DS428.P76 2002, (v5)
Procopius. DF572.P999 1967, (v5)
Procter, Ben H. Z473.H4.P76 1998, (v10)
Proctor, Michael C. F. QK926.P75 1996, (v1)
Proctor, Nick H. RA1229.P76 1996, (v2)
Proctor, Noble S. QL697.P76 1993, (v1)
Proctor, Robert E. AZ221.P76 1988, (v10)
Proctor, Robert. RC268.P77 1999, (v2)
  RC276.P76 1995, (v2)
Proctor, Sigmund Kluss. PR4537.P7 1966, (v3)
Proctor, William. Z1001.W58 1999, (v10)
Prodger, Phillip. QP401.P76 1998, (v1)
Proffer, Carl R. Z2503.P76 1990, (v10)
Proffer, Ellendea. PG3476.B78.Z8 1984, (v3)
Profillidis, V. A. (Vassilios A.). TF145.P76 2000, (v1)
Profio, A. Edward. R856.P76 1993, (v2)

Progoff, Ira. BF173.J85.P7 1969, (v2)
  BF173.P75, (v2)
Prokhovnik, Raia. B812.P77 1999, (v8)
Prokosch, Eduard. PD101.P7, (v3)
Prokosch, Frederic. PS3531.R78 A8, (v3)
  PS3531.R78 B3, (v3)
  PS3531.R78 I4, (v3)
  PS3531.R78 N5, (v3)
  PS3531.R78 S38, (v3)
  PS3531.R78 T3, (v3)
Prokurat, Michael. BX230.P76 1996, (v8)
Promey, Sally M. ND237.S3.A77 1999, (v9)
Propas, Sharon W. Z2019.P76 1992, (v10)
Propp, V. IA. GR202.P7513 1984, (v6)
Proser, Matthew N. PR2677.A36.P76 1995, (v3)
Proskouriakoff, Tatiana. F1435.P76 1993, (v4)
  F1435.3.A6.P7 1963, (v4)
Pross, Addy. QD476.P755 1995, (v1)
Pross, Christian. DS135.G332.P7613 1998, (v5)
Prosser, C. Ladd. QP31.P68 1961, (v1)
Prosser, Eleanor. PR643.M8.P7, (v3)
Prosser, Franklin P. TK7888.3.P77 1987, (v1)
Prosser, William Lloyd. KF1250.P7 1971, (v7)
Prothero, Donald R. QE692.8.P76 1994, (v1)
Prothero, Stephen R. GT3330.P76 2001, (v6)
Protzen, Jean-Pierre. F3429.1.O44.P76 1993, (v4)
Proudfoot, L. J. HT384.I66.P76 1995, (v6)
Proust, Marcel. PQ2631.P26 1932, (v3)
  PQ2631.R63.J4, (v3)
  PQ2631.R63.Z445413 1973, (v3)
  PQ2631.R63.Z48 1983, (v3)
Prouty, Charles Tyler. PR2828.P7, (v3)
Provence, Sally. BF723.I6.P76 1963, (v2)
Provenzo, Eugene F. LB1028.5.P739 1999, (v7)
  LC111.P83 1990, (v7)
Provost, Foster. Z8187.P76 1991, (v10)
Prown, Jules David. ND205.P74, (v9)
Prown, Katherine Hemple. PS3565.C57.Z837 2001, (v3)
Prucha, Francis Paul. E93.P9654 1984, (v4)
  E93.P9664, (v4)
  G1201.E1.P7 1990, (v6)
  KF8205.P75 1994, (v7)
  Z1236.P78 1987, (v10)
Pruden, Caroline. E835.P78 1998, (v4)
Prueitt, Melvin L. N7433.8.P7 1984, (v9)
Pruessen, Ronald W. E748.D868.P78 1982, (v4)
Pruett, Barbara J. PN1576.P78 1992, (v3)
Prugh, Thomas. HC79.E5 P748 1999, (v6)
Prunckun, Henry W. Z7164.T3.P78 1995, (v10)
Prunty, Jacinta. HV4088.D8.P78 1998, (v6)
Prus, Boleslaw. PG7158.G6L323 1996, (v3)
Prus, Robert C. HM291.P727 1996, (v6)
Prusek, Jaroslav. PL2302.P7, (v3)
Prussin, Labelle. NA7461.A1.P78 1995, (v9)
Prussing, John E. TL1050.P78 1993, (v1)
Pruter, Robert. ML3527.P78 1996, (v9)
  ML3537.P78 1991, (v9)
Prutky, Remedius. G161.H2 2nd ser., no. 174, (v6)
Pruys, Karl Hugo. DD262.P7813 1996, (v5)
Pryce-Jones, David. D802.F82.P376, (v5)
  DS36.77.P79 1989, (v5)
  PR6045.A97.Z76 1973, (v3)
  PR6066.R88.S2, (v3)
Pryde, Philip R. HC340.E5.P79 1991, (v6)
Pryke, Kenneth G. F1038.P83, (v4)
Pryor, Douglas W. HV6570.2.P77 1996, (v6)
Pryor, Frederic L. HC106.5.P79 1996, (v6)
  HC106.82.P79 2002, (v6)
  HJ7461.P7 1968b, (v6)
  HX550.A37.P79 1992, (v6)
Pryor, John H. VK55.P79 1988, (v10)
Pryse-Phillips, William. RC334.P79 1995, (v2)
Przeworski, Adam. HC244.P8 1991, (v6)
Przybyszewski, Boleslaw. DK4249.5.P7913 1997, (v5)
Przybyszewski, Linda. KF8745.H3.P79 1999, (v7)
Psacharopoulos, Nikos. PN2061.P74 1998, (v3)
Pu, Sung-ling. PL2722.U2.L513 1946, (v3)
  PL2722.U2 L52 1969, (v3)
Pucci, Joseph Michael. PN43.P83 1998, (v3)
Puckett, Anita. HN79.A127.P83 2000, (v6)

Puckett, John L. F217.A65.P83 1989, (v4)
Puerto, Cecilia. Z7963.A75.P84 1996, (v10)
Puertolas, Soledad. PQ6666.U35.B8713 1998, (v3)
Puett, Michael J. DS721.P794 2001, (v5)
Pugach, Marleen Carol. LC191.8.M58.P84 1998, (v7)
Pugel, Thomas A. HF1411.L536 2000, (v6)
Pugh, Herbert Lamont. VG227.P8.A3, (v10)
Pugh, Martin. DA560.P79 1982, (v5)
　HQ1593.P84 1992, (v6)
Pugh, Ronnie. ML420.T87.P84 1996, (v9)
Pugin, Augustus Welby Northmore. NA997.P9.A4
　1994, (v9)
Puglisi, Michael J. F67.P96 1991, (v4)
Pugsley, Anthony P. QP551.P83 1989, (v1)
Puig, Manuel. PQ7798.26.U4.B4, (v3)
　PQ7798.26.U4.B413x 1979, (v3)
　PQ7798.26.U4.T713 1981, (v3)
Pukui, Mary (Wiggin). PL6446.P795, (v3)
Pukui, Mary Kawena. DU622.P8, (v5)
　PL6446.P79, (v3)
　PL6446.P8, (v3)
Pulgram, Ernst. PC1075.P8 1969, (v3)
Pullan, Brian S. DG530.P84 1973b, (v5)
Pullen, L. Larry. BT738.15.P85 2000, (v8)
Pulleyblank, Edwin G. DS749.3.P8, (v5)
　PL1101.P85 1995, (v3)
Pullman, Wesley E. HV3181.P85 1995, (v6)
Pulos, Arthur J. NK1404.P85 1988, (v9)
　TS23.P84 1983, (v1)
Pulzer, Peter G.J. JN3971.A58.P85 1995, (v7)
Pumroy, Eric. Z6121.P85 1996, (v10)
Punch, Maurice. HV6768.P85 1996, (v6)
Pundik, Ron. DA47.9.J6.P86 1994, (v5)
Puniello, Francoise S. Z5949.U5.P86 1996, (v10)
Punter, David. PR408.G68.P8 1996, (v3)
　PR830.T3.P86 1998, (v3)
Punzo, Fred. QL434.P85 2000, (v1)
Purcell, Edward A. KF8858.P87 1992, (v7)
Purcell, Katherine. NK7398.F355.A4 1999, (v9)
Purcell, L. Edward. E46.5.P87 2000, (v4)
　E206.P87 1993, (v4)
Purcell, Victor William Williams Saunders.
　DS509.5.P8 1965, (v5)
Purcell-Gates, Victoria. LC152.A66.P87 1995, (v7)
　LC155.S22.P87 2000, (v7)
Purdie, Bob. DA990.U46.P86 1990, (v5)
Purdom, C. B. PR5367.P8 1963, (v3)
Purdy, James. PS3531.U426.C6, (v3)
　PS3531.U426.E8, (v3)
　PS3531.U426.M34, (v3)
　PS3531.U426.N4, (v3)
Purdy, Laura M. RG133.5.P87 1996, (v2)
Purdy, Richard Little. Z8386.5.P873 2002, (v10)
Purich, Daniel L. QP601.3.P87 2000, (v1)
Purinton, Marjean D. PR719.P65.P87 1994, (v3)
Puritz, Gerd. ML420.S388.P8 1993, (v9)
Purnell, Jennie. HD1531.M6.P87 1999, (v6)
Purpel, David E. LA217.P87 1989, (v7)
Pursell, Carroll W. T14.5.P87 1995, (v1)
Purtill, Richard L. BC108.P89, (v8)
Purtscher, Nora (von Wydenbruck).
　PT2635.I65.Z837, (v3)
Purver, Margery. Q41.L86.P86 1967a, (v1)
Purves, Dale. QP356.25.P87 1994, (v1)
　QP363.P87 1988, (v1)
Purvis, James D. Z3478.J4.P87 1988, (v10)
Purvis, Thomas L. E162.P86 1994, (v4)
　E188.P86 1999, (v4)
Pusey, James Reeve. PL2754.S5.Z8213 1998, (v3)
Pusey, Nathan Marsh. LB2325.P8, (v7)
Pusey, William Allen. RL46.P8, (v2)
Pushkarev, Boris. HE305.P87 1977, (v6)
Pushkarev, S. G. DK189.P813, (v5)
Pushkin, Aleksandr Sergeevich. PG3343.E8 1953,
　(v3)
　PG3347.A15 1983, (v3)
　PG3347.A2W6 1998, (v3)
Puskas, Julianna. E184.H95.P89 2000, (v4)
Pustz, Matthew. PN6725.P87 1999, (v3)
Put, Paul J. van der. QD151.2.P89 1998, (v1)
Putman, Rory. QL737.U55.P87 1988, (v1)

Putnam, Douglas T. GV706.5.P88 1999, (v6)
Putnam, George Haven. Z4.P99, (v10)
Putnam, Hilary. B29.P88 1992, (v8)
　B835.P88 1988, (v8)
　BC51.P88 1971, (v8)
　BD171.P875, (v8)
Putnam, Michael C. J. PA6825.P8, (v3)
Putnam, Robert D. JN5477.R35.P866 1993, (v7)
Putnam, Samuel. PQ9511.P8 1971, (v3)
Putnam, William Lowell. QB82.U62.F537 1994, (v1)
Putter, Ad. PR1972.G353.P87 1996, (v3)
Putterman, Louis G. HB171.5.P974 2001, (v6)
　HN740.Z9.C668 1993, (v6)
Puttick, Elizabeth. BL458.P88 1997, (v8)
Puttnam, David. PN1993.5.U6.P88 1998, (v3)
Puyana de Palacios, Alicia. HC165.P89 1982, (v6)
Pyatt, Sherman E. Z3608.R3.P93 1990, (v10)
　Z8464.44.P9 1986, (v10)
Pybus, Elizabeth. BJ1401.P93 1991, (v8)
Pycior, Julie Leininger. E847.2.P93 1997, (v4)
Pyddoke, Edward. CC75.P9, (v5)
Pye, Christopher. PR3017.P94 1990, (v3)
Pye, J. D. QC441.P94 2001, (v1)
Pye, Lucian W. DS778.M3.P93, (v5)
Pyle, David J. HC427.9.P95 1997, (v6)
Pyle, Ernie. D811.5.P92, (v5)
Pyle, Forest. PR468.R65.P95 1995, (v3)
Pyle, Howard. PZ8.1.A788P5, (v3)
　PZ8.1.R55P, (v3)
Pyle, Jean Larson. HD6138.P95 1990, (v6)
Pyle, Robert Michael. QL548.P94 1981, (v1)
Pyles, Marian S. PN1009.5.D43.P9 1988, (v3)
Pyles, Thomas. PE1075.P9, (v3)
Pym, Barbara. PR6066.Y58, (v3)
　PR6066.Y58.G5 1958, (v3)
Pyman, Avril. PG3015.5.S9.P95 1994, (v3)
Pynchon, Thomas. PS3566.Y55.C79 1986, (v3)
　PS3566.Y55.V2, (v3)
Pyne, Kathleen A. ND210.P96 1996, (v9)
Pyne, Stephen J. SD421.P94 1996, (v1)
　SD421.3.P96 1982, (v1)
Pyre, James Francis Augustin. PN35.W65 no. 12,
　(v3)
Pyrhonen, Heta. PN3448.D4.P96 1994, (v3)
Pyron, Darden Asbury. PS3525.I972.Z82 1991, (v3)
Pywell, Geoff. PN2193.E86.P98 1994, (v3)
Qasim, Abd al-Hakim. PJ7858.A76.M3513 1995, (v3)
Qian, Hao. DS715.Q513, (v5)
Qin, Duo. HB139.Q3 1993, (v6)
Quadagno, Jill S. HN59.Q28 1994, (v6)
Quah, Stella R. Z3285.Q33 1988, (v10)
Quaife, Milo Milton. F553.Q3, (v4)
Quale, G. Robina. HQ503.Q35 1988, (v6)
Quammen, David. QH541.5.I8.Q35 1996, (v1)
Quandt, William B. DS119.7.Q69 1993, (v5)
　DS128.183.Q36 1986, (v5)
Quantz, Johann Joachim. MT342.Q313 1985, (v9)
Quarles, Benjamin. E269.N3 Q3 1996, (v4)
　E449.D75 Q37 1997, (v4)
　E449.Q17, (v4)
　E457.2.Q3, (v4)
　E457.2.Q3 1991, (v4)
　E540.N3 Q3 1989, (v4)
Quataert, Donald. DR485 .Q37 2000, (v5)
Quattrocchi, Umberto. QK13.Q38 2000, (v1)
Quayd, Muhammad Yusuf. PJ7858.U3.H3713 1998,
　(v3)
Queen, Edward L. BL2525.Q44 2001, (v8)
Queen, Ellery. PS3533.U4 C6, (v3)
Queen, Sarah A. PL2470.Z7Q43 1996, (v3)
Queeney, Donna S. LC5219.Q84 1995, (v7)
Queinnec, Christian. QA76.73.L23.Q4613 1996, (v1)
Queiros, Eca de. PQ9261.E3 C42, (v3)
Queneau, Raymond. PQ2633.U43.A27 1985, (v3)
　PQ2633.U43.D413 1990, (v3)
　PQ2633.U43.D513 1977, (v3)
　PQ2633.U43.L6, (v3)
　PQ2633.U43.O513 1981, (v3)
　PQ2633.U43.P5, (v3)
　PQ2633.U43.S313 1993, (v3)
　PQ2633.U43.V613 1973, (v3)

Quennell, Peter. DA506.A1.Q4, (v5)
　ND497.H7.Q4 1955, (v9)
　PR2894.Q4, (v3)
　PR4382.Q42, (v3)
　PR6033.U4.S5, (v3)
Quesnay, Francois. HB153.Q55713, (v6)
Quester, George H. HE8700.6.Q47 1990, (v6)
Quetel, Claude. RC201.4.Q4813 1990, (v2)
Quevedo, Francisco de. PQ6422.A1 1911, (v3)
　PQ6422.A2 1916, (v3)
Quezada, J. Gilberto. F392.Z3 Q49 1999, (v4)
Quigley, Carroll. CB59.Q5, (v5)
Quigley, Christine. HQ1073.Q54 1994, (v6)
Quigley, Declan. GN491.4.Q54 1993, (v6)
Quigley, Harold Scott. DS518.Q46, (v5)
　DS775.Q49 1962, (v5)
Quigley, John B. DS119.7.Q722 1990, (v5)
Quigley, Thomas. ML134.B8.Q53 1998, (v9)
Quignard, Pascal. PQ2677.U486.S1813 1990, (v3)
Quiller-Couch, Arthur Thomas. PN511.Q5 1935, (v3)
　PR99.Q5 1896, (v3)
　PR99.Q53, (v3)
　PR99.Q62 1970, (v3)
　PR5194.A8 1963, (v3)
　PR5195.A3 .1945, (v3)
Quilliam, Neil. DS93.Q85 1999, (v5)
Quilliot, Roger. PQ2605.A3734.Z7313, (v3)
Quilter, Jeffrey. F3429.3.M7.Q56 1989, (v4)
Quimby, George Irving. E78.G7.Q49, (v4)
Quimby, Robert S. UA702.Q5 1968, (v10)
Quina, Kathryn. RC560.R36.Q56 1989, (v2)
Quinby, Lee. BJ352.Q56 1991, (v8)
Quincy, Josiah. E263.M4.Q72 1971, (v4)
Quine, Hector. MT580.Q56 1990, (v9)
Quine, W. V. B840.Q5, (v8)
　B945.Q51 1976, (v8)
　B945.Q53 P87 1992, (v8)
　B945.Q53.Q54 1987, (v8)
　BC51.Q5 1986, (v8)
　BC71.Q48 1963, (v8)
　BC71.Q5 1982, (v8)
　BC135.Q48 1951, (v8)
Quinlan, David. PN1998.2.Q56 1991, (v3)
　PN1998.2.Q56 1997, (v3)
　PN2285.Q56 1992, (v3)
Quinlan, Kieran. PS3566.E6912.Z832 1996, (v3)
Quinlan, Susan Canty. PQ9607.W6.Q5 1991, (v3)
Quinn, Arthur. E83.87.Q56 1997, (v4)
Quinn, Charlotte A. BP64.A37 Q56 2003, (v8)
Quinn, David B. G161.H2 2d ser., no. 104, (v6)
Quinn, Dennis Patrick. HD9710.U52.Q56 1988, (v6)
Quinn, Edward. PN44.5.Q56 1999, (v3)
Quinn, Frederick. HN380.7.A8.Q56 1998, (v6)
Quinn, Hartwell L. F396.C29.Q56 1990, (v4)
Quinn, John R. QL618.55.Q56 1994, (v1)
Quinn, Kenneth. PA6825.Q5, (v3)
Quinn, Patrick J. PR605.W65.Q56 1994, (v3)
Quinn, Susan. QD22.C8.Q56 1995, (v1)
Quinn, Warren. BJ1012.Q56 1993, (v8)
Quinn, William A. PR1882.Q56 1994, (v3)
Quinney, Laura. PR21.Q56 1995, (v3)
　PR585.D57.Q56 1999, (v3)
Quinones Keber, Eloise. F1219.56.C627.Q55 1995,
　(v4)
Quinones, Ricardo J. PN56.5.B74.Q56 1991, (v3)
Quint, Peter E. KK5096.Q56 1997, (v7)
Quintana, Manuel José. PQ6557.A1 1969, (v3)
Quintana, Ricardo. PR3726.Q53, (v3)
Quintelli-Neary, Marguerite. PR8807.F27.Q56 1997,
　(v3)
Quintero, Maria Cristina. PQ6107.Q56 1991, (v3)
Quintero, Ruben. PR3637.T4.Q56 1992, (v3)
Quintilian. PA6650.E5.M87 1987, (v3)
Quirarte, Jacinto. N6538.M4 Q57, (v9)
Quirk, James P. GV716.Q57 1992, (v6)
Quirk, Lawrence J. PN2287.D32.Q57 1990, (v3)
Quirk, Robert E. F1234.Q625 1973, (v4)
　F1788.22.C3.Q57 1993, (v4)
Quirk, Tom. PS1338.Q57 1997, (v3)
Quirk, William J. KF8748.Q57 1995, (v7)

Quiroga, Horacio. PQ8519.Q5.A23 1987, (v3)
 PQ8519.Q5.A6 1972, (v3)
Quiroga, Jose. PQ7297.P28.Z935 1998, (v3)
Quoirez, Francoise. PQ2633.U74B615, (v3)
Qvist, Per Olov. PN1993.5.S8.Q86 2000, (v3)
Raabe, Pamela. PR2017.F33.R3 1990, (v3)
Raabe, Peter B. BJ1595.5.R23 2001, (v8)
Raabe, Wilhelm Karl. PT2451.A2 1983, (v3)
Raack, R. C. DK273.R33 1995, (v5)
Raadschelders, J. C. N. JF1351.R25 1998, (v7)
Raaen, Aagot. F645.S2 R3 1994, (v4)
Raat, W. Dirk. F1221.T25.R33 1996, (v4)
Rabaey, Jan M. TK7874.65.R33 1996, (v1)
Raban, Sandra. DA229.R33 2000, (v5)
Rabasa, Jose. F799.R23 2000, (v4)
Rabate, Jean-Michel. PN56.M54.R33 1996, (v3)
 PN56.P92.R32 2001, (v3)
Rabb, Theodore K. DA391.1.S3.R33 1998, (v5)
Rabban, David M. KF4772.R33 1997, (v7)
Rabe, Barry George. TD1050.P64.R33 1994, (v1)
Rabe, David. PS3568.A23.B3, (v3)
 PS3568.A23.S85 1977, (v3)
Rabe, John. DS796.N2 R3313 1998, (v5)
Rabe, Stephen G. F1418.R24 1999, (v4)
Rabearivelo, Jean-Joseph. PQ3989.R23.A26 1975,
 (v3)
Rabelais, Francois. PQ1683.G5 1972, (v3)
 PQ1685.E5L4 1944, (v3)
Rabi`, Muhammad. HC415.25.R33 1988, (v6)
Rabin, Dan. TP568.D53 1998, (v1)
Rabinovich, Itamar. DS119.8.S95.R33 1998, (v5)
Rabinovitz, Lauren. PN1995.9.E96.R34 1991, (v3)
 PN1995.9.W6.R33 1998, (v3)
Rabinovitz, Rubin. PR6003.E282.Z7887 1984, (v3)
 PR6003.E282.Z78875 1992, (v3)
Rabinow, Paul. GN346.R3, (v6)
 QP606.D46.R33 1996, (v1)
Rabinowitch, Alexander. DK265.8.L4.R27 1976, (v5)
Rabinowitch, Eugene. CB151.R25, (v5)
Rabinowitz, Alan. HV91.R33 1990, (v6)
Rabinowitz, Dan. DS110.N28.R33 1997, (v5)
Rabinowitz, Howard N. E185.2.R23, (v4)
Rabinowitz, Paula. PN1995.9.D6.R34 1994, (v3)
Rabinowitz, Yaron S. RE336.R3 1993, (v2)
Rabkin, Eric S. PN56.F34.R3, (v3)
Rabkin, Jeremy A. KF5425.R33 1989, (v7)
Rabkin, Rhoda Pearl. F1788.R23 1991, (v4)
Rabon, Israel. PJ5129.R217.G313 1985, (v3)
Rabrenovic, Gordana. HN80.A33.R33 1996, (v6)
Rabson, Steve. PL733.57.W3.R33 1998, (v3)
Raby, Peter. PR4349.B7.Z89 1991, (v3)
Race, R. R. QP98.R3 1975, (v1)
Rachels, James. B818.R32 1990, (v8)
Rachleff, Peter J. HD5325.P152 1985.A877 1993, (v6)
Rachlin, Howard. BD418.3.R33 1994, (v8)
 BF448.R33 1989, (v2)
 BF632.R3 2000, (v2)
Rachlis, Eugene. HJ6645.R2, (v6)
Rachwald, Arthur R. DK4442.R33 1990, (v5)
Racine, Jean. PQ1888.E5.D5, (v3)
 PQ1891.A3.F7, (v3)
 PQ1898.A2.K55 1971, (v3)
 PQ1898.A44, (v3)
Racine, Michel. SB466.F82.P767 1987, (v1)
Racioppi, Linda. HQ1977.2.R33 1997, (v6)
Rackin, Phyllis. PR2982.R34, (v3)
 PR2983.R27, (v3)
Radano, Ronald Michael. ML419.B735.R3 1993, (v9)
Radcliffe, Ann (Ward). PR5202.I8 1968, (v3)
 PR5202.M8 1966, (v3)
Radcliffe, David Hill. PR2364.R33 1996, (v3)
Radcliffe, James. JA75.8.R33 2000, (v7)
Radcliffe-Brown, A. R. GN490.R3, (v6)
 GN494.R3, (v6)
Radding Murrieta, Cynthia. GN560.M6.R33 1997, (v6)
Radding, Charles. KJ399.R33 1988, (v7)
 NA390.R33 1992, (v9)
Rade, Lennart. QA41.R34 1995, (v1)
Radelet, Michael L. KF9756.R33 1992, (v7)
 Z5703.4.C36.R3 1988, (v10)

Rader, Benjamin G. GV742.3.R33 1984, (v6)
 GV863.A1 R33 2002, (v6)
 HB119.E5.R3, (v6)
Rader, Melvin Miller. BD31.R32 1969, (v8)
 BH21.R3 1979, (v8)
 BH201.R28, (v8)
 F891.R3 1998, (v4)
Rader, Ralph Wilson. PR5567.R3, (v3)
Radest, Howard B. B21.R273 1996, (v8)
 R725.5.R33 2000, (v2)
Radetsky, Peter. QR359.R33 1991, (v1)
 RC585.R275 1997, (v2)
Radetzki, Marian. HF1040.7.R33 1990, (v6)
Radford, Antony. NA2728.R34 1987, (v9)
Radhakrishnan, S. B130.R3, (v8)
 B131.R25 1952, (v8)
Radiguet, Raymond. PQ2635.A25.D5 1962, (v3)
Radin, Beryl. LB2807.R34 1988, (v7)
Radin, Paul. E99.W7.R142 1969, (v4)
 F2230.R3, (v4)
Radine, Lawrence B. U21.5.R32, (v10)
Radley, Kenneth. UB825.U54.R33 1989, (v10)
Rado, Lisa. PR888.A52, (v3)
Radoff, Morris Leon. F181.R3, (v4)
Radomski, James. ML420.G23.R33 2000, (v9)
Rados, David L. HF5415.R237 1996, (v6)
Radosh, Ronald. E744.R32, (v4)
 JK2316.R327 1996, (v7)
Radovich, Don. PN1998.3.R53.R34 1995, (v3)
Radway, Janice A. Z1003.2.R33 1997, (v10)
 Z1039.W65 R32 1984, (v10)
Radzinowicz, Mary Ann. PR3566.R3, (v3)
Rae, Murray. BT220.R34 1997, (v8)
Rae, Nicol C. JK2356.R24 1989, (v7)
Rae, Scott B. KF540.R34 1994, (v7)
Raeburn, Paul. SB123.25.U6.R34 1995, (v1)
Raeder, Erich. DD231.R17.A313, (v5)
Raeff, Marc. DK35.5.R34 1990, (v5)
Rafael, Vicente L. DS685.R24 2000, (v5)
Rafert, Stewart. E99.M48 R34 1996, (v4)
Raff, Diether. DD175.R3313 1988, (v5)
Raff, Rudolf A. QH390.R325 1996, (v1)
Raffat, Donné. PK6561.A4Z88 1985, (v3)
Raffel, Burton. PN241.R28 1994, (v3)
 PR1508.R3 1964, (v3)
Raffel, Jeffrey A. LC212.52.R34 1998, (v7)
Rafferty, Oliver. DA954.R34 1999, (v5)
Rafinesque, C. S. PS2673.R125.W6 1836a, (v3)
Rafter, Nicole Hahn. HV6047.R33 1997, (v6)
 PN1995.9.G3.R34 2000, (v3)
Raftery, Barry. DA931.R34 1994, (v5)
Ragan, David. PN1998.2.R34 1991, (v3)
Ragan, Ruth Moulton. F74.L7.R34 1991, (v4)
Ragan, William Burk. LB1570.R3 1977, (v7)
Ragatz, Lowell J. HC157.B8.R3 1963, (v6)
Raghavan, V. QK521.R34 1989, (v1)
 QK665.R34 1997, (v1)
 QK731.R26 2000, (v1)
Ragini Devi. GV1693.R25 1990, (v6)
Ragone, David V. TA418.52.R34 1995, (v1)
Ragsdale, Bruce A. HC107.V8.R33 1996, (v6)
Ragsdale, Hugh. DK186.2.R34 1988, (v5)
Ragsdale, Kenneth Baxter. F391.R14 1987, (v4)
Ragsdale, Lyn. JK518.R34 1996, (v7)
Ragussis, Michael. PR868.J4.R34 1995, (v3)
Rahaman, M.N. TP807.R28 1995, (v1)
Rahman, H. U. DS38.3.R35 1989, (v5)
Rahman, M. QA300.R312 2000, (v1)
 QA371.R28 1991, (v1)
Rahman, Mushtaqur. DS485.K27.R33 1996, (v5)
Rahn, Armin. TK7870.15.R34 1993, (v1)
Rahn, Suzanne. PS3503.A923.W637 1998, (v3)
Rahnama-Moghadam, Mashaalah. HF1413.R34 1995,
 (v6)
Rahner, Karl. BT75.2.R3313, (v8)
Rahv, Philip. PG3286.G74, (v3)
 PN511.R27, (v3)
 PN710.R327 1978, (v3)
Rai, Priya Muhar. Z7835.S64.R34 1989, (v10)
Raider, Mark A. DS149.5.U6.R35 1998, (v5)
Raiffa, Howard. HD58.6.R342 2002, (v6)

Railey, Kevin. PS3511.A86.Z94685 1999, (v3)
Railsback, Brian E. PS3537.T3234.Z844 1995, (v3)
Raimo, John. E187.5.R34, (v4)
Raine, Kathleen. PR4146.R32 1971, (v3)
Raines, Rebecca Robbins. UG573.R35 1996, (v10)
Rainey, Ada. F195.R23, (v4)
Rainey, Buck. PN2285.R35 1992, (v3)
Rainey, Lawrence S. PS310.M57.R35 1998, (v3)
Rainville, Earl David. QA371.R29 1981, (v1)
Rainwater, Catherine. PS374.I49.R35 1999, (v3)
Rainwater, Lee. E185.86.U54.R3, (v4)
Rais, Rasul Bux. DS371.2.R35 1994, (v5)
Raitt, A. W. PQ2362.Z5.R3 1970b, (v3)
Raja Rao. PR6035.A385 K3, (v3)
Rajadhyaksha, Ashish. PN1993.5.I8.R277 1999, (v3)
Rajagopal, Arvind. HE8700.76.I4, (v6)
Rajagopalachari, C. PL4758.9.R2595.R34 1968, (v3)
Rajagopalan, Swarna. DS341.R35 2001, (v5)
Rajam Aiyar, B. R. PL4758.9.R266K313 1998, (v3)
Rakesa, Mohana. PK2098.R36, (v3)
Rakove, Jack N. E342.R35 2002, (v4)
 KF4541.R35 1996, (v7)
Rakove, Milton L. F548.52.R34 1975, (v4)
Raleigh, John Henry. PR4024.R3, (v3)
Raleigh, Walter Alexander. PR3533.R35, (v3)
 PR3581.R3 1967, (v3)
Raleigh, Walter. PR2334.A17 1951, (v3)
 PR2334.A4.L3 1965, (v3)
Ralph, James R. F548.9.N4.R35 1993, (v4)
Ralston, Meredith L. HV4493.R35 1996, (v6)
Ram, Arie. TP1087.R36 1997, (v1)
Ram, Kalpana. DS432.M77.R36 1992, (v5)
Rama Rau, Santha. PR6035.A425.R4, (v3)
Rama, Angel. PQ7082.N7R343 1982, (v3)
Ramachandran, V. S. RC351.R24 1998, (v2)
Ramage, Douglas E. DS644.4.R34 1995, (v5)
Ramage, James A. E467.1.M87.R36 1999, (v4)
Ramage, Janet. TJ163.2.R345 1997, (v1)
Ramakrishnan, Dinakar. QA403.5.R327 1999, (v1)
Ramamoorthy, S. TD195.C5.R36 1997, (v1)
Raman Pillai, C. V. PL4718.9.R249M3713 1998, (v3)
Ramanathan, Suguna. PR6063.U7.Z83 1990, (v3)
Ramanujan Aiyangar, Srinivasa. QA3.R33 1985, (v1)
Ramanujan, A. K. GR305.R358 1997, (v6)
 PL2903.I4R36 1999, (v3)
 PL4663.E3.R32, (v3)
 PR9499.3.P36.A17 1995, (v3)
 PR9499.3.R36, (v3)
Ramaswamy, Sumathi. PL4758.9.R3528.P37 1997,
 (v3)
Ramazani, Jahan. PR508.E5.R36 1994, (v3)
Ramazani, Jahan. PR5908.D4.R36 1990, (v3)
Rambach, Pierre. BQ8965.4.R3513, (v8)
Ramet, Sabrina P. BL65.P7.R35 1998, (v8)
 BR738.6.R26 1987, (v8)
 DR1302.R36 1992, (v5)
 DR1308.R36 1992, (v5)
 HN373.5.R36 1991, (v6)
Ramirez, Bruno. E183.8.C2.R32 2001, (v4)
 HD8072.R34, (v6)
Ramirez, Elizabeth C. PN2270.M48.R36 1990, (v3)
Ramirez, Susan E. F3429.R35 1996, (v4)
Ramli, Linin. PJ7860.R36.B513 1994, (v3)
Rammohun Roy. DS475.2.R18 A25 1999, (v5)
Ramon y Cajal, Santiago. QM575.R343 1994, (v1)
Ramos, Alcida Rita. F2519.3.G6.R35 1998, (v4)
 F2520.1.Y3.R3413 1995, (v4)
Ramos, Julio. PQ7081.R38 1989, (v3)
Ramos, Samuel. F1210.R353, (v4)
Rampersad, Arnold. GV865.R6.R34 1997, (v6)
 PS3507.U147.Z85, (v3)
 PS3515.U274.Z698 1986, (v3)
Ramphele, Mamphela. DT1949.R36.A3 1996, (v5)
Rampton, Calvin L. F830.R36.A3 1989, (v4)
Rampton, David. PS3527.A15.Z88 1993, (v3)
Rampton, Sheldon. HD59.6.U6 R35 2001, (v6)
 RA644.C74.R35 1997, (v2)
Ramraj, Victor J. PR9199.3.R5.Z84 1983, (v3)
Ramraz-Raukh, Gilah. PJ5030.A7R36 1989, (v3)
 PJ5054.A755.Z84 1994, (v3)
Ramsaur, Ernest Edmondson. DR572.R3 1970, (v5)

Ramsay, Clay. DC195.S56.R36 1991, (v5)
Ramsay, David. F266.S53 no. 3-4, (v4)
Ramsay, Raylene L. PQ629.R36 1996, (v3)
Ramsbotham, Oliver. JX4481.R35 1996, (v7)
Ramsdell, Charles W. F391.R18 1970, (v4)
Ramsey, Janet L. BV4445.R36 1999, (v8)
Ramsey, Jarold. PM155.R35 1999, (v3)
Ramsey, Lee C. PR321.R35 1983, (v3)
Ramsey, Matthew. R504.R36 1988, (v2)
Ramsey, Patricia G. LC1099.3.R35 1989, (v7)
   LC1099.3.R36 1998, (v7)
Ramsey, Paul. BJ1231.R3, (v8)
   BJ1251.R284 1994, (v8)
   BR115.W2.R25, (v8)
   PR3424.R3, (v3)
Ramsey, Warren. PQ2323.L8.Z87, (v3)
Ramseyer, J. Mark. JQ1631.R36 1993, (v7)
Ranald, Margaret Loftus. PR2991.R36 1987, (v3)
   PR3187.R3 1989, (v3)
Rance, Nicholas. PR878.S44.R36 1991, (v3)
Ranciere, Jacques. JC423.R27813 1995, (v7)
Rancour-Laferriere, Daniel. DK33.R36 2000, (v5)
Rand Corporation. AS36.R332, (v10)
Rand McNally and Company. G1019.R22, (v6)
   G1021 .R15 1996, (v6)
   G1380.R35 1956, (v6)
Rand, Ayn. B945.R233 I67 1990, (v8)
   PS3535.A547.A6 1961, (v3)
   PS3535.A547 A68 1954, (v3)
   PS3535.A547 A9, (v3)
   PS3535.A547 F6 1943, (v3)
   PS3535.A547 W4 1959, (v3)
   PS3535.A547.Z476 1997, (v3)
   PS3535.A547.Z48 1995, (v3)
Rand, Benjamin. B41.B3 vol. 3, (v8)
Rand, Edward Kennard. CB351.R3 1957, (v5)
Rand, Harry. NB237.M3.A4 1989, (v9)
Rand, Paul. NC997.R27 1993, (v9)
Randall, Bernice. PE2835.R36 1988, (v3)
Randall, Charles E. E159.R36, (v4)
Randall, Clarence Belden. HC102.5.R3.A3, (v6)
Randall, Dale B. J. PR680.R36 1995, (v3)
Randall, Don. PR4858.I45, (v3)
Randall, Herbert. E185.93.M6.R36 2001, (v4)
Randall, J. G. E457.R212 2000, (v4)
   JK201.R3 1951, (v7)
Randall, John Herman. B52.R25, (v8)
   B803.R25, (v8)
   CB57.R32 1940, (v5)
Randall, Kenneth C. KF8858.R35 1990, (v7)
Randall, Laura. HD9574.B82.R36 1993, (v6)
Randall, Margaret. HQ1507.R37 1981, (v6)
   HX546.R35 1994, (v6)
Randall, Stephen J. HD9566.R36 1985, (v6)
Randall, Willard Sterne. E332.R196 1993, (v4)
Randhawa, Mohindar Singh. ND1002.R32, (v9)
Randi, James. BF1815.N8.R35 1990, (v2)
Randolph, Vance. F417.O9.R22, (v4)
Randolph, W. Alan. HD69.P75.R36 1988, (v6)
Ranft, Patricia. BV639.W7.R36 1998, (v8)
Rangaswamy, Padma. F548.9.E2.R36 2000, (v4)
Ranis, Gustav. HC59.7.R268 1991, (v6)
Rank, Mark R. HV91.R36 1994, (v6)
Rank, Otto. BF173.R35 1952, (v2)
   BL313.R3 1952, (v8)
   N71.R33, (v9)
   PN56.I55.R313 1991, (v3)
Ranke, Leopold von. D13.R32, (v5)
   D16.8.R29 1981, (v5)
   DD397.R25 1969, (v5)
Ranki, Vera. DS135.H9.R36 1999, (v5)
Rankin, David. BT91.R36 1995, (v8)
Rankin, H. D. D70.R36 1987, (v5)
Rankin, Robert H. VC303.R3, (v10)
Rankin, Sally H. RT90.R35 2000, (v2)
Rankin, Thomas Donald. HD6528.P42.E537 1990, (v6)
Rankin-Hill, Lesley M. F158.9.N4.R36 1997, (v4)
Ran-Moseley, Faye. PN1650.F66.R3 1993, (v3)
Ranney, Edward. F547.I13.R36 1998, (v4)
Rans, Geoffrey. PS1438.R3 1991, (v3)

Ransom, Harry Howe. JK468.I6.R3, (v7)
Ransom, John Crowe. PS3535.A635.A6 1969, (v3)
   PS3535.A635.C5 1924, (v3)
   PS3535.A635.Z48 1985, (v3)
   PS3535.A637.T8 1927, (v3)
Ransom, Roger L. E441.R3 1989, (v4)
   HC107.A13 R28 2001, (v6)
Ranstorp, Magnus. DS87.5.R367 1997, (v5)
Ranum, Orest A. DC123.3.R3 1963, (v5)
   DC124.4.R36 1993, (v5)
Rao, Aparna. DS432.B32.R36 1998, (v5)
Rao, V. S. SB611.R35 2000, (v1)
Rapaport, Herman. BH301.T77.R36 1997, (v8)
   PN98.D43.R37 2001, (v3)
Rapaport, Lynn. DS135.G332.R37 1997, (v5)
Rapf, Joanna E. PN2287.K4.R36 1995, (v3)
Raphael, D. D. BJ601.R3, (v8)
Raphael, Jody. HV6626.2.R37 2000, (v6)
Raphael, Matthew J. HV5032.W19.R36 2000, (v6)
Raphals, Lisa Ann. B5231.R37 1992, (v8)
Rapoport, Anatol. B820.R4 1971, (v8)
Rapoport, IA. L. DS135.R95.R3713 1991, (v5)
Rapp, Richard T. HC308.V4.R36, (v6)
Rapp, Stan. HF5415.R3245 1994, (v6)
Rappaport, Armin. E183.8.J3.R3, (v4)
Rappaport, Erika Diane. HF5415.33.E542.L667 2000, (v6)
Rappaport, George David. HG2613.P54.B45 1996, (v6)
Rappaport, Joanne. F2269.1.C93.R36 1994, (v4)
   F2270.2.P3.R36 1990, (v4)
Rappaport, R. QH605.R27 1996, (v1)
Rappaport, Roy A. BL600.R37 1999, (v8)
Rappaport, Steve Lee. HN398.L7.R37 1989, (v6)
Rappard, William E. DQ70.R322513 1984, (v5)
Rappe, Sara. B517.R36 1998, (v8)
Rapping, Elayne. PN1992.8.F5.R36 1992, (v3)
Rappole, John H. QL683.S75, (v1)
   QL685.7.R36 1995, (v1)
Rapport, Michael. DC158.8.R366 2000, (v5)
Rapport, Nigel. GN316.R37 2000, (v6)
   PR6011.O58.Z834 1994, (v3)
Rapson, Helen. QP101.4.R37 1982, (v1)
Rash, Nancy. ND237.B59.R37 1991, (v9)
Rashdall, Hastings. LA177.R25 1936, (v7)
Rashid, Ahmed. DS371.2.R367 2000, (v5)
Rashid, M. H. TK7881.15.R37 1993, (v1)
Rashkin, Elissa. PN1993.5.M4.R33 2001, (v3)
Rasler, Karen A. D31.R37 1994, (v5)
Rasmussen, Carl. BS630.R37 1989, (v8)
Rasmussen, Knud. PM64.Z95.E5 1961, (v3)
Rasmussen, R. Kent. PS1331.R37 1995, (v3)
Rasmussen, Randy. PN1998.3.K83.R37 2001, (v3)
Rasmussen, Shelley. QA276.R375 1991, (v1)
Rasmussen, Steen Eiler. NA2550.R313 1962, (v9)
   NA9090.R313, (v9)
Rasmussen, William M. S. E312.17.R37 1999, (v4)
Rasnake, Roger Neil. F2230.2.K4.R37 1988, (v4)
Rasor, Eugene L. D767.98.R37 1997, (v5)
   DA360.R37 1993, (v5)
   Z6207.W8.R36 1998, (v10)
   Z6207.W8.R37 1996, (v10)
   Z8068.78.R37 1998, (v10)
   Z8169.45.R37 2000, (v10)
Rasputin, Valentin Grigorevich. DK753.R3713 1996, (v5)
   PG3485.5.A85, (v3)
   PG3485.5.A85.A24 1989, (v3)
Rast, Joel. HC108.C4 R37 1999, (v6)
Ratchnevsky, Paul. DS22.R3713 1992, (v5)
Ratcliff, Carter. ND237.S3.R3 1982, (v9)
Ratcliffe, Krista. PS152.R33 1996, (v3)
Ratermanis, J B. PQ1956.R3, (v3)
Ratesh, Nestor. DR269.5.R38 1991, (v5)
Ratey, John J. QP360.R37 2001, (v1)
Rath, George. F645.R85 R37, (v4)
Rathbone, Belinda. TR140.E92.R38 1995, (v1)
Rathbone, Cristina. LC5131.R38 1998, (v7)
Rathbone, Richard. DT511.R28 2000, (v5)
Rathbun, John Wilbert. PN99.U5.R37, (v3)
Rathburn, Robert Charles. PR863.R3, (v3)

Rather, Dan. E855.R37 1974, (v4)
Rathjen, Frederick W. F392.P168 R37 1998, (v4)
Rathmann, Peggy. PZ7.R1936Of 1995, (v3)
Ratliff, Gerald Lee. PN2080.R39 1998, (v3)
Ratner, Carl. BF109.V95.R38 1991, (v2)
Ratner, Leonard G. ML195.R38 1980, (v9)
   ML196.R27 1992, (v9)
   MT6.R24 1977, (v9)
   MT50.R2, (v9)
Ratner, Steven R. K5301.R38 1997, (v7)
Rätsch, Christian. GR780.R3813 1992, (v6)
   RM666.C266R3813 2001, (v2)
Ratsey, Ernest A. VM532.R3 1957, (v10)
Rattigan, Neil. D743.23.R38 2001, (v5)
   PN1993.5.A8.R36 1991, (v3)
Rattigan, Terence. PR6035.A75.S4 1955, (v3)
Ratzsch, Delvin Lee. BL240.2.R335 2001, (v8)
Rauch, Georg von. DK511.B3.R3413, (v5)
Raun, Toivo U. DK503.54 .R38 2001, (v5)
Raup, David M. QB631.R38 1986, (v1)
   QE711.2.R37 1978, (v1)
   QH78.R38 1991, (v1)
Rausch, David A. BR1641.J83.R38 1991, (v8)
Rausch, Jane M. F2273.R37 1993, (v4)
   F2277.R29 1999, (v4)
Rauschning, Hermann. DD253.R38, (v5)
Ravage, John W. E185.925.R38 1997, (v4)
Raval, Suresh. PN81.R325 1998, (v3)
Ravel, Maurice. ML410.R23.A4 1990, (v9)
Raven, Alan. V800.R38, (v10)
Raven, Francis H. (Francis Harvey). TJ213.R38 1995, (v1)
Ravenhill, John. HC412.R365 2001, (v6)
Ravich, Samantha Fay. HC460.5.R38 2000, (v6)
Ravikovitch, Dalia. PJ5054.R265.A22 1989, (v3)
Ravindranath, B. QD79.C4.R38 1989, (v1)
Ravitch, Diane. LA209.2.R33 1983, (v7)
   LA339.N5.R38, (v7)
   LB3060.83.R38 1995, (v7)
Ravitch, Frank S. KF4162.R38 1999, (v7)
Rawley, James A. E433.R25, (v4)
   E457.R24 1996, (v4)
   E649.R28 1989, (v4)
Rawlings, Marjorie Kinnan. PS3535.A845.C7, (v3)
   PS3535.A845 Y9 1938, (v3)
Rawlins, Gregory J. E. QA76.9.C66.R39 1996, (v1)
   QA76.9.C66.R395 1997, (v1)
Rawlins, Jack P. PR5638.R3, (v3)
Rawlins, William K. HM132.5.R38 1991, (v6)
Rawls, John. JC578.R36925 1999, (v7)
   JC578.R3693 2001, (v7)
   JC578.R37 1993, (v7)
   JC578.R38 1999, (v7)
Rawls, Walton H. D522.25.R38 1988, (v5)
Rawlyk, George A. F1038.R38, (v4)
Rawnsley, Gary D. HE8697.45.G7.R39 1996, (v6)
   JZ1733.R39 1999, (v7)
Rawski, Evelyn Sakakida. DS754.R38 1998, (v5)
Rawson, Beryl. DG258.R38, (v5)
Rawson, Don C. JN6598.A1.R38 1995, (v7)
Rawson, Elizabeth. DG260.C5.R38 1983, (v5)
Rawson, Philip S. NB60.R36 1997, (v9)
Ray, Benjamin C. DT433.245.G35.R39 1991, (v5)
Ray, Celeste. F220.S3.R39 2001, (v4)
Ray, Christopher. BD632.R39 1991, (v8)
Ray, Dorothy Jean. E99.E7.R34 1996, (v4)
Ray, Gordon Norton. PR5631.R3, (v3)
   PR5631.R33 1972, (v3)
Ray, Man. TR647.R3813 1982, (v1)
Ray, Nicholas. PN1995.9.P7.R37 1993, (v3)
Ray, Reginald A. BQ7634.R39 2000, (v8)
Ray, Robert B. PN1995.R38 1995, (v3)
Ray, Robert H. PR2248.A3 1990, (v3)
   PR3508.R39 1995, (v3)
Ray, Ruth E. PE1479.A88.R39 2000, (v3)
Ray, Satyajit. PK1718.R3119, (v3)
Ray, William B. KF2765.1.R39 1990, (v7)
Ray, William. PQ648.R38 1990, (v3)
Rayack, Elton. R15.R26 1967, (v2)
Rayback, Joseph G. E420.R24, (v4)
Rayback, Robert J. E427.R3 1989, (v4)

Rayfield, Donald. DS785.P93.R38 1976b, (v5)
PG3458.R35 1998, (v3)
PG3458.Z8.R39 1999, (v3)
PK9160.R39 1994, (v3)
Raylor, Timothy. PR2411.E75.R38 2000, (v3)
Raymo, Chet. BL240.2.R36 1998, (v8)
Raymond, Andre. DT148.R3913 2000, (v5)
Raymond, Boris. DK35.5.R39 2000, (v5)
DK36.R39 1998, (v5)
Raymond, C. Elizabeth. F841.W56.R39 1992, (v4)
Raymond, Diane Christine. B819.E86 1990, (v8)
Raymond, Gino. DC35.R39 1998, (v5)
Raymond, Janice G. RG133.5.R38 1993, (v2)
Raymond, Joad. PN5115.R39 1996, (v3)
Raynal, M. QA76.9.D5.R3913 1988, (v1)
Raynal, Maurice. ND190.R39, (v9)
Rayner, Alice. PN1647.R39 1994, (v3)
PR631.R39 1987, (v3)
Rayner, Claire. PR6068.A949, (v3)
PR6068.A949.G6 1973, (v3)
Rayner, J. C. W. QA277.R395 1989, (v1)
Rayner, Jonathan. PN1998.3.W44.R39 1998, (v3)
Rayner, Keith. BF456.R2.R33 1989, (v2)
Rayner-Canham, Marelene F. QC16.B79.R39 1992, (v1)
QD20.R39 1998, (v1)
Raynor, William J. Q334.2.R39 1999, (v1)
Raz, Joseph. JA79.R39 1994, (v7)
Razina, T. M. NK975.R35 1990, (v9)
Rea, Robert Right. F334.M6.R33 1990, (v4)
Rea, William J. RB152.R38 1992, (v2)
Read, Anthony. D749.5.R8.R43 1988, (v5)
D757.9.B4.R43 1993, (v5)
DS479.R38 1998, (v5)
Read, Benedict. NB467.R4 1982, (v9)
Read, Christopher. DK265.R3718 1996, (v5)
DK266.R384 2001, (v5)
Read, Colin. F1032.R27 1982, (v4)
Read, Conyers. DA358.W2.R42 1978, (v5)
Z2018.R28 1959, (v10)
Read, David. PR2358.R38 2000, (v3)
Read, Donald. DA533.R37, (v5)
DA536.C6.R4 1968, (v5)
PN5111.R4.R43 1992, (v3)
Read, Gardner. ML455.R4, (v9)
MT35.R252 1990, (v9)
MT35.R253.M6, (v9)
MT35.R253.M9 1969, (v9)
MT70.R37 1969, (v9)
MT170.R38 1993, (v9)
Read, Herbert Edward. B819.R35, (v8)
BH21.R4 1960, (v8)
N66.R4 1965, (v9)
N6490.R4 1960, (v9)
NB198.R4, (v9)
NB1140.R4, (v9)
ND195.R4 1969, (v9)
PN511.R35 1963, (v3)
PN1031.R38 1948, (v3)
PR584.R4, (v3)
PR6035.E24 G74 1948, (v3)
PR6035.E24.H4 1963, (v3)
Read, Jacinda. PN1995.9.W6.R43 2000, (v3)
Read, Jan. DP102.R4 1975, (v5)
Read, Kay Almere. F1219.3.R38.R42 2000, (v4)
Read, Peter G. TS752.R44 1998, (v1)
Read, Piers Paul. CR4743.R4 1999, (v5)
Read, Stephen. BC71.R43 1994, (v8)
Reade, Charles. PR5210 1970, (v3)
PR5214.C55 1937, (v3)
Reader, Ian. BL2202.R43 1993, (v8)
BL2209.R42 1990, (v8)
BL2211.R44.R43 1998, (v8)
Reader, Keith. PN1998.3.B755.R43 2000, (v3)
Reading, Gerald Rufus Isaacs. HG6008.R4 1933, (v6)
Readings, Bill. LB2322.2.R42 1996, (v7)
Ready, John F. TA1677.R4 1997, (v1)
Reagan, Leslie J. HQ767.5.U5.R378 1997, (v6)
Reagan, Patrick D. HC106.3.R36 1999, (v6)
Reagan, Ronald. E838.5.R432 2001a, (v4)
E838.5.R435 1989, (v4)

E838.5.R435 1993, (v4)
E877.A3 1992, (v4)
J82.E5 1987, (v7)
Reagin, Nancy Ruth. HQ1623.R43 1995, (v6)
Real Academia Espanola. PC4111.A3 1931, (v3)
Reamer, Frederic G. HV10.5.R42 1990, (v6)
HV40.R35 1993, (v6)
Reams, Bernard D. KF42.2. 1994, (v7)
KF4529.R43 1988, (v7)
Reaney, Percy H. CS2505.R39 1997, (v5)
Reardon, Betty. JX1965.R39 1993, (v7)
Reardon, Carol. E181.R29 1990, (v4)
E475.53.R33 1997, (v4)
Reardon, John J. HD2785.R43 1992, (v6)
Rearick, Charles. DC33.7.R397 1997, (v5)
Rearick, William R. N6923.V36.A4 1988, (v9)
Reat, N. Ross. BQ266.R43 1994, (v8)
Reaves, Gerri. PS366.A88.R4 2001, (v3)
Reaves, Wendy Wick. NC1426.R3 1998, (v9)
Rebein, Robert. PS374.E95.R43 2001, (v3)
Rebellato, Dan. PR736.R35 1999, (v3)
Rebert, Paula. F786.R43 2001, (v4)
Reborn, Wayne A. PN721.R43 1995, (v3)
Rebolledo, Tey Diana. PS153.M4.R43 1995, (v3)
Rechcigl, Jack E. SB933.3.R436 1998, (v1)
Reck, Andrew J. B893.R4 1964, (v8)
Record, Jeffrey. UA23.R34 1988, (v10)
Reddaway, Peter. DK510.763.R43 2001, (v5)
Redden, Kenneth R. KF156.R42 1993, (v7)
Reddick, Allen Hilliard. PE1617.J7.R4 1990, (v3)
Reddick, John. PT2613.R338.Z78 1975, (v3)
Reddin, Paul. GV1833.R43 1999, (v6)
Redding, Arthur F. PS374.V53.R44 1998, (v3)
Reddy, B. Dayanand. QA320.R433 1998, (v1)
Reddy, William M. DC252.R38 1997, (v5)
Reder, Peter. HV6626.54.G7.R43 1993, (v6)
Redfield, Robert. F1376.R4, (v4)
Redford, Donald B. DT82.5.P19.R43 1992, (v5)
Redford, Emmette Shelburn. JK411.R43, (v7)
Redgrove, Peter. PR6035.E267.A17 1975, (v3)
Rediker, Marcus Buford. VK57.R43 1987, (v10)
Redish, Martin H. KF8700.R42 1991, (v7)
Redman, Barbara Klug. R727.4.R43 1999, (v2)
RT90.R43 2001, (v2)
Redman, Charles L. DS57.R4, (v5)
E78.A7.R44 1993, (v4)
Redman, Deborah A. HB71.R35 1991, (v6)
HB171.R415 1997, (v6)
Redman, Harry. PR3587.4.F8.R43 1994, (v3)
Redman, Nina. TX531.R44 2000, (v1)
Redmond, Kent C. UG633.R378 2000, (v10)
Redmont, Jane. BX2347.8.W6.R43 1992, (v8)
Reed, Adolph L. E185.97.D73.R44 1997, (v4)
Reed, Amy Louise. PR3502.E6.R4 1962, (v3)
Reed, Christopher Robert. E185.53.C5.R44 2000, (v4)
Reed, Cleota. NK4210.M42.R44 1987, (v9)
Reed, Donald R. C. BJ55.R44 1997, (v8)
Reed, Edward. BF353.R44 1996, (v2)
Reed, Harry A. E185.18.R44 1994, (v4)
Reed, James. HQ766.5.U5.R44, (v6)
Reed, John Robert. PR468.S6.R4, (v3)
PR4592.P76.R44 1995, (v3)
PR5778.P5.R44 1992, (v3)
Reed, John Shelton. BX5121.R44 1996, (v8)
F209.R44 1990, (v4)
Reed, John. DK265.R38 1967, (v5)
F1234.R32, (v4)
ML410.S3 R265 1997, (v9)
Reed, Joseph W. PN1993.5.U6.R44 1989, (v3)
Reed, Linda. E185.61.R306 1991, (v4)
Reed, Michael A. DA486.R43 1983, (v5)
Reed, Michael. QC20.R37 1972, (v1)
QC20.7.F84.R43 1980, (v1)
Reed, Nathaniel. F595.R37.A34, (v4)
Reed, Richard K. F2679.2.C5.R44 1995, (v4)
Reed, Robert M. PN1992.18.R44 1994, (v3)
Reed, Ronald F. B105.C45 R44 1999, (v8)
Reed, Sally Gardner. Z716.3.R43 2001, (v10)
Reed, Sue Welsh. NE650.D45.A4 1984, (v9)
Reed, Thomas A. QA76.6.R42 1988, (v1)
Reed, Thomas F. HD8146.5.R44 1996, (v6)

Reed, Thomas L. PR317.D42.R44 1990, (v3)
Reed-Danahay, Deborah. LC191.8.F8.R44 1996, (v7)
Reeder, John P. K3252.R44 1996, (v7)
Reeder, Red. U53.R4.A32, (v10)
Reeder, Roberta. PG3476.A324Z85 1994, (v3)
Reedy, George E. E184.I6.R44 1991, (v4)
E847.R36 1982, (v4)
Reel, A. Frank. D804.J33.Y36, (v5)
Reents-Budet, Dorie. F1435.3.P8.R44 1994, (v4)
Rees, Alan M. R733.C66 2001, (v2)
Rees, Christine. PR3546.R44 1989, (v3)
Rees, David. D767.2.R44 1997, (v5)
Rees, Ennis. PR2453.R4, (v3)
Rees, Gareth. G70.4.R435 1999, (v6)
G70.4.R44 1990, (v6)
QC32.R383 1994, (v1)
Rees, Joan. PR2216.R4, (v3)
PR2241.Z5.R4, (v3)
PR2342.A6.R38 1991, (v3)
Rees, Joseph V. TK9152.R427 1994, (v1)
Rees, M. H. QC879.R44 1989, (v1)
Rees, Martin J. QB981.R367 2000, (v1)
Rees, Samuel. PR6019.O53.Z86 1978, (v3)
Reese, Charles D. TH443.R432 2000, (v1)
Reese, Gregory L. Z682.4.M56 R44 1999, (v10)
Reese, Judy S. PR6045.O72.Z8653 1996, (v3)
Reese, Linda Williams. F699.R44 1997, (v4)
Reese, Roger R. UA772.R44 1996, (v10)
Reese, William J. LA222.R39 1995, (v7)
Reese, William L. B41.R43 1999, (v8)
Reeser, Linda Cherrey. HV40.8.U6.R44 1990, (v6)
Reesman, Jeanne Campbell. PS3523.O46.Z8665 1999, (v3)
Reesor, Margaret E. B528.R44 1989, (v8)
Reeve, C. D. C. B365.R44 1989, (v8)
JC71.P6.R43 1988, (v7)
Reeve, L. J. DA396.A2.R28 1989, (v5)
Reeve, Simon. HV6432.R42 1999, (v6)
Reeve, William C. PT2379.R37 1993, (v3)
Reeves, Byron. P96.A83.R44 1996, (v3)
Reeves, C. N. DT60.R397 2000, (v5)
DT87.4.R44 2001, (v5)
Reeves, Diane Lindsey. HQ778.7.U6.R44 1992, (v6)
Reeves, Eileen Adair. ND1460.A74.R44 1997, (v9)
Reeves, Floyd W. LD931.A3 vol.4, (v7)
Reeves, Jimmie Lynn. PN4888.T4.R44 1994, (v3)
Reeves, Nicholas. PN1993.5.E8.R43 1999, (v3)
Reeves, Richard. E842.R358 1993, (v4)
E866.R46, (v4)
Reeves, Robert. TL789.8.U5.R44 1994, (v1)
Reeves, T. Zane. HC60.5.R45 1988, (v6)
Reeves, Thomas C. E692.R43 1975, (v4)
E748.M143 R37, (v4)
Reff, Daniel T. E78.S7.R34 1991, (v4)
Regal, Martin S. PR6066.I53.Z77 1995, (v3)
Regal, Philip J. BC177.R345 1990, (v8)
Regalado, Samuel O. GV865.A1.R38 1998, (v6)
Regan, John. DA963.R44 1999, (v5)
Regan, Milton C. KF505.R43 1993, (v7)
KF509.R44 1998, (v7)
Regan, Priscilla M. JC596.2.U5.R44 1995, (v7)
Regan, Tom. HV4708.R43 1983, (v6)
HV4711.R366 2001, (v6)
Regelski, Thomas A. MT3.U5.R43, (v9)
Regens, James L. JK1991.R425 1995, (v7)
Regier, Cornelius C. E741.R34, (v4)
Regin, Deric. CB417.R4, (v5)
Regina, Karen. F497.C45 R44 1989, (v4)
Regini, Marino. HC240.R334 1995, (v6)
Regis, Edward. T174.7.R44 1995, (v1)
UG447.8.R44 1999, (v10)
Regnier, Philippe. HF3790.8.Z7.S556 1991, (v6)
Regosin, Richard L. PQ1643.R395 1996, (v3)
Reher, David Sven. HQ649.R44 1997, (v6)
Rehm, Rush. PA3131.R38 1994, (v3)
Rehman, Sajjad ur. Z668.R365 2000, (v10)
Rehnquist, William H. KF4750.R44 1998, (v7)
KF8742.R47 1987, (v7)
Rehrig, William H. ML102.B35.R4 1991, (v9)
Reich, Bernard. DS126.5.R385 2000, (v5)
Reich, Cary. E748.R673.R55 1996, (v4)

Reich, Howard. ML417.C67.R44 1993, (v9)
Reich, Michael. HV6401.R45 1991, (v6)
Reich, Nancy B. ML417.S4.R4 1985, (v9)
Reich, Robert B. HD8072.5.R45 2000, (v6)
Reich, Simon. HC286.5.R39 1990, (v6)
Reich, Wilhelm. BF109.R38.A3 1988, (v2)
Reich, Willi. ML410.S283.R43 1971b, (v9)
Reichardt, Mary R. PS1713.R44 1997, (v3)
    PS1713.R45 1992, (v3)
Reichenbach, Hans. BC135.R4, (v8)
    BD632.R413, (v8)
    QC6.R382, (v1)
Reichert, John. PR3562.R37 1992, (v3)
Reichheld, Frederick F. HF5415.5.R438 1996, (v6)
Reichl, Alexander J. HT168.N5.R45 1999, (v6)
Reichley, James. E855.R44, (v4)
Reichmann, James B. HV4708.R45 2000, (v6)
Reichstein, Andreas. F390.R3813 1989, (v4)
Reid, Brian Holden. U43.G7.R45 1987, (v10)
Reid, Constance. QA29.B447.R45 1993, (v1)
    QA29.R575.R45 1996, (v1)
Reid, Cornelius L. MT820.R365, (v9)
Reid, David. TA350.R295 2001, (v1)
Reid, Escott. F1034.3.R45.A3 1989, (v4)
Reid, Forrest. PR6035.E43 B2, (v3)
    PR6035.E43.D4, (v3)
    PR6035.E43 G3, (v3)
    PR6035.E43 R4, (v3)
    PR6035.E43 U5, (v3)
    PR6035.E43 Y6 1956, (v3)
Reid, Francis. PN2091.E4.R397 1995, (v3)
Reid, Gavin. LC4708.R45 1998, (v7)
Reid, Harry. F849.S43.R45 1998, (v4)
Reid, J. H. PT2603.O394.Z7297 1988, (v3)
Reid, Jane Davidson. NX650.M9.R45 1993, (v9)
Reid, John Cowie. PR4798.R4, (v3)
Reid, John Gilbert. DS773.R4, (v5)
Reid, John Phillip. KF4541.R45 1988, (v7)
    KF4881.R45 1989, (v7)
Reid, Louis Arnaud. BH201.R4 1973, (v8)
Reid, Mark. PN1995.9.N4.R45 1993, (v3)
Reid, Miles. QA564.R45 1988, (v1)
Reid, P. R. D805.G3.R35 1953, (v5)
Reid, Panthea. PR6045.O72.Z8654 1996, (v3)
Reid, Robert H. DS686.614.R44 1995, (v5)
Reid, Robert Lanier. PR2983.R39 2000, (v3)
Reid, Thomas. B1533.I2 1997, (v8)
Reid, William James. HV43.R383 1992, (v6)
Reid, William. E99.H2 R455 2000, (v4)
Reif, F. QC175.R43, (v1)
Reik, Theodor. BF173.R425, (v2)
    BF175.R4, (v2)
Reilly, Bernard F. DP138.3.R45 1998, (v5)
Reilly, Catherine W. Z2014.P7.R453 1994, (v10)
    Z2014.P7.R454 2000, (v10)
Reilly, Edward C. PS3559.R8.Z85 1991, (v3)
Reilly, John C. V815.3.R44, (v10)
Reilly, Patrick. PR3454.H7.R4 1991, (v3)
    PR6029.R8.N666 1989, (v3)
Reilly, Paul. NA967.R4 1977, (v9)
Reilly, Philip. HQ755.5.U5.R45 1991, (v6)
    QH431.R38 2000, (v1)
Reiman, Jeffrey H. HV8138.R42, (v6)
Reiman, Richard A. HV1431.R44 1992, (v6)
Reimer, Bennett. MT1.R435 1989, (v9)
Reimer, Michael J. DT154.A4.R45 1997, (v5)
Reimer, Robert C. PN1995.9.N36.R45 1992, (v3)
Rein, Monica Esti. LC92.A6.R45 1998, (v7)
Reinberg, Linda. PE3727.S7.R4 1991, (v3)
Reinders, Hans S. HV1568.R45 2000, (v6)
Reindl, Sheila M. RC552.B84.R45 2001, (v2)
Reinelt, Janelle G. PN739.S62.R45 1994, (v3)
Reiner, Robert. HV8195.A2.R44, (v6)
Reinert, Thomas. PR3537.P6.R44 1996, (v3)
Reines, Alvin Jay. BL99.R45 1987, (v8)
Reingold, Beth. JK8278.R45 2000, (v7)
Reingold, Nathan. Q127.U6.R397 1991, (v1)
Reinhard, David W. JK2356.R28 1983, (v7)
Reinhard, Herve. QA371.R34413 1986, (v1)
Reinhardt, Mark. JC585.R445 1997, (v7)
Reinharz, Jehuda. DS125.3.W45.R44 1993, (v5)

Reinharz, Peter. KFN5116.5.R45 1996, (v7)
Reinharz, Shulamit. HQ1180.R448 1992, (v6)
Reinicke, Wolfgang H. HG2491.R428 1995, (v6)
Reinier, Jacqueline S. HQ792.U5.R37 1996, (v6)
Reinisch, June Machover. HQ21.R415 1990, (v6)
Reis, Brian. Z5784.M9.R45 1997, (v10)
Reis, Elizabeth. HQ1438.N35.R45 1997, (v6)
Reis, Richard M. Q149.U5.R45 1997, (v1)
Reischauer, Edwin O. DS518.1.R43, (v5)
    DS707.R45, (v5)
    DS806.R35, (v5)
    DS835.R38 1970, (v5)
    DS835.R4 1953, (v5)
    E183.8.J3.R4 1965, (v4)
    PL882.R35, (v3)
Reischauer, Robert D. LB2824.R37, (v7)
Reisen, Abraham. PJ5129.R37.A26 1991, (v3)
Reiser, Christa. BF575.A5R45 1999, (v2)
Reiser, Stewart. UF535.I7.R44 1989, (v10)
Reisler, Mark. HD8081.M6.R44 1976, (v6)
Reisman, John M. RC467.R4 1976, (v2)
Reisman, Rosemary M. Canfield. Z1251.S7.R45 1998, (v10)
Reisner, Marc. HD1739.A17.R45 1986, (v6)
Reisner, Marc. SK354.H33.R45 1991, (v1)
Reiss, Edmund. Z8045.R45 1984, (v10)
Reiss, Edward. UG743.R44 1992, (v10)
Reiss, Mitchell. U264.R45 1995, (v10)
Reiss, Oscar. E185.18.R45 1997, (v4)
Reiss, Timothy J. PN49.R386 1992, (v3)
Reitan, E. A. JN1129.C7.R45 1997, (v7)
Reitano, Joanne R. HF1755.R38 1994, (v6)
Reiter, Andrea Ilse Maria. PN56.H55.R4513 2000, (v3)
Reiter, Frederick J. F2684.R34 1995, (v4)
Reiter, Yitzhak. KML271.35.R45 1996, (v7)
Reithmaier, L. W. (Lawrence W.). TL509.R44 1990, (v1)
Reitlinger, Gerald. DS135.E83.R4 1953, (v5)
Reitmeister, Louis Aaron. BD638.R4 1974, (v8)
Reitz, John R. QC670.R4 1979, (v1)
Reitz, Miriam. HV875.55.R45 1992, (v6)
Reitzes, Dietrich C. E185.82.R46, (v4)
Reizbaum, Marilyn. PR6019.O9.Z78433 1999, (v3)
Rejali, Darius M. HV8599.I7.R45 1994, (v6)
Rejwan, Nissim. DS119.7.R374 1998, (v5)
Reman, Edward. E105.R4, (v4)
Remarque, Erich Maria. PT2635.E68 I613 1929, (v3)
Rembert, James A. W. PR3728.T4.R46 1988, (v3)
Rembrandt Harmenszoon van Rijn. ND653.R4.A4 1999a, (v9)
Remington, Frederic. N6537.R4.A3 1988, (v9)
Remington, Robin Alison. D847.2.R45 1971, (v5)
Remington, Thomas F. JN6697.R46 2001, (v7)
Remini, Robert Vincent. E340.C6.R46 1991, (v4)
    E340.W4.R36 1997, (v4)
    E356.N5.R46 1999, (v4)
    E380.R4, (v4)
    E381.R415 1997, (v4)
    E382.R44 1981, (v4)
    E382.R45 1988, (v4)
    E387.R4, (v4)
    Z8443.R45 1991, (v10)
Remizov, Aleksei. PG3470.R4.A2 1985, (v3)
Remley, Mary L. Z7963.S6.R45 1991, (v10)
Remley, Paul G. PR203.R45 1996, (v3)
Remmer, Karen L. JL956.C58 R46 1989, (v7)
Remnick, David. DK288.R46 1993, (v5)
    DK510.763.R46 1997, (v5)
    GV1132.A44.R46 1998, (v6)
Rempel, Gerhard. DD253.5.R4 1989, (v5)
Rempel, William C. DS686.5.R43 1993, (v5)
Remy, Heinrich. QD151.R443, (v1)
Remy, Tristan. GV1828.R46 1997, (v6)
Renard, Jules. PQ2635.E48.H545 1966, (v3)
    PQ2635.E48Z533 1964, (v3)
Renard, Ronald D. HV5840.B93.R45 1996, (v6)
Renardy, Michael. QA374.R424 1993, (v1)
Renault, Mary. PR6035.E55 B8, (v3)
    PR6035.E55 C5, (v3)
    PR6035.E55 K5 1958, (v3)
    PR6035.E55 L3, (v3)

Renaux, Sigrid. PS2116.T83.R46 1993, (v3)
Rencher, Alvin C. QA276.R425 2000, (v1)
    QA278.R45 1995, (v1)
Rendall, Steven. PQ1643.R44 1992, (v3)
Rendell, Ruth. PR6068.R2, (v3)
Rendig, Victor V. S596.7.R46 1989, (v1)
Rendon, Laura I. LC4091.R42 1996, (v7)
Renehan, Edward. PS1226.R46 1992, (v3)
Renfrew, Colin. CC72.4.R46 1984, (v5)
    GN803.R46 1973, (v6)
Renfrew, John W. BF575.A3.R46 1997, (v2)
Rengert, George F. HV5825.R44 1996, (v6)
Rengger, N. J. JA83.R468 1995, (v7)
Renk, Kathleen J. PR9205.5.R46 1999, (v3)
Renker, Elizabeth. PS2388.A9.R46 1996, (v3)
Renne, Elisha P. DT515.45.Y67.R45 1995, (v5)
Renner, Hans. DB2216.R4613 1989, (v5)
Renner, Michael. GE140.R46 1996, (v6)
    HD9718.A2 R46 2000, (v6)
Rennert, Hugo Albert. PQ6469.R32, (v3)
Rennert, Maggie. DS107.4.R43, (v5)
Rennick, Robert M. F449.R46 1984, (v4)
Rennie, Neil. PN56.T7.R46 1995, (v3)
Reno, William. JQ1879.A15.R44 1998, (v7)
    JQ3121.A56.C64 1995, (v7)
Renouard, Yves. BX1270.R413, (v8)
Renouvin, Pierre. D421.R413 1969, (v5)
Rensch, Roslyn. ML1005.R43 1989, (v9)
Renshaw, Patrick. E741.R45 1996, (v4)
Renstrom, Peter G. KF156.R46 1991, (v7)
    KF8742.R48 2001, (v7)
Renteln, Alison Dundes. JC571.R47 1990, (v7)
Renton, Dave. DA586.R46 1999, (v5)
Rentschler, Eric. PN1995.9.N36.R46 1996, (v3)
Renwick Gallery. NK460.W3.R467 1998, (v9)
Renwick, W. L. PR447.R4 1963, (v3)
Renwick, William. MT59.R27 1995, (v9)
Renzi, Thomas C. PQ2469.Z5.R37 1998, (v3)
    PR5778.F55.R46 1992, (v3)
Repic, Oljan. RS403.R46 1998, (v2)
Repp, Kevin. DD228.5.R38 2000, (v5)
Reps, John William. F195.R34 1991, (v4)
    F353.R47 1994, (v4)
    Z5961.U5 R46 1984, (v10)
Resch, John Phillips. E259.R47 1999, (v4)
Resch, Margit. PT2685.O36.Z85 1997, (v3)
Rescher, Nicholas. B832.R42 2000, (v8)
    B945.R454 R37 1994, (v8)
    B2598.R46, (v8)
    BC126.R4, (v8)
    BD161.R468 1990, (v8)
    BD201.R47 1980, (v8)
    BD220.R49 1997, (v8)
    BD372.R47 1996, (v8)
    BD372.R475 2000, (v8)
    BD595.R47 1995, (v8)
    Q175.R393327 1999, (v1)
Resnick, Abraham. GF71.R47 2000, (v6)
Resnick, Lauren B. QA11.R47, (v1)
Resnick, Mitchel. QA76.58.R47 1994, (v1)
Resnick, Philip. F1088.R47 2000, (v4)
    JL27.R49 1991, (v7)
Resnick, Sidney I. QA274.R46 1992, (v1)
Resnik, Michael D. QA8.4.R473 1997, (v1)
Resnik, Susan. RC642.R47 1999, (v2)
Ressler, Everett M. HV873.R54 1988, (v6)
Restad, Penne L. GT4986.A1.R47 1995, (v6)
Restak, Richard M. RJ134.R47 1986, (v2)
Restall, Matthew. F1434.2.S63.R47 1997, (v4)
    F1435.R493 1998, (v4)
Restivo, Sal P. HM51.R42 1991, (v6)
Reston, James. PN4874.R447.A3 1991, (v3)
Restuccia, Frances L. PR6019.O9.Z78437 1989, (v3)
Retegan, Mihai. DR267.R47 2000, (v5)
Rethmann, Petra. DK759.K6, (v5)
Reti, Rudolph. MT40.R394.T6, (v9)
    MT40.R46, (v9)
Rettie, Dwight Fay. SB482.A4.R48 1995, (v1)
Rettinger, Michael. NA2800.R36 1988, (v9)
Reuben, Julie A. LA227.1.R48 1996, (v7)
Reubens, Beatrice G. HD5764.A6.R48, (v6)

Reuss, Richard A. ML3918.F65, **(v9)**
Reus-Smit, Christian. JZ1306.R48 1999, **(v7)**
Reutlinger, Shlomo. TX359.R48, **(v1)**
Revard, Stella Purce. PR3562.R4, **(v3)**
  PR3592.M96.R48 1997, **(v3)**
Reveley, W. Taylor. JK339.R48, **(v7)**
Reverand, Cedric D. PR3418.F5.R48 1988, **(v3)**
Reverdy, Pierre. PQ2635.E85.A17 1981, **(v3)**
Revest, Patricia. QP356.2.R49 1998, **(v1)**
Revesz, G. HC300.28.R48 1990, **(v6)**
Revill, David. ML410.C24.R5 1992, **(v9)**
Rewald, John. ND553.S5.R4 1946, **(v9)**
  ND1265.R4 1961, **(v9)**
Rex, Richard. DA332.R48 1993, **(v5)**
Rexford, Nancy E. GT2130.R48 2000, **(v6)**
Rexroth, Kenneth. PL884.R4, **(v3)**
  PL2658.E3R4, **(v3)**
  PS3535.E923.A16 1961, **(v3)**
  PS3535.E923.A17 1968, **(v3)**
  PS3535.E923.B4, **(v3)**
  PS3535.E923.B5, **(v3)**
  PS3535.E923.D7, **(v3)**
  PS3535.E923.P5, **(v3)**
  PS3535.E923.S5, **(v3)**
  PS3535.E923.Z487 1991, **(v3)**
  PS3535.E923.Z5, **(v3)**
Rey, Roselyne. RB127.R4913 1995, **(v2)**
Reyes, Luis. PN1995.9.H47.R49 1994, **(v3)**
Reyna, Ruth. B121.R46 1984, **(v8)**
Reyna, Stephen P. DT546.445.B34.R53 1990, **(v5)**
Reynaud, Paul. DC389.R433, **(v5)**
Reynolds, A. J. TA357.R49, **(v1)**
Reynolds, Andrew. JQ2720.A95 R48 1999, **(v7)**
Reynolds, Arthur J. HV743.C5, **(v6)**
Reynolds, Barbara. PC1640.R4, **(v3)**
Reynolds, Bede. BX4705.R446.A34, **(v8)**
Reynolds, Bertha Capen. HV28.R48 A3 1991, **(v6)**
Reynolds, Clark G. V25.R48 1989, **(v10)**
Reynolds, Colin S. QK935.R45 1984, **(v1)**
Reynolds, David K. RC480.5.R39, **(v2)**
Reynolds, David S. PS208.R49 1988, **(v3)**
  PS3231.R48 1995, **(v3)**
Reynolds, Donald M. N6450.R46, **(v9)**
  NB210.R49 1993, **(v9)**
Reynolds, Douglas Robertson. DS761.R47 1993, **(v5)**
Reynolds, Earle L. GV767.R47, **(v10)**
Reynolds, George W. M. PR5221.R35 W3 1975, **(v3)**
Reynolds, Graham. N6797.C63.A4 1996, **(v9)**
Reynolds, Guy. PS374.W6.R47 1999, **(v3)**
  PS3505.A87.Z813 1996, **(v3)**
Reynolds, James H. BF39.5.R49 1987, **(v2)**
Reynolds, John Elliott. QL737.C432, **(v1)**
  QL737.S63.R49 1991, **(v1)**
Reynolds, John J. Z2694.D7.R6 1998, **(v10)**
Reynolds, Josh. F74.G5 R49 2000, **(v4)**
Reynolds, Joshua. ND497.R4.W3 1973, **(v9)**
Reynolds, Katherine Chaddock. LA2317.R47.R49 1998, **(v7)**
Reynolds, L. D. Z40.R4 1974, **(v10)**
Reynolds, Lloyd George. HC59.7.R475 1985, **(v6)**
Reynolds, Matthew. PR585.N27, **(v3)**
Reynolds, Michael S. PS3515.E37.Z7546 1991, **(v3)**
  PS3515.E37.Z75466 1997, **(v3)**
  PS3515.E37.Z75469 1999, **(v3)**
Reynolds, Moira Davison. Q143.P2.R49 1994, **(v1)**
Reynolds, Pamela. DT2913.Z49.R49 1996, **(v5)**
Reynolds, Richard. PN6725.R48 1994, **(v3)**
Reynolds, Sian. Z243.G7.R49 1989, **(v10)**
Reynolds, Simon. ML82.R53 1995, **(v9)**
Reynolds, Verne. MT420.R49 1996, **(v9)**
Reynolds, Vernon. QL737.P9.R48, **(v1)**
Rezazadeh, Reza. JC423.R455 1991, **(v7)**
Rezendes, Paul. QL768.R49 1999, **(v1)**
Reznek, Lawrie. RC455.2.C4.R47 1987, **(v2)**
Rezun, Miron. DR1282.R49 1995, **(v5)**
  DR2087.R49 2001, **(v5)**
  DS79.7.R49 1992, **(v5)**
Rheingold, Howard. QA76.5.R467 2000, **(v1)**
Rhie, Marylin M. N8193.T5.R47 1991, **(v9)**
Rhines, Jesse Algeron. PN1995.9.N4.R52 1996, **(v3)**
Rhinesmith, Stephen H. HD62.4.R48 1996, **(v6)**

Rhoades, Gary. LB2331.72.R56 1998, **(v7)**
Rhoads, Edward J. M. DS761.2.R496 2000, **(v5)**
Rhoads, Robert A. LA229.R56 1998, **(v7)**
  LB2328.15.U6.R46 1996, **(v7)**
Rhode, Deborah L. KF297.R48 2000, **(v7)**
Rhodes James, Robert. DA564.R7.J3 1963, **(v5)**
  DA566.9.E28.R48 1987, **(v5)**
Rhodes, Colin. N6465.P74.R48 1994, **(v9)**
  N7432.5.A78.R49 2000, **(v9)**
Rhodes, Daniel. NK4360.R45, **(v9)**
Rhodes, Eugene Manlove. PS3535.H68 A6 1949, **(v3)**
Rhodes, Gale. QP551.R48 1993, **(v1)**
Rhodes, Joel P. DS559.62.U6.R47 2001, **(v5)**
Rhodes, Norman. PT8895.R47 1995, **(v3)**
Rhodes, Richard. HD9698.U52.R46 1993, **(v6)**
  HV6080.R46 1999, **(v6)**
  UG1282.A8.R46 1995, **(v10)**
Rhodes, Royal W. PR878.R5.R46 1995, **(v3)**
Rhoodie, Eschel M. K3243.R48 1989, **(v7)**
Rhyne, Elisabeth. HG4061.R48 1988, **(v6)**
Rhys, Jean. PR6035.H96.A15 1985, **(v3)**
  PR6035.H96 A33 1972, **(v3)**
  PR6035.H96 G6, **(v3)**
  PR6035.H96 W5 1966, **(v3)**
  PR6035.H96.Z48 1984, **(v3)**
Riahi-Belkaoui, Ahmed. HF5630.R53 1997, **(v6)**
  HF5657.R49 1995, **(v6)**
  HF5657.4.R526 1992, **(v6)**
  HF5686.C8.R457 1993, **(v6)**
  HF5686.I56.B443 1991, **(v6)**
Riall, Lucy. DG868.44.R53 1998, **(v5)**
Riasanovsky, Nicholas Valentine. DK40.R5 1984, **(v5)**
  DK132.R53 1985, **(v5)**
  DK210.R5, **(v5)**
  PR447.R48 1992, **(v3)**
Ribbans, Geoffrey. PQ6555.F7.R48 1997, **(v3)**
  PQ6555.Z5.R46 1993, **(v3)**
Ribbens, Jane. HQ769.R466 1994, **(v6)**
Ribeiro, Aileen. GT736.R53 1995, **(v6)**
Ribeiro, Darcy. F2510.R47713 2000, **(v4)**
Ribenboim, Paulo. QA241.R467 2000, **(v1)**
  QA244.R53 1999, **(v1)**
  QA246.R47 1988, **(v1)**
Ribner, Irving. PR658.H5.R5, **(v3)**
Ribowsky, Mark. GV865.G53 R53 1996, **(v6)**
  GV875.N35.R53 1995, **(v6)**
Ricalton, James. DS709.R49 1990, **(v5)**
Ricapito, Joseph V. PQ6324.Z5.R53 1996, **(v3)**
Ricardo, David. HB161.R485 1971, **(v6)**
Riccucci, Norma. HD8005.2.U5.R53 1990, **(v6)**
Rice, David Talbot. N6250.R46 1959a, **(v9)**
Rice, Edward E. U240.R53 1988, **(v10)**
Rice, Edward. G246.B8.R46 1990, **(v6)**
Rice, Elmer. PS3535.I224.L6, **(v3)**
  PS3535.I224.S45, **(v3)**
  PS3535.I224.Z5, **(v3)**
Rice, Elroy L. SB611.5.R53 1995, **(v1)**
Rice, Eugene F. B780.W5.R5 1973, **(v8)**
Rice, Jane. RM300.R53 2002, **(v2)**
Rice, John A. ML410.M9.R54 1991, **(v9)**
  ML410.S16.R53 1998, **(v9)**
Rice, John Steadman. RC569.5.C63.R5 1995, **(v2)**
Rice, Julian. E99.D1.R42 1992, **(v4)**
Rice, Marcelle Smith. PS3531.O936.Z86 2000, **(v3)**
Rice, Mary Kathleen. PQ6603.U4.Z837 1991, **(v3)**
Rice, Michael. DT83.R47 1999, **(v5)**
Rice, Mitchell F. RA448.5.N4.R52 1990, **(v2)**
Rice, Otis K. F241.R515 1993, **(v4)**
Rice, Prudence M. F1435.1.M22.R52 1987, **(v4)**
  NK3780.R53 1987, **(v9)**
Rice, Richard G. QA371.R37 1995, **(v1)**
Rice, Robyn. RT120.H65 M36 1995, **(v2)**
  RT120.H65R535 2001, **(v2)**
Rice, Tamara Talbot. DS27.R5, **(v5)**
  N6981.R52 1963, **(v9)**
Rice, Thomas Jackson. PR6019.O9.Z78455 1997, **(v3)**
  Z8984.2.R5 1984, **(v10)**
Rice, Timothy. ML3602.R5 1994, **(v9)**
Rich, Adrienne Cecile. HQ759.R53 1976, **(v6)**

PS3535.I233.A17 1975, **(v3)**
PS3535.I233.A83 2001, **(v3)**
PS3535.I233.D7 1978, **(v3)**
PS3535.I233.O6 1979, **(v3)**
PS3535.I233.W5, **(v3)**
Rich, B. Ruby. PN1995.9.W6.R47 1998, **(v3)**
Rich, Bennett Milton. HQ1064.U5.R512 1984, **(v6)**
Rich, Bruce. HG3881.5.W57.R53 1994, **(v6)**
Rich, David Alan. UB225.R9.R53 1998, **(v10)**
Rich, David Z. HB846.R53 1989, **(v6)**
Rich, Doris L. TL540.C646.R52 1993, **(v1)**
  TL540.E3.R53 1989, **(v1)**
Rich, E. E. F1060.R5 1961, **(v4)**
Rich, Jack C. NB1170.R5, **(v9)**
Rich, John Martin. LB1027.3.R53 1981, **(v7)**
Rich, Louise Dickinson. F19.R52, **(v4)**
Rich, Norman. D359.R48 1977, **(v5)**
  DD219.H6.R5, **(v5)**
  DD256.5.R473, **(v5)**
  DK215.R53 1985, **(v5)**
Rich, Pat Vickers. QE841.R5 1999, **(v1)**
Rich, Wilbur C. F574.D453.Y677 1989, **(v4)**
  LC90.M5.R53 1996, **(v7)**
Richard, Alfred Charles. PN1995.9.L37.R53 1993, **(v3)**
  PN1995.9.L37.R54 1994, **(v3)**
  PN1995.9.L37.R55 1992, **(v3)**
Richard, Carl J. JA84.U5.R48 1994, **(v7)**
Richard, Jean. DC91.R5313 1992, **(v5)**
Richard, Mark. BC181.R5 1990, **(v8)**
Richard, Oscar. D805.G3.R46 2000, **(v5)**
Richard, Yann. BP193.5.R5313 1995, **(v8)**
Richard-Allerdyce, Diane. PS3527.I865.Z86 1998, **(v3)**
Richards, A. J. SB413.P7.R53 1993, **(v1)**
Richards, Alan. HC415.15.R53 1996, **(v6)**
  HD2123.R5 1982, **(v6)**
Richards, Bernard Arthur. PR591.R5 1988, **(v3)**
Richards, Constance S. PR478.F45, **(v3)**
Richards, David A. J. KF4550.R475 1989, **(v7)**
  KF4754.5.R53 1998, **(v7)**
  KF4757.R5 1993, **(v7)**
Richards, David G. PT2617.E85.D437 1987, **(v3)**
Richards, David Gleyre. PT1828.B6.R5, **(v3)**
Richards, Denis. D786.R49 1974, **(v5)**
Richards, E. G. CE11.R5 1999, **(v5)**
Richards, Eric. HD1511.G7.R53 1982, **(v6)**
Richards, I. A. PN1031.R5 1970, **(v3)**
  PR6035.I337.N4, **(v3)**
Richards, Jack W. GV741.R47, **(v6)**
Richards, Jeffrey. BX970.R48, **(v8)**
  HN11.R49 1990, **(v6)**
  PN1995.9.N352.R53 1997, **(v3)**
  PN1998.3.D485.R53 1997, **(v3)**
Richards, K. S. GB1205.R5 1982, **(v6)**
Richards, Larry. PN1995.9.N4.R54 1998, **(v3)**
Richards, Leonard L. E377.R53 1986, **(v4)**
  E449.R5135 2000, **(v4)**
Richards, Mary Haskin Parker. F627.M66.R53 1996, **(v4)**
Richards, Michael D. D421.R47 2000, **(v5)**
Richards, Michael. JC599.S6.R53 1998, **(v7)**
Richards, Norvin. BJ1533.H93.R53 1992, **(v8)**
Richards, Pamela Spence. D810.S2.R53 1994, **(v5)**
Richards, Paul W. QK938.R34.R53 1996, **(v1)**
Richards, Phillip M. Z1229.N39.R53 2000, **(v10)**
Richards, Sandra. PN2582.W65.R5 1993, **(v3)**
Richards, Stanley. PR1259.D4.R5 1971, **(v3)**
Richards, Thomas. HC255.R53 1990, **(v6)**
Richards, Yevette. HD8073.S64, **(v6)**
Richardson, Alan W. B945.C163.L6336 1998, **(v8)**
Richardson, Alan. PR457.R456 1994, **(v3)**
Richardson, Bradley M. JQ1681.R5 1997, **(v7)**
Richardson, Brian. PR478.C38.R53 1997, **(v3)**
  Z155.R53 1994, **(v10)**
Richardson, Carl. PN1995.9.F54.R5 1992, **(v3)**
Richardson, D. H. S. QK537.R53 1981, **(v1)**
Richardson, Dorothy Miller. PR6035.I34 P5 1967, **(v3)**
Richardson, Edgar Preston. ND205.R53 1965, **(v9)**
Richardson, Frank M. U22.R57 1978, **(v10)**

Richardson, Gary A. PS332.R53 1993, **(v3)**
Richardson, Heather Cox. HC105.6.R53 1997, **(v6)**
Richardson, Henry Handel. PR6035.I354 F6, **(v3)**
  PR6035.I354 U5, **(v3)**
Richardson, J. S. DP94.R54 1996, **(v5)**
Richardson, Jim. Z3296.R53 1989, **(v10)**
Richardson, Joanna. DA538.A1.R5, **(v5)**
  PQ2293.R5, **(v3)**
  PQ2436.R5, **(v3)**
Richardson, Joe Martin. LC2851.F52.R5, **(v7)**
Richardson, John. N6853.P5.R56 1990, **(v9)**
  N7483.R52.A3 1999, **(v9)**
Richardson, Larry L. Z2235.A2 R5 1984, **(v10)**
Richardson, Lawrence. DG68.R5 1992, **(v5)**
  NA327.P6.R53 1988, **(v9)**
Richardson, Lewis Fry. U21.7.R48 1978, **(v10)**
  U21.7.R5, **(v10)**
Richardson, Philip. HC427.R45 1999, **(v6)**
Richardson, R. C. D13.R44 2000, **(v5)**
  DA403.R53 1977b, **(v5)**
  Z7165.G8.C46 1996, **(v10)**
Richardson, Richard C. LB2365.L38.R52 1983, **(v7)**
Richardson, Robert D. PS1631.R53 1995, **(v3)**
Richardson, S. D. HD9766.C52.R53 1990, **(v6)**
Richardson, Samuel. PR3660 1929 vols. 13-18, **(v3)**
  PR3661.P5 1970, **(v3)**
  PR3664.C3, **(v3)**
  PR3664.C4 1950, **(v3)**
  PR3664.C4 1985, **(v3)**
  PR3664.H57 1924, **(v3)**
Richardson, Stephen A. RC570.2.R53 1996, **(v2)**
Richardson, Theresa R. RJ501.A2.R53 1989, **(v2)**
Richardson, William D. JK421.R513 1997, **(v7)**
Richburg, Keith B. HN773.5.R53 1997, **(v6)**
Riche, Pierre. DC33.2.R5413, **(v5)**
  DC70.R5313 1993, **(v5)**
Richelson, Jeffrey. UB250.R53 1988, **(v10)**
  UG1523.R53 1990, **(v10)**
Richer, Jean. PQ2260.G36.Z763 1987, **(v3)**
Richetti, John J. PR858.H5.R53 1999, **(v3)**
  PR3407.R48 1987, **(v3)**
Richey, Robert W. LB1775.R52 1973, **(v7)**
Richey, William. PR4148.A35.R53 1996, **(v3)**
Richie, Alexandra. DD881.R5 1998, **(v5)**
Richie, Donald. PL781.E5.R5, **(v3)**
  PN1993.5.J3.R5 1971, **(v3)**
Richler, Mordecai. PR6068.I25.C6, **(v3)**
  PR9199.3.R5.Z468 1984, **(v3)**
  PR9199.3.R5.Z52 1975, **(v3)**
  PS3535.R399.SA2, **(v3)**
Richman, David. PR2981.R47 1990, **(v3)**
Richman, Irwin. F127.C3.R37 1998, **(v4)**
Richmond, Colin. DA240.R53 1990, **(v5)**
Richmond, Douglas W. F1234.R554 1983, **(v4)**
  F2847.P44.R53 1989, **(v4)**
Richmond, Hugh M. PR2821.R5 1989, **(v3)**
Richmond, Robert W. F681.R52 1999, **(v4)**
Richmond, Velma Bourgeois. PR1905.R5 1992, **(v3)**
  PR2065.G63.R53 1996, **(v3)**
  PR2981.5.R53 2000, **(v3)**
Richtarik, Marilynn J. PN2601.R53 1994, **(v3)**
Richter, Conrad. PS3535.I429 A7, **(v3)**
  PS3535.I429 A8 1966, **(v3)**
  PS3535.I429 F5, **(v3)**
  PS3535.I429 L5, **(v3)**
  PS3535.I429 S4, **(v3)**
  PS3535.I429 S5, **(v3)**
  PS3535.I429 T6, **(v3)**
  PS3535.I429 T7, **(v3)**
Richter, David H. PR830.T3.R53 1996, **(v3)**
Richter, Donald C. UG447.R498 1992, **(v10)**
Richter, Gisela Marie Augusta. N5760.R45, **(v9)**
  NB90.R54 1970, **(v9)**
Richter, Hans. ND1265.R5, **(v9)**
Richter, Harvena. PR6045.O72Z866, **(v3)**
Richter, Melvin. JA81.R495 1995, **(v7)**
Richter, Michael, Professor Dr. DA930.5.R53 1999, **(v5)**
Richter, Michael. DA930.R5313 1988, **(v5)**
Richter, William L. E668.R53 1996, **(v4)**
  F391.R54 1987, **(v4)**

F391.R543 1991, **(v4)**
  HE203.R54 1995, **(v6)**
Rickard, Clinton. E99.T9.R53 1973, **(v4)**
Rickard, John Nelson. D762.L63.R53 1999, **(v5)**
Rickard, John S. PR6019.O9.U6874 1999, **(v3)**
Rickards, Maurice. NC1280.R52 2001, **(v9)**
Rickel, Annette U. HV741.R54 1997, **(v6)**
Rickels, Milton. PS3061.T6.R5, **(v3)**
Rickenbacker, Eddie. E748.R4.A3, **(v4)**
Rickett, Harold William. QK115.R5, **(v1)**
Rickett, W. Allyn. DS777.57.R5, **(v5)**
Ricketts, Edward Flanders. QL138.R5 1985, **(v1)**
Ricketts, Harry. PR4856.R53 2000, **(v3)**
Ricketts, Norma B. E405.2.R53 1996, **(v4)**
Rickey, George. NB237.R5.R67, **(v9)**
Ricklefs, M. C. DS646.27.R536 1998, **(v5)**
Ricklefs, Robert E. QP86.R525 1995, **(v1)**
Rickman, Gregg J. HG3204.R53 1999, **(v6)**
Ricks, Beatrice. Z8562.58.R53, **(v10)**
Ricks, Christopher B. PR4809.H15.R54, **(v3)**
  PR5581.R54, **(v3)**
  PR6003.E282.Z7924 1993, **(v3)**
Ricks, David A. HD62.4.R53 1999, **(v6)**
Ricoeur, Paul. B2430.R553.C7513 1998, **(v8)**
  B2430.R553.D813 1991, **(v8)**
  B2430.R553.J8713 2000, **(v8)**
  BD241.R484, **(v8)**
  BL51.R43225 1995, **(v8)**
  PN212.R5213 1984, **(v3)**
Riddell, James A. PR2642.L5.R53 1995, **(v3)**
Riddell, Peter. DA589.7.R53 1990, **(v5)**
  HC256.6.R53 1985, **(v6)**
Riddick, John F. CT1503.R53 1998, **(v5)**
  Z3206.R5 1989, **(v10)**
Riddle, John M. RG137.45.R53 1997, **(v2)**
  RG137.5.R53 1992, **(v2)**
Riddle, Lawrence Melville. PQ1777.R5, **(v3)**
Ridenour, George M. PR5431.R5, **(v3)**
Ridge, George Ross. PQ287.R5, **(v3)**
Ridgely, Robert S. QL689.A1.R53 1989, **(v1)**
Ridgeon, Lloyd V. J. BP188.9.R53 1998, **(v8)**
Ridgway, Brunilde Sismondo. NB90.R56, **(v9)**
  NB90.R57, **(v9)**
Ridgway, Matthew Bunker. E745.R52 1974, **(v4)**
Ridinger, Robert B. Marks. Z3208.A8, **(v10)**
  Z5118.A6.R5 1993, **(v10)**
  Z7164.S42.R5 1990, **(v10)**
Ridington, Robin. E99.T77.R523 1990, **(v4)**
Ridley, Aaron. ML3847.R53 1995, **(v9)**
Ridley, Jane. DA564.B3.R53 1995, **(v5)**
Ridley, Jasper Godwin. DA334.A1.R52 1983, **(v5)**
  DA355.R53 1988, **(v5)**
  F1233.M45.R5 1992, **(v4)**
Ridley, Matt. QH431.R475 1999, **(v1)**
Ridley, Ronald T. DG63.R54 1992, **(v5)**
Ridolfi, Roberto. DG738.14.M2.R513, **(v5)**
Ridpath, Ian. QB63.R527 1998, **(v1)**
Riede, David G. NX547.6.R67.R53 1983, **(v9)**
  PR4024.R5 1988, **(v3)**
  PR5517.M82.R5, **(v3)**
Rieder, John. PR5892.S58.R54 1997, **(v3)**
Rieder, Jonathan. F128.68.C36.R54 1985, **(v4)**
Rieder, William. ND237.G32, **(v9)**
Riedman, Marianne. QL737.P6.R54 1990, **(v1)**
Riefenstahl, Leni. PN1998.3.R54.A3 1993, **(v3)**
Rieff, David. F319.M6.R537 1993, **(v4)**
Riegel, Emil Raymond. TP145.R54 1992, **(v1)**
Riegel, Robert Edgar. F591.R53 1971, **(v4)**
Rieger, Joerg. BT78.R48 2001, **(v8)**
Rieger, Rigomar. QH427.R54 1991, **(v1)**
Riegl, Alois. ND1319.R4513 1999, **(v9)**
Riehn, Richard K. DC235.R43 1990, **(v5)**
Rielly, Edward J. GV867.64.R52 2000, **(v6)**
Rieman, Timothy D. NK2407.R54 1993, **(v9)**
Riemann, Hugo. ML430.R563, **(v9)**
Riemenschneider, Tilman. NB588.R5.A4 1999, **(v9)**
Riemer, David R. HC110.P63.R49 1988, **(v6)**
Riemer, Neal. JC585.R535 1996, **(v7)**
Rierden, Andi. HV9475.C82.N537 1997, **(v6)**
Ries, Tomas. UA829.F5.R53 1988, **(v10)**
Riese, Hertha (Pataky). RJ499.R5, **(v2)**

Riese, Walther. RC338.R5, **(v2)**
Riesenberg, Felix. D773.B53, **(v5)**
Riesman, David. BF755.A5.R5, **(v2)**
  BF818.R5, **(v2)**
Riess, Steven A. GV583.R53 1984, **(v6)**
  GV583.R54 1989, **(v6)**
  GV706.5.R54 1995, **(v6)**
Rietbergen, P. J. A. N. D20.R42 1998, **(v5)**
Rietman, Ed. T174.7.R54 2001, **(v1)**
Rifaat, Alifa. PJ7860.I4128.A24 1983, **(v3)**
Riffaterre, Michael. PN3335.R5 1990, **(v3)**
Riffenburgh, Beau. PN4888.E97.R54 1993, **(v3)**
Rifkin, Jeremy. TP248.2.R54 1998, **(v1)**
Rifkin, Libbie. PS323.5.R53 2000, **(v3)**
Rigal, Laura. F158.44.R55 1998, **(v4)**
Rigby, Andrew. DS119.75.R54 1991, **(v5)**
Rigby, David W. T11.R565 2001, **(v1)**
Rigby, Peter. DT443.3.B38.R54 1992, **(v5)**
Rigby, S. H. D13.2.R54 1987, **(v5)**
  HN398.E5.R54 1995, **(v6)**
Riggs, David. PR2631.R54 1989, **(v3)**
Riggsby, Andrew M. KJA3340.R54 1999, **(v7)**
Righter, Robert W. F767.T3 R53 1982, **(v4)**
Righter, William. BH39.R5, **(v8)**
Rightmire, G. Philip. GN284.R54 1990, **(v6)**
Rigney, Barbara Hill. PR830.W62.R5, **(v3)**
Riis, Jacob A. CT275.R6.A29, **(v5)**
  HV4046.N6.R5 1969, **(v6)**
Riis, Thomas Laurence. ML1711.8.N3.R5 1989, **(v9)**
Riker, William H. JK274.R68 1965, **(v7)**
  UA42.R5, **(v10)**
Riley, Ann L. QH75.R535 1998, **(v1)**
Riley, B. F. F325.R57, **(v4)**
  F332.C7 R5 1964, **(v4)**
Riley, Charles M. TN23.R56, **(v1)**
Riley, Glenda. GV1157.O3.R55 1994, **(v6)**
  HQ834.R55 1991, **(v6)**
  HQ1438.G75.R55 1988, **(v6)**
Riley, J. P. DC236.R55 2000, **(v5)**
Riley, James Whitcomb. PS2700.F41, **(v3)**
  PS2706.A53 1973, **(v3)**
Riley, Jo. PN2871.5.R56 1997, **(v3)**
Riley, Jonathan. HB846.8.R55 1988, **(v6)**
Riley, K. F. QA401.R537 1997, **(v1)**
Riley, Michael O'Neal. PS3503.A923.Z85 1997, **(v3)**
Riley, Peter D. QH541.14.R556 1998, **(v1)**
Riley, Sam G. PN4871.R55 1998, **(v3)**
Riley, Woodbridge. B865.R5 1958, **(v8)**
Riley-Smith, Jonathan Simon Christopher. D157.R53 1987, **(v5)**
  D161.2.R485 1997, **(v5)**
  G1034.R5 1990, **(v6)**
Rilke, Rainer Maria. PT2635.I65.A224 1989, **(v3)**
  PT2635.I65.A8 1914, **(v3)**
  PT2635.I65.A83 1983, **(v3)**
  PT2635.I65.D82 1981, **(v3)**
  PT2635.I65D87313 1998, **(v3)**
  PT2635.I65.N413 1990, **(v3)**
  PT2635.I65.N4 1964, **(v3)**
  PT2635.I65.S613 1987, **(v3)**
  PT2635.I65.S723, **(v3)**
  PT2635.I65Z488 1987, **(v3)**
  PT2635.I65.Z514, **(v3)**
  PT2635.I65.Z5 1950, **(v3)**
Rimbaud, Arthur. PQ2387.R5A264 2002, **(v3)**
  PQ2387.R5A285 2001, **(v3)**
  PQ2387.R5.I4 1976, **(v3)**
  PQ2387.R5 1946, **(v3)**
Rimer, J. Thomas. PL715.R56 1988, **(v3)**
  PL717.R5 1988, **(v3)**
  PL747.55.R55, **(v3)**
  PL811.O7.Z83, **(v3)**
  PL832.I8.Z85, **(v3)**
Rimler, Walter. ML134.G29.R5 1991, **(v9)**
Rimlinger, Gaston V. HD7091.R48, **(v6)**
Rimmer, Douglas. HC1000.R56 1984, **(v6)**
Rimsky-Korsakov, Nikolay. MT70.R62 1964, **(v9)**
Rinderle, Walter. DD901.O2397.R56 1992, **(v5)**
Rindler, Wolfgang. QC6.R477, **(v1)**
  QC6.R48, **(v1)**
Rindos, David. GN799.A4 R56 1984, **(v6)**

Rinehart, Mary Roberts. PS3535.I73 F3, (v3)
Riney, Scott. E97.6.R35.R56 1999, (v4)
Ring, Jennifer. D804.3.R54 1997, (v5)
Ring, Malvin E. RK29.R54 1985, (v2)
Ringelblum, Emanuel. DS135.P6.R49513 1976, (v5)
Ringer, Alexander L. ML410.S283.R55 1990, (v9)
Ringius, Lasse. TD898.4, (v1)
Ringquist, Evan J. HC110.P55.R56 1993, (v6)
Ringrose, David R. HC385.R514 1996, (v6)
  HC388.M3.R56 1983, (v6)
Rings, Werner. D802.E9.R5613, (v5)
Rinhart, Floyd. TR375.R56 1999, (v1)
Rinn, Joseph Francis. BF1027.R5.A3, (v2)
Riordan, Cornelius H. LB3066.R56 1990, (v7)
Riordan, James. GV706.35.R56 1991, (v6)
Rios, Julian. PQ6668.I576.B313 1990, (v3)
Rios, Theodore. CT25.R56 2000, (v5)
Rios-Font, Wadda C. PQ6121.M4.R5 1997, (v3)
Rioux, Jean-Pierre. DC404.R5413 1987, (v5)
Rioux, Marcel. F1027.R53, (v4)
Riphenburg, Carol J. DS247.O65.R56 1998, (v5)
Ripley, Earle A. TD195.M5.R559 1996, (v1)
Ripley, John. PR2805.R56 1998, (v3)
  PR2808.R56, (v3)
Ripoll, Carlos. PQ7084.5.R5, (v3)
Rippin, Andrew. BP161.2.R53 1990, (v8)
Rippon, Stephen. DA670.S29.R57 1997, (v5)
Rips, Lance J. BF442.R56 1994, (v2)
Rise, Eric W. KF224.M29.R57 1995, (v7)
Risebero, Bill. NA642.R57 1983, (v9)
Rishell, Lyle. DS921.6.R57 1993, (v5)
Rising, Catharine. PR6005.O4.Z7878 1990, (v3)
Rising, George. E840.8.M3.R57 1997, (v4)
Risjord, Norman K. E338.R57, (v4)
Risse, Guenter B. RA964.R57 1999, (v2)
Risse-Kappen, Thomas. JX1417.R57 1995, (v7)
Rissler, Jane. SB123.57.R564 1996, (v1)
Risso, Patricia. DS340.R57 1995, (v5)
Rist, Ray C. LC2771.R57, (v7)
Ristaino, Marcia R. DS796.S484.R57 2001, (v5)
Ristelhueber, Rene. DR43.R513 1971, (v5)
Rister, Carl Coke. F697.P35, (v4)
  F702.N6 R5, (v4)
Ristoff, Dilvo I. PS3571.P4.R337 1988, (v3)
Ritchie, Adrian. PC2474.R58 1990, (v3)
Ritchie, Andrew. GV1051.T3.R58 1988, (v6)
Ritchie, Daniel E. PR438.R45.R58 1996, (v3)
Ritchie, David. QE521.R58 1994, (v1)
  TL789.R57 1994, (v1)
Ritchie, Donald A. PN4899.W3.R58 1991, (v3)
Ritchie, J. M. PT403.R54 1983, (v3)
Ritchie, James MacPherson. PT668.R5, (v3)
Rittenberg, Stephen Alan. DS392.N67.R57 1988, (v5)
Ritter, Charles F. E663.R57 1989, (v4)
Ritter, G. X. TA1634.R58 2001, (v1)
  TA1634.R58 1996, (v1)
Ritter, Harry. D13.R49 1986, (v5)
Ritter, Kurt W. E877.2.R58 1992, (v4)
Rittner, Barbara. LB2371.4.R58 1997, (v7)
Ritvo, Lucille B. BF173.R515 1990, (v2)
Ritz, Jean Georges. PR4161.B6.Z85, (v3)
Ritz, Wilfred J. KF8714.52.A16.R57 1990, (v7)
Riva, Joseph P. TN870.R53 1983, (v1)
Rivas, Angel de Saavedra. PQ6560.A17 1976, (v3)
Rivera, Jose A. HD1694.A3 1998, (v6)
Rivera, Jose Eustasio. PQ8179.R54 V7 1974, (v3)
Rivero, Albert J. PR3458.D7.R58 1989, (v3)
Rivers, Caryl. CT275.R62.A32, (v5)
  PN4784.O24.R58 1996, (v3)
Rivers, Isabel. PR532.R5, (v3)
  PR535.R4.R58 1994, (v3)
Rivers, Larry E. BX8444.F6, (v8)
  E445.F6, (v4)
Rivers, Larry. NC139.R56.A4 1979, (v9)
Rives, James Davidson. RD39.R58, (v2)
Riviere, Peter. F2554.B8.R59 1995, (v4)
Rivlin, Paul. HC415.25.R58 1992, (v6)
Rivlin, Paul. HC498.R58 2001, (v6)
Rizvi, Hasan Askari. JQ629.A38 C5865 2000, (v7)
Rizzuto, Ana-Maria. BF109.F74.R55 1998, (v2)
Roach, Catherine M. BD581.R59 2003, (v8)

Roach, John. Z6204.R62, (v10)
Roach, Joseph R. GT4211.N4.R63 1996, (v6)
Roadarmel, Gordon C. PK2141.E8.D4, (v3)
Roark, James L. E668.R64 1977, (v4)
Roaten, Darnell Higgins. PQ521.R6, (v3)
Roazen, Paul. BF109.F74.R632 1995, (v2)
  BF173.R5513 2001, (v2)
Roback, A. A. BF81.R6, (v2)
Robb, Carol S. HQ1381.R63 1995, (v6)
Robb, David Metheny. ND50.R6 1951a, (v9)
Robb, George. HV6771.G8.R63 1992, (v6)
Robb, H. Amanda. CS2485.R6 1995, (v5)
Robb, John S. PS2718.R62 S87 1962, (v3)
Robb, Peter. DS436.R63 2002, (v5)
  ND623.C26.R62 2000, (v9)
Robbe-Grillet, Alain. PQ2635.O117.D5413 1982, (v3)
  PQ2635.O117.G6, (v3)
Robbers, James E. RM666.H33.R6 1999, (v2)
Robbin, Tony. TA658.2.R63 1996, (v1)
Robbins, Edward. NA2700.R52 1994, (v9)
Robbins, J. Albert. Z6620.U5 M6 1977, (v10)
Robbins, Jill. B2430.L484.R63 1999, (v8)
Robbins, Keith. D727.R6, (v5)
  DA566.7.R547 1994, (v5)
  Z2020.R63 1996, (v10)
Robbins, Lionel Robbins. HB75.R526 1998, (v6)
  HB195.R6 1968, (v6)
  HC57.R57 1971, (v6)
Robbins, Paul R. RC537.R58 1993, (v2)
Robbins, Rossell Hope. PR1203.R58, (v3)
Robbins, Ruth. PR119.R63 1999, (v3)
Robe, Stanley Linn. PQ7297.A9.L638, (v3)
Roberge, Pierre R. TA418.74.R63 2000, (v1)
Roberson, Susan L. PS1623.S47.R63 1995, (v3)
Robert Gore Rifkind Center for German
  Expressionist Studies. N6868.5.E9.R6 1989, (v9)
Robert, Dana Lee. BV2610.R63 1996, (v8)
Robert, Paul. PC2625.R552 2001, (v3)
Roberto, Karen A. Z6664.P24, (v10)
Roberts, Adam. PN75.J36, (v3)
  PR4238.R596 1996, (v3)
  Z2014.P7.R67 1999, (v10)
Roberts, Adrian Clive. PT2638.N5.Z8484 1989, (v3)
Roberts, Andrew Michael. PR6005.O4.Z7879 2000,
  (v3)
Roberts, Brian. F865.R64 2000, (v4)
Roberts, Carolyn S. R726.R53 1996, (v2)
Roberts, Cecil E. U53.R59.A37, (v10)
Roberts, Charlotte A. R134.8.R62 1995, (v2)
Roberts, Clayton. DA375.R6, (v5)
Roberts, David Everett. B819.R57, (v8)
Roberts, David. HN385.R57, (v6)
Roberts, Diane. PS3511.A86.Z9614 1994, (v3)
Roberts, Dorothy E. HV741.R62 2002, (v6)
Roberts, E. C. F534.E59 R63 1991, (v4)
Roberts, Edward Baer. HC108.B65.R62 1991, (v6)
Roberts, Elfed Vaughan. DS796.H757.R64 1992, (v5)
Roberts, Elizabeth Madox. PS3535.O172 G7, (v3)
  PS3535.O172 H38, (v3)
  PS3535.O172 N6, (v3)
  PS3535.O172 T5, (v3)
Roberts, F. X. Z8572.4.R63 1995, (v10)
Roberts, Fred M. VM989.R6, (v4)
Roberts, Garyn C. PN6728.D53.R63 1993, (v3)
Roberts, Geoffrey K. D741.R53 1995, (v5)
  JN3971.A58R63 2000, (v7)
Roberts, Graham. PN1997.C452225, (v3)
Roberts, J. M. D20.R65 1993, (v5)
  D286.R63, (v5)
  DC141.R6, (v5)
  DC158.8.R62, (v5)
Roberts, James A. E263.N6.R59 1996, (v4)
Roberts, Jane. SB466.G8.R57 1997, (v1)
Roberts, Jeanne Addison. PR3039.R58 1991, (v3)
Roberts, Jennifer Tolbert. JC79.A8.R63 1994, (v7)
Roberts, Jerry. Z7408.L29.R63 1999, (v10)
Roberts, Joe. QA141.R63 1992, (v1)
Roberts, John L. QE36.R63 1982, (v1)
Roberts, John Richard. Z8237.R63 1982, (v10)
Roberts, John Storm. ML3477.R63 1999, (v9)
Roberts, John W. E806.R7216 1995, (v4)

Roberts, Jon H. LA636.7.R62 2000, (v7)
Roberts, Julian V. HV6789.R63 1997, (v6)
Roberts, Julian. B2521.R63 1988, (v8)
Roberts, K. B. R836.R63 1990, (v2)
Roberts, Katherine J. PR2343.R58 1993, (v3)
Roberts, Keith. PR6068.O15.C5 1976, (v3)
Roberts, Kenneth Lewis. PS3535.O176 A7 1947, (v3)
  PS3535.O176 B6, (v3)
  PS3535.O176 N6 1937, (v3)
  PS3535.O176 O4, (v3)
  PS3535.O176.R3, (v3)
Roberts, Kenneth M. JL2631.R6 1998, (v7)
Roberts, Michael. DL701.R63, (v5)
  PA6051.R64 1989, (v3)
  PR1195.H8.R56 1974, (v3)
Roberts, Moss. BL1900.L35 R628 2001, (v8)
Roberts, Nancy. PR830.F45.R63 1997, (v3)
Roberts, Neil. GF13.R6 1998, (v6)
  PR4688.R6 1975, (v3)
  PR5014.R63 1997, (v3)
Roberts, Norene A. F644.F2R63 1983, (v4)
Roberts, Patricia. Z6654.C69.R63 1990, (v10)
Roberts, Paul Craig. HC106.8.R6 1984, (v6)
  JC599.U5.R56 1995, (v7)
Roberts, Paul. ML410.D28.R56 1996, (v9)
  PE1111.R733, (v3)
Roberts, Penny. DC801.T87.R63 1996, (v5)
Roberts, Peter Deane. ML734.R6 1993, (v9)
Roberts, Peter. LB880.F732.R62 2000, (v7)
Roberts, Philip J. F761.R58 1994, (v4)
Roberts, Philip. PN2596.L7.R5173 1999, (v3)
Roberts, R. Ellis. PT8895.R6 1976, (v3)
Roberts, Randy. F390.R67 2001, (v4)
  GV583.R6 1989, (v6)
  PN2287.W454.R63 1995, (v3)
Roberts, Richard L. HC1035.R63 1987, (v6)
Roberts, Robert B. UA26.A45 1988, (v10)
Roberts, Robert North. JK468.E7.R558 1997, (v7)
  KF4568.R63 1988, (v7)
Roberts, Robert. HN398.S2.R6, (v6)
Roberts, Stephen Henry. HD1035.R6 1964, (v6)
Roberts, Thomas J. PN3503.R59 1990, (v3)
Roberts, Warren. N6853.D315.R63 1989, (v9)
  Z8490.5.R6 1982, (v10)
Roberts, Willard Lincoln. QE355.R6 1990, (v1)
Robertson, Alec. ML410.D99.R6 1974, (v9)
  ML3088.R62 1968, (v9)
Robertson, Allen. GV1601.R63 1990, (v6)
Robertson, Andrew W. PN239.P64.R63 1995, (v3)
Robertson, Bruce. ND237.H3435.R63 1995, (v9)
  ND237.H7.A4 1990, (v9)
Robertson, Charles L. D843.R623 1997, (v5)
Robertson, Claire C. DT433.545.K55.R63 1997, (v5)
Robertson, D. W. PR1924.R58, (v3)
Robertson, David. F279.C49.N473 1999, (v4)
  U24.R63 1987, (v10)
Robertson, Douglas S. QA76.9.C66.R618 1998, (v1)
Robertson, Frank C. F786.R66, (v4)
Robertson, Frederick Leslie. V27.R6 1968, (v10)
Robertson, J. M. PR2947.C5.R6, (v3)
Robertson, Jack. NX456.R59 1996, (v9)
Robertson, James C. PN1998.3.C87.R63 1993, (v3)
Robertson, James I. E467.1.J15.R63 1997, (v4)
  E492.3.R63 1988, (v4)
Robertson, Janet. GV199.9.R63 1990, (v6)
Robertson, Jennifer Ellen. GN635.J2.R62 1998, (v6)
Robertson, John G. PE1582.L3.R63 1991, (v3)
Robertson, John George. PT91.R7 1970, (v3)
Robertson, John. ML420.L38.R6 1991, (v9)
Robertson, Laurel. TX837.R6 1986, (v1)
Robertson, Leon S. RD93.8.R64 1998, (v2)
Robertson, Linda Kathryn. PR4692.E4.R63 1997, (v3)
Robertson, Matra. RC552.A5.R63 1992, (v2)
Robertson, Pamela. PN1995.9.W6.R52 1996, (v3)
Robertson, Priscilla Smith. HQ1588.R6 1982, (v6)
Robertson, Ritchie. DS135.G33.R53 1999, (v5)
Robertson, Robert Blackwood. SH381.R59, (v1)
Robertson, Scot. UG635.G7.R63 1995, (v10)
Robertson, Stuart. PE1075.R57 1954, (v3)
Robertson, William Spence. F1412.R65 1965, (v4)
  F1416.F7.R6 1967, (v4)

Robertson-Lorant, Laurie. PS2386.R635 1996, (v3)
Robeson, Paul. E185.97.R63.A25 1978, (v4)
  E185.97.R63.R58 2001, (v4)
Robey, Bryant. HB3505.R63 1985, (v6)
Robillard, Douglas. PS2388.A75.R63 1997, (v3)
Robin, Arthur L. RJ503.R63 1989, (v2)
Robin, Leon. B172.R63, (v8)
Robin, Martin. F1034.M314 1992, (v4)
Robin, Richard. PG2129.E5R63 1994, (v3)
Robin, Ron Theodore. D805.U5.R63 1995, (v5)
  E744.R63 2001, (v4)
Robinet, Isabelle. BL1910.R63 1997, (v8)
Robinet, Isabelle. BL1923.R6313 1993, (v8)
Robins, Ashley H. GN197.R6 1991, (v6)
Robins, C. Richard. QL621.5.R63 1986, (v1)
Robins, Elizabeth. F909.R65 1999, (v4)
Robins, Gay. N5350.R65 1994, (v9)
Robins-Mowry, Dorothy. HQ1762.R6 1983, (v6)
Robinson, Andrew. GB5014.R63 1993, (v6)
Robinson, Arthur Howard. GA201.R63 1982, (v6)
Robinson, Brooks. GV865.R58.A32, (v6)
Robinson, Bryan E. HQ756.R635 1988, (v6)
Robinson, Craig. PR6058.U37.Z85 1989, (v3)
Robinson, Daniel N. K5077.R63 1996, (v7)
Robinson, Daniel Sommer. B1401.R6 1979, (v8)
Robinson, David L. BF698.R8544 1996, (v2)
Robinson, David S. QP141.R535 1987, (v1)
Robinson, David. BX9833.R63 1985, (v8)
  DT541.65.R63 2000, (v5)
  PN1993.5.U6.R59 1996, (v3)
Robinson, Donald L. E446.R63, (v4)
Robinson, Douglas Hill. VG93.R6 1982, (v10)
Robinson, Edgar Eugene. E801.R57, (v4)
  PS3535.O25.A17 1937, (v3)
  PS3535.O25.A6 1965, (v3)
  PS3535.O25.C4, (v3)
  PS3535.O25.G6 1930, (v3)
  PS3535.O25.M3 1916, (v3)
  PS3535.O25.M33 1924, (v3)
  PS3535.O25.M35 1931a, (v3)
  PS3535.O25.N5 1932, (v3)
  PS3535.O25.T5, (v3)
  PS3535.O25.T75 1927b, (v3)
  PS3535.O25.V3 1914, (v3)
  PS3535.O25.Z53, (v3)
  PS3535.O25.Z536, (v3)
  PS3535.O25.Z54, (v3)
Robinson, Ella. PS144.S67.R63 1998, (v3)
Robinson, Elwyn B. F636.R6 1995, (v4)
Robinson, Francis. DS35.6.R6 1982, (v5)
Robinson, Frank M. PN3433.8.R58 1999, (v3)
Robinson, Frank. GV865.R59.A3 1975, (v6)
Robinson, Frazier. GV865.R596.A3 1999, (v6)
Robinson, Fred C. PR1588.R6 1985, (v3)
  Z2012.R6, (v10)
Robinson, Geoffrey. DS647.B2.R63 1995, (v5)
Robinson, Glen O. KF5402.R63 1991, (v7)
Robinson, Glenn E. HN660.Z9.E46 1997, (v6)
Robinson, Gordon. SD426.R63 1988, (v1)
Robinson, Guy. BD241.R594 1998, (v8)
Robinson, H. Basil. F1034.3.D5.R65 1989, (v4)
Robinson, Harlow. ML410.P865 R55 2002, (v9)
  ML429.H87.R6 1994, (v9)
Robinson, Henry Morton. PS3535.O257 C3, (v3)
Robinson, Howard. B828.45.R62 1994, (v8)
Robinson, I. S. DD143.R68 1999, (v5)
Robinson, Ian. PR751.R63 1998, (v3)
Robinson, Jackie. GV865.R6.A29 1972, (v6)
Robinson, Jacob. DS126.4.R6, (v5)
Robinson, Jane. Z6011.R65 1990, (v10)
Robinson, Jeffrey Cane. PR4837.R54 1998, (v3)
Robinson, Joan. HB97.5.R6 1967, (v6)
  HB201.R6 1969, (v6)
  HC59.7.R56, (v6)
  HC256.5.R644 1967, (v6)
Robinson, John Mansley. B188.R58, (v8)
Robinson, John Martin. DA28.35.N67.R63 1983, (v5)
Robinson, Judith Schiek. ZA5055.U6.R63 1998, (v10)
Robinson, Judith. Z473.H4.R62 1991, (v10)
Robinson, Laura. GV848.4.C2.R63 1998, (v6)
Robinson, Lillian S. HQ1426.R72 1986, (v6)

Robinson, Nancy M. RJ506.M4.R62 1976, (v2)
Robinson, Orrin W. PE124.R63 1992, (v3)
Robinson, Paul A. HQ18.3.R6, (v6)
  HQ75.2.R63 1999, (v6)
  ML1720.R6 1985, (v9)
Robinson, Paul H. KF9218.R634 1999, (v7)
  KF9219.R6 1995, (v7)
Robinson, Ray. GV939.R6 R56 1999, (v6)
Robinson, Richard. HC51.R615 1993, (v6)
Robinson, Roxana. N6537.O39.R64 1989, (v9)
Robinson, Sherry. E99.A6.R59 2000, (v4)
Robinson, Stanley L. TS155.R594 1991, (v1)
Robinson, W. Courtland. HV640.5.I5.R63 1998, (v6)
Robinson, Walter Stitt. F212.R62, (v4)
Robinson, William Henry. F786.R73, (v4)
Robinson, William I. E876.R63 1996, (v4)
Robiquet, Jean. DC159.R6 1960, (v5)
Robisheaux, Thomas Willard. HN458.L3.R63 1989, (v6)
Robison, Helen F. LB1169.R56, (v7)
Robison, Kevin. MT956.R63 2000, (v9)
Robison, Samuel Shelburne. V167.R6, (v10)
Robles, Emmanuel. PQ2635.O1845.A25, (v3)
Robnett, Belinda. E185.61.R685 1997, (v4)
Robson, Catherine. PR468.G5.R63 2001, (v3)
Robson, J. A. BD300.W93.R6 1961a, (v8)
Robson, L. L. DU470.R6 1983, (v5)
Rocchio, Vincent F. PN1993.5.I88.R59 1999, (v3)
  PN1995.9.N4.R59 2000, (v3)
Rochat, Philippe. BF719.R63 2001, (v2)
Roche, Alex F. QP84.R723 1992, (v1)
Roche, Anthony. PR8789.R62 1995, (v3)
Roche, Daniel. DC715.R6413 1987, (v5)
Roche, George Charles. LB2342.4.U6.R63 1994, (v7)
Roche, John Pearson. E184.A1.R6, (v4)
Roche, Maurice. HM216.R62 1992, (v6)
Rochester, John Wilmot. PR3669.R2. 1968, (v3)
  PR3669.R2.A83 1980, (v3)
Rochester, Stuart I. DS559.4.R63 1999, (v5)
Rochlin, Gene I. QA76.9.C66.R62 1997, (v1)
Rochlin, Harriet. F596.3.J5.R63 1984, (v4)
Rochlitz, Rainer. B3209.B584.R6313 1996, (v8)
Rochon, Thomas R. HM101.R56 1998, (v6)
Rock, David. F2848.R56 1993, (v4)
  F2848.R57, (v4)
  PT2662.E294, (v3)
Rock, Howard B. HD2346.U52.N5524, (v6)
Rock, Irvin. BF293.R63 1973, (v2)
Rock, Stephen R. D445.R58 1989, (v5)
Rock, William R. E806.R725 1988, (v4)
Rockaway, Robert A. F574.D49 J567 1986, (v4)
Rockefeller Brothers Fund. UA23.R6, (v10)
Rockett, Kevin. PN1993.5.I85.R6 1988, (v3)
Rockfellow, John Alexander. F811.R68 1955, (v4)
Rockmore, Tom. B2948.R62513 1993, (v8)
Rockmuller, Seth. KFN5648.Z9.R63 1993, (v7)
Rockoff, Hugh. HC110.W24.R6 1984, (v6)
Rockwell, John. ML420.S565 R6 1984, (v9)
Rodale, Robert. S494.5.A65.R63 1991, (v1)
Rodari, Florian. N7433.7.R6313 1988, (v9)
Rodd, Rosemary. HV4708.R63 1990, (v6)
Roddis, Louis H. VG228.L5.R6, (v10)
Roddy, Dennis. TK5104.R627 2001, (v1)
Roddy, Stephen. PL2437.R64 1998, (v3)
Rodenburg, Janet. DS632.T62.R63 1997, (v6)
Rodenwaldt, Gerhart. NA280.R63 1958, (v9)
Roderick, Melissa R. LC144.M4.R63 1993, (v7)
Rodger, N. A. M. DA70.R56 1998, (v5)
Rodger, Richard. Z7164.U7.R62 1996, (v10)
Rodgers, Andrew Denny. QK31.T7.R6, (v1)
Rodgers, Bradley A. VA65.M553.R64 1996, (v10)
Rodgers, Daniel T. HD8072.R76, (v6)
Rodgers, Eugene. G850 1928.B95.R63 1990, (v6)
Rodgers, Lawrence R. PS374.N4.R57 1997, (v3)
Rodgers, Marie E. Z5956.A47.R64 1998, (v10)
Rodgers, Nancy. QA9.R7264 2000, (v1)
Rodin, Auguste. N6853.R63.A4 1992, (v9)
Rodin, R. Scott. BT160.R57 1997, (v8)
Rodis-Lewis, Genevieve. B1873.R6313 1998, (v8)
Rodner, William S. ND497.T8.A4 1997, (v9)
Rodney, Walter. HC800.R62 1981, (v6)

Rodo, Jose Enrique. PQ8519.R6.A713 1988, (v3)
Rodowick, David Norman. PN1995.R619 1990, (v3)
  PN1995.R6194 1997, (v3)
Rodríguez Monegal, Emir. PQ7082.N7R62, (v3)
Rodriguez O., Jaime E. F1412.R68213 1998, (v4)
Rodríguez Pereyra, Gonzalo. B731.R63 2002, (v8)
Rodriguez, Barbara. PS366.A88.R63 1999, (v3)
Rodriguez, Ileana. PN849.C3.R7 1994, (v3)
  PQ7472.N7.R63 1996, (v3)
Rodriguez, Luis J. HV6439.U7.L77 1993, (v6)
Rodriguez, Mario. F1438.R684, (v4)
  F2323.M6.R68 1994, (v4)
Rodriguez-Luis, Julio. PQ7797.B635.Z9127 1991, (v3)
Rodriguez-Salgado, M. J. DD179.R62 1988, (v5)
Rodway, Allan Edwin. PR571.R6, (v3)
Rody, Caroline. PS153.N5.R59 2001, (v3)
Roe, Byron P. QC793.2.R64 1996, (v1)
Roe, Frank Gilbert. E98.H55.R6, (v4)
  QL737.U53R6 1970, (v1)
Roe, John. QA453.R66 1993, (v1)
Roe, Michael. JV9125.R64 1995, (v7)
Roe, Nicholas. PR5892.R27.R6 1988, (v3)
Roebuck, Julian B. LC2781.R64 1993, (v7)
Roeckelein, Jon E. BF31.R625 1998, (v2)
Roeder, Michael Thomas. ML1263.R64 1994, (v9)
Roeder, Philip G. JN6511.R44 1993, (v7)
Roeder, Ralph. F1233.J949. 1968, (v4)
Roederer, Juan G. ML3805.R74 1995, (v9)
Roelker, Nancy L. DC33.3.R64 1996, (v5)
Roell, Craig H. ML661.R64 1989, (v9)
Roelofs, H. Mark. JK271.R537 1992, (v7)
Roemer, John E. HB72.R63 1994, (v6)
  HB523.R63 1988, (v6)
Roemer, Michael. PN56.P53.R64 1995, (v3)
  PN1997.A1.R57 2001, (v3)
Roemer, Milton Irwin. RA393.R593 1991, (v2)
Roesch, Roberta. RC537.R63 2001, (v2)
Roessner, Jane. HT177.B6R64 2000, (v6)
Roethke, Theodore. PN1064.R6, (v3)
  PS3535.O39.I2, (v3)
  PS3535.O39.L6, (v3)
  PS3535.O39.O6 1941, (v3)
  PS3535.O39.P7, (v3)
  PS3535.O39.W3, (v3)
  PS3535.O39.W6 1958, (v3)
  PS3535.O39.Z54, (v3)
  PS3535.O39 1966, (v3)
Roett, Riordan. F2681.R62 1991, (v4)
Roetz, Heiner. BJ117.R64 1993, (v8)
Roetzel, Calvin J. BS2506.R595 1998, (v8)
Roff, Sue Rabbitt. DU780.R64 1991, (v5)
Roffe, David. DA190.D7.R64 2000, (v5)
Rogal, Samuel J. PR6025.A86.Z855 1996, (v3)
  PR6025.A86.Z857 1997, (v3)
Rogan, Helen. UB418.W65.R63 1981, (v10)
Rogers, A. J. TK5103.59.R64 2001, (v1)
Rogers, Adam. GE1.R64 1993, (v6)
Rogers, Allan. SB413.P4.R64 1995, (v1)
Rogers, Bogart. D602.R54 1996, (v5)
Rogers, Bonnie. RC966.R64 2001, (v2)
Rogers, Carl R. LB1051.R636, (v7)
  LB1051.R636 1983, (v7)
  RC480.5.R62, (v2)
  RC481.R59, (v2)
  RC481.R6, (v2)
  RC514.R63, (v2)
Rogers, Clifford J. DA233.R64 2000, (v5)
Rogers, Daniel E. JN3971.A979.R635 1995, (v7)
Rogers, Deborah D. Z8730.335.R64 1996, (v10)
Rogers, Deborah Webster. PR6039.O32.Z816, (v3)
Rogers, Earl M. Z5075.U5.R63 1989, (v10)
Rogers, Eric M. QC23.R68, (v1)
Rogers, George F. F286.R64 1984, (v4)
Rogers, George C. F269.R67, (v4)
  F277.G35 R6 1990, (v4)
Rogers, Glenn T. R121.R626 1997, (v2)
Rogers, John H. QB661.R64 1995, (v1)
Rogers, John James William. QE28.3.R64 1993, (v1)
Rogers, John. PR435.R64 1996, (v3)
Rogers, Katharine M. PR3777.R6, (v3)

Rogers, Lesley J. QL776.R64 2000, (v1)
  QP360.R628 2001, (v1)
Rogers, Martha E. RT42.R64, (v2)
  RT71.R6, (v2)
Rogers, Naomi. R747.H23.R64 1998, (v2)
Rogers, Nicholas. DA498.R63 1989, (v5)
Rogers, Pamela. Z7882.R64 1999, (v10)
Rogers, Pat. PR449.P66.R64 1985, (v3)
  PR3532.R64 1996, (v3)
Rogers, Paul P. D767.4.R62 1991, (v5)
Rogers, Randall. UG444.R64 1992, (v10)
Rogers, Robert F. DU647.R63 1995, (v5)
Rogers, Samuel. PQ2181.R6, (v3)
Rogers, Strudwick Marvin. KFA258.A1.R64 1995, (v7)
Rogers, Will. PN2287.R74.A25 1996, (v3)
Rogers, William Warren. F326.R85, (v4)
Rogers, William. BF311.R62 1995, (v2)
Rogge, O. John. BF634.R6, (v2)
Rogger, Hans. DK241.R63 1983, (v5)
Rogin, Michael Paul. E93.R8 1991, (v4)
  E748.M143.R57, (v4)
  PN1995.9.N4.R64 1996, (v3)
Rogister, John. DC133.4.R64 1995, (v5)
Rogler, Lloyd H. RC451.5.H57.R64 1989, (v2)
Rogner, Manfred. SF459.L5.R6313 1997, (v1)
Rogow, Arnold A. E302.6.H2.R64 1998, (v4)
Rogow, Roberta. PN3433.4.R64 1991, (v3)
Rogozinski, Jan. F1621.R72 1992, (v4)
Rohde, David W. JK1411.R64 1991, (v7)
Rohde, Ulrich L. TK7872.F73.R62 1997, (v1)
Rohl, John C. G. DD229.R6412813 1998, (v5)
  DD229.R6413 1994, (v5)
Rohler, Lloyd Earl. PS1638.R55 1995, (v3)
Rohlfs, Jeffrey H. HC110.H53 R64 2001, (v6)
Rohlfs, K. QB475.R63 1996, (v1)
Rohrbach, Peter T. Z6207.W8 R564 1994, (v10)
Rohrbough, Malcolm J. F484.3.R64, (v4)
  F784.A7 R64 2000, (v4)
Rohrich, Lutz. GR550.R613 1992, (v6)
Rohrs, Richard C. F705.G3 R63, (v4)
Rohrschneider, Robert. JN3971.A91.R655 1999, (v7)
Rohsenow, John Snowden. PL1273.R64 2002, (v3)
Ro'i, Yaacov. BP63.A34 R65 2000, (v8)
Rojankovsky, Feodor. PZ8.3.R65Fr 1955, (v3)
Rojas, Carlos. PQ6633.O594.J3713 1996, (v3)
  PQ6633.O594.J3813 1999, (v3)
Rojas, Fernando de. PQ6426.A1 1959, (v3)
  PQ6427.E56 1955, (v3)
Rojer, Olga Elaine. F3021.J5.R54 1989, (v4)
Rojo, Jerry. PN2071.P78.R65 2000, (v3)
Rokeach, Milton. BF378.A75.R57, (v2)
Rokem, Freddie. PN1879.H65R65 2000, (v3)
Roland Michel, Marianne. ND553.C4.R5613 1996,
  (v9)
Roland, Charles Pierce. F216.2.R64, (v4)
Rolfe, Frederick. PR5236.R27 D4, (v3)
  PR5236.R27 D6, (v3)
  PR5236.R27 D65 1963, (v3)
  PR5236.R27 H3 1969, (v3)
  PR5236.R27 N5 1958, (v3)
  PR5236.R27 S7, (v3)
Rolfs, Richard W. DD247.P3.R65 1996, (v5)
Rolfsrud, Erling Nicolai. CT253.R65 1987, (v5)
  F635.R6, (v4)
  F636.3.R6, (v4)
Roll, Eric. HC59.R626 1968, (v6)
Rolland, Romain. PQ2631.E25.Z76, (v3)
  PQ2635.O5.A78 1950, (v3)
Rolle, Andrew F. E415.9.F8.R65 1991, (v4)
Rolle, Richard. PR2135.A2.A6 1971, (v3)
Roller, Duane Emerson. QC252.R6, (v1)
  QC507.R7, (v1)
Roller, Matthew B. DG281.R65 2001, (v5)
Rollin, Betty. RC280.B8R64 2000, (v2)
Rollin, Lucy. PR990.R65 1999, (v3)
Rollin, Walter J. RC423.R65 2000, (v2)
Rollings, Willard H. E99.O8.R55 1992, (v4)
Rollins, Alden M. Z2340.R653 1991, (v10)
Rollins, Mark. BF367.R65 1989, (v4)
Rollins, Philip Ashton. F596.R75 1997, (v4)
Rollison, David. DA670.G5.R65 1992, (v5)

Rollo, Vera A. Foster. F181.8.R64 1999, (v4)
Rollock, Barbara. Z1037.R63 1992, (v10)
Rollyson, Carl E. PR6045.E8.Z85 1996, (v3)
  PS2386.A24 2001, (v3)
  PS3525.A4152.Z874 1991, (v3)
Rolston, David L. PL2415.R65 1997, (v3)
Rolston, David W. QA76.76.E95.R65 1988, (v1)
Rolston, Holmes. BJ1311.R65 1998, (v8)
  GF80.R64 1988, (v6)
Rølvaag, Ole Edvart. PT9150.R55 I22, (v3)
  PT9150.R55.P42, (v3)
  PT9150.R55 S52 1931, (v3)
  PT9150.R55 T62, (v3)
  PT9150.R55 L3, (v3)
Romain, William F. E99.H69 R65 2000, (v4)
Romaine-Davis, Ada. RD535.8.G53.R66 1991, (v2)
Romains, Jules. DC401.R62, (v5)
Roman, Eric. DB956.R66 1996, (v5)
Roman, James W. PN1992.2.R66 1996, (v3)
Roman, Judith. PS1669.F5.Z87 1990, (v3)
Roman, Margaret. PS2133.R6 1992, (v3)
Roman, Peter J. UA23.R663 1995, (v10)
Roman, Steven. QA268.R66 1997, (v1)
Romano, Anne T. HV8079.2.R76 1990, (v6)
Romanoff, Alexis Lawrence. CT275.R772.A33, (v5)
Romanov, B. A. DS783.7.R575, (v5)
Romanowitz, Harry Alex. TK7872.S4.R6, (v1)
Romanucci-Ross, Lola. DU520.R66 1985, (v5)
Romasco, Albert U. E801.R6, (v4)
Rombauer, Irma von Starkloff. TX715.R75 1975, (v1)
Romeiser, John Beals. Z8545.8.R66 1994, (v10)
Romer, Alfred Sherwood. QL605.R6 1959, (v1)
Romer, Alfred. QC773.R6, (v1)
Romero, Matias. E464.C672513 1991, (v4)
Romero, Patricia W. DT434.L35.R66 1997, (v5)
  HQ1800.5.R67 1998, (v6)
Romerstein, Herbert. UB271.R9.R66 1989, (v10)
Romig, Walter. F564.R6 1986, (v4)
Romilly, Jacqueline de. B288.R5513 1991, (v8)
  PA3055.R6513 1985, (v3)
Romine, Scott. PS261.R53 1999, (v3)
Romines, Ann. PS3545.I342.Z83 1997, (v3)
Romm, James S. D56.52.H45.R66 1998, (v5)
Rommel, Erwin. D766.82.R65, (v5)
Romney, Paul. JL27.R65 1999, (v7)
Romo, Harriett. LC2683.4.R65 1996, (v7)
Romo, Ricardo. F869.E18.R65 1983, (v4)
Romoli, Kathleen. F2263.R68, (v4)
Romp, Graham. HB144.R66 1997, (v6)
Ronald, Bruce W. F499.D257 R66 1981, (v4)
Ronan, Clifford. PR127.R66 1995, (v3)
Ronan, Colin A. Q125.R7426 1982, (v1)
Rona-Tas, Akos. HC300.24.R66 1997, (v6)
Ronda, James P. F592.7.R66 1984, (v4)
  F880.R68 1990, (v4)
Rondinelli, Dennis A. LC2605.R66 1990, (v7)
Rondot, Pierre. DS63.R6413 1961, (v5)
Ronen, Tammie. RC552.A5R664 2001, (v2)
  RJ505.C63R658 2002, (v2)
Roney, Lois. PR1868.K63.R66 1990, (v3)
Roney, R. Craig. LB1042.R64 2001, (v7)
Roniger, Luis. JC599.A7.R66 1999, (v7)
Ronning, C. Neale. F1783.M38.R7 1990, (v4)
Ronsard, Pierre de. PQ1674.A5.N6, (v3)
  PQ1676.S8 1970, (v3)
Rood, Karen Lane. PS3566.R697, (v3)
Rood, Tim. DF229.T6.R64 1998, (v5)
Roof, Judith. PN56.L45.R66 1991, (v3)
Roof, Wade Clark. BL2525.R654 1999, (v8)
Roolvink, Roelof. G1786.S1R6 1957, (v6)
Room, Adrian. BL715.R66 1997, (v8)
  G105.R66 1997, (v6)
  HC29.R66 1992, (v6)
  PR451.R66 1996, (v3)
  Z1041.R66 1998, (v10)
Rooney, Jim. HN80.N5.R66 1995, (v6)
Rooney, John F. GV583.R66, (v6)
Rooney, Ronald H. HV95.R69 1992, (v6)
Roorda, Eric. E183.8.D6.R59 1998, (v4)
Roosens, Eugeen. GN495.6.R66 1989, (v6)
Roosens, Laurent. Z7134.R66 1989, (v10)

Roosevelt, Archibald. UB271.U52.R66 1988, (v10)
Roosevelt, Eleanor. BJ1853.R65, (v8)
  E741.R66 1963, (v4)
  E807.1.R428 1975, (v4)
  F199.R66, (v4)
Roosevelt, Elliott. E807.R634 1975, (v4)
Roosevelt, Franklin D. E742.5.R576, (v4)
  E742.5.R65 1992, (v4)
  E748.S63.R7, (v4)
  E806.R7445 1970, (v4)
  E807.A4 1990, (v4)
  E807.R6483, (v4)
  E807.R649, (v4)
  E807.R656, (v4)
  J82.D6 1969, (v7)
  S930.R66 1972, (v1)
Roosevelt, James. E807.R657 1959, (v4)
Roosevelt, Theodore. E302.6.M7.R73, (v4)
  E360.R86 1987, (v4)
  E660.R72 1994, (v4)
  E660.R843, (v4)
  E660.R884 1970, (v4)
  E713.R69, (v4)
  E757.R794 1975, (v4)
  F2515.R78 1994, (v4)
  H35.R7 1970, (v6)
  JK1763.R67, (v7)
  PS2734.R5.H5 1967, (v3)
  SK33.R6, (v1)
  SK45.R748 1990, (v1)
  SK45.R75 1970, (v1)
  SK252.R64 1988, (v1)
  UA23.R7, (v10)
Root, Elihu. UA23.R75, (v10)
Root, Frank Albert. F591.R68 1970, (v4)
Root, Robert K. PR3009.R72, (v3)
Root, Robert L. PS3545.H5187.Z86 1999, (v3)
Root-Bernstein, Robert Scott. RC607.A26.R65 1993,
  (v2)
Rooth, Tim. HF1533.R59 1993, (v6)
Roozenburg, N. F. M. TS171.R65 1995, (v1)
Roper, Elmo. E743.R67, (v4)
Roper, Janice M. RT81.5.R66 2000, (v2)
Roper, John Herbert. E175.5.W66.R67 1987, (v4)
Roper, Jon. JC421.R627 1989, (v7)
Roper, William. PR1119.A2 no.197, (v3)
Ropp, Steve C. JL1648.R66 1982, (v7)
Ropp, Theodore. U39.R6, (v10)
Rorabaugh, W. J. F869.B5.R67 1989, (v4)
Rorem, Ned. ML410.R693 A27 2000, (v9)
Rorty, Richard. B945.R52 1991 Vol.3, (v8)
  B945.R52 1991 vol. 1, (v8)
Rosaldo, Michelle Zimbalist. HQ1206.R65, (v6)
Rosaldo, Renato. GN345.R667 1989, (v6)
Rosalsky, Mitch. ML102.P66.R67 2000, (v9)
Rosamond, Ben. JN15.R66 2000, (v7)
Rosand, Ellen. ML1733.8.V4.R67 1991, (v9)
Rosato, Donald V. TP1110.R66 2000, (v1)
Rosbottom, Ronald C. PQ1993.L22.L68, (v3)
Roscoe, Adrian A. PR9340.R6, (v3)
Rose, Anne C. E165.R7 1995, (v4)
  E169.1.R77515 1992, (v4)
Rose, Barbara. N6512.R63, (v9)
  N6512.R64, (v9)
  NB955.P63.A2337 1994, (v9)
  ND237.K677.A4 1983, (v9)
Rose, Burton David. RC630.R67 2001, (v2)
Rose, Dan. F158.9.N4.R67 1987, (v4)
Rose, Ellen Cronan. PR6054.R25.Z87 1980, (v3)
Rose, Fred. HN90.S6.R67 2000, (v6)
Rose, Gary L. JK516.R497 1997, (v7)
Rose, Gillian. GF50.R68 1993, (v6)
Rose, H. J. PA6003.R6 1996, (v3)
Rose, Jacqueline. PR21.R67 1996, (v3)
Rose, Kenneth D. HV5089.R67 1996, (v6)
Rose, Lisle Abbott. E813.R56 1999, (v4)
Rose, Mark H. HE355.R675, (v6)
Rose, Mark. PR2343.R6, (v3)
  PR2358.R66, (v3)
Rose, Mary Beth. PR658.L63.R6 1988, (v3)
Rose, Michael R. QP86.R59 1991, (v1)

Rose, Nancy Ellen. HD5713.6.U54.R67 1994, (v6)
Rose, Paul Lawrence. QC16.H35.R67 1998, (v1)
Rose, Peter Isaac. E184.A1.R719 1997, (v4)
Rose, Peter S. HG2491.R648 1997, (v6)
 HG2491.R664 1991, (v6)
Rose, Phyllis. HQ613.R67 1983, (v6)
 PR6045.O72.Z867, (v3)
Rose, R. B. DC187.8.R67 1978, (v5)
Rose, Saul. DS518.4.R6, (v5)
Rose, Sheldon D. RC489.C63.R67 1989, (v2)
Rose, Susan D. LC586.F85.R67 1988, (v7)
Rose, Tricia. ML3531.R67 1994, (v9)
Rose, William Ganson. F499.C657 R67 1990, (v4)
Rose, William. PT2328.R55, (v3)
Rose, Willie Lee Nichols. F277.B3.R6, (v4)
Rose-Ackerman, Susan. JF1081.R675 1999, (v7)
 K3585.4.R67 1995, (v7)
Roseberry, William. GN448.R48 1989, (v6)
Roseboom, Eugene Holloway. E183.R69 1979, (v4)
Rosefeldt, Paul. PN1821.R67 1995, (v3)
Rosefielde, Steven. UA770.R6 1982, (v10)
Rosegrant, Mark W. HN655.2.C6.C67 2000, (v6)
Rose-Innes, Alistair Christopher. QC612.S8.R6 1969, (v1)
Roseman, Marina. DS595.2.S3.R67 1991, (v5)
Rosen, Allen D. JC181.K4.R65 1993, (v7)
Rosen, Bernard Carl. HM221.R644 1998, (v6)
Rosen, Charles. ML195.R68 1997, (v9)
 ML196.R67 1995, (v9)
 ML1156.R67 1988, (v9)
 MT145.B42 R67 2002, (v9)
Rosen, David. ML410.V4.R73 1995, (v9)
 PR151.M46.R67 1993, (v3)
Rosen, Elliot A. E801.R65, (v4)
Rosen, George. HC430.6.R67 1985, (v6)
Rosen, Jay. PN4749.R668 1999, (v3)
Rosen, Jeffrey. KF1262.R67 2001, (v7)
Rosen, Joe. Q172.5.S95.R67, (v1)
 Q172.5.S95.R673 1995, (v1)
Rosen, Jonathan. BM504.R657 2000, (v8)
Rosen, Kenneth Mark. PS647.I5.M3 1975, (v3)
Rosen, Leora N. HV6570.7.R67 1996, (v6)
Rosen, Michael. HM101.R63 1996, (v6)
Rosen, Raymond. QP251.R626 1988, (v1)
Rosen, Robert N. F220.J5.R67 2000, (v4)
 F279.C457 R66 1994, (v4)
Rosen, Robert. QH325.R57 1991, (v1)
Rosen, Ruth. HQ144.R76 1982, (v6)
Rosen, Samuel. RF38.R67.A3, (v2)
Rosen, Stanley. B73.R67 1988, (v8)
 B791.R77 1989, (v8)
 B3313.A44.R67 1995, (v8)
Rosen, Stephen Peter. UA23.R758 1991, (v10)
 UA840.R67 1996, (v10)
Rosen, William. PR2983.R6, (v3)
Rosenak, Chuck. NK808.R6 1990, (v9)
Rosenau, James N. JX1391.R585 1990, (v7)
 JZ1251.R67 1997, (v7)
Rosenau, Pauline Marie. HM73.R59 1991, (v6)
Rosenbaum, Alan S. JX5436.R67 1993, (v7)
Rosenbaum, Jonathan. PN1993.5.U65.R575 2000, (v3)
Rosenbaum, Jonathan. PN1995.9.P6.R67 1997, (v3)
Rosenbaum, Robert A. CT782.R6, (v5)
Rosenbaum, Robert J. F790.M5 R67 1998, (v4)
Rosenbaum, S. P. PR478.B46.R673 1994, (v3)
Rosenbaum, Sidonia Carmen. PQ7082.P7.R6 1945a, (v3)
Rosenbaum, Walter A. HC110.E5 R665 2002, (v6)
Rosenberg, Alexander. B828.2.R66 2000, (v8)
 H61.R668 1988, (v6)
 Q175.R5475 2001, (v1)
Rosenberg, Bernard. ML1711.8.N3.R67 1993, (v9)
Rosenberg, Brian. PR4589.R6 1996, (v3)
Rosenberg, Bruce A. PN681.R67 1991, (v3)
Rosenberg, David. KF1250.R67 1995, (v7)
Rosenberg, Deena. ML410.G288.R67 1991, (v9)
Rosenberg, Edgar. PR151.J5.R6, (v3)
Rosenberg, Ellen MacGilvra. BX6462.7.R66 1989, (v8)
Rosenberg, Emily S. E744.R82 1982, (v4)

HF1455.R615 1999, (v6)
Rosenberg, Gerald N. KF8700.R66 1991, (v7)
Rosenberg, H. M. QC176.R67 1978, (v1)
 QC278.R6, (v1)
Rosenberg, Harold. N6490.R592, (v9)
 N7445.2.R66 1985, (v9)
Rosenberg, Isaac. PR6035.O67 1979b, (v3)
Rosenberg, Jakob. NC80.R6, (v9)
 NC715.R7, (v9)
Rosenberg, Jay F. BD241.R65, (v8)
Rosenberg, Jerome H. PR9199.3.A8.Z85 1984, (v3)
Rosenberg, Jerry Martin. DS119.76.R67 1997, (v5)
 HC94.R668 1995, (v6)
 HG4513.R67 1993, (v6)
 HG4910.R69 1982, (v6)
Rosenberg, John D. PR5263.R6, (v3)
Rosenberg, Martin. N7432.5.C6.R67 1995, (v9)
Rosenberg, Marvin. PR2807.R656 1992, (v3)
 PR2819.R65 1992, (v3)
 PR2829.R6 1961, (v3)
Rosenberg, Michael Roy. HG3823.R667 1996, (v6)
Rosenberg, Nathan. HC79.T4.R673 1982, (v6)
Rosenberg, Neil V. ML3520.R67 1985, (v9)
Rosenberg, Paul. TJ808.3.R67 1993, (v1)
Rosenberg, Pierre. ND553.C4.A413 1979, (v9)
Rosenberg, Robin L. F1436.8.S7.R67 1992, (v4)
Rosenberg, Rosalind. HQ1410.R67 1982, (v6)
Rosenberg, Shawn W. JA74.5.R67 1988, (v7)
Rosenberry, Lois Kimball Mathews. F95.R78, (v4)
Rosenblatt, Jason Philip. PR3562.R58 1994, (v3)
Rosenblatt, Louise M. PN45.R587, (v3)
Rosenblatt, Paul C. HQ1031.R69 1995, (v6)
Rosenbloom, David H. JF1601.R58 2000, (v7)
Rosenbloom, Joseph R. E184.J5.R63, (v4)
Rosenblum, Joseph. PN171.F6, (v3)
 Z4.R69 1995, (v10)
 Z8811.R68 1992, (v10)
Rosenblum, Naomi. TR15.R67 1984, (v1)
Rosenblum, Robert. N6425.N4.R65 1984, (v9)
 N6460 1900.R68 2000, (v9)
 N6494.C8.R67 1976b, (v9)
 N6512.R676 1999, (v9)
Rosenblum, Sandra P. ML705.R67 1988, (v9)
Rosenbrock, H. H. T14.R599 1990, (v1)
Rosendahl, Mona. HX160.P35.R67 1997, (v6)
Rosener, Werner. HD1531.5.R6713 1992, (v6)
Rosenfeld, Charles. QE523.S23.R67 1982, (v1)
Rosenfeld, Louis. TK5105.888.R67 1998, (v1)
Rosenfeld, Michel. K290.R67 1998, (v7)
 KF3464.R65 1991, (v7)
Rosenfeld, Natania. PR6045.O72.Z8672 2000, (v3)
Rosenfeld, Sidney. PT2635.O84Z83 2001, (v3)
Rosenfeld, Stuart A. HD3616.U48.A137 1992, (v6)
Rosenfield, John M. N7352.R67, (v9)
Rosengarten, Theodore. F277.B3.C487 1986, (v4)
Rosenman, Ellen Bayuk. PR6045.O72.Z86734 1995, (v3)
Rosenman, Samuel Irving. E807.R73 1972, (v4)
Rosenmeyer, Patricia A. PA3865.Z5.R67 1992, (v3)
Rosenmeyer, Thomas G. PA6686.R67 1989, (v3)
Rosenne, Shabtai. JX3695.I8 R67 1984, (v7)
Rosenof, Theodore. HB87.R67 1997, (v6)
Rosenrauch, Haiim Heinz Erich. PJ4567.R6 1966, (v3)
Rosenstein, Beryl J. RJ48.R67 1997, (v2)
Rosenstiel, Stephen F. RK666.R65 2001, (v2)
Rosenstone, Robert A. PN1995.2.R67 1995, (v3)
Rosenstone, Steven J. JK2007.R67 1983, (v7)
Rosenthal, Alan. JK1118.R676 1993, (v7)
 PN1995.9.D6.R65 1990, (v3)
Rosenthal, Bianca. PT2605.E4.Z729 1995, (v3)
Rosenthal, David. RB155.R77, (v2)
Rosenthal, Debra. U264.3.R68 1990, (v10)
Rosenthal, Earl E. NA5811.G7.R6, (v9)
Rosenthal, Franz. D198.2.R67 1968, (v5)
Rosenthal, James Aaron. HV875.55.R68 1992, (v6)
Rosenthal, Laura J. PR698.W6.R67 1996, (v3)
Rosenthal, M. L. PR601.R58 1983, (v3)
 PR601.R6, (v3)
 PR1225.R68, (v3)
 PR5907.R67 1994, (v3)

Rosenthal, Marilyn. PN1080.R65, (v3)
Rosenthal, Mark. ND588.K464.A4 1987a, (v9)
Rosenthal, Norman E. RC545.R67 1998, (v2)
Rosenthal, Rob. HV4506.S36.R67 1994, (v6)
Rosenthal, Steven T. E184.355.R67 2001, (v4)
Rosenus, Alan. F864.V2.R67 1995, (v4)
Rosenwaike, Ira. HB3527.N7.R66, (v6)
Rosenwald, Lawrence Alan. PS1631.R67 1988, (v3)
Rosenwein, Barbara H. JC116.I3.R67 1999, (v7)
Rosenzweig, Cynthia. S600.7.C54.R67 1998, (v1)
Rosenzweig, Michael L. QH541.15.S64.R67 1995, (v1)
Rosenzweig, Roy. E179.5.R67 1998, (v4)
 F128.65.C3.R67 1992, (v4)
Rosheim, Mark E. TJ211.R67 1994, (v1)
Roshwald, Aviel. DS63.R67 1990, (v5)
Roshwald, Mordecai. B29.R628 1999, (v8)
Rosinger, Lawrence Kaelter. DS777.53.R58 1945, (v5)
Roskies, David G. DS112.R755 1999, (v5)
 PJ5124.R67 1995, (v3)
Roskill, Mark W. N380.R66 1989, (v9)
Roskill, Stephen Wentworth. V25.R6 1962, (v10)
Rosner, David. RC774.R67 1991, (v2)
Rosnow, Ralph L. BF76.7.R67 2001, (v2)
Rosolowsky, Diane. DD260.5.R67 1987, (v5)
Rosow, La Vergne. Z5814.E59 R67 1996, (v10)
Ross, Alan O. RJ499.R66 1980, (v2)
Ross, Alan. PR6035.O673.A7, (v3)
Ross, Alexander. F880.R812 2000, (v4)
Ross, Andrew. E169.12.R675 1989, (v4)
Ross, Betsy McCaughey. E302.6.J7.M3, (v4)
Ross, Charles Derek. DA250.R76, (v5)
 DA258.R67, (v5)
Ross, Charles Kenyatta. GV955.5.N35.R67 1999, (v6)
Ross, Charles Stanley. PR428.C27.R67 1997, (v3)
Ross, Corey. HX280.5.A6.R67 2000, (v6)
Ross, Davis R. B. UB357.R67, (v10)
Ross, Earle Dudley. LA226.R65 1969, (v7)
Ross, Elizabeth Dale. LB1205.R67, (v7)
Ross, Ellen M. BT153.S8.R67 1997, (v8)
Ross, Eric B. HB863.R67 1998, (v6)
Ross, Ernest Carson. PR4865.L2.R6, (v3)
Ross, Graham. D424.R66 1983, (v5)
Ross, H. Laurence. HE5620.D7.R668 1992, (v6)
Ross, Heather L. HQ536.R66, (v6)
Ross, Ian K. QK603.R67, (v1)
Ross, Ian Simpson. HB103.S6.R67 1995, (v6)
Ross, Ivan A. RS164.R676 1999, (v2)
Ross, Jeffrey Ian. HV8141.R67 2000, (v6)
Ross, John Munder. HQ1090.R7 1994, (v6)
Ross, John. F1256.R7 1995, (v4)
 F1256.R72 2000, (v4)
Ross, Kristin. DC33.7.R65 1995, (v5)
Ross, Leslie. N7850.R67 1996, (v9)
Ross, Lillian. PS3535.O7479.V4, (v3)
Ross, M. J. G635.R6.R67 1994, (v6)
Ross, Mabel. TT847.R669 1988, (v1)
Ross, Malcolm Mackenzie. PR549.R4.R6, (v3)
Ross, Marc Howard. GN494.5.R67 1993, (v6)
Ross, Marilyn J. LC2781.R66 1998, (v7)
Ross, Robert J. S. HB501.R7456 1990, (v6)
Ross, Robert S. DS740.5.V5.R67 1988, (v5)
Ross, Ronald. PR6035.O854 R4, (v3)
Ross, Sinclair. PR6035.O76 L36 1968, (v3)
Ross, Stanley Robert. F1234.M244 1970, (v4)
 F1234.R85 1975, (v4)
Ross, Stephanie. SB457.6.R67 1998, (v1)
Ross, Stephen David. BD311.R67 1989, (v8)
Ross, Stephen M. PS3511.A86.Z9625 1989, (v3)
Ross, Steven J. PN1995.9.L28.R67 1998, (v3)
Ross, Steven Joseph. HC108.C5.R67 1985, (v6)
Ross, Steven T. UD215.R67 1996, (v10)
Ross, Stewart Halsey. D639.P7.U67 1996, (v5)
Ross, Susan A. BX2203.R65 1998, (v8)
Ross, Thomas Wynne. PR4623.A3.R67 1997, (v3)
Ross, Thomas. KF384.R67 1996, (v7)
Ross, W. D. B398.I3 R6, (v8)
 B485.R6 1995, (v8)
 BJ1011.R75, (v8)
Ross, Walter Sanford. RC276.R67 1987, (v2)

Ross, William G. KF4204.R67 1994, **(v7)**
  KF4575.R67 1994, **(v7)**
Rossabi, Morris. DS752.6.K83.R67 1988, **(v5)**
Rosse, Gerard. BT456.R6713 1987, **(v8)**
Rossel, Sven Hakon. PT7078.R6713 1982, **(v3)**
Rossell, Christine H. LC214.2.R66 1990, **(v7)**
Rosselli, John. ML290.4.R65 1991, **(v9)**
  ML410.B44 R77 1996, **(v9)**
  ML410.M9 R847 1998, **(v9)**
  ML410.V4.R74 2000, **(v9)**
  ML1460.R68 1992, **(v9)**
  ML1733.R78 1984, **(v9)**
Rosser, Gervase. DA685.W5.R67 1989, **(v5)**
Rosser, J. Barkley. BC135.R58 1978, **(v8)**
Rosser, John H. DF552.R67 2001, **(v5)**
Rosser, Sue Vilhauer. HQ1154.R744 1992, **(v6)**
Rossetti, Christina Georgina. PR5237.A1 1979, **(v3)**
  PR5237.A4 1998, **(v3)**
Rossetti, Dante Gabriel. PR5240.F14, **(v3)**
  PR5241.B3, **(v3)**
  PR5246.A4, **(v3)**
Rossetti, Louis Michael. RJ131.R66 1995, **(v2)**
Rossetti, William Michael. PR5249.R2.A799 1977, **(v3)**
  PR5249.R2.Z48 1990, **(v3)**
Rossi, Aldo. NA1123.R616.A4 1991, **(v9)**
Rossi, Alice S. HQ755.85.R67 1990, **(v6)**
  HQ1154.R745, **(v6)**
  HQ1154.R746, **(v6)**
  HQ1391.U5.R67 1982, **(v6)**
Rossi, Ernest E. F1406.R67 1992, **(v4)**
Rossi, Ferdinando. NA3750.R6713 1970, **(v9)**
Rossi, John P. GV867.64.R68 2000, **(v6)**
Rossi, John. SF515.5.S64.R67 1991, **(v1)**
Rossi, Nick. ML410.C57.R67 1999, **(v9)**
Rossi, Paolo. D16.8.R6813 1984, **(v5)**
Rossi, Peter Henry. HV4504.R67 1989, **(v6)**
  HV4505.R67 1989, **(v6)**
Rossignol, Rosalyn. PR1903.R67 1999, **(v3)**
Rossini, Christine. K50.R67 1998, **(v7)**
Rossinow, Douglas C. HN90.R3.R64 1998, **(v6)**
Rossiter, A. P. PR2976.R66 1989, **(v3)**
Rossiter, Clinton Lawrence. JK31.R58 1962a, **(v7)**
Rossiter, Evelyn. PJ1557.R67, **(v3)**
Rossiter, Margaret W. Q130.R68 1982, **(v1)**
Rosslyn, Felicity. PR3633.R67 1990, **(v3)**
Rossman, Douglas Athon. QL666.O636.R67 1996, **(v1)**
Rossol, Monona. RC963.6.A78.R67 1994, **(v2)**
  RC965.T54R668 2000, **(v2)**
Rosswurm, Steven. F158.44.R67 1987, **(v4)**
Rostand, Edmond. PQ2635.O7C913 1995, **(v3)**
  PQ2635.O7.C9 1898, **(v3)**
Rosteck, Thomas. E743.5.R717 1994, **(v4)**
Rosten, Leo Calvin. PS3535.O7577 E38, **(v3)**
  PS3535.O7577 R4, **(v3)**
Rostenberg, Leona. Z286.A55.R67, **(v10)**
  Z291.3.R67 2002, **(v10)**
Roston, Murray. PR428.A76.R67 1987, **(v3)**
  PR428.A76.R67 1990, **(v3)**
  PR3562.R6 1980, **(v3)**
Rostov, Charles I. NK2883.R67 1983, **(v9)**
Rostovtsev, Mikhail Ivanovich. DG271.R6 1957, **(v5)**
  D57.R8 1971, **(v5)**
Rostow, Eugene V. E183.7.R748 1993, **(v4)**
Rostow, W. W. E741.R67, **(v4)**
  HB75.R6724 1990, **(v6)**
  HB199.R66 1991, **(v6)**
Rosu, Anca. PS3537.T4753.Z7625 1995, **(v3)**
Roszak, Betty. HQ1154.R75, **(v6)**
Roszak, Theodore. CB428.R67, **(v5)**
  HN16.R63, **(v6)**
Rotberg, Robert I. DT776.R4.R66 1988, **(v5)**
Rotenberg, Robert Louis. HN418.V5.R68 1992, **(v6)**
  SB470.55.A9.R68 1995, **(v1)**
Rotenstreich, Nathan. D16.8.R842, **(v5)**
  JC330.R673 1988, **(v7)**
Roth, Barry. Z8048.R69 1996, **(v10)**
Roth, Cecil. DS124.R625 1992, **(v5)**
  DS135.E5.R62, **(v5)**
  DS135.I85.V4 1975, **(v5)**

Roth, Charles H. TK7868.L6R67 1992, **(v1)**
Roth, David Morris. F94.R67, **(v4)**
Roth, George J. KF283.R68 1991, **(v7)**
Roth, Harold David. BL1900.N45 R67 1999, **(v8)**
Roth, Henry. ML398.R68 1986, **(v9)**
  PS3535.O787.A6 1987, **(v3)**
Roth, John K. BJ21.R62 1991, **(v8)**
  BL2525.R68 1997, **(v8)**
Roth, Jonathan. DG89.R675 1998, **(v5)**
Roth, Joseph. PT2635.O84.R3x 1979, **(v3)**
Roth, Leland M. NA2500.R68 1993, **(v9)**
  NA7207.R68 1999, **(v9)**
Roth, Leon. B1849.R6, **(v8)**
Roth, Leon. B3998.R6 1963, **(v8)**
Roth, Mitchel P. HV7903.R67 2001, **(v6)**
  PN4784.W37.R68 1997, **(v6)**
Roth, Norman. DS135.S7.R68 1994, **(v5)**
Roth, Philip. PS3568.O855.G5, **(v3)**
  PS3568.O855.G6 1959, **(v3)**
  PS3568.O855.L4, **(v3)**
  PS3568.O855.M8, **(v3)**
  PS3568.O855.P67, **(v3)**
  PS3568.O855.P7, **(v3)**
Roth, Randolph A. F57.C7.R67 1987, **(v4)**
Roth, Robert J. B944.P72.R68 1998, **(v8)**
  B945.D44.R6 1963, **(v8)**
  BL51.R598, **(v8)**
Roth, Stacy Flora. D16.25.R68 1998, **(v5)**
Roth, William F. HF5549.5.J63.R62 1989, **(v6)**
Rothacher, Albrecht. HN730.Z9.E45 1993, **(v6)**
Rothblatt, Sheldon. LA636.R67 1997, **(v7)**
Rothenberg, Albert. BF408.R682 1990, **(v2)**
Rothenberg, Gunther Erich. U39.R65, **(v10)**
  UA853.I8.R67, **(v10)**
Rothenberg, Jerome. PM197.E3.R6, **(v3)**
Rothenberg, Lawrence S. JK1118.R68 1992, **(v7)**
Rothenberg, Marc. Z7405.H6.R67 1982, **(v10)**
Rothenberg, Paula S. E185.615.R68 2000, **(v4)**
Rothenberg, Winifred Barr. HC107.M4.R67 1992, **(v6)**
Rothermund, Dietmar. HB3717 1929.R658 1996, **(v6)**
Rothery, David A. QB401.R67 1992, **(v1)**
Rothko, Mark. ND237.R725.A4 1998, **(v9)**
Rothleder, Dianne. B945.R524.R68 1999, **(v8)**
Rothman, Barbara Katz. HQ759.R68 1989, **(v6)**
Rothman, David J. R723.5.R67 1991, **(v2)**
Rothman, Ellen K. HQ801.R85 1984, **(v6)**
Rothman, Hal K. GE197.R69 2000, **(v6)**
Rothman, Hal. F804.L6.R68 1992, **(v4)**
  G155.U6.R66 1998, **(v6)**
Rothman, Sheila M. RC310.R68 1994, **(v2)**
Rothschild, D. Aviva. Z5956.C6 R68 1995, **(v10)**
Rothschild, Deborah Menaker. GV1790.P34.R68 1991, **(v6)**
Rothschild, Emma. HB83.R68 2001, **(v6)**
Rothschild, Joseph. DJK4.S93 vol. 9, **(v5)**
  DJK50.R67 1989, **(v5)**
Rothschild, Kurt W. HD4909.R67 1967, **(v6)**
Rothschild, Miriam. QL31.R67.R63 1983, **(v1)**
  SB466.E9.R68 1997, **(v1)**
Rothstein, Bo. JN7995.S86.R68 1996, **(v7)**
Rothstein, Eric. PR502.R58 vol. 3, **(v3)**
  PR851.R6, **(v3)**
  PR3438.R6, **(v3)**
Rothstein, Jerome H. RJ499.R67, **(v2)**
Rothstein, Mark A. KF3570.R663 1989, **(v7)**
Rothstein, William Nathan. MT42.R84 1989, **(v9)**
Rothwell, Kenneth S. PR3093.R67 1999, **(v3)**
Rotman, Joseph J. QA3.P8 vol. 85, **(v1)**
  QA171.R668 1990, **(v1)**
Rotte, Joanna. PN2062.R68 2000, **(v3)**
Rottensteiner, Franz. PN6071.S33 R6, **(v3)**
Rotter, Andrew Jon. E183.8.I4.R63 2000, **(v4)**
Rottschaefer, William A. BJ1311.R68 1998, **(v8)**
Rotundo, E. Anthony. HQ1090.3.R69 1993, **(v6)**
Rotundo, Louis C. TL551.5.R68 1994, **(v1)**
Roudinesco, Elisabeth. BF109.L28.R6613 1997, **(v2)**
Rouge, Jean. VK16.R6413, **(v10)**
Rougeyron, Andre. D802.F8.R6213 1996, **(v5)**
Roulac, John. SB255.R68 1997, **(v1)**
Roulston, Christine. PN3495.R66 1998, **(v3)**
Roulston, David J. QC611.R86 1999, **(v1)**

Round, F.E. QK569.D54.R68 1990, **(v1)**
Round, Phillip H. F7.R69 1999, **(v4)**
Rountree, Helen C. E78.V7.R68 1997, **(v4)**
  E99.P85.R67 1990, **(v4)**
Rouquié, Alain. JL956.C58 R6813 1987, **(v7)**
Rourke, John T. JK570.R68 1983, **(v7)**
Rouse, Irving. F1619.2.T3.R68 1992, **(v4)**
Rouse, John E. SF197.R68, **(v1)**
Rouse, John. PT2603.R397.Z859 1989, **(v3)**
Rouse, Mary A. Z6.A96 1990, **(v10)**
Rousmaniere, John. GV775.R68 1998, **(v6)**
Rousmaniere, Kate. LB1775.3.N7.R68 1997, **(v7)**
Rousseau, J.-J. QD905.2.R6813 1998, **(v1)**
Rousseau, Jean-Jacques. JC179.R7 1971, **(v7)**
  JC179.R86 1978, **(v7)**
  PQ2034.A3 1990 vol. 7, **(v3)**
  PQ2039.A46, **(v3)**
  PQ2040.R5.E5 1979, **(v3)**
  PQ2040.R5 1948, **(v3)**
Rousselot, Jean. PQ441.R6, **(v3)**
Rousso, Henry. DC397.R7314 1991, **(v5)**
Rout, Kathleen. E185.97.C6.R68 1991, **(v4)**
Rout, Leslie B. F1419.B55.R68, **(v4)**
Routh, C. R. N. DA317.R68 1990, **(v5)**
Routley, Erik. BX5203.2.R65 1960, **(v8)**
  ML3131.R68, **(v9)**
Rouverol, Jean. PN1998.2.R68 2000, **(v3)**
Rouvez, Alain. DT353.5.E9.R68 1994, **(v5)**
Rouzer, Paul F. PL2261.R68 2001, **(v3)**
  PL2677.W45.Z87 1993, **(v3)**
Rovane, Carol A. BD450.R6538 1998, **(v8)**
Rovere, Richard Halworth. E743.R68 1980, **(v4)**
  E745.M3.R6, **(v4)**
Rovin, Jeff. PN3433.8.R68 1995, **(v3)**
Rovner, Julie. RA395.A3.R685 2000, **(v2)**
Rowan, Carl Thomas. E185.615.R65 1993, **(v4)**
Rowe, Alan J. HD30.213.R689 1996, **(v6)**
Rowe, Constance. JC179.V9.R6, **(v7)**
Rowe, David C. BF341.R68 1994, **(v2)**
Rowe, Donald W. PR1882.R68 1988, **(v3)**
Rowe, George E. PR2638.R68 1988, **(v3)**
  PR2717.R6, **(v3)**
Rowe, Glenn. QP406.R677 1994, **(v1)**
Rowe, John Carlos. PS169.I45.R69 2000, **(v3)**
  PS217.P64.R69 1997, **(v3)**
  PS2127.P6.R69 1998, **(v3)**
Rowe, Katherine. PR408.H35.R69 1999, **(v3)**
Rowe, Nicholas. PR3671.R5.A68 1974, **(v3)**
Rowe, Noel. QL737.P9.R675 1996, **(v1)**
Rowe, Peter G. HD7287.R68 1993, **(v6)**
  HT352.U6.R68 1991, **(v6)**
Rowe, Stephen C. HM216.R68 1989, **(v6)**
Rowe, William T. DS754.84.C45, **(v5)**
  HN740.H36.R69 1989, **(v6)**
Rowell, David L. S591.R68 1994, **(v1)**
Rowell, George. PN2596.L7.O766 1993, **(v3)**
  PR1271.R66 1972, **(v3)**
  PR1271.R68, **(v3)**
Rowell, Lewis Eugene. MT6.R87.M9 1992, **(v9)**
Rowell, Loring B. QP109.R68 1993, **(v1)**
Rowen, Herbert Harvey. DJ158.R693 1988, **(v5)**
Rowen, Hobart. HC106.6.R69 1994, **(v6)**
Rowen, Louis Halle. QA152.2.R68 1994, **(v1)**
Rowland, Benjamin. N5303.R68, **(v9)**
Rowland, C. K. KF8754.R69 1996, **(v7)**
Rowland, Christopher. BR148.R85 1988, **(v8)**
Rowland, David. MT227.R72 1993, **(v9)**
Rowland, Ingrid D. DG797.8.R68 1998, **(v5)**
Rowland, James R. TJ216.R67 1986, **(v1)**
Rowland, K. T. VM615.R85 1970b, **(v10)**
Rowland, Lawrence Sanders. F277.B3.R68 1996, **(v4)**
Rowland, Mary Canaga. R154.R767.A3 1994, **(v2)**
Rowland, Robin. ZA3075.R69 2000, **(v10)**
Rowland, Susan. PR888.D4.R68 2001, **(v3)**
Rowland, Thomas W. RJ133.R679 1996, **(v2)**
Rowland, Willard D. PN1992.6.R68 1983, **(v3)**
Rowlands, Ian H. QC879.7.R684 1995, **(v1)**
Rowlands, John. N6888.D8.A4 1988, **(v9)**
  ND588.H7.A4 1985, **(v9)**
Rowlands, Mark. BD418.3.R78 1999, **(v8)**
  HV4708.R69 1998, **(v6)**

Rowlandson, Mary White. E87.R894 1975b, **(v4)**
Rowley, Carl L. KFI1742.6.R69 1991, **(v7)**
Rowley, Charles Kershaw. KF336.R68 1991, **(v7)**
Rowley, George. ND1040.R6 1959, **(v9)**
Rowley, Gillian Gaye. PL819.O8.R68 2000, **(v3)**
Rowley, William D. E664.N4.R69 1996, **(v4)**
Rowling, J. K. PZ7.R79835Har 1998, **(v3)**
Rowlinson, Matthew Charles. PR5592.P74.R68 1994, **(v3)**
Rowse, A. L. DA27.R78, **(v5)**
　DA28.35.C45.R59, **(v5)**
　DA28.35.C45.R6, **(v5)**
　DA355.R67 1955a, **(v5)**
　DA356.R65 1951, **(v5)**
　DA578.R68, **(v5)**
　DA670.C8.R6 1969b, **(v5)**
　PR2894.R68 1963, **(v3)**
　PR2910.R76 1974, **(v3)**
Rowse, Arthur E. PN4784.T4.R69 2000, **(v3)**
Rowson. PS2736.R3 C51 1964, **(v3)**
　PS2736.R3.C5 1986, **(v3)**
Roy, Bimalendu Narayan. QC311.R675 1995, **(v1)**
Roy, Claude. PQ2635.O9644.T7, **(v3)**
Roy, Denny. JZ1734.R69 1998, **(v7)**
Roy, Donald H. E184.A1.R74 1996, **(v4)**
Roy, Gabrielle. PQ3919.R74.P4 1970, **(v3)**
Roy, Joaquin. KF4678.R69 2000, **(v7)**
Roy, Jules. PQ2635.O9654.V3, **(v3)**
Roy, Manisha. HQ1744.B4.R68, **(v6)**
Roy, Margaret. RX601.R59 1994, **(v2)**
Roy, R. RB127.R675 1992, **(v2)**
　RC569.5.C55.R69 1998, **(v2)**
Roy, Sumit. S494.5.I5.R66 1990, **(v1)**
Roy, Tirthankar. HC435.2.R67 2000, **(v6)**
Royal Academy of Arts (Great Britain). N6767.R66 1999, **(v9)**
Royal Institute of International Affairs. DA592.R65, **(v5)**
　DS49.R87 1958, **(v5)**
　DS518.1.R74, **(v5)**
　HC256.5.R69, **(v6)**
Royce, Josiah. B945.R61 1988, **(v8)**
　B945.R63.L6, **(v8)**
　B945.R63.M48 1998, **(v8)**
　B945.R63.R3 1958, **(v8)**
　BJ1533.L8.R6 1908a, **(v8)**
　BL530.R68 1968, **(v8)**
Royce, William F. SH331.R68 1996, **(v1)**
Royer, Ariela. RA644.5.R69 1998, **(v2)**
Royle, Trevor. PR8506.R69 1983, **(v3)**
　U102.R784 1989, **(v10)**
Royo, Sebastian. HD8588.R69 2000, **(v6)**
Royster, Charles. E468.9.R69 1991, **(v4)**
Royster, Jacqueline Jones. PE1405.U6.R68 2000, **(v3)**
Rozbicki, Michal. F184.R69 1988, **(v4)**
　F229.R86 1998, **(v4)**
Roze, Maris. T10.5.R65 2002, **(v1)**
Roze, Uldis. QL737.R652.R69 1989, **(v1)**
Rozell, Mark J. E872.R69 1989, **(v4)**
　E881.R69 1996, **(v4)**
　PN4888.P6.R69 1996, **(v3)**
Rozemond, Marleen. B1878.M55.R68 1998, **(v8)**
Rozen, Marvin E. HD31.R787 1991, **(v6)**
Rozenblit, Marsha L. DS135.A9.R69 2001, **(v5)**
Rozenfeld, B. A. QA685.R6713 1988, **(v1)**
Rozin, Mordechai. HV3193.G7.R69 1999, **(v6)**
Rozmovits, Linda. PR2825.R69 1998, **(v3)**
Ruan, Ming. DS778.T39.R813 1994, **(v5)**
Ruane, Joseph. DA990.U46.R83 1996, **(v5)**
Ruane, Kevin. UA646.R896 2000, **(v10)**
Ruark, Robert Chester. PS3535.U15.O43, **(v3)**
　PS3535.U15 S6, **(v3)**
　PS3535.U15 U38 1962, **(v3)**
Ruben, David-Hillel. BD237.R83 1990, **(v8)**
Rubenberg, Cheryl. HQ1728.7.R8 2001, **(v6)**
Rubenfeld, Jed. JC585.R82 2001, **(v7)**
Rubenstein, Albert Harold. HD45.R77 1989, **(v6)**
Rubenstein, Anne. PN6790.M48.R83 1998, **(v3)**
Rubenstein, Daniel Blake. HF5686.N3.R8 1994, **(v6)**
Rubenstein, James M. HD9710.U52.R83 1992, **(v6)**

Rubenstein, Jeffrey L. BM516.5.R83 1999, **(v8)**
Rubenstein, Jill. Z8802.R82, **(v10)**
Rubenstein, Roberta. PR6023.E833.Z87, **(v3)**
　PS374.D57.H66 2001, **(v3)**
Rubies, Joan-Pau. GN575.R83 2000, **(v6)**
Rubik, Margarete. PR635.W6.R83 1998, **(v3)**
Rubin, Barnett R. DS371.2.R8 1995, **(v5)**
　DS371.2.R82 1995, **(v5)**
Rubin, Barry M. DS119.7.R754 1994, **(v5)**
　DS119.76.R83 1999, **(v5)**
Rubin, David C. GR67.R83 1995, **(v6)**
Rubin, Herbert J. HN90.C6.R735 2000, **(v6)**
Rubin, James Henry. ND192.I4.R83 1999, **(v9)**
Rubin, Jay. PL726.63.C37.R8 1984, **(v3)**
Rubin, Jeffrey B. BQ4570.P76.R83 1996, **(v8)**
Rubin, Jeffrey W. JS2120.J84.R8 1997, **(v7)**
Rubin, Jerry. HN90.R3.R88, **(v6)**
Rubin, Julius H. BX8129.B65.R83 2000, **(v8)**
Rubin, Lillian B. HQ536.R8, **(v6)**
Rubin, Patricia Lee. N6921.F7.R47 1999, **(v9)**
Rubin, Rose M. HG179.R76 1997, **(v6)**
Rubin, Susan B. R725.5.R83 1998, **(v2)**
Rubin, Theodore Isaac. PS3568.U293.L565 1988, **(v3)**
Rubin, William Stanley. N6490.R77, **(v9)**
　N6494.S8.R8, **(v9)**
Rubin, Zick. HQ769.R7647, **(v6)**
Rubin-Dorsky, Jeffrey. PS2092.F53.R83 1988, **(v3)**
Rubins, Jack L. RC339.52.H67.R8, **(v2)**
Rubinstein, Alvin Z. D888.S65.R83 1988, **(v5)**
　DK68.7.T9.R83 1982, **(v5)**
Rubinstein, Artur. ML417.R79.A28, **(v9)**
　ML417.R79.A3, **(v9)**
Rubinstein, Charlotte Streifer. N6505.R8 1982, **(v9)**
　NB236.R8 1990, **(v9)**
Rubio, Manny. QL666.O69.R835 1998, **(v1)**
Rubio-Marin, Ruth. K3224.R83 2000, **(v7)**
Rublack, Ulinka. HV6973.R84 1999, **(v6)**
Rubulis, Aleksis. PH302.R8, **(v3)**
Ruby, Jay. GN347.R83 2000, **(v6)**
Ruby, Lionel. BC108.R77, **(v8)**
Ruby, Robert H. E78.N77.R8, **(v4)**
Ruch, William V. HD30.3.R823 1989, **(v6)**
Ruck, E. H. PQ203.5.A77.R83 1991, **(v3)**
Rucker, Rudy v. B. QA10.4.R83 1987, **(v1)**
Rudacille, Deborah. HV4915.R8 2000, **(v6)**
Rudat, Wolfgang E. H. PS3515.E37.S927 1990, **(v3)**
Rudd, Margaret Thomas. PQ6639.N3.Z835, **(v3)**
Ruddick, Nicholas. PR830.S35.R84 1992, **(v3)**
Ruddick, Nicholas. PR830.S35.R845 1993, **(v3)**
Rude, George F. E. DA512.W6.R8, **(v5)**
　DA682.R8, **(v5)**
　DC146.R6.R83 1976, **(v5)**
　DC148.R83 1988, **(v5)**
　DC158.8.R8, **(v5)**
　HM281.R8, **(v6)**
　HN438.P3.R8 1971, **(v6)**
Rudebusch, George. B318.E8.R83 1999, **(v8)**
Rudenstine, David. KF228.N52.R84 1996, **(v7)**
Ruder, Cynthia Ann. DK268.3.R83 1998, **(v5)**
Rudgers, David F. JK468.I6.R83 2000, **(v7)**
Rudgley, Richard. GN768.R83 1999, **(v6)**
Rudikoff, Sonya. PR6045.O72.Z8675 1999, **(v3)**
Rudin, Bo. TS1090.R83 1987, **(v1)**
Rudin, Ernst. PS374.M48.R83 1996, **(v3)**
Rudin, Ronald. F1024.R83 1997, **(v4)**
Rudin, Walter. QA300.R8 1964, **(v1)**
Rudko, Frances Howell. E302.6.M4.R83 1991, **(v4)**
　KF8742.R83 1988, **(v7)**
Rudman, Masha Kabakow. PN1009.A1.R8 1995, **(v3)**
Rudofsky, Bernard. NA9053.S7.R8, **(v9)**
Rudolf, Max. MT85.R8 1993, **(v9)**
Rudolph, Conrad. N6851.S29.R8 1990, **(v9)**
Rudolph, Donna Keyse. F2304.R8 1996, **(v4)**
Rudolph, Frederick. LA226.R72 1990, **(v7)**
　LB2361.5.R8, **(v7)**
Rudolph, Joseph R. TJ163.2.R84 1995, **(v1)**
Rudolph, Kurt. BT1390.R7713 1983, **(v8)**
Rudolph, Lloyd I. HC435.R77 1987, **(v6)**
Rudova, Larissa. PG3476.P27.Z815 1996, **(v3)**
Rudowski, Victor Anthony. JC143.M3946.R83 1992, **(v7)**

Rudwick, Elliott M. F549.E2.R8, **(v4)**
Rudwick, M. J. S. QE705.A1.R8 1976, **(v1)**
　QE881.R83 1997, **(v1)**
Rudy, John G. PR5892.P5.R83 1996, **(v3)**
Rudy, Kathy. HQ767.15.R83 1996, **(v6)**
Rudy, Willis. LA229.R85 1996, **(v7)**
Rue, John E. DS778.M3.R8, **(v5)**
Rue, Loyal D. BD171.R8 1994, **(v8)**
Rueckert, George L. UA12.5.R84 1998, **(v10)**
Rueckert, William H. PS3503.U6134.Z85 1994, **(v3)**
Ruedy, John. DT294.5.R84 1992, **(v5)**
Ruenes, Ramon. RF123.R84 1986, **(v2)**
Rueschemeyer, Dietrich. JC423.R78 1992, **(v7)**
Ruether, Rosemary Radford. BT704.R835 1998, **(v8)**
　BT707.7.R84 2000, **(v8)**
　HQ1237.R83 1995, **(v6)**
Ruf, Gregory A. HN733.R85 1998, **(v6)**
Rufer, Josef. ML444.R92 1979, **(v9)**
Ruff, Allen. Z473.C455.R84 1997, **(v10)**
Ruff, Willie. ML419.R84 A3 1991, **(v9)**
Ruffin, Bernard. PN6081.R84 1995, **(v3)**
Ruffin, Edmund. F230.R9316 1990, **(v4)**
Ruffner, Kevin Conley. E512.4.R84 1997, **(v4)**
Ruffo-Fiore, Silvia. Z8534.R83 1990, **(v10)**
Ruge, Friedrich. D770.R833, **(v5)**
Rugeley, Terry. F1435.3.W2.R84 1996, **(v4)**
Ruggie, John Gerard. E840.R78 1996, **(v4)**
Ruggiero, Kristin. F3011.C653.R83 1988, **(v4)**
Ruggiero, Vincenzo. HV6453.E9.R84 1996, **(v6)**
Ruggiers, Paul G. PR1874.R8, **(v3)**
Rugman, Alan M. HG4538.R82, **(v6)**
Rugoff, Milton. PR2248.R8 1962, **(v3)**
Ruhlen, Merritt. P116.R85 1994, **(v3)**
Ruiz Cabrero, Gabriel. NA1308.R84 2001, **(v9)**
Ruiz de Alarcon, Juan. PQ6431.R8 1957, **(v3)**
Ruiz, Arturo. DP53.I2.R813 1998, **(v5)**
Ruiz, Juan. PQ6430.A1 1972, **(v3)**
Ruiz, Ramon Eduardo. E183.8.M6.R83 1998, **(v4)**
　F1234.R9114 1980, **(v4)**
Ruiz, Teofilo F. HD2025.C325.R85 1994, **(v6)**
　HN583.R85 2001, **(v6)**
Ruiz, Vicki. E184.M5.R86 1998, **(v4)**
　HD6515.F72.U547 1987, **(v6)**
Rukeyser, Muriel. PS3535.U4.A17 1978, **(v3)**
　PS3535.U4.O75 1992, **(v3)**
Ruland, Vernon. BL80.2.R86 1998, **(v8)**
Rumbarger, John J. HV5089.R84 1989, **(v6)**
Rumberger, Russell W. HD6278.U5.R85, **(v6)**
Rumble, Patrick Allen. PN1998.3.P367.R86 1996, **(v3)**
Rumbold, Graham. RT85.R79 1999, **(v2)**
Rumbold, Valerie. PR3633.R84 1989, **(v3)**
Rummel, Erika. BR350.E7.R86 1989, **(v8)**
　PN175.R86 1995, **(v3)**
Rummel, Robert W. HE9803.T7.R86 1991, **(v6)**
Rumrich, John Peter. PR3562.R86 1987, **(v3)**
　PR3587.3.R85 1996, **(v3)**
Runciman, David. JC328.2.R86 1997, **(v7)**
Runciman, Steven. BX300.R86, **(v8)**
　BX410.R8, **(v8)**
　DF531.R8 1956, **(v5)**
　DG867.28.R8, **(v5)**
Runciman, W. G. HM24.R92 1983, **(v6)**
Rundell, John F. H51.R86 1987, **(v6)**
Rundell, Michael. GV917.R86 1995, **(v6)**
Runes, Dagobert D. B51.8.R8, **(v8)**
Running, Thorpe. PQ7082.P7.R86 1996, **(v3)**
Runte, Alfred. QH105.C2.R86 1990, **(v1)**
Runyan, William McKinley. BF38.5.R86 1982, **(v2)**
Runyon, Damon. PS3535.U52 G8, **(v3)**
Runyon, Randolph. PS3545.A748.Z864 1990, **(v3)**
Ruoff, A. LaVonne Brown. PM155.R86 1990, **(v3)**
Ruoff, Gene W. PR4034.S43.R86 1992, **(v3)**
　PR5888.R86 1989, **(v3)**
Ruokanen, Miikka. BX1787.R86 1992, **(v8)**
Rupke, Nicolaas A. QH31.O94.R86 1994, **(v1)**
Rupp, James M. N8845.S43.R87 1991, **(v9)**
Rupp, Leila J. D810.W7.R8, **(v5)**
Rupp, Leila J. HQ76.3.U5.R86 1999, **(v6)**
Rupp, Robert O. Z8324.18.R87 1997, **(v10)**
Ruppersburg, Hugh M. PS3545.A748.Z865 1990, **(v3)**
Ruppert, Edward E. QL362.R76 1994, **(v1)**

Rusaw, A. Carol. JF1525.O73.R87 1998, (v7)
Rusbridger, James. UB271.G7.R87 1991, (v10)
Rusche, Georg. HV8497.R85 1968, (v6)
Rusco, Elmer R. KF8205.R87 2000, (v7)
Ruse, Michael. HQ76.25.R87 1988, (v6)
  QH360.5.R874 1999, (v1)
  QH361.R87 1999, (v1)
  QH371.R77 1986, (v1)
Rush, Charles W. VM365.R8, (v10)
Rush, James R. HV5816.R87 1990, (v6)
Rush, Mark E. JK1347.R87 1993, (v7)
Rush, Sharon. HV875.64.R87 2000, (v6)
Rush, Theressa Gunnels. Z1229.N39.R87, (v10)
Rushdie, Salman. PR6068.U757E27 1994b, (v3)
  PR6068.U757H37 1990, (v3)
  PR6068.U757I4 1991, (v3)
  PR6068.U757.I4 1991, (v3)
  PR6068.U757.M5 1981, (v3)
  PR6068.U757M66 1995, (v3)
  PR6068.U757S27 1989, (v3)
Rushdy, Ashraf H. A. PR3588.R86 1992, (v3)
  PS374.N4.R87 2001, (v3)
  PS374.S58.R87 1999, (v3)
Rushing, W. Jackson. E98.A7.R87 1995, (v4)
Rushton, Alan R. RB155.R87 1994, (v2)
Rushton, Julian. ML410.E41.R87 1998, (v9)
  ML410.M9.R89 1993, (v9)
Rusi, Alpo. D860.R87 1997, (v5)
Rusinko, Susan. PR736.R87 1989, (v3)
Rusk, Dean. E748.R94.A3 1990, (v4)
Rusk, Howard Archibald. R154.R92.A3, (v2)
Rusk, Robert R. LA13.R85 1969, (v7)
Ruskin, John. NA1121.V4.R7 1981, (v9)
  NA2550.R7, (v9)
  PR5252.C48, (v3)
  PR5252.R6, (v3)
  PR5252.R64, (v3)
  PR5263.A2 1949, (v3)
  PR5263.A327, (v3)
  PR5263.A37, (v3)
  PR5263.A4 1991, (v3)
Russ, Charles V. J. PF3131.R8, (v3)
Russ, Joanna. PS3568.U763.F4, (v3)
Russ, John C. TA1637.R87 1999, (v1)
Russ, Michael. ML410.M97.R9 1992, (v9)
Russ, William Adam. DU627.2.R79 1992, (v5)
Russel, R. P. Z6664.A27.R87 1995, (v10)
Russell, A. D. RM409.R87 1990, (v2)
Russell, Alison. PS366.T73.R87 2000, (v3)
Russell, Bertrand. Q158.R8, (v1)
  AC8.R76, (v10)
  B72.R8, (v8)
  B72.R83 1959a, (v8)
  B1649.R91.C37, (v8)
  B1649.R91.E38, (v8)
  B1649.R91 1983, (v8)
  B1649.R93.B4, (v8)
  B1649.R93.E8, (v8)
  B1649.R93.L6, (v8)
  B1649.R93.O9 1927a, (v8)
  B1649.R93.U49, (v8)
  B1649.R96.O8 1929, (v8)
  BD21.R8 1959, (v8)
  BD161.R78, (v8)
  BF121.R8, (v2)
  BJ1481.R75 1971, (v8)
  BL240.R8, (v8)
  BL2780.R87 1957, (v8)
  D16.8.R95, (v5)
  D358.R8 1934a, (v5)
  D844.R89 1963b, (v5)
  JC433.R78, (v7)
  LB775.R83 1967, (v7)
  PR6035.U6, (v3)
  PR6035.U63.N58 1955, (v3)
  Q175.R86 1952a, (v1)
  QA9.R8 1970, (v1)
  QA9.R88 1938, (v1)
  QA681.R96 1956, (v1)
  QC6.R8 1958, (v1)
  QC6.R83 1954, (v1)

Russell, Charles M. F596.R92 1930, (v4)
Russell, Cheryl. E184.A1.R78 1998, (v4)
  HB849.49.R875 2000, (v6)
  HC79.C6 R 87 2001, (v6)
Russell, Conrad. DA395.R87 1991, (v5)
Russell, Conrad. DA415.R78 1990, (v5)
Russell, D. TK5105.5.R87 1989, (v1)
Russell, David R. PE1405.U6.R8 1991, (v3)
Russell, Denise. RC451.4.W6.R87 1994, (v2)
Russell, Diana E. H. HQ1236.5.S6.R87 1989, (v6)
  HV6561.R86 2000, (v6)
  HV6565.C2.R87 1984, (v6)
Russell, Dick. E185.86.R88 1998, (v4)
Russell, Edmund. QH545.C48, (v1)
Russell, Edward J. S591.R84 1988, (v1)
Russell, Ford. PN75.F7.R87 1998, (v3)
Russell, Francis. E786.R95, (v4)
Russell, Frank Santi. UB251.G8 R87 1999, (v10)
Russell, George William. PR6035.U7.Z54 1962, (v3)
Russell, Gillian. PN2594.R87 1995, (v3)
Russell, Greg. E377.R87 1995, (v4)
Russell, Gregory D. KF9725.R87 1994, (v7)
Russell, H. Diane. N6853.L64.R87 1982, (v9)
  NE962.W65.R87 1990, (v9)
Russell, Herbert K. PS3525.A83.Z86 2001, (v3)
Russell, J. Stephen. PR317.D7.R87 1988, (v3)
  PR1874.R87 1998, (v3)
Russell, James C. BR203.R87 1994, (v8)
Russell, James E. LA209.2.R864, (v7)
Russell, James M. F294.A857.R87 1988, (v4)
Russell, James W. E49.R87 1994, (v4)
Russell, John Malcolm. DS70.5.N47.R86 1998, (v5)
Russell, John. N6447.R87 1981, (v9)
Russell, Katheryn K. HV9950.R87 1998, (v6)
  Z5703.5.U5.R87 2000, (v10)
Russell, Ken. PN1994.R797 1994, (v3)
Russell, Louise B. HB3505.R87 1982, (v6)
Russell, Meg. KD4260.R87 2000, (v7)
Russell, Michael L. RC489.B4.R87 1986, (v2)
Russell, P. E. G286.H5 R879 2000, (v6)
Russell, Paul. PB1014.R87 1995, (v3)
Russell, Philip L. F1236.R88 1994, (v4)
  F1256.R88 1995, (v4)
Russell, Richard Joel. G126.R85 1961, (v6)
Russell, Ruth V. GV181.4.R87 2001, (v6)
Russell, Sharon A. PN1993.5.A35.R87 1998, (v3)
Russell, Theodore Pease. F472.O9.R87 1988, (v4)
Russell, William Felton. GV884.R86.A35, (v6)
  GV885.R82, (v6)
Russell-Wood, A. J. R. F2534.R87, (v4)
  F2659.N4.R86 1982, (v4)
Russett, Bruce M. E183.8.G7.R88 1963, (v4)
  JC423.R824 1993, (v7)
  UA23.R886 1990, (v10)
Russett, Cynthia Eagle. QH365.O8R87, (v1)
  QP81.5.R87 1989, (v1)
Russmann, Edna R. NB1296.2.R87 1989, (v9)
Russo, David J. E179.R97 2000, (v4)
Russo, Elena. PQ631.R87 1996, (v3)
Russo, John Paul. PR6035.I337.Z86 1989, (v3)
Russo, V. E. A. QH442.R87 1995, (v1)
Rust, Eric C. V64.G3.R87 1991, (v10)
Rust, Ezra Gardner. ML128.S17.R87 1996, (v9)
Rust, Val Dean. LA721.83.R87 1995, (v7)
  LA891.R87 1989, (v7)
Rustow, Alexander. CB88.R84213, (v5)
Ruthchild, Rochelle Goldberg. Z7964.S68.R88 1993, (v10)
Rutherford, Andrew. HV9960.G7.R87 1993, (v6)
  PR4388.R8, (v3)
  PR4857.R8, (v3)
Rutherford, Ernest. QC721.R94 1951, (v1)
Rutherford, Jonathan. BF175.5.M37.R87 1992, (v2)
Rutherford, R. B. B583.R88 1989, (v8)
Ruthven, Douglas M. TP156.A35.R8 1984, (v1)
Ruthven, K. K. PR21.R87 2001, (v3)
  PR77.R88 1984, (v3)
  PS3531.O82.Z813 1990, (v3)
Rutkow, Ira M. RD19.R88 1993, (v2)
Rutland, Robert Allen. E341.R87 1990, (v4)
  E342.R87 1981, (v4)

E342.R88 1997, (v4)
JK168.R8, (v7)
JK2316.R94 1995, (v7)
Rutland, William Rutland. PR4754.R8 1962, (v3)
Rutledge, Archibald Hamilton. F279.H25.R8, (v4)
Rutman, Darrett Bruce. F73.4.R8 1972, (v4)
Ruttan, Vernon W. HC79.T4.R88 2001, (v6)
Ruttenburg, Nancy. PS201.R85 1998, (v3)
Rutter, John W. QA567.R78 2000, (v1)
Rutter, Michael. HV9069.R92 1998, (v6)
Ruttkowski, Wolfgang Victor. PN44.5.R8 1980, (v3)
Ruud, Inger Marie. Z7963.J4 R88 1988, (v10)
Ruud, Jay. PR1924.R88 1992, (v3)
Ryals, Clyde de L. PR4231.R9 1993, (v3)
  PR4238.R86 1983, (v3)
  PR4238.R87, (v3)
Ryan, Alan. B1649.R94.R93 1988, (v8)
  HB701.R89 1987, (v6)
  HB701.R9 1984, (v6)
Ryan, Barbara. HQ1426.R93 1992, (v6)
Ryan, Cornelius. D756.5.N6.R9, (v5)
  D763.N4.R9, (v5)
Ryan, David. E183.7.R9645 2000, (v4)
Ryan, Dennis P. F73.9.I6 R9 1983, (v4)
Ryan, Frank. RC310.R9 1993, (v2)
Ryan, James G. HX84.B69.R93 1997, (v6)
Ryan, James R. DA16.R93 1997, (v5)
Ryan, Joan. KEN5929.T48.R93 1995, (v7)
Ryan, John Morris. F1523.R9, (v4)
Ryan, Judith. PT772.R9 1983, (v3)
  PT2635.I65.Z8528 1999, (v3)
Ryan, Karen L. PG3026.S3.R94 1995, (v3)
Ryan, Lawrence V. LB475.A7.R9, (v7)
Ryan, Marie-Laure. PN3355.R93 1991, (v3)
  Z1003.R97 2001, (v10)
Ryan, Mark A. UA835.R89 1989, (v10)
Ryan, Mark. DA963.R93 1994, (v5)
Ryan, Marleigh Grayer. PL806.T3 U43, (v3)
  PL817.S8.Z86, (v3)
Ryan, Mary P. HQ1391.U5.R9 1990, (v6)
Ryan, Michael. HA1444.R93 1990, (v6)
Ryan, Mick. HV9469.R93 1989, (v6)
Ryan, Pam Muñoz. PZ7.R9553Es 2000, (v3)
Ryan, Philip B. PN2601.R93 1992, (v3)
Ryan, Robert M. PR590.R93 1997, (v3)
Ryan, Timothy W. QA76.9.O35.R93 1997, (v1)
Ryan, William B. F. BS658.R93 1998, (v8)
Ryan, William. HN65.R9 1976, (v6)
Ryang, Sonia. DS832.7.K6.R93 1997, (v5)
Rybakov, Anatolii Naumovich. PG3476.R87.D4813 1988, (v3)
Rybczynski, Witold. GV174.R94 1991, (v6)
Rychlak, Joseph F. BF38.5.R9, (v2)
Rychlak, Ronald J. D810.C6.R95 2000, (v5)
Ryczek, William J. GV875.N18.R93 1992, (v6)
Rydell, Robert W. T395.5.U6.R934 2000, (v1)
Ryden, David K. JF1075.U6.R93 1996, (v7)
Ryder, John Douglas. TK23.R9 1984, (v1)
Ryder, John. B851.R93 1999, (v8)
Ryder, Mary Ruth. PS3505.A87.Z819 1990, (v3)
Ryding, Erik S. ML422.W27 R93 2001, (v9)
Ryding, Karin C. PJ6713.R93 1990, (v3)
Ryding, Sven-Olof. TD170.R83 1992, (v1)
Rye, Owen S. CC79.5.P6.R93, (v5)
Ryerson, Richard Alan. F158.4.R87, (v4)
Rykwert, Joseph. NA600.R94, (v9)
  NA2815.R95 1996, (v9)
Rylatt, R. M. F1060.9.R985 1991, (v4)
Ryle, Gilbert. B393.R9, (v8)
Rylestone, Anne L. PR5866.R95 1991, (v3)
Ryley, Robert M. PR3757.W7.R94 1984, (v3)
Rymer, Russ. RJ507.A29.R95 1993, (v2)
Rymer, Thomas. PR3671.R7 1971, (v3)
Ryokan. PL797.6.A29 1977, (v3)
  PL797.6.Z5.R8 1996, (v3)
Ryscavage, Paul. HC110.I5.R95 1998, (v6)
Ryskamp, Charles. PR3383.R9, (v3)
Rzepka, Charles J. PR4536.R94 1995, (v3)

Sa d¯ aw¯ i, Naw¯ al. PJ7862.A3M313 1985, **(v3)**
 PJ7862.A3M813 1988, **(v3)**
 PJ7862.A3W6 1983, **(v3)**
Sa d¯ i. PK6541.B2W5, **(v3)**
 PK6541.G2G6 1914, **(v3)**
Sa'adah, Anne. DC155.S23 1990, **(v5)**
 JN3971.A91.S23 1998, **(v7)**
Saadawi, Tarek N. TK5101.S13 1994, **(v1)**
Saalman, Howard. NA350.S2, **(v9)**
 NA1123.B8.S23 1993, **(v9)**
Saari, David J. JC585.S22 1995, **(v7)**
Saarinen, Eero. NA737.S28.S2 1968, **(v9)**
Saarinen, Eliel. NA9030.S2, **(v9)**
Saarni, Carolyn. BF710.S22 1999, **(v2)**
Saaty, Thomas L. CB158.S23 1990, **(v5)**
 QA7.S2, **(v1)**
Saba, Raul P. F3448.2.S23 1986, **(v4)**
Sabaliunas, Leonas. HX315.L77.S22 1990, **(v6)**
Sabaratnam, Lakshmanan. DS489.5.S26 2001, **(v5)**
Sabatine, Jean. PN2071.M6.S22 1995, **(v3)**
Sabato, Larry. JK1994.S23 1996, **(v7)**
 PN4888.P6.S236 2000, **(v3)**
Sabharwal, Gopa. DS452.S22, **(v5)**
Sabia, Debra. BX2347.72.N5.S23 1997, **(v8)**
Sabin, Edwin L. F592.C412 1995, **(v4)**
Sabin, Henry. F621.S12, **(v4)**
Sable, Martin Howard. F1401.C33.4, **(v4)**
Sableman, Mark. KF2750.S33 1997, **(v7)**
Sabloff, Annabelle. QL85.S22 2001, **(v1)**
Sabloff, Jeremy A. F1219.7.S33 1989, **(v4)**
Sabra, A. I. QC401.S3, **(v1)**
Sabra, Adam Abdelhamid. HC830.Z9 P625 2000, **(v6)**
Saccio, Peter. PR2982.S2, **(v3)**
Sacco, Nicola. HV6248.S3.A4 1971, **(v6)**
Sachar, Abram Leon. DS117.S3 1965, **(v5)**
Sachar, Howard Morley. DS62.9.S23 1969, **(v5)**
 DS119.6.S33 1999, **(v5)**
Sachar, Louis. PZ7.S1185Ho 1998, **(v3)**
Sachedina, Abdulaziz Abdulhussein. JC49.S162
 1988, **(v7)**
Sacher, Jack. ML1700.S13 1997, **(v9)**
Sachs, Carolyn E. HQ1240.S28 1996, **(v6)**
 S441.S25 1983, **(v7)**
Sachs, Curt. ML162.S14, **(v9)**
 ML437.S3, **(v9)**
 ML460.S24.H5, **(v9)**
 ML3797.S3, **(v9)**
 N5303.S2, **(v9)**
Sachs, Hans. PT1767.E5.L4, **(v3)**
Sachs, Harvey. ML417.R79.S23 1995, **(v9)**
 ML422.T67.S338 1991, **(v9)**
 ML422.T67 S34 1981, **(v9)**
Sachs, Jeffrey. HC340.3.S213 1993, **(v6)**
Sachs, Joe. Q151.A8.S23 1995, **(v1)**
Sachs, Murray. PQ1275.S2, **(v3)**
Sachs, Nelly. PT2637.A4184.A6 1967, **(v3)**
 PT2637.A4184.A6 1970, **(v3)**
Sachs, Paul J. NE940.S3, **(v9)**
Sachs, Robert Green. QC173.59.T53.S23 1987, **(v1)**
Sachs, Wolfgang. HC79.E5.S216 1998, **(v6)**
Sack, Allen L. GV351.S23 1998, **(v6)**
Sack, Daniel. BR115.N87 S23 2000, **(v8)**
Sack, Robert David. GF21.S33 1997, **(v6)**
 HB801.S23 1992, **(v6)**
Sacker, Hugh D. PT1688.S25, **(v3)**
Sackheim, George I. RT68.S23 1996, **(v2)**
Sacks, David Harris. HC258.B76.S23 1991, **(v6)**
Sacks, David. DF16.S23 1995, **(v5)**
Sacks, Michael Paul. HD5796.S23 1982, **(v6)**
Sacks, Peter M. PR509.E4.S23 1985, **(v3)**
Sacks, Peter. LB2331.S17 1996, **(v7)**
 LB3051.S22 1999, **(v7)**
Sackville-West, Edward. PR4536.S25 1936, **(v3)**
Sackville-West, V. PR3546.S3 1929, **(v3)**
 PR6037.A35.A6 1941, **(v3)**
 PR6037.A35 A64, **(v3)**
 PR6037.A35 D3, **(v3)**
 PR6037.A35 E15, **(v3)**
 PR6037.A35 E3, **(v3)**
 PR6037.A35 N6, **(v3)**
 PR6037.A35.Z497 1985, **(v3)**

Sadava, David E. QH581.2.S2 1993, **(v1)**
Sadawi, Nawal. PJ7862.A3.U3813 1989, **(v3)**
Sade. PQ2063.S3.A275, **(v3)**
 PQ2063.S3.A69 1969, **(v3)**
 PQ2063.S3 1972 t. 1, **(v3)**
Sadiku, Matthew N. O. QC760.S24 2000, **(v1)**
Sadiq, Muhammad. PK2155.S25, **(v3)**
Sadker, Myra. LC212.82.S27 1994, **(v7)**
Sadkovich, James J. DR1313.7.P73.S23 1998, **(v5)**
Sadleir, Randal. DT447.2.S34.A3 1999, **(v5)**
Sadler, Barry. U55.S25.A3, **(v10)**
Sadler, John Edward. LB475.C6.S2 1966, **(v7)**
Sadler, Lynn Veach. PR6052.R5816.Z87 1990, **(v3)**
Sadlier, Darlene J. PQ9033.S24 1989, **(v3)**
Sadlier, Darlene J. PQ9261.P417.Z835 1998, **(v3)**
Sadowski, Yahya M. HC498.9.D4 S23 1993, **(v6)**
Sadri, Ahmad. HM213.S22 1992, **(v6)**
Sadri, Houman A. JZ1315.S23 1997, **(v7)**
Sadrin, Anny. PR4592.P34.S23 1994, **(v3)**
Saenger, Paul Henry. Z1003.S13 1997, **(v10)**
Saenz, Mario. B1008.L53.S24 1999, **(v8)**
Saenz-Badillos, Angel. PJ4545.S2313 1993, **(v3)**
Saetevik, Sunneva. KJC6243.S23 1988, **(v7)**
Safa, Helen Icken. HD6114.S24 1995, **(v6)**
Safdar Mahmood. DS384.S2195 2000, **(v5)**
Saff, Donald. NE850.S23, **(v9)**
Saffle, Michael Benton. ML134.L7.S2 1991, **(v9)**
Saffle, Michael. ML134.W1 S24 2002, **(v9)**
Safire, William. E855.S23, **(v4)**
 JK9.S2 1993, **(v7)**
Safran, Gabriella. DS148.S34 2000, **(v5)**
Sagan, Carl. BF431.S19, **(v2)**
 Q173.S24 1997, **(v1)**
 Q175.S215 1995, **(v1)**
 QB44.2.S235 1995, **(v1)**
 QB721.S34 1985, **(v1)**
 QH325.S24 1992, **(v1)**
 QH545.N83.S24 1990, **(v1)**
Sagan, Leonard A. RA569.3.S24 1996, **(v2)**
Sagan, Scott Douglas. U264.S233 1995, **(v10)**
Sagarra, Eda. PT236.S55 1997, **(v3)**
Sagas, Ernesto. F1941.A1.S34 2000, **(v4)**
Sagdeev, R. Z. QC16.S24.A3 1994, **(v1)**
Sage, Andrew P. TA168.S15 2000, **(v1)**
Sage, George Harvey. GV706.5.S228 1998, **(v6)**
Sage, Leland L. F621.S15, **(v4)**
Sage, Lorna. PR111.S24 1999, **(v3)**
 PR6023.E833.Z878 1983, **(v3)**
Sagel, Jim. F801.2.S24 1991, **(v4)**
Sager, Eric W. HD8039.S4.O67 1989, **(v6)**
Saggers, Sherry. HV5198.S34 1998, **(v6)**
Saggs, H. W. F. DS57.S28 1989, **(v5)**
Sah, Chih-Tang. TK7871.85.S23 1991, **(v1)**
Saha, Santosh C. Z6465.U5 S24 1990, **(v10)**
Sahagun, Bernardino de. F1219.S1319, **(v4)**
 F1219.S132, **(v4)**
Saheb-Ettaba, Mouncef. PJ6307.S27, **(v3)**
Saher, P. J. B799.S32 1970, **(v8)**
Sahgal, Manmohini Zutshi. HQ1742.S235 1994, **(v6)**
Sahlins, Marshall David. DU626.O283.S35 1995, **(v5)**
 GN345.S24, **(v6)**
Sahlins, Peter. DC611.P985.S24 1989, **(v5)**
Sahliyeh, Emile F. DS110.W47.S24 1988, **(v5)**
Sahn, David E. HC800.S23 1997, **(v6)**
Sahnoun, Mohamed. DT407.S24 1994, **(v5)**
Said, Edward W. ML3845.S13 1991, **(v9)**
 PN81.S223 1983, **(v3)**
 PN98.P64.S35 2000, **(v3)**
 PN761.S28 1993, **(v3)**
Said, Rushdi. GB1361.S25 1993, **(v6)**
Saidel, Rochelle G. D804.175.N49.S25 1996, **(v5)**
Saidi, Ghulam Husayn. PK6561.S27.O6713 1996, **(v3)**
Saigyo. PL788.5.S213 1991, **(v3)**
 PL788.5.S22.E5 1978, **(v3)**
Saillet, Maurice. PQ2623.E386.Z83, **(v3)**
Sainsbury, Diane. HV1444.S35 1996, **(v6)**
Sainsbury, Keith. D749.S25 1985, **(v5)**
Sainsbury, Malcolm. QD331.S25 1992, **(v1)**
Sainsbury, R. M. BC135.S14 1991, **(v8)**
 BC199.P2 S25 1995, **(v8)**
Saint Exupery, Antoine de. D788.S3 1979, **(v5)**

 PQ2637.A274.C64 1979, **(v3)**
 PZ8.S14Li4, **(v3)**
Saint, Andrew. NA1995.S27 1983, **(v9)**
Saint-Amand, Pierre. PQ637.S43.S2513 1994, **(v3)**
Sainte-Beuve, Charles Augustin. PQ2391.Z2.S7, **(v3)**
Saint-Exupery, Antoine de. PQ2635.A274.C52, **(v3)**
 PQ2637.A274.C5, **(v3)**
 PQ2637.A274.L4 1944, **(v3)**
 PQ2637.A274.T43 1949, **(v3)**
 PQ2637.A274.Z52, **(v3)**
 PQ2637.A274P43713 1982, **(v3)**
Saint-John Perse. PQ2623.E386.A6 1960, **(v3)**
 PQ2623.E386.C3813, **(v3)**
 PQ2623.E386.E9 1973, **(v3)**
Saintsbury, George. PE1561.S3 1965, **(v3)**
 PQ119.S18, **(v3)**
 PQ631.S3, **(v3)**
 PR5294.A1 1969, **(v3)**
Saint-Simon, Louis de Rouvroy. DC130.S2.A1992,
 (v5)
Sainz de Robles, Federico Carlos. PQ6176.S23 1950,
 (v3)
Saito, Leland T. F869.M7.S25 1998, **(v4)**
Saito, Mokichi. PL816.A5.S4713 1989, **(v3)**
Saito, Sanki. PL838.A44.K63 1993, **(v3)**
Saivetz, Deborah. PN2287.A445.S25 2000, **(v3)**
Sajeva, Maurizio. SB438.S293 2000, **(v1)**
Sakanishi, Shio. PL888.S3 1960, **(v3)**
Sakawa, Masatoshi. QA402.5.S25 1993, **(v1)**
Sakharov, Andrei. CB427.S2313 1968, **(v5)**
 DK274.S276 1975, **(v5)**
 DK274.S277 1974, **(v5)**
Saki. PR6025.U675 1976, **(v3)**
Sakmyster, Thomas L. DB955.6.H67.S25 1994, **(v5)**
Salacrou, Armand. PQ2637.A48.T5, **(v3)**
Salamanca, J. R. PS3569.A458.E, **(v3)**
Salami, Mahmoud. PR6056.O85.Z84 1992, **(v3)**
Salamone, Frank A. F2520.1.Y3.S25 1997, **(v4)**
Salas, Elizabeth. UB419.M6.S25 1990, **(v10)**
Salazar, Norma. PQ7296.J6.Z84 1994, **(v3)**
Salazar-Carrillo, Jorge. HD9574.V42.S357 1994, **(v6)**
Saldivar, Jose David. PN843.S24 1991, **(v3)**
Saldivar-Hull, Sonia. PS374.M4837.S25 2000, **(v3)**
Sale, Maggie Montesinos. E447.S25 1997, **(v4)**
Sale, Roger. PR99.S25, **(v3)**
Salem, Dorothy C. E185.86.B543 1990 vol. 14, **(v4)**
Salem, Elie Adib. DS87.2.S24.A3 1995, **(v5)**
Salem, James M. Z5781.S16 1984, **(v10)**
Saler, Benson. TL789.5.N6.S25 1997, **(v1)**
Salerno, Joseph. B3245.F24 S24 2001, **(v8)**
Salerno, Roger A. Z8978.66.S24 1987, **(v10)**
Sales, Roger. PR2674.S19 1991, **(v3)**
Sales, William W. BP223.Z8.L5772 1994, **(v8)**
Saliba, Bonnie. HD1695.A165.S25 1987, **(v6)**
Saliba, John A. Z7835.C86.S34 1990, **(v10)**
Salibi, Kamal S. DS80.9.S26 1988, **(v5)**
 DS95.S24, **(v5)**
Salih, al-Tayyib. PJ7862.A564.M313 1989, **(v3)**
Salih, Halil Ibrahim. DS54.5.S24, **(v5)**
Salinas, Martin. E78.T4.S25 1990, **(v4)**
Salinas, Pedro. PQ6635.A32.A17 1953, **(v3)**
 PQ6635.A32A6 1991b, **(v3)**
 PQ6635.A32.V513 1993, **(v3)**
Salinger, J. D. PS3537.A426.C3 1951, **(v3)**
 PS3537.A426.F7 1991, **(v3)**
 PS3537.A426.N5 1959, **(v3)**
 PS3537.A426.R3 1963, **(v3)**
Salinger, Pierre. E841.S2, **(v4)**
Salins, Peter D. E169.1.S198 1996, **(v4)**
Salisbury, Harrison Evans. D764.3.L4.S2, **(v5)**
 DK267.S17 1961, **(v5)**
 PS3537.A428.N6, **(v3)**
Salisbury, Joyce E. HQ1127.S25 2001, **(v6)**
Salisbury, Neal. E78.N5.S24 1982, **(v4)**
Salisbury, Richard V. F1436.8.U6.S25 1989, **(v4)**
Salk, Jonas. Q175.S2326 1983, **(v1)**
Salkeld, Duncan. PR2992.M3.S22 1993, **(v3)**
Salkever, Stephen G. JC71.A7.S25 1990, **(v7)**
Salkey, Andrew. PR9216.S3 1972, **(v3)**
Salkey, Andrew. PR9327.5.S24, **(v3)**
Salkind, Neil J. HA29.S2365 2000, **(v6)**

Salles-Reese, Veronica. GR133.T57.S35 1997, **(v6)**
Salley, A. S. F272.S16, **(v4)**
Sallis, James F. R726.5.S25 1999, **(v2)**
Sallis, John,1938-. B395.S23 1996, **(v8)**
Sallis, John. B3313.G43.S24 1991, **(v8)**
Sallnow, Michael J. BL2590.P5.S25 1987, **(v8)**
Salmon, Edward Togo. DG221.5.S24 1982, **(v5)**
Salmon, J. B. DF261.C65.S24 1984, **(v5)**
Salmon, J. H. M. DC116.5.S25 1975b, **(v5)**
Salmon, Merrilee H. BC71.S25 1995, **(v8)**
Salmon, Patrick. DL83.S35 1997, **(v5)**
Salmon, Richard. PS2127.P6.S25 1997, **(v3)**
Salmon, Trevor C. UA829.I7.S25 1989, **(v10)**
Salmon, Wesley C. BC108.S2 1984, **(v8)**
  Q175.S23415 1984, **(v1)**
Salmond, Anne. DU423.F48.S25 1992, **(v5)**
Salmond, Anne. DU423.F48.S25 1997, **(v5)**
Salmond, John A. HD6509.M375.S25 1988, **(v6)**
  KF373.D87.S25 1990, **(v7)**
Salmonson, Jessica Amanda. HQ1115.S25 1991, **(v6)**
Salmore, Barbara G. JK3516.S35 1993, **(v7)**
Salokar, Rebecca Mae. KF5107.S25 1992, **(v7)**
Salomone, Rosemary C. LB1027.9.S26 2000, **(v7)**
Saloutos, Theodore. E184.G7.S29, **(v4)**
Salstrom, Paul. HC107.A127.S24 1994, **(v6)**
Salter, David F. GV709.S32 1996, **(v6)**
Salter, Elizabeth. PR2015.S3 1969, **(v3)**
Saltman, David. TS1105.S23, **(v1)**
Saltus, Edgar. BJ1477.S2 1925, **(v8)**
  PS2752.M5 1968, **(v3)**
  PS2752.P8, **(v3)**
Saltzman, Arthur M. PS379.S25 2000, **(v3)**
Salvadori, Mario George. TH845.S33 1980, **(v1)**
Salvaggio, Ruth. PN98.W64.S25 1999, **(v3)**
  PR449.W65.S25 1988, **(v3)**
Salvan, Jacques Leon. B2430.S34.S3, **(v8)**
Salvini, Roberto. NB170.S213, **(v9)**
Salwak, Dale. PR6001.M6.Z87 1992, **(v3)**
  PR6045.A249.Z87, **(v3)**
Salway, Peter. DA145.S26, **(v5)**
Salwen, Michael Brian. PN1991.3.C8.S25 1994, **(v3)**
  PN4930.S24 1991, **(v3)**
Salwolke, Scott. PN1998.3.R635.S26 1993, **(v3)**
Salyer, Lucy E. KF4845.S25 1995, **(v7)**
Salzberg, Hugh W. QD11.S23 1990, **(v1)**
Salzer, Felix. MT40.S2 1962, **(v9)**
Salzman, Eric. ML197.S17 2002, **(v9)**
Salzman, Harold. QA76.76.D47.S25 1994, **(v1)**
Salzman, Jack. PS659.S3, **(v3)**
Salzman, Paul. PR836.S24 1985, **(v3)**
Salzman, Philip Carl. DS269.B33, **(v5)**
Samar, Vincent Joseph. K240.S36 1998, **(v7)**
  KF1262.S26 1991, **(v7)**
Samarasinghe, S. W. R. de A. DS489.5.S33 1997, **(v5)**
Sambrook, Joseph. QH442.2.S26 2001, **(v1)**
Sambursky, Samuel. B528.S25, **(v8)**
Samek, Hana. E99.S54.S14 1987, **(v4)**
Samli, A. Coskun. HF5415.13.S24 1992, **(v6)**
  HF5415.135.S26 1996, **(v6)**
Samm̄ an, Gh̄ adah. PJ7862.A584B3913 1995, **(v3)**
  PJ7862.A584K313 1997, **(v3)**
Samman, Ghadah. PJ7862.A584.Q2613 1998, **(v3)**
Sammann, Patricia. GV443.A27 1998, **(v6)**
Sammet, Jean E. QA76.5.S213, **(v1)**
Sammons, Jeffrey L. PT2328.S2, **(v3)**
  PT2451.Z5.S18 1991, **(v3)**
Sammons, Jeffrey T. GV1125.S26 1988, **(v6)**
Sammons, Martha C. PR6023.E926.Z867 1999, **(v3)**
Sammons, Vivian O. Q141.B58 1990, **(v1)**
Samora, Julian. E184.M5 S25 1993, **(v4)**
Samora, Julian. F391.S22, **(v4)**
Sampath, Ursula. PT405.S287 1991, **(v3)**
Sampson, Anthony. DA589.7.S25 1982, **(v5)**
  DA592.S23 1972, **(v5)**
Sampson, Arthur William. SF85.S33, **(v1)**
Sampson, Curt. GV970.3.B75, **(v6)**
Sampson, Edward E. HM251.S2623 1991, **(v6)**
  LA186.S26, **(v6)**
Sampson, Geoffrey. PE1074.5.S364 1996, **(v3)**
Sampson, George. PR83.C3, **(v3)**
  PR85.S34 1970, **(v3)**

Sampson, Henry T. NC1766.5.A35.S26 1997, **(v9)**
  PN1995.9.N4.S2 1995, **(v3)**
Sampson, Robert J. HV9069.S246 1993, **(v6)**
Sampson, Ronald Victor. BD438.S25 1966, **(v8)**
Sams, Eric. MT115.W6 S3 1992, **(v9)**
  MT121.B73 S36 2000, **(v9)**
Samson, Claude. TJ211.35.S26 1990, **(v1)**
Samson, Danny. TS155.S16 1991, **(v1)**
Samson, Gloria Garrett. HV97.A64.S26 1996, **(v6)**
Samson, Jane. DU40.S26 1998, **(v5)**
Samson, John. PS2387.S19 1989, **(v3)**
Samuel, Maurice. CB63.T68.S3, **(v5)**
  DS126.S287, **(v5)**
  PJ5129.P4.Z96, **(v3)**
  PJ5129.R2.Z8, **(v3)**
Samuel, R. H. PT405.S3, **(v3)**
Samuels, Brian M. KF902.S26 1996, **(v7)**
Samuels, Ernest. N7483.B4.S25, **(v9)**
Samuels, Martin. D529.3.S26 1992, **(v5)**
  UA647.S182 1995, **(v10)**
Samuels, Peggy. E721.6.S19 1995, **(v4)**
  E757.S19 1997, **(v4)**
Samuels, Richard J. UA845.S327 1994, **(v10)**
Samuels, Robert. PN1998.3.H58.S26 1998, **(v3)**
Samuels, Shirley. PS374.H5.S26 1996, **(v3)**
Samuels, Wilfred D. PS3563.O8749.Z85 1990, **(v3)**
Samuelson, Norbert Max. B157.C65.S25 1994, **(v8)**
Samuelson, Paul Anthony. HB135.S24 1983, **(v6)**
Samway, Patrick H. PS3566.E6912.Z834 1997, **(v3)**
San Juan, E. D883.S16 1998, **(v5)**
  PL5531.S25 1996, **(v3)**
  PQ2613.I2.Z668 1988, **(v3)**
  PR5824.S3, **(v3)**
San Lazzaro, Gualtieri di. ND588.K5.S26, **(v9)**
Sanasarian, Eliz. BL2270.S26 2000, **(v8)**
Sanborn, Geoffrey. PS2388.I45.S26 1998, **(v3)**
Sanchez G., Gonzalo. HV6453.C75, **(v6)**
Sanchez, George J. F869.L89.M57 1993, **(v4)**
Sanchez, Joseph P. F799.S26 1997, **(v4)**
Sanchez, Magdalena S. DP183.S26 1998, **(v5)**
Sanchez, Pedro A. S599.9.T76.S26, **(v1)**
Sanchez, Reuben. PR3592.P7.S26 1997, **(v3)**
Sanchez, Rosaura. F864.S235 1995, **(v4)**
Sanchez, Sonia. PS3569.A468.L6, **(v3)**
  PS3569.A468.U53 1987, **(v3)**
Sanchez-Albornoz, Nicolas. HB3530.5.S2613, **(v6)**
Sanchez-H, Jose. PN1993.5.B5.S26 1999, **(v3)**
Sanchis, Luis E. QA248.S245 1996, **(v1)**
Sand, George. PQ2407.L913 1985, **(v3)**
  PQ2408.A1, **(v3)**
  PQ2409.M613 1999, **(v3)**
  PQ2411.P4.E5, **(v3)**
  PQ2412.A2 1945, **(v3)**
Sandage, Allan. QB851.S25, **(v1)**
Sandall, Roger. HQ2042.2.S26 2001, **(v6)**
Sandars, C. T. UA26.A2.S25 2000, **(v10)**
Sandars, N. K. DE73.2.S4.S26, **(v5)**
  N5310.S32, **(v9)**
Sanday, Peggy Reeves. HQ1075.S26, **(v6)**
  HV6561.S25 1990, **(v6)**
Sandbrook, Richard. HC800.S26 1985, **(v6)**
  JQ1879.A15 S27 2000, **(v7)**
Sandburg, Carl. E457.S215 1984, **(v4)**
  E457.3.S226, **(v4)**
  PS3537.A618. 1970, **(v3)**
  PS3537.A618.C5 1916, **(v3)**
  PS3537.A618.C7 1918, **(v3)**
  PS3537.A618.H63, **(v3)**
  PS3537.A618.P4 1936a, **(v3)**
  PS3537.A618.R4, **(v3)**
  PS3537.A618.S6 1942, **(v3)**
  PS3537.A618.Z5 1953, **(v3)**
  PS3537.A618.Z53, **(v3)**
Sandemose, Aksel. PT8950.S23 V32, **(v3)**
Sander, Alfred Dick. JK518.S26 1989, **(v7)**
Sanders, Andrew. PR83.S26 1994, **(v3)**
  PR4592.S58.S26 1999, **(v3)**
Sanders, Barry. PN6147.S26 1995, **(v3)**
Sanders, Charles Richard. PR6037.T73.Z8, **(v3)**
Sanders, David. PS3515.E7715.Z88 1990, **(v3)**
Sanders, E. P. BT301.2.S254 1993, **(v8)**

Sanders, Eve Rachele. PR658.S42.S26 1998, **(v3)**
Sanders, George. PN2598.S33.A3 1992, **(v3)**
Sanders, I. J. U760.S3, **(v10)**
Sanders, James. P96.S68.S26 2000, **(v3)**
Sanders, Julie. PR2642.P64.S26 1998, **(v3)**
Sanders, Marion K. R111.S25, **(v2)**
Sanders, Paula. DT146.S26 1994, **(v5)**
Sanders, Pete. RC552.E18.S26 1999, **(v2)**
Sanders, Rickie. HB1323.C52.U658 1998, **(v6)**
Sanders, Ronald. DS125.S284 1988, **(v5)**
Sanders, Wilbur. PR2839.S26 1987, **(v3)**
Sanders, William T. F1219.1.M53.S23, **(v4)**
Sanderson, James L. PR2242.D2.S2, **(v3)**
Sanderson, John. DA415.S26 1989, **(v5)**
Sanderson, R. T. QD467.S3, **(v1)**
Sanderson, Stephen K. GN360.S25 1990, **(v6)**
Sanderson, Steven E. HF1480.5.S33 1992, **(v6)**
Sanderson, Warren C. HB3633.A3.S26 1995, **(v6)**
Sandiford, Keith Albert. PR9340.S26 1988, **(v3)**
Sandige, Richard S. TK7868.L6.S26 1990, **(v1)**
Sandler, B. Z. TJ213.S1157 1999, **(v1)**
Sandler, Irving. N6512.S255 1988, **(v9)**
  ND212.5.A25.S2 1970, **(v9)**
Sandler, Stanley R. QD262.S24 1992, **(v1)**
  QD281.P6.S27, **(v1)**
Sandler, Stanley. D790.S26 1992, **(v5)**
Sandmel, Samuel. B689.Z7 S28, **(v8)**
  BM176.S26, **(v8)**
Sandmel, Samuel. BS1140.2.S2, **(v8)**
Sandmeyer, Elmer Clarence. F870.C5 S3 1991, **(v4)**
Sandner, David. PR990.S26 1996, **(v3)**
Sandoval, Annette. BX4656.5.S26 1996, **(v8)**
Sandoval, Salvador A. M. HD5353.S26 1993, **(v6)**
Sandoval-Sanchez, Alberto. PN2270.H57.S26 1999, **(v3)**
Sandoz, Ellis. JA84.U5.S26 1990, **(v7)**
Sandoz, Mari. F666.S34, **(v4)**
  PS3537.A667 M5, **(v3)**
Sandstrom, Alan R. F1221.N3.S258 1991, **(v4)**
Sandstrom, Flora. PR6037.A219 O8, **(v3)**
Sandved, Kjell Bloch. QK648.S32 1993, **(v1)**
Sanford, Charles L. E165.S25 1964a, **(v4)**
  E302.6.F8.S32, **(v4)**
Sanford, David H. BC199.C56 S26 2003, **(v8)**
Sanford, George. DK4030.S26 1994, **(v5)**
  Z2526.S26 1993, **(v10)**
Sanford, Mollie Dorsey. F666.S36 1976, **(v4)**
Sanford, Trent Elwood. NA720.S3 1971, **(v9)**
Sangalli, Arturo. QA76.9.S63.S26 1998, **(v1)**
Sanger, Abner. F44.K2.S26 1987, **(v4)**
Sanger, Clyde. DA822.M3.S36 1995, **(v5)**
Sangren, Paul Steven. DS799.9.T24.S36 1987, **(v5)**
Sanjek, Roger. F128.68.E53.S26 1998, **(v4)**
Sanjek, Russell. ML200.S263 1991, **(v9)**
  ML3477.S2 1996, **(v9)**
Sanjian, Gregory S. UF535.D44.S26 1988, **(v10)**
Sanneh, Lamin O. BL65.C8.S26 1996, **(v8)**
  BP64.A4.W367 1997, **(v8)**
Sano, Iwao Peter. D811.S3228 1997, **(v5)**
Sansom, George Bailey. DS821.S3 1943, **(v5)**
  DS835.S27, **(v5)**
Sansom, Robert L. HD2080.V5.S35, **(v6)**
Sansom, William. PR6037.A75 A15 1971, **(v3)**
  PR6037.A75 A3, **(v3)**
  PR6037.A75 B4, **(v3)**
  PR6037.A75 B6, **(v3)**
  PR6037.A75 C3, **(v3)**
  PR6037.A75 C6, **(v3)**
  PR6037.A75 L3, **(v3)**
  PR6037.A75 L59, **(v3)**
  PR6037.A75.S6, **(v3)**
  PR6037.A75 T63 1958, **(v3)**
Santamaria, Francisco Javier. PC4822.S3, **(v3)**
Santamarina, J. Carlos. TA331.S35 1998, **(v1)**
Santas, Gerasimos Xenophon. B398.L9.S26 1988, **(v8)**

Santayana, George. B945.S21 C59 1995, **(v8)**
B945.S21.C6, **(v8)**
B945.S21 E3 1936, **(v8)**
B945.S2 1986 vol. 1, **(v8)**
B945.S2 1986 vol. 5, **(v8)**
B945.S23.D5 1957, **(v8)**
B945.S23 L7 1998, **(v8)**
B945.S23.R38, **(v8)**
B945.S23.R4, **(v8)**
B945.S23.R42 1972, **(v8)**
B2528.E3.S3, **(v8)**
BD331.S3, **(v8)**
BD331.S33, **(v8)**
BT201.S263, **(v8)**
E169.1.S255, **(v4)**
PN511.S28, **(v3)**
PS2772.L3 1936, **(v3)**
PS2772.P6, **(v3)**
Santee, Ross. PS3537.A76W7 1981, **(v3)**
Santella, Andrew. F68.S25 2000, **(v4)**
Santi Leksukhum. ND1021.S26813 2000, **(v9)**
Santiago-Valles, Kelvin A. HV6872.S26 1994, **(v6)**
Santino, Jack. HD6515.R36.S26 1989, **(v6)**
Santner, Eric L. PN1993.5.G3.S33 1990, **(v3)**
Santoni, Pedro. E407.S26 1996, **(v4)**
Santoro, Gene. ML418.M45.S26 2000, **(v9)**
Santoro, Michael A. JC599.C6.S26 2000, **(v7)**
Santos, Boaventura de Sousa. K487.S3.S26 1995, **(v7)**
Santos, Miguel A. GF41.S17 1990, **(v6)**
Santos-Granero, Fernando. F3430.1.A54.S26 1991, **(v4)**
HC228.L6.S26 2000, **(v6)**
Santosuosso, Antonio. U29.S25 1997, **(v10)**
Santrock, John W. Z7204.S44.S26 1994, **(v10)**
Sapir, Edward. PM2031.S3, **(v3)**
Sapir, Jacques. UA770.S258 1991, **(v10)**
Sapiro, Virginia. HQ1236.S27 1983, **(v6)**
Sapolsky, Harvey M. V394.A7.S37 1990, **(v10)**
Sapon-Shevin, Mara. LC3993.9.S27 1994, **(v7)**
Sapoznik, Henry. ML3528.8.S26 1999, **(v9)**
Sapp, Jan. QH548.S26 1994, **(v1)**
Sappol, Michael. RA619.S37 2001, **(v2)**
Saragoza, Alex. HG185.M6.S27 1988, **(v6)**
Sarantakes, Nicholas Evan. DS889.16.S26 2000, **(v5)**
Sarasin, Lynne Celli. LB1060.S27 1999, **(v7)**
Sarason, Seymour Bernard. LA210.S34 1982, **(v7)**
LA217.S27 1990, **(v7)**
LB2805.S267 1995, **(v7)**
LB2806.36.S27 1998, **(v7)**
N71.S18 1990, **(v9)**
Saravanamuttoo, H. I. H. TJ778.S24 2001, **(v1)**
Sarbin, Theodore R. BF173.S326, **(v2)**
Sarewitz, Daniel R. Q127.U6.S25 1996, **(v1)**
Sareyan, Alex. RC443.S26 1994, **(v2)**
Sargeant, Amy. PN1998.3.P85S37 2000, **(v3)**
Sargeant, Kimon Howland. BR1640.S27 2000, **(v8)**
Sargent, Charles Sprague. QK481.S21 1961, **(v1)**
Sargent, John Singer. ND237.S3.A4 1998a, **(v9)**
Sargent, John. LA1151.S285 1968, **(v7)**
Sargent, Lyman Tower. Z2014.U84.S28 1988, **(v10)**
Sargent, Rose-Mary. Q143.B77.S27 1995, **(v1)**
Sargent, S. Stansfeld. BF131.S226 1965, **(v2)**
Saricks, Joyce G. Z711.5.S27 2001, **(v10)**
Sarkesian, Sam Charles. UA23.S275 1989, **(v10)**
Sarkonak, Ralph William. PQ2667.U4612, **(v3)**
Sarmiento, Domingo Faustino. F2846.S2185 1972, **(v4)**
F2846.S244 1916, **(v4)**
Sarmiento, Guillermo. QH130.S2713 1984, **(v1)**
Sarna, Jonathan D. E184.J5.S325 1997, **(v4)**
Z473.J46.S27 1989, **(v10)**
Sarnecky, Mary T. UH493.S27 1999, **(v10)**
Saroyan, William. PS3537.A826.A6 1958, **(v3)**
PS3537.A826 A7, **(v3)**
PS3537.A826 B6, **(v3)**
PS3537.A826.C3, **(v3)**
PS3537.A826 D3, **(v3)**
PS3537.A826 H8, **(v3)**
PS3537.A826 L38 1953, **(v3)**

PS3537.A826 M36 1956, **(v3)**
PS3537.A826 M9, **(v3)**
PS3537.A826 P3, **(v3)**
PS3537.A826 R6, **(v3)**
PS3537.A826 S23, **(v3)**
PS3537.A826.T43 1941, **(v3)**
PS3537.A826 T7, **(v3)**
PS3537.A826.W33 1991, **(v3)**
PS3537.A826 W5, **(v3)**
PS3537.A826.Z52, **(v3)**
PS3537.A826.Z525 1978b, **(v3)**
PS3537.A826.Z53, **(v3)**
PS3537.A826.Z532, **(v3)**
PS3537.A826.Z537 1969, **(v3)**
PS3537.A826.Z54, **(v3)**
PS3537.A826.Z543, **(v3)**
Sarra, Edith. PL741.2.S26 1999, **(v3)**
Sarraute, Nathalie. PQ2637.A783.T7, **(v3)**
Sarris, Greg. E99.P65.S27 1993, **(v4)**
Sarti, Roland. DG552.8.M3.S34 1997, **(v5)**
Sarton, George. Q125.S246, **(v1)**
Q125.S25 1956, **(v1)**
Q125.S323 1960, **(v1)**
Q125.S326, **(v1)**
Sarton, May. PS3537.A832.A17 1974, **(v3)**
PS3537.A832 B5, **(v3)**
PS3537.A832.C55, **(v3)**
PS3537.A832.C66 1994, **(v3)**
PS3537.A832.D8, **(v3)**
PS3537.A832.F3, **(v3)**
PS3537.A832 F8, **(v3)**
PS3537.A832.L3, **(v3)**
PS3537.A832.P55, **(v3)**
PS3537.A832 S4, **(v3)**
PS3537.A832 S56, **(v3)**
PS3537.A832.Z4667 1979, **(v3)**
PS3537.A832.Z48 1991, **(v3)**
PS3537.A832.Z52 1969, **(v3)**
PS3537.A832.Z524 1980, **(v3)**
PS3537.A832.Z526, **(v3)**
Sartori, Giovanni. JF2051.S26, **(v7)**
Sartre, Jean Paul. B819.S32, **(v8)**
B2430.S32.E53, **(v8)**
B2430.S33.C3213 1992, **(v8)**
B2430.S33.V4713 1992, **(v8)**
BF531.S314, **(v2)**
N67.S243, **(v9)**
PQ2191.Z5.S32, **(v3)**
PQ2637.A82.D5, **(v3)**
PQ2637.A82.D513 1960, **(v3)**
PQ2637.A82.S32, **(v3)**
PQ2637.A82.Z513, **(v3)**
B2430.S33 C713 1991, **(v8)**
Sartwell, Crispin. PS366.A35.S27 1998, **(v3)**
Sarup, Madan. B831.2.S27 1993, **(v8)**
Sarver, Stephanie L. PS163.S27 1999, **(v3)**
Sarzano, Frances. NC242.T3 . S3, **(v9)**
Sass, Louis Arnorsson. RC514.S316 1992, **(v2)**
Sassen, Saskia. JC327.S27 1996, **(v7)**
Sassi, Maria Michela. B187.M25 S2713 2001, **(v8)**
Sassoon, Anne Showstack. JC265.G68 S26 2000, **(v7)**
JC265.G68.S27 1980, **(v7)**
Sassoon, Rosemary. Z40.S27 1999, **(v10)**
Sassoon, Siegfried. D640.S3415, **(v5)**
PR6037.A86.A17 1961, **(v3)**
PR6037.A86.M4 1937, **(v3)**
PR6037.A86.Z52 1945, **(v3)**
PR6037.A86.Z53, **(v3)**
Sassower, Raphael. N72.S6.S29 2000, **(v9)**
T14.S268 1997, **(v1)**
Sather, Leland B. Z2621.S28 1987, **(v10)**
Satie, Erik. ML410.S196.A4 1988, **(v9)**
Satin, Morton. TP371.8.S28 1996, **(v1)**
Satinover, Jeffrey. QP360.5.S28 2001, **(v1)**
Sato, Haruo. PL838.A86.A28 1996, **(v3)**
Sato, Ikuya. HV6491.J3.S29 1991, **(v6)**
Sato, Naoshi. RK361.S2813 2000, **(v2)**
Sato, Ryuzo. E183.8.J3.S2413 1994, **(v4)**
Satterlee, Herbert Livingston. CT275.M6.S32, **(v5)**
Sattler, Cheryl L. HV6626.2.U5.S37 2000, **(v6)**

Satz, Ronald N. E93.S27 2002, **(v4)**
Saudan, Michel. NA8460.S2813 1988, **(v9)**
Sauer, Carl Ortwin. E121.S26, **(v4)**
G80.S35, **(v6)**
GF37.S3 1963, **(v6)**
S421.S3 1969, **(v1)**
Sauer, Elizabeth. PR3562.S314 1996, **(v3)**
Sauer, Jonathan D. QK101.S28 1988, **(v1)**
Sauerlander, Willibald. NB543.S31413 1973, **(v9)**
Sauers, Michael P. Z711.45.S28 2001, **(v10)**
Saul, Nigel. DA235.S26 1997, **(v5)**
Saul, Norman E. E183.8.R9.S383 1996, **(v4)**
E183.8.S65.S274 1991, **(v4)**
Saulnier, Verdun L. PQ261.S3, **(v3)**
Saum, Lewis O. E169.1.S268 1990, **(v4)**
Saunders, Kevin W. KF2750.S38 1996, **(v7)**
Saunders, Malcolm George. VA573.S3, **(v10)**
Saunders, Max. PR6011.O53.Z83 1996, **(v3)**
Saunders, Richard H. N7593.1.S28 1987, **(v9)**
N8214.5.U6.S28 1988, **(v9)**
ND1329.S63.S28 1995, **(v9)**
Saunders, Robert M. E767.1.S28 1998, **(v4)**
Saunders, Robert. KF8745.C27.S28 1997, **(v7)**
Saunders, Thomas J. PN1993.5.G3.S34 1994, **(v3)**
Saunders, Trevor J. HV8523.S28 1991, **(v6)**
Saunders, Vivien. GV966.S385 2000, **(v6)**
Saunt, Claudio. E99.C9.S28 1999, **(v4)**
Saussy, Haun. PL2264.S28 1993, **(v3)**
Sauvy, Alfred. HB871.S25213 1970, **(v6)**
Savage, Barbara Dianne. E185.61.S32 1999, **(v4)**
Savage, Candace Sherk. QC971.S28 1994, **(v1)**
Savage, Charles M. HD31.S322 1990, **(v6)**
Savage, David G. KF8742.S285 1993, **(v7)**
Savage, David. DS559.5.S29 1999, **(v5)**
Savage, Henry L. PR2065.G31.S3, **(v3)**
Savage, Henry. F277.S28.S3 1954, **(v4)**
Savage, James D. Q180.U5.S28 1999, **(v1)**
Savage, Richard. PR3671.S2A17 1962, **(v3)**
Savage, Robert J. G. QL708.5.S28 1986, **(v1)**
Savage, Sean J. E807.S28 1991, **(v4)**
E814.S28 1997, **(v4)**
Savage, William W. E169.12.S293 1990, **(v4)**
Savage-Rumbaugh, E. Sue. QL737.P96.S25 1986, **(v1)**
Savala, Refugio. F1221.Y3.S28, **(v4)**
Savelle, Max. F1030.S28 1968, **(v4)**
Savicki, Victor. HV713.S32 2002, **(v6)**
Savigliano, Marta. GV1796.T3.S28 1995, **(v6)**
Saville, Julia F. PR4803.H44.Z825 2000, **(v3)**
Savin-Williams, Ritch C. HQ76.25.S39 2001, **(v6)**
Savishinsky, Joel S. HQ1063.2.U6.S39 2000, **(v6)**
Savitch, H. V. HN65.S32 1979, **(v6)**
Savitt, William. HC59.7.S283 1995, **(v6)**
Savoie, Donald J. JL75.S28 1999, **(v7)**
Sawada, Janine Anderson. BJ971.S5 S29 1993, **(v8)**
Sawada, Mitziko. F128.9.J3.S29 1996, **(v4)**
Saward, Michael. JC423.S2748 1998, **(v7)**
Sawhney, Pravin. DS480.853.D383 2001, **(v5)**
Sawin, Clark T. QP187.S219, **(v1)**
Sawislak, Karen. F548.42.S29 1995, **(v4)**
Sawrey, Robert D. E668.S28 1992, **(v4)**
Sawyer, Birgit. DL61.S29 1993, **(v5)**
Sawyer, Donald T. QD181.O1.S18 1991, **(v1)**
QD553.S32 1995, **(v1)**
Sawyer, Jeffrey K. DC123.3.S39 1990, **(v5)**
Sawyer, John F. A. BS1515.2.S35 1996, **(v8)**
Sawyer, Roger. HD6231.S27 1988, **(v6)**
Sawyer, Thomas E. DS135.R92.S28, **(v5)**
Sax, Boria. HV4943.G3 S38 2000, **(v6)**
Saxby, Graham. TA1540.S36 1988, **(v1)**
Saxe, Stephen O. Z249.S23 1992, **(v10)**
Saxenian, AnnaLee. HC107.C22.N677 1994, **(v6)**
Saxonberg, Steven. HX240.7.A6 S29, **(v6)**
Saxonhouse, Arlene W. JC75.D36.S39 1996, **(v7)**
Saxton, Alexander. E184.A1.S28 1990, **(v4)**
Say, M. G. TK2711.S3 1983, **(v1)**
Sayegh, Fayez A. DS38.S37, **(v5)**
Sayegh, Kamal S. HD7305.A3.S38 1987, **(v6)**
Sayer, Derek. DB2063.S28 1998, **(v5)**
Sayers, Anthony M. JL193.S29 1999, **(v7)**

Sayers, Dorothy L. PR6037.A95 C55, **(v3)**
  PR6037.A95 G3, **(v3)**
  PR6037.A95 L6, **(v3)**
  PR6037.A95 N5, **(v3)**
  PR6037.A95 U498, **(v3)**
  PR6037.A95 U52 1955, **(v3)**
  PR6037.A95 W5, **(v3)**
Sayers, Janet. BF109.D48.S29 1991, **(v2)**
Sayers, Raymond S. PQ9523.N4.S3, **(v3)**
Sayers, Sean. JC71.P6 S39 1999, **(v7)**
Sayigh, Yazid. DS119.7.S3738 1997, **(v5)**
Sayler, James. Z1249.P7.S29 1996, **(v10)**
Sayre, Gordon M. PS173.I6.S29 1997, **(v3)**
Sayre, Henry M. NX504.S29 1989, **(v9)**
Sayre, James Kedzie. RS164.S1, **(v2)**
Sayre, Kenneth M. B395.S28 1995, **(v8)**
  BD215.S28 1997, **(v8)**
Sayre, Shay. HF5415.2.S29 2001, **(v6)**
Saywell, John T. F1053.S29, **(v4)**
Sayyad, Parviz. PK6561.S4.A23 1993, **(v3)**
Sbordoni, Valerio. QL542.S2613 1985b, **(v1)**
Sbragia, Alberta M. HJ3833.S26 1996, **(v6)**
Sbrega, John J. Z6207.W8.S29 1989, **(v10)**
Scaglione, Aldo D. GT3520.S34 1991, **(v6)**
Scalapino, Robert A. DS35.S347, **(v5)**
Scales, James R. F694.S28 1982, **(v4)**
Scalia, Antonin. KF4552.S28 1997, **(v7)**
Scalia, Laura J. KF4541.S32 1999, **(v7)**
Scally, M. Anthony. Z8983.4.S27 1985, **(v10)**
Scaltsas, T. B434.S32 1994, **(v8)**
Scammell, Michael. PG3488.O4.Z873 1984, **(v3)**
Scanlan, Phillip M. GC1212.N5.S33 1998, **(v6)**
Scanlan, Thomas. PS367.S33 1999, **(v3)**
Scanlon, Jennifer. E175.45.S27 1996, **(v4)**
  HC110.C6 S27 1995, **(v6)**
Scanlon, Thomas. BJ1411.S36 1998, **(v8)**
Scannell, Paddy. PN1991.3.G7.S28 1991, **(v3)**
Scarborough, Dorothy. PS3537.C16 W5, **(v3)**
Scarce, Rik. HC110.E5.S385 1990, **(v6)**
Scarf, Maggie. RC488.5.S28 1995, **(v2)**
Scarisbrick, J. J. DA332.S25 1968b, **(v5)**
Scarre, Christopher. DG274.S28 1995, **(v5)**
Scarrow, Susan E. JN1121.S33 1996, **(v7)**
Scarry, Elaine. BJ1409.S35 1985, **(v8)**
Sceats, Sarah. PR888.F65, **(v3)**
Sceve, Maurice. PQ1705.S5.D4 1966, **(v3)**
Schaaf, Fred. QB721.S365 1997, **(v1)**
Schaaf, Gregory. E93.M83.S33 1990, **(v4)**
Schaaf, Larry J. TR57.S32 1992, **(v1)**
Schaafsma, David. LB1576.S316 1993, **(v7)**
Schabas, Ezra. ML422.M125 S3 1994, **(v9)**
  ML422.T46.S3 1989, **(v9)**
Schabas, Margaret. HB103.J5.S33 1990, **(v6)**
Schabas, William. K5104.S335 1996, **(v7)**
  K5302.S32 2000, **(v7)**
Schaberg, William H. Z8628.85.S33 1995, **(v10)**
Schachner, Nathan. E310.S4 1970, **(v4)**
Schachter, Hindy Lauer. JK1764.S35 1997, **(v7)**
Schacter, Bernice Zeldin. TP248.2.S33 1999, **(v1)**
Schacter, Daniel L. BF371.S29 1996, **(v2)**
  BF376.S33 2001, **(v2)**
Schaefer, Arlington C. E59.L4 S32, **(v4)**
Schaefer, Christina K. CS44.S33 1996, **(v5)**
  CS49.S28 1997, **(v5)**
Schaefer, Claudia. PQ7203.S44 1996, **(v3)**
Schaefer, Michael W. PS374.C53.S33 1997, **(v3)**
Schaefer, Vincent J. QC863.S346, **(v1)**
Schaefer, William D. LA227.3.S32 1990, **(v7)**
Schaefer-Simmern, Henry. N71.S35, **(v9)**
Schaeffer, Jean-Marie. BH151.S3313 2000, **(v8)**
Schaeffer, Robert K. JC421.S33 1997, **(v7)**
Schafer, Edward H. DS749.3.S3, **(v5)**
  DS793.H3.S3 1970, **(v5)**
Schafer, Judith Kelleher. KFL401.6.S55.S33 1994, **(v7)**
Schafer, Jurgen. PE891.S34 1989, **(v3)**
Schafer, R. Murray. ML3805.S3, **(v9)**
Schafer, Roy. BF173.R63.S3, **(v2)**
Schafer, William John. PR9624.3.S33 1998, **(v3)**
Schaffer, Frederic Charles. JQ3396.A91.S34 1998, **(v7)**

Schaffer, Ronald. E780.S34 1991, **(v4)**
Schaffer, Talia. PR468.A33.S33 2000, **(v3)**
Schaffner, Bradley L. Z2506.S3 1995, **(v10)**
Schaffner, Kenneth F. R852.S32 1993, **(v2)**
Schafran, Lynn Hecht. KF8700.S326 1989, **(v7)**
Schalk, David L. DT295.S354 1991, **(v5)**
Schalkoff, Robert J. QA76.87.S3 1997, **(v1)**
Schaller, George B. QL737.C214.S28 1993, **(v1)**
Schaller, Michael. E183.8.C5.S325, **(v4)**
  E183.8.J3.S29 1985, **(v4)**
  E745.M3.S26 1989, **(v4)**
  E876.S29 1992, **(v4)**
Schama, Simon. DA130.S44 2000, **(v5)**
  DC148.S43 1989, **(v5)**
  GF50.S33 1995, **(v6)**
  ND653.R4.S24 1999, **(v9)**
Schamschula, Eleonore. GR105.5.S337 1996, **(v6)**
Schandorff, Esther Dech. Z7799.3.S22 1995, **(v10)**
Schanke, Robert A. PN2287.L3.S34 1992, **(v3)**
Schantz, Mark S. BR560.P86, **(v8)**
Schapiro, Barbara A. PN56.P92.S33 1994, **(v3)**
Schapiro, Leonard Bertram. JC481.S35, **(v7)**
Schapiro, Meyer. N6447.S33, **(v9)**
  N6537.S338.A4 2000, **(v9)**
  N6853.P5.S33 2000, **(v9)**
  N7832.S26, **(v9)**
  NB175.S28 1977b, **(v9)**
Schapsmeier, Edward L. E748.D557.S33 1985, **(v4)**
  S441.S36, **(v1)**
Scharchburg, Richard P. TL140.D83.S33 1993, **(v1)**
Scharf, Lois. HD6095.S3, **(v6)**
Scharfstein, Ben-Ami. B105.I533 S33 1993, **(v8)**
  B799.S37 1998, **(v8)**
  JA79.S3166 1995, **(v7)**
Scharnhorst, Gary. PS1833.S38 2000, **(v3)**
  PS3054.S33 1993, **(v3)**
  Z8388.65.S33 1995, **(v10)**
  Z8393.S3 1988, **(v10)**
Scharper, Stephen B. BT695.5.S27 1997, **(v8)**
Schattschneider, E. E. JK271.S23, **(v7)**
  JK2265.S35, **(v7)**
Schatz, Thomas. PN1993.5.U6.H55 1990 vol. 6, **(v3)**
  PN1993.5.U65.S3 1988, **(v3)**
Schaub, Danielle. PR9199.3.G26.Z88 1998, **(v3)**
Schaub, Diana J. PQ2011.L6.S33 1995, **(v3)**
Schechner Genuth, Sara. QB721.S367 1997, **(v1)**
Schechter, Susan. HV6250.4.W65.S33 1982, **(v6)**
Schechtman, Marya. BC199.I4.S33 1996, **(v8)**
Scheck, Raffael. DD231.T5.S34 1998, **(v5)**
Scheckel, Susan. E98.P99.S34 1998, **(v4)**
Scheerenberger, R. C. RC570.5.U6.S34 1987, **(v2)**
Scheese, Don. PS163.S34 1996, **(v3)**
Scheff, Thomas J. BF531.S35 1997, **(v2)**
Scheffer, Mechthild. RX615.F55S3413 2001, **(v2)**
Scheffer, Robert P. SB601.S28 1997, **(v1)**
Scheffler, Israel. BD220.S2 1982, **(v8)**
  BD418.3.S34 1997, **(v8)**
  LA132.S328 1985, **(v7)**
  LB7.S28 1966, **(v7)**
Scheffler, Samuel. BJ1012.S34 1992, **(v8)**
Scheflin, Alan W. KF9672.S34 1989, **(v7)**
Schehr, Lawrence R. PQ629.S33 1995, **(v3)**
Scheiber, Harry N. HE395.O34S34 1987, **(v6)**
Scheick, William J. PR878.R7.S34 1994, **(v3)**
  PR888.E73.S34 1990, **(v3)**
  PS153.P87.S34 1992, **(v3)**
  PS186.S34 1998, **(v3)**
Schein, Edgar H. HD58.7.S33 1992, **(v6)**
Scheiner, Georganne. PN1995.9.Y6.S34 2000, **(v3)**
Schelde, Per. PN1995.9.S26.S26 1993, **(v3)**
Schele, Linda. F1435.3.K55.S34 1990, **(v4)**
  F1435.3.S34.S34 1997, **(v4)**
Scheler, Max. BD431.S2753, **(v8)**
  BF575.S9.S32 1970, **(v2)**
  BJ1535.A6.S33, **(v8)**
Schell, Herbert Samuel. F651.S29 1975, **(v4)**
Schell, Orville. DS711.S288, **(v5)**
Schell, William. F1386.9.A5, **(v4)**
Schellenberg, James A. HM136.S282 1996, **(v6)**
Schellenberg, T. R. CD950.S29 1988, **(v5)**
  CD950.S3, **(v5)**

Schelling, Thomas C. U104.S33, **(v10)**
Scheman, Naomi. HQ1190.S34 1993, **(v6)**
Schenck, Mary Jane Stearns. PQ207.S34 1987, **(v3)**
Schenk, Edward T. QL353.S34 1956, **(v1)**
Schenk, George. SB433.55.S3 1997, **(v1)**
Schenk, Ronald. BH301.P78.S34 1992, **(v8)**
Schenken, Suzanne O'Dea. HQ1236.5.U6.S32 1999, **(v6)**
Schenker, Alexander M. PG25.S34 1995, **(v3)**
Schenker, Heinrich. MT40.S2912, **(v9)**
  MT40.S29213, **(v9)**
  MT55.S2413 1987, **(v9)**
  MT130.B43.S313 1992, **(v9)**
Scherer, F. M. HF1412.S3 1994, **(v6)**
Scherer, Jacques. PN1620.A1.S34 1994, **(v3)**
Scherer, Jennifer M. R726.S336 1999, **(v2)**
Scherer, Margaret Roseman. NA310.S4, **(v9)**
Scherk, John. QA154.2.S28 2000, **(v1)**
Scherr, Barry P. PG3465.S34 1988, **(v3)**
Scherzer, Kenneth A. HN80.N5.S27 1992, **(v6)**
Scheub, Harold. BL2400.S24 2000, **(v8)**
  GR358.S34 1998, **(v6)**
  GR359.S34 1996, **(v6)**
Scheuerman, William E. HM24.S356 1994, **(v6)**
Scheurer, Thierry. QA76.9.S88.S29 1994, **(v1)**
Schevill, Margot. F1435.3.T48.S34 1993, **(v4)**
Schiavone, Aldo. DG311.S35 2000, **(v5)**
Schiavone, Giuseppe. JZ4838.S344 2001, **(v7)**
Schick, Allen. HJ2051.S33 1990, **(v6)**
  HJ2051.S3424 2000, **(v6)**
  HJ2053.A1.S35, **(v6)**
Schick, Frank Leopold. CD3029.82.S35 1989, **(v5)**
Schick, Kathy Diane. GN799.T6.S35 1993, **(v6)**
Schick, Richard P. HD8008.S36, **(v6)**
Schickel, Richard. PN2287.B683.S3 1991, **(v3)**
Schider, Fritz. NC760.S32 1957, **(v9)**
Schiebinger, Londa L. Q130.S32 1989, **(v1)**
  QP81.5.S35 1993, **(v1)**
Schieder, Theodor. DD404.S28 1983, **(v5)**
Schieffelin, Edward L. DU740.S34 1991, **(v5)**
Schier, Steven E. HJ2052.S337 1992, **(v6)**
Schierbeek, Abraham. QH31.L55.S3, **(v1)**
Schiesser, W. E. TA347.D45.S34 1993, **(v1)**
Schiff, Daniel. TA340.S35 1996, **(v1)**
Schiff, Jacob H. CT275.S3442.A2, **(v5)**
Schiff, James A. PS3571.P4.Z873 1998, **(v3)**
Schiff, Joel L. QA432.S33 1999, **(v1)**
Schiff, Michel. BF431.S285 1986, **(v2)**
Schiffer, Michael B. CC80.S33, **(v5)**
  CC80.S335 1996, **(v5)**
  PN1991.3.U6.S35 1991, **(v3)**
  TL220.S34 1994, **(v1)**
Schiffhorst, Gerald J. PR3581.S34 1990, **(v3)**
Schiffrin, André. Z280.S18 2001, **(v10)**
Schiffrin, Harold Z. DS777.S33, **(v5)**
Schild, Georg. E183.8.S65.S33 1995, **(v4)**
  HG255.S2885 1995, **(v6)**
Schilit, Howard Mark. HF5681.B2.S3243 1993, **(v6)**
Schilit, Rebecca. HV5825.S36 1991, **(v6)**
Schiller, Anne. BL2123.N43.S35 1997, **(v8)**
Schiller, Dan. P90.S348 1996, **(v3)**
Schiller, F. C. S. B821.S3 1912, **(v8)**
Schiller, Friedrich. PT2465.B43, **(v3)**
  PT2465.B80, **(v3)**
  PT2473.A4.P3 1962, **(v3)**
  PT2473.K3.H5 1983, **(v3)**
  PT2473.M3.P3 1961, **(v3)**
Schiller, Gertrud. N7830.S3513 1971b, **(v9)**
Schiller, Wendy J. JK1161.S35 2000, **(v7)**
Schilling, Bernard Nicholas. PR468.S6.S4 1946, **(v3)**
  PR3416.A23.S3, **(v3)**
Schilling, Mark. PN1993.5.J3.S37 1999, **(v3)**
Schilling, Warner Roller. UA23.S33, **(v10)**
Schilpp, Paul Arthur. B1649.R94.S35 1952, **(v8)**
  B3216.Z34 S3 1958, **(v8)**
Schimmel, Annemarie. BF1623.P9.E55 1992, **(v2)**
  PJ827.S3313 1985, **(v3)**
  PK6416.S3513 1992, **(v3)**
Schimmel, Julie. ND237.P472.S35 1994, **(v9)**
Schimmelman, Janice Gayle. Z5941.S43 1999, **(v10)**
Schindler, Anton. ML410.B4 S3333 1996, **(v9)**

Schindler, Esther. TK7882.S65.S29 1996, (v1)
Schindler, John R. D569.I69, (v5)
Schindler, R. M. NA737.S35.A4 2001, (v9)
Schipper, Kristofer Marinus. BL1920.S2813 1993, (v8)
Schipper, Mineke. PL8010.S37 1990, (v3)
    PN6519.A6.S28 1991, (v3)
Schippers, Arie. PJ5024.S3 1994, (v3)
Schiralli, Martin. B831.2.S35 1999, (v8)
Schirmeister, Pamela. PS1638.S26 1999, (v3)
Schirmer, Gregory A. PR8761.S35 1998, (v3)
Schirmer, Walter F. PR2036.S413, (v3)
Schisgal, Murray. PS3569.C5.L8 1965, (v3)
Schivelbusch, Wolfgang. DD866.S3513 1998, (v5)
Schlag, Pierre. KF380.S32 1996, (v7)
Schlagel, Richard H. Q124.95.S35 1985, (v1)
    Q174.8.S335 1995, (v1)
Schlam, Carl C. PA6217.S27 1992, (v3)
Schlebecker, John T. S411.S34 1989, (v1)
    S441.S43, (v1)
Schlechty, Phillip C. LA217.S284 1990, (v7)
    LB2822.82.S34 2001, (v7)
Schlee, Gunther. GN659.K4.S35 1989, (v6)
Schlegel, Alice. HQ796.S4139 1991, (v6)
Schlegel, Christian. TK5102.96.S35 1997, (v1)
Schlegel, Dorothea von. PT2503.S55.A6513 1989, (v3)
Schlegel, Friedrich von. D16.8.S28 1888, (v5)
    PA3093.S3413 2001, (v3)
    PN45.S247, (v3)
Schlegel, John Henry. KF380.S34 1995, (v7)
Schlegel, Kip. KF9236.5.S35 1990, (v7)
Schlegel, Stuart A. DS666.T6.S36 1998, (v5)
Schleichkorn, Jay. RJ496.C4S348 1993, (v2)
Schleifer, Ronald. PN56.M54.S35 2000, (v3)
    PR471.S335 2000, (v3)
Schlereth, Thomas J. B802.S34, (v8)
Schlesinger, Allen B. QH308.2.S35 1994, (v1)
Schlesinger, Arthur Meier. B851.S37, (v8)
    E161.S25 1968, (v4)
    E175.5.S38, (v4)
    E178.H7165, (v4)
    E178.S33, (v4)
    E183.8.V5 S3 1968, (v4)
    E184.A1 S34 1998, (v4)
    E381.S38, (v4)
    E806.S34, (v4)
    E841.S3, (v4)
    JC481.S38, (v7)
    JK511.S35 1989, (v7)
Schlichting, Carl. QH546.S36 1998, (v1)
Schlichting, Hermann. TL574.B6, (v1)
Schlichting, Kurt C. TF302.N7, (v1)
Schlick, Mary Dodds. E78.C64.S35 1994, (v4)
Schloezer, Boris de. ML410.S5988.S313 1987, (v9)
Schloss, Marc R. DT549.45.B39.S35 1988, (v5)
Schloss, Patrick J. Q180.55.M4.S35 1999, (v1)
Schlossberg, Herbert. DA550.S3 2000, (v5)
Schlosser, W. QB62.7.S3713 1991, (v1)
Schlossman, Beryl. PN56.M54.S36 1999, (v3)
Schluchter, Wolfgang. B3361.Z7.S336 1996, (v8)
Schlueter, June. PT2668.A5.Z877 1981, (v3)
Schlueter, Paul. PR111.S34 1988, (v3)
Schmadel, Lutz D. QB651.S35 1999, (v1)
Schmalleger, Frank. Z5703.4.C73.S36 1991, (v10)
Schmalz, Rosemary. QA99.S33 1993, (v1)
Schmandt-Besserat, Denise. CJ4867.S364 1996, (v5)
Schmeckebier, Laurence Eli. N6555.S35, (v9)
Schmeckebier, Laurence Frederick. Z1223.Z7.S3 1969, (v10)
Schmid, Carol L. HN603.S35, (v6)
    P119.32.U6.S35 2001, (v3)
Schmid, Walter T. B366.S35 1998, (v8)
Schmid, Wolfram George. SB413.H73.S36 1991, (v1)
Schmidgall, Gary. ML3858.S373 1990, (v9)
Schmidheiny, Stephan. HD75.6.S35 1992, (v6)
Schmidhuber de la Mora, Guillermo. PQ7296.J6.Z874 2000, (v3)
Schmidt, Albert J. Q11.P612 vol. 181, (v1)
Schmidt, Albert-Marie. PQ1173.S37, (v3)
Schmidt, Arno. PT2638.M453.A15 1994, (v3)

    TX820.S355 1990, (v1)
Schmidt, David A. QA76.7.S345 1994, (v1)
Schmidt, David D. JF493.U6.S36 1989, (v7)
Schmidt, Diane. QH303.6.D38 2002, (v1)
Schmidt, Elizabeth. DT2913.S55.S36 1992, (v5)
Schmidt, Frederick W. BV676.S34 1996, (v8)
Schmidt, Hans. F1927.S35, (v4)
    VE25.B88.S36 1987, (v10)
Schmidt, Helmut. DD260.85.S3613 1989, (v5)
Schmidt, Helmut. UA646.3.S353 1962, (v10)
Schmidt, Henry C. F1210.S35, (v4)
Schmidt, John R. F548.5.D48.S35 1989, (v4)
Schmidt, Leigh Eric. BV4647.L56, (v8)
    GT4986.A1.S35 1995, (v6)
Schmidt, Mary Gwynne. HV1454.2.U6.S36 1990, (v6)
Schmidt, Michael. PR502.S35 1999, (v3)
Schmidt, Peter R. DT443.3.H39.S24 1997, (v5)
Schmidt, Peter. PS3545.E6.Z86 1991, (v3)
Schmidt, Regin. E743.5.S355 2000, (v4)
Schmidt, Samuel. F1236.S3613 1991, (v4)
Schmidt, Warren H. HD62.15.S363 1993, (v6)
Schmidt, Winsor C. KF553.S36 1995, (v7)
Schmidt-Nielsen, Knut. QL799.S34 1984, (v1)
    QP26.S33.A3 1998, (v1)
Schmidt-Nowara, Christopher. HT1078.S38 1999, (v6)
Schmidtz, David. BJ1012.S346 1995, (v8)
    HB846.5.S36 1991, (v6)
Schmink, Marianne. GF532.A4.S36 1992, (v6)
Schmitt, Bernadotte Everly. D465.S33 1970, (v5)
    D511.S28 1918, (v5)
    D521.S367 1984, (v5)
Schmitt, Cannon. PR868.T3.S33 1997, (v3)
Schmitt, Frederick F. BD171.S325 1995, (v8)
    BD215.S34 1991, (v8)
Schmitt, Fritz. PT103.S39, (v3)
Schmitt, Hans A. DD256.5.S3356 1997, (v5)
Schmitt, Jean Claude. GR135.S3613 1998, (v6)
Schmitt, Peter J. E169.1.S343 1990, (v4)
Schmitz, David F. E183.8.I8.S36 1988, (v4)
Schnaars, Steven P. HF5415.13.S345 1991, (v6)
Schnabel, Artur. ML417.S36.A3 1972, (v9)
Schnackenburg, Rudolf. BS2615.3.S313 1980, (v8)
Schnaiberg, Allan. HC79.E5.S29, (v6)
Schnapp, Alain. CC100.S3613 1997, (v5)
Schnapp, Jeffrey T. PN3206.A13 1996, (v3)
Schneewind, J. B. BJ604.S5.S36, (v8)
Schneidau, Herbert N. PR478.M6.S36 1991, (v3)
Schneider, Anne L. H97.S33 1997, (v6)
    HV9104.S323 1990, (v6)
Schneider, Ben Ross. JL2449.E9.S36 1991, (v7)
Schneider, Cathy Lisa. HV4076.S26.S36 1995, (v6)
Schneider, Dorothy. E441.S36 2000, (v4)
    HD6095.S34 1993, (v6)
Schneider, Elisabeth Wintersteen. PR4480.K83.S4 1966, (v3)
Schneider, Elizabeth M. KF9322.S36 2000, (v7)
Schneider, Eric C. HV9306.B7.S36 1991, (v6)
Schneider, Georg. Z1001.S353, (v10)
Schneider, Hermann. PD71.P33 10, (v3)
Schneider, James C. E806.S35 1989, (v4)
Schneider, Mark R. F73.9.N4.S36 1997, (v4)
Schneider, Mark. HB615.S353 1995, (v6)
    HJ9145.S36 1989, (v6)
    LB1027.9.S32 2000, (v7)
Schneider, Mary Jane. E78.N75 S36 1994, (v4)
Schneider, Mary W. PR4024.S295 1989, (v3)
Schneider, Mary-Jane. RA425.S28 2000, (v2)
Schneider, Paul. F72.C3 S34 2000, (v4)
Schneider, Pierre. N6853.M33.S3513 1984, (v9)
Schneider, Robert Alan. DC801.T726.S36 1989, (v5)
Schneider, Ronald M. F2508.S33 1996, (v4)
    F2521.S38 1991, (v4)
    F2538.2.S37, (v4)
Schneider, Stephen Henry. GE149.S36 1997, (v6)
    QC981.8.G56.S3 1989, (v1)
Schneider, Steve. NC1766.U52.W3737 1988, (v9)
Schneider, Steven P. PS3501.M6.Z85 1994, (v3)
Schneider-Hector, Dietmar. F802.W45.S35 1993, (v4)
Schneiderman, Rose. HD6079.S3, (v6)

Schneiders, Robert Kelley. GE155.M85.S36 1999, (v6)
Schneier, Bruce. QA76.9.A25, (v1)
Schneier, Marc. E185.97.K5.S595 1999, (v4)
Schneirov, Matthew. PN4877.S36 1994, (v3)
Schneirov, Richard. F548.42.S35 1998, (v4)
Schnell, Donald E. QK917.S36, (v1)
Schnell, Izhak. HD2346.I75.S56 1995, (v6)
Schneller, Robert John. E467.1.D13.S36 1996, (v4)
Schnitzler, Arthur. PT2638.N5.A2 1982, (v3)
    PT2638.N5 V5, (v3)
    PT2638.N5.W413 1992, (v3)
Schobert, Harold H. TP318.S37 1990, (v1)
Schobinger, Juan. E59.P42.S3613 2000, (v4)
Schoch, Richard W. PR3106.S36 1998, (v3)
Schodek, Daniel L. TA23.S36 1987, (v1)
Schodt, David W. F3738.S34 1987, (v4)
Schoeck, Richard J. PR1924.S37, (v3)
Schoeman, Elna. Z3608.A5.S35 1996, (v10)
Schoenbaum, David. E183.8.I7.S34 1993, (v4)
Schoenbaum, S. PR2717.S35 1970, (v3)
    PR2894.S3 1991, (v3)
    PR2894.S33 1977, (v3)
    PR2933.F64.S3, (v3)
Schoenbaum, Thomas J. E748.R94.S36 1988, (v4)
Schoenberg, Arnold. ML60.S374, (v9)
    MT40.S33.F8 1967b, (v9)
    MT50.S37413 1978b, (v9)
    MT50.S37417 1969, (v9)
Schoenberg, B. Mark. BF692.5.S36 1993, (v2)
Schoenberger, Karl. HD9940.U6.L457 2000, (v6)
Schoenbrod, David. KF5411.S36 1993, (v7)
Schoenbrun, David Lee. DT16.B2.S35 1998, (v5)
Schoenewolf, Gerald. BF692.15.S36 1989, (v2)
Schoenfeldt, Michael Carl. PR428.B63.S36 1999, (v3)
    PR3508.S36 1991, (v3)
Schofield, Janet Ward. LB1028.43.S34 1995, (v7)
Schofield, Malcolm. B205.Z7.S36, (v8)
Schofield, Robert E. BX9869.P8.S36 1997, (v8)
Schofield, Victoria. DS485.K25.S38 1996, (v5)
Schofield, William Henry. PR149.C5.S4 1970, (v3)
Scholem, Gershom Gerhard. BM526.S36413 1991, (v8)
    BM723.S35 1961, (v8)
    DS135.G33.S297, (v5)
Scholes, R. J. QH195.S6.S38 1993, (v1)
Scholes, Robert E. PN94.S25 1985, (v3)
    PN98.S46.S3 1982, (v3)
    PR830.S35.S3, (v3)
    Z1003.S3947 1999, (v10)
Scholte, Jan Aart. JZ1318.S36 2000, (v7)
Scholten, Joseph B. DF261.A2.S36 2000, (v5)
Scholz, Piotr O. HQ449.S364 2000, (v6)
Scholz, Sally J. B2137.S34 2001, (v8)
    B2430.B344 S36 2000, (v8)
Schom, Alan. DA88.5 1805.S36 1990, (v5)
    DC239.S36 1992, (v5)
    PQ2528.S36 1988, (v3)
Schonberg, Harold C. ML390.S393 1997, (v9)
    ML397.S3 1994, (v9)
    ML402.S387.G7, (v9)
Schonberg, Marcia. F491.3.S36 2000, (v4)
Schonberger, Richard. HD58.9.S36 1990, (v6)
Schonfeld, Martin. B2798.S315 2000, (v8)
Schoolcraft, Henry Rowe. E98.F6 S3 1999, (v4)
Schoolfield, George C. PD25.N6 no. 29, (v3)
Schoonover, Thomas David. F1436.8.G3.S3 1998, (v4)
    F1436.8.U6.S36 1991, (v4)
Schopenhauer, Arthur. B3114.E5.P3, (v8)
    B3118.E5.S38 1960, (v8)
Schopp, Claude. PQ2230.S3613 1988, (v3)
Schopp, Robert F. KF9246.S36 1998, (v7)
Schoppa, Leonard J. LA1311.82.S33 1993, (v7)
Schoppa, R. Keith. DS755.S294 2002, (v5)
    DS755.S635 2000, (v5)
    DS777.15.S53.S36 1995, (v5)
    DS793.H6443525.S36 1989, (v5)
Schor, Edith. PS3555.L625.Z876 1993, (v3)
Schor, Hilary Margo. PR4711.S36 1992, (v3)
Schor, Juliet. HD4904.6.S36 1991, (v6)

Schorer, Mark. PR4146.S4, (v3)
PS3537.C62 H4, (v3)
PS3537.C63 H6, (v3)
PS3537.C63 S8, (v3)
Schork, R. J. PR6019.O9.Z7478 1997, (v3)
PR6019.O9.Z79436 1998, (v3)
Schorr, Lisbeth B. HV91.S2945 1997, (v6)
Schorr, Thelma M. RT4.S375 1999, (v2)
Schorske, Carl E. DB851.S42 1979, (v5)
Schott, John R. G70.4.S36 1997, (v6)
Schott, Thomas Edwin. E467.1.S85.S36 1988, (v4)
Schottroff, Luise. BR195.W6.S3613 1995, (v8)
Schoub, B. D. RC607.A26.S3738 1999, (v2)
Schouls, Peter A. B1875.S368 2000, (v8)
Schoultz, Lars. F1418.S388 1998, (v4)
Schouvaloff, Alexander. PN2096.B337.S36 1991, (v3)
Schover, Leslie R. RC108.S38 1988, (v2)
Schrader, Barbel. NX550.A1.S2913 1988, (v9)
Schrader, Richard J. Z8563.5.S37 1998, (v10)
Schraeder, Peter J. DT30.5.S44 2000, (v5)
Schrag, Calvin O. B819.S37, (v8)
BD438.5.S37 1997, (v8)
BT103.S37 2002, (v8)
Schrag, Francis. LB1590.3.S36 1988, (v7)
Schrag, Philip G. KF4836.S37 2000, (v7)
Schrager, Samuel Alan. KF8915.S263 1999, (v7)
Schram, Stuart R. DS778.M3.S3 1967, (v5)
Schrank, Bernice. PR6029.C33.Z83 1996, (v3)
Schrank, Robert. HD8073.S34.A37, (v6)
HX84.S42.A3 1998, (v6)
Schratz, Paul R. V63.S38.A3 1988, (v10)
Schrecker, Ellen. E743.5.S37 1998, (v4)
Schrecker, John E. DS740.2.S33 1991, (v5)
Schreiber, Mae N. Z7164.C8.S33 1997, (v10)
Schreiber, William F. TA1632.S33 1993, (v1)
Schreiber, William Ildephonse. F500.M45.S3, (v4)
Schreiner, Claus. ML3575.B7.S313 1993, (v9)
Schreiner, Olive. PR9369.2.S37.Z48 1988, (v3)
Schrempp, Gregory Allen. BD511.S37 1992, (v8)
Schriber, Mary Suzanne. PS366.T73.S37 1997, (v3)
Schrijvers, Peter. D769.2.S34 1998, (v5)
Schroder, Ulrich E. QC173.65.S35 1990, (v1)
Schrodinger, Erwin. B118.S36, (v8)
QB500.S36, (v1)
QC311.S38 1952, (v1)
QH331.S3557, (v1)
Schroedel, Jean Reith. KF481.S37 2000, (v7)
Schroeder, Alan. JF2112.D43, (v7)
Schroeder, Gerald L. BS650.S35 1997, (v8)
Schroeder, John H. E182.P469 2001, (v4)
E415.2.S3, (v4)
Schroeder, M. R. QA241.S318 1997, (v1)
QC174.17.S9.S38 1990, (v1)
Schroeder, Paul W. D295.T73 1994, (v5)
D742.J3.S38, (v5)
Schroeder, Steven H. PR6045.O72.Z87474 1996, (v3)
Schroeder, Susan. F1219.76.P75.S37 1991, (v4)
Schroeder, Walter A. F472.S33 S37 2002, (v4)
Schubert, Frank N. F674.F7.S35 1993, (v4)
U52.O5 1995, (v10)
Schubert, Franz. ML54.6.S39.G515 1996, (v9)
ML410.S3.A413 1970b, (v9)
Schubert, Gerald. QE509.4.S38 2001, (v1)
Schubert, Glendon A. JA74.5.S356 1989, (v7)
Schubnell, Matthias. PS3563.O47.Z87 1985, (v3)
Schuchard, Ronald. PS3509.L43.Z86352 1999, (v3)
Schuck, Peter H. JV6465.S37 1998, (v7)
Schueler, G. F. B105.I56 S37 1995, (v8)
Schueller, Malini Johar. PS157.S38 1998, (v3)
Schueller, Wolfgang. TA658.S15 1996, (v1)
Schuetz, Janice E. KF220.S38 1988, (v7)
KF220.S383 1994, (v7)
Schuh, Randall T. QL521.S38 1995, (v1)
Schulberg, Budd Wilson. PS3537.C7114.Z5, (v3)
PS3537.C7114.D5, (v3)
PS3537.C7114 D5, (v3)
PS3537.C7114 S6, (v3)
PS3537.C7114 W3, (v3)
PS3537.C7114.W45 1941, (v3)
Schulenberg, David. ML193.S38 2001, (v9)
MT145.B14.S415 1992, (v9)

Schuler, Friedrich Engelbert. F1234.S378 1998, (v4)
Schulkin, Jay. BF311.S385 2000, (v2)
QP356.45.S38 1999, (v1)
Schull, William J. RA648.3.S38 1995, (v2)
Schuller, Gunther. ML3506.S35 1986, (v9)
ML3506.S36 1968 vol. 2, (v9)
MT85.S46 1997, (v9)
MT420.S35 1991, (v9)
Schulman, Bruce J. HC107.A13.S38 1991, (v6)
Schulte Nordholt, J. W. E175.9.S3613 1995, (v4)
E269.D88.S3813 1982, (v4)
Schulte, Regina. HV6979.O24.S3813 1994, (v6)
Schulten, Susan. G96.S36 2001, (v6)
Schulte-Sasse, Linda. PN1995.9.N36.S38 1996, (v3)
Schultheis, Eugenia Barnett. DS796.H25 S38 2000, (v5)
Schultz, Charles R. F865.S38 1999, (v4)
Schultz, David A. KF562.S385 1992, (v7)
KF8745.S33.S38 1996, (v7)
Schultz, Elizabeth A. PS2384.M62.S36 1995, (v3)
Schultz, Jack M. E99.S28.S37 1999, (v4)
Schultz, Margie. PN2287.D85.S38 1991, (v3)
Schultz, Nancy Lusignan. F74.C4 S35 2000, (v4)
Schultz, Theodore William. HB501.5.S3, (v6)
HC79.P6.S335 1993, (v6)
Schultze, Charles L. HB172.5.S365 1992, (v6)
Schultze, Quentin J. BV656.3.S385 1991, (v4)
Schulz, Ann. UA853.I7.S34 1989, (v10)
Schulz, Donald E. F1508.3.S34 1994, (v4)
Schulz, Dorothy Moses. HV8023.S28 1995, (v6)
Schulz, James H. HQ1064.A88.S38 1990, (v6)
Schulz, Max F. PR4484.S4, (v3)
PS3552.A75.Z88 1990, (v3)
Schulze, Franz. NA737.J6.S38 1994, (v9)
NA1088.M65.S38 1985, (v9)
Schulze, Hagen. DD204.S3413 1990, (v5)
JC131.S3813 1996, (v7)
Schulze, Kirsten E. DS119.8.L4.S38 1998, (v5)
Schulzinger, Robert D. E744.S399 1998, (v4)
E744.S3995 1984, (v4)
Schum, David A. BC171.S38 1994, (v8)
Schumacher, E. F. HB171.S384 1999, (v6)
Schumacher, John N. BX1656.S38, (v8)
Schumacher, Michael. ML420.O29.S43 1996, (v9)
Schumacher, Thomas L. NA1123.T4.S37 1991, (v9)
Schumaker, Paul. JS992.L8.S38 1991, (v7)
Schumann, Robert. ML410.S4 A124 1983, (v9)
Schumann, Willy. DD247.S384.A3 1991, (v5)
Schumm, Sandra J. PQ6055.S27 1999, (v3)
Schumpeter, Elizabeth Boody. HC462.S36, (v6)
Schumpeter, Joseph Alois. HB119.S35.S36 1990, (v6)
HB171.S385 1969, (v6)
HB175.S462, (v6)
Schuon, Frithjof. BD112.S22 1990, (v8)
Schuparra, Kurt. F866.2.S39 1998, (v4)
Schur, Edwin M. HQ1206.S443 1983, (v6)
Schürer, Emil. DS122.S422 1973, (v5)
Schurmann, Franz. DS777.55.S35 1968, (v5)
Schusky, Ernest Lester. GN407.4.S38 1989, (v6)
Schussler Fiorenza, Elisabeth. BR129.F56 1983, (v8)
BT303.2.S33 2000, (v8)
Schuster, Joseph F. KF4770.S38 1992, (v7)
Schutz, Alfred. B105.R3S34 1970, (v8)
B829.5.S38 1970, (v8)
B945.S354.A4 1989, (v8)
H61.S44, (v6)
Schutz, Bernard F. QC173.6.S38 1985, (v1)
Schutz, Heinrich. ML410.S35.A4 1990, (v9)
Schuursma, Ann Briegleb. ML128.E8.S4 1992, (v9)
Schwaab, Edleff H. DD247.H5.S347 1992, (v5)
Schwab, Gabriele. PR888.M63.S39 1994, (v3)
Schwab, James. GE197.S3 1994, (v6)
Schwab, Orrin. DS558.S39 1998, (v5)
Schwab, Peter. HC800.S389 2001, (v6)
HF1500.5.U5.S38 1999, (v6)
Schwab, Raymond. CB253.S3813 1984, (v5)
Schwabacher, Martin. F606.3.S39 1999, (v4)
Schwaber, Paul. PR6019.O9.U6916 1999, (v3)
Schwabl, Franz. QC174.12.S38713 1995, (v1)
Schwager, Edith. R119.S38 1991, (v2)

Schwandt, Thomas A. H61.S4435 2001, (v6)
Schwantes, Carlos A. F593.S339 1999, (v4)
F851.S34 1989, (v4)
Schwarcz, Vera. DS113.S377 1998, (v5)
DS778.C4966.S38 1992, (v5)
Schwartz, Alvin. PZ8.1.S399Sc 1981, (v3)
Schwartz, Arthur. HV43.S34, (v6)
Schwartz, Barry. E457.2.S38 2000, (v4)
GN365.9.S38 1986, (v6)
Schwartz, Barry. HC110.C6.S35 1994, (v6)
Schwartz, Barth David. PN1998.3.P367.S39 1992, (v3)
Schwartz, Benjamin Isadore. DS774.S37, (v5)
Schwartz, Bernard. JK31.S35, (v7)
KF228.B34.S39 1988, (v7)
KF352.S36 1993, (v7)
KF353.S27 1985, (v7)
KF4550.S335 1990, (v7)
KF4774.S34 1992, (v7)
KF8742.S29 1990, (v7)
KF8742.S323 1996, (v7)
KF8742.S39 1993, (v7)
KF8745.W3.S37 1983, (v7)
Schwartz, David B. HV1568.S38 1997, (v6)
Schwartz, David N. UA646.3.S38 1983, (v10)
Schwartz, Delmore. PS3537.C79.G4, (v3)
PS3537.C79.I5 1938, (v3)
PS3537.C79 S75, (v3)
PS3537.C79.S8, (v3)
PS3537.C79.V3, (v3)
PS3537.C79 W6, (v3)
Schwartz, E. A. E83.84.S39 1997, (v4)
Schwartz, Elliott. MT6.S354.M9, (v9)
Schwartz, Frank J. JQ1669.P7.S39 1998, (v7)
Schwartz, Herman. KF8700.S35 1988, (v7)
KJC5456.S39 2000, (v7)
Schwartz, Ira M. HV741.S367 1999, (v6)
Schwartz, Ira M. HV9104.S3286 1989, (v6)
Schwartz, Israel Jacob. PJ5129.S298.K413 1990, (v3)
Schwartz, Jeffrey H. QH366.2.S386 1999, (v1)
Schwartz, Joel. HV4044.S33 2000, (v6)
Schwartz, Joseph M. HX73.S385 1995, (v6)
Schwartz, Joseph. BF173.S387 1999, (v2)
Schwartz, Karen. HC60.5.S39 1991, (v6)
Schwartz, Lita Linzer. HQ814.S38 1997, (v6)
Schwartz, Marie Jenkins. E443.S39 2000, (v4)
Schwartz, Marilyn. PE1460.S474 1995, (v3)
Schwartz, Marvin. HC110.P63.S34 1988, (v6)
Schwartz, Mel M. TS227.2.S38, (v1)
Schwartz, Norman B. F1465.1.P47.S37 1990, (v4)
Schwartz, Peter. HD60.S39 1999, (v6)
Schwartz, Randal L. QA76.73.P22S37 2001, (v1)
Schwartz, Richard Alan. D843.S3365 1997, (v5)
DS79.72.S39 1998, (v5)
E169.12.S39 1997, (v4)
PN1998.3.A455.S38 2000, (v3)
Schwartz, Richard B. DA682.S38 1983, (v5)
Schwartz, Richard S. RK501.S436 1996, (v2)
Schwartz, Robert. B1339.S38 1994, (v8)
Schwartz, Ronald. PN1993.5.S7.S29 1991, (v3)
PN1995.9.L37.S38 1997, (v3)
PQ6144.S38 1976, (v3)
Schwartz, Rosalie. F1785.S38 1989, (v4)
Schwartz, Sally. F152.S34 1988, (v4)
Schwartz, Seymour I. E161.3.S39 2000, (v4)
F1528.S4 1992, (v4)
Schwartz, Stuart B. HT1126.S39 1992, (v6)
Schwartz, Susan E. PN6084.C556.S39 1998, (v3)
Schwartz, Thomas Alan. E183.8.G3.S513 1991, (v4)
Schwartz, Vanessa R. DC715.S39 1998, (v5)
Schwartz, William A. U264.S37 1990, (v10)
Schwartzkopf, William. KF902.S39 1992, (v7)
Schwartzman, David. QH343.4.S36 1999, (v1)
U263.S378 1988, (v10)
Schwartzman, Steven. QA5.S375 1994, (v1)
Schwartz-Nobel, Loretta. HC110.P6 S327 2002, (v6)
Schwarz, Arturo. ND553.D774.S3, (v9)
Schwarz, Balduin V. B29.S43, (v8)
Schwarz, Boris. ML300.5.S37 1983, (v9)
Schwarz, Cindy. QC793.24.S34 1992, (v1)

Schwarz, Daniel R. PN53.S38 1997, (v3)
PN56.H55.S35 1999, (v3)
PN81.S245 1991, (v3)
PR6019.O9.U692 1987, (v3)
PS3537.T4753.Z7647 1993, (v3)
Schwarz, Henry. DS428.S93 1997, (v5)
Schwarz, John E. HD8072.5.S39 1997, (v6)
Schwarz, Jordan A. E748.B32.S3, (v4)
E806.S358 1993, (v4)
Schwarz, Leo W. DS113.S38 1956, (v5)
Schwarz, Philip J. E445.V8.S38 2001, (v4)
KFV2801.6.S55.S386 1996, (v7)
KFV2801.6.S55.S39 1988, (v7)
Schwarz, Roberto. F2510.S39 1992, (v4)
Schwarz, Roger M. HD30.3.S373 2002, (v6)
Schwarz, Ted. PN4736.S38 1996, (v3)
Schwarz, Urs. E745.S35, (v4)
Schwarzbach, F. S. PR4584.S3, (v3)
Schwarzbach, Martin. QE22.W26.S3913 1986, (v1)
Schwarzer, Mitchell. NA2599.5.S38 1995, (v9)
Schwarzfuchs, Simon. BM652.S26 1993, (v8)
DS135.F82.S38, (v5)
Schwarzlose, Richard Allen. Z6951.S35 1987, (v10)
Schwarzmantel, J. J. JA83.S367 1998, (v7)
Schwebel, Andrew I. RC488.5.S384 1994, (v2)
Schweber, S. S. QC774.O56.S32 2000, (v1)
Schweickart, David. HB90.S379 1993, (v6)
Schweikart, Larry. HG2604.S39 1987, (v6)
Schweitzer, Albert. B3329.S52.E5 1949, (v8)
B3329.S52.E5 1965, (v8)
CT1098.S45.A282 1949, (v5)
CT1098.S45.A33 1949, (v5)
R722.32.S35.A4 1996, (v2)
Schweitzer, Glenn E. HV6431.S375 1998, (v6)
Schweizer, Harold. PN56.S742.S38 1996, (v3)
Schweizer, Peter. E183.8.S65.S34 1994, (v4)
Schwenger, Peter. PN3331.S444 1999, (v3)
Schweninger, Loren. E185.8.S39 1990, (v4)
Schwerdt, Lisa M. PR6017.S5.Z84 1989, (v3)
Schwerin, Alan. B1499.C38.S38 1989, (v8)
Schwerin, Jules Victor. ML420.J17.S4 1992, (v9)
Schwiebert, John E. PS3241.S39 1992, (v3)
Schwiebert, Valerie L. Z7164.O4.S38 1995, (v10)
Schwieder, Dorothy. F621.S38 1996, (v4)
F621.3.S39 2002, (v4)
F621.5.S38, (v4)
Schwieder, Elmer. BX8129.A6 S38, (v8)
Schwinger, Julian Seymour. QC173.59.S65.S39 1986, (v1)
Schwoerer, Lois G. DA452.S3, (v5)
Schyns, Jos. PL2422.S3 1965, (v3)
Sciabarra, Chris Matthew. B945.R234.S35 1995, (v8)
HX806.S34 1995, (v6)
Scigaj, Leonard M. PS310.N3.S38 1999, (v3)
Sclar, Elliott. HD3888.S35 2000, (v6)
Sclater, Neil. TJ181.S28 2001, (v1)
TK3305.S38 1991, (v1)
Sclove, Richard. JA80.S58 1995, (v7)
Scobie, Alexander. NA1068.5.N37.S26 1990, (v9)
Scobie, Ingrid Winther. E748.D677.S36 1992, (v4)
Scobie, James R. F2808.S42 1971, (v4)
HN270.B8.S3, (v6)
HN270.C67.S36 1988, (v6)
Scobie, Stephen. PN53.S385 1997, (v3)
Scoble, M. J. QL542.S39 1992, (v1)
Scoglio, Stefano. KF1262.S36 1998, (v7)
Scolnicov, Hanna. PN1590.W64.S36 1994, (v3)
Sconce, Jeffrey. P96.T42.S37 2000, (v3)
Scorer, R. S. QC921.S357, (v1)
Scott, A. C. DS721.S37, (v5)
PL2658.E5.S34, (v3)
Scott, Alan. HN373.5.S37 1990, (v6)
Scott, Allan W. TK7876.S36 1993, (v1)
Scott, Alwyn. QP411.S46 1995, (v1)
Scott, Andrew. QH501.S37 1988, (v1)
Scott, Anne Firor. HQ1412.S36 1984, (v6)
HQ1418.S38, (v6)
HQ1904.S28 1991, (v6)
Scott, Bonnie Kime. PR888.M63.S43 1995, (v3)
Scott, Charles E. BJ37.S35 1990, (v8)
BJ1031.S368 1996, (v8)

Scott, Clive. PC2511.S34 1998, (v3)
PQ471.F74.S33 1993, (v3)
Scott, Craig. QC395.2.S36 1998, (v1)
Scott, Daryl Michael. E185.625.S3 1997, (v4)
Scott, David Logan. HG4513.S37 1997, (v6)
Scott, Dominic. B398.L3 S36 1995, (v8)
Scott, Douglas D. E83.876.S28 1998, (v4)
Scott, Evelyn. PS3537.C89 E8, (v3)
PS3537.C89 N37 1977, (v3)
PS3537.C89 W3, (v3)
Scott, Franklin Daniel. DL5.S44, (v5)
DL59.S35 1950, (v5)
DL648.S36 1977, (v5)
Scott, G. E. BJ1031.S37 1990, (v8)
Scott, Geoffrey A. J. QK201.S25 1995, (v1)
Scott, Geoffrey. NA2500.S4 1924, (v9)
Scott, George Richard. GN209.S33 1997, (v6)
Scott, George Ryley. HV8613.S43, (v6)
Scott, George. JX1975.S36 1974, (v7)
Scott, Grant F. PR4838.A75.S36 1994, (v3)
Scott, H. M. DA510.S26 1990, (v5)
Scott, Harriet Fast. UA770.S355 1988, (v10)
Scott, Ian. DS796.H757.S43 1989, (v5)
Scott, James A. QL548.S381986, (v1)
Scott, James C. HD1513.A755.S36, (v6)
HM278.S37 1990, (v6)
Scott, Joan Wallach. HQ1616.S38 1996, (v6)
Scott, John Beldon. ND2757.R6.S38 1991, (v9)
Scott, John F. N6502.S367 1999, (v9)
Scott, John S. TA9.S35 1993, (v1)
Scott, John. DK781.M3 S35 1989, (v5)
Scott, Jonathan. DA375.S39 2000, (v5)
DA407.S6.S43 1988, (v5)
ND623.R7.S45 1995, (v9)
Scott, Julian. RJ53.A27S36 1999, (v2)
Scott, Katie. NK2049.P37.S33 1995, (v9)
Scott, L. V. UB345.G7.S28 1993, (v10)
Scott, Lawrence P. UG834.A37.S36 1994, (v10)
Scott, Mary Jane W. PR3733.S37 1988, (v3)
Scott, Mel. NA9127.S3.S3, (v9)
Scott, Michael. ML420.C18.S35 1992, (v9)
ML420.C259.S3 1988, (v9)
PR2880.A1.S34 1989, (v3)
Scott, Mona L. Z696.D7 S36 1998, (v10)
Scott, Paul. PR6069.C596.B4, (v3)
PR6069.C596.B5, (v3)
PR6069.C596.L6, (v3)
PR6069.C596.M3, (v3)
PR6069 C596 R3X, (v3)
Scott, Peter. BT738.S394 1994, (v8)
Scott, Phil. TL515.S412 1995, (v1)
Scott, Phillip A. PR888.M42.S26 1992, (v3)
Scott, Robert Gillam. NC703.S35, (v9)
Scott, Robert Lee. DS777.53.S38 1959, (v5)
Scott, Ronald M. RC967.S36 1995, (v2)
Scott, Ronald McLean. RC967.S356 1997, (v2)
Scott, Samuel F. UA702.S386 1998, (v10)
Scott, Shaunna L. HN79.K42.H377 1995, (v6)
Scott, Susan. RA650.6.A1.S36 2001, (v2)
Scott, Tom. BX4946.M8.S35 1989, (v8)
Scott, Virginia. PQ1852.S44 2000, (v3)
Scott, W. Richard. HM131.S3845 1995, (v6)
Scott, Walter. DC61.S43 1996, (v5)
PR5300.F12, (v3)
PR5305.E94, (v3)
PR5317.A5, (v3)
PR5317.B53 1993, (v3)
PR5317.G8, (v3)
PR5317.H4, (v3)
PR5319.A2.A44 1993, (v3)
PR5320.O4 1966, (v3)
PR5320.O4 1993, (v3)
PR5321.A1 1944, (v3)
PR5322.W4 1981, (v3)
PR5322.W4 vol. 17, (v3)
PR5334.A2 1950, (v3)
Scott, William B. NX511.N4.S38 1999, (v9)
Scott, William E. E842.9.S37 1999, (v4)
Scott, William R. DT387.8.S37 1992, (v5)
Scott, William T. QC518.S425, (v1)
Scoyen, Eivind T. F832.Z8S3, (v4)

Scragg, Leah. PR2997.P6.S37 1992, (v3)
Scranton, Margaret E. E183.8.P2.S37 1991, (v4)
Scranton, Robert Lorentz. NA270.S3, (v9)
Screech, M. A. PQ1694.S36, (v3)
Scribner, Charles. N6923.B5.S37 1991, (v9)
Z473.S39 1990, (v10)
Scribner, Robert W. BR307.S464 1994, (v8)
Scriven, Charles. BR115.C8.S37 1988, (v8)
Scriven, Michael. B2430.S34.S369 1999, (v8)
PQ2627.I95.Z87 1988, (v3)
Scriven, Paul. HV5825.S393 1992, (v6)
Scroggins, Daniel C. Z1049.A1.S38 1997, (v10)
Scruton, Roger. B791.S29 2001, (v8)
NA2500.S43, (v9)
Scudder, Townsend. PR4419.C5.S3, (v3)
Scudery, Madeleine de. PQ1922.A8 1973, (v3)
PQ1922.A1 1998, (v3)
Scull, Andrew T. RC450.G7.S284 1996, (v2)
Scullard, H. H. DG231.S35 1969, (v5)
DG250.S3, (v5)
DG254.S35 1970, (v5)
Scully, Crispian. RC815.S452 1999, (v2)
Scully, Gerald W. HD87.S38 1992, (v6)
Scully, Timothy. JL2698.A1.S38 1992, (v7)
Scully, Vincent Joseph. NA275.S3 1969, (v9)
NA680.S395, (v9)
NA705.S36, (v9)
NA737.K32.S38, (v9)
NA737.W7.S3, (v9)
NA7207.S38 1971, (v9)
Scura, Dorothy McInnis. Z8447.S38, (v10)
Seaborg, Glenn Theodore. QD172.T7.S38, (v1)
Seabrook, Charles. F292.C94S43 2002, (v4)
Seabrook, Jeremy. K5189.S43 2000, (v7)
Seabury, Caroline. F213.S42 1991, (v4)
Seabury, Paul. U21.2.S43 1989, (v10)
Seager, Joni. HC79.E5.S36 1993, (v6)
Seager, Richard Hughes. BL21.W8.S43 1995, (v8)
Seager, Robin. DG254.2.S4, (v5)
Seager, William. B105.C477 S42 1992, (v8)
Seagrave, Sterling. DS882.7.S29 1999, (v5)
Sealander, Judith. HV91.S3 1997, (v6)
Seale, Bobby. E185.615.S37, (v4)
Seale, Patrick. DS98.2.S4 1987, (v5)
Seale, William. F204.W5.S43 1986, (v4)
Sealey, Raphael. DF214.S45, (v5)
DF277.S315 1993, (v5)
KL4134 .S42 1990, (v7)
KL4345.S43 1994, (v7)
Sealock, Richard Burl. Z6824.S4 1982, (v10)
Sealts, Merton M. PS1615.A84.S43 1992, (v3)
Seaman, Ann Rowe. BV3785.S84.S43 1999, (v8)
Seaman, L. C. B. DA566.S4, (v5)
Searing, Donald. JN677.S43 1994, (v7)
Searing, Susan E. Z7961.S42 1985, (v10)
Searle, Eleanor. DC611.N856.S43 1988, (v5)
Searle, G. R. DA560.S39 1993, (v5)
DA570.S4 1971b, (v5)
HC255.S43 1998, (v6)
Searle, John R. B840.S4, (v8)
BD175.S43 1995, (v8)
BD418.3.S42 1998, (v8)
BD418.3.S43 1992, (v8)
BF161.S352 1984, (v2)
Sears, Alfred Byron. F495.W73 1998, (v4)
Sears, Francis Weston. QC21.2.S36 1987, (v1)
QC23.S3745, (v1)
Sears, Jean L. Z1223.Z7.S4 2001, (v10)
Sears, John F. E164.S43 1989, (v4)
Sears, Laurie Jo. PN1978.I53.S43 1996, (v3)
Sears, Louis Martin. E336.5.S42 1966, (v4)
Sears, Minnie Earl. ML128.S3.S31 1966, (v9)
ML128.S3.S31 Suppl., (v9)
Z695.S43 1986, (v10)
Sears, Paul Bigelow. S493.S4 1947, (v1)
Sears, Richard D. F459.B4.S43 1996, (v4)
Sears, Stephen W. E467.1.M2.S43 1988, (v4)
E473.6.S43 1992, (v4)
E475.35.S43 1996, (v4)
Seaward, Paul. DA445.S42 1989, (v5)
Seay, Albert. ML172.S4 1975, (v9)

Sebald, Hans. BF1576.S43 1995, (v2)
Sebald, Winfried Georg. PT2681.E18.A9413 1996, (v3)
Sebastian, Anton. Q124.8.S43 2001, (v1)
R121.S398 1999, (v2)
Sebastian, Mihail. DS135.R73.S38713 2000, (v5)
Sebba, Anne. PR6003.A35.Z87 1987, (v3)
Sebba, Leslie. HV6250.25.S42 1996, (v6)
Seccombe, Wally. HQ611.S43 1992, (v6)
Seckinger, Ron. F2536.S42 1984, (v4)
Secord, James A. QH363.S4 2000, (v1)
Secrest, Meryle. ML410.S6872.S43 1998, (v9)
Seddon, Keith. BD638.S43 1987, (v8)
Sedgewick, Robert. QA76.6.S435 1988, (v1)
Sedgwick, Alexander. DC33.3.S44 1998, (v5)
DC335.S4, (v5)
Sedgwick, Anne Douglas. PS3537.E22 T35, (v3)
Sedgwick, Ellery. PN4900.A7.S43 1994, (v3)
Sedgwick, P. H. BR115.C3.S43 1999, (v8)
Sedgwick, Peter R. B791.S39 2001, (v8)
Sedlar, Jean W. DJK4 .S93 vol. 3.JK46, (v5)
Sedley, Charles. PR3761.S4 1928, (v3)
Sedra, Adel S. TK7867.S39 1998, (v1)
Seech, Zachary. B52.7.S44 2000, (v8)
Seed, David. PR6019.O9.P6484 1992, (v3)
PS374.S35.S44 1999, (v3)
Seeger, Anthony. ML3575.B7.S36 1987, (v9)
Seeger, Pete. ML60.S444.I5, (v9)
Seekings, Jeremy. DT1963.S44 2000, (v5)
Seel, Cynthia. PS3565.C57.Z858 2001, (v3)
Seeley, Frank Friedeberg. PG3443.S37 1991, (v3)
Seeley, John Robert. DA16.S45 1971, (v5)
Seelig, Sharon Cadman. PR545.M4.S4 1981, (v3)
Seely, Bruce Edsall. TE23.S44 1987, (v1)
Seely, Robert. DK511.C37.S44 2001, (v5)
Seelye, John D. F74.P8.S44 1998, (v4)
Seery, John Evan. JA81.S39 1990, (v7)
Seeskin, Kenneth. BM610.S38 2000, (v8)
Segal Freilich, Ariel. F3619.M47.S45 1999, (v4)
Segal, Aaron. G1046.E27.S4 1993, (v6)
Segal, Arthur. NA335.M628.S44 1997, (v9)
Segal, Charles. PA25.M3 vol. 26, (v3)
PA3015.R5.O827 1989, (v3)
PA3973.B2.S56 1982, (v3)
PA4413.O7.S52 1993, (v3)
PA4417.S46 1995, (v3)
Segal, David R. UB323.S44 1989, (v10)
Segal, Erich. PA6585.S4, (v3)
Segal, Gerald. DU29.S43 1990, (v5)
Segal, Howard P. T21.S43 1994, (v1)
Segal, Jerome M. B105.A35 S44 1991, (v8)
Segal, Lynne. HQ1090.S43 1990, (v6)
Segal, Nancy L. BF723.T9S44 2000, (v2)
Segalen, Martine. DC611.B5783.S4413 1991, (v5)
Segall, Jeffrey. PR6019.O9.U693 1993, (v3)
Segaller, Stephen. TK5105.875.I57.S4 1998, (v1)
Segel, Harold B. PG3086.S44 1993, (v3)
PN1221.S4, (v3)
PN1655.S45 1998, (v3)
PN1972.S43 1995, (v3)
Segen, J. C. RC71.3.S424 2002, (v2)
Seger, Linda. PN1995.9.W6.S37 1996, (v3)
Segers, Mary C. BL2525.S44 1998, (v8)
Segrave, Kerry. HV6515.S44 1992, (v6)
HV6651.S44 2001, (v6)
ML3790.S385 1994, (v9)
PN1992.3.E78.S44 1998, (v3)
PN1992.8.F5.S45 1999, (v3)
PN1993.5.U6.S368 1997, (v3)
PN1993.5.U6.S37 1992, (v3)
PN2570.S4 1990, (v3)
Segre, Claudio G. DG575.B3.S44 1987, (v5)
Segre, Emilio. QC16.F46.S4, (v1)
QC16.S35.A3 1993, (v1)
QC721.S4475, (v1)
QC7.S435 1984, (v1)
Segre, Michael. Q127.I8.S44 1991, (v1)
Segrest, Mab. F220.A1.S38 1994, (v4)
Seguin, Juan Nepomuceno. F390.S465 1991, (v4)
Seguin, Robert. PS374.W64.S44 2001, (v3)
Sehlinger, Peter J. E748.B724 S44 2000, (v4)

Sei Shonagon. PL788.6.M3.E56 1967b, (v3)
Seib, Philip M. PN4784.T4.S45 2001, (v3)
PN4888.F69.S45 1997, (v3)
Seidel, Michael. GV865.D5.S46 1988, (v6)
Seidel, Michael. PR3403.Z5.S45 1991, (v3)
Seidelman, Harold. E99.E7.S38 1994, (v4)
Seidensticker, Edward. DS806.S43, (v5)
PL812.A4.Z88 3, (v3)
Seidler, Victor J. BJ1031.S42 1991, (v8)
DS143.S45 2000, (v5)
Seidman, Laurence S. HJ5715.U6.S45 1997, (v6)
Seidman, Naomi. PJ5113.b.S45 1997, (v3)
Seifer, Marc J. TK140.T4.S65 1996, (v1)
Seiffert, Ulrich. TL154.S3913 1991, (v1)
Seigfried, Charlene Haddock. B832.S45 1996, (v8)
Seinberg, Mark (Mark L.). TP248.16.S84 2001, (v1)
Seinfeld, John H. QC879.6.S45 1998, (v1)
Seiter, Ellen. HQ784.T68.S45 1993, (v6)
PN1992.3.U5.S35 1998, (v3)
Seitz, Frederick. TK7809.S45 1998, (v1)
Seitz, William Chapin. N6512.S335 1991, (v9)
Sekaquaptewa, Helen. E90.S45.A3, (v4)
Sekler, Eduard F. NA1053.J4.S44, (v9)
Selbin, Eric. F1414.2.S39 1993, (v4)
Selbourne, David. JC329.5.S45 2000, (v7)
Selby, John E. E263.V8.S45 1988, (v4)
Selcer, Richard F. F394.F7.S45 1991, (v4)
Selden, Raman. PN81.S365 1989, (v3)
Seldon, Arthur. HB501.S545 1990, (v6)
Seldon, W. Lynn. F239.3.S45 1999, (v4)
Selesky, Harold E. F97.S45 1990, (v4)
Self, Peter. JF1351.S44 1973, (v7)
Selgin, George A. HG1586.S38 1988, (v6)
Selic, Bran. QA76.54.S295 1994, (v1)
Selig, Robert L. PR4717.S4 1995, (v3)
PR6031.O74.D33365 1990, (v3)
Seligman, A. HM1251.S45 2000, (v6)
Seligman, Edwin Robert Anderson. D16.8.S46 1961, (v5)
Seligman, Kevin L. Z5691.S45 1996, (v10)
Seligman, Martin E. P. BF698.35.O57.S45 1995, (v2)
Seligman, Milton. HV888.5.S45 1989, (v6)
Seligmann, Matthew S. DD221.S38 2000, (v5)
DT1105.G3.S45 1998, (v5)
Seliktar, Ofira. JZ1480.A57I7 2000, (v7)
Selin, Helaine. Z7405.S6 S4 1992, (v10)
Selinger, Bernard. PS3562.E42.Z88 1988, (v3)
Sell, Louis. DR2053.M55 S45 2002, (v5)
Sell, Susan K. K1401.S455 1998, (v7)
Sell, T. M. HD9711.U63.B6364 2001, (v6)
Sellars, Wilfrid. BJ21.S4 1970, (v8)
Sellato, Bernard. DS646.32.P85.S4513 1994, (v5)
Sellek, Yoko. HD8728.5.S45 2001, (v6)
Sellerberg, Ann-Mari. HM22.G3.S493 1994, (v6)
Sellers, Charles Coleman. AM101.P496.S44, (v10)
Sellers, Charles Grier. HC105.S38 1991, (v6)
Sellers, Christopher C. RC967.S45 1997, (v2)
Sellers, Cleveland. E185.97.S44.A37, (v4)
Sellers, James Benson. E445.A3.S4, (v4)
Sells, A. Lytton. PR129.I8.S44 1971, (v3)
Sells, Scott P. RJ506.P63.S45 1998, (v2)
Selman, Robert L. RJ505.P33S45 1998, (v2)
Selnow, Gary W. H61.95.S45 1998, (v6)
PN1992.55.S4 1993, (v3)
Selsam, Howard. B809.8.S39, (v8)
Seltzer, George. ML3795.S36 1989, (v9)
Seltzer, Mark. HV6529.S45 1998, (v6)
Selvadurai, A. P. S. QA805.S45 2000, (v1)
Selver, Paul. DB217.M3.S4 1940, (v5)
Selvidge, Marla J. BS521.4.S45 1996, (v8)
Selwood, Dominic. CR4755.F7.S45 1999, (v5)
Selwyn, David. PR4038.L44.S45 1999, (v3)
Selz, Peter Howard. N6490.S37, (v9)
N7570.S38 1969, (v9)
NB237.C46.S46 1999, (v9)
ND568.5.E9.S45, (v9)
ND588.B37.S4 1996, (v9)
Selzer, Jack. PS3503.U6134.Z87 1996, (v3)
Semat, Henry. QC173.S315 1962, (v1)
Semelin, Jacques. D810.P76.S4613 1993, (v5)
Semkow, Brian. KNP99.5.S46 1992, (v7)

Semmel, Bernard. PR4692.P64.S46 1994, (v3)
Semmes, Clovis E. E185.5.N3815 Index, (v4)
E185.86.S46 1992, (v4)
Semonche, John E. KF8742.S444 1998, (v7)
Semple, J. G. QA564.S4, (v1)
Semyonova Tian-Shanskaia, Olga. HN523.S46 1993, (v6)
Sen, Amartya Kumar. JC575.S45 1992, (v7)
Sen, S. N. QC225.15.S46 1989, (v1)
Senak, Mark S. KF3803.A54.S46 1996, (v7)
Senarclens, Pierre de. D842.S4413 1995, (v5)
Senda, Akihiko. PN2921.S4413 1997, (v3)
Sendak, Maurice. PZ7.S47Wh, (v3)
Senden, Marius von. RE91.S413, (v2)
Sender, John. HN797.Z9.S645 1990, (v6)
Sender, Ramon Jose. PQ6635.E65.L82, (v3)
Sendich, Munir. Z8662.35.S46 1994, (v10)
Seneca, Lucius Annaeus. BJ214.S4 E73, (v8)
PA6156.S5.E6 1917, (v3)
PA6661.E7.A2 1988, (v3)
PA6666.A1 1992, (v3)
Senechal, Roberta. F549.S79.N47 1990, (v4)
Senelick, Laurence. PN2071.I47.S46 2000, (v3)
Senf, Carol A. PR6037.T617.D7865 1998, (v3)
Senghor, Leopold Sedar. PQ3989.S47.A17 1977, (v3)
PQ3989.S47.A17 1984, (v3)
SenGupta, Gunja. F686.S46 1996, (v4)
Senie, Harriet. NB198.S355 1992, (v9)
Senier, Siobhan. E98.C89.S46 2001, (v4)
Senior, Matthew. PQ615.S46 1994, (v3)
Senior, Olive. HQ1501.S46 1991, (v6)
Senkewicz, Robert M. F869.S357.S46 1985, (v4)
Senn, Alfred Erich. DK505.74.S46 1990, (v5)
Senn, Bryan. PN1995.9.F36.S46 1992, (v3)
Senn, Bryan. PN1995.9.H6.S44 1996, (v3)
Sennett, Richard. HQ557.C5.S45, (v6)
Seo, Audrey Yoshiko. ND1457.J32.L63 1998, (v9)
Serafine, Mary Louise. ML3838.S48 1988, (v9)
Serafini, Anthony. QC15.S437 1993, (v1)
Serafini, Anthony. QH305.S48 1993, (v1)
Serageldin, Ismail. NA1460.S44 1989, (v9)
Serber, R. QC773.A1.S47 1992, (v1)
Serbin, Andres. F2183.S4713 1990, (v4)
F2183.S48 1998, (v4)
Serbin, Ken. BX1466.2.S48 2000, (v8)
Sered, Susan Starr. BL458.S45 1994, (v8)
Seremetakis, C. Nadia. GT3251.A3.M367 1991, (v6)
Sereny, Gitta. DD247.S63.S47 1995, (v5)
Seret, Roberta. PR888.A74.S47 1992, (v3)
Serfaty, Simon. D1065.U5.S39 1997, (v5)
Sergeyev, Victor M. HV7015.15.S47 1998, (v6)
Sergiovanni, Thomas J. LB2805.S523 1996, (v7)
LB2805.S524 1992, (v7)
LB2822.S44 1984, (v7)
Serio, John N. Z8842.7.S47 1994, (v10)
Serling, Rod. PS3537.E654.P3, (v3)
Serlio, Sebastiano. NA2517.S5 1970, (v9)
Sernau, Scott. HD5731.A6.S47 1994, (v6)
Sernett, Milton C. BR563.N4.S474 1997, (v8)
Seron, Carroll. KF318.S47 1996, (v7)
Serow, William J. HQ1064.U5.S467 1990, (v6)
Serpell, James. SF411.5.S47 1996, (v1)
Serpell, Robert. LC191.8.Z33.S47 1993, (v7)
Serre, Jean Pierre. QA251.S4713 1987, (v1)
Serres, Michel. GE60.S4713 1995, (v6)
Serrin, William. F159.H7.S47 1992, (v4)
Servan-Schreiber, Jean Jacques. D1065.U5.S413, (v5)
Service, Robert W. PR6037.E72S6 1907b, (v3)
Service, Robert. DK254.L4.S4323 2000, (v5)
DK254.L4.S4324 1985, (v5)
DK266.S495 1998, (v5)
Servies, James Albert. Z1271.S47 1993, (v10)
Servos, John W. QD452.5.U6.S47 1990, (v1)
Sesonske, Alexander. BH21.S4, (v8)
Sessions, Patty Bartlett. F593.S45.A3 1997, (v4)
Sessions, Roger. ML60.S513, (v9)
Sessions, Roger. ML410.S473.A4 1992, (v9)
Sessions, William Lad. BL626.3.S47 1994, (v8)
Sesti, Giuseppe Maria. QB802.S4713 1991, (v1)
Seth, Ronald. UB271.J3.S4, (v10)

Seth, Vikram. PR9499.3.S38E67 1999, **(v3)**
  PR9499.3.S38P64 1995, **(v3)**
  PR9499.3.S38S83 1993, **(v3)**
Seton, Anya. PS3537.E787 D4, **(v3)**
  PS3537.E787 D7 1944, **(v3)**
  PS3537.E787 W5, **(v3)**
Seton, Ernest Thompson. QH31.5.S48.A36 1978, **(v1)**
Seton-Watson, Hugh. DK189 .S44 1988, **(v5)**
  DK223.S4, **(v5)**
  DR48.S38 1962, **(v5)**
  DR48.5.S4 1956, **(v5)**
Seton-Watson, R. W. D376.G7.S4 1972, **(v5)**
  DB48.S5, **(v5)**
  DB205.S4 1965, **(v5)**
  DR36.S5, **(v5)**
Setouchi, Harumi. PL861.E8.N313 1989, **(v3)**
Setterberg, Fred. RA566.5.N7.S48 1993, **(v2)**
Settle, William A. F594.J24 S47 1977, **(v4)**
Seung, T. K. B2799.E8.S53 1994, **(v8)**
Seuss. PZ8.3.G276Cat, **(v3)**
Seuss. PZ8.3.G276An, **(v3)**
Sevareid, Eric. E835.S4, **(v4)**
Sevastakis, Michael. PN1995.9.H6.S46 1993, **(v3)**
Severa, Joan L. GT610.S42 1995, **(v6)**
Severin, Dorothy Sherman. PQ6428.S44 1989, **(v3)**
Severin, Laura. PR6037.M43.Z84 1997, **(v3)**
Severin, Timothy. DS601.S4 1997, **(v5)**
Severini, Gino. ND623.S45.A2 1995, **(v9)**
Severson, Richard James. Z8047.7.S47 1996, **(v10)**
Sewall, Samuel. F67.S516 1973, **(v4)**
Seward, Desmond. DC137.1.S47 1981, **(v5)**
Seward, Robert. PN1991.3.I75.S49 1999, **(v3)**
Seward, Rudy Ray. HQ535.S44, **(v6)**
Sewell, Anna. PZ10.3.S38.Bl 1994, **(v3)**
Sewell, Elizabeth. PN1031.S475, **(v3)**
Sewell, Elizabeth. PR6037.E75.N9, **(v3)**
Sewell, Richard H. E415.7.S525 1988, **(v4)**
  E415.9.H15.S4 1965, **(v4)**
  E449.S49, **(v4)**
Sewter, A. C. N6415.B3.S4, **(v9)**
Sexton, Anne Harvey. PS3537.E915.Z53 1977, **(v3)**
Sexton, Anne. PS3537.E915.A17 1981, **(v3)**
  PS3537.E915.L5, **(v3)**
  PS3537.E915.W6, **(v3)**
Sexton, Conor. TK5105.55.S38 1995, **(v1)**
Sexton, Donal J. D810.S7.S428 1996, **(v5)**
Seydor, Paul. PN1998.3.P43.S48 1997, **(v3)**
Seyhan, Azade. PN491.5.S49 2001, **(v3)**
  PT361.S48 1992, **(v3)**
Seymour, Charles. D619.S435 1967, **(v5)**
  D644.S46, **(v5)**
Seymour, Elaine. LC148.2.S49 1997, **(v7)**
Seymour, Harold. GV863.A1.S48 1960, **(v6)**
Seymour, Miranda. PR6013.R35.Z777 1995, **(v3)**
Seymour, Nancy N. PL1171.S45 1989, **(v3)**
Seymour, Raymond Benedict. TP156.P6.S44 1990, **(v1)**
Seymour, Tryntje Van Ness. ND238.A4.S48 1988, **(v9)**
Seymour, Wendy. RD594.3.S497 1998, **(v2)**
Seymour-Smith, Martin. PR6013.R35.Z783 1983, **(v3)**
Seymour-Ure, Colin. PN5118.S39 1991, **(v3)**
Seyoum, Belay. HF1414.4.S49 2000, **(v6)**
Sgarbi, Vittorio. ND623.C3.S513 1994, **(v9)**
Sha, Richard C. PR468.A76.S53 1998, **(v3)**
Shabad, Theodore. DS777.55.S455, **(v5)**
Shabad, Theodore. DS777.55.S455 1972, **(v5)**
Shaban, Fuad. DS63.2.U5.S33 1991, **(v5)**
Shabana, Ahmed A. QA865.S49 1990, **(v1)**
Shabecoff, Philip. GE195.S43 1996, **(v6)**
Shabtai, Yaakov. PJ5054.S2643.S613 1987, **(v3)**
Shachtman, Tom. QC278.S48 1999, **(v1)**
Shackel, Paul A. F189.A647.S48 1993, **(v4)**
  F249.H2.S52 2000, **(v4)**
  F249.H2.S53 1996, **(v4)**
Shackelford, James F. TA403.S515 2000, **(v1)**
  TA403.4.S482 1995, **(v1)**
Shackleton, Ernst Henry. G850.1914.S52, **(v4)**
Shackleton, Robert. F199.S49, **(v4)**
  JC179.M8.S35 1961, **(v7)**
Shackley, Theodore. U241.S43, **(v10)**

Shade, Patrick. BD216.S43 2001, **(v8)**
Shade, William G. F230.S53 1996, **(v4)**
Shafer, Byron E. JK2317. 1983, **(v7)**
Shafer, D. Michael. E744.S475 1988, **(v4)**
Shafer, Yvonne. PS3573.I45677.Z87 1998, **(v3)**
Shaffer, Brian W. PR888.M63.S5 1993, **(v3)**
  PR6059.S5.Z87 1998, **(v3)**
Shaffer, Harry G. HC106.82.S5 1999, **(v6)**
Shaffer, Peter. PR6037.H23.A6 1982, **(v3)**
Shaffer, Thomas L. KF306.S45 1991, **(v7)**
Shaffer, William R. JN7543.S53 1998, **(v7)**
Shafqat, Saeed. JQ629.A38.C587 1997, **(v7)**
Shafritz, Jay M. PN6084.W35.S5 1990, **(v3)**
  U24.S47 1989, **(v10)**
Shah, Ghanshyam. HN683.S5 1990, **(v6)**
Shahan, Ewing Pope. B1674.W38.S5 1950, **(v8)**
Shahar, Shulamith. HQ792.E8.S53 1990, **(v6)**
Shaheen, Naseeb. PR3012.S48 1993, **(v3)**
  PR3012.S5 1989, **(v3)**
  PR3012.S53 1999, **(v3)**
Shahin, Emad Eldin. BP64.A4.N677 1997, **(v8)**
Shahn, Ben. N7445.S516, **(v9)**
  NC1075.S47.S6, **(v9)**
Shaikh, Farzana. DS479.S52 1989, **(v5)**
Shaiko, Ronald G. GE180.S42 1999, **(v6)**
Shain, Barry Alan. JA84.U5.S46 1994, **(v7)**
Shain, Yossi. E184.A1.S565 1999, **(v4)**
Shaked, Gershon. PJ5029.S5413 2000, **(v3)**
Shaker, Steven M. HD38.7.S48 1999, **(v6)**
Shakespeare, William. PR2750.B12.G87 2000, **(v3)**
  PR2752.C32, **(v3)**
  PR2754.E9 1974, **(v3)**
  PR2754.G74 1997, **(v3)**
  PR2754.P76 1998, **(v3)**
  PR2803.A1 1998, **(v3)**
  PR2807.A2.B43 1991, **(v3)**
  PR2818.A2.B7 1989, **(v3)**
  PR2819.A2.H24 1992, **(v3)**
  PR2828.A2.C69 1997, **(v3)**
  PR2832.A2.D65 1996, **(v3)**
  PR2833.A2, **(v3)**
  PR2848.A2.B6, **(v3)**
  PR2848.H78 1962, **(v3)**
  PR2859.A2.M45 1998, **(v3)**
  PR2878.J7.D3 1983, **(v3)**
  PR2878.K4.T3 1975, **(v3)**
  PR2892.F48 1998, **(v3)**
  PR2892.H55 1995, **(v3)**
  PR2892.S64, **(v3)**
Shakir, Evelyn. E184.A65.S48 1997, **(v4)**
Shalamov, Varlam Tikhonovich. PG3487.A592.K63 1980a, **(v3)**
Shale, Richard. PN1993.92.S53 1993, **(v3)**
Shalev, Aryeh. DS119.75.S4813 1991, **(v5)**
Shalev, Carmel. KF540.S53 1989, **(v7)**
Shalev, Michael. HD8660.A5.H584 1992, **(v6)**
Shalhope, Robert E. F59.B4.S53 1996, **(v4)**
Shalit, Ben. U22.3.S43 1988, **(v10)**
Shallenberger, David. BL65.H64.S53 1998, **(v8)**
Shames, Irving Herman. TA418.S48 1997, **(v1)**
Shames, Laurence. BJ1611.2.S43 1989, **(v8)**
Shammas, Anton. PJ5054.S414.A8913 1988, **(v3)**
Shammas, Carole. HC260.C6.S5 1990, **(v6)**
Shamos, Morris H. Q183.3.A1.S45 1995, **(v1)**
  QC7.S47, **(v1)**
Shampine, Lawrence F. QA297.A52 1997, **(v1)**
Shand, Alexander H. HB98.S483 1990, **(v6)**
Shand-Tucci, Douglass. N5220.G26.S48 1997, **(v9)**
  NA737.C7.S44 1995, **(v9)**
Shane, Ed. P92.U5.S48 2001, **(v3)**
Shane, Paul G. HV4505.S53 1996, **(v6)**
Shanefield, Daniel J. TK7881.S52 2001, **(v1)**
Shanes, Eric. NB933.B7.S52 1989, **(v9)**
Shange, Ntozake. PS3569.H3324.F6 1977, **(v3)**
Shankar, N. QA9.65.S53 1994, **(v1)**
Shankar, Ramamurti. QA300.S4315 1995, **(v1)**
Shankar, Ravi. ML338.S475.M9, **(v9)**
Shankar, Subramanian. PS366.T73.S53 2001, **(v3)**
Shankle, George Earlie. E155.S43 1970, **(v4)**
  E179.S545 1955, **(v4)**
Shanks, Hershel. BM487.S453 1998, **(v8)**

Shanley, Mary Lyndon. KD758.S47 1989, **(v7)**
Shannon, David Allen. JK2391.S6.S5 1955, **(v7)**
Shannon, Gary William. RA804.S54 1993, **(v2)**
Shannon, Lyle W. HV6795.R33.S5 1991, **(v6)**
Shannon, Magdaline W. F1927.P75.S5 1996, **(v4)**
Shannon, Michael Owen. Z2043.N6.S5 1991, **(v10)**
Shannon, Mike. GV742.4.S47 2002, **(v6)**
Shannon, Patrick. LB1573.S466 1989, **(v7)**
Shannon, Richard. DA560.S44 1992, **(v5)**
  DA563.4.S5 1984, **(v5)**
Shannon, Robert E. T57.62.S47, **(v1)**
Shannon, Robert M. PQ6490.H5.S53 1989, **(v3)**
Shannon, Robert Rennie. QC385.2.D47.S53 1997, **(v1)**
Shannon, Sandra Garrett. PS3573.I45677.Z88 1995, **(v3)**
Shannon, Thomas A. HQ759.5.S53 1988, **(v6)**
  QH442.S476 1999, **(v1)**
  QP251.S485 1988, **(v1)**
Shannon, Timothy J. E195.S53 2000, **(v4)**
Shantz, Homer Le Roy. S471.A35.S5, **(v1)**
Shao, Kuo-kang. DS778.A2.C467 1996, **(v5)**
Shapin, Steven. Q125.S5166 1996, **(v1)**
Shapin, Steven. Q175.52.G7.S48 1994, **(v1)**
Shapira, Anita. DS149.S497158 1992, **(v5)**
  DS151.K327.S52513 1984, **(v5)**
Shapiro, Ann-Louise. HV6046.S46 1996, **(v6)**
Shapiro, Arthur H. LC1201.S53 1999, **(v7)**
Shapiro, Barbara J. DA380.S53 1983, **(v5)**
  KD8371.S5 1991, **(v7)**
Shapiro, Barry M. DC194.S52 1993, **(v5)**
Shapiro, Bruce G. PN2071.P78.S53 1999, **(v3)**
  PT8876.S44 1990, **(v3)**
Shapiro, Carl. HC79.I55 S53 1999, **(v6)**
Shapiro, David L. KF4600.S53 1995, **(v7)**
Shapiro, David. NC139.J58.S5 1984, **(v9)**
Shapiro, Edward R. HM251.S459 1991, **(v6)**
Shapiro, Francine. RC489.E98.S53 1997, **(v2)**
Shapiro, Gilbert. DC141.3.A4.S53 1998, **(v5)**
Shapiro, H. A. NK4645.S47 1994, **(v9)**
Shapiro, Harry. ML3470.S48 1988b, **(v9)**
Shapiro, Henry D. F217.A65.S52, **(v4)**
Shapiro, Herbert. E185.2.S52 1988, **(v4)**
Shapiro, Ian. JC423.S465 1996, **(v7)**
Shapiro, James S. PN3235.S38 2000, **(v3)**
  PR651.S53 1991, **(v3)**
  PR2825.S44 1996, **(v3)**
Shapiro, Michael Edward. N6537.B53.S48 1993, **(v9)**
  N6537.R4.A4 1988, **(v9)**
Shapiro, Michael. HV741.S432 1999, **(v6)**
  PR3095.S524 1994, **(v3)**
Shapiro, Mitchell E. PN1992.3.U5.S54 1989, **(v3)**
Shapiro, Nat. ML395.S5 1975, **(v9)**
  ML3561.J3.S46 1966, **(v9)**
Shapiro, Stuart L. QB843.B55.S5 1983, **(v1)**
Shaplen, Robert. DS518.1.S47, **(v5)**
Shapley, Deborah. E840.8.M46.S47 1993, **(v4)**
Shapley, Harlow. Q111.S48 1965, **(v1)**
  QB3.S52, **(v1)**
  QB851.S47 1972, **(v1)**
  QC981.S5, **(v1)**
Shapo, Helene S. KF386.S44 2002, **(v7)**
Sharer, Robert J. F1435.3.A7.S53 1990, **(v4)**
Sharff, Stefan. PN1998.3.H58.S48 1991, **(v3)**
Sharkansky, Ira. BM390.S5112 2000, **(v8)**
Sharkansky, Ira. JQ1830.A56.S53 1997, **(v7)**
Sharlet, Robert S. KLA2070.S43 1992, **(v7)**
Sharma, Arvind. BL51.S49 1990, **(v8)**
  BL1151.3.S53 1998, **(v8)**
  BL1202.S385 1996, **(v8)**
Sharma, Hari D. TD793.S43 1994, **(v1)**
Sharma, Kanhaiyalal. HN690.Z9.S6438 1997, **(v6)**
Sharma, P. Vallabh. QE501.3.S48 1986, **(v1)**
  TA705.S515 1997, **(v1)**
Sharma, Ram Sharan. DS457.S445 2001, **(v5)**
Sharma, Shalendra D. HC435.2.S494 1999, **(v6)**
Sharman, Lyon. DS777.S5 1968, **(v5)**
Sharoni, Simona. HQ1728.5.Z8.W4773 1995, **(v6)**
Sharp, Alan. D644.S478 1991, **(v5)**
Sharp, Andrew. DU423.C57.S53 1990, **(v5)**

Sharp, Archibald. TL410.S5 1977, (v1)
Sharp, Dennis. NA680.S52 1972b, (v9)
Sharp, Elaine B. HN57.S49 1999, (v6)
Sharp, James Roger. E386.S5, (v4)
Sharp, Joanne P. PN4900.R3.S53 2000, (v3)
Sharp, Lesley Alexandra. DT469.M277.S358 1993, (v5)
Sharp, Maurice L. TA690.S44 1993, (v1)
Sharp, Mitchell. F1034.3.S53.A3 1994, (v4)
Sharp, Paul. DA589.8.S53 1997, (v5)
Sharp, Robert P. GB2403.2.S5 1988, (v6)
Sharp, Ronald A. PR4838.R4.S5, (v3)
Sharp, Samuel L. DK414.S45, (v5)
Sharpe, Charles C. RT42.S47 2001, (v2)
    T210.S53 2000, (v1)
Sharpe, Grant William. SD373.S56 1986, (v1)
Sharpe, Jenny. PR830.W6.S5 1993, (v3)
Sharpe, Kevin. DA375.S55 2000, (v5)
    DA396.A2.S48 1992, (v5)
    JN339.S53 2000, (v7)
Sharpe, Lesley. PT2492.S48 1991, (v3)
Sharpe, Mike. UG1240.S532 2001, (v10)
Sharpe, R. A. BD418.3.S5 1990, (v8)
Sharpe, Robert Boies. PR635.I7.S5, (v3)
Sharpe, Tony. PS3509.L43.Z86485 1991, (v3)
Sharpe, Tony. PS3537.T4753.Z7658 1999, (v3)
Sharq̄ aw̄ ̄i, Abd al-Raòhm̄ an. PJ7862.H27A813 1990, (v3)
Shasha, Dennis Elliott. QA76.2.A2.S53 1995, (v1)
Shastri, Gaurinath Bhattacharyya. PK2903.S5 1960, (v3)
Shatto, Susan. PR4556.S43 1988, (v3)
Shattuc, Jane. PN1998.3.F37.S52 1995, (v3)
Shattuck, Charles Harlen. PR3105.S5, (v3)
    PR3112.S5, (v3)
Shattuck, Gardiner H. BX5979.S53 2000, (v8)
Shattuck, George C. KF8228.O45.A3 1991, (v7)
Shattuck, Petra T. KF8205.S47 1990, (v7)
Shattuck, Roger. DC338.S48 1968, (v5)
    PN52.S53 1999, (v3)
    PN56.K64.S43 1996, (v3)
Shatz, Marilyn. BF721.S485 1994, (v2)
Shatzky, Joel. PS374.J48.C66 1997, (v3)
Shatzmiller, Joseph. DS135.F85.M377 1990, (v5)
    R694.S52 1994, (v2)
Shaughnessy, Edward L. PS3529.N5.Z79696 1997, (v3)
Shaughnessy, Mina P. PE1404.S5, (v3)
Shaull, Richard. BR1644.S46 2000, (v8)
Shava, Piniel Viriri. PR9358.2.B57.S54 1989, (v3)
Shaver, Robert. BJ1474.S43 1999, (v8)
Shaviro, Daniel N. HD7125.S526 2000, (v6)
Shavit, Arthur. QC311.S513 1995, (v1)
Shavit, David. DS33.4.U6.S46 1990, (v5)
    E183.8.R9.S487 1993, (v4)
    F1418.S494 1992, (v4)
Shavit, Jacob. DS150.R5.S52, (v5)
Shaw, Arnold. ML3477.S475 1987, (v9)
    ML3561.B63 S53, (v9)
Shaw, Bernard. DA913.S45 2001, (v5)
    ML286.8.L5.S44, (v9)
    MT100.W25.S5 1967, (v9)
    PN1994.S5183 1997, (v3)
    PN2596.L6.S48 1993, (v3)
    PR2976.S35 1971, (v3)
    PR5360 1930, (v3)
    PR5360.F48, (v3)
    PR5360.F51, (v3)
    PR5360.F61, (v3)
    PR5360.F62, (v3)
    PR5361.C39, (v3)
    PR5361.L3, (v3)
    PR5363.S3 1956, (v3)
    PR5365.A4 1959, (v3)
    PR5365.M9 1957, (v3)
    PR5365.U57 1928, (v3)
    PR5366.A4 1965, (v3)
    PR5366.A42 1952, (v3)
    PR5366.A463, (v3)
    PR5366.A48 1960, (v3)
    PR5366.A485 1995, (v3)

    PR5366.A5 1969, (v3)
    PT8895.S5 1958, (v3)
    PT8895.S53 1979, (v3)
Shaw, Bob. PR6069.H364.O85 1972a, (v3)
Shaw, Charles Bunsen. PS682.S5 1955, (v3)
Shaw, Donald Leslie. PQ7082.N7.S515 1998, (v3)
    PQ7389.C263.Z88 1985, (v3)
    PQ8549.G24.D6297, (v3)
Shaw, Eric. JN1129.L32.S456 1996, (v7)
Shaw, Gary. GV939.S43.A35, (v6)
Shaw, Harry E. PR868.R4.S53 1999, (v3)
Shaw, Irwin. PS3537.H384 A6 1961, (v3)
    PS3537.H384 L8, (v3)
    PS3537.H384 M5, (v3)
    PS3537.H384 T5, (v3)
    PS3537.H384 T7, (v3)
    PS3537.H384 T9, (v3)
    PS3537.H384 Y6, (v3)
Shaw, Marion. PR5592.S47.S5 1988, (v3)
    PR6005.H66.Z88 1991, (v3)
Shaw, Martin. UA10.S475 1991, (v10)
Shaw, Milton Clayton. TJ1280.S446 1996, (v1)
Shaw, Miranda Eberle. BQ8915.S53 1994, (v8)
Shaw, Patrick W. PS3505.A87.Z84 1992, (v3)
Shaw, Peter, 1936-. PS201.S48 1994, (v3)
Shaw, R. Paul. U21.2.S49 1989, (v10)
Shaw, Randy. HN65.S49 1996, (v6)
Shaw, Robert Gould. E513.5 54th.S53 1992, (v4)
Shaw, Stanford J. D804.3.S54 1993, (v5)
    DR440.S5, (v5)
    DS135.T8.S46 1991, (v5)
Shaw, Susan. TR287.S48 1983, (v1)
Shaw, W. David. PR508.E5.S5 1994, (v3)
Shaw, William. PR3533.S5 1974, (v3)
Shawcross, John T. PR431.S53 1991, (v3)
    PR3562.S48 1982, (v3)
    PR3565.S53 1988, (v3)
    PR3566.S47 2001, (v3)
    PR3581.S5 1993, (v3)
    Z8578.S52 1984, (v10)
    Z8578.S52 1984 Suppl, (v10)
Shawcross, Nancy M. TR183.S43 1997, (v1)
Shawcross, William. DS557.8.C3.S5, (v5)
Shawver, Lois. UB418.G38.S53 1995, (v10)
Shay, Anthony. GV1588.45.S5 2002, (v6)
Shay, Robert Paul. UA647.S37, (v10)
Shaykh, òHan̄ an. PJ7862.H356A7613 1998, (v3)
    PJ7862.H356B3713 1995, (v3)
    PJ7862.H356H5513 1994, (v3)
    PJ7862.H356I4613 2001, (v3)
    PJ7862.H356W66 1992, (v3)
Shayler, David. TL789.8.U6, (v1)
Shchepin, O. P. K3577.S5317 1989, (v7)
Shchutskii, IU. K. PL2464.Z7.S4713 1979, (v3)
Shea, Ann M. Z1318.N5.S54 1995, (v10)
Shea, Daniel M. JK2281.S49 1996, (v7)
Shea, Jonathan D. PB268.S46 1991, (v3)
Shea, Thomas F. PR6029.N56.Z87 1992, (v3)
Shea, William L. E473.17.S54 1992, (v4)
Sheahan, John. HC227.S435 1999, (v6)
Shearar, Cheryl. E78.N78 S446 2000, (v4)
Shearer, Alistair. BL1202.S39 1993, (v8)
Shearer, Barbara Smith. Z5942.S464 1983, (v10)
Shearer, Benjamin F. E155.S44 2002, (v4)
Shearer, David R. HD3616.S472.S5 1996, (v6)
Shearer, Peter M. QE534.2.S455 1999, (v1)
Shearer, W. M. SH346.S54 1992, (v1)
Shearman, John K. G. N6370.S48 1967, (v9)
    N6915.S54 1992, (v9)
Shedd, Joseph B. LB2805.S579 1991, (v7)
Sheed, Wilfrid. PR6069.H396.M3, (v3)
    PR6069.H396.M5, (v3)
    PR6069.H396.M6, (v3)
Sheehan, Bernard W. E78.V7.S53, (v4)
Sheehan, Jackie. HD8736.5.S465 1998, (v6)
Sheehan, James J. DD203.S48 1989, (v5)
    DD204.S53, (v5)
Sheehan, Michael. JX1318.S49 1996, (v7)
    PE1175.S45 2000, (v3)
Sheehan, Thomas J. GV436.S45, (v6)
    QK495.O64.S49 1994, (v1)

Sheehan, William. QB601.S54 1988, (v1)
    QB601.S543 1992, (v1)
    QB641.S4838 2001, (v1)
    QB641.S484 1996, (v1)
Sheehy, Edward John. VA63.M42.S54 1992, (v10)
Sheehy, Eugene P. Z1035.1.S43 1986, (v10)
Sheehy, Gail. E880.S54 1988, (v4)
Sheehy, Helen. PN2287.L2896.S54 1996, (v3)
Sheets-Johnstone, Maxine. B105.B64 S48 1994, (v8)
Sheffer, Martin S. KF4783.S54 1999, (v7)
    KF5060.A68.S53 1999, (v7)
Sheffrin, Steven M. HB172.5.S523 1983, (v6)
Shefrin, Hersh. HG4515.15.S53 2000, (v6)
Sheidley, Harlow W. F69.S44 1998, (v4)
Shekter, Robert J. VM321.S45, (v10)
Shelburne, Walter A. BF175.5.A72.S54 1988, (v2)
Shelby, Byron Bruce. GV53.S47 1986, (v6)
Shelden, Michael. PR6005.O393.Z95 1989, (v3)
    PR6013.R44.Z842 1995, (v3)
    PR6029.R8.Z7817 1991, (v3)
Sheldon, Garrett Ward. E332.2.S54 1991, (v4)
    JC211.M35 S44 2001, (v7)
Sheldon, George. F74.D4 S5 1895a, (v4)
Sheldon, Thomas. TK5102.S48 2001, (v1)
Shelford, W. O. VK1265.S45 1960, (v10)
Shell, Marc. PN51.S3637 1993, (v3)
Shellabarger, Samuel. DA501.C5.S52 1971, (v5)
    PS3537.H64 L6, (v3)
Sheller, Mimi. F1924.S54 2000, (v4)
Shelley, Bruce. U310.S483 1994, (v10)
Shelley, Louise I. HV8224.S376 1996, (v6)
Shelley, Mary Wollstonecraft. PR5397.A1 1996, (v3)
    PR5397.F7 1969, (v3)
    PR5398.A28 1947, (v3)
    PR5398.A4 1980, (v3)
    PR5401. 1985 vol. 9, (v3)
Shelley, Percy Bysshe. PR5400.F26, (v3)
    PR5402. 1972, (v3)
    PR5403.H8, (v3)
    PR5403.R4, (v3)
    PR5405.C48 1988, (v3)
    PR5431.A3 1964, (v3)
    PR5436.F6 1968, (v3)
Shelly, Judith Allen. RT86.3.S54 1988, (v2)
Shelton, Barrie. NA1550.S49 1999, (v9)
Shelton, George. B1248.E7 S54 1992, (v8)
Shelton, Hal T. E207.M7.S48 1994, (v4)
Shelton, Jo-Ann. HN10.R7 S45 1998, (v6)
Shelton, Napier. GB1227.G85.S48 1999, (v6)
Shelton, Suzanne. GV1785.S3.S53, (v6)
Shem, Samuel. HQ801.S5244 1998, (v6)
Shemek, Deanna. PQ4053.W6.S53 1998, (v3)
Shemesh, Haim. DS70.96.I72.S54 1992, (v5)
Shen, Raphael. HC340.19.S54 1996, (v6)
Shen, Tsung-lien. DS785.S43, (v5)
Shen, Tsung-wen. PL2801.N18.A24 1995, (v3)
Shenefield, John H. KF1650.S53 1993, (v7)
Sheng, Michael M. DS740.5.S65.S562 1997, (v5)
Shengold, Leonard. RC569.5.C55.S53 1999, (v2)
Shenkman, Richard. E176.1.S56 1999, (v4)
Shennan, Andrew. DC397.S47 1989, (v5)
Shenstone, William. PR3677.A1 1968, (v3)
Shentalinskii, Vitalii. PG2991.4.S4813 1996, (v3)
Shenton, Edward H. VM365.S42, (v10)
Shepard, Greg. GV346.S55 2003, (v6)
Shepard, Paul. HM206.S53, (v6)
Shepard, Richard F. PN4899.N42.T5685 1996, (v3)
Shephard, Roy F. GN66.S46 1990, (v4)
Shephard, Roy J. GN57.A73.S54 1996, (v6)
    QP86.S478 1997, (v1)
    QP301.S468 1994, (v1)
    QP301.S48 1977, (v1)
    QP301.S49, (v1)
Shepheard, Paul. NA2500.S47 1994, (v9)
Shepherd, James F. HF3025.S717, (v6)
Shepherd, Robin H. E. DB2244.7.S44 2000, (v5)
Shepherd, Simon. PR625.S54 1996, (v3)
    PR678.W6.S5 1981, (v3)
Shepley, James R. UF767.S4 1971, (v10)
Sheppard, Alice. NC1425.S54 1994, (v9)

Sheppard, Eric William. UA649.S52, (v10)
Sheppard, F. H. W. DA677.S54 1998, (v5)
  HC258.L6.S5 1971, (v6)
Sher, George. B105.J87.S54 1987, (v8)
  JA79.S42 1997, (v7)
Sher, Gila. BC71.S47 1991, (v8)
Sherbo, Arthur. PR635.S4.S5 1957, (v3)
  PR2968.S55 1992, (v3)
  PR3687.S7.Z8, (v3)
Sherburne, Donald W. B1674.W354.S45 1970, (v8)
  BD511.W515.S5, (v8)
Sherburne, John P. F786.S55 1988, (v4)
Sheridan, Eugene R. F137.M63.S47, (v4)
Sheridan, Frances Chamberlaine. PR3679.S5.A19
  1984, (v3)
Sheridan, James E. DS774.S54, (v5)
Sheridan, Kyoko. HC462.S47 1993, (v6)
Sheridan, Richard Brinsley. PR3680.A5.P7, (v3)
  PR3680.A5.R4 1962, (v3)
Sheridan, Thomas E. F811.S465 1995, (v4)
  F819.T99 M57 1986, (v4)
  GF517.C87.S54 1988, (v4)
Sheridan, Thomas. PR3687.S147.A17 1994, (v3)
Sheriff, John K. B945.P44.S47 1994, (v8)
Sheriff, Mary D. ND553.F7.S53 1990, (v9)
  ND1329.V53.S54 1996, (v9)
Sheriff, Robert E. TN269.S52417 1989, (v1)
Sherington, Geoffrey. HV887.G5.S47 1998, (v6)
Sherk, Warren M. PN1998.3.S43.S54 1998, (v3)
Sherlock, Philip Manderson. F1881.S5 1998, (v4)
Sherlock, Richard. RC86.95.S54 1988, (v2)
Sherman, A. J. DS126.S447 1998, (v5)
Sherman, Alvin F. PQ6533.Z5.S48 1992, (v3)
Sherman, Bernard D. ML457.S52 1997, (v9)
Sherman, Chris. ZA4450.S54 2001, (v10)
Sherman, Claire Richter. PC2875.S53 1995, (v3)
Sherman, Fraser A. PN1995.9.S26.S46 2000, (v3)
Sherman, Howard J. HB3711.S4722 1991, (v6)
  HX73.S499 1995, (v6)
Sherman, John W. F1234.S53 1997, (v4)
Sherman, Lawrence W. HV6626.2.S54 1992, (v6)
Sherman, Martin. JZ1253.S53 1998, (v7)
Sherman, Moshe D. BM750.S395 1996, (v8)
Sherman, Nancy. B491.E7 S44 1997, (v8)
Sherman, Richard B. KF224.W28.S48 1992, (v7)
Sherman, Roger. HD2757.2.S48 1989, (v6)
Sherman, Sandra. PR3408.E25.S54 1996, (v3)
Sherman, Sharon R. PN1995.9.D6.S494 1998, (v3)
Sherman, Steve. F32.3.S48 1999, (v4)
Sherman, Stuart Pratt. PS121.S5 1971, (v3)
Sherman, William C. F645.A1S54 1983, (v4)
Sherman, William H. Z8220.9.S48 1995, (v10)
Sherman, William T. E467.1.S55.A4 1999, (v4)
  E476.69.S57, (v4)
Shermer, Michael. BL240.2.S545 2000, (v8)
  D804.355.S54 2000, (v5)
  Q157.S48 1997, (v1)
Sherover, Charles M. JA71.S44 1989, (v7)
Sherr, Lynn. HQ1413.A55.S48 1995, (v6)
Sherraden, Jim. Z232.H38 S48 2001, (v10)
Sherratt, Andrew. GN803.S5 1997, (v6)
Sherrick, Julie. Z8386.5.S54 1998, (v10)
Sherrill, Martha. BQ734.S44 2000, (v8)
Sherrill, Robert. E847.S47, (v4)
  F216.2.S48, (v4)
  HV8059.S47, (v6)
Sherrill, Rowland A. PS374.P47.S54 2000, (v3)
Sherrow, Victoria. F491.3.S47 1998, (v4)
  GT499.S49 2001, (v6)
  GV709.S44 1996, (v6)
  HQ784.W3.S54 2000, (v6)
  U21.75.S54 1996, (v10)
Sherry, Clifford J. HV4764.S5 1994, (v6)
  QL82.S49 1998, (v1)
Sherry, Michael S. E743.S53 1995, (v4)
  UA23.S47 1977, (v10)
Sherry, Vincent B. PR6019.O9.U697 1995, (v3)
Sherry, Vincent. PS3531.O82.Z8348 1993, (v3)
Shershow, Scott Cutler. PN1972.S45 1995, (v3)
Sherwin, Byron L. BJ1287.A155.S54 2000, (v8)
Sherwin, Oscar. PR3493.S45, (v3)

Sherwin, Susan. R724.S48 1992, (v2)
Sherwin-White, A. N. JC85.C5S5 1973, (v7)
Sherwood, Dolly. NB237.H6.S53 1991, (v9)
Sherwood, John Darrell. DS920.2.U5.S53 1996, (v5)
Sherwood, Lyn A. GV1108.A1 S54 2002, (v6)
Sherwood, Robert E. PS3537.H825.A63 1939, (v3)
  PS3537.H825.I4 1936, (v3)
  PS3537.H825.P4 1936, (v3)
  PS3537.H825.R4 1932, (v3)
  PS3537.H825.S56, (v3)
  PS3537.H825.T45 1940a, (v3)
  PS3537.H825.W3 1930, (v3)
Sherwood, Roger. NA7126.S48, (v9)
Sherwood, Terry G. PR3507.T43.S48 1989, (v3)
Shesol, Jeff. E847.2.S48 1997, (v4)
Shetter, William Z. PF112.S5 1994, (v3)
Shevchenko, Taras. PG3948.S5K6113 1964, (v3)
Shevell, Richard Shepherd. TL570.S462 1989, (v1)
Shewring, Margaret. PR2820.S54 1996, (v3)
Shi, David E. E169.1.S5558 1995, (v4)
  E169.1.S556 1985, (v4)
Shi, Shumei. PL2303.S57 2001, (v3)
Shi, Tianjian. JQ1516.S53 1997, (v7)
Shiba, Shoji. HD62.15.S55 2001, (v6)
Shibley, Mark A. BR1642.U5.S456 1996, (v8)
Shick, J. Malcolm. QL377.C7.S33 1990, (v1)
Shideler, Ross. PN56.F37.S54 1999, (v3)
Shields, David Lyle. GV706.3.S54 1995, (v6)
Shields, Graham J. DP17.Z99 S54 1985, (v5)
Shields, Hugh. ML3654.S54 1993, (v9)
Shields, Rob. GF95.S55 1992, (v6)
Shiell, Timothy C. KF4772.S445 1998, (v7)
Shier, Douglas R. QA401.S465 2000, (v1)
Shiers, George. Z7711.S49 1997, (v10)
Shifflett, Andrew Eric. PR438.P65.S53 1998, (v3)
Shifflett, Crandall A. F217.A65.S54 1991, (v4)
Shiffrin, Steven H. KF4772.S448 1999, (v7)
  KF4772.S45 1990, (v7)
Shiga, Naoya. PL816.H5 A513, (v3)
Shigesada, Nanako. QH353.S54 1997, (v1)
Shigley, Joseph Edward. TJ230.S5 2001, (v1)
Shih ching. PL2997.S452.P6 1954, (v3)
  PL2997.S452.W3, (v3)
Shih, Chung-wen. PL2384.S5, (v3)
Shih, Yu-chung. DS759.S43, (v5)
Shikes, Ralph E. ND553.P55.S53, (v9)
Shiller, Robert J. HD61.S45 2003, (v6)
Shilling, Chris. HM110.S55 1993, (v6)
Shillingberg, Wm. B. F819.T6.S45 1999, (v4)
Shillingburg, Miriam Jones. PS1334.S55 1988, (v3)
Shillingsburg, Peter L. PR5631.S48 2001, (v3)
  PR5633.S5 1992, (v3)
Shiloah, Amnon. ML3195.S4 1992, (v9)
Shiloah, Amnon. ML3545.S486 1995, (v9)
Shim, Jae K. HB61.S466 1995, (v6)
  HD1365.S48 1996, (v6)
  HF1001.S525 1989, (v6)
Shimahara, Nobuo. LB2844.1.N4.S545 1995, (v7)
Shiman, Lilian Lewis. HQ1599.E5.S54 1992, (v6)
Shimazaki, Toson. PL816.H55.C413 1991, (v3)
  PL816.H55 H33, (v3)
  PL816.H55.Y613 1987, (v3)
Shimer, Hervey Woodburn. QE745.S48, (v1)
Shimomura, Junichi. NA7125.S5513 1992, (v9)
Shimoni, Yaacov. DS37.S53 1987, (v5)
Shimony, Annemarie Anrod. E99.I7.S53 1994, (v4)
Shin, Gi-Wook. DS916.55.S55 1996, (v5)
Shinagel, Michael. PR3407.S5, (v3)
Shindo, Charles J. NX650.L32.S53 1997, (v9)
Shiner, L. E. DC270.T6559.S47 1988, (v5)
Shinn, Charles Howard. F864.S58 1970, (v4)
Shinn, Larry D. BL1285.835.U6.S55 1987, (v8)
Shinn, Thelma S. PS374.W6.S56 1996, (v3)
Shinoda, Minoru. CB5.R4 57, (v5)
Shipan, Charles R. KF4575.S54 1997, (v7)
Shipler, David K. E185.615.S48 1997, (v4)
Shipley, Graham. DF235.S54 2000, (v5)
Shipley, Joseph Twadell. PE1571.S46 1984, (v3)
  PN41.S5 1970, (v3)
Shipley, Robert Morrill. TN980.S5 1951, (v1)
Shipman, Harry L. QB843.B55.S54 1980, (v1)

Shipman, Pat. GN284.6.S55 2001, (v6)
Shipman, Pat. QP88.2.S45 1985, (v1)
Shipps, Anthony W. PN6081.S44 1990, (v3)
Shipps, Jan. BX8611.S493 2000, (v8)
Shipton, Alyn. ML417.W15 S5 2002, (v9)
  ML419.G54.S55 1999, (v9)
  ML3506.S47 2001, (v9)
Shipway, Martin. DS550.S54 1996, (v5)
Shiraev, Eric. E183.8.S65.S544 2000, (v4)
Shirane, Haruo. PL788.4.G43.S464 1987, (v3)
Shirane, Haruo. PL794.4.Z5.S586 1998, (v3)
Shire, Helena Mennie. PR2363.S5, (v3)
Shirer, William L. D811.5.S5 1941, (v5)
  DD256.5.S48, (v5)
  PS3537.H913.Z4617 1976, (v3)
Shiri, Keith. PN1993.5.A35.S48 1992, (v3)
Shirin Tahir-Kheli. E183.8.P18.S5 1982, (v4)
Shirinian, Lorne. PS153.A75.S55 1990, (v3)
Shirk, George H. F692.S5 1974, (v4)
Shirk, Martha. HQ792.U5.S534 1999, (v6)
Shirlaw, Matthew. ML444.S55.T3 1955, (v9)
Shirley, James. PR3141.D8 1966, (v3)
  PR3144.C3 1986, (v3)
Shirley, Michael. F264.W8.S48 1994, (v4)
Shiu-hing, Lo. JQ1539.5.A91.S45 1997, (v7)
Shiva, Vandana. K1519.B54.S53 1997, (v7)
Shivel, Gail. Z5305.U5.S55 2000, (v10)
Shivers, Frank R. F189.B13 S46 1995, (v4)
Shivers, Jay Sanford. GV15.S533 1997, (v6)
  GV181.3.S55 1986, (v6)
  GV181.4.S54, (v6)
Shklar, Judith N. JA83.S52 1998, (v7)
  JA84.U5.S525 1998, (v7)
  JC179.R9.S55, (v7)
  PQ2012.S53 1987, (v3)
Shklovskii, Viktor Borisovich. PN3457.S4913 1990,
  (v3)
Shlaim, Avi. DD881.S46 1983, (v5)
  DS119.7.S4762 2000, (v5)
Shlain, Leonard. N70.S48 1991, (v9)
Shlapentokh, Dmitry. PN1993.5.R9.S436 1993, (v3)
Shlapentokh, Vladimir. DK276.S48 1990, (v5)
  HN523.5.S434 1989, (v6)
  JN6693.5.S8.S55 1997, (v7)
Shleifer, Andrei. HC340.12.S494 2000, (v6)
Shmanske, Stephen. HB846.5.S56 1991, (v6)
Shneiderman, Ben. QA76.6.S543, (v1)
Shneidman, Edwin S. RC569.S3848 2001, (v2)
Shneidman, N. N. PG3098.4.S47 1995, (v3)
Shoebridge, Michele. Z7511.S48 1992, (v10)
Shoemaker, Robert Brink. KD7876.S47 1991, (v7)
Shoemaker, Sydney. BD450.S46, (v8)
Shofner, Jerrell H. F316.S56, (v4)
Shogan, Robert. D753.S485 1995, (v5)
Shokeid, Moshe. F128.68.Q4.S56 1988, (v4)
Sholem Aleichem. PJ5129.R2 A15 1956, (v3)
  PJ5129.R2.A26 1984, (v3)
  PJ5129.R2.F83, (v3)
  PJ5129.R2.I5413 1948, (v3)
Sholokhov, Mikhail Aleksandrovich.
  PG3476.S52T4813 1989, (v3)
  PG3476.S52T4813 1996, (v3)
Sholom Aleichem. PJ5129.R2.B5413 1991, (v3)
Shomette, Donald. F187.C5 S47 1996, (v4)
  F187.C5 S48 1985, (v4)
Shomon, Joseph James. SK571.S48 1998, (v1)
Shonfield, Andrew. HC59.S494, (v6)
Shopkow, Leah. DC611.N856.S56 1997, (v5)
Shoptaw, John. PS3501.S475.Z86 1994, (v3)
Shor, Ira. LC191.4.S54 1986, (v7)
Shor, Ira. LC196.5.U6.S566 1996, (v7)
Shore, Bradd. GN502.S49 1996, (v6)
Shore, Cris. D2009.S54 2000, (v5)
Shore, Heather. HV9146.L65.S48 1999, (v6)
Shore, Peter. DA589.8.S56 2000, (v5)
Shore, Stephen. TR179.S56 1998, (v1)
Shorey, Paul. B395.S48, (v8)
Short, Brian. DA570.S47 1997, (v5)
Short, Bryan Collier. PS2388.T4.S46 1992, (v3)
Short, Douglas D. Z2012.S53, (v10)
Short, Michael. ML410.H748.S5 1990, (v9)

Short, Philip. DS778.M3.S548 2000, (v5)
Shorter, Clement King. PR4168.S38 1969, (v3)
Shorter, Edward. HD5374.S55, (v6)
  RC49.S354 1994, (v2)
  RC438.S54 1997, (v2)
Shorthouse, J. H. PR5451.J6, (v3)
Shortridge, James R. F351.S5 1989, (v4)
Shortt, Adam. F1008.S57, (v4)
Shostack, Albert L. HV1445.S47 2001, (v6)
Shostak, Marjorie. DT1058.K86, (v5)
Shosteck, Robert. F187.P8 S5, (v4)
Shotwell, James Thomson. D13.S5 1939, (v5)
Shover, John L. HD1761.S556, (v6)
Shover, Neal. HV6658.S54 1996, (v6)
Showalter, Elaine. PR115.S5, (v3)
  RC532.S46 1997, (v2)
Showell, Jak P. Mallmann. V859.G3.S5 1974, (v10)
  VA513.S52, (v10)
Shrader-Frechette, K. S. Q180.55.M67.S48 1994, (v1)
Shrake, Edwin. PS3569.H735B6 1997, (v3)
Shrimpton, Gordon Spencer. DF211.S47 1997, (v5)
Shriver, Donald W. BR115.P7.S514 1995, (v8)
Shroder, Maurice Z. PQ287.S48, (v3)
Shropshire, Kenneth L. GV706.32.S48 1996, (v6)
  GV734.5.S57 1990, (v6)
  GV734.5.S58 2003, (v6)
  KF299.E57 S57 1990, (v7)
Shrout, R. N. HV1569.5.S57 1991, (v6)
Shroyer, Jo Ann. QC789.2.U62L677 1998, (v1)
Shrum, Wesley. Z7407.D44 S57 1995, (v10)
Shryock, Andrew. DS153.55.B43.S57 1997, (v5)
Shryock, Henry S. HB881.S526 1976, (v6)
Shryock, Richard Harrison. R145.S45 1947, (v2)
  R148.S45, (v2)
Shu, Ch'ing-ch'un. PL2804.C5 Y45, (v3)
Shu, Frank H. QB461.S448 1991, (v1)
Shu, Yunzhong. PL2303.S625 2000, (v3)
Shubert, Adrian. GV1108.5.S58 1999, (v6)
  HD8039.M62.S68 1987, (v6)
Shubik, Martin. H61.25.S49 1982, (v6)
Shugar, Dana R. HQ1190.5.U6.S58 1995, (v6)
Shugar, Gershon J. QD65.S537 1990, (v1)
Shugart, H. H. QH541.15.M3.S56 1998, (v1)
Shuger, Debora K. BS500.S46 1994, (v8)
Shugg, Roger Wallace. F374.S58 1968, (v4)
Shui hu ch'uan. PL2694.S5.E52 1937, (v3)
Shuker, Roy. ML3470.S54 2001, (v9)
Shulimson, Jack. VE23.S52 1993, (v10)
Shull, Bernard. HG1722.S585 2001, (v6)
Shull, Michael S. D743.23.S55 1996, (v5)
  PN1995.75.S54 2000, (v3)
Shulman, Frank Joseph. Z3106.G65 Suppl. 2, (v10)
Shulman, George M. JC153.W63.S54 1989, (v7)
Shulman, James Lawrence. GV351.S48 2001, (v6)
Shulman, Lawrence. HV11.S493 1999, (v6)
Shulman, Mark R. VA58.S53 1995, (v10)
Shulman, Marshall Darrow. D844.S47, (v5)
  DK63.3.S368, (v5)
Shulman, Max. PS3537.H9919 B3, (v3)
  PS3537.H9919 M3 1951, (v3)
  PS3537.H9919 R3, (v3)
Shulman, Robert. PS228.C6.S58 2000, (v3)
Shulsky, Abram N. JF1525.I6.S49 1991, (v7)
Shultz, Gladys Denny. ML420.L7.S5, (v9)
Shultz, Richard H. UA770.S514 1988, (v10)
Shultz, Sandra J. RD97.S538 2000, (v2)
Shumacker, Harris B. RD598.S454 1992, (v2)
Shumaker, Arthur Wesley. PS283.I6S5, (v3)
Shuman, Cathy. PR468.E93.S48 2000, (v3)
Shuman, Jeffrey C. HD69.S8.S54 2001, (v6)
Shuman, Michael. E840.S48 1993, (v4)
  HC110.E5 S49 1998, (v6)
Shuman, R. Baird. LB2844.1.N4.S55 1989, (v7)
Shumway, Nicolas. F2843.S47 1991, (v4)
Shun, Kwong-loi. B128.M324.S48 1997, (v8)
Shupe, Anson D. BL2530.U6.S53, (v8)
Shurcliff, William A. QC441.S5 1964, (v1)
Shurgot, Michael W. PR3095.S58 1998, (v3)
Shurkin, Joel N. BF723.G5.S48 1992, (v2)
Shurts, John. KF8210.N37 S55 2000, (v7)
Shusterman, David. PR6037.N58.Z87, (v3)

Shusterman, Richard. BH39.S5256 1992, (v8)
Shute, Nevil. PR6027.O54 P32, (v3)
Shuter, Jane. DT61.S644 1999, (v5)
Shveælëtiser, Viktoriëila. PG3476.T75Z88213 1993, (v3)
Shvidkovskii, D. O. NA1196.S5613 1996, (v9)
Sia, Marian F. BT732.7.S53 1994, (v8)
Siani-Davies, Peter. DR205.R65 1998, (v5)
Siavelis, Peter. JL2619.S56 2000, (v7)
Sibiya, Christina. GN657.Z8.S5 1948, (v6)
Sibley, Charles Gald. QL678.S54 1990, (v1)
  QL696.5.S53 1991, (v1)
Sibley, David. GF121.S53 1995, (v6)
  QL681.S497 2000, (v1)
Sibley, Marilyn McAdams. HE554.H65S5 1968, (v6)
Sibley, Mulford Quickert. UB342.U5.S52, (v10)
Sibley, William F. PL816.H5.Z846, (v3)
Sicari, Stephen. PR6019.O9.U698 2001, (v3)
Sicari, Stephen. PS3531.O82.C2878 1991, (v3)
Sichel, Daniel E. HD9696.C63.U58339 1997, (v6)
Sicherman, Barbara. R154.H238.S53 1984, (v2)
Sicherman, Carol. PR9381.9.N45.Z87 1990, (v3)
Sichol, Marcia. U263.S53 1990, (v10)
Sicius, Francis J. PN4899.C4.C387 1990, (v3)
Sick, Gary. E875.S48 1992, (v4)
Sickels, Robert J. KF213.S66.S56 1988, (v7)
Sicker, Martin. DR473.S53 2001, (v5)
  DS38.2.S53 2000, (v5)
  DS62.2.S54 2000, (v5)
  DS62.8.S54 2001, (v5)
  DS119.7.S38195 1989, (v5)
  DS121.7.S53 2001, (v5)
  GN492.6.S53 1991, (v6)
Sickinger, James P. CD996.S53 1999, (v5)
Sidani, Souraya. RT85.5.S53 1998, (v2)
Sidanius, Jim. HM131.S5832 1999, (v6)
Sidbury, James. F234.R59.N477 1997, (v4)
Siddiquee, Noore Alam. JS7100.3.S53 1997, (v7)
Siddiqui, Ataullah. BP172.S53 1997, (v8)
Siddiqui, Kamal. JS7100.2.S53 2000, (v7)
Sidel, John Thayer. JS7303.A2.S55 1999, (v7)
Sidelle, Alan. B809.15.S56 1989, (v8)
Sidgwick, Henry. BJ71.S55 1960, (v8)
  BJ1008.S5 1981, (v8)
Sidgwick, Nevil Vincent. QD412.N1.S5 1966, (v1)
Sidhwa, Bapsi. PR9540.9.S53.A82 1993, (v3)
  PR9540.9.S53.I34 1991, (v3)
  PR9540.9.S53I34 1991, (v3)
Sidky, H. DS374.B28.S54 2000, (v3)
  GR530.S53 1997, (v6)
Sidney, Philip. PR2340.A5.F4, (v3)
  PR2340.A5.R5, (v3)
  PR2342.A5 1987, (v3)
Sieber, Roy. NB1091.65.S54 1987, (v9)
  NK2685.75.S53, (v9)
Siebert, William McC. TK454.S57 1986, (v1)
Sieden, Lloyd Steven. T49.5.S575 1989, (v1)
Siedentop, Larry. JN30.S47 2001, (v7)
Sieg, Katrin. PT668.S535 1994, (v3)
Siegan, Bernard H. K3165.S545 1994, (v7)
  KF5698.S55 1997, (v7)
Siegel, Ben. PJ5129.A8.Z926, (v3)
Siegel, Daniel M. QC670.S48 1991, (v1)
Siegel, Dorothy. LB2345.S54 1994, (v7)
Siegel, Frederick F. E741.S48 1984, (v4)
  HN80.N5.S54 1997, (v6)
Siegel, Irwin M., 1927-. RC930.S47 1998, (v2)
Siegel, Jacob S. HB849.4.S53 2002, (v6)
Siegel, James T. DS643.S54 1997, (v5)
Siegel, Katherine A. S. E183.8.S65.S56 1996, (v4)
Siegel, Marcia B. GV1623.S54, (v6)
  GV1783.S56 1979, (v6)
Siegel, Richard L. HD4903.S47 1994, (v6)
Siegel, Scott. PN1993.5.U6.S494 1990, (v3)
Siegelbaum, Lewis H. DK266.S5276 1992, (v5)
  HC340.S6.S515 1988, (v6)
Siegert, Bernhard. PN98.S46.S5413 1999, (v3)
Siegfried, Tom. QA76.S5159 2000, (v1)
Siegler, Robert S. BF723.C5.S53 1996, (v2)
Siegman, A. E. TA1675.S5 1986, (v1)
Siemann, Wolfram. DD207.S5413 1998, (v5)

Sienkewicz, Thomas J. BL304.S54 1997, (v8)
  Z7836.S54 1996, (v10)
Sienkiewicz, Henryk. PG7158.S4.O413 1991, (v3)
  PG7158.S4P313 1992, (v3)
  PG7158.S4 P33, (v3)
  PG7158.S4 P613, (v3)
  PG7158.S4.P627 1991, (v3)
  PG7158.S4Q43 1992, (v3)
Sierra, Judy. CS2377.S48 1997, (v5)
Sies, Luther F. PN1991.2.S57 2000, (v3)
Siewert, Charles P. B808.9.S54 1998, (v8)
Sifakis, Carl. HV6278.S54 2001, (v6)
  HV6441.S53 1999, (v6)
  HV6789.S537 2001, (v6)
Siff, Ezra Y. DS557.8.T6.S54 1999, (v5)
Sigal, Gale. PN691.S54 1996, (v3)
Sigal, Leon V. D821.U6.S54 1988, (v5)
Sigal, Peter Herman. F1435.3.R3.S54 2000, (v4)
Sigee, D. C. SB734.S54 1993, (v1)
Sigelman, Lee. E185.615.S55 1991, (v4)
Sigerist, Henry E. R151.S52, (v2)
Sigler, Barbara A. RF52.5.S54 1993, (v2)
Sigmund, Karl. QH313.S585 1993, (v1)
Sigmund, Paul E. JC183.8.C4.S57 1993, (v4)
Signorielli, Nancy. Z5633.V56.S56 1988, (v10)
Sigworth, Oliver F. PR3353.S5, (v3)
Sikainga, Ahmad Alawad. DT159.6.B34.S55 1991, (v5)
Siker, Jeffrey S. BJ1231.S45 1997, (v8)
Sikorsky, Igor Ivan. TL540.S54.A3 1967, (v1)
Sikov, Ed. PN1998.3.W56.S55 1998, (v3)
Silber, Laura. DR1313 .S55 1997, (v5)
Silber, Nina. E668.S57 1993, (v4)
Silbergeld, Jerome. ND1040.S47 1982, (v9)
Silberman, Arlene. LB1576.S43 1989, (v7)
Silberman, Bernard S. Z3301.S55, (v10)
Silberman, Marc. PN1993.5.G3.S54 1995, (v3)
Silberman, Neil Asher. CC101.I75.S57 1982, (v5)
Silberschatz, Abraham. QA76.76.O63S55825 2000, (v1)
  QA76.76.O63S5583 2002, (v1)
Silbey, Joel H. E338.S55 1985, (v4)
  E387.S64 2002, (v4)
Silcox, Harry C. F158.5.M55.S55 1989, (v4)
Silk, Joseph. QB981.S55 2001, (v1)
  QB981.S553 1994, (v1)
  QB981.S554 1994, (v1)
Silk, Leonard Solomon. HB501.S5896 1996, (v6)
Silk, Mark. PN4874.S513.A3 1995, (v3)
Silka, Linda. HM101.S54 1989, (v6)
  PS3569.I44.A79 1991, (v3)
  PS3569.I44.C4, (v3)
  PS3569.I44.S8, (v3)
Silla, Eric. RC154.8.M42.S56 1998, (v2)
Sillars, Stuart. PR471.S55 1999, (v3)
Silliphant, Leigh. HF5422.S54 1988, (v6)
Sillitoe, Alan. PR6037.I55.G4, (v3)
  PR6037.I55.K4 1962, (v3)
  PR6037.I55.L6 1960, (v3)
  PR6037.I55.S3, (v3)
  PR6037.I55.S4 1981, (v3)
Sillitoe, Paul. GN668.S55 1998, (v6)
  HN930.9.A8S55 2000, (v6)
Silman, Shlomo. RF294.S55 1991, (v2)
Silsby, Jill. QL520.S56 2001, (v1)
Silva Castro, Raul. PQ7997.S544.P3, (v3)
Silva, Eduardo da. F2659.N4.S47 1993, (v4)
Silva, Ruth Caridad. JK609.S5 1951, (v7)
Silver, A. David. HG4907.S46 1995, (v6)
Silver, A. I. F1027.S562 1982, (v4)
Silver, Alain. PN1995.9.F54.S58 1999, (v3)
  PN1995.9.V3.U77 1993, (v3)
Silver, Archie A. LC4705.S59 2002, (v7)
Silver, Arnold Jacques. PR5363.S33.S55 1993, (v3)
Silver, Brenda R. PR6045.O72.Z8764 1983, (v3)
Silver, Carole G. GR141.S55 1999, (v6)
Silver, Christopher. F234.R59.N48 1995, (v4)
Silver, Harold. LA631.7.S44 1983, (v7)
Silver, J. K. RC180.1.S56 2001, (v2)
Silver, Kenneth E. N6850.S56 1989, (v9)
Silver, Lee M. QH432.S56 1995, (v1)

Silver, Philip W. PQ6071.S55 1997, (v3)
Silver, Theodore. KF283.S57 1981, (v7)
Silver, Timothy. GF504.S67.S55 1990, (v6)
Silver, Victoria. PR3562.S54 2001, (v3)
Silverberg, Robert. PS3569.I472.T5, (v3)
Silverblatt, Art. P91.3.S527 1997, (v3)
Silverburg, Sanford R. Z3013.S54 1992, (v10)
Silverfarb, Daniel. DA47.9.I72.S56 1994, (v5)
Silverman, Bertram. HC340.12.S55 2000, (v6)
Silverman, Dan P. HD8450.S55 1998, (v6)
Silverman, Deborah Anders. GR111.P65.S55 2000, (v6)
Silverman, Eliane Leslau. HQ1459.A4.S55 1984, (v6)
Silverman, Helaine. F3429.1.N3.S55 1993, (v4)
    Z1209.2.P4.S55 1996, (v10)
Silverman, Kaja. PN1998.3.G63.S56 1998, (v3)
Silverman, Kenneth. F67.M43S57 1985, (v4)
    GV1545.H8.S55 1996, (v6)
    PS2631.S525 1991, (v3)
Silverman, Lisa. HV8599.F7, (v6)
Silverman, Mark P. QC21.2.S47 1993, (v1)
    QC173.4.A87.S55 2000, (v1)
    QC174.12.S525 1995, (v1)
Silverman, Milton. HD9674.D44.S54 1992, (v6)
Silverman, Phyllis R. BF723.D3.S58 2000, (v2)
Silverstein, Arthur M. RA644.I6.S54, (v2)
Silverstein, Gordon. KF4651.S72 1997, (v7)
Silverstein, Robert Milton. QD272.S6S55, (v1)
Silverstein, Shel. PS3569.I47224L5 1981, (v3)
Silverstein, Shel. PZ8.3.S5844Wh, (v3)
Silverstone, Paul H. VA61.S54 2001, (v10)
    VA61.S567 2001, (v10)
Silvert, Kalman H. F1410.S6 1966, (v4)
    F1421.T95 no.21, (v4)
Silverthorne, Elizabeth. PS2133.S56 1993, (v3)
    R692.S586 1997, (v2)
Silvertown, Jonathan W. QK910.S54 1993, (v1)
Silvester, P. P. TK153.S53 1990, (v1)
Silvester, Robert. Z5781.S55 1993, (v10)
Silz, Walter. PT2379.Z5.S5 1962, (v3)
Sim, Stuart. BH201.S49 1992, (v8)
Simai, Mihaly. JC362.S53 1994, (v7)
Simcox, E. J. PR5452.S27.Z47 1998, (v3)
Sime, Ruth Lewin. QC774.M4.S56 1996, (v1)
Simek, Rudolf. BD495.5.S5513 1996, (v8)
Simenon, Georges. PQ2637.I53 M178, (v3)
Simeone, James. F545.S56 2000, (v4)
Simiu, Emil. TA654.5.S55 1996, (v1)
Simkin, Tom. QE522.V92 1994, (v1)
Simkins, Francis Butler. F274.S57, (v4)
    F274.S583, (v4)
Simkins, Peter. D546.S56 1988, (v5)
Simmonds, Roy S. PS3537.T3234.Z8667 1996, (v3)
    Z8549.8.S55 1988, (v10)
Simmons, A. John. JC153.L87.S57 1993, (v7)
Simmons, Beth A. HF1411.S454 1994, (v6)
Simmons, Charles A. PN4882.5.S57 1998, (v3)
Simmons, Clare A. PR468.H57.S566 2000, (v3)
Simmons, Diane. PR9275.A583.K567 1994, (v3)
    PS3561.I52.Z88 1999, (v3)
Simmons, Harvey G. DC423.S556 1996, (v5)
Simmons, Jack. HE3018.S58 1991, (v6)
Simmons, John G. Q148.S55 1996, (v1)
Simmons, Keith. BC199.2.S56 1993, (v8)
Simmons, Marc. E83.88.S56 1997, (v4)
    F799.O587 1991, (v4)
Simmons, Peter J. (Peter John). QP356.Y68 1999, (v1)
Simmons, Philip E. PS374.P64.S5 1997, (v3)
Simmons, Virginia McConnell. E99.U8.S55 2000, (v4)
Simms, Brendan. DD420.S56 1997, (v5)
Simms, Bryan R. ML134.B46.S56 1996, (v9)
    ML197.S585 1996, (v9)
    ML410.S283.S45 2000, (v9)
Simms, William Gilmore. PS2843.G84 2001, (v3)
    PS2848.H3 1998, (v3)
    PS2848.S8 1968, (v3)
    PS2848.Y5 1937, (v3)
    PS2853.A4 1952, (v3)
Simon Diaz, Jose. Z2691.S54 1980, (v10)
Simon, Brian. LA631.82.S49 1991, (v7)

Simon, Claude. PQ2637.I547.G413 1989, (v3)
    PQ2637.I547.I513 1991, (v3)
Simon, Edith. DD404.S57 1963a, (v5)
Simon, George Thomas. ML3518.S55 1981, (v9)
Simon, Herbert Alexander. HB119.S47.A3 1991, (v6)
    HD31.S55 1976, (v6)
    HD69.D4.S49 1977, (v6)
    Q175.S564 1981, (v1)
Simon, James F. KF8745.D6 S55 1981, (v7)
Simon, Joan. ND237.R72484.S55 1991, (v9)
Simon, Julia. JC336.S47 2001, (v7)
Simon, Julian Lincoln. GE40.S55 1999, (v6)
    HB615.S55 1987, (v6)
    HB849.41.S548 2000, (v6)
    HB871.S57, (v6)
    HB871.S573 1996, (v6)
    HB3505.S52 1990, (v6)
    HD30.23.S56 2001, (v6)
Simon, Neil. PS3537.I663.A6 1971, (v3)
    PS3537.I663.O3, (v3)
Simon, Noel. QH541.S5345 1995, (v1)
Simon, Pierre Henri. PQ305.S5 1967, (v3)
    PQ671.S5, (v3)
    PQ2607.U53.Z84, (v3)
Simon, R. M. RC489.A7.S56 1992, (v2)
Simon, Randy. TK7872.S8.S55 1988, (v1)
Simon, Reeva S. DS79.S57 1986, (v5)
Simon, Rita James. KF9242.S48 1988, (v7)
Simon, Robert I. RC555.S57 1996, (v2)
Simon, Robert L. GV706.5.S56 1991, (v6)
Simon, Walter Michael. B831.S5, (v8)
    DD217.S5, (v5)
Simon, Walter. PL1171.S53 1947, (v3)
Simonds, Fred. QA76.9.A25.S35 1996, (v1)
Simonds, Peggy Munoz. PR2806.S56 1992, (v3)
Simonelli, Jeanne M. E99.N3.S55 1997, (v4)
Simonian, Lane. S934.M6.S55 1995, (v1)
Simons, Anna. DT407.S55 1995, (v5)
Simons, G. L. E840.S485 1998, (v4)
    JC599.I43.S56 1999, (v7)
    JC599.S33.S58 1998, (v7)
    JX1246.S47 1998, (v7)
    JX1977.S4563 1995, (v7)
Simons, H. J. DT1756.S53 1997, (v5)
Simons, Henry Calvert. HJ4652.S475, (v6)
Simons, Jack. QD462.S53 1997, (v1)
Simons, Linda Keir. Z6935.S56 1994, (v10)
Simons, Minot. Volume 1, 1966-1994. GV464.S55 1995, (v6)
Simonson, Harold Peter. PT9150.R55.Z86 1987, (v3)
Simonton, Dean Keith. BF109.A1S56 2002, (v2)
    BF412.S56 1994, (v2)
    D16.13.S58 1990, (v5)
    JK518.S56 1987, (v7)
Simonton, Deborah. HD6134.S54 1998, (v6)
Simosko, Vladimir. ML419.S52.S56 2000, (v9)
Simpson, A. W. B. KD671.A7.S56 1995, (v7)
Simpson, Amelia S. PN1992.6.S48 1993, (v3)
Simpson, Andrea Y. E185.615.S562 1998, (v4)
Simpson, Antony E. Z7164.A2 S53 1993, (v10)
Simpson, Bland. F262.A33.S56 1997, (v4)
Simpson, Brooks D. E175.5.A2.S56 1996, (v4)
    E668.S58 1998, (v4)
    E672.S6 1991, (v4)
Simpson, Christopher. UB276.S56 1994, (v10)
Simpson, Claude M. PS658.L6 1960, (v3)
Simpson, Evelyn Mary Spearing. PR2248.S5 1948, (v3)
Simpson, F. A. DC280.S6 1968, (v5)
Simpson, George Gaylord. QE711.S5, (v1)
    QL351.S5 1961, (v1)
    QL737.U6.S5, (v1)
Simpson, George. F1060.8.S552 1968, (v4)
Simpson, J. H. F826.S58 1983, (v4)
Simpson, Jacqueline. GR141.S59 2001, (v6)
Simpson, James. PR2017.L38.S56 1990, (v3)
Simpson, Jeffrey. F1034.2.S53, (v4)
Simpson, John E. QC939.L37.S56 1994, (v1)
Simpson, Lesley Byrd. F1226.S63 1966, (v4)
    F1411.S62 1950, (v4)
Simpson, Marc. ND237.H7.A4 1988, (v9)

Simpson, Martha Seif. Z718.1.S57 1992, (v10)
Simpson, Megan. PS310.L33.S56 2000, (v3)
Simpson, Michael. PR4392.D7.S55 1998, (v3)
Simpson, Peter. BX1378.5.S56 2001, (v8)
Simpson, Philip L. PN1995.9.S297.S56 2000, (v3)
Simpson, Ruth M. Rasey. F59.B4 S55 1993, (v4)
Simpson, Thomas K. QC665.E4.S554 1997, (v1)
Simpson, William Kelly. PJ1943.S5, (v3)
Sims, Edgar B. F247.A15 S5, (v4)
Sims, Harold. F1232.S56 1990, (v4)
Sims, Henry P. HD58.7.S584 1986, (v6)
Sims, James H. PR3592.R4S5, (v3)
Sims, John. BT1117.S55 1995, (v8)
Sims, Laura S. TX360.U6.S58 1998, (v1)
Sims, Robert Lewis. PQ8180.17.A73.Z92913 1992, (v3)
Sims, Ronald R. HF5387.S57 1994, (v6)
Simsion, Graeme C. QA76.9.D26S54 2001, (v1)
Simson, Otto Georg von. NA4830.S5 1962, (v9)
Sin Phe Mran. PL3988.T48.A45, (v3)
Sin, To-chol. JQ1729.A15.S55 1999, (v7)
Sinaiko, Herman L. PN81.S5274 1998, (v3)
Sinclair, Andrew. E786.S5, (v4)
    PR6069.I5.B7, (v3)
    PR6069.I5.M9, (v3)
    PR6069.I5.P3 1963, (v3)
    PR6069.I5.P7, (v3)
Sinclair, Barbara. JK1161.S56 1989, (v7)
    JK1411.S55 1995, (v7)
    JK1411.S56 1983, (v7)
    KF4945.S58 1997, (v7)
Sinclair, Brett Jason. R733.S56 1992, (v2)
Sinclair, May. PR6037.I73 D5 1970, (v3)
    PR6037.I73 M3, (v3)
Sinclair, R. K. JC79.A8.S56 1988, (v7)
Sinclair, Upton Beall. PS3537.I85.M4, (v3)
Sinclair, Upton. CT275.F68.S55 1937a, (v5)
    PS3537.I85 A65, (v3)
    PS3537.I85 B4, (v3)
    PS3537.I85 B6, (v3)
    PS3537.I85.C63, (v3)
    PS3537.I85 C64, (v3)
    PS3537.I85 D7, (v3)
    PS3537.I85.H4 1923, (v3)
    PS3537.I85 I9, (v3)
    PS3537.I85 J8 1951, (v3)
    PS3537.I85 K5, (v3)
    PS3537.I85 O2, (v3)
    PS3537.I85.O5 1927, (v3)
    PS3537.I85.P5 1970, (v3)
    PS3537.I85 P7, (v3)
    PS3537.I85 P75, (v3)
    PS3537.I85 R4, (v3)
    PS3537.I85 R6, (v3)
    PS3537.I85.S5 1924, (v3)
    PS3537.I85 S88, (v3)
    PS3537.I85 W5, (v3)
    PS3537.I85 W6, (v3)
    PS3537.I85.Z517, (v3)
    PS3537.I85.Z5 1969, (v3)
    PS3537.I85.Z54, (v3)
Sinden, Richard R. QP624.S56 1994, (v1)
Sindler, Allan P. F216.2.S5, (v4)
Sinfield, Alan. PR428.P6.S57 1992, (v3)
    PR739.H65.S56 1999, (v3)
Singal, Daniel Joseph. PS3511.A86.Z9686 1997, (v3)
Singer, Ben. PN1995.9.M45.S56 2001, (v3)
Singer, Beth J. JC571.S6285 1999, (v7)
Singer, Charles Joseph. R131.S55 1962, (v2)
Singer, Daniel. DC423.S565 1988, (v5)
Singer, David A. QA445.S55 1997, (v1)
Singer, Dorothy G. BF717.S514 1990, (v2)
Singer, Eleanor. PN4784.D57.S56 1993, (v3)
Singer, Hans Wolfgang. HC59.7.S4669 1993, (v6)
Singer, Irving. B945.S24 S56 2000, (v8)
    BD431.S578 1992, (v8)
    BD436.S5 1984, (v8)
    PN1995.S513 1998, (v3)

Singer, Isaac Bashevis. PJ5054.S572.Z513, (v3)
  PJ5129.S49 E8, (v3)
  PJ5129.S49 G52, (v3)
  PJ5129.S49 M3, (v3)
  PJ5129.S49 M35, (v3)
  PJ5129.S49 S3, (v3)
  PJ5129.S49 S55, (v3)
  PJ5129.S49 S7, (v3)
Singer, Israel Joshua. PJ5129.S5.B713 1980, (v3)
Singer, J. David. JX1291.S398 1990, (v7)
Singer, Jerome L. HQ784.T4.S56, (v6)
Singer, Linda R. KF9084.S57 1990, (v7)
Singer, Max. HC59.S5375 1987, (v6)
  JX1952.S6795 1993, (v7)
Singer, Michael J. (Michael John). S591.S555 2002, (v1)
Singer, Milton B. BL1220.S5 1981, (v8)
Singer, Peter. BJ51.S57 1981, (v8)
  BJ1012.S485 1997, (v8)
Singer, Robert T. N7353.5.S656 1998, (v9)
Singer, Stanley. QC966.S55, (v1)
Singerman, Robert. Z1002.S54 1996, (v10)
  Z6366.S526, (v10)
  Z7116.S55 1996, (v10)
Singh Mukerji, Vanita. PG1418.A6.Z85 1990, (v3)
Singh, Amar Kaur Jasbir. DS485.H6 S442 1988, (v5)
Singh, Chaitram. F2385.S56 1988, (v4)
Singh, D. S. Ranjit. DS650.5.S56 1997, (v5)
Singh, Gurcharan. QK95.S57 1999, (v1)
Singh, Gurdial. PK2659.S462A6613 1996, (v3)
Singh, Gurharpal. DS430.S543 2000, (v5)
Singh, Inderjit. HC430.6.S59 1990, (v6)
Singh, Jagjit. BD511.S5 1961, (v8)
Singh, K. Suresh. DS430.S545 1992, (v5)
Singh, Kavaljit. HG3881.S5372 2000, (v6)
Singh, Kelvin. F2121.S555 1994, (v4)
Singh, Khushwant. PR9499.3.K48.M3 1956, (v3)
Singh, Nanua. TS155.63.S56 1996, (v1)
Singh, Priyam. HV6250.4.W65.S54 1996, (v6)
Singh, R. S. SB731.S458 2001, (v1)
Singh, Robert. JK1415.S55 1998, (v7)
Singh, Sarup. PR635.F33.S56 1983, (v3)
Singh, Simon. QA244.S55 1997, (v1)
  Z103.S56 1999, (v10)
Singh, V. P. GB656.2.H9.S558 1997, (v6)
Singleton, Carl. Z3226.S56 1997, (v10)
Singleton, Frederick Bernard. DL1032.S55 1989, (v5)
  DR1246 .S56 1985, (v5)
Singleton, Jeff. HV91.S555 2000, (v6)
Singleton, Mary Ann. PR6023.E833.Z89, (v3)
Singleton, Ralph S. PN1993.45.S56 2000, (v3)
Singley, Carol J. PS3545.H16.Z878 1995, (v3)
Singley, Mark K. LB1059.S523 1989, (v7)
Sinha, Anil Kumar. TN693.I7.S485 1989, (v1)
Sinha, Anshu K. QE319.H5.S56 1989, (v1)
Sinha, Manisha. F273.S64 2000, (v4)
Sinha, Nirmal Chandra. DS786.S5423 1991, (v5)
Sinha, Ramesh P. HD6812.S56 1984, (v6)
Sinha, S. Prakash. K231.S57 1993, (v7)
Sinkankas, John. TS752.5.S56 1981, (v1)
Sinkin, Richard N. F1233.S56, (v4)
Sinkule, Barbara J. GE190.C6.S56 1995, (v6)
Sinn, Ulrich. GV23.S56 2000, (v6)
Sinnette, Elinor Des Verney. Z989.S36.S56 1989, (v10)
Sinnott, Edmund Ware. QH331.S5, (v1)
Sinnott, Roger W. QB65.S62 1997, (v1)
Sinnott-Armstrong, Walter. BJ1031.S55 1988, (v8)
Sinopoli, Richard C. JA84.U5.S555 1992, (v7)
Sinsheimer, Hermann. PR2825.S5 1963, (v3)
Siouris, George M. TJ213.S474443 1996, (v1)
Sipe, Thomas. ML410.B42.S57 1998, (v9)
Sipihr̄ī, Suhr̄āb. PK6561.S559A26 1988, (v3)
Siporin, Steve. NX504.S57 1992, (v9)
Sipple, William L. Z8830.8.S58 1984, (v10)
Siracusa, Joseph M. E744.S5637 1993, (v4)
Siraisi, Nancy G. R141.S546 1990, (v2)
Sircello, Guy. BD436.S54 1989, (v8)
Sire, H. J. A. CR4723.S5 1994, (v5)
Sire, James W. B823.3.S56 1997, (v8)
Siringo, Charles A. F391.S624.A37 1979, (v4)

Sirmans, Marion Eugene. F272.S5, (v4)
Sirovich, L. QA39.2.S525 1988, (v1)
Siry, Joseph. NA5235.O258.S58 1996, (v9)
  NA6233.C4.C387 1988, (v9)
Sisam, Celia. PR1203.S55, (v3)
Sisam, Kenneth. PR1585.S5, (v3)
Sisk, David W. PR888.D96.S57 1997, (v3)
Sisk, Timothy D. JQ1911.S57 1995, (v7)
Siskin, Clifford. PR448.S64.S57 1998, (v3)
Siskind, Aaron. F128.68.H3S57 1990, (v4)
  TR140.S54.A3, (v1)
Sisman, Elaine Rochelle. ML410.M9 S56 1993, (v9)
  MT90.S58 1993, (v9)
Sismondi, J.-C.-L. Simonde de. HB163.S613 1991, (v6)
Sissa, Giulia. BL782.S5713 2000, (v8)
Sissa, Giulia. DF93.S5313 1990, (v5)
Sisson, Charles Jasper. PR658.L6.S6, (v3)
Sitkoff, Harvard. E185.61.S596, (v4)
Sitney, P. Adams. PN1993.5.I88.S57 1995, (v3)
Sitte, Camillo. NA9030.S613 1965, (v9)
  NA9052.S5813 1979, (v9)
Sitter, John E. PR448.L66.S5 1982, (v3)
Sitter, L. U. de. QE501.S54 1964, (v1)
Sitton, John F. HT609.S57 1996, (v6)
Sitton, Thad. F392.N35.S57 1995, (v4)
Sitton, Tom. F866.H3473.S58 1992, (v4)
Sittser, Gerald Lawson. D744.5.U6.S58 1997, (v5)
Sitwell, Edith. CT775.S55 1957, (v5)
  PR3633.S5 1930a, (v3)
  PR6037.I8.A17 1954, (v3)
  PR6037.I8 I2 1938, (v3)
  PR6037.I8.M8, (v3)
Sitwell, Osbert. PR6037.I83.A17 1976b, (v3)
  PR6037.I83.P6 1963, (v3)
  PR6037.I83.Z5, (v3)
  PR6037.I83.Z515 1972, (v3)
  PR6037.I83.Z518 1962, (v3)
Sitwell, Sacheverell. BF1483.S5 1959, (v2)
  DA688.S58, (v5)
  NA1306.S5, (v9)
  PR6037.I85.A17 1936, (v3)
Siu, Paul C. P. HD8039.L32.U675 1987, (v6)
Sivan, Reuven. PJ4833.S56 1977, (v3)
Sivanandan, Ambalavaner. PR9440.9.S577.W44 1996, (v3)
Sivasankara Pillai, Thakazhi. PK2978.E5.S5x, (v3)
Sivasubramonian, S. HC440.I5.S58 2000, (v6)
Siverson, Randolph M. U21.2.S58 1991, (v10)
Sivin, Nathan. R601.S58 1995, (v2)
Six, Abigail Lee. PQ6613.O79.Z92 1990, (v3)
Sizer, Lyde Cullen. PS217.C58.S59 2000, (v3)
Sizer, Theodore R. LA222.S543 1996, (v7)
  LA222.S544 1992, (v7)
  LB1607.S54, (v7)
Sjoberg, Katarina. DS832.S66 1993, (v5)
Skaggs, Merrill Maguire. PS3505.A87.Z85 1990, (v3)
Skaine, Rosemarie. UB418.W65.S56 1999, (v10)
Skal, David J. PN1995.9.H6.S57 1993, (v3)
  PN1995.9.H6.S58 1998, (v3)
  PR6037.T617.D787 1990, (v3)
Skalnes, Lars S. JZ1252.S39 2000, (v7)
Skalnes, Tor. HC910.S58 1995, (v6)
Skandera-Trombley, Laura E. PS1332.S88 1994, (v3)
Skarbek, Janet L. HF5382.6.S53 2001, (v6)
Skaria, Ajay. DS485.D155 S55 1999, (v5)
Skarmeta, Antonio. PQ8098.29.K3.A2913 1991, (v3)
Skau, Michael. PS3505.O763.Z87 1999, (v3)
Skeat, Walter W. PE1667.S5, (v3)
Sked, Alan. DB80.S58 1989, (v5)
Skeen, Carl Edward. E359.3.S48 1999, (v4)
Skei, Hans H. PS3511.A86.Z9689 1999, (v3)
Skelly, Carole J. TX406.S57 1994, (v1)
Skelton, John. PR2346.S3 1983, (v3)
  PR2347.B66 1990, (v3)
Skelton, Oscar Douglas. F1033.L386, (v4)
Skelton, Robin. PR5533.S5, (v3)
Skelton, William B. UB413.S54 1992, (v10)
Skemp, Sheila L. F137.F82.S54 1990, (v4)
Skidelsky, Robert Jacob Alexander. DA574.M6.S55, (v5)

  HB103.K47.S57 1986, (v6)
Skidmore, David. E872.S556 1996, (v4)
Skidmore, Thomas E. F1413.S55 1984, (v4)
  F2538.S56, (v4)
  F2538.25.S58 1988, (v4)
  F2659.A1.S55, (v4)
Skidmore-Roth, Linda. RM666.H33S575 2001, (v2)
Skiena, Steven S. QA76.9.A43.S55 1998, (v1)
Skillicorn, David B. QA76.58.S59 1994, (v1)
Skilling, H. Gordon. DB2191.M38.S58 1994, (v5)
Skinner, B. F. BF109.S55.A33 1976, (v2)
  BF455.S53, (v2)
  BF698.9.C8.S57, (v2)
  PS3537.K527 W3, (v3)
  QP355.K57, (v1)
Skinner, Charles Edward. LB1051.S58 1959, (v7)
Skinner, Constance Lindsay. E173.C56 vol.18, (v4)
Skinner, Gillian. PR858.S45.S57 1999, (v3)
Skinner, John. PR9084.S58 1998, (v3)
Skinner, Patricia. HQ1147.I8.S58 2001, (v6)
  HT653.I8.S59 1995, (v6)
Skinner, Sidney. RX72.S556 2000, (v2)
Skjonsberg, Else. GN657.R4.S59 1989, (v6)
Sklair, Leslie. HD2755.5.S565 1991, (v6)
Sklair, Leslie. HD9734.M43.M497 1989, (v6)
Sklar, Kathryn Kish. HQ1413.B4.S54, (v6)
  HQ1413.K45.S58 1995, (v6)
Sklar, Lawrence. QC174.8.S55 1993, (v1)
Sklar, Martin J. HC110.C3.S58 1988, (v6)
Sklar, Richard L. JQ1879.A15 S545 2001, (v7)
  JQ3082.S57 1991, (v7)
Sklar, Robert. PN1993.5.A1.S55 1993, (v3)
  PN1995.9.M46.S56 1992, (v3)
Sklare, Marshall. E184.J5 S548 1979, (v4)
Skoblow, Jeffrey. PR8561.S55 2001, (v3)
Skocpol, Theda. HN57.S525 1995, (v6)
  HN65.S5635 2000, (v6)
  HV91.S56 1992, (v6)
Skogan, Wesley G. HV6791.S57 1990, (v6)
  HV7936.C83.S56 1997, (v6)
Skoller, Eleanor Honig. PN471.S55 1993, (v3)
Skolnick, Arlene S. HQ518.S56 1971, (v6)
  HQ535.S56 1991, (v6)
Skolnick, Jerome H. HV8141.S56 1993, (v6)
Skolnikoff, Eugene B. E744.S57, (v4)
Skorupski, John. B803.S54 1993, (v8)
Skotnicki, Andrew. HV9471.S59 2000, (v6)
Skousen, Mark. HB241.S63 1990, (v6)
Skowronek, Stephen. JK511.S55 1993, (v7)
Skowronski, Janislaw M. TJ213.S47475 1991, (v1)
Skran, Claudena M. HV640.4.E8.S57 1995, (v6)
Skrentny, John David. HF5549.5.A34.S57 1996, (v6)
Skreslet, Paula Youngman. Z3515.S57 2000, (v10)
Skulsky, Harold. PR545.M37.S58 1992, (v3)
  PR3562.S56 2000, (v3)
Skupsky, Donald S. KF1357.5.S59 1989, (v7)
Skura, Meredith Anne. PN98.P75.S58, (v3)
  PR3034.S58 1993, (v3)
Skutch, Alexander Frank. QH501.S54 2000, (v1)
  QL698.3.S553 1996, (v1)
Skvorecky, Josef. PG5038.S527.B383 1979, (v3)
Skyrms, Brian. BC91.S5 1986, (v8)
Slaatte, Howard Alexander. B395.S545 2000, (v8)
Slaby, Andrew Edmund. RJ506.S9.S53 1994, (v2)
Slack, Edward R. HV5840.C6.S54 2001, (v6)
Slack, James D. RA644.A25.S564 1998, (v2)
Slack, Paul. RA644.P7S65 1990, (v2)
Slack, Warner V. R858.S556 1997, (v2)
Slade, Bernard N. HF5415.153.S58 1993, (v6)
Slade, Doren L. F1221.N3.S55 1991, (v4)
Slade, Joseph W. HQ471.S59 2000, (v6)
  Z7164.P84.S56 2001, (v10)
Slade, Peter D. RC553.H3.S57 1988, (v2)
Slagle, Jay. E467.1.P56.S58 1996, (v4)
Slamet-Velsink, Ina E. DS641.S54 1995, (v5)
Slane, Andrea. PN1995.9.N36.S58 2001, (v3)
Slater, Candace. GR133.B62.A527 1994, (v6)
Slater, David. HC227.S55 1989, (v6)
Slater, Don. HM548.S55 2001, (v6)

Slater, John Clarke. QC174.1.S55 1968, (v1)
  QC174.12.S55, (v1)
  QC760.S55 1969, (v1)
Slater, Lauren. RC372.S576 2000, (v2)
Slater, Michael. PR4582.S4 1983, (v3)
Slater, P. J. B. QL751.S616 1999, (v1)
Slater, Philip Elliot. DF93.S55, (v5)
  HN65.S5649 1991, (v6)
Slater, Robert. HG172.S63.S58 1996, (v6)
Slatkin, Wendy. N43.S57 1985, (v9)
Slatta, Richard W. E20.S55 1997, (v4)
  E20.S57 1990, (v4)
  F2861.S53 1983, (v4)
Slattery, Dennis Patrick. PN56.B62.S59 2000, (v3)
Slattery, John Charles. TP156.T7S57 1999, (v1)
Slattery, William J. PN1998.3.K34.S63 1993, (v3)
Slaughter, Jane. D802.I8.S53 1997, (v5)
Slaughter, Sheila. LC67.6.S53 1997, (v7)
Slaughter, Thomas P. F159.C55.S58 1991, (v4)
Slavens, Thomas P. Z6201.S64 1994, (v10)
  Z7001.S57 1985, (v10)
Slavin, Morris. DC183.5.S58 1994, (v5)
Slavov, Atanas. PG1001.S53, (v3)
Slawson, David A. SB458.S66 1987, (v1)
Slay, Ben. HC340.3.S59 1994, (v6)
Slayter, Elizabeth M. QH205.2.S54 1993, (v1)
Sleap, Mike. GV706.5.S59 1998, (v6)
Sledd, James H. PE1617.J7.S7, (v3)
Sleeper, Barbara. QL737.C23.S5625 1995, (v1)
Sleeper, Jim. F128.9.N3.S54 1990, (v4)
Sleeper-Smith, Susan. E78.N76 S54 2001, (v4)
Sleight, Steve. GV811.S546 1999, (v6)
Slesnick, Daniel T. HC110.I5.S616 2001, (v6)
Slessarev, Helene. HV4045.S54 1997, (v6)
Slessor, Catherine. NA2542.35.S63 1997, (v9)
Slessor, John Cotesworth. UA11.S49, (v10)
Slethaug, Gordon. PS374.C4.S58 2000, (v3)
Slezkine, Yuri. GN673.S64 1994, (v6)
Slide, Anthony. PN1968.U5.S37 1994, (v3)
  PN1992.3.U5.S57 1991, (v3)
  PN1992.4.A2.S65 1996, (v3)
  PN1993.5.U6.S539 1998, (v3)
  PN1998.2.S548 1996, (v3)
  PN1998.3.W4.S65 1996, (v3)
  PN2285.S542 1998, (v3)
  Z1231.F4.S58 1995, (v10)
Slife, Brent D. BF41.S57 1995, (v2)
Slights, Camille Wells. PR2981.S55 1993, (v3)
Slipp, Samuel. BF175.5.F48.S55 1993, (v2)
Slive, Seymour. ND646.S55 1995, (v9)
Sloan, Alfred P. CT275.S5233.A3 1970, (v5)
  CT275.S5233.A35, (v5)
Sloan, Amy E. KF240.S66 2003, (v7)
Sloan, Barry. PR8891.N67, (v3)
Sloan, G. R. UA23.S5235 1988, (v10)
Sloan, Irving J. E877.2.R66 1990, (v4)
Sloan, Jane. PN1998.3.H58.S57 1993, (v3)
Sloan, John W. HC106.8.S574 1999, (v6)
Sloan, John. PR4525.D5.Z82 1995, (v3)
Sloan, W. David. PN4855.H57 1994 no. 1, (v3)
  Z6951.S54 1989, (v10)
Sloane, David Charles. GT3203.A2.S56 1991, (v6)
Sloane, Sarah. PN3377.C55.S59 2000, (v3)
Sloane, Thomas O. PN175.S59 1997, (v3)
Slobin, Mark. ML3195.S55 1989, (v9)
  ML3528.8.S58 2000, (v9)
Slocum, Robert B. Z1251.E1.S57 1994, (v10)
Slocum, Victor. VK140.S6.S6, (v10)
Slomanson, Joan Kanel. CT105.S63 1998, (v5)
Slomovitz, Albert Isaac. UH23.S56 1999, (v10)
Slomp, Gabriella. JC153.H66S56 2000, (v7)
Slomp, Hans. HD6658.5.S59 1996, (v6)
  HD8374.S57 1990, (v6)
Slonim, Marc. PG3022.S54 1977, (v3)
Slonim, Shlomo. DS109.93.S56 1998, (v5)
Slonimsky, Nicolas. ML65.S6, (v9)
  ML100.S637 1989, (v9)
  ML197.S634 1994, (v9)
  ML3785.S5 1965, (v9)
  MT45.S55, (v9)
Slote, Bernice. PN501.S55, (v3)

Slote, Michael A. BJ1012.S5165 1992, (v8)
Slotkin, Richard. E169.12.S57 1992, (v4)
Slotnick, Elliot E. KF8742.S56 1998, (v7)
Sluckin, W. LB1026.S56 1972, (v7)
Slusser, Robert M. DK268.S8.S48 1987, (v5)
Slyomovics, Susan. DS110.E645.S59 1998, (v5)
Slywotzky, Adrian J. HF5386.S6363 1997, (v6)
Smaby, Beverly Prior. F159.B5.S63 1988, (v4)
Smail, John. DA690.H17.S63 1994, (v5)
  HD9901.7.E54.S6 1999, (v6)
Small, Abner Ralph. E511.5 16th.S63 2000, (v4)
Small, Christopher. ML3556.S65 1987, (v9)
  ML3845.S628 1998, (v9)
Small, Graeme. DC611.B7747.C4437 1997, (v5)
Small, Helen. PR868.M46.S63 1996, (v3)
Small, Ian. PR75.S53 1991, (v3)
  PR5823.S63 1993, (v3)
  PR5823.S632 2000, (v3)
Small, Judy Jo. PS1541.Z5.S63 1990, (v3)
  PS3501.N4.Z845 1994, (v3)
Small, Melvin. E183.7.S515 1996, (v4)
  E855.S63 1999, (v4)
Small, Meredith F. QL737.P9.S595 1993, (v1)
  RJ61.S6345 1998, (v2)
Small, Robert. QB29.S6 1963, (v1)
Smalley, Donald Arthur. PR5687.S6 1969, (v3)
Smallman, Basil. ML410.S35.S6 2000, (v9)
  ML1165.S59 1994, (v9)
  ML1165.S6 1989, (v9)
Smallman, R.E. TN690.S56 1999, (v1)
Smart, Christopher. PR3687.S7.A6 1980, (v3)
Smart, J. J. C. B29.S53, (v8)
Smart, Julie. HV1568.S63 2001, (v6)
Smart, Ninian. B72.S64 1999, (v8)
  BL48.S591 1996, (v8)
  BL80.2.S593 1981, (v8)
Smart, Paul. JC585.S527 1990, (v7)
Smedley, Agnes. DS777.53.S5, (v5)
  DS778.C6.S5, (v5)
  HQ1737.S56 1976, (v6)
Smedley, Audrey. GN269.S63 1993, (v6)
Smeed, J. W. ML2829.S55 1987, (v9)
Smeed, J. W. PN57.D7.S48 1990, (v3)
Smeeton, Donald Dean. Z7830.S63 1988, (v10)
Smeins, Linda E. NA7571.S54 1999, (v9)
Smele, Jon. DK265.8.S5.S59 1996, (v5)
Smelik, Anneke. PN1995.9.W6.S54 1998, (v3)
Smernoff, Richard A. PQ2021.Z5.S65 1985, (v3)
Smialek, William. ML120.P6.S6 1989, (v9)
Smidt, Kristian. PR2981.S565 1993, (v3)
Smidt, Kristian. PR2983.S56 1990, (v3)
Smigel, Erwin Orson. KF297.S45 1969, (v7)
Smil, Vaclav. QH343.4.S65 1997, (v1)
  S651.S56 2001, (v1)
  TJ163.2.S618 1999, (v1)
  TJ163.5.S623 1994, (v1)
Smiley, Gene. HB3717 1929.S55 2002, (v6)
Smirnitskii, Alexandr Ivanovich. PG2640.S5 1959, (v3)
Smith, A. J. PR539.L7.S65 1985, (v3)
Smith, Adam. BJ1005.S59, (v8)
Smith, Adrian. PN5130.N4.S65 1996, (v3)
Smith, Alan G. HN981.C6.S63 1997, (v6)
Smith, Alan. HC244.S555 2000, (v6)
Smith, Albert A. TK6550.S49795 1998, (v1)
Smith, Alexander Hanchett. QK617.S56 1980, (v1)
Smith, Alison. PN1998.3.V368.S65 1998, (v3)
Smith, Allen. Z6208.O7.S54 1988, (v10)
Smith, Andrew B. GN645.S57 1992, (v6)
Smith, Andrew F. TX814.5.P66.S62 1999, (v1)
Smith, Angel. DP12.S59 1996, (v5)
Smith, Angela. PR9639.3.M258, (v3)
Smith, Anna Marie. DA125.A1.S597 1994, (v5)
Smith, Anthony D. JC311.S5388 1998, (v7)
Smith, B. Mark. HG4910.S5633 2001, (v6)
Smith, Barbara Herrnstein. PN1042.S65, (v3)
Smith, Barbara Lee. NK9212.S64 1991, (v9)
Smith, Barry. ML410.W2953.S6 1994, (v9)
Smith, Bernard. VM362.S56, (v10)
Smith, Betty. PS3537.M2895 T7 1947, (v3)
Smith, Bonnie G. D13.S567 1998, (v5)

  HQ1613.S54, (v6)
Smith, Bradley A. JK1991.S56 2001, (v7)
Smith, Bradley F. D804.G42.S64, (v5)
  D810.S7.S5544 1996, (v5)
Smith, Brenda. MT875.S63 1999, (v9)
Smith, Brian C. JA86.S594 1996, (v7)
Smith, Brian H. HC60.S548 1990, (v6)
Smith, Bruce D. GN799.A4.S52 1994, (v6)
Smith, Bruce R. PR428.H66.S6 1991, (v3)
  PR428.P65.S65 1999, (v3)
Smith, Bruce. NA737.G73.A4 1998, (v9)
Smith, C. Michael. RC489.R46.S64 1995, (v2)
Smith, C. Wayne. SB187.U6.S54 1995, (v1)
Smith, Catherine Parsons. ML410.S855 S65 2000, (v9)
Smith, Charles George. PR2997.P7.S4, (v3)
Smith, Charles H. Z7405.N38.S54 2000, (v10)
Smith, Charlotte (Turner). PR5453.S6 O4, (v3)
  PR3688.S4.D4 1997, (v3)
  PR3688.S4 E5 1971, (v3)
Smith, Christian. BR1642.U5.S623 2000, (v8)
  BT83.57.S64 1991, (v8)
  F1436.8.U6.S65 1996, (v4)
Smith, Christopher E. KF8700.S585 1991, (v7)
  KF8719.S55 1993, (v7)
  KF8745.S33.S65 1993, (v7)
  KF8792.S65 1990, (v7)
  KF9225.S64 1997, (v7)
Smith, Christopher J. HN733.5.S598 2000, (v6)
Smith, Christopher John. DG233.2.S63 1996, (v5)
Smith, Christopher. GN772.22.G7.S65 1992, (v6)
Smith, Clarence Jay. DK264.8.S5 1969, (v5)
Smith, Clint E. JZ1480.A57.M67 2000, (v7)
Smith, Colin. B2421.S6, (v8)
  PC4640.S595 1993, (v3)
Smith, Conrad. PN4888.D57.S63 1992, (v3)
Smith, Craig R. JC599.U5.S556 1989, (v7)
Smith, Crosbie. QC16.K3.S65 1989, (v1)
Smith, Curtis D. BF175.4.R44.S65 1990, (v2)
Smith, Dale Edwyna. F347.A5.S64 1999, (v4)
Smith, Dale O. U410.P1.S54 1988, (v10)
Smith, Dama Margaret. PS3537.M335 H6, (v3)
Smith, Dave. PN1999.W27.S6 1996, (v3)
Smith, David John. HN398.N6.S65 1991, (v6)
Smith, David L. DA415.S62 1994, (v5)
  TK454.2.S65 1994, (v1)
Smith, David Paul. E532.S65 1992, (v4)
Smith, David. BL1218.S62 1996, (v8)
  NB237.S567.G7, (v9)
Smith, Debra. HD69.T46 S65 2000, (v6)
Smith, Denis. F1034.S64 1988, (v4)
Smith, Donald L. TA418.9.T45.S65 1995, (v1)
Smith, Dorothy E. HM24.S53923 1990, (v6)
  HM51.S638 1987, (v6)
Smith, Douglas L. F215.S63 1988, (v4)
Smith, Duane A. F721.S65 1992, (v4)
  F781.T322S63, (v4)
Smith, Dwight La Vern. Z1361.N39 S53 1974, (v10)
Smith, E. A. DA536.G84.S65 1990, (v5)
Smith, E. Baldwin. NA2890.S6, (v9)
Smith, E. Timothy. JZ5584.U6.S63 1999, (v7)
Smith, Elbert B. E421.S65 1988, (v4)
  E436.S6, (v4)
Smith, Elsdon Coles. CS2481.S55, (v5)
Smith, Eric Ledell. PN2287.W46.S55 1992, (v3)
Smith, Erin A. PS374.D4.S65 2000, (v3)
Smith, F. G. Walton. GC24.S64, (v6)
Smith, F. Todd. E99.C12.S65 1995, (v4)
  E99.C12.S66 1996, (v4)
  E99.W6 S6 2000, (v4)
Smith, Frank. LB1060.S55 1998, (v7)
Smith, G. E. Kidder. NA705.S578 1996, (v9)
  NA1111.S5, (v9)
  NA1288.S6 1957, (v9)
  NA1348.S55, (v9)
Smith, Gaddis. E872.S66 1986, (v4)
Smith, Geddeth. PN2287.C595.S65 1996, (v3)
Smith, Gene. D741.S64 1987, (v5)
Smith, Gene. PN2285.S543 1992, (v3)
Smith, Geoff. QA174.2.S65 2000, (v1)
Smith, George Adam. DS107.S6 1932, (v5)

Smith, George Patrick. K3611.G46.S64 1993, (v7)
Smith, Graham. D810.N4.S6 1988, (v5)
Smith, Grahame. PR4581.S618 1996, (v3)
Smith, Grant H. (Grant Horace). TN413.N2S55 1998, (v1)
Smith, H. Allen. PS3537.M4655 A6355, (v3)
PS3537.M4655 M5, (v3)
Smith, Harmon L. PS3053.S65 1999, (v3)
Smith, Harold Frederick. Z6011.S5 1999, (v10)
Smith, Harold L. HQ1236.5.G3.S55 1998, (v6)
Smith, Hazel. F1528.S58 1992, (v4)
Smith, Hedrick. DK288.S59 1990, (v5)
JK271.S577 1988, (v7)
Smith, Helmut Walser. DD204.S57 1995, (v5)
Smith, Henry Nash. F591.S65 1971, (v4)
Smith, Hilda L. HQ1599.E5.S62 1982, (v6)
Smith, Huston. BL80.2.S645 1991, (v8)
BL80.2.S6455 1994, (v8)
BL240.2.S635 2001, (v8)
Smith, I. M. TA347.F5.S64 1997, (v1)
Smith, J. C. BF175.4.F45.S65 1996, (v2)
Smith, J. Clay. KF299.A35.S65 1993, (v7)
Smith, J. David. E184.A1.S655 1993, (v4)
Smith, J. F. PR3454.H7.S6 1993, (v3)
Smith, J. M. (Joseph Mauk). TP155.2.T45S58 2001, (v1)
Smith, J. W. HB95.S587 2000, (v6)
Smith, James Allen. JK468.C7.S65 1991, (v7)
Smith, James D. D. JX5173.S65 1995, (v7)
Smith, James Morton. E327.S59, (v4)
Smith, James R. QB281.S55 1996, (v1)
Smith, Jane S. RA644.P9.S553 1990, (v2)
Smith, Jay M. DC33.4.S55 1996, (v5)
Smith, Jean Edward. E672.S627 2001, (v4)
Smith, Jeanne Rosier. PS374.T7.S45 1997, (v3)
Smith, Jeff. ML2075.S65 1998, (v9)
U264.S585 1989, (v10)
Smith, Jeffery Alan. E302.6.B14.S65 1990, (v4)
Smith, John David. E441.S6555 1999, (v4)
Z7164.S6.S63 1982, (v10)
Smith, John Edwin. B851.S48, (v8)
Smith, John Hazel. Z8812.O8.S64 1988, (v10)
Smith, John K. H61.S5885 1989, (v6)
Smith, Joseph. BX8628.A3 1971, (v8)
D843.S547 2000, (v5)
Smith, Julia M. H. DC611.B856.S65 1992, (v5)
Smith, K. J. M. KD7850.S63 1998, (v7)
Smith, Karen Patricia. PR408.F34.S65 1993, (v3)
Smith, Kathleen E. DK266.3.S54 1996, (v5)
Smith, Kathryn. NA7238.L6, (v9)
Smith, Keith. GB5014.S6 1992, (v6)
Smith, Ken. DT1776.S63 1989, (v5)
Smith, Kerry Douglas. DS897.S3923, (v5)
Smith, Lacey Baldwin. BL626.5.S65 1997, (v8)
Smith, Laura J. Z1037.A2.S45 1992, (v10)
Smith, Lawrence A. TD897.845.S65 1995, (v1)
Smith, LeRoy W. PR4038.W6.S6 1983, (v3)
Smith, Les W. PN56.C67.S63 1996, (v3)
Smith, Lillian Eugenia. PS3537.M653 S7, (v3)
PS3537.M7 J6, (v3)
Smith, Lillian H. PN1009.A1.S6, (v3)
Smith, Logan Pearsall. PR6037.M5.Z5 1939, (v3)
Smith, Lois M. HQ1507.S63 1996, (v6)
Smith, M. G. DT515.9.K32.S65 1997, (v5)
Smith, M. L. R. DA963.S625 1995, (v5)
Smith, Madeline. Z8644.5.S63 2001, (v10)
Smith, Margaret (Bayard). F194.S65, (v4)
Smith, Margaret Charles. RG962.E98.S65 1996, (v2)
E748.S667.A3, (v4)
Smith, Marian Wesley. E51.C7 no. 36, (v4)
Smith, Mark A. JK467.S59 2000, (v7)
Smith, Mark J. JC11.S57 2000, (v7)
Smith, Mark M. E446.S65 1997, (v4)
Smith, Mark. D1065.E85, (v5)
Smith, Martha Nell. PS1541.Z5.S67 1992, (v3)
Smith, Marvin T. E99.C87414 S55 2000, (v4)
Smith, Maureen. HD9826.S65 1997, (v6)
Smith, Michael Ernest. F1219.73.S58 1996, (v4)
Smith, Michael French. DU740.42.S65 1994, (v5)
Smith, Michael Llewellyn. DF845.S4 1973, (v5)
Smith, Michael M. F705.M5 S63, (v4)

Smith, Michael P. HT119.S62 2000, (v6)
LA21.S6 1983, (v7)
Smith, Michael. BJ1031.S64 1995, (v8)
QD251.2.M37 2001, (v1)
Smith, Molly. PR658.P65.S65 1998, (v3)
PR2983.S57 1990, (v3)
Smith, Mortimer Brewster. LA209.2.S6, (v7)
Smith, Murray. PN1995.S536 1995, (v3)
Smith, Myron J. Z1245.S64 1983, (v10)
Z6207.W8.S564 1991, (v10)
Z6207.W8 S572 1990, (v10)
Z6724.I7 S63, (v10)
Z6835.U5 S62, (v10)
Z6835.U5 S63, (v10)
Z6835.U5 S6, (v10)
Smith, N. Craig. HF5415.32.S56 1990, (v6)
Smith, N. V. P85.C47.S64 1999, (v3)
Smith, Nancy R. N350.S67 1983, (v9)
Smith, Neal Edward. E840.8.S57 A3 1996, (v4)
Smith, Nelson Foot. F332.P5 S6 1980, (v4)
Smith, Noel W. GN811.S65 1992, (v6)
Smith, Otis Milton. KF373.S573, (v7)
Smith, P. Christopher. BC177.S64 1998, (v8)
Smith, Page. E208.S67, (v4)
E302.6.W64.S6, (v4)
LA226.S627 1990, (v7)
Smith, Pamela. GE42.S58 1997, (v6)
Smith, Patricia Juliana. PR888.L46.S66 1997, (v3)
Smith, Patricia. JC329.5.S64 1998, (v7)
Smith, Paul Chaat. E93.S655 1996, (v4)
Smith, Paul Julian. DP233.5.S65 2000, (v5)
PN1998.3.A46.S65 1994, (v3)
PQ6064.S65 1988, (v3)
PQ6073.H65.S45 1992, (v3)
PQ6613.A763Z88532 1998, (v3)
PQ6613.A763.Z88532 1998, (v3)
Smith, Paul. DA564.B3.S65 1996, (v5)
ND553.S52.S65 1997, (v9)
PN2287.E37.S6 1993, (v3)
Smith, Peter H. F1418.S645 1996, (v4)
F2848.S64, (v4)
HN120.Z9.E47, (v6)
Smith, Peter. Q172.5.C45.S55 1998, (v1)
Smith, Philip. HM621.S57 2001, (v6)
Smith, Phyllis. QC875.U72.P557 1993, (v1)
Smith, Quentin. BD111.S575 1995, (v8)
BD638.S64 1993, (v8)
Smith, R. A. QC611.S59 1978, (v1)
Smith, R. Martin. QD96.M3.S65 1999, (v1)
Smith, R. R. R. NB94.S63 1991, (v9)
Smith, Ralph Lee. ML1015.A6 S63 1997, (v9)
Smith, Raymond J. PR3346.C8.S55, (v3)
Smith, Raymond Thomas. F2368.S6 1962, (v4)
Smith, Rich. F869.L857.S58 1994, (v4)
Smith, Richard Candida. PN56.S9.S53 1999, (v3)
Smith, Richard D. ML420.M5595.S65 2000, (v9)
Smith, Richard Dean. PS2388.M4.S65 1991, (v3)
PS2388.S35.S63 1993, (v3)
Smith, Richard F. TK5102.94.S65 1997, (v1)
Smith, Richard Edwin. U35.S6, (v10)
Smith, Richard J. UA838.C4.S54, (v10)
Smith, Richard L. BX1795.H66.S65 1994, (v8)
Smith, Richard Norton. E312.29.S65 1993, (v4)
E748.D48.S65 1982, (v4)
E802.S68 1984, (v4)
PN4874.M48395.S64 1997, (v3)
Smith, Robert Charles. E185.615.S5815 2000, (v4)
Smith, Robert Freeman. F2178.U6.S65 1994, (v4)
Smith, Robert McClure. PS1541.Z5.S674 1996, (v3)
Smith, Robert W. QB500.267.S55 1989, (v1)
Smith, Roger C. VM83.S65 1993, (v10)
Smith, Roger Cletus. QH303.S6 1980, (v1)
Smith, Roger P. R859.7.D36.S54 2002, (v2)
Smith, Roger. Z7141.S65 1996, (v10)
Smith, Roger. Z7404.S64 1998, (v10)
Smith, Rogers M. KF4700.S63 1997, (v7)
Smith, Ronald A. GV351.S6 1988, (v6)
Smith, Ronald L. PN1583.S6 1992, (v3)
PS2625.S6 1990, (v3)
Smith, Ronn. PN2096.A1.S65 1991, (v3)
Smith, Ruth. ML410.H13.S58 1995, (v9)

Smith, Sam. E886.S65 1994, (v4)
Smith, Sherry Lynn. E78.W5.S67 1990, (v4)
Smith, Sidney. DS71.S75, (v5)
Smith, Simon C. DS596.6.S65 1995, (v5)
Smith, Stan. GV1002.8.S65 2002, (v6)
Smith, Stephen L. J. GV11.S57 1990, (v6)
Smith, Steven B. JC233.H46.S63 1989, (v7)
Smith, Steven D. KF4552.S63 1998, (v7)
KF4783.S64 1995, (v7)
Smith, Steven Rathgeb. HV95.S585 1993, (v6)
Smith, Steven S. JK1096.S58 1989, (v7)
JN6697.8.S63 2001, (v7)
Smith, Stevie. PR6037.M43.A17 1976, (v3)
Smith, Stewart. GV481.S6443 2001, (v6)
Smith, Susan Lynn. RA448.5.N4.S65 1995, (v2)
Smith, Susan M. QL696.P2615.S55 1991, (v1)
Smith, Suzanne E. ML3792.S65 1999, (v9)
Smith, Sydney. PR5456.A8, (v3)
Smith, Tara. BJ1012.S525 2000, (v8)
Smith, Terry. N6512.5.M63.S63 1993, (v9)
Smith, Thelma M. PQ143.U61, (v3)
Smith, Theresa C. HV9713.S59 1996, (v6)
Smith, Thomas Lynn. F2508.S6 1963, (v4)
Smith, Tim D. SH329.F56.S58 1994, (v1)
Smith, Tony. BJ1012.S53 1991, (v8)
DC401.S6, (v5)
E744.S588 1994, (v4)
HB241.S65 2000, (v6)
Smith, Valerie. PN1995.9.N4.S62 1998, (v3)
Smith, Vanessa. PN761.S65 1998, (v3)
Smith, Verity. PQ6641.A47.Z84, (v3)
Smith, Vivian Brian. PR9619.3.P27.Z8, (v3)
Smith, Walter Bedell. E183.8.R9.S6, (v4)
Smith, Warren W. DS786.S56 1996, (v5)
Smith, Wesley J. R724.S57 2000, (v2)
Smith, Wilbur A. PR9405.9.S5.B57 1997, (v3)
Smith, Wilfred Cantwell. DS38.S56, (v5)
Smith, William Anton. LA31.S63, (v7)
Smith, William C. HC175.S54 1989, (v6)
Smith, William Gardner. PS3569.M59 S8, (v3)
Smith, William H. QH545.A3.S64 1990, (v1)
Smith, William Stevenson. N5350.S5, (v9)
Smith, William. F122.S64 1972, (v4)
Smith, Wilson. BJ352.S56, (v8)
Smith, Woodruff D. DD204.S58 1991, (v5)
Smith, Zachary A. GB1019.S68 1989, (v6)
Smith-Cunnien, Susan L. R152.S58 1998, (v2)
Smitherman, Geneva. PE3102.N4.S63 1999, (v3)
PE3102.N4.S65 1994, (v3)
Smithers, Peter. PR3306.S55 1968, (v3)
Smith-Hefner, Nancy Joan. F73.9.K45.S65 1999, (v4)
Smithies, F. QA331.7.S63 1997, (v1)
Smithin, John N. HB172.5.S64 1990, (v6)
Smithsonian Institution. Q11.S79 1989, (v1)
Q11.S7 vol. 114, (v1)
QC61.S6 1920, (v1)
Z5883.S63 1991, (v10)
Smithwick, Noah. F389.S66 1983, (v4)
Smits, Alexander J. TA357.S517 1999, (v1)
Smits, Gregory. DS895.R95.S65 1999, (v5)
Smocovitis, Vassiliki Betty. QH361.S64 1996, (v1)
Smoke, Richard. UA23.S524 1984, (v10)
Smolansky, Oles M. DK68.7.I7.S56 1991, (v5)
Smollett, Tobias George. PR3694.A3 1988, (v3)
PR3694.E9 1929, (v3)
PR3694.H5 1989, (v3)
PR3694.H8 1990, (v3)
PR3694.L371 1973, (v3)
PR3694.P4, (v3)
PR3694.R6 1979, (v3)
PR3696.A5 1926 Suppl., (v3)
Smoodin, Eric Loren. NC1766.U5.S66 1993, (v9)
Smrekar, Claire. LC225.3.S64 1996, (v7)
Smulders, Sharon. PR5238.S68 1996, (v3)
Smullyan, Raymond M. QA9.6.S67 1994, (v1)
QA9.65.S68 1987, (v1)
QA9.65.S69 1992, (v1)
Smulyan, Susan. HE8698.S6 1994, (v6)
Smyer, Michael A. RC451.4.A5S66 1999, (v2)
Smyer, Richard I. PR6029.R8.A77 1988, (v3)
Smyers, Karen Ann. BL2211.I5.S69 1999, (v8)

Smyrl, Marc E. KF5060.S57 1988, (v7)
Smyser, W. R. HC286.8.S69 1992, (v6)
Smyth, A. L. Z8212.7.S5 1998, (v10)
Smyth, Alfred P. DA777.S68 1984, (v5)
  DA990.L5.S63 1982, (v5)
Smyth, Herbert Weir. PA254.S6 1968, (v3)
Smyth, James Desmond. QL391.P7S58 1983, (v1)
Smythe, William Ellsworth. F591.S662 1969, (v4)
Smythies, John R. RB170.S69 1998, (v2)
Snader, Joe. PR769.S64 2000, (v3)
  PR769.S64 2000, (v3)
Snaith, Anna. PR6045.O72.Z8768 2000, (v3)
Snapp, J. Russell. F212.S7.S65 1996, (v4)
Snare, Francis. BJ1012.S545 1992, (v8)
Snead, David L. E835.S57 1999, (v4)
Snead, Rodman E. G1046.C2.S6 1980, (v6)
  GB452.S64, (v6)
Sneed, M. Cannon. QD151.S69, (v1)
Snell, Bruno. B181.S6, (v8)
Snell, Daniel C. DS62.23.S65 1997, (v5)
Snell, K. D. M. Z2014.F4 S64 2002, (v10)
Snellgrove, David L. DS786.S6 1968b, (v5)
Snider, Alvin Martin. B1131.S65 1994, (v8)
Snipp, C. Matthew. E98.C3.S65 1989, (v4)
Snively, William Daniel. QP88.S63, (v1)
Snodgrass, Adrian. BQ5125.S8 S66 1985, (v8)
Snodgrass, Anthony M. DF77.S49 1987, (v5)
  DF222.S66, (v5)
  U805.S59, (v10)
Snodgrass, Chris. NC242.B3.S66 1995, (v9)
Snodgrass, Mary Ellen. BL70.S56 2001, (v8)
  BL581.U6, (v8)
  CT114.S56, (v5)
  PE1689.S675 1995, (v3)
  PN56.U8.S66 1995, (v3)
  PN980.S66 1998, (v3)
  PN6149.S2.S56 1996, (v3)
  PS169.F7.S65 1997, (v3)
  PS261.S515 1997, (v3)
  RT31.S66 1999, (v2)
Snodgrass, R. E. QL434.S43 1965, (v1)
Snook, Scott A. UG765.I72.S63 2000, (v10)
Snow, C. P. AZ361.S56 1969, (v10)
  PR5686.S5, (v3)
  PR6037.N58 A63, (v3)
  PR6037.N58 C58, (v3)
  PR6037.N58 C67 1964, (v3)
  PR6037.N58 H6, (v3)
  PR6037.N58 L5, (v3)
  PR6037.N58 M3, (v3)
  PR6037.N58 N4, (v3)
  PR6037.N58 S4 1958, (v3)
  PR6037.N58 S44, (v3)
  PR6037.N58 S8, (v3)
  PR6037.N58 T5, (v3)
Snow, Donald M. UA23.S52624 2000, (v10)
Snow, Edgar. D443.S588 1972, (v5)
  DS508.2.S56 1991, (v5)
  DS711.S57, (v5)
  DS775.S72 1968, (v5)
  DS777.55.S6, (v5)
  DS777.55.S6 1971, (v5)
  PL2658.E8.S66, (v5)
Snow, Ralph Linwood. VM301.P43.S66 1999, (v10)
Snow, Stephen Eddy. F74.P8.S68 1993, (v4)
Snowden, Frank M. DG738.7.S64 1989, (v5)
Snowiss, Sylvia. KF4575.S66 1990, (v7)
Snowman, A. Kenneth. NK5698.F3.S66 1979b, (v9)
Snyder Hook, Elizabeth. PT405.S56 2001, (v3)
Snyder, Bob. ML3830.S56 2000, (v9)
Snyder, Christopher A. DA140.S72 1998, (v5)
Snyder, Gary. PS3569.N88.N6 1992, (v3)
Snyder, Glenn Herald. UA11.S56, (v10)
Snyder, Graydon F. BR166.S58 1999, (v8)
Snyder, James. N5975.S58 1989, (v9)
  N6370.S6 1985, (v9)
  PA3067.S69 1989, (v3)
Snyder, John Parr. GA110.S576 1993, (v6)
Snyder, Katherine. RM300.S638 1999, (v2)
Snyder, Kerala J. ML410.B99.S6 1987, (v9)
Snyder, Lawrence D. ML128.S3 S66 1995, (v9)

Snyder, Lloyd R. QP519.9.H53.S69 1997, (v1)
Snyder, Louis Leo. D505.S7, (v5)
  D740.S65 1982, (v5)
  DD3.S55, (v5)
  JC311.S5484 1990, (v7)
  Z2241.N27.S65 1987, (v10)
Snyder, Margaret C. HQ1240.5.A35.S69 1995, (v6)
Snyder, Paula. HQ1587.S69 1992, (v6)
Snyder, Scott. DS935.65.S69 1999, (v5)
Snyder, Solomon H. QP552.E53.S68 1989, (v1)
Snyder, Stephen. PL812.A4.Z8837 2000, (v3)
So, Alvin Y. HC460.5.S63 1995, (v6)
So, Jenny F. NK1068.S596 1995, (v9)
Soal, S. G. BF1171.S6, (v2)
Soane, John. NA966.5.N4.S54 2000, (v9)
Sobel, Andrew Carl. HG4521.S71148 1994, (v6)
Sobel, Bernard. PN1967.S63, (v3)
Sobel, Dava. QB36.G2.S65 1999, (v1)
  QB225.S64 1995, (v1)
Sobel, David. GA130.S6 1998, (v6)
Sobel, Mechal. E185.93.V8.S64 1987, (v4)
Sobel, Robert. HC106.S676 1993b, (v6)
Soble, Alan. BD436.S59 1990, (v8)
Sobo, Elisa Janine. GR121.J2.S63 1993, (v6)
Sobol, Joseph Daniel. GR72.3.S62 1999, (v6)
Sobol, Richard B. KF228.A3.S6 1991, (v7)
Soboul, Albert. DC148.S5613 1975, (v5)
  DC158.8.S613, (v5)
Sobran, Joseph. PR2947.O9.S63 1997, (v3)
Soccio, Douglas J. BC108.B27 1998, (v8)
Sochen, June. E169.12.S63 1988, (v4)
  PN2285.S554 1999, (v3)
Society for General Microbiology. RA644.V55.S63 2001, (v2)
Society of General Physiologists. QP171.S67 1961, (v1)
Society of Naval Architects and Marine Engineers (US). VM23.S67, (v10)
Socken, Paul. PQ3919.2.P59.Z86 1993, (v3)
Socolofsky, Homer Edward. E701.S62 1987, (v4)
  F680.S63 1990, (v4)
Socolow, Susan Migden. HQ1460.5.S64 2000, (v6)
Socor, Barbara J. BF697.S672 1997, (v2)
Sodaro, Michael J. DK282.S63 1991, (v5)
Sofsky, Wolfgang. DD256.5.S5813 1997, (v5)
Sohnel, Otakar. QD547.S63 1992, (v1)
Soifer, Steven. F59.B9.S57 1991, (v4)
Soifer, Valeriaei. Q127.R9.S65 1994, (v1)
Soitos, Stephen F. PS648.D4.S577 1996, (v3)
Soja, Edward W. G70.S62 1989, (v6)
Sokal, Robert R. QH323.5.S63 1995, (v1)
Sokel, Walter Herbert. PT405.S6, (v3)
Sokol, Anthony Eugene. V25.S6, (v10)
  VA473.S63, (v10)
Sokol, B. J. PR2839.S65 1994, (v3)
  PR3028.S65 2000, (v3)
Sokol, Stanley S. N7255.P6.S65 2000, (v9)
Sokolnikoff, Ivan Stephen. QA433.S64 1964, (v1)
  QA931.S6 1956, (v1)
Sokoloff, Boris. B2247.S6, (v8)
Sokoloff, Naomi B. PN842.S6 1992, (v3)
Sokoloff, Natalie J. HD6054.2.U6.S65 1992, (v6)
Sokolovskii, Vasilii Danilovich. U162.S613 1975, (v10)
Sokolow, Anna. GV1782.62.B35.S65 1993, (v6)
Sokolow, Gary A. KF8203.6.S66 2000, (v7)
Sokolowski, Robert. B829.5.S576 2000, (v8)
Sokov, N. N. UA770.S6397 1999, (v10)
Solarz, Stephen J. DS673.U6 S65 1994, (v5)
Solberg, Carl. E748.H945.S65 1984, (v4)
Solbrig, Otto Thomas. GF75.S68 1994, (v6)
Solchanyk, Roman. DK508.57.R9.S65 2001, (v5)
Sole, Ricard V. QH501.S63 2000, (v1)
Sole-Leris, Amadeu. PQ6147.P3.S6, (v3)
Soley, Lawrence C. D810.P7.U53 1989, (v5)
Solimine, Michael E. KF5130.S66 1999, (v7)
Solinger, Dorothy J. HC427.92.S63 1993, (v6)
Solinger, Rickie. HQ999.U6.S65 1992, (v6)
Solis, Gary D. KF7657.5.S39.S65 1997, (v7)
Solle, Dorothee. BL625.S61513 2001, (v8)
Solmsen, Friedrich. PA25.C7 vol. 33, (v3)

Solnit, Albert J. HV875.55.S66 1992, (v6)
Sologub, Fyodor. PG3470.T4.M413 1983, (v3)
Solomey, Nickolas. QC793.5.N42.S658 1997, (v1)
Solomon, Alisa. PN1650.W65.S65 1997, (v3)
Solomon, Barbara Miller. LC1752.S65 1985, (v7)
Solomon, Clara. F374.S65.A3 1995, (v4)
Solomon, Eric. PS648.C54.F33, (v3)
Solomon, Gerald B. H. UA646.3.S654 1998, (v10)
Solomon, Hannah (Greenebaum). CT275.S59.A3, (v5)
Solomon, Harry M. PR3627.S64 1993, (v3)
  Z325.D68.S64 1996, (v10)
Solomon, Irvin D. HQ1426.S65 1989, (v6)
Solomon, Irving. RC501.4.S65 1992, (v2)
Solomon, Lewis D. HG540.S65 1996, (v6)
Solomon, Mark I. HX83.S665 1998, (v6)
Solomon, Maynard. ML410.B4.S64 1998, (v9)
  ML410.M9 S65 1995, (v9)
Solomon, Michael. PQ6412.M7.C637 1997, (v3)
Solomon, Norman. BM50.S65 1998, (v8)
Solomon, Pearl G. LB2806.15.S65 1998, (v7)
Solomon, Peter H. KLB1572.S64 2000, (v7)
  PQ2607.E834.Z88 1991, (v3)
Solomon, Philip. QP435.S6 1958, (v1)
Solomon, Robert C. B72.S654 1999, (v8)
  B72.S66 1996, (v8)
  BD436.S6 1988, (v8)
  HF5387.S612 1999, (v6)
  HF5387.S614 1992, (v6)
Solomon, Robert. HC59.S564 1999, (v6)
  HG3881.S5568 1999, (v6)
  HG3881.S5574 1977, (v6)
Solomon, Rovell Patrick. LC2804.2.O6.S66 1992, (v7)
Solomonson, Katherine. NA6233.C4.C466 2001, (v9)
Solomos, John. DA125.A1.S62 1989, (v5)
  DA125.N4.S65 1988, (v5)
  DA125.N4.S65 1995, (v5)
Solovev, Sergei Mikhailovich. DK40.S6213, (v5)
Soloveytchik, George. DQ17.S64 1982, (v5)
Solovyov, Vladimir Sergeyevich. B4262.E5.W69 2000, (v8)
Solow, Daniel. QA184.S645 1998, (v1)
Solow, Robert M. HD5707.S624 1990, (v6)
  HV95.S64 1998, (v6)
Solt, Leo F. BR377.S64 1990, (v8)
Soltow, Lee. HC110.W4.S64, (v6)
Solway, Diane. GV1785.N8.S66 1998, (v6)
Solzheniëtlsyn, Aleksandr Isaevich.
  PG3488.O4O3313 1995, (v3)
  PG3488.O4.A9, (v3)
  PG3488.O4.P41, (v3)
  PG3488.SO49.R1.E, (v3)
Somadeva Bhatta. PK3741.S7.E5 1968b, (v3)
Somer, Elizabeth. QP771.S66 1992, (v1)
Somers, Paul. Z5956.C3.S66 1998, (v10)
Somerset, J. A. B. PN2306.S77.S765 1991, (v3)
Somerville, E. OE. PR6037.O6 E9, (v3)
Somerville, Richard. QC879.7.S66 1996, (v1)
Somin, Ilya. DK265.4.S66 1996, (v5)
Somit, Albert. JA80.S596 1997, (v7)
Somjee, A. H. HD75.S65 1990, (v6)
Somjee, Geeta. HQ1743.S63 1989, (v6)
Somkin, Fred. E169.1.S68, (v4)
Sommer, Doris. PQ7082.N7S58 1991, (v3)
Sommer, Matthew Harvey. KNQ4200.S65 2000, (v7)
Sommerfeld, Arnold. QC20.S66, (v1)
Sommers, Albert T. HC106.5.S64 1993, (v6)
Sommers, Ira Brant. HV5833.N45, (v6)
Sommerville, C. John. HQ792.G7.S65 1992, (v6)
Sommerville, Ian. QA76.758.S657 2000, (v1)
Sompolinsky, Meier. DS135.E5.S56 1999, (v5)
Sonbol, Amira El Azhary. DT100.S66 2000, (v5)
Sondhaus, Lawrence. VA473.S66 1989, (v10)
  VA513.S66 1997, (v10)
Sone, Monica Itoi. F899.S49.J376 1979, (v4)
Sonenshein, Raphael. F869.L857.S66 1993, (v4)
Song, Cathy. PS3569.O6539L36 2001, (v3)
Songer, Donald R. KF8750.S66 2000, (v7)
Songer, Marcia. PS3561.E3755.Z89 2000, (v3)
Sonneborn, Liz. E77.S72 2001, (v4)
Sonnenberg, Rhonda. PN56.W3.S58 1998, (v3)
Sonnert, Gerhard. Q130.S66 1995, (v1)

Sonnichsen, C. L. F591.S67, (v4)
F806.S68 1984, (v4)
F819.T957.S66 1982, (v4)
Sonnino, Paul. D277.5.S66 1988, (v5)
Sonntag, Iliana L. Z1609.P6.S66 1998, (v10)
Sonsino, Rifat. BM723.S665 2000, (v8)
Sontag, Susan. PS3569.O55.B4, (v3)
TR183.S65 1977, (v1)
Sony Lab'Ou Tansi. PQ3989.2.S64.A813 1988, (v3)
Soofer, Robert M. UA646.S643 1988, (v10)
Soper, Kate. BD581.S67 1995, (v8)
Soper, Mary Ellen. Z1006.S595 1990, (v10)
Sorabji, Richard. B105.E46 S67 2000, (v8)
B187.M55.S67 1993, (v8)
BD638.S67 1983, (v8)
QC9.G8.S67 1988, (v1)
Sorel, Georges. HD6477.S523 1941, (v6)
Sorell, Tom. B67.S69 1991, (v8)
B1247.S63 1986, (v8)
BJ1012.S58 2000, (v8)
Soren, David. DS54.95.K68.S67 1988, (v5)
DT269.C35 S67 1990, (v5)
Sorensen, Robert M. TC172.S64 1993, (v1)
Sorensen, Roy A. B808.5.S667 1993, (v8)
Sorensen, Theodore C. E842.S57, (v4)
Sorensen, Villy. PT8175.S648.Ti, (v3)
Sorenson, David S. UA26.A2.S67 1998, (v10)
Sorenson, Herbert. LB1051.S645 1964, (v7)
Soriano, Osvaldo. PQ7798.29.O58.C813 1989, (v3)
Sorin, Gerald. E184.J5.S666 1997, (v4)
Sorkin, David Jan. BM194.S67 1996, (v8)
DS135.G33.S56 1987, (v5)
Sorlin, Per. KKV172.W58.S66 1999, (v7)
Sorlin, Pierre. PN1993.5.E8.S67 1991, (v3)
Sorman, Guy. HC59.7.S58913 1990, (v6)
Sorokin, Pitirim Aleksandrovich. BJ1474.S65, (v8)
BJ1474.S69 2002, (v8)
HM61.S673 1998, (v6)
HM299.S6 1968, (v6)
Soroos, Marvin S. GE170.S68 1997, (v6)
Soros, George. HB3722.S67 2000, (v6)
Sorrell, Roger D. BT695.5.S68 1988, (v8)
Sorri, Mari. BD214.5.S66 1989, (v8)
Sosa, Ernest. BD161.S647 1991, (v8)
Sosin, Jack M. KF4575.S67 1989, (v7)
Sosna, Morton. F215.S66, (v4)
Sosnick, Stephen H. HD1525.S63, (v6)
Sosnoski, James J. PN98.P67.S67 1995, (v3)
Soss, Joe. HV91.S6275 2000, (v6)
Soto, Francisco. PQ7390.A72.P437 1994, (v3)
PQ7390.A72.Z87 1998, (v3)
Soto, Hernando de. HB501.S778 2000, (v6)
Soto, Lourdes Diaz. LC3731.S647 1997, (v7)
Soucy, Robert. DC396.S66 1995, (v5)
Soudavar, Abolala. ND3241.S68 1992, (v9)
Souder, William. QL668.E2S737 2000, (v1)
Soueif, Ahdaf. PR6069.O78M37 2000, (v3)
Soufas, C. Christopher. PQ6085.S65 1989, (v3)
PQ6613.A763.Z8855 1996, (v3)
Soufas, Teresa Scott. PQ6055.S58 1997, (v3)
Soulé, Frank. F869.S357 S68 1998, (v4)
Soule, Judith D. S441.S757 1991, (v1)
Soule, Lesley Wade. PN2071.I47.S65 2000, (v3)
Soulen, R. Kendall. BT93.S35 1996, (v8)
Souljah, Sister. E185.86.S67 1994, (v4)
Sournia, Jean-Charles. HV5020.S6813 1990, (v6)
Sourvinou-Inwood, Christiane. DF78.S61 1991, (v5)
Sousa, Geraldo U. de. PR3069.E87.S68 1999, (v3)
Sousa, John Philip. ML410.S688.M3, (v9)
Soussloff, Catherine M. N71.S7 1997, (v9)
Soustelle, Jacques. F1219.S723 1962, (v4)
South Africa. DT1945.S56 1999, (v5)
South Carolina. F280.A1.S68 1997, (v4)
South, A. QL430.4.S66 1992, (v1)
South, David W. TJ184.S76 1995, (v1)
TL9.S64 1997, (v1)
South, Stanley A. F264.W8.S66 1999, (v4)
Southall, Aidan William. HT111.S63 1998, (v6)
Southam, B. C. PR4037.S59 1968, (v3)
Southard, Samuel. Z5725.S67 1991, (v10)
Southerland, Henry deLeon. F326.S73 1989, (v4)

Southern R. W. BX4700.A58.S59 1990, (v8)
Southern, Eileen. ML105.S67 1982, (v9)
ML3556.S738 2000, (v9)
ML3556.S74 1997, (v9)
Southern, Pat. DG279.S68 1998, (v5)
DG291.S68 1997, (v5)
Southern, R. W. CB351.S6 1953a, (v5)
Southern, Terry. PS3569.O8, (v3)
Southerne, Thomas. PR3699.S3.O6 1976, (v3)
Southey, Robert. F2524.S73, (v4)
PR5466.A4 1977, (v3)
Southgate, Beverley C. D16.8.S688 2000, (v5)
Southgate, Douglas DeWitt. SD414.L29.S68 1998, (v1)
Southwell, Robert. PR2349.S5.A14 1970, (v3)
Southwick, Charles H. GE105.S68 1996, (v6)
Southwick, Karen. QA76.2.M37.S68 1999, (v1)
Southwick, Leslie H. E175.1.S695 1998, (v4)
Southworth, Emma Dorothy Eliza Nevitte. PS2892.H5 1988, (v3)
Southworth, Herbert Rutledge. DP269.27.G8.S69, (v5)
Southworth, Susan. NA3503.S68, (v9)
Souza, Paulo Ney de. QA43.S695 1998, (v1)
Souza, Raymond D. PQ7389.C233.Z86 1996, (v3)
Sova, Dawn B. PN56.E7.S68 1998, (v3)
PN1995.9.W6.S68 1998, (v3)
PS2630.S68 2001, (v3)
Z658.U5.S69 1998, (v10)
Sowell, David. HD2346.C72.B657 1992, (v6)
Sowell, John. QH102.S69 2001, (v1)
Sowell, Thomas. B809.8.S5745 1985, (v8)
CB481.S58 1998, (v5)
E184.A1.S688, (v4)
HB171.S73 2000, (v6)
LA210.S65 1993, (v7)
LC2801.S64 1986, (v7)
Sowers, Robert. N7430.5.S69 1990, (v9)
Sowerwine, Charles. DC335.S66 2000, (v5)
Soyinka, Wole. DT30.5.S697 1999, (v5)
PL8010.S64, (v3)
PR9387.9.S6.I3 1968, (v3)
PR9387.9.S6.M36 1988, (v3)
PR9387.9.S6.Z466 1989, (v3)
PR9387.9.S6.Z473 1996, (v3)
PR9387.9.S6 1973, (v3)
Spache, George Daniel. LB1573.S792 1986, (v7)
Spacks, Patricia Ann (Meyer). PR3474.S67, (v3)
PR115.S6 1975, (v3)
PR858.P53.S63 1990, (v3)
PR1215.S75, (v3)
Spadaccini, Nicholas. PQ6351.S6 1993, (v3)
Spadafora, David. HN385.S73 1990, (v6)
Spaemann, Robert. BJ1114.S5413 1989, (v8)
Spaeth, Barbette Stanley. BL820.C5.S63 1996, (v8)
Spaeth, David A. NA1088.M65.S54 1985, (v9)
Spaeth, Harold J. KF8742.S59 1990, (v7)
Spaeth, Sigmund Gottfried. ML423.S74 A3 1977, (v9)
Spaethling, Robert. PF3117.S56, (v3)
Spahn, Mark. PL679.S68 1996, (v3)
Spahr, Juliana. PS310.L33.S63 2001, (v3)
Spain, August O. JC212.C3.S8, (v7)
Spain, Daphne. HQ1150.S68 1992, (v6)
HQ1421.S675 1996, (v6)
Spain, James W. DS380.P8 S66 1995, (v5)
Spalding, Frances. ND497.B44.S62 1983, (v9)
Spalding, Philip Anthony. PQ2631.R63.Z913, (v3)
Spalding, Phinizy. F289.O367, (v4)
Spandorfer, Merle. RC963.6.A78.S62 1993, (v2)
Spanel, Donald. NB1296.2.S63 1988, (v9)
Spanos, Nicholas J. RC455.2.F35.S67 1996, (v2)
Spanos, William V. PS2384.M62.S59 1995, (v3)
Spariosu, Mihai. PN521.S63 1997, (v3)
Spark, Clare. PS2387.S66 2001, (v3)
Spark, Muriel. PR4168.A4.S6 1954, (v3)
PR4173.S66 1960, (v3)
PR6037.P29.A, (v3)
PR6037.P29.B, (v3)
PR6037.P29.B3 1961, (v3)
PR6037.P29.D6 1966, (v3)
PR6037.P29.G5, (v3)

PR6037.P29.G6, (v3)
PR6037.P29.M4, (v3)
PR6037.P29.P7, (v3)
PR6037.P29.P8, (v3)
PR6037.P29.S8 1985, (v3)
PR6037.P29.Z463 1993, (v3)
PR6037.SP26.D8, (v3)
Sparke, Linda Siobhan. QB857.S63 2000, (v1)
Sparkes, A. W. B49.S63 1990, (v8)
Sparkes, Brian A. NK3840.S65 1991, (v9)
Sparkman, O. David. QD96.M3, (v1)
Sparks, Darrell. SB401.P4.S63 1992, (v1)
Sparks, Linda. Z5814.U7.S685 1993, (v10)
Z5814.U7.S69 1990, (v10)
Sparks, Paul. ML1015.M2 S63 1995, (v9)
Sparks, Sheila M. RT48.6.S66 1998, (v2)
Sparrow, Malcolm K. HV7935.S69 1994, (v6)
Sparshott, Francis Edward. BH39.S634 1982, (v8)
BH201.S6, (v8)
BJ1401.S77, (v8)
Spate, Virginia. ND553.M7.S7 1992, (v9)
Spaulding, Ernest Wilder. E302.6.C6.S7, (v4)
Spaulding, Frank Ellsworth. LA2317.S66.A3, (v7)
Spaulding, John H. F41.44.S732 1998, (v4)
Spaulding, Robert Kilburn. PC4075.S6, (v3)
Speaight, Robert. PR6003.E45.Z85 1970, (v3)
Spear, Allan H. F548.9.N3.S65, (v4)
Spear, Dorothea N. Z5771.2.S68 1978, (v10)
Spear, Elsa. F761.S65, (v4)
Spear, Joanna. HD9743.U6.S64 1995, (v6)
Spear, Joseph C. E856.S63 1984, (v4)
Spear, Thomas T. DT443.3.M47.S63 1997, (v5)
Spearing, A. C. PR311.S69 1987, (v3)
PR317.D7.S6, (v3)
Spears, George James. PR6025.U675.Z88, (v3)
Spears, Monroe Kirklyndorf. PR6001.U4.Z83, (v3)
PR6001.U4.Z84, (v3)
Spears, Richard A. PE2839.S64 2000, (v3)
PE2846.S64 2000, (v3)
Spears, Sally. V63.H86.S64 1998, (v10)
Specht, Harry. HV91.S6292 1994, (v6)
Speck, Bruce W. Z279.S64 1995, (v10)
Z5165.S67 1991, (v10)
Speck, W. A. DA452.S69 1988, (v5)
DA495.S73 1994, (v5)
DA498.S68, (v5)
Spector, David L. QH583.2.S64 1998, (v1)
Spector, Irwin. ML429.J2.S6 1990, (v9)
Spector, Leonard S. U264.S636 1988, (v10)
Spector, Rachel E. RA418.5.T73S64 2000, (v2)
Spector, Robert Donald. PR3534.S55 1997, (v3)
PR3697.S6, (v3)
PR3698.W6.S6 1994, (v3)
Spector, Robert. Z473.A485.S64 2000, (v10)
Spector, Ronald H. D767.S69 1985, (v5)
V53.S66 2001, (v10)
Spectorsky, A. C. G510.S69, (v6)
Speel, Erika. NK4998.5.S6 1998, (v9)
Speer, Albert. DD247.S63.A313 1970, (v5)
Speer, David C. RA790.5.S64 1998, (v2)
Spegele, Roger D. JX1394.S744 1996, (v7)
Spehr, Paul C. PN1998.L26 1976 Suppl., (v3)
Speidel, Michael. U35.S648 1994, (v10)
Speier, Hans. UA710.S56, (v10)
Speirs, John. PR311.S7 1957, (v3)
Speirs, Ronald. PT2621.A26.Z878 1997, (v3)
Speiser, Stuart M. KF300.S66 1993, (v7)
Spell, Jefferson Rea. PQ7082.N7.S6, (v3)
Spellberg, D. A. BP80.A52.S64 1994, (v8)
Spellman, Frank R. GB665.S64 1998, (v6)
Spellman, Paul N. TN872.T4, (v1)
Spelman, Elizabeth V. HQ1206.S666 1988, (v6)
Spence, Clark C. F731.S62 1978, (v4)
F731.S63, (v4)
F752.B55 S64 1999, (v4)
Spence, Gerry. KF384.S66 1990, (v7)
Spence, I. G. UA724.S64 1993, (v10)

Spence, Jonathan D. DS706.S62 1998, (v5)
DS736.S625 1992, (v5)
DS754.S65 1990, (v5)
DS754.74.T74 S64 2001, (v5)
DS758.23.H85.S64 1996, (v5)
DS774.S59 1981, (v5)
DS778.M3 S685 1999, (v5)
HQ1767.S63 1978, (v6)
Spencer, Charles D. TK7868.D5.S65 1990, (v1)
Spencer, Christopher. PR2825.S68 1988, (v3)
Spencer, Colin. TX392.S72 1996, (v1)
Spencer, Donald D. QA76.15.S64 1993, (v1)
Spencer, Edgar Winston. QE36.S64 2000, (v1)
Spencer, Elaine Glovka. HV8209.D87.S64 1992, (v6)
Spencer, Elizabeth. PS3537.P4454 L5, (v3)
PS3537.P45 F57, (v3)
Spencer, Frank. GN282.5.S63 1990, (v6)
GN282.5.S64 1990, (v6)
Spencer, Frederick Augustus Morland. BJ1231.S6, (v8)
Spencer, Hanna. PT2340.S64 1982, (v3)
Spencer, Hazelton. PR2894.S67, (v3)
PR3097.S7 1963, (v3)
Spencer, Herbert. AC8.S662 1977, (v10)
B1652.A2 1966, (v8)
HM51.S8112, (v6)
LB675.S79.K3, (v7)
Spencer, Jack. F210.S72 1999, (v4)
Spencer, Jane. PR3317.Z5.S64 2000, (v3)
PR4711.S67 1993, (v3)
Spencer, Jon Michael. BV313.S64 1992, (v8)
E184.A1.S7 1997, (v4)
ML3521.S63 1993, (v9)
ML3556.S8 1990, (v9)
ML3556.S63 1994, (v9)
Spencer, M. C. PQ2603.U73.Z89, (v3)
Spencer, Pam. Z1037.S7575 1994, (v10)
Spencer, Paul. DT433.545.M33.S64 1988, (v5)
GN658.S64 1998, (v6)
Spencer, Rainier. E184.A1.S73 1999, (v4)
Spencer, Theodore. PR2976.S65 1949, (v3)
Spender, Dale. HQ1206.S68 1982, (v6)
Spender, Dale. PN471.S64 1989, (v3)
Spender, Matthew. N6537.G65.S68 1999, (v9)
Spender, Stephen. DD43.S65, (v5)
PN771.S63 1971, (v3)
PN1136.S62 1955, (v3)
PR19.S6, (v3)
PR6023.A93.Z9175 1973, (v3)
PR6037.P47.A17 1955, (v3)
PR6037.P47.A17 1964, (v3)
PR6037.P47.A17 1986, (v3)
PR6037.P47 E5, (v3)
PR6037.P47.T5, (v3)
PR6037.P47.T7 1938, (v3)
PR6037.P47.Z5 1951, (v3)
Spenger, Wim van. DS493.9.N94.S64 2000, (v5)
Spengler, Joseph John. HB871.S6514, (v6)
Spengler, Oswald. CB83.S63 1991, (v5)
D443.S65, (v5)
Spenser, Daniela. F1228.5.S65.S64 1999, (v4)
Spenser, Edmund. PR235.R4, (v3)
PR2350. 1909 vol. 2-3, (v3)
PR2351.G65, (v3)
PR2351.R4 vol. 4, (v3)
PR2352.O74 1989, (v3)
PR2358.A3.H27 1977, (v3)
PR2360.A5 1997, (v3)
Sperber, A. M. PN4874.M89.S6 1998, (v3)
Sperber, Daniel. DS111.1.S74 1998, (v5)
Sperber, Jonathan. DD801.R682.S64 1991, (v5)
Sperber, Murray A. GV351.S63 2000, (v6)
Spergel, Irving A. HV6439.U5.S64 1995, (v6)
Sperling, Valerie. HQ1665.15.S685 1999, (v6)
Spero, Shubert. DS115.5.S64 2000, (v5)
Sperry, Roger Wolcott. QP360.S63 1983, (v1)
Sperry, Stuart M. PR5438.S65 1988, (v3)
Spevack, Marvin. PR2892.S62, (v3)
Speyer, Edward. QC21.2.S647 1994, (v1)
Speziale-Bagliacca, Roberto. PQ2246.M3.S66 1998, (v3)

Spicer, Edward Holland. E99.Y3.S615 1988, (v4)
F1221.Y3.S66, (v4)
Spicer, Joaneath A. ND651.U88.S67 1997, (v9)
Spicer, Paul. ML410.H886.S73 1998, (v9)
Spickard, Paul R. HQ1031.S75 1989, (v6)
Spiegel, Alan. PS3501.G35.Z894 1998, (v3)
Spiegel, Stanley. RJ504.S59 1989, (v2)
Spiegel, Steven L. DS63.2.U5.S62 1985, (v5)
Spiegelberg, Herbert. B829.5.S642, (v8)
BF204.5.S68, (v2)
Spiegelman, Mortimer. HB881.S68 1968, (v6)
Spiegelman, Willard. PR590.S66 1995, (v3)
Spielman, John P. DB853.S65 1993, (v5)
Spierenburg, Petrus Cornelis. GT129.S68 1991, (v6)
Spiers, Edward M. UA649.S73, (v10)
Spigel, Lynn. HQ520.S75 1992, (v6)
PN1992.6.S663 2001, (v3)
Spignesi, Angelyn. PR4167.J5.S65 1990, (v3)
Spike, John T. ND623.F5.A4 1997, (v9)
Spilka, Mark. PR6023.A93.Z918, (v3)
PR6023.A93.Z92, (v3)
PR6023.A93.Z923 1992, (v3)
Spillane, Joseph. HV5825.S597 2000, (v6)
Spiller, Robert Ernest. PS88.S6 1967, (v3)
Spindel, Donna. KFN7962.S65 1989, (v7)
Spinden, Herbert Joseph. F1435.3.A7.S75 1957, (v4)
Spindler, Frank MacDonald. F3736.S64 1987, (v4)
Spindler, George Dearborn. LB45.S64, (v7)
Spinella, Marcello. RC483.S65 2001, (v2)
Spinelli, Lawrence. E784.S68 1989, (v4)
Spingarn, Joel Elias. PR72.S7 1957, (v3)
Spink, John Stephenson. B1815.S68 1969, (v8)
Spinka, Matthew. BX4917.S7 1966, (v8)
Spinney, Robert G. D769.85.T21.N27 1998, (v5)
F548.3.S75 2000, (v4)
Spinosa, Charles. HM281.S635 1997, (v6)
Spinoza, Benedictus de. B3958.R3, (v8)
B3973.E5.E38, (v8)
Spinrad, Norman. PN3433.5.S65 1990, (v3)
Spinrad, Phoebe S. PR658.D4.S64 1987, (v3)
Spirn, Anne Whiston. SB472.S685 1998, (v1)
Spiro, Herbert J. JQ1872.S65 1974, (v7)
Spiro, Howard M. R726.5.S66 1998, (v2)
Spiro, Melford E. GN357.S68 1987, (v6)
GN635.B8.S63 1997, (v6)
LB1029.C5 S65 1965, (v7)
Spitta, Silvia. PQ7081.S72 1995, (v3)
Spittles, Brian. PR6005.O4.Z795 1992, (v3)
Spitz, Bob. ML420.D98.S6 1989, (v9)
Spitz, Elie Kaplan. BM635.7.S65 2000, (v8)
Spitz, Lewis William. CB359.S65, (v5)
Spitz, Rene A. RJ502.5.S65 1983, (v2)
Spitzberg, Irving J. F419.L7.S68 1987, (v4)
Spitzer, Alan B. DC256.8.S66 1987, (v5)
Spitzer, Leo. F3359.J47.S75 1998, (v4)
Spitzer, Lyman. QC718.S6 1962, (v1)
Spitzer, Manfred. QP363.3.S55 1999, (v1)
Spitzer, Robert J. HV7436.S68 1995, (v6)
JK585.S654 1992, (v7)
JK586.S67 1988, (v7)
Spivack, Bernard. PR2992.V5S6, (v3)
Spivack, Charlotte. PR153.M47.S67 1994, (v3)
Spivak, Burton. E331.S68, (v4)
Spivey, Nigel Jonathan. N5630.S65 1997, (v9)
Spivey, Ted Ray. PS3501.I5.Z87 1997, (v3)
Splittstoesser, Walter E. SB321.S645 1990, (v1)
Spock, Benjamin. BF721.S577 1961, (v2)
RJ61.S75, (v2)
RJ61.S76 1992, (v2)
Spodek, Bernard. LB1523.S66 1985, (v7)
Spoel, S. van der. QL123.S75 1983, (v1)
Spofford, Harriet Elizabeth Prescott. PS2896.B46 1989, (v3)
Spofford, Tim. F349.J13.S66 1988, (v4)
Spohn, William C. BS2417.E8.S67 1999, (v8)
Spolter, Pari. QC178.S66 1993, (v1)
Sponde, Jean de. PQ1705.S7.A6 1978, (v3)
Spongberg, Stephen A. SB435.65.S66 1990, (v1)
Sponsler, Claire. PR641.S66 1997, (v3)
Sponza, Lucio. Z2341.S66 1995, (v10)
Spooner, Mary Helen. F3100.S66 1994, (v4)

Spores, Ronald. F1219.S768, (v4)
F1221.M7.S66 1984, (v4)
Sporn, Paul. PN2270.F43.S66 1995, (v3)
Sporne, K. R. QK643.G99.S65, (v1)
Sposito, Garrison. S592.5.S656 1989, (v1)
Sposito, Garrison. S592.5.S66 1994, (v1)
Spottswood, Richard K. ML156.4.F5 S69 1990, (v9)
Spragens, Thomas A. JC423.S75 1990, (v7)
JC574.S6 1999, (v7)
Spragens, William C. E176.1.P82 1988, (v4)
PN4888.T4.S73 1995, (v3)
Sprague, Arthur Colby. PR3091.S65 1963, (v3)
Sprague, Claire. PR6045.O72.Z878, (v3)
Sprague, D. N. E99.M47.S66 1988, (v4)
Sprague, Marshall. F776.S76, (v4)
F784.C7 S8 1987, (v4)
Sprecher, David A. QA331.5.S68, (v1)
KZ1176.S68 1999, (v7)
Spreen, Otfried. RC386.6.N48S67 1998, (v2)
RC425.S675 2003, (v2)
Spreiregen, Paul D. NA9031.S65, (v9)
Sprent, Janet I. QR89.7.S67 1990, (v1)
Sprigge, Cecil J. S. B3614.C74.S6 1952a, (v8)
Sprigge, Timothy L. S. B945.S24 S65, (v8)
BJ1012.S595 1988, (v8)
Sprinchorn, Evert. PT9816.S64 1982, (v3)
Spring, Eileen. KD1500.S68 1993, (v7)
Spring, Joel H. LC89.S66 2002, (v7)
LC89.S663 1997, (v7)
LC191.S686 1998, (v7)
Spring, Justin. N6537.P63.S66 2000, (v9)
Springer, John Parris. PS374.M55.S67 2000, (v3)
Springer, Marlene. PR4757.S8.S67 1983, (v3)
Springhall, John. JV151.D67 2001, (v7)
Sprintzen, David. PQ2605.A3734.Z73627 1988, (v3)
Sprinzak, Ehud. HN660.Z9.V57 1999, (v6)
Spritzer, Lorraine Nelson. F291.3.H36.S67 1997, (v4)
Spronck, Lambert H. HF5667.S765 1983, (v6)
Sproule-Jones, Mark. JL65. 1993b, (v7)
Sproull, Natalie L. Q180.55.M4S67 1995, (v1)
Sprout, Harold Hance. E182.S79 1969, (v4)
Sproxton, Judy. PR6037.P29.Z89 1992, (v3)
Sprudzs, Adolf. JX1297.S68 1988, (v7)
Sprug, Joseph W. Z5983.F17 S67 1994, (v10)
Spruill, Julia Cherry. HQ1416.S65 1972, (v6)
Spufford, Margaret. PR972.S65 1982, (v3)
Spulber, Daniel F. HF5386.S7548 1998, (v6)
Spulber, Nicolas. HC106.5.S696 1995, (v6)
JC11.S69 1997, (v7)
Spuler, Bertold. DS19.S5613 1972, (v5)
Spurgeon, Caroline Frances Eleanor. PR1924 A2 1960, (v3)
PR3081.S64 1965, (v3)
Spurgin, Hugh. F82.W7.S68 1989, (v4)
Spurling, Hilary. PR6005.O3895.Z93 1984, (v3)
PR6069.C596.Z857 1991, (v3)
Spurlock, John C. HQ967.U6.S68 1988, (v6)
HQ1420.S68 1998, (v6)
Spurr, Barry. PR502.S78 1997, (v3)
Spurr, John. BX9334.2.S68 1998, (v8)
DA445.S68 2000, (v5)
Spurr, Stephen Hopkins. QK938.F6.S68 1980, (v1)
Spyer, Patricia. DS647.A78.S69 2000, (v5)
Squatriti, Paolo. HD1697.I8.S6 1998, (v6)
Squier, Charles L. PR3718.Z5.S6, (v3)
Squier, Susan Merrill. PR6045.O72.Z8785 1985, (v3)
Squires, G. L. QC174.15.S66 1995, (v1)
Squires, James D. PN4899.C4.S68 1993, (v3)
Sreenivasan, Gopal. JC153.L87.S68 1995, (v7)
Srinivas, Mysore Narasimhachar. HN690.R35.S74, (v6)
Ssu-ma, Chien. DS734.S75, (v5)
DS741.3.S6813 1994, (v5)
DS748.S7453, (v5)
St. Armand, Barton Levi. PS1541.Z5.S7 1984, (v3)
St. Aubyn, Giles. DA567.S24, (v5)
St. Clair, Guy. ZA3157.S23 1997, (v10)
St. Clair, William. PR4723.S7 1989, (v3)
St. George, Robert Blair. F7.S8 1998, (v4)
St. Jean, Yanick. E185.86.S695 1998, (v4)

St. John de Crevecoeur, J. Hector. E163.S73 1981, (v4)
F153.C923, (v4)
St. John, Ronald Bruce. DT223.3.S7 1998, (v5)
F3433.S7 1992, (v4)
St. Johns, Adela Rogers. HQ1412.S25, (v6)
St. Peter, Christine. PR8807.W6.S7 1999, (v3)
Staab, Andreas. DD290.29.S73 1998, (v5)
Staal, Frits. BC25.S76 1988, (v8)
Staar, Richard Felix. DK443.S7 1975, (v5)
Staats, Arthur W. BF199.S74 1996, (v2)
Stabb, Martin S. PQ7797.B635.Z9178 1991, (v3)
Stace, Clive A. QK306.S78 1997, (v1)
Stace, W. T. B56.S8, (v8)
BD111.S7, (v8)
BD161.S67, (v8)
Stacewicz, Richard. DS559.5.S72 1997, (v5)
Stacey, C. P. F1029.S73, (v4)
F1032.S78 1963, (v4)
Stacey, F. D. QC806.S65 1977, (v1)
Stacey, Jackie. PN1995.9.W6.S7 1994, (v3)
Stacey, Judith. HQ536.15.S26.S73 1990, (v6)
Stacey, Peter F. ML410.B773.S68 1987, (v9)
Stacey, William A. HQ809.3.U5.S77 1983, (v6)
Stachelhaus, Heiner. N6888.B463.S7413 1991, (v9)
Stachura, Peter D. DD244.S64 1993, (v5)
Stack, Carol B. E185.86.S6974 1996, (v4)
Stacton, David. PS3537.T1178.D3 1960a, (v3)
PS3537.T126.Ju, (v3)
Stacy, R. H. PN99.R9.S8, (v3)
Stadler, Karl R. DB91.S72 1971, (v5)
Stadler, Quandra Prettyman. PS647.A35.O97 1981, (v3)
Staël, Madame de (Anne-Louise-Germaine). DC146.S7.A25 2000, (v5)
Staelin, David H. QC461.S74 1994, (v1)
Stafford Smith, Bryan. TH1611.S59 1991, (v1)
Stafford, Barbara Maria. G468.S73 1984, (v6)
QP495.S73 1994, (v1)
Stafford, David. D753.S68 2000, (v5)
Stafford, Edward Peary. V210.S692, (v10)
Stafford, Fiona J. PR408.F34.S73 1994, (v3)
Stafford, Jean. PS3569.T2 B6, (v3)
PS3569.T2 C3, (v3)
PS3569.T2 C5, (v3)
PS3569.T2 C6, (v3)
PS3569.T2.M6, (v3)
Stafford, Pauline. DA160.S73 1997, (v5)
HQ1147.E85 S73 1998, (v6)
Stafford, William. ML410.M9 S815 1991, (v9)
Stagg, J. C. A. E357.S79 1983, (v4)
Staggenborg, Suzanne. HQ767.5.U5.S734 1991, (v6)
Stahl, Dean. PE1693.D4 2001, (v3)
Stahl, J. D. PS1342.E85.S7 1994, (v3)
Stahl, Saul. QA162.S73 1997, (v1)
QA269.S695 1999, (v1)
QA300.S882 1999, (v1)
QA685.S79 1993, (v1)
Staiger, Emil. PT2051.S67, (v3)
Staiger, Janet. PN1995.S6735 1992, (v3)
PN1995.9.A8.S69 2000, (v3)
PN1995.9.W6.S73 1995, (v3)
Staikos, K. Z723.S7313 2000, (v10)
Stainback, Robert D. RC1245.S73 1997, (v2)
Stainton, Leslie. PQ6613.A763.Z8856 1999, (v3)
Staiti, Paul J. N6537.M66.A4 1989, (v9)
Stakel, Susan. PQ1528.S17 1991, (v3)
Stakgold, Ivar. QA379.S72, (v1)
Staley, Allen. ND1354.5.S72 2001, (v9)
Staley, Lynn. PR2007.K4.Z75 1994, (v3)
Staley, Thomas F. PR6035.H96.Z87 1979, (v3)
PR6035.I34.Z93, (v3)
Stalheim, Ole H. V. SF623.S73 1994, (v1)
Stalin, Joseph. DK254.L4.S75 1942, (v5)
DK265.S668, (v5)
DK268.S75.A34 1970, (v5)
Stalker, Peter. HD6300.S734 2000, (v6)
Stallaerts, Robert. DH511.S73 1999, (v5)
DR1507.5 .S74 1995, (v5)
Stalley, R. A. NA350.S78 1999, (v9)
Stallings, Barbara. HC123.S83 2000, (v6)

HG5160.5.A3.S73 1987, (v6)
Stallings, William. QA76.76.O63S734 1998, (v1)
TK5105.S73 2000, (v1)
Stallman, R. W. PN81.S67, (v3)
Stallman, R. W. PR6005.O4.Z796, (v3)
Stalls, Clay. DP127.6.S7 1995, (v5)
Stallworthy, Jon. PR5907.S75, (v3)
PR6025.A316.Z944 1995, (v3)
Stalnaker, Robert. B831.5.S73 1999, (v8)
Staloff, Darren. F67.S8 1998, (v4)
Stalvey, Lois Mark. E185.61.S77, (v4)
Stam, Allan C. U21.2.S68 1996, (v10)
Stambaugh, John E. HT114.S7 1988, (v6)
Stambler, Irwin. ML102.F66.S7 1983, (v9)
Stamets, Paul. QK629.S77.S735 1996, (v1)
Stamm, Henry E. E99.S4.S73 1999, (v4)
Stamm, Laura. GV848.3.S7 2001, (v6)
Stammler, Wolfgang. PT238.S7 1950, (v3)
Stamp, L. Dudley. HF1025.S69 1973, (v6)
Stamp, Shelley. PN1995.9.W6.S75 2000, (v3)
Stampp, Kenneth M. E436.S78 1990, (v4)
E440.5.S78 1980, (v4)
E441.S8 1956b, (v4)
E458.S825, (v4)
F526.S84 1978, (v4)
Stanbury, Sarah. PR1972.G353.S7 1991, (v3)
Stancell, Steven. ML400.S7 1996, (v9)
Standage, Tom. QB36.A2, (v1)
Standifer, Leon C. DD257.S66 1997, (v5)
Standing Bear, Luther. E99.D1.S73 1975, (v4)
Stands In Timber, John. E99.C53 S7 1998, (v4)
Stanfield, D. P. QK495.G74, (v1)
Stanford, Craig B. GN281.4.S72 2001, (v6)
Stanford, Karin L. E185.97.J25.S73 1997, (v4)
Stang, Sondra J. PR6011.O53.Z9, (v3)
Stange, Margit. PS374.W6.S74 1998, (v3)
Stanhope, Marcia. RT98.S78197 2002, (v2)
RT98.S782 2000, (v2)
Stanier, Roger Y. QR41.S775 1963, (v1)
Staniland, Martin. DT38.7.S73 1991, (v5)
Stanish, Charles. F2230.1.P65.S74 1992, (v4)
Stanislawski, Michael. PJ5052.G6.Z86 1988, (v3)
Staniszkis, Jadwiga. DK4442.S72 1984, (v5)
Stanley, George Francis Gilman. F1030.9.S7, (v4)
F1063.S83 1989, (v4)
Stanley, H. Eugene. QC307.S7 1971b, (v1)
Stanley, Peter. UA649.32.I4.S73 1998, (v10)
Stanley, Robert. HJ4651.S73 1993, (v6)
Stanley, William Deane. HV6433.S2.S73 1996, (v6)
Stanlis, Peter J. JC176.B83.S72 1990, (v7)
Stannard, David E. E112.S82 1992, (v4)
GN875.H3.S73 1989, (v6)
Stannard, Martin. PR6045.A97.Z79 1987, (v3)
Stansfield, William D. QH309.S78 2000, (v1)
Stansky, Peter. DA685.B65.S73 1996, (v5)
NX543.S73 1994, (v9)
PR6029.R8.Z7898 1980, (v3)
Stanton, Andra Fischgrund. F1221.Z3.S68 1999, (v4)
Stanton, Elizabeth Cady. HQ1410.A2525 1997, (v6)
HQ1412.S72 1981, (v6)
JK1899.S7.A3 1971, (v7)
Stanton, Greta W. Z7164.M2.S73 1994, (v10)
Stanton, Robert Brewster. F788.S84, (v4)
F788.S845 1987, (v4)
Stanton, Shelby L. UA25.S767 1984, (v10)
Stanton, Stephen Sadler. PQ1222.S8, (v3)
Stanton, William Ragan. GN17.S75, (v6)
Stanwood, P. G. PR3757.W6.Z88 1998, (v3)
Stape, J. H. Z8976.485.S7 1988, (v10)
Stapledon, Olaf. PR6037.T18 T6, (v3)
Staples, William G. HN57.S68 1990, (v6)
Stapleton, Constance. TT23.S73 1988, (v1)
Stapleton, Kristin Eileen. HT147.C48.S76 2000, (v6)
Stapp, Andy. UB342.U5.S83, (v10)
Stapp, Henry P. QC174.12.S8 1993, (v1)
Star, Barbara. HQ809.3.U5.S777 1983, (v6)
Stares, Paul B. HV5801.S75 1996, (v6)
UG1523.S83 1985, (v10)
Stark, Andrew. JK468.E7 S73 2000, (v7)
Stark, Barbara L. F1219.1.V47.S69 1989, (v4)
Stark, David Charles. HD4140.7.S73 1998, (v6)

Stark, Frank M. P91.S68 1996, (v3)
Stark, Lucien. MT115.B73 S7 1998, (v9)
MT115.B73.S73 1995, (v9)
Stark, Oded. HD5856.D44.S73 1990, (v6)
Stark, Richard. PS3573.E9, (v3)
Stark, Rodney. BL48.S724 1987, (v8)
BR166.S75 1996, (v8)
Starker, Steven. BF632.S73 1989, (v2)
Starkey, Armstrong. E82.S7 1998, (v4)
Starkey, Brigid. JZ6045.S73 1999, (v7)
Starkey, Edward D. Z6370.S78 1990, (v10)
Starkey, Marion Lena. KFM2478.8.W5.S8 1989, (v7)
Starkie, Enid. PR129.F8.S8 1971, (v3)
Starkie, Walter. PQ6267.E6.S8, (v3)
Starko, Alane J. LB1062.S77 1994, (v7)
Starling, Ernest Henry. QP34.S75 1968, (v1)
Starnes, De Witt Talmage. PE1611.S68, (v3)
Starnes, John. HV7911.S75.A3 1998, (v6)
Starobinski, Jean. PQ1643.S74 1982, (v3)
Starr, Chester G. D59.S75 1974, (v5)
DG210.S8 1953, (v5)
HC37.S7, (v6)
JC73.S68 1986, (v7)
V39.S7 1975, (v10)
Starr, Douglas P. RM172.S728 1998, (v2)
Starr, George A. PR3406.S72, (v3)
Starr, John Bryan. DS778.M3.S76, (v5)
Starr, June. KKX120.S73 1992, (v7)
Starr, Kevin. F861.S82, (v4)
F866.S78 1997, (v4)
F867.S8 1985, (v4)
HB3717 1929.S73 1996, (v6)
Starr, Larry. ML410.I94 S7 1992, (v9)
Starr, Louis Morris. E609.S8 1987, (v4)
Starr, Rebecca. JK4274.5.S73 1998, (v7)
Starr, S. Frederick. F379.N56.G377 1989, (v4)
ML410.G68.S7 1995, (v9)
Starr, Stephen Z. E492.5.S7, (v4)
Starrett, Vincent. PS1097.Z5S7 1969, (v3)
Starrs, Paul F. SF196.U5.S7 1998, (v1)
Stassen, Harold Edward. E836.S69 1990, (v4)
Staten, Henry. PN56.D48.S83 1995, (v3)
Stathatos, Constantine C. Z8941.7.S82 1997, (v10)
Statius, P. Papinius. PA6156.S8 1928, (v3)
Statman, Meir. HD9666.5.S79 1983, (v6)
Staudenraus, P. J. E448.S78, (v4)
Staudinger, Hermann. QD22.S73.A313, (v1)
Staudt, Kathleen A. HC59.72.E44.S72 1991, (v6)
HD2346.U52.M497 1998, (v6)
Stauffer, Dietrich. QC20.S7413 1990, (v1)
Stauffer, Donald A. CT34.G7.S67, (v5)
PN1031.S78, (v3)
Stauffer, Russell G. LB1573.33.S72 1970, (v7)
Stavans, Ilan. PN57.C6.S7 1993, (v3)
PQ7207.D48.S83 1997, (v3)
PQ7797.C7145.Z795 1996, (v3)
Stave, Bruce M. KZ1176.S73 1998, (v7)
Stave, Shirley A. PR4757.M83.S73 1995, (v3)
Stave, Sondra Astor. LC214.2.S73 1995, (v7)
Staveley, E. S. JC73.S73, (v7)
Stavely, Keith W. F. F7.S83 1987, (v4)
Stavenhagen, Rodolfo. GN496.S7 1996, (v6)
Stavig, Mark. PR2527.S7, (v3)
Stavig, Mark. PR3072.S78 1995, (v3)
Stavrianos, Leften Stavros. CB428.S8, (v5)
D463.S7, (v5)
DR36.S83, (v5)
Stavy, Ruth. Q181.S694 2000, (v1)
Stead, Christina. PR6037.T225 A5 1978, (v3)
PR6037.T225 H67, (v3)
PR9619.3.S75 D3, (v3)
PR9619.3.S75 L5 1975, (v3)
PR9619.3.S75 M3 1969, (v3)
PR9619.3.S75 M5, (v3)
PR9619.3.S75.O25 1985, (v3)
PR9619.3.S75 P8, (v3)
Stead, Christopher. BR100.S754 1994, (v8)
Stead, Peter. PR6066.O77.Z88 1993, (v3)
Stead, W. Edward. HD75.6.S74 1996, (v6)
Steadman, David W. QH198.G3.S72 1988, (v1)

Author Index to Volumes 1-10

Steadman, John M. PR161.S8, **(v3)**
PR3592.E8.S84 1995, **(v3)**
Steane, J. B. ML1460.S73 1992, **(v9)**
PR2673.S75, **(v3)**
Steans, Jill. JZ1253.2.S74 1998, **(v7)**
Stearn, William T. (William Thomas). QK10.S7 1992, **(v1)**
Stearns, Marshall Winslow. GV1623.S67, **(v6)**
GV1624.7.A34 S74 1994, **(v6)**
Stearns, Maxwell L. KF8742.S745 2000, **(v7)**
Stearns, Monteagle. E840.S724 1996, **(v4)**
Stearns, Peter N. CB15.S74 1993, **(v5)**
D387.S7 1974, **(v5)**
HD2321.S74 1993, **(v6)**
RM222.2.S755 1997, **(v2)**
Stebbins, Chad. PN4874.A85.S74 1998, **(v3)**
Stebbins, Robert C. QL651.S783 1985, **(v1)**
QL667.S84 1995, **(v1)**
Stebbins, Theodore E. ND237.H39.A4 1999, **(v9)**
Stebner, Eleanor J. HV4196.C4S74 1997, **(v6)**
Stechow, Wolfgang. ND1359.S8, **(v9)**
Steck, Odil Hannes. BS1174.2.B3713 1998, **(v8)**
Stedman, Jane W. PR4714.S74 1996, **(v3)**
Stedman, John Gabriel. F2410.S815 1988, **(v4)**
Stedman, Thomas Lathrop. R121.S8 2000, **(v2)**
Steedman, Carolyn. LB775.M3172.S74 1990, **(v7)**
Steedman, Ian. HB801.S775 2001, **(v6)**
Steefel, Lawrence Dinkelspiel. DC292.S7, **(v5)**
DD491.S68.S8, **(v5)**
Steegmuller, Francis. PQ2601.P6.Z83, **(v3)**
Steegmuller, Francis. PQ2605.O15.Z86, **(v3)**
Steel, Duncan. CE6.S74 2000, **(v5)**
Steel, Gayla R. PR4757.F6.S73 1993, **(v3)**
Steele, Cassie Premo. PS151.S74 2000, **(v3)**
Steele, D. Gentry. GN70.S78 1988, **(v6)**
Steele, David Ramsay. HB101.V66.S73 1992, **(v6)**
Steele, E. D. DA536.P2.S74 1991, **(v5)**
Steele, E. J. QR184.S74 1998, **(v1)**
Steele, Elizabeth. Z8984.2.S74 1983, **(v10)**
Z8984.2.S743 1987, **(v10)**
Steele, G. R. HB101.H39.S73 1993, **(v6)**
Steele, Ian Kenneth. E82.S74 1994, **(v4)**
Steele, Janet E. PN4874.D3.S76 1993, **(v3)**
Steele, John M. QB175.S83 2000, **(v1)**
Steele, Ken. RC514.S754 2001, **(v2)**
Steele, Richard. PR3701.K4, **(v3)**
PR3702.B54, **(v3)**
PR3702.B55 1967, **(v3)**
PR3706.A43 1968, **(v3)**
Steele, Timothy. PE1505.S73 1999, **(v3)**
PN1059.F7.S74 1990, **(v3)**
Steele, Wilbur Daniel. PS3537.T2787 A6 1946, **(v3)**
PS3537.T2787 F8, **(v3)**
Steely, Mel. E840.8.G5.S74 2000, **(v4)**
Steen, Sara Jayne. PR2717.S74 1993, **(v3)**
Steensma, Robert C. PR3316.A5.Z87, **(v3)**
Steeples, Douglas W. F869.C146.S84 1999, **(v4)**
JK231.S74 1998, **(v7)**
Steer, John. ND621.V5.S83 1970, **(v9)**
Steeves, H. Leslie. PN5499.K4.S74 1997, **(v3)**
Stefan, Susan. KF480.S684 2001, **(v7)**
Stefansson, Vilhjalmur. G640.S75, **(v6)**
G670.1908.A52, **(v6)**
Steffan, Joseph. KF228.S74.S74 1993, **(v7)**
Steffen, Charles G. F187.B2.S74 1993, **(v4)**
Steffen, Jerome O. F592.C56.S74, **(v4)**
Steffen, Lloyd H. HV8698.S74 1998, **(v6)**
Steffen, Therese. PS3554.O884Z87 2001, **(v3)**
Steffens, Lincoln. HN57.S7 1968, **(v6)**
PS3537.T313.A4, **(v3)**
Steffy, J. Richard. VM144.S73 1994, **(v10)**
Steger, Manfred B. HM1281.S74 2000, **(v6)**
Stegner, Wallace Earle. PN6014.S74, **(v3)**
PS3537.T316 A4, **(v3)**
PS3537.T316.A6 1990, **(v3)**
PS3537.T316 B5, **(v3)**
PS3537.T316 C5, **(v3)**
PS3537.T316 S4, **(v3)**
PS3537.T316 S5, **(v3)**
PS3537.T316 W6, **(v3)**
PS3537.T316.Z474 1980, **(v3)**

Q143.P8.S8, **(v1)**
Stehle, Philip. QC7.S78 1994, **(v1)**
Steichen, Edward. TR140.S68.A25, **(v1)**
TR653 .S744 2000, **(v1)**
Steig, Michael. PR4583.S8, **(v3)**
Steigerwald, David. E743.S76 1994, **(v4)**
Steil, Janice M. Ingham. HQ536.S735 1997, **(v6)**
Stein, Arnold Sidney. PR2248.S7, **(v3)**
PR3508.S7, **(v3)**
Stein, Arthur A. JX1391.S76 1990, **(v7)**
Stein, Aurel. DS785.S83, **(v5)**
Stein, Benjamin. TH6010.S74 2000, **(v1)**
Stein, Burton. DS407.S82 1998, **(v5)**
Stein, Burton. DS485.M28.M867 1989, **(v5)**
Stein, David B. RJ506.H9.S68 1999, **(v2)**
Stein, Deborah J. MT120.S74 1996, **(v9)**
Stein, Donald G. RC387.5.B713 1995, **(v2)**
Stein, Edith Sarah. HV885.B7.S74 1994, **(v6)**
Stein, Edward. BD450.S747 1996, **(v8)**
Stein, Edwin. PR5892.A43.S78 1988, **(v3)**
Stein, George H. D757.85.S8, **(v5)**
Stein, Gertrude. ND553.P5.S76, **(v9)**
PS3537.T323.A19 1974, **(v3)**
PS3537.T323.A6 1969 vol. 3, **(v3)**
PS3537.T323.A6 1970, **(v3)**
PS3537.T323.A6 1971, **(v3)**
PS3537.T323.A6 1980, **(v3)**
PS3537.T323.A6 1993, **(v3)**
PS3537.T323.A6 vol. 1, **(v3)**
PS3537.T323.A6 vol. 2, **(v3)**
PS3537.T323.A6 vol.6, **(v3)**
PS3537.T323.A6 vol. 7, **(v3)**
PS3537.T323.A6 vol. 8, **(v3)**
PS3537.T323.B7, **(v3)**
PS3537.T323.C6 1926, **(v3)**
PS3537.T323.F56, **(v3)**
PS3537.T323.G37 1936, **(v3)**
PS3537.T323.G4 1968, **(v3)**
PS3537.T323 I23 1972, **(v3)**
PS3537.T323.L4 1935, **(v3)**
PS3537.T323 M3, **(v3)**
PS3537.T323.P6 1934, **(v3)**
PS3537.T323.T4 1914, **(v3)**
PS3537.T323 T48, **(v3)**
PS3537.T323.W3, **(v3)**
PS3537.T323.Z4974 1996, **(v3)**
PS3537.T323.Z5 1933, **(v3)**
PS3537.T323.Z53 1937, **(v3)**
PS3537.T323.Z547, **(v3)**
HC106.S79 1994, **(v6)**
Stein, Herbert. HJ257.S78 1996, **(v6)**
HJ2051.S74 1989, **(v6)**
Stein, Howard F. RA418.3.U6.S74 1990, **(v2)**
Stein, J. Stewart. TH9.S78 1993, **(v1)**
Stein, Jonathan B. UA23.S685 1984, **(v10)**
Stein, Jonathan Y. TK5102.9.S745 2000, **(v1)**
Stein, Judith. HD9515.S734 1998, **(v6)**
Stein, Karen F. PR9199.3.A8.Z896 1999, **(v3)**
Stein, Kevin. PS3573.R5358.Z88 1989, **(v3)**
Stein, Murray. BF173.S674 1998, **(v2)**
Stein, R. Conrad. F861.3.S69 1988, **(v4)**
Stein, Richard L. PR461.S78 1987, **(v3)**
Stein, Robert Louis. HD9115.F82.S74 1988, **(v6)**
Stein, Robert M. HJ275.S728 1995, **(v6)**
Stein, Ronald H. BF637.C6.S755 1990, **(v2)**
Stein, Ruth E. K. RC455.4.E46.S74 1991, **(v2)**
Stein, Sherman K. QA22.S85 1999, **(v1)**
QA93.S684 1996, **(v1)**
Stein, Stanley J. HC125.S76, **(v6)**
HF3685.S74 2000, **(v6)**
Stein, Stephen J. BX9766.S74 1992, **(v8)**
Stein, Steve. F3448.S73, **(v4)**
Steinbach, Robert H. F594.S823 1989, **(v4)**
Steinbeck, John. CT275.S6763.A3, **(v5)**
PS3537.T3234 A6, **(v3)**
PS3537.T3234 A6 1953, **(v3)**
PS3537.T3234 B8 1950, **(v3)**
PS3537.T3234 C3 1968, **(v3)**
PS3537.T3234.C8 1936b, **(v3)**
PS3537.T3234.E3 1952, **(v3)**
PS3537.T3234.G8 1939, **(v3)**

PS3537.T3234.G858 1989, **(v3)**
PS3537.T3234 I5, **(v3)**
PS3537.T3234.L6 1938, **(v3)**
PS3537.T3234.M6 1942, **(v3)**
PS3537.T3234 O2 1938, **(v3)**
PS3537.T3234 P3, **(v3)**
PS3537.T3234 P4, **(v3)**
PS3537.T3234 R4, **(v3)**
PS3537.T3234 S3, **(v3)**
PS3537.T3234 S9, **(v3)**
PS3537.T3234 S9, **(v3)**
PS3537.T3234 T65, **(v3)**
PS3537.T3234 W3, **(v3)**
PS3537.T3234 W5 1961, **(v3)**
PS3537.T3234.Z5 1969, **(v3)**
PS3537.T3234.Z53 1976, **(v3)**
PS3537.T3234.Z545, **(v3)**
UG633.S77, **(v10)**
Steinberg, Allen. KFX2137.S74 1989, **(v7)**
Steinberg, Blema S. DS558.S737 1996, **(v5)**
Steinberg, Danny D. B840.S82, **(v8)**
Steinberg, Esther R. LB1028.5.S72 1990, **(v7)**
Steinberg, Frances E. RC480.5.S675 1999, **(v2)**
Steinberg, Franz U. RB135.S73, **(v2)**
Steinberg, Jacob. PC871.E8.S8, **(v3)**
Steinberg, Jonathan. D804.3.S75 1990, **(v5)**
DQ17.S7 1996, **(v5)**
VA513.S74 1966, **(v10)**
Steinberg, Marc W. HD8399.E52.S73 1999, **(v6)**
Steinberg, Mark D. DK258.S74 1995, **(v5)**
Steinberg, Mark. Z244.6.S65.S84 1992, **(v10)**
Steinberg, Michael. ML1263.S74 1998, **(v9)**
MT125.S79 1995, **(v9)**
Steinberg, Raymond M. HV1461.S83 1983, **(v6)**
Steinberg, S. H. D11.S83 1986, **(v5)**
Steinberg, S. H. Z124.S8 1996, **(v10)**
Steinberg, Theodore L. PR2017.P74.S74 1990, **(v3)**
Steinberg, Warren. BF175.5.M37.S74 1993, **(v2)**
Steinberger, Peter J. K230.H432.S74 1988, **(v7)**
Steinbock, Bonnie. K642.S74 1992, **(v7)**
Steinbock, Dan. HF5415.1265.S735 2000, **(v6)**
Steinbrink, Jeffrey. PS1331.S75 1991, **(v3)**
Steinbruner, John D. JZ6005.S74 2000, **(v7)**
Steiner, Barry H. UA23.S687 1991, **(v10)**
Steiner, Bernard Christian. E340.T2.S8, **(v4)**
Steiner, Christopher Burghard. N7399.I8.S74 1994, **(v9)**
Steiner, Dale R. Z6205.S73 1993, **(v10)**
Steiner, Frederick R. S624.A1.S74 1990, **(v1)**
Steiner, George. BD638.S76 2001, **(v8)**
Steiner, George. PN511.S687 1967, **(v3)**
Steiner, Gilbert Yale. HQ536.S74, **(v6)**
Steiner, Zara S. D517.S816 1977, **(v5)**
Steinfeld, Robert J. K888.S74 1991, **(v7)**
Steinfirst, Susan. Z5981.S74 1992, **(v10)**
Steingass, Francis Joseph. PK6379.S7 1970, **(v3)**
Steingraber, Sandra. RC268.25.S74 1997, **(v2)**
Steinhardt, Arnold. ML398.G835 1998, **(v9)**
Steinhardt, Nancy Shatzman. NA6046.L5.S74 1997, **(v9)**
NA9265.S8 1990, **(v9)**
Steinhoff, William R. PR6029.R8.N67, **(v3)**
Steinlauf, Michael. DS135.P6.S76 1997, **(v5)**
Steinle, Pamela Hunt. PS3537.A426.C395 2000, **(v3)**
Steinman, David. TX356.S74 1995, **(v1)**
Steinmetz, David Curtis. BR315.S83 2001, **(v8)**
Steinmetz, Jean-Luc. PQ2387.R5.Z885 2001, **(v3)**
Steinmetz, Lee. E647.S85, **(v4)**
Steinmetz, Suzanne K. HQ1063.6.S74 1988, **(v6)**
Stella, Joseph. N6537.S73.A4 1990, **(v9)**
Stelling, Lucille Johnsen. F614.M6 S79 1988, **(v4)**
Stelljes, Mark E. RA1213.S73 2000, **(v2)**
Stelzig, Eugene L. PT2617.E85.Z937 1988, **(v3)**
Stempel, Tom. PN1992.7.S74 1992, **(v3)**
PN1995.9.A8.S73 2001, **(v3)**
Sten, Christopher. PS2388.T4.S74 1996, **(v3)**
Stenberg, Peter. PJ5120.7.H64.S74 1991, **(v3)**
Stenberger, Marten. DL661.S73 1963, **(v5)**
Stendhal, 1783-1842. DG805.B5715, **(v5)**

Stendhal. PQ2435.A8 1962, (v3)
  PQ2435.R7 1969, (v3)
  PQ2436.A2.J63, (v3)
Stengler, Mark. RZ440.S746 2001, (v2)
Stenius, Erik. BC135.W52.S8 1981, (v8)
Stent, Angela. DK67.5.G3.S77 1999, (v5)
Stepan, Alfred C. F2538.25.S79 1988, (v4)
  UA619.S7, (v10)
Stepansky, Paul E. BF575.A3.S76, (v2)
Stephan, Johannes. HC300.282.S74 1999, (v6)
Stephan, John J. D767.92.S835 1984, (v5)
  DK771.D3.S74 1994, (v5)
Stephan, Michael. BH301.P45.S74 1990, (v8)
Stephani, Hans. QC178.S8213 1982, (v1)
Stephen, Leslie. PR99.S7 1968, (v3)
  PR5473.S6.A815 1977, (v3)
Stephen, Lynn. F1221.Z3.S74 1991, (v4)
  HQ1240.5.L29.S74 1997, (v6)
Stephens, A. Ray. F386.S86 1989, (v4)
Stephens, Alexander Hamilton. E467.1.S85 A3 1998, (v4)
Stephens, Daniel B. GB1197.7.S74 1995, (v6)
Stephens, Donna M. LA2317.M578.S74 1990, (v7)
Stephens, Dorothy. PR539.N3.S74 1998, (v3)
Stephens, G. Lynn. RC553.A84.S74 2000, (v2)
Stephens, Gregory. E184.A1.S835 1999, (v4)
Stephens, Hal G. F788.S863 1987, (v4)
Stephens, James. PR6037.T4 C87, (v3)
  PR6037.T4 D4, (v3)
  PR6037.T4 H4, (v3)
  PR6037.T4 M3, (v3)
Stephens, John Russell. PN2594.S75 1991, (v3)
Stephens, John. PE1421.S674 1990, (v3)
Stephens, John. PN1009.A1.S82 1992, (v3)
Stephens, Michael L. PN1995.9.F54.S74 1995, (v3)
  PN1998.2.S73 1998, (v3)
Stephens, Thomas M. GN562.S74 1999, (v6)
Stephens, Trent D. RA1242.T5.G56 2000, (v2)
Stephens, W. P. BR346.S74 1992, (v8)
Stephenson, Bruce. QB361.S74 1994, (v1)
Stephenson, G. QA39.2.S745 1990, (v1)
Stephenson, G. M. HV6080.S83 1992, (v6)
Stephenson, Jill. HQ1623.S73 1975, (v6)
Stephenson, John B. HN79.A13.S82, (v6)
Stephenson, Marcia. F3320.1.W65.S74 1999, (v4)
Stephenson, Paul. DR39.S76 2000, (v5)
Stephenson, R. Bruce. HT168.S174.S74 1997, (v6)
Stephenson, Ralph L. TD897.5.S74 1998, (v1)
Stephenson, Steven L. QK635.A1.S73 1994, (v1)
Stephenson, Wendell Holmes. F208.2.S8 1969, (v4)
Steppe, Wolfhard. PR6019.O9.U725 1985, (v3)
Steptoe, Andrew. ML410.M9.S86 1988, (v9)
Sterba, James P. BJ1012.S69 2001, (v8)
Sterelny, Kim. QH331.S82 1999, (v1)
Sterling Publishing Company. G1025.S8 1960, (v6)
Sterling, Christopher H. HE8689.8.S7295 1984, (v6)
  Z5834.T4 S74 2000, (v10)
Stern, Alan. QB601.S76 1999, (v1)
Stern, Daniel N. BF719.S75 1985, (v2)
Stern, David. LC1037.6.C2.S74 1992, (v7)
  Z7141.S74 2000, (v10)
Stern, Fritz Richard. DD76.S72 1961, (v5)
  DD239.S74 1999, (v5)
Stern, Gerald M. KF228.P75 S7 1977, (v7)
Stern, J. P. PT2619.U43.Z87, (v3)
Stern, Jessica. HV6431.S74 1999, (v6)
Stern, Judy E. Q180.5.M67S74 1997, (v1)
Stern, Julia A. PS375.S74 1997, (v3)
Stern, Laura Ikins. KKH9851.86.S74 1994, (v7)
Stern, Lesley. PN1998.3.S39.S74 1995, (v3)
Stern, Madeleine B. PS1018.S74 1998, (v3)
Stern, Mark. E841.S75 1992, (v4)
Stern, Milton R. PS1862.S74 1991, (v3)
Stern, Peter A. Z1870.3.S7 1995, (v10)
Stern, Richard G. PS3569.T39.N3, (v3)
Stern, Robert A. M. NA680.S84 1988, (v9)
  NA735.N5.S727 1999, (v9)
  NA735.N5.S73 1983, (v9)
Stern, Robert N. Z7164.L1.S766 1996, (v10)
Stern, Robert W. DS341.S75 2001, (v5)
  DS463.S73 1993, (v5)

Stern, Robert. BD201.S73 2000, (v8)
Stern, William. PN1991.4.S83.A3, (v3)
Sternberg, Martin L. A. HV2475.S77 1998, (v6)
Sternberg, Patricia. HM254.S74 1989, (v6)
Sternberg, Robert J. BF311.S6778 1997, (v2)
  BF408.S76 1995, (v2)
  BF431.S7382 1990, (v2)
Sterne, Laurence. PR3710.F78, (v3)
  PR3714.S4 1968, (v3)
  PR3714.T7 1965, (v3)
Sternfeld, Robert. B3245.F24.S7, (v8)
Sternglass, Ernest J. QC171.2.S84 1997, (v1)
Sternglass, Marilyn S. PE1404.S824 1997, (v3)
Sternhell, Zeev. DS149.S69513 1998, (v5)
Sternlicht, Sanford V. PR6035.H96.Z88 1997, (v3)
  PR6037.A86.Z86 1993, (v3)
  PR6037.M43.Z875 1990, (v3)
  PR6037.P47.Z86 1992, (v3)
Sterritt, David. PN1998.3.H58.S74 1993, (v3)
  PS228.B6.S755 1998, (v3)
Stetkevych, Jaroslav. BL1685.S74 1996, (v8)
  PJ6075.S7, (v3)
Stetson, Brad. JC574.2.U6.S74 1998, (v7)
Stetson, Erlene. E185.97.T8.S74 1994, (v4)
Stettinius, Edward R. D734.C7 1970, (v5)
Stetz, Margaret D. PR830.H85, (v3)
Steuben Glass, inc. NK5112.C64, (v9)
Stevanovic, Bosiljka. Z2500.S8 1987, (v10)
Stevens, Anthony. BF458.S74 1999, (v2)
Stevens, Charles F. QC21.2.S688 1995, (v1)
Stevens, Denis. ML2800.S8 1961, (v9)
  ML2931.S8 1966a, (v9)
Stevens, Edward. BJ1031.S75 1997, (v8)
Stevens, Evelyn P. HD5331.A6.S75, (v6)
Stevens, Gwendolyn. BF95.S73 1982, (v2)
Stevens, James. PS3537.T839 H6, (v3)
Stevens, John D. PN4899.N4.S74 1991, (v3)
Stevens, John E. PN688.S75 1974, (v3)
Stevens, John. GV1114.35.S765 2001, (v6)
Stevens, Joseph E. E160.S72 1990, (v4)
  TC557.5.H6.S74 1988, (v1)
Stevens, Karl K. TA351.S73 1987, (v1)
Stevens, Keith G. BL1812.G63 S74 2001, (v8)
Stevens, Kenneth R. Z8387.97.S74 1998, (v10)
Stevens, Lauren R. PS3569.T42.D6, (v3)
Stevens, M. L. Tina. R724.S84 2000, (v2)
Stevens, Matthew. PN1993.45.S76 1993, (v3)
Stevens, Paul. HD9560.5.S755 1988, (v6)
Stevens, Richard. BF109.E7.S73 1983, (v2)
Stevens, Robert Bocking. KD7285.S74 1993, (v7)
Stevens, Roger T. QA76.64.S73 1994, (v1)
Stevens, Stanley F. GF696.N35.S74 1993, (v6)
Stevens, Thomas Wood. PS3537.T475W4 1938, (v3)
Stevens, Wallace. PN1055.S68, (v3)
Stevens, Wallace. PS3537.T4753.A6 1953, (v3)
  PS3537.T4753.H3 1931, (v3)
  PS3537.T4753.M3, (v3)
  PS3537.T4753.N6, (v3)
  PS3537.T4753.P3 1942, (v3)
  PS3537.T4753.T7, (v3)
  PS3537.T4753.Z53, (v3)
Stevens, William Oliver. F189.A6 S78, (v4)
Stevenson, Adlai E. E742.5.S74 1972, (v4)
  E835.S778, (v4)
  E837.5.S73 1971, (v4)
Stevenson, Brenda E. HN79.V82.L687 1996, (v6)
Stevenson, Charles L. BJ43.S8, (v8)
  BJ1012.S8 1975, (v8)
Stevenson, D. D621.F8.S75 1982, (v5)
Stevenson, D. (David), 1954-. D511.S815 1996, (v5)
  D511.S816 1988, (v5)
Stevenson, David Alan. VK1015.S7, (v10)
Stevenson, Elizabeth. F591.S827 1994, (v4)
Stevenson, F. J. S592.7.S73 1986, (v1)
Stevenson, James Earl. F394.M62, (v4)
Stevenson, Joan C. GN50.3.S74 1991, (v6)
Stevenson, Jonathan. DA990.U46.S774 1996, (v5)
Stevenson, Kay Gilliland. PR431.S74 2001, (v3)
Stevenson, Marc. E99.E7.S8265 1997, (v4)
Stevenson, Mary Lou Kohfeldt. PR4728.G5.Z625 1985, (v3)

Stevenson, Randall. PR888.M63.S74 1992, (v3)
Stevenson, Robert Louis. PR5480.F21, (v3)
  PR5482.C6 1950, (v3)
  PR5484.I7, (v3)
  PR5484.K5 1949, (v3)
  PR5484.M2, (v3)
  PR5485.A1, (v3)
  PR5486.A1 1883 (Rosenwald Coll), (v3)
  PR5493.A3 1997, (v3)
  PZ7.S8482.Tr25, (v3)
Stevenson, Warren. PR585.A49.S74 1996, (v3)
Stevenson, William R. BT736.2.S65 1987, (v8)
Stevick, Philip. PR826.S73, (v3)
Stevick, Robert David. Z107.S74 1994, (v10)
Steward, Dick. CR4595.U5 S78 2000, (v5)
  F466.S854 2000, (v4)
Steward, Helen. BD418.3.S74 1997, (v8)
Steward, Julian Haynes. E51.U6 no. 143, (v4)
  GN360.4.S73 1977, (v6)
Stewart, Alan. PR418.H8.S74 1997, (v3)
Stewart, Chuck. KF4754.5.A68, (v7)
Stewart, David B. NA1554.5.S74 1987, (v9)
Stewart, David Kenney. JL339.A45, (v7)
Stewart, David R. Z7751.B67 2003, (v10)
Stewart, David Wood. LC3746.S74 1993, (v7)
Stewart, Donald C. PE64.S39.S74 1997, (v3)
Stewart, Donald Henderson. E310.S8, (v4)
Stewart, Earl L. ML3556.S87 1998, (v9)
Stewart, Edgar Irving. F891.S87, (v4)
Stewart, Elinore (Pruitt). F761.S8 1961, (v4)
  F761.S82 1979, (v4)
Stewart, Garrett. PR878.A79.S74 1996, (v3)
  PR4594.S8, (v3)
Stewart, Gary. ML3502.5.S73 1992, (v9)
Stewart, George Rippey. E155.S79, (v4)
  F592.S797 1983, (v4)
  PS3537.T849 S8 1947, (v3)
Stewart, Gordon T. E183.8.C2.S74 1992, (v4)
Stewart, Harry E. PQ2613.E53.Z8853 1993, (v3)
  E98.T6.S74 1990, (v4)
Stewart, Ian. PR6069.T4588F58 2001, (v3)
  QA93.S736 1997, (v1)
  QA93.S737 1995, (v1)
  QH323.5.S74 1998, (v1)
  RC339.52.B48.S74 1992, (v2)
Stewart, J. I. M. PR461.S8, (v3)
  PR6037.T466 H3, (v3)
  PR6037.T466 L3, (v3)
  PR6037.T466 M3, (v3)
  PR6037.T466 M35 1959, (v3)
  PR6037.T466 S5, (v3)
Stewart, Jack. PR6023.A93.Z92397 1999, (v3)
Stewart, James B. KF300.S73 1983b, (v7)
Stewart, James Brewer. E446.S83 1996, (v4)
Stewart, John B. B1498.S8, (v8)
  JC176.H9.S74 1992, (v7)
Stewart, John Innes Mackintosh. PR6037.T466 A64, (v3)
Stewart, John L. ML410.K7365.S7 1991, (v9)
Stewart, John. DA16.S84 1996, (v5)
  G855.S74 1990, (v6)
  PN1998.2.S74 1994, (v3)
  PS3569.T465.C8, (v3)
  QB401.S74 1991, (v1)
Stewart, Kenneth L. F395.M5.S74 1993, (v4)
Stewart, Maaja A. PR4038.P6.S74 1993, (v3)
Stewart, Mary Lynn. DC271.L9.S74 1984, (v5)
Stewart, Mary White. RD539.8.S74 1998, (v2)
Stewart, Melville Y. BJ1401.S83 1993, (v8)
Stewart, Michael. DX223.S75 1997, (v5)
Stewart, Omer Call. E98.R3.S79 1987, (v4)
Stewart, Philip. NE647.2.S73 1992, (v9)
Stewart, Richard A. D766.7.I7.S74 1988, (v5)
Stewart, Robert Ernest. TN140.S8.S7, (v1)
Stewart, Stanley. PR3508.S73 1986, (v3)
Stewart, Wilson N. QE905.S73 1983, (v1)
Stewig, John W. PN147.5.S74 1995, (v3)
Stich, Stephen P. BD161.S685 1990, (v8)
  BD418.3.S75 1996, (v8)
  BF773.S75 1983, (v2)

Stichlmair, Johann. TP156.D5S85 1998, (v1)
Stick, David. F262.R4.S74 1983, (v4)
Stid, Daniel D. E766.S85 1998, (v4)
Stieglitz, Alfred. TR647.S84 1983, (v1)
Stiehm, Judith. UB418.W65.S75 1989, (v10)
Stierlin, Henri. F2230.1.A7.S7513 1984, (v4)
  NA6002.S8313 1998, (v9)
Stievater, Susan M. Z5938.S75 1991, (v10)
Stifter, Adalbert. PT2525.A1 1978, (v3)
Stigen, Terje. PT8950.S87, (v4)
Stigler, George Joseph. HB221.S82 1987, (v6)
  HB235.U6.S7, (v6)
  HD21.S815, (v6)
Stigler, Stephen M. QA276.15.S755 1999, (v1)
Stiglitz, Joseph E. HB90.S78 1994, (v6)
Stiles, T. J. F594.J27 S76 2002, (v4)
Stilgoe, John R. F72.C3.S79 1994, (v4)
  HT352.U6.S75 1988, (v6)
Still, Cecil C. RS172.N67.S75 1998, (v2)
Still, Clyfford. ND237.S78.A4 1979, (v9)
Still, Judith Anne. ML134.S8.S75 1996, (v9)
Still, Judith. HB501.S9154 1998, (v6)
Stilling, Roger. PR658.L63.S8, (v3)
Stillman, Damie. NA966.5.N4.S75 1988, (v9)
Stillman, John Maxson. QD11.S84 1960, (v1)
Stillman, Richard Joseph. JF1351.S84 1991, (v7)
Stillwell, John. QA39.2.S755 1998, (v1)
  QA155.S75 1994, (v1)
  QA611.S84, (v1)
  QA645.S75 1992, (v1)
Stiltner, Brian. BX1793.S75 1999, (v8)
Stilwell, Barbara M. BJ1471.S69 2000, (v8)
Stilwell, Hart. PS3537.T547U5 1985, (v3)
Stilwell, Joseph Warren. D767.6.S74 1972, (v5)
Stimson, Henry Lewis. E748.S883 A3 1971, (v4)
  F1526.S85, (v4)
Stimson, James A. HN90.P8 S84 1998, (v6)
Stinchcombe, Arthur L. HT1072.S75 1995, (v6)
Stine, Gerald James. RC607.A26S75 1998, (v2)
Stine, Sharon. LB3251.S696 1997, (v7)
Stinson, John J. PR6052.U638.Z89 1991, (v3)
Stinson, Russell. ML410.B13 S87 1996, (v9)
Stinton, Darrol. TL671.2.S77 1998, (v1)
  TL671.2.S773 1983, (v1)
Stirati, Antonella. HD4909.S7513 1994, (v6)
Stirling, Ian. QL737.C27.S726 1988, (v1)
Stirling, Monica. PT8119.S8 1965, (v3)
Stirzaker, David. QA273.S7534 1994, (v1)
  QA273.S75343 1999, (v1)
Stites, Richard. DK266.4.S75 1989, (v5)
  HQ1662.S735, (v6)
Stitt, Beverly A. Z5814.D5.S75 1994, (v10)
Stittle, John. HF5681.B2.S69 1997, (v6)
Stivale, Charles J. PN94.S75 1998, (v3)
Stiverson, Cynthia Zignego. Z5941.S695 1989, (v10)
Stock, A. G. PR5907.S84, (v3)
Stock, Catherine McNicol. HN79.S83.S76 1992, (v6)
  HN90.R3.S67 1996, (v6)
Stock, Irvin. PT2625.A44.Z852 1994, (v3)
Stock, Jonathan P. J. ML419.A32 S76 1996, (v9)
Stockdale, Melissa Kirschke. DK254.M52.S76 1996, (v5)
Stockel, H. Henrietta. E99.A6.S76 1991, (v4)
  E99.C68.S76 2000, (v4)
Stockhausen, Karlheinz. ML410.S858.A5 1989, (v9)
Stocking, George W. GN308.3.G7.S74 1995, (v6)
Stocking, Rachel L. BR1024.S79 2000, (v8)
Stocks, Kenneth. PS1541.Z5.S86 1988, (v3)
Stockton, Annis Boudinot. PS847.S4.A17 1995, (v3)
Stockton, D. L. JC79.A8.S74 1990, (v7)
Stockton, Frank Richard. PS2926.S38, (v3)
Stockton, Kathryn Bond. PR878.F45.S76 1994, (v3)
Stoddard, Charles Hatch. SD373.S79 1987, (v1)
Stoddard, Charles Warren. F862.S87, (v4)
Stoddard, Ellwyn R. F787.S76, (v4)
Stoddard, Henry Luther. E415.9.G8.S8, (v4)
Stoddard, Seneca Ray. F127.A2.S764 1997, (v4)
Stoddard, Whitney S. N6843.S7, (v9)
Stoddart, D. Michael. QP458.S77 1990, (v1)
Stoecker, Sally W. UA772.S824 1998, (v10)
Stoehr, Taylor. PS1889.S7, (v3)

Stoekl, Allan. DC33.7.S76 1992, (v5)
Stoesz, David. HV95.S824 2000, (v6)
Stoetzer, O. Carlos. KDZ1134.S7613 1993, (v7)
Stoianovich, Traian. DC36.9.S76, (v5)
  DR23.S758 1994, (v5)
Stoica, Ion. PC871.E3S7 1991, (v3)
Stoicheff, Peter. PS3531.O82.C2965 1995, (v3)
Stojanovic, Svetozar. DR1302.S7713 1997, (v5)
Stoker, Bram. PR6037.T617 D7 1975, (v3)
Stoker, Robert Phillip. JK325.S79 1991, (v7)
Stokes, Alec. TJ185.S74 1992, (v1)
Stokes, Douglas M. BF1031.S84 1997, (v2)
Stokes, Durward T. F277.D5 S85, (v4)
Stokes, Gale. DJK36.S85 1997, (v5)
  DJK50.S75 1993, (v5)
Stokes, John. PR5823.S68 1996, (v3)
Stokes, Mason Boyd. PS173.W46S76 2001, (v3)
  PS173.W46.S76 2001, (v3)
Stokes, Myra. PR4038.L3.S7 1991, (v3)
Stokes, Raymond G. HD9654.9.I5.S76 1988, (v6)
Stokes, Thomas Lunsford. F277.S3.S8, (v4)
Stokes, W. Royal. ML3506.S87 1991, (v9)
Stokke, Baard Richard. HF3628.A4.S7, (v6)
Stokker, Kathleen. DL532.S8 1995, (v5)
Stokoe, Frank Woodyer. PR719.G4.S8 1963, (v3)
Stokowski, Patricia A. GV14.5.S79 1994, (v6)
Stolberg, Benjamin. HD8055.C75.S7, (v6)
Stolberg, Mary M. HV7911.E37.S76 1998, (v6)
Stolcke, Verena. HD8039.C6382.B67 1988, (v6)
Stoler, Mark A. D769.1.S76 2000, (v5)
  E745.M37.S75 1989, (v4)
Stoll, Clifford. QA76.9.C66.S88 1995, (v1)
Stoll, David. BR1642.L29.S76 1990, (v8)
  F1466.5.S76 1993, (v4)
Stoll, Elmer Edgar. PN511.S69, (v3)
  PR2995.27 1968, (v3)
Stoll, Mark. BT695.5.S75 1997, (v8)
Stoll, Richard J. UA23.S822 1990, (v10)
Stoll, Robert Roth. QA248.S798, (v1)
Stolleis, Michael. KK190.S7613 1998, (v7)
Stoller, Paul. DT547.45.S65.S75 1989, (v5)
  DT547.45.S65.S765 1989, (v5)
Stoller, Robert J. HQ472.U6.S86 1991, (v6)
Stolley, Paul D. RA651.S75 1995, (v2)
Stolper, Carolyn L. NX765.S78 1989, (v9)
Stolper, Gustav. HC57.S75 1968, (v6)
Stolper, Wolfgang F. HB119.S35.S76 1994, (v6)
Stommel, Henry M. GC296.G9.S7 1965, (v6)
Stone Sweet, Alec. KJC5456.S757 2000, (v7)
Stone, Albert E. E169.12.S84 1992, (v4)
  PS228.W37.S76 1994, (v3)
  PS1339.S7 1961, (v3)
Stone, Andrea Joyce. F1435.1.N35.S76 1995, (v4)
Stone, Bailey. DC138.S76 1994, (v5)
Stone, Christopher D. HC79.E5.S75 1993, (v6)
Stone, Clarence N. F294.A857.S76 1989, (v4)
Stone, Daniel. DJK4.S93 vol. 4.K4188, (v5)
Stone, David R. UA770.S863 2000, (v10)
Stone, Desmond. ML410.W6975.S76 1996, (v9)
Stone, Donald David. PR4024.S83 1997, (v3)
Stone, Donald. PQ1227.S8, (v3)
Stone, Doris. F1434.S87, (v4)
Stone, Elizabeth Arnold. F767.U3 S8, (v4)
Stone, Glenn Davis. DT515.45.K64.S76 1996, (v5)
Stone, Glyn. DA47.9.P8.S76 1994, (v5)
Stone, Grace (Zaring). PS3537.T667 R4, (v3)
Stone, Gregory B. PN682.T76.S76 1994, (v3)
Stone, Harry. PR4588.S76 1994, (v3)
  PR4592.F35.S7, (v3)
Stone, I. F. B317.S76 1988, (v8)
Stone, Irving. F864.S7352 1999, (v4)
  KF373.D35.S74 1941, (v7)
  PS3523.O46Z9 1977, (v3)
  PS3537.T669 A62, (v3)
  PS3537 T669 I4 1945, (v3)
  PS3537.T669 L6, (v3)
  PS3537.T669 L8 1939, (v3)
  PS3537.T669 P7, (v3)
Stone, James Champion. LA226.S73, (v7)
Stone, James S. HQ1595.F27.S76 1994, (v6)
Stone, Jay. U43.G7.S76 1988, (v10)

Stone, Jon R. BR517.S76 1993, (v8)
Stone, Judith F. DC342.8.P35.S76 1996, (v5)
Stone, Judy. PN1995.9.P7.S75 1997, (v3)
Stone, Julius Frederick. F788.S87, (v4)
Stone, Kurt. MT35.S87, (v9)
Stone, L. Joseph. BF721.S82 1968, (v2)
Stone, Laurie. PN1969.C65.S76 1997, (v3)
Stone, Lawrence. CB203.S76, (v5)
  DA356.S8, (v5)
  NB463.S8, (v9)
Stone, Mary Isabella. PR3112.S76 1990, (v3)
Stone, Merlin. HF5415.S859, (v6)
Stone, Norman. D395.S77 1984, (v5)
  D550.S76, (v5)
Stone, Randall W. HC244.S743 2002, (v6)
  HF1421.S76 1996, (v6)
Stone, Richard D. KF2181.S76 1991, (v7)
Stone, Robert. PS3569.T6418.D6x, (v3)
Stone, Samuel Z. F1434.2.G68, (v4)
Stone, Wilfred Healey. PR6011.O58.Z845, (v3)
Stone, William J. GB1003.2.S76 1999, (v6)
Stone-Blackburn, Susan. PR9199.3.D3.Z8 1985, (v3)
Stonehouse, Bernard. QH84.1.S78 1989, (v1)
Stonehouse, Catherine. BV1475.2.S776 1998, (v8)
Stoneman, Richard. DF721.S76 1987, (v5)
Stonequist, Everett V. BF740.S8 1961, (v2)
Stoner, James Reist. KD671.S76 1992, (v7)
Stoner, K. Lynn. HQ1236.5.C9.S76 1991, (v6)
  Z7964.C85.S76 2000, (v10)
Stoner, Madeleine R. KF3742.S76 1995, (v7)
Stong, Philip Duffield. PS3537.T6894 S7 1932, (v3)
Stonich, Susan C. HC145.Z9.E57 1993, (v6)
Stopher, Peter R. HE305.S84, (v6)
Stoppard, Tom. PR6069.T6.O5 1981, (v3)
  PR6069.T6.R43 1983, (v3)
  PR6069.T6.T7 1975b, (v3)
Storey, David. PR6069.T65.A6 1980, (v3)
  PR6069.T65.A6 1984, (v3)
  PR6069.T65.F6, (v3)
  PR6069.T65.I5 1971, (v3)
  PR6069.T65.T5, (v3)
Storey, Edward. PR4453.C6.Z89 1982, (v3)
Storey, Graham. PR4558.S76 1991, (v3)
Storey, Mark. PR590.S86 1999, (v3)
  PR5466.S76 1997, (v3)
Storie, Monique Carriveau. Z4501.S76 1999, (v10)
Storing, Herbert J. JA37.S67, (v7)
Storm, Theodor. PT2528.A1 1987, (v3)
  PT2528.A12 1975, (v3)
Storm, William. PN1675.S76 1998, (v3)
Storoni Mazzolani, Lidia. DG82.S8613, (v5)
Storr, Anthony. BF637.S64.S65 1988, (v2)
  BL72.S76 1996, (v8)
  ML3830.S87 1992, (v9)
Storr, Robert. N6490.S7825 2000, (v9)
  N6537.C54.S75 1998, (v9)
Storrs, Ronald. D469.G7.S75, (v5)
Storry, Richard. DS882.S78, (v5)
Story, Jonathan. HG186.E8.S76 1997, (v6)
Story, Norah. PR9106.S7 1967, (v3)
Story, Ronald. HN80.B7.S76, (v6)
Stoskopf, Neal C. SB123.S89 1993, (v1)
Stotsky, Sandra. H62.5.U5.S76 1991, (v6)
  LB1573.S874 1999, (v7)
Stott, D. H. HV9069.S764 1982, (v6)
Stott, Jon C. PR9193.9.S76 1988, (v3)
  PS173.I6S76 1995, (v3)
Stott, Philip Anthony. QK101.S76, (v1)
Stott-Kendall, Pamela. RD539.8.S76 1994, (v2)
Stotzky, Irwin P. JL1090.S76 1997, (v7)
Stourton, Edward. BX1390.00S86 2000, (v8)
Stout, George Frederick. B1649.S863.M5, (v2)
Stout, Janis P. PS374.W6.S78 1998, (v3)
  PS3505.A87.Z863 2000, (v3)
  PS3531.O752.Z815 1995, (v3)
Stout, Jeffrey. BJ1012.S848 1988, (v8)
Stovall, Tyler Edward. DC718.A36.S76 1996, (v5)
Stove, D. C. B29.S815 1991, (v8)
Stover, John F. HE2751.S74, (v6)
Stow, Randolph. PR6037.T723.T68, (v3)

Stowe, Harriet Beecher. E449.S8959, (v4)
E449.S89592 1968b, (v4)
PS2954.D7, (v3)
PS2954.M5, (v3)
PS2954.O4 1966, (v3)
PS2954.U5 1853, (v3)
PS2954.U5 1969, (v3)
PS2956.A4 1967, (v3)
CS71.B4405 1970, (v5)
E176.S88, (v4)
Stowe, Richard S. PQ2230.S84, (v3)
Stowell, Daniel W. BR535.S76 1998, (v8)
Stowell, David O. HD5325.R2 1877.S76 1999, (v6)
Stoye, John. D274.M37.S88 1994, (v5)
Straayer, Chris. PN1995.9.H55.S77 1996, (v3)
Strachan, Hew. U43.E95.S76 1983, (v10)
Stracher, Cameron. KF299.I5.S77 1998, (v7)
Strachey, John. D415.S75 1962, (v5)
UA11.S8 1963, (v10)
Strachey, Lytton. CT104.S78, (v5)
DA355.S8 1928b, (v5)
DA554.S7 1969, (v5)
PQ119.S8 1969, (v3)
PR6037.T73.A6 1980, (v3)
Stradling, R. A. ML286.4.S85 1993, (v9)
VA583.S77 1992, (v10)
Straffin, Philip D. QA269.S77 1993, (v1)
Strahan, David B. LB1072.S87 1997, (v7)
Strahler, Arthur Newell. GB54.5.S8 1987, (v6)
Q158.5.S73 1992, (v1)
Straight, Michael Whitney. PS3569.T678.V4, (v3)
Strand, Bradford N. GV365.S76 1997, (v6)
GV436.5.S87 1993, (v6)
Strand, David. DS795.3.S82 1989, (v5)
Strandberg, Victor H. PS3565.Z5.Z87 1994, (v3)
Strang, Barbara M. H. PE1075.S85, (v3)
PE1112.S77 1968, (v3)
Strang, Ruth May. LB1050.5.S83, (v7)
Strang, Veronica. GF801.S77 1997, (v6)
Strang, William Strang. DA42.S85 1976, (v5)
Strange, P. G. RC386.S73 1992, (v2)
Strangeways, Ian. QE33.S79 2000, (v1)
Strasburger, Victor C. HQ799.2.M35.S87 1995, (v6)
Strassberg, Richard E. PL2717.U47.Z88 1983, (v3)
Strasser, Mark Philip. KF539.S77 1997, (v7)
Strasser, Susan. TX23.S77 1982, (v1)
Straszheim, Mahlon R. HE9786.S7, (v6)
Strathern, Paul. QD22.M43S87 2001, (v1)
Strathmann, Ernest Albert. DA86.22.R2.S86, (v5)
Stratton, David H. E748.F22.S77 1998, (v4)
Stratton, Joanna L. HQ1438.K2.S77, (v6)
Stratton-Porter, Gene. PS3531.O7345 F7 1977, (v3)
QH81.S8725 1996, (v1)
Straub, Kristina. PR3316.A4.Z79 1987, (v3)
Straub, Peter. PS3569.T6914, (v3)
Straus, Eugene. R154.Y24.S77 1998, (v2)
Straus, Joseph Nathan. ML197.S767 1990, (v9)
ML410.S4446.S77 1995, (v9)
MT40.S96 2000, (v9)
Straus, Lawrence Guy. GN836.C33.S77 1992, (v6)
Straus, Murray A. HQ770.4.S77 1994, (v6)
HQ809.3.U5.S87, (v6)
Straus, Nina Pelikan. PG3328.Z7.W657 1994, (v3)
Strauss, Alfred A. RJ499.S8, (v2)
Strauss, Anselm L. H61.S8824 1987, (v6)
HM24.S773 1993, (v6)
Strauss, Botho. PT2681.T6898, (v3)
PT2681.T6898.J8613 1995, (v3)
Strauss, Carol Ann. Z7164.G82.S74 1996, (v10)
Strauss, David. QB36.L849, (v1)
Strauss, Gerald. DD174.S87, (v5)
Strauss, Leo. B65.S8, (v8)
B757.L38.S7613 1995, (v8)
JA37.S7, (v7)
JA81.S75, (v7)
Strauss, Maurice Benjamin. R707.S75, (v2)
Strauss, Peter L. KF5402.S87 1989, (v7)
Strauss, Richard. ML410.S93 A372 1974, (v9)
Strauss, Richard. ML410.S93.A453, (v9)
Strausser, Jeffrey. KF298.S77 1997, (v7)
Strausz-Hupe, Robert. D15.S85.A3 1996, (v5)

Stravinsky, Igor Fedorovich. ML410.S932.A13 1970, (v9)
ML410.S932 A22 1962, (v9)
ML410.S932.A33 1980, (v9)
ML410.S932.A38, (v9)
Stravinsky, Igor. ML410.S932 A335 1982, (v9)
Stravinsky, Vera. ML410.S932.S787, (v9)
Strawson, Galen. B808.9.S73 1994, (v8)
BJ1461.S77 1986, (v8)
Strawson, John. D759.S77 1998, (v5)
Strawson, P. F. BC6.S8, (v8)
BD111.S78, (v8)
Strayer, Joseph Reese. DC92.S83, (v5)
HJ2646.S75 1972, (v6)
Strayhorn, Joseph M. RJ504.S77 1988, (v2)
Streatfeild, D. BD331.S82, (v8)
Street, Brian V. PR830.S63.S7, (v3)
Street, James Howell. PS3537.T8278 O36, (v3)
Street, John. JA75.7.S77 1997, (v7)
Street, Philip. QL754.S77 1976, (v1)
Street, Sarah. PN1993.5.G7.S75 1997, (v3)
Streeten, Paul. HC59.7.S859 1981, (v6)
Streeter, Stephen M. E183.8.G8.S785 2000, (v4)
Streetman, Ben G. TK7871.85.S77 2000, (v1)
Streissguth, Michael. ML420.A77.S77 1997, (v9)
Streitberger, W. R. PR649.M38.S77 1994, (v3)
Streitmatter, Janice. LC212.2.S77 1994, (v7)
Streitmatter, Rodger. HQ76.95.U5.S77 1995, (v6)
PN4888.I53.S77 1997, (v3)
Strenski, Ivan. DS135.F83.S84 1997, (v5)
Streshinsky, Shirley. QL31.A9.S77 1993, (v1)
Stretton, Timothy. KD734.S77 1998, (v7)
Stribling, T. S. PS3537.T836 C64, (v3)
PS3537.T836 F6, (v3)
PS3537.T836 S8, (v3)
Strich, Fritz. PT2166.S754 1971, (v3)
Strick, James Edgar. QH325.S85 2000, (v1)
Strickland, Edward. ML390.S942 1991, (v9)
Strickland, Matthew. DA60.S77 1996, (v5)
Strickland, Rennard. E77.2.S77 1997, (v4)
Strickland, William. BP223.Z8 L5776 1994, (v8)
Strickland-Hodge, Barry. R119.S773 1994, (v2)
Strieder, Jacob. HF442.F7.S745, (v6)
Strier, Franklin D. KF384.S78 1994, (v7)
Strier, Richard. PR428.H57.S77 1995, (v3)
PR3508.S75 1983, (v3)
Strijp, Ruud. Z3014.E85.S77 1992, (v10)
Strimple, Nick. ML1506.S76 2002, (v9)
Strindberg, August. PT9804.F3, (v3)
PT9804.J6, (v3)
PT9804.S86 1987, (v3)
PT9811.A3.J58, (v3)
PT9813.H42, (v3)
PT9813.T6, (v3)
PT9814.S3, (v3)
PT9814.Z6.B633, (v3)
Stringer, Arthur John Arbuthnott. PR6003.R4.Z75, (v3)
Stringfellow, Frank. PN56.I65.S77 1994, (v3)
Strobach, Nico. BD632.S645 1998, (v8)
Strobel, Margaret. HQ1593.S85 1991, (v6)
Strober, Deborah H. E842.L45 1993, (v4)
Strober, Gerald S. E856.S77 1994, (v4)
Strobl, Gerwin. DA47.2.S85 2000, (v5)
Stroble, Paul E. F549.V2.S77 1992, (v4)
Strocchia, Sharon T. GT3252.F56.S76 1992, (v6)
Strock, Herbert L. PN1995.9.P7.S77 2000, (v3)
Stroebe, Wolfgang. BF575.G7.S77 1987, (v2)
Stroebel, Leslie D. TR9.S88, (v1)
Strohl, Mitchell P. HE3005.S86 1993, (v6)
Strohm, Paul. DA245.S77 1998, (v5)
PR1933.S59.S77 1989, (v3)
Strohm, Reinhard. ML240.2.S87 1993, (v9)
Stroll, Avrum. B105.D4 S77 1998, (v8)
Strommenger, Eva. N5370.S713, (v9)
Stromseth, Jane E. UA646.3.S794 1988, (v10)
Strong, Carson. RG132.S75 1997, (v2)
Strong, Frank R. KF4575.S77 1997, (v7)
Strong, M. C. ML156.4.R6.S8 1998, (v9)
Strong, Robert A. E872.S79 2000, (v4)
G1000.2.S8 2000, (v6)

Strong, Roy C. ND1460.G37, (v9)
SB466.G75.E57, (v1)
Strong, Tracy B. JC179.R9.S77 1994, (v7)
Strong-Boag, Veronica Jane. PR9199.2.J64, (v3)
Stronge, W. J. TA354.S77 2000, (v1)
Stropus, Ruta K. KF283.S77 2001, (v7)
Strosberg, Eliane. N72.S3.S77 1999, (v9)
Strossen, Nadine. HQ472.U6.S87 1995, (v6)
Strother, Z. S. DT650.P46.S77 1997, (v5)
Stroud, Dorothy. NA997.S7.S76 1984, (v9)
SB470.B7.S7 1984, (v1)
Strouhal, Evzen. DT61.S92513 1992, (v5)
Stroup, Richard. HC103.7.S84 1983, (v6)
Strouse, Jean. CT275.J29.S77, (v5)
HQ1206.S86 1974, (v6)
Strout, Cushing. PS169.N35.S76 1990, (v3)
Strouthes, Daniel P. K487.P65.S77 1995, (v7)
Stroyan, K. D. QA3.P8 vol. 72, (v1)
QA303.5.D37.S77 1993, (v1)
Strozier, Charles B. E457.S897 1982, (v4)
Struever, Nancy S. BJ271.S77 1992, (v8)
Struik, Dirk Jan. QA21.S87 1967, (v1)
Strum, Philippa. HQ1728.5.Z8.W4775 1992, (v6)
KF8745.B67.S77 1993, (v7)
KF8745.B67.S78 1984, (v7)
Strum, Shirley C. QL737.P93.S79 1987, (v1)
Strunk, William. PE1408.S772 1979, (v3)
Struthers, James. HD7096.C2.S87 1983, (v6)
Struve, Gleb. PG3022.S82 1971, (v3)
Struve, Lynn A. DS753.2.S77 1998, (v5)
Struve, Walter. F395.G3.S7713 1996, (v4)
Stuart, Bruce S. KF266.S78 1990, (v7)
Stuart, David E. E99.P9.S83 2000, (v4)
Stuart, Granville. F731.S912 1977b, (v4)
Stuart, Jesse. PS3537.T92516 M4, (v3)
Stuart, Jesse. PS3537.T92516 T3, (v3)
Stuart, John David. QK149.S73 2001, (v1)
Stuart, John Leighton. DS775.S84, (v5)
Stuart, Paul. E77.S924 1987, (v4)
Stuart, Ralph. T55.S786 1997, (v1)
Stuart, Robert C. HD1492.R9.S74, (v6)
Stuart, Robert. F880.S927, (v4)
Stuart-Fox, Martin. DS555.5.S79 1997, (v5)
Stubbendieck, James L. SB193.3.N67.S88 1982, (v1)
Stubbings, Hilda Uren. PS2384.M62.S78 1992, (v3)
Stubbs, Jean. Z1511.S8 1996, (v10)
Stuckenschmidt, Hans Heinz. ML410.S283.S93 1977, (v9)
Stuckey, Charles F. N6853.M64.A4 1987, (v9)
ND553.M7.A4 1995b, (v9)
Stucky, Steven. ML410.L965.S8, (v9)
Studd, Stephen. ML410.S15.S78 1999, (v9)
Studdert-Kennedy, Gerald. DS480.4.S78 1991, (v5)
DS480.45.S72 1998, (v5)
Studlar, Gaylyn. PN1995.9.M46.S78 1996, (v3)
Studwell, William E. ML128.O4.S8 1989, (v9)
Stueben, Michael. QA11.S83 1998, (v1)
Stueck, William Whitney. DS918.S819 1995, (v5)
E183.8.K7.S88, (v4)
Stuempfle, Stephen. ML3486.T7.S78 1995, (v9)
Stuessy, Tod F. QK95.S78 1990, (v1)
Stuhler, Barbara. JK1881.S78 2000, (v7)
Stuhlinger, Ernst. TL781.85.V6.S78 1994, (v1)
Stuhr-Rommereim, Rebecca. Z5305.U5.S78 1997, (v10)
Stumm, Werner. GB855.S78 1995, (v6)
GB855.S79 1992, (v6)
Stump, Reva Juanita. PR4688.S8, (v3)
Stumpf, David K. UG1312.I2 S78 2000, (v10)
Stumpf, Harry P. KF8700.Z95.S78 1991, (v7)
Stupples, Peter. ND699.K88.S78 1989, (v9)
Sturcken, Frank. PN1992.3.U5.S87 1990, (v3)
Sturcken, H. Tracy. PQ6402.S8, (v3)
Sturges, Robert Stuart. PR1868.P3.S78 2000, (v3)
Sturgill, Claude C. D883.S79 1994, (v5)
Sturgis, Russell. NA31.S84 1966, (v9)
Sturm-Maddox, Sara. PQ1676.A63.S78 1999, (v3)
Sturrock, John. CT275.S898.A3 1993, (v5)
PQ671.S76 1969, (v3)
PQ2607.E834.V6385 1990, (v3)
Sturzenhofecker, G. DU740.42.S79 1998, (v5)

Stuster, Jack. Q180.55.P75.S78 1996, **(v1)**
Stutely, Richard. HF5695.S83 1993, **(v6)**
Stutley, Margaret. BL1105.S78 1984, **(v8)**
Styan, J. L. PN1655.S74, **(v3)**
  PN1861.S75 1968, **(v3)**
  PN2581.S89 1996, **(v3)**
Stych, F. S. Z8106.S79 1995, **(v10)**
Styer, Roger C. SB423.7.S88 1997, **(v1)**
Styron, William. PS3569.T9.I54 1993, **(v3)**
  PS3569.T9.L5, **(v3)**
  PS3569.T9.L6 1956, **(v3)**
  PS3569.T9.S4, **(v3)**
  PS3569.T9.S67, **(v3)**
Su, Shih. PL2685.A28, **(v3)**
  PL2685.A6 1994, **(v3)**
Su, Stanley Y. W. QA76.5.S86 1988, **(v1)**
Suarez, Ernest. PS3554.I32.Z87 1993, **(v3)**
Suarez, Jose I. PQ9697.A72.Z897 2000, **(v3)**
Suarez, Juan Antonio. PN1995.9.E96.S82 1996, **(v3)**
Suarez-Orozco, Carola. F870.M5.S83 1995, **(v4)**
Suarez-Villa, Luis. HC110.T4.S82 2000, **(v6)**
Subrahmanyam, Sanjay. DS484.65.S86 2001, **(v5)**
Subramuniya. BL1151.3.S93 1993, **(v8)**
Subtelny, Orest. DK508.51.S93 2000, **(v5)**
Suchantke, Andreas. GF90.S83 2001, **(v6)**
Suchlicki, Jaime. F1754.S83 1988, **(v4)**
Suchocki, Marjorie. BJ1406.S82 1988, **(v8)**
Suchoff, Benjamin. ML410.B26.S83 1995, **(v9)**
Suckiel, Ellen Kappy. B945.J24.S84 1996, **(v8)**
Suckling, John. PR3718.A1 1910, **(v3)**
  PR3718.A1 1960, **(v3)**
  PR3718.A1 1971, **(v3)**
Suckow, Ruth. PS3537.U34 B6, **(v3)**
  PS3537.U34 C65, **(v3)**
  PS3537.U34 I6, **(v3)**
  PS3537.U34 S6, **(v3)**
Sudalnik, James E. Z7711.S9 1994, **(v10)**
Sudetic, Chuck. DR1313.7.A85.S83 1998, **(v5)**
Sudhalter, Richard M. ML410.C327 S83 2002, **(v9)**
  ML3508.S85 1999, **(v9)**
Sudhir Chandra. PK2903.S785 1992, **(v3)**
Sudjic, Deyan. NA997.R64.S83 1995, **(v9)**
Sudraka. PK3798.S91.M713 1994, **(v3)**
Sue, Derald Wing. BF637.C6.S85, **(v2)**
Sue, Stanley. RC451.5.A75.S93 1982, **(v2)**
Suetonius, ca. 69-ca. 122. DG277.S7.T5 1957, **(v5)**
Suetonius. PA6701.E14.R65 1997, **(v3)**
Sugar, Peter F. DJK4.S93 vol. 5, **(v5)**
  DR37.S94, **(v5)**
Sugarman, Susan. BF723.P36.S84 1987, **(v2)**
Sugawara no Takasue no Musume. PL789.S8.H313 1983, **(v3)**
  PL789.S8.S2513, **(v3)**
Sugden, David E. G587.S93 1982, **(v6)**
Sugden, John Peter. GV1136.8.S84 1996, **(v6)**
Sugden, John. E99.S35 S83 2000, **(v4)**
  E99.S35 S86 1998, **(v4)**
Suggs, Jon Christian. KF4757.S84 2000, **(v7)**
Sugihara, Seishiro. D804.66.S84, **(v5)**
Sugimoto, Yoshio. HN723.S7 1997, **(v6)**
Sugiyama, Shinya. HF3826.S77 1988, **(v6)**
Sugrue, Thomas J. F574.D49.N4835 1996, **(v4)**
Suh, Nam P. TA174.S89 1990, **(v1)**
Suhl, Benjamin. PQ2637.A82.Z84 1990, **(v3)**
Sui Sin Far. PR9199.2.S93.M77 1995, **(v3)**
Sukenick, Ronald. PS3569.U33.N58x, **(v3)**
Sukhanov, N. N. DK265.7.S8813 1984, **(v5)**
Sukhwal, B. L. Z6004.P7.S85 1992, **(v10)**
Sukumar, R. QL737.P98.S95 1989, **(v1)**
Sulaiman, Khalid A. PJ7542.P35.S85 1984, **(v3)**
Suleman, Azmina. KE416.M55.S85 1998, **(v7)**
Suleri, Sara. PR9484.3.S85 1992, **(v3)**
Sullivan, Jean. PQ2679.U5.C313 1998, **(v3)**
Sullivan, Arthur. ML49.S9.A1 1996, **(v9)**
Sullivan, Bruce M. BL1105.S85 1997, **(v8)**
Sullivan, Claudia N. PN2071.M6.S8 1990, **(v3)**
Sullivan, David M. E591.S94 1997, **(v4)**
Sullivan, Deborah A. RD119.S85 2001, **(v2)**
  RG960.S85 1988, **(v2)**
Sullivan, Dolores P. LA2317.M2.S85 1994, **(v7)**
Sullivan, Ernest W. Z8237.S85 1993, **(v10)**

Sullivan, Garrett A. PR658.L35.S85 1998, **(v3)**
Sullivan, George. GV875.N4.S84 1997, **(v6)**
Sullivan, Gerald. GN635.I65 S948 1999, **(v6)**
Sullivan, Harry Stack. BF636.S77, **(v2)**
Sullivan, Henry W. PQ6358.R4.S8 1996, **(v3)**
Sullivan, James D. PS476.S85 1997, **(v3)**
Sullivan, John J. D756.5.N6.S85 1997, **(v5)**
Sullivan, John. DP302.B53.S85 1988, **(v5)**
Sullivan, Kevin. PR6019.O9.Z82, **(v3)**
Sullivan, Larry E. HV9469.S86 1990, **(v6)**
Sullivan, Lawrence Eugene. F2230.1.R3.S85 1988, **(v4)**
Sullivan, Lawrence R. DS777.2.S85 1997, **(v5)**
  F199.S94, **(v4)**
Sullivan, Louis H. NA2543.S6.S9 1989, **(v9)**
Sullivan, Megan. PR8891.N67.S75 1999, **(v3)**
Sullivan, Mercer L. HV9106.N6.S85 1989, **(v6)**
Sullivan, Michael J. JF51.S85 1996, **(v7)**
Sullivan, Michael. N7340.S9, **(v9)**
  N7345.S79 1996, **(v9)**
  N7429.S93 1989, **(v9)**
  ND1366.7.S93, **(v9)**
  ND1366.7.S94, **(v9)**
Sullivan, Neil J. GV416.N48.S85 2000, **(v6)**
Sullivan, Patricia Ann. HQ1391.U5.S85 1996, **(v6)**
Sullivan, Patricia. E185.61.S93 1996, **(v4)**
Sullivan, Robert R. JC263.G35.S86 1989, **(v7)**
Sullivan, Robert. E99.M19.S85 2000, **(v4)**
Sullivan, Robert. PR9199.3.M617.Z84 1996, **(v3)**
Sullivan, Roger J. B2799.E8.S83 1989, **(v8)**
Sullivan, Russell. GV1132.M3 S85 2002, **(v6)**
Sullivan, Shannon. B105.B64 S85 2001, **(v8)**
Sullivan, Stefan. B809.8.S8575 2001, **(v8)**
Sullivan, Walter. QE511.5.S93 1991, **(v1)**
Sullivan, William M. BJ1725.S85 1995, **(v8)**
Sullivan, Winnifred Fallers. KF4783.S85 1994, **(v7)**
Sullivan, Zohreh T. E184.I5.S85 2001, **(v4)**
Sulloway, Alison G. PR4037.S85 1989, **(v3)**
Sully, Melanie A. DB99.2.S85 1990, **(v5)**
  JN2031.F73.S85 1997, **(v7)**
Sultan, Stanley. PR478.M6.S8 1987, **(v3)**
Sulzberger, C. L. DC412.S8, **(v5)**
Sulzberger, Marina. CT275.S954.A4 1978, **(v5)**
Sumarsam. ML345.I5.S86 1995, **(v9)**
Summerfield, Henry. PR6035.U7.Z83, **(v3)**
Summerfield, M. A. GB401.5.S82 1991, **(v6)**
Summerfield, Penny. D810.W7.S84 1998, **(v5)**
Summerfield, Penny. HD6135.S86 1984, **(v6)**
Summerhayes, Martha. F811.S965, **(v4)**
Summerhill, Stephen J. E119.2.S86 2000, **(v4)**
Summers, Anne. UH495.G7.S86 1988, **(v10)**
Summers, Carol. DT2959.S86 1994, **(v5)**
Summers, Claude J. PR888.G34.S86 1990, **(v3)**
  PR2638.S69 1999, **(v3)**
  PR6011.O58.Z8464 1983, **(v3)**
Summers, David. BH39.S913 1987, **(v8)**
Summers, Mark W. E415.7.S96 1987, **(v4)**
  E668.S94 1993, **(v4)**
  PN4864.S86 1994, **(v3)**
Summers, Montague. PR447.S8, **(v3)**
Summers, Montague. PR830.T3.S9 1964, **(v3)**
Summerson, Robert S. KF386.S9 1972, **(v7)**
Summerson, John Newenham. NA964.S85 1977, **(v9)**
  NA970.S8 1978, **(v9)**
  NA997.N3.S85 1980, **(v9)**
  NA2563.S8 1998, **(v9)**
Summit, Jennifer. PR275.W6.S86 2000, **(v3)**
Sumner, Gregory D. E748.M147.S86 1996, **(v4)**
Sumner, Judith. QK99.A1, **(v1)**
Sumner, L. W. BJ1031.S86 1987, **(v8)**
Sumner, Rosemary. PR888.M63.S86 1999, **(v3)**
Sumners, Carolyn. QB721.S85 2000, **(v1)**
Sumption, Jonathan. DC83.3.S93 **(v5)**
  DC96.S86 1991, **(v5)**
Sumser, John. PN1992.8.D48.S86 1996, **(v3)**
Sun, Cecile Chu-chin. PL2308.5.N3.S86 1995, **(v3)**
Sun, Chaofen. PL1241.S86 1996, **(v3)**
Sun, S. F. QD381.8.S86 1994, **(v1)**
Sun, Xupei. PN4748.C5, **(v3)**
Sun, Yan. HX418.5.S87 1995, **(v6)**
Sun, Yat-sen. DS777.A25 1994, **(v5)**

  DS777.A55 1974, **(v5)**
  DS777.A55 1975, **(v5)**
  DS777.S8 1970, **(v5)**
  DS777.45.S82 1953, **(v5)**
Sun, You-Li. D742.C5.S85 1993, **(v5)**
Sunamura, Tsuguo. GB451.2.S86 1992, **(v6)**
Sundar, Nandini. DS485.B38.S86 1997, **(v5)**
Sundberg, Johan. MT821.S913 1987, **(v9)**
Sunderland, Lane V. KF4550.S83 1996, **(v7)**
Sundiata, I. K. DT620.9.F47.S86 1996, **(v5)**
Sundman, Per Olof. PT9876.29.U5.I513 1970, **(v3)**
Sundquist, Asebrit. PS173.I6.S87 1991, **(v3)**
Sundquist, Eric J. PS153.N5.S9 1993, **(v3)**
Sundquist, James L. JK1061.S93, **(v7)**
Sunstein, Cass R. HM851.S87 2001, **(v6)**
  JC591.S86 1993, **(v7)**
  K487.E3.S86 1997, **(v7)**
  KF3300.S86 1990, **(v7)**
  KF4549.S86 1993, **(v7)**
Sunstein, Emily W. PR5398.S86 1989, **(v3)**
Sun-tzu. U101.S932 1996, **(v10)**
  U101.S95 1963a, **(v10)**
Suny, Ronald Grigor. DK266.3.S86 1993, **(v5)**
  DK675.4.S86 1988, **(v5)**
Super, R. H. PR4873.S8, **(v3)**
  PR5686.S88 1988, **(v3)**
Supervielle, Jules. PQ2637.U6.A17 1947, **(v3)**
  PQ2637.U6.A6 1949, **(v3)**
Supplee, Patricia L. LC3981.S87 1990, **(v7)**
Suran, Bernard G. LC3965.S9 1983, **(v7)**
Suresh, S. (Subra). TA418.38.S87 1998, **(v1)**
Surette, Leon. PS3531.O82.Z848 1999, **(v3)**
Surits, E. IA. GV1785.A1.S7813 1990, **(v6)**
Suro, Roberto. E184.S75.S86 1998, **(v4)**
Surrey, Henry Howard. PR2370.A5.J6, **(v3)**
Surtees, Robert Smith. PR5499.S4 A7, **(v3)**
  PR5499.S4 J6 1968, **(v3)**
  PR5499.S4 M7, **(v3)**
Suski, Peter Marie. PL585.S8, **(v3)**
Suss, Elaine. RF291.35.S88 1999, **(v2)**
Sussekind, Flora. PQ9555.S8613 1997, **(v3)**
Susskind, Lawrence. K3585.4.S87 1993, **(v7)**
Susskind, Richard E. K87.S874 1996, **(v7)**
Sussman, Barry. HN90.P8.S88 1988, **(v6)**
Sussman, Charlotte. HC260.C6 S873 2000, **(v6)**
Sussman, George D. RJ216.S9 1982, **(v2)**
Sussman, Henry. PN771.S87 1990, **(v3)**
  PT2621.A26.P776 1993, **(v3)**
Sussman, Leonard R. LB2338.S88 1992, **(v7)**
Suster, Zeljan E. DR1232.S87 1998, **(v5)**
Sutcliff, Rosemary. PR6037.U936.S, **(v3)**
Sutcliffe, David, M. Ed. P40.5.B42.S88 1992, **(v3)**
Sutcliffe, Tom. ML1700.S9485 1996, **(v9)**
Sutcliffe, W. Dean. ML410.H4 S83 1992, **(v9)**
Suther, Marshall Edward. PR4480.S8, **(v3)**
  PR4483.S8 1960, **(v3)**
Sutherland, Anne. F1443.S88 1998, **(v4)**
Sutherland, Arthur E. KF292.H34.S9, **(v7)**
Sutherland, C. H. V. CJ1001.S76 1987, **(v5)**
Sutherland, Daniel E. E168.S957 1989, **(v4)**
  E474.85.S88 1998, **(v4)**
  E668.S96 1988, **(v4)**
  F232.C9.S88 1995, **(v4)**
Sutherland, James Runcieman. PE1075.5.S8, **(v3)**
  PR753.S8, **(v3)**
  PR931.S8, **(v3)**
  PR3407.S8, **(v3)**
Sutherland, Joan. ML420.S96.A3 1997, **(v9)**
Sutherland, John. PR871.S87 1989, **(v3)**
  PR878.P78.S89 1995, **(v3)**
  PR878.P78.S9, **(v3)**
  PR5716.S88 1990, **(v3)**
Sutherland, Lin. QE522.S87 1995, **(v1)**
Sutherland, Neil. Z7164.C5.S94 1992, **(v10)**
Sutherland, William J. QL752.S88 1996, **(v1)**
Sutiac, Dragoljub D. SB736.S836 1999, **(v1)**
Sutter, John Augustus. F865.S923, **(v4)**
Sutter, Robert G. DS779.27.S89 1996, **(v5)**
Suttles, Gerald D. HN80.C5.S97, **(v6)**
Sutton, David E. DF901.K25.S88 1998, **(v5)**

Sutton, Denys. ND237.W6.S83, (v9)
Sutton, H. Eldon. QH431.S94, (v1)
Sutton, John. HB135.S825 2000, (v6)
Sutton, John. HD2326.S88 1991, (v6)
Sutton, Marilyn. Z8164.S87 2000, (v10)
Sutton, Max Keith. PR4134.S9, (v3)
Sutton, Nina. RC438.6.B48.S8813 1996, (v2)
Sutton, Peter C. ND653.H75.A4 1998, (v9)
    ND1359.3.S88 1987, (v9)
Sutton, Robert P. HX632.S87 1994, (v6)
    KFV2801.5.S87 1989, (v7)
Sutton, Roberta Briggs. AI3.S85 1966 suppl., (v10)
Sutton, S. B. QK31.S15.S9, (v1)
Sutton, Sharon E. LC210.5.S88 1996, (v7)
Sutton, William R. BV3775.B2.S38 1998, (v8)
Sutton-Smith, Brian. BF717.S93 1997, (v2)
Sutzkever, Abraham. PJ5129.S86.A24 1991, (v3)
    PJ5129.S86.F513 1990, (v3)
Suutari, Raymond K. HG4521.S89 1996, (v6)
Suvorov, Viktor. UA772.S86 1982, (v10)
Suziedelis, Saulius. DK505.37.S89 1997, (v5)
Suzuki, Daisetz Teitaro. BL1442.Z4.S76, (v8)
    BL1483.S82 1963, (v8)
Suzuki, Koichi. E885.S89 1993, (v4)
Suzuki, Shunryu. BL1478.6.S9 1970, (v8)
Suzuki, Yoshio. HF1411.S8866 1989, (v6)
Svacha, Rostislav. NA1033.P7.S8313 1995, (v9)
Svanberg, S. QC454.A8.S85 1990, (v1)
Svanstrom, Ragnar. DL649.S8, (v5)
Svarverud, Rune. BJ117.S87 1998, (v8)
Sveiby, Karl Erik. HD53.S893 1997, (v6)
Svenonius, Elaine. Z666.5.S92 2000, (v10)
Swaan, A. de. HM73.S89 1990, (v6)
Swaan, Wim. N6320.S92 1977b, (v9)
Swabey, Marie Taylor (Collins). BC108.S9 1955, (v8)
    BH301.C7.S9 1970, (v8)
    JC423.S97, (v7)
Swaddle, T. W. QD151.5.S93 1997, (v1)
Swadener, Beth Blue. LB1139.3.K4, (v7)
Swados, Elizabeth. MT40.S98 1988, (v9)
Swados, Harvey. E169.12.S92 1973, (v4)
    PS3569.W2.C4, (v3)
    PS3569.W2.N5, (v3)
    PS3569.W2/W5x, (v3)
    PS3569.W22.F3, (v3)
    PS3569.W22.O5, (v3)
Swafford, Jan. ML410.B8 S93 1997, (v9)
Swagman, Charles F. HN664.Z9.C678 1988, (v6)
Swaim, Kathleen M. PR3330.A9.S93 1993, (v3)
Swain, Carol M. JK1323. 1993, (v7)
Swain, Tony. GN666.S93 1993, (v6)
    Z7834.A8.S82 1991, (v10)
Swales, Martin. PT747.E6.S9, (v3)
    PT763.S86, (v3)
    PT2525.Z5.S92 1984, (v3)
    PT2625.A44.B92 1991, (v3)
    PT2638.N5Z87, (v3)
Swaminathan, K. PL4758.9.S9.P5, (v3)
Swan, Carroll Judson. D570.9.S84, (v5)
Swan, James Gilchrist. F891.S97 1972, (v4)
Swan, Lester A. SB975.S92, (v1)
Swan, Oscar E. PG6112.S9 1983b, (v3)
    PG6129.E5S93 1986, (v3)
Swan, Robert O. PK2098.S7.Z93, (v3)
Swan, Susan Burrows. TT715.S9, (v1)
Swanborough, Gordon. UG1243.S9 1989, (v10)
Swann, Julian. KJV3747.S93 1995, (v7)
Swann, Marjorie. DA380.S93 2001, (v5)
Swann, Thomas Burnett. PR4613.D5.Z85, (v3)
Swann, William B. BF697.5.S46.S83 1996, (v2)
Swanson, Dorothy Collins. PN1992.55.S93 2000, (v3)
Swanson, G. A. HF5668.25.S93 1991, (v6)
    HJ9745.S92 1989, (v6)
Swanson, Judith A. JC596.S93 1992, (v7)
Swanson, R. N. BR750.S83 1989, (v8)
Swanson, Timothy M. QH75.S815 1994, (v1)
Swanson, Wayne R. KF228.D66.S93 1990, (v7)
Swanton, John Reed. E51.U6 no. 137, (v4)
    E51.U6 no. 145, (v4)
Swantz, Marja-Liisa. DT443.3.Z37.S93 1995, (v5)
Swardson, Harold Roland. PR549.R4.S9 1962a, (v3)

Swartz, David. HM22.F8.S93 1997, (v6)
Swartz, Jon David. PN1991.3.U6.S93 1993, (v3)
Swartz, Marc J. DT433.545.S93.S93 1991, (v5)
Swartz, Mark Evan. PS3503.A923.W6385 2000, (v3)
Swartz, Michael D. BM526.S93 1996, (v8)
Swartz, Omar. PS3521.E735.O537 1999, (v3)
Swartz, Robert J. BD143.S95, (v8)
Swash, Andy. QL345.G2, (v1)
Swasy, Alecia. HD9999.S74.P7674 1993, (v6)
Swatland, Andrew. JN621.S93 1996, (v7)
Sway, Marlene. DX201.S98 1988, (v5)
Swayne, Jeremy. RX72.S93 1998, (v2)
Swearer, Randolph. PR1583.S84 1990, (v3)
Swearingen, C. Jan. PA181.S9 1991, (v3)
Swearingen, James E. PR3714.T73.S9, (v3)
Swedenberg, H. T. PR437.S94, (v3)
    PR3422.A4, (v3)
Swedenborg, Emanuel. BX8712.A8.Z73 1984, (v8)
Sweeney, Edwin R. E99.A6.C577 1991, (v4)
Sweeney, Edwin R. E99.C68.M357 1998, (v4)
Sweeney, James Johnson. ND813.M5.S9 1969, (v9)
Sweeney, John A. H. NK2003.S9, (v9)
Sweeney, John J. HD8072.5.S84 1989, (v6)
Sweeney, Marvin A. BS1286.S94 2001, (v8)
Sweeney, Michael S. D799.U6.S834 2001, (v5)
Sweeney, Patricia E. CT3320.S85 1993, (v5)
Sweeney, Richard J. HB251.S94 1988, (v6)
Sweeney, Robert L. NA737.W7.S94 1994, (v9)
Sweeney, Wilma K. Z5814.C52.S84 1998, (v10)
Sweeny, Thomas William. F817.G52.S9, (v4)
Sweet, Frederick Arnold. ND237.C3.S9, (v9)
Sweet, Paul Robinson. DD422.H8.S93, (v5)
Sweet, Waldo E. GV21.S94 1987, (v6)
Sweeting, Adam W. PS253.N7.S94 1996, (v3)
Sweeting, Anthony. LA1134.H6.S84 1993, (v7)
Sweeting, Elizabeth. PR69.S8, (v3)
Sweetland, James H. Z1035.C5 2001, (v10)
Sweetman, David. N6853.T6.S93 1999, (v9)
Sweetman, John. N6764.S94 1988, (v9)
    UB58 1854-1856.S94 1984, (v10)
Sweetser, Richard S. TP492.7.S87 1996, (v1)
Sweezy, Paul Marlor. HB31.H37 v.63, (v6)
    HB501.M5.S9, (v6)
    HB501.S98 1976, (v6)
Swenson, Chester A. HF5415.127.S94 1990, (v6)
Swenson, James. DC138.S94 2000, (v5)
Swerdlow, Amy. JX1965.S94 1993, (v7)
Swetnam, Susan Hendricks. F755.M8.S84 1991, (v4)
Swetschinski, Daniel. DS135.N5.A684 2000, (v5)
Swiderski, Richard M. GN357.S85 1991, (v6)
Swidlicki, Andrzej. KKP40.P64.S95 1988, (v7)
Swietochowski, Tadeusz. DK695.4.S95 1995, (v5)
Swift, David Everett. BR563.N4.S97 1989, (v8)
Swift, Elaine K. JK1161.S95 1996, (v7)
Swift, Emerson Howland. N7831.S9 1970, (v9)
Swift, Jonathan. HG950.I8.S8 1935, (v6)
    PR3721.D3, (v3)
    PR3721.E4, (v3)
    PR3721.R63 1983, (v3)
    PR3722, (v3)
    PR3722.H3 1963, (v3)
    PR3724.G7 1980, (v3)
    PR3724.T3 1958, (v3)
    PR3726.A43 1975, (v3)
    PR3726.A5 1963, (v3)
    PR3726.A63, (v3)
Swift, Karen. HV873.S88 1995, (v6)
Swinburne, Algernon Charles. PR5500.F68, (v3)
    PR5502.S5 1960, (v3)
    PR5510.S95 1978, (v3)
    PR5510.S977.No 1963, (v3)
Swinburne, Richard. BC91.S96, (v8)
    BJ1451.S9 1989, (v8)
Swinnerton, Frank. PR6037.W85.N6, (v3)
Swire, Joseph. DR701.S5.S83 1971, (v5)
Swisher, Jacob Armstrong. F620.S92, (v4)
    F621.S9, (v4)
Switala, William J. E445.P3.S95 2001, (v4)
Swithinbank, Charles. G875.S95.A3 1997, (v6)
Switzer, Jacqueline Vaughn. GE197.S95 1997, (v6)
Switzer, Les. DT2400.C58.S95 1993, (v5)

Switzer, Teri R. Z7164.L1.S936 1997, (v10)
Swyripa, Frances. F1035.U5.S99 1993, (v4)
Sydenham, M. J. DC148.S985 1974b, (v5)
Sydnor, Charles S. F213.S92, (v4)
Sydnor, Charles W. D757.85.S95, (v4)
Sykes, Bryan. GN289.S94 2001, (v6)
Sykes, Christopher. DD247.T7.S95 1969, (v5)
    PR6045.A97.Z83 1975, (v3)
Sylos Labini, Paolo. HD75.S95 1984, (v6)
Sylvester, Christine. HQ1190.S95 1994, (v6)
    HQ1240.5.Z55, (v6)
Sylvester, David. ND497.B16.S93 2000, (v9)
Sylvester, Edward J. TP248.6.S94 1987, (v1)
Sylvester, Louise. Z2015.L49, (v10)
Syme, Ronald. DG209.S95 1979, (v5)
    DG254.S9 2002, (v5)
    PA6656.S9, (v3)
    PA6716.S9 1958, (v3)
Symeon, the New Theologian, Saint.
    BV5039.G7.S913, (v8)
Symington, Neville. BF175.4.R44.S94 1994, (v2)
Symonds, Craig L. E467.1.C58.S9 1997, (v4)
Symonds, John Addington. N6923.B9.S9 1928, (v9)
    PR5522.M3 1970, (v3)
    PR5523.A425 1984, (v3)
Symonds, Percival Mallon. BF698.S85, (v2)
Symons, Arthur. PR5528.A44 1989, (v3)
Symons, Julian. PR478.M6.S96 1987, (v3)
    PR6037.Y5 P5, (v3)
Symons, Michael. TX645.S97 2000, (v1)
Synge, J. L. QA433.S9 1969, (v1)
    QA807.S9 1959, (v1)
    QC6.S93 1965, (v1)
Synge, J. M. PR5530.A2 1935, (v3)
    PR5530.A2 1963, (v3)
    PR5533.A44 1983, (v3)
Sypher, Wylie. N6350.S9, (v9)
    N6370.S95, (v9)
    PR3069.T5.S9, (v3)
Syrett, David. D780.S96 1994, (v5)
    E271.S97 1998, (v4)
Syrotinski, Michael. PN94.S97 1998, (v3)
Szabo, Albert. NA7424.6.A1.S94 1991, (v9)
Szabo, Joyce M. E78.G73.S93 1994, (v4)
Szalay, Michael. PS228.M63.S93 2000, (v3)
Szasz, Ferenc Morton. F596.3.S3, (v4)
Szasz, Thomas Stephen. RA401.A3.S93 1992, (v2)
    RA418.3.U6S936 2001, (v2)
    RC437.5.S89 1992, (v2)
    RC437.5.S927 1984, (v2)
    RC455.S93, (v2)
Szatmary, David P. F69.S99, (v4)
Sze, S. M. TK7871.85.S988 1981, (v1)
    TK7871.85.S9883 2002, (v1)
Szekielda, Karl-Heinz. G70.6.S93 1988, (v6)
Szeri, A. Z. TJ1073.5.S97 1998, (v1)
Szigeti, Joseph. MT260.S99 1970, (v9)
Szirmai, J. A. Z269.3.M44.S95 1999, (v10)
Szkudlarek, Tomasz. LC71.S97 1993, (v7)
Szporluk, Roman. DK67.5 .U38, (v5)
Szuchman, Mark D. HN270.B8.S97 1988, (v6)
Szucs, Loretto Dennis. CD3026. 1988, (v5)
Szunyogh, Bela. U22.S953, (v10)
Szusterman, Celia. F2849.2.S98 1993, (v4)
Szwad, John F. Z5984.A44.S95, (v10)
Szymborska, Wislawa. PG7178.Z9A222 1998, (v3)
T᷿amir, Zakarῑyaᷓa. PJ7864.A384A25 1985, (v3)
Tien, Ju-k ang. BJ117.T44 1988, (v8)
Taaffe, Stephen R. D767.95.T316 1998, (v5)
Taagepera, Rein. DK503.54.T33 1993, (v5)
Tabbert, Russell. PE3101.A4.T3 1991, (v3)
Tabbi, Joseph. PS228.T42.T33 1995, (v3)
Taber, Gladys Bagg. S521.5.C8.T28, (v1)
Taber, Stephen Welton. QL568.F7, (v1)
Tabor, James D. BP605.B72.T33 1995, (v8)
Tabor, Michael. QA871.T33 1989, (v1)
Tabors, Patton O. PE1128.A2.T23 1997, (v3)
Tacitus, Cornelius. DG207.T2.C45, (v5)
    PA6156.T3 1951, (v3)
Tackett, Timothy. DC165.T33 1996, (v5)
Tadman, Michael. E442.T33 1996, (v4)

Tadros, Th. F. S587.73.S95.T33 1995, **(v1)**
Taff, Charles Albert. HE5623.T3 1986, **(v6)**
Taft, Philip. HD6508.T25, **(v6)**
  HD8055.A5.T3 1970, **(v6)**
Taft, Robert A. E748.T2.A3 1997, **(v4)**
Taft, William H. F194.T16, **(v4)**
  JF223.T3, **(v7)**
  KF1649.T34 1993, **(v7)**
Tafuri, Manfredo. NA500.T3313 1987, **(v9)**
  NA680.T2513, **(v9)**
  NA1118.T3413 1989, **(v9)**
Tager, Jack. HV6483.B6, **(v6)**
Tagore, Rabindranath. BL25.H5 1930, **(v8)**
  PK1718.T24.A28, **(v3)**
  PK1722.A2.B6 1976, **(v3)**
  PK1723.G5.E5 1985, **(v3)**
  PR6039.A2 1937, **(v3)**
  PR9499.3.T34A1125 1994, **(v3)**
Taha, Hamdy A. T57.6.T3 1992, **(v1)**
Taher, Bahaa'. PJ7864.A357.K4613 1996, **(v3)**
Taine, Hippolyte. PR93.T4 1965, **(v3)**
Tainer, Evelina M. HG4529.T34 1993, **(v6)**
Tainter, Joseph A. CB311.T245 1988, **(v5)**
Tait, Alan A. HJ5711.T36 1988, **(v6)**
Tait, L. Gordon. BV4647.P5, **(v8)**
Taiwo, Olufemi. K460.T35 1995, **(v7)**
Taiz, Lincoln. QK711.2.T35 1998, **(v1)**
Tajbakhsh, Kian. HT153.T27 2000, **(v6)**
Takabuki, Matsuo. DU627.83.T35.A3 1998, **(v5)**
Takagi, Midori. F234.R59.N485 1999, **(v4)**
Takaki, Ronald T. D769.T42 2000, **(v5)**
  E184.A1.T335 1993, **(v4)**
  E184.A1 T337 2000, **(v4)**
Takarl¯i, Fu®¯ad. PJ7864.A3744R3413 2001, **(v3)**
Takenaka, Heizo. HC462.95.T34 1991, **(v6)**
Takhtadzhian, A. L. QK101.T313 1986, **(v1)**
  QK495.A1.T35 1991, **(v1)**
Takkenberg, Alex. KMC567.T35 1998, **(v7)**
Takougang, Joseph. JQ3525.T35 1998, **(v7)**
Tal, Kali. BF175.5.P75.T35 1996, **(v2)**
Tal, Yisrael. UA853.I8T.3513 2000, **(v10)**
Talattof, Kamran. PK6415.5.T35 1999, **(v3)**
Talayesva, Don C. E99.H7.T25 1942, **(v4)**
Talbert, Ernest William. PR2976.T23, **(v3)**
Talbert, Richard J. A. JC85.S4.T17 1984, **(v7)**
Talbert, Roy. UB251.U5.T35 1991, **(v10)**
Talbot, David. TA462.T26 1998, **(v1)**
Talbot, Ethelbert. F761.T13, **(v4)**
Talbot, Ian. DS382.T35 1998, **(v5)**
  DS480.84.T287 2000, **(v5)**
Talbot, Michael. ML134.V7.T34 1988, **(v9)**
  ML410.A315.T37 1990, **(v9)**
  ML410.V82.T34 1993, **(v9)**
Talbott, Steve. QA76.9.C66.T26 1995, **(v1)**
Taliaferro, Charles. BL182.T35 1994, **(v8)**
Taliaferro, John. PS3503.U687.Z88 1999, **(v3)**
Tallett, Frank. D214.T35 1992, **(v5)**
Talley, Thomas Washington. GR111.A47.T36 1993, **(v6)**
Tallis, Raymond. BD418.3.T35 1991, **(v8)**
Tallmadge, Thomas Eddy. NA705.T3 1936, **(v9)**
  NA735.C4.T73, **(v9)**
Talocci, Mauro. CR101.T3413 1982, **(v5)**
Taly, Narendra. TG300.T28 1998, **(v1)**
Tam, Henry Benedict. HM216.T24 1998, **(v6)**
Tamadonfar, Mehran. JC49.T35 1989, **(v7)**
Tamayama, Kazuo. D767.6.T354 2000, **(v5)**
Tamayo, Rufino. ND259.T3.A4 1982, **(v9)**
Tambiah, Stanley Jeyaraja. GN345.T36 1990, **(v6)**
  HV6485.S64.T35 1996, **(v6)**
Tambling, Jeremy. PR4592.V56.T36 1995, **(v3)**
Tamburri, Anthony Julian. PS153.I8.T36 1998, **(v3)**
Tamen, Miguel. PN81.T3167 2000, **(v3)**
Taminiaux, Jacques. BH151.T36 1993, **(v8)**
Tamir, Yael. JC311.T295 1993, **(v7)**
Tamura, Eileen. DU624.7.J3.T36 1994, **(v5)**
Tamura, Linda. F882.H9.T36 1993, **(v4)**
Tan, Chester C. DS771.T3, **(v5)**
Tan, Chung. DS757.5.T28, **(v5)**
Tan, Gerald. HB3812.T36 2000, **(v6)**
Tan, Kok-Chor. JC574.T36 2000, **(v7)**

Tan, Soo Tang. QA7.2.T36 1999, **(v1)**
Tan, Sooi Beng. ML1751.M4.T34 1993, **(v9)**
Tanada, Yoshinori. SB942.T35 1993, **(v1)**
Tanaka, Kenneth Kenichi. BQ2025.H853 T36 1990, **(v8)**
Tanaka, Stefan. DS827.S3.T36 1993, **(v5)**
Tanaka, Toshiyuki. D805.I55.T3613 1996, **(v5)**
Tanaka, Yukiko. PL725.T36 2000, **(v3)**
Tanchis, Aldo. NK1535.M86.T3613 1987, **(v9)**
Tandeter, Enrique. HD9536.B63.P68513 1993, **(v6)**
Tanenbaum, Andrew S. TK5105.5.T36 1996, **(v1)**
Tanenhaus, Sam. E743.5.T36 1997, **(v4)**
Tanford, Charles. Q143.F8.T36 1989, **(v1)**
Tang, Hsien-tsu. PL2695.M8.E5 1980, **(v3)**
Tang, James Tuck-Hong. DA47.9.C6.T36 1992, **(v5)**
Tang, Kwong-Leung. HN720.5.A8, **(v6)**
Tang, Peter S. H. DR701.S86.T3, **(v5)**
Tang, Sheng-hao. DS777.55.T25, **(v5)**
Tang, Wenfang. DS779.23.T365 2000, **(v5)**
Tang, Xiaobing. DS764.23.L52.T36 1996, **(v5)**
Taniguchi, Yoshio. NA1559.T35.A4 1999, **(v9)**
Tanimoto, S. Q336.T36 1987, **(v1)**
Tanizaki, Junichiro. PL839.A7.N413 1990, **(v3)**
  PL839.A7.S4, **(v3)**
  PL898.T3.Ke, **(v3)**
  PL898.T3.M3, **(v3)**
  PL898.T3.T3 1955, **(v3)**
  PL898.T7.A8, **(v3)**
Tannehill, Ivan Ray. QC929.D8.T3, **(v1)**
  QC945.T82, **(v1)**
Tannenbaum, Edward R. DG551.T36, **(v5)**
  HN373.T33, **(v6)**
Tannenbaum, Frank. F1234.T13, **(v4)**
  F1234.T14 1971, **(v4)**
Tannenbaum, Judith. PN1101.T35 2000, **(v3)**
Tanner, B. K. QC176.T32 1995, **(v1)**
Tanner, Daniel. L13.J64.T36 1991, **(v7)**
Tanner, Duncan. JN1571.5.L28.T36 1990, **(v7)**
Tanner, Edward Everett. PS3570.A55.A8 1955, **(v3)**
Tanner, Faun McConkie. F834.M6T3 1976, **(v4)**
Tanner, J. M. RJ131.T29 1990, **(v2)**
Tanner, James T. F. PS3531.O752.Z825 1990, **(v3)**
Tanner, Jo A. PN2286.T36 1992, **(v3)**
Tanner, John S. PR3562.T36 1992, **(v3)**
Tanner, Laura E. PS374.V53.T35 1994, **(v3)**
Tanner, Laurel N. LD7501.C428.T36 1997, **(v7)**
Tanner, Marcus. DR1535.T36 1997, **(v5)**
Tanner, Michael. HV95.T36 1996, **(v6)**
Tanner, Nancy Makepeace. GN281.T36, **(v6)**
Tanner, Tony. PN56.3.V4.T36 1992, **(v3)**
  PS121.T36 2000, **(v3)**
  PS2127.P67.T36 1995, **(v3)**
Tanner, Vaino. DK459.5.T312, **(v5)**
Tannery, Claude. PQ2625.A716.Z943313 1991, **(v3)**
Tanselle, G. Thomas. Z1001.T255 1998, **(v10)**
Tansey, Stephen D. JA66.T35 1995, **(v7)**
Tansman, Alan. PL832.O33.Z85 1993, **(v3)**
Tanter, Raymond. DR48.6.T36 1999, **(v5)**
  E183.8.L4.T36 1990, **(v4)**
  HV6431.T39 1998, **(v6)**
Tanzi, Rudolph E. RC523.2.D43 2000, **(v2)**
Tanzi, Vito. HD87.T376 2000, **(v6)**
Tao, Jing-shen. DS751.T34 1988, **(v5)**
Tape, Walter. QC976.H15.T36 1994, **(v1)**
Taper, Bernard. GV1785.B32.T3 1984, **(v6)**
Tapie, Victor Lucien. DC123.T313 1975, **(v5)**
Taplin, Harry. TJ288.T37 1991, **(v1)**
Taplin, Oliver. PA3829.T36 1977, **(v3)**
Tapp, Hambleton. F456.T36, **(v4)**
Tapper, Richard. DS269.S53.T34 1997, **(v5)**
Tapscott, Don. HC79.I55.T368 1996, **(v6)**
Tapsell, R. F. D107.T36 1983, **(v5)**
Taragano, Martin. GV884.A1.T37 1991, **(v6)**
Taranath, Bungale S. TH845.T33 1988, **(v1)**
Taras, Ray. JN6752.T37 1995, **(v7)**
Tarazona-Sevillano, Gabriela. HV6433.P4.T37 1990, **(v6)**
Tarbell, Ida M. E169.1.H67 vol. 9, **(v4)**
Tarbox, Katherine. PR6056.O85.Z85 1988, **(v3)**
Tareke, Gebru. DT387.9.T34 1991, **(v5)**
Tarkhanov, Alexei. NA1188.T36 1992, **(v9)**

Tarkington, Booth. PS2972.Ax, **(v3)**
  PS2972.G5, **(v3)**
  PS2972.M3 1957, **(v3)**
  PS2972.W6 1925, **(v3)**
  PS2973.A4, **(v3)**
Tarle, Evgenii Viktorovich. DC235.T32 1971, **(v5)**
Tarling, Nicholas. DS518.4.T37, **(v5)**
  DS525.9.G7.T37 1996, **(v5)**
  DS526.4.T37 1993, **(v5)**
  DS526.7.T36 1998, **(v5)**
Tarlo, Emma. GT1460.T37 1996, **(v6)**
Tarn, W. W. U33.T3, **(v10)**
Tarock, Adam. DS318.85.T866 1998, **(v5)**
Tarr, Edward H. ML960.T3713 1988, **(v9)**
Tarr, G. Alan. KF4550.Z95.T37 1998, **(v7)**
Tarr, Joel A. E748.L892.T3, **(v4)**
Tarragó, Rafael E. Z6465.L29 T37 1994, **(v10)**
Tarrant, Harold. B395.T22 2000, **(v8)**
Tarrants, Thomas A. BV4935.T37.A33, **(v8)**
Tarski, Alfred. BC135.T35 1983, **(v8)**
  QA9.T28 1965, **(v1)**
Tart, Charles T. BF311.T28, **(v2)**
Tarter, Ralph E. TK7881.15.T362 1993, **(v1)**
Taruskin, Richard. ML300.T37 1997, **(v9)**
  ML410.M97.T37 1992, **(v9)**
  ML410.S932.T38 1996, **(v9)**
  ML457.T37 1995, **(v9)**
Tasaki, Hanama. PS3539.A68.L6, **(v3)**
Tasker, Yvonne. PN1995.9.S697.T37 1993, **(v3)**
  PN1995.9.W6.T36 1998, **(v3)**
Tatar, Maria M. PT921.T38 1987, **(v3)**
Tate, Allen. PN710.T33 1970, **(v3)**
  PS3539.A74.F3, **(v3)**
  PS3539.A74.F32 1977, **(v3)**
Tate, Carolyn Elaine. F1435.1.Y3.T38 1992, **(v4)**
Tate, Claudia. PS374.N4.T36 1998, **(v3)**
Tate, Mary Jo. PS3511.I9.Z459 1997, **(v3)**
Tate, Merze. E183.8.H3 T34 1980, **(v4)**
Tate, Michael L. F596.T36 1999, **(v4)**
Tatham, David. NC975.5.H65.T38 1992, **(v9)**
Tatla, Darshan Singh. Z3207.P8.T37 1995, **(v10)**
Tattersall, Ian. GN281.T357 1995, **(v6)**
  GN281.T36 1993, **(v6)**
  GN281.4.T39 2000, **(v6)**
  GN285.T37 1999, **(v6)**
Tattersall, James J. QA241.T35 1999, **(v1)**
Tatum, James. PA4494.C9.T38 1989, **(v3)**
Tatum, Jesse S. TJ163.2.T347 1995, **(v1)**
Tatum, W. Jeffrey. DG260.C63.T37 1999, **(v5)**
Taube, Herman. PJ5120.5.T33 1992, **(v3)**
Taube, Karl A. F1219.3.A7.T38 1988, **(v4)**
Tauber, Alfred I. QR181.T36 1994, **(v1)**
  R724.T38 1999, **(v2)**
Taubes, Timothy. BH39.T395 1993, **(v8)**
Taubman, William. DK275.K5 T38 2003, **(v5)**
Taufer, Alison. DA130.T38 1999, **(v5)**
Tausch, Arno. HD82.T33 1993, **(v6)**
Taussig, F. W. HB301.T22 1968, **(v6)**
Tavard, George H. BT88.T35 1978, **(v8)**
  BX9418.T38 2000, **(v8)**
Tavernier-Courbin, Jacqueline. PS3515.E37.Z8916 1991, **(v3)**
Tavernor, Robert. NA1123.A5.T38 1998, **(v9)**
Taves, Ann. BL53.T38 1999, **(v8)**
Tawa, Nicholas E. ML410.F75.T38 1997, **(v9)**
  ML3477.T42 1990, **(v9)**
Tawes, Leonard S. VK140.T3.A3, **(v10)**
Tawfiq, Sahar. PJ7864.A478.A6 1995, **(v3)**
Tawney, R. H. HB199.T35, **(v6)**
  HC251.T3 1963, **(v6)**
  HC427.8.T36 1966, **(v6)**
  HD594.T3, **(v6)**
Tax, Sol. F1434.T3, **(v4)**
Tayeb, Monir H. HF5549.5.M5.T39 1996, **(v6)**
Tayler, Irene. PR4169.T39 1990, **(v3)**
Tayler, R. J. QB791.35.T38 1991, **(v1)**
  QB808.T37 1994, **(v1)**
Taylor, A. E. B316.T33 1951, **(v8)**
  B395.T25 1956, **(v8)**
  BJ1011.T18 1937, **(v8)**

Taylor, A. J. P. D210.T3, (v5)
D359.T3, (v5)
D359.T33, (v5)
D387.T3 1970, (v5)
D741.T34 1962, (v5)
DA3.T36.A37 1983, (v5)
DA45.T3 1958, (v5)
DA566.T38 1965, (v5)
DB80.T382, (v5)
DD203.T3 1946, (v5)
DD218.T33 1955a, (v5)
Taylor, Alan R. DS63.2.U5.T39 1991, (v5)
Taylor, Alan. F24.T39 1990, (v4)
Taylor, Angus. HV4708.T39 1999, (v6)
Taylor, Anya. PR457.T39 1999, (v3)
Taylor, Archer. PT245.T3, (v3)
Z1041.T3, (v10)
Taylor, Arlene G. Z666.5.T39 1999, (v10)
Z693.W94 2000, (v10)
Taylor, Avril. HV5824.W6.T39 1993, (v6)
Taylor, B. N. QC39.T38, (v1)
Taylor, Barbara. HQ1206.T33 1983, (v6)
Taylor, Bayard. PS2993.A45, (v3)
Taylor, Benjamin. BF416.A1.T38 1995, (v2)
Taylor, Billy. ML700.T4 1982, (v9)
Taylor, Bob Pepperman. PS3057.P64.T39 1996, (v3)
Taylor, Bonnie B. KF4117.T39 1996, (v7)
Taylor, Brandon. N6490.T365 1995, (v9)
Taylor, Brian Brace. NA1053.C43.A4 1998, (v9)
NA1053.J4.T39 1987, (v9)
Taylor, Brian C. BV4501.2.T269 1996, (v8)
Taylor, Carl Cleveland. HD1761.T25 1971, (v6)
Taylor, Carl S. HV6439.U7.D68 1993, (v6)
Taylor, Carol. RT41.F882 2001, (v2)
Taylor, Carole Anne. PS374.N4.T38 2000, (v3)
Taylor, Charles Fayette. TJ785.T382 1985, (v1)
Taylor, Charles Lewis. HN25.T39 1983, (v6)
Taylor, Charles. BD450.T266 1989, (v8)
Taylor, Christopher. GF551.T39 1983, (v6)
Taylor, Clarence. LC214.23.N7.T39 1997, (v7)
Taylor, Claudia. QA303.T205 1989, (v1)
Taylor, Clyde. PN1995.9.N4.T38 1998, (v3)
Taylor, Colin F. E78.G73.T33 198, (v4)
Taylor, D. A. VM600.T38 1989, (v10)
Taylor, David D. DS485.K23.T39 2000, (v5)
Taylor, David. HV8195.T39 1997, (v6)
Taylor, Denis. QC795.T3 1957, (v1)
Taylor, Desmond. Z5917.W33 T39 1993, (v10)
Taylor, Diana. PN2451.T28 1997, (v3)
Taylor, E. G. R. VK549.T39 1971b, (v10)
Taylor, Edward. PS850.T2.A6 1960, (v3)
Taylor, Elizabeth. PR6039.A85.A6 1957, (v3)
Taylor, Elizabeth. PR6039.A85.Bl, (v3)
PR6039.A928.A8, (v3)
PR6039.A928.D4, (v3)
PR6039.A928.D43, (v3)
PR6039.A928.G3, (v3)
Taylor, Eric R. UG447.T393 1998, (v10)
Taylor, Francis Henry. N8380.T3 1948, (v9)
Taylor, Gary. BF175.5.C37, (v2)
PR2965.T39 1989, (v3)
PR3095.T39 1993, (v3)
Taylor, George Edward. DS777.53.T39, (v5)
Taylor, George Rogers. E384.7.T3, (v4)
Taylor, Gordon Rattray. CB478.T38 1970b, (v5)
QP360.T39 1979, (v1)
Taylor, Graham D. E93.T235, (v4)
HD9651.9.D8.T39 1984, (v6)
Taylor, Grant. E551.5 40th.T39 2000, (v4)
Taylor, Greg. PN1995.T339 1999, (v3)
Taylor, Helen. F216.2.T39 2001, (v4)
Taylor, Henry Osborn. PN671.T32 1957, (v3)
Taylor, Ian R. HN398.M27.T39 1996, (v6)
Taylor, Ina. PR4681.T37 1989, (v3)
Taylor, James L. PC5333.T3 1970, (v3)
Taylor, James Stephen. KD3311.T39 1989, (v7)
Taylor, James. DD256.5.T283 1987, (v5)
Taylor, Jane H. M. PQ1593.T39 2001, (v3)
Taylor, Jay. DS518.15.T38, (v5)
DS706.T39 1987, (v5)
DS799.82.C437, (v5)

Taylor, Jennifer. NA1605.A5.A4 1982, (v9)
Taylor, Jenny. PR4498.P8.T39 1988, (v3)
Taylor, Jeremy F. HG2491.T38 1989, (v6)
Taylor, Jeremy. PR3729.T13.A6 1930, (v3)
Taylor, Jill McLean. HQ798.T39 1995, (v6)
Taylor, Jim. GV1588.5.T39 1995, (v6)
Taylor, Joe Gray. E445.L8.T3, (v4)
F369.T29, (v4)
F375.T23, (v4)
Taylor, John A. DA591.A45, (v5)
Taylor, John F. RJ506.H9T383 2001, (v2)
Taylor, John Gerald. BF311.T354 1999, (v2)
Taylor, John R. QC39.T4 1997, (v1)
Taylor, John Russell. PR736.T3 1969b, (v3)
PR736.T34 1971, (v3)
Taylor, Joseph Henry. F594.T23, (v4)
Taylor, Kathleen. LC5225.L42 T39 2000, (v7)
Taylor, Kendall. ND237.E8.T39 1987, (v9)
Taylor, Lily Ross. DG81.T38, (v5)
Taylor, Linda J. Z8447.T39 1982, (v10)
Taylor, M. Brook. F1024.T39 1989, (v4)
Taylor, Mark C. B4378.S4.T38 2000, (v8)
Taylor, Maxwell D. E745.T317 1972, (v4)
UA23.T33, (v10)
Taylor, Michael Eugene. QA1.A647 vol. 115-117, (v1)
Taylor, Michael John Haddrick. UG628.T39 1988, (v10)
Taylor, Mildred D. PZ7.T21723Ro, (v3)
Taylor, Miles. DA560.T38 1995, (v5)
Taylor, Nick. QC16.G63, (v1)
Taylor, Owen M. F189.A6.T2, (v4)
Taylor, Patrick. F1609.5.T39 1989, (v4)
Taylor, Paul Beekman. PR1933.L6.T38 1996, (v3)
Taylor, Paul W. BD232.T33, (v8)
Taylor, Paul. GV1785.T39 A3 1999, (v6)
ND1403.N43.T39 1995, (v9)
QA39.2.T413 1999, (v1)
Taylor, Peter Hillsman. PS3539.A9633.L65, (v3)
PS3539.A9633.W5, (v3)
PS3539.A9633.W6, (v3)
Taylor, Peter K. DD801.H57.T39 1994, (v5)
Taylor, Peter O. QB521.4.T39 1991, (v1)
Taylor, Peter. DA990.U46.T37 1999, (v5)
Taylor, Philip Bates. JA37.T8 6-8, (v7)
Taylor, Philip M. PN1998.3.S65.T39 1992, (v3)
Taylor, Quintard. B3317.T39 1997, (v8)
Taylor, Quintard. F899.S49.N475 1994, (v4)
Taylor, Richard C. PR3494.T38 1993, (v3)
Taylor, Richard P. GT3150.T25 2000, (v6)
Taylor, Richard. BD111.T3, (v8)
BJ1012.T37 2000, (v8)
PR5908.D7.T38 1984, (v3)
Taylor, Robert E. (Robert Ellis). SF61.T39 2001, (v1)
Taylor, Robert J. QL758.T38 1984, (v1)
Taylor, Robert. HD6664.T4 1978, (v6)
Taylor, Rodney Leon. BL1852.T39 1990, (v8)
Taylor, Rogan P. GV943.9.F35.T39 1992, (v6)
Taylor, Ronald B. HD6515.A292.C38 1975, (v6)
Taylor, Ronald. PF3460.T3 1973, (v3)
PT401.T36 1980, (v3)
Taylor, Sandra C. DS559.8.W6.T39 1999, (v5)
Taylor, Simon. DD240.T36 1983, (v5)
Taylor, Stuart Ross. QB501.T25 1992, (v1)
Taylor, Susie King. E492.94 33rd.T3 1988, (v4)
Taylor, Telford. D727.T37 1979, (v5)
D756.5.B7.T3, (v5)
JX5437.8.T39 1992, (v7)
Taylor, Thomas J. Z5781.T25 1992, (v10)
Taylor, Victor E. BL65.P73.T38 2000, (v8)
Taylor, William L. HN65.T36, (v6)
Taylor, William N. RC1230.T42 1991, (v2)
Taylor, William Robert. F128.47.T19 1992, (v4)
Taylor, Zachary. E415.T24 1908a, (v4)
Taylor-Gooby, Peter. HV31.T39 1991, (v6)
Tchaikovsky, Peter Ilich. ML410.C4.A4 1993, (v9)
Te Brake, Wayne Ph. D231.T42 1998, (v5)
Teaford, Jon C. JS309.T4, (v7)
JS411.T43 1997, (v7)
Teague, Edward H. NA202.T4 1991, (v9)
Teague, Elizabeth. DK288.T43 1988, (v5)
Teague, Frances N. PR3091.T44 1991, (v3)

Teague, Lynn S. E78.S7.T48 1998, (v4)
Teahan, Sheila. PS2127.T4.T43 1995, (v3)
Teale, Edwin Way. QH31.T4.A3 1957, (v1)
QL467.T23 1944, (v1)
Tearle, John. PR3619.P5.Z88 1991, (v3)
Teasdale, Wayne. BL625.T43 1999, (v8)
Tebbel, John William. PN4832.T43 1991, (v3)
Z473.T4 1987, (v10)
Tebbit, Mark. K230.T43 A37 2000, (v7)
Tec, Nechama. DS135.P63.R848 1990, (v5)
Teck, Katherine. ML3460.T4 1989, (v9)
Tedesco, Janis. PR6069.C596.R3437 1985, (v3)
Tedlock, Barbara. F1465.2.Q5.T43 1982, (v4)
Tedlock, Dennis. E98.R3.T42 1975, (v4)
PM2711.Z95.E5 1972, (v3)
Tedlock, E. W. PR6023.A93.Z926, (v3)
Tedlow, Richard S. HF5415.1.T44 1990, (v6)
Teed, Peter. D419.T44 1992, (v5)
Teeple, Gary. HC59.T36 2000, (v6)
Teeter, Phyllis Anne. RJ506.H9.T44 1998, (v2)
Teets, Bruce E. Z8189.7.T38 1990, (v10)
Teeuw, A. PL5080.T4, (v3)
Teichgraeber, Richard F. PS1638.T44 1995, (v3)
Teichman, Jenny. BD21.T35 1999, (v8)
Teichman, Judith A. HD4014.T44 1995, (v6)
HD9574.M6.T45 1988, (v6)
Teichova, Alice. HC270.28.T45 1988, (v6)
Teilhard de Chardin, Pierre. B2430.T373.P5613 1999, (v8)
BR85.T3313 1971, (v8)
Teiser, Stephen F. BQ4485.T45 1994, (v8)
Teisseire, Paul Jose. TP983.T44513 1994, (v1)
Teitelbaum, Gene. KF8745.B67.T45 1988, (v7)
Teitelbaum, Michael S. JV6255.T45 1998, (v7)
Teitelman, Jodi L. Z6671.55.T45 1990, (v10)
Teitelman, Robert. Q127.U6.T384 1994, (v1)
Teiwes, Frederick C. DS777.75.T43 1999, (v5)
DS777.75.T442 1990, (v5)
DS778.L4725.T38 1996, (v5)
Teiwes, Helga. E99.H7.T25 1996, (v4)
Teixeira, Ruy A. JK1987.T45 1992, (v7)
Teja, Jesus F. de la. F394.S2.T4 1995, (v4)
Tejera, V. B935.T45 1996, (v8)
Tejirian, Edward J. RC465.T45 1990, (v2)
Tel, Gerard. QA76.9.D5.T44 1994, (v1)
Telban, Borut. DU740.42.T45 1998, (v5)
Teles, Steven Michael. HV699.T45 1996, (v6)
Teller, Edward. Q172.T44, (v1)
UF767.T4, (v10)
Teller, Walter Magnes. VK140.S6.T4, (v10)
Telotte, J. P. PN1995.9.S26.T46 1995, (v3)
Telushkin, Dvorah. PJ5129.S49.Z944 1997, (v3)
Telushkin, Joseph. PN6149.J4.T45 1992, (v3)
Temin, Peter. HB3717 1929.T45 1976, (v6)
HB3717 1929.T45 1989, (v6)
HC105.T4, (v6)
HE8846.A55.T44 1987, (v6)
Temkin, Larry S. HM146.T45 1993, (v6)
Temkin, Owsei. BD431.T19, (v8)
BL65.M4.T35 1991, (v8)
RC372.T45 1971, (v2)
Temkin, Samuel. QC243.T46, (v1)
Temko, Allan. NA5550.N7.T4, (v9)
Temmer, Mark J. PR3537.P5.T4 1988, (v3)
Temperley, Gladys. DA330.T4 1971, (v5)
Temperley, Harold William Vazeille. D383.T4 1966a, (v5)
DA522.C2.T3 1968, (v5)
Temperley, Nicholas. ML410.H4.T36 1991, (v9)
ML3131.T44, (v9)
Tempkin, Betty Bates. RC78.7.U4T46 1999, (v2)
Temple, Ruth Zabriskie. PR468.S9.T4, (v3)
PR473.T4, (v3)
Temple, William. PR3729.T2.F5 1963, (v3)
Templeman, Donald C. HC305.T357, (v6)
Templeton, Malcolm. DT107.83.T36 1994, (v5)
Ten Broek, Jacobus. E449.T4, (v4)
Ten Grotenhuis, Elizabeth. BQ5125.M3.T46 1999, (v8)
Ten, C. L. HV8675.T44 1987, (v6)
JC223.M66.T45, (v7)

Teng, Ssu-yu. DS740.2.T4, (v5)
DS759.T45, (v5)
DS759.5.T43, (v5)
Tennant, Alan. QL666.O6.T4565 2000, (v1)
Tennant, Paul. E78.B9.T46 1990, (v4)
Tennant, Richard A. HV2475.T46 1998, (v6)
Tennant, Richard B. HD9149.C42U68. 1971, (v6)
Tenner, Edward. T14.5.T459 1996, (v1)
Tennyson, Alfred Tennyson. PR5550.F07, (v3)
PR5550.F38, (v3)
PR5550.F69, (v3)
PR5550.F70, (v3)
PR5550.F87, (v3)
PR5558.A3.F7 1930, (v3)
PR5562.A1 1982, (v3)
PR5581.A4 1981, (v3)
Tennyson, Emily Sellwood Tennyson. PR5581.T39 1981, (v3)
Tennyson, G. B. PR4429.T4 1966, (v3)
Tentler, Leslie Woodcock. HD6095.T44, (v6)
Terborgh, John. QH541.5.R27.T47 1992, (v1)
Terborg-Penn, Rosalyn. JK1896.T47 1998, (v7)
Terchek, Ronald. DS481.G3.T43 1998, (v5)
JC574.T47 1997, (v7)
Terenzio, Stephanie C. NE539.M67.A4 1990, (v9)
Terhune, Alfred McKinley. PR4703.T4, (v3)
Terkel, Studs. BD444.T47 2001, (v8)
E806.T45, (v4)
E839.T47 1988, (v4)
Terman, Lewis Madison. LB1131.T53, (v7)
Terrace, Vincent. PN1991.9.T47 1998, (v3)
PN1992.3.U5.T46, (v3)
PN1992.8.P54.T46 1997, (v3)
PN1992.8.S4.T47 1991, (v3)
PN1992.8.S4.T48 1993, (v3)
Terraine, John. D786.T44 1985, (v5)
Terras, Victor. PG2950.T43 1991, (v3)
PG3056.T44 1998, (v3)
PG3325.I33.T47 1990, (v3)
Terrell, Carroll Franklin. PS3531.O82.C289, (v3)
Terrell, JoAnne Marie. BR563.N4.T39 1998, (v8)
Terres, John K. QL50.T4, (v1)
QL681.T43 1980, (v1)
Terrett, Nicholas K. RS419.T47 1998, (v2)
Terrie, Philip G. F127.A2.T43 1997, (v4)
Terriff, Terry. UA23.T43 1995, (v10)
Terrill, Ross. DS777.55.T4166 1992, (v5)
Terry, Charles Sanford. MT115.B17.T4, (v9)
MT115.B2 T38 1970, (v9)
Terry, Edith. HC415.W4 T47 2002, (v6)
Tersine, Richard J. TS161.T48, (v1)
Terzaghi, Karl. TA710.T39 1996, (v1)
Teschke, John P. D804.G4.T45 1998, (v5)
Tesich, Steve. PS3570.E8S8 1982, (v3)
Teske, Nathan. JK1764.T47 1997, (v7)
Teske, Paul Eric. HE7781.T444 1990, (v6)
Teskey, Gordon. PN56.A5.T47 1996, (v3)
Teson, Fernando R. KZ6369.T47 1988, (v7)
Tessitore, Aristide. B430.T47 1996, (v8)
Tessler, Mark A. DS119.7.T443 1994, (v5)
Tessler, Richard C. RC455.4.F3.T46 2000, (v2)
Tessmer, Arnold Lee. UG1125.E87.T47 1988, (v10)
Test, George A. PN6149.S2.T4 1991, (v3)
Tester, John R. QH105.M55.T47 1995, (v1)
Tester, Keith. HM101.T44 1994, (v6)
Tetel, Marcel. PQ1643.T4, (v3)
Tetlow, Wendolyn E. PS3515.E37.I538 1992, (v3)
Tewksbury, Donald George. DS775.T442, (v5)
Tey, Josephine. PR6025.A255.D2, (v3)
Thacher, James. R153.T32, (v2)
Thacker, Christopher. BH301.N3.T47 1983, (v8)
Thackeray, William Makepeace. PR5610.A1 1978, (v3)
PR5612 .A1.1950, (v3)
PR5614.A1 1996, (v3)
PR5616.A2.J47 1902, (v3)
PR5618.T5, (v3)
PR5631.A4 1980, (v3)
Thackston, W. M. PJ6307.T45 1994, (v3)
PK6235.T47 1993, (v3)
Thaddeus, Janice Farrar. PR3316.A4.Z795 2000, (v3)

Thagard, Paul. BD171.T45 2000, (v8)
BF316.6.T48 1996, (v2)
Thakur, Laxman S. BQ6331.T332 T43, (v8)
Thakur, Ramesh Chandra. DS480.853.T475 1994, (v5)
JQ231.T43 1995, (v7)
Thakur, Ravni. HQ1767.T43 1996, (v6)
Thaler, Paul. KF224.S485.T48 1997, (v7)
Thaler, Richard H. HB199.T47 1992, (v6)
Thane, Pat. HQ1064.G7.T44 2000, (v6)
Thant, U, 1909-1974. D839.7.T5.A35, (v5)
Thanvi, Ashraf Ali. BJ1292.W6.T4713 1990, (v8)
Thapar, Romila. DS451.T452 2000, (v5)
DS451.T465 2000, (v5)
Thapar, Valmik. QH193.S59.T48 1997, (v1)
Tharoor, Shashi. DS428.2.T47 1997, (v5)
PR9499.3.T535G7 1989, (v3)
PR9499.3.T535R56 2001, (v3)
PR9499.3.T535S5 1992, (v3)
Tharp, Louise Hall. CS71.P35 1949, (v5)
CS71.W26. 1956, (v5)
LB695.M35.T5, (v7)
Thatcher, Ian D. DK254.T6.T49 2000, (v5)
Thatcher, Margaret. DA591.T47 T476 1993, (v5)
Thawley, John. Z4001.T48 1997, (v10)
Thaxton, Ralph. HX417.5.T48 1997, (v6)
Thayer, John S. TD196.H43.T49 1995, (v1)
Thayer, Robert E. QP401.T42 1989, (v1)
Thayer, Theodore. E207.G9.T48, (v4)
Theado, Matt. PS3521.E735.Z9 2000, (v3)
Theall, Donald F. PR6019.O9.T48 1997, (v3)
Theberge, Nancy. GV848.6.W65, (v6)
Thebault, John. DD801.H57.T47 1995, (v5)
Theissen, Gerd. BT297.T4713 1998, (v8)
Thelen, David P. E876.T465 1996, (v4)
F586.T47, (v4)
Thelin, John R. GV351.T43 1994, (v6)
Theobald, Marjorie R. LC2482.T54 1996, (v7)
Theobald, Paul. LC5147.M55.T44 1995, (v7)
Theoharis, Athan G. HV7911.H6.T54 1988, (v6)
HV7911.H6.T545 1995, (v6)
HV8144.F43.T48 1999, (v6)
Theoharis, Theoharis Constantine. PT8895.T53 1996, (v3)
Theophanes. D17.T513 1982, (v5)
Theotocopuli, Dominico. ND813.T4.B7, (v9)
Theriot, Nancy M. HQ1418.T53 1996, (v6)
HQ1426.T48 1988, (v6)
Thernstrom, Stephan. HN65.T45, (v6)
HN80.B7.T45, (v6)
Theron, Stephen. BJ1012.T46 1987, (v8)
Theroux, Paul. PS3570.H4.C66 1977, (v3)
Theroux, Paul. PS3570.H4.F35x 1976, (v3)
Theroux, Phyllis. CT275.T523.A33, (v5)
Thevenaz. B829.5.T4, (v8)
Thibaudet, Albert. PQ281.T5, (v3)
Thibodeaux, Louis J. QD31.2.T47 1996, (v1)
Thiederman, Sondra B. HF5549.5.C6.T49 1991, (v6)
Thiele, Leslie Paul. JA71.T52 1997, (v7)
Thiemann, Ronald F. BR115.P7.T475 1996, (v8)
Thieme, John. PR9272.9.W3.Z85 1999, (v3)
Thienel, Phillip M. F349.V6.T48 1995, (v4)
Thigpen, Corbett H. RC555.T5, (v2)
Thiher, Allen. PN56.M45.T53 1999, (v3)
PN81.T45 1997, (v3)
PT2621.A26.Z9316 1990, (v3)
Thirion, Andre. PQ2639.H368.Z513 1975, (v3)
Thirring, Walter E. QC20.T4513, (v1)
Thirsk, Joan. HC260.I53.T48, (v6)
S455.T48 1997, (v1)
Thiselton, Anthony C. BD241.T46 1992, (v8)
Thistlethwaite, Frank. E178.T35, (v4)
Thody, Philip Malcolm Waller. D1051.T46 2000, (v5)
DC417.T485 1999, (v5)
PQ2631.R63.Z935 1988, (v3)
Thogmartin, Clyde. PN4748.F7.T47 1998, (v3)
Tholfsen, Trygve R. D299.T49 1984, (v5)
Thollander, Earl. F889.3.T48 1992, (v4)
Thom, Paul. PN1584.T48 1993, (v3)
Thomas Aquinas. B765.T5.D43E, (v8)
Thomas, A. M. E183.8.S6.T46 1997, (v4)

Thomas, Adolphe V. PC2460.T46 1974, (v3)
Thomas, Adrian. ML410.G6448.T5 1997, (v9)
Thomas, Alan G. Z8250.54.T47 1983, (v10)
Thomas, Alastair H. DL105.T46 1998, (v5)
Thomas, Alexander. RJ499.T53, (v2)
Thomas, Aquinas Saint. JC121.T42 2002, (v7)
BJ1400.T4813 1995, (v8)
BV4630.T473 1998, (v8)
K447.T45.A2 1988, (v7)
Thomas, Baylis. DS126.5.T495 1999, (v5)
Thomas, Benjamin Platt. E457.T427 1952, (v4)
E467.1.S8.T45, (v4)
Thomas, Brian J. Q179.97.T48 1998, (v1)
TK5105.875.I57.T48 1996, (v1)
Thomas, Brook. PS374.R37.T48 1997, (v3)
Thomas, Caitlin. PR6039.H52.Z86 1957, (v3)
Thomas, Chantal. DC137.1.T5613 1997, (v5)
Thomas, Charles Kenneth. PE1135.T5 1958, (v3)
Thomas, Clarke M. F159.P643.S38 1999, (v4)
Thomas, Claudia N. PR3637.W6.T48 1994, (v3)
Thomas, Colin. DA910.T39 1997, (v5)
Thomas, D. M. PR6070.H58.F4x 1979, (v3)
Thomas, Daniel H. CD1001.T4 1975, (v5)
Thomas, David Hurst. CC165.T48 1998, (v5)
E77.9.T54 2000, (v4)
Thomas, David Oswald. BJ604.P7.T47, (v8)
Thomas, David S. G. GB611.T48 1994, (v6)
Thomas, David. VM342.T46 1992, (v10)
Thomas, Deborah A. PR4591.T5 1982, (v3)
PR5642.S56.T48 1993, (v3)
Thomas, Donald Serrell. HV6949.E5.T48 1998, (v6)
Thomas, Dorothy. PS3539.H573M2 1933, (v3)
PS3539.H613.H6, (v3)
Thomas, Dylan. DA730.T44 1959, (v5)
PR6039.H52.A15 1984, (v3)
PR6039.H52.A17 1971, (v3)
PR6039.H52.A6 1954, (v3)
PR6039.H52.A621969, (v3)
PR6039.H52.B4 1963, (v3)
PR6039.H52.C48 1969, (v3)
PR6039.H52.D4, (v3)
PR6039.H52.P76 1955, (v3)
PR6039.H52.U6, (v3)
PR6039.H52.Z48 1985, (v3)
PR6039.H52.Z5 1940, (v3)
PR6039.H52.Z52 1967, (v3)
PR6039.H52 1953, (v3)
Thomas, E. G. QC32.T46 2000, (v1)
Thomas, E. J. BQ882.T45 2000, (v8)
Thomas, Eberle. Z8809.6.T56 1991, (v10)
Thomas, Edmund J. PN49.T447 1990, (v3)
Thomas, Edward. PR6039.H55.A17 1978, (v3)
Thomas, Emory M. E467.1.L4.T48 1995, (v4)
E487.T483 1979, (v4)
Thomas, Evan. E840.8.K4.T49 2000, (v4)
KF373.W466.T46 1991, (v7)
Thomas, Francis-Noel. PE1408.T4155 1994, (v3)
PN81.T47 1992, (v3)
Thomas, Frank. NC1766.U52.D58 1981, (v9)
Thomas, Frederic C. HV4140.C34.T45 1997, (v6)
Thomas, G. Scott. JK524.T44 1987, (v7)
Thomas, George C. KF9245.T48 1998, (v7)
Thomas, George E. LD4531.T56 1999, (v7)
NA737.F84.A4 1991, (v9)
NA737.P685.T48 2000, (v9)
Thomas, Gilbert Oliver. PR3383.T45 1948, (v3)
Thomas, Gillian. PR4984.M5.Z85 1985, (v3)
Thomas, Graham P. JN405.T56 1997, (v7)
Thomas, Graham Stuart. SB411.T4885 1994, (v1)
Thomas, H. Nigel. PS153.N5.T47 1988, (v3)
Thomas, Helen. PR448.S55.T48 2000, (v3)
Thomas, Hugh. DP269.T46 1977, (v5)
F1230.T48 1993, (v4)
HT985.T47 1997, (v6)
Thomas, Ian Q. R. D845.T48 1997, (v5)
Thomas, Isaiah. Z205.T56 1970b, (v10)
Thomas, J. J. HD2341.T52 1992, (v6)
Thomas, J. W. PD25.N6 no. 44, (v3)
Thomas, James D. JK4516.T49 1988, (v7)
Thomas, Jane. PR4757.W6.T48 1999, (v3)

Thomas, Jerry Bruce. F241.T47 1998, **(v4)**
Thomas, Jim. KF9731.T48 1988, **(v7)**
Thomas, John L. PS3537.T316.Z93 2000, **(v3)**
Thomas, Julian. GN776.22.G7.T48 1991, **(v6)**
Thomas, June Manning. HT177.D4.T56 1997, **(v6)**
Thomas, Keith. BR377.T48 1997, **(v8)**
Thomas, L. J. TN275.T48 1973b, **(v1)**
Thomas, Larry. TN802.T49 1992, **(v1)**
Thomas, Lorenzo. PS310.N4.T48 2000, **(v3)**
    PS310.N4T48 2000, **(v3)**
Thomas, Lowell Jackson. CT275.T554.A34, **(v5)**
Thomas, Lowell. DS786.T48 1959, **(v5)**
Thomas, Martin. D761.9.A1.T48 1998, **(v5)**
    DC59.8.G7, **(v5)**
Thomas, Michael Frederic. GB406.T47 1974, **(v6)**
    GB446.T46 1994, **(v6)**
Thomas, Milton Halsey. Z8228.T45 1962, **(v10)**
Thomas, Nicholas. DU700.T46 1990, **(v5)**
Thomas, Peter David Garner. DA512.W6.T55 1996, **(v5)**
    DA720.T482 1998, **(v5)**
    E215.3.T46 1987, **(v4)**
Thomas, Peter. QK475.T48 2000, **(v1)**
Thomas, R. Murray. BJ1408.5.T47 1995, **(v8)**
    BJ1408.5.T48 1993, **(v8)**
    LB1028.T446 1998, **(v7)**
Thomas, Raju G. C. JQ281.T56 1996, **(v7)**
Thomas, Richard Walter. F574.D49.N484 1992, **(v4)**
Thomas, Robert David. BX6995.T46 1994, **(v8)**
Thomas, Robert J. HD8039.L452.U67 1985, **(v6)**
Thomas, Ron. GV885.7.T46 2002, **(v6)**
Thomas, Ronald R. PR830.D4.T53 1999, **(v3)**
    PR878.P74.T48 1990, **(v4)**
Thomas, Rosalind. D58.T46 2000, **(v5)**
Thomas, Rosamund M. KD8024.T47 1990, **(v7)**
Thomas, S. Bernard. DS777.55.T45, **(v5)**
Thomas, Sandra P. RT42.T48 2002, **(v2)**
Thomas, Sue. PR6035.H96.Z9 1999, **(v3)**
Thomas, Veronica G. Z1361.N39 T49 2001, **(v10)**
Thomas, Vivian. PR3069.R6.T47 1989, **(v3)**
Thomas, William G. E468.9.T46 2001, **(v4)**
Thomason, Richmond H. BC135.T48, **(v8)**
Thombs, Dennis L. RC564.T55 1994, **(v2)**
Thomes, William Henry. PS3030.T65 O6 1892, **(v3)**
Thomison, Dennis. N6538.N5.T46 1991, **(v9)**
Thompson, Alvin O. F1621.T5 1997, **(v4)**
Thompson, Andrew. PR4692.I82.T47 1998, **(v3)**
Thompson, Ariadne. PS3539.H62.Oc7, **(v3)**
Thompson, Bradbury. Z116.A3.T45 1988, **(v10)**
Thompson, Bruce. PT2638.N5.Z894 1990, **(v3)**
Thompson, Claudia G. TS1120.5.T46 1992, **(v1)**
Thompson, Colin P. PQ6410.L3.T46 1988, **(v3)**
Thompson, Daniel Varney. ND1500.T5 1956, **(v9)**
Thompson, David E. TA174.T55 1999, **(v1)**
Thompson, David. F1060.7.T46 1994, **(v4)**
Thompson, Dawn. PR9188.T49 2000, **(v3)**
Thompson, Dennis F. JK1140.T48 1995, **(v7)**
Thompson, Donald. ML125.P8 T55 1991, **(v9)**
Thompson, Dorothy J. DT73.M5.T46 1988, **(v5)**
Thompson, E. A. D141.T5 1948, **(v5)**
    DG504.T46 1982, **(v5)**
Thompson, E. P. HD8388.T47, **(v6)**
    PR5083.T6 1977, **(v3)**
Thompson, Edward H. Z7164.O4.T5 1996, **(v10)**
Thompson, Edward Maunde. Z114.T472 1965, **(v10)**
Thompson, Ewa M. PG3011.T447 2000, **(v3)**
Thompson, F. M. L. DA550.T53 1988, **(v5)**
Thompson, Francis. PR99.T47, **(v3)**
Thompson, Francis. PR5650.A2.C6 1979, **(v3)**
Thompson, G. R. PS1892.H5.T47 1993, **(v3)**
Thompson, Graham R. QE33.T45 1999, **(v1)**
Thompson, Guy Llewelyn. DC725.T48 1991, **(v5)**
Thompson, Henry O. Z7772.C1.T46 1997, **(v10)**
    Z7772.D37.T48 1996, **(v10)**
    Z7772.J1.T48 1993, **(v10)**
Thompson, I. A. A. UB87.T48, **(v10)**
Thompson, Ian Bentley. HC276.2.T5, **(v6)**
Thompson, J. Kevin. RC552.A5.T49 1990, **(v2)**
Thompson, J. Lee. D544.T49 1999, **(v5)**
Thompson, J. M. DC203.T53 1952a, **(v5)**
Thompson, J. William. TH380.T46 2000, **(v1)**

Thompson, James A. U263.T46 1985, **(v10)**
Thompson, James R. QA279.T494 1999, **(v1)**
Thompson, James Westfall. D117.T53 1960, **(v5)**
    Z723.T47 1957, **(v10)**
Thompson, James. PR858.E37.T48 1996, **(v3)**
    PR4037.T48 1988, **(v3)**
Thompson, Jane L. LC5056.A3, **(v7)**
Thompson, John A. D632.T46 1987, **(v5)**
Thompson, John Eric Sidney. F1435.T497 1966, **(v4)**
Thompson, John Henry. F125.T5, **(v4)**
Thompson, John Herd. E183.8.C2.T46 1994, **(v4)**
Thompson, John M. D651.R8.T5, **(v5)**
Thompson, John. F699.T49 1986, **(v4)**
    PE1505.T46 1961, **(v3)**
Thompson, Jon. PR830.C74.T46 1993, **(v3)**
Thompson, Josiah. B4377.T514, **(v8)**
Thompson, Kathleen. F566.3.T48 1996, **(v4)**
Thompson, Kay. PZ7.T3716EI, **(v3)**
Thompson, Kenneth W. E176.1.P83 1982 vol. 4, **(v4)**
    E176.1.P83 1982 vol. 5, **(v4)**
    E176.1.P83 1982 vol. 7, **(v4)**
    E176.1.P83 1982 vol. 8, **(v4)**
    E176.1.P83 1982 v. 9, **(v4)**
Thompson, Kenneth. B2430.S34.T52 1984, **(v8)**
Thompson, Kristin. PN1996.T46 1999, **(v3)**
Thompson, Larry. RB155.8.T48 1994, **(v2)**
Thompson, Laurence G. BL1802.T5 1996, **(v8)**
    Z7757.C6.T55 1985, **(v10)**
Thompson, Lee Briscoe. PR9199.3.L56.Z894 1987, **(v3)**
Thompson, Leonard Monteath. DT1787.T48 1990, **(v5)**
Thompson, Lloyd A. DG190.T48 1989, **(v5)**
Thompson, Lynda M. PR756.W65.T48 2000, **(v3)**
Thompson, Mattie Crocker Thomas. F332.B3T5, **(v4)**
Thompson, Mildred I. E185.86.B543 1990 vol. 15, **(v4)**
Thompson, N. S. PR1874.T47 1996, **(v3)**
Thompson, Neil B. UA26.G675.T46, **(v10)**
Thompson, Nicola Diane. PR878.W6.T45 1996, **(v3)**
Thompson, Norma. JA81.T53 2001, **(v7)**
Thompson, Paul B. BJ52.5.T539 1998, **(v8)**
    HD9006.T49 1992, **(v6)**
Thompson, Paul Richard. HN389.T43 1992, **(v6)**
    NA997.B84.T45, **(v9)**
Thompson, Peter. E174.T47 2000, **(v4)**
Thompson, Peter. SB408.3.S645, **(v1)**
Thompson, Philip C. HD66.T48 1982, **(v6)**
Thompson, Raymond H. PR888.A76.T45 1985, **(v3)**
Thompson, Richard F. QP355.T45, **(v1)**
Thompson, Richard H. F1059.5.T689.C517 1989, **(v4)**
Thompson, Robert Grainger Ker. U240.T56 1966a, **(v10)**
Thompson, Robert J. PN1992.3.U5.T49 1996, **(v3)**
Thompson, Roger C. DU29.T48 1994, **(v5)**
Thompson, Roger. F15.B7.T46 1994, **(v4)**
Thompson, Scott M. E83.877.T56 2000, **(v4)**
Thompson, Stephen Andrew. TD223.T527 1999, **(v1)**
Thompson, Steven K. QA276.6.T58 1992, **(v1)**
Thompson, Thomas L. DS121.T48 1992, **(v5)**
Thompson, Thomas. RD598.T475, **(v2)**
Thompson, Virginia McLean. DS509.5.T45, **(v5)**
Thompson, Warren Simpson. HB871.T45 1965, **(v6)**
Thompson, Wayne C. DD84.T48 1994, **(v5)**
Thompson, William J. QA297.T5 1992, **(v1)**
    QA331.T385 1997, **(v1)**
Thompson, William Norman. E98.T77.T56 1996, **(v4)**
    GV1301.T47 2001, **(v6)**
    HV6710.T48 1994, **(v6)**
Thompson, William R. U21.2.T465 1988, **(v10)**
Thompson, Winfred Lee. KF4635.T48 1989, **(v7)**
Thoms, David. D760.8.M53.T47 1989, **(v5)**
Thoms, Peter. PR868.D4.T48 1998, **(v3)**
    PR4498.Q5.T4 1992, **(v3)**
Thomsett, Michael C. DD247.H5.T52 1997, **(v5)**
    ML108.T46 1989, **(v9)**
    PN6084.W35.T48 1997, **(v3)**
Thomson, Andrew. ML410.W648.T5 1987, **(v9)**
Thomson, Anne. BJ43.T47 1999, **(v8)**
Thomson, Dale C. F1034.3.S2.T48, **(v4)**
Thomson, David. D421.T58 1965, **(v5)**
    NA510.T56 1993, **(v9)**

PN1998.3.S395.T46 1992, **(v3)**
PN1998.3.W45.T56 1996, **(v3)**
Thomson, Derick S. PB1607.T5, **(v3)**
Thomson, Ellen Mazur. Z5956.D5.T46 1992, **(v10)**
Thomson, Garrett. B1296.T46 2001, **(v8)**
Thomson, Guy P. C. F1326.L83.T5 1998, **(v4)**
Thomson, J. DS709.T475 1982, **(v5)**
Thomson, J. A. K. PR127.T5, **(v3)**
    PR127.T55, **(v3)**
Thomson, J. J. QC711.T5 1969, **(v1)**
Thomson, J. K. J. D118.T49 1998, **(v5)**
Thomson, James. F1013.T45 1974, **(v4)**
    PR3732.L5, **(v3)**
    PR3732.S4 1981, **(v3)**
    PR3733.A45 1958, **(v3)**
Thomson, Judith Jarvis. B105.E7.T47, **(v8)**
    BJ55.T46 1990, **(v8)**
    BJ1012.T545 2001, **(v8)**
Thomson, Keith Stewart. QL638.L26.T46 1991, **(v1)**
    VM395.B38.T49 1995, **(v10)**
Thomson, Paul van K. PR5651.T55, **(v3)**
Thomson, Peter. PR2907.T48 1992, **(v3)**
Thomson, Rosemarie Garland. PS374.P44.T49 1997, **(v3)**
Thomson, Virgil. ML60.T515, **(v9)**
    ML410.T452.A4 1988, **(v9)**
    ML1406.T5 1989, **(v9)**
Thomson, William J. TP156.T7.T48 2000, **(v1)**
Thomson, William. H62.T465 2001, **(v6)**
Thomte, Reidar. BX4827.K5.T5 1969, **(v8)**
Thondup, Tulku. BQ7604.T47 1987, **(v8)**
Thone, Ruth Raymond. RC552.O25.T48 1997, **(v2)**
Thorburn, David. PR6005.O4.Z883, **(v3)**
Thoreau, Henry David. F27.P5.T43 1950, **(v4)**
    F72.C3.T4 1988, **(v4)**
    F72.M7.T5 1980, **(v4)**
    PS3041.B6 1964, **(v3)**
    PS3042.A7, **(v3)**
    PS3048.A1 1962, **(v3)**
    PS3053.A25 1971, **(v3)**
    PS3053.A26, **(v3)**
    PS3053.A27, **(v3)**
    PS3053.A3 1975, **(v3)**
Thoren, Victor E. QB36.B8.T49 1990, **(v1)**
Thörlind, Robert. JS7100.3.A3 T46 1999, **(v7)**
Thormählen, Marianne. PR3669.R2.T47 1993, **(v3)**
    PR4169.T47 1999, **(v3)**
Thorn, Colin E. GB401.5.T47 1988, **(v6)**
Thornburg, Mary K. Patterson. PR5397.F73.T48 1987, **(v3)**
Thornbury, Barbara E. PN2924.T526 1997, **(v3)**
Thornbury, William D. QE77.T5, **(v1)**
Thorndike, Edward L. LB1051.T52 1970, **(v7)**
    QL785.T5 2000, **(v1)**
Thorndike, Lynn. CB53.T5 1948, **(v5)**
    Q125.T52, **(v1)**
Thorndike, Robert Ladd. LB1131.T59 1961, **(v7)**
Thorne, Brian. RC339.52.R64.T48 1992, **(v2)**
Thorne, Kip S. QC6.T526 1994, **(v1)**
Thorne, Susan. BX7176.T46 1999, **(v8)**
Thorne, Tanis C. F598.T48 1996, **(v4)**
Thorne-Miller, Boyce. QH91.T45 1999, **(v1)**
Thornes, John B. GB400.4.T46 1977, **(v6)**
Thornhill, Randy. HV6558.T48 2000, **(v6)**
    QL468.7.T46 1983, **(v1)**
Thornton, A. P. JV1018.T5, **(v7)**
Thornton, Bruce S. DF78.T53 2000, **(v5)**
Thornton, Joe. RA1242.C436.T48 2000, **(v2)**
Thornton, John Kelly. DT31.T516 1992, **(v5)**
Thornton, Mark. HV5088.T48 1991, **(v6)**
Thornton, Richard C. E855.T52 2001, **(v4)**
Thornton, Robert D. R489.C9.T5, **(v2)**
Thornton, Russell. E59.P75.T48 1987, **(v4)**
    E99.C5.T48 1990, **(v4)**
Thornton, Tamara Plakins. F73.44.T48 1989, **(v4)**
    Z40.T46 1996, **(v10)**
Thornton, Weldon. PR6019.O9.P653 1994, **(v3)**
    PR6019.O9.U765 2000, **(v3)**
Thorp, Daniel B. F265.M7.T44 1989, **(v4)**
Thorp, Rosemary. HC125.T523 1998, **(v6)**
Thorpe, Andrew. JN1129.L32.T47 1997, **(v7)**

Thorpe, Clarence De Witt. PR590.T5 1957, **(v3)**
Thorpe, Earle E. E175.T5, **(v4)**
Thorpe, James Ernest. PB21.T5 1970, **(v3)**
  PR65.T5, **(v3)**
  PR751.T46 1987, **(v3)**
Thorpy, Michael J. RC547.Y34 2001, **(v2)**
Thorsen, Niels. E767.1.T47 1988, **(v4)**
Thorslev, Peter Larsen. PR4389.T45 1962, **(v3)**
Thoumi, Francisco E. HV5840.C7.T48 1995, **(v6)**
Thrapp, Dan L. F596.T515 1988, **(v4)**
Thrasher, Frederic Milton. HV6439.U7.C4 1936, **(v6)**
Throne, Mildred. F621.C252T45, **(v4)**
Thrower, Norman Joseph William. GA201.T47 1996, **(v6)**
Thrupp, Sylvia L. HF3510.L8.T4, **(v6)**
Thrush, Paul W. TN9.T5, **(v1)**
Thuan, Trinh Xuan. QB461.T5613 2001, **(v1)**
Thucydides. DF229.T5.C7 1951, **(v5)**
  DF229.T5.J6 1972, **(v5)**
  PA3405.58.T7 1942, **(v3)**
Thuery, Jacques. TK7876.T5313 1991, **(v1)**
Thuesen, Peter Johannes. BS455.T55 1999, **(v8)**
Thumann, Albert. TD892.T488 1990, **(v1)**
  TJ163.2.M425 1991, **(v1)**
  TJ163.235.T48 2001, **(v1)**
Thurber, James. NC1429.T48, **(v9)**
  PS3539.H94.A7, **(v3)**
  PS3539.H94.C7, **(v3)**
  PS3539.H94.L3, **(v3)**
  PS3539.H94.L4 1937, **(v3)**
  PS3539.H94.M3 1940, **(v3)**
  PS3539.H94.M5 1935, **(v3)**
  PS3539.H94.M9, **(v3)**
  PS3539.H94.T46, **(v3)**
  PS3539.H94.T5, **(v3)**
  PS3539.H94.T53, **(v3)**
  PS3539.H94.T54, **(v3)**
  PS3539.H94Z474 1999, **(v3)**
  PS3539.H94F3 1954, **(v3)**
Thurin, Erik Ingvar. PS3244.T48 1995, **(v3)**
Thurlow, Richard C. DA566.7.T55 1995, **(v5)**
Thurman, E. M. QD63.E88.T58 1998, **(v1)**
Thurman, Judith. PQ2605.O28.Z836 1999, **(v3)**
  PT8175.B545.Z89 1982, **(v3)**
Thurman, Wallace. PS3539.H957.B53, **(v3)**
  PS3539.H957.I5 1979, **(v3)**
Thurner, Dick. PE1175.T54 1993, **(v3)**
Thurner, Erika. D810.G9.T4813 1998, **(v5)**
Thurner, Mark. F3429.1.A45.T58 1997, **(v4)**
Thurow, Lester C. HB3730.T55 1996, **(v6)**
  HC59.T5157 1992, **(v6)**
  HJ2381.T53, **(v6)**
Thurston, Anne F. DS778.N53.T48 1991, **(v5)**
Thurston, Frederick. MT380.T5 1977, **(v9)**
Thurston, H. A. QA300.T48 1988, **(v1)**
Thurston, H. David. SB731.T48 1991, **(v1)**
Thurston, Robert W. DK267.T52 1996, **(v5)**
Thwaite, Ann. PR4725.G7.Z84 1984, **(v3)**
Thwaites, Reuben Gold. F519.T54 1999, **(v4)**
Tibbetts, John C. PN1997.85.T54 1998, **(v3)**
  PN1997.85.T544 2001, **(v3)**
Tibullus. PA6788.E5C3, **(v3)**
Ticciati, Robin. QC174.45.T53 1999, **(v1)**
Tice, George A. F144.P4.T5, **(v4)**
Tice, Karen Whitney. HV43.T43 1998, **(v6)**
Tice, Karin E. F1565.2.C8.T53 1995, **(v4)**
Tichi, Cecelia. HQ520.T53 1991, **(v6)**
  ML3524.T5 1994, **(v9)**
Tick, Judith. ML410.S4446 T5 1997, **(v9)**
Tickner, J. Ann. HQ1154.T53 2001, **(v6)**
  JX1391.T53 1992, **(v7)**
Tidwell, Mike. T10.5.T53 2000, **(v1)**
Tidwell, William A. E608.T53 1988, **(v4)**
Tieck, Ludwig. PT2536.A1 1963, **(v3)**
  PT2536.A1 1985, **(v3)**
  PT2537.G8 1974, **(v3)**
Tiedemann, Joseph S. F128.4.T54 1997, **(v4)**
Tiefer, Charles. E881.T54 1994, **(v4)**
Tiefer, Charles. KF4937.T54 1989, **(v7)**
Tieghem, Philippe van. PQ116.V3, **(v3)**
Tiemstra, Suzanne Spicer. ML128.C48.T5 1992, **(v9)**

Tiepolo, Giovanni Battista. NC257.T5.A4 1996e, **(v9)**
Tierney, Brian. D117.T6 1983, **(v5)**
Tierney, Nathan L. BJ1031.T54 1994, **(v8)**
Tierney, Patrick. F2520.1.Y3.T54 2000, **(v4)**
Tierney, William G. LA227.4.T54 1993, **(v7)**
Tiersten, Lisa. HC280.C6 T54 2001, **(v6)**
Tiffany, Daniel Newton. PN1271.T54 2000, **(v3)**
  PS3531.O82.Z865 1995, **(v3)**
Tiffin, John. LB1044.84.T54 1995, **(v7)**
Tifft, Larry. HV6626.2.T54 1993, **(v6)**
Tifft, Susan E. Z473.N44.T54 1999, **(v10)**
Tiger, Virginia. PR6013.O35.Z92, **(v3)**
Tigerman, Stanley. NA737.T49.T54 1989, **(v9)**
Tight, Malcolm. LC5215.T57 1996, **(v7)**
Tignor, Robert L. HC800.T52 1998, **(v6)**
  HC830.T54 1984, **(v6)**
Tikhonov, A. N. QC20.T543 1963a, **(v1)**
Tiles, Mary. B2430.B254.T55 1984, **(v8)**
Tileston, Donna Walker. LB1775.2.T54 2000, **(v7)**
Tilford, Gregory L. RS164.T556 1998, **(v2)**
Tillard, Francoise. ML410.H482.T513 1996, **(v9)**
Tiller, Veronica E. Velarde. E93.T55 1996, **(v4)**
Tillery, Tyrone. PS3525.A24785.Z89 1991, **(v3)**
Tillett, Margaret G. PQ2440.T5, **(v3)**
Tilley, Allen. BD450.T56 1995, **(v8)**
Tilley, Arthur Augustus. PQ233.T5 1968, **(v3)**
Tillich, Paul. BJ1251.T47, **(v8)**
  BJ1533.C8.T5, **(v8)**
  BL51.T58, **(v8)**
  BR100.T53, **(v8)**
  BR123.T54, **(v8)**
  BR127.T56, **(v8)**
  BR479.T5, **(v8)**
  BT21.2.T5 1968, **(v8)**
  BT28.T5, **(v8)**
  BT771.T54 1958, **(v8)**
  BV4253.T58, **(v8)**
  BX4817.T53, **(v8)**
Tillis, Steve. PN1631.T46 1998, **(v3)**
Tillman, David A. HD9750.5.T55 1985, **(v6)**
Tillman, Hoyt Cleveland. B127.C65 T55 1992, **(v8)**
  B128.C3474 T55 1994, **(v8)**
Tillman, Robert. HV6769.T55 1998, **(v6)**
Tillotson, Geoffrey. PR99.T54 1967, **(v3)**
  PR463.T5 1967, **(v3)**
  PR1134.T5, **(v3)**
  PR3634.T5 1950, **(v3)**
  PR3634.T52, **(v3)**
  PR5638.T5 1963, **(v3)**
Tilly, Charles. D214.T54 1993, **(v5)**
  HC79.I5.T388 1998, **(v6)**
  HN13.T54, **(v6)**
  HN425.T54, **(v6)**
  HD51110.2.U5.T548 1996, **(v6)**
Tillyard, E. M. W. PR99.T56, **(v3)**
  PR125.T55, **(v3)**
  PR2976.T55 1964, **(v3)**
  PR2976.T55, **(v3)**
  PR2982.T5 1964, **(v3)**
  PR3588.T62 1949, **(v3)**
  PR3588.T64 1951, **(v3)**
Tillyard, Eustace Mandeville Wetenhall. PR99.T57 1971, **(v3)**
  PR428.P5.T5 1944, **(v3)**
  PR3588.T614 1968, **(v3)**
Tilman, David. QK910.T55 1988, **(v1)**
Timberlake, Richard H. HG501.T59 1993, **(v6)**
Timbrell, Charles. ML724.T54 1999, **(v9)**
Timby, Barbara Kuhn. RT41.L67 2001, **(v2)**
  RT41.S38 2003, **(v2)**
Time-Life Books. ND212.T5, **(v9)**
Timerman, Jacobo. F1788.T5313 1990, **(v4)**
  F3100.T5413 1987, **(v4)**
Timilty, Joseph F. HV9468.T57.A3 1997, **(v6)**
Timm, Angelika. D819.G3.T56 1997, **(v5)**
Timmerman, John H. PS3509.L43.A6977 1994, **(v3)**
  PS3537.T3234.Z927 1990, **(v3)**
Timmerman, Kenneth R. UF505.I72.T56 1991, **(v10)**
Timmermans, Jean. QD291.T55, **(v1)**
Timmermans, Stefan. RC87.9.T56 1999, **(v2)**
Timmons, George. LB43.T56 1988, **(v7)**

Timmons, Mark. BJ37.T55 1999, **(v8)**
Timmons, Stuart. HQ75.8.H39.T56 1990, **(v6)**
Timms, Noel. HV12.T54 1982, **(v6)**
Timner, W. E. ML156.5.E45.T5 1988, **(v9)**
Timoshenko, Stephen. QA931.T55 1970, **(v1)**
  TA405.T52 1968, **(v1)**
Timrod, Henry. PS3070 .A2 6965, **(v3)**
  PS3071.C37, **(v3)**
  PS3071.P3, **(v3)**
Tinbergen, Jan. HB846.T56 1990, **(v6)**
Tinbergen, Niko. QL781.T58 1969, **(v1)**
Tindall, George Brown. F215.T59, **(v4)**
Tindall, James A. GB1197.7.T56 1999, **(v6)**
Tindall, William York. PN56.S9.T5 1955a, **(v3)**
  PR6019.O9.Z83, **(v3)**
  PR6039.H52.Z865, **(v3)**
Tiner, Ralph W. QK125.T55 1993, **(v1)**
Ting, Li. UA838.M5.T5, **(v10)**
Ting, Ling. PL2747.P5.A23 1989, **(v3)**
  PL2747.P5.T313 1984, **(v3)**
Tingen, Paul. ML419.D39.T56 2001, **(v9)**
Tingsten, Herbert. JF1001.T52 1975, **(v7)**
Tinker Salas, Miguel. F1346.T56 1997, **(v4)**
Tinker, George E. E98.M6.T56 1993, **(v4)**
Tinkle, Theresa Lynn. PR317.S48.T56 1996, **(v3)**
Tinkler, Penny. PN5124.J8.T56 1995, **(v3)**
Tinling, Marion. G200.T55 1989, **(v6)**
Tinterow, Gary. ND553.C8.A4 1996, **(v9)**
Tintner, Adeline R. PS2124.T55 1998, **(v3)**
  PS2124.T56 2000, **(v3)**
  PS2127.A75.T557 1993, **(v3)**
  PS2127.L5.T55 1991, **(v3)**
  PS2127.L5.T56 1989, **(v3)**
  PS3545.H16.Z8786 1999, **(v3)**
Tintoré, María José. PQ6503.A4R337 1987, **(v3)**
Tippett, Michael. ML60.T5533 1995, **(v9)**
Tipton, Frank B. HC240.T56 1987, **(v6)**
  HC460.5.T56 1998, **(v6)**
Tiptree, James. PS3570.I66.U6, **(v3)**
Tiratsoo, Nick. DA690.C75.T57 1990, **(v5)**
Tirion, Wil. G1000.2.T4 2001, **(v6)**
  QB65.T54 1998, **(v1)**
  QB65.T56 1996, **(v1)**
Tirman, John. UA23.T57 1989, **(v10)**
Tirpitz, Alfred von. DD231.T5.A3513 1970, **(v5)**
Tirro, Frank. ML3506.T57 1993, **(v9)**
Tiruneh, Andargachew. DT387.95.T57 1993, **(v5)**
Tischauser, Leslie Vincent. Z1361.N39.T57 1998, **(v10)**
Tischler, Alice. ML120.I75.T57 1988, **(v9)**
Tisdell, C. A. HD75.6.T565 1990, **(v6)**
Tise, Larry E. E302.1.T57 1998, **(v4)**
  E337.5.T57 1987, **(v4)**
Tishkov, Valerii Aleksandrovich. DK33.T54 1997, **(v5)**
Tismaneanu, Vladimir. DJK50 .T57 1992, **(v5)**
  JA84.E92.T57 1998, **(v7)**
Titelman, Gregory. PN6405.T57 1996, **(v3)**
Titmuss, Richard Morris. HN389.T58 1969, **(v6)**
Titon, Jeff Todd. ML3521.T58 1994, **(v9)**
Titterton, Robert J. ND237.S43715.T58 1997, **(v9)**
Tittler, Jonathan. PQ7798.26.U4.Z89 1993, **(v3)**
Tittler, Robert. DA315.T58 1998, **(v5)**
  HT133.T58 2001, **(v6)**
Titus, Charles. F182.T5, **(v4)**
Titus, James. E199.T63 1990, **(v4)**
Tiusanen, Timo. PT2607.U493.Z89, **(v3)**
Tiwari, Chitra K. UA830.T58 1989, **(v10)**
Tiwathia, Vijay. F2056.8.T59 1987, **(v4)**
Tober, James A. QL84.2.T62 1989, **(v1)**
Tobey, Ronald C. HD9685.U5.T63 1996, **(v6)**
Tobias, Henry Jack. F705.J5 T62, **(v4)**
  F805.J4.T63 1990, **(v4)**
Tobias, Michael. HV4764.T62 1999, **(v6)**
Tobias, Sheila. HQ1426.T64 1997, **(v6)**
  QA11.T67 1978, **(v1)**
Tobin, Beth Fowkes. PR868.P66.T63 1993, **(v3)**
Tobin, Graham A. GB5014.T63 1997, **(v6)**
Tobin, James Edward. Z2013.T62, **(v10)**
Tobin, James. HB99.7.T63 1987, **(v6)**
  PN4874.P88.T63 1997, **(v3)**

Tobin, Marvin Charles. QD95.T57, (v1)
Tobin, Patrick D. HV551.2.T63 1997, (v6)
Tobin, Robert Deam. PT321.T58 2000, (v3)
Toch, Hans. RC569.5.V55.T62 1989, (v2)
Toch, Thomas. LA217.T63 1991, (v1)
Tocqueville, Alexis de. DC138.T6313 1998, (v5)
  DC148.T683, (v5)
  DC270.T652 1949, (v5)
  E165.T5433 1971, (v4)
  JC229.T7713 1980, (v7)
  JC229.T775 2002, (v7)
  JK216.T713 2000b, (v7)
Todd, Alexandra Dundas. RC280.B7.T63 1994, (v2)
Todd, D. J. TS191.8.T63 1986, (v1)
Todd, Daniel. VA10.T63 1996, (v10)
  VM298.5.T62 1991, (v10)
Todd, David Keith. GB1003.2.T6 1980, (v6)
Todd, Francis Murray. PR5892.P8.T6, (v3)
Todd, Janet M. PN98.W64.T63 1988, (v3)
  PR858.W6.T58 1989, (v3)
  PR3317.Z5.T645 1997, (v3)
Todd, John. QA297.T58 1977, (v1)
Todd, Kim. QL86.T64 2001, (v1)
Todd, Loreto. PE2587.T6 1990, (v3)
  PM7891.T63 1984, (v3)
Todd, Mary. BX8061.M7.T63 2000, (v8)
Todd, R. Larry. ML410.M5.T64 1993, (v9)
Todd, Richard. PR6063.U7.Z924 1984, (v3)
Todd, Robert H. TS183.T63 1994, (v1)
Todd, S. C. KL4115.A75.T63 1993, (v7)
Todd, William B. Z8802.T63 1998, (v10)
Todhunter, Andrew. GV697.A1 T63 2000, (v6)
Todhunter, I. QB283.T63 1962, (v1)
Todorov, Tzvetan. BD241.T5813 1982, (v8)
  D802.F82.S21496813 1996, (v5)
  D804.3.T6313 1996, (v5)
  E123.T6313 1984, (v4)
  P99.T613 1982, (v3)
Toelken, Barre. PN1341.T64 1995, (v3)
Toer, Pramoedya Ananta. PL5089.T8.J4513 1994, (v3)
Toff, Nancy. ML935.T65 1996, (v9)
Toffler, Alvin. HN17.5.T64, (v6)
Toffoli, Tommaso. QA267.5.C45.T64 1987, (v1)
Toker, Leona. PG3026.C64T648 2000, (v3)
Tokes, Rudolf L. JN2066.T58 1996, (v7)
Toki, Zenmaro. PL871.T6, (v3)
Tolansky, S. TS753.T59, (v1)
Tolbert, Emory J. F869.L89.N38, (v4)
Tolchin, Martin. HC110.T4.T65 1992, (v6)
Toledano, Ehud R. HN786.A8.T65 1990, (v6)
  HT1316.T65 1998, (v6)
Toliver, Harold E. PR3508.T65 1993, (v3)
  PR3546.T6, (v3)
Tolkien, J. R. R. PR6039.O32.A6 1963, (v3)
  PR6039.O32.H6 1988, (v3)
  PR6039.O32.L6 1967, (v3)
  PR6039.O32.S5, (v3)
Toll, Nelly S. N6750.T58 1998, (v9)
Toll, William. F884.P89.J57 1982, (v4)
Toller, Ernst. PT2642.O65.A25 1935, (v3)
Tolles, Frederick Barnes. BX7631.2.T6, (v8)
Tolleson-Rinehart, Sue. F391.2.T64 1994, (v4)
Tolley, Howard. K110.I46.T65 1994, (v7)
Tollison, Robert D. HD9136.T65 1988, (v6)
  HD9349.S633.U67 1991, (v6)
  HV5735.T65 1991, (v6)
Tolliver, Joyce. PQ6629.A7.Z85 1998, (v3)
Tolnay, Stewart Emory. E185.92.T65 1999, (v4)
Tolstoy, Alexandra. PG3385.T53, (v3)
Tolstoy, Leo. LB675.T62.T65 2000, (v7)
  PG3366.A13K38 1990, (v3)
  PG3366.A6 M3, (v3)
  PG3366.V6 1996, (v3)
Tolzmann, Don Heinrich. F499.C59.G38 1987, (v4)
Tom, K. S. DS721.T59 1989, (v5)
Toma, Peter A. DB2763.T66 2001, (v5)
Tomajczyk, Stephen F. UA23.T647 1996, (v10)
Tomalin, Claire. PR5841.W8.Z84 1975, (v3)
Tomaselli, Keyan G. PN1993.5.S6.T58 1988, (v3)
Tomasello, Michael. QL737.P9.T65 1997, (v1)

Tomasevic, Nebojsa. DX118.T66 1988, (v5)
Tomasi, Wayne. TK5101.T625 2001, (v1)
Tomasko, Robert M. HD69.S5.T59 1990, (v6)
Tombs, Robert. DC317.T66 1981, (v5)
Tomczak, M. GC11.2.T66 1994, (v6)
Tomek, Ivan. QA76.9.A73.T65, (v1)
Tomes, Jason. DA566.9.B2.T66 1997, (v5)
Tomes, Jonathan P. KF3825.T655 1993, (v7)
Tomes, Robert R. DS558.T66 1998, (v5)
Tomich, Dale W. HT1108.M3.T66 1990, (v6)
Tomita, Mary Kimoto. E184.J3.T65 1995, (v4)
Tomkin, Shelley Lynne. HJ2051.T63 1998, (v6)
Tomkins, Adam. KD3989.3.T66 1998, (v7)
Tomkins, Calvin. ND237.L627.A74 1988, (v9)
Tomko, Linda J. GV1588.6.T66 1999, (v6)
Tomlan, Michael A. SB317.H64.T65 1992, (v1)
Tomlin, E. W. F. B72.T43 1968, (v8)
Tomlinson, Carol A. LB1031.T66 2000, (v7)
Tomlinson, Charles. PR6039.O349.P4, (v3)
Tomlinson, Gary. ML3858.T66 1999, (v9)
Tomlinson, H. M. PR6039.O35.D3, (v3)
  PR6039.T597.M8, (v3)
  PR6039.T597.T7, (v3)
Tomlinson, Harry. SB433.5.T66 1991, (v1)
Tomlinson, Jim. HD3616.G72.T66 1994, (v6)
Tomlinson, John. CB151.T56 1991, (v5)
Tomlinson, Louise M. LB2343.4.T6 1989, (v7)
Tommasini, Anthony. ML410.T452.T58 1997, (v9)
Tomory, William M. PR6029.D58.Z89, (v3)
Tompkins, E. Berkeley. E744.T6, (v4)
Tompkins, J. M. S. PR851.T6 1961, (v3)
Tompkins, Jane P. PS374.W4.T66 1992, (v3)
Tompkins, Joanne. E99.E7.T64 1998, (v4)
Tompkins, Sally Kress. NA735.W3.T65 1993, (v9)
Tompson, William J. DK275.K5.T66 1995, (v5)
Toms, Eric. BD331.T68, (v8)
Tomsho, Robert. HV645.T65 1987, (v6)
Tonelli, Alan E. QD381.T65 2001, (v1)
Tonelson, Alan. HF1713.T686 2000, (v6)
Tonetti, Claretta. PN1998.3.B48.T66 1995, (v3)
Tong, Y. L. QA273.6.T67 1990, (v1)
Tongzon, Jose L. HC441.T663 2002, (v6)
Tonias, Demetrios E. TG300.T66 1995, (v1)
Tonnessen, J. N. SH383.T6413 1982, (v1)
Tonry, Michael H. KF9685.T66 1996, (v7)
Toole, David. B828.3.T66 1998, (v8)
Toole, John Kennedy. PS3570.O54.C66 1980, (v3)
Toole, K. Ross. F731.T65, (v4)
Toole, K. Ross. F731.T66, (v4)
Tooley, Michael. BD541.T66 1987, (v8)
  BD638.T66 2000, (v8)
  HQ767.3.T66 1983, (v6)
Tooley, R. V. GA198.T66, (v6)
Toomer, Jean. PS3539.O478.A6 1993, (v3)
  PS3539.O478.A6 1996, (v3)
  PS3539.O478.E85 1991, (v3)
Topik, Steven. E183.8.B7.T66 1996, (v4)
  HC187.T558 1987, (v6)
Topitsch, Ernst. D754.S65.T6713 1987, (v5)
Toplin, Robert Brent. PN1995.9.H5.T66 1996, (v3)
Toponce, Alexander. F596.T65 1971, (v4)
Topsfield, L. T. PQ1448.T66, (v3)
Toraǎnska, Teresa. DK4438.T67 1987, (v5)
Torbert, Alice Coyle. F202.G3 T67, (v4)
Tordoff, William. JQ1875.T67 2002, (v7)
Torgovnick, Marianna. NX456.5.P7.T67 1990, (v9)
Torme, Mel. ML419.R52.T7 1991, (v9)
Tornqvist, Egil. PN2053.T57 1990, (v3)
Torok, Josef S. QA805.T67 2000, (v1)
Toropov, Brandon. E840.T57 2000, (v4)
Torp, Linda. LB1027.42.T67 1998, (v7)
Torrance, E. Paul. LB1537.T6, (v7)
Torrance, Richard. PL817.O36.Z88 1994, (v3)
Torrans, Thomas. F786.T68 2000, (v4)
Torre, Carlos de la. JL3081.T67 2000, (v7)
Torrence, Bruce F. QA76.95.T67 1999, (v1)
Torres Villarroel, Diego de. PQ6570.T6Z478 1985, (v3)
Torres, Andres. F128.9.N3.T67 1995, (v4)
Torres, Donald A. HV7965.T67 1987, (v6)
Torres, Kenneth C. SB319.625.T67 1989, (v1)

Torres-Rioseco, Arturo. PQ7081.T733 1960, (v3)
  PQ7082.N7.T582, (v3)
Torres-Rivas, Edelberto. F1439.5.T6713 1989, (v4)
  HC141.T6713 1993, (v6)
Torres-Saillant, Silvio. PN849.C3.T67 1997, (v3)
Torretti, Roberto. QC6.T653 1990, (v1)
Torrey, E. Fuller. BF175.T68 1992, (v2)
Tors, Ivan. QL31.T59.A37, (v1)
Torstrick, Rebecca L. DS110.A3.T67 2000, (v5)
Tortella Casares, Gabriel. HC385.T64313 2000, (v6)
Tortora, Gerard J. QP34.5.T68 1986, (v1)
Tory, Avraham. DS135.R93.K288 1990, (v5)
Toscano, Salvador. F1219.3.A7.T6 1984, (v4)
Tosches, Nick. GV1132.L53 T68 2000, (v6)
Toss, Brion. VM533.T58 1984, (v10)
Toth, Emily. PS1294.C63.T68 1990, (v3)
Toth, Gabor. QA154.2.T68 1998, (v1)
Toth, Istvan Gyorgy. LC156.H9, (v7)
Totman, Conrad D. DS835.T58, (v5)
  DS850.T68 1993, (v5)
  DS871.T6, (v5)
  DS881.3.T63, (v5)
Totten, Samuel. Z6207.G44.T67 1991, (v10)
Tottle, C. R. TN609.T68 1984, (v1)
Touchton, Judith G. LC1756.T68 1991, (v7)
Tough, Frank. E78.M25.T68 1996, (v4)
Toulmin, Stephen Edelston. BC177.T59 1984, (v8)
  BC177.T6 1958, (v8)
  BD638.T67 1983, (v8)
  BJ43.T6, (v8)
Toulouse-Lautrec, Henri de. NC1850.T6.J83, (v9)
  NE2451.T64, (v9)
Touma, Habib. ML348.T6913 1996, (v9)
Toumey, Christopher P. BS651.T59 1994, (v8)
Touraine, Alain. D210.T6813 1995, (v5)
  HM101.T6513 1988, (v6)
Tourgee, Albion Winegar. PS3087.B7 1969, (v3)
  PS3087.F6 1961, (v3)
Tourish, Dennis. HN17.T69 2000, (v6)
Tourneur, Cyril. PR3170.A5.N5 1963, (v3)
Tourtellot, Arthur Bernon. E302.6.F8.T7, (v4)
Toussaint, Eric. HJ8899.T6813 1999, (v6)
Toussaint, Manuel. N6553.T6813, (v9)
Tovee, Martin J. QP475.T68 1996, (v1)
Tovey, Donald Francis. MT140.T69, (v9)
  MT145.B42.T6 1976, (v9)
Tovias, Alfred. HC241.25.S6.T68 1990, (v6)
Towell, Larry. F1488.3.T68 1997, (v4)
Tower, Cynthia Crosson. HV6626.52.T693 2002, (v6)
Towns, W. Stuart. F215.T686 1999, (v4)
  PS407.T69 1998, (v3)
Townsend, Harvey Gates. B858.T6, (v8)
Townsend, Henry. ML419.T68.A3 1999, (v9)
Townsend, James Benjamin. PR4525.D5.Z83, (v3)
Townsend, Janet G. HQ1240.5.S63.T68 1995, (v6)
Townsend, Kenneth William. D810.I5.T69 2000, (v5)
Townsend, Mary Lee. PT3803.P8.T68 1992, (v3)
Townsend, Patricia K. GF41.T57 2000, (v6)
Townsend, Richard F. F1219.73.T68 1992, (v4)
Townshend, Charles. HV8195.A2.T68 1993, (v6)
Townson, Duncan. D842.T69 1999, (v5)
Townson, Nigel. JN8395.R4, (v7)
Towse, Ruth. ML3795.T66 1993, (v9)
Toy, Sidney. NA490.T63 1955, (v9)
Toynbee, Arnold Joseph. BL50.T69 1979, (v8)
  BR127.T6, (v8)
  CB63.T613, (v5)
  CB251.T69 1953a, (v5)
  CB251.T69 1960, (v5)
  CB428.T69 1971, (v5)
  DR476.T7, (v5)
  DS721.T67 1973, (v5)
  U21.T69, (v10)
Toynbee, J. M. C. DG103.T69, (v5)
  N5843.T6 1962, (v9)
Toynbee, Paget Jackson. PQ4333.T72 1968, (v3)
Toynbee, Philip. PR6039.O8.B3, (v3)
  PR6039.O8.P7, (v3)
  UA11.T6 1974, (v10)
Toyota Conference (12th : 1998 : Shizuoka-shi, Japan). SB123.57.T69 1998, (v1)

Trabue, Daniel. F454.T728, (v4)
Trace, Arther S. LA831.82.T7, (v7)
Tracey, Karen. PS374.F45.T73 2000, (v3)
Tracey, William R. HF5549.A23.T73 1991, (v6)
Trachtenberg, Alan. E169.1.T72 1982, (v4)
Trachtenberg, Joshua. DS145.T7, (v5)
Trachtenberg, Marc. D648.T72, (v5)
　D1058.T718 1999, (v5)
Trachtenberg, Marvin. NA9070.T73 1997, (v9)
Tracy, Honor. PR6070.R25.S8X, (v3)
Tracy, James D. BR290.T73 1999, (v8)
　DJ401.H64.T73 1990, (v5)
Tracy, James. HM278.T73 1996, (v6)
Tracy, Lane. HD58.7.T73 1989, (v6)
Tracy, Paul E. HV9104.T68 1996, (v6)
Tracy, Robert. GV1785.G7.T73 1997, (v6)
Tracy, Steven C. PS3515.U274.Z8 1988, (v3)
Trafzer, Clifford E. E83.859.T7 1982, (v4)
　E99.Y2.T73 1997, (v4)
Trager, Frank N. DS518.1.T7, (v5)
Trager, James. HQ1122.T73 1994, (v6)
　TX355.T72 1995, (v1)
Trager, Lillian. DT515.45.Y67.T73 2001, (v5)
Trahair, R. C. S. HX626.T73 1999, (v6)
Traherne, Thomas. PR3736.T7, (v3)
Traill, Nancy H. PN3377.5.F34.T73 1996, (v3)
Train, John. HG172.A2, (v6)
Trainor, Luke. DU115.T73 1994, (v5)
Traister, John E. TK3284.T75 1996, (v1)
Trakl, Georg. PT2642.R21 1938, (v3)
　PT2642.R22.A23 1988, (v3)
Tralbaut, Marc Edo. ND653.G7.T67453 1969, (v9)
Tralli, Nunzio. QC174.2.T7, (v1)
Trani, Eugene P. E785.T7, (v4)
Tran-Nam, Binh. HC444.T732 2002, (v6)
Trapnell, Judson B. BX4705.G6226, (v8)
Trapp, E. Philip. RJ499.A1.T7 1972, (v2)
Trask, Kerry A. F589.M2.T73 1995, (v4)
Trask, R. L. P216.T73 1996, (v3)
Trasko, Mary. GT2290.T73 1994, (v6)
Tratner, Michael. PR478.P64.T73 1995, (v3)
　PS228.C65.T73 2001, (v3)
Trattner, Walter I. HD6250.U3.T7, (v6)
　HV91.T7 1984, (v6)
Traub, J. F. QA267.7.T7 1998, (v1)
Traub, Valerie. HQ75.6.E5 T73 2002, (v6)
　PR3069.S45.T7 1992, (v6)
Traube, Alex. F804.L3.T7 1984, (v4)
Traubner, Richard. ML1900.T7 1983, (v9)
Traugott, John. PR3716.T74, (v3)
Trautmann, Thomas R. DS425.T68 1997, (v5)
Traven, B. PT3919.T7.S43, (v3)
Travers, Martin. PN761.T68 1998, (v3)
　PT2625.A44.Z922147 1992, (v3)
Travers, Timothy. D530.T73 1987, (v5)
Traversi, Derek Antona. PR1924.T67 1987, (v3)
　PR2976.T75 1969, (v3)
　PR2982.T7, (v3)
　PR2982.T72, (v3)
Travis, A. S. HD9660.D843.E858 1993, (v6)
Travis, Frederick F. E664.K344.T73 1990, (v4)
Travis, Molly Abel. PS379.T72 1998, (v3)
Travis, Peter W. PR644.C4.T7 1982, (v3)
Travisano, Thomas J. PS310.P63.T73 1999, (v3)
　PS3503.I785.Z88 1988, (v3)
Treadgold, Donald W. DK246.T65 1981, (v5)
Treadgold, Warren T. DF581.T73 1988, (v5)
Treadway, John D. DR1846.A9 T73 1983, (v5)
Treadwell, Edward Francis. F594.M62T73, (v4)
Treasure, G. R. R. DC130.M4.T73 1995, (v5)
Treat, John Whittier. PL830.B8.Z9 1988, (v3)
Trebat, Thomas J. HD4093.T727 1983, (v6)
Treckel, Paula A. HQ1416.T74 1996, (v6)
Tredell, Nicolas. PR6073.I44.Z87 1982, (v3)
Tree, Christina. F62.3.T74 1987, (v4)
Treece, Dave. F2519.3.P58.T73 2000, (v4)
Treece, Henry. PR6039.R38.D3, (v3)
　PR6039.R38.E4x, (v3)
　PR6039.R38.G6 1957, (v3)
　PR6039.R38.G7 1956, (v3)
Treese, Lorett. F152.T84 1992, (v4)

Trefethen, Lloyd N. QA184.T74 1997, (v1)
Trefil, James S. QB14.5.T74 1988, (v1)
　QB991.B54.T7 1983, (v1)
Trefousse, Hans Louis. E415.9.S84.T74 1997, (v4)
　E449.T79, (v4)
　E664.S39 T7 1998, (v4)
　E667.T74 1989, (v4)
Trefusis, Violet Keppel. PR6039.R39.Z493 1990, (v3)
Tregaskis, Richard. D767.98.T7 1955, (v5)
Tregear, T. R. DS711.T68 1966, (v5)
Treggiari, Susan. KJA2233.T74 1991, (v7)
Tregle, Joseph George. F374.T74 1999, (v4)
Trehane, Jennifer. SB413.C18.T675 1998, (v1)
Trehub, Arnold. QP376.T72 1991, (v1)
Treib, Marc. NA5230.N6.T74 1993, (v9)
Treiman, Rebecca. LB1526.T74 1993, (v7)
Treiman, Sam B. QC174.12.T73 1999, (v1)
Treitler, Leo. ML3845.T77 1989, (v9)
Trelawny, Edward John. PR5671.T5.A6 1974, (v3)
Trelease, Jim. LB1573.5.T68 2001, (v7)
Tremain, Mary. E445.D6 T7 1969, (v4)
Tremblay, Florent A. Z7004.G7.T74 1996, (v10)
Tremblay, Michel. PQ3919.2.T73.B4, (v3)
Tremper, Ellen. PR6045.O72.Z885 1998, (v3)
Trend, David. HN65.T7 1997, (v6)
Trend, J. B. DP48.T72 1965, (v5)
　PQ6077.T7, (v3)
Trenhaile, Alan S. GB451.2.T735 1997, (v6)
Trennert, Robert A. E97.6.P4.T74 1988, (v4)
Trent, James W. HV3006.A4.T74 1994, (v6)
Treptow, Kurt W. DR215.T74 1996, (v5)
Tressell, Robert. PR6039.R388 R3, (v3)
Trest, Warren A. UG626.2.A335.T74 2000, (v10)
Trevelyan, George Macaulay. DA32.T7487 1946, (v5)
　DA32.T749 1973, (v5)
　DA375.T7 1949, (v5)
　DA495.T7, (v5)
　DA565.B8.T8 1971, (v5)
Trevelyan, George Otto. DA506.F7.T87 1921, (v5)
Treverton, Gregory F. UB251.U5.T74 2001, (v10)
Trevett, Jeremy. DF233.8.A66.T74 1992, (v5)
Trevino, A. Javier. K366.T74 1998, (v7)
Trevor, William. PR6070.R4.B6, (v3)
　PR6070.R4.L6, (v3)
　PR6070.R4.O4 1964, (v3)
Trevor-Roper, H. R. D7.T79 1957, (v5)
　DD247.H5.T7 1971, (v5)
Trew, Simon. D802.Y8.T65 1997, (v5)
Trewartha, Glenn Thomas. QC981.T65 1980, (v1)
Trewin, J. C. PR3091.T72, (v3)
　PR3106.T7, (v3)
Trezise, Simon. ML410.D28.T7 1994, (v9)
Trezise, Thomas. PQ2603.E378.Z89 1990, (v3)
Trias Monge, Jose. F1971.T75 1997, (v4)
Triay, Victor Andres. HV640.5.C9.T74 1998, (v6)
Tribble, Alan C. QB500.25.T75 2000, (v1)
Tribble, Evelyn B. PR418.T48.T75 1993, (v3)
Tribe, Ivan M. ML421.S8 T7 1993, (v9)
Tribe, Laurence H. HQ767.5.U5.T73 1990, (v6)
Triber, Jayne E. F69.R43 T75 1998, (v4)
Tricard, Louise Mead. GV1060.8.T75 1996, (v6)
Trice, Harrison Miller. HD58.7.T74 1993, (v6)
Trickett, Edison J. LD7501.N374.T73 1991, (v7)
Tricomi, Albert H. PR421.T75 1996, (v3)
Triem, Eve. PS3539.R5.N63 1993, (v3)
Trierweiler, Steven J. RC467.8.T74 1998, (v2)
Trigg, Roger. BD450.T668 1999, (v8)
　BL51.T65 1998, (v8)
　Q175.T74 1993, (v1)
Trigger, Bruce G. CC75.T68 1978, (v5)
　CC115.C45.T74 1980, (v5)
Trigger, David S. GN667.Q4.T75 1991, (v6)
Triggs, J. H. [from old catalog]. F761.T83, (v4)
Trilling, Lionel. PN511.T76, (v3)
　PR4023.T7 1949, (v3)
　PS3539.R56.M5, (v3)
　PS3539.R56.M6 2000, (v3)
Trimble, Virginia. QB51.T75 1992, (v1)
Trimble, William F. V63.M57.T75 1994, (v10)
Trimiew, Darryl M. BJ1251.N523.T75 1993, (v8)
Trimpi, Helen P. Q11.C9 vol. 49, p. 1-339, (v1)

Trinh, T. Minh-Ha. PN1998.3.T76.A3 1992, (v3)
Trinka, Zena Irma. F636.T85, (v4)
Trinkaus, Charles Edward. CB361.T74 1983, (v5)
Trinkaus, Erik. GN285.T73 1993, (v6)
Trinkley, Michael. F279.G53.T75 1992, (v4)
Tripathi, Surya Kant. PK2098.T7.A27 1977, (v3)
Tripodi, Tony. HV11.T75, (v6)
Tripolitis, Antonia. BL722.T75 2001, (v8)
Tripp, Aili Mari. HC885.Z7.D377 1997, (v6)
Tripp, Anne Huber. HD5325.T42 1913.P387 1987, (v6)
Tripp, Steven Elliott. F234.L9.T75 1997, (v4)
Trites, Roberta Seelinger. PN3426.C5.T75 1997, (v3)
　PS374.A3.T75 2000, (v3)
Tritle, Lawrence A. HN650.5.Z9.V58 2000, (v6)
Trivieri, Larry. R733.T755 2001, (v2)
Trobisch, David. BS2320.T7613 2000, (v8)
　BS2655.C36.T76 1994, (v8)
Trobriand, Régis de. F655.T8413 1982, (v4)
Troccoli, Joan Carpenter. ND1441.5.T76 2000, (v9)
Trocki, Carl A. HN700.67.A8.T76 1990, (v6)
Trofimenkoff, Susan Mann. F1053.T84, (v4)
Troike, Rudolph C. Z7001.T78 1990, (v10)
Troitsky, M. S. TG300.T76 1994, (v1)
　TG380.T76 1990, (v1)
Troland, Leonard T. BF683.T7 1967, (v2)
Trolander, Judith Ann. HV4194.T74 1987, (v6)
Trollope, Anthony. E167.T8425 1869a, (v4)
　PR5682.B73, (v3)
　PR5684.A1, (v3)
　PR5684.A8 1981, (v3)
　PR5684.B3 1950, (v3)
　PR5684.B38 1985, (v3)
　PR5684.C5 1924, (v3)
　PR5684.CA16, (v3)
　PR5684.D6 1928, (v3)
　PR5684.D6 1931, (v3)
　PR5684.E7 1992, (v3)
　PR5684.F7, (v3)
　PR5684.F7 1984, (v3)
　PR5684.H4, (v3)
　PR5684.I8 1944, (v3)
　PR5684.J64, (v3)
　PR5684.K4 1929, (v3)
　PR5684.L3 1967, (v3)
　PR5684.M37 1982, (v3)
　PR5684.O4 1936, (v3)
　PR5684.O7 1950, (v3)
　PR5684.P39 1972, (v3)
　PR5684.P4 1951, (v3)
　PR5684.P7 1951, (v3)
　PR5684.R3 1980, (v3)
　PR5684.R34 1939, (v3)
　PR5684.S6 1939, (v3)
　PR5684.T5, (v3)
　PR5684.V5 1924, (v3)
　PR5684.W22 1952, (v3)
　PR5684.W38 1974, (v3)
　PR5686.A4 1983, (v3)
　PR5686.A5 1950, (v3)
Trollope, Frances Milton. E165.T84 1984, (v4)
Tromly, Frederic B. PR2677.T37.T76 1998, (v3)
Tromp, Marlene. PR878.M36, (v3)
Trompf, G. W. D16.8.T76, (v5)
Troper, Harold Martin. F1035.J5.T76 1989, (v4)
Tropman, John E. HC110.P6.T76 1998, (v6)
　HD62.5.T76 1989, (v6)
Tropp, Martin. PR830.T3.T76 1990, (v3)
Trosset, Carol. DA711.5.T76 1993, (v5)
Trotsky, Leon. DK254.L4.T7 1971, (v5)
　DK254.T6.A25 1963, (v5)
　DK254.T6.A48, (v5)
　DK265.T773 1957, (v5)
　DK267.T73, (v5)
　DK268.S8.T7 1968, (v5)
　DS775.T7 1966, (v5)
Trotter, Joe William. F520.6.N4.T76 1998, (v4)
　HD8039.M62.U66943 1990, (v6)
Trotter, Michael H. KF315.T76 1997, (v7)
Trotter, William R. DL1097.T76 1991, (v5)
　ML422.M59.T76 1995, (v9)
Troup, Calvin L. BR65.A62.T78 1999, (v8)

Trout, Andrew P. DC729.T76 1996, (v5)
Trout, Charles H. F73.5.T76, (v4)
Trout, Dennis E. PA6554.P5.Z89 1999, (v3)
Trowell, Kathleen Margaret. NB1080.T76, (v9)
Troy, Gil. JK524.T76 1991, (v7)
Troy, Nancy J. NK947.T76 1991, (v9)
Troyan, Michael. PN2287.G393.T76 1999, (v3)
Troyansky, David G. HQ1064.F7.T76 1989, (v6)
Troyat, Henri. PG3385.T8713, (v3)
    PQ2639.R78.A8 1938, (v3)
    PQ2639.R78.N4, (v3)
    PQ2639.R78.T3 1972, (v3)
Troyen, Carol. N6537.S523.A4 1987a, (v9)
Trubowitz, Peter. E183.7.T84 1998, (v4)
Trudeau, Noah Andre. E540.N3 T78 1998, (v4)
True, Michael. PS169.N65.T78 1995, (v3)
Trueba, Enrique T. E184.S75.T78 1999, (v4)
    LC2637.C2.C44 1993, (v7)
Trueblood, Elton. BD21.T7, (v8)
Truesdell, Matthew. DC278.T78 1997, (v5)
Truettner, William H. ND237.C35.T78 1979, (v9)
Truffaut, Francois. PN1994.T717 1993, (v3)
Trujillo, David M. TA342.T78 1997, (v1)
Truman, Harry S. E742.5.T6 1980a, (v4)
    E814.A327 1986, (v4)
    E814.A4 1982b, (v4)
    E814.A4 1983, (v4)
    J82.D7 1984, (v7)
    JC599.U5.T7, (v7)
Truman, Margaret. E814.T8 1984, (v4)
Trumbull, John. ND237.T8.A32 1970, (v9)
    PS852.A1 1968, (v3)
    PS852.P7 1962, (v3)
Trumbull, Robert. D811.5.T78, (v5)
Trump, Kenneth S. LB2866.5.T78 2000, (v7)
Trumpener, Katie. PR868.N356.T78 1997, (v3)
Trundle, Robert C. BD171.T69 1999, (v8)
Trunk, Isaiah. D810.J4.T7, (v5)
Trupin, Sophie. F645.J5T78 1988, (v4)
Truscott, Peter. DK510.763.T78 1997, (v5)
Trussell-Cullen, Alan. LA2124.T78 1996, (v7)
Trussler, Simon. PN2581.T78 1994, (v3)
Trusted, Jennifer. BD632.T78 1991, (v8)
Truxal, John G. TK5101.T79 1990, (v1)
Tryggvi J. Oleson. E105.O48, (v4)
Tryster, Hillel. PN1995.75.T79 1995, (v3)
Trzynadlowski, Andrzej. TK2785.T75 2001, (v1)
Tsagaris, Ellen M. PR6066.Y58.Z88 1998, (v3)
Tsai, Jung-fang. DS796.H757.T77 1993, (v5)
Tsai, Shih-shan Henry. DS753.6.M43 T75 2001, (v5)
Tsai, Ting-kan. PL2658.E3.T7 1991, (v3)
Tsang, Cheryl D. HD9696.63.U64.M538 2000, (v6)
Tsang, Chiu-sam. DS777.55.T73 1968, (v5)
Tsang, Steve Yui-Sang. DS796.H757.T735 1997, (v5)
Tsanoff, Radoslav Andrea. B72.T8 1953, (v8)
Tsao, Hsueh-chin. PL2727.S2.S713 1979, (v3)
Tsao, Kuan-lung. PL2912.A5335.A77 1996, (v3)
Tschernich, Rudy W. QE391.Z5.T73 1992, (v1)
Tschi˜zewskij, Dmitrij. PG3905.C513 1997, (v3)
Tschichold, Jan. Z116.T7513 1995, (v10)
Tseelon, Efrat. HQ1219.T74 1995, (v6)
Tseng, Wen-Shing. RC488.5.T79 1991, (v2)
Tsering Shakya. DS786.T679 1999, (v5)
Tsien, Tsuen-hsuin. Z45.T85, (v10)
Tsing, Anna Lowenhaupt. DS646.32.D9.T75 1993, (v5)
Tsivian, Yuri. PN1993.5.R9.T7713 1994, (v3)
Tso-chiu, Ming. PL2470.K8 1989, (v3)
Tsogas, George. K1705.T77 2001, (v7)
Tsonis, Panagiotis A. QP90.2.T76 1996, (v1)
Tsou, Tang. DS777.53.T866, (v5)
Tsoukalis, Loukas. HC241.2.T74 1991, (v6)
Tsouras, Peter. PN6084.W35.T75 1992, (v3)
Tsui, Chi. DS735.T75 1942, (v5)
Tsuji, Masatsugu. QA355.T77 1975, (v1)
Tsujimoto, Karen. N6537.B783.A4 1998, (v9)
    ND212.5.P67.T83 1982, (v9)
Tsukamoto, Zenryu. BQ636.T75713 1985, (v8)
Tsung, Pu. PL2912.U526.E93 1998, (v3)
Tsunoda, Ryusaku. DS821.T76, (v5)
Tsur, Samuel A. QH83.T77 1999, (v1)

Tsurutani, Taketsugu. UA845.T85 1981, (v10)
Tsushima, Yuko. PL862.S76.C413 1983, (v3)
Tsuzuki, Chushichi. DS881.9.T77 2000, (v5)
Tu, Fu. PL2997.T8.Z54 1929, (v3)
Tu, Wei-ming. BL1852.T8 1993, (v8)
Tuan, Yi-fu. BJ1031.T77 1989, (v8)
Tubb, Jonathan N. DS121.4.T83 1998, (v5)
Tucci, Giuseppe. BL1945.T5.T815, (v8)
    DS786.T7713, (v5)
    DS786.T8, (v5)
Tuccille, Jerome. HB119.G74 T83 2002, (v6)
Tuchman, Arleen. R511.B33.T8 1993, (v2)
Tuchman, Barbara Wertheim. D210.T89 1984, (v5)
    D530.T8, (v5)
    E271.T83 1988, (v4)
    E745.S68.T8, (v4)
Tuchman, Gaye. PR115.T8 1989, (v3)
Tucholsky, Kurt. PT2642.U4 1975, (v3)
Tuck, Richard. B1247.T8 1989, (v8)
Tucker, Barbara M. HD9860.S5.T83 1984, (v6)
Tucker, D. F. B. KF8748.T83 1995, (v7)
Tucker, David M. HN57.T77 1998, (v6)
    SB320.6.T83 1993, (v1)
Tucker, David. HV6431.T83 1997, (v6)
Tucker, George Holbert. PR4036.T83 1994, (v3)
Tucker, Herbert F. PR5592.R63.T83 1988, (v3)
Tucker, Irene. PR4658.A7, (v3)
Tucker, Judith E. KMC145.W64.T83 1998, (v7)
Tucker, Karen B. Westerfield. BX8337.T83 2001, (v8)
Tucker, Louis Leonard. F61.M43.T83 1995, (v4)
Tucker, Mark. ML410.E44 T8 1990, (v9)
Tucker, Paul Hayes. ND553.M7.T79 1995, (v9)
    ND553.M7.T83 1989, (v9)
Tucker, Phillip Thomas. E635.B36.T84 1992, (v4)
Tucker, Ray Thomas. E747.T933, (v4)
Tucker, Richard P. HD1417.T83 2000, (v6)
Tucker, Robert C. B3305.M74.T8 1972, (v8)
    DK268.S8.T85 1973, (v5)
    DK268.S8 T86 1990, (v5)
Tucker, Robert W. E332.45.T83 1990, (v4)
    E881.H46 1992, (v4)
    JX1295.U4 vol. 50, (v7)
    U21.T8, (v4)
Tucker, Spencer. D521.T83 1998, (v5)
    V895.T83 1993, (v10)
Tucker, Wallace H. QB472.T82 2001, (v1)
Tucker, William. HD7293.T77 1990, (v6)
Tucker, Wilson. PS3539.T799.L6 1969, (v3)
Tuckerman, Frederick Goddard. PS3104.T5 1965, (v3)
Tuckett, C. M. BS2331.T83 1987, (v8)
Tudge, Colin. GN281.T84 1996, (v6)
    QH83.T84 2000, (v1)
    QH437.T83 1995, (v1)
    QH437.T8333 2001, (v1)
    QH541.T819 1991, (v1)
    QL82.T83 1992, (v1)
Tugay, Emine Foat. CT1474.T8, (v5)
Tugwell, Franklin. HD9566.T85 1988, (v6)
Tugwell, Rexford G. E805.T8, (v4)
    H59.T8.A3, (v4)
    HC106.3.T78 1969, (v6)
Tulchinsky, Gerald J. J. F1035.J5.T85 1993, (v4)
Tulchinsky, Theodore H. RA425.T85 2000, (v2)
Tulis, Jeffrey. JK518.T84 1987, (v7)
Tullidge, Edward W[heelock]. F834.S2 T9, (v4)
Tullis, F. LaMond. HV5801.T78 1991, (v6)
Tulloch, John. PN1992.65.T85 1989, (v3)
Tully, Alan. JK99.N69.T85 1994, (v7)
Tully, Dennis. HC835.Z7.D377 1988, (v6)
Tully, James. JF1061.T85 1995, (v7)
Tuma, Keith. PR605.M63.T86 1998, (v3)
Tumarkin, Nina. DK254.L46.T85 1983, (v5)
Tunander, Ola. V55.N73.T86 1989, (v10)
Tung Chieh-yuan. PL2687.T9.H813 1976, (v3)
Tung, Louise Watanabe. Q123.T844 1993, (v1)
Tunick, Mark. K370.T86 1998, (v7)
    K5103.T86 1992, (v7)
Tunick, Susan. NA3511.N48.T86 1997, (v9)
Tunnard, Christopher. NA9105.T85, (v9)
    NA9108.T82, (v9)

Tunnell, James E. Z104.T89 1990, (v10)
Tunner, William H. UC333.T85 1985, (v10)
Tunstall, Jeremy. PN5117.T86 1995, (v3)
Tuohy, Frank. PR6070.U58.A3, (v3)
Tuohy, Thomas. DG975.F42.T86 1996, (v5)
Tuppen, John N. HC276.3.T86 1988, (v6)
Turabian, Kate L. LB2369.T8 1996, (v7)
Turbayne, Colin Murray. B840.T8 1970, (v8)
    BD418.3.T87 1991, (v8)
Turberville, Arthur Stanley. DA485.T77, (v5)
Turcan, Robert. BL805.T8713 1996, (v8)
Turcheneske, John Anthony. E99.C68.T87 1997, (v4)
Turco, Lewis. PN44.5.T87 1999, (v3)
Turcotte, Donald Lawson. QE33.2.M3.T87 1992, (v1)
    QE501.T83 2001, (v1)
Turek, Vojtech. QE721.T87 1989, (v1)
Turekian, Karl K. QC861.2.T87 1996, (v1)
Turgenev, Ivan Sergeevich. PG3420.O8.E5 1994, (v3)
    PG3421.A19.M3 1970, (v3)
    PG3421.A2A45 1994, (v3)
Turgeon, Mary Louise. RB145.T79 1999, (v2)
Turim, Maureen Cheryn. PN1998.3.O84.T87 1998, (v3)
Turino, Thomas. ML3503.Z55, (v9)
    ML3575.P4.T87 1993, (v9)
Turk, Eleanor L. DD90.T87 1999, (v5)
Turk, Richard W. E757.T87 1987, (v4)
Turkington, Carol. RA1224.5.T873 1999, (v2)
    RC848.H425.T87 1998, (v2)
    RF290.T93 2000, (v2)
Turkle, Sherry. QA76.9.C66T87 1995, (v1)
Turnbaugh, Douglas Blair. ND497.G68.T87 1987, (v9)
Turnbo, S. C. F417.W5 T87 1994, (v4)
Turnbull, Archibald Douglas. VG93.T8, (v10)
Turnbull, Colin M. GN654.T87, (v6)
Turnbull, Eleanor L. PQ6267.E3.T8 1968, (v3)
Turnbull, George Stanley. PN4897.O73T8, (v3)
Turnbull, Michael. ML420.G25.T87 1997, (v9)
Turnell, Martin. PQ527.T8 1971, (v3)
    PQ631.T83, (v3)
Turner, Charles. HM22.G3.W4587 1992, (v6)
Turner, Cheryl. PR858.W6.T8 1992, (v3)
Turner, Christy G. E78.S7.T877 1999, (v4)
Turner, Dorothea. PR6025.A473.Z9, (v3)
Turner, Edith L. B. DT3058.N44.T87 1992, (v5)
    E99.E7.T826 1996, (v4)
Turner, Edward T. GV1003.34.T87 1996, (v6)
Turner, Francis J. QE475.T89 1981, (v1)
Turner, Frederick Jackson. E175.5.T83.A43 1970, (v4)
    E178.A555 v.14, (v4)
    E179.5.T956 1962, (v4)
    E179.5.T958 1984, (v4)
    E338.T92 1965, (v4)
Turner, Frederick. BH39.T87 1992, (v8)
    PR3021.T87 1999, (v3)
Turner, George Edgar. E491.T95 1972, (v4)
Turner, George. PR9619.3.T868.D75 1987, (v3)
Turner, Gordon Brinkerhoff. U39.T87 1953, (v10)
    UA23.T84 1960a, (v10)
Turner, Harold W. Z7835.C86.T87 1977, (v10)
Turner, Harriet S. PQ6555.F73.T87 1992, (v3)
Turner, Henry Ashby. DD240.T8, (v5)
Turner, Henry Smith. F786.T9, (v4)
Turner, Herbert Hall. QB32.T92 1963, (v1)
Turner, Howard R. Q127.I742.T78 1997, (v1)
Turner, Hy B. PN4899.N4.T87 1999, (v3)
Turner, J. Rick. QA279.T86 2001, (v1)
Turner, J. Scott. QL756.T87 2000, (v1)
Turner, James. BL2757.T87 1985, (v8)
    PN4874.T79 1999, (v3)
Turner, Jeffrey S. HM132.T83 1996, (v6)
Turner, John. DA577.T86 1992, (v5)
Turner, Jonathan H. BF531.T87 2000, (v2)
Turner, Lowell. HD6483.T87 1991, (v6)
    HD8541.T87 1998, (v6)
Turner, Lynn W. F38.T87 1983, (v4)
Turner, Margaret. PR9192.6.N37.T87 1995, (v3)

Turner, Marjorie Shepherd. HB103.K47.T87 1993, **(v6)**
  HB103.R63.T87 1989, **(v6)**
Turner, Mark W. PR5688.P6.T87 1999, **(v3)**
Turner, Mark. PN49.T77 1996, **(v3)**
Turner, Martha A. PR830.S34.T87 1993, **(v3)**
Turner, Nancy J. QK100.A1.T87 1991, **(v1)**
Turner, Patricia. GR111.A47.T87 1993, **(v6)**
Turner, Paul. PR4753.T87 1998, **(v3)**
Turner, Peter R. QA297.T88 2001, **(v1)**
Turner, R. M. QK142.T87 1995, **(v1)**
Turner, R. Steven. QP491.T87 1994, **(v1)**
Turner, Ralph Lamar. PN1995.9.W4.T76 1999, **(v3)**
Turner, Richard. N6921.F7.T83 1997, **(v9)**
  N6923.L33.T87 1993, **(v9)**
Turner, Stansfield. U264.T87 1997, **(v10)**
Turner, Stephen P. HM22.U5.T87 1990, **(v6)**
Turner, Victor Witter. GN451.T87, **(v6)**
Turner, Wayne C. TJ163.2.T87 2001, **(v1)**
Turnock, David. DA850.T875 1995, **(v5)**
  GF645.E92.T87 1989, **(v6)**
Turow, Joseph. HF5813.U6.T85 1997, **(v6)**
Turow, Scott. KF373.T88 A33 1988, **(v7)**
Turshen, Meredeth. RA418.T915 1989, **(v2)**
Turville-Petre, Gabriel. PT7172.T83, **(v3)**
Turville-Petre, Thorlac. PE659.A6.T8, **(v3)**
  PR275.N29.T87 1996, **(v3)**
Tusa, Ann. DD881.T87 1997, **(v5)**
Tusa, Michael Charles. ML410.W3.T9 1991, **(v9)**
Tushnet, Mark V. KF4575.T87 1988, **(v7)**
  KF4575.T874 1999, **(v7)**
  KF4755.T87 1994, **(v7)**
  KF8745.M34.T87 1997, **(v7)**
  KF9725.T87 1994, **(v7)**
Tuska, Jon. F786.B54.T87 1983, **(v4)**
  PN1998.2.T8 1991, **(v3)**
Tusquets, Esther. PQ6670.U8.M513 1990, **(v3)**
Tussman, Malka Heifetz. PJ5129.T87.A25 1992, **(v3)**
Tuttle, Carolyn. HD6250.G7 T88 1999, **(v6)**
Tuttle, Frederick B. LC3993.T83 1988, **(v7)**
Tutuola, Amos. PR6070.U8.P3 1970, **(v3)**
Tuve, Rosemond. PR3588.T8, **(v3)**
Tuveson, Ernest Lee. PR3726.T86, **(v3)**
Tuzin, Donald F. DU740.42.T84 1997, **(v5)**
Tvede, Lars. HB3714.T84 1997, **(v6)**
Tveito, Aslak. QA377.T9 1998, **(v1)**
Tver, David F. GC9.T86, **(v6)**
  TN865.T83, **(v1)**
Tveter, Donald R. Q335.T9 1998, **(v1)**
Twain, Mark. F353.C6456 1950, **(v4)**
  F869.S3.C57, **(v4)**
  PS1300.F72 vol.2 1993, **(v3)**
  PS1300.F72 vol. 8, **(v3)**
  PS1302.N4, **(v3)**
  PS1302.T8 1980, **(v3)**
  PS1303.R37 1997, **(v3)**
  PS1305.A2.H4 1981, **(v3)**
  PS1308.A1 1960, **(v3)**
  PS1316.A1 1983, **(v3)**
  PS1317.B4 1980, **(v3)**
  PS1331.A3.F3, **(v3)**
  PS1331.A4 1987, **(v3)**
  PS1331.A4 1991, **(v3)**
Twentieth Century Fund. KF8776.T94 1988, **(v7)**
Tweton, D. Jerome. F612.O9.T84 1988, **(v4)**
  F636.T88, **(v4)**
T-W-Fiennes, Richard N. RA639.F53, **(v2)**
Twiname, B. Gayle. RT73.T94 1999, **(v2)**
Twing, Stephen W. JZ1479.T88 1998, **(v7)**
Twitchell, James B. CB358.T84 1989, **(v5)**
  HC110.C6.T89 1999, **(v6)**
Twitchell, Marshall Harvey. F375.T95 1989, **(v4)**
Twohey, Michael. JQ1510.T95 1999, **(v7)**
Twombly, Robert C. NA2707.S94.A4 2000, **(v9)**
Tworzecki, Hubert. JN6769.A45.T94 1996, **(v7)**
Twyning, John. PR8476.T95 1998, **(v3)**
Ty, Eleanor Rose. PR858.W6.T93 1998, **(v3)**
Tyack, David B. LA205.T9, **(v7)**
  LA216.T92 1995, **(v7)**
  LB2805.T9 1982, **(v7)**
  LB3066.T93 1990, **(v7)**

Tyckoson, David A. Z6033.E1 T9 1986, **(v10)**
Tye, Barbara Benham. LB2822.82.T94 2000, **(v7)**
  LC1090.T97 1992, **(v7)**
Tye, Michael. B808.9.T935 2003, **(v8)**
  BF161.T94 1989, **(v2)**
Tyerman, Christopher. DA176.T94 1988, **(v5)**
Tygiel, Jules. GV865.R6 T93 1997, **(v6)**
Tyldesley, Joyce A. DT61.T95 2000, **(v5)**
  DT87.45.T95 1998, **(v5)**
Tylecote, R. F. TN615.T94, **(v1)**
Tyler, Anne. PS3570.Y45.S4, **(v3)**
Tyler, Bruce Michael. NX512.3.A35.T95 1992, **(v9)**
Tyler, Daniel. E409.5.I72 T9, **(v4)**
Tyler, David Budlong. VM615.T9 1939, **(v10)**
Tyler, Gus. HD6515.C62.I558 1995, **(v6)**
Tyler, Hamilton A. QL561.P2.T82 1994, **(v1)**
Tyler, James. ML1015.G9.T95, **(v9)**
  ML1015.M2.T9 1989, **(v9)**
Tyler, Moses Coit. E302.6.H5.T94, **(v4)**
Tyler, Ronnie C. NE962.W48.T96 1994, **(v9)**
Tyler, Royall. PS855.T7.A16 1972, **(v3)**
  PS855.T7.C6 1970, **(v3)**
Tyler, S. Lyman. F1619.T83 1988, **(v4)**
Tyler, Tom R. K250.T95 1990, **(v7)**
Tymn, Marshall B. PR830.F3.T9, **(v3)**
Tymoczko, Maria. PR6019.O9.U748 1994, **(v3)**
Tyner, Kathleen R. LC149.5.T96 1998, **(v7)**
Tyrrell, Ian R. HV5227.T97 1991, **(v6)**
Tyson, Laura D'Andrea. HC110.H53.T94 1993, **(v6)**
Tyson, Neil De Grasse. QB982.T97 1994, **(v1)**
Tyson, Phyllis. BF713.T97 1990, **(v2)**
Tyson, Timothy B. F264.M75.T97 1999, **(v4)**
Tzeng, Oliver C. S. HV713.T94 1991, **(v6)**
Tzonis, Alexander. NA1313.C35.T9723 1999, **(v9)**
Tzou, Byron N. DS737.T96 1990, **(v5)**
Ubbelohde, Carl. F776.U195 2001, **(v4)**
Ubel, Peter A. RA410.5.U23 1999, **(v2)**
Uchill, Ida Libert. F785.J5U3 2000, **(v4)**
Uchino, Tatsuro. HC462.9.U2613 1983, **(v6)**
Udall, Nicholas. PR3176.U3.A7 1912, **(v3)**
Udall, Sharyn Rohlfsen. N6527.U3 1996, **(v9)**
Udall, Stewart L. E125.V3 U215 1995, **(v4)**
Udelson, Joseph H. PR5923.U34 1990, **(v3)**
Ueberhuber, Christoph W. QA297.U2413 1997, **(v1)**
Ueda, Akinari. PL794.8.H313, **(v3)**
  PL794.8.U35 1974, **(v3)**
  PL794.8.U52, **(v3)**
Ueda, Atsushi. NA7451.U3313 1990, **(v9)**
Ueda, Makoto. PL726.55.U28, **(v3)**
  PL733.55.U38 1983, **(v3)**
  PL794.4.Z5.U39 1992, **(v3)**
  PL794.7.U34 1998, **(v3)**
Ueda, Reed. LA222.U34 1987, **(v7)**
Uekert, Brenda K. D842.U35 1995, **(v5)**
Ugaki, Matome. D777.U3513 1991, **(v5)**
Ugalde, Luis Carlos. JL1265.U38 2000, **(v7)**
Uglow, Jennifer S. PR4681.U35 1987, **(v3)**
Uhlig, Helmut. TP248.E5.U37 1998, **(v1)**
Uhlin, Anders. JQ776.U35 1997, **(v7)**
Uhlmann, Anthony. PR6003.E282.Z86 1999, **(v3)**
Uhr, John. JQ4054.U57 1998, **(v7)**
Uitti, Karl D. PQ1448.U38 1995, **(v3)**
Ukadike, Nwachukwu Frank. PN1993.5.A35.U4 1994, **(v3)**
Ulack, Richard. G2360.U4 1989, **(v6)**
Ulam, Adam Bruno. DK221.U38 1977, **(v5)**
  DK246.U4, **(v5)**
  DK266.U49 1974, **(v5)**
  DK268.S8.U4 1973, **(v5)**
  DK274.U4 1983, **(v5)**
  DR370.U4 1971, **(v5)**
  E183.8.R9.U4 1971, **(v4)**
Ulanov, Ann Belford. HQ1206.U47, **(v6)**
Ulett, George A. RM184.U433 2002, **(v2)**
Ulich, Robert. BD431.U5, **(v8)**
  LA21.U4 1967, **(v7)**
  LB875.U6 1970, **(v7)**
Ullman, Dana. RX71.U46 1991, **(v2)**
  RX76.U467 1999, **(v2)**
Ullman, Edward Louis. G116.U44, **(v6)**
Ullman, James Ramsey. PS3541.L39.D3, **(v3)**

  PS3541.L39.W5, **(v3)**
Ullman, Jeffrey D. QA76.9.D3.U443 1988, **(v1)**
Ullman, Montague. BF1078.U44, **(v2)**
Ullman, Shimon. QP475.U44 1996, **(v1)**
Ullmann, Fritz. TP9.U57 1985, **(v1)**
Ullmann, Manfred. DS36.85.I8 no. 11, **(v5)**
Ullmann, Stephen. PQ635.U4, **(v3)**
Ullmann, Walter. CB361.U43, **(v5)**
  JA82.U4, **(v7)**
Ulloa, Antonio de. F2221.U45213 1975, **(v4)**
Ulloa, Miguel. QK600.35.U513 2000, **(v1)**
Ulmer, William Andrew. PR5442.L6.U46 1990, **(v3)**
Ulrich, David. HD57.7.U45 1999, **(v6)**
Ulrich, Deborah L. RT76.U46 1999, **(v2)**
Ulrich, Homer. ML1100.U4 1966, **(v9)**
  ML1200.U4, **(v9)**
Ulrich, Laurel. F8.U47 2001, **(v4)**
  F29.H15 U47 1991, **(v4)**
Ulrich, Lawrence P. R726.U39 1999, **(v2)**
Ulving, Tor. PL1201.U58 1997, **(v3)**
Uman, Martin A. QC966.U4 1987, **(v1)**
Umansky, Lauri. HQ1421.U43 1996, **(v6)**
Umapathy, Srinivasan. HG4028.B8.U46 1987, **(v6)**
Umble, Diane Zimmerman. BX8128.T45 U53 1996, **(v8)**
Umland, Rebecca A. PN1995.9.A75.U44 1996, **(v3)**
Umphlett, Wiley Lee. GV939.H38.U46 1992, **(v6)**
Unamuno, Miguel de. B4568.U53.D5 1954, **(v8)**
  PQ6352.U5 1938, **(v3)**
  PQ6639.N3.A25 1976 vol. 6, **(v3)**
  PQ6639.N3.A25 vol. 1, **(v3)**
  PQ6639.N3.A25 vol. 2, **(v3)**
  PQ6639.N3.A7 1947a, **(v3)**
  PQ6639.N3.S3 1933, **(v3)**
  PQ6639.N3 1995, **(v3)**
Underhill, Evelyn. BV5081.U55 1930, **(v8)**
  BV5082.U5, **(v8)**
Underhill, Lois Beachy. HQ1413.W66.U53 1995, **(v6)**
Underhill, Robert. E176.1.U5 1988, **(v4)**
Underhill, Ruth Murray. E99.P25.U5194, **(v4)**
  E99.P9.U314 1991, **(v4)**
  ML3557.U53 1976, **(v9)**
Underhill, Stefan. KF297.U53 1995, **(v7)**
Underwood, Doug. PN4734.U63 1993, **(v3)**
Underwood, Edna (Worthley). PE1574.G52, **(v3)**
Underwood, Jeffery S. UG633.U46 1991, **(v10)**
Undset, Sigrid. PT8950.U5, **(v3)**
  PT8950.U5, **(v3)**
  PT8950.UN2.K8, **(v3)**
Unekis, Joseph K. JK1029.U53 1984, **(v7)**
Unesco. ND1005.U5, **(v9)**
  ND1053.U5, **(v9)**
  ND2779.U5, **(v9)**
  ND2809.U5, **(v9)**
Ungar, Sheldon. U264.U53 1992, **(v10)**
Unger, Harlow G. PE64.W5.U54 1998, **(v3)**
Unger, Nancy C. E664.L16.U4 2000, **(v4)**
Unger, Peter K. BD450.U46 1990, **(v8)**
Unger, Richard. PT2359.H2.U44 1984, **(v3)**
Unger, Roberto Mangabeira. JC423.U49 1998, **(v7)**
Ungerer, Horst. HG930.5.U47 1997, **(v6)**
United Nations Environment Programme. G1046.J4 .M5 1997, **(v6)**
United Nations Population Fund. HB849.4.U55 1991, **(v6)**
United Nations. GE10.U54 1997, **(v6)**
  JX1977.A37.Y4, **(v7)**
  KZ5006.2.U55 1997, **(v7)**
United States Gymnastics Safety Association. GV461.U53 1979, **(v6)**
United States Lawn Tennis Association. GV990.U5 1972, **(v6)**
United States Military Academy. G1201.S1 .U5 1995, **(v6)**
United States Strategic Bombing Survey. UF767.U6 1946, **(v10)**

United States. CD3022.A45, (v5)
D734.A1.U57 1976, (v5)
E742.5.C75 1968, (v4)
E842.9.A55 1964b, (v4)
F1436.8.U6.U54 1984, (v4)
G1201.C8.U55 1975, (v6)
G1201.E2.U45 1953 (Map Div.), (v6)
G1540.U5 1955 (Map Div.), (v6)
G3701.K2 1974 .U5, (v6)
HV9103.A545 1968, (v6)
J10.D74 1975, (v7)
J80.A283 1962-1964, (v7)
J81.C62 1994, (v7)
J81.C66, (v7)
J82.C5 1889, (v7)
J82.D5 1974, (v7)
JK1010.A5 1989, (v7)
KF26.C693 1990, (v7)
KF26.E55 1996e, (v7)
KF26.F5 1997o, (v7)
KF26.F6 1993f, (v7)
KF26.F6 1995r, (v7)
KF26.G6735 1998b, (v7)
KF27.A33273 1993i, (v7)
KF27.E3 1995e, (v7)
KF27.E5546 1993n, (v7)
KF27.F645 1992e, (v7)
KF27.I5 1988, (v7)
L111.A783, (v7)
L112.U556 1997, (v7)
LA217.U49 1983, (v7)
PN4888.T4.U5 1990, (v3)
R724.U55 1982, (v2)
SB482.A3 1992, (v1)
U24.U56, (v10)
UB323.A5 1970, (v10)
UG633.A3763, (v10)
UG633.A3763 no. 127-101, (v10)
UG633.A3763 no. 163-2, (v10)
VG93.A79 1971, (v10)
Z1209.U5.U53 1984, (v10)
Z5313.U5.U54 2000, (v10)
Universitah ha-Ivrit bi-Yerushalayim. Z6372.U55 1990, (v10)
University of Chicago. BF408.C5, (v2)
University of Edinburgh. PR5333.E3, (v3)
University of Kansas. PD1514.S7, (v3)
University of London. DS33.1.L6, (v5)
Z3013.L7 1972, (v10)
University of Minnesota. Z1361.E4.U58 1991, (v10)
University of Oxford. PC2026.E8, (v3)
University of Pennsylvania. DT61.U55 1997, (v5)
Unklesbay, A. G. QE131.U54 1992, (v1)
Unnithan-Kumar, Maya. DS432.G7.U55 1997, (v5)
Uno, Chiyo. PL840.N58.I7613 1989, (v3)
Uno, Kimio. HF1602.15.J3.U56 1991, (v6)
Uno, Koji. PL840.N6.A24 1997, (v3)
Unrau, William E. E78.W5.U57 1996, (v4)
E99.K2.C878 1989, (v4)
Unruh, John David. F593.U67 1979, (v4)
Unruh, Vicky. PQ7081.U45 1994, (v3)
Unsworth, Walt. GV199.89.U57 1994, (v6)
Unterecker, John Eugene. PR5907.U5 1971, (v3)
Untermeyer, Louis. PR502.U5, (v3)
PR1175.U65 1955, (v3)
PR1224.U62 1962, (v3)
Unwin, P. T. H. SB387.7.U58 1991, (v1)
Unwin, Simon. NA2940.U58 2000, (v9)
Upchurch, David A. PR5819.U6 1992, (v3)
Upcraft, M. Lee. LB2343.F74 1989, (v7)
Updike, John. PS3541.P47.C4, (v3)
PS3541.UP2.M9, (v3)
PS3571.P4.A17 1977, (v3)
PS3571.P4.B4, (v3)
PS3571.P4.C3 1958, (v3)
PS3571.P4.C58, (v3)
PS3571.P4.C6, (v3)
PS3571.P4.H8 1983, (v3)
PS3571.P4.M3, (v3)
PS3571.P4.M5 1969, (v3)
PS3571.P4.M6 1975, (v3)

PS3571.P4.M7 1972, (v3)
PS3571.P4.O4, (v3)
PS3571.P4.P48, (v3)
PS3571.P4.P5, (v3)
PS3571.P4.P65 1959, (v3)
PS3571.P4.R23 1990, (v3)
PS3571.P4.R25 1981, (v3)
PS3571.P4.R29, (v3)
PS3571.P4.R3 1960b, (v3)
PS3571.P4.S3 1959, (v3)
PS3571.P4.W5 1984, (v3)
PS3571.P4.Z475 1989, (v3)
PS3571.P4T4, (v3)
Upgren, Arthur R. QB44.2.U554 1998, (v1)
Uphoff, Norman Thomas. HN981.C6.U66 1998, (v6)
Upp, E. L. TA357.5.M43.U66 1993, (v1)
Uppal, J. S. HC435.2.U64 1984, (v6)
Upton, Anthony F. DL727.U67 1998, (v5)
Upton, Clive. PE1705.U68 1996, (v3)
Upton, Joel M. ND673.C312.U68 1990, (v9)
Upton, Lee. PS310.A44.U67 1998, (v3)
PS3513.A7217.Z9 1991, (v3)
Urbach, Karina. DA565.R825.U72 1999, (v5)
Urban America (Organization). HN59.U7, (v6)
Urban, Greg. F2519.1.I25.U73 1996, (v4)
Urban, Michael E. JN6581.U72 1997, (v7)
Urban, Wayne J. LB2844.53.U6.U7 1982, (v7)
Urban, Wilbur Marshall. BD111.U7, (v8)
BD161.U7, (v8)
Urbanek, Mae Bobb. F759.U72 1988, (v4)
Urciuoli, Bonnie. F128.9.P85.U73 1996, (v4)
Urdan, Timothy C. QA276.12.U75 2001, (v1)
Urdang, Laurence. PE1460.U74 1988, (v3)
PE2832.U7 1992, (v3)
Urdang, Stephanie. HQ1799.U73 1989, (v6)
Ure, P. N. DF572.U73 1979, (v5)
Urey, Diane F. PQ6555.Z5.U74 1989, (v3)
Urfe, Honore d'. PQ1707.U7.A622513 1995, (v3)
Urgo, Joseph R. PS3505.A87.Z89 1995, (v3)
Uribe Uran, Victor. KHH207.U75 2000, (v7)
Uricchio, William. PN1995.9.S6.U75 1993, (v3)
Uris, Leon. PS3541.R46.B3, (v3)
PS3541.R46.E9, (v3)
Uriu, Robert M. HD3616.J33.U74 1996, (v6)
Urmson, J. O. B430.U76 1988, (v8)
B804.U7, (v8)
Urofsky, Melvin I. E664.B819.U7, (v4)
KF228.J64.U758 1997, (v7)
KF228.J64.U76 1991, (v7)
KF3827.E87.U755 2000, (v7)
KF8742.U76 1997, (v7)
KF8742.U764 2001, (v7)
KF8745.B67.U75, (v7)
Urquhart, Brian. E748.B885.U76 1993, (v4)
Urquhart, Diane. DA990.U46.U76 2000, (v5)
Uruburu, Paula M. PS169.G75.U78 1987, (v3)
Urwin, Derek W. D1051.U785 1997, (v5)
HC241.U78 1995, (v6)
Urwin, Gregory J. W. D767.99.W3.U78 1997, (v5)
Urzidil, Johannes. PT2621.A26.Z943, (v3)
Useem, Bert. HV9469.U84 1996, (v6)
HV9471.U84 1989, (v6)
Useem, Michael. HG4910.U83 1996, (v6)
Usner, Daniel H. E78.M75.U75 1998, (v4)
F352.U86 1992, (v4)
Usner, Donald J. F804.C48.U86 1995, (v4)
Ussher, Jane M. RC451.4.W6.U87 1992, (v2)
Ustinov, Peter. PR6041.S73.M6, (v3)
PR6041.S73.P5 1963a, (v3)
PR6041.S73.R6 1958, (v3)
Uthin Bunnyavong. PL4236.9.U838, (v3)
Utley, Francis Lee. CB365.U8, (v5)
Utley, Robert Marshall. E81.U747 1984, (v4)
E83.866.U87 1973, (v4)
E99.D1.S625 1993, (v4)
F391.U9 2002, (v4)
F802.L7.U86 1987, (v4)
UA25.U8, (v10)
Uttal, William R. BF241.U865 1998, (v2)
QP355.2.U88, (v1)
Utter, Glenn H. BR526.U88 1995, (v8)

KF3941.A68.U88 2000, (v7)
Utter, William T. F495.U87, (v4)
Utting, Peter. HD9018.D44.U88 1992, (v6)
Uviller, H. Richard. HV9950.U85 1999, (v6)
KF9223.U88 1996, (v7)
Uvin, Peter. DT450.435.U95 1998, (v5)
V̄emana. PL4780.9.V38A26 1995, (v3)
Vaccari, Oreste. PL535.V3 1951, (v3)
Vaccaro, Tony. DD257.2.V33 2001, (v5)
Vachon, Andre. F1030.V2813 1982, (v4)
Vaganay, Leon. BS2325.V3213 1991, (v8)
Vaggioli, Felice. DU420.16.V3413 2000, (v5)
Vagts, Alfred. U200.V3, (v10)
UA10.V3 1959, (v10)
Vahimagi, Tise. PN1992.3.G7.V34 1994, (v3)
Vaid, Krishna Baldev. PK2098.V22G8913 1994, (v3)
Vaidhyanathan, Siva. Z642.V35 2001, (v10)
Vaidyanathan, T. G. PN1995.V24 1996, (v3)
Vaihinger, Hans. B3354.V5.P6 1965, (v8)
Vail, Mark. ML1092.V25 1993, (v9)
Vaill, Amanda. ND237.M895.V35 1998, (v9)
Vaillant, George E. RC565.V332 1995, (v2)
Vainker, S. J. NK4165.V3 1991, (v9)
Vajda, S. QA241.V24 1989, (v1)
QA269.V28 1992, (v1)
Vakalopoulos, Apostolos E. DF631.B313 1970, (v5)
Vakhrameev, Vsevolod Andreevich. QE923.V35 1991, (v1)
Vaksberg, Arkadii. KM1.V35 S8 1991, (v7)
Valade, Roger M. Z1039.B56.V36 1995, (v10)
Valbuena Prat, Angel. PQ6032.V3 1982, (v3)
PQ6256.P5V3 1974, (v3)
Valcarcel Cases, Miguel. QD75.2.V35 2000, (v1)
Valcarcel, Carlos Daniel. F3444.T93 V14, (v4)
Valder, Peter. SB413.W57.V34 1995, (v1)
Valdes, Dennis Nodin. F614.S4.V35 2000, (v4)
Valdes, Guadalupe. PE1129.S8, (v3)
PE1129.S8V26 2001, (v3)
Valdes, Juan de. PC4073.V3, (v3)
Valdes, Juan Gabriel. HC192.V18 1995, (v6)
Vale, Brian. F2536.V16 1996, (v4)
Vale, Lawrence J. HD7288.78.U52.M48 2000, (v6)
NA4195.V35 1992, (v9)
Vale, M. G. A. DC96.V34 1990, (v5)
Vale, Thomas R. QH105.C2.V35 1998, (v1)
Valentine, Charles Wilfred. BF721.V25, (v2)
Valentine, Lisa Philips. E99.C6.V33 1995, (v4)
Valentine, Maggie. NA737.L42.V36 1994, (v9)
Valenzuela, Luisa. PQ7798.32.A48.A6 1988, (v3)
Valeo, Francis Ralph. E840.8.M25.V35 1999, (v4)
Valery, Paul. D363.V273 1951, (v5)
PQ2643.A26.A23, (v3)
PQ2643.A26.A25, (v3)
PQ2643.A26.S6 1946, (v3)
Valian, Virginia. HQ1237.V35 1998, (v6)
Valiant, Leslie. QP363.3.V35 1994, (v1)
Valiela, Ivan. Q180.A1, (v1)
QH541.5.S3.V34 1995, (v1)
Valiulis, Maryann Gialanella. DA965.M84.V35 1992, (v5)
Valkenier, Elizabeth Kridl. ND687.5.R4.V34, (v9)
ND699.R4.V3 1990, (v9)
Vall, Mark van de. HD6490.S6.V313, (v6)
Valle, Teresa del. GN549.B3.V3413 1994, (v6)
Valle-Inclan, Ramon del. PQ6641.A47.L813 1976, (v3)
Vallejo, Cesar. PQ8497.V35.A17 1978, (v3)
PQ8497.V35.H413 1990, (v3)
PQ8497.V35.T713 1992, (v3)
PQ8497.V35.T813 1988, (v3)
Vallentin, Antonina. ND623.L5.V25, (v9)
Vallieres, Pierre. F1027.V313 1971b, (v4)
Vallins, David. PR4487.P8.V35 1999, (v3)
Valmiki. BL1139.22.E54 1984, (v8)
PK3653.A2 M4, (v3)
Valsaraj, K. T. TD153.V35 2000, (v1)
Valsiner, Jaan. BF722.V34 1997, (v2)
Van Aken, Mark J. F3736.F5.V36 1989, (v4)
Van Aller, Christopher D. UA23.V23 2001, (v10)
Van Alstyne, Richard Warner. E179.5.V32, (v4)
Van Amerongen, C. T47.V35, (v1)

Van Anglen, Kevin P. PR3588.V36 1993, (v3)
Van Ausdale, Debra. HQ784.S56.V36 2001, (v6)
Van Belle, Douglas A. PN4736.B45 2000, (v3)
Van Bosse, John G. TK5103.8.V36 1998, (v1)
Van Brunt, Henry. NA710.V3 1969, (v9)
Van Buren, Martin. E387.A32 1973, (v4)
  JK2260.V3 1967, (v7)
Van Cleve, Thomas Curtis. DD151.V34, (v5)
Van Cott, Donna Lee. JL2281.V37 2000, (v7)
Van Creveld, Martin L. JC11.V35 1999, (v7)
  U27.V27 1989, (v10)
  U168.V36, (v10)
  U408.3.V36 1990, (v10)
  UA712.V256 1982, (v10)
  UA853.I8.V373 1998, (v10)
Van Cromphout, Gustaaf. PS1642.E8.V36 1999, (v3)
Van de Mieroop, Marc. DS69.5.V36 1997, (v5)
Van de Snepscheut, Jan L. A. QA76.6.S6163 1993, (v1)
Van de Ven, Hans J. JQ1519.A5.V36 1991, (v7)
Van de Water, Frederic Franklyn. E467.1.C99 V3 1988, (v4)
  F127.C6.V3, (v4)
Van de Wetering, Janwillem. BQ9294.4.J3 V3613 1999, (v8)
Van Deburg, William L. E185.86.V34 1997, (v4)
  E441.V23 1984, (v4)
Van der Bent, A. J. BX6.3.V36 1994, (v8)
Van der Does, Louise Q. Q141.V25 1999, (v1)
Van der Merwe, P. J. DT1813.V3613 1995, (v5)
Van der Merwe, Peter. ML3470.V36 1989, (v9)
Van der Vat, Dan. D770.V28 1988, (v5)
Van der Zee, Jacob. F630.B8 V2, (v4)
Van Deusen, Glyndon G. E340.C6.V3, (v4)
  E415.9.S4.V3, (v4)
Van Deusen, Kira. GV345.V35 2001, (v6)
Van Dine, S. S. PS3545.R846.B4, (v3)
Van Doren, Carl. E277.V23 1973, (v4)
  PR471.V3 1967, (v3)
  PR3726.V3, (v3)
  PS3543.A555.A6 1945, (v3)
  PS3543.A555.Z5 1936, (v3)
Van Doren, Mark. PN1111.V3, (v3)
  PR2976.V25 1953, (v3)
  PS1881.V3, (v3)
  PS3053.V3 1961, (v3)
  PS3543.A557.A17 1939, (v3)
  PS3543.A557.A17 1954, (v3)
  PS3543.A557.A17 1960, (v3)
  PS3543.A557.A17 1963, (v3)
  PS3543.A557.A6 1962 v.1-3, (v3)
  PS3543.A557.C43, (v3)
  PS3543.A557.H3, (v3)
  PS3543.A557.L27, (v3)
  PS3543.A557.N3, (v3)
  PS3543.A557.N6, (v3)
  PS3543.A557.T45, (v3)
  PS3543.A557.Z52, (v3)
Van Dormael, Armand. HG220.E85.V36 1997, (v6)
Van Dover, Cindy. QH541.5.D35.V34 2000, (v1)
Van Driesche, Jason. QH353.V36 2000, (v1)
Van Druten, John. PR6043.A4.B5 1951, (v3)
  PR6043.A4.I2, (v3)
  PR6043.A4.V5, (v3)
  PR6043.A4.Z52 1957, (v3)
  PS3543.A558.I2, (v3)
Van Dulken, Stephen. T19.V36 2001, (v1)
Van Dyke, Henry. PS3117.S7, (v3)
Van Dyke, Rachel. F144.N5, (v4)
Van Dyke, Vernon. JA84.U5.V36 1995, (v7)
Van Dyke, Vernon. JC585.V276, (v7)
Van Dyne, Susan R. PS3566.L27.Z947 1993, (v3)
Van Emden, Helmut Fritz. QH545.P4.V36 1996, (v1)
Van Erven, Eugene. PN2860.V36 1992, (v3)
Van Esterik, Penny. RJ216.V36 1989, (v2)
Van Evera, Stephen. U21.2.V34 1999, (v10)
Van Every, Dale. E310.V3, (v4)
Van Evra, Judith Page. HQ784.T4.V333 1990, (v6)
Van Fraassen, Bas C. B816.V36 2002, (v8)
  BD581.V27 1989, (v8)
Van Ghent, Dorothy (Bendon). PR821.V3, (v3)

  PR4838.H4.V36 1983, (v3)
Van Hear, Nicholas. JV6032.V36 1998, (v7)
Van Hecke, Gerald R. QD63.L3.V36 1998, (v1)
Van Hoogstraten, Nicholas. PN2277.N5.V36 1991, (v3)
Van Hook, Bailey. N6510.V35 1996, (v9)
Van Horn, Susan Householder. HQ1410.V36 1988, (v6)
Van Ingen, John Frederick. BJ1474.V36 1994, (v8)
Van Inwagen, Peter. BD111.V38 2002, (v8)
  BD311.V35 1990, (v8)
Van Kirk, Sylvia. F1060.V36 1983, (v4)
Van Kley, Dale K. DC158.2.V36 1996, (v5)
Van Maanen, John. GN307.7.V36 1988, (v6)
Van Ness, Peter. DS740.4.V34 1970, (v5)
Van Nostrand, Albert D. PN155.V3 1960, (v3)
Van Oudenaren, John. D1065.S65.V35 1991, (v5)
Van Praagh, David. DS578.32.K84.V36 1996, (v5)
Van Ravenswaay, Charles. F474.S275.V36 1991, (v4)
Van Rensburg, W. C. J. HD9506.A2.V36 1986, (v6)
Van Riper, Charles. RC423.V35 1996, (v2)
Van Sant, Ann Jessie. PR858.S615.V36 1993, (v3)
Van Sant, John E. E184.J3.V3 2000, (v4)
Van Scotter, Richard D. LA217.2.V36 1991, (v7)
Van Seters, John. DS62.2.V35 1983, (v5)
Van Sickle, Neil D. TL545.V3 1999, (v1)
Van Slyke, Lyman P. DS777.55.V36, (v5)
Van Soest, Peter J. SF95.V36 1994, (v1)
Van Staaveren, Jacob. DS894.59.V3485.V36 1994, (v5)
Van Tassel, Emily Field. KF5075.V36 1999, (v7)
Van Tuyll, Hubert P. UA23.V293 1998, (v10)
Van Vechten, Carl. PS3543.A653.B58, (v3)
  PS3543.A653.N5 1926, (v3)
  PS3543.A653.P3, (v3)
  PS3543.A653.P4, (v3)
  PS3543.A653.S65, (v3)
  PS3543.A653.T3, (v3)
  PS3543.A653.Z48 1987, (v3)
  PS3543.A653.Z5 1932, (v3)
Van Vlack, Lawrence H. TA403.V35 1989, (v1)
Van Vleck, Amelia Eileen. PC3304.V36 1990, (v3)
Van Voorst, Robert E. BT297.V36 2000, (v8)
Van Voris, Jacqueline. JK1899.C3 V25 1987, (v7)
Van Vugt, William E. E184.B7.V36 1999, (v4)
Van Wagenen, Jared. S451.N56.V25, (v1)
Van Whitlock, Rodney. Z5703.4.P75.V34 1999, (v10)
Van Wicklen, Janet. T11.V368 2001, (v1)
Van Willigen, John. Z5118.A54.V37 1991, (v10)
Van Wingerden, Sophia A. JN979.V36 1999, (v7)
Van Witsen, Leo. MT955.V36, (v9)
Van Wyk, Gary. NA7468.6.L4.V36 1998, (v9)
Van Wyk, J. J. Z7164.D2.V36 1997, (v10)
Van Wylen, Gord John. TJ265.V23 1994, (v1)
Van Young, Eric. F1232.V26 2001, (v4)
Van Zanten, David. NA1050.V358 1994, (v9)
  NA1050.V36 1987, (v9)
Van Zoeren, Steven Jay. PL2466.Z7V36 1991, (v3)
Vanbrugh, John. PR3737.P69 1973, (v3)
Vance, James E. TF23.V36 1995, (v1)
Vance, John A. PR3759.W2.Z93 1983, (v3)
  PR3777.V36 2000, (v3)
Vance, Laura Lee. BX6115.V36 1999, (v8)
Vance, Lucile E. N7525.V3 1966, (v9)
Vance, Norman. PR8711.V3 1990, (v3)
Vance, William L. NX503.7.V36 1989, (v9)
Vandecasteele, Carlo. QD139.T7.V355 1993, (v1)
Vanden Bossche, Chris. PR4437.A89.V36 1991, (v3)
Vanden, Harry E. JL1616.V36 1993, (v7)
Vandenbeld, John. QH197.V36 1988, (v1)
Vandenberg, Donald. LB880.V34.E34 1990, (v7)
Vandenbosch, Amry. DS518.1.V28, (v5)
Vandenbroucke, Lucien S. E840.4.V36 1993, (v4)
Vandeputte, Omer. PF95.V3 1995, (v3)
Vander Elst, Philip. PR6023.E926.Z92 1996, (v3)
Vander Wall, Stephen B. QL756.5.V36 1990, (v1)
Vander, Judith. ML3557.V36 1988, (v9)
Vanderbei, Robert J. T57.74.V36 2001, (v1)
Vanderbilt, Arthur T. KF352.V2.V35 1955, (v7)
Vanderbilt, Gloria (Morgan). CT275.V233.A28, (v5)
Vanderham, Paul. PR6019.O9.U756 1998, (v3)

VanderKam, James C. DS121.65.V36 2001, (v5)
Vanderkolk, Barbara Schwarz. HF5549.5.D39.V36 1991, (v6)
VanderLugt, Anthony. TA1632.V28 1992, (v1)
Vandermeer, John H. QH333.V36 1995, (v1)
Vandermeer, John H. S603.5.V36 1989, (v1)
VanderMeer, Philip R. F526.V26 1985, (v4)
Vandermerwe, Sandra. HF5415.5.V357 1999, (v6)
Vanderwerth, W. C. E98.O7.V33, (v4)
VanderWolk, William. PQ2250.V36 1990, (v3)
Vanderwood, Paul J. BR615.T65.V36 1998, (v8)
  F1234.V2 1987, (v4)
VanderZwaag, Harold J. GV346.V36 1984, (v6)
  GV706.V33, (v6)
  GV713.V35 1998, (v6)
Vandevelde, Kenneth J. K212.V36 1996, (v7)
Vandiver, Frank Everson. DS558.V38 1997, (v5)
Vandivier, Elizabeth L. Z7164.C81.V355 1996, (v10)
Vandkilde, Helle. TT205.V35 1996, (v1)
Vanek, Jaroslav. HD5650.V33, (v6)
  HD5650.V332, (v6)
VanEvery, Jo. HQ1206.V24 1995, (v6)
Vanger, Milton I. F2728.V27, (v4)
Vanhoozer, Kevin J. B2430.R554.V37 1990, (v8)
  BS476.V34 1998, (v8)
Vankeerberghen, Griet. BL1900.H825 V35 2001, (v8)
Vann, Richard T. DA125.Q34.V36 1991, (v5)
Vannoy, Dana. HQ536.V37 1989, (v6)
Vansina, Jan. DT19.7.V36.A3 1994, (v5)
Vanthoor, W. F. V. HC240.V258 2002, (v6)
  HG925.V3613 1997, (v6)
Varadarajan, V. S. QA151.V37 1998, (v1)
Vardy, Steven Bela. DB904.V37 1997, (v5)
Vardys, Vytas Stanley. DK505.54.V37 1997, (v5)
Varela, Felix. PQ7389.V38.J5313 1999, (v3)
Varenne, Jean. B132.Y6.V2913, (v8)
Varg, Paul A. BV3415.V37 1977, (v8)
  E310.7.V3, (v4)
Vargas Llosa, Alvaro. F3448.2.V365 1994, (v4)
Vargas Llosa, Mario. PQ8498.32.A65C413 1985, (v3)
  PQ8498.32.A65.C63, (v3)
  PQ8498.32.A65.E413 1990, (v3)
  PQ8498.32.A65.G813 1984, (v3)
  PQ8498.32.A65.H3413 1989, (v3)
  PQ8498.32.A65L5813 1996, (v3)
  PQ8498.32.A65P4913 1994, (v3)
Vargas, Zaragosa. HD8081.M6.V37 1993, (v6)
Varias, Alexander. HX896.P3.V37 1996, (v6)
Varley, H. Paul. PL747.25.W3.V37 1994, (v3)
Varley, John. PS3572.A724.O6 1977a, (v3)
Varma, Arvind. TP149.V36 1997, (v1)
Varma, Maha Devi. PK2098.V3.A913 1994, (v3)
Varnedoe, Kirk. N6447.V37 1990, (v9)
  ND237.P73.A4 1998, (v9)
  ND553.C243.V37 1987, (v9)
Varney, Andrew. PR448.S64.V37 1999, (v3)
Varon Gabai, Rafael. F3442.P776.V37 1997, (v4)
Varona, Verne. RC271.D52V37 2001, (v2)
Varro, Marcus Terentius. PA6792.A3 1938, (v3)
Varshney, Ashutosh. DS422.C64 V37 2002, (v5)
  HN690.Z9.C6846 1995, (v6)
Varshneya, Arun K. TP857.V37 1994., (v1)
Varty, Kenneth. Z6521.R73.V37 1998, (v10)
Vasari, Giorgio. N7420.V3 1960, (v9)
Vasey, Frank B. RD539.8.V38 1993, (v2)
Vasey, Ruth. PN1995.62.V37 1997, (v3)
Vasilyev, F.P. T57.74.V37 2001, (v1)
Vasquez, John A. B105.W3.V37 1993, (v8)
Vassallo, Peter. PR4392.I82.V37 1984, (v3)
Vassilian, Hamo B. Z3461.V38 1993, (v10)
Vassos, Basil H. TK7878.4.V37 1993, (v1)
Vasudevan Nair, M. T. PL4718.9.V32R3613 1997, (v3)
Vatikiotis, P. J. DF849.58.M48.V37 1998, (v5)
Vatikiotis, P. J. DT107.V38 1986, (v5)
Vatsyayana. HQ470.S3.V3 1962, (v6)
Vattimo, Gianni. B831.2.V3813 1992, (v8)
  BD241.V24513 1997, (v8)
Vauchez, André. BX2330.V3813 1997, (v8)
Vaughan, Alden T. F7.V32 1972b, (v4)
  PR2833.V38 1991, (v3)
Vaughan, Christopher C. RG525.V38 1996, (v2)

Vaughan, Dorothy Margaret. DR471.V38 1976, **(v5)**
Vaughan, Henry. PR3740.A2 1957, **(v3)**
 PR3740.A2 1964, **(v3)**
Vaughan, J.G. (John Griffith). SB175.V38 1997, **(v1)**
Vaughan, Mary K. LC92.M4.V38 1997, **(v7)**
Vaughan, Megan. R651.V38 1991b, **(v2)**
Vaughan, Olufemi. DT515.45.Y67.V38 2000, **(v5)**
Vaughan, Richard. DC611.B78.V35 1979, **(v5)**
 PR6043.A83 M6, **(v3)**
Vaughan, Susan C. BF698.35.O57.V38 2000, **(v2)**
Vaughan, Virginia Mason. PR2829.V38 1994, **(v3)**
Vaughan, William. N6757.V38 1999, **(v9)**
 ND567.5.R6.V38 1980, **(v9)**
Vaughn, Stephen. PN2287.R25.V38 1994, **(v3)**
Vaughn, William Preston. LC2802.S9.V38, **(v7)**
Vaux, Kenneth L. DS79.72.V37 1992, **(v5)**
Vaux, Roland de. DS110.Q8.V313 1973, **(v5)**
Vavilov, N. I. SB73.V3813 1992, **(v1)**
Vayda, Andrew Peter. GF51.V35, **(v6)**
Vazquez Gomez, Juana. F1205.V34 1997, **(v4)**
Veal, Anthony James. GV75.V398 1987, **(v6)**
Veatch, Henry Babcock. B21.S78 vol. 20, **(v8)**
 BJ37.V4, **(v8)**
Veatch, Robert M. R726.V4, **(v2)**
Veatch, Robert M. RD120.7.V43 2000, **(v2)**
Veblen, Thomas T. QK150.V38 1990, **(v1)**
Veblen, Thorstein. HB34.V38, **(v6)**
 HB34.V4 1990, **(v6)**
 HB171.V4, **(v6)**
 HB831.V4 2001, **(v6)**
 HC106.V4 1964, **(v6)**
 HC106.3.V4 1965, **(v6)**
 HF5351.V38 1935, **(v6)**
Vecsey, Christopher. E98.R3.V444 1997, **(v4)**
Vedder, Elihu. N6537.V43.A4 1979, **(v9)**
Vedung, Evert. H97.V4313 1997, **(v6)**
Veeck, Bill. GV865.V4.A3, **(v6)**
Veer, Peter van der. BL2015.N26.V44 1994, **(v8)**
Vega, Garcilaso de la. F3442.G2315, **(v4)**
Vega, Gina. HD30.28.V43 2000, **(v6)**
Vega, Lope de. PQ6438.A1 1916, **(v3)**
 PQ6438.A2 1946, **(v3)**
 PQ6457.A8 1973, **(v3)**
 PQ6459.A4 1991, **(v3)**
Vega, William. HV5824.Y68.V45 1998, **(v6)**
Vegetius Renatus, Flavius. U101.V14 1944, **(v10)**
Veidlinger, Jeffrey. PN3035.V45 2000, **(v3)**
 PN3035.V45 2000, **(v3)**
Veitch, Jonathan. PS3545.E8334.Z9 1997, **(v3)**
Veith, Gene Edward. BR99.74, **(v8)**
Veith, Richard. TK7882.I6.V445 1988, **(v1)**
Veit-Wild, Flora. PR9390.9.M3.Z94 1992, **(v3)**
Velarde-Mayol, Victor. B3212.Z7 V45 2000, **(v8)**
 B3279.H94 V45 2000, **(v8)**
Velasco, Sherry M. PN57.E68, **(v3)**
Velazquez de la Cadena, Mariano. PC4640.V5 1967, **(v3)**
Veldman, Meredith. DA589.4.V45 1994, **(v5)**
Velez de Escalante, Silvestre. F786.V513, **(v4)**
Velez-Ibanez, Carlos G. F790.M5.V45 1996, **(v4)**
Veliz, Claudio. F1408.3.V36 1994, **(v4)**
Vellas, Francois. G155.A1.V453 1995, **(v6)**
Velleman, Daniel J. QA9.V38 1994, **(v1)**
Veltmeyer, Henry. HN110.5.A8.V42 1999, **(v6)**
Ven, J. A. van der. BV1464.V45 1998, **(v8)**
Vena, Gary. PS3529.N5.I438 1988, **(v3)**
Venarde, Bruce L. BX4220.E85.V46 1997, **(v8)**
Venbrux, Eric. DU125.T5.V45 1995, **(v5)**
Vendelin, George D. TK7876.V47 1990, **(v1)**
Vendler, Helen Hennessy. PR4837.V43 1983, **(v3)**
 PR6058.E2.Z94 1998, **(v3)**
Venezky, Richard L. PE2817.V46 1999, **(v3)**
Venkataraman, K. TP913.V4, **(v1)**
Venkatesh, Sudhir Alladi. HD7288.78.U52.C476 2000, **(v6)**
Venn, Beth. ND1837.W94.A4 1998, **(v9)**
Venning, Timothy. DA425.V46 1995, **(v5)**
Ventris, Michael. CN362.V4, **(v5)**
Venturi, Franco. D289.V4613 1991, **(v5)**
 DG545.V4513 1989, **(v5)**
 DK189.V413, **(v5)**

Venturi, Lionello. ND170.V43 **(v9)**
 ND622.V4, **(v9)**
 ND1145.V4, **(v9)**
Venturi, Robert. NA2760.V46 1977, **(v9)**
Venturo, David F. PR3537.P58.V46 1999, **(v3)**
Ver Steeg, Clarence Lester. E302.6.M8.V4 1954, **(v4)**
Verastique, Bernardino. F1221.T3.V47 2000, **(v4)**
Verba, Cynthia. ML270.3.V47 1993, **(v9)**
Verba, Sidney. HN730.Z9.E49 1987, **(v6)**
 JC575.V47 1985, **(v7)**
 JK1764.V475 1995, **(v7)**
 JK2274.A3.V4, **(v7)**
Verbeke, Gerard. B528.V4 1983, **(v8)**
Vercors. PQ2603.R924.A8, **(v3)**
 PQ2603.R924.M3 1943, **(v3)**
Verdery, Katherine. HX373.5.V47 1996, **(v6)**
Verdeyen, Joseph Thomas. TA1675.V47 1995, **(v1)**
Verdi, Giuseppe. ML410.V4.A4 1994, **(v9)**
Verdi, Richard. ND553.P8.A4 1995, **(v9)**
Verdoia, Ken. F826.V47 1996, **(v4)**
Verdon, Frank P. GC63.C47.V47 1996, **(v6)**
Verdoorn, Frans. QK523.V47 1967, **(v1)**
Verduyn, Christl. PR9199.3.E5.Z93 1995, **(v3)**
Veremes, Thanos. DF802.V47 1995, **(v5)**
Verga, Giovanni. PQ4734.V5.M313 1975, **(v3)**
 PQ4734.V5.M4, **(v3)**
 PQ4734.V5.N62 1953, **(v3)**
 PQ4734.V5.SH, **(v3)**
Vergara, Camilo J. HN57.V47 1995, **(v6)**
Verheyen, Dirk. DD257.25.V47 1991, **(v5)**
Verhulst, F. QA372.V47 1990, **(v1)**
Verissimo, Erico. PQ9697.V298.T42 1951, **(v3)**
Verlaine, Paul. PQ2463.A6 1948, **(v3)**
 PQ2463.R6 1976, **(v3)**
Verma, Nirmal. PK2098.V43C7 1991, **(v3)**
 PK2098.V43L313 1997, **(v3)**
Vermeer, E. B. DS796.F86 V47 1991, **(v5)**
Vermeer, Johannes. ND653.V5.A4 1995, **(v9)**
Vermeij, Geerat J. QL403.V47 1993, **(v1)**
Vermeule, Cornelius Clarkson. NB86.V47 1981, **(v9)**
Vermeule, Emily. DF220.V4, **(v5)**
Vernadsky, George. DK38.V4413, **(v5)**
 DK40.V4 1933, **(v5)**
 DK72.V4, **(v5)**
Vernant, Jean Pierre. DF78.V4813 1982, **(v5)**
 PA3131.V413 1988, **(v3)**
Vernberg, F. John. QH541.5.C65, **(v1)**
Verne, Jules. PQ2469.T7.E56, **(v3)**
 PQ2469.V4E5 1993, **(v3)**
 PQ2469.V72 1959, **(v3)**
Verner, Andrew M. DK258.V44 1990, **(v5)**
Verney, Edmund Hope. F1089.V3.V47 1996, **(v4)**
Verney, Kevern. E185.61.V475 2000, **(v4)**
Vernez, Georges. LC213.2.V47 1999, **(v7)**
Vernon, Amelia Wallace. F279.M326.V47 1993, **(v4)**
Vernon, Jack A. RF293.8.V47 2001, **(v2)**
Vernon, James. JN216.V47 1993, **(v7)**
Verona, Sergiu. DK67.5.R6.V47 1992, **(v5)**
Verrier, Anthony. D785.V47 1968b, **(v5)**
Verschuur, Gerrit L. QB721.V48 1996, **(v1)**
 QC753.5.V47 1993, **(v1)**
Versenyi, Adam. PN2309.V46 1993, **(v3)**
Versluis, Arthur. B905.V47 1993, **(v8)**
 PS217.O33.V47 2001, **(v3)**
Versteegh, C. H. M. PJ6075.V46 1997, **(v3)**
Vertosick, Frank T. RB127.V47 2000, **(v2)**
Vertrees, Alan David. PN1997.G59.V47 1997, **(v3)**
Very, Jones. PS3126.D44 1993, **(v3)**
Vesalius, Andreas. QM25.V43, **(v1)**
Vesalius, Andreas. QM151.V4713 1999, **(v1)**
Veseth, Michael. HJ8003.V47 1990, **(v6)**
Vesilind, P. Aarne. TA157.V42 1998, **(v1)**
Vestal, Stanley. F591.V47, **(v4)**
 F591.V48, **(v4)**
 F592.C415, **(v4)**
 F689.D64 V47 1998, **(v4)**
 F786.V56, **(v4)**
Vestal, Theodore M. LC1090.V38 1994, **(v7)**
Vetlesen, Arne Johan. BJ1408.5.V48 1994, **(v8)**
Veyne, Paul. BL782.V4713 1988, **(v8)**
 PA6029.L6.V413 1988, **(v3)**

Viala, Alain. PQ241.V53 1985, **(v3)**
Vian, Boris. PQ2643.I152.B313 1967, **(v3)**
Vianna, Hermano. ML3465.V5313 1999, **(v9)**
Viano, Maurizio Sanzio. PN1998.3.P367.V5 1993, **(v3)**
Viau, Theophile de. PQ1933.A1 1951, **(v3)**
Vibert, Elizabeth. E78.C63.V52 1997, **(v4)**
Vice, Sue. PR888.H6.V53 2000, **(v3)**
Vicens Vives, Jaime. DP66.V513, **(v5)**
Vicente, Gil. PQ9251.A1 1979, **(v3)**
 PQ9251.A4.B4, **(v3)**
Vicentino, Nicola. MT5.5.V5313 1996, **(v9)**
Vicinus, Martha. HQ800.2.V53 1985, **(v6)**
 HQ1596.V5 1972, **(v6)**
Vickerman, Milton. E184.W54.V53 1999, **(v4)**
Vickers, Amy. TD388.V53 2001, **(v1)**
Vickers, Brian. PN175.V53 1988, **(v3)**
 PN1892.V45 vol. 1, **(v3)**
 PR2970.V5 1993, **(v3)**
 PR2976.V5, **(v3)**
Vickers, Daniel. F72.E7.V58 1994, **(v4)**
Vickers, Douglas. HB72.V498 1997, **(v6)**
Vickers, Ilse. PR3408.S35.V53 1996, **(v3)**
Vickers, Jill. HQ1236.5.C2.V53 1993, **(v6)**
Vickers, Miranda. DR941.V53 1995, **(v5)**
 DR978.3.V53 2000, **(v5)**
 DR2082.V53 1998, **(v5)**
Vickers, Roy. PR6043.I183, **(v3)**
Vickers, Scott B. E98.E85.V53 1998, **(v4)**
Vickery, Amanda. HQ1599.E5.V47 1998, **(v6)**
Vickery, Ann. PS228.F45.V54 2000, **(v3)**
Vickery, Donald M. RC81.V5 2001, **(v2)**
Victor, David G. QC981.8.G56, **(v1)**
Victor, Edward. LB1585.V46 1985, **(v7)**
Victor, George. DD247.H5.V48 1998, **(v5)**
Victor, Maurice. RC346.A3 2001, **(v2)**
Vida, Elizabeth M. PR4437.L5.V5 1993, **(v3)**
Vidal, Gore. PS3543.I26.A6214 1976, **(v3)**
 PS3543.I26.B4, **(v3)**
 PS3543.I26.B8, **(v3)**
 PS3543.I26.C5, **(v3)**
 PS3543.I26.J8, **(v3)**
 PS3543.I26.K3, **(v3)**
 PS3543.I26.L5 1984, **(v3)**
 PS3543.I26.M9, **(v3)**
 PS3543.I26.R6, **(v3)**
 PS3543.I26.R65 1962, **(v3)**
 PS3543.I26.S38, **(v3)**
 PS3543.I26.S4, **(v3)**
 PS3543.I26.T5, **(v3)**
 PS3543.I26.V5, **(v3)**
 PS3543.I26.Z474 1995, **(v3)**
Vidali, Gianfranco. QC611.92.V53 1993, **(v1)**
Vidal-Naquet, Pierre. DS102.5.V5313 1996, **(v5)**
Vidich, Arthur J. BR517.V47 1985, **(v8)**
Vidler, Anthony. PN56.A73.V53 1992, **(v3)**
Vidyakara. PK2971.H3 vol. 44, **(v3)**
Vieira, Mark. PN1995.62.V54 1999, **(v3)**
Vieira, Norman. KF8742.V54 1998, **(v7)**
Viera, Barbara L. GV1015.3.V54 1996, **(v6)**
Vierck, Elizabeth. HQ1064.U5.V494 1990, **(v6)**
Viereck, George Sylvester. E767.V52 1976, **(v4)**
 PS3543.I32.SA3, **(v3)**
Viereck, Peter Robert Edwin. JC501.V48, **(v7)**
Vietor, Karl. PT2177.V45, **(v3)**
Vietor, Richard H. K. HD3616.U46.V53 1994, **(v6)**
 HD9545.V54, **(v6)**
Vigarello, Georges. HV6569.F8, **(v6)**
Vigilante, Richard. PN4899.N42.D328 1994, **(v3)**
Vignaux, Paul. B721.V513 1959, **(v8)**
Vigny, Alfred de. PQ2474.C48 1973, **(v3)**
Vila, Anne C. PQ265.V48 1998, **(v3)**
Vila, Xavier Peter. PQ6641.A47.Z896 1994, **(v3)**
Vilar, Pierre. DP68.V5513 1967, **(v5)**
Vilas, Carlos Maria. F1528.V56 1989, **(v4)**
Vile, John R. KF4541.V55 1991, **(v7)**
 KF4550.V55 1993, **(v7)**
 KF4555.V55 1992, **(v7)**
 KF4555.V56 1993, **(v7)**
 KF4557.V55 1994, **(v7)**
 KF4557.V555 1996, **(v7)**
Villa, Brian Loring. D756.5.D5.V55 1989, **(v5)**

Villa, Dana Richard. JC251.A74.V55 1996, **(v7)**
  JC251.A74 V57 1999, **(v7)**
Villa, Raul. PS153.M4.V55 2000, **(v3)**
Villagra, Gaspar Perez de. PQ7296.V54.H5713 1992, **(v3)**
Villatoro, Jose Luis. F1465.P8785 1991, **(v4)**
Ville, Simon P. HE242.V54 1990, **(v6)**
Villedieu. PQ1794.D5.A65 1970, **(v3)**
Villee, Claude Alvin. QL47.2.V5 1984, **(v1)**
Villiers de L'Isle-Adam, Auguste. PQ2476.V4.A93 1970b, **(v3)**
Villiers, Alan John. G540.V646 **(v6)**
  SH281.V55, **(v1)**
  VK18.V5 1970, **(v10)**
Villoldo, Alberto. F3429.3.D79.V55, **(v4)**
Villon, Francois. PQ1590.A2 1964, **(v3)**
Vilmorin, Louise de. PQ2643.I517.M3, **(v3)**
Vinacke, Harold Monk. DS518.1.V43, **(v5)**
Vincent, Andrew. JC325.V55 1987, **(v7)**
Vincent, David. JN329.S4.V56 1998, **(v7)**
  LC156.A2, **(v7)**
Vincent, Deirdre. PT1980.V56 1992, **(v3)**
Vincent, John A. HV1461.V56 1995, **(v6)**
Vincent, Mary. DP17.V56 1994, **(v5)**
Vincent, Stephen A. E185.93.I4V56 1999, **(v4)**
Vincentelli, Moira. NK3780.V56 1999, **(v9)**
Vinding, Michael. DS493.9.T45 V65 1998, **(v5)**
Vine, Steven. PR4147.V5 1993, **(v3)**
  PR4173.V48 1998, **(v3)**
Vinen, Richard. DC404.V56 1995, **(v5)**
Vines, Alex. DT3394.V56 1991, **(v5)**
Vines, Lois. PQ2643.A26.Z84 1992, **(v3)**
Vines, Sherard. PR140.V5 1930a, **(v3)**
Vinogradoff, Paul. HC254.V48 1968b, **(v5)**
Vinogradov, Oleg. TJ175.V56 2000, **(v1)**
Vinovskis, Maris. HQ759.4.V55 1988, **(v6)**
  LC89.V55 1999, **(v7)**
Viola, Herman J. F591.V56 1987, **(v4)**
Viollet-le-Duc, Eugene-Emmanuel. NA2520.V813 1959, **(v9)**
Vipond, Mary. PN1991.3.C3.V56 1992, **(v3)**
Vipond, Robert Charles. JL27.V56 1990, **(v7)**
Viqueira Alban, Juan Pedro. F1386.2.V5713 1999, **(v4)**
Viramma. DS422.C3.V49613 1997, **(v5)**
Virchenko, N. O. QA231.V57 2001, **(v1)**
Vircondelet, Alain. PQ2607.U8245.Z9213 1994, **(v3)**
Virden, Jenel. D810.W7.V57 1996, **(v5)**
Virdung, Sebastian. MT5.5.V573.B8 1993, **(v9)**
Virgil. PA6105.S8V62 1969, **(v3)**
  PA6807.A5.F53 1983, **(v3)**
  PA6807.B7.F47 1999, **(v3)**
Virgin, Lawrence N. QA845.V57 2000, **(v1)**
Viroli, Maurizio. DG738.14.M2.V74 2000, **(v5)**
  JC143.M4.V523 1998, **(v7)**
  JF1051.V57 2002, **(v7)**
Viscusi, W. Kip. HV5765.V57 1992, **(v6)**
Visher, Emily B. HQ777.7.V57, **(v6)**
  RC488.5.V56 1988, **(v2)**
Vising, Johan. PC2942.V5 1970, **(v3)**
Visser, F. Th. PE1361.V5 1970, **(v3)**
Visser, H. HG221.V5415 1991, **(v6)**
Visser, Margaret. BJ2041.V57 1991, **(v8)**
Visser, Matt. QC173.6.V57 1995, **(v1)**
Vissing, Yvonne Marie. HV4505.V57 1996, **(v6)**
Viswanathan, Gauri. PR51.I4.V57 1989, **(v3)**
Vital, David. DS149.V515 1987, **(v5)**
Vitalis, Robert. HG5836.A3.V58 1995, **(v6)**
Vitanza, Victor J. PN183.V58 1997, **(v3)**
Vitoux, Frederic. PQ2607.E834.Z9513 1991, **(v3)**
Vitruvius Pollio. NA2515.V6135 1999, **(v9)**
Vitsaxis, Basile. BL1205.V5 1977, **(v8)**
Vitti, Antonio. PN1998.3.D417.V57 1996, **(v3)**
Vittorini, Elio. PQ4847.I77.C62, **(v3)**
Vittum, Patricia J. SB608.T87.V58 1999, **(v1)**
Vitz, Evelyn Birge. PQ155.D47.V58 1989, **(v3)**
  PQ205.V58 1999, **(v3)**
Vitz, Paul C. BL2747.3.V58 1999, **(v8)**
Vivas, Eliseo. B945.V54.A36, **(v8)**
  BH21.V55, **(v8)**
  PN45.V55 1972, **(v3)**

  PR6023.A93.Z94, **(v3)**
Vives, Juan Luis. B785.V63.D4713 2000, **(v8)**
Vivo, Jorge Abilio. F1215.V8, **(v4)**
Vizenor, Gerald Robert. E98.S67.V59 1994, **(v4)**
  E99.C6.V593 1984, **(v4)**
  PS153.I52.V59 1998, **(v3)**
Vizzard, William J. HV7436.V59 2000, **(v6)**
  HV8144.B87.V59 1997, **(v6)**
Vlach, John Michael. N6538.N5.V57, **(v9)**
Vlach, Norita. E184.G82.V57 1992, **(v4)**
Vlad, Roman. ML410.D138.V6 1977, **(v9)**
Vlasopolos, Anca. PE64.V57, **(v3)**
Vlastos, Gregory. B187.C7.V55, **(v8)**
  B317.V55, **(v8)**
  B395.V58 1981, **(v8)**
Vlietstra, J. TK5102.V55 2001, **(v1)**
  TK5102.V55 2001, **(v1)**
Vlock, Deborah. PR4592.P45.V58 1998, **(v3)**
Vo, Nhan Tri. HC444.V593 1990, **(v6)**
Voegelin, Eric. CB19.V58 1956, **(v5)**
Vogel, Arthur Israel. QD81.V6 1987, **(v1)**
Vogel, Arthur Israel. QD261.V63 1989, **(v1)**
Vogel, David. K3842.V64 1995, **(v7)**
Vogel, Ezra F. DS793.K7.V64 1989, **(v5)**
  HC460.5.V64 1991, **(v6)**
  HN723.5.V63, **(v6)**
Vogel, Jaroslav. ML410.J18.V712 1981, **(v9)**
Vogel, Lawrence. B3279.H48.S489 1994, **(v8)**
Vogel, Lise. HD6065.5.U6.D54 1993, **(v6)**
Vogel, Ronald K. JS451.F69.V64 1991, **(v7)**
Vogel, Steven. BD581.V57 1996, **(v8)**
Vogel, Steven. QH505.V63 1994, **(v1)**
Vogel, Susan Mullin. N7391.65.V63 1991, **(v9)**
Vogel, Virgil J. E98.M4 V6, **(v4)**
Vogeley, Nancy J. PQ7297.F37Z96 2001, **(v3)**
Vogelsang, W. J. DS358.V64 2002, **(v5)**
Voget, Fred W. E99.C92.D448 1995, **(v4)**
Vogler, John. K3585.4.V64 1995, **(v7)**
Vogler, Thomas A. PR4172.W73V6, **(v3)**
Voglino, Barbara. PS3529.N5.Z886 1999, **(v3)**
Vogt, Evon Zartman. F1435.V732 1994, **(v4)**
Vogt, W. Paul. HA17.V64 1993, **(v6)**
  LC1099.3.V64 1997, **(v7)**
Vohra, Ranbir. DS436.V6 2001, **(v5)**
Voigt, David Quentin. GV863.A1.V65 1983, **(v6)**
Voinovich, Vladimir. PG3489.4.I53.A25 1986, **(v3)**
  PG3489.4.I53.M6513 1987, **(v3)**
Voitle, Robert. PR3537.R4.V6, **(v3)**
Volbach, Wolfgang Fritz. N7832.V63, **(v9)**
Volcansek, Mary L. KF8782.C53.V65 1993, **(v7)**
Volcker, Paul A. HG3881.V65 1992, **(v6)**
Vold, George B. HV6035.V6 1986, **(v6)**
Volgy, Thomas J. JK1726.V65 2001, **(v7)**
Volkogonov, Dmitriæi Antonovich. DK254.L4 V587 1994, **(v5)**
  DK254.T6.V6513 1996, **(v5)**
  DK268.A1.V5813 1998, **(v5)**
  DK268.S8.V5613 1991, **(v5)**
Volkov, Solomon. DK557.V65 1995, **(v5)**
  PG3479.4.R64.Z93 1998, **(v3)**
Volo, James M. F213.V65 2000, **(v4)**
Volodine, Antoine. PQ2682.O436.N6613 1995, **(v3)**
Volpe, Vernon L. F484.3.V65 1990, **(v4)**
Voltaire. B42.V6 1924, **(v8)**
  PQ2082.C3.E5 1966, **(v3)**
  PQ2082.I5 1966, **(v3)**
  PQ2086.L4 1939, **(v3)**
Volti, Rudi. Q121.V65 1999, **(v1)**
Volz, Bridget Dealy. Z1037.V66 2000, **(v10)**
Von Baeyer, Hans Christian. QC318.M35.V66 1998, **(v1)**
Von Blum, Paul. N6505.V66 1982, **(v9)**
Von Braun, Joachim. HC800.Z9 F388 1999, **(v6)**
Von der Mehden, Fred R. DS525.9.M628.V66 1993, **(v5)**
Von Dohlen, Richard F. BJ1012.V66 1997, **(v8)**
Von Eckardt, Barbara. BF311.V624 1993, **(v2)**
Von Eckardt, Wolf. PR5823.V6 1987, **(v3)**
Von Eschen, Penny M. E185.615.V66 1997, **(v4)**
Von Frank, Albert J. PS1631.V66 1994, **(v3)**
Von Geldern, James. PN2724.V636 1993, **(v3)**

Von Glahn, Richard. HG1282.V66 1996, **(v6)**
Von Glinow, Mary Ann Young. HF5549.V75 1988, **(v6)**
Von Grunebaum, Gustave E. D199.3.V62 1961, **(v5)**
Von Gunden, Heidi. ML410.O5834.V6 1983, **(v9)**
Von Gunden, Kenneth. PN1998.2.V66 1991, **(v3)**
Von Hagen, Mark. UA770.V5492 1990, **(v10)**
Von Hippel, Karin. E840.V63 2000, **(v4)**
Von Hirsch, Andrew. KD8406.V66 1993, **(v7)**
Von Hoffman, Nicholas. KF373.C62.V66 1988, **(v7)**
Von Karman, Theodore. TL540.V67.A3, **(v1)**
Von Klemperer, Klemens. DD256.3.V673 1992, **(v5)**
Von Laue, Theodore H. D445.V73 1987, **(v5)**
  DK246 .V58 1993, **(v5)**
Von Mehren, Joan. PS2506.V66 1994, **(v3)**
Von Mises, Ludwig. HB71.V64 1969, **(v6)**
  HB101.V66.A35, **(v6)**
  HB175.V65 1966, **(v6)**
  JC585.V613, **(v7)**
Von Mises, Margit. HB101.V66.V66, **(v6)**
Von Neumann, John. QA76.V6, **(v1)**
  QA269.V65 1953, **(v1)**
  QC174.3.V613, **(v1)**
Von Seggern, David H. QA643.V67 1993, **(v1)**
Von Tunzelmann, G. N. HD82.V62 1995, **(v6)**
Vonnegut, Kurt. PS3572.O5.M6, **(v3)**
  PS3572.O5A6 1995, **(v3)**
  PS3572.O5G58 1999, **(v3)**
  PS3572.O5.G6 1965, **(v3)**
  PS3572.O5.P55x 1966, **(v3)**
  PS3572.O5.S58, **(v3)**
  PS3572.O5.S58 1976, **(v3)**
Voros, Gyorgyi. PS3537.T4753.Z83 1997, **(v3)**
Voss, Sarah. BD111.V67 1995, **(v8)**
Voyce, Arthur. NA1181.V69, **(v9)**
Voyles, Joseph B. PD75.V68 1992, **(v3)**
Vredenbregt, Jacob. DS644.5.V74 1999, **(v5)**
Vrettos, Athena. PR878.M42.V73 1995, **(v3)**
Vries, Hent de. B56.V75 1999, **(v8)**
Vries, J. de. HC324.V72 1997, **(v6)**
Vroman, A. J. BD555.V76 1999, **(v8)**
Vrooman, Jack Rochford. B1873.V7 1970, **(v8)**
Vryonis, Speros. DF545.V78, **(v5)**
Vuchic, Vukan R. HE4211.V83, **(v6)**
Vucinich, Alexander. AS262.A68.V79 1984, **(v10)**
Vuijsje, Herman. HN513.5.V8513 2000, **(v6)**
Vygotskii, L. S. BF706.V9413 1993, **(v2)**
  LB1051.V94513 1997, **(v7)**
Waal, Carla. PN2778.B65.W33 1990, **(v3)**
Waal, F. B. M. de. QL737.P96.W3 1997, **(v1)**
  QL737.P96.W3213 1998, **(v1)**
Wach, Joachim. BL25.L4 no. 4, **(v8)**
  BL41.W33 1988, **(v8)**
Wacher, J. S. DA145.W124 2000, **(v5)**
  DA145.W13 1975, **(v5)**
Wachman, Alan. DS799.847.W33 1994, **(v5)**
Wachsmann, Shelley. DE61.S43.W33 1998, **(v5)**
Wachtel, Andrew. PG2975.W33 1994, **(v3)**
Wachtel, Nathan. F3442.W313 1977b, **(v4)**
Wachtman, J. B. TA455.C43.W38 1996, **(v1)**
Wacker, Grant. BR1644.5.U6 W33 2001, **(v8)**
Wackernagel, Martin. N6921.F7.W313, **(v9)**
Waddan, Alex. HV95.W32 1997, **(v6)**
Waddell, Brian. E806.W17 2001, **(v4)**
Waddell, D. A. G. Z1911.W33 1990, **(v10)**
Waddell, Helen. PL3277.E3.W3 1935, **(v3)**
Waddell, Jack O. E98.S67 W3, **(v4)**
Waddell, Steve R. D810.L642.U653 1994, **(v5)**
Waddington, C. H. QH491.W3, **(v1)**
Waddington, Conrad Hal. BJ1311.W16 1961, **(v8)**
Waddington, Ivan. RC1230.W295 2000, **(v2)**
Wade, Barbara Ann. PS3527.E883.Z95 1998, **(v3)**
Wade, Bonnie C. ML338.W318 1998, **(v9)**
  ML338.W32, **(v9)**
Wade, Ira Owen. PQ2082.C4W3 1972, **(v3)**
Wade, Judy. F809.3.W33 1998, **(v4)**
Wade, Leslie A. PS3569.H394.Z97 1997, **(v3)**
Wade, Mason. F1027.W165, **(v4)**
Wade, Nicholas. BF241.W32 1991, **(v2)**
  BF241.W33 1990, **(v2)**
  QP475.W24 1998, **(v1)**
Wade, Peter. F2299.B55.W3 1993, **(v4)**

Wade, Rex A. DK265.W24 2000, (v5)
Wade, Richard C. F518.W15, (v4)
Wade, Stephen. PR6017.S5.Z89 1991, (v3)
Wade, Terence Leslie Brian. PG2106.W33 2000, (v3)
Wade-Gayles, Gloria Jean. PS153.N5.W26 1997, (v3)
Wadelington, Charles Weldon. LA2317.B598.W33 1999, (v7)
Wadler, Gary I. RC1230.W33 1989, (v2)
Wadsworth, Frank W. PR2937.W3, (v3)
Waelti-Walters, Jennifer R. PQ673.W34 1990, (v3)
Waerden, B. L. van der. QC174.1.W3 1968, (v1)
Wagaw, Teshome G. DS113.8.F34.W34 1993, (v5)
    LA1516.W33, (v7)
Wagener, Hans. PT2635.E68.Z94 1991, (v3)
    PT2647.E77.Z84 1993, (v3)
Wagenheim, Olga Jimenez de. F1973.W33 1997, (v4)
Wagenknecht, Edward. E757.W14, (v4)
    PN6071.S9 W3, (v3)
    PR821.W25 1954, (v3)
    PR1924.W3, (v3)
    PR5332.W34 1990, (v3)
    PS1881.W32 1989, (v3)
Wager, Jans B. PN1995.9.F44.W35 1999, (v3)
Waggoner, Dorothy. LC146.5.W34 1991, (v7)
Waggoner, Mark W. Z8069.2.W34 1990, (v10)
Wagley, Charles. E29.A1.W3, (v3)
    F2510.W26 1971, (v4)
Wagman, Morton. BF449.W34 2002, (v2)
    Q180.55.D57.W34 2000, (v1)
    Q335.W342 1999, (v1)
Wagner, Andrea. KF320.L4 W34 2001, (v7)
Wagner, Ann Louise. GV1623.W25 1997, (v6)
Wagner, Anne Middleton. N6512.W285 1996, (v9)
Wagner, David. HN90.M6.W34 1997, (v6)
    HV4505.W23 1993, (v6)
Wagner, Gerrit A. HD2755.5.W3213 1982, (v6)
Wagner, Gunther A. QE508.W34 1992, (v1)
Wagner, Harvey M. HD20.5.W34 1975, (v6)
Wagner, Henry N. QC795.W24 1989, (v1)
Wagner, Irmgard. PT1955.W34 1995, (v3)
Wagner, J. A. DA357.W34 1999, (v5)
Wagner, Kathrin M. PR9369.3.G6.Z96 1994, (v3)
Wagner, Otto. NA2707.W34.A4 1987, (v9)
Wagner, Richard E. HB846.8.W34 1989, (v6)
Wagner, Richard. ML50.W14.R32 1993, (v9)
    ML410.W1.A317 1988, (v9)
    ML410.W1.W146 1983, (v9)
    ML410.W11.W122, (v9)
Wagner, Robert B. LB2806.22.W34 1989, (v7)
Wagner, Rudolf G. BL1900.L35 W29 2000, (v8)
    PL2393.W34 1990, (v3)
    PL2413.W34 1992, (v3)
Wagner, Tony. LA222.W25 2000, (v7)
Wagner, Valeria. B105.A35.W33 1999, (v8)
Wagner, Warren Lambert. QK473.H4.W33 1990, (v1)
Wagner, William G. KLA542.W34 1994, (v7)
Wagner-Martin, Linda. PS3537.T323.Z87 1995, (v3)
    PS3545.H16.H688 1990, (v3)
    PS3566.L27.Z96 1987, (v3)
    PS3566.L27.Z964 1999, (v3)
    Z8396.3.W33, (v10)
Wagnleitner, Reinhold. DB91.2.W3413 1994, (v5)
Wagoner, Bob. BD436.W34 1997, (v8)
Wagoner, Jay J. F811.3.W33, (v4)
Wagy, Tom. F316.23.C65 W34 1985, (v4)
Wahl, Jean André. B819.W3313, (v8)
Wahl, Otto F. P96.M452.U68 1995, (v3)
Wahlbeck, Osten. DS59.K86.W34 1999, (v5)
Wahlstrom, Carl. LB2343.32.W353 1999, (v7)
Wahrig, Gerhard. PF3625.W2 2000, (v3)
Waibl, Elmar. B43.W29 1997, (v8)
Waid, Candace. PS3545.H16.Z89 1990, (v3)
Waife-Goldberg, Marie. PJ5129.R2.Z88, (v3)
Wailoo, Keith. RA645.S53.W35 2001, (v2)
Wain, John. PR99.W24, (v3)
    PR6045.A249.C6, (v3)
    PR6045.A249.L58xp, (v3)
    PR6045.A249.N8, (v3)
    PR6045.A249.W52, (v3)
    PR6045.A249.W6 1956, (v3)
    PR6045.A25.T7, (v3)

Waine, Barbara. HV248.W35 1991, (v6)
Wainscott, Ronald Harold. PN2266.3.W35 1997, (v3)
Wainstock, Dennis. D769.1.W35 1996, (v5)
Wainwright, A. Martin. DS480.45.W32 1994, (v5)
Wainwright, John William. PR6073.A354.R5 1984, (v3)
Wainwright, Jonathan Mayhew. D767.4.W3, (v5)
Wainwright, Stephen A. QH351.W25 1988, (v1)
Waite, Linda J. HQ536.W33 2000, (v6)
Waite, Peter B. F1032.W16 1967, (v4)
    F1033.M135, (v4)
    F1033.T473 1985, (v4)
    F1033.W15, (v4)
Waite, Robert G. L. DD229.W25 1998, (v5)
Waite, Robert George Leeson. DD238.W34, (v5)
Waites, Bernard. D546.W28 1987, (v5)
Waith, Eugene M. PR658.T7.W3 1962b, (v3)
Waitley, Douglas. TR140.J27.W35 1998, (v1)
Waits, William Burnell. GT4986.A1.W35 1993, (v6)
Waitzkin, Howard. RA418.W347 1991, (v2)
Wajcman, Judy. HD6054.3.W35 1998, (v6)
    HM221.W35 1991, (v6)
Wakefield, Dan. PS3573.A413.G6, (v3)
Wakefield, David. KNQ770.W35 1998, (v7)
Wakefield, Ernest Henry. TL220.W343 1994, (v1)
    TL220.W343 1998, (v1)
Wakefield, Wanda Ellen. U328.U5.W35 1997, (v10)
Wakelin, Derek. QR201.P27.W35 1996, (v1)
Wakeman, Frederic E. DS793.K7.W3, (v5)
    DS796.S2 W4 1995, (v5)
Wakeman, Rosemary. HT169.F72.T68 1997, (v6)
Wakeman, Sarah Rosetta. E628.W35 1994, (v4)
Waksman, Steve. ML1015.G9.W24 1999, (v9)
Walas, Stanley M. QA371.W29 1991, (v1)
Walbank, F. W. DF235.W3 1982, (v5)
    DG312.W3, (v5)
Walch, Timothy. LC501.W28 1996, (v7)
Walcott, Charles Eliot. JK552.W35 1995, (v7)
Walcott, Derek. PR6045.A26.D7, (v3)
    PR9272.9.W3.A17 1986, (v3)
    PR9272.9.W3.J6 1978, (v3)
    PR9272.9.W3.R4 1980, (v3)
    PR9272.9.W3.S7 1979, (v3)
Wald, Gayle. PS366.P37.W35 2000, (v3)
Wald, Kenneth D. BL2525.W35 2003, (v8)
Wald, Priscilla. E169.1.W25 1995, (v4)
Walden, Graham R. Z7164.P956.W33 1996, (v10)
    Z7164.P956 W34 1990, (v10)
    Z7164.S667 W35 2003, (v10)
Walden, R. QK981.5.W34 1989, (v1)
Walder, Andrew G. HD8736.5.W34 1986, (v6)
Walder, David. DS517.W34 1974, (v5)
Waldfogel, Jane. HV713.W27 1998, (v6)
Waldinger, Roger David. F128.9.N3.W32 1996, (v4)
Waldman, Carl. E76.2.W35 1999, (v4)
    E76.2.W36 1994, (v4)
    E77.W195 1985, (v4)
    E89.W35 2001, (v4)
Waldman, Diane. N6494.C6.W35 1992, (v9)
    N6537.D43.W35 1988, (v9)
    N6537.H577.A4 1989, (v9)
    NB497.C35.W3 1982, (v9)
Waldman, Harry. PN1998.W24 2000, (v3)
    PN1998.2.W37 1994, (v3)
    PN1998.2.W38 1995, (v3)
    PN1998.3.T64.W35 2001, (v3)
    UG743.W35 1988, (v10)
Waldmeir, Patti. DT1967.W35 1997, (v5)
Waldner, David. JC131.W36 1999, (v7)
Waldoff, Leon. PR5892.S38, (v3)
Waldram, James B. E78.P7.W35 1988, (v4)
Waldren, Jacqueline. DP402.D395.W3 1996, (v5)
Waldrep, Christopher. F456.W27 1993, (v4)
Waldron, Ann. PN4874.C27.W35 1993, (v3)
    PS3545.E6.Z934 1998, (v3)
Waldron, Arthur. DS777.36.W34 1995, (v5)
    DS793.G67 W25 1990, (v5)
Waldron, Jeremy. JC605.W36 1988, (v7)
Waldron, Mary. PR3779.Y4.Z95 1996, (v3)
Waldron, Peter. DK254.S595.W35 1998, (v5)
Waldrop, M. Mitchell. QA76.17.W35 2001, (v1)

Walens, Susann. HV8657.W35 1997, (v6)
Wales, Katie. PE1261.W35 1996, (v3)
    PR6019.O9.Z934 1991, (v3)
Wales, Nym. DS778.A1.S499, (v5)
Waley, Arthur. B126.W3, (v8)
    DS757.5.W3 1968, (v5)
    PL782.E3.W3 1956, (v3)
    PL884.W3, (v3)
    PL887.W3, (v3)
    PL2735.A5.Z94 1970, (v3)
    PL2997.L5.W23, (v3)
    PL2997.P7.W3, (v3)
    PL3277.E3.W37, (v3)
    PL3277.E3.W54, (v3)
Waley, Daniel Philip. DG975.S5.W35 1991, (v5)
Waley-Cohen, Joanna. DS793.S62.W22 1991, (v5)
Walford, E. John. ND653.R95.W35 1991, (v9)
Wali, K. C. QB36.C46.W35 1991, (v1)
Walicki, Andrzej. DK4358.W34 1994, (v5)
    HX39.W17 1995, (v6)
Waligorski, Conrad. HB119.A2.W18 1997, (v6)
    JC585.W28 1990, (v7)
Walker, A. Earl. RD593.W3, (v2)
Walker, Alan. GN284.W35 1996, (v6)
    ML410.L7 W27 1983, (v9)
Walker, Alice. PR3071.W3, (v3)
    PS3573.A425.C6 1982, (v3)
    PS3573.A425.I5x, (v3)
    PS3573.A425.M4 1986, (v3)
    PS3573.A425.Z467 1983, (v3)
Walker, Bonnie L. Z7164.O4.W28 1995, (v10)
Walker, C. B. F. PJ3193.W35 1987, (v3)
Walker, Cheryl. PS147.W27 1982, (v3)
    PS153.I52.W35 1997, (v3)
Walker, Clarence Earl. E185.625.W35 2001, (v4)
Walker, Danielle Medina. HD31.B7235 2003, (v6)
Walker, David H. PQ305.W34 1995, (v3)
Walker, David. DA715.W26, (v5)
Walker, Deward E. E78.I18 W342, (v4)
Walker, Donald E. Z7514.B3.W35 1995, (v10)
Walker, Dorothea. PR6037.P29.Z96 1988, (v3)
Walker, Franklin Dickerson. PS2473.W3 1963, (v3)
Walker, Greg. PR418.P65.W35 1996, (v3)
    PR649.P6.W35 1991, (v3)
    PR649.P6.W36 1998, (v3)
Walker, J. R. E99.O3.W172 1982, (v4)
Walker, J. Samuel. KF2138.W35 1992, (v7)
    TK9152.W35 2000, (v1)
Walker, Janet A. PL747.6.W34, (v3)
Walker, Janice R. PN171.F56.W35 1998, (v3)
Walker, Jearl. QC32.W2, (v1)
Walker, John Albert. N34.W34 1977, (v9)
    N72.M28.W34 1994, (v9)
    PN1995.9.A73.W3 1993, (v3)
Walker, John F. HC106.W15 1997, (v6)
Walker, John. N856.W33 1984, (v9)
Walker, Julia M. PR429.W64.W35 1998, (v3)
Walker, Juliet E. K. HD2344.5.U6.W35 1998, (v6)
Walker, Kenneth R. HD9046.C62.W335 1984, (v6)
Walker, Kim. PR113.W35 1996, (v3)
Walker, Laurence C. SD143.W285 1999, (v1)
Walker, Lenore E. HV6626.W345 1984, (v6)
Walker, Marcia L. GV745.W35 1992, (v6)
Walker, Mark. PN1995.9.V44.W35 1991, (v3)
    Q127.G3.W35 1995, (v1)
Walker, Martin. D842.W28 1994, (v5)
Walker, Nancy A. PN4879.W35 2000, (v3)
    PS152.W35 1995, (v3)
    PS2523.P9.Z95 1993, (v3)
Walker, Nancy E. KF479.W35 1999, (v7)
Walker, Paul. ML448.W25 2000, (v9)
Walker, R. B. J. JX1395.W33 1992, (v7)
Walker, Ralph Charles Sutherland. BD171.W28 1989, (v8)
Walker, Randi Jones. BX7260.N49, (v8)
Walker, Richard Louis. DS740.4.W23, (v5)
    DS777.55.W34, (v5)

Walker, Samuel. E185.615.W28 1998, **(v4)**
  JC599.U5.W28 1990, **(v7)**
  KF4741.W35 1992, **(v7)**
  KF9223.W254 1993, **(v7)**
  KF9345.W35 1994, **(v7)**
Walker, Steven F. BF175.5.M95.W35 1995, **(v2)**
Walker, Stuart H. GV811.W275 1998, **(v6)**
Walker, Sydney. RC455.4.B5.W35 1996, **(v2)**
Walker, Warren S. Z5917.S5.W35 1993, **(v10)**
Walker, Williston. BR145.W34 1985, **(v8)**
Walker-Hill, Helen. ML390.W16 2002, **(v9)**
Walker-Moffat, Wendy. LC3501.H56.W35 1995, **(v7)**
Walkowitz, Judith R. HQ185.A5.W34, **(v6)**
Wall, Cheryl A. PS153.N5.W33 1995, **(v3)**
Wall, Cynthia. PR8476.W35 1998, **(v3)**
Wall, Helena M. HN57.W27 1990, **(v6)**
Wall, Irwin M. DC404.W3513 1991, **(v5)**
Wall, Joseph Frazier. F621.W17, **(v4)**
Wall, Larry. QA76.73.P22W35 2000, **(v1)**
Wall, Patrick D. RB127.W355 2000, **(v2)**
Wall, Thomas Carl. B2430.L484.W35 1999, **(v8)**
Wallace, Alfred Russel. QL101.W18 1962, **(v1)**
Wallace, Anthony F. C. BF698.W29, **(v2)**
  E93.W18 1999, **(v4)**
Wallace, B. Alan. BQ7950.T754.B9338 1998, **(v8)**
Wallace, Barbara C. RC455.4.F3.W335 1996, **(v2)**
Wallace, Bruce. QH428.W35 1997, **(v1)**
Wallace, Bruce. QH430.W344 1992, **(v1)**
Wallace, Cornelia. F330.W28, **(v4)**
Wallace, Daniel J. RC924.5.L85.W35 2000, **(v2)**
Wallace, David Duncan. F269.W26, **(v4)**
Wallace, David Rains. SB484.C8.W35 1992, **(v1)**
Wallace, David. PR1933.P64.W35 1997, **(v3)**
Wallace, Diana. PR888.T76.W35 2000, **(v3)**
Wallace, George C. F330.W3.A35, **(v4)**
Wallace, George John. QL31.W27.A34, **(v1)**
Wallace, Henry Agard. SB191.M2W313 1988, **(v1)**
Wallace, Hugh N. F1090.5.W33, **(v4)**
Wallace, Ian. DD860.W24 1993, **(v5)**
Wallace, James D. BJ1031.W29 1996, **(v8)**
Wallace, Karl Richards. PR2208.W3, **(v3)**
Wallace, Lew. PS3134.B4 1992, **(v3)**
Wallace, M. Ann. RB37.5.W35 1998, **(v2)**
Wallace, Mark I. BT121.2.W32 1996, **(v8)**
Wallace, Patricia Ward. E748.S667.W35 1995, **(v4)**
Wallace, Paul A. W. F149.W25, **(v4)**
Wallace, Peter George. DC801.C657.W35 1995, **(v5)**
Wallace, R. Jay. BJ1451.W27 1994, **(v8)**
Wallace, Richard C. LB2805.W3236 1996, **(v7)**
Wallace, Robert K. PS2388.A75.W3 1992, **(v3)**
Wallace, Robert W. KL4115.A75 W35 1989, **(v7)**
Wallace, Ryland. DA722.W355 1991, **(v5)**
Wallace, Stephen R. HV687.W34 1984, **(v6)**
Wallace, Tara Ghoshal. PR4038.T4.W35 1994, **(v3)**
Wallace, William A. Q151.A8.W35 1996, **(v1)**
Wallace-Hadrill, Andrew. DG70.P7.W33 1994, **(v5)**
Wallace-Hadrill, J. M. D121.W3 1967, **(v5)**
  DC65.W3 1982, **(v5)**
Wallach, Bret. GF503.W35 1991, **(v6)**
Wallach, Geraldine P. LC4704.85.W35 1988, **(v7)**
Wallach, Glenn. HN90.I58.W35 1997, **(v6)**
Wallach, Janet. DS119.7.A6785.W35 1997, **(v5)**
Wallenrod, Reuben. PJ5020.W3, **(v3)**
Wallenstein, Peter. HJ384.W34 1987, **(v6)**
Waller, Altina L. HV6452.A128.W35 1988, **(v6)**
Waller, Bruce N. B808.67.W35 1998, **(v8)**
Waller, Douglas C. UG743.W355 1987, **(v10)**
Waller, Edmund. PR3750.A1 1645ab, **(v3)**
Waller, Gary F. PR2363.W35 1994, **(v3)**
  PR2399.W7.Z95 1993, **(v3)**
Waller, George Macgregor. E183.8.J3.W24, **(v4)**
Waller, Gregory A. PN1993.5.U743.W36 1995, **(v3)**
Waller, J. Michael. F1488.3.W35 1991, **(v4)**
Waller, James. E184.A1.W215 1998, **(v4)**
  E184.A1.W216 2000, **(v4)**
Waller, Margaret. PQ653.W35 1993, **(v3)**
Waller, Maureen. DA462.A3 W27 2003, **(v5)**
Waller, Susan. N43.W26 1991, **(v4)**
Wallerstein, Immanuel Maurice. HC51.W28 1974 vol.
  1, **(v6)**

Wallerstein, Judith S. HQ834.W356 2000, **(v6)**
  HQ834.W358 1989, **(v6)**
Wallerstein, Robert S. KF228.W413.W35 1998, **(v7)**
  RC489.P72.W35 1995, **(v2)**
Wallerstein, Ruth C. PR529.E4.W3, **(v3)**
Wallis, Allan D. HD7289.62.U6.W35 1991, **(v6)**
Wallis, L. W. Z250.W238 1990, **(v10)**
Wallis, Roy. BP605.S2.W34 1977, **(v8)**
Wallis, W. D. QA166.W314 2000, **(v1)**
Wallmann, Jeffrey M. PS374.W4.W27 1999, **(v3)**
Walls, Laura Dassow. PS3057.N3.D37 1995, **(v3)**
Wallulis, Jerald. BD241.W343 1990, **(v8)**
Wallwork, Ernest. BJ45.W35 1991, **(v8)**
Walmsley, Andrew S. F67.H982.W35 1999, **(v4)**
Waln, Nora. DS721.W3, **(v5)**
Walne, Graham. PN2091.S8.P76 1995, **(v3)**
Walpole, Horace. DA483.W2.A499, **(v5)**
  DA506.W2.A13 1963, **(v5)**
  PR3757.W2.C3, **(v3)**
  PR3757.W2.M5 1978, **(v3)**
Walpole, Hugh. PR6045.A34.C37, **(v3)**
  PR6045.A34.F6, **(v3)**
  PR6045.A34.F63, **(v3)**
  PR6045.A34 R6, **(v3)**
  PR6045.W165.J89, **(v3)**
Walrond-Skinner, Sue. RC475.7.W35 1986, **(v2)**
Walser, Martin. PT2685.A48.B713 1987, **(v3)**
  PT2685.A48.B7 1985, **(v3)**
  PT2685.A48.F48, **(v3)**
  PT2685.A48.F5513 1980x, **(v3)**
  PT2685.A48.S2713 1982, **(v3)**
  PT2685.A48.S4, **(v3)**
  PT2685.A48.S413 1985, **(v3)**
Walser, Robert. ML3534.W29 1993, **(v9)**
Walsh, Andrew D. BR115.E3.W33 2000, **(v8)**
Walsh, Claudette. Z8975.7.W34 1993, **(v10)**
Walsh, Dermot. DA995.L76.W35 2000, **(v5)**
Walsh, Frank. PN1995.5.W27 1996, **(v3)**
Walsh, Froma. RC489.F33.W34 1998, **(v2)**
Walsh, Gretchen. Z5634.A4.W35 1996, **(v10)**
Walsh, James J. B491.E7.W3, **(v8)**
Walsh, Jim. Z7165.U5.W27 1991, **(v10)**
Walsh, John Evangelist. GN282.5.W35 1996, **(v6)**
  PR4836.W275 1999, **(v3)**
  PS1541.Z5.W27 1991, **(v3)**
  PS2631.W28 1998, **(v3)**
Walsh, Kenneth. HD5364.5.A6.W34 1983, **(v6)**
Walsh, Lawrence E. E876.W33 1997, **(v4)**
Walsh, Lorena Seebach. F234.C35.W35 1997, **(v4)**
Walsh, Margaret. HE5623.W35 2000, **(v6)**
Walsh, Mary-Paula. Z7963.R45.W34 1999, **(v10)**
Walsh, P. G. PA6459.W37, **(v3)**
Walsh, Paddy. LB880.W26.E38 1993, **(v7)**
Walsh, Ronald A. TJ1185.W35 1994, **(v1)**
  TJ1185.W35 1999, **(v1)**
Walsh, Stephen. ML410.S932 W34 1988, **(v9)**
  ML410.S932 W345 1999, **(v9)**
Walsh, Thomas F. PS3531.O752.Z846 1992, **(v3)**
Walsh, William. PR9619.3.W5.Z94 1977, **(v3)**
Walshe, Maurice O'C. PT175.W27, **(v3)**
Walt, Stephen M. D21.3.W27 1996, **(v5)**
  JX4005.W335 1987, **(v7)**
Walter of Châtillon. PA8310.G3.A713 1996, **(v3)**
Walter, Andrew. HG3881.W268 1991, **(v6)**
Walter, Bruno. ML422.W27.A312, **(v9)**
  ML422.W27.A32, **(v9)**
Walter, Edward. HN90.R3.W36 1992, **(v6)**
Walter, Ingo. HG5422.W35 2000, **(v6)**
Walter, James. HC605.W436 1996, **(v6)**
Walter, John C. F128.5.J72.W35 1989, **(v4)**
Walter, Knut. F1527.W34 1993, **(v4)**
Walter, Richard J. JL2098.S6 W34, **(v7)**
Walter, Wolfgang. QA372.W244 1998, **(v1)**
Walters, Anna Lee. E98.A7.W32 1989, **(v4)**
Walters, E. Garrison. QA76.5.W287 2001, **(v1)**
Walters, Glenn D. HV6115.W35 1990, **(v6)**
Walters, Gregory J. Z7164.L6.W35 1994, **(v10)**
Walters, James E. SB439.8.W35 1992, **(v1)**
Walters, Kerry S. BL2747.4.W33 1992, **(v8)**
  E302.6.F8.W27 1999, **(v4)**
Walters, Michael. QL675.W32 1994, **(v1)**

Walters, Ronald G. E449.W2, **(v4)**
  HN64.W2136 1978, **(v6)**
Walters, Ronald W. JK1924.W34 1988, **(v7)**
  Z1361.N39.W285 2000, **(v10)**
Walters, Suzanna Danuta. HM101.W225 1995, **(v6)**
Walth, Brent. F881.35.M33.W35 1994, **(v4)**
Walthall, Anne. DS881.5.M323.W35 1998, **(v5)**
Walther, Eric H. E459.W25 1992, **(v4)**
Walther. PT1670.A1.K7 1936, **(v3)**
Waltke, Bruce K. PJ4707.W35 1990, **(v3)**
Walton, Clyde C. F541.W22, **(v4)**
Walton, Douglas N. B105.A35.W34 1989, **(v8)**
  BC175.W322 1999, **(v8)**
  BC175.W355 2000, **(v8)**
  BC177.W315 1997, **(v8)**
  BC177.W3215 1996, **(v8)**
  BC177.W322 1991, **(v8)**
  BC177.W324 1989, **(v8)**
  BC177.W3255 1999, **(v8)**
Walton, Evangeline. PS3573.A6.C48, **(v3)**
Walton, Geoffrey. PR545.M4.W3, **(v3)**
Walton, Harold F. QD79.C453.W35 1990, **(v1)**
Walton, Izaak. SH433.A1983 1983, **(v1)**
Walton, John. HN79.C22.O949 1991, **(v6)**
Walton, Kendall L. BH301.R47.W35 1990, **(v8)**
Walton, Priscilla L. PR5688.W6.W35 1995, **(v3)**
  PS374.D4.W35 1999, **(v3)**
Walton, Scott D. HC106.5.W32, **(v6)**
Walton, Susana. ML410.W292.W3 1988, **(v9)**
Walton, Whitney. HC280.C6 W35 1992, **(v6)**
Waltz, Kenneth Neal. JX1291.W37, **(v7)**
  JX1308.W3, **(v7)**
  JX1417.W3, **(v7)**
Walworth, Arthur. D645.W34 1986, **(v5)**
Walwyn, William. DA407.W35.A2 1989, **(v5)**
Walz, Robin. DC715.W26 2000, **(v5)**
Walzer, Kevin. PS309.N37.W35 1998, **(v3)**
Walzer, Michael. BD241.W345 1987, **(v8)**
  DC137.08.W34, **(v5)**
  JC328.3.W34, **(v7)**
  JC571.W147 1997, **(v7)**
  JC575.W35 1994, **(v7)**
Walzer, Richard. B741.W3, **(v8)**
Wambeke, A. van. S599.9.T76.W36 1991, **(v1)**
Wan, Ming. JC599.C49W36 2001, **(v7)**
Wandersee, Winifred D. HQ1426.W35 1988, **(v6)**
Wandycz, Piotr Stefan. DJK4.S93 vol. 7.K4349, **(v5)**
Wang, Ban. BH221.C6.W33 1997, **(v8)**
Wang, C. H. PL2466.Z7Y44, **(v3)**
Wang, Chengmian. DS753.6.H94 W35 1999, **(v5)**
Wang, Chi-chen. PL2658.E8.W28 1968, **(v3)**
  PL2658.E8.W3 1968, **(v3)**
Wang, Chu-Kia. TA683.2.W3 1998, **(v1)**
Wang, David D. DS793.S62 W24 1999, **(v5)**
  DS793.S62 W359 1999, **(v5)**
Wang, Enbao. DS796.H757.W36 1995, **(v5)**
Wang, Fang-yu. ND1049.C53.A4 1990, **(v9)**
Wang, Fan-shen. DS734.9.F8, **(v5)**
Wang, Gung-hsing. B126.W335 1946, **(v8)**
Wang, Gungwu. DS732.W346 2000, **(v5)**
  DS749.5.W3, **(v5)**
Wang, Hao. B808.5.W36 1986, **(v8)**
  QA29.G58.W357 1996, **(v1)**
Wang, James C. F. Z6464.M2.W36 1991, **(v10)**
Wang, Jessica. Q127.U6.W36 1999, **(v1)**
Wang, Joseph. QD115.W33 2000, **(v1)**
Wang, Meng. PL2919.M39.P8513 1989, **(v3)**
Wang, Q. Edward. DS734.7.W33 2001, **(v5)**
Wang, Qingxin Ken. DS849.C6.W358 2000, **(v5)**
Wang, Richard T. Z3106.W286 1997, **(v10)**
Wang, Shan K. (Shan Kuo). TH7687.W27 2000, **(v1)**
Wang, Shaoguang. DS796.W8.W36 1995, **(v5)**
Wang, Shih-fu. PL2693.H75.E5 1990, **(v3)**
  PL2693.H75E5 1968, **(v3)**
Wang, Shou-jen. B128.W4.E47, **(v8)**
Wang, Te-wei. PL2437.W37 1997, **(v3)**
  PL2442.W36 1992, **(v3)**
Wang, Wei. PL2676.A226 1991, **(v3)**
  PL2676.A285, **(v3)**
Wang, Y. C. DS721.W334, **(v5)**
Wang, Yi-tung. DS740.5.J3.W3, **(v5)**

Wangensteen, Owen Harding. RD19.W36, (v2)
Wankel, Charles. LA843.7.W36 1991, (v7)
Wann, T. W. BF20.W28, (v2)
Wanner, Susan Y. LB1631.W24 1994, (v7)
Wanniski, Jude. HB171.W22, (v6)
Warburg, Gabriel. DT156.4.W37 1992, (v5)
Warburg, Gerald Felix. JX1706.W37 1989, (v7)
Ward Jouve, Nicole. PN56.5.W64.W37 1998, (v3)
  PQ2605.O28.Z92 1987, (v3)
Ward, Adolphus William. DA45.W35 1970, (v5)
Ward, Alan J. DA962.W33, (v5)
  JN1411.W37 1994, (v7)
Ward, Andrew. ML421.J77.W37 2000, (v9)
Ward, Artemus. PS1141.N6, (v3)
Ward, Brian. ML3479.W37 1998, (v9)
Ward, Charles Eugene. PR3423.W3, (v3)
Ward, David. HV4044.W37 1989, (v6)
  PR9362.5.W37 1989, (v3)
Ward, Dederick C. Z6031.W35 1981, (v10)
Ward, Ed. ML3534.W33 1986, (v9)
Ward, Geoffrey C. E468.7.W26 1990, (v4)
  E807.W328 1989, (v4)
  GV863.A1.W37 1994, (v6)
Ward, H. Trawick. E78.N74.W37 1999, (v4)
Ward, Harry M. F454.S43.W37 1988, (v4)
  UB23.W3, (v10)
Ward, Humphry. PR5714.R63, (v3)
Ward, Jack. PN1992.4.A2.W37 1993, (v3)
Ward, John L. ND212.5.R4.W36 1989, (v9)
Ward, Jule DeJager. RJ216.W37 2000, (v2)
Ward, Keith. BL475.5.W37 1994, (v8)
Ward, Lawrence M. BF311.W2695 2002, (v2)
Ward, Margaret. DA958.M25.W37 1990, (v5)
Ward, Martha Coonfield. GN669.W37 1989, (v6)
Ward, Mary Jane. PS3545.A695.S6, (v3)
Ward, Nathaniel. PS858.W2.S5 1969, (v3)
Ward, Norman. F1034.G28.W37 1990, (v4)
Ward, Patricia Spain. R154.B3317.W37 1994, (v2)
Ward, Paul. DA650.W287 1998, (v5)
  QL737.C27.W385 1995, (v1)
Ward, Peter Douglas. QB54.W336 2000, (v1)
  QE721.2.E97, (v1)
  QE882.P8.W37 1997, (v1)
Ward, Peter M. HV4045.5.T4.W37 1999, (v6)
Ward, Philip. AZ999.W37 1989, (v10)
Ward, Samuel Ringgold. E449.W27 1968, (v4)
Ward, Samuel. E207.W26.A4, (v4)
Ward, Stephen A. TK7888.4.W37 1990, (v1)
Ward, W. Peter. GT2713.W37 1990, (v6)
Ward, W. Reginald. BV3777.E9.W37 1992, (v8)
Ward, William Henry. NA533.W2 1926, (v9)
Warde, Mary Jane. E99.C9.G78 1999, (v4)
Wardell, Steven. HQ799.J3.W37 1995, (v6)
Wardlaw, Alvia J. N6537.B52.A4 1995, (v9)
Wardle, David. LA631.W37 1974, (v7)
Wardle, Huon. F1895.K5, (v4)
Wardle, Peter. QK463.W385 1991, (v1)
Wardle, Ralph Martin. PR3493.W3 1969, (v3)
Wardle, Robert A. QL391.C4.W28 1968, (v1)
Wardman, Alan. PA4385.W3, (v3)
Ward-Perkins, J. B. NA310.W34, (v9)
Wardrop, Daneen. PS1541.Z5.W32 1996, (v3)
Ward-Smith, A. J. QP310.F5.W37 1984, (v1)
Ware, Alan. JF2011.W37 1996, (v7)
Ware, Chris. PN6727.W285, (v3)
Ware, Susan. E748.D49.W37 1987, (v4)
Ware, Vron. HQ1154.W37 1991, (v6)
Warford, Jeremy J. HC79.E5.W36 1997, (v6)
Wargin, Kathy-Jo. F567.W37 1999, (v4)
Warhaft, Z. TJ260.W217 1997, (v1)
Waring, Richard H. QH541.5.F6.W34 1998, (v1)
Waring, Stephen P. HD30.5.W37 1991, (v6)
Wark, McKenzie. HM258.W37 1994, (v6)
Warmbrunn, Werner. D802.B4.W37 1993, (v5)
Warmington, E. H. PA6156.A1 1935a, (v3)
Warnatz, J. QD516.W2813 2001, (v1)
Warneck, Peter. QC879.6.W37 1988, (v1)
Warner, Brigitte. MT1.W33 1991, (v9)
Warner, Carolyn M. BX1530.2.W37 2000, (v8)
Warner, Charles Dudley. PS3152.G6 1969, (v3)
  PS3152.T5, (v3)

Warner, Denis Ashton. DS517.W37, (v5)
Warner, Donald F. F1033.W32, (v4)
Warner, Edward L. UA770.W27 1977, (v10)
Warner, Elizabeth. ML3680.W33 1990, (v9)
Warner, Langdon. N7350.W3, (v9)
Warner, Marina. DC103.W27 1981, (v5)
Warner, Michael. HQ32.W367 1999, (v6)
  Z473.W36 1990, (v10)
Warner, Nicholas O. PS217.D75.W37 1997, (v3)
Warner, Rex. PR6045.A78.A65, (v3)
  PR6045.A78.I5, (v3)
  PR6045.A78.P76 1938, (v3)
  PR6045.A78.W5, (v3)
  PR6045.A78.W54 1938, (v3)
  PR6045.A78.Y6, (v3)
Warner, Robert Mark. CD3024.W37 1995, (v5)
Warner, Sam Bass. F73.3.W37 2001, (v4)
  F158.3.W18 1987, (v4)
Warner, Steven B. TS1548.5.W39 1995, (v1)
Warner, Sylvia Townsend. PR6045.A812.A6 1962,
  (v3)
  PR6045.A812.K5 1977, (v3)
  PR6045.A812.L6 1926, (v3)
  PR6045.A812.M5, (v3)
  PR6045.A812.W5, (v3)
Warner, W. Lloyd. LA210.W33, (v7)
Warner, William Beatty. PR858.P68.W37 1998, (v3)
  PR3664.C43.W3, (v3)
Warner-Vieyra, Myriam. PQ3989.2.W35.J8513 1987,
  (v3)
Warneryd, Karl Erik. HB822.W37 1999, (v6)
Warnicke, Retha M. DA333.B6.W37 1989, (v5)
  DA333.C54.W37 2000, (v5)
  HQ1596.W37 1983, (v6)
Warnier, Jean Dominique. QA76.W24313 1986, (v1)
  QA76.W24513, (v1)
Warnke, Georgia. HN59.2.W37 1999, (v6)
Warnock, John W. HD9018.D44.W37 1987, (v6)
  HF1766.W29 1988, (v6)
Warnock, Mary. B53.W35 1992, (v8)
  BF371.W385 1987, (v2)
  BJ319.W3 1978, (v8)
Warrack, John Hamilton. ML102.O6.W37 1992, (v9)
  ML410.W3.W26 1976, (v9)
Warren, Alan. DS392.W3.W37 2000, (v5)
Warren, Austin. B921.J24.W3, (v8)
  PN75.W3.A3 1995, (v3)
Warren, Charles. E301.W25, (v4)
  JK31.W35 1967, (v7)
  JK1561.W3 1937, (v7)
Warren, Christian. RA1231.L4.W37 2000, (v2)
Warren, Donald R. 1933-. LB2807.W33 1974, (v7)
Warren, Gretchen Ward. GV1788.W37 1989, (v6)
  GV1788.5.W27 1996, (v6)
Warren, Harris Gaylord. E801.W28 1980, (v4)
Warren, J. Benedict. F1306.W37 1985, (v4)
Warren, James Perrin. PS407.W37 1999, (v3)
  PS3238.W39 1990, (v3)
Warren, Joyce W. PS2523.P9.Z97 1992, (v3)
Warren, Karen. HQ1233.W297 2000, (v6)
Warren, Kay B. F1465.3.G6.W37 1998, (v4)
Warren, Larry. GV1785.H64.W37, (v6)
  GV1785.S59.W37 1990, (v6)
Warren, Mame. F181.W37 1984, (v4)
Warren, Mark. JC233.N52.W37 1988, (v7)
Warren, Mark. JC423.W326 2001, (v7)
Warren, Mary Anne. HQ751.W37 1985, (v6)
  R725.5.W37 1997, (v2)
Warren, Patricia. PN1993.5.G7.W327 1995, (v3)
Warren, Richard M. QP461.W27 1999, (v1)
Warren, Robert Penn. E451.W29, (v4)
  PS3545.A748.A17 1976b, (v3)
  PS3545.A748.A7 1953, (v3)
  PS3545.A748.A9 1959, (v3)
  PS3545.A748.B3, (v3)
  PS3545.A748.B4 1980, (v3)
  PS3545.A748.B7 1979, (v3)
  PS3545.A748.C3, (v3)
  PS3545.A748.C5, (v3)
  PS3545.A748.M4, (v3)
  PS3545.A748.N5, (v3)

  PS3545.A748.N6, (v3)
  PS3545.A748.P49, (v3)
  PS3545.A748.P7, (v3)
  PS3545.A748.S4, (v3)
  PS3545.A748.W5, (v3)
  PS3545.A748.W6 1950, (v3)
  PS3545.A748.Y6, (v3)
  PS3545.A748.Z48 2000, (v3)
Warren, Roger. PR3091.W37 1990, (v3)
Warren, Roland Leslie. F67.P64.W37 1991, (v4)
Warren, W. L. DA175.W36 1987, (v5)
  DA208.W33 1978b, (v5)
Warren, Warren S. QD475.W27 2000, (v1)
Warren, Wini. Q141.W367 1999, (v1)
Warrender, Howard. JC158.H66W3, (v7)
Warriner, Doreen. HD855.W3, (v6)
Warry, Wayne. E78.C2.W37 1998, (v4)
Warschauer, Mark. LC149.5.W37 1999, (v7)
Warshaw, Shirley Anne. JK611.W37 1996, (v7)
Warshofsky, Fred. QP86.W287 1999, (v1)
Wartenberg, Thomas E. HM136.W345 1990, (v6)
  PN1995.9.L6.W37 1999, (v3)
Wasby, Stephen L. KF4749.W37 1995, (v7)
Washburn, A. L. GB641.W37 1980, (v6)
Washburn, Dennis C. PL747.57.M577.W37 1995, (v3)
Washburn, Michael. BF204.7.W37 1995, (v2)
Washburn, Phil. BD21.W36 2001, (v8)
Washburn, Wilcomb E. E93.W27 1979, (v4)
Washington, Booker T. E185.W3146 1968, (v4)
  E185.97.W274, (v4)
  E185.97.W29 1969, (v4)
  E185.97.W3163, (v4)
Washington, Bryan R. PS159.E85.W37 1995, (v3)
Washington, George. E312.7. 1970, (v4)
  E312.8. 1976, (v4)
Washington, Linn. KF9223.W27 1995, (v7)
Washington, Valora. LC4091.W36 1995, (v7)
Wasiolek, Edward. PG3420.O83W37 1993, (v3)
Wasserman, David T. KFX2093.W37 1990, (v7)
Wasserman, Earl R. PR5438.W3, (v3)
Wasserman, George Russell. PR3338.W3, (v3)
Wasserman, Mark. HN120.C46.W39 1993, (v6)
Wasserman, Paul. AS8.W38, (v10)
Wasserman, Philip D. QA76.5.W353 1989, (v1)
Wassermann, Selma. LB1537.W34 1990, (v7)
Wasserstein, Bernard. DS109.93.W37 2001, (v5)
Wasserstrom, Jeffrey N. LA1134.S4.W37 1991, (v7)
Wasserstrom, Robert. F1219.1.C45.W37 1983, (v4)
Wassil-Grimm, Claudette. RC455.2.F35.W37 1995,
  (v2)
Wassink, Jan L. QL719.R63.W37 1993, (v1)
Wasson, D. DeWitt. ML3186.W2 1998, (v9)
Wasson, David Atwood. PS3157.W2.A6 1965, (v3)
Waste, Robert J. JS341.W379 1989, (v7)
Waswo, Richard. CB245.W28 1997, (v5)
  PR2216.W3, (v3)
Waterbury, John. HC830.W37 1983, (v6)
Waterfield, Gordon. DS70.88.L3.W3, (v5)
Waterford, Helen. DS135.G5.W338 1987, (v5)
Waterhouse, Keith. PR6073.A82.T43, (v3)
Waters, Catherine. PR4592.F36.W38 1997, (v3)
Waters, Chris. HX243.W38 1990, (v6)
Waters, David Watkin. VK549.W3, (v10)
Waters, Ethel. ML420.W24 A3 1992, (v9)
Waters, Frank. F788.W3, (v4)
Waters, Malcolm. HM22.U6.B448 1996, (v6)
Waters, T. Frederick. TS183.W38 1996, (v1)
Waters, Thomas F. F610.W37, (v4)
Waters, Tony. HV640.W335 2001, (v6)
Waterson, D. B. DU270.W38 1987, (v5)
Waterson, Jan. HV5137.W38 2000, (v6)
Waterston, Elizabeth. PR9185.3.W37 2001, (v3)
Watkin, David. NA645.5.E25.W37, (v9)
  NA961.W37 1979, (v9)
  NA997.S7.W38 1996, (v9)
Watkin, Julia. B4371.W38 2001, (v8)
Watkin, William. PS255.N5.W38 2001, (v3)
Watkins, Andrea. GV1588.W38 1990, (v6)
Watkins, Daniel P. PR4838.P6.W37 1989, (v3)
Watkins, Elizabeth Siegel. HQ766.5.U5.W325 1998,
  (v6)

Watkins, Evan. HM101.W278 1993, **(v6)**
Watkins, Glenn. ML197.W437 1994, **(v9)**
 ML410.G29 W4 1991, **(v9)**
Watkins, James. QP301.W34 1999, **(v1)**
Watkins, Joanne C. DS493.9.N94.W37 1996, **(v5)**
Watkins, Joe. E77.9.W37 2000, **(v4)**
Watkins, John C. KF9779.W38 1998, **(v7)**
Watkins, John. PR2367.L5.W38 1995, **(v3)**
Watkins, Kathleen Pullan. BF723.A75.W38 1987, **(v2)**
Watkins, Marilyn P. F897.L6.W38 1995, **(v4)**
Watkins, Mel. PN6231.N5.W38 1994, **(v3)**
Watkins, Peter. QC793.5.B62.W37 1986, **(v1)**
Watkins, Ronald. PR2995.W3 1950, **(v3)**
Watkins, S. Craig. PN1995.9.N4.W38 1998, **(v3)**
Watkins, Susan Cotts. HB991.W38 1991, **(v6)**
Watkins, T. H. F593.W32, **(v4)**
Watkins, W. B. C. PR2976.W3, **(v3)**
Watkinson, John. TK7881.4.W3834 1994, **(v1)**
Watkinson, Raymond. N6767.5.P7.W3 1970b, **(v9)**
Watkins-Owens, Irma. F128.9.C27.W38 1996, **(v4)**
Watlington, Patricia. F454.W3 1972, **(v4)**
Watras, Joseph. LC214.23.D29.W38 1997, **(v7)**
Watrous, James. NC735.W36, **(v9)**
 NE507.W37 1984, **(v4)**
Watson, Adam. JX1305.W38 1992, **(v7)**
Watson, Alan. K7030.W37 1992, **(v7)**
 KDZ546.W38 1989, **(v7)**
 KJA160.W38 1991, **(v7)**
 KJA3060.W37 1992, **(v7)**
Watson, Alaric. DG308.W37 1999, **(v5)**
Watson, Burton. PL2280.W3, **(v3)**
 PL2658.E3.W34, **(v3)**
Watson, Charles S. HD69.P75.W38 1996, **(v6)**
Watson, Curtis Brown. PR3007.W3, **(v3)**
Watson, Cynthia Ann. UA23.W364 1990, **(v10)**
Watson, David Robin. DC342.8.C6W34 1976, **(v5)**
Watson, David. PQ2603.E378.Z95 1990, **(v3)**
Watson, Derek. ML410.B88 W26 1996, **(v9)**
 ML410.L7 W35 2000, **(v9)**
 ML410.W1.W38 1981, **(v9)**
Watson, Donald G. PR2982.W38 1990, **(v3)**
Watson, G. Llewellyn. Z7961.W37 1990, **(v10)**
Watson, Geoffrey R. KMM707.W38 2000, **(v7)**
Watson, George Ronald. U35.W35 1969b, **(v10)**
Watson, George. Z2011.W3 1965, **(v10)**
Watson, Harry L. E381.W32 1990, **(v4)**
 F262.C9.W37, **(v4)**
Watson, J. R. BV312.W38 1997, **(v8)**
Watson, James D. QD341.A2.W315, **(v1)**
 QH431.W368 1970, **(v1)**
 QH438.W38 2000, **(v1)**
 QH442.W37, **(v1)**
 QH450.2.W37, **(v1)**
Watson, James G. PS3511.A86.Z985354 2000, **(v3)**
Watson, Jeanie. PR4487.F33.W3 1990, **(v3)**
Watson, John Broadus. BF199.W3 1958, **(v2)**
Watson, John Steven. DA505.W38, **(v5)**
Watson, Justin. BR526.W33 1997, **(v8)**
Watson, Lyall. BJ1406.W37 1995, **(v8)**
 QP458.W38 2000, **(v1)**
Watson, Martha. CT25.W28 1999, **(v5)**
Watson, Nicola J. PR868.P57.W38 1994, **(v3)**
Watson, Patty Jo. CC72.W37 1984, **(v5)**
Watson, Peter. N6447.W3 1992, **(v9)**
 U22.3.W37, **(v10)**
Watson, Robert Irving. BF81.W35 1968, **(v2)**
Watson, Robert. PN1993.7.W38 1990, **(v3)**
Watson, Sara Ruth. PR6007.A35.Z96, **(v3)**
Watson, Steven. NX504.W38 1991, **(v9)**
Watson, Thomas. PR2384.W5 1997, **(v3)**
Watson, Wallace Steadman. PN1998.3.F37.W38
 1996, **(v3)**
Watson, Wilbur H. R695.W38 1999, **(v2)**
Watson, William. DS715.W32 1966a, **(v5)**
 DS741.5.W3, **(v5)**
 N7343.W38 1995, **(v9)**
 NB1053.W34, **(v9)**
Watson-Watt, Robert Alexander. UG610.W28, **(v10)**
Watstein, Sarah. RC607.A26.W383 1998, **(v2)**
Watt, Alan H. T385.W3778 2000, **(v1)**
 T385.W38 1989, **(v1)**

Watt, Donald Cameron. D741.W36 1989, **(v5)**
Watt, Ian P. PN56.I57.W37 1996, **(v3)**
 PR4037.W35, **(v3)**
 PR6005.O4.Z923, **(v3)**
 PR6005.O4.Z9232 2000, **(v3)**
Watt, Stephen. PN1623.W35 1998, **(v3)**
 PR6019.O9.Z935 1991, **(v3)**
Watt, Tessa. PR428.C48.W38 1991, **(v3)**
Watt, W. Montgomery. D199.3.I8 no. 4, **(v5)**
 DS36.85.I8 no. 6, **(v5)**
 DS36.85.I8 no. 9, **(v5)**
Wattar, al-Tahir. PJ7870.A8.Z313 2000, **(v3)**
Wattenberg, Ben J. HN59.2.W38 1995, **(v6)**
Wattenberg, Martin P. JK2261.W38 1991, **(v7)**
Watters, Reginald Eyre. Z1375.W3 1972, **(v10)**
Watters, Thomas. PJ408.O7 new ser., vol. xiv, xv, **(v3)**
Watterson, Barbara. DT77.W35 1997, **(v5)**
Watterson, John Sayle. GV950.W28 2000, **(v6)**
Watts, Alan. B799.W34 1995, **(v8)**
 BD450.W3 1972, **(v8)**
Watts, Cedric Thomas. PR2807.W35 1988, **(v3)**
Watts, David. HC151.W375 1987, **(v6)**
Watts, Emily Stipes. PS173.B87.W3 1982, **(v3)**
Watts, Jerry Gafio. PS3555.L625.Z95 1994, **(v3)**
Watts, John Lovett. DA257.W38 1996, **(v5)**
Watts, Linda S. PS3537.T323.Z887 1999, **(v3)**
Watts, Michael. Z3236.W371986, **(v10)**
Watts, S. J. HN373.W37 1984, **(v6)**
Watts, Steven. E310.W37 1987, **(v4)**
 NC1766.U52.D5927 1997, **(v9)**
Watts, Thomas D. Z7721.W37 1986, **(v10)**
Wauchope, Piers. DA940.5.S27.W38 1992, **(v5)**
Wauchope, Robert. E61.W33, **(v4)**
Waugh, Alec. PR6045.A95.I8, **(v3)**
 PR6045.A95.Z52, **(v3)**
Waugh, Anne. RT69.W48 2001, **(v2)**
Waugh, Evelyn. PR6045.A97.A6 1983, **(v3)**
 PR6045.A97.B5, **(v3)**
 PR6045.A97.B7 1960, **(v3)**
 PR6045.A97.D4, **(v3)**
 PR6045.A97.E6, **(v3)**
 PR6045.A97.H3, **(v3)**
 PR6045.A97.H4 1950, **(v3)**
 PR6045.A97.L59 1953, **(v3)**
 PR6045.A97.L6 1977, **(v3)**
 PR6045.A97.M4, **(v3)**
 PR6045.A97.O7, **(v3)**
 PR6045.A97.P8, **(v3)**
 PR6045.A97.S3 1948, **(v3)**
 PR6045.A97.S37, **(v3)**
 PR6045.A97.S9 1966, **(v3)**
 PR6045.A97.T3 1971, **(v3)**
 PR6045.A97.V5, **(v3)**
 PR6045.A97.Z477 1984, **(v3)**
 PR6045.A97.Z498 1977, **(v3)**
 PR6045.A97.Z53 1980, **(v3)**
 PR6045.A97Z5, **(v3)**
Waugh, Joan. HV28.L66.W38 1997, **(v6)**
Waugh, Norah. TT504.W38, **(v1)**
Waugh, W. T. D102.M4 1980, vol. 4, **(v5)**
Waun, Maurine C. BR115.H6 W38 1999, **(v8)**
Wauzzinski, Robert A. T14.W33 2001, **(v1)**
Wawn, Andrew. PR468.V54, **(v3)**
Wawro, Geoffrey. DD438.W39 1996, **(v5)**
Wawro, Gregory J. JK1319.W38 2000, **(v7)**
Wax, Carol. NE1815.W38 1990, **(v9)**
Waxman, Barbara Frey. PS366.A88.W38 1997, **(v3)**
Waxman, Meyer. PJ5008.W323, **(v3)**
Waxman, Michael F. SB951.W396 1998, **(v1)**
Way, Douglas S. GB406.W39 1978, **(v6)**
Way, Frederick. F157.A5.W3, **(v4)**
Way, Lewis Malcolm. BF173.A55.W3, **(v2)**
Wayland, Robert L. HF5415.5.W39 1997, **(v6)**
Waylen, Georgina. JF60.W39 1996, **(v7)**
Wayne, Richard P. QC879.6.W39 1990, **(v1)**
 QD708.2.W39 1988, **(v1)**
Weales, Gerald Clifford. PR739.R4.W4 1961, **(v3)**
Weare, Walter B. HG8963.N9553W4 1993, **(v6)**
Wearing, Betsy. GV183.W43 1998, **(v6)**
Wearing, J. P. PN2596.L6.W3846 1991, **(v3)**
 Z8814.5.W4 1986, **(v10)**

Wearne, Phillip. E59.G6.W43 1996, **(v4)**
Weart, Spencer R. JC421.W43 1998, **(v7)**
Weatherall, D. J. R723.W355 1995, **(v2)**
Weatherall, M. RM45.W43 1990, **(v2)**
Weatherburn, Charles Ernest. QA276.W4 1961, **(v1)**
Weatherby, Harold L. PR2358.W38 1994, **(v3)**
Weatherford, J. McIver. E59.I53 W43 1988, **(v4)**
 E77.W418 1991, **(v4)**
Weatherford, Roy. BC141.W4 1982, **(v8)**
Weatherford, Willis Duke. LB2325.W38, **(v7)**
Weatherhead, A. Kingsley. PR888.P3, **(v3)**
 PR6013.R416.Z93, **(v3)**
Weathers, Shirley A. QK100.U6.W43 1998, **(v1)**
Weaver, Bruce L. Z5916.W43 1995, **(v10)**
Weaver, Frederick Stirton. HF1480.5.W43 2000, **(v6)**
Weaver, Glenn. F235.I8.W43 1988, **(v4)**
Weaver, Gordon. PS3573.E17.S9, **(v3)**
Weaver, Jace. KF373.B545.W43 1993, **(v7)**
Weaver, James H. HC79.E5.W43 1997, **(v6)**
Weaver, Martin E. NA105.W43 1993, **(v9)**
Weaver, Paul. PN4888.O25.W43 1994, **(v3)**
Weaver, R. Kent. HG229.5.W43 1988, **(v6)**
 HV95.W38 2000, **(v6)**
Weaver, Stewart Angas. DA3.H29.W43 1997, **(v5)**
 DA541.F54.W43 1987, **(v5)**
Webb, Barbara J. PN849.C3.W4 1992, **(v3)**
Webb, Clive. E184.36.A34.W43 2001, **(v4)**
Webb, D. A. SB413.S28.W43 1989, **(v1)**
Webb, Eugene J. H62.W38, **(v6)**
Webb, Geoffrey Fairbank. NA963.W4 1956, **(v9)**
Webb, James H. PS3573.E1955.F5, **(v3)**
Webb, Michael Gordon. HD9502.A2.W4 1980, **(v6)**
Webb, Samuel L. F326.W43 1997, **(v4)**
Webb, Stephen H. BL48.W313 1993, **(v8)**
Webb, Stephen. R134.8.W427 1995, **(v2)**
Webb, Walter Freeman. QL414.W42, **(v1)**
Webb, Walter Prescott. CB245.W4 1964, **(v5)**
 F591.W35 1981, **(v4)**
Webber, Elizabeth. PE1580.W33 1990, **(v3)**
 PN43.W384 1999, **(v3)**
Webber, Geoffrey. ML2929.W43 1996, **(v9)**
Webber, Jeremy H. A. JL27.W44 1994, **(v7)**
Webber, Joan. PR2248.W4, **(v3)**
 PR3562.W34, **(v3)**
Webber, Mark. DK293.W43 1996, **(v5)**
Webber, Roger. RA643.W37 1996, **(v2)**
Webber, Sabra Jean. GR353.52.Q53.W43 1991, **(v6)**
Weber, Carl Jefferson. PR4753.W27 1965, **(v3)**
Weber, Christian Oliver. LA93.W4, **(v7)**
Weber, David J. F800.W4 1982, **(v4)**
Weber, Devra. HD8039.C662.U68 1994, **(v6)**
Weber, Edward P. GE180.W43 1998, **(v6)**
Weber, Eugen Joseph. DC33.W37 1991, **(v5)**
 DC33.6.W43 1986, **(v5)**
 DC369.W36, **(v5)**
 DC389.W35 1994, **(v5)**
 HN426.W4 1976, **(v6)**
Weber, Lillian. LB885.W33.W33 1997, **(v7)**
Weber, Marvin J. TA1683.W44 2001, **(v1)**
Weber, Max. BL60.W433, **(v8)**
 BR115.C3 W413 2002b, **(v8)**
 H33.W3613, **(v6)**
 H61.W4, **(v6)**
 HB75.W5, **(v6)**
 HC31.W42213 1976, **(v6)**
Weber, Michael P. F155.3.L385.W42 1988, **(v4)**
Weber, Michael. GC1015.2.W43 1995, **(v6)**
Weber, Nicholas Fox. ND553.B23.W43 1999, **(v9)**
Weber, Ralf. NA2765.W39 1995, **(v9)**
Weber, Ralph Edward. Z103.W4, **(v10)**
Weber, Robert J. T212.W4 1992, **(v1)**
 TK7876.W42 2001, **(v1)**
Weber, Robert L. QC15.W4, **(v1)**
Weber, Ronald. PS88.W37 1997, **(v3)**
Weber, Thomas. DS480.45.W4 1997, **(v5)**
 JZ5584.I4.W43 1996, **(v7)**
Weber, William. ML286.3.W4 1992, **(v9)**
Websdale, Neil. HV6250.4.W65.W453 1998, **(v6)**
Webster, Anthony. DS526.4.W43 1998, **(v5)**
Webster, Arthur Gordon. QA371.W39, **(v1)**
Webster, Bruce. DA774.8.W4, **(v5)**

Webster, Charles K. F1416.G7.W4 1970, **(v4)**
Webster, Daniel. E337.8.W242 1990, **(v4)**
  E337.8.W365 1969, **(v4)**
Webster, Frank. QA76.W38 1986, **(v1)**
Webster, Graham. U35.W48 1985, **(v10)**
Webster, J. B. BJ1231.W42 1998, **(v8)**
Webster, John. PR3181.L8 1966, **(v3)**
  PR3184.D8 1969, **(v3)**
  PR3184.W5 1968, **(v3)**
  QK603.W4 1980, **(v1)**
Webster, Linda. HV6561.W45 1989, **(v6)**
Webster, Margaret. PR3091.W4 1955, **(v3)**
Webster, Noah. PE64.W5.A4, **(v3)**
Webster, Norman Edward. HF5601.A872.W4 1978, **(v6)**
Webster, R. S592.14.W4 1990, **(v1)**
Webster, Raymond B. Q141.W43 1999, **(v1)**
Webster, Robert. QE392.W37 1994, **(v1)**
Webster, Roger. PN86.W35 1996, **(v3)**
Webster, Yehudi O. LC1099.3.W43 1997, **(v7)**
Wechselblatt, Martin. PR3537.P6.W43 1998, **(v3)**
Wechsler, David. BF431.W35 1958, **(v2)**
  BF431.W35 1972, **(v2)**
  BF431.W37 1952, **(v2)**
Wechsler, Howard J. DS749.3.W36.W42, **(v5)**
Wechsler, Robert. PN241.W43 1998, **(v3)**
Weckert, John. QA76.9.M65.W43 1997, **(v1)**
Weckesser, Elden C. E457.5.W43 1991, **(v4)**
Weckmann, Luis. F1231.W3318 1992, **(v4)**
Wecter, Dixon. E161.W43 1970, **(v4)**
  E176.W4 1972, **(v4)**
Wedberg, Anders. B99.S82.W413 1982, **(v8)**
Wedborn, Helena. Z6207.E8 W38 1988, **(v10)**
Wedding, Mary Ellen. RB37.W42 1998, **(v2)**
Weddle, David. PN1998.3.P43.W44 1994, **(v3)**
Weddle, Meredith Baldwin. BX7639.W432001, **(v8)**
Weddle, Robert S. F296.W427 1991, **(v4)**
  F296.W43 1985, **(v4)**
  F394.S27 W43 1999, **(v4)**
Wedel, Janine R. HC244.W364 1998, **(v6)**
Wedemeyer, Albert C. D743.W4, **(v5)**
  UA23.W36934 1987, **(v10)**
Wedepohl, Karl Hans. QE515.W42, **(v1)**
Wedgwood, C. V. D7.W43, **(v5)**
  D8.W4, **(v5)**
  D13.W42, **(v5)**
  D16.8.W38 1960a, **(v5)**
  D258.W4, **(v5)**
  DA396.S8.W4 1970, **(v5)**
  DA405.W42 vol. 1, **(v5)**
  DA405.W42 vol. 2, **(v5)**
  DA426.W4, **(v5)**
  DA566.9.W4.W4, **(v5)**
  DC123.9.R5.W4, **(v5)**
  PR431.W4 1970, **(v3)**
Wedin, Michael V. B491.P8.W33 1988, **(v8)**
Weed, Frank. HV6250.3.U5.W44 1995, **(v6)**
Weed, Thurlow. E415.9.W39.W33, **(v4)**
Weeden, Robert B. QH105.A4.W44 1992, **(v1)**
Weegee. TR820.F45 1977, **(v1)**
Weekley, Carolyn J. ND237.H58.W44 1999, **(v9)**
Weeks, Jeffrey R. QA612.2.W44 1985, **(v1)**
Weeks, John M. Z1209.2.W47.A53 1994, **(v10)**
Weeks, John. HB98.2.W44 1989, **(v6)**
  HC1065.W44 1992, **(v6)**
Weeks, W. William. QH75.W43 1997, **(v1)**
Weeks, William Earl. F314.W44 1992, **(v4)**
Weems, M. L. E312.W3893, **(v4)**
Weems, Robert E. HC110.C6.W44 1998, **(v6)**
Weeramantry, C. G. KVU97.5.W44 1992, **(v7)**
Wegar, Katarina. HV875.55.W44 1997, **(v6)**
Wegener, Charles. BH39.W375 1992, **(v8)**
Wegener, Frank Corliss. LB885.W4 1974, **(v7)**
Wegener, Peter P. TL570.W4 1997, **(v1)**
  UF535.G3.W43 1996, **(v10)**
Wegman, William. N6537.W345.A4 1990, **(v9)**
Wehmann, Howard H. CD3045.W44 1989, **(v5)**
Wehr, Hans. PJ6640.W43 1976, **(v3)**
Wehr, Wesley. NX509.A1, **(v9)**
Wehrs, Donald R. PR9344.W44 2001, **(v3)**
Weibel, Ewald R. QP121.W395 1984, **(v1)**

Weick, Karl E. HD49.W45 2001, **(v6)**
Weideli, Walter. PT2603.R397.Z893, **(v3)**
Weidenbaum, Murray L. UA23.W36943 1992, **(v10)**
Weidensaul, Scott. QL696.F3, **(v1)**
Weidman, Jerome. PS3545.E449.B4, **(v3)**
  PS3545.E449.E5 1958, **(v3)**
  PS3545.E449.I, **(v3)**
Weiers, Margaret K. F1034.3.A2.W45 1995, **(v4)**
Weigand, Hermann John. PD25.N6 no.49, **(v3)**
  PN511.W42, **(v3)**
  PT1688.W43, **(v3)**
Weigand, Kate. HX546.W35 2001, **(v6)**
Weigel, Van B. HC79.B38.W45 1989, **(v6)**
Weigert, Stephen L. BR1430.W45 1996, **(v8)**
Weightman, Christine B. DC611.B781.W4 1989, **(v5)**
Weigle, Marta. BL226.W45 1989, **(v8)**
Weigley, Russell Frank. D761.W4, **(v5)**
  U39.W45 1991, **(v10)**
  UA25.W35 1984, **(v10)**
  UA25.W4, **(v10)**
Weihs, Jean Riddle. F1008.W44 1994, **(v4)**
Weil, Andre. QA241.W3418 1984, **(v1)**
Weil, Danny K. LC1099.3.W44 1998, **(v7)**
Weil, John A. QC763.W45 1994, **(v1)**
Weil, Rachel Judith. DA435.W37 2000, **(v5)**
Weil, Simone. B2430.W473.L3513, **(v8)**
  B2430.W473.L43, **(v8)**
  BV4817.W42, **(v8)**
Weil, Stephen E. AM7.W392 1995, **(v10)**
Weil, Thomas E. F2508.W44, **(v4)**
Weiler, Kathleen. LB2837.W445 1998, **(v7)**
Weiler, Michael. E877.2.R425 1992, **(v4)**
Weiler, Paul C. KF3989.W45 2000, **(v7)**
Weiler, Peter. DA585.B4.W44 1993, **(v5)**
  HD6490.F582.G78 1988, **(v6)**
Weimann, Gabriel. PN4784.T45.W45 1994, **(v3)**
Weimann, Robert. PR3034.W45 2000, **(v3)**
Weimer, Maryellen. LB2331.W37 1990, **(v7)**
Weinbaum, Marvin G. DS383.5.A3.W45 1994, **(v5)**
Weinbaum, Stanley Grauman. PS3545.E4636.M3, **(v3)**
Weinberg, Adam S. HN49.C6.W437 2000, **(v6)**
Weinberg, Alvin Martin. Q180.A1.W4, **(v1)**
Weinberg, Bennett Alan. QP801.C24, **(v1)**
Weinberg, Bernard. PQ4027.W4, **(v3)**
Weinberg, David H. DS143.W39 1996, **(v5)**
Weinberg, Gerhard L. D743.W424 1994, **(v5)**
  D754.R9.W4 1972, **(v5)**
Weinberg, H. Barbara. ND210.5.I4.W456 1994, **(v9)**
Weinberg, Julius R. B29.W4145, **(v8)**
Weinberg, Mark S. PN2266.5.W45 1992, **(v3)**
Weinberg, Meyer. LC214.2.W44 1983, **(v7)**
  Z1361.E4.W45 1990, **(v10)**
  Z7164.R12.W5 1992, **(v10)**
Weinberg, Robert A. RC267.W45 1996, **(v2)**
  RC268.48.W45 1984, **(v2)**
Weinberg, Robert S. GV706.4.W38 2003, **(v6)**
  GV735.W45 1990, **(v6)**
Weinberg, Robert. DK264.2.O3.W45 1993, **(v5)**
Weinberg, Steven. QB981.W48, **(v1)**
  QC793.2.W44 1983, **(v1)**
Weinberger, Barbara. HV8195.A2.W44 1990, **(v6)**
Weinbrot, Howard D. PR448.N38.W44 1993, **(v3)**
  PR935.W39 1988, **(v3)**
Weindling, Paul. RA652.W43 2000, **(v2)**
Weindruch, Richard. QP86.W45 1988, **(v1)**
Weiner, Alan R. Z6511.W44 1994, **(v10)**
Weiner, Amir. D744.55.W45 2001, **(v5)**
Weiner, Annette B. GN662.W45 1992, **(v6)**
Weiner, Dora B. R506.P3.W45 1993, **(v2)**
Weiner, Douglas R. GE199.R8.W45 1999, **(v6)**
  QH77.S626.W45 1988, **(v1)**
Weiner, Edward. HE308.W45 1999, **(v6)**
Weiner, Herbert. QP82.2.S8.W45 1992, **(v1)**
Weiner, James F. DU740.42.W4 1991, **(v5)**
Weiner, Jonathan. QL696.P246.W45 1994, **(v1)**
Weiner, Marc A. ML410.W19.W23 1995, **(v9)**
Weiner, Marli Frances. E445.S7.W45 1997, **(v4)**
Weiner, Myron E. HV41.W368 1990, **(v6)**
Weiner, Myron. HB2099.W44, **(v6)**
  HD6250.I42.W45 1991, **(v6)**

Weiner, Richard. P87.5.W45 1996, **(v3)**
Weiner, Robert. BF408.W384 2000, **(v2)**
Weiner, Stephen. Z5956.C6 W45 2001, **(v10)**
Weiner, Susan. PS2388.L36.W4 1992, **(v3)**
Weinfield, Henry. PR3502.E53.W45 1991, **(v3)**
Weinfurter, Stefan. DD143.W46 1999, **(v5)**
Weingartner, Rudolph H. LA226.W425 1992, **(v7)**
Weingreen, J. PJ4567.W4 1959, **(v3)**
Weinreich, Max. PJ5113.W3813, **(v3)**
Weinreich, Uriel. PJ5115.W4 1969, **(v3)**
Weinroth, Michelle. HX243.W45 1996, **(v6)**
Weinsheimer, Joel. BD241.W44 1991, **(v8)**
Weinstein, Allen. HG555.W44, **(v6)**
Weinstein, Allen. UB271.R9.W45 1999, **(v10)**
Weinstein, Brian. F1921.W45 1992, **(v4)**
  JQ3407.A2 W4, **(v7)**
Weinstein, David A. KF3180.Z9.W45 1991, **(v7)**
Weinstein, Edwin A. E767.W42, **(v4)**
Weinstein, Harvey. BF633.W45 1990, **(v2)**
Weinstein, James. E743.W44, **(v4)**
Weinstein, Martin. F2728.W43 1988, **(v4)**
Weinstein, Philip M. PS3511.A86.Z9855 1992, **(v3)**
Weinstein, Robert A. TR465.W44, **(v1)**
Weintraub, Dov. HD1491.P3.W38, **(v6)**
Weintraub, E. Roy. HB71.W397, **(v6)**
Weintraub, Sidney. HF1456.5.M6.W45 1990, **(v6)**
Weintraub, Stanley. PR5366.W42 1996, **(v3)**
  Z8814.5.W44 1992, **(v10)**
Weir, Alison. DA317.1.W45 1996, **(v5)**
  DA332.W45 2001, **(v5)**
  DA333.A2 W45 1991, **(v5)**
  DA355.W36 1998, **(v5)**
  DA787.D3 W45 2003, **(v5)**
Weir, David. PN51.W345 1997, **(v3)**
  PN56.D45.W45 1995, **(v3)**
Weir, Gary E. V55.U55.W45 2001, **(v10)**
  VA513.W255 1991, **(v10)**
Weir, Glenn. GV846.5.W45 1999, **(v6)**
Weir, Margaret. HD5724.W38 1991, **(v6)**
Weir, Neil. RF25.W45 1990, **(v2)**
Weir, Robert F. RJ253.5.W44 1984, **(v2)**
Weir, Robert M. F272.W46 1983, **(v4)**
Weis, Lois. LC2801.W36 1985, **(v7)**
  LC5051.W4 1990, **(v7)**
Weis, Ren. BX4891.2.W457 2001, **(v8)**
Weisberg, Arthur. MT75.W38 1993, **(v9)**
Weisberg, Gabriel P. N6847.5.R4.W44, **(v9)**
  ND457.W45 1992, **(v9)**
  Z5961.E8.W45 1998, **(v10)**
Weisberg, Jacob. JK271.W377 1996, **(v7)**
Weisberger, A. M. BJ1401.W45 1999, **(v8)**
Weisberger, Adam M. DS135.G33.W418 1997, **(v5)**
Weisberger, Bernard A. E747.W3 1994, **(v4)**
  HD9710.U52.D858, **(v6)**
Weisbrod, Burton Allen. HD2769.2.U6.W45 1988, **(v6)**
Weisbrot, Robert. BX7350.A4.W44 1983, **(v8)**
Weisburd, A. Mark. KZ6368.W45 1997, **(v7)**
Weischet, Wolfgang. S481.W45 1993, **(v1)**
Weisenburger, Steven. PS374.S2.W4 1995, **(v3)**
Weisenfeld, Judith. BV1393.B58.W45 1997, **(v8)**
Weisgall, Jonathan M. U264.3.W43 1994, **(v10)**
Weisinger, Kenneth D. PT2177.W4 1988, **(v3)**
Weiskel, Thomas. BH301.S7.W44, **(v8)**
Weisman, Avery D. RC489.E93.W45 1993, **(v2)**
Weisman, Brent Richards. F319.F54.W45 1992, **(v4)**
Weisman, Karen A. PR5438.W44 1994, **(v3)**
Weisman, Leslie. NA2543.W65.W45 1992, **(v9)**
Weismann, Elizabeth (Wilder). NB253.W4 1971, **(v9)**
  N6553.W44 1985, **(v9)**
Weismantel, Mary J. F3721.3.F7.W45 1988, **(v4)**
Weiss, Brad. DT443.3.H39.W45 1996, **(v5)**
Weiss, Daniel. PR6023.A93Z944, **(v3)**
Weiss, E.A. SB298.W44 2000, **(v1)**
Weiss, Jessica. HQ535.W435 2000, **(v6)**
Weiss, Joachim. QD79.C453.W4513 1995, **(v1)**
Weiss, John. DS146.G4.W43 1996, **(v5)**
  HC59.7.W454 1988, **(v6)**
Weiss, Judith A. PN2309.W45 1993, **(v3)**
Weiss, Kenneth M. RB155.W35 1993, **(v2)**
Weiss, Lawrence David. RA395.A3.W445 1997, **(v2)**
Weiss, Leonard W. HC106.W515 1980, **(v6)**

Weiss, Linda. HD87.W45 1998, **(v6)**
Weiss, M. Lynn. PS3537.T323.Z913 1998, **(v3)**
Weiss, Nancy J. E185.97.Y635.W45 1989, **(v4)**
Weiss, Noel S. RA652.2.C55W45 1996, **(v2)**
Weiss, Paul. B945.W396 B48, **(v8)**
   B945.W396.P5, **(v8)**
   B945.W396 P54 1996, **(v8)**
   BD21.W4, **(v8)**
Weiss, Peg. ND699.K3.W42 1995, **(v9)**
   ND699.K3.W43, **(v9)**
Weiss, Peter. PT2685.E5.A19 1968, **(v3)**
Weiss, Piero. ML90.W44, **(v9)**
Weiss, Raymond L. B759.M34.W45 1991, **(v8)**
Weiss, Richard. HN57.W45 1988, **(v6)**
Weiss, Robert Stuart. HQ777.4.W44, **(v6)**
   HQ1090.3.W45 1990, **(v6)**
Weiss, Roberto. AZ613.W4 1957, **(v10)**
Weiss, Roger D. RC568.C6.W46 1994, **(v2)**
Weiss, Roslyn. B368.W45 1998, **(v8)**
   B377.W45 2001, **(v8)**
Weiss, Steve. D752.8.W45 1996, **(v5)**
Weiss, Theodore Russell. PR2981.W45 1971, **(v3)**
Weiss, Thomas Fischer. QH631.W44 1996, **(v1)**
Weiss, Thomas George. JZ6374.W369.W45 1999, **(v7)**
Weiss, Wayne W. Z6671.2.T63 W45 1994, **(v10)**
Weissberg, Robert. HV91.W466 1999, **(v6)**
   JC571.W385 1998, **(v7)**
Weissberger, Arnold. QD251.W3683, **(v1)**
Weissbourd, Rick. HV741.W32 1996, **(v6)**
Weisse, Allen B. R723.W39 1998, **(v2)**
   R850.W45 1991, **(v2)**
Weisser, Susan Ostrov. PR868.W6.W36 1997, **(v3)**
Weissert, Carol S. RA395.A3.W45 1996, **(v2)**
Weisskopf, Victor Frederick. QC71.W443 1989, **(v1)**
Weissman, David. BD171.W44 1993, **(v8)**
Weissman, Harold H. HV40.W435 1983, **(v6)**
Weissman, Judith Reiter. TT387.W45 1987, **(v1)**
Weissman, Stephen M. PR4483.W4 1989, **(v3)**
Weissmark, Mona Sue. RC437.5.W46 1998, **(v2)**
Weisstein, Eric W. QA5.W45 1999, **(v1)**
Weitz, Eric D. HX280.5.A6.W385 1997, **(v6)**
Weitz, Morris. BD181.W384 1988, **(v8)**
Weitz, Raanan. HN17.5.W42, **(v6)**
Weitzenhoffer, Andre M. BF1141.W38, **(v2)**
Weitzmann, Kurt. N8187.W44 1978, **(v9)**
   ND2900.W4 1970, **(v9)**
   ND2930.W42, **(v9)**
   ND2930.W43, **(v9)**
Weitzner, Jacob. PJ5129.R2.Z885 1994, **(v3)**
Weizsacker, Ernst U. von. GE170.W4513 1994, **(v6)**
Weizsacker, Richard. DD260.65.W45.W442 1999, **(v5)**
Welborn, David M. JK901.W4, **(v7)**
Welby, T. Earle. PR5513.W4, **(v3)**
Welch, Cheryl B. JC229.T8 W45 2001, **(v7)**
Welch, Claude Emerson. JC599.A36.W45 1995, **(v7)**
Welch, David A. U21.2.W396 1993, **(v10)**
Welch, David. D639.P7.G396 2000, **(v5)**
   DD256.5.W4324 1993, **(v5)**
Welch, Don. BJ1725.W45 1994, **(v8)**
Welch, Evelyn S. N6915.W42 1997, **(v9)**
Welch, Holmes. BQ647.W44, **(v8)**
Welch, James. PS3573.E44.D4, **(v3)**
   PS3573.E44.W5, **(v3)**
Welch, Paula D. GV429.W44 1996, **(v6)**
Welch, Richard E. E696.W45 1988, **(v4)**
   E721.W4, **(v4)**
Welch, Rosanne. TL539.W395 1998, **(v1)**
Welch, Sharon D. BJ1275.W42 1989, **(v8)**
   E184.A1.W37 1999, **(v4)**
Welch, Susan. KF4155.W45 1998, **(v7)**
Welcher, Frank Johnson. E491.W43 1989, **(v4)**
Welchman, Kit. BF109.E7W45 2000, **(v2)**
Weld, Ralph Foster. E445.C7 W4, **(v4)**
Weldon, Fay. PR4037.W45 1985, **(v3)**
   PR6045.E8.Z88 1985, **(v3)**
Weldon, T. D. B2779.W4 1958, **(v8)**
Welford, W. T. QC355.2.W44 1981, **(v1)**
   QC355.2.W435 1991, **(v1)**
Wellbery, David E. PT1898.L8.W45 1996, **(v3)**
Wellek, Rene. PN85.W38, **(v3)**
   PR401.W4, **(v3)**

Wellen, Richard. JC574.W45 1996, **(v7)**
Weller, George. V210.W4, **(v10)**
Weller, Jac. U800.W4 1966, **(v10)**
Weller, Robert P. DS759.W455 1994, **(v5)**
Welles, Benjamin. E748.W442.W44 1997, **(v4)**
Welles, C. Bradford. CN405.W4, **(v5)**
Welles, Orson. PN1998.3.W45.A3 1992, **(v3)**
   PR2877.W45 1990, **(v3)**
Welles, Sumner. D748.W4, **(v5)**
Wellford, Harrison. KF6449.W45 1988, **(v7)**
Wellhofer, E. Spencer. DA560.W3 1996, **(v5)**
Wellington, Harry H. KF4575.W45 1991, **(v7)**
Wellington, J. J. Q181.W4416 2000, **(v1)**
Wellisch, Hans H. Z695.9.W45 1995, **(v10)**
Wellman, Francis Lewis. KF8920.W4 1997, **(v7)**
Wellman, James K. BX9211.C414.W48 1999, **(v8)**
Wellman, Kathleen Anne. R507.L193.W46 1992, **(v2)**
Wellmer, Albrecht. B63.W4213 1998, **(v8)**
Wellner, Alison Stein. GV191.4.W45 1997, **(v6)**
Wells, A. F. QD481.W44 1984, **(v1)**
Wells, Allen. F1376.W45 1996, **(v4)**
Wells, Charles. PR3069.R6.W44 1993, **(v3)**
Wells, Charlotte Catherine. JN2919.W45 1995, **(v7)**
Wells, D. G. QA93.W385 1995, **(v1)**
Wells, Daniel A. Z1225.W38 1996, **(v10)**
Wells, David F. BR115.C8.W43 1998, **(v8)**
Wells, Dianne. F452.W44 2002, **(v4)**
Wells, Edward R. GE10.W45 1997, **(v6)**
Wells, G. Margaret. TP692.3.W46 1999, **(v1)**
Wells, H. G. PR5772. 1985, **(v3)**
   PR5772. 1987, **(v3)**
   PR5772.D7, **(v3)**
   PR5772.T5 1960, **(v3)**
   PR5774.I5, **(v3)**
   PR5774.I8 1996, **(v3)**
   PR5774.K5, **(v3)**
   PR5774.K65 1984, **(v3)**
   PR5774.L6 1984, **(v3)**
   PR5774.S4, **(v3)**
   PR5774.T5 1987, **(v3)**
   PR5774.T5 1996b, **(v3)**
   PR5774.T66 1978, **(v3)**
   PR5774.T9, **(v3)**
   PR5774.W3 1993, **(v3)**
   PR5774.W6, **(v3)**
   PR5776.A34 1984, **(v3)**
Wells, Henry Willis. PR651.W4, **(v3)**
Wells, J. C. PE1711.W4, **(v3)**
Wells, Mark K. D786.W44 1995, **(v5)**
Wells, Mary Ann. E78.M73.W45 1994, **(v4)**
Wells, Miriam J. HD9259.S83.U648 1996, **(v6)**
Wells, Robert V. HB3501.W45, **(v6)**
Wells, Samuel F. E756.W44 1990, **(v4)**
Wells, Stanley W. PR3071.W44 1987, **(v3)**
Wells, Susan. PN212.W45 1996, **(v3)**
Wells, Susan. R692.W45 2001, **(v2)**
Wells, Tom Henderson. VA393.W45, **(v10)**
Wells-Barnett, Ida B. E185.97.B26.A3 1970, **(v4)**
   E185.97.W55.A3 1995, **(v4)**
   E185.97.W55.S68 1997, **(v4)**
Welmers, William Everett. PL8008.W4, **(v3)**
Welsbacher, Anne. F94.3.W44 1998, **(v4)**
   F621.3.W45 1998, **(v4)**
   F651.3.W45 1998, **(v4)**
Welsby, Derek A. DT159.9.N83.W45 1998, **(v5)**
Welsch, Roger L. E99.O4.W44, **(v4)**
Welsh, Alexander. PR2807.W39 2001, **(v3)**
   PR4556.W45 2000, **(v3)**
   PR4592.C56.W45 1971, **(v3)**
   PR4592.S38.W44 1987, **(v3)**
   PR5631.W4, **(v3)**
Welsh, Dominic. Z103.W46 1988, **(v10)**
Welsome, Eileen. RA1231.R2.W45 1999, **(v2)**
Welter, Rush. E165.W46, **(v4)**
Weltge-Wortmann, Sigrid. NK8950.B47.W46 1993, **(v9)**
Weltman, Sharon Aronofsky. PR5267.P6.W45 1998, **(v3)**
Welton, Donn. B3279.H94W453 2000, **(v8)**
Welty, Eudora. PS3545.E6.A153 1954, **(v3)**
   PS3545.E6.B7, **(v3)**

   PS3545.E6.C8 1941, **(v3)**
   PS3545.E6.D4 1946, **(v3)**
   PS3545.E6.G6, **(v3)**
   PS3545.E6.L6, **(v3)**
   PS3545.E6.O6, **(v3)**
   PS3545.E6.P6 1954, **(v3)**
   PS3545.E6.R6, **(v3)**
   PS3545.E6.W5, **(v3)**
   TR654.W422 1989, **(v1)**
Wendel, Frederick C. LB2831.82.W45 1996, **(v7)**
Wendt, Alexander. JZ1251.W46 1999, **(v7)**
Wenger, Andreas. UA23.W376 1997, **(v10)**
Wenger, Beth S. F128.9.J5.W46 1996, **(v4)**
Wengeroff, Pauline. DS135.R95.W313 2000, **(v5)**
Wengle, John L. GN33.W46 1988, **(v6)**
Wenke, John Paul. PS2388.A35.W46 1995, **(v3)**
Wenke, Robert J. GN740.W46 1996, **(v6)**
Wenocur, Stanley. HV91.W49 1989, **(v6)**
Went, Robert. HF1359.W46 2000, **(v6)**
Wentworth, Harold. PE2846.W4 1975, **(v3)**
Wentz, Richard E. BX9593.N4.W46 1997, **(v8)**
Wentzel, Donat G. QB521.W46 1989, **(v1)**
Wentzel, Wayne C. ML134.B175 W46 2001, **(v9)**
Wenz, Peter S. GE42.W458 2001, **(v6)**
   HB523.W46 1988, **(v6)**
Wepsiec, Jan. Z7164.S68 W46 1983, **(v10)**
Werbner, Pnina. DA690.M4.W47 1990, **(v5)**
Werfel, Alma (Schindler) Mahler. ML410.M23.W532 1969, **(v9)**
Werfel, Franz V. PT2647.E77.L5 1945, **(v3)**
Werhane, Patricia Hogue. B3376.W563.P637 1992, **(v8)**
   HB103.S6.W38 1991, **(v6)**
Werlich, David P. F3446.5.W47, **(v4)**
   F3447.T8.W47 1990, **(v4)**
Wermer, John. QA326.W47 1976, **(v1)**
Wernblad, Annette. PN1998.3.A45.W47 1992, **(v3)**
Werner, Craig Hansen. PR6019.O9.D885 1988, **(v3)**
   PS153.N5.W38 1994, **(v3)**
Werner, Emmy E. D810.C4.W45 2000, **(v5)**
Werner, Eric. ML166.W43 1970, **(v9)**
Werness, Hope B. E98.A7.W49 2000, **(v4)**
Wernham, R. B. DA355.W39, **(v5)**
   DA356.W47 1984, **(v5)**
   DA360.W37 1994, **(v5)**
Wernick, Andrew. HF5821.W46 1991, **(v6)**
Werrell, Kenneth P. D790.W378 1996, **(v5)**
Wert, Charles Allen. QC176.W45 1970, **(v1)**
Wertenbaker, Thomas Jefferson. F106.W52, **(v4)**
   F128.44.W4, **(v4)**
   F212.W5 1963, **(v4)**
Werth, Alexander. D764.W48 1965, **(v5)**
   DC373.G3.W4, **(v5)**
   DC396.W42 1966, **(v5)**
   DC412.W4, **(v5)**
   DK274.W4 1962, **(v5)**
Werth, Barry. PE64.A78, **(v3)**
   RS380.W47 1994, **(v2)**
Wertheim, Albert. PR9369.3.F8.Z95 2000, **(v3)**
Wertheim, Gunther K. QC490.W4 1964, **(v1)**
Wertheim, L. Jon. GV994.A1 W45 2001, **(v6)**
Wertheim, Margaret. QA76.9.C66.W48 1999, **(v1)**
   QC19.6.W47 1995, **(v1)**
Wertheim, Stanley. PS1449.C85.Z982 1994, **(v3)**
   PS1449.C85.Z9824 1997, **(v3)**
Wertheimer, Alan. BJ1474.5.W47 1996, **(v8)**
Wertheimer, Barbara M. HD6095.W47 1977, **(v6)**
Wertheimer, Eric. PS217.I47.W47 1999, **(v3)**
Wertheimer, Jack. BM205.W46 1993, **(v8)**
Wertz, Richard W. RG518.U5.W47 1989, **(v2)**
Wertz, Spencer K. GV706.W44 1991, **(v6)**
Wescott, Glenway. PS3545.E827.A7, **(v3)**
   PS3545.E827.G6, **(v3)**
   PS3545.E827.G7, **(v3)**
Weslager, C. A. E215.2.W47, **(v4)**
Wesley, Charles. PR3763.W4.A6 1963, **(v3)**
Wesley, Edgar Bruce. L13.N49.W4, **(v7)**
Wesley, John. BX8495.W5.A3 1987, **(v8)**
Wesley, Marilyn C. PS169.T74.W47 1999, **(v3)**
   PS3565.A8.Z96 1993, **(v3)**
Wesley, Michael. KZ6376.W47 1997, **(v7)**

Wesling, Donald. PN81.W447 1995, **(v3)**
Wess, Julius. QC174.17.S9.W47 1983, **(v1)**
Wesseling, H. L. DT28.W4713 1996, **(v5)**
Wesser, Robert F. E748.H88.W4, **(v4)**
Wessinger, Catherine Lowman. BL503.2.W47 2000, **(v8)**
Wesson, Robert G. QH366.2.W47 1991, **(v1)**
West, Allan M. L13.N49.W44, **(v7)**
West, Anthony C. PR6073.E76.F4, **(v3)**
  PR6073.E76.R4, **(v3)**
West, Anthony. PR5776.W46 1984, **(v3)**
  PR6045.E757.H4, **(v3)**
  PR6073.E782.T7, **(v3)**
West, Cornel. B944.P72.W47 1989, **(v8)**
West, D. J. HQ117.W57 1992, **(v6)**
West, Darrell M. JK1991.W47 2000, **(v7)**
West, David Alexander. PA6484.W4 1969, **(v3)**
West, David. B804.W389 1996, **(v8)**
West, Elliott. F591.W4527 1998, **(v4)**
  F721.W37, **(v4)**
West, Gilian. PR2997.P8.W47 1998, **(v3)**
West, Graham. TA705.2.W47 1990, **(v1)**
West, Guida. HV97.N34.W47, **(v6)**
West, James D. BH221.R93.W47, **(v8)**
West, James L. W. PS3569.T9.Z94 1998, **(v3)**
  Z479.W43 1988, **(v10)**
West, Jessamyn. BX7615.W4, **(v8)**
  PS3545.E8315.C7, **(v3)**
  PS3545.E8315.F7 1945, **(v3)**
  PS3545.E8315.L6, **(v3)**
  PS3545.E8315.M3, **(v3)**
  PS3545.E8315.W5, **(v3)**
  PS3545.E8315.Z516, **(v3)**
  PS3545.E8315.Z518, **(v3)**
  PS3545.E8315Z52, **(v3)**
West, John. DA1.W45 1962, **(v5)**
West, M. L. ML169.W5 1992, **(v9)**
West, Michael. PS217.P85.W47 2000, **(v3)**
West, Morris L. PR6045.E77.D3, **(v3)**
  PR6045.E77.D4, **(v3)**
  PR6045.E77 S5, **(v3)**
West, Nathanael. PS3545.E8334.D3, **(v3)**
West, Nigel. UB251.G7.W486 1988, **(v10)**
West, Patsy. E99.M615.W47 1998, **(v4)**
West, Paul. PR4381.W4, **(v3)**
West, Ray Benedict. BX8611.W4, **(v8)**
  PS374.S5.W37, **(v3)**
West, Rebecca. DA585.J6.W4, **(v5)**
  DR309.W47 1968, **(v5)**
  PN45.W45, **(v3)**
  PR6045.E8.A6 1977, **(v3)**
  PR6045.E8.B57 1966, **(v3)**
  PR6045.E8.F6, **(v3)**
  PR6045.E8.R4x 1980, **(v3)**
  PR6045.E8.T48 1985, **(v3)**
  PR6045.E8.T5 1985, **(v3)**
  PR6045.E8.Z464 1988, **(v3)**
  PR6045.E8.Z48 2000, **(v3)**
  PS2123.W4, **(v3)**
West, Richard S. E182.W45 1971, **(v4)**
  E591.W44, **(v4)**
West, Richard. DR1300.W47 1995, **(v5)**
  PR1905.W47 2000, **(v3)**
West, Robert Hunter. PR3592.A5.W4, **(v3)**
West, Robert W. PE1135.W4 1960, **(v3)**
West, Robin. KF4764.W47 1994, **(v7)**
West, Shearer. PN2061.W47 1991, **(v3)**
West, Thomas G. E302.1.W47 1997, **(v4)**
Westacott, Evalyn. B765.B24.W4 1974, **(v8)**
Westbrook, Deeanne. PS169.B36.W47 1996, **(v3)**
Westbrook, Robert B. JC251.D48.W47 1991, **(v7)**
Westcott, Cynthia. SB731.W47 2001, **(v1)**
Westcott, Edward Noyes. PS3159.W12.D3 1960, **(v3)**
Westcott, Wayne L. GV481.W47 2003, **(v6)**
Westerfield, Donald L. KF1183.W47 1993, **(v7)**
  KF5060.W457 1996, **(v7)**
Westerman, R. C. Z5111.W47 1994, **(v10)**
Westermann, Diedrich. PL8007.W4, **(v3)**
  PL8017.W43, **(v3)**
Westermarck, Edward Alexander. BJ1311.W5 1924, **(v8)**

Western Reserve University. RJ499.W42, **(v2)**
Western, David. QL84.6.K4.W47 1997, **(v1)**
Western, John. DT2405.C369.A28 1996, **(v5)**
Western, Samuel. HC107.W9 W47 2002, **(v6)**
Westervelt, Saundra Davis. HV6250.25.W47 1998, **(v6)**
Westfahl, Gary. PS374.S35.W43 1996, **(v3)**
  PS374.S35.W44 2000, **(v3)**
Westfall, Alfred Van Rensselaer. PR2971.U6.W4, **(v3)**
Westfall, Richard S. QC16.N7.W34 1993, **(v1)**
  QC16.N7.W35, **(v1)**
Westgard, James B. QC631.W47 1997, **(v1)**
Westheider, James E. DS559.8.B55.W47 1997, **(v5)**
Westin, Alan F. KF5060.W46 1990, **(v7)**
  KF8742.A5 W48 1978, **(v7)**
Westlake, Kenneth. TD795.4.W47 1995, **(v1)**
Westling, Louise Hutchings. PS374.L28.W47 1996, **(v3)**
Westlye, Mark Christopher. JK1965.W47 1991, **(v7)**
Westman, Daniel P. KF3471.W47 1991, **(v7)**
Westmoreland, Guy T. Z1361.W45, **(v10)**
Weston, Anthony. BJ1012.W447 2001, **(v8)**
Weston, Edward. TR140.W45.A3, **(v1)**
Weston, Kath. HQ76.3.U5.W48 1991, **(v6)**
Weston, Mary Ann. PN4888.I52.W47 1996, **(v3)**
Weston, Ruth D. PS3545.E6.Z97 1994, **(v3)**
Westphal, Merold. B4373.A4723.W47 1996, **(v8)**
Westrum, Dexter. PS3563.A3114.Z94 1991, **(v3)**
Westrum, Ron. UG1312.A6.W47 1999, **(v10)**
Westwater, Martha. PR888.Y68.W47 2000, **(v3)**
Westwood, J. N. HE1021.W47 1981, **(v6)**
Wethered, Herbert Newton. QH41.P78.W4 1937, **(v1)**
Wetherell, David. GN21.W43.W48 1990, **(v6)**
Wetherill, G. Barrie. TS156.8.W455 1990, **(v1)**
Wethey, Harold E. ND813.T4.W4, **(v9)**
Wetmore, Helen Cody. F594.B94 W48 2003, **(v4)**
Wetta, Frank Joseph. PN1995.9.W3.W48 1992, **(v3)**
Wetterau, Bruce. D9.W47 1994, **(v5)**
  JK274.W449 1995, **(v7)**
  JK2408.W48 1999, **(v7)**
Wetzel, C. Douglas. LB1044.75.W48 1994, **(v7)**
Wetzel, Robert G. QH96.W47 1983, **(v1)**
Wetzell, Richard F. HV6022.G3, **(v6)**
Wetzler, Peter. D767.2.W67 1998, **(v5)**
Wexler, Alice. RC394.H85.W49 1995, **(v2)**
Wexler, Joyce Piell. PR888.M63.W43 1997, **(v3)**
Wexler, Paul. DS134.W48 1996, **(v5)**
Wexman, Virginia Wright. PN1993.5.U6.W45 1993, **(v3)**
Weydt, Gunther. PT1732.W37, **(v3)**
Weyer, Edward Moffat. E99.E7.W48 1962, **(v4)**
Weyers, Wolfgang. RL46.W49 1998, **(v2)**
Weyl, Nathaniel. CB59.W4, **(v5)**
Weyland, Kurt Gerhard. HC165.W46 2002, **(v6)**
Weymar, Paul. DD259.7.A3.W413, **(v5)**
Whalen, D. Joel. HF5718.W467 1996, **(v6)**
Whalen, Jack. LA243.5.W48 1989, **(v7)**
Whalen, Lucille. K3240.4.W46 1989, **(v7)**
Whalen, Mollie. HV1445.W43 1996, **(v6)**
Whalen, Thomas J. F71.W49 2000, **(v4)**
Whalen-Bridge, John. PS374.P6.W47 1998, **(v3)**
Whalley, P. B. TJ265.W39 1992, **(v1)**
Wharton, David E. TA157.W448 1992, **(v1)**
Wharton, Edith Newbold (Jones). PS3545.H16.G6, **(v3)**
Wharton, Edith. D640.W5, **(v5)**
  NK2110.W5 1978, **(v9)**
  PS121.W43 1996, **(v3)**
  PS3545.H16.A6 1950, **(v3)**
  PS3545.H16.A7 1970, **(v3)**
  PS3545.H16.B4, **(v3)**
  PS3545.H16.C5, **(v3)**
  PS3545.H16.C8, **(v3)**
  PS3545.H16.E7, **(v3)**
  PS3545.H16.F37 1993, **(v3)**
  PS3545.H16.G5, **(v3)**
  PS3545.H16.G7, **(v3)**
  PS3545.H16.H6 1951, **(v3)**
  PS3545.H16.H8, **(v3)**
  PS3545.H16.M6, **(v3)**
  PS3545.H16.O5 1964, **(v3)**

  PS3545.H16.R4, **(v3)**
  PS3545.H16.S8, **(v3)**
  PS3545.H16.X5, **(v3)**
  PS3545.H16.Z5 1934, **(v3)**
Wharton, William. PS3573.H32.B5 1979, **(v3)**
Whatmore, Richard. HB105.S25, **(v6)**
Wheal, Elizabeth-Anne. D740.W47 1990, **(v5)**
Wheale, Nigel. PR438.P65.W75 1999, **(v3)**
Wheat, Carl I. GA405.W5, **(v6)**
Wheat, Leonard F. PN1997.T86, **(v3)**
Wheater, C. Philip. QA276.12.W52 2000, **(v1)**
Wheatley, Christopher J. PR8785, **(v3)**
Wheatley, Paul. HT384.I67.W48 2001, **(v6)**
Wheatley, Ronald. D771.W38 1958, **(v5)**
Wheaton, Bernard. DB2228.7.W47 1992, **(v5)**
Wheaton, Elizabeth. F264.G8.W48 1987, **(v4)**
Wheeler, Brannon M. BP134.P745 W48 2001, **(v8)**
Wheeler, Burton K. E748.W5.A3 1977, **(v4)**
Wheeler, Denice. F760.W47 1987, **(v4)**
Wheeler, Douglas L. DP675.W47, **(v5)**
Wheeler, Elizabeth A. PS374.C5.W48 2001, **(v3)**
Wheeler, Gerald E. E746.W5, **(v4)**
Wheeler, Helen Rippier. Z7963.A4.W54 1997, **(v10)**
Wheeler, J. Craig. QB843.S95, **(v1)**
Wheeler, James Scott. DA944.4.W48 1999, **(v5)**
Wheeler, John Archibald. Q158.5.W44 1994, **(v1)**
  QB334.W49 1990, **(v1)**
Wheeler, Kathleen M. PR888.W6.W44 1996, **(v3)**
Wheeler, Linda A. RG950.W48 2002, **(v2)**
Wheeler, Lynde Phelps. QC16.G5.W45 1962, **(v1)**
Wheeler, Marcus. PG2640.W5 1984, **(v3)**
Wheeler, Michael. PR468.D42.W4 1990, **(v3)**
Wheeler, Monroe. ND553.S7 F72, **(v9)**
Wheeler, Olin D. F592.7.W56 2002, **(v4)**
Wheeler, Robert Eric Mortimer. N5760.W5, **(v9)**
Wheeler, Roxann. DA125.A1.W448 2000, **(v5)**
Wheeler, Samuel C. B2430.D484.W475 2000, **(v8)**
Wheeler, Sara. G860.W48 1998, **(v6)**
Wheeler, Stanton. KF9685.W47 1988, **(v7)**
Wheeler, William Morton. QL496.W57, **(v1)**
Wheeler-Bennett, John Wheeler. DD231.H5.W5 1967, **(v5)**
Wheelock, Anne. LC213.2.W44 1992, **(v7)**
Wheelock, Arthur K. ND653.V5.W48 1995, **(v9)**
Wheelock, David C. HG2563.W44 1991, **(v6)**
Whelan, Bernadette. HC260.5.W477 2000, **(v6)**
Whelan, Elizabeth M. RC268.W528 1994, **(v2)**
Whelan, Frederick G. JQ224.W48 1996, **(v7)**
Whelan, Peter. PR6023.A93.R338 1988, **(v3)**
Whelan, Robert J. QH545.F5.W48 1995, **(v1)**
Whelehan, Imelda. HQ1190.W47 1995, **(v6)**
Whetten, Nathan Laselle. F1463.5.W5, **(v4)**
Whichard, Willis P. KF8745.I72 W48 2000, **(v7)**
Whiffen, Marcus. NA705.W473, **(v9)**
  NA735.W5.W47 vol. 1, **(v9)**
  NA735.W5.W47 vol. 2, **(v9)**
Whigham, Frank. PR658.S46.W38 1996, **(v3)**
Whigham, Thomas. Z1821.W55 1995, **(v10)**
Whipple, Fred Lawrence. QB601.W6 1968, **(v1)**
  QB601.W6 1981, **(v1)**
  QB721.4.W47 1985, **(v1)**
Whipple, Maurine. PS3545.H425.G5, **(v3)**
Whisenhunt, Donald W. PN2297.A78, **(v3)**
Whisnant, David E. F217.A65.W47 1983, **(v4)**
  F1523.8.W45 1995, **(v4)**
Whissen, Thomas R. PN761.W45 1989, **(v3)**
  PN1993.5.U6.W46 1998, **(v3)**
  PN3340.W48 1992, **(v3)**
Whistler, W. Arthur. SB407.W54 2000, **(v1)**
Whitaker, Arthur Preston. F1408.3.W5 1961, **(v4)**
  F1418.W6 1962, **(v4)**
  F1418.W62, **(v4)**
  F2232.2.U6.W47, **(v4)**
Whitaker, Donald P. DS706.W46, **(v5)**
Whitaker, Jerry C. TK7882.I6.W49 1994, **(v1)**
Whitaker, John O. QL715.W49 1996, **(v1)**
  QL719.E23.W49 1998, **(v1)**
Whitaker, Marian. Z674.25.W48 1989, **(v10)**
Whitaker, Reginald. F1034.2.W53 1994, **(v4)**
Whitaker, Richard E. BS425.W48 1988, **(v8)**
Whitaker, Stephen. QC320.W46 1977, **(v1)**

Whitaker, Thomas R. PR736.W53 1999, (v3)
Whitaker, Virgil Keeble. PR3000.W5, (v3)
Whitburn, Joel. ML156.4.P6.W497 1985, (v9)
  ML156.4.P6 W4977 1995, (v9)
Whitby, Kenny J. JK1924.W48 1997, (v7)
Whitcomb, Roger S. E183.7.W64 1998, (v4)
White Bull, Joseph. E99.D1.W66, (v4)
White, A. Sandri. PF5991.W5, (v3)
White, Barbara-Sue. DS796.H79.E189 1994, (v5)
White, Beatrice. PR2894.C442 1934, (v3)
White, Caramine. PR6054.O95, (v3)
White, Chappell. ML1263.W53 1992, (v9)
White, Christine A. HF3628.G7.W46 1993, (v6)
White, Christopher. N6973.R9.W48 1987, (v9)
  NE2054.5.R4.W44 1999, (v9)
White, David Gordon. BL1241.56.W47 1996, (v8)
White, Deborah Elise. PR457.W46 2000, (v3)
White, Deborah G. E185.86.W43875 1999, (v4)
White, Donald Wallace. E744.W538 1996, (v4)
White, Donna R. PS3562.E42.Z985 1999, (v3)
White, E. B. PS3545.H5187.A16 1977, (v3)
  PS3545.H5187.A6 1981, (v3)
  PS3545.H5187.P6, (v3)
  PS3545.H5187.Z48 1976, (v3)
  PZ7.W58277.Ch, (v3)
White, Edmund. PS3573.H463.N6, (v3)
White, Eric Walter. ML410.B853.W4 1970, (v9)
  ML1731.W58 1983, (v9)
White, Evelyn Davidson. ML128.C48.W5 1996, (v9)
White, Frank M. TJ260.W48 1984, (v1)
White, Frank. TL790.W48 1998, (v1)
White, G. Edward. KF379.W54 1994, (v7)
  KF4541.W48 2000, (v7)
  KF8745.H6 W47 1993, (v7)
White, G. J. DA206.W48 1999, (v5)
White, Geoffrey M. GN671.S6.W45 1992, (v6)
White, George W. DR38.2.W48 2000, (v5)
White, Gilbert F. GB70.W45, (v6)
White, Gordon. HC427.92.W494 1996, (v6)
White, Graham J. E748.W23.W48 1995, (v4)
White, Gregory L. BF575.J4.W48 1989, (v2)
White, Hayden V. PN50.W48 1999, (v3)
White, Helen Constance. PR1127.W5, (v3)
White, Hugh. PR275.N3, (v3)
White, James Boyd. JC328.2.W55 1994, (v7)
  KF250.W452 1985, (v7)
  PR3508.W48 1994, (v3)
White, James F. BX5013.E3.W5, (v8)
White, James W. HN723.W56 1995, (v6)
White, Jeremy J. B1499.K7.W45 1998, (v8)
White, John Albert. D558.W5, (v5)
White, John H. TF470.W45 1993, (v1)
White, John Kenneth. E877.2.W48 1998, (v4)
  E885.W48 1997, (v4)
White, Joseph L. E185.625.W46 1999, (v4)
White, Julie Anne. JC479.W48 2000, (v7)
White, K. D. S431.W46, (v1)
  S676.W5, (v1)
White, L. Michael. NA4817.W55 1990, (v9)
White, Landeg. PR9272.9.N32.Z97 1975, (v3)
White, Laura Amanda. F273.R52 1965, (v4)
White, Leonard Dupee. JK171.A1.W4 1978, (v7)
  JK180.W5, (v7)
White, Leslie A. CB19.W48 1969, (v5)
  CB311.W55, (v5)
  GN357.W47, (v6)
White, Lois. RT50.W457 2002, (v2)
  RT62.W455 2002, (v2)
White, Lynn T. DS778.7.W47 1989, (v5)
  HC427.92.W514 1998, (v6)
White, M. E. QE948.A1.W47 1990, (v1)
White, Matthew. MT955.W35 1999, (v9)
White, Merry I. HQ799.U65.W45 1993, (v6)
White, Michael J. JA71.W4558 1997, (v7)
White, Michael. QC16.H33.W45 1992, (v1)
  QC16.N7.W45 1997, (v1)
White, Mimi. PN1992.6.W43 1992, (v3)
White, Minor. TR647.W46.A2 1969, (v1)
White, Morton Gabriel. B29.W48 1982, (v8)
  B945.W474.A3 1999, (v8)
  BJ1461.W55 1993, (v8)

  D16.W59, (v5)
White, Newman Ivey. PR5431.W52, (v3)
  PR5433.W5 1966, (v3)
White, Nicholas J. DS596.6.W47 1996, (v5)
White, Nicholas P. B398.K7 W48, (v8)
  JC71.P6.W47, (v7)
White, Norman. PR4803.H44.Z924 1992, (v3)
White, Norval. F128.3.W48 1987, (v4)
White, Patricia. LC1011.W48 1996, (v7)
White, Patricia. PN1995.9.L48.W54 1999, (v3)
White, Patrick Cecil Telfer. E354.W5, (v4)
White, Patrick. PR9619.3.W5.A9, (v3)
  PR9619.3.W5.C6, (v3)
  PR9619.3.W5.E9, (v3)
  PR9619.3.W5.F7 1977, (v3)
  PR9619.3.W5.L5, (v3)
  PR9619.3.W5.R5, (v3)
  PR9619.3.W5.T7, (v3)
  PR9619.3.W5.T9 1980, (v3)
  PR9619.3.W5.V6, (v3)
  PR9619.3.W5.Z48 1996, (v3)
White, Peter. PA6047.W4 1993, (v3)
White, Phillip M. Z1209.W52 1995, (v10)
  Z1209.2.N67 W56 2000, (v10)
White, R. Kerry. PN2035.W48 1995, (v3)
White, R. S. PR418.N37.W48 1996, (v3)
White, Ray Lewis. PS3501.N4.W579 1990, (v3)
  Z1231.F4.W52 1988, (v10)
White, Reginald James. DA535.W45 1973, (v5)
White, Rhea A. Z6878.P8.W47 1990, (v10)
White, Richard E. QL581.W47 1983, (v1)
White, Richard. E99.A35.W48 1991, (v4)
  F591.W69 1991, (v4)
White, Robert W. DA959.W48 1992, (v5)
White, Samuel G. NA7207.W55 1998, (v9)
White, Sarah C. HQ1745.6.W54 1992, (v6)
White, Shane. E185.86.W4388 1998, (v4)
  F128.44.W54 1990, (v4)
White, Sol. GV863.A1.W448 1995, (v6)
White, Stephen A. B491.H36.W45 1992, (v8)
White, Stephen D. KJV1283.W48 1988, (v7)
White, Stephen K. HM22.G3.H348 1988, (v6)
  JA71.W456 1991, (v7)
White, Stephen L. BD418.W45 1991, (v8)
White, Stephen Solomon. B1649.S234.W5 1940, (v8)
White, Stephen. DK288.W46 1991, (v5)
  HV5515.15.W48 1996, (v6)
  JC474.W48 1987, (v7)
  JN6695.W48 2000, (v7)
  NA737.S639.W48 1993, (v9)
  NC1807.S65.W48 1988, (v9)
White, Stewart Edward. E173.C56 vol.25, (v4)
  PS3545.H6 B58, (v3)
  PS3545.H6 C55, (v3)
  PS3545.H6 S76, (v3)
  PS3545.H6 W4 1901, (v3)
  PS3545.H6.W6, (v3)
White, T. D. GN70.W45 2000, (v6)
White, T. H. PR6045.H2.E52, (v3)
  PR6045.H2 M5, (v3)
  PR6045.H2.O5, (v3)
  PR6045.H2.S9 1939, (v3)
White, Theodore Harold. D1051.W4, (v5)
  DS777.47.W5, (v5)
  E840.W5, (v4)
  E850.W5 1964, (v4)
  E851.W5, (v4)
White, William Allen. E792.W577 1986, (v4)
  PN4874.W52A3 1990, (v3)
White, William B. GB600.W47 1988, (v6)
White, William Hale. PR5795.W58.A1, (v3)
  PR5795.W7.C28, (v3)
  PR5795.W7.R49 1975, (v3)
White, William Lindsay. D811.W45, (v5)
White, William. Z8748.37.W455, (v10)
Whitecotton, Joseph W. F1221.Z3.W48, (v4)
Whitehead, Alfred North. B1674.W351.N6, (v8)
  B1674.W37.M6, (v8)
  BD41.W5, (v8)
  BD511.W5 1978, (v8)
  BL48.W35, (v8)

  CB53.W5, (v5)
  LB41.W64, (v7)
  LB875.W48, (v7)
  Q175.W62 1968, (v1)
  QA9.W5 1925, (v1)
Whitehead, David. DF82.W47 1986, (v5)
Whitehead, Frank S. PR4514.W48 1995, (v3)
Whitehead, Harriet. DU740.42.W465 2000, (v5)
Whitehead, Winifred. PN1009.A1.W495 1991, (v3)
Whitehill, Joseph. PS3545.H68.A2, (v3)
Whitehill, Walter Muir. F73.3.W57 1968, (v4)
  NA1303.W5, (v9)
  Z5961.U5.W5, (v10)
Whitehorne, Joseph W. A. E356.B2.W47 1996, (v4)
  E356.E5.W4 1992, (v4)
Whitehurst, Clinton H. HE745.W495 1983, (v6)
Whitehurst, Susan. F67.W495 2000, (v4)
Whiteley, Sheila. ML82.W48 2000, (v9)
Whiteley, Wilfred Howell. PL8013.E5.W4, (v3)
Whiteman, C. D. QC993.6.W48 2000, (v1)
Whiteman, David. JK1083.W48 1995, (v7)
Whiteman, Dorit Bader. RC451.4.H62.W48 1993, (v2)
Whitener, Scott. ML933.W52 1989, (v9)
Whiteside, Jonny. ML420.M13863.R36 1997, (v9)
Whiteside, Kerry H. JC261.M47.W48 1988, (v7)
Whitesitt, J. Eldon. QA266.W45, (v1)
Whitfield, Charles L. RC569.5.C63.W469 1991, (v2)
Whitfield, Eileen. PN2287.P5.W48 1997, (v3)
Whitfield, Peter. G81.W47 1998, (v6)
Whitfield, Peter. Q125.W59 1999, (v1)
Whitfield, Stephen J. E169.12.W47 1991, (v4)
  E185.61.W63 1988, (v4)
Whitford, Frank. N332.G33.B487 1984, (v9)
  N6999.K33.A4 1999c, (v9)
  NE1321.W47, (v9)
Whiting, Allen Suess. DS740.5.J3.W48 1989, (v5)
  DS740.5.R8.W5 1968, (v5)
Whiting, Anthony. PS3537.T4753.Z945 1996, (v3)
Whiting, Frederick. RF235.W5, (v2)
Whiting, Steven Moore. ML410.S196.W55 1999, (v9)
Whiting, Susan H. HC427.92.W52 2001, (v6)
Whiting, Van R. HG5162.W48 1992, (v6)
Whitley, A. Stewart. RC78.7.D53.W48 1999, (v2)
Whitley, Kathleen P. ND3327.G54.W55 2000, (v9)
Whitley, M. J. V820.W49 1995, (v10)
Whitley, Richard. HB501.W495 1999, (v6)
Whitlock, Brand. PS3545.H75J2 1982, (v3)
Whitlock, Flint. D769.31 45th.W45 1998, (v5)
Whitman, Jeffrey P. BD201.W54 1996, (v8)
Whitman, Marina von Neumann. HD2785.W46 1999, (v6)
Whitman, Mark. KF4155.W58 1998, (v7)
Whitman, Nicholas. F74.N5.W48 1994, (v4)
Whitman, Richard. KJE947.W46 1998, (v7)
Whitman, T. Stephen. E445.M3.W45 1997, (v4)
Whitman, Walt. PS3200.F48, (v3)
  PS3200.F49, (v3)
  PS3200.F68, (v3)
  PS3202. 1963, (v3)
  PS3203.B7, (v3)
  PS3203.V3, (v3)
  PS3204.L6 1989, (v3)
  PS3211.A1 1865, (v3)
  PS3231.A2 1972, (v3)
  PS3231.A23 1978, (v3)
  PS3231.A3 1961, (v3)
  PS3231.A364 1997, (v3)
  PS3231.A4 1990, (v3)
Whitmore, Philip. ML1263.W55 1991, (v9)
Whitmore, T. C. QH193.S6.W47 1984, (v1)
Whitnah, Donald Robert. HE206.3.W48 1998, (v6)
Whitney Museum of American Art. N6512.W46, (v9)
  N6512.W532 1999, (v9)
Whitney, Barry L. Z7850.W48 1993, (v10)
Whitney, Eleanor Searle. CT275.W5543.A3 1971, (v5)
Whitney, Ellen M. Z1277.W47 1995, (v10)
Whitney, Gordon Graham. GF503.W53 1994, (v6)
Whitney, Janet. HV8978.F7.W5 1972, (v6)
Whitney, Lois. PR448.P7.W5, (v3)
Whitney, Robert. F1787.W58 2001, (v4)
Whitson, Gene. TK452.W55 1996, (v1)

Whitson, Kathy J. PS153.I52.W47 1999, (v3)
Whitt, Margaret Earley. PS3564.A895.Z96 1999, (v3)
   PS3565.C57.Z94 1995, (v3)
Whittaker, C. R. DG59.A2.W5513 1994, (v5)
Whittaker, David J. JX1977.W4663 1995, (v7)
Whittaker, John C. GN799.T6.W446 1994, (v6)
Whittaker, Robert Harding. QH541.145.W47, (v1)
Whittemore, Charles Park. E207.S9.W5 1961, (v4)
Whittemore, Edward. PS3573.H557.Q7, (v3)
Whittemore, Lewis Bliss. LB885.M46.C48 1978, (v7)
Whittemore, Reed. PS129.W45 1992, (v3)
Whitten, David O. E185.97.D84 W48 1995, (v4)
Whitten, Norman E. F3722.1.C23.W48 1985, (v4)
   F3799.N4.W5, (v4)
Whitten, Phillip. GV837.W55 1994, (v6)
Whittick, Arnold. NA1088.M57.W5 1956, (v9)
Whittier, John Greenleaf. PS3250.F75, (v3)
   PS3252.C3, (v3)
   PS3281.A3 1975, (v3)
Whittier, Nancy. HQ1154.W49 1995, (v6)
Whittier-Ferguson, John. PR888.M63.W48 1996, (v3)
Whittington, Keith E. KF4552.W48 1999, (v7)
Whittington, Richard. HD30.28.W46 1993, (v6)
Whittle, Alasdair. GN776.2.A1.W46 1988, (v6)
Whittlesey, Lee H. F722.W59 1988, (v4)
Whittock, Trevor. PN1995.W45 1990, (v3)
Whittock, Trevor. PR1874.W5, (v3)
Whitton, Kenneth S. ML2829.W5 1984, (v9)
Whittow, Mark. DF556.W45 1996, (v5)
Whybrow, Peter C. RC537.W487 1997, (v2)
Whyte, Iain Boyd. NA1088.T33.W47 1982, (v9)
   NA2706.A9.W47 1989, (v9)
Whyte, Ian. DA850.W48 1991, (v5)
Whyte, Lancelot Law. BD646.W5, (v8)
   BD648.W47 1970, (v8)
Whyte, Martin King. HQ728.W526 1990, (v6)
Whyte, Susan Reynolds. GN659.U3.W59 1997, (v6)
Whyte, William Foote. H62.W457 1991, (v6)
Whyte, William Foote. HD31.W5136, (v6)
   HM22.U6.W48 1994, (v6)
Whyte, William Hollingsworth. BF697.W47, (v2)
Wiarda, Howard J. F1414.2.W49 1990, (v4)
   F1418.W648 1992, (v4)
   F1418.W6485 1995, (v4)
   F1418.W649 1987, (v4)
   F2178.S65.W52 1987, (v4)
Wice, Paul B. KF224.C375, (v7)
   KFN2316.M53.W53 1995, (v7)
Wicharaya, Tamasak. KF9685.W53 1995, (v7)
Wick, David. QC173.98.W53 1995, (v1)
Wick, Douglas A. F634.W53 1989, (v4)
Wickberg, Daniel. PS438.W47 1998, (v3)
Wicke, Jennifer. PR409.A38.W53 1988, (v3)
Wicke, Peter. ML3534.W5713 1990, (v9)
Wicker, Elmus. HG2481.W493 1996, (v6)
Wicker, Tom. E842.W54 1991, (v4)
   E856.W52 1995, (v4)
Wickett, Murray R. F705.A1 W53 2000, (v4)
Wickham, Chris. HN488.L82.W5313 1998, (v6)
Wickham-Crowley, Timothy P. JC491.W52 1991, (v7)
   JC491.W53 1992, (v7)
Wickins, P. L. HC800.W518 1986, (v6)
Wickman, Patricia R. E99.C9.W58 1999, (v4)
Wicks, David. GV855.3.W53 1995, (v6)
Wicks, Zeno W. TP1175.S6W56 1999, (v1)
Wicks-Nelson, Rita. RJ499.W45 2000, (v2)
Wickwar, W. Hardy. JF1411.W49 1991, (v7)
Widdess, Richard. ML338.2.W5 1995, (v9)
Widdicombe, Toby. PS3505.H3224.Z885 2001, (v3)
Widdifield, Stacie G. ND254.W54 1996, (v9)
Widdowson, Peter. PN45.W463 1999, (v3)
   PR4754.W465 1998, (v3)
Widenor, William C. E664.L7.W45, (v4)
Wider, Sarah Ann. PS1637.3.W44 2000, (v3)
Widlok, Thomas. DT1558.S38.W53 1999, (v5)
Widmaier, Eric P. QP33.W53 1998, (v1)
Widmer, Edward L. F128.44.W58 1999, (v4)
Widmer, Ellen. PL2698.C38.S539 1987, (v3)
Widmer, Kingsley. PR6023.A93.Z954, (v3)
   PR6023.A93.Z9542 1992, (v3)
Widmer, Kurt. BX8643.G63, (v8)

Widner, Jennifer A. DT433.584.W53 1992, (v5)
Wiebe, Donald. BL41.W47 1999, (v8)
Wiebe, Paul D. HD7361.A3.W53, (v6)
Wiebe, Robert H. E661.W58 1980, (v4)
   E743.W59, (v4)
Wiecek, William M. KF8742.W52 1988, (v7)
Wieck, Carl F. PS1305.W54 2000, (v3)
Wieck, Roger S. ND3363.A1.W54 1997, (v9)
Wieczynski, Joseph L. Z2510.3.W54 1996, (v10)
Wied, Maximilian. E78.G73 W53 2001, (v4)
Wiedemann, Barbara. PS3515.E596.Z95 1998, (v3)
Wiedemann, Thomas E. J. DG91.W54 1989, (v5)
Wiegand, Shirley A. Z678.82.W54 1994, (v10)
Wiegand, Wayne A. Z720.D5.W54 1996, (v10)
Wiegel, Robert L. GC201.W5, (v6)
Wiegersma, Nancy. HC681.W54 2000, (v6)
   HD1537.V5.W54 1988, (v6)
Wiehe, Vernon R. RC569.5.C55.W49 1996, (v2)
Wieland, Christoph Martin. PT2562.A1 1964, (v3)
Wieland, Sandra. RJ507.S49.W544 1998, (v2)
Wiener, Antje. KJE5124.W54 1998, (v7)
Wiener, Daniel N. RC438.6.E45.W54 1988, (v2)
Wiener, Joel H. DA45.W53, (v5)
   DA470.W48, (v5)
Wiener, Jon. E169.12.W49 1991, (v4)
   ML420.L38.W52 1999, (v9)
Wiener, Leo. PJ5120.W5 1972, (v3)
Wiener, Martin J. DA533.W59, (v5)
   HV6022.G7.W54 1990, (v6)
Wiener, Norbert. PS3573.I32.T4, (v3)
   Q175.W6516 1961, (v1)
   QA29.W497.A3, (v1)
   QA29.W497.A35, (v1)
   T15.W65 1993, (v1)
Wiener, Richard. QA76.73.J38.W53 2000, (v1)
Wiens, Herold J. DS730.W5 1954, (v5)
Wiens, John A. QL673.W523 1989, (v1)
Wiersbe, Warren W. BS537.W54 2000, (v8)
Wiersema, John Harry. SB107.W485 1999, (v1)
Wiersema, William H. HF5686.C8.W4476 1995, (v6)
Wierzbicka, Anna. BT380.2.W54 2001, (v8)
Wiese, Benno von. PT501.W5, (v3)
   PT671.W5 1967, (v3)
   PT745.W5, (v3)
   PT747.S6.W52, (v3)
Wiesel, Elie. PQ2683.I32.Z51713 1979, (v3)
Wiesenfarth, Joseph. PR830.S615.W54 1988, (v3)
Wiesenthal, Chris. PR868.M46.W54 1997, (v3)
Wiesenthal, Simon. DS135.A93.W53913 1989, (v5)
Wiesner, David. PZ7.W6367Th 2001, (v3)
Wiesner, Merry E. HQ1075.W526 2001, (v6)
   HQ1149.G3.W54 1986, (v6)
   HQ1587.W54 2000, (v6)
Wiet, Gaston. DS51.B3.W5, (v5)
Wigen, Karen. DS894.59.I53.W56 1995, (v5)
Wiget, Andrew. PM155.W54 1985, (v3)
Wigg, Philip R. LB1537.W3 2001, (v7)
Wiggershaus, Rolf. HM24.W48613 1994, (v6)
Wiggin, Kate Douglas Smith. PZ7.W638Re 1994, (v3)
Wiggins, David Kenneth. GV583.W545 1997, (v6)
Wiggins, David. BD232.W53 1998, (v8)
   BD236.W53 1980, (v8)
Wiggins, Gary. QD8.5.W54 1991, (v1)
Wiggins, Grant P. LB2806.15.W54 1998, (v7)
   LB3051.W494 1993, (v7)
   LB3051.W495 1998, (v7)
Wiggins, Melanie. D781.W54 1995, (v5)
Wiggins, Peter DeSa. PR2248.W48 2000, (v3)
Wiggins, Sarah Woolfolk. F326.W53, (v4)
Wigglesworth, Michael. PS871.A4 1989, (v3)
Wigglesworth, Vincent Brian. QL496.W62, (v1)
Wightwick, Jane. PJ6145.W44 1998, (v3)
Wigner, Eugene Paul. QC16.W52.A3 1992, (v1)
Wigoder, Geoffrey. DS115.W49 1991, (v5)
Wijdeveld, Paul. NA1011.5.W5.W55 1994, (v9)
Wikan, Unni. HN786.C3.W55 1996, (v6)
   HQ1731.Z8.S838 1982, (v6)
Wikander, Matthew H. PN2570.W55 1993, (v3)
Wilbanks, William. KF221.M8.W55 1990, (v7)
Wilber, Donald Newton. NA1483.W5, (v9)
Wilber, Ken. BD311.W54 1995, (v8)

BL73.W55 A3 1999, (v8)
Wilbert, Johannes. F2230.1.T63.W55 1987, (v4)
   F2319.2.W3.M55 1996, (v4)
Wilbur, C. Martin. DS734.9.W55 A3 1996, (v5)
   DS740.5.S65.W55 1989, (v5)
   DS777.47.W56, (v5)
Wilbur, Earl Morse. BX9831.W49 1945, (v8)
Wilburn, Reudene E. LB1117.W543 2000, (v7)
Wilcher, Robert. PR438.P65.W55 2001, (v3)
Wilcove, David Samuel. QL84.2.W53 1999, (v1)
Wilcox, Clyde. BR526.W53 1996, (v8)
   BT82.2.W54 1992, (v8)
Wilcox, Danny M. HV5045.W55 1998, (v6)
Wilcox, John C. PQ6055.W55 1997, (v3)
Wild, Alan. S591.W72 1993, (v1)
Wild, John Daniel. B395.W67 1964, (v8)
   B398.E8.W5, (v8)
   B819.W5, (v8)
   B835.W5, (v8)
Wildavsky, Aaron B. H61.W554, (v6)
   H91.W56 1988, (v6)
   HJ2051.W485 1984, (v6)
   JK511.W54 1991, (v7)
Wilde, Alan. PR6017.S5.Z9, (v3)
Wilde, Lawrence. B3305.M74.W4746 1998, (v8)
Wilde, Oscar. PR2935.W5 1958, (v3)
   PR5810.F66, (v3)
   PR5810.G00 2000, (v3)
   PR5811.A4, (v3)
   PR5812.M87 1989, (v3)
   PR5812.S55 1989, (v3)
   PR5818.H2 1952, (v3)
   PR5818.L6 1954, (v3)
   PR5819.A2.M979, (v3)
   PR5820.S2 1967, (v3)
   PR5823.A27 1962, (v3)
Wilder, Amos Niven. D640.W578 1994, (v5)
Wilder, Craig Steven. F129.B7.W56 2000, (v4)
Wilder, Laura Ingalls. PZ7.W6461Liv, (v3)
   PZ7.W6461Lo, (v3)
   PZ7.W6461Th, (v3)
Wilder, Robert Jay. GC11.2.W55 1998, (v6)
Wilder, Thornton. PS3545.I345.A19 1957, (v3)
   PS3545.I345.A6 1956, (v3)
   PS3545.I345.B7 1967, (v3)
   PS3545.I345.E35, (v3)
   PS3545.I345.I3, (v3)
   PS3545.I345.L6 1931, (v3)
   PS3545.I345.M4 1939, (v3)
   PS3545.I345.Z465 1985, (v3)
Wilderson, Paul W. F37.W46.W55 1994, (v4)
Wildes, Kevin Wm. R725.5.W55 2000, (v2)
Wildiers, N. M. BD518.D8.W5413 1982, (v8)
Wildman, Robert E. C. QP141.W485 2000, (v1)
Wilds, Elmer Harrison. LA11.W5 1970, (v7)
Wilenski, Reginald Howard. ND641.W5 1955a, (v9)
Wilensky, Harold L. HN17.5.W55 1975, (v6)
Wilentz, Gay Alden. PS153.N5.W48 1992, (v3)
Wilentz, Sean. HD8085.N53.W54 1984, (v6)
Wiles, David. PA3201.W55 1997, (v3)
Wiles, Maurice F. BT1350.W55 1996, (v8)
Wiley, Bell Irvin. E491.W69, (v4)
   E607.W48, (v4)
Wiley, Bell Irvin. E607.W5 1978, (v4)
Wiley, Elizabeth. PS2645.W55 1989, (v3)
Wiley, Joyce N. BP192.7.I7.W55 1992, (v8)
Wiley, Lori Sandford. LC311.W54 1998, (v7)
Wiley, Margaret Lenore. B1133.S4.W54 1968, (v8)
Wiley, Peter Booth. F869.S343 W55 2000, (v4)
Wilford, John Noble. GA105.3.W49 2000, (v6)
Wilhelm, Anthony G. JF799.W55 2000, (v7)
Wilhelm, Elliot. PN1995.9.F67.W56 1999, (v3)
Wilhelm, Hellmut. PL2464.Z7.W55, (v3)
Wilhelm, James J. PC3315.W5, (v3)
   PS3531.O82.Z893 1990, (v3)
Wilhelm, Jeffrey D. PN3171.W555 1998, (v3)
Wilhelm, Kate. PS3573.I434.W, (v3)
Wilhelm, Maria. D802.I8.W55 1988, (v5)
Wilinsky, Barbara. PN1993.5.U6.W496 2001, (v3)
Wilk, Richard R. F1465.2.K5.W55 1991, (v4)
Wilkas, Lenore. Z286.P4 W53 1994, (v10)

Wilken, Robert Louis. BT93.8.W55 1992, **(v8)**
Wilkening, M. TD885.5.R33.W55 1990, **(v1)**
Wilkes, Joanne. PR4383.W54 1999, **(v3)**
Wilkes, John. PR3765.W5317.Z52, **(v3)**
Wilkes, Paul. BX1406.2.W55 1996, **(v8)**
Wilkie, David S. G70.4.W438 1996, **(v6)**
Wilkie, Laurie A. F377.W5, **(v4)**
Wilkie, Tom. QB500.268.W55 1998, **(v1)**
Wilkins, Arnold J. RE48.W625 1995, **(v2)**
Wilkins, Burleigh Taylor. D15.B33.W5, **(v5)**
  D16.8.W597, **(v5)**
Wilkins, Esther M. RK60.5.W5 1999, **(v2)**
Wilkins, Frederick. F391.W67 1999, **(v4)**
Wilkins, Malcolm B. QK731.W45, **(v1)**
Wilkins, Nigel E. ML172.W58 1995, **(v9)**
Wilkins, Nigel E. PQ1322.W5, **(v3)**
Wilkins, Robert P. F636.W49, **(v4)**
Wilkins, Roger W. E185.97.W687.A35 1982, **(v4)**
Wilkins, Sally. GV1200.W55 2002, **(v3)**
Wilkins, Thurman. N6537.M6443.W55 1998, **(v9)**
  QH31.M78.W54 1995, **(v1)**
Wilkinson, Bertie. Z2017.W54, **(v10)**
Wilkinson, Charles F. KF5505.W55 1992, **(v7)**
  S932.W37.W55 1992, **(v1)**
Wilkinson, Charles F. Z1251.W5.W52 1989, **(v10)**
Wilkinson, Elizabeth M. PT2054.W54 1963, **(v3)**
Wilkinson, Endymion Porter. DS734.7.W5, **(v5)**
  DS735.W695 2000, **(v5)**
Wilkinson, J. Harvie. HM276.W497 1997, **(v6)**
Wilkinson, James D. D802.E9.W54, **(v5)**
Wilkinson, Kenneth P. HN59.2.W525 1991, **(v6)**
Wilkinson, Lise. R133.W459 1992, **(v2)**
Wilkinson, Marguerite Ogden Bigelow. PS3545.I4D5 1922, **(v3)**
Wilkinson, Paul F. G155.C35.W5 1997, **(v6)**
Wilkinson, Paul. HV6431.W564 2001, **(v6)**
Wilkinson, Richard H. DT68.8.W55 2000, **(v5)**
  N5350.W49 1992, **(v5)**
  N5350.W492 1994, **(v9)**
Wilkinson, Simon R. RJ47.53.W54 1988, **(v2)**
Wilkinson, Todd. GE180.W55 1998, **(v6)**
Wilkinson, Warren. E513.5 57th.W5 1990, **(v4)**
Will, Barbara. PS3537.T323Z925 2000, **(v3)**
Will, Clifford M. QC173.6.W55 1986, **(v1)**
Will, George F. E98.A3.W6 2002, **(v4)**
Willard, Charles Arthur. BC177.W544 1989, **(v8)**
  JC574.W55 1996, **(v7)**
Willard, Frances Elizabeth. CT3260.W56 1973, **(v5)**
Willard, Hobart Hurd. QD61.W67 1965, **(v1)**
Willbern, David. PR2997.P8.W55 1997, **(v3)**
Willborn, Steven L. K1770.W55 1989, **(v7)**
Willemen, Paul. PN1994.W458 1994, **(v3)**
Willems, Wim. DX145.W5513 1997, **(v5)**
Willett, Cynthia. BJ1395.W55 1995, **(v8)**
Willett, Frank. NB1097.W4.W55 1967b, **(v9)**
Willett, John. PT2603.R397.Z9 1968, **(v3)**
Willett, Ralph. DD257.2.W54 1989, **(v5)**
Willett, Ralph. PS374.D4.W55 1996, **(v3)**
Willett, Walter C. RA784.W55 2001, **(v2)**
Willett, Walter. QP141.W513 1990, **(v1)**
Willetts, R. F. DF221.C8.W54 1977b, **(v5)**
  DF261.C8.W49, **(v5)**
Willey, Basil. B1301.W5 1972, **(v8)**
  B1561.W55, **(v8)**
Willey, Gordon Randolph. E53.W5, **(v4)**
  F1435.W725 1987, **(v4)**
  GN739.W54, **(v6)**
William II, German Emperor, 1859-1941. DD229.A45, **(v5)**
William, of Ockham. BV629.W62213 1995, **(v8)**
William. B765.O32 E5 1990, **(v8)**
Williams, Alan Larson. PN1993.5.F7.W55 1992, **(v3)**
Williams, Alastair. ML3845.W59 1997, **(v9)**
Williams, Allan M. G155.C96W56 2000, **(v6)**
Williams, Andrew J. JX1391.W558 1998, **(v7)**
Williams, Angie. HM726.W56 2001, **(v6)**
Williams, Ann. DA195.W55 1995, **(v5)**
Williams, Anne. PR448.G6.W55 1995, **(v3)**
Williams, Arnold. PR641.W55, **(v3)**
Williams, Aubrey L. PR3368.R4.W5, **(v3)**
  PR3625.W5 1968, **(v3)**

Williams, Barbara J. F1219.56.C747.W55 1997, **(v4)**
Williams, Basil. DA483.P6.W5 1966a, **(v5)**
Williams, Bernard Arthur Owen. B1875.W56 1978, **(v8)**
Williams, Bruce Alan. H97.W544 1995, **(v6)**
Williams, Carol T. PN1992.8.S4.W55 1992, **(v3)**
Williams, Caroline. B1809.S85 W55 2001, **(v8)**
Williams, Carolyn D. PR3637.M36.W55 1993, **(v3)**
Williams, Carrington Bonsor. QL496.W64 1966, **(v1)**
Williams, Cecil J. E185.93.S7.W693 1995, **(v4)**
Williams, Charles G. S. PQ1925.W5, **(v3)**
Williams, Charles. PR6045.I5.A16 1958, **(v3)**
  PR6045.I5.A7, **(v3)**
  PR6045.I5.D4 1949, **(v3)**
  PR6045.I5.G7 1950, **(v3)**
  PR6045.I5.M3, **(v3)**
  PR6045.I5.P55 1951, **(v3)**
  PR6045.I5.S48 1950, **(v3)**
  PR6045.I5.W3 1949, **(v3)**
Williams, Christine L. HD6060.5.U5.W55 1989, **(v6)**
Williams, Christopher John Fards. BC199.I4.W55 1989, **(v8)**
Williams, Colin P. QA76.889.W55 2000, **(v1)**
  TK7888.3.W46 1998, **(v1)**
Williams, Craig A. GV558.W55 2001, **(v6)**
Williams, Dana A. Z1229.N39.W55 1998, **(v10)**
Williams, David. F290.W54 1993, **(v4)**
  PN682.M65.W55 1996, **(v3)**
Williams, Deborah Lindsay. PS374.F45.W55 2001, **(v3)**
Williams, Delores S. BT83.55.W55 1993, **(v8)**
Williams, Desmond. DA960.W48 1966a, **(v5)**
Williams, Donald C. HT384.U5.W55 2000, **(v5)**
Williams, Donna. RC553.A88.W55 1992, **(v2)**
Williams, Dyfri. NK7303.3.W55 1994, **(v9)**
Williams, E. W. TK7895.M4.W55 1994, **(v1)**
Williams, Emlyn. PR6045.I52.S6, **(v3)**
  PR6045.I52.Z5 1962, **(v3)**
  PR6045.I52 1961, **(v3)**
Williams, Eric Eustace. F2121.W517 1993, **(v4)**
  HC254.5.W5 1961, **(v6)**
Williams, Evelyn. KF373.W468.A3 1993, **(v7)**
Williams, Gary Jay. PR2827.W59 1997, **(v3)**
Williams, Gary. PS2018.W55 1999, **(v3)**
Williams, Geoffrey Lee. UA646.5.U5.S55, **(v10)**
Williams, George C. QH375.W52 1992, **(v1)**
Williams, George. HE9803.A4.W53 1994, **(v6)**
Williams, Geraint. JA81.W5 1991, **(v7)**
Williams, Gilbert Anthony. ML406.W56 1998, **(v9)**
Williams, Glanville Llewelyn. KD442.W54 2002, **(v7)**
Williams, Glyndwr. D20.W717 1997, **(v5)**
Williams, Gordon. PR428.S48.W54 1994, **(v3)**
Williams, Guy R. VM298.W48 1971, **(v10)**
Williams, Gwyn. PB2206.W64, **(v3)**
  PB2227.W5 1953, **(v3)**
  PB2246.W5, **(v3)**
Williams, H. P. QA402.5.W52 1993, **(v1)**
Williams, Henry. E185.6.W73, **(v4)**
Williams, Hiram Smith. E476.7.W55 1993, **(v4)**
Williams, Howard. JC481.W534 1988, **(v7)**
Williams, J. E. D. VK549.W55 1992, **(v10)**
Williams, James Thaxter. QC855.W55 1998, **(v1)**
Williams, James. B2430.L964W55 1998, **(v8)**
Williams, Jeannie. ML420.V367.W55 1999, **(v9)**
Williams, Jeffrey. PN3355.W58 1998, **(v3)**
Williams, Joanna Gottfried. NA6002.W5 1982, **(v9)**
Williams, John Alfred. PN2287.P77.W54 1991, **(v3)**
  PS3573.I4495.C3, **(v3)**
Williams, John B. PS2388.P5.W5 1991, **(v3)**
Williams, John Delane. QA276.W523 1996, **(v1)**
Williams, John Hoyt. F390.H84.W55 1992, **(v4)**
Williams, John Lee. F311.W65 1837a, **(v4)**
Williams, John R. PT2049.W55 1998, **(v3)**
Williams, John. ND3199.W54, **(v9)**
  PR5398.W55 2000, **(v3)**
  PR5881.W473 1996, **(v3)**
  PR5892.P64.W5 1989, **(v3)**
Williams, Jonathan. GA102.4.R44.W55 1995, **(v6)**
Williams, Juan. KF8745.M34.W55 1998, **(v7)**
Williams, Judith. PR4169.W48 1988, **(v3)**
Williams, Kathleen. PR3727.W5, **(v3)**

Williams, Kenneth L. QL666.O6.W455 1989, **(v1)**
Williams, Kimberly M. HV5824.W6.W55 1998, **(v6)**
Williams, L. O. TP359.H8.W54 1980, **(v1)**
Williams, Lea E. DS511.W66, **(v5)**
Williams, Leonard A. JC574.2.U6.W56 1997, **(v7)**
Williams, Linda. E185.625.W523 2001, **(v4)**
Williams, Lisa. PS3563.O8749.Z95 2000, **(v3)**
Williams, Lou Falkner. KF220.W537 1996, **(v7)**
Williams, Lynn Barstis. NE507.W53 1993, **(v9)**
Williams, Marc. HF1413.W54 1991, **(v6)**
Williams, Marcia L. LC5805.W55 1999, **(v7)**
Williams, Marie Sheppard. HV1555.M6.W55 1996, **(v6)**
Williams, Mark. PR9632.5.W55 1990, **(v3)**
  Z3008.L58.W55 1996, **(v10)**
Williams, Martin T. ML3506.W54 1980, **(v9)**
  ML3507.W53 1985, **(v9)**
  ML3507.W535 1989, **(v9)**
  ML3561.J3.W53 1979, **(v9)**
  ML3561.J3.W5317, **(v9)**
Williams, Meg Harris. PR508.I48.W5 1982, **(v3)**
Williams, Melissa S. JF1061.W55 1998, **(v7)**
Williams, Melvin D. E185.86.W4885 2000, **(v4)**
Williams, Michael Ann. GR108.W585 1995, **(v6)**
  GT225.N8.W55 1991, **(v6)**
Williams, Michael R. LB1139.35.P37.W54 1997, **(v7)**
  LC221.W55 1989, **(v7)**
Williams, Michael W. Z3508.P35.W55 1993, **(v10)**
Williams, Michael. BD161.W47 1999, **(v8)**
  BD161.W49 1991, **(v8)**
Williams, Neville. D209.W59 1994b, **(v5)**
Williams, Nicholas M. PR4148.U76.W55 1998, **(v3)**
Williams, Patricia J. KF4757.W53 1991, **(v7)**
Williams, Penry. DA355.W4835 1995, **(v5)**
Williams, Peter F. ML550.W38, **(v9)**
  MT145.B14.W53 1980, **(v9)**
Williams, Peter J. GB641.W55 1989, **(v6)**
Williams, Peter W. NA5205.W55 1997, **(v9)**
Williams, Peter. GV706.5.W54 1994, **(v6)**
Williams, Phil. Z6464.N65.W55 1994, **(v10)**
Williams, Philip F. PL2921.T72.Z95 1993, **(v3)**
Williams, Philip Maynard. DA566.9.G3.W54, **(v5)**
Williams, Philip Middleton. PN2277.N52.C579 1993, **(v3)**
Williams, R. J. P. QD33.W718 1999, **(v1)**
Williams, Raymond Brady. BR563.E27.W55 1996, **(v8)**
Williams, Raymond L. PQ7082.N7.W548 1998, **(v3)**
Williams, Raymond. DA566.4.W48, **(v5)**
  PR99.W67 1983, **(v3)**
  PR6029.R8.Z865, **(v3)**
Williams, Rhodri. DA570.W53 1991, **(v5)**
Williams, Richard E. E184.A1.W48 1990, **(v4)**
Williams, Robert A. E93.W755 1997, **(v4)**
  KF8205.W547 1990, **(v7)**
Williams, Robert Chadwell. N6981.W54, **(v9)**
  UB271.R9.F838 1987, **(v10)**
Williams, Robert. N6915.W525 1997, **(v9)**
Williams, Robin. Z246.W63 2001, **(v10)**
Williams, Roger Lawrence. DC304.5.W55 1993, **(v5)**
Williams, Roger M. E185.97.B75.W5 1971, **(v4)**
  ML420.W55 W5 1981, **(v9)**
Williams, Roger. F82.W64 1988, **(v4)**
Williams, Simon. PR2971.G3.W55 1990, **(v3)**
Williams, Stephen. CC125.N7.W55 1991, **(v5)**
  DF555.W55 1999, **(v5)**
  DG330.W55 1995, **(v5)**
Williams, Sue Rodwell. RM216.W682 2001, **(v2)**
Williams, Susan S. PS374.P43.W55 1997, **(v3)**
Williams, T. Harry. E467.W5, **(v4)**
  E467.1.B38.W5, **(v4)**
  E470.W78, **(v4)**
  E748.L86 W48 1981, **(v4)**
Williams, Tennessee. PS3545.I5365.A17 1956, **(v3)**
  PS3545.I5365.A19 1971, **(v3)**
  PS3545.I5365.A6 1984, **(v3)**
  PS3545.I5365.B3 1956, **(v3)**
  PS3545.I5365.C5 1983, **(v3)**
  PS3545.I5365.D7 1970, **(v3)**
  PS3545.I5365.E4, **(v3)**
  PS3545.I5365.G5 1949, **(v3)**

Williams, Tennessee *(cont.)*
PS3545.I5365.L6 1980, **(v3)**
PS3545.I5365.N5, **(v3)**
PS3545.I5365.O5 1967, **(v3)**
PS3545.I5365.O7, **(v3)**
PS3545.I5365.P4, **(v3)**
PS3545.I5365.R3 1988, **(v3)**
PS3545.I5365.R6, **(v3)**
PS3545.I5365.R6 1951, **(v3)**
PS3545.I5365.S64 1995, **(v3)**
PS3545.I5365.S83, **(v3)**
PS3545.I5365.S85 1948, **(v3)**
PS3545.I5365.S87 1959, **(v3)**
PS3545.I5365.T9, **(v3)**
PS3545.I5365.T95 1973, **(v3)**
PS3545.I5365.V5 1979, **(v3)**
PS3545.I5365.Z48 2000, **(v3)**
Williams, Theodore Samuel. GV865.W5.A3, **(v6)**
Williams, Thomas. PS3573.I456.H3, **(v3)**
Williams, Tony D. QL696.S473.W55 1995, **(v1)**
Williams, Tony. PN1995.9.H6.W46 1996, **(v3)**
PN1998.3.C664.W56 1997, **(v3)**
Williams, Trevor L. PR6019.O9.Z953 1997, **(v3)**
Williams, Vergil. HV9304.W54 1996, **(v6)**
Williams, Vernon J. GN21.B56.W55 1996, **(v6)**
Williams, W. H. A. ML3554.W77 1996, **(v9)**
PS3525.E43.Z914 1998, **(v3)**
Williams, Walter. HN60.W55 1998, **(v6)**
JA37.P9 no. 6, **(v7)**
Williams, William Appleman. E744.W56 1972, **(v4)**
HC105.W54, **(v6)**
Williams, William Carlos. PS3545.I544.A153, **(v3)**
PS3545.I544.A16 1954, **(v3)**
PS3545.I544.A17 1986, **(v3)**
PS3545.I544.A19 1961, **(v3)**
PS3545.I544.A6 1949, **(v3)**
PS3545.I544.B8 1952, **(v3)**
PS3545.I544.D4 1954, **(v3)**
PS3545.I544.G7, **(v3)**
PS3545.I544.I5 1967, **(v3)**
PS3545.I544.P3 1992, **(v3)**
PS3545.I544.W5 1967, **(v3)**
PS3545.I544.Z48 1984, **(v3)**
PS3545.I544.Z485 1989, **(v3)**
PS3545.I544.Z5, **(v3)**
PS3545.IL6.V9, **(v3)**
Williams, William Henry. E445.D3.W55 1996, **(v4)**
Williams-Myers, Albert James. F127.H8 W57 1994, **(v4)**
Williamson, Bill. HN385.5.W515 1990, **(v6)**
Williamson, Clark M. BT78.W585 1993, **(v8)**
Williamson, D. G. DD220.W48 1986, **(v5)**
DD238.W55 1990, **(v5)**
DD256.5.W49 1982, **(v5)**
Williamson, David. DA28.1.W523 1998, **(v5)**
Williamson, Edward C. F316.2.W54, **(v4)**
Williamson, George. PR541.W5 1958, **(v3)**
Williamson, Harold Francis. TS533.2.W37 1975, **(v1)**
Williamson, Henry Raymond. DS751.W35 1935, **(v5)**
Williamson, J. W. PN1995.9.M67.W54 1995, **(v3)**
Williamson, Jack. PS3545.I557.D3 1975, **(v3)**
Williamson, James R. HD2795.W68 1995, **(v6)**
Williamson, Jeffrey G. HT384.G7.W54 1990, **(v6)**
Williamson, Joel. E185.61.W738 1984, **(v4)**
E185.93.S7 W73 1975, **(v4)**
PS3511.A86.Z98574 1993, **(v3)**
Williamson, John B. HQ1064.U5.W5923 1985, **(v6)**
Williamson, Marilyn L. PR113.W55 1990, **(v3)**
Williamson, Mark. TL788.W54 2001, **(v1)**
Williamson, Miryam Ehrlich. RC927.3.W53 1996, **(v2)**
Williamson, Paul. NB180.W55 1995, **(v9)**
Williamson, Peter J. JC478.W5527 1989, **(v7)**
Williamson, Philip. DA566.9.B15.W56 1999, **(v5)**
Williamson, Robert Clifford. HN110.5.A8.W486 1997, **(v6)**
Williamson, Ronald. B689.Z7.W54 1989, **(v8)**
Williamson, Roxanne. NA1996.W48 1990, **(v9)**
Williamson, Samuel R. DB86.W515 1990, **(v5)**
UA23.W4593 1993, **(v10)**
Williamson, Sue. N7392.W55 1989, **(v9)**
Williamson, Tom. DA670.B695.W55 1997, **(v5)**

Willigan, J. Dennis. HB849.4.W54 1982, **(v6)**
Willingham, Warren W. LB3051.W4996 1997, **(v7)**
Willinsky, John. H61.8.W543 2000, **(v6)**
LB1631.W44 1984, **(v7)**
PE1617.O94.W55 1994, **(v3)**
Willis, Daniel. NA2543.S6.W525 1999, **(v9)**
Willis, Deborah. TR23 W55 2000, **(v1)**
Willis, F. Roy. DD257.2.W55, **(v5)**
Willis, H. Lee. TK1041.W55 2000, **(v1)**
Willis, J. H. Z232.H73.W54 1992, **(v10)**
Willis, Joe Don. GV481.2.W55 1992, **(v6)**
Willis, John C. F347.M6.W55 2000, **(v4)**
Willis, Mark R. Z711.W64 1999, **(v10)**
Willis, Nathaniel Parker. PS3322.B4 1970, **(v3)**
Willis, Parker B. HG2562.F8.W54 1972, **(v6)**
Willis, Paul E. GN345.W52 2001, **(v6)**
Willis, Susan. PR3093.W55 1991, **(v3)**
Willis, William James. PN4797.W528 1991, **(v3)**
Willius, Frederick A. RC681.C56, **(v2)**
Willmer, E. N. QP88.W5 1958, **(v1)**
Willmer, Pat. QL362.75.W55 1990, **(v1)**
Willmott, H. P. D743.W524 1990, **(v5)**
V25.W55 1981, **(v10)**
Willott, James F. QP356.25.V55 1999, **(v1)**
Willoughby, Barrett. PS3545.I6 R6, **(v3)**
Willoughby, Guy. PR5827.A35.W54 1993, **(v3)**
Willoughby, John. UA26.G3.W55 2001, **(v10)**
Willoughby, Lynn. BX5980.C6768 W55 1999, **(v8)**
F292.C4.W55 1999, **(v4)**
Willoughby, Malcolm Francis. D773.W48, **(v5)**
Wills, Charles. F566.3.W55 1996, **(v4)**
Wills, Christopher. QP376.W56 1993, **(v1)**
RB155.W54 1991, **(v2)**
Wills, David. PN85.W48 1995, **(v3)**
Wills, Garry. BX1765.2.W54 2000, **(v8)**
E221.W64, **(v4)**
E312.64.W54 1984, **(v4)**
E475.55.W54 1992, **(v4)**
E877.W55 1988, **(v4)**
HM141.W525 1994, **(v6)**
JC251.W554, **(v7)**
PR2823.W49 1995, **(v3)**
PR4453.C4.Z88, **(v3)**
E856.W53 1990, **(v4)**
Wills, Jeffrey. PA6142.Z5.W55 1996, **(v3)**
Wills, John E. D246.W55 2001, **(v5)**
DS734.W63 1994, **(v5)**
Willson, Beckles. E415.9.S58.W5, **(v4)**
Willson, James D. HG4026.H43 1981, **(v6)**
Willson, Meredith. ML422.W63.A3 1975, **(v9)**
Willson, Perry R. HD6073.E32.I818 1993, **(v6)**
Wilmarth, M. Grace. QE5.W5 1968, **(v1)**
Wilmer, Franke. GN380.W55 1993, **(v6)**
Wilmer, Harry A. RC480.5.W49 1987, **(v2)**
Wilmerding, John. N6505.W57 1991, **(v9)**
ND237.L27.A4 1988, **(v9)**
ND1351.5.W56 1994, **(v9)**
Wilmeth, Don B. PN1579.W5, **(v3)**
Wilmut, Ian. QH442.2.W545 1999, **(v1)**
Wilner, Joshua. PN603.W55 2000, **(v3)**
Wilpert, Gero von. PN41.W48, **(v3)**
Wilshire, Bruce W. B893.W55 2000, **(v8)**
Wilshire, Bruce W. RC569.5.D47.W55 1998, **(v2)**
Wilson, A. Jeyaratnam. DS489.8.W53 1988, **(v5)**
Wilson, A. N. BS2506.W54 1997, **(v8)**
DA562.W55 1989, **(v5)**
PR6003.E45.Z893 1984, **(v3)**
PR6023.E926.Z96 1990, **(v3)**
Wilson, Alexander. GF91.N7.W55 1992, **(v6)**
Wilson, Andrew J. DA990.U46.W488 1995, **(v5)**
Wilson, Andrew. DK508.45.W55 2000, **(v5)**
DK508.848.W55 1996, **(v5)**
Wilson, Angus. PQ2528.W5 1952a, **(v3)**
PR4856.W54 1978, **(v3)**
PR6045.I577.A7, **(v3)**
PR6045.I577.B5, **(v3)**
PR6045.I577.H4, **(v3)**
PR6045.I577.M5 1982, **(v3)**
PR6045.I577.M8 1956, **(v3)**
PR6045.I577.N6, **(v3)**
PR6045.I577.W5 1963, **(v3)**

Wilson, Arnold Talbot. D568.5.W6, **(v5)**
Wilson, August. PS3573.I45677.A6 1991, **(v3)**
Wilson, Brent. N108.W55 1997, **(v9)**
Wilson, Bruce L. LB1628.5.W55 1993, **(v7)**
Wilson, Bruce M. F1546.W55 1998, **(v4)**
Wilson, Bryan R. BL60.W543, **(v8)**
Wilson, C. Dwayne. Z7164.O7.W545 1997, **(v10)**
Wilson, C. H. HC254.5.W52, **(v6)**
Wilson, Carter A. E184.A1.W514 1996, **(v4)**
Wilson, Catherine. B67.W55 1995, **(v8)**
Wilson, Charles Morrow. SB111.W63, **(v1)**
Wilson, Charles. D228.W54, **(v5)**
Wilson, Chris. F804.S25.W55 1997, **(v4)**
Wilson, Christopher P. HV8138.W627 2000, **(v6)**
Wilson, Christopher. NA5453.W55 1990, **(v9)**
Wilson, Clyde Norman. F273.P53.W55 1990, **(v4)**
Z8140.62.W55 1990, **(v10)**
Wilson, Colin. BL580.W55 1996, **(v8)**
CB19.W53 1956a, **(v5)**
PR6073.I44.A3, **(v3)**
PR6073.I44.R5, **(v3)**
Wilson, Cynthia. RB152.W49 1993, **(v2)**
Wilson, David A. JC178.V2.W55 1988, **(v7)**
Wilson, David J. F2230.1.S7.W55 1999, **(v4)**
TD878.W53 1995, **(v1)**
Wilson, Derek A. G420.D7.W53 1977b, **(v6)**
HG1552.R8.W56 1988, **(v6)**
Wilson, Diana de Armas. PQ6327.P5.W55 1991, **(v3)**
Wilson, Dick. DS778.C593.W54 1984, **(v5)**
Wilson, Don W. F685.R648 1975, **(v4)**
Wilson, Dorothy Clarke. E99.O4 W54, **(v4)**
Wilson, Edmund. E169.W658 1971, **(v4)**
F124.W726 1971, **(v4)**
G469.W55, **(v6)**
PN511.W633 1947, **(v3)**
PN771.W55, **(v3)**
PR9153.W5, **(v3)**
PS3545.I6245.M4 1959, **(v3)**
PS3545.I6245.N5, **(v3)**
PS3545.I6245.Z465 1983, **(v3)**
PS3545.I6245.Z53, **(v3)**
PS3545.I6245.Z533, **(v3)**
PS3545.I6245.Z535 1980, **(v3)**
PS3545.I6245.Z536 1975, **(v3)**
PS3545.I6245.Z54 1977, **(v3)**
Wilson, Edward Osborne. B72.W54 1998, **(v8)**
BD581.W476 1996, **(v8)**
GN365.9.W54, **(v6)**
QH31.W64.A3 1994, **(v1)**
QH313.W55 1992, **(v1)**
QL496.W67 1990, **(v1)**
QL775.W54, **(v1)**
Wilson, Elizabeth A. M. PG2640.W54 1982, **(v3)**
Wilson, Elizabeth. HQ1593.W54 1980, **(v6)**
ML410.S53.W55 1994, **(v9)**
ML418.D85.W55 1999, **(v9)**
Wilson, Eunice. Z6207.W8.W54 1995, **(v10)**
Wilson, F. P. PR421.W5, **(v3)**
PR2673.W5, **(v3)**
Wilson, Frank R. QP334.W53 1998, **(v1)**
Wilson, George M. DS881.3.W55 1992, **(v5)**
Wilson, Greg. QA76.642.W553 1995, **(v1)**
Wilson, Harriet E. PS3334.W39.O9 1983, **(v3)**
Wilson, Howard Eugene. HV28.M3 W5, **(v6)**
Wilson, Ian. BT587.S4.W518 1998, **(v8)**
Wilson, J. QC673.W54 1983, **(v1)**
Wilson, Jack. QH331.W555 1999, **(v1)**
Wilson, James Q. BJ1012.W5375 1993, **(v8)**
HV6789.W53 1983, **(v4)**
JK421.W52 1989, **(v7)**
Wilson, Jason. PQ7297.P285.Z97 1986, **(v3)**
Wilson, Jean Moorcroft. PR6037.A86.Z9 1999, **(v3)**
Wilson, Jeremy. D568.4.L45.W55 1990, **(v5)**
Wilson, John Anthony Burgess. PR6052.U638.N6 1964, **(v3)**
Wilson, John Anthony Burgess. PR6073.I4678.C9, **(v3)**
Wilson, John Dover. PR2807.W47 1963, **(v3)**
PR2848.W5 1964, **(v3)**
PR2894.W57, **(v3)**
PR2981.W5, **(v3)**

Wilson, John Harold. PR437.W54 1967, (v3)
Wilson, John Howard. PR6045.A97.Z498 1996, (v3)
  PR6045.A97.Z498 1996, (v3)
Wilson, John K. LC89.W55 1995, (v7)
Wilson, John. DA565.C15.W54 1974, (v5)
  GV706.5.W55 1994, (v6)
Wilson, Keith. PR4757.D7.W55 1995, (v3)
Wilson, Kenneth G. PE2835.W55 1993, (v3)
Wilson, Laura. F394.L176 M388 1989, (v4)
Wilson, Lindsay B. R505.W55 1993, (v2)
Wilson, Lisa. F7.C36 1999, (v4)
Wilson, Louis Edward. DT510.43.K76.W55 1991, (v5)
Wilson, Luke. PR658.L38, (v3)
Wilson, Major L. E338.W684, (v4)
Wilson, Margaret. PQ6105.W5 1969, (v3)
  PQ6436.W54, (v3)
  PS3545.I63.A2, (v3)
Wilson, Mary Ann. PS3569.T2.Z93 1996, (v3)
Wilson, Michiko N. PL858.B3.Z95 1999, (v3)
Wilson, Milton Thomas. PR5438.W5, (v3)
Wilson, Myoung Chung. Z3317.W55 2000, (v10)
Wilson, Nick. GV865.A1.W55 2000, (v6)
Wilson, Norma. PS153.I52.W55 2001, (v3)
Wilson, Peter H. DAW1047.W55 2000, (v5)
  DD801.W76.W55 1995, (v5)
Wilson, Peter J. DT469.M277.T788 1992, (v5)
  GN360.W55 1988, (v6)
Wilson, Peter R. QB526.C9.W55 1994, (v1)
Wilson, R. M. PR1502.M4 ser. C, no. 2, (v3)
Wilson, R. M. S. HF5415.13.W547 1992, (v6)
Wilson, Raymond Jackson. Z479.W53 1989, (v10)
Wilson, Richard W. JA75.7.W553 1992, (v7)
Wilson, Richard. F1465.2.K5.W57 1995, (v4)
  NA7620.W55 2000, (v9)
  PR3024.W558 1993, (v3)
Wilson, Rob. DU18.W55 2000, (v5)
Wilson, Robert A. BD418.3.W54 1995, (v8)
Wilson, Rodney. HC415.24.W55 1995, (v6)
  HG3366.A6.W53 1983, (v6)
Wilson, Sandra. DS784.W55 2001, (v5)
Wilson, Scott. PR428.P6.W55 1995, (v3)
Wilson, Sharon Rose. PR9199.3.A8.Z95 1993, (v3)
Wilson, Sherrill D. F128.9.N3.W56 1994, (v4)
Wilson, Sloan. PS3573.I475.M3 1955, (v3)
Wilson, Suanna J. HV43.W518 1978, (v6)
Wilson, Thomas A. B5233.C6 W55 1995, (v8)
Wilson, Thomas C. Z678.9.W55 1998, (v10)
Wilson, William E. PQ6321.C7.Z9, (v3)
Wilson, William H. F394.D216.H369 1998, (v4)
Wilson, William J. E185.615.W545 1999, (v4)
  HV4045.W55 1987, (v4)
  HV4045.W553 1996, (v6)
Wilson, Woodrow. E312.W763 1969, (v4)
  E467.1.L4.W75, (v4)
  E660.W717, (v4)
  E660.W722, (v4)
  E742.5.W5, (v4)
  JK246.W82 1961, (v7)
  JK271.W6 1961, (v7)
  JK1061.W78 1981, (v7)
Wilson-Tagoe, Nana. PR9210.W55 1998, (v3)
Wilstach, Paul. F187.C5 W5, (v4)
Wilt, Alan F. D757.W545 1990, (v5)
Wilt, David E. PN1998.2.W5 1991, (v3)
Wilt, Judith. PR830.T3.W5, (v3)
  PR5014.W55, (v3)
  PR5341.W55 1985, (v3)
Wilton-Ely, John. N6923.P495.W54, (v9)
Wiltshire, John. PR3537.M4.W54 1990, (v3)
  PR4038.M4.W5 1992, (v3)
Wiltshire, Susan Ford. PA6825.W538 1989, (v3)
Wimsatt, James I. PR1912.A3.W56 1991, (v3)
Wimsatt, William K. PN80.5.E48, (v3)
  PN85.W49, (v3)
  PN1031.W517, (v3)
Winant, Howard. HC106.6.W56 1988, (v6)
Winch, Christopher. LB15.W54 1999, (v7)
  LC1042.5.W56 2000, (v7)
Winch, David M. HD6524.W56 1989, (v6)
Winch, Donald. HB103.A2.W56 1996, (v6)
  JC176.S63.W56, (v7)

Winch, Robert G. TK5101.W48 1993, (v1)
Winch, Samuel P. PN4784.T4.W56 1997, (v3)
Winchell, Constance M. Z1035.W79 1967, (v10)
Winchell, Mark Royden. PS29.B74.W56 1996, (v3)
  PS3507.A666.Z87 2000, (v3)
Winchell, Mary Edna. E78.A3.W5, (v4)
Winchester, Simon. QE22.S6W55 2001, (v1)
Winchilsea, Anne Kingsmill Finch. PR3765.W57.A17
  1979, (v3)
Wind, Herbert Warren. GV981.W5 1956, (v6)
Windass, Stan. UA646.W55 1988, (v10)
Windelband, W. B113.W613 1956, (v8)
Windels, Fernand. N5310.W764 1949, (v9)
Winders, James A. HQ1190.W56 1991, (v6)
Winders, Richard Bruce. E409.2.W56 1997, (v4)
  F390.W77 2002, (v4)
Windham, Laurie. HF5548.32.W56 2000, (v6)
Windhoff-Heritier, Adrienne. F128.55.W56 1992, (v4)
Windlesham, David James George Hennessy.
  HV9950.W56 1998, (v6)
Windley, Lathan A. E446.W73 1983, (v4)
Windrich, Elaine. PN4888.F69.W56 1992, (v3)
Windschuttle, Keith. D13.W624 1997, (v5)
Windt, Theodore. E841.W55 1990, (v4)
Winearls, Joan. Z6027.C22.O68 1991, (v10)
Wineburg, Robert J. HV530.W56 2001, (v6)
Winegar, Norman. RA413.W48 1998, (v2)
Winegardner, Duane L. S591.W73 1996, (v1)
Winegarten, Renee. PQ2603.E362.Z94 1988, (v3)
Winfield, Betty Houchin. E807.W58 1990, (v4)
Winfield, Gerald Freeman. DS721.W53 1950, (v5)
Winfree, Arthur T. QH527.W56 1987, (v1)
Winfrey, Carey. CT275.W58458.A34, (v5)
Wingell, Richard. ML3797.W54 2002, (v9)
Wingerson, Lois. QH438.7.W56 1998, (v1)
Wingert, Paul S. N5310.W766, (v9)
Wingfield Digby, George Frederick. NE642.B5.W5,
  (v9)
Wingfield, Paul. ML410.J18.W56 1992, (v9)
Wingfield-Stratford, Esme Cecil. DA566.W55, (v5)
Wingler, Hans Maria. N332.B38.W513, (v9)
Winham, Gilbert R. KF6668.C32 1988.W56 1988, (v7)
Winkelman, Michael. RZ401.W56 2000, (v2)
Winkelmann-Rhein, Gertraude. ND653.B75.W513,
  (v9)
Winkle, Kenneth J. F495.W65 1988, (v4)
Winkler, Allan M. UA23.W485 1993, (v10)
Winkler, Kenneth P. B1348.W56 1989, (v8)
Winkler, Max. CT275.W58465.A3, (v5)
Winks, Robin W. DA18.W52 1969, (v5)
  F1026.6.W56, (v4)
  F1035.N3.W5, (v4)
  HE2754.B5.W56 1991, (v6)
Winn, James Anderson. AZ182.W56 1998, (v10)
  ML3849.W58, (v9)
  PR3423.W5 1987, (v3)
  PR3427.L65.W56 1992, (v3)
Winn, Kenneth H. E184.M8.W56 1989, (v4)
Winner, Ellen. HQ773.5.W55 1996, (v6)
  NX165.W56 1982, (v9)
Winnick, Louis. F128.68.S94.W56 1990, (v4)
Winnicott, D. W. RJ499.W493 1996, (v2)
  RJ506.J88W56 1984, (v2)
Winny, James. B776.E5.W5 1976, (v8)
Winock, Michel. DC369.W5613 1998, (v5)
Winokur, Mark. PN1995.9.C55.W52 1996, (v3)
Winsbro, Bonnie C. PS151.W46 1993, (v3)
Winship, Michael. Z1225.B55 Index, (v10)
  Z1225.B55 Suppl., (v10)
Winskel, G. QA76.7.W555 1993, (v1)
Winslow, Barbara. HQ1595.P34.W56 1996, (v6)
Winslow, Charles D. HD31.W559 1994, (v6)
Winslow, Don. PS3573.I5326.C35 1999, (v3)
Winslow, Ola Elizabeth. F82.W855 1973, (v4)
  PR3331.W62, (v3)
Winslow, Richard Elliott. F44.P8.W55 1988, (v4)
Winslow, Thyra (Samter). PS3545.I7563.P5, (v3)
Winson, Gail. K3778.A12 W56 1990, (v7)
Winsor, Mary P. QL362.5.W56, (v1)
Winspear, Alban Dewes. B577.L64.W5, (v8)
Winstanley, Lilian. PR2807.W55, (v3)

Winstead, Karen A. BX4659.G7.W56 1997, (v8)
Winstedt, Richard Olof. PL5130.W5 1969, (v3)
Winston, Brian. PN1992.8.D6.W56 2000, (v3)
  PN1995.9.D6.W48 1995, (v3)
Winston, Diane H. BX9718.N7.W56 1999, (v8)
Winston, Judith E. QH83.W57 1999, (v1)
Winston, Mark L. SF523.3.W55 1998, (v1)
  SF538.5.A37.W56 1992, (v1)
Winston, Robert Paul. PN3448.D4.W55 1992, (v3)
Winston, Roger B. LB3227.5.W56 1993, (v7)
Wint, Guy. DS5.W5, (v5)
Winter, Bruce W. B288.W56 1996, (v8)
  BS2675.5.W56 2001, (v8)
Winter, Denis. D544.H29.W56 1991, (v5)
Winter, Ella. PR6045.I726.Z5, (v3)
Winter, Frank H. TL781.W55 1990, (v1)
Winter, J. M. D523.W578 1996, (v5)
  D523.W58 1995, (v5)
Winter, James H. GF551.W56 1999, (v6)
Winterbone, D. E. TJ265.W535 1997, (v1)
Winternitz, Emanuel. ML85.W58 1979, (v9)
  ML96.4.W5 1965, (v9)
Winters, Harold A. UA990.W45 1998, (v10)
Winters, John D. E565.W54, (v4)
Winters, L. Alan. HF1532.7.L25 1994, (v6)
Winters, Laura. PS3505.A87.Z9384 1993, (v3)
Winterson, Jeanette. PR6073.I558.S4 1990, (v3)
Winther, Sophus Keith. PS3545.I766 T3, (v3)
Winthrop, John. F67.W784 1996, (v4)
Winthrop, Robert H. GN307.W56 1991, (v6)
Wintle, Michael J. HC323.H643 2000, (v6)
Winton, Calhoun. PR3473.B6.W56 1993, (v3)
  PR3706.W5, (v3)
Winton, Harold R. U43.G7.W56 1988, (v10)
Winton, John. V182.W56 1983, (v10)
Wintrobe, Ronald. JC495.W55 1998, (v7)
Winzer, M. A. LC3965.W56 1993, (v7)
Wirenius, John F. KF4772.W57 2000, (v7)
Wires, Richard. PS3525.A6695.Z96 1990, (v3)
Wirls, Daniel. UA23.W486 1992, (v10)
Wirsing, Robert. UA853.P3.W57 1991, (v10)
Wirth, Arthur G. LC66.W57 1992, (v7)
Wirthmann, Alfred. GB446.W5713 2000, (v6)
Wirtschafter, Elise Kimerling. U771.W57 1990, (v10)
Wischnitzer, Saul. QC373.E4.W5, (v1)
Wisdom, J. O. BF173.W549 1991, (v2)
Wisdom, John. BD201.W55 1966, (v8)
Wise, Charles R. KF4945.W57 1991, (v7)
Wise, Claude Merton. PE1135.W57, (v3)
Wise, David H. QL458.4.W57 1993, (v1)
Wise, Gene. E175.W47 1980, (v4)
Wise, S. F. UG635.C2.W57, (v10)
Wise, Stephen R. E600.W57 1988, (v4)
Wise, Suzanne. Z7514.S72.W57 1994, (v10)
Wiseman, Carter. NA737.P365.W57 1990, (v9)
Wiseman, Frederick Matthew. E99.A13 W45 2001,
  (v4)
Wiseman, Jacqueline P. HV5132.W57 1991, (v6)
Wiseman, John A. JQ1879.A15 W57 1990, (v7)
  Z3559.W57 1992, (v10)
Wiseman, Susan. PR680.W57 1998, (v3)
Wisensale, Steven K. HD6066.U5.W57 2001, (v6)
Wisenthal, J. L. PR5368.H5.W57 1988, (v3)
Wiser, William. PS3573.I87.G74 1991, (v3)
Wish, Harvey. E175.W5, (v4)
Wishart, David J. E78.N3 W57 1994, (v4)
Wishnia, K. J. A. PQ8212.W57 1999, (v3)
Wishy, Bernard W. HQ792.U5.W5, (v6)
Wisse, Ruth R. PJ5129.P4.Z97 1991, (v3)
  PN842.W57 2000, (v3)
Wister, Owen. PS3345.V5 1930, (v3)
  PS3346.A3 1958, (v3)
Wistrich, Robert S. CT1063.W48 1982, (v5)
  DS135.A92.V583 1989, (v5)
  DS145.W542 1991, (v5)
Wit, H. C. D. de. QK98.W7213, (v1)
Witek, Terri. PS3523.O89.L538 1993, (v3)
Witemeyer, Hugh. PR4692.A66.W5, (v3)
Witherell, Julian W. Z3501.W57, (v10)
Witherell, Larry L. DA566.9.C76.W58 1997, (v5)
Witherington, Ben. BR195.W6.W58 1988, (v8)

Withers, Josephine. NB813.G6.W57, **(v9)**
Witherspoon, Gary. E99.N3.W678 1977, **(v4)**
  E99.N3.W68, **(v4)**
Withey, Lynne. DU20.W55 1987, **(v5)**
  E322.1.A38.W56, **(v4)**
Withington, Ann Fairfax. E209.W58 1991, **(v4)**
Withycombe, Elizabeth Gidley. CS2375.G7 W5 1977, **(v5)**
Witke, Roxane. DS778.C5374.W57, **(v5)**
Witkowski, Georg. PT651.W5 1910, **(v3)**
Witmer, Helen Leland. RJ499.W52, **(v2)**
Witt, Charlotte. B434.W58 1989, **(v8)**
  B434.W59 2003, **(v8)**
Witt, David L. N6535.T3.W58 1992, **(v9)**
Witt, Doris. E185.86.W58 1999, **(v4)**
Witt, Shirley Hill. PM197.E1.W5 1972b, **(v3)**
Wittcoff, Harold. TP247.W59 1996, **(v1)**
Witte, Bernd. PT2603.E455.Z95413 1991, **(v3)**
Witte, John F. HD5660.U5.W57, **(v6)**
Witte, John. KF4783.Z9.W58 2000, **(v7)**
Wittebols, James H. PN1992.77.M2854.W58 1998, **(v3)**
Wittek, Paul. PL125.W6 1956, **(v3)**
Wittels, Fritz. BF173.F85W46, **(v2)**
Witten, Marsha Grace. BR526.W58 1993, **(v8)**
Wittfogel, Karl August. DS751.W58 1949, **(v5)**
Wittgenstein, Ludwig. BC135.W5 1971, **(v8)**
  BF38.W764 1982, **(v2)**
  QA8.4.W5613 1978b, **(v1)**
Wittig, Joseph S. PR2015.W53 1997, **(v3)**
Wittke, Carl Frederick. F491.W78, **(v4)**
Wittkopf, Eugene R. E839.8.W57 1990, **(v4)**
Wittkower, Rudolf. N71.W54, **(v9)**
  NA520.W5 1965, **(v9)**
  NB1140.W57 1977b, **(v9)**
Wittman, Donald A. JC423.W499 1995, **(v7)**
Wittner, Lawrence S. JX1974.7.W575 1993, **(v7)**
Wittreich, Joseph Anthony. PR3587.3.W58 1987, **(v3)**
Wixson, Douglas C. PS3505.O53.Z95 1994, **(v3)**
Wixted, John Timothy. DS734.8.W58 1992, **(v5)**
Wlasuk, Peter. QB581.W63 2000, **(v1)**
Wlodkowski, Raymond J. LB1065.W58 1990, **(v7)**
Wober, J. M. PN1992.6.W64 1988, **(v3)**
Wodarski, John S. HV689.W62, **(v6)**
Wodehouse, P. G. PR6045.O53.C6 1938, **(v3)**
  PR6045.O53.M6, **(v3)**
  PR6045.O53.S, **(v3)**
  PR6045.O53.U6 1969, **(v3)**
  PR6045.O53.Z48 1990, **(v3)**
Wodin, Natascha. PT2685.O23.E3513 1992, **(v3)**
Woelfel, Norman. LA210.W6 1933a, **(v7)**
Woeste, Victoria Saker. KF1715.W64 1998, **(v7)**
Wofford, Harris. E841.W56 1992, **(v4)**
Wofford, Susanne Lindgren. PR2358.W6 1992, **(v3)**
Wogan-Browne, Jocelyn. PR275.W6.W64 2001, **(v3)**
Wohl, Ellen E. GB1227.S67, **(v6)**
Wohl, Robert. CB203.W63, **(v5)**
Wohletz, Kenneth. QE522.W64 1992, **(v1)**
Woiwode, Larry. PS3573.O4.B4, **(v3)**
Wojahn, Ellen. HD2746.5.W65 1988, **(v6)**
Wojciehowski, Dolora A. PN731.W65 1995, **(v3)**
Wojcik, Daniel. BR526.W65 1997, **(v8)**
Wojtowicz, Robert. NA737.M85.W66 1996, **(v9)**
Wolbrecht, Christina. HQ1236.5.U6.W63 2000, **(v6)**
Wolcott, Roger T. Z7831.W65 1990, **(v10)**
Wolf, Arthur P. GT2783.5.W65 1995, **(v6)**
Wolf, Carolyn E. Z1209.W82 Suppl., **(v10)**
Wolf, Charles. HB501.W89 1988, **(v6)**
Wolf, Christa. PT2685.O36.K313 1984, **(v3)**
  PT2685.O36.K338 1983, **(v3)**
  PT2685.O36.K513 1984, **(v3)**
  PT2685.O36.K5 1977, **(v3)**
  PT2685.O36.N313 1989, **(v3)**
  PT2685.O36.N3 1969, **(v3)**
Wolf, Diane L. HD6194.Z6.J388 1992, **(v6)**
Wolf, Eric R. GN29.W6, **(v6)**
  GN345.S74 2002, **(v6)**
Wolf, Jason. TK5103.4.W65 2001, **(v1)**
Wolf, John Baptist. DC129.W6 1968, **(v5)**
Wolf, Kenneth Baxter. DG847.14.W65 1995, **(v5)**
Wolf, Margery. GN345.W65 1992, **(v6)**

HQ668.95.W63, **(v6)**
Wolf, Naomi. HQ27.5.W65 1997, **(v6)**
  HQ1219.W65 1991, **(v6)**
Wolf, Paul R. TA545.W77 1994, **(v1)**
Wolf, Peter M. HT381.W65 1999, **(v6)**
Wolf, Stephanie Grauman. HN80.G46.W6, **(v6)**
Wolf, Susan R. BJ1461.W64 1990, **(v8)**
Wolfe, Alan. BJ352.W65 2001, **(v8)**
  HM24.W64 1993, **(v6)**
  HM216.W65 1989, **(v6)**
Wolfe, Bertram David. DK254.L4.W6 1964, **(v5)**
Wolfe, Cary. PS169.I53.W65 1993, **(v3)**
Wolfe, Charles K. ML420.L277.W6 1992, **(v9)**
  ML3524.W64 1999, **(v9)**
  ML3551.7.S68.W65 1997, **(v9)**
Wolfe, Christopher. KF4552.W63 1996, **(v7)**
Wolfe, Don Marion. PR3581.W6, **(v3)**
Wolfe, Gene. PS3573.O52.S45 1980, **(v3)**
Wolfe, Margaret Ripley. F444.K5.W65 1987, **(v4)**
  HQ1438.S63.W65 1995, **(v6)**
Wolfe, Marshall. HD78.W64 1996, **(v6)**
Wolfe, Peter. PL833.I7.Z926 1989, **(v3)**
  PR6056.O85.Z9 1976, **(v3)**
Wolfe, Richard J. Z271.W638 1990, **(v10)**
Wolfe, Rosalee Jean. T385.W6448 2000, **(v1)**
Wolfe, Thomas. PS3545.O337.F7, **(v3)**
  PS3545.O337.G66 1991, **(v3)**
  PS3545.O337.L6 1947, **(v3)**
  PS3545.O337.O18 2000, **(v3)**
  PS3545.O337.O4 1935, **(v3)**
  PS3545.O337.P37 1995, **(v3)**
  PS3545.O337.S6 1945, **(v3)**
  PS3545.O337.S7, **(v3)**
  PS3545.O337.W4 1939, **(v3)**
  PS3545.O337.W49 1983, **(v3)**
  PS3545.O337.Y6 1940, **(v3)**
  PS3545.O337.Z493 2000, **(v3)**
  PS3545.O337.Z54 1956, **(v3)**
  PS3545.O337.Z546 1954, **(v3)**
  PS3545.O337.Z552, **(v3)**
Wolfe, Tom. E169.02.W6, **(v4)**
  E169.1.W685, **(v4)**
Wolfensberger, Donald R. JK1021.W64 2000, **(v7)**
Wolferman, Kristie C. E99.O8 W65 1997, **(v4)**
Wolff, Christoph. ML410.B1.W79 1991, **(v9)**
  ML410.B1.W793 2000, **(v9)**
Wolff, David. DS796.H4 W64 1999, **(v5)**
Wolff, Edward A. QE49.5.W64 1974, **(v1)**
Wolff, Jonathan. JC571.N683.W65 1991, **(v7)**
Wolff, Konrad. ML705.W64 1990, **(v9)**
Wolff, Larry. DR1628.W65 2001, **(v5)**
Wolff, Peter H. BF702.P52.W6, **(v2)**
Wolff, Philippe. CB351.W613 1968, **(v5)**
Wolff, Robert Lee. DR48.5.W6 1974, **(v5)**
  PR878.R5.W6, **(v3)**
  PR4969.W6, **(v3)**
Wolff, Robert Paul. BD21.W64, **(v8)**
  BJ1431.W6 1969, **(v8)**
  JC578.R383.W64, **(v7)**
Wölfflin, Heinrich. N5300.W82, **(v9)**
  NA1115.W613 1966, **(v9)**
Wolffsohn, Michael. DS102.95.W65 1987, **(v5)**
Wolfgang, Charles H. LB3013.W62 1986, **(v7)**
Wolfgruber, Gernot. PT2685.O395.A9313 1999, **(v3)**
Wolfheim, Jaclyn H. QL737.P9.W64 1983, **(v1)**
Wolfram, Herwig. D137.W6213 1988, **(v5)**
  DG312.W6613 1997, **(v5)**
Wolfram, Stephen. QA76.95.W65 1999, **(v1)**
Wolfram, Sybil. BC71.W65 1989, **(v8)**
Wolfram, von Eschenbach, 12th cent. cn.
  PT1682.P6.S8 1975, **(v3)**
  PT1682.T6.E53 1988, **(v3)**
Wolfram, Walt. PE2808.W6, **(v3)**
  PE2927.O27.W65 1997, **(v3)**
Wolfreys, Julian. PR8477.W65 1998, **(v3)**
Wolfsfeld, Gadi. P95.8.W65 1997, **(v3)**
Wolfskill, George. E806.W67, **(v4)**
Wolfson, Harry Austryn. B689.Z7.W83, **(v8)**
  BT25.W63, **(v8)**
Wolfson, Nicholas. KF4772.W65 1997, **(v7)**
Wolfson, Richard. TK9145.W59 1993, **(v1)**

Wolfson, Susan J. PR590.W55 1997, **(v3)**
Wolfthal, Diane. ND635.W64 1989, **(v9)**
Wolin, Sheldon S. JC229.T8 W65 2001, **(v7)**
  JK261.W65 1989, **(v7)**
Woliver, Laura R. JS451.W65.W75 1993, **(v7)**
Wolk, Johannes van der. NC263.G56.W6513 1987, **(v9)**
Wolken, Jerome J. QP481.W58 1995, **(v1)**
Woll, Allen L. ML1711.W64 1989, **(v9)**
  Z5784.M9 W65 1987, **(v10)**
Woll, Josephine. PN1993.5.R9.W65 2000, **(v3)**
  Z2511.U5.W64 1983, **(v10)**
Wollaeger, Mark A. PR6005.O4.Z936 1990, **(v3)**
Wolle, Muriel Sibell. F776.W66 1974, **(v4)**
Wollen, Peter. NX456.W66 1993, **(v3)**
  PN1997.S5133.W67 1992, **(v3)**
Wollheim, Richard. BD418.3.W65 1993, **(v8)**
  BH39.W64 1980, **(v8)**
  ND1140.W78 1987, **(v9)**
Wollstein, Hans J. PN1998.2.W655 1999, **(v3)**
Wollstonecraft, Mary. HQ1596.W6 1975b, **(v6)**
  JC571.W87 1790a, **(v7)**
  PR5841.W8.A6 1977, **(v3)**
Wolman, Benjamin B. BF103.W6, **(v2)**
  RC49.W65 1988, **(v2)**
Wolman, Paul. HF1756.W65 1992, **(v6)**
Wolman, Richard. BL624.W66 2001, **(v8)**
Wolmark, Jenny. PN3433.6.W64 1994, **(v3)**
Woloch, Isser. DC155.W65 1994, **(v5)**
  DC203.9.W785 2001, **(v5)**
  UB359.F8.W64, **(v10)**
Wolosky, Shira. PN771.W65 1995, **(v3)**
Wolpert, L. QM603.W65 1991, **(v1)**
Wolpert, Stanley A. DS385.B45 W65 1993, **(v5)**
  DS385.J5.W64 1984, **(v5)**
  DS436.W66 2000, **(v5)**
Wolpin, Miles D. UA23.W63 1991, **(v10)**
Wolt, Jeffrey D. S594.W7 1994, **(v1)**
Wolters, Raymond. KF4757.W65 1996, **(v7)**
Wolterstorff, Nicholas. B1298.R4.W65 1996, **(v8)**
Wolton, Suke. D750.W35 2000, **(v5)**
Womach, Jasper. S411.W57 2000, **(v1)**
Womack, Carol Z. Z7164.F5.W86 1995, **(v10)**
Womack, James P. HD9710.A2.W65 1990, **(v6)**
Womack, John. F1234.W8, **(v4)**
Woman's home companion. TX715.W874 1955, **(v1)**
Women in Transition Inc. HQ834.W68 1975, **(v6)**
Wondolleck, Julia Marie. HD205.W66 1988, **(v6)**
Wong, Chun Wa. QC20.W66 1991, **(v1)**
Wong, David B. BJ1031.W65 1984, **(v8)**
Wong, Dominic W. S. QP601.W734 1995, **(v1)**
Wong, Eva. BL1910.W66 1997, **(v8)**
Wong, Glenn M. KF4166.W66 1994, **(v7)**
Wong, J. Y. DS760.W87 1998, **(v5)**
Wong, Jimmy. TD879.P4.W65 1997, **(v1)**
Wong, Jo Yung. TL240.W66 2001, **(v1)**
Wong, Kenneth K. HT123.W555 1990, **(v6)**
Wong, Roy Bin. DS735.W79 1997, **(v5)**
Wong, Sau-ling Cynthia. PS153.A84.W66 1993, **(v3)**
Wong, Wang-chi. PL1011.W65 1991, **(v3)**
Wong, Young-tsu. SB466.C53, **(v1)**
Wonham, Henry B. PS1292.C6.Z95 1998, **(v3)**
Woo, Deborah. HD8081.A8.W66 2000, **(v6)**
Woo, Henry K. H. HC427.92.W655 1991, **(v6)**
Wood, Allen W. B2799.E8.W59 1999, **(v8)**
Wood, Anthony. DA530.W58 1982, **(v5)**
Wood, Audrey. HD9706.6.G74, **(v6)**
Wood, Bret. PN1998.3.W45.W6 1990, **(v3)**
Wood, Bryce. F1418.W682 1985, **(v4)**
  F1418.W683, **(v4)**
  F2231.5.W6, **(v4)**
Wood, Charles T. DA176.W66 1988, **(v5)**
Wood, Christopher S. ND588.A4.W63 1993, **(v9)**
Wood, Corinne Shear. Z6664.L6.W66 1997, **(v10)**
Wood, David J. BF723.C5.W66 1988, **(v2)**
Wood, Derek N. C. PR3566.W66 2001, **(v3)**
Wood, Diane S. PQ1607.C65, **(v3)**
Wood, Donald N. HN90.M3.W63 1996, **(v6)**
Wood, Edwin Orin. F572.M16 W87, **(v4)**
Wood, Ellen Meiksins. HB501.W615 1999, **(v6)**
Wood, Gerald C. PS3511.O344.Z95 1999, **(v3)**

Wood, Gerald L. QL50.W82 1982, (v1)
Wood, Gordon S. JA84.U5W6 1972, (v7)
Wood, Harold Baker. TK5102.5.W67 1988, (v1)
Wood, Henry. PR5842.W8.E3 1984, (v3)
Wood, I. N. DC65.W48 1994, (v5)
Wood, James B. DC116.5.W66 1996, (v5)
Wood, James. HE8697.4.W66 1992, (v6)
Wood, Jane Roberts. PS3573.O5945T7 1995, (v3)
Wood, Joseph Sutherland. F4.W66 1997, (v4)
Wood, Marcus. PR936.W66 1994, (v3)
Wood, Mark David. HN90.S6.W66 2000, (v6)
Wood, Michael. PN3335.W66 1998, (v3)
  PS3527.A15.Z96 1995, (v3)
Wood, Nancy V. PE1417.W565 1998, (v3)
Wood, Nancy. DC363.W66 1999, (v5)
Wood, Norman K. RC815.W66 1997, (v2)
Wood, Peter H. E445.S7.W66, (v4)
  ND237.H7.A4 1988a, (v9)
Wood, Rebecca Theurer. TX369.W67 1988, (v1)
Wood, Robert Coldwell. JK518.W66 1993, (v7)
Wood, Robert E. BD111.W56 1990, (v8)
  BH81.W66 1999, (v8)
  PR2807.W59 1994, (v3)
Wood, Robert L. F897.O5.W626 1976, (v4)
Wood, Robin. PN1995.9.P6.W66 1998, (v3)
Wood, Rufus. PR2358.W65 1997, (v3)
Wood, Ruth Pirsig. PS374.P63.W66 1995, (v3)
Wood, Sarah. PR4231.W657 2001, (v3)
Wood, Sharon. PQ4055.W6.W66 1995, (v3)
Wood, W. J. E230.W66 1990, (v4)
Woodall, Brian. HD3861.J3.W66 1996, (v6)
Woodard, K. Komozi. E185.97.B23.W66 1999, (v4)
Woodberry, George Edward. PS3352.A5 1971, (v3)
Woodbridge, Frederick James Eugene. B485.W6, (v8)
Woodbridge, Hensley Charles. Z2695.A2.W66 1997, (v10)
Woodbridge, John D. DC135.C58.W66 1995, (v5)
Woodbridge, Linda. PR428.R63.W66 2001, (v3)
  PR429.W64.W66 1984, (v3)
Woodcock, George. F1216.W6 1975, (v4)
  PR6015.U9.Z96, (v3)
  PR6029.R8.Z9, (v3)
Woodcock, Raymond L. KF283.W66 1991, (v7)
Wooden, Warren W. PR2276.F7.Z93 1983, (v3)
Wooden, Wayne S. GV1834.5.W66 1996, (v6)
Woodfield, Ian. ML760.V55.W66 1984, (v9)
Woodfine, Philip. DA501.W2.W67 1998, (v5)
Woodford, Arthur M. VK597.U6.W66 1994, (v10)
Woodford, Frank B. E514.W6 1999, (v4)
Woodgate, G. K. QC173.W66 1980, (v1)
Woodham Smith, Cecil Blanche Fitz Gerald. DA536.C3.W6 1971, (v5)
Woodham, Jonathan M. NK1390.W59 1997, (v9)
Woodhead, A. G. CN350.W65 1992, (v5)
Woodhead, Peter. AM5.W66 1994, (v10)
Woodhouse, Arthur Sutherland Pigott. PR3588.W59, (v3)
Woodhouse, C. M. DF757 .W6 1991, (v5)
  DF836.K37.W66 1982, (v5)
Woodhouse, S. W. F697.W874 1992, (v4)
Woodhull, Victoria C. HN64.M393 1974, (v6)
Woodiwiss, Anthony. KF3390.W66 1990, (v7)
Woodiwiss, Michael. HV6707.U5.W66 1988, (v6)
Woodman, A. J. DG281.W66 1998, (v5)
Woodman, Harold D. HD9075.W58, (v6)
Woodman, Sue. R726.W655 1998, (v2)
Woodmansee, Martha. BH181.W66 1994, (v8)
Woodmason, Charles. F272.W77, (v4)
Woodring, Carl. PN70.W66 1999, (v3)
  PR468.A76.W6 1989, (v3)
  PR4487.P6W6, (v3)
  PR5881.W55, (v3)
Woodruff, Asahel Davis. LB1051.W72 1951, (v7)
Woodruff, Michael F. A. RD39.W66, (v2)
Woodruff, Paul. BJ1533.H8 W66 2001, (v8)
Woodruff-Pak, Diana S. QP360.W64 1997, (v1)
Woods, Christopher. SB434.W66 1992, (v1)
Woods, Donald R. TP155.7.W66 1995, (v1)
Woods, Gregory. PN56.H57.W66 1998, (v3)
  PR605.H65.W66 1987, (v3)

Woods, Harriett. HQ1236.5.U6.W69 1999, (v6)
Woods, James M. F411.W63 1987, (v4)
Woods, Jeannie Marlin. PN2287.H176.W66 1993, (v3)
Woods, L. Milton. CT269.W66 1991, (v5)
  F767.B4.W66 1997, (v4)
Woods, Leigh. PR3112.W66 1991, (v3)
Woods, Mary E. HV43.W64 2000, (v6)
Woods, Mary N. NA1996.W64 1999, (v9)
Woods, R. Grant. QA303.W66 1998, (v1)
Woods, Randall Bennett. E183.8.G7.W93 1990, (v4)
  E813.W58 1991, (v4)
Woods, Roger. DD240.W76 1996, (v5)
Woods, Susanne. PR2296.L27.Z95 1999, (v3)
Woods, Thomas A. HD1485.P5.W66 1991, (v6)
Woods, Thomas. B1607.W65, (v8)
Woods, Tiger. GV965.W743 2001, (v6)
Woods, Tim. NX456.5.P66.W66 1999, (v9)
Woodside, Arch G. HF6161.B4.W67 1996, (v6)
Woodside, Gayle. TD1030.W66 1993, (v1)
Woods-Marsden, Joanna. N7619.5.I8.W66 1998, (v9)
Woodson, Carter Godwin. E185.W8877 1969, (v4)
Woodson, Marie. RC439.W65 1994, (v2)
Woodsworth, J. S. F1035.A1.W6 1972, (v4)
Woodward, Bob. E861.W66, (v4)
  E881.W66 1991, (v4)
  E886.2.W66 1994, (v4)
  HG2565.W654 2001, (v6)
  KF8742.W66, (v7)
  UB251.U5.W66 1987, (v10)
Woodward, C. Vann. E185.61.W86 2002, (v4)
  E664.W337.W6 1973, (v4)
  E681.W83 1966, (v4)
  F215.W85, (v4)
Woodward, Claire. Z7835.M6 W66 2002, (v10)
Woodward, David R. D546.W59 1998, (v5)
Woodward, E. L. DA530.W6 1962, (v5)
Woodward, John B. VM740.W6, (v1)
Woodward, Kathleen M. PQ307.A47.W66 1991, (v3)
Woodward, Mary Dodge. F636.W66 1989, (v4)
Woodward, Ralph Lee. B1008.P6 W66, (v8)
  F1436.W66, (v4)
  F1466.45.C375.W66 1993, (v4)
Woodward, William E. E161.W65 1963, (v4)
Woodworth, Robert Sessions. BF105.W6 1964, (v2)
Woodworth, Steven E. E464.W66 2000, (v4)
  E467.1.D26.W8 1995, (v4)
  E467.1.D26.W82 1990, (v4)
  E470.4.W66 1998, (v4)
Woody, Bette. HD6057.5.U5.W66 1992, (v6)
Woody, Robert Henley. RC467.95.W66 1988, (v2)
  RC467.95.W663 1997, (v2)
Woody, Thomas. CB311.W66, (v5)
Wooldridge, Jeffrey M. HB139.W663 2002, (v6)
Woolery, George W. PN1992.8.C46.W6 1983, (v3)
Wooley, Wesley T. E744.W63 1988, (v4)
Woolf, D. R. DA1.W665 2000, (v5)
Woolf, Greg. DC33.2.W66 1998, (v5)
Woolf, Judith. PS2124.W6 1991, (v3)
Woolf, Leonard Sidney. PR6045.O68.H6 1963, (v3)
Woolf, Leonard. HC502.W6 1968b, (v6)
  PR6045.O68.Z5, (v3)
Woolf, Rosemary. PR643.M8.W66, (v3)
Woolf, S. J. D308.W66 1991, (v5)
Woolf, Virginia (Stephen). PR6045.O72.W3 1931, (v3)
  PN511.W72 1932a, (v3)
  PR6045.O72.A15 1985, (v3)
  PR6045.O72.A16 1967, (v3)
  PR6045.O72.A6 1986, (v3)
  PR6045.O72.B4, (v3)
  PR6045.O72.C3, (v3)
  PR6045.O72.D4 1942, (v3)
  PR6045.O72.F5 1976, (v3)
  PR6045.O72.H3 1944, (v3)
  PR6045.O72.J3 1965, (v3)
  PR6045.O72.M7 1990, (v3)
  PR6045.O72.O718 1984, (v3)
  PR6045.O72.T5 1938, (v3)
  PR6045.O72.T6, (v3)
  PR6045.O72.V68 1920, (v3)
  PR6045.O72.Y4 1937, (v3)
  PR6045.O72.Z473 1990, (v3)

  PR6045.O72.Z494 1977, (v3)
  PR6045.O72.Z496 1976b, (v3)
  PR6045.O72.Z5, (v3)
  PR6045.O72.Z53 1956a, (v3)
  PR6045.72.M6 1948, (v3)
Woolford, John. PR4231.W66 1996, (v3)
  PR4242.S9.W66 1988, (v3)
Woolfson, M. M. QD945.W59 1995, (v1)
Woollen, William Watson. F851.W78, (v4)
Woolley, Benjamin. BD331.W866 1992, (v8)
  QA29.L72, (v1)
Woolley, Lisa. PS285.C47.W66 2000, (v3)
Woolrych, Austin. DA415.W63 1987, (v5)
  DA425.W59 1982, (v5)
Woolson, Constance Fenimore. PS3360.A5B4, (v3)
  PS3361.W45 1988, (v3)
  PS3362.A5 1882, (v3)
Woolum, Janet. GV697.A1.W69 1992, (v6)
Woolverton, John Frederick. BX5881.W65 1984, (v8)
Wooster, Ralph A. E440.5.W9, (v4)
Wooster, Robert. E83.866.W66 1988, (v4)
  F391.W92 1987, (v4)
Wootton, R. J. QL639.8.W66 1992, (v1)
Worden, J. William. BF723.G75.W67 1996, (v2)
Worden, Mark. RJ503.W67 1991, (v2)
Wordsworth, Dorothy. PR5849.A6 1970, (v3)
  PR5849.A8 1941, (v3)
  PR5849.A8 1991, (v3)
Wordsworth, Mary. PR5881.A43, (v3)
Wordsworth, William. PR5850.F40, (v3)
  PR5851.O9 1974, (v3)
  PR5851.Z3, (v3)
  PR5852.G73 1998, (v3)
  PR5853.G54 1984, (v3)
  PR5853.K48 1989, (v3)
  PR5864.A2.D4 1959, (v3)
  PR5869.L9 1992, (v3)
Work in America Institute. HD5708.45.U6.W67 1984, (v6)
Workman, Herbert B. BX4905.W6 1966, (v8)
Workman, Samuel Klinger. PR297.W6 1972, (v3)
World Bank. HC244.W667 2000, (v6)
Worley, Leslie J. UE75.W67 1994, (v10)
Worley, Marvin L. UA25.W65 1959, (v10)
Wormser, René Albert. K150.W67 1982, (v7)
Worobec, Christine. HN530.R87.W67 1991, (v6)
Woronoff, Denis. DC148.F7 1984 vol. 3, (v5)
Woronoff, Jon. HN723.W673 1997, (v6)
Worrall, Anne. HV6046.W67 1990, (v6)
Worringer, Wilhelm. N68.W613, (v9)
  N6310.W6 1964a, (v9)
Worster, Donald. F786.W87, (v4)
  F788.P88, (v4)
  HC107.A17.W67 1985, (v6)
  QH541.W638 1985, (v1)
Worswick, G. D. N. HD5765.A6.W69 1991, (v6)
Worth, John E. E99.T55.W67 1998, (v4)
Worth, Katharine. PR701.W67 1992, (v3)
  PR6003.E282.Z965 1999, (v3)
Worthen, John. PR4483.W6 2001, (v3)
  PR6023.A93.Z955 1989, (v3)
  PR6023.A93.Z957 1991, (v3)
Worthen, William B. PR736.W64 1992, (v3)
Wortman, Andrze J. TJ825.W87 1983, (v1)
Wortman, William A. Z6519.W67 1995, (v10)
Wortzel, Larry M. DS754.15.W67 1999, (v5)
Wosh, Peter J. BV2370.A7.W674 1994, (v8)
Wou, Odoric Y. K. DS793.H5 W6 1994, (v5)
Wouk, Herman. PS3545.O98.C3, (v3)
  PS3545.O98.M6, (v3)
  PS3545.O98.W3, (v3)
Wray, James D. QB857.W73 1988, (v1)
Wrege, Charles D. T55.85.T38.W91 1991, (v1)
Wren, Daniel A. HC102.5.A2.W73 1998, (v6)
Wrenn, C. L. PE27.W7, (v3)
Wrenn, Lynette Boney. HD9093.U6.S688 1995, (v6)
Wrensch, Ruth D. SB351.H5.W74 1992, (v1)
Wright, A. D. BR430.W7 1982, (v8)
Wright, A. W. HD8393.C57.W74, (v6)
Wright, Albert Hazen. QL666.O6.W7, (v1)

Wright, Andrew H. PR3457.W7, (v3)
  PR6005.A77.Z8 1972, (v3)
Wright, Anna Allen. QL668.E2.W8 1949, (v1)
Wright, Arthur F. B126.W7, (v8)
  BQ632.W75 1990, (v8)
  DS749.2.W74 1978, (v5)
Wright, Austin McGiffert. PS3511.A86.A87 1990, (v3)
Wright, Bruce E. JL1602.W75 1995, (v7)
Wright, Charlotte M. PS374.W6.W74 2000, (v3)
Wright, Christopher. ND40.W75 1991, (v9)
Wright, Craig M. ML3027.8.P2.W7 1989, (v9)
Wright, Crispin. B840.W65 1993, (v8)
Wright, Dale S. BQ962.U33.W75 1998, (v8)
Wright, David E. E97.W96 1998, (v4)
Wright, David G. PR6019.O9.U7784 1991, (v3)
Wright, David. PR9881.W7, (v3)
Wright, Derek. PR9379.9.A7.Z98 1989, (v3)
  PR9387.9.S6.Z97 1993, (v3)
Wright, Donald R. DT532.23.W75 1997, (v5)
Wright, E. W. VK23.W8, (v10)
Wright, Elizabeth R. PQ6485.W75 2001, (v3)
Wright, Elizabeth. PT2603.R397.Z9825 1989, (v3)
Wright, Erik Olin. HT609.W698 1997, (v6)
Wright, Ernest Hunter. B2137.W7 1963, (v8)
Wright, Esmond. E661.W75 1996, (v4)
Wright, Frank Lloyd. NA680.W7, (v9)
  NA737.W7.A35 1992, (v9)
  NA737.W7.A48, (v9)
  NA737.W7.D7, (v9)
  NA2520.W85, (v9)
  NA6233.B3.P7, (v9)
  NA7208.W68, (v9)
  NA9050.W75 1945, (v9)
Wright, Frank. DA990.U46.W756 1996, (v5)
Wright, G. H. von. BD591.W74, (v8)
  BJ1401.W7 1963, (v8)
Wright, Gavin. HC107.A13.W68 1978, (v6)
Wright, George Thaddeus. PR3085.W75 1988, (v3)
Wright, Gordon. D743.W68 1968, (v5)
  DC385.W7 1967, (v5)
Wright, Gwendolyn. NA1590.2.M44.W75 1991, (v9)
Wright, Harold Bell. PS3545.R45.C3, (v3)
  PS3545.R45.W5, (v3)
Wright, Harrison M. JC359.W7, (v7)
Wright, Henry A. QH104.W74, (v1)
Wright, J. Edward. BM645.H43.W75 2000, (v8)
Wright, James Arlington. PS3573.R5358.A63 1990, (v3)
Wright, James D. HV4505.W75 1989, (v6)
  HV4505.W76 1998, (v6)
Wright, James Edward. F39.W75 1987, (v4)
  F781.W87, (v4)
Wright, James Leitch. E78.S65.W74, (v4)
Wright, Jay. PS3573.R5364.A6 1987, (v3)
Wright, Joanne. HV6431.W75 1991, (v6)
  HV8197.5.A3.W75 2000, (v6)
Wright, John B. F735.W75 1998, (v4)
Wright, John Kirtland. G3.A56.W7, (v6)
  G89.W7 1965, (v6)
Wright, John W. RA981.A2.S86 1995, (v2)
Wright, John. ML420.S8115.W74 1993, (v9)
Wright, Johnson Kent. JC179.M25.W75 1996, (v7)
Wright, Judith. PR9551.W73, (v3)
Wright, Katherine L. PR2831.W75 1997, (v3)
Wright, Kenneth R. TA52.W75 2000, (v1)
Wright, Larry. B809.2.W75 2001, (v8)
Wright, Lawrence. BF723.T9.W75 1997, (v2)
Wright, Louis B. DA320.W7, (v5)
  E162.W89, (v4)
  F269.W65 1976, (v4)
  PR421.W7 1980, (v3)
Wright, Marshall D. GV863.A1.W752 1996, (v6)
Wright, Muriel H. E78.O45.W7, (v4)
Wright, N. T. BS2398.W75 1992, (v8)
Wright, Nathalia. NB237.G8.W7, (v9)
  PS2388.B5.W7, (v3)
Wright, Nicholas. DC96.5.W75 1998, (v5)
Wright, Quincy. U21.W7, (v10)
Wright, R. George. KF4772.W75 1990, (v7)
Wright, R. Gerald. SB482.A4.W75 1991, (v1)
Wright, Richard A. HV9466.W85 1994, (v6)

Wright, Richard. PS3545.R815.EI, (v3)
  PS3545.R815.L3, (v3)
  PS3545.R815.L6, (v3)
  PS3545.R815.N, (v3)
  PS3545.R815.O9, (v3)
  PS3545.R815.U5 1969, (v3)
Wright, Robert K. UA25.W84 1983, (v10)
Wright, Robin B. DS63.1.W75 1985, (v5)
Wright, Robin. F2520.1.B35.W75 1998, (v4)
Wright, Ronald. E59.F53.W75 1992, (v4)
Wright, Sarah Bird. PS3545.H16.Z459 1998, (v3)
Wright, Simon. ML410.V76.W7 1992, (v9)
Wright, Stephen. HC1055.W75 1998, (v6)
Wright, Stuart T. Z8218.7.W75 1991, (v10)
  Z8862.7.W75 1988, (v10)
Wright, Sue. P119.32.E85.W75 2000, (v3)
Wright, Sylvia Hart. NA703.W75 1989, (v9)
Wright, T. R. PN49.W73 1988, (v3)
  PR4711.W75 1995, (v3)
  PR6023.A93.Z958 2000, (v3)
Wright, Talmadge. HV4505.W77 1997, (v6)
Wright, Thomas C. F1414.2.W75 1991, (v4)
Wright, Walter Francis. PR5014.W7, (v3)
Wright, Wilbur. TL540.W7.A25 2000, (v1)
Wright, Will. GF21.W75 1992, (v6)
Wright, William. TN413.N25.W8 1947, (v1)
Wright, Winthrop R. F2349.B55.W75 1990, (v4)
Wrightson, Keith. HC254.4.W74 2000, (v6)
Wrigley, Chris. DA566.9.L5.W76 1991, (v5)
Wrigley, Christopher. DT433.265.W75 1996, (v5)
Wrigley, Gordon. SB269.W75 1988, (v1)
Writers' Program of the Work Projects
  Administration in th. F761.W58, (v4)
  F774.3.W74 1973, (v4)
  F496.W96 1973, (v4)
Writers' Program. F124.W89 1974, (v4)
  F231.W88 1946, (v4)
  F241.W85 1974, (v4)
  F566.W9 1973, (v4)
  F586.W97 1954, (v4)
  F809.3.W7 1966, (v4)
Wrobel, David M. E179.5.W76 1993, (v4)
Wrobel, Paul. F574.D49.P78, (v4)
Wrobel, Piotr. DK4433.W76 1998, (v5)
Wroe, Ann. BS2520.P55.W76 2000, (v8)
Wroth, Mary. PR2399.W7.C68 1995, (v3)
Wroth, William. N7908.6.W76 1991, (v9)
Wu, Cheng-en. PL2697.H75.E596 1977, (v3)
Wu, Ching-tzu. PL2732.U22.J82 1972, (v3)
Wu, Duncan. PR736.W8 1995, (v3)
  PR5892.B6.W82 1995, (v3)
Wu, Fusheng. PL2321.W82 1998, (v3)
Wu, Hsin-hsing. DS799.847.W84 1994, (v5)
Wu, Jiahua. BH301.L3 W8 1995, (v8)
Wu, Kuang-ming. B5231.W846 1997, (v8)
Wu, Ningkun. CT1828.W785.A3 1993, (v5)
Wu, Qingyun. PN56.W6.F46 1995, (v3)
Wu, Silas H. L. DS754.4.C53.W8, (v5)
Wu, Yenna. PN56.5.W64.W8 1995, (v3)
Wu, Yu-Shan. HC427.92.W853 1994, (v6)
Wuketits, Franz M. BD177.W85 1990, (v8)
Wukovits, John F. GV567.W85 2000, (v6)
Wulf, Kathleen. LB1570.W85 1984, (v7)
Wulf, Maurice Marie Charles Joseph de. B734.W8
  1959, (v8)
Wulfinghoff, Donald. TJ163.3.W85 1999, (v1)
Wulfstan. PR1795.B4, (v3)
Wullschlager, Jackie. PT8119.W85 2000, (v3)
Wulpi, Donald J. TA460.W85 1999, (v1)
Wunder, Heide. HQ1623.W8513 1998, (v6)
Wunder, John R. KF8205.W86 1994, (v7)
Wuorinen, John Henry. DK458.W8 1931a, (v5)
Wurfel, David. JQ1402.W87 1988, (v7)
Wurmser, Leon. BF575.S45.W87, (v2)
Wurtele, Sandy K. HQ72.U53.W87 1992, (v6)
Wurzbach, Natascha. PR976.W85 1995, (v3)
Wurzburger, Walter S. BJ1285.W87 1994, (v8)
Wussow, Helen. PR888.W65.W87 1998, (v3)
Wuthnow, Robert. BL60.W87 1987, (v8)
  BL72.W88 2001, (v8)
  BL2525.W85 1998, (v8)

BL2525.W88 1988, (v8)
BL2530.U6.W87, (v8)
BR526.W88 1993, (v8)
HN13.W88 1989, (v6)
HN90.M6.W87 1996, (v6)
HN90.V64.W88 1991, (v6)
Wyatt, Charles. PS3573.Y19.L5 1995, (v3)
Wyatt, David K. LA1221.W9, (v7)
Wyatt, David. F870.A1.W93 1997, (v4)
  PS283.C2W9 1986, (v3)
Wyatt, Don J. B128.S514.W93 1996, (v8)
Wyatt, Gary. E78.B9.W93 1999, (v4)
Wyatt, Justin. PN1995.9.M29.W9 1994, (v3)
Wyatt, Thomas. PR2400.A5.R4 1981, (v3)
Wyatt-Brown, Bertram. E449.T18.W9, (v4)
  F209.W9 1982, (v4)
Wyatt-Walter, Holly. UA646.W95 1997, (v10)
Wycherley, R. E. NA9201.W85 1976, (v9)
Wycherley, William. PR3770.F67, (v3)
  PR3771.F7 1979, (v3)
  PR3774.C6 1975, (v3)
Wyckoff, D. Campbell. Z7849.W94 1995, (v10)
Wyckoff, Jerome. GB59.W9, (v6)
Wyckoff, William. F128.44.W93 1988, (v4)
  F781.W98 1999, (v4)
Wydick, Richard C. KF250.W9 1998, (v7)
Wye, Kenneth R. QL404.W955 1991, (v1)
Wyeth, Andrew. ND237.W93.S95, (v9)
Wyeth, N. C. ND237.W94.A3, (v9)
Wygoda, Hermann. DS135.P63.W945 1998, (v5)
Wylie, Diana. DT2458.N45.W95 1990, (v5)
Wylie, Elinor. PS3545.Y45.J4, (v3)
  PS3545.Y45.VE, (v3)
Wylie, Ian. PR4487.P6.W9 1989, (v3)
Wylie, J. C. U162.W9, (v10)
Wylie, James Hamilton. DA256.W8 1968, (v5)
Wylie, Kathryn. PN2071.G4.W95 1994, (v3)
Wylie, Laurence William. DC611.V357.W9 1964b, (v5)
  DC801.C43.W9, (v5)
Wylie, Philip. BJ1311.W9, (v8)
  PS3545.Y46.A65, (v3)
  PS3545.Y46.D5, (v3)
  PS3545.Y46.F5, (v3)
  PS3545.Y46.O6 1960, (v3)
  PS3545.Y46.T6, (v3)
  PS3545.Y46.T7, (v3)
Wylie, Ruth C. BF697.W92 1974, (v2)
Wyller, Arne A. B818.W95 1996, (v8)
Wyllie, Peter J. QE26.2.W9, (v1)
Wyly, M. Virginia. RJ51.D48.W94 1997, (v2)
Wyman, Donald. SB435.W9 1969, (v1)
  SB435.W92 1965, (v1)
  SB450.95.W96 1986, (v1)
Wyman, Mark. D808.W96 1988, (v5)
  F581.W96 1998, (v4)
Wyman, William Henry. Z8813.W982 1973, (v10)
Wymer, Rowland. PR3187.W95 1995, (v3)
Wyn Jones, David. ML410.B4.W97 1998, (v9)
Wynar, Bohdan S. Z2519.6.W96 2000, (v10)
Wynbrandt, James. RB155.5.W96 2000, (v2)
Wyndham, John. PR6015.A6425 M52, (v3)
Wynn, Charles M. Q172.5.P77W96 2001, (v1)
Wynne-Davies, Marion. PR149.A79.W96 1996, (v3)
Wynn-Williams, C. G. QB43.2.W96 1991, (v1)
Wyrick, Deborah Baker. PR3728.L33.W96 1988, (v3)
Wyschogrod, Edith. BJ1012.W97 1990, (v8)
  D13.W97 1998, (v5)
Wyse, Akintola J. G. DT516.7.W97 1990, (v5)
Wyss, Joh. PZ7.W996S5, (v3)
Wyszkowski, Charles. E184.J5.W97 1991, (v4)
X, Malcolm. E185.61.L577, (v4)
  E185.97.L5.A3, (v4)
Xanthakos, Petros P. TG300.X36 1994, (v1)
Xiong, Victor Cunrui. DS796.S55 X56 2000, (v5)
Xu, Yinong. HT169.C62.S999 2000, (v6)
Yablonka, Hanna. DS102.95.Y3313 1999, (v5)
Yablonskaya, Miuda. N6988.I14 1990, (v9)
Yablonsky, Lewis. HV6439.U5.Y3 1997, (v6)
Yachnin, Paul Edward. PR658.S46.Y33 1997, (v3)
Yack, Bernard. CB430.Y33 1997, (v5)

Yackle, Larry W. KF8858.Y33 1994, (v7)
 KFA588.Y33 1989, (v7)
Yadin, Yigael. DS110.M33.Y33, (v5)
 DS122.9.Y3, (v5)
Yaeger, Don. GV351.Y34 1991, (v6)
Yaeger, Patricia. PR119.Y34 1988, (v3)
 PS261.Y34 2000, (v3)
Yaffe, Martin D. PR2825.Y34 1997, (v3)
Yagoda, Ben. PN2287.R74.Y34 1993, (v3)
 PN4900.N35, (v3)
Yahil, Leni. D804.3.Y3413 1990, (v5)
Yahnke, Robert E. PN56.O4.Y35 1995, (v3)
Yaji, Hamman. DT515.77.Y35.A3 1995, (v5)
Yakan, Muhammad Zuhdi. DT15.Y35 1999, (v5)
Yakhlif, Yahya. PJ7874.A36.B813 1998, (v3)
Yakhontoff, Victor A. DS775.Y3 1972, (v5)
Yale university. BF721.Y3 1940, (v2)
Yale, William. DS62.Y3, (v5)
Yalom, Marilyn. DC145.Y35 1993, (v5)
Yamada, Isamu. QK360.Y3513 1997, (v1)
Yamamoto, Eric K. E184.A1.Y36 1999, (v4)
Yamamoto, Traise. PS153.J34.Y36 1999, (v3)
Yamanaka, Lois-Ann. PS3575.A434B58 1997, (v3)
Yamanouchi, Hisaaki. PL726.55.Y32, (v3)
Yamasaki, Minoru. NA737.Y3.A2 1979, (v9)
Yamayee, Zia A. TK1001.Y36 1994, (v1)
Yamazaki, James N. RJ43.Y36.A3 1995, (v2)
Yamazaki, Masakazu. PL865.A57.Z2813, (v3)
Yamigiwa, Joseph Koshimi. PL529.Y23 1959, (v3)
Yampolsky, Mariana. NA750.Y37 1993, (v9)
Yan, Jiaqi. DS778.7.Y4613 1996, (v5)
 JC273.Y46.Y36 1991, (v7)
Yanal, Robert J. B105.E46.Y37 1999, (v8)
Yancey, Dwayne. F231.3.W55.Y36 1988, (v4)
Yandell, Cathy M. PQ418.Y36 2000, (v3)
Yanez Cossio, Alicia. PQ8220.35.A5.B713 1999, (v3)
Yanez, Agustin. PQ7297.Y3.A67, (v3)
Yang, Anand A. JS7025.S27.Y36 1989, (v7)
Yang, Benjamin. DS777.5134.Y36 1990, (v5)
 DS778.T39.Y33 1997, (v5)
Yang, Dali L. HN740.Z9.C685 1996, (v6)
Yang, Fenggang. BR563.C45.Y36 1999, (v8)
Yang, Lan. PL2443.Y33 1998, (v3)
Yang, Lien-sheng. DS703.5.Y3, (v5)
Yang, Mu. PL2924.S47.A27 1998, (v3)
Yang, Rae. DS778.7.Y42 1997, (v5)
Yang, T. Y. TA645.Y36 1986, (v1)
Yang, Xiaokai. DS778.7.Y4313 1997, (v5)
Yankah, Kwesi. DT510.43.A53.Y35 1995, (v5)
Yankelovich, Daniel. HN59.Y33 1981, (v6)
 UA23.Y25 1988, (v10)
Yannakoudakis, E. J. QA76.9.D3.Y36 1988, (v1)
Yannella, Philip. PS3537.A618.Z885 1996, (v3)
Yannuzzi, Lawrence A. RE551.Y36 1995, (v2)
Yans-McLaughlin, Virginia. F129.B819.I89, (v4)
Yao, Hsin-chung. BL1852.Y36 2000, (v8)
Yao, Xinzhong. B127.J4 Y4 1996, (v8)
Yap, Chee-Keng. QA155.7.E4.Y36 2000, (v1)
Yapp, Malcolm. DS62.4.Y35 1987, (v5)
Yaquinto, Marilyn. PN1995.9.G3.Y37 1998, (v3)
Yarbro-Bejarano, Yvonne. PQ6490.H7.Y37 1994, (v3)
Yarbrough, Stephen R. P302.Y37 1999, (v3)
Yarbrough, Tinsley E. KF4770.Y37 1988, (v7)
 KF8742.Y37 2000, (v7)
 KF8745.H3.Y36 1995, (v7)
 KF8745.H33.Y37 1992, (v7)
Yardley, Jonathan. PS3523.A7.Z9, (v3)
Yarid, Nazik Saba. PJ7874.A77.T3713 1997, (v3)
Yarmolinsky, Adam. UA23.Y28 1971, (v10)
Yarnall, Judith. PN57.C52.Y37 1994, (v3)
Yarnold, Barbara M. KF3771.Y37 1995, (v7)
 KF8700.Y37 1992, (v7)
Yar-shater, Ehsan. PK6457.Y37 1998, (v3)
Yarwood, Doreen. NA957.Y37 1990, (v9)
 NA961.Y3 1967, (v9)
Yasar Kemal. PL248.Y275.Z9513 1999, (v3)
Yashar, Deborah J. JL1456.Y37 1997, (v7)
Yashpal. PK2098.Y3.A24, (v3)
Yasuda, Kenneth. PL768.H3.Y3, (v3)
Yasuoka, Shotaro. PL865.A7.A24 1984, (v3)
Yasutomo, Dennis T. HC60.Y372 1995, (v6)

Yates, Alayne. RC569.5.E94.Y38 1991, (v2)
Yates, Frances Amelia. PR2976.Y3, (v3)
Yates, JoAnne. HD30.3.Y38 1989, (v6)
Yates, Keith. D582.J8.Y38 2000, (v5)
Yates, Michael. KF3464.Y38 1994, (v7)
Yates, Nigel. BR763.K46.Y38 1994, (v8)
Yates, Norris Wilson. PS374.W4.Y38 1995, (v3)
Yates, Richard. PS3575.A83.E54 1982, (v3)
 PS3575.A83 R4, (v3)
Yates, Robin D. S. PL2677.W4.Z95 1988, (v3)
Yates, W. E. PT2265.Y34, (v3)
 PT3828.V5.Y38 1992, (v3)
Yates, Wilson. HB875.Y35, (v6)
Yau, John. ND588.P46.Y38 1993, (v9)
Yaws, Carl L. TP200.Y35 1999, (v1)
Yazbak, Mahmud. DS110.H28.Y39 1998, (v5)
Ye, Weili. LB2376.6.C6, (v7)
Yeager, Chuck. TL540.Y4A38 1985, (v1)
Yeager, Leland B. HB72.Y43 2001, (v6)
Yeager, Peter C. KF3775.Y4 1990, (v7)
Yeargers, Edward K. QH505.Y43 1992, (v1)
Yearley, Lee H. BJ1531.Y42 1990, (v8)
Yeats, Robert S. QE535.2.U6, (v1)
Yeats, W. B. PR5900.A2.F56 1989 vol. 1, (v3)
 PR5900.A3 1956, (v3)
 PR5900.A3 1957, (v3)
 PR5900.A4 1966, (v3)
 PR5900.A5 1961, (v3)
 PR5900.A5 1970, (v3)
 PR5902.M27 1959, (v3)
 PR5902.P4, (v3)
 PR5902.Y4, (v3)
 PR5904.U5 1995, (v3)
 PR5904.V53.Y4 1992, (v3)
 PR5904.W65 1995, (v3)
 PR5906.A538 1953, (v3)
Yee, Cordell D. K. PR6019.O9.Z97 1997, (v3)
Yee, Shirley J. E449.Y44 1992, (v4)
Yee, Sylvia Mei-ling. LB1737.U6.Y44 1990, (v7)
Yegul, Fikret K. DG97.Y45 1992, (v5)
 NA2310.I8.A448 1991, (v9)
Yeh, Michelle Mi-Hsi. PL2332.Y44 1991, (v3)
Yeh, Wen-hsin. DS793.C3.Y44 1996, (v5)
Yehoshua, Abraham B. PN49.Y4413 2000, (v3)
Yelin, Louise. PR9080.5.Y45 1998, (v3)
Yell, Mitchell L. KF4210.Y45 1998, (v7)
Yellin, Jean Fagan. HQ1423.Y45 1989, (v6)
Yellin, Victor Fell. ML410.C395.Y4 1990, (v9)
Yelling, J. A. HV4086.A3.Y45 1993, (v6)
Yellowitz, Irwin. HD8083.N7.Y4, (v6)
Yellowtail, Thomas. E99.C92.Y45 1991, (v4)
Yeltsin, Boris Nikolayevich. DK290.3.Y45, (v5)
Yen, Teh Fu. TD193.Y46 1999 vol. B, (v1)
Yenal, Edith. Z8693.7.Y45 1989, (v10)
Yentsch, Anne E. F189.A647.Y46 1994, (v4)
Yerushalmi, Yosef Hayim. BS580.M6.Y47 1991, (v8)
 DS102.C56 no. 1, (v5)
 DS115.5.Y47 1982, (v5)
Yerxa, Donald A. E746.Y47 1991, (v4)
Yetiv, Steven A. DS79.72.Y48 1997, (v5)
Yetman, David. F1221.M3.Y47 1998, (v4)
Yglesias, Helen. N6537.B55.A4 1989, (v9)
Yi, Hyong-gu. HC467.Y51395 1996, (v6)
Yi, Mu. DS779.32.Y5 1989, (v5)
Yick, Joseph K. S. DS777.542.Y53 1995, (v5)
Yin, Xiao-huang. PS153.C45.Y56 2000, (v3)
Yingling, Thomas E. PS3505.R272.Z93 1990, (v3)
Yip, Po-ching. PL1107.Y57 1996, (v3)
Yip, Wai-lim. PL1279.Y56 1993, (v3)
Yishai, Yael. DS126.5.I7 1987, (v5)
Yiu, Angela. PL812.A8.Z9665 1998, (v3)
YIVO Archives. Z6375.Y59 1998, (v10)
Yoder, Carroll. PQ3984.Y63 1990, (v3)
Yoder, Edwin. E175.9.Y63 1997, (v4)
 PN4874.A43.Y63 1995, (v3)
Yoder, Jennifer A. JN3971.A58.Y63 1999, (v7)
Yoder, John Charles. DT650.K33.Y63 1992, (v5)
Yoggy, Gary A. PN1992.8.W4.Y64 1995, (v3)
Yohannan, John D. PJ409.Y6, (v3)
Yohn, Susan M. BV2788.H56.Y64 1995, (v8)
Yokomitsu, Riichi. PL842.O5.O63, (v3)

Yokota-Murakami, Takayuki. PN57.D7.Y65 1998, (v3)
Yolton, John W. B1297.Y6 1968, (v8)
 B1297.Y64 1993, (v8)
 B1925.M25.Y64 1991, (v8)
 BD161.Y65 1996, (v8)
Yon, D. A. LB45.Y66 2000, (v7)
Yonay, Yuval P. HB99.5.Y66 1998, (v6)
Yoneyama, Lisa. D767.25.H6.Y66 1999, (v5)
Yoneyama, Shoko. LA1316.Y67 1999, (v7)
Yong, R. N. TD878.Y65 2001, (v1)
Yonge, Charlotte Mary. PR5912.H44 1997, (v3)
Yoon, Dae Kyu. KPA2020.Y66 1991, (v7)
York, Henry E. Z7161.Y75 1990, (v10)
York, Herbert F. QC16.Y67.A3 1995, (v1)
York, Michael. BP605.N48.Y67 1995, (v8)
York, R. A. PR888.T5.Y67 1999, (v3)
Yorke, Barbara. DA152.Y673 1995, (v5)
Yorke, James. DA687.L22, (v5)
Yorke, Valerie. DS63.2.S95.Y67 1988, (v5)
Yosano, Akiko. PL819.O8.M513 1987, (v3)
Yoshida, Kenko. PL791.6.T7.E48, (v3)
Yoshihara, Kunio. HC455.Y67 1985, (v6)
Yoshikawa, Eiji. PL898.Y62.H42, (v3)
Yoshikawa, Kojiro. PL2322.5.Y6713 1989, (v3)
 PL2323.Y613, (v3)
Yoshikawa, Tsuneo. TJ211.Y6713 1990, (v1)
Yoshimasu, Gozo. PL865.O713.T46 1987, (v3)
Yoshimi, Yoshiaki. D810.C698.Y6713 2000, (v5)
Yoshimoto, Mitsuhiro. PN1998.3.K87.Y67 2000, (v3)
Yost, Charles Woodruff. D443.Y63 (v5)
Yost, David S. UA646.3.Y674 1998, (v10)
 UG745.S65.Y67 1988, (v10)
Youens, Susan. ML410.S3.Y7 1992, (v9)
 ML410.S3.Y72 1997, (v9)
 ML410.S3.Y73 1996, (v9)
 ML410.W8.Y68 2000, (v9)
 ML410.W8.Y7 1992, (v9)
 MT115.S37.Y7 1991, (v9)
Young Bear, Ray A. E99.F7.Y688 1992, (v4)
Young Bear, Severt. E99.D1.Y688 1994, (v4)
Young, Al. PS3575.O68.S5, (v3)
 PS3575.O68.S6, (v3)
Young, Alan. ML394.Y68 1997, (v9)
 RC552.P67.Y68 1995, (v2)
Young, Allen M. SB268.C35.Y68 1994, (v1)
Young, Andrew McLaren. ND237.W6.A4 1980, (v9)
Young, Arthur Milton. PN57.T85.Y6, (v3)
Young, Arthur N. DS777.53.Y62, (v5)
Young, Arthur P. Z7757.U5.Y68 1992, (v10)
 Z7757.U5.Y69 1994, (v10)
Young, Bette Roth. PS2234.Y68 1995, (v3)
Young, Brian J. F1033.C46.Y68 1981, (v4)
Young, C. Walter. DS783.7.Y6, (v5)
 DS783.7.Y65 vol. 1, (v5)
Young, Clara Margaret (Candlin). PL3277.E4.Y6, (v3)
Young, Coleman A. F474.D453.Y68 1994, (v4)
Young, Crawford. JF60.Y67, (v7)
 JV246.Y68 1994, (v7)
Young, D. A. QD503.Y68 1991, (v1)
Young, David C. GV721.5.Y68 1996, (v6)
Young, David. BX5199.M3.Y68 1992, (v8)
 HE4491.C5.C8788 1998, (v6)
 PR2983.Y6 1990, (v3)
Young, Desmond. DD247.R57.Y68 1951, (v5)
Young, Donald F. TA357. Y68 2000, (v1)
Young, Donald J. D767.4.Y69 1992, (v5)
Young, Edward. PR3780.A2 1970, (v3)
Young, Elizabeth. PS217.C58.Y68 1999, (v3)
Young, Ernest P. DS777.2.Y68 1977, (v5)
Young, H. Peyton. HB72.Y68 1994, (v6)
Young, Hugo. DA591.T47 Y68 1989, (v5)
Young, J. Z. QL605.Y68 1981, (v1)
 QL739.2.Y68 1975, (v1)
Young, James Edward. D810.J4.Y58 1988, (v5)
 NA9330.G4.Y68 2000, (v9)
Young, James Harvey. KF3864.526.A16.Y68 1989,
 (v7)
 R730.Y68, (v2)
Young, James P. JC574.2.U6.Y68 1996, (v7)
Young, Jeffrey Robert. E445.G3.Y68 1999, (v4)
Young, Jeffrey S. T21.Y68 1998, (v1)

Young, Jeffrey T. HB103.S6.Y677 1997, **(v6)**
Young, John P. PN4897.C2Y6, **(v3)**
Young, John T. N8846.C6.Y68 1999, **(v9)**
Young, John W. D843.Y68 1996, **(v5)**
   D1053.Y68 1991, **(v5)**
   DC404.Y68 1990, **(v5)**
Young, John Wesley. P119.3.Y68 1991, **(v3)**
Young, Josiah U. BT30.A438.Y68 1993, **(v8)**
Young, Julian. B3279.H49.Y68 1997, **(v8)**
   B3318.A4.Y67 1992, **(v8)**
Young, Kate. HQ1240.Y68 1993, **(v6)**
Young, Katharine Galloway. GN298.Y68 1997, **(v6)**
Young, Kevin. HC445.5.Y68, **(v6)**
Young, Laura S. Z271.Y68 1995, **(v10)**
Young, Linda Wai Ling. PL1074.Y68 1994, **(v3)**
Young, Lisa. HQ1236.5.C2.Y68 2001, **(v6)**
Young, Louise. DS783.7.Y67 1998, **(v5)**
Young, Mary E. PS153.N5.Y64 1993, **(v3)**
Young, Matt. QC355.2.Y68 1986, **(v1)**
Young, Mel. E540.J5.Y68 1990, **(v4)**
Young, Michael B. DA391.Y68 2000, **(v5)**
Young, Michael L. HM261.Y684 1991, **(v6)**
Young, Nicholas. QA322.4.Y68 1988, **(v1)**
Young, Oran R. HC735.Y68 1992, **(v6)**
   KZ4110.P65.Y683 1998, **(v7)**
Young, Percy M. ML410.K732 Y7 1976, **(v9)**
Young, Peter R. P96.A75.Y68 1997, **(v3)**
Young, Philip. PS121.Y64 2000, **(v3)**
   PS2387.Y68 1993, **(v3)**
Young, Richard A. BT749.Y68 1999, **(v8)**
Young, Richard K. E99.U8.Y68 1997, **(v4)**
Young, Robert J. D742.F7.Y68 1996, **(v5)**
   DC373.B35.Y68 1991, **(v5)**
Young, Robert M. QA303.Y724 1992, **(v1)**
Young, Robert W. PM2007.Y724 1992, **(v3)**
Young, Robert. BS425.Y7 1955, **(v8)**
Young, Roland Arnold. JA37.Y6, **(v7)**
Young, Rosemary. Z711.2.Y68 1999, **(v10)**
Young, Steven B. QH84.1.Y68 1990, **(v1)**
Young, Sue. PE1519.Y68 1991, **(v3)**
Young, T. Kue. RA408.I49.Y68 1994, **(v2)**
Young, T. R. HM291.Y68 1990, **(v6)**
Young, Theodore Cuyler. PJ25.P7 v.15, **(v3)**
Young, Thomas Daniel. F209.Y68 1982, **(v4)**
Young, Timothy Wallace. LB1029.F7.Y58 1990, **(v7)**
Young, Virgil M. F746.3.Y68 2002, **(v4)**
Young, Virginia Heyer. F2106.Y64 1993, **(v4)**
Young, W. Murray. MT115.B2.Y7 1989, **(v9)**
Youngblood, Denise J. PN1993.5.R9.Y59 1999, **(v3)**
   PN1993.5.R9.Y6 1992, **(v3)**
Youngquist, Paul. PR4148.M45.Y6 1989, **(v3)**
Youniss, James. HQ796.Y583 1985, **(v6)**
Yount, George Calvert. F786.Y63, **(v4)**
Yount, Lisa. Q141.Y675 1999, **(v1)**
   TP248.23.Y684 2000, **(v1)**
Yount, Sylvia. N6537.P264.A4 1999, **(v9)**
Yourcenar, Marguerite. PQ2649.O8.C613, **(v3)**
Yousaf, Nahem. PR9369.3.L3.Z97 2001, **(v3)**
Youst, Lionel. E99.C8742.P479 1997, **(v4)**
Yovanovich, Gordana. PQ6147.P5.Y69 1999, **(v3)**
Yovel, Yirmiahu. B2949.J84.Y68 1998, **(v8)**
Yrigoyen, Charles. BX8211.H57 1996, **(v8)**
Yu, David C. Z7757.C6.Y83 1994, **(v10)**
Yu, Frederick T. C. DS777.57.Y78, **(v5)**
Yu, Henry. E184.O6 Y8 2001, **(v4)**
Yu, Hua. PL2928.H78.J66 1996, **(v3)**
Yu, Hyong-gi. PL937.E5.Y82 1952, **(v3)**
Yu, Lawrence. TX911.3.M27.Y82 1999, **(v1)**
Yu, Maochun. D810.S7.Y82 1996, **(v5)**
Yu, Peter Y. QC611.Y88 1996, **(v1)**
Yuan, Mei. PL2735.A5.I17 1997, **(v3)**
Yuasa, Yasuo. B127.C49 Y83 1993, **(v8)**
   BD450.Y8213 1987, **(v8)**
Yudkin, Jeremy. ML171.Y8 1989, **(v9)**
   MT6.Y86 U53 1999, **(v9)**
Yudkin, Simon. RJ42.G7.Y8, **(v2)**
Yudkoff, Alvin. PN2287.K64.Y83 1999, **(v3)**
Yue, Gang. PL2303.Y83 1999, **(v3)**
Yule, Andrew. PN1998.3.B64.Y8 1992, **(v3)**
Yung, Bell. ML1751.C4.Y9 1989, **(v9)**
Yung, Judy. F869.S39.C595 1995, **(v4)**

Yung, Y. L. QB603.A85.Y86 1999, **(v1)**
Yunker, James A. HB97.5.Y864 1997, **(v6)**
Yurchenco, Henrietta. ML410.G978.Y9, **(v9)**
Yusuf, Shahid. HT384.C6.Y87 1997, **(v6)**
Yusuf. PL55.U539.Y8713 1983, **(v3)**
Yuzna, Susan. PS3575.U95.H47 1996, **(v3)**
Zabalbeascoa, Anatxu. NA1308.Z33 1992, **(v9)**
Zabecki, David T. UF157.Z33 1994, **(v10)**
Zabeeh, Farhang. B1498.Z3, **(v8)**
Zabkar, Louis V. PJ1565.Z33 1988, **(v3)**
Zablocki, Benjamin David. HQ971.Z3, **(v6)**
Zabor, Rafi. PS3576.A157.B4 1997, **(v3)**
Zaborowska, Magdalena J. PS153.E37.Z33 1995, **(v3)**
Zabriskie, Edward Henry. E183.8.R9.Z3 1973, **(v4)**
Zacarias, Agostinho. UA855.6.Z37 1999, **(v10)**
Zacharias, Greg W. PS2124.Z33 1993, **(v3)**
Zachary, Joseph L. QA76.6.Z32 1996, **(v1)**
Zaczek, Barbara Maria. PR858.E65.Z33 1997, **(v3)**
Zadig, Ernest A. VM341.Z33 1985, **(v10)**
Zafar, Rafia. PS153.N5.Z34 1997, **(v3)**
Zagare, Frank C. U162.6.Z34 2000, **(v10)**
Zagorin, Perez. B1197.Z34 1998, **(v8)**
   D210.Z33 1982, **(v5)**
   DA395.Z3 1970, **(v5)**
   PR3592.P7.Z33 1992, **(v3)**
Zagorskaia, A. P. HF1002.Z25 1996, **(v6)**
Zagzebski, Linda Trinkaus. BD176.Z34 1996, **(v8)**
Zahan, Dominique. BL2400.Z2813, **(v8)**
Zahavi, Eliahu. TJ243.Z29 1996, **(v1)**
Zahedi, Dariush. DS318.825.Z34 2000, **(v5)**
Zahle, Erik. NK979.Z313, **(v9)**
Zaionchkovskii, Petr Andreevich. DK221.Z313, **(v5)**
Zaitsev, Pavlo. PG3948.S51.Z33 1988, **(v3)**
Zakaria, Fareed. E661.7.Z35 1998, **(v4)**
Zakaria, Rafiq. DS430.Z35 1995, **(v5)**
Zalabardo, Jose L. BC108.Z35 2000, **(v8)**
Zalewski, Waclaw. TA648.Z35 1998, **(v1)**
Zall, Paul M. PR1293.Z3, **(v3)**
Zaller, John. HM261.Z35 1992, **(v6)**
Zaman, Muhammad Qasim. BP185.Z36 2002, **(v8)**
Zamble, Edward. HV6089.Z36 1988, **(v6)**
Zamëïlatin, Evgeniæi Ivanovich. PG3476.Z34M913 1993, **(v3)**
Zamiatin, Evgenii Ivanovich. PG3476.Z34.A24, **(v3)**
Zamir, Meir. DS86.Z37 1997, **(v5)**
Zamora, Emilio. HD6517.T4.Z363 1993, **(v4)**
Zamoyski, Adam. DK4140.Z36 1988, **(v5)**
Zamponi, Lynda F. Z3707.Z36 1994, **(v10)**
Zanden, J. L. van. HD5792.Z36 1993, **(v6)**
Zander, Alvin Frederick. HN65.Z36 1990, **(v6)**
Zandvoort, Reinhard Willem. PE1630.Z3, **(v3)**
Zang, David. GV865.W34.Z35 1995, **(v6)**
Zanger, Abby E. DC128.5.Z36 1997, **(v5)**
Zangger, Eberhard. GN751.Z36 1992, **(v6)**
Zangwill, Israel. PR5922.C5 1998, **(v3)**
Zanine, Louis J. PS3507.R55.Z88 1993, **(v3)**
Zanker, Paul. DG70.P7.Z3613 1998, **(v5)**
Zantop, Susanne. PT363.N27.Z36 1997, **(v3)**
Zantwijk, R. A. M. van. F1219.76.S63.Z36 1985, **(v4)**
   F1221.T3.Z3 1967, **(v4)**
Zapf, Hermann. Z250.A2.Z379 1987, **(v10)**
Zaprudnik, Jan. DK507.37.Z37 1998, **(v5)**
   DK507.54.Z37 1993, **(v5)**
Zara, Louis. PS3549.A7.D3, **(v3)**
Zarb, Janet E. RJ505.C63.Z37 1992, **(v2)**
Zarefsky, David. E457.4.Z29 1990, **(v4)**
Zaretsky, Robert. DC611.G217.Z37 1995, **(v5)**
Zarin, Cynthia. PS3576.A69.S9 1989, **(v3)**
Zarit, Steven H. RC451.4.A5.Z374 1998, **(v2)**
Zarlino, Gioseffo. MT5.5.Z3813 1983, **(v9)**
Zarnowski, Frank. GV1060.7.Z36 1989, **(v6)**
Zarrilli, Phillip B. PN2884.5.K36.Z38 2000, **(v3)**
Zaslavskaia, T. I. DK288.Z37 1990, **(v5)**
Zaslavsky, Claudia. QA11.Z37 1994, **(v1)**
Zaslaw, Neal Alexander. MT145.M7.Z4 1990, **(v9)**
Zaslaw, Neal. ML410.M9.Z28 1989, **(v9)**
Zastoupil, Lynn. DS463.Z37 1994, **(v5)**
Zatarain, Michael. F376.3.D84.Z38 1990, **(v4)**
Zatlin, Phyllis. PN2635.Z38 1994, **(v3)**
   PQ2673.A46.Z97 2000, **(v3)**
Zatsiorsky, Vladimir M. GV711.5.Z38 1995, **(v6)**

QP303.Z38 1998, **(v1)**
Zavala, Iris M. PQ7081.Z38 1991, **(v3)**
Zavala, Silvio Arturo. F1410.Z3, **(v4)**
Zavarzadeh, Mas'ud. PN1995.9.P6.Z38 1991, **(v3)**
Zavattini, Cesare. DG975.L95.Z3813 1997, **(v5)**
Zayas y Sotomayor, María de. PQ6498.Z5.P3713 1997, **(v3)**
Zayas, Marius de. N6490.Z365 1996, **(v9)**
Zayyat, Latifah. PJ7876.A985.B3413 2001, **(v3)**
Zaza, Tony. TK7881.4.Z39 1991, **(v1)**
Zazove, Philip. R154.Z39.A3 1993, **(v2)**
Zbavitel, Dusan. PK1701.Z2, **(v3)**
Zborowski, Mark. DS112.Z37, **(v5)**
   RB127.Z2, **(v2)**
Zdatny, Steven M. HD2346.F8.Z38 1990, **(v6)**
Zea, Leopoldo. B1001.Z423, **(v8)**
Zebrowski, Ernest. GB5014.Z43 1997, **(v6)**
Zedner, Lucia. HV9649.E5.Z43 1991, **(v6)**
Zee, A. QC178.Z44 1989, **(v1)**
Zeeland, Steven. VB324.G38.Z44 1995, **(v10)**
   VE23.Z44 1996, **(v10)**
Zegart, Amy B. JK468.I6.Z43 1999, **(v7)**
Zeidan, Joseph T. PJ7525.2.Z45 1995, **(v3)**
Zeigler, Earle F. GV342.Z43 1989, **(v6)**
Zeiler, Thomas W. HF1379.Z45 1999, **(v6)**
   HF1455.Z45 1992, **(v6)**
Zeiller, Warren. QL737.S63.Z45 1992, **(v1)**
Zeitlin, Judith T. PL2722.U2.Z98 1993, **(v3)**
Zeitlin, Maurice. F3095.Z43 1984, **(v4)**
Zeitner, June Culp. TS752.Z45 1996, **(v1)**
Zeldin, Theodore. DC330.Z44, **(v5)**
Zeleza, Tiyambe. DT19.8.Z44 1997, **(v5)**
Zelikow, Philip. DD290.29.Z45 1995, **(v5)**
Zelinsky, Paul O. PZ8.Z38Rap 1997, **(v3)**
Zelinsky, Wilbur. E184.A1.Z45 2001, **(v4)**
   HB871.Z45, **(v6)**
Zelizer, Barbie. D804.32.Z45 1998, **(v5)**
   E842.9.Z45 1992, **(v4)**
Zelizer, Julian E. HJ2381.Z45 1998, **(v6)**
Zelizer, Viviana A. Rotman. HQ792.U5.Z45 1985, **(v6)**
Zell, Hans M. DT19.8.Z45 1997, **(v5)**
   PN849.A35.Z44 1983, **(v3)**
   PR9798.Z4, **(v3)**
   Z465.2.Z44 1995, **(v10)**
Zeller, Eduard. B265.Z413 1962, **(v8)**
   B338.Z413 1962, **(v8)**
   B505.Z413 1962, **(v8)**
Zelman, Walter A. RA413.5.U5.Z44 1998, **(v2)**
Zemach, Eddy M. BH39.Z444 1997, **(v8)**
Zemansky, Mark Waldo. QC254.2.Z45 1981, **(v1)**
Zembicki, Christine. TS155.Z39 1988, **(v1)**
Zemel, Carol M. ND653.G7.Z458 1997, **(v9)**
Zemtsov, Ilya. DK275.C45.Z46 1989, **(v5)**
Zenani, Nongenile Masithathu. GR359.2.X64.Z46 1992, **(v6)**
Zenkovich, V. P. GB451.Z4213 1967b, **(v6)**
Zenkovsky, Serge A. DK34.T8.Z4, **(v5)**
   PG3130.Z4, **(v3)**
Zepp, Ira G. BL2525.Z47 1997, **(v8)**
   BP161.2.Z46 2000, **(v8)**
Zerubavel, Eviatar. BD638.Z48 2003, **(v8)**
   BF323.S63.Z47 1997, **(v2)**
Zesmer, David M. PR166.Z4, **(v3)**
Zetler, Robert L. PE1475.Z4, **(v3)**
Zeuschner, Robert B. Z8136.15.Z48 1996, **(v10)**
Zevi, Bruno. NA2500.Z413, **(v9)**
Zhai, Qiang. DS777.8.Z388 2000, **(v5)**
Zhai, Zhenhua. DS778.Z47.A3 1993, **(v5)**
Zhan, Jun. DS740.5.T28 Z46 1993, **(v5)**
Zhang, Hsiao Yang. PR3109.C6.Z48 1996, **(v3)**
Zhang, Liang. DS779.32.L54 2001, **(v5)**
Zhang, Longxi. DS721.Z48 1999, **(v5)**
Zhang, Shu Guang. DS919.5.Z45 1995, **(v5)**
Zhang, Wei-Bin. BL1852.Z48 1999, **(v8)**
Zhang, Yingjin. PL2303.Z43 1996, **(v3)**
   PN1993.5.C4.Z53 1998, **(v3)**
Zhang, Yongjin. DS775.8.Z43 1991, **(v5)**
   DS777.8.Z39 1998, **(v5)**
Zhao, Suisheng. DS515.Z45 1997, **(v5)**
   JQ1522.Z43 1996, **(v7)**
Zheng, Shiping. JQ1519.A5.Z49 1997, **(v7)**

Zheng, Yi. DS793.K6 C4413 1996, **(v5)**
Zhong, Xueping. PL2303.Z48 2000, **(v3)**
Zhou, Xun. DS135.C5.R69 2001, **(v5)**
Zhou, Zhiping. PL1129.E5C436 1993, **(v3)**
  PL1129.E5C438 1992, **(v3)**
Zhu, Xiao Di. DS778.7.Z48 1998, **(v5)**
Ziebura, Gilbert. HC57.Z5413 1990, **(v6)**
Zieger, Robert H. D570.A1.Z54 2000, **(v5)**
Ziegfeld, Richard E. PN2287.Z5.Z54 1993, **(v3)**
Ziegler, Charles E. DS518.7.Z53 1993, **(v5)**
Ziegler, Irene. PS3576.I29325.R85 1999, **(v3)**
Ziegler, Philip. D760.8.L7.Z54 1995, **(v5)**
  DA89.1.M59 Z54, **(v5)**
Zielonka, Jan. D2009.Z54 1998, **(v5)**
Ziemer, Rodger E. TK5105.Z54 2002, **(v1)**
Zierdt-Warshaw, Linda. T36.Z54 2000, **(v1)**
Zietz, Dorothy. HV713.Z5 1969, **(v6)**
Zietz, Karyl Lynn. ML12.Z54 1999, **(v9)**
  ML13.Z54 1994, **(v9)**
Ziff, Larzer. BX7260.C79.Z5, **(v8)**
Zigerell, James. PR3605.O4.Z98 1983, **(v3)**
Zigler, Edward. LC4091.Z54 1992, **(v7)**
  RC570.Z54 1986, **(v2)**
Zigrosser, Carl. NE950.Z5, **(v9)**
Zijl, Wouter. TC176.Z55 1993, **(v1)**
Zilber, Jeremy. E185.615.Z55 2000, **(v4)**
Zilkha, Avraham. PJ4833.Z57 1989, **(v3)**
Zilversmit, Arthur. E446.Z5, **(v4)**
  LB1027.3.Z55 1993, **(v7)**
Ziman, J. M. Q125.Z56 1994, **(v1)**
  QC16.Z56.A3 1995, **(v1)**
  QC174.1.Z49, **(v1)**
  QC176.Z53 1972, **(v1)**
Zimbalist, Andrew S. GV351.Z56 1999, **(v6)**
  GV880.Z56 1992, **(v6)**
  HC147.Z44 1991, **(v6)**
Zimbardo, Rose A. PR934.Z56 1998, **(v3)**
  PR3776.Z5, **(v3)**
Zimbaro, Valerie P. PN56.A69.Z56 1996, **(v3)**
Zimdars-Swartz, Sandra. BT650.Z56 1991, **(v8)**
Zimmer, Carl. QH361.Z48 2001, **(v1)**
  QH371.5.Z55 1998, **(v1)**
Zimmer, Heinrich Robert. B131.Z52, **(v8)**
  N7301.Z49, **(v9)**
Zimmer, Paul. PS3576.I47.A6 1996, **(v3)**
Zimmerle, Winfried. TN870.5.Z56 1995, **(v1)**
Zimmerman, David. D810.S2.Z56 1996, **(v5)**
Zimmerman, Donald E. Q224.Z56 1995, **(v1)**
Zimmerman, Everett. PR858.H5.Z56 1996, **(v3)**
Zimmerman, Frederick Michael. HD58.8.Z55 1991, **(v6)**
Zimmerman, Jonathan. HV5128.U5.Z55 1999, **(v6)**
Zimmerman, Joseph Francis. JK2445.I57.Z55 1996, **(v7)**
  JS431.Z56 1999, **(v7)**
  KF4884.Z56 1997, **(v7)**
Zimmerman, Leo M. RD19.Z5 1967, **(v2)**
Zimmerman, Marc. Z1229.H57.Z55 1992, **(v10)**
Zimmerman, Martin B. HD9545.Z55, **(v6)**
Zimmerman, Michael. Q162.Z48 1995, **(v1)**
Zimmerman, Milhail. Q123.Z55 1992, **(v1)**
Zimmerman, Robert. QB500.262.Z56 2000, **(v1)**
Zimmermann, Matilde. F1527.F66Z56 2001, **(v4)**
Zimmermann, Patricia Rodden. PN1995.8.Z56 1995, **(v3)**
Zimmermann, T. C. Price. DG465.7.G56.Z56 1995, **(v5)**
Zimring, Franklin E. HV9469.Z56 1991, **(v6)**
  HV9471.Z55 1995, **(v6)**
  KF3941.Z56 1992, **(v7)**
Zinbarg, Edward D. BJ1188.Z56 2001, **(v8)**
Zinberg, Israel. PJ5008.Z5313, **(v3)**
Zindel, Paul. PS3576.I518.E3 1971b, **(v3)**
Zingo, Martha T. KF4772.Z46 1998, **(v7)**
Zink, Michel. PQ183.Z5513 1999, **(v3)**
Zinn, Howard. E175.5.Z25.A3 1994, **(v4)**
  E185.61.Z49 1965, **(v4)**
  E839.5.Z55 1990, **(v4)**
Zinnemann, Fred. PN1998.3.Z56.A3 1991, **(v3)**
Zinner, Paul E. DB215.Z55 1975, **(v5)**
  DB956.Z5, **(v5)**

Zinoman, Peter. HV9800.5.Z55 2001, **(v6)**
Zinoviev, Aleksandr. PG3490.I498.Z5, **(v3)**
Zinser, Charles I. GV191.4.Z56 1995, **(v6)**
Zinsser, Hans. RC199.1.Z54 1996, **(v2)**
Zinsser, Judith P. HQ1181.U5.Z56 1992, **(v6)**
Ziolkowski, Eric Jozef. BS1335.52.Z56 2001, **(v8)**
Ziolkowski, Jan M. PA8065.A54.Z55 1993, **(v3)**
Ziolkowski, Theodore. PN56.L33.Z56 1997, **(v3)**
  PN56.M54.Z56 1998, **(v3)**
  PN56.M95.Z56 2000, **(v3)**
  PT361.Z48 1990, **(v3)**
  PT772.Z5, **(v3)**
  PT2617.E85.Z989, **(v3)**
  PT2617.E85.Z99, **(v3)**
Zionkowski, Linda. PR551.Z56 2001, **(v3)**
Zipes, Jack David. GR550.Z56 1994, **(v6)**
  PD63.Z57 1988, **(v3)**
  PN1009.A1.Z57 2001, **(v3)**
  PN3437.Z57 1999, **(v3)**
Zipperstein, Steven J. DS151.G5.Z56 1993, **(v5)**
Zirakzadeh, Cyrus Ernesto. HN17.5.Z57 1997, **(v6)**
Ziring, Lawrence. DS61.Z58 1992, **(v5)**
  DS384.Z572 1997, **(v5)**
  JZ1161.P55 1995, **(v7)**
Zisk, Kimberly Marten. UA770.Z54 1993, **(v10)**
Zitner, Sheldon P. PR2801.Z58 1989, **(v3)**
Zito, George V. HN65.Z57 1993, **(v6)**
Zizek, Slavoj. B2894.W42.Z5 1997, **(v8)**
Zloch-Christy, Iliana. HC244.Z57 1994, **(v6)**
  HJ8615.Z57 1987, **(v6)**
  HJ8615.Z573 1991, **(v6)**
Zlotnick, Susan. PR448.I54.Z57 1998, **(v3)**
Zmora, Hillay. DD801.F566.Z57 1997, **(v5)**
  JC375.Z58 2000, **(v7)**
Zmora, Nurith. HV995.B2.Z46 1994, **(v6)**
Zmuda, Allison. LB1607.5.Z68 2001, **(v7)**
Zneimer, John. PR6029.F5.Z9, **(v3)**
Zobel, Hiller B. E215.4.Z6 1970, **(v4)**
Zocca, Louis Ralph. PR535.N3.Z6, **(v3)**
Zogbaum, Heidi. PT3919.T7.Z97 1992, **(v3)**
Zoghaib, Henri. PJ7876.O35.A24 1991, **(v3)**
Zohar, Danah. HM291.Z64 1994, **(v6)**
  QC174.12.Z64 1990, **(v1)**
Zohary, Daniel. GN799.A4.Z64 1988, **(v6)**
Zohary, Michael. BS665.Z64 1982, **(v8)**
Zohn, Harry. PT2621.R27.Z96 1997, **(v3)**
Zola, Emile. DC354.8.Z6513 1996, **(v5)**
  PQ2516.A38 1993, **(v3)**
  PQ2521.T3 1993, **(v3)**
Zola, Gary Phillip. F279.C49.J548 1994, **(v4)**
Zolberg, Vera L. N72.S6.Z65 1990, **(v9)**
Zolbrod, Paul G. PM168.Z65 1995, **(v3)**
Zollar, Ann Creighton. Z7164.D3.Z64 1993, **(v10)**
Zoller, Michael. BX1406.2.Z6513 1999, **(v8)**
Zollinger, Heinrich. QC495.Z65 1999, **(v1)**
Zolman, James F. QH323.5.Z64 1993, **(v1)**
Zombeck, Martin V. QB136.Z65 1990, **(v1)**
Zomlefer, Wendy B. QK115.Z65 1994, **(v1)**
Zonderman, Jon. RC862.I53.Z66 2000, **(v2)**
Zoninsein, Jonas. HB107.H55.Z66 1990, **(v6)**
Zonis, Marvin. HN740.Z9.E48, **(v6)**
Zonitch, Barbara. PR3316.A4.Z96 1997, **(v3)**
Zook, David Hartzler. U27.Z6, **(v10)**
Zook, Melinda S. DA435.Z66 1999, **(v5)**
Zopf, Paul E. HB1335.Z67 1992, **(v6)**
Zorach, Cecile. PE1099.Z6 1990, **(v3)**
Zorbaugh, Harvey Warren. F548.5.Z89, **(v4)**
Zornado, Joseph L. HQ767.9.Z67 2000, **(v6)**
Zorrilla, Jose. PQ6575.A17 1925, **(v3)**
Zoshchenko, Mikhail. PG3476.Z7.A6, **(v3)**
  PG3476.Z7.S3 1962, **(v3)**
Zubatsky, David S. Z2691.A1.Z85 1995, **(v10)**
Zubay, Geoffrey L. QH325.Z83 2000, **(v1)**
Zuber, William Physick. F390.Z815. 1971, **(v4)**
Zubkova, E. IU. HN523.5.Z8 1998, **(v6)**
Zubok, V. M. DK267.Z78 1996, **(v5)**
Zucchi, John. F1059.5.T689.I893 1988, **(v4)**
Zuccotti, Susan. DS135.F83.Z83 1993, **(v5)**
  DS135.I8.Z87 2000, **(v5)**
Zucker, A. E. E184.G3 Z8 1967, **(v4)**
Zucker, Ross. JC423.Z83 2001, **(v7)**

Zuckerman, Fredric Scott. HV8225.7.O54.Z83 1996, **(v6)**
Zuckerman, Marvin. BF698.Z825 1991, **(v2)**
Zuckerman, Mary Ellen. PN4879.Z83 1998, **(v3)**
Zuckert, Michael P. JC571.Z833 1996, **(v7)**
Zuker-Bujanowska, Liliana. D810.J4.Z8413, **(v5)**
Zukin, Sharon. HN59.2.Z85 1991, **(v6)**
Zulaika, Joseba. HN590.Z9.V59 1988, **(v6)**
  HV6431.Z85 1996, **(v6)**
Zumwalt, Elmo R. V63.Z85.A33 1976, **(v10)**
Zumwalt, Rosemary Levy. GN21.P37.Z86 1992, **(v6)**
Zung, Cecilia S. L. PL2357.Z8 1964, **(v3)**
Zunz, Olivier. HC108.D6.Z86 1982, **(v6)**
  HD2785.Z86 1990, **(v6)**
  HN57.Z83 1998, **(v6)**
Zupko, Ronald Edward. Q11.P612 vol. 186, **(v1)**
Zur Gathen, Joachim von. QA155.7.E4.Z87 1999, **(v1)**
Zur, Judith N. F1465.2.Q5.Z87 1998, **(v4)**
Zurbrugg, Nicholas. PR6003.E282.Z98 1988, **(v3)**
Zurcher, Bernard. N6853.B7.Z8713 1988, **(v9)**
Zurick, David. DS485.H6.Z87 1999, **(v5)**
Zurier, Rebecca. N6512.5.E4.Z87 1995, **(v9)**
  NC108.Z87 1988, **(v9)**
Zuriff, G. E. BF199.Z88 1985, **(v2)**
Zurita, Alonso de. F1219.Z943, **(v4)**
Zurndorfer, Harriet Thelma. Z3106.Z87 1995, **(v10)**
Zuroff, Efraim. D804.6.Z87 2000, **(v5)**
Zusne, Leonard. BF31.Z87 1987, **(v2)**
  BF109.A1.Z85 1984, **(v2)**
Zuzowski, Robert. JN96.A58.Z89 1998, **(v7)**
Zvelebil, Kamil. PL4758.Z9, **(v3)**
Zvirin, Stephanie. Z7164.Y8 Z95 1996, **(v10)**
Zwass, Adam. HB90.Z89 2002, **(v6)**
Zweibel, Kenneth. TK2960.Z945 1990, **(v1)**
Zweig, Arnold. PT2653.W4.A16 1959, **(v3)**
  PT2653.W4.S83, **(v3)**
Zweig, David. HN733.5.Z94 1997, **(v6)**
Zweig, Paul. PS3576.W4.A6 1989, **(v3)**
Zweig, Stefan. PT2653.W42.Z5 1953, **(v3)**
Zweigenhaft, Richard L. HN90.E4.Z94 1998, **(v6)**
  HN90.S65.Z94 1991, **(v6)**
Zweiger, Gary. QH447.Z94 2001, **(v1)**
Zweiniger-Bargielowska, Ina. HC256.4.Z94 2000, **(v6)**
Zwerdling, Alex. PR6029.R8.Z97, **(v3)**
Zwillinger, Daniel. QA371.Z88 1989, **(v1)**
Zwingli, Ulrich. BR346.A24, **(v8)**
Zwirn, Jerrold. Z1223.Z7.Z88 1996, **(v10)**

Subject Guide
to the
LC Classification Schedule

Academies and learned societies, AS, v10 - p5
    Directories and lists, AS8, v10 - p5
    International associations, congresses, conferences, etc. — General Works, AS2.5, v10 - p5
    Other associations, "funds," foundations, and institutions, AS911, v10 - p5
    Serial directories. Serial handbooks, AS2, v10 - p5
Aesthetics, BH, v8 - p105
    By region or country, A-Z, BH221, v8 - p109
    Collected works (nonserial) — Polyglot, BH21, v8 - p105
    Dictionaries. Encyclopedias, BH56, v8 - p107
    History — Medieval, BH131, v8 - p107
    History — Modern, BH151, v8 - p108
    History, BH81, v8 - p107
    Philosophy. Methodology. Relation to other topics — Special methods, BH41, v8 - p107
    Philosophy. Methodology. Relation to other topics, BH39, v8 - p105
    Special topics, A-Z, BH301, v8 - p110
Africa: Ghana, KRX, v7 - p198
Africa: Kenya, KSK, v7 - p198
Africa: Regional comparative and uniform law, KQC, v7 - p197
Africa: Rwanda, KTD, v7 - p198
Africa: South Africa, Republic of, KTL, v7 - p198
Africa: Zimbabwe, KTZ, v7 - p199
Agriculture (General), S, v1 - p371
    Agricultural ecology (General), S589.7, v1 - p376
    Encyclopedias and dictionaries, S411, v1 - p371
America, E16-135, v4 - p1
    Discovery of America and early explorations — General Works, E101, v4 - p78
    General — Social life and customs. Civilization. Intellectual life, E20, v4 - p1
    Indians of North America — Dictionaries. Directories. Guides to tribes, E76.2, v4 - p9
    Indians of North America — Historiography, E76.8, v4 - p10
    Indians of North America — Study and teaching, E76.6, v4 - p10
    North America — Description and travel, E41, v4 - p3
    North America — Dictionaries. Gazetteers. Geographic names, E35, v4 - p2
    North America — General Works, E38, v4 - p2
    North America — Geography, E40.5, v4 - p2
    North America — Social life customs. Civilization. Intellectual life, E40, v4 - p2
    Pre-Columbian America. The Indians — Archaeology of the Americans. Origin of the Indians in general, E61, v4 - p8
    Pre-Columbian America. The Indians — Dictionaries. Directories. Guides to tribes, E54.5, v4 - p5
    Pre-Columbian America. The Indians — General Works, E58, v4 - p5
    Pre-Columbian America. The Indians — Latin America (General), E65, v4 - p9
    Pre-Columbian America. The Indians — Museums. Exhibitions, E56, v4 - p5
    Pre-Columbian America. The Indians — Societies. Collections (Serial), E51, v4 - p4
    Pre-Columbian America. The Indians — Theory. Methods of investigation, E57, v4 - p5
    Pre-Columbian America. The Indians — Topics, A-Z, E59, v4 - p6
American Literature, PS, v3 - p670
    Collections of American literature — Selections. Anthologies, etc., PS507, v3 - p708
    Collections of American literature — Special classes of authors, A-Z, PS508, v3 - p708
    Collections of American literature — Special topics (Prose and verse), A-Z, PS509, v3 - p708
    Dictionaries. Encyclopedias, PS21, v3 - p670
    History of American literary history — Biography of historians of American literature, A-Z, PS29, v3 - p671
    History of American literary history — General Works, PS27, v3 - p671
    History of American literature — Collected essays, studies, etc., of individual authors, PS121, v3 - p672
    History of American literature — Other classes of authors, A-Z, PS153, v3 - p675
    History of American literature — Treatment of special classes, A-Z, PS173, v3 - p685
    Theory and principles of the study of American literature, PS25, v3 - p670
    Yearbooks, PS3, v3 - p670
Animal Culture, SF, v1 - p415
    Comprehensive works. Textbooks, SF61, v1 - p416
    Other special topics, A-Z, SF140, v1 - p417
Antarctica, KWX, v7 - p199
    General Works, KWX70, v7 - p199
Anthropology, GN, v6 - p37
    Addresses, essays, lectures, GN29, v6 - p39
    Biography — Collective, GN20, v6 - p38
    Biography — Individual, A-Z, GN21, v6 - p38
    By region or country, A-Z, GN17.3, v6 - p38
    Collected works (nonserial) — Individual authors, GN6-8, v6 - p37
    Communication of information — Anthropological archives, GN14, v6 - p37
    Congresses, GN3, v6 - p37
    Dictionaries. Encyclopedias, GN11, v6 - p37
    Ethnology. Social and cultural anthropology — Addresses, essays, lectures, GN325, v6 - p45

Ethnology. Social and cultural anthropology — Cultural traits, customs, and institutions, GN400-405, v6 - p48
Ethnology. Social and cultural anthropology — Dictionaries. Encyclopedias, GN307, v6 - p44
Ethnology. Social and cultural anthropology — General special (Special aspects of the subject as a whole), GN320, v6 - p45
Ethnology. Social and cultural anthropology — Juvenile works, GN333, v6 - p45
Ethnology. Social and cultural anthropology — Migrations of peoples (General), GN370, v6 - p48
General special (Special aspects of the subject as a whole), GN27, v6 - p39
General Works, treatises, and textbooks — 1871-1974, GN24, v6 - p39
General Works, treatises, and textbooks — 1975-, GN25, v6 - p39
History, GN17, v6 - p37
Philosophy. Relation to other topics. Methodology — Feminist anthropology, GN33.8, v6 - p40
Philosophy. Relation to other topics. Methodology — General Works, GN33, v6 - p39
Philosophy. Relation to other topics. Methodology — Other special methods, A-Z, GN34.3, v6 - p40
Physical anthropology. Somatology — Dictionaries. Encyclopedias, GN50.3, v6 - p40
Physical anthropology. Somatology — General special, GN62, v6 - p41
Physical anthropology. Somatology — General Works, GN60, v6 - p40
Physical anthropology. Somatology — History, GN50.4, v6 - p40
Physical anthropology. Somatology — Mummies, GN293, v6 - p43
Physical anthropology. Somatology — Social aspects of the human body, GN298, v6 - p43
Prehistoric archaeology — Dictionaries. Encyclopedias, GN710, v6 - p58
Prehistoric archaeology — General special, GN741, v6 - p59
Prehistoric archaeology — Pictorial works, GN746, v6 - p59
Societies, GN2, v6 - p37
Aquaculture. Fisheries. Angling, SH, v1 - p422
Archaeology, CC, v5 - p9
    Addresses, essays, lectures, CC173, v5 - p14
    Archaeology as a profession, CC107, v5 - p13
    Biography — Collective, CC110, v5 - p13
    Biography — Individual, A-Z, CC115, v5 - p13
    Collected works (nonserial) — Several authors, CC65, v5 - p9
    Dictionaries. Encyclopedias, CC70, v5 - p9
    General descriptive works — 1801-, CC165, v5 - p13
    General special, CC175, v5 - p14
    History of the science of archaeology — By region or country, A-Z, CC101-105, v5 - p12
    History of the science of archaeology — General Works, CC100, v5 - p12
    Philosophy. Theory — Classification, CC72.7, v5 - p10
    Philosophy. Theory — General Works, CC72, v5 - p10
    Philosophy. Theory — Social archaeology, CC72.4, v5 - p10
    Preservation, restoration, and conservation of antiquities. Antiquities and state — General Works, CC135, v5 - p13
Architecture, NA, v9 - p190
    Addresses, essays, lectures — Collections, NA2560, v9 - p226
    Addresses, essays, lectures — Single papers, NA2563, v9 - p226
    Aesthetics of cities. City planning and beautifying — General special, NA9050, v9 - p240
    Aesthetics of cities. City planning and beautifying — Special countries and cities, NA9105-9265, v9 - p242
    Architectural acoustics, NA2800, v9 - p228
    Architectural criticism — General Works, NA2599.5, v9 - p226
    Architectural decoration — Special countries, NA3503-3511, v9 - p229
    Architectural design — Composition. Proportion, NA2760, v9 - p228
    Architectural design — General Works, NA2750, v9 - p227
    Architectural design — Remodeling buildings for other use (General), NA2793, v9 - p228
    Architectural details, motives, etc. — Domes, NA2890, v9 - p229
    Architectural details, motives, etc. — General and miscellaneous, NA2840, v9 - p229
    Architectural drawing — By region or country, A-Z, NA2706, v9 - p226
    Architectural drawing — Special artists, A-Z, NA2707, v9 - p227
    Architecture as a profession, NA1995, v9 - p221
    Architecture in relation to special subjects — Architecture in relation to other subjects, A-Z, NA2543, v9 - p225
    Architecture in relation to special subjects — Environmental aspects of architecture, NA2542.35, v9 - p224
    Architecture in relation to special subjects — Human factors and architecture, NA2542.4, v9 - p225
    Architecture in relation to special subjects — Sustainable architecture, NA2542.36, v9 - p225
    Biography (Collective), NA40, v9 - p191
    Business management for architects, NA1996, v9 - p221
    Competitions — General and international, NA2335, v9 - p222
    Data processing. Computer-aided design, NA2728, v9 - p227
    Encyclopedias, dictionaries, glossaries, etc., NA31, v9 - p190
    General Works — General special, NA2540, v9 - p224
    General Works — Site planning, NA2540.5, v9 - p224

Architecture, NA *(cont.)*
General Works — Theory. Philosophy, NA2500, v9 - p223
History — Architecture of special countries, NA702, v9 - p198
History — General special, NA203, v9 - p191
History — General Works, NA200, v9 - p191
Orders of architecture — Works since 1800, NA2815, v9 - p228
Study and teaching. Research — Special countries, NA2127, v9 - p222
Women architects, NA1997, v9 - p222
Works for general readers, NA2550, v9 - p226
Armies: Organization, distribution, military situation, UA, v10 - p23
Armies of the world. Armies and navies of the world, UA15, v10 - p25
By region or country — America, UA21, v10 - p25
Civil defense — General Works, UA926, v10 - p45
Cost of armaments, budgets, estimates, etc., UA17, v10 - p25
Demobilization, UA917, v10 - p45
Disarmament inspection. Arms control and nuclear arms control verification, UA12.5, v10 - p24
Foreign military bases, UA15.5, v10 - p25
General Works, UA10, v10 - p23
Industrial mobilization for war and defense, UA18, v10 - p25
Military geography — General Works, UA990, v10 - p45
Military policy, UA11, v10 - p23
Mutual security programs, UA12, v10 - p24
National security, UA10.5, v10 - p23
Artillery, UF, v10 - p53
Field artillery — General Works, UF400, v10 - p53
Military explosives and pyrotechnics — General Works, UF860, v10 - p54
Ordnance material (Ordnance proper) — Ammunition, UF700, v10 - p54
Tactics. Maneuvers. Drill regulations — General Works, UF157, v10 - p53
Weapons systems — General Works, UF500, v10 - p53
Arts in general, NX, v9 - p320
Characters, persons, classes of persons, and ethnic groups — By name of character, person, class of persons, or ethnic group, A-Z, NX652, v9 - p327
Collected writings — Individual authors, NX65, v9 - p320
Collected writings — Several authors, NX60, v9 - p320
Criticism in the arts — General Works, NX640, v9 - p327
Directories — United States, NX110, v9 - p320
Economics of the arts, NX634, v9 - p327
History of the arts — Chronological lists, NX447.5, v9 - p322
History of the arts — Special countries, NX503-589, v9 - p323
History of the arts — Special movements, A-Z, NX600, v9 - p326
Interrelationships among the arts in general — General Works, NX170, v9 - p320
Patronage of the arts — Special regions or countries, A-Z, NX705.5, v9 - p328
Performance in the arts, NX212, v9 - p321
Psychology of the arts and the artist, NX165, v9 - p320
Special geographic areas and places as subjects, A-Z, NX653, v9 - p328
Special subjects or topics, A-Z, NX650, v9 - p327
The arts in relation to other subjects, A-Z, NX180, v9 - p320
Asia (General), KM, v7 - p194
Bibliography — Bibliography of bibliography, KM1, v7 - p194
Asia (Middle East. Southwest Asia): Israel, KMK, v7 - p195
Asia (Middle East. Southwest Asia): Jerusalem, KML, v7 - p195
State and religion — Religious trusts. Charities. Endowments (Waqf), etc., KML271.35, v7 - p195
Asia (Middle East. Southwest Asia): Jordan, KMM, v7 - p195
Asia (Middle East. Southwest Asia): Regional comparative and uniform law, KMC, v7 - p194
Asia (South Asia. Southeast Asia. East Asia): Cambodia, KNM, v7 - p195
Asia (South Asia. Southeast Asia. East Asia): China (People's Republic, 1949-), KNQ, v7 - p196
Asia (South Asia. Southeast Asia. East Asia): China (Republic, 1949-). Taiwan, KNP, v7 - p196
Asia (South Asia. Southeast Asia. East Asia): China, KNN, v7 - p195
Asia (South Asia. Southeast Asia. East Asia): Hong Kong, KNR, v7 - p196
Asia (South Asia. Southeast Asia. East Asia): India, KNS, v7 - p196
Asia (South Asia. Southeast Asia. East Asia): Japan, KNX, v7 - p197
Asia (South Asia. Southeast Asia. East Asia): Korea. South Korea, KPA, v7 - p197
Asia (South Asia. Southeast Asia. East Asia): Malaysia, KPG, v7 - p197
Asia (South Asia. Southeast Asia. East Asia): Pakistan, KPL, v7 - p197
Astronomy, QB, v1 - p98
Addresses, essays, lectures, QB51, v1 - p103
Astronomical photometry, QB135, v1 - p107
Atlases and charts, QB65, v1 - p106
Collected works (nonserial), QB3, v1 - p98
Cosmogony. Cosmology, QB980.5-991, v1 - p121
Dictionaries and encyclopedias, QB14, v1 - p98
Early works through 1700, QB41, v1 - p101
Elementary textbooks, QB45, v1 - p103
Extraterrestrial life, QB54, v1 - p104
Miscellany and curiosa, QB52, v1 - p104
Observers' handbooks, QB64, v1 - p105

Philosophy, QB14.5, v1 - p99
Societies, congresses, serial collections, yearbooks, QB1, v1 - p98
Space astronomy, QB136, v1 - p107
Special topics, A-Z, QB51.3, v1 - p104
Star catalogs, QB6, v1 - p98
Stargazers' guides, QB63, v1 - p105
Study and teaching. Research, QB61, v1 - p105
Atlases, G1000.2-2800, v6 - p9
Atlases of the moon, planets, etc. — Celestial atlases, G1000.2, v6 - p9
Bible, The, BS, v8 - p206
Biography, CT, v5 - p20
Autobiography, CT25, v5 - p20
Biography as an art or literary form — General Works, CT21, v5 - p20
Biography. By subject — Academicians. Scholars. Savants, CT3990, v5 - p26
History — By region or country, A-Z, CT34, v5 - p20
Book industries and trade, Z116-658, v10 - p79
Book design, Z116.A3, v10 - p79
Bookbinding — Special types of bindings, A-Z, Z269.3, v10 - p83
Bookselling and publishing — Bibliography, Z279, v10 - p83
Bookselling and publishing — Dictionaries. Encyclopedias, Z282.5, v10 - p83
Bookselling and publishing — Directories, Z282, v10 - p83
Bookselling and publishing — Special lines of business, A-Z, Z286, v10 - p83
Copyright — General Works, Z551, v10 - p86
Copyright — Special topics, A-Z, Z649, v10 - p87
Freedom of the press. Censorship — By region or country, A-Z, Z658, v10 - p87
Freedom of the press. Censorship — General Works, Z657, v10 - p87
Printing — Bibliography, Z117, v10 - p80
Printing — Collections. Series. Systematic encyclopedias, etc., Z118, v10 - p80
Printing — General Works, Z116.T7513, v10 - p79
Printing — Museums. Exhibitions, Z121, v10 - p80
Treatises on the modern printed book, Z116.A2, v10 - p79
Books (General). Writing. Paleography, Z4-114, v10 - p77
History of books and bookmaking — By region or country, A-Z, Z8, v10 - p78
History of books and bookmaking — General Works, Z4, v10 - p77
Manuscripts. Paleography — General Works, Z105, v10 - p79
Manuscripts. Paleography — Materials, instruments, etc., Z112, v10 - p79
Writing — Duplicating processes. Copying services, Z48, v10 - p78
Writing — General Works. History, Z40, v10 - p78
Botany, QK, v1 - p280
Dictionaries, QK9, v1 - p280
Indexes of plants, QK11, v1 - p280
Popular names, QK13, v1 - p280
Popular works, QK50, v1 - p281
Societies, congresses, serial collections, yearbooks, QK1, v1 - p280
Special topics, A-Z, QK46.5, v1 - p281
Terminology, notation, abbreviations, QK10, v1 - p280
Textbooks, QK47, v1 - p281
Vegetation mapping, QK63, v1 - p281
Bridge engineering, TG, v1 - p474
Floors, TG325.6, v1 - p475
British America, F1001-1123, v4 - p545
Canada — Biography, F1005, v4 - p545
Canada — Description and travel. Views — 1763-1866, F1013, v4 - p546
Canada — Elements in the population, F1035, v4 - p553
Canada — General Works, F1008, v4 - p545
Canada — Social life and customs. Civilization. Intellectual life, F1021-1021.2, v4 - p546
Buddhism, BQ, v8 - p183
Buddhism — Dictionaries (General), BQ130, v8 - p183
Doctrinal and systematic Buddhism — Special topics (nondoctrinal) and relations to special subjects, A-Z, BQ4570, v8 - p185
Encyclopedias (General), BQ128, v8 - p183
History — General special, BQ270, v8 - p183
Monasticism and monastic life. Sa.mgha (Order) — By region or country, A-Z, BQ6160, v8 - p186
Building construction, TH, v1 - p475
Building accidents and their prevention, TH443, v1 - p476
Building failures, errors, defects, etc., TH441, v1 - p476
Dictionaries and encyclopedias, TH9, v1 - p475
General special, TH153, v1 - p476
Cavalry. Armor, UE, v10 - p52
Chemical technology, TP, v1 - p533
Data processing, TP184, v1 - p536
Dictionaries and encyclopedias, TP9, v1 - p533
General special (Including municipal chemistry, safety measures, etc.), TP149-150, v1 - p533
Government and industrial laboratories, etc., General Works (Including organization, etc.), TP187, v1 - p536
Tables, pocketbooks, etc., TP151, v1 - p534

Chemistry, QD, v1 - p183
Addresses, essays, lectures, QD39, v1 - p188
Dictionaries, QD5, v1 - p184
Early works through 1761, QD27, v1 - p187
Elementary textbooks, QD33, v1 - p187
Encyclopedias, QD4, v1 - p184
Handbooks, tables, formulas, etc., QD65, v1 - p189
Nomenclature, terminology, notation, abbreviations, QD7, v1 - p184
Popular works, QD37, v1 - p187
Societies, congresses, serial collections, yearbooks, QD1, v1 - p183
Special topics, A-Z, QD39.3, v1 - p188
Christian denominations, BX, v8 - p233
Baptists — Dictionaries. Encyclopedias, BX6211, v8 - p247
Catholic Apostolic Church – Christadelphians, BX6600, v8 - p248
Catholic Church — Dictionaries. Encyclopedias, BX841, v8 - p235
Catholic Church — Forms of worship. Catholic practice, BX1969, v8 - p239
Catholic Church — Other special topics, A-Z, BX1795, v8 - p239
Christian Science — Christian Science healing, BX6950, v8 - p248
Church of England — Societies. Institutions, BX5013, v8 - p245
Church of God (Cleveland, Tenn.) — Periodicals, societies, directories, yearbooks, BX7032, v8 - p248
Church of South India, BX7066.5, v8 - p248
Church unity. Ecumenical movement. Interdenominational cooperation — Dictionaries. Encyclopedias, BX6.3, v8 - p233
Churches of Christ — Doctrines, creeds, catechisms, liturgy, ritual, sacraments, government, discipline, membership, BX7077, v8 - p248
Churches of Christ — Periodicals, societies, directories, yearbooks, BX7075, v8 - p248
Divine, Father (the man and his following), BX7350, v8 - p249
Dowieism. Christian Catholic Church — General Works. History, BX7415, v8 - p249
Episcopal Church. Protestant Episcopal Church in the United States of America — Movements and parties, BX5925, v8 - p246
Episcopal Church. Protestant Episcopal Church in the United States of America — Afro-Americans and the Episcopal Church, BX5979, v8 - p246
Friends - pGerman Baptist Brethren, BX7800, v8 - p250
Friends. Society of Friends. Quakers — Dictionaries. Encyclopedias, BX7611, v8 - p250
Friends. Society of Friends. Quakers — Other special topics, A-Z, BX7748, v8 - p250
Friends. Society of Friends. Quakers — Spiritual life, BX7738, v8 - p250
German Reformed Church - pLutheran churches, BX7990, v8 - p251
Lutheran churches — Dictionaries. Encyclopedias, BX8007, v8 - p251
Lutheran churches — Directories. Yearbooks. Almanacs. Calendars, BX8009, v8 - p251
Lutheran churches — Relations with other churches, A-Z, BX8063.7, v8 - p251
Mennonites — Individual branches of Mennonites, BX8129, v8 - p252
Mennonites — Special topics, A-Z, BX8128, v8 - p251
Methodism — Dictionaries. Encyclopedias, BX8211, v8 - p252
Methodism — Services. Ritual. Liturgy, BX8337, v8 - p252
Millennial Dawnists. Jehovah's Witnesses — General Works, BX8526, v8 - p253
Millennial Dawnists. Jehovah's Witnesses — Periodicals. Serials, BX8525, v8 - p253
Mormons. Church of Jesus Christ of Latter-Day Saints — Addresses, essays, lectures, BX8637, v8 - p253
Mormons. Church of Jesus Christ of Latter-Day Saints — Dictionaries. Encyclopedias, BX8605.5, v8 - p253
Orthodox Eastern Church — Dictionaries. Encyclopedias, BX230, v8 - p234
Other Protestant denominations — Arminians - pBaptists, BX6198, v8 - p247
Pentecostal churches — Afro-American Pentecostal Churches, BX8762.5, v8 - p254
Pentecostal churches — General Works, BX8762, v8 - p254
Protestantism — General special, BX4817, v8 - p244
Reformed or Calvinistic churches — Addresses, essays, lectures, BX9422.5, v8 - p256
Reformed or Calvinistic churches — Dictionaries. Encyclopedias, BX9406, v8 - p255
Reformed or Calvinistic churches — History, BX9415, v8 - p256
Schwenckfelder Church — pShakers — Segye Kidokkyo T'ongil Sillyong Hyophoe (Sun Myung Moon). Unification Church, BX9750, v8 - p256
Christianity, BR, v8 - p188
Biography — Religious biographies and confessions as a subject of study, BR1690, v8 - p205
Biography of Christian philosophers, BR102, v8 - p190
Christian antiquities. Archaeology. Museums — Other, BR132, v8 - p193
Christian theology — General Works, BR118, v8 - p192
Christianity in relation to special subjects, A-Z, BR115, v8 - p191
Ecclesiastical geography — Dictionaries, BR99, v8 - p190
Encyclopedias. Dictionaries, BR95, v8 - p189
General Works on Christianity — Addresses, essays, etc. (separates), BR123, v8 - p192
General Works on Christianity — Pamphlets, etc., BR125, v8 - p193
General Works on Christianity — Personal opinions, BR124, v8 - p193
Historiography. Methodology — General Works, BR138, v8 - p194
History — Christian denominations. Sects (General), BR157, v8 - p194
History — General special, BR148, v8 - p194

History — Jewish Christians, BR158, v8 - p194
History — Outlines, syllabi, tables, etc., BR149, v8 - p194
History — Popular works, BR150, v8 - p194
Literary history (General): Christian literature — General Works, BR117, v8 - p192
Movements transcending geographical and denominational lines and theological disciplines — Primitivism, BR1661, v8 - p205
Philosophy of Christianity. Philosophy and Christianity, BR100, v8 - p190
Relation of Christianity to other religious and philosophical systems — General Works, BR127, v8 - p193
Relation of Christianity to other religious and philosophical systems — Special, A-Z, BR128, v8 - p193
Sources of Christianity. Origins — General Works, BR129, v8 - p193
Classical Literature, PA3001-3043, v3 - p9
Literary history — Special topics, A-Z, PA3014, v3 - p9
Literary history — Collected essays, studies, etc., PA3003, v3 - p9
Literary history — General Works. Treatises, PA3001, v3 - p9
Literary history — Knowledge, treatment, and conception of special subjects, A-Z, PA3015, v3 - p9
Classical Philology, PA25-186, v3 - p8
Biography — Collective, PA83, v3 - p8
Biography — Individual, PA85, v3 - p8
Collections — Collected works, papers, etc., by individual authors, PA27, v3 - p8
Collections — Series of monographys; Collections of papers, etc. by various authors, PA25, v3 - p8
Criticism. Interpretation (Hermeneutics) — Language data processing, PA50, v3 - p8
Encyclopedias. Dictionaries. Indexes, PA31, v3 - p8
Etymology — Particular words, A-Z, PA430, v3 - p9
Greek philology and language, PA254-445, v3 - p8
Study and teaching. Research — By region or country, A-Z, PA78, v3 - p8
Style. Composition. Rhetoric — Treatises, PA401, v3 - p9
Collections. Series. Collected works, AC, v10 - p1
Colonies and Colonization, JV51-4235, v7 - p91
By region, hemisphere, continent — Eastern hemisphere, JV246, v7 - p91
Colonizing nations — France, JV1811-1835, v7 - p91
Colonizing nations — Germany, JV2018, v7 - p91
Colonizing nations — Great Britain, JV1011-1018, v7 - p91
Colonizing nations — Netherlands. Holland, JV2511, v7 - p91
Colonizing nations — Portugal, JV4235, v7 - p92
Colonizing nations — Spain, JV4062, v7 - p92
History — General Works, JV61, v7 - p91
Theory. Philosophy, JV51, v7 - p91
Commerce, HF, v6 - p269
Business — Applications for positions. Resumes. Employment portfolios, HF5383, v6 - p281
Business — Business organization and administration, HF5500.2-5500.3, v6 - p286
Business — General Works, treatises, and textbooks, HF5351, v6 - p281
Business — History, HF5343, v6 - p281
Business — Success in business, HF5386, v6 - p281
By region or country — Other regions or countries, HF3230.5-4055, v6 - p279
Commercial geography. Economic geography — General Works, HF1025, v6 - p270
Commodities. Commercial products — General Works, HF1040.7, v6 - p270
Commodities. Commercial products — Raw materials, HF1052, v6 - p270
Dictionaries. Encyclopedias — Bilingual and polyglot, HF1002, v6 - p270
Dictionaries. Encyclopedias — General, HF1001, v6 - p270
Export and international marketing, HF1009.5, v6 - p270
General Works — 1979-, HF1008, v6 - p270
Information services. Business information services — By region or country, A-Z, HF54.52, v6 - p269
Information services. Business information services — Electronic information resources, HF54.56, v6 - p269
Information services. Business information services — General Works, HF54.5, v6 - p269
International economic relations — Competition. International competition, HF1414, v6 - p273
International economic relations — Developing countries, HF1413, v6 - p272
International economic relations — Economic sanctions. Boycotts, HF1413.5, v6 - p273
International economic relations — General special, HF1412, v6 - p272
International economic relations — General Works, HF1359, v6 - p271
International economic relations — International commodity control, HF1428, v6 - p274
International economic relations — International economic integration, HF1418.5, v6 - p274
International economic relations — Nontariff trade barriers, HF1430, v6 - p274
International economic relations — North America, HF1452.5-1456.5, v6 - p274
International economic relations — Other regions or countries, HF1480.5-1613.4, v6 - p276
International economic relations — Trade adjustment assistance, HF1421, v6 - p274
International economic relations — Trade blocs, HF1418.7, v6 - p274
Tariff. Free trade. Protectionism — General Works, HF1713, v6 - p277
Tariff. Free trade. Protectionism — History, HF1711, v6 - p277

Commerce, HF (*cont.*)
Theory. Method, HF81, v6 - p269
Communities. Classes. Races, HT, v6 - p400
Classes — General Works, HT609, v6 - p405
Human settlements. Communities — General Works, HT65, v6 - p400
Races — General special, HT1523, v6 - p407
Races — General Works, HT1521, v6 - p407
Urban groups. The city. Urban sociology — Dictionaries. Encyclopedias, HT108.5, v6 - p400
Urban groups. The city. Urban sociology — General special, HT153, v6 - p401
Urban groups. The city. Urban sociology — General Works. "The city problem", HT151, v6 - p401
Urban groups. The city. Urban sociology — Suburban cities and towns, HT352, v6 - p403
Urban groups. The city. Urban sociology — The city as an economic factor. Urban economics, HT321, v6 - p403
Urban groups. The city. Urban sociology — Urban ecology, HT243, v6 - p403
Decorative arts. Applied arts. Decoration and ornament, NK, v9 - p308
Collected writings — Individual authors, NK27, v9 - p308
Decoration and ornament. Design — Dictionaries, NK1165, v9 - p311
Decoration and ornament. Design — Theory of ornament and design, K1505, v9 - p312
Dictionaries, NK30, v9 - p308
Furniture — Dictionaries. Encyclopedias, NK2205, v9 - p313
History — General Works, NK600, v9 - p308
History — Special countries, NK805-1073.5, v9 - p309
Museums, galleries, etc. — United States. By city and museum, A-Z, NK460, v9 - p308
Rugs. Carpets — Other countries, NK2883, v9 - p314
Dictionaries and other general reference works, AG, v10 - p2
Pictorial works (Views, events, etc.), AG250, v10 - p3
Wonders. Curiosities. Eccentric characters, fads, etc. — 1871-, AG243, v10 - p3
Diplomatics. Archives. Seals, CD, v5 - p14
Doctrinal theology, BT, v8 - p214
Authority — Church. Teaching office of the Church, BT91, v8 - p217
Authority — General Works, BT88, v8 - p217
Christology — General special, BT205, v8 - p219
Christology — History of Christological doctrines and study, BT198, v8 - p218
Christology — Topics (not otherwise provided for), A-Z, BT590, v8 - p221
Collected works — Several authors, BT10, v8 - p214
Creation — General Works, BT695.5, v8 - p221
Creation — Vegetarianism, BT749, v8 - p223
Creeds, confessions, covenants, etc. — General Works, BT990, v8 - p224
Doctrinal, dogmatic, systematic theology — Addresses, essays, sermons, etc., BT80, v8 - p216
Doctrinal, dogmatic, systematic theology — General special, BT78, v8 - p215
Doctrinal, dogmatic, systematic theology — Introductions. Prolegomena, etc., BT65, v8 - p215
Doctrinal, dogmatic, systematic theology — Popular works, BT77, v8 - p215
Eschatology. Last things — History, BT819.5, v8 - p223
God — History of doctrines concerning God, BT98, v8 - p218
Invisible world — Antichrist, BT985, v8 - p224
Judaism — General Works, BT93, v8 - p217
Palestine in Christianity. Palestinian liberation and Christianity, BT93.8, v8 - p217
Philosophy. Philosophical theology — General Works, BT40, v8 - p215
Drawing. Design. Illustration, NC, v9 - p252
Book jackets. Phonorecord jackets — Special countries, A-Z, NC1883, v9 - p259
Books of reproductions of drawings, NC1055-1115, v9 - p257
Collective biography, NC45, v9 - p252
Commercial art. Advertising art — Directories, NC999, v9 - p256
Commercial art. Advertising art — Economics of commercial art, NC1001.6, v9 - p256
Commercial art. Advertising art — General Works, NC997.L54-R27, v9 - p256
Commercial art. Advertising art — Special topics, A-Z, NC1002, v9 - p257
Drawing for reproduction — Illustration, NC960, v9 - p255
General Works — General special, NC715, v9 - p254
General Works — Theory of design, NC703, v9 - p254
History of drawing — Medieval, NC70, v9 - p252
History of drawing — Modern, NC80, v9 - p252
History of drawing — Special countries, NC108-287, v9 - p252
Posters — General special, NC1815, v9 - p259
Posters — Posters by special artists, NC1850, v9 - p259
Posters — Special countries, A-Z, NC1807, v9 - p258
Printed ephemera. Imagerie populaire — General Works, NC1280, v9 - p257
Special subjects (Technique, history and collections) — Art anatomy, NC760, v9 - p255
Technique — Studies for artists, NC735, v9 - p254
Dutch literature, PT5061-5926, v3 - p893
Afrikaans Literature, PT6510-6592, v3 - p894
Danish Literature, PT7663-8175, v3 - p897
Individual authors or works — 1961- , A-Z, PT5881.24, v3 - p894
Individual authors or works — 1961-, PT9876.29, v3 - p902

Individual sagas and historical works — Sagas relating to Denmark and Sweden, A-Z, PT7282, v3 - p896
Literary history and criticism — Societies, PT7103, v3 - p895
Norwegian Literature, PT8363-9150, v3 - p898
Scandinavian literature, PT7048-7094, v3 - p895
Swedish Literature, PT9263-9875, v3 - p900
Economic History and Conditions, HC, v6 - p140
Addresses, essays, lectures, HC12, v6 - p140
Biography — Collective, HC29, v6 - p140
By region or country — Africa (General) See HC800-1065, HC502-591, v6 - p190
By region or country — Arctic regions, HC735, v6 - p192
By region or country — Asia, HC412, v6 - p181
By region or country — Australia, HC603-605, v6 - p191
By region or country — Communist countries, HC704, v6 - p191
By region or country — Islamic countries, HC499, v6 - p190
By region or country — New Zealand, HC665, v6 - p191
By region or country — Tropics, HC695, v6 - p191
Congresses, HC13, v6 - p140
Dictionaries. Encyclopedias, HC15, v6 - p140
General Works, HC21, v6 - p140
Natural resources, HC85, v6 - p150
Societies. Serials, HC10, v6 - p140
Special topics, A-Z — Air pollution, HC79.A4, v6 - p146
Special topics, A-Z — Basic needs, HC79.B38, v6 - p146
Special topics, A-Z — Capital. Capital productivity. Infrastructure, HC79.C3, v6 - p146
Special topics, A-Z — Consumer demand. Consumers. Consumption, HC79.C6, v6 - p146
Special topics, A-Z — Consumer protection, HC79.C63, v6 - p147
Special topics, A-Z — Defense and disarmament. Economic impact of, HC79.D4, v6 - p147
Special topics, A-Z — Environmental policy and economic development. Sustainable development, HC79.E5, v6 - p147
Special topics, A-Z — Famines, HC79.F3, v6 - p148
Special topics, A-Z — High technology industries, HC79.H53, v6 - p148
Special topics, A-Z — Income. Income distribution. National income, HC79.I5, v6 - p148
Special topics, A-Z — Industrial productivity. Industrial efficiency, HC79.I52, v6 - p148
Special topics, A-Z — Information technology. Information economy, HC79.I55, v6 - p148
Special topics, A-Z — Pollution, HC79.P55, v6 - p149
Special topics, A-Z — Poor. Poverty, HC79.P6, v6 - p149
Special topics, A-Z — Saving and investment, HC79.S3, v6 - p149
Special topics, A-Z — Subsidies, HC79.S9, v6 - p149
Special topics, A-Z — Technological innovations. Technology transfer, HC79.T4, v6 - p149
Special topics, A-Z — Waste, HC79.W3, v6 - p150
Special topics, A-Z — Water pollution, HC79.W32, v6 - p150
Special topics, A-Z — Wealth, HC79.W4, v6 - p150
Theory. Method. Relation to other subjects, HC26, v6 - p140
Economic Theory. Demography, HB, v6 - p113
Business cycles. Economic fluctuations — By region or country, HB3743-3812, v6 - p139
Business cycles. Economic fluctuations — General Works, HB3711, v6 - p137
Business cycles. Economic fluctuations — History of theories, HB3714, v6 - p138
Business cycles. Economic fluctuations — Long waves. Kondratieff cycles, HB3729, v6 - p139
Demography. Population. Vital events — Addresses, essays, lectures, HB881, v6 - p133
Demography. Population. Vital events — By region or country, HB3501-3675, v6 - p136
Demography. Population. Vital events — By region or country, HB884, v6 - p134
Demography. Population. Vital events — Congresses, HB849, v6 - p131
Demography. Population. Vital events — Demographic transition, HB887, v6 - p134
Demography. Population. Vital events — Dictionaries. Encyclopedias, HB849.2, v6 - p131
Demography. Population. Vital events — General special, HB885, v6 - p134
Demography. Population. Vital events — Population assistance, HB884.5, v6 - p134
Demography. Population. Vital events — Population policy, HB883-883.5, v6 - p133
Economic theory — Capital. Capitalism, HB501-501.5, v6 - p127
Economic theory — Collected works (nonserial), HB31-34, v6 - p113
Economic theory — Competition. Monopolistic competition, HB238, v6 - p127
Economic theory — Dictionaries. Encyclopedias, HB61, v6 - p114
Economic theory — Economics of war, HB195, v6 - p126
Economic theory — General special, HB199, v6 - p126
Economic theory — Labor economics. Wages, HB301, v6 - p127
Economic theory — Production. Theory of the firm. Supply-side economics, HB241, v6 - p127
Economic theory — Rent, HB401, v6 - p127
Economic theory — Social choice, HB846.8, v6 - p131
Economic theory — Societies. Serials, HB1, v6 - p113
Economic theory — Terminology. Abbreviations. Notation, HB62, v6 - p114

Economic Theory. Demography, HB *(cont.)*
Economic theory — Wealth, HB251, v6 - p127
Education (General), L, v7 - p202
Directories of educational institutions — General, L900, v7 - p203
Yearbooks. By country, A-Z, L101, v7 - p203
Electrical engineering. Electronics. Nuclear engineering, TK, v1 - p490
Country divisions, TK23, v1 - p490
Dictionaries and encyclopedias, TK9, v1 - p490
Estimates, TK435, v1 - p491
General special (Including electro-mechanical transducers), TK153, v1 - p491
Insurance requirements, TK260, v1 - p491
Pocketbooks, tables, etc., TK151, v1 - p491
Safety measures (General), TK152, v1 - p491
Emigration and immigration. International migration, JV6021-9125, v7 - p92
Africa — South Africa. Republic of South Africa, JV8825, v7 - p94
Australia — General, JV9125, v7 - p94
Emigration — General Works, JV6091, v7 - p92
Europe — France, JV7925-7933, v7 - p93
Europe — General Works, JV7590, v7 - p93
Europe — Great Britain. England, JV7633-7685, v7 - p93
Europe — Italy, JV8131, v7 - p93
General Works, JV6035, v7 - p92
History — General, JV6021, v7 - p92
Immigration — Economic aspects, JV6217, v7 - p92
Immigration — Political aspects, JV6255, v7 - p92
Encyclopedias, AE, v10 - p1
History, method of use, etc., AE1, v10 - p1
Engineering (General). Civil engineering (General)., TA, v1 - p443
Country Divisions (general historical and descriptive literature, reports on public works, etc.), TA23-52, v1 - p443
Dictionaries and encyclopedias, TA9, v1 - p443
Engineering design, TA174, v1 - p446
Engineering economy, TA177.4, v1 - p446
Engineering instruments, meters, etc. Industrial instrumentation, TA165, v1 - p445
Engineering models, TA177, v1 - p446
Forensic engineering, TA219, v1 - p447
General Special, TA153, v1 - p444
Handbooks, manuals, etc., TA151, v1 - p444
Lasers in engineering, TA367.5, v1 - p451
Rock mechanics, TA706, v1 - p459
Symbols and abbreviations, TA11, v1 - p443
System failure, TA169.5, v1 - p446
Systems engineering, TA168, v1 - p445
Systems reliability, TA169, v1 - p446
Technical education. Technical, TA159, v1 - p445
English Literature, PR, v3 - p337
Criticism — Addresses, essays, lectures, PR61, v3 - p338
Criticism — Collections of essays in criticism, PR67, v3 - p
Criticism — History, PR63, v3 - p338
Criticism — Special topics, A-Z, PR65, v3 - p339
English literature: Provincial, local, etc. — England, PR8476-8489, v3 - p646
English literature: Provincial, local, etc. — English literature outside of Great Britain, PR9080-9084, v3 - p651
English literature: Provincial, local, etc. — Ireland, PR8706-8891, v3 - p647
English literature: Provincial, local, etc. — Scotland, PR8506-8655, v3 - p646
English literature: Provincial, local, etc. — Wales, PR8951-8964, v3 - p651
History of English literature — Collected essays, studies, etc., of individual authors, PR99, v3 - p339
History of English literature — Diaries, PR908, v3 - p409
History of English literature — Juvenile literature (General), PR990, v3 - p410
History of English literature — Other classes of authors, A-Z, PR120, v3 - p344
History of English literature — Women and literature. Feminine influence, PR119, v3 - p344
Literary history and criticism — Encyclopedias. Dictionaries, PR19, v3 - p337
Literary history and criticism — Literary research, PR56, v3 - p338
English Philology and Language, PE, v3 - p27
Anglo-Saxon. Old English — Philology, PE123, v3 - p30
English language — Dialects of Scotland (Dictionaries, etc., of obsolete, archaic words and provincialisms), PE2106, v3 - p43
English language — Linguistic geography, PE1700, v3 - p42
Middle English (ca. 1150 to 1500) — Philology, PE515, v3 - p30
Environmental Sciences, GE, v6 - p26
Biography — Collective, GE55, v6 - p27
Communication in environmental sciences — Environmental literature, GE35, v6 - p26
Communication in environmental sciences — General Works, GE30, v6 - p26
Dictionaries. Encyclopedias, GE10, v6 - p26
Environmental conditions. Environmental quality. Environmental indicators. Environmental degradation — General Works, GE140, v6 - p28
Environmental conditions. Environmental quality. Environmental indicators. Environmental degradation — Global environmental change, GE149, v6 - p28

Environmental education. Study and teaching. Research — General Works, GE70, v6 - p28
Environmental management — General Works, GE300, v6 - p31
Environmental policy — General Works, GE170, v6 - p29
Environmentalism. Green movement — General Works, GE195, v6 - p30
General Works, GE105, v6 - p28
Handbooks, manuals, etc., GE123, v6 - p28
Philosophy. Relation to other topics. Methodology — Environmental ethics, GE42, v6 - p27
Philosophy. Relation to other topics. Methodology — General Works, GE40, v6 - p27
Philosophy. Relation to other topics. Methodology — History, GE50, v6 - p27
Philosophy. Relation to other topics. Methodology — Special methods, A-Z, GE45, v6 - p27
Societies. Serials, GE1, v6 - p26
Vocational guidance, GE60, v6 - p27
Environmental Technology. Sanitary engineering, TD, v1 - p463
Dictionaries and encyclopedias, TD9, v1 - p463
Ethics, BJ10-1725, v8 - p111
Collected works (nonserial) — Polyglot, BJ21, v8 - p112
Communist ethics (20th century), BJ1390, v8 - p129
Comparative ethics, BJ69, v8 - p115
Dictionaries. Encyclopedias, BJ63, v8 - p115
Ethics of social groups, classes, etc. — Professional ethics, BJ1725, v8 - p139
Evolutionary and genetic ethics — History, BJ1298, v8 - p128
Feminist ethics, BJ1395, v8 - p129
Humanist ethics, BJ1360, v8 - p129
Individual ethics. Character. Virtue — General special, BJ1531, v8 - p137
Individual ethics. Character. Virtue — Special virtues, A-Z, BJ1533, v8 - p137
Philosophy. Methodology. Relation to other topics — Relation to aesthetics (Art, literature, etc.), BJ46, v8 - p113
Philosophy. Methodology. Relation to other topics — Relation to anthropology and culture, BJ52, v8 - p114
Philosophy. Methodology. Relation to other topics — Relation to agriculture, BJ52.5, v8 - p114
Philosophy. Methodology. Relation to other topics — Relation to biology, BJ58, v8 - p115
Philosophy. Methodology. Relation to other topics — Relation to cognitive science. Philosophy of mind, BJ45.5, v8 - p113
Philosophy. Methodology. Relation to other topics — Relation to history and sociology, BJ51, v8 - p114
Philosophy. Methodology. Relation to other topics — Relation to logic, BJ43, v8 - p113
Philosophy. Methodology. Relation to other topics — Relation to language, BJ44, v8 - p113
Philosophy. Methodology. Relation to other topics — Relation to law and politics, BJ55, v8 - p114
Philosophy. Methodology. Relation to other topics — Relation to psychology. Morale, BJ45, v8 - p113
Philosophy. Methodology. Relation to other topics — Relation to rhetoric, BJ42, v8 - p113
Philosophy. Methodology. Relation to other topics — Relation to religion and the supernatural, BJ47, v8 - p114
Philosophy. Methodology. Relation to other topics — Relation to science, BJ57, v8 - p115
Philosophy. Methodology. Relation to other topics, BJ37, v8 - p112
Religious ethics. The ethics of the religions — Buddhist ethics, BJ1289, v8 - p128
Religious ethics. The ethics of the religions — General Works, BJ1188, v8 - p125
Religious ethics. The ethics of the religions — Islamic ethics, BJ1291, v8 - p128
Socialist ethics, BJ1388, v8 - p129
Societies — International societies and movements, A-Z, BJ10, v8 - p111
Special topics — Altruism and egotism. Self-interest and egoism, BJ1474, v8 - p135
Special topics — Appropriateness, BJ1418.5, v8 - p132
Special topics — Conscience, BJ1471, v8 - p134
Special topics — Decision making, BJ1419, v8 - p132
Special topics — Emotivism, BJ1473, v8 - p135
Special topics — Exploitation, BJ1474.5, v8 - p135
Special topics — Forgiveness. Pardon, BJ1476, v8 - p135
Special topics — Guilt, BJ1471.5, v8 - p135
Special topics — Hedonism and asceticism. Renunciation, BJ1491, v8 - p136
Special topics — Optimism and pessimism, BJ1477, v8 - p135
Special topics — Other special topics in ethics, A-Z, BJ1500, v8 - p136
Special topics — Pain and suffering, BJ1409, v8 - p131
Special topics — Power over life and death, BJ1469, v8 - p134
Special topics — Revenge, BJ1490, v8 - p136
Special topics — Secrecy, BJ1429.5, v8 - p132
Special topics — Self-realization, BJ1470, v8 - p134
Special topics — Sympathy. Compassion. Caring, BJ1475, v8 - p135
Study and teaching. Research — General Works, BJ66, v8 - p115
Eurasia: Russia (Federation, 1992-), KLB, v7 - p194
Eurasia: Russia, Soviet Union. General, KLA, v7 - p193

Family. The, Marriage. Women, HQ, v6 - p351
Congresses, HQ7, v6 - p351
Dictionaries. Encyclopedias, HQ9, v6 - p351
Erotica — Pornography. Obscene literature, HQ471, v6 - p356
Life style, HQ2042-2044, v6 - p399
Men — General Works, HQ1090, v6 - p372
Men — Study and teaching. Men's studies. Research, HQ1088, v6 - p372
Sex role — By region or country, A-Z, HQ1075.5, v6 - p371
Sex role — General Works, HQ1075, v6 - p371
Sexual life — Emasculation. Eunuchs, etc., HQ449, v6 - p356
Sexual life — Sadism. Masochism. Fetishism, etc., HQ79, v6 - p355
Study and teaching. Research — By region or country, A-Z, HQ10.5, v6 - p351
Thanatology. Death. Dying — By region or country, A-Z, HQ1073.5, v6 - p371
Thanatology. Death. Dying — General Works, HQ1073, v6 - p371
The family. Marriage. Home — Adultery, HQ806, v6 - p367
The family. Marriage. Home — Brothers. Sisters, HQ759.96, v6 - p362
The family. Marriage. Home — Family demography, HQ759.98, v6 - p362
The family. Marriage. Home — Family violence, HQ809.3, v6 - p367
The family. Marriage. Home — Middle age, HQ1059.4-1059.5, v6 - p369
The family. Marriage. Home — Mixed marriages. Intermarriage. Interfaith marriage, HQ1031, v6 - p369
The family. Marriage. Home — Television and family, HQ520, v6 - p357
Women. Feminism — Congresses, HQ1106, v6 - p372
Women. Feminism — Dictionaries. Encyclopedias, HQ1115, v6 - p373
Women. Feminism — Feminist theory, HQ1190-1190.5, v6 - p377
Women. Feminism — General special (Special aspects of the subject as a whole), HQ1233, v6 - p380
Women. Feminism — Women and economics, HQ1381, v6 - p385
Women. Feminism — Women and religion, HQ1393-1394, v6 - p385
Women. Feminism — Women in science and the arts, HQ1397, v6 - p386
Fiction and Juvenile Belles Lettres, PZ, v3 - p902
Finance, HG, v6 - p292
Banking — Bank mergers, HG1722, v6 - p296
Banking — Theory. Method. Relations to other subjects, HG1586, v6 - p296
Biography, HG172, v6 - p292
Chivalry and knighthood (Orders, decorations, etc.) — By region or country, A-Z, CR4529, v5 - p17
Credit. Debt. Loans — General Works, HG3701, v6 - p298
Dictionaries. Encyclopedias, HG151, v6 - p292
Financial management. Business finance. Corporation finance — Chief financial officers, HG4027.35, v6 - p301
Financial management. Business finance. Corporation finance — General Works, HG4026, v6 - p300
Financial management. Business finance. Corporation finance — History, HG4017, v6 - p300
Financial management. Business finance. Corporation finance — International business enterprises, HG4027.5, v6 - p301
Financial management. Business finance. Corporation finance — Other topics, A-Z, HG4028, v6 - p301
Financial management. Business finance. Corporation finance — Small business finance, HG4027.7, v6 - p301
Flags, banners, and standards — General Works, CR101, v5 - p16
Foreign exchange. International finance — By region or country, HG3903-3915.5, v6 - p300
General Works — English, HG173, v6 - p292
Insurance — General special, HG8053, v6 - p304
Investment, capital formation, speculation — Capital market, HG4523, v6 - p302
Investment, capital formation, speculation — Charts, diagrams, etc., HG4638, v6 - p303
Investment, capital formation, speculation — Dictionaries. Encyclopedias, HG4513, v6 - p301
Investment, capital formation, speculation — Foreign investments, HG4538, v6 - p302
Investment, capital formation, speculation — General special, HG4528, v6 - p302
Investment, capital formation, speculation — General Works, HG4521, v6 - p301
Investment, capital formation, speculation — Handbooks, manuals, etc., HG4527, v6 - p302
Investment, capital formation, speculation — Investment analysis. Technical analysis, HG4529, v6 - p302
Investment, capital formation, speculation — Portfolio management. Asset allocation, HG4529.5, v6 - p302
Investment, capital formation, speculation — Prices. Values. Stock quotations, HG4636, v6 - p303
Money — Money supply, HG226.3, v6 - p293
Money — Dictionaries. Encyclopedias, HG216, v6 - p293
Money — General Works, HG221, v6 - p293
Money — Theory. Method. Relation to other subjects, HG220, v6 - p293
Personal finance, HG179, v6 - p292
Public and official heraldry — General Works, CR191, v5 - p17
Folklore, GR, v6 - p63
By subject — Demonology, GR530, v6 - p67
By subject — Medicine. Folk medicine, GR880, v6 - p68

Dictionaries. Encyclopedias, GR35, v6 - p63
Folk literature (General) — General Works, GR72, v6 - p63
Folk literature (General) — Performance, GR72.3, v6 - p64
General special (Special aspects of the subject as a whole), GR67, v6 - p63
Philosophy. Relation to other topics. Methodology — General Works, GR40, v6 - p63
Philosophy. Relation to other topics. Methodology — Relation to literature, GR41.3, v6 - p63
Study and teaching. Research — Fieldwork, GR45.5, v6 - p63
Forestry, SD, v1 - p411
General Works, SD373, v1 - p412
Special aspects of forestry, A-Z, SD387, v1 - p413
French Literature, PQ36-3989.2, v3 - p260
Literary history and criticism — Encyclopedias. Dictionaries, PQ41, v3 - p260
Literary history and criticism — Theory of the study of French literature, PQ45, v3 - p260
Genealogy, CS, v5 - p17
Directories, CS5, v5 - p17
General Works — American and English, CS9, v5 - p17
Personal and family names — General special, CS2309, v5 - p19
Personal and family names — General Works, CS2305, v5 - p19
Popular works — General special, CS21, v5 - p18
General bibliography, Z1001-1065, v10 - p96
Anonyms and pseudonyms — General bibliography, Z1041, v10 - p100
Best books — Book selection, reviews, etc., Z1035.A1, v10 - p98
Bibliography of bibliography. Books about books, Z1002, v10 - p96
Biography of bibliographers — Collective, Z1003.8, v10 - p97
Biography of bibliographers — Individual, A-Z, Z1004, v10 - p97
Books for other special classes, institutions, etc., A-Z, Z1039, v10 - p100
Books for the young — General Works, Z1037.A1, v10 - p99
Books for the young — Prize books, Z1037.A2, v10 - p99
Books for the young — Reference books for children, Z1037.9, v10 - p100
Choice of books. Books and reading — General Works, Z1003, v10 - p96
Collections, Z1009, v10 - p98
Dictionaries. Encyclopedias, Z1006, v10 - p97
History of bibliography — General Works, Z1001.3, v10 - p96
Introduction to bibliography. Theory, philosophy, psychology. Bibliography. Documentation, Z1001, v10 - p96
Reference books, Z1035.1, v10 - p99
Special classes of books — Imaginary books. Lost books. Forgeries, etc., Z1024, v10 - p98
Special classes of books — Other special classes, A-Z, Z1033, v10 - p98
General Legislative and Executive Papers, J, v7 - p1
Geography, G1-875, v6 - p(General)
Adventures, shipwrecks, buried treasures, etc. — General Works, G525, v6 - p7
Adventures, shipwrecks, buried treasures, etc. — Individual narratives. By explorer or traveler, or if better known, by name of ship, A-Z, G530, v6 - p7
Dictionaries. Encyclopedias, G63, v6 - p1
Geographical perception, G71.5, v6 - p2
Great cities of the world, G140, v6 - p4
Historical geography, G141, v6 - p4
History of discoveries, explorations, and travel — Collective biography, G200, v6 - p5
History of geography — General special, G81, v6 - p3
History of geography — General Works, G80, v6 - p2
Imaginary voyages, G560, v6 - p7
Mountaineering, G510, v6 - p7
Philosophy. Relation to other topics. Methodology — General Works, G70, v6 - p1
Seafaring life, ocean travel, etc. — General works, G540, v6 - p7
Seafaring life, ocean travel, etc. — Whaling voyages, G545, v6 - p7
Serials, G1, v6 - p1
Societies — United States, G3, v6 - p1
Study and teaching. Research — General special, G74, v6 - p2
Study and teaching. Research — General Works, G73, v6 - p2
Travel. Voyages and travels (General) — Collected works (nonserial), G161, v6 - p5
Travel. Voyages and travels (General) — Special topics, A-Z, G156.5, v6 - p5
Tropics, G515, v6 - p7
Geology, QE, v1 - p209
Addresses, essays, lectures, QE35, v1 - p211
Data Processing, QE48.8, v1 - p212
Dictionaries and Encyclopedias, QE5, v1 - p209
Field work, QE45, v1 - p212
Geological maps, QE36, v1 - p211
Instruments and apparatus, QE49.5, v1 - p212
Popular works, QE31, v1 - p210
Special aspects of the subject as a whole, QE33, v1 - p211
Special topics, A-Z, QE33.2, v1 - p211
German Literature, PT41-3919, v3 - p864
History of German literature — By country or language, A-Z, PT123, v3 - p865
History of German literature — Jewish authors, PT169, v3 - p866
History of German literature — Outlines, syllabi, tables, atlases, charts, questions and answers, etc., PT103-105, v3 - p865
History of German literature — Treatises in English, PT91, v3 - p865

German Literature, PT41-3919 *(cont.)*
History of German literature — Various aspects, forms, etc., PT129, v3 - p865
Literary history and criticism — Collections of essays in criticism, PT75, v3 - p865
Literary history and criticism — Encyclopedias. Dictionaries, PT41, v3 - p864
Provincial, local, colonial, etc. — By region, state, province, etc., PT3803, v3 - p893
Provincial, local, colonial, etc. — Germany (Democratic Republic, 1949-), PT3707-3740, v3 - p893
Germanic Philology and Languages, PD, v3 - p21
Greece, KKE, v7 - p192
Greek Literature, PA3055-4494, v3 - p10
Byzantine and modern Greek literature, PA5165-5610, v3 - p14
Individual authors to 600 A.D. — Anacreon, fl. 545-514 B.C., PA3865, v3 - p12
Individual authors to 600 A.D. — Bacchylides, ca. 505-ca. 450 B.C., PA3943, v3 - p12
Individual authors to 600 A.D. — Hesiodus, 8th (?) century B.C. and his school, PA4010, v3 - p13
Individual authors to 600 A.D. — Lic to Luc, PA4229, v3 - p13
Literary history — French, PA3055, v3 - p10
Literary history — Woman authors. Literary relations of women, PA3067, v3 - p10
Special periods — Modern, including Renaissance, PA5225, v3 - p14
Handicrafts. Arts and crafts, TT, v1 - p562
Directories, TT12, v1 - p562
History and country divisions (General Works on the crafts as practiced in particular regions or countries,manuals on how to duplicate craft articles from specific regions or countries), TT23-127, v1 - p562
Heraldry, CR, v5 - p16
Dictionaries. Encyclopedias, CR13, v5 - p16
General Works — 1801-, CR23, v5 - p16
Handbooks, manuals, etc., CR31, v5 - p16
Highway engineering. Roads and pavements, TE, v1 - p472
History (General), D, v5 - p26
Ancient history — Compends. Textbooks. Outlines. Syllabi. Questions, D59, v5 - p35
Ancient history — Works by classical historians, D58, v5 - p35
Chronological tables, etc. — Special, D11.5, v5 - p27
Chronological tables, etc., D11, v5 - p27
Collected works (Monographs, essays, etc.) — Individual authors, D7, v5 - p26
Collected works (Monographs, essays, etc.) — Several authors, D6, v5 - p26
Developing countries — General Works, D883, v5 - p87
Dictionaries, D9, v5 - p26
Historiography — By region or country, A-Z, D13.5, v5 - p28
Historiography — Criticism and reviews, D13.2, v5 - p28
Historiography — General Works, D13, v5 - p27
Medieval and modern history, 476- — General special, D104, v5 - p35
Medieval and modern history, 476- — General Works, D102, v5 - p35
Medieval history — Antiquities, D125, v5 - p36
Medieval history — Arab (Islamic) Empire, D198.2-199.3, v5 - p38
Medieval history — Dictionaries, D114, v5 - p36
Medieval history — Military and naval history, D128, v5 - p36
Medieval history — Social life and customs, D127, v5 - p36
Medieval history — Sources and documents. Collections. Chronicles, D113, v5 - p36
Military history — Dictionaries. Chronological tables, etc., D25.A2, v5 - p33
Military history — General special, D25.5, v5 - p34
Military history — General Works, D25.D86-25.K43, v5 - p34
Military history — Pamphlets, etc., D25.9, v5 - p34
Modern history, 1453- — Compends. Textbooks. Outlines, D209, v5 - p39
Modern history, 1453- — General special. Addresses, essays, lectures, D210, v5 - p39
Modern history, 1453- — General Works, D208, v5 - p39
Modern history, 1453- — Military history, D214, v5 - p39
Modern history, 1453- — Political and diplomatic history. European concert. Balance of power, D217, v5 - p39
Naval history, D27, v5 - p34
Pamphlets, etc., D8, v5 - p26
Period between world wars (1919-1939) — General special, D723, v5 - p54
Period between world wars (1919-1939) — General Works, D720, v5 - p54
Period between world wars (1919-1939) — Political and diplomatic history, D727, v5 - p55
Philosophy of history — Special topics, D16.9, v5 - p32
Political and diplomatic history — General special, D32, v5 - p34
Political and diplomatic history — General Works, D31, v5 - p34
Political and diplomatic history — Relations between Europe and individual countries, A-Z, D34, v5 - p34
Post-war history (1945-   ) — Congresses. Conferences, etc., D839.2, v5 - p83
Post-war history (1945-   ) — General special, D842, v5 - p84
Post-war history (1945-   ) — General Works, D840, v5 - p84
Post-war history (1945-   ) — Sources and documents, D839.3, v5 - p83
Societies. Serials, D1, v5 - p26
Sources and documents, D5, v5 - p26
Study and teaching — General special, D16.25, v5 - p30
Study and teaching — Special topics, A-Z, D16.255, v5 - p30
World histories — Chronicles and works written before 1525, D17, v5 - p32
World histories — Compends. Textbooks. Outlines. Syllabi. Questions, D21, v5 - p33

World histories — General special, D21.3, v5 - p33
World histories — General Works, 1801-, D20, v5 - p32
World histories — Historical geography, D21.5, v5 - p33
World War I (1914-1918) — Armistice of Compiegne, 1918, D641, v5 - p53
World War I (1914-1918) — Dictionaries, D510, v5 - p46
World War I (1914-1918) — General special, D523, v5 - p47
World War I (1914-1918) — General Works, D521, v5 - p46
World War I (1914-1918) — Historiography, D522.42, v5 - p47
World War I (1914-1918) — Motion pictures about the war, D522.23, v5 - p47
World War I (1914-1918) — Outlines, syllabi, tables, etc., D522.5, v5 - p47
World War I (1914-1918) — Personal narratives and other accounts, D640, v5 - p52
World War I (1914-1918) — Posters, D522.25, v5 - p47
World War I (1914-1918) — Sources and documents, D505, v5 - p45
World War II (1939-1945) — Congresses, conferences, etc., D734, v5 - p55
World War II (1939-1945) — Dictionaries, D740, v5 - p55
World War II (1939-1945) — General special, D744-744.7, v5 - p58
World War II (1939-1945) — General Works, D743, v5 - p56
World War II (1939-1945) — Historiography, D743.42, v5 - p57
World War II (1939-1945) — Motion pictures about the war, D743.23, v5 - p57
World War II (1939-1945) — Occupied territory, D802, v5 - p71
World War II (1939-1945) — Other special topics, A-Z, D810, v5 - p78
World War II (1939-1945) — Outlines, syllabi, tables, etc., D743.5, v5 - p57
World War II (1939-1945) — Pamphlets, addresses, sermons, etc., D743.9, v5 - p57
World War II (1939-1945) — Personal narratives and other accounts, D811-811.5, v5 - p82
World War II (1939-1945) — Pictorial works, D743.2, v5 - p57
World War II (1939-1945) — Posters, D743.25, v5 - p57
World War II (1939-1945) — Prisoners and prisons, D805-805.5, v5 - p76
World War II (1939-1945) — Sources and documents, D735, v5 - p55
History of Africa, DT, v5 - p344
Central Sub-Saharan Africa — General Works, DT351, v5 - p350
Central Sub-Saharan Africa — Social life and customs. Civilization. Intellectual life, DT352.4, v5 - p350
Egypt — Local antiquities, A-Z, DT73, v5 - p347
Egypt — Social life and customs. Civilization. Intellectual life, DT70, v5 - p347
Ethnography — General Works, DT15, v5 - p345
Ethnography — Individual elements in the population not limited to specific territorial divisions, A-Z, DT16, v5 - p345
Gazetteers. Dictionaries, etc. Guidebooks, DT2, v5 - p344
Geography, DT6.7, v5 - p344
History — Biography (Collective), DT18, v5 - p345
History — Dictionaries. Chronological tables, outlines, etc., DT17, v5 - p345
History — General Works, DT20, v5 - p345
History — Military history, DT21.5, v5 - p345
Social life and customs. Civilization. Intellectual life, DT14, v5 - p344
South Africa — Historical geography, DT1728, v5 - p361
Southern Africa, DT763.5-963.42, v5 - p360
Sudan. Anglo-Egyptian Sudan — Antiquities, DT154.8, v5 - p349
Swaziland — Gazetteers. Dictionaries, etc., DT2714, v5 - p363
West Africa. West Coast — Angola, DT611.8, v5 - p359
West Africa. West Coast — Ethnography, DT474.6, v5 - p355
Zambia. Northern Rhodesia — Gazetteers. Dictionaries, etc., DT3037, v5 - p364
History of Asia, DS, v5 - p248
Afghanistan — Gazetteers. Guidebooks, DS351, v5 - p285
Afghanistan — General Works, DS351.5, v5 - p285
Antiquities, DS11, v5 - p249
Arab countries — Ethnography, DS36.9, v5 - p252
Arab countries — Gazetteers. Guidebooks. Itineraries. Directories, etc., DS36.55, v5 - p251
Arab countries — General Works, DS36.7, v5 - p251
Arabian Peninsula. Saudi Arabia — General Works, DS204, v5 - p282
Bangladesh. East Pakistan — Social life and customs. Civilization. Intellectual life, DS393.8, v5 - p288
Bhutan — General Works, DS491.4, v5 - p295
China — Chinese in foreign countries (General), DS732, v5 - p314
China — Gazetteers. Dictionaries, etc. Guidebooks, DS705, v5 - p309
China — General Works, DS706, v5 - p309
China — General Works, DS735, v5 - p315
China — Geography, DS706.7, v5 - p310
China — Historical geography, DS706.5, v5 - p310
Collected works (nonserial), DS3, v5 - p248
Description and travel — 1492-1800, DS7, v5 - p249
Description and travel — 1801-1900, DS8, v5 - p249
Description and travel — 1901-1950, DS9, v5 - p249
Description and travel — 1951-, DS10, v5 - p249
Description and travel — Through 1491, DS6, v5 - p249
East Asia. The Far East — Antiquities, DS509, v5 - p297
East Asia. The Far East — Ethnography, DS509.5, v5 - p297
East Asia. The Far East — Social life and customs. Civilization. Intellectual life, DS509.3, v5 - p297
East Asia. The Far East — Sources and documents, DS503, v5 - p296

History of Africa, DT *(cont.)*
East Asia. The Far East — Yearbooks. Directories, etc., DS502, v5 - p296
Ethnography — General Works, DR24, v5 - p241
Ethnography — General Works, DS13, v5 - p249
Ethnography — National characteristics, DR24.5, v5 - p241
Ethnography — Other individual elements in the population, A-Z, DR27, v5 - p241
Gazetteers. Dictionaries, etc., DS4, v5 - p248
General Works, DS5, v5 - p248
Goa. Portuguese in India — General Works, DS498, v5 - p296
History — Balkan relations with individual regions or countries, A-Z, DR38.3, v5 - p241
History — Biography (Collective), DS32, v5 - p250
History — Dictionaries. Chronological tables, outlines, etc., DB35, v5 - p142
History — Dictionaries. Chronological tables, outlines, etc., DS31, v5 - p250
History — General special, DR37, v5 - p241
History — General special, DS33.1, v5 - p250
History — General Works, DS33, v5 - p250
History — Political and diplomatic history, DR38.2, v5 - p241
History of Austria, DB35-886, v5 - p142
History of Balkan Peninsula, DR, v5 - p241
History of Liechtenstein — General Works, DB886, v5 - p144
India (Bharat) — Gazetteers. Dictionaries. Directories, etc., DS405, v5 - p288
India (Bharat) — General Works, DS407, v5 - p288
Iraq (Assyria, Babylonia, Mesopotamia) — Ethnography, DS70.8, v5 - p260
Iraq (Assyria, Babylonia, Mesopotamia) — General Works, DS70.6, v5 - p259
Iraq (Assyria, Babylonia, Mesopotamia) — Social life and customs.Civilization, DS70.7, v5 - p260
Iraq (Assyria, Babylonia, Mesopotamia) — Sources and documents, DS68, v5 - p259
Israel (Palestine). The Jews — Directories, DS102.9, v5 - p264
Israel (Palestine). The Jews — Encyclopedias. Dictionaries, DS102.8, v5 - p264
Israel (Palestine). The Jews — General Works, DS102.95, v5 - p264
Israel (Palestine). The Jews — Historical geography. History of Palestine exploration, etc., DS108.9, v5 - p264
Israel (Palestine). The Jews — Regions, towns, etc., A-Z, DS110-110.5, v5 - p265
Israel (Palestine). The Jews — Sources and documents, DS102, v5 - p263
Japan — Gazetteers. Dictionaries, etc. Place names, DS805, v5 - p339
Japan — General Works, DS806, v5 - p339
Japan — Other cities, towns, etc., A-Z, DS897, v5 - p343
Jordan. Transjordan — Antiquities, DS153.3, v5 - p282
Lebanon (Phenicia) — General Works, DS80, v5 - p262
Lebanon (Phoenicia) — Philistines, DS90, v5 - p262
Lebanon (Phoenicia) — Regions, cities, etc., DS89, v5 - p262
Malay Archipelago — General Works. Description and travel, DS601, v5 - p306
Middle East. Southwestern Asia. Ancient Orient. Arab East. Near East — Societies. Serials, DS41, v5 - p253
Middle East. Southwestern Asia. Ancient Orient. Arab East. Near East — Sources and documents, DS42, v5 - p253
Middle East. Southwestern Asia. Ancient Orient. Arab East. Near East — Gazetteers. Guidebooks. Dictionaries. Directories, etc., DS43, v5 - p253
Middle East. Southwestern Asia. Ancient Orient. Arab East. Near East — General Works, DS44, v5 - p253
Middle East. Southwestern Asia. Ancient Orient. Arab East. Near East — Historical geography, DS44.9, v5 - p254
Middle East. Southwestern Asia. Ancient Orient. Arab East. Near East — Geography, DS44.96, v5 - p254
Middle East. Southwestern Asia. Ancient Orient. Arab East. Near East — Antiquities. Social antiquities, DS56, v5 - p255
Middle East. Southwestern Asia. Ancient Orient. Arab East. Near East — Social life and customs. Civilization. Intellectual life, DS57, v5 - p255
Nepal — Local history and description, A-Z, DS495.8, v5 - p296
Pakistan — Ethnography, DS380, v5 - p286
Pakistan — General Works, DS376.9, v5 - p286
Philippines — Social life and customs. Civilization. Intellectual life, DS663, v5 - p308
Romania — General Works, DR205, v5 - p242
Romania — General Works, DR217, v5 - p242
Social life and customs. Civilization. Intellectual life, DR23, v5 - p241
Social life and customs. Civilization. Intellectual life, DS12, v5 - p249
Societies. Serials, DS1, v5 - p248
Sources and documents, DS2, v5 - p248
Southeastern Asia — Antiquities, DS523, v5 - p301
Southeastern Asia — Ethnography, DS523.4, v5 - p301
Southeastern Asia — Social life and customs. Civilization. Intellectual life, DS523.2, v5 - p301
Southern Asia. Indian Ocean Region — Antiquities, DS338, v5 - p283
Southern Asia. Indian Ocean Region — Encyclopedias, DS334.9, v5 - p283
Southern Asia. Indian Ocean Region — Social life and customs. Civilization. Intellectual life, DS339, v5 - p284
Southern Asia. Indian Ocean Region — Societies. Sources and documents. Collections, DS331, v5 - p283
Syria — Antiquities, DS94.5, v5 - p263
Syria — Congresses, DS92.3, v5 - p262
Syria — Description and travel, DS94, v5 - p263

Syria — General Works, DS93, v5 - p263
Syria — Provinces, regions, cities, etc., A-Z, DS99, v5 - p263
The Islamic world — Congresses, DS35.32, v5 - p251
The Islamic world — Ethnography, DS35.625, v5 - p251
The Islamic world — Gazetteers. Guidebooks. Dictionaries. Directories, etc., DS35.53, v5 - p251
The Islamic world — General Works, DS35.6, v5 - p251
The Islamic world — Political history, DS35.69, v5 - p251
History of Central Europe, DAW, v5 - p142
General Works, DAW1009, v5 - p142
History of Civilization, CB, v5 - p1
By period — Prehistory, CB301, v5 - p5
Civilization and race — General special, CB197, v5 - p3
Civilization and race — General Works, CB195, v5 - p3
Collected works (nonserial) — Several authors, CB5, v5 - p1
Dictionaries. Encyclopedias, CB9, v5 - p1
Forecasts of future progress — Methodology, CB158, v5 - p3
General special, CB151, v5 - p2
Historiography — General Works, CB15, v5 - p1
Philosophy. Theory, CB19, v5 - p1
Relation to special topics — Symbolism and civilization, CB475, v5 - p9
Relation to special topics — Technology and civilization. Science and civilization, CB478, v5 - p9
Relation to special topics — War and civilization, CB481, v5 - p9
Relations to special topics, CB155, v5 - p3
Terrestrial evidence of interplanetary voyages. Influence of extraterrestrial life on human civilization, CB156, v5 - p3
History of Czechoslovakia, DB2005-2848, v5 - p145
Collected works (nonserial) — Several authors, DB2005, v5 - p145
Ethnography — General Works, DC34, v5 - p149
Ethnography — Individual elements in the population, A-Z, DC34.5, v5 - p149
Historical geography, DC20.5, v5 - p147
History — Compends, DC39, v5 - p150
History — Dictionaries. Chronological tables, outlines, etc., DC35, v5 - p149
History — General special, DC59.8, v5 - p150
History of France, DC, v5 - p147
Local history and description — Other cities, towns, etc., A-Z, DC801, v5 - p170
Local history and description — Regions, provinces, departments, etc., A-Z, DC611, v5 - p168
Pictorial works, DC20, v5 - p147
Slovakia — General Works, DB2711, v5 - p146
Social life and customs. Civilization. Intellectual life — General Works, DC33, v5 - p147
History of Eastern Europe (General), DJK, v5 - p208
Collected works (nonserial) — Several authors, DJK4, v5 - p208
History — Political history, DJK42, v5 - p209
Local history and description — Black Sea region, DJK61, v5 - p210
History of education, LA, v7 - p203
Biography — General collections, LA2301, v7 - p215
Collected works — Several authors, LA5, v7 - p203
General special, LA21, v7 - p204
General Works, LA11, v7 - p203
Historiography, LA9, v7 - p203
History of higher education — Early and medieval, LA177, v7 - p205
History of higher education — Student life, LA186, v7 - p205
Syllabi and topical outlines, LA14, v7 - p204
Textbooks, compends, etc., LA13, v7 - p204
History of Germany, DD, v5 - p170
Collected works — Individual authors, DD5, v5 - p170
Description and travel — 1946-, DD43, v5 - p171
Ethnography — General Works, DD74, v5 - p171
Ethnography — National characteristics, etc., DD76, v5 - p171
Gazetteers. Dictionaries, etc., DD14, v5 - p171
History — 1801-, DD89, v5 - p172
History — Compends, DD90, v5 - p172
History — Dictionaries. Chronological tables, outlines, etc., DD84, v5 - p171
Local history and description — States, provinces, regions, etc., A-Z, DD801, v5 - p184
Monumental and picturesque. Pictorial works, DD20, v5 - p171
Prussia — Local history and description, DD491, v5 - p184
Reunified Germany, 1990- — Foreign and general relations, DD290.3, v5 - p183
Reunified Germany, 1990- — General Works, DD290.25, v5 - p182
Reunified Germany, 1990- — Political history, DD290.29, v5 - p183
Reunified Germany, 1990- — Sources and documents, DD290.22, v5 - p182
Social life and customs. Civilization. Intellectual life — General Works, DD61, v5 - p171
Sources and documents. Collections, DD3, v5 - p170

History of Great Britain, DA, v5 - p90
British Empire. Commonwealth of Nations. The Commonwealth — Historical geography, DA13, v5 - p91
British Empire. Commonwealth of Nations. The Commonwealth — History, DA16, v5 - p91
England — Gazetteers. Dictionaries, etc., DA640, v5 - p127
England — General Works, DA27.5, v5 - p92
England — Guidebooks, DA650, v5 - p127
England — Historical geography, DA600, v5 - p126
England — Other cities, towns, etc., A-Z, DA690, v5 - p129
England — Place names, DA645, v5 - p127
England — Preservation of historic monuments, etc., DA655, v5 - p127
Historiography — Biography of historians, DA3, v5 - p91
Historiography — General Works, DA1, v5 - p90
Ireland — Cities, towns, etc., A-Z, DA995, v5 - p141
Ireland — Counties, regions, etc., A-Z, DA990, v5 - p139
Ireland — General Works, DA906, v5 - p133
Scotland — Cities, towns, etc., A-Z, DA890, v5 - p133
Scotland — Counties, regions, etc., A-Z, DA880, v5 - p133
Scotland — Sources and documents, DA755, v5 - p131
Wales — Compends, DA709, v5 - p130
Wales — Social life and customs. Civilization, DA711.5, v5 - p130

History of Greece, DF, v5 - p187
Ancient Greece — Dictionaries, DF16, v5 - p187
Ancient Greece — Sources and documents. Collections. Classical authors, DF12, v5 - p187
Medieval Greece. Byzantine Empire, 323-1453 — Military history, DF543, v5 - p193
Medieval Greece. Byzantine Empire, 323-1453 — Political history, DF545, v5 - p193
Modern Greece — General Works. Compends, DF717, v5 - p194
Modern Greece — Social life and customs. Civilization. Culture, DF741, v5 - p195

History of Gypsies, DX, v5 - p372
General Works, DX115, v5 - p372
History — Modern, DX145, v5 - p372
Popular works, DX118, v5 - p372

History of Hungary, DB904-958.3, v5 - p144
Gazetteers. Dictionaries, etc., DB904, v5 - p144
General Works, DB906, v5 - p145
History — Addresses, essays, lectures, DB925.3, v5 - p145
History — Compends, DB925.1, v5 - p145

History of Italy, DG, v5 - p196
Ancient Italy. Rome to 476 — Dictionaries, DG16, v5 - p196
Ancient Italy. Rome to 476 — Ethnography, DG190, v5 - p198
Ancient Italy. Rome to 476 — Sources and documents. Collections. Classical authors, DG13, v5 - p196
Cities (other than metropolitan), provinces, etc., A-Z, DG975, v5 - p207
Ethnography — General Works, DH491, v5 - p208
History of Belgium — Dictionaries. Chronological tables, outlines, etc., DH511, v5 - p208

History of law (Europe), KJ, v7 - p188
History of law. The ancient orient, KL, v7 - p193
History of Netherlands (Holland), DJ, v5 - p208
Local history and description — Provinces, regions, islands, etc., A-Z, DJ401, v5 - p208

History of Northern Europe. Scandinavia, DL, v5 - p233
Denmark — Gazetteers. Dictionaries, etc., DL105, v5 - p234
Description and travel — 1901-1950, DL10, v5 - p233
Description and travel — 1951-1980, DL11, v5 - p233
General Works, DL5, v5 - p233
Social life and customs. Civilization — General Works, DL30, v5 - p233
Sweden — Guidebooks, DL607, v5 - p234

History of Oceania (South Seas), DU, v5 - p364
Australia — Antiquities, DU106, v5 - p366
Australia — Gazetteers. Dictionaries, etc., DU90, v5 - p365
Australia — Historical geography, DU96.5, v5 - p366
Australia — Social life and customs. Civilization. Intellectual life, DU107, v5 - p366
General special, DU18, v5 - p365
General Works, DU17, v5 - p364
History — General Works, DU28.3, v5 - p365
History — Political and diplomatic history. Control of the Pacific. Colonies and possessions, DU29, v5 - p365
Melanesia (General), DU490, v5 - p368
Micronesia (General), DU500, v5 - p368
Polynesia (General), DU510, v5 - p368
Smaller island groups — Admiralty Islands, DU520, v5 - p368
Smaller island groups — Fiji Islands, DU600, v5 - p368
Smaller island groups — Marshall Islands, DU710, v5 - p370
Smaller island groups — New Hebrides. Vanuatu, DU760, v5 - p371
Smaller island groups — Pelew (Palau) Islands, DU780, v5 - p371
Smaller island groups — Samoan Islands, DU819, v5 - p371
Smaller island groups — Solomon Islands, DU850, v5 - p371
Smaller island groups — Tahiti and Society Islands, DU870, v5 - p372

Smaller island groups — Tonga Islands, DU880, v5 - p372
Smaller island groups —New Guinea, DU710, v5 - p370
Social life and customs. Civilization. Intellectual life, DU28, v5 - p365
South Sea description and travel. Voyages — 1898-1950, DU22, v5 - p365
South Sea description and travel. Voyages — General history of voyages and discoveries, DU19, v5 - p365
South Sea description and travel. Voyages — Through 1800, DU20, v5 - p365
Tasmania (Van Diemen's Land), DU470, v5 - p368

History of Portugal, DP517-702, v5 - p240
General Works, DP517, v5 - p240
History — Political and diplomatic history. Foreign, DP556, v5 - p240
Local history and description — Provinces, regions, etc., A-Z, DP702, v5 - p240
Social life and customs. Civilization — Through 1500, DP532.3, v5 - p240

History of Russia. Soviet Union. Former Soviet Republics, DK, v5 - p210
Description and travel — 1856-1900, DK26, v5 - p210
Ethnography — General Works, DK33, v5 - p211
Ethnography — Individual elements in the population, A-Z, DK34, v5 - p211
Finland, DK458-459.5, v5 - p225
Gazetteers. Dictionaries, etc., DK14, v5 - p210
Gazetteers. Dictionaries, etc., DK4030, v5 - p231
General Works, DK17, v5 - p210
General Works, DK4040, v5 - p231
History — Dictionaries. Chronological tables, outlines, etc., DK36, v5 - p212
History — Dictionaries. Chronological tables, outlines, etc., DK4123, v5 - p231
History — Elementary textbooks, DK41, v5 - p213
History — General Works, DK4140, v5 - p231
History of Poland, DK4030-4452, v5 - p225
Local history and description — Southern Soviet Union, DK509, v5 - p227
Poland, DK411-443, v5 - p225
Russians in foreign countries (General), DK35.5, v5 - p212
Social life and customs. Civilization — General Works, DK32, v5 - p210
Social life and customs. Civilization — Intellectual life, DK32.7, v5 - p211
Societies. Serials — Commonwealth of Independent States, DK1.5, v5 - p210
Sources and documents, DK3, v5 - p210

History of scholarship and learning. The humanities, AZ, v10 - p6
Philosophy. Theory — Value, aims, influences etc. Addresses, essays, lectures. Pamphlets, AZ103, v10 - p6
Popular errors and delusions, AZ999, v10 - p7
Study and teaching — By region or country, A-Z, AZ183, v10 - p6
Study and teaching — General Works, AZ182, v10 - p6

History of Spain, DP12-402, v5 - p235
Antiquities, DP44, v5 - p236
Description and travel — 1951-1980, DP43, v5 - p235
Ethnography — General Works, DP52, v5 - p236
Ethnography — Individual elements in the population, A-Z, DP53, v5 - p236
Gazetteers. Dictionaries, etc., DP12, v5 - p235
General Works, DP17, v5 - p235
Guidebooks, DP14, v5 - p
History — Compends, DP68, v5 - p236
History — Dictionaries. Chronological tables, outlines, etc., DP56, v5 - p236
History — Special topics (not A-Z), DP75, v5 - p236
Local history and description — Other cities, towns, etc., A-Z, DP402, v5 - p240
Local history and description — Provinces, regions, etc., A-Z, DP302, v5 - p239
Social life and customs. Civilization — General Works, DP48, v5 - p236

History of Switzerland, DQ, v5 - p240
General Works, DQ17, v5 - p240
History — Compends, DQ55, v5 - p240

History of the Greco-Roman World, DE, v5 - p186
Biography (Collective), DE7, v5 - p186
Dictionaries. Encyclopedias, DE5, v5 - p186
Ethnography — Individual elements in the population, A-Z, DE73.2, v5 - p187
Historiography — Biography of historians and archaeologists, DE9, v5 - p186
Historiography — General Works, DE8, v5 - p186

Home economics, TX, v1 - p564
Special countries, TX23, v1 - p565

Human Anatomy, QM, v1 - p337
Early works through 1800, QM21, v1 - p337
Pictorial works and atlases, QM25, v1 - p337
Special aspects of the subject as whole, QM28, v1 - p337

Human Ecology. Anthropogeography, GF, v6 - p32
Addresses, essays, lectures, GF49, v6 - p33
By region or country — Arctic regions, GF891, v6 - p37
By region or country — Asia, GF651, v6 - p36
By region or country — Tropic, GF895, v6 - p37
Climatic influences on humans, GF71, v6 - p34
Congresses, GF3, v6 - p32
Developing countries, GF900, v6 - p37
Dictionaries. Encyclopedias, GF4, v6 - p32
Environmental influences on humans, GF51, v6 - p33
Ethical, moral and religious aspects, GF80, v6 - p34
General special (Special aspects of the subject as a whole), GF50, v6 - p33

Human Ecology. Anthropogeography, GF *(cont.)*
Hazardous aspects of the environment, GF85, v6 - p34
History, GF13, v6 - p32
Human influences on the environment, GF75, v6 - p34
Humans and specific environments — Forests, GF54.5, v6 - p33
Humans and specific environments — Mountains, GF57, v6 - p34
Landscape assessment — By region or country, A-Z, GF91, v6 - p35
Landscape assessment — General Works, GF90, v6 - p34
Philosophy. Relation to other topics. Methodology — General Works, GF21, v6 - p32
Philosophy. Relation to other topics. Methodology — Special methods, A-Z, GF23, v6 - p33
Settlements — Cities. Urban sociology, GF125, v6 - p35
Settlements — Rural settlements. Rural geography, GF127, v6 - p35
Spatial studies, GF95, v6 - p35
Study and teaching. Research — General Works, GF26, v6 - p33
Hunting sports, SK, v1 - p426
Camping. Outdoor life, SK601, v1 - p429
Hydraulic engineering, TC, v1 - p462
Ocean engineering, TC1645-1665, v1 - p463
Hyperborean, Indian, and Artificial Languages, PM, v3 - p110
(General), PM101-108 American languages (Aboriginal) — Languages, v3 - p111
American languages (Aboriginal) — American languages north of Mexico, PM217-218, v3 - p112
American languages (Aboriginal) — American languages of British North America, PM238, v3 - p112
American languages (Aboriginal) — Literature, PM155-198, v3 - p111
American languages (Aboriginal) — Special languages of the United States and Canada (alphabetically), PM501, v3 - p112
American languages (Aboriginal) — Special languages of the United States and Canada, PM801-2711, v3 - p112
Language of Souther America and the West Indies — Special languages of South America and the West Indies, PM6308.6, v3 - p113
Languages of Mexico and Central America — Special languages of Mexico and Central America (alphabetically), PM3968.55-4068.6, v3 - p113
Mixed languages, PM7802-7895, v3 - p113
Indexes, AI, v10 - p3
By language of index — English, AI3, v10 - p3
Indexes to individual newspapers, A-Z, AI21, v10 - p3
Individual institutions: Asia, Africa,   Oceania, LG, v7 - p284
Asia — China, LG51, v7 - p284
Individual institutions: Europe, LF, v7 - p283
Individual institutions: United States, LD, v7 - p282
United States — California, College of. Oakland, California, LD729, v7 - p282
United States — New York (City). New School for Social Research, LD3837, v7 - p283
United States — New York. City University of New York, LD3835, v7 - p283
United States — Secondary schools, +elementary schools, and preschools. By place, A-Z, LD7501, v7 - p283
Indo-Iranian Philology and Literature, PK, v3 - p77
Armenian language and literature — Literature, PK8505-8831, v3 - p81
Middle Indo-Aryan dialects — Asoka inscriptions, PK1480, v3 - p77
Modern Indo-Aryan literature — History and collections, PK5416, v3 - p79
Sanskrit (Post-Vedic) literature — Individual authors or works, through 180790, PK3791, v3 - p79
Vedic literature, PK3406, v3 - p79
Industries. Land Use. Labor, HD, v6 - p195
Agricultural economics — Collective farms, HD1492, v6 - p217
Agricultural economics — Cooperative agriculture, HD1491, v6 - p217
Agricultural economics — Developing countries, HD1417, v6 - p216
Agricultural economics — Peasant proprietors, HD1513, v6 - p217
Economic development. Development economics. Economic growth — Congresses, HD73, v6 - p210
Economic development. Development economics. Economic growth — Collected works (nonserial), HD74-74.5, v6 - p210
Economic development. Development economics. Economic growth — History, HD78, v6 - p211
Industry — History, HD2321, v6 - p221
Industry — Theory. Relation to other subjects, HD2326, v6 - p221
Labor. Work. Working class — By industry or trade, A-Z, HD8039, v6 - p244
Labor. Work. Working class — Congresses, HD4813, v6 - p228
Labor. Work. Working class — Dictionaries. Encyclopedias, HD4839, v6 - p228
Labor. Work. Working class — General Works, HD4901, v6 - p228
Labor. Work. Working class — Human capital, HD4904.7, v6 - p229
Labor. Work. Working class — Leisure and work, HD4904.6, v6 - p229
Labor. Work. Working class — Professions (General). Professional employees, HD8038, v6 - p244
Labor. Work. Working class — Work and family, HD4904.25, v6 - p229
Land use — General Works, HD111, v6 - p212
Management. Industrial management — Bureaucracy, HD38.4, v6 - p200
Management. Industrial management — Business intelligence. Trade secrets, HD38.7, v6 - p200
Management. Industrial management — Business logistics, HD38.5, v6 - p200

Management. Industrial management — By region or country, A-Z, HD70, v6 - p209
Management. Industrial management — Competition, HD41, v6 - p201
Management. Industrial management — Conflict management, HD42, v6 - p201
Management. Industrial management — Dictionaries. Encyclopedias, HD30.15, v6 - p195
Management. Industrial management — Division of labor. Specialization, HD51, v6 - p201
Management. Industrial management — General special, HD38, v6 - p200
Management. Industrial management — Intellectual work. Intellectual capital, HD53, v6 - p201
Management. Industrial management — Leadership, HD57.7, v6 - p202
Management. Industrial management — Location of industry, HD58, v6 - p202
Management. Industrial management — Negotiation. Negotiation in business, HD58.6, v6 - p202
Management. Industrial management — Organizational behavior. Corporate culture, HD58.7, v6 - p203
Management. Industrial management — Organizational change. Organizational development, HD58.8, v6 - p203
Management. Industrial management — Organizational learning, HD58.82, v6 - p204
Management. Industrial management — Periodicals. Societies. Serials, HD28, v6 - p195
Management. Industrial management — Technological innovations, HD45, v6 - p201
Management. Industrial management, HD20.4-21, v6 - p195
Special industries and trades — Manufacturing industries, HD9720.1-9734, v6 - p259
Special industries and trades — Miscellaneous industries and trades, A-Z, HD9999, v6 - p261
Special industries and trades — Service industries (General), HD9980.5-9981.1, v6 - p261
Infantry, UD, v10 - p52
By region or country, UD59, v10 - p52
Information resources (General), ZA, v10 - p178
Information services. Information centers — General Works, ZA3157, v10 - p178
Information superhighway — By region or country, A-Z, ZA3250, v10 - p178
Information superhighway — General Works, ZA3225, v10 - p178
Research. How to find information — General Works, ZA3075, v10 - p178
Inscriptions. Epigraphy, CN, v5 - p16
International Law, JX, v7 - p94
International arbitration, organization, etc. — Study and teaching. Research, JX1904.5, v7 - p97
International arbitration, organization, etc. — Woman and peace movements, JX1965, v7 - p98
International law — Private international law. Conflict of laws, JX6731, v7 - p100
Study and teaching — By school, A-Z, JX1295, v7 - p94
Study and teaching — General Works, JX1291, v7 - p94
Study and teaching — Outlines. Syllabi, JX1297, v7 - p94
International Relations, JZ, v7 - p100
Dictionaries. Terms and phrases. Vocabulary., JZ1161, v7 - p100
Encyclopedias, JZ1160, v7 - p100
General Works, JZ1242, v7 - p100
International organizations and associations — Directories, JZ4838, v7 - p104
Non-military coercion — Reprisals, intervention, and sanctions, JZ6368-6373, v7 - p105
Promotion of peace. Peaceful change — By region or country, A-Z, JZ5584, v7 - p104
Promotion of peace. Peaceful change — General Works, JZ5538, v7 - p104
Promotion of peace. Peaceful change — History and theory of pacificism. By period, JZ5560, v7 - p104
Relation to other disciplines and topics — Gender theory and feminist theory in international relations, JZ1253.2, v7 - p101
Relation to other disciplines and topics — International economic policies and theories, JZ1252, v7 - p101
Relation to other disciplines and topics — Political and social psychology, JZ1253, v7 - p101
Relation to other disciplines and topics — Science and technology, JZ1254, v7 - p101
Relation to other disciplines and topics — Sociology of international relations and politics, JZ1251, v7 - p100
Scope of international relations. Political theory. Diplomacy — General Works, JZ1305, v7 - p101
The international community and its members. The state in international law, JZ4034, v7 - p104
Islam. Bahai Faith. Theosophy, etc., BP, v8 - p176
Bahai Faith — Dictionaries. Encyclopedias, BP327, v8 - p182
Islam — Dictionaries. Encyclopedias, BP40, v8 - p176
Islam — General special, BP163, v8 - p180
Islam — Islam and politics, BP173.7, v8 - p181
Islam — Islam and the state, BP173.6, v8 - p181
Islam — Topics not otherwise provided, A-Z, BP190.5, v8 - p181
Islam — Works against Islam and the Koran, BP169, v8 - p180
Other beliefs and movements — Dictionaries, BP601, v8 - p182
Other beliefs and movements — General Works, BP603, v8 - p182
Other beliefs and movements — Works. By movement, A-Z, BP605, v8 - p182
Theosophy — Special topics, A-Z, BP573, v8 - p182

Italian Literature, PQ4006-4847, v3 - p302
  Literary history and criticism — Encyclopedias. Dictionaries, PQ4006, v3 - p302
  Literary history and criticism — Relations to foreign literature, PQ4050, v3 - p302
  Literary history and criticism — Special classes, A-Z, PQ4055, v3 - p303
  Literary history and criticism — Special subjects, A-Z, PQ4053, v3 - p303
  Literary history and criticism — Women authors. Literary relations of women, PQ4063, v3 - p303
Italy, KKH, v7 - p192
  Trials — General collections, KKH38, v7 - p192
Journalism, PN4731-5648, v3 - p240
  Collections, extracts, etc. By subject, A-Z, PN6071, v3 - p255
  Comic books, strips, etc. — General Works, PN6710, v3 - p258
  Drama — Special classes of authors, PN6119.8, v3 - p257
  Fiction — English, PN6120.92, v3 - p257
  Fiction — Special. By subject or form, A-Z, PN6120.95, v3 - p257
  Journalism. The periodical press, etc. — Addresses, essays, lectures, PN4733, v3 - p240
  Journalism. The periodical press, etc. — General Works. Theory, scope, influence, etc., PN4731, v3 - p240
  Journalism. The periodical press, etc. — Journalism as a profession, PN4797, v3 - p243
  Poetry — By language, PN6101, v3 - p257
  Poetry — Poetry for children, PN6109.97, v3 - p257
  Poetry — Special. By subject or form, A-Z, PN6110, v3 - p257
  Quotations — Polyglot, PN6080, v3 - p255
  Wit and humor — Collections on special topics, A-Z, PN6231, v3 - p258
  Wit and humor — General Works. History, PN6147, v3 - p257
  Wit and humor — Special topics, A-Z, PN6149, v3 - p257
Judaism, BM, v8 - p169
  Biography — Collective, BM750, v8 - p175
  Biography — Individual, A-Z, BM755, v8 - p176
  Collected works — Individual authors, BM45, v8 - p169
  Collected works — Several authors, BM40, v8 - p169
  Dictionaries. Encyclopedias, BM50, v8 - p169
  Dogmatic Judaism — Conception of God, BM610, v8 - p174
  Dogmatic Judaism — Covenants. Covenant theology, BM612.5, v8 - p174
  Dogmatic Judaism — Man, BM627, v8 - p174
  Dogmatic Judaism — Other topics, A-Z, BM645, v8 - p174
  History — General special, BM157, v8 - p169
  Practical Judaism — Other special topics, A-Z, BM729, v8 - p175
  Pre-Talmudic Jewish literature (non-Biblical) — History and criticism, BM485, v8 - p171
  Relation of Judaism to special subject fields — Other, A-Z, BM538, v8 - p173
  Study and teaching — General special, BM71, v8 - p169
Languages of Eastern Asia, Africa, Oceania, PL, v3 - p82
  African languages and literature — Special languages (alphabetically), PL8233-8844, v3 - p110
  Chinese language and literature — Chinese language, PL1011-1455, v3 - p93
  Dravidian languages — Gondi, PL4633, v3 - p106
  Dravidian languages — Kurukh, PL4704, v3 - p106
  Dravidian languages — Malayalam (Malabar), PL4718-4718.9, v3 - p106
  Dravidian languages — Tamil (or Tamul), PL4758-4762, v3 - p106
  Dravidian languages, PL4609, v3 - p106
  Japanese language and literature — Japanese language, PL523-696, v3 - p83
  Korean language and literature — Korean language, PL918-937, v3 - p92
  Korean language and literature — Korean literature, PL957.5-992.62, v3 - p92
  Non-Aryan languages of India and Southeastern Asia in general, PL3508.5, v3 - p105
  Sino-Tibetan languages — Tibeto-Burman languages, PL3551, v3 - p105
  Tungus Manchu languages — Other languages, A-Z, PL481, v3 - p83
  Ural-Altaic languages — General, PL1, v3 - p82
Latin America, KG, v7 - p187
Latin America. Spanish America, F1205-3799, v4 - p563
  Central America — Antiquities. Indians (Ancient and modern) — General Works, F1434, v4 - p598
  Central America — Elements in the population, F1440, v4 - p606
  Central America — General Works, F1428, v4 - p598
  Central America — Societies. Collections, F1421, v4 - p597
  Latin America (General) — Gazetteers. Dictionaries. Geographic names, F1406, v4 - p585
  Latin America (General) — General Works, F1408, v4 - p585
  Latin America (General) — Social life and customs. Intellectual life, F1408.3, v4 - p585
  Latin America (General) — Societies. Collections, F1401, v4 - p584
  Mexico — Elements in the population, A-Z, F1392, v4 - p584
  Mexico — General Works, F1208, v4 - p563
  Mexico — Social life and customs. Civilization. Intellectual life, F1210, v4 - p563
  South America — Regions, F2216-2217, v4 - p627
  West Indies — Social life and customs. Civilization. Intellectual life, F1609.5, v4 - p616
Latin Philology and Language, PA2061-2802, v3 - p9
  Medieval Latin, PA2802, v3 - p9

  Study and teaching — General Works. History and method, PA2061, v3 - p9
Law in general. Comparative and uniform law. Jurisprudence, K, v7 - p105
  Bibliography — Library catalogs. Union lists, K40, v7 - p105
  Biography — Collective, K170, v7 - p106
  Comparative law. International uniform law — Birth control. Family planning. Population control, K2000, v7 - p110
  Comparative law. International uniform law — General Works, K559, v7 - p109
  Comparative law. International uniform law — Works on diverse aspects of a special subject and falling within several branches of the law. By subject, A-Z, K564, v7 - p109
  Comparative law. International uniform law — Public law, K3150, v7 - p111
  Dictionaries. Words and phrases — Bilingual. By language, A-Z, K52, v7 - p106
  Dictionaries. Words and phrases — Polyglot, K54, v7 - p106
  Dictionaries. Words and phrases — Unilingual, K50, v7 - p105
  Jurisprudence. Theory and philosophy of law — Bibliography, K201, v7 - p106
  Jurisprudence. Theory and philosophy of law — Encyclopedias, K204, v7 - p106
  Jurisprudence. Theory and philosophy of law — General Works. By author or title, A-Z, K230, v7 - p107
  Law societies. International bar associations — Particular law societies and international bar, K110, v7 - p106
  Maxims. Quotations, K58, v7 - p106
  Private international law. Conflict of laws — History, K7030, v7 - p115
  The legal profession — The lawyer and society, K117, v7 - p106
Law of Canada (British Columbia), KEB, v7 - p121
  Native peoples. Indians. Inuit — Other special topics, A-Z, KEB529.5, v7 - p121
Law of Canada (Northwest Territories), KEN, v7 - p121
  Native peoples. Indians. Inuit — General, KEN5929, v7 - p121
Law of Canada (Quebec), KEQ, v7 - p121
Law of Canada, KE, v7 - p120
  Native peoples. Indians. Inuit — Administration, KE7742, v7 - p120
  The legal profession — Particular classes of lawyers and types of careers, A-Z, KE332, v7 - p120
Law of England and Wales, KD, v7 - p115
  Common law, KD671, v7 - p116
  Constitutional law — General Works, KD3989.3, v7 - p118
  Criminal law — Administration of criminal justice. Reform of criminal law, enforcement, and procedure, KD7876, v7 - p118
  General and comprehensive works — Minor and popular works, KD662, v7 - p116
  History — General, KD532, v7 - p116
  Jurisprudence and philosophy of English law — General, KD640, v7 - p116
  Medical legislation — Artificial insemination. In vitro fertilization, KD3415, v7 - p118
  Social legislation — Birth control. Family planning. Population control, KD3340, v7 - p117
  Succession upon death — General, KD1500, v7 - p117
Law of France, KJV, v7 - p191
Law of Germany, KK, v7 - p191
  History of law. Rechts- und Verfassungsgeschichte — General, KK190, v7 - p191
Law of Ireland (Éire), KDK, v7 - p119
  Local laws — Cities, boroughs, towns, parishes, A-Z, KDK1930, v7 - p119
Law of nations, KZ, v7 - p199
  Encyclopedias, KZ1160, v7 - p200
  History, KZ1242, v7 - p200
  Legal research. Legal bibliography — General Works, KZ1234, v7 - p200
  Theory and principles — General Works, KZ1255, v7 - p200
Law of the Americas, Latin America and the West Indies, KDZ, v7 - p119
Law of the Sea, KZA, v7 - p202
  By region or country, A-Z, KZA1146, v7 - p202
Libraries, Z666-998, v10 - p88
  Booksellers' catalogs. Book prices — General Works, Z998, v10 - p96
  Library science. Information science — Bibliography, Z666, v10 - p88
  Library science. Information science — Classes of libraries, A-Z, Z675, v10 - p88
  Library science. Information science — Collected works (nonserial), Z674, v10 - p88
  Library science. Information science — Information organization, Z666.5, v10 - p88
  Library science. Information science — Library associations, Z673, v10 - p88
  Library science. Information science — Research, Z669.7, v10 - p88
  Library science. Information science — Shelving. Bookstacks, Z685, v10 - p90
  Library science. Information science — Statistical methods, Z669.8, v10 - p88
  Private libraries. Book collecting — Bibliography, Z988, v10 - p95
  Private libraries. Book collecting — Biography of book collectors, Z989, v10 - p95
  Private libraries. Book collecting — By region or country, A-Z, Z987.5, v10 - p95
  Private libraries. Book collecting — General Works, Z987, v10 - p95
Literature (General), PN1-1551, v3 - p113
  Authorship — Collections, PN137, v3 - p136
  Authorship — Dictionaries, PN141, v3 - p136
  Authorship — Early to 1800, PN144, v3 - p136
  Authorship — Imitation (in literature), PN166, v3 - p137
  Authorship — Literary landmarks. Home and haunts of authors, PN164, v3 - p137
  Authorship — Miscellany, PN165, v3 - p137
  Authorship — Other special topics, A-Z, PN171, v3 - p137
  Biography — Collective (more than one country), PN1583, v3 - p156
  Biography — Individual, A-Z, PN75, v3 - p128

Literature (General), PN1-1551 *(cont.)*

Broadcasting — By region or country, A-Z, PN1990.6, v3 - p163
Broadcasting — Dictionaries, PN1990.4, v3 - p163
Broadcasting — Special topics, A-Z, PN1990.9, v3 - p163
Collections — Collected essays of individual authors, PN1623, v3 - p157
Collections — Collected works, papers, essays, of individual authors, PN37, v3 - p114
Collections — Series. Monographs by different authors, PN35, v3 - p114
Collections — Various authors, PN1621, v3 - p157
Criticism — By region or country, A-Z, PN99, v3 - p135
Criticism — Congresses, PN80.5, v3 - p129
Criticism — Special topics. By subject, A-Z, PN98, v3 - p132
Criticism, PN1707, v3 - p159
Dictionaries, PN1625, v3 - p157
Dictionaries. Terminology, PN1579, v3 - p155
Digests of Literature. Synopses, etc., PN44, v3 - p115
Drama, PN1601-3307, v3 - p157
Dramatic representation. The theater — Biography of stage designers, PN2096, v3 - p217
Dramatic representation. The theater — College and school theatricals, PN3178, v3 - p232
Dramatic representation. The theater — Dictionaries. Terminology, PN2035, v3 - p213
Dramatic representation. The theater — Management, administration, production, and direction, PN2053, v3 - p214
Dramatic representation. The theater — Theatrical posters, PN2099, v3 - p218
Dramatic representation. The theater — Workers' theaters. Agitprop. Popular theater for community development, PN3305-3307, v3 - p233
Dramatic representation. The theater — The Jewish theater, PN3035, v3 - p232
Encyclopedias. Dictionaries — General, PN41, v3 - p114
Encyclopedias. Dictionaries — Miscellaneous and special, PN43, v3 - p114
General Works on the drama and the stage — 1801-, PN1655, v3 - p158
General Works, PN1584, v3 - p156
History — Origins of the drama, PN1737, v3 - p159
Indexes to children's plays, PN1627, v3 - p157
Literary history — Black literature (General), PN841, v3 - p148
Literary history — Jewish literature in various languages, PN842, v3 - p149
Literary history — Theory and method, PN441, v3 - p140
Literary research, PN73, v3 - p128
Motion pictures — Amateur motion pictures, PN1995.8, v3 - p186
Motion pictures — Anecdotes, facetiae, satire, PN1994.9, v3 - p182
Motion pictures — Authorship, scenario writing, etc., PN1996, v3 - p199
Motion pictures — Dictionaries, PN1993.45, v3 - p172
Motion pictures — General special, PN1995, v3 - p182
Motion pictures — General Works, PN1994, v3 - p181
Motion pictures — History, PN1993.5, v3 - p172
Motion pictures — Miscellaneous, PN1998, v3 - p200
Motion pictures — Museums, archives, exhibitions, festivals, etc., PN1993.4, v3 - p172
Motion pictures — Other special topics, A-Z, PN1995.9, v3 - p186
Motion pictures — Plays, scenarios, etc., PN1997-1997.85, v3 - p199
Motion pictures — Relation to ethics, etc., PN1995.5, v3 - p184
Motion pictures — Relation to history, PN1995.2, v3 - p184
Motion pictures — Relation to literature, PN1995.3, v3 - p184
Motion pictures — Relation to the arts, PN1995.25, v3 - p184
Motion pictures — Silent films, PN1995.75, v3 - p185
Motion pictures — Special corporations, A-Z, PN1999, v3 - p212
Motion pictures — Study and teaching, PN1993.7, v3 - p181
Motion pictures — Yearbooks, PN1993.3, v3 - p172
Museums, libraries, etc., PN1620, v3 - p157
Nonbroadcast video recordings — By region or country, A-Z, PN1992.934, v3 - p171
Nonbroadcast video recordings — Catalogs, PN1992.95, v3 - p172
Nonbroadcast video recordings — General Works, PN1992.935, v3 - p171
Performing arts as a profession, PN1580, v3 - p155
Periodicals — American and English, PN2, v3 - p113
Philosophy, aesthetics, scope, relations, etc. — General Works, PN1631, v3 - p157
Philosophy, aesthetics, scope, relations, etc. — Special topics, A-Z, PN1633, v3 - p157
Poetry — Dictionaries, PN1021, v3 - p152
Poetry — Miscellaneous essays, etc., PN1055, v3 - p153
Poetry — Poets on poetry. Anthologies in praise of poetry, etc., PN1064, v3 - p153
Poetry — Special topics, A-Z, PN1059, v3 - p153
Poetry — Study and teaching, PN1101, v3 - p154
Special topics, A-Z, PN1590, v3 - p156
Special types — Clowns, PN1955, v3 - p161
Special types — General Works, PN1892, v3 - p161
Special types — Monodrama, PN1936, v3 - p161
Special types — Religious plays, PN1880, v3 - p161
Study and teaching — General special, PN61, v3 - p128
Study and teaching — General Works, PN59, v3 - p128
Study and teaching. Research — General Works, PN1576, v3 - p155
Technique of dramatic composition — Character treatment, PN1689, v3 - p159
Technique of dramatic composition — Tragic effect. Tragic fault, poetic justice, etc., PN1675, v3 - p159
Terminology, PN44.5, v3 - p115
Theory. Philosophy. Esthetics — Forms of literature, PN45.5, v3 - p116
Theory. Philosophy. Esthetics — General Works. Ideals, content, etc. Plots, motives, PN45, v3 - p115

Literature on music, ML, v9 - p1

Bibliography — By region or country, A-Z, ML120, v9 - p9
Bibliography — By topic, A-Z, ML128, v9 - p11
Bibliography — Individual composers, A-Z, ML134, v9 - p15
Bibliography — Local, A-Z, ML125, v9 - p11
Bibliography — Other individuals, A-Z, ML134.5, v9 - p18
Dictionaries. Encyclopedias — By region or country, A-Z, ML101, v9 - p6
Dictionaries. Encyclopedias — By topic, A-Z, ML102, v9 - p6
Dictionaries. Encyclopedias — General Works, ML100, v9 - p5
Dictionaries. Encyclopedias — Pronouncing, ML109, v9 - p8
Dictionaries. Encyclopedias — Terminological, ML108, v9 - p8
Directories. Almanacs — International, ML12, v9 - p1
History and criticism — Interpretation. Performance practice, ML457, v9 - p76
History and criticism — Music of the Jews, ML3776, v9 - p107
History and criticism — Musical criticism, ML3785, v9 - p107
Music as a profession. Vocational guidance, ML3795, v9 - p108
Music librarianship — General Works, ML111, v9 - p8
Music printing and publishing — General Works, ML112, v9 - p8
Music trade — General Works, ML3790, v9 - p108
Music trade — Individual record companies and labels, A-Z, ML3792, v9 - p108
Philosophy and physics of music — General Works, ML3800, v9 - p110
Serials — United States, ML1, v9 - p1
Special aspects of the subject as a whole — Anecdotes, humor, etc., ML65, v9 - p4
Special aspects of the subject as a whole — Music in art. Musical instruments in art, ML85, v9 - p5
Special aspects of the subject as a whole — Pictorial works, ML89, v9 - p5
Special aspects of the subject as a whole — Topics not elsewhere provided for, ML63, v9 - p4
Special aspects of the subject as a whole — Women and music, ML82, v9 - p4
Special aspects of the subject as a whole — Writings of musicians (Collections), ML90, v9 - p5

Local Government. Municipal Government, JS, v7 - p88

Federal-city relations. State-local relations. Municipal home rule, JS113, v7 - p88
General Works, JS78, v7 - p88
History — Twentieth century, JS67, v7 - p88
Latin America, JS2061-2061.2, v7 - p89
Political participation. Neighborhood government, JS211, v7 - p88

Logic, BC, v8 - p72

Collected works (nonserial), BC6, v8 - p72
Deontic logic, BC145, v8 - p77
First-order logic, BC128, v8 - p75
History — Special topics, A-Z, BC21, v8 - p72
Logic of chance. Probability, BC141, v8 - p77
Many-valued logic, BC126, v8 - p75
Philosophy. Methodology. Relation to other topics — Other, BC57, v8 - p73
Philosophy. Methodology. Relation to other topics — Relation to ethics, BC55, v8 - p73
Philosophy. Methodology. Relation to other topics — Relation to speculative philosophy, BC51, v8 - p72
Philosophy. Methodology. Relation to other topics, BC50, v8 - p72
Special topics — Fallacies, BC175, v8 - p77
Special topics — Other special topics, A-Z, BC199-199.2, v8 - p79
Special topics — Proof, BC173, v8 - p77
Special topics — Propositions. Prediction. Judgment, BC181, v8 - p79
Special topics — Reasoning, argumentation, etc., BC177, v8 - p78
Special topics — Truth and error. Certitude, BC171, v8 - p77
Symbolic and mathematical logic — 1801-, BC135, v8 - p75

Maintenance and transportation, UC, v10 - p51

Supplies and stores — Contracts, UC267, v10 - p52

Manners and Customs (General), GT, v6 - p68

Costume. Dress. Fashion — Dictionaries. Encyclopedias, GT507, v6 - p69
Customs relating to private life — Family life. Home life, GT2420, v6 - p70
General Works, treatises, and textbooks — 1975-, GT76, v6 - p68
Household arts. Households — By region or country, A-Z, GT481, v6 - p69
Personal beauty, GT499, v6 - p69

Manufacturers, TS, v1 - p553

Country divisions, TS17.4-23, v1 - p553
Encyclopedias and dictionaries, TS9, v1 - p553
General special, TS149, v1 - p554
Juvenile works. Popular works, TS146, v1 - p554

Maps, G3701-9250, v6 - p14

Marines, VE, v10 - p70

Mathematical Geography. Cartography, GA, v6 - p15
Cartography — Cadastral mapping, GA109.5, v6 - p15
Cartography — Elementary map drawing and reading, GA130, v6 - p16
Cartography — General special (Special aspects of the subject as a whole), GA108.7, v6 - p15
Cartography — Topographic drawing, GA125, v6 - p16
Mathematical geography — General special (Special aspects of the subject as a whole), GA23, v6 - p15
Mathematics, QA, v1 - p28
Addresses, essays, lectures, QA7-7.2, v1 - p29
Collected works (nonserial), QA3, v1 - p28
Communication of mathematical information, QA42, v1 - p39
Dictionaries and encyclopedias, QA5, v1 - p29
Formulas, notation, abbreviations, QA41, v1 - p39
Handbooks, manuals, etc., QA40, v1 - p38
Mathematics as a profession, QA10.5, v1 - p32
Miscellany and curiosa, QA99, v1 - p61
Popular works, QA93, v1 - p59
Problems, exercises, examinations, QA43, v1 - p39
Societies, congresses, serial, QA1, v1 - p28
Study and teaching. Research, QA11, v1 - p32
Theory of errors. Least squares, QA275, v1 - p73
Women in mathematics. Women mathematicians, QA27.5, v1 - p35
Mechanical engineering and machinery, TJ, v1 - p478
Flow of fluids in pipes. Flowmeters, TJ935, v1 - p488
Machine parts, TJ243, v1 - p485
Power plants (General), TJ164, v1 - p480
Principles of mechanism. Kinematics of machinery, TJ175, v1 - p481
Medieval and Modern Latin Literature, PA8030-8555, v3 - p19
History and criticism — Special topics, A-Z, PA8030, v3 - p19
Special countries, A-Z, PA8045, v3 - p19
Mexico and Central America: Mexico, KGF, v7 - p187
Microbiology, QR, v1 - p366
Dictionaries and encyclopedias, QR9, v1 - p366
Pathogenic microorganisms.disease, A-Z, QR201, v1 - p369
Popular works, QR56, v1 - p367
Societies, congresses, serial collections, yearbooks, QR1, v1 - p366
Military administration, UB, v10 - p45
By region or country, UB23-87, v10 - p45
Civil law relating to the military, UB775, v10 - p51
Command and control systems, UB212, v10 - p46
Command of troops. Leadership, UB210, v10 - p46
Compulsory service. Conscription and exemption — General Works, UB340, v10 - p48
Intelligence — By region or country, A-Z, UB251, v10 - p46
Intelligence — General Works, UB250, v10 - p46
Military police. Gendarmes — By region or country, A-Z, UB825, v10 - p51
Military service as a profession, UB147, v10 - p46
Minorities, women, etc., in armed forces — General Works, UB416, v10 - p50
Prisons and prisoners — General Works, UB800, v10 - p51
Psychological warfare. Propaganda — General Works, UB275, v10 - p48
Staffs of armies — General Works, UB220, v10 - p46
Military engineering, UG23-612, v10 - p54
Air defenses — General Works, UG730, v10 - p58
Attack and defense. Siege warfare — Biological warfare. Bacterial warfare, UG447.8, v10 - p55
Attack and defense. Siege warfare — Tanks, armored cars, etc., UG446.5, v10 - p55
Ballistic missile defenses — General Works, UG740, v10 - p58
Biography — Individual, A-Z, UG128, v10 - p54
Biography — Individual, A-Z, UG626.2, v10 - p56
By region or country — Other regions or countries, A-Z, UG1525, v10 - p61
By region or country — Other regions or countries, A-Z, UG635, v10 - p58
By region or country — United States, UG1523, v10 - p60
Dictionaries. Encyclopedias, UG628, v10 - p56
Directed-energy weapons, UG486.5, v10 - p56
General Works, UG1520, v10 - p60
General Works, UG630, v10 - p56
Military architecture and building, UG460, v10 - p55
Military surveillance, UG475, v10 - p55
Space warfare. Interplanetary warfare, UG1530, v10 - p61
Tactics — By region or country, UG700, v10 - p58
Military science (General), U, v10 - p7
Addresses, essays, lectures, U19, v10 - p7
Army lists. By region or country, A-Z, U11, v10 - p7
Atomic warfare, U263, v10 - p19
Atomic weapons — General Works, U264, v10 - p20
Atomic weapons — Other regions or countries, A-Z, U264.5, v10 - p21
Biography — Collective, U51, v10 - p14
Commando tactics, U262, v10 - p18
Counterinsurgency. Counter-guerrilla warfare, U241, v10 - p18
Debarkation. Landing maneuvers, U200, v10 - p17
Dictionaries. Encyclopedias — General Works, U24, v10 - p10

General special, U104, v10 - p16
General Works — 1789-, U102, v10 - p15
General Works — Early through 1788, U101, v10 - p15
History of arms and armor — Armor, U825, v10 - p22
History of arms and armor — General Works, U800, v10 - p22
History of military science — By region or country, A-Z, U43, v10 - p14
History of military science — General Works, U27, v10 - p11
History of military science — Medieval, U37, v10 - p12
Joint operations. Combined operations, U260, v10 - p18
Logistics, U168, v10 - p17
Military sports — By region or country, A-Z, U328, v10 - p21
Military symbols and abbreviations, U26, v10 - p11
Popular works, U105, v10 - p16
Small wars. Guerrilla warfare. Indian fighting, U240, v10 - p17
Strategy — Deterrence, U162.6, v10 - p16
Strategy — Miscellaneous topics (not A-Z), U163, v10 - p17
Tactics — Special topics, A-Z, U167.5, v10 - p17
War games. Kriegsspiel — General Works, U310, v10 - p21
War. Philosophy. Military sociology — Ethics. Morale, U22, v10 - p10
War. Philosophy. Military sociology — Military psychology, U22.3, v10 - p10
Weapons of mass destruction, U793, v10 - p22
Minor services of navies, VG, v10 - p71
Naval aviation. Air service. Air warfare — General Works, VG90, v10 - p71
Naval aviation. Air service. Air warfare — Other regions or countries, A-Z, VG95, v10 - p71
Modern Languages. Celtic Languages, PB1-1607, v3 - p20
Literature — Encyclopedias. Dictionaries, PB2202, v3 - p21
Welsh. Cymric, PB2202-2369, v3 - p21
Motor vehicles. Aeronautics. Astronautics, TL, v1 - p515
Economic or applied geology and mineralogy, TN260, v1 - p527
Electrical engineering and equipment, TN343, v1 - p528
Marine mineral resources, TN264, v1 - p528
Metallic ores (General), TN265, v1 - p528
Mineral deposits. Metallic ore deposits, TN263, v1 - p527
Mining engineering. Metallurgy, TN, v1 - p526
Special countries (Including government reports on mineral resources and economic geology), TN23-115, v1 - p526
Museums. Collectors and collecting, AM, v10 - p3
Biography — Individual, A-Z, AM3.6, v10 - p3
Description and history of museums — Individual museums. By place, A-Z, AM101, v10 - p4
General special, AM7, v10 - p4
General Works — 1801-, AM5, v10 - p3
Periodicals, societies, collections, etc., AM1, v10 - p3
Musical instruction and study, MT, v9 - p114
Analysis and appreciation of musical works — Collections of music for analysis and appreciation, MT91, v9 - p123
Analysis and appreciation of musical works — General Works, MT90, v9 - p122
Analysis and appreciation of musical works — Individual composers, MT92, v9 - p123
Composition. Elements and techniques of music — Composition using mechanical devices or prescribed formulas, MT41, v9 - p118
Composition. Elements and techniques of music — Composition, MT40, v9 - p118
Composition. Elements and techniques of music — Continuo, MT49, v9 - p119
Composition. Elements and techniques of music — Counterpoint. Polyphony, MT55, v9 - p120
Composition. Elements and techniques of music — Electronic music. Computer music, MT56, v9 - p120
Composition. Elements and techniques of music — Harmony, MT50, v9 - p119
Composition. Elements and techniques of music — Rhythm, MT42, v9 - p119
Composition. Elements and techniques of music — Scales, MT45, v9 - p119
Conducting. Score reading and playing, MT85, v9 - p122
History and criticism — By region or country, A-Z, MT3, v9 - p115
Improvisation. Accompaniment. Transposition, MT68, v9 - p121
Instrumental techniques — General Works, MT170, v9 - p126
Interpretation, MT75, v9 - p122
Music theory — Early works to 1600, MT5.5, v9 - p115
Musical theater — Performing, MT956, v9 - p130
Musical theater — Production, MT955, v9 - p130
Notation — General Works, MT35, v9 - p117
Singing and vocal technique — General Works, MT820, v9 - p128
Singing and vocal technique — History of vocal instruction and study, MT823, v9 - p129
Singing and vocal technique — Interpretation, phrasing, expression, etc., MT892, v9 - p130
Singing and vocal technique — Physiology and care of the voice, MT821, v9 - p129
Specific systems and methods — Jaques-Dalcroze, MT22, v9 - p117
Theory and history of music education — General Works, MT1, v9 - p114
Tuning, MT165, v9 - p126

National bibliography, Z1201-4891, v10 - p101
America — Biobibliography of Americanists, Z1206, v10 - p101
America — General bibliography, Z1201, v10 - p101
America — Private libraries, and booksellers' catalogs of Americana, Z1207, v10 - p101
America — Saint Helena. Tristan da Cunha. Ascension Island, Z1946, v10 - p110
Europe — Commonwealth of Nations, Z2000.9, v10 - p111
Europe — Czechoslovakia. Czech Republic, Z2136-2137, v10 - p115
Europe — France, Z2171-2184, v10 - p115
Europe — General bibliography, Z2000, v10 - p110
Europe — Germany, Z2230-2241, v10 - p115
Europe — Great Britain and Ireland. England, Z2001-2014, v10 - p111
Europe — Greece, Z2281-2304, v10 - p115
Europe — Italy, Z2341-2360.3, v10 - p116
Europe — Mediterranean area, Z2260, v10 - p115
Europe — Rome. Roman Empire, Z2340, v10 - p116
Europe — Spain and Portugal. Spain, Z2691-2700, v10 - p117
Europe — Switzerland, Z2771, v10 - p118
Natural History (General), QH11-251, v1 - p231
Addresses, essays, lectures, QH311, v1 - p250
Addresses, essays, lectures, QH81, v1 - p239
Bioethics, QH332, v1 - p253
Biological invasions, QH353, v1 - p254
Biology (General), QH302.5-671, v1 - p248
Biometry. Biomathematics. Mathematical models, QH323.5, v1 - p250
Classification. Nomenclature, QH83, v1 - p240
Development. Morphogenesis, QH491, v1 - p268
Dictionaries and encyclopedias, QH13, v1 - p231
Dictionaries and encyclopedias, QH302.5, v1 - p248
Extinction (Biology), QH78, v1 - p239
General biochemistry of plants and animals, QH345, v1 - p253
General Works, treatises, and textbooks, QH303, v1 - p249
Geobiology. Biosphere, QH343.4, v1 - p253
Morphology, QH351, v1 - p253
Natural history illustration, QH46.5, v1 - p236
Origin and beginnings of life, QH325, v1 - p251
Philosophy of biology, QH331, v1 - p252
Popular works, QH309, v1 - p250
Popular works, QH45.5, v1 - p235
Population biology, QH352, v1 - p253
Pre-Linnaean works (through 1735), QH41, v1 - p235
Regeneration, QH499, v1 - p268
Social aspects of biology, QH333, v1 - p253
Special aspects of the subjectas a whole, QH313, v1 - p250
Voyages and expeditions, QH11, v1 - p231
Works about Linnaeus, QH44, v1 - p235
Naval administration, VB, v10 - p69
Intelligence — General Works, VB230, v10 - p69
Vocational guidance. The navy as a career. Job analysis, VB259, v10 - p69
Naval architecture. Shipbuilding. Marine engineering, VM, v10 - p73
Biography — Individual, A-Z, VM140, v10 - p74
Directories, VM12, v10 - p73
History — General Works, VM15, v10 - p74
History — Medieval, VM17, v10 - p74
Illustrations of ships of all kinds. Pictorial works, VM307, v10 - p75
Marine engineering — General Works, VM600, v10 - p77
Naval architecture (General) — General Works, 1861-, VM145, v10 - p75
Ship models. Steamboat models — General Works, VM298, v10 - p75
Shipbuilding industry. Shipyards — General Works, VM298.5, v10 - p75
Shipbuilding industry. Shipyards — Shipbuilding companies and shipyards, A-Z, VM301, v10 - p75
Special types of vessels — By construction or rigging, A-Z, VM311, v10 - p75
Special types of vessels — Hydrofoil boats, VM362, v10 - p76
Study and teaching — General Works, VM165, v10 - p75
Theory of the ship. Principles of naval architecture — General Works, VM156, v10 - p75
Naval maintenance, VC, v10 - p70
Naval ordnance, VF, v10 - p70
Collected works (nonserial), VF7, v10 - p70
Naval weapons systems — General Works, VF346, v10 - p71
Naval science (General), V, v10 - p62
Convoys, V182, v10 - p64
Dictionaries and encyclopedias — General, V23, v10 - p62
History and antiquities of naval science — By region or country, A-Z, V55, v10 - p63
History and antiquities of naval science — General Works, V27, v10 - p62
History and antiquities of naval science — Philosophy of history, V25, v10 - p62
Naval logistics, V179, v10 - p64
Naval strategy — General special, V165, v10 - p64
Naval tactics — General Works, V167, v10 - p64
Salutes. Honors. Ceremonies, V310, v10 - p64
Submarine warfare — General Works, V210, v10 - p64

War vessels: Construction, armament, etc. — General Works, V750, v10 - p64
Navies: Organization, distribution, naval situation, VA, v10 - p66
General Works, VA10, v10 - p66
Navies of the world — General Works, VA40, v10 - p66
Navigation. Merchant marine, VK, v10 - p71
Biography — Collective, VK139, v10 - p72
Biography — Individual, A-Z, VK140, v10 - p72
History, conditions, etc. — General Works, VK15, v10 - p71
Lighthouse service — History, VK1015, v10 - p73
Marine hydrography. Hydrographic surveying — By region or country, A-Z, VK597, v10 - p73
Science of navigation — History, VK549, v10 - p73
Seamanship — General Works, VK541, v10 - p72
Shipwrecks and fires — Submarine disasters, VK1265, v10 - p73
Numismatics, CJ, v5 - p15
Dictionaries. Encyclopedias — General Works, CJ67, v5 - p15
History — General Works, CJ59, v5 - p15
Oceanography, GC, v6 - p23
Dictionaries. Encyclopedias, GC9, v6 - p23
Elementary textbooks, GC16, v6 - p23
Estuarine oceanography — Congresses, GC96.5, v6 - p24
Estuarine oceanography — General Works, GC97, v6 - p24
General special (Special aspects of the subject as a whole), GC28, v6 - p24
General Works, treatises, and advanced textbooks — 1975-, GC11.2, v6 - p23
Handbooks, tables, etc., GC24, v6 - p24
Marine pollution. Sea water pollution — Congresses, GC1081, v6 - p25
Marine pollution. Sea water pollution — General Works, GC1085, v6 - p25
Ocean-atmosphere interaction — Methodology, GC190.5, v6 - p24
Oceanographic expeditions, GC63, v6 - p24
Oceanographic research — General Works, GC57, v6 - p24
Philosophy. Relation to other topics. Methodology — Special methods, A-Z, GC10.4, v6 - p23
Popular works, GC21, v6 - p24
Sea level — General Works, GC89, v6 - p24
Submarine topography — Ocean bottom. Ocean basin, GC87.2, v6 - p24
Underwater exploration — General Works, GC65, v6 - p24
Oriental Philology and Literature, PJ, v3 - p65
Arabic literature — By region or country, PJ8005-8453, v3 - p76
Arabic literature — Translations, PJ7694-7695, v3 - p74
Hebrew — Other languages used by Jews, PJ5089, v3 - p70
Languages — Encyclopedias. Dictionaries, PJ31, v3 - p65
Translations of Egyptian literature — Poetry, PJ1945, v3 - p67
Translations of Egyptian literature — Selections. Anthologies, etc., PJ1943, v3 - p66
Other services, UH, v10 - p61
Military unions. Union movements in armed forces — General Works, UH740, v10 - p62
Protection of morals and health, UH630, v10 - p61
Pacific area: Australia, KU, v7 - p199
Pacific area: Pacific area jurisdictions: Nauru, KVU, v7 - p199
Painting, ND, v9 - p259
Catalogues raisonnés (General), ND40, v9 - p259
Examination and conservation of paintings — Technical examination: Expertising, x-ray, micrography, etc., ND1635, v9 - p297
General Works — 1800-, ND1135, v9 - p292
General Works — Early works to 1800, ND1130, v9 - p292
General Works — Essays, lectures, etc., ND1150, v9 - p292
General Works — General special, ND1140, v9 - p292
History — General Works, ND50, v9 - p259
History — Islamic painting, ND198, v9 - p261
History — Special countries, ND205-457, v9 - p261
Illuminating of manuscripts and books — Biographical dictionaries, ND2890, v9 - p299
Illuminating of manuscripts and books — Dictionaries, ND2889, v9 - p299
Illuminating of manuscripts and books — Special techniques, A-Z, ND3327, v9 - p301
Mural painting — Special countries, ND2608-2880, v9 - p298
Other general catalogs of paintings. Indexes to paintings, ND45, v9 - p259
Painting in relation to other subjects, A-Z, ND1170, v9 - p292
Painting materials and methods — General. Technical manuals for artists, ND1500, v9 - p297
Painting materials and methods — Pigments, ND1510, v9 - p297
Technique. Styles. Materials and methods, ND1260-1265, v9 - p293
Personal bibliography, Z8015.6-8992, v10 - p162
A — Adams, John, Z8015.6, v10 - p162
A — Adams, John Q., Z8015.7, v10 - p162
A — Addison, Joseph, Z8015.87, v10 - p163
A — Alexander, Lloyd, Z8025.6, v10 - p163
A — Arthur, King, Z8045, v10 - p163
A — Asimov, Isaac, Z8045.59, v10 - p163
A — Augustinus, Aurelius, Saint, bp. of Hippo, Z8047.7, v10 - p163
A — Austen, Jane, Z8048, v10 - p163
B — Balfour, Arthur, Z8068.78, v10 - p163
B — Balzac, Honoré de, Z8069.2, v10 - p163

Personal bibliography, Z8015.6-8992 *(cont.)*
B — Beckett, Samuel, Z8086.37, v10 - p163
B — Benchley, Robert, Z8089.12, v10 - p163
B — Blackwood, Algernon, Z8102.23, v10 - p163
B — Boccaccio, Giovanni, Z8106, v10 - p163
B — Boethius, Z8106.3, v10 - p163
B — Boorstin, D.J., Z8109.16, v10 - p163
B — Boswell, James, Z8110.2, v10 - p164
B — Bradstreet, Annie, Z8113.6, v10 - p164
B — Braque, Georges, Z8115.66, v10 - p164
B — Bridges, R.S., Z8119.2, v10 - p164
B — Browning, Elizabeth (Barrett), Z8124.4, v10 - p164
B — Buero Vallejo, Antonio, Z8129.8, v10 - p164
B — Burchfield, Charles, Z8131.65, v10 - p164
B — Burroughs, E.R., Z8136.15, v10 - p164
B — Burroughs, W.S., Z8136.17, v10 - p164
B — Byron, G.G.N. Byron, 6th baron, Z8139, v10 - p164
C — Calhoun, J.C. (John Caldwell), Z8140.62, v10 - p164
C — Chaucer, Z8164, v10 - p164
C — Chisholm, Shirley, Z8167.47, v10 - p165
C — Churchill, Sir, W.L.S., Z8169.45, v10 - p165
C — Cleveland, Grover, Z8176.45, v10 - p165
C — Columbus, Z8187, v10 - p165
C — Conrad, Joseph, Z8189.7, v10 - p165
C — Cooper, J.F., Z8191.7, v10 - p165
C — Coward, Noel, Z8196.6, v10 - p165
C — Curzon, G.N., Z8206.58, v10 - p165
D — Dalton, John, Z8212.7, v10 - p166
D — Davie, Donald, Z8218.7, v10 - p166
D — Dee, John, Z8220.9, v10 - p166
D — Defoe, Daniel, Z8221, v10 - p166
D — Dewey, John, Z8228, v10 - p166
D — Dickens, Charles, Z8230, v10 - p166
D — Donne, John, Z8237, v10 - p166
D — Dostoevskii, F.M., Z8237.9, v10 - p166
D — Dürer, Albrecht, Z8246, v10 - p166
D — Duras, Marguerite, Z8250.3, v10 - p166
D — Durrell, Lawrence, Z8250.54, v10 - p167
E — Eden, Anthony, Z8254.74, v10 - p167
E — Edwards, Jonathan, Z8255.5, v10 - p167
E — Eliot, George, pseud, Z8259, v10 - p167
E — Eliot, T.S., Z8260.5, v10 - p167
F — Ford, Gerald, Z8308.34, v10 - p167
F — Forsyth, P.T., Z8309.4, v10 - p167
F — Franklin, Benjamin, Z8313, v10 - p167
F — Friel, Brian, Z8317.15, v10 - p167
F — Fulbright, James William, Z8318.22, v10 - p167
G — Gandhi, M.K., Z8322.7, v10 - p167
G — Garfield, J.A., Z8324.18, v10 - p167
G — Garland, Hamlin, Z8324.34, v10 - p167
G — Gauguin, Paul, Z8328.3, v10 - p167
G — Ginsberg, Allen, Z8342.5, v10 - p167
G — Grenville, George, Z8369.253, v10 - p168
G — Guillaume, de Lorris, Z8374.6478, v10 - p168
H — Harding, W.G., Z8386.2, v10 - p168
H — Hardy, Thomas, Z8386.5, v10 - p168
H — Harrison, W.H., Z8387.97, v10 - p168
H — Harte, Bret, Z8388.65, v10 - p168
H — Hawthorne, Nathaniel, Z8393, v10 - p168
H — Heaney, Seamus, Z8393.6, v10 - p168
H — Hemingway, Ernest, Z8396.3, v10 - p168
H — Hitler, Adolf, Z8409.6, v10 - p168
H — Holbein, Hans, the younger, Z8414, v10 - p168
H — Hughes, Langston, Z8423.3, v10 - p169
H — Hurston, Z.N., Z8428.66, v10 - p169
I — Ivanov, V.I., Z8442.65, v10 - p169
J — Jackson, Andrew, Z8443, v10 - p169
J — James, Henry, Z8447, v10 - p169
J — Jeanne d'Arc, Saint, Z8451, v10 - p169
J — Jesus Christ, Z8455, v10 - p169
J — Johnson, Andrew, Z8455.567, v10 - p169
J — Johnson, Samuel, 1709-1784, Z8455.8, v10 - p169
J — Jonson, Ben, Z8456.6, v10 - p169
K — Kavanagh, Patrick, Z8460.875, v10 - p169
K — Kennedy, J.F., Z8462.8, v10 - p170
K — King, M.L., Z8464.44, v10 - p170
K — Kosinski, J.N., Z8467.523, v10 - p170
L — Lawrence, D.H., Z8490.5, v10 - p170
L — Lawrence, T.E., Z8491.5, v10 - p170
L — Le Fanu, J.S., Z8492.7, v10 - p170
L — Lincoln, Abraham, Z8505, v10 - p170

L — Lispector, Clarice, Z8511.8, v10 - p170
M — Machiavelli, Niccolò, Z8534, v10 - p170
M — Malory, Sir Thomas, Z8545.5, v10 - p170
M — Malraux, André, Z8545.8, v10 - p170
M — Mann, Thomas, Z8547.41, v10 - p170
M — Mao, T^se-tung, Z8548.3, v10 - p170
M — March, William, Z8549.8, v10 - p171
M — Marlowe, Christopher, Z8550.4, v10 - p171
M — Matisse, Z8554.32, v10 - p171
M — McKinley, William, Z8561.18, v10 - p171
M — Melville, Herman, Z8562.58, v10 - p171
M — Mencken, H.L., Z8563.5, v10 - p171
M — Michener, James A., Z8572.4, v10 - p171
M — Milton, John, Z8578, v10 - p171
M — Monroe, James, Z8587.8, v10 - p171
M — Montgomery of Alamein, B.L.M., Z8591.3, v10 - p172
M — Moore, George, Z8592.6, v10 - p172
M — More, Sir Thomas, Saint, Z8592.8, v10 - p172
N — Naipaul, V.S. (Viviadha Surajprasad), Z8610.37, v10 - p172
N — Nasser, G.A., Z8614.74, v10 - p172
N — Nietsche, F.W., Z8628.85, v10 - p172
N — Nixon, R.M., Z8629.4, v10 - p172
O — Odets, Clifford, Z8641.13, v10 - p172
O — O'Neill, E.G., Z8644.5, v10 - p172
O — Oud, J.J.P., Z8648.43, v10 - p172
P — Pasternak, B.L., Z8662.35, v10 - p172
P — Peel, Robert, Sir, Z8667.8, v10 - p172
P — Piaget, Jean, Z8685.6, v10 - p172
P — Pisan, Christine de, Z8693.7, v10 - p172
P — Pitt, William, Z8694.5, v10 - p173
P — Poe, E.A., Z8699, v10 - p173
P — Pushkin, A.S., Z8718, v10 - p173
P — Pythagoras, Z8722.3, v10 - p173
R — Rabelais, François, Z8730, v10 - p173
R — Radcliffe, Ann, Z8730.335, v10 - p173
R — Robinson, E.A., Z8748.37, v10 - p173
R — Roosevelt, Eleanor, Z8757.27, v10 - p173
R — Rowse, A.L., Z8763.67, v10 - p173
R — Rush, Benjamin, Z8764.8, v10 - p173
S — Sarton, May, Z8784.43, v10 - p173
S — Scott, Sir Walter, Z8802, v10 - p173
S — Shaffer, Peter, Z8809.6, v10 - p174
S — Shaw, G.B., Z8814.5, v10 - p175
S — Sillitoe, Alan, Z8819.125, v10 - p175
S — Smith, Stevie, Z8822.32, v10 - p175
S — Spenser, Edmund, Z8830.8, v10 - p175
S — Spinoza, Benedictus de, Z8831, v10 - p175
S — Steinbeck, John, Z8839.4, v10 - p175
S — Stevens, Wallace, Z8842.7, v10 - p175
S — Stirling-Maxwell, Sir William bart, Z8847, v10 - p176
S — Sun, Yat-sen, Z8854.4, v10 - p176
S — Symons, Arthur, Z8857.6, v10 - p176
T — Taft, W.H., Z8857.88, v10 - p176
T — Talleyrand-Périgord, Charles Maurice de, prince de Bénévent, Z8858.5, v10 - p176
T — Taylor, P.H., Z8862.7, v10 - p176
T — Tennyson, Alfred Tennyson, baron, Z8866, v10 - p176
T — Trilling, Lionel, Z8885.48, v10 - p176
T — Truman, Harry, Z8888.9, v10 - p176
T — Tyler, John, Z8896, v10 - p176
U — Updike, John, Z8913.85, v10 - p176
V — Vicente, Gil, Z8941.7, v10 - p176
V — Vygotskii, L.S., Z8946.82, v10 - p176
W — Weber, Max, Z8957, v10 - p177
W — Wellington, A.W., Duke of, Z8963.8, v10 - p177
W — Wharton, E.N. (Jones), Z8969.2, v10 - p177
W — Whitman, Walt, Z8971.5, v10 - p177
W — Wilder, T.N., Z8975.7, v10 - p177
W — Williams, Tennessee, Z8976.424, v10 - p177
W — Wilson, Angus, Z8976.485, v10 - p177
W — Wilson, Woodrow, Z8976.9, v10 - p177
W — Windham, Donald, Z8977.35, v10 - p177
W — Wirth, Louis, Z8978.66, v10 - p177
W — Wittgenstein, Ludwig, Z8979.4, v10 - p177
W — Wolfe, Thomas, Z8980.45, v10 - p177
W — Woodson, C.G., Z8983.4, v10 - p177
W — Woolf, Virginia, Z8984.2, v10 - p178
W — Wright, Richard, Z8986.323, v10 - p178
X — X, Malcolm, Z8989.7, v10 - p178
X — Xenophon, Z8989.73, v10 - p178
Y — Yeats, W.B., Z8992, v10 - p178

Philology. Linguistics, P, v3 - p1
Addresses, essays, lectures, P49, v3 - p1
Biography of philologists — Individual, A-Z, P85, v3 - p1
Communication. Mass media — Dictionaries, P87.5, v3 - p1
Communication. Mass media — General Works, P91, v3 - p2
Communication. Mass media — General Works, P90, v3 - p1
Computational linguistics. Natural language processing — Special aspects, A-Z, P98.5, v3 - p4
History of philology — General Works, P61, v3 - p1
Indo-European (Indo-Germanic) philology — Proto-Indo-European language, P572, v3 - p7
Language. Linguistic theory. Comparative grammar — Groups of unrelated languages. General surveys of languages, P371, v3 - p7
Language. Linguistic theory. Comparative grammar — Play on words, P304, v3 - p7
Language. Linguistic theory. Comparative grammar — Translating and interpreting, P306, v3 - p7
Semiotics. Signs and symbols — General Works, P99, v3 - p4
Semiotics. Signs and symbols — Special aspects, A-Z, P99.4, v3 - p5
Study and teaching. Research — General, P51, v3 - p1

Philosophy (General), B, v8 - p1
Ancient (600 B.C.-430 A.D.) — Nature philosophy of the ancients, B118, v8 - p10
Authorship, B52.7, v8 - p4
Collected works (nonserial) — Addresses, essays, lectures, B29, v8 - p1
Collected works (nonserial) — English and American, B21, v8 - p1
Collective biography, B104, v8 - p7
Congresses, B20, v8 - p1
Curiosa. Miscellanea, B68, v8 - p6
Dictionaries — French and Belgian, B42, v8 - p3
Dictionaries — German, B43, v8 - p3
Dictionaries — International (Polyglot), B41, v8 - p3
Directories, B35, v8 - p2
Encyclopedias, B51, v8 - p3
General Works — Other. By language, A-Z, B99, v8 - p7
Historiography — General Works, B51.4, v8 - p3
Medieval (430-1450) — Collected works (nonserial), B720, v8 - p24
Medieval (430-1450) — European philosophers, B765, v8 - p26
Medieval (430-1450) — General Works, B721, v8 - p24
Modern (1450/1660-) — Collected works (nonserial), B790, v8 - p28
Modern (1450/1660-) — Comparative philosophy, B799, v8 - p29
Philosophy. Methodology. Relation to other topics — Electronic data processing, B54, v8 - p4
Philosophy. Methodology. Relation to other topics — General Works, B53, v8 - p4
Philosophy. Methodology. Relation to other topics — Relation to civilization, B59, v8 - p5
Philosophy. Methodology. Relation to other topics — Relation to law and political science, B65, v8 - p5
Philosophy. Methodology. Relation to other topics — Relation to social sciences. Relation to sociology, B63, v8 - p5
Philosophy. Methodology. Relation to other topics — Relation to science, B67, v8 - p5
Philosophy. Methodology. Relation to other topics — Relation to theology and religion, B56, v8 - p5
Pictorial works, B51.8, v8 - p3
Renaissance — By region or country, A-Z, B776, v8 - p27
Renaissance — General Works, B775, v8 - p27
Special topics, A-Z, B105, v8 - p7
Study and teaching. Research — General Works, B52, v8 - p4
Terminology. Nomenclature — General Works, B49, v8 - p3

Photography, TR, v1 - p545
Addresses, essays, lectures, TR185, v1 - p549
Composition, TR179, v1 - p548
Country divisions, TR23-57, v1 - p545
Dictionaries and encyclopedias, TR9, v1 - p545
Digital photography (Photo CDs), TR267, v1 - p549
Directories. Bluebooks, TR12, v1 - p545
Elementary works. Handbooks, manuals, etc., TR146, v1 - p548
History (General), TR15, v1 - p545
Photographers' reference handbooks, TR150, v1 - p548
Photographic amusements. Trick photography. Special effects, TR148, v1 - p548
Photographic criticism, TR187, v1 - p549
Psychology, aesthetics, etc. (Artistic photography), TR183, v1 - p548

Physical Geography, GB, v6 - p17
Congresses, GB3, v6 - p17
Dictionaries. Encyclopedias, GB10, v6 - p17
Elementary textbooks, GB55, v6 - p18
General special (Special aspects of the subject as a whole), GB70, v6 - p18
General Works, treatises, and advanced textbooks — 1975-, GB54.5, v6 - p17
Geomorphology. Landforms. Terrain — Climatic geomorphology, GB447, v6 - p19
Geomorphology. Landforms. Terrain — Congresses, GB400.2, v6 - p18
Geomorphology. Landforms. Terrain — Elementary textbooks, GB402, v6 - p18
Geomorphology. Landforms. Terrain — General special, GB406, v6 - p18
History, GB11, v6 - p17

Hydrology. Water — General special, GB665, v6 - p21
Hydrology. Water — Handbooks, tables, etc., GB662.5, v6 - p21
Hydrology. Water — Hydrologic cycle, GB848, v6 - p21
Hydrology. Water — Hydrological forecasting, GB845, v6 - p21
Hydrology. Water — Karst hydrology, GB843, v6 - p21
Hydrology. Water — Natural water chemistry, GB855, v6 - p21
Hydrology. Water — Popular works, GB671, v6 - p21
Natural disasters — General Works, GB5014, v6 - p23
Philosophy. Relation to other topics. Methodology — Special methods, A-Z, GB21.5, v6 - p17
Popular works, GB59, v6 - p18
Study and teaching. Research — General Works, GB23, v6 - p17

Physics, QC, v1 - p124
Collected works (nonserial), QC3, v1 - p124
Dictionaries and encyclopedias, QC5, v1 - p124
Elementary Textbooks, QC23, v1 - p135
Juvenile works, QC25, v1 - p136
Miscellany and curiosa, QC75, v1 - p139
Physics as a profession. Vocational guidance, QC29, v1 - p136
Popular works, QC24.5, v1 - p136
Recreations, home experiments, etc., QC26, v1 - p136
Special aspects of the subject as whole, QC28, v1 - p136

Physiology, QP, v1 - p339
Comparative physiology, QP33, v1 - p340
Dictionaries and encyclopedias, QP11, v1 - p340
Electrophysiology, QP341, v1 - p352
History, QP21, v1 - p340
Homeostasis, QP90.4, v1 - p345
Regeneration, QP90.2, v1 - p345
Societies, congresses, serial collections, yearbooks, QP1, v1 - p339
Special aspects of the subject as a whole, QP33.5, v1 - p341
Special topics, A-Z, QP33.6, v1 - p341

Plant culture, SB, v1 - p383
Encyclopedias and dictionaries, SB45, v1 - p383
Growth regulators, SB128, v1 - p386
New crops (General), SB160, v1 - p386
Nuts, SB401, v1 - p392
Parks and public reservations, SB481, v1 - p405
Physiology, SB112.5, v1 - p384
Special aspects of crops and plant culture as a whole, A-Z, SB106, v1 - p384

Poland, KKP, v7 - p193

Political Institutions and Public Administration (Asia, Arab and Islamic countries, Africa, Australia, New Zealand, Atlantic Ocean and Pacific Ocean islands), JQ, v7 - p79
Africa — Cameroon, JQ3521-3525, v7 - p87
Africa — Egypt. United Arab Republic, JQ3831, v7 - p87
Africa — Ethiopia. Abyssinia, JQ3752, v7 - p87
Africa — General, JQ1872-1879, v7 - p84
Africa — Morocco, JQ3949, v7 - p87
Africa — Namibia. Southwest Africa, JQ3543.5, v7 - p87
Africa — Rwanda, JQ3567, v7 - p87
Africa — Sudan, JQ3981, v7 - p87
Africa — Tanzania. Tanganyika. Zanzibar, JQ3519, v7 - p87
Asia — General Works, JQ24, v7 - p79
Australia — General, JQ4029-4098, v7 - p87
Pacific Area. Pacific Ocean islands — General Works, JQ5995, v7 - p87

Political Institutions and Public Administration (Canada, West Indies, Mexico, Central and South America), JL, v7 - p65
Canada, Latin America, etc. — Cuba, JL1010, v7 - p67
Canada, Latin America, etc. — Falkland Islands, JL698, v7 - p66
Canada, Latin America, etc. — Haiti, JL1090, v7 - p67
Canada, Latin America, etc. — Latin America, JL950-969, v7 - p66
Canada, Latin America, etc. — Mexico, JL1215-1298, v7 - p67
Canada, Latin America, etc. — Puerto Rico, JL1056, v7 - p67
Canada, Latin America, etc. — West Indies. Caribbean Area, JL599.5, v7 - p66

Political Institutions and Public Administration (Europe), JN, v7 - p70
Europe — European federation and integration, JN15, v7 - p70
Europe — Northern Ireland, JN1572, v7 - p74
Europe — Poland, JN6752-6769, v7 - p78
Europe — Russia (Federation), JN6690-6699, v7 - p77
Europe — Soviet Union. Russia. Former Soviet Republics, JN6511-6598, v7 - p77
Europe — Ukraine, JN6630-6639, v7 - p77

Political Institutions and Public Administration (General), JF, v7 - p37
General. Comparative government — Civil-military relations, JF195, v7 - p38
General. Comparative government — Developing countries, JF60, v7 - p38
General. Comparative government — Handbooks, manuals, etc., JF37, v7 - p37
Public administration — General Works. History, JF1341-1351, v7 - p41
Public administration — Military government, JF1820, v7 - p42
Public administration — Special topics, A-Z, JF1525, v7 - p41
Public administration — Study and teaching. Research, JF1338, v7 - p41

Political Institutions and Public Administration (United States), JK, v7 - p43
  United States — 1821-1865, JK216, v7 - p45
  United States — 1866-1898, JK231-246, v7 - p45
  United States — 20th century, JK251-274, v7 - p45
  United States — Addresses, essays, lectures, JK21, v7 - p43
  United States — Dictionaries. Encyclopedias, JK9, v7 - p43
  United States — General Works, JK31, v7 - p43
  United States — War and emergency powers, JK339, v7 - p47
Political Science (General), JA, v7 - p1
  Addresses, essays, lectures, JA38-41, v7 - p2
  Collections, JA37, v7 - p1
  Communication in politics. Political communication — By region or country, A-Z, JA85.2, v7 - p10
  Communication in politics. Political communication — General Works, JA85, v7 - p9
  Dictionaries. Encyclopedias — English, JA61, v7 - p2
  Dictionaries. Encyclopedias — Other languages, A-Z, JA64, v7 - p2
  General Works — English, JA66, v7 - p2
  General Works — German, JA68, v7 - p2
  History of political science — Ancient and medieval (to 1500/1600), JA82, v7 - p7
  History of political science — By region or country, A-Z, JA84, v7 - p7
  History of political science — General Works, JA81, v7 - p6
  History of political science — Modern, JA83, v7 - p7
  Study and teaching. Research — By region or country, A-Z, JA88, v7 - p10
  Study and teaching. Research — General Works, JA86, v7 - p10
  Theory. Method. Scope. Relations to other subjects — General Works, JA71, v7 - p2
  Theory. Method. Scope. Relations to other subjects — Mathematical methods. Quantitative analysis, JA73, v7 - p3
  Theory. Method. Scope. Relations to other subjects — Relation to psychology. Political psychology, JA74-74.5, v7 - p3
  Theory. Method. Scope. Relations to other subjects — Relation to law, JA75, v7 - p4
  Theory. Method. Scope. Relations to other subjects — Relation to culture. Political culture, JA75.7, v7 - p4
  Theory. Method. Scope. Relations to other subjects — Relation to ecology. Political ecology, JA75.8, v7 - p5
  Theory. Method. Scope. Relations to other subjects — Relation to sociology. Political sociology, JA76, v7 - p5
  Theory. Method. Scope. Relations to other subjects — Relation to economics, JA77, v7 - p5
  Theory. Method. Scope. Relations to other subjects — Relation to ethics. Political ethics, JA79, v7 - p5
  Theory. Method. Scope. Relations to other subjects — Relation to science, JA80, v7 - p6
  Yearbooks, JA51, v7 - p2
Political Theory, JC, v7 - p10
  State. Theories of the state — Allegiance. Loyalty, JC328, v7 - p22
  State. Theories of the state — Ancient state. Political theory in antiquity, JC51, v7 - p11
  State. Theories of the state — Civil society, JC337, v7 - p24
  State. Theories of the state — Consensus. Consent of the governed, JC328.2, v7 - p22
  State. Theories of the state — General Works, JC11, v7 - p10
  State. Theories of the state — Islamic state, JC49, v7 - p10
  State. Theories of the state — Nature, entity, concept of the state, JC325, v7 - p21
  State. Theories of the state — Opposition. Resistance of government. Civil disobedience, JC328.3, v7 - p22
  State. Theories of the state — Political anthropology, JC21, v7 - p10
  State. Theories of the state — Political leadership, JC330.3, v7 - p23
  State. Theories of the state — Political obligation, JC329.5, v7 - p22
  State. Theories of the state — Power, JC330, v7 - p23
  State. Theories of the state — Public interest. Common good, JC330.15, v7 - p23
  State. Theories of the state — Social and evolutionary theories of the state, JC336, v7 - p23
  State. Theories of the state — Sovereignty, JC327, v7 - p21
  State. Theories of the state — Stability, JC330.2, v7 - p23
  State. Theories of the state — Violence. Political violence, JC328.6, v7 - p22
Portuguese Literature, PQ9011-9900, v3 - p334
  History and criticism — Women authors. Literary relations of women, PQ9033, v3 - p334
  Individual authors — Individual authors and works, 1701-1960, A-Z, PQ9261, v3 - p335
Practical theology, BV, v8 - p225
  Evangelism. Revivals — History of revivals and evangelistic work, BV3773, v8 - p229
  Practical religion. The Christian life — History, BV4490, v8 - p230
  Practical religion. The Christian life — Collections, BV4495, v8 - p230
Print media, NE, v9 - p301
  Lithography — Collections in book form, NE2451, v9 - p308
  Monotype (Printmaking) — By region or country, A-Z, NE2245, v9 - p307
  Printmaking and engraving — Collections of prints in book form, NE940-950, v9 - p305
Prose, PN3321-3503, v3 - p233
  Diaries, PN4390, v3 - p239

  Essays, PN4500, v3 - p239
  Oratory, PN4055-4500, v3 - p239
  Oratory. Elocution, etc. — By region or country, A-Z, PN4055, v3 - p239
  Prose. Prose fiction — General Works, PN3353, v3 - p234
Psychology, BF11-891, v2 - p1
  Affection. Feeling. Emotion, BF511, v2 - p33
  Behaviorism. Neobehaviorism. Behavioral Psychology, BF199, v2 - p18
  By region or country, A-Z, BF108, v2 - p6
  Character, BF818, v2 - p53
  Cognitive psychology, BF201, v2 - p18
  Collected works (nonserial), BF21, v2 - p1
  Congresses, BF20, v2 - p1
  Dictionaries. Encyclopedias, BF1407, v2 - p56
  Dictionaries. Encyclopedias, BF31, v2 - p1
  Directories, BF30, v2 - p1
  Ethics in psychology and in psychological research, BF76.4, v2 - p4
  Feminist psychology, BF201.4, v2 - p18
  Gestalt psychology. Gestalt perception, BF203, v2 - p18
  Humanistic psychology, BF204, v2 - p19
  Occult sciences, BF1407-2050, v2 - p56
  Parapsychology, BF1025-1389, v2 - p53
  Phenomenological psychology. Existential psychology, BF204.5, v2 - p19
  Philosophy. Relation to other topics, BF38, v2 - p2
  Psychological tests and testing, BF176, v2 - p17
  Psychology of belief, faith, etc., BF773, v2 - p52
  Psychology of other special subjects, A-Z, BF789, v2 - p52
  Psychology of values, meaning, BF778, v2 - p52
  Psychotropic drugs and other substances, BF207, v2 - p19
  Research, BF76.5, v2 - p4
  Societies, BF11, v2 - p1
  Transpersonal psychology, BF204.7, v2 - p19
Public Finance, HJ, v6 - p305
  Budget. Income and expenditure — General Works, HJ2005, v6 - p307
  By region or country — Developing countries, HJ1620, v6 - p307
  Expenditures. Government spending — General Works, HJ7461, v6 - p310
  General Works — 1701-, HJ141, v6 - p305
  General Works — Fiscal policy, HJ192-192.5, v6 - p305
  Public accounting. Auditing — Data processing, HJ9745, v6 - p312
  Public debts — History, HJ8003, v6 - p311
  Revenue. Taxation. Internal revenue — Illicit distilling and taxation. Moonshining, HJ5021, v6 - p310
  Revenue. Taxation. Internal revenue — Inflation and taxation, HJ2351, v6 - p308
  Revenue. Taxation. Internal revenue — Internal Revenue Service, HJ5018, v6 - p310
  Revenue. Taxation. Internal revenue — Tax evasion, HJ2348.6, v6 - p308
  Revenue. Taxation. Internal revenue — Taxation. Administration and procedure, HJ3252, v6 - p309
Railroad engineering and operation, TF, v1 - p473
  Country divisions, TF23-25, v1 - p473
Recreation. Leisure, GV, v6 - p73
  Circuses, spectacles, etc. — Wild West shows, GV1833, v6 - p107
  Dancing — Addresses, essays, lectures, GV1599, v6 - p102
  Dancing — Dance criticism. Appreciation, GV1600, v6 - p102
  Dancing — Dancing in motion pictures, television, etc., GV1779, v6 - p104
  Dancing — Dictionaries. Encyclopedias, GV1585, v6 - p101
  Dancing — General special (Special aspects of the subject as a whole), GV1595, v6 - p102
  Dancing — Special dances, A-Z, GV1796, v6 - p106
  Dictionaries. Encyclopedias, GV11, v6 - p73
  Games and amusements — General Works, GV1201, v6 - p100
  Games and amusements — History, GV1200, v6 - p100
  Games and amusements — Peep shows, GV1525, v6 - p101
  Games and amusements — Social aspects. Relation to sociology, GV1201.38, v6 - p100
  General special (Special aspects of the subject as a whole), GV181.3, v6 - p74
  General Works, treatises, and textbooks — American and English, 1976-, GV174, v6 - p74
  General Works, treatises, and textbooks — American, through 1975, GV171, v6 - p74
  Hiking. Pedestrian tours — By region or country, GV199.42, v6 - p76
  History — General Works, GV15, v6 - p74
  Outdoor life. Outdoor recreation — General Works, GV191.6, v6 - p76
  Outdoor life. Outdoor recreation — Orienteering, GV200.4, v6 - p77
  Philosophy. Relation to other topics — General Works, GV14, v6 - p73
  Philosophy. Relation to other topics — Relation to sociology, GV14.45, v6 - p73
  Physical education and training — General Works, treatises, and textbooks, GV341, v6 - p77
  Physical education and training — Movement education, GV452, v6 - p81
  Physical education and training — Organization and administration, GV343.5, v6 - p78
  Physical education and training — Safety measures. Accident prevention, GV344, v6 - p78
  Physical education and training — School athletics. Intramural and interscholastic athletics, GV346, v6 - p78

Recreation. Leisure, GV *(cont.)*

Physical education and training — Value of physical training in schools and colleges, GV345, v6 - p78

Recreation for special classes of persons — Girls and women, GV183, v6 - p75

Recreation leadership — General Works, GV181.4, v6 - p75

Recreational areas and facilities. Recreation centers — Financial and business aspects, GV182.15, v6 - p75

Recreational areas and facilities. Recreation centers — General Works, GV182, v6 - p75

Sports — Addresses, essays, lectures, GV707, v6 - p87

Sports — Biography of sports personalities, GV697, v6 - p84

Sports — Coaching, GV711, v6 - p88

Sports — Dictionaries. Encyclopedias, GV567, v6 - p82

Sports — General special (Special aspects of the subject as a whole), GV706.8, v6 - p87

Sports — Rules (Collections), GV731, v6 - p89

Sports — Sports records and statistics. Champions, GV741, v6 - p89

Sports — Training and conditioning, GV711.5, v6 - p88

Sports — Umpires. Sports officiating, GV735, v6 - p89

Sports sciences — General Works, GV558, v6 - p81

Study and teaching. Research, GV14.5, v6 - p74

Regional comparative and uniform law (Europe), KJC, v7 - p189

Constitutional law — Constitutional courts and procedure, KJC5456, v7 - p190

Constitutional law — General Works. Treatises, KJC4445, v7 - p189

Environmental law — Environmental planning. Conservation of natural resources, KJC6243, v7 - p190

Legal research. Legal bibliography — General Works, KJC76, v7 - p189

Regional organization and integration (Europe), KJE, v7 - p190

The European Communities. Community law — Compends, outlines, etc., KJE949, v7 - p190

The European Communities. Community law — General Works. Treatises, KJE947, v7 - p190

Religions. Mythology. Rationalism, BL, v8 - p140

Religion — Addresses, essays, lectures, BL50, v8 - p142

Religion — Apostasy, BL639.5, v8 - p155

Religion — Biography of students and historians, A-Z, BL43, v8 - p142

Religion — Computer network resources, BL37, v8 - p141

Religion — Congresses, BL21, v8 - p140

Religion — Dictionaries. Encyclopedias, BL31, v8 - p141

Religion — Directories, BL35, v8 - p141

Religion — General Works, BL48, v8 - p142

Religion — Philosophy of religion. Philosophy and religion, BL51, v8 - p143

Religion — Prophets and prophecy, BL633, v8 - p155

Religion — Religion and sociology, BL60, v8 - p144

Religion — Religion in relation to other subjects, A-Z, BL65, v8 - p145

Religion — Religious liberty, BL640, v8 - p155

Religion — Study of comparative religion. Historiography. Methodology, BL41, v8 - p141

Roman law, KJA, v7 - p188

Criminal law and procedure — General, KJA3340, v7 - p189

General Works, KJA147, v7 - p188

Public law — State and religion, KJA3060, v7 - p189

Roman law compared with other legal systems — General Works, KJA160, v7 - p188

Roman Literature, PA6003-6825, v3 - p14

Individual authors — Boethius, Anicius Manlius Severinus, d. 524 (525?) A.D., PA6231, v3 - p16

Individual authors — Caesar, C. Julius, 100-44 B.C., PA6246, v3 - p16

Individual authors — Pa... to Pers..., PA6554, v3 - p17

Literary history — Treatment and conception of special subjects, A-Z, PA6029, v3 - p15

Poetry — General, PA6047, v3 - p15

Translations — Anthologies. Selections, PA6164, v3 - p15

Translations — Poetry, PA6165, v3 - p15

Romanic Philology and Languages, PC, v3 - p21

Science (General), Q, v1 - p1

Addresses, essays, lectures, Q171, v1 - p16

Dictionaries, Q123, v1 - p3

Early works through 1800, Q151-157, v1 - p14

Encyclopedias., Q121, v1 - p3

Handbooks, tables, formulas, etc., Q199, v1 - p25

Instruments and apparatus, Q184.5-185, v1 - p25

Miscellany and curiosa, Q173, v1 - p17

Nomenclature, terminology, notation, abbreviation, Q179, v1 - p22

Popular works, Q162, v1 - p16

Science as a profession, Q147-149, v1 - p14

Scientific ethics, Q175.37, v1 - p21

Scientific illustration, Q222, v1 - p25

Scientific Literature, Q225.5, v1 - p26

Social Aspects, Q175.5-175.55, v1 - p21

Special aspects of the subject as a whole, Q172, v1 - p16

Special Topics, A-Z, Q172.5, v1 - p16

Study and teaching, Q181-183.3, v1 - p24

Translating services, Q124, v1 - p4

Women in science, Q130, v1 - p10

Sculpture, NB, v9 - p244

General Works — Relation to other arts. Sculpture and architecture, NB1137, v9 - p250

History — General Works, NB60, v9 - p244

History — Medieval sculpture, NB170, v9 - p245

History — Special countries, NB205-210, v9 - p246

Indexes to sculpture, NB36, v9 - p244

Sculpture in special materials — Metals, NB1220, v9 - p251

Sculpture materials, NB1202, v9 - p251

Technique, NB1170, v9 - p251

Slavic. Baltic. Albanian, PG, v3 - p48

Collections of Russian literature — Special classes of authors, A-Z, PG3203, v3 - p53

Individual authors and works, 18th century — Karamzin, Nikolai Mikhailovich, 1766-1826, PG3314, v3 - p54

Individual authors, 1961- — A, PG3478, v3 - p61

Individual authors, 1961- — Bf-Bz, PG3479.4, v3 - p61

Individual authors, 1961- — D, PG3479.6, v3 - p61

Individual authors, 1961- — Ra-Rn, PG3485.5, v3 - p61

Individual authors, 1961- — Sh, PG3487, v3 - p61

Individual authors, 1961- — Si-Sz, PG3488, v3 - p61

Individual authors, 1961- — Vo, PG3489.4, v3 - p62

Individual authors, 1961- — Zb-Zz, PG3490, v3 - p62

Literary history and criticism — Encyclopedias. Dictionaries, PG2940, v3 - p50

Social History and Conditions. Social Problems.Social Reform, HN, v6 - p325

By region or country — America, HN50, v6 - p328

Congresses, HN3, v6 - p325

History — Medieval, HN11, v6 - p325

Special topics (not otherwise provided for), A-Z, HN49, v6 - p327

Statistics. Social indicators. Quality of life, HN25, v6 - p327

Study and teaching. Research, HN29, v6 - p327

Theory. Method. Relation to other subjects — General Works, HN28, v6 - p327

Social pathology. Social and public welfare. Criminology, HV, v6 - p407

Addresses, essays, lectures, HV37, v6 - p409

Alcoholism. Intemperance. Temperance reform — Addresses, essays, lectures, HV5047, v6 - p431

Alcoholism. Intemperance. Temperance reform — Alcohol and the family. Children of alcoholics, HV5132, v6 - p432

Alcoholism. Intemperance. Temperance reform — Alcohol and women, HV5137, v6 - p432

Alcoholism. Intemperance. Temperance reform — Alcohol and youth, HV5135, v6 - p432

Alcoholism. Intemperance. Temperance reform — Alcoholism and the child, HV5133, v6 - p432

Alcoholism. Intemperance. Temperance reform — Psychology of alcoholism, HV5045, v6 - p431

Alcoholism. Intemperance. Temperance reform — Societies (International), HV5006, v6 - p430

Biography — Individual, A-Z, HV28, v6 - p408

Charity fairs, bazaars, etc., HV544, v6 - p414

Criminal justice administration — Prevention of crime, methods, etc., HV7431, v6 - p449

Criminal justice administration — Research, HV7419.5, v6 - p449

Criminology — Encyclopedias. Dictionaries, HV6017, v6 - p437

Criminology — General special (Special aspects of the subject as a whole), HV6030, v6 - p437

Criminology — Research, HV6024.5, v6 - p437

Criminology — Theory and methodology, HV6018, v6 - p437

Data processing — General Works, HV29.2, v6 - p408

Dictionaries. Encyclopedias, HV12, v6 - p408

Drug habits. Drug abuse — Dictionaries. Encyclopedias, HV5804, v6 - p434

Drug habits. Drug abuse — Drugs and special classes of persons, A-Z, HV5824, v6 - p434

Drug habits. Drug abuse — General Works, HV5801, v6 - p434

Emergency management, HV551.2, v6 - p415

Free professional services — Other, A-Z, HV696, v6 - p417

Handbooks, manuals, etc., HV35, v6 - p409

History of philanthropy — General, HV16, v6 - p408

Refugee problems — Church work with refugees, including the sanctuary movement, HV645, v6 - p416

Social service. Social work. Charity organization and practice — General Works, HV40, v6 - p409

Social service. Social work. Charity organization and practice — General special, HV41, v6 - p409

Social service. Social work. Charity organization and practice — Social group work, HV45, v6 - p410

Social work as a profession, HV10.5, v6 - p407

Study and teaching. Research. Schools. Social work education — General Works, HV11, v6 - p407

Social pathology. Social and public welfare. Criminology, HV *(cont.)*
Substance abuse — Societies. Serials, HV4997, v6 - p430
The church and charity, HV530, v6 - p414
Tobacco habit — Other general (not A-Z), HV5735, v6 - p433
Treatises — 1871-, HV31, v6 - p408
Women and charity, HV541, v6 - p414
Social Sciences (General), H, v6 - p107
Biography — Individual, A-Z, H59, v6 - p108
Collected works, H31-35, v6 - p107
Communication of information — Computer networks, H61.95, v6 - p110
Communication of information — General Works, H61.8, v6 - p110
Dictionaries. Encyclopedias — English, H41, v6 - p108
General special, H91, v6 - p111
General Works — 1871-1975, H83, v6 - p111
General Works — 1976-, H85, v6 - p111
History — By region or country, A-Z, H53, v6 - p108
History — General Works, H51, v6 - p108
Public policy (General). Policy sciences — General Works, H97, v6 - p111
Schools. Institutes of social sciences, H67, v6 - p111
Study and teaching. Research, H62-62.5, v6 - p110
Theory. Method. Relation to other subjects — Data processing, H61.3, v6 - p110
Theory. Method. Relation to other subjects — Forecasting in the social sciences, H61.4, v6 - p110
Theory. Method. Relation to other subjects — General Works, H61, v6 - p109
Theory. Method. Relation to other subjects — Interviewing. Focused group interviewing, H61.28, v6 - p110
Theory. Method. Relation to other subjects — Mathematics. Mathematical models, H61.25, v6 - p110
Theory. Method. Relation to other subjects — Relation to philosophy. Social philosophy, H61.15, v6 - p110
Social usages. Etiquette, BJ1853-2122, v8 - p140
Etiquette of entertaining. Duties of host and hostess. Hospitality — Table etiquette, BJ2041, v8 - p140
General Works — Other languages, A-Z, BJ2007, v8 - p140
Religious etiquette — General Works, BJ2010, v8 - p140
Socialism. Communism. Anarchism, HX, v6 - p461
Anarchism — Biography (Collective), HX830, v6 - p466
Communism and religion. Socialism and religion, HX536, v6 - p464
Communism and society. Socialism and society, HX542, v6 - p464
Communism and women. Socialism and women. Communism/socialism and the family, HX546, v6 - p465
Communism/socialism and science, HX541, v6 - p464
Communism/socialism in relation to other topics, A-Z, HX550, v6 - p465
Dictionaries. Encyclopedias, HX17, v6 - p461
General Works — 1981-, HX73, v6 - p462
History — General Works, HX21, v6 - p461
Societies. Associations, HX11, v6 - p461
Special topics, A-Z, HX518, v6 - p464
Utopias. The ideal state — General Works. History, HX806, v6 - p465
Societies: Secret, Benevolent, etc., HS, v6 - p399
Secret societies — By region or country, HS310, v6 - p399
Sociology, HM, v6 - p312
Association. Mutuality. Social groups — General Works, HM131, v6 - p318
Association. Mutuality. Social groups — Interpersonal relations, HM132, v6 - p318
Association. Mutuality. Social groups — Sociology of friendship, HM132.5, v6 - p319
Biography — Individual, A-Z, HM479, v6 - p324
By region or country — Islamic countries, HM511, v6 - p324
Congresses, HM13, v6 - p312
Culture — General Works, HM621, v6 - p324
Culture — Subculture, HM646, v6 - p324
Culture. Progress — General Works, HM101, v6 - p317
Culture. Progress — Historical sociology, HM104, v6 - p317
Culture. Progress — Human body, HM110, v6 - p317
Dictionaries. Encyclopedias, HM17, v6 - p312
Dictionaries. Encyclopedias, HM425, v6 - p323
General special, HM73, v6 - p316
General Works — English, HM51, v6 - p316
General Works — German, HM57, v6 - p316
General Works — Italian, HM59, v6 - p316
General Works — Other European languages, HM61, v6 - p316
General Works — Other languages, A-Z, HM606, v6 - p324
History — By region or country, A-Z, HM22, v6 - p313
History — General Works, HM19, v6 - p312
Individualism. Differentiation. Struggle — Equality, HM146, v6 - p319
Individualism. Differentiation. Struggle — General Works, HM136, v6 - p319
Individualism. Differentiation. Struggle — The great man. Leadership. Prestige, HM141, v6 - p319
Miscellaneous special, HM299, v6 - p323
Research, HM48, v6 - p315
Social control — Social ethics, HM665, v6 - p324
Social control — Social norms, HM676, v6 - p324

Social elements, forces, laws — Economic, HM211, v6 - p320
Social elements, forces, laws — Intellectual, HM213, v6 - p320
Social elements, forces, laws — Moral, HM216, v6 - p320
Social elements, forces, laws — Technological, HM221, v6 - p320
Social psychology — Communication, HM258, v6 - p321
Social psychology — General Works, HM1033, v6 - p325
Social psychology — General Works, HM251, v6 - p320
Social psychology — Other special, HM291, v6 - p323
Social psychology — Passive resistance, HM278, v6 - p322
Social psychology — Public opinion, HM261, v6 - p321
Social psychology — Public relations. Publicity. Propaganda, HM263, v6 - p321
Social psychology — Risk perception. Risk assessment, HM256, v6 - p321
Social psychology — Social influence, HM259, v6 - p321
Social psychology — Sociodrama, HM254, v6 - p321
Study and teaching — By region or country, A-Z, HM47, v6 - p315
Theory. Method. Relation to other subjects — General Works, HM24, v6 - p314
Theory. Method. Relation to other subjects — Relation to economics, HM35, v6 - p315
Theory. Method. Relation to other subjects — Relation to history and geography, HM36, v6 - p315
Theory. Method. Relation to other subjects — Relation to philosophy, HM26, v6 - p315
Theory. Method. Relation to other subjects — Relation to psychology, HM27, v6 - p315
Theory. Method. Relation to other subjects — Relation to war, HM36.5, v6 - p315
Theory. Method. Relations to other subjects — Relation to economics, HM548, v6 - p324
Unity. Solidarity, HM126, v6 - p317
South America: Argentina, KHA, v7 - p188
South America: Colombia, KHH, v7 - p188
Spain, KKT, v7 - p193
Autonomous communities and provinces (Provincias) — Castilla-León. Castile, KKT6053.4, v7 - p193
Spanish Literature, PQ6006-8549, v3 - p304
Collections of Spanish literature — Selections from women authors, PQ6173, v3 - p309
Collections of Spanish literature — Selections. Anthologies, etc., PQ6172, v3 - p309
Collections of Spanish literature — Special periods, PQ6174, v3 - p309
Literary history and criticism — Encyclopedias. Dictionaries, PQ6006, v3 - p304
Special aspects of education, LC, v7 - p257
Education and travel, LC6681, v7 - p282
Education extension. Adult education. Continuing education — Encyclopedias. Dictionaries, LC5211, v7 - p280
Education extension. Adult education. Continuing education — General Works, LC5215, v7 - p280
Education extension. Adult education. Continuing education — General special, LC5219, v7 - p280
Education extension. Adult education. Continuing education — Special topics, A-Z, LC5225, v7 - p280
Education of special classes of persons — Other ethnic groups, A-Z, LC3650, v7 - p274
Education of special classes of persons — Racially mixed people, LC3621, v7 - p274
Speculative philosophy, BD, v8 - p80
Cosmology — Addresses, essays, lectures, BD523, v8 - p101
Cosmology — Miscellaneous speculations. Curiosa, etc., BD701, v8 - p104
Epistemology. Theory of knowledge — Analogy, BD190, v8 - p87
Epistemology. Theory of knowledge — Authority, BD209, v8 - p88
Epistemology. Theory of knowledge — Belief. Faith, BD215, v8 - p88
Epistemology. Theory of knowledge — Body. Somatic aspects, BD214.5, v8 - p88
Epistemology. Theory of knowledge — Collected works (nonserial), BD143, v8 - p82
Epistemology. Theory of knowledge — Comparison. Resemblance. Identity, BD236, v8 - p90
Epistemology. Theory of knowledge — Criterion, BD182, v8 - p87
Epistemology. Theory of knowledge — Epistemology and ethics. Intellectual virtues, BD176, v8 - p86
Epistemology. Theory of knowledge — Epistemology and evolution, BD177, v8 - p86
Epistemology. Theory of knowledge — Epistemology and sociology. Sociology of knowledge, BD175, v8 - p85
Epistemology. Theory of knowledge — Explanation, BD237, v8 - p90
Epistemology. Theory of knowledge — Hope, BD216, v8 - p89
Epistemology. Theory of knowledge — Inquiry, BD183, v8 - p87
Epistemology. Theory of knowledge — Justification, BD212, v8 - p88
Epistemology. Theory of knowledge — Limits of knowledge, BD201, v8 - p87
Epistemology. Theory of knowledge — Objectivity, BD220, v8 - p89
Epistemology. Theory of knowledge — Origins and sources of knowledge, BD181, v8 - p87
Epistemology. Theory of knowledge — Relativity of knowledge, BD221, v8 - p89
Epistemology. Theory of knowledge — Senses and sensation, BD214, v8 - p88
Epistemology. Theory of knowledge — Truth. Error. Certitude, etc., BD171, v8 - p85
Epistemology. Theory of knowledge — Value. Worth, BD232, v8 - p89
Epistemology. Theory of knowledge — Verification. Empirical verification. Verifiability, BD212.5, v8 - p88
Epistemology. Theory of knowledge— Memory, BD181.7, v8 - p87

Speculative philosophy, BD *(cont.)*
General philosophical works — Addresses, essays, lectures, BD41, v8 - p81
Metaphysics — Elementary textbooks. Outlines, syllabi, etc., BD131, v8 - p82
Methodology — Heuristic, BD260, v8 - p92
Methodology — Interdisciplinary approach to knowledge, BD255, v8 - p92
Ontology — Becoming. Process, BD372, v8 - p93
Ontology — Being. Nature of reality. Substance. First philosophy, BD331, v8 - p92
Ontology — Birth, BD443, v8 - p98
Ontology — Change, BD373, v8 - p93
Ontology — Division, BD390, v8 - p93
Ontology — Finite and infinite, BD411, v8 - p94
Ontology — Holes, BD399, v8 - p94
Ontology — Love, BD436, v8 - p97
Ontology — Perspective, BD348, v8 - p93
Ontology — Philosophical anthropology, BD450, v8 - p98
Ontology — Power, BD438, v8 - p97
Ontology — Self, BD438.5, v8 - p97
Ontology — Self-deception, BD439, v8 - p97
Ontology — Unity and plurality, BD394, v8 - p93
Ontology — Whole and parts (Philosophy). "Ganzheit", BD396, v8 - p93
Statistics, HA, v6 - p112
Communication of information — General Works, HA33, v6 - p112
Congresses, HA12.5, v6 - p112
Dictionaries. Encyclopedias, HA17, v6 - p112
Statistical services. Statistical bureaus — By region or country, A-Z, HA37, v6 - p113
Statistical services. Statistical bureaus— International, HA36, v6 - p113
Theory and method of social science statistics — General Works, HA29, v6 - p112
Theory and method of social science statistics — Regression. Correlation, HA31.3, v6 - p112
Theory and method of social science statistics — Spatial analysis, HA30.6, v6 - p112
Subject bibliography, Z5052-7991, v10 - p123
Aerospace technology — By region or country, A-Z, Z5065, v10 - p123
Agriculture — General bibliography, Z5071, v10 - p123
Agriculture — Local, A-Z, Z5075, v10 - p123
Agriculture — Special topics, A-Z, Z5074, v10 - p123
Anthropology and ethnology — General bibliography, Z5111, v10 - p123
Anthropology and ethnology — Special topics, A-Z, Z5118, v10 - p123
Archaeology — General bibliography, Z5131, v10 - p124
Archaeology — Special topics, A-Z, Z5133, v10 - p124
Archives. Records, Z5140, v10 - p124
Authorship (General), Z5165, v10 - p124
Automobiles. Automobile travel. Motor vehicles — General bibliography, Z5170, v10 - p124
Biography. Genealogy. Heraldry — By class, A-Z, Z5304, v10 - p124
Biography. Genealogy. Heraldry — By region or country, A-Z, Z5305, v10 - p124
Biography. Genealogy. Heraldry — Catalogs, Z5319, v10 - p125
Biography. Genealogy. Heraldry — General bibliography, Z5301, v10 - p124
Biology — Special topics, A-Z, Z5322, v10 - p125
Botany — General bibliography, Z5351, v10 - p125
Chemistry, Z5524, v10 - p125
Civilization — Medieval, Z5579.5, v10 - p125
Civilization — Modern, Z5579.6, v10 - p125
Communication. Mass media, Z5630-5634, v10 - p126
Computer science. Electronic data processing — General bibliography, Z5640, v10 - p126
Computer science. Electronic data processing — Special topics, A-Z, Z5643, v10 - p126
Costume, Z5691-5694, v10 - p126
Criminology — Bibliography of bibliographies, Z5703, v10 - p126
Criminology — By region or country, A-Z, Z5703.5, v10 - p127
Criminology — Special topics, A-Z, Z5703.4, v10 - p126
Days. Holidays. Festivals. Birthdays — General bibliography, Z5710, v10 - p127
Deaf-mutes, Z5721, v10 - p127
Death, Z5725, v10 - p127
Directories — General, Z5771, v10 - p127
Domestic economy. Home economics — Special topics, A-Z, Z5776, v10 - p127
Drama. Theater, Z5781-5784, v10 - p127
Education — By region or country, A-Z, Z5815, v10 - p129
Education — General bibliography, Z5811, v10 - p128
Education — Periodicals. Societies, Z5813, v10 - p128
Education — Special disciplines and subjects, A-Z, Z5818, v10 - p129
Education — Special topics, A-Z, Z5814, v10 - p128
Education — Teaching aids, Z5817.2, v10 - p129
Electricity — Special topics, A-Z, Z5834, v10 - p130
Encyclopedias — General, Z5848, v10 - p130
Engineering — Special topics, A-Z, Z5853, v10 - p130
Environment (General and human). Human ecology — General bibliography, Z5861, v10 - p130
Environment (General and human). Human ecology — Other special topics, A-Z, Z5863, v10 - p130
Erotic literature, facetiae, curiosa, etc. — General bibliography, Z5865, v10 - p130

Erotic literature, facetiae, curiosa, etc. — Special topics, A-Z, Z5866, v10 - p131
Exhibitions, Z5883, v10 - p131
Fiction — General bibliography, Z5916, v10 - p131
Fiction — Special topics, A-Z, Z5917, v10 - p131
Fine arts (Visual arts). The arts (General) — Biobibliography, Z5938, v10 - p132
Fine arts (Visual arts). The arts (General) — By region or country, A-Z, Z5961, v10 - p134
Fine arts (Visual arts). The arts (General) — General bibliography, Z5931, v10 - p132
Fine arts (Visual arts). The arts (General) — Periodicals. Societies, Z5937, v10 - p132
Fine arts (Visual arts). The arts (General) — Special aspects or movements, A-Z, Z5936, v10 - p132
Fine arts (Visual arts). The arts (General) — Special topics (not otherwise provided for), A-Z, Z5956, v10 - p133
Folklore, Z5981-5984, v10 - p134
Forecasting, Z5990, v10 - p134
Gardening. Horticulture. Floriculture. Landscape gardening and architecture — By region or country, A-Z, Z5996.5, v10 - p135
Geography and travels. Maps. Cartography — Bibliography of bibliography, Z6001.A1, v10 - p135
Geography and travels. Maps. Cartography — Catalogs, Z6009, v10 - p135
Geography and travels. Maps. Cartography — Local. By region, physical feature, etc.,, Z6005, v10 - p135
Geography and travels. Maps. Cartography — Special topics, A-Z, Z6004, v10 - p135
Geology. Mineralogy. Paleontology, Z6031-6033, v10 - p135
Gymnastics. Physical education, Z6121, v10 - p136
History — General bibliography, Z6201.A55-S64, v10 - p136
History — Periodicals. Societies, Z6205, v10 - p136
History — Special historical events, movements, etc., A-Z, Z6207, v10 - p136
History — Special methodological topics, A-Z, Z6208, v10 - p137
Hospitality industry. Hotels, Z6250, v10 - p137
Humanities, Z6265, v10 - p137
International law and relations — Foreign relations. By region or country, A-Z, Z6465, v10 - p139
International law and relations — General bibliography, Z6461, v10 - p138
International law and relations — Special topics, A-Z, Z6464, v10 - p139
Jews — Catalogs, Z6375, v10 - p138
Jews — General bibliography, Z6366, v10 - p138
Jews — Other special topics, A-Z, Z6374, v10 - p138
Literature — General bibliography, Z6511, v10 - p139
Literature — Special subjects, A-Z, Z6514, v10 - p140
Manuscripts — By region or country, A-Z, Z6620, v10 - p141
Manuscripts — Catalogs of manuscript collections in specific libraries. By name of library, A-Z, Z6621, v10 - p141
Mathematics — Periodicals. Societies, Z6653, v10 - p141
Mathematics — Special topics, A-Z, Z6654, v10 - p141
Medicine — Biography, Z6660.5, v10 - p141
Medicine — By region or country, A-Z, Z6661, v10 - p141
Medicine — General bibliography, Z6658.I54, v10 - p141
Medicine — Geriatrics, Z6671.55, v10 - p142
Medicine — Internal medicine. Diseases and manifestations, A-Z, Z6664, v10 - p141
Medicine — Other, A-Z, Z6675, v10 - p142
Metals. Metallurgy — General bibliography, Z6678, v10 - p142
Meteorology — Special topics, A-Z, Z6683, v10 - p143
Military science — Local, A-Z, Z6725, v10 - p143
Military science — Special topics, A-Z, Z6724, v10 - p143
Names, Z6824, v10 - p143
Naval science — Local, A-Z, Z6835, v10 - p143
Occultism — Special topics, A-Z, Z6878, v10 - p143
Performing arts, Z6935, v10 - p144
Periodicals, newspapers, and other serials — Catalogs of libraries. Union lists, Z6945, v10 - p144
Periodicals, newspapers, and other serials — General bibliography, Z6941, v10 - p144
Periodicals, newspapers, and other serials — Journalism, Z6940, v10 - p144
Periodicals, newspapers, and other serials — Special topics, A-Z, Z6944, v10 - p144
Philology and linguistics — General bibliography, Z7001, v10 - p145
Philology and linguistics — Special topics, A-Z, Z7004, v10 - p145
Philosophy, Z7125-7128, v10 - p145
Photography — General bibliography, Z7134, v10 - p146
Physics — Special topics, A-Z, Z7144, v10 - p146
Physics, Z7141, v10 - p146
Poetry — Special topics, A-Z, Z7156, v10 - p146
Political and social sciences — Bibliography of bibliography, Z7161.A1, v10 - p146
Political and social sciences — By region or country, A-Z, Z7165, v10 - p151
Political and social sciences — General bibliography, Z7161.C17-Y75, v10 - p146
Political and social sciences — General special, Z7161.A15, v10 - p146
Political and social sciences — Special topics, A-Z, Z7164, v10 - p147
Political and social sciences — Theory, method, etc., Z7161.A2, v10 - p146
Psychology, Z7201-7204, v10 - p152
Radio — By region or country, A-Z, Z7224, v10 - p152
Radio — General bibliography, Z7221, v10 - p152
Railroads — Bibliography of bibliography, Z7231, v10 - p152

Subject bibliography, Z5052-7991 *(cont.)*

Science. Natural history — Bibliography of early works, Z7402, v10 - p153

Science. Natural history — Biobibliography, Z7404, v10 - p153

Science. Natural history — General bibliography, Z7401, v10 - p152

Science. Natural history — Natural history. By region or country, A-Z, Z7408, v10 - p153

Science. Natural history — Periodicals. Societies, Z7403, v10 - p153

Science. Natural history — Science. By region or country, A-Z, Z7407, v10 - p153

Science. Natural history — Special topics, A-Z, Z7405, v10 - p153

Sports. Amusements. Recreation, Z7511-7515, v10 - p154

Statistics, Z7551-7554, v10 - p154

Suicide, Z7615, v10 - p154

Television, Z7711, v10 - p154

Temperance, Z7721, v10 - p155

Theology and religion — Angels, Z7763, v10 - p156

Theology and religion — By region or country, A-Z, Z7757, v10 - p156

Theology and religion — Christian unity, Z7845.1, v10 - p160

Theology and religion — Christianity and culture, Z7776.6, v10 - p157

Theology and religion — Christianity and the arts, Z7776.68, v10 - p157

Theology and religion — Church and state. Religion and state, Z7776.72, v10 - p157

Theology and religion — Church, Z7776.7, v10 - p157

Theology and religion — City churches, Z7782, v10 - p157

Theology and religion — Emotions, Z7785, v10 - p157

Theology and religion — End of the world, Z7786, v10 - p157

Theology and religion — Future life, Z7794, v10 - p157

Theology and religion — General bibliography, Z7751, v10 - p155

Theology and religion — Glossolalia, Z7798, v10 - p157

Theology and religion — Holy Spirit, Z7799.3, v10 - p158

Theology and religion — Liberation theology, Z7809, v10 - p158

Theology and religion — Liturgy. Prayer books, Z7813, v10 - p158

Theology and religion — Mysticism (Theology), Z7819, v10 - p158

Theology and religion — Periodicals. Directories. Yearbooks, Z7753, v10 - p155

Theology and religion — Reformation and Counter-Reformation, Z7830, v10 - p158

Theology and religion — Religion and sociology, Z7831, v10 - p158

Theology and religion — Revivals, Z7836.7, v10 - p159

Theology and religion — Sects, churches, movements, heresies (Christian), A-Z, Z7845, v10 - p159

Theology and religion — Sunday schools. Religious education in secular schools, Z7849, v10 - p160

Theology and religion — Theodicy, Z7850, v10 - p160

Tobacco. Smoking, Z7882, v10 - p160

Useful arts and applied science. Technology, Z7911-7914, v10 - p160

Women, Z7961-7964, v10 - p160

Zoology — General bibliography, Z7991, v10 - p162

Sweden, KKV, v7 - p193

Technical Chronology. Calendar, CE, v5 - p15

General Works — 1801-, CE11, v5 - p15

History — General Works, CE6, v5 - p15

Medieval and modern — Medieval, CE59, v5 - p15

Medieval and modern — Reform of the calendar, CE73, v5 - p15

Technology (General), T, v1 - p431

Addresses, essays, lectures, T185, v1 - p441

Communication of technical information, T10.5, v1 - p431

Dictionaries and encyclopedias, T9, v1 - p431

Industrial archaeology, T37, v1 - p436

Industrial directories - pGeneral Works, T11.95, v1 - p432

Industrial research. Research and development, T175, v1 - p441

Nanotechnology, T174.7, v1 - p441

Philosophy. Theory. Classification. Methodology, T14, v1 - p432

Social aspects, T14.5, v1 - p433

Women in technology, T36, v1 - p436

Theory and practice of education, LB, v7 - p216

Addresses, essays, lectures. Pamphlets, LB41, v7 - p217

Child study — Addresses, essays, lectures. Pamphlets, LB1119, v7 - p231

Child study — Adolescence, LB1135, v7 - p231

Child study — Behavioral assessment of children, LB1124, v7 - p231

Child study — General special, LB1117, v7 - p231

Child study — General Works, LB1115, v7 - p230

Child study — Play, games, etc., LB1137, v7 - p231

Child study — Special, A-Z, LB1139, v7 - p231

Comparative education, LB43, v7 - p218

Early childhood education — Curricula, LB1139.4, v7 - p232

Early childhood education — General Works, LB1139.23, v7 - p232

Early childhood education — Individual areas of study, A-Z, LB1139.5, v7 - p232

Early childhood education — Special aspects and methods, A-Z, LB1139.35, v7 - p232

Education and training of teachers and administrators — General Works, LB1707, v7 - p239

Education and training of teachers and administrators — Mentors, LB1731.4, v7 - p240

Education and training of teachers and administrators — Professional aspects of teaching and school administration. Vocational guidance, LB1775, v7 - p240

Education and training of teachers and administrators — Student teachers. Student teaching, LB2157, v7 - p242

Educational anthropology, LB45, v7 - p218

Educational psychology — Formal discipline. Transfer of training, LB1059, v7 - p229

Educational psychology — General Works, LB1051, v7 - p228

Educational psychology — Group behavior, LB1084, v7 - p230

Educational psychology —Individuality, LB1083, v7 - p230

Elementary or public school education. Elementary school teaching — General Works, LB1555, v7 - p234

Elementary or public school education. Elementary school teaching — Rural schools. Rural education. Education of children in rural areas, LB1567, v7 - p234

General Works — 1991-, LB14.7, v7 - p217

General Works — Encyclopedias and dictionaries, LB15, v7 - p217

General Works — Modern comprehensive works. Systematic encyclopedias. Handbooks, LB17, v7 - p217

Higher education — Academic degrees, LB2381, v7 - p248

Higher education — Addresses, essays, lectures. Pamphlets, LB2325, v7 - p243

Higher education — Finance. Income and expenditure. Accounting, LB2341.98, v7 - p246

Higher education — General special, LB2324, v7 - p242

Higher education — Periodicals, LB2300, v7 - p242

Higher education — Preparation of theses, LB2369, v7 - p247

Higher education — Research, LB2326.3, v7 - p243

Higher education — Technology. Information technology, LB2395.7, v7 - p248

Higher education — Yearbooks, LB2310, v7 - p242

Kindergarten — Miscellaneous, LB1195, v7 - p233

Preschool education. Nursery schools — Individual areas of study, A-Z, LB1140.5, v7 - p233

Preschool education. Nursery schools — Periodicals, societies, etc., LB1140, v7 - p232

School architecture and equipment. School physical facilities. Campus planning — Vandalism, LB3249, v7 - p256

School hygiene. School health services — By region or country, A-Z, LB3409, v7 - p256

School life. Student manners and customs — Political activity, LB3610, v7 - p257

Secondary education. High school teaching — General Works, LB1607, v7 - p238

Secondary education. High school teaching — Junior high schools. Middle schools. Intermediate schools. Middle school teaching, LB1623, v7 - p238

Systems of individual educators and writers — Counter-Reformation, LB375, v7 - p218

Systems of individual educators and writers — Early Christian and medieval, LB125, v7 - p218

Teaching (Principles and practice) — Active learning, LB1027.23, v7 - p222

Teaching (Principles and practice) — Choice of school, LB1027.9, v7 - p223

Teaching (Principles and practice) — Communication in education. Authorship, LB1033.5, v7 - p226

Teaching (Principles and practice) — Computer conferencing, LB1044.875, v7 - p227

Teaching (Principles and practice) — Computer network resources, LB1044.87, v7 - p226

Teaching (Principles and practice) — Experimental methods, LB1027.3, v7 - p222

Teaching (Principles and practice) — Experimental studies in educational theory and practice, LB1026, v7 - p222

Teaching (Principles and practice) — General special, LB1027, v7 - p222

Teaching (Principles and practice) — Group work, LB1032, v7 - p225

Teaching (Principles and practice) — Individual instruction, LB1031, v7 - p225

Teaching (Principles and practice) — Mastery learning, LB1031.4, v7 - p225

Teaching (Principles and practice) — Peer-group tutoring of students, LB1031.5, v7 - p225

Teaching (Principles and practice) — Problem-based learning, LB1027.42, v7 - p222

Teaching (Principles and practice) — Stories and storytelling, LB1042, v7 - p226

Teaching (Principles and practice) — Teacher-student relationships, LB1033, v7 - p225

Teaching (Principles and practice) — Technology. Educational technology, LB1028.3, v7 - p224

Transportation and Communications, HE, v6 - p261

Air transportation. Airlines — Government policy. Aeronautics and state, HE9777.7, v6 - p268

Automotive transportation — General Works, HE5611, v6 - p265

Automotive transportation — Special, A-Z, HE5620, v6 - p265

Bicycles — General Works, HE5736, v6 - p265

By region or country — Other regions or countries, HE242, v6 - p262

Government policy (General), HE193, v6 - p261

Information superhighway — By region or country, A-Z, HE7572, v6 - p266

Passenger traffic (General), HE199.9, v6 - p261

Railroads — History, HE1021, v6 - p263

Telecommunication industry. Telegraph — General Works, HE7631, v6 - p266

Telecommunication industry. Telegraph — Government policy. Telecommunication policy, HE7645, v6 - p266

Traffic engineering — By subject, A-Z, HE336, v6 - p262

Traffic engineering — General Works, HE333, v6 - p262

Transportation and Communications, HE *(cont.)*
Urban transportation — By region or country, HE308-310, v6 - p262
Urban transportation — General Works, HE305, v6 - p262
Turkey, KKX, v7 - p193
History of law — General Works. Treatises, KKX120, v7 - p193
United States (Alabama), KFA, v7 - p184
United States (California, Connecticut), KFC, v7 - p184
Food. Drugs. Cosmetics — Drug law....Narcotics. Cosmetics, KFC632, v7 - p184
United States (Cities), KFX, v7 - p187
Chicago, Illinois — Juvenile criminal law and procedure. Administration of juvenile justice, KFX1248, v7 - p187
United States (Confederate States of America), KFZ, v7 - p187
Constitutional law — General principles, KFZ9002, v7 - p187
United States (General), KF, v7 - p121
Administrative organization and procedure — The administrative process. Regulatory agencies, KF5406-5425, v7 - p168
Associations — General, KF1355, v7 - p141
Bibliography — General, KF1, v7 - p121
Civil service. Government officials and employees — State civil service, KF5390, v7 - p168
Civil trials — Particular trials. By plaintiff, A-Z, KF228, v7 - p125
Collections — Individual authors, A-Z, KF213, v7 - p123
Common law in the United States, KF394, v7 - p137
Community legal services. Legal aid. Legal services to the poor — General. National organizations, KF336, v7 - p132
Constitutional law — Amending process, KF4555, v7 - p156
Constitutional law — National territory. Noncontiguous territories, KF4635, v7 - p158
Constitutional law — Separation of powers. Delegation of powers, KF4565, v7 - p156
Contracts — General and comprehensive works, KF801, v7 - p139
Control of social activities — Sports. Prizefighting. Horse racing, KF3989, v7 - p150
Courts. Procedure — Administration of justice. Organization of the judiciary, KF8700, v7 - p172
Criminal law — Administration of criminal justice. Reform of criminal law, enforcement, and procedure, KF9223-9223.4, v7 - p180
Criminal procedure — Arrest and commitment. Rights of suspects, KF9625, v7 - p182
Criminal procedure — Execution of sentence, KF9725-9731, v7 - p183
Criminal procedure — Pardon, KF9695, v7 - p183
Criminal trials — General collections, KF220, v7 - p123
Criminal trials — Particular offenses, A-Z, KF221, v7 - p124
Criticism. Legal reform. General administration of justice, KF384, v7 - p135
Directories — By specialization, A-Z, KF195, v7 - p123
Encyclopedias, KF154, v7 - p122
Equity — Treatises, KF399, v7 - p137
General and comprehensive works — Casebooks. Readings. Treatises, KF385, v7 - p136
General and comprehensive works — Compends. Courses of study, KF386, v7 - p136
General and comprehensive works — Minor and popular works, KF387, v7 - p136
General and comprehensive works — Works for particular groups of users, A-Z, KF390, v7 - p136
General and comprehensive works — Works on diverse legal aspects of a particular subject and falling within several branches of the law, A-Z, KF390.5, v7 - p137
Indians — Particular groups or tribes, A-Z, KF8228, v7 - p171
Jurisprudence and philosophy of American law. General doctrines of American legal institutions — Rule of law in the United States, KF382, v7 - p135
Law dictionaries. Words and phrases, KF156, v7 - p122
Law reporting, KF255, v7 - p127
Law societies, A-Z, KF294, v7 - p129
Legal composition and draftsmanship — Brief writing, KF251, v7 - p127
Legal composition and draftsmanship — General Works, KF250, v7 - p127
Legal education — Directories, KF266, v7 - p127
Legal education — Particular law schools, A-Z, KF292, v7 - p129
Legal education — Prelaw-school education. Admission to law school, KF285, v7 - p128
Legal education — Yearbooks. Annual and periodical surveys, KF265, v7 - p127
Legal maxims. Quotations, KF159, v7 - p123
Legal research. Legal bibliography — Electronic data processing. Information retrieval, KF242, v7 - p126
Legal research. Legal bibliography — General, KF240, v7 - p126
Medical legislation — General, KF3821, v7 - p148
Medical legislation — Human reproductive technology, KF3830, v7 - p149
Medical legislation — Patients' rights, KF3823, v7 - p148
Medical legislation — Special topics, A-Z, KF3827, v7 - p148
Medical legislation — The mentally ill, KF3828, v7 - p149
National emblem. Flag. Seal. Seat of government. National anthem, KF5150, v7 - p168
Negotiated settlement. Compromise, KF9084, v7 - p180
Other bibliographic aids. Tables of popular names, KF90, v7 - p122
Police and power of the police. Federal and comparative state law — General, KF5399, v7 - p168
Public health. Sanitation — General, KF3775, v7 - p147

Public health. Sanitation — Other public health hazards and measures, A-Z, KF3816, v7 - p148
Public property. Public restraints on private property — Eminent domain, KF5599, v7 - p169
Regulation of industry, trade, and commerce. Occupational law — General. Comprehensive, KF1600, v7 - p141
Social legislation — General, KF3300, v7 - p144
The legal profession — General. Law as a career, KF297, v7 - p129
The legal profession — Particular aspects. The lawyer and society, KF298, v7 - p130
The legal profession — Particular classes of lawyers and types of careers, A-Z, KF299, v7 - p130
United States (Georgia), KFG, v7 - p184
United States (Hawaii), KFH, v7 - p184
United States (Illinois), KFI, v7 - p184
United States (Louisiana), KFL, v7 - p185
United States (Maryland, Massachusetts, Michigan, Missouri), KFM, v7 - p185
History — General, KFM7878, v7 - p185
History — Special topics, A-Z, KFM2478.8, v7 - p185
United States (Nebraska, New Jersey, New Mexico, New York, North Carolina), KFN, v7 - p185
Constitutional law — History, KFN5681, v7 - p186
Indians, KFN5940, v7 - p186
Juvenile criminal law and procedure. Administration of juvenile justice — General, KFN6195, v7 - p186
Public property. Public restraints on private property — Land grants, KFN4055, v7 - p185
Succession upon death — General, KFN5200, v7 - p185
United States (Oklahoma), KFO, v7 - p186
Indians — General, KFO1705, v7 - p186
United States (Pennsylvania), KFP, v7 - p186
Medical legislation — General, KFP360, v7 - p186
United States (Virginia), KFV, v7 - p186
United States Local History, F2.3-970, v4 - p325
Alabama — Biography (Collective). Genealogy (Collective), F325, v4 - p411
Alabama — Cities, towns, etc., A-Z, F334, v4 - p415
Alabama — Elements in the population, F335, v4 - p415
Alabama — Gazetteers. Dictionaries. Geographic names, F324, v4 - p410
Alabama — General Works. Histories, F326, v4 - p411
Alabama — Historic monuments (General). Illustrative material, F327, v4 - p412
Alabama — Pamphlets, addresses, essays, F326.5, v4 - p412
Alabama — Regions, countries, etc., A-Z, F332, v4 - p413
Alaska — Bering Sea and Aleutian Islands, F951, v4 - p545
Alaska — Cities, towns, etc., A-Z, F914, v4 - p545
Alaska — General Works. Histories, F904, v4 - p544
Alaska — Klondike River and Valley, F931, v4 - p545
Alaska — Pamphlets, addresses, essays, F904.5, v4 - p544
Alaska — Regions, counties, etc., A-Z, F912, v4 - p545
Arizona — Antiquities, F813, v4 - p518
Arizona — Biography (Collective).Genealogy (Collective), F810, v4 - p516
Arizona — Cities, towns, etc., A-Z, F819, v4 - p519
Arizona — Elements in the population, F820, v4 - p520
Arizona — Gazetteers. Dictionaries. Geographic names, F809, v4 - p516
Arizona — General Works. Histories, F811, v4 - p517
Arizona — Guidebooks, F809.3, v4 - p516
Arizona — Historic monuments (General). Illustrative material, F812, v4 - p518
Arizona — Juvenile works, F811.3, v4 - p518
Arizona — Pamphlets, addresses, essays, F811.5, v4 - p518
Arizona — Regions, counties, etc., A-Z, F817, v4 - p518
Arizona — Societies. Collections, F806, v4 - p516
Arkansas — Biography (Collective). Genealogy (Collective), F410, v4 - p435
Arkansas — Cities, towns, etc., A-Z, F419, v4 - p437
Arkansas — Elements in the population, F420, v4 - p437
Arkansas — General Works. Histories, F411, v4 - p435
Arkansas — Pamphlets, addresses, essays, F411.5, v4 - p436
Arkansas — Regions, counties, etc., A-Z, F417, v4 - p436
Arkansas — Societies. Collections, F406, v4 - p435
Atlantic coast of North America. Middle Atlantic States, F106, v4 - p345
California — Anecdotes, legends, pageants, etc., F861.6, v4 - p528
California — Antiquities (Non-Indian), F863, v4 - p528
California — Biography (Collective). Genealogy (Collective), F860, v4 - p527
California — Cities, towns, etc., A-Z, F869, v4 - p533
California — Elements in the population, F870, v4 - p538
California — Gazetteers. Dictionaries. Geographic names, F859, v4 - p526
California — General Works. Histories, F861, v4 - p527
California — Guidebooks, F859.3, v4 - p527
California — Historic monuments (General). Illustrative material, F862, v4 - p528
California — Juvenile works, F861.3, v4 - p527
California — Pamphlets, addresses, essays, etc., F861.5, v4 - p528
California — Regions, counties, etc., A-Z, F868, v4 - p532
California — Southern California, F867, v4 - p532
Colorado — Antiquities (Non-Indian), F778, v4 - p503

United States Local History, F2.3-970 *(cont.)*

Colorado — Cities, towns, etc., A-Z, F784, v4 - p505
Colorado — Elements in the population, F785, v4 - p505
Colorado — Gazetteers. Dictionaries. Geographic names, F774, v4 - p502
Colorado — General Works. Histories, F776, v4 - p503
Colorado — Guidebooks, F774.3, v4 - p502
Colorado — Historic monuments (General). Illustrative material, F777, v4 - p503
Colorado — Juvenile works, F776.3, v4 - p503
Colorado — Regions, counties, etc., A-Z, F782, v4 - p504
Connecticut — Cities, towns, etc. A-Z, F104, v4 - p345
Connecticut — General Works. Histories, F94, v4 - p344
Connecticut — Historic monuments (General). Illustrative material, F95, v4 - p344
Connecticut — Juvenile works, F94.3, v4 - p344
Delaware — General Works. Histories, F164, v4 - p366
Delaware — Historic monuments (General). Illustrative material, F165, v4 - p367
Delaware — Juvenile works, F164.3, v4 - p367
District of Columbia. Washington — Biography (Collective). Genealogy (Collective), F193, v4 - p372
District of Columbia. Washington — Buildings, F204, v4 - p376
District of Columbia. Washington — General Works. Histories, F194, v4 - p372
District of Columbia. Washington — Guidebooks, F192.3, v4 - p372
District of Columbia. Washington — Historic monuments. Illustrative material, F195, v4 - p373
District of Columbia. Washington — Political and social life, F196, v4 - p373
District of Columbia. Washington — Regions, suburbs, etc., A-Z, F202, v4 - p375
Florida — Cities, towns, etc., A-Z, F319, v4 - p408
Florida — Elements in the population, F320, v4 - p410
Florida — General Works. Histories, F311, v4 - p406
Florida — Guidebooks, F309.3, v4 - p406
Florida — Historic monuments (General). Illustrative material, F312, v4 - p406
Florida — Pamphlets, addresses, essays, etc., F311.5, v4 - p406
Florida — Regions, countries, etc., A-Z, F317, v4 - p408
Georgia — Cities, towns, etc., A-Z, F294, v4 - p404
Georgia — Elements in the population, F295, v4 - p405
Georgia — General Works. Histories, F286, v4 - p401
Georgia — Historic monuments (General). Illustrative material, F287, v4 - p401
Georgia — Regions, counties, etc., A-Z, F292, v4 - p403
Gulf States, F296, v4 - p405
Idaho — Elements in the population, F755, v4 - p499
Idaho — General Works. Histories, F746, v4 - p498
Idaho — Juvenile works, F746.3, v4 - p498
Idaho — Regions, counties, etc., A-Z, F752, v4 - p499
Illinois — Antiquities (Non-Indian), F543, v4 - p454
Illinois — Elements in the population, F550, v4 - p461
Illinois — Gazetteers. Dictionaries. Geographic names, F539, v4 - p454
Illinois — General Works. Histories, F541, v4 - p454
Illinois — Guidebooks, F539.3, v4 - p454
Illinois — Other cities, towns, etc., A-Z, F549, v4 - p459
Illinois — Regions, counties, etc., A-Z, F547, v4 - p455
Indiana — Biography (Collective). Genealogy (Collective), F525, v4 - p452
Indiana — Cities, towns, etc., A-Z, F534, v4 - p453
Indiana — Elements in the population, F535, v4 - p453
Indiana — Gazetteers. Dictionaries. Geographic names, F524, v4 - p452
Indiana — General Works. Histories, F526, v4 - p452
Indiana — Guidebooks, F524.3, v4 - p452
Indiana — Historic monuments (General). Illustrative material, F527, v4 - p453
Indiana — Juvenile works, F526.3, v4 - p453
Indiana — Pamphlets, addresses, essays, F526.5, v4 - p453
Insular possessions of the United States (General), F970, v4 - p545
Iowa — Antiquities (Non-Indian), F623, v4 - p485
Iowa — Biography (Collective). Genealogy (Collective), F620, v4 - p483
Iowa — Cities, towns, etc., A-Z, F629, v4 - p485
Iowa — Elements in the population, F630, v4 - p485
Iowa — General Works. Histories, F621, v4 - p483
Iowa — Historic monuments (General). Illustrative material, F622, v4 - p485
Iowa — Juvenile works, F621.3, v4 - p484
Iowa — Pamphlets, addresses, essays, F621.5, v4 - p484
Iowa — Regions, counties, etc., A-Z, F627, v4 - p485
Iowa — Societies. Collections, F616, v4 - p483
Kansas — Biography (Collective). Genealogy (Collective), F680, v4 - p491
Kansas — Cities, towns, etc., A-Z, F689, v4 - p492
Kansas — Elements in the population, F690, v4 - p492
Kansas — General Works. Histories, F681, v4 - p491
Kansas — Guidebooks, F679.3, v4 - p491
Kansas — Juvenile works, F681.3, v4 - p491
Kansas — Regions, counties, etc., A-Z, F687, v4 - p492
Kentucky — Antiquities (Non-Indian), F453, v4 - p440
Kentucky — Biography (Collective). Genealogy (Collective), F450, v4 - p439
Kentucky — Cities, towns, etc., A-Z, F459, v4 - p442
Kentucky — Gazetteers. Dictionaries. Geographic names, F449, v4 - p439
Kentucky — General Works. Histories, F451, v4 - p439

Kentucky — Historic monuments (General). Illustrative material, F452, v4 - p440
Kentucky — Regions, counties, etc., A-Z, F457, v4 - p442
Louisiana — Antiquities (Non-Indian), F371, v4 - p420
Louisiana — Biography (Collective). Genealogy (Collective), F368, v4 - p420
Louisiana — Cities, towns, etc., A-Z, F379, v4 - p422
Louisiana — Elements in the population, F380, v4 - p424
Louisiana — General Works. Histories, F369, v4 - p420
Louisiana — Guidebooks, F367.3, v4 - p420
Louisiana — Regions, parishes, etc., A-Z, F377, v4 - p422
Maine — Cities, towns, etc., A-Z, F29, v4 - p329
Maine — General Works. Histories, F19, v4 - p328
Maine — Pamphlets, addresses, 328essays, etc., F19.5, v4 - p328
Maine — Regions, counties, etc., A-Z, F27, v4 - p328
Maryland — Cities, towns, etc., A-Z, F189, v4 - p371
Maryland — Gazetteers. Dictionaries. Geographic names, F179, v4 - p367
Maryland — General Works. Histories, F181, v4 - p367
Maryland — Geography, F181.8, v4 - p368
Maryland — Guidebooks, F179.3, v4 - p367
Maryland — Historic monuments (General). Illustrative material, F182, v4 - p368
Maryland — Pamphlets, addresses, essays, etc., F181.5, v4 - p368
Maryland — Regions, counties, etc., A-Z, F187, v4 - p369
Massachusetts — Anecdotes, legends, pageants, etc., F64.6, v4 - p332
Massachusetts — Elements in the population, F75, v4 - p342
Massachusetts — General Works. Histories, F64, v4 - p332
Massachusetts — Guidebooks, F62.3, v4 - p332
Massachusetts — Other cities and towns, etc., A-Z, F74, v4 - p340
Massachusetts — Regions, counties, etc., A-Z, F72, v4 - p336
Massachusetts — Societies. Collections, F61, v4 - p332
Michigan — Cities, towns, etc., A-Z, F574, v4 - p463
Michigan — Gazetteers. Dictionaries. Geographic names, F564, v4 - p461
Michigan — General Works. Histories, F566, v4 - p461
Michigan — Historic monuments (General). Illustrative material, F567, v4 - p462
Michigan — Juvenile works, F566.3, v4 - p462
Michigan — Pamphlets, addresses, essays, F566.5, v4 - p462
Michigan — Regions, counties, etc., A-Z, F572, v4 - p463
Minnesota — Anecdotes, legends, pageants, etc., F606.6, v4 - p481
Minnesota — Biography (Collective). Genealogy (Collective), F605, v4 - p480
Minnesota — Cities, towns, etc., A-Z, F614, v4 - p482
Minnesota — Elements in the population, F615, v4 - p482
Minnesota — Gazetteers. Dictionaries. Geographic names, F604, v4 - p480
Minnesota — General Works. Histories, F606, v4 - p481
Minnesota — Guidebooks, F604.3, v4 - p480
Minnesota — Historic monuments (General). Illustrative material, F607, v4 - p481
Minnesota — Juvenile works, F606.3, v4 - p481
Minnesota — Pamphlets, addresses, essays, F606.5, v4 - p481
Minnesota — Regions, counties, etc., A-Z, F612, v4 - p482
Mississippi — Cities, towns, etc., A-Z, F349, v4 - p418
Mississippi — Elements in the population, F350, v4 - p418
Mississippi — General Works. Histories, F341, v4 - p416
Mississippi — Pamphlets, addresses, essays, F341.5, v4 - p416
Mississippi — Regions, countries, etc., A-Z, F347, v4 - p417
Mississippi River and Valley. Middle West — 1803-1865, F353, v4 - p419
Mississippi River and Valley. Middle West — 1865-1950, F354, v4 - p419
Mississippi River and Valley. Middle West — 1951-, F355, v4 - p419
Mississippi River and Valley. Middle West — Early to 1803, F352, v4 - p418
Mississippi River and Valley. Middle West — Elements in the population, F358-358.2, v4 - p419
Mississippi River and Valley. Middle West — General Works, F351, v4 - p418
Missouri — Cities, towns, etc., A-Z, F474, v4 - p444
Missouri — Elements in the population, F475, v4 - p445
Missouri — General Works. Histories, F466, v4 - p443
Missouri — Pamphlets, addresses, essays, etc., F466.5, v4 - p443
Missouri — Regions, counties, etc., A-Z, F472, v4 - p444
Missouri River and Valley, F598, v4 - p479
Montana — Cities, towns, etc., A-Z, F739, v4 - p498
Montana — General Works. Histories, F731, v4 - p496
Montana — Historic monuments (General). Illustrative material, F732, v4 - p497
Montana — Pamphlets, addresses, essays, etc., F731.5, v4 - p497
Montana — Regions, counties, etc., A-Z, F737, v4 - p497
Nebraska — Cities, towns, etc., A-Z, F674, v4 - p490
Nebraska — Gazetteers. Dictionaries. Geographic names, F664, v4 - p489
Nebraska — General Works. Histories, F666, v4 - p489
Nebraska — Pamphlets, addresses, essays, F666.5, v4 - p490
Nebraska — Regions, counties, etc., A-Z, F672, v4 - p490
Nebraska — Societies. Collections, F661, v4 - p489
Nevada — Cities, towns, etc., A-Z, F849, v4 - p523
Nevada — Elements in the population, F850, v4 - p524
Nevada — General Works. Histories, F841, v4 - p523
Nevada — Guidebooks, F839.3, v4 - p523
Nevada — Pamphlets, addresses, essays, F841.5, v4 - p523
Nevada — Regions, counties, etc., A-Z, F847, v4 - p523

United States Local History, F2.3-970 *(cont.)*

New England — Antiquities (Non-Indian), F6, v4 - p325
New England — Elements in the population, F15, v4 - p328
New England — Guidebooks, F2.3, v4 - p325
New England — Historic monuments (General). Illustrative material, F5, v4 - p325
New England — Juvenile works, F4, v4 - p325
New England — Regions, A-Z, F12, v4 - p328
New Hampshire — Cities, towns, etc., A-Z, F44, v4 - p330
New Hampshire — Gazetteers. Dictionaries. Geographic names, F32, v4 - p329
New Hampshire — Guidebooks, F32.3, v4 - p329
New Hampshire — Regions, countries, etc., A-Z, F42, v4 - p330
New Jersey — Cities, towns, etc., A-Z, F144, v4 - p359
New Jersey — Elements in the population, F145, v4 - p360
New Jersey — Pamphlets, addresses, essays, etc., F134.5, v4 - p358
New Jersey — Regions, counties, etc., A-Z, F142, v4 - p359
New Mexico — Cities, towns, etc., A-Z, F804, v4 - p515
New Mexico — Elements in the population, F805, v4 - p515
New Mexico — General Works. Histories, F796, v4 - p513
New Mexico — Guidebooks, F794.3, v4 - p513
New Mexico — Historic monuments (General). Illustrative material, F797, v4 - p513
New Mexico — Pamphlets, addresses, essays, F796.5, v4 - p513
New Mexico — Regions, counties, etc., A-Z, F802, v4 - p515
New York — Biography (Collective). Genealogy (Collective), F118, v4 - p346
New York — Elements in the population, F130, v4 - p358
New York — General Works. Histories, F119, v4 - p346
New York — Other cities, towns, etc., A-Z, F129, v4 - p357
New York — Regions, counties, etc., A-Z, F127, v4 - p348
New York — Societies. Collections, F116, v4 - p346
North Carolina — Cities, towns, etc., A-Z, F264, v4 - p394
North Carolina — Elements in the population, F265, v4 - p395
North Carolina — General Works. Histories, F254, v4 - p392
North Carolina — Historic monuments (General). Illustrative material, F255, v4 - p392
North Carolina — Pamphlets, addresses, essays, etc., F254.5, v4 - p392
North Carolina — Regions, counties, etc., A-Z, F262, v4 - p393
North Dakota — Biography (Collective). Genealogy (Collective), F635, v4 - p486
North Dakota — Cities, towns, A-Z, F644, v4 - p487
North Dakota — Elements in the population, F645, v4 - p487
North Dakota — Gazetteers. Dictionaries. Geographic names, F634, v4 - p485
North Dakota — General Works. Histories, F636, v4 - p486
North Dakota — Historic monuments (General). Illustrative material, F637, v4 - p487
North Dakota — Juvenile works, F636.3, v4 - p487
North Dakota — Pamphlets, addresses, essays, etc., F636.5, v4 - p487
North Dakota — Regions, counties, etc., A-Z, F642, v4 - p487
Ohio — Cities, towns, etc., A-Z, F499, v4 - p449
Ohio — Elements in the population, F500, v4 - p450
Ohio — Gazetteers. Dictionaries. Geographic names, F489, v4 - p447
Ohio — General Works, F491, v4 - p447
Ohio — Guidebooks, F489.3, v4 - p447
Ohio — Historic monuments (General). Illustrative material, F492, v4 - p448
Ohio — Juvenile works, F491.3, v4 - p447
Ohio — Pamphlets, addresses, essays, etc., F491.5, v4 - p447
Ohio — Regions, counties, etc., A-Z, F497, v4 - p448
Ohio — Societies. Collections, F486, v4 - p446
Ohio River and Valley — General Works, F516, v4 - p451
Oklahoma — Biography (Collective). Genealogy (Collective), F693, v4 - p492
Oklahoma — Cities, towns, etc., A-Z, F704, v4 - p494
Oklahoma — Elements in the population, F705, v4 - p495
Oklahoma — Gazetteers. Dictionaries. Geographic names, F692, v4 - p492
Oklahoma — General Works. Histories, F694, v4 - p492
Oklahoma — Pamphlets, addresses, essays, etc., F694.5, v4 - p493
Oklahoma — Regions, counties, etc., A-Z, F702, v4 - p494
Oklahoma — Societies. Collections, F691, v4 - p492
Old Northwest. Northwest Territory — General Works. Histories, F479, v4 - p446
Old Southwest. Lower Mississippi Valley, F396, v4 - p435
Oregon — Cities, towns, etc., A-Z, F884, v4 - p540
Oregon — Gazetteers. Dictionaries. Geographic names, F874, v4 - p539
Oregon — Guidebooks, F874.3, v4 - p539
Oregon — Historic monuments (General). Illustrative material, F877, v4 - p539
Oregon — Pamphlets, addresses, essays, F876.5, v4 - p539
Oregon — Regions, counties, etc., A-Z, F882, v4 - p540
Pennsylvania — Elements in the population, F160, v4 - p366
Pennsylvania — Gazetteers. Dictionaries. Geographic names, F147, v4 - p360
Pennsylvania — General Works. Histories, F149, v4 - p360
Pennsylvania — Other cities, towns, etc., A-Z, F159, v4 - p365
Pennsylvania — Pamphlets, addresses, essays, etc., F149.5, v4 - p360
Pennsylvania — Regions, counties, etc., A-Z, F157, v4 - p361
Rhode Island — Biography (Collective). Genealogy (Collective), F78, v4 - p343
Rhode Island — Cities, towns, etc., A-Z, F89, v4 - p344
Rhode Island — General Works. Histories, F79, v4 - p343
Rhode Island — Pamphlets, addresses, essays, etc., F79.5, v4 - p343
Rhode Island — Societies. Collections, F76, v4 - p342

Rocky Mountains. Rocky Mountains in the United States — Yellowstone National Park, F722, v4 - p496
Rocky Mountains. Rocky Mountains in the United States, F721, v4 - p495
South Carolina — Cities, towns, etc., A-Z, F279, v4 - p399
South Carolina — Elements in the population, F280, v4 - p401
South Carolina — General Works. Histories, F269, v4 - p395
South Carolina — Historic monuments (General). Illustrative material, F270, v4 - p395
South Carolina — Pamphlets, addresses, essays, etc., F269.5, v4 - p395
South Carolina — Regions, countries, etc., A-Z, F277, v4 - p398
South Carolina — Societies. Collections, F266, v4 - p395
South Dakota — Cities, towns, etc., A-Z, F659, v4 - p489
South Dakota — General Works. Histories, F651, v4 - p488
South Dakota — Juvenile works, F651.3, v4 - p488
South Dakota — Pamphlets, addresses, essays, F651.5, v4 - p488
South Dakota — Periodicals. Societies. Collections, F646, v4 - p488
South Dakota — Regions, counties, etc., A-Z, F657, v4 - p489
Tennessee — Cities, towns, etc., A-Z, F444, v4 - p438
Tennessee — General Works. Histories, F436, v4 - p437
Tennessee — Historic monuments (General). Illustrative material, F437, v4 - p438
Tennessee — Pamphlets, addresses, essays, F436.5, v4 - p438
Tennessee — Regions, counties, etc., A-Z, F443, v4 - p438
Texas — Cities, towns, etc., A-Z, F394, v4 - p432
Texas — Elements in the population, F395, v4 - p434
Texas — Gazetteers. Dictionaries. Geographic names, F384, v4 - p425
Texas — Guidebooks, F384.3, v4 - p425
Texas — Historic monuments (General). Illustrative material, F387, v4 - p425
Texas — Pamphlets, addresses, essays, F386.5, v4 - p425
Texas — Regions, counties, etc., A-Z, F392, v4 - p431
Texas — Study and teaching, F386, v4 - p425
The Lake region. Great Lakes — General Works, F551, v4 - p461
The Lake region. Great Lakes — Lake Erie, F555, v4 - p461
The Lake region. Great Lakes — Lake Huron, F554, v4 - p461
The Lake region. Great Lakes — Lake Michigan, F553, v4 - p461
The Lake region. Great Lakes — Lake Superior, F552, v4 - p461
The New Southwest. Southwestern States — 1848-1950, F786, v4 - p506
The New Southwest. Southwestern States — 1951-, F787, v4 - p510
The New Southwest. Southwestern States — Colorado River, Canyon, and Valley, F788, v4 - p510
The New Southwest. Southwestern States — Elements in the population, F790, v4 - p512
The New Southwest. Southwestern States — Four Corners Region, F788.5, v4 - p511
The New Southwest. Southwestern States — Great Basin, F789, v4 - p511
The Northwest, F597, v4 - p479
The Pacific States — Cascade Range, F851.7, v4 - p526
The Pacific States — Exploring expeditions to the Pacific coast before 1800, F851.5, v4 - p525
The Pacific States — General Works, F851, v4 - p524
The South. South Atlantic States — Biography (Collective). Genealogy (Collective), F208, v4 - p376
The South. South Atlantic States — Dictionaries and encyclopedias of history, F207.7, v4 - p376
The South. South Atlantic States — Elements in the population, F220, v4 - p385
The South. South Atlantic States — General Works. Histories, F209, v4 - p377
The South. South Atlantic States — Historic monuments (General). Illustrative material, F210, v4 - p378
The South. South Atlantic States — Historiography, F208.2, v4 - p376
The South. South Atlantic States — Pamphlets, addresses, essays, etc., F209.5, v4 - p377
The South. South Atlantic States — Regions, A-Z, F217, v4 - p384
The South. South Atlantic States — Societies. Collections, F206, v4 - p376
The West. Trans-Mississippi Region. Great Plains — Biography (Collective). Genealogy (Collective), F590.5, v4 - p466
The West. Trans-Mississippi Region. Great Plains — By period, F592, v4 - p470
The West. Trans-Mississippi Region. Great Plains — Frontier and pioneer life. Ranch life, cowboys, cattle trails, etc., F596, v4 - p477
The West. Trans-Mississippi Region. Great Plains — General Works. Histories, F591, v4 - p466
The West. Trans-Mississippi Region. Great Plains — Historic monuments (General). Illustrative material, F590.7, v4 - p466
Utah — Biography (Collective). Genealogy (Collective), F825, v4 - p520
Utah — Cities, towns, etc., A-Z, F834, v4 - p522
Utah — Elements in the population, F835, v4 - p522
Utah — Gazetteers. Dictionaries. Geographic names, F824, v4 - p520
Utah — General Works. Histories, F826, v4 - p520
Utah — Juvenile works, F826.3, v4 - p521
Utah — Pamphlets, addresses, essays, etc., F826.5, v4 - p522
Utah — Regions, counties, etc., A-Z, F832, v4 - p522
Utah — Societies. Collections, F821, v4 - p520
Vermont — Cities, towns, etc., A-Z, F59, v4 - p331
Vermont — General Works. Histories, F49, v4 - p331
Vermont — Guidebooks, F47.3, v4 - p331

United States Local History, F2.3-970 (cont.)
Vermont — Pamphlets, addresses, essays, etc., F49.5, v4 - p331
Vermont — Regions, counties, etc., A-Z, F57, v4 - p331
Vermont — Societies. Collections, F46, v4 - p331
Virginia — Biography (Collective). Genealogy (Collective), F225, v4 - p385
Virginia — Cities, towns, etc., A-Z, F234, v4 - p388
Virginia — Elements in the population, F235, v4 - p389
Virginia — General Works. Histories, F226, v4 - p385
Virginia — Historic monuments (General). Illustrative material, F227, v4 - p386
Virginia — Pamphlets, addresses, essays, etc., F226.5, v4 - p386
Virginia — Regions, counties, etc., A-Z, F232, v4 - p388
Washington — Cities, towns, etc., A-Z, F899, v4 - p543
Washington — Elements in the population, F900, v4 - p543
Washington — Gazetteers. Dictionaries. Geographic names, F889, v4 - p541
Washington — General Works. Histories, F891, v4 - p541
Washington — Guidebooks, F889.3, v4 - p541
Washington — Historic monuments (General). Illustrative material, F892, v4 - p542
Washington — Pamphlets, addresses, essays, F891.5, v4 - p542
Washington — Region, counties, etc., A-Z, F897, v4 - p542
West Florida, F301, v4 - p406
West Virginia — Cities, towns, etc., A-Z, F249, v4 - p391
West Virginia — Gazetteers. Dictionaries. Geographic names, F239, v4 - p390
West Virginia — General Works. Histories, F241, v4 - p390
West Virginia — Guidebooks, F239.3, v4 - p390
West Virginia — Historic monuments (General). Illustrative material, F242, v4 - p391
West Virginia — Pamphlets, addresses, essays, etc., F241.5, v4 - p391
West Virginia — Periodicals. Societies. Collections, F236, v4 - p390
West Virginia — Regions, counties, etc., A-Z, F247, v4 - p391
Wisconsin — Cities, towns, etc., A-Z, F589, v4 - p466
Wisconsin — General Works. Histories, F581, v4 - p465
Wisconsin — Pamphlets, addresses, essays, F581.5, v4 - p465
Wisconsin — Regions, counties, etc., A-Z, F587, v4 - p466
Wisconsin — Societies. Collections, F576, v4 - p464
Wyoming — Biography (Collective). Genealogy (Collective), F760, v4 - p499
Wyoming — Cities, towns, etc., A-Z, F769, v4 - p502
Wyoming — Gazetteers. Dictionaries. Geographic names, F759, v4 - p499
Wyoming — General Works. Histories, F761, v4 - p500
Wyoming — Guidebooks, F759.3, v4 - p499
Wyoming — Pamphlets, addresses, essays, etc., F761.5, v4 - p501
Wyoming — Regions, counties, etc., A-Z, F767, v4 - p501
United States, E154-888, v4 - p81
Colonial history, 1607-1775 — Collections. Collected works, E187, v4 - p169
Colonial history, 1607-1775 — General Works, E188, v4 - p170
Colonial history, 1607-1775 — Minor works, E189, v4 - p170
General — Antiquities (non-Indian), E159.5, v4 - p82
General — Gazetteers, E154, v4 - p81
General — General Works, E156, v4 - p82
General — Geographic names, E155, v4 - p81
General — Geography, E161.3, v4 - p84
General — Guidebooks. Handbooks, E158, v4 - p82
General — Historic monuments (General), E159, v4 - p82
General — National and state parks and reservations (Collective descriptive works), E160, v4 - p83
General — Social life and customs (General), E161, v4 - p83
History — Chronology. Chronological tables, etc., E174.5, v4 - p97
History — Dictionaries and encyclopedias, E174, v4 - p97
History — Historical geography, E179.5, v4 - p106
History — Military history, E181, v4 - p108
History — Naval history (United States Navy and Marine Corps), E182, v4 - p108
History — Philosophy of American history, E175.9, v4 - p100
History — Societies, E172, v4 - p96
History — Sources and documents. Collections. Collected works, E173, v4 - p96
History — Study and teaching, E175.8, v4 - p100
Late nineteenth century, 1865-1900 — Diplomatic history. Foreign and general relations, E661.7, v4 - p253
Late nineteenth century, 1865-1900 — General Works, E661, v4 - p252
Later twentieth century, 1961- — Dictionaries and encyclopedias, E838.6, v4 - p300
Later twentieth century, 1961- — General Works, E839, v4 - p300
Later twentieth century, 1961- — Military, naval and air force history, E840.4, v4 - p304
Revolution to the Civil War, 1775/1783-1861 — Collected works of American statesmen (Revolutionary group), A-Z, E302, v4 - p180
Revolution to the Civil War, 1775/1783-1861 — General Works, E301, v4 - p179
Revolution to the Civil War, 1775/1783-1861 — Political history, E302.1, v4 - p181
The Civil War, 1861-1865 — Army life. The private soldier, E607, v4 - p248
The Civil War, 1861-1865 — Collections.Collected works, E464, v4 - p227
The Civil War, 1861-1865 — Press. Censorship, E609, v4 - p249
The Civil War, 1861-1865 — Religion in the armed forces (North and South), E635, v4 - p250
The Civil War, 1861-1865 — Secret Service. Signal Corps, E608, v4 - p249
The Civil War, 1861-1865 — Women's work, E628, v4 - p250

The Revolution, 1775-1783 — Collections. Collected works, E203, v4 - p171
The Revolution, 1775-1783 — Declaration of Independence, E221, v4 - p175
The Revolution, 1775-1783 — Diplomatic history. Treaty of Paris, 1783, E249, v4 - p176
The Revolution, 1775-1783 — General special, E209, v4 - p173
The Revolution, 1775-1783 — General Works.History (General), E208, v4 - p173
The Revolution, 1775-1783 — Participation by race, ethnic group, religious group, etc., A-Z, E269, v4 - p178
The Revolution, 1775-1783 — Women and the war, E276, v4 - p178
Twentieth century — 1919-1933. Harding-Coolidge-Hoover era. "The twenties", E784, v4 - p286
Twentieth century — Addresses, essays, lectures, etc. (Collected), E742, v4 - p262
Twentieth century — Collected works of American statesmen, A-Z, E742.5, v4 - p262
Twentieth century — Dictionaries and encyclopedias, E740.7, v4 - p261
Twentieth century — Diplomatic history. Foreign relations, E768, v4 - p286
Twentieth century — General Works, E741, v4 - p261
Twentieth century — Internal history during World War I, E780, v4 - p286
Twentieth century — Military history, E745, v4 - p272
Twentieth century — Naval history, E746, v4 - p273
Uralic. Basque, PH, v3 - p64
Visual art, N, v9 - p131
Art collectors, patrons, etc., N8380, v9 - p189
Art criticism — General special, N7454-7476, v9 - p182
Art criticism — Historiography, N7480, v9 - p182
Art criticism — Popular works on art appreciation, N7477, v9 - p182
Art critics and historians; historiography, N8375, v9 - p188
Artists' marks and monograms, N45, v9 - p132
Communication of information — Computer network resources, N59, v9 - p132
Communication of information — Information services, N58, v9 - p132
Dictionaries, N33, v9 - p131
Economics of art, N8600, v9 - p189
Encyclopedias, N31, v9 - p131
Exhibitions — General Works. History. Organization, etc., N4395, v9 - p140
General special — Comparative art, N7428.5, v9 - p180
General special — Ethnic art (General), N7429.4, v9 - p180
General special, N7428, v9 - p179
General Works — Early works to 1800, N7420, v9 - p179
History — General special, N5303, v9 - p141
History — General Works, N5300, v9 - p140
History — Special countries, N6501, v9 - p151
Indexes to illustrations (General). Repertoires, N7525, v9 - p183
Miscellaneous genres and media, not limited by time period, style, place, or subject matter — Assemblage. Collage. Found objects, N7433.7, v9 - p181
Popular works, N7438, v9 - p181
Special subjects of art — Choice of subject. Titles. Themes and motives, N7560, v9 - p183
Special subjects of art — Iconography. Iconology, N7565, v9 - p183
Study and teaching. Research — General Works, N85, v9 - p136
Technique, composition, etc. — General special, N7430.5, v9 - p180
Terminology, N34, v9 - p131
West Germanic Philology and Languages, PF, v3 - p44
West Indies. Caribbean area: Antigua and Barbuda, KGK, v7 - p188
West Indies. Caribbean area: Cuba, KGN, v7 - p188
General — General Works. Treatises, KGN327, v7 - p188
Yearbooks. Almanacs. Directories, AY, v10 - p6
Yugoslavia, DR309-370, v5 - p243
Turkey — General Works, DR417, v5 - p243
Turkey — Social life and customs. Civilization, DR432, v5 - p243
Zoology, QL, v1 - p301
Animal introduction, QL86, v1 - p305
Animals and civilization. Human-animal relationships, QL85, v1 - p305
Dictionaries, QL9, v1 - p301
Encyclopedias, QL7, v1 - p301
Poisonous animals. Dangerous animals, QL100, v1 - p305
Popular works, QL50, v1 - p303
Societies, congresses, serial collections, yearbooks, QL1, v1 - p301
Zoological illustrating, QL46.5, v1 - p302